# Langenscheidt Pocket German Dictionary

**German – English**
**English – German**

includes new German spelling

edited by the
Langenscheidt editorial staff

**Langenscheidt**

New York · Berlin · Munich · Vienna · Zurich

Neither the presence nor the absence of a designation indicating that any entered word constitutes a trademark should be regarded as affecting the legal status thereof.

This dictionary uses the standardised German spelling system as of 2006.

1. 2. 3. 4. 5. 11 10 09 08 07


Printed in Germany

# Preface

This new dictionary of English and German is a tool with more than 55,000 references for those who work with these languages at beginner's or intermediate level.

Languages are in a constant process of change. Therefore many words which have entered German and English in the last few years have been included in the vocabulary, e.g. *abgasfrei*, *Blog*, *chatten*, *DVD-Player*, *Handynummer*, *Kanzlerin*, *Lauschangriff*, *SMS*, *Vogelgrippe*; *blog*, *cell (phone)*, *chat*, *coach class*, *digital camera*, *Internet access*, *low-calorie*, *snowboarding*, *text message*.

The easy-to-read, clearly laid out typography with all the headwords in blue makes for good readability and allows the user to find words and expressions and their translations more quickly. The **new German spelling** has been used and detailed notes for the user have been included.

The A–Z part of this dictionary contains many important German and English proper names and abbreviations. Another feature is the special quick-reference sections listing the States of Germany and Austria and the Cantons of Switzerland, German weights and measures, examples of German declension and conjugation and alphabetical lists of German and English irregular verbs.

Designed for the widest possible variety of uses, this dictionary will be of great value to students, teachers and tourists, and will find a place in home and office libraries alike.

# Contents

# How to use this dictionary

This dictionary endeavors to do everything it can to help you find the words and translations you are looking for as quickly and as easily as possible.

To enable you to get the most out of your dictionary, you will be shown exactly where and how to find the information that will help you choose the right translation in every situation – whether at school or at home, in your profession, when writing letters, or in everyday conversation.

## 1. German and English headwords

**1.1** When you are looking for a particular word it is important to know that the dictionary entries are arranged in strict **alphabetical order:**

A**a**l – a**b**
b**e**ugen – b**i**egen
ha**y** – ha**z**e

In the German-English section the letters **ä**, **ö** and **ü** are treated on the same basis as **a**, **o** and **u**. **ß** is treated as **ss**.

**1.2** Besides the headwords and their derivatives and compounds, the past tense and past participle of irregular German verbs are also given as individual entries in alphabetical order in the German-English section, e.g. **ging, gegangen.**

**1.3** Many German and English proper names and abbreviations are included in the vocabulary.

**1.4** How then do you go about finding a particular word? Take a look at the words in bold print at the top of each page. These are the so-called **catchwords** and they serve as a guide to tracing your word as quickly as possible. The catchword on the top left gives you the first headword on the left-hand page, while the one on the top right gives you the last word on the right-hand page, e.g.

**Griechenland – gut**

**1.5** What about entries comprising hyphenated expressions or two or more words, such as **DVD-Player, left-handed** or **mass media?** Expressions of this kind are treated in the same way as single words and thus appear in strict alphabetical order. Should you be unable to find a compound in the dictionary, just break it down into its components and look these up separately. In this way the meaning of many compound expressions can be derived indirectly.

When using the dictionary you will notice many 'word families', or groups of words stemming from a common root, which have been collated within one article in order to save space:

**Einkaufs... – ~bummel – ~preis – ~wagen – ~zentrum**
**amend – amendment – amends**

## 2. Spelling

**2.1** Where American and British spelling of a word differs, the American spelling is given first as in

**center,** *Br* **centre**
**center** (*Br* **centre**) **forward**
**dialog,** *Br* **dialogue**
**analy|ze,** *Br* **-se** etc.

or in the English-German section as a separate headword, e.g. **theater, defense** etc.

A 'u' or an 'l' in parentheses in a word also indicates variant spellings:

**colo(u)red** means: American **colored,** British **coloured**
**travel(l)er** means: American **traveler,** British **traveller**

**2.2** Word division in a German word is possible after each syllable, e.g.

**ein-hül-len, Zu-cker, ba-cken, tes-ten**

In the English-German section the centered dots within a headword indicate syllabification breaks.

## 3. The different typefaces and their functions

**3.1 Bold type** is used for the German and English headwords and for Arabic numerals separating different parts of speech (nouns, transitive and intransitive verbs, adjectives and adverbs etc.) and different grammatical forms of a word:

**bieten 1.** *v/t* ... **2.** *v/i* ...
**hängen 1.** *v/i* (*irr, ge-, h*) hang (***an*** *dat* on...); **2.** *v/t* (*ge-, h*) hang (***an*** *acc* on)
**feed 1.** Futter *n* ; ... **2.** *v/t* füttern

**3.2** *Italics* are used for

a) grammatical and other abbreviations: *v/t*, *v/i*, *adj*, *adv*, *appr*, *fig* etc.
b) gender labels (masculine, feminine and neuter): *m*, *f*, *n*
c) grammatical references in brackets in the German-English section
d) any additional information preceding or following a translation (including dative or accusative objects):

**knacken** *v/t and v/i ... twig*: snap; *fire, radio*: crackle
**Etikett** *n* ... label (*a. fig*)
**Gedanke** *m* (*-n; -n*) ...
**geben** (*irr, ge-, h*) ...
**befolgen** ... follow, take (*advice*); observe (*rule etc*)
**file** ... *Briefe etc* ablegen
**labored** schwerfällig (*style etc*); mühsam (*breathing etc*)

**3.3** ***Boldface italics*** are used for phraseology etc., notes on German grammar and prepositions taken by the headword:

**Lage** *f* ... ***in der ~ sein zu*** *inf* be able to *inf*
**BLZ** ... *abbr of* ***Bankleitzahl***
**abheben** (*irr*, ***heben***, *sep, -ge-, h*)
**abfahren** ... (*irr*, ***fahren***, *sep, -ge-, sein*) leave, depart (*both*: ***nach*** for)
**line** ... ***hold the ~*** TEL bleiben Sie am Apparat
**agree** ... sich einigen (***on*** über *acc*)

**3.4** Normal type is used for translations of the headwords.

## 4. Pronunciation

When you have found the headword you are looking for in the German-English section, you will notice that very often this word is followed by certain symbols enclosed in square brackets. This is the phonetic transcription of the word, which tells you how it is pronounced. And one phonetic alphabet has come to be used internationally, namely that of the International Phonetic Association. This phonetic system is known by the abbreviation **IPA.** The symbols used in this dictionary are listed in the following tables on page 9 and 10.

**4.1** The length of vowels is indicated by [ː] following the vowel symbol.

**4.1.1** Stress is indicated by ['] or [ˌ] preceding the stressed syllable. ['] stands for strong stress, [ˌ] for weak stress:

**Kabel** ['kaːbəl] – **Kabine** [ka'biːnə]
**'nachsehen – Be'sitz – be'sprechen**
**Jus'tizminisˌterium – Mi'nisterpräsiˌdent**

**4.1.2** The glottal stop [ˀ] is the forced stop between one word or syllable and a following one beginning with a vowel, as in

**Analphabet** [anˀalfa'beːt]
**beeindrucken** [bə'ˀaindrʊkən]

**4.2** No transcription of compounds is given if the parts appear as separate entries. Each individual part should be looked up, as with

**'Blumenbeet** (= **Blume** and **Beet**)

## 4.3 Guide to pronunciation for the German-English section

### A. Vowels

[a] as in French *carte*: ***Mann*** [man]
[aː] as in *father*: ***Wagen*** ['vaːgən]
[e] as in *bed*: ***Tenor*** [te'noːɐ]
[eː] resembles the first sound in English [eɪ]: ***Weg*** [veːk]
[ə] unstressed e as in *ago*: ***Bitte*** ['bɪtə]
[ɛ] as in *fair*: ***männlich*** ['mɛnlɪç], ***Geld*** [gɛlt]
[ɛː] same sound but long: ***zählen*** ['tsɛːlən]
[ɪ] as in *it*: ***Wind*** [vɪnt]
[i] short, otherwise like [iː]: ***Kapital*** [kapi'taːl]
[iː] long, as in *meet*: ***Vieh*** [fiː]
[ɔ] as in *long*: ***Ort*** [ɔrt]
[o] as in *molest*: ***Moral*** [mo'raːl]
[oː] resembles the English sound in *go* [gəʊ] but without the [ʊ]: ***Boot*** [boːt]
[øː] as in French *feu*. The sound may be acquired by saying [e] through closely rounded lips: ***schön*** [ʃøːn]
[ø] same sound but short: ***ökumenisch*** [øku'meːnɪʃ]
[œ] as in French *neuf*. The sound resembles the English vowel in *her*. Lips, however, must be well rounded as for [ɒ]: ***öffnen*** ['œfnən]
[ʊ] as in *book*: ***Mutter*** ['mʊtɐ]
[u] short, otherwise like [uː]: ***Musik*** [mu'ziːk]
[uː] long, as in *boot*: ***Uhr*** [uːɐ]
[ʏ] short, opener than [yː]: ***Hütte*** ['hʏtə]
[y] almost like the French u as in *sur*. It may be acquired by saying [ɪ] through fairly closely rounded lips: ***Büro*** [by'roː]
[yː] same sound but long: ***führen*** ['fyːrən]

### B. Diphthongs

[aɪ] as in like: ***Mai*** [maɪ]
[aʊ] as in *mouse*: ***Maus*** [maʊs]
[ɔʏ] as in *boy*: ***Beute*** ['bɔʏtə], ***Läufer*** ['lɔʏfɐ]

### C. Consonants

[b] as in *better*: ***besser*** ['bɛsɐ]

[d] as in *dance*: ***du*** [duː]

[f] as in *find*: ***finden*** ['fɪndən], ***Vater*** ['faːtɐ], ***Philosoph*** [filo'zoːf]

[g] as in *gold*: ***Gold*** [gɔlt]

[ʒ] as in *measure*: ***Genie*** [ʒe'niː]

[h] as in *house* but not aspirated: ***Haus*** [haʊs]

[ç] an approximation to this sound may be acquired by assuming the mouth-configuration for [ɪ] and emitting a strong current of breath: ***Licht*** [lɪçt], ***Mönch*** [mœnç], ***lustig*** ['lʊstɪç]

[x] as in Scottish *loch*, Whereas [ç] is pronounced at the front of the mouth, [x] is pronounced in the throat: ***Loch*** [lɔx]

[j] as in *year*: ***ja*** [jaː]

[k] as in *kick*: ***keck*** [kɛk], ***Tag*** [taːk], ***Chronik*** ['kroːnɪk], ***Café*** [ka'feː]

[l] as in *lump*. Pronounced like English initial "clear l": ***lassen*** ['lasən]

[m] as in *mouse*: ***Maus*** [maʊs]

[n] as in *not*: ***nein*** [naɪn]

[ŋ] as in *sing*, *drink*: ***singen*** ['zɪŋən], ***trinken*** ['trɪŋkən]

[p] as in *pass*: ***Pass*** [pas], ***Trieb*** [triːp], ***obgleich*** [ɔp'glaɪç]

[r] as in *rot*. There are two pronunciations: the frontal or lingual r: ***rot*** [roːt] and the uvular r [ʁ] (unknown in the

English language): ***Mauer*** ['mauɐ]

[s] as in *miss*. Unvoiced when final, doubled, or next a voiceless consonant: ***Glas*** [gla:s], ***Masse*** ['masə], ***Mast*** [mast], ***nass*** [nas]

[z] as in *zero*. S voiced when initial in a word or syllable: ***Sohn*** [zo:n], ***Rose*** ['ro:zə]

[ʃ] as in *ship*: ***Schiff*** [ʃɪf], ***Charme*** [ʃarm], ***Spiel*** [ʃpi:l], ***Stein*** [ʃtaın]

[t] as in *tea*: ***Tee*** [te:], ***Thron*** [tro:n], ***Stadt*** [ʃtat], ***Bad*** [ba:t], ***Findling*** ['fɪntlɪŋ], ***Wind*** [vɪnt]

[v] as in *vast*: ***Vase*** ['va:ze], ***Winter*** ['vɪntɐ]

[ã, ɛ̃, õ] are nasalized vowels. Examples: ***Ensemble*** [ã'sã:bəl], ***Terrain*** [tɛ'rɛ̃:], ***Bonbon*** [bõ'bõ:]

## 4.3.1 Phonetic changes in plurals

| singular | | plural | | example |
|---|---|---|---|---|
| -g | [-k] | -ge | [-gə] | Flug – Flüge |
| -d | [-t] | -de | [-də] | Grund – Gründe, Abend – Abende |
| -b | [-p] | -be | [-bə] | Stab – Stäbe |
| -s | [-s] | -se | [-zə] | Los – Lose |
| -ch | [-x] | -che | [-çə] | Bach – Bäche |
| -iv | [-i:f] | -ive | [-i:və] | Stativ – Stative |

## 4.3.2 The German alphabet

a [a:], b [be:], c [tse:], d [de:], e [e:], f [ɛf], g [ge:], h [ha:], i [i:], j [jɔt], k [ka:], l [ɛl], m [ɛm], n [ɛn], o [o:], p [pe:], q [ku:], r [ɛr], s [ɛs], t [te:], u [u:], v [fau], w [ve:], x [ɪks], y ['ʏpsilɔn], z [tsɛt]

## 4.3.3 List of suffixes

The German suffixes are not transcribed unless they are parts of headwords.

| | |
|---|---|
| -bar | [-ba:ɐ] |
| -chen | [-çən] |
| -d | [-t] |
| -de | [-də] |
| -ei | [-aı] |
| -en | [-ən] |
| -end | [-ənt] |
| -er | [-ɐ] |
| -haft | [-haft] |
| -heit | [-haıt] |
| -icht | [-ɪçt] |
| -ie | [-i:] |
| -ieren | [-i:rən] |
| -ig | [-ɪç] |
| -ik | [-ɪk] |
| -in | [-ɪn] |
| -isch | [-ɪʃ] |
| -ist | [-ɪst] |
| -keit | [-kaıt] |
| -lich | [-lɪç] |
| -ling | [-lɪŋ] |
| -losigkeit | [-lo:zɪçkaıt] |
| -nis | [-nɪs] |
| -sal | [-za:l] |
| -sam | [-za:m] |
| -schaft | [-ʃaft] |
| -sieren | [-zi:rən] |
| -ste | [-stə] |
| -tät | [-tɛ:t] |
| -tum | [-tu:m] |
| -ung | [-ʊŋ] |
| -ungs- | [-ʊŋs-] |
| -wärts | [-vɛrts] |

## 5. The tilde (~)

**5.1** A symbol you will repeatedly come across in the dictionary articles is the so-called tilde (~), which serves as a replacement mark. For reasons of space, related words are often combined in groups with the help of the tilde. In these cases, the tilde represents either the complete headword or that part of the word up to a vertical line (|):

**Ski ... ~fahrer(in)** (= ***Skifahrer***, ***Skifahrerin***)
**Ess|löffel ... ~stäbchen** (= ***Essstäbchen***)
**jet ... ~ engine** (= ***jet engine***)
**natural| resources ... ~ science** (= ***natural science***)

**5.2** In the case of the phrases in boldface italics, the tilde represents the headword immediately preceding, which itself may also have been formed with the help of a tilde:

**kommen ...** ***zu spät ~*** (= ***kommen***)
**ange|bracht ... ~gossen ...** ***wie ~*** (= ***angegossen***) ***sitzen***
**foreign ... ~** (= ***foreign***) ***affairs***
**break ...** ***take a ~*** (= ***break***)

**6. Abbreviations** of grammatical terms and subject areas are designed to help the user choose the appropriate headword or translation of a word.

Words which are predominantly used in British English are marked by the abbreviation *Br*:

**Bürgersteig** *m* sidewalk, *Br* pavement
**girl guide** *Br* Pfadfinderin *f*

## List of abbreviations

| | |
|---|---|
| *a.* | *also*, auch |
| *abbr* | *abbreviation*, Abkürzung |
| *acc* | *accusative* (*case*), Akkusativ |
| *adj* | *adjective*, Adjektiv |
| *adv* | *adverb*, Adverb |
| AGR | *agriculture*, Landwirtschaft |
| *Am* | *American English*, amerikanisches Englisch |
| ANAT | *anatomy*, Anatomie |
| *appr* | *approximately*, etwa |
| ARCH | *architecture*, Architektur |
| *art* | *article*, Artikel |
| ASTR | *astrology*, Astrologie; *astronomy*, Astronomie |
| *attr* | *attributively* , attributiv |
| AVIAT | *aviation*, Luftfahrt |
| BIOL | *biology*, Biologie |
| BOT | *botany*, Botanik |
| *Br* | *British English*, britisches Englisch |
| CHEM | *chemistry*, Chemie |
| *cj* | *conjunction*, Konjunktion |
| *coll* | *collectively*, als Sammelwort |
| *comp* | *comparative*, Komparativ |
| *contp* | *contemptuously*, verächtlich |
| *cpds* | *compounds*, Zusammensetzungen |
| *dat* | *dative* (*case*), Dativ |
| ECON | *economy*, Wirtschaft |
| *e-e* | *a*(*n*), eine |
| e.g. | *for example*, zum Beispiel |
| ELECTR | *electrical engineering*, Elektrotechnik |
| *e-m* | *einem*, to a(n) |
| *e-n* | *einen*, a(n) |
| *e-r* | *einer*, of a(n), to a(n) |
| *e-s* | *eines*, of a(n) |
| *esp.* | *especially*, besonders |
| et., *et.* | etwas, *something* |
| *etc* | *et cetera*, *and so on*, usw., und so weiter |
| F | *colloquial*, umgangssprachlich |
| *f* | *feminine*, weiblich |
| *fig* | *figuratively*, übertragen |

| | |
|---|---|
| GASTR | *gastronomy*, Kochkunst |
| *gen* | *genitive* (*case*), Genitiv |
| GEOGR | *geography*, Geografie |
| GEOL | *geology*, Geologie |
| *ger* | *gerund*, Gerundium |
| GR | *grammar*, Grammatik |
| *h* | *haben*, have |
| *hist* | *historically*, historisch |
| HIST | *history*, Geschichte |
| HUMOR | *humorous*, humorvoll |
| *impers* | *impersonal*, unpersönlich |
| *indef* | *indefinite*, unbestimmt |
| *inf* | *infinitive* (*mood*), Infinitiv |
| *int* | *interjection*, Interjektion |
| *interr* | *interrogative*, fragend |
| *irr* | *irregular*, unregelmäßig |
| IT | *information technology*, Informationstechnologie |
| *j-m* | *jemandem*, to someone |
| *j-n* | *jemanden*, someone |
| *j-s* | *jemandes*, someone's |
| JUR | *jurisprudence*, Recht |
| LING | *linguistics*, Sprachwissenschaft |
| *lit* | *literary*, nur in der Schriftsprache vorkommend |
| *m* | *masculine*, männlich |
| MAR | *maritime term*, Schifffahrt |
| MATH | *mathematics*, Mathematik |
| *m-e* | *my*, meine |
| MED | *medicine*, Medizin |
| METEOR | *meteorology*, Meteorologie |
| MIL | *military term*, militärisch |
| MOT | *motoring*, Kraftfahrwesen |
| *m-r* | *meiner*, of my, to my |
| *mst* | *mostly* , *usually*, meistens |
| MUS | *music*, Musik |
| *n* | *neuter*, sächlich |
| *neg!* | *negative*, *usually considered offensive*, kann als beleidigend empfunden werden |
| *nom* | *nominative* (*case*), Nominativ |
| *num* | *numeral*, Zahlwort |

| | |
|---|---|
| OPT | *optics*, Optik |
| O.S., *o.s.* | *oneself*, sich |
| PAINT | *painting*, Malerei |
| PARL | *parliamentary term*, parlamentarischer Ausdruck |
| *pass* | *passive voice*, Passiv |
| PED | *pedagogy*, Schulwesen |
| *pers* | *personal*, persönlich |
| PHARM | *pharmacy*, Pharmazie |
| PHIL | *philosophy*, Philosophie |
| PHOT | *photography*, Fotografie |
| PHYS | *physics*, Physik |
| *pl* | *plural*, Plural |
| POET | *poetry*, Dichtung |
| POL | *politics*, Politik |
| POSS | *possessive*, besitzanzeigend |
| POST | *post and telecommunications*, Postwesen |
| *pp* | *past participle*, Partizip Perfekt |
| *pred* | *predicative*, prädikativ |
| *pres* | *present*, Präsens |
| *pres p* | *present participle*, Partizip Präsens |
| *pret* | *preterit(e)*, Präteritum |
| PRINT | *printing*, Druckwesen |
| *pron* | *pronoun*, Pronomen |
| *prp* | *preposition*, Präposition |
| PSYCH | *psychology*, Psychologie |
| RAIL | *railroad*, *railway*, Eisenbahn |
| *refl* | *reflexive*, reflexiv |
| REL | *religion*, Religion |
| RHET | *rhetoric*, Rhetorik |
| *s-e* | *seine*, his, one's |
| *sep* | *separable*, abtrennbar |
| *sg* | *singular*, Singular |
| *sl* | *slang*, Slang |
| *s-m* | *seinem*, to his, to one's |
| *s-n* | *seinen*, his, one's |
| s.o., *s.o.* | *someone*, jemand(en) |
| SPORT | *sports*, Sport |
| *s-r* | *seiner*, of his, of one's, to his, to one's |
| *s-s* | *seines*, of his, of one's |
| s.th., *s.th.* | *something*, etwas |
| *su* | *substantive*, Substantiv |
| *subj* | *subjunctive* (*mood*), Konjunktiv |
| *sup* | *superlative*, Superlativ |
| TECH | *technology*, Technik |
| TEL | *telephony*, Telefon; *telecommunications*, Telekommunikation |
| THEA | *theater*, Theater |
| TV | *television*, Fernsehen |
| u., *u.* | *und*, and |
| UNIV | *university*, Hochschulwesen |
| V | *vulgar*, vulgär, unanständig |
| *v/aux* | *auxiliary verb*, Hilfsverb |
| *vb* | *verb*, Verb |
| VET | *veterinary medicine*, Veterinärmedizin, Tiermedizin |
| *v/i* | *intransitive verb*, intransitives Verb |
| *v/refl* | *reflexive verb*, reflexives Verb |
| *v/t* | *transitive verb*, transitives Verb |
| ZO | *zoology*, Zoologie |
| → | *see*, *refer to*, siehe |
| ® | *registered trademark*, eingetragene Marke |

## 7. Translations and phraseology

After the boldface headword in the German-English section, the phonetic transcription of this word, its part of speech label, and its grammar, we finally come to the most important part of the entry: **the translation(s).**

**7.1** It is quite rare for a headword to be given just one translation. Usually a word will have several related translations, which are separated by a **comma.**

**7.2** Different senses of a word are indicated by

a) **semicolons:**

**Fest** ... celebration; party; REL festival
**balance** ... Waage *f*; Gleichgewicht *n*

b) italics for **definitions:**

**Läufer** ... runner (*a . carpet* ); *chess*: bishop
**call** ... Berufung *f* (***to*** in *ein Amt*; auf *einen Lehrstuhl*)
**cake** ... Tafel *f Schokolade*, Stück *n Seife*

c) **abbreviations** of subject areas:

**Bug** *m* ... MAR bow; AVIAT nose
**Gespräch** *n* talk (*a.* POL); ... TEL call
**daisy** BOT Gänseblümchen *n*
**duck** ... ZO Ente *f*

**7.2.1** Where a word has fundamentally different meanings, it very often appears as two or more separate entries distinguished by **exponents** or raised figures:

**betreten**[1] *v/t* ... step on; enter
**betreten**[2] *adj* embarrassed
**Bauer**[1] *m* ... farmer
**Bauer**[2] *n*, *m* ... (bird)cage
**chap**[1] ... Riss *m*
**chap**[2] ... *Br* F Bursche *m*

This does not apply to senses which have directly evolved from the primary meaning of the word.

**7.3** When a headword can be several different parts of speech, these are distinguished by boldface **Arabic numerals** (see also the section on p.7, paragraph 3.1 concerning the different typefaces):

**geräuschlos** 1. *adj* noiseless (*adjective*)
2. without a sound (*adverb*)

**work** 1. Arbeit *f* (*noun*)
2. *v/i* arbeiten (*verb*)

**green** 1. grün (*adjective*)
2. Grün *n* (*noun*)

**7.3.1** In the German-English section boldface Arabic numerals are also used to distinguish between transitive, intransitive and reflexive verbs (if this affects their translation) and to show that where there is a change of meaning a verb may be differently conjugated:

**fahren** (*irr*, *ge-*) **1.** *v/i* (*sein*) go; *bus etc*: run; ... **2.** *v/t* (*h*) drive (*car etc*) ...

If grammatical indications come before the subdivision they refer to all translations that follow:

**bauen** (*ge-*, *h*) **1.** *v/t* build ...; **2.** *fig v/i*: ~ ***auf*** ...

**7.3.2** Boldface Arabic numerals are also used to indicate the different meanings of nouns which can occur in more than one gender and to show that where there is a change of meaning a noun may be differently inflected:

**Halfter 1.** *m*, *n* (*-s*; -) halter; **2.** *n* (*-s*; -), *f* (-; *-n*) holster

**7.4 Illustrative phrases** in boldface italics are generally given within the respective categories of the dictionary article:

**baden 1.** *v/i* ... ~ ***gehen*** go swimming; **2.** *v/t* ...
**good 1.** ... ***real*** ~ F echt gut (= *adjective* ); **2.** ... ***for*** ~ für immer (= *noun*)

## 8. Grammatical references

Knowing what to do with the grammatical information available in the dictionary will enable the user to get the most out of this dictionary.

**8.1 verbs** (see the list of irregular German verbs on page 654).

Verbs have been treated in the following ways:

a) **bändigen** *v/t* (*ge-*, *h*)

The past participle of this word is formed by means of the prefix *ge-* and the auxiliary verb *haben*: ***er hat gebändigt.***

b) **abfassen** *v/t* (*sep*, *-ge-*, *h*)

In conjugation the prefix *ab* must be separated from the primary verb *fassen*: ***sie fasst ab***; ***sie hat abgefasst.***

c) **finden** *v/t* (*irr*, *ge-*, *h*)

*irr* following a verb means that it is an irregular verb. The principal parts of this particular word can be found as an individual headword in the main part of the German-English section and in the list of irregular German verbs on page 654: ***sie fand***; ***sie hat gefunden.***

d) **abfallen** *v/i* (*irr*, ***fallen***, *sep*, *-ge-*, *sein*)

A reference such as *irr*, ***fallen*** indicates that the compound word ***abfallen*** is conjugated in exactly the same way as the primary verb ***fallen*** as given in the list of irregular German verbs on page 654: ***er fiel ab***; ***er ist abgefallen.***

e) **senden** *v/t* ([*irr*,] *ge-*, *h*)

The square brackets indicate that ***senden*** can be treated as a regular or an irregular verb: ***sie sandte*** or ***sie sendete***; ***sie hat gesandt*** or ***sie hat gesendet.***

## 8.2 nouns

The inflectional forms (*genitive singular*; *nominative plural*) follow immediately after the indication of gender. No forms are given for compounds if the parts appear as separate headwords.

The horizontal stroke replaces the part of the word which remains unchanged in the inflection:

**Affäre** *f* (-; *-n*)
**Keks** *m*, *n* (*-es*; *-e*)
**Bau** *m* (-[*e*]*s*; *Bauten*)
**Blatt** *n* (-[*e*]*s*; *Blätter* ['blɛtɐ])

The inflectional forms of German nouns ending in ***-in*** are given in the following ways:

**Ärztin** *f* (-; *-nen*)
**Chemiker(in)** (*-s*; -/-; *-nen*) = **Chemiker** *m* (*-s*; -) and **Chemikerin** *f* (-; *-nen*)

### 8.3 Prepositions

If, for instance, a headword (verb, adjective or noun) is governed by certain prepositions, these are given in boldface italics and in brackets together with their English or German translations and placed next to the appropriate translation. If the German or English preposition is the same for all or several translations, it is given only once before or after the first translation and then also applies to the translations which follow it:

**abrücken ... 1.** *v/t* (*h*) move away (***von*** from)
**befestigen** *v/t* (*no -ge-, h*) fasten (***an*** *dat* to), fix (to), attach (to)
**dissent ... 2.** anderer Meinung sein (***from*** als)
**dissimilar** (***to***) unähnlich (*dat*); verschieden (von)

With German prepositions which can take the dative or the accusative, the case is given in brackets:

**fürchten ...** ***sich ~*** **...** be afraid (***vor*** *dat* of)
**bauen ... ~** ***auf*** (*acc*) rely *or* count on

We hope that this somewhat lengthy introduction has shown you that this dictionary contains a great deal more than simple one-to-one translations, and that you are now well-equipped to make the most of all it has to offer.

# GERMAN – ENGLISH

# A

**à** [a] *prp* ***5 Karten ~ 20 Euro*** 5 tickets at 20 euros each *or* a piece
**Aal** [aːl] *m* (-[*e*]*s*; -*e*) zo eel
**aalen** ['aːlən] *v/refl* (*ge-*, *h*) ***sich in der Sonne ~*** bask in the sun
**'aal'glatt** *fig adj* (as) slippery as an eel
**Aas** [aːs] *n* (-[*e*]*s*) *no pl* carrion; F *contp pl* ***Äser*** beast, *sl* bastard
**'Aasgeier** *m* zo vulture (*a. fig*)
**ab** [ap] *prp and adv*: ***München ~ 13.55*** departure from Munich (at) 1.55; ***~ 7 Uhr*** from 7 o'clock (on); ***~ morgen*** (***1. März***) starting tomorrow (March 1st); ***von jetzt ~*** from now on; ***~ und zu*** now and then; ***ein Film ~ 18*** an X (-rated) film; ***ein Knopf ist ~*** a button has come off
**'abarbeiten** *v/t* (*sep*, *-ge-*, *h*) work out *or* off (*debts*); ***sich ~*** wear o.s. out
**Abart** ['apˀart] *f* (-; *en*) variety
**abartig** ['apˀartɪç] *adj* abnormal
**Abb.** *abbr of* ***Abbildung*** fig., illustration
**'Abbau** *m* (-[*e*]*s*; *no pl*) mining; TECH dismantling; *fig* overcoming (*of prejudices etc*); reduction (*of expenditure, staff etc*); **'abbauen** *v/t* (*sep*, *-ge-*, *h*) mine; TECH dismantle; *fig* overcome (*prejudices etc*); reduce (*expenditure, staff etc*); ***sich ~*** BIOL break down
**'abbeißen** *v/t* (*irr*, ***beißen***, *sep*, *-ge-*, *h*) bite off
**'abbeizen** *v/t* (*sep*, *-ge-*, *h*) remove *old paint etc* with corrosives
**'abbekommen** *v/t* (*irr*, ***kommen***, *sep*, *no -ge-*, *h*) get off; ***s-n Teil*** *or* ***et. ~*** get one's share; ***et. ~*** *fig* get hurt, get damaged
**'abberufen** *v/t* (*irr*, ***rufen***, *sep*, *no -ge-*, *h*), **'Abberufung** *f* recall
**'abbestellen** *v/t* (*sep*, *no -ge-*, *h*) cancel one's subscription (*or* order) for
**'Abbestellung** *f* cancellation
**'abbiegen** *v/i* (*irr*, ***biegen***, *sep*, *-ge-*, *sein*) turn (off); ***nach rechts*** (***links***) ***~*** turn right (left)
**'abbilden** *v/t* (*sep*, *-ge-*, *h*) show, depict
**'Abbildung** *f* (-; *-en*) picture, illustration
**'Abbitte** *f* apology; ***j-m ~ leisten wegen*** apologize to s.o. for
**'abblasen** F *v/t* (*irr*, ***blasen***, *sep*, *-ge-*, *h*) call off, cancel
**'abblättern** *v/i* (*sep*, *-ge-*, *sein*) *paint etc*: flake off
**'abblenden** **1.** *v/t* (*sep*, *-ge-*, *h*) dim **2.** *v/i* MOT dim (*Br* dip) the headlights
**'Abblendlicht** *n* MOT dimmed (*Br* dipped) headlights *pl*, low beam
**'abbrechen** *v/t* (*irr*, ***brechen***, *sep*, *-ge-*) **1.** *v/t* (*h*) break off (*a. fig*); pull down, demolish (*building etc*); strike (*camp, tent*) **2.** *v/i* (*sein*) break off; (*h*) *fig* stop; 'abbremsen *v/t* (*sep*, *-ge-*, *h*) slow down; **'abbrennen** *v/t* (*irr*, ***brennen***, *sep*, *-ge-*) **1.** *v/i* (*sein*) burn down **2.** *v/t* (*h*) burn down (*building etc*); let *or* set off (*fireworks*); **'abbringen** *v/t* (*irr*, ***bringen***, *sep*, *-ge-*, *h*) ***j-n von e-r Sache ~*** talk s.o. out of (doing) s.th.; ***j-n vom Thema ~*** get s.o. off a subject
**'Abbruch** *m* (-[*e*]*s*; *no pl*) breaking off; demolition; **'abbruchreif** *adj* derelict, due for demolition
**'abbuchen** *v/t* (*sep*, *-ge-*, *h*) debit (***von*** to); **'Abbuchung** *f* debit
**'abbürsten** *v/t* (*sep*, *-ge-*, *h*) brush off (*dust etc*); brush (*coat etc*)
**Abc** [aːbeː'tseː] *n* (-; *no pl*) ABC, alphabet; **ABC-Waffen** *pl* MIL nuclear, biological and chemical weapons
**'abdanken** *v/i* (*sep*, *-ge-*, *h*) resign; *king etc*: abdicate; **'Abdankung** *f* (-; *-en*) resignation; abdication
**'abdecken** *v/t* (*sep*, *-ge-*, *h*) uncover; untile (*roof*); unroof (*house*); clear (*the table*); ECON cover (up)
**'abdichten** *v/t* (*sep*, *-ge-*, *h*) TECH seal
**'abdrängen** *v/t* (*sep*, *-ge-*, *h*) push aside
**'abdrehen** **1.** *v/t* (*sep*, *-ge-*, *h*) turn *or* switch off (*light, water etc*) **2.** *v/i* (*a. sein*) *ship, plane*: change one's course
**'Abdruck** *m* print, mark
**'abdrucken** *v/t* (*sep*, *-ge-*, *h*) print
**'abdrücken** (*sep*, *-ge-*, *h*) **1.** *v/t* fire (*gun*) **2.** *v/i* pull the trigger
**Abend** ['aːbənt] *m* (*-s*; *-e*) evening; ***am ~*** in the evening, at night; ***heute ~*** tonight; ***morgen*** (***gestern***) ***~*** tomorrow (last) night; → ***bunt***, ***essen***; **~brot** *n* (-[*e*]*s*; *no pl*), **~essen** *n* supper, dinner, *Br a.* high tea; **~kasse** *f* THEA *etc* box

office; **~kleid** *n* evening dress *or* gown; **~kurs** *m* evening classes *pl*

ˈ**Abendland** *n* (-[*e*]*s*; *no pl*) West, Occident; ˈ**abendländisch** [ˈaːbəntlɛndɪʃ] *adj* Western, Occidental

ˈ**Abendmahl** *n* (-[*e*]*s*; *no pl*) *the* (Holy) Communion, *the* Lord's Supper; ***das ~ empfangen*** receive Communion

**abends** [ˈaːbənts] *adv* in the evening, at night; ***dienstags ~*** (on) Tuesday evenings

ˈ**Abendschule** *f* evening classes *pl*, night school

**Abenteuer** [ˈaːbəntɔʏɐ] *n* (-*s*; -) adventure (*a. in cpds …ferien, …spielplatz*)

ˈ**abenteuerlich** *adj* adventurous; *fig* risky; fantastic

**Abenteurer** [ˈaːbəntɔʏrɐ] *m* (-*s*; -) adventurer; ˈ**Abenteurerin** [ˈaːbəntɔʏrərɪn] *f* (-; -*nen*) adventuress

**aber** [ˈaːbɐ] *cj and adv* but; ***oder ~*** or else; **~, ~!** now then!; ***~ nein!*** not at all!

ˈ**Aberglaube** *m* superstition

**abergläubisch** [ˈaːbɐglɔʏbɪʃ] *adj* superstitious

ˈ**aberkennen** *v/t* (*irr*, ***kennen***, *sep*, *no -ge-*, *h*) ***j-m et. ~*** deprive s.o. of s.th. (*a.* JUR); ˈ**Aberkennung** *f* (-; -*en*) deprivation (*a.* JUR)

**abermalig** [ˈaːbɐmaːlɪç] *adj* repeated

**abermals** [ˈaːbɐmaːls] *adv* once more *or* again

ˈ**aberˈtausend** *adj*: ***tausende und ~e*** thousands upon thousands

ˈ**abfahren** (*irr*, ***fahren***, *sep*, *-ge-*) **1.** *v/i* (*sein*) leave, depart (*both*: ***nach*** for); F (***voll***) ***~ auf*** (*acc*) really go for **2.** *v/t* (*h*) carry *or* cart away

ˈ**Abfahrt** *f* departure (***nach*** for), start (for); *skiing*: descent

ˈ**Abfahrts|lauf** *m* downhill skiing (*or* race); **~zeit** *f* (time of) departure

ˈ**Abfall** *m* waste, refuse, garbage, trash, *Br a.* rubbish; **~beseitigung** *f* waste disposal; **~eimer** *m* → ***Mülleimer***

ˈ**abfallen** *v/i* (*irr*, ***fallen***, *sep*, *-ge-*, *sein*) fall (off); *terrain*: slope (down); *fig* fall away (***von*** from); *esp* POL secede (from); ***vom Glauben ~*** renounce one's faith; ***~ gegen*** compare badly with

ˈ**abfällig 1.** *adj* derogatory **2.** *adv*: ***~ von j-m sprechen*** run s.o. down

ˈ**Abfallpro,dukt** *n* waste product

ˈ**abfälschen** *v/t* (*sep*, *-ge-*, *h*) SPORT deflect; ˈ**abfangen** *v/t* (*irr*, ***fangen***, *sep*, *-ge-*, *h*) catch, intercept; MOT, AVIAT right; ˈ**abfärben** *v/i* (*sep*, *-ge-*, *h*) *color etc*: run, *material*: *a.* bleed; *fig* ***~ auf*** (*acc*) rub off on; ˈ**abfassen** *v/t* (*sep*, *-ge-*, *h*) compose, word, write

ˈ**abfertigen** *v/t* (*sep*, *-ge-*, *h*) dispatch; *customs*: clear; serve (*customers*); check in (*passengers etc*); ***j-n kurz ~*** be short with s.o.; ˈ**Abfertigung** *f* dispatch; clearance; check-in

ˈ**abfeuern** *v/t* (*sep*, *-ge-*, *h*) fire (off); launch (*rocket*)

ˈ**abfinden** *v/t* (*irr*, ***finden***, *sep*, *-ge-*, *h*) ECON pay off (*creditor*); buy out (*partner*); compensate; ***sich mit e-r Sache ~*** put up with s.th.; ˈ**Abfindung** *f* (-; -*en*) ECON satisfaction; compensation

ˈ**abflachen** *v/t and v/refl* (*sep*, *-ge-*, *h*) flatten; ˈ**abflauen** *v/i* (*sep*, *-ge-*, *sein*) *wind etc*: drop (*a. fig*); ˈ**abfliegen** *v/i* (*irr*, ***fliegen***, *sep*, *-ge-*, *sein*) AVIAT leave, depart; ˈ**abfließen** *v/i* (*irr*, ***fließen***, *sep*, *-ge-*, *sein*) flow off, drain (off *or* away)

ˈ**Abflug** *m* AVIAT departure

ˈ**Abfluss** *m* (-*es*; *Abflüsse*) *no pl* flowing off; TECH drain

ˈ**Abflussrohr** *n* wastepipe, drain(pipe)

ˈ**abfragen** *v/t* (*sep*, *-ge-*, *h*) quiz *or* question *s.o.* (***über*** *acc* about), test *s.o.* orally

**Abfuhr** [ˈapfuːɐ] *f* (-; -*en*) removal; ***j-m e-e ~ erteilen*** rebuff (F SPORT lick) s.o.

ˈ**abführen** (*sep*, *-ge-*, *h*) **1.** *v/t* lead *or* take away; ECON pay (over) (***an*** *acc* to); **2.** *v/i* MED move one's bowels; act as a laxative; ˈ**abführend** *adj*, ˈ**Abführmittel** *n* MED laxative

ˈ**abfüllen** *v/t* (*sep*, *-ge-*, *h*) bottle; can

ˈ**Abgabe** *f* (-; -*n*) *no pl* handing in; SPORT pass; ECON rate; duty

ˈ**abgabenfrei** *adj* tax-free

ˈ**abgabenpflichtig** *adj* dutiable

ˈ**Abgang** *m* (-[*e*]*s*; *Abgänge*) *no pl* departure; *Am* graduation, *Br* school-leaving; THEA exit (*a. fig*); SPORT dismount; **Abgänger** [ˈapgɛŋɐ] *m* (-*s*; -) *Am* graduate, *Br* school-leaver

ˈ**Abgas** *n* waste gas; *pl* emission(s *pl*); MOT exhaust fumes *pl*

ˈ**abgasfrei** *adj* emission-free

ˈ**Abgasuntersuchung** *f* MOT *Am* emissions test, *Br* exhaust emission test

ˈ**abgearbeitet** *adj* worn out

'**abgeben** *v/t* (*irr*, ***geben***, *sep*, *-ge-*, *h*) leave (***bei*** with); hand in; deposit (*one's baggage etc*), hand over (*ticket etc*) (***an*** *acc* to); cast (*vote*); pass (*ball*); *give* off, emit (*heat etc*); make (*offer, statement etc*); ***j-m et. ~ von*** share s.th. with s.o.; ***sich ~ mit*** concern o.s. with *s.th.*, associate with *s.o.*

'**abge|brannt** *adj* burnt down; F *fig* broke; **~brüht** *fig adj* hard-boiled; **~droschen** *adj* hackneyed; **~fahren** *adj tires*: worn out; **~griffen** *adj* worn; **~hackt** *fig adj* disjointed; **~hangen** *adj*: ***gut ~es Fleisch*** well-hung meat; **~härtet** *adj* hardened (***gegen*** to)

'**abgehen** *v/i* (*irr*, ***gehen***, *sep*, *-ge-*, *sein*) *train etc*: leave; *mail, goods*: get off; THEA go off (stage); *button etc*: come off; *path etc*: branch off; ***von der Schule ~*** leave school; ***~ von*** drop (*plan etc*); ***von s-r Meinung ~*** change one's mind *or* opinion; ***ihm geht … ab*** he lacks …; ***gut ~*** end well, pass off well

'**abge|hetzt**, **~kämpft** *adj* exhausted, worn out; **~kartet** ['apgəkartət] F *adj*: ***~e Sache*** put-up job; **~legen** *adj* remote, distant; **~macht** *adj* fixed; ***~!*** it's a deal!; **~magert** *adj* emaciated; **~neigt** *adj*: ***e-r Sache ~ sein*** be averse to s.th.; ***ich wäre nicht ~, et. zu tun*** I wouldn't mind doing s.th.; **~nutzt** *adj* worn out

**Abgeordnete** ['apgəˀɔrdnətə] *m*, *f* (*-n*; *-n*) *Am* representative, congress|man (-woman), *Br* Member of Parliament (*abbr* MP); '**Abgeordnetenhaus** *n Am* House of Representatives, *Br* House of Commons

'**abgepackt** *adj* prepack(ag)ed

'**abgeschieden** *adj* secluded

'**Abgeschiedenheit** *f* (*-*; *no pl*) seclusion

'**abge|schlossen** *adj* completed; ***~e Wohnung*** self-contained apartment (*Br* flat); **~sehen** *adj*: ***~ von*** aside (*Br a.* apart) from; ***ganz ~ von*** not to mention, let alone; **~spannt** *adj* exhausted, weary; **~standen** *adj* stale; **~storben** *adj* dead (*tree etc*); numb (*leg etc*); **~stumpft** *adj* insensitive, indifferent (***gegen*** to); **~tragen**, **~wetzt** *adj* worn out; threadbare, shabby

**abgewöhnen** *v/t* (*sep*, *-ge-*, *h*) ***j-m et. ~*** make s.o. give up s.th.; ***sich*** (*dat*) ***das Rauchen ~*** stop *or* give up smoking

'**Abgott** *m* idol (*a. fig*); **abgöttisch** ['apgœtɪʃ] *adv*: ***j-n ~ lieben*** idolize s.o.

'**abgrasen** *v/t* (*sep*, *-ge-*, *h*) graze; *fig* scour

'**abgrenzen** *v/t* (*sep*, *-ge-*, *h*) mark off; delimit (***gegen*** from)

'**Abgrund** *m* abyss, chasm, gulf (*all a. fig*); ***am Rande des ~s*** *fig* on the brink of disaster; '**abgrund'tief** *adj* abysmal

'**abgucken** F *v/t* (*sep*, *-ge-*, *h*) ***j-m et. ~*** learn s.th. from (watching) s.o.; → ***abschreiben***

'**Abguss** *m* cast

'**abhaben** F *v/t* (*irr*, ***haben***, *sep*, *-ge-*, *h*) ***willst du et. ~?*** do you want some (of it)? '**abhacken** *v/t* (*sep*, *-ge-*, *h*) chop *or* cut off; '**abhaken** *v/t* (*sep*, *-ge-*, *h*) check (*Br* tick) off; F forget; '**abhalten** *v/t* (*irr*, ***halten***, *sep*, *-ge-*, *h*) hold (*meeting etc*); ***j-n von der Arbeit ~*** keep s.o. from his work; ***j-n davon ~, et. zu tun*** keep s.o. from doing s.th.

'**abhandeln** *v/t* (*sep*, *-ge-*, *h*) treat (*subject etc*); ***j-m et. ~*** make a deal with s.o. for s.th.; '**Abhandlung** *f* treatise (***über*** *acc* on)

'**Abhang** *m* slope

'**abhängen**[1] *v/t* (*sep*, *-ge-*, *h*) take down (*picture etc*); RAIL *etc* uncouple; F shake *s.o.* off

'**abhängen**[2] *v/i* (*irr*, ***hängen***, *sep*, *-ge-*, *h*) ***~ von*** depend on; ***das hängt davon ab*** that depends

**abhängig** ['aphɛŋɪç] *adj*: ***~ von*** dependent on; *a.* addicted to *drugs etc*

'**Abhängigkeit** *f* (*-*; *-en*) dependence (***von*** on); addiction (to)

'**abhärten** *v/t* (*sep*, *-ge-*, *h*) ***sich ~*** harden o.s. (***gegen*** to)

'**abhauen** (*irr*, ***hauen***, *sep*, *-ge-*) **1.** *v/t* (*h*) cut *or* chop off **2.** F *v/i* (*sein*) make off (***mit*** with), run away (with); ***hau ab!*** beat it!, scram!

'**abheben** (*irr*, ***heben***, *sep*, *-ge-*, *h*) **1.** *v/t* lift *or* take off; pick up (*receiver*); (with)draw (*money*); cut (*cards*); ***sich ~*** stand out (***von*** among, from), *fig a.* contrast with **2.** *v/i* cut the cards; answer the phone; *plane*: take (*esp rocket*: lift) off

'**abheften** *v/t* (*sep*, *-ge-*, *h*) file

'**abheilen** *v/i* (*sep*, *-ge-*, *sein*) heal (up)

'**abhetzen** *v/refl* (*sep*, *-ge-*, *h*) wear o.s.

out

ˈ**Abhilfe** *f* remedy; **~ *schaffen*** take remedial measures

ˈ**Abholdienst** *m* pickup service

ˈ**abholen** *v/t* (*sep*, *-ge-*, *h*) pick up, collect; ***j-n von der Bahn* ~** meet s.o. at the station; ˈ**abholzen** *v/t* (*sep*, *-ge-*, *h*) fell, cut down (*trees*); deforest (*area*); ˈ*abhorchen v/t* (*sep*, *-ge-*, *h*) MED auscultate, sound; ˈ**abhören** *v/t* (*sep*, *-ge-*, *h*) listen in on, tap (*telephone conversation*), F bug; → ***abfragen***

ˈ**Abhörgerät** *n* bugging device, F bug

**Abitur** [abiˈtuːɐ] *n* (*-s*; *-e*) school-leaving examination (qualifying for university entrance)

ˈ**abjagen** *v/t* (*sep*, *-ge-*, *h*) ***j-m et.* ~** recover s.th. from s.o.; ˈ**abkanzeln** F *v/t* (*sep*, *-ge-*, *h*) tell *s.o.* off; ˈ**abkaufen** *v/t* (*sep*, *-ge-*, *h*) ***j-m et.* ~** buy s.th. from s.o.

**Abkehr** [ˈapkeːɐ] *f* (*-*; *no pl*) break (***von*** with); ˈ**abkehren** *v/refl* (*sep*, *-ge-*, *h*) ***sich* ~ *von*** turn away from

ˈ**abklingen** *v/i* (*irr*, ***klingen***, *sep*, *-ge-*, *sein*) fade away; *pain etc*: ease off

ˈ**abklopfen** *v/t* (*sep*, *-ge-*, *h*) MED sound

ˈ**abknallen** F *v/t* (*sep*, *-ge-*, *h*) pick off

ˈ**abknicken** *v/t* (*sep*, *-ge-*, *h*) snap *or* break off; bend

ˈ**abkochen** *v/t* (*sep*, *-ge-*, *h*) boil

ˈ**abkommanˌdieren** *v/t* (*sep*, *no -ge-*, *h*) MIL detach (***zu*** for)

ˈ**abkommen** *v/i* (*irr*, ***kommen***, *sep*, *-ge-*, *sein*) **~ *von*** get off; drop (*plan etc*); ***vom Thema* ~** stray from the point; → ***Weg***

ˈ**Abkommen** *n* (*-s*; *-*) agreement, treaty; ***ein* ~ *schließen*** make an agreement

**Abkömmling** [ˈapkœmlɪŋ] *m* (*-s*; *-e*) descendant

ˈ**abkoppeln** *v/t* (*sep*, *-ge-*, *h*) uncouple (***von*** from); undock (*spacecraft*)

ˈ**abkratzen** (*sep*, *-ge-*) **1.** *v/t* (*h*) scrape off **2.** F *v/i* (*sein*) kick the bucket

ˈ**abkühlen** *v/t and v/refl* (*sep*, *-ge-*, *h*) cool down (*a. fig*)

ˈ**Abkühlung** *f* cooling

ˈ**abkürzen** *v/t* (*sep*, *-ge-*, *h*) shorten; abbreviate; ***den Weg* ~** take a short cut

ˈ**Abkürzung** *f* abbreviation; short cut

ˈ**abladen** *v/t* (*irr*, ***laden***, *sep*, *-ge-*, *h*) unload; dump (*waste etc*)

ˈ**Ablage** *f* (*-*; *-n*) *no pl* filing; filing tray; *Swiss* → ***Zweigstelle***

ˈ**ablagern** (*sep*, *-ge-*, *h*) **1.** *v/t* season (*wood*); let *wine* age; GEOL *etc* deposit; ***sich* ~** settle, be deposited **2.** *v/i* (*a. sein*) season; age; ˈ**Ablagerung** *f* (*-*; *-en*) CHEM, GEOL deposit, sediment

ˈ**ablassen** (*irr*, ***lassen***, *sep*, *-ge-*, *h*) **1.** *v/t* drain off (*liquid*); let off (*steam*); drain (*pond etc*) **2.** *v/i*: ***von et.* (*j-m*) ~** stop doing s.th. (leave s.o. alone)

ˈ**Ablauf** *m* (*-[e]s*; *Abläufe*) course; process; order of events; *no pl* expiration, *Br* expiry; → ***Abfluss***

ˈ**ablaufen** (*irr*, ***laufen***, *sep*, *-ge-*) **1.** *v/i* (*sein*) *water etc*: run off; *performance etc*: go, proceed; come to an end; *period*, *passport etc*: expire; *time*, *record*, *tape*: run out; *clock*: run down; ***gut* ~** turn out well **2.** *v/t* (*h*) wear down

ˈ**ablecken** *v/t* (*sep*, *-ge-*, *h*) lick (off)

ˈ**ablegen** (*sep*, *-ge-*, *h*) **1.** *v/t* take off (*clothes*); file (*letters etc*); give up (*habit etc*); take (*examination*, *oath*); ***abgelegte Kleider*** cast-offs *pl* **2.** *v/i* take off one's (hat and) coat; MAR put out, sail

ˈ**Ableger** *m* (*-s*; *-*) BOT layer; offshoot (*a. fig*)

ˈ**ablehnen** *v/t* (*sep*, *-ge-*, *h*) refuse; turn down (*application etc*); PARL reject; object to; condemn; **~d** *adj* negative

ˈ**Ablehnung** *f* (*-*; *-en*) refusal; rejection; objection (*gen* to)

ˈ**ableiten** *v/t* (*sep*, *-ge-*, *h*) divert; LING, MATH derive (***aus*** *dat*, ***von*** from) (*a. fig*)

ˈ**Ableitung** *f* diversion; LING, MATH derivation (*a. fig*)

ˈ**ablenken** *v/t* (*sep*, *-ge-*, *h*) divert (***von*** from); *soccer*: turn away (*ball*); deflect (*rays etc*); ***j-n von der Arbeit* ~** distract s.o. from his work; ***er lässt sich leicht* ~** he is easily diverted

ˈ**Ablenkung** *f* diversion

ˈ**ablesen** *v/t* (*irr*, ***lesen***, *sep*, *-ge-*, *h*) read

ˈ**abliefern** *v/t* (*sep*, *-ge-*, *h*) deliver (***bei*** to, at); hand over (to)

ˈ**ablösbar** *adj* detachable; ˈ**ablösen** *v/t* (*sep*, *-ge-*, *h*) detach; take off; take *s.o.'s* place, take over from *s.o.*; *esp* MIL relieve; replace; ***sich* ~** take turns (*driving etc*); ˈ**Ablösesumme** *f* SPORT transfer fee; ˈ**Ablösung** *f* relief

ˈ**abmachen** *v/t* (*sep*, *-ge-*, *h*) remove, take off; settle, arrange

ˈ**Abmachung** *f* (*-*; *-en*) arrangement, agreement, deal

**'abmagern** *v/i* (*sep*, *-ge-*, *sein*) get thin
**'Abmagerung** *f* (-; *-en*) emaciation
**'Abmagerungskur** *f* slimming diet
**'abmähen** *v/t* (*sep*, *-ge-*, *h*) mow
**'abmalen** *v/t* (*sep*, *-ge-*, *h*) copy
**'Abmarsch** *m* (-[*e*]*s*; *no pl*) start; MIL marching off; **'abmar,schieren** *v/i* (*sep*, *no -ge-*, *sein*) start; MIL march off
**'abmelden** *v/t* (*sep*, *-ge-*, *h*) cancel the registration of (*car etc*); cancel s.o.'s membership (*in a club etc*); give notice of s.o.'s withdrawal (from school); ***sich ~*** give notice of change of address; report off duty; **'Abmeldung** *f* notice of withdrawal; notice of change of address
**'abmessen** *v/t* (*irr*, ***messen***, *sep*, *-ge-*, *h*) measure; **'Abmessung** *f* measurement; *pl* dimensions
**'abmon,tieren** *v/t* (*sep*, *no -ge-*, *h*) take off; take down; TECH dismantle
**'abmühen** *v/refl* (*sep*, *-ge-*, *h*) work very hard; try hard (*to do s.th.*); struggle (***mit*** with)
**'abnagen** *v/t* (*sep*, *-ge-*, *h*) gnaw (at)
**Abnahme** ['apna:mə] *f* (-; *-n*) reduction, decrease; loss (*a. of weight*); ECON purchase; TECH acceptance
**'abnehmbar** *adj* removable
**'abnehmen** (*irr*, ***nehmen***, *sep*, *-ge-*, *h*) **1.** *v/t* take off (*a.* MED), remove; pick up (*receiver*); TECH accept; ECON buy; ***j-m et. ~*** take s.th. (away) from s.o. **2.** *v/i* decrease, diminish; lose weight; answer the phone; *moon*: wane
**'Abnehmer** *m* (*-s*; -) buyer; customer
**'Abneigung** *f* (***gegen***) dislike (of, for); aversion (to)
**abnorm** [ap'nɔrm] *adj* abnormal; exceptional, unusual; **Abnormität** [apnɔrmi'tɛ:t] *f* (-; *-en*) abnormality
**'abnutzen**, **'abnützen** *v/t and v/refl* (*sep*, *-ge-*, *h*) wear out
**'Abnutzung**, **'Abnützung** *f* (-; *no pl*) wear (and tear) (*a. fig*)
**Abonnement** [abɔnə'mã:] *n* (*-s*; *-s*) subscription (***auf*** *acc* to); **Abonnent** [abɔ'nɛnt] *m* (*-en*; *-en*) subscriber; THEA season-ticket holder; **abonnieren** [abɔ'ni:rən] *v/t* (*no -ge-*, *h*) subscribe to
**Abordnung** *f* (-; *-en*) delegation
**Abort** [a'bɔrt] *m* (-[*e*]*s*; *-e*) lavatory, toilet

**'abpassen** *v/t* (*sep*, *-ge-*, *h*) watch *or* wait for (*s.o.*, *s.th.*); waylay *s.o.* (*a. fig*)
**'abpfeifen** *v/t and v/i* (*irr*, ***pfeifen***, *sep*, *-ge-*, *h*) SPORT blow the final whistle; stop the game
**'abplagen** *v/refl* (*sep*, *-ge-*, *h*) struggle (***mit*** with)
**'abprallen** *v/i* (*sep*, *-ge-*, *sein*) rebound, bounce (off); *bullet*: ricochet
**'abputzen** *v/t* (*sep*, *-ge-*, *h*) wipe off; clean
**'abraten** *v/i* (*irr*, ***raten***, *sep*, *-ge-*, *h*) ***j-m ~ von*** advise *or* warn s.o. against
**'abräumen** *v/t* (*sep*, *-ge-*, *h*) clear away; clear (*the table*)
**'abrea,gieren** *v/t* (*sep*, *no -ge-*, *h*) work off (*one's anger etc*) (***an*** *dat* on); ***sich ~*** F let off steam
**'abrechnen** (*sep*, *-ge-*, *h*) **1.** *v/t* deduct, subtract; claim (*expenses*) **2.** *v/i*: ***mit j-m ~*** settle accounts (*fig a.* get even) with s.o.; **'Abrechnung** *f* settlement; F *fig* showdown
**'abreiben** *v/t* (*irr*, ***reiben***, *sep*, *-ge-*, *h*) rub off; rub down (*body*); polish
**'Abreise** *f* departure (***nach*** for)
**'abreisen** *v/i* (*sep*, *-ge-*, *sein*) depart, leave, start, set out (*all*: ***nach*** for)
**'Abreisetag** *m* day of departure
**'abreißen** (*irr*, ***reißen***, *sep*, *-ge-*) **1.** *v/t* (*h*) tear *or* pull off; pull down (*building*) **2.** *v/i* (*sein*) break; *button etc*: come off
**'Abreißka,lender** *m* tear-off calendar
**'abrichten** *v/t* (*sep*, *-ge-*, *h*) train (*animal*), *a.* break *a horse* in
**'abriegeln** *v/t* (*sep*, *-ge-*, *h*) block off, cordon off
**'Abriss** *m* (*-es*; *-e*) (*no pl*) demolition; outline, summary
**'abrollen** *v/i* (*sep*, *-ge-*, *sein*) *and v/t* (*h*) unroll (*a. fig*)
**'abrücken** (*sep*, *-ge-*) **1.** *v/t* (*h*) move away (***von*** from); **2.** *v/i* (*sein*) draw away (***von*** from); MIL march off
**'Abruf** *m*: ***auf ~*** ECON on call
**'abrufen** *v/t* (*irr*, ***rufen***, *sep*, *-ge-*, *h*) call away; IT recall, fetch, retrieve
**'abrunden** *v/t* (*sep*, *-ge-*, *h*) round (off)
**'abrupfen** *v/t* (*sep*, *-ge-*, *h*) pluck (off)
**abrupt** [ap'rʊpt] *adj* abrupt
**'abrüsten** *v/i* (*sep*, *-ge-*, *h*) MIL disarm
**'Abrüstung** *f* (-; *no pl*) MIL disarmament
**'abrutschen** *v/i* (*sep*, *-ge-*, *sein*) slide down; slip (off) (***von*** from)

**ABS** [aːbeːˈɛs] → ***Antiblockiersystem***

**Absage** [ˈapzaːgə] *f* (-; *-n*) refusal; cancellation; ˈ**absagen** (*sep*, *-ge-*, *h*) **1.** *v/t* call off, cancel (*event etc*) **2.** *v/i* call off; ***j-m ~ a.*** cancel one's appointment with s.o.; decline (the invitation)

ˈ**absägen** *v/t* (*sep*, *-ge-*, *h*) saw off; F *fig* oust, sack *s.o.*

ˈ**absahnen** F *v/i* (*sep*, *-ge-*, *h*) cash in

ˈ**Absatz** *m* paragraph; ECON sales *pl*; *shoe*: heel; *stairs*: landing

ˈ**abschaben** *v/t* (*sep*, *-ge-*, *h*) scrape off

ˈ**abschaffen** *v/t* (*sep*, *-ge-*, *h*) do away with, abolish; repeal (*law*); put an end to (*abuses etc*); ˈ**Abschaffung** *f* (-; *no pl*) abolition; repeal

ˈ**abschalten** (*sep*, *-ge-*, *h*) **1.** *v/t* switch *or* turn off **2.** F *v/i* relax, switch off

ˈ**abschätzen** *v/t* (*sep*, *-ge-*, *h*) estimate; assess; size up; **abschätzig** [ˈapʃɛtsɪç] *adj* contemptuous; derogatory

**Abschaum** *m* (*-s*; *no pl*) scum (*a. fig*)

ˈ**Abscheu** *m* (*-s*; *no pl*) disgust (***vor, gegen*** at, for); ***e-n ~ haben vor*** abhor, detest; ***~ erregend*** → ***abscheuerregend***; ˈ**abscheuerregend** *adj* revolting, repulsive

**ab**ˈ**scheulich** *adj* abominable, despicable (*a. person*), *a.* atrocious (*crime*)

ˈ**abschicken** *v/t* (*sep*, *-ge-*, *h*) → ***absenden***

ˈ**abschieben** *fig v/t* (*irr*, ***schieben***, *sep*, *-ge-*, *h*) push away; get rid of; deport; ***et. auf j-n ~*** shove s.th. off on (to) s.o.

**Abschied** [ˈapʃiːt] *m* (*-[e]s*; *-e*) parting, farewell; ***~ nehmen*** (***von***) say goodbye (to), take leave (of); ***s-n ~ nehmen*** resign, retire

ˈ**Abschiedsfeier** *f* farewell party

ˈ**Abschiedskuss** *m* goodbye kiss

ˈ**abschießen** *v/t* (*irr*, ***schießen***, *sep*, *-ge-*, *h*) shoot off (AVIAT down); launch (*rocket*); shoot, kill (*deer*); F pick *s.o.* off; *fig* oust; get rid of *s.o.*

ˈ**abschirmen** *v/t* (*sep*, *-ge-*, *h*) shield (***gegen*** from); *fig* protect (***gegen*** against, from); ˈ**Abschirmung** *f* (-; *-en*) shield, screen; *fig* protection

ˈ**abschlachten** *v/t* (*sep*, *-ge-*, *h*) slaughter (*a. fig*)

ˈ**Abschlag** *m* SPORT kickout; ECON down payment; ˈ**abschlagen** *v/t* (*irr*, ***schlagen***, *sep*, *-ge-*, *h*) knock off; cut off (*head*); cut down (*tree*); refuse (*request etc*), turn *s.th.* down

ˈ**abschleifen** *v/t* (*irr*, ***schleifen***, *sep*, *-ge-*, *h*) grind off; sand(paper), smooth

ˈ**Abschleppdienst** *m* MOT emergency road (*Br* breakdown) service

ˈ**abschleppen** *v/t* (*sep*, *-ge-*, *h*) MOT (give *s.o.* a) tow; *police*: tow away

ˈ**Abschlepp|seil** *n* towrope; **~wagen** *m Am* tow truck, *Br* breakdown lorry

ˈ**abschließen** (*irr*, ***schließen***, *sep*, *-ge-*, *h*) **1.** *v/t* lock (up); close, finish; complete; take out (*insurance*); conclude (*research etc*); ***e-n Handel ~*** strike a bargain; ***sich ~*** shut o.s. off; → ***Wette*** **2.** *v/i* close, finish; **~d 1.** *adj* concluding; final **2.** *adv*: ***~ sagte er*** he concluded by saying

ˈ**Abschluss** *m* conclusion, close; **~prüfung** *f* final examination, finals *pl*, *esp Am a.* graduation; ***s-e ~ machen*** graduate (***an*** *dat* from); **~zeugnis** *n Am* diploma, *Br* school-leaving certificate

ˈ**abschmecken** *v/t* (*sep*, *-ge-*, *h*) season

ˈ**abschmieren** *v/t* (*sep*, *-ge-*, *h*) TECH lubricate, grease

ˈ**abschminken** *v/t* (*sep*, *-ge-*, *h*) ***sich ~*** remove one's make-up

ˈ**abschnallen** *v/t* (*sep*, *-ge-*, *h*) undo; take off (*skis*); ***sich ~*** MOT, AVIAT unfasten one's seat belt

ˈ**abschneiden** (*irr*, ***schneiden***, *sep*, *-ge-*, *h*) **1.** *v/t* cut (off) (*a. fig*); ***j-m das Wort ~*** cut s.o. short **2.** *v/i*: ***gut ~*** come off well

ˈ**Abschnitt** *m* passage, section (*of book etc*); paragraph; MATH, BIOL segment; period (*of time*), stage (*of journey*), phase (*of development*); coupon, slip, stub (*of check etc*)

ˈ**abschnittweise** *adv* section by section

ˈ**abschrauben** *v/t* (*sep*, *-ge-*, *h*) unscrew

ˈ**abschrecken** *v/t* (*sep*, *-ge-*, *h*) deter (***von*** from); GASTR douse *eggs etc* with cold water; **~d** *adj* deterrent; ***~es Beispiel*** warning example

ˈ**Abschreckung** *f* (-; *-en*) deterrence

ˈ**abschreiben** *v/t* (*irr*, ***schreiben***, *sep*, *-ge-*, *h*) copy; PED crib; ECON write off (*a.* F *fig*); ˈ**Abschrift** *f* copy, duplicate

ˈ**abschürfen** *v/t* (*sep*, *-ge-*, *h*) graze

ˈ**Abschürfung** *f* (-; *-en*) abrasion

**Abschuss** *m* launch(ing) (*of rocket*); AVIAT shooting down, downing; kill;

**~basis** *f* MIL launching base
**abschüssig** ['apʃʏsɪç] *adj* sloping; steep
'**Abschussliste** F *f*: ***auf der ~ stehen*** be on the hit list
'**Abschussrampe** *f* MIL launching pad
'**abschütteln** *v/t* (*sep*, *-ge-*, *h*) shake off
'**abschwächen** *v/t* (*sep*, *-ge-*, *h*) lessen, diminish
'**abschweifen** *fig v/i* (*sep*, *-ge-*, *sein*) digress (***von*** from)
'**Abschweifung** *f* (-; *-en*) digression
**absehbar** ['apzeːbaːɐ] *adj* foreseeable; ***in ~er*** (***auf ~e***) ***Zeit*** in the (for the) foreseeable future
'**absehen** *v/t* (*irr*, ***sehen***, *sep*, *-ge-*, *h*) foresee; ***es ist kein Ende abzusehen*** there is no end in sight; ***es abgesehen haben auf*** (*acc*) be after; ***~ von*** refrain from
'**abseilen** *v/refl* (*sep*, *-ge-*, *h*) descend by a rope, *Br a.* abseil; F make a getaway
**abseits** ['apzaɪts] *adv and prp* away *or* remote from
'**Abseitsfalle** *f soccer*: offside trap
**abseitsstehen** *v/i* (*irr*, ***stehen***, *sep*, *-ge-*, *h*) *soccer*: be offside; *fig* be left out
'**absenden** *v/t* ([*irr*, ***senden***,] *sep*, *-ge-*, *h*) send (off), dispatch; mail, *esp Br* post (*letter etc*)
'**Absender** *m* (*-s*; -) sender
**absetzbar** ['apzɛtsbaːɐ] *adj*: ***steuerlich ~*** deductible from tax
'**absetzen** (*sep*, *-ge-*, *h*) **1.** *v/t* take off (*hat*, *glasses etc*); set *or* put down (*bag etc*); drop (*passenger*); dismiss (*employee*); THEA, *film*: take off; deduct (*from tax*); depose (*king etc*); ECON sell; ***sich ~*** CHEM, GEOL settle, be deposited **2.** *v/i*: ***ohne abzusetzen*** without stopping
'**Absetzung** *f* (-; *-en*) dismissal; deposition; THEA, *film*: withdrawal
'**Absicht** *f* (-; *-en*) intention; ***mit ~*** on purpose; '**absichtlich 1.** *adj* intentional **2.** *adv* on purpose
'**absitzen** (*irr*, ***sitzen***, *sep*, *-ge-*) **1.** *v/i* (*sein*) dismount (***von*** from); **2.** *v/t* (*h*) serve (*sentence*); F sit out (*play etc*)
**absolut** [apzo'luːt] *adj* absolute
**Absolvent** [apzɔl'vɛnt] *m* (*-en*; *-en*), **Absol'ventin** *f* (-; *-nen*) graduate; **absolvieren** [apzɔl'viːrən] *v/t* (*no -ge-*, *h*) attend (*school*); complete (*studies*); graduate from (*college etc*)
'**absondern** *v/t* (*sep*, *-ge-*, *h*) separate; MED, BIOL secrete; ***sich ~*** cut o.s. off (***von*** from); '**Absonderung** *f* (-; *-en*) separation; MED, BIOL secretion
**absorbieren** [apzɔr'biːrən] *v/t* (*no -ge-*, *h*) absorb (*a. fig*)
'**abspeichern** *v/t* (*sep*, *-ge-*, *h*) IT store, save
**abspenstig** ['apʃpɛnstɪç] *adj*: ***j-m die Freundin ~ machen*** steal s.o.'s girlfriend
**absperren** *v/t* (*sep*, *-ge-*, *h*) lock; turn off (*water*, *gas etc*); block off (*road*); cordon off; '**Absperrung** *f* (-; *-en*) barrier; cordon
'**abspielen** *v/t* (*sep*, *-ge-*, *h*) play (*record etc*); SPORT pass (*the ball*); ***sich ~*** happen, take place
'**Absprache** *f* agreement
'**absprechen** *v/t* (*irr*, ***sprechen***, *sep*, *-ge-*, *h*) agree upon; arrange; ***j-m die Fähigkeit*** *etc* ***~*** dispute s.o.'s ability *etc*
'**abspringen** *v/i* (*irr*, ***springen***, *sep*, *-ge-*, *sein*) jump off; AVIAT jump, bail out; *fig* back out (***von*** of)
'**Absprung** *m* jump; SPORT take-off; *fig* ***den ~ schaffen*** make it
'**abspülen** *v/t* (*sep*, *-ge-*, *h*) rinse; wash up
**abstammen** *v/i* (*sep*, *no past participle*) be descended (***von*** from); CHEM, LING derive; '**Abstammung** *f* (-; *no pl*) descent; derivation; '**Abstammungslehre** *f* theory of the origin of species
'**Abstand** *m* distance (*a. fig*); interval; ***~ halten*** keep one's distance; *fig* ***mit ~*** by far
**abstatten** ['apʃtatən] *v/t* (*sep*, *-ge-*, *h*) ***j-m e-n Besuch ~*** pay a visit to s.o.
'**abstauben** *v/t* (*sep*, *-ge-*, *h*) dust; F *fig* sponge; swipe
'**Abstauber** F *m* (*-s*; -), '**Abstaubertor** *n* SPORT opportunist goal
'**abstechen** (*irr*, ***stechen***, *sep*, *-ge-*, *h*) **1.** *v/t* stick (*pig etc*) **2.** *v/i* contrast (***von*** with); '**Abstecher** *m* (*-s*; -) side-trip, excursion (*a. fig*)
'**abstecken** *v/t* (*sep*, *-ge-*, *h*) mark out
'**abstehen** *v/i* (*irr*, ***stehen***, *sep*, *-ge-*, *h*) stick out, protrude; → ***abgestanden***
'**absteigen** *v/i* (*irr*, ***steigen***, *sep*, *-ge-*, *sein*) get off (*a horse etc*); climb down;

stay (***in*** *dat* at); SPORT *Am* be moved down to a lower division, *Br* be relegated; '**Absteiger** *m* (*-s*; -) SPORT *Br* relegated club

'**abstellen** *v/t* (*sep*, *-ge-*, *h*) put down; leave (*s.th. with s.o.*); turn off (*gas etc*); park (*car*); *fig* put an end to *s.th.*

'**Abstellgleis** *n* RAIL siding; ***j-n aufs ~ schieben*** F push s.o. aside

'**Abstellraum** *m* storeroom

'**abstempeln** *v/t* (*sep*, *-ge-*, *h*) stamp

'**absterben** *v/i* (*irr*, ***sterben***, *sep*, *-ge-*, *sein*) die off; *limb*: go numb

**Abstieg** ['apʃtiːk] *m* (*-[e]s*; *-e*) descent; *fig* decline; SPORT *Br* relegation

'**abstimmen** *v/i* (*sep*, *-ge-*, *h*) vote (***über*** *acc* on)

'**Abstimmung** *f* vote; *radio*: tuning

**Abstinenzler** [apsti'nɛntslɐ] *m* (*-s*; -) teetotal(l)er

'**Abstoß** *m* SPORT goal-kick

'**abstoßen** *v/t* (*irr*, ***stoßen***, *sep*, *-ge-*, *h*) repel; MED reject; push off (*boat*); F get rid of *s.th.*; **~d** *fig adj* repulsive

**abstrakt** [ap'strakt] *adj* abstract

'**abstreiten** *v/t* (*irr*, ***streiten***, *sep*, *-ge-*, *h*) deny

'**Abstrich** *m* MED smear; *pl* ECON cuts; *fig* reservations

'**abstufen** *v/t* (*sep*, *-ge-*, *h*) graduate; gradate (*colors*)

'**abstumpfen** (*sep*, *-ge-*) **1.** *v/t* (*h*) blunt, dull (*a. fig*) **2.** *fig v/i* (*sein*) become unfeeling

'**Absturz** *m*, '**abstürzen** *v/i* (*sep*, *-ge-*, *sein*) fall; AVIAT, IT crash

'**absuchen** *v/t* (*sep*, *-ge-*, *h*) search (***nach*** for)

**absurd** [ap'zʊrt] *adj* absurd, preposterous

**Abszess** [aps'tsɛs] *m* (*-es*; *-e*) MED abscess

**Abt** [apt] *m* (*-[e]s*; *Äbte* ['ɛptə]) REL abbot

'**abtasten** *v/t* (*sep*, *-ge-*, *h*) feel (for); MED palpate; frisk; TECH, IT scan

'**abtauen** *v/t* (*sep*, *-ge-*, *h*) defrost

**Abtei** [ap'tai] *f* (-; *-en*) REL abbey

**Abteil** [ap'tail] *n* (*-[e]s*; *-e*) RAIL compartment

'**abteilen** *v/t* (*sep*, *-ge-*, *h*) divide; ARCH partition off

**Ab'teilung** *f* (-; *-en*) department (*a.* ECON); ward (*of hospital*); MIL detachment; **Ab'teilungsleiter** *m* head of (a) department; *Am* floorwalker, *Br* shopwalker

**Äbtissin** [ɛp'tɪsɪn] *f* (-; *-nen*) REL abbess

'**abtöten** *v/t* (*sep*, *-ge-*, *h*) kill (*bacteria etc*); *fig* deaden (*feelings etc*)

'**abtragen** *v/t* (*irr*, ***tragen***, *sep*, *-ge-*, *h*) wear out (*clothes*); clear away (*dishes etc*); pay off (*debt*)

'**Abtrans,port** *m* transportation

'**abtreiben** (*irr*, ***treiben***, *sep*, *-ge-*) **1.** *v/i* MED (*h*) have an abortion; MAR, AVIAT (*sein*) be blown off course **2.** *v/t* (*h*) MED abort; '**Abtreibung** *f* (-; *-en*) abortion; ***e-e ~ vornehmen*** perform an abortion

'**abtrennen** *v/t* (*sep*, *-ge-*, *h*) detach; separate; MED sever

'**abtreten** (*irr*, ***treten***, *sep*, *-ge-*) **1.** *v/t* (*h*) wear down (*heels*); wipe (*one's feet*); *fig* give up (***an*** *acc* to); **2.** *v/i* (*sein*) resign; THEA; exit; '**Abtreter** *m* (*-s*; -) doormat

'**abtrocknen** (*sep*, *-ge-*, *h*) **1.** *v/t* dry; ***sich ~*** dry o.s. off **2.** *v/i* dry the dishes, *Br a.* dry up

**abtrünnig** ['aptrʏnɪç] *adj* unfaithful, disloyal; '**Abtrünnige** ['aptrʏnɪgə] *m*, *f* (*-n*; *-n*) renegade, turncoat

**abtun** *v/t* (*irr*, ***tun***, *sep*, *-ge-*, *h*) dismiss (***als*** as), brush *s.o.*, *s.th.* aside

**abwägen** ['apvɛːgən] *v/t* (*irr*, ***wägen***, *sep*, *-ge-*, *h*) weigh (***gegen*** against)

'**abwählen** *v/t* (*sep*, *-ge-*, *h*) vote out

'**abwälzen** *v/t* (*sep*, *-ge-*, *h*) ***et. auf j-n ~*** shove s.th. off on (to) s.o.

'**abwandeln** *v/t* (*sep*, *-ge-*, *h*) vary, modify

'**abwandern** *v/i* (*sep*, *-ge-*, *sein*) migrate (***von*** from; ***nach*** to); '**Abwanderung** *f* migration

'**Abwandlung** *f* modification, variation

'**Abwärme** *f* TECH waste heat

**Abwart** ['apvart] *m* (*-s*; *-e*) *Swiss* → ***Hausmeister***

'**abwarten** (*sep*, *-ge-*, *h*) **1.** *v/t* wait for, await **2.** *v/i* wait; ***warten wir ab!*** let's wait and see!; ***wart nur ab!*** just wait!

**abwärts** ['apvɛrts] *adv* down, downward(s)

**Abwasch** ['apvaʃ] *m* (*-[e]s*; *no pl*) ***den ~ machen*** do the washing-up

'**abwaschbar** *adj* washable

'**abwaschen** (*irr*, ***waschen***, *sep*, *-ge-*, *h*) **1.** *v/t* wash off **2.** *v/i* do the dishes, *Br a.*

wash up
'**Abwaschwasser** *n* dishwater
'**Abwasser** *n* TECH waste water, sewage; **~aufbereitung** *f* TECH sewage treatment
'**abwechseln** *v/i* (*sep*, *-ge-*, *h*) alternate; ***sich mit j-m ~*** take turns (***bei et.*** at [doing] s.th.); **~d** *adv* by turns
'**Abwechslung** *f* (-; *-en*) change; ***zur ~*** for a change; '**abwechslungsreich** *adj* varied; colo(u)rful
'**Abweg** *m*: ***auf ~e geraten*** go astray
**abwegig** ['apve:gɪç] *adj* absurd, unrealistic
'**Abwehr** *f* (-; *no pl*) defen|se, *Br* -ce (*a.* SPORT); warding off (*of blow etc*); save (*of ball*)
'**abwehren** *v/t* (*sep*, *-ge-*, *h*) ward off (*blow etc*); beat off; SPORT block
'**Abwehr|fehler** *m* SPORT defensive error; **~kräfte** *pl* MED resistance; **~spieler** *m* SPORT defender; **~stoffe** *pl* MED antibodies
'**abweichen** *v/i* (*irr*, ***weichen***, *sep*, *-ge-*, *sein*) deviate (***von*** from); digress
'**Abweichung** *f* (-; *-en*) deviation
'**abweisen** *v/t* (*irr*, ***weisen***, *sep*, *-ge-*, *h*) turn away; rebuff; decline, turn down (*request*, *offer etc*); **~d** *adj* unfriendly
'**abwenden** *v/t* ([*irr*, ***wenden***,] *sep*, *-ge-*, *h*) turn away (*a.* ***sich ~***) (***von*** from); avert (*tragedy etc*)
'**abwerfen** *v/t* (*irr*, ***werfen***, *sep*, *-ge-*, *h*) throw off; AVIAT drop; BOT shed (*leaves*); ECON yield (*profit*)
'**abwerten** *v/t* (*sep*, *-ge-*, *h*) ECON devalue; **~d** *fig adj* disparaging
'**Abwertung** *f* ECON devaluation
'**abwesend** *adj* absent
'**Abwesenheit** *f* (-; *no pl*) absence
**abwickeln** *v/t* (*sep*, *-ge-*, *h*) unwind; ECON handle; transact (*business*)
'**abwiegen** *v/t* (*irr*, ***wiegen***, *sep*, *-ge-*, *h*) weigh (out)
'**abwimmeln** F *v/t* (*sep*, *-ge-*, *h*) ***j-n ~*** get rid of s.o., give s.o. the elbow
'**abwischen** *v/t* (*sep*, *-ge-*, *h*) wipe (off)
'**Abwurf** *m* dropping; *soccer*: throw-out
'**abwürgen** F *v/t* (*sep*, *-ge-*, *h*) MOT stall; *fig* stifle; '**abzahlen** *v/t* (*sep*, *-ge-*, *h*) make *monthly etc* payments for; pay off; '**abzählen** *v/t* (*sep*, *-ge-*, *h*) count
'**Abzahlung** *f*: ***et. auf ~ kaufen*** *Am* buy s.th. on the instalment plan (*Br* on hire purchase)
'**abzapfen** *v/t* (*sep*, *-ge-*, *h*) tap, draw off
'**Abzeichen** *n* badge; medal
'**abzeichnen** *v/t* (*sep*, *-ge-*, *h*) copy, draw; sign, initial; ***sich ~*** (begin to) show; stand out (***gegen*** against)
'**Abziehbild** *n* *Am* decal, *Br* transfer
'**abziehen** (*irr*, ***ziehen***, *sep*, *-ge-*) **1.** *v/t* (*h*) take off, remove; MATH subtract; strip (*bed*); take out (*key*); ***das Fell ~*** skin **2.** *v/i* (*sein*) go away; MIL withdraw; *smoke*: escape; *storm*, *clouds*: move off
'**Abzug** *m* ECON deduction; discount; MIL withdrawal; PRINT copy; PHOT print; *gun*: trigger; TECH vent, outlet; cooker hood
**abzüglich** ['aptsy:klɪç] *prp* less, minus
'**abzweigen** (*sep*, *-ge-*) **1.** *v/t* (*h*) divert (*resources etc*) (***für*** to); **2.** *v/i* (*sein*) *path etc*: branch off
'**Abzweigung** *f* (-; *-en*) junction
**ach** [ax] *int* oh!; ***~ je!*** oh dear!; ***~ so!*** I see; ***~ was!*** *surprised*: really?, *annoyed*: of course not!, nonsense!
**Achse** ['aksə] *f* (-; *-n*) TECH axle; MATH *etc* axis; F ***auf ~ sein*** be on the move
**Achsel** ['aksəl] *f* (-; *-n*) ANAT shoulder; ***die ~n zucken*** shrug one's shoulders
'**Achselhöhle** *f* ANAT armpit
'**Achsenbruch** *m* MOT broken axle
**acht** [axt] *adj* eight; ***heute in ~ Tagen*** a week from today, *esp Br* today week; (***heute***) ***vor ~ Tagen*** a week ago (today)
**Acht** *f*: ***~ geben*** → ***achtgeben***; ***außer ~ lassen*** disregard; ***sich in ~ nehmen*** be careful, look *or* watch out (***vor*** *dat* for)
**achte** ['axtə] *adj* eighth
'**achteckig** *adj* octagonal
**Achtel** ['axtəl] *n* (*-s*; -) eighth (part)
**achten** (*ge-*, *h*) **1.** *v/t* respect **2.** *v/i*: ***~ auf*** (*acc*) pay attention to; keep an eye on; watch; be careful with; ***darauf ~, dass*** see to it that
**ächten** ['ɛçtən] *v/t* (*ge-*, *h*) ban; *esp* HIST outlaw
**Achter** ['axtɐ] *m* (*-s*; -) *rowing*: eight
'**Achterbahn** *f* roller coaster
'**achtfach** *adj and adv* eightfold
**achtgeben** *v/i* (*irr*, ***geben***, *sep*, *-ge-*, *h*) be careful; pay attention (***auf*** *acc* to); take care (***auf*** *acc* of); ***gib acht!*** look *or* watch out!, be careful!
'**achtlos** *adj* careless, heedless
'**Achtung** *f* (-; *no pl*) respect (***vor*** *dat*

for); ~! look out!; MIL attention!; ~! ~! attention please!; ~! **Fertig! Los!** On your marks! Get set! Go!; ~ **Stufe!** *Am* caution: step!, *Br* mind the step!

**'achtzehn** *adj* eighteen

**'achtzehnte** *adj* eighteenth

**achtzig** ['axtsıç] *adj* eighty; **die ~er Jahre** the eighties; **~ste** *adj* eightieth

**ächzen** ['ɛçtsən] *v/i* (*ge-*, *h*) groan (**vor** *dat* with)

**Acker** ['akɐ] *m* (*-s*; *Äcker* ['ɛkɐ]) field; **~bau** *m* (*-[e]s*; *no pl*) agriculture; farming; ~ **und Viehzucht** crop and stock farming; **~land** *n* (*-[e]s*; *no pl*) farmland

**'ackern** F *v/i* (*ge-*, *h*) slog (away)

**Adapter** [a'daptɐ] *m* (*-s*; *-*) TECH adapter

**addieren** [a'di:rən] *v/t* (*no -ge-*, *h*) add (up); **Addition** [adi'tsio:n] *f* (*-*; *-en*) addition, adding up

**Adel** ['a:dəl] *m* (*-s*; *no pl*) aristocracy

**'adeln** *v/t* (*ge-*, *h*) ennoble (*a. fig*); *Br* knight

**Ader** ['a:dɐ] *f* (*-*; *-n*) ANAT blood vessel, vein

**Adjektiv** ['atjɛkti:f] *n* (*-s*; *-e*) LING adjective

**Adler** ['a:dlɐ] *m* (*-s*; *-*) ZO eagle

**adlig** ['a:dlıç] *adj* noble; **Adlige** ['a:dlıgə] *m*, *f* (*-n*; *-n*) noble|man (-woman)

**Admiral** [atmi'ra:l] *m* (*-s*; *-e*) MAR admiral

**adoptieren** [adɔp'ti:rən] *v/t* (*no -ge-*, *h*) adopt; **Adoptivkind** [adɔp'ti:fkınt] *n* adopted child

**Adressbuch** [a'drɛsbu:x] *n* directory

**Adresse** [a'drɛsə] *f* (*-*; *-n*) address

**adressieren** [adrɛ'si:rən] *v/t* (*no -ge-*, *h*) address (**an** *acc* to)

**Advent** [at'vɛnt] *m* (*-[e]s*; *no pl*) REL Advent; Advent Sunday

**Ad'ventszeit** *f* Christmas season

**Adverb** [at'vɛrp] *n* (*-s*; *Adverbien* [at'vɛrbĭən]) LING adverb

**Aerobic** [ɛ'ro:bık] *n* (*-s*; *no pl*) aerobics

**Affäre** [a'fɛ:rə] *f* (*-*; *-n*) affair

**Affe** ['afə] *m* (*-n*; *-n*) ZO monkey; ape

**Affekt** [a'fɛkt] *m* (*-[e]s*; *-e*) **im ~** in the heat of passion (*a.* JUR)

**affektiert** [afɛk'ti:ɐt] *adj* affected

**Afrika** ['a:frika] Africa; **Afrikaner** [afri'ka:nɐ] *m* (*-s*; *-*), **Afri'kanerin** [afri'ka:nərın] *f* (*-*; *-nen*), **afri'kanisch** *adj* African

**After** ['aftɐ] *m* (*-s*; *-*) ANAT anus

**AG** *abbr of* **Aktiengesellschaft** *Am* (stock) corporation, *Br* PLC, public limited company

**Agent** [a'gɛnt] *m* (*-en*; *-en*), **A'gentin** *f* (*-*; *-nen*) agent; POL (secret) agent

**Agentur** [agɛn'tu:ɐ] *f* (*-*; *-en*) agency

**Aggression** [agrɛ'sĭo:n] *f* (*-*; *-en*) aggression; **aggressiv** [agrɛ'si:f] *adj* aggressive; **Aggressivität** [agrɛsivi'tɛ:t] *f* (*-*; *no pl*) aggressiveness

**Agitator** [agi'ta:to:ɐ] *m* (*-s*; *-en* [agita'to:rən]) agitator

**ah** [a:] *int* ah!

**äh** [ɛ:] *int* er; *disgusted*: ugh!

**aha** [a'ha] *int* I see!, oh!

**A'ha-Erlebnis** *n* aha-experience

**Ahn** [a:n] *m* (*-[e]s*; *-en*; *-en*) ancestor, *pl a.* forefathers

**ähneln** ['ɛ:nəln] *v/i* (*ge-*, *h*) resemble, look like

**ahnen** ['a:nən] *v/t* (*ge-*, *h*) suspect; foresee, know

**ähnlich** ['ɛ:nlıç] *adj* similar (*dat* to); **j-m ~ sehen** look like s.o.

**'Ähnlichkeit** *f* (*-*; *-en*) likeness, resemblance, similarity (**mit** to)

**'Ahnung** *f* (*-*; *-en*) presentiment, *a.* foreboding; notion, idea; **ich habe keine ~** I have no idea; **'ahnungslos** *adj* unsuspecting, innocent

**Ahorn** ['a:hɔrn] *m* (*-s*, *-e*) BOT maple

**Ähre** ['ɛ:rə] *f* (*-*; *-n*) BOT ear; spike

**Aids** [eıdz] *n* (*-*; *no pl*) MED AIDS

**'Aids|-Kranke** *m*, *f* MED AIDS victim *or* sufferer; **~test** *m* MED AIDS test

**Airbag** ['ɛəbæg] *m* (*-s*; *-s*) MOT airbag

**Akademie** [akade'mi:] *f* (*-*; *-n*) academy, college; **Akademiker(in)** [aka'de:mikɐ, aka'de:mikərın] *m(f)* (*-s*; *-/-*; *-nen*) university graduate; **akademisch** [aka'de:mıʃ] *adj* academic

**akklimatisieren** [aklimati'zi:rən] *v/refl* (*no -ge-*, *h*) acclimatize (**an** *acc* to)

**Akkord** [a'kɔrt] *m* (*-[e]s*; *-e*) MUS chord; **im ~** ECON by the piece *or* job; **~arbeit** *f* ECON piecework; **~arbeiter(in)** ECON pieceworker

**Akkordeon** [a'kɔrdeɔn] *n* (*-s*; *-s*) MUS accordion

**Ak'kordlohn** *m* ECON piece wages

**Akku** ['aku] F *m* (*-s*; *-s*), **Akkumulator** [akumu'la:to:ɐ] *m* (*-s*; *-en* [akumula'to:rən]) TECH (storage) battery, *Br a.*

accumulator
**Akkusativ** ['akuzati:f] *m* (*-s*; *-e*) LING accusative (case)
**Akne** ['aknə] *f* (-; *-n*) MED acne
**Akrobat** [akro'ba:t] *m* (*-en*; *-en*), **Akro'batin** *f* (-; *-nen*) acrobat; **akro'batisch** *adj* acrobatic
**Akt** [akt] *m* (-[*e*]*s*; *-e*) act(ion); THEA act; PAINT, PHOT nude
**Akte** ['aktə] *f* (-; *-n*) file; *pl.* files, records; ***zu den ~n legen*** file
**'Akten|deckel** *m* folder; **~koffer** *m* attaché case; **~ordner** *m* file; **~tasche** *f* briefcase; **~zeichen** *n* reference (number)
**Aktie** ['aktsĭə] *f* (-; *-n*) ECON share, *esp Am* stock; **'Aktiengesellschaft** *f Am* corporation, *Br* joint-stock company
**Aktion** [ak'tsĭo:n] *f* (-; *-en*) campaign, drive; MIL *ect* operation; ***in ~*** in action
**Aktionär** [aktsĭo'nɛ:ɐ] *m* (*-s*; *-e*), **Aktio'närin** *f* (-; *-nen*) ECON shareholder, *esp Am* stockholder
**aktiv** [ak'ti:f] *adj* active
**Aktiv** ['akti:f] *n* (*-s*; *no pl*) LING active voice; **aktivieren** *v/t* (*no -ge-*, *h*) activate; **Aktivist** [akti'vist] *m* (*-en*; *-en*) *esp* POL activist
**Ak'tivurlaub** *m* activity vacation
**aktualisieren** [aktŭali'zi:rən] *v/t* (*no -ge-*, *h*) update
**aktuell** [aktŭ'ɛl] *adj* topical; current; up-to-date; TV, *radio*: ***e-e ~e Sendung*** a current affairs *or* news feature
**Akupunktur** [akupʊŋk'tu:ɐ] *f* (-; *-en*) MED acupuncture
**Akustik** [a'kʊstɪk] *f* (-; *no pl*) acoustics
**a'kustisch** *adj* acoustic
**akut** [a'ku:t] *adj* urgent (*problem etc*); *a.* MED acute
**Akzent** [ak'tsɛnt] *m* (-[*e*]*s*; *-e*) accent; stress (*a. fig*)
**akzeptabel** [aktsɛp'ta:bəl] *adj* acceptable; reasonable (*price etc*)
**akzeptieren** [aktsɛp'ti:rən] *v/t* (*no -ge-*, *h*) accept
**Alarm** [a'larm] *m* (-[*e*]*s*; *-e*) alarm; ***~ schlagen*** sound the alarm; **~anlage** *f* alarm system; **~bereitschaft** *f*: ***in ~*** on standby, on the alert
**alarmieren** [alar'mi:rən] *v/t* (*no -ge-*, *h*) call; alert; **~d** *adj* alarming
**albern** ['albɐn] *adj* silly, foolish
**Album** ['albʊm] *n* (*-s*; *Alben* ['albən]) album (*a. record*)
**Algebra** ['algəbra] *f* (-; *no pl*) MATH algebra
**Algen** ['algən] *pl* BOT algae; **~pest** *f* plague of algae, algal bloom
**Alibi** ['a:libi] *n* (*-s*; *-s*) JUR alibi
**Alimente** [ali'mɛntə] *pl* JUR alimony
**Alkohol** ['alkoho:l] *m* (*-s*; *no pl*) alcohol; **'alkoholfrei** *adj* nonalcoholic, soft; **Alkoholiker(in)** [alko'ho:likɐ, alko'ho:likərɪn] *m*(*f*) (*-s*; *-/-*; *-nen*) alcoholic; **alko'holisch** *adj* alcoholic; **Alkoholismus** [alkoho'lɪsmʊs] *m* (-; *no pl*) alcoholism; **alkoholsüchtig** *adj* addicted to alcohol; **Alkoholtest** *m* alcohol test, *Br* breathalyser® test
**All** *n* (*-s*; *no pl*) universe; (outer) space
**alle**[1] ['alə] *indef pron and adj* all; ***~s*** (***Beliebige***) anything; ***~*** (***Leute***) everybody; anybody; ***~ beide*** both of them; ***wir ~*** all of us; ***~s in ~m*** all in all; ***auf ~ Fälle*** in any case; ***~ drei Tage*** every three days; → ***Art, Gute, vor***;
**alle**[2] ['alə] F *adj*: ***~ sein*** be all gone; ***mein Geld ist ~*** I'm out of money
**Allee** [a'le:] *f* (-; *-n*) avenue
**allein** [a'lain] *adj and adv* alone; lonely; by o.s.; ***ganz ~*** all alone; ***er hat es ganz ~ gemacht*** he did it all by himself; ***~ stehend*** → ***alleinstehend***
**Al'lein|erziehende** *m*, *f* (*-n*; *-n*) single parent; **~gang** *m*: ***im ~*** single-handedly, solo
**alleinig** [a'lainɪç] *adj* sole
**Al'leinsein** *n* (*-s*; *no pl*) loneliness
**alleinstehend** *adj* single
**Allerbeste** ['alɐ'bɛstə]: ***der*** (***die, das***) ***~*** the best of all, the very best
**allerdings** ['alɐ'dɪŋs] *adv* however, though; ***~!*** certainly!, *esp Am* F sure!
**'aller'erste** *adj* very first
**Allergie** [alɛr'gi:] *f* (-; *-n*) MED allergy (***gegen*** to); **allergisch** [a'lɛrgɪʃ] *adj* allergic (***gegen*** to)
**'aller'hand** F *adj* a good deal (of); ***das ist ja ~!*** that's a bit much!
**'Aller'heiligen** *n* REL All Saints' Day
**allerlei** ['alɐ'lai] *adj* all kinds *or* sorts of
**'aller|'letzte** *adj* last of all, very last; **~'liebst** **1.** *adj* (most) lovely **2.** *adv*: ***am ~en mögen*** like best of all; **~'meiste** *adj* (by far the) most; **~'nächste** *adj* very next; ***in ~r Zeit*** in the very near future; **~'neu(e)ste** *adj* very latest

'**Aller'seelen** *n* REL All Souls' Day
**allerseits** ['alɐ'zaits] *adv* F: ***Tag~!*** hi, everybody!
'**aller'wenigst** *adv*: ***am ~en*** least of all
**alles** everything
**allesamt** ['alə'zamt] *adv* all together
'**allge'mein** **1.** *adj* general; common; universal **2.** *adv*: ***im Allgemeinen*** in general, generally; ***~ verständlich*** intelligible (to all), popular
**Allge'mein|arzt** *m*, **Allge'meinärztin** *f Br* GP, *Am* family practitioner; **~bildung** *f* general education
'**Allge'meinheit** *f* (-; *no pl*) (general) public
**allgemeinver'ständlich** *adj* → ***allgemein***
**All'heilmittel** *n* cure-all (*a. fig*)
**Allianz** [a'ljants] *f* (-; *-en*) alliance
**Alligator** [ali'ga:to:ɐ] *m* (*-s*; *-en*) alligator
**Alliierte** [ali'i:ɐtə]: ***die ~n*** *pl* POL the Allies
'**all|'jährlich** *adv* every year; ***~ stattfindend*** annual; **~'mächtig** *adj* omnipotent; Almighty (*God*)
**allmählich** [al'mɛ:lɪç] **1.** *adj* gradual **2.** *adv* gradually
'**Allradantrieb** *m* MOT four-wheel drive
**allseitig** ['alzaitɪç] *adv*: ***~ interessiert sein*** have all-round interests
'**Alltag** *m* everyday life
'**all|'täglich** *adj* everyday; *fig a.* ordinary; **~'wissend** *adj* omniscient
'**allzu** *adv* (all) too; ***~ viel*** too much
**Alm** [alm] *f* (-; *-en*) alpine pasture, alp
**Almosen** ['almo:zən] *n* (*-s*; -) alms
'**Alpdruck** *m* (-[*e*]*s*; *no pl*) nightmare (*a. fig*)
**Alphabet** [alfa'be:t] *n* (-[*e*]*s*; *-e*) alphabet; **alpha'betisch** *adj* alphabetical
**alpin** [al'pi:n] *adj* alpine
'**Alptraum** *m* nightmare (*a. fig*)
**als** [als] *cj time*: when; while; *after comp*: than; ***~ ich ankam*** when I arrived; ***~ Kind*** (***Geschenk***) as a child (present); ***älter ~*** older than; ***~ ob*** as if, as though; ***nichts ~*** nothing but
**also** ['alzo] *cj* so, therefore; F well, you know; ***~ gut!*** very well (then)!, all right (then)!; ***~ doch*** so … after all; ***du willst ~ gehen*** *etc?* so you want to go *etc?*
**alt** [alt] *adj* old; HIST ancient; classical (*language*); ***ein 12 Jahre ~er Junge*** a twelve-year-old boy
**Alt** *m* (*-s*; *no pl*) MUS alto
**Altar** [al'ta:ɐ] *m* (*-s*; *Altäre* [al'tɛ:rə]) REL altar
'**Alte** *m*, *f* (*-n*; *-n*) ***der ~*** the old man (*a. fig*); the boss; ***die ~*** the old woman (*a. fig*); ***die ~n*** *pl* the old
'**Altenheim** *n* → ***Altersheim***
'**Altenpfleger(in)** geriatric nurse
**Alter** ['altɐ] *n* (*-s*; *no pl*) age; old age; ***im ~ von …*** at the age of …; ***er ist in deinem ~*** he's your age
**älter** ['ɛltɐ] *adj* older; ***mein ~er Bruder*** my elder brother; ***ein ~er Herr*** an elderly gentleman
'**altern** *v/i* (*ge-*, *sein*) grow old, age
**alternativ** [altɛrna'ti:f] *adj* alternative; POL ecological, green; *a.* counter-culture (*movement etc*)
**Alternative**[1] [altɛrna'ti:və] *f* (-; *-n*) alternative; option, choice
**Alterna'tive**[2] *m*, *f* (*-n*; *-n*) ecologist, member of the counterculture movement
'**Alters|grenze** *f* age limit; retirement age; **~heim** *n* old people's home; **~rente** *f* old-age pension; **~schwäche** *f* (-; *no pl*) infirmity; ***an ~ sterben*** die of old age; **~versorgung** *f* old age pension (scheme)
'**Altertum** *n* (*-s*; *no pl*) antiquity
'**Altglascon,tainer** *m Am* glass recycling bin, *Br* bottle bank
'**altklug** *adj* precocious
'**Altlasten** *pl* residual pollution
'**Altme,tall** *n* scrap (metal)
'**altmodisch** *adj* old-fashioned
'**Altöl** *n* waste oil
'**Altpa,pier** *n* waste paper
'**altsprachlich** *adj*: ***~es Gymnasium*** *appr* classical secondary school
'**Altstadt** *f* old town; **~sa,nierung** *f* town-cent|er (*Br* -re) rehabilitation
'**Altwarenhändler** *m* second-hand dealer
**Alt'weibersommer** *m* Indian summer; gossamer
**Aluminium** [alu'mi:njʊm] *n* (*-s*; *no pl*) alumin(i)um
**am** [am] *prp* at the (*window etc*); *time*: in the (*morning etc*); at the (*weekend etc*); on (*Sunday etc*); ***~ 1. Mai*** on May 1st; ***~ Tage*** during the day; ***~ Himmel*** in the sky; ***~ meisten*** most; ***~ Leben*** alive

**Amateur** [ama'tøːɐ] *m* (*-s*; *-e*) amateur; **~funker** *m* radio amateur, F radio ham
**Amboss** ['ambɔs] *m* (*-es*; *-e*) anvil
**ambulant** [ambu'lant] *adv*: **~ *behandelt werden*** MED get outpatient treatment
**Ambulanz** [ambu'lants] *f* (-; *-en*) MED outpatients' department; MOT ambulance
**Ameise** ['aːmaizə] *f* (-; *-n*) ZO ant
**'Ameisenhaufen** *m* ZO anthill
**Amerika** [a'meːrika] America
**Amerikaner** [ameri'kaːnɐ] *m* (*-s*; -), **Ameri'kanerin** [ameri'kaːnərɪn] *f* (-; *-nen*), **ameri'kanisch** *adj* American
**Amnestie** [amnɛs'tiː] *f* (-; *-n*), **amnes'tieren** *v/t* (*no -ge-*, *h*) JUR amnesty
**Amok** ['aːmɔk] *m*: **~ *laufen*** run amok
**Ampel** ['ampəl] *f* (-; *-n*) traffic light(s)
**Amphibie** [am'fiːbjə] *f* (-; *-n*) ZO amphibian
**Ampulle** [am'pʊlə] *f* (-; *-n*) ampoule
**Amputation** [amputa'tsjoːn] *f* (-; *-en*) MED amputation; **amputieren** [ampu'tiːrən] *v/t* (*no -ge-*, *h*) MED amputate
**Amsel** ['amzəl] *f* (-; *-n*) ZO blackbird
**Amt** [amt] *n* (*-[e]s*; *Ämter* ['ɛmtɐ]) office, department, *esp Am* bureau; position; duty, function; TEL exchange
**'amtlich** *adj* official
**'Amts|arzt** *m* medical examiner (*Br* officer); **~einführung** *f* inauguration; **~geheimnis** *n* official secret; **~geschäfte** *pl* official duties; **~zeichen** *n* TEL dial (*Br* dialling) tone; **~zeit** *f* term (of office)
**Amulett** [amu'lɛt] *n* (*-[e]s*; *-e*) amulet, (lucky) charm
**amüsant** [amy'zant] *adj* amusing, entertaining
**amüsieren** [amy'ziːrən] *v/t* (*no -ge-*, *h*) amuse; ***sich* ~** enjoy o.s., have a good time; ***sich* ~ *über*** (*acc*) laugh at
**an** [an] **1.** *prp*: **~ *der Themse* (*Küste, Wand*)** on the Thames (coast, wall); **~ *s-m Schreibtisch*** at his desk; **~ *der Hand*** by the hand; **~ *der Arbeit*** at work; **~ *den Hausaufgaben sitzen*** sit over one's homework; ***et. schicken* ~** (*acc*) send s.th. to; ***sich lehnen* ~** (*acc*) lean against; **~ *die Tür*** *etc* ***klopfen*** knock at the door *etc*; **~ *e-m Sonntagmorgen*** on a Sunday morning; **~ *dem Tag, ...*** on the day ...; **~ *Weihnachten*** *etc* at Christmas *etc*; → ***Mangel, Stelle, sterben*** **2.** *adv* on (*a. light etc*); ***von jetzt* (*da, heute*) ~** from now (that time, today) on; ***München* ~ *16.45*** arrival Munich 4.45 p.m.
**Anabolikum** [ana'boːlikum] *n* (*-s*; *-ka*) PHARM anabolic steroid
**analog** [ana'loːk] *adj* analogous
**Ana'log...** *in cpds* analog(ue) (*computer etc*)
**Analphabet** [anˀalfa'beːt] *m* (*-en*; *-en*), **Analpha'betin** *f* (-; *-nen*) illiterate (person)
**Analyse** [ana'lyːzə] *f* (-; *-n*) analysis
**analysieren** [analy'ziːrən] *v/t* (*no -ge-*, *h*) analy|ze, *Br* -se
**Ananas** ['ananas] *f* (-; -, *-se*) BOT pineapple
**Anarchie** [anar'çiː] *f* (-; *-n*) anarchy
**Anatomie** [anato'miː] *f* (-; *-n*) anatomy
**anatomisch** [ana'toːmɪʃ] *adj* anatomical
**'anbahnen** *v/t* (*sep*, *-ge-*, *h*) pave the way for; ***sich* ~** be developing; be impending
**'Anbau** *m* (*-[e]s*; *-ten*) AGR (*no pl*) cultivation; ARCH annex, extension
**'anbauen** *v/t* (*sep*, *-ge-*, *h*) AGR cultivate, grow; ARCH add (***an*** *acc* to), build on
**'anbehalten** *v/t* (*irr*, ***halten***, *sep*, *no -ge-*, *h*) keep on
**an'bei** *adv* ECON enclosed
**'anbeißen** (*irr*, ***beißen***, *sep*, *-ge-*, *h*) **1.** *v/t* take a bite of **2.** *v/i fish*: bite; *fig* take the bait; **'anbellen** *v/t* (*sep*, *-ge-*, *h*) bark at; **'anbeten** *v/t* (*sep*, *-ge-*, *h*) adore, worship (*a. fig*)
**'Anbetracht** *m*: ***in* ~ (*dessen, dass*)** considering (that)
**'anbetteln** *v/t* (*sep*, *-ge-*, *h*) ***j-n um et.* ~** beg s.o. for s.th.; **anbiedern** ['anbiːdɐn] *v/refl* (*sep*, *-ge-*, *h*) curry favo(u)r (***bei*** with); **'anbieten** *v/t* (*irr*, ***bieten***, *sep*, *-ge-*, *h*) offer; **'anbinden** *v/t* (*irr*, ***binden***, *sep*, *-ge-*, *h*) tie up; **~ *an*** (*acc or dat*) tie to
**'Anblick** *m* sight; **'anblicken** *v/t* (*sep*, *-ge-*, *h*) look at; glance at
**'anbohren** *v/t* (*sep*, *-ge-*, *h*) tap
**'anbrechen** (*irr*, ***brechen***, *sep*, *-ge-*) **1.** *v/t* (*h*) break into (*supplies*); open **2.** *v/i* (*sein*) begin; *day*: break; *night*: fall
**'anbrennen** *v/i* (*irr*, ***brennen***, *sep*, *-ge-*, *sein*) burn (*a.* **~ *lassen***)
**'anbringen** *v/t* (*irr*, ***bringen***, *sep*, *-ge-*, *h*)

fix (***an*** *dat* to)
'**Anbruch** *m* (-[*e*]*s*; *no pl*) beginning; ***bei ~ der Nacht*** at nightfall
'**anbrüllen** *v/t* (*sep*, *-ge-*, *h*) roar at
**Andacht** ['andaxt] *f* (-; *-en*) REL (*no pl*) devotion; service; prayers
**andächtig** ['andɛçtɪç] *adj* REL devout
'**andauern** *v/i* (*sep*, *-ge-*, *h*) continue, go on, last; **~d** *adj and adv* → ***dauernd***
'**Andenken** *n* (*-s*; -) keepsake; souvenir (*both*: ***an*** *acc* of); ***zum ~ an*** (*acc*) in memory of
**andere** ['andərə] *adj and indef pron* other; different; ***mit ~n Worten*** in other words; ***am ~n Morgen*** the next morning; ***et.*** (***nichts***) ***~s*** s.th. (nothing) else; ***nichts ~s als*** nothing but; ***die ~n*** the others; ***alle ~n*** everybody else
**andererseits** ['andərɐ'zaits] *adv* on the other hand
**ändern** ['ɛndɐn] *v/t* (*ge-*, *h*) change; alter (*clothes*); ***ich kann es nicht ~*** I can't help it; ***sich ~*** change
'**andern'falls** *adv* otherwise
**anders** ['andɐs] *adv* different(ly); ***jemand ~*** somebody else; ***~ werden*** change; ***~ sein*** (***als***) be different (from); ***es geht nicht ~*** there is no other way; **~herum 1.** *adv* the other way round **2.** F *adj* queer; **~wo**(**hin**) *adv* elsewhere
**anderthalb** ['andɐt'halp] *adj* one and a half
'**Änderung** *f* (-; *-en*) change; alteration
'**andeuten** *v/t* (*sep*, *-ge-*, *h*) hint (at), suggest; indicate; ***j-m ~, dass*** give s.o. a hint that
'**Andeutung** *f* (-; *-en*) hint, suggestion
'**Andrang** *m* (-[*e*]*s*; *no pl*) crush; ECON rush (***nach*** for), run (***zu, nach*** on)
'**andrehen** *v/t* (*sep*, *-ge-*, *h*) turn on; F ***j-m et. ~*** fob s.th. off on s.o.
'**androhen** *v/t* (*sep*, *-ge-*, *h*) ***j-m et. ~*** threaten s.o. with s.th.
'**aneignen** *v/refl* (*sep*, *-ge-*, *h*) acquire; *esp* JUR appropriate
**anei'nander** *adv tie etc* together; ***~ denken*** think of each other; ***~geraten*** *v/t* (*irr*, ***geraten***, *sep*, *sein*) clash (***mit*** with)
**Anekdote** [anɛk'doːtə] *f* (-; *-n*) anecdote
'**anekeln** *v/t* (*sep*, *-ge-*, *h*) disgust, sicken; ***es ekelt mich an*** it makes me sick
'**anerkannt** *adj* acknowledged, recognized
'**anerkennen** *v/t* (*irr*, ***kennen***, *sep*, *no -ge-*, *h*) acknowledge, recognize; appreciate; **~d** *adj* appreciative
'**Anerkennung** *f* (-; *-en*) acknowledg(e)ment, recognition; appreciation
'**anfahren** (*irr*, ***fahren***, *sep*, *-ge-*) **1.** *v/i* (*sein*) start **2.** *v/t* (*h*) deliver; MOT *etc* hit, *car etc*: *a.* run into; *fig* ***j-n ~*** jump on s.o.; '**Anfahrt** *f* journey, ride
'**Anfall** *m* MED fit, attack
'**anfallen** *v/t* (*irr*, ***fallen***, *sep*, *-ge-*, *h*) attack, assault; *dog*: go for
'**anfällig** *adj* delicate; ***~ für*** susceptible to
'**Anfang** *m* beginning, start; ***am ~*** at the beginning; ***~ Mai*** early in May; ***~ nächsten Jahres*** early next year; ***~ der neunziger Jahre*** in the early nineties; ***er ist ~ 20*** he is in his early twenties; ***von ~ an*** from the beginning *or* start;
'**anfangen** *v/t and v/i* (*irr*, ***fangen***, *sep*, *-ge-*, *h*) begin, start; do;
'**Anfänger** *m* (*-s*; -), '**Anfängerin** *f* (-; *-nen*) beginner
'**anfangs** *adv* at first
'**Anfangs|buchstabe** *m* initial (letter); ***großer ~*** capital (letter); **~stadium** *n*: ***im ~*** at an early stage
'**anfassen** *v/t* (*sep*, *-ge-*, *h*) touch; take (hold of); ***sich ~*** take each other by the hands; F ***zum Anfassen*** everyman's
'**anfechtbar** *adj* contestable;
'**anfechten** *v/t* (*irr*, ***fechten***, *sep*, *-ge-*, *h*) contest; '**Anfechtung** *f* (-; *-en*) contesting
'**anfertigen** *v/t* (*sep*, *-ge-*, *h*) make, manufacture
'**anfeuchten** *v/t* (*sep*, *-ge-*, *h*) moisten
'**anfeuern** *fig v/t* (*sep*, *-ge-*, *h*) cheer
'**anflehen** *v/t* (*sep*, *-ge-*, *h*) implore
'**anfliegen** *v/t* (*irr*, ***fliegen***, *sep*, *-ge-*, *h*) AVIAT approach; fly (regularly) to
'**Anflug** *m* AVIAT approach; *fig* touch
'**anfordern** *v/t* (*sep*, *-ge-*, *h*) demand; request; '**Anforderung** *f* (-; *-en*) demand; request; *pl* requirements, qualifications
'**Anfrage** *f* (-; *-n*) inquiry
'**anfragen** *v/i* (*sep*, *-ge-*, *h*) inquire (***bei j-m nach et.*** of s.o. about s.th.)
'**anfreunden** *v/refl* (*sep*, *-ge-*, *h*) make friends (***mit*** with)
'**anfühlen** *v/refl* (*sep*, *-ge-*, *h*) feel; ***es***

***fühlt sich weich an*** it feels soft
'**anführen** *v/t* (*sep*, *-ge-*, *h*) lead; state; F fool; '**Anführer(in)** leader
'**Anführungszeichen** *pl* quotation marks, inverted commas
'**Angabe** *f* (-; *-n*) statement; indication; F big talk; *tennis*: service; *pl* information, data; TECH specifications
'**angeben** (*irr*, ***geben***, *sep*, *-ge-*, *h*) **1.** *v/t* give, state; *customs*: declare; indicate; quote (*price*) **2.** *v/i* F *fig* brag, show off; *tennis*: serve; '**Angeber** F *m* (*-s*; -) braggart, show-off; **Angeberei** [ange:bə'rai] F *f* (-; *no pl*) bragging, showing off
**angeblich** ['ange:plɪç] *adj* alleged; ***~ ist er*** ... he is said to be ...
'**angeboren** *adj* innate, inborn; MED congenital
'**Angebot** *n* (-[*e*]*s*, *-e*) offer (*a.* ECON); ***~ und Nachfrage*** supply and demand
'**ange|bracht** *adj* appropriate; **~bunden** *adj*: ***kurz ~*** curt; **~gossen** F *adj*: ***wie ~ sitzen*** fit like a glove; **~heitert** *adj* tipsy, *Br a.* (slightly) merry
'**angehen** (*irr*, ***gehen***, *sep*, *-ge-*, *sein*) **1.** F *v/i light etc*: go on **2.** *v/t* concern; ***das geht dich nichts an*** that is none of your business; **~d** *adj* future; ***~er Arzt*** doctor-to-be
'**angehören** *v/i* (*sep*, *no -ge-*, *h*) belong to; '**Angehörige** *m*, *f* (*-n*; *-n*) relative; member; ***die nächsten ~n*** the next of kin
'**Angeklagte** *m*, *f* (*-n*; *-n*) JUR defendant
**Angel** ['aŋəl] *f* (-; *-n*) fishing tackle; TECH hinge
'**Angelegenheit** *f* (-; *-en*) matter, affair
**angelehnt** *adj door etc*: ajar
'**angelernt** *adj* semi-skilled (*worker*)
'**Angelhaken** *m* fishhook
'**angeln** (*ge-*, *h*) **1.** *v/i* (***nach*** for) fish, angle (*both a. fig*) **2.** *v/t* catch, hook
'**Angelrute** *f* fishing rod
**Angelsachse** ['aŋəlzaksə] *m* (*-n*; *-n*), **angelsächsisch** ['aŋəlzɛksɪʃ] *adj* Anglo-Saxon
'**Angelschein** *m* fishing permit
'**Angelschnur** *f* fishing line
**angemessen** *adj* proper, suitable; just (*punishment*); reasonable (*price*)
'**angenehm** *adj* pleasant, agreeable; ***~!*** pleased to meet you
'**ange|nommen** *cj* (let's) suppose, supposing; **~regt** *adj* animated; lively; **~schrieben** *adj*: ***bei j-m gut*** (***schlecht***) ***~ sein*** be in s.o.'s good (bad) books; **~sehen** *adj* respected
'**angesichts** *prp* (*gen*) in view of
'**Angestellte** *m*, *f* (*-n*; *-n*) employee (***bei*** with), *pl* the staff
'**ange|tan** *adj*: ***ganz ~ sein von*** be taken with; **~trunken** *adj* (slightly) drunk; ***in ~em Zustand*** under the influence of alcohol; **~wandt** *adj* applied; **~wiesen** *adj*: ***~ auf*** (*acc*) dependent (up)on
'**angewöhnen** *v/t* (*sep*, *no -ge-*, *h*) ***sich*** (***j-m***) ***~, et. zu tun*** get (s.o.) used to doing s.th.; ***sich das Rauchen ~*** take to smoking; '**Angewohnheit** *f* habit
**Angina** [aŋ'gi:na] *f* (-; *-nen*) MED tonsillitis
'**angleichen** *v/t* (*irr*, ***gleichen***, *sep*, *-ge-*, *h*) adjust (***an*** *acc* to)
**Angler** ['aŋlɐ] *m* (*-s*; -) angler
**Anglist** [aŋ'glɪst] *m* (*-en*; *-en*), **An'glistin** *f* (-; *-nen*) student of (*or* graduate in) English
'**angreifen** *v/t* (*irr*, ***greifen***, *sep*, *-ge-*, *h*) attack (*a.* SPORT *and fig*); affect (*health etc*); touch (*supplies*)
'**Angreifer** *m* (*-s*; -) attacker, SPORT *a.* offensive player; *esp* POL aggressor
'**angrenzend** *adj* adjacent (***an*** *acc* to)
'**Angriff** *m* attack (*a.* SPORT *and fig*); MIL assault, charge; ***in ~ nehmen*** set about
'**angriffslustig** *adj* aggressive
**Angst** [aŋst] *f* (-; *Ängste* ['ɛŋstə]) fear (***vor*** *dat* of); ***~ haben*** (***vor*** *dat*) be afraid *or* scared (of); ***j-m ~ einjagen*** frighten *or* scare s.o.; (***hab***) ***keine Angst!*** don't be afraid!; **~hase** F *m* chicken
**ängstigen** ['ɛŋstɪgən] *v/t* (*ge-*, *h*) frighten, scare; ***sich ~*** be afraid (***vor*** *dat* of); be worried (***um*** about)
**ängstlich** ['ɛŋstlɪç] *adj* timid, fearful; anxious
'**anhaben** F *v/t* (*irr*, ***haben***, *sep*, *-ge-*, *h*) have on (*a. light etc*), *a.* wear, be wearing (*dress etc*)
'**anhalten** (*irr*, ***halten***, *sep*, *-ge-*, *h*) **1.** *v/t* stop; ***den Atem ~*** hold one's breath **2.** *v/i* stop; continue; **~d** *adj* continual
'**Anhalter** *m* (*-s*; -) hitchhiker; F ***per ~ fahren*** hitchhike
'**Anhaltspunkt** *m* clue
**an'hand** *prp* (*gen*) by means of
'**Anhang** *m* appendix; (*no pl*) relations;
'**anhängen** *v/t* (*sep*, *-ge-*, *h*) add; hang

up; RAIL, MOT couple (**an** *acc* to); 'Anhänger *m* (-*s*; -) follower, supporter (*a.* SPORT); pendant; label, tag; MOT trailer; 'anhänglich *adj* affectionate; *contp* clinging

'**anhäufen** *v/t and v/refl* (*sep*, -*ge*-, *h*) heap up, accumulate

'**Anhäufung** *f* (-; -*en*) accumulation

'**anheben** *v/t* (*irr*, **heben**, *sep*, -*ge*-, *h*) lift, raise (*a. price*); MOT jack up

'**anheften** *v/t* (*sep*, -*ge*-, *h*) attach, tack (*both*: **an** *acc* to)

**Anhieb** *m*: ***auf*** **~** on the first try

'**anhimmeln** F *v/t* (*sep*, -*ge*-, *h*) idolize, worship

'**Anhöhe** *f* rise, hill, elevation

**anhören** *v/t* (*sep*, -*ge*-, *h*) listen to; ***mit*** **~** overhear; ***es hört sich ... an*** it sounds ...; '**Anhörung** *f* (-; -*en*) hearing

**animieren** [ani'mi:rən] *v/t* (*no -ge-*, *h*) encourage; stimulate

'**ankämpfen** *v/i* (*sep*, -*ge*-, *h*) **~ *gegen*** fight *s.th.*

'**Ankauf** *m* purchase

**Anker** ['aŋkɐ] *m* (-*s*; -) MAR anchor; ***vor*~ *gehen*** drop anchor

'**ankern** *v/i* (*ge*-, *h*) MAR anchor

'**anketten** *v/t* (*sep*, -*ge*-, *h*) chain up

'**Anklage** *f* (-; *no pl*) JUR accusation, charge (*a. fig*); '**anklagen** *v/t* (*sep*, -*ge*-, *h*) JUR accuse (***wegen*** of), charge (with) (*both a. fig.*)

'**anklammern** *v/t* (*sep*, -*ge*-, *h*) clip *s.th.* on; ***sich*** **~** (***an*** *acc*) cling (to)

**Anklang** *m*: **~ *finden*** meet with approval

'**ankleben** *v/t* (*sep*, -*ge*-, *h*) stick on (**an** *dat or acc* to)

'**anklicken** *v/t* (*sep*, -*ge*-, *h*) IT click

'**anklopfen** *v/i* (*sep*, -*ge*-, *h*) knock (**an** *dat or acc* at)

'**anknipsen** *v/t* (*sep*, -*ge*-, *h*) switch on

'**anknüpfen** *v/t* (*sep*, -*ge*-, *h*) tie (**an** *acc* to); *fig* begin; ***Beziehungen*** **~** (***zu***) establish contacts (with)

'**ankommen** *v/i* (*irr*, **kommen**, *sep*, -*ge*-, *sein*) arrive; ***nicht gegen j-n*** **~** be no match for s.o.; ***es kommt*** (***ganz***) ***darauf an*** it (all) depends; ***es kommt darauf an, dass*** what matters is; ***darauf kommt es nicht an*** that doesn't matter; ***es darauf*** **~ *lassen*** take a chance; ***gut*** **~** (***bei***) *fig* go down well (with)

'**ankündigen** *v/t* (*sep*, -*ge*-, *h*) announce; advertise; '**Ankündigung** *f* announcement; advertisement

**Ankunft** ['ankʊnft] *f* (-; *no pl*) arrival

'**anlächeln**, '**anlachen** *v/t* (*sep*, -*ge*-, *h*) smile at

'**Anlage** *f* arrangement; facility; plant; TECH system; (stereo *etc*) set; ECON investment; enclosure; *fig* gift; *pl* park, gardens; ***sanitäre*** **~*n*** sanitary facilities

**Anlass** ['anlas] *m* (-*es*; *Anlässe* ['anlɛsə]) occasion; cause

'**anlassen** *v/t* (*irr*, **lassen**, *sep*, -*ge*-, *h*) MOT start; F keep on, leave on (*a. light etc*); '**Anlasser** *m* (-*s*; -) MOT starter

**anlässlich** ['anlɛslɪç] *prp* (*gen*) on the occasion of

'**Anlauf** *m* SPORT run-up; *fig* start

'**anlaufen** (*irr*, **laufen**, *sep*, -*ge*-) **1.** *v/i* (*sein*) run up; *fig* start; *metal*: tarnish; *glasses etc*: steam up **2.** *v/t* (*h*) MAR call *or* touch at

'**anlegen** (*sep*, -*ge*-, *h*) **1.** *v/t* put on (*dress etc*); lay out (garden *etc*); build (*road etc*); invest (*money*); found (*town etc*); MED apply (*dressing etc*); lay in (*supplies*); ***sich mit j-m*** **~** pick a quarrel with s.o. **2.** *v/i* MAR land; moor; ***es*** **~ *auf*** (*acc*) aim at; '**Anleger** *m* (-*s*; -) ECON investor; MAR landing stage

'**anlehnen** *v/t* (*sep*, -*ge*-, *h*) lean (**an** *acc* against); leave *door etc* ajar; ***sich*** **~ *an*** (*acc*) lean against, *fig* lean on *s.o.*

**Anleihe** ['anlaiə] *f* (-; -*n*) ECON loan

'**Anleitung** *f* (-; -*en*) guidance, instruction; *written* instructions

'**Anliegen** *n* (-*s*; -) request; message (*of a film etc*)

**Anlieger** ['anli:gɐ] *m* (-*s*; -) resident

'**anlocken** *v/t* (*sep*, -*ge*-, *h*) attract, lure

'**anmachen** *v/t* (*sep*, -*ge*-, *h*) light (*fire etc*); turn on (*light etc*); dress (*salad*); F chat *s.o.* up; turn *s.o.* on

'**anmalen** *v/t* (*sep*, -*ge*-, *h*) paint

'**Anmarsch** *m*: ***im*** **~** on the way

**anmaßen** *v/t* (*sep*, -*ge*-, *h*) ***sich*** **~** assume; claim (*right*); ***sich*** **~, *et. zu tun*** presume to do s.th.; **~d** *adj* arrogant

'**anmelden** *v/t* (*sep*, -*ge*-, *h*) announce (*visitor*); register (*birth etc*); *customs*: declare; ***sich*** **~** enrol(l) (*for classes etc*); register (*at a hotel*); ***sich*** **~ *bei*** make an appointment with (*doctor etc*)

'**Anmeldung** *f* announcement; registration, enrol(l)ment

'**anmerken** *v/t* (*sep*, *-ge-*, *h*) ***j-m et.*** **~** notice s.th. in s.o.; ***sich et.*** (***nichts***) **~** ***lassen*** (not) let it show; '**Anmerkung** *f* (-; *-en*) note; annotation, footnote
**Anmut** ['anmu:t] *f* (-; *no pl*) grace
'**anmutig** *adj* graceful
'**annähen** *v/t* (*sep*, *-ge-*, *h*) sew on (***an*** *acc* to)
'**annähernd** *adv* approximately
'**Annäherung** *f* (-; *-en*) approach (***an*** *acc* to); '**Annäherungsversuche** *pl* advances, F pass
**Annahme** ['anna:mə] *f* (-; *-n*) (*no pl*) acceptance (*a. fig*); assumption
'**annehmbar** *adj* acceptable; reasonable (*price etc*); '**annehmen** *v/t* (*irr*, ***nehmen***, *sep*, *-ge-*, *h*) accept; suppose; adopt (*child*, *name*); take (*ball*); take on (*color*, *look etc*); ***sich e-r Sache*** *or* ***j-s*** **~** take care of s.th. *or* s.o.; '**Annehmlichkeiten** *pl* comforts, amenities
**Annonce** [a'nõ:sə] *f* (-; *-n*) advertisement
**annullieren** [anʊ'li:rən] *v/t* (*no -ge-*, *h*) annul; ECON cancel
**anöden** ['anˀø:dən] F *v/t* (*sep*, *-ge-*, *h*) bore *s.o.* to death
**anonym** [ano'ny:m] *adj* anonymous
**Anonymität** [anonymi'tɛ:t] *f* (-; *no pl*) anonymity
**Anorak** ['anorak] *m* (*-s*; *-s*) anorak
'**anordnen** *v/t* (*sep*, *-ge-*, *h*) arrange; give order(s), order; '**Anordnung** *f* (-; *-en*) arrangement; direction, order
'**anorganisch** *adj* CHEM inorganic
'**anpacken** F *fig* (*sep*, *-ge-*, *h*) **1.** *v/t* tackle **2.** *v/i*: ***mit*** **~** lend a hand
'**anpassen** *v/t* (*sep*, *-ge-*, *h*) adapt, adjust (*both a.* ***sich*** **~**) (*dat*, ***an*** *acc* to)
'**Anpassung** *f* (-; *-en*) adaptation, adjustment
'**anpassungsfähig** *adj* adaptable
'**Anpassungsfähigkeit** *f* adaptability
'**Anpfiff** *m* SPORT starting whistle; F *fig* dressing-down
'**anpflanzen** *v/t* (*sep*, *-ge-*, *h*) cultivate, plant; '**Anpflanzung** *f* cultivation
'**anpöbeln** *v/t* (*sep*, *-ge-*, *h*) accost; shout abuse at; **anprangern** ['anpraŋɐn] *v/t* (*sep*, *-ge-*, *h*) denounce; '**anpreisen** *v/t* (*irr*, ***preisen***, *sep*, *-ge-*, *h*) push; plug; 'anpro,bieren *v/t* (*no -ge-*, *h*) try on; '**anpumpen** F *v/t* (*sep*, *-ge-*, *h*) touch *s.o.* (***um*** for); '**anraten** *v/t* (*irr*, ***raten***, *sep*, *-ge-*, *h*) advise; '**anrechnen** *v/t* (*sep*, *-ge-*, *h*) charge; allow
'**Anrecht** *n*: ***ein*** **~** ***haben auf*** (*acc*) be entitled to
'**Anrede** *f* address; '**anreden** *v/t* (*sep*, *-ge-*, *h*) address (***mit Namen*** by name)
'**anregen** *v/t* (*sep*, *-ge-*, *h*) stimulate; suggest; **~d** *adj* stimulating
'**Anregung** *f* stimulation; suggestion
'**Anregungsmittel** *n* PHARM stimulant
'**Anreise** *f* (*Anfahrt*) journey; (*Ankunft*) arrival
'**anreisen** *v/i* (*sep*, *-ge-*, *sein*) arrive
'**Anreisetag** *m* day of arrival
'**Anreiz** *m* incentive
'**anrichten** *v/t* (*sep*, *-ge-*, *h*) GASTR prepare, dress; cause, do (*damage etc*)
**anrüchig** ['anryçıç] *adj* disreputable
'**Anruf** *m* call (*a.* TEL); **~beantworter** *m* TEL answering machine
'**anrufen** *v/t* (*irr*, ***rufen***, *sep*, *-ge-*, *h*) TEL call *or* ring up, phone
'**anrühren** *v/t* (*sep*, *-ge-*, *h*) touch; mix
'**Ansage** *f* announcement; '**ansagen** *v/t* (*sep*, *-ge-*, *h*) announce; **Ansager** ['anza:gɐ] *m* (*-s*; -), **Ansagerin** ['anza:gərın] *f* (-; *-nen*) announcer
'**ansammeln** *v/t and v/refl* (*sep*, *-ge-*, *h*) accumulate; '**Ansammlung** *f* collection, accumulation; crowd
'**Ansatz** *m* start (***zu*** of); attempt (***zu*** at); approach; TECH attachment; MATH set--up; *pl* first signs
'**anschaffen** *v/t* (*sep*, *-ge-*, *h*) get; ***sich et.*** **~** buy *or* get (o.s.) s.th.
'**Anschaffung** *f* (-; *-en*) purchase, buy
'**anschauen** *v/t* (*sep*, *-ge-*, *h*) → ***ansehen***; '**anschaulich** *adj* graphic (*account etc*); '**Anschauung** *f* (-; *-en*) (***von***) view (of), opinion (about, of)
'**Anschauungsmateri,al** *n* PED visual aids
'**Anschein** *m* (-[*e*]*s*; *no pl*) appearance; ***allem*** **~** ***nach*** to all appearances; ***den*** **~** ***erwecken, als*** (***ob***) give the impression of …; '**anscheinend** *adv* apparently
'**anschieben** *v/t* (*irr*, ***shieben***, *sep*, *-ge-*, *h*) give a push (*a.* MOT)
'**Anschlag** *m* attack; poster; bill, notice; *typewriter*: stroke; MUS, *swimming*: touch; ***e-n*** **~** ***auf j-n verüben*** make an attempt on s.o.'s life; **~brett** *n* bulletin (*esp Br* notice) board

**'anschlagen** (*irr*, ***schlagen***, *sep*, *-ge-*, *h*) **1.** *v/t* post; MUS strike; chip (*cup etc*) **2.** *v/i dog*: bark; take (effect) (*a.* MED); *swimming*: touch the wall

**'anschließen** *v/t* (*irr*, ***schließen***, *sep*, *-ge-*, *h*) ELECTR, TECH connect; ***sich ~*** follow; agree with; ***sich j-m*** *or* ***e-r Sache ~*** join s.o. or s.th.; **~d 1.** *adj* following **2.** *adv* then, afterwards

**'Anschluss** *m* connection; ***im ~ an*** (*acc*) following; ***~ finden*** (***bei***) make contact *or* friends (with); ***~ bekommen*** TEL get through

**'anschmiegen** *v/refl* (*sep*, *-ge-*, *h*) snuggle up (***an*** *acc* to)

**'anschmiegsam** *adj* affectionate

**'anschnallen** *v/t* (*sep*, *-ge-*, *h*) strap on, put on (*a. ski*); ***sich ~*** AVIAT, MOT fasten one's seat belt; **'anschnauzen** F *v/t* (*sep*, *-ge-*, *h*) tell *s.o.* off, *Am a.* bawl *s.o.* out; **'anschneiden** *v/t* (*irr*, ***schneiden***, *sep*, *-ge-*, *h*) cut; *fig* bring up; **'anschrauben** *v/t* (*sep*, *-ge-*, *h*) screw on (***an*** *acc* to); **'anschreiben** *v/t* (*irr*, ***schreiben***, *sep*, *-ge-*, *h*) write on the (black)board; ***j-n ~*** write to s.o.; (***et.***) ***~ lassen*** buy (s.th.) on credit; → ***angeschrieben***; **'anschreien** *v/t* (*irr*, ***schreien***, *sep*, *-ge-*, *h*) shout at

**'Anschrift** *f* address

**'Anschuldigung** *f* (-; *-en*) accusation

**'anschwellen** *v/i* (*irr*, ***schwellen***, *sep*, *-ge-*, *sein*) swell (*a. fig*); **'anschwemmen** *v/t* (*sep*, *-ge-*, *h*) wash ashore

**'ansehen** *v/t* (*irr*, ***sehen***, *sep*, *-ge-*, *h*) look at, have *or* take a look at; watch; see (*all a.* ***sich*** [*dat*] ***~***); ***~ als*** look upon as; ***et. mit ~*** watch *or* witness s.th.; ***man sieht ihm an, dass ...*** one can see that ...; **'Ansehen** *n* (*-s*; *no pl*) reputation

**ansehnlich** ['anze:nlɪç] *adj* considerable

**'anseilen** *v/t and v/refl* (*sep*, *-ge-*, *h*) rope

**'ansetzen** (*sep*, *-ge-*, *h*) **1.** *v/t* put (***an*** *acc* to); put on, add; fix, set (*date etc*); ***Fett*** *etc* ***~*** put on weight *etc* **2.** *v/i*: ***~ zu*** prepare for (*landing etc*)

**'Ansicht** *f* (-; *-en*) view, *a.* opinion, *a.* sight; ***der ~ sein, dass ...*** be of the opinion that ...; ***meiner ~ nach*** in my opinion; ***zur ~*** ECON on approval

**'Ansichts|karte** *f* picture postcard; **~sache** *f* matter of opinion

**'anspannen** *v/t* (*sep*, *-ge-*, *h*) strain

**'Anspannung** *f* (-; *-en*) strain, exertion

**'anspielen** *v/i* (*sep*, *-ge-*, *h*) *soccer*: kick off; ***~ auf*** (*acc*) allude to, hint at

**'Anspielung** *f* (-; *-en*) allusion, hint

**'anspitzen** *v/t* (*sep*, *-ge-*, *h*) sharpen

**'Ansporn** *m* (-[*e*]*s*; *no pl*) incentive

**'anspornen** *v/t* (*sep*, *-ge-*, *h*) encourage, spur *s.o.* on

**'Ansprache** *f* address, speech; ***e-e ~ halten*** deliver an address

**'ansprechen** *v/t* (*irr*, ***sprechen***, *sep*, *-ge-*, *h*) address, speak to; *fig* appeal to; **~d** *adj* attractive

**'Ansprechpartner** *m* s.o. to talk to, contact

**'anspringen** (*irr*, ***springen***, *sep*, *-ge-*) **1.** *v/i* (*sein*) *engine*: start **2.** *v/t* (*h*) jump (up)on

**'anspritzen** *v/t* (*sep*, *-ge-*, *h*) spatter

**'Anspruch** *m* claim (***auf*** *acc* to) (*a.* JUR); ***~ haben auf*** (*acc*) be entitled to; ***~ erheben auf*** (*acc*) claim; ***Zeit in ~ nehmen*** take up time

**'anspruchslos** *adj* modest; light, undemanding (*reading etc*); *contp* trivial

**'anspruchsvoll** *adj* demanding; sophisticated, refined (*tastes etc*)

**Anstalt** ['anʃtalt] *f* (-; *-en*) establishment, institution; mental hospital; ***~en machen zu*** get ready for

**'Anstand** *m* (-[*e*]*s*; *no pl*) decency; manners; **'anständig** *adj* decent (*a. fig*)

**'anstandslos** *adv* unhesitatingly; without difficulty

**'anstarren** *v/t* (*sep*, *-ge-*, *h*) stare at

**an'statt** *prp* (*gen*) *and cj* instead of

**'anstechen** *v/t* (*irr*, ***stechen***, *sep*, *-ge-*, *h*) tap (*barrel*)

**'anstecken** *v/t* (*sep*, *-ge-*, *h*) stick on; put on (*ring*); light; set fire to; MED infect; ***sich bei j-m ~*** MED catch s.th. from s.o.; **~d** *adj* MED infectious, contagious, catching (*all a. fig*)

**'Anstecknadel** *f* pin, button

**'Ansteckung** *f* (-; *no pl*) MED infection, contagion

**'anstehen** *v/i* (*irr*, ***stehen***, *sep*, *-ge-*, *h*) (***nach*** for) stand in line, *Br* queue up

**'ansteigen** *v/i* (*irr*, ***steigen***, *sep*, *-ge-*, *sein*) rise

**'anstellen** *v/t* (*sep*, *-ge-*, *h*) engage, employ; TV *etc*: turn on; MOT start; F be up to (*s.th. illegal etc*); make (*inquiries etc*);

***sich ~*** line up (***nach*** for), *Br* queue up (for); F (make a) fuss

ˈ**Anstellung** *f* job, position; ***e-e ~ finden*** find employment

**Anstieg** [ˈanʃtiːk] *m* (-[*e*]*s*; *no pl*) rise, increase

ˈ**anstiften** *v/t* (*sep*, *-ge-*, *h*) incite

ˈ**Anstifter** *m* instigator

ˈ**Anstiftung** *f* incitement

ˈ**anstimmen** *v/t* (*sep*, *-ge-*, *h*) MUS strike up

ˈ**Anstoß** *m soccer*: kickoff; *fig* initiative, impulse; offen|se, *Br* -ce; ***~ erregen*** give offense (***bei*** to); ***~ nehmen an*** take offense at; ***den ~ zu et. geben*** start s.th., initiate s.th.; ˈ**anstoßen** (*irr*, ***stoßen***, *sep*, *-ge-*) **1.** *v/t* (*h*) nudge *s.o.* **2.** *v/i* (*sein*) knock, bump; (*h*) clink glasses; ***~ auf*** (*acc*) drink to *s.o. or s.th.*

**anstößig** [ˈanʃtøːsɪç] *adj* offensive

ˈ**anstrahlen** *v/t* (*sep*, *-ge-*, *h*) illuminate; beam at *s.o.*

ˈ**anstreichen** *v/t* (*irr*, ***streichen***, *sep*, *-ge-*, *h*) paint; PED mark (*mistakes etc*)

ˈ**Anstreicher** *m* (house)painter

ˈ**anstrengen** *v/refl* (*sep*, *-ge-*, *h*) try (hard), make an effort; **~d** *adj* strenuous, hard

ˈ**Anstrengung** *f* (-; *-en*) exertion, strain; effort

**Ansturm** *fig m* (-[*e*]*s*; *no pl*) rush (***auf*** *acc* for)

ˈ**Anteil** *m* share (*a.* ECON), portion; ***~ nehmen an*** (*dat*) take an interest in; sympathize with; **~nahme** [ˈannaːmə] *f* (-; *no pl*) sympathy; interest

**Antenne** [anˈtɛnə] *f* (-; *-n*) antenna, *Br* aerial

**Anti...**, **anti...** *in cpds* anti...

**Anti|alkoˈholiker** *m* teetotal(l)er; **~ˈbabypille** F *f* birth control pill, F the pill; **~ˈbiotikum** *n* MED antibiotic; **~blo-ˈckiersysˌtem** *n* MOT anti-lock braking system

**antik** [anˈtiːk] *adj* antique, HIST *a.* ancient; **Anˈtike** *f* (-; *no pl*) ancient world

ˈ**Antikörper** *m* MED antibody

**Antilope** [antiˈloːpə] *f* (-; *-n*) ZO antelope

**Antipathie** [antipaˈtiː] *f* (-; *-n*) antipathy

**Antiquariat** [antikvaˈrjaːt] *n* (-[*e*]*s*; *-e*) second-hand bookshop

**antiquarisch** [antiˈkvaːrɪʃ] *adj and adv* second-hand

**Antiquitäten** [antikviˈtɛːtən] *pl* antiques; **~laden** *m* antique shop

**Antisemit** [antizeˈmiːt] *m* (*-en*; *-en*) anti-Semite; **antiseˈmitisch** *adj* anti-Semitic; **Antisemitismus** [antizemiˈtɪsmʊs] *m* (-; *no pl*) anti-Semitism

**Antrag** [ˈantraːk] *m* (-[*e*]*s*; *Anträge* [ˈantrɛːgə]) application; PARL motion; proposal; ***~ stellen auf*** (*acc*) make an application for; PARL move for; **~steller(in)** [ˈantraːkʃtɛlɐ, ˈantraːkʃtɛlərɪn] *m* (*-s*; *-/-*; *-nen*) applicant; PARL mover

ˈ**antreiben** (*irr*, ***treiben***, *sep*, *-ge-*) **1.** *v/t* (*h*) TECH drive; urge *s.o.* (on) **2.** *v/i* (*sein*) float ashore

ˈ**antreten** (*irr*, ***treten***, *sep*, *-ge-*) **1.** *v/t* (*h*) enter upon (*office etc*); take up (*position*); set out on (*journey*) **2.** *v/i* (*sein*) take one's place; MIL line up

ˈ**Antrieb** *m* TECH drive (*a. fig*), propulsion; *fig* motive, impulse; ***aus eigenem ~*** of one's own accord

ˈ**antun** *v/t* (*irr*, ***tun***, *sep*, *-ge-*, *h*) ***j-m et. ~*** do s.th. to s.o.; ***sich et. ~*** lay hands on o.s.

**Antwort** [ˈantvɔrt] *f* (-; *-en*) answer (***auf*** *acc* to), reply (to)

ˈ**antworten** *v/i* (*ge-*, *h*) answer (***j-m*** s.o., ***auf et.*** s.th.), reply (to s.o. *or* s.th.)

ˈ**anvertrauen** *v/t* (*sep*, *no -ge-*, *h*) ***j-m et. ~*** (en)trust s.o. with s.th.; confide s.th. to s.o.

ˈ**anwachsen** *v/i* (*irr*, ***wachsen***, *sep*, *-ge-*, *sein*) BOT take root; *fig* increase

**Anwalt** [ˈanvalt] *m* (-[*e*]*s*; *Anwälte* [ˈanvɛltə]) → ***Rechtsanwalt***

ˈ**Anwärter** *m* candidate (***auf*** *acc* for)

ˈ**anweisen** *v/t* (*irr*, ***weisen***, *sep*, *-ge-*, *h*) instruct; direct, order

ˈ**Anweisung** *f* instruction; order

ˈ**anwenden** *v/t* ([irr, ***wenden***,] *sep*, *-ge-*, *h*) use; apply (***auf*** *acc* to)

ˈ**Anwendung** *f* use; application

ˈ**anwerben** *v/t* (*irr*, ***werben***, *sep*, *-ge-*, *h*) recruit (*a. fig*)

ˈ**Anwesen** *n* (*-s*; -) estate; property

ˈ**anwesend** *adj* present

ˈ**Anwesenheit** *f* (-; *no pl*) presence; PED attendance; ***die ~ feststellen*** call the roll; ˈ**Anwesenheitsliste** *f* attendance record (*Br* list)

**anwidern** [ˈanviːdɐn] *v/t* (*sep*, *-ge-*, *h*) make *s.o.* sick

ˈ**Anzahl** *f* (-; *no pl*) number, quantity

**'anzahlen** *v/t* (*sep*, *-ge-*, *h*) pay on account; **'Anzahlung** *f* down payment
**'anzapfen** *v/t* (*sep*, *-ge-*, *h*) tap
**'Anzeichen** *n* symptom (*a.* MED), sign
**Anzeige** ['antsaigə] *f* (-; *-n*) advertisement; announcement; JUR information; IT display; TECH reading
**'anzeigen** *v/t* (*sep*, *-ge-*, *h*) announce; report to the police; TECH indicate, show
**'anziehen** *v/t* (*irr*, ***ziehen***, *sep*, *-ge-*, *h*) put on (*dress etc*); dress *s.o.*; *fig* attract, draw; tighten (*screw*); pull (*lever etc*); ***sich ~*** get dressed; dress; **~d** *adj* attractive
**'Anziehung** *f* (-; *no pl*), **'Anziehungskraft** *f* (-; *no pl*) PHYS attraction, *fig a.* appeal
**'Anzug** *m* suit
**anzüglich** ['antsy:klıç] *adj* suggestive (*joke*); personal, offensive (*remark etc*)
**'anzünden** *v/t* (*sep*, *-ge-*, *h*) light; set on fire
**apart** [a'part] *adj* striking
**Apartment** [a'partmənt] *n* (*-s*; *-s*) studio (apartment *or Br* flat)
**apathisch** [a'pa:tıʃ] *adj* apathetic
**Apfel** ['apfəl] *m* (*-s*; *Äpfel* ['ɛpfəl]) BOT apple; **~mus** *n* GASTR apple sauce
**Apfelsine** [apfəl'zi:nə] *f* (-; *-n*) BOT orange
**'Apfelwein** *m* cider
**Apostel** [a'pɔstəl] *m* (*-s*; -) REL apostle
**Apostroph** [apo'strɔf] *m* (*-s*; *-e*) apostrophe
**Apotheke** [apo'te:kə] *f* (-; *-n*) pharmacy, drugstore, *Br* chemist's
**Apotheker** [apo'te:kɐ] *m* (*-s*; -), **Apo'thekerin** *f* (-; *-nen*) pharmacist, druggist, *Br* chemist
**App.** *abbr of* ***Apparat*** TEL ext., extension
**Apparat** [apa'ra:t] *m* (-[*e*]*s*; *-e*) apparatus; device; (tele)phone; radio; TV set; camera; POL *etc* machine(ry); ***am ~!*** TEL speaking!; ***am ~ bleiben*** TEL hold the line
**Appell** [a'pɛl] *m* (*-s*; *-e*) appeal (***an*** *acc* to); MIL roll call
**appellieren** [apɛ'li:rən] *v/i* (*no -ge-*, *h*) (make an) appeal (***an*** *acc* to)
**Appetit** [ape'ti:t] *m* (-[*e*]*s*; *no pl*) appetite (***auf*** *acc* for); ***~ auf et. haben*** feel like s.th.; ***guten ~!*** enjoy your meal!
**appe'titanregend** *adj* appetizing
**Appe'tithappen** *m* GASTR appetizer
**appe'titlich** *adj* appetizing, savo(u)ry, *fig a.* inviting
**applaudieren** [aplau'di:rən] *v/i* (*no -ge-*, *h*) applaud; **Applaus** [a'plaus] *m* (*-es*; *no pl*) applause
**Aprikose** [apri'ko:zə] *f* (-; *-n*) BOT apricot
**April** [a'prıl] *m* (-[*s*]; *no pl*) April; ***~! ~!*** April fool!
**Aqua|jogging** ['akvadʒɔgıŋ] *n* (*-s*; *no pl*) SPORT aqua jogging; **~planing** [akva'pla:nıŋ] *n* (-[*s*]; *no pl*) MOT hydroplaning, *Br* aquaplaning
**Aquarell** [akva'rɛl] *n* (*-s*; *-e*) watercolo(u)r
**Aquarium** [a'kva:rjʊm] *n* (*-s*; *-ien*) aquarium
**Äquator** [ɛ'kva:to:ɐ] *m* (*-s*; *no pl*) equator
**Ära** ['ɛ:ra] *f* (-; *no pl*) era
**Araber** ['arabɐ] *m* (*-s*; -), **Araberin** ['arabərın] *f* (-; *-nen*) Arab
**arabisch** [a'ra:bıʃ] *adj* Arabian; Arabic
**Arbeit** ['arbait] *f* (-; *-en*) work, ECON, POL *a.* labo(u)r; employment, job; PED test; *scientific etc* paper; workmanship; ***bei der ~*** at work; ***zur ~ gehen*** *or* ***fahren*** go to work; ***gute ~ leisten*** make a good job of it; ***sich an die ~ machen*** set to work; **'arbeiten** *v/i* (*ge-*, *h*) work (***an*** *dat* at, on)
**'Arbeiter** *m* (*-s*; -), **'Arbeiterin** *f* (-; *-nen*) worker
**'Arbeitgeber** *m* (*-s*; -) employer
**'Arbeitnehmer** *m* (*-s*; -) employee
**'Arbeits|agentur** *f Am* (un)employment agency, *Br* employment agency; **~amt** *n Am* employment office, *Br* job centre; **~blatt** *n* PED worksheet; **~erlaubnis** *f* green card, *Br* work permit
**'arbeitsfähig** *adj* fit for work
**'Arbeits|gang** *m* TECH operation; **~gemeinschaft** *f* work *or* study group; **~gericht** *n* JUR labor court, *Br* industrial tribunal; **~hose** *f* overalls; **~kleidung** *f* working clothes; **~kräfte** *pl* workers, labo(u)r
**'arbeitslos** *adj* unemployed, out of work; **'Arbeitslose** *m*, *f* (*-n*; *-n*) ***die ~n*** *pl* the unemployed
**'Arbeitslosengeld** *n* unemployment compensation (*Br* benefit); ***~ beziehen*** F be on the dole
**'Arbeitslosigkeit** *f* (-; *no pl*) unemploy-

ment
'**Arbeits|markt** *m* labo(u)r market; **~mi'nister** *m Am* Secretary of Labor; *Br* Minister of Labour; **~niederlegung** *f* strike, walkout; **~pause** *f* break, intermission; **~platz** *m* workplace; job
'**arbeitsscheu** *adj* work-shy
'**Arbeits|speicher** *m* IT main memory; **~suche** *f*: ***er ist auf ~*** he is looking for a job; **~süchtige** *m, f* workaholic; **~tag** *m* workday
'**arbeitsunfähig** *adj* unfit for work; *permanently* disabled
'**Arbeits|weise** *f* method (of working); **~zeit** *f* (***gleitende*** flexible) working hours; **~zeitverkürzung** *f* fewer working hours; **~zimmer** *n* study
**Archäologe** [arçɛo'lo:gə] *m* (*-n*; *-n*) arch(a)eologist; **Archäologie** [arçɛolo'gi:] *f* (*-*; *no pl*) arch(a)eology; **Archäo'login** *f* (*-*; *-nen*) arch(a)eologist
**Arche** ['arçə] *f* (*-*; *-n*) ark; ***die ~ Noah*** Noah's ark
**Architekt** [arçi'tɛkt] *m* (*-en*; *-en*), **Archi'tektin** *f* (*-*; *-nen*) architect; **architektonisch** [arçitɛk'to:nɪʃ] *adj* architectural; **Architektur** [arçitɛk'tu:ɐ] *f* (*-*; *-en*) architecture
**Archiv** [ar'çi:f] *n* (*-s*; *-e*) archives; record office
**Arena** [a're:na] *f* (*-*; *-nen*) ring
**Ärger** ['ɛrgɐ] *m* (*-s*; *no pl*) anger (***über*** *acc* at); trouble; F ***j-m ~ machen*** cause s.o. trouble; '**ärgerlich** *adj* angry (***über, auf*** *acc* at *s.th.*; with *s.o.*); annoying; '**ärgern** *v/t* (*ge-*, *h*) annoy; ***sich ~*** be annoyed (***über*** *acc* at, about *s.th.*, with *s.o.*); '**Ärgernis** *n* (*-ses*; *-se*) nuisance
**arglos** ['arklo:s] *adj* innocent
**Argwohn** ['arkvo:n] *m* (*-[e]s*; *no pl*) suspicion (***gegen*** of)
**argwöhnisch** ['arkvø:nɪʃ] *adj* suspicious
**Arie** ['a:rjə] *f* (*-*; *-n*) MUS aria
**Aristokratie** [arɪstokra'ti:] *f* (*-*; *-n*) aristocracy
**arm** [arm] *adj* poor; ***die Armen*** the poor
**Arm** *m* (*-[e]s*; *-e*) ANAT arm; GEOGR branch; F ***j-n auf den ~ nehmen*** pull s.o.'s leg
**Armaturen** [arma'tu:rən] *pl* TECH instruments; (plumbing) fixtures; **~brett** *n* MOT dashboard
'**Armband** *n* bracelet
'**Armbanduhr** *f* wrist-watch
**Armee** [ar'me:] *f* (*-*; *-n*) MIL armed forces; army
**Ärmel** ['ɛrməl] *m* (*-s*; *-*) sleeve
**ärmlich** ['ɛrmlɪç] *adj* poor (*a. fig*); shabby
'**Armreif(en)** *m* bangle
'**armselig** *adj* wretched, miserable
**Armut** ['armu:t] *f* (*-*; *no pl*) poverty; ***~ an*** (*dat*) lack of
**Aroma** [a'ro:ma] *n* (*-s*; *-men*) flavo(u)r; aroma
**Arrest** [a'rɛst] *m* (*-[e]s*; *-e*) PED detention; ***~ bekommen*** be kept in
**arrogant** [aro'gant] *adj* arrogant, conceited
**Arsch** [arʃ] V *m* (*-es*; *Ärsche* ['ɛrʃə]) ass, *Br* arse; **~loch** V *n* asshole, *Br* arsehole
**Art** [art] *f* (*-*; *-en*) way, manner; kind, sort; BIOL species; ***auf diese ~*** (in) this way; ***e-e ~ …*** a sort of …; ***Geräte aller ~*** all kinds *or* sorts of tools
'**Artenschutz** *m* protection of endangered species
**Arterie** [ar'te:rjə] *f* (*-*; *-n*) ANAT artery
**Ar'terienverkalkung** *f* MED arteriosclerosis
**Arthritis** [ar'tri:tɪs] *f* (*-*; *-tiden*) MED arthritis
**artig** ['artɪç] *adj* good, well-behaved; ***sei ~!*** be good!, be a good boy (*or* girl)!
**Artikel** [ar'ti:kəl] *m* (*-s*; *-*) article
**Artillerie** ['artɪləri:] *f* (*-*; *no pl*) MIL artillery
**Artist** [ar'tɪst] *m* (*-en*; *-en*), **Ar'tistin** *f* (*-*; *-nen*) acrobat, (circus) performer
**Arznei** [a:ɐts'nai] *f* (*-*; *-en*), **~mittel** *n* medicine, drug
**Arzt** [a:ɐtst] *m* (*-es*; *Ärzte* ['ɛ:ɐtstə]) doctor, physician; **Ärztin** ['ɛ:ɐtstɪn] *f* (*-*; *-nen*) (lady) doctor *or* physician
'**ärztlich** *adj* medical; ***sich ~ behandeln lassen*** undergo treatment
**As** [as] *n* (*-*; *-*) MUS A flat
**Asbest** [as'bɛst] *m* (*-[e]s*; *-e*) asbestos
**Asche** ['aʃə] *f* (*-*; *-n*) ash(es)
'**Aschen|bahn** *f* SPORT cinder-track, MOT dirt track; **~becher** *m* ashtray
**Ascher'mittwoch** *m* Ash Wednesday
**äsen** ['ɛ:zən] *v/i* (*ge-*, *h*) HUNT feed, browse
**Asiat** [a'zja:t] *m* (*-en*; *-en*), **Asi'atin** *f* (*-*; *-nen*) Asian; **asi'atisch** *adj* Asian, Asi-

atic; **Asien** ['aːzjən] *n (-s; no pl)* Asia
**Asket** [as'keːt] *m (-en; -en)*, **as'ketisch** *adj* ascetic
**'asozial** *adj* antisocial
**Asphalt** [as'falt] *m (-s; -e)* asphalt
**asphaltieren** [asfal'tiːrən] *v/t (no -ge-, h)* (cover with) asphalt
**Ass** [as] *n (-es; -e)* ace *(a. tennis and fig)*
**aß** [aːs] *pret of* ***essen***
**Assistent** [asɪs'tɛnt] *m (-en; -en)*, **Assis'tentin** *f (-; -nen)* assistant
**Assis'tenzarzt** *m Am* intern, *Br* houseman
**Ast** [ast] *m (-es; Äste* ['ɛstə]) BOT branch
**Astronaut** [astro'naut] *m (-en; -en)*, **Astro'nautin** *f (-; -nen)* astronaut
**Astronom** [astro'noːm] *m (-en; -en)* astronomer; **Astronomie** [astrono'miː] *f (-; no pl)* astronomy
**ASU** ['aːzu] *abbr of* ***Abgas-Sonder-Untersuchung*** MOT *Am* emissions test, *Br* exhaust emission test
**Asyl** [a'zyːl] *n (-s; -e)* asylum; **Asylant** [azy'lant] *m (-en; -en)*, **Asy'lantin** *f (-; -nen)* asylum seeker, (political) refugee
**A'syl|bewerber(in)** asylum seeker; **~recht** *n* right of (political) asylum
**Atelier** [ate'ljeː] *n (-s; -s)* studio
**Atem** ['aːtəm] *m (-s; no pl)* breath; ***außer~*** out of breath; ***(tief) ~ holen*** take a (deep) breath; **'atemberaubend** *adj* breathtaking; **'Atemgerät** *n* MED respirator; **'atemlos** *adj* breathless; **'Atempause** *f* F breather; **'Atemzug** *m* breath
**Äther** ['ɛːtɐ] *m (-s; no pl)* CHEM ether; *radio etc:* air
**Athlet** [at'leːt] *m (-en; -en)*, **Ath'letin** *f (-; -nen)* SPORT athlete
**ath'letisch** *adj* athletic
**Atlas** ['atlas] *m (-ses; -se, Atlanten)* atlas
**atmen** ['aːtmən] *v/i and v/t (ge-, h)* breathe
**Atmosphäre** [atmo'sfɛːrə] *f (-; -n)* atmosphere
**'Atmung** *f (-; no pl)* breathing, respiration
**Atoll** [a'tɔl] *n (-s; -e)* atoll
**Atom** [a'toːm] *n (-s; -e)* atom
**A'tom...** *in cpds -energie, -forschung, -kraft, -krieg, -müll, -rakete, -reaktor, -waffen etc* nuclear ...
**atomar** [ato'maːɐ] *adj* atomic, nuclear
**A'tombombe** *f* MIL atom(ic) bomb
**A'tomkern** *m* PHYS (atomic) nucleus
**a'tomwaffenfrei** *adj* nuclear-free
**Attentat** ['atəntaːt] *n (-[e]s; -e)* assassination attempt, attempt on *s.o.'s* life; ***Opfer e-s ~s werden*** be assassinated
**'Attentäter** *m (-s; -)* assassin
**Attest** [a'tɛst] *n (-[e]s; -e)* (doctor's) certificate
**Attraktion** [atrak'tsjoːn] *f (-; -en)* attraction; **attraktiv** [atrak'tiːf] *adj* attractive
**Attrappe** [a'trapə] *f (-; -n)* dummy
**Attribut** [atri'buːt] *n (-[e]s; -e)* LING attribute *(a. fig)*
**ätzend** ['ɛtsənt] *adj* corrosive, caustic *(a. fig)*; F gross; ***das ist echt ~*** it's the pits
**au** [au] *int* ouch!; ***~ fein!*** oh, good!
**Aubergine** [obɛr'ʒiːnə] *f (-; -n)* BOT eggplant, *Br* aubergine
**auch** [aux] *cj* also, too, as well; ***ich ~*** so am *(or* do) I, F me too; ***~ nicht*** not ... either; ***wenn ~*** even if; ***wo ~ (immer)*** wherever; ***ist es ~ wahr?*** is it really true?
**Audienz** [au'djɛnts] *f (-; -en)* audience *(**bei** with)*
**auf** [auf] *prp (dat and acc) and adv* on; in; at; open; up; ***~ Seite 20*** on page 20; ***~ der Straße*** on *(Br* in) the street; on the road; ***~ der Welt*** in the world; ***~ See*** at sea; ***~ dem Lande*** in the country; ***~ dem Bahnhof*** *etc* at the station *etc*; ***~ Urlaub*** on vacation; ***die Uhr stellen ~*** *(acc)* set the watch to; ***~ deutsch*** in German; ***~ deinen Wunsch*** at your request; ***~ die Sekunde genau*** to the second; ***~ und ab*** up and down
**'auf|arbeiten** *v/t (sep, -ge-, h)* catch up on *(backlog)*; refurbish; **~atmen** *v/i (sep, -ge-, h)* heave a sigh of relief
**'Aufbau** *m (-[e]s; no pl)* building (up); structure; **'aufbauen** *v/t (sep, -ge-, h)* build (up) *(a. fig)*; set up; construct
**'auf|bauschen** *v/t (sep, -ge-, h)* exaggerate; **~bekommen** *v/t (irr,* ***kommen****, sep, no -ge-, h)* get *door etc* open; be given *(a task etc)*; **~bereiten** *v/t (sep, no -ge-, h)* process, clean, treat; **~bessern** *v/t (sep, -ge-, h)* raise *(salary etc)*; **~bewahren** *v/t (sep, no -ge-, h)* keep; **~bieten** *v/t (irr,* ***bieten****, sep, -ge-, h)* muster; **~blasen** *v/t (irr,* ***blasen****, sep,*

*-ge-, h)* blow up; **~bleiben** *v/i (irr,* ***bleiben****, sep, -ge-, sein)* stay up; *door etc*: remain open; **~blenden** *v/i (sep, -ge-, h)* MOT turn the headlights up; **~blicken** *v/i (sep, -ge-, h)* look up (***zu*** at) *(a. fig)*; **~blitzen** *v/i (sep, -ge-, h, sein)* flash *(a. fig)*

'**aufbrausen** *v/i (sep, -ge-, sein)* fly into a temper; **~d** *adj* irascible

'**aufbrechen** *(irr,* ***brechen****, sep, -ge-)* **1.** *v/t (h)* break *or* force open **2.** *v/i (sein)* burst open; *fig* leave (***nach*** for)

'**aufbringen** *v/t (irr,* ***bringen****, sep, -ge-, h)* raise *(money)*; muster *(courage etc)*; start *(fashion etc)*; → ***aufgebracht***

'**Aufbruch** *m (-[e]s; no pl)* departure, start

'**auf|brühen** *v/t (sep, -ge-, h)* make; **~bürden** *v/t (sep, -ge-, h)* ***j-m et. ~*** burden s.o. with s.th.; **~decken** *v/t (sep, -ge-, h)* uncover; **~drängen** *v/t (sep, -ge-, h)* ***j-m et. ~*** force s.th. on s.o.; ***sich j-m ~*** impose on s.o.; ***sich ~*** *fig* suggest itself; **~drehen** F *(sep, -ge-, h)* **1.** *v/t* turn on **2.** *v/i* MOT step on the gas

'**aufdringlich** *adj* obtrusive

'**Aufdruck** *m* imprint; *on stamps*: overprint, surcharge

**aufei'nander** *adv* on top of each other; one after another; ***~folgend*** *adj* successive

**Aufenthalt** ['aufɛnthalt] *m (-[e]s; -e)* stay; RAIL stop

'**Aufenthalts|genehmigung** *f* residence permit; **~raum** *m* lounge, recreation room

'**auferstehen** *v/i (irr,* ***stehen****, sep, no -ge-, sein)* rise (from the dead)

'**Auferstehung** *f (-; -en)* REL resurrection

'**aufessen** *v/t (irr,* ***essen****, sep, -ge-, h)* eat up

'**auffahren** *v/i (irr,* ***fahren****, sep, -ge-, sein)* crash (***auf*** *acc* into); *fig* start up; '**Auffahrt** *f* approach; driveway, *Br* drive; '**Auffahrunfall** *m* MOT rear-end collision; pileup

'**auffallen** *v/i (irr,* ***fallen****, sep, -ge-, sein)* attract attention; ***j-m ~*** strike s.o.

'**auffallend**, '**auffällig** *adj* striking; conspicuous; flashy *(clothes)*

'**auffangen** *v/t (irr,* ***fangen****, sep, -ge-, h)* catch *(a. fig)*

'**auffassen** *v/t (sep, -ge-, h)* understand (***als*** as)

'**Auffassung** *f* view; interpretation

'**auffinden** *v/t (irr,* ***finden****, sep, -ge-, h)* find, discover

'**auffordern** *v/t (sep, -ge-, h)* ***j-n ~, et. zu tun*** ask *(or* tell) s.o. to do s.th.

'**Aufforderung** *f* request; demand

'**auffrischen** *v/t (sep, -ge-, h)* freshen up; brush up

'**aufführen** *v/t (sep, -ge-, h)* THEA *etc* perform, present; state; ***sich ~*** behave

'**Aufführung** *f* THEA *etc* performance; *film*: showing

'**Aufgabe** *f* task, job; duty; PED task, assignment; MATH problem; *fig* surrender; ***es sich zur ~ machen*** make it one's business

'**Aufgang** *m* staircase; AST rising

'**aufgeben** *(irr,* ***geben****, sep, -ge-, h)* **1.** *v/t* give up; mail, send, *Br* post; check *(baggage)*; PED set, give, assign *(homework etc)*; ECON place *(order etc)* **2.** *v/i* give up *or* in

'**aufge|bracht** *adj* furious; **~dreht** F *adj* excited; **~dunsen** ['aufgədʊnzən] *adj* puffed(-up)

'**aufgehen** *v/i (irr,* ***gehen****, sep, -ge-, sein)* open; *sun, dough etc*: rise; MATH come out even; ***in Flammen ~*** go up in flames

'**aufge|hoben** *fig adj*: ***gut ~ sein bei*** be in good hands with; **~legt** *adj*: ***zu et. ~ sein*** feel like (doing) s.th.; ***gut (schlecht) ~*** in a good (bad) mood; **~regt** *adj* excited; nervous; **~schlossen** *fig adj* open-minded; ***~ für*** open to; **~weckt** *fig adj* bright

'**aufgreifen** *v/t (irr,* ***greifen****, sep, -ge-, h)* pick up

**auf'grund** *(gen)* because of

'**auf|haben** F *v/t (irr,* ***haben****, sep, -ge-, h)* have on, wear; PED have *homework etc* to do; **~halten** *v/t (irr,* ***halten****, sep, -ge-, h)* stop, hold up *(a. traffic, thief etc)*; keep open; ***sich ~ (bei j-m)*** stay (with s.o.); **~hängen** *v/t (sep, -ge-, h)* hang (up); ***j-n ~*** hang s.o.; **~heben** *v/t (irr,* ***heben****, sep, -ge-, h)* pick up; keep; abolish *(law etc)*; break up *(meeting etc)*; ***sich gegenseitig ~*** neutralize each other; → ***aufgehoben***

'**Aufheben** *n (-s; no pl)* ***viel ~s machen*** make a fuss (***von*** about)

'**auf|heitern** *v/t (sep, -ge-, h)* cheer up;

***sich ~*** *weather*: clear up; **~helfen** *v/i* (*irr*, ***helfen***, *sep*, *-ge-*, *h*) help *s.o.* up; **~hellen** *v/t and v/refl* (*sep*, *-ge-*, *h*) brighten; **~hetzen** *v/t* (*sep*, *-ge-*, *h*) ***j-n ~ gegen*** set s.o. against; **~holen** (*sep*, *-ge-*, *h*) **1.** *v/t* make up for **2.** *v/i* catch up (***gegen*** with); **~horchen** *v/i* (*sep*, *-ge-*, *h*) prick (up) one's ears; ***~ lassen*** make *s.o.* sit up; **~hören** *v/i* (*sep*, *-ge-*, *h*) stop, end, finish, quit; ***mit et. ~*** stop (doing) s.th.; ***hör(t) auf!*** stop it!; **~kaufen** *v/t* (*sep*, *-ge-*, *h*) buy up

'**aufklären** *v/t* (*sep*, *-ge-*, *h*) clear up, *a.* solve (*crime*); ***j-n ~ über*** (*acc*) inform s.o. about; ***j-n (sexuell) ~*** F tell s.o. the facts of life; '**Aufklärung** *f* (-; *no pl*) clearing up, solution; information; sex education; PHILOS Enlightenment; MIL reconnaissance

'**aufkleben** *v/t* (*sep*, *-ge-*, *h*) paste *or* stick on; '**Aufkleber** *m* (*-s*; -) sticker

'**aufknöpfen** *v/t* (*sep*, *-ge-*, *h*) unbutton

'**aufkommen** *v/i* (*irr*, ***kommen***, *sep*, *-ge-*, *sein*) come up; come into fashion *or* use; *rumo(u)r etc*: arise; ***~ für*** pay (for)

'**Aufladegerät** *n* charger

'**aufladen** *v/t* (*irr*, ***laden***, *sep*, *-ge-*, *h*) load; ELECTR charge; (*prepaid card etc*) top up

'**Auflage** *f* edition; circulation

'**auf|lassen** F *v/t* (*irr*, ***lassen***, *sep*, *-ge-*, *h*) leave *door etc* open; keep *one's hat etc* on; **~lauern** *v/i* (*sep*, *-ge-*, *h*) ***j-m ~*** waylay s.o.

'**Auflauf** *m* crowd; GASTR soufflé, pudding

'**auf|laufen** *v/i* (*irr*, ***laufen***, *sep*, *-ge-*, *sein*) MAR run aground; **~leben** *v/i* (*sep*, *-ge-*, *sein*) *a.* ***(wieder) ~ lassen*** revive; **~legen** (*sep*, *-ge-*, *h*) **1.** *v/t* put on, lay on **2.** *v/i* TEL hang up

'**auflehnen** *v/t and v/refl* (*sep*, *-ge-*, *h*) lean (***auf*** *acc* on); ***sich ~*** rebel, revolt (***gegen*** against); '**Auflehnung** *f* (-; *-en*) rebellion, revolt

'**auf|lesen** *v/t* (*irr*, ***lesen***, *sep*, *-ge-*, *h*) pick up (*a. fig*); **~leuchten** *v/i* (*sep*, *-ge-*, *h*) flash (up); **~listen** *v/t* (*sep*, *-ge-*, *h*) list (a. IT); **~lockern** *v/t* (*sep*, *-ge-*, *h*) loosen up; *fig* liven up

'**auflösen** *v/t* (*sep*, *-ge-*, *h*) dissolve; solve (*a.* MATH); disintegrate; '**Auflösung** *f* (dis)solution; disintegration

'**aufmachen** F *v/t* (*sep*, *-ge-*, *h*) open; ***sich ~*** set out; '**Aufmachung** *f* (-; *-en*) get-up

'**aufmerksam** *adj* attentive (***auf*** *acc* to); thoughtful; ***j-n ~ machen auf*** (*acc*) call s.o.'s attention to

'**Aufmerksamkeit** *f* (-; *-en*) (*no pl*) attention; (*gift*) small present

'**aufmuntern** *v/t* (*sep*, *-ge-*, *h*) encourage; cheer up

**Aufnahme** ['aufnaːmə] *f* (-; *-n*) taking up; reception (*a.* MED *etc*); admission; photo(graph); recording; *film*: shooting

'**aufnahmefähig** *adj* receptive (***für*** of)

'**Aufnahme|gebühr** *f* admission fee; **~prüfung** *f* entrance exam(ination)

'**aufnehmen** *v/t* (*irr*, ***nehmen***, *sep*, *-ge-*, *h*) take up (*a. post etc*); pick up; put *s.o.* up; hold; take *s.th.* in; receive; PED *etc* admit; PHOT take a picture of; record; take (*the ball*); ***es ~ mit*** be a match for

'**aufpassen** *v/i* (*sep*, *-ge-*, *h*) pay attention; take care; ***~ auf*** (*acc*) take care of, look after; keep an eye on; ***pass auf!*** look out!

'**Aufprall** *m* (-[*e*]*s*; *no pl*) impact

'**aufprallen** *v/i* (*sep*, *-ge-*, *sein*) ***~ auf*** (*dat or acc*) hit

'**aufpumpen** *v/t* (*sep*, *-ge-*, *h*) pump up

'**aufputschen** *v/t* (*sep*, *-ge-*, *h*) pep up

'**Aufputschmittel** *n* PHARM stimulant, pep pill

'**auf|raffen** *v/refl* (*sep*, *-ge-*, *h*) ***sich ~ zu*** bring o.s. to *do s.th.*; **~räumen** *v/t* (*sep*, *-ge-*, *h*) tidy up; clear

'**aufrecht** *adj and adv* upright (*a. fig*); **~erhalten** *v/t* (*irr*, ***halten***, *sep*, *no -ge-*, *h*) maintain, keep up

'**aufregen** *v/t* (*sep*, *-ge-*, *h*) excite, upset; ***sich ~*** get excited *or* upset (***über*** *acc* about); **~d** *adj* exciting

'**Aufregung** *f* excitement; fuss

'**aufreiben** *fig v/t* (*irr*, ***reiben***, *sep*, *-ge-*, *h*) wear down; **~d** *adj* stressful

'**aufreißen** *v/t* (*irr*, ***reißen***, *sep*, *-ge-*, *h*) tear open; fling *door etc* open; open *one's eyes* wide; F pick *s.o.* up

'**aufreizend** *adj* provocative

'**aufrichten** *v/t* (*sep*, *-ge-*, *h*) put up, raise; ***sich ~*** straighten up; sit up

'**aufrichtig** *adj* sincere; frank

'**Aufrichtigkeit** *f* (-; *no pl*) sincerity; frankness

'**Aufriss** *m* (*-es*; *-e*) ARCH elevation

'**aufrollen** *v/t and v/refl* (*sep*, *-ge-*, *h*) roll up

'**Aufruf** *m* call; appeal (***zu*** for)

'**aufrufen** *v/t* (*irr*, ***rufen***, *sep*, *-ge-*, *h*) call on

**Aufruhr** ['aufruːɐ] *m* (*-s*; *no pl*) revolt; riot; turmoil; '**Aufrührer** *m* (*-s*; *-*) rebel; rioter; **aufrührerisch** ['aufryːrərɪʃ] *adj* rebellious

'**aufrunden** *v/t* (*sep*, *-ge-*, *h*) round off

'**aufrüsten** *v/t and v/i* (*sep*, *-ge-*, *h*) (re)-arm; '**Aufrüstung** *f* (re)armament

'**auf|rütteln** *fig v/t* (*sep*, *-ge-*, *h*) shake up, rouse; **~sagen** *v/t* (*sep*, *-ge-*, *h*) say; *a.* recite (*poem*)

**aufsässig** ['aufzɛsɪç] *adj* rebellious

'**Aufsatz** *m* PED essay, *Am a.* theme; (*newspaper etc*) article; TECH top

'**auf|saugen** *v/t* (*sep*, *-ge-*, *h*) absorb (*a. fig*); **~scheuern** *v/t* (*sep*, *-ge-*, *h*) chafe; **~schichten** *v/t* (*sep*, *-ge-*, *h*) pile up; **~schieben** *fig v/t* (*irr*, ***schieben***, *sep*, *-ge-*, *h*) put off, postpone; delay

'**Aufschlag** *m* impact; ECON extra charge; lapel; cuff, *Br* turnup; *tennis*: service; '**aufschlagen** (*irr*, ***schlagen***, *sep*, *-ge-*, *h*) **1.** *v/t* open (*book*, *eyes etc*); pitch (*tent*); cut (*one's knee etc*); ***Seite 3 ~*** open at page 3 **2.** *v/i tennis*: serve; ***auf dem Boden ~*** hit the ground

'**auf|schließen** *v/t* (*irr*, ***schließen***, *sep*, *-ge-*, *h*) unlock, open; **~schlitzen** *v/t* (*sep*, *-ge-*, *h*) slit *or* rip open

'**Aufschluss** *m* information (***über*** *acc* on)

'**auf|schnappen** F *fig v/t* (*sep*, *-ge-*, *h*) pick up; **~schneiden** (*irr*, ***schneiden***, *sep*, *-ge-*, *h*) **1.** *v/t* cut open; GASTR cut up **2.** F *fig v/i* brag, boast, talk big

'**Aufschnitt** *m* (*-[e]s*; *no pl*) GASTR cold cuts, *Br* (slices of) cold meat

'**auf|schnüren** *v/t* (*sep*, *-ge-*, *h*) untie; unlace; **~schrauben** *v/t* (*sep*, *-ge-*, *h*) unscrew; **~schrecken** (*sep*, *-ge-*) **1.** *v/t* (*h*) startle **2.** *v/i* (*sein*) start (up)

'**Aufschrei** *m* yell; scream, outcry (*a. fig*)

'**auf|schreiben** *v/t* (*irr*, ***schreiben***, *sep*, *-ge-*, *h*) write down; **~schreien** *v/i* (*irr*, ***schreien***, *sep*, *-ge-*, *h*) cry out, scream

'**Aufschrift** *f* inscription

'**Aufschub** *m* postponement; delay; adjournment; respite

'**Aufschwung** *m* SPORT swing-up; *esp* ECON recovery, upswing; boom

'**Aufsehen** *n* (*-s*; *no pl*) ***~ erregen*** attract attention; cause a sensation; ***~ erregend*** → ***aufsehenerregend***; '**aufsehenerregend** *adj* sensational

'**Aufseher** *m* (*-s*; *-*), '**Aufseherin** *f* (*-*; *-nen*) guard

'**aufsetzen** (*sep*, *-ge-*, *h*) **1.** *v/t* put on; draw up (*letter etc*); ***sich ~*** sit up **2.** *v/i* AVIAT touch down

'**Aufsetzer** *m* (*-s*; *-*) SPORT awkward bouncing ball

'**Aufsicht** *f* (*-*; *no pl*) supervision, control; ***~ führen*** PED *etc* be on (break) duty; proctor, *Br* invigilate

'**Aufsichts|behörde** *f* supervisory board; **~rat** *m* ECON board of directors; supervisory board

'**auf|sitzen** *v/i* (*irr*, ***sitzen***, *sep*, *-ge-*, *sein*) mount; **~spannen** *v/t* (*sep*, *-ge-*, *h*) stretch; put up (*umbrella*); spread; **~sparen** *v/t* (*sep*, *-ge-*, *h*) save; **~sperren** *v/t* (*sep*, *-ge-*, *h*) unlock; F open wide; **~spielen** *v/refl* (*sep*, *-ge-*, *h*) show off; ***sich ~ als*** play; **~spießen** *v/t* (*sep*, *-ge-*, *h*) spear, skewer; *animal*: gore; **~springen** *v/i* (*irr*, ***springen***, *sep*, *-ge-*, *sein*) jump up; *door etc*: fly open; *lips etc*: chap; **~spüren** *v/t* (*sep*, *-ge-*, *h*) track down; **~stacheln** *v/t* (*sep*, *-ge-*, *h*) goad (*s.o. into doing s.th.*); **~stampfen** *v/i* (*sep*, *-ge-*, *h*) stamp (one's foot)

'**Aufstand** *m* revolt, rebellion

'**Aufständische** *m*, *f* (*-n*; *-n*) rebel

'**auf|stapeln** *v/t* (*sep*, *-ge-*, *h*) pile up; **~stechen** *v/t* (*irr*, ***stechen***, *sep*, *-ge-*, *h*) puncture, prick open; MED lance; **~stecken** *v/t* (*sep*, *-ge-*, *h*) put up (*hair*); F *fig* give up; **~stehen** *v/i* (*irr*, ***stehen***, *sep*, *-ge-*, *sein*) get up, rise; **~steigen** *v/i* (*irr*, ***steigen***, *sep*, *-ge-*, *sein*) rise (*a. fig*); get on (*horse*, *bicycle*); be promoted; SPORT *Am a.* be moved up to a higher division

'**aufstellen** *v/t* (*sep*, *-ge-*, *h*) set up, put up; post (*guard*); set (*trap*, *record etc*); nominate *s.o.*; draw up (*table*, *list etc*)

'**Aufstellung** *f* putting up; nomination; list; SPORT line-up

**Aufstieg** ['aufʃtiːk] *m* (*-[e]s*; *-e*) ascent, *fig a.* rise

'**auf|stöbern** *fig v/t* (*sep*, *-ge-*, *h*) ferret out; **~stoßen** (*irr*, ***stoßen***, *sep*, *-ge-*, *h*) **1.** *v/t* push open **2.** *v/i* belch; **~stützen** *v/refl* (*sep*, *-ge-*, *h*) lean (***auf*** *acc or dat* on); **~suchen** *v/t* (*sep*, *-ge-*, *h*) visit; see

'**Auftakt** *m* MUS upbeat; *fig* prelude

'**auf|tanken** *v/t* (*sep*, *-ge-*, *h*) fill up; MOT, AVIAT refuel; **~tauchen** *v/i* (*sep*, *-ge-*, *sein*) appear; MAR surface; **~tauen** *v/t* (*sep*, *-ge-*, *h*) thaw; GASTR defrost; **~teilen** *v/t* (*sep*, *-ge-*, *h*) divide (up)

**Auftrag** ['auftra:k] *m* (-[*e*]*s*; *Aufträge* ['auftrɛ:gə]) instructions, order (*a.* ECON); MIL mission; ***im ~ von*** on behalf of; **auftragen** *v/t* (*irr*, ***tragen***, *sep*, *-ge-*, *h*) serve (up) (*food*); apply (*paint*); ***j-m et. ~*** ask (*or* tell) s.o. to do s.th; F ***dick ~*** exaggerate; '**Auftraggeber** *m* (-*s*; -) principal; customer

'**auf|treffen** *v/i* (*irr*, ***treffen***, *sep*, *-ge-*, *sein*) strike, hit; **~treiben** F *v/t* (*irr*, ***treiben***, *sep*, *-ge-*, *h*) get hold of; raise (*money*); **~trennen** *v/t* (*sep*, *-ge-*, *h*) undo (*seam*), cut open; **~treten** *v/i* (*irr*, ***treten***, *sep*, *-ge-*, *sein*) THEA *etc* appear (***als*** *as*); behave, act; occur

'**Auftreten** *n* (-*s*; *no pl*) appearance; behavio(u)r; occurrence

'**Auftrieb** *m* (-[*e*]*s*; *no pl*) PHYS buoyancy (*a. fig*); AVIAT lift; *fig* impetus

'**Auftritt** *m* THEA entrance

'**auf|tun** *v/refl* (*irr*, ***tun***, *sep*, *-ge-*, *h*) open (*a. fig*); *abyss*: yawn; **~türmen** *v/t* (*sep*, *-ge-*, *h*) pile *or* heap up; ***sich ~*** pile up; **~wachen** *v/i* (*sep*, *-ge-*, *sein*) wake up; **~wachsen** *v/i* (*irr*, ***wachsen***, *sep*, *-ge-*, *sein*) grow up

**Aufwand** ['aufvant] *m* (-[*e*]*s*; *no pl*) expenditure (***an*** *dat* of), *a.* expense; pomp

**aufwändig** ['aufvɛndɪç] *adj* costly; extravagant (*lifestyle*)

'**aufwärmen** *v/t* (*sep*, *-ge-*, *h*) warm up; F *fig contp* bring up

**aufwärts** ['aufvɛrts] *adv* upward(s); ***~gehen*** *v/i* (*irr*, ***gehen***, *sep*, *-ge-*, *sein*) *fig* improve

'**auf|wecken** *v/t* (*sep*, *-ge-*, *h*) wake (up); **~weichen** *v/t* (*sep*, *-ge-*, *h*) soften; soak; **~weisen** *v/t* (*irr*, ***weisen***, *sep*, *-ge-*, *h*) show, have; **~wenden** *v/t* ([*irr*, ***wenden***,] *sep*, *-ge-*, *h*) spend (***für*** on); ***Mühe ~*** take pains

**aufwendig** → ***aufwändig***

'**aufwerfen** *v/t* (*irr*, ***werfen***, *sep*, *-ge-*, *h*) raise (*question etc*)

'**aufwerten** *v/t* (*sep*, *-ge-*, *h*) ECON revalue; *fig* increase the value of

'**Aufwertung** *f* revaluation

'**aufwickeln** *v/t and v/refl* (*sep*, *-ge-*, *h*) wind up, roll up; put *hair* in curlers

**aufwiegeln** ['aufvi:gəln] *v/t* (*sep*, *-ge-*, *h*) stir up, incite, instigate

'**aufwiegen** *v/t* (*irr*, ***wiegen***, *sep*, *-ge-*, *h*) make up for

**Aufwiegler** ['aufvi:glɐ] *m* (-*s*; -) agitator; instigator

'**Aufwind** *m* upwind; ***im ~*** *fig* on the upswing

'**auf|wirbeln** *v/t* (*sep*, *-ge-*, *h*) whirl up; *fig* (***viel***) ***Staub ~*** make (quite) a stir; **~wischen** *v/t* (*sep*, *-ge-*, *h*) wipe up; **~wühlen** *fig v/t* (*sep*, *-ge-*, *h*) stir, move

'**aufzählen** *v/t* (*sep*, *-ge-*, *h*) name (one by one), list; '**Aufzählung** *f* enumeration, list

'**aufzeichnen** *v/t* (*sep*, *-ge-*, *h*) TV, *radio etc*: record, tape; draw; '**Aufzeichnung** *f* recording; *pl* notes

'**aufzeigen** *v/t* (*sep*, *-ge-*, *h*) show; demonstrate; point out (*mistake etc*)

'**aufziehen** (*irr*, ***ziehen***, *sep*, *-ge-*) **1.** *v/t* (*h*) draw *or* pull up; (pull) open; bring up (*child*); wind (up) (*clock*); mount (*photo etc*); ***j-n ~*** tease s.o. **2.** *v/i* (*sein*) come up; '**Aufzug** *m* elevator, *Br* lift; THEA act; F *contp* get-up

'**aufzwingen** *v/t* (*irr*, ***zwingen***, *sep*, *-ge-*, *h*) ***j-m et. ~*** force s.th. upon s.o.

**Augapfel** ['auk'apfəl] *m* ANAT eyeball

**Auge** ['augə] *n* (-*s*; -*n*) ANAT eye; ***ein blaues ~*** a black eye; ***mit bloßem ~*** with the naked eye; ***mit verbundenen ~n*** blindfold; ***in meinen ~n*** in my view; ***mit anderen ~n*** in a different light; ***aus den ~n verlieren*** lose sight of; ***ein ~ zudrücken*** turn a blind eye; ***unter vier ~n*** in private; F ***ins ~ gehen*** go wrong

'**Augenarzt** *m* eye specialist

'**Augenblick** *m* moment, instant

'**augenblicklich** **1.** *adj* present; immediate; momentary **2.** *adv* at present, at the moment; immediately

'**Augen|braue** *f* eyebrow; **~licht** *n* (-[*e*]*s*; *no pl*) eyesight; **~lid** *n* eyelid; **~maß** *n*: ***ein gutes ~*** a sure eye; ***nach dem ~*** by the eye; **~merk** *n*: ***sein ~ richten auf*** (*acc*) turn one's attention to, *fig a.* have in view; **~schein** *m* (-*s*; *no pl*) appearance; ***in ~ nehmen*** examine, inspect; **~zeuge** *m* eyewitness

**August** [au'gust] *m* (-; *no pl*) August

**Auktion** [auk'tsjo:n] *f* (-; *-en*) auction

**Auktionator** [auktsjo'na:to:ɐ] *m* (*-s*; *-en* [auktsjona'to:rən]) auctioneer

**Aula** ['aula] *f* (-; *-s*, *Aulen*) auditorium, *Br* (assembly) hall

**aus** [aus] *prp* (*dat*) *and adv mst* out of, from; of (*silk etc*); out of (*spite etc*); *light etc*: out, off; *play etc*: over, finished; SPORT out; ***~ dem Fenster*** *etc* out of the window *etc*; ***~ München*** from Munich; ***~ Holz*** (made) of wood; ***~ Mitleid*** out of pity; ***~ Spaß*** for fun; ***~ Versehen*** by mistake; ***~ diesem Grunde*** for this reason; ***von hier ~*** from here; F ***von mir ~!*** I don't care!; ***~ der Mode*** out of fashion; F ***~ sein*** be over; be out; ***~ sein auf*** (*acc*) be out for; be after (*s.o.'s money etc*); ***die Schule*** (***das Spiel***) ***ist ~*** school (the game) is over; ***einl~*** TECH on / off

**Aus** *n*: ***im ~*** *ball*: out of play

'**aus|arbeiten** *v/t* (*sep*, *-ge-*, *h*) work out; prepare; **~arten** *v/i* (*sep*, *-ge-*, *sein*) get out of hand; **~atmen** *v/t and v/i* (*sep*, *-ge-*, *h*) breathe out; **~baden** F *v/t* (*sep*, *-ge-*, *h*) ***et. ~ müssen*** take the rap for s.th.

'**Ausbau** *m* (*-[e]s*; *no pl*) extension; completion; removal; '**ausbauen** *v/t* (*sep*, *-ge-*, *h*) extend; complete; remove; improve; '**ausbaufähig** *adj*: ***et. ist ~*** there is potential for growth *or* development

'**ausbessern** *v/t* (*sep*, *-ge-*, *h*) mend, repair, F *a.* fix; '**Ausbesserung** *f* (-; *-en*) repair(ing)

'**Ausbeute** *f* (-; *no pl*) gain, profit; yield; '**ausbeuten** *v/t* (*sep*, *-ge-*, *h*) exploit (*a. contp*); '**Ausbeutung** *f* (-; *no pl*) exploitation

'**ausbilden** *v/t* (*sep*, *-ge-*, *h*) train, instruct; ***j-n ~ zu*** train s.o. to be

'**Ausbilder** *m* (*-s*; -) instructor

'**Ausbildung** *f* (-; *-en*) training, instruction

'**ausbleiben** *v/i* (*irr*, ***bleiben***, *sep*, *-ge-*, *sein*) stay out; fail to come; ***es konnte nicht ~*** it was inevitable

'**Ausblick** *m* view (***auf*** *acc* of); *fig* outlook (*for*)

'**ausbrechen** *v/i* (*irr*, ***brechen***, *sep*, *-ge-*, *sein*) break out (*a. fig*); ***in Tränen ~*** burst into tears; '**Ausbrecher** *m* (*-s*; -) escaped prisoner

'**ausbreiten** *v/t* (*sep*, *-ge-*, *h*) spread (out); ***sich ~*** spread; '**Ausbreitung** *f* (-; *no pl*) spreading

'**ausbrennen** *v/t* (*irr*, ***brennen***, *sep*, *-ge-*, *sein*) burn out

'**Ausbruch** *m* escape, breakout; outbreak (*of fire etc*); eruption (*of volcano*); (out)burst (*of resentment etc*)

'**ausbrüten** *v/t* (*sep*, *-ge-*, *h*) hatch (*a. fig*)

'**Ausdauer** *f* perseverance, stamina, *esp* SPORT *a.* staying power; '**ausdauernd** *adj* persevering; SPORT tireless

'**ausdehnen** *v/t and v/refl* (*sep*, *-ge-*, *h*) stretch; *fig* expand, extend

'**Ausdehnung** *f* expansion; extension

'**ausdenken** *v/t* (*irr*, ***denken***, *sep*, *-ge-*, *h*) think *s.th.* up; invent (*a. fig*)

'**Ausdruck** *m* expression, term; IT printout; '**ausdrucken** *v/t* (*sep*, *-ge-*, *h*) IT print out

'**ausdrücken** *v/t* (*sep*, *-ge-*, *h*) stub out (*cigarette etc*); *fig* express

**ausdrücklich** ['ausdrʏklɪç] *adj* express, explicit

'**ausdrucks|los** *adj* expressionless, blank; **~voll** *adj* expressive

'**Ausdrucksweise** *f* language, style

'**Ausdünstung** *f* (-; *-en*) exhalation; perspiration; odo(u)r

**auseinander** [ausˀai'nandɐ] *adv* apart; separate(d); ***~bringen*** *v/t* (*irr*, ***bringen***, *sep*, *-ge-*, *h*) separate, ***~gehen*** *v/i* (*irr*, ***gehen***, *sep*, *-ge-*, *sein*) part; *meeting etc*: break up; *opinions etc*: differ; *married couple*: separate; ***~halten*** *v/t* (*irr*, ***halten***, *sep*, *-ge-*, *h*) tell apart; ***~nehmen*** *v/t* (*irr*, ***nehmen***, *sep*, *-ge-*, *h*) take apart (*a. fig*); ***~setzen*** *v/t* (*irr*, ***setzen***, *sep*, *-ge-*, *h*) explain; ***sich ~ setzen mit*** *v/refl* deal with; argue with *s.o.*

**Ausei'nandersetzung** *f* (-; *-en*) argument

'**auserlesen** *adj* choice, exquisite

'**ausfahren** (*irr*, ***fahren***, *sep*, *-ge-*) **1.** *v/i* (*sein*) go for a drive *or* ride **2.** *v/t* (*h*) take *s.o.* out; AVIAT extend (*landing gear*); '**Ausfahrt** *f* drive, ride; MOT exit

'**Ausfall** *m* TECH, MOT, SPORT failure; loss

'**ausfallen** *v/i* (*irr*, ***fallen***, *sep*, *-ge-*, *sein*) fall out; not take place, be cancelled; TECH, MOT break down, fail; ***gut*** *etc* ***~*** turn out well *etc*; ***~ lassen*** cancel;

***die Schule fällt aus*** there is no school

'**ausfallend**, '**ausfällig** *adj* insulting

'**ausfertigen** *v/t* (*sep*, *-ge-*, *h*) draw up (*contract etc*); make out (*check etc*)

'**Ausfertigung** *f* drawing up; copy; ***in doppelter ~*** in duplicate

'**ausfindig** *adj*: ***~ machen*** find

**ausflippen** ['ausflɪpən] F *v/i* (*sep*, *-ge-*, *sein*) freak out

**Ausflüchte** ['ausflʏçtə] *pl* excuses

'**Ausflug** *m* trip, excursion, outing

**Ausflügler** ['ausfly:klɐ] *m* (*-s*; *-*) day tripper

'**Ausfluss** *m* TECH outlet; MED discharge

'**aus|fragen** *v/t* (*sep*, *-ge-*, *h*) question (***über*** *acc* about); sound out; **~fransen** *v/i* (*sep*, *-ge-*, *sein*) fray; **~fressen** F *v/t* (*irr*, ***fressen***, *sep*, *-ge-*, *h*) ***et. ~*** be up to no good

**Ausfuhr** ['ausfu:ɐ] *f* (*-*; *-en*) ECON export (-ation); '**ausführbar** *adj* practicable; '**ausführen** *v/t* (*sep*, *-ge-*, *h*) take *s.o.* out; carry out (*task etc*); ECON export; explain

**ausführlich** ['ausfy:ɐlɪç] **1.** *adj* detailed; comprehensive **2.** *adv* in detail; '**Ausführlichkeit** *f*: ***in aller ~*** in great detail

'**Ausführung** *f* execution, performance; type, model, design

'**ausfüllen** *v/t* (*sep*, *-ge-*, *h*) fill out (*Br* in) (*form*)

'**Ausgabe** *f* distribution; edition; expense; issue; IT output

'**Ausgang** *m* exit, way out; end; result, outcome; TECH, ELECTR output, outlet

'**Ausgangs|punkt** *m* starting point; **~sperre** *f* POL curfew

'**ausgeben** *v/t* (*irr*, ***geben***, *sep*, *-ge-*, *h*) give out; spend; F ***j-m e-n ~*** buy s.o. a drink; ***sich ~ als*** pass o.s. off as

'**ausge|beult** *adj* baggy; **~bildet** *adj* trained, skilled; **~bucht** *adj* booked up; **~dehnt** *adj* extensive; **~dient** *adj*: ***~ haben*** *fig* have had its day; **~fallen** *adj* odd, unusual; **~glichen** *adj* (well-) balanced

'**ausgehen** *v/i* (*irr*, ***gehen***, *sep*, *-ge-*, *sein*) go out; end; *hair*: fall out; *money*, *supplies*: run out; ***leer ~*** get nothing; ***~ von*** start from *or* at; come from; ***davon ~, dass*** assume that; ***ihm ging das Geld aus*** he ran out of money

'**ausge|kocht** *fig adj* cunning; out-and-out (*villain etc*); **~lassen** *fig adj* cheerful; hilarious; ***~ sein*** be in high spirits; **~macht** *adj* agreed(-on); downright (*nonsense*); **~prägt** *adj* marked, pronounced; **~rechnet** *adv*: ***~ er*** he of all people; ***~ heute*** today of all days; **~schlossen** *adj* out of the question; **~storben** *adj* extinct; **~sucht** *adj* select, choice; **~wachsen** *adj* fullgrown; **~wogen** *adj* (well-)balanced; **~zeichnet** *adj* excellent

**ausgiebig** ['ausgi:bɪç] *adj* extensive, thorough; substantial (*meal*)

'**ausgießen** *v/t* (*irr*, ***gießen***, *sep*, *-ge-*, *h*) pour out

'**Ausgleich** *m* (*-[e]s*; *no pl*) compensation; SPORT even score, *Br* equalization; *tennis*: deuce; '**ausgleichen** *v/t and v/i* (*irr*, ***gleichen***, *sep*, *-ge-*, *h*) compensate; equalize (*Br a.* SPORT); ECON balance; SPORT make the score even

'**Ausgleichs|sport** *m* remedial exercises; **~tor** *n*, **~treffer** *m* SPORT tying point, *Br* equalizer

'**ausgraben** *v/t* (*irr*, ***graben***, *sep*, *-ge-*, *h*) dig out *or* up (*a. fig*)

'**Ausgrabungen** *pl* excavations

'**ausgrenzen** *v/t* (*sep*, *-ge-*, *h*) isolate

'**Ausguss** *m* (kitchen) sink

'**aushalten** (*irr*, ***halten***, *sep*, *-ge-*, *h*) **1.** *v/t* bear, stand; keep (*mistress etc*); ***nicht auszuhalten sein*** be unbearable **2.** *v/i* hold out

**aushändigen** ['aushɛndɪgən] *v/t* (*sep*, *-ge-*, *h*) hand over

'**Aushang** *m* notice; bulletin

'**aushängen** *v/t* (*sep*, *-ge-*, *h*) hang out, put up; unhinge (*door*)

'**aus|heben** *v/t* (*irr*, ***heben***, *sep*, *-ge-*, *h*) dig (*trench*); raid (*place etc*); **~helfen** *v/i* (*irr*, ***helfen***, *sep*, *-ge-*, *h*) help out

'**Aushilfe** *f* (temporary) help

'**Aushilfs...** *in cpds -kellner etc*: temporary

'**aus|holen** *v/i* (*sep*, *-ge-*, *h*) ***zum Schlag ~*** swing (to strike); *fig* ***weit ~*** go far back; **~horchen** *v/t* (*sep*, *-ge-*, *h*) sound (***über*** *acc* on); **~hungern** *v/t* (*sep*, *-ge-*, *h*) starve out; **~kennen** *v/refl* (*irr*, ***kennen***, *sep*, *-ge-*, *h*) ***sich ~*** (***in*** *dat*) know one's way (about); *fig* know a lot (about); **~klingen** *v/i* (*irr*, ***klingen***, *sep*, *-ge-*, *sein*) draw to a close; **~klopfen** *v/t* (*sep*, *-ge-*, *h*) knock out; **~kom-**

men *v/i* (*irr*, ***kommen***, *sep*, *-ge-*, *sein*) get by; ~ ***mit*** manage with *s.th.*; get along with *s.o.*

**Auskunft** ['auskʊnft] *f* (-; *Auskünfte* ['auskʏnftə]) information; (*no pl*) information desk; TEL inquiries

'**aus|lachen** *v/t* (*sep*, *-ge-*, *h*) laugh at (***wegen*** for); **~laden** *v/t* (*irr*, ***laden***, *sep*, *-ge-*, *h*) unload

'**Auslage** *f* window display; *pl* expenses

'**Ausland** *n* (-[*e*]*s*; *no pl*) ***das ~*** foreign countries; ***ins ~, im ~*** abroad

**Ausländer** ['auslɛndɐ] *m* (-*s*; -) foreigner; **~feindlichkeit** *f* hostility to foreigners, xenophobia

**Ausländerin** ['auslɛndərɪn] *f* (-; *-nen*) foreigner

**ausländisch** ['auslɛndɪʃ] *adj* foreign

'**Auslands|gespräch** *n* international call; **~korrespondent**(in) foreign correspondent

'**auslassen** *v/t* (*irr*, ***lassen***, *sep*, *-ge-*, *h*) leave out; melt (*butter etc*); let out (*seam*); ***s-n Zorn an j-m ~*** take it out on s.o.; ***sich ~ über*** (*acc*) express o.s. on

'**Auslassung** *f* (-; *-en*) omission

'**Auslassungszeichen** *n* LING apostrophe

'**Auslauf** *m* room to move about; *dog*: exercise; '**auslaufen** *v/i* (*irr*, ***laufen***, *sep*, *-ge-*, *sein*) MAR leave port; *pot etc*: leak; *liquid etc*: run out; '**Ausläufer** *m* METEOR ridge, trough; *pl* GEOGR foothills; '**Auslaufmo,dell** *n* ECON close-out (*Br* phase-out) model

'**auslegen** *v/t* (*sep*, *-ge-*, *h*) lay out; carpet; line (*with paper etc*); display (*goods*); interpret (*text etc*); advance (*money*)

'**Auslegung** *f* (-; *-en*) interpretation

'**aus|leihen** *v/t* (*irr*, ***leihen***, *sep*, *-ge-*, *h*) lend (out), loan; ***sich*** (*dat*) ***et. ~*** borrow s.th.; **~lernen** *v/i* (*sep*, *-ge-*, *h*) complete one's training; ***man lernt nie aus*** we live and learn

'**Auslese** *f* choice, selection; *fig* pick

'**auslesen** *v/t* (*irr*, ***lesen***, *sep*, *-ge-*, *h*) pick out, select; finish (*book etc*)

'**ausliefern** *v/t* (*sep*, *-ge-*, *h*) hand *or* turn over, deliver (up); POL extradite; '**Auslieferung** *f* delivery; extradition

'**aus|liegen** *v/i* (*irr*, ***liegen***, *sep*, *-ge-*, *h*) be laid out; **~löschen** *v/t* (*sep*, *-ge-*, *h*) put out; *fig* wipe out; **~losen** *v/t* (*sep*, *-ge-*, *h*) draw (lots) for

'**auslösen** *v/t* (*sep*, *-ge-*, *h*) TECH release; ransom, redeem; cause, start, trigger *s.th.* off; '**Auslöser** *m* (PHOT shutter) release; trigger

'**ausmachen** *v/t* (*sep*, *-ge-*, *h*) put out (*fire*); turn off (*light etc*); arrange (*date etc*); agree on (*price etc*); make up; amount to; settle (*dispute*); sight, spot; ***macht es Ihnen et. aus*** (, ***wenn***...) **?** do you mind (if ...)?; ***es macht mir nichts aus*** I don't mind; ***das macht*** (***gar***) ***nichts aus*** that doesn't matter (at all)

'**ausmalen** *v/t* (*sep*, *-ge-*, *h*) paint; ***sich et. ~*** imagine s.th.

'**Ausmaß** *n* extent; *pl* proportions

**aus|merzen** ['ausmɛrtsən] *v/t* (*sep*, *-ge-*, *h*) eliminate; **~messen** *v/t* (*irr*, ***messen***, *sep*, *-ge-*, *h*) measure

**Ausnahme** ['ausna:mə] *f* (-; *-n*) exception; **~zustand** *m* POL state of emergency

'**ausnahmslos** *adv* without exception

'**ausnahmsweise** *adv* by way of exception; just this once

'**ausnehmen** *v/t* (*irr*, ***nehmen***, *sep*, *-ge-*, *h*) clean (*chicken etc*); except; F *contp* fleece *s.o.*; **~d** *adv* exceptionally

'**aus|nutzen** *v/t* (*sep*, *-ge-*, *h*) use; take advantage of (*a. contp*); exploit; **~packen** (*sep*, *-ge-*, *h*) **1.** *v/t* unpack **2.** F *v/i* talk; **~pfeifen** *v/t* (*irr*, ***pfeifen***, *sep*, *-ge-*, *h*) boo, hiss; **~plaudern** *v/t* (*sep*, *-ge-*, *h*) blab out; **~plündern** *v/t* (*sep*, *-ge-*, *h*) plunder, rob; **~pro,bieren** *v/t* (*sep*, *no -ge-*, *h*) try (out), test

'**Auspuff** *m* MOT exhaust; **~gase** *pl* MOT exhaust fumes; **~rohr** *n* MOT exhaust pipe; **~topf** *m* MOT muffler, *Br* silencer

'**aus|quar,tieren** *v/t* (*sep*, *no -ge-*, *h*) move out; **~ra,dieren** *v/t* (*sep*, *no -ge-*, *h*) erase; *fig* wipe out; **~ran,gieren** *v/t* (*sep*, *no -ge-*, *h*) discard; **~rauben** *v/t* (*sep*, *-ge-*, *h*) rob; **~räumen** *v/t* (*sep*, *-ge-*, *h*) empty; clear out (*room etc*); *fig* clear up (*doubt etc*); **~rechnen** *v/t* (*sep*, *-ge-*, *h*) work out

'**Ausrede** *f* excuse

'**ausreden** (*sep*, *-ge-*, *h*) **1.** *v/i* finish speaking; ***j-n ~ lassen*** hear s.o. out **2.** *v/t*: ***j-m et. ~*** talk s.o. out of s.th.

'**ausreichen** *v/t* (*sep*, *-ge-*, *h*) be enough; **~d** *adj* sufficient, enough; *grade*: (barely) passing, only average, weak, D

**'Ausreise** *f* departure; **'ausreisen** *v/i* (*sep*, *-ge-*, *sein*) leave (a *or* one's country); **'Ausreisevisum** *n* exit visa

**'ausreißen** (*irr*, ***reißen***, *sep*, *-ge-*) **1.** *v/t* (*h*) pull *or* tear out **2.** F *v/i* (*sein*) run away; **'Ausreißer** *m* (*-s*; *-*) runaway

**'aus|renken** *v/t* (*sep*, *-ge-*, *h*) MED dislocate; **~richten** *v/t* (*sep*, *-ge-*, *h*) tell *s.o. s.th.*; deliver (*message*); accomplish; arrange (*party etc*); ***richte ihr e-n Gruß von mir aus!*** give her my regards!; ***kann ich et. ~?*** can I take a message

**'ausrotten** *v/t* (*sep*, *-ge-*, *h*) exterminate

**'Ausrottung** *f* (*-*; *-en*) extermination

**'ausrücken** *v/i* (*sep*, *-ge-*, *sein*) F run away; MIL march out

**'Ausruf** *m* cry, shout; **'ausrufen** *v/t* (*irr*, ***rufen***, *sep*, *-ge-*, *h*) cry, shout, exclaim; call out (*name*); POL proclaim; **'Ausrufung** *f* (*-*; *-en*) POL proclamation; 'Ausrufungszeichen *n* LING exclamation mark

**'ausruhen** *v/i*, *v/t and v/refl* (*sep*, *-ge-*, *h*) rest

**'ausrüsten** *v/t* (*sep*, *-ge-*, *h*) equip; **'Ausrüstung** *f* equipment

**'ausrutschen** *v/i* (*sep*, *-ge-*, *sein*) slip

**'Aussage** *f* statement; JUR evidence

**'aussagen** *v/t* (*sep*, *-ge-*, *h*) state, declare; JUR testify

**ausschalten** *v/t* (*sep*, *-ge-*, *h*) switch off; *fig* eliminate

**'Ausschau** *f*: ***~ halten nach*** → **'ausschauen** *v/i* (*sep*, *-ge-*, *h*) ***~ nach*** look out for, watch out for

**'ausscheiden** (*irr*, ***scheiden***, *sep*, *-ge-*) **1.** *v/i* (*sein*) be ruled out; SPORT *etc* drop out (***aus*** *dat* of); retire (***aus*** *dat* from *office etc*); ***~ aus*** (*dat*) leave (*a firm etc*) **2.** *v/t* (*h*) eliminate; MED *etc* secrete, exude; **'Ausscheidung** *f* elimination (*a.* SPORT); MED secretion

**'Ausscheidungs...** *in cpds ...spiel etc*: SPORT qualifying ...

**'aus|schlachten** *fig v/t* (*sep*, *-ge-*, *h*) salvage, *Br a.* cannibalize; *contp* exploit; **~schlafen** (*irr*, ***schlafen***, *sep*, *-ge-*, *h*) **1.** *v/i* sleep in **2.** *v/t* sleep off

**'Ausschlag** *m* MED rash; TECH deflection; ***den ~ geben*** decide it

**'ausschlagen** (*irr*, ***schlagen***, *sep*, *-ge-*, *h*) **1.** *v/t* knock out (*tooth etc*); *fig* refuse, decline (*offer etc*) **2.** *v/i horse*: kick; BOT bud; TECH deflect

**'ausschlaggebend** *adj* decisive

**'ausschließen** *v/t* (*irr*, ***schließen***, *sep*, *-ge-*, *h*) lock out; *fig* exclude; expel; SPORT disqualify

**'ausschließlich** *adj* exclusive

**'Ausschluss** *m* exclusion; expulsion; SPORT disqualification; ***unter ~ der Öffentlichkeit*** in closed session

**'aus|schmücken** *v/t* (*sep*, *-ge-*, *h*) decorate; *fig* embellish; **~schneiden** *v/t* (*irr*, ***schneiden***, *sep*, *-ge-*, *h*) cut out

**'Ausschnitt** *m clothing*: neck; (*press*) clipping (*Br* cutting); *fig* part; extract; ***mit tiefem ~*** low-necked

**'ausschreiben** *v/t* (*irr*, ***schreiben***, *sep*, *-ge-*, *h*) write out (*a. check etc*); advertise (*post etc*); **'Ausschreibung** *f* advertisement

**'Ausschreitungen** *pl* violence, riots

**'Ausschuss** *m* committee, board; TECH (*no pl*) refuse, waste, rejects

**'aus|schütteln** *v/t* (*sep*, *-ge-*, *h*) shake out; **~schütten** *v/t* (*sep*, *-ge-*, *h*) pour out (*a. fig*); spill; ECON pay; ***sich vor Lachen ~*** split one's sides

**'ausschweifend** *adj* dissolute

**'Ausschweifung** *f* (*-*; *-en*) debauchery, excess

**'aussehen** *v/i* (*irr*, ***sehen***, *sep*, *-ge-*, *h*) look; ***krank*** (***traurig***) ***~*** look ill (sad); ***~ wie ...*** look like ...; ***wie sieht er aus?*** what does he look like? **'Aussehen** *n* (*-s*; *no pl*) look(s), appearance

**außen** ['ausən] *adv* outside; ***nach ~*** (***hin***) outward(s); *fig* outwardly

**'Außenbordmotor** *m* outboard motor

**aussenden** *v/t* ([*irr*, ***senden***,] *sep*, *-ge-*, *h*) send out

**'Außen|dienst** *m* field service; **~handel** *m* foreign trade; **~mi,nister** *m Am* Secretary of State, *Br* Foreign Secretary; **~minis,terium** *n Am* State Department, *Br* Foreign Office; **~poli,tik** *f* foreign affairs; foreign policy

**'außenpo,litisch** *adj* foreign-policy

**'Außenseite** *f* outside

**Außenseiter** ['ausənzaitɐ] *m* (*-s*; *-*) outsider

**'Außen|spiegel** *m* MOT outside rearview mirror; **~stände** *pl* ECON receivables; **~stelle** *f* branch; **~stürmer** *m* SPORT winger; **~welt** *f* outside world

**außer** ['ausɐ] **1.** *prp* (*dat*) out of; aside

from, *Br* beside(s); except; **~ sich sein** be beside o.s. (**vor Freude** with joy); **alle ~ e-m** all but one; → **Betrieb, Gefahr** **2.** *cj*: **~ dass** except that; **~ wenn** unless

'**außerdem** *cj* besides, moreover

**äußere** ['ɔʏsərə] *adj* exterior, outer, outward; '**Äußere** *n* (*-n*; *no pl*) exterior, outside; (outward) appearance

'**außergewöhnlich** *adj* unusual

'**außerhalb** *prp* (*gen*) *and adv* outside; out of; beyond

'**außerirdisch** *adj* extraterrestrial

'**äußerlich** *adj* external, outward

'**Äußerlichkeit** *f* (-; *-en*) formality; minor detail

**äußern** ['ɔʏsɐn] *v/t* (*ge-*, *h*) utter, express; **sich ~** say s.th.; **sich ~ zu** *or* **über** (*acc*) express o.s. on

'**außer'ordentlich** *adj* extraordinary

'**außerplanmäßig** *adj* unscheduled

**äußerst** ['ɔʏsɐst] **1.** *adj* outermost; *fig* extreme; **im ~en Fall** at (the) worst; at (the) most **2.** *adv* extremely

**außer'stande** *adj*: **~ sein** be unable

'**Äußerung** *f* (-; *-en*) utterance, remark

'**aussetzen** (*sep*, *-ge-*, *h*) **1.** *v/t* abandon; expose (*dat* to); **et. auszusetzen haben an** (*dat*) find fault with **2.** *v/i* stop, break off; MOT, TECH fail

'**Aussicht** *f* view (**auf** *acc* of); *fig* prospect (of), chance (**auf Erfolg** of success); '**aussichtslos** *adj* hopeless, desperate; '**Aussichtspunkt** *m* vantage point; '**aussichtsreich** *adj* promising; '**Aussichtsturm** *m* lookout tower

'**Aussiedler** *m* resettler, evacuee

'**aussitzen** *v/t* (*irr*, **sitzen**, *sep*, *-ge-*, *h*) sit *s.th.* out

**aussöhnen** ['auszøːnən] *v/refl* (*sep*, *-ge-*, *h*) **sich ~ (mit)** become reconciled (with), F make it up (with)

'**Aussöhnung** *f* (-; *-en*) reconciliation

'**aus|sor,tieren** *v/t* (*sep*, *no -ge-*, *h*) sort out; **~spannen** (*sep*, *-ge-*, *h*) **1.** *v/t* unharness **2.** *fig v/i* (take a) rest, relax

'**aussperren** *v/t* (*sep*, *-ge-*, *h*) lock out (*a.* ECON); '**Aussperrung** *f* (-; *-en*) ECON lock-out

'**aus|spielen** (*sep*, *-ge-*, *h*) **1.** *v/t* play; **j-n gegen j-n ~** play s.o. off against s.o. **2.** *v/i card game*: lead; **er hat ausgespielt** *fig* he is done for; **~spio,nieren** *v/t* (*sep*, *no -ge-*, *h*) spy out

'**Aussprache** *f* pronunciation; discussion; *private* heart-to-heart (talk)

'**aussprechen** *v/t* (*irr*, **sprechen**, *sep*, *-ge-*, *h*) pronounce; express; **sich ~ für** (**gegen**) speak for (against); **sich mit j-m gründlich ~** have a heart-to--heart talk with s.o.

'**Ausspruch** *m* saying; remark

'**aus|spucken** *v/i and v/t* (*sep*, *-ge-*, *h*) spit out; **~spülen** *v/t* (*sep*, *-ge-*, *h*) rinse

'**Ausstand** *m* strike, F walkout

'**ausstatten** *v/t* (*sep*, *-ge-*, *h*) fit out, equip, furnish; '**Ausstatung** *f* (-; *-en*) equipment, furnishings; design

'**aus|stechen** *v/t* (*irr*, **stechen**, *sep*, *-ge-*, *h*) GASTR cut out (*a. fig*); put out (*eyes*); **~stehen** (*irr*, **stehen**, *sep*, *-ge-*, *h*) **1.** *v/t* stand, endure; F **ich kann ihn** (**es**) **nicht ~** I can't stand him (it) **2.** *v/i*: (**noch**) **~** be outstanding *or* overdue

'**aussteigen** *v/i* (*irr*, **steigen**, *sep*, *-ge-*, *sien*) get out (**aus** *dat* of); (*a.* **~ aus** *dat*) get off *a bus, train*; F *fig* drop out; '**Aussteiger** F *m* (*-s*; -) drop-out

'**ausstellen** *v/t* (*sep*, *-ge-*, *h*) exhibit, display, show; make out (*check etc*); issue (*passport*); '**Aussteller** *m* (*-s*; -) exhibitor; issuer; drawer (*of check*)

'**Ausstellung** *f* exhibition, show

'**aussterben** *v/i* (*irr*, **sterben**, *sep*, *-ge-*, *sein*) die out, become extinct (*both a. fig*)

'**Aussteuer** *f* trousseau; dowry

'**aussteuern** *v/t* (*sep*, *-ge-*, *h*) ELECTR modulate; '**Aussteuerung** *f* ELECTR modulation; level control

**Ausstieg** ['ausʃtiːk] *m* (*-[e]s*; *-e*) exit; *fig* withdrawal (**aus** *dat* from)

'**ausstopfen** *v/t* (*sep*, *-ge-*, *h*) stuff; pad

'**Ausstoß** *m* TECH, PHYS discharge, ejection; ECON output

'**ausstoßen** *v/t* (*irr*, **stoßen**, *sep*, *-ge-*, *h*) TECH, PHYS give off, eject, emit; ECON turn out; give (*cry, sigh*); expel

'**aus|strahlen** *v/t* (*sep*, *-ge-*, *h*) radiate (*happiness etc*); TV, *radio*: broadcast, transmit; '**Ausstrahlung** *f* radiation; broadcast; *fig* magnetism, charisma

'**aus|strecken** *v/t* (*sep*, *-ge-*, *h*) stretch (out); **~streichen** *v/t* (*irr*, **streichen**, *sep*, *-ge-*, *h*) strike out; **~strömen** *v/i* (*sep*, *-ge-*, *sein*) escape (**aus** *dat* from); **~suchen** *v/t* (*sep*, *-ge-*, *h*) choose, pick

'**Austausch** *m* (*-[e]s*; *no pl*) exchange

'**austauschbar** *adj* exchangeable

'**austauschen** *v/t* (*sep*, *-ge-*, *h*) exchange (***gegen*** for)
'**Austauschschüler(in)** exchange student
'**austeilen** *v/t* (*sep*, *-ge-*, *h*) distribute, hand out; deal (out) (*cards*, *blows*)
**Auster** ['austɐ] *f* (-; *-n*) zo oyster
'**austragen** *v/t* (*irr*, ***tragen***, *sep*, *-ge-*, *h*) deliver (*mail*); settle (*dispute etc*); hold (*contest etc*); ***das Kind ~*** have the baby
'**Austragungsort** *m* SPORT venue
**Australien** [aus'tra:ljən] Australia
**Australier** [aus'tra:ljɐ] *m* (*-s*; -), **Australierin** [aus'tra:ljərɪn] *f* (-; *-nen*), **aust'ralisch** *adj* Australian
'**aus|treiben** *v/t* (*irr*, ***treiben***, *sep*, *-ge-*, *h*) exorcise; F ***j-m et. ~*** cure s.o. of s.th.; **~treten** (*irr*, ***treten***, *sep*, *-ge-*) **1.** *v/t* (*h*) tread *or* stamp out (*fire*); wear out (*shoes*) **2.** *v/i* (*sein*) escape (***aus*** *dat* from); F go to the bathroom (*Br* toilet); ***~ aus*** (*dat*) leave (*a club etc*); resign from; **~trinken** *v/t* (*irr*, ***trinken***, *sep*, *-ge-*, *h*) drink up; empty
'**Austritt** *m* leaving; resignation; escape
'**austrocknen** *v/t* (*sep*, *-ge-*, *h*) *and v/i* (*sein*) dry up
'**ausüben** *v/t* (*sep*, *-ge-*, *h*) practi|ce, *Br* -se; hold (*office*); exercise (*power etc*); exert (*pressure etc*); '**Ausübung** *f* (-; *no pl*) practice; exercise
'**Ausverkauf** *m* ECON (clearance) sale
'**ausverkauft** *adj* ECON, THEA sold out; ***vor ~em Haus spielen*** play to a full house
'**Auswahl** *f* choice, selection (*both a.* ECON); SPORT representative team
'**auswählen** *v/t* (*sep*, *-ge-*, *h*) choose, select
'**Auswanderer** *m* emigrant
'**auswandern** *v/i* (*sep*, *-ge-*, *sein*) emigrate; '**Auswanderung** *f* emigration
**auswärtig** ['ausvɛrtɪç] *adj* out-of-town; POL foreign
'**auswärts** *adv* out of town
'**Auswärts|sieg** *m* SPORT away victory; **~spiel** *n* SPORT away game
'**auswechseln** *v/t* (*sep*, *-ge-*, *h*) exchange (***gegen*** for); change (*tire*); replace; ***A gegen B ~*** SPORT substitute B for A; ***wie ausgewechselt*** (like) a different person; '**Auswechselspieler** *m* SPORT substitute
'**Ausweg** *m* way out; '**ausweglos** *adj* hopeless; '**Ausweglosigkeit** *f* (-; *no pl*) hopelessness
'**ausweichen** *v/i* (*irr*, ***weichen***, *sep*, *-ge-*, *sein*) make way (*dat* for); *fig* avoid *s.o.*; evade (*question*); **~d** *adj* evasive
'**ausweinen** *v/refl* (*sep*, *-ge-*, *h*) have a good cry
**Ausweis** ['ausvais] *m* (*-es*; *-e*) identification (card); card
'**ausweisen** *v/t* (*irr*, ***weisen***, *sep*, *-ge-*, *h*) expel; ***sich ~*** identify o.s.
'**Ausweispa,piere** *pl* documents
'**Ausweisung** *f* (-; *-en*) expulsion
'**ausweiten** *fig v/t* (*sep*, *-ge-*, *h*) expand
'**auswendig** *adv* by heart; ***et. ~ können*** know s.th. by heart; ***~ lernen*** memorize; learn by heart
'**auswerfen** *v/t* (*irr*, ***werfen***, *sep*, *-ge-*, *h*) throw out; cast (*anchor*); TECH eject
'**auswerten** *v/t* (*sep*, *-ge-*, *h*) evaluate, analyze, interpret; utilize, exploit; '**Auswertung** *f* evaluation; utilization
'**auswickeln** *v/t* (*sep*, *-ge-*, *h*) unwrap
'**auswirken** *v/refl* (*sep*, *-ge-*, *h*) ***sich ~ auf*** (*acc*) affect; ***sich positiv ~*** have a favo(u)rable effect; '**Auswirkung** *f* effect
'**auswischen** *v/t* (*sep*, *-ge-*, *h*) wipe out
'**auswringen** *v/t* (*irr*, ***wringen***, *sep*, *-ge-*, *h*) wring out
'**Auswuchs** *m* (*-es*; *Auswüchse* ['ausvy:ksə]) excrescence; *fig pl* excesses
'**aus|wuchten** *v/t* (*sep*, *-ge-*, *h*) TECH balance: **~zahlen** *v/t* (*sep*, *-ge-*, *h*) pay (out); pay *s.o.* off; ***sich ~*** pay; **~zählen** *v/t* (*sep*, *-ge-*, *h*) count; *boxing*: count out
'**Auszahlung** *f* payment; paying off
'**auszeichnen** *v/t* (*sep*, *-ge-*, *h*) price, mark (out) (*goods*); ***sich ~*** distinguish o.s.; ***j-n mit et. ~*** award s.th. to s.o.; '**Auszeichnung** *f* marking; *fig* distinction, hono(u)r; award; decoration
'**ausziehen** (*irr*, ***ziehen***, *sep*, *-ge-*) **1.** *v/t* (*h*) take off (*coat etc*); pull out (*table etc*); ***sich ~*** undress **2.** *v/i* (*sein*) move out
'**Auszubildende** *m*, *f* (*-n*; *-n*) apprentice, trainee
'**Auszug** *m* move, removal; extract, excerpt; statement (of account)
**authentisch** [au'tɛntɪʃ] *adj* authentic, genuine
**Autismus** [au'tɪsmʊs] *m* PSYCH autism
**autistisch** [au'tɪstɪʃ] *adj* PSYCH autistic

**Auto** ['auto] *n* (*-s*; *-s*) car, auto(mobile); (***mit dem***) ~ ***fahren*** drive, go by car
'**Autobahn** *f Am* expressway, *Br* motorway; ~**dreieck** *n* interchange; ~**gebühr** *f* toll; ~**kreuz** *n* interchange
**Autobiogra'phie** *f* autobiography
'**Auto|bombe** *f* car bomb; ~**bus** *m* → ***Bus***; ~**fähre** *f* car ferry; ~**fahrer(in)** motorist, driver; ~**fahrt** *f* drive; ~**friedhof** F *m* car dump, auto junkyard
**Autogramm** [auto'gram] *n* autograph; ~**jäger** *m* autograph hunter
'**Auto|karte** *f* road map; ~**kino** *n* drive-in theater (*Br* cinema)
**Automat** [auto'maːt] *m* (*-en*; *-en*) vending (*Br a.* slot) machine; TECH robot; → ***Spielautomat***; **Automatik** [auto'maːtɪk] *f* (*-*; *no pl*) automatic (system *or* control); MOT automatic transmission; automatic; **Automation** [automa'tsjoːn] *f* (*-*; *no pl*) automation; **auto'matisch** *adj* automatic
'**Autome,chaniker** *m* car mechanic
**autonom** [auto'noːm] *adj* autonomous
'**Autonummer** *f* license (*Br* licence) number
**Autor** ['autoːɐ] *m* (*-s*; *-en* [au'toːrən]) author
'**Autorepara,turwerkstatt** *f* garage, car repair shop
**Autorin** [au'toːrɪn] *f* (*-*; *-nen*) author(ess)
**autorisieren** [autori'ziːrən] *v/t* (*no -ge-*, *h*) authorize; **autoritär** [autori'tɛːɐ] *adj* authoritarian; **Autorität** [autori'tɛːt] *f* (*-*; *-en*) authority
'**Auto|tele,fon** *n* car phone; ~**vermietung** *f* car rental (*Br* hire) service; ~**waschanlage** *f* car wash
**Axt** [akst] *f* (*-*; *Äxte* ['ɛkstə]) ax(e)

# B

**Baby** ['beːbi] *n* (*-s*; *-s*) baby; ~**bett** *n* crib, *Br* cot; ~**fläschchen** *n* baby's bottle; ~**nahrung** *f* baby food; ~**sitter(in)** babysitter; ~**sitz** *m* child seat; ~**wickelraum** *m* baby-changing room
**Bach** [bax] *m* (*-[e]s*; *Bäche* ['bɛçə]) brook, stream, *Am a.* creek
'**Backblech** *n* baking sheet
'**Backbord** *n* (*-s*; *no pl*) MAR port
**Backe** ['bakə] *f* (*-*; *-n*) ANAT cheek
**backen** *v/t and v/i* ([*irr*, ***backen***,] *-ge-*, *h*) bake
'**Backenzahn** *m* ANAT molar (tooth)
**Bäcker** ['bɛkɐ] *m* (*-s*; *-*) baker; ***beim*** ~ at the baker's; **Bäckerei** [bɛkə'rai] *f* (*-*; *-en*) bakery, baker's (shop)
'**Back|form** *f* baking tin; ~**hendl** ['bakhɛndl] *Austrian n* (*-s*; *-n*) fried chicken; ~**obst** *n* dried fruit; ~**ofen** *m* oven; ~**pflaume** *f* prune; ~**pulver** *n* baking powder; ~**stein** *m* brick
**backte** ['baktə] *pret of* ***backen***
'**Backwaren** *pl* breads and pastries
**Bad** [baːt] *n* (*-[e]*; *Bäder* ['bɛːdɐ]) bath; swim; bathroom; → ***Badeort***; ***ein*** ~ ***nehmen*** → ***baden*** *1*
'**Bade|anstalt** *f* swimming pool, public baths; ~**anzug** *m* swimsuit; ~**hose** *f* bathing trunks; ~**kappe** *f* bathing cap; ~**mantel** *m* bathrobe; ~**meister** *m* pool *or* bath attendant
**baden** ['baːdən] (*ge-*, *h*) **1.** *v/i* bathe, take *or* have a bath; swim; ~ ***gehen*** go swimming **2.** *v/t* bathe (*a.* MED); *Br a.* bath
'**Bade|ort** *m* seaside (*or* health) resort; ~**sachen** *Pl* swimming things; ~**schaum** *m* bubble bath, bath foam; ~**tuch** *n* bath towel; ~**wanne** *f* bathtub; ~**zeug** *n* swimming gear; ~**zimmer** *n* bathroom
**Badminton** ['bɛtmɪntn] *n* (*-*; *no pl*) badminton
**baff** [baf] *adj*: F ~ ***sein*** be flabbergasted
**Bagatelle** [baga'tɛlə] *f* (*-*; *-n*) trifle
**Baga'tellschaden** *m* superficial damage
**Bagger** ['bagɐ] *m* (*-s*; *-*) TECH excavator; dredge(r); '**baggern** *v/i* (*ge-*, *h*) TECH excavate; dredge
**Bahn** [baːn] *f* (*-*; *-en*) railroad, *Br* railway; train; way, path, course; SPORT track; ***mit der*** ~ by rail; ~ ***frei!*** make way!; *cpds* → *a.* ***Eisenbahn***
'**bahnbrechend** *adj* epoch-making
**BahnCard**® [baːn'kaːt] *f* (*-*; *-s*) rail card (*allowing 50% or 25% reduction on*

B

*tickets)*

'**Bahndamm** *m* railroad (*Br* railway) embankment

'**bahnen** *v/t (ge-, h)* ***den Weg ~*** clear the way (*dat* for *s.o. or s.th.*); ***sich e-n Weg ~*** force *or* work one's way

'**Bahn|hof** *m* (railroad, *Br* railway) station; **~linie** *f* railroad (*Br* railway) line; **~steig** ['ba:nʃtaik] *m (-[e]s; -e)* platform; **~übergang** *m* grade (*Br* level) crossing

**Bahre** ['ba:rə] *f (-; -n)* stretcher; bier

**Baisse** ['bɛ:sə] *f (-; -n)* ECON fall, slump

**Bakterien** [bak'te:rjən] *pl* MED bacteria, germs

**balancieren** [bala͂'si:rən] *v/t and v/i (no -ge-, h)* balance

**bald** [balt] *adv* soon; F almost, nearly; ***so ~ wie möglich*** as soon as possible

**baldig** ['baldɪç] *adj* speedy; ***~e Antwort*** ECON early reply; ***auf (ein) ~es Wiedersehen!*** see you again soon!

**balgen** ['balgən] *v/refl (ge-, h)* scuffle (**um** for)

**Balken** ['balkən] *m (-s; -)* beam

**Balkon** [bal'kɔŋ] *m (-s; -s, -e* [bal'ko:nə]) balcony; **~tür** *f* French window

**Ball** [bal] *m (-[e]s; Bälle* ['bɛlə]) ball; dance; ***am ~ sein*** SPORT have the ball; ***am ~ bleiben*** *fig* stick to it

**Ballade** [ba'la:də] *f (-; -n)* ballad

**Ballast** ['balast] *m (-[e]s; no pl)* ballast, *fig a.* burden; **~stoffe** *pl* MED roughage, bulk

**ballen** ['balən] *v/t (ge-, h)* clench (*fist*)

'**Ballen** *m (-s; -)* bale; ANAT ball

**Ballett** [ba'lɛt] *n (-[e]s; -e)* ballet

**Ballon** [ba'lɔŋ] *m (-s; -s)* balloon

'**Ballungs|raum** *m*, **~zentrum** *n* congested area, conurbation

**Balsam** ['balza:m] *m (-s; no pl)* balm

**Bambus** ['bambʊs] *m (-ses, -; -se)* BOT bamboo; **~rohr** *n* BOT bamboo (cane)

**banal** [ba'na:l] *adj* banal, trite

**Banane** [ba'na:nə] *f (-; -n)* BOT banana

**Banause** [ba'nauzə] *m (-n; -n)* philistine

**band** [bant] *pret of* ***binden***

**Band**[1] *n (-[e]s; Bänder* ['bɛndɐ]) ribbon; tape; (*hat*) band; ANAT ligament; *fig* tie, link; ***auf ~ aufnehmen*** tape; ***am laufenden ~*** *fig* continuously

**Band**[2] *m (-[e]s; Bände* ['bɛndə]) volume

**Bandage** [ban'da:ʒə] *f (-; -n)* bandage

**bandagieren** [banda'ʒi:rən] *v/t (no -ge-, h)* bandage (up)

'**Bandbreite** *f* ELECTR bandwidth; *fig* range

**Bande** ['bandə] *f (-; -n)* gang; *billiards*: cushions; *ice hockey*: boards; *bowling*: gutter

'**Bänderriss** *m* MED torn ligament

**bändigen** ['bɛndigən] *v/t (ge-, h)* tame (*a. fig*); restrain, control (*children etc*)

**Bandit** [ban'di:t] *m (-en; -en)* bandit, outlaw

'**Band|maß** *n* tape measure; **~scheibe** *f* ANAT (intervertebral) disk (*Br* disc); **~scheibenschaden** *m*, **~scheibenvorfall** *m* MED slipped disk; **~wurm** *m* ZO tapeworm

**bange** ['baŋə] *adj* afraid; anxious

'**Bange** *f*: ***j-m ~ machen*** frighten *or* scare s.o.; ***keine ~!*** (have) no fear!

'**bangen** *v/i (ge-, h)* be anxious *or* worried (**um** about)

**Bank**[1] [baŋk] *f (-; Bänke* ['bɛŋkə]) bench; F ***durch die ~*** without exception; ***auf die lange ~ schieben*** put off

**Bank**[2] *f (-; -en)* bank; ***auf der ~*** in the bank

'**Bankangestellte** *m, f* bank clerk *or* employee

'**Bankauto͵mat** *m* → ***Geldautomat***

**Bankett** [baŋ'kɛt] *n (-[e]s; -e)* banquet

'**Bankgeschäfte** *pl* banking transactions

**Bankier** [baŋ'kje:] *m (-s; -s)* banker

'**Bank|konto** *n* bank(ing) account; **~leitzahl** *f* A.B.A. number, *Br* bank (sorting) code; **~note** *f* bill, *Br* (bank) note; **~raub** *m* bank robbery

**bankrott** [baŋ'krɔt] *adj* ECON bankrupt

**Bank'rott** *m (-[e]s; -e)* ECON bankruptcy; ***~ machen*** go bankrupt

'**Bankverbindung** *f* account(s), account details

**Bann** [ban] *m (-[e]s; no pl)* ban; spell

'**bannen** *v/t (ge-, h)* ward off; **(*wie*) *gebannt*** spellbound

**Banner** ['banɐ] *n (-s; -)* banner (*a. fig*)

**bar** [ba:ɐ] *adj* (in) cash; ***gegen ~*** for cash

**Bar** *f (-; -s)* bar; nightclub

**Bär** [bɛ:ɐ] *m (-en; -en)* ZO bear

**Baracke** [ba'rakə] *f (-; -n)* hut; *contp* shack

**Barbar** [bar'ba:ɐ] *m (-en; -en)* barbarian; **barbarisch** [bar'ba:rɪʃ] *adj* barbarous, *a.* atrocious (*crime etc*)

'**Bardame** *f* barmaid
'**barfuß** *adj and adv* barefoot
**barg** [bark] *pret of* ***bergen***
'**Bargeld** *n* cash
'**bargeldlos** *adj* noncash
'**Barhocker** *m* bar stool
**Bariton** ['ba:ritɔn] *m* (*-s*; *-e* ['ba:rito:nə]) MUS baritone
**Barkasse** [bar'kasə] *f* (-; *-n*) MAR launch
**barm'herzig** *adj* merciful; charitable
**Barm'herzigkeit** *f* (-; *no pl*) mercy; charity
'**Barmixer** *m* barman
**Barometer** [baro'me:tɐ] *n* (*-s*; -) barometer
**Baron** [ba'ro:n] *m* (*-s*; *-e*) baron
**Ba'ronin** *f* (-; *-nen*) baroness
**Barren** ['barən] *m* (*-s*; -) bar, ingot, *a. gold, silver* bullion; SPORT parallel bars
**Barriere** [ba'rje:rə] *f* (-; *-n*) barrier
**Barrikade** [bari'ka:də] *f* (-; *-n*) barricade
**barsch** [barʃ] *adj* rough, gruff, brusque
**Barsch** *m* (*-[e]s*; *-e*) ZO perch
'**Barscheck** *m* (negotiable) check, *Br* open cheque
**barst** [barst] *pret of* ***bersten***
**Bart** [ba:ɐt] *m* (*-[e]s*; *Bärte* ['bɛ:ɐtə]) beard; TECH bit; ***sich e-n ~ wachsen lassen*** grow a beard
**bärtig** ['bɛ:ɐtɪç] *adj* bearded
'**Barzahlung** *f* cash payment
**Basar** [ba'za:ɐ] *m* (*-s*; *-e*) bazaar
**Base** ['ba:zə] *f* (-; *-n*) cousin; CHEM base
**basieren** [ba'zi:rən] *v/i* (*no -ge-, h*) ***~ auf*** (*dat*) be based on
**Basis** ['ba:zɪs] *f* (-; *Basen*) basis; MIL, ARCH base
**Baskenmütze** ['baskənmʏtsə] *f* beret
**Bass** [bas] *m* (*-es*; *Bässe* ['bɛsə]) MUS bass
**Bassin** [ba'se͂:] *n* (*-s*; *-s*) basin; (swimming) pool
**Bassist** [ba'sɪst] *m* (*-en*; *-en*) MUS bass singer *or* player
**Bast** [bast] *m* (*-[e]s*; *-e*) bast; HUNT velvet
**Bastard** ['bastart] *m* (*-s*; *-e*) BIOL hybrid; mongrel; V bastard
**basteln** ['bastəln] (*ge-, h*) **1.** *v/i* make *or* repair things o.s. **2.** *v/t* build, make
**Bastler** ['bastlɐ] *m* (*-s*; -) home handyman, do-it-yourselfer
**bat** [ba:t] *pret of* ***bitten***
**Batik** ['ba:tɪk] *m* (*-s*; *-en*), *f* (-; *-en*) batik
**Batist** [ba'tɪst] *m* (*-[e]s*; *-e*) cambric
**Batterie** [batə'ri:] *f* (-; *-n*) ELECTR, MIL battery
**Bau** [bau] *m* (*-[e]s*; *Bauten*) (*no pl*) building, construction; build, frame; building; ZO (*pl Baue*) hole, den; ***im ~*** under construction; **~arbeiten** *pl* construction work; road works; **~arbeiter** *m* construction worker; **~art** *f* style (of construction); type, model
**Bauch** [baux] *m* (*-[e]s*; *Bäuche* ['bɔʏçə]) belly (*a. fig*); ANAT abdomen; F tummy
'**bauchig** *adj* bulgy
'**Bauch|landung** *f* AVIAT belly landing; **~redner** *m* ventriloquist; **~schmerzen** *pl* stomachache; **~tanz** *m* belly dancing
**bauen** ['bauən] (*ge-, h*) **1.** *v/t* build, construct, *a.* make (*furniture etc*) **2.** *fig v/i*: ***~ auf*** (*acc*) rely *or* count on
**Bauer**[1] ['bauɐ] *m* (*-n*; *-n*) farmer; *chess*: pawn
'**Bauer**[2] *n, m* (*-s*; -) (bird)cage
**Bäuerin** ['bɔʏərɪn] *f* (-; *-nen*) farmer's wife; farmer
**bäuerlich** ['bɔʏɐlɪç] *adj* rural; rustic
'**Bauern|fänger** *contp m* trickster, conman; **~haus** *n* farmhouse; **~hof** *m* farm; **~möbel** *pl* rustic furniture
'**baufällig** *adj* dilapidated
'**Bau|firma** *f* builders and contractors; **~genehmigung** *f* building permit; **~gerüst** *n* scaffold(ing); **~herr** *m* owner; **~holz** *n* lumber, *Br a.* timber; **~inge,nieur** *m* civil engineer; **~jahr** *n* year of construction; ***~ 1995*** 1995 model; **~kasten** *m* box of building blocks (*Br* bricks); TECH construction set; kit; **~leiter** *m* building supervisor
'**baulich** *adj* structural
**Baum** [baum] *m* (*-[e]s*; *Bäume* ['bɔʏmə]) BOT tree
'**Baumarkt** *m* do-it-yourself superstore
**baumeln** ['bauməln] *v/i* (*ge-, h*) dangle, swing; ***mit den Beinen ~*** dangle one's legs
'**Baum|schule** *f* nursery; **~stamm** *m* trunk; log; **~wolle** *f* cotton
'**Bau|plan** *m* architectural drawing; blueprints; **~platz** *m* building site
**Bausch** [bauʃ] *m* (*-[e]s*; *-e*) wad, ball; ***in ~ und Bogen*** lock, stock and barrel
'**Bausparkasse** *f* building and loan association, *Br* building society
'**Bau|stein** *m* brick; (building) block; *fig*

element; **~stelle** *f* building site; MOT construction zone, *Br* roadworks; **~stil** *m* (architectural) style; **~stoff** *m* building material; **~techniker** *m* engineer; **~teil** *n* component (part), unit, module; **~unternehmer** *m* building contractor; **~vorschriften** *pl* building regulations; **~werk** *n* building; **~zaun** *m* hoarding; **~zeichner** *m* draftsman, *Br* draughtsman

**Bayer** ['baiɐ] *m* (*-n*; *-n*), **Bayerin** ['baiərɪn] *f* (-; *-nen*), **bay(e)risch** ['bai(ə)rɪʃ] *adj* Bavarian; **Bayern** ['baiɐn] Bavaria

**Bazillus** [ba'tsɪlʊs] *m* (-; *-len*) MED bacillus, germ

**beabsichtigen** [bə'ʔapzɪçtɪgən] *v/t* (*no -ge-*, *h*) intend, plan; ***es war beabsichtigt*** it was intentional

**be'achten** *v/t* (*no -ge-*, *h*) pay attention to; observe, follow (*rule etc*); ***~ Sie, dass …*** note that …; ***nicht ~*** take no notice of; disregard; **be'achtlich** *adj* remarkable; considerable

**Be'achtung** *f* (-; *no pl*) attention; consideration; observance

**Beamte** [bə'ʔamtə] *m* (*-n*; *-n*), **Be'amtin** *f* (-; *-nen*) official; (*police etc*) officer; civil servant

**be'ängstigend** *adj* alarming

**beanspruchen** [bə'ʔanʃprʊxən] *v/t* (*no -ge-*, *h*) claim; take up (*time etc*); TECH stress; **Be'anspruchung** *f* (-; *-en*) claim; TECH stress, strain (*a. fig*)

**beanstanden** [bə'ʔanʃtandən] *v/t* (*no -ge-*, *h*) complain about; object to

**beantragen** [bə'ʔantra:gən] *v/t* (*no -ge-*, *h*) apply for; JUR, PARL move (for); propose

**be'antworten** *v/t* (*no -ge-*, *h*) answer, reply to

**be'arbeiten** *v/t* (*no -ge-*, *h*) work; AGR till; hew (*stone*); process; be in charge of (*a case etc*); treat (*subject*); revise; THEA adapt (***nach*** from); *esp* MUS arrange; F ***j-n ~*** work on s.o.

**Be'arbeitung** *f* (-; *-en*) working; revision; THEA adaptation; *esp* MUS arrangement; TECH processing, treatment

**be'atmen** *v/t* (*no -ge-*, *h*) MED give artificial respiration to *s.o.*

**beaufsichtigen** [bə'ʔaufzɪçtɪgən] *v/t* (*no -ge-*, *h*) supervise; look after; **Be'aufsichtigung** *f* (-; *-en*) supervision; looking after

**be'auftragen** *v/t* (*no -ge-*, *h*) commission; instruct; ***~ mit*** put *s.o.* in charge of; **Beauftragte** [bə'ʔauftra:ktə] *m*, *f* (*-n*; *-n*) agent; representative; commissioner

**be'bauen** *v/t* (*no -ge-*, *h*) build on; AGR cultivate

**beben** ['be:bən] *v/i* (*ge-*, *h*) shake, tremble; shiver (*all*: ***vor*** with); *earth*: quake

**bebildern** [bə'bɪldɐn] *v/t* (*no -ge-*, *h*) illustrate

**Becher** ['bɛçɐ] *m* (*-s*; -) cup, mug

**Becken** ['bɛkən] *n* (*-s*; -) basin, bowl; pool; ANAT pelvis; MUS cymbal(s)

**bedacht** [bə'daxt] *adj*: ***darauf ~ sein zu inf*** be anxious to *inf*

**bedächtig** [bə'dɛçtɪç] *adj* deliberate; measured

**bedang** [bə'daŋ] *pret of* ***bedingen***

**be'danken** *v/refl* (*no -ge-*, *h*) ***sich bei j-m für et. ~*** thank s.o. for s.th.

**Bedarf** [bə'darf] *m* (*-[e]s*; *no pl*) need (***an*** *dat* of), want (of); ECON demand (for); ***bei ~*** if necessary

**Be'darfshaltestelle** *f* request stop

**bedauerlich** [bə'dauɐlɪç] *adj* regrettable; **be'dauerlicher'weise** *adv* unfortunately

**be'dauern** *v/t* (*no -ge-*, *h*) feel *or* be sorry for *s.o.*, pity *s.o.*; regret *s.th.*; **Be'dauern** *n* (*-s*; *no pl*) regret (***über*** *acc* at); **be'dauernswert** *adj* pitiable, deplorable

**be'decken** *v/t* (*no -ge-*, *h*) cover

**be'deckt** *adj* METEOR overcast

**be'denken** *v/t* (*irr*, ***denken***, *no -ge-*, *h*) consider, think *s.th.* over; **Be'denken** *pl* doubts; scruples; objections

**be'denkenlos** *adv* unhesitatingly; without scruples

**be'denklich** *adj* doubtful; serious, critical; alarming

**Be'denkzeit** *f*: ***e-e Stunde ~*** one hour to think it over

**be'deuten** *v/t* (*no -ge-*, *h*) mean; **~d** *adj* important; considerable; distinguished

**Be'deutung** *f* (-; *-en*) meaning; importance; **be'deutungslos** *adj* insignificant; meaningless; **be'deutungsvoll** *adj* significant; meaningful

**be'dienen** (*no -ge-*, *h*) **1.** *v/t* serve, wait on *s.o.*; TECH operate, work; ***sich ~*** help o.s.; ~ ***Sie sich!*** help yourself! **2.** *v/i* serve; wait (at table); *card games*: follow suit; **Be'dienung** *f* (-; *-en*) (*no pl*) service; waiter, waitress; shop assistant, clerk; TECH operation, control; **Be'dienungsanleitung** *f* operating instructions

**bedingen** [bə'dɪŋən] *v/t* ([*irr*,] *no -ge-*, *h*) require; cause; imply, involve; **be'dingt** *adj*: ~ ***durch*** caused by, due to

**Be'dingung** *f* (-; *-en*) condition; *pl* ECON terms; requirements; conditions; ***unter einer*** ~ on one condition

**be'dingungslos** *adj* unconditional

**be'drängen** *v/t* (*no -ge-*, *h*) press (hard)

**be'drohen** *v/t* (*no -ge-*, *h*) threaten, menace; **be'drohlich** *adj* threatening; **Be'drohung** *f* threat, menace (*gen* to)

**be'drücken** *v/t* (*no -ge-*, *h*) depress, sadden

**bedungen** [bə'duŋən] *pp of* ***bedingen***

**Bedürfnis** [bə'dʏrfnɪs] *n* (*-ses*; *-se*) need, necessity (***für, nach*** for); ~**anstalt** *f* comfort station, *Br* public convenience (*or* toilets)

**be'dürftig** *adj* needy, poor

**be'eilen** *v/refl* (*no -ge-*, *h*) hurry (up)

**beeindrucken** [bə'ʔaindrʊkən] *v/t* (*no -ge-*, *h*) impress

**beeinflussen** [bə'ʔainflʊsən] *v/t* (*no -ge-*, *h*) influence; affect

**beeinträchtigen** [bə'ʔaintrɛçtɪgən] *v/t* (*no -ge-*, *h*) affect, impair

**be'end(ig)en** *v/t* (*no -ge-*, *h*) (bring to an) end, finish, conclude, close

**beengen** [bə'ɛŋən] *v/t* (*no -ge-*, *h*) make *s.o.* (feel) uncomfortable; **be'engt** *adj*: ~ ***wohnen*** live in cramped quarters

**be'erben** *v/t* (*no -ge-*, *h*) ***j-n*** ~ be s.o.'s heir

**beerdigen** [bə'ʔeːɐdɪgən] *v/t* (*no -ge-*, *h*) bury; **Be'erdigung** *f* (-; *-en*) burial, funeral

**Beere** ['beːrə] *f* (-; *-n*) BOT berry; grape

**Beet** [beːt] *n* (-[*e*]*s*; *-e*) bed, patch

**befähigen** [bə'fɛːɪgən] *v/t* (*no -ge-*, *h*) enable; qualify (***für, zu*** for); **be'fähigt** *adj* (cap)able; ***zu et.*** ~ fit *or* qualified for s.th.; **Be'fähigung** *f* (-; *no pl*) qualification(s), (cap)ability

**befahl** [bə'faːl] *pret of* ***befehlen***

**be'fahrbar** *adj* passable, practicable; MAR navigable

**be'fahren** *v/t* (*irr*, ***fahren***, *no -ge-*, *h*) drive *or* travel on; MAR navigate

**be'fallen** *v/t* (*irr*, ***fallen***, *no -ge-*, *h*) attack, seize (*a. fig*)

**be'fangen** *adj* self-conscious; prejudiced, JUR *a.* bias(s)ed

**Be'fangenheit** *f* (-; *no pl*) self-consciousness; JUR bias, prejudice

**be'fassen** *v/refl* (*no -ge-*, *h*) ***sich*** ~ ***mit*** engage *or* occupy o.s. with; work on *s.th.*; deal with *s.o.*, *s.th.*

**Befehl** [bə'feːl] *m* (-[*e*]*s*; *-e*) order; command (***über*** *acc* of); **be'fehlen** *v/t* (*irr*, *no -ge-*, *h*) order; command

**Be'fehlshaber** *m* (*-s*; -) MIL commander

**be'festigen** *v/t* (*no -ge-*, *h*) fasten (***an*** *dat* to), fix (to), attach (to); MIL fortify; **Be'festigung** *f* (-; *-en*) fixing, fastening; MIL fortification

**be'feuchten** *v/t* (*no -ge-*, *h*) moisten, damp

**be'finden** *v/refl* (*irr*, ***finden***, *no -ge-*, *h*) be (situated); **Be'finden** *n* (*-s*; *no pl*) (state of) health

**be'flecken** *v/t* (*no -ge-*, *h*) stain; *fig a.* sully

**befohlen** [bə'foːlən] *pp of* ***befehlen***

**be'folgen** *v/t* (*no -ge-*, *h*) follow, take (*advice*); observe (*rule etc*); REL keep; **Be'folgung** *f* (-; *no pl*) following; observance

**be'fördern** *v/t* (*no -ge-*, *h*) carry, transport; haul, ship; promote (***zu*** to)

**Be'förderung** *f* (-; *-en*) (*no pl*) transport (-ation); shipment; promotion

**be'fragen** *v/t* (*no -ge-*, *h*) question, interview

**be'freien** *v/t* (*no -ge-*, *h*) free, liberate; rescue; exempt (***von*** from); **Be'freiung** *f* (-; *no pl*) liberation; exemption

**Befremden** [bə'frɛmdən] *n* (*-s*; *no pl*) irritation, displeasure; **be'fremdet** *adj* irritated, displeased

**befreunden** [bə'frɔyndən] *v/refl* (*no -ge-*, *h*) ***sich*** ~ ***mit*** make friends with; *fig* warm to; **be'freundet** *adj* friendly; ~ ***sein*** be friends

**befriedigen** [bə'friːdɪgən] *v/t* (*no -ge-*, *h*) satisfy; ***sich selbst*** ~ masturbate; ~**d** *adj* satisfactory; *grade*: fair

**befriedigt** [bə'friːdɪçt] *adj* satisfied, pleased

**Be'friedigung** *f* (-; *no pl*) satisfaction

**be'fristet** *adj* limited (***auf*** *acc* to), tem-

B

porary

**be'fruchten** *v/t* (*no -ge-, h*) BIOL fertilize, inseminate; **Be'fruchtung** *f* (-; *-en*) BIOL fertilization, insemination

**Befugnis** [bə'fu:knɪs] *f* (-; *-se*) authority; *esp* JUR competence; **befugt** [bə'fu:kt] *adj* authorized; competent

**be'fühlen** *v/t* (*no -ge-, h*) feel, touch

**Be'fund** *m* finding(s) (*a.* MED, JUR)

**be'fürchten** *v/t* (*no -ge-, h*) fear, be afraid of; suspect; **Be'fürchtung** *f* (-; *-en*) fear, suspicion

**befürworten** [bə'fy:ɐvɔrtən] *v/t* (*no -ge-, h*) advocate, speak *or* plead for; **Be'fürworter** *m* (*-s*; -) advocate

**begabt** [bə'ga:pt] *adj* gifted, talented

**Be'gabung** *f* (-; *-en*) gift, talent(s)

**begann** [bə'gan] *pret of* ***beginnen***

**be'geben** *v/refl* (*irr*, ***geben***, *no -ge-, h*) ***sich in Gefahr ~*** expose o.s. to danger

**Be'gebenheit** *f* (-; *-en*) incident, event

**begegnen** [bə'ge:gnən] *v/i* (*no -ge-, sein*) meet (*a. fig* ***mit*** with); ***sich ~*** meet

**Be'gegnung** *f* (-; *-en*) meeting, encounter (*a.* SPORT)

**be'gehen** *v/t* (*irr*, ***gehen***, *no -ge-, h*) walk (on); celebrate (*birthday etc*); commit (*crime*); make (*mistake*); ***ein Unrecht ~*** do wrong

**begehren** [bə'ge:rən] *v/t* (*no -ge-, h*) desire; **be'gehrenswert** *adj* desirable

**be'gehrlich** *adj* desirous, covetous

**begehrt** [bə'ge:ɐt] *adj* (very) popular, (much) in demand

**begeistern** [bə'gaistɐn] *v/t* (*no -ge-, h*) fill with enthusiasm; carry away (*audience*); ***sich ~ für*** be enthusiastic about

**be'geistert** *adj* enthusiastic

**Be'geisterung** *f* (-; *no pl*) enthusiasm

**Begierde** [bə'gi:ɐdə] *f* (-; *-n*) desire (***nach*** for), appetite (for)

**be'gierig** *adj* greedy; eager (***nach, auf*** *acc* for; ***zu*** *inf* to *inf*)

**be'gießen** *v/t* (*irr*, ***gießen***, *no -ge-, h*) water; GASTR baste; F *fig* celebrate *s.th.* (with a drink)

**Beginn** [bə'gɪn] *m* (-[*e*]*s*; *no pl*) beginning, start; ***zu ~*** at the beginning

**be'ginnen** *v/t and v/i* (*irr*, *no -ge-, h*) begin, start

**beglaubigen** [bə'glaubɪgən] *v/t* (*no -ge-, h*) attest, certify; **Be'glaubigung** *f* (-; *-en*) attestation, certification

**be'gleichen** *v/t* (*irr*, ***gleichen***, *no -ge-, h*) pay, settle

**be'gleiten** *v/t* (*no -ge-, h*) accompany (*a.* MUS ***auf*** *dat* on); ***j-n nach Hause ~*** see s.o. home; **Be'gleiter(in)** (*-s*; *-/-*; *-nen*) companion; MUS accompanist

**Be'gleit|erscheinung** *f* concomitant; MED side effect; **~schreiben** *n* covering letter

**Be'gleitung** *f* (-; *-en*) company; *esp* MIL escort; MUS accompaniment

**be'glückwünschen** *v/t* (*no -ge-, h*) congratulate (***zu*** on)

**begnadigen** [bə'gna:dɪgən] *v/t* (*no -ge-, h*), **Be'gnadigung** *f* (-; *-en*) JUR pardon; amnesty

**begnügen** [bə'gny:gən] *v/refl* (*no -ge-, h*) ***sich ~ mit*** be satisfied with; make do with

**begonnen** [bə'gɔnən] *pp of* ***beginnen***

**be'graben** *v/t* (*irr*, ***graben***, *no -ge-, h*) bury (*a. fig*); **Begräbnis** [bə'grɛ:pnɪs] *n* (*-ses*; *-se*) burial; funeral

**begradigen** [bə'gra:dɪgən] *v/t* (*no -ge-, h*) straighten

**be'greifen** *v/t* (*irr*, ***greifen***, *no -ge-, h*) comprehend, understand

**be'greiflich** *adj* understandable

**be'grenzen** *v/t* (*no -ge-, h*) limit, restrict (***auf*** *acc* to); **be'grenzt** *adj* limited

**Be'griff** *m* (-[*e*]*s*; *-e*) idea, notion; term (*a.* MATH); ***im ~ sein zu*** *inf* be about to *inf*; **be'griffsstutzig** *contp adj* F slow on the uptake

**be'gründen** *v/t* (*no -ge-, h*) give reasons for; **be'gründet** *adj* well-founded, justified; **Be'gründung** *f* (-; *-en*) reasons, arguments

**be'grünen** *v/t* (*no -ge-, h*) landscape

**be'grüßen** *v/t* (*no -ge-, h*) greet, welcome (*a. fig*); **Be'grüßung** *f* (-; *-en*) greeting, welcome

**begünstigen** [bə'gʏnstɪgən] *v/t* (*no -ge-, h*) favo(u)r

**be'gutachten** *v/t* (*no -ge-, h*) give an (expert's) opinion on; examine; ***~ lassen*** obtain expert opinion on

**begütert** [bə'gy:tɐt] *adj* wealthy

**be'haart** *adj* hairy

**behäbig** [bə'hɛ:bɪç] *adj* slow; portly

**be'haftet** *adj*: ***mit Fehlern ~*** flawed

**behagen** [bə'ha:gən] *v/i* (*no -ge-, h*) ***j-m ~*** please *or* suit s.o.; **Be'hagen** *n* (*-s*; *no pl*) pleasure, enjoyment; **behaglich** [bə'ha:klɪç] *adj* comfortable; cozy,

B

snug

**be'halten** *v/t* (*irr*, ***halten***, *no -ge-*, *h*) keep (*fig* ***für sich*** to o.s.); remember

**Behälter** [bə'hɛltɐ] *m* (*-s*; -) container, receptacle

**be'handeln** *v/t* (*no -ge-*, *h*) handle; treat (*a.* MED); ***sich*** (***ärztlich***) ***~ lassen*** undergo (medical) treatment

**Be'handlung** *f* (-; *-en*) handling; *a.* MED treatment

**beharren** [bə'harən] *v/i* (*no -ge-*, *h*) insist (***auf*** *dat* on)

**be'harrlich** *adj* persistent

**behaupten** [bə'hauptən] *v/t* (*no -ge-*, *h*) claim; pretend; **Be'hauptung** *f* (-; *-en*) statement, claim

**be'heben** *v/t* (*irr*, ***heben***, *no -ge-*, *h*) repair (*damage etc*)

**be'heizen** *v/t* (*no -ge-*, *h*) heat

**be'helfen** *v/refl* (*irr*, ***helfen***, *no -ge-*, *h*) ***sich ~ mit*** make do with; ***sich ~ ohne*** do without

**Be'helfs...** *in cpds mst* temporary

**beherbergen** [bə'hɛrbɛrgən] *v/t* (*no -ge-*, *h*) accommodate

**be'herrschen** *v/t* (*no -ge-*, *h*) rule (over), govern; ECON dominate, control; have (a good) command of (*language*); ***sich ~*** control o.s.; **Be'herrschung** *f* (-; *no pl*) command, control

**beherzigen** [bə'hɛrtsɪgən] *v/t* (*no -ge-*, *h*) take to heart, mind

**be'hilflich** *adj*: ***j-m ~ sein*** help s.o. (***bei*** with, in)

**be'hindern** *v/t* (*no -ge-*, *h*) hinder; obstruct (*a.* SPORT); **be'hindert** *adj* MED handicapped; disabled

**Be'hinderung** *f* (-; *-en*) obstruction; MED handicap

**Behörde** [bə'hø:ɐdə] *f* (-; *-n*) authority, *mst the* authorities; board

**be'hüten** *v/t* (*no -ge-*, *h*) guard (***vor*** *dat* from)

**behutsam** [bə'hu:tza:m] *adj* careful; gentle

**bei** [bai] *prp* (*dat*) near; at; with; by; *time*: during; at; ***~ München*** near Munich; ***wohnen ~*** stay (*or* live) with; ***~ mir*** (***ihr***) at my (her) place; ***~ uns*** (***zu Hause***) at home; ***arbeiten ~*** work for; ***e-e Stelle ~*** a job with; ***~ der Marine*** in the navy; ***~ Familie Müller*** at the Müllers'; ***~ Müller*** c/o Müller; ***ich habe kein Geld ~ mir*** I have no money with *or* on me; ***~ e-r Tasse Tee*** over a cup of tea; ***wir haben Englisch ~ Herrn X*** we have Mr X for English; ***~ Licht*** by light; ***~ Tag*** during the day; ***~ Nacht*** (***Sonnenaufgang***) at night (sunrise); ***~ s-r Geburt*** at his birth; ***~ Regen*** (***Gefahr***) in case of rain (danger); ***~ 100 Grad*** at a hundred degrees; → ***Arbeit, beim, weit***

**'beibehalten** *v/t* (*irr*, ***halten***, *sep*, *no -ge-*, *h*) keep up, retain

**'beibringen** *v/t* (*irr*, ***bringen***, *sep*, *no -ge-*, *h*) teach; tell; inflict (*dat* on)

**Beichte** ['baiçtə] *f* (-; *-n*) REL confession

**'beichten** *v/t and v/i* (*ge-*, *h*) REL confess (*a. fig*)

**'Beichtstuhl** *m* REL confessional

**beide** ['baidə] *adj and pron* both; ***m-e ~n Brüder*** my two brothers; ***wir ~*** the two of us; both of us; ***keiner von ~n*** neither of them; ***30 ~*** *tennis*: 30 all

**beiei'nander** *adv* together

**'Beifahrer** *m* front(-seat) passenger

**'Beifall** *m* (-[*e*]*s*; *no pl*) applause; *fig* approval

**'Beifallssturm** *m* (standing) ovation

**'beifügen** *v/t* (*sep*, *-ge-*, *h*) enclose (*dat* with)

**beige** [be:ʃ] *adj* beige

**'beigeben** (*irr*, ***geben***, *sep*, *-ge-*, *h*) **1.** *v/t* add **2.** F *v/i*: ***klein ~*** knuckle under

**'Bei|geschmack** *m* smack (***von*** of) (*a. fig*); **~hilfe** *f* aid, allowance; JUR aiding and abetting

**Beil** [bail] *n* (-[*e*]*s*; *-e*) hatchet; ax(e)

**'Beilage** *f* supplement; GASTR side dish; vegetables

**'beiläufig** *adj* casual

**'beilegen** *v/t* (*sep*, *-ge-*, *h*) add (*dat* to); enclose (with); settle (*dispute*)

**'Beilegung** *f* (-; *-en*) settlement

**'Beileid** *n* (-[*e*]*s*; *no pl*) condolence; ***herzliches ~*** my deepest sympathy

**'beiliegen** *v/i* (*irr*, ***liegen***, *sep*, *-ge-*, *h*) be enclosed (*dat* with)

**beim** [baim] *prp*: ***~ Bäcker*** at the baker's; ***~ Sprechen*** *etc* while speaking *etc*; ***~ Spielen*** at play; → *a.* ***bei***

**'beimessen** *v/t* (*irr*, ***messen***, *sep*, *-ge-*, *h*) attach *importance etc* (*dat* to)

**Bein** [bain] *n* (-[*e*]*s*; *-e*) ANAT leg; bone

**beinah(e)** ['baina:(ə)] *adv* almost, nearly

**'Beinbruch** *m* MED fracture of the leg

**'beipflichten** *v/i* (*sep*, *-ge-*, *h*) agree (*dat*

B

with)
**be'irren** *v/t* (*no -ge-*, *h*) confuse
**beisammen** [bai'zamən] *adv* together
**Bei'sammensein** *n*: ***geselliges ~*** get-together
**'Beischlaf** *m* JUR sexual intercourse
**bei'seite** *adv* aside; ***~schaffen*** *v/t* (*sep*, *-ge-*, *h*) remove; liquidate *s.o.*
**'beisetzen** *v/t* (*sep*, *-ge-*, *h*) bury
**'Beisetzung** *f* (*-*; *-en*) funeral
**'Beispiel** *n* (*-[e]s*; *-e*) example; ***zum ~*** for example, for instance; ***sich an j-m ein ~ nehmen*** follow s.o.'s example
**'beispiel|haft** *adj* exemplary; **~los** *adj* unprecedented, unparalleled
**'beispielsweise** *adv* such as
**beißen** ['baisən] *v/t and v/i* (*irr*, *-ge-*, *h*) bite (*a. fig*); ***sich ~*** *colors*: clash; **~d** *adj* biting, pungent (*both a. fig*)
**'Beistand** *m* (*-[e]s*; *no pl*) assistance
**'bei|stehen** *v/i* (*irr*, ***stehen***, *sep*, *-ge-*, *h*) ***j-m ~*** assist *or* help s.o.; **~steuern** *v/t* (*sep*, *-ge-*, *h*) contribute (***zu*** to)
**Beitrag** ['baitra:k] *m* (*-[e]s*; *Beiträge* ['baitrε:gə]) contribution; dues, *Br* subscription; **'beitragen** *v/t* (*irr*, ***tragen***, *sep*, *-ge-*, *h*) contribute (***zu*** to)
**'beitreten** *v/i* (*irr*, ***treten***, *sep*, *-ge-*, *sein*) join; **'Beitritt** *m* (*-[e]s*; *-e*) joining
**'Beiwagen** *m* MOT sidecar
**bei'zeiten** *adv* early, in good time
**beizen** ['baitsən] *v/t* (*ge-*, *h*) stain (*wood*); pickle (*meat*)
**bejahen** [bə'ja:ən] *v/t* (*no -ge-*, *h*) answer in the affirmative, affirm; **~d** *adj* affirmative
**be'kämpfen** *v/t* (*no -ge-*, *h*) fight (against)
**bekannt** [bə'kant] *adj* (well-)known; familiar; ***et. ~ geben*** announce s.th.; ***j-n mit j-m ~ machen*** introduce s.o. to s.o.; **Be'kannte** *m*, *f* (*-n*; *-n*) acquaintance, *mst* friend
**be'kanntgeben** *v/t* (*irr*, ***geben***, *sep*, *-ge-*, *h*) → ***bekannt***
**be'kanntlich** *adv* as you know
**be'kanntmachen** *v/t* (*sep*, *-ge-*, *h*) → ***bekannt***; **Be'kanntmachung** *f* (*-*; *-en*) announcement
**Be'kanntschaft** *f* (*-*; *-en*) acquaintance
**be'kehren** *v/t* (*no -ge-*, *h*) convert
**be'kennen** *v/t* (*irr*, ***kennen***, *no -ge-*, *h*) confess (*a.* REL); admit; ***sich schuldig ~*** JUR plead guilty; ***sich ~ zu*** profess *s.th.*; claim responsibility for; **Be'kennerbrief** *m* letter claiming responsibility
**Be'kenntnis** *n* (*-ses*; *-se*) confession, REL *a.* denomination
**be'klagen** *v/t* (*no -ge-*, *h*) deplore; ***sich ~*** complain (***über*** *acc* about)
**be'klagenswert** *adj* deplorable
**be'kleben** *v/t* (*no -ge-*, *h*) stick (*or* paste) on *s.th.*; ***mit Etiketten ~*** label *s.th.*
**be'kleckern** F *v/t* (*no -ge-*, *h*) stain; ***sich ~ mit*** spill *s.th.* over o.s.
**Be'kleidung** *f* (*-*; *-en*) clothing, clothes
**be'kommen** (*irr*, ***kommen***, *no -ge-*) **1.** *v/t* (*h*) get, receive; MED catch; be having (*baby*) **2.** *v/i* (*sein*) ***j-m*** (***gut***) **~** agree with s.o.; **bekömmlich** [bə'kœmlıç] *adj* wholesome
**be'kräftigen** *v/t* (*no -ge-*, *h*) confirm
**be'kreuzigen** *v/refl* (*no -ge-*, *h*) cross o.s.
**bekümmert** [bə'kʏmɐt] *adj* worried
**be'laden** *v/t* (*irr*, ***laden***, *no -ge-*, *h*) load, *fig a.* burden
**Belag** [bə'la:k] *m* (*-[e]s*; *Beläge* [bə'lε:gə]) covering; TECH coat(ing); MOT lining; (*road*) surface; MED fur; plaque; GASTR topping; spread; (sandwich) filling
**be'lagern** *v/t* (*no -ge-*, *h*) MIL besiege (*a. fig*); **Be'lagerung** *f* (*-*; *-en*) MIL siege
**be'langlos** *adj* irrelevant
**be'lassen** *v/t* (*irr*, ***lassen***, *no -ge-*, *h*) leave; ***es dabei ~*** leave it at that
**be'lastbar** *adj* resistant to strain *or* stress; TECH loadable; **be'lasten** *v/t* (*no -ge-*, *h*) load; *fig* burden; JUR incriminate; pollute; damage; ***j-s Konto ~ mit*** charge *s.th.* to s.o.'s account
**belästigen** [bə'lεstıgən] *v/t* (*no -ge-*, *h*) molest; annoy; disturb, bother; **Be'lästigung** *f* (*-*; *-en*) molestation; annoyance; disturbance
**Be'lastung** *f* (*-*; *-en*) load (*a.* TECH); *fig* burden; strain; stress; JUR incrimination; pollution, contamination
**Be'lastungszeuge** *m* JUR witness for the prosecution
**be'laufen** *v/refl* (*irr*, ***laufen***, *no -ge-*, *h*) ***sich ~ auf*** (*acc*) amount to
**be'lauschen** *v/t* (*no -ge-*, *h*) eavesdrop on
**be'leben** *fig v/t* (*no -ge-*, *h*) stimulate; **~d** *adj* stimulating
**belebt** [bə'le:pt] *adj* busy, crowded

**Beleg** [bə'leːk] *m* (-[*e*]*s*; -*e*) proof; receipt; document; **be'legen** *v/t* (*no -ge-, h*) cover; reserve (*seat*); prove; enrol(l) for, take (*classes*); GASTR put s.th. on; ***den ersten*** *etc* ***Platz ~*** SPORT take first *etc* place
**Be'legschaft** *f* (-; -*en*) staff
**be'legt** *adj* taken, occupied; *hotel etc*: full; TEL busy, *Br* engaged; MED coated; ***~es Brot*** sandwich
**be'lehren** *v/t* (*no -ge-, h*) teach, instruct, inform; ***sich ~ lassen*** take advice
**beleidigen** [bə'laidɪgən] *v/t* (*no -ge-, h*) offend (*a. fig*), insult; **~d** *adj* offensive, insulting
**Be'leidigung** *f* (-; -*en*) offense, *Br* offence, insult
**be'lesen** *adj* well-read
**be'leuchten** *v/t* (*no -ge-, h*) light (up), illuminate (*a. fig*); *fig* throw light on
**Be'leuchtung** *f* (-; -*en*) light(ing); illumination
**Belgien** ['bɛlgjən] Belgium; **Belgier** ['bɛlgjɐ] *m* (-*s*; -), **Belgierin** ['bɛlgjərɪn] *f* (-; -*nen*), **'belgisch** *adj* Belgian
**be'lichten** *v/t* (*no -ge-, h*) PHOT expose
**Be'lichtungsmesser** *m* PHOT exposure meter
**Be'lieben** *n*: ***nach ~*** at will
**beliebig** [bə'liːbɪç] *adj* any; optional; ***jeder ~e*** anyone
**beliebt** [bə'liːpt] *adj* popular (***bei*** with)
**Be'liebtheit** *f* (-; *no pl*) popularity
**be'liefern** *v/t* (*no -ge-, h*) supply, furnish (***mit*** with); **Be'lieferung** *f* supply
**bellen** ['bɛlən] *v/i* (*ge-, h*) bark (*a. fig*)
**be'lohnen** *v/t* (*no -ge-, h*) reward
**Be'lohnung** *f* (-; -*en*) reward; ***zur ~*** as a reward
**be'lügen** *v/t* (*irr*, ***lügen***, *no -ge-, h*) ***j-n ~*** lie to s.o.
**belustigen** [bə'lʊstɪgən] *v/t* (*no -ge-, h*) amuse; **belustigt** [bə'lʊstɪçt] *adj* amused; **Be'lustigung** *f* (-; -*en*) amusement
**bemächtigen** [bə'mɛçtɪgən] *v/refl* (*no -ge-, h*) get hold of, seize
**be'malen** *v/t* (*no -ge-, h*) paint
**bemängeln** [bə'mɛŋəln] *v/t* (*no -ge-, h*) find fault with
**bemannt** [bə'mant] *adj* manned
**be'merkbar** *adj* noticeable; ***sich ~ machen*** draw attention to o.s.; begin to show; **be'merken** *v/t* (*no -ge-, h*) notice; remark; **be'merkenswert** *adj* remarkable; **Be'merkung** *f* (-; -*en*) remark (***über*** *acc* about)
**be'mitleiden** *v/t* (*no -ge-, h*) pity, feel sorry for; **be'mitleidenswert** *adj* pitiable
**be'mühen** *v/refl* (*no -ge-, h*) try (hard); ***sich ~ um*** try to get *s.th.*; try to help *s.o.*; ***bitte ~ Sie sich nicht!*** please don't bother; **Be'mühung** *f* (-; -*en*) effort; ***danke für Ihre ~en!*** thank you for your trouble
**be'muttern** *v/t* (*no -ge-, h*) mother *s.o.*
**be'nachbart** *adj* neighbo(u)ring
**benachrichtigen** [bə'naːxrɪçtɪgən] *v/t* (*no -ge-, h*) inform, notify
**Be'nachrichtigung** *f* (-; -*en*) information, notification
**benachteiligen** [bə'naːxtailɪgən] *v/t* (*no -ge-, h*) place *s.o.* at a disadvantage; discriminate against *s.o.*; **benachteiligt** [bə'naːxtailɪçt] *adj* disadvantaged; ***die Benachteiligten*** the underprivileged; **Be'nachteiligung** *f* (-; -*en*) disadvantage; discrimination
**be'nehmen** *v/refl* (*irr*, ***nehmen***, *no -ge-, h*) behave (o.s.); **Be'nehmen** *n* (-*s*; *no pl*) behavio(u)r; manners
**be'neiden** *v/t* (*no -ge-, h*) ***j-n um et. ~*** envy s.o. s.th.
**be'neidenswert** *adj* enviable
**BENELUX** ['beːnelʊks] *abbr of* ***Belgien, Niederlande, Luxemburg*** Belgium, the Netherlands and Luxembourg
**be'nennen** *v/t* (*irr*, ***nennen***, *no -ge-, h*) name
**Bengel** ['bɛŋəl] *m* (-*s*; -) (little) rascal, urchin
**benommen** [bə'nɔmən] *adj* dazed, F dopey
**be'noten** *v/t* (*no -ge-, h*) grade, *Br* mark
**be'nötigen** *v/t* (*no -ge-, h*) need, want, require
**be'nutzen** *v/t* (*no -ge-, h*) use
**Be'nutzer** *m* (-*s*; -) user
**be'nutzerfreundlich** *adj* user-friendly
**Be'nutzeroberfläche** *f* IT user interface
**Be'nutzung** *f* use
**Benzin** [bɛn'tsiːn] *n* (-*s*; -*e*) gasoline, F gas, *Br* petrol
**beobachten** [bə'ʔoːbaxtən] *v/t* (*no -ge-, h*) watch; observe
**Be'obachter** *m* (-*s*; -) observer

B

**Be'obachtung** *f* (-; *-en*) observation
**be'pflanzen** *v/t* (*no -ge-, h*) plant (***mit*** with)
**bequem** [bə'kveːm] *adj* comfortable; easy; lazy; **be'quemen** *v/refl* (*no -ge-, h*) ***sich ~ zu*** *inf* bring o.s. to *inf*
**Be'quemlichkeit** *f* (-; *-en*) comfort; ***alle ~en*** all conveniences; (*no pl*) laziness
**be'raten** *v/t* (*irr*, ***raten***, *no -ge-, h*) advise *s.o.*; debate, discuss *s.th.*; ***sich ~*** confer (***mit j-m*** with s.o.; ***über et.*** on s.th.); **Be'rater** *m* (*-s*; -) adviser, consultant; **Be'ratung** *f* (-; *-en*) advice (*a.* MED); debate; consultation, conference; **Be'ratungsstelle** *f* counsel(l)ing center (*Br* centre)
**be'rauben** *v/t* (*no -ge-, h*) rob
**be'rauschend** *adj* intoxicating; F *fig* ***nicht gerade ~!*** not so hot!; **be'rauscht** *fig adj*: ***~ von*** drunk with
**be'rechnen** *v/t* (*no -ge-, h*) calculate; ECON charge (***zu*** at); **~d** *adj* calculating
**Be'rechnung** *f* calculation (*a. fig*)
**berechtigen** [bə'rɛçtɪgən] *v/t*: ***j-n ~ zu*** entitle (*or* authorize) s.o. to; **berechtigt** [bə'rɛçtɪçt] *adj* entitled (***zu*** to); authorized (to); legitimate; **Be'rechtigung** *f* (-; *no pl*) right (***zu*** to); authority
**Beredsamkeit** [bə'reːtzaːmkait] *f* (-; *no pl*) eloquence
**beredt** [bə'reːt] *adj* eloquent (*a. fig*)
**Be'reich** *m* (-[*e*]*s*; *-e*) area; range; field
**bereichern** [bə'raiçɐn] *v/t* (*no -ge-, h*) enrich; ***sich ~*** get rich (***an*** *dat* on); **Be'reicherung** [bə'raiçərʊŋ] *f* (-; *no pl*) enrichment
**Be'reifung** *f* (-; *-en*) (set of) tires (*Br* tyres)
**be'reinigen** *v/t* (*no -ge-, h*) settle
**be'reisen** *v/t* (*no -ge-, h*) tour; cover
**bereit** [bə'rait] *adj* ready, prepared; willing; **be'reiten** *v/t* (*no -ge-, h*) prepare; cause; **be'reithalten** *v/t* (*irr*, ***halten***, *sep, -ge-, h*) have *s.th.* ready; ***sich ~*** stand by; **be'reits** *adv* already; **Be'reitschaft** *f* (-; *no pl*) readiness; ***in ~*** on standby; **Be'reitschaftsdienst** *m*: ***~ haben*** *doctor etc*: be on call; **be'reitstellen** *v/t* (*sep, -ge-, h*) provide; **be'reitwillig** *adj* ready, willing
**be'reuen** *v/t* (*no -ge-, h*) repent (of); regret
**Berg** [bɛrk] *m* (-[*e*]*s*; *-e*) mountain; ***~e von*** F loads of; ***die Haare standen ihm zu ~e*** his hair stood on end
**berg'ab** *adv* downhill (*a. fig*)
**'Bergarbeiter** *m* miner
**berg'auf** *adv* uphill
**'Berg|bahn** *f* mountain railroad (*Br* railway); **~bau** *m* (-[*e*]*s*; *no pl*) mining
**bergen** ['bɛrgən] *v/t* (*irr, ge- h*) rescue, save *s.o.*; salvage *s.th.*; recover (*body*)
**'Bergführer** *m* mountain guide
**bergig** ['bɛrgɪç] *adj* mountainous
**'Berg|kette** *f* mountain range; **~mann** *m* (-[*e*]*s*; *-leute*) miner; **~rutsch** *m* landslide; **~schuhe** *pl* mountain(eering) boots; **~spitze** *f* (mountain) peak; **~steigen** *n* mountaineering, (mountain) climbing; **~steiger** *m* (*-s*; -) mountaineer, (mountain) climber
**'Bergung** *f* (-; *-en*) recovery; rescue
**'Bergungsarbeiten** *pl* rescue work; salvage operations
**'Bergwacht** *f* alpine rescue service
**'Bergwerk** *n* mine
**Bericht** [bə'rɪçt] *m* (-[*e*]*s*; *-e*) report (***über*** *acc* on), account (of)
**be'richten** *v/t and v/i* (*no -ge-, h*) report (***über*** *acc* on); ***j-m et. ~*** inform s.o. of s.th.; tell s.o. about s.th.
**Be'richt|erstatter** *m* (*-s*; -) reporter; correspondent; **~erstattung** *f* (-; *-en*) report(ing)
**berichtigen** [bə'rɪçtɪgən] *v/t* (*no -ge-, h*) correct; **Be'richtigung** *f* (-; *-en*) correction
**be'rieseln** *v/t* (*no -ge-, h*) sprinkle
**Bernstein** ['bɛrnʃtain] *m* (*-s*; *no pl*) amber
**bersten** ['bɛrstən] *v/i* (*irr, -ge-, sein*) burst (*fig* ***vor*** *dat* with)
**berüchtigt** [bə'rʏçtɪçt] *adj* notorious (***wegen*** for)
**berücksichtigen** [bə'rʏkzɪçtɪgən] *v/t* (*no -ge-, h*) take into consideration; ***nicht ~*** disregard
**Be'rücksichtigung** *f*: ***unter ~*** (*gen*) in consideration of
**Be'ruf** *m* (-[*e*]*s*; *-e*) job, occupation; trade; profession; **be'rufen** *v/t* (*irr*, ***rufen***, *no -ge-, h*) appoint (***zu*** [as] *s.o.*; to *s.th.*); ***sich ~ auf*** (*acc*) refer to
**be'ruflich** *adj* professional; ***~ unterwegs*** away on business
**Be'rufs...** *in cpds ...sportler etc*: profes-

sional …; ~**ausbildung** *f* vocational (*or* professional) training; ~**berater** *m* careers advisor; ~**beratung** *f* careers guidance; ~**bezeichnung** *f* job designation *or* title; ~**kleidung** *f* work clothes; ~**krankheit** *f* occupational disease; ~**schule** *f* vocational school

**be'rufstätig** *adj*: ~ ***sein*** (go to) work, have a job; **Be'rufstätige** *m, f* (*-n*; *-n*) working person, *pl* working people

**Be'rufsverkehr** *m* rush-hour traffic

**Be'rufung** *f* (-; *-en*) appointment (***zu*** to); JUR appeal (***bei*** to); ***unter ~ auf*** (*acc*) with reference to; on the grounds of

**be'ruhen** *v/i* (*no -ge-*, *h*) ~ ***auf*** (*dat*) be based on; ***et. auf sich ~ lassen*** let s.th. rest

**beruhigen** [bə'ruːɪgən] *v/t* (*no -ge-*, *h*) quiet(en), calm, soothe; reassure *s.o.*; ***sich ~*** calm down; ~**d** *adj* reassuring; MED sedative

**Be'ruhigung** *f* (-; *-en*) calming (down); soothing; relief; **Be'ruhigungsmittel** *n* MED sedative; tranquil(l)izer

**berühmt** [bə'ryːmt] *adj* famous (***wegen*** for); **Be'rühmtheit** *f* (-; *-en*) (*no pl*) fame; celebrity, star

**be'rühren** *v/t* (*no -ge-*, *h*) touch (*a. fig*); concern; **Be'rührung** *f* (-; *-en*) touch; ***in ~ kommen*** come into contact

**Be'rührungs|angst** *f* fear of contact; ~**punkt** *m* point of contact

**besänftigen** [bə'zɛnftɪgən] *v/t* (*no -ge-*, *h*) appease, calm, soothe

**Be'satzung** *f* (-; *-en*) AVIAT, MAR crew; MIL occupying forces

**Be'satzungs|macht** *f* MIL occupying power; ~**truppen** *pl* MIL occupying forces

**be'saufen** F *v/refl* (*irr*, ***saufen***, *no -ge-*, *h*) get drunk, get bombed

**be'schädigen** *v/t* (*no -ge-*, *h*) damage

**Be'schädigung** *f* (-; *-en*) damage

**be'schaffen** *v/t* (*no -ge-*, *h*) provide, get; raise (*money*); **Be'schaffenheit** *f* (-; *no pl*) state, condition

**beschäftigen** [bə'ʃɛftɪgən] *v/t* (*no -ge-*, *h*) employ; keep *s.o.* busy; ***sich ~*** occupy o.s.; **beschäftigt** [bə'ʃɛftɪçt] *adj* busy, occupied; **Be'schäftigte** *m, f* (*-n*; *-n*) employed person, *pl* employed people; **Be'schäftigung** *f* (-; *-en*) employment; occupation

**be'schämen** *v/t* (*no -ge-*, *h*) shame *s.o.*, make *s.o.* feel ashamed; ~**d** *adj* shameful; humiliating

**be'schämt** *adj* ashamed (***über*** *acc* of)

**be'schatten** *fig v/t* (*no -ge-*, *h*) shadow, F tail

**Bescheid** [bə'ʃait] *m* (-[*e*]*s*; *-e*) answer; JUR decision; information (***über*** *acc* on, about); ***sagen Sie mir ~*** let me know; (***gut***) ***~ wissen über*** (*acc*) know all about

**be'scheiden** *adj* modest (*a. fig*); humble; **Be'scheidenheit** *f* (-; *no pl*) modesty

**bescheinigen** [bə'ʃainɪgən] *v/t* (*no -ge-*, *h*) certify

**Be'scheinigung** *f* (-; *-en*) (*no pl*) certification; certificate

**be'scheißen** V *v/t* (*irr*, ***scheißen***, *no -ge-*, *h*) cheat; ***j-n ~ um*** do s.o. out of

**be'schenken** *v/t* (*no -ge-*, *h*) ***j-n*** (***reich***) ~ give s.o. (shower s.o. with) presents

**Be'scherung** *f* (-; *-en*) distribution of (Christmas) presents; F *fig* mess

**be'schichten** *v/t* (*no -ge-*, *h*) TECH coat

**Be'schichtung** *f* (-; *-en*) TECH coat

**be'schießen** *v/t* (*irr*, ***schießen***, *no -ge-*, *h*) MIL fire *or* shoot at; bombard (*a.* PHYS), shell

**be'schimpfen** *v/t* (*no -ge-*, *h*) abuse, insult; swear at; **Be'schimpfung** *f* (-; *-en*) abuse, insult

**be'schissen** V *adj* lousy, rotten

**Be'schlag** *m* TECH metal fitting(s); ***in ~ nehmen*** *fig* monopolize *s.o.*; bag; occupy; **be'schlagen** (*irr*, ***schlagen***, *no -ge-*) **1.** *v/t* (*h*) cover; TECH fit, mount; shoe (*horse*) **2.** *v/i* (*sein*) *window etc*: steam up **3.** *adj* steamed-up; *fig* well-versed (***auf, in*** *dat* in)

**Be'schlagnahme** [bə'ʃlaːknaːmə] *f* (-; *-n*) confiscation; **be'schlagnahmen** *v/t* (*no -ge-*, *h*) confiscate

**beschleunigen** [bə'ʃlɔynɪgən] *v/t and v/i* (*no -ge-*, *h*) accelerate, speed up; **Be'schleunigung** *f* (-; *-en*) acceleration

**be'schließen** *v/t* (*irr*, ***schließen***, *no -ge-*, *h*) decide (on); pass (*law*); conclude; **Be'schluss** *m* decision

**be'schmieren** *v/t* (*no -ge-*, *h*) smear, soil; scrawl all over; cover *wall etc* with graffiti; spread (*toast etc*)

**be'schmutzen** *v/t* (*no -ge-*, *h*) soil (*a.*

B

*fig*), dirty
**be'schneiden** *v/t* (*irr*, ***schneiden***, *no -ge-*, *h*) clip, cut (*a. fig*); prune; MED circumcise
**be'schönigen** [bə'ʃøːnɪgən] *v/t* (*no -ge-*, *h*) gloss over
**beschränken** [bə'ʃrɛŋkən] *v/t* (*no -ge-*, *h*) confine, limit, restrict; ***sich ~ auf*** (*acc*) confine o.s. to; **be'schränkt** *adj* limited; *contp* dense; narrow-minded
**Be'schränkung** *f* (-; *-en*) limitation, restriction
**be'schreiben** *v/t* (*irr*, ***schreiben***, *no -ge-*, *h*) describe; write on
**Be'schreibung** *f* (-; *-en*) description
**be'schriften** *v/t* (*no -ge-*, *h*) inscribe; mark (*goods*); **Be'schriftung** *f* (-; *-en*) inscription
**beschuldigen** [bə'ʃʊldɪgən] *v/t* (*no -ge-*, *h*) blame; ***j-n e-r Sache ~*** accuse s.o. of s.th. (*a.* JUR); **Be'schuldigung** *f* (-; *-en*) accusation
**be'schummeln** F *v/t* (*no -ge-*, *h*) cheat
**Be'schuss** *m*: ***unter ~*** MIL under fire
**be'schützen** *v/t* (*no -ge-*, *h*) protect, shelter, guard (***vor*** *dat* from)
**Be'schützer** *m* (*-s*; -) protector
**Beschwerde** [bə'ʃveːɐdə] *f* (-; *-n*) complaint (***über*** *acc* about; ***bei*** to); *pl* MED complaints, trouble
**beschweren** [bə'ʃveːrən] *v/t* (*no -ge-*, *h*) weight *s.th.*; ***sich ~*** complain (***über*** *acc* about; ***bei*** to)
**be'schwerlich** *adj* hard, arduous
**beschwichtigen** [bə'ʃvɪçtɪgən] *v/t* (*no -ge-*, *h*) appease (*a.* POL), calm
**be'schwindeln** *v/t* (*no -ge-*, *h*) tell a fib *or* lie; cheat
**beschwingt** [bə'ʃvɪŋt] *adj* buoyant; MUS lively, swinging
**beschwipst** [bə'ʃvɪpst] F *adj* tipsy
**be'schwören** *v/t* (*irr*, ***schwören***, *no -ge-*, *h*) swear to; implore; conjure up
**beseitigen** [bə'zaitɪgən] *v/t* (*no -ge-*, *h*) remove (*a. s.o.*), *a.* dispose of (*waste etc*); eliminate; POL liquidate
**Be'seitigung** *f* (-; *no pl*) removal; disposal; elimination
**Besen** ['beːzən] *m* (*-s*; -) broom
**'Besenstiel** *m* broomstick
**besessen** [bə'zesən] *adj* obsessed (***von*** by, with); ***wie ~*** like mad
**be'setzen** *v/t* (*no -ge-*, *h*) occupy (*a.* MIL); fill (*post etc*); THEA cast; trim; squat in; **be'setzt** *adj* occupied; *seat*: taken; *bus etc*: full up; TEL busy, *Br* engaged; **Be'setztzeichen** *n* TEL busy signal, *Br* engaged tone; **Be'setzung** *f* (-; *-en*) THEA cast; MIL occupation
**besichtigen** [bə'zɪçtɪgən] *v/t* (*no -ge-*, *h*) visit, see the sights of; inspect
**Be'sichtigung** *f* (-; *-en*) sightseeing; visit (*gen* to); inspection (of)
**be'siedeln** *v/t* (*no -ge-*, *h*) settle; colonize; populate; **be'siedelt** *adj*: ***dicht*** (***dünn***) ~ densely (sparsely) populated;
**Be'siedlung** *f* (-; *-en*) settlement; colonization; population
**be'siegeln** *v/t* (*no -ge-*, *h*) seal
**be'siegen** *v/t* (*no -ge-*, *h*) defeat, beat; conquer (*a. fig*)
**besinnen** *v/refl* (*irr*, ***sinnen***, *no -ge-*, *h*) remember; think (***auf*** *acc* about); ***sich anders ~*** change one's mind
**be'sinnlich** *adj* contemplative
**Be'sinnung** *f* (-; *no pl*) MED consciousness; (***wieder***) ***zur ~ kommen*** MED come round; *fig* come to one's senses
**be'sinnungslos** *adj* MED unconscious
**Be'sitz** *m* (*-es*; *no pl*) possession; property; ***~ ergreifen von*** take possession of; **be'sitzanzeigend** *adj* LING possessive; **be'sitzen** *v/t* (*irr*, ***sitzen***, *no -ge-*, *h*) possess, own; **Be'sitzer** *m* (*-s*; -) possessor, owner; ***den ~ wechseln*** change hands
**besoffen** [bə'zɔfən] F *adj* drunk, plastered, stoned
**besohlen** [bə'zoːlən] *v/t* (*no -ge-*, *h*) ***~ lassen*** have (re)soled
**Be'soldung** *f* (-; *-en*) pay; salary
**besondere** [bə'zɔndərə] *adj* special, particular; peculiar
**Be'sonderheit** *f* (-; *-en*) peculiarity
**be'sonders** *adv* especially, particularly; chiefly, mainly
**be'sonnen** *adj* prudent, level-headed
**be'sorgen** *v/t* (*no -ge-*, *h*) get, buy; → ***erledigen***; **Be'sorgnis** [bə'zɔrknɪs] *f* (-; *-se*) concern, alarm, anxiety (***über*** *acc* about, at); ***~ erregend*** → ***besorgniserregend***; **be'sorgniserregend** *adj* alarming; **besorgt** [bə'zɔrkt] *adj* worried, concerned; **Be'sorgung** *f* (-; *-en*) ***~en machen*** go shopping
**be'spielen** *v/t* (*no -ge-*, *h*) make a recording on
**be'spitzeln** *v/t* (*no -ge-*, *h*) spy on *s.o.*

**be'sprechen** *v/t* (*irr*, ***sprechen***, *no -ge-*, *h*) discuss, talk *s.th.* over; review (*book etc*); **Be'sprechung** *f* (-; *-en*) discussion, talk(s); meeting, conference; review

**be'spritzen** *v/t* (*no -ge-*, *h*) spatter

**besser** ['bɛsɐ] *adj and adv* better; ***es ist ~, wir fragen ihn*** we had better ask him; ***immer ~*** better and better; ***es geht ihm ~*** he is better; ***oder ~ gesagt*** or rather; ***es ~ wissen*** know better; ***es ~ machen als*** do better than; ***~ ist ~*** just to be on the safe side

**'bessern** *v/refl* (*ge-*, *h*) improve, get better; **'Besserung** *f* (-; *no pl*) improvement; ***auf dem Wege der ~*** on the way to recovery; ***gute ~!*** get better soon

**Besserwisser** ['bɛsɐvɪsɐ] *m* (*-s*; -) F smart aleck

**Be'stand** *m* (*no pl*) (continued) existence; stock; ***~ haben*** last, be lasting

**be'ständig** *adj* constant, steady (*a. character*); settled; ***...beständig*** *in cpds* ...-resistant, ...proof

**Be'standsaufnahme** *f* ECON stocktaking (*a. fig*); ***~ machen*** take stock (*a. fig*)

**Be'standteil** *m* part, component

**be'stärken** *v/t* (*no -ge-*, *h*) confirm, strengthen, encourage (***in*** *dat* in)

**bestätigen** [bə'ʃtɛːtɪgən] *v/t* (*no -ge-*, *h*) confirm; certify; acknowledge (*receipt*); ***sich ~*** prove (to be) true; come true; ***sich bestätigt fühlen*** feel affirmed; **Be'stätigung** *f* (-; *-en*) confirmation; certificate; acknowledg(e)ment; letter of confirmation

**bestatten** [bə'ʃtatən] *v/t* (*no -ge-*, *h*) bury; **Be'stattungsinsti,tut** *n* funeral home, *Br* undertakers

**be'stäuben** *v/t* (*no -ge-*, *h*) dust; BOT pollinate

**beste** ['bɛstə] *adj and adv* best; ***am ~n*** best; ***welches gefällt dir am ~n?*** which one do you like best?; ***am ~n nehmen Sie den Bus*** it would be best to take a bus; **Beste** *m*, *f* (*-n*; *-n*), *n* (*-n*; *no pl*) *the* best; ***das ~ geben*** do one's best; ***das ~ machen aus*** make the best of; ***(nur) zu deinem ~n*** for your own good

**be'stechen** *v/t* (*irr*, ***stechen***, *no -ge-*, *h*) bribe; fascinate (***durch*** by)

**be'stechlich** *adj* corrupt

**Be'stechung** *f* (-; *-en*) bribery, corruption; **Be'stechungsgeld** *n* bribe

**Besteck** [bə'ʃtɛk] *n* (*-[e]s*; *-e*) (set of) knife, fork and spoon; cutlery

**be'stehen** (*irr*, ***stehen***, *no -ge-*, *h*) **1.** *v/t* pass (*examination etc*) **2.** *v/i* be, exist; ***~ auf*** (*dat*) insist on; ***~ aus (in)*** (*dat*) consist of (in); ***~ bleiben*** last, survive

**Be'stehen** *n* (*-s*; *no pl*) existence

**be'stehlen** *v/t* (*irr*, ***stehlen***, *no -ge-*, *h*) ***j-n ~*** steal s.o.'s money *etc*

**be'steigen** *v/t* (*irr*, ***steigen***, *no -ge-*, *h*) climb; get on *a bus etc*; ascend (*the throne*)

**be'stellen** *v/t* (*no -ge-*, *h*) order; book (*room etc*); reserve (*seat etc*); call (*taxi*); give, send (*message etc*); AGR cultivate; ***kann ich et. ~?*** can I take a message?; ***~ Sie ihm bitte, ...*** please tell him ...

**Be'stellschein** *m* ECON order form

**Be'stellung** *f* (-; *-en*) booking; reservation; ECON order; ***auf ~*** to order

**'bestenfalls** *adv* at best

**'bestens** *adv* very well

**bestialisch** [bɛs'tjaːlɪʃ] *adj fig* bestial

**Bestie** ['bɛstjə] *f* (-; *-n*) beast, *fig a.* brute

**be'stimmen** *v/t* (*no -ge-*, *h*) determine, decide; define; choose, pick; ***zu ~ haben*** be in charge, F be the boss; ***bestimmt für*** meant for; **be'stimmt** **1.** *adj* determined, firm; LING definite (*article*); ***~e Dinge*** certain things **2.** *adv* certainly; ***ganz ~*** definitely; ***er ist ~ ...*** he must be ...; **Be'stimmung** *f* (-; *-en*) regulation; destiny

**Be'stimmungsort** *m* destination

**'Bestleistung** *f* SPORT (personal) record

**be'strafen** *v/t* (*no -ge-*, *h*) punish

**Be'strafung** *f* (-; *-en*) punishment

**be'strahlen** *v/t* (*no -ge-*, *h*) irradiate (*a.* MED); **Be'strahlung** *f* (-; *-en*) irradiation; MED ray treatment, radiotherapy

**be'streichen** *v/t* (*irr*, ***streichen***, *no -ge-*, *h*) spread; **be'streiten** *v/t* (*irr*, ***streiten***, *no -ge-*, *h*) challenge; deny; pay for, finance; **be'streuen** *v/t* (*no -ge-*, *h*) sprinkle (***mit*** with); **be'stürmen** *v/t* (*no -ge-*, *h*) urge; bombard

**be'stürzt** *adj* dismayed (***über*** *acc* at); **Be'stürzung** *f* (-; *no pl*) consternation, dismay

**Besuch** [bə'zuːx] *m* (*-[e]s*; *-e*) visit (*gen*, ***bei, in*** *dat* to); call (***bei*** on; ***in*** *dat* at); attendance (*gen* at); ***~ haben*** have company *or* guests; **be'suchen** *v/t*

B

(*no -ge-, h*) visit; call on, (go to) see; look *s.o.* up; attend (*meeting etc*); go to (*pub etc*); **Be'sucher(in)** (*-s; -/-; -nen*) visitor, guest; **Be'suchszeit** *f* visiting hours; **be'sucht** *adj*: ***gut*** (***schlecht***) ~ well (poorly) attended; much (little) frequented

**betagt** [bə'ta:kt] *adj* aged

**be'tasten** *v/t* (*no -ge-, h*) touch, feel

**be'tätigen** *v/t* (*no -ge-, h*) TECH operate; apply (*brake*); ***sich ~*** be active

**Be'tätigung** *f* (*-; -en*) activity

**betäuben** [bə'tɔʏbən] *v/t* (*no -ge-, h*) stun (*a. fig*), daze; MED an(a)esthetize

**Be'täubung** *f* (*-; -en*) MED an(a)esthetization; an(a)esthesia; *fig* daze, stupor

**Be'täubungsmittel** *n* MED an(a)esthetic; narcotic

**Bete** ['be:tə] *f* (*-; -n*) ***rote ~*** BOT beet, *Br* beetroot

**beteiligen** [bə'tailɪgən] *v/t* (*no -ge-, h*) ***j-n ~*** give s.o. a share (***an*** *dat* in); ***sich ~*** take part (***an*** *dat*, ***bei*** in), participate (in) (*a.* JUR); **beteiligt** [bə'tailɪçt] *adj* concerned; ***~ sein an*** (*dat*) be involved in; ECON have a share in; **Be'teiligung** *f* (*-; -en*) participation (*a.* JUR, ECON); involvement; share (*a.* ECON)

**beten** ['be:tən] *v/i* (*ge-, h*) pray (***um*** for), say one's prayers; say grace

**beteuern** [bə'tɔʏɐn] *v/t* (*no -ge-, h*) protest (*one's innocence etc*)

**Beton** [be'tɔŋ] *m* (*-s; -s, -e* [be'to:nə]) concrete

**betonen** [bə'to:nən] *v/t* (*no -ge-, h*) stress, *fig a.* emphasize

**betonieren** [beto'ni:rən] *v/t* (*no -ge-, h*) (cover with) concrete

**Be'tonung** *f* (*-; -en*) stress; *fig* emphasis

**betören** [bə'tø:rən] *v/t* (*no -ge-, h*) infatuate, bewitch

**Betr.** *abbr of* ***betrifft*** re

**Betracht** [bə'traxt] *m*: ***in ~ ziehen*** take into consideration; ***nicht in ~ kommen*** be out of the question

**be'trachten** *v/t* (*no -ge-, h*) look at, *fig a.* view; ***~ als*** look upon *or* regard as, consider; **Be'trachter** *m* (*-s; -*) viewer

**beträchtlich** [bə'trɛçtlɪç] *adj* considerable

**Be'trachtung** *f* (*-; -en*) view; ***bei näherer ~*** on closer inspection

**Betrag** [bə'tra:k] *m* (*-[e]s; Beträge* [bə'trɛ:gə]) amount, sum; **be'tragen** (*irr,* ***tragen***, *no -ge-, h*) **1.** *v/t* amount to **2.** *v/refl* behave (o.s.); **Be'tragen** *n* (*-s; no pl*) behavio(u)r, conduct

**be'trauen** *v/t* (*no -ge-, h*) entrust (***mit*** with)

**be'treffen** *v/t* (*irr,* ***treffen***, *no -ge-, h*) concern; refer to; ***was ... betrifft*** as for ..., as to ...; ***betrifft*** (*abbr* ***Betr.***) re; ***~d*** *adj* concerning; ***die ~en Personen*** *etc* the people *etc* concerned

**be'treiben** *v/t* (*irr,* ***treiben***, *no -ge-, h*) operate, run; go in for (*sport etc*)

**be'treten**[1] *v/t* (*irr,* ***treten***, *no -ge-, h*) step on; enter; ***Betreten*** (***des Rasens***) ***verboten!*** keep out! (keep off the grass!)

**be'treten**[2] *adj* embarrassed

**betreuen** [bə'trɔʏən] *v/t* (*no -ge-, h*) look after, take care of; **Be'treuung** *f* (*-; no pl*) care (*gen* of, for)

**Betrieb** [bə'tri:p] *m* (*-[e]s; -e*) business, firm, company; (*no pl*) operation, running; (*no pl*) rush; ***in ~ sein*** (***setzen***) be in (put into) operation; ***außer ~*** out of order; ***im Geschäft war viel ~*** the shop was very busy

**Be'triebs|anleitung** *f* operating instructions; ***~berater*** *m* business consultant; ***~ferien*** *pl* company (*Br a.* works) holiday; ***~fest*** *n* annual company fête; ***~kapi,tal*** *n* working capital; ***~klima*** *n* working atmosphere; ***~kosten*** *pl* operating costs; ***~leitung*** *f* management; ***~rat*** *m* works council

**be'triebssicher** *adj* safe to operate

**Be'triebs|störung** *f* TECH breakdown; ***~sys,tem*** *n* IT operating system; ***~unfall*** *m* industrial accident; ***~wirtschaft*** *f* business administration

**be'trinken** *v/refl* (*irr,* ***trinken***, *no -ge-, h*) get drunk

**betroffen** [bə'trɔfən] *adj* affected, concerned; dismayed, shocked; **Be'troffenheit** *f* (*-; no pl*) dismay, shock

**betrübt** [bə'try:pt] *adj* sad, grieved (***über*** *acc* at)

**Betrug** [bə'tru:k] *m* (*-[e]s; no pl*) cheat; JUR fraud; deceit; **be'trügen** *v/t* (*irr,* ***trügen***, *no -ge-, h*) deceive; cheat (***beim Kartenspiel*** at cards); swindle, trick (***um et.*** out of s.th.); be unfaithful to; **Be'trüger(in)** (*-s; -/-; -nen*) swindler, trickster

**betrunken** [bə'trʊŋkən] *adj* drunken; ~

***sein*** be drunk
**Be'trunkene** *m, f (-n; -n)* drunk
**Bett** [bɛt] *n (-[e]s; -en)* bed; ***am ~*** at the bedside; ***ins ~ gehen*** (***bringen***) go (put) to bed; **~bezug** *m* comforter case, *Br* duvet cover; **~decke** *f* blanket; quilt
**betteln** ['bɛtəln] *v/i (ge-, h)* beg (***um*** for)
**'Bettgestell** *n* bedstead
**bettlägerig** ['bɛtlɛːgərɪç] *adj* bedridden
**'Bettlaken** *n* sheet
**Bettler** ['bɛtlɐ] *m (-s; -)* beggar
**Bett|nässer** ['bɛtnɛsɐ] *m (-s; -)* MED bed wetter; **~ruhe** *f* bed rest; ***j-m ~ verordnen*** tell s.o. to stay in bed; **~vorleger** *m* bedside rug; **~wäsche** *f* bed linen; **~zeug** *n* bedding, bedclothes
**beugen** ['bɔʏgən] *v/t (ge-, h)* bend; LING inflect; ***sich ~*** (***vor*** *dat* to) bend, bow
**Beule** ['bɔʏlə] *f (-; -n)* MED bump; MOT dent
**beunruhigen** [bə'ʔʊnruːɪgən] *v/t (no -ge-, h)* alarm, worry
**beurlauben** [bə'ʔuːɐlaubən] *v/t* give *s.o.* leave *or* time off; suspend; ***sich ~ lassen*** ask for leave; **beurlaubt** [bə'ʔuːɐlaupt] *adj* on leave
**be'urteilen** *v/t (no -ge-, h)* judge (***nach*** by); rate; **Be'urteilung** *f (-; -en)* judg(e)ment; evaluation
**Beute** ['bɔʏtə] *f (-; no pl)* booty, loot; ZO prey (*a. fig*); HUNT bag; *fig a.* victim
**Beutel** ['bɔʏtəl] *m (-s; -)* bag; pouch
**bevölkern** [bə'fœlkɐn] *v/t (no -ge-, h)* populate; **be'völkert** *adj* → ***besiedelt***; **Be'völkerung** *f (-; -en)* population
**bevollmächtigen** [bə'fɔlmɛçtɪgən] *v/t (no -ge-, h)* authorize
**be'vor** *cj* before
**bevor|munden** [bə'foːɐmʊndən] *v/t (no -ge-, h)* patronize; **~stehen** *v/i (irr,* ***stehen****, sep, -ge-, h)* be approaching; lie ahead; be imminent; ***j-m ~*** be in store for s.o., await s.o.
**bevorzugen** [bə'foːɐtsuːgən] *v/t (no -ge-, h)* prefer; favo(u)r; **Be'vorzugung** *f (-; -en)* preferential treatment
**be'wachen** *v/t (no -ge-, h)* guard, watch over; **Be'wacher** *m (-s; -)* guard; SPORT marker; **Be'wachung** *f (-; -en) (no pl)* guarding; SPORT marking; guard
**bewaffnen** [bə'vafnən] *v/t (no -ge-, h)* arm (*a. fig*); **Be'waffnung** *f (-; -en)* armament; arms
**be'wahren** *v/t (no -ge-, h)* keep; ***~ vor*** (*dat*) keep *or* save from
**be'währen** *v/refl (no -ge-, h)* prove successful; ***sich ~ als*** prove to be
**bewährt** [bə'vɛːɐt] *adj* (well-)tried, reliable; experienced; **Be'währung** *f (-; -en)* JUR probation
**Be'währungs|frist** *f* JUR (period of) probation; **~helfer** *m* JUR probation officer; **~probe** *f* (acid) test
**bewaldet** [bə'valdət] *adj* wooded, woody
**bewältigen** [bə'vɛltɪgən] *v/t (no -ge-, h)* manage, cope with; cover (*distance*)
**be'wandert** *adj* (well-)versed (***in*** *dat* in)
**be'wässern** *v/t (no -ge-, h)* irrigate; **Be'wässerung** *f (-; -en)* irrigation
**bewegen** [bə'veːgən] *v/t and v/refl (no -ge-, h)* move (*a. fig*); ***nicht ~!*** don't move!; (*irr*) ***j-n zu et. ~*** get s.o. to do s.th.
**Be'weggrund** *m* motive
**beweglich** [bə'veːklɪç] *adj* movable; agile; flexible; TECH moving (*parts*); **Be'weglichkeit** *f (-; no pl)* mobility; agility; **be'wegt** *adj* rough (*sea*); choked (*voice*); eventful (*life*); *fig* moved, touched; **Be'wegung** *f (-; -en)* movement (*a.* POL); motion (*a.* PHYS); exercise; *fig* emotion; ***in ~ setzen*** set in motion; **Be'wegungsfreiheit** *f (-; no pl)* freedom of movement (*fig a.* of action); **be'wegungslos** *adj* motionless
**Beweis** [bə'vais] *m (-es; -e)* proof (***für*** of); **~(e)** evidence (*esp* JUR)
**be'weisen** *v/t (irr,* ***weisen****, no -ge-, h)* prove; show
**Be'weismittel** *n* JUR (piece of) evidence
**Be'weisstück** *n* (piece of) evidence, JUR exhibit
**be'wenden** *v/i*: ***es dabei ~ lassen*** leave it at that
**be'werben** *v/refl (irr,* ***werben****, no -ge-, h)* ***sich ~ um*** apply for; **Be'wer-ber(in)** *(-s; -/-; -nen)* applicant; **Be'werbung** *f (-; -en)* application; **Be'werbungsschreiben** *n* (letter of) application
**be'werten** *v/t (no -ge-, h)* assess; judge; **Be'wertung** *f (-; -en)* assessment
**bewilligen** [bə'vɪlɪgən] *v/t (no -ge-, h)* grant, allow; **be'wirken** *v/t (no -ge-,*

B

*h*) cause; **bewirten** [bə'vɪrtən] *v/t* (*no -ge-, h*) entertain
**be'wirtschaften** *v/t* (*no -ge-, h*) run; AGR farm; **be'wirtschaftet** *adj* open (to the public)
**Be'wirtung** *f* (-; *-en*) catering; service; hospitality
**bewog** [bə'voːk] *pret of* ***bewegen***
**bewogen** [bə'voːgən] *pp of* ***bewegen***
**be'wohnen** *v/t* (*no -ge-, h*) live in; inhabit; **Be'wohner(in)** (*-s; -/-; -nen*) inhabitant; occupant; **be'wohnt** *adj* inhabited; occupied
**bewölken** [bə'vœlkən] *v/refl* (*no -ge-, h*) METEOR cloud over (*a. fig*); **be'wölkt** *adj* METEOR cloudy, overcast
**Be'wölkung** *f* (-; *no pl*) METEOR clouds
**Bewunderer** [bə'vʊndərɐ] *m* (*-s*; -) admirer; **be'wundern** *v/t* (*no -ge-, h*) admire (***wegen*** for); **be'wundernswert** *adj* admirable; **Be'wunderung** *f* (-; *no pl*) admiration
**bewusst** [bə'vʊst] *adj* conscious; intentional; ***sich e-r Sache ~ sein*** be conscious *or* aware of s.th., realize s.th.; ***j-m et. ~ machen*** make s.o. realize s.th.
**be'wusstlos** *adj* MED unconscious
**be'wusstmachen** *v/t* → ***bewusst***
**Be'wusstsein** *n* (*-s; no pl*) MED consciousness; ***bei ~*** conscious
**be'zahlen** *v/t* (*no -ge-, h*) pay; pay for (*a. fig*); **be'zahlt** *adj*: ***~er Urlaub*** paid leave; ***es macht sich ~*** it pays; **Be'zahlung** *f* (-; *no pl*) payment; pay
**be'zaubern** *v/t* (*no -ge-, h*) charm; **~d** *adj* charming, F sweet, darling
**be'zeichnen** *v/t* (*no -ge-, h*) ***~ als*** call, describe as; **~d** *adj* characteristic, typical (***für*** of)
**Be'zeichnung** *f* (-; *-en*) name, term
**be'zeugen** *v/t* (*no -ge-, h*) JUR testify to
**be'ziehen** *v/t* (*irr,* ***ziehen****, no -ge-, h*) cover; put clean sheets on (*bed*); move into; receive; subscribe to (*paper etc*); ***~ auf*** (*acc*) relate to; ***sich ~*** cloud over; ***sich ~ auf*** (*acc*) refer to; **Be'ziehung** *f* (-; *-en*) relation (***zu*** to *s.th.*; with *s.o.*); connection (***zu*** with); relationship; respect; ***~en haben*** have connections
**be'ziehungsweise** *cj* respectively; or; or rather
**Bezirk** [bə'tsɪrk] *m* (*-[e]s; -e*) precinct, *Br a.* district
**Bezug** [bə'tsuːk] *m* (*-[e]s; Bezüge* [bə'tsyːgə]) cover(ing); case, slip; (*no pl*) ECON purchase; subscription (*gen* to); *pl* earnings; ***~ nehmen auf*** (*acc*) refer to; ***in ~ auf*** (*acc*) → ***bezüglich***
**bezüglich** [bə'tsyːklɪç] *prp* (*gen*) regarding, concerning
**Be'zugs|per,son** *f* PSYCH person to relate to, role model; **~punkt** *m* reference point; **~quelle** *f* source (of supply)
**be'zwecken** *v/t* (*no -ge-, h*) aim at, intend; **be'zweifeln** *v/t* (*no -ge-, h*) doubt, question; **be'zwingen** *v/t* (*irr,* ***zwingen****, no -ge-, h*) conquer, defeat
**Bibel** ['biːbəl] *f* (-; *-n*) Bible
**Biber** ['biːbɐ] *m* (*-s*; -) ZO beaver
**Bibliothek** [biblio'teːk] *f* (-; *-en*) library
**Bibliothekar** [bibliote'kaːɐ] *m* (*-s; -e*), **Bibliothe'karin** *f* (-; *-nen*) librarian
**biblisch** ['biːblɪʃ] *adj* biblical
**bieder** ['biːdɐ] *adj* honest; square
**biegen** ['biːgən] *v/t* (*irr, ge-, h*) *and v/i* (*sein*) bend (*a.* ***sich ~***), *road*: *a.* turn; ***um die Ecke ~*** turn (round) the corner
**biegsam** ['biːkzaːm] *adj* flexible
**'Biegung** *f* (-; *-en*) curve
**Biene** ['biːnə] *f* (-; *-n*) ZO bee
**'Bienen|königin** *f* ZO queen (bee); **~korb** *m*, **~stock** *m* (bee)hive; **~wachs** *n* beeswax
**Bier** [biːɐ] *n* (*-[e]s; -e*) beer; ***~ vom Faß*** draft (*Br* draught) beer; **~deckel** *m* coaster, beer mat; **~krug** *m* beer mug, stein
**Biest** [biːst] F *fig n* (*-[e]s; -er*) beast; (***kleines***) ***~*** brat, little devil, stinker
**bieten** ['biːtən] (*irr, ge-, h*) **1.** *v/t* offer; ***sich ~*** present itself **2.** *v/i auction*: (make a) bid
**Bigamie** [biga'miː] *f* (-; *-n*) bigamy
**Bikini** [bi'kiːni] *m* (*-s; -s*) bikini
**Bilanz** [bi'lants] *f* (-; *-en*) ECON balance; *fig* result; ***~ ziehen aus*** (*dat*) *fig* take stock of
**Bild** [bɪlt] *n* (*-[e]s; -er* ['bɪldɐ]) picture; image; ***sich ein ~ machen von*** get an idea of; **~ausfall** *m* TV blackout; **~bericht** *m* photo(graphic) essay (*Br* report)
**bilden** ['bɪldən] *v/t* (*ge-, h*) form (*a.* ***sich ~***); shape; *fig* educate (***sich*** o.s.); be, constitute
**'Bilderbuch** *n* picture book

**'Bildfläche** *f*: F ***auf der ~ erscheinen*** (***von der ~ verschwinden***) appear on (disappear from) the scene

**'Bildhauer** *m* (-*s*; -), **'Bildhauerin** *f* (-; -*nen*) sculptor

**'bildlich** *adj* graphic; figurative

**'Bildnis** *n* (-*ses*; -*se*) portrait

**'Bildplatte** *f* videodisk (*Br* -disc)

**'Bildröhre** *f* picture tube

**'Bildschirm** *m* TV screen, IT *a.* display, monitor; **~schoner** *m* (-*s*; -) screen saver; **~text** *m* videotext, *Br* viewdata

**'bild'schön** *adj* most beautiful

**'Bildung** *f* (-; -*en*) (*no pl*) education; formation

**'Bildungs...** *in cpds* ...*chancen*, ...*reform*, ...*urlaub etc*: educational ...; **~lücke** *f* gap in one's knowledge

**'Bildunterschrift** *f* caption

**Billard** ['bɪljart] *n* (-*s*; -*e*) billiards, pool; **~kugel** *f* billiard ball; **~stock** *m* cue

**Billett** [bɪl'jɛt] *n* (-[*e*]*s*; -*e*) *Swiss* ticket

**billig** ['bɪlɪç] *adj* cheap (*a. contp*), inexpensive

**billigen** ['bɪlɪgən] *v/t* (*ge-*, *h*) approve of; **'Billigung** *f* (-; *no pl*) approval

**Billion** [bɪ'ljoːn] *f* (-; -*en*) trillion

**bimmeln** ['bɪməln] F *v/i* (*ge-*, *h*) jingle; TEL ring

**binär** [bi'nɛːɐ] *adj* MATH, PHYS *etc* binary

**Binde** ['bɪndə] *f* (-; -*n*) bandage; sling; → ***Damenbinde***; **~gewebe** *n* ANAT connective tissue; **~glied** *n* (connecting) link

**'Bindehaut** *f* ANAT conjunctiva; **~entzündung** *f* MED conjunctivitis

**binden** (*irr*, *ge-*, *h*) **1.** *v/t* bind (*a. book*), tie (***an*** *acc* to); make (*wreath etc*); knot (*tie*); ***sich ~*** bind *or* commit o.s. **2.** *v/i* bind

**'Bindestrich** *m* LING hyphen

**'Bindewort** *n* LING conjunction

**Bindfaden** ['bɪntfaːdən] *m* string

**'Bindung** *f* (-; -*en*) tie, link, bond; *skiing*: binding

**Binnen|hafen** ['bɪnənhaːfən] *m* inland port; **~handel** *m* domestic trade; **~markt** *m*: ***Europäischer ~*** European single market; **~schifffahrt** *f* inland navigation; **~verkehr** *m* inland traffic *or* transport

**Binse** ['bɪnzə] *f* (-; -*n*) BOT rush

**'Binsenweisheit** *f* (-; -*en*) truism

**Bio..., bio...** [bio-] *in cpds* ...*chemie*, ...*dynamisch*, ...*sphäre etc*: bio...

**Biografie, Biographie** [biogra'fiː] *f* (-; -*n*) biography

**bio'grafisch, bio'graphisch** *adj* biographic(al)

**Bioladen** ['biːolaːdən] *m* health food shop *or* store

**Biologe** [bio'loːgə] *m* (-*n*; -*n*) biologist

**Biologie** [biolo'giː] *f* (-; *no pl*) biology

**Bio'login** *f* (-; -*nen*) biologist

**biologisch** [bio'loːgɪʃ] *adj* biological; AGR organic; ***~ abbaubar*** biodegradable

**'Biorhythmus** *m* biorhythms

**'Biotechnik** *f* (-; *no pl*) biotechnology

**Biotop** [bio'toːp] *n* (-*s*; -*e*) biotope

**Birke** ['bɪrkə] *f* (-; -*n*) BOT birch (tree)

**Birne** ['bɪrnə] *f* (-; -*n*) BOT pear; ELECTR (light) bulb

**bis** [bɪs] *prp* (*acc*) *and adv and cj time*: till, until, (up) to; *space*: (up) to, as far as; ***von ... ~ ...*** from ... to ...; ***~ auf*** (*acc*) except; ***~ zu*** up to; ***~ später!*** see you later!; ***~ jetzt*** up to now, so far; ***~ Montag*** by Monday; ***zwei ~ drei*** two or three; ***wie weit ist es ~ ...?*** how far is it to ...?

**Bischof** ['bɪʃɔf] *m* (-*s*; *Bischöfe* ['bɪʃœfə]) REL bishop

**bisexuell** [bizɛ'ksuɛl] *adj* bisexual

**bis'her** *adv* up to now, so far; ***wie ~*** as before

**bisherig** [bɪs'heːrɪç] *adj* previous

**Biskuit** [bɪs'kviːt] *n* (-[*e*]*s*; -*e*) sponge cake (mix)

**biss** [bɪs] *pret of* ***beißen***

**Biss** *m* (-*es*; -*e*) bite (*a. fig*)

**bisschen** ['bɪsçən] *adj and adv*: ***ein ~*** a little, a (little) bit (of); ***nicht ein ~*** not in the least

**Bissen** ['bɪsən] *m* (-*s*; -) bite; ***keinen ~*** not a thing

**bissig** ['bɪsɪç] *adj fig* cutting; ***ein ~er Hund*** a dog that bites; ***Vorsicht, ~er Hund!*** beware of the dog!

**Bistum** ['bɪstuːm] *n* (-*s*; *Bistümer* ['bɪstyːmɐ]) REL bishopric, diocese

**bis'weilen** *adv* at times, now and then

**Bit** [bɪt] *n* (-[*s*]; -[*s*]) IT bit

**bitte** ['bɪtə] *adv* please; ***~ nicht!*** please don't!; ***~ (schön)!*** that's all right, not at all, you're welcome; here you are; (***wie***) ***~?*** pardon?; ***~ sehr?*** can I help you?; **'Bitte** *f* (-; -*n*) request (***um*** for);

B

***ich habe e-e ~ (an dich)*** I have a favo(u)r to ask of you; '**bitten** *v/t (irr, ge-, h)* ***j-n um et. ~*** ask s.o. for s.th.; ***darf ich ~?*** may I have (the pleasure of) this dance?; → ***Erlaubnis***

**bitter** ['bɪtɐ] *adj* bitter (*a. fig*), *a.* biting (*cold*); ~'**kalt** *adj* bitterly cold

**blähen** ['blɛːən] *v/refl (ge-, h)* swell

'**Blähungen** *pl* MED flatulence, *Br a.* wind

**blamabel** [bla'maːbəl] *adj* embarrassing; **Blamage** [bla'maːʒə] *f (-; -n)* disgrace, shame; **blamieren** [bla'miːrən] *v/t (no -ge-, h)* ***j-n ~*** make s.o. look like a fool; ***sich ~*** make a fool of o.s.

**blank** [blaŋk] *adj* shining, shiny, bright; polished; F broke

**Blanko...** ['blaŋko] *in cpds* ECON blank

**Bläschen** ['blɛːsçən] *n (-s; -)* MED vesicle, small blister

**Blase** ['blaːzə] *f (-; -n)* bubble; ANAT bladder; MED blister

'**Blasebalg** *m* (pair of) bellows

'**blasen** *v/t (irr, ge-, h)* blow (*a.* MUS)

'**Blas|instru,ment** *n* MUS wind instrument; ~**ka,pelle** *f* brass band; ~**rohr** *n* blowpipe

**blass** [blas] *adj* pale (***vor*** with); ***~ werden*** turn pale; **Blässe** ['blɛsə] *f (-; no pl)* paleness, pallor

**Blatt** [blat] *n (-[e]s; Blätter* ['blɛtɐ]*)* BOT leaf; piece, sheet (*a.* MUS); (news)paper; *card games*: hand; **blättern** ['blɛtɐn] *v/i (ge-, h)* ***~ in*** *(dat)* leaf through

'**Blätterteig** *m* puff pastry

**blau** [blau] *adj* blue; F loaded, stoned; ***~es Auge*** black eye; ***~er Fleck*** bruise; ***Fahrt ins Blaue*** mystery tour

**blauäugig** ['blauɔʏgɪç] *adj* blue-eyed; *fig* starry-eyed

'**Blaubeere** *f* BOT blueberry, *Br* bilberry

'**blaugrau** *adj* bluish-gray (*Br* -grey)

'**Blauhelme** *pl* MIL UN soldiers

**bläulich** ['blɔʏlɪç] *adj* bluish

'**Blaulicht** *n (-[e]s; -er)* flashing light(s)

'**blaumachen** F *v/i (sep, -ge-, h)* stay away from work *or* school

'**Blausäure** *f* CHEM prussic acid

**Blech** [blɛç] *n (-[e]s; -e)* sheet metal; *in cpds ...dach, ...löffel etc*: tin ...; *...instrument*: MUS brass ...

'**Blech|büchse**, ~**dose** *f* can, *Br a.* tin

'**blechen** F *v/t and v/i (ge-, h)* shell out

'**Blechschaden** *m* MOT bodywork damage

**Blei** [blai] *n (-[e]s; -e)* lead; ***aus ~*** leaden

**Bleibe** ['blaibə] *f (-; -n)* place to stay

'**bleiben** *v/i (irr, ge-, sein)* stay, remain; ***~ bei*** stick to; F ***et. ~ lassen*** not do s.th.; ***lass das ~!*** stop that!; ***das wirst du schön ~ lassen!*** you'll do nothing of the sort!; → ***Apparat, ruhig***; ~**d** *adj* lasting, permanent

'**bleibenlassen** *v/i* → ***bleiben***

**bleich** [blaiç] *adj* pale (***vor*** *dat* with)

'**bleichen** *v/t ([irr,] ge-, h)* bleach

**bleiern** ['blaiɐn] *adj* lead(en *fig*)

'**bleifrei** *adj* MOT unleaded

'**Bleistift** *m* pencil; ~**spitzer** *m* pencil sharpener

**Blende** ['blɛndə] *f (-; -n)* blind; PHOT aperture; ***(bei) ~ 8*** (at) f-8

'**blenden** *v/t (ge-, h)* blind, dazzle (*both a. fig*); ~**d** *adj* dazzling (*a. fig*); brilliant; ***~ aussehen*** look great

'**blendfrei** *adj* OPT antiglare

**blich** [blɪç] *pret of* ***bleichen***

**Blick** [blɪk] *m (-[e]s; -e)* look (***auf*** *acc* at); view (of); ***flüchtiger ~*** glance; ***auf den ersten ~*** at first sight; '**blicken** *v/i (ge-, h)* look, glance (*both*: ***auf*** *acc*, ***nach*** at)

'**Blickfang** *m* eye-catcher

'**Blickfeld** *n* field of vision

**blieb** [bliːp] *pret of* ***bleiben***

**blies** [bliːs] *pret of* ***blasen***

**blind** [blɪnt] *adj* blind (*a. fig* ***gegen, für*** to; ***vor*** *dat* with); dull (*mirror etc*); ***~er Alarm*** false alarm; ***~er Passagier*** stowaway; ***auf e-m Auge ~*** blind in one eye; ***ein Blinder*** a blind man; ***e-e Blinde*** a blind woman; ***die Blinden*** the blind

'**Blinddarm** *m* ANAT appendix; ~**entzündung** *f* MED appendicitis; ~**operati,on** *f* MED appendectomy

**Blinden|hund** ['blɪndənhʊnt] *m* seeing eye (*Br* guide) dog; ~**schrift** *f* braille

**Blindgänger** ['blɪntgɛŋɐ] *m (-s; -)* MIL dud

'**Blindheit** *f (-; no pl)* blindness

**blindlings** ['blɪntlɪŋs] *adv* blindly

'**Blindschleiche** *f* ZO blindworm

**blinken** ['blɪŋkən] *v/i (ge-, h)* sparkle, shine; twinkle; flash (a signal); MOT indicate; **Blinker** ['blɪŋkɐ] *m (-s; -)* MOT turn signal, *Br* indicator

**blinzeln** ['blɪntsəln] *v/i (ge-, h)* blink (one's eyes)

**Blitz** [blɪts] *m* (*-es*; *-e*) (flash of) lightning; PHOT flash; **~ableiter** *m* (*-s*; *-*) lightning conductor
'**blitzen** *v/i* (*ge-*, *h*) flash; ***es blitzt*** it's lightening
'**Blitz|gerät** *n* PHOT (electronic) flash; **~lampe** *f* PHOT flashbulb; flash cube; **~licht** *n* (*-[e]s*; *-er*) PHOT flash(light); **~schlag** *m* lightning stroke
'**blitz'schnell** *adj and adv* like a flash; *attr* split-second
**Block** [blɔk] *m* (*-[e]s*; *Blöcke* ['blœkə]) block; POL, ECON bloc; (*writing*) pad
**Blockade** [blɔ'ka:də] *f* (*-*; *-n*) MAR, MIL blockade
'**Blockflöte** *f* recorder
'**Blockhaus** *n* log cabin
**blockieren** [blɔ'ki:rən] *v/t and v/i* (*no -ge-*, *h*) block; MOT lock
'**Blockschrift** *f* block letters
**blöde** ['blø:də] F *adj* silly, stupid
'**blödeln** *v/i* (*ge-*, *h*) fool *or* clown around
**Blödheit** ['blø:thait] *f* (*-*; *no pl*) stupidity
'**Blödsinn** F *m* (*-[e]s*; *no pl*) rubbish, nonsense
'**blödsinnig** F *adj* stupid, idiotic
**Blog** [blɔk] *m*, *n* (*-s*; *-s*) blog
**blöken** ['blø:kən] *v/i* (*ge-*, *h*) zo bleat
**blond** [blɔnt] *adj* blond, fair
**Blondine** [blɔn'di:nə] *f* (*-*; *-n*) blonde
**bloß** [blo:s] **1.** *adj* bare; naked (*eye*); mere; ***~ legen*** *v/t* (*sep*, *-ge-*, *h*) lay bare, expose **2.** *adv* only, just, merely
**Blöße** ['blø:sə] *f* (*-*; *-n*) nakedness; ***sich e-e ~ geben*** lay o.s. open to attack *or* criticism
'**bloß|legen** *v/t* → ***bloß***; **~stellen** *v/t* (*sep*, *-ge-*, *h*) expose, compromise, unmask; ***sich ~*** compromise o.s.
**blühen** ['bly:ən] *v/i* (*ge-*, *h*) (be in) bloom; (be in) blossom; *fig* flourish
**Blume** ['blu:mə] *f* (*-*; *-n*) flower; GASTR bouquet; head, froth
'**Blumen|beet** *n* flowerbed; **~händler** *m* florist; **~kohl** *m* BOT cauliflower; **~laden** *m* flower shop, florist's; **~strauß** *m* bunch of flowers; bouquet; **~topf** *m* flowerpot; **~vase** *f* vase
**Bluse** ['blu:zə] *f* (*-*; *-n*) blouse
**Blut** [blu:t] *n* (*-[e]s*; *no pl*) blood
'**blutarm** *adj* MED an(a)emic (*a. fig*)
'**Blut|armut** *f* MED an(a)emia; **~bad** *n* massacre; **~bahn** *f* ANAT bloodstream; **~bank** *f* (*-*; *-en*) MED blood bank
'**blutbefleckt** *adj* bloodstained
'**Blut|bild** *n* MED blood count; **~blase** *f* MED blood blister; **~druck** *m* MED blood pressure
**Blüte** ['bly:tə] *f* (*-*; *-n*) flower; bloom (*a. fig*); blossom; *fig* height, heyday; ***in*** (***voller***) ***~*** in (full) bloom
'**Blutegel** *m* zo leech
'**bluten** *v/i* (*ge-*, *h*) bleed (***aus*** *dat* from)
'**Blüten|blatt** *n* petal; **~staub** *m* pollen
**Bluter** ['blu:tɐ] *m* (*-s*; *-*) MED h(a)emophiliac
'**Blut|erguss** *m* bruise; MED h(a)ematoma; **~gefäß** *n* ANAT blood vessel; **~gerinnsel** *n* MED blood clot; **~gruppe** *f* MED blood group; **~hund** *m* zo bloodhound
'**blutig** *adj* bloody; ***~er Anfänger*** rank beginner, F greenhorn
'**Blut|körperchen** *n* MED blood corpuscle; **~kreislauf** *m* MED (blood) circulation; **~lache** *f* pool of blood
'**blutleer** *adj* bloodless
'**Blutprobe** *f* MED blood test
**blutrünstig** ['blu:trʏnstɪç] *adj* bloodthirsty, gory
'**Blutschande** *f* JUR incest
'**Blutspender** *m* blood donor
'**Blutsverwandte** *m*, *f* blood relation
'**Blutübertragung** *f* MED blood transfusion
'**Blutung** *f* (*-*; *-en*) MED bleeding, h(a)emorrhage
'**blutunterlaufen** *adj* bloodshot
'**Blut|vergießen** *n* (*-s*; *no pl*) bloodshed; **~vergiftung** *f* MED blood poisoning; **~wurst** *f* black sausage (*Br* pudding)
**BLZ** [be:ɛl'tsɛt] *abbr of* ***Bankleitzahl*** A.B.A. number, *Br* bank (sorting) code
**Bö** [bø:] *f* (*-*; *-en*) gust, squall
**Bob** [bɔp] *m* (*-s*; *-s*) bob(sled); **~bahn** *f* bob run; **~fahrer** *m* bobber
**Bock** [bɔk] *m* (*-[e]s*; *Böcke* ['bœkə]) zo buck; he-goat, billy-goat; ram; SPORT buck; F ***e-n ~ schießen*** (make a) blunder; F ***keinen*** (*or* ***null***) ***~ auf et. haben*** have zero interest in s.th.
'**bocken** *v/i* (*ge-*, *h*) buck; sulk
'**bockig** *adj* obstinate; sulky
'**Bockspringen** *n* leapfrog
**Boden** ['bo:dən] *m* (*-s*; *Böden* ['bø:dən]) ground; AGR soil; bottom; floor; attic

B

**'Boden|perso,nal** *n* AVIAT ground crew; **~schätze** *pl* mineral resources; **~stati,on** *f* AVIAT ground control; **~turnen** *n* floor exercises
**Body** ['bɔdi] *m* (*-s*; *-s*) bodysuit
**bog** [bo:k] *pret of* ***biegen***
**Bogen** ['bo:gən] *m* (*-s*; *Bögen* ['bø:gən]) bend, curve; MATH arc; ARCH arch; *skiing*: turn; bow; sheet; **~schießen** *n* archery; **~schütze** *m* archer
**Bohle** ['bo:lə] *f* (*-*; *-n*) plank
**Bohne** ['bo:nə] *f* (*-*; *-n*) BOT bean; ***grüne ~n*** green (*Br a.* French) beans
**'Bohnenstange** *f* beanpole (*a.* F)
**bohnern** ['bo:nɐn] *v/t* (*ge-*, *h*) polish, wax; **'Bohnerwachs** *n* floor polish
**bohren** ['bo:rən] *v/t* (*ge-*, *h*) bore, drill (*a. dentist*); **~d** *fig adj* piercing (*look*); insistent (*questions etc*)
**Bohrer** ['bo:rɐ] *m* (*-s*; *-*) TECH drill
**'Bohr|insel** *f* oil rig; **~loch** *n* borehole, well(head); **~ma,schine** *f* (electric) drill; **~turm** *m* derrick
**'Bohrung** *f* (*-*; *-en*) drilling; bore
**Boje** ['bo:jə] *f* (*-*; *-n*) MAR buoy
**Bolzen** ['bɔltsən] *m* (*-s*; *-*) TECH bolt
**bombardieren** [bɔmbar'di:rən] *v/t* (*no -ge-*, *h*) bomb; *fig* bombard
**Bombe** ['bɔmbə] *f* (*-*; *-n*) bomb; *fig* bombshell
**'Bomben|angriff** *m* air raid; **~anschlag** *m* bomb attack; **~erfolg** F *m* roaring success; THEA *etc* smash hit; **~geschäft** F *n* super deal
**'Bombenleger** *m* (*-s*; *-*) bomber
**'bombensicher** *adj* bombproof
**Bomber** ['bɔmbɐ] F *m* (*-s*; *-*) MIL bomber (*a.* SPORT)
**Bon** [bɔŋ] *m* (*-s*; *-s*) coupon, voucher
**Bonbon** [bɔŋ'bɔŋ] *m*, *n* (*-s*; *-s*) candy, *Br* sweet
**Boot** [bo:t] *n* (*-[e]s*; *-e*) boat
**'Bootsmann** *m* (*-[e]s*; *-leute*) boatswain
**Bord**[1] [bɔrt] *n* (*-[e]s*; *-e*) shelf
**Bord**[2] *m*: ***an ~*** AVIAT, MAR on board; ***über ~*** MAR overboard; ***von ~ gehen*** MAR disembark
**Bordell** [bɔr'dɛl] *n* (*-s*; *-e*) brothel, F whorehouse
**'Bordkarte** *f* AVIAT boarding pass
**'Bordstein** *m* curb, *Br* kerb
**borgen** ['bɔrgən] *v/t* (*ge-*, *h*) borrow; ***sich et. von j-m ~*** borrow s.th. from s.o.; ***j-m et. ~*** lend s.th. to s.o.
**Borke** ['bɔrkə] *f* (*-*; *-n*) BOT bark
**borniert** [bɔr'ni:ɐt] *adj* narrow-minded
**Börse** ['bœrzə] *f* (*-*; *-n*) ECON stock exchange
**'Börsen|bericht** *m* market report; **~kurs** *m* quotation; **~makler** *m* stockbroker; **~speku,lant** *m* stock-jobber
**Borste** ['bɔrstə] *f* (*-*; *-n*) bristle
**'borstig** *adj* bristly
**Borte** ['bɔrtə] *f* (*-*; *-n*) border; braid, lace
**bösartig** ['bø:sartɪç] *adj* vicious; MED malignant
**Böschung** ['bœʃʊŋ] *f* (*-*; *-en*) slope, bank; RAIL embankment
**böse** ['bø:zə] *adj* bad, evil, wicked; angry (***über*** *acc* about; ***auf j-n*** with s.o.), mad (***auf*** *acc* at); ***er meint es nicht ~*** he means no harm
**'Böse** *n* (*-n*; *no pl*) (the) evil
**'Bösewicht** *m* (*-[e]s*; *-er*) villain
**boshaft** ['bo:shaft] *adj* malicious
**Bosheit** ['bo:shait] *f* (*-*; *no pl*) malice
**'böswillig** *adj* malicious, JUR *a.* wil(l)ful
**bot** [bo:t] *pret of* ***bieten***
**Botanik** [bo'ta:nɪk] *f* (*-*; *no pl*) botany
**Bo'taniker** *m* (*-s*; *-*) botanist
**bo'tanisch** *adj* botanical
**Bote** ['bo:tə] *m* (*-n*; *-n*) messenger
**'Botengang** *m* errand; ***Botengänge machen*** run errands
**Botschaft** ['bo:tʃaft] *f* (*-*; *-en*) message; POL embassy
**'Botschafter** *m* (*-s*; *-*) POL ambassador (***in*** *dat* to); **'Botschafterin** *f* (*-*; *-nen*) POL ambassadress (***in*** *dat* to)
**Bottich** ['bɔtɪç] *m* (*-s*; *-e*) tub, vat
**Bouillon** [bʊl'jɔŋ] *f* (*-*; *-s*) consommé, bouillon, broth
**Boulevard|blatt** [bulə'va:ɐblat] *n*, **~zeitung** *f* tabloid
**Bowle** ['bo:lə] *f* (*-*; *-n*) (cold) punch; bowl
**boxen** ['bɔksən] (*ge-*, *h*) **1.** *v/i* box **2.** *v/t* punch; **'Boxen** *n* (*-s*; *no pl*) boxing; **Boxer** ['bɔksɐ] *m* (*-s*; *-*) boxer
**'Box|handschuh** *m* boxing glove; **~kampf** *m* boxing match, fight; **~sport** *m* boxing
**Boykott** [bɔʏ'kɔt] *m* (*-[e]s*; *-e*), **boykottieren** [bɔʏkɔ'ti:rən] *v/t* (*no -ge-*, *h*) boycott
**brach** [bra:x] *pret of* ***brechen***
**brachliegend** *adj* AGR fallow
**brachte** ['braxtə] *pret of* ***bringen***

**Branche** ['brã:ʃə] *f* (-; *-n*) ECON line (of business); '**Branchenverzeichnis** *n* TEL yellow pages

**Brand** [brant] *m* (-[*e*]*s*; *Brände* ['brɛndə]) fire; ***in ~ geraten*** catch fire; ***in ~ stecken*** set fire to; **~blase** *f* MED blister

**branden** ['brandən] *v/i* (*ge-*, *sein*) surge (***gegen*** against)

'**Brand|fleck** *m* burn; **~mal** *n* brand

'**brandmarken** *fig v/t* (*ge-*, *h*) brand, stigmatize

'**Brand|mauer** *f* fire wall; **~stätte** *f*, **~stelle** *f* scene of fire; **~stifter** *m* arsonist; **~stiftung** *f* arson

'**Brandung** *f* (-; *no pl*) surf, surge, breakers

'**Brandwunde** *f* MED burn; scald

**brannte** ['brantə] *pret of* ***brennen***

'**Branntwein** *m* brandy, spirits

**braten** ['bra:tən] *v/t* (*irr*, *ge-*, *h*) roast; grill, broil; fry; ***am Spieß ~*** roast on a spit, barbecue

'**Braten** *m* (-*s*; -) roast (meat); joint; **~fett** *n* dripping; **~soße** *f* gravy

'**Brat|fisch** *m* fried fish; **~huhn** *n* roast chicken; **~kar,toffeln** *pl* fried potatoes; **~ofen** *m* oven; **~pfanne** *f* frying pan

**Bratsche** ['bra:tʃə] *f* (-; *-n*) MUS viola

'**Bratwurst** *f* grilled sausage

**Brauch** [braux] *m* (-[*e*]*s*; *Bräuche* ['brɔʏçə]) custom; habit, practice

'**brauchbar** *adj* useful

'**brauchen** *v/t* (*ge-*, *h*) need; require; take (*time*); use; ***wie lange wird er ~?*** how long will it take him?; ***du brauchst es nur zu sagen*** just say the word; ***ihr braucht es nicht zu tun*** you don't have to do it; ***er hätte nicht zu kommen ~*** he need not have come

**brauen** ['brauən] *v/t* (*ge-*, *h*) brew

**Brauerei** [brauə'rai] *f* (-; *-en*) brewery

**braun** [braun] *adj* brown; (sun)tanned; ***~ werden*** (get a) tan

**Bräune** ['brɔʏnə] *f* (-; *no pl*) (sun)tan

'**bräunen** (*ge-*, *h*) **1.** *v/t* brown, tan **2.** *v/i* (get a) tan

'**Braunkohle** *f* brown coal, lignite

'**bräunlich** *adj* brownish

**Brause** ['brauzə] *f* (-; *-n*) shower; → ***Limonade***; '**brausen** *v/i* (*ge-*, *h*) roar; (*sein*) rush; (*h*) → ***duschen***

**Braut** [braut] *f* (-; *Bräute* ['brɔʏtə]) bride; fiancée; **Bräutigam** ['brɔʏtɪgam] *m* (-*s*; *-e*) (bride)groom; fiancé

'**Braut|jungfer** *f* bridesmaid; **~kleid** *n* wedding-dress; **~paar** *n* bride and (bride)groom; engaged couple

**brav** [bra:f] *adj* good; honest; ***sei(d) ~!*** be good!

**BRD** [be:ˀɛr'de:] *abbr of* ***Bundesrepublik Deutschland*** FRG, Federal Republic of Germany

**brechen** ['brɛçən] (*irr*, *ge-*) **1.** *v/t* (*h*) break (*a. fig*); MED vomit; ***sich ~*** OPT be refracted; ***sich den Arm ~*** break one's arm **2.** *v/i* (*h*) MED vomit, F throw up, *Br a.* be sick; ***mit j-m ~*** break with s.o; ***~d voll*** crammed, packed; (*sein*) break, get broken, fracture

'**Brechreiz** *m* MED nausea

'**Brechstange** *f* crowbar

'**Brechung** *f* (-; *-en*) OPT refraction

**Brei** [brai] *m* (-[*e*]*s*; *-e*) pulp, mash; pap; porridge; pudding

'**breiig** *adj* pulpy, mushy

**breit** [brait] *adj* wide; broad (*a. fig*)

'**breitbeinig** *adj* with legs (wide) apart

**Breite** ['braitə] *f* (-; *-n*) width, breadth; ASTR, GEOGR latitude

'**breiten** *v/t* (*ge-*, *h*) spread

'**Breiten|grad** *m* degree of latitude; **~kreis** *m* parallel (of latitude)

**breitmachen** *v/refl* (*sep*, *-ge-*, *h*): ***sich ~*** F spread o.s., take up room

'**Breitwand** *f film*: wide screen

**Bremsbelag** ['brɛmsbəla:k] *m* brake lining

**Bremse** ['brɛmzə] *f* (-; *-n*) TECH brake; ZO gadfly; '**bremsen** (*ge-*, *h*) **1.** *v/i* MOT brake, put on the brake(s); slow down **2.** *v/t* MOT brake; *fig* curb

'**Brems|licht** *n* (-[*e*]*s*; *-er*) MOT stop light; **~pe,dal** *n* MOT brake pedal; **~spur** *f* MOT skid marks; **~weg** *m* MOT stopping distance

'**brennbar** *adj* combustible; (in)flammable; **brennen** ['brɛnən] (*irr*, *ge-*, *h*) **1.** *v/t* burn; distil(l) (*whisky etc*); bake (*bricks*) **2.** *v/i* burn; be on fire; *wound*, *eyes*: smart, burn; F ***darauf ~ zu*** *inf* be dying to *inf*; ***es brennt!*** fire!; **Brenner** ['brɛnɐ] *m* (-*s*; -) burner

'**Brenn|holz** *n* firewood; **~materi,al** *n* fuel; **~nessel** *f* BOT (stinging) nettle; **~punkt** *m* focus, focal point; **~spiritus** *m* methylated spirit; **~stab** *m* TECH fuel rod; **~stoff** *m* fuel

B

**brenzlig** ['brɛntslɪç] *adj* burnt; *fig* hot
**Bresche** ['brɛʃə] *f* (-; *-n*) breach (*a. fig*), gap
**Brett** [brɛt] *n* (-[*e*]*s*; *-er*) board
'**Bretterzaun** *m* wooden fence
'**Brettspiel** *n* board game
**Brezel** ['breːtsəl] *f* (-; *-n*) pretzel
**Brief** [briːf] *m* (-[*e*]*s*; *-e*) letter; **~beschwerer** *m* (*-s*; -) paperweight; **~bogen** *m* sheet of (note)paper; **~freund(in)** pen pal (*Br* friend); **~kasten** *m* mailbox, *Br* letterbox
'**brieflich** *adj and adv* by letter
'**Brief|marke** *f* (postage) stamp; **~markensammlung** *f* stamp collection; **~öffner** *m* letter opener, *Br* paper knife; **~pa,pier** *n* stationery; **~tasche** *f* wallet; **~taube** *f* ZO carrier pigeon; **~träger(in)** (*-s*; *-/-*; *-nen*) mailman (mailwoman), *Br* postman (postwoman); **~umschlag** *m* envelope; **~wahl** *f* postal vote; **~wechsel** *m* correspondence
**briet** [briːt] *pret of* ***braten***
**Brikett** [bri'kɛt] *n* (*-s*; *-s*) briquet(te)
**brillant** [brɪl'jant] *adj* brilliant
**Bril'lant** *m* (*-en*; *-en*) (cut) diamond
**Bril'lantring** *m* diamond ring
**Brille** ['brɪlə] *f* (-; *-n*) (pair of) glasses, spectacles; goggles; toilet seat
'**Brillen|etui** *n* eyeglass (*Br* spectacle) case; **~träger(in)** (*-s*; *-/-*; *-nen*) ***~ sein*** wear glasses
**bringen** ['brɪŋən] *v/t* (*irr, ge-, h*) bring; take; cause; make (*sacrifice*); yield (*profit*); ***j-n nach Hause ~*** see (*or* take) s.o. home; ***in Ordnung ~*** put in order; ***das bringt mich auf e-e Idee*** that gives me an idea; ***j-n dazu ~, et. zu tun*** get s.o. to do s.th.; ***et. mit sich ~*** involve s.th.; ***j-n um et. ~*** deprive s.o. of s.th.; ***j-n zum Lachen ~*** make s.o. laugh; ***j-n wieder zu sich ~*** bring s.o. round; ***es zu et.*** (***nichts***) ***~*** go far (get nowhere); F ***es ~*** make it; ***das bringt nichts*** it's no use
**Brise** ['briːzə] *f* (-; *-n*) breeze
**Brite** ['brɪtə] *m* (*-n*; *-n*), '**Britin** *f* (-; *-nen*) Briton; ***die Briten*** *pl* the British
'**britisch** *adj* British
**bröckeln** ['brœkəln] *v/i* (*ge-, h, sein*) crumble
**Brocken** ['brɔkən] *m* (*-s*; -) piece; lump; rock; GASTR chunk; morsel; ***ein paar ~ Englisch*** a few scraps of English; F ***ein harter ~*** a hard nut to crack
**Brombeere** ['brɔmbeːrə] *f* BOT blackberry
**Bronchitis** [brɔn'çiːtɪs] *f* (-; *-tiden* [brɔnçi'tiːdən]) MED bronchitis
**Bronze** ['broːsə] *f* (-; *-n*) bronze; **~zeit** *f* (-; *no pl*) HIST Bronze Age
**Brosche** ['brɔʃə] *f* (-; *-n*) brooch, pin
**broschiert** [brɔ'ʃiːɐt] *adj* paperback
**Broschüre** [brɔ'ʃyːrə] *f* (-; *-n*) pamphlet; brochure
**Brot** [broːt] *n* (-[*e*]*s*; *-e*) bread; sandwich; ***ein*** (***Laib***) ***~*** a loaf (of bread); ***e-e Scheibe ~*** a slice of bread; ***sein ~ verdienen*** earn one's living
**Brötchen** ['brøːtçən] *n* (*-s*; -) roll
'**Brot|rinde** *f* crust; **~(schneide)ma,schine** *f* bread cutter
**Bruch** [brʊx] *m* (-[*e*]*s*; *Brüche* ['brʏçə]) break; MED fracture; hernia; MATH fraction; GEOL fault; *fig* breach (*of promise etc*); JUR violation; ***zu ~ gehen*** be wrecked; **~bude** F *f* dump, hovel
**brüchig** ['brʏçɪç] *adj* brittle
'**Bruch|landung** *f* AVIAT crash landing; **~rechnung** *f* MATH fractional arithmetic, F fractions
'**bruchsicher** *adj* breakproof
'**Bruch|strich** *m* MATH fraction bar; **~stück** *n* fragment; **~teil** *m* fraction; ***im ~ e-r Sekunde*** in a split second; **~zahl** *f* MATH fraction(al) number
**Brücke** ['brʏkə] *f* (-; *-n*) bridge (*a.* SPORT); rug; '**Brückenpfeiler** *m* pier
**Bruder** ['bruːdɐ] *m* (*-s*; *Brüder* ['bryːdɐ]) brother (*a.* REL); **~krieg** *m* civil war
**brüderlich** ['bryːdɐlɪç] **1.** *adj* brotherly **2.** *adv*: ***~ teilen*** share and share alike
'**Brüderlichkeit** *f* (-; *no pl*) brotherhood
'**Brüderschaft** *f*: ***~ trinken*** *agree to use the familiar 'du' form of address*
**Brühe** ['bryːə] *f* (-; *-n*) broth; stock; F dishwater; slops; F filthy water, bilge
'**Brühwürfel** *m* beef cube
**brüllen** ['brʏlən] *v/i* (*ge-, h*) roar (***vor Lachen*** with laughter); ZO bellow; F bawl; ***~des Gelächter*** roars of laughter
**brummen** ['brʊmən] *v/i* (*ge-, h*) growl; ZO hum, buzz (*a. engine etc*); *head*: be buzzing; '**brummig** *adj* grumpy
**brünett** [bry'nɛt] *adj* brunette, dark-haired
**Brunnen** ['brʊnən] *m* (*-s*; -) well, spring,

fountain

**Brunstzeit** ['brʊnsttsait] *f* ZO rutting season

**Brust** [brʊst] *f* (-; *Brüste* ['brʏstə]) ANAT (*no pl*) chest; breast(s), bosom; **~bein** *n* ANAT breastbone; **~beutel** *m* neck pouch, *Br* money bag

**brüsten** ['brʏstən] *v/refl* (*ge-*, *h*) boast, brag (***mit*** of)

'**Brust|kasten** *m*, **~korb** *m* ANAT chest, thorax; **~schwimmen** *n* breaststroke

'**Brüstung** *f* (-; *-en*) parapet

'**Brustwarze** *f* ANAT nipple

**Brut** [bruːt] *f* (-; *-en*) ZO brooding; brood (*a*. F), hatch; fry

**brutal** [bruˈtaːl] *adj* brutal; **Brutalität** [brutaliˈtɛːt] *f* (-; *-en*) brutality

'**Brutappa,rat** *m* ZO incubator

**brüten** ['bryːtən] *v/i* (*ge-*, *h*) ZO brood, sit (on eggs); **~ *über*** (*dat*) *fig* brood over

'**Brutkasten** *m* MED incubator

**brutto** ['brʊto] *adv* ECON gross

'**Brutto|einkommen** *n* ECON gross earnings; **~sozi,alpro,dukt** *n* ECON gross national product

**Bube** ['buːbə] *m* (-*n*; -*n*) boy, lad; *card game*: knave, jack

**Buch** [buːx] *n* (-[*e*]*s*; *Bücher* ['byːçɐ]) book; **~binder** *m* (-*s*; -) (book)binder; **~drucker** *m* printer; **~druckerei** *f* print shop, *Br* printing office

**Buche** ['buːxə] *f* (-; -*n*) BOT beech

'**buchen** *v/t* (*ge-*, *h*) book; ECON enter

**Bücherbord** ['byːçɐbɔrt] *n* bookshelf

**Bücherei** [byːçəˈrai] *f* (-; *-en*) library

'**Bücherre,gal** *n* bookshelf

'**Bücherschrank** *m* bookcase

'**Buch|fink** *m* ZO chaffinch; **~halter(in)** bookkeeper; **~haltung** *f* (-; *no pl*) bookkeeping; **~händler(in)** bookseller; **~handlung** *f* bookstore, *Br* bookshop; **~macher** *m* bookmaker

**Büchse** ['bʏksə] *f* (-; -*n*) can, *Br* tin; box; rifle

'**Büchsen|fleisch** *n* canned (*Br* tinned) meat; **~öffner** *m* can (*Br* tin) opener

**Buchstabe** ['buːxʃtaːbə] *m* (-*n*; -*n*) letter; ***großer*** (***kleiner***) **~** capital (small) letter; **buchstabieren** [buːxʃtaˈbiːrən] *v/t* (*no -ge-*, *h*) spell; **buchstäblich** ['buːxʃtɛːplɪç] *adv* literally

'**Buchstütze** *f* bookend

**Bucht** ['bʊxt] *f* (-; *-en*) bay; creek, inlet

'**Buchung** *f* (-; *-en*) booking; ECON entry

**Buckel** ['bʊkəl] *m* (-*s*; -) hump, hunch; ***e-n ~ machen*** hump *or* hunch one's back

**bücken** ['bʏkən] *v/refl* (*ge-*, *h*) bend (down), stoop

**bucklig** ['bʊklɪç] *adj* hunchbacked

**Bucklige** ['bʊklɪgə] *m*, *f* (-*n*; -*n*) hunchback

**Bückling** ['bʏklɪŋ] *m* (-*s*; -*e*) smoked herring, *Br* kipper

**Buddhismus** [bʊˈdɪsmʊs] *m* (-; *no pl*) Buddhism; **Buddhist** [bʊˈdɪst] *m* (-*en*; -*en*), **bud'dhistisch** *adj* Buddhist

**Bude** ['buːdə] *f* (-*n*; -*n*) stall, booth; hut; F pad, *Br* digs; *contp* shack, dump, hole

**Budget** [bʏˈdʒeː] *n* (-*s*; -*s*) budget

**Büfett** [byˈfɛt] *n* (-[*e*]*s*; -*s*, -*e*) counter, bar, buffet; sideboard, cupboard; ***kaltes* ~** GASTR cold buffet (meal)

**Büffel** ['bʏfəl] *m* (-*s*; -) ZO buffalo

'**büffeln** F *v/i* (*ge-*, *h*) grind, cram, swot

**Bug** [buːk] *m* (-[*e*]*s*; -*e*) MAR bow; AVIAT nose; ZO, GASTR shoulder

**Bügel** ['byːgəl] *m* (-*s*; -) hanger; bow; **~brett** *n* ironing board; **~eisen** *n* iron; **~falte** *f* crease

'**bügelfrei** *adj* no(n)-iron

'**bügeln** *v/t* (*ge-*, *h*) iron, press

**buh** [buː] *int* boo!

**buhen** ['buːən] *v/i* (*ge-*, *h*) boo

**Bühne** ['byːnə] *f* (-; -*n*) stage, *fig a.* scene

'**Bühnen|bild** *n* (stage) set(ting); **~bildner(in)** (-*s*; -/-; -*nen*) stage designer

'**Buhrufe** *pl* boos

**Bullauge** ['bʊlaugə] *n* MAR porthole

'**Bulldogge** *f* ZO bulldog

**Bulle** ['bʊlə] *m* (-*n*; -*n*) ZO bull (*a. fig*); F *contp* cop, *pl the* fuzz

**Bummel** ['bʊməl] F *m* (-*s*; -) stroll; **Bummelei** [bʊməˈlai] *f* (-; *no pl*) F *contp* dawdling; slackness; '**bummeln** F *v/i* (*ge-*, *sein*) stroll, saunter; (*ge-*, *h*) *contp* dawdle; ECON go slow; '**Bummelstreik** *m* ECON slowdown, *Br* go-slow (strike); **Bummler** ['bʊmlɐ] F *m* (-*s*; -) stroller; *contp* dawdler, slowpoke, *Br* slowcoach

**bumsen** ['bʊmzən] *v/i and v/t* (*ge-*, *h*) F → ***krachen***; V screw

**Bund**[1] [bʊnt] *m* (-[*e*]*s*; *Bünde* ['bʏndə]) union, federation, alliance; association; (waist)band; ***der* ~** POL the Federal Government; F → ***Bundeswehr***

**Bund**[2] *n* (-[*e*]*s*; -*e*) bundle; bunch
**Bündel** ['bʏndəl] *n* (-*s*; -) bundle
'**bündeln** *v/t* (*ge*-, *h*) bundle (up)
**Bundes...** ['bʊndəs-] *in cpds* Federal ...; German ...; **~bahn** *f* Federal Railroad(s); **~genosse** *m* ally; **~kanzler**(**in**) Federal Chancellor; **~land** *n appr* (federal) state, Land; **~liga** *f* SPORT First Division; **~präsi,dent** *m* Federal President; **~rat** *m* Bundesrat, Upper House of German Parliament; **~repu,blik** *f* Federal Republic; **~staat** *m* federal state; confederation; **~straße** *f* Federal Highway; **~tag** *m* (-[*e*]*s*; *no pl*) Bundestag, Lower House of German Parliament; **~trainer** *m* coach of the (German) national team; **~verfassungsgericht** *n* Federal Constitutional Court, *Am appr* Supreme Court; **~wehr** *f* (-; *no pl*) MIL (German Federal) Armed Forces
**bündig** ['bʏndɪç] *adj* TECH flush; ***kurz und ~*** terse(ly); point-blank
**Bündnis** ['bʏntnɪs] *n* (-*ses*; -*se*) alliance
**Bunker** ['bʊŋkɐ] *m* (-*s*; -) air-raid shelter, bunker
**bunt** [bʊnt] *adj* colo(u)red; multicolo(u)red; colo(u)rful (*a. fig*); varied; ***~er Abend*** evening of entertainment; F ***mir wird's zu ~*** that's all I can take
'**Buntstift** *m* colo(u)red pencil, crayon
**Bürde** ['bʏrdə] *f* (-; -*n*) burden (***für j-n*** to s.o.)
**Burg** [bʊrk] *f* (-; -*en*) castle
**Bürge** ['bʏrgə] *m* (-*n*; -*n*) JUR guarantor (*a. fig*); '**bürgen** *v/i* (*ge*-, *h*) ***für j-n ~*** JUR stand surety for s.o.; ***für et. ~*** guarantee s.th.
**Bürger** ['bʏrgɐ] *m* (-*s*; -), '**Bürgerin** *f* (-; -*nen*) citizen; **~initia,tive** *f* (citizen's *or* local) action group; **~krieg** *m* civil war
'**bürgerlich** *adj* civil; middle-class; *esp contp* bourgeois; ***~e Küche*** home cooking; '**Bürgerliche** *m*, *f* (-*n*; -*n*) commoner
'**Bürger|meister** *m* mayor; **~rechte** *pl* civil rights; **~steig** ['bʏrgɐʃtaik] *m* (-[*e*]*s*; -*e*) sidewalk, *Br* pavement
'**Bürgschaft** *f* (-; -*en*) JUR surety; bail
**Büro** [by'roː] *n* (-*s*; -*s*) office; **~angestellte** *m*, *f* (-*n*; -*n*) clerk, office worker; **~klammer** *f* (paper) clip
**Bürokrat** [byro'kraːt] *m* (-*en*; -*en*) bureaucrat; **Bürokratie** [byrokra'tiː] *f* (-; -*n*) bureaucracy; *contp* red tape
**Bü'rostunden** *pl* office hours
**Bursche** ['bʊrʃə] *m* (-*n*; -*n*) fellow, guy
**burschikos** [bʊrʃi'koːs] *adj* (tom)boyish, pert
**Bürste** ['bʏrstə] *f* (-; -*n*) brush
'**bürsten** *v/t* (*ge*-, *h*) brush
'**Bürstenschnitt** *m* crew cut
**Bus** [bʊs] *m* (-*ses*; -*se*) bus; coach
**Busch** [bʊʃ] *m* (-[*e*]*s*; *Büsche* ['bʏʃə]) BOT bush, shrub
**Büschel** ['bʏʃəl] *n* (-*s*; -) bunch; tuft
'**buschig** *adj* bushy
**Busen** ['buːzən] *m* (-*s*; -) ANAT bosom, breast(s)
'**Busfahrer** *m* bus driver
'**Bushaltestelle** *f* bus stop
**Bussard** ['bʊsart] *m* (-*s*; -*e*) ZO buzzard
**Buße** ['buːsə] *f* (-; -*n*) REL penance; repentance; ***~ tun*** do penanc
**büßen** ['byːsən] *v/t* (*ge*-, *h*) pay *or* suffer for *s.th.*; REL repent
'**Bußgeld** *n* fine, penalty
'**Bußtag** *m* REL day of repentance
**Büste** ['byːstə] *f* (-; -*n*) bust
'**Büstenhalter** *m* bra
**Butter** ['bʊtɐ] *f* (-; *no pl*) butter; **~blume** *f* BOT buttercup; **~brot** *n* (slice *or* piece of) bread and butter; F ***für ein ~*** for a song; **~brotpa,pier** *n* greaseproof paper; **~dose** *f* butter dish; **~milch** *f* buttermilk
**b.w.** *abbr of* ***bitte wenden*** PTO, please turn over
**bzw.** *abbr of* ***beziehungsweise*** resp., respectively

# C

**C** *abbr of* ***Celsius*** C, Celsius, centigrade
**ca.** *abbr of* ***circa*** approx., approximately
**Café** [ka'feː] *n* (*-s*; *-s*) café, coffee house
**Cafeteria** [kafetəˈriːa] *f* (*-*; *-s or -ien*) cafeteria
**campen** ['kɛmpən] *v/i* (*ge-*, *h*) camp
**Camper** ['kɛmpɐ] *m* (*-s*; *-*) camper
**Camping...** ['kɛmpɪŋ-] *in cpds* *...bett*, *...tisch etc* camp ...; **~bus** *m* camper (van *Br*); **~platz** *m* campground, *Br* campsite
**Cappuccino** [kapʊ'tʃiːno] *m* (*-[s]*; *-[s]*) cappuccino
**Casino** [ka'ziːno] *n* → ***Kasino***
**Catcher** ['kɛtʃɐ] *m* (*-s*; *-*) wrestler
**C'D** [tseː'deː] *f* (*-*; *-s*) CD, compact disk (*Br* disc); **C'D-Brenner** *m* CD burner, CD writer; **C'D-Player** *m* CD player; **CD-'ROM** CD-ROM; **CD-'ROM-Laufwerk** *n* CD-ROM drive; **C'D-Spieler** *m* CD player
**Cellist** [tʃɛ'lɪst] *m* (*-en*; *-en*), **Cel'listin** *f* (*-*; *-nen*) MUS cellist
**Cello** ['tʃɛlo] *n* (*-s*; *-s*, *Celli*) MUS Cello
**Celsius** ['tsɛlzjʊs] ***5 Grad ~*** (*abbr* ***5° C***) five degrees centigrade *or* Celsius
**Cembalo** ['tʃɛmbalo] *n* (*-s*; *-s*, *-li*) MUS harpsichord
**Champagner®** [ʃam'panjɐ] *m* (*-s*; *-*) champagne
**Champignon** ['ʃampɪnjɔŋ] *m* (*-s*; *-s*) BOT mushroom
**Chance** ['ʃaːsə] *f* (*-*; *-n*) chance; ***die ~n stehen gleich*** (***3 zu 1***) the odds are even (three to one); **'Chancengleichheit** *f* equal opportunities
**Chaos** ['kaːɔs] *n* (*-*; *no pl*) chaos
**Chaot** [ka'oːt] *m* (*-en*; *-en*) chaotic person; POL anarchist, *pl a.* lunatic fringe
**cha'otisch** *adj* chaotic
**Charakter** [ka'raktɐ] *m* (*-s*; *-e* [karak'teːrə]) character, nature; **charakterisieren** [karakteri'ziːrən] *v/t* (*no -ge-*, *h*) characterize, describe (***als*** as); **charakteristisch** [karakte'rɪstɪʃ] *adj* characteristic, typical (***für*** of); **Cha'rakterzug** *m* trait
**charmant** [ʃar'mant] *adj* charming
**Charme** [ʃarm] *m* (*-s*; *no pl*) charm
**Charterflug** ['tʃartərfluːk] *m* (*-[e]s*; *-flüge*) charter flight
**chartern** ['tʃartɐn] *v/t* (*ge-*, *h*) charter
**Chassis** [ʃa'siː] *n* (*-*; *-*) TECH chassis
**Chat** [tʃɛt] *m* (*-s*; *-s*) IT chat
**chatten** ['tʃɛtən] *v/t* (*ge-*, *h*) IT chat
**Chauffeur** [ʃɔ'føːɐ] *m* (*-s*; *-e*) chauffeur, driver
**Chauvi** ['ʃoːvi] *m* (*-s*; *-s*) F male chauvinist (pig)
**Chauvinismus** [ʃovi'nɪsmʊs] *m* (*-*; *no pl*) chauvinism, POL *a.* jingoism
**checken** ['tʃɛkən] *v/t* (*ge-*, *h*) check; F (*understand*) get
**Chef** [ʃɛf] *m* (*-s*; *-s*) head, chief, F boss; **~arzt** *m* medical director, *Br* senior consultant; **~sekre,tärin** *f* executive secretary
**Chemie** [çe'miː] *f* (*-*; *no pl*) chemistry; **~faser** *f* synthetic fiber (*Br* fibre)
**Chemikalien** [çemi'kaːljən] *pl* chemicals; **Chemiker(in)** ['çeːmikɐ, 'çeːmikərɪn] *m(f)* (*-s*; *-/-*; *-nen*) (analytical) chemist; **chemisch** ['çeːmɪʃ] *adj* chemical; ***~e Reinigung*** dry cleaning
**Chemothera'pie** [çemotera'piː] *f* MED chemotherapy
**Chiffre** ['ʃɪfrə] *f* (*-*; *-n*) code, cipher; box (number); **chiffrieren** [ʃɪ'friːrən] *v/t* (*no -ge-*, *h*) (en)code
**China** ['çiːna] China; **Chinese** [çi'neːzə] *m* (*-n*; *-n*), **Chi'nesin** *f* (*-*; *-nen*), **chi'nesisch** *adj* Chinese
**Chinin** [çi'niːn] *n* (*-s*; *no pl*) PHARM quinine
**Chip** [tʃɪp] *m* (*-s*; *-s*) *a.* IT chip; GASTR *pl* chips, *Br* crisps
**Chirurg** [çi'rʊrk] *m* (*-en*; *-en*) surgeon
**Chirurgie** [çirʊr'giː] *f* (*-*; *-n*) surgery
**Chirurgin** [çi'rʊrgɪn] *f* (*-*; *-nen*) surgeon
**chirurgisch** [çi'rʊrgɪʃ] *adj* surgical
**Chlor** [kloːɐ] *n* (*-s*; *no pl*) CHEM chlorine
**chloren** ['kloːrən] *v/t* (*ge-*, *h*) chlorinate
**Cholera** ['koːlera] *f* (*-*; *no pl*) MED cholera; **cholerisch** [ko'leːrɪʃ] *adj* choleric
**Cholesterin** [çolɛste'riːn] *n* (*-s*; *no pl*) MED cholesterol
**Chor** [koːɐ] *m* (*-[e]s*; *Chöre* ['køːrə]) MUS choir (*a.* ARCH); ***im ~*** in chorus
**Choral** [ko'raːl] *m* (*-s*; *Choräle* [ko-

'rɛːlə]) MUS, REL chorale, hymn

**Christ** [krɪst] *m* (*-en*; *-en*) REL Christian; **~baum** *m* Christmas tree

**'Christenheit**: ***die ~*** REL Christendom

**'Christentum** *n* (*-s*; *no pl*) REL Christianity

**Christin** ['krɪstɪn] *f* (*-*; *-nen*) REL Christian

**'Christkind** *n* Infant Jesus; Father Christmas, Santa Claus

**'christlich** *adj* REL Christian

**Christus** ['krɪstʊs] REL Christ; ***vor ~*** B.C.; ***nach ~*** A.D.

**Chrom** [kroːm] *n* (*-s*; *no pl*) chrome, CHEM *a.* chromium

**Chromosom** [kromo'zoːm] *n* (*-s*; *-en*) BIOL chromosome

**Chronik** ['kroːnɪk] *f* (*-*; *-en*) chronicle

**chronisch** ['kroːnɪʃ] *adj* MED chronic

**chronologisch** [krono'loːgɪʃ] *adj* chronological

**circa** → ***zirka***

**City** ['sɪtɪ] *f* (*-*; *-s*) downtown, (city) center, *Br* centre

**Clique** ['klɪkə] *f* (*-*; *-n*) F group, set; *contp* clique

**Clou** [kluː] F *m* (*-s*; *-s*) highlight, climax; ***der ~ daran*** the whole point of it

**Compact Disc**, **Compact Disk** ['kɔmpæktdɪsk] *f* (*-*; *-s*) compact disk (*Br* disc)

**Computer** [kɔm'pjuːtɐ] *m* (*-s*; *-*) computer; **~ausdruck** *m* computer printout

**com'puter|gesteuert** *adj* computer-controlled; **~gestützt** *adj* computer-aided

**Com'putergrafik** *f* computer graphics

**computerisieren** [kɔmpjutəri'ziːrən] *v/t* (*no -ge-*, *h*) computerize

**Com'puter|spiel** *n* computer game; **~virus** *m* computer virus

**Conférencier** [koˌferaˌ'sjeː] *m* (*-s*; *-s*) master of ceremonies, F emcee, MC, *Br* compère

**Cord** *etc* → ***Kord*** *etc*

**Couch** [kautʃ] *f* (*-*; *-s*) couch

**Coupé** [ku'peː] *n* (*-s*; *-s*) MOT coupé

**Coupon** → ***Kupon***

**Cousin** [ku'zɛˌː] *m* (*-s*; *-s*), **Cousine** [ku'ziːnə] *f* (*-*; *-n*) cousin

**Creme** [kreːm] *f* (*-*; *-s*) cream (*a. fig*)

**Curry** ['kari] *m* (*-s*; *-s*) curry powder

**Cursor** ['kɜːsə] *m* (*-s*; *-s*) IT cursor

# D

**da** [daː] **1.** *adv space*: there; here; *time*: then, at that time; ***~ drüben*** (***draußen***, ***hinten***) over (out, back) there; ***von ~ aus*** from there; ***das ... ~*** that ... (over there); ***~ kommt er*** here he comes; ***~ bin ich*** here I am; ***~ sein*** be there; exist; ***ist noch ... ~?*** is any ... left?; ***noch nie ~ gewesen*** unprecedented; ***er ist gleich wieder ~*** he'll be right back; ***von ~ an*** *or* ***ab*** from then on **2.** *cj* as, since, because

**'dabehalten** *v/t* (*irr*, ***halten***, *sep*, *no -ge-*, *h*) keep; ***j-n ~*** keep s.o. in

**dabei** [da'bai] *adv* there, present; near *or* close by; at the same time; included with it; ***~ sein*** be there; take part; be in on it; ***ich bin ~!*** count me in!; ***er ist gerade ~ zu gehen*** he's just leaving; ***es ist nichts ~*** there's nothing to it; there's no harm in it; ***was ist schon ~?*** (so) what of it?; ***lassen wir es ~!*** let's leave it at that!; **~bleiben** *v/i* (*irr*, ***bleiben***, *sep*, *-ge-*, *sein*) stick to it; **~haben** F *v/t* (*irr*, ***haben***, *sep*, *-ge-*, *h*) have with (*or* on) one

**'dableiben** *v/i* (*irr*, ***bleiben***, *sep*, *-ge-*, *sein*) stay

**Dach** [dax] *n* (*-[e]s*; *Dächer* ['dɛçɐ]) roof

**'Dach|boden** *m* attic; **~decker** ['daxdekɐ] *m* (*-s*; *-*) roofer; **~fenster** *n* dormer window; **~gepäckträger** *m* MOT roof-rack

**'Dachgeschoss** *n*, **'Dachgeschoß** *Austrian n* attic; **~wohnung** *f* loft apartment, *Br* attic flat

**'Dach|kammer** *f* garret; **~luke** *f* skylight; **~pappe** *f* roofing felt; **~rinne** *f* gutter

**Dachs** [daks] *m* (*-es*; *-e*) ZO badger

**'Dachstuhl** *m* roof framework

**dachte** ['daxtə] *pret of* ***denken***

**'Dachterˌrasse** *f* roof terrace

'**Dachverband** *m* ECON *etc* umbrella organization
**Dackel** ['dakəl] *m* (*-s*; -) ZO dachshund
'**dadurch** *adv and cj* this *or* that way; for this reason, so; **~, *dass*** due to the fact that
**dafür** [da'fy:ɐ] *adv* for it, for that; instead; in return, in exchange; ***~ sein*** be in favo(u)r of it; ***er kann nichts ~*** it is not his fault; ***~ sorgen, dass*** see to it that
**da'gegen** *adv and cj* against it; however, on the other hand; ***~ sein*** be against (*or* opposed to) it; ***haben Sie et. ~, dass ich …?*** do you mind if I …?; ***wenn Sie nichts ~ haben*** if you don't mind; ***… ist nichts ~*** … can't compare
**da'heim** *adv* at home
'**daher** *adv and cj* from there; that's why
**da'hin** *adv* there, to that place; gone, past; ***bis ~*** till then; up to there
**da'hinten** *adv* back there
**da'hinter** *adv* behind it; ***es steckt nichts ~*** there is nothing to it; F ***~ kommen*** find out (about it)
'**dalassen** F *v/t* (*irr*, ***lassen***, *sep*, *-ge-*, *h*) leave behind
**damalig** ['da:ma:lıç] *adj* then
**damals** ['da:ma:ls] *adv* then, at that time
**Dame** ['da:mə] *f* (-; *-n*) lady; partner; *cards*, *chess*: queen; checkers, *Br* draughts
'**Damen…** *in cpds* ladies' …; SPORT women's …; **~binde** *f* sanitary napkin (*Br* towel)
'**damenhaft** *adj* ladylike
'**Damen|toi,lette** *f* ladies' room (*Br* toilet), *the* ladies; **~wahl** *f* ladies' choice
**damit 1.** ['da:mıt] *adv* with it *or* that; by it, with it; ***was will er ~ sagen?*** what's he trying to say?; ***wie steht es ~?*** how about it?; ***~ einverstanden sein*** have no objections **2.** [da'mıt] *cj* so that; in order to *inf*; ***~ nicht*** so as not to *inf*
**Damm** [dam] *m* (-[*e*]*s*; *Dämme* ['dɛmə]) dam; embankment
**dämmerig** ['dɛmərıç] *adj* dim
'**Dämmerlicht** *n* (-[*e*]*s*; *no pl*) twilight
**dämmern** ['dɛmɐn] *v/i* (*ge-*, *h*) dawn (*a.* F ***j-m*** on s.o.); get dark *or* dusky
'**Dämmerung** *f* (-; *-en*) dusk; dawn
**Dämon** ['dɛ:mɔn] *m* (*-s*; *-en* [dɛ'mo:nən]) demon; **dämonisch** [dɛ'mo:nıʃ] *adj* demoniac(al)
**Dampf** [dampf] *m* (-[*e*]*s*; *Dämpfe* ['dɛmpfə]) steam; PHYS vapo(u)r
'**dampfen** *v/i* (*ge-*, *h and sein*) steam
**dämpfen** ['dɛmpfən] *v/t* (*ge-*, *h*) deaden; muffle (*voice*); soften (*light*, *sound*, *blow*); GASTR steam, stew; steam-iron; *fig* put a damper on; curb (*a.* ECON)
**Dampfer** ['dampfɐ] *m* (*-s*; -) steamer, steamship
'**Dampf|kochtopf** *m* pressure cooker; **~ma,schine** *f* steam engine; **~schiff** *n* steamer, steamship
**da'nach** *adv* after it *or* that; afterwards; for it; according to it; ***ich fragte ihn ~*** I asked him about it; F ***mir ist nicht ~*** I don't feel like it
**Däne** ['dɛ:nə] *m* (*-n*; *-n*) Dane
**da'neben** *adv* next to it, beside it; besides, as well, at the same time; beside the mark; **~benehmen** F *v/refl* (*irr*, ***nehmen***, *sep*, *no -ge-*, *h*) step out of line; **~gehen** F *v/i* (*irr*, ***gehen***, *sep*, *-ge-*, *sien*) miss (the target); F misfire
'**Dänemark** Denmark
**Dänin** ['dɛ:nın] *f* (-; *-nen*) Danish woman *or* girl; '**dänisch** *adj* Danish
**dank** [daŋk] *prp* (*gen*) thanks to
**Dank** *m* (-[*e*]*s*; *no pl*) thanks; ***Gott sei ~!*** thank God!; ***vielen ~!*** many thanks!
'**dankbar** *adj* grateful (***j-m*** to s.o.); rewarding (*task etc*)
'**Dankbarkeit** *f* (-; *no pl*) gratitude
'**danken** *v/i* (*ge-*, *h*) thank (***j-m für et.*** s.o. for s.th.); ***danke*** (***schön***) thank you (very much); (***nein,***) ***danke*** no, thank you; ***nichts zu ~*** not at all
**dann** [dan] *adv* then; ***~ und wann*** (every) now and then
**daran** [da'ran] *adv* on it; *die*, *think etc* of it; *believe etc* in it; *suffer etc* from it; → ***liegen***
**darauf** [da'rauf] *adv* on (top of) it; after (that); *listen*, *drink etc* to it; *proud etc* of it; *wait etc* for it; ***am Tage ~*** the day after; ***zwei Jahre ~*** two years later; ***~ kommt es an*** that's what matters
**darauf'hin** *adv* after that; as a result
**daraus** [da'raus] *adv* from (*or* out of) it; ***was ist ~ geworden?*** what has become of it?; ***~ wird nichts!*** F nothing doing!
**Darbietung** ['da:ɐbi:tʊŋ] *f* (-; *-en*) presentation; performance
**darin** [da'rın] *adv* in it; ['da:rın] in that

**darlegen** ['da:ɐle:gən] *v/t* (*sep*, *-ge-*, *h*) explain, set out
**Darlehen** ['da:ɐle:ən] *n* (*-s*; *-*) loan; ***ein~ geben*** grant a loan
**Darm** [darm] *m* (*-[e]s*; *Därme* ['dɛrmə]) ANAT bowel(s), intestine(s); GASTR skin; **~grippe** *f* MED intestinal flu
D
**darstellen** ['da:ɐʃtɛlən] *v/t* (*sep*, *-ge-*, *h*) represent, show, depict; describe; THEA play, do; trace, graph; '**Darsteller(in)** (*-s*; *-/-*; *-nen*) THEA performer, actor (actress); '**Darstellung** *f* (*-*; *-en*) representation; description; account; portrayal
**darüber** [da'ry:bɐ] *adv* over *or* above it; across it; in the meantime; *write*, *talk etc* about it; ***... und ~*** ... and more; ***~ werden Jahre vergehen*** that will take years
**darum** [da'rʊm] *adv and cj* (a)round it; because of it, that's why; ***~ bitten*** ask for it; → ***gehen***
**darunter** [da'rʊntɐ] *adv* under *or* below it, underneath; among them; including; ***... und ~*** ... and less; ***was verstehst du ~?*** what do you understand by it?
**das** [das] → ***der***
'**Dasein** *n* (*-s*; *no pl*) life, existence
**dass** [das] *cj* that; so (that); ***es sei denn, ~*** unless; ***nicht ~ ich wüsste*** not that I know of
'**dastehen** *v/i* (*irr*, ***stehen***, *sep*, *-ge-*, *h*) stand (there)
**Datei** [da'tai] *f* (*-*; *-en*) IT file; **~verwaltung** *f* IT file management
**Daten** ['da:tən] *pl* data (*a.* IT), facts; particulars; **~bank** *f* (*-*; *-en*) database, data bank; **~schutz** *m* JUR data protection; **~speicher** *m* data memory *or* storage; **~träger** *m* data medium *or* carrier; **~übertragung** *f* data transfer; **~verarbeitung** *f* data processing
**datieren** [da'ti:rən] *v/t and v/i* (*no -ge-*, *h*) date
**Dativ** ['da:ti:f] *m* (*-s*; *-e*) dative (case)
**Dattel** ['datəl] *f* (*-*; *-n*) BOT date
**Datum** ['da:tʊm] *n* (*-s*; *Daten* ['da:tən]) date; ***welches ~ haben wir heute?*** what's the date today?
**Dauer** ['daʊɐ] *f* (*-*; *no pl*) duration; continuance; ***auf die ~*** in the long run; ***für die ~ von*** for a period *or* term of; ***von ~ sein*** last; **~arbeitslosigkeit** *f* long-term unemployment; **~auftrag** *m* ECON standing order; **~geschwindigkeit** *f* MOT *etc* cruising speed
'**dauerhaft** *adj* lasting; durable
'**Dauer|karte** *f* season ticket; **~lauf** *m* SPORT jogging; ***im ~*** at a jog; **~lutscher** *m* lollipop
**dauern** *v/i* (*ge-*, *h*) last, take; → ***lange***
'**Dauerwelle** *f* permanent, *Br* perm
**Daumen** ['daumən] *m* (*-s*; *-*) ANAT thumb; F ***j-m den ~ halten*** keep one's fingers crossed (for s.o.); ***am ~ lutschen*** suck one's thumb
**Daunen** ['daunən] *pl* down
'**Daunendecke** *f* eiderdown
**da'von** *adv* (away) from it; by it; about it; away; of it *or* them; ***et. ~ haben*** get s.th. out of it; ***das kommt ~!*** there you are!, that will teach you!; **~kommen** *v/i* (*irr*, ***kommen***, *sep*, *-ge-*, *sein*) escape, get away; **~laufen** *v/i* (*irr*, ***laufen***, *sep*, *-ge-*, *sein*) run away
**da'vor** *adv* before it; in front of it; *be afraid*, *warn s.o. etc* of it
**da'zu** *adv* for it, for that purpose; in addition; ***noch ~*** into the bargain; ***~ ist es da*** that's what it's there for; ***Salat ~?*** a salad with it?; → ***kommen, Lust***; **~gehören** *v/i* (*sep*, *no -ge-*, *h*) belong to it, be part of it; **~gehörig** *adj* belonging to it; **~kommen** *v/i* (*irr*, ***kommen***, *sep*, *-ge-*, *sein*) join *s.o.*; be added
**da'zwischen** *adv* between (them); in between; among them; **~kommen** *v/i* (*irr*, ***kommen***, *sep*, *-ge-*, *sein*) intervene, happen; ***wenn nichts dazwischenkommt*** if all goes well
**DB** [de:'be:] *abbr of* ***Deutsche Bahn*** German Rail
**dealen** ['di:lən] *v/i* (*ge-*, *h*) F push drugs
**Dealer** ['di:lɐ] *m* (*-s*; *-*) drug dealer, F pusher
**Debatte** [de'batə] *f* (*-*; *-n*) debate
**debattieren** [deba'ti:rən] *v/i* (*no -ge-*, *h*) debate (***über*** *acc* on)
**Debüt** [de'by:] *n* (*-s*; *-s*) debut; ***sein ~ geben*** make your debut
**dechiffrieren** [deʃɪ'fri:rən] *v/t* (*no -ge-*, *h*) decipher, decode
**Deck** [dɛk] *n* (*-[e]s*; *-s*) MAR deck
**Decke** ['dɛkə] *f* (*-*; *-n*) blanket; quilt; ARCH ceiling
**Deckel** ['dɛkəl] *m* (*-s*; *-*) lid, cover, top
'**decken** *v/t and v/i* (*ge-*, *h*) cover (*a.* ZO), SPORT *a.* mark; ***sich ~*** (***mit***) coincide

(with); → ***Tisch***
**'Deckung** *f* (-; *no pl*) cover; *boxing*: guard; ***in ~ gehen*** take cover
**defekt** [de'fɛkt] *adj* defective, faulty; TECH out of order; **De'fekt** *m* (-[*e*]*s*; -*e*) defect, fault
**defensiv** [defɛn'si:f] *adj*, **Defensive** [defɛn'zi:və] *f* (-; *no pl*) defensive
**definieren** [defi'ni:rən] *v/t* (*no -ge-*, *h*) define; **Definition** [defini'tsjo:n] *f* (-; -*en*) definition
**Defizit** ['de:fitsɪt] *n* (-*s*; -*e*) deficit; deficiency
**Degen** ['de:gən] *m* (-*s*; -) sword; *fencing*: épée
**degradieren** [degra'di:rən] *v/t* (*no -ge-*, *h*) degrade (*a. fig*)
**dehnbar** ['de:nba:ɐ] *adj* flexible, elastic (*a. fig*); **dehnen** ['de:nən] *v/t* (*ge-*, *h*) stretch (*a. fig*)
**Deich** [daiç] *m* (-[*e*]*s*; -*e*) dike
**Deichsel** ['daiksəl] *f* (-; -*n*) pole, shaft
**dein** [dain] *poss pron* your; ***~er, ~e, ~(e)s*** yours; **deinerseits** ['dainɐ'zaits] *adv* on your part; **deines'gleichen** ['dainəsglaiçən] *pron contp* the likes of you
**deinetwegen** ['dainət'veːgən] *adv* for your sake; because of you
**Dekan** [de'ka:n] *m* (-*s*; -*e*), **De'kanin** *f* (-; -*nen*) REL, UNIV dean
**Deklination** [deklina'tsjo:n] *f* (-; -*en*) LING declension; **deklinieren** [dekli'ni:rən] *v/t* (*no -ge-*, *h*) decline
**Dekolleté** [dekɔl'te:] *n* (-*s*; -*s*) low neckline
**Dekorateur** [dekora'tø:ɐ] *m* (-*s*; -*e*), **Dekora'teurin** *f* (-; -*nen*) decorator; window dresser; **Dekoration** [dekora'tsjo:n] *f* (-; -*en*) decoration; (window) display; THEA scenery; **dekorativ** [dekora'ti:f] *adj* decorative; **dekorieren** [deko'ri:rən] *v/t* (*no -ge-*, *h*) decorate; dress
**Delfin** → ***Delphin***
**delikat** [deli'ka:t] *adj* delicious, exquisite; *fig* delicate, ticklish
**Delikatesse** [delika'tɛsə] *f* (-; -*n*) delicacy; **Delika'tessenladen** *m* delicatessen, F deli
**Delphin** [dɛl'fi:n] *m* (-*s*; -*e*) ZO dolphin
**Dementi** [de'mɛnti] *n* (-*s*; -*s*) (official) denial; **dementieren** [demɛn'ti:rən] *v/t* (*no -ge-*, *h*) deny (officially)
**dementsprechend**, **demgemäß** ['de:mgəmɛ:s] *adv* accordingly
**'demnach** *adv* according to that
**'demnächst** *adv* shortly, before long
**Demo** ['de:mo] F *f* (-; -*s*) demo
**Demokrat** [demo'kra:t] *m* (-*en*; -*en*) democrat; **Demokratie** [demokra'ti:] *f* (-; -*n*) democracy; **Demo'kratin** *f* (-; -*nen*) democrat; **demo'kratisch** *adj* democratic
**demolieren** [demo'li:rən] *v/t* (*no -ge-*, *h*) demolish, wreck
**Demonstrant** [demɔn'strant] *m* (-*en*; -*en*), **Demon'strantin** *f* (-; -*nen*) demonstrator; **Demonstration** [demɔnstra'tsjo:n] *f* (-; -*en*) demonstration; **demonstrieren** [demɔn'stri:rən] *v/t and v/i* (*no -ge-*, *h*) demonstrate
**demontieren** [demɔn'ti:rən] *v/t* (*no -ge-*, *h*) dismantle
**demoralisieren** [demorali'zi:rən] *v/t* (*no -ge-*, *h*) demoralize
**Demoskopie** [demosko'pi:] *f* (-; -*n*) public opinion research
**Demut** ['de:mu:t] *f* (-; *no pl*) humility, humbleness; **demütig** ['de:my:tɪç] *adj* humble; **demütigen** ['de:my:tɪgən] *v/t* (*ge-*, *h*) humiliate; **'Demütigung** *f* (-; -*en*) humiliation
**denkbar** ['dɛŋkba:ɐ] **1.** *adj* conceivable **2.** *adv*: ***~ einfach*** most simple
**denken** ['dɛŋkən] *v/t and v/i* (*irr*, *ge-*, *h*) think (***an*** *acc*, ***über*** *acc* of, about); ***daran ~*** (***zu*** *inf*) remember (to *inf*)
**'Denkfa,brik** *f* think tank
**'Denkmal** *n* monument; memorial
**'denkwürdig** *adj* memorable
**denn** [dɛn] *cj and adv* for, because; ***es sei ~, dass*** unless; ***mehr ~ je*** more than ever; **dennoch** ['dɛnnɔx] *cj* yet, still, nevertheless
**Denunziant** [denʊn'tsjant] *m* (-*en*; -*en*) informer; **denunzieren** [denʊn'tsi:rən] *v/t* (*no -ge-*, *h*) inform on *or* against
**Deodorant** [deˀodo'rant] *n* (-*s*; -*e*, -*s*) deodorant
**Deponie** [depo'ni:] *f* (-; -*n*) dump, waste disposal site
**deponieren** [depo'ni:rən] *v/t* (*no -ge-*, *h*) deposit, leave
**Depot** [de'po:] *n* (-*s*; -*s*) depot (*a.* MIL); *Swiss*: deposit
**Depression** [deprɛ'sjo:n] *f* (-; -*en*) de-

D

pression (*a.* ECON)
**depressiv** [deprɛ'siːf] *adj* depressive
**deprimieren** [depri'miːrən] *v/t* (*no -ge-, h*) depress; **~d** *adj* depressing
**deprimiert** [depri'miːɐt] *adj* depressed
**der** [deːɐ], **die** [diː], **das** [das] **1.** *art* the **2.** *dem pron* that, this; he, she, it; ***die*** *pl* these, those, they **3.** *rel pron* who, which, that; '**derartig 1.** *adv* so (much); like that **2.** *adj* such (as this)
**derb** [dɛrp] *adj* coarse; tough, sturdy
'**der'gleichen** *dem pron*: ***nichts ~*** nothing of the kind
**derjenige** ['deːɐjeːnɪgə], **diejenige** ['diːjeːnɪgə], **dasjenige** ['dasjeːnɪgə] *dem pron* the one; ***diejenigen*** *pl* the ones, those
**dermaßen** ['deːɐ'maːsən] *adv* so (much), like that
**Dermatologe** [dɛrmato'loːgə] *m* (*-n*; *-n*), **Dermato'login** *f* (*-*; *-nen*) dermatologist **derselbe** [dɛr'zɛlbə], **dieselbe** [diː'zɛlbə], **dasselbe** [das'zɛlbə] *dem pron* the same
**Deserteur** [dezɛr'tøːɐ] *m* (*-s*; *-e*) MIL deserter; **desertieren** [dezɛr'tiːrən] *v/i* (*no -ge-, sein*) MIL desert
**deshalb** ['dɛs'halp] *cj and adv* therefore, for that reason, that is why, so
**Desinfektionsmittel** [dɛsʔɪnfɛk'tsjoːnsmɪtəl] *n* MED disinfectant
**desinfizieren** [dɛsʔɪnfi'tsiːrən] *v/t* (*no -ge-, h*) MED disinfect
'**Desinteresse** *n* (*-s*; *no pl*) indifference
'**desinteres,siert** *adj* uninterested, indifferent
**destillieren** [dɛstɪ'liːrən] *v/t* (*no -ge-, h*) distil(l)
**desto** ['dɛsto] *cj and adv* → ***je***
'**des'wegen** *cj and adv* → ***deshalb***
**Detail** [de'tai] *n* (*-s*; *-s*) detail
**detailliert** [deta'jiːɐt] *adj* detailed
**Detektiv** [detɛk'tiːf] *m* (*-s*; *-e*) detective
**deuten** ['dɔytən] (*ge-, h*) **1.** *v/t* interpret **2.** *v/i*: ***~ auf*** (*acc*) point at
'**deutlich** *adj* clear, distinct, plain
**deutsch** [dɔytʃ] *adj* German; ***auf Deutsch*** in German
'**Deutsche** *m, f* (*-n*; *-n*) German
'**Deutschland** Germany
**Devise** [de'viːzə] *f* (*-*; *-n*) motto
**De'visen** *pl* ECON foreign currency
**Dezember** [de'tsɛmbɐ] *m* (*-[s]*; *-*) December
**dezent** [de'tsɛnt] *adj* discreet, unobtrusive; conservative (*clothes etc*); soft (*music etc*)
**Dezimal...** [detsi'maːl-] MATH *in cpds ...bruch, ...system etc*: decimal ...; **~stelle** *f* MATH decimal (place)
**DGB** [deːgeː'beː] *abbr of* ***Deutscher Gewerkschaftsbund*** Federation of German Trade Unions
**d. h.** *abbr of* ***das heißt*** i. e., that is
**Dia** ['diːa] *n* (*-s*; *-s*) PHOT slide
**Diagnose** [dia'gnoːzə] *f* (*-*; *-n*) diagnosis
**diagonal** [diago'naːl] *adj*, **Diago'nale** *f* (*-*; *-n*) diagonal
**Dialekt** [dia'lɛkt] *m* (*-[e]s*; *-e*) dialect
**Dialog** [dia'loːk] *m* (*-[e]s*; *-e*) dialog, *Br* dialogue
**Diamant** [dia'mant] *m* (*-en*; *-en*) diamond
'**Diapro,jektor** *m* slide projector
**Diät** [di'ɛːt] *f* (*-*; *-en*) diet; ***e-e ~ machen*** (***Diät leben***) be on (keep to) a diet
**Di'äten** *pl* PARL allowance
**dich** [dɪç] *pers pron* you; **~ (*selbst*)** yourself
**dicht** [dɪçt] **1.** *adj* dense, *a.* thick (*fog*); heavy (*traffic*); F closed, shut **2.** *adv*: ***~ an*** (*dat*) *or* ***bei*** close to
'**dichten** *v/t and v/i* (*ge-, h*) write (poetry); **Dichter(in)** ['dɪçtɐ, 'dɪçtərɪn] *m(f)* (*-s*; *-/-*; *-nen*) poet; writer; **dichterisch** ['dɪçtərɪʃ] *adj* poetic; ***~e Freiheit*** poetic licen|se, *Br* -ce
'**dichthalten** F *v/i* (*irr*, ***halten***, *sep*, *-ge-, h*) keep mum
'**Dichtung**[1] *f* (*-*; *-en*) TECH seal(ing)
'**Dichtung**[2] *f* (*-*; *-en*) poetry
**dick** [dɪk] *adj* thick; fat; ***es macht ~*** it's fattening
'**Dicke** *f* (*-*; *-n*) thickness; fatness;
'**dickfellig** F *adj* thick-skinned
'**dickflüssig** *adj* thick; TECH viscous
**Dickicht** ['dɪkɪçt] *n* (*-[e]s*; *-e*) thicket
'**Dick|kopf** *m* stubborn *or* pig-headed person; **~milch** *f* soured milk
**Dieb** [diːp] *m* (*-[e]s*; *-e* ['diːbə]), **Diebin** ['diːbɪn] *f* (*-*; *-nen*) thief
**diebisch** ['diːbɪʃ] *adj* thievish; *fig* malicious (*glee etc*)
**Diebstahl** ['diːpʃtaːl] *m* (*-[e]s*; *-stähle* ['diːpʃtɛːlə]) theft; JUR *mst* larceny
**Diele** ['diːlə] *f* (*-*; *-n*) board, plank; hallway, *Br a.* hall
**dienen** ['diːnən] *v/i* (*ge-, h*) serve (***j-m***

s.o.; ***als*** as); **Diener** ['diːnɐ] *m* (*-s*; *-*) servant; *fig* bow (***vor*** *dat* to)
**Dienst** [diːnst] *m* (*-[e]s*; *-e*) service; work; ***~ haben*** be on duty; ***im*** (***außer***) **~** on (off) duty; ***~ tuend*** on duty; **~...** *in cpds ...wagen, ...wohnung etc*: official ..., company ..., business ...
**'Dienstag** *m* (*-[e]s*; *-e*) Tuesday
**'Dienstalter** *n* seniority, length of service
**'dienstbereit** *adj* on duty
**diensteifrig** *adj* (*contp* over-)eager
**'Dienstgrad** *m* grade, rank (*a.* MIL)
**'Dienstleistung** *f* service
**'dienstlich** *adj* official
**'Dienstreise** *f* business trip
**'Dienststunden** *pl* office hours
**'Dienstweg** *m* official channels
**dies** [diːs], **dieser** ['diːzɐ], **diese** ['diːzə], **dieses** ['diːzəs] *dem pron* this; this one; ***diese*** *pl* these
**diesig** ['diːzɪç] *adj* hazy, misty
**diesjährig** ['diːsjɛːrɪç] *adj* this year's
**'diesmal** *adv* this time
**diesseits** ['diːszaits] *prp* (*gen*) on this side of; **'Diesseits** *n* (*-*; *no pl*) this life *or* world
**Dietrich** ['diːtrɪç] *m* (*-s*; *-e*) TECH picklock, skeleton key
**Differenz** [dɪfə'rɛnts] *f* (*-*; *-en*) difference; disagreement
**differenzieren** [dɪfərɛn'tsiːrən] *v/i* (*no -ge-*, *h*) distinguish
**Digital...** [digi'taːl] *in cpds ...anzeige, ...uhr etc*: digital ...
**Diktat** [dɪk'taːt] *n* (*-[e]s*; *-e*) dictation; **Diktator** [dɪk'taːtoːɐ] *m* (*-s*; *-en*) [dɪkta'toːrən] dictator; **diktatorisch** [dɪkta'toːrɪʃ] *adj* dictatorial; **Diktatur** [dɪkta'tuːɐ] *f* (*-*; *-en*) dictatorship; **diktieren** [dɪk'tiːrən] *v/t and v/i* (*no -ge-*, *h*) dictate
**Dik'tiergerät** *n* Dictaphone®
**Dilettant** [dilɛ'tant] *m* (*-en*; *-en*) amateur; **dilet'tantisch** *adj* amateurish
**DIN**® [diːn] *abbr of* ***Deutsches Institut für Normung*** German Institute for Standardization
**Ding** [dɪŋ] *n* (*-[e]s*; *-e*) thing; ***vor allen ~en*** above all; F ***ein ~ drehen*** pull a job
**'Dings(bums)** *m, f, n*, **Dingsda** *m, f, n* F thingamajig, whatchamacallit
**Dinosaurier** [dino'zaurjɐ] *m* (*-s*; *-*) ZO dinosaur

**Dioxid** ['diːˀɔksyːt] *n* (*-s*; *-e*) CHEM dioxide
**Dioxin** [diɔ'ksiːn] *n* (*-s*; *-e*) CHEM dioxin
**Diphtherie** [dɪfte'riː] *f* (*-*; *-n*) MED diphtheria
**Diplom** [di'ploːm] *n* (*-s*; *-e*) diploma, degree; **~...** *in cpds ...ingenieur etc*: qualified ..., graduate ...
**Diplomat** [diplo'maːt] *m* (*-en*; *-en*) diplomat; **Diplomatie** [diploma'tiː] *f* (*-*; *no pl*) diplomacy; **Diplo'matin** *f* (*-*; *-nen*) diplomat; **diplo'matisch** *adj* diplomatic (*a. fig*)
**dir** [diːɐ] *pers pron* (to) you; **~** (***selbst***) yourself
**direkt** [di'rɛkt] **1.** *adj* direct; TV live **2.** *adv* direct; *fig* directly, right; TV live; ***~ gegenüber*** (***von***) right across
**Direktion** [dirɛk'tsjoːn] *f* (*-*; *-en*) management
**Direktor** [di'rɛktoːɐ] *m* (*-s*; *-en* [dirɛk'toːrən]) director, manager; PED principal, *Br* headmaster; **Direktorin** [dirɛk'toːrɪn] (*-*; *-nen*) director, manager; PED principal, *Br* headmistress
**Di'rektübertragung** *f* TV live transmission *or* broadcast
**Dirigent** [diri'gɛnt] *m* (*-en*; *-en*) conductor; **dirigieren** [diri'giːrən] *v/t and v/i* (*no -ge-*, *h*) MUS conduct; *fig* direct
**Dirne** ['dɪrnə] *f* (*-*; *-n*) prostitute, whore
**Discman**® *m* (*-s*; *-men*) portable CD player, Discman®
**Disharmo'nie** [dɪsharmo'niː] *f* MUS dissonance (*a. fig*); **dishar'monisch** *adj* MUS discordant
**Diskette** [dɪs'kɛtə] *f* (*-*; *-n*) diskette, floppy (disk); **Dis'kettenlaufwerk** *n* disk drive
**Disko** ['dɪsko] *f* (*-*; *-s*) disco
**Diskont** [dɪs'kɔnt] *m* (*-s*; *-e*) ECON discount
**Diskothek** [dɪsko'teːk] (*-*; *-en*) disco, discotheque
**diskret** [dɪs'kreːt] *adj* discreet; **Diskretion** [dɪskre'tsjoːn] *f* (*-*; *no pl*) discretion
**diskriminieren** [dɪskrimi'niːrən] *v/t* (*no -ge-*, *h*) discriminate against
**Diskrimi'nierung** *f* (*-*; *-en*) discrimination (***von*** against)
**Diskussion** [dɪskʊ'sjoːn] *f* (*-*; *-en*) discussion, debate
**Diskussi'ons|leiter** *m* (panel) chair-

man; **~runde** *f*, **~teilnehmer** *pl* panel
**Diskuswerfen** ['dɪskʊsvɛrfən] *n* (*-s; no pl*) SPORT discus throwing
**diskutieren** [dɪsku'tiːrən] *v/t and v/i* (*no -ge-, h*) discuss
D
**Disqualifikati'on** *f* SPORT disqualification (***wegen*** for); **disqualifi'zieren** *v/t* (*no -ge-, h*) SPORT disqualify
**Dissident** [dɪsi'dɛnt] *m* (*-en; -en*), **Dissi'dentin** *f* (*-; -nen*) POL dissident
**Distanz** [dɪs'tants] *f* (*-; -en*) distance
**distanzieren** [dɪstan'tsiːrən] *v/refl* (*no -ge-, h*) distance o.s. (***von*** from)
**Distel** ['dɪstəl] *f* (*-; -n*) BOT thistle
**Distrikt** [dɪs'trɪkt] *m* (*-[e]s; -e*) district
**Disziplin** [dɪstsi'pliːn] *f* (*-; -en*) (*no pl*) discipline; SPORT event; **diszipliniert** [dɪstsipli'niːɐt] *adj* disciplined
**divers** [di'vɛrs] *adj* various; several
**Dividende** [divi'dɛndə] *f* (*-; -n*) ECON dividend
**dividieren** [divi'diːrən] *v/t* (*no -ge-, h*) MATH divide (***durch*** by)
**Division** [divi'zjoːn] *f* (*-; -en*) MATH, MIL division
**DJH** [deːjɔt'haː] *abbr of* ***Deutsches Jugendherbergswerk*** German Youth Hostel Association
**DM** [deː'ɛm] *abbr of* ***Deutsche Mark*** *hist* (*former monetary unit of Germany*) German mark(s)
**doch** [dɔx] *cj and adv* but, however, yet; ***kommst du nicht*** (***mit***) ***? - ~!*** aren't you coming? - (oh) yes, I am!; ***ich war es nicht - ~!*** I didn't do it - yes, you did!; ***er kam also ~?*** so he did come after all?; ***du kommst ~?*** you're coming, aren't you?; ***kommen Sie ~ herein!*** do come in!; ***wenn ~ ...!*** if only ...!
**Docht** [dɔxt] *m* (*-[e]s; -e*) wick
**Dock** [dɔk] *n* (*-s; -s*) MAR dock
**Dogge** ['dɔgə] *f* (*-; -n*) ZO mastiff; Great Dane
**Dogma** ['dɔgma] *n* (*-s; Dogmen* ['dɔgmən]) dogma; **dogmatisch** [dɔg'maːtɪʃ] *adj* dogmatic
**Dohle** ['doːlə] *f* (*-; -n*) ZO (jack)daw
**Doktor** ['dɔktoːɐ] *m* (*-s; -en* [dɔk'toːrən]) doctor; UNIV doctor's degree; **~arbeit** *f* UNIV (doctoral *or* PhD) thesis
**Dokument** [doku'mɛnt] *n* (*-[e]s; -e*) document
**Dokumentar...** [dokumɛn'taːɐ-] *in cpds ...spiel etc*: documentary ...; **~film** *m* documentary (film)
**Dolch** [dɔlç] *m* (*-[e]s; -e*) dagger
**Dollar** ['dɔlar] *m* (*-[s]; -s*) dollar
**dolmetschen** ['dɔlmɛtʃən] *v/i* (*ge-, h*) interpret; '**Dolmetscher(in)** (*-s; -/-; -nen*) interpreter
**Dom** [doːm] *m* (*-[e]s; -e*) cathedral
**dominierend** [domi'niːrənt] *adj* (pre-)dominant
**Dompteur** [dɔmp'tøːɐ] *m* (*-s; -e*), **Dompteuse** [dɔmp'tøːzə] *f* (*-; -n*) animal tamer *or* trainer
**Donner** ['dɔnɐ] *m* (*-s; no pl*) thunder
'**donnern** *v/i* (*ge-, h*) thunder (*a. fig*)
'**Donnerstag** *m* (*-[e]s; -e*) Thursday
'**Donnerwetter** F *n* (*-s; -*) dressing-down; ***~!*** wow!
**doof** [doːf] F *adj* stupid, dumb
**Doppel** ['dɔpəl] *n* (*-s; -*) duplicate; *tennis etc*: doubles; *~... in cpds ...bett, ...zimmer etc*: double ...
**Doppeldecker** ['dɔpəldɛkɐ] *m* (*-s; -*) AVIAT biplane; MOT double-decker (bus)
**Doppelgänger** ['dɔpəlgɛŋɐ] *m* (*-s; -*) double, look-alike
'**Doppelhaus** *n* duplex, *Br* pair of semis; **~hälfte** *f* semidetached (house)
'**Doppel|pass** *m soccer*: wall pass; **~punkt** *m* LING colon; **~stecker** *m* ELECTR two-way adapter
**doppelt** *adj* double; ***~ so viel*** (***wie***) twice as much (as)
'**Doppelverdiener** *pl* two-income family
**Dorf** [dɔrf] *n* (*-[e]s; Dörfer* ['dœrfɐ]) village; **~bewohner** *m* villager
**Dorn** [dɔrn] *m* (*-[e]s; -en*) BOT thorn (*a. fig*); TECH tongue; spike
'**dornig** *adj* thorny (*a. fig*)
**Dorsch** [dɔrʃ] m (*-[e]s; -e*) ZO cod(fish)
**dort** [dɔrt] *adv* there
'**dorther** *adv* from there
'**dorthin** *adv* there
**Dose** ['doːzə] *f* (*-; -n*) can, *Br a.* tin
'**Dosen...** *in cpds* canned, *Br a.* tinned
**dösen** ['døːzən] F *v/i* (*ge-, h*) doze
'**Dosenöffner** *m* can (*Br* tin) opener
**Dosis** ['doːzɪs] *f* (*-; Dosen*) MED dose
**Dotter** ['dɔtɐ] *m, n* (*-s; -*) yolk
**Double** ['duːbəl] *n* (*-s; -s*) *film*: stunt man (*or* woman)
**Dozent** [do'tsɛnt] *m* (*-en; -en*), **Do'zentin** *f* (*-; -nen*) (university) lecturer, assistant professor

**Dr.** *abbr of* ***Doktor*** Dr., Doctor
**Drache** ['draxə] *m* (*-n*; *-n*) dragon
'**Drachen** *m* (*-s*; *-*) kite; SPORT hang glider; ***e-n ~ steigen lassen*** fly a kite; **~fliegen** *n* SPORT hang gliding
**Draht** [dra:t] *m* (*-[e]s*; *Drähte* ['drɛ:tə]) wire; F ***auf ~ sein*** be on the ball
**drahtig** ['dra:tɪç] *fig adj* wiry
'**drahtlos** *adj* wireless
'**Drahtseil** *n* TECH cable; *circus*: tightrope; **~bahn** *f* cable railway
'**Drahtzieher** *fig m* (*-s*; *-*) wirepuller
**drall** [dral] *adj* buxom, strapping
**Drall** *m* (*-[e]s*; *no pl*) twist, spin
**Drama** ['dra:ma] *n* (*-s*; *Dramen*) drama
**Dramatiker** [dra'ma:tikɐ] *m* (*-s*; *-*) dramatist, playwright
**dra'matisch** *adj* dramatic
**dran** [dran] F *adv* → ***daran***; ***du bist ~*** it's your turn; *fig* you're in for it
**drang** [draŋ] *pret of* ***dringen***
**Drang** *m* (*-[e]s*; *no pl*) urge, drive (***nach*** for)
**drängeln** ['drɛŋəln] F *v/t and v/i* (*ge-*, *h*) push, shove
**drängen** ['drɛŋən] *v/t and v/i* (*ge-*, *h*) push, shove; ***j-n zu et. ~*** press *or* urge s.o. to do s.th.; ***sich ~*** press; force one's way; **~d** *adj* pressing
'**drankommen** F *v/i* (*irr*, ***kommen***, *sep*, *-ge-*, *sein*) have one's turn; ***als erster ~*** be first
**drastisch** ['drastɪʃ] *adj* drastic
**drauf** [drauf] F *adv* → ***darauf***; ***~ und dran sein, et. zu tun*** be just about to do s.th.; **Draufgänger** ['draufgɛŋɐ] *m* (*-s*; *-*) daredevil
**draus** [draus] F *adv* → ***daraus***
**draußen** ['drausən] *adv* outside; outdoors; ***da ~*** out there; ***bleib(t) ~!*** keep out!
**drechseln** ['drɛksəln] *v/t* (*ge-*, *h*) turn (on a lathe)
**Drechsler** ['drɛkslɐ] *m* (*-s*; *-*) turner
**Dreck** [drɛk] F *m* (*-[e]s*; *no pl*) dirt; filth (*a. fig*); mud; *fig* trash; **dreckig** ['drɛkɪç] F *adj* dirty; filthy (*both a. fig*)
**Dreh|arbeiten** ['dre:arbaitən] *pl film*: shooting; **~bank** *f* (*-*; *-bänke*) TECH lathe
'**drehbar** *adj* revolving, rotating
'**Drehbuch** *n film*: script
**drehen** ['dre:ən] *v/t* (*ge-*, *h*) turn; *film*: shoot; roll; ***sich ~*** turn, rotate; spin; ***sich ~ um*** *fig* be about; → ***Ding***
**Dreher** ['dre:ɐ] *m* (*-s*; *-*) TECH turner
'**Dreh|kreuz** *n* turnstile; **~orgel** *f* barrel organ; **~ort** *m film*: location; **~strom** *m* ELECTR three-phase current; **~stuhl** *m* swivel chair; **~tür** *f* revolving door
'**Drehung** *f* (*-*; *-en*) turn; rotation
'**Drehzahl** *f* TECH (number of) revolutions; **~messer** *m* MOT rev(olution) counter
**drei** [drai] *adj* three
**Drei** *f* (*-*; *-en*) three; *grade*: fair, C
'**drei|beinig** *adj* three-legged; **~dimensio'nal** *adj* three-dimensional
'**Dreieck** *n* (*-[e]s*; *-e*) triangle
'**dreieckig** *adj* triangular
**dreierlei** ['draiɐ'lai] *adj* three kinds of
'**dreifach** *adj* threefold, triple
'**Drei|gang...** TECH *in cpds* three-speed ...; **~kampf** *m* SPORT triathlon; **~rad** *n* tricycle; **~satz** *m* (*-es*; *no pl*) MATH rule of three; **~sprung** *m* (*-[e]s*; *no pl*) SPORT triple jump
**dreißig** ['draisɪç] *adj* thirty
'**dreißigste** *adj* thirtieth
**dreist** [draist] *adj* brazen, impertinent
**dreistufig** ['draiʃtu:fɪç] *adj* three-stage
'**dreizehn(te)** *adj* thirteen(th)
**Dresche** ['drɛʃə] F *f* (*-*; *no pl*) thrashing
'**dreschen** *v/t and v/i* (*irr*, *ge-*, *h*) AGR thresh; thrash; '**Dreschma,schine** *f* AGR threshing machine
**dressieren** [drɛ'si:rən] *v/t* (*no -ge-*, *h*) train
**Dressman** ['drɛsmən] *m* (*-s*; *-men*) male model
**Dressur** [drɛ'su:ɐ] *f* (*-*; *-en*) training; act; **~reiten** *n* dressage
**dribbeln** ['drɪbəln] *v/i* (*ge-*, *h*), **Dribbling** *n* (*-s*; *-s*) SPORT dribble
**drillen** ['drɪlən] *v/t* (*ge-*, *h*) MIL drill (*a. fig*)
**Drillinge** ['drɪlɪŋə] *pl* triplets
**drin** [drɪn] F *adv* → ***darin***; ***das ist nicht ~!*** no way!
**dringen** ['drɪŋən] *v/i* (*irr*, *ge-*, *h*) ***~ auf*** (*acc*) insist on; ***~ aus*** come from; ***~ durch*** force one's way through, penetrate, pierce; ***~ in*** (*acc*) penetrate into; ***darauf ~, dass*** urge that; **~d** *adj* urgent, pressing; strong (*suspicion etc*)
**drinnen** ['drɪnən] F *adv* inside; indoors
**dritte** ['drɪtə] *adj* third; ***wir sind zu dritt*** there are three of us; ***die Dritte Welt*** the Third World; '**Drittel** *n* (*-s*; *-*) third;

'**drittens** *adv* thirdly; '**Dritte-Welt-Laden** *m* third world shop
**Droge** ['dro:gə] *f* (-; *-n*) drug
'**drogenabhängig** *adj* addicted to drugs; ~ ***sein*** be a drug addict
'**Drogen|abhängige** *m*, *f* (*-n*; *-n*) drug addict; ~**missbrauch** *m* drug abuse
'**drogensüchtig** → ***drogenabhängig***
'**Drogentote** *m*, *f* drug victim
**Drogerie** [drogə'ri:] *f* (-; *-n*) drugstore, *Br* chemist's (shop)
**Drogist** [dro'gɪst] *m* (*-en*; *-en*), **Dro'gistin** *f* (-; *-nen*) chemist
**drohen** ['dro:ən] *v/i* (*ge-*, *h*) threaten, menace
**dröhnen** ['drø:nən] *v/i* (*ge-*, *h*) roar
'**Drohung** *f* (-; *-en*) threat (***gegen*** to)
**drollig** ['drɔlɪç] *adj* funny, droll
**Dromedar** [dromə'da:ɐ] *n* (*-s*; *-e*) ZO dromedary
**drosch** [drɔʃ] *pret of* ***dreschen***
**Drossel** ['drɔsəl] *f* (-; *-n*) ZO thrush
'**drosseln** *v/t* (*ge-*, *h*) TECH throttle
**drüben** ['dry:bən] *adv* over there (*a. fig*)
**drüber** ['drybɐ] F *adv* → ***darüber, drunter***
**Druck** [drʊk] *m* (*-[e]s*; *-e*) pressure; printing; print
'**Druckbuchstabe** *m* block letter
**Drückeberger** ['drʏkəbɛrgɐ] F *m* (*-s*; -) shirker
'**drucken** *v/t* (*ge-*, *h*) print; ***et.*** ~ ***lassen*** have s.th. printed *or* published
**drücken** ['drʏkən] (*ge-*, *h*) **1.** *v/t* press; push; *fig* force down; ***j-m die Hand*** ~ shake hands with s.o. **2.** *v/i* pinch **3.** F *v/refl*: ***sich vor et.*** ~ shirk (doing) s.th.; ~**d** *adj* heavy, oppressive
**Drucker** ['drʊkɐ] *m* (*-s*; -) printer (*a.* IT)
**Drücker** ['drʏkɐ] *m* (*-s*; -) latch; trigger; F hawker
**Druckerei** [drʊkə'rai] *f* (-; *-en*) printers
'**Druck|fehler** *m* misprint; ~**kammer** *f* pressurized cabin; ~**knopf** *m* snap fastener, *Br* press stud; TECH (push) button; ~**luft** *f* TECH compressed air; ~**sache** *f* printed (*or* second-class) matter; ~**schrift** *f* block letters; ~**taste** *f* TECH push button
**drunter** ['drʊntɐ] F *adv* → ***darunter***; ***es ging*** ~ ***und drüber*** it was absolutely chaotic
**Drüse** ['dry:zə] *f* (-; *-n*) ANAT gland
**Dschungel** ['dʒʊŋəl] *m* (*-s*; -) jungle (*a. fig*)
**Dschunke** ['dʒʊŋkə] *f* (-; *-n*) MAR junk
**du** [du:] *pers pron* you
**Dübel** ['dy:bəl] *m* (*-s*; -), '**dübeln** *v/t* (*ge-*, *h*) TECH dowel
**ducken** ['dʊkən] *v/refl* (*ge-*, *h*) duck; *fig* cringe (***vor*** *dat* before); crouch
**Duckmäuser** ['dʊkmɔyzɐ] *m* (*-s*; -) coward; yes-man
**Dudelsack** ['du:dəlzak] *m* MUS bagpipes
**Duell** [du'ɛl] *n* (*-s*; *-e*) duel; **duellieren** [duɛ'li:rən] *v/refl* (*no -ge-*, *h*) fight a duel
**Duett** [du'ɛt] *n* (*-[e]s*; *-e*) MUS duet
**Duft** [dʊft] *m* (*-[e]s*; *Düfte* ['dʏftə]) scent, fragrance, smell (***nach*** of); '**duften** *v/i* (*ge-*, *h*) smell (***nach*** of); '**duftend** *adj* fragrant; '**duftig** *adj* dainty
**dulden** ['dʊldən] *v/t* (*ge-*, *h*) tolerate, put up with; suffer
**duldsam** ['dʊltza:m] *adj* tolerant
**dumm** [dʊm] *adj* stupid, F dumb
'**Dummheit** *f* (-; *-en*) (*no pl*) stupidity, ignorance; stupid *or* foolish thing
'**Dummkopf** *m contp* fool, blockhead
**dumpf** [dʊmpf] *adj* dull; *fig* vague
**Düne** ['dy:nə] *f* (-; *-n*) (sand) dune
**Dung** [dʊŋ] *m* (*-[e]s*; *no pl*) dung, manure
**düngen** ['dʏŋən] *v/t* (*ge-*, *h*) fertilize; manure; **Dünger** ['dʏŋɐ] *m* (*-s*; -) fertilizer; manure
**dunkel** ['dʊŋkəl] *adj* dark (*a. fig*)
'**Dunkelheit** *f* (-; *no pl*) dark(ness)
'**Dunkel|kammer** *f* PHOT darkroom; ~**ziffer** *f* number of unreported cases
**dünn** [dʏn] *adj* thin; weak (*coffee etc*)
**Dunst** [dʊnst] *m* (*-[e]s*; *Dünste* ['dʏnstə]) haze, mist; CHEM vapo(u)r; **dünsten** ['dʏnstən] *v/t* (*ge-*, *h*) GASTR stew, braise; '**dunstig** *adj* hazy, misty
**Duplikat** [dupli'ka:t] *n* (*-[e]s*; *-e*) duplicate; copy
**Dur** [du:ɐ] *n* (-; *no pl*) MUS major (key)
**durch** [dʊrç] *prp* (*acc*) *and adv* through; across; MATH divided by; GASTR (well) done; ~ ***j-n*** (***et.***) by s.o. (s.th.); ~ ***und*** ~ through and through
'**durcharbeiten** (*sep*, *-ge-*, *h*) **1.** *v/t* study thoroughly; ***sich*** ~ ***durch*** work (one's way) through a *text etc* **2.** *v/i* work without a break

**durch'aus** *adv* absolutely, quite; **~ *nicht*** by no means
**'durchblättern** *v/t* (*sep*, *-ge-*, *h*) leaf *or* thumb through
**'Durchblick** *fig m* grasp *of s.th.*
**'durchblicken** *v/i* (*sep*, *-ge-*, *h*) look through; **~ *lassen*** give to understand; ***ich blicke* (*da*) *nicht durch*** I don't get it
**durch'bohren** *v/t* (*no -ge-*, *h*) pierce; perforate
**'durchbraten** *v/t* (*irr*, ***braten***, *sep*, *-ge-*, *h*) roast thoroughly
**'durchbrechen**[1] (*irr*, ***brechen***, *sep*, *-ge-*) **1.** *v/t* (*h*) break (in two) **2.** *v/i* (*sein*) break through *or* apart
**durch'brechen**[2] *v/t* (*irr*, ***brechen***, *no -ge-*, *h*) break through
**'durch|brennen** *v/i* (*irr*, ***brennen***, *sep*, *-ge-*, *sein*) ELECTR blow; *reactor*: melt down; F run away
**'durchbringen** *v/t* (*irr*, ***bringen***, *sep*, *-ge-*, *h*) get (MED pull) *s.o.* through; go through *one's money*; support (*family*)
**'Durchbruch** *m* breakthrough (*a. fig*)
**durch'dacht** *adj* (well) thought-out
**'durchdrehen** (*sep*, *-ge-*, *h*) **1.** *v/i wheels*: spin; F *fig* crack up, flip **2.** *v/t* GASTR grind, *Br* mince
**'durchdringend** *adj* piercing
**durchei'nander** *adv* confused; (in) a mess; **~*bringen*** *v/t* (*irr*, ***bringen***, *sep*, *-ge-*, *h*) confuse, mix up; mess up; **Durchei'nander** *n* (*-s*; *no pl*) confusion, mess
**durch'fahren**[1] *v/t* (*irr*, ***fahren***, *no -ge-*, *h*) go (*or* pass, drive) through
**'durchfahren**[2] *v/i* (*irr*, ***fahren***, *sep*, *-ge-*, *sein*) go (*or* pass, drive) through
**'Durchfahrt** *f* passage; **~ *verboten*** no thoroughfare
**'Durchfall** *m* MED diarrh(o)ea
**'durch|fallen** *v/i* (*irr*, ***fallen***, *sep*, *-ge-*, *sein*) fall through; fail, F flunk (*test etc*); F be a flop; ***j-n ~ lassen*** fail (F flunk) s.o.; **~fragen** *v/refl* (*sep*, *-ge-*, *h*) ask one's way (***nach, zu*** to)
**'durchführbar** *adj* practicable, feasible
**'durchführen** *v/t* (*sep*, *-ge-*, *h*) carry out, do
**'Durchgang** *m* passage
**'Durchgangs...** *in cpds ...verkehr etc*: through ...; *...lager etc*: transit ...
**'durchgebraten** *adj* well done
**'durchgehen** (*irr*, ***gehen***, *sep*, *-ge-*, *sein*) **1.** *v/i* go through (*a.* RAIL *and* PARL); *fig* run away (***mit*** with); *horse*: bolt **2.** *v/t* go *or* look through; **~ *lassen*** tolerate; **~d** *adj* continuous; **~*er Zug*** through train; **~ *geöffnet*** open all day
**'durchgreifen** *fig v/i* (*irr*, ***greifen***, *sep*, *-ge-*, *h*) take drastic measures; **~d** *adj* drastic; radical
**'durchhalten** (*irr*, ***halten***, *sep*, *-ge-*, *h*) **1.** *v/t* keep up **2.** *v/i* hold out
**'durchhängen** *v/i* (*irr*, ***hängen***, *sep*, *-ge-*, *h*) sag; F have a low
**'durchkämpfen** *v/t* (*sep*, *-ge-*, *h*) fight out; ***sich ~*** fight one's way through
**'durchkommen** *v/i* (*irr*, ***kommen***, *sep*, *-ge-*, *sein*) come through (*a.* MED); get through; get along; get away (***mit e-r Lüge*** *etc* with a lie *etc*)
**durch'kreuzen** *v/t* (*no -ge-*, *h*) cross, thwart
**'durchlassen** *v/t* (*irr*, ***lassen***, *sep*, *-ge-*, *h*) let pass, let through
**'durchlässig** *adj* permeable (***für*** to)
**'durchlaufen**[1] (*irr*, ***laufen***, *sep*, *-ge-*) **1.** *v/i* (*sein*) run through **2.** *v/t* (*h*) wear through
**durch'laufen**[2] *v/t* (*irr*, ***laufen***, *no -ge-*, *h*) pass through
**'Durchlauferhitzer** *m* (*-s*; *-*) (instant) water heater, *Br a.* geyser
**'durchlesen** *v/t* (*irr*, ***lesen***, *sep*, *-ge-*, *h*) read through
**durch|'leuchten** *v/t* (*no -ge-*, *h*) MED X-ray; *fig* screen; **~löchern** [dʊrç'lœçɐn] *v/t* (*no -ge-*, *h*) perforate, make holes in
**'durchmachen** F *v/t* (*sep*, *-ge-*, *h*) go through; ***viel ~*** suffer a lot; ***die Nacht ~*** make a night of it
**'Durchmesser** *m* (*-s*; *-*) diameter
**durch'nässen** *v/t* (*no -ge-*, *h*) soak
**'durchnehmen** *v/t* (*irr*, ***nehmen***, *sep*, *-ge-*, *h*) PED do, deal with
**'durchpausen** *v/t* (*sep*, *-ge-*, *h*) trace
**durch'queren** *v/t* (*no*, *-ge-*, *h*) cross
**'Durchreiche** *f* (*-*; *-n*) hatch
**'Durchreise** *f*: ***ich bin nur auf der ~*** I'm only passing through; **'durchreisen** *v/i* (*sep*, *-ge-*, *sein*) travel through
**'Durchreisevisum** *n* transit visa
**'durch|reißen** (*irr*, ***reißen***, *sep*, *-ge-*) **1.** *v/t* (*h*) tear (in two) **2.** *v/i* (*sein*) tear,

break; **~ringen** *v/refl* (*irr*, ***ringen***, *sep*, *-ge-*, *h*) ***sich ~, et. zu tun*** bring o.s. to do s.th.
'**Durchsage** *f* announcement
**durch'schauen** *v/t* (*no -ge-*, *h*) see through *s.o. or s.th.*
'**durchscheinen** *v/i* (*irr*, ***scheinen***, *sep*, *-ge-*, *h*) shine through; **~d** *adj* transparent
'**durchscheuern** *v/t* (*sep*, *-ge-*, *h*) chafe; wear through
'**durchschlafen** *v/i* (*irr*, ***schlafen***, *sep*, *-ge-*, *h*) sleep through
'**Durchschlag** *m* (carbon) copy
**durch'schlagen**[1] *v/t* (*irr*, ***schlagen***, *no -ge-*, *h*) cut in two; *bullet etc*: go through, pierce
'**durchschlagen**[2] (*irr*, ***schlagen***, *sep*, *-ge-*) **1.** *v/refl* (*h*): ***sich ~ nach*** make one's way to **2.** *v/i* (*sein*) come through (*a. fig*); **~d** *adj* sweeping; effective
'**Durch|schlagpa,pier** *n* carbon paper; **~schlagskraft** *fig f* force, impact
'**durchschneiden** *v/t* (*irr*, ***schneiden***, *sep*, *-ge-*, *h*) cut (through)
'**Durchschnitt** *m* average; ***im*** (***über, unter dem***) **~** on an (above, below) average; ***im ~ betragen*** (***verdienen*** *etc*) average
'**durchschnittlich** **1.** *adj* average; ordinary **2.** *adv* on an average
'**Durchschnitts...** *in cpds* average ...
'**Durchschrift** *f* (carbon) copy
'**durch|sehen** *v/t* (*irr*, ***sehen***, *sep*, *-ge-*, *h*) look *or* go through; check; **~setzen** *v/t* (*sep*, *-ge-*, *h*) put (*or* push) *s.th.* through; ***s-n Kopf ~*** have one's way; ***sich ~*** get one's way; be successful; ***sich ~ können*** have authority (***bei*** over)
**durch'setzt** *adj*: ***~ mit*** interspersed with
'**durchsichtig** *adj* transparent (*a. fig*); clear; see-through
'**durchsickern** *v/i* (*sep*, *-ge-*, *sein*) seep through; *fig* leak out
'**durchstarten** *v/i* (*sep*, *-ge-*, *sein*) AVIAT climb and reaccelerate
**durch'stechen** *v/t* (*irr*, ***stechen***, *no -ge-*, *h*) pierce
'**durch|stecken** *v/t* (*sep*, *-ge-*, *h*) stick through; **~stehen** *v/t* (*irr*, ***stehen***, *sep*, *-ge-*, *h*) go through
**durch'stoßen** *v/t* (*irr*, ***stoßen***, *no -ge-*, *h*) break through
'**durchstreichen** *v/t* (*irr*, ***streichen***, *sep*, *-ge-*, *h*) cross out
**durch'suchen** *v/t* (*no -ge-*, *h*) search, F frisk; **Durch'suchung** *f* (-; *-en*) search; **Durch'suchungsbefehl** *m* search warrant
**durch|trieben** [durç'tri:bən] *adj* cunning, sly; **~'wachsen** *adj* GASTR streaky
'**Durchwahl** *f* (-; *no pl*) TEL direct dial(l)ing; '**durchwählen** *v/i* (*sep*, *-ge-*, *h*) TEL dial direct
**durchweg** ['durçvɛk] *adv* without exception
**durch'weicht** *adj* soaked, drenched
**durch'wühlen** *v/t* (*no -ge-*, *h*) rummage through
'**durch|zählen** *v/t* (*sep*, *-ge-*, *h*) count off (*Br* up); **~ziehen** (*irr*, ***ziehen***, *sep*, *-ge-*) **1.** *v/i* (*sein*) pass through **2.** *v/t* (*h*) pull *s.th.* through; *fig* carry *s.th.* through (to the end)
**durch'zucken** *v/t* (*no -ge-*, *h*) flash through
'**Durchzug** *m* (-[*e*]*s*; *no pl*) draft, *Br* draught
**dürfen** ['dʏrfən] **1.** *v/aux* (*irr*, *no -ge-*, *h*) be allowed *or* permitted to *inf*; ***darf ich gehen?*** may I go?; ***ja***(, ***du darfst***) yes, you may; ***du darfst nicht*** you must not, you aren't allowed to; ***dürfte ich ...?*** could I ...?; ***das dürfte genügen*** that should be enough **2.** *v/i* (*irr*, *ge-*, *h*) ***er darf*** (***nicht***) he is (not) allowed to *inf*
**durfte** ['durftə] *pret of* ***dürfen***
**dürftig** ['dʏrftɪç] *adj* poor; scanty
**dürr** [dʏr] *adj* dry; barren, arid; skinny
**Dürre** ['dʏrə] *f* (-; *-n*) drought; (*no pl*) barrenness
**Durst** [durst] *m* (-[*e*]*s*; *no pl*) thirst (***auf*** *acc* for); ***~ haben*** be thirsty
'**durstig** *adj* thirsty
**Dusche** ['duʃə] *f* (-; *-n*) shower
'**duschen** *v/refl and v/i* (*ge-*, *h*) have *or* take a shower
**Düse** ['dy:zə] *f* (-; *-n*) TECH nozzle; jet
'**düsen** F *v/i* (*ge-*, *sein*) jet
'**Düsen|antrieb** *m* jet propulsion; ***mit ~*** jet-propelled; **~flugzeug** *n* jet (plane); **~jäger** *m* MIL jet fighter; **~triebwerk** *n* jet engine
**düster** ['dy:stɐ] *adj* dark, gloomy (*both a. fig*); dim (*light*); *fig* dismal
**Dutzend** ['dutsənt] *n* (*-s*; *-e*) dozen
'**dutzendweise** *adv* by the dozen

**duzen** ['du:tsən] *v/t* (*ge-, h*) use the familiar 'du' with s.o.; ***sich ~*** be on 'du' terms
**DVD** [de:fau'de:] *abbr of* ***Digital Versatile Disk*** DVD; **~-Player** *m* (*-s; -*) DVD player; **~-Rekorder** *m* (*-s; -*) DVD recorder
**Dynamik** [dy'na:mɪk] *f* (*-; no pl*) PHYS dynamics; *fig* dynamism
**dy'namisch** *adj* dynamic
**Dynamit** [dyna'mi:t] *n* (*-s; no pl*) dynamite
**Dynamo** [dy'an:mo] *m* (*-s; -s*) ELECTR dynamo, generator
**D-Zug** ['de:tsu:k] *m* express train

# E

**Ebbe** ['ɛbə] *f* (*-; -n*) ebb, low tide
**eben** ['e:bən] **1.** *adj* even; flat; MATH plane; ***zu ~er Erde*** on the first (*Br* ground) floor **2.** *adv* just; ***an ~ dem Tag*** on that very day; ***so ist es ~*** that's the way it is; ***gerade ~ so*** *or* ***noch*** just barely
**'Ebenbild** *n* image
**ebenbürtig** ['e:bənbʏrtɪç] *adj*: ***j-m ~ sein*** be a match for s.o., be s.o.'s equal
**Ebene** ['e:bənə] *f* (*-; -n*) GEOGR plain; MATH plane; *fig* level
**'ebenerdig** *adj and adv* at street level; on the first (*Br* ground) floor
**'ebenfalls** *adv* as well, too
**'Ebenholz** *n* ebony
**'Ebenmaß** *n* (*-es; no pl*) symmetry; harmony; regularity; **'ebenmäßig** *adj* symmetrical; harmonious; regular
**'ebenso** *adv and cj* just as; as well; ***~ wie*** in the same way as; ***~ gern, ~ gut*** just as well; ***~ sehr, ~ viel*** just as much; ***~ wenig*** just as little *or* few
**Eber** ['e:bɐ] *m* (*-s; -*) ZO boar
**ebnen** ['e:bnən] *v/t* (*ge-, h*) even, level; *fig* smooth
**Echo** ['ɛço] *n* (*-s; -s*) echo; *fig* response
**echt** [ɛçt] *adj* genuine (*a. fig*), real; true; pure; fast (*color*); authentic; F ***~ gut*** real good; **'Echtheit** *f* (*-; no pl*) genuineness; authenticity
**Eckball** ['ɛkbal] *m* SPORT corner (kick)
**Ecke** ['ɛkə] *f* (*-; -n*) corner; edge; SPORT ***lange*** (***kurze***) ***~*** far (near) corner; → ***Eckball***; **eckig** ['ɛkɪç] *adj* square, angular; *fig* awkward
**'Eckzahn** *m* canine tooth
**Economyclass** [i'kɔnəmikla:s] *f* (*-; no pl*) coach (class)
**edel** ['e:dəl] *adj* noble; MIN precious
**'Edelme,tall** *n* precious metal
**'Edelstahl** *m* stainless steel
**'Edelstein** *m* precious stone; gem
**EDV** [e:de:'fau] *abbr of* ***Elektronische Datenverarbeitung*** electronic data processing
**Efeu** ['e:fɔʏ] *m* (*-s; no pl*) BOT ivy
**Effekt** [ɛ'fɛkt] *m* (*-[e]s; -e*) effect
**effektiv** [ɛfɛk'ti:f] **1.** *adj* effective **2.** *adv* actually; **Effektivität** [ɛfɛktivi'tɛ:t] *f* (*-; no pl*) effectiveness
**ef'fektvoll** *adj* effective, striking
**Effet** [ɛ'fe:] *m* (*-s; -s*) SPORT spin
**EG** [e:'ge:] *hist abbr of* ***Europäische Gemeinschaft*** EC, European Community
**egal** [e'ga:l] F *adj*: ***~ ob*** (***warum, wer*** *etc*) no matter if (why, who, *etc*); ***das ist ~*** it doesn't matter; ***das ist mir ~*** I don't care, it's all the same to me
**Egge** ['ɛgə] *f* (*-; -n*), **'eggen** *v/t* (*ge-, h*) AGR harrow
**Egoismus** [ego'ɪsmʊs] *m* (*-; no pl*) ego(t)ism; **Egoist(in)** [ego'ɪst(ɪn)] (*-en; -en/-; -nen*) ego(t)ist; **ego'istisch** *adj* selfish, ego(t)istic(al)
**ehe** ['e:ə] *cj* before; ***nicht ~*** not until
**Ehe** ['e:ə] *f* (*-; -n*) marriage (***mit*** to); **~beratung** *f* marriage counseling (*Br* guidance)
**'Ehe|bruch** *m* adultery; **~frau** *f* wife; **~leute** *pl* married couple
**'ehelich** *adj* conjugal; JUR legitimate
**ehemalig** ['e:əma:lɪç] *adj* former, ex-…
**ehemals** ['e:əma:ls] *adv* formerly
**'Ehemann** *m* husband
**'Ehepaar** *n* (married) couple
**eher** ['e:ɐ] *adv* earlier, sooner; ***je ~, desto lieber*** the sooner the better; ***nicht ~ als*** not until *or* before

'**Ehering** *m* wedding ring
**ehrbar** ['eːɐbaːɐ] *adj* respectable
**Ehre** ['eːrə] *f* (-; *-n*) hono(u)r; ***zu ~n*** (***von***) in hono(u)r of
'**ehren** *v/t* (*ge-*, *h*) hono(u)r; respect
'**ehrenamtlich** *adj* honorary
'**Ehren|bürger** *m* honorary citizen; **~doktor** *m* UNIV honorary doctor; **~gast** *m* guest of hono(u)r; **~kodex** *m* code of hono(u)r; **~mann** *m* man of hono(u)r; **~mitglied** *n* honorary member; **~platz** *m* place of hono(u)r; **~rechte** *pl* civil rights; **~rettung** *f* rehabilitation
'**ehrenrührig** *adj* defamatory
'**Ehren|runde** *f esp* SPORT lap of hono(u)r; **~sache** *f* point of hono(u)r; **~tor** *n*, **~treffer** *m* SPORT consolation goal
'**ehrenwert** *adj* hono(u)rable
'**Ehrenwort** *n* (-[*e*]*s*; *-e*) word of hono(u)r; F **~!** cross my heart!
**ehrerbietig** ['eːɐˀɛɐbiːtɪç] *adj* respectful
**Ehrfurcht** ['eːɐfʊrçt] *f* (-; *no pl*) respect (***vor*** *dat* for); awe (of); ***~ gebietend*** awe-inspiring, awesome; **ehrfürchtig** ['eːɐfʏrçtɪç] *adj* respectful
'**Ehrgefühl** *n* (-[*e*]*s*; *no pl*) sense of hono(u)r
'**Ehrgeiz** *m* ambition; '**ehrgeizig** *adj* ambitious
'**ehrlich** *adj* honest; frank; fair; '**Ehrlichkeit** *f* (-; *no pl*) honesty; fairness
'**Ehrung** *f* (-; *-en*) hono(u)r(ing)
'**ehrwürdig** *adj* venerable
**Ei** [ai] *n* (-[*e*]*s*; *Eier* ['aiɐ]) egg; V *pl* balls
**Eiche** ['aiçə] *f* (-; *-n*) oak(-tree)
**Eichel** ['aiçəl] *f* (-; *-n*) BOT acorn; *card games*: club(s); ANAT glans (penis)
**eichen** ['aiçən] *v/t* (*ge-*, *h*) ga(u)ge
**Eichhörnchen** ['aiçhœrnçən] *n* (*-s*; -) ZO squirrel
**Eid** [ait] *m* (-[*e*]*s*; *-e*) oath; ***e-n ~ ablegen*** take an oath
**Eidechse** ['aidɛksə] *f* (-; *-n*) ZO lizard
**eidesstattlich** ['aidəsʃtatlɪç] *adj*: ***~e Erklärung*** JUR statutory declaration
'**Eidotter** *m*, *n* (egg) yolk
'**Eier|becher** *m* eggcup; **~kuchen** *m* pancake; **~li,kör** *m* eggnog; **~schale** *f* eggshell; **~stock** *m* ANAT ovary; **~uhr** *f* egg timer

**Eifer** ['aifɐ] *m* (*-s*; *no pl*) zeal, eagerness; ***glühender ~*** ardo(u)r
'**Eifersucht** *f* (-; *no pl*) jealousy
'**eifersüchtig** *adj* jealous (***auf*** *acc* of)
**eifrig** *adj* eager, zealous; ardent
'**Eigelb** *n* (-[*e*]*s*; *-e*) (egg) yolk
**eigen** ['aigən] *adj* own, of one's own; peculiar; particular, F fussy; **...eigen** *in cpds staatseigen etc*: ...-owned
'**Eigenart** *f* peculiarity
'**eigenartig** *adj* peculiar; strange
'**Eigenbedarf** *m* personal needs
'**Eigengewicht** *n* dead weight
**eigenhändig** ['aigənhɛndɪç] **1.** *adj* personal **2.** *adv* personally, with one's own hands
'**Eigen|heim** *n* home (of one's own); **~liebe** *f* self-love; **~lob** *n* self-praise
'**eigenmächtig** *adj* arbitrary
'**Eigenname** *m* proper noun
'**Eigennutz** *m* (*-es*; *no pl*) self-interest
**eigennützig** ['aigənnʏtsɪç] *adj* selfish
'**eigens** *adv* (e)specially, expressly
'**Eigenschaft** *f* (-; *-en*) quality; TECH, PHYS, CHEM property; ***in s-r ~ als*** in his capacity as; '**Eigenschaftswort** *n* (-[*e*]*s*; *-wörter*) LING adjective
'**Eigensinn** *m* (-[*e*]*s*; *no pl*) stubbornness; '**eigensinnig** *adj* stubborn, obstinate
**eigentlich** ['aigəntlɪç] **1.** *adj* actual, true, real; exact **2.** *adv* actually, really; originally
'**Eigentor** *n* SPORT own goal (*a. fig*)
'**Eigentum** *n* (-[*e*]*s*; *no pl*) property
**Eigentümer** ['aɪgəntyːmɐ] *m* (*-s*; -), '**Eigentümerin** *f* (-; *-nen*) owner, proprietor (proprietress)
**eigentümlich** ['aigəntyːmlɪç] *adj* peculiar; strange, odd; '**Eigentümlichkeit** *f* (-; *-en*) peculiarity
'**Eigentumswohnung** *f* condominium, F condo, *Br* owner-occupied flat
'**eigenwillig** *adj* wil(l)ful; individual, original (*style etc*)
**eignen** ['aignən] *v/refl* (*ge-*, *h*) ***sich ~ für*** be suited *or* fit for; '**Eignung** *f* (-; *no pl*) suitability; aptitude, qualification
'**Eignungs|prüfung** *f*, **~test** *m* aptitude test
**Eil|bote** ['ailboːtə] *m*: ***durch ~n*** by special delivery; **~brief** *m* special delivery (*Br* express) letter
**Eile** ['ailə] *f* (-; *no pl*) haste, hurry; '**eilen**

*v/i* (*ge-*, *sein*) hurry, hasten, rush; (*ge-*, *h*) be urgent; **'eilig** *adj* hurried, hasty; urgent; ***es ~ haben*** be in a hurry
**Eimer** ['aimɐ] *m* (*-s*; *-*) bucket, pail
**ein** [ain] **1.** *adj* one **2.** *indef art* a, an **3.** *adv*: "**ein/aus**" "on / off"; ***~ und aus gehen*** come and go; ***nicht mehr ~ noch aus wissen*** be at one's wits' end
**einander** [ai'nandɐ] *pron* each other, one another
**'einarbeiten** *v/t* (*sep*, *-ge-*, *h*) train, acquaint *s.o.* with his work, F break *s.o.* in; ***sich ~*** work o.s. in
**'einarmig** ['ainarmɪç] *adj* one-armed
**einäschern** ['ainˀɛʃɐn] *v/t* (*sep*, *-ge-*, *h*) cremate; **Einäscherung** ['ainˀɛʃərʊŋ] *f* (*-*; *-en*) cremation
**'einatmen** *v/t* (*sep*, *-ge-*, *h*) inhale, breathe
**einäugig** ['ainɔʏgɪç] *adj* one-eyed
**'Einbahnstraße** *f* one-way street
**einbalsamieren** ['ainbalzamiːrən] *v/t* (*no -ge-*, *h*) embalm
**'Einband** *m* (*-*[*e*]*s*; *-bände*) binding, cover
**'Einbau** *m* (*-*[*e*]*s*; *-bauten*) installation, fitting; ***~...*** *in cpds ...möbel etc*: built-in ...; **'einbauen** *v/t* (*sep*, *-ge-*, *h*) build in, instal(l), fit
**'einberufen** *v/t* (*irr*, ***rufen***, *sep*, *no -ge-*, *h*) MIL draft, *Br* call up; call (*meeting etc*); **'Einberufung** *f* (*-*; *-en*) MIL draft, *Br* call-up
**'ein|beziehen** *v/t* (*irr*, ***ziehen***, *sep*, *no -ge-*, *h*) include; **~biegen** *v/i* (*irr*, ***biegen***, *sep*, *-ge-*, *sein*) turn (***in*** *acc* into)
**'einbilden** *v/refl* (*sep*, *-ge-*, *h*) imagine; ***sich et. ~ auf*** (*acc*) be conceited about
**'Einbildung** *f* (*-*; *no pl*) imagination, fancy; conceit
**'einblenden** *v/t* (*sep*, *-ge-*, *h*) TV fade in
**'Einblick** *m* insight (***in*** *acc* into)
**'einbrechen** *v/i* (*irr*, ***brechen***, *sep*, *-ge-*, *sein*) collapse; *winter*: set in; ***~ in*** (*acc*) break into, burgle; fall through (the ice); **'Einbrecher** *m* (*-s*; *-*) burglar
**'einbringen** *v/t* (*irr*, ***bringen***, *sep*, *-ge-*, *h*) bring in; yield (*profit etc*)
**'Einbruch** *m* burglary; ***bei ~ der Nacht*** at nightfall
**einbürgern** ['ainbʏrgɐn] *v/t* (*sep*, *-ge-*, *h*) naturalize; ***sich ~*** *fig* come into use
**'Einbürgerung** *f* (*-*; *-en*) naturalization
**'Einbuße** *f* (*-*; *-n*) loss
**'einbüßen** *v/t* (*sep*, *-ge-*, *h*) lose
**eindämmen** ['aindɛmən] *v/t* (*sep*, *-ge-*, *h*) dam (up), *fig a.* get under control
**'eindecken** *fig v/t* (*sep*, *-ge-*, *h*) provide (***mit*** with)
**'eindeutig** ['aindɔʏtɪç] *adj* clear
**'eindrehen** *v/t* (*sep*, *-ge-*, *h*) put *hair* in curlers
**'eindringen** *v/i* (*irr*, ***dringen***, *sep*, *-ge-*, *sein*) ***~ in*** (*acc*) enter (*a. fig*); force one's way into; MIL invade; **'eindringlich** *adj* urgent; **'Eindringling** *m* (*-s*; *-e*) intruder; MIL invader
**'Eindruck** *m* impression; **'eindrücken** *v/t* (*sep*, *-ge-*, *h*) break *or* push in
**'eindrucksvoll** *adj* impressive
**eineiig** ['ainˀaiɪç] *adj* identical (*twins*)
**'einein'halb** *adj* one and a half
**einengen** ['ainˀɛŋən] *v/t* (*sep*, *-ge-*, *h*) confine, restrict
**einer** ['ainɐ], **eine** ['ainə], **ein(e)s** ['ain(ə)s] *indef pron* one
**'Einer** *m* (*-s*; *-*) MATH unit; *rowing*: single sculls
**einerlei** ['ainɐ'lai] *adj*: ***ganz ~*** all the same; ***~ ob*** no matter if; **'Einer'lei** *n*: ***das tägliche ~*** the daily grind *or* rut
**'einer'seits** *adv* on the one hand
**'einfach** *adj* simple; easy; plain; one-way (*Br* single) (*ticket*)
**'Einfachheit** *f* (*-*; *no pl*) simplicity
**einfädeln** ['ainfɛːdəln] *v/t* (*sep*, *-ge-*, *h*) thread; F start, set afoot; MOT merge
**'einfahren** (*irr*, ***fahren***, *sep*, *-ge-*) **1.** *v/t* (*h*) MOT run in; bring in (*harvest*) **2.** *v/i* (*sein*) come in, RAIL *a.* pull in
**'Einfahrt** *f* entrance, way in
**'Einfall** *m* idea; MIL invasion
**'einfallen** *v/i* (*irr*, ***fallen***, *sep*, *-ge-*, *sein*) fall in; collapse; MUS join in; ***~ in*** (*acc*) MIL invade; ***ihm fiel ein, dass*** it came to his mind that; ***mir fällt nichts ein*** I have no ideas; ***es fällt mir nicht ein*** I can't think of it; ***dabei fällt mir ein*** that reminds me; ***was fällt dir ein?*** what's the idea?
**einfältig** ['ainfɛltɪç] *adj* simple-minded; stupid
**Einfa'milienhaus** *n* detached house
**'einfarbig** *adj* solid-colored, *Br* self-coloured
**'ein|fassen** *v/t* (*sep*, *-ge-*, *h*) border; **~fetten** *v/t* (*sep*, *-ge-*, *h*) grease; **~finden** *v/refl* (*irr*, ***finden***, *sep*, *-ge-*, *h*) appear,

E

arrive; **~flechten** *fig v/t* (*irr*, ***flechten***, *sep*, *-ge-*, *h*) work in; **~fliegen** *v/t* (*irr*, ***fliegen***, *sep*, *-ge-*, *h*) fly in; **~fließen** *v/i* (*irr*, ***fließen***, *sep*, *-ge-*, *sein*) *fig* ***et. ~ lassen*** slip s.th. in; **~flößen** *v/t* (*sep*, *-ge-*, *h*) pour (***j-m*** into s.o.'s mouth); *fig* fill with (*awe etc*)

'**Einfluss** *fig m* influence

'**einflussreich** *adj* influential

**einförmig** ['ainfœrmıç] *adj* uniform

'**einfrieren** (*irr*, ***frieren***, *sep*, *-ge-*) **1.** *v/i* (*sein*) freeze (in) **2.** *v/t* (*h*) freeze (*a. fig*)

'**einfügen** *v/t* (*sep*, *-ge-*, *h*) put in; *fig* insert; ***sich ~*** fit in; adjust (o.s.) (***in*** *acc* to); '**Einfügetaste** *f* IT insert key

**einfühlsam** ['ainfy:lza:m] *adj* sympathetic; '**Einfühlungsvermögen** *n* (*-s*; *no pl*) empathy

**Einfuhr** ['ainfu:ɐ] *f* (*-*; *-en*) ECON (*no pl*) importation; import

'**einführen** *v/t* (*sep*, *-ge-*, *h*) introduce; instal(l); ECON import

'**Einfuhrstopp** *m* ECON import ban

'**Einführung** *f* (*-*; *-en*) introduction

'**Einführungs...** *in cpds ...kurs*, *...preis etc*: introductory ...

'**Eingabe** *f* petition; IT input; **~taste** *f* IT enter *or* return key

'**Eingang** *m* entrance; ECON arrival; receipt; '**eingängig** *adj* catchy (*tune etc*)

'**eingangs** *adv* at the beginning

'**eingeben** *v/t* (*irr*, ***geben***, *sep*, *-ge-*, *h*) MED administer (*dat* to); IT feed, enter

'**eingebildet** *adj* imaginary; conceited (***auf*** *acc* of)

'**Eingeborene** *m*, *f* (*-n*; *-n*) native

'**Eingebung** *f* (*-*; *-en*) inspiration; impulse

'**eingefallen** *adj* sunken, hollow

'**eingefleischt** *adj* confirmed

'**eingehen** (*irr*, ***gehen***, *sep*, *-ge-*, *sein*) **1.** *v/i* ECON come in, arrive; BOT, ZO die; *fabric*: shrink; ***~ auf*** (*acc*) agree to; go into (*detail*); listen to *s.o.* **2.** *v/t* enter into (*a contract etc*); make (*a bet*); take (*a risk etc*); **~d** *adj* thorough; detailed

'**eingemacht** *adj* preserved

**eingemeinden** ['aingəmaindən] *v/t* (*sep*, *no -ge-*, *h*) incorporate (***in*** *acc* into)

'**einge|nommen** *adj* partial (***für*** to); prejudiced (***gegen*** against); ***von sich ~*** full of o.s.; **~schlossen** *adj* locked in; trapped; ECON included; **~schnappt** F *adj* in a huff; **~schrieben** *adj* registered; **~spielt** *adj*: (***gut***) ***aufeinander ~ sein*** work well together, be a good team; **~stellt** *adj*: ***~ auf*** (*acc*) prepared for; ***~ gegen*** opposed to

**Eingeweide** ['aingəvaidə] *pl* ANAT intestines, guts

'**Eingeweihte** *m*, *f* (*-n*; *-n*) insider

'**eingewöhnen** *v/refl* (*sep*, *no -ge-*, *h*) ***sich ~ in*** (*acc*) get used to, settle in

'**eingießen** *v/t* (*irr*, ***gießen***, *sep*, *-ge-*, *h*) pour

**eingleisig** ['ainglaizıç] *adj* single-track

'**eingliedern** *v/t* (*sep*, *-ge-*, *h*) integrate

'**Eingliederung** *f* integration

'**ein|graben** *v/t* (*irr*, ***graben***, *sep*, *-ge-*, *h*) bury; **~gra,vieren** *v/t* (*sep*, *no -ge-*, *h*) engrave

'**eingreifen** *v/i* (*irr*, ***greifen***, *sep*, *-ge-*, *h*) step in, interfere; '**Eingriff** *m* intervention, interference; MED operation

'**einhaken** *v/t* (*sep*, *-ge-*, *h*) hook in; ***sich ~*** link arms, take s.o.'s arm

'**Einhalt** *m*: ***~ gebieten*** put a stop (*dat* to); '**einhalten** *v/t* (*irr*, ***halten***, *sep*, *-ge-*, *h*) keep

'**einhängen** (*sep*, *-ge-*, *h*) **1.** *v/t* hang in; TEL hang up (*receiver*); ***sich ~*** → ***einhaken*** **2.** *v/i* TEL hang up

'**einheimisch** *adj* native, local; ECON home, domestic; '**Einheimische** *m*, *f* (*-n*; *-n*) local, native

'**Einheit** *f* (*-*; *-en*) unit; POL unity

'**einheitlich** *adj* uniform; homogeneous

'**Einheits...** *in cpds ...preis etc*: standard

**einhellig** ['ainhɛlıç] *adj* unanimous

'**einholen** *v/t* (*sep*, *-ge-*, *h*) catch up with (*a. fig*); make up for *lost time*; make (*inquiries*) (***über*** *acc* about); seek (*advice*) (***bei*** from); ask for *permission etc*; strike (*sail*); ***~ gehen*** go shopping

'**Einhorn** *n* MYTH unicorn

'**einhüllen** *v/t* (*sep*, *-ge-*, *h*) wrap (up); *fig* shroud

**einig** ['ainıç] *adj*: ***sich ~ sein*** agree; ***sich nicht ~ sein*** disagree, differ

**einige** ['ainıgə] *indef pron* some, a few, several

**einigen** ['ainıgən] *v/t* (*ge-*, *h*) ***sich ~ über*** (*acc*) agree on

**einigermaßen** ['ainıgɐ'ma:sən] *adv* quite, fairly; not too bad

'**einiges** *indef pron* some, something; quite a lot

'**Einigkeit** *f* (-; *no pl*) unity; agreement

'**Einigung** *f* (-; *-en*) agreement, settlement; POL unification

'**einjagen** *v/t* (*sep*, *-ge-*, *h*) ***j-m e-n Schrecken ~*** give s.o. a fright, frighten *or* scare s.o.

**einjährig** ['ainjɛːrɪç] *adj* one-year-old; ***~e Pflanze*** annual

'**einkalku,lieren** *v/t* (*no -ge-*, *h*) take into account, allow for

'**Einkauf** *m* purchase; ***Einkäufe machen*** → ***einkaufen*** 2; '**einkaufen** (*sep*, *-ge-*, *h*) **1.** *v/t* buy, ECON *a.* purchase **2.** *v/i* go shopping

'**Einkaufs...** *in cpds* shopping ...; **~bummel** *m* shopping spree; **~preis** *m* ECON purchase price; **~wagen** *m* grocery *or* shopping cart, *Br* (supermarket) trolley; **~zentrum** *n* (shopping) mall, *Br* shopping centre

'**ein|kehren** *v/i* (*sep*, *-ge-*, *sein*) stop (***in*** *dat* at); **~klammern** *v/t* (*sep*, *-ge-*, *h*) put in brackets

'**Einklang** *m* (-[*e*]*s*; *no pl*) MUS unison; *fig* harmony

'**ein|kleiden** *v/t* (*sep*, *-ge-*, *h*) clothe (*a. fig*); **~klemmen** *v/t* (*sep*, *-ge-*, *h*) squeeze, jam; ***eingeklemmt sein*** be stuck, be jammed; **~kochen** (*sep*, *-ge-*) **1.** *v/t* (*h*) preserve **2.** *v/i* (*sein*) boil down

'**Einkommen** *n* (*-s*; -) income; **~steuererklärung** *f* income-tax return

'**einkreisen** *v/t* (*sep*, *-ge-*, *h*) encircle, surround

**Einkünfte** ['ainkʏnftə] *pl* income

'**einladen** *v/t* (*irr*, ***laden***, *sep*, *-ge-*, *h*) invite; load; **~d** *adj* inviting

'**Einladung** *f* (-; *-en*) invitation

'**Einlage** *f* (-; *-n*) ECON investment; MED arch support; THEA, MUS interlude

**Einlass** ['ainlas] *m* (*-es*; *no pl*) admission, admittance; '**einlassen** *v/t* (*irr*, ***lassen***, *sep*, *-ge-*, *h*) let in; run (*a bath*); ***sich ~ auf*** (*acc*) get involved in; let o.s. in for; agree to; ***sich mit j-m ~*** get involved with s.o.

'**Einlauf** *m* SPORT finish; MED enema

'**einlaufen** (*irr*, ***laufen***, *sep*, *-ge-*) **1.** *v/i* (*sein*) come in (*a.* SPORT); *water*: run in; MAR enter port; *fabric*: shrink **2.** *v/t* (*h*) break *new shoes* in; ***sich ~*** warm up

'**einleben** *v/refl* (*sep*, *-ge-*, *h*) settle in

'**einlegen** *v/t* (*sep*, *-ge-*, *h*) put in; set (*hair*); GASTR pickle; MOT change into

'**Einlegesohle** *f* insole

'**einleiten** *v/t* (*sep*, *-ge-*, *h*) start; introduce; MED induce; TECH dump, discharge (*sewage*); **~d** *adj* introductory

'**Einleitung** *f* introduction

'**ein|lenken** *v/i* (*sep*, *-ge-*, *h*) come round; **~leuchten** *v/i* (*sep*, *-ge-*, *h*) be evident, be obvious; ***das leuchtet mir*** (***nicht***) ***ein*** that makes (doesn't make) sense to me; **~liefern** *v/t* (*sep*, *-ge-*, *h*) take (***ins Gefängnis*** to prison; ***in die Klinik*** to [the] hospital); **~lösen** *v/t* (*sep*, *-ge-*, *h*) redeem; cash (*check*); **~machen** *v/t* (*sep*, *-ge-*, *h*) preserve

'**einmal** *adv* once; some *or* one day, sometime; ***auf ~*** suddenly; at the same time, at once; ***noch ~*** once more *or* again; ***noch ~ so ...*** (***wie***) twice as ... (as); ***es war ~*** once (upon a time) there was; ***haben Sie schon ~ ...?*** have you ever ...?; ***schon ~ dort gewesen sein*** have been there before; ***nicht ~*** not even

'**Einmal...** *in cpds* disposable ...

**Einmal'eins** *n* (-; *no pl*) multiplication table

**einmalig** ['ainmaːlɪç] *adj* single; *fig* unique; F fabulous

'**Einmann...** *in cpds* one-man ...

'**Einmarsch** *m* entry; MIL invasion

'**einmar,schieren** *v/i* (*no -ge-*, *sein*) march in; ***~ in*** (*acc*) MIL invade

'**einmischen** *v/refl* (*sep*, *-ge-*, *h*) meddle (***in*** *acc* in, with), interfere (with)

'**Einmündung** *f* junction

**einmütig** ['ainmyːtɪç] *adj* unanimous

'**Einmütigkeit** *f* (-; *no pl*) unanimity

**Einnahmen** ['ainnaːmən] *pl* takings, receipts; '**einnehmen** *v/t* (*irr*, ***nehmen***, *sep*, *-ge-*, *h*) take (*a.* MIL); earn, make; '**einnehmend** *adj* engaging

'**einnicken** *v/i* (*sep*, *-ge-*, *sein*) doze off

'**einnisten** *v/refl* (*sep*, *-ge-*, *h*) ***sich bei j-m ~*** park o.s. on s.o.

'**Einöde** *f* (-; *-n*) desert, wilderness

'**ein|ordnen** *v/t* (*sep*, *-ge-*, *h*) put in its proper place; file; ***sich ~*** MOT get in lane; **~packen** *v/t* (*sep*, *-ge-*, *h*) pack (up); wrap up; **~parken** *v/t and v/i* (*sep*, *-ge-*, *h*) park (between two cars); **~pferchen** *v/t* (*sep*, *-ge-*, *h*) pen in; coop up; **~pflanzen** *v/t* (*sep*, *-ge-*, *h*) plant; *fig* implant (*a.* MED); **~planen** *v/t* (*sep*, *-ge-*, *h*) allow for; **~prägen** *v/t* (*sep*, *-ge-*, *h*) impress; ***sich et. ~*** keep s.th. in mind; memorize s.th.; **~quartieren** F *v/t* (*no -ge-*, *h*) put *s.o.* up (***bei j-m*** at s.o.'s place); ***sich ~ bei*** (*dat*) move in with; **~rahmen** *v/t* (*sep*, *-ge-*, *h*) frame; **~räumen** *v/t* (*sep*, *-ge-*, *h*) put away; furnish; *fig* grant, concede; **~reden** (*sep*, *-ge-*, *h*) **1.** *v/t*: ***j-m et. ~*** talk s.o. into (believing) s.th. **2.** *v/i*: ***auf j-n ~*** keep on at s.o.; **~reiben** *v/t* (*irr*, ***reiben***, *sep*, *-ge-*, *h*) rub; **~reichen** *v/t* (*sep*, *-ge-*, *h*) hand *or* send in; **~reihen** *v/t* (*sep*, *-ge-*, *h*) place (among); ***sich ~*** take one's place

**einreihig** ['ainraiiç] *adj* single-breasted

'**Einreise** *f* entry (*a. in cpds*)

'**einreisen** *v/i* (*sep*, *-ge-*, *sein*) enter (***in ein Land*** a country)

'**ein|reißen** (*irr*, ***reißen***, *sep*, *-ge-*) **1.** *v/t* (*h*) tear; pull down **2.** *v/i* (*sein*) tear; *fig* spread; **~renken** *v/t* (*sep*, *-ge-*, *h*) MED set; *fig* straighten out

'**einrichten** *v/t* (*sep*, *-ge-*, *h*) furnish; establish; arrange; ***sich ~*** furnish one's home; ***sich ~ auf*** (*acc*) prepare for; '**Einrichtung** *f* (-; *-en*) furnishings; fittings; TECH installation(s), facilities; institution, facility

'**einrücken** (*sep*, *-ge-*) **1.** *v/i* (*sein*) MIL join the forces; march in **2.** *v/t* (*h*) PRINT indent

**eins** [ains] *pron and adj* one; one thing; ***es ist alles ~*** it's all the same (thing)

**Eins** *f* (-; *-en*) one; *grade*: excellent, A

**einsam** ['ainza:m] *adj* lonely, lonesome; solitary; '**Einsamkeit** *f* (-; *no pl*) loneliness; solitude

'**einsammeln** *v/t* (*sep*, *-ge-*, *h*) collect

'**Einsatz** *m* TECH inset, insert; stake(s) (*a. fig*); MUS entry; *fig* effort(s), zeal; use, employment; MIL action, mission; deployment; ***im ~*** in action; ***unter ~ des Lebens*** at the risk of one's life

'**einsatz|bereit** *adj* ready for action; **~freudig** *adj* dynamic, zealous

'**einschalten** *v/t* (*sep*, *-ge-*, *h*) ELECTR switch *or* turn on; call *s.o.* in; ***sich ~*** step in; '**Einschaltquote** *f* TV rating

'**ein|schärfen** *v/t* (*sep*, *-ge-*, *h*) urge (***j-m et.*** s.o. to do s.th.); **~schätzen** *v/t* (*sep*, *-ge-*, *h*) estimate; judge, rate; ***falsch ~*** misjudge; **~schenken** *v/t* (*sep*, *-ge-*, *h*) pour (out); **~schicken** *v/t* (*sep*, *-ge-*, *h*) send in; **~schieben** *v/t* (*irr*, ***schieben***, *sep*, *-ge-*, *h*) slip in; insert

**einschl.** *abbr of* ***einschließlich*** incl., including

'**ein|schlafen** *v/i* (*irr*, ***schlafen***, *sep*, *-ge-*, *sein*) fall asleep, go to sleep; **~schläfern** ['ainʃlɛ:fɐn] *v/t* (*sep*, *-ge-*, *h*) put to sleep

'**Einschlag** *m* strike, impact; *fig* touch

'**einschlagen** (*irr*, ***schlagen***, *sep*, *-ge-*, *h*) **1.** *v/t* knock in (*or* out); break (in), smash; wrap up; take (*road etc*); turn (*wheels*); → ***Laufbahn* 2.** *v/i lightning etc*: strike; *fig* be a success

**einschlägig** ['ainʃlɛ:gıç] *adj* relevant

'**ein|schleusen** *fig v/t* (*sep*, *-ge-*, *h*) infiltrate (***in*** *acc* into); **~schließen** *v/t* (*irr*, ***schließen***, *sep*, *-ge-*, *h*) lock in *or* up; enclose; MIL surround, encircle; *fig* include; **~schließlich** *prp* (*gen*) including, … included; **~schmeicheln** *v/refl* (*sep*, *-ge-*, *h*) ***sich ~ bei*** ingratiate o.s. with; **~schnappen** *v/i* (*sep*, *-ge-*, *sein*) snap shut; *fig* go into a huff; → ***eingeschnappt***

'**einschneidend** *fig adj* drastic; far-reaching; '**Einschnitt** *m* cut; notch; *fig* break

'**einschränken** *v/t* (*sep*, *-ge-*, *h*) restrict, reduce (*both*: ***auf*** *acc* to); cut down on; ***sich ~*** economize; '**Einschränkung** *f* (-; *-en*) restriction, reduction, cut; ***ohne ~*** without reservation

'**Einschreibebrief** *m* registered letter

'**einschreiben** *v/t* (*irr*, ***schreiben***, *sep*, *-ge-*, *h*) enter; book; enrol(l) (*a.* MIL); ***(sich) ~ lassen (für)*** enrol(l) (o.s.) (for)

'**einschreiten** *fig v/i* (*irr*, ***schreiten***, *sep*, *-ge-*, *sein*) step in, intervene; ***~ (gegen)*** take (legal) measures (against)

'**einschüchtern** *v/t* (*sep*, *-ge-*, *h*) intimidate; bully; '**Einschüchterung** *f* (-; *-en*) intimidation

'**einschulen** *v/t* (*sep*, *-ge-*, *h*) ***eingeschult werden*** start school

'**Einschuss** *m* bullet hole

'**einschweißen** *v/t* (*sep*, *-ge-*, *h*) shrink-wrap

'**einsegnen** *v/t* (*sep*, *-ge-*, *h*) REL consecrate; confirm; '**Einsegnung** *f* (-; *-en*) REL consecration; confirmation

'**einsehen** *v/t* (*irr*, ***sehen***, *sep*, *-ge-*, *h*) see, realize; ***das sehe ich nicht ein!*** I don't see why!; '**Einsehen** *n*: ***ein ~ ha-***

***ben*** show some understanding
**'einseifen** *v/t* (*sep*, *-ge-*, *h*) soap; lather; F *fig* ***j-n ~*** take s.o. for a ride
**einseitig** ['ainzaitɪç] *adj* one-sided; MED, POL, JUR unilateral
**'einsenden** *v/t* ([*irr*, ***senden***,] *sep*, *-ge-*, *h*) send in; **'Einsendeschluss** *m* closing date (for entries)
**'einsetzen** (*sep*, *-ge-*, *h*) **1.** *v/t* put in, insert; appoint; use, employ; TECH put into service; ECON invest, stake; bet; risk; ***sich ~*** try hard, make an effort; ***sich ~ für*** stand up for **2.** *v/i* set in, start
**'Einsicht** *f* (-; *-en*) insight; (*no pl*) understanding; ***zur ~ kommen*** listen to reason; ***~ nehmen in*** (*acc*) take a look at; **'einsichtig** *adj* understanding; reasonable
**'Einsiedler** *m* (*-s*; -) hermit
**einsilbig** ['ainzɪlbɪç] *adj* monosyllabic; *fig* taciturn
**'ein|spannen** *v/t* (*sep*, *-ge-*, *h*) harness; TECH clamp, fix; F rope *s.o.* in; **~sparen** *v/t* (*sep*, *-ge-*, *h*) save, economize on; **~sperren** *v/t* (*sep*, *-ge-*, *h*) lock *or* shut up; **~spielen** *v/t* (*sep*, *-ge-*, *h*) bring in; ***sich ~*** warm up; *fig* get going; → ***eingespielt***
**'Einspielergebnisse** *pl film*: box office returns
**'einspringen** *v/i* (*irr*, ***springen***, *sep*, *-ge-*, *sein*) ***für j-n ~*** take s.o.'s place
**'Einspritz...** *in cpds* MOT fuel-injection
**'Einspruch** *m* objection (*a.* JUR), protest; POL veto; appeal
**einspurig** ['ainʃpu:rɪç] *adj* RAIL single-track; MOT single-lane
**einst** [ainst] *adv* once, at one time
**'Einstand** *m* start; *tennis*: deuce
**'ein|stecken** *v/t* (*sep*, *-ge-*, *h*) pocket (*a. fig*); ELECTR plug in; mail, post; *fig* take; **~stehen** *v/i* (*irr*, ***stehen***, *sep*, *-ge-*, *h*) ***~ für*** stand up for; **~steigen** *v/i* (*irr*, ***steigen***, *sep*, *-ge-*, *sein*) get in; get on (*bus etc*); ***alles ~!*** RAIL all aboard!; **~stellen** *v/t* (*sep*, *-ge-*, *h*) engage, employ, hire; give up; stop; SPORT equal; TECH adjust (***auf*** *acc* to); *radio*: tune in (to); OPT, PHOT focus (on); ***die Arbeit ~*** (go on) strike, walk out; ***das Feuer ~*** MIL cease fire; ***sich ~ auf*** (*acc*) adjust to; be prepared for
**'Einstellung** *f* attitude (***zu*** towards); employment; cessation; TECH adjustment; OPT, PHOT focus(s)ing; *film*: take
**'Einstellungsgespräch** *n* interview
**Einstieg** ['ainʃti:k] *m* (-[*e*]*s*; *-e*) entrance, entry (*a.* POL, ECON)
**'Einstiegsdroge** *f* gateway drug
**einstig** ['ainstɪç] *adj* former, one-time
**'einstimmen** *v/i* (*sep*, *-ge-*, *h*) MUS join in
**einstimmig** ['ainʃtɪmɪç] *adj* unanimous
**einstöckig** ['ainʃtœkɪç] *adj* one-storied, *Br* one-storey(ed)
**'ein|stu,dieren** *v/t* (*no -ge-*, *h*) THEA rehearse; **~stufen** *v/t* (*sep*, *-ge-*, *h*) grade, rate
**einstufig** ['ainʃtu:fɪç] *adj* single-stage
**'Einstufungsprüfung** *f* placement test
**'Einsturz** *m*, **'einstürzen** *v/i* (*sep*, *-ge-*, *sein*) collapse
**'einst'weilen** *adv* for the present
**einstweilig** ['ainstvailɪç] *adj* temporary
**'ein|tauschen** *v/t* (*sep*, *-ge-*, *h*) exchange (***gegen*** for); **~teilen** *v/t* (*sep*, *-ge-*, *h*) divide (***in*** *acc* into); organize
**einteilig** ['aintailɪç] *adj* one-piece
**'Einteilung** *f* (-; *-en*) division; organization; arrangement
**eintönig** ['aintø:nɪç] *adj* monotonous
**'Eintönigkeit** *f* (-; *no pl*) monotony
**'Eintopf** *m* GASTR stew
**'Eintracht** *f* (-; *no pl*) harmony, unity
**'einträchtig** *adj* harmonious, peaceful
**Eintrag** ['aintra:k] *m* (-[*e*]*s*; *Einträge* ['aintrɛ:gə]) entry (*a.* ECON), registration; **'eintragen** *v/t* (*irr*, ***tragen***, *sep*, *-ge-*, *h*) enter (***in*** *acc* in); register (***bei*** with); enrol(l) (with); *fig* earn; ***sich ~*** register, *hotel*: *a.* check in
**einträglich** ['aintrɛ:klɪç] *adj* profitable
**'ein|treffen** *v/i* (*irr*, ***treffen***, *sep*, *-ge-*, *sein*) arrive; happen; come true; **~treiben** *fig v/t* (*irr*, ***treiben***, *sep*, *-ge-*, *h*) collect; **~treten** (*irr*, ***treten***, *sep*, *-ge-*) **1.** *v/i* (*sein*) enter; happen, take place; ***~ für*** stand up for, support; ***~ in*** (*acc*) join (*club etc*) **2.** *v/t* (*h*) kick in (*door etc*); ***sich et. ~*** run s.th. into one's foot
**'Eintritt** *m* entry; admission; ***~ frei!*** admission free!; ***~ verboten!*** keep out!
**'Eintritts|geld** *n* entrance *or* admission (fee); **~karte** *f* (admission) ticket
**'einüben** *v/t* (*sep*, *-ge-*, *h*) practise; rehearse
**'einverstanden** *adj*: ***~ sein*** agree (***mit*** to); ***~!*** agreed!; **'Einverständnis** *n* (*-ses*; *no pl*) agreement

**Einwand** ['ainvant] *m* (-[*e*]*s*; *Einwände* ['ainvɛndə]) objection (***gegen*** to)
'**Einwanderer** *m*, '**Einwanderin** *f* immigrant; '**einwandern** *v/t* (*sep*, *-ge-*, *sein*) immigrate; '**Einwanderung** *f* immigration
'**einwandfrei** *adj* perfect, faultless
**einwärts** ['ainvɛrts] *adv* inward(s)
'**Einweg...** *...rasierer*, *...spritze etc*: disposable; **~flasche** *f* non-returnable bottle; **~packung** *f* throwaway pack
'**einweichen** *v/t* (*sep*, *-ge-*, *h*) soak
'**einweihen** *v/t* (*sep*, *-ge-*, *h*) dedicate, *Br* inaugurate; ***j-n ~ in*** (*acc*) F let s.o. in on; '**Einweihung** *f* (-; *-en*) dedication, *Br* inauguration
'**einweisen** *v/t* (*irr*, ***weisen***, *sep*, *-ge-*, *h*) ***j-n ~ in*** (*acc*) send (*esp* JUR commit) s.o. to; instruct s.o. in, brief s.o. on
'**einwenden** *v/t* ([*irr*, ***wenden***,] *sep*, *-ge-*, *h*) object (***gegen*** to)
'**Einwendung** *f* (-; *-en*) objection
'**einwerfen** *v/t* (*irr*, ***werfen***, *sep*, *-ge-*, *h*) throw in (*a. fig*, SPORT *a. v/i*); break (*window*); mail, *Br* post; insert (*coin*)
'**einwickeln** *v/t* (*sep*, *-ge-*, *h*) wrap (up); F take *s.o.* in
'**Einwickelpa,pier** *n* wrapping-paper
**einwilligen** ['ainvɪlɪgən] *v/i* (*sep*, *-ge-*, *h*) consent (***in*** *acc* to), agree (to)
'**Einwilligung** *f* (-; *-en*) consent (***in*** *acc* to), agreement
'**einwirken** *v/i* (*sep*, *-ge-*, *h*) **~ *auf*** (*acc*) act (up)on; *fig* work on *s.o.*
'**Einwirkung** *f* effect, influence
**Einwohner** ['ainvo:nɐ] *m* (*-s*; -), '**Einwohnerin** *f* (-; *-nen*) inhabitant; '**Einwohnermeldeamt** *n* registration office
'**Einwurf** *m* slot; SPORT throw-in
'**Einzahl** *f* (-; *no pl*) LING singular
'**einzahlen** *v/t* (*sep*, *-ge-*, *h*) pay in
'**Einzahlung** *f* payment, deposit
**einzäunen** ['aintsɔynən] *v/t* (*sep*, *-ge-*, *h*) fence in
**Einzel** ['aintsəl] *n* (*-s*; -) *tennis*: singles
'**Einzel...** *in cpds ...bett*, *...zimmer etc*: single ...; **~fall** *m* special case; **~gänger** ['aintsəlgɛŋɐ] *m* (*-s*; -) F loner; **~haft** *f* solitary confinement; **~handel** *m* retail trade; **~händler** *m* retailer; **~haus** *n* detached house
'**Einzelheit** *f* (-; *-en*) detail
'**einzeln** *adj* single; odd (*shoe etc*); ***Einzelne*** *pl* several, some; ***der Einzelne*** the individual; **~ *eintreten*** enter one at a time; **~ *angeben*** specify; ***im Einzelnen*** in detail; ***jeder Einzelne*** each and every one
'**einziehen** (*irr*, ***ziehen***, *sep*, *-ge-*) **1.** *v/t* (*h*) draw in; *esp* TECH retract; duck; strike (*sail etc*); MIL draft, *Br* call up; confiscate; withdraw (*license etc*); make (*inquiries*) **2.** *v/i* (*sein*) move in; march in; soak in
**einzig** ['aintsɪç] *adj* only; single; ***kein Einziger ...*** not a single ...; ***das Einzige*** the only thing; ***der*** (***die***) ***Einzige*** the only one; **~artig** *adj* unique, singular
'**Einzug** *m* moving in; entry
**Eis** [ais] *n* (*-es*; *no pl*) ice; GASTR ice cream; **~ *am Stiel*** ice lolly; **~bahn** *f* skating rink; **~bär** *m* ZO polar bear; **~becher** *m* sundae; **~bein** *n* GASTR (pickled) pork knuckles; **~berg** *m* iceberg; **~brecher** *m* (*-s*; -) MAR icebreaker; **~diele** *f* ice-cream parlo(u)r
**Eisen** ['aizən] *n* (*-s*; -) iron
'**Eisenbahn** *f* railroad, *Br* railway; train set; **Eisenbahner** ['aizənba:nɐ] *m* (*-s*; -) railroadman, *Br* railwayman
'**Eisenbahnwagen** *m* (railroad) car, *Br* coach, railway carriage
'**Eisen|erz** *n* iron ore; **~gießerei** *f* iron foundry; **~hütte** *f* TECH ironworks
'**Eisenwaren** *pl* hardware, ironware; **~handlung** *f* hardware store, *Br* ironmonger's
**eisern** ['aizɐn] *adj* iron (*a. fig*), of iron
'**eisgekühlt** *adj* iced
'**Eishockey** *n* hockey, *Br* ice hockey
**eisig** ['aizɪç] *adj* icy (*a. fig*)
'**eis'kalt** *adj* ice-cold
'**Eiskunst|lauf** *m* (-[*e*]*s*; *no pl*) figure skating; **~läufer**(**in**) figure skater
'**Eis|meer** *n* polar sea; **~re,vue** *f* ice show; **~schnelllauf** *m* speed skating; **~scholle** *f* ice floe; **~verkäufer** *m* iceman; **~würfel** *m* ice cube; **~zapfen** *m* icicle; **~zeit** *f* (-; *no pl*) GEOL ice age
**eitel** ['aitəl] *adj* vain; '**Eitelkeit** *f* (-; *no pl*) vanity
**Eiter** ['aitɐ] *m* (*-s*; *no pl*) MED pus
'**Eiterbeule** *f* MED abscess, boil
'**eitern** *v/i* (*ge-*, *h*) MED fester
**eitrig** ['aitrɪç] *adj* MED purulent, festering
'**Eiweiß** *n* (*-es*; *no pl*) white of egg; BIOL

protein

'**eiweiß|arm** *adj* low in protein, low-protein; **~reich** *adj* rich in protein, high-protein

'**Eizelle** *f* BIOL egg cell, ovum

**Ekel** ['e:kəl] **1.** *m* (*-s; no pl*) disgust (***vor*** *dat* at), loathing (for); ***~ erregend*** → ***ekelhaft*** **2.** F *n* (*-s;* -) beast; **ekelerregend** *adj* → ***ekelhaft***

'**ekelhaft**, '**ek(e)lig** *adj* sickening, disgusting, repulsive

'**ekeln** *v/refl and v/impers* (*ge-, h*) ***ich ekle mich davor*** it makes me sick

**Ekstase** [ɛk'sta:zə] *f* (*-; -n*) ecstasy

**Elan** [e'la:n] *m* (*-s; no pl*) vigo(u)r

**elastisch** [e'lastɪʃ] *adj* elastic, flexible

**Elch** [ɛlç] *m* (*-[e]s; -e*) ZO elk; moose

**Elefant** [ele'fant] *m* (*-en; -en*) ZO elephant; **Ele'fantenhochzeit** F *f* ECON jumbo merger

**elegant** [ele'gant] *adj* elegant

**Eleganz** [ele'gants] *f* (*-; no pl*) elegance

**Elektriker** [e'lɛktrɪkɐ] *m* (*-s;* -) electrician; **elektrisch** [e'lɛktrɪʃ] *adj* electrical; electric; **elektrisieren** [elɛktri'zi:rən] *v/t* (*no -ge-, h*) electrify

**Elektrizität** [elɛktritsi'tɛ:t] *f* (*-; no pl*) electricity; **Elektrizi'tätswerk** *n* (electric) power station

**Elektrogerät** [e'lɛktrogərɛ:t] *n* electric appliance

**Elektronik** [elɛk'tro:nɪk] *f* electronics; electronic system; **elektronisch** [elɛk'tro:nɪʃ] *adj* electronic

**E'lektrora,sierer** *m* (*-s;* -) electric razor

**Elektro|'technik** *f* electrical engineering; **~'techniker** *m* electrical engineer

**Element** [ele'mɛnt] *n* (*-[e]s; -e*) element

**elementar** [elemɛn'ta:ɐ] *adj* elementary

**elend** ['e:lɛnt] *adj* miserable

'**Elend** *n* (*-s; no pl*) misery

'**Elendsviertel** *n* slum

**elf** [ɛlf] *adj* eleven

**Elf** *f* (*-; -en*) eleven; *soccer:* team

**Elfe** ['ɛlfə] *f* (*-; -n*) elf, fairy

'**Elfenbein** *n* ivory

**Elf'meter** *m* (*-s;* -) *soccer:* penalty; **~punkt** *m* penalty spot; **~schießen** *n* penalty shoot-out

'**elfte** *adj* eleventh

**Elite** [e'li:tə] *f* (*-; -n*) elite

**Ellbogen** ['ɛlbo:gən] *m* ANAT elbow

**Elster** ['ɛlstɐ] *f* (*-; -n*) ZO magpie

**elterlich** ['ɛltɐlɪç] *adj* parental

**Eltern** ['ɛltɐn] *pl* parents

'**Elternhaus** *n* (one's parents') home

'**elternlos** *adj* orphan(ed)

'**Eltern|teil** *m* parent; **~vertretung** *f appr* Parent-Teacher Association; **~zeit** *f* parental leave

**Email** [e'mai] *n* (*-s; -s*), **Emaille** [e'maljə] *f* (*-; -n*) enamel

**Emanzipation** [emantsipa'tsjo:n] *f* (*-; -en*) emancipation; women's lib (-eration); **emanzipieren** [emantsi'pi:rən] *v/refl* (*no -ge-, h*) become emancipated

**Embargo** [ɛm'bargo] *n* (*-s; -s*) ECON embargo

**Embolie** [ɛmbo'li:] *f* (*-; -n*) MED embolism

**Embryo** ['ɛmbryo] *m* (*-s; -en* [ɛmbry'o:nən]) BIOL embryo

**Emigrant** [emi'grant] *m* (*-en; -en*), **Emi'grantin** *f* (*-; -nen*) emigrant, *esp* POL refugee; **Emigration** [emigra'tsjo:n] *f* (*-; -en*) emigration; ***in der ~*** in exile; **emigrieren** [emi'gri:rən] *v/i* (*no -ge-, sein*) emigrate

**Emission** [emɪ'sjo:n] *f* (*-; -en*) PHYS emission; ECON issue

**empfahl** [ɛm'pfa:l] *pret of* ***empfehlen***

**Empfang** [ɛm'pfaŋ] *m* (*-[e]s; Empfänge* [ɛm'pfɛŋə]) reception (*a. radio, hotel*), welcome; receipt (***nach, bei*** on)

**emp'fangen** *v/t* (*irr,* ***fangen****, no -ge-, h*) receive; welcome; **Emp'fänger(in)** (*-s; -/-; -nen*) receiver (*m a. radio*); addressee

**emp'fänglich** *adj* susceptible (***für*** to)

**Empfängnis** [ɛm'pfɛŋnɪs] *f* (*-; no pl*) MED conception; **~verhütung** *f* MED contraception, birth control

**Emp'fangs|bescheinigung** *f* receipt; **~dame** *f* receptionist

**empfehlen** [ɛm'pfe:lən] *v/t* (*irr, no -ge-, h*) recommend; **emp'fehlenswert** *adj* advisable; **Emp'fehlung** *f* (*-; -en*) recommendation

**empfinden** [ɛm'pfɪndən] *v/t* (*irr,* ***finden****, no -ge-, h*) feel (***als*** … to be …); **empfindlich** [ɛm'pfɪntlɪç] *adj* sensitive (***für, gegen*** to) (*a.* PHOT, CHEM); tender, delicate; touchy; irritable (*a.* MED); severe (*punishment etc*); ***~e Stelle*** sore spot

**Emp'findlichkeit** *f* (*-; -en*) sensitivity;

PHOT speed; delicacy; touchiness
**empfindsam** [ɛm'pfɪntza:m] *adj* sensitive
**Emp'findung** *f* (-; *-en*) sensation; perception; feeling, emotion
**empfohlen** [ɛm'pfo:lən] *pp of* ***empfehlen***
**empor** [ɛm'po:ɐ] *adv* up, upward(s)
**empören** [ɛm'pø:rən] *v/t* (*no -ge-, h*) outrage; shock; ***sich ~*** (***über*** *acc*) be outraged *or* shocked (at); **~d** *adj* shocking, outrageous
**Emporkömmling** [ɛm'po:ɐkœmlɪŋ] *contp m* (*-s*; *-e*) upstart
**empört** [ɛm'pø:ɐt] *adj* indignant (***über*** *acc* at), shocked (at); **Em'pörung** *f* (-; *no pl*) indignation
**Ende** ['ɛndə] *n* (*-s*; *no pl*) end; *film*: ending; ***am ~*** at the end; in the end, finally; ***zu ~*** over; *time*: up; ***zu ~ gehen*** come to an end; ***zu ~ lesen*** finish reading; ***er ist ~ zwanzig*** he is in his late twenties; ***~ Mai*** at the end of May; ***~ der achtziger Jahre*** in the late eighties; *radio*: ***~!*** over!; **'enden** *v/i* (*ge-, h*) (come to an) end; stop, finish; F ***~ als*** end up as
**'Endergebnis** *n* final result
**'endgültig** *adj* final, definitive
**Endlagerung** ['ɛntla:gərʊŋ] *f* final disposal (*of radioactive waste*)
**'endlich** *adv* finally, at last
**'endlos** *adj* endless
**'End|runde** *f*, **~spiel** *n* SPORT final(s); **~spurt** *m* SPORT final spurt (*a. fig*); **~stati,on** *f* RAIL terminus, terminal; **~summe** *f* (sum) total
**'Endung** *f* (-; *-en*) LING ending
**Energie** [enɛr'gi:] *f* (-; *-n*) energy; TECH, ELECTR power; ***~sparen*** *n* energy saving, conservation of energy
**ener'giebewusst** *adj* energy-conscious
**Ener'giekrise** *f* energy crisis
**ener'gielos** *adj* lacking in energy
**Ener'gie|quelle** *f* source of energy; **~versorgung** *f* power supply
**energisch** [e'nɛrgɪʃ] *adj* energetic, vigorous
**eng** [ɛŋ] *adj* narrow; tight; cramped; *fig* close; ***~ beieinander*** close(ly) together
**Engagement** [ã̃gaʒə'mã:] *n* (*-s*; *-s*) THEA *etc* engagement; POL commitment; **engagieren** [ãga'ʒi:rən] *v/t* (*no -ge-, h*) engage; ***sich ~ für*** be very involved in; **engagiert** [ãga'ʒi:ɐt] *adj* involved, committed
**Enge** ['ɛŋə] *f* (-; *no pl*) narrowness; cramped conditions; ***in die ~ treiben*** drive into a corner
**Engel** ['ɛŋəl] *m* (-s; -) angel
**'England** England; **Engländer** ['ɛŋlɛndɐ] *m* (*-s*; -) Englishman; ***die ~*** *pl* the English; **Engländerin** ['ɛŋlɛndərɪn] *f* (-; *-nen*) Englishwoman
**'englisch** *adj* English; ***auf Englisch*** in English
**'Englischunterricht** *m* English lesson(s) *or* class(es); teaching of English
**'Engpass** *m* bottleneck (*a. fig*)
**engstirnig** ['ɛŋʃtɪrnɪç] *adj* narrow-minded
**Enkel** ['ɛŋkəl] *m* (*-s*; -) grandchild; grandson
**'Enkelin** *f* (-; *-nen*) granddaughter
**enorm** [e'nɔrm] *adj* enormous; F terrific
**Ensemble** [ã'sã:bl] *n* (*-s*; *-s*) THEA company; cast
**entarten** [ɛnt'ʔa:ɐtən] *v/i* (*no -ge-, sein*), **ent'artet** *adj* degenerate; **Ent'artung** *f* (-; *-en*) degeneration
**entbehren** [ɛnt'be:rən] *v/t* (*no -ge-, h*) do without; spare; miss; **entbehrlich** [ɛnt'be:ɐlɪç] *adj* dispensable; superfluous; **Ent'behrung** *f* (-; *-en*) want, privation
**ent'binden** (*irr*, ***binden***, *no -ge-, h*) **1.** *v/i* MED have the baby **2.** *v/t*: ***j-n ~ von*** *fig* relieve s.o. of; ***entbunden werden von*** MED give birth to
**Ent'bindung** *f* (-; *-en*) MED delivery
**Ent'bindungsstati,on** *f* MED maternity ward
**entblößen** [ɛnt'blø:sən] *v/t* (*no -ge-, h*) bare, uncover
**ent'decken** *v/t* (*no -ge-, h*) discover
**Ent'decker** *m* (*-s*; -), **Ent'deckerin** *f* (-; *-nen*) discoverer
**Ent'deckung** *f* (-; *-en*) discovery
**Ente** ['ɛntə] *f* (-; *-n*) zo duck; F *fig* hoax
**ent'ehren** *v/t* (*no -ge-, h*) dishono(u)r
**enteignen** [ɛnt'ʔaignən] *v/t* (*no -ge-, h*) expropriate; dispossess *s.o.*
**Ent'eignung** *f* (-; *-en*) expropriation; dispossession
**ent'erben** *v/t* (*no -ge-, h*) disinherit
**entern** ['ɛntɐn] *v/t* (*ge-, h*) MAR board
**ent|fachen** [ɛnt'faxən] *v/t* (*no -ge-, h*) kindle, *fig a.* rouse; **~fallen** *v/i* (*irr*, ***fallen***, *no -ge-, sein*) be cancelled; ***~ auf***

(*acc*) fall to s.o. ('s share); ***es ist mir ~*** it has slipped my memory; **~falten** *v/t* (*no -ge-, h*) unfold; *fig* develop; ***sich ~*** unfold; *fig* develop (***zu*** into)
**entfernen** [ɛnt'fɛrnən] *v/t* (*no -ge-, h*) remove (*a. fig*); ***sich ~*** leave; **ent'fernt** *adj* distant (*a. fig*); ***weit (zehn Meilen) ~*** far (10 miles) away; **Ent'fernung** *f* (-; *-en*) distance; removal
**Ent'fernungsmesser** *m* (*-s*; -) PHOT range finder
**ent'flammbar** *adj* (in)flammable
**entfremden** [ɛnt'frɛmdən] *v/t* (*no -ge-, h*) estrange (*dat* from); **Ent'fremdung** *f* (-; *-en*) estrangement, alienation
**ent'führen** *v/t* (*no -ge-, h*) kidnap; AVIAT hijack; **Ent'führer** *m* (*-s*; -) kidnapper; AVIAT hijacker; **Ent'führung** *f* (-; *-en*) kidnapping; AVIAT hijacking
**ent'gegen** *prp* (*dat*) *and adv* contrary to; toward(s); **~gehen** *v/i* (*irr,* ***gehen***, *sep, -ge-, sein*) go to meet
**ent'gegengesetzt** *adj* opposite
**ent'gegenkommen** *v/i* (*irr,* ***kommen***, *sep, -ge-, sein*) come to meet; *fig* ***j-m ~*** meet s.o. halfway; **~d** *fig adj* obliging
**ent'gegen|nehmen** *v/t* (*irr,* ***nehmen***, *sep, -ge-, h*) accept, receive; **~sehen** *v/i* (*irr,* ***sehen***, *sep, -ge-, h*) await; look forward to *s.th.*; **~setzen** *v/t* (*sep, -ge-, h*) ***j-m Widerstand ~*** put up resistance to s.o.; **~treten** *v/i* (*irr,* ***treten***, *sep, -ge-, sein*) walk towards; oppose; face
**entgegnen** [ɛnt'ge:gnən] *v/i* (*no -ge-, h*) reply, answer; retort
**Ent'gegnung** *f* (-; *-en*) reply; retort
**ent'gehen** *v/i* (*irr,* ***gehen***, *no -ge-, sein*) escape; miss
**entgeistert** [ɛnt'gaistɐt] *adj* aghast
**Entgelt** [ɛnt'gɛlt] *n* (*-[e]s*; *-e*) remuneration; fee
**ent|giften** [ɛnt'gɪftən] *v/t* (*no -ge-, h*) decontaminate; **~gleisen** [ɛnt'glaizən] *v/i* (*no -ge-, sein*) RAIL be derailed; *fig* blunder; **~'gleiten** *fig v/i* (*irr,* ***gleiten***, *no -ge-, sein*) get out of control; **~gräten** [ɛnt'grɛ:tən] *v/t* (*no -ge-, h*) bone, fil(l)et
**ent'halten** *v/t* (*irr,* ***halten***, *no -ge-, h*) contain, hold; include; ***sich ~*** (*gen*) abstain *or* refrain from; **ent'haltsam** *adj* abstinent; moderate; **Ent'haltsamkeit** *f* (-; *no pl*) abstinence; moderation
**Ent'haltung** *f* (-; *-en*) abstention
**ent'härten** *v/t* (*no -ge-, h*) soften
**enthaupten** [ɛnt'hauptən] *v/t* (*no -ge-, h*) behead, decapitate
**ent'hüllen** *v/t* (*no -ge-, h*) uncover; unveil; *fig* reveal, disclose; **Ent'hüllung** *f* (-; *-en*) unveiling; *fig* revelation, disclosure
**Enthusiasmus** [ɛntu'zjasmʊs] *m* (-; *no pl*) enthusiasm; **Enthusiast(in)** [ɛntu'zjast(-ɪn)] (*-en, -en*/-; *-nen*) enthusiast; *film*, SPORT F fan; **enthusi'astisch** *adj* enthusiastic
**ent|'kleiden** *v/t and v/refl* (*no -ge-, h*) undress, strip; **~'kommen** *v/i* (*irr,* ***kommen***, *no -ge-, sein*) escape (*dat* from); **~'korken** *v/t* (*no -ge-, h*) uncork
**entkräften** [ɛnt'krɛftən] *v/t* (*no -ge-, h*) weaken (*a. fig*); **Ent'kräftung** *f* (-; *-en*) weakening, exhaustion
**ent'laden** *v/t* (*irr,* ***laden***, *no -ge-, h*) unload; *esp* ELECTR discharge; ***sich ~*** *esp* ELECTR discharge; *fig* explode
**Ent'ladung** *f* (-; *-en*) unloading; *esp* ELECTR discharge; *fig* explosion
**ent'lang** *prp* (*dat*) *and adv* along; ***hier ~, bitte!*** this way, please!; ***die Straße*** *etc* ***~*** along the street *etc*
**entlarven** [ɛnt'larfən] *v/t* (*no -ge-, h*) unmask, expose
**ent'lassen** *v/t* (*irr,* ***lassen***, *no -ge-, h*) dismiss, F fire, give *s.o.* the sack; MED discharge; JUR release
**Ent'lassung** *f* (-; *-en*) dismissal; MED discharge; JUR release
**ent'lasten** *v/t* (*no -ge-, h*) relieve *s.o.* of some of his work; JUR exonerate, clear *s.o.* of a charge; ***den Verkehr ~*** relieve the traffic congestion; **Ent'lastung** *f* (-; *-en*) relief; JUR exoneration
**Ent'lastungszeuge** *m* JUR witness for the defense (*Br* defence)
**ent'laufen** *v/i* (*irr,* ***laufen***, *no -ge-, sein*) run away (*dat* from)
**ent'legen** *adj* remote, distant
**ent|'locken** *v/t* (*no -ge-, h*) draw, elicit (*dat* from); **~'lohnen** *v/t* (*no -ge-, h*) pay (off); **~'lüften** *v/t* (*no -ge-, h*) ventilate; **~machten** [ɛnt'maxtən] *v/t* (*no -ge-, h*) deprive *s.o.* of *his* power; **~militarisieren** [ɛntmilitari'zi:rən] *v/t* (*no -ge-, h*) demilitarize; **~mündigen** [ɛnt'myndɪgən] *v/t* (*no -ge-, h*) JUR place under disability; **~mutigen** [ɛnt'mu:tɪgən] *v/t* (*no -ge-, h*) discourage;

~'**nehmen** *v/t* (*irr*, ***nehmen***, *no -ge-*, *h*) take (*dat* from); ~ ***aus*** (with-)draw from; *fig* gather *or* learn from; ~'**puppen** *v/refl* (*no -ge-*, *h*) ***sich ~ als*** turn out to be; ~'**rahmen** *v/t* (*no -ge-*, *h*) skim; ~'**reißen** *v/t* (*irr*, ***reißen***, *no -ge-*, *h*) snatch (away) (*dat* from); ~'**rinnen** *v/i* (*irr*, ***rinnen***, *no -ge-*, *sein*) escape (*dat* from); ~'**rollen** *v/t* (*no -ge-*, *h*) unroll

E

**ent'rüsten** *v/t* (*no -ge-*, *h*) fill with indignation; ***sich ~*** become indignant (***über*** *acc* at *s.th.*, with *s.o.*); **ent'rüstet** *adj* indignant (***über*** *acc* at *s.th.*, with *s.o.*;)

**Ent'rüstung** *f* (-; *-en*) indignation

**Entsafter** [ɛnt'zaftɐ] *m* (*-s*; -) juice extractor

**ent'salzen** *v/t* (*no -ge-*, *h*) desalinize

**ent'schädigen** *v/t* (*no -ge-*, *h*) compensate; **Ent'schädigung** *f* (-; *-en*) compensation

**ent'schärfen** *v/t* (*no -ge-*, *h*) defuse (*a. fig*)

**ent'scheiden** *v/t and v/i and v/refl* (*irr*, ***scheiden***, *no -ge-*, *h*) decide (***für*** on, in favo[u]r of; ***gegen*** against); settle; ***er kann sich nicht ~*** he can't make up his mind; ~**d** *adj* decisive; crucial

**Ent'scheidung** *f* (-; *-en*) decision

**entschieden** [ɛnt'ʃiːdən] *adj* decided, determined, resolute; ~ ***dafür*** strongly in favo(u)r of it; **Ent'schiedenheit** *f* (-; *no pl*) determination

**ent'schließen** *v/refl* (*irr*, ***schließen***, *no -ge-*, *h*) decide, determine, make up one's mind; **Ent'schließung** *f* (-; *-en*) POL resolution

**entschlossen** [ɛnt'ʃlɔsən] *adj* determined, resolute; **Ent'schlossenheit** *f* (-; *no pl*) determination, resoluteness

**Ent'schluss** *m* decision, resolution

**entschlüsseln** [ɛnt'ʃlʏsəln] *v/t* (*no -ge-*, *h*) decipher, decode

**entschuldigen** [ɛnt'ʃʊldɪgən] *v/t* (*no -ge-*, *h*) excuse; ***sich ~*** apologize (***bei*** to; ***für*** for); excuse o.s.; ~ ***Sie!*** (I'm) sorry!; excuse me!; **Ent'schuldigung** *f* (-; *-en*) excuse; apology; ***um ~ bitten*** apologize; ~***!*** (I'm) sorry!; excuse me!

**ent'setzen** *v/t* (*no -ge-*, *h*) shock; horrify; **Ent'setzen** *n* (*-s*; *no pl*) horror, terror; **ent'setzlich** *adj* horrible, dreadful, terrible; atrocious; **ent'setzt** *adj* shocked; horrified

**ent|'sichern** *v/t* (*no -ge-*, *h*) release the safety catch of; ~'**sinnen** *v/refl* (*irr*, ***sinnen***, *no -ge-*, *h*) remember, recall

**ent'sorgen** *v/t* (*no -ge-*, *h*) dispose of

**Ent'sorgung** *f* (-; *-en*) (waste) disposal

**ent'spannen** *v/t and v/refl* (*no -ge-*, *h*) relax; ***sich ~*** *a.* take it easy; *fig* ease (up); **ent'spannt** *adj* relaxed

**Ent'spannung** *f* (-; *-en*) relaxation; POL détente

**ent'spiegelt** *adj* OPT non-glare

**ent'sprechen** *v/i* (*irr*, ***sprechen***, *no -ge-*, *h*) correspond to; answer to *a description*; meet (*requirements etc*); ~**d** *adj* corresponding (*dat* to); appropriate

**Ent'sprechung** *f* (-; *-en*) equivalent

**ent'springen** *v/i* (*irr*, ***springen***, *no -ge-*, *sein*) *river*: rise

**entstehen** *v/i* (*irr*, ***stehen***, *no -ge-*, *sein*) come into being; arise; emerge, develop; ~ ***aus*** originate from

**Ent'stehung** *f* (-; *-en*) origin

**ent'stellen** *v/t* (*no -ge-*, *h*) disfigure, deform; *fig* distort; **Ent'stellung** *f* (-; *-en*) disfigurement, deformation, distortion (*a. fig*)

**entstört** [ɛnt'ʃtøːɐt] *adj* ELECTR interference-free

**ent'täuschen** *v/t* (*no -ge-*, *h*) disappoint; **Ent'täuschung** *f* (-; *-en*) disappointment

**entwaffnen** [ɛnt'vafnən] *v/t* (*no -ge-*, *h*) disarm

**Ent'warnung** *f* all clear (signal)

**ent'wässern** *v/t* (*no -ge-*, *h*) drain; **Ent'wässerung** *f* (-; *-en*) drainage; CHEM dehydration

**'entweder** *cj*: ~ ... ***oder*** either … or

**ent|'weichen** *v/i* (*irr*, ***weichen***, *no -ge-*, *sein*) escape (***aus*** from); ~'**weihen** *v/t* (*no -ge-*, *h*) desecrate; ~'**wenden** *v/t* (*no -ge-*, *h*) pilfer, steal; ~'**werfen** *v/t* (*irr*, ***werfen***, *no -ge-*, *h*) design; draw up

**ent'werten** *v/t* (*no -ge-*, *h*) lower the value of (*a. fig*); cancel; **Ent'wertung** *f* (-; *-en*) devaluation; cancellation

**ent'wickeln** *v/t and v/refl* (*no -ge-*, *h*) develop (*a.* PHOT) (***zu*** into); **Ent'wicklung** *f* (-; *-en*) development, BIOL *a.* evolution; adolescence, age of puberty

**Ent'wicklungs|helfer** *m*, ~**helferin** *f* POL, ECON development aid volunteer; Peace Corps volunteer, *Br* VSO work-

er; **~hilfe** *f* development aid; **~land** *n* POL developing country
**ent|wirren** [ɛnt'vɪrən] *v/t (no -ge-, h)* disentangle *(a. fig)*; **~'wischen** *v/i (no -ge-, sein)* get away
**ent'würdigend** *adj* degrading
**Ent'wurf** *m* outline, (rough) draft, plan; design; sketch
**ent|'wurzeln** *v/t (no -ge-, h)* uproot; **~'ziehen** *v/t (irr,* ***ziehen****, no -ge-, h)* take away *(dat* from); revoke *(license etc)*; deprive of *rights etc*; CHEM extract; ***sich j-m (e-r Sache) ~*** evade s.o. (s.th.)
**Ent'ziehungs|anstalt** *f* substance *(Br* drug) abuse clinic; **~kur** *f* detoxi(fi)cation (treatment), *a.* F drying out
**entziffern** [ɛnt'tsɪfɐn] *v/t (no -ge-, h)* decipher, make out
**ent'zücken** *v/t (no -ge-, h)* charm, delight; **Ent'zücken** *n (-s; no pl)* delight; **ent'zückend** *adj* delightful, charming, F sweet; **ent'zückt** *adj* delighted (***über*** *acc,* ***von*** at, with)
**Ent'zug** *m* withdrawal; revocation
**Ent'zugserscheinung** *f* MED withdrawal symptom
**entzündbar** [ɛnt'tsʏntba:ɐ] *adj* (in-) flammable; **ent'zünden** *v/refl (no -ge-, h)* catch fire; MED become inflamed; **Ent'zündung** *f (-; -en)* MED inflammation
**ent'zwei** *adv* in two, to pieces
**Enzyklopädie** [ɛntsyklopɛ'di:] *f (-; -n)* encyclop(a)edia
**Epidemie** [epide'mi:] *f (-; -n)* MED epidemic (disease)
**Epilog** [epi'lo:k] *m (-[e]s; -e* [epi'lo:gə]) epilog, *Br* epilogue
**episch** ['e:pɪʃ] *adj* epic
**Episode** [epi'zo:də] *f (-; -n)* episode
**Epoche** [e'pɔxə] *f (-; -n)* epoch, period, era
**Epos** ['e:pɔs] *n (-; Epen* ['e:pən]) epic (poem)
**er** [e:ɐ] *pers pron* he; it
**Er'achten** *n*: ***meines ~s*** in my opinion
**Erbanlage** ['ɛrpˀanla:gə] *f* BIOL genes, genetic code
**erbarmen** [ɛɐ'barmən] *v/refl (no -ge-, h)* ***sich j-s ~*** take pity on s.o.
**erbärmlich** [ɛɐ'bɛrmlɪç] *adj* pitiful, pitiable; miserable; mean
**er'barmungslos** *adj* pitiless, merciless
**er'bauen** *v/t (no -ge-, h)* build, construct; **Er'bauer** *m (-s; -)* builder, constructor
**er'baulich** *adj* edifying; **Er'bauung** *fig f (-; -en)* edification, uplift
**Erbe** ['ɛrbə] **1.** *m (-n; -n)* heir **2.** *n (-s; no pl)* inheritance, heritage
**erben** ['ɛrbən] *v/t (ge-, h)* inherit
**erbeuten** [ɛɐ'bɔʏtən] *v/t (no -ge-, h)* MIL capture; *thief*: get away with
**'Erbfaktor** *m* BIOL gene
**Erbin** ['ɛrbɪn] *f (-; -nen)* heir, heiress
**er'bitten** *v/t (irr,* ***bitten****, no -ge-, h)* ask for, request
**erbittert** [ɛɐ'bɪtɐt] *adj* fierce, furious
**'Erbkrankheit** *f* MED hereditary disease
**erblich** ['ɛrplɪç] *adj* hereditary
**er'blicken** *v/t (no -ge-, h)* see, catch sight of
**erblinden** [ɛɐ'blɪndən] *v/i (no -ge-, sein)* go blind
**er'brechen** *v/t and v/refl (irr,* ***brechen****, no -ge-, h)* MED vomit
**Erbschaft** ['ɛrpʃaft] *f (-; -en)* inheritance, heritage
**Erbse** ['ɛrpsə] *f (-; -n)* BOT pea; **(*grüne*) *~n*** green peas
**'Erbstück** *n* heirloom
**Erd|apfel** ['e:ɐtapfəl] *Austrian m* potato; **~ball** *m (-[e]s; no pl)* globe; **~beben** *n (-s; -)* earthquake; **~beere** *f* BOT strawberry; **~boden** *m* earth, ground
**Erde** ['e:ɐdə] *f (-; -n) (no pl)* earth; ground, soil; → ***eben***; **'erden** *v/t (ge-, h)* ELECTR earth, ground
**erdenklich** [ɛɐ'dɛŋklɪç] *adj* imaginable
**Erd|gas** ['e:ɐtga:s] *n* natural gas; **~geschoss** *n*, **~geschoß** *Austrian n* first *(Br* ground) floor
**er'dichten** *v/t (no -ge-, h)* invent, make up; **er'dichtet** *adj* invented, made-up
**erdig** ['e:ɐdɪç] *adj* earthy
**'Erd|klumpen** *m* clod, lump of earth; **~kruste** *f* earth's crust; **~kugel** *f* globe; **~kunde** *f (-; no pl)* geography; **~leitung** *f* ELECTR ground *(Br* earth) connection; underground pipe(line); **~nuss** *f* BOT peanut; **~öl** *n* (mineral) oil, petroleum; **~reich** *n* ground, earth
**erdreisten** [ɛɐ'draistən] *v/refl (no -ge-, h)* F have the nerve
**er'drosseln** *v/t (no -ge-, h)* throttle
**er'drücken** *v/t (no -ge-, h)* crush (to death); **~d** *fig adj* overwhelming
**'Erd|rutsch** *m (-[e]s; -e)* landslide *(a.*

E

POL); **~teil** *m* GEOGR continent
**er'dulden** *v/t* (*no -ge-*, *h*) suffer, endure
**'Erdumlaufbahn** *f* earth orbit
**'Erdung** *f* (-; *-en*) ELECTR grounding, *Br* earthing
**'Erdwärme** *f* GEOL geothermal energy
**er'eifern** *v/refl* (*no -ge-*, *h*) get excited
**ereignen** [ɛɐ'ʔaignən] *v/refl* (*no -ge-*, *h*) happen, occur; **Ereignis** [ɛɐ'ʔaignɪs] *n* (*-ses*; *-se*) event, occurrence
**er'eignisreich** *adj* eventful
**Erektion** [erɛk'tsjoːn] *f* (-; *-en*) erection
**Eremit** [ere'miːt] *m* (*-en*; *-en*) hermit, anchorite
**er'fahren**[1] *v/t* (*irr*, ***fahren***, *no -ge-*, *h*) hear; learn; experience
**er'fahren**[2] *adj* experienced
**Er'fahrung** *f* (-; *-en*) (work) experience
**Er'fahrungsaustausch** *m* exchange of experience; **er'fahrungsgemäß** *adv* as experience shows
**er'fassen** *v/t* (*no -ge-*, *h*) grasp; record, register; cover, include; IT collect
**er'finden** *v/t* (*irr*, ***finden***, *no -ge-*, *h*) invent; **Er'finder(in)** (*-s*; *-/-*; *-nen*) inventor; **erfinderisch** [ɛɐ'fɪndərɪʃ] *adj* inventive; **Er'findung** *f* (-; *-en*) invention; **Er'findungskraft** *f* (-; *no pl*) inventiveness
**Erfolg** [ɛɐ'fɔlk] *m* (-[*e*]*s*; *-e*) success; result; ***viel ~!*** good luck!; ***~ versprechend*** promising; **er'folgen** *v/i* (*no -ge-*, *sein*) happen, take place; **er'folglos** *adj* unsuccessful; futile; **Er'folglosigkeit** *f* (-; *no pl*) lack of success; **er'folgreich** *adj* successful; **Er'folgserlebnis** *n* sense of achievement
**erforderlich** [ɛɐ'fɔrdɐlɪç] *adj* necessary, required; **er'fordern** *v/t* (*no -ge-*, *h*) require, demand; **Erfordernis** [ɛɐ'fɔrdɐnɪs] *n* (*-ses*; *-se*) requirement, demand
**er'forschen** *v/t* (*no -ge-*, *h*) explore; investigate, study; **Er'forscher** *m* explorer; **Er'forschung** *f* exploration
**er'freuen** *v/t* (*no -ge-*, *h*) please
**erfreulich** [ɛɐ'frɔylɪç] *adj* pleasing, pleasant; gratifying
**er'freut** *adj* pleased (***über*** *acc* at, about); ***sehr ~!*** pleased to meet you
**er'frieren** *v/i* (*irr*, ***frieren***, *no -ge-*, *sein*) freeze to death; **Er'frierung** *f* (-; *-en*) MED frostbite
**er'frischen** *v/t and v/refl* (*no -ge-*, *h*) refresh (o.s.); **~d** *adj* refreshing
**Er'frischung** *f* (-; *-en*) refreshment
**erfroren** [ɛɐ'froːrən] *adj* frostbitten; BOT killed by frost
**er'füllen** *fig v/t* (*no -ge-*, *h*) fulfil(l); keep (*promise etc*); serve (*purpose etc*); meet (*requirements etc*); ***~ mit*** fill with; ***sich ~*** be fulfilled, come true; **Er'füllung** *f* (-; *-en*) fulfil(l)ment; ***in ~ gehen*** come true
**ergänzen** [ɛɐ'gɛntsən] *v/t* (*no -ge-*, *h*) complement (***einander*** each other); supplement, add; **~d** *adj* complementary, supplementary
**Er'gänzung** *f* (-; *-en*) completion; supplement, addition
**ergattern** [ɛɐ'gatɐn] F *v/t* (*no -ge-*, *h*) (manage to) get hold of
**er'geben** (*irr*, ***geben***, *no -ge-*, *h*) **1.** *v/t* amount *or* come to **2.** *v/refl* surrender; *fig* arise; ***sich ~ aus*** result from; ***sich ~ in*** (*acc*) resign o.s. to
**Er'gebenheit** *f* (-; *no pl*) devotion
**Ergebnis** [ɛɐ'geːpnɪs] *n* (*-ses*; *-se*) result, SPORT *a.* score; outcome
**er'gebnislos** *adj* without result
**er'gehen** *v/i* (*irr*, ***gehen***, *no -ge-*, *sein*) *order etc*: be issued (***an*** *acc* to); ***wie ist es dir ergangen?*** how did things go with you?; ***et. über sich ~ lassen*** (patiently) endure s.th.
**ergiebig** [ɛɐ'giːbɪç] *adj* productive, rich; **Er'giebigkeit** *f* (-; *no pl*) (high) yield; productiveness
**er'gießen** *v/refl* (*irr*, ***gießen***, *no -ge-*, *h*) ***sich ~ über*** (*acc*) pour down on
**er'grauen** *v/i* (*no -ge-*, *sein*) turn gray (*Br* grey)
**er'greifen** *v/t* (*irr*, ***greifen***, *no -ge-*, *h*) seize, grasp, take hold of; take (*measures etc*); take up; *fig* move, touch
**ergriffen** [ɛɐ'grɪfən] *fig adj* moved
**Er'griffenheit** *f* (-; *no pl*) emotion
**er'gründen** *v/t* (*no -ge-*, *h*) find out, fathom
**er'haben** *adj* raised, elevated; *fig* sublime; ***~ sein über*** (*acc*) be above
**er'halten**[1] *v/t* (*irr*, ***halten***, *no -ge-*, *h*) get, receive; keep, preserve; protect; support, maintain (*family etc*)
**er'halten**[2] *adj*: ***gut ~*** in good condition
**erhältlich** [ɛɐ'hɛltlɪç] *adj* obtainable, available
**Er'haltung** *f* (-; *no pl*) preservation; up-

keep
**er'hängen** *v/t* (*no -ge-, h*) hang (**sich** o.s.)
**er'heben** *v/t* (*irr*, **heben**, *no -ge-, h*) raise (*a. voice*), lift; **sich ~** rise up (**gegen** against)
**erheblich** [ɛɐ'heːplɪç] *adj* considerable
**Er'hebung** *f* (-; *-en*) survey; revolt
**erheitern** [ɛɐ'haitɐn] *v/t* (*no -ge-, h*) cheer up, amuse; **erhellen** [ɛɐ'hɛlən] *v/t* (*no -ge-, h*) light up; *fig* throw light upon; **erhitzen** [ɛɐ'hɪtsən] *v/t* (*no -ge-, h*) heat; **sich ~** get hot; **er'hoffen** *v/t* (*no -ge-, h*) hope for
**erhöhen** [ɛɐ'høːən] *v/t* (*no -ge-, h*) raise; increase; **Er'höhung** *f* (-; *-en*) increase
**er'holen** *v/refl* (*no -ge-, h*) recover; relax, rest; **erholsam** [ɛɐ'hoːlzaːm] *adj* restful, relaxing; **Er'holung** *f* (-; *no pl*) recovery; relaxation
**Er'holungsheim** *n* rest home
**erinnern** [ɛɐ'ʔɪnɐn] *v/t* (*no -ge-, h*) **j-n ~ an** (*acc*) remind s.o. of; **sich ~ an** (*acc*) remember, recall; **Erinnerung** [ɛɐ'ɪnərʊŋ] *f* (-; *-en*) memory (**an** *acc* of); remembrance, souvenir; keepsake; **zur ~ an** (*acc*) in memory of
**erkalten** [ɛɐ'kaltən] *v/i* (*no -ge-, sein*) cool down (*a. fig*)
**erkälten** [ɛɐ'kɛltən] *v/refl* (*no -ge-, h*) **sich ~** catch (a) cold; (**stark**) **erkältet sein** have a (bad) cold; **Er'kältung** *f* (-; *-en*) cold
**erkennbar** [ɛɐ'kɛnbaːɐ] *adj* recognizable; **er'kennen** *v/t* (*irr*, **kennen**, *no -ge-, h*) recognize (**an** *dat* by), know (by); see, realize; **er'kenntlich** *adj*: **sich** (**j-m**) **~ zeigen** show (s.o.) one's gratitude; **Er'kenntnis** *f* (-; *-se*) realization; discovery; *pl* findings
**Er'kennungs|dienst** *m* (police) records department; **~melo,die** *f* signature tune; **~zeichen** *n* badge; AVIAT markings
**Erker** ['ɛrkɐ] *m* (*-s*; -) ARCH bay; **~fenster** *n* ARCH bay window
**er'klären** *v/t* (*no -ge-, h*) explain (**j-m** to s.o.); declare; **j-n** (*offiziell*) **für ... ~** pronounce s.o. ...; **~d** *adj* explanatory
**erklärlich** [ɛɐ'klɛːɐlɪç] *adj* explainable; **er'klärt** *adj* declared; **Er'klärung** *f* (-; *-en*) explanation; declaration; definition; **e-e ~ abgeben** make a statement
**er'klingen** *v/i* (*irr*, **klingen**, *no -ge-, sein*) (re)sound, ring (out)
**erkranken** [ɛɐ'kraŋkən] *v/i* (*no -ge-, sein*) fall ill, get sick; **~ an** (*dat*) get; **Er'krankung** *f* (-; *-en*) illness, sickness
**erkunden** [ɛɐ'kʊndən] *v/t* (*no -ge-, h*) explore
**erkundigen** [ɛɐ'kʊndɪgən] *v/refl* (*no -ge-, h*) inquire (**nach** about *s.th.*; after *s.o.*); make inquiries (about); **sich** (**bei j-m**) **nach dem Weg ~** ask (s.o.) the way; **Er'kundigung** *f* (-; *-en*) inquiry
**Er'kundung** *f* (-; *-en*) exploration; MIL reconnaissance
**Erlagschein** [ɛɐ'laːkʃain] *Austrian m* money-order form
**er'lahmen** *v/i* (*no -ge-, sein*) flag
**Erlass** [ɛɐ'las] *m* (*-es*; *-e*) decree; JUR remission; **er'lassen** *v/t* (*irr*, **lassen**, *no -ge-, h*) issue; enact (*bill etc*); **j-m et. ~** release s.o. from s.th.
**erlauben** [ɛɐ'laubən] *v/t* (*no -ge-, h*) allow, permit; **sich et. ~** permit o.s. (*or* dare) to do s.th.; treat o.s. to s.th.
**Erlaubnis** [ɛɐ'laupnɪs] *f* (-; *no pl*) permission; authority; **um ~ bitten** ask s.o.'s permission; **~schein** *m* permit
**erläutern** [ɛɐ'lɔʏtɐn] *v/t* (*no -ge-, h*) explain, illustrate; **Er'läuterung** *f* (-; *-en*) explanation; annotation
**Erle** ['ɛrlə] *f* (-; *-n*) BOT alder
**er'leben** *v/t* (*no -ge-, h*) experience; go through; see; have; **das werden wir nicht mehr ~** we won't live to see that
**Erlebnis** [ɛɐ'leːpnɪs] *n* (*-ses*; *-se*) experience; adventure
**er'lebnisreich** *adj* eventful
**erledigen** [ɛɐ'leːdɪgən] *v/t* (*no -ge-, h*) take care of, do, handle; settle; F finish *s.o.* (*a.* SPORT); do *s.o.* in; **erledigt** [ɛɐ'leːdɪçt] *adj* finished, settled; F worn out; F **der ist ~!** he is done for
**Er'ledigung** *f* (-; *-en*) (*no pl*) settlement; *pl* things to do, shopping
**er'legen** *v/t* (*no -ge-, h*) HUNT shoot
**erleichtern** [ɛɐ'laiçtɐn] *v/t* (*no -ge-, h*) ease, relieve; **er'leichtert** *adj* relieved; **Erleichterung** [ɛɐ'laiçtərʊŋ] *f* (-; *no pl*) relief (**über** *acc* at)
**er'leiden** *v/t* (*irr*, **leiden**, *no -ge-, h*) suffer
**er'lesen** *adj* choice, select
**er'leuchten** *v/t* (*no -ge-, h*) illuminate
**er'liegen** *v/i* (*irr*, **liegen**, *no -ge-, sein*) succumb to

**Er'liegen** *n*: ***zum ~ kommen*** (***bringen***) come (bring) to a standstill
**erlogen** [ɛɐ'lo:gən] *adj* false; ***~ sein*** be a lie
**Erlös** [ɛɐ'lø:s] *m* (*-es*; *-e*) proceeds; profit(s)
**erlosch** [ɛɐ'lɔʃ] *pret of* ***erlöschen***
**erloschen** [ɛɐ'lɔʃən] **1.** *pp of* ***erlöschen*** **2.** *adj* extinct (*volcano*)
**er'löschen** *v/i* (*irr*, *no -ge-*, *sein*) go out; *fig* die; JUR lapse, expire
**er'lösen** *v/t* (*no -ge-*, *h*) deliver, free (*both*: ***von*** from); **Erlöser** [ɛɐ'lø:zɐ] *m* (*-s*; *no pl*) REL Savio(u)r; **Er'lösung** *f* (-; *no pl*) REL salvation; relief
**ermächtigen** [ɛɐ'mɛçtɪgən] *v/t* (*no -ge-*, *h*) authorize; **Er'mächtigung** *f* (-; *-en*) authorization; authority
**er'mahnen** *v/t* (*no -ge-*, *h*) admonish; reprove, warn (*a.* SPORT)
**Er'mahnung** *f* (-; *-en*) admonition; warning; *esp* SPORT (first) caution
**Er'mangelung** *f*: ***in ~*** (*gen*) for want of
**ermäßigt** [ɛɐ'mɛ:sɪçt] *adj* reduced, cut; **Er'mäßigung** *f* (-; *-en*) reduction, cut
**er'messen** *v/t* (*irr*, ***messen***, *no -ge-*, *h*) assess; judge; **Er'messen** *n* (*-s*; *no pl*) discretion; ***nach eigenem ~*** at one's own discretion
**er'mitteln** (*no -ge-*, *h*) **1.** *v/t* find out; determine **2.** *v/i esp* JUR investigate; **Er'mittlung** *f* (-; *-en*) finding; JUR investigation
**er'möglichen** *v/t* (*no -ge-*, *h*) make possible
**er'morden** *v/t* (*no -ge-*, *h*) murder; *esp* POL assassinate; **Er'mordung** *f* (-; *-en*) murder; *esp* POL assassination
**ermüden** [ɛɐ'my:dən] (*no -ge-*) **1.** *v/t* (*h*) tire, fatigue **2.** *v/i* (*sein*) tire, get tired, fatigue (*a.* TECH); **Er'müdung** *f* (-; *no pl*) fatigue, tiredness
**er'muntern** [ɛɐ'mʊntɐn] *v/t* (*no -ge-*, *h*) encourage; stimulate; **Er'munterung** *f* (-; *-en*) encouragement; incentive
**ermutigen** [ɛɐ'mu:tɪgən] *v/t* (*no -ge-*, *h*) encourage; **~d** *adj* encouraging
**Er'mutigung** *f* (-; *-en*) encouragement
**er'nähren** *v/t* (*no -ge-*, *h*) feed; support (*family etc*); ***sich ~ von*** live on; **Er'nährer** *m* (*-s*; -) breadwinner, supporter; **Er'nährung** *f* (-; *no pl*) nutrition, food, diet
**er'nennen** *v/t* (*irr*, ***nennen***, *no -ge-*, *h*) ***j-n ~ zu*** appoint s.o. (to be)
**Er'nennung** *f* (-; *-en*) appointment
**erneuern** [ɛɐ'nɔʏɐn] *v/t* (*no -ge-*, *h*) renew; **Er'neuerung** *f* (-; *-en*) renewal
**er'neut** **1.** *adj* renewed **2.** *adv* once more
**erniedrigen** [ɛɐ'ni:drɪgən] *v/t* (*no -ge-*, *h*) humiliate; ***sich ~*** degrade o.s.
**Er'niedrigung** *f* (-; *-en*) humiliation
**ernst** [ɛrnst] *adj* serious, earnest; ***~ nehmen*** take *s.o. or s.th.* seriously
**Ernst** *m* (*-es*; *no pl*) seriousness, earnest; ***im ~***(?) seriously(?); ***ist das dein ~?*** are you serious?
**'ernsthaft**, **'ernstlich** *adj* serious
**Ernte** ['ɛrntə] *f* (-; *-n*) harvest; crop(s)
**'Erntedankfest** *n* Thanksgiving (Day), *Br* harvest festival
**'ernten** *v/t* (*ge-*, *h*) harvest, reap (*a. fig*)
**er'nüchtern** *v/t* (*no -ge-*, *h*) sober, *fig a.* disillusion; **Er'nüchterung** *f* (-; *-en*) sobering up; *fig* disillusionment
**Eroberer** [ɛɐ'ˀo:bərɐ] *m* (*-s*; -) conqueror; **erobern** [ɛɐ'ˀo:bɐn] *v/t* (*no -ge-*, *h*) conquer; **Er'oberung** *f* (-; *-en*) conquest (*a. fig*)
**er'öffnen** *v/t* (*no -ge-*, *h*) open; inaugurate; disclose *s.th.* (***j-m*** to s.o.)
**Er'öffnung** *f* (-; *-en*) opening; inauguration; disclosure
**erörtern** [ɛɐ'ˀœrtɐn] *v/t* (*no -ge-*, *h*) discuss; **Er'örterung** *f* (-; *-en*) discussion
**Erotik** [e'ro:tɪk] *f* (-; *no pl*) eroticism
**erotisch** [e'ro:tɪʃ] *adj* erotic
**er'pressen** *v/t* (*no -ge-*, *h*) blackmail; extort; **Er'presser(in)** (*-s*; *-/-*; *-nen*) blackmailer; **Er'pressung** *f* (-; *-en*) blackmail(ing); extortion
**er'proben** *v/t* (*no -ge-*, *h*) try, test
**er'raten** *v/t* (*irr*, ***raten***, *no -ge-*, *h*) guess
**er'rechnen** *v/t* (*no -ge-*, *h*) calculate, work *s.th.* out
**erregbar** [ɛɐ're:kba:ɐ] *adj* excitable; irritable
**er'regen** *v/t* (*no -ge-*, *h*) excite, *sexually*: *a.* arouse; *fig* rouse; cause; ***sich ~*** get excited; **~d** *adj* exciting, thrilling
**Er'reger** *m* (*-s*; -) MED germ, virus
**Er'regung** *f* (-; *-en*) excitement
**erreichbar** [ɛɐ'raiçba:ɐ] *adj* within reach (*a. fig*); available; ***leicht ~*** within easy reach; ***nicht ~*** out of reach; not available; **er'reichen** *v/t* (*no -ge-*, *h*) reach; catch (*train etc*); ***es ~, dass ...*** succeed in *doing s.th.*; ***et. ~*** get some-

where; ***telefonisch zu ~ sein*** have a (*Br* be on the) phone
**er'richten** *v/t* (*no -ge-, h*) put up, erect; *fig* found, *esp* ECON set up
**Er'richtung** *f* (-; *-en*) erection; *fig* establishment
**er'ringen** *v/t* (*irr*, ***ringen***, *no -ge-, h*) win, gain; achieve
**er'röten** *v/i* (*no -ge-, sein*) blush
**Errungenschaft** [ɛɐ'rʊŋənʃaft] *f* (-; *-en*) achievement; ***m-e neueste ~*** my latest acquisition
**Ersatz** [ɛɐ'zats] *m* (*-es*; *no pl*) replacement; substitute; surrogate; compensation; damages; ***als ~ für*** in exchange for; **~dienst** *m* → ***Zivildienst***; **~mann** *m* (-[*e*]*s*; *-leute*) substitute (*a.* SPORT); **~mine** *f* refill; **~reifen** *m* MOT spare tire (*Br* tyre); **~spieler** *m* SPORT substitute; **~teil** *n* TECH spare part
**er'schaffen** *v/t* (*irr*, ***schaffen***, *no -ge-, h*) create
**er'schallen** *v/i* ([*irr*, ***schallen***,] *no -ge-, sein*) (re)sound, ring (out)
**er'scheinen** *v/i* (*irr*, ***scheinen***, *no -ge-, sein*) appear, F turn up; be published; **Er'scheinen** *n* (*-s*; *no pl*) appearance; publication; **Er'scheinung** *f* (-; *-en*) appearance; apparition; phenomenon
**er'schießen** *v/t* (*irr*, ***schießen***, *no -ge-, h*) shoot (dead); **erschlaffen** [ɛɐ'ʃlafən] *v/i* (*no -ge-, sein*) go limp; *fig* weaken; **er'schlagen** *v/t* (*irr*, ***schlagen***, *no -ge-, h*) kill; **er'schließen** *v/t* (*irr*, ***schließen***, *no -ge-, h*) open up; develop
**erschollen** [ɛɐ'ʃɔlən] *pp of* ***erschallen***
**er'schöpfen** *v/t* (*no -ge-, h*) exhaust; **er'schöpft** *adj* exhausted
**Er'schöpfung** *f* (-; *no pl*) exhaustion
**erschrak** [ɛɐ'ʃraːk] *pret of* ***erschrecken*** 2
**er'schrecken** **1.** *v/t* (*no -ge-, h*) frighten, scare **2.** *v/i* (*irr*, *no -ge-, sein*) be frightened (***über*** *acc* at); **~d** *adj* alarming; terrible
**erschrocken** [ɛɐ'ʃrɔkən] *pp of* ***erschrecken*** 2
**erschüttern** [ɛɐ'ʃʏtɐn] *v/t* (*no -ge-, h*) shake; *fig a.* shock; *fig* move
**Er'schütterung** *f* (-; *-en*) shock (*a. fig*); TECH vibration
**erschweren** [ɛɐ'ʃveːrən] *v/t* (*no -ge-, h*) make more difficult; aggravate
**er'schwindeln** *v/t* (*no -ge-, h*) obtain *s.th.* by fraud; (***sich***) ***et. von j-m ~*** swindle s.o. out of s.th.
**er'schwingen** *v/t* (*irr*, ***schwingen***, *no -ge-, h*) afford; **er'schwinglich** *adj* within one's means, affordable; reasonable (*price*)
**er'sehen** *v/t* (*irr*, ***sehen***, *no -ge-, h*) see, learn, gather (*all*: ***aus*** from)
**ersetzbar** [ɛɐ'zɛtsbaːɐ] *adj* replaceable; reparable; **er'setzen** *v/t* (*no -ge-, h*) replace (***durch*** by); compensate for; ***j-m et. ~*** reimburse s.o. for s.th.
**er'sichtlich** *adj* evident, obvious
**er'sparen** *v/t* (*no -ge-, h*) save; ***j-m et. ~*** spare s.o. s.th.
**Ersparnisse** [ɛɐ'ʃpaːɐnɪsə] *pl* savings
**erst** [eːɐst] *adv* first; at first; ***~ jetzt*** (***gestern***) only now (yesterday); ***~ nächste Woche*** not before *or* until next week; ***es ist ~ neun Uhr*** it's only nine o'clock; ***eben ~*** just (now); ***~ recht*** all the more; ***~ recht nicht*** even less; → ***einmal***
**er'starren** *v/i* (*no -ge-, sein*) stiffen; *fig* freeze; **er'starrt** *adj* stiff; numb
**erstatten** [ɛɐ'ʃtatən] *v/t* (*no -ge-, h*) refund, reimburse (***j-m et.*** s.o. for s.th.); ***Bericht ~*** (give a) report (***über*** *acc* on); ***Anzeige ~*** report to the police
**'Erstaufführung** *f* THEA first night *or* performance, premiere, *film*: *a.* first run
**er'staunen** *v/t* (*no -ge-, h*) surprise, astonish; **Er'staunen** *n* (*-s*; *no pl*) surprise, astonishment; ***in ~*** (***ver***)***setzen*** astonish; **er'staunlich** *adj* surprising, astonishing; **er'staunt** *adj* astonished
**'Erstausgabe** *f* first edition
**'erst'beste** *adj* first; any old
**'erste** *adj* first; ***auf den ~n Blick*** at first sight; ***fürs Erste*** for the time being; ***als Erste***(***r***) first; ***zum ~n Mal***(***e***) for the first time; ***am Ersten*** on the first
**er'stechen** *v/t* (*irr*, ***stechen***, *no -ge-, h*) stab
**'erstens** *adv* first(ly), in the first place
**'Erstere**: ***der*** (***die, das***) ***~*** the former
**er'sticken** *v/t* (*no -ge-, h*) *and v/i* (*sein*) choke, suffocate; **Er'stickung** *f* (-; *no pl*) suffocation
**erst|klassig** ['eːɐstklasɪç] *adj* first-class, F *a.* super; **~malig** ['eːɐstmaːlɪç] *adj* first; **~mals** ['eːɐstmaːls] *adv* for

the first time
**er'streben** *v/t* (*no -ge-, h*) strive after
**er'strebenswert** *adj* desirable
**er'strecken** *v/refl* (*no -ge-, h*) extend, stretch (***bis, auf*** *acc* to; ***über*** *acc* over); ***sich ~ über*** (*acc*) *a.* cover
**'Erstschlag** *m* MIL first strike
**er'suchen** *v/t* (*no -ge-, h*) request
**er'tappen** *v/t* (*no -ge-, h*) catch; → ***Tat***
**er'tönen** *v/i* (*no -ge-, sein*) (re)sound
**Ertrag** [ɛɐ'tra:k] *m* (-[*e*]*s*; *Erträge* [ɛɐ'trɛ:gə]) AGR yield, produce, TECH *a.* output; ECON proceeds, returns
**er'tragen** *v/t* (*irr*, ***tragen***, *no -ge-, h*) bear, endure; stand
**erträglich** [ɛɐ'trɛ:klɪç] *adj* bearable, tolerable
**er'tränken** *v/t* (*no -ge-, h*) drown
**er'trinken** *v/i* (*irr*, ***trinken***, *no -ge-, sein*) drown
**erübrigen** [ɛɐ'ʔy:brɪgən] *v/t* (*no -ge-, h*) spare; ***sich ~*** be unnecessary
**Erw.** *abbr of* ***Erwachsene(r)*** adult(s)
**er'wachen** *v/i* (*no -ge-, sein*) wake (up); *esp fig* awake, awaken
**er'wachsen**[1] *v/i* (*irr*, ***wachsen***, *no -ge-, sein*) arise (***aus*** from)
**er'wachsen**[2] *adj* grown-up, adult
**Er'wachsene** *m, f* (*-n; -n*) adult; ***nur für ~!*** adults only!; **Er'wachsenenbildung** *f* adult education
**erwägen** [ɛɐ'vɛ:gən] *v/t* (*irr*, ***wägen***, *no -ge-, h*) consider, think *s.th.* over; **Er'wägung** *f* (-; *-en*) consideration; ***in ~ ziehen*** take into consideration
**erwähnen** [ɛɐ'vɛ:nən] *v/t* (*no -ge-, h*) mention; **Er'wähnung** *f* (-; *-en*) mention(ing)
**er'wärmen** *v/t and v/refl* (*no -ge-, h*) warm (up); *fig* ***sich ~ für*** warm to
**Er'wärmung** *f* (-; *-en*) warming up; ***~ der Erdatmosphäre*** global warming
**er'warten** *v/t* (*no -ge-, h*) expect; wait for, await; **Er'wartung** *f* (-; *-en*) expectation, anticipation
**er'wartungsvoll** *adj and adv* full of expectation, expectant(ly)
**er'wecken** *fig v/t* (*no -ge-, h*) awaken; arouse; → ***Anschein***
**er'weisen** *v/t* (*irr*, ***weisen***, *no -ge-, h*) do (*service etc*); show (*respect etc*); ***sich ~ als*** prove to be
**erweitern** [ɛɐ'vaitɐn] *v/t and v/refl* (*no -ge-, h*) extend, enlarge; *esp* ECON expand; **Er'weiterung** *f* (-; *-en*) extension, enlargement, expansion
**Erwerb** [ɛɐ'vɛrp] *m* (-[*e*]*s*; *-e*) acquisition; purchase; income; **er'werben** *v/t* (*irr*, ***werben***, *no -ge-, h*) acquire (*a. fig*); purchase
**er'werbs|los** *adj* unemployed; **~tätig** *adj* (gainfully) employed, working; **~unfähig** *adj* unable to work
**Er'werbung** *f* (-; *-en*) acquisition; purchase
**erwidern** [ɛɐ'vi:dɐn] *v/t* (*no -ge-, h*) reply, answer; return (*visit etc*)
**Er'widerung** *f* (-; *-en*) reply, answer; return
**er'wischen** *v/t* (*no -ge-, h*) catch, get; ***ihn hat's erwischt*** he's had it
**er'wünscht** *adj* desired; desirable; welcome
**er'würgen** *v/t* (*no -ge-, h*) strangle
**Erz** [e:ɐts] *n* (*-es; -e*) ore
**er'zählen** *v/t* (*no -ge-, h*) tell; narrate; ***man hat mir erzählt*** I was told
**Er'zähler** *m* (*-s*; -), **Er'zählerin** *f* (-; *-nen*) narrator
**Er'zählung** *f* (-; *-en*) (short) story, tale
**'Erzbischof** *m* REL archbishop
**'Erzbistum** *n* REL archbishopric
**'Erzengel** *m* REL archangel
**er'zeugen** *v/t* (*no -ge-, h*) ECON produce (*a. fig*); TECH make, manufacture; ELECTR generate; *fig* cause, create; **Er'zeuger** *m* (*-s*; -) ECON producer; **Er'zeugnis** *n* (*-ses; -se*) ECON product (*a. fig*); **Er'zeugung** *f* (-; *-en*) ECON production
**er'ziehen** *v/t* (*irr*, ***ziehen***, *no -ge-, h*) bring up, raise; educate; ***j-n zu et. ~*** teach s.o. to be *or* to do s.th.
**Erzieher** [ɛɐ'tsi:ɐ] *m* (*-s*; -), **Erzieherin** [ɛɐ'tsi:ərɪn] *f* (-; *-nen*) educator; teacher; (qualified) kindergarten teacher; **er'zieherisch** *adj* educational, pedagogic(al); **Er'ziehung** *f* (-; *no pl*) upbringing; education
**Er'ziehungs|anstalt** *f* reform (*Br* approved) school; **~berechtigte** *m, f* (*-n; -n*) parent or guardian; **~wesen** *n* (*-s; no pl*) educational system
**er'zielen** *v/t* (*no -ge-, h*) achieve; SPORT score
**erzogen** [ɛɐ'tso:gən] *adj*: ***gut ~ sein*** be well-bred; ***schlecht ~ sein*** be ill-bred
**er'zwingen** *v/t* (*irr*, ***zwingen***, *no -ge-, h*)

(en)force
**es** [ɛs] *pers pron* it; he; she; ~ ***gibt*** there is, there are; ***ich bin*** ~ it's me; ***ich hoffe*** ~ I hope so; ***ich kann*** ~ I can (do it)
**Esche** ['ɛʃə] *f* (-; *-n*) BOT ash (tree)
**Esel** ['eːzəl] *m* (*-s*; -) ZO donkey, ass (*a.* F)
'**Eselsbrücke** *f* mnemonic
'**Eselsohr** *fig n* dog-ear
**Eskorte** [ɛs'kɔrtə] *f* (-; *-n*) MIL escort, MAR *a.* convoy
**essbar** ['ɛsbaːɐ] *adj* eatable; edible
**essen** ['ɛsən] *v/t and v/i* (*irr, ge-, h*) eat; ***zu Mittag*** ~ (have) lunch; ***zu Abend*** ~ have supper (*or* dinner); ~ ***gehen*** eat *or* dine out; '**Essen** *n* (*-s*; -) food; meal; dish; dinner
'**Essens|marke** *f* meal ticket; ~**zeit** *f* lunchtime; dinner *or* supper time
**Essig** ['ɛsɪç] *m* (*-s*; *-e*) vinegar
'**Essiggurke** *f* pickled gherkin, pickle
**Ess|löffel** *m* tablespoon; ~**stäbchen** *pl* chopsticks; ~**tisch** *m* dining table; ~**zimmer** *n* dining room
**Estrich** ['ɛstrɪç] *m* (*-s*; *-e*) ARCH flooring, subfloor; *Swiss*: loft, attic, garret
**etablieren** [eta'bliːrən] *v/refl* (*no -ge-, h*) establish o.s.
**Etage** [e'taːʒə] *f* (-; *-n*) floor, stor(e)y; ***auf der ersten*** ~ on the second (*Br* first) floor; **E'tagenbett** *n* bunk bed
**Etappe** [e'tapə] *f* (-; *-n*) stage, SPORT *a.* leg
**Etat** [e'taː] *m* (*-s*; *-s*) budget
**Ethik** ['eːtɪk] *f* (-; *no pl*) ethics
**ethisch** ['eːtɪʃ] *adj* ethical
**ethnisch** ['ɛtnɪʃ] *adj* ethnic
**Etikett** [eti'kɛt] *n* (*-[e]s*; *-e[n]*) label (*a. fig*); (price) tag; **Eti'kette** *f* (-; *-n*) etiquette; **etikettieren** [etikɛ'tiːrən] *v/t* (*no -ge-, h*) label
**etliche** ['ɛtlɪçə] *indef pron* several, quite a few
**Etui** [ɛt'viː] *n* (*-s*; *-s*) case
**etwa** ['ɛtva] *adv* about, around; perhaps, by any chance; ***nicht*** ~, ***dass*** not that; **etwaig** ['ɛtvaɪç] *adj* any
**etwas** ['ɛtvas] **1.** *indef pron* something; anything **2.** *adj* some; any **3.** *adv* a little, somewhat
**EU** [eː'uː] *abbr of* ***Europäische Union*** EU, European Union
**euch** [ɔʏç] *pers pron* you; ~ (***selbst***) yourselves; **euer** ['ɔʏɐ] *poss pron* your; ***der*** (***die, das***) ***Eu***(***e***)***re*** yours
**Eule** ['ɔʏlə] *f* (-; *-n*) ZO owl; ~***n nach Athen tragen*** carry coals to Newcastle
**euresgleichen** ['ɔʏrəs'glaɪçən] *pron* people like you, F *contp* the likes of you
**Euro...** ['ɔʏro] *in cpds ...cheque etc*: Euro...
**Europa** [ɔʏ'roːpa] Europe; ~... *in cpds* European; **Europäer** [ɔʏro'pɛːɐ] *m* (*-s*; -), **Europäerin** [ɔʏro'pɛːərɪn] *f* (-; *-nen*), **euro'päisch** *adj* European; ***Europäische Gemeinschaft*** European Community
**Euter** ['ɔʏtɐ] *n* (*-s*; -) udder
**ev.** *abbr of* ***evangelisch*** Prot., Protestant
**evakuieren** [evaku'iːrən] *v/t* (*no -ge-, h*) evacuate
**evangelisch** [evaŋ'geːlɪʃ] *adj* REL Protestant; ~***-lutherisch*** Lutheran
**Evangelium** [evaŋ'geːljʊm] *n* (*-s*; *-lien*) Gospel
**eventuell** [evɛntu'ɛl] **1.** *adj* possible **2.** *adv* possibly, perhaps
**evtl.** *abbr of* ***eventuell*** poss., possibly
**ewig** ['eːvɪç] *adj* eternal; F constant, endless; ***auf*** ~ for ever; '**Ewigkeit** *f* (-; *no pl*) eternity; F ***eine*** ~ (for) ages
**exakt** [ɛ'ksakt] *adj* exact, precise
**Ex'aktheit** *f* (-; *no pl*) exactness, precision
**Examen** [ɛ'ksaːmən] *n* (*-s*; *Examina* [ɛ'ksaːmina]) exam, examination
**Exekutive** [ɛkseku'tiːvə] *f* (-; *-n*) POL executive (power)
**Exemplar** [ɛksɛm'plaːɐ] *n* (*-s*; *-e*) specimen; copy
**exerzieren** [ɛksɛr'tsiːrən] *v/i* (*no -ge-, h*) MIL drill
**Exil** [ɛ'ksiːl] *n* (*-s*; *-e*) exile
**Existenz** [ɛksɪs'tɛnts] *f* (-; *-en*) existence; living, livelihood; ~**kampf** *m* struggle for survival; ~**minimum** *n* subsistence level
**existieren** [ɛksɪs'tiːrən] *v/i* (*no -ge-, h*) exist; live (***von*** on)
**exklusiv** [ɛksklu'ziːf] *adj* exclusive, select
**exotisch** [ɛ'ksoːtɪʃ] *adj* exotic
**Expansion** [ɛkspan'zjoːn] *f* (-; *-en*) expansion
**Expedition** [ɛkspedi'tsjoːn] *f* (-; *-en*) expedition
**Experiment** [ɛksperi'mɛnt] *n* (*-[e]s*; *-e*), **experimentieren** [ɛksperimɛn'tiːrən]

E

*v/i* (*no -ge-*, *h*) experiment
**Experte** [ɛks'pɛrtə] *m* (*-n*; *-n*), **Ex'pertin** *f* (*-*; *-nen*) expert (***für*** on)
**explodieren** [ɛksplo'di:rən] *v/i* (*no -ge-*, *sein*) explode (*a. fig*), burst; **Explosion** [ɛksplo'zjo:n] *f* (*-*; *-en*) explosion (*a. fig*); **explosiv** [ɛksplo'zi:f] *adj* explosive
**Export** [ɛks'pɔrt] *m* (*-[e]s*; *-e*) (*no pl*) export(ation); exports
**exportieren** [ɛkspɔr'ti:rən] *v/t* (*no -ge-*, *h*) export
**Express** [ɛks'prɛs] *m* (*-es*; *no pl*) RAIL express; ***per ~*** by special delivery, *Br* express
**extra** ['ɛkstra] *adv* extra; separately; F on purpose; ***~ für dich*** especially for you
**Extra** *n* (*-s*; *-s*), **~blatt** *n* extra
**Extrakt** [ɛks'trakt] *m* (*-[e]s*; *-e*) extract
**extravagant** [ɛkstrava'gant] *adj* flamboyant
**extrem** [ɛks'tre:m] *adj*, **Ex'trem** *n* (*-s*; *-e*) extreme; **Extremist(in)** [ɛkstre'mɪst(ɪn)] (*-en*; *-en/-*; *-nen*), **extre'mistisch** *adj* extremist, ultra
**Exzellenz** [ɛkstsɛ'lɛnts] *f* (*-*; *-en*) Excellency
**exzentrisch** [ɛks'tsɛntrɪʃ] *adj* eccentric
**Exzess** [ɛks'tsɛs] *m* (*-ses*; *-se*) excess

# F

**Fa.** *abbr of* ***Firma*** firm; Messrs.
**Fabel** ['fa:bəl] *f* (*-*; *-n*) fable (*a. fig*)
**'fabelhaft** *adj* fantastic, wonderful
**Fabrik** [fa'bri:k] *f* (*-*; *-en*) factory, works, shop; **Fabrikant** [fabri'kant] *m* (*-en*; *-en*) factory owner; manufacturer
**Fa'brikarbeiter** *m* factory worker
**Fabrikat** [fabri'ka:t] *n* (*-[e]s*; *-e*) make, brand; product
**Fabrikation** [fabrika'tsjo:n] *f* (*-*; *-en*) manufacturing, production
**Fabrikati'onsfehler** *m* flaw
**Fa'brik|besitzer** *m* factory owner; **~ware** *f* manufactured product(s)
**Fach** [fax] *n* (*-[e]s*; *Fächer* ['fɛçɐ]) compartment; pigeonhole; shelf; PED, UNIV subject; → ***Fachgebiet***; **~arbeiter** *m* skilled worker; **~arzt** *m*, **~ärztin** *f* specialist (***für*** in); **~ausbildung** *f* professional training; **~ausdruck** *m* technical term; **~buch** *n* specialist book
**Fächer** ['fɛçɐ] *m* (*-s*; *-*) fan
**'Fach|frau** *f* expert; **~gebiet** *n* line, field; trade, business; **~geschäft** *n* dealer (specializing in …); **~hochschule** *f* *appr* (technial) college, *esp Br* polytechnic; **~kenntnisse** *pl* specialized knowledge
**'fachkundig** *adj* competent, expert
**'fachlich** *adj* professional, specialized
**'Fach|litera,tur** *f* specialized literature; **~mann** *m* (*-[e]s*; *-leute*) expert
**fachmännisch** ['faxmɛnɪʃ] *adj* expert
**'Fachschule** *f* technical school *or* college
**fachsimpeln** ['faxzɪmpəln] *v/i* (*ge-*, *h*) talk shop
**'Fach|werk** *n* framework; **~werkhaus** *n* half-timbered house; **~zeitschrift** *f* (professional *or* specialist) journal
**Fackel** ['fakəl] *f* (*-*; *-n*) torch; **~zug** *m* torchlight procession
**fade** ['fa:də] *adj* GASTR tasteless, flat; stale; *fig* dull, boring
**Faden** ['fa:dən] *m* (*-s*; *Fäden* ['fɛ:dən]) thread (*a. fig*); **'fadenscheinig** *adj* threadbare; *fig* flimsy (*excuse etc*)
**fähig** ['fɛ:ɪç] *adj* capable (***zu*** of [*doing*] *s.th.*), able (to *do s.th.*); **'Fähigkeit** *f* (*-*; *-en*) (cap)ability; talent, gift
**fahl** [fa:l] *adj* pale; ashen (*face*)
**fahnden** ['fa:ndən] *v/i* (*ge-*, *h*) search (***nach*** for); **'Fahndung** *f* (*-*; *-en*) search; 'Fahndungsliste *f* wanted list
**Fahne** ['fa:nə] *f* (*-*; *-n*) flag; *mst fig* banner; F ***e-e ~ haben*** reek of alcohol
**'Fahnen|flucht** *f* (*-*; *no pl*) MIL desertion; **~stange** *f* flagpole, flagstaff
**Fahrbahn** ['fa:ɐba:n] *f* road(way), pavement; MOT lane
**'fahrbar** *adj* mobile
**Fähre** ['fɛ:rə] *f* (*-*; *-n*) ferry(boat)
**fahren** ['fa:rən] (*irr*, *ge-*) **1.** *v/i* (*sein*) go; *bus etc*: run; leave; MOT drive; ride; ***mit dem Auto*** (***Zug, Bus*** *etc*) ***~*** go by car (train, bus *etc*); ***über e-e Brücke*** *etc*

~ cross a bridge *etc*; ***mit der Hand über et.*** ~ run one's hand over s.th.; ***was ist denn in dich gefahren?*** what's got into you? **2.** *v/t* (*h*) drive (*car etc*); ride (*bicycle etc*); carry

**Fahrer** ['fa:rɐ] *m* (-*s*; -) driver; **~flucht** *f* hit-and-run offense (*Br* offence)

'**Fahrerin** *f* (-; -*nen*) driver

**Fahr|gast** ['fa:ɐgast] *m* passenger; **~geld** *n* fare; **~gelegenheit** *f* means of transport(ation); **~gemeinschaft** *f* car pool; **~gestell** *n* MOT chassis; AVIAT → ***Fahrwerk***; **~karte** *f* ticket

'**Fahrkarten|auto,mat** *m* ticket machine; **~entwerter** *m* (-*s*; -) ticket-cancel(l)ing machine; **~schalter** *m* ticket window

'**fahrlässig** *adj* careless, reckless (*a.* JUR); ***grob*** ~ grossly negligent

'**Fahrlehrer** *m* driving instructor

'**Fahrplan** *m* timetable, schedule

'**fahrplanmäßig 1.** *adj* scheduled **2.** *adv* according to schedule; on time

'**Fahr|preis** *m* fare; **~prüfung** *f* driving test; **~rad** *n* bicycle, F bike; **~schein** *m* ticket; **~schule** *f* driving school; **~schüler** *m* MOT student driver, *Br* learner (driver); PED non-local student; **~stuhl** *m* elevator, *Br* lift; **~stunde** *f* driving lesson

**Fahrt** [fa:ɐt] *f* (-; -*en*) ride, MOT *a.* drive; trip, journey, MAR voyage, cruise; speed (*a.* MOT); ***in voller*** ~ at full speed

**Fährte** ['fɛ:ɐtə] *f* (-; -*n*) track (*a. fig*)

'**Fahrtenschreiber** *m* MOT tachograph

'**Fahrwasser** *n* MAR fairway

'**Fahrwerk** *n* AVIAT landing gear

'**Fahrzeug** *n* (-[*e*]*s*; -*e*) vehicle

**Fairness** ['fɛ:ɐnɪs] *f* (-; *no pl*) fair play

**Faktor** ['fakto:ɐ] *m* (-*s*; -*en* [fak'to:rən]) factor

**Fakultät** [fakʊl'tɛ:t] *f* (-; -*en*) UNIV faculty, department

**Falke** ['falkə] *m* (-*n*; -*n*) ZO hawk, falcon

**Fall** [fal] *m* (-[*e*]*s*; *Fälle* ['fɛlə]) fall; LING, JUR, MED case; ***auf jeden*** ~ in any case; ***auf keinen*** ~ on no account; ***für den*** ~, ***dass ...*** in case ...; ***gesetzt den*** ~, ***dass*** suppose (that); ***zu*** ~ ***bringen*** *fig* defeat

**Falle** ['falə] *f* (-; -*n*) trap (*a. fig*)

**fallen** ['falən] *v/i* (*irr, ge-, sein*) fall (*a. rain etc*), drop; ~ ***lassen*** drop (*a. fig*); MIL be killed (in action); ***ein Tor fiel*** SPORT a goal was scored

**fällen** ['fɛlən] *v/t* (*ge-, h*) fell, cut down (*tree*); JUR pass (*sentence*); make (*a decision etc*)

'**fallenlassen** ['faləlasən] *v/i* (*irr*, **fallen**, *no ge-, h*) *fig* drop

**fällig** ['fɛlɪç] *adj* due; payable

'**Fall|obst** *n* windfall; **~rückzieher** *m soccer*: overhead kick

**falls** [fals] *cj* if, in case; ~ ***nicht*** unless

'**Fallschirm** *m* parachute; **~jäger** *m* MIL paratrooper; **~springen** *n* MIL parachuting; SPORT skydiving; **~springer** *m* MIL parachutist; SPORT skydiver

'**Falltür** *f* trapdoor

**falsch** [falʃ] *adj and adv* wrong; false (*a. fig*); forged; ~ ***gehen*** *watch*: be wrong; ***et.*** ~ ***aussprechen*** (***schreiben, verstehen*** *etc*) mispronounce (misspell, misunderstand *etc*) s.th.; ~ ***verbunden!*** TEL sorry, wrong number

**fälschen** ['fɛlʃən] *v/t* (*ge-, h*) forge, fake; counterfeit; '**Fälscher** *m* (-*s*; -) forger

'**Falsch|geld** *n* counterfeit *or* false money; **~spieler** *m* cheat

'**Fälschung** *f* (-; -*en*) forgery; counterfeit; '**fälschungssicher** *adj* forgery-proof

**Falt...** ['falt-] *in cpds ...bett, ...boot etc*: folding ...; **Falte** ['faltə] *f* (-; -n) fold; wrinkle; pleat; crease; '**falten** *v/t* (*ge-, h*) fold; '**Faltenrock** *m* pleated skirt

**Falter** ['faltɐ] *m* (-*s*; -) ZO butterfly

**faltig** ['faltɪç] *adj* wrinkled

**familiär** [fami'ljɛ:ɐ] *adj* personal; informal; ***~e Probleme*** family problems

**Familie** [fa'mi:ljə] *f* (-; -*n*) family (*a.* ZO, BOT)

**Fa'milien|angelegenheit** *f* family affair; **~anschluss** *m*: ~ ***haben*** live as one of the family; **~name** *m* family (*or* last) name, surname; **~packung** *f* family size (package); **~planung** *f* family planning; **~stand** *m* marital status; **~vater** *m* family man

**Fanatiker** [fa'na:tikɐ] *m* (-*s*; -), **Fa'natikerin** *f* (-; -*nen*), **fa'natisch** *adj* fanatic; **Fanatismus** [fana'tɪsmʊs] *m* (-; *no pl*) fanaticism

**fand** [fant] *pret of* ***finden***

**Fang** [faŋ] *m* (-[*e*]*s*; *Fänge* ['fɛŋə]) catch (*a. fig*); '**fangen** *v/t* (*irr, ge-, h*) catch (*a. fig*); ***sich wieder*** ~ get a grip on o.s. again; ***Fangen spielen*** play tag (*Br*

catch); '**Fangzahn** *m* ZO fang
**Fantasie** [fanta'ziː] *f* (-; *-n*) imagination; fantasy; **fanta'sielos** *adj* unimaginative; **fanta'sieren** *v/i* (*no -ge-*, *h*) daydream; MED be delirious; F talk nonsense; **fanta'sievoll** *adj* imaginative; **Fantast** [fan'tast] *m* (*-en*; *-en*) dreamer; **fan'tastisch** *adj* fantastic, F *a.* great, terrific
**Farbband** ['farpbant] *n* (typewriter) ribbon
**Farbe** ['farbə] *f* (-; *-n*) colo(u)r; paint; complexion; tan; *card games*: suit
'**farbecht** *adj* colo(u)r-fast
**färben** ['fɛrbən] *v/t* (*ge-*, *h*) dye; *esp fig* colo(u)r; ***sich rot ~*** turn red; → ***abfärben***
'**farben|blind** *adj* colo(u)r-blind; **~froh, ~prächtig** *adj* colo(u)rful
'**Farb|fernsehen** *n* colo(u)r television; **~fernseher** *m* colo(u)r TV set; **~film** *m* colo(u)r film; **~foto** *n* colo(u)r photo
**farbig** ['farbɪç] *adj* colo(u)red; stained (*glass*); *fig* colo(u)rful; **Farbige** ['farbɪgə] *m, f* (*-n*; *-n*) → ***Schwarze***
'**Farbkasten** *m* paintbox
'**farblos** *adj* colo(u)rless (*a. fig*)
'**Farbstift** *m* colo(u)red pencil, crayon
'**Farbstoff** *m* dye; GASTR colo(u)ring
'**Farbton** *m* shade, tint
'**Färbung** *f* (-; *-en*) colo(u)ring; hue
**Farnkraut** ['farnkraut] *n* BOT fern
**Fasan** [fa'zaːn] *m* (*-[e]s*; *-e[n]*) ZO pheasant
**Faschismus** [fa'ʃɪsmʊs] *m* (-; *no pl*) POL fascism; **Faschist** [fa'ʃɪst] *m* (*-en*; *-en*), **fa'schistisch** *adj* POL fascist
**faseln** ['faːzəln] F *v/i* (*ge-*, *h*) drivel
**Faser** ['faːzɐ] *f* (-; *-n*) fiber, *Br* fibre; grain; **faserig** ['faːzərɪç] *adj* fibrous; '**fasern** *v/i* (*ge-*, *h*) fray
**Fass** [fas] *n* (*-es*; *Fässer* ['fɛsɐ]) cask, barrel; ***vom ~*** on tap
**Fassade** [fa'saːdə] *f* (-; *-n*) ARCH facade, front (*a. fig*)
'**Fassbier** *n* draft (*Br* draught) beer
**fassen** ['fasən] (*ge-*, *h*) **1.** *v/t* take hold of, grasp; seize; catch (*criminal*); hold, take; set (*jewels*); *fig* grasp, understand; pluck up (*courage*); make (*a decision*); ***sich ~*** compose o.s.; ***sich kurz ~*** be brief; ***es ist nicht zu ~*** that's incredible **2.** *v/i*: ***~ nach*** reach for
'**Fassung** *f* (-; *-en*) setting; frame (*of glasses*); ELECTR socket; draft(ing); wording, version; (*no pl*) composure; ***die ~ verlieren*** lose one's composure; ***j-n aus der ~ bringen*** put s.o. out
'**fassungslos** *adj* stunned; speechless
'**Fassungsvermögen** *n* capacity
**fast** [fast] *adv* almost, nearly; ***~ nie*** (***nichts***) hardly ever (anything)
**fasten** ['fastən] *v/i* (*ge-*, *h*) fast
'**Fastenzeit** *f* REL Lent
'**Fastnacht** *f* → ***Karneval***
**fatal** [fa'taːl] *adj* unfortunate; awkward; disastrous
**fauchen** ['fauxən] *v/i* (*ge-*, *h*) ZO hiss
**faul** [faul] *adj* rotten, bad, GASTR *a.* spoiled; *fig* lazy; F fishy; ***~e Ausrede*** lame excuse; '**faulen** *v/i* (*ge-*, *h*, *sein*) rot, go bad; decay
**faulenzen** ['faulɛntsən] *v/i* (*ge-*, *h*) laze, loaf (about); '**Faulenzer**(**in**) ['faulɛntsɐ, 'faulɛntsərɪn] (*-s*; *-/-*; *-nen*) lazybones; *contp* loafer
'**Faulheit** *f* (-; *no pl*) laziness
**faulig** ['faulɪç] *adj* rotten
**Fäulnis** ['fɔʏlnɪs] *f* (-; *no pl*) rottenness, decay (*a. fig*)
'**Faulpelz** F *m* → ***Faulenzer***
'**Faultier** *n* ZO sloth
**Faust** [faust] *f* (-; *Fäuste* ['fɔʏstə]) fist; ***auf eigene ~*** on one's own initiative; **~handschuh** *m* mitten; **~regel** *f* (***als ~*** as a) rule of thumb; **~schlag** *m* punch
**Favorit** [favo'riːt] *m* (*-en*; *-en*), **Favo'ritin** *f* (-; *-nen*) favo(u)rite
**Fax** [faks] *n* (-; *-[e]*) fax; fax machine
**faxen** ['faksən] *v/i and v/t* (*ge-*, *h*) fax, send a fax (to)
'**Faxgerät** *n* fax machine
**FCKW** [ɛftseːkaː'veː] *abbr of* ***Fluorchlorkohlenwasserstoff*** chlorofluorocarbon, CFC
**Feber** ['feːbɐ] *Austrian m* (*-s*; -), **Februar** ['feːbruaːɐ] *m* (*-s*; *-e*) February
**fechten** ['fɛçtən] *v/i* (*irr, ge-*, *h*) SPORT fence; *fig* fight; '**Fechten** *n* (*-s*; *no pl*) SPORT fencing; **Fechter**(**in**) ['fɛçtɐ, 'fɛçtərɪn] *m*(*f*) (*-s*; *-/-*; *-nen*) SPORT fencer
**Feder** ['feːdɐ] *f* (-; *-n*) feather; plume; nib; TECH spring; **~ball** *m* SPORT badminton; shuttlecock; **~bett** *n* comforter, *Br* duvet; **~gewicht** *n* SPORT featherweight; **~halter** *m* penholder
'**feder'leicht** *adj* (as) light as a feather

**Federmäppchen** ['feːdɐmɛpçən] *n* (*-s*; *-*) pencil case
'**federn** (*ge-*, *h*) **1.** *v/i* be springy **2.** *v/t* TECH spring; **~d** *adj* springy, elastic
'**Federstrich** *m* stroke of the pen
**Federung** ['feːdərʊŋ] *f* (*-*; *-en*) springs; MOT suspension; ***e-e gute ~ haben*** be well sprung
'**Federzeichnung** *f* pen-and-ink drawing
**Fee** [feː] *f* (*-*; *-n*) fairy
**fegen** ['feːgən] *v/t* (*ge-*, *h*) *and fig v/i* (*sein*) sweep
**fehl** [feːl] *adj*: ***~ am Platze*** out of place
'**Fehlbetrag** *m* deficit
'**fehlen** *v/i* (*ge-*, *h*) be missing; be absent; ***ihm fehlt*** (***es an***) … he is lacking …; ***du fehlst uns*** we miss you; ***was dir fehlt, ist …*** what you need is …; ***was fehlt Ihnen?*** what's wrong with you?
**Fehler** ['feːlɐ] *m* (*-s*; *-*) mistake; fault, TECH *a.* defect, flaw; IT error
'**fehlerfrei** *adj* faultless, flawless
'**fehlerhaft** *adj* faulty; full of mistakes; TECH defective
'**Fehlermeldung** *f* IT error message
'**Fehl|ernährung** *f* malnutrition; **~geburt** *f* MED miscarriage; **~griff** *m* mistake; wrong choice
'**Fehlschlag** *m* failure; '**fehlschlagen** *v/i* (*irr*, ***schlagen***, *sep*, *-ge-*, *sein*) fail
'**Fehl|start** *m* false start; **~tritt** *m* slip; *fig* lapse; **~zündung** *f* MOT backfire (*a.* ***~ haben***)
**Feier** ['faiɐ] *f* (*-*; *-n*) celebration; party
'**Feierabend** *m* end of a day's work; closing time; evening (at home); ***~ machen*** finish (work), F knock off; ***nach ~*** after work
'**feierlich** *adj* solemn; festive
'**Feierlichkeit** *f* (*-*; *-en*) (*no pl*) solemnity; ceremony
'**feiern** *v/t and v/i* (*ge-*, *h*) celebrate; have a party
'**Feiertag** *m* holiday; ***gesetzlicher ~*** public (*or* legal, *Br a.* bank) holiday
**feig** [faik], **feige** ['faigə] *adj* cowardly; ***~ sein*** be a coward
**Feige** ['faigə] *f* (*-*; *-n*) BOT *fig*
'**Feigheit** *f* (*-*; *no pl*) cowardice
'**Feigling** *m* (*-s*; *-e*) coward
**Feile** ['failə] *f* (*-*; *-n*), '**feilen** *v/t and v/i* (*ge-*, *h*) file
**feilschen** ['failʃən] *v/i* (*ge-*, *h*) haggle (***um*** about, over)
**fein** [fain] *adj* fine; choice, excellent; keen (*ear*); delicate; distinguished, F posh; ***~!*** good!, okay!
**Feind** [faint] *m* (*-[e]s*; *-e* ['faində]) enemy (*a. fig*); **~bild** *n* enemy image
**Feindin** ['faindɪn] *f* (*-*; *-nen*) enemy
'**feindlich** *adj* hostile; MIL enemy
'**Feindschaft** *f* (*-*; *no pl*) hostility
'**feindselig** *adj* hostile (***gegen*** to)
'**Feindseligkeit** *f* (*-*; *no pl*) hostility
**feinfühlig** ['fainfyːlɪç] *adj* sensitive
'**Feingefühl** *n* (*-[e]s*; *no pl*) sensitiveness
'**Feinheit** *f* (*-*; *-en*) (*no pl*) fineness; keenness; delicacy; *pl* niceties
'**Fein|kostgeschäft** *n* delicatessen; **~me,chaniker** *m* precision mechanic
'**Feinschmecker** *m* (*-s*; *-*) gourmet
**feist** [faist] *adj* fat, stout
**Feld** [fɛlt] *n* (*-[e]s*; *-er* ['fɛldɐ]) field (*a. fig*); *chess*: square; **~arbeit** *f* AGR work in the fields; fieldwork; **~bett** *n* cot, *Br* camp bed; **~flasche** *f* water bottle, canteen; **~lerche** *f* ZO skylark; **~marschall** *m* MIL field marshal
**Feldstecher** ['fɛltʃtɛçɐ] *m* (*-s*; *-*) field glasses
**Feldwebel** ['fɛltveːbəl] *m* (*-s*; *-*) MIL sergeant
'**Feldzug** *m* MIL campaign (*a. fig*)
**Felge** ['fɛlgə] *f* (*-*; *-n*) rim; SPORT circle
**Fell** [fɛl] *n* (*-[e]s*; *-e*) ZO coat; skin, fur
**Fels** [fɛls] *m* (*-en*; *-en*) rock
'**Felsbrocken** *m* boulder
**Felsen** ['fɛlzən] *m* (*-s*; *-*) rock
**felsig** ['fɛlzɪç] *adj* rocky
'**Felsspalte** *f* crevice
'**Felsvorsprung** *m* ledge
**feminin** [femi'niːn] *adj* feminine (*a.* LING); *contp* effeminate; **Feminismus** [femi'nɪsmʊs] *m* (*-*; *no pl*) feminism; **Feministin** [femi'nɪstɪn] *f* (*-*; *-nen*), **femi'nistisch** *adj* feminist
**Fenchel** ['fɛnçəl] *m* (*-s*; *no pl*) BOT fennel
**Fenster** ['fɛnstɐ] *n* (*-s*; *-*) window; **~bank** *f* (*-*; *-bänke*), **~brett** *n* windowsill; **~flügel** *m* casement; **~laden** *m* shutter; **~rahmen** *m* window frame; **~scheibe** *f* (window)pane
**Ferien** ['feːrjən] *pl* vacation, *esp Br* holiday(s *pl*); ***~ haben*** be on vacation; **~haus** *n* vacation home, cottage; **~la-**

F

**ger** *n* summer camp; **~wohnung** *f* vacation rental, *Br* holiday apartment
**Ferkel** ['fɛrkəl] *n* (*-s*; *-*) ZO piglet; F pig
**fern** [fɛrn] *adj and adv* far(away), far-off, distant; ***von ~*** from a distance
'**Fernamt** *n* telephone exchange
'**Fernbedienung** *f* remote control
'**fernbleiben** *v/i* (*irr*, ***bleiben***, *sep*, *-ge-*, *sein*) stay away (*dat* from)
**Ferne** ['fɛrnə] *f* (*-*; *no pl*) distance; ***aus der ~*** from a distance
**ferner** ['fɛrnɐ] *adv* further(more); in addition, also
'**Fern|fahrer** *m* long-haul truck driver, F trucker, *Br* long-distance lorry driver; **~gespräch** *n* TEL long-distance call
'**ferngesteuert** *adj* remote-controlled; MIL guided (*missile etc*)
'**Fernglas** *n* binoculars
'**fernhalten** *v/t* (*irr*, ***halten***, *sep*, *-ge-*, *h*) keep away (***von*** from)
**Fern|heizung** *f* district heating; **~kurs** *m* correspondence course; **~laster** F *m* (*-s*; *-*) MOT longhaul truck, *Br* long-distance lorry; **~lenkung** *f* remote control; **~licht** *n* MOT full (*or* high) beam
'**fernliegen** *v/i* (*irr*, ***liegen***, *sep*, *-ge-*, *h*): ***es liegt mir fern zu*** far be it from me to
'**Fernmelde|satel,lit** *m* communications satellite; **~technik** *f*, **~wesen** *n* (*-s*; *no pl*) telecommunications
'**Fern|rohr** *n* telescope; **~schreiben** *n*, **~schreiber** *m* telex
'**fernsehen** *v/i* (*irr*, ***sehen***, *sep*, *-ge-*, *h*) watch television; '**Fernsehen** *n* (*-s*; *no pl*) television (***im*** on); '**Fernseher** F *m* (*-s*; *-*) TV (set); TV viewer
'**Fernseh|schirm** *m* (TV) screen; **~sendung** *f* TV program(me)
'**Fernsteuerung** *f* remote control
'**Fernverkehr** *m* long-distance traffic
**Ferse** ['fɛrzə] *f* (*-*; *-n*) ANAT heel (*a. fig*)
**fertig** ['fɛrtɪç] *adj* ready; finished; ***~ bringen*** manage; *iro* be capable of; ***~ machen*** finish (*a.* F *s.o.*); get *s.th.* ready; F give *s.o.* hell, do *s.o.* in; ***sich ~ machen*** get ready; ***(mit et.) ~ sein*** have finished (s.th.); ***mit** et.* ***~ werden*** cope with *a problem etc*; F ***völlig ~*** dead beat
'**fertigbringen** *v/t* (*irr*, ***bringen***, *sep*, *-ge-*, *h*) → ***fertig***
'**Fertig|gericht** *n* ready(-to-serve) meal; **~haus** *n* prefabricated house, F prefab
'**Fertigkeit** *f* (*-*; *-en*) skill
'**fertigmachen** *v/t* (*irr*, ***bringen***, *sep*, *-ge-*, *h*) → ***fertig***
'**Fertigstellung** *f* (*-*; *no pl*) completion
'**fertigwerden** *v/t* (*irr*, ***bringen***, *sep*, *-ge-*, *sein*) → ***fertig***
**fesch** [fɛʃ] *Austrian adj* smart, chic
**Fessel** ['fɛsəl] *f* (*-*; *-n*) shackle (*a. fig*); ANAT ankle; '**fesseln** *v/t* (*ge-*, *h*) bind, tie (up); *fig* fascinate
**fest** [fɛst] *adj* firm (*a. fig*); solid; fast; *fig* fixed (*date etc*); sound (*sleep*); steady (*girlfriend etc*); ***~ schlafen*** be fast asleep
**Fest** *n* (*-[e]s*; *-e*) celebration; party; REL festival, feast; → ***froh***
'**festbinden** *v/t* (*irr*, ***binden***, *sep*, *-ge-*, *h*) fasten, tie (***an*** *dat* to)
'**Festessen** *n* banquet, feast
'**festfahren** *v/refl* (*irr*, ***fahren***, *sep*, *-ge-*, *h*) get stuck
'**Festhalle** *f* (festival) hall
'**festhalten** (*irr*, ***halten***, *sep*, *-ge-*, *h*) **1.** *v/i*: ***~ an*** (*dat*) stick to **2.** *v/t* hold on to; hold *s.o. or s.th.* tight; ***sich ~ an*** (*dat*) hold on to
**festigen** ['fɛstɪgən] *v/t* (*ge-*, *h*) strengthen; ***sich ~*** grow firm *or* strong
**Festigkeit** ['fɛstɪçkait] *f* (*-*; *no pl*) firmness; strength
'**Festland** *n* mainland; *the* Continent
'**festlegen** *v/t* (*sep*, *-ge-*, *h*) fix, set; ***sich ~ auf*** (*acc*) commit o.s. to *s.th.*
'**festlich** *adj* festive
'**festmachen** *v/t* (*sep*, *-ge-*, *h*) fasten, fix (***an*** *dat* to); MAR moor; ECON fix
**Festnahme** ['fɛstna:mə] *f* (*-*; *-n*), '**festnehmen** *v/t* (*irr*, ***nehmen***, *sep*, *-ge-*, *h*) arrest
'**Festplatte** *f* IT hard disk
'**fest|schrauben** *v/t* (*sep*, *-ge-*, *h*) screw (on) tight; **~setzen** *v/t* (*sep*, *-ge-*, *h*) fix; **~sitzen** *v/i* (*irr*, ***sitzen***, *sep*, *-ge-*, *h*) be stuck; be (left) stranded
'**Festspiele** *pl* festival
'**feststehen** *v/i* (*irr*, ***stehen***, *sep*, *-ge-*, *h*) be certain; *date etc*: be fixed; **~d** *adj* established (*fact etc*); set (*phrase etc*)
'**feststellen** *v/t* (*sep*, *-ge-*, *h*) find (out); establish; see, notice; state; TECH lock, arrest; '**Feststellung** *f* (*-*; *-en*) finding(s); realization; statement
'**Festtag** *m* holiday; REL religious holiday; F red-letter day
'**Festung** *f* (*-*; *-en*) fortress

'**Festzug** *m* procession
**fett** [fɛt] *adj* fat (*a. fig*); PRINT bold; **~ gedruckt** boldface, in bold type (*or* print); **Fett** *n* (-[*e*]*s*; -*e*) fat; dripping; shortening; TECH grease; '**fettarm** *adj* low-fat, *pred* low in fat; '**Fettfleck** *m* grease spot; **fettig** ['fɛtɪç] *adj* greasy
'**Fettnäpfchen** *n*: ***ins ~ treten*** put one's foot in it
**Fetzen** ['fɛtsən] *m* (-*s*; -) shred; rag; scrap (*of paper etc*)
**feucht** [fɔʏçt] *adj* moist, damp; humid
**Feuchtigkeit** ['fɔʏçtɪçkait] *f* (-; *no pl*) moisture; dampness; humidity
**feudal** [fɔʏ'da:l] *adj* POL feudal; F posh, *Br* swish
**Feuer** ['fɔʏɐ] *n* (-*s*; -) fire (*a. fig*); ***j-m ~ geben*** give s.o. a light; ***~ fangen*** catch fire; *fig* fall for *s.o.*; **~a͵larm** *m* fire alarm; **~bestattung** *f* cremation
'**feuerfest** *adj* fireproof, fire-resistant
'**Feuergefahr** *f* danger of fire
'**feuergefährlich** *adj* inflammable
'**Feuer|leiter** *f* fire escape; **~löscher** ['fɔʏɐlœʃɐ] *m* (-*s*; -) fire extinguisher; **~melder** ['fɔʏɐmɛldɐ] *m* (-*s*; -) fire alarm
**feuern** ['fɔʏɐn] *v/i and v/t* (*ge-*, *h*) fire (*a.* F *s.o.*)
'**feuer'rot** *adj* blazing red; crimson
'**Feuer|schiff** *n* lightship; **~stein** *m* flint; **~wache** *f* fire station; **~waffe** *f* firearm, gun; **~wehr** *f* (-; -*en*) fire brigade (*or* department); fire truck (*Br* engine); **~wehrmann** *m* (-[*e*]*s*, -*männer*, -*leute*) fireman, fire fighter; **~werk** *n* fireworks; **~werkskörper** *m* firework, firecracker; **~zeug** *n* (cigarette) lighter
**feurig** ['fɔʏrɪç] *adj* fiery, ardent
**Fiasko** ['fjasko] *n* (-*s*; -*s*) fiasco, (complete) failure
**Fibel** ['fi:bəl] *f* (-; -*n*) primer, first reader
**Fiber** ['fi:bɐ] *f* fiber, *Br* fibre; **~glas** *n* fiberglass, *Br* fibreglass
**Fichte** ['fɪçtə] *f* (-; -*n*) BOT spruce, F *mst* pine *or* fir (tree)
**ficken** ['fɪkən] V *v/i and v/t* (*ge-*, *h*) fuck
**Fieber** ['fi:bɐ] *n* (-*s*; *no pl*) MED temperature, fever (*a. fig*); ***~ haben*** (***messen***) have a (take *s.o.'s*) temperature; ***~ senkend*** MED antipyretic
'**fieberhaft** *adj* MED feverish (*a. fig*)
'**fiebern** *v/i* (*ge-*, *h*) MED have *or* run a temperature; ***~ nach*** *fig* crave for
'**Fieberthermo͵meter** *n* fever (*Br* clinical) thermometer
**fiel** [fi:l] *pret of* ***fallen***
**fies** [fi:s] F *adj* mean, nasty
**Figur** [fi'gu:ɐ] *f* (-; -*en*) figure
**Filet** [fi'le:] *n* (-*s*; -*s*) GASTR fil(l)et
**Filiale** [fi'lja:lə] *f* (-; -*n*) branch
**Film** [film] *m* (-[*e*]*s*; -*e*) film; movie, *esp Br* (motion) picture; *the* movies, *Br the* cinema; **~aufnahme** *f* filming, shooting; take, shot
**filmen** ['filmən] (*ge-*, *h*) **1.** *v/t* film, shoot **2.** *v/i* make a film
'**Film|gesellschaft** *f* motion-picture (*Br* film) company; **~kamera** *f* motion-picture (*Br* film) camera; **~kas͵sette** *f* film magazine, cartridge; **~pro͵jektor** *m* film (*or* movie) projector; **~regis͵seur** *m* film director; **~schauspieler(in)** film (*or* screen, movie) actor (actress); **~studio** *n* film studio(s); **~the͵ater** *n* → ***Kino***; **~verleih** *m* film distributors; **~vorführer** *m* (-*s*; -) projectionist
**Filter** ['fɪltɐ] *m*, *esp* TECH *n* (-*s*; -) filter
'**Filterkaffee** *m* filter coffee
'**filtern** *v/t* (*ge-*, *h*) filter
'**Filterziga͵rette** *f* filter(-tipped) cigarette, filter tip
**Filz** [fɪlts] *m* (-*es*; -*e*) felt; F POL corruption, sleaze; '**filzen** F *v/t* (*ge-*, *h*) frisk
'**Filz|schreiber** ['fɪltsʃraibɐ] *m* (-*s*; -), **~stift** *m* felt(-tipped) pen
**Finale** [fi'na:lə] *n* (-*s*; -) finale; SPORT final(s)
**Finanz|amt** [fi'nantsʔamt] *n* tax office; Internal (*Br* Inland) Revenue; **~beamte** *m* tax officer
**Finanzen** [fi'nantsən] *pl* finances
**finanziell** [finan'tsjɛl] *adj* financial
**finanzieren** [finan'tsi:rən] *v/t* (*no -ge-*, *h*) finance
**Fi'nanz|mi͵nister** *m* minister of finance; Secretary of the Treasury, *Br* Chancellor of the Exchequer; **~minis͵terium** *n* ministry of finance; Treasury Department, *Br* Treasury; **~wesen** *n* (-*s*; *no pl*) finance
**Findelkind** ['fɪndəlkɪnt] *n* JUR foundling
**finden** *v/t* (*irr*, *ge-*, *h*) find; think, believe; ***ich finde ihn nett*** I think he's nice; ***wie ~ Sie …?*** how do you like …?; ***~ Sie*** (***nicht***)***?*** do (don't) you think so?;

***das wird sich ~*** we'll see
**Finder** ['fɪndɐ] *m* (*-s*; *-*) finder
'**Finderlohn** *m* finder's reward
**findig** ['fɪndɪç] *adj* clever
**fing** [fɪŋ] *pret of* ***fangen***
**Finger** ['fɪŋɐ] *m* (*-s*; *-*) ANAT finger; **~abdruck** *m* fingerprint; **~fertigkeit** *f* (*-*; *no pl*) manual skill; **~hut** *m* thimble; BOT foxglove; **~nagel** *m* ANAT fingernail; **~spitze** *f* fingertip; **~spitzengefühl** *n* (*-[e]s*; *no pl*) sure instinct; tact
**fingiert** [fɪŋ'giːɐt] *adj* faked; fictitious
**Fink** [fɪŋk] *m* (*-en*; *-en*) ZO finch
**Finne** ['fɪnə] *m* (*-n*; *-n*), **Finnin** ['fɪnɪn] *f* (*-*; *-nen*) Finn; '**finnisch** *adj* Finnish
**Finnland** ['fɪnlant] Finland
**finster** ['fɪnstɐ] *adj* dark, gloomy; *fig* grim; shady
'**Finsternis** *f* (*-*; *-se*) darkness, gloom
**Finte** ['fɪntə] *f* (*-*; *-n*) trick; SPORT feint
**Firma** ['fɪrma] (*-*; *-men*) firm, company
**firmen** ['fɪrmən] *v/t* (*ge-*, *h*) REL confirm
'**Firmung** *f* (*-*; *-en*) REL confirmation
**First** [fɪrst] *m* (*-[e]s*; *-e*) ARCH ridge
**Fisch** [fɪʃ] *m* (*-[e]s*; *-e*) ZO fish; *pl* ASTR Pisces; ***er ist*** (***ein***) ***~*** he's (a) Pisces
'**Fischdampfer** *m* trawler
**fischen** ['fɪʃən] *v/t and v/i* (*ge-*, *h*) fish
**Fischer** ['fɪʃɐ] *m* (*-s*; *-*) fisherman; **~...** *in cpds ...boot*, *...dorf etc*: fishing ...
**Fischerei** [fɪʃə'rai] *f* (*-*; *no pl*) fishing
'**Fisch|fang** *m* (*-[e]s*; *no pl*) fishing; **~gräte** *f* fishbone; **~grätenmuster** *n* herring-bone (pattern); **~gründe** *pl* fishing grounds; **~händler** *m* fish dealer, *esp Br* fishmonger; **~kutter** *m* smack; **~laich** *m* spawn; **~stäbchen** *n* GASTR fish stick (*Br* finger); **~zucht** *f* fish farming; **~zug** *m* catch, haul (*both a. fig*)
**Fisole** [fi'zoːlə] *Austrian f* (*-*; *-n*) BOT string bean
**Fistel** ['fɪstəl] *f* (*-*; *-n*) MED fistula
'**Fistelstimme** *f* falsetto
**fit** [fɪt] *adj* fit; ***sich ~ halten*** keep fit
'**Fitness** *f* (*-*; *no pl*) fitness; **~center** *n* health club, fitness center, gym
**fix** [fɪks] *adj* ECON fixed; F quick; F smart, bright; F ***~ und fertig sein*** be dead beat; be a nervous wreck; ***~e Idee*** PSYCH obsession
**fixen** ['fɪksən] F *v/i* (*ge-*, *h*) shoot, fix; be a junkie; **Fixer** ['fɪksɐ] F *m* (*-s*; *-*) junkie, mainliner
**fixieren** [fɪ'ksiːrən] *v/t* (*no -ge-*, *h*) fix (*a.* PHOT); stare at *s.o.*
'**Fixstern** *m* ASTR fixed star
**FKK** [ɛfkaː'kaː] *abbr of* ***Freikörperkultur*** nudism
**FK'K-Strand** *m* nudist beach
**flach** [flax] *adj* flat; level, even, plane; *fig* shallow
**Fläche** ['flɛçə] *f* (*-*; *-n*) surface (*a.* MATH); area (*a.* MATH); expanse, space
'**flächendeckend** *adj* exhaustive
'**Flächen|inhalt** *m* MATH (surface) area; **~maß** *n* square *or* surface measure
'**Flachland** *n* (*-[e]s*; *no pl*) lowland, plain
**Flachs** [flaks] *m* (*-es*; *no pl*) BOT flax
**flackern** ['flakɐn] *v/i* (*ge-*, *h*) flicker
**Fladenbrot** ['flaːdənbroːt] *n* round flat bread (*or* loaf)
**Flagge** ['flagə] *f* (*-*; *-n*) flag
'**flaggen** *v/i* (*ge-*, *h*) fly a flag *or* flags
**Flak** [flak] *f* (*-*; *-*) MIL anti-aircraft gun
**Flamme** ['flamə] *f* (*-*; *-n*) flame (*a. fig*)
**Flanell** [fla'nɛl] *m* (*-s*; *-e*) flannel
**Flanke** ['flaŋkə] *f* (*-*; *-n*) flank, side; *soccer*: cross; SPORT flank vault
**flankieren** [flaŋ'kiːrən] *v/t* (*no -ge-*, *h*) flank
**Flasche** ['flaʃə] *f* (*-*; *-n*) bottle; baby's bottle; F *contp* dead loss
'**Flaschen|bier** *n* bottled beer; **~hals** *m* neck of a bottle; **~öffner** *m* bottle opener; **~pfand** *n* (bottle) deposit; **~zug** *m* TECH block and tackle, pulley
**flatterhaft** ['flatɐhaft] *adj* fickle, flighty
**flattern** ['flatɐn] *v/i* (*ge-*, *sein*) flutter; TECH (*h*) wobble
**flau** [flau] *adj* queasy; *fig* flat; ECON slack
**Flaum** [flaum] *m* (*-[e]s*; *no pl*) down, fluff, fuzz
**Flausch** [flauʃ] *m* (*-es*; *-e*) fleece
**flauschig** ['flauʃɪç] *adj* fleecy, fluffy
**Flausen** ['flauzən] F *pl* (funny) ideas
**Flaute** ['flautə] *f* (*-*; *-n*) MAR calm; ECON slack period
**Flechte** ['flɛçtə] *f* (*-*; *-n*) plait, braid; BOT, MED lichen; '**flechten** *v/t* (*irr*, *ge-*, *h*) plait, braid (*hair*); weave (*basket*)
**Fleck** [flɛk] *m* (*-[e]s*; *-e*) stain, mark; speck; dot; blot(ch); *fig* place, spot; patch; ***blauer ~*** bruise; ***vom ~ weg*** on the spot; ***nicht vom ~ kommen*** not get anywhere; '**Flecken** *m* → ***Fleck***

ˈ**Fleckenentferner** *m* stain remover
ˈ**fleckenlos** *adj* spotless (*a. fig*)
**fleckig** [ˈflɛkɪç] *adj* spotted; stained
**Fledermaus** [ˈfleːdɐmaus] *f* zo bat
**Flegel** [ˈfleːgəl] *m* (*-s*; -) lout, boor
ˈ**flegelhaft** *adj* loutish
ˈ**Flegeljahre** *pl* awkward age
ˈ**flegeln** F *contp v/refl* (*ge-*, *h*) lounge
**flehen** [ˈfleːən] *v/i* (*ge-*, *h*) beg; pray (***um*** for); **flehentlich** [ˈfleːəntlɪç] *adj* imploring, entreating
**Fleisch** [flaiʃ] *n* (*-[e]s*; *no pl*) flesh (*a. fig*); GASTR meat; **~*fressend*** → ***fleischfressend***; **~brühe** *f* (meat) broth, consommé
**Fleischer** [ˈflaiʃɐ] *m* (*-s*; -) butcher
**Fleischerei** [flaiʃəˈrai] *f* (-; *-en*) butcher's (shop)
ˈ**fleischfressend** *adj* BOT, ZO carnivorous
**Fleischhauer** [ˈflaiʃhauɐ] *Austrian m* (*-s*; -) butcher
**fleischig** [ˈflaiʃɪç] *adj* fleshy
ˈ**Fleisch|klößchen** *n* (*-s*; -) meatball; **~konˌserven** *pl* canned (*Br* tinned) meat
ˈ**fleischlos** *adj* meatless
ˈ**Fleischwolf** *m* meat grinder, *Br* mincer
**Fleiß** [flais] *m* (*-es*; *no pl*) diligence, hard work; **fleißig** [ˈflaisɪç] *adj* diligent, hard-working; **~ *sein*** work hard
**fletschen** [ˈflɛtʃən] *v/t* (*ge-*, *h*) bare
**flexibel** [flɛˈksiːbəl] *adj* flexible
**Flexibilität** [flɛksibiliˈtɛːt] *f* (-; *no pl*) flexibility
**flicken** [ˈflɪkən] *v/t* (*ge-*, *h*) mend, repair, *a. fig* patch (up); ˈ**Flicken** *m* (*-s*; -) patch; ˈ**Flickwerk** *n* patchwork (*a. fig*); ˈ**Flickzeug** *n* TECH repair kit
**Flieder** [ˈfliːdɐ] *m* (*-s*; -) BOT lilac
**Fliege** [ˈfliːgə] *f* (-; *-n*) zo fly; bow tie
ˈ**fliegen** *v/i* (*irr*, *ge-*, *sein*) *and v/t* (*h*) fly (*a.* **~ *lassen***); F fall; F be fired, F get the sack; be kicked out *of school*; F **~ *auf*** (*acc*) really go for; F ***in die Luft* ~** blow up
ˈ**Fliegen** *n* (*-s*; *no pl*) flying; aviation
ˈ**Fliegen|fänger** *m* flypaper; **~fenster** *n* flyscreen; **~gewicht** *n* SPORT flyweight; **~gitter** *n* wire mesh (screen); **~klatsche** *f* flyswatter; **~pilz** *m* BOT fly agaric
**Flieger** [ˈfliːgɐ] *m* (*-s*; -) MIL airman; F plane; *cycling*: sprinter; **~aˌlarm** *m* air-raid warning
**fliehen** [ˈfliːən] *v/i* (*irr*, *ge-*, *sein*) flee, run away (*both*: ***vor*** *dat* from)
ˈ**Fliehkraft** *f* PHYS centrifugal force
**Fliese** [ˈfliːzə] *f* (-; *-n*), ˈ**fliesen** *v/t* (*ge-*, *h*) tile; ˈ**Fliesenleger** *m* (*-s*; -) tiler
**Fließband** [ˈfliːsbant] *n* (*-[e]s*; *-bänder*) TECH assembly line; conveyor belt
**fließen** [ˈfliːsən] *v/i* (*irr*, *ge-*, *sein*) flow (*a. fig*); run; **~d 1.** *adj* flowing; running; LING fluent **2.** *adv*: ***er spricht* ~ *Englisch*** he speaks English fluently *or* fluent English
ˈ**Fließheck** *n* MOT fastback
**flimmern** [ˈflɪmɐn] *v/i* (*ge-*, *h*) shimmer; *film*: flicker
**flink** [flɪŋk] *adj* quick, nimble
**Flinte** [ˈflɪntə] *f* (-; *-n*) shotgun; F gun
**Flipper** [ˈflɪpɐ] F *m* (*-s*; -) pinball machine; ˈ**flippern** *v/i* (*ge-*, *h*) play pinball
**Flirt** [flœrt] *m* (*-s*; *-s*) flirtation
**flirten** [ˈflœrtən] *v/i* (*ge-*, *h*) flirt
**Flittchen** [ˈflɪtçən] F *n* (*-s*; -) floozie
**Flitter** [ˈflɪtɐ] *m* (*-s*; -) tinsel (*a. fig*), spangles; **~wochen** *pl* honeymoon
**flitzen** [ˈflɪtsən] F *v/i* (*ge-*, *sein*) flit, whizz, shoot
**flocht** [flɔxt] *pret of* ***flechten***
**Flocke** [ˈflɔkə] *f* (-; *-n*) flake
**flockig** [ˈflɔkɪç] *adj* fluffy, flaky
**flog** [floːk] *pret of* ***fliegen***
**floh** [floː] *pret of* ***fliehen***
**Floh** *m* (*-[e]s*; *Flöhe* [ˈfløːə]) zo flea
ˈ**Flohmarkt** *m* flea market
**Florett** [floˈrɛt] *n* (*-[e]s*; *-e*) foil
**florieren** [floˈriːrən] *v/i* (*no -ge-*, *h*) flourish, prosper
**Floskel** [ˈflɔskəl] *f* (-; *-n*) empty *or* cliché(d) phrase
**floss** [flɔs] *pret of* ***fließen***
**Floß** [floːs] *n* (*-es*; *Flöße* [ˈfløːsə]) raft, float
**Flosse** [ˈflɔsə] *f* (-; *-n*) zo fin, *a.* SPORT flipper
**Flöte** [ˈfløːtə] *f* (-; *-n*) MUS flute; recorder
**flott** [flɔt] *adj* brisk (*pace*); F smart, chic; MAR afloat
**Flotte** [ˈflɔtə] *f* (-; *-n*) MAR fleet; navy
ˈ**Flottenstützpunkt** *m* MIL naval base
**Fluch** [fluːx] *m* (*-[e]s*; *Flüche* [ˈflyːçə]) curse; swear word; **fluchen** [ˈfluːxən] *v/i* (*ge-*, *h*) swear, curse
**Flucht** [flʊxt] *f* (-; *-en*) flight (***vor*** *dat* from); escape, getaway (***aus*** *dat* from)
ˈ**fluchtartig** *adv* hastily

'**Fluchtauto** *n* getaway car

**flüchten** ['flʏçtən] *v/i* (*ge-*, *sein*) flee (***nach, zu*** to), run away; escape, get away; **flüchtig** ['flʏçtɪç] *adj* quick; superficial; careless; fugitive, *criminal etc*: on the run, at large; ***~er Blick*** glance; ***~er Eindruck*** glimpse

'**Flüchtigkeitsfehler** *m* slip

**Flüchtling** ['flʏçtlɪŋ] *m* fugitive; POL refugee

'**Flüchtlingslager** *n* refugee camp

**Flug** [flu:k] *m* (-[*e*]*s*; *Flüge* ['fly:gə]) flight; ***im ~(e)*** rapidly, quickly; **~abwehrra,kete** *f* MIL anti-aircraft missile; **~bahn** *f* trajectory; **~ball** *m tennis*: volley; **~begleiter(in)** flight attendant; **~blatt** *n* handbill, leaflet; **~dienst** *m* air service

**Flügel** ['fly:gəl] *m* (*-s*; -) ZO wing (*a.* SPORT); TECH blade; *windmill*: sail; MUS grand piano; **~mutter** *f* TECH wing nut; **~schraube** *f* TECH thumb screw; **~stürmer** *m* SPORT wing forward; **~tür** *f* folding door

'**Fluggast** *m* (air) passenger

**flügge** ['flʏgə] *adj* full-fledged

'**Flug|gesellschaft** *f* airline; **~hafen** *m* airport; **~linie** *f* air route; → ***Fluggesellschaft***; **~lotse** *m* air traffic controller; **~nummer** *f* flight number; **~plan** *m* flight schedule; **~platz** *m* airfield, airport; **~schein** *m* (flight) ticket; **~schreiber** *m* (*-s*; -) flight recorder, black box; **~sicherung** *f* air traffic control; **~ticket** *n* (flight) ticket; **~verbindung** *f* flight connection; **~verkehr** *m* air traffic; **~zeit** *f* flying time

'**Flugzeug** *n* (-[*e*]*s*; *-e*) (air)plane, aircraft, *Br a.* aeroplane; ***mit dem ~*** by air *or* plane; **~absturz** *m* air *or* plane crash; **~entführung** *f* hijacking, skyjacking; **~halle** *f* hangar; **~träger** *m* MAR MIL aircraft carrier

**Flunder** ['flʊndɐ] *f* (-; *-n*) ZO flounder

**flunkern** ['flʊŋkɐn] *v/i* (*ge-*, *h*) fib; brag

**Fluor** ['flu:o:ɐ] *n* (*-s*; *no pl*) CHEM fluorine; fluoride

'**Fluorchlorkohlenwasserstoff** *m* CHEM chlorofluorocarbon, CFC

**Flur** [flu:ɐ] *m* (-[*e*]*s*; *-e*) hall; corridor

**Fluss** [flʊs] *m* (*-es*; *Flüsse* ['flʏsə]) river; stream; ***im ~*** *fig* in (a state of) flux

**fluss'abwärts** *adv* downstream

**fluss'aufwärts** *adv* upstream

'**Flussbett** *n* river bed

**flüssig** ['flʏsɪç] *adj* liquid; melted; *fig* fluent; ECON available; '**Flüssigkeit** *f* (-; *-en*) liquid; (*no pl*) liquidity; *fig* fluency; '**Flüssigkris,tallanzeige** *f* liquid crystal display, LCD; '**Flüssigseife** *f* liquid soap

'**Fluss|lauf** *m* course of a river; **~pferd** *n* ZO hippopotamus, F hippo; **~ufer** *n* riverbank, riverside

**flüstern** ['flʏstɐn] *v/i and v/t* (*ge-*, *h*) whisper

**Flut** [flu:t] *f* (-; *-en*) flood (*a. fig*); high tide; ***es ist ~*** the tide is in; **~licht** *n* floodlights; **~welle** *f* tidal wave

**focht** [fɔxt] *pret of* ***fechten***

**Fohlen** ['fo:lən] *n* (*-s*; -) ZO foal; colt; filly

**Föhn**[1] [fø:n] *m* (-[*e*]*s*; *-e*) hairdrier

**Föhn**[2] *m* (-[*e*]*s*; *-e*) METEOR foehn, föhn

**föhnen** ['fø:nən] *v/t* (*ge-*, *h*) blow-dry

**Folge** ['fɔlgə] *f* (-; *-n*) result, consequence; effect; succession; order; series; TV *etc*: sequel, episode; aftermath; MED aftereffect

**folgen** ['fɔlgən] *v/i* (*ge-*, *sein*) follow; obey; ***hieraus folgt, dass*** from this it follows that; ***wie folgt*** as follows; **~d** *adj* following, subsequent

**folgendermaßen** ['fɔlgəndɐ'ma:sən] *adv* as follows

'**folgenschwer** *adj* momentous

'**folgerichtig** *adj* logical; consistent

**folgern** ['fɔlgɐn] *v/t* (*ge-*, *h*) conclude (***aus*** *dat* from); **Folgerung** ['fɔlgərʊŋ] *f* (-; *-en*) conclusion

**folglich** ['fɔlklɪç] *cj* consequently, thus, therefore

**folgsam** ['fɔlkza:m] *adj* obedient

**Folie** ['fo:ljə] *f* (-; *-n*) foil; transparency

**Folter** ['fɔltɐ] *f* (-; *-n*) torture; ***auf die ~ spannen*** tantalize; '**foltern** *v/t* (*ge-*, *h*) torture, *fig a.* torment

**Fön**® *m* → ***Föhn***[1]

**Fonds** [fõ:] *m* (-; -) ECON fund

**fönen** *v/t* → ***föhnen***

**Fontäne** [fɔn'tɛ:nə] *f* (-; *-n*) jet, spout; gush

**Förder|band** ['fœrdɐbant] *n* TECH conveyor belt; **~korb** *m mining*: cage

**fordern** ['fɔrdɐn] *v/t* (*ge-*, *h*) demand, *esp* JUR *a.* claim; ECON ask, charge

**fördern** ['fœrdɐn] *v/t* (*ge-*, *h*) promote; support (*a.* UNIV), sponsor; PED tutor, provide remedial classes for; TECH mine

**Forderung** ['fɔrdərʊŋ] *f* (-; *-en*) demand; claim (*a.* JUR); ECON charge

**Förderung** ['fœrdərʊŋ] *f* (-; *-en*) promotion, advancement; support, sponsorship; UNIV *etc*: grant; PED tutoring, remedial classes; TECH mining

**Forelle** [fo'rɛlə] *f* (-; *-n*) zo trout

**Form** [fɔrm] *f* (-; *-en*) form, shape, SPORT *a.* condition; TECH mo(u)ld; ***gut in*** ~ in great form; **formal** [fɔr'maːl] *adj* formal; **Formalität** [fɔrmali'tɛːt] *f* (-; *-en*) formality

**Format** [fɔr'maːt] *n* (-[*e*]*s*; *-e*) size; format; *fig* caliber, *Br* calibre

**formatieren** [fɔrma'tiːrən] *v/t* (*no -ge-*, *h*) IT format; **Forma'tierung** *f* (-; *-en*) IT formatting

**Formel** ['fɔrməl] *f* (-; *-n*) formula

**formell** [fɔr'mɛl] *adj* formal

**formen** ['fɔrmən] *v/t* (*ge-*, *h*) shape, form; *fig* mo(u)ld

'**Formfehler** *m* irregularity

**formieren** [fɔr'miːrən] *v/t and v/refl* (*no -ge-*, *h*) form (up)

**förmlich** ['fœrmlɪç] **1.** *adj* formal; *fig* regular **2.** *adv* formally; *fig* literally

'**formlos** *adj* shapeless; *fig* informal

'**formschön** *adj* well-designed

**Formular** [fɔrmu'laːɐ] *n* (*-s*; *-e*) form, blank

**formulieren** [fɔrmu'liːrən] *v/t* (*no -ge-*, *h*) word, phrase; formulate; express

**Formu'lierung** *f* (-; *-en*) wording, phrasing; formulation; expression, phrase

**forsch** [fɔrʃ] *adj* dashing

**forschen** ['fɔrʃən] *v/i* (*ge-*, *h*) research, do research; ~ ***nach*** search for

**Forscher** ['fɔrʃɐ] *m* (*-s*; -), '**Forscherin** *f* (-; *-nen*) explorer; (research) scientist; **Forschung** ['fɔrʃʊŋ] *f* (-; *-en*) research (work)

**Forst** [fɔrst] *m* (-[*e*]*s*; *-e*[*n*]) forest

**Förster** ['fœrstɐ] *m* (*-s*; -) forester; forest ranger

'**Forstwirtschaft** *f* (-; *no pl*) forestry

**fort** [fɔrt] *adv* off, away; gone; missing

**Fort** [foːɐ] *n* (*-s*; *-s*) MIL fort

'**fortbestehen** *v/i* (*irr*, ***stehen***, *sep*, *no -ge-*, *h*) continue

'**fortbewegen** *v/refl* (*sep*, *no -ge-*, *h*) move; '**Fortbewegung** *f* moving; (loco)motion

'**Fortbildung** *f* (-, *no pl*) further education *or* training

'**fort|fahren** *v/i* (*irr*, ***fahren***, *sep*, *-ge-*) (*sein*) leave, go away, MOT *a.* drive off; (*h*) continue, go *or* keep on (***et. zu tun*** doing s.th.); **~führen** *v/t* (*sep*, *-ge-*, *h*) continue, carry on; **~gehen** *v/i* (*irr*, ***gehen***, *sep*, *-ge-*, *sein*) go away, leave

'**fortgeschritten** *adj* advanced

'**fortlaufend** *adj* consecutive, successive

'**fortpflanzen** *v/refl* (*sep*, *-ge-*, *h*) BIOL reproduce; *fig* spread; '**Fortpflanzung** *f* BIOL reproduction

'**fortschreiten** *v/i* (*irr*, ***schreiten***, *sep*, *-ge-*, *sein*) advance, proceed, progress; **~d** *adj* progressive

'**Fortschritt** *m* progress

'**fortschrittlich** *adj* progressive

'**fortsetzen** *v/t* (*sep*, *-ge-*, *h*) continue, go on with; '**Fortsetzung** *f* (-; *-en*) continuation; *film etc*: sequel; ~ ***folgt*** to be continued; '**Fortsetzungsro,man** *m* serialized novel

'**fortwährend** *adj* continual, constant

**fossil** [fɔ'siːl] *adj*, **Fos'sil** *n* (*-s*; *-ien*) GEOL fossil (*a. fig* F)

**Foto** ['foːto] *n* (*-s*; *-s*) photo(graph); ***ein ~ machen*** (***von***) take a photo (of)

'**Fotoalbum** *n* photo album

'**Fotoappa,rat** *m* camera

**Fotograf** [foto'graːf] *m* (*-en*; *-en*) photographer; **Fotografie** [fotogra'fiː] *f* (-; *-n*) (*no pl*) photography; photograph, picture; **fotografieren** [fotogra'fiːrən] *v/t and v/i* (*no -ge-*, *h*) take a photo(graph) *or* picture (of); ***sich ~ lassen*** have one's picture taken; **Foto'grafin** *f* (-; *-nen*) photographer

'**Fotohandy** *n* camera phone

**Fotoko'pie** *f* photocopy; **fotoko'pieren** *v/t* (*no -ge-*, *h*) (photo)copy

'**Fotomo,dell** *n* model

'**Fotozelle** *f* photoelectric cell

**Fotze** ['fɔtsə] V *f* (-; *-n*) cunt

**Foul** [faul] *n* (*-s*; *-s*) SPORT foul; **foulen** ['faulən] *v/t and v/i* (*ge-*, *h*) SPORT foul

**Foyer** [foa'jeː] *n* (*-s*; *-s*) foyer, lobby, lounge

**Fr.** *abbr of* ***Frau*** Mrs, Ms

**Fracht** [fraxt] *f* (-; *-en*) freight, load, MAR, AVIAT *a.* cargo; ECON freight, *Br* carriage; **~brief** *m* RAIL bill of lading (*a.* MAR), *Br* consignment note

F

**Frachter** ['fraxtɐ] *m* (-*s*; -) MAR freighter
**Frack** [frak] *m* (-[*e*]*s*; *Fräcke* ['frɛkə]) tails, tailcoat
**Frage** ['fra:gə] *f* (-; -*n*) question; ***e-e ~ stellen*** ask a question; → ***infrage***
'**Fragebogen** *m* question(n)aire
'**fragen** *v/t and v/i* (*ge-*, *h*) ask (***nach*** for; ***wegen*** about); ***nach dem Weg*** (***der Zeit***) ~ ask the way (time); ***sich ~*** wonder
'**Frage|wort** *n* LING interrogative; **~zeichen** *n* LING question mark
**fraglich** ['fra:klɪç] *adj* doubtful, uncertain; ... in question
**fraglos** ['fra:klo:s] *adv* undoubtedly, unquestionably
**Fragment** [fra'gmɛnt] *n* (-[*e*]*s*; -*e*) fragment
**fragwürdig** ['fra:kvʏrdɪç] *adj* dubious, F shady
**Fraktion** [frak'tsjo:n] *f* (-; -*en*) (parliamentary) group *or* party
**Frakti'onsführer** *m* PARL floor leader, *Br* chief whip
**Franc** [frã:] *m* (-; -*s*), **Franken** ['fraŋkən] *m* (-; -) franc
**frankieren** [fraŋ'ki:rən] *v/t* (*no -ge-*, *h*) stamp; frank
**Frankreich** ['fraŋkraiç] France
**Franse** ['franzə] *f* (-; -*n*) fringe
**fransig** ['franzɪç] *adj* frayed
**Franzose** [fran'tso:zə] *m* (-*n*; -*n*) Frenchman; ***die ~n*** *pl* the French
**Französin** [fran'tsø:zɪn] *f* (-; -*nen*) Frenchwoman
**französisch** [fran'tsø:zɪʃ] *adj* French
**fraß** [fra:s] *pret of* ***fressen***
**Fraß** F *contp m* (-*es*; *no pl*) muck
**Fratze** ['fratsə] *f* (-; -*n*) grimace
**Frau** [frau] *f* (-; -*en*) woman; wife; ***~ X*** Mrs (*or* Ms) X
**Frauchen** ['frauçən] *n* mistress (*of dog*)
'**Frauen|arzt** *m*, **~ärztin** *f* gyn(a)ecologist; **~bewegung** *f*: ***die ~*** POL women's lib(eration)
'**frauenfeindlich** *adj* sexist
'**Frauen|haus** *n* women's shelter (*Br* refuge); **~klinik** *f* gyn(a)ecological hospital; **~rechtlerin** ['frauənrɛçtlərɪn] *f* (-; -*nen*) feminist
**Fräulein** ['frɔʏlain] *n* (-*s*; -) Miss
'**fraulich** *adj* womanly, feminine
**frech** [frɛç] *adj* sassy, *Br* cheeky
'**Frechheit** *f* (-; *no pl*) F *Br* cheek
**Freeclimbing** ['fri:klaɪmiŋ] *n* (-*s*; *no pl*) free climbing
**frei** [frai] *adj* free (***von*** from, of); independent; freelance; vacant; candid, frank; SPORT unmarked; ***ein ~er Tag*** a day off; ***morgen haben wir ~*** there is no school tomorrow; ***im Freien*** outdoors; → ***Fuß***; ***sich ~ machen*** undress; ***sich ~ machen von*** free o.s. from; → *a.* ***freibekommen, freigeben, freihaben***; ***~ halten*** keep clear (*exit*), → ***freihalten***
'**Freibad** *n* open-air swimming-pool
'**freibekommen** *v/t* (*irr*, ***kommen***, *sep*, *no -ge-*, *h*) get *a day etc* off
'**freiberuflich** *adj* freelance, self-employed
'**Freiexem,plar** *n* free copy
'**Freigabe** *f* (-; *no pl*) release
'**freigeben** (*irr*, ***geben***, *sep*, *-ge-*, *h*) **1.** *v/t* release; ***e-n Tag*** *etc* ~ give a day *etc* off **2.** *v/i*: ***j-m ~*** give s.o. time off
**freigebig** ['fraige:bɪç] *adj* generous
'**Freigepäck** *n* AVIAT baggage allowance
'**freihaben** F *v/i* (*irr*, ***haben***, *sep*, *-ge-*, *h*) have a day off (*Br a.* a holiday)
'**Freihafen** *m* free port
'**freihalten** *v/t* (*irr*, ***halten***, *sep*, *-ge-*, *h*) keep, save (*seat etc*); treat (*s.o.*)
'**Frei|handel** *m* free trade; **~handelszone** *f* free trade area
**freihändig** ['fraihɛndɪç] *adv* with no hands
'**Freiheit** *f* (-; -*en*) freedom, liberty; ***sich ~en herausnehmen gegen*** take liberties with
'**Freiheitsstrafe** *f* JUR prison sentence
'**Freikarte** *f* free ticket
'**freikaufen** *v/t* (*sep*, *-ge-*, *h*) ransom
'**Freikörperkul,tur** *f* (-; *no pl*) nudism
'**freilassen** *v/t* (*irr*, ***lassen***, *sep*, *-ge-*, *h*) release, set free; '**Freilassung** *f* (-; -*en*) release
'**Freilauf** *m* freewheel (*a.* ***im ~ fahren***)
'**freilich** *adv* indeed, of course
'**Freilicht...** *in cpds* open-air ...
'**freimachen** *v/t* (*sep*, *-ge-*, *h*) *post*: stamp; ***sich ~*** undress; ***sich ~ von*** free o.s. from; → ***frei***; → ***Oberkörper***
'**Freimaurer** *m* freemason
**freimütig** ['fraimy:tɪç] *adj* candid, frank
'**freischaffend** *adj* freelance
'**freischwimmen** *v/refl* (*irr*, ***schwimmen***, *sep*, *-ge-*, *h*) pass a 15-minute

swimming test
'**Freisprechanlage** *f* hands-free kit
'**freisprechen** *v/t* (*irr*, ***sprechen***, *sep*, *-ge-*, *h*) *esp* REL absolve (***von*** from); JUR acquit (of); '**Freispruch** *m* JUR acquittal
'**Freistaat** *m* POL free state
'**frei|stehen** *v/i* (*irr*, ***stehen***, *sep*, *-ge-*, *h*) be unoccupied; SPORT be unmarked; ***es steht dir frei zu*** *inf* you are free to *inf*; **~stellen** *v/t* (*sep*, *-ge-*, *h*) ***j-n ~*** exempt s.o. (***von*** from) (*a.* MIL); ***j-m et. ~*** leave s.th. (up) to s.o.
'**Frei|stil** *m* freestyle; **~stoß** *m soccer*: free kick; **~stunde** *f* PED free period; **~tag** *m* Friday; **~tod** *m* suicide; **~treppe** *f* outdoor stairs; **~wild** *fig n* fair game
'**freiwillig** *adj* voluntary; ***sich ~ melden*** volunteer (***zu*** for); **Freiwillige** ['fraivɪlɪgə] *m*, *f* (*-n*; *-n*) volunteer
'**Freizeit** *f* free *or* leisure time; **~gestaltung** *f* leisure-time activities; **~kleidung** *f* leisurewear; **~park** *m* amusement park; **~zentrum** *n* leisure center (*Br* centre)
'**freizügig** *adj* permissive; *film etc*: explicit
**fremd** [frɛmt] *adj* strange; foreign; unknown; ***ich bin auch ~ hier*** I'm a stranger here myself; '**fremdartig** *adj* strange, exotic; **Fremde** ['frɛmdə] *m*, *f* (*-n*; *-n*) stranger; foreigner
'**Fremden|führer** *m*, **~führerin** *f* (*-*; *-nen*) (tourist) guide; **~hass** *m* xenophobia; **~legi,on** *f* Foreign Legion; **~verkehr** *m* tourism; **~verkehrsbü,ro** *n* tourist office; **~zimmer** *n* guest room; **~ (*zu vermieten*)** rooms to let
'**fremdgehen** F *v/i* (*irr*, ***gehen***, *sep*, *-ge-*, *sein*) be unfaithful (to one's wife *or* husband), play around
'**Fremd|körper** *m* MED foreign body; *fig* alien element; **~sprache** *f* foreign language; **~sprachensekre,tärin** *f* bilingual secretary
'**fremd|sprachig**, **~sprachlich** *adj* foreign-language
'**Fremdwort** *n* (*-[e]s*; *-wörter*) foreign word
**Frequenz** [fre'kvɛnts] *f* (*-*; *-en*) PHYS frequency
**Fresse** ['frɛsə] V *f* (*-*; *-n*) big (fat) mouth
'**fressen** *v/t* (*irr*, *ge-*, *h*) zo eat, feed on; F gobble (up); *fig* devour
**Freude** ['frɔʏdə] *f* (*-*; *-n*) joy, delight; pleasure; ***~ haben an*** (*dat*) take pleasure in
'**Freuden|geschrei** *n* shouts of joy, cheers; **~haus** F *n* brothel; **~tränen** *pl* tears of joy
'**freudestrahlend** *adj* radiant (with joy)
**freudig** ['frɔʏdɪç] *adj* joyful, cheerful; happy (*event etc*)
**freudlos** ['frɔʏtlo:s] *adj* joyless, cheerless
**freuen** ['frɔʏən] *v/t* (*ge-*, *h*) ***es freut mich, dass*** I'm glad *or* pleased (that); ***sich ~ über*** (*acc*) be pleased *or* glad about; ***sich ~ auf*** (*acc*) look forward to
**Freund** [frɔʏnt] *m* (*-[e]s*; *-e* ['frɔʏndə]) friend; boyfriend; **Freundin** ['frɔʏndɪn] *f* (*-*; *-nen*) friend; girlfriend
'**freundlich** *adj* friendly, kind, nice; *fig* cheerful (*room etc*); '**Freundlichkeit** *f* (*-*; *no pl*) friendliness, kindness
'**Freundschaft** *f* (*-*; *-en*) friendship; ***~ schließen*** make friends
'**freundschaftlich** *adj* friendly
'**Freundschaftsspiel** *n* SPORT friendly (game)
**Frevel** ['fre:fəl] *m* (*-s*; *-*) outrage (***an*** *dat*, ***gegen*** on)
**Frieden** ['fri:dən] *m* (*-s*; *no pl*) peace; ***im ~*** in peacetime; ***lass mich in ~!*** leave me alone!
'**Friedens|bewegung** *f* peace movement; **~forschung** *f* peace studies; **~verhandlungen** *pl* peace negotiations *or* talks; **~vertrag** *m* peace treaty
**friedfertig** ['fri:tfɛrtɪç] *adj* peaceable
'**Friedhof** *m* cemetery, graveyard
'**friedlich** *adj* peaceful
'**friedliebend** *adj* peace-loving
**frieren** ['fri:rən] *v/i* (*irr*, *ge-*, *h*) freeze; ***ich friere*** I am *or* feel cold; I'm freezing
**Fries** [fri:s] *m* (*-es*; *-e*) ARCH frieze
**Frikadelle** [frika'dɛlə] *f* (*-*; *-n*) meatball
**frisch** [frɪʃ] *adj* fresh; clean (*shirt etc*); ***~ gestrichen!*** wet (*or* fresh) paint!
**Frische** ['frɪʃə] *f* (*-*; *no pl*) freshness
'**Frischhalte|beutel** *m* polythene bag; **~folie** *f* plastic wrap, *Br.* cling film
**Friseur** [fri'zø:ʀ] *m* (*-s*; *-e*) hairdresser; barber; **~sa,lon** *m* hairdresser's (shop), barber's shop
**Friseuse** [fri'zø:zə] *f* (*-*; *-n*) hairdresser
**frisieren** [fri'zi:rən] *v/t* (*no -ge-*, *h*) do *s.o.'s* hair; F MOT soup up

F

**Frisör** *etc* → ***Friseur*** *etc*
**Frist** [frɪst] *f* (-; *-en*) (fixed) period of time; deadline; extension (*a.* ECON)
**fristen** ['frɪstən] *v/t* (*ge-*, *h*) ***sein Dasein*** ~ scrape a living
'**fristlos** *adj* without notice
**Frisur** [fri'zuːɐ] *f* (-; *-en*) hairstyle, hairdo
**Fritten** ['frɪtən] F *pl* fries, *Br* chips; **frittieren** [fri'tiːrən] *v/t* (*no -ge-*, *h*) deep fry
**frivol** [fri'voːl] *adj* frivolous; suggestive
**froh** [froː] *adj* glad (***über*** *acc* about); cheerful; happy; ***~es Fest!*** happy holiday!; Merry Christmas!
**fröhlich** ['frøːlɪç] *adj* cheerful, happy; merry; '**Fröhlichkeit** *f* (-; *no pl*) cheerfulness, merriment
**fromm** [frɔm] *adj* pious, devout; meek; steady (*horse*); ***~er Wunsch*** pious hope
**Frömmigkeit** ['frœmɪçkait] *f* (-; *no pl*) religiousness, piety
**Fronleichnam** [froːn'laiçnaːm] *m* (-[*e*]*s*; *no pl*) REL Corpus Christi
**Front** [frɔnt] *f* (-; *-en*) front (*a. fig*), ARCH *a.* face, MIL *a.* line; ***in ~ liegen*** SPORT be ahead
**frontal** [frɔn'taːl] *adj* MOT head-on
**Fron'talzusammenstoß** *m* MOT head-on collision
'**Frontantrieb** *m* MOT front-wheel drive
**fror** [froːɐ] *pret of* ***frieren***
**Frosch** [frɔʃ] *m* (-[*e*]*s*; *Frösche* ['frœʃə]) ZO frog; **~mann** *m* frogman; **~perspek,tive** *f* worm's-eye view
**Frost** [frɔst] *m* (-[*e*]*s*; *Fröste* ['frœstə]) frost; **~beule** *f* chilblain
**frösteln** ['frœstəln] *v/i* (*ge-*, *h*) feel chilly, shiver (*a. fig*)
'**frostig** *adj* frosty, *fig a.* chilly
'**Frostschutzmittel** *n* MOT antifreeze
**Frottee** [frɔ'teː] *n*, *m* (-[*s*]; *-s*) terry (-cloth); **frottieren** [frɔ'tiːrən] *v/t* (*no -ge-*, *h*) rub down
**Frucht** [frʊxt] *f* (-; *Früchte* ['frʏçtə]) BOT fruit (*a. fig*); '**fruchtbar** *adj* BIOL fertile, *esp fig a.* fruitful; '**Fruchtbarkeit** *f* (-; *no pl*) fertility; *fig* fruitfulness
'**fruchtlos** *adj* fruitless, futile
'**Fruchtsaft** *m* fruit juice
**früh** [fryː] *adj and adv* early; ***zu ~ kommen*** be early; ***~ genug*** soon enough; ***heute*** (***morgen***) ~ this (tomorrow) morning; '**Frühaufsteher** *m* (-*s*; -) early riser (F bird); **Frühe** ['fryːə] *f*: ***in aller ~*** (very) early in the morning
**früher** ['fryːɐ] **1.** *adj* former; previous **2.** *adv* in former times, at one time; ***~ oder später*** sooner or later; ***ich habe ~ (einmal)*** ... I used to ...
'**frühestens** *adv* at the earliest
'**Früh|geburt** *f* MED premature birth; premature baby; **~jahr** *n* spring; **~jahrsputz** *m* spring cleaning
**früh'morgens** *adv* early in the morning
'**frühreif** *adj* precocious
'**Frühstück** *n* breakfast (***zum*** for)
'**frühstücken** *v/i* (*ge-*, *h*) (have) breakfast
**Frust** [frʊst] F *m* (-[*e*]*s*; *no pl*) frustration
**Frustration** [frʊstra'tsjoːn] *f* (-; *-en*) frustration; **frustrieren** [frʊs'triːrən] *v/t* (*no -ge-*, *h*) frustrate
**frz.** *abbr of* ***französisch*** Fr., French
**Fuchs** [fʊks] *m* (-*es*; *Füchse* ['fʏksə]) ZO fox (*a. fig*); sorrel; **~jagd** *f* foxhunt(ing); **~schwanz** *m* TECH handsaw
'**fuchs'teufels'wild** F *adj* hopping mad
**fuchteln** ['fʊxtəln] *v/i* (*ge-*, *h*) ***~ mit*** wave *s.th.* around
**Fuge** ['fuːgə] *f* (-; *-n*) TECH joint; MUS fugue
**fügen** ['fyːgən] *v/refl* (*ge-*, *h*) submit (***in*** *acc*, *dat* to *s.th.*)
**fühlbar** ['fyːlbaːɐ] *fig adj* noticeable; considerable; **fühlen** ['fyːlən] *v/t and v/i and v/refl* (*ge-*, *h*) feel, *fig a.* sense; ***sich wohl ~*** → ***wohlfühlen***
**Fühler** ['fyːlɐ] *m* (-*s*; -) ZO feeler (*a. fig*)
**fuhr** [fuːɐ] *pret of* ***fahren***
**führen** ['fyːrən] (*ge-*, *h*) **1.** *v/t* lead; guide; take; run, manage; ECON sell, deal in; keep (*account*, *books etc*); have (*a talk etc*); bear (*name etc*); MIL command; ***j-n ~ durch*** show s.o. round; ***sich ~*** conduct o.s. **2.** *v/i* lead (***zu*** to, *a. fig*), SPORT *a.* be leading, be ahead; **~d** *adj* leading
**Führer** ['fyːrɐ] *m* (-*s*; -) leader (*a.* POL); guide; head, chief; guide(book)
'**Führerschein** *m* MOT driver's license, *Br* driving licence
'**Führung** *f* (-; *-en*) (*no pl*) leadership, control; ECON management; (guided) tour; ***gute ~*** good conduct; ***in ~ gehen*** (***sein***) SPORT take (be in) the lead;

'**Führungszeugnis** *n* certificate of (good) conduct
**Fuhrunternehmen** ['fuːɐ?ʊntɐneːmən] *n* trucking company, *Br* haulage contractors
'**Fuhrwerk** *n* horse-drawn vehicle
**Fülle** ['fʏlə] *f* (-; *no pl*) crush; *fig* wealth, abundance; GASTR body
'**füllen** *v/t and v/refl* (*ge-*, *h*) fill (*a.* MED), stuff (*a.* GASTR)
**Füller** ['fʏlɐ] *m* (-*s*; -), '**Füllfederhalter** *m* fountain pen
**füllig** ['fʏlɪç] *adj* stout, portly
'**Füllung** *f* (-; -*en*) filling (*a.* MED), stuffing (*a.* GASTR)
**fummeln** ['fʊməln] F *v/i* (*ge-*, *h*) fiddle, tinker (*both*: ***an*** *dat* with); F grope
**Fund** [fʊnt] *m* (-[*e*]*s*; -*e* ['fʊndə]) discovery; find
**Fundament** [fʊnda'mɛnt] *n* (-[*e*]*s*; -*e*) ARCH foundation(s), *fig a.* basis
**Fundamentalist** [fʊndamɛnta'lɪst] *m* (-*en*; -*en*) fundamentalist
'**Fundbüˌro** *n* lost and found (office), *Br* lost-property office
'**Fundgrube** *fig f* treasure trove
**Fundi** ['fʊndi] F *m* (-*s*; -*s*) POL radical Green
**fundiert** [fʊn'diːɐt] *adj* well-founded (*argument etc*); sound (*knowledge*)
**fünf** [fʏnf] *adj* five; *grade*: F, N, *Br* fail, poor, E; '**Fünfeck** *n* (-[*e*]*s*; -*e*) pentagon; '**fünffach** *adj* fivefold
'**Fünfkampf** *m* SPORT pentathlon
'**Fünflinge** *pl* quintuplets
'**fünfte** *adj* fifth; '**Fünftel** *n* (-*s*; -) fifth
'**fünftens** *adv* fifth(ly), in the fifth place
'**fünfzehn(te)** *adj* fifteen(th)
**fünfzig** ['fʏnftsɪç] *adj* fifty
'**fünfzigste** *adj* fiftieth
**fungieren** [fʊŋ'giːrən] *v/i* (*no -ge-*, *h*) **~ *als*** act as, function as
**Funk** [fʊŋk] *m* (-*s*; *no pl*) radio; ***über*** *or* ***durch* ~** by radio
'**Funkamaˌteur** *m* radio ham
**Funke** ['fʊŋkə] *m* (-*n*; -*n*) spark; *fig a.* glimmer; **funkeln** ['fʊŋkəln] *v/i* (*ge-*, *h*) sparkle, glitter; twinkle
'**funken** *v/t* (*ge-*, *h*) radio, transmit
**Funker** ['fʊŋkɐ] *m* (-*s*; -) radio operator
'**Funk|gerät** *n* radio set; **~haus** *n* broadcasting center (*Br* centre); **~sigˌnal** *n* radio signal; **~spruch** *m* radio message; **~statiˌon** *f* radio station; **~streife** *f* (radio) patrol car; **~teleˌfon** *n* cellular phone
**Funktion** [fʊŋk'tsjoːn] *f* (-; -*en*) function; **Funktionär** [fʊŋktsjo'nɛːɐ] *m* (-*s*; -*e*) functionary, official (*a.* SPORT); **funktionieren** [fʊŋktsjo'niːrən] *v/i* (*no -ge-*, *h*) work
'**Funkturm** *m* radio tower
'**Funkverkehr** *m* radio communication
**für** [fyːɐ] *prp* (*acc*) for; in favo(u)r of; on behalf of; **~ *immer*** forever; ***Tag* ~ *Tag*** day by day; ***Wort* ~ *Wort*** word by word; ***jeder* ~ *sich*** everyone by himself; ***was* ~ ...?** what (kind *or* sort of) ...?; ***das Für und Wider*** the pros and cons
**Furche** ['fʊrçə] *f* (-; -*n*) furrow; rut
**Furcht** [fʊrçt] *f* (-; *no pl*) fear, dread (*both*: ***vor*** *dat* of); ***aus*~(, *dass*)** for fear (that); **~ *erregend* → *furchterregend***
'**furchtbar** *adj* terrible, awful
**fürchten** ['fʏrçtən] *v/t and v/i* (*ge-*, *h*) fear, be afraid of; dread; **~ *um*** fear for; ***sich* ~** be scared; be afraid (***vor*** *dat* of); ***ich fürchte***, ... I'm afraid ...
**fürchterlich** ['fʏrçtɐlɪç] → ***furchtbar***
'**furcht|erregend** *adj* frightening; **~los** *adj* fearless; **~sam** *adj* timid
**füreiˈnander** *adv* for each other
**Furnier** [fʊr'niːɐ] *n* (-[*e*]*s*; -*e*), **furnieren** [fʊr'niːrən] *v/t* (*no -ge-*, *h*) veneer
'**Fürsorge** *f* (-; *no pl*) care; ***öffentliche* ~** (public) welfare (work); **~empfänger** *m* social security beneficiary
**fürsorglich** ['fyːɐzɔrklɪç] *adj* considerate
'**Für|sprache** *f* intercession (***für*** for; ***bei*** with); **~sprech** *m* (-[*e*]*s*; -*e*) *Swiss*: lawyer; **~sprecher(in)** advocate (*a. fig*)
**Fürst** [fʏrst] *m* (-*en*; -*en*) prince
'**Fürstentum** *n* (-*s*; -*tümer* ['fʏrstəntyːmɐ]) principality
'**Fürstin** *f* (-; -*nen*) princess
'**fürstlich** *adj* princely (*a. fig*)
**Furt** [fʊrt] *f* (-; -*en*) ford
**Furunkel** [fu'rʊŋkəl] *m* (-*s*; -) MED boil, furuncle
'**Fürwort** *n* (-[*e*]*s*; -*wörter*) LING pronoun
**Furz** [fʊrts] *m* (-*es*; -*e*), '**furzen** *v/i* (*ge-*, *h*) fart
**Fusion** [fu'zjoːn] *f* (-; -*en*) ECON merger, amalgamation
**fusionieren** [fuzjo'niːrən] *v/i* (*no -ge-*, *h*) ECON merge, amalgamate
**Fuß** [fuːs] *m* (-*es*; *Füße*) ['fyːsə] ANAT

F

foot; stand; stem; ***zu ~*** on foot; ***zu ~ gehen*** walk; ***gut zu ~ sein*** be a good walker; ***~ fassen*** become established; ***auf freiem ~*** at large
**'Fußball** *m* (*no pl*) soccer, *Br* football; soccer ball, *Br* football
**Fußballer** ['fu:sbalɐ] *m* (*-s*; *-*) footballer
**'Fußball|feld** *n* football field; **~rowdy** *m* (football) hooligan; **~spiel** *n* soccer *or* football match; **~spieler(in)** football player, footballer; **~toto** *n* football pools
**'Fußboden** *m* floor; flooring; **~heizung** *f* underfloor heating
**'Fußbremse** *f* MOT footbrake
**Fussel** ['fʊsəl] *f* (*-*; *-n*), *m* (*-s*; *-[n]*) piece of lint (*Br* fluff); *pl* lint, *Br* fluff; **'fusselig** ['fʊsəlɪç] *adj* linty, *Br* covered in fluff; **'fusseln** *v/i* (*ge-*, *h*) shed a lot of lint (*Br* fluff), F mo(u)lt
**Fußgänger** ['fu:sgɛŋɐ] *m* (*-s*; *-*), **'Fußgängerin** *f* (*-*; *-nen*) pedestrian; **'Fußgängerzone** *f* (pedestrian *or* shopping) mall, *Br* pedestrian precinct
**'Fußgeher** *Austrian m* → ***Fußgänger***
**'Fuß|gelenk** *n* ANAT ankle; **~matte** *f* doormat; **~note** *f* footnote; **~pflege** *f* pedicure; MED podiatry, *Br.* chiropody; **~pfleger(in)** podiatrist, *Br* chiropodist; **~pilz** *m* MED athlete's foot; **~sohle** *f* ANAT sole (of the foot); **~spur** *f* footprint; track; **~stapfen** *pl*: ***in j-s ~ treten*** follow in s.o.'s footsteps; **~tritt** *m* kick; **~weg** *m* foothpath; ***e-e Stunde ~*** an hour's walk
**Futter**[1] ['fʊtɐ] *n* (*-s*; *no pl*) AGR feed, fodder, food
**'Futter**[2] *n* (*-s*; *-*) lining
**Futteral** [fʊtə'ra:l] *n* (*-s*; *-e*) case; cover
**füttern**[1] ['fʏtɐn] *v/t* (*ge-*, *h*) AGR feed
**'füttern**[2] *v/t* (*ge-*, *h*) line
**'Futternapf** *m* (feeding) bowl
**Fütterung** ['fʏtərʊŋ] *f* (*-*; *-en*) feeding (time)
**Futur** [fu'tu:ɐ] *n* (*-s*; *-e*) future (*a.* LING)

# G

**gab** [ga:p] *pret of* ***geben***
**Gabe** ['ga:bə] *f* (*-*; *-n*) gift, present; MED dose; *fig* talent, gift; ***milde ~*** alms
**Gabel** ['ga:bəl] *f* (*-*; *-n*) fork; TEL cradle
**'gabeln** *v/refl* (*ge-*, *h*) fork, branch
**Gabelstapler** ['ga:bəlʃta:plɐ] *m* (*-s*; *-*) TECH fork-lift (truck)
**Gabelung** ['ga:bəlʊŋ] *f* (*-*; *-en*) fork(ing)
**gackern** ['gakɐn] *v/i* (*ge-*, *h*) cluck, cackle (*a. fig*)
**gaffen** ['gafən] *v/i* (*ge-*, *h*) gawk, gawp, F rubberneck; **Gaffer** ['gafɐ] *m* (*-s*; *-*) F rubberneck(er), *Br* nosy parker
**Gage** ['ga:ʒə] *f* (*-*; *-n*) fee
**gähnen** ['gɛ:nən] *v/i* (*ge-*, *h*) yawn
**Gala** ['ga:la] *f* (*-*; *-s*) gala
**galant** [ga'lant] *adj* gallant, courteous
**Galeere** [ga'le:rə] *f* (*-*; *-n*) MAR galley
**Galerie** [galə'ri:] *f* (*-*; *-n*) gallery
**Galgen** ['galgən] *m* (*-s*; *-*) gallows; **~frist** *f* reprieve; **~hu,mor** *m* gallows humo(u)r; **~vogel** F *m* crook
**Galle** ['galə] *f* (*-*; *-n*) ANAT gall; bile
**'Gallen|blase** *f* ANAT gall bladder; **~stein** *m* MED gallstone
**Gallert** ['galɐt] *n* (*-[es]*; *-e*), **Gallerte** [ga'lɛrtə] *f* (*-*; *-n*) jelly
**Galopp** [ga'lɔp] *m* (*-s*; *-s*, *-e*) gallop
**galoppieren** [galɔ'pi:rən] *v/i* (*no -ge-*, *sein*) gallop
**galt** [galt] *pret of* ***gelten***
**gammeln** ['gaməln] F *v/i* (*ge-*, *h*) loaf (about), bum around; **Gammler(in)** ['gamlɐ, 'gamlərɪn] *m(f)* F (*-s*; *-/-*; *-nen*) loafer, bum
**Gämse** ['gɛmzə] *f* (*-*; *-n*) ZO chamois
**gang** [gaŋ] *adj*: ***~ und gäbe*** nothing unusual, (quite) usual
**Gang** [gaŋ] *m* (*-[e]s*; *Gänge* ['gɛŋə]) walk, gait, way *s.o.* walks; ARCH passage, *a.* AVIAT *etc* aisle; corridor; MOT gear; GASTR course; ***et. in ~ bringen*** get s.th. going, start s.th.; ***in ~ kommen*** get started; ***im ~(e) sein*** be (going) on, be in progress; ***in vollem ~(e)*** in full swing
**gängeln** ['gɛŋəln] *v/t* (*ge-*, *h*) lead *s.o.* by the nose
**gängig** ['gɛŋɪç] *adj* current; ECON sal(e)able

'**Gangschaltung** *f* MOT gears
**Ganove** [ga'noːvə] F *m* (*-n*; *-n*) crook
**Gans** [gans] *f* (-; *Gänse* ['gɛnzə]) ZO goose
**Gänse|blümchen** ['gɛnzəblyːmçən] *n* BOT daisy; **~braten** *m* roast goose; **~haut** *f* (-; *no pl*) gooseflesh; ***dabei kriege ich e-e ~*** F it gives me the creeps; **~marsch** *m* (-[*e*]*s*; *no pl*) single *or* Indian file
**Gänserich** ['gɛnzərɪç] *m* (*-s*; *-e*) ZO gander
**ganz** [gants] **1.** *adj* whole, entire, total; F undamaged; full (*hour etc*); ***den ~en Tag*** all day; ***die ~e Zeit*** all the time; ***auf der ~en Welt*** all over the world; ***sein ~es Geld*** all his money **2.** *adv* completely, totally; very; quite, rather, fairly; ***~ allein*** all by oneself; ***~ aus Holz*** *etc* all wood *etc*; ***~ und gar*** completely, totally; ***~ und gar nicht*** not at all, by no means; ***~ wie du willst*** just as you like; ***nicht ~*** not quite; → ***voll***
**Ganze** ['gantsə] *n* (*-n*; *no pl*) whole; ***das ~*** the whole thing; ***im ~n*** in all, altogether; ***im großen und ~n*** on the whole; ***aufs ~ gehen*** go all out
**gänzlich** ['gɛntslɪç] *adv* completely, entirely
'**Ganztags|beschäftigung** *f* full-time job; **~schule** *f* all-day school(ing)
**gar** [gaːɐ] **1.** *adj* GASTR done **2.** *adv*: ***~ nicht*** not at all; ***~ nichts*** nothing at all; ***~ zu ...*** (a bit) too ...
**Garage** [ga'raːʒə] *f* (-; *-n*) garage
**Garantie** [garan'tiː] *f* (-; *-n*) guarantee, *esp* ECON warranty; **garantieren** [garan'tiːrən] *v/t and v/i* (*no -ge-*, *h*) guarantee (***für et.*** s.th.)
**Garbe** ['garbə] *f* (-; *-n*) AGR sheaf
**Garde** ['gardə] *f* (-; *-n*) guard; MIL (the) Guards
**Garderobe** [gardə'roːbə] *f* (-; *-n*) (*no pl*) wardrobe, clothes; checkroom, *Br* cloakroom; THEA dressing room
**Garde'roben|frau** *f* checkroom (*Br* cloakroom) attendant; **~marke** *f* coat check (*Br* cloakroom) ticket; **~ständer** *m* coat stand *or* rack
**Gardine** [gar'diːnə] *f* (-; *-n*) curtain
**Gar'dinenstange** *f* curtain rod
**gären** ['gɛːrən] *v/i* ([*irr*,] *ge-*, *h*, *sein*) ferment, work
**Garn** [garn] *n* (-[*e*]*s*; *-e*) yarn; thread; cotton
**Garnele** [gar'neːlə] *f* (-; *-n*) ZO shrimp; prawn
**garnieren** [gar'niːrən] *v/t* (*no -ge-*, *h*) garnish (*a. fig*)
**Garnison** [garni'zoːn] *f* (-; *-en*) MIL garrison, post
**Garnitur** [garni'tuːɐ] *f* (-, *-en*) set; suite
**Garten** ['gartən] *m* (*-s*; *Gärten* ['gɛrtən]) garden; **~arbeit** *f* gardening; **~bau** *m* (-[*e*]*s*; *no pl*) horticulture; **~erde** *f* (garden) mo(u)ld; **~fest** *n* garden party; **~geräte** *pl* gardening tools; **~haus** *n* summerhouse; **~lo,kal** *n* beer garden; outdoor restaurant; **~schere** *f* pruning shears; **~stadt** *f* garden city; **~zwerg** *m* (garden) gnome
**Gärtner** ['gɛrtnɐ] *m* (*-s*; -) gardener
**Gärtnerei** [gɛrtnə'rai] *f* (-; *-en*) truck farm, *Br* market garden
'**Gärtnerin** *f* (-; *-nen*) gardener
**Gärung** ['gɛːrʊŋ] *f* (-; *-en*) fermentation
**Gas** [gaːs] *n* (*-es*; *-e* ['gaːzə]) gas; ***~ geben*** MOT accelerate, F step on the gas
**gasförmig** ['gaːsfœrmɪç] *adj* gaseous
'**Gas|hahn** *m* gas valve (*or* cock, *Br* tap); **~heizung** *f* gas heating; **~herd** *m* gas cooker *or* stove; **~kammer** *f* gas chamber; **~la,terne** *f* gas (street) lamp; **~leitung** *f* gas main; **~maske** *f* gas mask; **~ofen** *m* gas stove; **~pe,dal** *n* MOT gas pedal, *Br* accelerator (pedal)
**Gasse** ['gasə] *f* (-; *-n*) lane, alley
**Gast** [gast] *m* (-[*e*]*s*; *Gäste* ['gɛstə]) guest; visitor; customer
'**Gastarbeiter** *m*, '**Gastarbeiterin** *f* foreign worker
**Gästebuch** ['gɛstəbuːx] *n* visitors' book
'**Gästezimmer** *n* guest (*or* spare) room
'**gastfreundlich** *adj* hospitable
'**Gastfreundschaft** *f* hospitality
**Gastgeber** ['gastgeːbɐ] *m* (*-s*; -) host
**Gastgeberin** ['gastgeːbərɪn] *f* (-; *-nen*) hostess
'**Gast|haus** *n*, **~hof** *m* restaurant, inn
**gastieren** [gas'tiːrən] *v/i* (*no -ge-*, *h*) give performances; THEA guest, give a guest performance
'**gastlich** *adj* hospitable
'**Gast|mannschaft** *f* SPORT visiting team; **~spiel** *n* THEA guest performance; **~stätte** *f* restaurant; **~stube** *f* taproom; restaurant; **~wirt** *m* landlord;

G

~**wirtschaft** *f* restaurant, inn
'**Gaswerk** *n* TECH gasworks
'**Gaszähler** *m* TECH gas meter
**Gatte** ['gatə] *m* (*-n*; *-n*) husband
**Gatter** ['gatɐ] *n* (*-s*; -) fence; gate
**Gattin** ['gatɪn] *f* (-; *-nen*) wife
**Gattung** ['gatʊŋ] *f* (-; *-en*) type, class, sort; BIOL genus; species
**GAU** [gau] (ABBR *of* ***größter anzunehmender Unfall***) *m* (-[*s*]; *no pl*) worst case scenario, *Br* maximum credible accident, MCA
**Gaul** [gaul] *m* (-[*e*]*s*; *Gäule* ['gɔylə]) nag
**Gaumen** ['gaumən] *m* (*-s*; -) ANAT palate
**Gauner** ['gaunɐ] *m* (*-s*; -), '**Gaunerin** *f* (-; *-nen*) F crook
**Gaze** ['ga:zə] *f* (-; *-n*) gauze
**Gazelle** [ga'tsɛlə] *f* (-; *-n*) ZO gazelle
**geb.** *abbr of* ***geboren*** b., born
**Gebäck** [gə'bɛk] *n* (-[*e*]*s*; *-e*) pastry; cookies, *Br* biscuits
**ge'backen** *pp of* ***backen***
**Gebälk** [gə'bɛlk] *n* (-[*e*]*s*; *-e*) timberwork, beams
**gebar** [gə'ba:ɐ] *pret of* ***gebären***
**Gebärde** [gə'bɛ:ɐdə] *f* (-; *-n*) gesture
**ge'bärden** *v/refl* (*no -ge-*, *h*) behave, act (***wie*** like)
**gebären** [gə'bɛ:rən] *v/t* (*irr*, *no -ge-*, *h*) give birth to; **Gebärmutter** [gə'bɛ:ɐmʊtɐ] *f* ANAT uterus, womb
**Gebäude** [gə'bɔydə] *n* (*-s*; -) building, structure
**Ge'beine** *pl* bones, mortal remains
**geben** ['ge:bən] *v/t* (*irr*, *ge-*, *h*) give (***j-m et.*** s.o. s.th.); hand, pass; deal (*cards*); make; ***sich ~*** pass; get better; ***von sich ~*** utter, let out; ***j-m die Schuld ~*** blame s.o.; ***es gibt*** there is, there are; ***was gibt es?*** what's up?; what's for *lunch etc?*; TV *etc* what's on?; ***das gibt's nicht*** that can't be true; that's out
**Gebet** [gə'be:t] *n* (-[*e*]*s*; *-e*) prayer
**ge'beten** *pp of* ***bitten***
**Gebiet** [gə'bi:t] *n* (-[*e*]*s*; *-e*) region, area; *esp* POL territory; *fig* field
**ge'bieterisch** *adj* imperious
**ge'bietsweise** *adv* regionally; ***~ Regen*** local showers
**Gebilde** [gə'bɪldə] *n* (*-s*; -) thing, object
**gebildet** [gə'bɪldət] *adj* educated
**Gebirge** [gə'bɪrgə] *n* (*-s*; -) mountains
**gebirgig** [gə'bɪrgɪç] *adj* mountainous
**Ge'birgs|bewohner** *m* mountain-dweller; ~**zug** *m* mountain range
**Ge'biss** *n* (*-es*; *-e*) (set of) teeth; (set of) false teeth, denture(s)
**ge'bissen** *pp of* ***beißen***
**Gebläse** [gə'blɛ:zə] *n* (*-s*; -) TECH blower, (MOT air) fan
**ge'blasen** *pp of* ***blasen***
**geblichen** [gə'blɪçən] *pp of* ***bleichen***
**geblieben** [gə'bli:bən] *pp of* ***bleiben***
**geblümt** [gə'bly:mt] *adj* floral
**gebogen** [gə'bo:gən] **1.** *pp of* ***biegen*** **2.** *adj* bent, curved
**geboren** [gə'bo:rən] **1.** *pp of* ***gebären*** **2.** *adj* born; ***~e Smith*** née Smith; ***ich bin am … ~*** I was born on the …
**geborgen** [gə'bɔrgən] **1.** *pp of* ***bergen*** **2.** *adj* safe, secure; **Ge'borgenheit** *f* (-; *no pl*) safety, security
**geborsten** [gə'bɔrstən] *pp of* ***bersten***
**Gebot** [gə'bo:t] *n* (-[*e*]*s*; *-e*) REL commandment; *fig* rule; necessity; *auction etc*: bid
**geboten** [gə'bo:tən] *pp of* ***bieten***
**gebracht** [gə'braxt] *pp of* ***bringen***
**gebrannt** [gə'brant] *pp of* ***brennen***
**ge'braten** *pp of* ***braten***
**Ge'brauch** *m* (-[*e*]*s*; *no pl*) use; application; **ge'brauchen** *v/t* (*no -ge-*, *h*) use; employ; ***gut*** (***nicht***) ***zu ~ sein*** be useful (useless); ***ich könnte … ~*** I could do with …; **gebräuchlich** [gə'brɔyçlɪç] *adj* in use; common, usual; current
**Ge'brauchsanweisung** *f* directions *or* instructions for use
**ge'brauchsfertig** *adj* ready for use; instant (*coffee etc*)
**Ge'brauchsgrafiker** *m* commercial artist
**ge'braucht** *adj* used, ECON *a.* second-hand
**Ge'brauchtwagen** *m* MOT used *or* second-hand car; ~**händler** *m* used car dealer
**Ge'brechen** *n* (*-s*; -) defect, handicap
**gebrechlich** [gə'brɛçlɪç] *adj* frail; infirm; **Ge'brechlichkeit** *f* (-; *no pl*) frailty; infirmity
**gebrochen** [gə'brɔxən] *pp of* ***brechen***
**Ge'brüder** *pl* brothers
**Gebrüll** [gə'brʏl] *n* (-[*e*]*s*; *no pl*) roar(-ing)
**Gebühr** [gə'by:ɐ] *f* (-; *-en*) charge (*a.* TEL), fee; postage; due; **gebührend** [gə'by:rənt] *adj* due; proper

**ge'bühren|frei** *adj* free of charge; TEL toll-free, *Br* nonchargeable; **~pflichtig** *adj* chargeable; ***~e Straße*** toll road; ***~e Verwarnung*** fine
**gebunden** [gə'bʊndən] **1.** *pp of* ***binden*** **2.** *adj* bound, *fig a.* tied
**Geburt** [gə'buːɐt] *f* (-; *-en*) birth
**Ge'burten|kon,trolle** *f*, **~regelung** *f* birth control
**ge'burten|schwach** *adj* low-birthrate; **~stark** *adj*: ***~e Jahrgänge*** baby boom
**Ge'burtenziffer** *f* birthrate
**gebürtig** [gə'bʏrtɪç] *adj* by birth
**Ge'burts|anzeige** *f* birth announcement; **~datum** *n* date of birth; **~fehler** *m* congenital defect; **~helfer(in)** obstetrician; **~jahr** *n* year of birth; **~land** *n* native country; **~ort** *m* birthplace; **~tag** *m* birthday; **~tagsfeier** *f* birthday party; **~tagskind** *n* birthday boy (*or* girl); **~urkunde** *f* birth certificate
**Gebüsch** [gə'bʏʃ] *n* (-[*e*]*s*; *-e*) bushes, shrubbery
**gedacht** [gə'daxt] *pp of* ***denken***
**Gedächtnis** [gə'dɛçtnɪs] *n* (*-ses*; *-se*) memory; ***aus dem ~*** from memory; ***zum ~ an*** (*acc*) in memory (*or* commemoration) of; ***im ~ behalten*** keep in mind, remember; **~lücke** *f* memory lapse; **~schwund** *m* MED amnesia; blackout; **~stütze** *f* memory aid
**Gedanke** [gə'daŋkə] *m* (*-n*; *-n*) thought; idea; ***was für ein ~!*** what an idea!; ***in ~n*** absorbed in thought; absent-minded; ***sich ~n machen über*** (*acc*) think about; be worried *or* concerned about; ***j-s ~n lesen*** read s.o.'s mind
**Ge'danken|austausch** *m* exchange of ideas; **~gang** *m* train of thought
**ge'dankenlos** *adj* thoughtless
**Ge'danken|strich** *m* dash; **~übertragung** *f* telepathy
**Gedeck** [gə'dɛk] *n* (-[*e*]*s*; *-e*) cover; ***ein ~ auflegen*** set a place
**gedeihen** [gə'daiən] *v/i* (*irr*, *no -ge-*, *sein*) thrive, prosper; grow; flourish
**ge'denken** *v/i* (*irr*, ***denken***, *no -ge-*, *h*) (*gen*) think of; commemorate; mention
**Gedenk|feier** [gə'dɛŋkfaiɐ] *f* commemoration; **~mi,nute** *f*: ***e-e ~*** a moment's (*Br* minute's) silence; **~stätte** *f*, **~stein** *m* memorial; **~tafel** *f* plaque
**Gedicht** [gə'dɪçt] *n* (-[*e*]*s*; *-e*) poem
**gediegen** [gə'diːgən] *adj* solid; tasteful
**gedieh** [gə'diː] *pret of* ***gedeihen***
**gediehen** [gə'diːən] *pp of* ***gedeihen***
**Gedränge** [gə'drɛŋə] *n* (*-s*; -) crowd, F crush; **ge'drängt** *fig adj* concise
**gedroschen** [gə'drɔʃən] *pp of* ***dreschen***
**ge'drückt** *fig adj* depressed
**gedrungen** [gə'drʊŋən] **1.** *pp of* ***dringen*** **2.** *adj* squat, stocky; thickset
**Geduld** [gə'dʊlt] *f* (-; *no pl*) patience; **ge'dulden** *v/refl* (*no -ge-*, *h*) wait (patiently); **geduldig** [gə'dʊldɪç] *adj* patient; **Ge'duldspiel** *n* puzzle (*a. fig*)
**gedurft** [gə'dʊrft] *pp of* ***dürfen***
**geehrt** [gə'ʔeːɐt] *adj* hono(u)red; ***Sehr ~er Herr N.*** Dear Mr N.
**geeignet** [gə'ʔaignət] *adj* suitable; suited, qualified; right
**Gefahr** [gə'faːɐ] *f* (-; *-en*) danger; threat; risk; ***auf eigene ~*** at one's own risk; ***außer ~*** out of danger, safe
**gefährden** [gə'fɛːɐdən] *v/t* (*no -ge-*, *h*) endanger; risk, jeopardize
**ge'fahren** *pp of* ***fahren***
**gefährlich** [gə'fɛːɐlɪç] *adj* dangerous; risky
**ge'fahrlos** *adj* without risk, safe
**Gefährte** [gə'fɛːɐtə] *m* (*-n*; *-n*), **Ge'fährtin** *f* (-; *-nen*) companion
**Gefälle** [gə'fɛlə] *n* (*-s*; -) fall, slope, descent; gradient (*a.* PHYS)
**ge'fallen 1.** *pp of* ***fallen*** **2.** *v/i* (*irr*, ***fallen***, *no -ge-*, *h*) please; ***es gefällt mir (nicht)*** I (don't) like it; ***wie gefällt dir …?*** how do you like …?; ***sich et. ~ lassen*** put up with s.th.
**Ge'fallen**[1] *m* (*-s*; -) favo(u)r; ***j-n um e-n ~ bitten*** ask a favo(u)r of s.o.
**Ge'fallen**[2] *n*: ***~ finden an*** (*dat*) enjoy, like
**ge'fällig** *adj* pleasant, agreeable; obliging, kind; ***j-m ~ sein*** do s.o. a favo(u)r
**Ge'fälligkeit** *f* (-; *-en*) (*no pl*) kindness; favo(u)r
**ge'fangen 1.** *pp of* ***fangen*** **2.** *adj* captive; imprisoned; ***~ halten*** keep *s.o.* prisoner; ***~ nehmen*** take *s.o.* prisoner; *fig* captivate; **Ge'fangene** *m*, *f* (*-n*; *-n*) prisoner; convict; **Ge'fangennahme** *f* (-; *no pl*) capture; **Ge'fangenschaft** *f* (-; *no pl*) captivity, imprisonment; ***in ~ sein*** be a prisoner of war
**Gefängnis** [gə'fɛŋnɪs] *n* (*-ses*; *-se*) prison, jail, *Br a.* gaol; ***ins ~ kommen*** go to

G

jail *or* prison; **~di͵rektor** *m* governor, warden; **~strafe** *f* (sentence *or* term of) imprisonment; **~wärter** *m* prison guard
**Gefäß** [gəˈfɛːs] *n* (*-es*; *-e*) vessel (*a.* ANAT), container
**gefasst** [gəˈfast] *adj* composed; **~ auf** (*acc*) prepared for
**Gefecht** [gəˈfɛçt] *n* (*-[e]s*; *-e*) MIL combat, action
**gefedert** [gəˈfeːdɐt] *adj*: ***gut ~ sein*** MOT have good suspension
**gefeit** [gəˈfait] *adj*: ***~ gegen*** immune to
**Gefieder** [gəˈfiːdɐ] *n* (*-s*; -) ZO plumage, feathers
**geflochten** [gəˈflɔxtən] *pp of* ***flechten***
**geflogen** [gəˈfloːgən] *pp of* ***fliegen***
**geflohen** [gəˈfloːən] *pp of* ***fliehen***
**geflossen** [gəˈflɔsən] *pp of* ***fließen***
**Geˈflügel** *n* (*-s*; *no pl*) poultry
**geˈflügelt** *adj*: ***~es Wort*** saying
**gefochten** [gəˈfɔxtən] *pp of* ***fechten***
**Geˈfolge** *n* (*-s*; -) entourage, retinue, train; **Gefolgschaft** [gəˈfɔlkʃaft] *f* (-; *-en*) followers
**gefragt** [gəˈfraːkt] *adj* in demand, popular
**gefräßig** [gəˈfrɛːsɪç] *adj* greedy, voracious
**Gefreite** [gəˈfraitə] *m* (*-n*; *-n*) MIL private first class, *Br* lance corporal
**geˈfressen** *pp of* ***fressen***
**geˈfrieren** *v/i* (*irr*, ***frieren***, *no -ge-*, *sein*) freeze
**Gefrierfach** [gəˈfriːɐfax] *n* freezer, freezing compartment
**geˈfriergetrocknet** *adj* freeze-dried
**Geˈfrier|punkt** *m* freezing point; **~truhe** *f* freezer, deep-freeze
**gefroren** [gəˈfroːrən] *pp of* ***frieren***
**Geˈfrorene** *Austrian n* (*-n*; *no pl*) ice cream
**Gefüge** [gəˈfyːgə] *n* (*-s*; -) structure, texture
**gefügig** [gəˈfyːgɪç] *adj* pliant
**Geˈfügigkeit** *f* (-; *no pl*) pliancy
**Gefühl** [gəˈfyːl] *n* (*-[e]s*; *-e*) feeling; sense; sensation; emotion; **geˈfühllos** *adj* insensible, numb; unfeeling, heartless; **geˈfühlsbetont** *adj* (highly) emotional; **geˈfühlvoll** *adj* (full of) feeling; tender; sentimental
**gefunden** [gəˈfʊndən] *pp of* ***finden***
**gegangen** [gəˈgaŋən] *pp of* ***gehen***
**gegeben** [gəˈgeːbən] *pp of* ***geben***
**gegen** [ˈgeːgən] *prp* (*acc*) against, JUR, SPORT *a.* versus; about, around; (in return) for; MED *etc* for; compared with
**ˈGegen...** *in cpds ...aktion*, *...angriff*, *...argument*, *...frage etc*: counter-...; **~besuch** *m* return visit
**Gegend** [ˈgeːgənt] *f* (-; *-en*) region, area; countryside; neighbo(u)rhood
**gegeneiˈnander** *adv* against one another *or* each other
**ˈGegen|fahrbahn** *f* MOT opposite *or* oncoming lane; **~gewicht** *n* counterweight; ***ein ~ bilden zu et.*** counterbalance s.th.; **~kandi͵dat** *m* rival candidate; **~leistung** *f* quid pro quo; ***als ~*** in return; **~licht** *n* (*-[e]s*; *no pl*) PHOT back light; ***im*** *or* ***bei ~*** against the light; **~maßnahme** *f* countermeasure; **~mittel** *n* MED antidote (*a. fig*); **~par͵tei** *f* other side; POL opposition; SPORT opposite side; **~richtung** *f* opposite direction
**ˈGegensatz** *m* contrast; opposite; ***im ~ zu*** in contrast to *or* with; **gegensätzlich** [ˈgeːgənzɛtslɪç] *adj* contrary, opposite
**ˈGegenseite** *f* opposite side
**gegenseitig** [ˈgeːgənzaitɪç] *adj* mutual
**ˈGegenseitigkeit** *f*: ***auf ~ beruhen*** be mutual
**ˈGegen|spieler** *m*, **~spielerin** *f* SPORT opponent (*a. fig*); **~sprechanlage** *f* intercom (system)
**ˈGegenstand** *m* object (*a. fig*); *fig* subject; **gegenständlich** [ˈgeːgənʃtɛntlɪç] *adj art*: representational; **ˈgegenstandslos** *adj* invalid; irrelevant; *art*: abstract, nonrepresentational
**ˈGegen|stimme** *f* PARL vote against, no; ***nur drei ~n*** only three noes; **~stück** *n* counterpart
**ˈGegenteil** *n* opposite; ***im ~*** on the contrary; **ˈgegenteilig** *adj* contrary, opposite
**gegenˈüber** *adv and prp* (*dat*) opposite; *fig* to, toward(s); compared with
**Gegenˈüber** *n* (*-s*; -) person opposite; neighbo(u)r across the street
**gegenˈüberstehen** *v/i* (*irr*, ***stehen***, *sep*, *-ge-*, *h*) face, be faced with
**Gegenˈüberstellung** *f* confrontation
**ˈGegenverkehr** *m* oncoming traffic

**Gegenwart** ['ge:gənvart] *f* (-; *no pl*) present (time); presence; LING present (tense)

**gegenwärtig** ['ge:gənvɛrtɪç] **1.** *adj* present, current **2.** *adv* at present

**Gegen|wehr** ['ge:gənve:ɐ] *f* (-; *no pl*) resistance; **~wert** *m* equivalent (value); **~wind** *m* head wind

'**gegenzeichnen** *v/t* (*sep, -ge-, h*) countersign

'**Gegenzug** *m* countermove; RAIL train coming from the opposite direction

**gegessen** [gə'gɛsən] *pp of* ***essen***

**geglichen** [gə'glɪçən] *pp of* ***gleichen***

**geglitten** [gə'glɪtən] *pp of* ***gleiten***

**geglommen** [gə'glɔmən] *pp of* ***glimmen***

**Gegner** ['ge:gnɐ] *m* (*-s*; -), '**Gegnerin** *f* (-; *-nen*) opponent (*a.* SPORT), adversary; MIL enemy

'**gegnerisch** *adj* opposing; MIL (of the) enemy, hostile

'**Gegnerschaft** *f* (-; *-en*) opposition

**gegolten** [gə'gɔltən] *pp of* ***gelten***

**gegoren** [gə'go:rən] *pp of* ***gären***

**gegossen** [gə'gɔsən] *pp of* ***gießen***

**ge'graben** *pp of* ***graben***

**gegriffen** [gə'grɪfən] *pp of* ***greifen***

**gehabt** [gə'ha:pt] *pp of* ***haben***

**Gehackte** [gə'haktə] *n* → ***Hackfleisch***

**Gehalt** [gə'halt] **1.** *m* (-[*e*]*s*; *-e*) content **2.** *n* (-[*e*]*s*; *Gehälter* [gə'hɛltɐ]) salary

**ge'halten** *pp of* ***halten***

**Ge'halts|empfänger** *m* salaried employee; **~erhöhung** *f* raise, *Br* increase *or* rise in salary

**ge'haltvoll** *adj* substantial; nutritious

**gehangen** [gə'haŋən] *pp of* ***hängen*** 1

**gehässig** [gə'hɛsɪç] *adj* malicious, spiteful; **Ge'hässigkeit** *f* (-; *no pl*) malice, spite(fulness)

**ge'hauen** *pp of* ***hauen***

**Gehäuse** [gə'hɔʏzə] *n* (*-s*; -) case, box; TECH casing; ZO shell; BOT core

**Gehege** [gə'he:gə] *n* (*-s*; -) enclosure

**geheim** [gə'haim] *adj* secret; ***et. ~ halten*** keep s.th. (a) secret

**Ge'heim|a,gent** *m* secret agent; **~dienst** *m* secret service

**Geheimnis** [gə'haimnɪs] *n* (*-ses*; *-se*) secret; mystery

**ge'heimnisvoll** *adj* mysterious

**Ge'heim|nummer** *f* TEL unlisted (*Br* ex-directory) number; **~poli,zei** *f* secret police; **~schrift** *f* code, cipher

**ge'heißen** *pp of* **heißen**

**gehemmt** [gə'hɛmt] *adj* inhibited, self-conscious

**gehen** ['ge:ən] *v/i* (*irr, ge-, sein*) go; walk; leave; TECH work (*a. fig*); ECON sell; *fig* last; ***einkaufen*** (***schwimmen***) **~** go shopping (swimming); **~ *wir!*** let's go!; ***wie geht es dir*** (***Ihnen***)***?*** how are you?; ***es geht mir gut*** (***schlecht***) I'm fine (not feeling well); **~ *in*** (*acc*) go into; **~ *nach*** *road etc*: lead to; *window etc*: face; *fig* go *or* judge by; ***das geht nicht*** that's impossible; ***das geht schon*** that's o.k.; ***es geht nichts über*** (*acc*) ***...*** there is nothing like ...; ***worum geht es?*** what is it about?; ***darum geht es*** (***nicht***) that's (not) the point; ***sich ~ lassen*** let o.s. go

'**gehenlassen** *v/refl* (*irr*, ***lassen***, *sep, no -ge-, h*) → ***gehen***

**geheuer** [gə'hɔʏɐ] *adj*: ***nicht*** (***ganz***) **~** eerie, creepy, F fishy

**Geheul** [gə'hɔʏl] *n* (-[*e*]*s*; *no pl*) howling

**Ge'hirn** *n* (-[*e*]*s*; *-e*) ANAT brain(s); **~erschütterung** *f* MED concussion (of the brain); **~schlag** *m* MED (cerebral) apoplexy; **~wäsche** *f* brainwashing

**gehoben** [gə'ho:bən] **1.** *pp of* ***heben*** **2.** *adj* elevated; high(er); ***~e Stimmung*** high spirits

**Gehöft** [gə'hœft] *n* (-[*e*]*s*; *-e*) farm (-stead)

**geholfen** [gə'hɔlfən] *pp of* ***helfen***

**Gehölz** [gə'hœlts] *n* (*-es*; *-e*) wood, coppice, copse

**Gehör** [gə'hø:ɐ] *n* (-[*e*]*s*; *-e*) (sense of) hearing; ear; ***nach dem ~*** by ear; ***sich ~ verschaffen*** make o.s. heard

**ge'horchen** *v/i* (*no -ge-, h*) obey; ***nicht ~*** disobey

**ge'hören** *v/i* (*no -ge-, h*) belong (*dat or* ***zu*** to); ***gehört dir das?*** is this yours?; ***es gehört sich*** (***nicht***) it is proper *or* right (not done); ***das gehört nicht hierher*** that's not to the point

**ge'hörig** **1.** *adj* due, proper; necessary; decent; ***zu et. ~*** belonging to s.th. **2.** *adv* properly, thoroughly

**ge'hörlos** *adj* deaf; ***die Gehörlosen*** the deaf

**gehorsam** [gə'ho:ɐza:m] *adj* obedient

**Ge'horsam** *m* (*-s*; *no pl*) obedience

'**Gehsteig** *m*, '**Gehweg** *m* sidewalk, *Br*

pavement
**Geier** ['gaiɐ] *m* (-*s*; -) ZO vulture, buzzard
**Geige** ['gaigə] *f* (-; -*n*) MUS violin, F fiddle; (***auf der***) **~ *spielen*** play (on) the violin
'**Geigen|bogen** *m* MUS (violin) bow; **~kasten** *m* MUS violin case
'**Geiger** ['gaigɐ] *m* (-*s*; -), **Geigerin** ['gaigərɪn] *f* (-; -*nen*) MUS violinist
'**Geigerzähler** *m* PHYS Geiger counter
**geil** [gail] *adj* V hot, horny; *contp* lecherous, lewd; BOT rank; F awesome, *Br* brill, ace
**Geisel** ['gaizəl] *f* (-; -*n*) hostage; **~nehmer** ['gaizəlne:mɐ] *m* (-*s*; -) kidnap(p)er
**Geißel** ['gaisəl] *fig f* (-; -*n*) scourge
**Geist** [gaist] *m* (-[*e*]*s*; -*er*) (*no pl*) spirit; soul; mind; intellect; wit; ghost; ***der Heilige*** **~** REL the Holy Ghost *or* Spirit
**Geister|bahn** ['gaistɐba:n] *f* tunnel of horror, *Br* ghost train; **~fahrer** F *m* MOT wrong-way driver
'**geisterhaft** *adj* ghostly
'**geistesabwesend** *adj* absent-minded
'**Geistes|arbeiter** *m* brainworker; **~blitz** *m* brainstorm, *Br* brainwave
'**Geistesgegenwart** *f* presence of mind; '**geistesgegenwärtig** *adj* alert; quick-witted
'**geistesgestört** *adj* mentally disturbed, deranged
'**geisteskrank** *adj* mentally ill
'**Geisteskrankheit** *f* mental illness
'**geistesschwach** *adj* feeble-minded
'**Geisteswissenschaften** *pl the* arts, *the* humanities
'**Geisteszustand** *m* mental state
**geistig** ['gaistɪç] *adj* mental; intellectual; spiritual; **~ *behindert*** mentally handicapped
'**geistlich** *adj* religious; spiritual; ecclesiastical; clerical; '**Geistliche** *m* (-*n*; -*n*) clergyman; priest; minister; ***die* ~*n*** the clergy
'**geistlos** *adj* trivial, inane, silly
'**geistreich**, '**geistvoll** *adj* witty, clever
**Geiz** [gaits] *m* (-*es*; *no pl*) stinginess
'**Geizhals** *m* miser, niggard
**geizig** ['gaitsɪç] *adj* stingy, miserly
**Ge'jammer** F *n* (-*s*; *no pl*) wailing, complaining
**gekannt** [gə'kant] *pp of* ***kennen***
**Gekläff** [gə'klɛf] F *n* (-[*e*]*s*; *no pl*) yapping
**Geklapper** [gə'klapɐ] F *n* (-*s*; *no pl*) clatter(ing)
**Geklimper** F *n* (-*s*; *no pl*) tinkling
**geklungen** [gə'klʊŋən] *pp of* ***klingen***
**gekniffen** [gə'knɪfən] *pp of* ***kneifen***
**ge'kommen** *pp of* ***kommen***
**gekonnt** [gə'kɔnt] **1.** *pp of* ***können*** **2.** *adj* masterly
**gekränkt** [gə'krɛŋkt] *adj* hurt, offended
**Gekritzel** [gə'krɪtsəl] *contp n* (-*s*; *no pl*) scrawl, scribble
**gekrochen** [gə'krɔxən] *pp of* ***kriechen***
**gekünstelt** [gə'kʏnstəlt] *adj* affected; artificial
**Gelächter** [gə'lɛçtɐ] *n* (-*s*; *no pl*) laughter
**ge'laden** *pp of* ***laden***
**Ge'lage** *n* (-*s*; -) feast; carouse
**Gelände** [gə'lɛndə] *n* (-*s*; -) area, country, ground; site; ***auf dem*** **~** on the premises; **~...** *in cpds …lauf, …ritt, …wagen etc*: cross-country …
**Geländer** [gə'lɛndɐ] *n* (-*s*; -) banisters; handrail, rail(ing); parapet
**ge'lang** *pret of* ***gelingen***
**ge'langen** *v/i* (*no -ge-, sein*) **~ *an*** (*acc*) *or* ***nach*** reach, arrive at, get *or* come to; **~ *in*** (*acc*) get *or* come into; *fig* ***zu et.*** **~** gain *or* win *or* achieve s.th.
**ge'lassen** **1.** *pp of* ***lassen*** **2.** *adj* calm, composed, cool
**Gelatine** [ʒela'ti:nə] *f* (-; *no pl*) gelatin(e)
**ge'laufen** *pp of* ***laufen***
**ge'läufig** *adj* common, current; familiar
**gelaunt** [gə'launt] *adj*: ***schlecht*** (***gut***) **~ *sein*** be in a bad (good) mood
**gelb** [gɛlp] *adj* yellow
'**gelblich** *adj* yellowish
'**Gelbsucht** *f* (-; *no pl*) MED jaundice
**Geld** [gɛlt] *n* (-[*e*]*s*; -*er* ['gɛldɐ]) money; ***zu* ~ *machen*** turn into cash
'**Geld|angelegenheiten** *pl* money *or* financial matters *or* affairs; **~anlage** *f* investment; **~ausgabe** *f* expense; **~auto,mat** *m* automatic teller machine, ATM, autoteller, *Br* cash dispenser; **~beutel** *m*, **~börse** *f* purse; **~buße** *f* fine, penalty; **~geber(in)** [gɛltge:bɐ, gɛltge:bərɪn] (-*s*; -/-; -*nen*) financial backer; investor

'**geldgierig** *adj* greedy for money

'**Geld|knappheit** *f*, **~mangel** *m* lack of money; ECON (financial) stringency; **~mittel** *pl* funds, means, resources; **~schein** *m* bill, *Br* (bank)note; **~schrank** *m* safe; **~sendung** *f* remittance; **~strafe** *f* fine; **~stück** *n* coin; **~verlegenheit** *f* financial embarrassment; **~verschwendung** *f* waste of money; **~waschanlage** *f* money laundering scheme; **~wechsel** *m* exchange of money; **~wechselautomat** *m*, **~wechsler** ['gɛltvɛkslɐ] *m* (*-s*; -) change machine

**Gelee** [ʒe'le:] *n*, *m* (*-s*; *-s*) jelly; gel

**ge'legen 1.** *pp of* ***liegen*** **2.** *adj* situated, located; *fig* convenient, opportune; **Ge'legenheit** *f* (-; *-en*) occasion; opportunity, chance; ***bei ~*** on occasion

**Ge'legenheits|arbeit** *f* casual *or* odd job; **~arbeiter** *m* casual labo(u)rer, odd-job man; **~kauf** *m* bargain

**gelegentlich** [gə'le:gəntlıç] *adv* occasionally

**gelehrig** [gə'le:rıç] *adj* docile

**Gelehrsamkeit** [gə'le:ɐza:mkait] *f* (-; *no pl*) learning; **gelehrt** [gə'le:ɐt] *adj* learned; **Ge'lehrte** *m, f* (*-n*; *-n*) scholar, learned man *or* woman

**Geleise** [gə'laizə] *n* → ***Gleis***

**Geleit** [gə'lait] *n* (*-[e]s*; *-e*) escort

**ge'leiten** *v/t* (*no -ge-*, *h*) accompany, conduct, escort

**Ge'leitzug** *m* MAR, MIL convoy

**Gelenk** [gə'lɛŋk] *n* (*-[e]s*; *-e*) ANAT, TECH joint; **ge'lenkig** *adj* flexible (*a.* TECH); lithe, supple

**gelernt** [gə'lɛrnt] *adj* skilled, trained

**ge'lesen** *pp of* ***lesen***

**geliebt** [gə'li:pt] *adj* (be)loved, dear

**Ge'liebte 1.** *m* (*-n*; *-n*) lover **2.** *f* (*-n*; *-n*) mistress

**geliehen** [gə'li:ən] *pp of* ***leihen***

**gelingen** [gə'lıŋən] *v/i* (*irr, no -ge-, sein*) succeed, manage; turn out well; ***es gelang mir, et. zu tun*** I succeeded in doing (I managed to do) s.th.; **Ge'lingen** *n* (*-s*; *no pl*) success; ***gutes ~!*** good luck!

**gelitten** [gə'lıtən] *pp of* ***leiden***

**gelogen** [gə'lo:gən] *pp of* ***lügen***

**gelten** ['gɛltən] *v/i and v/t* (*irr, ge-, h*) be worth; *fig* count for; be valid; SPORT count; ECON be effective; ***~ für*** apply to; ***~ als*** be regarded *or* looked upon as, be considered *or* supposed to be; ***~ lassen*** accept (***als*** as); **~d** *adj* accepted; ***~ machen*** assert; ***s-n Einfluss*** (***bei j-m***) ***~ machen*** bring one's influence to bear (on s.o.)

'**Geltung** *f* (-; *no pl*) prestige; weight; ***zur ~ kommen*** show to advantage

'**Geltungsbedürfnis** *n* (*-ses*; *no pl*) need for recognition

**Gelübde** [gə'lʏpdə] *n* (*-s*; -) vow

**gelungen** [gə'lʊŋən] **1.** *pp of* ***gelingen*** **2.** *adj* successful, a success

**gemächlich** [gə'mɛ:çlıç] *adj* leisurely

**ge'mahlen** *pp of* ***mahlen***

**Gemälde** [gə'mɛ:ldə] *n* (*-s*; -) painting, picture; **~gale,rie** *f* art (*or* picture) gallery

**gemäß** [gə'mɛ:s] *prp* (*dat*) according to

**gemäßigt** [gə'mɛ:sıçt] *adj* moderate; temperate (*climate etc*)

**gemein** [gə'main] *adj* mean; dirty, filthy (*joke etc*); BOT, ZO common

**Gemeinde** [gə'maində] *f* (-; *-n*) POL municipality; local government; REL parish; congregation; **~rat** *m* (member of the) city (*Br* local) council; **~rätin** [gə'maindərɛ:tın] *f* (-; *-nen*) member of the city (*Br* local) council; **~steuern** *pl* local taxes, *Br* (local) rates

**ge'meingefährlich** *adj*: ***~er Mensch*** public enemy

**Ge'meinheit** *f* (-; *-en*) (*no pl*) meanness; mean thing (to do *or* say), F dirty trick

**gemeinnützig** [gə'mainnʏtsıç] *adj* non-profit, *Br* non-profitmaking

**Ge'meinplatz** *m* commonplace

**ge'meinsam 1.** *adj* common, joint; mutual **2.** *adv* together

**Ge'meinschaft** *f* (-; *-en*) community

**Ge'meinschafts|arbeit** *f* teamwork; **~kunde** *f* (-; *no pl*) PED social studies; **~produkti,on** *f* coproduction; **~raum** *m* recreation room, lounge

**Ge'meinsinn** *m* (*-[e]s*; *no pl*) public spirit; (sense of) solidarity

**ge'meinverständlich** *adj* popular

**Ge'meinwohl** *n* public welfare

**ge'messen 1.** *pp of* ***messen*** **2.** *adj* measured; formal; grave

**Gemetzel** [gə'mɛtsəl] *n* (*-s*; -) slaughter, massacre

**gemieden** [gə'mi:dən] *pp of* ***meiden***

G

**Gemisch** [gəˈmɪʃ] *n* (-[*e*]*s*; -*e*) mixture (*a.* CHEM)
**gemocht** [gəˈmɔxt] *pp of* ***mögen***
**gemolken** [gəˈmɔlkən] *pp of* ***melken***
**Gemse** → ***Gämse***
**Gemurmel** [gəˈmʊrməl] *n* (-*s*; *no pl*) murmur, mutter
**Gemüse** [gəˈmyːzə] *n* (-*s*; -) vegetable(s); greens; **~händler** *m* greengrocer('s)
**gemusst** [gəˈmʊst] *pp of* ***müssen***
**Gemüt** [gəˈmyːt] *n* (-[*e*]*s*; -*er*) mind, soul; heart; nature, mentality
**geˈmütlich** *adj* comfortable, snug, cozy, *Br* cosy; peaceful, pleasant, relaxed; ***mach es dir ~*** make yourself at home; **Geˈmütlichkeit** *f* (-; *no pl*) snugness, coziness, *Br* cosiness; cozy (*Br* cosy) *or* relaxed atmosphere
**Geˈmütsbewegung** *f* emotion
**geˈmütskrank** *adj* emotionally disturbed
**Geˈmütszustand** *m* state of mind
**Gen** [geːn] *n* (-*s*; -*e*) BIOL gene
**genannt** [gəˈnant] *pp of* ***nennen***
**genas** [gəˈnaːs] *pret of* ***genesen*** 1
**genau** [gəˈnau] **1.** *adj* exact, precise, accurate; careful, close; strict; ***Genaueres*** further details **2.** *adv*: ***~ um 10 Uhr*** at 10 o'clock sharp; ***~ der ...*** that very ...; ***~ zuhören*** listen closely; ***es ~ nehmen*** (***mit et.***) be particular (about s.th.); **Geˈnauigkeit** *f* (-; *no pl*) accuracy, precision, exactness
**geˈnauso** *adv* → ***ebenso***
**genehmigen** [gəˈneːmɪgən] *v/t* (*no -ge-, h*) permit, allow; approve
**Geˈnehmigung** *f* (-; -*en*) permission; approval; permit; licen|se, *Br* -ce
**geneigt** [gəˈnaikt] *adj* inclined (***zu*** to)
**General** [genəˈraːl] *m* (-*s*; *Generäle* [genəˈrɛːlə]) MIL general; **~diˌrektor** *m* ECON president, *Br* chairman; **~konsul** *m* consul general; **~konsuˌlat** *n* consulate general; **~probe** *f* THEA dress rehearsal; **~sekreˌtär** *m* secretary-general; **~stab** *m* MIL general staff; **~streik** *m* general strike; **~versammlung** *f* general meeting; **~vertreter** *m* ECON sole agent
**Generation** [genəraˈtsjoːn] *f* (-; -*en*) generation; **Generatiˈonenkonˌflikt** *m* generation gap
**Generator** [genəˈraːtoːɐ] *m* (-*s*; -*en* [genəraˈtoːrən]) ELECTR generator
**generell** [genəˈrɛl] *adj* general, universal
**genesen** [gəˈneːzən] **1.** *v/i* (*irr, no -ge-, sein*) recover (***von*** from), get well **2.** *pp of* ***genesen*** 1
**Geˈnesung** *f* (-; *no pl*) recovery
**Genetik** [geˈneːtɪk] *f* (-; *no pl*) BIOL genetics; **geˈnetisch** *adj* BIOL genetic; ***~er Fingerabdruck*** genetic fingerprint
**genial** [geˈnjaːl] *adj* brilliant, of genius
**Genialität** [genjaliˈtɛːt] *f* (-; *no pl*) genius
**Genick** [gəˈnɪk] *n* (-[*e*]*s*; -*e*) ANAT (back *or* nape of the) neck
**Genie** [ʒeˈniː] *n* (-*s*; -*s*) genius
**genieren** [ʒeˈniːrən] *v/refl* (*no -ge-, h*) be embarrassed
**genießen** [gəˈniːsən] *v/t* (*irr, no -ge-, h*) enjoy
**Genießer** [gəˈniːsɐ] *m* (-*s*; -) gourmet
**Genitiv** [ˈgeːnitiːf] *m* (-*s*; -*e*) LING genitive *or* possessive (case)
**genommen** [gəˈnɔmən] *pp of* ***nehmen***
**genormt** [gəˈnɔrmt] *adj* standardized
**genoss** [gəˈnɔs] *pret of* ***genießen***
**Genosse** [gəˈnɔsə] *m* (-*n*; -*n*) POL comrade; F pal, buddy, *Br* mate
**genossen** [gəˈnɔsən] *pp of* ***genießen***
**Geˈnossenschaft** *f* (-; -*en*) cooperative
**Geˈnossin** *f* (-; -*nen*) POL comrade
**ˈGentechnik** *f*, **ˈGentechnoloˌgie** *f* genetic engineering
**genug** [gəˈnuːk] *adj* enough, sufficient
**Genüge** [gəˈnyːgə] *f*: ***zur ~*** (well) enough, sufficiently
**geˈnügen** *v/i* (*no -ge-, h*) be enough, be sufficient; ***das genügt*** that will do; **~d** *adj* enough, sufficient; plenty of
**genügsam** [gəˈnyːkzaːm] *adj* easily satisfied; frugal; modest; **Geˈnügsamkeit** *f* (-; *no pl*) modesty; frugality
**Geˈnugtuung** *f* (-; *no pl*) satisfaction
**Genus** [ˈgeːnʊs] *n* (-; *Genera* [ˈgeːnera]) LING gender
**Genuss** [gəˈnʊs] *m* (-*es*; *Genüsse* [gəˈnʏsə]) pleasure; (*no pl*) consumption; ***ein ~*** a real treat; *food*: *a.* delicious; **~mittel** *n* excise item, *Br* (semi-)luxury
**Geografie**, **Geographie** [geograˈfiː] *f* (-; *no pl*) geography; **geografisch**, **geographisch** [geoˈgraːfɪʃ] *adj* geographic(al)

**Geologe** [geo'lo:gə] *m* (*-n*; *-n*) geologist; **Geologie** [geolo'gi:] *f* (-; *no pl*) geology; **Geo'login** *f* (-; *-nen*) geologist; **geologisch** [geo'lo:gɪʃ] *adj* geologic(al)

**Geometrie** [geome'tri:] *f* (-; *no pl*) geometry; **geometrisch** [geo'me:trɪʃ] *adj* geometric(al)

**Gepäck** [gə'pɛk] *n* (*-[e]s*; *no pl*) baggage, luggage; **~ablage** *f* baggage (*or* luggage) rack; **~aufbewahrung** *f* baggage room, *Br* left-luggage office; **~kon,trolle** *f* baggage check, *Br* luggage inspection; **~schalter** *m* baggage (*or* luggage) counter; **~schein** *m* baggage check, *Br* luggage ticket; **~träger** *m* porter; *bicycle*: carrier

**gepanzert** [gə'pantsɐt] *adj* MOT armo(u)red

**Gepard** ['ge:part] *m* (*-s*; *-e*) zo cheetah

**gepfiffen** [gə'pfɪfən] *pp of* ***pfeifen***

**gepflegt** [gə'pfle:kt] *adj* well-groomed, neat; *fig* cultivated

**Gepflogenheit** [gə'pflo:gənhait] *f* (-; *-en*) habit, custom

**Geplapper** [gə'plapɐ] F *n* (*-s*; *no pl*) babbling, chatter(ing)

**Geplauder** [gə'plaudɐ] *n* (*-s*; *no pl*) chat (-ting)

**Gepolter** [gə'pɔltɐ] *n* (*-s*; *no pl*) rumble

**gepriesen** [gə'pri:zən] *pp of* ***preisen***

**Gequassel** [gə'kvasəl] F *n* (*-s*; *no pl*), **Gequatsche** [gə'kvatʃə] F *n* (*-s*; *no pl*) blather, blabber

**gequollen** [gə'kvɔlən] *pp of* ***quellen***

**gerade** [gə'ra:də] **1.** *adj* straight (*a. fig*); even (*number*); direct; upright, erect (*posture*) **2.** *adv* just; ***nicht ~*** not exactly; ***das ist es ja ~!*** that's just it!; ***~ deshalb*** that's just why; ***~ rechtzeitig*** just in time; ***warum ~ ich?*** why me of all people?; ***da wir ~ von ... sprechen*** speaking of ...; **Ge'rade** *f* (*-n*; *-n*) MATH (straight) line; SPORT straight; ***linke*** (***rechte***) ***~*** *boxing*: straight left (right)

**gerade|'aus** *adv* straight on *or* ahead; **~he'raus** *adj* straightforward, frank

**ge'radestehen** *v/i* (*irr*, ***stehen***, *sep*, *-ge-*, *h*) stand straight; ***~ für*** answer for

**ge'radewegs** *adv* straight, directly

**ge'radezu** *adv* simply

**gerannt** [gə'rant] *pp of* ***rennen***

**Gerät** [gə'rɛ:t] *n* (*-[e]s*; *-e*) device; F gadget; appliance; (kitchen) utensil; *radio*, TV set; *coll*, *a.* SPORT *etc* equipment; SPORT apparatus; TECH tool; instrument

**ge'raten** **1.** *pp of* ***raten*** **2.** *v/i* (*irr*, ***raten***, *no -ge-*, *sein*) turn out (***gut*** well); ***~ an*** (*acc*) come across; ***~ in*** (*acc*) get into; ***in Brand ~*** catch fire

**Ge'räteturnen** *n* apparatus gymnastics

**Ge'ratewohl** *n*: ***aufs ~*** at random

**geräumig** [gə'rɔʏmɪç] *adj* spacious, roomy

**Geräusch** [gə'rɔʏʃ] *n* (*-[e]s*; *-e*) sound, noise; **ge'räuschlos** **1.** *adj* noiseless (*a.* TECH); **2.** *adv* without a sound; **ge'räuschvoll** *adj* noisy

**gerben** ['gɛrbən] *v/t* (*ge-*, *h*) tan

**Gerberei** [gɛrbə'rai] *f* (-; *-en*) tannery

**ge'recht** *adj* just, fair; (*j-m*, *e-r Sache*) ***~ werden*** do justice to; meet (*demands etc*); **Ge'rechtigkeit** *f* (-; *no pl*) justice

**Ge'rede** F *n* (*-s*; *no pl*) talk; gossip

**gereizt** [gə'raitst] *adj* irritable

**Ge'reiztheit** *f* (-; *no pl*) irritability

**Gericht**[1] [gə'rɪçt] *n* (*-[e]s*; *-e*) GASTR dish

**Ge'richt**[2] *n* (*-[e]s*; *-e*) JUR court; ***vor ~ stehen*** (***stellen***) stand (bring to) trial; ***vor ~ gehen*** go to court

**ge'richtlich** *adj* JUR judicial, legal

**Ge'richtsbarkeit** *f* (-; *no pl*) JUR jurisdiction

**Ge'richts|gebäude** *n* JUR law court(s), courthouse; **~hof** *m* JUR law court; **~medi,zin** *f* JUR forensic medicine; **~saal** *m* JUR courtroom; **~verfahren** *n* JUR lawsuit; **~verhandlung** *f* JUR hearing; trial; **~vollzieher** [gə'rɪçtsfɔltsi:ɐ] *m* (*-s*; *-*) JUR marshal, *Br* bailiff

**gerieben** [gə'ri:bən] *pp of* ***reiben***

**gering** [gə'rɪŋ] *adj* little, small; slight, minor; low; ***~ schätzen*** think little of

**ge'ringfügig** *adj* slight, minor; petty

**ge'ring|schätzen** *v/t* (*sep*, *-ge-*, *h*) → ***gering***; **~schätzig** [gə'rɪŋʃɛtsɪç] *adj* contemptuous

**ge'ringst** *adj* least; ***nicht im Geringsten*** not in the least

**ge'rinnen** *v/i* (*irr*, ***rinnen***, *no -ge-*, *sein*) coagulate; curdle; clot

**Ge'rippe** *n* (*-s*; *-*) skeleton (*a. fig*); TECH framework

**gerissen** [gə'rɪsən] **1.** *pp of* ***reißen*** **2.** F *adj* cunning, smart

**geritten** [gə'rɪtən] *pp of* ***reiten***

G

**germanisch** [gɛr'maːnɪʃ] *adj* Germanic; **Germanist(in)** [gɛrma'nɪst(ɪn)] (*-en*; *-en*/-; *-nen*) student of (*or* graduate in) German

**gern** [gɛrn] *adv* willingly, gladly; ***et.*** (***sehr***) ***~ tun*** like (love) to do s.th. *or* doing s.th.; ***ich möchte ~*** I'd like (to); ***~ geschehen!*** not at all, (you're) welcome

**gernhaben** *v/t* (*irr*, ***haben***, *sep*, *-ge-*, *h*) like, be fond of;

**gerochen** [gə'rɔxən] *pp of* ***riechen***

**Geröll** [gə'rœl] *n* (*-[e]s*; *-e*) scree; boulders

**geronnen** [gə'rɔnən] *pp of* ***rinnen***

**Gerste** ['gɛrstə] *f* (-; *-n*) BOT barley

**'Gerstenkorn** *n* MED sty(e)

**Gerte** ['gɛrtə] *f* (-; *-n*) switch, rod, twig

**Geruch** [gə'rʊx] *m* (*-[e]s*; *Gerüche* [gə'rʏçə]) smell; odo(u)r; scent

**ge'ruchlos** *adj* odo(u)rless

**Ge'ruchssinn** *m* (sense of) smell

**Gerücht** [gə'rʏçt] *n* (*-[e]s*; *-e*) rumo(u)r

**ge'rufen** *pp of* ***rufen***

**gerührt** [gə'ryːʁt] *adj* touched, moved

**Gerümpel** [gə'rʏmpəl] *n* (*-s*; *no pl*) lumber, junk

**Gerundium** [ge'rʊndiʊm] *n* (*-s*; *-ien*) LING gerund

**gerungen** [gə'rʊŋən] *pp of* ***ringen***

**Gerüst** [gə'rʏst] *n* (*-[e]s*; *-e*) frame(-work); scaffold(ing); stage

**ge'salzen** *pp of* ***salzen***

**gesamt** [gə'zamt] *adj* whole, entire, total, all

**Ge'samt...** *in cpds ...ergebnis etc*: *mst* total ...; **~ausgabe** *f* complete edition; **~schule** *f* comprehensive school

**gesandt** [gə'zant] *pp of* ***senden***

**Gesandte** [gə'zantə] *m, f* (*-n*; *-n*) POL envoy; **Ge'sandtschaft** *f* (-; *-en*) legation, mission

**Gesang** [gə'zaŋ] *m* (*-[e]s*; *Gesänge* [gə'zɛŋə]) singing; song; voice; **~buch** *n* REL hymn book; **~(s)lehrer(in)** singing teacher; **~verein** *m* choral society, glee club

**Gesäß** [gə'zɛːs] *n* (*-es*; *-e*) ANAT buttocks, bottom

**ge'schaffen** *pp of* ***schaffen***[1]

**Geschäft** [gə'ʃɛft] *n* (*-[e]s*; *-e*) business; store, *Br* shop; bargain

**ge'schäftig** *adj* busy, active

**Ge'schäftigkeit** *f* (-; *no pl*) activity

**ge'schäftlich 1.** *adj* business ...; commercial **2.** *adv* on business

**Ge'schäfts|brief** *m* business letter; **~frau** *f* businesswoman; **~freund** *m* business friend; **~führer(in)** managing director; (*of shop*) manager; **~inhaber(in)** proprietor; **~leitung** *f* executive board; **~mann** *m* businessman

**ge'schäftsmäßig** *adj* businesslike

**Ge'schäfts|ordnung** *f* PARL standing orders; rules (of procedure); **~partner(in)** (business) partner; **~räume** *pl* (business) premises; **~reise** *f* business trip; **~schluss** *m* closing time; ***nach ~ a.*** after business hours; **~stelle** *f* office; **~straße** *f* shopping street

**'ge'schäftstüchtig** *adj* efficient, smart

**Ge'schäfts|verbindung** *f* business connection; **~viertel** *n* commercial district; downtown; **~zeit** *f* office *or* business hours; **~zweig** *m* branch *or* line (of business)

**geschah** [gə'ʃaː] *pret of* ***geschehen*** 1

**geschehen** [gə'ʃeːən] **1.** *v/i* (*irr*, *no -ge-*, *sein*) happen, occur, take place; be done; ***es geschieht ihm recht*** it serves him right **2.** *pp of* ***geschehen*** 1

**gescheit** [gə'ʃait] *adj* clever, bright, F brainy

**Geschenk** [gə'ʃɛŋk] *n* (*-[e]s*; *-e*) present, gift; **~gutschein** *m* gift voucher; **~packung** *f* gift box; **~papier** *n* gift wrap

**Geschichte** [gə'ʃɪçtə] *f* (-; *-n*) story; (*no pl*) history; F business, thing

**ge'schichtlich** *adj* historical

**Ge'schichts|schreiber** *m* (*-s*; -), **~wissenschaftler** *m* historian

**Geschick** [gə'ʃɪk] *n* (*-[e]s*; *-e*) fate, destiny; → **Ge'schicklichkeit** *f* (-; *no pl*) skill; dexterity; **ge'schickt** *adj* skil(l)ful, skilled; dext(e)rous; clever

**geschieden** [gə'ʃiːdən] **1.** *pp of* ***scheiden*** **2.** *adj* divorced, *marriage*: dissolved

**geschienen** [gə'ʃiːnən] *pp of* ***scheinen***

**Geschirr** [gə'ʃɪr] *n* (*-[e]s*; *-e*) dishes, china; (*no pl*) kitchen utensils, pots and pans, crockery; harness; ***~ spülen*** wash *or* do the dishes

**Ge'schirrspüler** *m* (*-s*; -) dishwasher

**geschissen** [gə'ʃɪsən] *pp of* ***scheißen***

**ge'schlafen** *pp of* ***schlafen***

**ge'schlagen** *pp of* ***schlagen***

**Geschlecht** [gəˈʃlɛçt] *n* (-[*e*]*s*; -*er*) (*no pl*) sex; kind, species; family, line(age); generation; LING gender

**Geˈschlechts|krankheit** *f* MED sexually transmitted disease, venereal disease; **~teile** *pl* genitals; **~trieb** *m* sexual instinct *or* urge; **~verkehr** *m* (sexual) intercourse; **~wort** *n* LING article

**geschlichen** [gəˈʃlɪçən] *pp of* ***schleichen***

**geschliffen** [gəˈʃlɪfən] **1.** *pp of* ***schleifen²*** **2.** *adj* cut; *fig* polished

**geschlossen** [gəˈʃlɔsən] **1.** *pp of* ***schließen*** **2.** *adj* closed

**geschlungen** [gəˈʃlʊŋən] *pp of* ***schlingen***

**Geschmack** [gəˈʃmak] *m* (-[*e*]*s*; *Geschmäcke* [gəˈʃmɛkə]) taste (*a. fig*); flavo(u)r; **~ *finden an*** (*dat*) develop a taste for; **geˈschmacklos** *adj a. fig* tasteless; **Geˈschmacklosigkeit** *f* (-; *no pl*) tastelessness; **Geˈschmack(s)sache** *f* matter of taste; **geˈschmackvoll** *adj* tasteful, in good taste

**geschmeidig** [gəˈʃmaidɪç] *adj* supple, pliant

**geschmissen** [gəˈʃmɪsən] *pp of* ***schmeißen***

**geschmolzen** [gəˈʃmɔltsən] *pp of* ***schmelzen***

**geschnitten** [gəˈʃnɪtən] *pp of* ***schneiden***

**geschoben** [gəˈʃoːbən] *pp of* ***schieben***

**Geschöpf** [gəˈʃœpf] *n* (-[*e*]*s*; -*e*) creature

**geschoren** [gəˈʃoːrən] *pp of* ***scheren***

**Geschoss** [gəˈʃɔs] *n* (-*es*; -*e*), **Geschoß** [gəˈʃoːs] *Austrian n* (-*es*; -*e*) projectile, missile; stor(e)y, floor

**geˈschossen** *pp of* ***schießen***

**Geˈschrei** F *n* (-*s*; *no pl*) shouting, yelling; screams; crying; *fig* fuss

**geschrieben** [gəˈʃriːbən] *pp of* ***schreiben***

**geschrie(e)n** [gəˈʃriː(ə)n] *pp of* ***schreien***

**geschritten** [gəˈʃrɪtən] *pp of* ***schreiten***

**geschunden** [gəˈʃʊndən] *pp of* ***schinden***

**Geschütz** [gəˈʃʏts] *n* (-*es*; -*e*) MIL gun, cannon

**Geschwader** [gəˈʃvaːdɐ] *n* (-*s*; -) MIL MAR squadron; AVIAT group, *Br* wing

**Geschwätz** [gəˈʃvɛts] F *n* (-*es*; *no pl*) chatter, babble; gossip; *fig* nonsense

**geˈschwätzig** *adj* talkative; gossipy

**geschweige** [gəˈʃvaigə] *cj*: **~ (*denn*)** let alone

**geschwiegen** [gəˈʃviːgən] *pp of* ***schweigen***

**geschwind** [gəˈʃvɪnt] *adj* quick, swift

**Geschwindigkeit** [gəˈʃvɪndɪçkait] *f* (-; -*en*) speed; fastness, quickness; PHYS velocity; ***mit e-r ~ von ...*** at a speed *or* rate of ...

**Geˈschwindigkeits|begrenzung** *f* speed limit; **~überschreitung** *f* MOT speeding

**Geschwister** [gəˈʃvɪstɐ] *pl* brother(s) and sister(s); JUR siblings

**geschwollen** [gəˈʃvɔlən] **1.** *pp of* ***schwellen*** 1 **2.** *adj* MED swollen; *fig* bombastic, pretentious, pompous

**geschwommen** [gəˈʃvɔmən] *pp of* ***schwimmen***

**geschworen** [gəˈʃvoːrən] *pp of* ***schwören***; **Geˈschworene** *m, f* (-*n*; -*n*) member of a jury; ***die ~n*** the jury

**Geschwulst** [gəˈʃvʊlst] *f* (-; *Geschwülste* [gəˈʃvʏlstə]) MED growth, tumo(u)r

**geschwunden** [gəˈʃvʊndən] *pp of* ***schwinden***

**geschwungen** [gəˈʃvʊŋən] *pp of* ***schwingen***

**Geschwür** [gəˈʃvyːɐ] *n* (-*s*; -*e*) MED abscess, ulcer

**geˈsehen** *pp of* ***sehen***

**Geselchte** [gəˈzɛlçtə] *Austrian n* (-*n*; *no pl*) GASTR smoked meat

**Geselle** [gəˈzɛlə] *m* (-*n*; -*n*) journeyman

**geˈsellen** *v/refl* (*no -ge-, h*) ***sich zu j-m ~*** join s.o.

**geˈsellig** *adj* sociable; zo *etc* social; ***~es Beisammensein*** get-together

**Geˈsellin** *f* (-; -*nen*) trained woman *hairdresser etc*, journeywoman

**Gesellschaft** [gəˈzɛlʃaft] *f* (-; -*en*) society; company; party; ECON company, corporation; ***j-m ~ leisten*** keep s.o. company

**geˈsellschaftlich** *adj* social

**Geˈsellschafts...** *in cpds ...kritik, ...ordnung etc*: social ...; **~spiel** *n* parlo(u)r game; **~tanz** *m* ballroom dance

**gesessen** [gəˈzɛsən] *pp of* ***sitzen***

**Gesetz** [gəˈzɛts] *n* (-*es*; -*e*) JUR law; act;

**~buch** *n* JUR code (of law); **~entwurf** *m* PARL bill
**ge'setzgebend** *adj* JUR legislative
**Ge'setzgeber** *m* (*-s*; -) JUR legislator
**Ge'setzgebung** *f* (-; *-en*) JUR legislation
**ge'setzlich 1.** *adj* legal; lawful **2.** *adv*: **~ *geschützt*** JUR patented, registered
**ge'setzlos** *adj* lawless
**ge'setzmäßig** *adj* legal, lawful
**gesetzt** [gə'zɛtst] **1.** *adj* staid, dignified; mature (*age*) **2.** *cj*: ***~ den Fall*(*, dass*) ...** supposing (that)
**ge'setzwidrig** *adj* illegal, unlawful
**Gesicht** [gə'zɪçt] *n* (*-[e]s*; *-er*) face; ***zu ~ bekommen*** catch sight of
**Ge'sichts|ausdruck** *m* look, expression; **~creme** *f* face cream; **~farbe** *f* complexion; **~punkt** *m* point of view, aspect, angle; **~wasser** *n* toner; **~zug** *m* feature
**Gesindel** [gə'zɪndəl] *n* (*-s*; *no pl*) trash, *the* riff-raff
**gesinnt** [gə'zɪnt] *adj* minded; ***j-m feindlich ~ sein*** be ill-disposed towards s.o.
**Ge'sinnung** *f* (-; *-en*) mind; attitude; POL conviction(s)
**ge'sinnungslos** *adj* unprincipled
**ge'sinnungstreu** *adj* loyal
**Ge'sinnungswechsel** *m* about-face, *Br* about-turn
**gesittet** [gə'zɪtət] *adj* civilized, well-mannered
**gesoffen** [gə'zɔfən] *pp of* ***saufen***
**gesogen** [gə'zo:gən] *pp of* ***saugen***
**gesotten** [gə'zɔtən] *pp of* ***sieden***
**gespalten** [gə'ʃpaltən] *pp of* ***spalten***
**Gespann** [gə'ʃpan] *n* (*-[e]s*; *-e*) team (*a. fig*)
**gespannt** [gə'ʃpant] *adj* tense (*a. fig*); ***~ sein auf*** (*acc*) be anxious to see; ***ich bin ~, ob*** (***wie***) I wonder if (how)
**Gespenst** [gə'ʃpɛnst] *n* (*-[e]s*; *-er*) ghost, apparition, *esp fig* specter, *Br* spectre
**ge'spenstisch** *adj* ghostly, F spooky
**gespie(e)n** [gə'ʃpi:(ə)n] *pp of* ***speien***
**Gespinst** [gə'ʃpɪnst] *n* (*-[e]s*; *-e*) web, tissue (*both a. fig*)
**gesponnen** [gə'ʃpɔnən] *pp of* ***spinnen***
**Gespött** [gə'ʃpœt] *n* (*-[e]s*; *no pl*) mockery, ridicule; ***j-n zum ~ machen*** make a laughingstock of s.o.
**Gespräch** [gə'ʃprɛ:ç] *n* (*-[e]s*; *-e*) talk (*a.* POL), conversation; TEL call
**ge'sprächig** *adj* talkative
**gesprochen** [gə'ʃprɔxən] *pp of* ***sprechen***
**gesprossen** [gə'ʃprɔsən] *pp of* ***sprießen***
**gesprungen** [gə'ʃprʊŋən] *pp of* ***springen***
**Gespür** [gə'ʃpy:ɐ] *n* (*-s*; *no pl*) flair, nose
**Gestalt** [gə'ʃtalt] *f* (-; *-en*) shape, form; figure; **ge'stalten** *v/t* (*no -ge-*, *h*) arrange; design; **Ge'staltung** *f* (-; *-en*) arrangement; design; decoration
**gestanden** [gə'ʃtandən] *pp of* ***stehen***
**ge'ständig** *adj*: ***~ sein*** confess; have confessed
**Geständnis** [gə'ʃtɛntnɪs] *n* (*-ses*; *-se*) confession (*a. fig*)
**Gestank** [gə'ʃtaŋk] *m* (*-[e]s*; *no pl*) stench, stink
**gestatten** [gə'ʃtatən] *v/t* (*no -ge-*, *h*) allow, permit
**Geste** ['gɛstə] *f* (-; *-n*) gesture (*a. fig*)
**ge'stehen** *v/t and v/i* (*irr*, ***stehen***, *no -ge-*, *h*) confess
**Ge'stein** *n* (*-[e]s*; *-e*) rock, stone
**Gestell** [gə'ʃtɛl] *n* (*-[e]s*; *-e*) stand, base, pedestal; shelves; frame
**gestern** ['gɛstɐn] *adv* yesterday; ***~ Abend*** last night
**gestiegen** [gə'ʃti:gən] *pp of* ***steigen***
**gestochen** [gə'ʃtɔxən] *pp of* ***stechen***
**gestohlen** [gə'ʃto:lən] *pp of* ***stehlen***
**gestorben** [gə'ʃtɔrbən] *pp of* ***sterben***
**ge'stoßen** *pp of* ***stoßen***
**gestreift** [gə'ʃtraift] *adj* striped
**gestrichen** [gə'ʃtrɪçən] *pp of* ***streichen***
**gestrig** ['gɛstrɪç] *adj* yesterday's, of yesterday
**gestritten** [gə'ʃtrɪtən] *pp of* ***streiten***
**Gestrüpp** [gə'ʃtrʏp] *n* (*-[e]s*; *-e*) brushwood, undergrowth; *fig* jungle, maze
**gestunken** [gə'ʃtʊŋkən] *pp of* ***stinken***
**Gestüt** [gə'ʃty:t] *n* (*-[e]s*; *-e*) stud
**Gesuch** [gə'zu:x] *n* (*-[e]s*; *-e*) application, request
**gesund** [gə'zʊnt] *adj* healthy; healthful, *fig a.* sound; ***~er Menschenverstand*** common sense; (***wieder***) ***~ werden*** get well (again), recover; **Ge'sundheit** *f* (-; *no pl*) health; ***auf j-s ~ trinken*** drink to s.o.'s health; ***~!*** bless you!; **ge'sundheitlich 1.** *adj*: ***~er Zustand*** state of health; ***aus ~en Grün-***

***den*** for health reasons **2.** *adv*: ***~ geht es ihm gut*** he is in good health
**Ge'sundheitsamt** *n* Public Health Department (*Br* Office)
**ge'sundheitsschädlich** *adj* bad for one's health
**Ge'sundheits|zeugnis** *n* health certificate; **~zustand** *m* state of health
**gesungen** [gə'zʊŋən] *pp of* ***singen***
**gesunken** [gə'zʊŋkən] *pp of* ***sinken***
**getan** [gə'taːn] *pp of* ***tun***
**Getöse** [gə'tøːzə] *n* (*-s*; *no pl*) din, (deafening) noise
**ge'tragen** *pp of* ***tragen***
**Getränk** [gə'trɛŋk] *n* (*-[e]s*; *-e*) drink, beverage; **Ge'tränkeauto,mat** *m* drinks machine
**Getreide** [gə'traidə] *n* (*-s*; *-*) cereals, grain, *Br a.* corn; **~ernte** *f* grain harvest (*or* crop)
**ge'treten** *pp of* ***treten***
**Getriebe** [gə'triːbə] *n* (*-s*; *-*) MOT transmission
**ge'trieben** [gə'triːbən] *pp of* ***treiben***
**getroffen** [gə'trɔfən] *pp of* ***treffen***
**getrogen** [gə'troːgən] *pp of* ***trügen***
**getrost** [gə'troːst] *adv* safely
**getrunken** [gə'trʊŋkən] *pp of* ***trinken***
**Getue** [gə'tuːə] F *n* (*-s*; *no pl*) fuss
**Getümmel** [gə'tʏməl] *n* (*-s*; *-*) turmoil
**Gewächs** [gə'vɛks] *n* (*-es*; *-e*) plant; MED growth
**ge'wachsen** **1.** *pp of* ***wachsen***[1] **2.** *fig adj*: ***j-m ~ sein*** be a match for s.o.; ***e-r Sache ~ sein*** be equal to s.th., be able to cope with s.th.
**Ge'wächshaus** *n* greenhouse, hothouse
**gewagt** [gə'vaːkt] *adj* daring; *fig* risqué
**gewählt** [gə'vɛːlt] *adj* refined
**Gewähr** [gə'vɛːɐ] *f*: ***~ übernehmen*** (***für***) guarantee; **ge'währen** *v/t* (*no -ge-*, *h*) grant, allow; **ge'währleisten** *v/t* (*no -ge-*, *h*) guarantee
**Gewahrsam** [gə'vaːɐzaːm] *m*: ***et.*** (***j-n***) ***in ~ nehmen*** take s.th. in safekeeping (s.o. into custody)
**Gewalt** [gə'valt] *f* (*-*; *-en*) (*no pl*) force, violence; power; ***mit ~*** by force; ***höhere ~*** act of God; ***häusliche ~*** domestic violence; ***in s-e ~ bringen*** seize by force; ***die ~ verlieren über*** (*acc*) lose control over; **~herrschaft** *f* tyranny
**ge'waltig** *adj* powerful, mighty; enormous
**ge'waltlos** *adj* nonviolent; **Ge'waltlosigkeit** *f* (*-*; *no pl*) nonviolence
**ge'waltsam** **1.** *adj* violent **2.** *adv* by force; ***~ öffnen*** force open
**ge'walttätig** *adj* violent
**Ge'walttätigkeit** *f* (*-*; *-en*) (*no pl*) violence; act of violence
**Ge'waltverbrechen** *n* crime of violence
**Gewand** [gə'vant] *n* (*-[e]s*; *Gewänder* [gə'vɛndɐ]) robe, gown; REL vestment
**gewandt** [gə'vant] **1.** *pp of* ***wenden*** (*v/refl*) **2.** *adj* nimble; skil(l)ful; clever
**Ge'wandtheit** *f* (*-*; *no pl*) nimbleness; skill; ease
**gewann** [gə'van] *pret of* ***gewinnen***
**ge'waschen** *pp of* ***waschen***
**Gewässer** [gə'vɛsɐ] *n* (*-s*; *-*) body of water; *pl* waters
**Gewebe** [gə'veːbə] *n* (*-s*; *-*) fabric; BIOL tissue
**Gewehr** [gə'veːɐ] *n* (*-[e]s*; *-e*) gun; rifle; shotgun; **~kolben** *m* (rifle) butt; **~lauf** *m* (rifle *or* gun) barrel
**Geweih** [gə'vai] *n* (*-[e]s*; *-e*) ZO antlers, horns
**Gewerbe** [gə'vɛrbə] *n* (*-s*; *-*) trade, business; **~schein** *m* trade licen|se, *Br* -ce
**gewerblich** [gə'vɛrplɪç] *adj* commercial, industrial; **gewerbsmäßig** [gə'vɛrpsmɛːsɪç] *adj* professional
**Gewerkschaft** [gə'vɛrkʃaft] *f* (*-*; *-en*) labor union, *Br* (trade) union
**Ge'werkschaft(l)er** *m* (*-s*; *-*), **Ge'werkschaft(l)erin** *f* (*-*; *-nen*) labor (*Br* trade) unionist; **ge'werkschaftlich** *adj*, **Ge'werkschafts...** *in cpds* labor (*Br* trade) union ...
**ge'wesen** *pp of* ***sein***[1]
**gewichen** [gə'vɪçən] *pp of* ***weichen***
**Gewicht** [gə'vɪçt] *n* (*-[e]s*; *-e*) weight; importance; ***~ legen auf*** (*acc*) stress
**gewiesen** [gə'viːzən] *pp of* ***weisen***
**gewillt** [gə'vɪlt] *adj* willing, ready
**Gewimmel** [gə'vɪməl] *n* (*-s*; *no pl*) throng
**Gewinde** [gə'vɪndə] *n* (*-s*; *-*) TECH thread; ***ein ~ bohren in*** (*acc*) tap
**Gewinn** [gə'vɪn] *m* (*-[e]s*; *-e*) ECON profit (*a. fig*); gain(s); prize; winnings; ***~ bringend*** → ***gewinnbringend***
**ge'winnbringend** *adj* profitable
**ge'winnen** *v/t and v/i* (*irr*, *no -ge-*, *h*)

win; gain; **~d** *fig adj* winning, engaging
**Gewinner** [gə'vɪnɐ] *m* (*-s*; -), **Ge'winnerin** *f* (-; *-nen*) winner
**Ge'winnzahl** *f* winning number
**Gewirr** [gə'vɪr] *n* (*-[e]s*; *no pl*) tangle; maze
**gewiss** [gə'vɪs] **1.** *adj* certain **2.** *adv* certainly
**Ge'wissen** *n* (*-s*; -) conscience
**ge'wissenhaft** *adj* conscientious
**ge'wissenlos** *adj* unscrupulous
**Ge'wissens|bisse** *pl* pricks *or* pangs of conscience; **~frage** *f* question of conscience; **~gründe** *pl*: ***aus ~n*** for reasons of conscience
**Ge'wissheit** *f* (-; *no pl*) certainty; ***mit ~*** *know etc* for certain *or* sure
**Gewitter** [gə'vɪtɐ] *n* (*-s*; -) thunderstorm; **~regen** *m* thundershower; **~wolke** *f* thundercloud
**gewoben** [gə'vo:bən] *pp of* ***weben***
**gewogen** [gə'vo:gən] *pp of* ***wiegen***[1] *and* ***wägen***
**gewöhnen** [gə'vø:nən] *v/t and v/refl* (*no -ge-*, *h*) ***sich (j-n) ~ an*** (*acc*) get (s.o.) used to; **Gewohnheit** [gə'vo:nhait] *f* (-; *-en*) habit (***et. zu tun*** of doing s.th.); **ge'wohnheitsmäßig** *adj* habitual
**gewöhnlich** [gə'vø:nlɪç] *adj* common, ordinary, usual; vulgar, F common
**gewohnt** [gə'vo:nt] *adj* usual; ***et.*** (***zu tun***) ***~ sein*** be used *or* accustomed to (doing) s.th.
**Gewölbe** [gə'vœlbə] *n* (*-s*; -) vault
**gewölbt** [gə'vœlpt] *adj* arched
**gewonnen** [gə'vɔnən] *pp of* ***gewinnen***
**geworben** [gə'vɔrbən] *pp of* ***werben***
**geworden** [gə'vɔrdən] *pp of* ***werden***
**geworfen** [gə'vɔrfən] *pp of* ***werfen***
**gewrungen** [gə'vrʊŋən] *pp of* ***wringen***
**Gewühl** [gə'vy:l] *n* (*-[e]s*; *no pl*) crowd, crush
**gewunden** [gə'vʊndən] **1.** *pp of* ***winden*** **2.** *adj* winding
**Gewürz** [gə'vʏrts] *n* (*-es*; *-e*) spice; **~gurke** *f* pickle(d gherkin)
**gewusst** [gə'vʊst] *pp of* ***wissen***
**gezackt** [gə'tsakt] *adj* jagged, serrated
**Ge'zeiten** *pl* tide(s)
**Gezeter** [gə'tse:tɐ] *contp n* (*-s*; *no pl*) (shrill) clamo(u)r; nagging
**geziert** [gə'tsi:ɐt] *adj* affected
**gezogen** [gə'tso:gən] *pp of* ***ziehen***
**Gezwitscher** [gə'tsvɪtʃɐ] *n* (*-s*; *no pl*) chirp(ing), twitter(ing)
**gezwungen** [gə'tsvʊŋən] **1.** *pp of* ***zwingen*** **2.** *adj* forced, unnatural
**Gicht** [gɪçt] *f* (-; *no pl*) MED gout
**Giebel** ['gi:bəl] *m* (*-s*; -) gable
**Gier** [gi:ɐ] *f* (-; *no pl*) greed(iness) (***nach*** for); **gierig** ['gi:rɪç] *adj* greedy (***nach, auf*** *acc* for, after)
**gießen** ['gi:sən] *v/t and v/i* (*irr, ge-, h*) pour; TECH cast; water
**Gieße'rei** *f* (-; *-en*) TECH foundry
**'Gießkanne** *f* watering pot (*Br* can)
**Gift** [gɪft] *n* (*-[e]s*; *-e*) poison, ZO *a.* venom (*a. fig*); **'giftig** *adj* poisonous; venomous (*a. fig*); poisoned; MED toxic
**'Gift|müll** *m* toxic waste; **~mülldepo,nie** *f* toxic waste dump; **~schlange** *f* ZO poisonous *or* venomous snake; **~stoff** *m* poisonous *or* toxic substance; pollutant; **~zahn** *m* ZO poison fang
**Gigant** [gi'gant] *m* (*-en*; *-en*) giant
**gi'gantisch** *adj* gigantic
**ging** [gɪŋ] *pret of* ***gehen***
**Gipfel** ['gɪpfəl] *m* (*-s*; -) top, peak, summit, *fig a.* height; **~konfe,renz** *f* POL summit (meeting *or* conference)
**'gipfeln** *v/i* (*ge-, h*) culminate (***in*** *dat* in)
**Gips** [gɪps] *m* (*-es*; *-e*) plaster (of Paris); ***in ~*** MED in (a) plaster (cast); **~abdruck** *m*, **~abguss** *m* plaster cast
**'gipsen** *v/t* (*ge-, h*) plaster (*a.* F MED)
**'Gipsverband** *m* MED plaster cast
**Giraffe** [gi'rafə] *f* (-; *-n*) ZO giraffe
**Girlande** [gɪr'landə] *f* (-; *-n*) garland, festoon
**Girokonto** ['ʒi:rokɔnto] *n* checking (*or* current) account; postal check (*Br* giro) account
**Gischt** [gɪʃt] *m* (*-[e]s*; *-e*), *f* (-; *-en*) (sea) spray, spindrift
**Gitarre** [gi'tarə] *f* (-; *-n*) MUS guitar
**Gitarrist** [gita'rɪst] *m* (*-en*; *-en*) guitarist
**Gitter** ['gɪtɐ] *n* (*-s*; -) lattice; grating; F ***hinter ~n*** (***sitzen***) (be) behind bars
**'Gitterbett** *n* crib, *Br* cot
**'Gitterfenster** *n* lattice (window)
**Glanz** [glants] *m* (*-es*; *no pl*) shine, gloss (*a.* TECH), luster, *Br* lustre, brilliance (*a. fig*); *fig* splendo(u)r, glamo(u)r
**glänzen** ['glɛntsən] *v/i* (*ge-, h*) shine, gleam; glitter, glisten; **~d** *adj* shining, shiny, bright; PHOT glossy; *fig* brilliant, excellent

'**Glanz|leistung** *f* brilliant achievement; **~zeit** *f* heyday
**Glas** [glaːs] *n* (*-es*; *Gläser* ['glɛːzɐ]) glass
**Glaser** ['glaːzɐ] *m* (*-s*; -) glazier
**gläsern** ['glɛːzɐn] *adj* (of) glass
'**Glas|faser** *f*, **~fiber** *f* glass fiber (*Br* fibre); **~hütte** *f* TECH glassworks
**glasieren** [gla'ziːrən] *v/t* (*no -ge-*, *h*) glaze; GASTR ice, frost
**glasig** ['glaːzɪç] *adj* glassy
'**glasklar** *adj* crystal-clear (*a. fig*)
'**Glasscheibe** *f* (glass) pane
**Glasur** [gla'zuːɐ] *f* (-; *-en*) glaze; GASTR icing
**glatt** [glat] *adj* smooth (*a. fig*); slippery; *fig* clear; **Glätte** ['glɛtə] *f* (-; *no pl*) smoothness (*a. fig*); slipperiness
'**Glatteis** *n* (glare, *Br* black) ice; ***es herrscht*** **~** the roads are icy; F ***j-n aufs*** **~** ***führen*** mislead s.o.
**glätten** ['glɛtən] *v/t* (*ge-*, *h*) smooth; *Swiss*: → ***bügeln***
'**glattgehen** *v/i* (*irr*, *sep*, *-ge-*, *sein*) F work (out well), go (off) well
**Glatze** ['glatsə] *f* (-; *-n*) bald head; ***e-e*** **~** ***haben*** be bald
**Glaube** ['glaubə] *m* (*-ns*; *no pl*) belief, *esp* REL faith (*both*: ***an*** *acc* in)
'**glauben** *v/t and v/i* (*ge-*, *h*) believe; think, guess; **~** ***an*** (*acc*) believe in (*a.* REL)
'**Glaubens|bekenntnis** *n* REL creed, profession *or* confession of faith; **~lehre** *f*, **~satz** *m* dogma, doctrine
**glaubhaft** ['glauphaft] *adj* credible, plausible
**gläubig** ['glɔʏbɪç] *adj* religious; devout; ***die Gläubigen*** the faithful
**Gläubiger** ['glɔʏbɪgɐ] *m* (*-s*; -), '**Gläubigerin** *f* (-; *-nen*) ECON creditor
'**glaubwürdig** *adj* credible; reliable
**gleich** [glaiç] **1.** *adj* same; equal (*right etc*); ***auf die ~e Art*** (in) the same way; ***zur ~en Zeit*** at the same time; ***das ist mir*** **~** it's all the same to me; ***ganz ~, wann*** *etc* no matter when *etc*; ***das Gleiche*** the same; (***ist***) **~ …** MATH equals …, is …; **~** ***bleibend*** → ***gleichbleibend***; **~** ***gesinnt*** like-minded; **~** ***lautend*** → ***gleichlautend*** **2.** *adv* equally, alike; at once, right away; in a moment *or* minute; **~** ***groß*** (***alt***) of the same size (age); **~** ***nach*** (***neben***) right after (next to); **~** ***gegenüber*** just opposite *or* across the street; ***es ist ~ 5 Uhr*** it's almost 5 o'clock; **~** ***aussehen*** (***gekleidet sein***) look (be dressed) alike; ***bis ~!*** see you soon *or* later!; **gleichaltrig** ['glaiçˀaltrɪç] *adj* (of) the same age
'**gleichberechtigt** *adj* equal, having equal rights; '**Gleichberechtigung** *f* (-; *no pl*) equal rights
'**gleichbleibend** *adj* constant, steady
'**gleichen** *v/i* (*irr*, *ge-*, *h*) (*dat*) be *or* look like
'**gleichfalls** *adv* also, likewise; ***danke, ~!*** (thanks,) the same to you
**gleichförmig** ['glaiçfœrmɪç] *adj* uniform
'**Gleichgewicht** *n* (*-[e]s*; *no pl*) balance (*a. fig*)
'**gleichgültig** *adj* indifferent (***gegen*** to); careless; ***das*** (***er***) ***ist mir*** **~** I don't care (for him); '**Gleichgültigkeit** *f* (-; *no pl*) indifference
'**Gleichheit** *f* (-; *no pl*) equality
'**gleichkommen** *v/i* (*irr*, ***kommen***, *sep*, *-ge-*, *sein*) ***e-r Sache*** **~** amount to s.th.; ***j-m*** **~** equal s.o. (***an*** *dat* in)
'**gleichlautend** *adj* identical
'**gleichmäßig** *adj* regular; constant; even
**gleichnamig** ['glaiçnaːmɪç] *adj* of the same name
'**Gleichnis** *n* (*-ses*; *-se*) parable
'**gleichsam** *adv* as it were, so to speak
**gleichseitig** ['glaiçzaitɪç] *adj* MATH equilateral
'**gleich|setzen**, **~stellen** *v/t* (*sep*, *-ge-*, *h*) equate (*dat* to, with); put *s.o.* on an equal footing (with)
'**Gleichstrom** *m* ELECTR direct current
'**Gleichung** *f* (-; *-en*) MATH equation
'**gleichwertig** *adj* equally good; ***j-m*** **~** ***sein*** be a match for s.o. (*a.* SPORT)
'**gleichzeitig** *adj* simultaneous; ***beide*** **~** both at the same time
**Gleis** [glais] *n* (*-es*; *-e*) RAIL rail(s), track(s), line; platform, gate
**gleiten** ['glaitən] *v/i* (*irr*, *ge-*, *sein*) glide, slide; **~d** *adj*: ***~e Arbeitszeit*** flexible working hours, flextime, *Br a.* flexitime
'**Gleitflug** *m* glide
'**Gleitschirm|fliegen** *n* paragliding; **~flieger** *m* paraglider
**Gletscher** ['glɛtʃɐ] *m* (*-s*; -) glacier; **~spalte** *f* crevasse

**glich** [glıç] *pret of* ***gleichen***
**Glied** [gliːt] *n* (*-es*; *Glieder* [ˈgliːdɐ]) ANAT limb; penis; TECH link
**gliedern** [ˈgliːdɐn] *v/t* (*ge-*, *h*) structure; divide (***in*** *acc* into)
**Gliederung** [ˈgliːdərʊŋ] *f* (-; *-en*) structure, arrangement; outline
ˈ**Gliedmaßen** *pl* ANAT limbs, extremities
**glimmen** [ˈglımən] *v/i* ([*irr*,] *ge-*, *h*) glow; smo(u)lder
ˈ**Glimmstängel** F *m* (*-s*; -) cigarette, *Br sl* fag
**glimpflich** [ˈglımpflıç] **1.** *adj* lenient, mild **2.** *adv*: ~ ***davonkommen*** get off lightly
**glitschig** [ˈglıtʃıç] *adj* slippery
**glitt** [glıt] *pret of* ***gleiten***
**glitzern** [ˈglıtsɐn] *v/i* (*ge-*, *h*) glitter, sparkle, glint
**global** [gloˈbaːl] *adj* global
**Globus** [ˈgloːbʊs] *m* (-[*ses*]; *-se*) globe
**Glocke** [ˈglɔkə] *f* (-; *-n*) bell
ˈ**Glocken|blume** *f* bluebell; **~spiel** *n* chimes; **~turm** *m* bell tower, belfry
**glomm** [glɔm] *pret of* ***glimmen***
**glorreich** [ˈgloːɐraiç] *adj* glorious
**Glotze** [ˈglɔtsə] F *f* (-; *-n*) TV *the* tube, *Br* goggle box; ˈ**glotzen** F *v/i* (*ge-*, *h*) goggle, gape, stare
**Glück** [glʏk] *n* (-[*e*]*s*; *no pl*) (good) luck, fortune; happiness; ~ ***haben*** be lucky; ***zum*** ~ fortunately; ***viel*** ~***!*** good luck!
**Glucke** [ˈglʊkə] *f* (-; *-n*) ZO sitting hen; *fig* hen
**gluckern** [ˈglʊkɐn] *v/i* (*ge-*, *h*) gurgle
ˈ**glücklich** *adj* happy; ~***er Zufall*** lucky chance
ˈ**glücklicherˈweise** *adv* fortunately
ˈ**Glücks|bringer** *m* (*-s*; -) lucky charm; **~fall** *m* lucky chance; **~pfennig** *m* lucky penny; **~pilz** *m* lucky fellow; **~spiel** *n* game of chance; *coll* gambling; **~spieler** *m* gambler; **~tag** *m* lucky day
ˈ**glückstrahlend** *adj* radiant
ˈ**Glückwunsch** *m* congratulations; ***herzlichen*** ~***!*** congratulations!; happy birthday!
**Glühbirne** [ˈglyːbırnə] *f* ELECTR light bulb
**glühen** [ˈglyːən] *v/i* (*ge-*, *h*) glow (*a. fig*)
**glühend** [ˈglyːənt] *adj* glowing; red-hot (*iron*); *fig* burning; ~ ***heiß*** blazing hot
ˈ**Glühwein** *m* mulled wine
**Glut** [gluːt] *f* (-; *-en*) (glowing) fire; embers; live coals; *fig* ardo(u)r
ˈ**Gluthitze** *f* blazing heat
**GmbH** [geːˀɛmbeːˈhaː] *abbr of* ***Gesellschaft mit beschränkter Haftung*** private limited liability company
**Gnade** [ˈgnaːdə] *f* (-; *-n*) mercy, *esp* REL *a.* grace; favo(u)r
ˈ**Gnaden|frist** *f* reprieve; **~gesuch** *n* JUR petition for mercy
ˈ**gnadenlos** *adj* merciless
**gnädig** [ˈgnɛːdıç] *adj* gracious; *esp* REL merciful
**Gold** [gɔlt] *n* (-[*e*]*s*; *no pl*) gold; **~barren** *m* gold bar *or* ingot; *coll* bullion
**golden** [ˈgɔldən] *adj* gold; *fig* golden
ˈ**Goldfisch** *m* ZO goldfish
ˈ**goldgelb** *adj* golden (yellow)
ˈ**Gold|gräber** [ˈgɔltgrɛːbɐ] *m* (*-s*; -) gold digger; **~grube** *fig f* goldmine, bonanza
**goldig** [ˈgɔldıç] F *adj* sweet, lovely, cute
ˈ**Gold|mine** *f* goldmine; **~münze** *f* gold coin; **~schmied** *m* goldsmith; **~stück** *n* gold coin
**Golf**[1] [gɔlf] *m* (-[*e*]*s*; *-e*) GEOGR gulf
**Golf**[2] *n* (*-s*; *no pl*) SPORT golf; **~platz** *m* golf course; **~schläger** *m* golf club; **~spieler** *m* golfer
**Gondel** [ˈgɔndəl] *f* (-; *-n*) gondola; cabin
**Gong** [gɔŋ] *m* (*-s*; *-s*) gong
**gönnen** [ˈgœnən] *v/t* (*ge-*, *h*) ***j-m et.*** ~ not (be)grudge s.o. s.th.; ***j-m et. nicht*** ~ (be)grudge s.o. s.th.; ***sich et.*** ~ allow o.s. s.th., treat o.s. to s.th.
**gönnerhaft** [ˈgœnɐhaft] *adj* patronizing
**gor** [goːɐ] *pret of* ***gären***
**Gorilla** [goˈrıla] *m* (*-s*; *-s*) ZO gorilla
**goss** [gɔs] *pret of* ***gießen***
**Gosse** [ˈgɔsə] *f* (-; *-n*) gutter (*a. fig*)
**Gotik** [ˈgoːtık] *f* (-; *no pl*) ARCH Gothic style *or* period; ˈ**gotisch** *adj* Gothic
**Gott** [gɔt] *m* (-[*e*]*s*; *Götter* [ˈgœtɐ]) REL God, Lord; MYTH god; ~ ***sei Dank***(!) thank God(!); ***um*** ~***es Willen!*** for heaven's sake!; ˈ**gottergeben** *adj* resigned (to the will of God)
ˈ**Gottesdienst** *m* REL (divine) service
**gottesfürchtig** [ˈgɔtəsfʏrçtıç] *adj* god-fearing
**Gotteslästerer** [ˈgɔtəslɛstərɐ] *m* (*-s*; -) blasphemer; ˈ**Gotteslästerung** *f* (-; *-en*) blasphemy
ˈ**Gottheit** *f* (-; *-en*) deity, divinity
**Göttin** [ˈgœtın] *f* (-; *-nen*) goddess

**'göttlich** ['gœtlɪç] *adj* divine
**gott'lob** *int* thank God *or* goodness!
**'gottlos** *adj* godless, wicked
**'gottverlassen** F *adj* godforsaken
**'Gottvertrauen** *n* trust in God
**Götze** ['gœtsə] *m* (*-n*; *-n*), **'Götzenbild** *n* idol
**Gouverneur** [guvɛr'nøːɐ] *m* (*-s*; *-e*) governor
**Grab** [graːp] *n* (*-[e]s*; *Gräber* ['grɛːbɐ]) grave; tomb
**graben** ['graːbən] *v/t and v/i* (*irr*, *ge-*, *h*) dig, zo *a.* burrow; **'Graben** *m* (*-s*; *Gräben* ['grɛːbən]) ditch; MIL trench
**'Grab|mal** *n* monument; tomb; **~rede** *f* funeral address; **~schrift** *f* epitaph; **~stätte** *f* burial place; grave, tomb; **~stein** *m* tombstone, gravestone
**Grad** [graːt] *m* (*-[e]s*; *-e*) degree; MIL *etc* rank, grade; ***15 ~ Kälte*** 15 degrees below zero; **~einteilung** *f* graduation
**graduell** [gra'duɛl] *adj* in degree
**Graf** [graːf] *m* (*-en*; *-en*) count, *Br* earl
**Graffiti** [gra'fiːti] *pl* graffiti
**Grafik** ['graːfɪk] *f* (*-*; *-en*) (*no pl*) graphic arts; print; MATH, TECH graph, diagram; (*no pl*) art(work), illustrations; (*no pl*) IT graphics
**'Grafiker** *m* (*-s*; *-*), **'Grafikerin** *f* (*-*; *-nen*) graphic artist
**Gräfin** ['grɛːfɪn] *f* (*-*; *-nen*) countess
**grafisch** ['graːfɪʃ] *adj* graphic
**Grafologie** *f* → ***Graphologie***
**'Grafschaft** *f* (*-*; *-en*) county
**Gramm** [gram] *n* (*-s*; *-e*) gram
**Grammatik** [gra'matɪk] *f* (*-*; *-en*) grammar; **gram'matisch** *adj* grammatical
**Granat** [gra'naːt] *m* (*-[e]s*; *-e*) MIN garnet
**Gra'nate** *f* (*-*; *-n*) MIL shell
**Gra'nat|splitter** *m* MIL shell splinter; **~werfer** *m* MIL mortar
**grandios** [gran'djoːs] *adj* magnificent, grand
**Granit** [gra'niːt] *m* (*-s*; *-e*) granite
**Graphik** *f etc* → ***Grafik*** *etc*
**Graphologie** [grafolo'giː] *f* (*-*; *no pl*) graphology
**Gras** [graːs] *n* (*-es*; *Gräser* ['grɛːzɐ]) grass; **grasen** ['graːzən] *v/i* (*ge-*, *h*) graze; **'Grashalm** *m* blade of grass
**grassieren** [gra'siːrən] *v/i* (*no -ge-*, *h*) rage, be rife
**grässlich** ['grɛslɪç] *adj* hideous, atrocious
**Gräte** ['grɛːtə] *f* (*-*; *-n*) (fish)bone
**Gratifikation** [gratifika'tsjoːn] *f* (*-*; *-en*) gratuity, bonus
**gratis** ['graːtɪs] *adv* free (of charge)
**Grätsche** ['grɛːtʃə] *f* (*-*; *-n*), **'grätschen** *v/i* (*ge-*, *h*) straddle; *soccer*: stride tackle
**Gratulant** [gratu'lant] *m* (*-en*; *-en*), **Gratu'lantin** *f* (*-*; *-nen*) congratulator; **Gratulation** [gratula'tsjoːn] *f* (*-*; *-en*) congratulation; **gratulieren** [gratu'liːrən] *v/i* (*no -ge-*, *h*) congratulate (***j-m zu et.*** s.o. on s.th.); ***j-m zum Geburtstag ~*** wish s.o. many happy returns (of the day)
**grau** [grau] *adj* gray, *Br* grey
**'Graubrot** *n* rye bread
**Gräuel** ['grɔʏəl] *m* (*-s*; *-*) horror
**'Gräueltat** *f* atrocity
**'grauen** *v/i* (*ge-*, *h*) ***mir graut es vor*** (*dat*) I dread (the thought of)
**'Grauen** *n* (*-s*; *-*) horror
**'grauenhaft**, **'grauenvoll** *adj* horrible, horrifying
**Graupel** ['graupəl] *f* (*-*; *-n*) sleet, soft hail
**grausam** ['grauzaːm] *adj* cruel
**'Grausamkeit** *f* (*-*; *-en*) cruelty
**grausig** ['grauzɪç] *adj* → ***grauenhaft***
**'Grauzone** *f fig* gray (*Br* grey) area
**gravieren** [gra'viːrən] *v/t* (*no -ge-*, *h*) engrave; **~d** *adj* serious
**Gravur** [gra'vuːɐ] *f* (*-*; *-en*) engraving
**Grazie** ['graːtsjə] *f* (*-*; *no pl*) grace
**graziös** [gra'tsjøːs] *adj* graceful
**greifen** ['graifən] (*irr*, *ge-*, *h*) **1.** *v/t* seize, grasp, grab, take *or* catch hold of **2.** *v/i fig* take effect; ***~ nach*** reach for; grasp at
**Greis** [grais] *m* (*-es*; *-e*) (very) old man; **greisenhaft** ['graizənhaft] *adj* senile (*a.* MED); **Greisin** ['graizɪn] *f* (*-*; *-nen*) (very) old woman
**grell** [grɛl] *adj* glaring; shrill
**Grenze** ['grɛntsə] *f* (*-*; *-n*) border; boundary; *fig* limit; **'grenzen** *v/i* (*ge-*, *h*) ***~ an*** (*acc*) border on
**'grenzenlos** *adj* boundless
**'Grenz|fall** *m* borderline case; **~land** *n* borderland, frontier; **~linie** *f* borderline, POL demarcation line; **~stein** *m* boundary stone; **~übergang** *m* frontier crossing (point), checkpoint
**Greuel** *m* → ***Gräuel***
**Grieche** ['griːçə] *m* (*-n*; *-n*) Greek;

G

**'Griechenland** Greece; **'Griechin** *f* (-; *-nen*), **'griechisch** *adj* Greek

**Grieß** [gri:s] *m* (*-es*; *-e*) semolina

**griff** [grɪf] *pret of* ***greifen***

**Griff** *m* (-[*e*]*s*; *-e*) grip, grasp; handle

**'griffbereit** *adj* at hand, handy

**Grill** [grɪl] *m* (*-s*; *-s*) grill

**Grille** ['grɪlə] *f* (-; *-n*) zo cricket

**'grillen** *v/t* (*ge-*, *h*) grill, barbecue

**Grimasse** [gri'masə] *f* (-; *-n*) grimace; ***~n schneiden*** pull faces

**grimmig** ['grɪmɪç] *adj* grim

**grinsen** ['grɪnzən] *v/i* (*ge-*, *h*) grin (***über*** *acc* at); ***höhnisch*** *or* ***spöttisch ~*** (***über*** *acc*) sneer (at); **'Grinsen** *n* (*-s*; *no pl*) grin; ***höhnisches*** *or* ***spöttisches ~*** sneer

**Grippe** ['grɪpə] *f* (-; *-n*) MED influenza, F flu

**Grips** [grɪps] F *m* (*-es*; *no pl*) brains

**grob** [gro:p] **1.** *adj* coarse (*a. fig*); *fig* gross; crude; rude; rough **2.** *adv*: ***~ geschätzt*** at a rough estimate

**'Grobheit** *f* (-; *no pl*) coarseness; roughness; rudeness

**grölen** ['grø:lən] F *v/t and v/i* (*ge-*, *h*) bawl

**Groll** [grɔl] *m* (-[*e*]*s*; *no pl*) grudge, ill will; **'grollen** *v/i* (*ge-*, *h*) ***j-m ~*** bear s.o. a grudge

**Groschen** ['grɔʃən] *m* (*-s*; -) *hist* (*former monetary unit of Austria*) groschen; F ten-pfennig piece, ten pfennigs

**groß** [gro:s] *adj* big; large (*a. family*); tall; grown-up; F big (*brother etc*); *fig* great (*a. fun*, *trouble*, *pain etc*); capital (*letter*); ***~es Geld*** bills, *Br* notes; ***~e Ferien*** summer vacation, *Br* summer holiday(s); ***Groß und Klein*** young and old; ***im Großen und Ganzen*** on the whole; F ***~ in et. sein*** be great at (doing) s.th.; ***wie ~ ist es?*** what size is it?; ***wie ~ bist du?*** how tall are you?

**'großartig** *adj* great, F *a.* terrific

**'Großaufnahme** *f film*: close-up

**Größe** ['grø:sə] *f* (-; *-n*) size; height; *esp* MATH quantity; *fig* greatness; celebrity

**'Großeltern** *pl* grandparents

**'großen'teils** *adv* to a large *or* great extent, largely

**'Größenwahn** *m* megalomania (*a. fig*)

**'Groß|fa,milie** *f* extended family; **~handel** *m* ECON wholesale (trade); **~händler** *m* ECON wholesale dealer, wholesaler; **~handlung** *f* ECON wholesale business; **~indus,trie** *f* big industry; big business; **~industri,elle** *m* big industrialist, F tycoon; **~macht** *f* POL great power; **~markt** *m* ECON hypermarket; wholesale market; **~maul** F *n* braggart; **~mutter** *f* grandmother; **~raum** *m* conurbation, metropolitan area; ***der ~ München*** Greater Munich, the Greater Munich area; **~raumflugzeug** *n* wide-bodied jet

**'großschreiben** *v/t* (*irr*, ***schreiben***, *sep*, *-ge-*, *h*) capitalize; **'Großschreibung** *f* (use of) capitalization

**großsprecherisch** ['gro:sʃprɛçərɪʃ] *adj* boastful

**großspurig** ['gro:sʃpu:rɪç] *adj* arrogant

**'Großstadt** *f* big city; **'großstädtisch** *adj* of *or* in a big city, urban

**'größten'teils** *adv* mostly, mainly

**'großtun** *v/i* (*irr*, ***tun***, *sep*, *-ge-*, *h*) show off; ***sich mit et. ~*** brag about s.th.

**'Großvater** *m* grandfather

**'Großverdiener** *m* (*-s*; -) big earner

**'Großwild** *n* big game

**'großziehen** *v/t* (*irr*, ***ziehen***, *sep*, *-ge-*, *h*) raise, rear; bring up

**'großzügig** *adj* generous, liberal; … on a large scale; spacious

**'Großzügigkeit** *f* (-; *no pl*) generosity, liberality; spaciousness

**grotesk** [gro'tɛsk] *adj* grotesque

**Grotte** ['grɔtə] *f* (-; *-n*) grotto

**grub** [gru:p] *pret of* ***graben***

**Grübchen** ['gry:pçən] *n* (*-s*; -) dimple

**Grube** ['gru:bə] *f* (-; *-n*) pit; mine

**Grübelei** [gry:bə'lai] *f* (-; *-en*) pondering, musing

**grübeln** ['gry:bəln] *v/i* (*ge-*, *h*) ponder, muse (***über*** *acc* on, over)

**Gruft** [grʊft] *f* (-; *Grüfte* ['grʏftə]) tomb, vault

**grün** [gry:n] *adj* green; **Grün** *n* (*-s*; -) green; ***im ~en*** in the country

**'Grünanlage** *f* park

**Grund** [grʊnt] *m* (-[*e*]*s*; *Gründe* ['grʏndə]) reason; cause; ground, AGR *a.* soil; bottom; ***~ und Boden*** property, land; ***aus diesem ~(e)*** for this reason; ***von ~ auf*** entirely; ***im ~e*** (***genommen***) actually, basically; → ***aufgrund***; → ***zugrunde***

**'Grund…** *in cpds …bedeutung*, *…be-*

*dingung, …regel, …prinzip, …wortschatz etc*: *mst* basic …; **~begriffe** *pl* basics, fundamentals; **~besitz** *m* property, land; **~besitzer** *m* landowner

**gründen** ['grʏndən] *v/t (ge-, h)* found (*a. family*), set up, establish; ***sich ~ auf*** (*dat*) be based *or* founded on

**Gründer** ['grʏndɐ] *m (-s; -)*, '**Gründerin** *f (-; -nen)* founder

'**grund'falsch** *adj* absolutely wrong

'**Grund|fläche** *f* MATH base; ARCH area; **~gedanke** *m* basic idea; **~geschwindigkeit** *f* AVIAT ground speed; **~gesetz** *n* POL Basic (Constitutional) Law (for the Federal Republic of Germany); **~lage** *f* foundation, *fig a.* basis; *pl* (basic) elements

'**grundlegend** *adj* fundamental, basic

**gründlich** ['grʏntlɪç] *adj* thorough

'**Grundlinie** *f tennis etc*: base line

'**grundlos** *adj* groundless, unfounded

'**Grundmauer** *f* foundation

**Grün'donnerstag** *m* REL Maundy *or* Holy Thursday

'**Grund|rechnungsart** *f* MATH basic arithmetical operation; **~riss** *m* ARCH ground plan; **~satz** *m* principle

**grundsätzlich** ['grʊntzɛtslɪç] **1.** *adj* fundamental **2.** *adv*: ***ich bin ~ dagegen*** I am against it on principle

'**Grund|schule** *f* elementary (*or* grade) school, *Br* primary (*or* junior) school; **~stein** *m* ARCH foundation stone; *fig* foundations; **~stück** *n* plot (of land), lot; (building) site; premises; **~stücksmakler** *m* realtor, *Br* real estate agent

'**Gründung** *f (-; -en)* foundation, establishment, setting up

'**grundver'schieden** *adj* totally different

'**Grund|wasser** *n* ground water; **~zahl** *f* cardinal number; **~zug** *m* main feature, characteristic

**Grüne** ['gry:nə] *m, f (-n; -n)* POL Green

'**Grünfläche** *f* green space

'**grünlich** *adj* greenish

'**Grünspan** *m (-[e]s; no pl)* verdigris

**grunzen** ['grʊntsən] *v/i and v/t (ge-, h)* grunt

**Gruppe** ['grʊpə] *f (-; -n)* group

'**Gruppenreise** *f* group tour

**gruppieren** [grʊ'pi:rən] *v/t (no -ge-, h)* group, arrange in groups; ***sich ~*** form groups

**Grusel…** ['gru:zəl-] *in cpds …film etc*: horror …; '**gruselig** *adj* eerie, creepy; spine-chilling; '**gruseln** *v/t and v/refl (ge-, h)* ***es gruselt mich*** F it gives me the creeps

**Gruß** [gru:s] *m (-es; Grüße* ['gry:sə]*)* greeting(s); MIL salute; ***viele Grüße an*** (*acc*) … give my regards (*or* love) to …; ***mit freundlichen Grüßen*** yours sincerely; ***herzliche Grüße*** best wishes; love

**grüßen** ['gry:sən] *v/t (ge-, h)* greet, F say hello to; MIL salute; ***~ Sie ihn von mir*** give my regards (*or* love) to him

**gucken** ['gʊkən] *v/i (ge-, h)* look

'**Guckloch** *n* peephole

**Güggeli** ['gʏgəli] *n (-s; -) Swiss* chicken

**gültig** ['gʏltɪç] *adj* valid; current

'**Gültigkeit** *f (-; no pl)* validity; ***s-e ~ verlieren*** expire

**Gummi** ['gʊmi] *m, n (-s; -[s])* rubber; **~band** *n (-[e]s; -bänder)* rubber (*esp Br a.* elastic) band; **~bärchen** *pl* gummy bears; **~baum** *m* BOT rubber tree; rubber plant

**gummieren** [gʊ'mi:rən] *v/t (no -ge-, h)* gum

'**Gummi|knüppel** *m* truncheon; **~stiefel** *m* rubber boot, *esp Br* wellington (boot); **~zug** *m* elastic

**Gunst** [gʊnst] *f (-; no pl)* favo(u)r, goodwill; → ***zugunsten***

**günstig** ['gʏnstɪç] *adj* favo(u)rable (***für*** to); convenient; ***im ~sten Fall*** at best; ***~e Gelegenheit*** chance

**Gurgel** ['gʊrgəl] *f (-; -n)* throat; ***j-m an die ~ springen*** fly at s.o.'s throat; '**gurgeln** *v/i (ge-, h)* MED gargle

**Gurke** ['gʊrkə] *f (-; -n)* BOT cucumber

**gurren** ['gʊrən] *v/i (ge-, h)* ZO coo

**Gurt** [gʊrt] *m (-[e]s; -e)* belt (*a.* MOT *and* AVIAT); strap

**Gürtel** ['gʏrtəl] *m (-s; -)* belt; **~reifen** *m* MOT radial (tire, *Br* tyre)

**GUS** [gʊs, ge:ʔu:'ʔɛs] *abbr of* ***Gemeinschaft Unabhängiger Staaten*** CIS, Commonwealth of Independent States

**Guss** [gʊs] *m (-es; Güsse* ['gʏsə]*)* downpour; TECH casting; GASTR icing; *fig* ***aus e-m ~*** of a piece; '**Gusseisen** *n* cast iron; '**gusseisern** *adj* cast-iron

**gut** [gu:t] **1.** *adj* good; fine; ***ganz ~*** not bad; ***also ~!*** all right (then)!; ***schon ~!*** never mind!; (***wieder***) ***~ werden***

G

come right (again), be all right; ***~e Reise!*** have a nice trip!; ***sei bitte so ~ und …*** would you be so good as to *or* good enough to …; ***in et. ~ sein*** be good at (doing) s.th. **2.** *adv* well; *look*, *taste etc* good; ***du hast es ~*** you are lucky; ***es ist ~ möglich*** it may well be; ***es gefällt mir ~*** I (do) like it; ***~ gebaut*** well-built; ***~ gelaunt*** in a good mood; ***~ gemacht!*** well done!; ***mach's ~!*** take care (of yourself)!; ***~ gehen*** go (off) well, work out well *or* all right; ***wenn alles ~ geht*** if nothing goes wrong; ***mir geht es ~*** I'm (doing) well; **Gut** *n* (-[*e*]*s*; *Güter* ['gyːtɐ]) estate; *pl* goods

'**Gutachten** *n* (-*s*; -) (expert) opinion; certificate; **Gutachter** ['guːtʔaxtɐ] *m* (-*s*; -) expert

'**gutartig** *adj* good-natured; MED benign

**Gutdünken** ['guːtdʏŋkən] *n*: ***nach ~*** at one's discretion

**Gute** ['guːtə] *n* (-*n*; *no pl*) good; ***~s tun*** do good; ***alles ~!*** all the best!, good luck!

**Güte** ['gyːtə] *f* (-; *no pl*) goodness, kindness; ECON quality; F ***meine ~!*** good gracious!

**Güter|bahnhof** ['gyːtɐbaːnhoːf] *m* freight depot, *Br* goods station; **~gemeinschaft** *f* JUR community of property; **~trennung** *f* JUR separation of property; **~verkehr** *m* freight (*Br* goods) traffic; **~wagen** *m* freight car, *Br* goods wag(g)on; **~zug** *m* freight (*Br* goods) train

'**gutgläubig** *adj* credulous

'**Guthaben** *n* (-*s*; -) ECON credit (balance)

'**gutheißen** *v/t* (*irr*, ***heißen***, *sep*, -*ge*-, *h*) approve (of)

'**gutherzig** *adj* kind(-hearted)

**gütig** ['gyːtɪç] *adj* good, kind(ly)

**gütlich** ['gyːtlɪç] *adv*: ***sich ~ einigen*** come to an amicable settlement

'**gutmachen** *v/t* (*sep*, -*ge*-, *h*) make up for, repay

**gutmütig** ['guːtmyːtɪç] *adj* good-natured

'**Gutmütigkeit** *f* (-; *no pl*) good nature

'**Gutsbesitzer** *m*, '**Gutsbesitzerin** *f* (-; -*nen*) estate owner

'**Gutschein** *m* coupon, *esp Br* voucher

'**gutschreiben** *v/t* (*irr*, ***schreiben***, *sep*, -*ge*-, *h*) ***j-m et. ~*** credit s.th. to s.o.'s account; '**Gutschrift** *f* credit

'**Gutshaus** *n* manor (house)

'**Gutshof** *m* estate, manor

'**gutstehen** *v/refl* (*irr*, ***stehen***, *sep*, -*ge*-, *h*): ***sich ~*** be well off; F ***sich gut mit j-m stehen → stehen***

'**Gutsverwalter** *m* steward, manager

'**gutwillig** *adj* willing

**Gymnasium** [gʏm'naːzjʊm] *n* (-*s*; -*ien*) high school, *Br appr* grammar school

**Gymnastik** [gʏm'nastɪk] *f* (-; *no pl*) exercises, gymnastics; **gym'nastisch** *adj*: ***~e Übungen*** physical exercises

**Gynäkologe** [gynɛko'loːgə] *m* (-*n*; -*n*), **Gynäko'login** *f* (-; -*nen*) MED gyn(a)ecologist

# H

**Haar** [haːɐ] *n* (-[*e*]*s*; -*e* ['haːrə]) hair; ***sich die ~e kämmen (schneiden lassen)*** comb one's hair (have one's hair cut); ***sich aufs ~ gleichen*** look absolutely identical; ***um ein ~*** by a hair's breadth

'**Haarausfall** *m* loss of hair

'**Haarbürste** *f* hairbrush

**haaren** ['haːrən] *v/i and v/refl* (*ge*-, *h*) zo lose its hair; *fur*: shed hairs

'**Haaresbreite** *f*: ***um ~*** by a hair's breadth

'**haarfein** *adj* (as) fine as a hair

'**Haarfestiger** *m* (-*s*; -) setting lotion

'**Haargefäß** *n* ANAT capillary (vessel)

'**haargenau** F *adv* precisely; **(*stimmt*) *~!*** dead right!

**haarig** ['haːrɪç] *adj* hairy

'**haarklein** F *adv* to the last detail

'**Haar|klemme** *f* bobby pin, *Br* hair clip; **~nadel** *f* hairpin; **~nadelkurve** *f* hairpin bend; **~netz** *n* hair-net

'**haarscharf** F *adv* by a hair's breadth

'**Haar|schnitt** *m* haircut; **~spalterei** *f* (-; *no pl*) hair-splitting; **~spange** *f* barrette, *Br* (hair) slide; **~spray** *m*, *n* hairspray

'**haarsträubend** *adj* hair-raising

'**Haar|teil** *n* hairpiece; **~trockner** *m* hair dryer; **~wäsche** *f*, **~waschmittel** *n* shampoo; **~wasser** *n* hair tonic; **~wuchs** *m*: ***starken ~ haben*** have a lot of hair; **~wuchsmittel** *n* hair restorer

**haben** ['ha:bən] *v/t* (*irr*, *ge-*, *h*) have (got); ***Hunger ~*** be hungry; ***Durst ~*** be thirsty; ***Ferien*** (***Urlaub***) ***~*** be on vacation (*Br* holiday); ***er hat Geburtstag*** it's his birthday; ***welche Farbe hat ...?*** what colo(u)r is ...?; ***zu ~ sein*** be available; F ***sich ~*** make a fuss; F ***was hast du?*** what's the matter with you?; F ***da ~ wir's!*** there we are!; → ***Datum***

'**Haben** *n* (*-s*; *no pl*) ECON credit

**Habgier** ['ha:pgi:ɐ] *f* greed(iness)

'**habgierig** *adj* greedy

**Habicht** ['ha:bɪçt] *m* (*-s*; *-e*) ZO hawk

'**Habseligkeiten** *pl* belongings

**Hacke** ['hakə] *f* (*-*; *-n*) AGR hoe; (pick-) axe; ANAT heel; '**hacken** *v/t* (*ge-*, *h*) chop; AGR hoe; ZO peck

'**Hackentrick** *m soccer*: backheeler

**Hacker** ['hakɐ] *m* (*-s*; *-*) IT hacker

'**Hack|fleisch** *n* ground (*Br* minced) meat; **~ordnung** *f* ZO pecking order

**Hafen** ['ha:fən] *m* (*-s*; *Häfen* ['hɛ:fən]) harbo(u)r, port; **~arbeiter** *m* docker, longshoreman; **~stadt** *f* (sea)port

**Hafer** ['ha:fɐ] *m* (*-s*; *-*) BOT oats; **~brei** *m* oatmeal, *Br* porridge; **~flocken** *pl* (rolled) oats; **~schleim** *m* gruel

**Haft** [haft] *f* (*-*; *no pl*) JUR confinement, imprisonment; ***in ~*** under arrest

'**haftbar** *adj* responsible, JUR liable

'**Haftbefehl** *m* JUR warrant of arrest

'**haften** *v/i* (*ge-*, *h*) stick, adhere (***an*** *dat* to); ***~ für*** JUR answer for, be liable for

**Häftling** ['hɛftlɪŋ] *m* (*-s*; *-e*) prisoner, convict

'**Haftpflicht** *f* JUR liability; **~versicherung** *f* liability insurance; MOT third party insurance

'**Haftung** *f* (*-*; *-en*) responsibility, JUR liability; ***mit beschränkter ~*** limited

**Hagel** ['ha:gəl] *m* (*-s*; *no pl*) hail, *fig a.* shower, volley; '**Hagelkorn** *n* hailstone; '**hageln** *v/i* (*ge-*, *h*) hail (*a. fig*); '**Hagelschauer** *m* hail shower

**hager** ['ha:gɐ] *adj* lean, gaunt, haggard

**Hahn** [ha:n] *m* (*-*[*e*]*s*; *Hähne* ['hɛ:nə]) ZO cock, rooster; TECH (water) tap, faucet

**Hähnchen** ['hɛ:nçən] *n* (*-s*; *-*) ZO chicken

'**Hahnenkamm** *m* ZO cockscomb

**Hai** [hai] *m* (*-*[*e*]*s*; *-e*), **~fisch** *m* ZO shark

**häkeln** ['hɛ:kəln] *v/t and v/i* (*ge-*, *h*) crochet

**Haken** ['ha:kən] *m* (*-s*; *-*) hook (*a. boxing*), peg; check, *Br* tick; F snag, catch

'**Hakenkreuz** *n* swastika

**halb** [halp] *adj and adv* half; ***e-e ~e Stunde*** half an hour; ***ein ~es Pfund*** half a pound; ***zum ~en Preis*** at half-price; ***auf ~em Wege*** (***entgegenkommen***) (meet) halfway; ***~ so viel*** half as much; F (***mit j-m***) ***halbe-halbe machen*** go halves *or* fifty-fifty (with s.o.); ***~ gar*** GASTR underdone

'**Halbbruder** *m* half-brother

'**Halbdunkel** *n* semi-darkness

**Halbe** ['halbə] *f* (*-n*; *-n*) pint (of beer)

'**halbfett** *adj* GASTR medium-fat; PRINT semi-bold

'**Halbfi,nale** *n* SPORT semifinal

'**Halbgott** *m* demigod

'**halbherzig** *adj* half-hearted

**halbieren** [hal'bi:rən] *v/t* (*no -ge-*, *h*) halve; MATH bisect

'**Halbinsel** *f* peninsula

'**Halbjahr** *n* six months; **halbjährig** ['halpjɛ:rɪç] *adj* six-month; '**halbjährlich** **1.** *adj* half-yearly **2.** *adv* half-yearly, twice a year

'**Halbkreis** *m* semicircle

'**Halbkugel** *f* hemisphere

'**halblaut** **1.** *adj* low, subdued **2.** *adv* in an undertone

'**Halbleiter** *m* ELECTR semiconductor

'**halbmast** *adv* (at) half-mast

'**Halb|mond** *m* half-moon, crescent; **~pensi,on** *f* (*-*; *no pl*) *esp Br* half board; **~schlaf** *m* doze; **~schuh** *m* (low) shoe; **~schwester** *f* half-sister

'**halbtags** *adv*: ***~ arbeiten*** work part-time; '**Halbtagsarbeit** *f* (*-*; *no pl*) part-time job; '**Halbtagskraft** *f* part-time worker, F part-timer

**halbwegs** ['halpve:ks] *adv* reasonably

**Halbwüchsige** ['halpvy:ksɪgə] *m*, *f* (*-n*; *-n*) adolescent

'**Halbzeit** *f* SPORT half (time); **~stand** *m* SPORT half-time score

**Halde** ['haldə] *f* (*-*; *-n*) slope; dump

**half** [half] *pret of* ***helfen***

**Hälfte** ['hɛlftə] *f* (-; -*n*) half; ***die ~ von*** half of
**Halfter** ['halftɐ] **1.** *m*, *n* (-*s*; -) halter **2.** *n* (-*s*; -), *f* (-; -*n*) holster
**Halle** ['halə] *f* (-; -*n*) hall; lounge; ***in der ~*** SPORT *etc* indoors
'**hallen** *v/i* (*ge-*, *h*) resound, reverberate
'**Hallenbad** *n* indoor swimming pool
'**Hallensport** *m* indoor sports
**Halm** [halm] *m* (-[*e*]*s*; -*e*) BOT blade; ha(u)lm, stalk; straw
**Hals** [hals] *m* (-*es*; *Hälse* ['hɛlzə]) ANAT neck; throat; ***~ über Kopf*** helter-skelter; F ***sich vom ~ schaffen*** get rid of; F ***es hängt mir zum ~(e) (he)raus*** I'm fed up with it; *fig* ***bis zum ~*** up to one's neck; **~band** *n* (-[*e*]*s*; -*bänder*) necklace; collar; **~entzündung** *f* MED sore throat; **~kette** *f* necklace; **~schmerzen** *pl*: ***~ haben*** have a sore throat
**halsstarrig** ['halsʃtarıç] *adj* stubborn, obstinate
'**Halstuch** *n* neckerchief; scarf
**Halt** *m* (-[*e*]*s*; -*e*, -*s*) (*no pl*) hold; support (*a. fig*); *fig* stability; stop
**halt** [halt] *int* stop!, MIL halt!
'**haltbar** *adj* durable; GASTR not perishable; *fig* tenable; ***~ bis ...*** best before ...
'**Haltbarkeitsdatum** *n* best-by (*or* best-before) date
**halten** ['haltən] (*irr*, *ge-*, *h*) **1.** *v/t* hold; keep (*animal*, *promise etc*); make (*speech*); give (*lecture*); take (*Br a.* in) *a paper etc*; SPORT save; ***~ für*** regard as; (mis)take for; ***viel (wenig) ~ von*** think highly (little) of; ***sich ~*** last; GASTR keep; ***sich gut ~*** *fig* do well; ***sich ~ an*** (*acc*) keep to **2.** *v/i* hold, last; stop, halt; *ice*: bear; *rope etc*: hold; ***~ zu*** stand by, F stick to; **Halter(in)** ['haltɐ, 'haltərin] *m(f)* (-*s*; -/-; -*nen*) owner; TECH holder
'**Haltestelle** *f* stop, RAIL *a.* station
'**Halteverbot** *n* MOT no stopping (area)
'**haltlos** *adj* unsteady; *fig* baseless
'**haltmachen** *v/i* (*sep*, -*ge*-, *h*) stop; *fig* ***vor nichts ~*** stop at nothing
'**Haltung** *f* (-; -*en*) posture; *fig* attitude (***zu*** towards)
**hämisch** ['hɛːmıʃ] *adj* malicious, sneering
**Hammel** ['haməl] *m* (-*s*; -) ZO wether
'**Hammelfleisch** *n* GASTR mutton
**Hammer** ['hamɐ] *m* (-*s*; *Hämmer* ['hɛmɐ]) hammer (*a.* SPORT); **hämmern** ['hɛmɐn] *v/t and v/i* (*ge-*, *h*) hammer
**Hämorrhoiden, Hämorriden** [hɛmɔro-'iːdən] *pl* MED h(a)emorrhoids, F *Br* piles
**Hampelmann** ['hampəlman] *m* jumping jack
**Hamster** ['hamstɐ] *m* (-*s*; -) ZO hamster
'**hamstern** *v/t and v/i* (*ge-*, *h*) hoard
**Hand** [hant] *f* (-; *Hände* ['hɛndə]) hand; ***von ~, mit der ~*** by hand; ***an ~ von*** (*or gen*) by means of; ***zur ~*** at hand; ***aus erster (zweiter) ~*** first-hand (second-hand); ***an die ~ nehmen*** take by the hand; ***sich die ~ geben*** shake hands; ***aus der ~ legen*** lay aside; ***~ breit*** → ***handbreit***; ***~ voll*** → ***handvoll***; ***Hände hoch (weg)!*** hands up (off)!; **~arbeit** *f* (*no pl*) manual labo(u)r; needlework; ***es ist ~*** it is handmade; **~ball** *m* SPORT (European) handball; **~betrieb** *m* TECH manual operation; **~breit** *f* (-; -) hand's breadth; **~bremse** *f* MOT handbrake; **~buch** *n* manual, handbook
**Händedruck** ['hɛndədrʊk] *m* (-[*e*]*s*; -*drücke*) handshake
**Handel** ['handəl] *m* (-*s*; *no pl*) commerce, business; trade; market; transaction, deal, bargain; ***~ treiben*** ECON trade (***mit*** with *s.o.*); '**handeln** *v/i* (*ge-*, *h*) act, take action; bargain (***um*** for), haggle (over); ***mit j-m ~*** ECON trade with s.o.; ***~ mit*** deal in; ***~ von*** deal with, be about; ***es handelt sich um*** it concerns, it is about; it is a matter of
'**Handels|abkommen** *n* trade agreement; **~bank** *f* (-; -*banken*) commercial bank; **~bi,lanz** *f* balance of trade
'**handelseinig** *adj*: ***~ werden*** come to terms
'**Handels|gesellschaft** *f* (trading) company; **~kammer** *f* chamber of commerce; **~schiff** *n* merchant ship; **~schule** *f* commercial school; **~vertreter** *m* (traveling) salesman, *Br* sales representative; **~ware** *f* commodity, merchandise
'**Hand|feger** ['hantfeːgɐ] *m* (-*s*; -) hand-brush; **~fertigkeit** *f* manual skill
'**handfest** *adj* solid
'**Handfläche** *f* ANAT palm
'**handgearbeitet** *adj* handmade

'**Hand|gelenk** *n* ANAT wrist; **~gepäck** *n* hand baggage (*Br* luggage); **~gra,nate** *f* MIL hand grenade

**handgreiflich** ['hantgraiflıç] *adj*: **~ *werden*** turn violent, get tough

'**handhaben** *v/t* (*ge-*, *h*) handle, manage; TECH operate

**Händler** ['hɛndlɐ] *m* (*-s*; -), '**Händlerin** *f* (-; *-nen*) dealer, trader

'**handlich** *adj* handy, manageable

**Handlung** ['handlʊŋ] *f* (-; *-en*) act, action; *film etc*: story, plot

'**Handlungs|reisende** *m* sales representative, travel(l)ing salesman; **~weise** *f* conduct, behavio(u)r

'**Hand|rücken** *m* ANAT back of the hand; **~schellen** *pl* handcuffs; ***j-m ~ anlegen*** handcuff s.o.; **~schlag** *m* handshake; **~schrift** *f* hand(writing)

'**handschriftlich** *adj* handwritten

'**Hand|schuh** *m* glove; **~spiel** *n soccer*: hand ball; **~stand** *m* handstand; **~tasche** *f* handbag, purse; **~tuch** *n* towel; **~voll** *f* handful; **~wagen** *m* handcart; **~werk** *n* craft, trade

**Handwerker** ['hantvɛrkɐ] *m* (*-s*; -) craftsman; workman

'**Handwerkszeug** *n* (kit of) tools

'**Handwurzel** *f* ANAT wrist

**Handy** ['hɛndi] *n* (*-s*; *-s*) *Br* mobile (phone), *Am* cell (phone); **~nummer** *f Br* mobile number, *Am* cell phone number

**Hanf** [hanf] *m* (*-es*; *no pl*) BOT hemp; cannabis

**Hang** [haŋ] *m* (*-[e]s*; *Hänge* ['hɛŋə]) slope; (*no pl*) *fig* inclination (***zu*** for), tendency (towards)

**Hänge|brücke** ['hɛŋəbrʏkə] *f* suspension bridge; **~lampe** *f* hanging lamp; **~matte** *f* hammock

**hängen** ['hɛŋən] **1.** *v/i* (*irr*, *ge-*, *h*) hang (***an*** *dat* on *the wall etc*; from *the ceiling etc*); ***~ bleiben*** get stuck (*a. fig*); ***~ bleiben an*** (*dat*) get caught on; ***~ an*** (*dat*) be fond of; be devoted to; ***alles, woran ich hänge*** everything that is dear to me **2.** *v/t* (*ge-*, *h*) hang (***an*** *acc* on); **~bleiben** *v/i* (*irr*, **bleiben**, *sep*, *-ge-*, *sein*) *fig* get stuck; → ***hängen***

**hänseln** ['hɛnzəln] *v/t* (*ge-*, *h*) tease (***wegen*** about)

**Hanswurst** [hans'vʊrst] *m* (*-[e]s*; *-e*) fool, clown

**Hantel** ['hantəl] *f* (-; *-n*) dumbbell

**hantieren** [han'tiːrən] *v/i* (*no -ge-*, *h*) ***~ mit*** handle; ***~ an*** (*dat*) fiddle about with

**Happen** ['hapən] *m* (*-s*; -) morsel, bite; snack

**Hardware** ['hɑːdwɛə] *f* (-; *-s*) IT hardware

**Harfe** ['harfə] *f* (-; *-n*) MUS harp

**Harfenist** [harfə'nıst] *m* (*-en*; *-en*), **Harfe'nistin** *f* (-; *-nen*) MUS harpist

**Harke** ['harkə] *f* (-; *-n*), '**harken** *v/t* (*ge-*, *h*) rake

**harmlos** ['harmloːs] *adj* harmless

**Harmonie** [harmo'niː] *f* (-; *-n*) harmony (*a.* MUS); **harmo'nieren** *v/i* (*no -ge-*, *h*) harmonize (***mit*** with); **harmonisch** [har'moːnıʃ] *adj* harmonious

**Harn** [harn] *m* (*-[e]s*; *-e*) MED urine

'**Harnblase** *f* ANAT (urinary) bladder

'**Harnröhre** *f* ANAT urethra

**Harpune** [har'puːnə] *f* (-; *-n*) harpoon

**harpunieren** [harpu'niːrən] *v/t* (*no -ge-*, *h*) harpoon

**hart** [hart] **1.** *adj* hard, F *a.* tough; SPORT rough; severe; ***~ gekocht*** hard-boiled **2.** *adv* hard

**Härte** ['hɛrtə] *f* (-; *-n*) hardness; toughness; roughness; severity; *esp* JUR hardship; **~fall** *m* case of hardship

'**härten** *v/t* (*ge-*, *h*) harden

'**Hartfaserplatte** *f* hardboard

'**Hartgeld** *n* coin(s)

**hartgesotten** ['hartgəzɔtən] *adj* hard-boiled

'**hartherzig** *adj* hard-hearted

**hartnäckig** ['hartnɛkıç] *adj* stubborn, obstinate; persistent

**Harz** [haːɐts] *n* (*-es*; *-e*) resin; rosin

'**harzig** *adj* resinous

**Hasch** [haʃ] F *n* (*-s*; *no pl*) hash

'**haschen** F *v/i* (*ge-*, *h*) smoke hash

**Haschisch** ['haʃıʃ] *n* (*-[s]*; *no pl*) hashish

**Hase** ['haːzə] *m* (*-n*; *-n*) ZO hare

**Haselmaus** ['haːzəlmaus] *f* ZO dormouse

'**Haselnuss** *f* BOT hazelnut

'**Hasenscharte** *f* MED harelip

**Hass** [has] *m* (*-es*; *no pl*) hatred, hate (***auf*** *acc*, ***gegen*** of, for)

**hassen** ['hasən] *v/t* (*ge-*, *h*) hate

**hässlich** ['hɛslıç] *adj* ugly, *fig a.* nasty

**Hast** [hast] *f* (-; *no pl*) hurry, haste; rush

**hasten** ['hastən] *v/i* (*ge-*, *sein*) hurry,

hasten, rush
'**hastig** *adj* hasty, hurried
**hätscheln** ['hɛːtʃəln] *v/t* (*ge-*, *h*) fondle; *contp* pamper
**hatte** ['hatə] *pret of* ***haben***
**Haube** ['haubə] *f* (-; *-n*) bonnet (*a. Br* MOT); cap; ZO crest; MOT hood
**Hauch** [haux] *m* (-[*e*]*s*; *-e*) breath; whiff; *fig* touch, trace; **hauchen** ['hauxən] *v/t* (*ge-*, *h*) breathe
**hauen** F *v/t* ([*irr*,] *ge-*, *h*) hit, beat, thrash; TECH hew; ***sich ~*** (have a) fight
**Haufen** ['haufən] *m* (*-s*; -) heap, pile (*both a.* F); F crowd; **häufen** ['hɔʏfən] *v/t* (*ge-*, *h*) heap (up), pile (up); ***sich ~*** *fig* become more frequent, be on the increase; **häufig** ['hɔʏfiç] **1.** *adj* frequent **2.** *adv* frequently, often
**Haupt** [haupt] *n* (-[*e*]*s*; *Häupter* ['hɔʏptɐ]) head, *fig a.* leader; **~bahnhof** *m* main *or* central station; **~beschäftigung** *f* chief occupation; **~bestandteil** *m* chief ingredient; **~darsteller(in)** leading actor (actress), lead
**Häuptelsa͵lat** ['hɔʏptəlzalaːt] *Austrian m* BOT lettuce
'**Haupt|fach** *n* UNIV major, *Br* main subject; **~film** *m* feature (film); **~gericht** *n* GASTR main course; **~gewinn** *m* first prize; **~grund** *m* main reason; **~leitung** *f* TECH main
**Häuptling** ['hɔʏptlɪŋ] *m* (*-s*; *-e*) chief
'**Haupt|mann** *m* (-[*e*]*s*; *-leute*) MIL captain; **~me͵nü** *n* IT main menu; **~merkmal** *n* chief characteristic; **~per͵son** F *f* center (*Br* centre) of attention; **~quar͵tier** *n* headquarters; **~rolle** *f* THEA *etc* lead(ing part)
'**Hauptsache** *f* main thing *or* point
'**hauptsächlich** *adj* main, chief, principal
'**Haupt|satz** *m* LING main clause; **~sendezeit** *f* TV prime time, *Br* peak time (*or* viewing hours); **~speicher** *m* IT main memory; **~stadt** *f* capital; **~straße** *f* main street; main road; **~verkehrsstraße** *f* arterial road; **~verkehrszeit** *f* rush *or* peak hour(s); **~versammlung** *f* general meeting; **~wohnsitz** *m* main place of residence; **~wort** *n* (-[*e*]*s*; *-wörter*) LING noun
**Haus** [haus] *n* (*-es*; *Häuser* ['hɔʏzɐ]) house; building; ***zu ~e*** at home, in; ***nach ~e kommen*** (***bringen***) come *or* get (take) home; **~angestellte** *m*, *f* domestic (servant); **~apo͵theke** *f* medicine cabinet; **~arbeit** *f* housework; **~arzt** *m*, **~ärztin** *f* family doctor; **~aufgaben** *pl* PED homework, assignment; ***s-e ~ machen*** *a. fig* do one's homework; **~bar** *f* cocktail cabinet; **~besetzer** *m* (*-s*; -) squatter; **~besetzung** *f* squatting; **~besitzer** *m* house owner; **~einweihung** *f* house-warming (party)
**hausen** ['hauzən] *v/i* (*ge-*, *h*) live; *fig* play havoc
'**Hausflur** *m* (entrance) hall, hallway
'**Hausfrau** *f* housewife
'**Hausfriedensbruch** *m* JUR trespass
'**hausgemacht** *adj* homemade
'**Haushalt** *m* (-[*e*]*s*; *-e*) household; PARL budget; (***j-m***) ***den ~ führen*** keep house (for s.o.); **Haushälterin** ['haushɛltərɪn] *f* (-; *-nen*) housekeeper
'**Haushalts|geld** *n* housekeeping money; **~plan** *m* PARL budget; **~waren** *pl* household articles
'**Haus|herr** *m* head of the household; host; **~herrin** *f* lady of the house; hostess
'**haushoch** *adj* huge; crushing (*defeat etc*)
**hausieren** [hau'ziːrən] *v/i* (*no -ge-*, *h*) peddle, hawk (***mit et.*** s.th.) (*a. fig*); **Hau'sierer** *m* (*-s*; -) pedlar, hawker
**häuslich** ['hɔʏslɪç] *adj* domestic; home-loving
'**Haus|mädchen** *n* (house)maid; **~mann** *m* house husband; **~mannskost** *f* plain fare; **~meister** *m* caretaker, janitor; **~mittel** *n* household remedy; **~ordnung** *f* house rules; **~rat** *m* (-[*e*]*s*; *no pl*) household effects; **~schlüssel** *m* front-door key; **~schuh** *m* slipper
**Hausse** ['hoːs(ə)] *f* (-; *-n*) ECON rise, boom
'**Haus|suchung** *f* (-; *-en*) house search; **~tier** *n* domestic animal; **~tür** *f* front door; **~verwaltung** *f* property management; **~wirt** *m* landlord; **~wirtin** *f* landlady; **~wirtschaft** *f* (-; *no pl*) housekeeping; **~wirtschaftslehre** *f* domestic science, home economics; **~wirtschaftsschule** *f* domestic science (*or* home economics) school
**Haut** [haut] *f* (-; *Häute* ['hɔʏtə]) skin; complexion; ***bis auf die ~ durchnässt***

H

soaked to the skin; **~abschürfung** *f* MED abrasion; **~arzt** *m*, **~ärztin** *f* dermatologist; **~ausschlag** *m* MED rash
**'hauteng** *adj* skin-tight
**'Haut|farbe** *f* colo(u)r of the skin; complexion; **~krankheit** *f* skin disease; **~pflege** *f* skin care; **~schere** *f* cuticle scissors
**Hbf.** *abbr of* ***Hauptbahnhof*** cent. sta., central station
**H-Bombe** ['ha:bɔmbə] *f* MIL H-bomb
**Hebamme** ['he:pʔamə] *f* (-; *-n*) midwife
**Hebebühne** ['he:bəby:nə] *f* MOT car hoist
**Hebel** ['he:bəl] *m* (-*s*; -) TECH lever
**heben** ['he:bən] *v/t* (*irr*, *ge-*, *h*) lift, raise (*a. fig*); heave; hoist; *fig a.* improve; ***sich ~*** rise, go up
**Hecht** [hɛçt] *m* (-[*e*]*s*; *-e*) ZO pike
**'hechten** *v/i* (*ge-*, *sein*) dive (***nach*** for); SPORT do a long-fly
**Heck** [hɛk] *n* (-[*e*]*s*; *-e*) MAR stern; AVIAT tail; MOT rear
**Hecke** ['hɛkə] *f* (-; *-n*) BOT hedge
**'Heckenrose** *f* BOT dogrose
**'Heckenschütze** *m* MIL sniper
**'Heckscheibe** *f* MOT rear window
**Heer** [he:ɐ] *n* (-[*e*]*s*; *-e*) MIL army, *fig a.* host
**Hefe** ['he:fə] *f* (-; *-n*) yeast
**Heft** [hɛft] *n* (-[*e*]*s*; *-e*) notebook; exercise book; booklet; issue, number
**heften** ['hɛftən] *v/t* (*ge-*, *h*) fix, fasten, attach (***an*** *acc* to); pin (to); tack, baste; stitch
**Hefter** ['hɛftɐ] *m* (-*s*; -) stapler; file
**heftig** ['hɛftɪç] *adj* violent, fierce; heavy
**'Heftklammer** *f* staple
**'Heftpflaster** *n* bandage, Band Aid®, *Br* (adhesive *or* sticking) plaster
**Hehl** [he:l] *n*: ***kein ~ aus et. machen*** make no secret of s.th.
**Hehler** ['he:lɐ] *m* (-*s*; -) JUR receiver of stolen goods, *sl* fence
**Hehlerei** [he:lə'rai] *f* (-; *-en*) JUR receiving stolen goods
**Heide**[1] ['haidə] *m* (*-n*; *-n*) REL heathen
**'Heide**[2] *f* (-; *-n*) heath(land)
**'Heidekraut** *n* (-[*e*]*s*; *no pl*) BOT heather, heath
**'Heiden|angst** F *f*: ***e-e ~ haben*** be scared stiff; **~geld** F *n*: ***ein ~*** a fortune; **~lärm** F *m*: ***ein ~*** a hell of a noise; **~spaß** F *m*: ***e-n ~ haben*** have a ball
**'Heidentum** *n* (-*s*; *no pl*) REL heathenism; **Heidin** ['haidɪn] *f* (-; *-nen*), **'heidnisch** ['haidnɪʃ] *adj* REL heathen
**heikel** ['haikəl] *adj* delicate, tricky; tender; F fussy
**heil** [hail] *adj* safe, unhurt; undamaged, whole, intact; **Heil** *n* (-*s*; *no pl*) REL grace
**Heiland** ['hailant] *m* (-[*e*]*s*; *no pl*) REL Savio(u)r, Redeemer
**'Heilbad** *n* health resort, spa
**'heilbar** *adj* curable
**heilen** ['hailən] **1.** *v/t* (*ge-*, *h*) cure **2.** *v/i* (*ge-*, *sein*) heal (up)
**'Heilgym,nastik** *f* physiotherapy
**heilig** ['hailɪç] *adj* REL holy; sacred (*a. fig*)
**Heilig'abend** *m* Christmas Eve
**Heilige** ['hailɪgə] *m*, *f* (*-n*; *-n*) REL saint
**heiligen** ['hailɪgən] *v/t* (*ge-*, *h*) REL sanctify (*a. fig*), hallow
**'heiligsprechen** *v/t* (*irr*, ***sprechen***, *sep*, *-ge-*, *h*) canonize
**'Heiligtum** *n* (-*s*; *-tümer* ['hailɪçty:mɐ]) REL sanctuary, shrine
**'Heilkraft** *f* healing *or* curative power; **'heilkräftig** *adj* curative
**'Heilkraut** *n* BOT medicinal herb
**'heillos** *fig adj* utter, hopeless
**'Heil|mittel** *n* remedy, cure (*both a. fig*); **~praktiker(in)** ['hailpraktikɐ, 'hailpraktikərɪn] (-*s*; -/-; *-nen*) nonmedical practitioner; **~quelle** *f* (medicinal) mineral spring
**'heilsam** *fig adj* salutary
**'Heilsar,mee** *f* Salvation Army
**'Heilung** *f* (-; *-en*) cure; healing
**heim** [haim] *adv* home
**Heim** *n* (-[*e*]*s*; *-e*) (*no pl*) home; hostel; **Heim...** *in cpds ...mannschaft*, *...sieg*, *...spiel etc*: home
**Heimat** ['haima:t] *f* (-; *no pl*) home; home country; home town; ***in der*** (***meiner***) ***~*** at home; **'heimatlos** *adj* homeless; **'Heimatstadt** *f* home town; 'Heimatvertriebene *m*, *f* expellee
**heimisch** ['haimɪʃ] *adj* home, domestic; BOT, ZO *etc* native; *fig* homelike, hom(e)y; ***sich ~ fühlen*** feel at home
**Heimkehr** ['haimke:ɐ] *f* (-; *no pl*) return (home); **'heimkehren** *v/i* (*sep*, *-ge-*, *sein*) return home, come back
**'heimlich** *adj* secret; **'Heimlichkeit** *f* (-;

H

*-en*) (*no pl*) secrecy; *pl* secrets
'**Heimreise** *f* journey home
'**heimsuchen** *v/t* (*sep*, *-ge-*, *h*) strike
'**heimtückisch** *adj* insidious (*a.* MED); treacherous
**heimwärts** ['haimvɛrts] *adv* homeward(s)
'**Heimweg** *m* way home
'**Heimweh** *n* (*-s*; *no pl*) homesickness; *~ **haben*** be homesick
**Heimwerker** ['haimvɛrkɐ] *m* (*-s*; *-*) do-it-yourselfer
**Heirat** ['haira:t] *f* (*-*; *-en*) marriage
**heiraten** ['haira:tən] *v/t and v/i* (*ge-*, *h*) marry, get married (to)
'**Heirats|antrag** *m* proposal (of marriage); ***j-m e-n ~ machen*** propose to s.o.; **~schwindler** *m* marriage impostor; **~vermittler(in)** (*-s*; *-/-*; *-nen*) marriage broker; **~vermittlung** *f* marriage bureau
**heiser** ['haizɐ] *adj* hoarse, husky
'**Heiserkeit** *f* (*-*; *no pl*) hoarseness, huskiness
**heiß** [hais] *adj* hot, *fig a.* passionate, ardent; ***mir ist ~*** I am *or* feel hot
**heißen** ['haisən] *v/i* (*irr*, *ge-*, *h*) be called; mean; ***wie ~ Sie?*** what's your name?; ***wie heißt das?*** what do you call this?; ***was heißt … auf Englisch?*** what is … in English?; ***es heißt im Text*** it says in the text; ***das heißt*** that is (*abbr* **d. h.** i. e.)
**heiter** ['haitɐ] *adj* cheerful; humorous (*film etc*); METEOR fair; *fig* ***aus ~em Himmel*** out of the blue; '**Heiterkeit** *f* (*-*; *no pl*) cheerfulness; amusement
**heizbar** ['haitsba:ɐ] *adj* heated; **heizen** ['haitsən] *v/t and v/i* (*ge-*, *h*) heat; ***mit Kohlen ~*** burn coal; **Heizer** ['haitsɐ] *m* (*-s*; *-*) MAR, RAIL stoker
'**Heiz|kessel** *m* boiler; **~kissen** *n* electric cushion; **~körper** *m* radiator; **~kraftwerk** *n* thermal power-station; **~materi,al** *n* fuel; **~öl** *n* fuel oil
'**Heizung** *f* (*-*; *-en*) heating
**Held** [hɛlt] *m* (*-en*; *-en* ['hɛldən]) hero
**heldenhaft** ['hɛldənhaft] *adj* heroic
'**Heldentat** *f* heroic deed
'**Heldentum** *n* (*-s*; *no pl*) heroism
**Heldin** ['hɛldɪn] *f* (*-*; *-nen*) heroine
**helfen** ['hɛlfən] *v/i* (*irr*, *ge-*, *h*) help, aid; assist; ***j-m bei et. ~*** help s.o. with *or* in (doing) s.th.; ***~ gegen*** MED *etc* be good for; ***er weiß sich zu ~*** he can manage; ***es hilft nichts*** it's no use
**Helfer** ['hɛlfɐ] *m* (*-s*; *-*), '**Helferin** *f* (*-*; *-nen*) helper, assistant
'**Helfershelfer** *contp m* accomplice
**hell** [hɛl] *adj* bright (*light*, *flame etc*); light (*color etc*); light-colo(u)red (*dress etc*); clear (*voice etc*); pale (*beer*); *fig* bright, clever; ***es wird schon ~*** it's getting light already; **~blau** *adj* light blue; **~blond** *adj* very fair; **~hörig** *adj* quick of hearing; ARCH poorly soundproofed; ***~ werden*** prick up one's ears
'**Hellseher** *m* (*-s*; *-*), '**Hellseherin** *f* (*-*; *-nen*) clairvoyant
**Helm** [hɛlm] *m* (*-[e]s*; *-e*) helmet
**Hemd** [hɛmt] *n* (*-[e]s*; *-en* ['hɛmdən]) shirt; vest; **~bluse** *f* shirt; **~blusenkleid** *n* shirtwaist, *Br* shirt-waister
**Hemisphäre** [hemi'sfɛ:rə] *f* (*-*; *-n*) hemisphere
**hemmen** ['hɛmən] *v/t* (*ge-*, *h*) check, stop; hamper; '**Hemmung** *f* (*-*; *-en*) PSYCH inhibition; scruple
'**hemmungslos** *adj* unrestrained; unscrupulous
**Hengst** [hɛŋst] *m* (*-[e]s*; *-e*) ZO stallion
**Henkel** ['hɛŋkəl] *m* (*-s*; *-*) handle
**Henker** ['hɛŋkɐ] *m* (*-s*; *-*) hangman, executioner
**Henne** ['hɛnə] *f* (*-*; *-n*) ZO hen
**her** [he:ɐ] *adv* here; ***das ist lange ~*** that was a long time ago
**herab** [hɛ'rap] *adv* down; **~lassen** *fig v/refl* (*irr*, **lassen**, *sep*, *-ge-*, *h*) condescend; **~lassend** *adj* condescending; **~sehen** *fig v/i* (*irr*, **sehen**, *sep*, *-ge-*, *h*) ***~ auf*** (*acc*) look down upon; **~setzen** *v/t* (*sep*, *-ge-*, *h*) reduce; *fig* disparage
**heran** [hɛ'ran] *adv* close, near; ***~ an*** (*acc*) up *or* near to; **~gehen** *v/i* (*irr*, **gehen**, *sep*, *-ge-*, *sein*) ***~ an*** (*acc*) walk up to; *fig* set about *a task etc*; **~kommen** *v/i* (*irr*, **kommen**, *sep*, *-ge-*, *sein*) come near (*a. fig*); **~wachsen** *v/i* (*irr*, **wachsen**, *sep*, *-ge-*, *sein*) grow (up) (***zu*** into)
**He'ranwachsende** *m*, *f* (*-n*; *-n*) adolescent
**he'ranwinken** *v/t* (*sep*, *-ge-*, *h*) hail (*taxi etc*)
**herauf** [hɛ'rauf] *adv* up (here); upstairs; **~beschwören** *v/t* (*irr*, **schwören**, *sep*, *no -ge-*, *h*) call up; bring on, provoke
**heraus** [hɛ'raus] *adv* out; *fig* ***aus*** (*dat*)

**... ~** out of ...; ***zum Fenster ~*** out of the window; **~ *mit der Sprache!*** speak out!, out with it!; **~bekommen** *v/t* (*irr*, **kommen**, *sep*, *no -ge-*, *h*) get out; get back (*change*); *fig* find out; **~bringen** *v/t* (*irr*, **bringen**, *sep*, *-ge-*, *h*) bring out; PRINT publish; THEA stage; *fig* find out; **~finden** (*irr*, **finden**, *sep*, *-ge-*, *h*) **1.** *v/t* find; *fig* find out, discover **2.** *v/i* find one's way out

**He'rausforderer** *m* (*-s*; *-*) challenger; **he'rausfordern** *v/t* (*sep*, *-ge-*, *h*) challenge; provoke, F ask for it; **He'rausforderung** *f* challenge; provocation

**he'rausgeben** *v/t* (*irr*, **geben**, *sep*, *-ge-*, *h*) give back; give up; PRINT publish; issue; give change (***auf*** *acc* for); **He'rausgeber(in)** [hɛ'rausge:bɐ, hɛ'rausge:bərɪn] *m(f)* (*-s*; *-/-*; *-nen*) publisher

**he'raus|kommen** *v/i* (*irr*, **kommen**, *sep*, *-ge-*, *sein*) come out; *book*: be published; *stamps*: be issued; **~ *aus*** get out of; F ***groß ~*** be a great success; **~nehmen** *v/t* (*irr*, **nehmen**, *sep*, *-ge-*, *h*) take out; SPORT take *s.o.* off the team; *fig* ***sich et. ~*** take liberties, go too far; **~putzen** *v/t and v/refl* (*sep*, *-ge-*, *h*) spruce (o.s.) up; **~reden** *v/refl* (*sep*, *-ge-*, *h*) make excuses; talk one's way out; **~stellen** *v/t* (*sep*, *-ge-*, *h*) put out; *fig* emphasize; ***sich ~ als*** turn out *or* prove to be; **~strecken** *v/t* (*sep*, *-ge-*, *h*) stick out; **~suchen** *v/t* (*sep*, *-ge-*, *h*) pick out; ***j-m et. ~*** find s.o. s.th.

**herb** [hɛrp] *adj* tart; dry (*wine etc*); *fig* harsh; bitter

**her'bei** *adv* up, over, here; **~eilen** *v/i* (*sep*, *-ge-*, *sein*) come running up; **~führen** *fig v/t* (*sep*, *-ge-*, *h*) cause, bring about

**Herberge** ['hɛrbɛrgə] *f* (*-*; *-n*) inn; lodging; hostel

**Herbst** [hɛrpst] *m* (*-[e]s*; *-e*) fall, autumn

**Herd** [he:ɐt] *m* (*-[e]s*; *-e* ['he:ɐdə]) cooker, stove; *fig* center, *Br* centre; MED focus, seat

**Herde** ['he:ɐdə] *f* (*-*; *-n*) ZO herd (*a. fig contp*); flock (*of sheep, geese etc*)

**herein** [hɛ'rain] *adv* in (here); **~!** come in!; **~brechen** *v/i* (*irr*, **brechen**, *sep*, *-ge-*, *sein*) *night*: fall; **~ *über*** (*acc*) befall *s.o.*; **~fallen** F *v/i* (*irr*, **fallen**, *sep*, *-ge-*, *sein*) be taken in (***auf*** *acc* by); **~legen** F *v/t* (*sep*, *-ge-*, *h*) take *s.o.* in

**'herfallen** *v/i* (*irr*, **fallen**, *sep*, *-ge-*, *sein*) **~ *über*** (*acc*) attack (*a. fig*)

**'Hergang** *m*: ***j-m den ~ schildern*** tell s.o. what happened

**'hergeben** *v/t* (*irr*, **geben**, *sep*, *-ge-*, *h*) give up, part with; ***sich ~ zu*** lend o.s. to

**Hering** ['he:rɪŋ] *m* (*-s*; *-e*) ZO herring

**'herkommen** *v/i* (*irr*, **kommen**, *sep*, *-ge-*, *sein*) come (here); **~ *von*** come from, *fig a.* be caused by

**herkömmlich** ['he:ɐkœmlɪç] *adj* conventional (*a.* MIL)

**Herkunft** ['he:ɐkʊnft] *f* (*-*; *no pl*) origin; birth, descent

**heroisch** [he'ro:ɪʃ] *adj* heroic

**Herr** [hɛr] *m* (*-n*; *-en*) gentleman; master; REL *the* Lord; **~ *Brown*** Mr Brown; **~ *der Lage*** master of the situation

**'Herren|bekleidung** *f* menswear; **~doppel** *n tennis*: men's doubles; **~einzel** *n tennis*: men's singles

**'herrenlos** *adj* abandoned; stray (*dog*)

**'Herrentoi,lette** *f* men's restroom (*Br* toilet *or* lavatory)

**'herrichten** *v/t* (*sep*, *-ge-*, *h*) get ready, F fix

**herrisch** ['hɛrɪʃ] *adj* imperious

**herrlich** ['hɛrlɪç] *adj* marvel(l)ous, wonderful, F fantastic; **'Herrlichkeit** *f* (*-*; *-en*) glory

**'Herrschaft** *f* (*-*; *no pl*) rule, power, control (*a. fig*) (***über*** *acc* over); ***die ~ verlieren über*** (*acc*) lose control of

**herrschen** ['hɛrʃən] *v/i* (*ge-*, *h*) rule; ***es herrschte ...*** there was ...; **Herrscher(in)** ['hɛrʃɐ, 'hɛrʃərɪn] *m(f)* (*-s*; *-/-*; *-nen*) ruler; sovereign, monarch; **'herrschsüchtig** *adj* domineering, F bossy

**'herrühren** *v/i* (*sep*, *-ge-*, *h*) **~ *von*** come from, be due to

**'herstellen** *v/t* (*sep*, *-ge-*, *h*) make, produce; *fig* establish; **'Herstellung** *f* (*-*; *no pl*) production; *fig* establishment; **'Herstellungskosten** *pl* production cost(s)

**herüber** [hɛ'ry:bɐ] *adv* over (here), across

**herum** [hɛ'rʊm] *adv* (a)round; F ***anders ~*** the other way round; **~führen** *v/t* (*sep*, *-ge-*, *h*) ***j-n*** (***in der Stadt*** *etc*) **~** show s.o.

(a)round (the town *etc*); ~**kommen** F *v/i* (*irr*, **kommen**, *sep*, *-ge-*, *sein*) (**weit** *or* **viel**) ~ get around; **um et.** ~ *fig* get (a)round s.th.; ~**kriegen** F *v/t* (*sep*, *-ge-*, *h*) **j-n zu et.** ~ get s.o. round to (doing) s.th.; ~**lungern** F *v/i* (*sep*, *-ge-*, *h*) loaf *or* hang around; ~**reichen** *v/t* (*sep*, *-ge-*, *h*) pass *or* hand round; ~**sprechen** *v/refl* (*irr*, **sprechen**, *sep*, *-ge-*, *h*) get around; ~**treiben** F *v/refl* (*irr*, **treiben**, *sep*, *-ge-*, *h*) gad *or* knock about

**He'rumtreiber** F *m* (*-s*; -), **He'rumtreiberin** F *f* (-; *-nen*) tramp, loafer

**herunter** [hɛ'rʊntɐ] *adv* down; downstairs; ~**gekommen** *adj* run-down; seedy, shabby; ~**hauen** F *v/t* (*sep*, *-ge-*, *h*) **j-m e-e** ~ smack *or* slap s.o. ('s face); ~**machen** F *v/t* (*sep*, *-ge-*, *h*) run *s.o. or s.th.* down; ~**spielen** F *v/t* (*sep*, *-ge-*, *h*) play *s.th.* down

**hervor** [hɛɐ'foːɐ] *adv* out of *or* from, forth; ~**bringen** *v/t* (*irr*, **bringen**, *sep*, *-ge-*, *h*) bring out, produce (*a. fig*); yield; utter; ~**gehen** *v/i* (*irr*, **gehen**, *sep*, *-ge-*, *sein*) ~ **aus** (*dat*) follow from; **als Sieger** ~ come off victorious; ~**heben** *v/t* (*irr*, **heben**, *sep*, *-ge-*, *h*) stress, emphasize; ~**ragend** *adj* outstanding, excellent, superior; prominent, eminent; ~**rufen** *v/t* (*irr*, **rufen**, *sep*, *-ge-*, *h*) cause, bring about; create; ~**stechend** *adj* striking; ~**tretend** *adj* prominent; protruding, bulging; ~**tun** *v/refl* (*irr*, **tun**, *sep*, *-ge-*, *h*) distinguish o.s. (**als** as)

**Herz** [hɛrts] *n* (*-ens*; *-en*) ANAT heart (*a. fig*); *cards*: heart(s); **j-m das** ~ **brechen** break s.o.'s heart; **sich ein** ~ **fassen** take heart; **mit ganzem** ~**en** whole-heartedly; **schweren** ~**ens** with a heavy heart; **sich et. zu** ~**en nehmen** take s.th. to heart; **es nicht übers** ~ **bringen zu** *inf* not have the heart to *inf*; **et. auf dem** ~**en haben** have s.th. on one's mind; **ins** ~ **schließen** take to one's heart; ~**anfall** *m* heart attack

'**Herzens|lust** *f*: **nach** ~ to one's heart's content; ~**wunsch** *m* heart's desire, dearest wish

'**Herzfehler** *m* cardiac defect

'**herzhaft** *adj* hearty; savo(u)ry

'**herzig** *adj* sweet, lovely, cute

'**Herz|in,farkt** *m* MED cardiac infarct (-ion), F *mst* heart attack, coronary; ~**klopfen** *n* (*-s*; *no pl*) palpitation; **er hatte** ~ (**vor** *dat*) his heart was throbbing (with)

'**herzkrank** *adj* suffering from (a) heart disease

'**herzlich 1.** *adj* cordial, hearty; warm, friendly **2.** *adv*: ~ **gern** with pleasure

'**herzlos** *adj* heartless

**Herzog** ['hɛrtsoːk] *m* (*-s*; *Herzöge* ['hɛrtsøːgə]) duke; **Herzogin** ['hɛrtsoːgɪn] *f* (-; *-nen*) duchess

'**Herz|schlag** *m* heartbeat; MED heart failure; ~**schrittmacher** *m* MED (cardiac) pacemaker; ~**transplantati,on** *f* MED heart transplant

'**herzzerreißend** *adj* heart-rending

**heterosexuell** [heterozɛksu'ɛl] *adj* heterosexual

**Hetze** ['hɛtsə] *f* (-; *no pl*) hurry, rush; POL *etc* agitation, campaign(ing) (**gegen** against); '**hetzen 1.** *v/t* (*ge-*, *h*) rush; ZO hunt, chase; **e-n Hund auf j-n** ~ set a dog on s.o. **2.** *v/i* (*ge-*, *sein*) hurry, rush; (*ge-*, *h*) POL *etc* agitate (**gegen** against); '**hetzerisch** *adj* inflammatory; '**Hetzjagd** *f* hunt(ing), chase (*a. fig*); *fig* rush; '**Hetzkam,pagne** *f* POL smear campaign

**Heu** [hɔʏ] *n* (-[*e*]*s*; *no pl*) hay

'**Heuboden** *m* hayloft

**Heuchelei** [hɔʏçə'lai] *f* (-; *-en*) hypocrisy; cant; **heucheln** ['hɔʏçəln] *v/i and v/t* (*ge-*, *h*) feign, simulate; **Heuchler(in)** ['hɔʏçlɐ (-lərɪn)] (*-s*; -/-; *-nen*) hypocrite; **heuchlerisch** ['hɔʏçlərɪʃ] *adj* hypocritical

**heuer** ['hɔʏɐ] *Austrian adv* this year

**Heuer** ['hɔʏɐ] *f* (-; *-n*) MAR pay; '**heuern** *v/t* (*ge-*, *h*) hire, MAR *a.* sign on

**heulen** ['hɔʏlən] *v/i* (*ge-*, *h*) howl; F *contp* bawl; MOT roar; *siren*: whine

'**Heuschnupfen** *m* MED hay fever

'**Heuschrecke** *f* (-; *-n*) ZO grasshopper; locust

**heute** ['hɔʏtə] *adv* today; ~ **Abend** this evening, tonight; ~ **früh**, ~ **Morgen** this morning; ~ **in acht Tagen** a week from now; ~ **vor acht Tagen** a week ago today; **heutig** ['hɔʏtɪç] *adj* today's; of today, present(-day); '**heutzutage** *adv* nowadays, these days

**Hexe** ['hɛksə] *f* (-; *-n*) witch (*a. fig*); **alte** ~ (old) hag; '**hexen** *v/i* (*ge-*, *h*) practice

witchcraft; F work miracles
'**Hexen|kessel** *m* inferno; **~schuss** *m* (*-es; no pl*) MED lumbago
**hieb** [hi:p] *pret of* ***hauen***
**Hieb** [hi:p] *m* (*-[e]s; -e* ['hi:bə]) blow, stroke; punch; lash, cut; *pl* beating; thrashing
**hielt** [hi:lt] *pret of* ***halten***
**hier** [hi:ɐ] *adv* here, in this place; present; **~ *entlang!*** this way!
**hieran** ['hi:'ran] *adv* from *or* in this; **hierauf** ['hi:'rauf] *adv* on it *or* this; after this, then; **hieraus** ['hi:'raus] *adv* from *or* out of this; '**hier'bei** *adv* here, in this case; on this occasion; '**hier'durch** *adv* by this, hereby, this way; '**hier'für** *adv* for this; '**hier'her** *adv* (over) here, this way; ***bis*~** so far; **hierin** ['hi:'rın] *adv* in this; '**hier'mit** *adv* with this; '**hier'nach** *adv* after this; according to this; **hierüber** ['hi:'ry:bɐ] *adv* about this (subject); **hierunter** ['hi:'rʊntɐ] *adv* under this; among these; *understand etc* by this *or* that; '**hier'von** *adv* of *or* from this; '**hier'zu** *adv* for this; to this
**hiesig** ['hi:zıç] *adj* local; ***ein Hiesiger*** one of the locals
**hieß** [hi:s] *pret of* ***heißen***
**Hilfe** ['hılfə] *f* (*-; -n*) help; aid (*a.* ECON), assistance (*a.* MED), relief (***für*** to); ***Erste* ~** first aid; ***um* ~ *rufen*** cry for help; **~*!*** help!; → ***mithilfe***; **~me,nü** *n* IT help menu; **~ruf** *m* call (*or* cry) for help; **~stellung** *f* support (*a. fig*)
'**hilf|los** *adj* helpless; **~reich** *adj* helpful
'**Hilfsakti,on** *f* relief action
'**Hilfsarbeiter** *m*, '**Hilfsarbeiterin** *f* unskilled worker
'**hilfsbedürftig** *adj* needy
'**hilfsbereit** *adj* helpful, ready to help; '**Hilfsbereitschaft** *f* (*-; no pl*) readiness to help, helpfulness
'**Hilfs|mittel** *n* aid, TECH *a.* device; **~organisati,on** *f* relief organization; **~verb** *n* LING auxiliary (verb)
**Himbeere** ['hımbe:rə] *f* BOT raspberry
**Himmel** ['hıməl] *m* (*-s; -*) sky; REL heaven (*a. fig*); ***um* ~*s willen*** for Heaven's sake; → ***heiter***
'**Himmelfahrt** REL Ascension (Day)
'**Himmels|körper** *m* AST celestial body; **~richtung** *f* direction; cardinal point
**himmlisch** ['hımlıʃ] *adj* heavenly, *fig a.* marvel(l)ous
**hin** [hın] **1.** *adv* there; ***bis* ~ *zu*** as far as; ***noch lange* ~** still a long way off; ***auf s-e Bitte*** (***s-n Rat***) **~** at his request (advice); **~ *und her*** to and fro, back and forth; **~ *und wieder*** now and then; **~ *und zurück*** there and back; RAIL round trip, round-trip ticket, *esp Br* return (ticket) **2.** F *pred adj* ruined; done for; gone
**hi'nab** *adv* → ***hinunter***
'**hinarbeiten** *v/i* (*sep, -ge-, h*) **~ *auf*** (*acc*) work towards
**hi'nauf** *adv* up (there); upstairs; ***die Straße*** *etc* **~** up the street *etc*; **~gehen** *v/i* (*irr*, ***gehen***, *sep, -ge-, sein*) go up, *fig a.* rise
**hi'naus** *adv* out; ***aus ...* ~** out of ...; ***in*** (*acc*) ***...* ~** out into ...; **~ (*mit dir*)*!*** (get) out!, out you go!; **~gehen** *v/i* (*irr*, ***gehen***, *sep, -ge-, sein*) go out(side); **~ *über*** (*acc*) go beyond; **~ *auf*** (*acc*) *window etc*: look out onto; **~laufen** *v/i* (*irr*, ***laufen***, *sep, -ge-, sein*) run out(side); **~ *auf*** (*acc*) come *or* amount to; **~schieben** *v/t* (*irr*, ***schieben***, *sep, -ge-, h*) put off, postpone; **~stellen** *v/t* (*sep, -ge-, h*) SPORT send *s.o.* off (the field); **~werfen** *v/t* (*irr*, ***werfen***, *sep, -ge-, h*) throw out (***aus*** of), *fig a.* kick out; (give *s.o.* the) sack, fire; **~wollen** *v/i* (*sep, -ge-, h*) **~ *auf*** (*acc*) aim (*or* drive *or* get) at; ***hoch* ~** aim high
'**Hinblick** *m*: ***im* ~ *auf*** (*acc*) in view of, with regard to
'**hinbringen** *v/t* (*irr*, ***bringen***, *sep, -ge-, h*) take there
**hinderlich** ['hındɐlıç] *adj* hindering, impeding; ***j-m* ~ *sein*** be in s.o.'s way
**hindern** ['hındɐn] *v/t* (*ge-, h*) hinder, hamper; **~ *an*** (*dat*) prevent from
**Hindernis** ['hındɐnıs] *n* (*-ses; -se*) obstacle (*a. fig*); **~rennen** *n* steeplechase
**Hindu** ['hındu] *m* (*-[s]; -[s]*) Hindu
**Hinduismus** [hındu'ısmʊs] *m* (*-; no pl*) hinduism
**hin'durch** *adv* through; ***das ganze Jahr*** *etc* **~** throughout the year *etc*
**hi'nein** *adv* in; **~ *mit dir!*** in you go!; **~gehen** *v/i* (*irr*, ***gehen***, *sep, -ge-, sein*) go in; **~ *in*** (*acc*) go into
'**hinfallen** *v/i* (*irr*, ***fallen***, *sep, -ge-, sein*) fall (down)
'**hinfällig** *adj* frail, infirm; invalid
**hing** [hıŋ] *pret of* ***hängen*** 1

H

'**Hingabe** *f* (-; *no pl*) devotion (***an*** *acc* to); '**hingeben** *v/t* (*irr*, ***geben***, *sep*, *-ge-*, *h*) give (up); ***sich ~*** (*dat*) give o.s. to; devote o.s. to
'**hinhalten** *v/t* (*irr*, ***halten***, *sep*, *-ge-*, *h*) hold out; ***j-n ~*** put s.o. off
**hinken** ['hɪŋkən] *v/i* (*ge-*, *h*) (walk with a) limp; (*ge-*, *sein*) limp
'**hin|kommen** *v/i* (*irr*, ***kommen***, *sep*, *-ge-*, *sein*) get there; **~kriegen** F *v/t* (*sep*, *-ge-*, *h*) manage
'**hinlänglich** *adj* sufficient
'**hin|legen** *v/t* (*sep*, *-ge-*, *h*) lay *or* put down; ***sich ~*** lie down; **~nehmen** *v/t* (*irr*, ***nehmen***, *sep*, *-ge-*, *h*) put up with
'**hinreißen** *v/t* (*irr*, ***reißen***, *sep*, *-ge-*, *h*) carry away; **~d** *adj* entrancing; breathtaking
'**hinrichten** *v/t* (*sep*, *-ge-*, *h*) execute; '**Hinrichtung** *f* (-; *-en*) execution
'**hinsetzen** *v/t* (*sep*, *-ge-*, *h*) set *or* put down; ***sich ~*** sit down
'**Hinsicht** *f* (-; *no pl*) respect; ***in gewisser ~*** in a way; '**hinsichtlich** *prp* (*gen*) with respect *or* regard to
'**Hinspiel** *n* SPORT first leg
'**hinstellen** *v/t* (*sep*, *-ge-*, *h*) put (down); ***~ als*** make *s.o. or s.th.* appear to be
**hinten** ['hɪntən] *adv* at the back; MOT in the back; ***von ~*** from behind
**hinter** ['hɪntɐ] *prp* (*dat*) behind
'**Hinter...** *in cpds ...achse*, *...eingang*, *...rad etc*: rear ...; **~bein** *n* hind leg
**Hinterbliebenen** [hɪntɐ'bli:bənən] *pl the* bereaved; *esp* JUR surviving dependents
**hinterei'nander** *adv* one after the other; ***dreimal ~*** three times in a row
'**Hintergedanke** *m* ulterior motive
**hinter'gehen** *v/t* (*irr*, ***gehen***, *no -ge-*, *h*) deceive
'**Hintergrund** *m* background (*a. fig*)
'**Hinterhalt** *m* ambush; **hinterhältig** ['hɪntɐhɛltɪç] *adj* insidious, underhand(ed)
'**Hinterhaus** *n* rear building
**hinter'her** *adv* behind, after; afterwards
'**Hinterhof** *m* backyard
'**Hinterkopf** *m* back of the head
**hinter'lassen** *v/t* (*irr*, ***lassen***, *no -ge-*, *h*) leave (behind); **Hinter'lassenschaft** *f* (-; *-en*) property (left), estate
**hinter'legen** *v/t* (*no -ge-*, *h*) deposit (***bei*** with)
'**Hinterlist** *f* deceit(fulness); (underhanded) trick; '**hinterlistig** *adj* deceitful; underhand(ed)
'**Hintermann** *m* person (car *etc*) behind (one); *fig mst pl* person behind the scenes, brain(s), mastermind
'**Hintern** F *m* (*-s*; -) bottom, backside, behind, *Br* bum
**hinterrücks** ['hɪntɐrʏks] *adv* from behind
'**Hinter|seite** *f* back; **~teil** F *n* → ***Hintern***; **~treppe** *f* back stairs; **~tür** *f* back door
**hinter'ziehen** *v/t* (*irr*, ***ziehen***, *no -ge-*, *h*) evade (*taxes*)
'**Hinterzimmer** *n* back room
**hi'nüber** *adv* over, across; ***~ sein*** F be ruined; GASTR be spoilt
**hi'nunter** *adv* down; downstairs; ***die Straße ~*** down the road
**Hinweg** ['hɪnve:k] *m* way there
**hinweg** [hɪn'vɛk] *adv*: ***über*** (*acc*) ***... ~*** over ...; **~kommen** *v/i* (*irr*, ***kommen*** *sep*, *-ge-*, *sein*) ***~ über*** (*acc*) get over; **~sehen** *v/i* (*irr*, ***sehen***, *sep*, *-ge-*, *h*) ***~ über*** (*acc*) ignore; **~setzen** *v/refl* (*sep*, *-ge-*, *h*) ***sich ~ über*** (*acc*) ignore, disregard
**Hinweis** ['hɪnvais] *m* (*-es*; *-e*) reference (***auf*** *acc* to); hint, tip (as to, regarding); indication (of), clue (as to); '**hinweisen** (*irr*, ***weisen***, *sep*, *-ge-*, *h*) **1.** *v/t*: ***j-n ~ auf*** (*acc*) draw *or* call s.o.'s attention to **2.** *v/i*: ***~ auf*** (*acc*) point at *or* to, indicate; *fig* point out, indicate; hint at
'**Hinweis|schild** *n*, **~tafel** *f* sign, notice
'**hin|werfen** *v/t* (*irr*, ***werfen***, *sep*, *-ge-*, *h*) throw down; **~ziehen** *v/refl* (*irr*, ***ziehen***, *sep*, *-ge-*, *h*) extend (***bis zu*** to), stretch (to); drag on
**hin'zu|fügen** *v/t* (*sep*, *-ge-*, *h*) add (***zu*** to) (*a. fig*); **~kommen** *v/i* (*irr*, ***kommen***, *sep*, *-ge-*, *sein*) be added; ***hinzu kommt, dass*** add to this ..., and what is more, ...; **~ziehen** *v/t* (*irr*, ***ziehen***, *sep*, *-ge-*, *h*) call in, consult
**Hirn** [hɪrn] *n* (-[*e*]*s*; *-e*) ANAT brain; *fig* brain(s), mind; **~gespinst** *n* fantasy
**Hirsch** [hɪrʃ] *m* (-[*e*]*s*; *-e*) ZO stag; **~geweih** *n* ZO antlers; **~kuh** *f* ZO hind
**Hirse** ['hɪrzə] *f* (-; *-n*) BOT millet
**Hirte** ['hɪrtə] *m* (*-n*; *-n*) herdsman; shepherd (*a. fig*)
**hissen** ['hɪsən] *v/t* (*ge-*, *h*) hoist

**Historiker** [hɪs'toːrikɐ] *m* (*-s*; -), **His'torikerin** *f* (-; *-nen*) historian; **his'torisch** *adj* historical; historic (*event etc*)
**Hitliste** ['hɪtlɪstə] *f* top 40 *etc*, charts
**Hitze** ['hɪtsə] *f* (-; *no pl*) heat
'**Hitzewelle** *f* heat wave
'**hitzig** *adj* hot-tempered, peppery; heated (*debate etc*)
'**Hitzkopf** *m* hothead
'**Hitzschlag** *m* MED heatstroke
**HIV|-negativ** [haːʔiːfau'neːgatiːf] *adj* MED HIV negative; **~-positiv** *adj* MED HIV positive; **~-Positive** *m, f* (*-n*; *-n*) MED HIV carrier
**H-Milch** ['haːmɪlç] *f Br* long-life milk
**hob** [hoːp] *pret of* ***heben***
**Hobby** ['hɔbi] *n* (*-s*; *-s*) hobby
'**Hobby...** *in cpds* amateur ...
**Hobel** ['hoːbəl] *m* (*-s*; -) TECH plane
'**Hobelbank** *f* (-; *-bänke*) TECH carpenter's bench
'**hobeln** *v/t* (*ge-*, *h*) TECH plane
**hoch** [hoːx] *adj and adv* high; tall; *fig* heavy (*fine etc*); distinguished (*guest*); great, old (*age*); deep (*snow*); ***10 ~ 4*** MATH 10 to the power of 4; ***3000 Meter ~*** *fly etc* at an altitude of 3,000 meters; ***in hohem Maße*** highly, greatly; ***~ verschuldet*** heavily in debt; F ***das ist mir zu ~*** that's above me
**Hoch** *n* (*-s*; *-s*) METEOR high (*a. fig*)
'**Hochachtung** *f* (deep) respect (***vor*** *dat* for); '**hochachtungsvoll** *adv* Yours sincerely
'**Hoch|bau** *m* (*-[e]s*; *no pl*) ***Hoch- und Tiefbau*** structural and civil engineering; **~betrieb** F *m* (*-[e]s*; *no pl*) rush
'**hochdeutsch** *adj* High *or* standard German
'**Hoch|druck** *m* high pressure (*a. fig*); **~ebene** *f* plateau, tableland; **~form** *f*: ***in ~*** in top form *or* shape; **~fre,quenz** *f* ELECTR high frequency; **~gebirge** *n* high mountains; **~genuss** *m* real treat
'**hochgezüchtet** *adj* ZO, TECH highbred, TECH *a.* sophisticated; MOT tuned up, F souped up
**hochhackig** ['hoːxhakɪç] *adj* high-heeled
'**Hoch|haus** *n* high rise, tower block; **~konjunk,tur** *f* ECON boom; **~land** *n* highlands; **~leistungs...** *in cpds* *...sport etc*: high-performance ...
'**Hochmut** *m* arrogance; **hochmütig** ['hoːxmyːtɪç] *adj* arrogant
'**Hochofen** *m* TECH blast furnace
'**hochpro,zentig** *adj* high-proof
'**Hoch|rechnung** *f* projection; POL computer prediction; **~sai,son** *f* peak (*or* height of the) season; **~schulabschluss** *m* degree; **~schulausbildung** *f* higher education; **~schule** *f* university; college; academy; **~seefischerei** *f* deep-sea fishing; **~sommer** *m* midsummer; **~spannung** *f* ELECTR high tension (*a. fig*) *or* voltage; **~sprung** *m* SPORT high jump
**höchst** [høːçst] **1.** *adj* highest, *fig a.* supreme; extreme **2.** *adv* highly, most, extremely; '**Höchst...** *in cpds mst* maximum ..., top ...
**Hochstapler** ['hoːxʃtaːplɐ] *m* (*-s*; -), '**Hochstaplerin** *f* (-; *-nen*) impostor, swindler
'**höchstens** *adv* at (the) most, at best
'**Höchst|form** *f* SPORT top form *or* shape; **~geschwindigkeit** *f* top speed (***mit*** at); speed limit; **~leistung** *f* SPORT record (performance); TECH maximum output; **~maß** *n* maximum (***an*** *dat* of)
'**höchstwahr'scheinlich** *adv* most likely *or* probably
'**Hochtechnolo,gie** *f* high technology, hi tech
'**hochtrabend** *adj* pompous
'**Hochverrat** *m* high treason
'**Hochwasser** *n* high tide; flood
**hochwertig** ['hoːxveːɐtɪç] *adj* high-grade, high-quality
**Hochzeit** ['hɔxtsait] *f* (-; *-en*) wedding
'**Hochzeits...** *in cpds ...geschenk*, *...kleid*, *...tag etc*: wedding ...; **~reise** *f* honeymoon
**Hocke** ['hɔkə] *f* (-; *-n*) crouch, squat
'**hocken** *v/i* (*ge-*, *h*) squat, crouch; F sit
**Hocker** ['hɔkɐ] *m* (*-s*; -) stool
**Höcker** ['hœkɐ] *m* (*-s*; -) ZO hump
**Hockey** ['hɔki] *n* (*-s*; *no pl*) SPORT field hockey, *Br* hockey
**Hoden** ['hoːdən] *m* (*-s*; -) ANAT testicle
**Hof** [hoːf] *m* (*-[e]s*; *Höfe* ['høːfə]) yard; AGR farm; court(yard); court; **~dame** *f* lady-in-waiting
**hoffen** ['hɔfən] *v/i and v/t* (*ge-*, *h*) hope (***auf*** *acc* for); trust (in); ***das Beste ~*** hope for the best; ***ich hoffe es*** I hope so; ***ich hoffe nicht, ich will es nicht ~*** I

hope not; 'hoffentlich *adv* I hope, let's hope, hopefully; '**Hoffnung** *f* (-; -*en*) hope (**auf** *acc* of); ***sich ~en machen*** have hopes; ***die ~ aufgeben*** lose hope
'**hoffnungslos** *adj* hopeless
'**hoffnungsvoll** *adj* hopeful; promising
**höflich** ['hø:flɪç] *adj* polite, courteous (**zu** to); '**Höflichkeit** *f* (-; *no pl*) politeness, courtesy
**Höhe** ['hø:ə] *f* (-; -*n*) height; AVIAT, MATH, ASTR, GEOGR altitude; peak (*a. fig*); *fig* amount; level; extent (*of damage etc*); MUS pitch; ***auf gleicher ~ mit*** on a level with; ***in die ~*** up; F ***ich bin nicht ganz auf der ~*** I'm not feeling up to the mark
**Hoheit** ['ho:hait] *f* (-; *no pl*) POL sovereignty; Highness
'**Hoheits|gebiet** *n* territory; **~gewässer** *pl* territorial waters; **~zeichen** *n* national emblem
'**Höhen|luft** *f* mountain air; **~messer** *m* altimeter; **~ruder** *n* AVIAT elevator; **~sonne®** *f* MED ultraviolet lamp, sunlamp; **~zug** *m* mountain chain
'**Höhepunkt** *m* climax, culmination, height, peak; highlight
**hohl** [ho:l] *adj* hollow (*a. fig*)
**Höhle** ['hø:lə] *f* (-; -*n*) cave, cavern; ZO hole, burrow; den, lair
'**Hohl|maß** *n* measure of capacity; **~raum** *m* hollow, cavity; **~spiegel** *m* concave mirror
**Hohn** [ho:n] *m* (-[*e*]*s*; *no pl*) derision, scorn; '**Hohngelächter** *n* jeers, jeering laughter; **höhnisch** ['hø:nɪʃ] *adj* derisive, scornful; ***~es Lächeln*** sneer
**holen** ['ho:lən] *v/t* (*ge-*, *h*) (go and) get, fetch, go for; draw (*breath*); call (*s.o., the police etc*); ***~ lassen*** send for; ***sich ~*** catch, get (*a cold etc*); seek (*advice*)
**Holland** ['hɔlant] Holland, *the* Netherlands; **Holländer** ['hɔlɛndɐ] *m* (-*s*; -) Dutchman; **Hol'länderin** ['hɔlɛndərɪn] *f* (-; -*nen*) Dutchwoman; '**holländisch** *adj* Dutch
**Hölle** ['hœlə] *f* (-; *no pl*) hell
'**Höllenlärm** F *m a* hell of a noise
**Holler** ['hɔlɐ] *Austrian m* (-*s*; -) BOT elder
**höllisch** ['hœlɪʃ] *adj* infernal, F hellish
**holperig** ['hɔlpərɪç] *adj* bumpy (*a. fig*), rough, uneven; *fig* clumsy (*style etc*)
**holpern** ['hɔlpɐn] *v/i* (*ge-*, *sein*) jolt, bump; *fig* be bumpy
**Holunder** [ho'lʊndɐ] *m* (-*s*; -) BOT elder
**Holz** [hɔlts] *n* (-*es*; *Hölzer* ['hœltsɐ]) wood; lumber, *Br a.* timber; ***aus ~*** (made) of wood, wooden; ***~ hacken*** chop wood; **~blasinstru,ment** *n* MUS woodwind (instrument)
**hölzern** ['hœltsɐn] *adj* wooden, *fig a.* clumsy
'**Holz|fäller** ['hɔltsfɛlɐ] *m* (-*s*; -) woodcutter, lumberjack; **~hammer** *m* mallet; *fig* sledgehammer
**holzig** ['hɔltsɪç] *adj* woody; stringy
'**Holz|kohle** *f* charcoal; **~schnitt** *m* woodcut; **~schnitzer** *m* wood carver; **~schuh** *m* clog; **~weg** *fig m*: ***auf dem ~ sein*** be barking up the wrong tree; **~wolle** *f* wood shavings, excelsior; **~wurm** *m* ZO woodworm
**homöopathisch** [homøo'pa:tɪʃ] *adj* hom(o)eopathic
**homosexuell** [homozɛ'ksuɛl] *adj* homosexual
**Honig** ['ho:nɪç] *m* (-*s*; -*e*) honey
'**Honigwabe** *f* honeycomb
**Honorar** [hono'ra:ɐ] *n* (-*s*; -*e*) fee
**honorieren** [hono'ri:rən] *v/t* (*no -ge-*, *h*) pay (a fee to); *fig* appreciate, reward
**Hopfen** ['hɔpfən] *m* (-*s*; -) BOT hop; *brewing*: hops
**hoppla** ['hɔpla] *int* (wh)oops!
**hopsen** ['hɔpsən] F *v/i* (*ge-*, *sein*) hop, jump
**Hörappa,rat** ['hø:ɐˀapara:t] *m* hearing aid
**hörbar** ['hø:ɐba:ɐ] *adj* audible
**horchen** ['hɔrçən] *v/i* (*ge-*, *h*) listen (**auf** *acc* to); eavesdrop; **Horcher** ['hɔrçɐ] *m* (-*s*; -) eavesdropper
**Horde** ['hɔrdə] *f* (-; -*n*) horde (*a.* ZO), *contp a.* mob, gang
**hören** ['hø:rən] *v/i and v/t* (*ge-*, *h*) hear; listen to; obey, listen; ***~ auf*** (*acc*) listen to; ***von j-m ~*** hear from (*or* of, about) s.o.; ***er hört schwer*** his hearing is bad; ***hör*(*t*) *mal!*** listen!; look (here)!; ***nun*** *or* ***also hör*(*t*) *mal!*** wait a minute!, now look *or* listen here!; **Hörer** ['hø:rɐ] *m* (-*s*; -) listener; TEL receiver; '**Hörerin** ['hø:rərɪn] *f* (-; -*nen*) listener
**Hör|fehler** ['hø:ɐfe:lɐ] *m* MED hearing defect; **~gerät** *n* hearing aid
**hörig** ['hø:rɪç] *adj*: ***j-m ~ sein*** be s.o.'s slave
**Horizont** [hori'tsɔnt] *m* (-[*e*]*s*; -*e*) hori-

H

zon (*a. fig*); ***s-n ~ erweitern*** broaden one's mind; ***das geht über meinen ~*** that's beyond me; **horizontal** [horitsɔn'ta:l] *adj* horizontal

**Hormon** [hɔr'mo:n] *n* (*-s; -e*) hormone

**Horn** [hɔrn] *n* (*-[e]s; Hörner* ['hœrnɐ]) horn; **~haut** *f* horny skin, callus(es); ANAT cornea

**Hornisse** [hɔr'nisə] *f* (*-; -n*) ZO hornet

**Horoskop** [horo'sko:p] *n* (*-s; -e*) horoscope

**Hör|rohr** ['hø:ɐro:ɐ] *n* MED stethoscope; **~saal** *m* lecture hall, auditorium; **~spiel** *n* radio play; **~weite** *f*: ***in*** (***außer***) **~** within (out of) earshot

**Höschen** ['hø:sçən] *n* (*-s; -*) panties

**Hose** ['ho:zə] *f* (*-; -n*) (***e-e ~*** a pair of) pants, *Br* trousers; slacks; shorts

'**Hosen|anzug** *m* pants (*Br* trouser) suit; **~schlitz** *m* fly; **~tasche** *f* trouser pocket; **~träger** *pl* (a pair of) suspenders *or Br* braces

**Hospital** [hɔspi'ta:l] *n* (*-s; -täler* [hɔspi'tɛ:lɐ]) hospital

**Hostie** ['hɔstjə] *f* (*-; -n*) REL host

**Hotel** [ho'tɛl] *n* (*-s; -s*) hotel; **~di,rektor** *m* hotel manager; **~fach** *n* (*-[e]s; no pl*) hotel business; **~zimmer** *n* hotel room

**HP** *abbr of* ***Halbpension*** half-board

**Hr**(**n**). *abbr of* ***Herrn*** Mr

**Hubraum** ['hu:praum] *m* MOT cubic capacity

**hübsch** [hʏpʃ] *adj* pretty, nice (-looking), cute; *fig* nice, lovely

**Hubschrauber** ['hu:pʃraubɐ] *m* (*-s; -*) helicopter; **~landeplatz** *m* heliport

**Huf** [hu:f] *m* (*-[e]s; -e*) ZO hoof

'**Hufeisen** *n* horseshoe

**Hüfte** ['hʏftə] *f* (*-; -n*) ANAT hip

'**Hüftgelenk** *n* ANAT hip joint

'**Hüftgürtel** *m* girdle

**Hügel** ['hy:gəl] *m* (*-s; -*) hill; '**hügelig** *adj* hilly; '**Hügelland** *n* downs

**Huhn** [hu:n] *n* (*-[e]s; Hühner* ['hy:nɐ]) ZO chicken; hen; **Hühnchen** ['hy:nçən] *n* (*-s; -*) chicken; F ***mit j-m ein ~ zu rupfen haben*** have a bone to pick with s.o.

'**Hühner|auge** *n* MED corn; **~brühe** *f* chicken broth; **~ei** *n* hen's egg; **~farm** *f* poultry *or* chicken farm; **~hof** *m* poultry *or* chicken yard; **~leiter** *f* chicken ladder; **~stall** *m* henhouse

**huldigen** ['hʊldɪgən] *v/i* (*ge-, h*) pay homage to; *fig* indulge in

**Hülle** ['hʏlə] *f* (*-; -n*) cover(ing), wrap (-ping); jacket, *Br* sleeve; sheath; ***in ~ und Fülle*** in abundance; '**hüllen** *v/t* (*ge-, h*) **~** ***in*** (*acc*) wrap (up) in, cover in

**Hülse** ['hʏlzə] *f* (*-; -n*) BOT pod; husk; TECH case; '**Hülsenfrüchte** *pl* pulse

**human** [hu'ma:n] *adj* humane

**humanitär** [humani'tɛ:ɐ] *adj* humanitarian; **Humanität** [humani'tɛ:t] *f* (*-; no pl*) humanity

**Hummel** ['hʊməl] *f* (*-; -n*) ZO bumblebee

**Hummer** ['hʊmɐ] *m* (*-s; -*) ZO lobster

**Humor** [hu'mo:ɐ] *m* (*-s; no pl*) humo(u)r; (***keinen***) **~** ***haben*** have a (no) sense of humo(u)r; **Humorist** [humo'rɪst] *m* (*-en; -en*) humorist; **humo'ristisch**, **hu'morvoll** *adj* humorous

**humpeln** ['hʊmpəln] *v/i* (*ge-, h*) hobble; (*ge-, sein*) limp

**Hund** [hʊnt] *m* (*-[e]s; -e*) ZO dog

**Hunde|hütte** ['hʊndəhʏtə] *f* doghouse, *Br* kennel; **~kuchen** *m* dog biscuit; **~leine** *f* lead, leash

'**hunde'müde** *adj* dog-tired

**hundert** ['hʊndɐt] *adj* a *or* one hundred; ***zu hunderten*** by the hundreds

'**hundertfach** *adj* hundredfold

**Hundert'jahrfeier** *f* centenary, centennial; **hundertjährig** ['hʊndɐtjɛ:rɪç] *adj* a hundred years old; a hundred years of

'**hundertste** *adj* hundredth

**Hündin** ['hʏndɪn] *f* (*-; -nen*) ZO bitch

**hündisch** ['hʏndɪʃ] *adj* doglike, slavish

**Hüne** ['hy:nə] *m* (*-n; -n*) giant

'**Hünengrab** *n* dolmen

**Hunger** ['hʊŋɐ] *m* (*-s; no pl*) hunger; ***~ bekommen*** get hungry; ***~ haben*** be hungry; ***vor ~ sterben*** die of starvation, starve to death

'**Hungerlohn** *m* starvation wages

'**hungern** *v/i* (*ge-, h*) go hungry, starve

'**Hungersnot** *f* famine

'**Hungerstreik** *m* hunger strike

'**Hungertod** *m* (death from) starvation

**hungrig** ['hʊŋrɪç] *adj* hungry (***nach, auf*** *acc* for)

**Hupe** ['hu:pə] *f* (*-; -n*) MOT horn

'**hupen** *v/i* (*ge-, h*) MOT sound one's horn, hoot, honk

**hüpfen** ['hʏpfən] *v/i* (*ge, sein*) hop, skip; *ball etc*: bounce

**Hürde** ['hʏrdə] *f* (*-; -n*) hurdle, *fig a.* ob-

stacle; zo fold, pen
'**Hürdenlauf** *m* SPORT hurdles
'**Hürdenläufer** *m*, '**Hürdenläuferin** *f* SPORT hurdler
**Hure** ['hu:rə] *f* (-; *-n*) whore, prostitute
**huschen** ['hʊʃən] *v/i* (*ge-*, *sein*) flit, dart
**hüsteln** ['hy:stəln] *v/i* (*ge-*, *h*) cough slightly; *iro* hem; **husten** ['hu:stən] *v/i* (*ge-*, *h*), '**Husten** *m* (*-s*; *no pl*) cough
'**Husten|bon**,**bon** *m*, *n* cough drop; **~saft** *m* PHARM cough syrup
**Hut**[1] [hu:t] *m* (*-[e]s*; *Hüte* ['hy:tə]) hat; ***den ~ aufsetzen*** (***abnehmen***) put on (take off) one's hat
**Hut**[2] *f*: ***auf der ~ sein*** be on one's guard (***vor*** *dat* against)
**hüten** ['hy:tən] *v/t* (*ge-*, *h*) guard, protect, watch over; zo herd, mind; look after; ***das Bett ~*** be confined to (one's) bed; ***sich ~ vor*** (*dat*) beware of; ***sich ~, et. zu tun*** be careful not to do s.th.
'**Hutkrempe** *f* (hat) brim
**hutschen** ['hʊtʃən] *Austrian v/t and v/i* → ***schaukeln***
**Hütte** ['hʏtə] *f* (-; *-n*) hut; *contp* shack; cottage, cabin; mountain hut; TECH ironworks
**Hyäne** ['hyɛ:nə] *f* (-; *-n*) zo hy(a)ena
**Hyazinthe** [hya'tsɪntə] *f* (-; *-n*) BOT hyacinth
**Hydrant** [hy'drant] *m* (*-en*; *-en*) hydrant
**hydraulisch** [hy'draulɪʃ] *adj* hydraulic
**Hydrokultur** ['hy:drokʊltu:ɐ] *f* hydroponics
**Hygiene** [hy'gje:nə] *f* (-; *no pl*) hygiene
**hygienisch** [hy'gje:nɪʃ] *adj* hygienic
**Hypnose** [hʏp'no:zə] *f* (-; *-n*) hypnosis; **Hypnotiseur** [hʏpnoti'zø:ɐ] *m* (*-s*; *-e*) hypnotist; **hypnotisieren** [hʏpnoti'zi:rən] *v/t* (*no -ge-*, *h*) hypnotize
**Hypotenuse** [hypote'nu:zə] *f* (-; *-n*) MATH hypotenuse
**Hypothek** [hypo'te:k] *f* (-; *-en*) ECON mortgage; ***e-e ~ aufnehmen*** take out a mortgage
**Hypothese** [hypo'te:zə] *f* (-; *-n*) hypothesis, supposition; **hypothetisch** [hypo'te:tɪʃ] *adj* hypothetical
**Hysterie** [hʏste'ri:] *f* (-; *-n*) hysteria
**hysterisch** [hʏs'te:rɪʃ] *adj* hysterical

# I

**i. A.** *abbr of* ***im Auftrag*** p. p., per procuration
**ICE**® [i:tse:'ʔe:] *abbr of* ***Intercityexpresszug*** intercity express (train)
**ich** [ɪç] *pers pron* I; ***~ selbst*** (I) myself; ***~ bin's*** it's me
**ideal** [ide'a:l] *adj*, **Ide'al** *n* (*-s*; *-e*) ideal; **Idealismus** [idea'lɪsmʊs] *m* (-; *no pl*) idealism; **Idea'list(in)** (*-en*; *-en*/-; *-nen*) idealist
**Idee** [i'de:] *f* (-; *-n*) idea
**identifizieren** [idɛntifi'tsi:rən] *v/t* (*no -ge-*, *h*) identify; ***sich ~ mit*** identify with; **identisch** [i'dɛntɪʃ] *adj* identical
**Identitätskarte** [idɛnti'tɛ:tskartə] *Austrian f* identity card
**Ideologe** [ideo'lo:gə] *m* (*-n*; *-n*) ideologist; **Ideologie** [ideolo'gi:] *f* (-; *-n*) ideology; **ideo'logisch** *adj* ideological
**idiomatisch** [idio'ma:tɪʃ] *adj* LING idiomatic; ***~er Ausdruck*** idiom
**Idiot** [i'djo:t] *m* (*-en*; *-en*) idiot
**Idi'otenhügel** F *m skiing*: nursery slope
**idi'otisch** *adj* idiotic
**Idol** [i'do:l] *n* (*-s*; *-e*) idol
**Idyll** [i'dʏl] *n* (*-s*; *-e*), **I'dylle** *f* (-; *-n*) idyl(l); **i'dyllisch** *adj* idyllic
**Igel** ['i:gəl] *m* (*-s*; -) zo hedgehog
**Iglu** ['i:glu] *m* (*-s*; *-s*) igloo
**ignorieren** [ɪgno'ri:rən] *v/t* (*no -ge-*, *h*) ignore, disregard
**i. H.** *abbr of* ***im Hause*** on the premises
**ihr** [i:ɐ] *poss pron* her; *pl* their; ***Ihr*** your; **ihrerseits** ['i:rɐzaits] *adv* on her (*pl* their) part; **ihresgleichen** ['i:rəsglaiçən] *indef pron* her (*pl* their) equals, people like herself (*pl* themselves); **ihretwegen** ['i:rətvegən] *adv* for her (*pl* their) sake
**Ikone** [i'ko:nə] *f* (-; *-n*) icon
**illegal** ['ɪlega:l] *adj* JUR illegal
**illegitim** [ɪlegi'ti:m] *adj* JUR illegitimate
**Illusion** [ɪlu'zjo:n] *f* (-; *-en*) illusion
**illusorisch** [ɪlu'zo:rɪʃ] *adj* illusory
**Illustration** [ɪlʊstra'tsjo:n] *f* (-; *-en*) illustration; **illustrieren** [ɪlʊs'tri:rən]

*v/t* (*no -ge-*, *h*) illustrate; **Illustrierte** [ɪlʊsˈtriːɐtə] *f* (*-n*; *-n*) magazine

**im** [ɪm] *prep* in the; **~ *Bett*** in bed; **~ *Kino** etc* at the cinema *etc*; **~ *Erdgeschoss*** on the first (*Br* ground) floor; **~ *Mai*** in May; **~ *Jahre 1997*** in (the year) 1997; **~ *Stehen*** (while) standing up; **→ *in***

**imaginär** [imagiˈnɛːɐ] *adj* imaginary

**Imbiss** [ˈɪmbɪs] *m* (*-es*; *-e*) snack

**ˈImbissstube** *f* snack bar

**imitieren** [imiˈtiːrən] *v/t* (*no -ge-*, *h*) imitate

**Imker** [ˈɪmkɐ] *m* (*-s*; *-*) beekeeper

**immatrikulieren** [ɪmatrikuˈliːrən] *v/t and v/refl* (*no -ge-*, *h*) UNIV enrol(l), register

**immer** [ˈɪmɐ] *adv* always, all the time; **~ *mehr*** more and more; **~ *wieder*** again and again; ***für* ~** for ever, for good

**ˈImmergrün** *n* BOT evergreen

**ˈimmerˈhin** *adv* after all

**ˈimmerˈzu** *adv* all the time, constantly

**Immigrant** [ɪmiˈgrant] *m* (*-en*; *-en*), **Immiˈgrantin** *f* (*-*; *-nen*) immigrant

**Immissionen** [ɪmɪˈsjoːnən] *pl* (harmful effects of) noise, pollutants *etc*

**Immobilien** [ɪmoˈbiːliən] *pl* real estate; **~makler** *m* realtor, real estate agent

**immun** [ɪˈmuːn] *adj* immune (***gegen*** to, against, from); **~ *machen*** → **immunisieren** [ɪmuniˈziːrən] *v/t* (*no -ge-*, *h*) immunize; **Immunität** [ɪmuniˈtɛːt] *f* (*-*; *no pl*) immunity; **Imˈmunschwäche** *f* (*-*; *-n*) MED immunodeficiency; **Imˈmunsystem** *n* (*-s*; *-e*) MED immune system

**Imperativ** [ˈɪmperatiːf] *m* (*-s*; *-e*) LING imperative (mood)

**Imperfekt** [ˈɪmpɛrfɛkt] *n* (*-s*; *-e*) LING past (tense)

**Imperialismus** [ɪmperjaˈlɪsmʊs] *m* (*-*; *no pl*) imperialism; **Imperialist** [ɪmperjaˈlɪst] *m* (*-en*; *-en*), **imperiaˈlistisch** *adj* imperialist

**impfen** [ˈɪmpfən] *v/t* (*ge-*, *h*) MED vaccinate

**ˈImpf|pass** *m* MED vaccination card; **~schein** *m* MED vaccination certificate; **~stoff** *m* MED vaccine, serum

**ˈImpfung** *f* (*-*; *-en*) MED vaccination

**imponieren** [ɪmpoˈniːrən] *v/i* (*no -ge-*, *h*) ***j-m* ~** impress s.o.

**Import** [ɪmˈpɔrt] *m* (*-[e]s*; *-e*) ECON import(ation); **Importeur** [ɪmpɔrˈtøːɐ] *m* (*-s*; *-e*) ECON importer; **importieren** [ɪmpɔrˈtiːrən] *v/t* (*no -ge-*, *h*) ECON import

**imposant** [ɪmpoˈzant] *adj* impressive, imposing

**imprägnieren** [ɪmprɛˈgniːrən] *v/t* (*no -ge-*, *h*), **imprägniert** [ɪmprɛˈgniːɐt] *adj* waterproof

**improvisieren** [ɪmproviˈziːrən] *v/t and v/i* (*no -ge-*, *h*) improvise

**Impuls** [ɪmˈpʊls] *m* (*-es*; *-e*) impulse; stimulus

**impulsiv** [ɪmpʊlˈziːf] *adj* impulsive

**imstande** [ɪmˈʃtandə] *adj*: **~ *sein zu** inf* be capable of *ger*

**in** [ɪn] *prp* (*dat and acc*) **1.** in, at; within, inside; into, in; ***überall* ~** all over; **~ *der Stadt*** in town; **~ *der Schule*** at school; **~ *die Schule*** to school; ***~s Kino*** to the cinema; ***~s Bett*** to bed; ***warst du schon mal* ~ ...?** have you ever been to ...?; → ***im*** **2.** in, at, during; **~ *dieser*** (***der nächsten***) ***Woche*** this (next) week; **~ *diesem Alter*** (***Augenblick***) at this age (moment); **~ *der Nacht*** at night; ***heute* ~ *acht Tagen*** a week from now; ***heute* ~ *e-m Jahr*** this time next year; → ***im*** **3.** in, at; ***gut sein* ~** (*dat*) be good at; **~ *Eile*** in a hurry; **~ *Behandlung*** (***Reparatur***) under treatment (repair); ***~s Deutsche*** into German; → ***im*** **4.** F **~ *sein*** be in

**ˈInbegriff** *m* epitome

**ˈinbegriffen** *adj* ECON included

**inˈdem** *cj* while, as; by *doing s.th.*

**Inder** [ˈɪndɐ] *m* (*-s*; *-*), **Inderin** [ˈɪndərɪn] *f* (*-*; *-nen*) Indian

**Indian** [ˈɪndjaːn] *Austrian m* (*-s*; *-e*) ZO turkey (cock)

**Indianer** [ɪnˈdjaːnɐ] *m* (*-s*; *-*), **Indianerin** [ɪnˈdjaːnərɪn] *f* (*-*; *-nen*) Native American, (American) Indian

**Indien** [ˈɪndjən] India

**Indikativ** [ˈɪndikatiːf] *m* (*-s*; *-e*) LING indicative (mood)

**indirekt** [ˈɪndirɛkt] *adj* indirect, LING *a.* reported

**indisch** [ˈɪndɪʃ] *adj* Indian

**indiskret** [ˈɪndɪskreːt] *adj* indiscreet

**Indiskretion** [ɪndɪskreˈtsjoːn] *f* (*-*; *-en*) indiscretion

**indiskutabel** [ɪndɪskuˈtaːbəl] *adj* out of the question

I

**individuell** [ɪndivi'duɛl] *adj*, **Individuum** [ɪndi'vi:duʊm] *n (-s; -en)* individual
**indiz** [ɪn'di:ts] *n (-es; -ien)* indication, sign; *pl* JUR circumstantial evidence
**industrialisieren** [ɪndʊstriali'zi:rən] *v/t (no -ge-, h)* industrialize; **Industriali'sierung** *f (-; no pl)* industrialization
**Industrie** [ɪndʊs'tri:] *f (-; -n)* industry
**Indus'triegebiet** *n* industrial area
**industriell** [ɪndʊstri'ɛl] *adj* industrial
**Industri'elle** *m (-n; -n)* industrialist
**inei'nander** *adv* into one another; **~ verliebt** in love with each other; **~greifen** *v/t (irr,* **greifen**, *sep, -ge-, h)* TECH interlock *(a. fig)*
**Infanterie** ['ɪnfantəri:] *f (-; -n)* MIL infantry; **Infanterist** ['ɪnfantərɪst] *m (-en; -en)* MIL infantryman
**Infektion** [ɪnfɛk'tsjo:n] *f (-; -en)* MED infection; **Infekti'onskrankheit** *f* infectious disease
**Infinitiv** ['ɪnfiniti:f] *m (-s; -e)* LING infinitive (mood)
**infizieren** [ɪnfi'tsi:rən] *v/t (no -ge-, h)* MED infect
**Inflation** [ɪnfla'tsjo:n] *f (-; -en)* inflation
**in'folge** *prp (gen)* owing to, due to
**infolge'dessen** *adv* consequently
**Informatik** [ɪnfɔr'ma:tɪk] *f (-; no pl)* computer science; **Infor'matiker(in)** [ɪnfɔr'ma:tikɐ, ɪnfɔr'ma:tikərɪn] *m(f) (-s; -/-; -nen)* computer scientist
**Information** [ɪnfɔrma'tsjo:n] *f (-; -en)* information; ***die neuesten ~en*** the latest information
**informieren** [ɪnfɔr'mi:rən] *v/t (no -ge-, h)* inform; ***falsch ~*** misinform
**in'frage**: ***~ stellen*** question; put in jeopardy; ***~ kommen*** be possible *(person:* eligible); ***nicht ~ kommen*** be out of the question
**infrarot** ['ɪnfraro:t] *adj* PHYS infrared
**'Infrastruk,tur** *f* infrastructure
**Ing.** *abbr of* ***Ingenieur*** eng., engineer
**Ingenieur** [ɪnʒe'njø:ɐ] *m (-s; -e)*, **Inge'nieurin** [ɪnʒe'njø:rɪn] *f (-; -nen)* engineer
**Ingwer** ['ɪŋvɐ] *m (-s; no pl)* ginger
**Inhaber** ['ɪnha:bɐ] *m (-s; -)*, **'Inhaberin** *f (-; -nen)* owner, proprietor (proprietress); holder
**Inhalt** ['ɪnhalt] *m (-[e]s; -e)* contents; volume, capacity; *fig* meaning
**'Inhalts|angabe** *f* summary; **~verzeichnis** *n* table of contents
**Initiative** [initsja'ti:və] *f (-; -n)* initiative; ***die ~ ergreifen*** take the initiative
**inklusive** [ɪnklu'zi:və] *prp* ECON including
**inkonsequent** ['ɪnkɔnzekvɛnt] *adj* inconsistent
**In-'Kraft-Treten** *n (-s; no pl)* coming into force, taking effect
**'Inland** *n (-[e]s; no pl)* home (country); **~flug** *m* domestic *(or* internal) flight
**inländisch** ['ɪnlɛndɪʃ] *adj* domestic, home, inland
**Inlett** ['ɪnlɛt] *n (-[e]s; -e)* ticking
**in'mitten** *prp (gen)* in the middle of
**innen** ['ɪnən] *adv* inside; ***nach ~*** inwards
**'Innen|archi,tekt** *m*, **~archi,tektin** *f* interior designer; **~architek,tur** *f* interior design; **~mi,nister(in)** minister of the interior; Secretary of the Interior, *Br* Home Secretary; **~minis,terium** *n* ministry of the interior; Department of the Interior, *Br* Home Office; **~poli,tik** *f* domestic politics
**'innenpo,litisch** *adj* domestic, internal
**'Innenseite** *f*: ***auf der ~*** (on the) inside
**'Innenstadt** *f* downtown, (city *or* town) center *or Br* centre
**inner** ['ɪnɐ] *adj* inside; *fig* inner; MED, POL internal; **Innere** ['ɪnərə] *n (-n; no pl)* interior, inside
**Innereien** [ɪnə'raiən] *pl* GASTR offal
**'innerhalb** *prp (gen)* within
**'innerlich** *adj* internal *(a.* MED)
**innert** ['ɪnɐt] *Swiss prp (gen or dat)* within
**innig** ['ɪnɪç] *adj* tender, affectionate
**Innung** ['ɪnʊŋ] *f (-; -en)* guild
**'inoffiziell** *adj* unofficial
**ins** [ɪns] → ***in***
**Insasse** ['ɪnzasə] *m (-n; -n)* inmate; MOT passenger; **'Insassenversicherung** *f* MOT passenger insurance; **'Insassin** *f (-; -nen)* inmate; MOT passenger
**insbe'sondere** *adv* (e)specially
**'Inschrift** *f* inscription, legend
**Insekt** [ɪn'zɛkt] *n (-s; -en)* ZO insect, bug
**In'sektenstich** *m* insect bite
**Insel** ['ɪnzəl] *f (-; -n)* island
**'Inselbewohner** *m* islander
**Inserat** [ɪnze'ra:t] *n (-[e]s; -e)* advertisement, F ad; **inserieren** [ɪnze'ri:rən] *v/t*

*and v/i (no -ge-, h)* advertise
**insge'heim** *adv* secretly
**insge'samt** *adv* altogether, in all
**inso'fern 1.** *adv* as far as that goes **2.** *cj*: **~ als** in so far as
**Inspektion** [ɪnspɛk'tsjoːn] *f (-; -en)* inspection; MOT service
**Inspektor** [ɪn'spɛktoːɐ] *m (-s; -en* [ɪnspɛk'toːrən]), **Inspek'torin** *f (-; -nen)* inspector
**inspizieren** [ɪnspi'tsiːrən] *v/t (no -ge-, h)* inspect
**Installateur** [ɪnstala'tøːɐ] *m (-s; -e)* plumber; (gas *or* electrical) fitter
**installieren** [ɪnsta'liːrən] *v/t (no -ge-, h)* put in, fit, instal(l)
**instand** [ɪn'ʃtant] *adv*: **~ halten** keep in good condition *or* repair; TECH maintain; **~ setzen** repair
**In'standhaltung** *f (-; no pl)* maintenance
**'inständig** *adv*: **j-n ~ bitten** implore s.o.
**In'standsetzung** *f (-; -en)* repair
**Instanz** [ɪn'stants] *f (-; -en)* authority; JUR instance
**Instinkt** [ɪn'stɪŋkt] *m (-[e]s; -e)* instinct
**instinktiv** [ɪnstɪŋk'tiːf] *adv* instinctively
**Institut** [ɪnsti'tuːt] *n (-[e]s; -e)* institute
**Institution** [ɪnstitu'tsjoːn] *f (-; -en)* institution
**Instrument** [ɪnstru'mɛnt] *n (-[e]s; -e)* instrument
**inszenieren** [ɪnstse'niːrən] *v/t (no -ge-, h)* (put on) stage; *film*: direct; *fig* stage
**Insze'nierung** *f (-; -en)* production
**intellektuell** [ɪntɛlɛk'tuɛl] *adj*, **Intellektu'elle** *m, f (-n; -n)* intellectual, F highbrow
**intelligent** [ɪntɛli'gɛnt] *adj* intelligent
**Intelligenz** [ɪntɛli'gɛnts] *f (-; -en)* intelligence; **~quoti,ent** *m* I.Q.
**Intendant** [ɪntɛn'dant] *m (-en; -en)*, **Inten'dantin** *f (-; -nen)* THEA *etc* director
**intensiv** [ɪntɛn'ziːf] *adj* intensive; intense; **Inten'sivkurs** *m* crash course
**interessant** [ɪntərɛ'sant] *adj* interesting; **Interesse** [ɪntə'rɛsə] *n (-s; -n)* interest (**an** *dat*, **für** in)
**Inte'ressengebiet** *n* field of interest
**Interessent** [ɪntərɛ'sɛnt] *m (-en; -en)*, **Interes'sentin** *f (-; -nen)* interested person; ECON prospect, *Br* prospective buyer
**interessieren** [ɪntərɛ'siːrən] *v/t (no -ge-, h)* interest (**für** in); **sich ~ für** take an interest in; be interested in
**intern** [ɪn'tɛrn] *adj* internal
**Internat** [ɪntɐ'naːt] *n (-[e]s; -e)* boarding school
**internatio'nal** [ɪntɐnatsjo'naːl] *adj* international
**Internet** ['ɪntɐnɛt] *n (-[s]; no pl)* Internet
**Internist** [ɪntɐ'nɪst] *m (-en; -en)*, **Inter'nistin** *f (-; -nen)* MED internist
**Interpretation** [ɪntɐpreta'tsjoːn] *f (-; -en)* interpretation; analysis
**interpretieren** [ɪntɐpre'tiːrən] *v/t (no -ge-, h)* interpret, ana|lyze, *Br* -lyse
**Interpunktion** [ɪntɐpʊŋk'tsjoːn] *f (-; no pl)* punctuation
**Intervall** [ɪntɐ'val] *n (-[e]s; -e)* interval
**intervenieren** [ɪntɐve'niːrən] *v/i (no -ge-, h)* intervene
**Interview** ['ɪntɐvjuː] *n (-s; -s)*, **interviewen** [ɪntɐ'vjuːən] *v/t (no -ge-, h)* interview
**intim** [ɪn'tiːm] *adj* intimate (**mit** with) (*a. sexually*); **Intimität** [ɪntimi'tɛːt] *f (-; no pl)* intimacy; **In'timsphäre** *f* privacy
**intolerant** ['ɪntolerant] *adj* intolerant (**gegen** of); **Intoleranz** ['ɪntolerants] *f (-; no pl)* intolerance
**intransitiv** ['ɪntranzitiːf] *adj* LING intransitive
**Intrige** [ɪn'triːgə] *f (-; -n)* intrigue, scheme, plot; **intrigieren** [ɪntri'giːrən] *v/i (no -ge-, h)* (plot and) scheme
**Invalide** [ɪnva'liːdə] *m (-n; -n)* invalid; **Inva'lidenrente** *f* disability pension
**Invalidität** [ɪnvalidi'tɛːt] *f (-; no pl)* disablement, disability
**Inventar** [ɪnvɛn'taːɐ] *n (-s; -e)* inventory, stock
**Inventur** [ɪnvɛn'tuːɐ] *f (-; -en)* ECON stocktaking; **~ machen** take stock
**investieren** [ɪnvɛs'tiːrən] *v/t (no -ge-, h)* ECON invest (*a. fig*); **Investition** [ɪnvɛsti'tsjoːn] *f (-; -en)* ECON investment
**inwiefern** [ɪnvi'fɛrn] *cj and adv* in what respect *or* way
**inwie'weit** *cj and adv* to what extent
**'Inzucht** *f* inbreeding
**in'zwischen** *adv* meanwhile, in the meantime; by now
**irdisch** ['ɪrdɪʃ] *adj* earthly, worldly

I

**Ire** ['i:rə] *m* (*-n*; *-n*) Irishman; *pl* the Irish
**irgend** ['ɪrgənt] *adv in cpds*: some…; any…; ***wenn ~ möglich*** if at all possible; ***wenn du ~ kannst*** if you possibly can; F ***~ so ein …*** some …; **~'ein(e)** *indef pron* some(one); any(one); **~'ein(e)s** *indef pron* some; any; **~etwas** something; anything; **~jemand** someone, somebody; anyone, anybody; **~'wann** *adv* sometime (or other); (at) any time; **~'wie** *adv* somehow (or other); **~'wo** *adv* somewhere; anywhere
**Irin** ['i:rɪn] *f* (*-*; *-nen*) Irishwoman; **irisch** ['i:rɪʃ] *adj* Irish; **Irland** ['ɪrlant] Ireland
**Ironie** [iro'ni:] *f* (*-*; *no pl*) irony
**ironisch** [i'ro:nɪʃ] *adj* ironic(al)
**irre** ['ɪrə] *adj* mad, crazy, insane; confused; F super, terrific
**'Irre** *m*, *f* (*-n*; *-n*) madman (madwoman), lunatic; ***wie ein ~r*** like mad *or* a madman
**'irreführen** *v/t* (*sep*, *-ge-*, *h*) mislead, lead astray; **~d** *adj* misleading
**'irre|gehen** *v/i* (*irr*, **gehen**, *sep*, *-ge-*, *sein*) go astray, *fig a.* be wrong; **~machen** *v/t* (*sep*, *-ge-*, *h*) confuse
**irren** ['ɪrən] **1.** *v/refl* (*ge-*, *h*) be wrong, be mistaken; ***sich ~*** be wrong; ***sich in et. ~*** get s.th. wrong **2.** *v/i* (*ge-*, *sein*) wander, stray, err
**irritieren** [ɪri'ti:rən] *v/t* (*no -ge-*, *h*) irritate; F confuse
**'Irrlicht** *n* (*-[e]s*; *-er*) will-o'-the-wisp
**'Irrsinn** *m* (*-[e]s*; *no pl*) madness
**'irrsinnig** *adj* insane, mad; F terrific
**Irrtum** ['ɪrtu:m] *m* (*-s*; *Irrtümer* ['ɪrty:mɐ]) error, mistake; ***im ~ sein*** be mistaken; **'irrtümlich** *adv* by mistake
**Ischias** ['ɪʃjas] *m*, *n*, *f* (*-*; *no pl*) MED sciatica
**Islam** [ɪs'la:m] *m* (*-[s]*; *no pl*) Islam
**Island** ['i:slant] Iceland
**Isländer** ['i:slɛndɐ] *m* (*-s*; *-*), **'Isländerin** ['i:slɛndərɪn] *f* (*-*; *-nen*) Icelander
**'isländisch** *adj* Icelandic
**Isolierband** [izo'li:ɐbant] *n* (*-[e]s*; *-bänder*) insulating tape; **isolieren** [izo'li:rən] *v/t* (*no -ge-*, *h*) isolate; ELECTR, TECH insulate; **Iso'lierstati,on** *f* MED isolation ward; **Iso'lierung** *f* (*-*; *-en*) isolation; ELECTR, TECH insulation
**Israel** ['ɪsrae:l] Israel
**Israeli** [ɪsra'e:li] *m* (*-[s]*; *-[s]*), *f* (*-*; *-[s]*), **israelisch** [ɪsra'e:lɪʃ] *adj* Israeli
**Italien** [i'ta:ljən] Italy; **Italiener** [ita'lje:nɐ] *m* (*-s*; *-*), **Itali'enerin** [ita'lje:nərɪn] *f* (*-*; *-nen*), **itali'enisch** *adj* Italian

# J

**ja** [ja:] *adv* yes, F *a.* yeah; PARL yea, aye; ***wenn ~*** if so; ***da ist er ~!*** well, there he is!; ***ich sagte es Ihnen ~*** I told you so; ***ich bin ~ (schließlich) …*** after all, I am …; ***tut es 'ja nicht!*** don't you dare do it!; ***sei 'ja vorsichtig!*** do be careful!; ***vergessen Sie es 'ja nicht!*** be sure not to forget it!; ***~, weißt du nicht?*** why, don't you know?; ***du kommst doch, ~?*** you're coming, aren't you?
**Jacht** [jaxt] *f* (*-*; *-en*) MAR yacht
**Jacke** ['jakə] *f* (*-*; *-n*) jacket; coat
**Jackett** [ʒa'kɛt] *n* (*-s*; *-s*) jacket, coat
**Jagd** [ja:kt] *f* (*-*; *-en*) hunt(ing) (*a. fig*); shoot(ing); *fig* chase; → ***Jagdrevier***; ***auf (die) ~ gehen*** go hunting *or* shooting; ***~ machen auf*** (*acc*) hunt (for); *a.* chase *s.o.*; **~aufseher** *m* gamekeeper; **~flugzeug** *n* MIL fighter (plane); **~hund** *m* ZO hound; **~hütte** *f* (hunting) lodge; **~re,vier** *n* hunting ground; **~schein** *m* hunting *or* shooting licen|se, *Br* -ce
**jagen** ['ja:gən] *v/t and v/i* (*ge-*, *h*) hunt; shoot; *fig* race, dash; hunt, chase; ***j-n aus dem Haus*** *etc* ***~*** drive *or* chase s.o. out of the house *etc*
**Jäger** ['jɛ:gɐ] *m* (*-s*; *-*) hunter, huntsman
**Jaguar** ['ja:gua:ɐ] *m* (*-s*; *-e*) ZO jaguar
**jäh** [jɛ:] *adj* sudden; steep
**Jahr** [ja:ɐ] *n* (*-[e]s*; *-e* ['ja:rə]) year; ***ein drei viertel ~*** nine months; ***einmal im ~*** once a year; ***im ~e 1995*** in (the year) 1995; ***ein 10 ~e altes Auto*** a ten-year-old car; ***mit 18 ~en, im Alter von 18 ~en*** at (the age of) eighteen; ***heute vor e-m ~*** a year ago today; ***die 80er-Jahre*** the eighties

**jahr'aus** *adv*: ***~, jahrein*** year in, year out; year after year
**'Jahrbuch** *n* yearbook, annual
**jahrelang** ['ja:rəlaŋ] **1.** *adj* longstanding, (many) years of **2.** *adv* for (many) years
**Jahres...** ['ja:rəs-] *in cpds ...bericht, ...bilanz, ...einkommen etc*: annual ...; **~anfang** *m* beginning of the year; **~ende** *n* end of the year; **~tag** *m* anniversary; **~wechsel** *m* turn of the year; **~zahl** *f* date, year; **~zeit** *f* season, time of (the) year
**'Jahrgang** *m* age group; PED year, class (***1995*** of '95); GASTR vintage
**Jahr'hundert** *n* (*-s*; *-e*) century; **~wende** *f* turn of the century
**jährlich** ['jɛ:ɐlɪç] **1.** *adj* annual, yearly **2.** *adv* every year, yearly, once a year
**'Jahrmarkt** *m* fair
**Jahr'tausend** *n* (*-s*; *-e*) millennium
**Jahr'zehnt** *n* (*-[e]s*; *-e*) decade
**'Jähzorn** *m* violent (fit of) temper
**'jähzornig** *adj* hot-tempered
**Jalousie** [ʒalu'zi:] *f* (*-*; *-n*) (venetian) blind
**Jammer** ['jamɐ] *m* (*-s*; *no pl*) misery; ***es ist ein ~*** it is a pity; **jämmerlich** ['jɛmɐlɪç] *adj* miserable, wretched; pitiful, sorry; ***~ versagen*** fail miserably; **'jammern** *v/i* (*ge-*, *h*) moan, lament (***über*** *acc* over, about); complain (of, about); **jammer'schade** *adj*: ***es ist ~, dass*** it's a crying shame that
**Janker** ['jaŋkɐ] *Austrian m* (*-s*; *-*) jacket
**Jänner** ['jɛnɐ] *Austrian m* (*-s*; *-*), **Januar** ['janua:ɐ] *m* (*-[s]*; *-e*) January
**Japan** ['ja:pan] Japan; **Japaner** [ja'pa:nɐ] *m* (*-s*; *-*), **Ja'panerin** [ja'pa:nərɪn] *f* (*-*; *-nen*), **ja'panisch** *adj* Japanese
**Jargon** [ʒar'go͂:] *m* (*-s*; *-s*) jargon; slang
**'Jastimme** *f* PARL aye, yea
**jäten** ['jɛ:tən] *v/t* (*ge-*, *h*) weed
**Jauche** ['jauxə] *f* (*-*; *-n*) liquid manure
**jauchzen** ['jauxtsən] *v/i* (*ge-*, *h*) shout for *or* with joy; exult, rejoice
**Jause** ['jauzə] *Austrian f* (*-*; *-n*) snack
**ja'wohl** *adv* (that's) right, (yes,) indeed
**je** [je:] *adv and cj* ever; each; per; ***der beste Film, den ich ~ gesehen habe*** the best film I have ever seen; ***~ zwei*** (***Pfund***) two (pounds) each; ***drei Euro ~ Kilo*** three euros per kilo; ***~ nach Größe*** (***Geschmack***) according to size (taste); ***~ nachdem***(, ***wie***) it depends (on how); ***~ ..., desto ...*** the ... the ...
**Jeans** [dʒi:nz] *pl*, *a. f* (*-*; *-*) (***e-e ~*** a pair of) jeans; **~jacke** *f* denim jacket
**jede** ['je:də], **jeder** ['je:dɐ], **jedes** ['je:dəs] *indef pron* every; any; each; either; ***jeder weiß*** (***das***) everybody knows; ***du kannst jeden fragen*** (you can) ask anyone; ***jeder von uns*** (***euch***) each of us (you); ***jeder, der*** whoever; ***jeden zweiten Tag*** every other day; ***jeden Augenblick*** any moment now; ***jedes Mal*** every time; ***jedes Mal wenn*** whenever
**'jeden'falls** *adv* in any case, anyhow
**'jedermann** *indef pron* everyone, everybody
**'jeder'zeit** *adv* any time, always
**je'doch** *cj* however
**je'her** *adv*: ***von ~*** always
**jemals** ['je:ma:ls] *adv* ever
**jemand** ['je:mant] *indef pron* someone, somebody; anyone, anybody
**jene** ['je:nə], **jener** ['je:nɐ], **jenes** ['je:nəs] *dem pron* that (one); *pl* those; ***dies und jenes*** this and that
**jenseitig** ['je:nzaitɪç] *adj* opposite
**jenseits** ['je:nzaits] *adv and prp* (*gen*) on the other side (of), beyond (*a. fig*)
**'Jenseits** *n* (*-*; *no pl*) next world, hereafter
**jetzig** ['jɛtsɪç] *adj* present; existing
**jetzt** [jɛtst] *adv* now, at present; ***bis ~*** up to now, so far; ***erst ~*** only now; ***~ gleich*** right now *or* away; ***von ~ an*** from now on
**jeweilig** ['je:'vailɪç] *adj* respective
**jeweils** ['je:'vails] *adv* each; at a time
**Jh.** *abbr of* ***Jahrhundert*** cent., century
**Jochbein** ['jɔxbain] *n* ANAT cheekbone
**Jockei** ['dʒɔke] *m* (*-s*; *-s*) jockey
**Jod** [jo:t] *n* (*-[e]s*; *no pl*) CHEM iodine
**jodeln** ['jo:dəln] *v/i* (*ge-*, *h*) yodel
**Joga** → ***Yoga***
**joggen** ['dʒɔgən] *v/i* (*ge-*, *h*) jog
**Jogger** ['dʒɔgɐ] *m* (*-s*; *-*) jogger
**Jogging** ['dʒɔgɪŋ] *n* (*-s*; *no pl*) jogging; **~anzug** *m* tracksuit; **~hose** *f* tracksuit trousers
**Joghurt**, **Jogurt** ['jo:gʊrt] *m*, *n* (*-[s]*; *-[s]*) yog(h)urt, yoghourt
**Johannisbeere** [jo'hanɪsbe:rə] *f*: ***rote ~*** redcurrant; ***schwarze ~*** blackcurrant

**johlen** ['jo:lən] *v/i (ge-, h)* howl, yell
**Jolle** ['jɔlə] *f (-; -n)* MAR dinghy
**Jongleur** [ʒo-'glø:ɐ] *m (-s; -e)* juggler
**jonglieren** [ʒo-'gli:rən] *v/t and v/i (no -ge-, h)* juggle
**Joule** [dʒu:l] *n (-[s]; -)* PHYS joule
**Journalismus** [ʒʊrna'lɪsmʊs] *m (-; no pl)* journalism; **Journalist(in)** [ʒʊrna'lɪst(ɪn)] *(-en; -en/-; -nen)* journalist
**jr.** → ***jun.***
**Jubel** ['ju:bəl] *m (-s; no pl)* cheering, cheers; rejoicing; '**jubeln** *v/i (ge-, h)* cheer, shout for joy; rejoice
**Jubiläum** [jubi'lɛ:ʊm] *n (-s; -läen)* anniversary; ***50-jähriges ~*** fiftieth anniversary, (golden) jubilee
**jucken** ['jʊkən] *v/t and v/i (ge-, h)* itch; ***es juckt mich am ...*** my ... itches
**Jude** ['ju:də] *m (-n; -n)* Jewish person; ***er ist ~*** he is Jewish; **Jüdin** ['jy:dɪn] *f (-; -nen)* Jewish woman *or* girl; ***sie ist ~*** she is Jewish; **jüdisch** ['jy:dɪʃ] *adj* Jewish
**Judo** ['ju:do] *n (-[s]; no pl)* SPORT judo
**Jugend** ['ju:gənt] *f (-; no pl)* youth; ***die ~*** young people; **~amt** *n* youth welfare office; **~arbeitslosigkeit** *f* youth unemployment
'**jugendfrei** *adj*: ***~er Film*** G(-rated) (*Br* U(-rated)) film; ***nicht ~*** X-rated
'**Jugend|fürsorge** *f* youth welfare; **~gericht** *n* JUR juvenile court; **~herberge** *f* youth hostel; **~klub** *m* youth club; **~kriminali,tät** *f* juvenile delinquency
'**jugendlich** *adj* youthful, young
'**Jugendliche** *m, f (-n; -n)* young person, *m a.* youth, JUR *a.* juvenile
'**Jugend|stil** *m (-s; no pl)* Art Nouveau; **~strafanstalt** *f* detention center (*Br* centre), reformatory; **~verbot** *n* for adults only; → ***jugendfrei***; **~zentrum** *n* youth center (*Br* centre)
**Juli** ['ju:li] *m (-[s]; -s)* July
**Jumbojet** ['jʊmbojɛt] *m* jumbo (jet)
**jun.** *abbr of* ***junior*** Jun., jun., Jnr., Jr., junior
**jung** [jʊŋ] *adj* young
**Junge**[1] ['jʊŋə] *m (-n; -n)* boy; lad; *cards*: jack, knave
'**Junge**[2] *n (-n; -n)* ZO young; puppy; kitten; cub; ***~ bekommen*** *or* ***werfen*** have young
'**jungenhaft** *adj* boyish
'**Jungenstreich** *m* boyish prank
**jünger** ['jʏŋɐ] *adj* younger
'**Jünger** *m (-s; -)* REL disciple (*a. fig*)
'**Jungfern|fahrt** *f* MAR maiden voyage; **~flug** *m* AVIAT maiden flight
'**Jung|frau** *f* virgin; ASTR Virgo; ***er ist ~*** he's (a) Virgo; **~geselle** *m* bachelor, single (man); **~gesellin** *f* bachelor girl, single (woman); *esp* JUR spinster
**jüngste** ['jʏŋstə] *adj* youngest; *fig* latest; ***in ~r Zeit*** lately, recently; ***das Jüngste Gericht*** the Last Judg(e)ment; ***der Jüngste Tag*** Doomsday
**Juni** ['ju:ni] *m (-[s]; -s)* June
**junior** ['ju:njo:ɐ] *adj*, '**Junior** *m (-s; -en* [ju'njo:rən]), **Juni'orin** *f (-; -nen)* junior (*a.* SPORT)
**Jupe** [ʒy:p] *Swiss m (-s; -s)* skirt
**Jura** ['ju:ra]: ***~ studieren*** study (the) law
**juridisch** [ju'ri:dɪʃ] *Austrian* → ***juristisch***; **Jurist(in)** [ju'rɪst(ɪn)] *(-en; -en/-; -nen)* lawyer; law student; ju'**ristisch** *adj* legal
**Jurorenkomitee** [ju'ro:rənkomite:] *Austrian n* → ***Jury***
**Jury** [ʒy'ri:] *f (-; -s)* jury
**justieren** [jʊs'ti:rən] *v/t (no -ge-, h)* TECH adjust, set
**Justiz** [jʊs'ti:ts] *f (-; no pl)* (administration of) justice, (the) law; **~beamte** *m* judicial officer; **~irrtum** *m* error of justice; **~mi,nister** *m* minister of justice; Attorney General, *Br* Lord Chancellor; **~minis,terium** *n* ministry of justice; Department of Justice
**Jute** ['ju:tə] *f (-; no pl)* jute
**Juwel** [ju've:l] *m, n (-s; -en)* jewel, gem (*both a. fig*); *pl* jewel(le)ry
**Juwelier** [juve'li:ɐ] *m (-s; -e)* jewel(l)er

# K

**Kabarett** [kaba'rɛt] *n* (-*s*; -*s*) (political) revue
**Kabel** ['ka:bəl] *n* (-*s*; -) cable
'**Kabelfernsehen** *n* cable TV
**Kabeljau** ['ka:bəljau] *m* (-*s*; -*e*, -*s*) ZO cod(fish)
**Kabine** [ka'bi:nə] *f* (-; -*n*) cabin; cubicle; SPORT dressing room; TECH car; TEL *etc* booth; **Ka'binenbahn** *f* cable railway
**Kabinett** [kabi'nɛt] *n* (-*s*; -*e*) POL cabinet
**Kabis** ['ka:bɪs] *Swiss m* (-; *no pl*) green cabbage
**Kabriolett** [kabrio'lɛt] *n* (-*s*; -*s*) MOT convertible
**Kachel** ['kaxəl] *f* (-; -*n*), '**kacheln** *v/t* (*ge*-, *h*) tile; '**Kachelofen** *m* tiled stove
**Kadaver** [ka'da:vɐ] *m* (-*s*; -) carcass
**Kadett** [ka'dɛt] *m* (-*en*; -*en*) MIL cadet
**Käfer** ['kɛ:fɐ] *m* (-*s*; -) ZO beetle, bug
**Kaffee** ['kafe] *m* (-*s*; -*s*) coffee; **~ *kochen*** make coffee; **~ *mit Milch*** white coffee; **~auto,mat** *m* coffee machine; **~bohne** *f* coffee bean; **~haus** [ka-'fe:haus] *Austrian n* café, coffee house; **~kanne** *f* coffee pot; **~ma,schine** *f* cofffeemaker; **~mühle** *f* coffee grinder
**Käfig** ['kɛ:fɪç] *m* (-*s*; -*e*) cage (*a. fig*)
**kahl** [ka:l] *adj* bald; *fig* bare (*rock, wall etc*); barren, bleak (*landscape*)
**Kahn** [ka:n] *m* (-[*e*]*s*; *Kähne* ['kɛ:nə]) boat; barge
**Kai** [kai] *m* (-*s*; -*s*) quay, wharf
**Kaiser** ['kaizɐ] *m* (-*s*; -) emperor
**Kaiserin** ['kaizərɪn] *f* (-; -*nen*) empress
'**Kaiserreich** *n* empire
**Kajüte** [ka'jy:tə] *f* (-; -*n*) MAR cabin
**Kakao** [ka'kau] *m* (-*s*; -*s*) cocoa; (hot) chocolate; chocolate milk
**Kaktee** [kak'te:] *f* (-; -*n*), **Kaktus** ['kaktʊs] *m* (-; *Kakteen*) BOT cactus
**Kalb** [kalp] *n* (-[*e*]*s*; *Kälber* ['kɛlbɐ]) ZO calf; **kalben** ['kalbən] *v/i* (*ge*-, *h*) calve
'**Kalbfleisch** *n* veal
'**Kalbs|braten** *m* roast veal; **~schnitzel** *n* veal cutlet; escalope (of veal)
**Kaldaunen** [kal'daunən] *pl* GASTR tripe
**Kalender** [ka'lɛndɐ] *m* (-*s*; -) calendar; **~jahr** *n* calendar year
**Kali** ['ka:li] *n* (-*s*; *no pl*) CHEM potash
**Kaliber** [ka'li:bɐ] *n* (-*s*; -) caliber, *Br* calibre (*a. fig*)
**Kalk** [kalk] *m* (-[*e*]*s*; -*e*) lime; GEOL limestone, chalk; MED calcium; '**kalken** *v/t* (*ge*-, *h*) whitewash; AGR lime; '**kalkig** *adj* limy; '**Kalkstein** *m* limestone
**Kalorie** [kalo'ri:] *f* (-; -*n*) calorie
**kalo'rien|arm** *adj*, **~redu,ziert** *adj* low-calorie, low in calories; **~reich** *adj* high-calorie, high *or* rich in calories
**kalt** [kalt] *adj* cold; ***mir ist ~*** I'm cold; ***es*** (***mir***) ***wird ~*** it's (I'm) getting cold; **~ *bleiben*** *fig* keep (one's) cool; ***das lässt mich kalt*** that leaves me cold
**kaltblütig** ['kaltbly:tɪç] **1.** *adj* cold-blooded (*a. fig*) **2.** *adv* in cold blood
**Kälte** ['kɛltə] *f* (-; *no pl*) cold; *fig* coldness; ***vor ~ zittern*** shiver with cold; ***fünf Grad ~*** five degrees below zero; **~einbruch** *m* cold snap; **~grad** *m* degree below zero; **~peri,ode** *f* cold spell
'**kaltmachen** F *v/t* (*sep*, -*ge*-, *h*) bump off
**kam** [ka:m] *pret of* ***kommen***
**Kamee** [ka'me:ə] *f* (-; -*n*) cameo
**Kamel** [ka'me:l] *n* (-*s*; -*e*) ZO camel
**Ka'melhaar** *n* (-[*e*]*s*; *no pl*) camelhair
**Kamera** ['kamәra] *f* (-; -*s*) camera
**Kamerad** [kamə'ra:t] *m* (-*en*; -*en* [kamə'ra:dən]) companion, F mate, pal, buddy; **Kameradin** [kamə'ra:dɪn] *f* (-; -*nen*) companion
**Kame'radschaft** *f* (-; *no pl*) comradeship
'**Kameramann** *m* cameraman
'**Kamerare,korder** *m* (-*s*; -) camcorder
**Kamille** [ka'mɪlə] *f* (-; -*n*) BOT camomile
**Kamin** [ka'mi:n] *m* (-*s*; -*e*) fireplace; chimney (*a.* MOUNT); ***am ~*** by the fire (-side); **~kehrer** [ka'mi:nke:rɐ] *m* (-*s*; -) chimney sweep; **~sims** *m*, *n* mantelpiece
**Kamm** [kam] *m* (-[*e*]*s*; *Kämme* ['kɛmə]) comb, ZO *a.* crest (*a. fig*)
**kämmen** ['kɛmən] *v/t* (*ge*-, *h*) comb; ***sich*** (***die Haare***) **~** comb one's hair
**Kammer** ['kamɐ] *f* (-; -*n*) (small) room; storeroom, closet; garret; POL, ECON chamber; JUR division
'**Kammermu,sik** *f* chamber music
'**Kammgarn** *n* worsted (yarn)
**Kampagne** [kam'panjə] *f* (-; -*n*) cam-

K

paign

**Kampf** [kampf] *m* (-[*e*]*s*; *Kämpfe* ['kɛmpfə]) fight (*a. fig*), struggle (*a. fig*), *esp* MIL combat, battle (*a. fig*); SPORT contest, match; *boxing*: fight, bout; *fig* conflict; '**kampfbereit** *adj* ready for battle (MIL combat); **kämpfen** ['kɛmpfən] *v/i* (*ge-*, *h*) fight (***gegen*** against; ***mit*** with; ***um*** for) (*a. fig*); struggle (*a. fig*); *fig* contend, wrestle

**Kampfer** ['kampfɐ] *m* (-*s*; *no pl*) CHEM camphor

**Kämpfer** ['kɛmpfɐ] *m* (-*s*; -), '**Kämpferin** *f* (-; -*nen*) fighter (*a. fig*); **kämpferisch** ['kɛmpfərɪʃ] *adj* fighting, aggressive

'**Kampf|flugzeug** *n* MIL combat aircraft; **~kraft** *f* (-; *no pl*) fighting strength; **~richter** *m* SPORT judge; **~sportarten** *pl* martial arts

**Kanada** ['kanada] Canada; **Kanadier** [ka'naːdjɐ] *m* (-*s*; -), **Ka'nadierin** [ka'naːdjərɪn] *f* (-; -*nen*), **ka'nadisch** *adj* Canadian

**Kanal** [ka'naːl] *m* (-*s*; *Kanäle* [ka'nɛːlə]) canal; channel (*a.* TV, TECH, *fig*); sewer, drain; ***der ~*** the (English) Channel

**Kanalisation** [kanaliza'tsjoːn] *f* (-; -*en*) sewerage (system); canalization

**kanalisieren** [kanali'ziːrən] *v/t* (*no -ge-*, *h*) sewer; canalize; *fig* channel

**Ka'naltunnel** *m* Channel Tunnel, F Chunnel

**Kanarienvogel** [ka'naːrjənfoːgəl] *m* canary

**Kandidat** [kandi'daːt] *m* (-*en*; -*en*), **Kandi'datin** *f* (-; -*nen*) candidate; **Kandidatur** [kandida'tuːɐ] *f* (-; -*en*) candidacy, *Br a.* candidature; **kandidieren** [kandi'diːrən] *v/i* (*no -ge-*, *h*) stand *or* run for election; ***~ für ...*** run for the office of ...

**Känguru**, **Känguruh** ['kɛŋguru] *n* (-*s*; -*s*) ZO kangaroo

**Kaninchen** [ka'niːnçən] *n* (-*s*; -) ZO rabbit

**Kanister** [ka'nɪstɐ] *m* (-*s*; -) (fuel) can

**Kanne** ['kanə] *f* (-; -*n*) pot; can

**Kannibale** [kani'baːlə] *m* (-*n*; -*n*) cannibal

**kannte** ['kantə] *pret of* ***kennen***

**Kanon** ['kaːnɔn] *m* (-*s*; -*s*) MUS canon

**Kanone** [ka'noːnə] *f* (-; -*n*) MIL gun; cannon; F ace, *esp* SPORT *a.* crack

**Kante** ['kantə] *f* (-; -*n*) edge; '**kanten** *v/t* (*ge-*, *h*) set on edge; tilt; edge (*skis*)

'**Kanten** *m* (-*s*; -) crust

**kantig** ['kantɪç] *adj* angular, square(d)

**Kantine** [kan'tiːnə] *f* (-; -*n*) canteen

**Kanton** [kan'toːn] *m* (-*s*; -*e*) POL canton

**Kanu** ['kaːnu] *n* (-*s*; -*s*) canoe

**Kanüle** [ka'nyːlə] *f* (-; -*n*) MED cannula, (drain) tube

**Kanzel** ['kantsəl] *f* (-; -*n*) REL pulpit; AVIAT cockpit

**Kanzlei** [kants'lai] *f* (-; -*en*) office

**Kanzler** ['kantslɐ] *m* (-*s*; -) chancellor

**Kanzlerin** ['kantslərɪn] *f* (-; -*nen*) chancellor

**Kap** [kap] *n* (-*s*; -*s*) cape, headland

**Kapazität** [kapatsi'tɛːt] *f* (-; -*en*) capacity; *fig* authority

**Kapelle** [ka'pɛlə] *f* (-; -*n*) REL chapel; MUS band

**Ka'pellmeister** *m* MUS conductor

**kapern** ['kaːpɐn] *v/t* (*ge-*, *h*) MAR capture, seize

**kapieren** [ka'piːrən] F *v/t* (*no -ge-*, *h*) get; ***kapiert?*** got it?

**Kapital** [kapi'taːl] *n* (-*s*; -*e*, -*ien*) ECON capital, funds; **~anlage** *f* investment

**Kapitalismus** [kapita'lɪsmus] *m* (-; *no pl*) capitalism; **Kapita'list** *m* (-*en*; -*en*), **kapita'listisch** *adj* capitalist

**Kapi'talverbrechen** *n* capital crime, JUR felony

**Kapitän** [kapi'tɛːn] *m* (-*s*; -*e*) captain (*a.* SPORT)

**Kapitel** [ka'pɪtəl] *n* (-*s*; -) chapter (*a. fig*); F *fig* story

**Kapitulation** [kapitula'tsjoːn] *f* (-; -*en*) capitulation, surrender (*a. fig*)

**kapitulieren** [kapitu'liːrən] *v/i* (*no -ge-*, *h*) capitulate, surrender (*a. fig*)

**Kaplan** [ka'plaːn] *m* (-*s*; *Kapläne* [ka'plɛːnə]) REL curate

**Kappe** ['kapə] *f* (-; -*n*) cap, TECH *a.* top, hood; '**kappen** *v/t* (*ge-*, *h*) cut (*rope*); lop, top (*tree*)

**Kapsel** ['kapsəl] *f* (-; -*n*) capsule

**kaputt** [ka'pʊt] F *adj* broken (*a. fig*); TECH out of order; *fig* dead beat; ruined; ***~ machen*** F *v/t* (*sep*, *-ge-*, *h*) break, wreck (*a. fig*), ruin; *fig* → ***~machen***; **~gehen** F *v/i* (*irr*, ***gehen***, *sep*, *-ge-*, *sein*) break; MOT *etc* break down; *fig* break up; **~machen** *v/t* (*sep*, *-ge-*, *h*) F *fig* wreck, ruin

**Kapuze** [ka'puːtsə] *f* (-; *-n*) hood; cowl
**Karabiner** [kara'biːnɐ] *m* (*-s*; -) carbine; **~haken** *m* karabiner, snaplink
**Karaffe** [ka'rafə] *f* (-; *-n*) decanter
**Karambolage** [karambo'laːʒə] *f* (-; *-n*) collision, crash
**Karat** [ka'raːt] *n* (-[*e*]*s*; *-e*) carat
**Karate** [ka'raːtə] *n* (-[*s*]; *no pl*) SPORT karate
**Karawane** [kara'vaːnə] *f* (-; *-n*) caravan
**Kardinal** [kardi'naːl] *m* (*-s*; *Kardinäle* [kardi'nɛːlə]) REL cardinal
**Karfiol** [kar'fjoːl] *Austrian m* (*-s*; *no pl*) BOT cauliflower
**Kar'freitag** [kaːɐ'fraitaːk] *m* REL Good Friday
**karg** [kark], **kärglich** ['kɛrklıç] *adj* mealg|er, *Br* -re, scanty; frugal; poor
**kariert** [ka'riːɐt] *adj* checked, checkered, *Br* chequered; squared
**Karies** ['kaːrjɛs] *f* (-; *no pl*) MED (dental) caries
**Karikatur** [karika'tuːɐ] *f* (-; *-en*) *mst* cartoon, *esp fig* caricature; **Karikaturist** [karikatu'rıst] *m* (*-en*; *-en*) cartoonist
**karikieren** [kari'kiːrən] *v/t* (*no -ge-*, *h*) caricature
**Karneval** ['karnəval] *m* (*-s*; *-e*, *-s*) carnival
**Karo** ['kaːro] *n* (*-s*; *-s*) square, check; *cards*: diamonds
**Karosserie** [karɔsə'riː] *f* (-; *-n*) MOT body
**Karotte** [ka'rɔtə] *f* (-; *-n*) BOT carrot
**Karpfen** ['karpfən] *m* (*-s*; -) ZO carp
**Karre** ['karə] *f* (-; *-n*), **'Karren** *m* (*-s*; -) cart; wheelbarrow; F MOT jalopy
**Karriere** [ka'rjeːrə] *f* (-; *-n*) career; ***~ machen*** work one's way up, get to the top
**Karte** ['kartə] *f* (-; *-n*) card; ticket; GEOGR map; chart; GASTR menu; ***gute*** (***schlechte***) ***~n*** a good (bad) hand
**Kartei** [kar'tai] *f* (-; *-en*) card index; **~karte** *f* index *or* file card
**'Karten|haus** *n* house of cards (*a. fig*); MAR chartroom; **~spiel** *n* card game; deck (*Br* pack) of cards; **~tele,fon** *n* cardphone; **~vorverkauf** *m* advance booking; box office
**Kartoffel** [kar'tɔfəl] *f* (-; *-n*) BOT potato; **~brei** *m* mashed potatoes; **~chips** *pl* (potato) chips, *Br* crisps; **~kloß** *m*, **~knödel** *m* potato dumpling; **~puffer** *m* potato fritter; **~schalen** *pl* potato peelings; **~schäler** *m* potato peeler
**Karton** [kar'tɔŋ] *m* (*-s*; *-s*) cardboard; pasteboard; cardboard box
**Karussell** [karʊ'sɛl] *n* (*-s*; *-s*) roundabout, car(r)ousel, merry-go-round
**Karwoche** ['kaːɐvɔxə] *f* REL Holy Week
**Kaschmir** ['kaʃmiːɐ] *m* (*-s*; *-e*) cashmere
**Käse** ['kɛːzə] *m* (*-s*; -) cheese
**Kaserne** [ka'zɛrnə] *f* (-; *-n*) barracks
**Ka'sernenhof** *m* barrack square
**käsig** ['kɛːzıç] *adj* cheesy; pasty
**Kasino** [ka'ziːno] *n* (*-s*; *-s*) casino; MIL (officers') mess
**Kasperle** ['kaspɐlə] *n*, *m* (*-s*; -) Punch; **~the,ater** *n* Punch and Judy show
**Kassa** ['kasa] *Austrian f* (-; *Kassen*), **Kasse** ['kasə] *f* (-; *-n*) till; cash register; checkout (counter); cash desk; cashier's counter; THEA *etc* box office; F ***gut*** (***knapp***) ***bei Kasse sein*** be flush (be a bit hard up)
**'Kassen|beleg** *m*, **~bon** *m* sales slip, *Br* receipt; **~erfolg** *m* THEA *etc* box-office success; **~pati,ent** *m* MED health plan (*Am* medicaid, *Br* NHS) patient; **~schlager** F *m* blockbuster; **~wart** ['kasənvart] *m* (-[*e*]*s*; *-e*) treasurer
**Kassette** [ka'sɛtə] *f* (-; *-n*) box, case; MUS, TV, PHOT *etc* cassette; casket
**Kas'setten...** *in cpds ...rekorder etc*: cassette ...
**kassieren** [ka'siːrən] *v/t and v/i* (*no -ge-*, *h*) collect, take (the money)
**Kassierer** [ka'siːrɐ] *m* (*-s*; -), **Kas'siererin** *f* (-; *-nen*) cashier; teller; collector
**Kastanie** [kas'taːnjə] *f* (-; *-n*) BOT chestnut
**Kasten** ['kastən] *m* (*-s*; *Kästen* ['kɛstən]) box (*a.* F TV, SPORT *etc*); case; chest
**kastrieren** [kas'triːrən] *v/t* (*no -ge-*, *h*) MED, VET castrate
**Kasus** ['kaːzʊs] *m* (-; -) LING case
**Katalog** [kata'loːk] *m* (-[*e*]*s*; *-e*) catalog(ue *Br*)
**Katalysator** [kataly'zaːtoːɐ] *m* (*-s*; *-en* [katalyza'toːrən]) CHEM catalyst; MOT catalytic converter
**Katapult** [kata'pʊlt] *m*, *n* (-[*e*]*s*; *-e*), **katapultieren** [katapʊl'tiːrən] *v/t* (*no -ge-*, *h*) catapult
**katastrophal** [katastro'faːl] *adj* disastrous (*a. fig*); **Katastrophe** [katas-

'tro:fə] *f* (-; *-n*) catastrophe, disaster (*a. fig*)
**Kata'strophen|gebiet** *n* disaster area; **~schutz** *m* disaster control
**Katechismus** [katɛ'çɪsmʊs] *m* (-; *-men*) REL catechism
**Kategorie** [katego'ri:] *f* (-; *-n*) category
**Kater** ['ka:tɐ] *m* (*-s*; -) ZO male cat, tomcat; F hangover
**kath.** *abbr of* ***katholisch*** Cath., Catholic
**Kathedrale** [kate'dra:lə] *f* (-; *-n*) cathedral
**Katholik** [kato'li:k] *m* (*-en*; *-en*), **Katho'likin** *f* (-; *-nen*), **katholisch** [ka'to:lɪʃ] *adj* (Roman) Catholic
**Kätzchen** ['kɛtsçən] *n* (*-s*; -) ZO kitten, pussy (*a.* BOT)
**Katze** ['katsə] *f* (-; *-n*) ZO cat; kitten
**Kauderwelsch** ['kaudɐvɛlʃ] *n* (*-[s]*; *no pl*) gibberish
**kauen** ['kauən] *v/t and v/i* (*ge-*, *h*) chew
**kauern** ['kauɐn] *v/i and v/refl* (*ge-*, *h*) crouch, squat
**Kauf** [kauf] *m* (*-[e]s*; *Käufe* ['kɔʏfə]) purchase (*a.* ECON), F buy; purchasing, buying; ***ein guter ~*** a bargain, F a good buy; ***zum ~ anbieten*** offer for sale
'**kaufen** *v/t* (*ge-*, *h*) buy (*a. fig*), purchase
**Käufer** ['kɔʏfɐ] *m* (*-s*; -), '**Käuferin** *f* (-; *-nen*) buyer; customer
'**Kauffrau** *f* (-; *-en*) businesswoman
'**Kauf|haus** *n* department store; **~kraft** *f* (-; *no pl*) ECON purchasing power
**käuflich** ['kɔʏflɪç] *adj* for sale; *fig* venal
'**Kaufmann** *m* (*-[e]s*; *-leute*) businessman; dealer, trader, merchant; storekeeper, *Br mst* shopkeeper; grocer
**kaufmännisch** ['kaufmɛnɪʃ] *adj* commercial, business; ***~er Angestellter*** clerk
'**Kaufvertrag** *m* contract of sale
'**Kaugummi** *m* (*-s*; *-s*) chewing gum
**kaum** [kaum] *adv* hardly; ***~ zu glauben*** hard to believe
**Kaution** [kau'tsjo:n] *f* (-; *-en*) security; JUR bail
**Kautschuk** ['kautʃʊk] *m* (*-s*; *-e*) (india) rubber
**Kavalier** [kava'li:ɐ] *m* (*-s*; *-e*) gentleman
**Kaviar** ['ka:vjar] *m* (*-s*; *-e*) caviar(e)
**keck** [kɛk] *adj* cheeky, saucy, pert
**Kegel** ['ke:gəl] *m* (*-s*; -) skittle, pin; MATH, TECH cone; **~bahn** *f* bowling (*esp Br* skittle) alley
'**kegelförmig** ['ke:gəlfœrmɪç] *adj* conical
'**Kegelkugel** *f* bowling (*esp Br* skittle) ball
'**kegeln** *v/i* (*ge-*, *h*) bowl, go bowling, *esp Br* play (at) skittles *or* ninepins
**Kehle** ['ke:lə] *f* (-; *-n*) ANAT throat
'**Kehlkopf** *m* ANAT larynx
**Kehre** ['ke:rə] *f* (-; *-n*) (sharp) bend
'**kehren** *v/t* (*ge-*, *h*) sweep; ***j-m den Rücken ~*** turn one's back on s.o.
**Kehricht** ['ke:rɪçt] *m* (*-s*; *no pl*) sweepings; **~schaufel** *f* dustpan
**kehrtmachen** ['ke:ɐtmaxən] *v/i* (*sep*, *-ge-*, *h*) turn back
**keifen** ['kaifən] *v/i* (*ge-*, *h*) nag, bitch
**Keil** [kail] *m* (*-[e]s*; *-e*) wedge; gusset
**Keiler** ['kailɐ] *m* (*-s*; -) ZO wild boar
'**Keilriemen** *m* MOT fan belt
**Keim** [kaim] *m* (*-[e]s*; *-e*) BIOL, MED germ; BOT bud, sprout; *fig* seed(s)
'**keimen** *v/i* (*ge-*, *h*) BOT germinate, sprout; *fig* form, grow; stir
'**keimfrei** *adj* MED sterile
'**keimtötend** *adj* MED germicidal
'**Keimzelle** *f* BIOL germ cell
**kein** [kain] *indef pron* **1.** *adj*: **~(e)** no, not any; ***~ anderer*** no one else; ***~(e) … mehr*** not any more …; ***~ Geld*** (***~e Zeit***) ***mehr*** no money (time) left; ***~ Kind mehr*** no longer a child **2.** *su*: **~er, ~e, ~(e)s** none, no one, nobody; ***~er von beiden*** neither (of the two); ***~er von uns*** none of us; '**keines'falls** *adv* by no means, under no circumstances; '**keineswegs** [kainəs've:ks] *adv* by no means, not in the least; '**keinmal** *adv* not once, not a single time
**Keks** [ke:ks] *m*, *n* (*-es*, *-e*) cookie, *Br* biscuit
**Kelch** [kɛlç] *m* (*-[e]s*; *-e*) cup (*a.* BOT); REL chalice
**Kelle** ['kɛlə] *f* (-; *-n*) GASTR ladle, scoop; TECH trowel; signaling disk
**Keller** ['kɛlɐ] *m* (*-s*; -) cellar; → **~geschoss** *n*, **~geschoß** *Austrian n* basement; **~wohnung** *f* basement (apartment, *esp Br* flat)
**Kellner** ['kɛlnɐ] *m* (*-s*; -) waiter
**Kellnerin** ['kɛlnərɪn] *f* (-; *-nen*) waitress
**keltern** ['kɛltɐn] *v/t* (*ge-*, *h*) press
**kennen** ['kɛnən] *v/t* (*irr*, *ge-*, *h*) know, be acquainted with; ***~ lernen*** → ***kennenlernen***

K

**'kennenlernen** *v/t* (*sep*, *-ge-*, *h*) get to know, become acquainted with; meet *s.o.*; ***als ich ihn kennenlernte*** when I first met him

**Kenner** ['kɛnɐ] *m* (*-s*; -), **'Kennerin** *f* (-; *-nen*) expert; **kenntlich** ['kɛntlɪç] *adj* recognizable (***an*** *dat* by); **Kenntnis** *f* (-; *-se*) knowledge; ***gute ~se in*** (*dat*) a good knowledge of

**'Kennwort** *n* password

**'Kennzeichen** *n* mark, sign; (distinguishing) feature, characteristic; MOT license (*Br* registration) number

**'kennzeichnen** *v/t* (*ge-*, *h*) mark; *fig* characterize

**kentern** ['kɛntɐn] *v/i* (*ge-*, *sein*) MAR capsize

**Keramik** [ke'ra:mɪk] *f* (-; *-en*) ceramics

**Kerbe** ['kɛrbə] *f* (-; *-n*) notch

**Kerker** ['kɛrkɐ] *m* (*-s*; -) dungeon

**Kerl** [kɛrl] F *m* (*-s*; *-e*) fellow, guy; ***armer ~*** poor devil; ***ein anständiger ~*** a decent sort

**Kern** [kɛrn] *m* (*-[e]s*; *-e*) BOT pip, seed, stone, kernel; TECH core (*a. fig*); PHYS nucleus; *~... in cpds ...energie*, *...forschung*, *...physik*, *...reaktor*, *...technik etc*: nuclear ...; **~fach** *n* PED basic subject; **~fa,milie** *f* nuclear family; **~gehäuse** *n* BOT core

**'kernge'sund** *adj* F (as) sound as a bell

**kernig** ['kɛrnɪç] *adj* full of seeds (*Br* pips); *fig* robust; pithy

**'Kernkraft** *f* PHYS nuclear power; **~gegner** *m* anti-nuclear activist; **~werk** *n* nuclear power station *or* plant

**'kernlos** *adj* BOT seedless

**'Kernspaltung** *f* PHYS nuclear fission

**'Kernwaffen** *pl* MIL nuclear weapons; **'kernwaffenfrei** *adj*: ***~e Zone*** MIL nuclear-free zone; **'Kernwaffenversuch** *m* MIL nuclear test

**'Kernzeit** *f* ECON core time

**Kerze** ['kɛrtsə] *f* (-; *-n*) candle; SPORT shoulder stand

**kess** [kɛs] F *adj* cheeky, saucy, pert

**Kessel** ['kɛsəl] *m* (*-s*; -) kettle; TECH boiler; tank

**Kette** ['kɛtə] *f* (-; *-n*) chain (*a. fig*); necklace; ***e-e ~ bilden*** form a line

**'Ketten...** *in cpds ...antrieb*, *...laden*, *...rauchen*, *...raucher*, *...reaktion etc*: chain ...

**'ketten** *v/t* (*ge-*, *h*) chain (***an*** *acc* to)

**'Kettenfahrzeug** *n* tracked vehicle

**Ketzer** ['kɛtsɐ] *m* (*-s*; -) heretic

**Ketzerei** [kɛtsə'rai] *f* (-; *-en*) heresy

**keuchen** ['kɔʏçən] *v/i* (*ge-*, *h*) pant, gasp

**'Keuchhusten** *m* MED whooping cough

**Keule** ['kɔʏlə] *f* (-; *-n*) club; GASTR leg

**keusch** [kɔʏʃ] *adj* chaste

**'Keuschheit** *f* (-; *no pl*) chastity

**Kfz** [ka:ʔɛf'tsɛt] *abbr of* ***Kraftfahrzeug*** motor vehicle; **Kf'z-Brief** *m*, **Kf'z-Schein** *m* vehicle registration document; **Kf'z-Steuer** *f* road *or* automobile tax; **Kf'z-Werkstatt** *f* garage

**KG** [ka:'ge:] *abbr of* ***Kommanditgesellschaft*** ECON limited partnership

**kichern** ['kɪçɐn] *v/i* (*ge-*, *h*) giggle

**Kiebitz** ['ki:bɪts] *m* (*-es*; *-e*) ZO peewit, lapwing; F kibitzer

**Kiefer**[1] ['ki:fɐ] *m* (*-s*; -) ANAT jaw(bone)

**'Kiefer**[2] *f* (-; *-n*) BOT pine(tree)

**Kiel** [ki:l] *m* (*-[e]s*; *-e*) MAR keel; **~flosse** *f* AVIAT tail fin; **~raum** *m* MAR bilge; **~wasser** *n* (*-s*; -) MAR wake (*a. fig*)

**Kieme** ['ki:mə] *f* (*-n*; *-n*) ZO gill

**Kies** [ki:s] *m* (*-es*; *-e*) gravel (*a.* ***mit ~ bestreuen***); F dough

**Kiesel** ['ki:zəl] *m* (*-s*; -) pebble

**Kilo** ['ki:lo] *n* (*-s*; -) → ***Kilogramm***

**Kilo|'gramm** [kilo'gram] *n* kilogram(me); **~hertz** [kilo'hɛrts] *n* (-; -) kilohertz; **~'meter** *m* kilometer, *Br* kilometre; **~'watt** *n* ELECTR kilowatt

**Kind** [kɪnt] *n* (*-[e]s*; *-er* ['kɪndɐ]) child; ***ein ~ erwarten*** be expecting a baby

**'Kinder|arzt** *m*, **~ärztin** *f* p(a)ediatrician; **~garten** *m* kindergarten, nursery school; **~gärtnerin** ['kɪndɐgɛrtnərɪn] *f* (-; *-nen*) nursery-school *or* kindergarten teacher; **~geld** *n* child benefit; **~hort** ['kɪndɐhɔrt] *m* (*-[e]s*; *-e*), **~krippe** *f* day nursery; **~lähmung** *f* MED polio(-myelitis)

**'kinderlieb** *adj* fond of children

**'kinderlos** *adj* childless

**'Kinder|mädchen** *n* nurse(maid), nanny; **~spiel** *fig n*: ***ein ~ sein*** be child's play; **~stube** *fig f* manners, upbringing; **~wagen** *m* baby carriage, buggy, *Br* pram; **~zimmer** *n* children's room

**Kindes|alter** ['kɪndəsʔaltɐ] *n* childhood; infancy; **~entführung** *f* kidnap(p)ing; **~misshandlung** *f* child abuse

**'Kindheit** *f* (-; *no pl*) (***von ~ an*** from) childhood

K

**kindisch** ['kɪndɪʃ] *adj* childish
**'kindlich** *adj* childlike
**Kinn** [kɪn] *n* (-[*e*]*s*; -*e*) ANAT chin; **~backe** *f*, **~backen** *m* (-*s*; -) ANAT jaw(-bone); **~haken** *m boxing*: hook (to the chin), uppercut
**Kino** ['kiːno] *n* (-*s*; -*s*) (*no pl*) motion pictures, *esp Br* cinema, F *the* movies; movie theater, *esp Br* cinema
**'Kinobesucher** *m*, **'Kinogänger** ['kiːnogɛŋɐ] *m* (-*s*; -) moviegoer, *Br* cinemagoer
**Kippe** ['kɪpə] *f* (-; -*n*) F butt, *esp Br* stub; SPORT upstart
**'kippen 1.** *v/i* (*ge-*, *sein*) tip *or* topple (over) **2.** *v/t* (*ge-*, *h*) tilt, tip over *or* up
**Kirche** ['kɪrçə] *f* (-; -*n*) church; ***in die ~ gehen*** go to church
**'Kirchen|buch** *n* parish register; **~diener** *m* sexton; **~gemeinde** *f* parish; **~jahr** *n* Church *or* ecclesiastical year; **~lied** *n* hymn; **~mu,sik** *f* sacred *or* church music; **~schiff** *n* ARCH nave; **~steuer** *f* church tax; **~stuhl** *m* pew; **~tag** *m* church congress
**'Kirchgang** *m* churchgoing; **Kirchgänger** ['kɪrçgɛŋɐ] *m* (-*s*; -) churchgoer
**'kirchlich** *adj* church, ecclesiastical
**'Kirchturm** *m* steeple; spire; church tower
**Kirsche** ['kɪrʃə] *f* (-; -*n*) BOT cherry
**Kissen** ['kɪsən] *n* (-*s*; -) pillow; cushion; **~bezug** *m*, **~hülle** *f* pillowcase, pillowslip
**Kiste** ['kɪstə] *f* (-; -*n*) box, chest; crate
**Kitsch** [kɪtʃ] *m* (-[*e*]*s*; *no pl*) kitsch; trash; F slush
**'kitschig** *adj* kitschy; trashy; slushy
**Kitt** [kɪt] *m* (-[*e*]*s*; -*e*) cement; putty
**Kittel** ['kɪtəl] *m* (-*s*; -) smock; overall; MED (white) coat
**'kitten** *v/t* (*ge-*, *h*) cement; putty
**Kitzel** ['kɪtsəl] *m* (-*s*; -) tickle, *fig a.* thrill, kick; **'kitzeln** *v/i and v/t* (*ge-*, *h*) tickle; **Kitzler** ['kɪtslɐ] *m* (-*s*; -) ANAT clitoris; **kitzlig** ['kɪtslɪç] *adj* ticklish (*a. fig*)
**kläffen** ['klɛfən] *v/i* (*ge-*, *h*) yap, yelp
**klaffend** ['klafənt] *adj* gaping; yawning
**Klage** ['klaːgə] *f* (-; -*n*) complaint; lament; JUR action, (law)suit
**'klagen** *v/i* (*ge-*, *h*) complain (***über*** *acc* of, about; ***bei*** to); lament; JUR go to court; ***gegen j-n ~*** JUR sue s.o.
**Kläger** ['klɛːgɐ] *m* (-*s*; -), **'Klägerin** *f* (-; -*nen*) JUR plaintiff
**kläglich** ['klɛːklɪç] → ***jämmerlich***
**Klamauk** [kla'mauk] *m* (-*s*; *no pl*) racket; THEA *etc* slapstick
**klamm** [klam] *adj* numb; clammy
**Klammer** ['klamɐ] *f* (-; -*n*) TECH cramp, clamp; clip; clothespin, *Br* (clothes) peg; MED brace; MATH, PRINT bracket(s); **'klammern** *v/t* (*ge-*, *h*) fasten *or* clip together; ***sich ~ an*** (*acc*) cling to
**klang** [klaŋ] *pret of* ***klingen***
**Klang** *m* (-[*e*]*s*; *Klänge* ['klɛŋə]) sound; tone; clink; ringing
**'klangvoll** *adj* sonorous; *fig* illustrious
**Klappe** ['klapə] *f* (-; -*n*) flap; hinged lid; MOT tailgate, *Br* tailboard; TECH, BOT, ANAT valve; F trap; **'klappen** (*ge-*, *h*) **1.** *v/t*: ***nach oben ~*** lift up, raise; put *or* fold up; ***nach unten ~*** lower, put down; ***es lässt sich*** (***nach hinten***) ***~*** it folds (backward) **2.** *v/i* clap, clack; F work, work out (well)
**Klapper** ['klapɐ] *f* (-; -*n*) rattle
**'klappern** *v/i* (*ge-*, *h*) clatter, rattle (***mit et.*** s.th.)
**'Klapperschlange** *f* ZO rattlesnake
**Klapp|fahrrad** ['klapfaːraːt] *n* folding bicycle; **~fenster** *n* top-hung window; **~messer** *n* jack knife, clasp knife
**klapprig** ['klaprɪç] *adj* MOT rattly, ramshackle; F shaky
**'Klappsitz** *m* folding *or* tip-up seat
**'Klappstuhl** *m* folding chair
**'Klapptisch** *m* folding table
**Klaps** [klaps] *m* (-*es*; -*e*) slap, pat; smack
**klar** [klaːɐ] *adj* clear (*a. fig*); ***ist dir ~, dass …?*** do you realize that …?; ***das ist mir*** (***nicht ganz***) ***~*** I (don't quite) understand; (***na***) ***~!*** of course!; ***alles ~?*** everything okay?
**Kläranlage** ['klɛːɐˀanlaːgə] *f* sewage works
**klären** ['klɛːrən] *v/t* (*ge-*, *h*) TECH purify, treat; *fig* clear up; settle; SPORT clear
**'Klarheit** *f* (-; *no pl*) clearness, *fig a.* clarity
**Klarinette** [klari'nɛtə] *f* (-; -*n*) MUS clarinet
**'Klarsicht...** *in cpds* transparent
**Klasse** ['klasə] *f* (-; -*n*) class (*a.* POL), PED *a.* grade, *Br* form; classroom; F ***klasse sein*** be super, be fantastic
**'Klassen|arbeit** *f* (classroom) test;

**~buch** *n* classbook, *Br* (class) register; **~kame,rad** *m* classmate; **~lehrer(in)** homeroom teacher, *Br* form teacher, *a.* form master (mistress); **~sprecher** *m* class representative; **~zimmer** *n* classroom

**klassifizieren** [klasifi'tsi:rən] *v/t* (*no -ge-, h*) classify; '**Klassifi'zierung** *f* (-; *-en*) classification

**Klassiker** ['klasikɐ] *m* (*-s*; -) classic

**klassisch** ['klasɪʃ] *adj* classic(al)

**Klatsch** [klatʃ] F *m* (*-es*; *no pl*) gossip

'**Klatschbase** *f* gossip

'**klatschen** *v/i and v/t* (*ge-, h*) clap, applaud; F slap, bang; splash; F gossip; ***in die Hände ~*** clap one's hands

'**klatschhaft** *adj* gossipy

'**Klatschmaul** F *n* (old) gossip

'**klatsch'nass** F *adj* soaking wet

**klauben** ['klaubən] *Austrian v/t* (*ge-, h*) pick; gather

**Klaue** ['klauə] *f* (-; *-n*) ZO claw; *pl fig* clutches

**klauen** ['klauən] F *v/t* (*ge-, h*) pinch

**Klausel** ['klauzəl] *f* (-; *-n*) JUR clause; condition

**Klausur** [klau'zu:ɐ] *f* (-; *-en*) test (paper), exam(ination)

**Klavier** [kla'vi:ɐ] *n* (*-s*; *-e*) MUS piano; ***~ spielen*** play the piano; **~kon,zert** *n* MUS piano concerto; piano recital

**Klebeband** ['kle:bəbant] *n* (-[*e*]*s*; *-bänder*) adhesive tape; **kleben** ['kle:bən] (*ge-, h*) **1.** *v/t* glue, paste; stick **2.** *v/i* stick, cling (***an*** *dat* to) (*a. fig*); **klebrig** ['kle:brɪç] *adj* sticky

**Kleb|stoff** ['kle:pʃtɔf] *m* adhesive; glue; **~streifen** *m* adhesive tape

**kleckern** ['klɛkɐn] F (*ge-, h*) **1.** *v/i* make a mess **2.** *v/t* spill

**Klecks** [klɛks] F *m* (*-es*; *-e*) (ink)blot; blob; **klecksen** ['klɛksən] F *v/i* (*ge-, h*) blot, make blots

**Klee** [kle:] *m* (*-s*; *no pl*) BOT clover

'**Kleeblatt** *n* cloverleaf

**Kleid** [klait] *n* (-[*e*]*s*; *-er* ['klaidɐ]) dress; *pl* clothes; **kleiden** ['klaidən] *v/t* (*ge-, h*) dress, clothe; ***j-n gut ~*** suit s.o.; ***sich gut*** *etc* **~** dress well *etc*

**Kleider|bügel** ['klaidɐby:gəl] *m* (coat) hanger; **~bürste** *f* clothes brush; **~haken** *m* coat hook; **~schrank** *m* wardrobe; **~ständer** *m* coat stand; **~stoff** *m* dress material

'**kleidsam** *adj* becoming

'**Kleidung** *f* (-; *no pl*) clothes, clothing

'**Kleidungsstück** *n* article of clothing

**Kleie** ['klaiə] *f* (-; *-n*) AGR bran

**klein** [klain] *adj* small, *esp* F little (*a. finger, brother*); short; ***von ~ auf*** from an early age; ***ein ~ wenig*** a little bit; ***Groß und Klein*** young and old; ***die Kleinen*** the little ones; ***~ schneiden*** cut up (into small pieces)

'**Klein|anzeige** *f* want ad, *Br* small ad; **~bildkamera** *f* 35 mm camera; **~fa,milie** *f* nuclear family; **~geld** *n* (small) change; **~holz** *n* matchwood

**Kleinigkeit** ['klainɪçkait] *f* (-; *-en*) little thing, trifle; little something; ***e-e ~ sein*** be nothing, be child's play

'**Kleinkind** *n* baby, infant

'**Kleinkram** F *m* odds and ends

'**kleinlaut** *adj* subdued

'**kleinlich** *adj* small-minded, petty; mean; pedantic, fussy

'**kleinschneiden** *v/t* (*irr*, ***schneiden***, *sep, -ge-, h*) → ***klein***

'**Kleinstadt** *f* small town; '**kleinstädtisch** *adj* small-town, provincial

'**Kleintrans,porter** *m* MOT pick-up

'**Kleinwagen** *m* MOT small *or* compact car, F runabout

**Kleister** ['klaistɐ] *m* (*-s*; -) paste

**Klemme** ['klɛmə] *f* (-; *-n*) TECH clamp; (hair) clip; F ***in der ~ sitzen*** be in a fix *or* tight spot; '**klemmen** *v/i and v/t* (*ge-, h*) jam; stick; be stuck, be jammed; ***sich ~*** jam one's finger *or* hand

**Klempner** ['klɛmpnɐ] *m* (*-s*; -) plumber

**Klepper** ['klɛpɐ] *m* (*-s*; -) ZO nag

**Klerus** ['kle:rʊs] *m* (-; *no pl*) REL clergy

**Klette** ['klɛtə] *f* (-; *-n*) BOT bur(r); *fig* leech

**klettern** ['klɛtɐn] *v/i* (*ge-, sein*) climb; ***auf e-n Baum ~*** climb (up) a tree

'**Kletterpflanze** *f* BOT climber

**Klient** [kli'ɛnt] *m* (*-en*; *-en*), **Kli'entin** *f* (-; *-nen*) client

**Klima** ['kli:ma] *n* (*-s*; *-s*) climate, *fig a.* atmosphere

'**Klimaanlage** *f* air-conditioning

**klimatisch** [kli'ma:tɪʃ] *adj* climatic

**klimpern** ['klɪmpɐn] *v/i* (*ge-, h*) jingle, chink (***mit et.*** s.th.); F MUS strum (away) (***auf*** *dat* on)

K

**Klinge** ['klɪŋə] *f* (-; *-n*) blade
**Klingel** ['klɪŋəl] *f* (-; *-n*) bell
'**Klingelknopf** *m* bell (push)
'**klingeln** *v/i* (*ge-*, *h*) ring (the bell); ***es klingelt*** the (door)bell is ringing
'**klingen** *v/i* (*irr*, *ge-*, *h*) sound; *bell*, *metal etc*: ring; *glasses etc*: clink
**Klinik** ['kli:nɪk] *f* (-; *-en*) hospital; clinic
**klinisch** ['kli:nɪʃ] *adj* clinical
**Klinke** ['klɪŋkə] *f* (-; *-n*) (door) handle
**Klippe** ['klɪpə] *f* (-; *-n*) cliff, rock(s); *fig* obstacle
**klirren** ['klɪrən] *v/i* (*ge-*, *h*) *window*: rattle; *glasses etc*: clink; *broken glass*: tinkle; *swords*: clash; *keys*, *coins*: jingle
**Klischee** [kli'ʃe:] *n* (*-s*; *-s*) cliché
**klobig** ['klo:bɪç] *adj* bulky, clumsy
**klopfen** ['klɔpfən] (*ge-*, *h*) **1.** *v/i heart etc*: beat, throb; knock (***an*** *acc* at, on); tap; pat; ***es klopft*** there's a knock at the door **2.** *v/t* beat; knock; drive (*nail etc*)
**Klosett** [klo'zɛt] *n* (*-s*; *-s*) lavatory, toilet
**Kloß** [klo:s] *m* (*-es*; *Klöße* ['klø:sə]) clod, lump (*a. fig*); GASTR dumpling
**Kloster** ['klo:stɐ] *n* (*-s*; *Klöster* ['klø:stɐ]) REL monastery; convent
**Klotz** [klɔts] *m* (*-es*; *Klötze* ['klœtsə]) block; log
**Klub** [klʊb] *m* (*-s*; *-s*) club
'**Klubsessel** *m* lounge chair
**Kluft** [klʊft] *f* (-; *Klüfte* ['klʏftə]) gap (*a. fig*); abyss
**klug** [klu:k] *adj* intelligent, clever, F bright, smart; wise; ***daraus*** (***aus ihm***) ***werde ich nicht ~*** I don't know what to make of it (him)
'**Klugheit** *f* (-; *no pl*) intelligence, cleverness, F brains; good sense; knowledge
**Klumpen** ['klʊmpən] *m* (*-s*; -) lump; clod; nugget; '**Klumpfuß** *m* MED club foot; '**klumpig** *adj* lumpy; cloddish
**knabbern** ['knabɐn] *v/t and v/i* (*ge-*, *h*) nibble, gnaw
**Knabe** ['kna:bə] *m* (*-n*; *-n*) boy
'**knabenhaft** *adj* boyish
**Knäckebrot** ['knɛkəbro:t] *n* crispbread
**knacken** ['knakən] *v/t and v/i* (*ge-*, *h*) crack; *twig*: snap; *fire*, *radio*: crackle
**Knacks** F *m* (*-es*; *-e*) crack; *fig* defect
**Knall** [knal] *m* (*-[e]s*; *-e*) bang; crack, report; pop; F ***e-n ~ haben*** be nuts
'**Knallbon**,**bon** *m*, *n* cracker
'**knallen** *v/i and v/t* (*ge-*, *h*) bang; slam; crack; pop; F crash (***gegen*** into); F ***j-m e-e ~*** slap s.o.('s face)
'**knallig** F *adj* flashy, loud
'**Knallkörper** *m* firecracker
**knapp** [knap] *adj* scarce; scanty, meager, *Br* meagre (*food*, *pay etc*); bare (*a. majority etc*); limited (*time etc*); narrow (*escape etc*); tight (*dress etc*); brief; ***~ an Geld*** (***Zeit*** *etc*) short of money (time *etc*); ***mit ~er Not*** only just, barely
**Knappe** ['knapə] *m* (*-n*; *-n*) miner
'**knapphalten** *v/t* (*irr*, **halten**, *sep*, *-ge-*, *h*): ***j-n ~*** keep s.o. short
'**Knappheit** *f* (-; *no pl*) shortage
**Knarre** ['knarə] *f* (-; *-n*) rattle; F gun
'**knarren** *v/i* (*ge-*, *h*) creak
**Knast** [knast] F *m* (*-[e]s*; *Knäste* ['knɛstə]) *sl* clink
**knattern** ['knatɐn] *v/i* (*ge-*, *h*) crackle; MOT roar
**Knäuel** ['knɔʏəl] *m*, *n* (*-s*; -) ball; tangle
**Knauf** [knauf] *m* (*-[e]s*; *Knäufe* ['knɔʏfə]) knob; pommel
**knaus(e)rig** ['knauz(ə)rɪç] F *adj* stingy
**knautschen** ['knautʃən] *v/t and v/i* (*ge-*, *h*) crumple
'**Knautschzone** *f* MOT crumple zone
**Knebel** ['kne:bəl] *m* (*-s*; -), '**knebeln** *v/t* (*ge-*, *h*) gag (*a. fig*)
**kneifen** ['knaifən] *v/t and v/i* (*irr*, *ge-*, *h*) pinch (***j-m in den Arm*** s.o.'s arm); F chicken out; '**Kneifzange** *f* pincers
**Kneipe** ['knaipə] F *f* (-; *-n*) saloon, bar, *esp Br* pub
**kneten** ['kne:tən] *v/t* (*ge-*, *h*) knead; mo(u)ld; '**Knetmasse** *f* Plasticine®, Play-Doh®
**Knick** [knɪk] *m* (*-[e]s*; *-e*, *-s*) fold, crease; bend; '**knicken** *v/t* (*ge-*, *h*) fold, crease; bend; break; ***nicht ~!*** do not bend!
**Knicks** [knɪks] *m* (*-es*; *-e*) curts(e)y; ***e-n ~ machen*** → '**knicksen** *v/i* (*ge-*, *h*) curts(e)y (***vor*** *dat* to)
**Knie** [kni:] *n* (*-s*; - ['kni:ə, kni:]) ANAT knee; **~beuge** *f* SPORT knee bend; **~kehle** *f* ANAT hollow of the knee
**knien** [kni:n] *v/i* (*ge-*, *h*) kneel, be on one's knees (***vor*** *dat* before)
'**Kniescheibe** *f* ANAT kneecap
'**Kniestrumpf** *m* knee(-length) sock
**kniff** [knɪf] *pret of* ***kneifen***
**Kniff** *m* (*-[e]s*; *-e*) crease, fold; pinch; trick, knack
**kniff(e)lig** ['knɪf(ə)lɪç] *adj* tricky

**knipsen** ['knɪpsən] *v/t and v/i* (*ge-*, *h*) F PHOT take a picture (of); punch, clip
**Knirps** [knɪrps] *m* (*-es*; *-e*) little guy
**knirschen** ['knɪrʃən] *v/i* (*ge-*, *h*) crunch; ***mit den Zähnen*** **~** grind *or* gnash one's teeth
**knistern** ['knɪstɐn] *v/i* (*ge-*, *h*) crackle; rustle
**knittern** ['knɪtɐn] *v/t and v/i* (*ge-*, *h*) crumple, crease, wrinkle
**Knoblauch** ['kno:plaux] *m* (*-[e]s*; *no pl*) BOT garlic
**Knöchel** ['knœçəl] *m* (*-s*; *-*) ANAT ankle; knuckle
**Knochen** ['knɔxən] *m* (*-s*; *-*) ANAT bone
'**Knochenbruch** *m* MED fracture
**knochig** ['knɔxɪç] *adj* bony
**Knödel** ['knø:dəl] *m* (*-s*; *-*) dumpling
**Knolle** ['knɔlə] *f* (*-*; *-n*) BOT tuber; bulb
**Knopf** [knɔpf] *m* (*-es*; *Knöpfe* ['knœpfə]), **knöpfen** ['knœpfən] *v/t* (*ge-*, *h*) button
'**Knopfloch** *n* buttonhole
**Knorpel** ['knɔrpəl] *m* (*-s*; *-*) GASTR gristle; ANAT cartilage
**knorrig** ['knɔrɪç] *adj* gnarled, knotted
**Knospe** ['knɔspə] *f* (*-*; *-n*), '**knospen** *v/i* (*ge-*, *h*) BOT bud
**knoten** [kno:tən] *v/t* (*ge-*, *h*) knot, make a knot in; '**Knoten** *m* (*-s*; *-*) knot (*a. fig*); '**Knotenpunkt** *m* center, *Br* centre; RAIL junction
**knüllen** ['knʏlən] *v/t and v/i* (*ge-*, *h*) crumple
**Knüller** ['knʏlɐ] F *m* (*-s*; *-*) smash (hit); scoop
**knüpfen** ['knʏpfən] *v/t* (*ge-*, *h*) tie; weave
**Knüppel** ['knʏpəl] *m* (*-s*; *-*) stick, cudgel; truncheon; **~schaltung** *f* floor shift
**knurren** ['knʊrən] *v/i* (*ge-*, *h*) growl, snarl; *fig* grumble (***über*** *acc* at); *stomach*: rumble
**knusp(e)rig** ['knʊsp(ə)rɪç] *adj* crisp, crunchy
**knutschen** ['knu:tʃən] F *v/i* (*ge-*, *h*) pet, neck, smooch
**k.o.** [ka:'ʔo:] *adj* knocked out; *fig* beat
**Koalition** [koali'tsjo:n] *f* (*-*; *-en*) *esp* POL coalition; ***Große*** **~** grand coalition
**Kobold** ['ko:bɔlt] *m* (*-[e]s*; *-e*) (hob)goblin, imp (*a. fig*)
**Koch** [kɔx] *m* (*-[e]s*; *Köche* ['kœçə]) cook; chef; **~buch** *n* cookbook, *Br* cookery book
'**kochen** (*ge-*, *h*) **1.** *v/t* cook; boil (*eggs etc*); make (*coffee etc*) **2.** *v/i* cook, do the cooking; boil (*a. fig*); ***gut*** **~** be a good cook; F ***vor Wut*** **~** boil with rage; **~*d heiß*** boiling hot
**Kocher** ['kɔxɐ] *m* (*-s*; *-*) ELECTR cooker
**Köchin** ['kœçɪn] *f* (*-*; *-nen*) cook; chef
'**Koch|löffel** *m* (wooden) spoon; **~nische** *f* kitchenette; **~platte** *f* hotplate; **~salz** *n* common salt; **~topf** *m* saucepan, pot
**Köder** ['kø:dɐ] *m* (*-s*; *-*) bait, decoy (*both a. fig*), lure; '**ködern** *v/t* (*ge-*, *h*) bait, decoy (*both a. fig*)
**Kodex** ['ko:dɛks] *m* (*-es*; *-*, *-e*) code
**kodieren** [ko'di:rən] *v/t* (*no -ge-*, *h*) (en)code; **Ko'dierung** *f* (*-*; *-en*) (en)coding
**Koffein** [kɔfe'i:n] *n* (*-s*; *no pl*) caffeine
**Koffer** ['kɔfɐ] *m* (*-s*; *-*) (suit)case; trunk; **~radio** *n* portable (radio); **~raum** *m* MOT trunk, *Br* booth
**Kognak®** ['kɔnjak] *m* (*-s*; *-s*) cognac® *brandy from the Cognac region in France*
**Kohl** [ko:l] *m* (*-[e]s*; *-e*) BOT cabbage
**Kohle** ['ko:lə] *f* (*-*; *-n*) coal; ELECTR carbon; F dough
'**Kohlehy,drat** *n* carbohydrate
'**Kohlen...** *in cpds ...dioxid etc*: CHEM carbon ...; **~bergwerk** *n* coalmine, colliery; **~ofen** *m* coal-burning stove
'**Kohlensäure** *f* CHEM carbonic acid; GASTR F fizz; '**kohlensäurehaltig** *adj* carbonated, F fizzy
'**Kohlen|stoff** *m* CHEM carbon; **~wasserstoff** *m* CHEM hydrocarbon
'**Kohle|pa,pier** *n* carbon paper; **~zeichnung** *f* charcoal drawing
**Kohlrabi** [ko:l'ra:bi] *m* (*-s*; *-s*) BOT kohlrabi
**Koje** ['ko:jə] *f* (*-*; *-n*) MAR berth, bunk
**Kokain** [koka'i:n] *n* (*-s*; *no pl*) cocaine
**kokettieren** [kokɛ'ti:rən] *v/i* (*no -ge-*, *h*) flirt; *fig* **~ *mit*** toy with
**Kokosnuss** ['ko:kɔsnʊs] *f* BOT coconut
**Koks** [ko:ks] *m* (*-es*; *no pl*) coke; F dough; *sl* coke, snow
**Kolben** ['kɔlbən] *m* (*-s*; *-*) butt; TECH piston; **~stange** *f* TECH piston rod
**Kolibri** ['ko:libri] *m* (*-s*; *-s*) ZO humming bird
**Kolleg** [kɔ'le:k] *n* (*-s*; *-s*) UNIV course (of lectures)

K

**Kollege** [kɔ'leːgə] *m* (*-n*; *-n*), **Kol'legin** *f* (*-*; *-nen*) colleague
**Kollegium** [kɔ'leːgjʊm] *n* (*-s*; *-ien*) UNIV faculty, *Br* teaching staff
**Kollekte** [kɔ'lɛktə] *f* (*-*; *-n*) REL collection
**Kollektion** [kɔlɛk'tsjoːn] *f* (*-*; *-en*) ECON collection; range
**kollektiv** [kɔlɛk'tiːf] *adj*, **Kollek'tiv** *n* (*-s*; *-e*) collective (*a. in cpds*)
**Koller** ['kɔlɐ] F *m* (*-s*; *-*) fit; rage
**kollidieren** [kɔli'diːrən] *v/i* (*no -ge-*, *sein*) collide; **Kollision** [kɔli'zjoːn] *f* (*-*; *-en*) collision, *fig a.* clash, conflict
**Kölnischwasser** ['kœlnɪʃvasɐ] *n* (*-s*; *-*) (eau de) cologne
**Kolonie** [kolo'niː] *f* (*-*; *-n*) colony
**kolonisieren** [koloni'ziːrən] *v/t* (*no -ge-*, *h*) colonize; **Koloni'sierung** *f* (*-*; *-en*) colonization
**Kolonne** [ko'lɔnə] *f* (*-*; *-n*) column; MIL convoy; gang, crew
**Koloss** [ko'lɔs] *m* (*-es*; *-e*) colossus, *fig a.* giant (of a man)
**kolossal** [kolɔ'saːl] *adj* gigantic

**Kombi** ['kɔmbi] *m* (*-[s]*; *-s*) MOT station wagon, *Br* estate (car)
**Kombination** [kɔmbina'tsjoːn] *f* (*-*; *-en*) combination; set; coveralls, *Br* overalls; flying suit; *soccer*: combined move
**kombinieren** [kɔmbi'niːrən] (*no -ge-*, *h*) **1.** *v/t* combine **2.** *v/i* reason
**Kombüse** [kɔm'byːzə] *f* (*-*; *-n*) MAR galley
**Komet** [ko'meːt] *m* (*-en*; *-en*) ASTR comet
**Komfort** [kɔm'foːɐ] *m* (*-s*; *no pl*) (modern) conveniences; luxury
**komfortabel** [kɔmfɔr'taːbəl] *adj* comfortable; well-appointed; luxurious
**Komik** ['koːmɪk] *f* (*-*; *no pl*) humo(u)r; comic effect; **Komiker** ['koːmikɐ] *m* (*-s*; *-*) comedian; **komisch** ['koːmɪʃ] *adj* comic(al), funny; strange, odd
**Komitee** [komi'teː] *n* (*-s*; *-s*) committee
**Komma** ['kɔma] *n* (*-s*; *-s*, *-ta*) comma; ***sechs ~ vier*** six point four
**Kommandant** [kɔman'dant] *m* (*-en*; *-en*), **Kommandeur** [kɔman'døːɐ] *m* (*-s*; *-e*) MIL commander, commanding officer; **kommandieren** [kɔman'diːrən] *v/i and v/t* (*no -ge-*, *h*) command, be in command of; **Kommando** [kɔ'mando] *n* (*-s*; *-s*) command; order; MIL commando; **Kom'mandobrücke** *f* MAR (navigating) bridge
**kommen** ['kɔmən] *v/i* (*irr*, *ge-*, *sein*) come; arrive; get; reach; ***zu spät ~*** be late; ***weit ~*** get far; ***zur Schule ~*** start school; ***ins Gefängnis ~*** go to jail; ***~ lassen*** send for *s.o.*, call *s.o.*; order *s.th.*; ***~ auf*** (*acc*) think of, hit upon; remember; ***hinter et. ~*** find s.th. out; ***um et. ~*** lose s.th.; miss s.th.; ***zu et. ~*** come by s.th.; ***wieder zu sich ~*** come round *or* to; ***wohin kommt …?*** where does … go?; ***daher kommt es, dass*** that's why; ***woher kommt es, dass …?*** why is it that …?, F how come …?
**Kommentar** [kɔmɛn'taːɐ] *m* (*-s*; *-e*) commentary; ***kein ~!*** no comment
**Kommentator** [kɔmɛn'taːtoːɐ] *m* (*-s*; *-en* [kɔmɛnta'toːrən]), **Kommentatorin** [kɔmɛnta'toːrɪn] *f* (*-*; *-nen*) commentator
**kommentieren** [kɔmɛn'tiːrən] *v/t* (*no -ge-*, *h*) comment (on)
**kommerzialisieren** [kɔmɛrtsjali'ziːrən] *v/t* (*no -ge-*, *h*) commercialize
**Kommissar** [kɔmɪ'saːɐ] *m* (*-s*; *-e*) commissioner; superintendent
**Kommission** [kɔmɪ'sjoːn] *f* (*-*; *-en*) commission; committee
**Kommode** [kɔ'moːdə] *f* (*-*; *-n*) bureau, *Br* chest (of drawers)
**Kommunal…** [kɔmu'naːl-] *in cpds …politik etc*: local …; **Kommune** [kɔ'muːnə] *f* (*-*; *-n*) commune
**Kommunikation** [kɔmunika'tsjoːn] *f* (*-*; *no pl*) communication
**Kommunion** [kɔmu'njoːn] *f* (*-*; *-en*) REL (Holy) Communion
**Kommunismus** [kɔmu'nɪsmʊs] *m* (*-*; *no pl*) POL communism; **Kommunist** [kɔmu'nɪst] *m* (*-en*; *-en*), **Kommu'nistin** *f* (*-*; *-nen*), **kommu'nistisch** *adj* POL communist
**Komödie** [ko'møːdjə] *f* (*-*; *-n*) comedy; ***~ spielen*** put on an act, play-act
**kompakt** [kɔm'pakt] *adj* compact
**Kom'paktanlage** *f* stereo system, music center (*Br* centre)
**Kompanie** [kɔmpa'niː] *f* (*-*; *-n*) MIL company
**Kompass** ['kɔmpas] *m* (*-es*; *-e*) compass
**kompatibel** [kɔmpa'tiːbəl] *adj* compatible (*a.* IT)
**komplett** [kɔm'plɛt] *adj* complete

**Komplex** [kɔm'plɛks] *m* (*-es*; *-e*) complex (*a.* PSYCH)

**Kompliment** [kɔmpli'mɛnt] *n* (*-[e]s*; *-e*) compliment; ***j-m ein ~ machen*** pay s.o. a compliment

**Komplize** [kɔm'pliːtsə] *m* (*-n*; *-n*) accomplice

**komplizieren** [kɔmpli'tsiːrən] *v/t* (*no -ge-*, *h*) complicate; **kompliziert** [kɔmpli'tsiːɐt] *adj* complicated, complex

**Kom'plizin** *f* (*-*; *-nen*) accomplice

**Komplott** [kɔm'plɔt] *n* (*-[e]s*; *-e*) plot, conspiracy

**komponieren** [kɔmpo'niːrən] *v/t and v/i* (*no -ge-*, *h*) MUS compose; write; **Komponist** [kɔmpo'nɪst] *m* (*-en*; *-en*) MUS composer; **Komposition** [kɔmpozi'tsjoːn] *f* (*-*; *-en*) MUS composition

**Kompott** [kɔm'pɔt] *n* (*-[e]s*; *-e*) GASTR compot(e), stewed fruit

**Kompresse** [kɔm'prɛsə] *f* (*-*; *-n*) MED compress

**komprimieren** [kɔmpri'miːrən] *v/t* (*no -ge-*, *h*) compress

**Kompromiss** [kɔmpro'mɪs] *m* (*-es*; *-e*) compromise; **kompro'misslos** *adj* uncompromising

**kompromittieren** [kɔmpromɪ'tiːrən] *v/t* (*no -ge-*, *h*) compromise (***sich*** o.s.); **~d** *adj* compromising

**Kondensator** [kɔndɛn'zaːtoːɐ] *m* (*-s*; *-en* [kɔndɛnza'toːrən]) ELECTR capacitor; TECH condenser; **kondensieren** [kɔndɛn'ziːrən] *v/t* (*no -ge-*, *h*) condense

**Kondensmilch** [kɔn'dɛnsmɪlç] *f* condensed milk

**Kondition** [kɔndi'tsjoːn] *f* (*-*; *-en*) condition; (*no pl*) SPORT condition, shape, form; ***gute ~*** (great) stamina

**konditional** [kɔnditsjo'naːl] *adj* LING conditional

**Konditi'onstraining** *n* fitness training

**Konditor** [kɔn'diːtoːɐ] *m* (*-s*; *-en* [kɔndi'toːrən]) confectioner, pastrycook

**Konditorei** [kɔndito'rai] *f* (*-*; *-en*) cake shop; café, tearoom; **~waren** *pl* confectionery

**Kondom** [kɔn'doːm] *n*, *m* (*-s*; *-e*) condom

**Kondukteur** [kɔndʊk'tøːɐ] *Swiss m* (*-s*; *-e*) → ***Schaffner***

**Konfekt** [kɔn'fɛkt] *n* (*-[e]s*; *-e*) sweets, chocolates

**Konfektion** [kɔnfɛk'tsjoːn] *f* (*-*; *no pl*) ready-made clothing; **Konfekti'ons...** *in cpds* ready-made ..., off-the-peg ...

**Konferenz** [kɔnfe'rɛnts] *f* (*-*; *-en*) conference

**Konfession** [kɔnfɛ'sjoːn] *f* (*-*; *-en*) religion, denomination; **konfessionell** [kɔnfɛsjo'nɛl] *adj* confessional, denominational; **Konfessi'onsschule** *f* denominational school

**Konfirmand** [kɔnfɪr'mant] *m* (*-en*; *-en*), **Konfir'mandin** *f* (*-*; *-nen*) REL confirmand; **Konfirmation** [kɔnfɪrma'tsjoːn] *f* (*-*; *-en*) REL confirmation; **konfirmieren** [kɔnfɪr'miːrən] *v/t* (*no -ge-*, *h*) confirm

**konfiszieren** [kɔnfɪs'tsiːrən] *v/t* (*no -ge-*, *h*) JUR confiscate

**Konfitüre** [kɔnfi'tyːrə] *f* (*-*; *-n*) jam

**Konflikt** [kɔn'flɪkt] *m* (*-[e]s*; *-e*) conflict

**konfrontieren** [kɔnfrɔn'tiːrən] *v/t* (*no -ge-*, *h*) confront

**konfus** [kɔn'fuːs] *adj* confused, mixed-up

**Kongress** [kɔn'grɛs] *m* (*-es*; *-e*) convention, *Br* congress

**König** ['køːnɪç] *m* (*-s*; *-e*) king

**Königin** ['køːnɪgɪn] *f* (*-*; *-nen*) queen

**königlich** ['køːnɪklɪç] *adj* royal

**Königreich** ['køːnɪkraiç] *n* kingdom

**Konjugation** [kɔnjuga'tsjoːn] *f* (*-*; *-en*) LING conjugation; **konjugieren** [kɔnju'giːrən] *v/t* (*no -ge-*, *h*) LING conjugate

**Konjunktiv** ['kɔnjʊŋktiːf] *m* (*-s*; *-e*) LING subjunctive (mood)

**Konjunktur** [kɔnjʊŋk'tuːɐ] *f* (*-*; *-en*) economic situation

**konkret** [kɔn'kreːt] *adj* concrete

**Konkurrent** [kɔnkʊ'rɛnt] *m* (*-en*; *-en*), **Konkur'rentin** *f* (*-*; *-nen*) competitor, rival; **Konkurrenz** [kɔnkʊ'rɛnts] *f* (*-*; *no pl*) competition; ***die ~*** one's competitors; ***außer ~*** not competing; → ***konkurrenzlos***

**konkur'renzfähig** *adj* competitive

**Konkur'renzkampf** *m* competition

**konkur'renzlos** *adj* without competition, unrival(l)ed

**konkurrieren** [kɔnkʊ'riːrən] *v/i* (*no -ge-*, *h*) compete

**Konkurs** [kɔn'kʊrs] *m* (*-es*; *-e*) ECON, JUR bankruptcy; ***in ~ gehen*** go bankrupt;

**~masse** *f* JUR bankrupt's estate
**können** ['kœnən] *v/t and v/i (irr, ge-, h), v/aux (irr, no -ge-, h)* can, be able to; may, be allowed to; ***kann ich gehen*** *etc?* can *or* may I go *etc?*; ***du kannst nicht*** you cannot *or* can't; ***ich kann nicht mehr*** I can't go on; I can't manage *or* eat any more; ***es kann sein*** it may be; ***ich kann nichts dafür*** it's not my fault; ***e-e Sprache ~*** know *or* speak a language
'**Können** *n (-s; no pl)* ability, skill
**Könner** ['kœnɐ] *m (-s; -)*, '**Könnerin** *f (-; -nen)* master, expert; *esp* SPORT ace, crack
**konnte** ['kɔntə] *pret of* ***können***
**konsequent** [kɔnze'kvɛnt] *adj* consistent; **Konsequenz** [kɔnze'kvɛnts] *f (-; -en) (no pl)* consistency; consequence
**konservativ** [kɔnzɛrva'ti:f] *adj* conservative
**Konserven** [kɔn'zɛrvən] *pl* canned (*Br a.* tinned) foods; **~büchse** *f*, **~dose** *f* can, *Br a.* tin; **~fa,brik** *f* cannery
**konservieren** [kɔnzɛr'vi:rən] *v/t (no -ge-, h)* preserve; **Konser'vierungsmittel** *n* preservative
**Konsonant** [kɔnzɔ'nant] *m (-en; -en)* LING consonant
**konstruieren** [kɔnstru'i:rən] *v/t (no -ge-, h)* construct; design
**Konstrukteur** [kɔnstrʊk'tø:ɐ] *m (-s; -e)* TECH designer; **Konstruktion** [kɔnstrʊk'tsjo:n] *f (-; -en)* construction
**Konsul** ['kɔnzʊl] *m (-s; -n)* consul
**Konsulat** [kɔnzu'la:t] *n (-[e]s; -e)* consulate
**konsultieren** [kɔnzʊl'ti:rən] *v/t (no -ge-, h)* consult
**Konsum**[1] [kɔn'zu:m] *m (-s; no pl)* consumption
**Konsum**[2] ['kɔnzu:m] *m (-s; -s)* cooperative (society *or* store), F co-op
**Konsument** [kɔnzu'mɛnt] *m (-en; -en)*, **Konsu'mentin** *f (-; -nen)* consumer; **Kon'sumgesellschaft** *f* consumer society; **konsumieren** [kɔnzu'mi:rən] *v/t (no -ge-, h)* consume
**Kontakt** [kɔn'takt] *m (-[e]s; -e)* contact (*a.* ELECTR); ***~ aufnehmen*** get in touch; ***~ haben*** *or* ***in ~ stehen mit*** be in contact *or* touch with; ***den ~ verlieren*** lose touch; **kon'taktfreudig** *adj* sociable
**Kon'taktlinsen** *pl* OPT contact lenses
**Konter** ['kɔntɐ] *m (-s; -)*, '**kontern** *v/i (ge-, h)* counter (*a. fig*)
**Kontinent** [kɔnti'nɛnt] *m (-[e]s; -e)* continent
**Konto** ['kɔnto] *n (-s; Konten)* account
'**Kontoauszug** *m* (bank) statement
**Kontrast** [kɔn'trast] *m (-[e]s; -e)* contrast (*a.* PHOT, TV *etc*)
**Kontrolle** [kɔn'trɔlə] *f (-; -n)* control; supervision; check(up)
**Kontrolleur** [kɔntrɔ'lø:ɐ] *m (-s; -e)*, **Kontrol'leurin** *f (-; -nen)* inspector, RAIL *a.* conductor
**kontrollieren** [kɔntrɔ'li:rən] *v/t (no -ge-, h)* check; check up on *s.o.*; control
**Kon'trollpunkt** *m* checkpoint
**Kontroverse** [kɔntro'vɛrzə] *f (-; -n)* controversy
**konventionell** [kɔnvɛntsjo'nɛl] *adj* conventional
**Konversation** [kɔnvɛrza'tsjo:n] *f (-; -en)* conversation; **Konversati'onslexikon** *n* encyclop(a)edia
**Konzentration** [kɔntsɛntra'tsjo:n] *f (-; -en)* concentration
**Konzentrati'onslager** *n* concentration camp
**konzentrieren** [kɔntsɛn'tri:rən] *v/t and v/refl (no -ge-, h)* concentrate; ***sich auf et. ~*** concentrate on s.th.
**Konzept** [kɔn'tsɛpt] *n (-[e]s; -e)* (rough) draft; conception; ***j-n aus dem ~ bringen*** put s.o. out
**Konzern** [kɔn'tsɛrn] *m (-[e]s; -e)* ECON combine, group
**Konzert** [kɔn'tsɛrt] *n (-[e]s; -e)* MUS concert; concerto; **~halle** *f*, **~saal** *m* concert hall, auditorium
**Konzession** [kɔntsɛ'sjo:n] *f (-; -en)* concession; license, *Br* licence
**Kopf** [kɔpf] *m (-[e]s; Köpfe* ['kœpfə]) head (*a. fig*); top; *fig a.* brains, mind; ***~ hoch!*** chin up!; ***j-m über den ~ wachsen*** outgrow s.o.; *fig* be too much for s.o.; ***sich den ~ zerbrechen*** (***über*** *acc*) rack one's brains (over); ***sich et. aus dem ~ schlagen*** put s.th. out of one's mind; ***~ an ~*** neck and neck; **~ball** *m* SPORT header; headed goal; **~bedeckung** *f* headgear; ***ohne ~*** bareheaded
**köpfen** ['kœpfən] *v/t (ge-, h)* behead, decapitate; SPORT head (***ins Tor*** home)

'**Kopf|ende** *n* head; **~hörer** *pl* headphones; **~jäger** *m* headhunter; **~kissen** *n* pillow
'**kopflos** *adj* headless; *fig* panicky
'**Kopf|rechnen** *n* mental arithmetic; **~sa,lat** *m* BOT lettuce; **~schmerzen** *pl* headache; **~sprung** *m* SPORT header; **~stand** *m* SPORT headstand; **~tuch** *n* scarf, (head)kerchief
**kopf'über** *adv* headfirst (*a. fig*)
'**Kopfweh** *n* → ***Kopfschmerzen***
'**Kopfzerbrechen** *n*: ***j-m ~ machen*** give s.o. a headache
**Kopie** [ko'pi:] *f* (-; *-n*), **ko'pieren** *v/t* (*no -ge-*, *h*) copy; **Kopiergerät** [ko'pi:ɐgərɛ:t] *n* copier
**Koppel**[1] ['kɔpəl] *f* (-; *-n*) paddock
'**Koppel**[2] *n* (*-s*; -) MIL belt
'**koppeln** *v/t* (*ge-*, *h*) couple; dock
**Koralle** [ko'ralə] *f* (-; *-n*) ZO coral
**Korb** [kɔrp] *m* (*-[e]s*; *Körbe* ['kœrbə]) basket
**Kord** [kɔrt] *m* (*-[e]s*; *-e*) corduroy
**Kordel** ['kɔrdəl] *f* (-; *-n*) cord
'**Kordhose** *f* corduroys
**Korinthe** [ko'rɪntə] *f* (-; *-n*) currant
**Kork** [kɔrk] *m* (*-[e]s*; *-e*) BOT cork
'**Korkeiche** *f* BOT cork oak
**Korken** ['kɔrkən] *m* (*-s*; -) cork; **~zieher** ['kɔrkəntsi:ɐ] *m* (*-s*; -) corkscrew
**Korn**[1] [kɔrn] *n* (*-[e]s*; *Körner* ['kœrnɐ]) BOT grain; seed; (*no pl*) grain, *Br a.* corn; (*pl -e*) TECH front sight
**Korn**[2] F *m* (*-[e]s*; *-e*) (grain) schnapps
**körnig** ['kœrnɪç] *adj* grainy
**Körper** ['kœrpɐ] *m* (*-s*; -) body (*a.* PHYS, CHEM), MATH *a.* solid, **~bau** *m* (*-[e]s*; *no pl*) build, physique
'**körperbehindert** *adj* (physically) disabled *or* handicapped
'**Körper|geruch** *m* body odo(u)r, BO; **~größe** *f* height; **~kraft** *f* physical strength
'**körperlich** *adj* physical
'**Körperpflege** *f* personal hygiene
'**Körperschaft** *f* (-; *-en*) corporation, (corporate) body
'**Körper|teil** *m* part of the body; **~verletzung** *f* JUR bodily injury
**korrekt** [kɔ'rɛkt] *adj* correct
**Korrektur** [kɔrɛk'tu:ɐ] *f* (-; *-en*) correction; PED *etc* grading, *Br* marking
**Korrespondent** [kɔrɛspɔn'dɛnt] *m* (*-en*; *-en*), **Korrespon'dentin** *f* (-; *-nen*) correspondent; **Korrespondenz** [kɔrɛspɔn'dɛnts] *f* (-; *-en*) correspondence; **korrespondieren** [kɔrɛspɔn'di:rən] *v/i* (*no -ge-*, *h*) correspond (***mit*** with)
**Korridor** ['kɔrido:ɐ] *m* (*-s*; *-e*) corridor; hall
**korrigieren** [kɔri'gi:rən] *v/t* (*no -ge-*, *h*) correct; PED *etc* grade, *Br* mark
**korrupt** [kɔ'rʊpt] *adj* corrupt(ed)
**Korruption** [kɔrʊp'tsjo:n] *f* (-; *-en*) corruption
**Korsett** [kɔr'zɛt] *n* (*-s*; *-s*) corset (*a. fig*)
**Kosename** ['ko:zəna:mə] *m* pet name
**Kosmetik** [kɔs'me:tɪk] *f* (-; *no pl*) beauty culture; cosmetics, toiletries
**Kosmetikerin** [kɔs'me:tikərɪn] *f* (-; *-nen*) beautician, cosmetician
**Kost** [kɔst] *f* (-; *no pl*) food, diet; board
'**kostbar** *adj* precious, valuable; costly
'**Kostbarkeit** *f* (-; *-en*) precious object, treasure (*a. fig*)
**kosten**[1] ['kɔstən] *v/t* (*ge-*, *h*) cost, be; *fig* take (*time etc*); ***was or wie viel kostet ...?*** how much it ...?
'**kosten**[2] *v/t* (*ge-*, *h*) taste, try
'**Kosten** *pl* cost(s); price; expenses; charges; ***auf j-s ~*** at s.o.'s expense
'**kostenlos** **1.** *adj* free **2.** *adv* free of charge
**köstlich** ['kœstlɪç] *adj* delicious; *fig* priceless; ***sich ~ amüsieren*** have great fun, F have a ball
'**Kostprobe** *f* taste, sample (*a. fig*)
'**kostspielig** *adj* expensive, costly
**Kostüm** [kɔs'ty:m] *n* (*-s*; *-e*) costume, dress; suit; **~fest** *n* fancy-dress ball
**Kot** [ko:t] *m* (*-[e]s*; *no pl*) excrement, ZO *a.* droppings
**Kotelett** [kotə'lɛt] *n* (*-s*; *-s*) chop, cutlet
**Koteletten** [kotə'lɛtən] *pl* sideburns
'**Kotflügel** *m* MOT fender, *Br* wing
**kotzen** ['kɔtsən] V *v/i* (*ge-*, *h*) puke
**Krabbe** ['krabə] *f* (-; *-n*) ZO shrimp; prawn
**krabbeln** ['krabəln] *v/i* (*ge-*, *sein*) crawl
**Krach** [krax] *m* (*-[e]s*; *Kräche* ['krɛçə]) crash, bang; (*no pl*) noise; F quarrel, fight
'**krachen** *v/i* (*ge-*, *h*) crack, bang, crash
**Kracher** ['kraxɐ] *m* (*-s*; -) (fire)cracker
**krächzen** ['krɛçtsən] *v/t and v/i* (*ge-*, *h*) croak
**Kraft** [kraft] *f* (-; *Kräfte* ['krɛftə])

K

strength, force (*a.* POL), power (*a.* ELECTR, TECH, POL); ***in ~ sein (setzen, treten)*** JUR *etc* be in (put into, come into) force; **~brühe** *f* GASTR consommé, clear soup; **~fahrer(in)** driver, motorist; **~fahrzeug** *n* motor vehicle

**kräftig** ['krɛftɪç] *adj* strong (*a. fig*), powerful; substantial (*food*); good

'**kraftlos** *adj* weak, feeble

'**Kraft|probe** *f* test of strength; **~stoff** *m* MOT fuel; **~verschwendung** *f* waste of energy; **~werk** *n* power station

**Kragen** ['kra:gən] *m* (*-s*; *-*) collar

**Krähe** ['krɛ:ə] *f* (*-*; *-n*) ZO crow

**krähen** ['krɛ:ən] *v/i* (*ge-*, *h*) crow

**Krake** ['kra:kə] *m* (*-n*; *-n*) ZO octopus

**Kralle** ['kralə] *f* (*-*; *-n*) ZO claw (*a. fig*)

'**krallen** *v/refl* (*ge-*, *h*) cling (***an*** *acc* on), clutch (at)

**Kram** [kra:m] F *m* (*-[e]s*; *no pl*) stuff, (one's) things

**Krampf** [krampf] *m* (*-[e]s*; *Krämpfe* ['krɛmpfə]) MED cramp; spasm, convulsion; **~ader** *f* MED varicose vein

'**krampfhaft** *fig adj* forced (*smile etc*); desperate (*attempt etc*)

**Kran** [kra:n] *m* (*-[e]s*; *Kräne* ['krɛ:nə]) TECH crane

**Kranich** ['kra:nɪç] *m* (*-s*; *-e*) ZO crane

**krank** [kraŋk] *adj* ill, sick; ***~ werden*** get sick, *Br* fall ill; '**Kranke** *m, f* (*-n*; *-n*) sick person, patient; ***die ~n*** the sick

**kränken** ['krɛŋkən] *v/t* (*ge-*, *h*) hurt (*s.o.'s* feelings), offend

'**Kranken|bett** *n* sickbed; **~geld** *n* sickness benefit; **~gym|nastik** *f* physiotherapy; **~haus** *n* hospital; **~kasse** *f* health insurance scheme; ***in e-r ~ sein*** be a member of a health insurance scheme *or* plan; **~pflege** *f* nursing; **~pfleger** *m* male nurse; **~schein** *m* health insurance certificate; **~schwester** *f* nurse; **~versicherung** *f* health insurance; **~wagen** *m* ambulance; **~zimmer** *n* sickroom

'**krankhaft** *adj* morbid (*a. fig*)

'**Krankheit** *f* (*-*; *-en*) illness, sickness, disease

'**Krankheitsserreger** *m* germ

**kränklich** ['krɛŋklɪç] *adj* sickly, ailing

**Kränkung** ['krɛŋkʊŋ] *f* (*-*; *-en*) insult, offense, *Br* offence

**Kranz** [krants] *m* (*-es*; *Kränze* ['krɛntsə]) wreath; *fig* ring, circle

**krass** [kras] *adj* crass, gross; blunt

**Krater** ['kra:tɐ] *m* (*-s*; *-*) crater

**kratzen** ['kratsən] *v/t and v/refl* (*ge-*, *h*) scratch (o.s.); scrape (***von*** off)

**Kratzer** ['kratsɐ] *m* (*-s*; *-*) scratch (*a.* MED)

**kraulen** ['kraulən] **1.** *v/t* (*ge-*, *h*) stroke; run one's fingers through **2.** *v/i* (*ge-*, *sein*) SPORT do the crawl

**kraus** [kraus] *adj* curly (*hair*); wrinkled

**Krause** ['krauzə] *f* (*-*; *-n*) ruff; friz(z)

**kräuseln** ['krɔʏzəln] *v/t and v/refl* (*ge-*, *h*) curl, friz(z); *water*: ripple

**Kraut** [kraut] *n* (*-[e]s*; *Kräuter* ['krɔʏtɐ]) BOT herb; tops, leaves; cabbage

**Krawall** [kra'val] *m* (*-s*; *-e*) riot; F row, racket

**Krawatte** [kra'vatə] *f* (*-*; *-n*) tie

**kreativ** [krea'ti:f] *adj* creative

**Kreativität** [kreativi'tɛ:t] *f* (*-*; *no pl*) creativity

**Kreatur** [krea'tu:ɐ] *f* (*-*; *-en*) creature

**Krebs** [kre:ps] *m* ZO crayfish; MED cancer; AST Cancer; ***sie ist (ein) ~*** she's (a) Cancer; ***~ erregend → krebserregend***

**Krebs...** MED cancerous; **krebserregend** *adj* MED carcinogenic; **~geschwulst** *f* MED carcinoma; **~kranke** *m, f* cancer patient

**Kredit** [kre'di:t] *m* (*-[e]s*; *-e*) ECON credit; loan; **~karte** *f* credit card, *pl coll* F plastic money

**Kreide** ['kraidə] *f* (*-*; *-n*) chalk; crayon

**Kreis** [krais] *m* (*-es*; *-e*) circle (*a. fig*); POL district, county; **~bahn** *f* AST orbit

**kreischen** ['kraiʃən] *v/i* (*ge-*, *h*) screech; squeal

**Kreisel** ['kraizəl] *m* (*-s*; *-*) (spinning) top; PHYS gyro(scope); '**kreiseln** *v/i* (*ge-*, *h*, *sein*) spin around

**kreisen** ['kraizən] *v/i* (*ge-*, *h*, *sein*) (move in a) circle, revolve, rotate; circulate

**kreisförmig** ['kraisfœrmɪç] *adj* circular

'**Kreislauf** *m* MED, ECON circulation; BIOL cycle (*a. fig*), TECH, ELECTR *a.* circuit; **~störungen** *pl* MED circulatory trouble

'**Kreis|säge** *f* circular saw; **~verkehr** *m* traffic circle, *Br* roundabout

**Krempe** ['krɛmpə] *f* (*-*; *-n*) brim

**Kren** [kre:n] *Austrian m* (*-[e]s*; *no pl*) GASTR horseradish

**Krepp** [krɛp] *m* (*-s*; *-s*) crepe

**Kreuz** [krɔʏts] *n* (*-es*; *-e*) cross (*a. fig*); ANAT (small of the) back; *cards*: club(s);

MUS sharp; ***über ~*** crosswise; F ***j-n aufs ~ legen*** take s.o. in; **kreuzen** ['krɔʏtsən] **1.** *v/t and v/refl (ge-, h)* cross; clash **2.** *v/i (ge-, sein)* MAR cruise
**Kreuzer** ['krɔʏtsɐ] *m (-s; -)* MAR cruiser
'**Kreuzfahrer** *m* HIST crusader
'**Kreuzfahrt** *f* MAR cruise
**kreuzigen** ['krɔʏtsɪgən] *v/t (ge-, h)* crucify; '**Kreuzigung** *f (-; -en)* crucifixion
'**Kreuzotter** *f* zo adder
'**Kreuzschmerzen** *pl* backache
'**Kreuzung** *f (-; -en)* RAIL, MOT crossing, junction; intersection, crossroads; BIOL cross(breed)ing; cross(breed); *fig* cross
'**Kreuzverhör** *n* JUR cross-examination; ***ins ~ nehmen*** cross-examine
'**kreuzweise** *adv* crosswise, crossways
'**Kreuz|worträtsel** *n* crossword (puzzle); **~zug** HIST *m* crusade
**kriechen** ['kri:çən] *v/i (irr, ge-, sein)* creep, crawl; *fig* ***vor j-m ~*** toady to s.o.
**Kriecher** ['kri:çɐ] *contp m (-s; -)* toady
'**Kriechspur** *f* MOT slow lane
**Krieg** [kri:k] *m (-[e]s; -e* ['kri:gə]) war; ***~ führen gegen*** be at war with
**kriegen** ['kri:gən] F *v/t (ge-, h)* get; catch
**Krieger** ['kri:gɐ] *m (-s; -)* warrior
'**Kriegerdenkmal** *n* war memorial
**kriegerisch** ['kri:gərɪʃ] *adj* warlike, martial
'**Kriegführung** *f (-; no pl)* warfare
'**Kriegs|beil** *fig n*: ***das ~ begraben*** bury the hatchet; **~dienstverweigerer** *m (-s; -)* conscientious objector; **~erklärung** *f* declaration of war; **~gefangene** *m* prisoner of war, P.O.W.; **~gefangenschaft** *f* captivity; **~recht** *n* JUR martial law; **~schauplatz** *m* theater (*Br* theatre) of war; **~schiff** *n* warship; **~teilnehmer** *m* (war) veteran, *Br* ex-serviceman; **~verbrechen** *n* war crime; **~verbrecher** *m* war criminal
**Krimi** ['kri:mi] F *m (-s; -s)* (crime) thriller, detective novel
**Kriminal|beamte** [krimi'na:lbəʔamtə] *m* detective, plain-clothesman; **~polizei** *f* criminal investigation department; **~roman** *m* → ***Krimi***
**kriminell** [krimi'nɛl] adj, **Krimi'nelle** *m, f (-n; -n)* criminal
**Krippe** ['krɪpə] *f (-; -n)* crib, manger (*a.* REL); REL crèche, *Br* crib
**Krise** ['kri:zə] *f (-; -n)* crisis
'**Krisenherd** *m esp* POL trouble spot
**Kristall**[1] [krɪs'tal] *m (-s; -e)* crystal
**Kris'tall**[2] *n (s; no pl)*, **~glas** *n* crystal
**kristallisieren** [krɪstali'zi:rən] *v/i and v/refl (no -ge-, h)* crystallize
**Kriterium** [kri'te:rjʊm] *n (-s; -ien)* criterion (***für*** of)
**Kritik** [kri'ti:k] *f (-; -en)* criticism; THEA, MUS *etc* review, critique; ***gute ~en*** a good press; ***~ üben an*** *(dat)* criticize; **Kritiker(in)** ['kri:tikɐ, 'kri:tikərɪn] *m(f) (-s; -/-; -nen)* critic; **kri'tiklos** *adj* uncritical; **kritisch** ['kri:tɪʃ] *adj* critical (*a. fig*) (***gegenüber*** of); **kritisieren** [kriti'zi:rən] *v/t (no -ge-, h)* criticize
**kritzeln** ['krɪtsəln] *v/t and v/i (ge-, h)* scrawl, scribble
**kroch** [krɔx] *pret of* ***kriechen***
**Krokodil** [kroko'di:l] *n (-s; -e)* zo crocodile
**Krone** ['kro:nə] *f (-; -n)* crown; coronet
**krönen** ['krø:nən] *v/t (ge-, h)* crown; ***j-n zum König ~*** crown s.o. king
'**Kronleuchter** *m* chandelier
'**Kronprinz** *m* crown prince
'**Kronprin,zessin** *f* crown princess
'**Krönung** *f (-; -en)* coronation; *fig* crowning event, climax, high point
**Kropf** [krɔpf] *m (-[e]s; Kröpfe* ['krœpfə]) MED goiter, *Br* goitre; zo crop
**Kröte** ['krø:tə] *f (-; -n)* zo toad
**Krücke** ['krʏkə] *f (-; -n)* crutch
**Krug** [kru:k] *m (-[e]s; Krüge* ['kry:gə]) jug, pitcher; mug, stein; tankard
**Krümel** ['kry:məl] *m (-s; -)* crumb
**krümelig** ['kry:məlɪç] *adj* crumbly
'**krümeln** *v/t and v/i (ge-, h)* crumble
**krumm** [krʊm] *adj* crooked (*a. fig*), bent
**krummbeinig** ['krʊmbainɪç] *adj* bow-legged
**krümmen** ['krʏmən] *v/t (ge-, h)* bend (*a.* TECH), crook; ***sich ~*** bend; writhe (with pain); '**Krümmung** *f (-; -en)* bend, curve; GEOGR, MATH, MED curvature
**Krüppel** ['krʏpəl] *m (-s; -)* cripple
**Kruste** ['krʊstə] *f (-; -n)* crust
**Kto.** *abbr of* ***Konto*** a/c, account
**Kübel** ['ky:bəl] *m (-s; -)* bucket, pail; tub
**Kubik|meter** [ku'bi:kme:tɐ] *n, m* cubic meter (*Br* metre); **~wurzel** *f* MATH cube root
**Küche** ['kʏçə] *f (-; -n)* kitchen; GASTR cooking, cuisine; ***kalte (warme) ~*** cold (hot) meals

K

**Kuchen** ['ku:xən] *m* (*-s*; *-*) cake; tart, pie
'**Küchen|geräte** *pl* kitchen utensils (*or* appliances); **~geschirr** *n* kitchen crockery, kitchenware; **~herd** *m* cooker; **~schrank** *m* (kitchen) cupboard
**Kuckuck** ['kʊkʊk] *m* (*-s*; *-s*) ZO cuckoo
**Kufe** ['ku:fə] *f* (*-*; *-n*) runner; AVIAT skid
**Kugel** ['ku:gəl] *f* (*-*; *-n*) ball; bullet; MATH, GEOGR sphere; SPORT shot
**kugelförmig** ['ku:gəlfœrmɪç] *adj* ball-shaped, *esp* ASTR, MATH spheric(al)
'**Kugelgelenk** *n* TECH, ANAT ball (and socket) joint
'**Kugellager** *n* TECH ball bearing
'**kugeln** *v/i* (*ge-*, *sein*) *and v/t* (*h*) roll
**Kugelschreiber** ['ku:gəlʃraibɐ] *m* (*-s*; *-*) ballpoint (pen)
'**kugelsicher** *adj* bulletproof
'**Kugelstoßen** *n* (*-s*; *no pl*) SPORT shot put(ting); **Kugelstoßer** ['ku:gəlʃto:sɐ] *m* (*-s*; *-*), **Kugelstoßerin** ['ku:gəlʃto:sərɪn] *f* (*-*; *-nen*) SPORT shot-putter
**Kuh** [ku:] *f* (*-*; *Kühe* ['ky:ə]) ZO cow
**kühl** [ky:l] *adj* cool (*a. fig*); '**Kühle** *f* (*-*; *no pl*) cool(ness); '**kühlen** *v/t* (*ge-*, *h*) cool; chill; refrigerate; refresh
**Kühler** ['ky:lɐ] *m* (*-s*; *-*) MOT radiator
'**Kühlerhaube** *f* MOT hood, *Br* bonnet
'**Kühlmittel** *n* coolant
'**Kühlraum** *m* cold-storage room
'**Kühlschrank** *m* fridge, refrigerator
'**Kühltruhe** *f* deep-freeze, freezer
'**Kühlwasser** *n* MOT cooling water
**kühn** [ky:n] *adj* bold
'**Kühnheit** *f* (*-*; *no pl*) boldness
'**Kuhstall** *m* cowshed
**Küken** ['ky:kən] *n* (*-s*; *-*) ZO chick (*a. fig*)
**Kukuruz** ['kʊkurʊts] *Austrian m* → ***Mais***
**Kuli** ['ku:li] F *m* (*-s*; *-s*) ballpoint
**Kulissen** [ku'lɪsən] *pl* THEA wings; scenery; ***hinter den ~*** backstage, *esp fig* behind the scenes
**Kult** [kʊlt] *m* (*-[e]s*; *-e*) cult; rite, ritual (act)
**kultivieren** [kʊlti'vi:rən] *v/t* (*no -ge-*, *h*) cultivate
**Kultur** [kʊl'tu:ɐ] *f* (*-*; *-en*) culture (*a.* BIOL), civilization; AGR cultivation
**Kul'turbeutel** *m* toilet bag
**kulturell** [kʊltu'rɛl] *adj* cultural
**Kul'tur|geschichte** *f* history of civilization; **~zentrum** *n* cultural center (*Br* centre)
**Kultusmi,nister** ['kʊltʊsminɪstɐ] *m* minister of education and cultural affairs
**Kummer** ['kʊmɐ] *m* (*-s*; *no pl*) grief, sorrow; trouble, worry; ***~ haben mit*** have trouble *or* problems with
**kümmerlich** ['kʏmɐlɪç] *adj* miserable; poor, scanty; **kümmern** ['kʏmɐn] *v/refl and v/t* (*ge-*, *h*) ***sich ~ um*** look after, take care of, mind; care *or* worry about, be interested in
**Kumpel** ['kʊmpəl] *m* (*-s*; *-*) miner; F mate, buddy, pal
**Kunde** ['kʊndə] *m* (*-n*; *-n*) customer, client; '**Kundendienst** *m* after-sales service; (customer) service; service department; TECH servicing
**Kundgebung** ['kʊntge:bʊŋ] *f* (*-*; *-en*) meeting, rally, demonstration
**kündigen** ['kʏndɪgən] *v/i and v/t* (*ge-*, *h*) cancel; ***j-m ~*** give s.o. his / her / one's notice; dismiss s.o., F sack *or* fire s.o.
'**Kündigung** *f* (*-*; *-en*) cancellation; (period of) notice
**Kundin** ['kʊndɪn] *f* (*-*; *-nen*) customer, client
**Kundschaft** ['kʊntʃaft] *f* (*-*; *-en*) customers, clients
**Kunst** [kʊnst] *f* (*-*; *Künste* ['kʏnstə]) art; skill; **~...** *in cpds* ...*herz*, ...*leder*, ...*licht etc*: artificial ...; **~akade,mie** *f* academy of arts; **~ausstellung** *f* art exhibition; **~dünger** *m* AGR artificial fertilizer; **~erziehung** *f* PED art (education); **~faser** *f* man-made *or* synthetic fiber (*Br* fibre); **~fehler** *m* professional blunder; **~fliegen** *n* stunt flying, aerobatics; **~geschichte** *f* history of art; **~gewerbe** *n*, **~handwerk** *n* arts and crafts
**Künstler** ['kʏnstlɐ] *m* (*-s*; *-*), **Künstlerin** ['kʏnstlərɪn] *f* (*-*; *-nen*) artist, MUS, THEA *a.* performer
**künstlerisch** ['kʏnstlərɪʃ] *adj* artistic
**künstlich** ['kʏnstlɪç] *adj* artificial; false; synthetic; man-made
'**Kunst|schwimmen** *n* water ballet; **~seide** *f* rayon; **~springen** *n* springboard diving; **~stoff** *m* plastic; **~stück** *n* trick, stunt, *esp fig* feat; **~turnen** *n* gymnastics; **~turner** *m* gymnast
'**kunstvoll** *adj* artistic; elaborate
'**Kunstwerk** *n* work of art
**Kupfer** ['kʊpfɐ] *n* (*-s*; *no pl*) copper (***aus***

K

of); **~stich** *m* copperplate (engraving)
**Kupon** [ku'poː] *m* (*-s*; *-s*) coupon
**Kuppe** ['kʊpə] *f* (*-*; *-n*) (rounded) hilltop; ANAT head
**Kuppel** ['kʊpəl] *f* (*-*; *-n*) ARCH dome; cupola
**Kuppelei** [kʊpə'lai] *f* (*-*; *-en*) JUR procuring
'**kuppeln** *v/i* (*ge-*, *h*) MOT put the clutch in *or* out; **Kupplung** ['kʊplʊŋ] *f* (*-*; *-en*) MOT clutch
**Kur** [kuːɐ] *f* (*-*; *-en*) course of treatment; cure
**Kür** [kyːɐ] *f* (*-*; *-en*) SPORT free skating; free exercises
**Kurbel** ['kʊrbəl] *f* (*-*; *-n*) crank, handle; '**kurbeln** *v/t* (*ge-*, *h*) crank; wind (up *etc*); '**Kurbelwelle** *f* TECH crankshaft
**Kürbis** ['kʏrbɪs] *m* (*-ses*; *-se*) BOT pumpkin, gourd, squash
'**Kurgast** *m* visitor
**kurieren** [ku'riːrən] *v/t* (*no -ge-*, *h*) cure (***von*** of)
**kurios** [ku'rjoːs] *adj* curious, odd, strange
'**Kürlauf** *m* SPORT free skating
'**Kurort** *m* health resort, spa
**Kurpfuscher** ['kuːɐpfʊʃɐ] *m* (*-s*; *-*) quack (doctor)
**Kurs** [kʊrs] *m* (*-es*; *-e*) AVIAT, MAR course (*a. fig*); PED *etc* class(es); ECON (exchange) rate; (stock) price
**Kürschner** ['kʏrʃnɐ] *m* (*-s*; *-*) furrier
**kursieren** [kʊr'ziːrən] *v/i* (*no -ge-*, *h*) circulate (*a. fig*)
**Kurve** ['kʊrvə] *f* (*-*; *-n*) curve (*a.* MATH *and fig*); bend, turn; '**kurvenreich** *adj* winding, full of bends; F curvaceous
**kurz** [kʊrts] *adj* short; brief; ***~e Hose*** shorts; (***bis***) ***vor ~em*** (until) recently; (***erst***) ***seit ~em*** (only) for a short time; ***~ vorher*** (***darauf***) shortly before (after[wards]); ***~ vor uns*** just ahead of us; ***~ nacheinander*** in quick succession; ***~ fortgehen*** *etc* go away for a short time *or* a moment; ***~ gesagt*** in short; ***zu ~ kommen*** go short; ***~ angebunden*** curt
'**Kurzarbeit** *f* ECON short time
'**kurzarbeiten** *v/i* (*sep*, *ge-*, *h*) ECON work short time
**kurzatmig** ['kʊrtsʔaːtmɪç] *adj* short of breath
**Kürze** ['kʏrtsə] *f* (*-*; *no pl*) shortness; brevity; ***in ~*** soon, shortly, before long
'**kürzen** *v/t* (*ge-*, *h*) shorten (***um*** by); abridge; cut, reduce (*a.* MATH)
**kurzerhand** ['kʊrtsɐ'hant] *adv* without hesitation, on the spot
'**kurzfassen** *v/refl* (*sep*, *-ge-*, *h*): ***sich ~*** be brief, put it briefly
'**kurzfristig** **1.** *adj* short-term **2.** *adv* at short notice
'**Kurzgeschichte** *f* short story
**kurzlebig** ['kʊrtsleːbɪç] *adj* short-lived
**kürzlich** ['kʏrtslɪç] *adv* recently, not long ago
'**Kurz|nachrichten** *pl* news summary; **~schluss** *m* ELECTR short circuit, F short; **~schrift** *f* shorthand
'**kurzsichtig** *adj* nearsighted, *Br* shortsighted
'**Kurzstrecke** *f* short distance
'**Kürzung** *f* (*-*; *-en*) cut, reduction (*a.* MATH)
'**Kurzwaren** *pl* notions, *Br* haberdashery
**kurzweilig** ['kʊrtsvailɪç] *adj* entertaining
'**Kurzwelle** *f* PHYS, *radio*: short wave
**kuschelig** ['kʊʃəlɪç] F *adj* cozy, *Br* cosy, snug; **kuscheln** ['kʊʃəln] *v/refl* (*ge-*, *h*) snuggle, cuddle (***an*** *acc* up to; ***in*** *acc* in)
**Kusine** *f* → ***Cousine***
**Kuss** [kʊs] *m* (*-es*; *Küsse* ['kʏsə]) kiss
'**kussecht** *adj* kiss-proof
**küssen** ['kʏsən] *v/t* (*ge-*, *h*) kiss
**Küste** ['kʏstə] *f* (*-*; *-n*) coast, shore; ***an der ~*** on the coast; ***an die ~*** ashore
'**Küsten|gewässer** *pl* coastal waters; **~schifffahrt** *f* coastal shipping; **~schutz** *m*, **~wache** *f* coast guard
**Küster** ['kʏstɐ] *m* (*-s*; *-*) REL verger, sexton
**Kutsche** ['kʊtʃə] *f* (*-*; *-n*) carriage, coach; **Kutscher** ['kʊtʃɐ] *m* (*-s*; *-*) coachman
**Kutte** ['kʊtə] *f* (*-*; *-n*) (monk's) habit
**Kutteln** ['kʊtəln] *pl* GASTR tripe
**Kutter** ['kʊtɐ] *m* (*-s*; *-*) MAR cutter
**Kuvert** [ku'veːɐ] *n* (*-s*; *-s*) envelope
**Kybernetik** [kybɛr'neːtɪk] *f* (*-*; *no pl*) cybernetics

K

# L

**labil** [la'bi:l] *adj* unstable

**Labor** [la'bo:ɐ] *n* (*-s*; *-e*) laboratory, F lab; **Laborant(in)** [labo'rant(ɪn)] (*-en*; *-en*/-; *-nen*) laboratory assistant

**Labyrinth** [laby'rɪnt] *n* (-[*e*]*s*; *-e*) labyrinth, maze (*both a. fig*)

**Lache** ['laxə] *f* (-; *-n*) pool, puddle

**lächeln** ['lɛçəln] *v/i* (*ge-*, *h*), '**Lächeln** *n* (*-s*; *no pl*) smile

**lachen** ['laxən] *v/i* (*ge-*, *h*) laugh (***über*** *acc* at); '**Lachen** *n* (*-s*; *no pl*) laugh (-ter); ***j-n zum ~ bringen*** make s.o. laugh; **lächerlich** ['lɛçɐlɪç] *adj* ridiculous; ***~ machen*** ridicule, make fun of; ***sich ~ machen*** make a fool of o.s.

**Lachs** [laks] *m* (*-es*; *-e*) ZO salmon

**Lack** [lak] *m* (-[*e*]*s*; *-e*) varnish; lacquer; MOT paint(work)

**lackieren** [la'ki:rən] *v/t* (*no -ge-*, *h*) varnish; lacquer; paint (*a.* MOT)

'**Lackschuhe** *pl* patent-leather shoes

**Ladefläche** ['la:dəflɛçə] *f* loading space

'**Ladegerät** *n* ELECTR battery charger

'**Ladehemmung** *f* MIL jam

**laden** ['la:dən] *v/t* (*irr*, *ge-*, *h*) load; ELECTR charge; IT boot (up); *fig* ***et. auf sich ~*** burden o.s. with s.th.

'**Laden** *m* (*-s*; *Läden* ['lɛ:dən]) store, *Br* shop; shutter; **~dieb** *m* shoplifter; **~diebstahl** *m* shoplifting; **~inhaber** *m* storekeeper, *Br* shopkeeper; **~kasse** *f* till; **~schluss** *m* closing time; ***nach ~*** after hours; **~tisch** *m* counter

'**Laderampe** *f* loading platform *or* ramp

'**Laderaum** *m* loading space; MAR hold

'**Ladung** *f* (-; *-en*) load, freight; AVIAT, MAR cargo; ELECTR, MIL charge; ***e-e ~ ...*** a load of ...

**lag** [la:k] *pret of* ***liegen***

**Lage** ['la:gə] *f* (-; *-n*) situation, position (*both a. fig*); location; layer; round (*of beer etc*); ***in schöner*** (***ruhiger***) ***~*** beautifully (peacefully) situated; ***in der ~ sein zu*** *inf* be able to *inf*, be in a position to *inf*

**Lager** ['la:gɐ] *n* (*-s*; -) bed; camp (*a. fig*); ECON stock, store; GEOL deposit; TECH bearing; ***et. auf ~ haben*** have s.th. in store (*a. fig for s.o.*); **~feuer** *n* campfire; **~haus** *n* warehouse

'**lagern** (*ge-*, *h*) **1.** *v/i* camp; ECON be stored **2.** *v/t* store, keep; MED lay, rest; ***kühl ~*** keep in a cool place

'**Lagerraum** *m* storeroom

**Lagerung** ['la:gərʊŋ] *f* (-; *no pl*) storage

**Lagune** [la'gu:nə] *f* (-; *-n*) lagoon

**lahm** [la:m] *adj* lame; **lahmen** ['la:mən] *v/i* (*ge-*, *h*) be lame (***auf*** *dat* in)

**lähmen** ['lɛ:mən] *v/t* (*ge-*, *h*) paralyze, *Br* paralyse; bring *traffic etc* to a standstill

'**lahmlegen** *v/t* (*sep*, *-ge-*, *h*) → ***lähmen***;

'**Lähmung** *f* (-; *-en*) MED paralysis

**Laib** [laip] *m* (-[*e*]*s*; *-e* ['laibə]) loaf

**Laich** [laiç] *m* (-[*e*]*s*; *-e*), **laichen** ['laiçən] *v/i* (*ge-*, *h*) spawn

**Laie** ['laɪə] *m* (*-n*; *-n*) layman; amateur

'**laienhaft** *adj* amateurish

'**Laienspiel** *n* amateur play

**Laken** ['la:kən] *n* (*-s*; -) sheet; bath towel

**Lakritze** [la'krɪtsə] *f* (-; *-n*) liquorice

**lallen** ['lalən] *v/i and v/t* (*ge-*, *h*) speak drunkenly; *baby*: babble

**Lamm** [lam] *n* (-[*e*]*s*; *Lämmer* ['lɛmɐ]) ZO lamb; **~fell** *n* lambskin

**Lampe** ['lampə] *f* (-; *-n*) lamp, light; bulb

'**Lampenfieber** *n* stage fright

'**Lampenschirm** *m* lampshade

**Lampion** [lam'pjo͂:] *m* (*-s*; *-s*) Chinese lantern

**Land** [lant] *n* (-[*e*]*s*; *Länder* ['lɛndɐ]) land; country; AGR ground, soil; ECON land, property; ***an ~ gehen*** MAR go ashore; ***auf dem ~e*** in the country; ***aufs ~ fahren*** go into the country; ***außer ~es gehen*** go abroad; **~arbeiter** *m* farmhand; **~bevölkerung** *f* country *or* rural population

**Landebahn** ['landəba:n] *f* AVIAT runway

**land'einwärts** *adv* up-country, inland

**landen** ['landən] *v/i* (*ge-*, *sein*) land; *fig* ***~ in*** (*dat*) end up in

'**Landenge** *f* neck of land, isthmus

'**Landeplatz** *m* AVIAT landing field

**Länderspiel** ['lɛndɐʃpi:l] *n* SPORT international match

'**Landes|grenze** *f* national border; **~innere** *n* interior; **~re͵gierung** *f* Land (*Austrian* Provincial) government;

L

**~sprache** *f* national language
'**landesüblich** *adj* customary
'**Landesverrat** *m* treason
'**Land|flucht** *f* rural exodus; **~friedensbruch** *m* JUR breach of the public peace; **~gericht** *n* JUR *appr* regional superior court; **~haus** *n* country house, cottage; **~karte** *f* map; **~kreis** *m* district
'**landläufig** *adj* customary, current, common
**ländlich** ['lɛntlɪç] *adj* rural; rustic
'**Land|rat** *m*, **~rätin** ['lantrɛːtɪn] *f* (-; *-nen*) *appr* District Administrator
'**Landschaft** *f* (-; *-en*) countryside; scenery; *esp* PAINT landscape
'**landschaftlich** *adj* scenic
'**Landsmann** *m* (-[*e*]*s*; *-leute*) (fellow) countryman; **Landsmännin** ['lantsmɛnɪn] *f* (-; *-nen*) fellow countrywoman
'**Land|straße** *f* country (*or* ordinary) road; **~streicher(in)** tramp; **~streitkräfte** *pl* MIL land forces; **~tag** *m* Land parliament
'**Landung** *f* (-; *-en*) landing, AVIAT *a.* touchdown
'**Landungssteg** *m* MAR gangway
'**Land|vermesser** ['lantfɛɐmɛsɐ] *m* (*-s*; -) land surveyor; **~vermessung** *f* (-; *-en*) land surveying; **~weg** *m*: ***auf dem ~e*** by land; **~wirt(in)** farmer
'**Landwirtschaft** *f* (-; *no pl*) agriculture, farming; '**landwirtschaftlich** *adj* agricultural
'**Landzunge** *f* GEOGR promontory, spit
**lang** [laŋ] *adj and adv* long; F tall; ***drei Jahre*** (***einige Zeit***) **~** for three years (some time); ***den ganzen Tag ~*** all day long; ***seit ~em*** for a long time; ***vor ~er Zeit*** (a) long (time) ago; ***über kurz oder ~*** sooner or later; ***~ ersehnt*** long-hoped-for; ***~ erwartet*** long-awaited; ***gleich ~*** the same length
**langatmig** ['laŋʔaːtmɪç] *adj* long-winded
**lange** ['laŋə] *adv* (for a) long (time); ***es ist schon ~ her***(, ***seit***) it has been a long time (since); (***noch***) ***nicht ~ her*** not long ago; ***noch ~ hin*** still a long way off; ***es dauert nicht ~*** it won't take long; ***ich bleibe nicht ~ fort*** I won't be long; ***wie ~ noch?*** how much longer?
**Länge** ['lɛŋə] *f* (-; *-n*) length; GEOGR longitude; ***der ~ nach*** (at) full length; (***sich***) ***in die ~ ziehen*** stretch (*a. fig*)
**langen** ['laŋən] F *v/i* (*ge-*, *h*) reach (***nach*** for); be enough; ***mir langt es*** I've had enough, *fig a.* I'm sick of it
'**Längen|grad** *m* GEOGR degree of longitude; **~maß** *n* linear measure
'**Langeweile** *f* (-; *no pl*) boredom; ***~ haben*** be bored; ***aus ~*** to pass the time
'**langfristig** *adj* long-term
**langjährig** ['laŋjɛːrɪç] *adj* long-standing; ***~e Erfahrung*** many years of experience
'**Langlauf** *m* (-[*e*]*s*; *no pl*) SPORT cross--country (skiing)
**langlebig** ['laŋleːbɪç] *adj* long-lived
**länglich** ['lɛŋlɪç] *adj* longish, oblong
**längs** [lɛŋs] **1.** *prp* (*gen*) along(side) **2.** *adv* lengthwise
'**langsam** *adj* slow; ***~er werden*** *or* ***fahren*** slow down
'**Langschläfer** ['laŋʃlɛːfɐ] *m* (*-s*; -), **~schläferin** ['laŋʃlɛːfərɪn] *f* (-; *-nen*) late riser
**längst** [lɛŋst] *adv* long ago *or* before; ***~ vorbei*** long past; ***ich weiß es ~*** I have known it for a long time; **längstens** ['lɛŋstəns] *adv* at (the) most
'**Langstrecken...** *in cpds* long-distance ...; AVIAT, MIL long-range ...
'**langweilen** *v/t* (*ge-*, *h*) bore; ***sich ~*** be bored; **langweilig** ['laŋvailɪç] *adj* boring, dull
'**Langwelle** *f* PHYS, *radio*: long wave
**langwierig** ['laŋviːrɪç] *adj* lengthy, protracted (*a.* MED)
**Lanze** ['lantsə] *f* (-; *-n*) lance, spear
**Lappalie** [la'paːljə] *f* (-; *-n*) trifle
**Lappen** ['lapən] *m* (*-s*; -) (piece of) cloth; rag (*a. fig*)
**läppisch** ['lɛpɪʃ] *adj* silly; ridiculous
**Lärche** ['lɛrçə] *f* (-; *-n*) BOT larch
**Lärm** [lɛrm] *m* (*-s*; *no pl*) noise
**lärmen** ['lɛrmən] *v/i* (*ge-*, *h*) be noisy; **~d** *adj* noisy
**Larve** ['larfə] *f* (-; *-n*) mask; ZO larva
**las** [laːs] *pret of* ***lesen***
**lasch** [laʃ] F *adj* slack, lax
**Lasche** ['laʃə] *f* (-; *-n*) flap; tongue
**Laser** ['leːzɐ] *m* (*-s*; -) PHYS laser; **~drucker** *m* IT laser printer; **~strahl** *m* PHYS laser beam; **~technik** *f* laser technology
**lassen** ['lasən] *v/t* (*irr*, *ge-*, *h*) *and v/aux*

L

(*irr, no -ge-, h*) let, leave; ***j-n et. tun ~*** let s.o. do s.th.; allow s.o. to do s.th.; make s.o. do s.th.; ***j-n (et.) zu Hause ~*** leave s.o. (s.th.) at home; ***j-n allein (in Ruhe) ~*** leave s.o. alone; ***sich die Haare schneiden ~*** have *or* get one's hair cut; ***sein Leben ~ (für)*** lose (give) one's life (for); ***rufen ~*** send for, call in; ***es lässt sich machen*** it can be done; ***lass alles so, wie (wo) es ist*** leave everything as (where) it is; ***er kann das Rauchen** etc **nicht ~*** he can't stop smoking *etc*; ***lass das!*** stop it! → ***grüßen, kommen***

**lässig** ['lɛsɪç] *adj* casual; careless

**Last** [last] *f* (-; *-en*) load, burden, weight (*all a. fig*); ***j-m zur ~ fallen*** be a burden to s.o.; ***j-m et. zur ~ legen*** charge s.o. with s.th.; **lasten** ['lastən] *v/i* (*ge-, h*) ***~ auf*** (*dat*) *a. fig* weigh *or* rest (up)on

**'Lastenaufzug** *m* freight elevator, *Br* goods lift

**Laster**[1] ['lastɐ] *m* (*-s*; -) → ***Lastwagen***

**'Laster**[2] *n* (*-s*; -) vice

**lästern** ['lɛstɐn] *v/i* (*ge-, h*) ***~ über*** (*acc*) run down

**lästig** ['lɛstɪç] *adj* troublesome, annoying; ***(j-m) ~ sein*** be a nuisance (to s.o.)

**'Last|kahn** *m* barge; **~tier** *n* pack animal; **~wagen** *m* MOT truck, *Br a.* lorry; **~wagenfahrer** *m* MOT truck (*Br a.* lorry) driver, trucker

**Latein** [la'tain] *n* (*-s*; *no pl*) Latin

**La'teina,merika** Latin America; **La'teinameri,kaner(in)**, **la'teinameri,kanisch** *adj* Latin American

**la'teinisch** *adj* Latin

**Laterne** [la'tɛrnə] *f* (-; *-n*) lantern; streetlight

**La'ternenpfahl** *m* lamppost

**Latte** ['latə] *f* (-; *-n*) lath; pale; SPORT bar

**'Lattenzaun** *m* paling, picket fence

**Lätzchen** ['lɛtsçən] *n* (*-s*; -) bib

**Laub** [laup] *n* (*-[e]s*; *no pl*) foliage, leaves; **'Laubbaum** *m* deciduous tree

**Laube** ['laubə] *f* (-; *-n*) arbo(u)r

**'Laubfrosch** *m* ZO tree frog

**'Laubsäge** *f* fretsaw

**Lauch** [laux] *m* (*-[e]s*; *-e*) BOT leek

**Lauer** ['lauɐ] *f*: ***auf der ~ liegen** or **sein*** lie in wait; **'lauern** *v/i* (*ge-, h*) lurk; ***~ auf*** (*acc*) lie in wait for

**Lauf** [lauf] *m* (*-[e]s*; *Läufe* ['lɔyfə]) run; course; *gun*: barrel; ***im ~(e) der Zeit*** in the course of time; **~bahn** *f* career; **~diszi,plin** *f* SPORT track event

**laufen** ['laufən] *v/i and v/t* (*irr, ge-, sein*) run (*a.* TECH, MOT, ECON); walk; *fig* work, run; ***j-n ~ lassen*** let s.o. go; let s.o. off; **~d 1.** *fig adj* present, current (*a.* ECON); continual; ***auf dem Laufenden sein*** be up to date **2.** *adv* continuously; regularly; always

**'laufenlassen** *v/t* (*irr*, **lassen**, *sep*, *no -ge-, h*) → ***laufen***

**Läufer** ['lɔyfɐ] *m* (*-s*; -) runner (*a. carpet*); *chess*: bishop; **'Läuferin** *f* (-; *-nen*) runner

**'Lauf|gitter** *n* playpen; **~masche** *f* run, *Br* ladder; **~schuhe** *pl* walking shoes; SPORT trainers; **~steg** *m* footbridge; TECH, *fashion*: catwalk; MAR gangway

**Lauge** ['laugə] *f* (-; *-n*) suds; CHEM lye

**Laune** ['launə] *f* (-; *-n*) mood, temper; ***gute (schlechte) ~ haben*** be in a good (bad) mood *or* temper; **launenhaft**, **'launisch** *adj* moody; bad-tempered

**Laus** [laus] *f* (-; *Läuse* ['lɔyzə]) ZO louse

**Lauschangriff** ['lauʃʔaŋgrɪf] *m* bugging operation; **lauschen** ['lauʃən] *v/i* (*ge-, h*) listen (*dat* to); eavesdrop

**lauschig** ['lauʃɪç] *adj* snug, cozy, *Br* cosy

**laut**[1] [laut] **1.** *adj* loud; noisy **2.** *adv* loud(ly); ***~ vorlesen*** read (out) aloud; ***(sprich) ~er, bitte!*** speak up, please!

**laut**[2] *prp* (*gen or dat*) according to

**Laut** *m* (*-[e]s*; *-e*) sound, noise

**lauten** ['lautən] *v/i* (*ge-, h*) read; be

**läuten** ['lɔytən] *v/i and v/t* (*ge-, h*) ring; ***es läutet (an der Tür)*** the (door)bell is ringing

**lauter** ['lautɐ] *adv* sheer (*nonsense etc*); nothing but; (so) many

**'lautlos** *adj* silent, soundless; hushed

**'Lautschrift** *f* phonetic transcription

**'Lautsprecher** *m* TECH (loud)speaker

**'Lautstärke** *f* loudness, ELECTR *a.* (sound) volume; ***mit voller ~*** (at) full blast; **~regler** *m* volume control

**lauwarm** ['lauvarm] *adj* lukewarm (*a. fig*)

**Lava** ['laːva] *f* (-; *Laven*) GEOL lava

**Lavabo** [la'vaːbo] *Swiss n* → ***Waschbecken***

**Lavendel** [la'vɛndəl] *m* (*-s*; -) BOT lavender

**Lawine** [la'viːnə] *f* (-; *-n*) avalanche

**Lazarett** [latsa'rɛt] *n* (-[*e*]*s*; -*e*) (military) hospital

**leben** ['le:bən] (*ge*-, *h*) **1.** *v/i* live; be alive; ***von et. ~*** live on s.th. **2.** *v/t* live; 'Leben *n* (-*s*; -) life; ***am ~ bleiben*** stay alive; survive; ***am ~ sein*** be alive; ***sich das ~ nehmen*** take one's (own) life, commit suicide; ***ums ~ kommen*** lose one's life, be killed; ***um sein ~ laufen*** (***kämpfen***) run (fight) for one's life; ***das tägliche ~*** everyday life; ***mein ~ lang*** all my life; '**lebend** *adj* living; **lebendig** [le'bɛndɪç] *adj* living, alive; *fig* lively

'**Lebens|abend** *m* old age, the last years of one's life; **~bedingungen** *pl* living conditions; **~dauer** *f* life-span; TECH (service) life; **~erfahrung** *f* experience of life; **~erwartung** *f* life expectancy

'**lebensfähig** *adj* MED viable (*a. fig*)

'**Lebensgefahr** *f* mortal danger; ***in*** (***unter***) ***~*** in danger (at the risk) of one's life; '**lebensgefährlich** *adj* dangerous (to life), perilous

'**lebensgroß** *adj* life-size(d)

'**Lebensgröße** *f*: ***e-e Statue in ~*** a life-size(d) statue

'**Lebenshaltungskosten** *pl* cost of living

'**lebenslänglich 1.** *adj* lifelong; ***~e Freiheitsstrafe*** JUR life sentence **2.** *adv* for life

'**Lebenslauf** *m* personal record, curriculum vitae

'**lebenslustig** *adj* fond of life

'**Lebensmittel** *pl* food(stuffs); groceries; **~geschäft** *n* grocery, supermarket

'**lebensmüde** *adj* tired of life

'**Lebens|notwendigkeit** *f* vital necessity; **~retter(in)** lifesaver, rescuer; **~standard** *m* standard of living; **~unterhalt** *m* livelihood; ***s-n ~ verdienen*** earn one's living (***als*** as; ***mit*** out of, by); **~versicherung** *f* life insurance; **~weise** *f* way of life

'**lebenswichtig** *adj* vital, essential

'**Lebenszeichen** *n* sign of life

'**Lebenszeit** *f* lifetime; ***auf ~*** for life

**Leber** ['le:bɐ] *f* (-; -*n*) ANAT liver; **~fleck** *m* mole; **~tran** *m* cod-liver oil

'**Lebewesen** *n* living being, creature

**lebhaft** ['le:phaft] *adj* lively; heavy (*traffic etc*)

'**Lebkuchen** *m* gingerbread

'**leblos** *adj* lifeless (*a. fig*)

'**Lebzeiten** *pl*: ***zu s-n ~*** in his lifetime

**lechzen** ['lɛçtsən] *v/i* (*ge*-, *h*) ***~ nach*** thirst for

**leck** [lɛk] *adj* leaking, leaky

**Leck** *n* (-[*e*]*s*; -*s*) leak

**lecken**[1] ['lɛkən] *v/t and v/i* (*ge*-, *h*) *a.* ***~ an*** (*dat*) lick

'**lecken**[2] *v/i* (*ge*-, *h*) leak

**lecker** ['lɛkɐ] *adj* delicious, tasty, F yummy; '**Leckerbissen** *m* delicacy, treat (*a. fig*)

**Leder** ['le:dɐ] *n* (-*s*; -) leather; '**ledern** *adj* leather(n); '**Lederwaren** *pl* leather goods

**ledig** ['le:dɪç] *adj* single, unmarried

**lediglich** ['le:dɪklɪç] *adv* only, merely

**Lee** [le:] *f* (-; *no pl*) MAR lee; ***nach ~*** leeward

**leer** [le:ɐ] **1.** *adj* empty (*a. fig*); vacant (*house etc*); blank (*page etc*); ELECTR dead, *Br* flat; ***~ stehend*** unoccupied, vacant **2.** *adv*: ***~ laufen*** TECH idle; **Leere** ['le:rə] *f* (-; *no pl*) emptiness (*a. fig*); '**leeren** *v/t and v/refl* (*ge*-, *h*) empty; '**Leergut** *n* empties; '**Leerlauf** *m* TECH idling; neutral (gear); *fig* running on the spot; '**Leertaste** *f* space bar; '**Leerung** *f* (-; -*en*) *post* collection

**legal** [le'ga:l] *adj* legal, lawful

**legalisieren** [legali'zi:rən] *v/t* (*no -ge-*, *h*) legalize; **Legali'sierung** *f* (-; -*en*) legalization

**Legasthenie** [legaste'ni:] *f* (-; -*n*) PSYCH dyslexia, F word blindness

**Legastheniker** [legas'te:nikɐ] *m* (-*s*; -), **Legas'thenikerin** *f* (-; -*nen*) PSYCH dyslexic

**legen** ['le:gən] *v/t and v/i* (*ge*-, *h*) lay (*a. eggs*); place, put; set (*hair*); ***sich ~*** lie down; *fig* calm down; *pain*: wear off

**Legende** [le'gɛndə] *f* (-; -*n*) legend

**leger** [le'ʒe:ɐ] *adj* casual, informal

**Legislative** [legɪsla'ti:və] *f* (-; -*n*) legislative power

**legitim** [legi'ti:m] *adj* legitimate

**Lehm** [le:m] *m* (-[*e*]*s*; -*e*) loam; clay

**lehmig** ['le:mɪç] *adj* loamy, F muddy

**Lehne** ['le:nə] *f* (-; -*n*) back(rest); arm(-rest); '**lehnen** *v/t and v/i* lean (*a.* ***sich ~***) rest (***an*** *acc*, ***gegen*** against; ***auf*** *acc* on); ***sich aus dem Fenster ~*** lean out of the window; '**Lehnsessel** *m*, '**Lehnstuhl** *m* armchair, easy chair

L

**Lehrbuch** ['leːɐbuːx] *n* textbook
**Lehre** ['leːrə] *f* (-; -*n*) science; theory; REL, POL teachings, doctrine; moral; ECON apprenticeship; ***in der ~ sein*** be apprenticed (***bei*** to); ***das wird ihm e-e ~ sein*** that will teach him a lesson
'**lehren** *v/t* (*ge-*, *h*) teach, instruct; show
**Lehrer** ['leːrɐ] *m* (-*s*; -) teacher, instructor, *Br a.* master; **~ausbildung** *f* teacher training
**Lehrerin** ['leːrərɪn] *f* (-; -*nen*) (lady) teacher, *Br a.* mistress
'**Lehrer|kol,legium** *n* (teaching) staff; **~zimmer** *n* staff *or* teachers' room
'**Lehr|gang** *m* course (of instruction *or* study); training course; **~jahr** *n* year (of apprenticeship)
**Lehrling** ['leːɐlɪŋ] *m* (-*s*; -*e*) apprentice, trainee
'**Lehr|meister** *m*, **~meisterin** *f* master; *fig* teacher; **~mittel** *pl* teaching aids; **~plan** *m* curriculum, syllabus; **~probe** *f* demonstration lesson
'**lehrreich** *adj* informative, instructive
'**Lehr|stelle** *f* apprenticeship; vacancy for an apprentice; **~stuhl** *m* professorship; **~tochter** *Swiss f* apprentice; **~vertrag** *m* indenture(s); **~zeit** *f* apprenticeship
**Leib** [laip] *m* (-[*e*]*s*; *Leiber* ['laibɐ]) body; belly, ANAT abdomen; stomach; ***bei lebendigem ~e*** alive; ***mit ~ und Seele*** (with) heart and soul
'**Leibgericht** *n* GASTR favo(u)rite dish
**leibhaftig** [laip'haftɪç] *adj*: ***der ~e Teufel*** the devil incarnate; ***~es Ebenbild*** living image; ***ich sehe ihn noch ~ vor mir*** I can see him (before me) now
'**leiblich** *adj* physical
'**Leib|rente** *f* life annuity; **~wache** *f*, **~wächter** *m* bodyguard; **~wäsche** *f* underwear
**Leiche** ['laiçə] *f* (-; -*n*) (dead) body, corpse
'**leichen'blass** *adj* deadly pale
'**Leichen|halle** *f* mortuary; **~schauhaus** *n* morgue; **~verbrennung** *f* cremation; **~wagen** *m* hearse
**leicht** [laiçt] *adj* light (*a. fig*); easy, simple; slight, minor; TECH light(weight); ***~ möglich*** quite possible; ***~ gekränkt*** easily offended; ***es fällt mir*** (***nicht***) ***~*** (***zu*** *inf*) I find it easy (difficult) (to *inf*); ***das ist ~ gesagt*** it's not as easy as that; ***es geht ~ kaputt*** it breaks easily; ***~ verständlich*** easy to understand
'**Leicht|ath,let** *m* SPORT (track-and-field) athlete; **~ath,letik** *f* SPORT track and field (events), athletics; **~ath,letin** *f* SPORT (track-and-field) athlete; **~gewicht** *n* SPORT lightweight
'**leichtgläubig** *adj* credulous
**Leichtigkeit** ['laiçtɪçkait] *f*: ***mit ~*** easily, with ease
**leichtlebig** ['laiçtleːbɪç] *adj* happy-go-lucky
'**Leichtme,tall** *n* light metal
'**leichtnehmen** *v/t* (*irr*, ***nehmen***, *sep*, *-ge-*, *h*): ***et. ~*** not worry about s.th.; make light of s.th.; ***nimm's leicht!*** never mind!, don't worry about it!
'**Leichtsinn** *m* (-[*e*]*s*; *no pl*) carelessness; recklessness; '**leichtsinnig** *adj* careless; reckless
'**leichtverständlich** *adj* → ***leicht***
**Leid** [lait] *n* (-[*e*]*s*; *no pl*) sorrow, grief; pain; ***es tut mir ~*** I'm sorry (***um*** for; ***wegen*** about; ***dass ich zu spät komme*** for being late)
**leiden** ['laidən] *v/t and v/i* (*irr*, *ge-*, *h*) suffer (***an*** *dat*, ***unter*** *dat* from); ***j-n gut ~ können*** like s.o.; ***ich kann ... nicht ~*** I don't like ...; I can't stand ...; '**Leiden** *n* (-*s*; -) suffering(s); MED disease
'**Leidenschaft** *f* (-; -*en*) passion
'**leidenschaftlich** *adj* passionate; vehement
'**Leidensgenosse** *m*, '**Leidensgenossin** *f* fellow sufferer
**leider** ['laidɐ] *adv* unfortunately; ***~ ja*** (***nein***) I'm afraid so (not)
'**leidlich** *adj* passable, F so-so
'**Leidtragende** *m, f* (-*n*; -*n*) mourner; ***er ist der ~ dabei*** he is the one who suffers for it
'**Leidwesen** *n*: ***zu m-m ~*** to my regret
**Leierkasten** ['laiɐkastən] *m* barrel organ; **~mann** *m* organ grinder
**leiern** ['laiɐn] *v/i and v/t* (*ge-*, *h*) crank (up); *fig* drone
**Leihbücherei** ['laibyːçərai] *f* public library
**leihen** ['laiən] *v/t* (*irr*, *ge-*, *h*) lend; rent (*Br* hire) out; borrow (***von*** from); rent, hire
'**Leih|gebühr** *f* rental, lending fee; **~haus** *n* pawnshop, pawnbroker's

(shop); **~mutter** F *f* surrogate mother; **~wagen** *m* MOT rented (*Br* hire) car
'**leihweise** *adv* on loan
**Leim** [laim] *m* (-[*e*]*s*; -*e*), **leimen** ['laimən] *v/t* (*ge-*, *h*) glue
**Leine** ['lainə] *f* (-; -*n*) line; lead, leash
**Leinen** ['lainən] *n* (-*s*; -) linen; canvas; ***in ~ gebunden*** clothbound
'**Leinenschuh** *m* canvas shoe
'**Lein|samen** *m* BOT linseed; **~tuch** *n* (linen) sheet; **~wand** *f* linen; PAINT canvas; screen
**leise** ['laizə] *adj* quiet, *a.* low, soft (*voice, a. music etc*); *fig* slight, faint; ***~r stellen*** turn (the volume) down
**Leiste** ['laistə] *f* (-; -*n*) ledge; ANAT groin
'**leisten** *v/t* (*ge-*, *h*) do, work; achieve, accomplish; render (*service etc*); take (*oath*); ***gute Arbeit ~*** do a good job; ***sich et. ~*** treat o.s. to s.th.; ***ich kann es mir (nicht) ~*** I can('t) afford it
'**Leistung** *f* (-; -*en*) performance; achievement, PED *a.* (piece of) work, result, TECH *a.* output; service; benefit
'**Leistungsdruck** *m* (-[*e*]*s*; *no pl*) pressure, stress
'**leistungsfähig** *adj* efficient; (physically) fit; '**Leistungsfähigkeit** *f* (-; *no pl*) efficiency (*a.* TECH, ECON); fitness
'**Leistungs|kon,trolle** *f* (achievement *or* proficiency) test; **~kurs** *m* PED *appr* special subject; **~sport** *m* competitive sport(s)
**Leitar,tikel** ['laitˀartiːkəl] *m* editorial, *esp Br* leader, leading article
**leiten** ['laitən] *v/t* (*ge-*, *h*) lead, guide (*a. fig*), conduct (*a.* PHYS, MUS); run (*a.* PED), be in charge of, manage; TV *etc* direct; host; **~d** *adj* leading; PHYS conductive; ***~e Stellung*** key position; ***~er Angestellter*** executive
**Leiter**[1] ['laitɐ] *f* (-; -*n*) ladder
'**Leiter**[2] *m* (-*s*; -) leader; conductor (*a.* PHYS, MUS); ECON *etc* head, manager; chairman; → ***Schulleiter***
**Leiterin** ['laitərın] *f* (-; -*nen*) leader; head; chairwoman
'**Leit|faden** *m* manual, guide; **~planke** *f* MOT guardrail, *Br* crash barrier; **~spruch** *m* motto
'**Leitung** *f* (-; -*en*) ECON management; head office; administration; chairmanship; organization; THEA *etc* direction; TECH main, pipe(s); ELECTR, TEL line; ***die ~ haben*** be in charge; ***unter der ~ von*** MUS conducted by
'**Leitungsrohr** *n* pipe
'**Leitungswasser** *n* tap water
**Lektion** [lɛk'tsjoːn] *f* (-; -*en*) lesson
**Lektüre** [lɛk'tyːrə] *f* (-; -*n*) reading (matter); PED reader
**Lende** ['lɛndə] *f* (-; -*n*) ANAT loin; GASTR sirloin
**lenken** ['lɛŋkən] *v/t* (*ge-*, *h*) steer, drive; *fig* guide *s.o.*; direct (*traffic etc*)
**Lenker** ['lɛŋkɐ] *m* (-*s*; -) handlebar
'**Lenkrad** *n* MOT steering wheel
'**Lenkung** *f* (-; -*en*) MOT steering (system)
**Leopard** [leo'part] *m* (-*en*; -*en*) ZO leopard
**Lerche** ['lɛrçə] *f* (-; -*n*) ZO lark
**lernen** ['lɛrnən] *v/t and v/i* (*ge-*, *h*) learn; study; ***er lernt leicht*** he is a quick learner; ***lesen ~*** learn (how) to read
'**Lernmittelfreiheit** *f* free books *etc*
**lesbar** ['leːsbaːɐ] *adj* readable
**Lesbierin** ['lɛsbjərın] *f* (-; -*nen*), **lesbisch** ['lɛsbıʃ] *adj* lesbian
**Lesebuch** ['leːzəbuːx] *n* reader
'**Leselampe** *f* reading lamp
**lesen** ['leːzən] *v/i and v/t* (*irr*, *ge-*, *h*) read; AGR harvest
'**lesenswert** *adj* worth reading
**Leser** ['leːzɐ] *m* (-*s*; -) reader
'**Leseratte** F *f* bookworm
'**Leserbrief** *m* letter to the editor
'**Leserin** *f* (-; -nen) reader
'**leserlich** *adj* legible
'**Lesestoff** *m* reading matter
'**Lesezeichen** *n* bookmark
'**Lesung** *f* (-; -*en*) reading (*a.* PARL)
**Letzt** [lɛtst] *f*: ***zu guter ~*** in the end
**letzte** ['lɛtstə] *adj* last; latest; ***zum ~n Mal(e)*** for the last time; ***in ~r Zeit*** recently; ***als Letzter ankommen*** *etc* arrive *etc* last; ***Letzter sein*** be last (*a.* SPORT); ***das ist das Letzte!*** that's the limit!; '**letztens** *adv* finally; ***erst ~*** just recently; **letztere** ['lɛtstərə] *adj* latter; ***der (die, das) Letztere*** the latter
**Leuchtanzeige** ['lɔʏçtˀantsaigə] *f* luminous *or* LED display light; **leuchten** ['lɔʏçtən] *v/i* (*ge-*, *h*) shine; glow; '**Leuchten** *n* (-*s*; *no pl*) shining; glow; '**leuchtend** *adj* shining (*a. fig*); bright; **Leuchter** ['lɔʏçtɐ] *m* (-*s*; -) candlestick
'**Leucht|farbe** *f* luminous paint; **~reklame** *f* neon sign(s); **~(stoff)röhre** *f*

L

ELECTR fluorescent lamp; **~turm** *m* lighthouse; **~ziffer** *f* luminous figure
**leugnen** ['lɔʏgnən] *v/t and v/i* (*ge-*, *h*) deny (***et. getan zu haben*** having done s.th.)
**Leute** ['lɔʏtə] *pl* people, F folks
**Leutnant** ['lɔʏtnant] *m* (*-s*; *-s*) MIL second lieutenant
**Lexikon** ['lɛksikɔn] *n* (*-s*; *-ka*, *-ken*) encyclop(a)edia; dictionary
**Libelle** [li'bɛlə] *f* (*-*; *-n*) ZO dragonfly
**liberal** [libe'ra:l] *adj* liberal
**Libero** ['li:bero] *m* (*-s*; *-s*) *soccer*: sweeper
**licht** ['lɪçt] *adj* bright; *fig* lucid
**Licht** *n* (*-[e]s*; *-er* ['lɪçtɐ]) light; (*no pl*) brightness; **~ *machen*** switch *or* turn on the light(s)
'**Licht|bild** *n* photo(graph); slide; **~bildervortrag** *m* slide lecture; **~blick** *m* ray of hope; bright moment
'**lichtempfindlich** *adj* sensitive to light; PHOT sensitive; '**Lichtempfindlichkeit** *f* (light) sensitivity; PHOT speed
**lichten** ['lɪçtən] *v/t* (*ge-*, *h*) clear; ***den Anker* ~** MAR weigh anchor; ***sich* ~** get thin(ner); *fig* be thinning (out)
'**Licht|geschwindigkeit** *f* speed of light; **~hupe** *f* MOT (headlight) flash(er); ***die* ~ *betätigen*** flash one's lights; **~jahr** *n* light year; **~ma,schine** *f* MOT generator; **~orgel** *f* colo(u)r organ; **~pause** *f* blueprint; **~schacht** *m* well; **~schalter** *m* (light) switch
'**lichtscheu** *fig adj* shady
'**Licht|schutzfaktor** *m* sun protection factor, SPF; **~strahl** *m* ray *or* beam of light (*a. fig*)
'**Lichtung** *f* (*-*; *-en*) clearing
**Lid** [li:t] *n* (*-[e]s*; *Lider* ['li:dɐ]) ANAT (eye)lid; **~schatten** *m* eye shadow
**lieb** [li:p] *adj* dear; sweet; nice, kind; good; **~ *gewinnen*** get fond of; **~ *haben*** love, be fond of; **Liebe** ['li:bə] *f* (*-*; *no pl*) love (***zu*** of, for); ***aus* ~ *zu*** out of love for; **~ *auf den ersten Blick*** love at first sight; '**lieben** *v/t* (*ge-*, *h*) love, *a.* be in love with *s.o.*; make love to
'**liebenswert** *adj* lovable, charming, sweet
'**liebenswürdig** *adj* kind; '**Liebenswürdigkeit** *f* (*-*; *no pl*) kindness
**lieber** ['li:bɐ] *adv* rather, sooner; **~ *haben*** prefer, like better; ***ich möchte* ~ (*nicht*) ...** I'd rather (not) ...; ***du solltest* ~ (*nicht*) ...** you had better (not) ...
'**Liebes|brief** *m* love letter; **~erklärung** *f*: ***j-m e-e* ~ *machen*** declare one's love to s.o.; **~kummer** *m*: **~ *haben*** be lovesick; **~paar** *n* lovers
'**liebevoll** *adj* loving, affectionate
'**liebgewinnen** *v/t* (*irr*, ***gewinnen***, *sep*, *h*) → ***lieb***
'**liebhaben** *v/t* (*irr*, ***haben***, *sep*, *-ge-*, *h*) → ***lieb***; **Liebhaber** ['li:pha:bɐ] *m* (*-s*; *-*) lover (*a. fig*); **~...** *in cpds ...preis*, *...stück etc*: collector's ...; **Liebhaberei** [li:pha:bə'rai] *f* (*-*; *-en*) hobby
**Liebkosung** [li:p'ko:zʊŋ] *f* (*-*; *-en*) caress
'**lieblich** *adj* lovely, charming, sweet (*a. wine*)
'**Liebling** *m* (*-s*; *-e*) darling; favo(u)rite
'**Lieblings...** *in cpds mst* favo(u)rite
'**lieblos** *adj* unloving, cold; unkind (*words etc*); *fig* careless
**Lied** [li:t] *n* (*-[e]s*; *-er* ['li:dɐ]) song; tune
**liederlich** ['li:dɐlɪç] *adj* slovenly, sloppy
**Liedermacher** ['li:dɐmaxɐ] *m* (*-s*; *-*) singer-songwriter
**lief** [li:f] *pret of* ***laufen***
**Lieferant** [lifə'rant] *m* (*-en*; *-en*) ECON supplier; **lieferbar** ['li:fɐba:ɐ] *adj* ECON available; '**Lieferfrist** *f* ECON term of delivery; **liefern** ['li:fɐn] *v/t* (*ge-*, *h*) ECON deliver; ***j-m et.* ~** supply s.o. with s.th.; **Lieferung** ['li:fərʊŋ] *f* (*-*; *-en*) ECON delivery; supply
'**Lieferwagen** *m* MOT (delivery) van
**Liege** ['li:gə] *f* (*-*; *-n*) couch
**liegen** ['li:gən] *v/i* (*irr*, *ge-*, *h*) lie, *a.* be (situated); (***krank***) ***im Bett* ~** be (ill) in bed; ***nach Osten*** (***der Straße***) **~** face east (the street); ***daran liegt es***(, ***dass***) that's (the reason) why; ***es*** (***er***) ***liegt mir nicht*** F it (he) is not my cup of tea; ***mir liegt viel*** (***wenig***) ***daran*** it means a lot (doesn't mean much) to me; **~ *bleiben*** stay in bed; be left behind; **~ *lassen*** leave (behind); F ***j-n links* ~ *lassen*** ignore s.o., give s.o. the cold shoulder
'**liegenbleiben** *v/i* (*irr*, ***bleiben***, *sep*, *-ge-*, *sein*) → ***liegen***; **~lassen** *v/i* (*irr*, ***lassen***, *sep*, *no -ge-*, *h*) → ***liegen***
'**Liege|sitz** *m* reclining seat; **~stuhl** *m* deckchair; **~stütz** *m* (*-es*; *-e*) SPORT

L

push-up, *Br* press-up; **~wagen** *m* RAIL couchette
**lieh** [liː] *pret of* ***leihen***
**ließ** [liːs] *pret of* ***lassen***
**Lift** [lɪft] *m* (-[*e*]*s*; -*e*, -*s*) elevator, *Br* lift; ski lift
**Liga** ['liːga] *f* (-; *Ligen*) league, SPORT *a.* division
**Likör** [li'køːɐ] *m* (-*s*; -*e*) liqueur
**lila** ['liːla] *adj* purple, violet
**Lilie** ['liːljə] *f* (-; -*n*) BOT lily
**Liliputaner** [lilipu'taːnɐ] *m* (-*s*; -) dwarf, midget
**Limonade** [limo'naːdə] *f* (-; -*n*) pop; lemon soda, *Br* lemonade
**Limousine** [limu'ziːnə] *f* (-; -*n*) MOT sedan, *Br* saloon car; limousine
**Linde** ['lɪndə] *f* (-; -*n*) BOT lime (tree), linden
**lindern** ['lɪndɐn] *v/t* (*ge*-, *h*) relieve, ease, alleviate; **Linderung** ['lɪndərʊŋ] *f* (-; *no pl*) relief, alleviation
**Lineal** [line'aːl] *n* (-*s*; -*e*) ruler
**Linie** ['liːnjə] *f* (-; -*n*) line; ***auf s-e ~ achten*** watch one's weight
'**Linien|flug** *m* AVIAT scheduled flight; **~richter** *m* SPORT linesman
'**linientreu** *adj* POL: ***~ sein*** follow the party line
**linieren** [li'niːrən], **liniieren** [lini'iːrən] *v/t* (*no -ge-*, *h*) rule, line
**linke** ['lɪŋkə] *adj* left (*a.* POL); ***auf der ~n Seite*** on the left(-hand side); '**Linke** *m*, *f* (-*n*; -*n*) POL leftist, left-winger
**linkisch** ['lɪŋkɪʃ] *adj* awkward, clumsy
**links** [lɪŋks] *adv* on the left (*a.* POL); on the wrong side; ***nach ~*** (to the) left; ***~ von*** to the left of
**Links...** *in cpds ...verkehr etc*: left-hand
**Links'außen** *m* (-; -) SPORT outside left, left wing
**Linkshänder** ['lɪŋkshɛndɐ] *m* (-*s*; -), '**Linkshänderin** *f* (-; -*nen*) left-hander
'**Linksradi,kale** *m*, *f* (-*n*; -*n*) POL left-wing extremist
**Linse** ['lɪnzə] *f* (-; -*n*) BOT lentil; OPT lens
**Lippe** ['lɪpə] *f* (-; -*n*) ANAT lip
'**Lippenstift** *m* lipstick
**liquidieren** [likvi'diːrən] *v/t* (*no -ge-*, *h*) ECON liquidate (*a.* POL)
**lispeln** ['lɪspəln] *v/i* (*ge*-, *h*) (have a) lisp
**List** [lɪst] *f* (-; -*en*) trick; (*no pl*) cunning
**Liste** ['lɪstə] *f* (-; -*n*) list; roll
**listig** ['lɪstɪç] *adj* cunning, tricky, sly
**Liter** ['liːtɐ] *n*, *m* (-*s*; -) liter, *Br* litre
**literarisch** [lɪtə'raːrɪʃ] *adj* literary
**Literatur** [lɪtəra'tuːɐ] *f* (-; -*en*) literature; **~...** *in cpds ...kritik etc*: *mst* literary
**Litfaßsäule** ['lɪtfaszɔʏlə] *f* advertising pillar
**litt** [lɪt] *pret of* ***leiden***
**Lizenz** [li'tsɛnts] *f* (-; -*en*) license, *Br* licence
**Lkw, LKW** ['ɛlkave] *m* (-[*s*]; -) *abbr of* ***Lastkraftwagen*** truck, *Br a.* lorry
**Lob** [loːp] *n* (-[*e*]*s*; *no pl*), **loben** ['loːbən] *v/t* (*ge*-, *h*) praise; '**lobenswert** *adj* praiseworthy, laudable
**Loch** [lɔx] *n* (-[*e*]*s*; *Löcher* ['lœçɐ]) hole (*a. fig*); puncture; **lochen** ['lɔxən] *v/t* (*ge*-, *h*) punch (*a.* TECH); **Locher** ['lɔxɐ] *m* (-*s*; -) punch
**Locke** ['lɔkə] *f* (-; -*n*) curl; lock
**locken**[1] ['lɔkən] *v/t and v/refl* (*ge*-, *h*) curl
**locken**[2] *v/t* (*ge*-, *h*) lure, entice, *fig a.* attract, tempt
'**Locken|kopf** *m* curly head; **~wickler** ['lɔkənvɪklɐ] *m* (-*s*; -) curler, roller
**locker** ['lɔkɐ] *adj* loose; slack; *fig* relaxed; '**lockern** *v/t* (*ge*-, *h*) loosen, slacken; relax (*a. fig*); ***sich ~*** loosen, (be)come loose; SPORT limber up; *fig* relax
**lockig** ['lɔkɪç] *adj* curly, curled
'**Lockvogel** *m* decoy (*a. fig*)
**lodern** ['loːdɐn] *v/i* (*ge*-, *h*) blaze, flare
**Löffel** ['lœfəl] *m* (-*s*; -) spoon; ladle
'**löffeln** *v/t* (*ge*-, *h*) spoon up
**log** [loːk] *pret of* ***lügen***
**Logbuch** ['lɔkbuːx] *n* MAR log
**Loge** ['loːʒə] *f* (-; -*n*) THEA box; lodge
**Logik** ['loːgɪk] *f* (-; *no pl*) logic
**logisch** ['loːgɪʃ] *adj* logical
'**logischer'weise** *adv* obviously
**Lohn** [loːn] *m* (-[*e*]*s*; *Löhne* ['løːnə]) ECON wages, pay(ment); *fig* reward; **~empfänger** *m* wageworker, *Br* wage earner
**lohnen** ['loːnən] *v/refl* (*ge*-, *h*) be worth (-while), pay; ***es*** (***die Mühe***) ***lohnt sich*** it's worth it (the trouble); ***das Buch*** (***der Film***) ***lohnt sich*** the book (film) is worth reading (seeing); **~d** *adj* paying; *fig* rewarding
'**Lohn|erhöhung** *f* raise, *Br* increase in

wages, rise; **~steuer** *f* income tax; **~stopp** *m* wage freeze

**Loipe** ['lɔʏpə] *f* (-; -*n*) (cross-country) course

**Lok** [lɔk] *f* (-; -*s*) → ***Lokomotive***

**Lokal** [lo'ka:l] *n* (-*s*; -*e*) restaurant; bar, saloon, *esp Br* pub

**Lo'kal...** *in cpds mst* local

**Lokführer** *m* RAIL engineer, *Br* train driver

**Lokomotive** [lokomo'ti:və] *f* (-; -*n*) RAIL engine

**Lorbeer** ['lɔrbe:ɐ] *m* (-*s*; -*en*) BOT laurel; GASTR bay leaf

**Lore** ['lo:rə] *f* (-; -*n*) TECH tipcart

**los** [lo:s] *adj and adv* off; *dog etc*: loose; ***~ sein*** be rid of; ***was ist ~?*** what's the matter?, F what's up?; what's going on (here)?; ***hier ist nicht viel ~*** there's nothing much going on here; F ***da ist was ~!*** that's where the action is!; F ***also ~!*** okay, let's go!

**Los** [lo:s] *n* (-*es*; -*e* ['lo:zə]) lot, *fig a.* fate; (lottery) ticket, number

**'losbinden** *v/t* (*irr*, ***binden***, *sep*, -*ge*-, *h*) untie

**Löschblatt** ['lœʃblat] *n* blotting paper

**löschen** ['lœʃən] *v/t* (*ge*-, *h*) extinguish, put out; quench (*thirst*); blot (*ink*); wipe off *the blackboard*; erase, IT *a.* delete; slake (*lime*); MAR unload

**'Löschpa,pier** *n* blotting paper

**lose** ['lo:zə] *adj* loose

**Lösegeld** ['lø:zəgɛlt] *n* ransom

**losen** ['lo:zən] *v/i* (*ge*-, *h*) draw lots (***um*** for)

**lösen** ['lø:zən] *v/t* (*ge*-, *h*) undo (*knot etc*); loosen, relax; TECH release; take off; solve (*problem etc*); settle (*conflict etc*); buy, get (*ticket etc*); dissolve (*a.* CHEM); ***sich ~*** come loose *or* undone; *fig* free o.s. (***von*** from)

**'los|fahren** *v/i* (*irr*, ***fahren***, *sep*, -*ge*-, *sein*) leave; drive off; **~gehen** *v/i* (*irr*, ***gehen***, *sep*, -*ge*-, *sein*) leave; start, begin; *shot etc*: go off; ***auf j-n ~*** go for s.o.; ***ich gehe jetzt los*** I'm off now; **~ketten** *v/t* (*sep*, -*ge*-, *h*) unchain; **~kommen** *v/i* (*irr*, ***kommen***, *sep*, -*ge*-, *sein*) get away (***von*** from); **~lassen** *v/t* (*irr*, ***lassen***, *sep*, -*ge*-, *h*) let go; ***den Hund ~ auf*** (*acc*) set the dog on; **~legen** F *v/i* (*sep*, -*ge*-, *h*) get cracking

**löslich** ['lø:slıç] *adj* CHEM soluble

**'los|machen** *v/t* (*sep*, -*ge*-, *h*) → ***lösen***; **~reißen** *v/t* (*irr*, ***reißen***, *sep*, -*ge*-, *h*) tear off; ***sich ~*** break away; *esp fig* tear o.s. away (*both*: ***von*** from); **~sagen** *v/refl* (*sep*, -*ge*-, *h*) ***sich ~ von*** break with; **~schlagen** *v/i* (*irr*, ***schlagen***, *sep*, -*ge*-, *h*) strike (***auf j-n*** out at s.o.); **~schnallen** *v/t* (*sep*, -*ge*-, *h*) unbuckle; ***sich ~*** MOT, AVIAT unfasten one's seat belt; **~stürzen** *v/i* (*sep*, -*ge*-, *sein*) ***~ auf*** (*acc*) rush at

**Losung** ['lo:zʊŋ] *f* (-; -*en*) MIL password; *fig* slogan

**Lösung** ['lø:zʊŋ] *f* (-; -*en*) solution (*a. fig*); settlement

**'Lösungsmittel** *n* solvent

**'loswerden** *v/t* (*irr*, ***werden***, *sep*, -*ge*-, *sein*) get rid of; spend (*money*); lose

**'losziehen** *v/i* (*irr*, ***ziehen***, *sep*, -*ge*-, *sein*) set out, take off, march away

**Lot** [lo:t] *n* (-[*e*]*s*; -*e*) plumbline

**löten** ['lø:tən] *v/t* (*ge*-, *h*) TECH solder

**Lotion** [lo'tsjo:n] *f* (-; -*en*) lotion

**Lotse** ['lo:tsə] *m* (-*n*; -*n*), **'lotsen** *v/t* (*ge*-, *h*) MAR pilot

**Lotterie** [lɔtə'ri:] *f* (-; -*n*) lottery; **~gewinn** *m* prize; **~los** *n* lottery ticket

**Lotto** ['lɔto] *n* (-*s*; -*s*) lotto, bingo; *Br* national lottery; *in Germany*: Lotto; (***im***) ***~ spielen*** do Lotto; **~schein** *m* Lotto coupon; **~ziehung** *f* Lotto draw

**Löwe** ['lø:və] *m*(-*n*; -*n*) ZO lion; AST Leo; ***er ist*** (***ein***) ***~*** he's (a) Leo

**'Löwenzahn** *m* BOT dandelion

**Löwin** ['lø:vın] *f* (-; -*nen*) ZO lioness

**loyal** [loa'ja:l] *adj* loyal, faithful

**Luchs** [lʊks] *m* (-*es*; -*e*) ZO lynx

**Lücke** ['lʏkə] *f* (-; -*n*) gap (*a. fig*); **'Lückenbüßer** *m* stopgap; **'lückenhaft** *adj* full of gaps; *fig* incomplete; **'lückenlos** *adj* without a gap; *fig* complete; **'Lückentest** *m* PSYCH completion *or* fill-in test

**lud** [lu:t] *pret of* ***laden***

**Luft** [lʊft] *f* (-; *no pl*) air; ***an der frischen ~*** (out) in the fresh air; (***frische***) ***~ schöpfen*** get a breath of fresh air; ***die ~ anhalten*** catch (*esp fig a.* hold) one's breath; ***tief ~ holen*** take a deep breath; ***in die ~ sprengen*** (F ***fliegen***) blow up

**'Luft|angriff** *m* air raid; **~ballon** *m* balloon; **~bild** *n* aerial photograph *or* view; **~blase** *f* air bubble; **~brücke** *f*

airlift
'**luftdicht** *adj* airtight
'**Luftdruck** *m* (-[*e*]*s*; *no pl*) PHYS, TECH air pressure
**lüften** ['lʏftən] *v/t and v/i* (*ge-*, *h*) air, ventilate; *fig* reveal
'**Luft|fahrt** *f* (-; *no pl*) aviation, aeronautics; **~feuchtigkeit** *f* (atmospheric) humidity; **~gewehr** *n* airgun
'**luftig** *adj* airy; breezy; light (*dress etc*)
'**Luft|kissen** *n* air cushion; **~kissenfahrzeug** *n* hovercraft; **~krankheit** *f* air-sickness; **~krieg** *m* air warfare; **~kurort** *m* (climatic) health resort
'**luftleer** *adj*: ***~er Raum*** vacuum
'**Luft|linie** *f*: ***50 km ~*** 50 km as the crow flies; **~post** *f* air mail; **~pumpe** *f* air pump; bicycle pump; **~röhre** *f* ANAT windpipe, trachea; **~schlange** *f* streamer; **~schloss** *n* castle in the air; **~sprünge** *pl*: ***~ machen vor Freude*** jump for joy
'**Lüftung** *f* (-; *-en*) airing; TECH ventilation
'**Luft|veränderung** *f* change of air; **~verkehr** *m* air traffic; **~verschmutzung** *f* air pollution; **~waffe** *f* MIL air force; **~weg** *m*: ***auf dem ~*** by air; **~zug** *m* draft, *Br* draught
**Lüge** ['ly:gə] *f* (-; *-n*) lie; '**lügen** *v/i* (*irr*, *ge-*, *h*) lie, tell a lie *or* lies; ***das ist gelogen*** that's a lie; **Lügner(in)** ['ly:gnɐ, 'ly:gnərɪn] *m*(*f*) (*-s*; *-/-*; *-nen*) liar; **lügnerisch** ['ly:gnərɪʃ] *adj* false
**Luke** ['lu:kə] *f* (-; *-n*) hatch; skylight
**Lümmel** ['lʏməl] F *m* (*-s*; -) rascal
**lumpen** ['lʊmpən] F *v/t*: ***sich nicht ~ lassen*** be generous
'**Lumpen** *m* (*-s*; -) rag; ***in ~*** in rags
**lumpig** ['lʊmpɪç] F *adj*: ***für ~e zwei Euro*** for a paltry two euros
**Lunge** ['lʊŋə] *f* (-; *-n*) ANAT lungs; (***auf***) ***~ rauchen*** inhale
'**Lungen|entzündung** *f* MED pneumonia; **~flügel** *m* ANAT lung; **~zug** *m*: ***e-n ~ machen*** inhale
**Lupe** ['lu:pə] *f* (-; *-n*) magnifying glass; ***unter die ~ nehmen*** scrutinize (closely)
**Lust** [lʊst] *f* (-; *Lüste* ['lʏstə]) (*no pl*) desire, interest; pleasure, delight; lust; ***~ haben auf et.*** (***et. zu tun***) feel like (doing) s.th.; ***hättest du ~ auszugehen?*** would you like to go out?, how about going out?; ***ich habe keine ~*** I don't feel like it, I'm not in the mood for it; ***die ~ an et. verlieren*** (***j-m die ~ an et. nehmen***) (make s.o.) lose all interest in s.th.
**lüstern** ['lʏstɐn] *adj* greedy (***nach*** for)
**lustig** ['lʊstɪç] *adj* funny; cheerful; ***er ist sehr ~*** he is full of fun; ***es war sehr ~*** it was great fun; ***sich ~ machen über*** (*acc*) make fun of
'**lustlos** *adj* listless, indifferent
'**Lustmord** *m* sex murder
'**Lustspiel** *n* THEA comedy
**lutschen** ['lʊtʃən] *v/i and v/t* (*ge-*, *h*) suck
**Luv** [lu:f] *f* (-; *no pl*) MAR windward, weather side
**luxuriös** [lʊksu'rjø:s] *adj* luxurious
**Luxus** ['lʊksʊs] *m* (-; *no pl*) luxury; **~ar,tikel** *m* luxury (article); **~ausführung** *f* deluxe version; **~ho,tel** *n* five-star (*or* luxury) hotel
**Lymphdrüse** ['lʏmfdry:zə] *f* ANAT lymph gland
**lynchen** ['lʏnçən] *v/t* (*ge-*, *h*) lynch
**Lyrik** ['ly:rɪk] *f* (-; *no pl*) poetry
**Lyriker** ['ly:rikɐ] *m* (*-s*; -), '**Lyrikerin** *f* (-; *-nen*) (lyric) poet
**lyrisch** ['ly:rɪʃ] *adj* lyrical (*a. fig*)

M

# M

**machbar** ['maxba:ɐ] *adj* feasible
**machen** ['maxən] *v/t* (*ge-*, *h*) do; make; GASTR make, prepare; fix (*a. fig*); be, come to, amount to; take, pass (*test etc*); make, go on (*a trip etc*); ***Hausaufgaben ~*** do one's homework; ***da*** (***-gegen***) ***kann man nichts ~*** it can't be helped; ***mach, was du willst!*** do as you please!; (***nun***) ***mach mal*** *or* ***schon!*** hurry up!, come on *or* along now!; ***mach's gut!*** take care (of yourself)!, good luck!; (***das***) ***macht nichts***

it doesn't matter; ***mach dir nichts d-(a)raus!*** never mind!, don't worry!; ***das macht mir nichts aus*** I don't mind *or* care; ***was*** *or* ***wie viel macht das?*** how much is it?; ***sich et.*** (***nichts***) ***~ aus*** (not) care about; (not) care for
'**Machenschaften** *pl* machinations; ***unsaubere ~*** sleaze (*esp* POL)
**Macher** ['maxɐ] *m* (*-s*; -) man of action, doer
**Macho** ['matʃo] *m* (*-s*; *-s*) macho
**Macht** [maxt] *f* (-; *Mächte* ['mɛçtə]) power (***über*** *acc* of); ***an der ~*** in power; ***mit aller ~*** with all one's might
**Machthaber** ['maxtha:bɐ] *m* (*-s*; -) POL ruler
**mächtig** ['mɛçtɪç] *adj* powerful, mighty (*a.* F); enormous, huge
'**Machtkampf** *m* struggle for power
'**machtlos** *adj* powerless
'**Macht|missbrauch** *m* abuse of power; **~poli,tik** *f* power politics; **~übernahme** *f* takeover; **~wechsel** *m* transition of power
**Mädchen** ['mɛ:tçən] *n* (*-s*; -) girl; maid
'**mädchenhaft** *adj* girlish
'**Mädchen|name** *m* girl's name; maiden name; **~schule** *f* girls' school
**Made** ['ma:də] *f* (-; *-n*) ZO maggot; worm
**Mädel** ['mɛ:dəl] *n* (*-s*; *-s*) girl
'**madig** *adj* maggoty, worm-eaten; F'**madigmachen** *v/t* (*sep*, *-ge-*, *h*): F ***j-m et. ~*** spoil s.th. for s.o.
**Magazin** [maga'tsi:n] *n* (*-s*; *-e*) magazine (*a.* MIL, PHOT, TV); store(room), warehouse
**Magd** [ma:kt] *f* (-; *Mägde* ['mɛ:ktə]) (female) farmhand
**Magen** ['ma:gən] *m* (*-s*; *Mägen* ['mɛ:gən]) ANAT stomach; **~beschwerden** *pl* MED stomach trouble; **~geschwür** *n* MED (stomach) ulcer; **~schmerzen** *pl* stomachache
**mager** ['ma:gɐ] *adj* lean, thin, skinny; GASTR low-fat (*cheese*), lean (*meat*), skim (*milk*); *fig* meager, *Br* meagre
**Magie** [ma'gi:] *f* (-; *no pl*) magic
**magisch** ['ma:gɪʃ] *adj* magic(al)
**Magister** [ma'gɪstɐ] *m* (*-s*; -) UNIV Master of Arts *or* Science; *Austrian* → ***Apotheker***
**Magistrat** [magɪs'tra:t] *m* (*-[e]s*; *-e*) municipal council
**Magnet** [ma'gne:t] *m* (*-[e]s*, *-en*; *-e[n]*) magnet (*a. fig*); **~...** *in cpds ...band, ...feld, ...nadel etc*: magnetic ...
**mag'netisch** *adj* magnetic (*a. fig*)
**magnetisieren** [magneti'zi:rən] *v/t* (*no -ge-*, *h*) magnetize
**Mahagoni** [maha'go:ni] *n* (*-s*; *no pl*) mahogany
**Mähdrescher** ['mɛ:drɛʃɐ] *m* (*-s*; -) AGR combine (harvester); **mähen** ['mɛ:ən] *v/t* (*ge-*, *h*) mow; cut; AGR reap
**mahlen** ['ma:lən] *v/t* (*irr*, *ge-*, *h*) grind; mill
'**Mahlzeit** *f* (-; *-en*) meal; feed(ing)
**Mähne** ['mɛ:nə] *f* (-; *-n*) ZO mane (*a.* F)
**mahnen** ['ma:nən] *v/t* (*ge-*, *h*) remind; ECON send *s.o.* a reminder
'**Mahngebühr** *f* reminder fee
'**Mahnmal** *n* memorial
'**Mahnung** *f* (-; *-en*) reminder
**Mai** [mai] *m* (*-[e]s*; *-e*) May; ***der Erste ~*** May Day; **~baum** *m* maypole; **~glöckchen** *n* BOT lily of the valley; **~käfer** *m* ZO cockchafer
**Mais** [mais] *m* (*-es*; *-e*) BOT corn, *Br* maize
**Majestät** [majɛs'tɛ:t] *f*: ***Seine*** (***Ihre, Eure***) ***~*** His (Her, Your) Majesty
**majes'tätisch** *adj* majestic
**Majonäse** *f* → ***Mayonnaise***
**Major** [ma'jo:ɐ] *m* (*-s*; *-e*) MIL major
**makaber** [ma'ka:bɐ] *adj* macabre
**Makel** ['ma:kəl] *m* (*-s*; -) blemish (*a. fig*)
**mäkelig** ['mɛ:kəlɪç] F *adj* picky, *esp Br* choos(e)y
'**makellos** *adj* immaculate (*a. fig*)
**mäkeln** ['mɛ:kəln] F *v/i* (*ge-*, *h*) carp, pick, nag (***an*** *dat* at)
**Makler** ['ma:klɐ] *m* (*-s*; -) ECON real estate agent; broker; **~gebühr** *f* fee, commission
'**Maklerin** *f* (-; *-nen*) ECON → ***Makler***
**mal** [ma:l] *adv* MATH times, multiplied by; by; F → ***einmal***; ***12 ~ 5 ist*** (***gleich***) ***60*** 12 times *or* multiplied by 5 is *or* equals 60; ***ein 7 ~ 4 Meter großes Zimmer*** a room 7 meters by 4
**Mal**[1] *n* (*-[e]s*; *-e*) time; ***zum ersten*** (***letzten***) ***~(e)*** for the first (last) time; ***mit e-m ~(e)*** all of a sudden; ***ein für alle ~(e)*** once and for all
**Mal**[2] *n* mark
**malen** ['ma:lən] *v/t* (*ge-*, *h*) paint
**Maler** ['ma:lɐ] *m* (*-s*; -) painter
**Malerei** [ma:lə'rai] *f* (-; *-en*) painting

M

**Malerin** ['maːlərın] *f* (-; *-nen*) (woman) painter
'**malerisch** *fig adj* picturesque
'**Malkasten** *m* paintbox
'**malnehmen** → ***multiplizieren***
**Malz** [malts] *n* (*-es*; *no pl*) malt
'**Malzbier** *n* malt beer
**Mama** ['mama] F *f* (-; *-s*) mom(my), *Br* mum(my)
**Mammut** ['mamʊt] *n* (*-s*; *-e*, *-s*) ZO mammoth
**man** [man] *indef pron* you, one; they, people; ***wie schreibt ~ das?*** how do you spell it?; ***~ sagt, dass*** they *or* people say (that); ***~ hat mir gesagt*** I was told
**Manager** ['mɛnɪdʒɐ] *m* (*-s*; -), '**Managerin** *f* (-; *-nen*) ECON executive; SPORT manager
**manch** [manç], **~er** ['mançɐ], **~e** ['mançə], **~es** ['mançəs] *indef pron* (*mst pl*) some; quite a few, many
'**manchmal** *adv* sometimes, occasionally
**Mandant** [man'dant] *m* (*-en*; *-en*), **Man'dantin** *f* (-; *-nen*) JUR client
**Mandarine** [manda'riːnə] *f* (-; *-n*) BOT tangerine
**Mandat** [man'daːt] *n* (*-[e]s*; *-e*) POL mandate; seat; **Mandatar** [manda'taːɐ] *Austrian m* → ***Abgeordnete***
**Mandel** ['mandəl] *f* (-; *-n*) BOT almond; ANAT tonsil; **~entzündung** *f* MED tonsillitis
**Manege** [ma'neːʒə] *f* (-; *-n*) (circus) ring
**Mangel**[1] ['maŋəl] *m* (*-s*; *Mängel* ['mɛŋəl]) (*no pl*) lack (***an*** *dat* of), shortage; TECH defect, fault; shortcoming; ***aus ~ an*** (*dat*) for lack of
'**Mangel**[2] *f* (-; *-n*) mangle
'**mangelhaft** *adj* poor (*quality etc*); defective (*goods etc*); PED poor, unsatisfactory, failing
'**mangeln** *v/t* (*ge-*, *h*) mangle
'**mangels** *prp* (*gen*) for lack *or* want of
'**Mangelware** *f*: ***~ sein*** be scarce
**Manie** [ma'niː] *f* (-; *-n*) mania (*a. fig*)
**Manieren** [ma'niːrən] *pl* manners
**manierlich** [ma'niːɐlɪç] *adv*: ***sich ~ betragen*** behave (decently)
**Manifest** [mani'fɛst] *n* (*-[e]s*; *-e*) manifesto
**manipulieren** [manipu'liːrən] *v/t* (*no -ge-*, *h*) manipulate
**Mann** [man] *m* (*-[e]s*; *Männer* ['mɛnɐ]) man; husband
**Männchen** ['mɛnçən] *n* (*-s*; -) ZO male
'**Manndeckung** *f* SPORT man-to-man marking
**Mannequin** ['manəkɛ̃ː] *n* (*-s*; *-s*) model
**mannigfach** ['manɪçfax], '**mannigfaltig** *adj* many and various
**männlich** ['mɛnlɪç] *adj* BIOL male; masculine (*a.* LING)
'**Mannschaft** *f* (-; *-en*) SPORT team; MAR, AVIAT crew
**Manöver** [ma'nøːvɐ] *n* (*-s*; -), **manövrieren** [manø'vriːrən] *v/i* (*no -ge-*, *h*) maneuver, *Br* manoeuvre
**Mansarde** [man'zardə] *f* (-; *-n*) room *or* apartment in the attic
**Manschette** [man'ʃɛtə] *f* (-; *-n*) cuff; TECH gasket
**Man'schettenknopf** *m* cuff-link
**Mantel** ['mantəl] *m* (*-s*; *Mäntel* ['mɛntəl]) coat; *tire*: casing, *bicycle*: tire (*Br* tyre) cover; TECH jacket, shell
**Manuskript** [manu'skrɪpt] *n* (*-[e]s*; *-e*) manuscript; copy
**Mappe** ['mapə] *f* (-; *-n*) briefcase; school bag, satchel; folder
**Märchen** ['mɛːɐçən] *n* (*-s*; -) fairytale (*a. fig*); **~land** *n* (*-[e]s*; *no pl*) fairyland
**Marder** ['mardɐ] *m* (*-s*; -) ZO marten
**Margarine** [marga'riːnə] *f* (-; *no pl*) margarine
**Margerite** [margə'riːtə] *f* (-; *-n*) BOT marguerite
**Marienkäfer** [ma'riːənkɛːfɐ] *m* ZO lady bug, *Br* ladybird
**Marihuana** [mari'huaːna] *n* (*-s*; *no pl*) marijuana, *sl* grass; **~ziga,rette** *f sl* joint
**Marille** [ma'rɪlə] *Austrian f* (-; *-n*) BOT apricot
**Marine** [ma'riːnə] *f* (-; *-n*) MIL navy
**ma'rineblau** *adj* navy blue
**Marionette** [marjo'nɛtə] *f* (-; *-n*) puppet (*a. fig*); **Mario'nettenthe,ater** *n* puppet show
**Mark**[1] *n* (*-[e]s*; *no pl*) marrow; BOT pulp
**Mark**[2] [mark] *f* (-; -) *hist* (*former monetary unit of Germany*) mark
**Marke** ['markə] *f* (-; *-n*) ECON brand; TECH make; trademark; stamp; badge, tag; mark; **markieren** [mar'kiːrən] *v/t* (*no -ge-*, *h*) mark (*a.* SPORT); F *fig* act; **Mar'kierung** *f* (-; *-en*) mark
**Markise** [mar'kiːzə] *f* (-; *-n*) awning, sun

M

blind

**Markt** [markt] *m* (-[*e*]*s*; *Märkte* ['mɛrktə]) ECON market; ***auf den ~ bringen*** put on the market; **~platz** *m* market place; **~wirtschaft** *f* market economy

**Marmelade** [marmə'la:də] *f* (-; *-n*) jam

**Marmor** ['marmo:ɐ] *m* (-*s*; *-e*) marble

**Marsch**[1] [marʃ] *m* (-[*e*]*s*; *Märsche* ['mɛrʃə]) march (*a.* MUS)

**Marsch**[2] *f* (-; *-en*) GEOGR marsh, fen

**Marschall** ['marʃal] *m* (-*s*; *Marschälle* ['marʃɛlə]) MIL marshal

'**Marschbefehl** *m* MIL marching orders

**marschieren** [mar'ʃi:rən] *v/i* (*no -ge-*, *sein*) march

**Marsmensch** ['marsmɛnʃ] *m* Martian

**Marter** ['martɐ] *f* (-; *-n*) torture

'**martern** *v/t* (*ge-*, *h*) torture

'**Marterpfahl** *m* stake

**Martinshorn** ['marti:nshɔrn] *n* (police *etc*) siren

**Märtyrer** ['mɛrtyrɐ] *m* (-*s*; -), '**Märtyrerin** ['mɛrtyrərɪn] *f* (-; *-nen*) martyr (*a. fig*)

**Marxismus** [mar'ksɪsmʊs] *m* (-; *no pl*) POL Marxism; **Marxist** [mar'ksɪst] *m* (-*en*; *-en*), **mar'xistisch** *adj* POL Marxist

**März** [mɛrts] *m* (-[*es*]; *-e*) March

**Marzipan** [martsi'pa:n] *n* (-*s*; *-e*) marzipan

**Masche** ['maʃə] *f* (-; *-n*) stitch; mesh; F trick

'**Maschendraht** *m* wire netting

**Maschine** [ma'ʃi:nə] *f* (-; *-n*) machine; MOT engine; AVIAT plane; motorcycle

**Ma'schinen|bau** *m* (-[*e*]*s*; *no pl*) mechanical engineering; **~gewehr** *n* MIL machinegun

**ma'schinenlesbar** *adj* machine-readable

**Ma'schinen|öl** *n* engine oil; **~pis,tole** *f* MIL submachine gun, machine pistol; **~schaden** *m* engine trouble *or* failure; **~schlosser** *m* (engine) fitter

**Masern** ['ma:zɐn] *pl* MED measles

**Maserung** ['ma:zərʊŋ] *f* (-; *-en*) grain

**Maske** ['maskə] *f* (-; *-n*) mask (*a.* IT)

'**Maskenball** *m* fancy-dress ball

**Maskenbildner** ['maskənbɪldnɐ] *m* (-*s*; -), '**Maskenbildnerin** *f* (-; *-nen*) THEA *etc* make-up artist

**maskieren** [mas'ki:rən] *v/t* (*no -ge-*, *h*) mask; ***sich ~*** put on a mask

**maskulin** [masku'li:n] *adj* masculine (*a.* LING)

**maß** [ma:s] *pret of* ***messen***

**Maß**[1] *n* (-*es*; *-e*) measure (***für*** of); dimensions, measurements, size; *fig* extent, degree; ***~e und Gewichte*** weights and measures; ***nach ~*** (***gemacht***) made to measure; ***in gewissem*** (***hohem***) ***~e*** to a certain (high) degree; ***in zunehmendem ~e*** increasingly; ***~ halten*** → ***maßhalten***

**Maß**[2] *f* (-; -[*e*]) liter (*Br* litre) of beer

**Massage** [ma'sa:ʒə] *f* (-; *-n*) massage

**Massaker** [ma'sa:kɐ] *n* (-*s*; -) massacre

**Masse** ['masə] *f* (-; *-n*) mass; substance; bulk; F ***e-e ~*** *Geld etc* loads *or* heaps of; ***die*** (***breite***) ***~***, POL ***die ~n*** *pl* the masses

'**Maßeinheit** *f* unit of measure(ment)

'**Massen...** *in cpds ...medien, ...mörder etc*: mass ...; **~andrang** *m* crush

'**massenhaft** F *adv* masses *or* loads of

'**Massen|karambo,lage** *f* MOT pileup; **~produkti,on** *f* ECON mass production

**Masseur** [ma'sø:ɐ] *m* (-*s*; *-e*) masseur

**Masseurin** [ma'sø:rɪn] *f* (-; *-nen*), **Masseuse** [ma'sø:zə] *f* (-; *-n*) masseuse

'**maßgebend**, **maßgeblich** ['ma:sge:plɪç] *adj* authoritative

'**maßhalten** *v/i* (*irr*, ***halten***, *sep*, *-ge-*, *h*) be moderate (***in*** *dat* in)

**massieren** [ma'si:rən] *v/t* (*no -ge-*, *h*) massage

**massig** ['masɪç] *adj* massive, bulky

**mäßig** ['mɛ:sɪç] *adj* moderate; poor

**mäßigen** ['mɛ:sɪgən] *v/t and v/refl* (*ge-*, *h*) moderate; '**Mäßigung** *f* (-; *no pl*) moderation; restraint

**massiv** [ma'si:f] *adj* solid

**Mas'siv** *n* (-*s*; *-e*) GEOL massif

'**Maßkrug** *m* beer mug, stein

'**maßlos** *adj* immoderate; gross (*exaggeration*)

**Maßnahme** ['ma:sna:mə] *f* (-; *-n*) measure, step

'**Maßregel** *f* rule; '**maßregeln** *v/t* (*ge-*, *h*) reprimand; discipline

'**Maßstab** *m* scale; *fig* standard; ***im ~ 1:10*** on the scale of 1:10

**maßstabgetreu** *adj* true to scale

'**maßvoll** *adj* moderate

**Mast**[1] [mast] *m* (-[*e*]*s*; *-en*) MAR, TECH mast

**Mast**[2] *f* (-; *-en*) AGR fattening

'**Mastdarm** *m* ANAT rectum

M

**mästen** ['mɛstən] *v/t* (*ge-*, *h*) AGR fatten; F stuff *s.o.*
**masturbieren** [mastʊr'biːrən] *v/i* (*no -ge-*, *h*) masturbate
**Match** [mɛtʃ] *n* (*-[e]s*; *-s*, *-e*) game, *Br* match; **~ball** *m tennis*: match point
**Material** [mate'rjaːl] *n* (*-s*; *-ien*) material (*a. fig*); TECH materials
**Materialismus** [materja'lɪsmʊs] *m* (*-*; *no pl*) PHILOS materialism; **Materialist** [materja'lɪst] *m* (*-en*; *-en*) materialist; **materia'listisch** *adj* materialistic
**Materie** [ma'teːrjə] *f* (*-*; *-n*) matter (*a. fig*); *fig* subject (matter); **materiell** [mate'rjɛl] *adj* material
**Mathematik** [matema'tiːk] *f* (*-*; *no pl*) mathematics; **Mathematiker** [mate'maːtikɐ] *m* (*-s*; *-*) mathematician; **mathe'matisch** *adj* mathematical
**Matinee** [mati'neː] *f* (*-*; *-n*) THEA *etc* morning performance
**Matratze** [ma'tratsə] *f* (*-*; *-n*) mattress
**Matrize** [ma'triːtsə] *f* (*-*; *-n*) stencil
**Matrose** [ma'troːzə] *m* (*-n*; *-n*) MAR sailor, seaman
**Matsch** [matʃ] F *m* (*-[e]s*; *no pl*) mud, slush; **'matschig** *adj* muddy, slushy
**matt** [mat] *adj* weak; exhausted, worn out; dull, pale (*color*); PHOT mat(t); frosted (*glass*); *chess*: checkmate
**Matte** ['matə] *f* (*-*; *-n*) mat
**Mattigkeit** ['matɪçkait] *f* (*-*; *no pl*) exhaustion, weakness
**'Mattscheibe** *f* screen; PHOT focus(s)ing screen; F (boob) tube, *Br* telly, box
**Matura** [ma'tuːra] *Austrian*, *Swiss f* → ***Abitur***
**Mauer** ['mauɐ] *f* (*-*; *-n*) wall; **~blümchen** *fig n* wallflower
**'mauern** *v/i* (*ge-*, *h*) lay bricks
**Mauerwerk** *n* (*-[e]s*; *no pl*) masonry, brickwork
**Maul** [maul] *n* (*-[e]s*; *Mäuler* ['mɔylɐ]) zo mouth; *sl* ***halt's ~!*** shut up!
**maulen** ['maulən] F *v/i* (*ge-*, *h*) grumble, sulk, pout
**'Maul|korb** *m* muzzle (*a. fig*); **~tier** *n* mule; **~wurf** *m* zo mole; **~wurfshaufen** *m*, **~wurfshügel** *m* molehill
**Maurer** ['maurɐ] *m* (*-s*; *-*) bricklayer; **~kelle** *f* trowel; **~meister** *m* master bricklayer
**Maus** [maus] *f* (*-*; *Mäuse* ['mɔyzə]) zo mouse (*a.* IT)
**'Mausefalle** ['mauzəfalə] *f* mousetrap
**Mauser** ['mauzɐ] *f* (*-*; *no pl*) zo mo(u)lt (-ing); ***in der ~ sein*** be mo(u)lting
**Maut** [maut] *Austrian f* (*-*; *-en*) toll; **~straße** *f* turnpike, toll road
**maximal** [maksi'maːl] **1.** *adj* maximum **2.** *adv* at (the) most; **Maximum** ['maksimʊm] *n* (*-s*; *-ma*) maximum
**Mayonnaise** [majɔ'nɛːzə] *f* (*-*; *-n*) GASTR mayonnaise
**Mäzen** [mɛ'tseːn] *m* (*-s*; *-e*) patron; SPORT sponsor
**Mechanik** [me'çaːnɪk] *f* (*-*; *-en*) (*no pl*) PHYS mechanics; TECH mechanism; **Mechaniker** [me'çaːnikɐ] *m* (*-s*; *-*) mechanic; **mechanisch** [me'çaːnɪʃ] *adj* TECH mechanical; **mechanisieren** [meçani'ziːrən] *v/t* (*no -ge-*, *h*) mechanize; **Mechani'sierung** *f* (*-*; *-en*) mechanization; **Mechanismus** [meça'nɪsmʊs] *m* (*-*; *-men*) TECH mechanism; works
**meckern** ['mɛkɐn] *v/i* (*ge-*, *h*) zo bleat; F grumble, bitch (***über*** *acc* at, about)
**Medaille** [me'daljə] *f* (*-*; *-n*) medal
**Me'daillengewinner** *m* medal(l)ist
**Medaillon** [medal'joː] *n* (*-s*; *-s*) locket
**Medien** ['meːdjən] *pl* mass media; teaching aids; audio-visual aids
**Medikament** [medika'mɛnt] *n* (*-[e]s*; *-e*) drug; medicine
**meditieren** [medi'tiːrən] *v/i* (*no -ge-*, *h*) meditate (***über*** *acc* on)
**Medizin** [medi'tsiːn] *f* (*-*; *-en*) (*no pl*) (science of) medicine; medicine, remedy (***gegen*** for)
**Mediziner** [medi'tsiːnɐ] *m* (*-s*; *-*), **Medi'zinerin** *f* (*-*; *-nen*) (medical) doctor; UNIV medical student
**medizinisch** [medi'tsiːnɪʃ] *adj* medical
**Meer** [meːɐ] *n* (*-[e]s*; *-e* ['meːrə]) sea (*a. fig*), ocean; **~enge** *f* GEOGR straits
**Meeres|boden** ['meːrəsboːdən] *m* seabed; **~früchte** *pl* GASTR seafood; **~spiegel** *m* sea level
**'Meerjungfrau** *f* MYTH mermaid
**'Meerrettich** *m* (*-s*; *-e*) horseradish
**Meerschweinchen** ['meːɐʃvainçən] *n* (*-s*; *-*) zo guinea pig
**Megabyte** [mega'bait] *n* IT megabyte
**Mehl** [meːl] *n* (*-[e]s*; *-e*) flour; meal
**mehlig** ['meːlɪç] *adj* mealy
**'Mehlspeise** *Austrian f* sweet (dish)
**mehr** [meːɐ] *indef pron and adv* more;

M

***immer ~*** more and more; ***nicht ~*** no longer, not any longer (*or* more); ***noch ~*** even more; ***es ist kein … ~ da*** there isn't any … left
**mehrdeutig** ['meːɐdɔʏtɪç] *adj* ambiguous
**mehrere** ['meːrərə] *adj and indef pron* several
'**Mehrheit** *f* (-; *-en*) majority
'**Mehrkosten** *pl* extra costs
'**mehrmals** *adv* several times
'**Mehr|wegflasche** *f* returnable (*or* deposit) bottle; **~wertsteuer** *f* ECON value-added tax (*abbr* VAT); **~zahl** *f* (-; *no pl*) majority; LING plural (form)
'**Mehrzweck…** *in cpds …fahrzeug etc*: multi-purpose …
**meiden** ['maidən] *v/t* (*irr, ge-, h*) avoid
**Meile** ['mailə] *f* (-; *-n*) mile
'**meilenweit** *adv* (for) miles
**mein** [main] *poss pron and adj* my; ***das ist ~er*** (***~e, ~[e]s***) that's mine
'**Meineid** *m* JUR perjury
**meinen** ['mainən] *v/t* (*ge-, h*) think, believe; mean; say; ***~ Sie wirklich?*** do you (really) think so?; ***wie ~ Sie das?*** what do you mean by that?; ***sie ~ es gut*** they mean well; ***ich habe es nicht so gemeint*** I didn't mean it; ***wie ~ Sie?*** (I beg your) pardon?
'**meinetwegen** ['mainətvegən] *adv* for my sake; because of me; F I don't mind *or* care!
'**Meinung** *f* (-; *-en*) opinion (***über*** *acc*, ***von*** about, of); ***meiner ~ nach*** in my opinion; ***der ~ sein, dass*** be of the opinion that, feel *or* believe that; ***s-e ~ äußern*** express one's opinion; ***s-e ~ ändern*** change one's mind; ***ich bin Ihrer*** (***anderer***) ***~*** I (don't) agree with you; ***j-m die ~ sagen*** give s.o. a piece of one's mind
'**Meinungs|austausch** *m* exchange of views (***über*** *acc* on); **~forscher** *m* pollster; **~freiheit** *f* (-; *no pl*) freedom of speech *or* opinion; **~umfrage** *f* opinion poll; **~verschiedenheit** *f* disagreement (***über*** *acc* about)
**Meise** ['maizə] *f* (-; *-n*) ZO titmouse
**Meißel** ['maisəl] *m* (*-s*; -) chisel
'**meißeln** *v/t and v/i* (*ge-, h*) chisel, carve
**meist** [maist] **1.** *adj* most; ***das ~e*** (***davon***) most of it; ***die ~en*** (***von ihnen***) most of them; ***die ~en Leute*** most people; ***die ~e Zeit*** most of the time **2.** *adv* → ***meistens***; ***am ~en*** (the) most; most (of all); **meistens** ['maistəns] *adv* usually; most of the time
**Meister** ['maistɐ] *m* (*-s*; -) master (*a. fig*); SPORT champion, F champ
'**meisterhaft 1.** *adj* masterly **2.** *adv* in a masterly manner *or* way
'**Meisterin** *f* (-; *-nen*) master (*a. fig*); SPORT champion
**meistern** ['maistɐn] *v/t* (*ge-, h*) master
'**Meisterschaft** *f* (-; *-en*) (*no pl*) mastery; SPORT championship, cup; title
'**Meister|stück** *n*, **~werk** *n* masterpiece
**Melancholie** [melaŋko'liː] *f* (-; *-n*) melancholy; **melancholisch** [melaŋ'koːlɪʃ] *adj* melancholy; ***~ sein*** feel depressed, F have the blues
**Melange** [me'laːʒə] *Austrian f* (-; *-n*) coffee with milk
**melden** ['mɛldən] (*ge-, h*) **1.** *v/t* report *s.th. or s.o.* (***bei*** to); *radio etc*: announce, report; ***j-m et. ~*** notify s.o. of s.th. **2.** *v/refl*: ***sich ~*** report (***bei*** to, ***für, zu*** for); register (***bei*** with); PED *etc*: put up one's hand; TEL answer the phone; SPORT enter (***für, zu*** for); volunteer (***für, zu*** for)
'**Meldung** *f* (-; *-en*) report, news, announcement; information, notice; notification; registration (***bei*** with); SPORT entry (***für, zu*** for)
**melken** ['mɛlkən] *v/t* ([*irr*,] *ge-, h*) milk
**Melodie** [melo'diː] *f* (-; *-n*) MUS melody, tune; **melodisch** [me'loːdɪʃ] *adj* MUS melodious, melodic
**Melone** [me'loːnə] *f* (-; *-n*) BOT melon; F derby, *Br* bowler (hat)
**Memoiren** [me'moaːrən] *pl* memoirs
**Menge** ['mɛŋə] *f* (-; *-n*) amount, quantity; MATH set; F ***e-e ~ Geld*** plenty (*or* lots) of money; → ***Menschenmenge***
'**Mengenlehre** *f* (-; *no pl*) MATH set theory; PED new math(ematics)
**Mensa** ['mɛnza] *f* (-; *-s, Mensen*) cafeteria, *Br* refectory, canteen
**Mensch** [mɛnʃ] *m* (*-en*; *-en*) human being; man; person, individual; *pl* people; mankind; ***kein ~*** nobody; ***~!*** wow!
**Menschen|affe** *m* ZO ape; **~fresser** *m* cannibal; **~freund** *m* philanthropist; **~handel** *m* slave trade; **~kenntnis** *f*: ***~ haben*** know human nature; **~leben** *n* human life

M

'**menschenleer** *adj* deserted
'**Menschen|menge** *f* crowd; **~rechte** *pl* human rights; **~seele** *f*: ***keine ~*** not a (living) soul
'**menschenunwürdig** *adj* degrading; *housing etc*: unfit for human beings
'**Menschen|verstand** *m*: ***gesunder ~*** common sense; **~würde** *f* human dignity
**Menschheit**: ***die ~*** mankind, the human race
'**menschlich** *adj* human; humane
'**Menschlichkeit** *f* (-; *no pl*) humanity
**Menstruation** [mɛnstrua'tsjoːn] *f* (-; *-en*) MED menstruation
**Mentalität** [mɛntali'tɛːt] *f* (-; *-en*) mentality
**Menü** [me'nyː] *n* (*-s*; *-s*) set meal (*or* lunch); IT menu
**Meridian** [meri'djaːn] *m* (*-s*; *-e*) GEOGR, ASTR meridian
**merkbar** ['mɛrkbaːɐ] *adj* marked, distinct; noticeable; '**Merkblatt** *n* leaflet; **merken** ['mɛrkən] *v/t* (*ge-*, *h*) notice; feel; find (out), discover; ***sich et. ~*** remember s.th., keep *or* bear s.th. in mind; '**merklich** *adj* → ***merkbar***; '**Merkmal** *n* sign; feature, trait
'**merkwürdig** *adj* strange, odd, curious
'**merkwürdiger'weise** *adv* strangely enough
**messbar** ['mɛsbaːɐ] *adj* measurable
'**Messbecher** *m* measuring cup
**Messe** ['mɛsə] *f* (-; *-n*) ECON fair; REL mass; MIL, MAR mess
**messen** ['mɛsən] *v/t* (*irr*, *ge-*, *h*) measure; take (*temperature etc*); ***sich nicht mit j-m ~ können*** be no match for s.o.; ***gemessen an*** (*dat*) compared with
**Messer** ['mɛsɐ] *n* (*-s*; -) knife; ***bis aufs ~*** to the knife; ***auf des ~s Schneide stehen*** be on a razor edge, be touch and go (***ob*** whether)
**Messerstecherei** [mɛsɐʃtɛçə'rai] *f* (-; *-en*) knife fight
'**Messerstich** *m* stab (with a knife)
**Messing** ['mɛsɪŋ] *n* (*-s*; *-e*) brass
'**Messinstru,ment** *n* measuring instrument
'**Messung** *f* (-; *-en*) measuring; reading
**Metall** [me'tal] *n* (*-s*; *-e*) metal
**metallen** [me'talən], **me'tallisch** *adj* metallic
**Me'tallwaren** *pl* hardware
**Metamorphose** [metamɔr'foːzə] *f* (-; *-n*) metamorphosis
**Metastase** [meta'staːzə] *f* (-; *-n*) MED metastasis
**Meteor** [mete'oːɐ] *m* (*-s*; *-e*) ASTR meteor
**Meteorit** [meteo'riːt] *m* (*-en*; *-e[n]*) ASTR meteorite
**Meteorologe** [meteoro'loːgə] *m* (*-n*; *-n*) meteorologist; **Meteorologie** [meteorolo'giː] *f* (-; *no pl*) meteorology; **Meteoro'login** *f* (-; *-nen*) meteorologist
**Meter** ['meːtɐ] *n*, *m* (*-s*; -) meter, *Br* metre; **~maß** *n* tape measure
**Methode** [me'toːdə] *f* (-; *-n*) method, TECH *a.* technique; **methodisch** [me'toːdɪʃ] *adj* methodical
**metrisch** ['meːtrɪʃ] *adj* metric; ***~es Maßsystem*** metric system
**Metropole** [metro'poːlə] *f* (-; *-n*) metropolis
**Metzger** ['mɛtsgɐ] *m* (*-s*; -) butcher
**Metzgerei** [mɛtsgə'rai] *f* (-; *-en*) butcher's (shop)
**Meute** ['mɔʏtə] *f* (-; *-n*) pack (of hounds); *fig* mob, pack
**Meuterei** [mɔʏtə'rai] *f* (-; *-en*) mutiny; **Meuterer** ['mɔʏtərɐ] *m* (*-s*; -) mutineer; **meutern** ['mɔʏtɐn] *v/i* (*ge-*, *h*) mutiny (***gegen*** against)
**MEZ** *abbr of* ***Mitteleuropäische Zeit*** CET, Central European Time
**miau** [mi'au] *int* ZO meow, *Br* miaow
**miauen** [mi'auən] *v/i* (*no -ge-*, *h*) ZO meow, *Br* miaow
**mich** [mɪç] *pers pron* me; ***~ (selbst)*** myself
**mied** [miːt] *pret of* ***meiden***
**Mieder** ['miːdɐ] *n* (*-s*; -) corset(s); bodice; **~höschen** *n* pantie girdle; **~waren** *pl* foundation garments
**Miene** ['miːnə] *f* (-; *-n*) expression, look, air; ***gute ~ zum bösen Spiel machen*** grin and bear it
**mies** [miːs] F *adj* rotten, lousy
**Miete** ['miːtə] *f* (-; *-n*) rent; hire charge; ***zur ~ wohnen*** be a tenant; lodge (***bei*** with); '**mieten** *v/t* (*ge-*, *h*) rent; (take on) lease; AVIAT, MAR charter; ***ein Auto etc ~*** rent (*Br* hire) a car *etc*; **Mieter(in)** ['miːtɐ, 'miːtərɪn] *m(f)* (*-s*; *-/-*; *-nen*) tenant, lodger
'**Mietshaus** *n* apartment building *or* house, *Br* block of flats, tenement

M

**'Mietvertrag** *m* lease (contract)
**'Mietwohnung** *f* apartment, *Br* (rented) flat
**Migräne** [mi'grɛːnə] *f* (-; *-n*) MED migraine
**Mikro** ['miːkro] F *n* (*-s*; *-s*) mike
**Mikro...** ['miːkro-] *in cpds ...chip, ...computer, ...elektronik, ...film, ...prozessor etc*: micro...
**Mikrofon** [mikro'foːn] *n* (*-s*; *-e*) microphone
**Mikroskop** [mikro'skoːp] *n* (*-s*; *-e*) microscope; **mikro'skopisch** *adj* microscopic(al)
**Mikrowelle** ['miːkrovɛlə] F *f*, **'Mikrowellenherd** *m* microwave oven
**Milbe** ['mɪlbə] *f* (-; *-n*) ZO mite
**Milch** [mɪlç] *f* (-; *no pl*) milk; **~geschäft** *n* dairy, creamery; **~glas** *n* frosted glass
**milchig** ['mɪlçɪç] *adj* milky
**'Milch|kaffee** *m* white coffee; **~kännchen** *n* (milk) jug; **~kanne** *f* milk can; **~mann** F *m* milkman; **~mixgetränk** *n* milk shake; **~pro,dukte** *pl* dairy products; **~pulver** *n* powdered milk; **~reis** *m* rice pudding; **~straße** *f* ASTR Milky Way, Galaxy; **~tüte** *f* milk carton; **~wirtschaft** *f* dairy farming; **~zahn** *m* milk tooth
**mild** [mɪlt] *adj* mild, soft; gentle
**milde** ['mɪldə] *adv* mildly; **~ *ausgedrückt*** to put it mildly
**'Milde** *f* (-; *no pl*) mildness, gentleness; leniency, mercy
**mildern** ['mɪldɐn] *v/t* (*ge-, h*) lessen, soften; **~d** *adj*: ***~e Umstände*** JUR mitigating circumstances
**'mildtätig** *adj* charitable
**Milieu** [mi'ljøː] *n* (*-s*; *-s*) environment; social background
**Militär** [mili'tɛːɐ] *n* (*-s*; *no pl*) *the* military, armed forces; army; **~dienst** *m* (*-[e]s*; *no pl*) military service; **~dikta,tur** *f* military dictatorship; **~gericht** *n* court martial
**militärisch** [mili'tɛːrɪʃ] *adj* military
**Militarismus** [milita'rɪsmʊs] *m* (-; *no pl*) militarism; **Militarist** [milita'rɪst] *m* (*-en*; *-en*) militarist; **milita'ristisch** *adj* militaristic
**'Mili'tärre'gierung** *f* military government
**Milliarde** [mɪ'ljardə] *f* (-; *-n*) billion, *Br old use a.* a thousand million(s)
**Millimeter** ['mɪlimeːtɐ] *n, m* (*-s*; -) millimet|er, *Br* -re; **~pa,pier** *n* graph paper
**Million** [mɪ'lioːn] *f* (-; *-en*) million
**Millionär** [mɪljo'nɛːɐ] *m* (*-s*; *-e*), **Millio'närin** *f* (-; *-nen*) millionaire
**Milz** [mɪlts] *f* (-; *no pl*) ANAT spleen
**Mimik** ['miːmɪk] *f* (-; *no pl*) facial expression
**minder** ['mɪndɐ] **1.** *adj* → ***geringer, weniger*** **2.** *adv* less; ***nicht ~*** no less
**'Minderheit** *f* (-; *-en*) minority
**minderjährig** ['mɪndɐjɛːrɪç] *adj*: ***~ sein*** be under age, be a minor; **Minderjährige** ['mɪndɐjɛːrɪgə] *m, f* (*-n*; *-n*) minor
**'Minderjährigkeit** *f* (-; *no pl*) minority
**'minderwertig** *adj* inferior, of inferior quality; **'Minderwertigkeit** *f* (-; *no pl*) inferiority; ECON inferior quality
**'Minderwertigkeitskom,plex** *m* PSYCH inferiority complex
**mindest** ['mɪndəst] *adj* least; ***das Mindeste*** the (very) least; ***nicht im Mindesten*** not in the least, not at all
**'Mindest...** *in cpds ...alter, ...einkommen, ...lohn etc*: minimum...
**mindestens** ['mɪndəstəns] *adv* at least
**'Mindest|haltbarkeitsdatum** *n* pull date, *Br* best-before (*or* best-by, sell-by) date; **~maß** *n* minimum; ***auf ein ~ herabsetzen*** reduce to a minimum
**Mine** ['miːnə] *f* (-; *-n*) mine (*a.* MAR, MIL); lead; cartridge; refill
**Mineral** [minəˈraːl] *n* (*-s*; *-e*, *-ien*) mineral; **Mineralogie** [mineralo'giː] *f* (-; *no pl*) mineralogy
**Mine'ralöl** *n* mineral oil
**Mine'ralwasser** *n* mineral water
**Miniatur** [minja'tuːɐ] *f* (-; *-en*) miniature
**Minigolf** ['mɪnigɔlf] *n* miniature (*Br* crazy) golf
**minimal** [mini'maːl] *adj, adv* minimal; minimum; at least; **Minimum** ['miːnimʊm] *n* (*-s*; *-ma*) minimum
**Minirock** ['mɪnirɔk] *m* miniskirt
**Minister** [mi'nɪstɐ] *m* (*-s*; -), **Mi'nisterin** *f* (-; *-nen*) minister, secretary, *Br a.* secretary of state
**Ministerium** [minɪs'teːriʊm] *n* (*-s*; *-ien*) ministry, department, *Br a.* office
**Mi'nisterpräsi,dent** *m*, **Mi'nisterpräsi,dentin** *f* prime minister
**minus** ['miːnʊs] *adv* MATH minus; ***bei 10 Grad ~*** at 10 degrees below zero
**Minute** [mi'nuːtə] *f* (-; *-n*) minute

**Mi'nutenzeiger** *m* minute hand
**Mio** *abbr of **Million(en)*** m, million
**mir** [miːɐ] *pers pron* (to) me
**Mischbatte,rie** ['mɪʃbatəriː] *f* mixing faucet, *Br* mixer tap
**'Mischbrot** *n* wheat and rye bread
**mischen** ['mɪʃən] *v/t* (*ge-, h*) mix; blend (*tea etc*); shuffle (*cards*); ***sich ~*** mingle *or* mix (***unter*** with)
**'Mischling** *m* (*-s; -e*) *esp contp* half-caste; BOT, ZO hybrid; mongrel
**'Mischmasch** F *m* (*-[e]s; -e*) hotchpotch, jumble
**'Misch|ma,schine** *f* TECH mixer; **~pult** *n radio*, TV: mixer, mixing console
**'Mischung** *f* (*-; -en*) mixture; blend; assortment
**'Mischwald** *m* mixed forest
**miserabel** [mizə'raːbəl] F *adj* lousy, rotten
**miss'achten** [mɪsʔ'axtən] *v/t* (*no -ge-, h*) disregard, ignore; despise
**Miss'achtung** *f* disregard; contempt; neglect (*all*: *gen* of)
**'Missbildung** *f* (*-; -en*) deformity, malformation
**miss'billigen** *v/t* (*no -ge-, h*) disapprove of
**'Missbrauch** *m* abuse (*a.* JUR); misuse; **miss'brauchen** *v/t* (*no -ge-, h*) abuse; misuse
**miss'deuten** *v/t* (*no -ge-, h*) misinterpret
**'Misserfolg** *m* failure; F flop
**'Missernte** *f* bad harvest, crop failure
**miss'fallen** *v/i* (*irr, **fallen**, no -ge-, h*) ***j-m ~*** displease s.o.; **'Missfallen** *n* (*-s; no pl*) displeasure, dislike
**'missgebildet** *adj* deformed, malformed; **'Missgeburt** *f* deformed child *or* animal; freak
**'Missgeschick** *n* (*-[e]s; -e*) mishap
**miss'glücken** *v/i* (*no -ge-, sein*) fail
**miss'gönnen** *v/t* (*no -ge-, h*) ***j-m et. ~*** envy s.o. s.th.
**'Missgriff** *m* mistake
**miss'handeln** *v/t* (*no -ge-, h*) ill-treat, maltreat (*a. fig*); batter
**Miss'handlung** *f* ill-treatment, maltreatment, *esp* JUR assault and battery
**Mission** [mɪ'sjoːn] *f* (*-; -en*) mission (*a.* POL *and fig*); **Missionar(in)** [mɪsjo'naːɐ, mɪsjo'naːrɪn] *m(f)* (*-s; -e/-; -nen*) missionary
**'Missklang** *m* dissonance, discord (*both a. fig*)
**'Misskre,dit** *m* discredit
**misslang** [mɪs'laŋ] *pret of **misslingen***; **misslingen** [mɪs'lɪŋən] *v/i* (*irr, no -ge-, sein*) fail; **misslungen** [mɪs'lʊŋən] *pp of **misslingen***; ***das ist mir ~*** I've bungled it
**'missmutig** *adj* bad-tempered, grumpy, glum
**miss'raten 1.** *v/i* (*irr, **raten**, no -ge-, sein*) fail; turn out badly **2.** *adj* wayward
**miss'trauen** *v/i* (*no -ge-, h*) distrust; **'Misstrauen** *n* (*-s; no pl*) distrust, suspicion (*both*: ***gegenüber*** of)
**'Misstrauens|antrag** *m* PARL motion of no confidence; **~votum** *n* PARL vote of no confidence
**misstrauisch** ['mɪstrauɪʃ] *adj* distrustful, suspicious
**'Missverhältnis** *n* disproportion
**'Missverständnis** *n* (*-ses; -se*) misunderstanding; **'missverstehen** *v/t* (*irr, **stehen**, no -ge-, h*) misunderstand
**'Misswahl** *f* beauty contest *or* competition
**Mist** [mɪst] *m* (*-[e]s; no p*) AGR dung, manure; F trash, rubbish
**'Mistbeet** *n* AGR hotbed
**Mistel** ['mɪstəl] *f* (*-; -n*) BOT mistletoe
**'Mistgabel** *f* AGR dung fork
**'Misthaufen** *m* AGR manure heap
**mit** [mɪt] *prp* (*dat*) *and adv* with; ***~ Gewalt*** by force; ***~ Absicht*** on purpose; ***~ dem Auto*** (***der Bahn*** *etc*) by car (train *etc*); ***~ 20 Jahren*** at (the age of) 20; ***~ 100 Stundenkilometern*** at 100 kilometers per hour; ***~ einem Mal(e)*** all of a sudden; (all) at the same time; ***~ lauter Stimme*** in a loud voice; ***~ anderen Worten*** in other words; ***ein Mann ~ dem Namen ...*** a man by the name of ...; ***j-n ~ Namen kennen*** know s.o. by name; ***~ der Grund dafür, dass*** one of the reasons why; ***~ der Beste*** one of the best
**'Mitarbeit** *f* cooperation; assistance; PED activity, class participation
**'Mitarbeiter** *m*, **'Mitarbeiterin** *f* colleague; employee; assistant; ***freie(r) Mitarbeiter(in)*** freelance
**'mit|bekommen** F *v/t* (*irr, **kommen**, sep, no -ge-, h*) get; catch; **~benutzen** *v/t* (*sep, no -ge-, h*) share

M

'**Mit|bestimmungsrecht** *n* (right of) codetermination, worker participation; **~bewerber(in)** (rival) competitor; fellow applicant; **~bewohner(in)** roommate, *Br* flatmate

'**mitbringen** *v/t* (*irr*, ***bringen***, *sep*, *-ge-*, *h*) bring *s.th. or s.o.* with one; ***j-m et. ~*** bring s.o. s.th.; **Mitbringsel** ['mɪtbrɪŋzəl] F *n* (*-s*; -) little present; souvenir

'**Mitbürger** *m*, '**Mitbürgerin** *f* fellow citizen

**mitei'nander** *adv* with each other, with one another; together, jointly

'**miterleben** *v/t* (*sep*, *no -ge-*, *h*) live to see

'**Mitesser** *m* MED blackhead

'**mitfahren** *v/i* (*irr*, ***fahren***, *sep*, *-ge-*, *sein*) ***mit j-m ~*** drive *or* go with s.o.; ***j-n ~ lassen*** give s.o. a lift

'**Mitfahr|gelegenheit** *f* lift; **~zen,trale** *f* car pool(ing) service

'**mitfühlend** *adj* sympathetic

'**mitgeben** *v/t* (*irr*, ***geben***, *sep*, *-ge-*, *h*) ***j-m et. ~*** give s.o. s.th. (to take along)

'**Mitgefühl** *n* (-[*e*]*s*; *no pl*) sympathy

'**mitgehen** *v/i* (*irr*, ***gehen***, *sep*, *-ge-*, *sein*) ***mit j-m ~*** go *or* come along with s.o.; F ***et. ~ lassen*** walk off with s.th.

'**Mitgift** *f* (-; *-en*) dowry

'**Mitglied** *n* member (***bei*** of)

'**Mitgliedsbeitrag** *m* subscription

'**Mitgliedschaft** *f* (-; *-en*) membership

'**mithaben** *v/t* (*irr*, ***haben***, *sep*, *-ge-*, *h*) ***ich habe kein Geld mit*** I haven't got any money with me *or* on me

'**Mithilfe** *f* (-; *no pl*) assistance, help, cooperation (***bei*** in; ***von*** of)

**mit'hilfe** *prp*: ***~ von*** (*or gen*) with the help of, *fig a.* by means of

'**mithören** *v/t* (*sep*, *-ge-*, *h*) listen in to; overhear

'**Mitinhaber** *m*, '**Mitinhaberin** *f* joint owner

'**mitkommen** *v/i* (*irr*, ***kommen***, *sep*, *-ge-*, *sein*) come along (***mit*** with); *fig* keep pace (***mit*** with), follow; PED get on, keep up (with the class)

'**Mitlaut** *m* LING consonant

'**Mitleid** *n* (-[*e*]*s*; *no pl*) pity (***mit*** for); ***aus ~*** out of pity; ***~ haben mit*** feel sorry for

**mitleidig** ['mɪtlaidɪç] *adj* compassionate, sympathetic

'**mitleidslos** *adj* pitiless

'**mitmachen** (*sep*, *-ge-*, *h*) **1.** *v/i* join in **2.** *v/t* take part in; follow (*a fashion etc*); F go through

'**Mitmenschen**: ***die ~*** one's fellow human beings; people

'**mitnehmen** *v/t* (*irr*, ***nehmen***, *sep*, *-ge-*, *h*) take *s.th. or s.o.* with one; ***j-n (im Auto) ~*** give s.o. a lift

'**mitreden** *v/t* (*sep*, *-ge-*, *h*) ***et. mitzureden haben*** (***bei***) have a say (in)

'**mitreißen** *v/t* (*irr*, ***reißen***, *sep*, *-ge-*, *h*) drag along; *fig* carry away (*mst passive*); **~d** *fig adj* electrifying (*speech etc*)

'**mitschneiden** *v/t* (*irr*, ***schneiden***, *sep*, *-ge-*, *h*) *radio*, TV record, tape(-record)

'**mitschreiben** (*irr*, ***schreiben***, *sep*, *-ge-*, *h*) **1.** *v/t* take down; take, do (*a test*) **2.** *v/i* take notes

'**Mitschuld** *f* (-; *no pl*) partial responsibility; '**mitschuldig** *adj*: ***~ sein*** be partly to blame (***an*** *dat* for)

'**Mitschüler** *m*, '**Mitschülerin** *f* classmate; schoolmate, fellow student

'**mitspielen** *v/i* (*sep*, *-ge-*, *h*) SPORT, MUS play; join in *a game etc*; ***in e-m Film*** *etc* ***~*** be *or* appear in a film *etc*

'**Mitspieler** *m*, '**Mitspielerin** *f* partner, SPORT *a.* team-mate

**Mittag** ['mɪtaːk] *m* (*-s*; *-e*) noon, midday; ***heute ~*** at noon today; ***zu ~ essen*** (have) lunch; **~essen** *n* lunch; ***was gibt es zum ~?*** what's for lunch?

'**mittags** *adv* at noon; ***12 Uhr ~*** 12 o'clock noon

'**Mittags|pause** *f* lunch break; **~ruhe** *f* midday rest; **~schlaf** *m* after-dinner nap; **~zeit** *f* lunchtime

**Mitte** ['mɪtə] *f* (-; *no pl*) middle; center, *Br* centre (*a.* POL); ***~ Juli*** in the middle of July; ***~ dreißig*** in one's mid thirties

'**mitteilen** *v/t* (*sep*, *-ge-*, *h*) ***j-m et. ~*** inform s.o. of s.th.; '**mitteilsam** *adj* communicative; '**Mitteilung** *f* (-; *-en*) report; information, message

**Mittel** ['mɪtəl] *n* (*-s*; -) means, way; measure; PHARM remedy (***gegen*** for) (*a. fig*); average; MATH mean; PHYS medium; *pl* means, money

'**Mittelalter** *n* (*-s*; *no pl*) Middle Ages

'**mittelalterlich** *adj* medi(a)eval

'**Mittel|ding** *n* cross (***zwischen*** between); **~feld** *n* SPORT midfield; **~feldspieler(in)** midfield player, midfielder; **~finger** *m* ANAT middle finger

**'mittelfristig** *adj* medium-term
**'Mittelgewicht** *n* (-[*e*]*s*; *no pl*) SPORT middleweight (class)
**'mittelgroß** *adj* of medium height; medium-sized
**'Mittel|klasse** *f* middle class (*a.* MOT); **~linie** *f* SPORT halfway line
**'mittellos** *adj* without means
**'mittelmäßig** *adj* average
**'Mittelpunkt** *m* center, *Br* centre (*a. fig*)
**'mittels** *prp* (*gen*) by (means of), through
**'Mittelschule** *f* → ***Realschule***
**'Mittel|strecke** *f* SPORT middle distance; **~streckenra,kete** *f* MIL medium-range missile; **~streifen** *m* MOT median strip, *Br* central reservation; **~stufe** *f* PED junior highschool, *Br* middle school; **~stürmer(in)** SPORT center (*Br* centre) forward; **~weg** *m* middle course; **~welle** *f radio*: medium wave (*abbr* AM); **~wort** *n* (-[*e*]*s*; *-wörter*) LING participle
**mitten** ['mɪtən] *adv*: ***~ in*** (***auf, unter*** *dat*) in the midst *or* middle of
**mitten'drin** F *adv* right in the middle
**mitten'durch** F *adv* right through (the middle); right in two
**Mitternacht** ['mɪtɐnaxt] *f* midnight
**mittlere** ['mɪtlərə] *adj* middle, central; average, medium
**mittlerweile** ['mɪtlɐ'vailə] *adv* meanwhile, (in the) meantime
**Mittwoch** ['mɪtvɔx] *m* (-[*s*]; *-e*) Wednesday
**mit'unter** *adv* now and then
**'Mitverantwortung** *f* share of the responsibility
**'mitwirken** *v/i* (*sep*, *-ge-*, *h*) take part (***bei*** in); **'Mitwirkende** *m*, *f* (*-n*; *-n*) THEA, MUS performer; *pl* THEA the cast; 'Mitwirkung *f* (-; *no pl*) participation
**'Mixbecher** *m* shaker
**mixen** ['mɪksən] *v/t* (*ge-*, *h*) mix
**Mixer** ['mɪksɐ] *m* (*-s*; -) mixer; **'Mixgetränk** *n* mixed drink, cocktail, shake
**Möbel** ['mø:bəl] *pl* furniture; **~speditі,on** *f* removal firm; **~stück** *n* piece of furniture; **~wagen** *m* moving (*Br* furniture) van
**mobil** [mo'bi:l] *adj* mobile; ***~ machen*** MIL mobilize
**Mobiliar** [mobi'lja:ɐ] *n* (*-s*; *no pl*) furniture
**Mo'biltele,fon** *n* mobile phone
**möblieren** [mø'bli:rən] *v/t* (*no -ge-*, *h*) furnish
**mochte** ['mɔxtə] *pret of* ***mögen***
**Mode** ['mo:də] *f* (-; *-n*) fashion; ***in ~*** in fashion; ***~ sein*** be in fashion, F be in; ***die neueste ~*** the latest fashion; ***mit der ~ gehen*** follow the fashion; ***in*** (***aus der***) ***~ kommen*** come into (go out of) fashion
**Modell** [mo'dɛl] *n* (*-s*; *-e*) model; ***j-m ~ stehen*** *or* ***sitzen*** pose *or* sit for s.o.; **~bau** *m* model construction; **~baukasten** *m* model construction kit; **~eisenbahn** *f* model railway
**modellieren** [modɛ'li:rən] *v/t* (*no -ge-*, *h*) model
**Modem** ['mo:dɛm] *m*, *n* (*-s*; *-s*) IT modem
**'Modenschau** *f* fashion show
**Moderator** [mode'ra:to:ɐ] *m* (*-s*; *-en* [modera'to:rən]), **Modera'torin** *f* (-; *-nen*) TV *etc* presenter, host, anchorman (anchorwoman)
**moderieren** [mode'ri:rən] *v/t* (*no -ge-*, *h*) TV *etc* present, host
**moderig** ['mo:dərɪç] *adj* musty, mo(u)ldy
**modern**[1] ['mo:dɐn] *v/i* (*ge-*, *h*, *sein*) mo(u)ld, rot, decay
**modern**[2] [mo'dɛrn] *adj* modern; fashionable
**modernisieren** [modɛrni'zi:rən] *v/t* (*no -ge-*, *h*) modernize, bring up to date
**'Mode|schmuck** *m* costume jewel(le)ry; **~schöpfer(in)** fashion designer; **~waren** *pl* fashionwear; **~wort** *n* (-[*e*]*s*; *-wörter*) vogue word, F in word; **~zeichner(in)** fashion designer; **~zeitschrift** *f* fashion magazine
**modisch** ['mo:dɪʃ] *adj* fashionable, stylish
**Modul**[1] [mo'du:l] *n* (*-s*; *-e*) IT module
**Modul**[2] ['mo:dʊl] *m* (*-s*; *-n*) MATH, TECH module
**Mofa** ['mo:fa] *n* (*-s*; *-s*) (small) moped, motorized bicycle
**mogeln** ['mo:gəln] F *v/i* (*ge-*, *h*) cheat; crib
**mögen** ['mø:gən] *v/t* (*irr*, *ge-*, *h*) *and v/aux* (*irr*, *no -ge-*, *h*) like; ***er mag sie*** (***nicht***) he likes (doesn't like) her; ***lieber ~*** like better, prefer; ***nicht ~*** dislike; ***was möchten Sie?*** what would you

M

like?; ***ich möchte, dass du es weißt*** I'd like you to know (it); ***ich möchte lieber bleiben*** I'd rather stay; ***es mag sein*** (, ***dass***) it may be (that)

**möglich** ['mø:klıç] **1.** *adj* possible; ***alle ~en*** all sorts of; ***sein Möglichstes tun*** do what one can; do one's utmost; ***nicht ~!*** you don't say (so)!; ***so bald*** (***schnell, oft***) ***wie ~*** as soon (quickly, often) as possible **2.** *adv*: ***~st bald*** *etc* as soon *etc* as possible; **'möglicher'weise** *adv* possibly; **'Möglichkeit** *f* (-; *-en*) possibility; opportunity; chance; ***nach ~*** if possible

**Mohammedaner** [mohame'da:nɐ] *m* (*-s*; -),**mohamme'danisch** *adj* Muslim

**Mohn** [mo:n] *m* (-[*e*]*s*; *-e*) BOT poppy

**Möhre** ['mø:rə] *f* (-; *-n*), **Mohrrübe** ['mo:ɐry:bə] *f* BOT carrot

**Molch** [mɔlç] *m* (-[*e*]*s*; *-e*) ZO salamander

**Mole** ['mo:lə] *f* (-; *-n*) MAR mole, jetty

**Molekül** [mole'ky:l] *n* (*-s*; *-e*) CHEM molecule

**molk** [mɔlk] *pret of* ***melken***

**Molkerei** [mɔlkə'rai] *f* (-; *-en*) dairy

**Moll** [mɔl] *n* (-; *no pl*) MUS minor (key); ***a-Moll*** A minor

**mollig** ['mɔlıç] F *adj* snug, cozy, *Br* cosy; plump, chubby

**Moment** [mo'mɛnt] *m* (-[*e*]*s*; *-e*) moment; (***e-n***) ***~ bitte!*** just a moment please!; ***im ~*** at the moment

**Monarch** [mo'narç] *m* (*-en*; *-en*) monarch; **Monarchie** [monar'çi:] *f* (-; *-n*) monarchy; **Monarchin** [mo'narçın] *f* (-; *-nen*) monarch; **Monarchist** [monar'çıst] *m* (*-en*; *-en*) monarchist

**Monat** ['mo:nat] *m* (-[*e*]*s*; *-e*) month; ***zweimal im*** *or* ***pro ~*** twice a month

**'monatelang** *adv* for months

**'monatlich** *adj and adv* monthly

**'Monats|binde** *f* sanitary napkin (*Br* towel); **~karte** *f* commuter ticket, *Br* (monthly) season ticket

**Mönch** [mœnç] *m* (-[*e*]*s*; *-e*) monk; friar

**Mond** [mo:nt] *m* (-[*e*]*s*; *-e* ['mo:ndə]) moon; **~finsternis** *f* lunar eclipse

**'mondhell** *adj* moonlit

**'Mond|landefähre** *f* lunar module; **~landung** *f* moon landing; **~oberfläche** *f* moon surface, lunar soil; **~schein** *m* (-[*e*]*s*; *no pl*) moonlight; **~sichel** *f* crescent; **~umkreisung** *f*, **~umlaufbahn** *f* lunar orbit

**Monitor** ['mo:nito:ɐ] *m* (*-s*; *-en* [moni'to:rən]) TV *etc* monitor

**Monolog** [mono'lo:k] *m* (-[*e*]*s*; *-e*) monolog(ue *Br*)

**Monopol** [mono'po:l] *n* (*-s*; *-e*) ECON monopoly

**monoton** [mono'to:n] *adj* monotonous

**Monotonie** [monoto'ni:] *f* (-; *-n*) monotony

**Monoxid** ['mo:nɔksi:t] *n* CHEM monoxide

**Monster** ['mɔnstɐ] *n* (*-s*; -) monster

**Montag** ['mo:nta:k] *m* (-[*e*]*s*; *-e*) Monday

**Montage** [mɔn'ta:ʒə] *f* (-; *-n*) TECH assembly; installation; ***auf ~ sein*** be away on a field job; **~band** *n* (-[*e*]*s*; *-bänder*) TECH assembly line; **~halle** *f* TECH assembly shop

**Monteur** [mɔn'tø:ɐ] *m* (*-s*; *-e*) TECH fitter; *esp* MOT, AVIAT mechanic

**montieren** [mɔn'ti:rən] *v/t* (*no -ge-*, *h*) TECH assemble; fit, attach; instal(l)

**Moor** [mo:ɐ] *n* (-[*e*]*s*; *-e*) bog, moor (-land); **moorig** ['mo:rıç] *adj* boggy

**Moos** [mo:s] *n* (*-es*; *-e*) BOT moss

**moosig** ['mo:zıç] *adj* mossy

**Moped** ['mo:pɛt] *n* (*-s*; *-s*) moped

**Mops** [mɔps] *m* (*-es*; *Möpse* ['mœpsə]) ZO pug(dog)

**Moral** [mo'ra:l] *f* (-; *no pl*) morals, moral standards; MIL *etc* morale; **mo'ralisch** *adj* moral; **moralisieren** [morali'zi:rən] *v/i* (*no -ge-*, *h*) moralize

**Morast** [mo'rast] *m* (-[*e*]*s*; *-e*) morass; mire, mud

**Mord** [mɔrt] *m* (-[*e*]*s*; *-e* ['mɔrdə]) murder (***an*** *dat* of); ***e-n ~ begehen*** commit murder; **~anschlag** *m esp* POL assassination attempt

**Mörder** ['mœrdɐ] *m* (*-s*; -), **'Mörderin** *f* (-; *-nen*) murderer; (hired) killer; *esp* POL assassin

**'Mord|kommissi,on** *f* homicide division, *Br* murder squad; **~pro,zess** *m* JUR murder trial

**'Mords|angst** F *f*: ***e-e ~ haben*** be scared stiff; **~glück** F *n* stupendous luck; **~kerl** F *m* devil of a fellow; **~wut** F *f*: ***e-e ~ haben*** be in a hell of a rage

**'Mord|verdacht** *m* suspicion of murder; **~versuch** *m* attempted murder

**morgen** ['mɔrgən] *adv* tomorrow; ~

M

***Abend*** (***früh***) tomorrow night (morning); **~ *Mittag*** at noon tomorrow; **~ *in e-r Woche*** a week from tomorrow; **~ *um diese Zeit*** this time tomorrow; ***... von ~*** tomorrow's ..., ... of tomorrow
'**Morgen** *m* (*-s*; -) morning; AGR acre; ***heute ~*** this morning; ***am*** (***frühen***) **~** (early) in the morning; ***am nächsten ~*** the next morning; **~essen** *Swiss n* breakfast; **~grauen** *n* dawn; ***im*** *or* ***bei ~*** at dawn; **~land** *n* (*-[e]s*; *no pl*) Orient; **~mantel** *m*, **~rock** *m* dressing gown
'**morgens** *adv* in the morning; ***von ~ bis abends*** from morning till night
**morgig** ['mɔrgɪç] *adj* tomorrow's ...
**Morphium** ['mɔrfjʊm] *n* (*-s*; *no pl*) PHARM morphine
**morsch** [mɔrʃ] *adj* rotten; **~ *werden*** rot
**Morsealpha,bet** ['mɔrzəalfabe:t] *n* Morse code
**Mörser** ['mœrzɐ] *m* (*-s*; -) mortar (*a.* MIL)
'**Morsezeichen** *n* Morse signal
**Mörtel** ['mœrtəl] *m* (*-s*; -) mortar
**Mosaik** [moza'i:k] *n* (*-s*; *-en*) mosaic
**Mosa'ikstein** *m* piece
**Moschee** [mɔ'ʃe:] *f* (-; *-n*) mosque
**Moskito** [mɔs'ki:to] *m* (*-s*; *-s*) ZO mosquito
**Moslem** ['mɔslɛm] *m* (*-s*; *-s*), **moslemisch** [mɔs'le:mɪʃ] *adj*, **Moslime** [mɔs'li:mə] *f* (-; *-n*) Muslim
**Most** [mɔst] *m* (*-[e]s*; *-e*) grape juice; cider
**Motiv** [mo'ti:f] *n* (*-s*; *-e*) motive; PAINT, MUS motif; **Motivation** [motiva'tsjo:n] *f* (-; *-en*) motivation; **motivieren** [moti'vi:rən] *v/t* (*no -ge-*, *h*) motivate
**Motor** ['mo:to:ɐ, mo'to:ɐ] *m* (*-s*; *-en* [mo'to:rən]) motor, engine; **~boot** *n* motor boat; **~haube** *f* hood, *Br* bonnet
**motorisieren** [motori'zi:rən] *v/t* (*no -ge-*, *h*) motorize
'**Motor|leistung** *f* (engine) performance; **~rad** *n* motorcycle, F motorbike; **~ *fahren*** ride a motorcycle; **~radfahrer(in)** motorcyclist, biker; **~roller** *m* (motor) scooter; **~säge** *f* power saw; **~schaden** *m* engine trouble (*or* failure)
**Motte** ['mɔtə] *f* (-; *-n*) ZO moth
'**Mottenkugel** *f* mothball
'**mottenzerfressen** *adj* moth-eaten
**Motto** ['mɔto] *n* (*-s*; *-s*) motto
**Möwe** ['mø:və] *f* (-; *-n*) ZO (sea)gull
**Mücke** ['mʏkə] *f* (-; *-n*) ZO gnat, midge, mosquito; ***aus e-r ~ e-n Elefanten machen*** make a mountain out of a molehill; '**Mückenstich** *m* gnat bite
**müde** ['my:də] *adj* tired; weary; sleepy; **~ *sein*** (***werden***) be (get) tired (*fig* ***e-r Sache*** of s.th.)
'**Müdigkeit** *f* (-; *no pl*) tiredness
**Muff** [mʊf] *m* (*-[e]s*; *-e*) muff
**Muffe** ['mʊfə] *f* (-; *-n*) TECH sleeve, socket
**Muffel** ['mʊfəl] F *m* (*-s*; -) sourpuss
**muff(e)lig** ['mʊf(ə)lɪç], **muffig** ['mʊfɪç] F *adj* musty; *contp* sulky, sullen
**Mühe** ['my:ə] *f* (-; *-n*) trouble; effort; difficulty (***mit*** with *s.th.*); (***nicht***) ***der ~ wert*** (not) worth the trouble; ***j-m ~ machen*** give s.o. trouble; ***sich ~ geben*** try hard; ***sich die ~ sparen*** save o.s. the trouble; ***mit ~ und Not*** (just) barely
'**mühelos** *adv* without difficulty
**mühen** ['my:ən] *v/refl* (*ge-*, *h*) struggle, work hard
'**mühevoll** *adj* laborious
**Mühle** ['my:lə] *f* (-; *-n*) mill; morris
**Mühsal** ['my:za:l] *f* (-; *-e*) toil
**mühsam** ['my:za:m], '**mühselig** **1.** *adj* laborious **2.** *adv* with difficulty
**Mulatte** [mu'latə] *m* (*-n*; *-n*), **Mu'lattin** *f* (-; *-nen*) mulatto
**Mulde** ['mʊldə] *f* (-; *-n*) hollow
**Mull** [mʊl] *m* (*-[e]s*; *-e*) muslin; *esp* MED gauze
**Müll** [mʏl] *m* (*-s*; *no pl*) garbage, trash, *Br* refuse, rubbish; **~abfuhr** *f* garbage (*Br* refuse) collection; **~beseitigung** *f* waste disposal; **~beutel** *m* garbage bag, *Br* dustbin liner
'**Mullbinde** *f* MED gauze bandage
'**Müll|con,tainer** *m* garbage (*Br* rubbish) skip; **~depo,nie** *f* dump; **~eimer** *m* garbage can, *Br* dustbin; **~fahrer** *m* garbage man, *Br* dustman; **~halde** *f* dump; **~haufen** *m* garbage (*Br* rubbish) heap; **~kippe** *f* dump; **~schlucker** *m* garbage (*Br* refuse) chute; **~tonne** *f* garbage can, *Br* dustbin; **~verbrennungsanlage** *f* (waste) incineration plant; **~wagen** *m* garbage truck, *Br* dustcart
**Multiplikation** [mʊltiplika'tsjo:n] *f* (-; *-en*) MATH multiplication; **multiplizieren** [mʊltipli'tsi:rən] *v/t* (*no -ge-*, *h*)

MATH multiply (***mit*** by)
**Mumie** ['muːmjə] *f* (-; *-n*) mummy
**Mumps** [mʊmps] *m*, *f* (-; *no pl*) MED mumps
**Mund** [mʊnt] *m* (-[*e*]*s*; *Münder* ['mʏndɐ]) mouth; F ***den ~ vollnehmen*** talk big; ***halt den ~!*** shut up!; **~art** *f* dialect
**münden** ['mʏndən] *v/i* (*ge-*, *h*, *sein*) ***~ in*** (*acc*) *river etc*: flow into; *road etc*: lead into
'**Mundgeruch** *m* bad breath
'**Mundharˌmonika** *f* MUS mouth organ, harmonica
**mündig** ['mʏndɪç] *adj* emancipated; ~ (***werden***) JUR (come) of age
**mündlich** ['mʏntlɪç] *adj* oral; verbal
'**Mundstück** *n* mouthpiece; tip
'**Mündung** *f* (-; *-en*) *river*: mouth; *gun*: muzzle
'**Mund|wasser** *n* mouthwash; **~werk** F *n*: ***ein loses ~*** a loose tongue; **~winkel** *m* corner of the mouth
'**Mund-zu-'Mund-Beatmung** *f* (-; *-en*) MED mouth-to-mouth resuscitation, F kiss of life
**Munition** [muni'tsjoːn] *f* (-; *-en*) ammunition
**munkeln** ['mʊŋkəln] F *v/t* (*ge-*, *h*) ***man munkelt, dass*** rumo(u)r has it that
**Münster** ['mʏnstɐ] *n* (-*s*; -) cathedral, minster
**munter** ['mʊntɐ] *adj* awake; lively; merry
**Münze** ['mʏntsə] *f* (-; *-n*) coin; medal
'**Münz|einwurf** *m* (coin) slot; **~fernsprecher** *m* pay phone; **~tank(autoˌmat)** *m* coin-operated (gas, *Br* petrol) pump; **~wechsler** *m* (-s; -) change machine
**mürbe** ['mʏrbə] *adj* tender; brittle; GASTR crisp; '**Mürbeteig** *m* short pastry; shortcake
**Murmel** ['mʊrməl] *f* (-; *-n*) marble
'**murmeln** *v/t and v/i* (*ge-*, *h*) murmur
'**Murmeltier** *n* ZO marmot
**murren** ['mʊrən] *v/i* (*ge-*, *h*) complain (***über*** *acc* about)
**mürrisch** ['mʏrɪʃ] *adj* sullen; grumpy
**Mus** [muːs] *n* (*-es*; *-e*) mush; stewed fruit
**Muschel** ['mʊʃəl] *f* (-; *-n*) ZO mussel; shell
**Museum** [mu'zeːʊm] *n* (-*s*; *Museen*) museum
**Musik** [mu'ziːk] *f* (-; *no pl*) music
**musikalisch** [muzi'kaːlɪʃ] *adj* musical
**Mu'sik|anlage** *f* hi-fi *or* stereo set; **~autoˌmat** *m*, **~box** *f* juke box
**Musiker** ['muːzikɐ] *m* (-*s*; -), '**Musikerin** *f* (-; *-nen*) musician
**Mu'sik|instruˌment** *n* musical instrument; **~kaˌpelle** *f* band; **~kasˌsette** *f* music cassette; **~lehrer(in)** music teacher; **~stunde** *f* music lesson
**musisch** ['muːzɪʃ] *adv*: ***~ interessiert*** (***begabt***) fond of (gifted for) fine arts and music
**musizieren** [muzi'tsiːrən] *v/i* (*no -ge-*, *h*) make music
**Muskat** [mʊs'kaːt] *m* (-[*e*]*s*; *-e*), **~nuss** *f* BOT nutmeg
**Muskel** ['mʊskəl] *m* (-*s*; *-n*) ANAT muscle; **~kater** F *m* aching muscles; **~zerrung** *f* MED pulled muscle
**muskulös** [mʊsku'løːs] *adj* muscular, brawny
**Müsli** ['myːsli] *n* (-*s*; -) GASTR granola, *Br* muesli
**Muss** *n* (-; *no pl*) necessity; ***es ist ein ~*** it is a must
**Muße** ['muːsə] *f* (-; *no pl*) leisure; spare time
**müssen** ['mʏsən] *v/i* (*irr*, *ge-*, *h*) *and v/aux* (*irr*, *no -ge-*, *h*) must, have (got) to; ***du musst den Film sehen!*** you must see the film!; ***ich muss jetzt*** (***m-e***) ***Hausaufgaben machen*** I have (got) to do my homework now; ***sie muss krank sein*** she must be ill; ***du musst es nicht tun*** you need not do it; ***das müsstest du*** (***doch***) ***wissen*** you ought to know (that); ***sie müsste zu Hause sein*** she should (ought to) be (at) home; ***das müsste schön sein!*** that would be nice!; ***du hättest ihm helfen ~*** you ought to have helped him
**müßig** ['myːsɪç] *adj* idle; useless
**musste** ['mʊstə] *pret of* ***müssen***
**Muster** ['mʊstɐ] *n* (-*s*; -) pattern; sample; model
'**muster|gültig**, **~haft** *adj* exemplary; ***sich ~ benehmen*** behave perfectly
'**Musterhaus** *n* showhouse
'**mustern** *v/t* (*ge-*, *h*) eye *s.o.*; size *s.o.* up; MIL ***gemustert werden*** F have one's medical; **Musterung** ['mʊstərʊŋ] *f* (-; *-en*) MIL medical (examination for military service)
**Mut** [muːt] *m* (-[*e*]*s*; *no pl*) courage; ***j-m***

~ ***machen*** encourage s.o.; ***den*** ~ ***verlieren*** lose courage; → ***zumute***
**mutig** ['mu:tɪç] *adj* courageous, brave
'**mutlos** *adj* discouraged
'**mutmaßen** *v/t* (*ge-*, *h*) speculate
'**mutmaßlich** *adj* probable; presumed
'**Mutprobe** *f* test of courage
**Mutter** ['mʊtɐ] *f* (-; *Mütter* ['mʏtɐ]) mother; TECH nut; ~**boden** *m*, ~**erde** *f* AGR topsoil
**mütterlich** ['mʏtɐlɪç] *adj* motherly
'**mütterlicherseits** *adv*: ***Onkel*** *etc* ~ maternal uncle *etc*
'**Mutterliebe** *f* motherly love
'**mutterlos** *adj* motherless
'**Mutter|mal** *n* birthmark, mole; ~**milch** *f* mother's milk; ~**schaftsurlaub** *m* maternity leave; ~**schutz** *m* JUR legal protection of expectant and nursing mothers; ~**söhnchen** *contp n* sissy; ~**sprache** *f* mother tongue; ~**sprachler** ['mʊtɐʃpra:xlɐ] *m* (*-s*; -) native speaker; ~**tag** *m* Mother's Day
**Mutti** ['mʊti] F *f* (-; *-s*) mom(my), *esp Br* mum(my)
'**mutwillig** *adj* wanton
**Mütze** ['mʏtsə] *f* (-; *-n*) cap
**MwSt** *abbr of* ***Mehrwertsteuer*** VAT, value-added tax
**mysteriös** [mʏste'rjø:s] adj mysterious
**mystisch** ['mʏstɪʃ] *adj* mystic(al)
**mythisch** ['my:tɪʃ] *adj* mythical
**Mythologie** [mytolo'gi:] *f* (-; *-n*) mythology
**Mythos** ['my:tɔs] *m* (-; *Mythen*) myth

# N

**N** *abbr of* ***Nord*(*en*)** N, north
**na** [na] *int* well; ~ ***und?*** so what?; ~ ***gut!*** all right then; ~ ***ja*** (oh) well; ~(, ~)***!*** come on!, come now!; ~ ***so*** (***et***)***was!*** what do you know!, *Br* I say!; ~, ***dann nicht!*** oh, forget it!; ~ ***also!*** there you are!; ~, ***warte!*** just you wait!
**Nabe** ['na:bə] *f* (-; *-n*) TECH hub
**Nabel** ['na:bəl] *m* (*-s*; -) ANAT navel
'**Nabelschnur** *f* ANAT umbilical chord
**nach** [na:x] *prp* (*dat*) *and adv* to, toward(s), for; after; *time*: after, past; according to, by; ~ ***Hause*** home; ***abfahren*** ~ leave for; ~ ***rechts*** (***Süden***) to the right (south); ~ ***oben*** up(stairs); ~ ***unten*** down(stairs); ~ ***vorn*** (***hinten***) to the front (back); ***der Reihe*** ~ one after the other; ***s-e Uhr*** ~ ***dem Radio stellen*** set one's watch by the radio; ~ ***m-r Uhr*** by my watch; ***suchen*** (***fragen***) ~ look (ask) for; ~ ***Gewicht*** (***Zeit***) by weight (the hour); ***riechen*** (***schmecken***) ~ smell (taste) of; ~ ***und*** ~ gradually; ~ ***wie vor*** as before, still
**nachahmen** ['na:xa:mən] *v/t* (*sep*, *-ge-*, *h*) imitate, copy; take off
'**Nachahmung** *f* (-; *-en*) imitation
**Nachbar** ['naxba:ɐ] *m* (*-n*; *-n*), '**Nachbarin** *f* (-; *-nen*) neighbo(u)r; '**Nachbarschaft** *f* (-; *no pl*) neighbo(u)rhood, vicinity
'**Nachbau** *m* (-[*e*]*s*; *-ten*) TECH reproduction; '**nachbauen** *v/t* (*sep*, *-ge-*, *h*) copy, reproduce
'**Nachbildung** *f* (-; *-en*) copy, imitation; replica; dummy
'**nachblicken** *v/i* (*sep*, *-ge-*, *h*) look after
**nach'dem** *cj* after, when; ***je*** ~ ***wie*** depending on how
'**nachdenken** *v/i* (*irr*, ***denken***, *sep*, *-ge-*, *h*) think; ~ ***über*** (*acc*) think about, think *s.th.* over
'**nachdenklich** *adj* thoughtful; ***es macht e-n*** ~ it makes you think
'**Nachdruck**[1] *m* (-[*e*]*s*; *no pl*) emphasis, stress
'**Nachdruck**[2] (-[*e*]*s*; *-e*) reprint
'**nachdrucken** *v/t* (*sep*, *-ge-*, *h*) reprint
**nachdrücklich** ['na:xdrʏklɪç] *adj* emphatic; forceful; ~ ***raten*** (***empfehlen***) advise (recommend) strongly
'**nacheifern** *v/i* (*sep*, *-ge-*, *h*) ***j-m*** ~ emulate s.o.
**nachei'nander** *adv* one after the other, in (*or* by) turns
'**nacherzählen** *v/t* (*sep*, *no -ge-*, *h*) retell; '**Nacherzählung** *f* (-; *-en*) PED reproduction
'**Nachfolge** *f* (-; *no pl*) succession; ***j-s*** ~ ***antreten*** succeed s.o.; '**nachfolgen** *v/i*

N

(*sep*, *-ge-*, *sein*) (*dat*) succeed *s.o.*; 'Nachfolger(in) ['na:xfɔlgɐ, 'na:xfɔlgərɪn] (*-s*; *-/-*; *-nen*) successor

'**nachforschen** *v/i* (*sep*, *-ge-*, *h*) investigate; '**Nachforschung** *f* (-; *-en*) investigation, inquiry

'**Nachfrage** *f* (-; *-n*) inquiry; ECON demand; '**nachfragen** *v/i* (*sep*, *-ge-*, *h*) inquire, ask

'**nach|fühlen** *v/t* (*sep*, *-ge-*, *h*) ***j-m et.*** ~ understand how s.o. feels; **~füllen** *v/t* (*sep*, *-ge-*, *h*) refill; **~geben** *v/i* (*irr*, ***geben***, *sep*, *-ge-*, *h*) give (way); *fig* give in

'**Nachgebühr** *f* (-; *-en*) *post* surcharge

'**nachgehen** *v/i* (*irr*, ***gehen***, *sep*, *-ge-*, *sein*) follow (*a. fig*); *watch*: be slow; ***e-r Sache*** ~ investigate s.th.; ***s-r Arbeit*** ~ go about one's work

'**Nachgeschmack** *m* (*-[e]s*; *no pl*) aftertaste (*a. fig*)

**nachgiebig** ['na:xgi:bɪç] *adj* yielding, soft (*both a. fig*); '**Nachgiebigkeit** *f* (-; *no pl*) yieldingness, softness (*both a. fig*)

**nachhaltig** ['na:xhaltɪç] *adj* lasting, enduring

**nach'hause** → ***Haus***

**nach'her** *adv* afterwards; ***bis ~!*** see you later!, so long!

'**Nachhilfe** *f* help, assistance; PED → **~stunden** *pl*, **~unterricht** *m* PED private lesson(s), coaching

'**nachholen** *v/t* (*sep*, *-ge-*, *h*) make up for, catch up on

'**Nachkomme** *m* (*-n*; *-n*) descendant, *pl esp* JUR issue; '**nachkommen** *v/i* (*irr*, ***kommen***, *sep*, *-ge-*, *sein*) follow, come later; (*dat*) comply with

'**Nachkriegs...** *in cpds* postwar ...

**Nachlass** ['na:xlas] *m* (*-es*; *-lässe* ['na:xlɛsə]) ECON reduction, discount; JUR estate

'**nachlassen** *v/i* (*irr*, ***lassen***, *sep*, *-ge-*, *h*) decrease, diminish, go down; *effect etc*: wear off; *student etc*: slacken one's effort; *interest etc*: flag; *health etc*: fail, deteriorate

'**nachlässig** *adj* careless, negligent

'**nach|laufen** *v/i* (*irr*, ***laufen***, *sep*, *-ge-*, *sein*) run after; **~lesen** *v/t* (*irr*, ***lesen***, *sep*, *-ge-*, *h*) look up; **~machen** *v/t* (*sep*, *-ge-*, *h*) imitate, copy; counterfeit, forge

'**Nachmittag** *m* afternoon; ***heute*** ~ this afternoon

'**nachmittags** *adv* in the afternoon

**Nachnahme** ['na:xna:mə] *f* (-; *-n*) ECON cash on delivery; ***per ~ schicken*** send C.O.D.

'**Nach|name** *m* surname, last (*or* family) name; **~porto** *n* surcharge

'**nachprüfen** *v/t* (*sep*, *-ge-*, *h*) check (up), make sure (of)

'**nachrechnen** *v/t* (*sep*, *-ge-*, *h*) check

'**Nachrede** *f*: ***üble*** ~ malicious gossip; JUR defamation (of character), slander

**Nachricht** ['na:xrɪçt] *f* (-; *-en*) news; message; report; information, notice; *pl* news (report), newscast; ***e-e gute*** (***schlechte***) ~ good (bad) news; ***Sie hören ~en*** here is the news

'**Nachrichten|dienst** *m* news service; MIL intelligence service; **~satel,lit** *m* communications satellite; **~sprecher(in)** newscaster, *esp Br* newsreader; **~technik** *f* telecommunications

'**Nachruf** *m* obituary

'**nach|rüsten** *v/i* (*sep*, *-ge-*, *h*) POL, MIL close the armament gap; **~sagen** *v/t* (*sep*, *-ge-*, *h*) ***j-m Schlechtes ~*** speak badly of s.o.; ***man sagt ihm nach, dass er ...*** he is said to *inf*

'**Nachsai,son** *f* off-peak season; ***in der ~*** out of season

'**nachschlagen** (*irr*, ***schlagen***, *sep*, *-ge-*, *h*) **1.** *v/t* look up **2.** *v/i*: ***~ in*** (*dat*) consult; '**Nachschlagewerk** *n* reference book

'**Nach|schlüssel** *m* duplicate (*or* skeleton) key; **~schrift** *f* postcript; dictation; **~schub** *m esp* MIL supplies

'**nach|sehen** (*irr*, ***sehen***, *sep*, *- ge-*, *h*) **1.** *v/i* follow with one's eyes; (have a) look; ***~ ob*** (go and) see whether **2.** *v/t* look *or* go over *or* through; correct, mark; *check* (*a.* TECH); **~senden** *v/t* ([*irr*, ***senden***,] *sep*, *-ge-*, *h*) send on, forward; ***bitte ~!*** *post* please forward!

'**Nachsilbe** *f* LING suffix

'**nachsitzen** *v/i* (*irr*, ***sitzen***, *sep*, *-ge-*, *h*) stay in (after school), be kept in; ***~ lassen*** keep in, detain

'**Nachspann** *m* (*-[e]s*; *-e*) *film*: credits *pl*

'**Nachspiel** *n* sequel, consequences

'**nachspielen** *v/i* (*sep*, *-ge-*, *h*) SPORT ***5 Minuten ~ lassen*** allow 5 minutes for injury time; '**Nachspielzeit** *f esp soccer*: injury time

'**nach|spio,nieren** *v/i* (*no -ge-*, *h*) spy

(up)on; **~sprechen** *v/t* (*irr*, ***sprechen***, *sep*, *-ge-*, *h*) ***j-m et. ~*** say *or* repeat s.th. after s.o.

**nächst'beste** [nɛːçst'bɛstə] *adj* first, F any old; next-best, second-best

**nächste** ['nɛːçstə] *adj* next; nearest (*a. relative*); ***in den ~n Tagen*** (***Jahren***) in the next few days (years); ***in ~r Zeit*** in the near future; ***was kommt als Nächstes?*** what comes next?; ***der Nächste, bitte!*** next please!

**'nachstehen** *v/i* (*irr*, ***stehen***, *sep*, *-ge-*, *h*) ***j-m in nichts ~*** be in no way inferior to s.o.

**'nachstellen** (*sep*, *-ge-*, *h*) **1.** *v/t* put back (*watch*); TECH (re)adjust **2.** *v/i*: ***j-m ~*** be after s.o.; **'Nachstellung** *f* (-; *-en*) persecution

**'Nächstenliebe** *f* charity

**Nacht** [naxt] *f* (-; *Nächte* ['nɛçtə]) night; ***Tag und ~*** night and day; ***die ganze ~*** all night (long); ***heute Nacht*** tonight; last night

**'Nachtdienst** *m* night duty; ***~ haben*** PHARM be open all night

**'Nachteil** *m* disadvantage, drawback; ***im ~ sein*** be at a disadvantage (***gegenüber*** compared with); **nachteilig** ['naːxtailɪç] *adj* disadvantageous

**'Nacht|essen** *Swiss n* → ***Abendbrot***; **~falter** *m* ZO moth; **~hemd** *n* nightgown, nightdress, F nightie; nightshirt

**Nachtigall** ['naxtigal] *f* (-; *-en*) ZO nightingale

**'Nachtisch** *m* (-[*e*]*s*; *no pl*) dessert; sweet

**nächtlich** ['nɛçtlɪç] *adj* nightly; at *or* by night

**'Nachtlo,kal** *n* nightclub

**Nachtrag** ['naːxtraːk] *m* (-[*e*]*s*; *-träge* ['naːxtrɛːgə]) supplement; **'nachtragen** *fig v/t* (*irr*, ***tragen***, *sep*, *-ge-*, *h*) ***j-m et. ~*** bear s.o. a grudge; **'nachtragend** *adj* unforgiving; **nachträglich** ['naːxtrɛːklɪç] *adj* additional; later; belated

**nachts** *adv* at night, in the night(time)

**'Nachtschicht** *f* night shift; ***~ haben*** be on night shift

**'nachtschlafend** *adj*: ***zu ~er Zeit*** in the middle of the night

**'Nachttisch** *m* bedside table

**'Nachttopf** *m* chamber pot

**'Nachtwächter** *m* night watchman

**'nachwachsen** *v/i* (*irr*, ***wachsen***, *sep*, *-ge-*, *sein*) grow again

**'Nachwahl** *f* PARL special election, *Br* by-election

**Nachweis** ['naːxvais] *m* (*-es*; *-e*) proof, evidence; **'nachweisbar** *adj* demonstrable; *esp* CHEM *etc* detectable

**'nachweisen** *v/t* (*irr*, ***weisen***, *sep*, *-ge-*, *h*) prove; *esp* CHEM *etc* detect

**'nachweislich** *adv* as can be proved

**'Nach|welt** *f* (-; *no pl*) posterity; **~wirkung** *f* aftereffect(s), *pl a.* aftermath; **~wort** *n* (-[*e*]*s*; *-worte*) epilog(ue)

**'Nachwuchs** *m* (*-es*; *no pl*) young talent, F new blood; **~...** *in cpds ...autor, ...schauspieler etc*: talented *or* promising young ..., up-and-coming ...

**'nach|zahlen** *v/t* (*sep*, *-ge-*, *h*) pay extra; **~zählen** *v/t* (*sep*, *-ge-*, *h*) count over (again), check

**'Nachzahlung** *f* additional *or* extra payment

**Nachzügler** ['naːxtsyːklɐ] *m* (*-s*; -) straggler, latecomer

**Nacken** ['nakən] *m* (*-s*; -) ANAT (back *or* nape of the) neck; **~stütze** *f* headrest

**nackt** [nakt] *adj* naked; *esp* PAINT, PHOT nude; bare (*a. fig*); *fig* plain; ***völlig ~*** stark naked; ***sich ~ ausziehen*** strip; ***~ baden*** swim in the nude; ***j-n ~ malen*** paint s.o. in the nude

**Nadel** ['naːdəl] *f* (-; *-n*) needle; pin; brooch; **~baum** *m* BOT conifer(ous tree); **~öhr** *n* eye of a needle; **~stich** *m* pinprick (*a. fig*)

**Nagel** ['naːgəl] *m* (*-s*; *Nägel* ['nɛːgəl]) nail; ***an den Nägeln kauen*** bite one's nails; **~lack** *m* nail varnish *or* polish

**'nageln** *v/t* (*ge-*, *h*) nail (***an*** *acc*, ***auf*** *acc* to)

**'nagel'neu** F *adj* brand-new

**'Nagelpflege** *f* manicure

**nagen** ['naːgən] (*ge-*, *h*) **1.** *v/i* gnaw (***an*** *dat* at); ***an e-m Knochen ~*** pick a bone **2.** *v/t* gnaw; **'Nagetier** *n* ZO rodent

**'Nahaufnahme** *f* PHOT *etc* close-up

**nahe** [naːə] *adj* near, close (***bei*** to); nearby; ***~ kommen*** (*dat*) come close to; *fig* → ***nahekommen***; → ***nahelegen***; → ***naheliegen***; → ***naheliegend***; **Nähe** ['nɛːə] *f* (-; *no pl*) nearness; neighbo(u)rhood, vicinity; ***in der ~ des Bahnhofs*** near the station; ***ganz in der ~*** quite near, close by; ***in deiner***

N

~ near you
**nahegehen** *v/i* (*irr*, ***gehen***, *sep*, *-ge-*, *sein*): ***j-m*** ~ affect s.o. deeply
'**nahekommen** *v/i* (*irr*, ***kommen***, *sep*, *-ge-*, *sein*) *fig* come close to
'**nahelegen** *v/t* (*sep*, *-ge-*, *h*) suggest
'**naheliegen** *v/i* (*irr*, ***liegen***, *sep*, *-ge-*, *h*) seem likely; '**naheliegend** *adj* likely, obvious
**nahen** ['na:ən] *v/i* (*ge-*, *sein*) approach
**nähen** ['nɛ:ən] *v/t and v/i* (*ge-*, *h*) sew; make
**Nähere** ['nɛ:ərə] *n* (*-n*; *no pl*) details, particulars
**nähern** ['nɛ:ɐn] *v/refl* (*ge-*, *h*) approach, get near(er) *or* close(r) (*dat* to)
'**nahezu** *adv* nearly, almost
'**Nähgarn** *n* (sewing) cotton
'**Nahkampf** *m* MIL close combat
**nahm** [na:m] *pret of* ***nehmen***
'**Nähma,schine** *f* sewing machine
'**Nähnadel** *f* (sewing) needle
**nähren** ['nɛ:rən] *v/t* (*ge-*, *h*) feed; *fig* nurture
**nahrhaft** ['na:ɐhaft] *adj* nutritious, nourishing
**Nährstoff** ['nɛ:ɐʃtɔf] *m* nutrient
**Nahrung** ['na:rʊŋ] *f* (*-*; *no pl*) food, nourishment; AGR feed; diet
'**Nahrungsmittel** *pl* food(stuffs)
**Nährwert** ['nɛ:ɐve:ɐt] *m* nutritional value
**Naht** [na:t] *f* (*-*; *Nähte* ['nɛ:tə]) seam; MED suture
'**Nahverkehr** *m* local traffic; '**Nahverkehrszug** *m* local *or* commuter train
'**Nähzeug** *n* sewing kit
**naiv** [na'i:f] *adj* naive; **Naivität** [naivi'tɛ:t] *f* (*-*; *no pl*) naivety
**Name** ['na:mə] *m* (*-ns*; *-n*) name; ***im ~n von*** on behalf of; ***nur dem ~n nach*** in name only; '**namenlos** *adj* nameless, *fig a.* unspeakable; '**namens** *adv* by (the) name of, named, called
'**Namens|tag** *m* name day; **~vetter** *m* namesake; **~zug** *m* signature
**namentlich** ['na:məntlɪç] *adj and adv* by name
**nämlich** ['nɛ:mlɪç] *adv* that is (to say), namely; you see *or* know
**nannte** ['nantə] *pret of* ***nennen***
**Napf** [napf] *m* (*-[e]s*; *Näpfe* ['nɛpfə]) bowl, basin
**Narbe** ['narbə] *f* (*-*; *-n*) scar
**narbig** ['narbɪç] *adj* scarred
**Narkose** [nar'ko:zə] *f* (*-*; *-n*) MED an(a)esthesia; ***in*** ~ under an an(a)esthetic
**Narr** [nar] *m* (*-en*; *-en*) fool; ***j-n zum ~en halten*** fool s.o.; '**narrensicher** *adj* foolproof; **närrisch** ['nɛrɪʃ] *adj* foolish; ~ ***vor*** (*dat*) mad with
**Narzisse** [nar'tsɪsə] *f* (*-*; *-n*) BOT daffodil
**nasal** [na'za:l] *adj* nasal
**naschen** ['naʃən] *v/i and v/t* (*ge-*, *h*) nibble (***an*** *dat* at); ***gern*** ~ have a sweet tooth; **Naschereien** [naʃə'raiən] *pl* dainties, goodies, sweets; '**naschhaft** *adj* sweet-toothed
**Nase** ['na:zə] *f* (*-*; *-n*) ANAT nose (*a. fig*); ***sich die ~ putzen*** blow one's nose; ***in der ~ bohren*** pick one's nose; F ***die ~ voll haben*** (***von***) be fed up (with)
'**Nasen|bluten** *n* MED nosebleed; **~loch** *n* nostril; **~spitze** *f* tip of the nose
**Nashorn** *n* ZO rhinoceros, F rhino
**nass** [nas] *adj* wet; ***triefend*** ~ soaking (wet); **Nässe** ['nɛsə] *f* (*-*; *no pl*) wet (-ness); '**nässen** (*ge-*, *h*) **1.** *v/t* wet **2.** *v/i* MED weep
'**nasskalt** *adj* damp and cold, raw
**Nation** [na'tsjo:n] *f* (*-*; *-en*) nation
**national** [natsjo'na:l] *adj* national
**Natio'nalhymne** *f* national anthem
**Nationalismus** [natsjona'lɪsmʊs] *m* (*-*; *no pl*) nationalism; **Nationalität** [natsjonali'tɛ:t] *f* (*-*; *-en*) nationality
**Natio'nal|mannschaft** *f* SPORT national team; **~park** *m* national park
**Natio'nalsozia,lismus** *m* HIST National Socialism, *contp* Nazism; **Natio'nalsozia,list** *m*, **natio'nalsozia,listisch** *adj* HIST National Socialist, *contp* Nazi
**Natter** ['natɐ] *f* (*-*; *-n*) ZO adder, viper (*a. fig*)
**Natur** [na'tu:ɐ] *f* (*-*; *-en*) nature; ***von*** ~ (***aus***) by nature
**Naturalismus** [natura'lɪsmʊs] *m* (*-*; *no pl*) naturalism
**Na'tur|ereignis** *n*, **~erscheinung** *f* natural phenomenon; **~forscher** *m* naturalist; **~geschichte** *f* natural history; **~gesetz** *n* law of nature
**na'turgetreu** *adj* true to life; lifelike
**Na'turkata,strophe** *f* (natural) catastrophe *or* disaster, act of God
**natürlich** [na'ty:ɐlɪç] **1.** *adj* natural **2.**

N

*adv* naturally, of course

**Na'tur|schätze** *pl* natural resources; **~schutz** *m* nature conservation; ***unter ~*** protected; **~schützer** [na'tu:ɐʃʏtsɐ] *m (-s; -)* conservationist; **~schutzgebiet** *n* nature reserve; national park; **~wissenschaft** *f* (natural) science

**n. Chr.** *abbr of* ***nach Christus*** AD, Anno Domini

**Nebel** ['ne:bəl] *m (-s; -)* fog; mist; haze; smoke; **~horn** *n* foghorn; **~leuchte** *f* MOT fog light

**neben** ['ne:bən] *prp (dat and acc)* beside, next to; besides, apart from; compared with; ***~ anderem*** among other things; ***setz dich ~ mich*** sit by me *or* by my side

**neben'an** *adv* next door

**neben'bei** *adv* in addition, at the same time; ***~ (gesagt)*** by the way

**'Nebenberuf** *m* second job, sideline; **'nebenberuflich** *adv* as a sideline

**Nebenbuhler** ['ne:bənbu:lɐ] *m (-s; -)*, **'Nebenbuhlerin** *f (-; -nen)* rival

**'nebenei'nander** *adv* side by side; next (door) to each other; ***~ bestehen*** coexist

**'Neben|einkünfte** *pl*, **~einnahmen** *pl* extra money; **~fach** *n* PED *etc* minor (subject), *Br* subsidiary subject; **~fluss** *m* tributary; **~gebäude** *n* next-door *or* adjoining building; annex(e); **~haus** *n* house next door; **~kosten** *pl* extras; **~mann** *m*: ***dein ~*** the person next to you; **~pro,dukt** *n* by-product; **~rolle** *f* THEA supporting role, minor part (*a. fig*); cameo (role); **~sache** *f* minor matter; ***das ist ~*** that's of little *or* no importance

**'nebensächlich** *adj* unimportant

**'Neben|satz** *m* LING subordinate clause; **~stelle** *f* TEL extension; **~straße** *f* side street; minor road; **~strecke** *f* RAIL branch line; **~tisch** *m* next table; **~verdienst** *m* extra earnings; **~wirkung** *f* side effect; **~zimmer** *n* adjoining room

**neblig** ['ne:blɪç] *adj* foggy; misty; hazy

**necken** ['nɛkən] *v/t (ge-, h)* tease

**Neckerei** [nɛkə'rai] *f (-; -en)* teasing

**'neckisch** *adj* playful, teasing

**Neffe** ['nɛfə] *m (-n; -n)* nephew

**negativ** ['ne:gati:f] *adj* negative

**'Negativ** *n (-s; -e)* PHOT negative

**nehmen** ['ne:mən] *v/t (irr, ge-, h)* take (*a.* ***sich ~***); ***j-m et. ~*** take s.th. (away) from s.o. (*a. fig*); ***sich e-n Tag frei ~*** take a day off; ***j-n an die Hand ~*** take s.o. by the hand

**Neid** [nait] *m (-es; no pl)* envy; ***reiner ~*** sheer envy; **neidisch** ['naidɪʃ] *adj* envious (***auf*** *acc* of)

**Neige** ['naigə] *f*: ***zur ~ gehen*** draw to its close; run out

**'neigen** *(ge-, h)* **1.** *v/t and refl* bend, incline **2.** *v/i*: ***zu et. ~*** tend to (do) s.th.

**'Neigung** *f (-; -en)* inclination (*a. fig*), slope, incline; *fig* tendency

**nein** [nain] *adv* no

**Nektar** ['nɛkta:ɐ] *m (-s; -e)* BOT nectar

**Nelke** ['nɛlkə] *f (-; -n)* BOT carnation; GASTR clove

**nennen** ['nɛnən] *v/t (irr, ge-, h)* name, call; mention; ***sich ~*** call o.s., be called; ***man nennt ihn ...*** he is called ...; ***das nenne ich ...!*** that's what I call ...!

**'nennenswert** *adj* worth mentioning

**Nenner** ['nɛnɐ] *m (-s; -)* MATH denominator

**'Nennwert** *m* ECON nominal *or* face value; ***zum ~*** at par

**Neo..., neo...** [neo-] *in cpds ...faschist etc*: neo-...

**Neon** ['ne:ɔn] *n (-s; no pl)* CHEM neon

**'Neonröhre** *f* neon tube

**Nepp** [nɛp] F *m (-s; no pl)* rip-off

**neppen** ['nɛpən] F *v/t (ge-, h)* fleece, rip *s.o.* off

**Nerv** [nɛrf] *m (-s; -en)* ANAT nerve; ***j-m auf die ~en fallen*** *or* ***gehen*** get on s.o.'s nerves; ***die ~en behalten*** (***verlieren***) keep (lose) one's head

**nerven** ['nɛrfən] F *v/t and v/i (ge-, h)* be a pain in the neck (***j-n*** to s.o.)

**'Nervenarzt** *m*, **'Nervenärztin** *f* neurologist

**'nervenaufreibend** *adj* nerve-racking

**'Nerven|belastung** *f* nervous strain; **~kitzel** *m* thrill, F kick(s)

**'nervenkrank** *adj* mentally ill

**'Nerven|säge** F *f* pain in the neck; **~sys,tem** *n* nervous system; **~zusammenbruch** *m* nervous breakdown

**nervös** [nɛr'vø:s] *adj* nervous

**Nervosität** [nɛrvozi'tɛ:t] *f (-; no pl)* nervousness

**Nerz** [nɛrts] *m (-es; -e)* ZO mink

**Nessel** ['nɛsəl] *f (-; -n)* BOT nettle

**Nest** [nɛst] *n (-[e]s; -er* ['nɛstɐ]*)* ZO nest;

F *contp* one-horse town
**nett** [nɛt] *adj* nice; kind; ***so ~ sein und et.*** (*or* ***et. zu***) ***tun*** be so kind as to do s.th.
**netto** ['nɛto] *adv* ECON net
**Netz** [nɛts] *n* (*-es*; *-e*) net; RAIL, TEL, IT network; ELECTR mains; **~haut** *f* ANAT retina; **~karte** *f* RAIL area season ticket
**neu** [nɔʏ] *adj* new; fresh; *fig* modern; ***neuere Sprachen*** modern languages; ***neueste Nachrichten*** (***Mode***) latest news (fashion); ***von neuem*** anew, afresh; ***seit neu***(***st***)***em*** since (very) recently; ***viel Neues*** a lot of new things; ***was gibt es Neues?*** what's the news?, what's new?; '**neuartig** *adj* novel
'**Neubau** *m* (-[*e*]*s*; *-ten*) new building; **~gebiet** *n* new housing estate
**neuerdings** ['nɔʏɐ'dɪŋs] *adv* lately, recently
**Neuerer** ['nɔʏərɐ] *m* (*-s*; -) innovator; '**Neuerung** *f* (-; *-en*) innovation
'**Neugestaltung** *f* reorganization, reformation
'**Neugier** *f*, **Neugierde** ['nɔʏgiːɐdə] *f* (-; *no pl*) curiosity; '**neugierig** *adj* curious (***auf*** *acc* about); F *contp* nos(e)y; ***ich bin ~, ob*** I wonder if; **Neugierige** ['nɔʏgiːrɪgə] *contp pl* rubbernecks
'**Neuheit** *f* (-; *-en*) novelty
**Neuigkeit** ['nɔʏɪçkait] *f* (-; *-en*) (piece of) news
'**Neujahr** *n* New Year('s Day); ***Prost ~!*** Happy New Year!
'**neulich** *adv* the other day
**Neuling** ['nɔʏlɪŋ] *m* (*-s*; *-e*) newcomer, F greenhorn
'**neumodisch** *contp adj* newfangled
'**Neumond** *m* new moon
**neun** [nɔʏn] *adj* nine; '**neunte** *adj* ninth; '**Neuntel** *n* (*-s*; -) ninth (part); '**neuntens** *adv* ninthly; '**neunzehn** *adj* nineteen; '**neunzehnte** *adj* nineteenth; '**neunzig** *adj* ninety; '**neunzigste** *adj* ninetieth
**Neurose** [nɔʏ'roːzə] *f* (-; *-n*) MED neurosis; **neurotisch** [nɔʏ'roːtɪʃ] *adj* MED neurotic
'**neusprachlich** *adj* modern-language
**neutral** [nɔʏ'traːl] *adj* neutral
**Neutralität** [nɔʏtrali'tɛːt] *f* (-; *no pl*) neutrality
**Neutronen...** [nɔʏ'troːnən-] PHYS *in cpds ...bombe etc*: neutron ...
**Neutrum** ['nɔʏtrʊm] *n* (*-s*; *-tra*) LING neuter
'**Neuverfilmung** *f* remake
'**neuwertig** *adj* as good as new
'**Neuzeit** *f* (-; *no pl*) modern times
**nicht** [nɪçt] *adv* not; ***überhaupt ~*** not at all; ***~*** (***ein***)***mal, gar ~ erst*** not even; ***~ mehr*** not any more *or* longer; ***sie ist nett*** (***wohnt hier***), ***~*** (***wahr***)***?*** she's nice (lives here), isn't (doesn't) she?; ***~ so ... wie*** not as ... as; ***noch ~*** not yet; ***~ besser*** (***als***) no (*or* not any) better (than); ***ich*** (***auch***) ***~*** I don't *or* I'm not (either); (***bitte***) ***~!*** (please) don't!
'**Nicht...** *in cpds ...mitglied, ...schwimmer etc*: *mst* non-...; **~beachtung** *f* disregard; non-observance
**Nichte** ['nɪçtə] *f* (-; *-n*) niece
**nichtig** ['nɪçtɪç] *adj* trivial; JUR void, invalid
'**Nichtraucher** *m*, '**Nichtraucherin** *f* non-smoker
**nichts** *indef pron* nothing, not anything; ***~*** (***anderes***) ***als*** nothing but; ***gar ~*** nothing at all; F ***das ist ~*** that's no good; ***~ sagend*** meaningless; **Nichts** *n* (*-s*; *no pl*) nothing(ness); ***aus dem ~*** *appear etc* from nowhere; *build etc* from nothing
**nichtsdesto'weniger** *adv* nevertheless
**nichtsnutzig** ['nɪçtsnʊtsɪç] *adj* good-for-nothing, worthless
'**nichtssagend** *adj* meaningless
**Nichtstuer** ['nɪçtstuːɐ] *m* (*-s*; -) do-nothing, F bum
**nicken** ['nɪkən] *v/i* (*ge-*, *h*) nod (one's head)
**nie** [niː] *adv* never, at no time; ***fast ~*** hardly ever; ***~ und nimmer*** never ever
**nieder** ['niːdɐ] **1.** *adj* low **2.** *adv* down
'**Niedergang** *m* (-[*e*]*s*; *no pl*) decline
'**niedergeschlagen** *adj* depressed, (feeling) down
'**Niederlage** *f* defeat, F beating
'**niederlassen** *v/refl* (*irr*, ***lassen***, *sep*, *-ge-*, *h*) settle (down); ECON set up (***als*** as); '**Niederlassung** *f* (-; *-en*) ECON establishment; branch
'**nieder|legen** *v/t* (*sep*, *-ge-*, *h*) lay down (*a. office etc*); ***die Arbeit ~*** (go on) strike, down tools, F walk out; ***sich ~*** lie down; go to bed; **~metzeln** *v/t* (*sep*, *-ge-*, *h*) massacre
'**Niederschlag** *m* METEOR rain(fall);

PHYS fallout; CHEM precipitate; *boxing*: knock-down; '**niederschlagen** *v/t* (*irr*, ***schlagen***, *sep*, *-ge-*, *h*) knock down; cast down (*eyes*); *fig* put down (*revolt etc*); JUR quash; ***sich ~*** CHEM precipitate
'**niederschmettern** *fig v/t* (*sep*, *-ge-*, *h*) shatter, crush
'**niederträchtig** *adj* base, mean
**Niederung** ['ni:dərʊŋ] *f* (-; *-en*) lowland(s)
**niedlich** ['ni:tlɪç] *adj* pretty, sweet, cute
**niedrig** ['ni:drɪç] *adj* low (*a. fig*); *fig* light (*sentence etc*); ***~ fliegen*** fly low
**niemals** ['ni:ma:ls] → ***nie***
**niemand** ['ni:mant] *indef pron* nobody, no one, not anybody; ***~ von ihnen*** none of them; '**Niemandsland** *n* (-[*e*]*s*; *no pl*) no-man's-land
**Niere** ['ni:rə] *f* (-; *-n*) ANAT kidney
**nieseln** ['ni:zəln] *v/i* (*ge-*, *h*) drizzle
'**Nieselregen** *m* drizzle
**niesen** ['ni:zən] *v/i* (*ge-*, *h*) sneeze
**Niete**[1] ['ni:tə] *f* (-; *-n*) TECH rivet
'**Niete**[2] *f* (-; *-n*) blank; F failure
**Nikolaustag** ['nɪkolausta:k] *m* St. Nicholas' Day
**Nikotin** [niko'ti:n] *n* (*-s*; *no pl*) CHEM nicotine
**Nilpferd** ['ni:lpfe:ɐt] *n* ZO hippopotamus, F hippo
**Nippel** ['nɪpəl] *m* (*-s*; -) TECH nipple
**nippen** ['nɪpən] *v/i* (*ge-*, *h*) sip (***an*** *dat* at)
**nirgends** ['nɪrgənts] *adv* nowhere
**Nische** ['ni:ʃə] *f* (-; *-n*) niche, recess
**nisten** ['nɪstən] *v/i* (*ge-*, *h*) ZO nest
'**Nistplatz** *m* ZO nesting place
**Niveau** [ni'vo:] *n* (*-s*; *-s*) level, *fig a.* standard
**Nixe** ['nɪksə] *f* (-; *-n*) water nymph, mermaid
**noch** [nɔx] *adv* still; ***~ nicht*** not yet; ***~ nie*** never before; ***er hat nur ~ 5 Euro*** (***Minuten***) he has only 5 euros (minutes) left; (***sonst***) ***~ et.?*** anything else?; ***ich möchte ~ et.*** (***Tee***) I'd like some more (tea); ***~ ein(e, -n)…, bitte*** another …, please; ***~ einmal*** once more *or* again; ***~ zwei Stunden*** another two hours, two hours to go; ***~ besser*** (***schlimmer***) even better (worse); ***~ gestern*** only yesterday; ***und wenn es ~ so … ist*** however (*or* no matter how) … it may be
**nochmalig** ['nɔxma:lɪç] *adj* new, renewed
'**nochmals** *adv* once more *or* again
**Nockerl** ['nɔkɐl] *Austrian n* (*-s*; *-n*) GASTR small dumpling
**Nomade** [no'ma:də] *m* (*-n*; *-n*), **No'madin** *f* (-; *-nen*) nomad
**Nominativ** ['no:minati:f] *m* (*-s*; *-e*) LING nominative (case)
**nominieren** [nomi'ni:rən] *v/t* (*no -ge-*, *h*) nominate
**Nonne** ['nɔnə] *f* (-; *-n*) REL nun
'**Nonnenkloster** *n* REL convent
**Norden** ['nɔrdən] *m* (*-s*; *no pl*) north; ***nach ~*** north(wards); **nordisch** ['nɔrdɪʃ] *adj* northern; SPORT ***~e Kombination*** Nordic Combined
**nördlich** ['nœrtlɪç] **1.** *adj* north(ern); northerly **2.** *adv*: ***~ von*** north of
**Nordlicht** ['nɔrtlɪçt] *n* (-[*e*]*s*; *-er*) ASTR northern lights
**Nord'osten** *m* northeast; **nord'östlich** *adj* northeast(ern); northeasterly
'**Nordpol** *m* North Pole
**Nord'westen** *m* northwest
**nord'westlich** *adj* northwest(ern); northwesterly
'**Nordwind** *m* north wind
**nörgeln** ['nœrgəln] *v/i* (*ge-*, *h*) nag (***an*** *dat* at)
**Nörgler** ['nœrglɐ] *m* (*-s*; -), '**Nörglerin** *f* (-; *-nen*) nagger
**Norm** [nɔrm] *f* (-; *-en*) standard, norm
**normal** [nɔr'ma:l] *adj* normal; F ***nicht ganz ~*** not quite right in the head
**Nor'mal…** *esp* TECH *in cpds …maß, …zeit etc*: standard …; **~ben'zin** *n* regular (gas, *Br* petrol)
**normalerweise** [nɔr'ma:lɐ'vaizə] *adv* normally, usually
**normalisieren** [nɔrmali'zi:rən] *v/refl* (*no -ge-*, *h*) return to normal
**normen** ['nɔrmən] *v/t* (*ge-*, *h*) standardize
**Norwegen** ['nɔrve:gən] Norway
**Norweger** ['nɔrve:gɐ] *m* (*-s*; -), '**Norwegerin** ['nɔrve:gərɪn] *f* (-; *-nen*), '**norwegisch** *adj* Norwegian
**Not** [no:t] *f* (-; *Nöte* ['nø:tə]) need; want; poverty; hardship, misery; difficulty; emergency; distress; ***~ leidend*** needy; ***in ~ sein*** be in trouble; ***zur ~*** if need be, if necessary
**Notar** [no'ta:ɐ] *m* (*-s*; *-e*), **No'tarin** *f* (-; *-nen*) JUR notary (public)

N

**'Not|aufnahme** *f* MED emergency room, *Br* casualty; **~ausgang** *m* emergency exit; **~behelf** *m* (-[*e*]*s*; -*e*) makeshift, expedient; **~bremse** *f* emergency brake; **~dienst** *m* emergency duty

**'notdürftig** *adj* scanty; temporary

**Note** ['no:tə] *f* (-; -*n*) note (*a.* MUS *and* POL); ECON bill, *esp Br* (bank)note; PED grade, *Br* mark; *pl* MUS (sheet) music; ***~n lesen*** read music

**Notebook** ['noutbʊk] *n* (-*s*; -*s*) IT notebook

**'Notendurchschnitt** *m* PED *etc* average

**'Notenständer** *m* music stand

**'Notfall** *m* emergency

**'notfalls** *adv* if necessary

**'notgedrungen** *adv*: ***et. ~ tun*** be forced to do s.th.

**notieren** [no'ti:rən] *v/t* (*no -ge-, h*) make a note of, note (down); ECON quote

**nötig** ['nø:tɪç] *adj* necessary; ***~ haben*** need; ***~ brauchen*** need badly; ***das Nötigste*** the (bare) necessities *or* essentials; **nötigen** ['nø:tɪgən] *v/t* (*ge-, h*) force, compel; press, urge; **'Nötigung** *f* (-; -*en*) coercion; JUR intimidation

**Notiz** [no'ti:ts] *f* (-; -*en*) note; ***keine ~ nehmen von*** take no notice of, ignore; ***sich ~en machen*** take notes; **~block** *m* memo pad, *Br* notepad; **~buch** *n* notebook

**'Notlage** *f* awkward (*or* difficult) situation; difficulties; emergency

**'notlanden** *v/i* (*-ge-, sein*) AVIAT make an emergency landing; **'Notlandung** *f* AVIAT emergency landing

**'Notlösung** *f* expedient

**'Notlüge** *f* white lie

**notorisch** [no'to:rɪʃ] *adj* notorious

**'Not|ruf** *m* TEL emergency call; **~rufsäule** *f* TEL emergency phone; **~sig,nal** *n* emergency *or* distress signal; **~stand** *m* state of (national) emergency; **~standsgebiet** *n* disaster area; ECON depressed area; **~standsgesetze** *pl* POL emergency laws; **~verband** *m* MED emergency dressing

**'Notwehr** *f* (-; *no pl*) JUR self-defense, *Br* self-defence

**'notwendig** *adj* necessary

**'Notwendigkeit** *f* (-; -*en*) necessity

**'Notzucht** *f* (-; *no pl*) JUR rape

**Novelle** [no'vɛlə] *f* (-; -*n*) novella; PARL amendment

**November** [no'vɛmbɐ] *m* (-[*s*]; -) November

**Nr.** *abbr of* ***Nummer*** No., no., number

**Nu** [nu:] *m*: ***im ~*** in no time

**Nuance** ['nya~:sə] *f* shade

**nüchtern** ['nʏçtɐn] *adj* sober (*a. fig*); matter-of-fact; ***auf ~en Magen*** on an empty stomach; ***~ werden*** (***machen***) sober up

**'Nüchternheit** *f* (-; *no pl*) sobriety

**Nudel** ['nu:dəl] *f* (-; -*n*) noodle

**nuklear** [nukle'a:ɐ] *adj* nuclear

**null** [nʊl] *adj* zero, *Br* nought; TEL 0; SPORT nil, nothing; *tennis*: love; ***~ Grad*** zero degrees; ***~ Fehler*** no mistakes; ***gleich Null sein*** be nil

**'Null|di,ät** *f* low-calorie (*or* F starvation) diet; **~punkt** *m* zero (point *or fig* level); **~ta,rif** *m* free fare(s); ***zum ~*** free (of charge)

**Numerus clausus** ['nu:merʊs 'klauzʊs] *m* (-; *no pl*) UNIV restricted admission(s)

**Nummer** ['nʊmɐ] *f* (-; -*n*) number; issue; size; **nummerieren** [nʊmə'ri:rən] *v/t* (*no -ge-, h*) number

**'Nummernschild** *n* MOT license plate, *Br* numberplate

**nun** [nu:n] *adv* now; well

**nur** [nu:ɐ] *adv* only, just; merely; nothing but; ***er tut ~ so*** he's just pretending; ***~ so*** (***zum Spaß***) just for fun; ***warte ~!*** just you wait!; ***mach ~!, ~ zu!*** go ahead!; → ***Erwachsene***

**Nuss** [nʊs] *f* (-; *Nüsse* ['nʏsə]) BOT nut; **~baum** *m* walnut (tree); **~knacker** *m* nutcracker; **~schale** *f* nutshell

**Nüstern** ['nʏstɐn] *pl* ZO nostrils

**Nutte** ['nʊtə] F *f* (-; -*n*) hooker, *sl* tart

**Nutzanwendung** ['nʊtsˀanvɛndʊŋ] *f* practical application; **'nutzbar** *adj* usable; ***~ machen*** utilize; exploit; harness; **'nutzbringend** *adj* profitable, useful

**nütze** ['nʏtsə] *adj* useful; ***zu nichts ~ sein*** be (of) no use; be good for nothing

**Nutzen** ['nʊtsən] *m* (-*s*; -) use; profit, gain; advantage; ***~ ziehen aus*** (*dat*) benefit *or* profit from *or* by; ***zum ~ von*** (*or gen*) for the benefit of

**'nutzen, 'nützen** (*ge-, h*) **1.** *v/i*: ***j-m ~*** be of use to s.o.; ***es nützt nichts*** (***es zu tun***) it's no use (doing it) **2.** *v/t* use, make use of; take advantage of

**nützlich** ['nʏtslɪç] *adj* useful, helpful; advantageous; ***sich ~ machen*** make o.s. useful
'**nutzlos** *adj* useless, (of) no use
'**Nutzung** *f* (-; *-en*) use, utilization
**Nylon**® ['nailɔn] *n* (*-s*; *no pl*) nylon®; **~strümpfe** *pl* nylon® stockings
**Nymphe** ['nʏmfə] *f* (-; *-n*) nymph

# O

**O** *abbr of* **Osten** E, east
**o** *int* oh!; ***o weh!*** oh dear!
**o. Ä.** *abbr of* **oder Ähnliche(s)** or the like
**Oase** [o'a:zə] *f* (-; *-n*) oasis (*a. fig*)
**ob** [ɔp] *cj* whether, if; ***als ~*** as if, as though; ***und ~!*** and how!, you bet!
**Obacht** ['o:baxt] *f*: ***~ geben auf*** (*acc*) pay attention to; (***gib***) ***~!*** watch out!
**Obdach** ['ɔpdax] *n* (-[*e*]*s*; *no pl*) shelter
'**obdachlos** *adj* homeless, without shelter; '**Obdachlose** *m, f* (*-n*; *-n*) homeless person; '**Obdachlosenaˌsyl** *n* shelter for the homeless
**Obduktion** [ɔpdʊk'tsjo:n] *f* (-; *-en*) MED autopsy
**obduzieren** [ɔpdu'tsi:rən] *v/t* (*no -ge-, h*) MED perform an autopsy on
**oben** ['o:bən] *adv* above; up; on (the) top; at the top (*a. fig*); on the surface; upstairs; ***da ~*** up there; ***von ~ bis unten*** from top to bottom (*or* toe); ***links ~*** (at the) top left; ***siehe ~*** see above; F ***~ ohne*** topless; ***von ~ herab*** *fig* patronizing(ly), condescending(ly); ***~ erwähnt*** *or* ***genannt*** above-mentioned; **~'an** *adv* at the top; **~'auf** *adv* on the top; on the surface; F feeling great; **~'drein** *adv* besides, into the bargain, at that; **~'hin** *adv* superficially
**Ober** ['o:bɐ] *m* (*-s*; -) waiter
'**Ober|arm** *m* ANAT upper arm; **~arzt** *m*, **~ärztin** *f* assistant medical director; **~befehl** *m* MIL supreme command; **~begriff** *n* generic term; **~bürgermeister** *m* mayor, *Br* Lord Mayor
**obere** ['o:bərə] *adj* upper, top, *fig a.* superior
'**Oberfläche** *f* surface (*a. fig*) (**an** *dat* on); '**oberflächlich** *adj* superficial
'**oberhalb** *prp* (*gen*) above
'**Ober|hand** *f*: ***die ~ gewinnen*** (***über*** *acc*) get the upper hand (of); **~haupt** *n* head, chief; **~haus** *n* (*-es*; *no pl*) *Br* PARL House of Lords; **~hemd** *n* shirt; **~herrschaft** *f* (-; *no pl*) supremacy
**Oberin** ['o:bərɪn] *f* (-; *-nen*) REL Mother Superior
'**oberirdisch** *adj* above ground; ELECTR overhead
'**Ober|kellner** *m* head waiter; **~kiefer** *m* ANAT upper jaw; **~körper** *m* upper part of the body; ***den ~ frei machen*** strip to the waist; **~leder** *n* uppers; **~leitung** *f* chief management; ELECTR overhead contact line; **~lippe** *f* ANAT upper lip
**Obers** ['o:bɐs] *Austrian n* (-; *no pl*) GASTR cream
'**Oberschenkel** *m* ANAT thigh
'**Oberschule** *f appr* highschool, *Br* grammar school
**Oberst** ['o:bɐst] *m* (*-en*; *-en*) MIL colonel
**oberste** ['o:bɐstə] *adj* up(per)most, top (-most); highest; *fig* chief, first
'**Ober|stufe** *f appr* senior highschool, *Br appr* senior classes; **~teil** *n* top
**ob'gleich** *cj* (al)though
**Obhut** ['ɔphu:t] *f* (-; *no pl*) care, charge; ***in s-e ~ nehmen*** take care *or* charge of
**obig** ['o:bɪç] *adj* above(-mentioned)
**Objekt** [ɔp'jɛkt] *n* (-[*e*]*s*; *-e*) object (*a.* LING); ECON property
**objektiv** [ɔpjɛk'ti:f] *adj* objective; impartial, unbias(s)ed
**Objek'tiv** *n* (*-s*; *-e*) PHOT (object) lens
**Objektivität** [ɔpjɛktivi'tɛ:t] *f* (-; *no pl*) objectivity; impartiality
**Oblate** [o'bla:tə] *f* (-; *-n*) wafer; REL host
**obligatorisch** [obliga'to:rɪʃ] *adj* compulsory
**Oboe** [o'bo:ə] *f* (-; *-n*) MUS oboe
**Oboist** [obo'ɪst] *m* (*-en*; *-en*) MUS oboist
**Observatorium** [ɔpzɛrva'to:rjʊm] *n* (*-s*; *-ien*) ASTR observatory
**Obst** [o:pst] *n* (-[*e*]*s*; *no pl*) fruit; **~garten** *m* orchard; **~konˌserven** *pl* canned fruit; **~laden** *m* fruit store, *esp Br* fruiterer's (shop); **~torte** *f*

fruit pie (*Br* flan)
**obszön** [ɔps'tsøːn] *adj* obscene, filthy
**ob'wohl** *cj* (al)though
**Occasion** [ɔka'zjoːn] *Swiss f* (-; *-en*) bargain, good buy
**Ochse** ['ɔksə] *m* (*-n*; *-n*) ZO ox, bullock; F blockhead
**od.** *abbr of* ***oder*** or
**öde** ['øːdə] *adj* deserted, desolate; waste; *fig* dull, dreary, tedious
**oder** ['oːdɐ] *cj* or; ***~ aber*** or else, otherwise; ***~ vielmehr*** or rather; ***~ so*** or so; ***er kommt doch, ~?*** he's coming, isn't he?; ***du kennst ihn ja nicht, ~ doch?*** you don't know him, or do you?
**Ofen** ['oːfən] *m* (*-s*; *Öfen* ['øːfən]) stove; oven; TECH furnace; **~heizung** *f* stove heating; **~rohr** *n* stovepipe
**offen** ['ɔfən] **1.** *adj* open (*a. fig*); vacant (*post*); *fig* frank **2.** *adv*: ***~ gesagt*** frankly (speaking); ***~ s-e Meinung sagen*** speak one's mind (freely); ***~ stehen*** be open; ECON be outstanding
**'offenbar** *adj* obvious, evident; apparent; **offenbaren** [ɔfən'baːrən] *v/t* (*ge-*, *h*) reveal, disclose, show; **Offen'barung** *f* (-; *-en*) revelation
**'Offenheit** *f* (-; *no pl*) openness, frankness
**'offenherzig** *adj* open-hearted, frank, candid; *fig* revealing (*dress*)
**'offensichtlich** *adj* → ***offenbar***
**offensiv** [ɔfɛn'ziːf] adj, **Offensive** [ɔfɛn'ziːvə] *f* (-; *-n*) offensive
**'offenstehen** *v/i* (*irr*, ***stehen***, *sep*, *-ge-*, *h*): ***j-m ~*** *fig* be open to s.o.
**öffentlich** ['œfəntlɪç] *adj* public; ***~e Verkehrsmittel*** *pl* public transport; ***~e Schulen*** *pl* public (*Br* state) schools; ***~ auftreten*** appear in public
**'Öffentlichkeit** *f* (-; *no pl*) *the* public; ***in aller ~*** in public, openly; ***an die ~ bringen*** make public
**offiziell** [ɔfi'tsjɛl] *adj* official
**Offizier** [ɔfi'tsiːɐ] *m* (*-s*; *-e*) MIL (commissioned) officer
**öffnen** ['œfnən] *v/t and v/refl* (*ge-*, *h*) open; **Öffner** ['œfnɐ] *m* (*-s*; -) opener; **'Öffnung** *f* (-; *-en*) opening
**'Öffnungszeiten** *pl* business *or* office hours
**oft** [ɔft] *adv* often, frequently
**oh** [oː] *int* o(h)!
**ohne** ['oːnə] *prp* (*acc*) *and cj* without; ***~ mich!*** count me out!; ***~ ein Wort*** (***zu sagen***) without (saying) a word
**ohne|'gleichen** *adv* unequal(l)ed, unparalleled; **~'hin** *adv* anyhow, anyway
**Ohnmacht** ['oːnmaxt] *f* (-; *-en*) MED unconsciousness; *fig* helplessness; ***in ~ fallen*** faint, pass out; **'ohnmächtig** *adj* MED unconscious; *fig* helpless; ***~ werden*** faint, pass out
**Ohr** [oːɐ] *n* (-[*e*]*s*; *-en* ['oːrən]) ANAT ear; F ***j-n übers ~ hauen*** cheat s.o.; ***bis über die ~en verliebt*** (***verschuldet***) head over heels in love (over your head in debt)
**Öhr** [øːɐ] *n* (-[*e*]*s*; *-e* ['øːrə]) eye
**Ohrenarzt** ['oːrənˀaːɐtst] *m* ear specialist
**'ohrenbetäubend** *adj* deafening
**'Ohren|schmerzen** *pl* earache; **~schützer** *pl* earmuffs; **~zeuge** *m* earwitness
**'Ohrfeige** *f* slap in the face (*a. fig*); **ohrfeigen** ['oːɐfaigən] *v/t* (*ge-*, *h*) ***j-n ~*** slap s.o.'s face
**'Ohr|läppchen** ['oːɐlɛpçən] *n* (*-s*; -) ANAT earlobe; **~ring** *m* earring
**oje** [o'jeː] *int* oh dear!, dear me!
**Ökologe** [øko'loːgə] *m* (*-n*; *-n*) ecologist; **Ökologie** [økolo'giː] *f* (-; *no pl*) ecology; **ökologisch** [øko'loːgɪʃ] *adj* ecological
**Ökonomie** [økono'miː] *f* (-; *no pl*) economy; ECON economics; **ökonomisch** [øko'noːmɪʃ] *adj* economical; ECON economic
**Ökosys,tem** ['øːkozʏsteːm] *n* ecosystem
**Oktave** [ɔk'taːvə] *f* (-; *-n*) MUS octave
**Oktober** [ɔk'toːbɐ] *m* (-[*s*]; -) October
**ökumenisch** [øku'meːnɪʃ] *adj* REL ecumenical
**Öl** [øːl] *n* (-[*e*]*s*; *Öle*) oil; petroleum; ***nach ~ bohren*** drill for oil; ***auf ~ stoßen*** strike oil; **'Ölbaum** *m* BOT olive (tree)
**Oldtimer** ['ouldtaɪmə] *m* (*-s*; -) MOT veteran car
**ölen** ['øːlən] *v/t* (*ge-*, *h*) oil, TECH *a.* lubricate
**'Öl|farbe** *f* oil (paint); **~feld** *n* oilfield; **~förderland** *n* oil-producing country; **~förderung** *f* oil production; **~gemälde** *n* oil painting; **~heizung** *f* oil heating
**ölig** ['øːlɪç] *adj* oily, greasy (*both a. fig*)

**oliv** [o'liːf] *adj* olive
**Olive** [o'liːvə] *f* (-; *-n*) BOT olive
'**Öl|leitung** *f* (oil) pipeline; **~messtab** *m* MOT dipstick; **~pest** *f* oil pollution; **~quelle** *f* oil well; **~sar,dine** *f* canned (*Br a.* tinned) sardine; **~stand** *m* oil level; **~tanker** *m* MAR oil tanker; **~teppich** *m* oil slick
'**Ölung** *f* (-; *no pl*) oiling, TECH *a.* lubrication; ***Letzte ~*** REL extreme unction
'**Öl|wanne** *f* MOT oil pan, *Br* sump; **~wechsel** *m* MOT oil change
**Olympia…** [o'lympja-] *in cpds …mannschaft, …medaille etc*: Olympic …
**Olympiade** [olym'pjaːdə] *f* (-; *-n*) SPORT Olympic Games, Olympics
'**Ölzeug** *n* oilskins
**Oma** ['oːma] F *f* (-; *-s*) grandma
**Omi** ['oːmi] F *f* (-; *-s*) granny
**Omnibus** ['ɔmnibʊs] *m* → ***Bus***
**onanieren** [ona'niːrən] *v/i* (*no -ge-*, *h*) masturbate
**Onkel** ['ɔŋkəl] *m* (*-s*; -) uncle
**Online…** ['ɔnlain-] IT online …
**Opa** ['oːpa] F *m* (*-s*; *-s*) grandpa
**Oper** ['oːpɐ] *f* (-; *-n*) MUS opera; opera (house)
**Operation** [opəra'tsjoːn] *f* (-; *-en*) MED operation; ***e-e ~ vornehmen*** perform an operation; **Operati'onssaal** *m* MED operating room (*Br* theatre)
**Operette** [opə'rɛtə] *f* (-; *-n*) MUS operetta
**operieren** [opə'riːrən] (*no -ge-*, *h*) **1.** *v/t* MED ***j-n ~*** operate on s.o. (***wegen*** for); ***operiert werden*** be operated on, have an operation; ***sich ~ lassen*** undergo an operation **2.** *v/i* MED, MIL operate; proceed
'**Opernsänger(in)** opera singer
**Opfer** ['ɔpfɐ] *n* (*-s*; -) sacrifice; offering; victim; ***ein ~ bringen*** make a sacrifice; (*dat*) ***zum ~ fallen*** fall victim to
'**opfern** *v/t and v/i* (*ge-*, *h*) sacrifice
**Opium** ['oːpjʊm] *n* (*-s*; *no pl*) opium
**Opposition** [ɔpozi'tsjoːn] *f* (-; *-en*) opposition (*a.* PARL)
**Optik** ['ɔptik] *f* (-; *no pl*) optics; PHOT optical system
**Optiker** ['ɔptikɐ] *m* (*-s*; -), '**Optikerin** *f* (-; *-nen*) optician
**optimal** [ɔpti'maːl] *adj* optimum, best
**Optimismus** [ɔpti'mɪsmʊs] *m* (-; *no pl*) optimism; **Optimist(in)** [ɔpti'mɪst(ɪn)] (*-en*; *-en*/-; *-nen*) optimist; **opti'mistisch** *adj* optimistic
**Option** [ɔp'tsjoːn] *f* (-; *-en*) option
**optisch** ['ɔptɪʃ] *adj* optical
**Orange** [o'raːʒə] *f* (-; *-n*) BOT orange
**Orchester** [ɔr'kɛstɐ] *n* (*-s*; -) MUS orchestra
**Orchidee** [ɔrçi'deː] *f* (-; *-n*) bot orchid
**Orden** ['ɔrdən] *m* (*-s*; -) medal, decoration; *esp* REL order
'**Ordensschwester** *f* REL sister, nun
**ordentlich** ['ɔrdəntlɪç] **1.** *adj* tidy, neat, orderly; proper; thorough; decent (*a.* F); respectable; full (*member etc*); JUR ordinary; reasonable (*performance etc*); F good, sound **2.** *adv*: ***s-e Sache ~ machen*** do a good job; ***sich ~ benehmen*** (***anziehen***) behave (dress) properly *or* decently
**ordinär** [ɔrdi'nɛːɐ] *adj* vulgar; common
**ordnen** ['ɔrdnən] *v/t* (*ge-*, *h*) put in order; arrange, sort (out); file; settle
**Ordner** ['ɔrdnɐ] *m* (*-s*; -) file; folder; attendant, guard
'**Ordnung** *f* (-; *no pl*) order; orderliness, tidiness; arrangement; system, set-up; class; ***in ~*** all right; TECH *etc* in (good) order; ***in ~ bringen*** put right (*a. fig*); tidy up; repair, fix (*a. fig*); (***in***) ***~ halten*** keep (in) order; ***et. ist nicht in ~*** (***mit***) there is s.th. wrong (with)
'**ordnungsgemäß** **1.** *adj* correct, regular **2.** *adv* duly, properly
'**Ordnungs|strafe** *f* JUR fine, penalty; **~zahl** *f* MATH ordinal number
**Organ** [ɔr'gaːn] *n* (*-s*; *-e*) organ; **~empfänger** *m* MED organ recipient; **~handel** *m* sale of (transplant) organs
**Organisation** [ɔrganiza'tsjoːn] *f* (-; *-en*) organization; **Organisator** [ɔrgani'zaːtoːɐ] *m* (*-s*; *-en* [ɔrganiza'toːrən]) organizer; **Organisa'torin** *f* (-; *-nen*) organizer; **organisatorisch** [ɔrganiza'toːrɪʃ] *adj* organizational
**organisch** [ɔr'gaːnɪʃ] *adj* organic
**organisieren** [ɔrgani'ziːrən] *v/t* organize; F get (hold of); ***sich ~*** organize; ECON unionize; **organisiert** [ɔrgani'ziːɐt] *adj* organized; ECON unionized
**Organismus** [ɔrga'nɪsmʊs] *m* (-; *-men*) BIOL organism
**Organist** [ɔrga'nɪst] *m* (*-en*; *-en*), **Orga'nistin** *f* (-; *-nen*) MUS organist
**Or'ganspender** *m* MED (organ) donor
**Orgasmus** [ɔr'gasmʊs] *m* (-; *-men*) or-

gasm

**Orgel** ['ɔrgəl] *f* (-; *-n*) MUS organ

'**Orgelpfeife** *f* MUS organ pipe

**Orgie** ['ɔrgjə] *f* (-; *-n*) orgy

**Orientale** [orjɛn'ta:lə] *m* (*-n*; *-n*), **Orien'talin** *f* (-; *-nen*), **orien'talisch** *adj* oriental

**orientieren** [orjɛn'ti:rən] *v/t* (*no -ge-*, *h*) inform (***über*** *acc* about), brief (on); ***sich ~*** orient(ate) o.s. (*a. fig*) (***nach*** by); inform o.s.; **Orien'tierung** *f* (-; *no pl*) orientation, *fig a.* information; ***die ~ verlieren*** lose one's bearings

**Orien'tierungssinn** *m* (-[*e*]*s*; *no pl*) sense of direction

**original** [origi'na:l] *adj* original; real, genuine; TV live; **Origi'nal** *n* (*-s*; *-e*) original; *fig* real (*or* quite a) character

**Origi'nal...** *in cpds ...aufnahme*, *...ausgabe etc*: original ...; **~übertragung** *f* live broadcast *or* program(me)

**originell** [origi'nɛl] *adj* original; ingenious; witty

**Orkan** [ɔr'ka:n] *m* (-[*e*]*s*; *-e*) hurricane

**or'kanartig** *adj* violent; *fig* thunderous

**Ort** [ɔrt] *m* (-[*e*]*s*; *-e*) place; village, (small) town; spot, point; scene; ***vor ~*** *mining*: at the (pit) face; *fig* in the field, on the spot

**orten** ['ɔrtən] *v/t* (*ge-*, *h*) locate, spot

**orthodox** [ɔrto'dɔks] *adj* orthodox

**Orthographie** [ɔrtogra'fi:] *f* (-; *-n*) orthography

**Orthopäde** [ɔrto'pɛ:də] *m* (*-n*; *-n*), **Ortho'pädin** *f* (-; *-nen*) MED ortho-p(a)edic specialist

**örtlich** ['œrtlıç] *adj* local

'**Ortsbestimmung** *f* AVIAT, MAR location; LING adverb of place

'**Ortschaft** *f* → ***Ort***

'**Ortsgespräch** *n* TEL local call

'**Ortskenntnis** *f*: ***~ besitzen*** know a place

'**Ortsnetz** *n* TEL local exchange

'**Ortszeit** *f* local time

**Öse** ['ø:zə] *f* (-; *-n*) eye; eyelet

**Ostblock** ['ɔstblɔk] *m* (-[*e*]*s*; *no pl*) HIST POL East(ern) Bloc

**Osten** ['ɔstən] *m* (*-s*; *no pl*) east; POL *the* East; ***nach ~*** east(wards)

**Oster|ei** ['o:stɐˀai] *n* Easter egg; **~hase** *m* Easter bunny *or* rabbit

**Ostern** ['o:stɐn] *n* (-; -) Easter (***zu, an*** at); ***frohe ~!*** Happy Easter!

**Österreicher** ['ø:stəraiçɐ] *m* (*-s*; -), '**Österreicherin** ['ø:stəraiçərın] *f* (-; *-nen*), '**österreichisch** *adj* Austrian

**östlich** ['œstlıç] **1.** *adj* east(ern); easterly **2.** *adv*: ***~ von*** (to the) east of

**ostwärts** ['ɔstvɛrts] *adv* east(wards)

'**Ostwind** *m* east wind

**Otter** ['ɔtɐ] zo **1.** *m* (*-s*; -) otter **2.** *f* (-; *-n*) adder, viper

**outen** ['autən] *v/t* (*ge-*, *h*) out

**Ouvertüre** [uvɛr'ty:rə] *f* (-; *-n*) MUS overture

**oval** [o'va:l] adj, **O'val** *n* (*-s*; *-e*) oval

**Oxid** [ɔ'ksi:t] *n* (-[*e*]*s*; *-e* [ɔ'ksi:də]) CHEM oxide; **oxidieren** [ɔksi'di:rən] *v/t* (*no -ge-*, *h*) *and v/i* (*h*, *sein*) CHEM oxidize; **Oxyd** *n* → ***Oxid***

**Ozean** ['o:tsea:n] *m* (*-s*; *-e*) ocean, sea

**Ozon** [o'tso:n] *n* (*-s*; *no pl*) CHEM ozone

**o'zonfreundlich** *adj* ozone-friendly

**O'zon|loch** *n* ozone hole; **~schicht** *f* ozone layer; **~schild** *m* ozone shield; **~werte** *pl* ozone levels

# P

**paar** [pa:ɐ] *indef pron*: ***ein ~*** a few, some, F a couple of; ***ein ~ Mal*** a few times

**Paar** *n* (-[*e*]*s*; *-e*) pair; couple; ***ein ~ (neue) Schuhe*** a (new) pair of shoes

**paaren** ['pa:rən] *v/t and v/refl* (*ge-*, *h*) zo mate; *fig* combine

'**Paarlauf** *m* SPORT pair skating

'**Paarung** *f* (-; *-en*) zo mating, copulation; SPORT matching

'**paarweise** *adv* in pairs, in twos

**Pacht** [paxt] *f* (-; *-en*) lease; rent

'**pachten** *v/t* (*ge-*, *h*) (take on) lease

**Pächter** ['pɛçtɐ] *m* (*-s*; -), '**Pächterin** *f* (-; *-nen*) leaseholder; AGR tenant

'**Pacht|vertrag** *m* lease; **~zins** *m* rent

**Pack**[1] [pak] *m* → ***Packen***

**Pack**[2] *contp n* (-[*e*]*s*; *no pl*) rabble

**Päckchen** ['pɛkçən] *n* (*-s*; -) pack, *Br*

packet; small parcel; **packen** ['pakən] *v/t and v/i* (*ge-, h*) pack; make up (*parcel etc*); grab, seize (***an*** *dat* by); *fig* grip; '**Packen** *m* (*-s; -*) pack, pile (*a. fig*); **Packer** ['pakɐ] *m* (*-s; -*) packer; removal man; '**Packpa,pier** *n* packing *or* brown paper; '**Packung** *f* (*-; -en*) package, box; pack, *Br* packet

**Pädagoge** [pɛda'go:gə] *m* (*-n; -n*), **Päda'gogin** *f* (*-; -nen*) teacher; education(al)ist

**päda'gogisch** *adj* pedagogic, educational; ***~e Hochschule*** college of education

**Paddel** ['padəl] *n* (*-s; -*) paddle

'**Paddelboot** *n* canoe

'**paddeln** *v/i* (*ge-, h, sein*) paddle, canoe

**Page** ['pa:ʒə] *m* (*-n; -n*) page(boy)

**Paket** [pa'ke:t] *n* (*-[e]s; -e*) package; parcel; **~karte** *f* parcel post slip, *Br* parcel mailing form; **~post** *f* parcel post; **~schalter** *m* parcel counter; **~zustellung** *f* parcel delivery

**Pakt** [pakt] *m* (*-[e]s; -e*) POL pact

**Palast** [pa'last] *m* (*-[e]s; Paläste* [pa'lɛstə]) palace

**Palme** ['palmə] *f* (*-; -n*) BOT palm (tree)

**Palm'sonntag** *m* REL Palm Sunday

**Pampelmuse** ['pampəlmu:zə] *f* (*-; -n*) BOT grapefruit

**paniert** [pa'ni:ɐt] *adj* GASTR breaded

**Panik** ['pa:nɪk] *f* (*-; -en*) panic; ***in ~ geraten*** (***versetzen***) panic; ***in ~*** panic-stricken, F panicky; **panisch** ['pa:nɪʃ] *adj*: ***~e Angst*** mortal terror

**Panne** ['panə] *f* (*-; -n*) breakdown, MOT *a.* engine trouble; *fig* mishap

'**Pannenhilfe** *f* MOT breakdown service

**Panter, Panther** ['pantɐ] *m* (*-s; -*) ZO panther

**Pantoffel** [pan'tɔfəl] *m* (*-s; -n*) slipper; **~held** F *m* henpecked husband

**Pantomime** [panto'mi:mə] THEA **1.** *f* (*-; -n*) mime, dumb show **2.** *m* (*-n; -n*) mime (artist); **panto'mimisch** *adv*: ***~ darstellen*** mime

**Panzer** ['pantsɐ] *m* (*-s; -*) armo(u)r (*a. fig*); MIL tank; ZO shell; **~glas** *n* bulletproof glass

'**panzern** *v/t* (*ge-, h*) armo(u)r; → ***gepanzert***

'**Panzerschrank** *m* safe

**Panzerung** ['pantsərʊŋ] *f* (*-; -en*) armo(u)r plating

**Papa** [pa'pa:] F *m* (*-s; -s*) dad(dy), pa

**Papagei** [papa'gai] *m* (*-en; -en*) ZO parrot

**Papeterie** [papɛtə'ri:] *Swiss f* (*-; -n*) stationer('s shop)

**Papier** [pa'pi:ɐ] *n* (*-s; -e*) paper; *pl* papers, documents; identification (paper)

**Pa'pier...** *in cpds ...geld, ...handtuch, ...serviette, ...tüte etc*: *mst* paper ...; **~geschäft** *n* stationer('s store, *Br* shop); **~korb** *m* wastepaper basket; **~krieg** F *m* red tape; **~schnitzel** *pl* scraps of paper; **~waren** *pl* stationery

**Pappe** ['papə] *f* (*-; -n*) cardboard, pasteboard

**Pappel** ['papəl] *f* (*-; -n*) BOT poplar

'**Papp|kar,ton** *m* cardboard box, carton; **~teller** *m* paper plate

**Paprika** ['paprika] *m* (*-s; -[s]*) BOT sweet pepper; (*no pl*) GASTR paprika

**Papst** [pa:pst] *m* (*-[e]s; Päpste* ['pɛ:pstə]) pope; '**päpstlich** *adj* papal

**Parade** [pa'ra:də] *f* (*-; -n*) parade; *soccer etc*: save; *boxing, fencing*: parry

**Paradeiser** [para'daizɐ] *Austrian m* (*-s; -*) BOT tomato

**Paradies** [para'di:s] *n* (*-es; -e*) paradise

**paradiesisch** [para'di:zɪʃ] *fig adj* heavenly, delightful

**paradox** [para'dɔks] *adj* paradoxical

**Paragraph** [para'gra:f] *m* (*-en; -en*) JUR article, section; paragraph

**parallel** [para'le:l] adj, **Paral'lele** *f* (*-; -n*) parallel

**Parasit** [para'zi:t] *m* (*-en; -en*) parasite

**Parfüm** [par'fy:m] *n* (*-s; -s*) perfume, *Br a.* scent; **Parfümerie** [parfymə'ri:] *f* (*-; -n*) perfumery; **parfümieren** [parfy'mi:rən] *v/t* (*no -ge-, h*) perfume, scent; ***sich ~*** put on perfume

**parieren** [pa'ri:rən] *v/t and v/i* (*no -ge-, h*) SPORT parry, *fig a.* counter (***mit*** with); pull up (*horse*); obey

**Park** [park] *m* (*-s; -s*) park

**parken** ['parkən] *v/i and v/t* (*ge-, h*) MOT park; ***Parken verboten!*** no parking!

**Parkett** [par'kɛt] *n* (*-[e]s; -e, -s*) parquet (floor); THEA orchestra, *Br* stalls; dance floor

'**Park|gebühr** *f* parking fee; **~(hoch)haus** *n* parking garage, *Br* multi-storey car park

**parkieren** [par'ki:rən] *Swiss v/t and v/i*

P

→ ***parken***

**'Park|kralle** *f* wheel clamp; **~lücke** *f* parking space; **~platz** *m* parking lot, *Br* car park; → ***Parklücke***; ***e-n ~ suchen*** (***finden***) look for (find) somewhere to park the car; **~scheibe** *f* parking disk (*Br* disc); **~sünder** *m* parking offender; **~uhr** *f* MOT parking meter; **~wächter** *m* park keeper; MOT parking lot (*Br* car park) attendant

**Parlament** [parla'mɛnt] *n* (-[*e*]*s*; -*e*) parliament; **parlamentarisch** [parlamɛn'ta:rɪʃ] *adj* parliamentary

**Parodie** [paro'di:] *f* (-; -*n*), **paro'dieren** *v/t* (*no -ge-, h*) parody

**Parole** [pa'ro:lə] *f* (-*n*; -*n*) MIL password; *fig* watchword, POL *a.* slogan

**Partei** [par'tai] *f* (-; -*en*) party (*a.* POL); ***j-s ~ ergreifen*** take sides with s.o., side with s.o.; **par'teiisch** *adj* partial (***für*** to); prejudiced (***gegen*** against)

**par'teilos** *adj* POL independent

**Par'tei|mitglied** *n* POL party member; **~pro,gramm** *n* POL platform; **~tag** *m* POL convention; **~zugehörigkeit** *f* POL party membership

**Parterre** [par'tɛrə] *n* (-*s*; -*s*) first (*Br* ground) floor

**Partie** [par'ti:] *f* (-; -*n*) game, SPORT *a.* match; part, passage (*a.* MUS); ***e-e gute*** *etc* ***~ sein*** be a good *etc* match

**Partisan** [parti'za:n] *m* (-*s*; -*en*; -*en*), **Parti'sanin** *f* (-; -*nen*) MIL partisan, guerilla

**Partitur** [parti'tu:ɐ] *f* (-; -*en*) MUS score

**Partizip** [parti'tsi:p] *n* (-*s*; -*ien*) LING participle

**Partner** ['partnɐ] *m* (-*s*; -), **'Partnerin** *f* (-; -*nen*) partner

**'Partnerschaft** *f* (-; -*en*) partnership

**'Partnerstadt** *f* twin town

**paschen** ['paʃən] *Austrian v/t and v/i* (*ge-, h*) smuggle; **Pascher** ['paʃɐ] *Austrian m* (-*s*; -) smuggler

**Pass** [pas] *m* (-*es*; *Pässe* ['pɛsə]) passport; SPORT, GEOGR pass; ***langer ~*** SPORT long ball

**Passage** [pa'sa:ʒə] *f* (-; -*n*) passage

**Passagier** [pasa'ʒi:ɐ] *m* (-*s*; -*e*) passenger; **~flugzeug** *n* passenger plane; airliner

**Passa'gierin** *f* (-; -*nen*) passenger

**Passah** ['pasa] *n* (-*s*; *no pl*), **'Passahfest** *n* REL Passover

**Passant** [pa'sant] *m* (-*en*; -*en*), **Pas'santin** *f* (-; -*nen*) passerby

**'Passbild** *n* passport photo(graph)

**passen** ['pasən] *v/i* (*ge-, h*) fit (***j-m*** s.o.; ***auf*** *or* ***für*** *or* ***zu et.*** s.th.); suit (***j-m*** s.o.), be convenient; *cards*, SPORT pass; ***~ zu*** go with, match; ***sie ~ gut zueinander*** they are well suited to each other; ***passt es Ihnen morgen?*** would tomorrow suit you *or* be all right (with you)?; ***das*** (***es***) ***passt mir gar nicht*** I don't like that (him) at all; ***das passt*** (***nicht***) ***zu ihm*** that's just like him (not like him, not his style); **~d** *adj* fitting; matching; suitable, right

**passierbar** [pa'si:ɐba:ɐ] *adj* passable

**passieren** [pa'si:rən] (*no -ge-*) **1.** *v/i* (*sein*) happen **2.** *v/t* (*h*) pass (through)

**Pas'sierschein** *m* pass, permit

**Passion** [pa'sjo:n] *f* (-; -*en*) passion; REL Passion

**passiv** ['pasi:f] *adj* passive

**'Passiv** *n* (-*s*; *no pl*) LING passive (voice)

**Paste** ['pastə] *f* (-; -*n*) paste

**Pastell** [pas'tɛl] *n* (-[*e*]*s*; -*e*) PAINT pastel

**Pastete** [pas'te:tə] *f* (-; -*n*) GASTR pie

**Pate** ['pa:tə] *m* (-*n*; -*n*) godfather; **'Patenkind** *n* godchild

**'Patenschaft** *f* (-; -*en*) sponsorship

**Patent** [pa'tɛnt] *n* (-[*e*]*s*; -*e*) patent; MIL commission; **~amt** *n* patent office; **~anwalt** *m* JUR patent agent

**patentieren** [patɛn'ti:rən] *v/t* (*no -ge-, h*) patent; (***sich***) ***et. ~ lassen*** take out a patent for s.th.

**Pa'tentinhaber** *m* patentee

**pathetisch** [pa'te:tɪʃ] *adj* pompous

**Patient** [pa'tsjɛnt] *m* (-*en*; -*en*), **Pa'tientin** *f* (-; -*nen*) MED patient

**Patin** ['pa:tɪn] *f* (-; -*nen*) godmother

**Patriot** [patri'o:t] *m* (-*en*; -*en*) patriot

**patri'otisch** *adj* patriotic

**Patrone** [pa'tro:nə] *f* (-; -*n*) cartridge

**Patrouille** [pa'trʊljə] *f* (-; -*n*) MIL patrol; **patroullieren** [patrʊl'ji:rən] *v/i* (*no -ge-, h*) MIL patrol

**Patsche** ['patʃə] F *f*: ***in der ~ sitzen*** be in a fix *or* jam

**'patschen** F *v/i* (*ge-, h*) (s)plash

**'patsch'nass** *adj* soaking wet

**patzen** ['patsən] F *v/i* (*ge-, h*), **Patzer** ['patsɐ] F *m* (-*s*; -) blunder

**Pauke** ['paukə] *f* (-; -*n*) MUS bass drum; kettledrum

P

'**pauken** F *v/i and v/t* (*ge-*, *h*) cram
**Pauschale** [pau'ʃaːlə] *f* (-; *-n*) lump sum
**Pau'schal|gebühr** *f* flat rate; **~reise** *f* package tour; **~urteil** *n* sweeping judg(e)ment
**Pause**[1] ['pauzə] *f* (-; *-n*) recess, *Br* break, *esp* THEA, SPORT intermission, *Br* interval; pause; rest (*a.* MUS)
'**Pause**[2] *f* (-; *-n*) TECH tracing
'**pausen** *v/t* (*ge-*, *h*) TECH trace
'**pausenlos** *adj* uninterrupted, nonstop
'**Pausenzeichen** *n radio*: interval signal; PED bell
**pausieren** [pau'ziːrən] *v/i* (*no -ge-*, *h*) pause, rest
**Pavian** ['paːvjaːn] *m* (*-s*; *-e*) zo baboon
**Pavillon** ['pavɪljɔŋ] *m* (*-s*; *-s*) pavilion
**Pazifist** [patsi'fɪst] *m* (*-en*; *-en*), **Pazi'fistin** *f* (-; *-nen*), **pazi'fistisch** *adj* pacifist
**PC** [peː'tseː] *m* (-[*s*]; -[*s*]) *abbr of* ***personal computer*** PC
**Pech** [pɛç] *n* (*-s*; *no pl*) pitch; F bad luck; **~strähne** F *f* run of bad luck; **~vogel** F *m* unlucky fellow
**pedantisch** [pe'dantɪʃ] *adj* pedantic, fussy
**Pegel** ['peːgəl] *m* (*-s*; -) level (*a. fig*)
**peilen** ['pailən] *v/t* (*ge-*, *h*) sound
**peinigen** ['painɪgən] *v/t* (*ge-*, *h*) torment
**Peiniger** ['painɪgɐ] *m* (*-s*; -) tormentor
**peinlich** ['painlɪç] *adj* embarrassing; ***~ genau*** meticulous (***bei, in*** *dat* in); ***es war mir ~*** I was *or* felt embarrassed
**Peitsche** ['paitʃə] *f* (-; *-n*), '**peitschen** *v/t* (*ge-*, *h*) whip
'**Peitschenhieb** *m* lash
**Pelle** ['pɛlə] *f* (-; *-n*) skin; peel; '**pellen** *v/t* (*ge-*, *h*) peel; '**Pellkar,toffeln** *pl* potatoes (boiled) in their jackets
**Pelz** [pɛlts] *m* (*-es*; *-e*) fur; skin
'**pelzgefüttert** *adj* fur-lined
'**Pelzgeschäft** *n* fur(rier's) store (*Br* shop)
**pelzig** ['pɛltsɪç] *adj* furry; MED furred
'**Pelzmantel** *m* fur coat
'**Pelztiere** *pl* furred animals, furs
**Pendel** ['pɛndəl] *n* (*-s*; -) pendulum
'**pendeln** *v/i* (*ge-*, *h*) swing; RAIL *etc* shuttle; commute
'**Pendeltür** *f* swing door
'**Pendelverkehr** *m* RAIL *etc* shuttle service; commuter traffic; **Pendler(in)** ['pɛndlɐ, 'pɛndlərɪn] *m(f)* (*-s*; *-/-*; *-nen*) RAIL *etc* commuter
**Penis** ['peːnɪs] *m* (*-s*; *-se*) ANAT penis
**Penner** ['pɛnɐ] F *m* (*-s*; -) tramp, bum
**Pension** [pa͂'sjoːn] *f* (-; *-en*) (old age) pension; boarding-house, private hotel; ***in ~ sein*** be retired; **Pensionär(in)** [pa͂sjo'nɛːɐ, pa͂sjo'nɛːrɪn] *m(f)* (*-s*; *-e*/-; *-nen*) (old age) pensioner; boarder; **Pensionat** [pa͂sjo'naːt] *n* (-[*e*]*s*; *-e*) boarding school
**pensionieren** [pa͂sjo'niːrən] *v/t* (*no -ge-*, *h*) pension (off); ***sich ~ lassen*** retire; **Pensio'nierung** *f* (-; *-en*) retirement
**Pensionist** [pa͂sjo'nɪst] *Austrian, Swiss m* (*-en*; *-en*) (old age) pensioner
**Pensi'onsgast** *m* boarder
**Pensum** ['pɛnzʊm] *n* (*-s*; *Pensen*, *Pensa*) (work) quota, stint
**per** [pɛr] *prp* (*acc*) per; by
**perfekt** [pɛr'fɛkt] *adj* perfect; ***~ machen*** settle
'**Perfekt** *n* (*-s*; *-e*) LING present perfect
**Pergament** [pɛrga'mɛnt] *n* (-[*e*]*s*; *-e*) parchment
**Periode** [pe'rjoːdə] *f* (-; *-n*) period, MED *a.* menstruation
**periodisch** [pe'rjoːdɪʃ] *adj* periodic(al)
**Peripherie** [perife'riː] *f* (-; *-n*) periphery, outskirts; **~geräte** *pl* IT peripheral equipment
**Perle** ['pɛrlə] *f* (-; *-n*) pearl; bead
'**perlen** *v/i* (*ge-*, *h*) sparkle, bubble
'**Perlenkette** *f* pearl necklace
'**Perlmuschel** *f* zo pearl oyster
**Perlmutt** ['pɛrlmʊt] *n* (*-s*; *no pl*) mother-of-pearl
**Perron** [pɛ'ro͂ː] *m* (*-s*; *-s*) *Swiss* platform
**Perser** ['pɛrzɐ] *m* (*-s*; -) Persian; Persian carpet; **Perserin** ['pɛrzərɪn] *f* (-; *-nen*) Persian (woman); **Persien** ['pɛrzjən] Persia; **persisch** ['pɛrzɪʃ] *adj* Persian
**Person** [pɛr'zoːn] *f* (-; *-en*) person, THEA *etc a.* character; ***ein Tisch für drei ~en*** a table for three
**Personal** [pɛrzo'naːl] *n* (*-s*; *no pl*) staff, personnel; ***zu wenig ~ haben*** be understaffed; **~abbau** *m* staff reduction; **~abteilung** *f* personnel department; **~ausweis** *m* identity card; **~chef** *m* staff manager
**Personalien** [pɛrzo'naːljən] *pl* particulars, personal data

P

**Perso'nalpro͵nomen** *n* LING personal pronoun

**Per'sonen|(kraft)wagen** (*abbr* ***PKW***) *m* (*Br a.* motor)car, auto(mobile); **~zug** *m* passenger train; local *or* commuter train

**personifizieren** [pɛrzonifi'tsiːrən] *v/t* (*no -ge-, h*) personify

**persönlich** [pɛr'zøːnlɪç] *adj* personal

**Per'sönlichkeit** *f* (-; *-en*) personality

**Perücke** [pe'rʏkə] *f* (-; *-n*) wig

**pervers** [pɛr'vɛrs] *adj* perverted; ***~er Mensch*** pervert

**Pessimismus** [pɛsi'mɪsmʊs] *m* (-; *no pl*) pessimism; **Pessimist(in)** [pɛsi'mɪst(ɪn)] (*-en; -en/-; -nen*) pessimist; **pessi'mistisch** *adj* pessimistic

**Pest** [pɛst] *f* (-; *no pl*) MED plague

**Pestizid** [pɛsti'tsiːt] *n* (*-s; -e*) pesticide

**Petersilie** [peːtɐ'ziːljə] *f* (-; *-n*) BOT parsley

**Petroleum** [pe'troːleʊm] *n* (*-s; no pl*) kerosene, *Br* paraffin; **~lampe** *f* kerosene (*Br* paraffin) lamp

**petzen** ['pɛtsən] F *v/i* (*ge-, h*) tell tales, *Br a.* sneak

**Pfad** [pfaːt] *m* (*-[e]s; -e* ['pfaːdə]) path, track; **~finder** *m* boy scout; **~finderin** ['pfaːtfɪndərɪn] *f* (-; *-nen*) girl scout, *Br* girl guide

**Pfahl** [pfaːl] *m* (*-[e]s; Pfähle* ['pfɛːlə]) stake; post; pole

**Pfand** [pfant] *n* (*-[e]s; Pfänder* ['pfɛndɐ]) security; pawn, pledge; deposit; forfeit

**'Pfandbrief** *m* ECON mortgage bond

**pfänden** ['pfɛndən] *v/t* (*ge-, h*) seize

**'Pfandhaus** *n* → ***Leihhaus***

**Pfandleiher** ['pfantlaiɐ] *m* (*-s; -*) pawnbroker

**'Pfandschein** *m* pawn ticket

**'Pfändung** *f* (-; *-en*) JUR seizure

**Pfanne** ['pfanə] *f* (-; *-n*) pan, skillet

**'Pfannkuchen** *m* pancake

**Pfarrbezirk** ['pfarbətsɪrk] *m* parish

**Pfarrer** ['pfarɐ] *m* (*-s; -*) vicar; pastor; (parish) priest

**'Pfarr|gemeinde** *f* parish; **~haus** *n* parsonage; rectory, vicarage; **~kirche** *f* parish church

**Pfau** [pfau] *m* (*-[e]s; -en*) ZO peacock

**Pfeffer** ['pfɛfɐ] *m* (*-s; -*) pepper; **~kuchen** *m* gingerbread; **~minze** ['pfɛfɐmɪntsə] *f* (-; *no pl*) BOT peppermint

**'pfeffern** *v/t* (*ge-, h*) pepper

**'Pfefferstreuer** *m* (*-s; -*) pepper caster

**pfeffrig** ['pfɛfrɪç] *adj* peppery

**Pfeife** ['pfaifə] *f* (-; *-n*) whistle; pipe (*a.* MUS); **'pfeifen** *v/i and v/t* (*irr, ge-, h*) whistle (***j-m*** to s.o.); F ***~ auf*** (*acc*) not give a damn about

**Pfeil** [pfail] *m* (*-[e]s; -e*) arrow

**Pfeiler** ['pfailɐ] *m* (*-s; -*) pillar; pier

**Pfennig** ['pfɛnɪç] *m* (*-s; -e*) *hist* (*former monetary unit of Germany*) pfennig; *fig* penny

**Pferch** [pfɛrç] *m* (*-[e]s; -e*) fold, pen

**'pferchen** *v/t* (*ge-, h*) cram (***in*** *acc* into)

**Pferd** [pfeːɐrt] *n* (*-[e]s; -e*) ZO horse (*a.* SPORT); ***zu ~e*** on horseback

**Pferde|geschirr** ['pfeːɐdəgəʃɪr] *n* harness; **~koppel** *f* paddock; **~rennen** *n* horserace; **~stall** *m* stable; **~stärke** *f* TECH horsepower; **~wagen** *m* (horse-drawn) carriage

**pfiff** [pfɪf] *pret of* ***pfeifen***

**Pfiff** *m* (*-[e]s; -e*) whistle

**pfiffig** ['pfɪçɪç] *adj* smart

**Pfingsten** ['pfɪŋstən] *n* (-; -) REL Pentecost, *Br* Whitsun (***zu, an*** at)

**Pfingst'montag** *m* REL Whit Monday

**'Pfingstrose** *f* BOT peony

**Pfingst'sonntag** *m* REL Pentecost, *Br* Whit Sunday

**Pfirsich** ['pfɪrzɪç] *m* (*-s; -e*) BOT peach

**Pflanze** ['pflantsə] *f* (-; *-n*) plant; ***~n fressend*** ZO herbivorous

**'pflanzen** *v/t* (*ge-, h*) plant

**'Pflanzenfett** *n* vegetable fat

**'pflanzlich** *adj* vegetable

**'Pflanzung** *f* (-; *-en*) plantation

**Pflaster** ['pflastɐ] *n* (*-s; -*) pavement; MED Band-Aid®, *Br* plaster

**'pflastern** *v/t* (*ge-, h*) pave

**'Pflasterstein** *m* paving stone

**Pflaume** ['pflaumə] *f* (-; *-n*) BOT plum

**Pflege** ['pfleːgə] *f* (-; *no pl*) care; MED nursing; *fig* cultivation; TECH maintenance; ***j-n in ~ nehmen*** take s.o. into one's care; **~...** *in cpds ...eltern, ...kind, ...sohn etc*: foster ...; *...heim, ...kosten, ...personal etc*: nursing ...

**'pflegebedürftig** *adj* needing care

**'Pflegefall** *m* constant-care patient

**'pflegeleicht** *adj* wash-and-wear, easy-care

**'pflegen** *v/t* (*ge-, h*) care for, look after, *esp* MED *a.* nurse; TECH maintain; *fig* cultivate; keep up (*custom etc*); **sie pflegte zu sagen** she used to *or* would say; **Pfleger** ['pfle:gɐ] *m* (-*s*; -) male nurse; **Pflegerin** ['pfle:gərɪn] *f* (-; -*nen*) nurse; '**Pflegestelle** *f* nursing place

**Pflicht** [pflɪçt] *f* (-; -*en*) duty (**gegen** to); SPORT compulsory events

'**pflichtbewusst** *adj* conscientious

'**Pflicht|bewusstsein** *n* sense of duty; **~erfüllung** *f* performance of one's duty; **~fach** *n* PED compulsory subject

'**pflicht|gemäß**, **~getreu** *adj* dutiful; **~vergessen** *adv*: **~ handeln** neglect one's duty

'**Pflichtversicherung** *f* compulsory insurance

**Pflock** ['pflɔk] *m* (-[*e*]*s*; *Pflöcke* ['pflœkə]) peg, pin; plug

**pflücken** ['pflʏkən] *v/t* (*ge-*, *h*) pick, gather

**Pflug** [pflu:k] *m* (-[*e*]*s*; *Pflüge* ['pfly:gə]), **pflügen** ['pfly:gən] *v/t and v/i* (*ge-*, *h*) plow, *Br* plough

**Pforte** ['pfɔrtə] *f* (-; -*n*) gate, door, entrance; **Pförtner** ['pfœrtnɐ] *m* (-*s*; -) doorman, doorkeeper, porter

**Pfosten** ['pfɔstən] *m* (-*s*; -) post

**Pfote** ['pfo:tə] *f* (-; -*n*) ZO paw (*a.* F)

**pfropfen** ['pfrɔpfən] *v/t* (*ge-*, *h*) stopper; cork; plug; AGR graft; F cram, stuff

'**Pfropfen** *m* (-*s*; -) stopper; cork; plug; MED clot

**pfui** [pfui] *int* ugh!; *audience*: boo!

**Pfund** [pfʊnt] *n* (-[*e*]*s*; -*e* ['pfʊndə]) pound (*453,59 g*); pound (sterling); **10 ~** ten pounds

'**pfundweise** *adv* by the pound

**pfuschen** ['pfʊʃən] F *v/i* (*ge-*, *h*), **Pfuscherei** [pfʊʃə'rai] F *f* (-; -*en*) bungle, botch

**Pfütze** ['pfʏtsə] *f* (-; -*n*) puddle, pool

**Phänomen** [fɛno'me:n] *n* (-*s*; -*e*) phenomenon; **phänomenal** [fɛnome'na:l] *adj* phenomenal

**Phantasie** *etc* → ***Fantasie*** *etc*

**pharmazeutisch** [farma'tsɔʏtɪʃ] *adj* pharmaceutic(al)

**Phase** ['fa:zə] *f* (-; -*n*) phase (*a.* ELECTR), stage

**Philosoph** [filo'zo:f] *m* (-*en*; -*en*) philosopher; **Philosophie** [filozo'fi:] *f* (-; -*n*) philosophy; **philosophieren** [filozo'fi:rən] *v/i* (*no -ge-*, *h*) philosophize (**über** *acc* on); **Philo'sophin** *f* (-; -*nen*) (woman) philosopher; **philosophisch** [filo'zo:fɪʃ] *adj* philosophical

**phlegmatisch** [flɛ'gma:tɪʃ] *adj* phlegmatic

**Phonetik** [fo'ne:tɪk] *f* (-; *no pl*) phonetics; **pho'netisch** *adj* phonetic

**Phosphor** ['fɔsfo:ɐ] *m* (-*s*; -*e*) CHEM phosphorus

**Photo...** → ***Foto...***

**Phrase** ['fra:zə] *contp f* (-; -*n*) cliché (phrase)

**Physik** [fy'zi:k] *f* (-; *no pl*) physics

**physikalisch** [fyzi'ka:lɪʃ] *adj* physical

**Physiker** ['fy:zikɐ] *m* (-*s*; -), '**Physikerin** *f* (-; -*nen*) physicist

**physisch** ['fy:zɪʃ] *adj* physical

**Pianist** [pja'nɪst] *m* (-*en*; -*en*), **Pia'nistin** *f* (-; -*nen*) MUS pianist

**Piano** ['pja:no] *n* (-*s*; -*s*) MUS piano

**Picke** ['pɪkə] *f* (-; -*n*) TECH pick(axe)

**Pickel**[1] ['pɪkəl] *m* (-*s*; -) TECH pick(axe)

'**Pickel**[2] *m* (-*s*; -) MED pimple; **pickelig** ['pɪkəlɪç] *adj* MED pimpled, pimply

**picken** ['pɪkən] *v/i and v/t* (*ge-*, *h*) ZO peck, pick

**Picknick** ['pɪknɪk] *n* (-*s*; -*e*, -*s*) picnic

'**picknicken** *v/i* (*ge-*, *h*) (have a) picnic

**piekfein** ['pi:kfain] F *adj* posh

**piep(s)en** ['pi:p(s)ən] *v/i* (*ge-*, *h*) chirp, cheep; ELECTR bleep

**Pietät** [pje'tɛ:t] *f* (-; *no pl*) reverence; piety; **pie'tätlos** *adj* irreverent; **pie'tätvoll** *adj* reverent

**Pik** [pi:k] *n* (-[*s*]; -[*s*]) *cards*: spade(s)

**pikant** [pi'kant] *adj* piquant, spicy (*both a. fig*)

**Pilger** ['pɪlgɐ] *m* (-*s*; -) pilgrim; '**Pilgerfahrt** *f* pilgrimage; '**Pilgerin** *f* (-; -*nen*) pilgrim; '**pilgern** *v/i* (*ge-*, *sein*) (go on a) pilgrimage

**Pille** ['pɪlə] *f* (-; -*n*) pill; F ***die ~ nehmen*** be on the pill

**Pilot** [pi'lo:t] *m* (-*en*; -*en*), **Pi'lotin** *f* (-; -*nen*) pilot

**Pilz** [pɪlts] *m* (-*es*; -*e*) BOT mushroom (*a. fig*); toadstool; MED fungus; ***~e suchen*** (***gehen***) go mushrooming

**Pinguin** ['pɪŋgui:n] *m* (-*s*; -*e*) ZO penguin

**pinkeln** ['pɪŋkəln] F *v/i* (*ge-*, *h*) (have a) pee, piddle

**Pinsel** ['pɪnzəl] *m* (-*s*; -) (paint)brush

P

'**Pinselstrich** *m* brushstroke
**Pinzette** [pɪn'tsɛtə] *f* (-; *-n*) tweezers
**Pionier** [pjo'niːɐ] *m* (*-s*; *-e*) pioneer, MIL *a.* engineer
**Pirat** [pi'raːt] *m* (*-en*; *-en*) pirate
**Pisse** ['pɪsə] V *f* (-; *no pl*), '**pissen** V *v/i* (*ge-*, *h*) piss
**Piste** ['pɪstə] *f* (-; *-n*) course; AVIAT runway
**Pistole** [pɪs'toːlə] *f* (-; *-n*) pistol, gun
**Pkw, PKW** ['peːkaːveː] *abbr of* ***Personenkraftwagen*** (*Br a.* motor)car, automobile
**Plache** ['plaxə] *Austrian f* (-; *-n*) awning, tarpaulin
**placieren** *etc* → ***platzieren*** *etc*
**plädieren** [plɛ'diːrən] *v/i* (*no -ge-*, *h*) JUR plead (***für*** for); **Plädoyer** [plɛdoa'jeː] *n* (*-s*; *-s*) JUR final speech, pleading
**Plage** ['plaːgə] *f* (-; *-n*) trouble, misery; plague; nuisance, F pest; '**plagen** *v/t* (*ge-*, *h*) trouble; bother; pester; ***sich ~*** toil, drudge
**Plakat** [pla'kaːt] *n* (-[*e*]*s*; *-e*) poster, placard, bill
**Plakette** [pla'kɛtə] *f* (-; *-n*) plaque, badge
**Plan** [plaːn] *m* (-[*e*]*s*; *Pläne* ['plɛːnə]) plan; intention
**Plane** ['plaːnə] *f* (-; *-n*) awning, tarpaulin
'**planen** *v/t* (*ge-*, *h*) plan, make plans for
**Planet** [pla'neːt] *m* (*-en*; *-en*) ASTR planet
**planieren** [pla'niːrən] *v/t* (*no -ge-*, *h*) TECH level, plane, grade
**Planke** ['plaŋkə] *f* (-; *-n*) plank, (thick) board
**plänkeln** ['plɛŋkəln] *v/i* (*ge-*, *h*) skirmish
'**planlos** *adj* without plan; aimless
'**planmäßig 1.** *adj* scheduled (*arrival etc*) **2.** *adv* according to plan
**Plan(t)schbecken** ['planʃbɛkən] *n* paddling pool
**plan(t)schen** ['planʃən] *v/i* (*ge-*, *h*) splash
**Plantage** [plan'taːʒə] *f* (-; *-n*) plantation
**Plappermaul** ['plapɐmaul] F *n* chatterbox
**plappern** ['plapɐn] F *v/i* (*ge-*, *h*) chatter, prattle, babble, jabber
**plärren** ['plɛrən] F *v/i and v/t* (*ge-*, *h*) blubber; bawl; *radio*: blare
**Plastik**[1] ['plastɪk] *f* (-; *-en*) sculpture
'**Plastik**[2] *n* (*-s*; *no pl*) plastic; ***~...*** *in cpds ...besteck etc*: plastic ...
**plastisch** ['plastɪʃ] *adj* plastic; three-dimensional; *fig* graphic
**Platin** ['plaːtiːn] *n* (*-s*; *no pl*) platinum
**plätschern** ['plɛtʃɐn] *v/i* (*ge-*, *h*) ripple (*a. fig*), splash
**platt** [plat] *adj* flat, level, even; *fig* trite; F flabbergasted
**Platte** ['platə] *f* (-; *-n*) sheet, plate; slab; board; panel; MUS record, disk, *Br* disc; IT disk; GASTR dish; F bald pate; ***kalte ~*** GASTR plate of cold cuts (*Br* meats)
**plätten** ['plɛtən] *v/t* (*ge-*, *h*) iron, press
'**Platten|spieler** *m* record player; **~teller** *m* turntable
'**Plattform** *f* platform
'**Plattfuß** *m* MED flat foot
'**Plattheit** *fig f* (-; *-en*) triviality; platitude
**Plättli** ['plɛtli] *Swiss n* (*-s*; *-s*) tile
**Platz** [plats] *m* (*-es*; *Plätze* ['plɛtsə]) place, spot; site; room, space; square; circus; seat; ***es ist*** (***nicht***) ***genug ~*** there's (there isn't) enough room; ***~ machen für*** make room for; make way for; ***~ nehmen*** take a seat, sit down; ***ist dieser ~ noch frei?*** is this seat taken?; ***j-n vom ~ stellen*** SPORT send s.o. off; ***auf eigenem ~*** SPORT at home; ***auf die Plätze, fertig, los!*** SPORT on your marks, get set, go!
'**Platz|anweiser** *m* (*-s*; -) usher; **~anweiserin** *f* (-; *-nen*) usherette
**Plätzchen** ['plɛtsçən] *n* (*-s*; -) (little) place, spot; GASTR cookie, *Br* biscuit
**platzen** ['platsən] *v/i* (*ge-*, *sein*) burst (*a. fig*); crack, split; explode (*a. fig* ***vor*** *dat* with), blow up; F come to grief *or* nothing, fall through, blow up, *sl* go phut; break up
**platzieren** [pla'tsiːrən] *v/t* (*no -ge-*, *h*) place; ***sich ~*** SPORT be placed
**Plat'zierung** *f* (-; *-en*) place, placing
'**Platzkarte** *f* reservation (ticket)
**Plätzli** ['plɛtsli] *Swiss n* (*-s*; -) cutlet
'**Platz|pa,trone** *f* blank (cartridge); **~regen** *m* cloudburst, downpour; **~reser,vierung** *f* seat reservation; **~verweis** *m*: ***e-n ~ erhalten*** SPORT be sent off; **~wart** *m* (*-s*; *-e*) SPORT groundkeeper, *Br* groundsman; **~wunde** *f* MED cut, laceration
**Plauderei** [plaudə'rai] *f* (-; *-en*) chat
**plaudern** ['plaudɐn] *v/i* (*ge-*, *h*) (have a) chat

P

**plauschen** ['plauʃən] *Austrian v/i* (have a) chat
**pleite** ['plaitə] F *adj* broke
'**Pleite** F *f* (-; -*n*) bankruptcy; *fig* flop; **pleitegehen** go broke
**Plombe** ['plɔmbə] *f* (-; -*n*) TECH seal; MED filling; **plombieren** [plɔm'bi:rən] *v/t* (*no -ge-*, *h*) TECH seal; MED fill
**plötzlich** ['plœtslıç] **1.** *adj* sudden **2.** *adv* suddenly, all of a sudden
**plump** [plʊmp] *adj* clumsy; **plumps** *int* thud, plop; **plumpsen** ['plʊmpsən] *v/i* (*ge-*, *sein*) thud, plop, flop
**Plunder** ['plʊndɐ] F *m* (-*s*; *no pl*) trash, junk
**Plünderer** ['plʏndərɐ] *m* (-*s*; -) looter, plunderer; **plündern** ['plʏndɐn] *v/i and v/t* (*ge-*, *h*) plunder, loot
**Plural** ['plu:ra:l] *m* (-*s*; -*e*) LING plural
**plus** [plʊs] *adv* plus
**Plusquamperfekt** ['plʊskvampɛrfɛkt] *n* (-*s*; -*e*) LING past perfect
**Pneu** [pnɔʏ] *Swiss m* (-*s*; -*s*) tire, *Br* tyre
**Po** [po:] F *m* (-*s*; -*s*) bottom, behind
**Pöbel** ['pø:bəl] *m* (-*s*; *no pl*) mob, rabble
**pochen** ['pɔxən] *v/i* (*ge-*, *h*) knock, rap (*both*: ***an*** *acc* at)
**Pocke** ['pɔkə] *f* (-; -*n*) MED pock
'**Pocken** *pl* MED smallpox; **~impfung** *f* MED smallpox vaccination
**Podest** [po'dɛst] *n*, *m* (-[*e*]*s*; -*e*) platform; *fig* pedestal
**Podium** ['po:djʊm] *n* (-*s*; -*ien*) podium, platform; '**Podiumsdiskussi͵on** *f* panel discussion
**Poesie** [poe'zi:] *f* (-; -*n*) poetry
**Poet** [po'e:t] *m* (-*en*; -*en*), **Po'etin** *f* (-; -*nen*) poet
**poetisch** [po'e:tıʃ] *adj* poetic(al)
**Pointe** ['poɛ̃:tə] *f* (-; -*n*) point, punch line
**Pokal** [po'ka:l] *m* (-*s*; -*e*) goblet; SPORT cup; **~endspiel** *n* SPORT cup final; **~sieger** *m* SPORT cup winner; **~spiel** *n* SPORT cup tie
**pökeln** ['pø:kəln] *v/t* (*ge-*, *h*) salt
**Pol** [po:l] *m* (-*s*; -*e*) GEOGR pole
**polar** [po'la:ɐ] *adj* polar
**Pole** ['po:lə] *m* (-*n*; -*n*) Pole
**Polemik** [po'le:mık] *f* (-; -*en*) polemic(s); **po'lemisch** *adj* polemic(al)
**polemisieren** [polemi'zi:rən] *v/i* (*no -ge-*, *h*) polemize
'**Polen** Poland
**Police** [po'li:sə] *f* (-; -*n*) policy
**Polier** [po'li:ɐ] *m* (-*s*; -*e*) TECH foreman
**polieren** [po'li:rən] *v/t* (*no -ge-*, *h*) polish
**Polin** ['po:lın] *f* (-; -*nen*) Pole, Polish woman
**Politik** [poli'ti:k] *f* (-; *no pl*) politics; policy (*a. fig*); **Politiker(in)** [po'li:tikɐ, po'li:tikərın] *m*(*f*) (-*s*; -/-; -*nen*) politician; **politisch** [po'li:tıʃ] *adj* political; **politisieren** [politi'zi:rən] *v/i* (*no -ge-*, *h*) talk politics
**Polizei** [poli'tsai] *f* (-; *no pl*) police; **~auto** *n* police car; **~beamt|e** *m*, **-in** *f* police officer
**poli'zeilich** *adj* (of *or* by the) police
**Poli'zei|prä͵sidium** *n* police headquarters; **~re͵vier** *n* police station; precinct, *Br* district; **~schutz** *m*: ***unter ~*** under police guard; **~streife** *f* police patrol; **~stunde** *f* closing time; **~wache** *f* police station
**Polizist** [poli'tsıst] *m* (-*en*; -*en*) policeman; **Poli'zistin** *f* (-; -*nen*) policewoman
**polnisch** ['pɔlnıʃ] *adj* Polish
**Polster** ['pɔlstɐ] *n* (-*s*; -) upholstery; cushion; pad(ding); *fig* bolster; **~garni͵tur** *f* three-piece suite; **~möbel** *pl* upholstered furniture
'**polstern** *v/t* (*ge-*, *h*) upholster; pad
'**Polster|sessel** *m* easy chair, armchair; **~stuhl** *m* upholstered chair
**Polsterung** ['pɔlstərʊŋ] *f* (-; -*en*) upholstery; padding
**poltern** ['pɔltɐn] *v/i* (*ge-*, *h*) rumble; *fig* bluster
**Pommes frites** [pɔm'frıt] *pl* French fries, French fried potatoes, *Br* chips
**Pomp** [pɔmp] *m* (-[*e*]*s*; *no pl*) pomp
**pompös** [pɔm'pø:s] *adj* showy
**Pony**[1] ['pɔni] *n* (-*s*; -*s*) ZO pony
'**Pony**[2] *m* (-*s*; -*s*) fringe, bangs
**Popgruppe** ['pɔpgrʊpə] *f* MUS pop group
'**Popmu͵sik** *f* pop music
**populär** [popu'lɛ:ɐ] *adj* popular
**Popularität** [populari'tɛ:t] *f* (-; *no pl*) popularity
**Pore** ['po:rə] *f* (-; -*n*) pore
**Porno** ['pɔrno] F *m* (-*s*; -*s*), **~film** *m* porn (film), blue movie; **~heft** *n* porn magazine
**porös** [po'rø:s] *adj* porous
**Portemonnaie** [pɔrtmɔ'ne:] *n* (-*s*; -*s*)

P

purse
**Portier** [pɔr'tjeː] *m* (-*s*; -*s*) doorman, porter
**Portion** [pɔr'tsjoːn] *f* (-; -*en*) portion, share; helping, serving
**Portmonee** *n* → ***Portemonnaie***
**Porto** ['pɔrto] *n* (-*s*; -*s*, -*ti*) postage
**Porträt** [pɔr'trɛː] *n* (-*s*; -*s*) portrait
**porträtieren** [pɔrtrɛ'tiːrən] *v/t* (*no -ge-*, *h*) portray
**Portugal** ['pɔrtugal] Portugal
**Portugiese** [pɔrtu'giːzə] *m* (-*n*; -*n*), **Portu'giesin** *f* (-; -*nen*), **portu'giesisch** *adj* Portuguese
**Porzellan** [pɔrtsɛ'laːn] *n* (-*s*; -*e*) china, porcelain
**Posaune** [po'zaunə] *f* (-; -*n*) MUS trombone; *fig* trumpet
**Pose** ['poːzə] *f* (-; -*n*) pose, attitude
**Position** [pozi'tsjoːn] *f* (-; -*en*) position (*a. fig*)
**positiv** ['poːzitiːf] *adj* positive
**possessiv** [pɔsɛ'siːf] *adj* LING possessive; **Posses'sivpro,nomen** *n* LING possessive pronoun
**Post®** [pɔst] *f* (-; *no pl*) mail, *esp Br* post; letters; ***mit der Post®*** by post *or* mail; **Postamt** *n* post office; **Postanweisung** *f* money order; **Postbote** *m* mailman, *Br* postman
**Posten** ['pɔstən] *m* (-*s*; -) post; job, position; MIL sentry; ECON item; lot, parcel
'**Postfach** *n* (PO) box
**postieren** [pɔs'tiːrən] *v/t* (*no -ge-*, *h*) post, station, place; ***sich ~*** station o.s.
'**Postkarte** *f* postcard
'**Postkutsche** *f* stagecoach
'**postlagernd** *adj* (in care of) general delivery, *Br* poste restante
'**Post|leitzahl** *f* zip code, *Br* post(al) code; **~sparbuch** *n* post-office savings book; **~stempel** *m* postmark
'**postwendend** *adv* by return mail, *Br* by return (of post)
'**Post|wertzeichen** *n* (postage) stamp; **~zustellung** *f* postal *or* mail delivery
**Potenz** [po'tɛnts] *f* (-; -*en*) (*no pl*) MED potency; MATH power
**Pracht** [praxt] *f* (-; *no pl*) splendo(u)r, magnificence
**prächtig** ['prɛçtɪç] *adj* splendid, magnificent, *fig a.* great, super
**Prädikat** [prɛdi'kaːt] *n* (-[*e*]*s*; -*e*) LING predicate
**prägen** ['prɛːgən] *v/t* (*ge-*, *h*) stamp, coin (*a. fig*)
**prahlen** ['praːlən] *v/i* (*ge-*, *h*) brag, boast (*both*: ***mit*** of), talk big, show off; **Prahler** ['praːlɐ] *m* (-*s*; -) boaster, braggart; **Prahlerei** [praːlə'rai] *f* (-; -*en*) boasting, bragging; '**prahlerisch** *adj* boastful; showy
**Praktikant** [prakti'kant] *m* (-*en*; -*en*), **Prakti'kantin** *f* (-; -*nen*) trainee; **Praktiken** ['praktikən] *pl* practices; '**Praktikum** *n* (-*s*; -*ka*) practical training; '**praktisch 1.** *adj* practical; useful, handy; ***~er Arzt*** general practitioner **2.** *adv* practically; virtually; **praktizieren** [prakti'tsiːrən] *v/t* (*no -ge-*, *h*) practice (*Br* practise) medicine *or* law
**Prälat** [prɛ'laːt] *m* (-*en*; -*en*) REL prelate
**Praline** [pra'liːnə] *f* (-; -*n*) chocolate
**prall** [pral] *adj* tight; well-rounded; bulging; blazing (*sun*)
**prallen** ['pralən] *v/i* (*ge-*, *sein*) ***~ gegen*** (*or* ***auf*** *acc*) crash *or* bump into
**Prämie** ['prɛːmjə] *f* (-; -*n*) premium; prize; bonus; **prämieren** [prɛ'miːrən], **prämiieren** [prɛmi'iːrən] *v/t* (*no -ge-*, *h*) award a prize to
**Pranke** ['praŋkə] *f* (-; -*n*) ZO paw (*a.* F)
**Präparat** [prɛpa'raːt] *n* (-[*e*]*s*; -*e*) preparation
**präparieren** [prɛpa'riːrən] *v/t* (*no -ge-*, *h*) prepare; MED, BOT, ZO dissect
**Präposition** [prɛpozi'tsjoːn] *f* (-; -*en*) LING preposition
**Prärie** [prɛ'riː] *f* (-; -*n*) prairie
**Präsens** ['prɛːzɛns] *n* (-; -*sentia* [prɛ'zɛntsja]) LING present (tense)
**präsentieren** [prɛzɛn'tiːrən] *v/t* (*no -ge-*, *h*) present; offer
**Präservativ** [prɛzɛrva'tiːf] *n* (-*s*; -*e*) condom
**Präsident** [prɛzi'dɛnt] *m* (-*en*; -*en*), **Präsi'dentin** *f* (-; -*nen*) president; chairman (chairwoman); **präsidieren** [prɛzi'diːrən] *v/i* preside (***in*** *dat* over)
**Präsidium** [prɛ'ziːdjʊm] *n* (-*s*; -*ien*) presidency
**prasseln** ['prasəln] *v/i* (*ge-*, *h*) *rain etc*: patter; *fire*: crackle
**Präteritum** [prɛ'teːritʊm] *n* (-*s*; -*ta*) LING past (tense)
**Praxis** ['praksɪs] *f* (-; *Praxen*) (*no pl*) practice (*a.* MED, JUR); MED doctor's of-

P

fice, *Br* surgery
**Präzedenzfall** [prɛtse'dɛntsfal] *m* precedent
**präzis** [prɛ'tsiːs], **präzise** [prɛ'tsiːzə] *adj* precise; **Präzision** [prɛtsi'zjoːn] *f* (-; *no pl*) precision
**predigen** ['preːdɪgən] *v/i and v/t* (*ge-, h*) preach
**Prediger** ['preːdɪgɐ] *m* (*-s*; -), '**Predigerin** *f* (-; *-nen*) preacher
**Predigt** ['preːdɪçt] *f* (-; *-en*) sermon
**Preis** [prais] *m* (*-es*; *-e*) price (*a. fig*); prize; *film etc*: award; reward; ***um jeden ~*** at all costs
'**Preisausschreiben** *n* competition
**Preiselbeere** ['praizəlbeːrə] *f* BOT cranberry
**preisen** ['praizən] *v/t* (*irr, ge-, h*) praise
'**Preiserhöhung** *f* rise *or* increase in price(s)
'**preisgeben** *v/t* (*irr*, ***geben***, *sep, -ge-, h*) abandon; reveal, give away
'**preisgekrönt** *adj* prize-winning; *film etc*: award-winning
'**Preis|gericht** *n* jury; **~lage** *f* price range; **~liste** *f* price list; **~nachlass** *m* discount; **~rätsel** *n* competition; **~richter(in)** judge; **~schild** *n* price tag; **~stopp** *m* price freeze; **~träger(in)** prizewinner
'**preiswert** *adj* cheap
**prellen** ['prɛlən] *v/t* (*ge-, h*) *fig* cheat (***um*** out of); ***sich et. ~*** MED bruise s.th.; '**Prellung** *f* (-; *-en*) MED contusion, bruise
**Premiere** [prə'mjeːrə] *f* (-; *-n*) THEA *etc* first night, première
**Premiermi,nister** [prə'mjeːminɪstɐ] *m*, **Pre'miermi,nisterin** [prə'mjeːminɪstərɪn] *f* prime minister
**Presse** ['prɛsə] *f* (-; *-n*) (*no pl*) press; squeezer; **~...** *in cpds ...agentur, ...konferenz, ...fotograf etc*: press ...; **~freiheit** *f* freedom of the press; **~meldung** *f* news item
'**pressen** *v/t* (*ge-, h*) press; squeeze
'**Presse|tri,büne** *f* press box; **~vertreter** *m* reporter
'**Pressluft** *f* compressed air; **~...** *in cpds ...bohrer, ...hammer etc*: pneumatic ...
**Prestige** [prɛs'tiːʒə] *n* (*-s*; *no pl*) prestige; **~verlust** *m* loss of prestige *or* face
**Preuße** ['prɔʏsə] *m* (*-n*; *-n*), '**Preußin** *f* (-; *-nen*), '**preußisch** *adj* Prussian
**prickeln** ['prɪkəln] *v/i* (*ge-, h*) prickle; tingle
**pries** [priːs] *pret of **preisen***
**Priester** ['priːstɐ] *m* (*-s*; -) priest; **Priesterin** ['priːstərɪn] *f* (-; *-nen*) priestess; '**priesterlich** *adj* priestly
**prima** ['priːma] F *adj* great, super
**primär** [pri'mɛːɐ] *adj* primary
**Primar|arzt** [pri'maːɐʔaːɐtst] *Austrian m* → ***Oberarzt***; **~schule** *Swiss f* → ***Grundschule***
**Primel** ['priːməl] *f* (-; *-n*) BOT primrose
**primitiv** [primi'tiːf] *adj* primitive
**Prinz** [prɪnts] *m* (*-en*; *-en*) prince
**Prinzessin** [prɪn'tsɛsɪn] *f* (-; *-nen*) princess
'**Prinzgemahl** *m* prince consort
**Prinzip** [prɪn'tsiːp] *n* (*-s*; *-ien*) principle (***aus*** on; ***im*** in); **prinzipiell** [prɪntsi'pjɛl] *adv* as a matter of principle
**Prise** ['priːzə] *f* (-; *-n*) ***e-e ~ Salz*** *etc* a pinch of salt *etc*
**Prisma** ['prɪsma] *n* (*-s*; *-men*) prism
**Pritsche** ['prɪtʃə] *f* (-; *-n*) plank bed; MOT platform
**privat** [pri'vaːt] *adj* private; personal
**Pri'vat...** *in cpds ...leben, ...schule, ...detektiv etc*: private ...; **~angelegenheit** *f* personal *or* private matter *or* affair; ***das ist m-e ~*** that's my own business
**Privileg** [privi'leːk] *n* (*-[e]s*; *-gien* [privi'leːgjən]) privilege
**pro** [proː] *prp* (*acc*) per; ***2 Euro ~ Stück*** two euros each
**Pro** *n*: ***das ~ und Kontra*** the pros and cons
**Probe** ['proːbə] *f* (-; *-n*) trial, test; sample; THEA rehearsal; MATH proof; ***auf ~*** on probation; ***auf die ~ stellen*** put to the test; **~a,larm** *m* test alarm, fire drill; **~aufnahmen** *pl film*: screen test; **~fahrt** *f* test drive; **~flug** *m* test flight
'**proben** *v/i and v/t* (*ge-, h*) THEA *etc* rehearse
'**probeweise** *adv* on trial; on probation
'**Probezeit** *f* (time of) probation
**probieren** [pro'biːrən] *v/t* (*no -ge-, h*) try; taste
**Problem** [pro'bleːm] *n* (*-s*; *-e*) problem
**problematisch** [proble'maːtɪʃ] *adj* problematic(al)
**Produkt** [pro'dʊkt] *n* (*-[e]s*; *-e*) product (*a.* MATH); result

P

**Produktion** [produk'tsjo:n] *f* (-; *-en*) production; output
**produktiv** [produk'ti:f] *adj* productive
**Produktivität** [produktivi'tɛ:t] *f* (-; *no pl*) productivity
**Produzent** [produ'tsɛnt] *m* (*-en*; *-en*), **Produ'zentin** *f* (-; *-nen*) producer; **produzieren** [produ'tsi:rən] *v/t* (*no -ge-*, *h*) produce
**professionell** [profɛsjo'nɛl] *adj* professional
**Professor** [pro'fɛso:ɐ] *m* (*-s*; *-en* [profɛ'so:rən]), **Profes'sorin** *f* (-; *-nen*) professor
**Professur** [profɛ'su:ɐ] *f* (-; *-en*) professorship, chair (***für*** of)
**Profi** ['pro:fi] *m* (*-s*; *-s*) pro; *~... in cpds ...boxer, ...fußballer etc*: professional
**Profil** [pro'fi:l] *n* (*-s*; *-e*) profile; MOT tread; **profilieren** [profi'li:rən] *v/refl* (*no -ge-*, *h*) distinguish o.s.
**Profit** [pro'fi:t] *m* (*-[e]s*; *-e*) profit
**profitieren** [profi'ti:rən] *v/i* (*no -ge-*, *h*) profit (***von*** *or* ***bei et.*** from *or* by s.th.)
**Prognose** [pro'gno:zə] *f* (-; *-n*) prediction; METEOR forecast; MED prognosis
**Programm** [pro'gram] *n* (*-s*; *-e*) program(me *Br*), TV *a.* channel; IT program; **~fehler** *m* IT program error, bug
**programmieren** [progra'mi:rən] *v/t* (*no -ge-*, *h*) program (*a.* IT)
**Programmierer** [progra'mi:rɐ] *m* (*-s*; -), **Program'miererin** *f* (-; *-nen*) IT programmer
**Projekt** [pro'jɛkt] *n* (*-[e]s*; *-e*) project
**Projektion** [projɛk'tsjo:n] *f* (-; *-en*) projection; **Projektor** [pro'jɛkto:ɐ] *m* (*-s*; *-en* [projɛk'to:rən]) projector
**proklamieren** [prokla'mi:rən] *v/t* (*no -ge-*, *h*) proclaim
**Prokurist** [proku'rɪst] *m* (*-en*; *-en*), **Proku'ristin** *f* (-; *-nen*) authorized signatory
**Proletarier** [prole'ta:rjɐ] *m* (*-s*; -), **proletarisch** [prole'ta:rɪʃ] *adj* proletarian
**Prolog** [pro'lo:k] *m* (*-[e]s*; *-e*) prologue
**Promillegrenze** [pro'mɪləgrɛntsə] *f* (blood) alcohol limit
**prominent** [promi'nɛnt] *adj* prominent
**Prominenz** [promi'nɛnts] *f* (-; *no pl*) notables; high society
**Promotion** [promo'tsjo:n] *f* (-; *-en*) UNIV doctorate; **promovieren** [promo'vi:rən] *v/i* (*no -ge-*, *h*) do one's doctorate
**prompt** [prɔmpt] *adj* prompt; quick
**Pronomen** [pro'no:mən] *n* (*-s*; *-mina*) LING pronoun
**Propeller** [pro'pɛlɐ] *m* (*-s*; -) propeller
**Prophet** [pro'fe:t] *m* (*-en*; *-en*) prophet; **pro'phetisch** *adj* prophetic
**prophezeien** [profe'tsaiən] *v/t* (*no -ge-*, *h*) prophesy, predict; **Prophe'zeiung** *f* (-; *-en*) prophecy, prediction
**Proportion** [propɔr'tsjo:n] *f* (-; *-en*) proportion
**Proporz** [pro'pɔrts] *m* (*-es*; *-e*) POL proportional representation
**Prosa** ['pro:za] *f* (-; *no pl*) prose
**Prospekt** [pro'spɛkt] *m* (*-[e]s*; *-e*) prospectus; brochure, pamphlet
**prost** [pro:st] *int* cheers!
**Prostituierte** [prostitu'i:ɐtə] *f* (*-n*; *-n*) prostitute
**Protest** [pro'tɛst] *m* (*-[e]s*; *-e*) protest; ***aus ~*** in (*or* as a) protest
**Protestant** [protɛs'tant] *m* (*-en*; *-en*), **Protes'tantin** *f* (-; *-nen*), **protes'tantisch** *adj* REL Protestant
**protestieren** [protɛs'ti:rən] *v/i* (*no -ge-*, *h*) protest
**Prothese** [pro'te:zə] *f* (-; *-n*) MED artificial limb; denture
**Protokoll** [proto'kɔl] *n* (*-s*; *-e*) record, minutes; protocol; ***(das) ~ führen*** take *or* keep the minutes; ***zu ~ nehmen*** JUR record; **~führer** *m* keeper of the minutes
**protokollieren** [protokɔ'li:rən] *v/t and v/i* (*no -ge-*, *h*) take the minutes (of); JUR record
**protzen** ['prɔtsən] F *v/i* (*ge-*, *h*) show off (***mit et.*** s.th.)
**protzig** ['prɔtsɪç] *adj* showy, flashy
**Proviant** [pro'vjant] *m* (*-s*; *no pl*) provisions, food
**Provinz** [pro'vɪnts] *f* (-; *-en*) province; *fig* country; **provinziell** [provɪn'tsjɛl] *adj* provincial (*a. contp*)
**Provision** [provi'zjo:n] *f* (-; *-en*) ECON commission
**provisorisch** [provi'zo:rɪʃ] *adj* provisional, temporary
**provozieren** [provo'tsi:rən] *v/t* (*no -ge-*, *h*) provoke
**Prozent** [pro'tsɛnt] *n* (*-[e]s*; *-e*) per cent; F *pl* discount; **~satz** *m* percentage
**prozentual** [protsɛn'tua:l] *adj* propor-

P

tional; ***~er Anteil*** percentage

**Prozess** [pro'tsɛs] *m* (*-es*; *-e*) process (*a.* TECH, CHEM *etc*); JUR action; lawsuit, case; trial; ***j-m den ~ machen*** take s.o. to court; ***e-n ~ gewinnen*** (***verlieren***) win (lose) a case; **prozessieren** [protsɛ'siːrən] *v/i* (*no -ge-, h*) JUR go to court; ***gegen j-n ~*** bring an action against s.o., take s.o. to court

**Prozession** [protsɛ'sjoːn] *f* (*-; -en*) procession

**Prozessor** [pro'tsɛsoːɐ] *m* (*-s; -en* [protsɛ'soːrən]) IT processor

**prüde** ['pryːdə] *adj* prudish; ***~ sein*** be a prude

**prüfen** ['pryːfən] *v/t* (*ge-, h*) PED *etc* examine, test (*a.* TECH); check; inspect (*a.* TECH); *fig* consider; **~d** *adj* searching

**Prüfer** ['pryːfɐ] *m* (*-s; -*), '**Prüferin** *f* (*-; -nen*) PED *etc* examiner; *esp* TECH tester

**Prüfling** ['pryːflɪŋ] *m* (*-s; -e*) candidate

'**Prüfstein** *m* touchstone (***für*** of)

'**Prüfung** *f* (*-; -en*) examination, F exam; test; check(ing), inspection; ***e-e ~ machen*** (***bestehen, nicht bestehen***) take (pass, fail) an exam(ination)

'**Prüfungsarbeit** *f* examination *or* test paper

**Prügel** ['pryːgəl] F *pl* (***e-e Tracht***) ***~ bekommen*** get a (good) beating *or* hiding *or* thrashing; **Prüge'lei** F *f* (*-; -en*) fight; '**prügeln** F *v/t* (*ge-, h*) beat, flog; ***sich ~*** (have a) fight; '**Prügelstrafe** *f* corporal punishment

**Prunk** [prʊŋk] *m* (*-[e]s; no pl*) splendo(u)r, pomp; '**prunkvoll** *adj* splendid, magnificent

**PS** [peː'ʔɛs] *abbr of* ***Pferdestärke*** horsepower, HP

**Psalm** [psalm] *m* (*-s; -en*) REL psalm

**Pseudonym** [psɔʏdo'nyːm] *n* (*-s; -e*) pseudonym

**pst** [pst] *int* sh!, ssh!; psst!

**Psyche** ['psyːçə] *f* (*-; -n*) mind, psyche

**Psychiater** [psy'çjaːtɐ] *m* (*-s; -*), **Psy'chiaterin** *f* (*-; -nen*) psychiatrist; **psychiatrisch** [psy'çjaːtrɪʃ] *adj* psychiatric

**psychisch** ['psyːçɪʃ] *adj* mental, MED *a.* psychic

**Psychoana'lyse** ['psyçoanalyːzə] *f* psychoanalysis

**Psychologe** [psyço'loːgə] *m* (*-n; -n*) psychologist (*a. fig*); **Psychologie** [psyçolo'giː] *f* (*-; no pl*) psychology; **Psycho'login** *f* (*-; -nen*) psychologist; **psycho'logisch** *adj* psychological

**Psychose** [psy'çoːzə] *f* (*-; -n*) MED psychosis

**psychosomatisch** [psyçozo'maːtɪʃ] *adj* MED psychosomatic

**Pubertät** [pubɛr'tɛːt] *f* (*-; no pl*) puberty

**Publikum** ['puːblikʊm] *n* (*-s; no pl*) audience, TV *a.* viewers, *radio*: *a.* listeners; SPORT crowd, spectators; ECON customers; public

**publizieren** [publi'tsiːrən] *v/t* (*no -ge-, h*) publish

**Pudding** ['pʊdɪŋ] *m* (*-s; -e, -s*) pudding, *esp Br* blancmange

**Pudel** ['puːdəl] *m* (*-s; -*) ZO poodle

**Puder** ['puːdɐ] *m* (*-s; -*) powder

'**Puderdose** *f* powder compact

'**pudern** *v/t* (*ge-, h*) powder; ***sich ~*** powder one's face

'**Puderzucker** *m* confectioner's (*Br* icing) sugar

**Puff**[1] [pʊf] F *m* (*-s; -s*) brothel

**Puff**[2] *m* (*-[e]s; Püffe* ['pʏfə]) hump; poke

**Puffer** ['pʊfɐ] *m* (*-s; -*) RAIL buffer (*a. fig*)

'**Puffmais** *m* popcorn

**Pulli** ['pʊli] F *m* (*-s; -s*) (light) sweater

**Pullover** [pʊ'loːvɐ] *m* (*-s; -*) sweater, pullover

**Puls** [pʊls] *m* (*-es; -e*) MED pulse; pulse rate; **~ader** *f* ANAT artery

**pulsieren** [pʊl'ziːrən] *v/i* (*no -ge-, h*) MED pulsate (*a. fig*)

**Pult** [pʊlt] *n* (*-[e]s; -e*) desk

**Pulver** ['pʊlvɐ] *n* (*-s; -*) powder; F cash, *sl* dough; **pulv(e)rig** ['pʊlv(ə)rɪç] *adj* powdery; **pulverisieren** [pʊlveri'ziːrən] *v/t* (*no -ge-, h*) pulverize

'**Pulverkaffee** *m* instant coffee

'**Pulverschnee** *m* powder snow

**pumm(e)lig** ['pʊm(ə)lɪç] F *adj* chubby, plump, tubby

**Pumpe** ['pʊmpə] *f* (*-; -n*) TECH pump

'**pumpen** *v/i and v/t* TECH pump; F lend; borrow

**Punker** ['paŋkɐ] F *m* (*-s; -*), '**Punkerin** *f* (*-; -nen*) punk

**Punkt** [pʊŋkt] *m* (*-[e]s; -e*) point (*a. fig*); dot; full stop, period; *fig* spot, place; ***um ~ zehn*** (***Uhr***) at ten (o'clock) sharp; ***nach ~en gewinnen*** *etc* SPORT win *etc* on points

**punktieren** [puŋk'tiːrən] *v/t* (*no -ge-, h*) dot; MED puncture

**pünktlich** ['pʏŋktlɪç] *adj* punctual; **~ sein** be on time; '**Pünktlichkeit** *f* (-; *no pl*) punctuality

'**Punkt|sieger** *m* SPORT winner on points; **~spiel** *n* SPORT league game

**Pupille** [pu'pɪlə] *f* (-; -*n*) ANAT pupil

**Puppe** ['pʊpə] *f* (-; -*n*) doll, F *a.* chick; THEA puppet (*a. fig*); MOT dummy; ZO chrysalis, pupa

'**Puppen|spiel** *n* puppet show; **~stube** *f* doll's house; **~wagen** *m* doll carriage, *Br* doll's pram

**pur** [puːɐ] *adj* pure (*a. fig*); *whisky etc*: straight, *Br* neat

**Purpur** ['pʊrpʊr] *m* (-*s*; *no pl*) crimson

'**purpurrot** *adj* crimson

**Purzelbaum** ['pʊrtsəlbaum] *m* somersault; ***e-n ~ schlagen*** turn a somersault

**purzeln** ['pʊrtsəln] *v/i* (*ge-, sein*) tumble

**Pute** ['puːtə] *f* (-; -*n*) ZO turkey (hen)

**Puter** ['puːtɐ] *m* (-*s*; -) ZO turkey (cock)

**Putsch** [pʊtʃ] *m* (-[*e*]*s*; -*e*) putsch, coup (d'état); '**putschen** *v/i* (*ge-, h*) revolt, make a putsch

**Putz** [pʊts] *m* (-*es*; *no pl*) ARCH plaster (-ing); ***unter ~*** ELECTR concealed

**putzen** ['pʊtsən] (*ge-, h*) **1.** *v/t* clean; polish; wipe; ***sich die Nase ~*** blow one's nose; ***sich die Zähne ~*** brush one's teeth **2.** *v/i* do the cleaning; **~ (*gehen*)** work as a cleaner

'**Putzfrau** *f* cleaner, cleaning woman *or* lady

**putzig** ['pʊtsɪç] *adj* funny, cute

'**Putzlappen** *m* cleaning rag

'**Putzmittel** *n* clean(s)er; polish

**Puzzle** ['pazəl] *n* (-*s*; -*s*) jigsaw (puzzle)

**Pyjama** [py'dʒaːma] *m* (-*s*; -*s*) pajamas, *Br* pyjamas

**Pyramide** [pyra'miːdə] *f* (-; -*n*) pyramid

# Q

**Quacksalber** ['kvakzalbɐ] *m* (-*s*; -) quack (doctor)

**Quadrat** [kva'draːt] *n* (-[*e*]*s*; -*e*) square; ***ins ~ erheben*** MATH square; **~...** *in cpds …meile, …meter, …wurzel, …zahl etc*: square …; **qua'dratisch** *adj* square; MATH quadratic

**quaken** ['kvaːkən] *v/i* (*ge-, h*) *duck*: quack; *frog*: croak

**quäken** ['kvɛːkən] *v/i* (*ge-, h*) squeak

**Qual** [kvaːl] *f* (-; -*en*) pain, torment, agony; anguish

**quälen** ['kvɛːlən] *v/t* (*ge-, h*) torment (*a. fig*); torture; *fig* pester, plague

**Qualifikation** [kvalifika'tsjoːn] *f* (-; -*en*) qualification; **Qualifikati'ons...** *in cpds …spiel etc*: qualifying …

**qualifizieren** [kvalifi'tsiːrən] *v/t and v/refl* (*no -ge-, h*) qualify

**Qualität** [kvali'tɛːt] *f* (-; -*en*) quality

**qualitativ** [kvalita'tiːf] *adj and adv* in quality

**Quali'täts...** *in cpds …arbeit, …waren etc*: high-quality …

**Qualm** [kvalm] *m* (-[*e*]*s*; *no pl*) (thick) smoke; **qualmen** ['kvalmən] *v/i* (*ge-, h*) smoke; F be a heavy smoker

'**qualvoll** *adj* very painful; agonizing

**Quantität** [kvanti'tɛːt] *f* (-; -*en*) quantity; **quantitativ** [kvantita'tiːf] *adj and adv* in quantity

**Quantum** ['kvantʊm] *n* (-*s*; *Quanten*) amount, *fig a.* share

**Quarantäne** [karan'tɛːnə] *f* (-; -*n*) **(*unter ~ stellen*** put in) quarantine

**Quark** [kvark] *m* (-*s*; *no pl*) curd, cottage cheese

**Quartal** [kvar'taːl] *n* (-*s*; -*e*) quarter (of a year)

**Quartett** [kvar'tɛt] *n* (-[*e*]*s*; -*e*) MUS quartet(te)

**Quartier** [kvar'tiːɐ] *n* (-*s*; -*e*) accommodation; *Swiss*: quarter

**Quarz** [kvaːɐts] *m* (-*es*; -*e*) MIN quartz

**Quatsch** [kvatʃ] F *m* (-[*e*]*s*; *no pl*) nonsense, rubbish, *sl* rot, crap, bullshit; ***~ machen*** fool around; joke, F kid

**quatschen** ['kvatʃən] F *v/i* (*ge-, h*) talk rubbish; chat

**Quecksilber** ['kvɛkzɪlbɐ] *n* (-*s*; *no pl*) mercury, quicksilver

**Quelle** ['kvɛlə] *f* (-; -*n*) spring, source (*a.*

*fig*), well, *fig a.* origin; '**quellen** *v/i* (*irr, ge-, sein*) pour (***aus*** from)
'**Quellenangabe** *f* reference
**quengeln** ['kvɛŋəln] F *v/i* (*ge-, h*) whine
**quer** [kveːɐ] *adv* across; crosswise; ***kreuz und ~*** all over the place; ***kreuz und ~ durch Deutschland fahren*** travel all over Germany; **Quere** ['kveːrə] *f*: F ***j-m in die ~ kommen*** get in s.o.'s way
**Querfeld'einlauf** *m* SPORT cross-country race
'**Querlatte** *f* SPORT crossbar
'**Querschläger** *m* MIL ricochet
'**Querschnitt** *m* cross-section (*a. fig*)
'**querschnitt(s)gelähmt** *adj* MED paraplegic
'**Querstraße** *f* intersecting road; ***zweite ~ rechts*** second turning on the right
**Querulant** [kveru'lant] *m* (*-en; -en*), **Queru'lantin** *f* (*-; -nen*) querulous person
**quetschen** ['kvɛtʃən] *v/t and v/refl* (*ge-, h*) squeeze; MED bruise (o.s.)
'**Quetschung** *f* (*-; -en*) MED bruise
**quiek(s)en** ['kviːk(s)ən] *v/i* (*ge-, h*) squeak, squeal
**quietschen** ['kviːtʃən] *v/i* (*ge-, h*) squeal; screech; squeak, creak
**quitt** [kvɪt] *adj*: ***mit j-m ~ sein*** be quits *or* even with s.o. (*a. fig*)
**quittieren** [kvɪ'tiːrən] *v/t* (*no -ge-, h*) ECON give a receipt for
'**Quittung** *f* (*-; -en*) receipt; *fig* answer
**quoll** [kvɔl] *pret of* ***quellen***
**Quote** ['kvoːtə] *f* (*-; -n*) quota; share; rate
'**Quotenregelung** *f* quota system
**Quotient** [kvo'tsjɛnt] *m* (*-en; -en*) MATH quotient

# R

**Rabatt** [ra'bat] *m* (*-[e]s; -e*) ECON discount, rebate
**Rabe** ['raːbə] *m* (*-n; -n*) ZO raven
**rabiat** [ra'bjaːt] *adj* rough, tough
**Rache** ['raxə] *f* (*-; no pl*) revenge; ***aus ~ für*** in revenge for
**Rachen** ['raxən] *m* (*-s; -*) ANAT throat
**rächen** ['rɛçən] *v/t* (*ge-, h*) avenge *s.th.*; revenge *s.o.*; ***sich an j-m für et. ~*** revenge o.s. *or* take revenge on s.o. for s.th.; **Rächer** ['rɛçɐ] *m* (*-s; -*) avenger
**rachsüchtig** ['raxzʏçtɪç] *adj* revengeful, vindictive
**Rad** [raːt] *n* (*-[e]s; Räder* ['rɛːdɐ]) wheel; bicycle, F bike; ***~ fahren*** cycle, ride a bicycle, F bike; ***ein ~ schlagen*** *peacock*: spread its tail; SPORT turn a (cart)wheel
**Radar** [ra'daːɐ] *m, n* (*-s; -e*) radar; **~falle** *f* MOT speed trap; **~kon,trolle** *f* MOT radar speed check; **~schirm** *m* radar screen; **~stati,on** *f* radar station
**radeln** ['raːdəln] F *v/i* (*ge-, sein*) bike
**Rädelsführer** ['rɛːdəlsfyːrɐ] *m* ringleader
**Räderwerk** ['rɛːdɐvɛrk] *n* TECH gearing
'**Radfahrer** *m* (*-s; -*), '**Radfahrerin** *f* (*-; -nen*) cyclist
**radieren** [ra'diːrən] *v/t* (*no -ge-, h*) erase, rub out; *art*: etch
**Radiergummi** [ra'diːɐgʊmi] *m* eraser, *Br a.* rubber
**Ra'dierung** *f* (*-; -en*) *art*: etching
**Radieschen** [ra'diːsçən] *n* (*-s; -*) BOT (red) radish
**radikal** [radi'kaːl] *adj*, **Radi'kale** *m, f* (*-n; -n*) radical; **Radikalismus** [radika'lɪsmʊs] *m* (*-; no pl*) radicalism
**Radio** ['raːdjo] *n* (*-s; -s*) radio; ***im ~*** on the radio; ***~ hören*** listen to the radio
**radioak'tiv** [radjoak'tiːf] *adj* PHYS radioactive; ***~er Niederschlag*** fall-out
**Radioaktivi'tät** *f* (*-; no pl*) radioactivity
'**Radiowecker** *m* clock radio
**Radius** ['raːdjʊs] *m* (*-s; Radien*) radius
'**Rad|kappe** *f* hubcap; **~rennbahn** *f* cycling track; **~rennen** *n* cycle race; **~sport** *m* cycling; **~sportler** *m* cyclist; **~weg** *m* cycle track *or* path, bikeway
**raffen** ['rafən] *v/t* (*ge-, h*) gather up; ***an sich ~*** grab
**Raffinerie** [rafinə'riː] *f* (*-; -n*) CHEM refinery
**Raffinesse** [rafi'nɛsə] *f* (*-; -n*) (*no pl*) shrewdness; refinement
**raffiniert** [rafi'niːɐt] *adj* refined (*a. fig*);

*fig* shrewd, clever

**ragen** ['ra:gən] *v/i* (*ge-*, *h*) tower (up), rise (high)

**Rahe** ['ra:ə] *f* (-; *-n*) MAR yard

**Rahm** [ra:m] *m* (-[*e*]*s*; *no pl*) cream

**rahmen** ['ra:mən] *v/t* (*ge-*, *h*) frame; PHOT mount; '**Rahmen** *m* (*-s*; -) frame; *fig* framework; setting; scope; ***aus dem ~ fallen*** be out of the ordinary

**Rakete** [ra'ke:tə] *f* (-; *-n*) rocket, MIL *a.* missile; ***ferngelenkte ~*** guided missile; ***e-e ~ abfeuern*** (***starten***) launch a rocket *or* missile

**Ra'keten|antrieb** *m* rocket propulsion; ***mit ~*** rocket-propelled; **~basis** *f* MIL rocket *or* missile base *or* site

**rammen** ['ramən] *v/t* (*ge-*, *h*) ram; MOT *etc* hit, collide with

**Rampe** ['rampə] *f* (-; *-n*) (loading) ramp

'**Rampenlicht** *n* (-[*e*]*s*; *no pl*) THEA footlights; *fig* limelight

**Ramsch** [ramʃ] F *m* (*-es*; *no pl*) junk

**Rand** [rant] *m* (-[*e*]*s*; *Ränder* ['rɛndɐ]) edge, border; brink (*a. fig*); rim; brim; margin; ***am ~(e) des Ruins*** *etc* on the brink of ruin *etc*

**randalieren** [randa'li:rən] *v/i* (*no -ge-*, *h*) kick up a racket; **Randalierer** [randa'li:rɐ] *m* (*-s*; -) rowdy, hooligan

'**Rand|bemerkung** *f* marginal note; *fig* comment; **~gruppe** *f* fringe group

'**randlos** *adj* rimless

'**Randstreifen** *m* MOT shoulder

**rang** [raŋ] *pret of* ***ringen***

**Rang** *m* (-[*e*]*s*; *Ränge* ['rɛŋə]) position, rank (*a.* MIL); THEA balcony, *Br* circle; *pl* SPORT terraces

**rangieren** [raŋ'ʒi:rən] (*no -ge-*, *h*) **1.** *v/t* RAIL switch, *Br* shunt **2.** *fig v/i* rank (***vor j-m*** before s.o.)

'**Rangordnung** *f* hierarchy

**Ranke** ['raŋkə] *f* (-; *-n*) BOT tendril

'**ranken** *v/refl* (*ge-*, *h*) BOT creep, climb

**rann** [ran] *pret of* ***rinnen***

**rannte** ['rantə] *pret of* ***rennen***

**Ranzen** ['rantsən] *m* (*-s*; -) knapsack; satchel

**ranzig** ['rantsɪç] *adj* rancid, rank

**Rappe** ['rapə] *m* (*-n*; *-n*) ZO black horse

**rar** [ra:ɐ] *adj* rare, scarce

**Rarität** [rari'tɛ:t] *f* (-; *-en*) curiosity; (*no pl*) rarity

**rasch** [raʃ] *adj* quick, swift; prompt

**rascheln** ['raʃəln] *v/i* (*ge-*, *h*) rustle

**rasen** ['ra:zən] *v/i* (*ge-*, *sein*) F MOT race, tear, speed; (*ge-*, *h*) rage; ***~ vor Begeisterung*** roar with enthusiasm

'**Rasen** *m* (*-s*; -) lawn, grass

'**rasend** *adj* breakneck; raging; agonizing; splitting; thunderous

'**Rasen|mäher** *m* lawn mower; **~platz** *m* lawn; *tennis*: grass court

**Raserei** [ra:zə'rai] *f* (-; *-en*) (*no pl*) frenzied rage; frenzy, madness; F MOT reckless driving

**Rasier|appa,rat** [ra'zi:ɐapara:t] *m* (safety) razor; *esp* ***elektrischer ~*** shaver; **~creme** *f* shaving cream

**rasieren** [ra'zi:rən] *v/t and v/refl* (*no -ge-*, *h*) shave

**Ra'sier|klinge** *f* razor blade; **~messer** *n* (straight) razor; **~pinsel** *m* shaving brush; **~seife** *f* shaving soap; **~wasser** *n* aftershave (lotion)

**Rasse** ['rasə] *f* (-; *-n*) race; ZO breed

'**Rassehund** *m* ZO pedigree dog

**Rassel** ['rasəl] *f* (-; *-n*), '**rasseln** *v/i* (*ge-*, *h*) rattle

'**Rassen...** *in cpds ...diskriminierung*, *...konflikt*, *...probleme etc*: *mst* racial ...; **~trennung** *f* POL (racial) segregation; HIST apartheid; **~unruhen** *pl* race riots

**rassig** ['rasɪç] *adj* classy

**rassisch** ['rasɪʃ] *adj* racial

**Rassismus** [ra'sɪsmʊs] *m* (-; *no pl*) POL racism; **Ras'sist(in)** (*-en*; *-en*/-; *-nen*), **ras'sistisch** *adj* POL racist

**Rast** [rast] *f* (-; *-en*) rest, stop; break; **rasten** ['rastən] *v/i* (*ge-*, *h*) rest, stop, take a break; '**rastlos** *adj* restless

'**Rastplatz** *m* resting place; MOT rest area, *Br* lay-by

'**Raststätte** *f* MOT service area

**Rasur** [ra'zu:ɐ] *f* (-; *-en*) shave

**Rat** [ra:t] *m* (-[*e*]*s*; *Räte* ['rɛ:tə]) (*no pl*) (piece of) advice; council; ***j-n um ~ fragen*** ask s.o.'s advice; ***j-s ~ befolgen*** take s.o.'s advice

**Rate** ['ra:tə] *f* (-; *-n*) rate; ECON instal(l)-ment; ***auf ~n*** by instal(l)ments

**raten** ['ra:tən] *v/t and v/i* (*irr*, *ge-*, *h*) advise; guess; solve; ***j-m zu et. ~*** advise s.o. to do s.th.; ***rate mal!*** (have a) guess!

'**Ratenzahlung** *f* → ***Abzahlung***

'**Rateteam** *n* TV *etc* panel

**Ratgeber** ['ra:tge:bɐ] *m* (*-s*; -),

R

ˈ**Ratgeberin** *f* (-; *-nen*) adviser, counsel(l)or; *m* guide (***über*** *acc* to)
ˈ**Rathaus** *n* city (*Br* town) hall
**ratifizieren** [ratifiˈtsiːrən] *v/t* (*no -ge-, h*) ratify
**Ration** [raˈtsjoːn] *f* (-; *-en*) ration
**rational** [ratsjoˈnaːl] *adj* rational
**rationell** [ratsjoˈnɛl] *adj* efficient; economical
**rationieren** [ratsjoˈniːrən] *v/t* (*no -ge-, h*) ration
ˈ**ratlos** *adj* at a loss
ˈ**ratsam** *adj* advisable, wise
ˈ**Ratschlag** *m* piece of advice; ***ein paar gute Ratschläge*** some good advice
**Rätsel** [ˈrɛːtsəl] *n* (*-s*; -) puzzle; riddle (*both a. fig*); mystery
ˈ**rätselhaft** *adj* puzzling; mysterious
**Ratte** [ˈratə] *f* (-; *-n*) ZO rat (*a. contp*)
**rattern** [ˈratɐn] *v/i* (*ge-, h, sein*) rattle, clatter
**rau** [rau] *adj* rough, rugged (*both a. fig*); harsh; chapped; sore
**Raub** [raup] *m* (*-[e]s*; *no pl*) robbery; loot, booty; prey; **~bau** *m* (*-[e]s*; *no pl*) overexploitation (***an*** *dat* of); **~ *mit s-r Gesundheit treiben*** ruin one's health
**rauben** [ˈraubən] *v/t* (*ge-, h*) rob, steal; kidnap; ***j-m et. ~*** rob s.o. of s.th. (*a. fig*)
**Räuber** [ˈrɔʏbɐ] *m* (*-s*; -) robber
ˈ**Raub|fisch** *m* predatory fish; **~mord** *m* murder with robbery; **~mörder** *m* murderer and robber; **~tier** *n* beast of prey; **~überfall** *m* holdup, (armed) robbery; mugging; **~vogel** *m* bird of prey; **~zug** *m* raid
**Rauch** [raux] *m* (*-[e]s*; *no pl*) smoke; CHEM *etc* fume; **rauchen** [ˈrauxən] *v/i and v/t* (*ge-, h*) smoke; CHEM *etc* fume; ***Rauchen verboten!*** no smoking; ***Pfeife ~*** smoke a pipe; **Raucher(in)** [ˈrauxɐ, ˈrauxərɪn] *m(f)* (*-s*; *-/-*; *-nen*) smoker (*m a.* RAIL)
**Räucher...** [ˈrɔʏçɐ-] *in cpds ...aal, ...speck etc*: smoked ...
ˈ**räuchern** *v/t* (*ge-, h*) smoke
ˈ**Räucherstäbchen** *n* joss stick
ˈ**Rauchfahne** *f* trail of smoke
**rauchig** [ˈrauxɪç] *adj* smoky
ˈ**Rauch|waren** *pl* tobacco products; furs; **~zeichen** *n* smoke signal
**Räude** [ˈrɔʏdə] *f* (-; *-n*) VET mange
ˈ**räudig** *adj* VET mangy
**raufen** [ˈraufən] (*ge-, h*) **1.** *v/t*: ***sich die Haare ~*** tear one's hair **2.** *v/i* fight, scuffle; **Rauferei** [raufəˈrai] *f* (-; *-en*) fight, scuffle
**Raum** [raum] *m* (*-[e]s*; *Räume* [ˈrɔʏmə]) room; space; area; (outer) space; **~anzug** *m* spacesuit; **~deckung** *f* SPORT zone marking
**räumen** [ˈrɔʏmən] *v/t* (*ge-, h*) leave, move out of; check out of; clear (***von*** of); evacuate (*a.* MIL); ***s-e Sachen in ... (acc) ~*** put one's things (away) in ...
ˈ**Raum|fähre** *f* space shuttle; **~fahrer** F *m* spaceman; **~fahrt** *f* (-; *no pl*) space travel *or* flight; astronautics; **~fahrt...** *in cpds ...technik, ...zentrum etc*: space ...; **~flug** *m* space flight; **~inhalt** *m* volume; **~kapsel** *f* space capsule; **~laˌbor** *n* space lab
**räumlich** [ˈrɔʏmlɪç] *adj* three-dimensional
ˈ**Raum|schiff** *n* spacecraft; spaceship; **~sonde** *f* space probe; **~statiˌon** *f* space station
ˈ**Räumung** *f* (-; *-en*) clearance; evacuation (*a.* MIL); JUR eviction
ˈ**Räumungsverkauf** *m* ECON clearance sale
**raunen** [ˈraunən] *v/i* (*ge-, h*) whisper, murmur
**Raupe** [ˈraupə] *f* (-; *-n*) ZO caterpillar, TECH *a.* track; ˈ**Raupenschlepper** *m* MOT caterpillar® tractor
ˈ**Raureif** *m* hoarfrost
**raus** [raus] F *int* get out (of here)!
**Rausch** [rauʃ] *m* (*-es*; *Räusche* [ˈrɔʏʃə]) drunkenness, intoxication; F high; *fig* ecstasy; ***e-n ~ haben*** be drunk; ***s-n ~ ausschlafen*** sleep it off
**rauschen** [ˈrauʃən] *v/i* (*ge-, h*) *water etc*: rush; *brook*: murmur; *storm*: roar; (*ge-, sein*) sweep; **~d** *adj* thunderous (*applause*); ***~es Fest*** lavish celebration
ˈ**Rauschgift** *n* drug(s), narcotic(s); **~dezerˌnat** *n* narcotics *or* drugs squad; **~handel** *m* drug traffic(king); **~händler** *m* drug trafficker, F pusher
**räuspern** [ˈrɔʏspɐn] *v/refl* (*ge-, h*) clear one's throat
**Razzia** [ˈratsja] *f* (-; *-ien*) raid, roundup
**Reagenzglas** [reaˈgɛntsglaːs] *n* CHEM test tube
**reagieren** [reaˈgiːrən] *v/i* (*no -ge-, h*) CHEM, MED react (***auf*** *acc* to), *fig a.* re-

R

spond (to); **Reaktion** [reak'tsjo:n] *f* (-; -*en*) CHEM, MED, PHYS, POL reaction (***auf*** *acc* to), *fig a.* response (to)
**Reaktor** [re'akto:ɐ] *m* (-*s*; -*en* [reak'to:rən]) PHYS (nuclear *or* atomic) reactor
**real** [re'a:l] *adj* real; concrete
**realisieren** [reali'zi:rən] *v/t* (*no -ge-*, *h*) realize
**Realismus** [rea'lɪsmʊs] *m* (-; *no pl*) realism; **rea'listisch** *adj* realistic
**Realität** [reali'tɛ:t] *f* (-; *no pl*) reality
**Re'alschule** *f appr.* (junior) highschool, *Br* secondary (modern) school
**Rebe** ['re:bə] *f* (-; -*n*) BOT vine
**Rebell** [re'bɛl] *m* (-*en*; -*en*) rebel
**rebellieren** [rebɛ'li:rən] *v/i* (*no -ge-*, *h*) rebel, revolt, rise (*all*: ***gegen*** against)
**Re'bellin** *f* (-; -*nen*) rebel
**re'bellisch** *adj* rebellious
**Rebhuhn** ['re:phu:n] *n* ZO partridge
**'Rebstock** *m* BOT vine
**Rechen** ['rɛçən] *m* (-*s*; -), **'rechen** *v/t* (*ge-*, *h*) rake
**'Rechen|aufgabe** *f* MATH (arithmetical) problem; **~fehler** *m* MATH arithmetical error, miscalculation; **~ma,schine** *f* calculator; computer
**'Rechenschaft** *f*: ***~ ablegen über*** (*acc*) account for; ***zur ~ ziehen*** call to account (***wegen*** for)
**'Rechen|schieber** *m* MATH slide rule; **~werk** *n* IT arithmetic unit; **~zentrum** *n* computer center (*Br* centre)
**rechnen** ['rɛçnən] *v/i and v/t* (*ge-*, *h*) calculate, reckon; work out, do sums; count; ***~ mit*** *fig* expect; count on; ***mit mir kannst du nicht ~!*** count me out!
**'Rechnen** *n* (-*s*; *no pl*) arithmetic
**Rechner** ['rɛçnɐ] *m* (-*s*; -) calculator; computer
**rechnerisch** ['rɛçnərɪʃ] *adj* arithmetical
**'Rechnung** *f* (-; -*en*) MATH calculation; problem, sum; ECON invoice, bill, check; ***die ~, bitte!*** can I have the check, please?; ***das geht auf m-e ~*** that's on me
**recht** [rɛçt] **1.** *adj* right; correct; POL right-wing; ***auf der ~en Seite*** on the right(-hand side); ***mir ist es ~*** I don't mind **2.** *adv* right(ly), correctly; rather, quite; ***ich weiß nicht ~*** I don't really know; ***es geschieht ihm ~*** it serves him right; ***erst ~*** all the more; ***erst ~ nicht*** even less; ***du kommst gerade ~*** (***zu***) you're just in time (for); ***j-m ~ geben*** agree with s.o.; ***~ haben*** be right
**Recht** *n* (-[*e*]*s*; -*e*) right, claim (*both*: ***auf*** *acc* to); (*no pl*) JUR law; justice; ***gleiches ~*** equal rights; ***~ haben → recht***; ***j-m ~ geben → recht***; ***im ~ sein*** be in the right; ***er hat es mit*** (***vollem***) ***~ getan*** he was (perfectly) right to do so; ***ein ~ auf et. haben*** be entitled to s.th.
**'Rechteck** *n* (-[*e*]*s*; -*e*) rectangle
**'rechteckig** *adj* rectangular
**'rechtfertigen** *v/t* (*ge-*, *h*) justify
**'Rechtfertigung** *f* (-; -*en*) justification
**'rechtlich** *adj* JUR legal
**'rechtlos** *adj* without rights; outcast
**'rechtmäßig** *adj* JUR lawful; legitimate; legal; **'Rechtmäßigkeit** *f* (-; *no pl*) JUR lawfulness, legitimacy
**rechts** [rɛçts] *adv* on the right(-hand side); ***nach ~*** to the right
**Rechts...** *in cpds* POL right-wing ...; **~anspruch** *m* legal claim (***auf*** *acc* to); **~anwalt** *m*, **~anwältin** ['rɛçtsanvɛltɪn] *f* (-; -*nen*) lawyer
**Rechts'außen** *m* (-; -) *soccer*: outside right
**'rechtschaffen** *adj* honest
**'Recht|schreibfehler** *m* spelling mistake; **~schreibung** *f* (-; *no pl*) spelling, orthography
**'rechtsextre,mistisch** *adj* POL extreme right
**'Rechtsfall** *m* JUR (law) case
**Rechtshänder** ['rɛçtshɛndɐ] *m* (-*s*; -), **'Rechtshänderin** *f* (-; -*nen*) right-handed person; ***sie ist Rechtshänderin*** she is right-handed
**'Rechtsprechung** *f* (-; *no pl*) jurisdiction
**'rechtsradi,kal** *adj* POL extreme right-wing
**'Rechtsschutz** *m* legal protection; legal costs insurance
**'rechtswidrig** *adj* JUR illegal, unlawful
**'rechtwink(e)lig** *adj* rectangular
**'rechtzeitig** **1.** *adj* punctual **2.** *adv* in time (***zu*** for)
**Reck** [rɛk] *n* (-[*e*]*s*; -*e*) horizontal bar
**recken** ['rɛkən] *v/t* (*ge-*, *h*) stretch; ***sich ~*** stretch o.s.
**recyceln** [ri'saikəln] *v/t* (*no -ge-*, *h*) recycle; **Recyclingpa,pier** [ri-

R

'saiklıŋpapiːɐ] *n* recycled paper
**Redakteur** [redak'tøːɐ] *m* (*-s*; *-e*), **Redak'teurin** *f* (*-*; *-nen*) editor
**Redaktion** [redak'tsjoːn] *f* (*-*; *-en*) (*no pl*) editing; editorial staff, editors; editorial office *or* department
**redaktionell** [redaktsjo'nɛl] *adj* editorial
**Rede** ['reːdə] *f* (*-*; *-n*) speech, address; talk (***von*** of); ***e-e ~ halten*** make a speech; ***direkte*** (***indirekte***) ***~*** LING direct (reported *or* indirect) speech; ***j-n zur ~ stellen*** take s.o. to task; ***nicht der ~ wert*** not worth mentioning
'**redegewandt** *adj* eloquent
**reden** ['reːdən] *v/i and v/t* (*ge-*, *h*) talk, speak (*both*: ***mit*** to; ***über*** *acc* about, of); ***ich möchte mit dir ~*** I'd like to talk to you; ***die Leute ~*** people talk; ***j-n zum Reden bringen*** make s.o. talk
'**Redensart** *f* saying, phrase
**redlich** ['reːtlıç] *adj* upright, honest; ***sich ~(e) Mühe geben*** do one's best
**Redner** ['reːdnɐ] *m* (*-s*; *-*), '**Rednerin** *f* (*-*; *-nen*) speaker
'**Rednerpult** *n* speaker's desk
**redselig** ['reːtzeːlıç] *adj* talkative
**reduzieren** [redu'tsiːrən] *v/t* (*no -ge-*, *h*) reduce (***auf*** *acc* to)
**Reeder** ['reːdɐ] *m* (*-s*; *-*) shipowner
**Reederei** [reːdə'rai] *f* (*-*; *-en*) shipping company
**reell** [re'ɛl] *adj* reasonable, fair (*price*); real (*chance*); solid (*firm*)
**Referat** [refe'raːt] *n* (*-[e]s*; *-e*) paper; report; lecture; ***ein ~ halten*** read a paper
**Referendar** [referɛn'daːɐ] *m* (*-s*; *-e*), **Referen'darin** *f* (*-*; *-nen*) *appr* trainee teacher
**Referent** [refe'rɛnt] *m* (*-en*; *-en*), **Refe'rentin** *f* (*-*; *-nen*) speaker; **Referenz** [refe'rɛnts] *f* (*-*; *-en*) reference; **referieren** [refe'riːrən] *v/i* (*no -ge-*, *h*) (give a) report *or* lecture (***über*** *acc* on)
**reflektieren** [reflɛk'tiːrən] *v/t and v/i* (*no -ge-*, *h*) reflect (*fig* ***über*** *acc* [up]on)
**Reflex** [re'flɛks] *m* (*-es*; *-e*) reflex
**reflexiv** [reflɛ'ksiːf] *adj* LING reflexive
**Reform** [re'fɔrm] *f* (*-*; *-en*) reform
**Reformator** [refɔr'maːtoːɐ] *m* (*-s*; *-en* [refɔrma'toːrən]), **Reformer**(**in**) [re'fɔrmɐ, re'fɔrmərın] *m*(*f*) (*-s*; *-/-*; *-nen*) reformer
**Re'formhaus** *n* health food store (*Br* shop)
**reformieren** [refɔr'miːrən] *v/t* (*no -ge-*, *h*) reform
**Refrain** [rə'frɛ̃ː] *m* (*-s*; *-s*) refrain, chorus
**Regal** [re'gaːl] *n* (*-s*; *-e*) shelf (unit), shelves
**rege** ['reːgə] *adj* lively; busy; active
**Regel** ['reːgəl] *f* (*-*; *-n*) rule; MED period, menstruation; ***in der ~*** as a rule
'**regelmäßig** *adj* regular
**regeln** ['reːgəln] *v/t* (*ge-*, *h*) regulate, TECH *a.* adjust; ECON settle
'**regelrecht** *adj* regular (*a.* F)
'**Regeltechnik** *f* control engineering
'**Regelung** *f* (*-*; *-en*) regulation; adjustment; ECON settlement; TECH control
'**regelwidrig** *adj* against the rule(s); SPORT unfair; ***~es Spiel*** foul play
**regen** ['reːgən] *v/t and v/refl* (*ge-*, *h*) move, stir
'**Regen** *m* (*-s*; *-*) rain; ***starker ~*** heavy rain(fall); **~bogen** *m* rainbow; **~bogenhaut** *f* ANAT iris; **~guss** *m* (heavy) shower, downpour; **~mantel** *m* raincoat; **~schauer** *m* shower; **~schirm** *m* umbrella; **~tag** *m* rainy day; **~tropfen** *m* raindrop; **~wald** *m* rain forest; **~wasser** *n* rainwater; **~wetter** *n* rainy weather; **~wurm** *m* ZO earthworm; **~zeit** *f* rainy season, the rains
**Regie** [re'ʒiː] *f* (*-*; *no pl*) THEA, *film etc*: direction; ***unter der ~ von*** directed by
**Re'gieanweisung** *f* stage direction
**regieren** [re'giːrən] (*no -ge-*, *h*) **1.** *v/i* reign **2.** *v/t* govern (*a.* LING), rule
**Re'gierung** *f* (*-*; *-en*) government, administration; reign
**Re'gierungs|bezirk** *m* administrative district; **~chef** *m* head of government; **~wechsel** *m* change of government
**Regime** [re'ʒiːm] *n* (*-s*; *-*) POL regime
**Re'gimekritiker** *m* POL dissident
**Regiment** [regi'mɛnt] *n* (*-[e]s*; *-er*) (*no pl*) rule (*a. fig*); MIL regiment
**Regisseur** [reʒı'søːɐ] *m* (*-s*; *-e*), **Regis'seurin** *f* (*-*; *-nen*) THEA, *film etc*: director, THEA *Br a.* producer
**Register** [re'gıstɐ] *n* (*-s*; *-*) register (*a.* MUS), record; index; **registrieren** [regıs'triːrən] *v/t* (*no -ge-*, *h*) register, record; *fig* note; **Registrierkasse** [regıs'triːɐkasə] *f* cash register
**Reglement** [reglə'mɑ̃ː] *n* (*-s*; *-s*) regu-

lation, order, rule
**Regler** ['re:glɐ] *m* (*-s*; -) TECH control
**regnen** ['re:gnən] *v/i* (*ge-*, *h*) rain (*a. fig*); ***es regnet in Strömen*** it's pouring with rain; '**regnerisch** *adj* rainy
**regulär** [regu'lɛ:ɐ] *adj* regular; normal
**regulierbar** [regu'li:ɐba:ɐ] *adj* adjustable; controllable
**regulieren** [regu'li:rən] *v/t* (*no -ge-*, *h*) regulate, adjust; control
'**Regung** *f* (-; *-en*) movement, motion; emotion; impulse
'**regungslos** *adj* motionless
**Reh** [re:] *n* (*-[e]s*; *-e*) ZO deer, roe; doe; GASTR venison
**rehabilitieren** [rehabili'ti:rən] *v/t* (*no -ge-*, *h*) rehabilitate
'**Reh|bock** *m* ZO (roe)buck; **~keule** *f* GASTR leg of venison; **~kitz** *n* ZO fawn
**Reibe** ['raibə] *f* (-; *-n*), **Reibeisen** ['raipˀaizən] *n* (*-s*; -) grater, rasp
**reiben** ['raibən] *v/i and v/t* (*irr*, *ge-*, *h*) rub; grate, grind; ***sich die Augen*** (***Hände***) **~** rub one's eyes (hands)
'**Reibung** *f* (-; *-en*) TECH *etc* friction
'**reibungslos** *adj* TECH *etc* frictionless; *fig* smooth
**reich** [raiç] *adj* rich (***an*** *dat* in), wealthy; abundant
**Reich** *n* (*-[e]s*; *-e*) empire, kingdom (*a.* REL, BOT, ZO); *fig* world
**reichen** ['raiçən] (*ge-*, *h*) **1.** *v/t* reach; hand, pass; give, hold out (*one's hand*); **2.** *v/i* last, do; ***~ bis*** reach *or* come up to; ***das reicht*** that will do; F ***mir reicht's!*** I've had enough
'**reichhaltig** *adj* rich
'**reichlich 1.** *adj* rich, plentiful; plenty of **2.** *adv* rather; generously
'**Reichtum** *m* (*-s*; *no pl*) wealth (***an*** *dat* of) (*a. fig*)
'**Reichweite** *f* reach; AVIAT, MIL *etc* range; ***in*** (***außer***) (***j-s***) **~** within (out of) (s.o.'s) reach
**reif** [raif] *adj* ripe, *esp fig* mature
**Reif** *m* (*-[e]s*; *no pl*) white frost, hoarfrost
**Reife** ['raifə] *f* (-; *no pl*) ripeness, *esp fig* maturity; '**reifen** *v/i* (*ge-*, *sein*) ripen, mature (*both a. fig*)
**Reifen** ['raifən] *m* (*-s*; -) hoop; MOT *etc* tire, *Br* tyre; **~panne** *f* MOT flat tire (*Br* tyre), puncture, F flat
'**Reifeprüfung** *f* → ***Abitur***
'**reiflich** *adj* careful
**Reihe** ['raiə] *f* (-; *-n*) line, row; number; series; ***der ~ nach*** in turn; ***ich bin an der ~*** it's my turn
'**Reihenfolge** *f* order
'**Reihenhaus** *n* row (*Br* terraced) house
'**reihenweise** *adv* in rows; F *fig* by the dozen
**Reiher** ['raiɐ] *m* (*-s*; -) ZO heron
**Reim** [raim] *m* (*-[e]s*; *-e*) rhyme
**reimen** ['raimən] *v/t and v/refl* (*ge-*, *h*) rhyme (***auf*** *acc* with)
**rein** [rain] *adj* pure (*a. fig*); clean; *fig* clear (*conscience*); plain (*truth*); mere, sheer, nothing but
'**Reinfall** F *m* flop; let-down
'**Reingewinn** *m* ECON net profit
'**reinhauen** F *v/i* (*sep*, *-ge-*, *h*) tuck in
'**Reinheit** *f* (-; *no pl*) purity (*a. fig*); cleanness
**reinigen** ['rainɪgən] *v/t* (*ge-*, *h*) clean; cleanse (*a.* MED); dry-clean; *fig* purify
'**Reinigung** *f* (-; *-en*) clean(s)ing; *fig* purification; (dry) cleaners; ***chemische ~*** dry cleaning; dry cleaner's
'**Reinigungsmittel** *n* cleaning agent, cleaner, detergent
'**reinlich** *adj* clean; cleanly
'**reinrassig** *adj* ZO purebred, pedigree; thoroughbred
'**Reinschrift** *f* fair copy
**Reis** [rais] *m* (*-es*; *-e*) BOT rice
**Reise** ['raizə] *f* (-; *-n*) trip; journey; tour; MAR voyage; ***auf ~n sein*** be travel(l)ing; ***e-e ~ machen*** take a trip; ***gute ~!*** have a nice trip!; **~andenken** *n* souvenir; **~bü,ro** *n* travel agency *or* bureau; **~führer** *m* guide(book); **~gesellschaft** *f* tourist party; tour operator; **~kosten** *pl* travel(l)ing expenses; **~krankheit** *f* travel sickness; **~leiter(in)** tour guide *or* manager, *Br* courier
'**reisen** *v/i* (*ge-*, *sein*) travel; ***durch Frankreich ~*** tour France; ***ins Ausland ~*** go abroad; '**Reisende** *m*, *f* (*-n*; *-n*) travel(l)er; tourist; passenger
'**Reise|pass** *m* passport; **~scheck** *m* travel(l)er's check (*Br* cheque); **~tasche** *f* travel(l)ing bag, holdall
**Reisig** ['raizɪç] *n* (*-s*; *no pl*) brushwood
**Reißbrett** ['raisbrɛt] *n* drawing board
**reißen** ['raisən] (*irr*, *ge-*) **1.** *v/t* (*h*) tear (***in Stücke*** to pieces), rip; pull, drag; ZO kill; F crack (*jokes*); SPORT knock down;

R

***an sich*** ~ seize, snatch, grab **2.** *v/i* (*sein*) break, burst; ***sich um et.*** ~ scramble for (*or* to get) s.th.; **~d** *adj* torrential

**Reißer** ['raisɐ] F *m* (-*s*; -) thriller; hit

**reißerisch** ['raisərɪʃ] *adj* sensational, loud

'**Reiß|verschluss** *m* zipper; ***den ~ an et. öffnen*** (***schließen***) unzip (zip up) s.th.; **~zwecke** *f* thumbtack, *Br* drawing pin

**reiten** ['raitən] (*irr, ge-*) **1.** *v/i* (*sein*) ride, go on horseback **2.** *v/t* (*h*) ride

'**Reiten** *n* (-*s*; *no pl*) horseback riding

**Reiter** ['raitɐ] *m* (-*s*; -) rider, horseman

**Reiterin** ['raitərɪn] *f* (-; -*nen*) rider, horsewoman

'**Reitpferd** *n* saddle *or* riding horse

**Reiz** [raits] *m* (-*es*; -*e*) charm, attraction, appeal; thrill; MED, PSYCH stimulus; (***für j-n***) ***den ~ verlieren*** lose one's appeal (for s.o.); '**reizbar** *adj* irritable, excitable; **reizen** ['raitsən] (*ge-, h*) **1.** *v/t* irritate (*a.* MED), annoy; ZO bait; provoke; appeal to, attract; tempt; challenge **2.** *v/i cards*: bid; '**reizend** *adj* charming, delightful; lovely, sweet, cute; '**reizlos** *adj* unattractive

'**Reizung** *f* (-; -*en*) irritation (*a.* MED)

'**reizvoll** *adj* attractive; challenging

'**Reizwort** *n* (-[*e*]*s*; -*wörter*) emotive word

**rekeln** ['rɛːkəln] F *v/refl* (*ge-, h*) loll

**Reklamation** [reklama'tsjoːn] *f* (-; -*en*) complaint

**Reklame** [re'klaːmə] *f* (-; -*n*) advertising, publicity; advertisement, F ad; ***~ machen für*** advertise, promote

**reklamieren** [rekla'miːrən] *v/i* (*no -ge-, h*) complain (***wegen*** about), protest (against)

**Rekord** [re'kɔrt] *m* (-[*e*]*s*; -*e*) record; ***e-n ~ aufstellen*** set *or* establish a record

**Rekrut** [re'kruːt] *m* (-*en*; -*en*) MIL recruit

**rekrutieren** [rekru'tiːrən] *v/t* (*no -ge-, h*) recruit

**Rektor** ['rɛktoːɐ] *m* (-*s*; -*en* [rɛk'toːrən]) principal, *Br* headmaster; UNIV president, *Br* rector; **Rektorin** [rɛk'toːrɪn] *f* (-; -*nen*) principal, *Br* headmistress; UNIV president, *Br* rector

**relativ** [rela'tiːf] *adj* relative

**Relief** [re'ljɛf] *n* (-*s*; -*s*) relief

**Religion** [reli'gjoːn] *f* (-; -*en*) religion

**religiös** [reli'gjøːs] *adj* religious

**Reling** ['reːlɪŋ] *f* (-; -*s*) MAR rail

**Reliquie** [re'liːkvjə] *f* (-; -*n*) relic

**Rempelei** [rɛmpə'lai] F *f* (-; -*en*), **rempeln** ['rɛmpəln] F *v/t* (*ge-, h*) jostle

**Rennbahn** ['rɛnbaːn] *f* racecourse, racetrack; cycling track

'**Rennboot** *n* racing boat; speedboat

**rennen** ['rɛnən] *v/i and v/t* (*irr, ge-, sein*) run; '**Rennen** *n* (-*s*; -) race (*a. fig*); heat

'**Renn|fahrer** *m*, **~fahrerin** *f* racing driver; racing cyclist; **~läufer** *m* ski racer; **~pferd** *n* racehorse, racer; **~rad** *n* racing bicycle, racer; **~sport** *m* racing; **~stall** *m* racing stable; **~wagen** *m* race (*Br* racing) car, racer

**renommiert** [renɔ'miːɐt] *adj* renowned

**renovieren** [reno'viːrən] *v/t* (*no -ge-, h*) renovate, F do up; redecorate

**rentabel** [rɛn'taːbəl] *adj* ECON profitable, paying

**Rente** ['rɛntə] *f* (-; -*n*) (old age) pension; ***in ~ gehen*** retire

'**Renten|alter** *n* retirement age; **~versicherung** *f* pension scheme

**Rentier** ['rɛntiːɐ] *n* (-*s*; -*e*) ZO reindeer

**rentieren** [rɛn'tiːrən] *v/refl* (*no -ge-, h*) ECON pay; *fig* be worth it

**Rentner** ['rɛntnɐ] *m* (-*s*; -), '**Rentnerin** ['rɛntnərɪn] *f* (-; -*nen*) (old age) pensioner

**Reparatur** [repara'tuːɐ] *f* (-; -*en*) repair; **~werkstatt** *f* repair shop; MOT garage

**reparieren** [repa'riːrən] *v/t* (*no -ge-, h*) repair, mend, F fix

**Reportage** [repɔr'taːʒə] *f* (-; -*n*) report

**Reporter** [re'pɔrtɐ] *m* (-*s*; -), **Re'porterin** *f* (-; -*nen*) reporter

**Repräsentant** [reprɛzɛn'tant] *m* (-*en*; -*en*) representative; **Repräsentantenhaus** *n* PARL House of Representatives; **Repräsen'tantin** *f* (-; -*nen*) representative; **repräsentieren** [reprɛzɛn'tiːrən] *v/t* (*no -ge-, h*) represent

**Repressalie** [reprɛ'saːljə] *f* (-; -*n*) reprisal

**Reproduktion** [reproduk'tsjoːn] *f* (-; -*en*) reproduction, print

**reproduzieren** [reprodu'tsiːrən] *v/t* (*no -ge-, h*) reproduce

**Reptil** [rɛp'tiːl] *n* (-*s*; -*ien*) ZO reptile

**Republik** [repu'bliːk] *f* (-; -*en*) republic

**Republikaner** [republi'kaːnɐ] *m* (-*s*; -), **Republi'kanerin** *f* (-; -*nen*), **republi'kanisch** *adj* POL republican

**Reservat** [rezɛr'vaːt] *n* (-[*e*]*s*; -*e*) (p)re-

R

serve; reservation

**Reserve** [re'zɛrvə] *f* (-; *-n*) reserve (*a.* MIL); **~...** *in cpds ...kanister, ...rad etc*: spare ...

**reservieren** [rezɛr'vi:rən] *v/t* (*no -ge-, h*) reserve (*a.* **~ *lassen***); ***j-m e-n Platz* ~** keep *or* save a seat for s.o.; **reserviert** [rezɛr'vi:ɐt] *adj* reserved (*a. fig*); aloof; **Reser'viertheit** *f* (-; *no pl*) aloofness

**Residenz** [rezi'dɛnts] *f* (-; *-en*) residence

**Resignation** [rezɪgna'tsjo:n] *f* (-; *no pl*) resignation; **resignieren** [rezɪ'gni:rən] *v/i* (*no -ge-, h*) give up; **resigniert** [rezɪ'gni:ɐt] *adj* resigned

**Resoziali'sierung** *f* (-; *-en*) rehabilitation

**Respekt** [re'spɛkt] *m* (-[*e*]*s*; *no pl*) respect (***vor*** *dat* for); **respektieren** [respɛk'ti:rən] *v/t* (*no -ge-, h*) respect

**re'spektlos** *adj* irreverent, disrespectful; **re'spektvoll** *adj* respectful

**Ressort** [rɛ'so:ɐ] *n* (*-s*; *-s*) department, province

**Rest** [rɛst] *m* (-[*e*]*s*; *-e*) rest; *pl* remains, remnants; GASTR leftovers; F ***das gab ihm den* ~** that finished him (off)

**Restaurant** [rɛsto'rã:] *n* (*-s*; *-s*) restaurant

**restaurieren** [rɛsto'ri:rən] *v/t* (*no -ge-, h*) restore

**'Restbetrag** *m* remainder

**'restlich** *adj* remaining

**'restlos** *adv* completely

**Resultat** [rezʊl'ta:t] *n* (-[*e*]*s*; *-e*) result (*a.* SPORT), outcome

**Retorte** [re'tɔrtə] *f* (-; *-n*) CHEM retort

**Re'tortenbaby** F *n* test-tube baby

**retten** ['rɛtən] *v/t* (*ge-, h*) save, rescue (*both*: ***aus*** *dat*, ***vor*** *dat* from)

**Retter** ['rɛtɐ] *m* (*-s*; -), **'Retterin** *f* (-; *-nen*) rescuer

**Rettich** ['rɛtɪç] *m* (*-s*; *-e*) BOT radish

**'Rettung** *f* (-; *-en*) rescue (***aus*** *dat*, ***vor*** *dat* from); ***das war s-e* ~** that saved him

**'Rettungs|boot** *n* lifeboat; **~mannschaft** *f* rescue party; **~ring** *m* life belt, life buoy; **~schwimmer** *m* lifeguard

**Reue** ['rɔʏə] *f* (-; *no pl*) remorse, repentance (*both*: ***über*** *acc* for)

**reumütig** ['rɔʏmy:tɪç] *adj* repentant

**Revanche** [re'vã:ʃ(ə)] *f* (-; *-n*) revenge

**revanchieren** [revã'ʃi:rən] *v/refl* (*no -ge-, h*) have one's revenge (***bei, an*** *dat* on); make it up (***bei j-m*** to s.o.)

**Revers** [re've:ɐ] *n, m* (-; -) lapel

**revidieren** [revi'di:rən] *v/t* (*no -ge-, h*) revise; ECON audit

**Revier** [re'vi:ɐ] *n* (*-s*; *-e*) district; ZO territory (*a. fig*); → ***Polizeirevier***

**Revision** [revi'zjo:n] *f* (-; *-en*) revision; ECON audit; JUR appeal

**Revolte** [re'vɔltə] *f* (-; *-n*), **revoltieren** [revɔl'ti:rən] *v/i* (*no -ge-, h*) revolt

**Revolution** [revolu'tsjo:n] *f* (-; *-en*) revolution; **revolutionär** [revolutsjo'nɛ:ɐ] *adj*, **Revolutio'när(in)** (*-s*; *-e*/-; *-nen*) revolutionary

**Revolver** [re'vɔlvɐ] *m* (*-s*; -) revolver, F gun

**Revue** [re'vy:] *f* (-; *-n*) THEA (musical) show

**Rezept** [re'tsɛpt] *n* (-[*e*]*s*; *-e*) MED prescription; GASTR recipe (*a. fig*)

**Rezession** [retsɛ'sjo:n] *f* (-; *-en*) ECON recession

**Rhabarber** [ra'barbɐ] *m* (*-s*; *no pl*) BOT rhubarb

**rhetorisch** [re'to:rɪʃ] *adj* rhetorical

**Rheuma** ['rɔʏma] *n* (*-s*; *no pl*) MED rheumatism

**rhythmisch** ['rʏtmɪʃ] *adj* rhythmic(al)

**Rhythmus** ['rʏtmʊs] *m* (-; *-men*) rhythm

**Ribisel** ['ri:bi:zəl] *Austrian f* (-; -[*n*]) → ***Johannisbeere***

**richten** ['rɪçtən] *v/t* (*ge-, h*) fix; get *s.th.* ready, prepare; do (*room, one's hair*); (***sich***) **~ *an*** (*acc*) address (o.s.) to; put *a question* to; **~ *auf*** (*acc*) direct *or* turn to; point *or* aim *camera, gun etc* at; **~ *gegen*** direct against; ***sich* ~ *nach*** go by, act according to; follow (*fashion etc*); depend on; ***ich richte mich ganz nach dir*** I leave it to you

**Richter(in)** ['rɪçtɐ, 'rɪçtərɪn] *m*(*f*) (*-s*; *-/-*; *-nen*) judge

**'richterlich** *adj* judicial

**'Richtgeschwindigkeit** *f* MOT recommended speed

**richtig** ['rɪçtɪç] **1.** *adj* right; correct, proper; true; real **2.** *adv*: **~ *nett*** (***böse***) really nice (angry); ***et.* ~ *machen*** do s.th. right; ***m-e Uhr geht* ~** my watch is right

**'Richtigkeit** *f* (-; *no pl*) correctness

**richtigstellen** *v/t* (*sep, -ge-, h*) *fig* put *or* set right

**'Richt|linien** *pl* guidelines; **~preis** *m*

R

ECON recommended price
'**Richtung** *f* (-; *-en*) direction; POL leaning; PAINT *etc* style; '**richtungslos** *adj* aimless, disorient(at)ed
'**richtungweisend** *adj* pioneering
**rieb** [ri:p] *pret of* ***reiben***
**riechen** ['ri:çən] *v/i and v/t* (*irr, ge-, h*) smell (***nach*** of; ***an*** *dat* at)
**rief** [ri:f] *pret of* ***rufen***
**Riegel** ['ri:gəl] *m* (*-s*; -) bolt, bar
**Riemen** ['ri:mən] *m* (*-s*; -) strap; TECH belt; MAR oar
**Riese** ['ri:zə] *m* (*-n*; *-n*) giant (*a. fig*)
**rieseln** ['ri:zəln] *v/i* (*ge-, sein*) trickle; *rain*: drizzle; *snow*: fall gently
'**Riesen...** *in cpds mst* giant ..., gigantic ..., enormous ...; **~erfolg** *m* huge success, *film etc*: *a.* smash hit
'**riesengroß**, '**riesenhaft** → ***riesig***
'**Riesenrad** *n* Ferris wheel
**riesig** ['ri:zıç] *adj* enormous, gigantic, giant
'**Riesin** *f* (-; *-nen*) giantess (*a. fig*)
**riet** [ri:t] *pret of* ***raten***
**Riff** [rıf] *n* (*-[e]s*; *-e*) GEOGR reef
**Rille** ['rılə] *f* (-; *-n*) groove
**Rind** [rınt] *n* (*-[e]s*; *-er* ['rındɐ]) ZO cow, *pl* cattle; GASTR beef
**Rinde** ['rındə] *f* (-; *-n*) BOT bark; GASTR rind; crust
**Rinder|braten** ['rındɐbra:tən] *m* roast beef; **~herde** *f* herd of cattle
'**Rind|fleisch** *n* GASTR beef; **~(s)leder** *n* cowhide; **~vieh** *n* ZO cattle
**Ring** [rıŋ] *m* (*-[e]s*; *-e*) ring (*a. fig*); MOT ring road; *subway etc*: circle (line)
'**Ringbuch** *n* loose-leaf *or* ring binder
**ringeln** ['rıŋəln] *v/refl* (*ge-, h*) curl, coil (*a.* ZO)
'**Ringelnatter** *f* ZO grass snake
'**Ringelspiel** *Austrian n* → ***Karussell***
**ringen** ['rıŋən] (*irr, ge-, h*) **1.** *v/i* SPORT wrestle (***mit*** with), *fig a.* struggle (against, with; ***um*** for); ***nach Atem ~*** gasp (for breath) **2.** *v/t* wring
'**Ringen** *n* (*-s*; *no pl*) SPORT wrestling
**Ringer** ['rıŋɐ] *m* (*-s*; -) SPORT wrestler
**ringförmig** ['rıŋfœrmıç] *adj* circular
'**Ringkampf** *m* SPORT wrestling match
'**Ringrichter** *m* SPORT referee
**rings** *adv*: ***~ um*** around
'**ringshe'rum**, '**rings'um**, '**ringsum'her** *adv* all around; everywhere
**Rinne** ['rınə] *f* (-; *-n*) groove, channel; gutter; '**rinnen** *v/i* (*irr, ge-, sein*) run; flow, stream; **Rinnsal** ['rınza:l] *n* (*-s*; *-e*) trickle
'**Rinnstein** *m* gutter
**Rippe** ['rıpə] *f* (-; *-n*) ANAT rib
'**Rippenfell** *n* ANAT pleura; **~entzündung** *f* MED pleurisy
'**Rippenstoß** *m* nudge in the ribs
**Risiko** ['ri:ziko] *n* (*-s*; *-s*, *-ken*) risk; ***ein (kein) ~ eingehen*** take a risk (no risks); ***auf eigenes ~*** at one's own risk
**riskant** [rıs'kant] *adj* risky
**riskieren** [rıs'ki:rən] *v/t* (*no -ge-, h*) risk
**riss** [rıs] *pret of* ***reißen***
**Riss** *m* (*-es*; *-e*) tear, rip, split (*a. fig*); crack; MED chap, laceration; **rissig** ['rısıç] *adj* chapped; cracky, cracked
**Rist** [rıst] *m* (*-es*; *-e*) ANAT instep
**ritt** [rıt] *pret of* ***reiten***
**Ritt** *m* (*-[e]s*; *-e*) ride (on horseback)
**Ritter** ['rıtɐ] *m* (*-s*; -) knight; ***j-n zum ~ schlagen*** knight s.o.
'**ritterlich** *fig adj* chivalrous
**Ritz** [rıts] *m* (*-es*; *-e*), **Ritze** ['rıtsə] *f* (-; *-n*) crack, chink; gap
**Rivale** [ri'va:lə] *m* (*-n*; *-n*), **Ri'valin** *f* (-; *-nen*) rival; **rivalisieren** [rivali'zi:rən] *v/i* (*no -ge-, h*) compete; **Rivalität** [rivali'tɛ:t] *f* (-; *-en*) rivalry
**rk.**, **r.-k.** *abbr of* ***römisch-katholisch*** RC, Roman Catholic
**Robbe** ['rɔbə] *f* (-; *-n*) ZO seal
**Robe** ['ro:bə] *f* (-; *-n*) robe, gown
**Roboter** ['rɔbɔtɐ] *m* (*-s*; -) robot
**robust** [ro'bʊst] *adj* robust, strong, tough
**roch** [rɔx] *pret of* ***riechen***
**röcheln** ['rœçəln] (*ge-, h*) **1.** *v/i* moan **2.** *v/t* gasp
**Rock** [rɔk] *m* (*-[e]s*; *Röcke* ['rœkə]) skirt
**Rodelbahn** ['ro:dəlba:n] *f* toboggan run
**rodeln** ['ro:dəln] *v/i* (*ge-, sein*) sled(ge), coast; SPORT toboggan
'**Rodelschlitten** *m* sled(ge); toboggan
**roden** ['ro:dən] *v/t* (*ge-, h*) clear; stub
**Rogen** ['ro:gən] *m* (*-s*; -) (hard) roe
**Roggen** ['rɔgən] *m* (*-s*; -) BOT rye
**roh** [ro:] *adj* raw; rough; *fig* brutal; ***mit ~er Gewalt*** with brute force
'**Rohbau** *m* (*-[e]s*; *-ten*) carcass
'**Rohkost** *f* raw vegetables and fruit
'**Rohling** *m* (*-s*; *-e*) TECH blank; *fig* brute
'**Rohmateri,al** *n* raw material

R

'**Rohöl** *n* crude (oil)
**Rohr** [roːɐ] *n* (-[*e*]*s*; -*e* ['roːrə]) TECH pipe, tube; duct; BOT reed; cane
**Röhre** ['røːrə] *f* (-; -*n*) pipe, tube (*a.* TV), TV *etc* valve
'**Rohr|leitung** *f* duct, pipe(s); plumbing; pipeline; **~stock** *m* cane; **~zucker** *m* cane sugar
'**Rohstoff** *m* raw material
**Rollbahn** ['rɔlbaːn] *f* AVIAT runway
**Rolle** ['rɔlə] *f* (-; -*n*) roll (*a.* SPORT), TECH *a.* roller; coil; caster, castor; THEA part, role (*both a. fig*); ***e-e ~ Garn*** a spool of thread, *Br* a reel of cotton; ***das spielt keine ~*** that doesn't matter, that makes no difference; ***Geld spielt k-e ~*** money is no object
'**rollen** *v/i* (*ge-, sein*) *and v/t* (*ge-, h*) roll
**Roller** ['rɔlɐ] *m* (-*s*; -) (motor) scooter
'**Roll|film** *m* PHOT roll film; **~kragen** *m* turtleneck, *esp Br* polo neck; **~laden** *m* rolling shutter
**Rollo** ['rɔlo] *n* (-*s*; -*s*) shades, *Br* (roller) blind
'**Rollschuh** *m* roller skate; ***~ laufen*** roller-skate; **~bahn** *f* roller-skating rink; **~läufer** *m* roller skater
'**Rollstuhl** *m* wheelchair
'**Rolltreppe** *f* escalator
**Roman** [ro'maːn] *m* (-*s*; -*e*) novel
**Romanik** [ro'maːnɪk] *f* (-; *no pl*) ARCH Romanesque (style *or* period)
**romanisch** [ro'maːnɪʃ] *adj* LING Romance; ARCH Romanesque
**Romanist** [roma'nɪst] *m* (-*en*; -*en*), **Roma'nistin** *f* (-; -*nen*) student of Romance languages
**Ro'manschriftsteller** *m*, **Ro'manschriftstellerin** *f* novelist
**Romantik** [ro'mantɪk] *f* (-; *no pl*) romance; HIST Romanticism
**romantisch** [ro'mantɪʃ] *adj* romantic
**Römer** ['røːmɐ] *m* (-*s*; -), '**Römerin** *f* (-; -*nen*), **römisch** ['røːmɪʃ] *adj* Roman
**Rommee** ['rɔme] *n* (-*s*; -*s*) rummy
**röntgen** ['rœntgən] *v/t* (*ge-, h*) MED X-ray
'**Röntgen|appa,rat** *m* MED X-ray apparatus; **~aufnahme** *f*, **~bild** *n* MED X-ray; **~strahlen** *pl* PHYS X-rays; **~untersuchung** *f* MED X-ray
**rosa** ['roːza] *adj* pink; *fig* rose-colo(u)red; **Rose** ['roːzə] *f* (-; -*n*) BOT rose
'**Rosenkohl** *m* BOT Brussels sprouts
'**Rosenkranz** *m* REL rosary
**rosig** ['roːzɪç] *adj* rosy (*a. fig*)
**Rosine** [ro'ziːnə] *f* (-; -*n*) raisin
'**Rosshaar** *n* (-[*e*]*s*; *no pl*) horsehair
**Rost** [rɔst] *m* (-[*e*]*s*; -*e*) (*no pl*) CHEM rust; TECH grate; GASTR grid(iron), grill; **rosten** ['rɔstən] *v/i* (*ge-, sein*) rust
**rösten** ['rœstən] *v/t* (*ge-, h*) roast (*a.* F); toast; fry
'**Rostfleck** *m* rust stain; '**rostfrei** *adj* rustproof, stainless; '**rostig** *adj* rusty
**rot** [roːt] *adj* red (*a.* POL); ***~ glühend*** red-hot; ***~ werden*** blush; ***in den ~en Zahlen*** ECON in the red
**Rot** *n* (-*s*; -) red; ***die Ampel steht auf ~*** the lights are red; ***bei ~*** at red
'**rotblond** *adj* sandy(-haired)
**Röte** ['røːtə] *f* (-; *no pl*) redness, red (colo[u]r); *fig* blush
**Röteln** ['røːtəln] *pl* MED German measles
**röten** ['røːtən] *v/refl* (*ge-, h*) redden; flush
'**rothaarig** *adj* red-haired
'**Rothaarige** *m, f* (-*n*; -*n*) redhead
**rotieren** [ro'tiːrən] *v/i* (*no -ge-, h*) rotate
'**Rotkehlchen** *n* (-*s*; -) ZO robin
'**Rotkohl** *m* BOT red cabbage
**rötlich** ['røːtlɪç] *adj* reddish
'**Rot|stift** *m* red crayon *or* pencil; **~wein** *m* red wine; **~wild** *n* ZO (red) deer
**Rotznase** ['rɔtsnaːzə] F *f* snotty nose
**Route** ['ruːtə] *f* (-; -*n*) route
**Routine** [ru'tiːnə] *f* (-; *no pl*) routine; experience; **~sache** *f* routine (matter)
**routiniert** [ruti'niːɐt] *adj* experienced
**Rübe** ['ryːbə] *f* (-; -*n*) BOT turnip; (sugar) beet
**Rubin** [ru'biːn] *m* (-*s*; -*e*) MIN ruby
**Rübli** ['ryːpli] *Swiss n* (-*s*; -) BOT carrot
**Rubrik** [ru'briːk] *f* (-; -*en*) heading; column
**Ruck** [rʊk] *m* (-[*e*]*s*; -*e*) jerk, jolt, start; *fig* POL swing
**Rückantwortschein** ['rʏkantvɔrtʃain] *m* reply coupon
'**ruckartig** *adj* jerky, abrupt
'**rückbezüglich** *adj* LING reflexive
'**Rückblende** *f* flashback (***auf*** *acc* to)
'**Rückblick** *m* review (***auf*** *acc* of); ***im ~*** in retrospect
**rücken** ['rʏkən] **1.** *v/t* (*ge-, h*) move, shift, push **2.** *v/i* (*ge-, sein*) move; move over; ***näher ~*** approach

R

ˈ**Rücken** *m* (-*s*; -) ANAT back (*a. fig*); **~deckung** *fig f* backing, support; **~lehne** *f* back(rest); **~mark** *n* ANAT spinal cord; **~schmerzen** *pl* backache; **~schwimmen** *n* backstroke; **~wind** *m* following wind, tailwind; **~wirbel** *m* ANAT dorsal vertebra

ˈ**Rück|erstattung** *f* (-; -*en*) refund; **~fahrkarte** *f* round-trip ticket, *Br a.* return (ticket); **~fahrt** *f* return trip; ***auf der ~*** on the way back; **~fall** *m* relapse

ˈ**rückfällig** *adj*: ***~ werden*** relapse

ˈ**Rückflug** *m* return flight

ˈ**Rückgabe** *f* (-; *no pl*) return

ˈ**Rückgang** *m* drop, fall; ECON recession

ˈ**rückgängig** *adj*: ***~ machen*** cancel

ˈ**Rück|gewinnung** *f* (-; *no pl*) recovery; **~grat** *n* ANAT spine, backbone (*both a. fig*); **~halt** *m* (-[*e*]*s*; *no pl*) support; **~hand** *f*, **~handschlag** *m tennis*: backhand; **~kauf** *m* ECON repurchase

**Rückkehr** [ˈrʏkkeːɐ] *f* (-; *no pl*) return; ***nach s-r ~ aus ...*** on his return from ...

ˈ**Rück|kopplung** *f* ELECTR feedback (*a. fig*); **~lage** *f* (-; -*n*) reserve(s); savings; **~lauf** *m* TECH rewind

ˈ**rückläufig** *adj* falling, downward

ˈ**Rücklicht** *n* (-[*e*]*s*; -*er*) MOT rear light, taillight

**rücklings** [ˈrʏklɪŋs] *adv* backward(s); from behind

ˈ**Rückporto** *n* return postage

ˈ**Rückreise** *f* → ***Rückfahrt***

**Rucksack** [ˈrʊkzak] *m* rucksack, backpack; **~touˌrismus** *m* backpacking; **~touˌrist** *m* backpacker

ˈ**Rück|schlag** *m* SPORT return; *fig* setback; **~schluss** *m* conclusion; **~schritt** *m fig* step back(ward); **~seite** *f* back; reverse; flip side; **~sendung** *f* return

ˈ**Rücksicht** *f* (-; -*en*) consideration, regard; ***aus*** (***ohne***) ***~ auf*** (*acc*) out of (without any) consideration *or* regard for; ***~ nehmen auf*** (*acc*) show consideration for; ˈ**rücksichtslos** *adj* inconsiderate (***gegen*** of), thoughtless (of); ruthless; reckless; ˈ**rücksichtsvoll** *adj* considerate (***gegen*** of), thoughtful

ˈ**Rück|sitz** *m* MOT back seat; **~spiegel** *m* MOT rear-view mirror; **~spiel** *n* SPORT return match; **~stand** *m* CHEM residue; ***mit der Arbeit*** (***e-m Tor***) ***im ~ sein*** be behind with one's work (down by one goal)

ˈ**rückständig** *adj* backward; underdeveloped; ***~e Miete*** arrears of rent

ˈ**Rück|stau** *m* MOT tailback; **~stelltaste** *f* backspace key; **~tritt** *m* resignation; withdrawal; TECH → **~trittbremse** *f* coaster (*Br* back-pedal) brake

**rückwärts** [ˈrʏkvɛrts] *adv* backward(s); ***~ aus*** (*dat*) ***... fahren*** back out of ...; ***~ in*** (*acc*) ***... fahren*** back into ...

ˈ**Rückwärtsgang** *m* MOT reverse (gear)

ˈ**Rückweg** *m* way back

ˈ**ruckweise** *adv* jerkily, in jerks

ˈ**rückwirkend** *adj* retroactive

ˈ**Rück|wirkung** *f* reaction (***auf*** *acc* upon); **~zahlung** *f* repayment; **~zieher** *m* (-*s*; -) *soccer*: overhead kick; F ***e-n ~ machen*** back (*or* chicken) out (***von*** of); **~zug** *m* retreat

**Rüde** [ˈryːdə] *m* (-*n*; -*n*) ZO male (dog *ect*)

**Rudel** [ˈruːdəl] *n* (-*s*; -) ZO pack; herd

**Ruder** [ˈruːdɐ] *n* (-*s*; -) AVIAT, MAR rudder; SPORT oar; ***am ~*** at the helm (*a. fig*); **~boot** *n* rowing boat, rowboat

**Ruderer** [ˈruːdərɐ] *m* (-*s*; -) rower, oarsman; ˈ**Ruderin** *f* (-; -*nen*) rower, oarswoman; ˈ**rudern** *v/i and v/t* (*ge-*, *h*) row

ˈ**Ruder|reˌgatta** *f* (rowing) regatta, boat race; **~sport** *m* rowing

**Ruf** [ruːf] *m* (-[*e*]*s*; -*e*) call (*a. fig*); cry, shout; *fig* reputation; ˈ**rufen** *v/i and v/t* (*irr*, *ge-*, *h*) call (*a. doctor etc*); cry, shout; ***~ nach*** call for (*a. fig*); ***~ lassen*** send for; ***um Hilfe ~*** call *or* cry for help

ˈ**Rufnummer** *f* telephone number

ˈ**Rufweite** *f*: ***in*** (***außer***) ***~*** within (out of) call(ing distance)

**Rüge** [ˈryːgə] *f* (-; -*n*) reproof, reproach (*both*: ***wegen*** for); ˈ**rügen** *v/t* (*ge-*, *h*) reprove, reproach

**Ruhe** [ˈruːə] *f* (-; *no pl*) quiet, calm; silence; rest; peace; calm(ness); ***zur ~ kommen*** come to rest; ***j-n in ~ lassen*** leave s.o. in peace; ***lass mich in ~!*** leave me alone!; ***et. in ~ tun*** take one's time (doing s.th.); ***die ~ behalten*** F keep (one's) cool, play it cool; ***sich zur ~ setzen*** retire; ***~, bitte!*** (be) quiet, please!; ˈ**ruhelos** *adj* restless

ˈ**ruhen** *v/i* (*ge-*, *h*) rest (***auf*** *dat* on)

ˈ**Ruhe|pause** *f* break; **~stand** *m* (-[*e*]*s*; *no pl*) retirement; **~tag** *m* a day's rest; ***Montag ~*** closed on Mondays

**ruhig** [ˈruːɪç] *adj* quiet; silent; calm;

cool; TECH smooth; **~ bleiben** F keep (one's) cool, play it cool
**Ruhm** [ruːm] *m* (-[*e*]*s*; *no pl*) fame, *esp* POL, MIL *etc* glory; **rühmen** [ˈryːmən] *v/t* (*ge-*, *h*) praise (**wegen** for); **sich e-r Sache ~** boast of s.th.; **rühmlich** [ˈryːmlɪç] *adj* laudable, praiseworthy
ˈ**ruhmlos** *adj* inglorious
ˈ**ruhmreich** *adj* glorious
**Ruhr** [ruːɐ] *f* (-; *no pl*) MED dysentery
**Rühreier** [ˈryːɐʔaiɐ] *pl* scrambled eggs
**rühren** [ˈryːrən] *v/t* (*ge-*, *h*) stir; move (*a. fig*); *fig* touch, affect; **das rührt mich gar nicht** that leaves me cold; **rührt euch!** MIL (stand) at ease!; **~d** *fig adj* touching, moving; very kind
**rührig** [ˈryːrɪç] *adj* active, busy
**rührselig** [ˈryːɐzeːlɪç] *adj* sentimental
ˈ**Rührung** *f* (-; *no pl*) emotion
**Ruin** [ruˈiːn] *m* (-*s*; *no pl*) ruin
**Ruine** [ruˈiːnə] *f* (-; -*n*) ruin
**ruinieren** [ruiˈniːrən] *v/t* (*no -ge-*, *h*) ruin
**rülpsen** [ˈrʏlpsən] *v/i* (*ge-*, *h*), **Rülpser** [ˈrʏlpsɐ] *m* (-*s*; -) belch
**Rumäne** [ruˈmɛːnə] *m* (-*n*; -*n*) Romanian; **Rumänien** Romania; **Ruˈmänin** *f* (-; -*nen*), **ruˈmänisch** *adj* Romanian
**Rummel** [ˈrʊməl] F *m* (-*s*; *no pl*) (hustle and) bustle; F ballyhoo; **~platz** F *m* amusement park, fairground
**rumoren** [ruˈmoːrən] *v/i* (*no -ge-*, *h*) rumble
**Rumpelkammer** [ˈrʊmpəlkamɐ] F *f* lumber room
**rumpeln** [ˈrʊmpəln] F *v/i* (*ge-*, *h*, *sein*) rumble
**Rumpf** [rʊmpf] *m* (-*es*; *Rümpfe* [ˈrʏmpfə]) ANAT trunk; MAR hull; AVIAT fuselage
**rümpfen** [ˈrʏmpfən] *v/t* (*ge-*, *h*) **die Nase ~** turn up one's nose (**über** *acc* at), sneer (at)
**rund** [rʊnt] **1.** *adj* round (*a. fig*) **2.** *adv* about; **~ um** (a)round; ˈ**Rundblick** *m* panorama; **Runde** [ˈrʊndə] *f* (-; -*n*) round (*a. fig and* SPORT); *racing*: lap; **s-e ~ machen in** (*dat*) patrol; **die ~ machen** go the round(s)
ˈ**Rundfahrt** *f* tour (**durch** round)
ˈ**Rundfunk** *m* (-*s*; *no pl*) radio; broadcasting corporation; **im ~** on the radio; **im ~ übertragen** *or* **senden** broadcast; **~hörer(in)** listener, *pl a.* (radio) audience; **~sender** *m* broadcasting *or* radio station
ˈ**Rundgang** *m* tour (**durch** of)
ˈ**rundheˈraus** *adv* frankly, plainly
ˈ**rundheˈrum** *adv* all around
ˈ**rundlich** *adj* plump, chubby
ˈ**Rund|reise** *f* tour (**durch** of); **~schau** *f* review; **~schreiben** *n* circular (letter); **~spruch** *Swiss m* → **Rundfunk**
ˈ**Rundung** *f* (-; -*en*) curve
**rundweg** [rʊntˈvɛk] *adv* flatly, plainly
**runter** [ˈrʊntɐ] F *adv* → **herunter**
**Runzel** [ˈrʊntsəl] *f* (-; -*n*) wrinkle
**runz(e)lig** [ˈrʊnts(ə)lɪç] *adj* wrinkled
ˈ**runzeln** *v/t* (*ge-*, *h*) **die Stirn ~** frown (**über** *acc* at)
**Rüpel** [ˈryːpəl] *m* (-*s*; -) lout
**rupfen** [ˈrʊpfən] *v/t* (*ge-*, *h*) pluck
**Rüsche** [ˈryːʃə] *f* (-; -*n*) frill, ruffle
**Ruß** [ˈruːs] *m* (-*es*; *no pl*) soot
**Russe** [ˈrʊsə] *m* (-*n*; -*n*) Russian
**Rüssel** [ˈrʏsəl] *m* (-*s*; -) ZO trunk; snout
**rußen** [ˈruːsən] *v/i* (*ge-*, *h*) smoke
**rußig** [ˈruːsɪç] *adj* sooty
**Russin** [ˈrʊsɪn] *f* (-; -*nen*), **russisch** [ˈrʊsɪʃ] *adj* Russian
ˈ**Russland** Russia
**rüsten** [ˈrʏstən] (*ge-*, *h*) **1.** *v/i* MIL arm **2.** *v/refl* get ready, prepare (**zu, für** for); arm o.s. (**gegen** for)
**rüstig** [ˈrʏstɪç] *adj* vigorous, sprightly
**rustikal** [rʊstiˈkaːl] *adj* rustic
ˈ**Rüstung** *f* (-; -*en*) MIL armament; armo(u)r
ˈ**Rüstungs|indusˌtrie** *f* armament industry; **~wettlauf** *m* arms race
ˈ**Rüstzeug** *n* equipment
**Rute** [ˈruːtə] *f* (-; -*n*) rod (*a. fig*), switch
**Rutschbahn** [ˈrʊtʃbaːn] *f*, **Rutsche** [ˈrʊtʃə] *f* (-; -*n*) slide, chute; ˈ**rutschen** *v/i* (*ge-*, *sein*) slide, slip; glide; MOT *etc* skid; **rutschig** [ˈrʊtʃɪç] *adj* slippery
ˈ**rutschsicher** *adj* MOT *etc* non-skid
**rütteln** [ˈrʏtəln] (*ge-*, *h*) **1.** *v/t* shake **2.** *v/i* jolt; **an der Tür ~** rattle at the door

# S

**S** *abbr of* ***Süd(en)*** S, south
**S.** *abbr of* ***Seite*** p., page
**s.** *abbr of* ***siehe*** see
**Saal** [zaːl] *m* (-[*e*]*s*; *Säle* ['zɛːlə]) hall
**Saat** [zaːt] *f* (-; *-en*) (*no pl*) sowing; seed(s) (*a. fig*); crop(s)
**Sabbat** ['zabat] *m* (-*s*; -*e*) sabbath (day)
**sabbern** ['zabɐn] F *v/i* (*ge-*, *h*) slobber, slaver
**Säbel** ['zɛːbəl] *m* (-*s*; -) saber, *Br* sabre (*a.* SPORT), sword; '**säbeln** F *v/t* (*ge-*, *h*) cut, hack
**Sabotage** [zabo'taːʒə] *f* (-; *-n*) sabotage; **Saboteur** [zabo'tøːɐ] *m* (-*s*; -*e*) saboteur; **sabotieren** [zabo'tiːrən] *v/t* (*no -ge-*, *h*) sabotage
**Sach|bearbeiter** ['zaxbəˀarbaitɐ] *m*, **~bearbeiterin** ['zaxbəˀarbaitərın] *f* official in charge; **~beschädigung** *f* damage to property; **~buch** *n* specialized book, *pl coll* nonfiction
'**sachdienlich** *adj*: ***~e Hinweise*** relevant information
**Sache** ['zaxə] *f* (-; *-n*) thing; matter, business; issue, problem, question; cause; JUR matter, case; *pl* things, clothes; ***zur ~ kommen*** (***bei der ~ bleiben***) come (keep) to the point; ***nicht zur ~ gehören*** be irrelevant
'**sachgerecht** *adj* proper
'**Sachkenntnis** *f* expert knowledge
'**sachkundig** *adj* expert
'**sachlich** *adj* matter-of-fact, businesslike; unbias(s)ed, objective; practical, technical; ***~ richtig*** factually correct
**sächlich** ['zɛçlıç] *adj* LING neuter
'**Sachre,gister** *n* (subject) index
'**Sachschaden** *m* damage to property
**sacht** [zaxt] *adj* soft, gentle; slow
'**Sach|verhalt** *m* (-[*e*]*s*; -*e*) facts (of the case); **~verstand** *m* know-how; **~verständige** *m*, *f* (-*n*; -*n*) expert; JUR expert witness; **~wert** *m* (-[*e*]*s*; *no pl*) real value; **~zwänge** *pl* inherent necessities
**Sack** [zak] *m* (-[*e*]*s*; *Säcke* ['zɛkə]) sack, bag; V balls; **sacken** ['zakən] F *v/i* (*ge-*, *sein*) sink; '**Sackgasse** *f* blind alley (*a. fig*), dead end (*a. fig*), *fig* impasse
**Sadismus** [za'dısmʊs] *m* (-; *no pl*) sadism; **Sadist** [za'dıst] *m* (-*en*; -*en*) sadist; **sa'distisch** *adj* sadistic
**säen** ['zɛːən] *v/t and v/i* (*ge-*, *h*) sow (*a. fig*)
**Safari** [za'faːri] *f* (-; -*s*) safari; **~park** *m* wildlife reserve, safari park
**Saft** [zaft] *m* (-[*e*]*s*; *Säfte* ['zɛftə]) juice; BOT sap (*both a. fig*); **saftig** ['zaftıç] *adj* juicy (*a. fig*); lush; F fancy (*prices etc*)
**Sage** ['zaːgə] *f* (-; *-n*) legend, myth
**Säge** ['zɛːgə] *f* (-; *-n*) saw
'**Sägemehl** *n* sawdust
**sagen** ['zaːgən] *v/i and v/t* (*ge-*, *h*) say; ***j-m et. ~*** tell s.o. s.th.; ***die Wahrheit ~*** tell the truth; ***er lässt dir ~*** he asked me to tell you; ***~ wir …*** (let's) say …; ***man sagt, er sei reich*** he is said to be rich; ***er lässt sich nichts ~*** he will not listen to reason; ***das hat nichts zu ~*** it doesn't matter; ***et.*** (***nichts***) ***zu ~ haben*** (***bei***) have a say (no say) (in); ***das sagt mir nichts*** it doesn't mean anything to me; ***unter uns gesagt*** between you and me
**sägen** ['zɛːgən] *v/t and v/i* (*ge-*, *h*) saw
'**sagenhaft** *adj* legendary; F fabulous, incredible, fantastic
'**Sägespäne** *pl* sawdust
'**Sägewerk** *n* sawmill
**sah** [zaː] *pret of* ***sehen***
**Sahne** ['zaːnə] *f* (-; *no pl*) cream
**Saison** [zɛ'zõː] *f* (-; -*s*) season; ***in der ~*** in season
**sai'sonbedingt** *adj* seasonal
**Saite** ['zaitə] *f* (-; *-n*) MUS string, chord (*a. fig*); '**Saiteninstru,ment** *n* MUS string(ed) instrument
**Sakko** ['zako] *m*, *n* (-*s*; -*s*) (sports) jacket, sport(s) coat
**Sakristei** [zakrıs'tai] *f* (-; *-en*) REL vestry, sacristy
**Salat** [za'laːt] *m* (-[*e*]*s*; -*e*) BOT lettuce; GASTR salad; **~sauce** *f* salad dressing
**Salbe** ['zalbə] *f* (-; *-n*) ointment
'**Salbung** *f* (-; *-en*) unction
'**salbungsvoll** *adj* unctuous
**Saldo** ['zaldo] *m* (-*s*; -*s*, -*di*) ECON balance
**Salon** [za'lõː] *m* (-*s*; -*s*) salon; MAR saloon; drawing room
**salopp** [za'lɔp] *adj* casual; *contp* sloppy

**Salpeter** [zal'peːtɐ] *m* (*-s*; *no pl*) CHEM salt|peter (*Br* -petre), niter, *Br* nitre
**Salto** ['zalto] *m* (*-s*; *-s*, *-ti*) somersault
**Salut** [za'luːt] *m* (*-[e]s*; *-e*) MIL salute; **~ *schießen*** fire a salute
**salutieren** [zalu'tiːrən] *v/i* (*no -ge-*, *h*) MIL (give a) salute
**Salve** ['zalvə] *f* (*-*; *-n*) MIL volley (*a. fig*); salute
**Salz** [zalts] *n* (*-es*; *-e*) salt
**'Salzbergwerk** *n* salt mine
**salzen** ['zaltsən] *v/t* (*[irr,] ge-*, *h*) salt
**salzfrei** ['zaltsfrai] *adj* salt-free, no-salt *diet*
**salzig** ['zaltsɪç] *adj* salty
**'Salz|kar,toffeln** *pl* boiled potatoes; **~säure** *f* (*-*; *no pl*) CHEM hydrochloric acid; **~stange** *f* pretzel (*Br* salt) stick; **~streuer** *m* (*-s*; *-*) salt shaker, *Br* salt cellar; **~wasser** *n* salt water
**Same** ['zaːmə] *m* (*-n*; *-n*), **'Samen** *m* (*-s*-*-*) BOT seed (*a. fig*); BIOL sperm, semen
**'Samen|bank** *f* (*-*; *-en*) MED, VET sperm bank; **~erguss** *m* ejaculation; **~korn** *n* BOT seedcorn
**Sammel...** ['zaməl-] *in cpds ...begriff*, *...bestellung*, *...konto etc*: collective ...; **~büchse** *f* collecting box
**'sammeln** *v/t* (*ge-*, *h*) collect; gather, pick; accumulate; ***sich* ~** assemble; *fig* compose o.s.
**Sammler** ['zamlɐ] *m* (*-s*; *-*), **'Sammlerin** *f* (*-*; *-nen*) collector
**'Sammlung** *f* (*-*; *-en*) collection
**Samstag** ['zamstaːk] *m* (*-[e]s*; *-e*) Saturday
**samt** [zamt] *prp* (*dat*) together *or* along with
**Samt** *m* (*-[e]s*; *-e*) velvet
**sämtlich** ['zɛmtlɪç] *adj*: **~e** *pl* all the; the complete *works etc*
**Sanatorium** [zana'toːrjʊm] *n* (*-s*; *-ien*) sanatorium, sanitarium
**Sand** [zant] *m* (*-[e]s*; *-e*) sand
**Sandale** [zan'daːlə] *f* (*-*; *-n*) sandal
**Sandalette** [zanda'lɛtə] *f* (*-*; *-n*) high-heeled sandal
**'Sand|bahn** *f* SPORT dirt track; **~bank** *f* (*-*; *-bänke*) sandbank; **~boden** *m* sandy soil; **~burg** *f* sandcastle
**sandig** ['zandɪç] *adj* sandy
**'Sand|mann** *m*, **~männchen** *n* sandman; **~pa,pier** *n* sandpaper; **~sack** *m* sand bag; **~stein** *m* sandstone; **~strand** *m* sandy beach
**sandte** ['zantə] *pret of* ***senden***
**'Sanduhr** *f* hourglass
**sanft** [zanft] *adj* gentle, soft; mild; easy (*death*)
**sanftmütig** ['zanftmyːtɪç] *adj* gentle, mild
**sang** [zaŋ] *pret of* ***singen***
**Sänger** ['zɛŋɐ] *m* (*-s*; *-*), **Sängerin** ['zɛŋərɪn] *f* (*-*; *-nen*) singer
**sanieren** [za'niːrən] *v/t* (*no -ge-*, *h*) redevelop (*a.* ECON), rehabilitate (*a.* ARCH)
**Sa'nierung** *f* (*-*; *-en*) redevelopment, rehabilitation; **Sa'nierungsgebiet** *n* redevelopment area
**sanitär** [zani'tɛːɐ] *adj* sanitary
**Sanitäter** [zani'tɛːtɐ] *m* (*-s*; *-*) paramedic; MIL medic, *Br* medical orderly
**sank** [zaŋk] *pret of* ***sinken***
**Sankt** [zaŋkt] Saint, ABBR St
**Sardelle** [zar'dɛlə] *f* (*-*; *-n*) ZO anchovy
**Sardine** [zar'diːnə] *f* (*-*; *-n*) ZO sardine
**Sarg** [zark] *m* (*-[e]s*; *Särge* ['zɛrgə]) casket, *esp Br* coffin
**Sarkasmus** [zar'kasmʊs] *m* (*-*; *no pl*) sarcasm; **sar'kastisch** *adj* sarcastic
**saß** [zaːs] *pret of* ***sitzen***
**Satan** ['zaːtan] *m* (*-s*; *-e*) Satan; *fig* devil
**Satellit** [zatɛ'liːt] *m* (*-en*; *-en*) satellite (*a. fig*); ***über* ~** by *or* via satellite
**Satel'liten...** *in cpds ...bild*, *...staat*, *...stadt*, *...-TV*: satellite ...
**Satin** [za'tɛ̃ː] *m* (*-s*; *-s*) satin; sateen
**Satire** [za'tiːrə] *f* (*-*; *-n*) satire (***auf*** *acc* upon); **Satiriker** [za'tiːrikɐ] *m* (*-s*; *-*) satirist; **sa'tirisch** *adj* satiric(al)
**satt** [zat] *adj* F full (up); ***ich bin* ~** I've had enough, F I'm full (up); ***sich* ~ *essen*** eat one's fill (***an*** *dat* of)
**Sattel** ['zatəl] *m* (*-s*; *Sättel* ['zɛtəl]) saddle; **'satteln** *v/t* (*ge-*, *h*) saddle; **'Sattelschlepper** *m* MOT semi-trailer truck, *Br* articulated lorry
**'satthaben** *v/t* (*irr*, ***haben***, *sep*, *-ge-*, *h*) F be tired *or* F sick of, be fed up with
**sättigen** ['zɛtɪgən] (*ge-*, *h*) **1.** *v/t* satisfy; feed; CHEM, PHYS saturate **2.** *v/i* be substantial, be filling; **'Sättigung** *f* (*-*; *-en*) satiety; CHEM, ECON saturation (*a. fig*)
**Sattler** ['zatlɐ] *m* (*-s*; *-*) saddler
**Sattlerei** [zatlə'rai] *f* (*-*; *-en*) saddlery
**Satz** [zats] *m* (*-es*; *Sätze* ['zɛtsə]) leap; LING sentence; *tennis etc*: set; ECON rate; MUS movement; **~aussage** *f* LING

predicate; **~bau** *m* (-[*e*]*s*; *no pl*) LING syntax; construction; **~gegenstand** *m* LING subject
**Satzung** ['zatsʊŋ] *f* (-; *-en*) statute
'**Satzzeichen** *n* LING punctuation mark
**Sau** [zau] *f* (-; *Säue* ['zɔʏə]) ZO sow; HUNT wild sow; F swine, pig
**sauber** ['zaubɐ] *adj* clean (*a.* F fig); pure; neat (*a. fig*), tidy; decent; *iro* fine, nice; **~ *halten*** keep clean (***sich*** o.s.); **~ *machen*** clean (up); '**Sauberkeit** *f* (-; *no pl*) clean(li)ness; tidiness, neatness; purity; decency; '**saubermachen** *v/t and v/i* (*sep*, *-ge-*, *h*) → ***sauber***; **säubern** ['zɔʏbɐn] *v/t* (*ge-*, *h*) clean (up); cleanse (*a.* MED)
**sauer** ['zauɐ] *adj* sour (*a. fig*), acid (*a.* CHEM); GASTR pickled; F mad (***auf*** *acc* at), cross (with); **~ *werden*** turn sour; F get mad; ***saurer Regen*** acid rain
**säuerlich** ['zɔʏɐlɪç] *adj* sharp; F wry
'**Sauerstoff** *m* (-[*e*]*s*; *no pl*) CHEM oxygen; **~gerät** *n* MED oxygen apparatus; **~zelt** *n* MED oxygen tent
'**Sauerteig** *m* leaven
**saufen** ['zaufən] *v/t and v/i* (*irr*, *ge-*, *h*) ZO drink; F booze; **Säufer(in)** ['zɔʏfɐ, 'zɔʏfərɪn] *m*(*f*) F (*-s*; *-/-*; *-nen*) drunkard, F boozer
**saugen** ['zaugən] *v/i and v/t* ([*irr*,] *ge-*, *h*) suck (***an et.*** [at] s.th.)
**säugen** ['zɔʏgən] *v/t* (*ge-*, *h*) suckle (*a.* ZO), nurse, breastfeed
'**Säugetier** *n* mammal
**saugfähig** ['zaukfɛːɪç] *adj* absorbent
**Säugling** ['zɔʏklɪŋ] *m* (*-s*; *-e*) baby, infant
'**Säuglings|heim** *n* (baby) nursery; **~pflege** *f* infant care; **~schwester** *f* baby nurse; **~stati,on** *f* neonatal care unit; **~sterblichkeit** *f* infant mortality
**Säule** ['zɔʏlə] *f* (-; *-n*) column; pillar (*a. fig*); '**Säulengang** *m* colonnade
**Saum** [zaum] *m* (-[*e*]*s*; *Säume* ['zɔʏmə]) hem(line); seam; **säumen** ['zɔʏmən] *v/t* (*ge-*, *h*) hem; border, edge; line
**Sauna** ['zauna] *f* (-; *-s*, *Saunen*) sauna
**Säure** ['zɔʏrə] *f* (-; *-n*) CHEM acid
**säurehaltig** ['zɔʏrəhaltɪç] *adj* acid
**sausen** ['zauzən] *v/i* (*ge-*, *sein*) F rush, dash; (*ge-*, *h*) *ears*: buzz; *wind*: howl
'**Saustall** *m* pigsty (*a.* F *contp*)
**Saxophon** [zakso'foːn] *n* (*-s*; *-e*) MUS saxophone, F sax
**S-Bahn** ['ɛsbaːn] *f* rapid transit, *Br* suburban train
**Schabe** ['ʃaːbə] *f* (-; *-n*) ZO cockroach
'**schaben** *v/t* (*ge-*, *h*) scrape (***von*** from)
**schäbig** ['ʃɛːbɪç] *adj* shabby, *fig a.* mean
**Schablone** [ʃa'bloːnə] *f* (-; *-n*) stencil; *fig* stereotype
**Schach** [ʃax] *n* (*-s*; *no pl*) chess; **~*!*** check!; **~ *und matt!*** checkmate!; ***j-n in ~ halten*** keep s.o. in check; **~brett** *n* chessboard; **~feld** *n* square; **~fi,gur** *f* chessman, piece
**schach'matt** *adj*: ***j-n ~ setzen*** checkmate s.o.
'**Schachspiel** *n* (game of) chess; chessboard and men
**Schacht** [ʃaxt] *m* (-[*e*]*s*; *Schächte* ['ʃɛçtə]) shaft, *mining*: *a.* pit
**Schachtel** ['ʃaxtəl] *f* (-; *-n*) box; carton; ***e-e ~ Zigaretten*** a pack (*esp Br* packet) of cigarettes
'**Schachzug** *m* move (*a. fig*)
**schade** ['ʃaːdə] *pred adj*: ***es ist ~*** it's a pity; ***wie ~!*** what a pity *or* shame!; ***zu ~ sein für*** be too good for
**Schädel** ['ʃɛːdəl] *m* (*-s*; -) ANAT skull; **~bruch** *m* MED fracture of the skull
**schaden** ['ʃaːdən] *v/i* (*ge-*, *h*) damage, do damage to, harm, hurt; ***der Gesundheit ~*** be bad for one's health; ***das schadet nichts*** it doesn't matter; ***es könnte ihm nicht ~*** it wouldn't hurt him
'**Schaden** *m* (*-s*; *Schäden* ['ʃɛːdən]) damage (***an*** *dat* to); *esp* TECH trouble, defect (*a.* MED); *fig* disadvantage; ECON loss; ***j-m ~ zufügen*** do s.o. harm; **~ersatz** *m* damages; **~ *leisten*** pay damages; **~freude** *f*: **~ *empfinden über*** (*acc*) gloat over
'**schadenfroh** *adv* gloatingly
**schadhaft** ['ʃaːthaft] *adj* damaged; defective, faulty; leaking (*pipes*)
**schädigen** ['ʃɛːdɪgən] *v/t* (*ge-*, *h*) damage, harm
**schädlich** ['ʃɛːtlɪç] *adj* harmful, injurious; bad (for your health)
**Schädling** ['ʃɛːtlɪŋ] *m* (*-s*; *-e*) BIOL pest
'**Schädlings|bekämpfung** *f* pest control; **~bekämpfungsmittel** *n* pesticide
**Schadstoff** ['ʃaːtʃtɔf] *m* harmful substance; pollutant
'**schadstoffarm** *adj* MOT low-emission

**Schaf** [ʃaːf] *n* (-[*e*]*s*; -*e*) zo sheep
'**Schafbock** *m* zo ram
**Schäfer** ['ʃɛːfɐ] *m* (-*s*; -) shepherd; **~hund** *m* sheepdog; ***Deutscher~*** German shepherd, *esp Br* Alsatian
'**Schaffell** *n* sheepskin; zo fleece
**schaffen**[1] ['ʃafən] *v/t* (*irr*, *ge-*, *h*) create
'**schaffen**[2] (*ge-*, *h*) **1.** *v/t* cause, bring about; manage, get *s.th.* done; take; ***es ~*** make it, *a.* succeed **2.** *v/i* work; ***j-m zu ~ machen*** cause s.o. trouble; ***sich zu ~ machen an*** (*dat*) tamper with
**Schaffner** ['ʃafnɐ] *m* (-*s*; -), '**Schaffnerin** *f* (-; -*nen*) conductor; *Br* RAIL guard
**Schafott** [ʃa'fɔt] *n* (-[*e*]*s*; -*e*) scaffold
**Schaft** [ʃaft] *m* (-[*e*]*s*; *Schäfte* ['ʃɛftə]) shaft; stock; shank; leg
'**Schafwolle** *f* sheep's wool
'**Schafzucht** *f* sheep breeding
**schäkern** ['ʃɛːkɐn] *v/i* (*ge-*, *h*) joke; flirt
**schal** [ʃaːl] *adj* stale, flat, *fig a.* empty
**Schal** *m* (-*s*; -*s*) scarf
**Schale** ['ʃaːlə] *f* (-; -*n*) bowl, dish; GASTR shell; peel, skin; **schälen** ['ʃɛːlən] *v/t* (*ge-*, *h*) peel, pare; ***sich ~*** *skin*: peel (off)
**Schall** [ʃal] *m* (-[*e*]*s*; -*e*) sound; **~dämpfer** *m* silencer (*a. Br* MOT), MOT muffler
'**schalldicht** *adj* soundproof
**schallen** ['ʃalən] *v/i* ([*irr*,] *ge-*, *h*) sound; ring (out); ***~des Gelächter*** roars of laughter
'**Schall|geschwindigkeit** *f* speed of sound; **~mauer** *f* sound barrier; **~platte** *f* record, disk, *Br* disc; **~welle** *f* PHYS sound wave
**schalten** ['ʃaltən] *v/i and v/t* (*ge-*, *h*) switch, turn; MOT shift (*esp Br* change) gear; F get it; react; **Schalter** ['ʃaltɐ] *m* (-*s*; -) counter; RAIL ticket window; AVIAT desk; ELECTR switch
'**Schalt|hebel** *m* MOT gear lever; TECH, AVIAT control lever; ELECTR switch lever; **~jahr** *n* leap year; **~tafel** *f* ELECTR switchboard, control panel; **~uhr** *f* time switch
'**Schaltung** *f* (-; -*en*) MOT gearshift; ELECTR circuit
**Scham** [ʃaːm] *f* (-; *no pl*) shame; ***vor~*** with shame; **schämen** ['ʃɛːmən] *v/refl* (*ge-*, *h*) be *or* feel ashamed (*gen*, ***wegen*** of); ***du solltest dich*** (***was***) ***~!*** you ought to be ashamed of yourself!

'**Scham|gefühl** *n* (-[*e*]*s*; *no pl*) sense of shame; **~haare** *pl* pubic hair
'**schamhaft** *adj* bashful
'**schamlos** *adj* shameless; indecent
**Schande** ['ʃandə] *f* (-; *no pl*) shame, disgrace; **schänden** ['ʃɛndən] *v/t* (*ge-*, *h*) disgrace; desecrate; rape
**Schandfleck** ['ʃantflɛk] *m* eyesore
**schändlich** ['ʃɛntlɪç] *adj* disgraceful
'**Schandtat** *f* atrocity
**Schanze** ['ʃantsə] *f* (-; -*n*) SPORT ski jump
**Schar** [ʃaːɐ] *f* (-; -*en* ['ʃaːrən]) troop, band; F horde; crowd; zo flock
'**scharen** *v/refl* (*ge-*, *h*) ***sich ~ um*** gather round
**scharf** [ʃarf] *adj* sharp (*a. fig*), PHOT *a.* in focus; clear; savage, fierce (*dog*); live (*ammunition*), armed (*bomb etc*); GASTR hot; F hot, sexy; F ***~ sein auf*** (*acc*) be keen on; ***~ (ein)stellen*** PHOT focus; F ***~e Sachen*** hard liquor
**Schärfe** ['ʃɛrfə] *f* (-; -*n*) sharpness (*a.* PHOT); *fig* severity, fierceness
'**schärfen** *v/t* (*ge-*, *h*) sharpen
'**Scharf|richter** *m* executioner; **~schütze** *m* sharpshooter; sniper
'**scharfsichtig** *adj* sharp-sighted; *fig* clear-sighted
'**Scharfsinn** *m* (-[*e*]*s*; *no pl*) acumen
'**scharfsinnig** *adj* sharp-witted, shrewd
'**scharfstellen** *v/t* (*sep*, *-ge-*, *h*) → ***scharf***
**Scharlach** ['ʃarlax] *m* (-*s*; *no pl*) scarlet; MED scarlet fever
'**scharlachrot** *adj* scarlet
**Scharlatan** ['ʃarlatan] *m* (-*s*; -*e*) charlatan, fraud
**Scharnier** [ʃar'niːɐ] *n* (-*s*; -*e*) TECH hinge
**Schärpe** ['ʃɛrpə] *f* (-; -*n*) sash
**scharren** ['ʃarən] *v/i* (*ge-*, *h*) scrape, scratch
**schartig** ['ʃartɪç] *adj* jagged, notchy
**Schaschlik** ['ʃaʃlɪk] *m*, *n* (-*s*; -*s*) GASTR shish kebab
**Schatten** ['ʃatən] *m* (-*s*; -) shadow (*a. fig*); shade; ***im ~*** in the shade
'**schattenhaft** *adj* shadowy
**Schattierung** [ʃa'tiːrʊŋ] *f* (-; -*en*) shade; *fig* colo(u)r
**schattig** ['ʃatɪç] *adj* shady
**Schatz** [ʃats] *m* (-*es*; *Schätze* ['ʃɛtsə]) treasure; *fig* darling; **~amt** *n* POL Treasury Department, *Br* Treasury
**schätzen** ['ʃɛtsən] *v/t* (*ge-*, *h*) estimate,

S

value (*both*: ***auf*** *acc* at); appreciate; think highly of; F reckon, guess

'**Schatz|kammer** *f* treasury (*a. fig*); **~kanzler** *m* Chancellor of the Exchequer; **~meister(in)** treasurer

'**Schätzung** *f* (-; *-en*) estimate; valuation

**Schau** [ʃau] *f* (-; *-en*) show, exhibition; ***zur ~ stellen*** exhibit, display

**Schauder** ['ʃaudɐ] *m* (*-s*; -) shudder

'**schauderhaft** *adj* horrible, dreadful

'**schaudern** *v/i* (*ge-*, *h*) shudder, shiver (*both*: **vor** *dat* with)

**schauen** ['ʃauən] *v/i* (*ge-*, *h*) look (***auf*** *acc* at)

**Schauer** ['ʃauɐ] *m* (*-s*; -) METEOR shower; shudder, shiver; **~geschichte** *f* horror story (*a. fig*)

'**schauerlich** *adj* dreadful, horrible

**Schaufel** ['ʃaufəl] *f* (-; *-n*) shovel; dustpan; '**schaufeln** *v/t* (*ge-*, *h*) shovel; dig

'**Schaufenster** *n* shop window; **~auslage** *f* window display; **~bummel** *m*: ***e-n ~ machen*** go window-shopping; **~dekorati,on** *f* window dressing

**Schaukel** ['ʃaukəl] *f* (-; *-n*) swing

'**schaukeln** (*ge-*, *h*) **1.** *v/i* swing; *boat etc*: rock **2.** *v/t* rock

'**Schaukel|pferd** *n* rocking horse; **~stuhl** *m* rocking chair, rocker

**Schaulustige** ['ʃaulustɪgə] *pl* (curious) onlookers, F rubbernecks

**Schaum** [ʃaum] *m* (*-[e]s*; *Schäume* ['ʃɔʏmə]) foam; GASTR froth, head; lather; spray; **schäumen** ['ʃɔʏmən] *v/i* (*ge-*, *h*) foam (*a. fig*), froth; lather; spray

'**Schaumgummi** *m* foam rubber

**schaumig** ['ʃaumɪç] *adj* foamy, frothy

'**Schaumlöscher** *m* foam extinguisher

'**Schauplatz** *m* scene

'**Schaupro,zess** *m* JUR show trial

**schaurig** ['ʃaurɪç] *adj* creepy; horrible

'**Schauspiel** *n* THEA play; *fig* spectacle

'**Schauspieler(in)** actor (actress)

'**Schauspielschule** *f* drama school

**Schausteller** ['ʃauʃtɛlɐ] *m* (*-s*; -) showman

**Scheck** [ʃɛk] *m* (*-s*; *-s*) ECON check, *Br* cheque; **~heft** *n* checkbook, *Br* chequebook

**scheckig** ['ʃɛkɪç] *adj* spotty

'**Scheckkarte** *f* check cashing (*Br* cheque) card

**scheffeln** ['ʃɛfəln] F *v/t* (*ge-*, *h*) rake in

**Scheibe** ['ʃaibə] *f* (-; *-n*) disk, *Br* disc; slice; pane; target

'**Scheiben|bremse** *f* MOT disk (*Br* disc) brake; **~wischer** *m* MOT windshield (*Br* windscreen) wiper

**Scheide** ['ʃaidə] *f* (-; *-n*) sheath; scabbard; ANAT vagina; '**scheiden** (*irr*, *ge-*, -) **1.** *v/t* (*h*) separate, part (*both*: **von** from); divorce; ***sich ~ lassen*** get a divorce, ***von j-m***: divorce s.o. **2.** *v/i* (*sein*) part; ***~ aus*** (*dat*) retire from

'**Scheideweg** *m* crossroads

'**Scheidung** *f* (-; *-en*) divorce

'**Scheidungsklage** *f* JUR divorce suit

**Schein**[1] [ʃain] *m* (*-[e]s*; *-e*) certificate; blank, *Br* form; bill, *Br* note

**Schein**[2] *m* (*-[e]s*; *no pl*) light; *fig* appearance; ***et.*** (***nur***) ***zum ~ tun*** (only) pretend to do s.th.

'**scheinbar** *adj* seeming, apparent

**scheinen** ['ʃainən] *v/i* (*irr*, *ge-*, *h*) shine; *fig* seem, appear, look

'**scheinheilig** *adj* hypocritical

'**Scheinwerfer** *m* searchlight; MOT headlight; THEA spotlight

**Scheiß...** ['ʃais-] V *in cpds* damn ..., fucking ..., *esp Br* bloody ...

**Scheiße** ['ʃaisə] V *f* (-; *no pl*), '**scheißen** V *v/i* (*irr*, *ge-*, *h*) shit, crap

**Scheit** [ʃait] *n* (*-[e]s*; *-e*) piece of wood

**Scheitel** ['ʃaitəl] *m* (*-s*; -) parting

'**scheiteln** *v/t* (*ge-*, *h*) part

**Scheiterhaufen** ['ʃaitɐhaufən] *m* pyre; HIST stake

**scheitern** ['ʃaitɐn] *v/i* (*ge-*, *sein*) fail, go wrong

**Schelle** ['ʃɛlə] *f* (-; *-n*) (little) bell; TECH clamp, clip

**Schellfisch** ['ʃɛlfɪʃ] *m* zo haddock

**Schelm** [ʃɛlm] *m* (*-[e]s*; *-e*) rascal

**schelmisch** ['ʃɛlmɪʃ] *adj* impish

**Schema** ['ʃeːma] *n* (*-s*; *-s*, *-ta*) pattern, system; **schematisch** [ʃe'maːtɪʃ] *adj* schematic; mechanical

**Schemel** ['ʃeːməl] *m* (*-s*; -) stool

**schemenhaft** ['ʃeːmənhaft] *adj* shadowy

**Schenkel** ['ʃɛŋkəl] *m* (*-s*; -) ANAT thigh; shank; MATH leg

**schenken** ['ʃɛŋkən] *v/t* (*ge-*, *h*) give (as a present) (***zu*** for)

'**Schenkung** *f* (-; *-en*) JUR donation

**Scherbe** ['ʃɛrbə] *f* (-; *-n*), '**Scherben** *m* (*-s*; -) (broken) piece, fragment

S

**Schere** ['ʃeːrə] *f* (-; *-n*) scissors; zo claw
**scheren**[1] ['ʃeːrən] *v/t* (*irr*, *ge-*, *h*) zo shear; BOT clip; cut
'**scheren**[2] *v/refl* (*ge-*, *h*) ***sich ~ um*** bother about
**Scherereien** [ʃeːrə'raiən] *pl* trouble, bother
**Schermaus** ['ʃeːɐmaus] *Austrian f* zo mole
**Scherz** [ʃɛrts] *m* (*-es*; *-e*) joke; ***im*** (***zum***) ~ for fun; **scherzen** ['ʃɛrtsən] *v/i* (*ge-*, *h*) joke (***über*** *acc* at); '**scherzhaft** *adj* joking; ***~ gemeint*** meant as a joke
**scheu** [ʃɔʏ] *adj* shy (*a.* zo); bashful; ***~ machen*** frighten; **Scheu** *f* (-; *no pl*) shyness; awe; **scheuen** ['ʃɔʏən] (*ge-*, *h*) **1.** *v/i* shy (***vor*** *dat* at), take fright (at) **2.** *v/t* shun, avoid; fear; ***sich ~, et. zu tun*** be afraid of doing s.th.
**scheuern** ['ʃɔʏɐn] *v/t and v/i* (*ge-*, *h*) scrub, scour; chafe
'**Scheuertuch** *n* floor cloth
'**Scheuklappen** *pl* blinders, *Br* blinkers (*both a. fig*)
'**scheumachen** *v/t* (*sep*, *-ge-*, *h*) → ***scheu***
**Scheune** ['ʃɔʏnə] *f* (-; *-n*) barn
**Scheusal** ['ʃɔʏzaːl] *n* (*-s*; *-e*) monster (*a. fig*); *fig* beast
**scheußlich** ['ʃɔʏslɪç] *adj* horrible (*a.* F), atrocious
**Schicht** [ʃɪçt] *f* (-; *-en*) layer; coat; film; ECON shift; class; **schichten** ['ʃɪçtən] *v/t* (*ge-*, *h*) arrange in layers, pile up
'**schichtweise** *adv* in layers
**schick** [ʃɪk] *adj* smart, chic, stylish
**schicken** ['ʃɪkən] *v/t* (*ge-*, *h*) send (***nach, zu*** to); ***das schickt sich nicht*** that isn't done
**Schickeria** [ʃɪkə'riːa] F *f* (-; *no pl*) smart set, beautiful people, trendies
**Schickimicki** [ʃɪki'mɪki] F *contp m* (*-s*; *-s*) trendy
**Schicksal** ['ʃɪkzaːl] *n* (*-s*; *-e*) fate, destiny; lot
**Schiebe|dach** ['ʃiːbədax] *n* MOT sliding roof, sunroof; **~fenster** *n* sliding window; sash window
**schieben** ['ʃiːbən] *v/t* (*irr*, *ge-*, *h*) push
**Schieber** ['ʃiːbɐ] *m* (*-s*; -) TECH slide; bolt; F profiteer
'**Schiebetür** *f* sliding door
'**Schiebung** F *f* (-; *-en*) swindle, fix (*a.* SPORT)

S

**schied** [ʃiːt] *pret of* ***scheiden***
'**Schiedsrichter** ['ʃiːtsrɪçtɐ] *m*, '**Schiedsrichterin** *f soccer*: referee; *tennis*: umpire; judge, *esp pl a.* jury
**schief** [ʃiːf] *adj* crooked, not straight; sloping, oblique (*a.* MATH); leaning; *fig* false
**Schiefer** ['ʃiːfɐ] *m* (*-s*; -) GEOL slate
'**Schiefertafel** *f* slate
'**schiefgehen** *v/i* (*irr*, ***gehen***, *sep*, *-ge-*, *sein*) F go wrong
**schielen** ['ʃiːlən] *v/i* (*ge-*, *h*) squint, be cross-eyed
**schien** [ʃiːn] *pret of* ***scheinen***
**Schienbein** ['ʃiːnbain] *n* ANAT shin (-bone)
**Schiene** ['ʃiːnə] *f* (-; *-n*) TECH *etc* rail; MED splint
'**schienen** *v/t* (*ge-*, *h*) MED splint
**Schießbude** ['ʃiːsbuːdə] *f* shooting gallery
**schießen** ['ʃiːsən] *v/i and v/t* (*irr*, *ge-*, *h*) shoot, fire (*both*: ***auf*** *acc* at); SPORT score; **Schießerei** [ʃiːsə'rai] *f* (-; *-en*) shooting; gunfight
'**Schieß|pulver** *n* gunpowder; **~scharte** *f* MIL loophole, embrasure; **~scheibe** *f* target; **~stand** *m* shooting range
**Schiff** [ʃɪf] *n* (*-[e]s*; *-e*) MAR ship, boat; ARCH nave; ***mit dem ~*** by boat
**Schiffahrt** *f* → ***Schifffahrt***
'**schiffbar** *adj* navigable
'**Schiffbau** *m* (*-[e]s*; *no pl*) shipbuilding
'**Schiffbruch** *m* shipwreck (*a. fig*); ***~ erleiden*** be shipwrecked
**Schiffer** ['ʃɪfɐ] *m* (*-s*; -) sailor; skipper
'**Schifffahrt** *f* (-; *no pl*) shipping, navigation
'**Schiffs|junge** *m* ship's boy; **~ladung** *f* shipload; cargo; **~schraube** *f* (ship's) propeller; **~werft** *f* shipyard
**Schikane** [ʃi'kaːnə] *f* (-; *-n*) *a. pl* harassment; ***aus reiner ~*** out of sheer spite; F ***mit allen ~n*** with all the trimmings
**schikanieren** [ʃika'niːrən] *v/t* (*no -ge-*, *h*) harass; bully
**Schild**[1] [ʃɪlt] *n* (*-[e]s*; *-er* ['ʃɪldɐ]) sign, plate
**Schild**[2] *m* (*-[e]s*; *-e*) shield
'**Schilddrüse** *f* ANAT thyroid (gland)
**schildern** ['ʃɪldɐn] *v/t* (*ge-*, *h*) describe; depict, portray
**Schilderung** ['ʃɪldərʊŋ] *f* (-; *-en*) description, portrayal; account

'**Schildkröte** *f* zo tortoise; turtle
**Schilf** [ʃɪlf] *n* (-[*e*]*s*; *no pl*) BOT reed(s)
**schillern** ['ʃɪlɐn] *v/i* (*ge-*, *h*) be iridescent; **~d** *adj* iridescent; *fig* dubious
**Schimmel** ['ʃɪməl] *m* zo white horse; BOT mo(u)ld; **schimm(e)lig** ['ʃɪm(ə)lɪç] *adj* mo(u)ldy, musty; '**schimmeln** *v/i* (*ge-*, *h*, *sein*) go mo(u)ldy
**Schimmer** ['ʃɪmɐ] *m* (*-s*; -) glimmer (*a. fig*), gleam, *fig a.* trace, touch
'**schimmern** *v/i* (*ge-*, *h*) shimmer, glimmer, gleam
**Schimpanse** [ʃɪm'panzə] *m* (*-n*; *-n*) zo chimpanzee
**schimpfen** ['ʃɪmpfən] *v/i and v/t* (*ge-*, *h*) scold (***mit j-m*** s.o.); F tell *s.o.* off, bawl *s.o.* out; ***~ über*** (*acc*) complain about
'**Schimpfwort** *n* swearword
**Schindel** ['ʃɪndəl] *f* (-; *-n*) shingle
**schinden** ['ʃɪndən] *v/t* (*irr*, *ge-*, *h*) maltreat; slave-drive; ***sich ~*** drudge, slave away; **Schinder** ['ʃɪndɐ] *m* (*-s*; -) slave driver; **Schinderei** [ʃɪndə'rai] *f* (-; *-en*) slavery, drudgery
**Schinken** ['ʃɪŋkən] *m* (*-s*; -) ham
**Schippe** ['ʃɪpə] *f* (-; *-n*), '**schippen** *v/t* (*ge-*, *h*) shovel
**Schirm** [ʃɪrm] *m* (-[*e*]*s*; *-e*) umbrella; sunshade; TV, IT *etc*: screen; shade; peak, visor; **~herr(in)** patron, sponsor; **~herrschaft** *f* patronage, sponsorship; ***unter der ~ von*** under the auspices of; **~mütze** *f* peaked cap; **~ständer** *m* umbrella stand
**schiss** [ʃɪs] *pret of* scheißen
**Schlacht** [ʃlaxt] *f* (-; *-en*) battle (***bei*** of)
'**schlachten** *v/t* (*ge-*, *h*) slaughter, kill, butcher
**Schlachter** ['ʃlaxtɐ] *m* (*-s*; -) butcher
'**Schlacht|feld** *n* MIL battlefield, battleground; **~haus** *n*, **~hof** *m* slaughterhouse; **~plan** *m* MIL plan of action (*a. fig*); **~schiff** *n* MIL battleship
**Schlacke** ['ʃlakə] *f* (-; *-n*) cinders; GEOL, METALL slag
**Schlaf** [ʃla:f] *m* (-[*e*]*s*; *no pl*) sleep; ***e-n leichten*** (***festen***) ***~ haben*** be a light (sound) sleeper; F *fig* ***im ~*** blindfold
'**Schlafanzug** *m* pajamas, *Br* pyjamas
**Schläfe** ['ʃlɛ:fə] *f* (-; *-n*) ANAT temple
**schlafen** ['ʃla:fən] *v/i* (*irr*, *ge-*, *h*) sleep (*a. fig*); ***~ gehen, sich ~ legen*** go to bed; ***fest ~*** be fast asleep; ***j-n ~ legen*** put s.o. to bed *or* to sleep

**schlaff** [ʃlaf] *adj* slack (*a. fig*); flabby; limp
'**Schlaf|gelegenheit** *f* sleeping accommodation; **~krankheit** *f* MED sleeping sickness; **~lied** *n* lullaby
'**schlaflos** *adj* sleepless
'**Schlaflosigkeit** *f* (-; *no pl*) sleeplessness, MED insomnia
'**Schlafmittel** *n* MED sleeping pill(s)
'**Schlafmütze** *fig f* sleepyhead; slowpoke, *Br* slowcoach
**schläfrig** ['ʃlɛ:frɪç] *adj* sleepy, drowsy
'**Schlaf|saal** *m* dormitory; **~sack** *m* sleeping bag; **~ta,blette** *f* sleeping pill
'**schlaftrunken** *adj* (very) drowsy
'**Schlaf|wagen** *m* RAIL sleeping car, sleeper; **~wandler(in)** [ʃla:fvandlɐ, ʃla:fvandlərɪn] (*-s*; *-/-*; *-nen*) sleepwalker, somnambulist; **~zimmer** *n* bedroom
**Schlag** [ʃla:k] *m* (-[*e*]*s*; *Schläge* ['ʃlɛ:gə]) blow (*a. fig*); slap; punch; pat, tap; *a. tennis*: stroke; ELECTR shock (*a. fig*); MED beat; *pl* beating; → ***Schlaganfall***; **~ader** *f* ANAT artery; **~anfall** *m* MED (apoplectic) stroke
'**schlagartig** **1.** *adj* sudden, abrupt **2.** *adv* all of a sudden, abruptly
'**Schlagbaum** *m* barrier
'**Schlagbohrer** *m* TECH percussion drill
**schlagen** ['ʃla:gən] (*irr*, *ge-*, *h*) **1.** *v/t* hit, beat (*a.* GASTR *and fig*), strike, knock; fell, cut (down); ***sich ~*** fight (***um*** over); ***sich geschlagen geben*** admit defeat **2.** *v/i* hit, beat (*a. heart etc*), strike (*a. clock*), knock; ***an*** *or* ***gegen et. ~*** hit s.th., bump *or* crash into s.th.
**Schlager** ['ʃla:gɐ] *m* (*-s*; -) MUS hit (*a. fig*), (pop) song
**Schläger** ['ʃlɛ:gɐ] *m* (*-s*; -) *tennis etc*: racket; *table tennis*, *cricket*, *baseball*: bat; *golf*: club; *hockey*: stick; *contp* thug; **Schlägerei** [ʃlɛ:gə'rai] *f* (-; *-en*) fight, brawl
'**schlagfertig** *adj* quick-witted; ***~e Antwort*** (witty) repartee
'**Schlag|instru,ment** *n* MUS percussion instrument; **~kraft** *f* (-; *no pl*) striking power (*a.* MIL); **~loch** *n* pot-hole; **~obers** *Austrian n*, **~sahne** *f* whipped cream; **~seite** *f* MAR list; ***~ haben*** be listing; **~stock** *m* baton, truncheon; **~wort** *n* catchword, slogan; **~zeile** *f* headline
'**Schlagzeug** *n* MUS drums
**Schlagzeuger** ['ʃla:ktsɔʏgɐ] *m* (*-s*; -)

S

MUS drummer
**schlaksig** ['ʃla:ksɪç] *adj* lanky, gangling
**Schlamm** [ʃlam] *m* (-[*e*]*s*; -*e*) mud
**schlammig** ['ʃlamɪç] *adj* muddy
**Schlampe** ['ʃlampə] F *f* (-; -*n*) slut
**schlampig** ['ʃlampɪç] F *adj* sloppy
**schlang** [ʃlaŋ] *pret of* ***schlingen***
**Schlange** ['ʃlaŋə] *f* (-; -*n*) ZO snake, serpent (*a. fig*); *fig* line, *esp Br* queue; ***~ stehen*** line up, stand in line, *esp Br* queue (up) (***nach*** for); **schlängeln** ['ʃlɛŋəln] *v/refl* (*ge-*, *h*) wind *or* weave (one's way), *person*: worm one's way
'**Schlangen|linie** *f* serpentine line; ***in ~n fahren*** weave
**schlank** [ʃlaŋk] *adj* slim, slender; ***j-n ~ machen*** make s.o. look slim; ***~e Unternehmensstruktur*** ECON lean management; '**Schlankheitskur** *f*: ***e-e ~ machen*** be slimming; '**schlankmachen** *v/t* (*sep*, *-ge-*, *h*): ***j-n ~*** → ***schlank***
**schlapp** [ʃlap] F *adj* worn out; weak; **Schlappe** ['ʃlapə] F *f* (-; -*n*) setback, beating; '**schlappmachen** F *v/i* (*sep*, *-ge-*, *h*) flake out; '**Schlappschwanz** F *m* weakling, wimp
**schlau** [ʃlau] *adj* clever, smart, bright; sly, cunning, crafty
**Schlauch** [ʃlaux] *m* (-[*e*]*s*; *Schläuche* ['ʃlɔʏçə]) tube; hose; **~boot** *n* (inflatable *or* rubber) dinghy
**Schlaufe** ['ʃlaufə] *f* (-; -*n*) loop
**schlecht** [ʃlɛçt] *adj* bad; poor; ***mir ist*** (***wird***) **~** I feel (I'm getting) sick to my stomach; ***~ aussehen*** look ill; ***sich ~ fühlen*** feel bad; ***~ werden*** GASTR go bad; ***es geht ihm sehr ~*** he is in a bad way; ***~ gelaunt*** in a bad temper *or* mood, bad-tempered; F ***j-n ~ machen*** run s.o. down, backbite s.o.
'**schlechtmachen** *v/t* (*sep*, *-ge-*, *h*): F ***j-n ~ machen*** run s.o. down, backbite s.o.
**schleichen** ['ʃlaiçən] *v/i* (*irr*, *ge-*, *sein*) creep (*a. fig*), sneak; '**Schleichweg** *m* secret path; '**Schleichwerbung** *f* plugging; ***für et. ~ machen*** plug s.th.
**Schleier** ['ʃlaiɐ] *m* (-*s*; -) veil (*a. fig*); haze; '**schleierhaft** *adj*: F ***es ist mir ~*** it's a mystery to me
**Schleife** ['ʃlaifə] *f* (-; -*n*) bow; ribbon; AVIAT, IT, ELECTR, GEOGR loop
**schleifen**[1] ['ʃlaifən] *v/t and v/i* (*ge-*, *h*) drag (along); rub
'**schleifen**[2] *v/t* (*irr*, *ge-*, *h*) grind (*a.* TECH), sharpen; sand(paper); cut; F drill *s.o.* hard
**Schleifer** ['ʃlaifɐ] *m* (-*s*; -), '**Schleifma,schine** *f* TECH grinder
'**Schleifpa,pier** *n* sandpaper
'**Schleifstein** *m* grindstone; whetstone
**Schleim** [ʃlaim] *m* (-[*e*]*s*; -*e*) slime; MED mucus; '**Schleimhaut** *f* ANAT mucous membrane; **schleimig** ['ʃlaimɪç] *adj* slimy (*a. fig*); MED mucous
**schlemmen** ['ʃlɛmən] *v/i* (*ge-*, *h*) feast
**schlendern** ['ʃlɛndɐn] *v/i* (*ge-*, *sein*) stroll, saunter, amble
**schlenkern** ['ʃlɛŋkɐn] *v/i and v/t* (*ge-*, *h*) dangle, swing (***mit den Armen*** one's arms)
**schleppen** ['ʃlɛpən] *v/t* (*ge-*, *h*) drag (*a. fig*); MOT, MAR tow; ***sich ~*** drag (on); **~d** *adj* dragging; *fig* drawling
**Schlepper** ['ʃlɛpɐ] *m* (-*s*; -) MAR tug; MOT tractor
'**Schlepp|lift** *m* T-bar (lift), drag lift, ski tow; **~tau** *n* tow-rope; ***im*** (***ins***) **~** in tow (*a. fig*)
**Schleuder** ['ʃlɔʏdɐ] *f* (-; -*n*) catapult, slingshot; TECH spin drier
'**schleudern** (*ge-*, *h*) **1.** *v/t* fling, hurl (*both a. fig*); spin-dry **2.** *v/i* MOT skid
'**Schleudersitz** *m* AVIAT ejection (*esp Br* ejector) seat
**schleunigst** ['ʃlɔʏnɪçst] *adv* immediately
**Schleuse** ['ʃlɔʏzə] *f* (-; -*n*) sluice; lock
**schlich** [ʃlɪç] *pret of* ***schleichen***
**schlicht** [ʃlɪçt] *adj* plain, simple
**schlichten** ['ʃlɪçtən] *v/t* (*ge-*, *h*) settle
'**Schlichtung** *f* (-; -*en*) settlement
**schlief** [ʃli:f] *pret of* ***schlafen***
**schließen** ['ʃli:sən] *v/t and v/i* (*irr*, *ge-*, *h*) shut, close (down); *fig* close, finish; ***~ aus*** (*dat*) conclude from; ***nach ... zu ~*** judging by ...
**Schließfach** ['ʃli:sfax] *n* safe-deposit box; RAIL *etc*: (left luggage) locker
**schließlich** ['ʃli:slɪç] *adv* finally; eventually, in the end; after all
**schliff** [ʃlɪf] *pret of* ***schleifen***[2]
**Schliff** *m* (-[*e*]*s*; -*e*) cut; polish (*a. fig*)
**schlimm** [ʃlɪm] *adj* bad; awful; ***das ist nicht*** *or* ***halb so ~*** it's not as bad as that; ***das Schlimme daran*** the bad thing about it
'**schlimmsten'falls** *adv* at (the) worst
**Schlinge** ['ʃlɪŋə] *f* (-; -*n*) loop; noose;

HUNT snare (*a. fig*); MED sling
**Schlingel** ['ʃlɪŋəl] *m* (*-s*; -) rascal
**schlingen** ['ʃlɪŋən] *v/t* (*irr, ge-, h*) wind, twist; tie; wrap (***um*** [a]round); gobble; ***sich um et. ~*** wind (a)round s.th.
**schlingern** ['ʃlɪŋɐn] *v/i* (*ge-, h*) MAR roll
'**Schlingpflanze** *f* BOT creeper, climber
**Schlips** [ʃlɪps] *m* (*-es; -e*) necktie, *esp Br* tie
**schlitteln** ['ʃlɪtəln] *Swiss v/i* (*ge-, sein*) go sledging, go tobogganing
**Schlitten** ['ʃlɪtən] *m* (*-s*; -) sled, *Br* sledge; sleigh; SPORT toboggan; ***~ fahren*** go sledging, go tobogganing
**Schlittschuh** ['ʃlɪtʃuː] *m* ice-skate (*a.* ***~ laufen***); **~läufer(in)** ice-skater
**Schlitz** [ʃlɪts] *m* (*-es; -e*) slit; slot
**schlitzen** ['ʃlɪtsən] (*v/t ge-, h*) slit, slash
**schloss** [ʃlɔs] *pret of* ***schließen***
**Schloss** *n* (*-es; Schlösser* ['ʃlœsɐ]) TECH lock; ARCH castle, palace; ***ins ~ fallen*** *door*: slam shut; ***hinter ~ und Riegel*** locked up, under lock and key
**Schlosser** ['ʃlɔsɐ] *m* (*-s*; -) metalworker; locksmith; **Schlosserei** [ʃlɔsə'rai] *f* (-; *-en*) metalwork shop
**schlottern** ['ʃlɔtɐn] *v/i* (*ge-, h*) shake, tremble (*both*: ***vor*** *dat* with); bag
**Schlucht** [ʃlʊxt] *f* (-; *-en*) canyon, gorge, ravine
**schluchzen** ['ʃlʊxtsən] *v/i* (*ge-, h*), **Schluchzer** ['ʃlʊxtsɐ] *m* (*-s*; -) sob
**Schluck** [ʃlʊk] *m* (*-[e]s; -e*) draught, swallow; sip; gulp; '**Schluckauf** *m* (*-s; no pl*) hiccups; **(*e-n*) *~ haben*** have (the) hiccups; **schlucken** ['ʃlʊkən] *v/t and v/i* (*ge-, h*) swallow (*a. fig*)
'**Schluckimpfung** *f* MED oral vaccination
**schlug** [ʃluːk] *pret of* ***schlagen***
**Schlummer** ['ʃlʊmɐ] *m* (*-s; no pl*) slumber; '**schlummern** *v/i* (*ge-, h*) lie asleep; *fig* slumber
**schlüpfen** ['ʃlʏpfən] *v/i* (*ge-, sein*) slip, slide; ZO hatch (out); **Schlüpfer** ['ʃlʏpfɐ] *m* (*-s*; -) briefs, panties
**schlüpfrig** ['ʃlʏpfrɪç] *adj* slippery; *contp* risqué, off-colo(u)r
**Schlupfwinkel** ['ʃlʊpfvɪŋkəl] *m* hiding place
**schlurfen** ['ʃlʊrfən] *v/i* (*ge-, sein*) shuffle (along)
**schlürfen** ['ʃlʏrfən] *v/t and v/i* (*ge-, h*) slurp
**Schluss** [ʃlʊs] *m* (*-es; no pl*) end; conclusion; ending; ***~ machen*** finish; break up; ***~ machen mit*** stop *s.th.*, put an end to *s.th.*; ***zum ~*** finally; **(*ganz*) *bis zum ~*** to the (very) end; ***~ für heute!*** that's all for today!
**Schlüssel** ['ʃlʏsəl] *m* (*-s*; -) key (***für, zu*** to); **~bein** *n* ANAT collarbone; **~blume** *f* BOT cowslip, primrose; **~bund** *m, n* bunch of keys; **~kind** F *n* latchkey child; **~loch** *n* keyhole; **~wort** *n* keyword, IT *a.* password
'**Schlussfolgerung** *f* conclusion
**schlüssig** ['ʃlʏsɪç] *adj* conclusive; ***sich ~ werden*** make up one's mind (***über*** *acc* about)
'**Schluss|licht** *n* MOT *etc*: tail-light; **~pfiff** *m* SPORT final whistle; **~phase** *f* final stage(s); **~verkauf** *m* ECON (end-of-season) sale
**schmächtig** ['ʃmɛçtɪç] *adj* slight, thin, frail
**schmackhaft** ['ʃmakhaft] *adj* tasty
**schmal** [ʃmaːl] *adj* narrow; thin, slender (*a. fig*); **schmälern** ['ʃmɛːlɐn] *v/t* (*ge-, h*) detract from
'**Schmalfilm** *m* cinefilm
'**Schmalspur** *f* RAIL narrow ga(u)ge
'**Schmalspur...** *fig in cpds* small-time ...
**Schmalz** [ʃmalts] *n* (*-es; -e*) grease; lard
**schmalzig** ['ʃmaltsɪç] F *adj* schmaltzy, mushy, *Br* soapy
**schmarotzen** [ʃma'rɔtsən] F *v/i* (*no -ge-, h*) sponge (***bei*** on)
**Schmarotzer** [ʃma'rɔtsɐ] *m* (*-s*; -) BOT, ZO parasite, *fig a.* sponger
**schmatzen** ['ʃmatsən] *v/i* smack (one's lips), eat noisily
**schmecken** ['ʃmɛkən] *v/i and v/t* (*ge-, h*) taste (***nach*** of); ***gut*** (***schlecht***) ***~*** taste good (bad); (***wie***) ***schmeckt dir ...?*** (how) do you like ...? (*a. fig*); ***es schmeckt süß*** (***nach nichts***) it has a sweet (no) taste
**Schmeichelei** [ʃmaiçə'lai] *f* (-; *-en*) flattery; '**schmeichelhaft** *adj* flattering; '**schmeicheln** *v/i* (*ge-, h*) flatter (***j-m*** s.o.); **Schmeichler(in)** ['ʃmaiçlɐ, 'ʃmaiçlərɪn] *m(f)* (*-s; -/-; -nen*) flatterer; **schmeichlerisch** ['ʃmaiçlərɪʃ] *adj* flattering
**schmeißen** ['ʃmaisən] F *v/t and v/i* (*irr, ge-, h*) throw, chuck; slam; ***mit Geld um***

S

***sich* ~** throw one's money about
'**Schmeißfliege** *f* zo blowfly, bluebottle
**schmelzen** ['ʃmɛltsən] *v/i* (*irr, ge-, sein*) *and v/t* (*h*) melt; thaw; TECH smelt
'**Schmelz|ofen** *m* (s)melting furnace; **~tiegel** *m* melting pot (*a. fig*)
**Schmerz** [ʃmɛrts] *m* (*-es; -en*) pain (*a. fig*), ache; *fig* grief, sorrow
**schmerzen** ['ʃmɛrtsən] *v/i and v/t* (*ge-, h*) hurt (*a. fig*), ache; *esp fig* pain
'**schmerzfrei** *adj* without pain
'**schmerzhaft** *adj* painful
'**schmerzlich** *adj* painful, sad
'**schmerzlos** *adj* painless
'**Schmerzmittel** *n* PHARM painkiller
'**schmerzstillend** *adj* painkilling
**Schmetterling** ['ʃmɛtɐlɪŋ] *m* (*-s; -e*) zo butterfly
**schmettern** ['ʃmɛtɐn] (*ge-, h*) **1.** *v/t* smash (*a. tennis*); F MUS belt out **2.** *v/i* (*sein*) crash, slam; MUS blare
**Schmied** [ʃmiːt] *m* (*-[e]s; -e*) (black)-smith; **Schmiede** ['ʃmiːdə] *f* (*-; -n*) forge, smithy; '**Schmiedeeisen** *n* wrought iron; '**schmieden** *v/t* (*ge-, h*) forge; *fig* make (*plans etc*)
**schmiegen** ['ʃmiːgən] *v/refl* (*ge-, h*) ***sich* ~ *an*** (*acc*) snuggle up to; *dress etc*: cling to
**Schmiere** ['ʃmiːrə] *f* (*-; -n*) grease
'**schmieren** *v/t* (*ge-, h*) TECH grease, oil, lubricate; spread (*butter etc*); *contp* scribble, scrawl; **Schmiererei** [ʃmiːrə'rai] *f* (*-; -en*) scrawl; graffiti
**schmierig** ['ʃmiːrɪç] *adj* greasy; dirty; filthy; *contp* slimy
**Schmiermittel** ['ʃmiːɐmɪtəl] *n* TECH lubricant
**Schminke** ['ʃmɪŋkə] *f* (*-; -n*) make-up (*a.* THEA); '**schminken** *v/t* (*ge-, h*) make *s.o.* up; ***sich* ~** make o.s. *or* one's face up
**Schmirgelpa|pier** ['ʃmɪrgəlpapiːɐ] *n* emery paper
**schmiss** [ʃmɪs] *pret of* ***schmeißen***
**schmollen** ['ʃmɔlən] *v/i* (*ge-, h*) sulk, be sulky, pout
**schmolz** [ʃmɔlts] *pret of* ***schmelzen***
**schmoren** ['ʃmoːrən] *v/t and v/i* (*ge-, h*) GASTR braise, stew (*a. fig*)
**Schmuck** [ʃmʊk] *m* (*-[e]s; no pl*) jewel(le)ry, jewels; decoration(s), ornament(s); **schmücken** ['ʃmʏkən] *v/t* (*ge-, h*) decorate; '**schmucklos** *adj* unadorned; plain; '**Schmuckstück** *n* piece of jewel(le)ry; *fig* gem
**Schmuggel** ['ʃmʊgəl] *m* (*-; no pl*), **Schmuggelei** [ʃmʊgə'lai] *f* (*-; -en*) smuggling; '**schmuggeln** *v/t and v/i* (*ge-, h*) smuggle; '**Schmuggelware** *f* smuggled goods; **Schmuggler** ['ʃmʊglɐ] *m* (*-s; -*) smuggler
**schmunzeln** ['ʃmʊntsəln] *v/i* (*ge-, h*) smile to o.s.
**schmusen** ['ʃmuːzən] F *v/i* (*ge-, h*) (kiss and) cuddle, smooch
**Schmutz** [ʃmʊts] *m* (*-es; no pl*) dirt, filth, *fig a.* smut; **~fleck** *m* smudge
**schmutzig** ['ʃmʊtsɪç] *adj* dirty, filthy (*both a. fig*); **~ *werden, sich* ~ *machen*** get dirty
**Schnabel** ['ʃnaːbəl] *m* (*-s; Schnäbel* ['ʃnɛːbəl]) zo bill, beak
**Schnalle** ['ʃnalə] *f* (*-; -n*) buckle
'**schnallen** *v/t* (*ge-, h*) buckle; ***et.* ~ *an*** (*acc*) strap s.th. to
**schnalzen** ['ʃnaltsən] *v/i* (*ge-, h*) snap one's fingers; click one's tongue
**schnappen** ['ʃnapən] (*ge-, h*) **1.** *v/i* snap, snatch (*both*: ***nach*** at); F ***nach Luft* ~** gasp for breath **2.** F *v/t* catch
'**Schnappschuss** *m* PHOT snapshot
**Schnaps** [ʃnaps] *m* (*-es; Schnäpse* ['ʃnɛpsə]) spirits, schnapps, F booze
**schnarchen** ['ʃnarçən] *v/i* (*ge-, h*) snore
**schnarren** ['ʃnarən] *v/i* (*ge-, h*) rattle; *voice*: rasp
**schnattern** ['ʃnatɐn] *v/i* (*ge-, h*) zo cackle; chatter (*a.* F)
**schnauben** ['ʃnaubən] *v/i and v/t* (*ge-, h*) snort; ***sich die Nase* ~** blow one's nose
**schnaufen** ['ʃnaufən] *v/i* (*ge-, h*) breathe hard, pant, puff
**Schnauze** ['ʃnautsə] *f* (*-; -n*) zo snout, mouth, muzzle; F AVIAT, MOT nose; TECH spout; V trap, kisser; V ***die* ~ *halten*** keep one's trap shut
**Schnecke** ['ʃnɛkə] *f* (*-; -n*) zo snail; slug
'**Schnecken|haus** *n* zo snail shell; **~tempo** *n*: ***im* ~** at a snail's pace
**Schnee** [ʃneː] *m* (*-s; no pl*) snow (*a. sl*); **~ *räumen*** remove snow; **~ball** *m* snowball; **~ballschlacht** *f* snowball fight
'**schneebedeckt** *adj* snow-capped
'**Schnee|fall** *m* snowfall; **~flocke** *f* snowflake; **~gestöber** ['ʃneːgəʃtøːbɐ] *n* (*-s; -*) snow flurry; **~glöckchen** *n*

BOT snowdrop; **~grenze** *f* snow line; **~mann** *m* snowman; **~matsch** *m* slush; **~mo͵bil** *n* snowmobile; **~pflug** *m* snowplow, *Br* snowplough; **~regen** *m* sleet; **~sturm** *m* snowstorm, blizzard; **~verwehung** *f* snowdrift
**ˈschneeˈweiß** *adj* snow-white
**Schneewittchen** [ʃneːˈvɪtçən] *n* (*-s*; *no pl*) Snow White
**Schneid** [ʃnait] F *m* (*-[e]s*; *no pl*) grit, guts; **~brenner** *m* TECH cutting torch
**Schneide** [ˈʃnaidə] *f* (*-*; *-n*) edge
**ˈschneiden** *v/t and v/i* (*irr*, *ge-*, *h*) cut (*a. fig*), *film etc*: *a.* edit; GASTR carve
**Schneider** [ˈʃnaidɐ] *m* (*-s*; *-*) tailor; **Schneiderei** [ʃnaidəˈrai] *f* (*-*; *-en*) (*no pl*) tailoring, dressmaking; tailor's *or* dressmaker's shop; **ˈSchneiderin** *f* (*-*; *-nen*) dressmaker; seamstress; **ˈschneidern** *v/i and v/t* (*ge-*, *h*) do dressmaking; make, sew
**ˈSchneidezahn** *m* incisor
**schneidig** [ˈʃnaidɪç] *adj* dashing; smart
**schneien** [ˈʃnaiən] *v/i* (*ge-*, *h*) snow
**schnell** [ʃnɛl] *adj* fast, quick; prompt; rapid; ***es geht ~*** it won't take long; (***mach***[***t***]) ***~!*** hurry up!
**ˈSchnell...** *in cpds …dienst*, *…paket*, *…zug etc*: *mst* express …
**schnellen** [ˈʃnɛlən] *v/t* (*ge-*, *h*) *and v/i* (*ge-*, *sein*) shoot, spring
**ˈSchnellhefter** *m* folder
**Schnelligkeit** [ˈʃnɛlɪçkait] *f* (*-*; *no pl*) speed; quickness, rapidity
**ˈSchnell|imbiss** *m* snack bar; **~straße** *f* expressway, thruway, *Br* motorway
**schnetzeln** [ˈʃnɛtsəln] *esp Swiss v/t* (*ge-*, *h*) GASTR chop up
**schnippisch** [ˈʃnɪpɪʃ] *adj* sassy, pert
**schnipsen** [ˈʃnɪpsən] *v/i* (*ge-*, *h*) snap one's fingers
**schnitt** [ʃnɪt] *pret of* ***schneiden***
**Schnitt** *m* (*-[e]s*; *-e*) cut (*a. fig*); average
**ˈSchnittblumen** *pl* cut flowers
**Schnitte** [ˈʃnɪtə] *f* (*-*; *-n*) slice; open sandwich
**schnittig** [ˈʃnɪtɪç] *adj* stylish; MOT sleek
**Schnitt|lauch** *m* BOT chives; **~muster** *n* pattern; **~punkt** *m* (point of) intersection; **~stelle** *f film etc*: cut; IT interface; **~wunde** *f* MED cut
**Schnitzel**[1] [ˈʃnɪtsəl] *n* (*-s*; *-*) GASTR cutlet; ***Wiener ~*** schnitzel
**ˈSchnitzel**[2] *n*, *m* (*-s*; *-*) chip; scrap
**schnitzen** [ˈʃnɪtsən] *v/t* (*ge-*, *h*) carve, cut (in wood); **Schnitzer** [ˈʃnɪtsɐ] *m* (*-s*; *-*) (wood) carver; **Schnitzerei** [ʃnɪtsəˈrai] *f* (*-*; *-en*) (wood) carving
**Schnorchel** [ˈʃnɔrçəl] *m* (*-s*; *-*), **ˈschnorcheln** *v/i* (*ge-*, *h*) snorkel
**Schnörkel** [ˈʃnœrkəl] *m* (*-s*; *-*) flourish; ARCH scroll
**schnorren** [ˈʃnɔrən] F *v/t* (*ge-*, *h*) mooch, *Br* cadge
**schnüffeln** [ˈʃnʏfəln] *v/i* (*ge-*, *h*) sniff (***an*** *dat* at); F snoop (about *or* around)
**Schnuller** [ˈʃnʊlɐ] *m* (*-s*; *-*) pacifier, *Br* dummy
**Schnulze** [ˈʃnʊltsə] F *f* (*-*; *-n*) tearjerker; schmal(t)zy song
**ˈSchnulzensänger** F *m*, **ˈSchnulzensängerin** *f* crooner
**schnulzig** [ˈʃnʊltsɪç] F *adj* schmal(t)zy
**Schnupfen** [ˈʃnʊpfən] *m* (*-s*; *-*) MED cold; ***e-n ~ haben*** (***bekommen***) have a (catch [a]) cold
**ˈSchnupftabak** *m* snuff
**schnuppern** [ˈʃnʊpɐn] *v/i* (*ge-*, *h*) sniff (***an et.*** [at] s.th.)
**Schnur** [ʃnuːɐ] *f* (*-*; *Schnüre* [ˈʃnyːrə]) string, cord; ELECTR flex
**Schnürchen** [ˈʃnyːɐçən] *n*: ***wie am ~*** like clockwork
**schnüren** [ˈʃnyːrən] *v/t* (*ge-*, *h*) lace (up); tie up
**ˈschnurgerade** *adv* dead straight
**ˈschnurlos** *adj*: ***~es Telefon*** cordless phone
**Schnürlsamt** [ˈʃnyːɐlzamt] *Austrian m* corduroy
**Schnurrbart** [ˈʃnʊrbaːɐt] *m* m(o)ustache
**schnurren** [ˈʃnʊrən] *v/i* (*ge-*, *h*) purr
**Schnür|schuh** [ˈʃnyːɐʃuː] *m* laced shoe; **~senkel** [ˈʃnyːɐzɛŋkəl] *m* (*-s*; *-*) shoestring, *Br* shoelace
**schnurstracks** [ˈʃnuːɐˈʃtraks] *adv* direct(ly), straight; straight away
**schob** [ʃoːp] *pret of* ***schieben***
**Schober** [ˈʃoːbɐ] *m* (*-s*; *-*) haystack, hayrick; barn
**Schock** [ʃɔk] *m* (*-[e]s*; *-s*) MED shock; ***unter ~ stehen*** be in (a state of) shock
**schocken** [ˈʃɔkən] F *v/t* (*ge-*, *h*) shock
**schockieren** [ʃɔˈkiːrən] *v/t* (*no -ge-*, *h*) shock
**Schokolade** [ʃokoˈlaːdə] *f* (*-*; *-n*) chocolate; ***e-e Tafel ~*** a bar of chocolate

**scholl** [ʃɔl] *pret of* ***schallen***
**Scholle** ['ʃɔlə] *f* (-; *-n*) clod; (ice)floe; zo flounder, *Br* plaice
**schon** [ʃoːn] *adv* already; ever; even; **~ *damals*** even then; **~ *1968*** as early as 1968; **~ *der Gedanke*** the very idea; ***ist sie ~ da* (*zurück*)?** has she come (is she back) yet?; ***habt ihr ~ gegessen?*** have you eaten yet?; ***bist du ~ einmal dort gewesen?*** have you ever been there?; ***ich wohne hier ~ seit zwei Jahren*** I've been living here for two years now; ***ich kenne ihn ~, aber*** I do know him, but; ***er macht das ~*** he'll do it all right; **~ *gut!*** never mind!, all right!
**schön** [ʃøːn] **1.** *adj* beautiful, lovely; METEOR *a.* fine, fair; nice (*a.* F *iro*); (***na,***) **~** all right **2.** *adv*: **~ *warm* (*kühl*)** nice and warm (cool); ***ganz ~ teuer* (*schnell*)** pretty expensive (fast); ***j-n ganz ~ erschrecken* (*überraschen*)** give s.o. quite a start (surprise)
**schonen** ['ʃoːnən] *v/t* (*ge-, h*) take care of, go easy on (*a.* TECH); spare; ***sich ~*** take it easy; save o.s. *or* one's strength; **~d** **1.** *adj* gentle; mild **2.** *adv*: **~ *umgehen mit*** take (good) care of; handle with care; go easy on
'**Schönheit** *f* (-; *-en*) beauty
'**Schönheitspflege** *f* beauty care
'**Schonung** *f* (-; *-en*) (*no pl*) (good) care; rest; preservation; tree nursery
'**schonungslos** *adj* relentless, brutal
**schöpfen** ['ʃœpfən] *v/t* (*ge-, h*) scoop, ladle; draw (*water*); → ***Luft, Verdacht***
**Schöpfer** ['ʃœpfɐ] *m* (*-s*; -), '**Schöpferin** *f* (-; *-nen*) creator
**schöpferisch** ['ʃœpfərɪʃ] *adj* creative
'**Schöpfung** *f* (-; *-en*) creation
**schor** [ʃoːɐ] *pret of* ***scheren***
**Schorf** [ʃɔrf] *m* (-[*e*]*s*; *-e*) MED scab
**Schornstein** ['ʃɔrnʃtain] *m* chimney; MAR, RAIL funnel; **~feger** *m* chimney sweep
**schoss** [ʃɔs] *pret of* ***schießen***
**Schoß** [ʃoːs] *m* (*-es*; *Schöße* ['ʃøːsə]) lap; womb
**Schote** ['ʃoːtə] *f* (-; *-n*) BOT pod, husk
**Schotte** ['ʃɔtə] *m* (*-n*; *-n*) Scot(sman); *pl* the Scots, the Scottish (people)
**Schotter** ['ʃɔtɐ] *m* (*-s*; -) gravel, road metal
**Schottin** ['ʃɔtɪn] *f* (-; *-nen*) Scotswoman
'**schottisch** *adj* Scots, Scottish; Scotch
'**Schottland** Scotland
**schräg** [ʃrɛːk] **1.** *adj* slanting, sloping, oblique; diagonal **2.** *adv*: **~ *gegenüber*** diagonally opposite
**Schramme** ['ʃramə] *f* (-; *-n*), '**schrammen** *v/t and v/i* (*ge-, h*) scratch (*a.* MED)
**Schrank** [ʃraŋk] *m* (-[*e*]*s*; *Schränke* ['ʃrɛŋkə]) cupboard; closet; wardrobe
**Schranke** ['ʃraŋkə] *f* (-; *-n*) barrier (*a. fig*), RAIL *a.* gate; JUR bar; *pl* limits, bounds
'**schrankenlos** *fig adj* boundless
'**Schrankenwärter** *m* RAIL gatekeeper
'**Schrankwand** *f* wall units
**Schraube** ['ʃraubə] *f* (-; *-n*), '**schrauben** *v/t* (*ge-, h*) TECH screw
'**Schrauben|schlüssel** *m* TECH spanner, wrench; **~zieher** *m* TECH screwdriver
**Schraubstock** ['ʃraupʃtɔk] *m* vise, *Br* vice
**Schreck** [ʃrɛk] *m* (-[*e*]*s*; *-e*) fright, shock; ***j-m e-n ~ einjagen*** give s.o. a fright, scare s.o.
**Schrecken** ['ʃrɛkən] *m* (*-s*; -) terror, fright; horror(s); '**Schreckensnachricht** *f* dreadful news
'**schreckhaft** *adj* jumpy; skittish
'**schrecklich** *adj* awful, terrible; horrible, dreadful, atrocious
**Schrei** [ʃrai] *m* (-[*e*]*s*; *-e*) cry, shout, yell, scream (*all*: ***um, nach*** for)
**schreiben** ['ʃraibən] *v/t and v/i* (*irr, ge-, h*) write (***j-m*** to s.o.; ***über*** *acc* about); type; spell; ***falsch ~*** misspell; ***wie schreibt man …?*** how do you spell …?
'**Schreiben** *n* (*-s*; -) letter
'**Schreib|fehler** *m* spelling mistake; **~heft** *n* exercise book; **~kraft** *f* typist; **~ma,schine** *f* typewriter; **~materi,al** *n* writing materials, stationery; **~schutz** *m* IT write *or* file protection; **~tisch** *m* desk
'**Schreibung** *f* (-; *-en*) spelling
'**Schreibwaren** *pl* stationery; **~geschäft** *n* stationer's, stationery shop
'**Schreibzen,trale** *f* typing pool
**schreien** ['ʃraiən] *v/i and v/t* (*irr, ge-, h*) cry, shout, yell, scream (*all*: ***um, nach*** [out] for); **~ *vor Schmerz* (*Angst*)** cry out with pain (in terror); ***es war***

***zum Schreien*** it was a scream; **~d** *fig adj* loud (*colors*); flagrant (*abuse etc*), glaring (*injustices etc*)
**Schreiner** ['ʃrainɐ] *m* (-*s*; -) → ***Tischler***
**schreiten** ['ʃraitən] *v/i* (*irr*, *ge-*, *sein*) stride
**schrie** [ʃriː] *pret of* ***schreien***
**schrieb** [ʃriːp] *pret of* ***schreiben***
**Schrift** [ʃrɪft] *f* (-; -*en*) (hand)writing, hand; PRINT type; character, letter; *pl* works, writings; ***die Heilige ~*** REL the Scriptures; **~art** *f* script; PRINT typeface; **~deutsch** *n* standard German
'**schriftlich** *adj* written; ***~ übersetzen*** translate in writing
**Schriftsteller** ['ʃrɪftʃtɛlɐ] *m* (-*s*; -), '**Schriftstellerin** *f* (-; -*nen*) author, writer
'**Schrift|verkehr** *m*, **~wechsel** *m* correspondence; **~zeichen** *n* character, letter
**schrill** [ʃrɪl] *adj* shrill (*a. fig*), piercing
**schritt** [ʃrɪt] *pret of* ***schreiten***
**Schritt** *m* (-[*e*]*s*; -*e*) step (*a. fig*); pace; *fig* ***~e unternehmen*** take steps; ***~ fahren!*** MOT dead slow; **~macher** *m* SPORT pacemaker (*a.* MED), pacesetter
'**schrittweise** *adv* step by step, gradually
**schroff** [ʃrɔf] *adj* steep; jagged; *fig* gruff
**Schrot** [ʃroːt] *m*, *n* (-[*e*]*s*; -*e*) (*no pl*) coarse meal; HUNT (small) shot; pellet; **~flinte** *f* shotgun
**Schrott** [ʃrɔt] *m* (-[*e*]*s*; -*e*) scrap (metal)
'**Schrotthaufen** *m* scrap heap
'**Schrottplatz** *m* scrapyard
**schrubben** ['ʃrʊbən] *v/t* (*ge-*, *h*) scrub, scour
**schrumpfen** ['ʃrʊmpfən] *v/i* (*ge-*, *sein*) shrink
**Schub** [ʃuːp] *m* (-[*e*]*s*; *Schübe* ['ʃyːbə]) → ***Schubkraft***; **~fach** *n* drawer; **~karren** *m* wheelbarrow; **~kasten** *m* drawer; **~kraft** *f* PHYS, TECH thrust; **~lade** *f* drawer
**Schubs** [ʃʊps] F *m* (-*es*; -*e*), **schubsen** ['ʃʊpsən] F *v/t* (*ge-*, *h*) push
**schüchtern** ['ʃʏçtɐn] *adj* shy, bashful
'**Schüchternheit** *f* (-; *no pl*) shyness, bashfulness
**schuf** [ʃuːf] *pret of* ***schaffen***[1]
**Schuft** [ʃʊft] *m* (-[*e*]*s*; -*e*) *contp* bastard
**schuften** ['ʃʊftən] F *v/i* (*ge-*, *h*) slave away, drudge

**Schuh** [ʃuː] *m* (-[*e*]*s*; -*e*) shoe; ***j-m et. in die ~e schieben*** put the blame for s.th. on s.o.; **~anzieher** *m* shoehorn; **~creme** *f* shoe polish; **~geschäft** *n* shoe store (*Br* shop); **~löffel** *m* shoehorn; **~macher** *m* shoemaker; **~putzer** ['ʃuːpʊtsɐ] *m* (-*s*; -) shoeshine boy
'**Schul|abbrecher** *m* (-*s*; -) dropout; **~abgänger** ['ʃuːlapgɛŋɐ] *m* (-*s*; -) school leaver; **~amt** *n* school board, *Br* education authority; **~arbeit** *f* schoolwork; *pl* homework; **~besuch** *m* (school) attendance; **~bildung** *f* education; **~buch** *n* textbook
**Schuld** [ʃʊlt] *f* (-; -*en* ['ʃʊldən]) (*no pl*) JUR guilt, *esp* REL sin; *mst pl* debt; ***j-m die ~*** (***an et.***) ***geben*** blame s.o. (for s.th.); ***es ist*** (***nicht***) ***deine ~*** it is(n't) your fault; ***~en haben*** (***machen***) be in (run into) debt; → ***zuschulden***; '**schuldbewusst** *adj*: ***~e Miene*** guilty look; **schulden** ['ʃʊldən] *v/t* (*ge-*, *h*) ***j-m et. ~*** owe s.o. s.th.; **schuldig** ['ʃʊldɪç] *adj esp* JUR guilty (***an*** *dat* of); responsible *or* to blame (for); ***j-m et. ~ sein*** owe s.o. s.th.; **Schuldige** ['ʃʊldɪgə] *m*, *f* (-*n*; -*n*) culprit; JUR guilty person, offender
'**schuldlos** *adj* innocent
**Schuldner** ['ʃʊldnɐ] *m* (-*s*; -); '**Schuldnerin** *f* (-; -*nen*) debtor
'**Schuldschein** *m* ECON promissory note, IOU (= I owe you)
**Schule** ['ʃuːlə] *f* (-; -*n*) school (*a. fig*); ***höhere ~*** *appr* (senior) high school, *Br* secondary school; ***auf*** *or* ***in der ~*** at school; ***in die*** *or* ***zur ~ gehen*** (***kommen***) go to (start) school
'**schulen** *v/t* (*ge-*, *h*) train, school
**Schüler** ['ʃyːlɐ] *m* (-*s*; -) student, schoolboy, *esp Br a.* pupil; **~austausch** *m* student exchange (program[me])
**Schülerin** ['ʃyːlərɪn] *f* (-; -*nen*) student, schoolgirl, *esp Br a.* pupil
'**Schülervertretung** *f appr* student government (*Br* council)
'**Schul|ferien** *pl* vacation, *Br* holidays; **~fernsehen** *n* educational TV; **~funk** *m* schools programmes; **~gebäude** *n* school (building); **~geld** *n* school fee(s), tuition; **~heft** *n* exercise book; **~hof** *m* school yard, playground; **~kame,rad** *m* schoolfellow; **~leiter** *m* principal, *Br* headmaster, head teach-

S

er; **~leiterin** *f* principal, *Br* headmistress; **~mappe** *f* schoolbag; satchel; **~ordnung** *f* school regulations

'**schulpflichtig** *adj*: ***~es Kind*** school--age child

'**Schul|schiff** *n* training ship; **~schluss** *m* end of school (*or* term); ***nach ~*** after school; **~schwänzer** ['ʃuːlʃvɛntsɐ] *m* (*-s*; -) truant; **~stunde** *f* lesson, class, period; **~tasche** *f* schoolbag

**Schulter** ['ʃʊltɐ] *f* (-; *-n*) ANAT shoulder

'**Schulterblatt** *n* ANAT shoulder-blade

'**schulterfrei** *adj* strapless

'**schultern** *v/t* (*ge-*, *h*) shoulder

'**Schultertasche** *f* shoulder bag

'**Schulwesen** *n* (*-s*; *no pl*) education(al system)

**schummeln** ['ʃʊməln] F *v/i* (*ge-*, *h*) cheat

**Schund** [ʃʊnt] *m* (-[*e*]*s*; *no pl*) trash, rubbish, junk

**schund** [ʃʊnt] *pret of* ***schinden***

**Schuppe** ['ʃʊpə] *f* (-; *-n*) ZO scale; *pl* MED dandruff

'**Schuppen** *m* (*-s*; -) shed, *esp* F *contp* shack

**schuppig** ['ʃʊpɪç] *adj* ZO scaly

**schüren** ['ʃyːrən] *v/t* (*ge-*, *h*) stir up (*a. fig*)

**schürfen** ['ʃʏrfən] *v/i* (*ge-*, *h*) prospect (***nach*** for)

'**Schürfwunde** *f* MED graze, abrasion

**Schurke** ['ʃʊrkə] *m* (*-n*; *-n*) *esp* THEA *etc* villain

**Schurwolle** ['ʃuːɐvɔlə] *f* virgin wool

**Schürze** ['ʃʏrtsə] *f* (-; *-n*) apron

**Schuss** [ʃʊs] *m* (*-es*; *Schüsse* ['ʃʏsə]) shot; GASTR dash; SPORT shot, *soccer*: *a.* strike; *skiing*: schuss (*a.* ***~ fahren***); *sl* shot, fix; F ***gut in ~ sein*** be in good shape

**Schüssel** ['ʃʏsəl] *f* (-; *-n*) bowl, dish; basin

'**Schuss|waffe** *f* firearm; **~wunde** *f* MED gunshot *or* bullet wound

**Schuster** ['ʃuːstɐ] *m* (*-s*; -) shoemaker

**Schutt** [ʃʊt] *m* (-[*e*]*s*; *no pl*) rubble, debris

'**Schüttelfrost** *m* MED shivering fit, *the* shivers

**schütteln** ['ʃʏtəln] *v/t* (*ge-*, *h*) shake

**schütten** ['ʃʏtən] *v/t* (*ge-*, *h*) pour; throw

**Schutz** [ʃʊts] *m* (*-es*; *no pl*) protection (***gegen, vor*** *dat* against), defense, *Br* defence (against, from); shelter (from); safeguard (against); cover; **~blech** *n* fender, *Br* mudguard; **~brille** *f* goggles

**Schütze** ['ʃʏtsə] *m* (*-n*; *-n*) MIL rifleman; hunter; SPORT scorer; ASTR Sagittarius; ***er ist (ein) ~*** he's (a) Sagittarius; ***ein guter ~*** a good shot

**schützen** ['ʃʏtsən] *v/t* (*ge-*, *h*) protect (***gegen, vor*** *dat* against, from), defend (against, from), guard (against, from); shelter (from); safeguard

'**Schutzengel** *m* guardian angel

'**Schützengraben** *m* MIL trench

'**Schutzgeld** *n* protection money; **~erpressung** *f* protection racket

'**Schutz|haft** *f* JUR protective custody; **~heilige** *m*, *f* patron (saint); **~impfung** *f* MED protective inoculation; vaccination; **~kleidung** *f* protective clothing

**Schützling** ['ʃʏtslɪŋ] *m* (*-s*; *-e*) protégé(e)

'**schutzlos** *adj* unprotected; defenseless, *Br* defenceless

'**Schutz|maßnahme** *f* safety measure; **~pa,tron** *m* REL patron (saint); **~umschlag** *m* dust cover; **~zoll** *m* ECON protective duty (*or* tariff)

**schwach** [ʃvax] *adj* weak (*a. fig*); poor; faint; delicate, frail; ***schwächer werden*** grow weak; decline; fail; fade

**Schwäche** ['ʃvɛçə] *f* weakness (*a. fig*); MED infirmity; *fig* drawback, shortcoming; ***e-e ~ haben für*** be partial to; '**schwächen** *v/t* (*ge-*, *h*) weaken (*a. fig*); lessen; '**schwächlich** *adj* weakly, feeble; delicate, frail; '**Schwächling** *m* (*-s*; *-e*) weakling (*a. fig*), softy, sissy

'**schwachsinnig** *adj* feeble-minded; F stupid, idiotic

'**Schwachstrom** *m* ELECTR low-voltage current

**Schwager** ['ʃvaːgɐ] *m* (*-s*; *Schwäger* ['ʃvɛːgɐ]) brother-in-law; **Schwägerin** ['ʃvɛːgərɪn] *f* (-; *-nen*) sister-in-law

**Schwalbe** ['ʃvalbə] *f* (-; *-n*) ZO swallow; *soccer*: dive

**Schwall** [ʃval] *m* (-[*e*]*s*; *-e*) gush, *esp fig a.* torrent

**schwamm** [ʃvam] *pret of* ***schwimmen***

**Schwamm** *m* (-[*e*]*s*; *Schwämme* ['ʃvɛmə]) sponge; BOT fungus; F dry rot

**Schwammerl** ['ʃvamɐl] *Austrian m* (*-s*; -[*n*]) → ***Pilz***

S

**schwammig** ['ʃvamɪç] *adj* spongy; puffy; *fig* woolly
**Schwan** [ʃvaːn] *m* (-[*e*]*s*; *Schwäne* ['ʃvɛːnə]) zo swan
**schwand** [ʃvant] *pret of* ***schwinden***
**schwang** [ʃvaŋ] *pret of* ***schwingen***
**schwanger** ['ʃvaŋɐ] *adj* pregnant
'**Schwangerschaft** *f* (-; *-en*) pregnancy; '**Schwangerschaftsabbruch** *m* abortion
**schwanken** ['ʃvaŋkən] *v/i* (*ge-*, *h*) sway, roll (*a.* MAR); stagger; *fig* ~ ***zwischen … und …*** waver between … and …; *prices*: range from … to …; '**Schwankung** *f* (-; *-en*) change, variation (*a.* ECON)
**Schwanz** [ʃvants] *m* (*-es*; *Schwänze* ['ʃvɛntsə]) zo tail (*a.* AVIAT, ASTR); V cock
**schwänzen** ['ʃvɛntsən] *v/i and v/t* (*ge-*, *h*) (***die Schule***) ~ play truant (F hooky)
**Schwarm** [ʃvarm] *m* (-[*e*]*s*; *Schwärme* ['ʃvɛrmə]) swarm; crowd, F bunch; zo shoal, school; F dream; idol
**schwärmen** ['ʃvɛrmən] *v/i* (*ge-*, *sein*) zo swarm; (*ge-*, *h*) ~ ***für*** be mad about; dream of; have a crush on *s.o.*; ~ ***von*** rave about
**Schwarte** ['ʃvartə] *f* (-; *-n*) rind; F *contp* (old) tome
**schwarz** [ʃvarts] *adj* black (*a. fig*); ***Schwarzes Brett*** bulletin board, *Br* notice board; ~ ***auf weiß*** in black and white
'**Schwarzarbeit** *f* (-; *no pl*) illicit work
'**Schwarzbrot** *n* rye bread
**Schwarze** ['ʃvartsə] *m*, *f* (*-n*; *-n*) black (man *or* woman); *pl* the Blacks
**schwärzen** ['ʃvɛrtsən] *v/t* (*ge-*, *h*) blacken
'**Schwarz|fahrer** *m* fare dodger; ~**händler** *m* black marketeer; ~**markt** *m* black market; ~**seher** *m* pessimist; (TV) license (*Br* licence) dodger
**Schwarz'weiß…** *in cpds …film*, *…fernseher etc*: black-and-white …
**schwatzen** ['ʃvatsən], **schwätzen** ['ʃvɛtsən] *v/i* (*ge-*, *h*) chat(ter); PED talk
**Schwätzer** ['ʃvɛtsɐ] *contp m* (*-s*; *-*), '**Schwätzerin** *f* (-; *-nen*) loudmouth
**schwatzhaft** ['ʃvatshaft] *adj* chatty
**Schwebe|bahn** ['ʃveːbəbaːn] *f* cableway, ropeway; ~**balken** *m* SPORT beam
**schweben** ['ʃveːbən] *v/i* (*ge-*, *h*) be suspended; zo, AVIAT hover (*a. fig*); glide; *esp* JUR be pending; ***in Gefahr*** ~ be in danger
**Schwede** ['ʃveːdə] *m* (*-n*; *-n*) Swede
**Schweden** ['ʃveːdən] Sweden
**Schwedin** ['ʃveːdɪn] *f* (-; *-nen*) Swede
'**schwedisch** *adj* Swedish
**Schwefel** ['ʃveːfəl] *m* (*-s*; *no pl*) CHEM sulfur, *Br* sulphur; ~**säure** *f* CHEM sulfuric (*Br* sulphuric) acid
**Schweif** [ʃvaif] *m* (-[*e*]*s*; *-e*) zo tail (*a.* ASTR); **schweifen** ['ʃvaifən] *v/i* (*ge-*, *sein*) wander (*a. fig*), roam
**schweigen** ['ʃvaigən] *v/i* (*irr*, *ge-*, *h*) be silent; '**Schweigen** *n* (*-s*; *no pl*) silence; '**schweigend** *adj* silent
**schweigsam** ['ʃvaikzaːm] *adj* quiet, taciturn, reticent
**Schwein** [ʃvain] *n* (-[*e*]*s*; *-e*) zo pig, hog; F *contp* (filthy) pig; swine, bastard; F ~ ***haben*** be lucky; '**Schweinebraten** *m* roast pork; '**Schweinefleisch** *n* pork; **Schweinerei** [ʃvainə'rai] F *f* (-; *-en*) mess; *fig* dirty trick; dirty *or* crying shame; filth(y story *or* joke)
'**Schweinestall** *m* pigsty (*a. fig*)
'**schweinisch** F *adj* filthy, obscene
'**Schweinsleder** *n* pigskin
**Schweiß** [ʃvais] *m* (*-es*; *no pl*) sweat, perspiration
**schweißen** *v/t* (*ge-*, *h*) TECH weld
**Schweißer** *m* (*-s*; *-*) TECH welder
'**schweißgebadet** *adj* soaked in sweat
'**Schweißgeruch** *m* body odo(u)r, BO
**Schweiz** [ʃvaits] Switzerland
**Schweizer** ['ʃvaitsɐ] *m* (*-s*; *-*), *adj* Swiss
**Schweizerin** ['ʃvaitsərɪn] *f* (-; *-nen*) Swiss woman *or* girl
**schweizerisch** ['ʃvaitsərɪʃ] *adj* Swiss
**schwelen** ['ʃveːlən] *v/i* (*ge-*, *h*) smo(u)lder (*a. fig*)
**schwelgen** ['ʃvɛlgən] *v/i* (*ge-*, *h*) ~ ***in*** (*dat*) revel in
**Schwelle** ['ʃvɛlə] *f* (-; *-n*) threshold (*a. fig*); RAIL tie, *Br* sleeper
'**schwellen 1.** *v/i* (*irr*, *ge-*, *sein*) swell **2.** *v/t* (*ge-*, *h*) swell
'**Schwellung** *f* (-; *-en*) MED swelling
**Schwemme** ['ʃvɛmə] *f* (-; *-n*) ECON glut, oversupply; '**schwemmen** *v/t* (*ge-*, *h*) ***an Land*** ~ wash ashore
**Schwengel** ['ʃvɛŋəl] *m* (*-s*; *-*) clapper; handle
**schwenken** ['ʃvɛŋkən] *v/t* (*ge-*, *h*) *and v/i* (*ge-*, *sein*) swing, wave

S

**schwer** [ʃveːɐ] **1.** *adj* heavy; *fig* difficult, hard; GASTR strong, rich; MED *etc* serious, severe; heavy, violent (*storm etc*); **~e Zeiten** hard times; **es ~ haben** have a bad time; **100 Pfund ~ sein** weigh a hundred pounds **2.** *adv*: **~ arbeiten** work hard; → **schwerfallen**; → **hören**; **~ beschädigt** → **schwerbeschädigt**; **~ verdaulich** indigestible, heavy (*both a. fig*); **~ verständlich** difficult *or* hard to understand; **~ verwundet** seriously wounded

'**schwerbeschädigt** *adj* seriously disabled

**Schwere** ['ʃveːrə] *f* (-; *no pl*) weight (*a. fig*); *fig* seriousness

'**schwerfallen** *v/i* (*irr*, **fallen**, *sep*, *-ge-*, *sein*): **j-m ~** be difficult for s.o.; **es fällt ihm schwer zu ...** he finds it difficult to ...

'**schwerfällig** *adj* awkward, clumsy

'**Schwergewicht** *n* (-[*e*]*s*; *no pl*) heavyweight; *fig* (main) emphasis

'**schwerhörig** *adj* hard of hearing

'**Schwer|indus,trie** *f* heavy industry; **~kraft** *f* (-; *no pl*) PHYS gravity; **~me,tall** *n* heavy metal

**schwermütig** ['ʃveːɐmyːtɪç] *adj* melancholy; **~ sein** have the blues

'**Schwerpunkt** *m* center (*Br* centre) of gravity; *fig* (main) emphasis

**Schwert** [ʃveːɐt] *n* (-[*e*]*s*; *-er*) sword

'**Schwerverbrecher** *m* dangerous criminal, JUR felon

'**schwer|verdaulich** *adj* → **schwer**; **~verständlich** *adj* → **schwer**; **~ver,wundet** *adj* → **schwer**

'**schwerwiegend** *fig adj* weighty, serious

**Schwester** ['ʃvɛstɐ] *f* (-; *-n*) sister, REL *a.* nun; MED nurse

**schwieg** [ʃviːk] *pret of* **schweigen**

**Schwieger...** ['ʃviːgɐ-] *in cpds ...eltern*, *...mutter*, *...sohn etc*: ...-in-law

**Schwiele** ['ʃviːlə] *f* (-; *-n*) MED callus

**schwielig** ['ʃviːlɪç] *adj* horny

**schwierig** ['ʃviːrɪç] *adj* difficult, hard

'**Schwierigkeit** *f* (-; *-en*) difficulty, trouble; **in ~en geraten** get *or* run into trouble; **~en haben, et. zu tun** have difficulty in doing s.th.

**Schwimmbad** ['ʃvɪmbaːt] *n* (indoor) swimming pool; **schwimmen** ['ʃvɪmən] *v/i* (*irr*, *ge-*, *sein*) swim; float; **~ gehen** go swimming

'**Schwimm|flosse** *f* swimfin, *Br* flipper; **~gürtel** *m* swimming belt; **~haut** *f* ZO web; **~lehrer** *m* swimming instructor; **~weste** *f* life jacket

**Schwindel** ['ʃvɪndəl] *m* (*-s*; *no pl*) MED giddiness, dizziness; F swindle, fraud; **~ erregend** dizzy; '**schwindeler,regend** *adj* dizzy

'**schwindeln** F *v/i* (*ge-*, *h*) fib, tell fibs

**schwinden** ['ʃvɪndən] *v/i* (*irr*, *ge-*, *sein*) dwindle, decline

**Schwindler** ['ʃvɪndlɐ] F *m* (*-s*; *-*), '**Schwindlerin** *f* (-; *-nen*) swindler, crook; liar

**schwindlig** ['ʃvɪndlɪç] *adj* MED dizzy, giddy; **mir ist ~** I feel dizzy

**Schwinge** ['ʃvɪŋə] *f* (-; *-n*) ZO wing

'**schwingen** *v/i and v/t* (*irr*, *ge-*, *h*) swing; wave; PHYS oscillate; vibrate

'**Schwingung** *f* (-; *-en*) PHYS oscillation; vibration

**Schwips** [ʃvɪps] F *m*: **e-n ~ haben** be tipsy

**schwirren** ['ʃvɪrən] *v/i* (*ge-*, *sein*) whirr, whizz, *esp* ZO buzz (*a. fig*); (*ge-*, *h*) **mir schwirrt der Kopf** my head is buzzing

**schwitzen** ['ʃvɪtsən] *v/i* (*ge-*, *h*) sweat, perspire

**schwoll** [ʃvɔl] *pret of* **schwellen** 1

**schwor** [ʃvoːɐ] *pret of* **schwören**

**schwören** ['ʃvøːrən] *v/t and v/i* (*irr*, *ge-*, *h*) swear; JUR take an *or* the oath; *fig* **~ auf** (*acc*) swear by

**schwul** [ʃvuːl] F *adj* gay; *contp* queer

**schwül** [ʃvyːl] *adj* sultry (*a. fig*), close

**schwülstig** ['ʃvʏlstɪç] *adj* bombastic, pompous

**Schwung** [ʃvʊŋ] *m* (-[*e*]*s*; *Schwünge* ['ʃvʏŋə]) swing; *fig* verve, pep; drive; **in ~ kommen** get going; **et. in ~ bringen** get s.th. going; '**schwungvoll** *adj* full of energy *or* verve; MUS swinging

**Schwur** [ʃvuːɐ] *m* (-[*e*]*s*; *Schwüre* ['ʃvyːrə]) oath; **~gericht** *n* JUR jury court

**sechs** [zɛks] *adj* six; *grade*: F, *Br a.* poor; '**Sechseck** *n* (-[*e*]*s*; *-e*) hexagon; '**sechseckig** *adj* hexagonal; '**sechsfach** *adj* sixfold; '**sechsmal** *adv* six times; **Sechs'tagerennen** *n* SPORT six-day race; **sechstägig** ['zɛkstɛːgɪç] *adj* lasting *or* of six days; '**sechste** *adj* sixth; **Sechstel** ['zɛkstəl] *n* (-*s*; -) sixth (part); '**sechstens** *adv* sixthly, in the sixth place; **sechzehn(te)** ['zɛçtseːn(tə)] *adj* sixteen(th); **sechzig** ['zɛçtsɪç] *adj* sixty; '**sechzigste** *adj* sixtieth

**See**¹ [zeː] *m* (-*s*; -*n*) lake

**See**² *f* (-; *no pl*) sea, ocean; ***auf ~*** at sea; ***auf hoher ~*** on the high seas; ***an der ~*** at the seaside; ***zur ~ gehen*** (***fahren***) go to sea (be a sailor); ***in ~ stechen*** put to sea; **~bad** *n* seaside resort; **~fahrt** *f* navigation; **~gang** *m* (-[*e*]*s*; *no pl*): ***hoher ~*** heavy sea; **~hafen** *m* seaport; **~hund** *m* ZO seal; **~karte** *f* nautical chart

'**seekrank** *adj* seasick

'**Seekrankheit** *f* seasickness

**Seele** ['zeːlə] *f* (-; -*n*) soul (*a. fig*)

'**seelenlos** *adj* soulless

'**Seelenruhe** *f* peace of mind; ***in aller ~*** as cool as you please

**seelisch** ['zeːlɪʃ] *adj* mental

'**Seelsorge** *f* (-; *no pl*) pastoral care

**Seelsorger** ['zeːlzɔrgɐ] *m* (-*s*; -), '**Seelsorgerin** *f* (-; -*nen*) pastor

'**See|macht** *f* sea power; **~mann** *m* (-[*e*]*s*; -*leute*) seaman, sailor; **~meile** *f* nautical mile; **~not** *f* (-; *no pl*) distress (at sea); **~notkreuzer** *m* MAR rescue cruiser; **~räuber** *m* pirate; **~reise** *f* voyage, cruise; **~rose** *f* BOT water lily; **~sack** *m* kit bag; **~schlacht** *f* MIL naval battle; **~streitkräfte** *pl* MIL naval forces, navy

'**seetüchtig** *adj* seaworthy

'**See|warte** *f* naval observatory; **~weg** *m* sea route; ***auf dem ~*** by sea; **~zeichen** *n* seamark; **~zunge** *f* ZO sole

**Segel** ['zeːgəl] *n* (-*s*; -) sail; **~boot** *n* sailboat, *Br* sailing boat; **~fliegen** *n* gliding; **~flugzeug** *n* glider

'**segeln** *v/i* (*ge*-, *sein*) sail, SPORT *a.* yacht

'**Segel|schiff** *n* sailing ship; sailing vessel; **~sport** *m* sailing, yachting; **~tuch** *n* canvas, sailcloth

**Segen** ['zeːgən] *m* (-*s*; -) blessing (*a. fig*)

**Segler** ['zeːglɐ] *m* (-*s*; -) yachtsman

**Seglerin** ['zeːglərɪn] *f* (-; -*nen*) yachtswoman

**segnen** ['zeːgnən] *v/t* (*ge*-, *h*) bless

'**Segnung** *f* (-; -*nen*) blessing

**Sehbeteiligung** ['zeːbətailɪgʊŋ] *f* (TV) ratings

**sehen** ['zeːən] *v/i and v/t* (*irr*, *ge*-, *h*) see; watch; notice; ***~ nach*** look after; look for; ***sich ~ lassen*** show up; ***das sieht man*** (***kaum***) it (hardly) shows; ***siehst du*** (you) see; I told you; ***siehe oben*** (***unten, Seite …***) see above (below, page …); '**sehenlassen** *v/refl* (*irr*, ***lassen***, *sep*, *no -ge-*, *h*) → ***sehen***; '**sehenswert** *adj* worth seeing; '**Sehenswürdigkeit** *f* (-; -*en*) place *etc* worth seeing, sight, *pl* sights

'**Sehkraft** *f* (-; *no pl*) eyesight, vision

**Sehne** ['zeːnə] *f* (-; -*n*) ANAT sinew; string

**sehnen** ['zeːnən] *v/refl* (*ge*-, *h*) long (***nach*** for), yearn (for); ***sich danach ~ zu*** *inf* be longing to *inf*

'**Sehnerv** *m* ANAT optic nerve

**sehnig** ['zeːnɪç] *adj* sinewy, GASTR *a.* stringy

**sehnlichst** ['zeːnlɪçst] *adj* dearest

'**Sehnsucht** *f*, '**sehnsüchtig** *adj* longing, yearning

**sehr** [zeːɐ] *adv before adj and adv*: very; *with verbs*: very much, greatly

'**Sehtest** *m* sight test

**seicht** [zaiçt] *adj* shallow (*a. fig*)

**Seide** ['zaidə] *f* (-; -*n*), '**seiden** *adj* silk

'**Seidenpa͵pier** *n* tissue paper

'**Seidenraupe** *f* ZO silkworm

**seidig** ['zaidɪç] *adj* silky

**Seife** ['zaifə] *f* (-; -*n*) soap

'**Seifen|blase** *f* soap bubble; **~lauge** *f* (soap)suds; **~oper** *f* TV soap opera; **~schale** *f* soap dish; **~schaum** *m* lather

**seifig** ['zaifɪç] *adj* soapy

**Seil** [zail] *n* (-[*e*]*s*; -*e*) rope

'**Seilbahn** *f* cable railway

'**seilspringen** *v/i* (*only inf*) skip

**sein**¹ [zain] *v/i* (*irr*, *ge*-, *sein*) be; exist; ***et. ~ lassen*** stop *or* quit (doing) s.th.

**sein**² *poss pron* his, her, its; ***~er, ~e, ~(e)s*** his, hers

**Sein** *n* (-*s*; *no pl*) being; existence

**seiner|seits** ['zainɐzaits] *adv* for his part; **~'zeit** *adv* then, in those days

**seines'gleichen** ['zainəsglaiçən] *pron* his equals

**seinet'wegen** ['zainətveːgən] → ***meinetwegen***

'**seinlassen** *v/t* (*irr*, *sep*, -*ge*-, *h*): ***et. ~*** → ***sein***

**seit** [zait] *prp and cj* since; ***~ 2002*** since 2002; ***~ drei Jahren*** for three years (now); ***~ langem*** (***kurzem***) for a long

S

(short) time; ~'**dem** **1.** *adv* since then, since that time, ever since **2.** *cj* since
**Seite** ['zaitə] *f* (-; -*n*) side (*a. fig*); page; ***auf der linken ~*** on the left(-hand side); *fig* ***auf der e-n*** (***anderen***) ***~*** on the one (other) hand
'**Seiten|ansicht** *f* side view, profile; ~**blick** *m* sidelong glance; ~**hieb** *m* sideswipe; ~**linie** *f esp soccer*: touchline
**seitens** ['zaitəns] *prp* (*gen*) on the part of, by
'**Seitensprung** F *m*: ***e-n ~ machen*** cheat (on one's wife *or* husband)
'**Seitenstechen** *n* (-*s*; *no pl*) MED a stitch (in the side)
'**seitlich** *adj* side ..., at the side(s)
**seitwärts** ['zaitvɛrts] *adv* sideways, to the side
**Sekretär** [zekre'tɛːɐ] *m* (-*s*; -*e*) secretary; bureau; **Sekretariat** [zekreta'rjaːt] *n* (-[*e*]*s*; -*e*) (secretary's) office; **Sekretärin** [zekre'tɛːrɪn] *f* (-; -*nen*) secretary
**Sekt** [zɛkt] *m* (-[*e*]*s*; -*e*) sparkling wine
**Sekte** ['zɛktə] *f* (-; -*n*) sect
**Sektion** [zɛk'tsjoːn] *f* (-; -*en*) section; MED autopsy
**Sektor** ['zɛktoːɐ] *m* (-*s*; -*en* [zɛk'toːrən]) sector; *fig* field
**Sekunde** [ze'kʊndə] *f* (-; -*n*) second; ***auf die ~*** to the second
**Se'kundenzeiger** *m* second(s) hand
**selbe** ['zɛlbə] *adj* same
**selber** ['zɛlbɐ] *pron* → ***selbst 1***
**selbst** [zɛlbst] **1.** *pron*: ***ich*** (***du*** *etc*) ***~*** I (you *etc*) myself (yourself *etc*); ***mach es ~*** do it yourself; ***et. ~ tun*** do s.th. by oneself; ***von ~*** by itself; ***~ gemacht*** homemade **2.** *adv* even
'**Selbstachtung** *f* self-respect
'**selbständig** *etc* → ***selbstständig*** *etc*
'**Selbstbedienung** *f* self-service; ~**sladen** *m* self-service store (*Br* shop)
'**Selbst|befriedigung** *f* masturbation; ~**beherrschung** *f* self-control; ~**bestimmung** *f* self-determination
'**selbstbewusst** *adj* self-confident, self-assured; '**Selbstbewusstsein** *n* self-confidence
'**Selbst|bildnis** *n* self-portrait; ~**erhaltungstrieb** *m* survival instinct; ~**erkenntnis** *f* (-; *no pl*) self-knowledge
'**selbstgerecht** *adj* self-righteous
'**Selbst|hilfe** *f* self-help; ~**hilfegruppe** *f* self-help group; ~**kostenpreis** *m*: ***zum ~*** ECON at cost (price)
'**selbstkritisch** *adj* self-critical
'**Selbstlaut** *m* LING vowel
'**selbstlos** *adj* unselfish
'**Selbst|mord** *m*, ~**mörder**(**in**) suicide
'**selbstmörderisch** *adj* suicidal
'**selbstsicher** *adj* self-confident, self-assured
'**selbstständig** *adj* independent, self-reliant; self-employed; '**Selbstständigkeit** *f* (-; *no pl*) independence
'**Selbststudium** *n* (-*s*; *no pl*) self-study
'**selbst|süchtig** *adj* selfish, ego(t)istic(al); ~**tätig** *adj* automatic
'**Selbsttäuschung** *f* self-deception
'**selbstverständlich** **1.** *adj* natural; ***das ist ~*** that's a matter of course **2.** *adv* of course, naturally; ***~!*** *a.* by all means!; '**Selbstverständlichkeit** *f* (-; -*en*) matter of course
'**Selbst|verteidigung** *f* self-defense, *Br* self-defence; ~**vertrauen** *n* self-confidence, self-reliance; ~**verwaltung** *f* self-government, autonomy
'**selbstzufrieden** *adj* self-satisfied
**selchen** ['zɛlçən] *Austrian* → ***räuchern***
**selig** ['zeːlɪç] *adj* REL blessed; late; *fig* overjoyed
**Sellerie** ['zɛləri] *m* (-*s*; -[*s*]), *f* (-; -) BOT celeriac; celery
**selten** ['zɛltən] **1.** *adj* rare; ***~ sein*** be rare, be scarce **2.** *adv* rarely, seldom
'**Seltenheit** *f* (-; *no pl*) rarity
**seltsam** ['zɛltzaːm] *adj* strange, odd
**Semester** [ze'mɛstɐ] *n* (-*s*; -) UNIV semester, *esp Br* term
**Semikolon** [zemi'koːlɔn] *n* (-*s*; -*s*) LING semicolon
**Seminar** [zemi'naːɐ] *n* (-*s*; -*e*) UNIV department; seminar; REL seminary; teacher training college
**sen.** *abbr of* ***senior*** sen., Sen., Sr, Snr, senior
**Senat** [ze'naːt] *m* (-[*e*]*s*; -*e*) senate
**Senator** [ze'naːtoːɐ] *m* (-*s*; -*en* [zena'toːrən]), **Sena'torin** *f* (-; -*nen*) senator
**Sendemast** *m* ELECTR mast
**senden** ['zɛndən] *v/t* ([*irr*,] *ge*-, *h*) send (***mit der Post***® by mail, *Br* by post); ELECTR broadcast, transmit, *a.* televise
**Sender** ['zɛndɐ] *m* (-*s*; -) radio *or* television station; ELECTR transmitter

S

**'Sende|reihe** *f* TV *or* radio series; **~schluss** *m* close-down, F sign-off; **~zeichen** *n* call letters (*Br* sign); **~zeit** *f* air time

**'Sendung** *f* (-; *-en*) broadcast, program (-me), *a.* telecast; ECON consignment, shipment; ***auf ~ sein*** be on the air

**Senf** [zɛnf] *m* (-[*e*]*s*; *-e*) mustard (*a.* BOT)

**senil** [ze'ni:l] *adj* senile; **Senilität** [zenili'tɛ:t] *f* (-; *no pl*) senility

**Senior** ['ze:njo:ɐ] **1.** *m* (*-s*; *-en* [ze-'njo:rən]) senior (*a.* SPORT); senior citizen **2.** *adj* senior

**Seni'orenheim** *n* old people's home

**Seni'orin** *f* (-; *-nen*) senior citizen

**Senke** ['zɛŋkə] *f* (-; *-n*) GEOGR depression, hollow; **'senken** *v/t* (*ge-*, *h*) lower (*a. one's voice*), *a.* bow (*one's head*); ECON *a.* reduce, cut; ***sich ~*** drop, go *or* come down

**'senkrecht** *adj* vertical

**Sensation** [zɛnza'tsjo:n] *f* (-; *-en*) sensation; **sensationell** [zɛnzatsjo'nɛl] *adj*, **Sensati'ons…** *in cpds …blatt etc*: sensational (…)

**Sense** ['zɛnzə] *f* (-; *-n*) AGR scythe

**sensibel** [zɛn'zi:bəl] *adj* sensitive

**sensibilisieren** [zɛnzibili'zi:rən] *v/t* (*no -ge-*, *h*) sensitize (***für*** to)

**sentimental** [zɛntimɛn'ta:l] *adj* sentimental; **Sentimentalität** [zɛntimɛntali'tɛ:t] *f* (-; *-en*) sentimentality

**September** [zɛp'tɛmbɐ] *m* (-[*s*]; -) September

**Serenade** [zere'na:də] *f* (-; *-n*) MUS serenade

**Serie** ['ze:rjə] *f* (-; *-n*) series, TV *etc a.* serial; set; ***in ~*** *produce etc* in series

**'serienmäßig** *adj* series(-produced); standard

**'Serien|nummer** *f* serial number; **~wagen** *m* MOT standard-type car

**seriös** [ze'rjø:s] *adj* respectable; honest; serious

**Serum** ['ze:rum] *n* (*-s*; *-ren*, *-ra*) serum

**Service**[1] [zɛr'vi:s] *n* (-[*s*]; -) set; service

**Service**[2] ['zø:ɐvɪs] *m*, *n* (-; *-s*) service

**servieren** [zɛr'vi:rən] *v/t* (*no -ge-*, *h*) serve; **Serviererin** [zɛr'vi:rərɪn] *f* (-; *-nen*) waitress; **Serviertochter** [zɛr-'vi:ɐtɔxtɐ] *Swiss f* waitress

**Serviette** [zɛr'vjɛtə] *f* (-; *-n*) napkin, *esp Br* serviette

**Servo|bremse** ['zɛrvobrɛmzə] *f* MOT servo *or* power brake; **~lenkung** *f* MOT servo(-assisted) *or* power steering

**Sessel** ['zɛsəl] *m* (*-s*; -) armchair, easy chair; **~lift** *m* chair lift

**sesshaft** ['zɛshaft] *adj*: ***~ werden*** settle (down)

**Set** [zɛt] *n*, *m* (*-s*; *-s*) place mat

**setzen** ['zɛtsən] *v/t and v/i* (*ge-*, *h*) put, set (*a.* PRINT, AGR, MAR), AGR *a.* plant; place; seat *s.o.*; ***~ über*** (*acc*) jump over; cross (*river*); ***~ auf*** (*acc*) bet on, back; ***sich ~*** sit down; CHEM *etc* settle; ***sich ~ auf*** (*acc*) get on, mount; ***sich ~ in*** (*acc*) get into; ***sich zu j-m ~*** sit beside *or* with s.o.; ***~ Sie sich bitte!*** take *or* have a seat!

**Setzer** ['zɛtsɐ] *m* (*-s*; -) PRINT compositor, typesetter; **Setzerei** [zɛtsə'rai] *f* (-; *-en*) PRINT composing room

**Seuche** ['zɔʏçə] *f* (-; *-n*) epidemic (disease)

**seufzen** ['zɔʏftsən] *v/i* (*ge-*, *h*), **Seufzer** ['zɔʏftsɐ] *m* (*-s*; -) sigh

**Sexismus** [zɛ'ksɪsmus] *m* (-; *no pl*) sexism; **Sexist** [zɛ'ksɪst] *m* (*-en*; *-en*), **se'xistisch** *adj* sexist

**Sexual…** [zɛ'ksua:l-] *in cpds …erziehung*, *…leben*, *…trieb etc*: sex(ual) …; **~verbrechen** *n* sex crime

**sexuell** [zɛ'ksuɛl] *adj* sexual; ***~e Belästigung*** (sexual) harassment

**sexy** ['zɛksi] *adj* sexy

**sezieren** [ze'tsi:rən] *v/t* (*no -ge-*, *h*) MED dissect (*a. fig*); perform an autopsy on

**Showgeschäft** ['ʃougəʃɛft] *n* (-[*e*]*s*; *no pl*) show business

**sich** [zɪç] *refl pron* oneself; himself, herself, itself; *pl* themselves; yourself, *pl* yourselves; ***~ ansehen*** look at oneself; look at each other

**Sichel** ['zɪçəl] *f* (-; *-n*) AGR sickle; ASTR crescent

**sicher** ['zɪçɐ] **1.** *adj* safe (***vor*** *dat* from), secure (from); *esp* TECH proof (***gegen*** against); *fig* certain, sure; reliable; **(*sich*) *~ sein*** be sure (***e-r Sache*** of s.th.; ***dass*** that); **2.** *adv* safely; ***~!*** of course, sure(ly); certainly; probably; ***du hast*** (***bist***) ***~ …*** you must have (be) …

**'Sicherheit** *f* (-; *-en*) (*no pl*) security (*a.* MIL, POL, ECON); safety (*a.* TECH); *fig* certainty; skill; **(*sich*) *in ~ bringen*** get to

S

safety; ECON cover

'**Sicherheits...** *esp* TECH *in cpds ...glas, ...nadel, ...schloss etc*: safety ...; **~gurt** *m* seat belt, safety belt; **~maßnahme** *f* safety (POL security) measure

'**sicherlich** *adv* → **sicher** 2

'**sichern** *v/t* (*ge-, h*) protect, safeguard; secure (*a.* MIL, TECH); IT save; ***sich ~*** secure o.s. (***gegen, vor*** *dat* against, from); '**sicherstellen** *v/t* (*sep, -ge-, h*) secure; guarantee; **Sicherung** ['zɪçərʊŋ] *f* (-; *-en*) securing; safeguard(-ing); TECH safety device; ELECTR fuse

'**Sicherungs|kasten** *m* ELECTR fuse box; **~ko,pie** *f* IT backup; ***e-e ~ machen*** (***von***) back up

**Sicht** [zɪçt] *f* (-; *no pl*) visibility; view; ***in ~ kommen*** come into sight *or* view; ***auf lange ~*** in the long run; '**sichtbar** *adj* visible; **sichten** ['zɪçtən] *v/t* (*ge-, h*) sight; *fig* sort (through *or* out)

'**Sichtkarte** *f* season ticket

'**sichtlich** *adv* visibly

'**Sichtweite** *f* visibility; ***in*** (***außer***) ***~*** within (out of) sight

**sickern** ['zɪkɐn] *v/i* (*ge-, sein*) trickle, ooze, seep

**sie** [ziː] *pers pron* she; it; *pl* they; ***Sie*** you

**Sieb** [ziːp] *n* (-[*e*]*s*; *-e*) sieve; strainer

**sieben**[1] ['ziːbən] *v/t* (*ge-, h*) sieve, sift

'**sieben**[2] *adj* seven

**Sieben'meter** *m* SPORT penalty shot *or* throw

**siebte** ['ziːptə] *adj*, '**Siebtel** *n* (-*s*; -) seventh; **siebzehn(te)** ['ziːptseːntə] *adj* seventeen(th); **siebzig** ['ziːptsɪç] *adj* seventy; '**siebzigste** *adj* seventieth

**siedeln** ['ziːdəln] *v/i* (*ge-, h*) settle

**sieden** ['ziːdən] *v/t and v/i* ([*irr*,] *ge-, h*) boil, simmer

'**Siedepunkt** *m* boiling point (*a. fig*)

**Siedler** ['ziːdlɐ] *m* (-*s*; -) settler

**Siedlung** ['ziːdlʊŋ] *f* (-; *-en*) settlement; housing development

**Sieg** [ziːk] *m* (-[*e*]*s*; *-e*) victory, SPORT *a.* win

**Siegel** ['ziːgəl] *n* (-*s*; -) seal, signet

'**Siegellack** *m* sealing wax

'**siegeln** *v/t* (*ge-, h*) seal

**siegen** ['ziːgən] *v/i* (*ge-, h*) win

**Sieger** ['ziːgɐ] *m* (-*s*; -), **Siegerin** ['ziːgərɪn] *f* (-; *-nen*) winner

'**siegreich** *adj* winning; victorious

**Signal** [zɪ'gnaːl] *n* (-*s*; *-e*), **signalisieren** [zɪgnali'ziːrən] *v/t* (*no -ge-, h*) signal

**signieren** [zɪ'gniːrən] *v/t* (*no -ge-, h*) sign

**Silbe** ['zɪlbə] *f* (-; *-n*) syllable

'**Silbentrennung** *f* LING syllabification

**Silber** ['zɪlbɐ] *n* (-*s*; *no pl*) silver; silverware; '**silbergrau** *adj* silver-gray (*Br* -grey); '**Silberhochzeit** *f* silver wedding; '**silbern** *adj* silver

**Silhouette** [zi'luɛtə] *f* (-; *-n*) silhouette; skyline

**Silikon** [zili'koːn] *n* (-*s*; *-e*) CHEM silicone

**Silizium** [zi'liːtsjʊm] *n* (-*s*; *no pl*) CHEM silicon

**Silvester** [zɪl'vɛstɐ] *n* (-*s*; -) New Year's Eve

**Sims** [zɪms] *m, n* (-*es*; *-e*) ledge; windowsill

**simulieren** [zimu'liːrən] *v/t and v/i* TECH *etc* simulate; sham

**simultan** [zimʊl'taːn] *adj* simultaneous

**Sinfonie** [zɪnfo'niː] *f* (-; *-n*) MUS symphony

**singen** ['zɪŋən] *v/t and v/i* (*irr, ge-, h*) sing (***richtig*** [***falsch***] in [out of] tune)

**Singular** ['zɪŋgulaːɐ] *m* (-*s*; *-e*) LING singular

**Singvogel** ['zɪŋfoːgəl] *m* ZO songbird

**sinken** ['zɪŋkən] *v/i* (*irr, ge-, sein*) sink (*a. fig*), go down (*a.* ECON), ASTR *a.* set; *prices etc*: fall, drop

**Sinn** [zɪn] *m* (-[*e*]*s*; *-e*) sense (***für*** of); mind; meaning; point, idea; ***im ~ haben*** have in mind; ***es hat keinen ~*** (***zu warten*** *etc*) it's no use *or* good (waiting *etc*); '**Sinnbild** *n* symbol

'**sinnentstellend** *adj* distorting

**Sinnes|organ** ['zɪnəsˀɔrgaːn] *n* sense organ; **~täuschung** *f* hallucination; **~wandel** *m* change of mind

'**sinnlich** *adj* sensuous; sensory; sensual; '**Sinnlichkeit** *f* (-; *no pl*) sensuality

'**sinnlos** *adj* senseless; useless

'**sinnverwandt** *adj* synonymous

'**sinnvoll** *adj* meaningful; useful; wise, sensible

**Sintflut** ['zɪntfluːt] *f the* Flood

**Sippe** ['zɪpə] *f* (-; *-n*) (extended) family, clan

**Sirene** [zi'reːnə] *f* (-; *-n*) siren

**Sirup** ['ziːrʊp] *m* (-*s*; *-e*) sirup, *Br* syrup; treacle, molasses

**Sitte** ['zɪtə] *f* (-; *-n*) custom, tradition; *pl* morals; manners

'**Sittenlosigkeit** *f* (-; *no pl*) immorality
'**Sittenpoli,zei** *f* vice squad
'**sittenwidrig** *adj* immoral
'**Sittlichkeitsverbrechen** *n* sex crime
**Situation** [zitua'tsjo:n] *f* (-; *-en*) situation; position
**Sitz** [zɪts] *m* (*-es*; *-e*) seat; fit; **~blo,ckade** *f* sit-down demonstration
**sitzen** ['zɪtsən] *v/i* (*irr*, *ge-*, *h*) sit (***an*** *dat* at; ***auf*** *dat* on); be; fit; F do time; ***~ bleiben*** keep one's seat; PED have to repeat a year; F ***~ bleiben auf*** (*dat*) be left with; F ***j-n ~ lassen*** leave s.o. in the lurch, let s.o. down
'**sitzen|bleiben** *v/i* (*irr*, ***bleiben***, *sep*, *-ge-*, *sein*) → ***sitzen***; **~lassen** *v/i* (*irr*, ***lassen***, *sep*, *no -ge-*, *sein*) *a. fig* → ***sitzen***
'**Sitzplatz** *m* seat
'**Sitzstreik** *m* sit-down strike
'**Sitzung** *f* (-; *-en*) session (*a.* PARL), meeting, conference
**Skala** ['ska:la] *f* (-; *-en*) scale, *fig a.* range
**Skalp** [skalp] *m* (*-s*; *-e*), **skalpieren** [skal'pi:rən] *v/t* (*no -ge-*, *h*) scalp
**Skandal** [skan'da:l] *m* (*-s*; *-e*) scandal; ***ein ~ sein*** be scandalous; **skandalös** [skanda'lø:s] *adj* scandalous, shocking
**Skelett** [ske'lɛt] *n* (*-[e]s*; *-e*) skeleton
**Skepsis** ['skɛpsɪs] *f* (-; *no pl*) skepticism, *Br* scepticism; **Skeptiker** ['skɛptikɐ] *m* (*-s*; -) skeptic, *Br* sceptic; **skeptisch** ['skɛptɪʃ] *adj* skeptical, *Br* sceptical
**Ski** [ʃi:] *m* (*-s*; *-er* ['ʃi:ɐ]) ski; ***~ laufen*** *or* ***fahren*** ski; **~brille** *f* ski goggles; **~fahren** *n* skiing; **~fahrer(in)** skier; **~fliegen** *n* ski flying; **~gebiet** *n* skiing area; **~kurs** *m* skiing course; **~läufer(in)** skier; **~lehrer(in)** ski instructor; **~lift** *m* ski lift; **~schuh** *m* ski boot; **~sport** *m* skiing; **~springen** *n* ski jumping; **~stock** *m* ski pole
**Skizze** ['skɪtsə] *f* (-; *-n*), **skizzieren** [skɪ'tsi:rən] *v/t* (*no -ge-*, *h*) sketch
**Sklave** ['skla:və] *m* (*-n*; *-n*) slave (*a. fig*); **Sklaverei** [skla:və'rai] *f* (-; *no pl*) slavery; '**Sklavin** *f* (-; *-nen*) slave (*a. fig*); '**sklavisch** *adj* slavish (*a. fig*)
**Skonto** ['skɔnto] *m*, *n* (*-s*; *-s*) ECON (cash) discount
**Skorpion** [skɔr'pjo:n] *m* (*-s*; *-e*) ZO scorpion; ASTR Scorpio; ***er ist*** (***ein***) ***~*** he's (a) Scorpio

**Skrupel** ['skru:pəl] *m* (*-s*; -) scruple, qualm; '**skrupellos** *adj* unscrupulous
**Skulptur** [skʊlp'tu:ɐ] *f* (-; *-en*) sculpture
**Slalom** ['sla:lɔm] *m* (*-s*; *-s*) slalom
**Slawe** ['sla:və] *m* (*-n*; *-n*), '**Slawin** *f* (-; *-nen*) Slav; '**slawisch** *adj* Slav(ic)
**Slip** [slɪp] *m* (*-s*; *-s*) briefs, panties
'**Slipeinlage** *f* panty liner
**Slipper** ['slɪpɐ] *m* (*-s*; -) loafer, *esp Br* slip-on (shoe)
**Slowake** [slo'va:kə] *m* (*-n*; *-n*) Slovak
**Slowakei** [slova'kai] *f* Slovakia
**Slo'wakin** *f* (-; *-nen*), **slo'wakisch** *adj* Slovak
**Smaragd** [sma'rakt] *m* (*-[e]s*; *-e*) MIN, **sma'ragdgrün** *adj* emerald
**Smiley** ['smaili] *n* (*-s*; *-s*) smiley
**Smog** [smɔk] *m* (*-[s]*; *-s*) smog; **Smogalarm** *m* smog alert
**Smoking** ['smo:kɪŋ] *m* (*-s*; *-s*) tuxedo, *Br* dinner jacket
**SMS** [ɛsɛm'ɛs] *f* (-; -) text (message); ***ich schicke dir eine ~*** I'll text you, I'll send you a text (message)
**Snob** [snɔp] *m* (*-s*; *-s*) snob; **Snobismus** [sno'bɪsmʊs] *m* (-; *no pl*) snobbery; **sno'bistisch** *adj* snobbish
**Snowboard** ['sno:bo:ɐt] *n* (*-s*; *-s*) snowboard; **Snowboardfahren** *n* snowboarding
**so** [zo:] **1.** *adv* so; like this *or* that, this *or* that way; thus; such; (***nicht***) ***~ groß wie*** (not) as big as; ***~ ein***(***e***) such a; ***~ sehr*** so (F that) much; ***und ~ weiter*** and so on; ***oder ~ et.*** or s.th. like that; ***oder ~*** or so; ***~, fangen wir an!*** well *or* all right, let's begin!; F ***~ weit sein*** be ready; ***es ist ~ weit*** it's time; ***~ genannt*** so-called; ***doppelt ~ viel*** twice as much; ***~ viel wie möglich*** as much as possible **2.** *cj* so, therefore; ***~ dass*** so that **3.** *int*: ***~!*** all right!, o.k.!; that's it!; ***ach ~!*** I see
**s.o.** *abbr of* ***siehe oben*** see above
**so'bald** [zo'balt] *cj* as soon as
**Socke** ['zɔkə] *f* (-; *-n*) sock
**Sockel** ['zɔkəl] *m* (*-s*; -) base; pedestal
**Sodbrennen** ['zo:tbrɛnən] *n* (*-s*; *no pl*) MED heartburn
**soeben** [zo'e:bən] *adv* just (now)
**Sofa** ['zo:fa] *n* (*-s*; *-s*) sofa, settee, davenport
**sofern** [zo'fɛrn] *cj* if, provided that; ***~ nicht*** unless
**soff** [zɔf] *pret of* ***saufen***

**sofort** [zo'fɔrt] *adv* at once, immediately, right away
**So'fortbildkamera** *f* PHOT instant camera
**Software** ['zɔftwɛːɐ] *f* IT software; **~pa,ket** *n* software package
**sog** [zoːk] *pret of* ***saugen***
**Sog** *m* (-[*e*]*s*; -*e*) suction, MAR *a.* wake
**sogar** [zo'gaːɐ] *adv* even
**sogenannt** ['zoːgənant] *adj* so-called
**Sohle** ['zoːlə] *f* (-; -*n*) sole; *mining*: floor
**Sohn** [zoːn] *m* (-[*e*]*s*; *Söhne* ['zøːnə]) son
**Sojabohne** ['zoːjaboːnə] *f* BOT soybean
**so'lange** [zo'laŋə] *cj* as long as
**Solar…** [zo'laːɐ-] *in cpds …energie etc*: solar …
**solch** [zɔlç] *dem pron* such, like this *or* that
**Sold** [zɔlt] *m* (-[*e*]*s*; -*e*) MIL pay
**Soldat** [zɔl'daːt] *m* (-*en*; -*en*), **Sol'datin** *f* (-; -*nen*) soldier
**Söldner** ['zœldnɐ] *m* (-*s*; -) MIL mercenary
**Sole** ['zoːlə] *f* (-; -*n*) brine, salt water
**solidarisch** [zoli'daːrɪʃ] *adj*: ***sich ~ erklären mit*** declare one's solidarity with
**solide** [zo'liːdə] *adj* solid, *fig a.* sound; reasonable (*prices*); steady (*person*)
**Solist** [zo'lɪst] *m* (-*en*; -*en*), **So'listin** *f* (-; -*nen*) soloist
**Soll** [zɔl] *n* (-[*s*]; -[*s*]) ECON debit; target, quota; ***~ und Haben*** debit and credit
**sollen** ['zɔlən] *v/i* (*ge-*, *h*) *and v/aux* (*irr*, *no -ge-*, *h*) be to; be supposed to; (***was***) ***soll ich …?*** (what) shall I …?; ***du solltest*** (***nicht***) ***…*** you should(n't) …; you ought(n't) to; ***was soll das?*** what's the idea?
**Solo** ['zoːlo] *n* (-*s*, -*s*, *Soli*) *esp* MUS solo; SPORT solo attempt *etc*
**so'mit** [zo'mɪt] *cj* thus, so, consequently
**Sommer** ['zɔmɐ] *m* (-*s*; -) summer (time); ***im ~*** in (the) summer; **~ferien** *pl* summer vacation (*Br* holidays); **~frische** *f* summer resort
**'sommerlich** *adj* summery
**'Sommersprosse** *f* freckle
**'sommersprossig** *adj* freckled
**'Sommerzeit** *f* summertime; daylight saving (*Br* summer) time
**Sonate** [zo'naːtə] *f* (-; -*n*) MUS sonata
**Sonde** ['zɔndə] *f* (-; -*n*) probe (*a.* MED)
**Sonder…** ['zɔndɐ-] *in cpds …angebot*, *…ausgabe*, *…flug*, *…preis*, *…wunsch*, *…zug etc*: special …
**'sonderbar** *adj* strange, F funny
**'Sonderling** *m* (-*s*; -*e*) eccentric
**'Sondermüll** *m* hazardous (*or* special toxic) waste; **~depo,nie** *f* special waste dump
**sondern** ['zɔndɐn] *cj* but; ***nicht nur …, ~ auch …*** not only … but also …
**'Sonderschule** *f* special school (for the handicapped *etc*)
**Sonnabend** ['zɔnˀaːbənt] *m* Saturday
**Sonne** ['zɔnə] *f* (-; -*n*) sun
**sonnen** ['zɔnən] *v/refl* (*ge-*, *h*) sunbathe
**'Sonnenaufgang** *m* (***bei ~*** at) sunrise
**'Sonnen|bad** *n*: ***ein ~ nehmen*** sunbathe; **~bank** *f* (-; -*bänke*) sunbed; **~blume** *f* BOT sunflower; **~brand** *m* sunburn; **~bräune** *f* suntan; **~brille** *f* sunglasses; **~creme** *f* suntan lotion, *Br* sun cream; **~ener,gie** *f* solar energy; **~finsternis** *f* solar eclipse
**'sonnen'klar** F *adj* (as) clear as daylight
**'Sonnen|kol,lektor** *m* solar panel; **~licht** *n* (-[*e*]*s*, *no pl*) sunlight; **~öl** *n* suntan oil; **~schein** *m* sunshine; **~schirm** *m* sunshade; **~schutz** *m* suntan lotion; **~seite** *f* sunny side (*a. fig*); **~stich** *m* sunstroke; **~strahl** *m* sunbeam; **~sys,tem** *n* solar system; **~uhr** *f* sundial; **~untergang** *m* sunset
**sonnig** ['zɔnɪç] *adj* sunny (*a. fig*)
**Sonntag** ['zɔntaːk] *m* Sunday; (***am***) ***~*** on Sunday; **'sonntags** *adv* on Sundays
**'Sonntagsfahrer** *contp m* MOT Sunday driver
**sonst** [zɔnst] *adv* else; otherwise, or (else); normally, usually; ***~ noch et.*** (***jemand***)***?*** anything (anyone) else?; ***~ noch Fragen?*** any other questions?; ***~ nichts*** nothing else; ***alles wie ~*** everything as usual; ***nichts ist wie ~*** nothing is as it used to be; **'sonstig** *adj* other
**Sopran** [zo'praːn] *m* (-*s*; -*e*) MUS, **Sopranistin** [zopra'nɪstɪn] *f* (-; -*nen*) MUS soprano
**Sorge** ['zɔrgə] *f* (-; -*n*) worry; sorrow; trouble; care; ***sich ~n machen*** (***um***) worry *or* be worried (about); ***keine ~!*** don't worry!; **sorgen** ['zɔrgən] (*ge-*, *h*) **1.** *v/i*: ***~ für*** care for, take care of; ***dafür ~, dass*** see (to it) that **2.** *v/refl*: ***sich ~ um*** worry *or* be worried about
**'Sorgenkind** *n* problem child

S

**Sorgfalt** ['zɔrkfalt] *f* (-; *no pl*) care
**sorgfältig** ['zɔrkfɛltɪç] *adj* careful
**sorglos** ['zɔrkloːs] *adj* carefree; careless
**Sorte** ['zɔrtə] *f* (-; *-n*) sort, kind, type; **sortieren** [zɔr'tiːrən] *v/t* (*no -ge-, h*) sort; arrange; **Sortiment** [zɔrti'mɛnt] *n* (-[*e*]*s*; *-e*) ECON assortment
**Soße** ['zoːsə] *f* (-; *-n*) sauce; gravy
**sott** [zɔt] *pret of* ***sieden***
**Souffleur** [zu'fløːɐ] *m* (*-s*; *-e*), **Souffleuse** [zu'fløːzə] *f* (-; *-n*) THEA prompter; **soufflieren** [zu'fliːrən] *v/i* (*no -ge-, h*) THEA prompt (***j-m*** s.o.)
**souverän** [zuvə'rɛːn] *adj* POL sovereign
**Souveränität** [zuvərɛni'tɛːt] *f* (-; *no pl*) POL sovereignty
**so'viel** [zo'fiːl] *cj* as far as; → ***so***; **so'weit** *cj* as far as; → ***so***; **so'wie** *cj* as well as, and … as well; as soon as; **sowie'so** *adv* anyway, anyhow, in any case
**so'wohl** [zo'voːl] *cj*: ***~ Lehrer als (auch) Schüler*** both teachers and students
**sozial** [zo'tsjaːl] *adj* social
**Sozi'al…** *in cpds …arbeiter, …demokrat, …versicherung etc*: social …; **~hilfe** *f* welfare, *Br* social security; ***~ beziehen*** be on welfare (*Br* social security)
**Sozialismus** [zotsja'lɪsmʊs] *m* (-; *no pl*) socialism; **Sozialist(in)** (*-en*/-; *-en* / *-nen*), **sozia'listisch** *adj* socialist
**Sozi'alkunde** *f* PED social studies
**Sozi'alstaat** *m* welfare state
**Soziologe** [zotsjo'loːgə] *m* (*-n*; *-n*) sociologist; **Soziologie** [zotsjolo'giː] *f* (-; *no pl*) sociology; **Sozio'login** *f* (-; *-nen*) sociologist; **soziologisch** [zotsjo'loːgɪʃ] *adj* sociological
**sozu'sagen** *adv* so to speak
**Spagat** [ʃpa'gaːt] *m*: ***~ machen*** do the splits
**Spalier** [ʃpa'liːɐ] *n* (*-s*; *-e*) BOT espalier; MIL *etc* lane
**Spalt** [ʃpalt] *m* (-[*e*]*s*; *-e*) crack, gap; **Spalte** ['ʃpaltə] *f* (-; *-n*) → ***Spalt***; PRINT column; '**spalten** *v/t* ([*irr*,] *ge-, h*) split (*a. fig*); POL divide; ***sich ~*** split (up); '**Spaltung** *f* (-; *-en*) split(ting); PHYS fission; *fig* split; POL division
**Span** [ʃpaːn] *m* (-[*e*]*s*; *Späne* ['ʃpɛːnə]) chip; *pl* TECH shavings
**Spange** ['ʃpaŋə] *f* (-; *-n*) clasp
**Spaniel** ['ʃpaːnjəl] *m* (*-s*; *-s*) ZO spaniel
**Spanien** ['ʃpaːnjən] Spain
**Spanier** ['ʃpaːnjɐ] *m* (*-s*; -), **Spanierin** ['ʃpaːnjərɪn] *f* (-; *-nen*) Spaniard
**spanisch** ['ʃpaːnɪʃ] *adj* Spanish
**spann** [ʃpan] *pret of* ***spinnen***
**Spann** *m* (-[*e*]*s*; *-e*) ANAT instep
**Spanne** ['ʃpanə] *f* (-; *-n*) span
'**spannen** (*ge-, h*) **1.** *v/t* stretch, tighten; put up (*line*); cock (*gun*); draw, bend (*bow*) **2.** *v/i* be (too) tight; **~d** *adj* exciting, thrilling, gripping
'**Spannung** *f* (-; *-en*) tension (*a.* TECH, POL, PSYCH); ELECTR voltage; *fig* suspense, excitement
'**Spannweite** *f* span, *fig a.* range
**Spar|buch** ['ʃpaːɐbuːx] *n* savings book; **~büchse** *f esp Br* money box
**sparen** ['ʃpaːrən] *v/i and v/t* (*ge-, h*) save; economize; ***~ für*** *or* ***auf*** (*acc*) save up for; **Sparer(in)** ['ʃpaːrɐ, 'ʃpaːrərɪn] *m*(*f*) (*-s*; *-/-*; *-nen*) saver
**Spargel** ['ʃpargəl] *m* (*-s*; -) BOT asparagus
'**Sparkasse** *f* savings bank
'**Sparkonto** *n* savings account
**spärlich** ['ʃpɛːɐlɪç] *adj* sparse, scant; scanty; poor (*attendance*)
**sparsam** ['ʃpaːɐzaːm] *adj* economical (***mit*** of); ***~ leben*** lead a frugal life; ***~ umgehen mit*** use sparingly; go easy on
'**Sparsamkeit** *f* (-; *no pl*) economy
'**Sparschwein(chen)** *n* piggy bank
**Spaß** [ʃpaːs] *m* (*-es*; *Späße* ['ʃpɛːsə]), *Austrian a.* **Spass** fun; joke; ***aus (nur zum) ~*** (just) for fun; ***es macht viel (keinen) ~*** it's great (no) fun; ***j-m den ~ verderben*** spoil s.o.'s fun; ***er macht nur ~*** he is only joking (F kidding); ***keinen ~ verstehen*** have no sense of humo(u)r
**spaßen** ['ʃpaːsən] *v/i* (*ge-, h*) joke
**spaßig** ['ʃpaːsɪç] *adj* funny
'**Spaßvogel** *m* joker
**spät** [ʃpɛːt] *adj and adv* late; ***am ~en Nachmittag*** late in the afternoon; ***wie ~ ist es?*** what time is it?; ***von früh bis ~*** from morning till night; ***(fünf Minuten) zu ~ kommen*** be (five minutes) late; ***bis ~er!*** see you (later)!; → ***früher***
**Spaten** ['ʃpaːtən] *m* (*-s*; -) spade
'**spätestens** *adv* at the latest
**Spatz** [ʃpats] *m* (*-en*; *-en*) ZO sparrow
**spazieren** [ʃpa'tsiːrən]: ***~ fahren*** go (take *s.o.*) for a drive; take *s.o.* out; ***~ gehen*** go for a walk

S

**Spazierfahrt** [ʃpa'tsiːɐfaːɐt] *f* drive, ride

**Spa'ziergang** *m* walk; ***e-n ~ machen*** go for a walk; **Spa'ziergänger(in)** [ʃpa'tsiːɐgɛŋɐ, ʃpa'tsiːɐgɛŋərɪn] (*-s*; *-/-*; *-nen*) walker

**Specht** [ʃpɛçt] *m* (*-[e]s*; *-e*) ZO woodpecker

**Speck** [ʃpɛk] *m* (*-[e]s*; *-e*) bacon

**speckig** ['ʃpɛkɪç] *fig adj* greasy

**Spediteur** [ʃpedi'tøːɐ] *m* (*-s*; *-e*) shipping agent; remover

**Spedition** [ʃpedi'tsjoːn] *f* (*-*; *-en*) shipping agency; moving (*Br* removal) firm

**Speer** [ʃpeːɐ] *m* (*-[e]s*; *-e*) spear; SPORT javelin

**Speiche** ['ʃpaiçə] *f* (*-*; *-n*) spoke

**Speichel** ['ʃpaiçəl] *m* (*-s*; *no pl*) saliva, spit

**Speicher** ['ʃpaiçɐ] *m* (*-s*; *-*) storehouse; tank, reservoir; ARCH attic; IT memory, store; **~dichte** *f* IT bit density; **~kapazi,tät** *f* IT memory capacity

'**speichern** *v/t* (*ge-*, *h*) store (up)

**Speicherung** ['ʃpaiçərʊŋ] *f* (*-*; *-en*) storage

**speien** ['ʃpaiən] *v/t* (*irr*, *ge-*, *h*) spit; spout; *volcano etc*: belch

**Speise** ['ʃpaizə] *f* (*-*; *-n*) food; dish; **~eis** *n* ice cream; **~kammer** *f* larder, pantry; **~karte** *f* menu

'**speisen** (*ge-*, *h*) **1.** *v/i* dine **2.** *v/t* feed (*a.* ELECTR *etc*)

'**Speise|röhre** *f* ANAT gullet; **~saal** *m* dining hall; **~wagen** *m* RAIL diner, *esp Br* dining car

**Spekulant** [ʃpeku'lant] *m* (*-en*; *-en*) ECON speculator

**Spekulation** [ʃpekula'tsjoːn] *f* (*-*; *-en*) speculation, ECON *a.* venture

**spekulieren** [ʃpeku'liːrən] *v/i* (*no -ge-*, *h*) ECON speculate (***auf*** *acc* on; ***mit*** in)

**Spende** ['ʃpɛndə] *f* (*-*; *-n*) gift; contribution; donation; '**spenden** *v/t* (*ge-*, *h*) give (*a. fig*); donate (*a.* MED); **Spender** ['ʃpɛndɐ] *m* (*-s*; *-*) giver; donor (*a.* MED), **Spenderin** *f* (*-*; *-nen*) donor (*a.* MED)

**spendieren** [ʃpɛn'diːrən] *v/t* (*no -ge-*, *h*) ***j-m et. ~*** treat s.o. to s.th.

**Spengler** ['ʃpɛŋlɐ] *Austrian m* → ***Klempner***

**Sperling** ['ʃpɛrlɪŋ] *m* (*-s*; *-e*) ZO sparrow

**Sperre** ['ʃpɛrə] *f* (*-*; *-n*) barrier, RAIL *a.* gate; *fig* stop; TECH lock(ing device); barricade; SPORT suspension; PSYCH mental block; ECON embargo

'**sperren** *v/t* (*ge-*, *h*) close; ECON embargo; cut off; stop (*check*); SPORT suspend; obstruct; ***~ in*** (*acc*) lock (up) in

'**Sperr|holz** *n* plywood; **~müllabfuhr** *f* removal of bulky refuse

'**Sperrung** *f* (*-*; *-en*) closing

**Spesen** ['ʃpeːzən] *pl* expenses

**Spezi** ['ʃpeːtsi] F *m* (*-s*; *-[s]*) buddy, pal

**Spezial|ausbildung** [ʃpe'tsjaːlʔausbɪldʊŋ] *f* special training; **~gebiet** *n* special field, special(i)ty; **~geschäft** *n* specialized shop *or* store

**spezialisieren** [ʃpetsjali'ziːrən] *v/refl* (*no -ge-*, *h*) specialize (***auf*** *acc* in); **Spezialist(in)** [ʃpetsja'lɪst(ɪn)] (*-en*; *-en/-*; *-nen*) specialist; **Spezialität** [ʃpetsjali'tɛːt] *f* (*-*; *-en*) special(i)ty;

**speziell** [ʃpe'tsjɛl] *adj* specific, particular

**spezifisch** [ʃpe'tsiːfɪʃ] *adj* specific; ***~es Gewicht*** specific gravity

**Sphäre** ['sfɛːrə] *f* (*-*; *-n*) sphere (*a. fig*)

**spicken** ['ʃpɪkən] (*ge-*, *h*) **1.** *v/t* GASTR lard (*a. fig*) **2.** F *v/i* PED crib

**spie** [ʃpiː] *pret of* ***speien***

**Spiegel** ['ʃpiːgəl] *m* (*-s*; *-*) mirror (*a. fig*)

'**Spiegelbild** *n* reflection (*a. fig*)

'**Spiegelei** *n* GASTR fried egg

'**spiegel'glatt** *adj* glassy; icy

'**spiegeln** *v/i and v/t* (*ge-*, *h*) reflect (*a. fig*); shine; ***sich ~*** be reflected (*a. fig*)

'**Spiegelung** *f* (*-*; *-en*) reflection

**Spiel** [ʃpiːl] *n* (*-[e]s*; *-e*) game (*a. fig*); match; play (*a.* THEA *etc*); gambling; *fig* gamble; ***auf dem ~ stehen*** be at stake; ***aufs ~ setzen*** risk; '**Spielca,sino** *n* casino; **spielen** ['ʃpiːlən] *v/i and v/t* (*ge-*, *h*) play (*a. fig*) (***um*** for); THEA act; perform; gamble; do (*the pools etc*); ***Klavier*** *etc* ***~*** play the piano *etc*; '**spielend** *fig adv* easily; **Spieler** ['ʃpiːlɐ] *m* (*-s*; *-*), **Spielerin** ['ʃpiːlərɪn] *f* (*-*; *-nen*) player; gambler

'**Spiel|feld** *n* (playing) field, pitch; **~film** *m* feature film; **~halle** *f* amusement arcade, game room; **~kame,rad(in)** playmate; **~karte** *f* playing card; **~ka,sino** *n* casino; **~marke** *f* counter, chip; **~plan** *m* THEA *etc* program(me); **~platz** *m* playground; **~raum** *fig m* play, scope; **~regel** *f* rule (of the game); **~sachen**

S

*pl* toys; **~stand** *m* score; **~uhr** *f* music (*Br* musical) box; **~verderber(in)** (*-s*; *-/-*; *-nen*) spoilsport; **~waren** *pl* toys; **~zeit** *f* THEA, SPORT season; playing (*film*: running) time

'**Spielzeug** *n* toy(s); **~...** *in cpds ...pistole etc*: toy ...

**Spieß** [ʃpiːs] *m* (*-es*; *-e*) MIL spear; GASTR spit; skewer

**spießen** ['ʃpiːsən] *v/t* (*ge-, h*) skewer

**Spießer** ['ʃpiːsɐ] F *contp m* (*-s*; -), '**spießig** F *contp adj* philistine

**Spinat** [ʃpi'naːt] *m* (*-[e]s*; *-e*) BOT spinach

**Spind** [ʃpɪnt] *n, m* (*-[e]s*; *-e*) locker

**Spindel** ['ʃpɪndəl] *f* (*-*; *-n*) spindle

**Spinne** ['ʃpɪnə] *f* (*-*; *-n*) ZO spider

'**spinnen** (*irr, ge-, h*) **1.** *v/t* spin (*a. fig*) **2.** F *contp v/i* be nuts; talk nonsense

**Spinner** ['ʃpɪnɐ] *m* (*-s*; -), '**Spinnerin** *f* (*-*; *-nen*) spinner; F *contp* nut, crackpot

'**Spinnrad** *n* spinning wheel

'**Spinnwebe** *f* (*-*; *-n*) cobweb

**Spion** [ʃpjoːn] *m* (*-s*; *-e*) spy

**Spionage** [ʃpjo'naːʒə] *f* (*-*; *no pl*) espionage; **spionieren** [ʃpjo'niːrən] *v/i* (*no -ge-, h*) spy; F snoop

**Spi'onin** *f* (*-*; *-nen*) spy

**Spirale** [ʃpi'raːlə] *f* (*-*; *-n*), **spiralförmig** [ʃpi'raːlfœrmɪç] *adj* spiral

**Spirituosen** [ʃpiri'tuoːzən] *pl* spirits

**Spiritus** ['ʃpiːritʊs] *m* spirit

**Spital** [ʃpi'taːl] *Austrian, Swiss n* (*-s*; *Spitäler* [ʃpi'tɛːlɐ]) hospital

**spitz** [ʃpɪts] *adj* pointed (*a. fig*); MATH acute; ***~e Zunge*** sharp tongue

'**Spitzbogen** *m* ARCH pointed arch

**Spitze** ['ʃpɪtsə] *f* (*-*; *-n*) point; tip; ARCH spire; BOT, GEOGR top; head (*a. fig*); lace; F MOT top speed; ***spitze sein*** F be super, be (the) tops; ***an der ~*** at the top (*a. fig*)

**Spitzel** ['ʃpɪtsəl] *m* (*-s*; -) informer, F stoolpigeon

**spitzen** ['ʃpɪtsən] *v/t* (*ge-, h*) point, sharpen; purse; ZO prick up (*its ears*)

'**Spitzen...** *in cpds* top ...; hi-tech ...; **~technolo,gie** *f* high technology, hi tech

'**spitzfindig** *adj* quibbling

'**Spitzfindigkeit** *f* (*-*; *-en*) subtlety

'**Spitzhacke** *f* pickax(e), pick

'**Spitzname** *m* nickname

**Splitter** ['ʃplɪtɐ] *m* (*-s*; -), '**splittern** *v/i* (*ge-, h, sein*) splinter

'**splitter'nackt** F *adj* stark naked

**sponsern** ['ʃpɔnzɐn] *v/t* (*ge-, h*) sponsor

**Sponsor** ['ʃpɔnzɐ] *m* (*-s*; *-en* [ʃpɔn-'zoːrən]) sponsor

**spontan** [ʃpɔn'taːn] *adj* spontaneous

**Sporen** ['ʃpoːrən] *pl* spurs (*a.* ZO); BIOL spores

**Sport** [ʃpɔrt] *m* (*-[e]s*; *no pl*) sport(s); PED physical education; ***~ treiben*** do sports

'**Sport...** *in cpds ...ereignis, ...geschäft, ...hemd, ...verein, ...zentrum etc*: *mst* sports ...; **~kleidung** *f* sportswear

'**Sportler** ['ʃpɔrtlɐ] *m* (*-s*; -), **Sportlerin** ['ʃpɔrtlərɪn] *f* (*-*; *-nen*) athlete

'**sportlich** *adj* athletic; casual, sporty

'**Sport|nachrichten** *pl* sports news; **~platz** *m* sports grounds; **~tauchen** *n* scuba diving; **~wagen** *m* stroller, *Br* pushchair; MOT sports car

**Spott** [ʃpɔt] *m* (*-[e]s, no pl*) mockery; derision

'**spott'billig** F *adj* dirt cheap

**spotten** ['ʃpɔtən] *v/i* (*ge-, h*) mock (***über*** *acc* at), scoff (at); make fun (of)

**Spötter** ['ʃpœtɐ] *m* (*-s*; -) mocker, scoffer; '**spöttisch** *adj* mocking, derisive

'**Spottpreis** *m*: ***für e-n ~*** dirt cheap

**sprach** [ʃpraːx] *pret of* ***sprechen***

**Sprache** ['ʃpraːxə] *f* (*-*; *-n*) language (*a. fig*); speech; ***zur ~ kommen*** (***bringen***) come up (bring *s.th.* up)

'**Sprach|fehler** *m* speech defect; **~gebrauch** *m* usage; **~lehrer(in)** language teacher

'**sprachlich** **1.** *adj* language ... **2.** *adv*: ***~ richtig*** grammatically correct

'**sprachlos** *adj* speechless

'**Sprach|rohr** *fig n* mouthpiece; **~unterricht** *m* language teaching; **~wissenschaft** *f* linguistics

**sprang** [ʃpraŋ] *pret of* ***springen***

**Spraydose** ['ʃpreːdoːzə] *f* spray can, aerosol (can)

**Sprechanlage** ['ʃprɛçanlaːgə] *f* intercom

**sprechen** ['ʃprɛçən] *v/t and v/i* (*irr, ge-, h*) speak (***j-n, mit j-m*** to s.o.); talk (to) (*both*: ***über*** *acc*, ***von*** about, of); ***nicht zu ~ sein*** be busy; **Sprecher(in)** ['ʃprɛçɐ, 'ʃprɛçərɪn] *m(f)* (*-s*; *-/-*; *-nen*) speaker; announcer; spokesman (spokeswoman); '**Sprechstunde** *f* of-

S

fice hours; MED office (*Br* consulting) hours, *Br* surgery; '**Sprechzimmer** *n* office, *Br a.* consulting room
**spreizen** ['ʃpraitsən] *v/t* (*ge-, h*) spread
**sprengen** ['ʃprɛŋən] *v/t* (*ge-, h*) blow up; blast; sprinkle; water; *fig* break up
'**Sprengkopf** *m* MIL warhead
'**Sprengstoff** *m* MIL explosive
'**Sprengung** *f* (-; *-en*) blasting; blowing up
**sprenkeln** ['ʃprɛŋkəln] *v/t* (*ge-, h*) speck(le), spot, dot
**Spreu** [ʃprɔy] *f* (-; *no pl*) chaff (*a. fig*)
**Sprichwort** ['ʃprɪçvɔrt] *n* proverb, saying
'**sprichwörtlich** *adj* proverbial (*a. fig*)
**sprießen** ['ʃpri:sən] *v/i* (*irr, ge-, sein*) BOT sprout
'**Springbrunnen** *m* fountain
**springen** ['ʃprɪŋən] *v/i* (*irr, ge-, sein*) jump, leap; *ball etc*: bounce; SPORT dive; *glass etc*: crack; break; burst; ***in die Höhe*** (***zur Seite***) **~** jump up (aside)
**Springer** ['ʃprɪŋɐ] *m* (*-s*; -) jumper; diver; *chess*: knight
'**Springflut** *f* spring tide
'**Springreiten** *n* show jumping
**Spritze** ['ʃprɪtsə] *f* (-; *-n*) MED injection, F shot; syringe; '**spritzen 1.** *v/i and v/t* (*ge-, h*) splash; spray (*a.* TECH, AGR); MED inject; give *s.o.* an injection of **2.** *v/i* (*ge-, sein*) spatter; gush (***aus*** from); **Spritzer** ['ʃprɪtsɐ] *m* (*-s*; -) splash; dash
'**Spritzpis,tole** *f* TECH spray gun
'**Spritztour** F *f* MOT spin
**spröde** ['ʃprø:də] *adj* brittle (*a. fig*); rough
**spross** [ʃprɔs] *pret of* ***sprießen***
**Sprosse** ['ʃprɔsə] *f* (-; *-n*) rung
**Spruch** [ʃprʊx] *m* (-[*e*]*s*; *Sprüche* ['ʃprʏçə]) saying; decision; **~band** *n* banner
**Sprudel** ['ʃpru:dəl] *m* (*-s*; -) mineral water; '**sprudeln** *v/i* (*ge-, sein*) bubble
**Sprühdose** ['ʃpry:do:zə] *f* spray can, aerosol (can); **sprühen** ['ʃpry:ən] *v/t and v/i* (*ge-, h*) spray; throw out (*sparks*)
'**Sprühregen** *m* drizzle
**Sprung** [ʃprʊŋ] *m* (-[*e*]*s*; *Sprünge* ['ʃprʏŋə]) jump, leap; SPORT dive; crack, fissure; **~brett** *n* SPORT diving board; springboard; *fig* stepping stone; **~schanze** *f* ski jump
**Spucke** ['ʃpʊkə] F *f* (-; *no pl*) spit
'**spucken** *v/i and v/t* (*ge-, h*) spit; F throw up
**Spuk** [ʃpu:k] *m* (-[*e*]*s*; *-e*) apparition, ghost; **spuken** ['ʃpu:kən] *v/i* (*ge-, h*) **~ *in*** (*dat*) haunt; ***hier spukt es*** this place is haunted
**Spule** ['ʃpu:lə] *f* (-; *-n*) spool, reel; bobbin; ELECTR coil; '**spulen** *v/t* (*ge-, h*) spool, wind, reel
**spülen** ['ʃpy:lən] *v/t and v/i* (*ge-, h*) wash up, do the dishes; rinse; flush the toilet
'**Spülma,schine** *f* dishwasher
**Spur** [ʃpu:ɐ] *f* (-; *-en*) track(s); trail; print; lane; trace (*a. fig*); ***j-m auf der ~ sein*** be on s.o.'s trail; **spüren** ['ʃpy:rən] *v/t* (*ge-, h*) feel, sense; notice
'**spurlos** *adv* without leaving a trace
'**Spurweite** *f* RAIL ga(u)ge; MOT track
**St.** *abbr of* ***Sankt*** St, Saint
**Staat** [ʃta:t] *m* (-[*e*]*s*; *-en*) state; POL government; '**Staatenbund** *m* confederacy, confederation; '**staatenlos** *adj* stateless; '**staatlich 1.** *adj* state ...; public, national **2.** *adv*: **~ *geprüft*** qualified, registered
'**Staats|angehörige** *m, f* national, citizen, subject; **~angehörigkeit** *f* (-; *no pl*) nationality; **~anwalt** *m* JUR district attorney, *Br* (public) prosecutor; **~besuch** *m* official *or* state visit; **~bürger(in)** citizen; **~chef** *m* head of state; **~dienst** *m* civil (*or* public) service
'**staatseigen** *adj* state-owned
'**Staatsfeind** *m* public enemy
'**Staats|haushalt** *m* budget; **~kasse** *f* treasury; **~mann** *m* statesman; **~oberhaupt** *n* head of (the) state; **~sekre,tär(in)** undersecretary of state; **~streich** *m* coup d'état; **~vertrag** *m* treaty; **~wissenschaft** *f* political science
**Stab** [ʃta:p] *m* (-[*e*]*s*; *Stäbe* ['ʃtɛ:bə]) staff (*a. fig*); bar; SPORT, MUS baton; SPORT pole
**Stäbchen** ['ʃtɛ:pçən] *pl* chopstick
'**Stabhochsprung** *m* SPORT pole vault
**stabil** [ʃta'bi:l] *adj* stable (*a.* ECON, POL); solid, strong; sound; **stabilisieren** [ʃtabili'zi:rən] *v/t* (*no -ge-, h*) stabilize; **Stabilität** [ʃtabili'tɛ:t] *f* (-; *no pl*) stability
**stach** [ʃta:x] *pret of* ***stechen***
**Stachel** ['ʃtaxəl] *m* (*-s*; *-n*) BOT, ZO spine, prick; ZO sting; **~beere** *f* BOT gooseberry; **~draht** *m* barbed wire

**stachelig** ['ʃtaxəlɪç] *adj* prickly
'**Stachelschwein** *n* zo porcupine
**Stadel** ['ʃta:dəl] *Austrian m* (*-s*; *-[n]*) barn
**Stadion** ['ʃta:djɔn] *n* (*-s*; *-ien*) stadium
**Stadium** ['ʃta:djʊm] *n* (*-s*; *-ien*) stage, phase
**Stadt** [ʃtat] *f* (-; *Städte* ['ʃtɛ:tə]) town; city; ***die ~ Berlin*** the city of Berlin; ***in die ~ fahren*** go downtown, *esp Br* go (in)to town; **~bahn** *f* urban railway
**Städter** ['ʃtɛ:tɐ] *m* (*-s*; -), '**Städterin** *f* (-; *-nen*) city dweller, F townie, *often contp* city slicker
'**Stadt|gebiet** *n* urban area; **~gespräch** *fig n* talk of the town
**städtisch** ['ʃɛ:tɪʃ] *adj* urban; POL municipal
'**Stadt|plan** *m* city map; **~rand** *m* outskirts; **~rat** *m* town council; city councilman, *Br* town council(l)or; **~rundfahrt** *f* sightseeing tour; **~streicher**(**in**) city vagrant; **~teil** *m*, **~viertel** *n* quarter
**Staffel** ['ʃtafəl] *f* (-; *-n*) SPORT relay race *or* team; MIL, AVIAT squadron
**Staffelei** [ʃtafə'lai] *f* (-; *-en*) PAINT easel
'**staffeln** *v/t* (*ge-*, *h*) grade, scale
**stahl** [ʃta:l] *pret of* ***stehlen***
**Stahl** *m* (*-[e]s*; *Stähle* ['ʃtɛ:lə]) steel
'**Stahlwerk** *n* steelworks
**stak** [ʃta:k] *pret of* ***stecken*** 2
**Stall** [ʃtal] *m* (*-[e]s*; *Ställe* ['ʃtɛlə]) stable
'**Stallknecht** *m* stableman
**Stamm** [ʃtam] *m* (*-[e]s*; *Stämme* ['ʃtɛmə]) BOT stem (*a.* LING), trunk; tribe, stock; *fig* regulars; ***~... in cpds ...gast, ...kunde, ...spieler etc***: regular ...; **~baum** *m* family tree; zo pedigree
**stammeln** ['ʃtaməln] *v/t* (*ge-*, *h*) stammer
**stammen** ['ʃtamən] *v/i* (*ge-*, *h*) ***~ aus*** (***von***) come from; be from; ***~ von*** *work of art etc*: be by
'**Stammformen** *pl* LING principal parts, *mst* tenses
**stämmig** ['ʃtɛmɪç] *adj* sturdy; stout
'**Stammkneipe** F *f Br* local
**stampfen** ['ʃtampfən] (*ge-*, *h*) **1.** *v/t* mash **2.** *v/i* stamp (***mit dem Fuß*** one's foot)
**stand** [ʃtant] *pret of* ***stehen***
**Stand** *m* (*-[e]s*; *Stände* ['ʃtɛndə]) (*no pl*) stand(ing), standing *or* upright position; footing, foothold; ASTR position; TECH *etc*: height, level (*a. fig*); reading; SPORT score; *racing*: standings; *fig* state; social standing, status; stand, stall; class; profession; ***auf den neuesten ~ bringen*** bring up to date; ***e-n schweren ~ haben*** have a hard time (of it); → ***außerstande***; → ***imstande***; → ***instand***; → ***zustande***
**Standard** ['ʃtandart] *m* (*-s*; *-s*) standard
'**Standbild** *n* statue
**Ständchen** ['ʃtɛntçən] *n* (*-s*; -) MUS serenade
**Ständer** ['ʃtɛndɐ] *m* (*-s*; -) stand; rack
**Standesamt** ['ʃtandəsamt] *n* marriage license bureau, *Br* registry office; '**standesamtlich** *adj*: ***~e Trauung*** civil marriage; '**Standesbeamt|e** *m*, **-in** *f* civil magistrate, *Br* registrar
'**Standfoto** *n* still
'**standhaft** *adj* steadfast, firm; ***~ bleiben*** resist temptation
'**standhalten** *v/i* (*irr*, ***halten***, *sep*, *-ge-*, *h*) withstand, resist
**ständig** ['ʃtɛndɪç] *adj* constant; permanent (*address*)
'**Stand|licht** *n* (*-[e]s*; *no pl*) MOT parking light; **~ort** *m* position; location; MIL post, garrison; **~pauke** F *f*: ***j-m e-e ~ halten*** give s.o. a talking-to; **~platz** *m* stand; **~punkt** *m* (point of) view, standpoint; **~spur** *f* MOT (*Br* hard) shoulder; **~uhr** *f* grandfather clock
**Stange** ['ʃtaŋə] *f* (-; *-n*) pole; staff; rod, bar; carton (*of cigarettes*)
**Stängel** ['ʃtɛŋəl] *m* (*-s*; -) BOT stalk, stem
**stank** [ʃtaŋk] *pret of* ***stinken***
**Stanniol** [ʃta'njo:l] *n* (*-s*; *-e*) tin foil
**Stanze** ['ʃtantsə] *f* (-; *-n*), '**stanzen** *v/t* (*ge-*, *h*) TECH punch
**Stapel** ['ʃta:pəl] *m* (*-s*; -) pile, stack; heap; ***vom ~ lassen*** MAR launch (*a. fig*); ***vom ~ laufen*** MAR be launched
'**Stapellauf** *m* MAR launch
'**stapeln** *v/t* (*ge-*, *h*) pile (up), stack
**stapfen** ['ʃtapfən] *v/i* (*ge-*, *sein*) trudge
**Star**[1] [ʃta:ɐ] *m* (*-[e]s*; *-e*) zo starling; MED cataract
**Star**[2] *m* (*-s*; *-s*) THEA *etc*: star
**starb** [ʃtarp] *pret of* ***sterben***
**stark** [ʃtark] **1.** *adj* strong (*a.* GASTR); powerful; *fig* heavy; F super, great **2.** *adv*: ***~ beeindruckt*** greatly impressed; ***~ beschädigt*** badly damaged; **Stärke** ['ʃtɛrkə] *f* (-; *-n*) (*no pl*) strength, pow-

er; intensity; degree; CHEM starch; **'stärken** *v/t* (*ge-*, *h*) strengthen (*a. fig*); starch; ***sich ~*** take some refreshment; **'Starkstrom** *m* ELECTR high-voltage (*or* heavy) current; **Stärkung** *f* (-; *-en*) strengthening; refreshment; **'Stärkungsmittel** *n* MED tonic

**starr** [ʃtar] *adj* stiff; rigid (*a.* TECH); frozen (*face*); ***~er Blick*** (fixed) stare; ***~ vor Kälte*** (***Entsetzen***) frozen (scared) stiff; **'starren** *v/i* (*ge-*, *h*) stare (***auf*** *acc* at); **starrköpfig** ['ʃtarkœpfɪç] *adj* stubborn, obstinate; **'Starrsinn** *m* (-[*e*]*s*; *no pl*) stubbornness, obstinacy

**Start** [ʃtart] *m* (-[*e*]*s*; *-s*) start (*a. fig*); AVIAT take-off; *rocket*: lift-off

**'Startbahn** *f* AVIAT runway

**'startbereit** *adj* ready to start; AVIAT ready for take-off

**starten** ['ʃtartən] *v/i* (*ge-*, *sein*) *and v/t* (*ge-*, *h*) start (*a.* F); AVIAT take off; lift off; launch (*a. fig*)

**Station** [ʃta'tsjo:n] *f* (-; *-en*) station; MED ward; **stationär** [ʃtatsjo'nɛ:ɐ] *adj*: ***~er Patient*** MED in-patient; **stationieren** [ʃtatsjo'ni:rən] *v/t* (*no -ge-*, *h*) MIL station; deploy; **Stationsvorsteher** *m* RAIL stationmaster

**Statist** [ʃta'tɪst] *m* (*-en*; *-en*) THEA extra

**Statistik** [ʃta'tɪstɪk] *f* (-; *-en*) statistics; **Sta'tistiker** [ʃta'tɪstikɐ] *m* (*-s*; -) statistician; **sta'tistisch** *adj* statistical

**Stativ** [ʃta'ti:f] *n* (*-s*; *-e*) PHOT tripod

**statt** [ʃtat] *prp* instead of; ***~ et. zu tun*** instead of doing s.th.; ***~'dessen*** instead

**Stätte** ['ʃtɛtə] *f* (-; *-n*) place; scene

**'stattfinden** *v/i* (*irr*, ***finden***, *sep*, *-ge-*, *h*) take place; happen

**'stattlich** *adj* imposing; handsome

**Statue** ['ʃta:tuə] *f* (-; *-n*) statue

**Statur** [ʃta'tu:ɐ] *f* (-; *-en*) build

**Status** ['ʃta:tʊs] *m* (-; -) state; status; **~sym,bol** *n* status symbol; **~zeile** *f* IT status line

**Stau** [ʃtau] *m* (-[*e*]*s*; *-s*, *-e*) MOT traffic jam *or* congestion

**Staub** [ʃtaup] *m* (-[*e*]*s*; TECH *-e*, *Stäube* ['ʃtɔʏbə]) dust (*a.* ***~ wischen***)

**'Staubecken** *n* reservoir

**stauben** ['ʃtaubən] *v/i* (*ge-*, *h*) give off *or* make dust; **staubig** ['ʃtaubɪç] *adj* dusty; **'staubsaugen** *v/i and v/t* (*ge-*, *h*) vacuum, F *Br* hoover; **'Staubsauger** *m* vacuum cleaner, F *Br* hoover; **'Staubtuch** *n* duster

**'Staudamm** *m* dam

**Staude** ['ʃtaudə] *f* (-; *-n*) BOT herbacious plant

**stauen** ['ʃtauən] *v/t* (*ge-*, *h*) dam up; ***sich ~*** MOT *etc* be stacked up

**staunen** ['ʃtaunən] *v/i* (*ge-*, *h*) be astonished *or* surprised (***über*** *acc* at)

**'Staunen** *n* (*-s*; *no pl*) astonishment, amazement

**Staupe** ['ʃtaupə] *f* (-; *-n*) VET distemper

**'Stausee** *m* reservoir

**stechen** ['ʃtɛçən] *v/i and v/t* (*irr*, *ge-*, *h*) prick; ZO sting, bite; stab; pierce; ***mit et. ~ in*** (*acc*) stick s.th. in(to); ***sich ~*** prick o.s.; **~d** *fig adj* piercing (*look*); stabbing (*pain*)

**'Stechuhr** *f* time clock

**Steckbrief** ['ʃtɛkbri:f] *m* JUR „wanted" poster

**'steckbrieflich** *adv*: ***er wird ~ gesucht*** JUR a warrant is out against him

**'Steckdose** *f* ELECTR (wall) socket

**stecken** ['ʃtɛkən] (*ge-*, *h*) **1.** *v/t* stick; put; *esp* TECH insert (***in*** *acc* into); pin (***an*** *acc* to, on); AGR set, plant **2.** *v/i* ([*irr*]) be; stick, be stuck; ***~ bleiben*** get stuck; **'steckenbleiben** *v/i* (*irr*, ***bleiben***, *sep*, *-ge-*, *sein*) *fig* get stuck

**'Steckenpferd** *n* hobby horse; *fig* hobby

**Stecker** ['ʃtɛkɐ] *m* (*-s*; -) ELECTR plug

**'Steck|kon,takt** *m* ELECTR plug (connection); **~nadel** *f* pin; **~platz** *m* IT slot

**Steg** [ʃte:k] *m* (-[*e*]*s*; *-e*) footbridge

**Stegreif** ['ʃte:kraif] *m*: ***aus dem ~*** extempore, ad-lib; ***aus dem ~ sprechen*** *or* ***spielen*** *etc* extemporize, ad-lib

**stehen** ['ʃte:ən] *v/i* (*irr*, *ge-*, *h*) stand; be; stand up; ***es steht ihr*** it suits (*or* looks well on) her; ***wie steht es*** (*or* ***das Spiel***)***?*** what's the score?; ***hier steht, dass*** it says here that; ***wo steht das?*** where does it say so *or* that?; ***wie steht es mit ...?*** what about ...?; F ***darauf stehe ich*** it turns me on; ***~ bleiben*** stop; *esp* TECH come to a standstill (*a. fig*); ***~ lassen*** leave (untouched); leave behind; ***alles ~ und liegen lassen*** drop everything; ***sich e-n Bart ~ lassen*** grow a beard

**'stehen|bleiben** *v/i* (*irr*, ***bleiben***, *sep*, *-ge-*, *sein*) → ***stehen***; **~lassen** *v/t* (*irr*,

S

***lassen***, *sep*, *no -ge-*, *h*) → ***stehen***
'**Steh|kragen** *m* stand-up collar; **~lampe** *f* floor (*Br* standard) lamp; **~leiter** *f* step ladder
**stehlen** ['ʃteːlən] *v/t and v/i* (*irr*, *ge-*, *h*) steal (*a. fig* ***sich ~***)
'**Stehplatz** *m* standing ticket; *pl* standing room
**steif** [ʃtaif] *adj* stiff (***vor*** *dat* with)
**Steigbügel** ['ʃtaikbyːgəl] *m* stirrup
**steigen** ['ʃtaigən] *v/i* (*irr*, *ge-*, *sein*) go, step; climb (*a.* AVIAT); *fig* rise, go up; ***~ in*** (***auf***) (*acc*) get on (*bus*, *bike etc*); ***~ aus*** (***von***) get off (*bus*, *horse etc*); ***aus dem Bett ~*** get out of bed
**steigern** ['ʃtaigɐn] *v/t* (*ge-*, *h*) raise, increase; heighten; improve; LING compare; ***sich ~*** improve, get better
**Steigerung** ['ʃtaigərʊŋ] *f* (-; *-en*) rise, increase; heightening; improvement; LING comparison
'**Steigung** *f* (-; *-en*) gradient; slope
**steil** [ʃtail] *adj* steep (*a. fig*)
**Stein** [ʃtain] *m* (-[*e*]*s*; *-e*) stone (*a.* BOT, MED), rock; **~bock** *m* ZO rock goat; ASTR Capricorn; ***er ist*** (***ein***) ***~*** he's (a) Capricorn; **~bruch** *m* quarry
**steinern** ['ʃtainɐn] *adj* (of) stone; *fig* stony
'**Steingut** *n* (-[*e*]*s*; *-e*) earthenware
**steinig** ['ʃtainɪç] *adj* stony
**steinigen** ['ʃtainɪgən] *v/t* (*ge-*, *h*) stone
'**Steinkohle** *f* (hard) coal
**Steinmetz** ['ʃtainmɛts] *m* (*-en*; *-en*) stonemason
'**Steinzeit** *f* (-; *no pl*) Stone Age
**Stellage** [ʃtɛ'laːʒə] *Austrian f* (-; *-n*) stand, rack, shelf
**Stelle** ['ʃtɛlə] *f* (-; *-n*) place; spot; point; job; authority; MATH figure; ***freie ~*** vacancy, opening; ***auf der*** (***zur***) ***~*** on the spot; ***an erster ~ stehen*** (***kommen***) be (come) first; ***an j-s ~*** in s.o.'s place; ***ich an deiner ~*** if I were you
'**stellen** *v/t* (*ge-*, *h*) put; set (*trap*, *clock*, *task etc*); turn (*up*, *down etc*); ask (*question*); provide; corner, hunt down (*criminal etc*); ***sich ~*** give o.s. up, turn o.s. in; ***sich gegen*** (***hinter***) ***j-n ~*** *fig* oppose (back) s.o.; ***sich schlafend*** *etc* ***~*** pretend to be asleep *etc*; ***stell dich dorthin!*** (go and) stand over there!
'**Stellen|angebot** *n* vacancy; ***ich habe ein ~*** I was offered a job; **~anzeige** *f* job ad(vertisement), employment ad; **~gesuch** *n* application for a job
'**stellenweise** *adv* partly, in places
'**Stellung** *f* (-; *-en*) position; post, job; ***~ nehmen zu*** comment on, give one's opinion of; **~nahme** ['ʃtɛlʊŋnaːmə] *f* (-; *-n*) comment, opinion (*both*: ***zu*** on)
'**stellungslos** *adj* unemployed, jobless
'**stellvertretend** *adj* acting, deputy, vice-…; '**Stellvertreter(in)** (*-s*; *-/-*; *-nen*) representative; deputy
**Stelze** ['ʃtɛltsə] *f* (-; *-n*) stilt
'**stelzen** *v/i* (*ge-*, *sein*) stalk
**stemmen** ['ʃtɛmən] *v/t* (*ge-*, *h*) lift (*weight*); ***sich ~ gegen*** press o.s. against; *fig* resist *or* oppose *s.th.*
**Stempel** ['ʃtɛmpəl] *m* (*-s*; -) stamp; postmark; hallmark; BOT pistil
'**Stempelkissen** *n* ink pad
'**stempeln** (*ge-*, *h*) **1.** *v/t* stamp; cancel; hallmark **2.** F *v/i*: ***~ gehen*** be on the dole
**Stengel** → ***Stängel***
**Stenografie** [ʃtenogra'fiː] *f* (-; *-n*) shorthand; **stenogra'fieren** *v/t* (*no -ge-*, *h*) take down in shorthand
**Stenogramm** [ʃteno'gram] *n* (-[*e*]*s*; *-e*) shorthand notes; **Stenotypistin** [ʃtenoty'pɪstɪn] *f* (-; *-nen*) shorthand typist
**Steppdecke** ['ʃtɛpdɛkə] *f* quilt; **steppen** ['ʃtɛpən] (*ge-*, *h*) **1.** *v/t* quilt; stitch **2.** *v/i* tap dance; '**Stepptanz** *m* tap dancing
**Sterbebett** ['ʃtɛrbəbɛt] *n* deathbed
'**Sterbeklinik** *f* MED hospice
**sterben** ['ʃtɛrbən] *v/i* (*irr*, *ge-*, *sein*) die (***an*** *dat* of) (*a. fig*); ***im Sterben liegen*** be dying
**sterblich** ['ʃtɛrplɪç] *adj* mortal
'**Sterblichkeit** *f* (-; *no pl*) mortality
**Stereo** ['ʃteːreo] *n* (*-s*; *-s*) stereo
**steril** [ʃte'riːl] *adj* sterile; **Sterilisation** [ʃteriliza'tsjoːn] *f* (-; *-en*) sterilization; **sterilisieren** [ʃterili'ziːrən] *v/t* (*no -ge-*, *h*) sterilize
**Stern** [ʃtɛrn] *m* (-[*e*]*s*; *-e*) star (*a. fig*)
'**Sternbild** *n* ASTR constellation; sign of the zodiac
'**Sternchen** *n* (*-s*; -) PRINT asterisk
'**Sternenbanner** *n* Star-Spangled Banner, Stars and Stripes
'**Sternenhimmel** *m* starry sky
'**sternklar** *adj* starry

'**Stern|kunde** *f* (-; *no pl*) astronomy; **~schnuppe** *f* (-; *-n*) shooting *or* falling star; **~warte** *f* (-; *-n*) observatory
**stetig** ['ʃteːtɪç] *adj* continual, constant; steady; **stets** [ʃteːts] *adv* always
**Steuer**[1] ['ʃtɔʏɐ] *n* (*-s*; -) MOT (steering) wheel; MAR helm, rudder
'**Steuer**[2] *f* (-; *-n*) tax (***auf*** *acc* on)
'**Steuer|beamte** *m* revenue officer; **~berater** *m* tax adviser
'**Steuerbord** *n* MAR starboard
'**Steuer|erklärung** *f* tax return; **~ermäßigung** *f* tax allowance
'**steuerfrei** *adj* tax-free
'**Steuerhinterziehung** *f* tax evasion
'**Steuer|knüppel** *m* AVIAT control column *or* stick; **~mann** *m* MAR helmsman; *rowing*: cox, coxswain
'**steuern** *v/t and v/i* (*ge-*, *h*) steer, AVIAT, MAR *a.* navigate, pilot, MOT *a.* drive; TECH control (*a. fig*); *fig* direct
'**steuerpflichtig** *adj* taxable
'**Steuerrad** *n* MOT steering wheel
'**Steuerruder** *n* MAR helm, rudder
'**Steuersenkung** *f* tax reduction
**Steuerung** ['ʃtɔʏərʊŋ] *f* (-; *-en*) steering (system); ELECTR, TECH control (*a. fig*)
'**Steuerzahler** *m*, '**Steuerzahlerin** *f* taxpayer
**Stich** [ʃtɪç] *m* (-[*e*]*s*; *-e*) prick; ZO sting, bite; stab; stitch; *cards*: trick; engraving; ***im ~ lassen*** desert *or* abandon *s.o.*, *s.th.*, leave *s.o.* in the lurch, let *s.o.* down
**Stichelei** [ʃtɪçə'lai] F *f* (-; *-en*) dig, gibe
**sticheln** ['ʃɪçəln] F *v/i* (*ge-*, *h*) make digs, gibe (***gegen*** at)
'**Stichflamme** *f* jet of flame
'**stichhaltig** *adj* valid, sound; watertight; ***nicht ~ sein*** F not hold water
'**Stich|probe** *f* spot check; **~tag** *m* cutoff date; deadline; **~wahl** *f* POL run-off; **~wort** *n* (-[*e*]*s*; *-e*) THEA cue; (-[*e*]*s*; *-wörter*) headword; ***~e*** *pl* notes; ***das Wichtigste in ~en*** an outline of the main points; **~wortverzeichnis** *n* index; **~wunde** *f* MED stab
**sticken** ['ʃtɪkən] *v/t and v/i* (*ge-*, *h*) embroider; **Stickerei** [ʃtɪkə'rai] *f* (-; *-en*) embroidery
**stickig** ['ʃtɪkɪç] *adj* stuffy
'**Stickstoff** *m* (-[*e*]*s*; *no pl*) CHEM nitrogen
**Stief...** [ʃtiːf-] *in cpds ...mutter etc*: step...
**Stiefel** ['ʃtiːfəl] *m* (*-s*; -) boot
**Stiefmütterchen** ['ʃtiːfmʏtɐçən] *n* (*-s*; -) BOT pansy
**stieg** [ʃtiːk] *pret of* ***steigen***
**Stiege** ['ʃtiːgə] *Austrian f* (-; *-n*) → ***Treppe***
**Stiel** [ʃtiːl] *m* (-[*e*]*s*; *-e*) handle; stick; stem; BOT stalk
**Stier** [ʃtiːɐ] *m* (-[*e*]*s*; *-e*) ZO bull; ASTR Taurus; ***er ist*** (***ein***) ~ he's (a) Taurus
'**Stierkampf** *m* bullfight
**stieß** [ʃtiːs] *pret of* ***stoßen***
**Stift** [ʃtɪft] *m* (-[*e*]*s*; *-e*) pen; pencil; crayon; TECH pin; peg
**stiften** ['ʃtɪftən] *v/t* (*ge-*, *h*) donate; *fig* cause; '**Stiftung** *f* (-; *-en*) donation
**Stil** [ʃtiːl] *m* (-[*e*]*s*; *-e*) style (*a. fig*); ***in großem ~*** in (grand) style; *fig* on a large scale; **stilistisch** [ʃti'lɪstɪʃ] *adj* stylistic
**still** [ʃtɪl] *adj* quiet, silent; still; ***sei***(***d***) ***~!*** be quiet!; ***halt ~!*** keep still!; ***sich ~ verhalten*** keep quiet (*or* still)
**Stille** ['ʃtɪlə] *f* (-; *no pl*) silence, quiet (-ness); ***in aller ~*** quietly; secretly
**Stilleben** *n* → ***Stillleben***
**stillen** ['ʃtɪlən] *v/t* (*ge-*, *h*) nurse, breastfeed; *fig* relieve (*pain*); satisfy (*curiosity etc*); quench (*one's thirst*)
'**stillhalten** *v/i* (*irr*, ***halten***, *sep*, *-ge-*, *h*) keep still
'**Stillleben** *n* PAINT still life
'**stilllegen** *v/t* (*sep*, *-ge-*, *h*) close down
'**stillos** *adj* lacking style, tasteless
'**stillschweigend** *adj* tacit
'**Stillstand** *m* (-[*e*]*s*; *no pl*) standstill, stop, *fig a.* stagnation (*a.* ECON); deadlock; '**stillstehen** *v/i* (*irr*, ***stehen***, *sep*, *-ge-*, *h*) (have) stop(ped), (have) come to a standstill
'**Stilmöbel** *pl* period furniture
'**stilvoll** *adj* stylish; ***~ sein*** have style
'**Stimmband** *n* ANAT vocal cord
'**stimmberechtigt** *adj* entitled to vote
**Stimme** ['ʃtɪmə] *f* (-; *-n*) voice; POL vote; ***sich der ~ enthalten*** abstain
'**stimmen** (*ge-*, *h*) **1.** *v/i* be right, be true, be correct; POL vote (***für*** for; ***gegen*** against); ***es stimmt et. nicht*** (***damit*** *or* ***mit ihm***) there's s.th. wrong (with it *or* him); **2.** *v/t* MUS tune; ***j-n traurig*** *etc* ***~*** make s.o. sad *etc*
'**Stimmenthaltung** *f* abstention

S

ˈ**Stimmrecht** *n* right to vote
ˈ**Stimmung** *f* (-; *-en*) mood; atmosphere; feeling
ˈ**stimmungsvoll** *adj* atmospheric
ˈ**Stimmzettel** *m* ballot (paper)
**stinken** [ˈʃtɪŋkən] *v/i* (*irr, ge-, h*) stink (*a. fig*) (***nach*** of)
**Stipendium** [ʃtiˈpɛndjʊm] *n* (*-s; -ien*) UNIV scholarship, grant
**stippen** [ˈʃtɪpən] *v/t* (*ge-, h*) dip
ˈ**Stippviˌsite** F *f* flying visit
**Stirn** [ʃtɪrn] *f* (-; *-en*) ANAT forehead; ***die ~ runzeln*** frown
**stöbern** [ˈʃtøːbɐn] F *v/i* (*ge-, h*) rummage (about)
**stochern** [ˈʃtɔxɐn] *v/i* (*ge-, h*) ***im Feuer ~*** poke the fire; ***im Essen ~*** pick at one's food; ***in den Zähnen ~*** pick one's teeth
**Stock** [ʃtɔk] *m* (-[*e*]*s*; *Stöcke* [ˈʃtœkə]) stick; cane; ARCH stor(e)y, floor; ***im ersten ~*** on the second (*Br* first) floor
ˈ**stockˈdunkel** F *adj* pitch-dark
**stocken** [ˈʃtɔkən] *v/i* (*ge-, h*) stop (short); falter; *traffic*: be jammed; **~d** **1.** *adj* halting **2.** *adv*: ***~ lesen*** stumble through a text; ***~ sprechen*** speak haltingly
ˈ**Stockfleck** *m* mo(u)ld stain
ˈ**Stockung** *f* (-; *-en*) holdup, delay
ˈ**Stockwerk** *n* stor(e)y, floor
**Stoff** [ʃtɔf] *m* (-[*e*]*s*; *-e*) material, stuff (*a.* F); fabric, textile; cloth; CHEM, PHYS *etc* substance; *fig* subject (matter)
ˈ**stofflich** *adj* material
ˈ**Stofftier** *n* soft toy animal
ˈ**Stoffwechsel** *m* BIOL metabolism
**stöhnen** [ˈʃtøːnən] *v/i* (*ge-, h*) groan, moan (*a. fig*)
**Stollen** [ˈʃtɔlən] *m* (*-s*; -) tunnel, gallery
**stolpern** [ˈʃtɔlpɐn] *v/i* (*ge-, sein*) stumble (***über*** *acc* over), trip (over) (*both a. fig*)
**stolz** [ʃtɔlts] *adj* proud (***auf*** *acc* of)
**Stolz** *m* (*-es; no pl*) pride (***auf*** *acc* in)
**stolzieren** [ʃtɔlˈtsiːrən] *v/i* (*no -ge-, sein*) strut, stalk
**stopfen** [ˈʃtɔpfən] *v/t* (*ge-, h*) darn, mend; stuff, fill (*a. pipe*)
**Stoppel** [ˈʃtɔpəl] *f* (-; *-n*) stubble
ˈ**Stoppelbart** F *m* stubbly beard
ˈ**stoppelig** *adj* stubbly, bristly
ˈ**Stoppelzieher** *Austrian m* corkscrew
**stoppen** [ˈʃtɔpən] *v/i and v/t* (*ge-, h*) stop (*a. fig*); *esp* SPORT time
ˈ**Stopp|licht** *n* (-[*e*]*s*; *-er*) MOT stop light; **~schild** *n* stop sign; **~uhr** *f* stopwatch
**Stöpsel** [ˈʃtœpsəl] *m* (*-s*; -) stopper; plug
**Storch** [ʃtɔrç] *m* (-[*e*]*s*; *Störche* [ˈʃtœrçəl]) ZO stork
**stören** [ˈʃtøːrən] *v/t and v/i* (*ge-, h*) disturb; trouble; bother, annoy; be in the way; ***lassen Sie sich nicht ~!*** don't let me disturb you!; ***darf ich Sie kurz ~?*** may I trouble you for a minute?; ***es*** (***er***) ***stört mich nicht*** it (he) doesn't bother me, I don't mind (him); ***stört es Sie***(, ***wenn ich rauche***)***?*** do you mind (my smoking *or* if I smoke)?
ˈ**Störenfried** [ˈʃtøːrənfriːt] *m* (-[*e*]*s*; *-e*) troublemaker; intruder
**Störfall** [ˈʃtøːɐfal] *m* TECH accident
**störrisch** [ˈʃtœrɪʃ] *adj* stubborn, obstinate
ˈ**Störung** *f* (-; *-en*) disturbance; trouble (*a.* TECH); TECH breakdown; TV, *radio*: interference
**Stoß** [ʃtoːs] *m* (*-es*; *Stöße* [ˈʃtøːsə]) push, shove; thrust; kick; butt; blow, knock; shock; MOT jolt; bump, *esp* TECH, PHYS impact; pile, stack; ˈ**Stoßdämpfer** *m* MOT shock absorber; **stoßen** [ˈʃtoːsən] *v/t* (*irr, ge-, h*) *and v/i* (*sein*) push, shove; thrust; kick; butt; knock, strike; pound; ***~ gegen*** *or* ***an*** (*acc*) bump *or* run into *or* against; ***sich den Kopf ~*** (***an*** *dat*) knock one's head (against); ***~ auf*** (*acc*) strike (*oil etc*); *fig* come across; meet with; ˈ**stoßgesichert** *adj* shockproof, shock-resistant; ˈ**Stoßstange** *f* MOT bumper; ˈ**Stoßzahn** *m* ZO tusk; ˈ**Stoßzeit** *f* rush hour, peak hours
**stottern** [ˈʃtɔtɐn] *v/i and v/t* (*ge-, h*) stutter
**Str.** *abbr of* ***Straße*** St, Street; Rd, Road
ˈ**Strafanstalt** *f* prison, penitentiary; ˈ**strafbar** *adj* punishable, penal; ***sich ~ machen*** commit an offense (*Br* offence); **Strafe** [ˈʃtraːfə] *f* (-; *-n*) punishment; JUR, ECON, SPORT penalty (*a. fig*); fine; ***30 Euro ~ zahlen müssen*** be fined 30 euros; ***zur ~*** as a punishment; ˈstrafen *v/t* (*ge-, h*) punish
**straff** [ʃtraf] *adj* tight; *fig* strict
ˈ**straffrei** *adj*: ***~ ausgehen*** go unpunished

S

'**Straf|gefangene** *m, f* prisoner, convict; **~gesetz** *n* criminal law
**sträflich** ['ʃtrɛːflɪç] **1.** *adj* inexcusable **2.** *adv*: **~ *vernachlässigen*** neglect badly
'**Straf|mi,nute** *f* SPORT penalty minute; **~pro,zess** *m* JUR criminal action, trial; **~raum** *m* SPORT penalty area (F box); **~stoß** *m* SPORT penalty kick; **~tat** *f* JUR criminal offense (*Br* offence); crime; **~zettel** *m* ticket
**Strahl** [ʃtraːl] *m* (-[*e*]*s*, *-en*) ray (*a. fig*); beam; flash; jet; **strahlen** ['ʃtraːlən] *v/i* (*ge-*, *h*) radiate; shine (brightly); *fig* beam (***vor*** with); '**Strahlen...** *in cpds* PHYS *...schutz etc*: radiation ...
'**Strahlung** *f* (-; *-en*) PHYS radiation
**Strähne** ['ʃtrɛːnə] *f* (-; *-n*) strand; streak
**stramm** [ʃtram] *adj* tight; **~stehen** MIL stand to attention
**strampeln** ['ʃtrampəln] *v/i* (*ge-*, *h*) kick
**Strand** [ʃtrant] *m* (-[*e*]*s*; *Strände* ['ʃtrɛndə]) beach; ***am ~*** on the beach
**stranden** ['ʃtrandən] *v/i* (*ge-*, *sein*) MAR strand; *fig* fail
'**Strand|gut** *n* flotsam and jetsam (*a. fig*); **~korb** *m* roofed wicker beach chair
**Strang** [ʃtraŋ] *m* (-[*e*]*s*; *Stränge* ['ʃtrɛŋə]) rope; *esp* ANAT cord
**Strapaze** [ʃtra'paːtsə] *f* (-; *-n*) strain, exertion, hardship; **strapazieren** [ʃtrapa'tsiːrən] *v/t* (*no -ge-*, *h*) wear *s.o. or s.th.* out, be hard on; **strapazierfähig** *adj* longwearing, *Br* hardwearing
**strapaziös** [ʃtrapa'tsjøːs] *adj* strenuous
**Straße** ['ʃtraːsə] *f* (-; *-n*) road; street; GEOGR strait; ***auf der ~*** on the road; on (*Br a.* in) the street
'**Straßen|arbeiten** *pl* roadworks; **~bahn** *f* streetcar, *Br* tram; **~ca,fé** *n* sidewalk (*Br* pavement) café; **~karte** *f* road map; **~kehrer** ['ʃtraːsənkeːrɐ] *m* (*-s*; -) street sweeper; **~kreuzung** *f* crossroads; intersection; **~lage** *f* MOT roadholding; **~rand** *m* roadside; ***am ~*** at *or* by the roadside; **~sperre** *f* road block
**strategisch** [ʃtra'teːgɪʃ] *adj* strategic
**sträuben** ['ʃtrɔʏbən] *v/t and v/refl* (*ge-*, *h*) ruffle (up); bristle (up); ***sich ~ gegen*** struggle against
**Strauch** [ʃtraux] *m* (-[*e*]*s*; *Sträucher* ['ʃtrɔʏçɐ]) BOT shrub, bush
**straucheln** ['ʃtrauxəln] *v/i* (*ge-*, *sein*) stumble
**Strauß**[1] [ʃtraus] *m* (*-es*; *-e*) ZO ostrich
**Strauß**[2] *m* (*-es*; *Sträuße* ['ʃtrɔʏsə]) bunch, bouquet
**Strebe** ['ʃtreːbə] *f* (-; *-n*) prop, stay (*a.* AVIAT, MAR); '**streben** *v/i* (*ge-*, *h*) strive (***nach*** for, after); **Streber** ['ʃtreːbɐ] *m* (*-s*; -) pusher; PED *etc* grind, *Br* swot; **strebsam** ['ʃtreːpzaːm] *adj* ambitious
**Strecke** ['ʃtrɛkə] *f* (-; *-n*) distance (*a.* SPORT, MATH), way; route; RAIL line; SPORT course; stretch; ***zur ~ bringen*** kill; *esp fig* hunt down; '**strecken** *v/t* (*ge-*, *h*) stretch (out), extend
**Streich** [ʃtraiç] *m* (-[*e*]*s*; *-e*) trick, prank, practical joke; ***j-m e-n ~ spielen*** play a trick *or* joke on s.o.
**streicheln** ['ʃtraiçəln] *v/t* (*ge-*, *h*) stroke, caress
**streichen** ['ʃtraiçən] *v/t and v/i* (*irr*, *ge-*, *h*) paint; spread; cross out; cancel; MAR strike; MUS bow; ***mit der Hand ~ über*** (*acc*) run one's hand over; ***~ durch*** roam (*acc*); **Streicher**(**in**) ['ʃtraiçɐ, 'ʃtraiçərɪn] *m*(*f*) (*-s*; *-/-*; *-nen*) MUS string player, *pl the* strings
'**Streich|holz** *n* match; **~instru,ment** *n* MUS string instrument; **~or,chester** *n* MUS string orchestra
'**Streichung** *f* (-; *-en*) cancellation; cut
**Streife** ['ʃtraifə] *f* (-; *-n*) patrol; ***auf ~ gehen*** go on patrol; ***auf ~ sein in*** (*dat*) patrol
'**streifen** *v/t and v/i* (*ge-*, *h*) touch, brush (against); MOT scrape against; graze; slip (***von*** off); *fig* touch on; ***~ durch*** roam (*acc*), wander through
'**Streifen** *m* (*-s*; -) stripe; strip
'**Streifenwagen** *m* squad (*Br* patrol) car
'**Streifschuss** *m* MED graze
'**Streifzug** *m* tour (***durch*** of)
**Streik** [ʃtraik] *m* (-[*e*]*s*; *-s*) strike, walkout
'**Streikbrecher** *m* strikebreaker, *Br* blackleg, *contp* scab
**streiken** ['ʃtraikən] *v/i* (*ge-*, *h*) (go *or* be on) strike; F *fig* refuse (to work etc)
'**Streikende** *m, f* (*-n*; *-n*) striker
'**Streikposten** *m* picket
**Streit** [ʃtrait] *m* (-[*e*]*s*; *-e*) quarrel; argument; fight; POL *etc* dispute; ***~ anfangen*** pick a fight *or* quarrel; ***~ suchen*** be looking for trouble; **streiten** ['ʃtraitən] *v/i and v/refl* (*irr*, *ge-*, *h*) quarrel,

S

argue, fight (*all*: ***wegen, über*** *acc* about, over); ***sich ~ um*** fight for
ˈ**Streitfrage** *f* (point at) issue
**streitig** [ˈʃtraitɪç] *adj*: ***j-m et. ~ machen*** dispute s.o.'s right to s.th.
ˈ**Streitkräfte** *pl* MIL (armed) forces
ˈ**streitsüchtig** *adj* quarrelsome
**streng** [ʃtrɛŋ] *adj* strict; severe; harsh; rigid; ***~ genommen*** strictly speaking
**Strenge** [ˈʃtrɛŋə] *f* (-; *no pl*) strictness; severity; harshness; rigidity
ˈ**strenggläubig** *adj* REL orthodox
**Stress** [ʃtrɛs] *m* (-*es*; *no pl*) stress; ***im ~*** under stress
**Streu** [ʃtrɔʏ] *f* (-; -*en*) AGR litter
ˈ**streuen** *v/t and v/i* (*ge-*, *h*) scatter (*a.* PHYS); spread; sprinkle; grit
**streunen** [ˈʃtrɔynən] *v/i* (*ge-*, *sein*), **~d** *adj* stray
**strich** [ʃtrɪç] *pret of* ***streichen***
**Strich** *m* (-[*e*]*s*; -*e*) line; stroke; F red-light district; F ***auf den ~ gehen*** walk the streets; **~junge** F *m* male prostitute; **~kode** *m* bar code
ˈ**strichweise** *adv* in parts; ***~ Regen*** scattered showers
**Strick** [ʃtrɪk] *m* (-[*e*]*s*; -*e*) cord; rope
**stricken** [ˈʃtrɪkən] *v/t and v/i* (*ge-*, *h*) knit
ˈ**Strick|jacke** *f* cardigan; **~leiter** *f* rope ladder; **~nadel** *f* knitting needle; **~waren** *pl* knitwear; **~zeug** *n* knitting (things)
**Striemen** [ˈʃtriːmən] *m* (-*s*; -) welt, weal
**stritt** [ʃtrɪt] *pret of* ***streiten***
**strittig** [ˈʃtrɪtɪç] *adj* controversial; ***~er Punkt*** point at issue
**Stroh** [ʃtroː] *n* (-[*e*]*s*; *no pl*) straw; thatch; **~dach** *n* thatch(ed) roof; **~halm** *m* straw; **~hut** *m* straw hat; **~witwe** F *f* grass widow; **~witwer** F *m* grass widower
**Strom** [ʃtroːm] *m* (-[*e*]*s*; *Ströme* [ˈʃtrøːmə]) (large) river; current (*a.* ELECTR); ***ein ~ von*** a stream of (*a. fig*); ***es gießt in Strömen*** it's pouring (with rain)
**stromˈab(wärts)** *adv* downstream
**stromˈauf(wärts)** *adv* upstream
ˈ**Stromausfall** *m* ELECTR power failure, blackout
**strömen** [ˈʃtrøːmən] *v/i* (*ge-*, *sein*) stream (*a. fig*), flow, run; pour (*a. fig*)
ˈ**Stromkreis** *m* ELECTR circuit
ˈ**stromlinienförmig** *adj* streamlined
ˈ**Stromschnelle** *f* (-; -*n*) GEOGR rapid
ˈ**Stromstärke** *f* ELECTR amperage
ˈ**Strömung** *f* (-; -*en*) current, *fig a.* trend
**Strophe** [ˈʃtroːfə] *f* (-; -*n*) stanza, verse
**strotzen** [ˈʃtrɔtsən] *v/i* (*ge-*, *h*) ***~ von*** be full of, abound with; ***~ vor*** (*dat*) be bursting with
**Strudel** [ˈʃtruːdəl] *m* (-*s*; -) whirlpool (*a. fig*), eddy
**Struktur** [ʃtrʊkˈtuːɐ] *f* (-; -*en*) structure, pattern
**Strumpf** [ʃtrʊmpf] *m* (-[*e*]*s*; *Strümpfe* [ˈʃtrʏmpfə]) stocking
ˈ**Strumpfhose** *f* pantyhose, *Br* tights
**struppig** [ˈʃtrʊpɪç] *adj* shaggy
**Stück** [ʃtʏk] *n* (-[*e*]*s*; -*e*) piece; part; lump; AGR head (*a. pl*); THEA play; ***2 Euro das ~*** 2 euros each; ***im*** *or* ***am ~*** in one piece; ***in ~e schlagen*** (***reißen***) smash (tear) to pieces; ˈ**stückweise** *adv* bit by bit (*a. fig*); ECON by the piece
**Student** [ʃtuˈdɛnt] *m* (-*en*; -*en*), **Stuˈdentin** *f* (-; -*nen*) student; **Studie** [ˈʃtuːdjə] *f* (-; -*n*) study (***über*** *acc* of); ˈ**Studienplatz** *m* university *or* college place; **studieren** [ʃtuˈdiːrən] *v/t and v/i* (*no -ge-*, *h*) study, be a student (of) (***an*** *dat* at); **Studium** [ˈʃtuːdjʊm] *n* (-*s*; -*ien*) studies
**Stufe** [ˈʃtuːfə] *f* (-; -*n*) step; level; stage
ˈ**Stufenbarren** *m* SPORT uneven parallel bars
**Stuhl** [ʃtuːl] *m* (-[*e*]*s*; *Stühle* [ˈʃtyːlə]) chair; MED stool; **~gang** *m* (-[*e*]*s*; *no pl*) MED (bowel) movement; **~lehne** *f* back of a chair
**stülpen** [ˈʃtʏlpən] *v/t* (*ge-*, *h*) put (***auf*** *acc*, ***über*** *acc* over, on)
**stumm** [ʃtʊm] *adj* dumb, mute; *fig* silent
**Stummel** [ˈʃtʊməl] *m* (-*s*; -) stub, stump, butt
ˈ**Stummfilm** *m* silent film
**Stümper** [ˈʃtʏmpɐ] F *m* (-*s*; -) bungler
**stumpf** [ʃtʊmpf] *adj* blunt, dull (*a. fig*)
**Stumpf** *m* (-[*e*]*s*; *Stümpfe* [ˈʃtʏmpfə]) stump, stub
ˈ**stumpfsinnig** *adj* dull; monotonous
**Stunde** [ˈʃtʊndə] *f* (-; -*n*) hour; PED class, lesson; period
ˈ**Stundenkiloˌmeter** *m* kilometer (*Br* kilometre) per hour
ˈ**stundenlang** **1.** *adj*: ***nach ~em Warten*** after hours of waiting **2.** *adv* for hours

(and hours)
'**Stunden|lohn** *m* hourly wage; **~plan** *m* schedule, *Br* timetable
'**stundenweise** *adv* by the hour
'**Stundenzeiger** *m* hour hand
**stündlich** ['ʃtʏntlɪç] **1.** *adj* hourly **2.** *adv* hourly, every hour
**Stupsnase** ['ʃtʊpsnaːzə] F *f* snub nose
**stur** [ʃtuːɐ] F *adj* pigheaded
**Sturm** [ʃtʊrm] *m* (-[*e*]*s*; *Stürme* ['ʃtʏrmə]) storm (*a. fig*); **stürmen** ['ʃtʏrmən] *v/t* (*ge-*, *h*) *and v/i* (*ge-*, *sein*) storm; SPORT attack; rush; **Stürmer(in)** ['ʃtʏrmɐ, -'ʃtʏrmərɪn] *m(f)* (*-s*; *-/-*; *-nen*) SPORT forward; *esp soccer*: striker; **stürmisch** ['ʃtʏrmɪʃ] *adj* stormy; *fig* wild, vehement
**Sturz** [ʃtʊrts] *m* (*-es*; *Stürze* ['ʃtʏrtsə]) fall (*a. fig*); POL etc: overthrow
**stürzen** ['ʃtʏrtsən] **1.** *v/i* (*ge-*, *sein*) fall; crash; rush, dash; ***schwer ~*** have a bad fall **2.** *v/t* (*ge-*, *h*) throw; POL etc: overthrow; ***j-n ins Unglück ~*** ruin s.o.; ***sich stürzen aus*** throw o.s. out of; ***sich ~ auf*** (*acc*) throw o.s. at
'**Sturzflug** *m* AVIAT nosedive
'**Sturzhelm** *m* crash helmet
**Stute** ['ʃtuːtə] *f* (-; *-n*) zo mare
**Stütze** ['ʃtʏtsə] *f* (-; *-n*) support, prop; *fig a.* aid
**stutzen** ['ʃtʊtsən] (*ge-*, *h*) **1.** *v/t* trim, clip **2.** *v/i* stop short; (begin to) wonder
**stützen** ['ʃtʏtsən] *v/t* (*ge-*, *h*) support (*a. fig*); ***sich ~ auf*** (*acc*) lean on; *fig* be based on
'**Stütz|pfeiler** *m* ARCH supporting column; **~punkt** *m* MIL base (*a. fig*)
**Styropor**® [ʃtyro'poːɐ] *n* (*-s*; *no pl*) Styrofoam®, *Br* polystyrene®
**s. u.** *abbr of* ***siehe unten*** see below
**Subjekt** [zʊp'jɛkt] *n* (-[*e*]*s*; *-e*) LING subject; *contp* character
**subjektiv** [zʊpjɛk'tiːf] *adj* subjective
**Substantiv** ['zʊpstantiːf] *n* (*-s*; *-e*) LING noun
**Substanz** [zʊp'stants] *f* (-; *-en*) substance (*a. fig*)
**subtrahieren** [zʊptra'hiːrən] *v/t* (*no -ge-*, *h*) MATH subtract; **Subtraktion** [zʊptrak'tsjoːn] *f* (-; *-en*) MATH subtraction
**subventionieren** [zʊpvɛntsjo'niːrən] *v/t* (*no -ge-*, *h*) subsidize
**Suche** ['zuːxə] *f* (-; *no pl*) search (***nach*** for); ***auf der ~ nach*** in search of;
'**suchen** *v/t and v/i* (*ge-*, *h*) look for; search for; ***gesucht: ...*** wanted: ...; ***was hat er hier zu ~?*** what's he doing here?; ***er hat hier nichts zu ~*** he has no business to be here; **Sucher** ['zuːxɐ] *m* (*-s*; -) PHOT viewfinder
**Sucht** [zʊxt] *f* (-; *Süchte* ['zʏçtə]) addiction (***nach*** to); mania (for); **süchtig** ['zʏçtɪç] *adj*: ***~ sein*** be addicted to *drugs etc*, be a *drug etc* addict; **Süchtige** ['zʏçtɪgə] *m*, *f* (*-n*; *-n*) addict
**Süden** ['zyːdən] *m* (*-s*; *no pl*) south; ***nach ~*** south(wards)
**Südfrüchte** ['zyːtfrʏçtə] *pl* tropical *or* southern fruits
'**südlich** **1.** *adj* south(ern); southerly **2.** *adv*: ***~ von*** (to the) south of
**Süd'osten** *m* southeast; **süd'östlich** *adj* southeast(ern); southeasterly
'**Südpol** *m* South Pole
'**südwärts** ['zyːdvɛrts] *adv* southward(s)
**Süd'westen** *m* southwest; **süd'westlich** *adj* southwest(ern); southwesterly
'**Südwind** *m* south wind
**Sülze** ['zʏltsə] *f* (-; *-n*) GASTR jellied meat
**Summe** ['zʊmə] *f* (-; *-n*) sum (*a. fig*); amount; (sum) total
**summen** ['zʊmən] *v/i and v/t* (*ge-*, *h*) buzz, hum
**summieren** [zʊ'miːrən] *v/refl* (*no -ge-*, *h*) add up (***auf*** *acc* to)
**Sumpf** [zʊmpf] *m* (*-es*; *Sümpfe* ['zʏmpfə]) swamp, bog
'**sumpfig** *adj* swampy, marshy
**Sünde** ['zʏndə] *f* (-; *-n*) sin (*a. fig*)
'**Sündenbock** F *m* scapegoat
**Sünder** ['zʏndɐ] *m* (*-s*; -), '**Sünderin** *f* (-; *-nen*) sinner
**sündig** ['zʏndɪç] *adj* sinful; **sündigen** ['zʏndɪgən] *v/i* (*ge-*, *h*) (commit a) sin
**Super...** ['zuːpɐ-] *in cpds ...macht etc*: *mst* super...
'**Super** *n* (*-s*; *no pl*), **~ben,zin** *n* super *or* premium (gasoline), *Br* four-star (petrol)
**Superlativ** ['zuːpɐlatiːf] *m* (*-s*; *-e*) LING superlative (*a. fig*)
'**Supermarkt** *m* supermarket
**Suppe** ['zʊpə] *f* (-; *-n*) soup
'**Suppen...** *in cpds ...löffel, ...teller, ...küche etc*: soup ...

S

**Surfbrett** ['zøːɐfbrɛt] *n* sail board; surfboard; '**surfen** *v/i* (*ge-*, *h*) surf
**surren** ['zʊrən] *v/i* (*ge-*, *h*) whirr; buzz
**süß** [zyːs] *adj* sweet, sugary (*both a. fig*)
**Süße** ['zyːsə] *f* (-; *no pl*) sweetness
'**süßen** *v/t* (*ge-*, *h*) sweeten
**Süßigkeiten** ['zyːsɪçkaitən] *pl* sweets, candy
'**süßlich** *adj* sweetish; *contp* mawkish, sugary
'**süß'sauer** *adj* GASTR sweet-and-sour
'**Süßstoff** *m* sweetener
'**Süßwasser** *n* fresh water
**Symbol** [zʏm'boːl] *n* (*-s*; *-e*) symbol; **Symbolik** [zʏm'boːlɪk] *f* (-; *no pl*) symbolism; **sym'bolisch** *adj* symbolic(al)
**Symmetrie** [zʏme'triː] *f* (-; *-n*) symmetry; **symmetrisch** [zʏ'meːtrɪʃ] *adj* symmetric(al)
**Sympathie** [zʏmpa'tiː] *f* (-; *-n*) liking (***für*** for); sympathy; **Sympathisant(in)** [zʏmpati'zant(ɪn)] (*-en*; *-en*/-; *-nen*) sympathizer; **sympathisch** [zʏm'paːtɪʃ] *adj* nice, likable; ***er ist mir ~*** I like him
**Symphonie** [zʏmfo'niː] *f* (-; *-n*) *etc* → ***Sinfonie***
**Symptom** [zʏmp'toːm] *n* (*-s*; *-e*) symptom
**Synagoge** [zyna'goːgə] *f* (-; *-n*) synagogue
**synchron** [zʏn'kroːn] *adj* TECH synchronous; **synchronisieren** [zʏnkroni'ziːrən] *v/t* (*no -ge-*, *h*) synchronize; *film etc*: dub
**synonym** [zyno'nyːm] *adj* synonymous
**Syno'nym** *n* (*-s*; *-e*) synonym
**Synthese** [zʏn'teːzə] *f* (-; *-n*) synthesis
**synthetisch** [zʏn'teːtɪʃ] *adj* synthetic
**System** [zʏs'teːm] *n* (*-s*; *-e*) system
**systematisch** [zʏste'maːtɪʃ] *adj* systematic, methodical
**Sys'temfehler** *m* IT system error
**Szene** ['stseːnə] *f* (-; *-n*) scene (*a. fig*)
**Szenerie** [stsenə'riː] *f* (-; *-n*) scenery; setting

# T

**Tabak** ['taːbak] *m* (*-s*; *-e*) tobacco; **~geschäft** *n* tobacconist's; **~waren** *pl* tobacco products
**Tabelle** [ta'bɛlə] *f* (-; *-n*) table (*a.* MATH, SPORT)
**Ta'bellen|kalkulati,on** *f* IT spreadsheet; **~platz** *m* SPORT position
**Tablett** [ta'blɛt] *n* (-[*e*]*s*; *-s*) tray
**Tablette** [ta'blɛtə] *f* (-; *-n*) tablet
**tabu** [ta'buː] *adj*, **Ta'bu** *n* (*-s*; *-s*) taboo
**Tabulator** [tabu'laːtoːɐ] *m* (*-s*; *-en* [tabula'toːrən]) tabulator
**Tachometer** [taxo'meːtɐ] *m*, *n* (*-s*; -) MOT speedometer
**Tadel** ['taːdəl] *m* (*-s*; -) blame; censure, reproof, rebuke; '**tadellos** *adj* faultless; blameless; excellent; perfect
'**tadeln** *v/t* (*ge-*, *h*) criticize, blame; censure, reprove, rebuke (*all*: ***wegen*** for)
**Tafel** ['taːfəl] *f* PED *etc*: blackboard; (bulletin, *esp Br* notice) board; sign; tablet, plaque; GASTR bar (*of chocolate*)
**täfeln** ['tɛːfəln] *v/t* (*ge-*, *h*) panel
'**Täfelung** *f* (-; *-en*) panel(l)ing
**Taft** [taft] *m* (-[*e*]*s*; *-e*) taffeta
**Tag** [taːk] *m* (-[*e*]*s*; *-e* ['taːgə]) day; daylight; ***welchen ~ haben wir heute?*** what day is it today?; ***heute*** (***morgen***) ***in 14 ~en*** two weeks from today (tomorrow); ***e-s ~es*** one day; ***den ganzen ~*** all day; ***am ~e*** during the day; ***~ und Nacht*** night and day; ***am helllichten ~*** in broad daylight; ***ein freier ~*** a day off; ***guten ~!*** hello!, hi!; how do you do?; (***j-m***) ***guten ~ sagen*** say hello (to s.o.); F ***sie hat ihre ~e*** she has her period; ***unter ~e*** underground; → ***zutage***
**Tage|bau** ['taːgəbau] *m* (-[*e*]*s*; *-e*) opencast mining; **~buch** *n* diary; ***~ führen*** keep a diary
'**tagelang** *adv* for days
'**tagen** *v/i* (*ge-*, *h*) meet, hold a meeting; JUR be in session
'**Tages|anbruch** *m*: ***bei ~*** at daybreak, at dawn; **~gespräch** *n* talk of the day; **~karte** *f* day ticket; GASTR menu for the day; **~licht** *n* (-[*e*]*s*; *no pl*) daylight; **~mutter** *f* childminder; **~ordnung** *f* agenda; **~stätte** *f* day care center (*Br*

centre); **~tour** *f* day trip; **~zeit** *f* time of day; ***zu jeder ~*** at any hour; **~zeitung** *f* daily (paper)

'**tageweise** *adv* by the day

**täglich** ['tɛːklɪç] *adj and adv* daily

'**Tagschicht** *f* ECON day shift

'**tagsüber** *adv* during the day

'**Tagung** *f* (-; *-en*) conference

**Taille** ['taljə] *f* (-; *-n*) waist; waistline

**tailliert** [ta'jiːɐt] *adj* waisted, tapered

**Takelage** [takə'laːʒə] *f* (-; *-n*) MAR rigging

**Takt** [takt] *m* (*-[e]s*; *-e*) (*no pl*) MUS time, measure, beat; MUS bar; MOT stroke; (*no pl*) tact; ***den ~ halten*** MUS keep time

**Taktik** ['taktɪk] *f* (-; *-en*) MIL tactics (*a. fig*); '**taktisch** *adj* tactical

'**taktlos** *adj* tactless

'**Taktstock** *m* MUS baton

'**Taktstrich** *m* MUS bar

'**taktvoll** *adj* tactful

**Tal** [taːl] *n* (*-[e]s*; *Täler* ['tɛːlɐ]) valley

**Talar** [ta'laːɐ] *m* (*-s*; *-e*) robe, gown

**Talent** [ta'lɛnt] *n* (*-[e]s*; *-e*) talent (*a. person*), gift; **talentiert** [talɛn'tiːɐt] *adj* talented, gifted

**Talg** [talk] *m* (*-[e]s*; *-e*) tallow; GASTR suet

**Talisman** ['taːlɪsman] *m* (*-s*; *-e*) talisman, charm

**Talk|master** ['tɔːkmaːstɐ] *m* (*-s*; -) TV talk (*Br* chat) show host; **~show** ['tɔːkʃoʊ] *f* (-; *-s*) TV talk (*Br* chat) show

'**Talsperre** *f* dam, barrage

**Tampon** ['tampɔn] *m* (*-s*; *-s*) tampon

**Tandler** ['tandlɐ] *Austrian m* (*-s*; -) second-hand dealer

**Tang** [taŋ] *m* (*-[e]s*; *-e*) BOT seaweed

**Tank** [taŋk] *m* (*-s*; *-s*) tank; **tanken** ['taŋkən] *v/t* (*ge-*, *h*) get some gasoline (*Br* petrol), fill up; **Tanker** ['taŋkɐ] *m* (*-s*; -) MAR tanker; '**Tankstelle** *f* filling (*or* gas, *Br* petrol) station; '**Tankwart** *m* (*-[e]s*; *-e*) gas station (*Br* petrol pump) attendant

**Tanne** ['tanə] *f* (-; *-n*) BOT fir (tree)

'**Tannenbaum** *m* Christmas tree

'**Tannenzapfen** *m* BOT fir cone

**Tante** ['tantə] *f* (-; *-n*) aunt; ***~ Lindy*** Aunt Lindy; **~-Emma-Laden** F *m* mom-and-pop store, *Br* corner shop

**Tantiemen** [ta‿'tjeːmən] *pl* royalties

**Tanz** [tants] *m* (*-es*; *Tänze* ['tɛntsə]), **tanzen** ['tantsən] *v/i* (*ge-*, *h*, *sein*) *and v/t* (*ge-*, *h*) dance; **Tänzer** ['tɛntsɐ] *m* (*-s*; -), **Tänzerin** ['tɛntsərɪn] *f* (-; *-nen*) dancer

'**Tanz|fläche** *f* dance floor; **~kurs** *m* dancing lessons; **~mu,sik** *f* dance music; **~schule** *f* dancing school

**Tapete** [ta'peːtə] *f* (-; *-n*), **tapezieren** [tape'tsiːrən] *v/t* (*no -ge-*, *h*) wallpaper

**tapfer** ['tapfɐ] *adj* brave; courageous

'**Tapferkeit** *f* (-; *no pl*) bravery; courage

**Tarif** [ta'riːf] *m* (*-[e]s*; *-e*) rate(s), tariff; (wage) scale; **~lohn** *m* standard wage(s); **~verhandlungen** *pl* wage negotiations, collective bargaining

**tarnen** ['tarnən] *v/t* (*ge-*, *h*) camouflage; *fig* disguise

'**Tarnung** *f* (-; *-en*) camouflage

**Tasche** ['taʃə] *f* (-; *-n*) bag; pocket

'**Taschen|buch** *n* paperback; **~dieb** *m* pickpocket; **~geld** *n* allowance, *Br* pocket money; **~lampe** *f* flashlight, *Br* torch; **~messer** *n* penknife, pocketknife; **~rechner** *m* pocket calculator; **~schirm** *m* telescopic umbrella; **~tuch** *n* handkerchief, F hankie; **~uhr** *f* pocket watch

**Tasse** ['tasə] *f* (-; *-n*) cup; ***e-e ~ Tee*** *etc* a cup of tea *etc*

**Tastatur** [tasta'tuːɐ] *f* (-; *-en*) keyboard, keys; **Taste** ['tastə] *f* (-; *-n*) key

**tasten** ['tastən] (*ge-*, *h*) **1.** *v/i* grope (***nach*** for), feel (for); fumble (for) **2.** *v/t* touch, feel; ***sich ~*** feel *or* grope (*a. fig*) one's way

'**Tastentele,fon** *n* push-button phone

'**Tastsinn** *m* (*-[e]s*; *no pl*) sense of touch

**tat** [taːt] *pret of* ***tun***

**Tat** *f* (-; *-en*) act, deed; action; JUR offense, *Br* offence; ***j-n auf frischer ~ ertappen*** catch s.o. in the act

'**tatenlos** *adj* inactive, passive

**Täter** ['tɛːtɐ] *m* (*-s*; -), '**Täterin** *f* (-; *-nen*) culprit; JUR offender

**tätig** ['tɛːtɪç] *adj* active; busy; ***~ sein bei*** be employed with; ***~ werden*** act, take action; '**Tätigkeit** *f* (-; *-en*) activity; work; occupation, job

'**Tatkraft** *f* (-; *no pl*) energy

'**tatkräftig** *adj* energetic, active

**tätlich** ['tɛːtlɪç] *adj* violent; ***~ werden gegen*** assault; '**Tätlichkeiten** *pl* (acts of) violence; JUR assault (and battery)

'**Tatort** *m* JUR scene of the crime

**tätowieren** [tɛto'viːrən] *v/t* (*no -ge-*, *h*), **Täto'wierung** *f* (-; *-en*) tattoo

'**Tatsache** *f* fact
'**tatsächlich 1.** *adj* actual, real **2.** *adv* actually, in fact; really
**tätscheln** ['tɛːtʃəln] *v/t* (*ge-*, *h*) pat, pet
**Tatze** ['tatsə] *f* (-; *-n*) ZO paw (*a. fig*)
**Tau**[1] [tau] *n* (*-[e]s*; *-e*) rope
**Tau**[2] *m* (*-[e]s*; *no pl*) dew
**taub** [taup] *adj* deaf (*fig* ***gegen*** to); numb, benumbed
**Taube** ['taubə] *f* (-; *-n*) ZO pigeon; *esp fig* dove; '**Taubenschlag** *m* pigeonhouse
'**Taubheit** *f* (-; *no pl*) deafness; numbness
'**taubstumm** *adj* deaf-and-dumb
'**Taubstumme** *m*, *f* (*-n*; *-n*) deaf mute
**tauchen** ['tauxən] **1.** *v/i* (*ge-*, *h*, *sein*) dive (***nach*** for); SPORT skin-dive; *submarine*: *a.* submerge; stay underwater **2.** *v/t* (*h*) dip (***in*** *acc* into); duck; **Taucher** ['tauxɐ] *m* (*-s*; -) (SPORT skin) diver; '**Tauchsport** *m* skin diving
**tauen** ['tauən] *v/i* (*ge-*, *sein*) *and v/t* (*ge-*, *h*) thaw, melt
**Taufe** ['taufə] *f* (-; *-n*) baptism, christening; '**taufen** *v/t* (*ge-*, *h*) baptize, christen; '**Taufpate** *m* godfather; '**Taufpatin** *f* godmother; '**Taufschein** *m* certificate of baptism
**taugen** ['taugən] *v/i* (*ge-*, *h*) be good *or* fit *or* of use *or* suited (*all*: ***zu, für*** for); ***nichts ~*** be no good; F ***taugt es was?*** is it any good?; **tauglich** ['tauklɪç] *adj esp* MIL fit (for service)
**Taumel** ['tauməl] *m* (*-s*; *no pl*) dizziness; rapture, ecstasy; '**taumelig** *adj* dizzy; '**taumeln** *v/i* (*ge-*, *sein*) stagger, reel
**Tausch** [tauʃ] *m* (*-[e]s*; *-e*) exchange, F swap; **tauschen** ['tauʃən] *v/t* (*ge-*, *h*) exchange, F swap (*both*: ***gegen*** for); switch; change; ***ich möchte nicht mit ihm ~*** I wouldn't like to be in his shoes
**täuschen** ['tɔʏʃən] *v/t* (*ge-*, *h*) deceive, fool; delude; cheat; *a.* SPORT feint; ***sich ~*** deceive o.s.; be mistaken; ***sich ~ lassen von*** be taken in by; ***~de Ähnlichkeit*** striking similarity; '**Täuschung** *f* (-; *-en*) deception; delusion; JUR deceit; *a.* PED cheating
**tausend** ['tauzənt] *adj* a thousand
'**tausendst** *adj* thousandth
'**Tausendstel** *n* (*-s*; -) thousandth (part)
'**Tautropfen** *m* dewdrop
'**Tauwetter** *n* thaw
'**Tauziehen** *n* (*-s*; *no pl*) SPORT tug-of-war (*a. fig*)
**Taxi** ['taksi] *n* (*-s*; *-s*) taxi(cab), cab
**taxieren** [ta'ksiːrən] *v/t* (*no -ge-*, *h*) rate, estimate (***auf*** *acc* at)
'**Taxistand** *m* cabstand, *esp Br* taxi rank
**Technik** ['tɛçnɪk] *f* (-; *-en*) (*no pl*) technology, engineering; technique (*a.* SPORT *etc*), MUS execution
**Techniker** ['tɛçnikɐ] *m* (*-s*; -), '**Technikerin** *f* (-; *-nen*) engineer; technician (*a.* SPORT *etc*)
**technisch** ['tɛçnɪʃ] *adj* technical; technological; ***~e Hochschule*** school *etc* of technology
**Technologie** [tɛçnolo'giː] *f* (-; *-n*) technology; **technologisch** [tɛçno'loːgɪʃ] *adj* technological
**Tee** [teː] *m* (*-s*; *-s*) tea; ***(e-n) ~ trinken*** have some tea; ***(e-n) ~ machen*** *or* ***kochen*** make some tea; **~beutel** *m* teabag; **~kanne** *f* teapot; **~löffel** *m* teaspoon
**Teer** [teːɐ] *m* (*-[e]s*; *-e*), **teeren** ['teːrən] *v/t* (*ge-*, *h*) tar
'**Teesieb** *n* tea strainer
'**Teetasse** *f* teacup
**Teich** [taiç] *m* (*-[e]s*; *-e*) pool, pond
**Teig** [taik] *m* (*-[e]s*; *-e*) dough, paste
**teigig** ['taigɪç] *adj* doughy, pasty
'**Teigwaren** *pl* pasta
**Teil** [tail] *m*, *n* (*-[e]s*; *-e*) part; portion, share; component; ***zum ~*** partly, in part; *~... in cpds ...erfolg etc*: partial ...
'**teilbar** *adj* divisible
'**Teilchen** *n* (*-s*; -) particle
**teilen** ['tailən] *v/t* (*ge-*, *h*) divide; share
'**teilhaben** *v/i* (*irr*, ***haben***, *sep*, *-ge-*, *h*) ***~ an*** (*dat*) (have a) share in; '**Teilhaber**(**in**) ['tailhaːbɐ (-bərɪn)] (*-s*; *-/-*; *-nen*) ECON partner
'**Teilnahme** ['tailnaːmə] *f* (-; *no pl*) participation (***an*** *dat* in); *fig* interest (in); sympathy (for)
'**teilnahmslos** *adj* indifferent; *esp* MED apathetic; '**Teilnahmslosigkeit** *f* (-; *no pl*) indifference; apathy
'**teilnehmen** *v/i* (*irr*, ***nehmen***, *sep*, *-ge-*, *h*) ***~ an*** (*dat*) take part *or* participate in; share (in); '**Teilnehmer**(**in**) ['tailneːmɐ (-mərɪn)] (*-s*; *-/-*; *-nen*) participant; UNIV student; SPORT competitor
**teils** *adv* partly
'**Teilstrecke** *f* stage, leg
'**Teilung** *f* (-; *-en*) division

**'teilweise** *adv* partly, in part
**'Teilzahlung** *f* → ***Abzahlung, Rate***
**Teint** [tɛ̃ː] *m* (*-s*; *-s*) complexion
**Tel.** *abbr of* ***Telefon*** tel., telephone
**Telefon** [tele'foːn] *n* (*-s*; *-e*) telephone, phone; ***am ~*** on the (tele)phone; ***~ haben*** have a (*Br* be on the) (tele)phone; ***ans ~ gehen*** answer the (tele)phone; **~anruf** *m* (tele)phone call; **~anschluss** *m* telephone connection; **~appa,rat** *m* telephone, phone
**Telefonat** [telefo'naːt] *n* (*-[e]s*; *-e*) → ***Telefongespräch***
**Tele'fon|buch** *n* telephone directory, phone book; **~gebühr** *f* telephone charge; **~gespräch** *n* (tele)phone call
**telefonieren** [telefo'niːrən] *v/i* (*no -ge-, h*) (tele)phone; be on the phone; ***mit j-m ~*** talk to s.o. on the phone
**telefonisch** [tele'foːnɪʃ] **1.** *adj* telephonic, telephone … **2.** *adv* by (tele)phone, over the (tele)phone
**Tele'fon|karte** *f* phonecard; **~leitung** *f* telephone line; **~netz** *n* telephone network; **~nummer** *f* (tele)phone number; **~zelle** *f* (tele)phone booth, *esp Br* (tele)phone box, *Br* call box; **~zen,trale** *f* switchboard
**Telegramm** [tele'gram] *n* (*-s*; *-e*) telegram, wire, cable(gram)
**Teleobjektiv** ['teːləɔpjɛktiːf] *n* telephoto lens
**Telephon** *n* → ***Telefon***
**Teletext** ['teːlətɛkst] *m* teletext
**Teller** ['tɛlɐ] *m* (*-s*; *-*) plate; **~wäscher** ['tɛlɐvɛʃɐ] *m* (*-s*; *-*) dishwasher
**Tempel** ['tɛmpəl] *m* (*-s*; *-*) temple
**Temperament** [tɛmpəra'mɛnt] *n* (*-[e]s*; *-e*) temper(ament); life, F pep
**tempera'ment|los** *adj* lifeless, dull; **~voll** *adj* full of life *or* F pep
**Temperatur** [tɛmpəra'tuːɐ] *f* (*-*; *-en*) temperature; ***j-s ~ messen*** take s.o.'s temperature
**Tempo** ['tɛmpo] *n* (*-s*; *-s, -pi*) speed; MUS time; ***mit ~*** … at a speed of … an hour
**Tendenz** [tɛn'dɛnts] *f* (*-*; *-en*) tendency, trend; leaning; **tendenziös** [tɛndɛn'tsjøːs] *adj* tendentious; **tendieren** [tɛn'diːrən] *v/i* (*no -ge-, h*) tend (***zu*** towards; ***dazu, et. zu tun*** to do s.th.)
**Tennis** ['tɛnɪs] *n* (*-*; *no pl*) tennis; **~platz** *m* tennis court; **~schläger** *m* tennis racket; **~spieler(in)** tennis player
**Tenor** [te'noːɐ] *m* (*-s*; *Tenöre* [te'nøːrə]) MUS tenor
**Teppich** ['tɛpɪç] *m* (*-s*; *-e*) carpet
**'Teppichboden** *m* fitted carpet, wall-to--wall carpeting
**Termin** [tɛr'miːn] *m* (*-s*; *-e*) date; deadline; engagement; ***e-n ~ vereinbaren*** (***einhalten, absagen***) make (keep, cancel) an appointment
**Terminal** ['tøːɐminəl] *m, n* (*-s*; *-s*) AVIAT terminal; *n* (*-s*; *-s*) IT terminal
**Terrasse** [tɛ'rasə] *f* (*-*; *-n*) terrace
**ter'rassenförmig** [tɛ'rasənfœrmɪç] *adj* terraced, in terraces
**Terrine** [tɛ'riːnə] *f* (*-*; *-n*) tureen
**Territorium** [tɛri'toːrjʊm] *n* (*-s*; *-ien*) territory
**Terror** ['tɛroːɐ] *m* (*-s*; *no pl*) terror
**terrorisieren** [tɛrori'ziːrən] *v/t* (*no -ge-, h*) terrorize
**Terrorismus** [tɛro'rɪsmʊs] *m* (*-*; *no pl*) terrorism; **Terrorist(in)** [tɛro'rɪst(ɪn)] (*-en*; *-en/-*; *-nen*), **terro'ristisch** *adj* terrorist
**Testament** [tɛsta'mɛnt] *n* (*-[e]s*; *-e*) (last) will; JUR last will and testament
**testamentarisch** [tɛstamɛn'taːrɪʃ] *adv* by will
**Testa'mentsvollstrecker** *m* executor
**Testbild** ['tɛstbɪlt] *n* TV test card
**testen** ['tɛstən] *v/t* (*no -ge-, h*) test
**'Testpi,lot** *m* test pilot
**Tetanus** ['teːtanʊs] *m* (*-*; *no pl*) MED tetanus
**teuer** ['tɔʏɐ] *adj* expensive; ***wie ~ ist es?*** how much is it?
**Teufel** ['tɔʏfəl] *m* (*-s*; *-*) devil (*a. fig*); ***wer*** (***wo, was***) ***zum ~ …?*** who (where, what) the hell …? **'Teufelskerl** F *m* devil of a fellow; **'Teufelskreis** *m* vicious circle; **teuflisch** ['tɔʏflɪʃ] *adj* devilish, diabolic(al)
**Text** [tɛkst] *m* (*-[e]s*; *-e*) text; MUS words, lyrics
**Texter** ['tɛkstɐ] *m* (*-s*; *-*), **'Texterin** *f* (*-*; *-nen*) MUS songwriter
**Textil…** [tɛks'tiːl-] *in cpds* textile …
**Textilien** [tɛks'tiːljən] *pl* textiles
**'Textverarbeitung** *f* word processing
**Theater** [te'aːtɐ] *n* (*-s*; *-*) theater, *Br* theatre; F ***~ machen*** (***um***) make a fuss (about); **~besucher** *m* theatergoer, *Br* theatregoer; **~karte** *f* theater (*Br* theatre) ticket; **~kasse** *f* box office;

T

**~stück** *n* play
**Thema** ['te:ma] *n* (*-s*; *Themen*) subject, topic; MUS theme; ***das ~ wechseln*** change the subject
**Theologe** [teo'lo:gə] *m* (*-n*; *-n*) theologian; **Theologie** [teolo'gi:] *f* (*-*; *-n*) theology; **Theo'login** *f* (*-*; *-nen*) theologian; **theo'logisch** *adj* theological
**Theoretiker** [teo're:tikɐ] *m* (*-s*; *-*) theorist; **theo'retisch** *adj* theoretical
**Theorie** [teo'ri:] *f* (*-*; *-n*) theory
**Therapeut** [tera'pɔyt] *m* (*-en*; *-en*), **Thera'peutin** *f* (*-*; *-nen*) therapist; **Therapie** [tera'pi:] *f* (*-*; *-n*) therapy
**Thermometer** [tɛrmo'me:tɐ] *n* (*-s*; *-*) thermometer
**Thermosflasche®** ['tɛrmɔsflaʃə] *f* thermos®
**These** ['te:zə] *f* (*-*; *-n*) thesis
**Thon** [to:n] *Swiss m* (*-s*; *-s*) tuna (fish)
**Thrombose** [trɔm'bo:zə] *f* (*-*; *-n*) MED thrombosis
**Thron** [tro:n] *m* (*-[e]s*; *-e*) throne
**'Thronfolger** ['tro:nfɔlgɐ] *m* (*-s*; *-*), **'Thronfolgerin** ['tro:nfɔlgərɪn] *f* (*-*; *-nen*) successor to the throne
**Thunfisch** ['tu:nfɪʃ] *m* tuna (fish)
**Tick** [tɪk] F *m* (*-[e]s*; *-s*) quirk
**ticken** ['tɪkən] *v/i* (*ge-*, *h*) tick
**Tiebreak, Tie-Break** ['taɪbreɪk] *m*, *n* *tennis*: tiebreak(er)
**tief** [ti:f] *adj* deep (*a. fig*); low
**Tief** *n* (*-s*; *-s*) METEOR depression (*a.* PSYCH, ECON), low (*a. fig*)
**Tiefe** ['ti:fə] *f* (*-*; *-n*) depth (*a. fig*)
**'Tief|ebene** *f* lowland(s); **~flieger** *m* low-flying air plane; **~gang** *m* MAR draft, *Br* draught; *fig* depth; **~ga,rage** *f* parking *or* underground garage, *Br* underground car park
**'tiefgekühlt** *adj* deep-frozen
**'Tiefkühl|fach** *n* freezing compartment; **~kost** *f* frozen foods; **~schrank** *m*, **~truhe** *f* freezer, deep-freeze
**Tier** [ti:ɐ] *n* (*-[e]s*; *-e*) animal; F ***hohes ~*** bigwig, big shot; **~arzt** *m*, **-ärztin** *f* veterinarian, *Br* veterinary surgeon, F vet; **~freund** *m* animal lover; **~garten** *m* → ***Zoo***; **~heim** *n* animal shelter
**tierisch** ['ti:rɪʃ] *adj* animal; *fig* bestial, brutish
**'Tierkreis** *m* ASTR zodiac; **~zeichen** *n* sign of the zodiac
**'Tiermedi,zin** *f* veterinary medicine
**Tierquäle'rei** *f* cruelty to animals
**'Tier|reich** *n* animal kingdom; **~schutz** *m* protection of animals; **~schutzverein** *m* society for the prevention of cruelty to animals; **~versuch** *m* MED experiment with animals
**Tiger** ['ti:gɐ] *m* (*-s*; *-*) ZO tiger
**Tigerin** ['ti:gərɪn] *f* (*-*; *-nen*) ZO tigress
**tilgen** ['tɪlgən] *v/t* (*ge-*, *h*) ECON pay off
**Tinte** ['tɪntə] *f* (*-*; *-n*) ink
**'Tintenfisch** *m* ZO squid
**Tipp** [tɪp] *m* (*-s*; *-s*) hint, tip; tip-off; ***j-m e-n ~ geben*** tip s.o. off
**tippen** ['tɪpən] *v/i and v/t* (*ge-*, *h*) tap; type; F guess; do *lotto etc*
**Tisch** [tɪʃ] *m* (*-[e]s*; *-e*) table; ***am ~ sitzen*** sit at the table; ***bei ~*** at table; ***den ~ decken*** (***abräumen***) lay (clear) the table; **~decke** *f* tablecloth; **~gebet** *n* REL grace: ***das ~ sprechen*** say grace
**Tischler** ['tɪʃlɐ] *m* (*-s*; *-*) joiner; cabinet-maker
**'Tisch|platte** *f* tabletop; **~tennis** *n* table tennis; **~tuch** *n* tablecloth
**Titel** ['ti:təl] *m* (*-s*; *-*) title; **~bild** *n* cover picture; **~blatt** *n*, **~seite** *f* title page; cover, front page
**Toast** [to:st] *m* (*-[e]s*; *-s*), **toasten** ['to:stən] *v/t* (*ge-*, *h*) toast
**toben** ['to:bən] *v/i* (*ge-*, *h*) rage (*a. fig*); romp; **tobsüchtig** ['to:pzʏçtɪç] *adj* raving mad; **'Tobsuchtsanfall** *m* tantrum
**Tochter** ['tɔxtɐ] *f* (*-*; *Töchter* ['tœçtɐ]) daughter; **~gesellschaft** *f* ECON subsidiary (company)
**Tod** [to:t] *m* (*-[e]s*; *no pl*) death (*a. fig*) (***durch*** from); **tod...** *in cpds ...ernst, ...müde, ...sicher*: dead ...
**Todes|ängste** ['to:dəsɛŋstə] *pl*: ***~ ausstehen*** be scared to death; **~anzeige** *f* obituary (notice); **~fall** *m* (case of) death; **~kampf** *m* agony; **~opfer** *n* casualty; **~strafe** *f* JUR capital punishment; death penalty; **~ursache** *f* cause of death; **~urteil** *n* JUR death sentence
**'Todfeind** *m* deadly enemy
**'tod'krank** *adj* mortally ill
**tödlich** ['tø:tlɪç] *adj* fatal; deadly; *esp fig* mortal
**'Todsünde** *f* mortal *or* deadly sin
**Toilette** [toa'lɛtə] *f* (*-*; *-n*) bathroom, *Br* toilet, lavatory; *pl* rest rooms, *Br* ladies' *or* men's rooms

**Toi'letten...** *in cpds ...papier, ...seife etc*: toilet ...; **~tisch** *m* dressing table
**tolerant** [tole'rant] *adj* tolerant (***gegen*** of, towards); **Toleranz** [tole'rants] *f* (-; -*en*) tolerance (*a.* TECH); **tolerieren** [tole'ri:rən] *v/t* (*no -ge-*, *h*) tolerate
**toll** [tɔl] *adj* wild; F great, fantastic
**'tollkühn** *adj* daredevil
**'Tollwut** *f* VET rabies; **'tollwütig** ['tɔlvy:tɪç] *adj* VET rabid
**Tomate** [to'ma:tə] *f* (-; -*n*) BOT tomato
**Ton**[1] [to:n] *m* (-[*e*]*s*; -*e*) clay
**Ton**[2] *m* (-[*e*]*s*; *Töne* ['tø:nə]) tone (*a.* MUS, PAINT), PAINT *a.* shade; sound (*a.* TV, *film*); note; stress; ***kein ~*** not a word; **~art** *f* MUS key; **~band** *n* (-[*e*]*s*; -*bänder*) (recording) tape; **~bandgerät** *n* tape recorder
**tönen** ['tø:nən] (*ge-*, *h*) **1.** *v/i* sound, ring **2.** *v/t* tinge, tint, shade
**'Ton|fall** *m* tone (of voice); accent; **~film** *m* sound film; **~kopf** *m* ELECTR (magnetic) head; **~lage** *f* MUS pitch; **~leiter** *f* MUS scale
**Tonne** ['tɔnə] *f* (-; -*n*) barrel; (metric) ton
**'Tontechniker** *m* sound engineer
**'Tönung** *f* (-; -*en*) tint, tinge, shade
**Topf** [tɔpf] *m* (-[*e*]*s*; *Töpfe* ['tœpfə]) pot; saucepan
**Topfen** ['tɔpfən] *Austrian m* (-*s*; *no pl*) GASTR curd(s)
**Töpfer** ['tœpfɐ] *m* (-*s*; -) potter
**Töpferei** [tœpfə'rai] *f* (-; -*en*) pottery
**'Töpferin** *f* (-; -*nen*) potter
**'Töpferscheibe** *f* potter's wheel
**'Töpferware** *f* pottery, earthenware
**Tor** [to:ɐ] *n* (-[*e*]*s*; -*e*) gate; *soccer etc*: goal; ***ein ~ schießen*** score (a goal); ***im ~ stehen*** keep goal
**Torf** [tɔrf] *m* (-[*e*]*s*; -*e*) peat
**'Torfmull** *m* peat dust
**'Torhüter** ['to:ɐhy:tɐ] *m* → ***Torwart***
**torkeln** ['tɔrkəln] F *v/i* (*ge-*, *h*, *sein*) reel, stagger
**'Torlatte** *f* SPORT crossbar
**'Torlinie** *f* SPORT goal line
**torpedieren** [tɔrpe'di:rən] *v/t* (*no -ge-*, *h*) MIL torpedo (*a. fig*)
**'Tor|pfosten** *m* SPORT goalpost; **~raum** *m* SPORT goalmouth; **~schuss** *m* SPORT shot at goal; **~schütze** *m* SPORT scorer
**Torte** ['tɔrtə] *f* (-; -*n*) pie, *esp Br* flan; cream cake, gateau
**'Torwart** ['to:ɐvart] *m* (-[*e*]*s*; -*e*) SPORT goalkeeper, F goalie
**tosen** ['to:zən] *v/i* (*ge-*, *h*) roar; thunder; **~d** *adj* thunderous (*applause*)
**tot** [to:t] *adj* dead (*a. fig*); late; ***~ geboren*** MED stillborn; ***~ umfallen*** drop dead
**total** [to'ta:l] *adj* total, complete
**totalitär** [totali'tɛ:ɐ] *adj* POL totalitarian
**'Tote** *m*, *f* (-*n*; -*n*) dead man *or* woman; (dead) body, corpse; *mst pl* casualty; *pl the* dead; **töten** ['tø:tən] *v/t* (*ge-*, *h*) kill
**'Totenbett** *n* deathbed
**'toten'blass** *adj* deadly pale
**'Toten|gräber** ['to:təngrɛ:bɐ] *m* (-*s*; -) gravedigger; **~kopf** *m* skull; skull and crossbones; **~maske** *f* death mask; **~messe** *f* REL mass for the dead, requiem (*a.* MUS); **~schädel** *m* skull; **~schein** *m* death certificate
**'toten'still** *adj* deathly still
**'totlachen** F *v/refl* (*sep*, *-ge-*, *h*) kill o.s. laughing
**Toto** ['to:to] *m*, F *n* (-*s*; -*s*) football pools
**'Totschlag** *m* (-[*e*]*s*; *no pl*) JUR manslaughter; **'totschlagen** *v/t* (*irr*, ***schlagen***, *sep*, *-ge-*, *h*) kill; ***j-n ~*** beat s.o. to death; ***die Zeit ~*** kill time
**'totschweigen** *v/t* (*irr*, ***schweigen***, *sep*, *-ge-*, *h*) hush up
**Toupet** [tu'pe:] *n* (-*s*; -*s*) toupee
**toupieren** [tu'pi:rən] *v/t* (*no -ge-*, *h*) *Br* backcomb
**Tour** [tu:ɐ] *f* (-; -*en*) tour (***durch*** of), trip; excursion; TECH turn, revolution; ***auf ~en kommen*** MOT pick up speed; F ***krumme ~en*** underhand methods
**Touren...** ['tu:rən-] *in cpds ...rad etc*: touring ...
**Tourismus** [tu'rɪsmʊs] *m* (-; *no pl*) tourism; **~geschäft** *n* tourist industry
**Tourist** [tu'rɪst] *m* (-*en*; -*en*), **Tou'ristin** *f* (-; -*nen*) tourist; **tou'ristisch** *adj* touristic
**Tournee** [tʊr'ne:] *f* (-; -*s*, -*n*) tour; ***auf ~ gehen*** go on tour
**Trab** [tra:p] *m* (-[*e*]*s*; *no pl*) trot
**Trabant** [tra'bant] *m* (-*en*; -*en*) ASTR satellite; **Tra'bantenstadt** *f* satellite town
**traben** ['tra:bən] *v/i* (*ge-*, *sein*) trot
**Traber** ['tra:bɐ] *m* (-*s*; -) ZO trotter
**'Trabrennen** *n* trotting race
**Tracht** [traxt] *f* (-; -*en*) costume; uniform; dress; F ***e-e ~ Prügel*** a thrashing
**trächtig** ['trɛçtɪç] *adj* ZO with young,

pregnant
**Tradition** [tradi'tsjo:n] *f* (-; *-en*) tradition; **traditionell** [traditsjo'nɛl] *adj* traditional
**traf** [tra:f] *pret of* ***treffen***
**Trafik** [tra'fɪk] *Austrian f* (-; *-en*) → ***Tabakgeschäft***; **Trafikant** [trafi'kant] *Austrian m* (*-en*; *-en*) tobacconist
**Tragbahre** ['tra:kba:rə] *f* stretcher
'**tragbar** *adj* portable; wearable; *fig* bearable; *person*: acceptable
**Trage** ['tra:gə] *f* (-; *-n*) stretcher
**träge** ['trɛ:gə] *adj* lazy, indolent; PHYS inert (*a. fig*)
**tragen** [tra:gən] (*irr, ge-, h*) **1.** *v/t* carry; wear; *fig* bear; ***sich gut ~*** wear well **2.** *v/i* BOT bear fruit; *fig* hold; **~d** *adj* ARCH supporting; THEA leading
**Träger** ['trɛ:gɐ] *m* (*-s*; -) carrier; porter; (shoulder) strap; TECH support; ARCH girder; *fig* bearer
'**trägerlos** *adj* strapless
'**Tragetasche** *f* carrier bag; carrycot
'**tragfähig** *adj* load-bearing; *fig* sound
'**Tragfläche** *f* AVIAT wing
**Trägheit** ['trɛ:khait] *f* (-; *no pl*) laziness, indolence; PHYS inertia (*a. fig*)
**Tragik** ['tra:gɪk] *f* (-; *no pl*) tragedy
**tragisch** ['tra:gɪʃ] *adj* tragic
**Tragödie** [tra'gø:djə] *f* (-; *-n*) tragedy
'**Tragriemen** *m* strap; sling
'**Tragweite** *f* range; *fig* significance
**Trainer** ['trɛ:nɐ] *m* (*-s*; -), '**Trainerin** *f* (-; *-nen*) SPORT trainer, coach; **trainieren** [trɛ'ni:rən] *v/i and v/t* (*no -ge-, h*) SPORT train, coach
'**Training** *n* (*-s*; *-s*) training
'**Trainingsanzug** *m* track suit
**Traktor** ['trakto:ɐ] *m* (*-s*; *-en* [trak'to:rən]) MOT tractor
**trällern** ['trɛlɐn] *v/t and v/i* (*ge-, h*) warble, trill
**Tram** [tram] *Austrian f* (-; *-s*), *Swiss n* (*-s*; *-s*) streetcar, *Br* tram
**trampeln** ['trampəln] *v/i* (*ge-, h*) trample, stamp
'**Trampelpfad** *m* beaten track
**trampen** ['trɛmpən] *v/i* (*ge-, sein*) hitchhike; **Tramper(in)** ['trɛmpɐ, 'trɛmpərɪn] (*-s*; *-/-*; *-nen*) hitchhiker
**Träne** ['trɛ:nə] *f* (-; *-n*) tear; ***in ~n ausbrechen*** burst into tears; '**tränen** *v/i* (*ge-, h*) water; '**Tränengas** *n* tear gas
**trank** [traŋk] *pret of* ***trinken***
**Tränke** ['trɛŋkə] *f* (-; *-n*) watering place
'**tränken** *v/t* (*ge-, h*) zo water; soak, drench
**Transfer** [trans'fe:ɐ] *m* (*-s*; *-s*) transfer (*a.* SPORT)
**Transformator** [transfɔr'ma:to:ɐ] *m* (*-s*; *-en* [transfɔrma'to:rən]) ELECTR transformer
**Transfusion** [transfu'zjo:n] *f* (-; *-en*) MED transfusion
**Transistor** [tran'zɪsto:ɐ] *m* (*-s*; *-en* [tranzɪs'to:rən]) ELECTR transistor
**Transit** [tran'zi:t] *m* (*-s*; *-e*) transit
**transitiv** ['tranziti:f] *adj* LING transitive
**transparent** [transpa'rɛnt] *adj* transparent
**Transpa'rent** *n* (*-[e]s*; *-e*) banner
**Transplantation** [transplanta'tsjo:n] *f* (-; *-en*), **transplantieren** [transplan'ti:rən] *v/t* (*no -ge-, h*) MED transplant
**Transport** [trans'pɔrt] *m* (*-[e]s*; *-e*) transport; shipment; **transportabel** [transpɔr'ta:bəl], **trans'portfähig** *adj* transportable; **transportieren** [transpɔr'ti:rən] *v/t* (*no -ge-, h*) transport, ship, carry, MOT *a.* haul
**Trans'port|mittel** *n* (means of) transport(ation); **~unternehmen** *n* hauler, *Br* haulier
**Trapez** [tra'pe:ts] *n* (*-es*; *-e*) MATH trapezoid, *Br* trapezium; SPORT trapeze
**trappeln** ['trapəln] *v/i* (*ge-, sein*) clatter; patter
**trat** [tra:t] *pret of* ***treten***
**Traube** ['traubə] *f* (-; *-n*) BOT bunch of grapes; grape; *pl* grapes; *fig* cluster
**Traubensaft** *m* grape juice
'**Traubenzucker** *m* glucose
**trauen** ['trauən] (*ge-, h*) **1.** *v/t* marry **2.** *v/i* trust (***j-m*** s.o.); ***sich ~, et. zu tun*** dare (to) do s.th.; ***ich traute meinen Augen nicht*** I couldn't believe my eyes
**Trauer** ['trauɐ] *f* (-; *no pl*) grief, sorrow; mourning; ***in ~*** in mourning; **~fall** *m* death; **~feier** *f* funeral service; **~marsch** *m* MUS funeral march
'**trauern** *v/i* (*ge-, h*) mourn (***um*** for)
'**Trauerrede** *f* funeral oration
'**Trauerzug** *m* funeral procession
**träufeln** ['trɔʏfəln] *v/t* (*ge-, h*) drip, trickle
**Traum** [traum] *m* (*-[e]s*; *Träume* ['trɔʏmə]) dream (*a. fig*); **~...** *in cpds* *...beruf, ...mann etc*: dream ..., ... of

one's dreams; **träumen** ['trɔʏmən] *v/i and v/t* (*ge-*, *h*) dream (*a. fig*) (**von** about, of); **schlecht ~** have bad dreams; **Träumer** ['trɔʏmɐ] *m* (*-s*; *-*) dreamer (*a. fig*); **Träumerei** [trɔʏmə'rai] *fig f* (day)dream(s), reverie (*a.* MUS)

**träumerisch** ['trɔʏmərɪʃ] *adj* dreamy

**traurig** ['traurɪç] *adj* sad (**über** *acc*, **wegen** about)

'**Traurigkeit** *f* (*-*; *no pl*) sadness

**Trauring** ['traurɪŋ] *m* wedding ring

'**Trauschein** *m* marriage certificate

'**Trauung** *f* (*-*; *-en*) marriage, wedding

'**Trauzeuge** *m*, '**Trauzeugin** *f* witness to a marriage

**Trecker** ['trɛkɐ] *m* (*-s*; *-*) MOT tractor

**Treff** [trɛf] F *m* (*-s*; *-s*) meeting place

**treffen** ['trɛfən] *v/t and v/i* (*irr, ge-*, *h*) hit (*a. fig*); hurt; meet *s.o.*; take (*measures etc*); **nicht ~** miss; **sich ~** (**mit j-m**) meet (s.o.); **gut ~** PHOT *etc*: capture well; '**Treffen** *n* (*-s*; *-*) meeting; '**treffend 1.** *adj* apt (*remark etc*) **2.** *adv*: **~ gesagt** well put; **Treffer** ['trɛfɐ] *m* (*-s*; *-*) hit (*a. fig*); SPORT goal; win; '**Treffpunkt** *m* meeting place

**Treibeis** ['traipˀais] *n* drift ice

**treiben** ['traibən] (*irr, ge-*) **1.** *v/t* (*h*) drive (*a.* TECH *and fig*); SPORT *etc*: do; push, press *s.o.*; BOT put forth; F do, be up to **2.** *v/i* (*sein*) drift (*a. fig*), float; BOT shoot (up); **sich ~ lassen** drift along (*a. fig*); **~de Kraft** driving force; '**Treiben** *n* (*-s*; *no pl*) doings, goingson; **geschäftiges ~** bustle

'**treibenlassen** *v/refl* (*irr*, **lassen**, *sep*, *no -ge-*, *h*) → **treiben**

'**Treib|haus** *n* hothouse; **~hausef,fekt** *m* greenhouse effect; **~holz** *n* driftwood; **~riemen** *m* TECH driving belt; **~sand** *m* quicksand; **~stoff** *m* fuel

**trennen** ['trɛnən] *v/t* (*ge-*, *h*) separate; sever; part; divide (*a.* LING, POL); segregate; TEL disconnect; **sich ~** separate (**von** from), part (*a. fig*); **sich ~ von** part with *s.th.*; leave *s.o.*; '**Trennung** *f* (*-*; *-en*) separation; division; segregation

'**Trennwand** *f* partition

**Treppe** ['trɛpə] *f* (*-*; *-n*) staircase, stairs

'**Treppen|absatz** *m* landing; **~geländer** *n* banisters; **~haus** *n* staircase; hall

**Tresor** [tre'zoːɐ] *m* (*-s*; *-e*) safe; strongroom, vault

**treten** ['treːtən] *v/i and v/t* (*irr*, *ge-*, *h*) kick; step (**aus** out of; **in** *acc* into; **auf** *acc* on[to]); pedal (away)

**treu** [trɔʏ] *adj* faithful (*a. fig*); loyal; devoted; **Treue** ['trɔʏə] *f* (*-*; *no pl*) fidelity, faithfulness, loyalty

'**Treuhänder(in)** ['trɔʏhɛndɐ, 'trɔʏhɛndərɪn] *m*(*f*) (*-s*; *-/-*; *-nen*) JUR trustee

'**treulos** *adj* faithless, disloyal, unfaithful (*all*: **gegen** to)

**Tribüne** [tri'byːnə] *f* (*-*; *-n*) platform; stand

**Trichter** ['trɪçtɐ] *m* (*-s*; *-*) funnel; crater

**Trick** [trɪk] *m* (*-s*; *-s*) trick; **~aufnahme** *f* trick shot; **~betrüger(in)** confidence trickster

**trieb** [triːp] *pret of* **treiben**

**Trieb** *m* (*-[e]s*; *-e* ['triːbə]) BOT (young) shoot, sprout; *fig* impulse, drive; sex drive; **~feder** *f* mainspring (*a. fig*)

**triefen** ['triːfən] *v/i* (*ge-*, *h*) drip, be dripping (**von** with)

**triftig** ['trɪftɪç] *adj* weighty; good

**Trikot** [tri'koː] *n* (*-s*; *-s*) SPORT shirt, jersey; leotard

**Triller** ['trɪlɐ] *m* (*-s*; *-*) MUS trill; '**trillern** *v/i and v/t* (*ge-*, *h*) trill; ZO warble

**trimmen** ['trɪmən] *v/refl* (*ge-*, *h*) keep fit

'**Trimmpfad** *m* fitness trail

**trinkbar** ['trɪŋkbaːɐ] *adj* drinkable

**trinken** ['trɪŋkən] *v/t and v/i* (*irr*, *ge-*, *h*) drink (**auf** *acc* to); have; **et. zu ~** a drink; **Trinker(in)** ['trɪŋkɐ (-kərɪn)] (*-s*; *-/-*; *-nen*) drinker, alcoholic

'**Trink|geld** *n* tip; **j-m** (**zwei Euro**) **~ geben** tip s.o. (two euros); **~spruch** *m* toast; **~wasser** *n* drinking water

**Trio** ['triːo] *n* (*-s*; *-s*) MUS trio (*a. fig*)

**trippeln** ['trɪpəln] *v/i* (*ge-*, *sein*) mince

**Tripper** ['trɪpɐ] *m* (*-s*; *-*) MED gonorrh(o)ea

**Tritt** [trɪt] *m* (*-[e]s*; *-e*) kick; step

'**Trittbrett** *n* step; MOT running board

'**Trittleiter** *f* stepladder

**Triumph** [tri'ʊmf] *m* (*-[e]s*; *-e*) triumph

**triumphal** [triʊm'faːl] *adj* triumphant

**triumphieren** [triʊm'fiːrən] *v/i* (*no -ge-*, *h*) triumph (**über** *acc* over)

**trocken** ['trɔkən] *adj* dry (*a. fig*)

'**Trocken...** *in cpds* dried ...; drying ...

'**Trockenhaube** *f* hairdryer

'**Trockenheit** *f* (*-*; *no pl*) dryness; AGR drought

'**trockenlegen** *v/t* (*sep*, *-ge-*, *h*) drain; change (*a baby*)
**trocknen** ['trɔknən] *v/t* (*ge-*, *h*) *and v/i* (*sein*) dry
**Trockner** ['trɔknɐ] *m* (*-s*; *-*) dryer
**Troddel** ['trɔdəl] *f* (*-*; *-n*) tassel
**Trödel** ['trøːdəl] *m* (*-s*; *no pl*) junk
**trödeln** ['trøːdəln] *v/i* (*ge-*, *h*) dawdle
**Trödler** ['trøːdlɐ] *m* (*-s*; *-*) junk dealer; dawdler
**trog** [troːk] *pret of* ***trügen***
**Trog** *m* (*-[e]s*; *Tröge* ['trøːgə]) trough
**Trommel** ['trɔməl] *f* (*-*; *-n*) MUS drum (*a.* TECH); **~fell** *n* ANAT eardrum
'**trommeln** *v/i and v/t* (*ge-*, *h*) drum
**Trommler** ['trɔmlɐ] *m* (*-s*; *-*) drummer
**Trompete** [trɔm'peːtə] *f* (*-*; *-n*) MUS trumpet; **trom'peten** *v/i and v/t* (*no -ge-*, *h*) trumpet (*a.* ZO); **Trompeter** [trɔm'peːtɐ] *m* (*-s*; *-*) trumpeter
**Tropen** ['troːpən]: ***die ~*** *pl* the tropics
'**Tropen...** *in cpds* tropical ...
**Tropf** [trɔpf] *m* (*-[e]s*; *Tröpfe* ['trœpfə]) MED drip
**Tröpfchen** ['trœpfçən] *n* (*-s*; *-*) droplet
**tröpfeln** ['trœpfəln] *v/i and v/t* (*ge-*, *h*) drip; ***es tröpfelt*** it's spitting
**tropfen** ['trɔpfən] *v/i and v/t* (*ge-*, *h*) drip, drop; '**Tropfen** *m* (*-s*; *-*) drop (*a. fig*); ***ein ~ auf den heißen Stein*** a drop in the bucket; '**tropfenweise** *adv* in drops, drop by drop
**Trophäe** [tro'fɛːə] *f* (*-*; *-n*) trophy (*a. fig*)
**tropisch** ['troːpɪʃ] *adj* tropical
**Trosse** ['trɔsə] *f* (*-*; *-n*) cable
**Trost** [troːst] *m* (*-[e]s*; *no pl*) comfort, consolation; ***ein schwacher ~*** cold comfort
**trösten** ['trøːstən] *v/t* (*ge-*, *h*) comfort, console; ***sich ~*** console o.s. (***mit*** with)
**tröstlich** ['trøːstlɪç] *adj* comforting
'**trostlos** *adj* miserable; desolate
**Trott** [trɔt] *m* (*-[e]s*; *-e*) trot; F ***der alte ~*** the old routine
**Trottel** ['trɔtəl] F *m* (*-s*; *-*) dope
**trottelig** ['trɔtəlɪç] F *adj* dopey
**trotten** ['trɔtən] *v/i* (*ge-*, *sein*) trot
**Trottinett** ['trɔtinɛt] *Swiss n* (*-s*; *-e*) scooter
**Trottoir** [trɔ'toaːɐ] *Swiss n* (*-s*; *-e*, *-s*) sidewalk, *Br* pavement
**trotz** [trɔts] *prp* (*gen*) in spite of, despite
**Trotz** *m* (*-es*; *no pl*) defiance; ***j-m zum ~*** to spite s.o.
'**trotzdem** *adv* in spite of it, nevertheless, F anyhow, anyway
**trotzen** ['trɔtsən] *v/i* (*ge-*, *h*) defy (*dat s.o. or s.th.*); sulk
**trotzig** ['trɔtsɪç] *adj* defiant; sulky
**trüb** [tryːp], **trübe** ['tryːbə] *adj* cloudy; muddy; dim; dull, *fig a.* gloomy
**Trubel** ['truːbəl] *m* (*-s*; *no pl*) (hustle and) bustle
**trüben** ['tryːbən] *v/t* (*ge-*, *h*) cloud; *fig* spoil, mar
**Trübsal** ['tryːpzaːl] *f*: ***~ blasen*** mope
'**trübselig** *adj* sad, gloomy; dreary
'**Trübsinn** *m* (*-[e]s*; *no pl*) melancholy, gloom, low spirits; '**trübsinnig** *adj* melancholy, gloomy
**trug** [truːk] *pret of* ***tragen***
**trügen** ['tryːgən] (*irr*, *ge-*, *h*) **1.** *v/t* deceive **2.** *v/i* be deceptive
**trügerisch** ['tryːgərɪʃ] *adj* deceptive
'**Trugschluss** *m* fallacy
**Truhe** ['truːə] *f* (*-*; *-n*) chest
**Trümmer** ['trʏmɐ] *pl* ruins; debris; pieces, bits
**Trumpf** [trʊmpf] *m* (*-[e]s*; *Trümpfe* ['trʏmpfə]) trump (card) (*a. fig*); ***~ sein*** be trumps; *fig* ***s-n ~ ausspielen*** play one's trump card
**Trunkenheit** ['trʊŋkənhait] *f* (*-*; *no pl*) *esp* JUR; ***~ am Steuer*** drunk (*Br* drink) driving
'**Trunksucht** *f* (*-*; *no pl*) alcoholism
**Trupp** [trʊp] *m* (*-s*; *-s*) band, party; group; **Truppe** ['trʊpə] *f* (*-*; *-n*) MIL troop, *pl* troops, forces; THEA company, troupe
'**Truppen|gattung** *f* MIL branch (of service); **~übungsplatz** *m* training area
**Truthahn** ['truːthaːn] *m* ZO turkey
**Tscheche** ['tʃɛçə] *m* (*-n*; *-n*) Czech; **Tschechien** ['tʃɛçjən] Czech Republic; '**Tschechin** *f* (*-*; *-nen*) Czech; '**tschechisch** *adj* Czech; ***Tschechische Republik*** Czech Republic
**Tube** ['tuːbə] *f* (*-*; *-n*) tube
**Tuberkulose** [tubɛrku'loːzə] *f* (*-*; *-n*) MED tuberculosis
**Tuch** [tuːx] *n* (*-[e]s*) (*pl -e*) cloth; (*pl Tücher* ['tyːçɐ]) scarf
'**Tuchfühlung** *f*: ***auf ~*** in close contact
**tüchtig** ['tʏçtɪç] *adj* (cap)able, competent; skil(l)ful; efficient; F *fig* good
'**Tüchtigkeit** *f* (*-*; *no pl*) (cap)ability, qualities; skill; efficiency

**tückisch** ['tʏkɪʃ] *adj* malicious; MED insidious; treacherous
**tüfteln** ['tʏftəln] F *v/i (ge-, h)* puzzle (***an*** *dat* over)
**Tugend** ['tu:gənt] *f (-; -en)* virtue (*a. fig*)
**Tulpe** ['tʊlpə] *f (-; -n)* BOT tulip
**Tumor** ['tu:mo:ɐ] *m (-s; -en* [tu'mo:rən]) MED tumo(u)r
**Tümpel** ['tʏmpəl] *m (-s; -)* pool
**Tumult** [tu'mʊlt] *m (-[e]s; -e)* tumult, uproar
**tun** [tu:n] *v/t and v/i (irr, ge-, h)* do; take (*a step etc*); F put; ***zu ~ haben*** have work to do; be busy; ***ich weiß*** (***nicht***), ***was ich ~ soll*** *or* ***muss*** I (don't) know what to do; ***so ~, als ob*** pretend to *inf*
**Tünche** ['tʏnçə] *f (-; -n)*, '**tünchen** *v/t (ge-, h)* whitewash
**Tunfisch** *m* → ***Thunfisch***
**Tunke** ['tʊŋkə] *f (-; -n)* sauce
**Tunnel** ['tʊnəl] *m (-s; -)* tunnel
**Tüpfelchen** ['tʏpfəlçən] *n*: ***das ~ auf dem i*** the icing on the cake
**tupfen** ['tʊpfən] *v/t (ge-, h)* dab
'**Tupfen** *m (-s; -)* dot, spot
**Tupfer** ['tʊpfɐ] *m (-s; -)* MED swab
**Tür** [ty:ɐ] *f (-; -en* ['ty:rən]) door (*a. fig*); ***die ~(en) knallen*** slam the door(s); F ***j-n vor die ~ setzen*** throw s.o. out; ***Tag der offenen ~*** open house (*Br* day)
**Turban** ['tʊrba:n] *m (-s; -e)* turban
**Turbine** [tʊr'bi:nə] *f (-; -n)* TECH turbine
**Turbolader** ['tʊrbola:dɐ] *m (-s; -)* MOT turbo(charger)
**Türke** ['tʏrkə] *m (-n; -n)* Turk; **Türkei** [tʏr'kai] *f* Turkey; **Türkin** ['tʏrkɪn] *f (-; -nen)* Turk(ish woman); '**türkisch** *adj* Turkish
'**Tür|klingel** *f* doorbell; **~klinke** *f* door handle; **~knauf** *m* doorknob
**Turm** [tʊrm] *m (-[e]s; Türme* ['tʏrmə]) tower; steeple; *chess*: castle, rook
**türmen** ['tʏrmən] *v/t (ge-, h)* pile up (*a.* ***sich ~***)
'**Turmspitze** *f* spire
'**Turmspringen** *n* SPORT platform diving
**turnen** ['tʊrnən] *v/i (ge-, h)* SPORT do gymnastics; '**Turnen** *n (-s; no pl)* SPORT gymnastics; PED physical education (*abbr* PE); **Turner** ['tʊrnɐ] *m (-s; -)*, **Turnerin** ['tʊrnərɪn] *f (-; -nen)* SPORT gymnast
'**Turnhalle** *f* gymnasium, F gym
'**Turnhemd** *n* gym shirt
'**Turnhose** *f* gym shorts
**Turnier** [tʊr'ni:ɐ] *n (-s; -e)* tournament
**Tur'niertanz** *m* ballroom dancing
'**Turn|lehrer(in)** gym(nastics) *or* PE teacher; **~schuh** *m* sneaker, *Br* trainer; **~verein** *m* gymnastics club
'**Tür|pfosten** *m* doorpost; **~rahmen** *m* doorframe; **~schild** *n* doorplate; **~sprechanlage** *f* entryphone
**Tusche** ['tʊʃə] *f (-; -n)* Indian ink; watercolo(u)r
'**Tuschkasten** *m* paintbox
**Tüte** ['ty:tə] *f (-; -n)* (paper *or* plastic) bag; ***e-e ~ ...*** a bag of ...
**TÜV** [tʏf] *abbr of* ***Technischer Überwachungs-Verein*** *Br appr* MOT (test), compulsory car inspection; (***nicht***) ***durch den ~ kommen*** pass (fail) its *or* one's MOT
**Typ** [ty:p] *m (-s; -en)* type; model; F fellow, guy; **Type** ['ty:pə] *f (-; -n)* TECH type; F character
**Typhus** ['ty:fʊs] *m (-; no pl)* MED typhoid (fever)
**typisch** ['ty:pɪʃ] *adj* typical (***für*** of)
**Tyrann** [ty'ran] *m (-en; -en)* tyrant
**Tyrannei** [tyra'nai] *f (-; -en)* tyranny
**tyrannisch** [ty'ranɪʃ] *adj* tyrannical
**tyrannisieren** [tyrani'zi:rən] *v/t (no -ge-, h)* tyrannize, bully

# U

**u. a.** *abbr of* ***unter anderem*** among other things; ***und andere*** and others
**U-Bahn** ['u:ba:n] *f* underground, subway, *in London*: tube
**übel** ['y:bəl] *adj* bad; ***mir ist ~*** I feel sick; ***et. ~ nehmen*** be offended by s.th.; ***~ riechend*** foul-smelling, foul
'**Übel** *n (-s; -)* evil
'**Übelkeit** *f (-; -en)* nausea
'**übelnehmen** *v/t (irr,* ***nehmen****, sep, -ge-, h)* → ***übel***
'**Übeltäter** *m*, '**Übeltäterin** *f esp iro* cul-

prit

**üben** ['y:bən] *v/t and v/i (ge-, h)* practice, *Br* practise; ***Klavier*** *etc* **~** practice the piano *etc*

**über** ['y:bɐ] *prp (dat or acc)* over; above *(a. fig)*; more than; across; *fig* about, of, *lecture etc a.* on; ***sprechen*** **(*nachdenken*** *etc)* **~** *(acc)* talk (think *etc*) about; **~ *Nacht bleiben*** stay overnight; **~ *München nach Rom*** to Rome via Munich

**über'all** *adv* everywhere; **~ *in ...*** *(dat) a.* throughout ..., all over ...

**über'anstrengen** *v/t and v/refl (no -ge-, h)* overstrain (o.s.)

**über'arbeiten** *v/t (no -ge-, h)* revise; ***sich*** **~** overwork o.s.

**'überaus** *adv* most, extremely

**'überbelichten** *v/t (no -ge-, h)* PHOT overexpose

**über'bieten** *v/t (irr, **bieten**, no -ge-, h) at auction*: outbid (***um*** by); *fig* beat, *a.* outdo *s.o.*

**'Überblick** *m* view; *fig* overview (***über*** *acc* of); general idea, outline

**über|'blicken** *v/t (no -ge-, h)* overlook; *fig* be able to calculate

**über'bringen** *v/t (irr, **bringen**, no -ge-, h)* deliver; **Über'bringer(in)** *(-s; -/-; -nen)* ECON bearer

**über|'brücken** *v/t (no -ge-, h)* bridge *(a. fig)*; **~dacht** [y:bɐ'daxt] *adj* roofed, covered; **~'dauern** *v/t (no -ge-, h)* outlast, survive; **~'denken** *v/t (irr, **denken**, no -ge-, h)* think *s.th.* over

**'überdimensio,nal** *adj* oversized

**'Überdosis** *f* MED overdose

**'überdrüssig** ['y:bɐdrʏsɪç] *adj*: **~ *sein*** be weary *or* sick *(gen* of)

**'über|durchschnittlich** *adj* above--average; **~eifrig** *adj* overzealous

**über'eilen** *v/t (no -ge-, h)* rush; ***nichts*** **~!** don't rush things!; **über'eilt** *adj* rash, hasty

**überei'nander** *adv* on top of each other; *talk etc* about one another; **~schlagen** *v/t (irr, **schlagen**, sep, -ge-, h)*: ***die Beine*** **~** cross one's legs

**über'einkommen** *v/i (irr, **kommen**, sep, -ge-, sein)* agree; **Über'einkommen** *n (-s; -)*, **Über'einkunft** *f (-; -künfte)* agreement

**über'einstimmen** *v/i (sep, -ge-, h)* tally, correspond (with); ***mit j-m*** **~** agree with s.o. (***in*** *dat* on); **Über'einstimmung** *f (-; -en)* agreement; correspondence; ***in*** **~ *mit*** in accordance with

**über'fahren** *v/t (irr, **fahren**, no -ge-, h)* run *s.o.* over, knock *s.o.* down

**'Überfahrt** *f* MAR crossing

**'Überfall** *m* assault (***auf*** *acc* on); hold-up (on, of); mugging (of); MIL raid (on); invasion (of); **über'fallen** *v/t (irr, **fallen**, no -ge-, h)* attack, assault; hold up; mug; MIL raid; invade

**'überfällig** *adj* overdue

**über'fliegen** *v/t (irr, **fliegen**, no -ge-, h)* fly over *or* across; *fig* glance over, skim (through)

**'überfließen** *v/i (irr, **fließen**, sep, -ge-, sein)* overflow

**'Überfluss** *m (-es; no pl)* abundance (***an*** *dat* of); affluence; ***im*** **~ *haben*** abound in; **'überflüssig** *adj* superfluous

**über|'fluten** *v/t (no -ge-, h)* flood *(a. fig)*; **~'fordern** *v/t (no -ge-, h)* overtax

**überfragt** [y:bɐ'fra:kt] *adj*: F ***da bin ich*** **~** you've got me there

**über'führen** *v/t (no -ge-, h)* transport; JUR convict (***e-r Tat*** of a crime)

**Über'führung** *f (-; -en)* transfer; JUR conviction; MOT overpass, *Br* flyover; footbridge

**über'füllt** *adj* overcrowded, packed

**über'füttern** *v/t (no -ge-, h)* overfeed

**'Übergang** *m* crossing; *fig* transition

**über'geben** *v/t (irr, **geben**, no -ge-, h)* hand over; MIL surrender; ***sich*** **~** vomit

**über'gehen**[1] *v/t (irr, **gehen**, no -ge-, h)* pass over, ignore

**'übergehen**[2] *v/i (irr, **gehen**, sep, -ge-, sein)* pass (***zu*** on to); **~ *in*** *(acc)* change *or* turn (in)to

**'übergeschnappt** F *adj* cracked

**'Übergewicht** *n* (**~ *haben*** be) overweight; *fig* predominance

**'übergewichtig** *adj* overweight

**'überglücklich** *adj* overjoyed

**'übergreifen** *v/i (irr, **greifen**, sep, -ge-, h)* **~ *auf*** *(acc)* spread to

**'Übergriff** *m* infringement (***auf*** *acc* of); (act of) violence

**'Übergröße** *f* outsize; ***in*** **~n** outsized, oversize(d)

**über'handnehmen** *v/i (irr, **nehmen**, sep, -ge-, h)* become rampant

**über'häufen** *v/t (no -ge-, h)* swamp; shower

U

**über'haupt** *adv* ... at all; anyway; ~ ***nicht*** (***nichts***) not (nothing) at all
**überheblich** [y:bɐ'he:plɪç] *adj* arrogant
**Über'heblichkeit** *f* (-; *no pl*) arrogance
**über|'hitzen** *v/t* (*no -ge-, h*) overheat (*a. fig*); **~höht** [y:bɐ'hø:t] *adj* excessive; **~'holen** *v/t* (*no -ge-, h*) pass, overtake (*a.* SPORT); TECH overhaul, service; **~'holt** *adj* outdated, antiquated; **~'hören** *v/t* (*no -ge-, h*) miss, not catch *or* get; ignore
**'überirdisch** *adj* supernatural
**über'kleben** *v/t* (*no -ge-, h*) paste up, cover
**'überkochen** *v/i* (*sep, -ge-, sein*) boil over
**über|'kommen** *v/t* (*irr,* ***kommen***, *no -ge-, h*) ***... überkam ihn*** he was seized with *or* overcome by ...; **~'laden** *v/t* (*irr,* ***laden***, *no -ge-, h*) overload (*a.* ELECTR); *fig* clutter; **~'lassen** *v/t* (*irr,* ***lassen***, *no -ge-, h*) ***j-m et. ~*** let s.o. have s.th., leave s.th. to s.o. (*a. fig*); ***j-n sich selbst ~*** leave s.o. to himself; ***j-n s-m Schicksal ~*** leave s.o. to his fate; **~'lasten** *v/t* (*no -ge-, h*) overload (*a.* ELECTR); *fig* overburden
**'überlaufen**[1] *v/i* (*irr,* ***laufen***, *sep, -ge-, sein*) run *or* flow over; MIL desert
**über'laufen**[2] *v/t* (*irr,* ***laufen***, *no -ge-, h*) ***es überlief mich heiß und kalt*** I went hot and cold
**über'laufen**[3] *adj* overcrowded
**'Überläufer** *m* MIL deserter; POL defector
**über'leben** *v/t and v/i* (*no -ge-, h*) survive (*a. fig*); live through *s.th.*
**Über'lebende** *m, f* (*-n; -n*) survivor
**'überlebensgroß** *adj* larger than life
**über'legen**[1] *v/t and v/i* (*no -ge-, h*) think about *s.th.*, think *s.th.* over; consider; ***lassen Sie mich ~*** let me think; ***ich habe es mir*** (***anders***) ***überlegt*** I've made up (changed) my mind
**über'legen**[2] *adj* superior (***j-m*** to s.o.)
**Über'legenheit** *f* (-; *no pl*) superiority
**über'legt** *adj* deliberate; prudent
**Über'legung** *f* (-; *-en*) consideration, reflection
**'überleiten** *v/i* (*sep, -ge-, h*) ~ ***zu*** lead up *or* over to
**über'liefern** *v/t* (*no -ge-, h*) hand down, pass on; **Über'lieferung** *f* (-; *-en*) tradition

**über'listen** *v/t* (*no -ge-, h*) outwit
**'Übermacht** *f* (-; *no pl*) superiority; *esp* MIL superior forces; ***in der ~ sein*** be superior in numbers; **'übermächtig** *adj* superior; *fig* overpowering
**'Übermaß** *n* (*-es; no pl*) excess (***an*** *dat* of); **'übermäßig** *adj* excessive
**'übermenschlich** *adj* superhuman
**über'mitteln** *v/t* (*no -ge-, h*) convey
**'übermorgen** *adv* the day after tomorrow
**über'müdet** *adj* overtired
**'übermütig** ['y:bɐmy:tɪç] *adj* high-spirited
**'übernächst** *adj the* next but one; **~e** ***Woche*** the week after next
**übernachten** [y:bɐ'naxtən] *v/i* (*no -ge-, h*) stay overnight (***bei j-m*** at s.o.'s [house], with s.o.), spend the night (at, with)
**Über'nachtung** *f* (-; *-en*) night; ~ ***und Frühstück*** bed and breakfast
**Übernahme** ['y:bɐna:mə] *f* (-; *-n*) taking (over); adoption
**'überna,türlich** *adj* supernatural
**über'nehmen** *v/t* (*irr,* ***nehmen***, *no -ge-, h*) take over; adopt; take (*responsibility etc*); undertake *to do*
**über'prüfen** *v/t* (*no -ge-, h*) check, examine; verify; *esp* POL screen
**Über'prüfung** *f* check, examination; verification; screening
**über|'queren** *v/t* (*no -ge-, h*) cross; **~'ragen** *v/t* (*no -ge-, h*) tower above (*a. fig*); **~'ragend** *adj* outstanding
**überraschen** [y:bɐ'raʃən] *v/t* (*no -ge-, h*) surprise; ***j-n bei et. ~*** *a.* catch s.o. doing s.th.; **Über'raschung** *f* (-; *-en*) surprise
**über'reden** *v/t* (*no -ge-, h*) persuade (***et. zu tun*** to do s.th.); ***j-n zu et. ~*** talk s.o. into (doing) s.th.; **Über'redung** *f* (-; *no pl*) persuasion
**'überregio,nal** *adj* national
**über|'reichen** *v/t* (*no -ge-, h*) present, hand *s.th.* over (*dat* to); **~'reizen** *v/t* (*no -ge-, h*) overexcite; **~'reizt** *adj* overwrought, F on edge
**'Überrest** *m* remains; *pl* relics; GASTR leftovers
**über|'rumpeln** *v/t* (*no -ge-, h*) (take *s.o.* by) surprise; **~'runden** *v/t* (*no -ge-, h*) SPORT lap
**übersät** [y:bɐ'zɛ:t] *adj*: ~ ***mit*** strewn

with *garbage*; studded with *stars*

**übersättigt** [yːbɐˈzɛtɪçt] *adj* sated, surfeited

ˈ**Überschall…** *in cpds* supersonic …

**über|ˈschatten** *v/t* (*no -ge-, h*) overshadow (*a. fig*); **~ˈschätzen** *v/t* (*no -ge-, h*) overrate, overestimate

ˈ**Überschlag** *m* AVIAT loop; SPORT somersault; ECON rough estimate

ˈ**überschlagen**[1] (*irr*, ***schlagen***, *sep, -ge-*) **1.** *v/t* (*h*) cross (*one's legs*); **2.** *v/i* (*sein*) *fig* **~ *in*** (*acc*) turn into

**überˈschlagen**[2] (*no -ge-, h*) **1.** *v/t* skip; ECON make a rough estimate of **2.** *v/refl* turn (right) over; go head over heels; *voice*: break

ˈ**überschnappen** F *v/i* (*no -ge-, sein*) crack up

**über|ˈschneiden** *v/refl* (*irr*, ***schneiden***, *no -ge-, h*) overlap (*a. fig*); intersect; **~ˈschreiben** *v/t* (*irr*, ***schreiben***, *no -ge-, h*) make *s.th.* over (*dat* to); **~ˈschreiten** *v/t* (*irr*, ***schreiten***, *no -ge-, h*) cross; *fig* go beyond; pass; break (*the speed limit etc*)

ˈ**Überschrift** *f* heading, title; headline; caption

ˈ**Überschuss** *m*, ˈ**überschüssig** [ˈyːbɐʃʏsɪç] *adj* surplus

**überˈschütten** *v/t* (*no -ge-, h*) **~ *mit*** cover with; shower with; heap *s.th.* on

ˈ**überschwänglich** [ˈyːbɐʃvɛŋlɪç] *adj* effusive

**überˈschwemmen** *v/t* (*no -ge-, h*), **Überˈschwemmung** *f* (-; *-en*) flood

ˈ**überschwenglich** → ***überschwänglich***

ˈ**Übersee**: ***in*** (***nach***) **~** oversea

**überˈsehen** *v/t* (*irr*, ***sehen***, *no -ge-, h*) overlook; ignore

**überˈsetzen**[1] *v/t* (*no -ge-, h*) translate (***in*** *acc* into)

ˈ**übersetzen**[2] (*sep, -ge-*) **1.** *v/i* (*h, sein*) cross (***über e-n Fluss*** a river); **2.** *v/t* (*h*) take over

**Übersetzer** [yːbɐˈzɛtsɐ] *m* (*-s*; -), **Überˈsetzerin** *f* (-; *-nen*) translator

**Überˈsetzung** *f* (-; *-en*) translation (***aus*** *dat* from; ***in*** *acc* into)

ˈ**Übersicht** *f* (-; *-en*) overview (***über*** *acc* of); outline, summary

ˈ**übersichtlich** *adj* clear(ly arranged)

ˈ**übersiedeln** *v/i* (*sep, -ge-, sein*) move (***nach*** to); ˈ**Übersied(e)lung** *f* move

**überˈspannen** *v/t* (*no -ge-, h*) span

**überˈspannt** *fig adj* eccentric; extravagant

**überˈspielen** *v/t* (*no -ge-, h*) record; tape; *fig* cover up

**überˈspitzt** *adj* exaggerated

**überˈspringen** *v/t* (*irr*, ***springen***, *no -ge-, h*) jump (over), *esp* SPORT *a.* clear; *fig* skip

**überˈstehen**[1] *v/t* (*irr*, ***stehen***, *no -ge-, h*) get over; survive (*a. fig*), live through

ˈ**überstehen**[2] *v/i* (*irr*, ***stehen***, *sep, -ge-, h*) jut out

**über|ˈsteigen** *fig v/t* (*irr*, ***steigen***, *no -ge-, h*) exceed; **~ˈstimmen** *v/t* (*no -ge-, h*) outvote

ˈ**über|streifen** *v/t* (*sep, -ge-, h*) slip *s.th.* on; **~strömen** *v/i* (*sep, -ge-, sein*) overflow (***vor*** *dat* with)

ˈ**Überstunden** *pl* overtime; **~ *machen*** work overtime

**über|ˈstürzen** *v/t* (*no -ge-, h*) ***et.* ~** rush things; ***sich* ~** *events*: follow in rapid succession; **~ˈstürzt** *adj* (over)hasty; rash; **~ˈteuert** *adj* overpriced; **~ˈtönen** *v/t* (*no -ge-, h*) drown (out)

**überˈtragbar** *adj* transferable; MED contagious

**überˈtragen**[1] *adj* figurative

**überˈtragen**[2] *v/t* (*irr*, ***tragen***, *no -ge-, h*) broadcast, *a.* televise; translate; MED, TECH transmit; MED transfuse (*blood*); JUR, ECON transfer

**Überˈtragung** *f* (-; *-en*) *radio*, TV broadcast; transmission; translation; MED transfusion; JUR, ECON transfer

**überˈtreffen** *v/t* (*irr*, ***treffen***, *no -ge-, h*) outstrip, outdo, surpass, beat

**überˈtreiben** *v/i and v/t* (*irr*, ***treiben***, *no -ge-, h*) exaggerate; overdo

**Überˈtreibung** *f* (-; *-en*) exaggeration

ˈ**übertreten**[1] *v/i* (*irr*, ***treten***, *sep, -ge-, sein*) **~ *zu*** go over to, REL convert to

**überˈtreten**[2] (*irr*, ***treten***, *no -ge-, h*) **1.** *v/t* break, violate **2.** *v/i* SPORT foul (a jump *or* throw); **Überˈtretung** *f* (-; *-en*) violation, JUR *a.* offen|se, *Br* -ce

ˈ**Übertritt** *m* change (***zu*** to); REL, POL conversion (to)

**übervölkert** [yːbɐˈfœlkɐt] *adj* overpopulated

**überˈwachen** *v/t* (*no -ge-, h*) supervise, oversee; control; observe

**Überˈwachung** *f* (-; *-en*) supervision,

control; observance; surveillance

**überwältigen** [yːbɐˈvɛltɪɡən] *v/t* (*no -ge-, h*) overwhelm, overpower, *fig a.* overcome; **~d** *adj* overwhelming, overpowering

**überˈweisen** *v/t* (*irr*, ***weisen***, *no -ge-, h*) ECON transfer (***an j-n*** to s.o.'s account); remit; MED refer (***an*** *acc* to)

**Überˈweisung** *f* (-; *-en*) ECON transfer; remittance; MED referral

**ˈüberwerfen**[1] *v/t* (*irr*, ***werfen***, *sep, -ge-, h*) slip *s.th.* on

**überˈwerfen**[2] *v/refl* (*irr*, ***werfen***, *no -ge-, h*) ***sich ~*** (***mit j-m***) fall out with each other (with s.o.)

**überˈwiegen** *v/i* (*irr*, ***wiegen***, *no -ge-, h*) predominate; **~d** *adj* predominant; vast (*majority*)

**über|ˈwinden** *v/t* (*irr*, ***winden***, *no -ge-, h*) overcome (*a. fig*); defeat; ***sich ~ zu*** *inf* bring o.s. to *inf*; **~wintern** [yːbɐˈvɪntɐn] *v/i* (*no -ge-, h*) spend the winter (***in*** *dat* in); **~ˈwuchern** *v/t* (*no -ge-, h*) overgrow

**ˈÜberzahl** *f* (-; *no pl*) majority; ***in der ~ sein*** outnumber *s.o.*

**überˈzeugen** *v/t* (*no -ge-, h*) convince (***von*** of), persuade; ***sich ~, dass*** make sure that; ***sich selbst ~*** (go and) see for o.s.; **überzeugt** [yːbɐˈtsɔʏkt] *adj* convinced; ***~ sein*** *a.* be *or* feel (quite) sure; **Überˈzeugung** *f* (-; *-en*) conviction

**ˈüberziehen**[1] *v/t* (*irr*, ***ziehen***, *sep, -ge-, h*) put *s.th.* on

**überˈziehen**[2] *v/t* (*irr*, ***ziehen***, *no, -ge-, h*) TECH *etc* cover; ECON overdraw

**Überˈziehungskreˌdit** *m* ECON overdraft (facility)

**ˈÜberzug** *m* cover; coat(ing)

**üblich** [ˈyːplɪç] *adj* usual, normal; ***es ist ~*** it's the custom; ***wie ~*** as usual

**ˈU-Boot** *n* submarine

**übrig** [ˈyːbrɪç] *adj* remaining; ***die Übrigen*** *pl* the others, the rest; ***~ sein*** (***haben***) be (have) left; ***~ bleiben*** be left, remain; ***es bleibt mir nichts anderes ~*** (***als zu*** *inf*) there is nothing else I can do (but *inf*); ***~ lassen*** leave

**übrigens** [ˈyːbrɪɡəns] *adv* by the way

**ˈübriglassen** *v/i* (*irr*, ***lassen***, *sep, -ge-, sein*) (*a. fig*) → ***übrig***

**Übung** [ˈyːbʊŋ] *f* (-; *-en*) exercise; practice; ***in*** (***aus der***) ***~*** in (out of) practice

**Ufer** [ˈuːfɐ] *n* (*-s*; -) shore; bank; ***ans ~*** ashore

**Uhr** [uːɐ] *f* (-; *-en* [ˈuːrən]) clock; watch; ***um vier ~*** at four o'clock

**ˈUhr|armband** *n* watchstrap; **~macher** *m* (*-s*; -) watchmaker; **~werk** *n* clockwork; **~zeiger** *m* hand; **~zeigersinn** *m*: ***im ~*** clockwise; ***entgegen dem ~*** counterclockwise, *Br* anticlockwise

**Uhu** [ˈuːhu] *m* (*-s*; *-s*) ZO eagle owl

**UKW** [uːkaːˈveː] *abbr of* ***Ultrakurzwelle*** VHF, very high frequency

**Ulk** [ʊlk] *m* (*-s*; *-e*) joke; hoax

**ulkig** [ˈʊlkɪç] *adj* funny

**Ulme** [ˈʊlmə] *f* (-; *-n*) BOT elm

**Ultimatum** [ʊltiˈmaːtʊm] *n* (*-s*; *-ten*) ultimatum; ***j-m ein ~ stellen*** deliver an ultimatum to s.o.

**um** [ʊm] *prp* (*acc*) *and cj* (a)round; at; about, around; ***~ Geld*** for money; ***~ e-e Stunde*** (***10 cm***) by an hour (10 cm); ***~ … willen*** for the sake of …; ***~ zu*** *inf* (in order) to *inf*; ***~ sein*** F be over; ***die Zeit ist ~*** time's up; → ***umso***

**umarmen** [ʊmˈʔarmən] *v/t* (*no -ge-, h*) (*a.* ***sich ~***) embrace, hug

**Umˈarmung** *f* (-; *-en*) embrace, hug

**ˈUmbau** *m* (-[*e*]*s*; *-e, -ten*) rebuilding, reconstruction; **ˈumbauen** *v/t* (*sep, -ge-, h*) rebuild, reconstruct

**ˈum|binden** *v/t* (*irr*, ***binden***, *sep, -ge-, h*) put *s.th.* on; **~blättern** *v/i* (*sep, -ge-, h*) turn (over) the page; **~bringen** *v/t* (*irr*, ***bringen***, *sep, -ge-, h*) kill; ***sich ~*** kill o.s.; **~buchen** *v/t* (*sep, -ge-, h*) change; ECON transfer (***auf*** *acc* to); **~denken** *v/i* (*irr*, ***denken***, *sep, -ge-, h*) change one's way of thinking; **~dispoˌnieren** *v/i* (*sep, no -ge-, h*) change one's plans; **~drehen** *v/t* (*sep, -ge-, h*) turn (round); ***sich ~*** turn round

**Umˈdrehung** *f* (-; *-en*) turn; PHYS, TECH rotation, revolution

**umeiˈnander** *adv care etc* about *or* for each other

**ˈumfahren**[1] *v/t* (*irr*, ***fahren***, *sep, -ge-, h*) run down

**umˈfahren**[2] *v/t* (*irr*, ***fahren***, *no -ge-, h*) drive (MAR sail) round

**ˈumfallen** *v/i* (*irr*, ***fallen***, *sep, -ge-, sein*) fall down *or* over; collapse; ***tot ~*** drop dead

**ˈUmfang** *m* circumference; size; extent; ***in großem ~*** on a large scale

**ˈumfangreich** *adj* extensive; volumi-

nous
**um'fassen** *fig v/t* (*no -ge-*, *h*) cover; include; **~d** *adj* comprehensive; complete
**'umformen** *v/t* (*sep*, *-ge-*, *h*) turn, change; ELECTR, LING, MATH *a.* transform, convert (*all*: ***in*** *acc* [in]to)
**'Umformer** *m* (*-s*; *-*) ELECTR converter
**'Umfrage** *f* opinion poll
**'Umgang** *m* (*-[e]s*; *no pl*) company; ***~ haben mit*** associate with; ***beim ~ mit*** when dealing with
**'umgänglich** ['ʊmgɛŋlɪç] *adj* sociable
**'Umgangs|formen** *pl* manners; **~sprache** *f* colloquial speech; ***die englische ~*** colloquial English
**um'geben** *v/t* (*irr*, ***geben***, *no -ge-*, *h*) surround (***mit*** with); **Um'gebung** *f* (*-*; *-en*) surroundings; environment
**'umgehen**[1] *v/i* (*irr*, ***gehen***, *sep*, *-ge-*, *sein*) ***~ mit*** deal with, handle; ***~ können mit*** have a way with, be good with
**um'gehen**[2] *v/t* (*irr*, ***gehen***, *no -ge-*, *h*) avoid; bypass
**'umgehend** *adv* immediately
**Um'gehungsstraße** *f* bypass; beltway, *Br* ring road
**umgekehrt** ['ʊmgəkeːɐt] **1.** *adj* reverse; opposite; (***genau***) **~** (just) the other way round **2.** *adv* the other way round; ***und ~*** and vice versa
**'umgraben** *v/t* (*irr*, ***graben***, *sep*, *-ge-*, *h*) dig (up), break up
**'Umhang** *m* cape; **'umhängen** *v/t* (*sep*, *-ge-*, *h*) put around *or* over s.o.'s shoulders *etc*; rehang
**'umhauen** *v/t* (*irr*, ***hauen***, *sep*, *-ge-*, *h*) fell, cut down; F knock *s.o.* out
**um'her** *adv* (a)round, about
**um'herstreifen** *v/i* (*sep*, *-ge-*, *sein*) roam *or* wander around
**'umkehren** (*sep*, *-ge-*) **1.** *v/i* (*sein*) turn back **2.** *v/t* (*h*) reverse
**'Umkehrung** *f* (*-*; *-en*) reversal (*a. fig*)
**'umkippen** (*sep*, *-ge-*) **1.** *v/t* (*h*) tip over, upset **2.** *v/i* (*sein*) fall down *or* over, overturn
**um'klammern** *v/t* (*no -ge-*, *h*), **Um'klammerung** *f* (*-*; *-en*) clasp, clutch, clench
**'Umkleide|ka,bine** *f* changing cubicle; **~raum** *m esp* SPORT changing *or* locker room; THEA dressing room
**'umkommen** *v/i* (*irr*, ***kommen***, *sep*, *-ge-*, *sein*) be killed (***bei*** in), die (in); F ***~ vor*** (*dat*) be dying with
**'Umkreis** *m*: ***im ~ von*** within a radius of;
**um'kreisen** *v/t* (*no -ge-*, *h*) circle; ASTR revolve around; *satellite etc*: orbit
**'umkrempeln** *v/t* (*sep*, *-ge-*, *h*) roll up
**'Umlauf** *m* circulation; PHYS, TECH rotation; ECON circular; ***im*** (***in***) ***~ sein*** (***bringen***) be in (put into) circulation, circulate; **~bahn** *f* ASTR orbit
**'um|laufen** *v/i* (*irr*, ***laufen***, *sep*, *-ge-*, *sein*) circulate; **~legen** *v/t* (*sep*, *-ge-*, *h*) put on; move; share (*expenses etc*); TECH pull; F do *s.o.* in, bump *s.o.* off
**'umleiten** *v/t* (*sep*, *-ge-*, *h*) divert; **'Umleitung** *f* (*-*; *-en*) detour, *Br* diversion
**'umliegend** *adj* surrounding
**'umpacken** *v/t* (*sep*, *-ge-*, *h*) repack
**'umpflanzen** *v/t* (*sep*, *-ge-*, *h*) repot
**umranden** [ʊm'randən] *v/t* (*no -ge-*, *h*), **Um'randung** *f* (*-*; *-en*) edge, border
**'umräumen** *v/t* (*sep*, *-ge-*, *h*) rearrange
**'umrechnen** *v/t* (*sep*, *-ge-*, *h*) convert (***in*** *acc* into); **'Umrechnung** *f* (*-*; *-en*) conversion; **'Umrechnungskurs** *m* exchange rate
**'umreißen** *v/t* (*irr*, ***reißen***, *sep*, *-ge-*, *h*) knock *s.o.* down
**um'ringen** *v/t* (*no -ge-*, *h*) surround
**'Umriss** *m* outline (*a. fig*), contour
**'um|rühren** *v/t* (*sep*, *-ge-*, *h*) stir; **~rüsten** *v/t* (*sep*, *-ge-*, *h*) TECH convert (***auf*** *acc* to); **~satteln** F *v/i* (*sep*, *-ge-*, *h*) ***~ von ... auf*** (*acc*) ... switch from ... to ...
**'Umsatz** *m* ECON sales
**'umschalten** *v/t and v/i* (*sep*, *-ge-*, *h*) switch (over) (***auf*** *acc* to) (*a. fig*)
**'Umschlag** *m* envelope; cover, wrapper; jacket; cuff, *Br* turn-up; MED compress; ECON handling; **'umschlagen** (*irr*, ***schlagen***, *sep*, *-ge-*) **1.** *v/t* (*h*) cut down, fell; turn up; turn down; ECON handle **2.** *v/i* (*sein*) turn over; *fig* change (suddenly)
**'Umschlagplatz** *m* trading center (*Br* centre)
**'umschnallen** *v/t* (*sep*, *-ge-*, *h*) buckle on
**'umschreiben**[1] *v/t* (*irr*, ***schreiben***, *sep*, *-ge-*, *h*) rewrite
**um'schreiben**[2] *v/t* (*irr*, ***schreiben***, *no -ge-*, *h*) paraphrase
**Um'schreibung** *f* (*-*; *-en*) paraphrase
**'Umschrift** *f* transcription

'**umschulen** *v/t* (*sep*, *-ge-*, *h*) retrain; transfer to another school
**umschwärmt** [ʊm'ʃvɛrmt] *adj* idolized
'**Umschwung** *m* (drastic) change, *esp* POL *a.* swing
**um'segeln** *v/t* (*no -ge-*, *h*) sail round; circumnavigate
'**um|sehen** *v/refl* (*irr*, ***sehen***, *sep*, *-ge-*, *h*) look around (***in e-m Laden*** a shop; ***nach*** for); look back (***nach*** at); ***sich ~ nach*** be looking for; **~setzen** *v/t* (*sep*, *-ge-*, *h*) move (*a.* PED); ECON sell; ***~ in*** (*acc*) convert (in)to; ***in die Tat ~*** put into action; ***sich ~*** change places
'**umsiedeln** *v/i* (*sep*, *-ge-*, *sein*) *and v/t* (*h*) resettle; → ***umziehen***
'**Umsied(e)lung** *f* (-; *-en*) resettlement
'**Umsiedler** *m* (*-s*; -) resettler
'**umso 1.** ***je später*** *etc*, ***~ schlechter*** *etc* the later *etc* the worse *etc* **2.** ***~ besser*** so much the better
**um'sonst** *adv* free (of charge), for nothing; F for free; *fig* in vain
**um'spannen** *v/t* (*no -ge-*, *h*) span (*a. fig*)
'**umspringen** *v/i* (*irr*, ***springen***, *sep*, *-ge-*, *sein*) shift, change (suddenly) (*a. fig*); ***~ mit*** treat (badly)
'**Umstand** *m* circumstance; fact; detail; ***unter diesen*** (***keinen***) ***Umständen*** under the (no) circumstances; ***unter Umständen*** possibly; ***keine Umstände machen*** not cause *s.o.* any trouble; not go to any trouble; no put o.s. out; ***in anderen Umständen sein*** be expecting
**umständlich** ['ʊmʃtɛntlɪç] *adj* awkward; complicated; long-winded; ***das ist*** (***mir***) ***viel zu ~*** that's far too much trouble (for me)
'**Umstands|kleid** *n* maternity dress; **~wort** *n* (-[*e*]*s*; *-wörter*) LING adverb
'**Umstehende**: ***die ~n*** *pl* the bystanders
'**umsteigen** *v/i* (*irr*, ***steigen***, *sep*, *-ge-*, *sein*) change (***nach*** for), RAIL *a.* change trains (for)
'**umstellen** *v/t* (*sep*, *-ge-*, *h*) change (***auf*** *acc* to), make a change *or* changes in, *esp* TECH *a.* switch (over) (to), convert (to); adjust (to); rearrange (*a. furniture*), reorganize; reset (*watch*); ***sich ~ auf*** (*acc*) change *or* switch (over) to; adjust (o.s.) to, get used to
'**Umstellung** *f* (-; *-en*) change; switch, conversion; adjustment; rearrangement, reorganization
'**umstimmen** *v/t* (*sep*, *-ge-*, *h*) ***j-n ~*** change s.o.'s mind
'**umstoßen** *v/t* (*irr*, ***stoßen***, *sep*, *-ge-*, *h*) knock over, upset (*a. fig*)
**umstritten** [ʊm'ʃtrɪtən] *adj* controversial
'**Umsturz** *m* overthrow; '**umstürzen** *v/i* (*sep*, *-ge-*, *sein*) overturn, fall over
'**Umtausch** *m*, '**umtauschen** *v/t* (*sep*, *-ge-*, *h*) exchange (***gegen*** for)
'**umwälzend** *adj* revolutionary
'**Umwälzung** *f* (-; *-en*) radical change
'**umwandeln** *v/t* (*sep*, *-ge-*, *h*) turn (***in*** *acc* into), transform (into), *esp* CHEM, ELECTR, PHYS *a.* convert ([in]to)
'**Umwandlung** *f* (-; *-en*) transformation, conversion
'**Umweg** *m* roundabout route *or* way (*a. fig*), *esp* MOT *a.* detour; ***ein ~ von 10 Minuten*** ten minutes out of the way; *fig* ***auf ~en*** in a roundabout way
'**Umwelt** *f* (-; *no pl*) environment
'**Umwelt...** *in cpds mst* environmental ...; **~forschung** *f* ecology
'**umwelt|freundlich** *adj* environment friendly, non-polluting; **~schädlich** *adj* harmful, noxious, polluting
'**Umwelt|schutz** *m* conservation, environmental protection, pollution control; **~schützer** *m* environmentalist, conservationist; **~schutzpa,pier** *n* recycled paper; **~sünder** *m* (environmental) polluter; **~verschmutzer** *m* (*-s*; -) polluter; **~verschmutzung** *f* (environmental) pollution; **~zerstörung** *f* ecocide
'**umziehen** (*irr*, ***ziehen***, *sep -ge-*) **1.** *v/i* (*sein*) move (***nach*** to); **2.** *v/refl* (*h*) change (one's clothes)
**umzingeln** [ʊm'tsɪŋəln] *v/t* (*no -ge-*, *h*) surround, encircle
'**Umzug** *m* move (***nach*** to), removal (to); parade
**unabhängig** ['ʊnaphɛŋɪç] *adj* independent (***von*** of); ***~ davon, ob*** (***was***) regardless of whether (what);
'**Unabhängigkeit** *f* (-; *no pl*) independence (***von*** from)
'**unabsichtlich** *adj* unintentional; ***et. ~ tun*** do s.th. by mistake
**unab'wendbar** *adj* inevitable
'**unachtsam** *adj* careless, negligent
'**Unachtsamkeit** *f* (-; *no pl*) careless-

ness, negligence
**unan'fechtbar** *adj* incontestable
**'un|angebracht** *adj* inappropriate; **~ sein** be out of place; **~angemessen** *adj* unreasonable; inadequate; **~angenehm** *adj* unpleasant; embarrassing
**unan'nehmbar** *adj* unacceptable
**Unannehmlichkeiten** ['ʊnˀanneːmlɪkkaitən] *pl* trouble, difficulties
**'unansehnlich** *adj* unsightly
**'unanständig** *adj* indecent, obscene
**unan'tastbar** *adj* inviolable
**'unappetitlich** *adj* unappetizing
**Unart** ['ʊnˀart] *f* (-; *-en*) bad habit
**'unartig** *adj* naughty, bad
**'unaufdringlich** *adj* unobtrusive
**'unauffällig** *adj* inconspicuous, unobtrusive
**unauf'findbar** *adj* not to be found, untraceable
**'unaufgefordert** *adv* without being asked, of one's own accord
**unaufhörlich** [ʊnˀauf'høːɐlɪç] *adj* continuous
**'unaufmerksam** *adj* inattentive
**'Unaufmerksamkeit** *f* (-; *no pl*) inattention, inattentiveness
**'unaufrichtig** *adj* insincere
**unaus|löschlich** [ʊnˀaus'lœʃlɪç] *adj* indelible; **~stehlich** [ʊnˀaus'ʃteːlɪç] *adj* unbearable
**'unbarmherzig** *adj* merciless
**'un|beabsichtigt** *adj* unintentional; **~beachtet** *adj* unnoticed; **~beaufsichtigt** *adj* unattended; **~bebaut** *adj* undeveloped; **~bedacht** ['ʊnbədaxt] *adj* thoughtless; **~bedenklich 1.** *adj* safe **2.** *adv* without hesitation; **~bedeutend** *adj* insignificant; minor; **~bedingt 1.** *adj* unconditional, absolute **2.** *adv* by all means, absolutely; *need etc* badly; **~befahrbar** *adj* impassable; **~befangen** *adj* unprejudiced, unbias(s)ed; unembarrassed; **~befriedigend** *adj* unsatisfactory; **~befriedigt** *adj* dissatisfied; **~begabt** *adj* untalented; **~begreiflich** *adj* inconceivable, incomprehensible; **~begrenzt** *adj* unlimited, boundless; **~begründet** *adj* unfounded
**'Unbehagen** *n* (*-s*; *no pl*) uneasiness, discomfort; **'unbehaglich** *adj* uneasy, uncomfortable
**unbehelligt** [ʊnbə'hɛlɪçt] *adj* unmolested
**'un|beherrscht** *adj* uncontrolled, lacking self-control; **~beholfen** ['ʊnbəhɔlfən] *adj* clumsy, awkward; **~beirrt** *adj* unwavering; **~bekannt** *adj* unknown
**'Unbekannte** *f* (-; *-n*) MATH unknown quantity
**'un|bekümmert** *adj* light-hearted, cheerful; **~belehrbar** *adj*: ***er ist ~*** he'll never learn; **~beliebt** *adj* unpopular; ***er ist überall ~*** nobody likes him; **~bemannt** *adj* unmanned; **~bemerkt** *adj* unnoticed; **~benutzt** *adj* unused; **~bequem** *adj* uncomfortable; inconvenient; **~berechenbar** *adj* unpredictable; **~berechtigt** *adj* unauthorized; unjustified; **~beschädigt** *adj* undamaged; **~bescheiden** *adj* immodest
**un|be'schränkt** *adj* unlimited; absolute (*power*); **~beschreiblich** ['ʊnbə'ʃraiplɪç] *adj* indescribable; **~be'sehen** *adv* unseen; **~besiegbar** ['ʊnbə'ziːkbaːɐ] *adj* invincible
**'un|besonnen** *adj* thoughtless, imprudent; rash; **~be'spielbar** *adj* SPORT unplayable; **~beständig** *adj* unstable; METEOR changeable, unsettled; **~bestätigt** *adj* unconfirmed
**unbe'stechlich** *adj* incorruptible
**'unbestimmt** *adj* indefinite (*a.* LING); uncertain; vague
**un|be'streitbar** *adj* indisputable; **~bestritten** [ʊnbə'ʃtrɪtən] *adj* undisputed
**'un|beteiligt** *adj* not involved; indifferent; **~betont** *adj* unstressed
**unbeugsam** [ʊn'bɔʏkzaːm] *adj* inflexible
**'un|bewacht** *adj* unwatched, unguarded (*a. fig*); **~bewaffnet** *adj* unarmed; **~beweglich** *adj* immovable; motionless
**unbe'wohnbar** *adj* uninhabitable
**'unbewohnt** *adj* uninhabited; unoccupied, vacant
**'unbewusst** *adj* unconscious
**unbe'zahlbar** *fig adj* invaluable, priceless; **'unbezahlt** *adj* unpaid
**'unblutig 1.** *adj* bloodless **2.** *adv* without bloodshed
**'unbrauchbar** *adj* useless
**und** [ʊnt] *cj* and; F ***na ~?*** so what?
**'undankbar** *adj* ungrateful (***gegen*** to); thankless; **'Undankbarkeit** *f* (-; *no pl*) ingratitude, ungratefulness
**undefi'nierbar** *adj* undefinable
**un'denkbar** *adj* unthinkable

'**undeutlich** *adj* indistinct; inarticulate; *fig* vague
'**undicht** *adj* leaky
'**unduldsam** *adj* intolerant; '**Unduldsamkeit** *f* (-; *no pl*) intolerance
**undurch|'dringlich** *adj* impenetrable; ~'**führbar** *adj* impracticable
'**undurch|lässig** *adj* impervious, impermeable; ~**sichtig** *adj* opaque; *fig* mysterious
'**uneben** *adj* uneven; '**Unebenheit** *f* (-; *no pl*) unevenness; (-; *-en*) bump
'**unecht** *adj* false; artificial; imitation ...; F *contp* fake, phon(e)y
'**unehelich** *adj* illegitimate
'**unehrenhaft** *adj* dishono(u)rable
'**unehrlich** *adj* dishonest
'**uneigennützig** *adj* unselfish
'**uneinig** *adj*: (***sich***) ~ ***sein*** disagree (***über*** *acc* on); '**Uneinigkeit** *f* (-; *no pl*) disagreement; dissension
**unein'nehmbar** *adj* impregnable
'**un|empfänglich** *adj* insusceptible (***für*** to); ~**empfindlich** *adj* insensitive (***gegen*** to)
**un'endlich** *adj* infinite; endless, never-ending; **Un'endlichkeit** *f* (-; *no pl*) infinity (*a. fig*)
**unent|behrlich** [ʊnʔɛnt'beːɐlɪç] *adj* indispensable; ~**geltlich** [ʊnʔɛnt'gɛltlɪç] *adj and adv* free (of charge)
'**unentschieden** *adj* undecided; ~ ***enden*** SPORT end in a draw *or* tie; ***es steht*** ~ the score is even; '**Unentschieden** *n* (*-s*; -) SPORT draw, tie
'**unentschlossen** *adj* irresolute
**unent'schuldbar** *adj* inexcusable
**unentwegt** [ʊnʔɛnt'veːkt] *adv* untiringly; continuously
'**un|erfahren** *adj* inexperienced; ~**erfreulich** *adj* unpleasant; ~**erfüllt** *adj* unfulfilled; ~**ergiebig** *adj* unproductive; ~**erheblich** *adj* irrelevant (***für*** to); insignificant
**unerhört** ['ʊnʔɛːɐ'høːɐt] *adj* outrageous
'**un|erkannt** *adj* unrecognized; ~**erklärlich** *adj* inexplicable; ~**erlässlich** *adj* essential, indispensable; ~**erlaubt** *adj* unallowed; unauthorized; ~**erledigt** *adj* unsettled (*a.* ECON)
**uner'messlich** *adj* immeasurable
**unermüdlich** [ʊnʔɛɐ'myːtlɪç] *adj* indefatigable; untiring
**uner'reichbar** *adj* inaccessible; *esp fig* unattainable; **uner'reicht** *adj* unequal(l)ed
**unersättlich** [ʊnʔɛɐ'zɛtlɪç] *adj* insatiable
'**unerschlossen** *adj* undeveloped
**uner|schöpflich** [ʊnʔɛɐ'ʃœpflɪç] *adj* inexhaustible; ~**schütterlich** [ʊnʔɛɐ'ʃʏtɐlɪç] *adj* imperturbable; ~**schwinglich** [ʊnʔɛɐ'ʃvɪŋlɪç] *adj* exorbitant; ***für j-n*** ~ ***sein*** be beyond s.o.'s means; ~**setzlich** [ʊnʔɛɐ'zɛtslɪç] *adj* irreplaceable; ~**träglich** [ʊnʔɛɐ'trɛːklɪç] *adj* unbearable
'**unerwartet** *adj* unexpected
'**unerwünscht** *adj* unwanted
'**unfähig** *adj* incompetent; incapable (***zu tun*** of doing), unable (to *inf*)
'**Unfähigkeit** *f* (-; *no pl*) incompetence; incapacity, inability
'**Unfall** *m* accident; crash
'**Unfallstelle** *f* scene of the accident
**un'fehlbar** *adj* infallible (*a.* REL); unfailing
**unförmig** ['ʊnfœrmɪç] *adj* shapeless; misshapen; monstrous
'**unfrankiert** *adj* unstamped
'**unfrei** *adj* not free; *post* unpaid
'**unfreiwillig** *adj* involuntary; unconscious (*humor*)
'**unfreundlich** *adj* unfriendly (***zu*** to), unkind (to); *fig* cheerless
'**Unfrieden** *m* (*-s*; *no pl*) discord; ~ ***stiften*** make mischief
'**unfruchtbar** *adj* infertile; '**Unfruchtbarkeit** *f* (-; *no pl*) infertility
**Unfug** ['ʊnfuːk] *m* (-[*e*]*s*; *no pl*) nonsense; ~ ***treiben*** be up to mischief, fool around
**Ungar** ['ʊŋgar] *m* (*-n*; *-n*), '**Ungarin** *f* (-; *-nen*), '**ungarisch** *adj* Hungarian; '**Ungarn** Hungary
'**ungastlich** *adj* inhospitable
'**un|geachtet** *prp* (*gen*) regardless of; despite; ~**geahnt** *adj* unthought-of; ~**gebeten** *adj* uninvited, unasked; ~**gebildet** *adj* uneducated; ~**geboren** *adj* unborn; ~**gebräuchlich** *adj* uncommon, unusual; ~**gebührlich** ['ʊngəbyːɐlɪç] *adj* unseemly; ~**gebunden** *fig adj* free, independent; ***frei und*** ~ footloose and fancy-free; ~**gedeckt** *adj* ECON uncovered; SPORT unmarked

U

'**Ungeduld** *f* (-; *no pl*) impatience
'**ungeduldig** *adj* impatient
'**ungeeignet** *adj* unfit; unqualified; inappropriate
**ungefähr** ['ʊngəfɛːɐ] **1.** *adj* approximate; rough **2.** *adv* approximately, roughly, about, around, … or so; ***so ~*** something like that
'**ungefährlich** *adj* harmless; safe
'**ungeheuer** *adj* enormous (*a. fig*), huge, vast
'**Ungeheuer** *n* (*-s*; *-*) monster (*a. fig*)
**unge'heuerlich** *adj* monstrous
'**ungehindert** *adj and adv* unhindered
'**ungehobelt** *fig adj* uncouth, rough
'**ungehörig** *adj* improper, unseemly
'**ungehorsam** *adj* disobedient
**Ungehorsam** *m* (*-s*; *no pl*) disobedience
'**un|gekocht** *adj* uncooked; **~gekünstelt** *adj* unaffected; **~gekürzt** *adj* unabridged; **~gelegen** *adj* inconvenient; ***j-m ~ kommen*** be inconvenient for s.o.
**ungelenk** ['ʊngəlɛŋk] *adj* awkward, clumsy
'**ungelernt** *adj* unskilled
'**ungemütlich** *adj* uncomfortable; F ***~ werden*** get nasty
'**ungenau** *adj* inaccurate; *fig* vague; '**Ungenauigkeit** *f* (-; *-en*) inaccuracy
**ungeniert** ['ʊnʒeniːɐt] *adj* uninhibited
'**un|genießbar** *adj* uneatable; undrinkable; F unbearable; **~genügend** *adj* insufficient; PED poor, unsatisfactory; *grade*: *a.* F; **~gepflegt** *adj* neglected; untidy, unkempt; **~gerade** *adj* uneven; odd; **~gerecht** *adj* unfair, unjust
'**Ungerechtigkeit** *f* (-; *no pl*) injustice, unfairness
'**ungern** *adv* unwillingly; ***et. ~ tun*** hate *or* not like to do s.th.
'**un|geschehen** *adj*: ***~ machen*** undo; **~geschickt** *adj* awkward, clumsy; **~geschliffen** *adj* uncut (*diamond etc*); unpolished (*a. fig*); **~geschminkt** *adj* without make-up; *fig* unvarnished, plain (*truth*); **~gesetzlich** *adj* illegal, unlawful; **~gestört** *adj* undisturbed; **~gestraft** *adj*: ***~ davonkommen*** get off unpunished (F scot-free); **~gesund** *adj* unhealthy (*a. fig*); **~geteilt** *adj* undivided (*a. fig*)
**Ungetüm** ['ʊngətyːm] *n* (*-s*; *-e*) monster, *fig a.* monstrosity
'**ungewiss** *adj* uncertain; ***j-n im Ungewissen lassen*** keep s.o. in the dark (***über*** *acc* about); '**Ungewissheit** *f* (-; *no pl*) uncertainty
'**ungewöhnlich** *adj* unusual
'**ungewohnt** *adj* strange, unfamiliar;
**Ungeziefer** ['ʊngətsiːfɐ] *n* (*-s*; *no pl*) vermin
'**ungezogen** *adj* naughty, bad; spoilt
'**ungezwungen** *adj* relaxed, informal; easygoing
'**ungläubig** *adj* incredulous, unbelieving (*a.* REL)
**unglaublich** [ʊn'glauplɪç] *adj* incredible, unbelievable
'**unglaubwürdig** *adj* implausible; unreliable (*witness etc*)
'**ungleich** *adj* unequal, different; unlike; **~mäßig** *adj* uneven; irregular
'**Unglück** *n* (-[*e*]*s*; *-e*) (*no pl*) bad luck, misfortune; misery; accident; disaster; 'unglücklich *adj* unhappy, miserable; unfortunate; '**unglücklicher'weise** *adv* unfortunately
'**ungültig** *adj* invalid; ***für ~ erklären*** JUR invalidate
'**Ungunst** *f*: ***zu ~en → zuungunsten***; '**ungünstig** *adj* unfavo(u)rable; disadvantageous
'**ungut** *adj*: ***~es Gefühl*** misgivings (***bei et.*** about s.th.); ***nichts für ~!*** no offense (*Br* offence) meant!
'**unhaltbar** *adj* untenable; intolerable; SPORT unstoppable
'**unhandlich** *adj* unwieldy
'**unhar͵monisch** *adj* MUS discordant
'**Unheil** *n* (*-s*; *no pl*) mischief; evil; disaster; '**unheilbar** *adj* MED incurable
'**unheilvoll** *adj* disastrous; sinister
'**unheimlich** *adj* creepy, spooky, eerie; F tremendous; F ***~ gut*** terrific, fantastic
'**unhöflich** *adj* impolite; rude
'**Unhöflichkeit** *f* (-; *no pl*) impoliteness; rudeness
**un'hörbar** *adj* inaudible
'**unhygienisch** *adj* insanitary
**Uniform** [uni'fɔrm] *f* (-; *-en*) uniform
'**uninteressant** *adj* uninteresting
**uninteressiert** ['ʊnˀɪntərɛsiːɐt] *adj* uninterested (***an*** *dat* in)
**Union** [u'njoːn] *f* (-; *-en*) union
**Universität** [univɛrzi'tɛːt] *f* (-; *-en*) university

**Universum** [uni'vɛrzʊm] *n* (*-s*; *no pl*) universe
**Unke** ['ʊŋkə] *f* (-; *-n*) zo toad
'**unkenntlich** *adj* unrecognizable
'**Unkenntnis** *f* (-; *no pl*) ignorance
'**unklar** *adj* unclear; uncertain; confused, muddled; ***im Unklaren sein*** (***lassen***) be (leave *s.o.*) in the dark
'**unklug** *adj* imprudent, unwise
'**Unkosten** *pl* expenses, costs
'**Unkraut** *n* (-[*e*]*s*; *no pl*) weed(s); ***~ jäten*** weed (the garden)
**unkündbar** ['ʊnkʏntbaːɐ] *adj* permanent (*post*)
'**unlängst** *adv* lately, recently
'**unleserlich** *adj* illegible
'**unlogisch** *adj* illogical
**un'lösbar** *adj* insoluble
'**unmännlich** *adj* unmanly, effeminate
'**unmäßig** *adj* excessive
'**Unmenge** *f* vast quantity *or* number(s) (***von*** of), F loads (of), tons (of)
'**Unmensch** *m* monster, brute
'**unmenschlich** *adj* inhuman, cruel
'**Unmenschlichkeit** *f* (-; *-en*) (*no pl*) inhumanity; cruelty
**un'merklich** *adj* imperceptible
'**unmissverständlich** *adj* unmistakable
'**unmittelbar 1.** *adj* immediate, direct **2.** *adv*: ***~ nach*** (***hinter***) right after (behind)
'**unmöbliert** *adj* unfurnished
'**unmodern** *adj* out of fashion *or* style
'**unmöglich 1.** *adj* impossible **2.** *adv*: ***ich kann es ~ tun*** I can't possibly do it
'**unmoralisch** *adj* immoral
'**unmündig** *adj* JUR under age
'**unmusikalisch** *adj* unmusical
'**unnachahmlich** *adj* inimitable
'**unnachgiebig** *adj* unyielding
'**unnachsichtig** *adj* strict, severe
**unnahbar** [ʊn'naːbaːɐ] *adj* standoffish, cold
'**unnatürlich** *adj* unnatural (*a. fig*); affected
'**unnötig** *adj* unnecessary, needless
**unnütz** ['ʊnnʏts] *adj* useless
'**unordentlich** *adj* untidy; ***~ sein*** *room etc*: be (in) a mess; '**Unordnung** *f* (-; *no pl*) disorder, mess
'**unparteiisch** *adj* impartial, unbias(s)ed; '**Unparteiische** *m*, *f* (*-n*; *-n*) SPORT referee
'**unpassend** *adj* unsuitable; improper; inappropriate
'**unpassierbar** *adj* impassable
**unpässlich** ['ʊnpɛslɪç] *adj* indisposed
'**unpersönlich** *adj* impersonal (*a.* LING)
'**unpolitisch** *adj* unpolitical
'**unpraktisch** *adj* impractical
'**unpünktlich** *adj* unpunctual
'**unrecht** *adj* wrong; ***~ haben*** be wrong; ***j-m ~ tun*** do s.o. wrong; '**Unrecht** *n* (-[*e*]*s*; *no pl*) injustice, wrong; ***zu ~*** wrong(ful)ly; ***~ haben → unrecht***; ***~ tun → unrecht***
'**unrechtmäßig** *adj* unlawful
'**unregelmäßig** *adj* irregular (*a.* LING)
'**Unregelmäßigkeit** *f* (-; *-en*) irregularity
'**unreif** *adj* unripe; *fig* immature
'**Unreife** *fig f* immaturity
'**unrein** *adj* unclean; impure (*a.* REL)
'**Unreinheit** *f* (-; *-en*) impurity
'**unrichtig** *adj* incorrect, wrong
'**Unruhe** *f* (-; *-n*) (*no pl*) restlessness, unrest (*a.* POL); anxiety, alarm; *pl* disturbances, riots
'**unruhig** *adj* restless; uneasy; worried, alarmed; MAR rough
**uns** [ʊns] *pers pron* (to) us; each other; ***~*** (***selbst***) (to) ourselves; ***ein Freund von ~*** a friend of ours
'**un|sachgemäß** *adj* improper; **~sachlich** *adj* unobjective; **~sanft** *adj* rude, rough; **~sauber** *adj* unclean, *esp fig a.* impure; SPORT unfair; *fig* underhand; **~schädlich** *adj* harmless; **~scharf** *adj* PHOT blurred, out of focus
**un'schätzbar** *adj* inestimable, invaluable
'**un|scheinbar** *adj* inconspicuous; plain; **~schlüssig** *adj* irresolute; undecided; **~schön** *adj* unsightly; *fig* unpleasant
'**Unschuld** *f* (-; *no pl*) innocence; *fig* virginity
'**unschuldig** *adj* innocent (***an*** *dat* of)
'**unselbstständig** *adj* dependent on others; '**Unselbstständigkeit** *f* lack of independence, dependence on others
**unser** ['ʊnzɐ] *poss pron* our; ***~er, ~e, ~es*** ours
'**unsicher** *adj* unsafe, insecure; self-conscious; uncertain; '**Unsicherheit** *f* (-; *-en*) (*no pl*) insecurity, unsafeness;

U

self-consciousness; uncertainty
'**unsichtbar** *adj* invisible
'**Unsinn** *m* (-[*e*]*s*; *no pl*) nonsense
'**unsinnig** *adj* nonsensical, stupid; absurd
'**Unsitte** *f* bad habit; abuse
'**unsittlich** *adj* immoral, indecent
'**unsozial** *adj* unsocial
'**unsportlich** *adj* unathletic; *fig* unfair
'**unsterblich 1.** *adj* immortal (*a. fig*) **2.** *adv*: **~ *verliebt*** madly in love (***in*** *acc* with); '**Unsterblichkeit** *f* immortality
'**Unstimmigkeit** *f* (-; -*en*) discrepancy; *pl* disagreements
'**unsympathisch** *adj* disagreeable; ***er*** (***es***) ***ist mir* ~** I don't like him (it)
'**untätig** *adj* inactive; idle; '**Untätigkeit** *f* (-; *no pl*) inactivity
'**untauglich** *adj* unfit (*a.* MIL); incompetent
**un'teilbar** *adj* indivisible
**unten** ['ʊntən] *adv* (down) below, down (*a.* ***nach* ~**); downstairs; **~ *auf*** (*dat*) at the bottom of *the page etc*; ***siehe* ~** see below; ***von oben bis* ~** from top to bottom
**unter** ['ʊntɐ] *prp* under; below (*a. fig*); among; *fig* less than; **~ *anderem*** among other things; **~ *uns*** (***gesagt***) between you and me; **~ *Wasser*** underwater
'**Unterarm** *m* ANAT forearm
'**unter|belichtet** *adj* PHOT underexposed; **~besetzt** *adj* understaffed
'**Unterbewusstsein** *n* subconscious; ***im* ~** subconsciously
**unter|'bieten** *v/t* (*irr*, ***bieten***, *no -ge-*, *h*) underbid; undercut; beat (*record*); **~'binden** *fig v/t* (*irr*, ***binden***, *no -ge-*, *h*) put a stop to; prevent
**unter'brechen** *v/t* (*irr*, ***brechen***, *no -ge-*, *h*) interrupt; **Unter'brechung** *f* (-; -*en*) interruption
'**unterbringen** *v/i* (*irr*, ***bringen***, *sep*, *-ge-*, *h*) accommodate, put *s.o.* up; find a place for, put (***in*** *acc* into); '**Unterbringung** *f* (-; -*en*) accommodation
**unter'dessen** *adv* in the meantime, meanwhile
**unter'drücken** *v/t* (*no -ge-*, *h*) oppress; suppress; **Unter'drücker** *m* (-*s*; -) oppressor; **Unter'drückung** *f* (-; -*en*) oppression; suppression
**untere** ['ʊntərə] *adj* lower (*a. fig*)
'**unterentwickelt** *adj* underdeveloped
'**unterernährt** *adj* undernourished, underfed; '**Unterernährung** *f* (-; *no pl*) undernourishment, malnutrition
**Unter'führung** *f* (-; -*en*) underpass, *Br a.* subway
'**Untergang** *m* ASTR setting; MAR sinking; *fig* downfall; decline; fall; '**untergehen** *v/i* (*irr*, ***gehen***, *sep*, *-ge-*, *sein*) go down (*a. fig*), ASTR *a.* set, MAR *a.* sink
'**untergeordnet** *adj* subordinate, inferior; secondary
'**Untergewicht** *n* (-[*e*]*s*; *no pl*), '**untergewichtig** *adj* underweight
**unter'graben** *fig v/t* (*irr*, ***graben***, *no -ge-*, *h*) undermine
'**Untergrund** *m* subsoil; POL underground; ***in den* ~ *gehen*** go underground; **~bahn** *f* → ***U-Bahn***
'**unterhalb** *prp* (*gen*) below, under
'**Unterhalt** *m* (-[*e*]*s*; *no pl*) support, maintenance (*a.* JUR); **unter'halten** *v/t* (*irr*, ***halten***, *no -ge-*, *h*) entertain; support; ***sich* ~** (***mit***) talk (to, with); ***sich*** (***gut***) **~** enjoy o.s., have a good time; **unter'haltsam** *adj* entertaining; **Unter'haltung** *f* (-; -*en*) talk, conversation; entertainment; **Unter'haltungsindus,trie** *f* show business
'**Unter|händler** *m* negotiator; **~haus** *n* (-*es*; *no pl*) *Br* PARL House of Commons; **~hemd** *n* undershirt, *Br* vest; **~holz** *n* (-*es*; *no pl*) undergrowth; **~hose** *f* shorts, *esp Br* underpants, panties, *Br* pants; ***e-e lange* ~, *lange* ~*n*** (a pair of) long johns
'**unterirdisch** *adj* underground
'**Unterkiefer** *m* ANAT lower jaw
'**Unterkleid** *n* slip
'**unterkommen** *v/i* (*irr*, ***kommen***, *sep*, *-ge-*, *sein*) find accommodation; find work *or* a job (***bei*** with)
**Unterkunft** ['ʊntɐkʊnft] *f* (-; -*künfte* ['ʊntɐkʏnftə]) accommodation, lodging(s); MIL quarters; **~ *und Verpflegung*** board and lodging
'**Unterlage** *f* TECH base; *pl* documents; data
**unter'lassen** *v/t* (*irr*, ***lassen***, *no -ge-*, *h*) omit, fail to do *s.th.*; stop *or* quit doing *s.th.*; **Unter'lassung** *f* (-; -*en*) omission (*a.* JUR)

**'unterlegen**[1] *v/t (sep, -ge-, h)* underlay
**unter'legen**[2] *adj* inferior (*dat* to)
**Unter'legenheit** *f (-; no pl)* inferiority
**'Unterleib** *m* ANAT abdomen, belly
**unter'liegen** *v/i (irr,* ***liegen****, no -ge-, sein)* be defeated (***j-m*** by s.o.), lose (to s.o.); *fig* be subject to
**'Unterlippe** *f* ANAT lower lip
**'Untermieter** *m*, **'Untermieterin** *f* roomer, *Br* lodger
**unter'nehmen** *v/t (irr,* ***nehmen****, no -ge-, h)* make, take, go on *a trip etc*; ***et. ~*** do s.th. (***gegen*** about *s.th.*), take action (against *s.o.*); **Unter'nehmen** *n (-s; -)* firm, business; venture; undertaking, enterprise; MIL operation; **Unter'nehmensberater(in)** management consultant; **Unter'nehmer** *m (-s; -)* businessman, entrepreneur; employer; **Unter'nehmerin** *f (-; -nen)* businesswoman; **unter'nehmungslustig** *adj* active, dynamic; adventurous
**'Unteroffizier** *m* MIL non-commissioned officer
**'unterordnen** *v/t and v/refl (sep, -ge-, h)* subordinate (o.s.) (*dat* to)
**Unter'redung** *f (-; -en)* talk(s)
**Unterricht** ['ʊntɐrɪçt] *m (-[e]s; no pl)* instruction, teaching; PED school, classes, lessons; **unter'richten** *v/i and v/t (no -ge-, h)* teach; give lessons; inform (***über*** *acc* of); **'Unterrichtsstunde** *f* lesson, PED *a.* class, period
**'Unterrock** *m* slip
**unter'sagen** *v/t (no -ge-, h)* prohibit
**unter'schätzen** *v/t (no -ge-, h)* underestimate; underrate
**unter'scheiden** *v/t and v/i (irr,* ***scheiden****, no -ge-, h)* distinguish (***zwischen*** between; ***von*** from); tell apart; ***sich ~*** differ (***von*** from; ***in*** *dat* in; ***durch*** by); **Unter'scheidung** *f (-; -en)* distinction; **Unterschied** ['ʊntɐʃiːt] *m (-[e]s; -e)* difference; ***im ~ zu*** unlike, as opposed to; **'unterschiedlich** *adj* different; varying
**unter'schlagen** *v/t (irr,* ***schlagen****, no -ge-, h)* embezzle; **Unter'schlagung** *f (-; -en)* embezzlement
**Unterschlupf** ['ʊntɐʃlʊpf] *m (-[e]s; no pl)* hiding place
**unter'schreiben** *v/t and v/i (irr,* ***schreiben****, no -ge-, h)* sign
**'Unterschrift** *f* signature; caption
**'Unterseeboot** *n* → ***U-Boot***
**Untersetzer** ['ʊntɐzɛtsɐ] *m (-s; -)* coaster; saucer
**unter'setzt** *adj* thickset, stocky
**'Unterstand** *m* shelter, MIL *a.* dugout
**unter'stehen** *(irr,* ***stehen****, no -ge-, h)* **1.** *v/i (dat)* be under (the control of) **2.** *v/refl* dare; ***~ Sie sich (et. zu tun)!*** don't you dare ([to] do s.th.)!
**'unterstellen**[1] *v/t (sep, -ge-, h)* put *s.th.* in; store; ***sich ~*** take shelter
**unter'stellen**[2] *v/t (no -ge-, h)* assume; ***j-m ~, dass er ...*** insinuate that s.o. ...; **Unter'stellung** *f (-; -en)* insinuation
**unter'streichen** *v/t (irr,* ***streichen****, no -ge-, h)* underline (*a. fig*)
**unter'stützen** *v/t (no -ge-, h)* support; back (up); **Unter'stützung** *f (-; -en)* support; aid; welfare (payments)
**unter'suchen** *v/t (no -ge-, h)* examine (*a.* MED), investigate (*a.* JUR); search; CHEM analyze; **Unter'suchung** *f (-; -en)* examination (*a.* MED), investigation (*a.* JUR), *a.* (medical) checkup; CHEM analysis
**Unter'suchungs|gefangene** *m, f* JUR prisoner on remand; **~gefängnis** *n* JUR remand prison; **~haft** *f*: ***in ~ sein*** JUR be on remand; **~richter** *m* JUR examining magistrate
**Untertan** ['ʊntɐtaːn] *m (-s; -en)* subject
**'Untertasse** *f* saucer
**'untertauchen** *(sep, -ge-)* **1.** *v/i (sein)* dive, submerge; *fig* disappear; *esp* POL go underground **2.** *v/t (h)* duck
**'Unterteil** *n, m* lower part, bottom
**unter'teilen** *v/t (no -ge-, h)* subdivide; **Unter'teilung** *f (-; -en)* subdivision
**'Untertitel** *m* subtitle, *film*: *a.* caption
**'Unterton** *m* undertone
**Unter'treibung** *f (-; -en)* understatement
**'untervermieten** *v/t (no -ge-, h)* sublet
**unter'wandern** *v/t (no -ge-, h)* infiltrate
**'Unterwäsche** *f* underwear
**'Unterwasser...** *in cpds* underwater ...
**unterwegs** [ʊntɐ'veːks] *adv* on the *or* one's way (***nach*** to)
**unter'weisen** *v/t (irr,* ***weisen****, no -ge-, h)* instruct; **Unter'weisung** *f (-; -en)* instruction
**'Unterwelt** *f (-; no pl)* underworld
**unter'werfen** *v/t (irr,* ***werfen****, no -ge-, h)* subject (*dat* to); subjugate; ***sich ~*** sub-

mit (to); **Unter'werfung** *f* (-; -*en*) subjection; submission (***unter*** *acc* to)
**unterwürfig** [ʊntɐ'vʏrfɪç] *adj* servile
**unter'zeichnen** *v/t* (*no -ge-, h*) sign; **Unter'zeichnete** *m, f* (-*n*; -*n*) *the* undersigned; **Unter'zeichnung** *f* (-; -*en*) signing
**'unterziehen**[1] *v/t* (*irr,* ***ziehen****, sep, -ge-, h*) put *s.th.* on underneath
**unter'ziehen**[2] *v/t* (*irr,* ***ziehen****, no -ge-, h*) ***sich*** *e-r Behandlung, Prüfung etc* **~** undergo (*treatment etc*), take (*an examination etc*)
**'Untiefe** *f* shallow, shoal
**un|'tragbar** *adj* unbearable, intolerable; **~'trennbar** *adj* inseparable
**'untreu** *adj* unfaithful (*dat* to)
**un|'tröstlich** *adj* inconsolable; **~trüglich** [ʊn'try:klɪç] *adj* unmistakable
**'Untugend** *f* vice, bad habit
**'unüber|legt** *adj* thoughtless; **~sichtlich** *adj* blind (*bend etc*)
**unüber|trefflich** [ʊnʔy:bɐ'trɛflɪç] *adj* unsurpassable, matchless; **~troffen** [ʊnʔy:bɐ'trɔfən] *adj* unequal(l)ed; **~windlich** [ʊnʔy:bɐ'vɪntlɪç] *adj* insuperable, invincible
**unum|gänglich** [ʊnʔʊm'gɛŋlɪç] *adj* inevitable; **~schränkt** [ʊnʔʊm'ʃrɛŋkt] *adj* unlimited; POL absolute; **~stritten** [ʊnʔʊm'ʃtrɪtən] *adj* undisputed; **~wunden** [ʊnʔʊm'vʊndən] *adv* straight out, frankly
**ununterbrochen** ['ʊnʔʊntɐbrɔxən] *adj* uninterrupted; continuous
**un|ver'änderlich** *adj* unchanging; **~ver'antwortlich** *adj* irresponsible; **~ver'besserlich** *adj* incorrigible; **~ver'bindlich** *adj* noncommittal, ECON not binding; **~ver'daulich** *adj* indigestible (*a. fig*)
**'unverdient** *adj* undeserved
**'unverdünnt** *adj* undiluted; straight
**unver'einbar** *adj* incompatible
**'unverfälscht** *adj* unadulterated
**'unverfänglich** *adj* harmless
**'unverfroren** *adj* brazen, impertinent
**'unvergänglich** *adj* immortal, eternal
**unver'gesslich** *adj* unforgettable
**'unver'gleichlich** *adj* incomparable
**'unverhältnismäßig** *adv* disproportionately; **~ *hoch*** excessive
**'unverheiratet** *adj* unmarried, single
**unverhofft** ['ʊnfɛɐhɔft] *adj* unhoped-for; unexpected
**unverhohlen** ['ʊnfɛɐho:lən] *adj* undisguised, open
**'unverkäuflich** *adj* not for sale; unsal(e)able
**unver'kennbar** *adj* unmistakable
**'unverletzt** *adj* unhurt
**unvermeidlich** [ʊnfɛɐ'maitlɪç] *adj* inevitable
**'unvermindert** *adj* undiminished
**'unvermittelt** *adj* abrupt, sudden
**'Unvermögen** *n* (-*s*; *no pl*) inability, incapacity
**'unvermutet** *adj* unexpected
**'unvernünftig** *adj* unreasonable; foolish
**'unverschämt** *adj* rude, impertinent; outrageous (*price etc*); **'Unverschämtheit** *f* (-; -*en*) impertinence; ***die* ~ *haben zu*** *inf* have the nerve to *inf*
**'unverschuldet** *adj* through no fault of one's own
**unversehens** ['ʊnfɛɐze:əns] *adv* unexpectedly, all of a sudden
**'un|versehrt** *adj* unhurt; undamaged; **~versöhnlich** *adj* irreconcilable (*a. fig*), implacable; **~versorgt** *adj* unprovided for; **~verständlich** *adj* unintelligible; ***es ist mir* ~** I can't see how *or* why, F it beats me; **~versucht** *adj*: ***nichts* ~ *lassen*** leave nothing undone
**unver'wundbar** *adj* invulnerable
**unver|wüstlich** [ʊnfɛɐ'vy:stlɪç] *adj* indestructible; **~zeihlich** [ʊnfɛɐ'tsailɪç] *adj* inexcusable; **~züglich** [ʊnfɛɐ'tsy:klɪç] **1.** *adj* immediate, prompt **2.** *adv* immediately, without delay
**'unvollendet** *adj* unfinished
**'unvollkommen** *adj* imperfect
**'unvollständig** *adj* incomplete
**'unvorbereitet** *adj* unprepared
**'unvoreingenommen** *adj* unprejudiced, unbias(s)ed
**'unvorhergesehen** *adj* unforeseen
**'unvorhersehbar** *adj* unforeseeable
**'unvorsichtig** *adj* careless; **'Unvorsichtigkeit** *f* (-; *no pl*) carelessness
**unvor'stellbar** *adj* unthinkable
**'unvorteilhaft** *adj* unbecoming
**'unwahr** *adj* untrue; **'Unwahrheit** *f* untruth; **'unwahrscheinlich** *adj* improbable, unlikely; F fantastic

**unwegsam** ['ʊnveːkzaːm] *adj* difficult, rough (*terrain*)
**unweigerlich** [ʊn'vaigɐlɪç] *adv* inevitably
'**unweit** *prp* (*gen*) not far from
'**Unwetter** *n* (*-s*; -) disastrous (thunder)-storm
'**unwichtig** *adj* unimportant
**unwider|legbar** [ʊnviːdɐ'leːkbaːɐ] *adj* irrefutable; **~ruflich** [ʊnviːdɐ'ruːflɪç] *adj* irrevocable; **~stehlich** [ʊnviːdɐ'ʃteːlɪç] *adj* irresistible
'**Unwille(n)** *m* indignation (***über** acc* at); '**unwillig** *adj* indignant (***über** acc* at); unwilling, reluctant
'**unwillkürlich** *adj* involuntary
'**unwirklich** *adj* unreal
'**unwirksam** *adj* ineffective
**unwirsch** ['ʊnvɪrʃ] *adj* surly, gruff
**unwirtlich** ['ʊnvɪrtlɪç] *adj* inhospitable
'**unwirtschaftlich** *adj* uneconomic(al)
'**unwissend** *adj* ignorant
'**Unwissenheit** *f* (*-; no pl*) ignorance
'**unwohl** *adj* unwell; uneasy
'**unwürdig** *adj* unworthy (*gen* of)
**unzählig** [ʊn'tsɛːlɪç] *adj* innumerable, countless
**unzer'brechlich** *adj* unbreakable
**unzer'reißbar** *adj* untearable
**unzer'störbar** *adj* indestructible
**unzer'trennlich** *adj* inseparable
'**Unzucht** *f* (*-; no pl*) sexual offense (*Br* offence); '**unzüchtig** *adj* indecent; obscene
'**unzufrieden** *adj* discontent(ed) (***mit*** with), dissatisfied (with); '**Unzufriedenheit** *f* discontent, dissatisfaction
'**unzugänglich** *adj* inaccessible
'**unzulänglich** *adj* inadequate
'**unzulässig** *adj* inadmissible
**unzu'mutbar** *adj* unacceptable; unreasonable
'**unzurechnungsfähig** *adj* JUR irresponsible; '**Unzurechnungsfähigkeit** *f* (*-; no pl*) JUR irresponsibility
'**unzureichend** *adj* insufficient
'**unzusammenhängend** *adj* incoherent
'**unzuverlässig** *adj* unreliable, untrustworthy; uncertain
**üppig** ['ʏpɪç] *adj* luxuriant, lush (*both a. fig*); voluptuous, luscious; opulent; rich
**uralt** ['uːɐˀalt] *adj* ancient (*a. iro*)
**Uran** [u'raːn] *n* (*-s; no pl*) uranium
'**Uraufführung** *f* première, first performance (*film*: showing)
**urbar** ['uːɐbaːɐ] *adj* arable; ***~ machen*** cultivate; reclaim
'**Urbevölkerung** *f*, '**Ureinwohner** *pl* aboriginal inhabitants; *in Australia*: Aborigines
'**Urenkel** *m* great-grandson
'**Urenkelin** *f* great-granddaughter
'**Urgroß...** *in cpds ...eltern, ...mutter, ...vater*: great-grand...
**Urheberrecht** ['uːɐheːbɐrɛçt] *n* copyright (***an** dat* on, for)
**Urin** [u'riːn] *m* (*-s; -e*) urine; **urinieren** [uri'niːrən] *v/i* (*no -ge-, h*) urinate
**Urkunde** ['uːɐkʊndə] *f* (*-; -n*) document; diploma; '**Urkundenfälschung** *f* forgery of documents
**Urlaub** ['uːɐlaup] *m* (*-[e]s; -e*) vacation, *Br* holiday(s); MIL leave; ***in** or **im ~ sein*** (***auf ~ gehen***) be (go) on vacation (*Br* holiday); ***e-n Tag*** (***ein paar Tage***) ***~ nehmen*** take a day (a few days) off; **Urlauber(in)** ['uːɐlaubɐ, 'uːɐlaubərɪn] *m(f)* (*-s; -/-; -nen*) vacationist, vacationer, *Br* holidaymaker
**Urne** ['ʊrnə] *f* (*-; -n*) urn; ballot box
'**Ursache** *f* (*-; -n*) cause; reason; ***keine ~!*** not at all, you're welcome
'**Ursprung** *m* origin
**ursprünglich** ['uːɐʃprʏŋlɪç] *adj* original; natural, unspoilt
**Urteil** ['ʊrtail] *n* (*-[e]s; -e*) judg(e)ment; JUR sentence; ***sich ein ~ bilden*** form a judg(e)ment (***über** acc* about)
'**urteilen** *v/i* (*ge-, h*) judge (***über j-n, et.*** s.o., s.th.; ***nach*** by)
'**Urwald** *m* primeval forest; jungle
**urwüchsig** ['uːɐvyːksɪç] *adj* coarse, earthy
'**Urzeit** *f* prehistoric times
**usw.** *abbr of **und so weiter*** etc, and so on
**Utensilien** [utɛn'ziːljən] *pl* utensils
**Utopie** [uto'piː] *f* (*-; -n*) illusion
**utopisch** [u'toːpɪʃ] *adj* utopian; fantastic

# V

**Vagabund** [vaga'bʊnt] *m* (*-en*; *-en*) vagabond, tramp, F bum
**vage** ['va:gə] *adj* vague
**Vakuum** ['va:kuʊm] *n* (*-s*; *-kua*, *-kuen*) vacuum
**Vampir** ['vampi:ɐ] *m* (*-s*; *-e*) ZO vampire (*a. fig*)
**Vanille** [va'nɪljə] *f* (*-*; *no pl*) vanilla
**variabel** [va'rja:bəl] *adj* variable
**Variante** [va'rjantə] *f* (*-*; *-n*) variant
**Variation** [varja'tsio:n] *f* (*-*; *-en*) variation
**Varietee**, *a.* **Varieté** [varje'te:] *n* (*-s*; *-s*) vaudeville, *Br* variety theatre, music hall
**variieren** [vari'i:rən] *v/i and v/t* (*no -ge-*, *h*) vary
**Vase** ['va:zə] *f* (*-*; *-n*) vase
**Vater** ['fa:tɐ] *m* (*-s*; *Väter* ['fɛ:tɐ]) father
**'Vaterland** *n* native country
**'Vaterlandsliebe** *f* patriotism
**väterlich** ['fɛ:tɐlɪç] *adj* fatherly, paternal
**'Vaterschaft** *f* (*-*; *-en*) JUR paternity
**'Vater'unser** *n* (*-s*; *-*) REL Lord's Prayer
**V-Ausschnitt** ['fauʔausʃnɪt] *m* V-neck
**v. Chr.** *abbr of* ***vor Christus*** BC, before Christ
**Vegetarier** [vege'ta:rjɐ] *m* (*-s*; *-*), **Vege'tarierin** *f* (*-*; *-nen*), **vegetarisch** [vege'ta:rɪʃ] *adj* vegetarian
**Vegetation** [vegeta'tsjo:n] *f* (*-*; *-en*) vegetation; **vegetieren** [vege'ti:rən] *v/i* (*no -ge-*, *h*) vegetate
**Veilchen** ['failçən] *n* (*-s*; *-*) BOT violet
**Velo** ['ve:lo] *Swiss n* (*-s*; *-s*) bicycle, F bike
**Ventil** [vɛn'ti:l] *n* (*-s*; *-e*) TECH valve; *fig* vent, outlet
**Ventilation** [vɛntila'tsjo:n] *f* (*-*; *-en*) ventilation; **Ventilator** [vɛnti'la:to:ɐ] *m* (*-s*; *-en* [vɛntila'to:rən]) fan
**verabreden** [fɛɐ'ʔapre:dən] *v/t* (*no -ge-*, *h*) agree (up)on, arrange; appoint, fix; ***sich ~*** make a date (*or* an appointment) (***mit*** with); **Ver'abredung** *f* (*-*; *-en*) appointment; date
**ver'abreichen** *v/t* (*no -ge-*, *h*) give; MED administer; **ver'abscheuen** *v/t* (*no -ge-*, *h*) loathe, detest
**verabschieden** [fɛɐ'ʔapʃi:dən] *v/t* (*no -ge-*, *h*) say goodbye to (*a.* ***sich ~ von***); dismiss; JUR pass; **Ver'abschiedung** *f* (*-*; *-en*) dismissal; JUR passing
**ver'achten** *v/t* (*no -ge-*, *h*) despise; **verächtlich** [fɛɐ'ʔɛçtlɪç] *adj* contemptuous; **Ver'achtung** *f* (*-*; *no pl*) contempt
**verallgemeinern** [fɛɐ'ʔalgə'mainɐn] *v/t* (*no -ge-*, *h*) generalize
**ver'altet** *adj* antiquated, out of date
**Veranda** [ve'randa] *f* (*-*; *-den*) porch, *Br* veranda(h)
**veränderlich** [fɛɐ'ʔɛndɐlɪç] *adj* changeable (*a.* METEOR), variable (*a.* MATH, LING); **ver'ändern** *v/t and v/refl* (*no -ge-*, *h*), **Ver'änderung** *f* change
**verängstigt** [fɛɐ'ʔɛŋstɪçt] *adj* frightened, scared
**ver'anlagen** *v/t* (*no -ge-*, *h*) ECON assess; **veranlagt** [fɛɐ'ʔanla:kt] *adj* inclined (***zu, für*** to); ***künstlerisch*** (***musikalisch***) ***~ sein*** have a gift *or* bent for art (music); **Ver'anlagung** *f* (*-*; *-en*) (pre)disposition (*a.* MED); talent, gift; ECON assessment
**ver'anlassen** *v/t* (*no -ge-*, *h*) make arrangements (*or* arrange) for *s.th.*; ***j-n zu et. ~*** make s.o. do s.th.
**Ver'anlassung** *f* (*-*; *-en*) cause (***zu*** for)
**ver|'anschaulichen** *v/t* (*no -ge-*, *h*) illustrate; **~'anschlagen** *v/t* (*no -ge-*, *h*) estimate (***auf*** *acc* at)
**ver'anstalten** *v/t* (*no -ge-*, *h*) arrange, organize; hold, give (*concert*, *party etc*); **Ver'anstaltung** *f* (*-*; *-en*) event, SPORT *a.* meet, *Br* meeting
**ver'antworten** *v/t* (*no -ge-*, *h*) take the responsibility for; **ver'antwortlich** *adj* responsible; ***j-n ~ machen für*** hold s.o. responsible for; **Ver'antwortung** *f* (*-*; *no pl*) responsibility; ***auf eigene ~*** at one's own risk; ***j-n zur ~ ziehen*** call s.o. to account; **Ver'antwortungsgefühl** *n* (*-[e]s*; *no pl*) sense of responsibility; **ver'antwortungslos** *adj* irresponsible
**ver|'arbeiten** *v/t* (*no -ge-*, *h*) process; *fig* digest; ***et. ~ zu*** manufacture (*or* make) s.th. into; **~'ärgern** *v/t* (*no -ge-*, *h*) make

*s.o.* angry, annoy
**ver'armt** *adj* impoverished
**ver'arschen** *v/t* (*no -ge-, h*) ***j-n*** **~** take the piss out of s.o.
**Verb** [vɛrp] *n* (*-s; -en* ['vɛrbən]) LING verb
**Verband** [fɛɐ'bant] *m* (*-es; Verbände* [fɛɐ'bɛndə]) MED dressing, bandage; ECON association; MIL formation, unit; **~(s)kasten** *m* MED first-aid kit *or* box; **~(s)zeug** *n* MED dressing material
**ver'bannen** *v/t* (*no -ge-, h*) banish (*a. fig*), exile; **Ver'bannung** *f* (*-; -en*) banishment, exile
**verbarrika'dieren** *v/t* (*no -ge-, h*) barricade; block
**ver'bergen** *v/t* (*irr,* ***bergen****, no -ge-, h*) hide (*a.* ***sich*** **~**), conceal
**ver'bessern** *v/t* (*no -ge-, h*) improve; correct; **Ver'besserung** *f* (*-; -en*) improvement; correction
**ver'beugen** *v/refl* (*no -ge-, h*), **Ver'beugung** *f* (*-; -en*) bow (***vor*** to)
**ver|'biegen** *v/t* (*irr,* ***biegen****, no -ge-, h*) twist; **~'bieten** *v/t* (*irr,* ***bieten****, no -ge-, h*) forbid; prohibit; → ***verboten***
**ver'billigen** *v/t* (*no -ge-, h*) reduce in price; **verbilligt** [fɛɐ'bɪlɪçt] *adj* reduced, at reduced prices
**verbinden** *v/t* (*irr,* ***binden****, no -ge-, h*) MED dress, bandage; bandage *s.o.* up; *a.* TECH connect, join, link (up); TEL put *s.o.* through (***mit*** to); combine (*a.* CHEM ***sich*** **~**); *fig* unite; associate; ***j-m die Augen*** **~** blindfold s.o.; ***damit sind beträchtliche Kosten verbunden*** that involves considerable cost(s *pl*); ***falsch verbunden!*** wrong number!
**verbindlich** [fɛɐ'bɪntlɪç] *adj* obligatory, compulsory (*a.* PED); obliging
**Ver'bindlichkeit** *f* (*-; -en*) (*no pl*) obligingness; *pl* ECON liabilities
**Ver'bindung** *f* (*-; -en*) connection; combination; CHEM compound; UNIV fraternity, *Br* society; ***sich in*** **~** ***setzen mit*** get in touch with; ***in*** **~** ***stehen*** (***bleiben***) be (keep) in touch
**verbissen** [fɛɐ'bɪsən] *adj* dogged
**ver'bittert** *adj* bitter, embittered
**verblassen** [fɛɐ'blasən] *v/i* (*no -ge-, sein*) fade (*a. fig*)
**Verbleib** [fɛɐ'blaip] *m* (*-[e]s; no pl*) whereabouts; **ver'bleiben** *v/i* (*irr,* ***bleiben****, no -ge-, sein*) remain
**verbleit** [fɛɐ'blait] *adj* leaded
**ver'blendet** *fig adj* blind
**Ver'blendung** *fig f* (*-; -en*) blindness
**verblichen** [fɛɐ'blɪçən] *adj* faded
**verblüffen** [fɛɐ'blʏfən] *v/t* (*no -ge-, h*) amaze, F flabbergast
**Ver'blüffung** *f* (*-; -en*) amazement
**ver'blühen** *v/i* (*no -ge-, sein*) fade, wither (*both a. fig*)
**ver'bluten** *v/i* (*no -ge-, sein*) MED bleed to death
**verborgen** [fɛɐ'bɔrgən] *adj* hidden, concealed; ***im Verborgenen*** in secret
**Verbot** [fɛɐ'bo:t] *n* (*-[e]s; -e*) prohibition, ban (on *s.th.*); **ver'boten** *adj*: ***Rauchen*** **~** no smoking
**Ver'brauch** *m* (*-[e]s; no pl*) consumption (***an*** *dat* of); **ver'brauchen** *v/t* (*no -ge-, h*) consume, use up
**Verbraucher** [fɛɐ'brauxɐ] *m* (*-s; -*), **Ver'braucherin** *f* (*-; -nen*) consumer; **~schutz** *m* consumer protection
**Ver'brechen** *n* (*-s; -*) crime; ***ein*** **~** ***begehen*** commit a crime; **Ver'brecher(in)** (*-s; -/-; -nen*), **ver'brecherisch** *adj* criminal
**ver'breiten** *v/t and v/refl* (*no -ge-, h*) spread (***in*** *dat*, ***über*** *acc* over, through); circulate
**verbreitern** [fɛɐ'braitɐn] *v/t and v/refl* (*no -ge-, h*) widen, broaden
**Ver'breitung** *f* (*-; no pl*) spread(ing); circulation
**ver'brennen** *v/i* (*irr,* ***brennen****, no -ge-, sein*) *and v/t* (*h*) burn (up); cremate
**Ver'brennung** *f* (*-; -en*) burning; cremation; TECH combustion; MED burn
**ver'bringen** *v/t* (*irr,* ***bringen****, no -ge-, h*) spend, pass
**verbrüdern** [fɛɐ'bry:dɐn] *v/refl* (*no -ge-, h*) fraternize; **Verbrüderung** [fɛɐ'bry:dərʊŋ] *f* (*-; -en*) fraternization
**ver'brühen** *v/t* (*no -ge-, h*) scald
**ver'buchen** *v/t* (*no -ge-, h*) book
**verbünden** [fɛɐ'bʏndən] *v/refl* (*no -ge-, h*) ally o.s. (***mit*** to, with)
**Ver'bündete** *m, f* (*-n; -n*) ally (*a. fig*)
**ver'bürgen** *v/refl* (*no -ge-, h*) ***sich*** **~** ***für*** vouch for, guarantee
**ver'büßen** *v/t* (*no -ge-, h*) ***e-e Strafe*** **~** serve a sentence, serve time
**verchromt** [fɛɐ'kro:mt] *adj* chromium-plated

**Verdacht** [fɛɐ'daxt] *m* (-[*e*]*s*; -*e*) suspicion; ***~ schöpfen*** become suspicious

**verdächtig** [fɛɐ'dɛçtɪç] *adj* suspicious, suspect; **Verdächtige** [fɛɐ'dɛçtɪɡə] *m, f* (-*n*; -*n*) suspect; **ver'dächtigen** *v/t* (*no -ge-, h*) suspect (***j-n e-r Tat*** s.o. of [doing] s.th.); **Ver'dächtigung** *f* (-; -*en*) suspicion

**verdammen** [fɛɐ'damən] *v/t* (*no -ge-, h*) condemn (***zu*** to), damn (*a.* REL); **Ver'dammnis** *f* (-; *no pl*) REL damnation; **ver'dammt 1.** *adj* damned, F *a.* damn, darn(ed), *Br sl a.* bloody; F ***~ (noch mal)!*** damn (it)! **2.** *adv*: ***~ gut*** *etc* damn (*Br sl a.* bloody) good *etc*; **Ver'dammung** *f* (-; -*en*) condemnation; REL damnation

**ver'dampfen** *v/t* (*no -ge-, h*) and *v/i* (*sein*) evaporate

**ver'danken** *v/t* (*no -ge-, h*) ***j-m*** (***e-m Umstand***) ***et. ~*** owe s.th. to s.o. (s.th.)

**verdarb** [fɛɐ'darp] *pret of* ***verderben***

**verdauen** [fɛɐ'dauən] *v/t* (*no -ge-, h*) digest (*a. fig*)

**ver'daulich** *adj* digestible; ***leicht*** (***schwer***) ***~*** easy (hard) to digest

**Ver'dauung** *f* (-; *no pl*) digestion

**Ver'deck** *n* (-[*e*]*s*; -*e*) top; **ver'decken** *v/t* (*no -ge-, h*) cover (up) (*a. fig*)

**ver'denken** *v/t* (*irr*, ***denken***, *no -ge-, h*) ***ich kann es ihm nicht ~*** (, ***dass er …***) I can't blame him (for *doing*)

**verderben** [fɛɐ'dɛrbən] (*irr, no -ge-*) **1.** *v/i* (*sein*) spoil (*a. fig*); GASTR go bad **2.** *v/t* (*h*) spoil (*a. fig*), ruin; ***sich den Magen ~*** upset one's stomach

**Ver'derben** *n* (-*s*; *no pl*) ruin

**verderblich** [fɛɐ'dɛrplɪç] *adj* perishable; ***leicht ~e Lebensmittel*** perishables

**ver'dichten** *v/t* (*no -ge-, h*) compress, condense

**ver'dienen** *v/t* (*no -ge-, h*) earn, make; *fig* deserve

**Ver'dienst**[1] *m* (-[*e*]*s*; -*e*) earnings; salary; wages; gain, profit

**Ver'dienst**[2] *n* (-[*e*]*s*; -*e*) merit; ***es ist sein ~, dass*** it is thanks to him that

**ver'dient** *adj* (well-)deserved

**ver'doppeln** *v/t and v/refl* (*no -ge-, h*) double

**verdorben** [fɛɐ'dɔrbən] **1.** *pp of* ***verderben*** **2.** *adj* GASTR spoilt, bad (*both a. fig*); MED upset

**ver|dorren** [fɛɐ'dɔrən] *v/i* (*no -ge-, sein*) wither, dry up; **~'drängen** *v/t* (*no -ge-, h*) supplant, supersede; replace; PHYS displace; PSYCH repress, suppress; **~'drehen** *v/t* (*no -ge-, h*) twist, *fig a.* distort; ***die Augen ~*** roll one's eyes; ***j-m den Kopf ~*** turn s.o.'s head; **~'dreht** F *fig adj* mixed up; **~'dreifachen** *v/t and v/refl* (*no -ge-, h*) treble, triple

**verdrießen** [fɛɐ'driːsən] *v/t* (*irr, no -ge-, h*) annoy; **verdrießlich** [fɛɐ'driːslɪç] *adj* glum, morose, sullen; **verdross** [fɛɐ'drɔs] *pret of* ***verdrießen***; **verdrossen** [fɛɐ'drɔsən] **1.** *pp of* ***verdrießen*** **2.** *adj* grumpy, sullen; **Verdruss** [fɛɐ'drʊs] *m* (-*es*; -*e*) annoyance

**ver'dummen** (*no -ge-*) **1.** *v/t* (*h*) make stupid, stultify **2.** *v/i* (*sein*) become stultified

**ver'dunkeln** *v/t and v/refl* (*no -ge-, h*) darken; black out; *fig* obscure

**Ver'dunk(e)lung** *f* (-; -*en*) darkening; blackout; JUR collusion

**ver'dünnen** *v/t* (*no -ge-, h*) dilute

**ver'dunsten** *v/i* (*no -ge-, sein*) evaporate

**ver'dursten** *v/i* (*no -ge-, sein*) die of thirst

**verdutzt** [fɛɐ'dʊtst] *adj* puzzled

**ver'edeln** *v/t* (*no -ge-, h*) BOT graft; TECH process, refine; **Ver'ed(e)lung** *f* (-; -*en*) BOT grafting; TECH processing, refinement

**ver'ehren** *v/t* (*no -ge-, h*) admire; adore, worship (*both a. fig*), *esp* REL *a.* revere, venerate; **Ver'ehrer(in)** (-*s*; -/-; -*nen*) admirer, *esp film etc*: *a.* fan; **Ver'ehrung** *f* (-; *no pl*) admiration; adoration, worship; *esp* REL reverence, veneration

**vereidigen** [fɛɐ'ʔaidɪɡən] *v/t* (*no -ge-, h*) swear *s.o.* in; JUR put *s.o.* under an oath

**Verein** [fɛɐ'ʔain] *m* (-[*e*]*s*; -*e*) club (*a.* SPORT); society, association

**vereinbar** [fɛɐ'ʔainbaːɐ] *adj* compatible (***mit*** with); **vereinbaren** [fɛɐ'ʔainbaːrən] *v/t* (*no -ge-, h*) agree (up)on, arrange; **Ver'einbarung** *f* (-; -*en*) agreement, arrangement

**ver'einen** → ***vereinigen***

**ver'einfachen** *v/t* (*no -ge-, h*) simplify

**Ver'einfachung** *f* (-; -*en*) simplification

**ver'einheitlichen** *v/t* (*no -ge-, h*) standardize

**ver'einigen** *v/t and v/refl (no -ge-, h)* unite (***zu*** into); combine, join

**Ver'einigung** *f (-; -en)* union; combination; alliance

**ver'einsamen** *v/i (no -ge-, sein)* become lonely *or* isolated

**vereinzelt** [fɛɐ'ˀaintsəlt] *adj* occasional, odd; ***~ Regen*** scattered showers

**ver\|'eiteln** *v/t (no -ge-, h)* prevent; frustrate; **~'enden** *v/i (no -ge-, sein) esp zo* die, perish; **~'engen** *v/t and v/refl (no -ge-, h)* narrow

**ver'erben** *v/t (no -ge-, h)* ***j-m et. ~*** leave (BIOL transmit) s.th. to s.o.; ***sich ~ (auf*** *acc)* be passed on *or* down (to) (*a.* BIOL *and fig*); **Ver'erbung** *f (-; no pl)* BIOL heredity; **Ver'erbungslehre** *f* BIOL genetics

**verewigen** [fɛɐ'ˀeːvɪɡən] *v/t (no -ge-, h)* immortalize

**ver'fahren** *(irr,* ***fahren****, no -ge-)* **1.** *v/i (sein)* proceed; ***~ mit*** deal with **2.** *v/refl (h)* MOT get lost

**Ver'fahren** *n (-s; -)* procedure, method, *esp* TECH *a.* technique, way; JUR (legal) proceedings (***gegen*** against)

**Ver'fall** *m (-[e]s; no pl)* decay (*a. fig*); dilapidation; *fig* decline; ECON *etc* expiry; **ver'fallen** *(irr,* ***fallen****, no -ge-, sein)* **1.** *v/i* decay (*a. fig*), dilapidate; *esp fig* decline; ECON expire; MED waste away; become addicted to; (***wieder***) ***~ in*** *(acc)* fall (back) into; ***~ auf*** *(acc)* hit (up)on **2.** *adj* decayed; dilapidated; **Ver'fallsdatum** *n* expiry date; GASTR pull date, *Br* best-before (*or* best-by) date; PHARM sell-by date

**ver'fälschen** *v/t (no -ge-, h)* falsify; distort; GASTR adulterate

**verfänglich** [fɛɐ'fɛŋlɪç] *adj* delicate, tricky; embarrassing, compromising

**ver'färben** *v/refl (no -ge-, h)* discolo(u)r

**ver'fassen** *v/t (no -ge-, h)* write

**Verfasser** [fɛɐ'fasɐ] *m (-s; -)*, **Ver'fasserin** *f (-; -nen)* author

**Ver'fassung** *f (-; -en)* state (of health *or* of mind), condition; POL constitution

**ver'fassungs\|mäßig** *adj* POL constitutional; **~widrig** *adj* unconstitutional

**ver'faulen** *v/i (no -ge-, sein)* rot, decay

**ver'fechten** *v/t (irr,* ***fechten****, no -ge-, h)*, **Ver'fechter(in)** *(-s; -/-; -nen)* advocate

**ver'fehlen** *v/t (no -ge-, h)* miss (***sich*** each other); **Ver'fehlung** *f (-; -en)* offense, *Br* offence

**verfeinden** [fɛɐ'faindən] *v/refl (no -ge-, h)* become enemies; **ver'feindet** *adj* hostile; ***~ sein*** be enemies

**verfeinern** [fɛɐ'fainɐn] *v/t and v/refl (no -ge-, h)* refine

**ver'filmen** *v/t (no -ge-, h)* film; **Ver'filmung** *f (-; -en)* filming; film version

**ver'flechten** *v/t (irr,* ***flechten****, no -ge-, h)* intertwine (*a.* ***sich ~***)

**ver'fluchen** *v/t (no -ge-, h)* curse

**ver'flucht** → ***verdammt***

**ver'folgen** *v/t (no -ge-, h)* pursue (*a. fig*); chase, hunt (*both a. fig*); POL, REL persecute; follow (*track etc*); *fear etc*: haunt *s.o.*; ***j-n gerichtlich ~*** prosecute s.o.; **Verfolger** [fɛɐ'fɔlɡɐ] *m (-s; -)* pursuer; persecutor; **Ver'folgung** *f (-; -en)* pursuit (*a. cycling*); chase, hunt; persecution; ***gerichtliche ~*** prosecution

**ver'frachten** *v/t (no -ge-, h)* freight, ship; F bundle *s.o., s.th.* (***in*** *acc* into)

**verfremden** [fɛɐ'frɛmdən] *v/t (no -ge-, h) esp art*: alienate

**ver'früht** *adj* premature

**verfügbar** [fɛɐ'fyːkbaːɐ] *adj* available;

**ver'fügen** *(no -ge-, h)* **1.** *v/t* decree, order **2.** *v/i*: ***~ über*** *(acc)* have at one's disposal; **Ver'fügung** *f (-; -en)* decree, order; *(no pl)* disposal; ***j-m zur ~ stehen*** (***stellen***) be (place) at s.o. 's disposal

**ver'führen** *v/t (no -ge-, h)* seduce (***et. zu tun*** into doing s.th.); **Ver'führer** *m (-s; -)* seducer; **Ver'führerin** *f (-; -nen)* seductress; **ver'führerisch** *adj* seductive; tempting; **Ver'führung** *f (-; -en)* seduction

**vergangen** [fɛɐ'ɡaŋən] *adj* gone, past; ***im ~en Jahr*** last year; **Ver'gangenheit** *f (-; no pl)* past; LING past tense

**vergänglich** [fɛɐ'ɡɛŋlɪç] *adj* transitory, transient

**vergasen** [fɛɐ'ɡaːzən] *v/t (no -ge-, h)* gas; CHEM gasify; **Vergaser** [fɛɐ'ɡaːzɐ] *m (-s; -)* MOT carburet(t)or

**vergaß** [fɛɐ'ɡaːs] *pret of* ***vergessen***

**ver'geben** *v/t (irr,* ***geben****, no -ge-, h)* give away (*a. fig*); award (*prize etc*); forgive; **ver'gebens** *adv* in vain; **vergeblich** [fɛɐ'ɡeːplɪç] **1.** *adj* futile **2.** *adv* in vain; **Ver'gebung** *f (-; -en)* forgiveness, pardon

V

**ver'gehen** (*irr*, ***gehen***, *no -ge-*, *sein*) **1.** *v/i time etc*: go by, pass; *pain*, *effect etc*: wear off; **~ vor** (*dat*) be dying with; ***wie die Zeit vergeht!*** how time flies! **2.** *v/refl* ***sich ~ an*** (*dat*) violate; rape
**Vergehen** *n* (*-s*; -) JUR offen|se, *Br* -ce
**ver'gelten** *v/t* (*irr*, ***gelten***, *no -ge-*, *h*) repay; reward; **Ver'geltung** *f* (-; *-en*) retaliation (*a.* MIL)
**vergessen** [fɛɐ'gɛsən] **1.** *v/t* (*irr*, *no -ge-*, *h*) forget; leave **2.** *pp of* ***vergessen*** 1; **Ver'gessenheit** *f*: ***in ~ geraten*** fall into oblivion; **vergesslich** [fɛɐ'gɛslɪç] *adj* forgetful
**vergeuden** [fɛɐ'gɔʏdən] *v/t* (*no -ge-*, *h*), **Ver'geudung** *f* (-; *-en*) waste
**vergewaltigen** [fɛɐgə'valtɪgən] *v/t* (*no -ge-*, *h*) rape, violate (*a. fig*)
**Verge'waltigung** *f* (-; *-en*) rape, violation (*a. fig*)
**vergewissern** [fɛɐgə'vɪsɐn] *v/refl* (*no -ge-*, *h*) make sure (***e-r Sache*** of s.th.; ***ob*** whether; ***dass*** that)
**ver'gießen** *v/t* (*irr*, ***gießen***, *no -ge-*, *h*) shed (*blood*, *tears*); spill
**ver'giften** *v/t* (*no -ge-*, *h*) poison (*a. fig*); contaminate; **Ver'giftung** *f* (-; *-en*) poisoning (*a. fig*); contamination
**ver'gittert** *adj* barred (*window etc*)
**Ver'gleich** *m* (-[*e*]*s*; *-e*) comparison; JUR compromise; **ver'gleichbar** *adj* comparable (***mit*** to, with); **ver'gleichen** *v/t* (*irr*, ***gleichen***, *no -ge-*, *h*) compare (***mit*** with *or* to); ***... ist nicht zu ~ mit*** ... cannot be compared to; ... cannot compare with; ***verglichen mit*** compared to *or* with; **ver'gleichsweise** *adv* comparatively, relatively
**ver'glühen** *v/i* (*no -ge-*, *sein*) burn out (*or* up)
**vergnügen** [fɛɐ'gny:gən] *v/refl* (*no -ge-*, *h*) enjoy o.s. (***mit et.*** doing s.th.)
**Ver'gnügen** *n* (*-s*; -) pleasure, enjoyment, fun; ***mit ~*** with pleasure; ***viel ~!*** have fun!, have a good time!
**vergnügt** [fɛɐ'gny:kt] *adj* cheerful
**Ver'gnügung** *f* (-; *-en*) pleasure, amusement, entertainment
**Ver'gnügungspark** *m* amusement park
**ver'gnügungssüchtig** *adj* pleasure-seeking
**Ver'gnügungsviertel** *n* nightlife district
**ver|'golden** *v/t* (*no -ge-*, *h*) gild; **~'göttern** [fɛɐ'gœtɐn] *v/t* (*no -ge-*, *h*) idolize, adore; **~'graben** *v/t* (*irr*, ***graben***, *no -ge-*, *h*) bury (*a. fig*)
**ver'greifen** *v/refl* (*irr*, ***greifen***, *no -ge-*, *h*) ***sich ~ an*** (*dat*) lay hands on
**vergriffen** [fɛɐ'grɪfən] *adj* out of print
**vergrößern** [fɛɐ'grø:sɐn] *v/t* (*no -ge-*, *h*) enlarge (*a.* PHOT); increase; OPT magnify; ***sich ~*** increase, grow, expand; **Ver'größerung** *f* (-; *-en*) increase; PHOT enlargement; OPT magnification; **Ver'größerungsglas** *n* OPT magnifying glass
**Vergünstigung** [fɛɐ'gʏnstɪgʊŋ] *f* (-; *-en*) privilege
**vergüten** [fɛɐ'gy:tən] *v/t* (*no -ge-*, *h*) reimburse, pay (for); **Ver'gütung** *f* (-; *-en*) reimbursement
**ver'haften** *v/t* (*no -ge-*, *h*), **Ver'haftung** *f* (-; *-en*) arrest
**ver'halten**¹ *v/refl* (*irr*, ***halten***, *no -ge-*, *h*) behave, conduct o.s., act; ***sich ruhig ~*** keep quiet
**ver'halten**² *adj* restrained; subdued
**Ver'halten** *n* (*-s*; *no pl*) behavio(u)r, conduct; **Ver'haltensforschung** *f* behavio(u)ral science; **ver'haltensgestört** *adj* disturbed, maladjusted
**Verhältnis** [fɛɐ'hɛltnɪs] *n* (*-ses*; *-se*) relationship, relations; attitude; proportion, relation, *esp* MATH ratio; F affair; *pl* circumstances, conditions; ***über j-s ~se*** beyond s.o.'s means; **ver'hältnismäßig** *adv* comparatively, relatively
**Ver'hältniswort** *n* (-[*e*]*s*; *-wörter*) LING preposition
**ver'handeln** *no* (*-ge-*, *h*) **1.** *v/i* negotiate **2.** *v/t* JUR hear; **Ver'handlung** *f* (-; *-en*) negotiation, talk; JUR hearing; trial; **Ver'handlungsbasis** *f* ECON asking price
**ver'hängen** *v/t* (*no -ge-*, *h*) cover (***mit*** with); impose (***über*** *acc* on)
**Verhängnis** [fɛɐ'hɛŋnɪs] *n* (*-ses*; *-se*) fate; disaster; **ver'hängnisvoll** *adj* fatal, disastrous
**verharmlosen** [fɛɐ'harmlo:zən] *v/t* (*no -ge-*, *h*) play *s.th.* down
**verhärmt** [fɛɐ'hɛrmt] *adj* careworn
**ver'hasst** *adj* hated; hateful
**ver'hätscheln** *v/t* (*no -ge-*, *h*) coddle, pamper, spoil

**ver'hauen** F *v/t* (*no -ge-, h*) spank
**verheerend** [fɛɐ'heːrənt] *adj* disastrous
**ver'heilen** *v/i* (*no -ge-, sein*) heal (up)
**verheimlichen** [fɛɐ'haimlɪçən] *v/t* (*no -ge-, h*) hide, conceal
**ver'heiraten** *v/t* (*no -ge-, h*) marry (*s.o.* off) (***mit*** to); ***sich ~*** get married
**ver'heiratet** *adj* married (***mit*** to)
**ver'heißungsvoll** *adj* promising
**ver'helfen** *v/i* (*irr*, ***helfen***, *no -ge-, h*) ***j-m zu et. ~*** help s.o. to get s.th.
**ver'herrlichen** *v/t* (*no -ge-, h*) glorify, *contp a.* idolize; **Ver'herrlichung** *f* (*-; -en*) glorification
**ver'hexen** *v/t* (*no -ge-, h*) bewitch
**ver'hindern** *v/t* (*no -ge-, h*) prevent (***dass j. et. tut*** s.o. from doing s.th.); **ver'hindert** *adj* unable to come; F ***ein ~er ...*** a would-be ...; **Ver'hinderung** *f* (*-; -en*) prevention
**ver'höhnen** *v/t* (*no -ge-, h*) deride, mock (at), jeer (at)
**Verhör** [fɛɐ'høːɐ] *n* (*-[e]s; -e*) JUR interrogation; **ver'hören** (*no -ge-, h*) **1.** *v/t* interrogate, question **2.** *v/refl* get it wrong
**ver'hüllen** *v/t* (*no -ge-, h*) cover, veil
**ver'hungern** *v/i* (*no -ge-, sein*) die of hunger, starve (to death)
**Ver'hungern** *n* (*-s; no pl*) starvation
**ver'hüten** *v/t* (*no -ge-, h*) prevent
**Ver'hütung** *f* (*-; -en*) prevention
**Ver'hütungsmittel** *n* MED contraceptive
**ver'irren** *v/refl* (*no -ge-, h*) get lost, lose one's way, go astray (*a. fig*)
**Ver'irrung** *f* (*-; -en*) aberration
**ver'jagen** *v/t* (*no -ge-, h*) chase *or* drive away
**verjähren** [fɛɐ'jɛːrən] *v/i* (*no -ge-, sein*) JUR come under the statute of limitations; **ver'jährt** *adj* JUR statute-barred
**verjüngen** [fɛɐ'jʏŋən] *v/t* (*no -ge-, h*) make *s.o.* (look) younger, rejuvenate; ***sich ~*** ARCH, TECH taper (off)
**ver'kabeln** *v/t* (*no -ge-, h*) ELECTR cable
**Ver'kauf** *m* sale; **ver'kaufen** *v/t* (*no -ge-, h*) sell; ***zu ~*** for sale; ***sich gut ~*** sell well; **Ver'käufer** *m* (*-s; -*) (sales)clerk, salesman, *Br* shop assistant; ECON seller; **Ver'käuferin** *f* (*-; -nen*) (sales)clerk, saleslady, *Br* shop assistant; **ver'käuflich** *adj* for sale; ***schwer ~*** hard to sell
**Verkehr** [fɛɐ'keːɐ] *m* (*-s; no pl*) traffic; transportation, *Br* transport; *fig* contact, dealings; intercourse; circulation; ***starker*** (***schwacher***) ***~*** heavy (light) traffic; **ver'kehren** (*no -ge-, h*) **1.** *v/i bus etc*: run; ***~ in*** (*dat*) frequent; ***~ mit*** associate *or* mix with; have intercourse with **2.** *v/t* turn (***in*** *acc* into); ***ins Gegenteil ~*** reverse
**Ver'kehrs|ader** *f* arterial road; **~ampel** *f* traffic light(s); **~behinderung** *f* hold--up, delay; JUR obstruction of traffic; **~de,likt** *n* traffic offense (*Br* offence); **~flugzeug** *n* airliner; **~funk** *m* traffic bulletin; **~insel** *f* traffic island; **~meldung** *f* traffic announcement, flash; **~mi,nister** *m* minister of transportation; **~minis,terium** *n* ministry of transportation; **~mittel** *n* means of transportation; ***öffentliche ~*** public transportation; **~opfer** *n* road casualty; **~poli,zei** *f* traffic police; **~rowdy** *m* F road hog
**ver'kehrssicher** *adj* MOT roadworthy
**Ver'kehrs|sicherheit** *f* MOT road safety; roadworthiness; **~stau** *m* traffic jam; **~sünder(in)** F traffic offender; **~teilnehmer(in)** road user; **~unfall** *m* traffic accident; (car) crash; **~unterricht** *m* traffic instruction; **~zeichen** *n* traffic sign
**ver'kehrt** *adj and adv* wrong; upside down; inside out
**ver|'kennen** *v/t* (*irr*, ***kennen***, *no -ge-, h*) mistake, misjudge; **~'klagen** *v/t* (*no -ge-, h*) JUR sue (***auf*** *acc*, ***wegen*** for); **~'klappen** *v/t* (*no -ge-, h*) dump (into the sea); **~'kleben** *v/t* (*no -ge-, h*) glue (together)
**ver'kleiden** *v/t* (*no -ge-, h*) disguise (***als*** as), dress *s.o.* up (as); TECH cover, (en)case; panel; ***sich ~*** disguise o.s., dress (o.s.) up; **Ver'kleidung** *f* (*-; -en*) disguise; TECH cover, encasement; panel(l)ing; MOT fairing
**verkleinern** [fɛɐ'klainɐn] *v/t* (*no -ge-, h*) make smaller, reduce, diminish; **Ver'kleinerung** [fɛɐ'klainərʊŋ] *f* (*-; -en*) reduction
**ver'klingen** *v/i* (*irr*, ***klingen***, *no -ge-, sein*) die away
**ver'knallt** F *adj*: ***~ sein in*** (*acc*) be madly in love with, have a crush on
**ver|'knoten** *v/t* (*no -ge-, h*) knot; **~'knüpfen** *v/t* (*no -ge-, h*) knot together;

V

*fig* connect, combine; ~'**kohlen** *v/i* (*no -ge-, sein*) char; ~'**kommen 1.** *v/i* (*irr,* ***kommen****, no -ge-, sein*) become run-down *or* dilapidated; go to seed; GASTR go bad **2.** *adj* run-down, dilapidated; neglected; depraved, rotten (to the core); ~'**korken** *v/t* (*no -ge-, h*) cork (up); ~'**körpern** *v/t* (*no -ge-, h*) personify; embody; *esp* THEA impersonate; ~'**kriechen** *v/refl* (*irr,* ***kriechen****, no -ge-, h*) hide; ~'**krümmt** *adj* crooked, curved (*a.* MED); ~'**krüppelt** *adj* crippled; ~'**kümmern** *v/i* (*no -ge-, sein*) BIOL become stunted; ~'**kümmert** *adj* BIOL stunted

**verkünden** [fɛɐ'kʏndən] *v/t* (*no -ge-, h*) announce; proclaim; JUR pronounce; REL preach; **Ver'kündung** *f* (-; *-en*) announcement; proclamation; JUR pronouncement; REL preaching

**ver|'kürzen** *v/t* (*no -ge-, h*) shorten; reduce; ~'**laden** *v/t* (*irr,* ***laden****, no -ge-, h*) load (***auf*** *acc* onto; ***in*** *acc* into)

**Verlag** [fɛɐ'la:k] *m* (-[*e*]*s*; *-e* [fɛɐ'la:gə]) publishing house *or* company, publisher(s)

**ver'lagern** *v/t and v/refl* (*no -ge-, h*) shift (***auf*** *acc* to)

**ver'langen** *v/t* (*no -ge-, h*) ask for; demand; claim; charge; take, call for; **Ver'langen** *n* (*-s*; -) desire (***nach*** for); longing (for), yearning (for); ***auf*** ~ by request; ECON on demand

**verlängern** [fɛɐ'lɛŋɐn] *v/t* (*no -ge-, h*) lengthen, make longer; prolong, extend (*a.* ECON); **Verlängerung** [fɛɐ'lɛŋərʊŋ] *f* (-; *-en*) lengthening; prolongation, extension; SPORT overtime, *Br* extra time

**ver'langsamen** *v/t and v/refl* (*no -ge-, h*) slacken, slow down (*both a. fig*)

**ver'lassen** (*irr,* ***lassen****, no -ge-, h*) **1.** *v/t* leave; abandon, desert **2.** *v/refl*: ***sich*** ~ ***auf*** (*acc*) rely *or* depend on

**verlässlich** [fɛɐ'lɛslɪç] *adj* reliable, dependable

**Ver'lauf** *m* course; **ver'laufen** (*irr,* ***laufen****, no -ge-*) **1.** *v/i* (*sein*) run; go; end (up) **2.** *v/refl* (*h*) get lost, lose one's way

**ver'leben** *v/t* (*no -ge-, h*) spend; have

**ver'legen**[1] *v/t* (*no -ge-, h*) move; mislay; TECH lay; put off, postpone; publish

**ver'legen**[2] *adj* embarrassed

**Ver'legenheit** *f* (-; *-en*) (*no pl*) embarrassment; embarrassing situation

**Verleger** [fɛɐ'le:gɐ] *m* (*-s*; -), **Ver'legerin** *f* (-; *-nen*) publisher

**Verleih** [fɛɐ'lai] *m* (-[*e*]*s*; *-e*) (*no pl*) hire, rental; *film*: distributor(s)

**ver'leihen** *v/t* (*irr,* ***leihen****, no -ge-, h*) lend, loan; MOT *etc* rent (*Br* hire) out; award (*prize etc*); grant (*privilege etc*); **Ver'leihung** *f* (-; *-en*) award(ing), presentation; grant(ing)

**ver'leiten** *v/t* (*no -ge-, h*) ***j-n zu et.*** ~ make s.o. do s.th., lead s.o. to do s.th.

**ver'lernen** *v/t* (*no -ge-, h*) forget

**ver'lesen** (*irr,* ***lesen****, no -ge-, h*) **1.** *v/t* read (*or* call) out **2.** *v/refl* make a slip (in reading); misread *s.th.*

**verletzen** [fɛɐ'lɛtsən] *v/t* (*no -ge-, h*) hurt, injure, *fig a.* offend; ***sich*** ~ hurt o.s., get hurt; ~**d** *adj* offensive

**Ver'letzte** *m, f* (*-n*; *-n*) injured person; *pl the* injured; **Ver'letzung** *f* (-; *-en*) injury, *esp pl a.* hurt; JUR violation

**ver'leugnen** *v/t* (*no -ge-, h*) deny; renounce

**verleumden** [fɛɐ'lɔʏmdən] *v/t* (*no -ge-, h*) defame; JUR slander, libel; **ver'leumderisch** *adj* JUR slanderous, libel(l)ous; **Ver'leumdung** *f* (-; *-en*) JUR slander; libel

**ver'lieben** *v/refl* (*no -ge-, h*) fall in love (***in*** *acc* with); **verliebt** [fɛɐ'li:pt] *adj* in love (***in*** *acc* with); amorous (*look etc*); **Ver'liebte** *m, f* (*-n*; *-n*) lover

**verlieren** [fɛɐ'li:rən] *v/t and v/i* (*irr, no -ge-, h*) lose; **Ver'lierer(in)** (*-s*; -/-; *-nen*) loser

**ver'loben** *v/refl* (*no -ge-, h*) get engaged (***mit*** to); **Verlobte** [fɛɐ'lo:ptə] **1.** *m* (*-n*; *-n*) fiancé **2.** *f* (*-n*; *-n*) fiancée; **Ver'lobung** *f* (-; *-en*) engagement

**ver'locken** *v/t* (*no -ge-, h*) tempt; ~**d** *adj* tempting

**Ver'lockung** *f* (-; *-en*) temptation

**verlogen** [fɛɐ'lo:gən] *adj* untruthful, lying

**verlor** [fɛɐ'lo:ɐ] *pret of* ***verlieren***

**verloren** [fɛɐ'lo:rən] **1.** *pp of* ***verlieren*** **2.** *adj* lost; wasted; ~ ***gehen*** be *or* get lost; **ver'lorengehen** *v/i* (*irr,* ***gehen****, sep, -ge-, sein*) → ***verloren***

**ver'losen** *v/t* (*no -ge-, h*) raffle (off); **Ver'losung** *f* (-; *-en*) raffle

**Verlust** [fɛɐ'lʊst] *m* (-[*e*]*s*; *-e*) loss (*a. fig*); *pl esp* MIL casualties

**ver'machen** *v/t* (*no -ge-, h*) leave, will
**Vermächtnis** [fɛɐ'mɛçtnɪs] *n* (*-ses; -se*) legacy (*a. fig*)
**ver'markten** *v/t* (*no -ge-, h*) market, merchandize; **Ver'marktung** *f* (*-; -en*) marketing, merchandizing
**ver'mehren** *v/t and v/refl* increase (***um*** by), multiply (by) (*a.* BIOL); BIOL reproduce, *esp* ZO *a.* breed; **Ver'mehrung** *f* (*-; -en*) increase; BIOL reproduction
**vermeidbar** [fɛɐ'maitbaːɐ] *adj* avoidable; **ver'meiden** *v/t* (*irr,* ***meiden****, no -ge-, h*) avoid
**vermeintlich** [fɛɐ'maintɪç] *adj* supposed, alleged
**ver'mengen** *v/t* (*no -ge-, h*) mix, mingle, blend
**Vermerk** [fɛɐ'mɛrk] *m* (*-[e]s; -e*) note
**ver'merken** *v/t* (*no -ge-, h*) make a note of
**ver'messen**[1] *v/t* (*irr,* ***messen****, no -ge-, h*) measure; survey
**ver'messen**[2] *adj* presumptuous
**Ver'messung** *f* (*-; -en*) measuring; survey(ing)
**ver'mieten** *v/t* (*no -ge-, h*) let, rent, lease (out); rent (*Br* hire) out (*cars etc*); ***zu ~*** for rent, *Br* to let, for hire
**Ver'mieter** *n* (*-s; -*) landlord
**Ver'mieterin** *f* (*-; -nen*) landlady
**Ver'mietung** *f* (*-; -en*) letting, renting
**ver'mischen** *v/t and v/refl* (*no -ge-, h*) mix, mingle, blend (***mit*** with); **ver'mischt** *adj* mixed; miscellaneous
**vermissen** [fɛɐ'mɪsən] *v/t* (*no -ge-, h*) miss; **ver'misst** *adj* missing; ***die Vermissten*** *pl* the missing
**ver'mitteln** (*no -ge-, h*) **1.** *v/t* arrange; give, convey (*impression etc*); ***j-m et. ~*** get *or* find s.o. s.th. **2.** *v/i* mediate (***zwischen*** between); **Ver'mittler** *m* (*-s; -*) mediator, go-between; ECON agent, broker; **Ver'mittlung** *f* (*-; -en*) mediation; arrangement; agency, office; (telephone) exchange; operator
**ver'modern** *v/i* (*no -ge-, sein*) rot, mo(u)lder
**Ver'mögen** *n* (*-s; -*) fortune, property, possessions; ECON assets
**ver'mögend** *adj* well-to-do, well-off
**vermummen** [fɛɐ'mumən] *v/refl* (*no -ge-, h*) mask o.s., disguise o.s.
**vermuten** [fɛɐ'muːtən] *v/t* (*no -ge-, h*) suppose, expect, think, guess; **ver'mutlich** *adv* probably; **Ver'mutung** *f* (*-; -en*) supposition; speculation
**vernachlässigen** [fɛɐ'naːxlɛsɪgən] *v/t* (*no -ge-, h*), **Ver'nachlässigung** *f* (*-; -en*) neglect
**ver'narben** *v/i* (*no -ge-, sein*) scar over; *fig* heal
**ver'narrt** *adj*: ***~ in*** (*acc*) mad *or* crazy about
**ver'nehmen** *v/t* (*irr,* ***nehmen****, no -ge-, h*) JUR question, interrogate
**ver'nehmlich** *adj* clear, distinct
**Ver'nehmung** *f* (*-; -en*) JUR interrogation, examination
**ver'neigen** *v/refl* (*no -ge-, h*), **Ver'neigung** *f* (*-; -en*) bow (***vor*** *dat* to) (*a. fig*)
**ver'neinen** (*no -ge-, h*) **1.** *v/t* deny **2.** *v/i* say no, answer in the negative; **~d** *adj* negative
**Ver'neinung** *f* (*-; -en*) denial, negative (*a.* LING)
**ver'nichten** *v/t* (*no -ge-, h*) destroy; **~d** *adj* devastating (*a. fig*); crushing
**Ver'nichtung** *f* (*-; -en*) destruction; extermination
**Vernunft** [fɛɐ'nunft] *f* (*-; no pl*) reason; ***~ annehmen*** listen to reason; ***j-n zur ~ bringen*** bring s.o. to reason
**vernünftig** [fɛɐ'nʏnftɪç] *adj* sensible, reasonable (*a.* ECON); F decent
**ver'öden** *v/i* (*no -ge-, sein*) become deserted
**ver'öffentlichen** *v/t* (*no -ge-, h*) publish; **Ver'öffentlichung** *f* (*-; -en*) publication
**ver'ordnen** *v/t* (*no -ge-, h*) order, MED *a.* prescribe (***gegen*** for); **Ver'ordnung** *f* (*-; -en*) order; MED prescription
**ver'pachten** *v/t* (*no -ge-, h*) lease
**Ver'pächter** *m* lessor
**ver'packen** *v/t* (*no -ge-, h*) pack (up); TECH package; wrap up
**Ver'packung** *f* (*-; -en*) pack(ag)ing; wrapping; **Ver'packungsmüll** *m* superfluous packaging
**ver|'passen** *v/t* (*no -ge-, h*) miss; **~'patzen** F *v/t* (*no -ge-, h*) mess up, spoil; **~pesten** [fɛɐ'pɛstən] *v/t* (*no -ge-, h*) pollute, foul, contaminate; stink up (*Br* out); **~'petzen** F *v/t* (*no -ge-, h*) ***j-n ~*** tell on s.o. (***bei*** to); **~'pfänden** *v/t* (*no -ge-, h*) pawn; *fig* pledge
**ver'pflanzen** *v/t* (*no -ge-, h*), **Ver'pflanzung** *f* (*-; -en*) transplant (*a.* MED)

**ver'pflegen** *v/t* (*no -ge-*, *h*) feed
**Ver'pflegung** *f* (-; *-en*) food
**ver'pflichten** *v/t* (*no -ge-*, *h*) oblige; engage; ***sich ~, et. zu tun*** undertake (ECON agree) to do s.th.; **ver'pflichtet** *adj*: ***~ sein*** (***sich ~ fühlen***) ***et. zu tun*** be (feel) obliged to do s.th.; **Ver'pflichtung** *f* (-; *-en*) obligation; duty; ECON, JUR liability; engagement, commitment
**ver'pfuschen** F *v/t* (*no -ge-*, *h*) bungle, botch
**ver'plappern** *v/refl* (*no -ge-*, *h*) blab
**verpönt** [fɛɐ'pø:nt] *adj* taboo
**ver'prügeln** F *v/t* (*no -ge-*, *h*) beat *s.o.* up
**Ver'putz** *m* (*-es*; *no pl*), **ver'putzen** *v/t* (*no -ge-*, *h*) ARCH plaster
**verquollen** [fɛɐ'kvɔlən] *adj face etc*: puffy, swollen; *wood*: warped
**Verrat** [fɛɐ'ra:t] *m* (*-[e]s*; *no pl*) betrayal (***an*** *dat* of); treachery (to); JUR treason (to); **ver'raten** *v/t* (*irr*, ***raten***, *no -ge-*, *h*) betray, give away (*both a. fig*); ***sich ~*** betray o.s., give o.s. away
**Verräter** [fɛɐ'rɛ:tɐ] *m* (*-s*; -), **Ver'räterin** *f* (-; *-nen*) traitor
**verräterisch** [fɛɐ'rɛ:tərɪʃ] *adj* treacherous; *fig* telltale
**ver'rechnen** (*no -ge-*, *h*) **1.** *v/t* offset (***mit*** against); **2.** *v/refl* miscalculate, make a mistake (*a. fig*); ***sich um zwei Euro ~*** be two euros out
**Ver'rechnungsscheck** *m* ECON voucher check, *Br* crossed cheque
**ver'regnet** *adj* rainy
**ver'reisen** *v/i* (*no -ge-*, *sein*) go away (***geschäftlich*** on business); **ver'reist** *adj* away (***geschäftlich*** on business)
**verrenken** [fɛɐ'rɛŋkən] *v/t* (*no -ge-*, *h*) MED dislocate, luxate; ***sich et. ~*** MED dislocate s.th.; ***sich den Hals ~*** crane one's neck; **Ver'renkung** *f* (-; *-en*) MED dislocation, luxation
**ver'richten** *v/t* (*no -ge-*, *h*) do, perform, carry out
**ver'riegeln** *v/t* (*no -ge-*, *h*) bolt, bar
**verringern** [fɛɐ'rɪŋɐn] *v/t* (*no -ge-*, *h*) decrease, lessen (*both a.* ***sich ~***), reduce, cut down; **Ver'ringerung** *f* (-; *-en*) reduction, decrease
**ver'rosten** *v/t* (*no -ge-*, *sein*) rust, get rusty (*a. fig*)
**verrotten** [fɛɐ'rɔtən] *v/i* (*no -ge-*, *sein*) rot; **ver'rottet** *adj* rotten
**ver'rücken** *v/t* (*no -ge-*, *h*) move, shift
**ver'rückt** *adj* mad, crazy (*both a. fig* ***nach*** about); ***wie ~*** like mad; ***~ werden*** go mad, go crazy; ***j-n ~ machen*** drive s.o. mad; **Ver'rückte** *m*, *f* (*-n*; *-n*) madman (madwoman), lunatic, maniac (*all a.* F); **Ver'rücktheit** *f* (-; *-en*) (*no pl*) madness, craziness; crazy thing
**Ver'ruf** *m*: ***in ~ bringen*** bring discredit (up)on; ***in ~ kommen*** get into discredit
**ver'rufen** *adj* disreputable, notorious
**ver'rutschen** *v/i* (*no -ge-*, *sein*) slip, get out of place
**Vers** [fɛrs] *m* (*-es*; *-e* ['fɛrzə]) verse; line
**ver'sagen** (*no -ge-*, *h*) **1.** *v/i* fail (*a.* MED), MOT *etc a.* break down; *gun etc*: misfire **2.** *v/t* deny, refuse; **Ver'sagen** *n* (*-s*; *no pl*) failure; **Ver'sager** *m* (*-s*; -) failure
**ver'salzen** *v/t* (*no -ge-*, *h*) oversalt
**ver'sammeln** *v/t* (*no -ge-*, *h*) gather, assemble; ***sich ~*** *a.* meet; **Ver'sammlung** *f* (-; *-en*) assembly, meeting
**Versand** [fɛɐ'zant] *m* (*-[e]s*; *no pl*) dispatch, shipment; ***~...*** *in cpds ...haus, ...katalog etc*: mail-order ...
**ver'säumen** *v/t* (*no -ge-*, *h*) miss; ***~ et. zu tun*** fail to do s.th.; **Versäumnis** [fɛɐ'zɔʏmnɪs] *n* (*-ses*; *-se*) omission
**ver|'schaffen** *v/t* (*no -ge-*, *h*) get, find; ***sich ~*** *a.* obtain; **~'schämt** *adj* bashful; **~'schanzen** *v/refl* (*no -ge-*, *h*) entrench o.s. (*a. fig* ***hinter*** behind); **~'schärfen** *v/t* (*no -ge-*, *h*) aggravate; tighten up; increase; ***sich ~*** get worse; **~'schenken** *v/t* (*no -ge-*, *h*) give away (*a. fig*); **~'scherzen** *v/t* (*no -ge-*, *h*) forfeit; **~'scheuchen** *v/t* (*no -ge-*, *h*) chase away (*a. fig*); **~'schicken** *v/t* (*no -ge-*, *h*) send off, *esp* ECON *a.* dispatch
**ver'schieben** *v/t* (*irr*, ***schieben***, *no -ge-*, *h*) move, shift (*a.* ***sich ~***); postpone, put off; **Ver'schiebung** *f* (-; *-en*) shift(ing); postponement
**verschieden** [fɛɐ'ʃi:dən] *adj* different (***von*** from); ***~e ...*** *pl* various ..., several...; **~artig** *adj* different; various
**Ver'schiedenheit** *f* (-; *-en*) difference
**ver'schiedentlich** *adv* repeatedly
**ver'schiffen** *v/t* (*no -ge-*, *h*) ship
**Ver'schiffung** *f* (-; *-en*) shipment
**ver|'schimmeln** *v/i* (*no -ge-*, *sein*) get mo(u)ldy; **~'schlafen** (*irr*, ***schlafen***, *no -ge-*, *h*) **1.** *v/i* oversleep **2.** *v/t* sleep through **3.** *adj* sleepy (*a. fig*)

V

**Ver'schlag** *m* shed
**ver'schlagen**[1] *v/t* (*irr*, ***schlagen***, *no -ge-*, *h*) ***j-m den Atem ~*** take s.o.'s breath away; ***j-m die Sprache ~*** leave s.o. speechless; ***es hat ihn nach X ~*** he ended up in X
**ver'schlagen**[2] *adj* sly, cunning
**verschlechtern** [fɛɐ'ʃlɛçtɐn] *v/t and v/refl* (*no -ge-*, *h*) make (*refl* get) worse, worsen, deteriorate
**Ver'schlechterung** *f* (-; *-en*) deterioration; change for the worse
**ver'schleiern** *v/t* (*no -ge-*, *h*) veil (*a. fig*)
**Verschleiß** [fɛɐ'ʃlais] *m* (*-es*; *no pl*) wear (and tear); **ver'schleißen** *v/t* (*irr*, *no -ge-*, *h*) wear out
**ver|'schleppen** *v/t* (*no -ge-*, *h*) carry off; POL displace; draw out, delay; MED neglect; **~'schleudern** *v/t* (*no -ge-*, *h*) waste; ECON sell dirt cheap; **~'schließen** *v/t* (*irr*, ***schließen***, *no -ge-*, *h*) close (*a. fig one's eyes*); lock (up)
**ver'schlingen** *v/t* (*irr*, ***schlingen***, *no -ge-*, *h*) devour (*a. fig*); gulp (down)
**verschliss** [fɛɐ'ʃlɪs] *pret of* ***verschleißen***; **verschlissen** [fɛɐ'ʃlɪsən] *pp of* ***verschleißen***
**verschlossen** [fɛɐ'ʃlɔsən] *adj* closed; *fig* aloof, reserved; **Ver'schlossenheit** *f* (-; *no pl*) aloofness
**ver'schlucken** (*no -ge-*, *h*) **1.** *v/t* swallow (*fig* up); **2.** *v/refl* choke; ***ich habe mich verschluckt*** it went down the wrong way
**Ver'schluss** *m* fastener; clasp; catch; lock; cover, lid; cap, top; PHOT shutter; ***unter ~*** under lock and key
**ver'schlüsseln** *v/t* (*no -ge-*, *h*) (en)code, (en)cipher
**verschmähen** [fɛɐ'ʃmɛːən] *v/t* (*no -ge-*, *h*) disdain, scorn
**ver'schmelzen** *v/i* (*irr*, ***schmelzen***, *no -ge-*, *sein*) *and v/t* (*h*) merge, fuse (*both a.* ECON, POL *etc*), melt; **Ver'schmelzung** *f* (-; *-en*) fusion (*a. fig*)
**ver|'schmerzen** *v/t* (*no -ge-*, *h*) get over *s.th.*; **~'schmieren** *v/t* (*no -ge-*, *h*) smear, smudge
**verschmitzt** [fɛɐ'ʃmɪtst] *adj* mischievous
**ver|'schmutzen** (*no -ge-*) **1.** *v/t* (*h*) soil, dirty; pollute **2.** *v/i* (*sein*) get dirty; get polluted; **~'schnaufen** F *v/i and v/refl* (*no -ge-*, *h*) stop for breath
**ver'schneit** *adj* snow-covered, snowy
**Ver'schnitt** *m* blend; waste
**verschnupft** [fɛɐ'ʃnʊpft] *adj*: **~ *sein*** MED have a cold; F be in a huff
**ver'schnüren** *v/t* (*no -ge-*, *h*) tie up
**verschollen** [fɛɐ'ʃɔlən] *adj* missing; JUR presumed dead
**ver'schonen** *v/t* (*no -ge-*, *h*) spare; ***j-n mit et. ~*** spare s.o. s.th.
**verschönern** [fɛɐ'ʃøːnɐn] *v/t* (*no -ge-*, *h*) embellish; **Verschönerung** [fɛɐ'ʃøːnərʊŋ] *f* (-; *-en*) embellishment
**verschossen** [fɛɐ'ʃɔsən] *adj* faded; F ***~ sein in*** (*acc*) have a crush on
**verschränken** [fɛɐ'ʃrɛŋkən] *v/t* (*no -ge-*, *h*) fold; cross (*one's legs*)
**ver'schreiben** (*irr*, ***schreiben***, *no -ge-*, *h*) **1.** *v/t* MED prescribe (***gegen*** for); **2.** *v/refl* make a slip of the pen
**ver'schreibungspflichtig** *adj* PHARM available on prescription only
**verschroben** [fɛɐ'ʃroːbən] *adj* eccentric, odd
**ver'schrotten** *v/t* (*no -ge-*, *h*) scrap
**ver'schüchtert** *adj* intimidated
**ver'schulden** *v/t* (*no -ge-*, *h*) be responsible for, cause, be the cause of; ***sich ~*** get into debt; **ver'schuldet** *adj* in debt
**ver'schütten** *v/t* (*no -ge-*, *h*) spill; bury *s.o.* (alive)
**verschwägert** [fɛɐ'ʃvɛːgɐt] *adj* related by marriage
**ver'schweigen** *v/t* (*irr*, ***schweigen***, *no -ge-*, *h*) keep *s.th.* a secret, hide
**verschwenden** [fɛɐ'ʃvɛndən] *v/t* (*no -ge-*, *h*) waste; **Verschwender** [fɛɐ'ʃvɛndɐ] *m* (*-s*; -) spendthrift; **verschwenderisch** [fɛɐ'ʃvɛndərɪʃ] *adj* wasteful, extravagant; lavish; **Ver'schwendung** *f* (-; *-en*) waste
**verschwiegen** [fɛɐ'ʃviːgən] *adj* discreet; hidden, secret; **Ver'schwiegenheit** *f* (-; *no pl*) secrecy, discretion
**ver'schwimmen** *v/i* (*irr*, ***schwimmen***, *no -ge-*, *sein*) become blurred
**ver'schwinden** *v/i* (*irr*, ***schwinden***, *no -ge-*, *sein*) disappear, vanish; F ***verschwinde!*** beat it!; **Ver'schwinden** *n* (*-s*; *no pl*) disappearance
**verschwommen** [fɛɐ'ʃvɔmən] *adj* blurred (*a.* PHOT), *fig a.* vague, hazy
**ver'schwören** *v/refl* (*irr*, ***schwören***, *no*

V

-*ge*-, *h*) conspire, plot; **Verschwörer** [fɛɐ'ʃvøːrɐ] *m* (-*s*; -) conspirator; **Ver'schwörung** *f* (-; -*en*) conspiracy, plot
**verschwunden** [fɛɐ'ʃvʊndən] *adj* missing
**ver'sehen** (*irr*, ***sehen***, *no -ge-*, *h*) **1.** *v/t* hold (*an office etc*); ***~ mit*** provide with **2.** *v/refl* make a mistake; **Ver'sehen** *n* (-*s*; -) mistake, error; ***aus ~*** → **versehentlich** [fɛɐ'zeːəntlɪç] *adv* by mistake, unintentionally
**Versehrte** [fɛɐ'zeːɐtə] *m, f* (-*n*; -*n*) disabled person
**ver|'sengen** *v/t* (*no -ge-*, *h*) singe, scorch; **~'senken** *v/t* (*no -ge-*, *h*) sink; ***sich ~ in*** (*acc*) become absorbed in
**versessen** [fɛɐ'zɛsən] *adj*: ***~ auf*** (*acc*) keen on, mad *or* crazy about
**ver'setzen** *v/t* (*no -ge-*, *h*) move, shift; transfer; PED promote, *Br* move *s.o.* up; give (*s.o. a kick etc*); pawn; AGR transplant; F ***j-n ~*** stand s.o. up; ***j-n in die Lage ~ zu*** *inf* put s.o. in a position to *inf*, enable s.o. to *inf*; ***sich in j-s Lage ~*** put o.s. in s.o.'s place; **Ver'setzung** *f* (-; -*en*) transfer; PED promotion
**ver'seuchen** *v/t* (*no -ge-*, *h*) contaminate; **Ver'seuchung** *f* (-; -*en*) contamination
**ver'sichern** *v/t* (*no -ge-*, *h*) ECON insure (***bei*** with); assure (***j-m et.*** s.o. of s.th.), assert; ***sich ~*** insure o.s.; make sure (***dass*** that); **Ver'sicherte** *m, f* (-*n*; -*n*) *the* insured; **Ver'sicherung** *f* (-; -*en*) insurance; assurance, assertion
**Ver'sicherungs|gesellschaft** *f* insurance company; **~po,lice** *f*, **~schein** *m* insurance policy
**ver|'sickern** *v/i* (*no -ge-*, *sein*) trickle away; **~'siegeln** *v/t* (*no -ge-*, *h*) seal; **~'siegen** *v/i* (*no -ge-*, *sein*) dry up, run dry; **~'silbern** *v/t* (*no -ge-*, *h*) silver-plate; F turn *s.th.* into cash; **~'sinken** *v/i* (*irr*, ***sinken***, *no -ge-*, *sein*) sink; → ***versunken***
**Version** [vɛr'zjoːn] *f* (-; -*en*) version
**'Versmaß** *n* meter, *Br* metre
**versöhnen** [fɛɐ'zøːnən] *v/t* (*no -ge-*, *h*) reconcile; ***sich*** (***wieder***) ***~*** make it up (***mit*** with); **ver'söhnlich** *adj* conciliatory; **Ver'söhnung** *f* (-; -*en*) reconciliation; *esp* POL appeasement
**ver'sorgen** *v/t* (*no -ge-*, *h*) provide (***mit*** with), supply (with); support; take care of, look after; **Ver'sorgung** *f* (-; *no pl*) supply (***mit*** with); support; care
**ver'späten** *v/refl* (*no -ge-*, *h*) be late; **ver'spätet** *adj* belated, late, RAIL *etc a.* delayed; **Ver'spätung** *f* (-; -*en*) being *or* coming late, RAIL *etc* delay; ***20 Minuten ~ haben*** be 20 minutes late
**ver'speisen** *v/t* (*no -ge-*, *h*) eat (up)
**ver'sperren** *v/t* (*no -ge-*, *h*) bar, block (up), obstruct (*a. view*); lock
**ver'spielen** *v/t* (*no -ge-*, *h*) lose; **ver'spielt** *adj* playful
**ver'spotten** *v/t* (*no -ge-*, *h*) make fun of, ridicule
**ver'sprechen** (*irr*, ***sprechen***, *no -ge-*, *h*) **1.** *v/t* promise (*a. fig*); ***sich zu viel ~*** (***von***) expect too much (of) **2.** *v/refl* make a mistake *or* slip; **Ver'sprechen** *n* (-*s*; -) promise; ***ein ~ geben*** (***halten, brechen***) make (keep, break) a promise; **Ver'sprecher** F *m* (-*s*; -) slip (of the tongue)
**ver'staatlichen** *v/t* (*no -ge-*, *h*) ECON nationalize; **Ver'staatlichung** *f* (-; -*en*) ECON nationalization
**Verstädterung** [fɛɐ'ʃtɛːtərʊŋ] *f* (-; -*en*) urbanization
**Verstand** [fɛɐ'ʃtant] *m* (-[*e*]*s*; *no pl*) mind, intellect; reason, (common) sense; intelligence, brains; ***nicht bei ~*** out of one's mind, not in one's right mind; ***den ~ verlieren*** go out of one's mind; **verstandesmäßig** [fɛɐ'ʃtandəsmɛːsɪç] *adj* rational
**ver'ständig** *adj* reasonable, sensible
**verständigen** [fɛɐ'ʃtɛndɪgən] *v/t* (*no -ge-*, *h*) inform (***von*** of), notify (of); call (*doctor, police etc*); ***sich ~*** communicate; come to an agreement (***über*** *acc* on); **Ver'ständigung** *f* (-; *no pl*) communication (*a.* TEL); agreement
**verständlich** [fɛɐ'ʃtɛntlɪç] *adj* audible; intelligible; comprehensible; understandable; ***schwer*** (***leicht***) ***~*** difficult (easy) to understand; ***j-m et. ~ machen*** make s.th. clear to s.o.; ***sich ~ machen*** make o.s. understood
**Verständnis** [fɛɐ'ʃtɛntnɪs] *n* (-*ses*; *no pl*) comprehension, understanding; sympathy; (***viel***) ***~ haben*** be (very) understanding; ***~ haben für*** understand; appreciate
**ver'ständnislos** *adj* uncomprehend-

ing; blank (*look etc*)
**ver'ständnisvoll** *adj* understanding, sympathetic; knowing (*look etc*)
**ver'stärken** *v/t* (*no -ge-, h*) reinforce (*a.* TECH, MIL); strengthen (*a.* TECH); *radio,* PHYS amplify; intensify; **Ver'stärker** *m* (*-s; -*) amplifier; **Ver'stärkung** *f* (*-; -en*) strengthening; reinforcement(s MIL); amplification; intensification
**ver'stauben** *v/i* (*no -ge-, sein*) get dusty
**verstauchen** [fɛɐ'ʃtauxən] *v/t* (*no -ge-, h*), **Ver'stauchung** *f* (*-; -en*) MED sprain
**ver'stauen** *v/t* (*no -ge-, h*) stow away
**Versteck** [fɛɐ'ʃtɛk] *n* (*-[e]s; -e*) hiding place, hideout, hideaway
**ver'stecken** *v/t and v/refl* (*no -ge-, h*) hide (*a. fig*); ***Verstecken spielen*** play (at) hide-and-seek
**ver'stehen** *v/t* (*irr,* ***stehen***, *no -ge-, h*) understand, F get; catch; see; realize; know; ***es ~ zu*** *inf* know how to *inf*; ***zu ~ geben*** give *s.o.* to understand, suggest; ***ich verstehe!*** I see!; ***falsch ~*** misunderstand; ***was ~ Sie unter ...?*** what do you mean *or* understand by ...?; ***sich*** **(*gut*)** ***~*** get along (well) (***mit*** with); ***es versteht sich von selbst*** it goes without saying
**ver'steifen** (*no -ge-, h*) **1.** *v/t* stiffen (*a.* ***sich ~***); TECH strut, brace **2.** *v/refl*: ***sich auf et. ~*** insist on (doing) s.th.
**ver'steigern** *v/t* (*no -ge-, h*) auction off
**Ver'steigerung** *f* (*-; -en*) auction (sale)
**ver'steinern** *v/i* (*no -ge-, sein*) petrify (*a. fig*)
**ver'stellbar** *adj* adjustable
**ver'stellen** *v/t* (*no -ge-, h*) block; move; set *s.th.* wrong *or* the wrong way; TECH adjust, regulate; disguise (*one's voice etc*); ***sich ~*** pretend
**Ver'stellung** *f* (*-; no pl*) disguise, make-believe, (false) show
**ver'steuern** *v/t* (*no -ge-, h*) pay duty *or* tax on
**verstiegen** [fɛɐ'ʃtiːgən] *adj* high-flown
**ver'stimmen** *v/t* (*no -ge-, h*) MUS put out of tune; *fig* annoy; **ver'stimmt** *adj* annoyed; MUS out of tune; MED upset; **Ver'stimmung** *f* (*-; -en*) annoyance
**ver|stockt** [fɛɐ'ʃtɔkt] *adj* stubborn, obstinate; **~stohlen** [fɛɐ'ʃtoːlən] *adj* furtive, stealthy
**ver'stopfen** *v/t* (*no -ge-, h*) plug (up); block, jam; MED constipate; **ver'stopft** *adj* MED constipated; **Ver'stopfung** *f* (*-; -en*) block(age); MED constipation
**verstorben** [fɛɐ'ʃtɔrbən] *adj* late, deceased; **Ver'storbene** *m, f* (*-n; -n*) *the* deceased; ***die ~n*** the deceased
**verstört** [fɛɐ'ʃtøːɐt] *adj* upset; distracted; wild (*look etc*)
**Ver'stoß** *m* offense, *Br* offence (***gegen*** against), violation (of)
**ver'stoßen** (*irr,* ***stoßen***, *no -ge-, h*) **1.** *v/t* expel (***aus*** from); disown **2.** *v/i*: ***~ gegen*** offend against, violate
**ver'strahlt** *adj* (radioactively) contaminated
**ver'streichen** (*irr,* ***streichen***, *no -ge-*) **1.** *v/i* (*sein*) *time*: pass, go by; *date*: expire **2.** *v/t* (*h*) spread
**ver'streuen** *v/t* (*no -ge-, h*) scatter
**verstümmeln** [fɛɐ'ʃtʏməln] *v/t* (*no -ge-, h*) mutilate (*a. fig*); **Ver'stümmelung** *f* (*-; -en*) mutilation (*a. fig*)
**ver'stummen** *v/i* (*no -ge-, sein*) grow silent; stop; die down
**Versuch** [fɛɐ'zuːx] *m* (*-[e]s; -e*) attempt, try; trial, test; PHYS experiment; ***mit et.*** **(*j-m*)** ***e-n ~ machen*** give s.th. (s.o.) a try; **ver'suchen** *v/t* (*no -ge-, h*) try, attempt; taste; REL tempt; ***es ~*** have a try (at it)
**Ver'suchs...** *in cpds ...bohrung etc*: test ..., trial ...; **~ka,ninchen** *n* guinea pig; **~stadium** *n* experimental stage; **~tier** *n* laboratory *or* test animal
**ver'suchsweise** *adv* by way of trial
**Ver'suchung** *f* (*-; -en*) temptation; ***j-n in ~ führen*** tempt s.o.
**versunken** [fɛɐ'zʊŋkən] *fig adj*: ***~ in*** (*acc*) absorbed *or* lost in
**ver'süßen** *v/t* (*no -ge-, h*) sweeten
**ver'tagen** *v/t and v/refl* (*no -ge-, h*) adjourn; **Ver'tagung** *f* (*-; -en*) adjournment
**ver'tauschen** *v/t* (*no -ge-, h*) exchange (***mit*** for)
**verteidigen** [fɛɐ'taidɪgən] *v/t* (*no -ge-, h*) defend (***sich*** o.s.); **Verteidiger(in)** [fɛɐ'taidɪgɐ (-gərɪn)] (*-s; -/-; -nen*) defender, SPORT *a.* back; *fig* advocate; **Ver'teidigung** *f* (*-; -en*) defense, *Br* defence
**Ver'teidigungs...** *in cpds ...politik etc*: *mst* defense ..., *Br* defence ...; **~mi,nister** *m* Secretary of Defense, *Br* Minister of Defence; **~minis,terium**

V

*n* Department of Defense, *Br* Ministry of Defence

**ver'teilen** *v/t* (*no -ge-, h*) distribute; hand out; **Ver'teiler** *m* (*-s; -*) distributor; **Ver'teilung** *f* (*-; -en*) distribution

**ver'tiefen** *v/t and v/refl* (*no -ge-, h*) deepen (*a. fig*); ***sich ~ in*** (*acc*) become absorbed in; **Ver'tiefung** *f* (*-; -en*) hollow, depression, dent; *fig* deepening

**vertikal** [vɛrti'ka:l] *adj*, **Verti'kale** *f* (*-; -n*) vertical

**ver'tilgen** *v/t* (*no -ge-, h*) exterminate; F consume; **Ver'tilgung** *f* (*-; no pl*) extermination

**vertonen** [fɛɐ'to:nən] *v/t* (*no -ge-, h*) set to music

**Vertrag** [fɛɐ'tra:k] *m* (*-[e]s; Verträge* [fɛɐ'trɛ:gə]) contract; POL treaty

**ver'tragen** *v/t* (*irr, **tragen**, no -ge-, h*) endure, bear, stand; ***ich kann ... nicht ~*** ... doesn't agree with me; I can't stand ...; ***er kann viel ~*** he can take a lot; he can hold his drink; F ***ich*** (***es***) ***könnte ... ~*** I (it) could do with ...; ***sich*** (***gut***) ***~*** get along (well) (***mit*** with); ***sich wieder ~*** make it up

**ver'traglich** *adv* by contract

**verträglich** [fɛɐ'trɛ:klıç] *adj* easy to get on with; GASTR (easily) digestible

**ver'trauen** *v/i* (*no -ge-, h*) trust (***auf*** *acc* in); **Ver'trauen** *n* (*-s; no pl*) confidence, trust, faith; ***im ~*** (***gesagt***) between you and me; ***wenig ~ erweckend aussehen*** inspire little confidence

**Ver'trauens|frage** *f*: ***die ~ stellen*** PARL ask for a vote of confidence; **~sache** *f*: ***das ist ~*** that is a matter of confidence; **~stellung** *f* position of trust

**ver'trauensvoll** *adj* trustful, trusting

**Ver'trauensvotum** *n* PARL vote of confidence

**ver'trauenswürdig** *adj* trustworthy

**ver'traulich** *adj* confidential; familiar

**ver'traut** *adj* familiar; close

**Ver'traute** *m, f* (*-n; -n*) confidant(e *f*)

**Ver'trautheit** *f* (*-; no pl*) familiarity

**ver'treiben** *v/t* (*irr, **treiben**, no -ge-, h*) drive *or* chase away (*a. fig*); pass (*the time*); ECON sell; ***~ aus*** drive out of; **Ver'treibung** *f* (*-; -en*) expulsion (***aus*** from)

**ver'treten** *v/t* (*irr, **treten**, no -ge-, h*) substitute for, replace, stand in for; POL, ECON represent, PARL *a.* sit for; JUR act for *s.o.*; ***j-s Sache ~*** JUR plead s.o.'s cause; ***die Ansicht ~, dass*** argue that; ***sich den Fuß ~*** sprain one's ankle; F ***sich die Beine ~*** stretch one's legs

**Ver'treter** *m* (*-s; -*), **Ver'treterin** *f* (*-; -nen*) substitute, deputy; POL, ECON representative, ECON *a.* agent; MED locum

**Ver'tretung** *f* (*-; -en*) substitution, replacement; substitute, stand-in, *a.* supply teacher; ECON, POL representation

**Vertrieb** [fɛɐ'tri:p] *m* (*-[e]s; no pl*) ECON sale, distribution

**Vertriebene** [fɛɐ'tri:bənə] *m, f* (*-n; -n*) POL expellee, refugee

**ver|'trocknen** *v/i* (*no -ge-, sein*) dry up; **~'trödeln** F *v/t* (*no -ge-, h*) dawdle away, waste; **~'trösten** *v/t* (*no -ge-, h*) put *s.o.* off; **~'tuschen** F *v/t* (*no -ge-, h*) cover up; **~'übeln** *v/t* (*no -ge-, h*) take amiss; ***ich kann es ihr nicht ~*** I can't blame her for it; **~'üben** *v/t* (*no -ge-, h*) commit

**verunglücken** [fɛɐ'ˀʊnglʏkən] *v/i* (*no -ge-, sein*) have an accident; *fig* go wrong; ***tödlich ~*** die in an accident

**ver'ursachen** *v/t* (*no -ge-, h*) cause

**ver'urteilen** *v/t* (*no -ge-, h*) condemn (***zu*** to) (*a. fig*), sentence (to), convict (***wegen*** of); **Ver'urteilung** *f* (*-; -en*) condemnation (*a. fig*)

**ver'vielfachen** *v/t* (*no -ge-, h*) multiply

**vervielfältigen** [fɛɐ'fi:lfɛltıgən] *v/t* (*no -ge-, h*) copy, duplicate; **Ver'vielfältigung** *f* (*-; -en*) duplication; copy

**ver'vollkommnen** *v/t* (*no -ge-, h*) perfect; improve

**vervollständigen** [fɛɐ'fɔlʃtɛndıgən] *v/t* (*no -ge-, h*) complete

**ver|'wachsen** *adj* MED deformed, crippled; *fig* ***~ mit*** deeply rooted in, bound up with; **~'wackelt** F *adj* PHOT blurred

**ver'wahren** *v/t* (*no -ge-, h*) keep (in a safe place); ***sich ~ gegen*** protest against

**verwahrlost** [fɛɐ'va:ɐlo:st] *adj* uncared-for, neglected

**ver'walten** *v/t* (*no -ge-, h*) manage, *esp* POL *a.* administer; **Ver'walter** *m* (*-s; -*) manager; administrator; **Ver'waltung** *f* (*-; -en*) administration, management; **Ver'waltungs...** *in cpds ...gericht, ...kosten etc*: administrative ...

**ver'wandeln** *v/t* (*no -ge-, h*) change, turn (*both a.* ***sich ~***), *esp* PHYS, CHEM *a.* transform, convert (*all:* ***in*** *acc* into); **Ver'wandlung** *f* (-; *-en*) change, transformation; conversion

**verwandt** [fɛɐ'vant] *adj* related (***mit*** to); **Ver'wandte** *m, f* (*-n; -n*) relative; (***alle***) ***m-e ~n*** (all) my relatives *or* relations; ***der nächste ~*** the next of kin; **Ver'wandtschaft** *f* (-; *-en*) relationship; (*no pl*) relations

**ver'warnen** *v/t* (*no -ge-, h*) *Br* caution; SPORT book; **Ver'warnung** *f* (-; *-en*) *Br* caution; SPORT booking

**ver'waschen** *adj* washed-out

**ver'wässern** *v/t* (*no -ge-, h*) water down (*a. fig*)

**ver'wechseln** *v/t* (*no -ge-, h*) confuse (***mit*** with), mix up (with), mistake (for)

**Ver'wechs(e)lung** *f* (-; *-en*) mistake, F mix-up

**ver'wegen** *adj* daring, bold

**Ver'wegenheit** *f* (-; *no pl*) boldness, daring

**ver'weichlicht** *adj* soft

**ver'weigern** *v/t* (*no -ge-, h*) refuse; disobey; **Ver'weigerung** *f* (-; *-en*) denial, refusal

**ver'weilen** *v/i* (*no -ge-, h*) stay; *fig* rest

**Verweis** [fɛɐ'vais] *m* (*-es; -e*) reprimand, reproof; reference (***auf*** *acc* to)

**ver'weisen** *v/t* (*irr,* ***weisen***, *no -ge-, h*) refer (***auf*** *acc,* ***an*** *acc* to); expel (*gen* from)

**ver'welken** *v/i* (*no -ge-, sein*) wither, *fig a.* fade

**ver'wenden** *v/t* (*no -ge-, h*) use; spend (*time etc*) (***auf*** *acc* on); **Ver'wendung** *f* (-; *-en*) use; ***keine ~ haben für*** have no use for

**ver'werfen** *v/t* (*irr,* ***werfen***, *no -ge-, h*) drop, give up; reject

**ver'werten** *v/t* (*no -ge-, h*) use, make use of

**verwesen** [fɛɐ've:zən] *v/i* (*no -ge-, sein*), **Ver'wesung** *f* (-; *no pl*) decay

**ver'wickeln** *fig v/t* (*no -ge-, h*) involve; ***sich ~ in*** (*acc*) get caught in; **ver'wickelt** *fig adj* complicated; ***~ sein*** (***werden***) ***in*** (*acc*) be (get) involved in; **Ver'wicklung** *fig f* (-; *-en*) involvement; complication

**ver'wildern** *v/i* (*no -ge-, sein*) grow (*or* run) wild; **ver'wildert** *adj* wild (*a. fig*), overgrown

**ver'winden** *v/t* (*irr,* ***winden***, *no -ge-, h*) get over *s.th.*

**ver'wirklichen** *v/t* (*no -ge-, h*) realize; ***sich ~*** come true; ***sich selbst ~*** fulfil(l) o.s.; **Ver'wirklichung** *f* (-; *-en*) realization

**ver'wirren** *v/t* (*no -ge-, h*) tangle (up); *fig* confuse; **ver'wirrt** *fig adj* confused; **Ver'wirrung** *fig f* (-; *-en*) confusion

**ver'wischen** *v/t* (*no -ge-, h*) blur (*a. fig*); cover (*track etc*)

**verwittern** [fɛɐ'vɪtɐn] *v/i* (*no -ge-, sein*) GEOL weather

**ver'witwet** *adj* widowed

**verwöhnen** [fɛɐ'vø:nən] *v/t* (*no -ge-, h*) spoil; **ver'wöhnt** *adj* spoilt

**verworren** [fɛɐ'vɔrən] *adj* confused, muddled; complicated

**verwundbar** [fɛɐ'vʊntba:ɐ] *adj* vulnerable (*a. fig*); **ver'wunden** *v/t* (*no -ge-, h*) wound

**ver'wunderlich** *adj* surprising

**Verwunderung** [fɛɐ'vʊndərʊŋ] *f* (-; *no pl*) (***zu m-r*** *etc* ***~*** to my *etc*) surprise

**Ver'wundete** *m, f* (*-n; -n*) wounded (person), casualty

**Ver'wundung** *f* (-; *-en*) wound, injury

**ver'wünschen** *v/t* (*no -ge-, h*), **Ver'wünschung** *f* (-; *-en*) curse

**ver'wüsten** *v/t* (*no -ge-, h*) lay waste, devastate, ravage; **Ver'wüstung** *f* (-; *-en*) devastation, ravage

**ver|'zählen** *v/refl* (*no -ge-, h*) count wrong; **~'zaubern** *v/t* (*no -ge-, h*) enchant, *fig a.* charm; ***~ in*** (*acc*) turn into; **~'zehren** *v/t* (*no -ge-, h*) consume (*a. fig*)

**ver'zeichnen** *v/t* (*no -ge-, h*) record, keep a record of, list; *fig* achieve; suffer; **Ver'zeichnis** *n* (*-ses; -se*) list, catalog(ue); record, register; index

**verzeihen** [fɛɐ'tsaiən] *v/t and v/i* (*irr, no -ge-, h*) forgive *s.o.*; pardon, excuse *s.th.*; **ver'zeihlich** *adj* pardonable; **Ver'zeihung** *f* (-; *no pl*) pardon; (***j-n***) ***um ~ bitten*** apologize (to s.o.); ***~!*** (I'm) sorry!; excuse me!

**ver'zerren** *v/t* (*no -ge-, h*) distort (*a. fig*); ***sich ~*** become distorted

**Ver'zerrung** *f* (-; *-en*) distortion

**Verzicht** [fɛɐ'tsɪçt] *m* (-[*e*]*s*; *-e*) renunciation (***auf*** *acc* of); *mst* giving up, doing without *etc*

V

**ver'zichten** *v/i* (*no -ge-, h*) ~ ***auf*** (*acc*) do without; give up; renounce (*a.* JUR)
**verzieh** [fɛɐ'tsiː] *pret of* ***verzeihen***
**ver'ziehen** (*irr,* ***ziehen****, no -ge-*) **1.** *v/i* (*sein*) move (***nach*** to); **2.** *v/t* (*h*) spoil; ***das Gesicht*** ~ make a face; ***sich*** ~ *wood*: warp; *storm etc*: pass (over); F disappear **3.** *pp of* ***verzeihen***
**ver'zieren** *v/t* (*no -ge-, h*) decorate
**Ver'zierung** *f* (-; *-en*) decoration, ornament
**ver'zinsen** *v/t* (*no -ge-, h*) pay interest on; ***sich*** ~ yield interest
**Ver'zinsung** *f* (-; *-en*) interest
**ver'zögern** *v/t* (*no -ge-, h*) delay; ***sich*** ~ be delayed; **Ver'zögerung** *f* (-; *-en*) delay
**ver'zollen** *v/t* (*no -ge-, h*) pay duty on; ***et.*** (***nichts***) ***zu*** ~ ***haben*** have s.th. (nothing) to declare
**verzückt** [fɛɐ'tsʏkt] *adj* ecstatic; **Ver'zückung** *f* (-; *-en*) ecstasy; ***in*** ~ ***geraten*** go into ecstasies *or* raptures (***wegen, über*** *acc* over)
**Verzug** [fɛɐ'tsuːk] *m* (-[*e*]*s*; *no pl*) delay; ECON default
**ver'zweifeln** *v/i* (*no -ge-, h*) despair (***an*** *dat* of); **ver'zweifelt** *adj* desperate, despairing
**Ver'zweiflung** *f* (-; *no pl*) despair; ***j-n zur*** ~ ***bringen*** drive s.o. to despair
**verzweigen** [fɛɐ'tsvaigən] *v/refl* (*no -ge-, h*) branch
**verzwickt** [fɛɐ'tsvɪkt] F *adj* tricky
**Veteran** [vete'raːn] *m* (*-en*; *-en*) MIL veteran (*a. fig*)
**Veterinär** [veteri'nɛːɐ] *m* (*-s*; *-e*), **Veteri'närin** *f* (-; *-nen*) veterinarian, *Br* veterinary surgeon, F vet
**Veto** ['veːto] *n* (*-s*; *-s*) veto; (***s***)***ein*** ~ ***einlegen gegen*** veto
**Vetter** ['fɛtɐ] *m* (*-s*; *-n*) cousin
**'Vetternwirtschaft** *f* (-; *no pl*) nepotism
**vgl.** *abbr of* ***vergleiche*** cf., confer
**VHS** *abbr of* ***Volkshochschule*** adult education program(me); adult evening classes
**Vibration** [vibra'tsjoːn] *f* (-; *-en*) vibration; **vibrieren** [vi'briːrən] *v/i* (*no -ge-, h*) vibrate
**Video** ['viːdeo] *n* (*-s*; *-s*) video (*a. in cpds …aufnahme, …clip, …kamera, …kassette, …recorder etc*); ***auf*** ~ ***aufnehmen*** video(tape), tape; **~band** *n* videotape; **~text** *m* teletext
**Videothek** [video'teːk] *f* (-; *-en*) video (-tape) library; video store (*Br* shop)
**Vieh** [fiː] *n* (-[*e*]*s*; *no pl*) cattle; ***20 Stück*** ~ 20 head of cattle; **~bestand** *m* livestock; **~händler** *m* cattle dealer
**'viehisch** *contp adj* bestial, brutal
**'Vieh|markt** *m* cattle market; **~zucht** *f* cattle breeding, stockbreeding; **~züchter** *m* cattle breeder, stockbreeder
**viel** [fiːl] *adj and adv* a lot (of), plenty (of), F lots of; ~***e*** many; ***nicht*** ~ not much; ***nicht*** ~***e*** not many; ***sehr*** ~ a great deal (of); ***sehr*** ~***e*** very many, a lot (of); ***das*** ~***e Geld*** all that money; ***ziemlich*** ~ quite a lot (of); ***ziemlich*** ~***e*** quite a few; ~ ***besser*** much better; ~ ***teurer*** much more expensive; ***e-r zu*** ~ one too many; ~ ***zu*** ~ far too much; ~ ***zu wenig*** not nearly enough; ~ ***lieber*** much rather; ***wie*** ~ how much (*pl* many); ~ ***beschäftigt*** very busy; ~ ***sagend*** meaningful; ~ ***versprechend*** promising; **'vieldeutig** [-dɔʏtɪç] *adj* ambiguous; **vielerlei** ['fiːlɐ'lai] *adj* all kinds *or* sorts of; **'vielfach 1.** *adj* multiple **2.** *adv* in many cases, (very) often; **'Vielfalt** *f* (-; *no pl*) (great) variety (*gen* of); **'vielfarbig** *adj* multicolo(u)red
**vielleicht** [fi'laiçt] *adv* perhaps, maybe; ~ ***ist er …*** he may *or* might be …
**'vielmals** *adv*: (***ich***) ***danke*** (***Ihnen***) ~ thank you very much; ***entschuldigen Sie*** ~ I'm very sorry, I do apologize
**viel'mehr** *cj* rather
**'viel|sagend** *adj* meaningful; **~seitig** ['fiːlzaitɪç] *adj* versatile
**'Vielseitigkeit** *f* (-; *no pl*) versatility
**'vielversprechend** *adj* promising
**vier** [fiːɐ] *adj* four; ***zu viert sein*** be four; ***auf allen*** ~***en*** on all fours; ***unter*** ~ ***Augen*** in private, privately
**'Vierbeiner** [-bainɐ] *m* (*-s*; -) ZO quadruped, four-legged animal
**'vierbeinig** *adj* four-legged
**'Viereck** *n* quadrangle, quadrilateral
**'viereckig** *adj* quadrangular, square
**Vierer** ['fiːrɐ] *m* (*-s*; -) *rowing*: four
**'vierfach** *adj* fourfold; ~***e Ausfertigung*** four copies
**'vierfüßig** ['fiːɐfyːsɪç] *adj* four-footed
**'Vierfüßler** ['fiːɐfyːslɐ] *m* (*-s*; -) ZO quadruped
**'vierhändig** ['fiːɐhɛndɪç] *adj* MUS four-

handed
'**vierjährig** ['fi:ɐjɛ:rɪç] *adj* four-year--old, of four
**Vierlinge** ['fi:ɐlɪŋə] *pl* quadruplets, quads
'**viermal** *adv* four times
'**Vierradantrieb** *m* MOT four-wheel drive
'**vierseitig** ['fi:ɐzaitɪç] *adj* MATH quadrilateral
'**vierspurig** ['fi:ɐʃpu:rɪç] *adj* MOT four--lane
'**vierstöckig** ['fi:ɐʃtœkɪç] *adj* four-storied, *Br* four-storey …
'**Viertaktmotor** *m* four-stroke engine
**vierte** ['fi:ɐtə] *adj* fourth
**Viertel** ['fɪrtəl] *n* (*-s*; -) fourth (part); quarter; **(*ein*) ~ *vor* (*nach*)** (a) quarter to (past); **~fi,nale** *n* SPORT quarter finals
**Viertel'jahr** *n* three months
'**vierteljährlich 1.** *adj* quarterly **2.** *adv* every three months, quarterly
**vierteln** ['fɪrtəln] *v/t* (*ge-, h*) quarter
'**Viertel|note** *f* MUS quarter note, *Br* crotchet; **~pfund** *n* quarter of a pound
**Viertel'stunde** *f* quarter of an hour
**viertens** ['fi:ɐtəns] *adv* fourthly
**vierzehn** ['fɪrtse:n] *adj* fourteen; **~ *Tage*** two weeks, *esp Br a.* a fortnight
'**vierzehnte** *adj* fourteenth
**vierzig** ['fɪrtsɪç] *adj* forty
'**vierzigste** *adj* fortieth
**Villa** ['vɪla] *f* (-; *Villen*) villa
**violett** [vio'lɛt] *adj* violet, purple
**Violine** [vio'li:nə] *f* (-; *-n*) MUS violin
**Virtuelle Realität** [vɪr'tuɛlə] *f* virtual reality, Cyberspace
**virtuos** [vɪr'tuo:s] *adj* virtuoso …, masterly; **Virtuose** [vɪr'tuo:zə] *m* (*-n*; *-n*) virtuoso; **Virtuosität** [vɪrtuozi'tɛ:t] *f* (-; *no pl*) virtuosity
**Virus** ['vi:rʊs] *n*, *m* (-; *Viren*) MED virus
**Visier** [vi'zi:ɐ] *n* (*-s*; *-e*) sights; visor
**Vision** [vi'zjo:n] *f* (-; *-en*) vision
**Visite** [vi'zi:tə] *f* (-; *-n*) MED round
**Vi'sitenkarte** *f* (visiting) card
**Visum** ['vi:zʊm] *n* (*-s*; *Visa*) visa
**vital** [vi'ta:l] *adj* vigorous; **Vitalität** [vitali'tɛ:t] *f* (-; *no pl*) vigo(u)r
**Vitamin** [vita'mi:n] *n* (*-s*; *-e*) vitamin
**Vitrine** [vi'tri:nə] *f* (-; *-n*) (glass) cabinet; showcase
**Vize…** ['fi:tsə-] *in cpds* vice(-)…
**Vogel** ['fo:gəl] *m* (*-s*; *Vögel* ['fø:gəl]) ZO bird
'**Vogelbauer** *n* birdcage
'**vogelfrei** *adj* outlawed
'**Vogel|futter** *n* birdseed; **~grippe** *f* bird flu, avian flu; **~käfig** *m* birdcage; **~kunde** *f* ornithology
**vögeln** ['fø:gəln] V *v/t and v/i* (*ge-, h*) screw
'**Vogel|nest** *n* bird's nest; **~perspektive** *f* bird's-eye view; **~scheuche** *f* scarecrow (*a. fig*); **~schutzgebiet** *n* bird sanctuary; **~warte** *f* ornithological station; **~zug** *m* bird migration
**Vokabel** [vo'ka:bəl] *f* (-; *-n*) word; *pl* → **Vokabular** [vokabu'la:ɐ] *n* (*-s*; *-e*) vocabulary
**Vokal** [vo'ka:l] *m* (*-s*; *-e*) LING vowel
**Volant** [vo'lã:] *Austrian m* → ***Lenkrad***
**Volk** [fɔlk] *n* (-[*e*]*s*; *Völker* ['fœlkɐ]) people, nation; *the* people; ZO swarm; ***ein Mann aus dem ~e*** a man of the people
**Völker|kunde** ['fœlkɐkʊndə] *f* ethnology; **~mord** *m* genocide; **~recht** *n* (-[*e*]*s*; *no pl*) international law; **~wanderung** *f* migration of peoples; F mass exodus
'**Volks|abstimmung** *f* POL referendum; **~fest** *n* funfair; **~hochschule** *f* adult evening classes; **~lied** *n* folk song; **~mund** *m*: ***im* ~** in the vernacular; **~mu,sik** *f* folk music; **~repu,blik** *f* people's republic; **~schule** HIST *f* → ***Grundschule***; **~sport** *m* popular sport; **~sprache** *f* vernacular; **~stamm** *m* tribe, race; **~tanz** *m* folk dance; **~tracht** *f* national costume
'**volkstümlich** ['fɔlksty:mlɪç] *adj* popular, folk …; traditional
'**Volks|versammlung** *f* public meeting; **~wirt** *m* economist; **~wirtschaft** *f* (national) economy; → **~wirtschaftslehre** *f* economics; **~zählung** *f* census
**voll** [fɔl] **1.** *adj* full (*a. fig*); full up (*a.* F); F plastered; thick, rich (*hair*); ***~er*** full of, filled with, *a.* covered with *dirt etc* **2.** *adv* fully; completely, totally, wholly; *pay etc* in full, the full price; *hit etc* full, straight, right; ***~ entwickelt*** fully developed; **(*nicht*) *für ~ nehmen*** (not) take seriously
'**vollauf** *adv* perfectly, quite
'**vollauto,matisch** *adj* fully automatic
'**Vollbart** *m* (full) beard
'**Vollbeschäftigung** *f* full employment
'**Vollblut…** *in cpds* full-blooded (*a. fig*)
'**Vollblüter** ['fɔlbly:tɐ] *m* (*-s*; -) ZO thor-

oughbred
**voll'bringen** *v/t* (*irr*, ***bringen***, *no -ge-*, *h*) accomplish, achieve; perform
**'Volldampf** *m* full steam; F ***mit ~*** (at) full blast
**voll'enden** *v/t* (*no -ge-*, *h*) finish, complete; **voll'endet** *adj* completed; *fig* perfect; **vollends** ['fɔlɛnts] *adv* completely; **Voll'endung** *f* (-; *no pl*) finishing, completion; *fig* perfection
**voll'führen** *v/t* (*no -ge-*, *h*) perform
**'vollfüllen** *v/t* (*sep*, *-ge-*, *h*) (***gießen***) fill (up)
**'Vollgas** *n* (*-es*; *no pl*) MOT full throttle; ***~ geben*** F step on it
**völlig** ['fœlɪç] **1.** *adj* complete, absolute, total **2.** *adv* completely; ***~ unmöglich*** absolutely impossible
**'volljährig** ['fɔljɛːrɪç] *adj* JUR ***~ sein*** (***werden***) be (come) of age; ***noch nicht ~*** under age; **'Volljährigkeit** *f* (-; *no pl*) JUR majority
**voll'kommen** *adj* perfect; → ***völlig***
**Voll'kommenheit** *f* (-; *no pl*) perfection
**'Vollkornbrot** *n* wholemeal bread
**'vollmachen** *v/t* (*sep*, *-ge-*, *h*) fill (up); F soil, dirty; ***um das Unglück voll zu machen*** to crown it all
**Voll|macht** *f* (-; *-en*) full power(s), authority; JUR power of attorney; ***~ haben*** be authorized; **~milch** *f* full-cream milk; **~mond** *m* full moon
**'vollpacken** *v/t* (*sep*, *-ge-*, *h*) load (***mit*** with) (*a. fig*)
**'Vollpensi,on** *f* full board
**'vollschlank** *adj* plump
**'vollständig** *adj* complete; → ***völlig***
**'vollstopfen** *v/t* (*sep*, *-ge-*, *h*) stuff, *fig a.* cram, pack (*all*: ***mit*** with)
**voll'strecken** *v/t* (*no -ge-*, *h*) JUR execute; **Voll'streckung** *f* (-; *-en*) JUR execution
**'volltanken** *v/t* (*sep*, *-ge-*, *h*): ***bitte ~!*** MOT fill her up, please!
**'Voll|treffer** *m* direct hit; bull's eye (*a. fig*); **~versammlung** *f* plenary session
**'vollwertig** *adj* full
**'Vollwertkost** *f* wholefoods
**vollzählig** ['fɔltsɛːlɪç] *adj* complete
**voll'ziehen** *v/t* (*irr*, ***ziehen***, *no -ge-*, *h*) execute; perform; ***sich ~*** take place; **Voll'ziehung** *f* (-; *no pl*), **Voll'zug** *m* (-[*e*]*s*; *no pl*) execution
**Volontär** [volɔn'tɛːɐ] *m* (*-s*; *-e*), **Volon'tärin** *f* (-; *-nen*) unpaid trainee
**Volt** [vɔlt] *n* (-; -) ELECTR volt
**Volumen** [vo'luːmən] *n* (*-s*; -, *-mina*) volume; size
**von** [fɔn] *prp* from; *instead of gen*: of; *passive*: by; about *s.o. or s.th.*; ***südlich ~*** south of; ***weit ~*** far from; ***~ Hamburg*** from Hamburg; ***~ nun an*** from now on; ***ein Freund ~ mir*** a friend of mine; ***die Freunde ~ Alice*** Alice's friends; ***ein Brief*** (***Geschenk***) ***~ Tom*** a letter (gift) from Tom; ***ein Buch*** (***Bild***) ***~ Orwell*** (***Picasso***) a book (painting) by Orwell (Picasso); ***der König*** (***Bürgermeister*** *etc*) ***~ …*** the King (Mayor *etc*) of …; ***ein Kind ~ 10 Jahren*** a child of ten; ***müde ~ der Arbeit*** tired from work; ***es war nett*** (***gemein***) ***~ dir*** it was nice (mean) of you; ***reden*** (***hören***) ***~*** talk (hear) about *or* of; ***~ Beruf*** (***Geburt***) by profession (birth); ***~ selbst*** by itself; ***~ mir aus!*** I don't mind *or* care
**von'stattengehen** *v/i* (*irr*, ***gehen***, *sep*, *-ge-*, *sein*) go, come off
**vor** [foːɐ] *prp* (*dat and acc*) in front of; outside; before; … ago; with, for; ***~ der Klasse*** in front of the class; ***~ der Schule*** in front of *or* outside the school; before school; ***~ kurzem*** (***e-r Stunde***) a short time (an hour) ago; ***5 Minuten ~ 12*** five (minutes) to twelve; ***~ j-m liegen*** be *or* lie ahead of s.o. (*a. fig and* SPORT); ***~ sich hin*** *smile etc* to o.s.; ***sicher ~*** safe from; ***~ Kälte*** with cold; ***~ Angst*** for fear; ***~ allem*** above all; ***~ sich gehen*** go on, happen
**'Vorabend** *m* eve (*a. fig*)
**'Vorahnung** *f* presentiment, foreboding
**voran** [fo'ran] *adv* at the head (*dat* of), in front (of), before; ***Kopf ~*** head first; **~gehen** *v/i* (*irr*, ***gehen***, *sep*, *-ge-*, *sein*) go in front *or* first; *esp fig* lead the way; **~kommen** *v/i* (*irr*, ***kommen***, *sep*, *-ge-*, *sein*) get on *or* along (*a. fig*), make headway
**'Voranzeige** *f* preannouncement; *film*: trailer
**'vorarbeiten** *v/i* (*sep*, *-ge-*, *h*) work in advance; *fig* pave the way
**'Vorarbeiter** *m* foreman
**voraus** [fo'raus] *adv* ahead (*dat* of); ***im Voraus*** in advance, beforehand
**vo'rausgehen** *v/i* (*irr*, ***gehen***, *sep*, *-ge-*,

*sein*) precede; → ***vorangehen***
**vo'rausgesetzt** *cj*: **~, *dass*** provided that
**Vo'raussage** *f* (-; *-n*) prediction; METEOR forecast; **vo'raussagen** *v/t* (*sep*, *-ge-*, *h*) predict; forecast
**vo'raus|schicken** *v/t* (*sep*, *-ge-*, *h*) send on ahead; **~sehen** *v/t* (*irr*, ***sehen***, *sep*, *-ge-*, *h*) foresee, see *s.th.* coming
**vo'raussetzen** *v/t* (*sep*, *-ge-*, *h*) assume; take *s.th.* for granted
**Vo'raussetzung** *f* (-; *-en*) condition, prerequisite; assumption; ***die ~en erfüllen*** meet the requirements
**Vo'raussicht** *f* (-; *no pl*) foresight; ***aller ~ nach*** in all probability
**vo'raussichtlich** *adv* probably; ***er kommt ~ morgen*** he is expected to arrive tomorrow
**Vo'rauszahlung** *f* advance payment
**'Vorbedeutung** *f* omen
**'Vorbedingung** *f* prerequisite
**Vorbehalt** ['foːɐbəhalt] *m* (-[*e*]*s*; *-e*) reservation; **'vorbehalten 1.** *v/t* (*irr*, ***halten***, *sep*, *no -ge-*, *h*) ***sich*** (***das Recht***) ***~ zu*** *inf* reserve the right to *inf* **2.** *adj* reserved; **'vorbehaltlos 1.** *adj* unconditional **2.** *adv* without reservation
**vor'bei** *adv time*: over, past; finished; gone; *space*: past, by; ***jetzt ist alles ~*** it's all over now; ***~!*** missed!; **~fahren** *v/i* (*irr*, ***fahren***, *sep*, *-ge-*, *sein*) go (*or* drive) past (***an*** *dat s.o. or s.th.*), pass (*s.o. or s.th.*); **~gehen** *v/i* (*irr*, ***gehen***, *sep*, *-ge-*, *sein*) walk past; *a. fig* go by, pass; *shot etc*: miss; **~ kommen** *v/i* (*irr*, ***kommen***, *sep*, *-ge-*, *sein*) pass (***an*** *dat s.th.*); get past (*an obstacle etc*); F drop in (***bei j-m*** on s.o.); *fig* avoid; **~lassen** *v/t* (*irr*, ***lassen***, *sep*, *-ge-*, *h*) let *s.o.* pass
**'Vorbemerkung** *f* preliminary remark
**'vorbereiten** *v/t and v/refl* (*sep*, *no -ge-*, *h*) prepare (***auf*** *acc* for); **'Vorbereitung** *f* (-; *-en*) preparation (***auf*** *acc* for)
**'vorbestellen** *v/t* (*sep*, *no -ge-*, *h*) book (*or* order) in advance; reserve (*room*, *seat etc*); **'Vorbestellung** *f* (-; *-en*) advance booking; reservation

**'vorbestraft** *adj*: ***~ sein*** have a police record
**'vorbeugen** (*sep*, *-ge-*, *h*) **1.** *v/i* prevent (***e-r Sache*** s.th.); **2.** *v/refl* bend forward; **~d** *adj* preventive, MED *a.* prophylactic
**'Vorbeugung** *f* (-; *-en*) prevention
**'Vorbild** *n* model, pattern; (***j-m***) ***ein ~ sein*** set an example (to s.o.); ***sich j-n zum ~ nehmen*** follow s.o.'s example
**'vorbildlich** *adj* exemplary
**'Vorbildung** *f* education(al background)
**'vor|bringen** *v/t* (*irr*, ***bringen***, *sep*, *-ge-*, *h*) bring forward; say, state; **~da,tieren** *v/t* (*no -ge-*, *h*) antedate; postdate
**Vorder...** ['fɔrdɐ-] *in cpds …achse*, *…rad*, *…sitz*, *…tür*, *…zahn etc*: front …
**vordere** ['fɔrdərə] *adj* front
**'Vorder|grund** *m* foreground (*a. fig*); **~mann** *m*: ***mein ~*** the man *or* boy in front of me; **~seite** *f* front (side); head
**'vor|dränge(l)n** *v/refl* (*sep*, *-ge-*, *h*) cut into line, *Br* jump the queue; **~dringen** *v/i* (*irr*, ***dringen***, *sep*, *-ge-*, *sein*) advance; **~** (***bis***) ***zu*** work one's way through to (*a. fig*)
**'Vordruck** *m* (-[*e*]*s*; *-e*) form, blank
**'voreilig** *adj* hasty, rash, precipitate; ***~e Schlüsse ziehen*** jump to conclusions
**'voreingenommen** *adj* prejudiced, bias(s)ed; **'Voreingenommenheit** *f* (-; *no pl*) prejudice, bias
**'vorenthalten** *v/t* (*irr*, ***halten***, *sep*, *no -ge-*, *h*) keep back, withhold (*both*: ***j-m et.*** s.th. from s.o.)
**'Vorentscheidung** *f* preliminary decision
**'vorerst** *adv* for the present, for the time being
**Vorfahr** ['foːɐfaːɐ] *m* (*-en*; *-en*) ancestor
**'vorfahren** *v/i* (*irr*, ***fahren***, *sep*, *-ge-*, *sein*) drive up (*or* on); **'Vorfahrt** *f* (-; *no pl*) right of way, priority
**'Vorfall** *m* incident, occurrence, event
**'vor|fallen** *v/i* (*irr*, ***fallen***, *sep*, *-ge-*, *sein*) happen, occur; **~finden** *v/t* (*irr*, ***finden***, *sep*, *-ge-*, *h*) find
**'Vorfreude** *f* anticipation
**'vorführen** *v/t* (*sep*, *-ge-*, *h*) show, present; perform (*trick etc*); demonstrate; JUR bring (***j-m*** before s.o.); **'Vorführer** *m* demonstrator; **'Vorführung** *f* presentation, show(ing); performance; demonstration; JUR production
**'Vorführwagen** *m* MOT demonstrator, *Br* demonstration car
**'Vorgabe** *f* handicap
**'Vorgang** *m* event, occurrence, happen-

ing; file, record(s); BIOL, TECH process; ***e-n ~ schildern*** give an account of what happened; **Vorgänger(in)** ['foːɐgɛŋɐ, 'foːɐgɛŋərɪn] *m(f)* (*-s*; *-/-*; *-nen*) predecessor

**'Vorgarten** *m* front yard (*Br* garden)

**'vorgeben** *v/t* (*irr*, ***geben***, *sep*, *-ge-*, *h*) SPORT give; *fig* use *s.th.* as a pretext

**'Vorgebirge** *n* foothills

**'vorgefasst** *adj* preconceived

**'vorgefertigt** *adj* prefabricated

**'Vorgefühl** *n* presentiment

**'vorgehen** *v/i* (*irr*, ***gehen***, *sep*, *-ge-*, *sein*) go on; come first; act; JUR sue (***gegen j-n*** s.o.); proceed; *watch*: be fast; **'Vorgehen** *n* (*-s*; *no pl*) procedure

**'vorgeschichtlich** *adj* prehistoric

**'Vor|geschmack** *m* foretaste (***auf*** *acc* of); **~gesetzte** *m*, *f* (*-n*; *-n*) superior, F boss

**'vorgestern** *adv* the day before yesterday

**'vorgreifen** *v/i* (*irr*, ***greifen***, *sep*, *-ge-*, *h*) anticipate *s.o. or s.th.*

**'vorhaben** *v/t* (*irr*, ***haben***, *sep*, *-ge-*, *h*) plan, intend; ***haben Sie heute Abend et. vor?*** have you anything on tonight?; ***was hat er jetzt wieder vor?*** what is he up to now?; **'Vorhaben** *n* (*-s*; *-*) plan(s), intention; TECH, ECON *a.* project

**'Vorhalle** *f* (entrance) hall, lobby

**'vorhalten** (*irr*, ***halten***, *sep*, *-ge-*, *h*) **1.** *v/t*: ***j-m et. ~*** hold s.th. in front of s.o.; *fig* blame s.o. for (doing) s.th. **2.** *v/i* last; **'Vorhaltungen** *pl* reproaches; ***j-m ~ machen*** (***für et.***) reproach s.o. (with s.th., for being …)

**'Vorhand** *f* (*-*; *no pl*) *tennis*: forehand

**vorhanden** [foːɐ'handən] *adj* available; in existence; ***~ sein*** exist; ***es ist nichts mehr ~*** there's nothing left; **Vor'handensein** *n* (*-s*; *no pl*) existence

**'Vorhang** *m* curtain

**'Vorhängeschloss** *n* padlock

**vor'her** *adv* before, earlier; in advance, beforehand

**vor'herbestimmen** *v/t* (*sep*, *no -ge-*, *h*) predetermine

**vorherig** [foːɐ'heːrɪç] *adj* previous

**'Vorherrschaft** *f* (*-*; *no pl*) predominance; **'vorherrschen** *v/i* (*sep*, *-ge-*, *h*) predominate, prevail; **'vorherrschend** *adj* predominant, prevailing

**vor'hersehbar** *adj* foreseeable

**vor'hersehen** *v/t* (*irr*, ***sehen***, *sep*, *-ge-*, *h*) foresee

**vor'hin** *adv* a (little) while ago

**'Vorhut** *f* (*-*; *-en*) MIL vanguard

**vorig** ['foːrɪç] *adj* last; former, previous

**vorjährig** ['foːɐjɛːrɪç] *adj* of last year, last year' …

**'Vorkämpfer** *m*, **'Vorkämpferin** *f* champion, pioneer

**Vorkehrungen** ['foːɐkeːrʊŋən] *pl*: ***~ treffen*** take precautions

**'Vorkenntnisse** *pl* previous knowledge *or* experience (***in*** *dat* of)

**'vorkommen** *v/i* (*irr*, ***kommen***, *sep*, *-ge-*, *sein*) be found; happen; ***es kommt mir … vor*** it seems … to me

**'Vorkommen** *n* (*-s*; *-*) MIN deposit(s)

**Vorkommnis** ['foːɐkɔmnɪs] *n* (*-ses*; *-se*) occurrence, incident, event

**'Vorkriegs…** *in cpds* prewar …

**'vorladen** *v/t* (*irr*, ***laden***, *sep*, *-ge-*, *h*) JUR summon; **'Vorladung** *f* (*-*; *-en*) JUR summons

**'Vorlage** *f* model; pattern; copy; presentation; PARL bill; *soccer etc*: pass

**'vorlassen** *v/t* (*irr*, ***lassen***, *sep*, *-ge-*, *h*) let *s.o.* go first; let *s.o.* pass; ***vorgelassen werden*** be admitted (***bei*** to)

**'Vorlauf** *m recorder*: fast-forward; SPORT (preliminary) heat; **'Vorläufer** *m* forerunner, precursor; **'vorläufig** **1.** *adj* provisional, temporary **2.** *adv* for the present, for the time being

**'vorlaut** *adj* pert, cheeky

**'Vorleben** *n* (*-s*; *no pl*) former life, past

**'vorlegen** *v/t* (*sep*, *-ge-*, *h*) present; produce; show

**'Vorleger** *m* (*-s*; *-*) rug; mat

**'vorlesen** *v/t* (*irr*, ***lesen***, *sep*, *-ge-*, *h*) read out (aloud); ***j-m et. ~*** read s.th. to s.o.; **'Vorlesung** *f* (*-*; *-en*) lecture (***über*** *acc* on; ***vor*** *dat* to); ***e-e ~ halten*** (give a) lecture

**'vorletzte** *adj* last but one; ***~ Nacht*** (***Woche***) the night (week) before last

**'Vorliebe** *f* (*-*; *-n*) preference, special liking

**'vorliebnehmen** *v/i* (*irr*, ***nehmen***, *sep*, *-ge-*, *h*) ***mit*** make do with

**'vorliegen** *v/i* (*irr*, ***liegen***, *sep*, *-ge-*, *h*) ***es liegen*** (***keine***) ***… vor*** there are (no) …; ***was liegt gegen ihn vor?*** what is he charged with?; **~d** *adj* present, in question

'**vor|lügen** *v/t* (*irr*, ***lügen***, *sep*, *-ge-*, *h*) ***j-m et.*** ~ tell s.o. lies; **~machen** *v/t* (*sep*, *-ge-*, *h*) ***j-m et.*** ~ show s.th. to s.o., show s.o. how to do s.th.; *fig* fool s.o.

'**Vormachtstellung** *f* supremacy

'**Vormarsch** *m* MIL advance (*a. fig*)

'**vormerken** *v/t* (*sep*, *-ge-*, *h*) ***j-n*** ~ put s.o.'s name down

'**Vormittag** *m* morning; ***heute*** ~ this morning

'**vormittags** *adv* in the morning; ***sonntags*** ~ on Sunday mornings

'**Vormund** *m* (-[*e*]*s*; *-e*) JUR guardian; **~schaft** *f* (-; *-en*) JUR guardianship

**vorn** [fɔrn] *adv* in front; ***nach*** ~ forward; ***von*** ~ from the front; from the beginning; ***j-n von ~(e) sehen*** see s.o.'s face; ***noch einmal von ~(e) (anfangen)*** (start) all over again

'**Vorname** *m* first *or* Christian name, forename

**vornehm** ['foːɐneːm] *adj* distinguished; noble; fashionable, exclusive, F smart, posh; ***die ~e Gesellschaft*** (high) society; ~ ***tun*** put on airs

'**vornehmen** *v/t* (*irr*, ***nehmen***, *sep*, *-ge-*, *h*) carry out, do; make (*changes etc*); ***sich et.*** ~ decide *or* resolve to do s.th.; make plans for s.th.; ***sich fest vorgenommen haben zu*** *inf* have the firm intention to *inf*, be determined to *inf*

'**vornherein** *adv*: ***von*** ~ from the start *or* beginning

'**Vorort** *m* suburb

'**Vorposten** *m* outpost (*a.* MIL)

'**vorprogram,mieren** *v/t* (*sep*, *no -ge-*, *sein*) (pre)program(me); *fig* ***das war vorprogrammiert*** that was bound to happen

'**Vorrang** *m* (-[*e*]*s*; *no pl*) precedence (***vor*** *dat* over), priority (over)

'**Vorrat** *m* (-[*e*]*s*; *-räte*) store, stock, supply (*all*: ***an*** *dat* of); GASTR provisions; ECON resources, reserves; ***e-n ~ anlegen an*** (*dat*) stockpile; **vorrätig** ['foːɐreːtɪç] *adj* available; ECON in stock

'**Vorrecht** *n* privilege

'**Vorredner** *m* previous speaker

'**Vorrichtung** *f* TECH device

'**vorrücken** (*sep*, *-ge-*) **1.** *v/t* (*h*) move forward **2.** *v/i* (*sein*) advance

'**Vorrunde** *f* SPORT preliminary round

'**vorsagen** *v/i* (*sep*, *-ge-*, *h*) ***j-m*** ~ prompt s.o.

'**Vorsai,son** *f* off-peak season

'**Vorsatz** *m* resolution; intention; JUR intent; **vorsätzlich** ['foːɐzɛtslɪç] *adj* intentional; *esp* JUR wil(l)ful

'**Vorschau** *f* preview (***auf*** *acc* of), *film*, TV *a.* trailer

'**Vorschein** *m*: ***zum ~ bringen*** produce; *fig* bring out; ***zum ~ kommen*** appear; *fig* come to light

'**vor|schieben** *v/t* (*irr*, ***schieben***, *sep*, *-ge-*, *h*) push forward; slip (*bolt*); *fig* use as a pretext; **~schießen** F *v/t* (*irr*, ***schießen***, *sep*, *-ge-*, *h*) advance (*money*)

'**Vorschlag** *m* suggestion, proposal (*a.* PARL *etc*); ***den ~ machen*** → '**vorschlagen** *v/t* (*irr*, ***schlagen***, *sep*, *-ge-*, *h*) suggest, propose

'**Vorschlussrunde** *f* SPORT semifinal

'**vorschnell** *adj* hasty, rash

'**vorschreiben** *fig v/t* (*irr*, ***schreiben***, *sep*, *-ge-*, *h*) prescribe; tell; ***ich lasse mir nichts*** ~ I won't be dictated to; '**Vorschrift** *f* rule, regulation; instruction, direction; ***Dienst nach ~ machen*** work to rule

'**vorschrifts|mäßig** *adj* correct, proper; **~widrig** *adj and adv* contrary to regulations

'**Vorschub** *m*: ***~ leisten*** (*dat*) encourage; JUR aid and abet

'**Vorschul…** *in cpds* pre-school …

'**Vorschule** *f* preschool

'**Vorschuss** *m* advance

'**vorschützen** *v/t* (*sep*, *-ge-*, *h*) use *s.th.* as a pretext

'**vorsehen** (*irr*, ***sehen***, *sep*, *-ge-*, *h*) **1.** *v/t* plan; JUR provide; ~ ***für*** intend (*or* designate) for **2.** *v/refl* be careful, take care, watch out (***vor*** *dat* for)

'**Vorsehung** *f* (-; *no pl*) providence

'**vorsetzen** *v/t* (*sep*, *-ge-*, *h*) ***j-m et.*** ~ put s.th. before s.o.; offer s.o. s.th.

'**Vorsicht** *f* (-; *no pl*) caution, care; ***~!*** look *or* watch out!, (be) careful!; ***~, Stufe!*** mind the step!; '**vorsichtig** *adj* careful, cautious; '**vorsichtshalber** ['foːɐzɪçtshalbɐ] *adv* to be on the safe side; '**Vorsichtsmaßnahme** *f* precaution, precautionary measure; ***~n treffen*** take precautions

'**Vorsilbe** *f* LING prefix

V

'**vorsingen** *v/t and v/i* (*irr*, ***singen***, *sep*, *-ge-*, *h*) ***j-m et. ~*** sing s.th. to s.o.; (have an) audition
'**Vorsitz** *m* chair(manship), presidency; ***den ~ haben*** (***übernehmen***) be in (take) the chair, preside (***bei*** over, at)
'**Vorsitzende** *m*, *f* (*-n*; *-n*) chairman (chairwoman), president
'**Vorsorge** *f* (*-*; *no pl*) precaution; ***~ treffen*** take precautions; **~untersuchung** *f* MED preventive checkup
'**vorsorglich 1.** *adj* precautionary **2.** *adv* as a precaution
'**Vorspann** *m* (*-[e]s*; *-e*) *film etc*: credits
'**Vorspeise** *f* hors d'œuvre, *Br* starter
'**Vorspiel** *n* MUS prelude (*a. fig*); foreplay; '**vorspielen** *v/t* (*sep*, *-ge-*, *h*) ***j-m et. ~*** play s.th. to s.o.
'**vorsprechen** (*irr*, ***sprechen***, *sep*, *-ge-*, *h*) **1.** *v/t* pronounce (***j-m*** for s.o.); **2.** *v/i* call (***bei*** at); THEA (have an) audition
'**vorspringen** *fig v/i* (*irr*, ***springen***, *sep*, *-ge-*, *sein*) project, protrude (*both a.* ARCH); '**Vorsprung** *m* ARCH projection; SPORT lead; ***e-n ~ haben*** be leading (***von*** by); *esp fig* ***e-n ~ von zwei Jahren haben*** be two years ahead
'**Vorstadt** *f* suburb
'**Vorstand** *m* ECON board (of directors); managing committee (*of a club etc*)
'**vorstehen** *v/i* (*irr*, ***stehen***, *sep*, *-ge-*, *h*) project, protrude
'**vorstellen** *v/t* (*sep*, *-ge-*, *h*) introduce (***sich*** o.s.; ***j-n j-m*** s.o. to s.o.); put *watch* forward (***um*** by); *fig* mean; ***sich et.*** (***j-n als …***) ***~*** imagine s.th. (s.o. as …); ***so stelle ich mir … vor*** that's my idea of …; ***sich ~ bei*** have an interview with *a firm etc*; '**Vorstellung** *f* (*-*; *-en*) introduction; interview; THEA performance, *film etc*: *a.* show; idea; expectation
'**Vorstellungs|kraft** *f* (*-*; *no pl*), **~vermögen** *n* (*-s*; *no pl*) imagination
**Vorstopper** ['foːɐʃtɔpɐ] *m* (*-s*; *-*) SPORT center (*Br* centre) back
'**Vorstoß** *m* MIL advance; *fig* attempt
'**Vorstrafe** *f* previous conviction
'**vorstrecken** *v/t* (*sep*, *-ge-*, *h*) advance (*money*)
'**Vorstufe** *f* preliminary stage
'**vortäuschen** *v/t* (*sep*, *-ge-*, *h*) feign, fake
'**Vorteil** *m* advantage (*a.* SPORT); benefit, profit; ***die ~e und Nachteile*** the pros and cons; '**vorteilhaft** *adj* advantageous, profitable; '**Vorteilsregel** *f* SPORT advantage rule
**Vortrag** ['foːɐtraːk] *m* (*-[e]s*; *Vorträge* ['foːɐtrɛːgə]) talk, *esp* UNIV lecture; MUS *etc* recital; ***e-n ~ halten*** give a talk *or* lecture (***vor*** *dat* to; ***über*** *acc* on)
'**vortragen** *v/t* (*irr*, ***tragen***, *sep*, *-ge-*, *h*) express, state; MUS *etc* perform, play; recite (*poem etc*)
'**vortreten** *v/i* (*irr*, ***treten***, *sep*, *-ge-*, *sein*) step forward; *fig* protrude, stick out
'**Vortritt** *m* (*-[e]s*; *no pl*) precedence; ***j-m den ~ lassen*** let s.o. go first
**vorüber** [fo'ryːbɐ] *adv*: ***~ sein*** be over; **~gehen** *v/i* (*irr*, ***gehen***, *sep*, *-ge-*, *sein*) pass, go by; **~gehend** *adj* temporary
'**Vorübung** *f* preparatory exercise
'**Voruntersuchung** *f* JUR, MED preliminary examination
'**Vorurteil** *n* prejudice; '**vorurteilslos** *adj* unprejudiced, unbias(s)ed
'**Vorverkauf** *m* THEA advance booking
'**vorverlegen** *v/t* (*sep*, *no -ge-*, *h*) advance
'**Vorwahl** *f* TEL area (*Br* STD *or* dialling) code; POL primary, *Br* preliminary election
'**Vorwand** *m* pretext, excuse
**vorwärts** ['foːɐvɛrts] *adv* forward, on(-ward), ahead; ***~!*** come on!, let's go!; '**vorwärtskommen** *v/i* (*irr*, ***kommen***, *sep*, *-ge-*, *sein*) make headway (*a. fig*)
**vorweg** [foːɐ'vɛk] *adv* beforehand
**vor'wegnehmen** *v/t* (*irr*, ***nehmen***, *sep*, *-ge-*, *h*) anticipate
'**vor|weisen** *v/t* (*irr*, ***weisen***, *sep*, *-ge-*, *h*) produce, show; ***et. ~ können*** boast s.th.; **~werfen** *fig v/t* (*irr*, ***werfen***, *sep*, *-ge-*, *h*) ***j-m et. ~*** reproach s.o. with s.th.
'**vorwiegend** *adv* predominantly, chiefly, mainly, mostly
'**vorwitzig** *adj* cheeky, pert
'**Vorwort** *n* (*-[e]s*; *-e*) foreword; preface
'**Vorwurf** *m* reproach; ***j-m Vorwürfe machen*** (***wegen***) reproach s.o. (for); '**vorwurfsvoll** *adj* reproachful
'**Vorzeichen** *n* omen, sign (*a.* MATH)
'**vorzeigen** *v/t* (*sep*, *-ge-*, *h*) show; produce
'**vorzeitig** *adj* premature, early
'**vorziehen** *v/t* (*irr*, ***ziehen***, *sep*, *-ge-*, *h*) draw; *fig* prefer

ˈ**Vorzimmer** *n* anteroom; outer office; *Austrian* → ***Hausflur***
ˈ**Vorzug** *m* advantage; merit
**vorzüglich** [foːɐˈtsyːklɪç] *adj* excellent, exquisite
ˈ**vorzugsweise** *adv* preferably
**Votum** [ˈvoːtʊm] *n* (*-s*; *-ta*, *-ten*) vote
**VP** *abbr of* ***Vollpension*** full board; (full) board and lodging
**vulgär** [vʊlˈgɛːɐ] *adj* vulgar
**Vulkan** [vʊlˈkaːn] *m* (*-s*; *-e*) volcano; **~ausbruch** *m* volcanic eruption
**vulˈkanisch** *adj* volcanic

# W

**W** *abbr of* ***West(en)*** W, west; ***Watt*** W, watt(s)
**Waage** [ˈvaːgə] *f* (*-*; *-n*) scale(s *Br*); balance; ASTR Libra; ***sich die ~ halten*** balance each other; ***er ist*** (***e-e***) **~** he's (a) Libra; ˈ**waagerecht** *adj* horizontal
**Waagschale** [ˈvaːkʃaːlə] *f* scale
**Wabe** [ˈvaːbə] *f* (*-*; *-n*) honeycomb
**wach** [vax] *adj* awake; **~ *rütteln*** rouse; *fig* → ***wachrütteln***; **~ *werden*** wake (up), *esp fig* → ***wachwerden***
**Wache** [ˈvaxə] *f* (*-*; *-n*) guard (*a.* MIL); sentry; MAR, MED *etc* watch; police station; **~ *haben*** be on guard (MAR watch); **~ *halten*** keep watch; ˈ**wachen** *v/i* (*ge-*, *h*) (keep) watch (***über*** *acc* over)
ˈ**Wachhund** *m* watchdog
ˈ**Wachmann** *m* (*-[e]s*; *-männer*, *-leute*) watchman; *Austrian* → ***Polizist***
**Wacholder** [vaˈxɔldɐ] *m* (*-s*; *-*) BOT juniper
ˈ**wach|rufen** *v/t* (*irr*, ***rufen***, *sep*, *-ge-*, *h*) call up, evoke; **~rütteln** *v/t* (*sep*, *-ge-*, *h*) *fig* rouse (*a. fig*)
**Wachs** [vaks] *n* (*-es*; *-e*) wax
**wachsam** [ˈvaxzaːm] *adj* watchful, on one's guard, vigilant; ˈ**Wachsamkeit** *f* (*-*; *no pl*) watchfulness, vigilance
**wachsen**[1] [ˈvaksən] *v/i* (*irr*, *ge-*, *sein*) grow (*a.* ***sich ~ lassen***), *fig a.* increase
ˈ**wachsen**[2] *v/t* (*ge-*, *h*) wax
ˈ**Wachs|fiˌgurenkabiˌnett** *n* waxworks; **~tuch** *n* oilcloth
ˈ**Wachstum** *n* (*-s*; *no pl*) growth, *fig a.* increase
**Wachtel** [ˈvaxtəl] *f* (*-*; *-n*) ZO quail
**Wächter** [ˈvɛçtɐ] *m* (*-s*; *-*) guard
ˈ**Wachtmeister** *m* (*-s*; *no pl*) patrolman, *Br* (police) constable
ˈ**Wach(t)turm** *m* watchtower
ˈ**wachwerden** *v/i* (*irr*, ***werden***, *sep*, *-ge-*, *sein*) *fig* awake; → ***wach***
**wackelig** [ˈvakəlɪç] *adj* shaky (*a. fig*); loose (*tooth*); ˈ**wackeln** *v/i* (*ge-*, *h*) shake; *table etc*: wobble; *tooth*: be loose; PHOT move; **~ *mit*** waggle
**Wade** [ˈvaːdə] *f* (*-*; *-n*) ANAT calf
**Waffe** [ˈvafə] *f* (*-*; *-n*) weapon (*a. fig*), *pl a.* arms
**Waffel** [ˈvafəl] *f* (*-*; *-n*) waffle; wafer
ˈ**Waffen|gewalt** *f*: ***mit ~*** by force of arms; **~schein** *m* gun license (*Br* licence); **~stillstand** *m* armistice (*a. fig*); truce
**wagen** [ˈvaːgən] *v/t* (*ge-*, *h*) dare; risk; ***sich ~*** venture
ˈ**Wagen** *m* (*-s*; *-*) MOT car; RAIL car, *Br* carriage
**wägen** [ˈvɛːgən] *lit v/t* (*irr*, *ge-*, *h*) weigh (*one's words etc*)
ˈ**Wagen|heber** *m* TECH jack; **~ladung** *f* cartload
**Waggon** [vaˈgoː] *m* (*-s*, *-s*) (railroad) car, *Br* (railway) carriage; freight car, *Br* goods waggon
**Wagnis** [ˈvaːknɪs] *n* (*-ses*; *-se*) venture, risk
**Waˈgon** *m* → ***Waggon***
**Wahl** [vaːl] *f* (*-*; *-en*) choice; alternative; selection; POL election; voting, poll; vote; ***die ~ haben*** (***s-e ~ treffen***) have the (make one's) choice; ***keine*** (***andere***) **~ *haben*** have no choice *or* alternative; ˈ**wahlberechtigt** *adj* POL entitled to vote; ˈ**Wahlbeteiligung** *f* POL poll, (voter) turnout; ***hohe*** (***niedrige***) **~** heavy (light) poll; ˈ**Wahlbezirk** *m* → ***Wahlkreis***
**wählen** [ˈvɛːlən] *v/t and v/i* (*ge-*, *h*) choose, pick, select; POL vote (for); elect; TEL dial; ˈ**Wähler** *m* (*-s*; *-*) voter
ˈ**Wahlergebnis** *n* election result
**wählerisch** [ˈvɛːlərɪʃ] *adj* F picky (***in*** *dat*

about), *esp Br* choos(e)y
'**Wählerschaft** *f* (-; *-en*) electorate, voters
'**Wahl|fach** *n* PED *etc* elective, optional subject; **~ka,bine** *f* voting (*esp Br* polling) booth; **~kampf** *m* election campaign; **~kreis** *m* electoral district, *Br* constituency; **~lo,kal** *n* polling place (*Br* station)
'**wahllos** *adj* indiscriminate
'**Wahl|pro,gramm** *n* election platform; **~recht** *n* (-[*e*]*s*; *no pl*) (right to) vote, suffrage, franchise; **~rede** *f* election speech
'**Wählscheibe** *f* TEL dial
'**Wahl|sieg** *m* election victory; **~sieger** *m* election winner; **~spruch** *m* motto; **~urne** *f* ballot box; **~versammlung** *f* election rally
'**Wahnsinn** *m* (-[*e*]*s*; *no pl*) madness (*a.* F), insanity
'**wahnsinnig 1.** *adj* mad (*a.* F), insane, F *a.* crazy; F awful, terrible **2.** F *adv* terribly, awfully; madly (*in love*)
'**Wahnsinnige** *m*, *f* (*-n*; *-n*) madman (madwoman), lunatic, maniac (*all a.* F)
'**Wahnvorstellung** *f* delusion, hallucination
**wahr** [vaːɐ] *adj* true; real; genuine
**wahren** ['vaːrən] *v/t* (*ge-*, *h*) protect; ***den Schein ~*** keep up appearances
**während** ['vɛːrənt] **1.** *prp* (*gen*) during **2.** *cj* while; whereas
'**wahrhaft, wahr'haftig** *adv* really, truly
'**Wahrheit** *f* (-; *-en*) truth
'**wahrheits|gemäß, ~getreu** *adj* true, truthful; **~liebend** *adj* truthful
**wahrnehmbar** ['vaːɐneːmbaːɐ] *adj* noticeable, perceptible; '**wahrnehmen** *v/t* (*irr*, ***nehmen***, *sep*, *-ge-*, *h*) perceive, notice; seize, take (*chance etc*); look after (*s.o.'s interests etc*); '**Wahrnehmung** *f* (-; *-en*) perception
'**wahrsagen** *v/i* (sep, -ge-, h) ***j-m ~*** tell s.o. his fortune; ***sich ~ lassen*** have one's fortune told; '**Wahrsager(in)** ['vaːɐzaːgɐ, 'vaːɐzaːgərɪn] *m* (*f*) (*-s*; *-/-*; *-nen*) fortune-teller
**wahr'scheinlich 1.** *adj* probable, likely **2.** *adv* probably, (very *or* most) likely; ***~ gewinnt er*** (***nicht***) he is (not) likely to win; **Wahr'scheinlichkeit** *f* (-; *-en*) probability, likelihood
**Währung** ['vɛːrʊŋ] *f* (-; *-en*) currency
'**Währungs...** *in cpds ...politik*, *...reform etc*: monetary ...
'**Wahrzeichen** *n* landmark
**Waise** ['vaizə] *f* (-; *-n*) orphan
'**Waisenhaus** *n* orphanage
**Wal** [vaːl] *m* (-[*e*]*s*; *-e*) ZO whale
**Wald** [valt] *m* (-[*e*]*s*; *Wälder* ['vɛldɐ]) wood(s), forest; **~brand** *m* forest fire
'**waldreich** *adj* wooded
'**Waldsterben** *n* dying of forests
'**Walfang** *m* whaling
'**Walfänger** *m* whaler
**Walkman**® *m* (*-s*; *-men*) personal stereo, Walkman®
**Wall** [val] *m* (-[*e*]*s*; *Wälle* ['vɛlə]) mound; MIL rampart
**Wallach** ['valax] *m* (-[*e*]*s*; *-e*) ZO gelding
**wallen** ['valən] *v/i* (*ge-*, *sein*) flow
'**Wallfahrer** *m*, '**Wallfahrerin** *f* pilgrim
'**Wallfahrt** *f* pilgrimage
'**Walnuss** *f* BOT walnut
'**Walross** *n* ZO walrus
**Walze** ['valtsə] *f* (-; *-n*) roller; cylinder; TECH, MUS barrel
'**walzen** *v/t* (*ge-*, *h*) roll (*a.* TECH)
**wälzen** ['vɛltsən] *v/t* (*ge-*, *h*) roll (*a.* ***sich ~***); *fig* turn *s.th.* over in one's mind
**Walzer** ['valtsɐ] *m* (*-s*; -) MUS waltz (*a.* ***~ tanzen***)
**wand** [vant] *pret of* ***winden***
**Wand** *f* (-; *Wände* ['vɛndə]) wall, *fig a.* barrier
**Wandale** [van'daːlə] *m* (*-n*; *-n*) vandal; **Wandalismus** [vanda'lɪsmʊs] *m* (-; *no pl*) vandalism
**Wandel** ['vandəl] *m* (*-s*; *no pl*), '**wandeln** *v/t and v/refl* (*ge-*, *h*) change
**Wanderer** ['vandərɐ] *m* (*-s*; -), '**Wanderin** *f* (-; *-nen*) hiker
**wandern** ['vandɐn] *v/i* (*ge-*, *sein*) hike; ramble (about); *eyes etc*: roam, wander
'**Wander|po,kal** *m* challenge cup; **~preis** *m* challenge trophy; **~schuhe** *pl* walking shoes; **~tag** *m* (school) outing *or* excursion
'**Wanderung** *f* (-; *-en*) walking tour, hike; ZO *etc* migration
'**Wand|gemälde** *n* mural; **~ka,lender** *m* wall calendar; **~karte** *f* wallchart
**Wandlung** ['vandlʊŋ] *f* (-; *-en*) change
'**Wand|schrank** *m* closet, *Br* built-in cupboard; **~tafel** *f* blackboard
**wandte** ['vantə] *pret of* ***wenden***
'**Wandteppich** *m* tapestry

**Wange** ['vaŋə] *f* (-; *-n*) ANAT cheek
**Wankelmotor** ['vaŋkəlmoːtoːɐ] *m* rotary piston *or* Wankel engine
**wankelmütig** ['vaŋkəlmyːtɪç] *adj* fickle
**wanken** ['vaŋkən] *v/i* (*ge-, sein*) stagger, reel; *fig* rock
**wann** [van] *interr adv* when, (at) what time; ***seit ~?*** (for) how long?, since when?
**Wanne** ['vanə] *f* (-; *-n*) tub (*a.* F); bath (-tub)
**Wanze** ['vantsə] *f* (-; *-n*) zo bug (*a.* F)
**Wapitihirsch** [va'piːtihɪrʃ] *m* zo elk
**Wappen** ['vapən] *n* (*-s*; -) (coat of) arms
'**Wappenkunde** *f* heraldry
**wappnen** ['vapnən] *fig v/refl* (*ge-, h*) arm o.s.
**war** [vaːɐ] *pret of* ***sein***[1]
**warb** [varp] *pret of* ***werben***
**Ware** ['vaːrə] *f* (-; *-n*) *coll mst* goods; article; product
'**Waren|haus** *n* department store; **~lager** *n* stock; **~probe** *f* sample; **~zeichen** *n* trademark
**warf** [varf] *pret of* ***werfen***
**warm** [varm] *adj* warm (*a. fig*); GASTR hot; ***schön ~*** nice and warm; ***~ halten*** keep warm; ***~ machen*** warm (up)
**Wärme** ['vɛrmə] *f* (-; *no pl*) warmth; PHYS heat; **~iso,lierung** *f* heat insulation
'**wärmen** *v/t* (*ge-, h*) warm
'**Wärmflasche** *f* hot-water bottle
'**warmherzig** *adj* warm-hearted
'**warmmachen** *v/t* (*sep, -ge-, h*) → ***warm***
**Warm'wasser|bereiter** *m* (*-s*; -) water heater; **~versorgung** *f* hot-water supply
'**Warn|blinkanlage** *f* MOT warning flasher; **~dreieck** *n* MOT warning triangle
**warnen** ['varnən] *v/t* (*ge-, h*) warn (***vor*** *dat* of, against); ***j-n davor ~, et. zu tun*** warn s.o. not to do s.th.
'**Warn|schild** *n* danger sign; **~sig,nal** *n* warning signal; **~streik** *m* token strike
'**Warnung** *f* (-; *-en*) warning
'**Warteliste** *f* waiting list
**warten**[1] ['vartən] *v/i* (*ge-, h*) wait (***auf*** *acc* for); *j-n* ***~ lassen*** keep *s.o.* waiting
'**warten**[2] *v/t* (*ge-, h*) TECH service, maintain
**Wärter** ['vɛrtɐ] *m* (*-s*; -), '**Wärterin** *f* (-; *-nen*) attendant; zo keeper
'**Warte|saal** *m*, **~zimmer** *n* waiting room
'**Wartung** *f* (-; *-en*) TECH maintenance
**warum** [va'rʊm] *interr adv* why
**Warze** ['vartsə] *f* (-; *-n*) MED wart
**was** [vas] **1.** *interr pron* what; ***~ gibt's?*** what is it?, F what's up?; what's for lunch *etc?*; ***~ soll's?*** so what?; ***~ machen Sie?*** what are you doing?; what do you do?; ***~ kostet …?*** how much is …?; ***~ für …?*** what kind *or* sort of …?; ***~ für e-e Farbe*** (***Größe***)***?*** what colo(u)r (size)?; ***~ für ein Unsinn*** what nonsense!; ***~ für e-e gute Idee!*** what a good idea! **2.** *rel pron* what; ***~*** (***auch***) ***immer*** whatever; ***alles, ~ ich habe*** (***brauche***) all I have (need); ***ich weiß nicht, ~ ich tun*** (***sagen***) ***soll*** I don't know what to do (say); ***…, ~ mich ärgerte…***, which made me angry **3.** F *indef pron* → ***etwas***
**waschbar** ['vaʃbaːɐ] *adj* washable
'**Waschbecken** *n* washbowl, *Br* washbasin
**Wäsche** ['vɛʃə] *f* (-; *-n*) washing; (*no pl*) laundry; linen; underwear; ***in der ~*** in the wash; ***schmutzige ~ waschen*** wash one's dirty linen in public
'**waschecht** *adj* washable; fast (*color*); *fig* trueborn, genuine
'**Wäsche|klammer** *f* clothespin, *Br* clothes peg; **~leine** *f* clothesline
**waschen** ['vaʃən] *v/t and v/refl* (*irr, ge-, h*) wash; ***sich die Haare*** (***Hände***) ***~*** wash one's hair (hands)
**Wäscherei** [vɛʃə'rai] *f* (-; *-en*) laundry
'**Wasch|lappen** *m* washcloth, *Br* flannel, facecloth; **~ma,schine** *f* washing machine, F washer
'**waschma,schinenfest** *adj* machine-washable
**Wasch|mittel** *n*, **~pulver** *n* washing powder; **~raum** *m* lavatory, washroom; **~sa,lon** *m* laundromat, *Br* launderette; **~straße** *f* MOT car wash
**Wasser** ['vasɐ] *n* (*-s*; -) water; **~ball** *m* beach ball; SPORT water polo; **~bett** *n* water bed; **~dampf** *m* steam
'**wasserdicht** *adj* waterproof; *esp* MAR watertight (*a. fig*)
'**Wasser|fall** *m* waterfall; falls; **~farbe** *f* water colo(u)r; **~flugzeug** *n* seaplane; **~graben** *m* SPORT water jump; **~hahn** *m* tap, faucet
**wässerig** ['vɛsərɪç] *adj* watery; ***j-m den Mund ~ machen*** make s.o.'s mouth wa-

ter

'**Wasser|kessel** *m* kettle; **~klo,sett** *n* water closet, W.C.; **~kraft** *f* (-; *no pl*) water power; **~kraftwerk** *n* hydroelectric power station *or* plant; **~lauf** *m* watercourse; **~leitung** *f* waterpipe(s); **~mangel** *m* (-*s*; *no pl*) water shortage; **~mann** *m* (-[*e*]*s*; *no pl*) ASTR Aquarius; ***er ist* (*ein*) ~** he's (an) Aquarius

'**wassern** *v/i* (*ge-*, *h*) AVIAT touch down on water; *spacecraft*: splash down

**wässern** ['vɛsɐn] *v/t* (*ge-*, *h*) water; AGR irrigate; GASTR soak; PHOT rinse

'**Wasserpflanze** *f* BOT aquatic plant

'**Wasserrohr** *n* TECH water pipe

'**Wasserscheide** *f* GEOGR watershed

'**wasserscheu** *adj* afraid of water

'**Wasser|ski 1.** *m* water ski **2.** *n* (-*s*; *no pl*) water skiing; ***~ fahren*** water-ski; **~spiegel** *m* water level; **~sport** *m* water *or* aquatic sports, aquatics; **~spülung** *f* TECH flushing cistern; ***Toilette mit ~*** (flush) toilet, W.C.; **~stand** *m* water level; **~stoff** *m* (-[*e*]*s*; *no pl*) CHEM hydrogen; **~stoffbombe** *f* MIL hydrogen bomb, H-bomb; **~strahl** *m* jet of water; **~straße** *f* waterway; **~tier** *n* aquatic animal; **~verschmutzung** *f* water pollution; **~versorgung** *f* water supply; **~waage** *f* (*Br* spirit) level; **~weg** *m* waterway; ***auf dem ~*** by water; **~welle** *f* water wave; **~werk(e)** *n*(*pl*) waterworks; **~zeichen** *n* watermark

**waten** ['va:tən] *v/i* (*ge-*, *sein*) wade

**watscheln** ['va:tʃəln] *v/i* (*ge-*, *sein*) waddle

**Watt**¹ [vat] *n* (-*s*; -) ELECTR watt

**Watt**² *n* (-[*e*]*s*; -*en*) GEOGR mud flats

**Watte** ['vatə] *f* (-; -*n*) cotton wool

**wattiert** [va'ti:ɐt] *adj* padded; quilted

**weben** ['ve:bən] *v/t and v/i* ([*irr*,] *ge-*, *h*) weave; **Weber** ['ve:bɐ] *m* (-*s*; -) weaver; **Weberei** [ve:bə'rai] *f* (-; -*en*) weaving mill; '**Weberin** *f* (-; -*nen*) weaver; **Webstuhl** ['ve:pʃtu:l] *m* loom

**Wechsel** ['vɛksəl] *m* (-*s*; -) change; exchange; ECON bill of exchange; allowance; '**Wechselgeld** *n* (small) change

**wechselhaft** *adj* changeable

'**Wechseljahre** *pl* MED menopause

'**Wechselkurs** *m* ECON exchange rate

'**wechseln** *v/t and v/i* (*ge-*, *h*) change; exchange; vary; **~d** *adj* varying

'**wechselseitig** ['vɛksəlzaitɪç] *adj* mutual, reciprocal

'**Wechsel|strom** *m* ELECTR alternating current; **~stube** *f* ECON exchange office; **~wirkung** *f* interaction

**wecken** ['vɛkən] *v/t* (*ge-*, *h*) wake (up), F call; *fig* awaken (*memories etc*); rouse (*s.o.'s curiosity etc*)

**Wecker** ['vɛkɐ] *m* (-*s*; -) alarm (clock)

**wedeln** ['ve:dəln] *v/i* (*ge-*, *h*) wave (***mit et.*** s.th.); *skiing*: wedel; ***mit dem Schwanz ~*** wag its tail

**weder** ['ve:dɐ] *cj*: ***~ … noch …*** neither … nor …

**Weg** [ve:k] *m* (- [*e*]*s*; -*e* ['ve:gə]) way (*a. fig*); road (*a. fig*); path; route; walk; ***auf friedlichem* (*legalem*) *~e*** by peaceful (legal) means; ***j-m aus dem ~ gehen*** get (*fig* keep) out of s.o.'s way; ***j-n aus dem ~ räumen*** put s.o. out of the way; ***vom ~ abkommen*** lose one's way; → ***halb***

**weg** [vɛk] *adv* away; gone; off; F in raptures (***von*** over, about); ***Finger ~!*** (keep your) hands off!; ***nichts wie ~!*** let's get out of here!; F ***~ sein*** be out; **~bleiben** F *v/i* (*irr*, ***bleiben***, *sep*, *-ge-*, *sein*) stay away; be left out; **~bringen** F *v/t* (*irr*, ***bringen***, *sep*, *-ge-*, *h*) take away; ***~ von*** get *s.o.* away from

**wegen** ['vegən] *prp* (*gen*) because of; for the sake of; due *or* owing to; JUR for

**wegfahren** ['vɛkfa:rən] (*irr*, ***fahren***, *sep*, *-ge-*) **1.** *v/i* (*sein*) leave **2.** *v/t* (*h*) take away, remove

'**wegfallen** *v/i* (*irr*, ***fallen***, *sep*, *-ge-*, *sein*) be dropped; stop, be stopped

**Weggang** ['vɛkgaŋ] *m* (-[*e*]*s*; *no pl*) leaving; '**weggehen** *v/i* (*irr*, ***gehen***, *sep*, *-ge-*, *sein*) go away (*a. fig*), leave; *stain etc*: come off; ECON sell

**weg|jagen** ['vɛkja:gən] *v/t* (*sep*, *-ge-*, *h*) drive *or* chase away; **~kommen** F *v/i* (*irr*, ***kommen***, *sep*, *-ge-*, *sein*) get away; get lost; ***gut ~*** come off well; ***mach, dass du wegkommst!*** get out of here!, *sl* get lost!; **~lassen** *v/t* (*irr*, ***lassen***, *sep*, *-ge-*, *h*) let *s.o.* go; leave *s.th.* out; **~laufen** *v/i* (*irr*, ***laufen***, *sep*, *-ge-*, *sein*) run away ([***vor***] ***j-m*** from s.o.) (*a. fig*); **~legen** *v/t* (*sep*, *-ge-*, *h*) put away; **~nehmen** *v/t* (*irr*, ***nehmen***, *sep*, *-ge-*, *h*) take away (***von*** from); take up (*room*, *time*); steal (*a. s.o.'s girlfriend etc*); ***j-m et. ~*** take s.th. (away) from s.o.; **~räumen**

*v/t* (*sep*, *-ge-*, *h*) clear away, remove; **~schaffen** *v/t* (*sep*, *-ge-*, *h*) remove; **~schicken** *v/t* (*sep*, *-ge-*, *h*) send away *or* off; **~sehen** *v/i* (*irr*, ***sehen***, *sep*, *-ge-*, *h*) look away; **~setzen** *v/t* (*sep*, *-ge-*, *h*) move

**Wegweiser** ['veːkvaizɐ] *m* (*-s*; -) signpost; *fig* guide

**Wegwerf...** ['vɛkvɛrf-] *in cpds ...geschirr*, *...besteck*, *...rasierer etc*: throwaway ..., disposable ...; *...flasche etc*: non-returnable ...; '**wegwerfen** *v/t* (*irr*, ***werfen***, *sep*, *-ge-*, *h*) throw away

**weg|wischen** ['vɛkvɪʃən] *v/t* (*sep*, *-ge-*, *h*) wipe off; **~ziehen** (*irr*, ***ziehen***, *sep*, *-ge-*) **1.** *v/i* (*sein*) move away **2.** *v/t* (*h*) pull away

**weh** [veː] *adv*: ***~ tun*** → ***wehtun***

**wehen** ['veːən] *v/i* (*ge-*, *h*) blow; wave

'**Wehen** *pl* MED labo(u)r

**wehmütig** ['veːmyːtɪç] *adj* melancholy; wistful

**Wehr**[1] [veːɐ] *n* (*-[e]s*; *-e* ['veːrə]) weir

**Wehr**[2] *f*: ***sich zur ~ setzen*** → ***wehren***

'**Wehrdienst** *m* (*-[e]s*; *no pl*) military service; **~verweigerer** *m* (*-s*; -) conscientious objector

**wehren** ['veːrən] *v/refl* (*ge-*, *h*) defend o.s. (***gegen*** against), fight (*a. fig* ***gegen et.*** s.th.); '**wehrlos** *adj* defenseless, *Br* defenceless; *fig* helpless

'**Wehrpflicht** *f* (-; *no pl*) compulsory military service; '**wehrpflichtig** *adj* liable to military service; '**Wehrpflichtige** *m* (*-n*; *-n*) draftee, *Br* conscript

'**wehtun** hurt (***j-m*** s.o.; *fig* s.o.'s feelings); be aching; ***sich*** (***am Finger***) ***~*** hurt o.s. (hurt one's finger)

**Weib** [vaip] *n* (*-[e]s*; *-er* ['vaibɐ]) *contp* woman; bitch; '**Weibchen** *n* (*-s*; -) ZO female; **weibisch** ['vaibɪʃ] *adj* effeminate, F sissy; '**weiblich** *adj* female; feminine (*a.* LING)

**weich** [vaiç] *adj* soft (*a. fig*), tender; GASTR done; soft-boiled (*egg*); ***~ werden*** soften; *fig* give in

**Weiche** ['vaɪçə] *f* (-; *-n*) RAIL switch, points

**weichen** ['vaɪçən] *v/i* (*irr*, *ge-*, *sein*) give way (*dat* to), yield (to); go (away)

'**weichlich** *adj* soft, effeminate, F sissy

'**Weichling** *m* (*-s*; *-e*) weakling, F softy, sissy

'**weichmachen** *v/t* (*sep*, *-ge-*, *h*): F ***j-n ~*** soften s.o. up

'**Weichspüler** *m* (*-s*; -) fabric softener

'**Weichtier** *n* ZO mollusk, *Br* mollusc

**Weide**[1] ['vaidə] *f* (-; *-n*) BOT willow

'**Weide**[2] *f* (-; *-n*) AGR pasture; ***auf die*** (***der***) ***~*** to (at) pasture; '**Weideland** *n* pasture(land), range; '**weiden** *v/t and v/i* (*ge-*, *h*) graze, pasture; *fig* ***sich ~ an*** (*dat*) feast on; *contp* gloat over

**weigern** ['vaigɐn] *v/refl* (*ge-*, *h*) refuse

**Weigerung** ['vaigərʊŋ] *f* (-; *-en*) refusal

**Weihe** ['vaiə] *f* (-; *-n*) REL consecration; ordination; '**weihen** *v/t* (*ge-*, *h*) consecrate; ***zum Priester ~*** ordain *s.o.* priest

**Weiher** ['vaiɐ] *m* (*-s*; -) pond

**Weihnachten** ['vainaxtən] *n* (-; -) Christmas, F Xmas

'**Weihnachts|abend** *m* Christmas Eve; **~baum** *m* Christmas tree; **~einkäufe** *pl* Christmas shopping; **~geschenk** *n* Christmas present; **~lied** *n* (Christmas) carol; **~mann** *m* Father Christmas, Santa Claus; **~markt** *m* Christmas fair; **~tag** *m* Christmas Day; ***zweiter ~*** day after Christmas, *esp Br* Boxing Day; **~zeit** *f* Christmas season

'**Weih|rauch** *m* REL incense; **~wasser** *n* (*-s*; *no pl*) REL holy water

**weil** [vail] *cj* because; since, as

'**Weilchen** *n*: ***ein ~*** a little while

**Weile** ['vailə] *f*: ***e-e ~*** a while

**Wein** [vain] *m* (*-[e]s*; *-e*) wine; BOT vine; **~(an)bau** *m* (*-[e]s*; *no pl*) wine growing; **~beere** *f* grape; **~berg** *m* vineyard; **~brand** *m* brandy

**weinen** ['vainən] *v/i* (*ge-*, *h*) cry (***vor*** *dat* with; ***nach*** for; ***wegen*** about, over); weep (***um*** for, over; ***über*** *acc* at; ***vor*** *dat* for, with); **weinerlich** ['vainɐlɪç] *adj* tearful; whining

'**Wein|fass** *n* wine cask *or* barrel; **~flasche** *f* wine bottle; **~händler** *m* wine merchant; **~hauer** *Austrian m* → ***Winzer***; **~karte** *f* wine list; **~keller** *m* wine cellar *or* vault, vaults; **~kellerei** *f* winery; **~kenner** *m* wine connoisseur; **~lese** *f* vintage; **~presse** *f* wine press; **~probe** *f* wine tasting; **~rebe** *f* BOT vine

'**weinrot** *adj* claret

'**Weinstock** *m* BOT vine

'**Weintraube** *f* → ***Traube***

**weise** ['vaizə] *adj* wise

'**Weise** *f* (-; *-n*) way; MUS tune; ***auf diese***

W

(***die gleiche***) ~ this (the same) way; ***auf m-e*** (***s-e***) ~ my (his) way
**weisen** ['vaizən] *v/t and v/i* (*irr, ge-, h*) show; ***j-n von der Schule ~*** expel s.o. from school; ~ ***auf*** (*acc*) point to *or* at; ***von sich ~*** reject; repudiate
**Weisheit** ['vaishait] *f* (-; *-en*) wisdom; ***mit s-r ~ am Ende sein*** be at one's wit's end
'**Weisheitszahn** *m* wisdom tooth
**weismachen** ['vaismaxən] F *v/t*: ***j-m ~, dass*** make s.o. believe that; ***du kannst mir nichts ~*** you can't fool me
**weiß** [vais] *adj* white; ~ ***werden*** *or* ***machen*** whiten; '**Weißbrot** *n* white bread; '**Weiße** *m, f* (*-n; -n*) white, white man (woman), *pl the* whites
'**weißen** *v/t* (*ge-, h*) whitewash
'**Weißkohl** *m*, '**Weißkraut** *n* BOT (green, *Br* white) cabbage
'**weißlich** *adj* whitish
'**weißmachen** *v/t* (*sep, -ge-, h*) → ***weiß***
'**Weißwein** *m* white wine
**Weisung** ['vaizʊŋ] *f* (-; *-en*) instruction, directive
**weit** [vait] **1.** *adj* wide, *clothes*: *a.* big; long (*way, trip etc*) **2.** *adv* far, a long way (*a. time and fig*); ~ ***weg*** far away (***von*** from); ***von ~em*** from a distance; ~ ***und breit*** far and wide; ***bei ~em*** by far; ***bei ~em nicht so …*** not nearly as …; ~ ***über*** (*acc*) well over; ~ ***besser*** far *or* much better; ***zu ~ gehen*** go too far; ***es ~ bringen*** go far; ***wir haben es ~ gebracht*** we have come a long way; ~ ***blickend*** *fig* farsighted; ~ ***reichend*** far-reaching; ~ ***verbreitet*** widespread
'**weit'ab** *adv* far away (***von*** from)
'**weit'aus** *adv* (by) far, much
**Weite** ['vaitə] *f* (-; *-n*) width; vastness, expanse; *esp* SPORT distance
'**weiten** *v/t and v/refl* (*ge-, h*) widen
**weiter** ['vaitɐ] *adv* on, further; (***mach***) ***~!*** go on!; (***geh***) ***~!*** move on!; ***und so ~*** and so on *or* forth, et cetera; ***nichts ~*** nothing else; **~arbeiten** *v/i* (*sep, -ge-, h*) go on working; **~bilden** *v/refl* (*sep, -ge-, h*) improve one's knowledge; continue one's education *or* training
'**Weiterbildung** *f* (-; *no pl*) further education *or* training
**weitere** ['vaitərə] *adj* further, additional; ***alles Weitere*** the rest; ***bis auf ~s*** until further notice; ***ohne ~s*** easily; ***Weiteres*** more, (further) details
'**weiter|geben** *v/t* (*irr,* ***geben***, *sep, -ge-, h*) pass (*dat*, ***an*** *acc* to) (*a. fig*); **~gehen** *v/i* (*irr,* ***gehen***, *sep, -ge-, sein*) move on; *fig* continue, go on
'**weiter'hin** *adv* further(more); ***et. ~ tun*** go on doing s.th., continue to do s.th.
'**weiter|kommen** *v/i* (*irr,* ***kommen***, *sep, -ge-, sein*) get on (*fig* in life); **~leben** *v/i* (*sep, -ge-, h*) live on, *fig a.* survive; **~machen** *v/t and v/i* (*sep, -ge-, h*) go *or* carry on, continue
'**Weiterverkauf** *m* resale
'**weit|gehend** **1.** *adj* considerable **2.** *adv* largely; **~läufig** *adj* spacious; distant (*relative*); **~sichtig** *adj* MED farsighted (*a. fig*), *Br* longsighted
'**Weitsprung** *m* broad (*Br* long) jump
'**Weitwinkelobjek,tiv** *n* PHOT wide-angle lens
**Weizen** ['vaitsən] *m* (*-s*; -) BOT wheat
**welche** ['vɛlçə], **welcher** ['vɛlçɐ], **welches** ['vɛlçəs] **1.** *interr pron* what, which; ***welcher?*** which one?; ***welcher von beiden?*** which of the two? **2.** *rel pron* who, that; which, that **3.** F ***welche*** *indef pron* some, any
**welk** [vɛlk] *adj* faded, withered; flabby
**welken** ['vɛlkən] *v/i* (*ge-, sein*) fade, wither
**Wellblech** ['vɛlblɛç] *n* corrugated iron
**Welle** ['vɛlə] *f* (-; *-n*) wave (*a.* PHYS *and fig*); TECH shaft; '**wellen** *v/t and v/refl* (*ge-, h*) wave
'**Wellenlänge** *f* ELECTR wavelength
'**Wellensittich** ['vɛlənzɪtɪç] *m* (*-s*; *-e*) ZO budgerigar, F budgie
**wellig** ['vɛlɪç] *adj* wavy
**Welt** [vɛlt] *f* (-; *-en*) world; ***die ganze ~*** the whole world; ***auf der ganzen ~*** all over *or* throughout the world; ***das beste*** *etc* … ***der ~*** the best *etc* … in the world, the world's best *etc* …; ***zur ~ kommen*** be born; ***zur ~ bringen*** give birth to
'**Weltall** *n* universe
'**weltberühmt** *adj* world-famous
**Weltergewicht** ['vɛltɐgəvɪçt] *n* (-[*e*]*s*; *no pl*), '**Weltergewichtler** *m* (*-s*; -) SPORT welterweight
'**weltfremd** *adj* naive, unrealistic
'**Weltfriede(n)** *m* world peace
'**Weltgeschichte** *f* world history
'**weltklug** *adj* worldlywise

'**Weltkrieg** *m* world war; ***der Zweite ~*** World War II
'**Weltkugel** *f* globe
'**weltlich** *adj* worldly
'**Welt|litera,tur** *f* world literature; **~macht** *f* POL world power; **~markt** *m* ECON world market; **~meer** *n* ocean; **~meister(in)** world champion; **~meisterschaft** *f* world championship; *esp soccer*: World Cup; **~raum** *m* (-[*e*]*s*; *no pl*) (outer) space; **~reich** *n* empire; **~reise** *f* world trip; **~re,kord** *m* world record; **~stadt** *f* metropolis; **~untergang** *m* end of the world
'**weltweit** *adj* worldwide
'**Weltwirtschaft** *f* world economy
'**Weltwirtschaftskrise** *f* worldwide economic crisis
'**Weltwunder** *n* wonder of the world
**Wende** ['vɛndə] *f* (-; *-n*) turn (*a. swimming*); change; **~kreis** *m* ASTR, GEOGR tropic; MOT turning circle
**Wendeltreppe** ['vɛndəltrɛpə] *f* spiral staircase
'**wenden** *v/t and v/i* (*ge-, h*) *and v/refl* ([*irr*,] *ge-, h*) turn (***nach*** to; ***gegen*** against); MOT turn (round); GASTR turn over; ***sich an j-n um Hilfe ~*** turn to s.o. for help; ***bitte ~*** please turn over, pto
'**Wendepunkt** *m* turning point
**wendig** ['vɛndɪç] *adj* MOT, MAR maneuverable, *Br* manoeuvrable; *fig* nimble
'**Wendung** *f* (-; *-en*) turn, *fig a.* change; expression, phrase
**wenig** ['ve:nɪç] *indef pron and adv* little; **~(*e*)** *pl* few; ***nur ~e*** only few; only a few; (***in***) ***~er als*** (in) less than; ***am ~sten*** least of all; ***er spricht ~*** he doesn't talk much; (***nur***) ***ein*** (***klein***) ***~*** (just) a little (bit)
'**wenigstens** *adv* at least
**wenn** [vɛn] *cj* when; if; ***~ ... nicht*** if ... not, unless; ***~ auch*** (al)though, even though; ***wie*** *or* ***als ~*** as though, as if; ***~ ich nur ... wäre!*** if only I were ...!; ***~ auch noch so ...*** no matter how ...; ***und ~ nun ...?*** what if ...?
**wer** [ve:ɐ] **1.** *interr pron* who, which; ***~ von euch?*** which of you? **2.** *rel pron* who; ***~ auch*** (***immer***) who(so)ever **3.** F *indef pron* somebody, anybody
**Werbe|abteilung** ['vɛrbəaptailʊŋ] *f* publicity department; **~agen,tur** *f* advertising agency; **~feldzug** *m* advertising campaign; **~fernsehen** *n* commercial television; **~film** *m* promotion(al) film; **~funk** *m* radio commercials
**werben** ['vɛrbən] (*irr, ge-, h*) **1.** *v/i* advertise (***für et.*** s.th.), promote (s.th.), give *s.th. or s.o.* publicity; *esp* POL make propaganda (***für*** for), canvass (for); ***~ um*** court (*a. fig*) **2.** *v/t* recruit; canvass, solicit
'**Werbesendung** *f*, '**Werbespot** ['vɛrbəspɔt] *m* (*-s*; *-s*) (TV) commercial
'**Werbung** *f* (-; *no pl*) advertising, (sales) promotion; *a.* POL *etc* publicity, propaganda; recruitment; ***~ machen für et.*** advertise s.th.
**Werdegang** ['ve:ɐdəgaŋ] *m* career
**werden** ['ve:ɐdən] *v/i* (*irr, ge-, sein*) *and v/aux* become, get; turn, go; grow; turn out; ***wir ~*** we will (*or* shall), we are going to; ***geliebt ~*** be loved (***von*** by); ***was willst du ~?*** what do you want to be?; ***mir wird schlecht*** I'm going to be sick; F ***es wird schon wieder*** (***~***) it'll be all right
**werfen** ['vɛrfən] *v/i and v/t* (*irr, ge-, h*) throw (*a.* ZO) ([***mit***] ***et. nach*** s.th. at); drop (*bombs*); cast (*shadow*)
**Werft** [vɛrft] *f* (-; *-en*) MAR shipyard, dockyard
**Werk** [vɛrk] *n* (-[*e*]*s*; *-e*) work, deed; TECH mechanism; ECON works, factory; ***ans ~ gehen*** set *or* go to work; **~bank** *f* (-; *-bänke*) TECH workbench; **~meister** *m* TECH foreman
'**Werkstatt** *f* (-; *-stätten*) workshop; MOT garage
'**Werktag** *m* workday
'**werktags** *adv* on workdays
'**werktätig** *adj* working
'**Werkzeug** *n* tool (*a. fig*); *coll* tools; instrument; **~macher** *m* toolmaker
**wert** [ve:ɐt] *adj* worth; ***die Mühe*** (***e-n Versuch***) ***~*** worth the trouble (a try); *fig* ***nichts ~*** no good; **Wert** *m* (-[*e*]*s*; *-e*) value, *esp fig a.* worth; use; *pl* data, figures; ***... im ~(e) von 20 Dollar*** 20 dollars' worth of ...; ***großen ~ legen auf*** (*acc*) set great store by
**werten** ['ve:ɐtən] *v/t* (*ge-, h*) value; *a.* SPORT rate, judge
'**Wertgegenstand** *m* article of value
'**wertlos** *adj* worthless
'**Wertpa,piere** *pl* securities
'**Wertsachen** *pl* valuables

**'Wertung** *f* (-; *-en*) valuation; *a.* SPORT rating, judging; score, points
**'wertvoll** *adj* valuable
**Wesen** ['veːzən] *n* (*-s*; -) being, creature; *fig* essence; nature, character
**'wesentlich** *adj* essential; considerable; ***im Wesentlichen*** on the whole
**weshalb** [vɛs'halp] *interr adv* → ***warum***
**Wespe** ['vɛspə] *f* (-; *-n*) ZO wasp
**Weste** ['vɛstə] *f* (-; *-n*) vest, *Br* waistcoat
**Westen** ['vɛstən] *m* (*-s*; *no pl*) west; POL West
**Western** ['vɛstɐn] *m* (*-s*; -) western
**'westlich 1.** *adj* western; westerly; POL West(ern) **2.** *adv*: ***~ von*** (to the) west of
**'Westwind** *m* west(erly) wind
**Wettbewerb** ['vɛtbəvɛrp] *m* (*-[e]s*; *-e*) competition (*a.* ECON), contest
**'Wettbü,ro** *n* betting office
**Wette** ['vɛtə] *f* (-; *-n*) bet; ***e-e ~ abschließen*** make a bet; ***um die ~ laufen*** *etc* race (***mit j-m*** s.o.)
**'wetteifern** *v/i* (*ge-*, *h*) compete (***mit*** with; ***um*** for)
**'wetten** *v/i and v/t* (*ge-*, *h*) bet; ***mit j-m um 10 Dollar ~*** bet s.o. ten dollars; ***~ auf*** (*acc*) bet on, back
**Wetter** ['vɛtɐ] *n* (*-s*; -) weather
**'Wetterbericht** *m* weather report
**'Wetterfahne** *f* weather vane
**'wetterfest** *adj* weatherproof
**'Wetter|karte** *f* weather chart; **~lage** *f* weather situation; **~leuchten** *n* sheet lightning; **~vorhersage** *f* weather forecast; **~warte** *f* weather station
**'Wett|kampf** *m* competition, contest; **~kämpfer(in)** contestant, competitor; **~lauf** *m* race (*a. fig* ***mit*** against); **~läufer(in)** runner
**'wettmachen** *v/t* (*sep*, *-ge-*, *h*) make up for
**'Wettrennen** *n* race
**'Wettrüsten** *n* (*-s*; *no pl*) arms race
**'Wettstreit** *m* contest, competition
**wetzen** ['vɛtsən] *v/t* (*ge-*, *h*) whet, sharpen
**wich** [vɪç] *pret of* ***weichen***
**wichtig** ['vɪçtɪç] *adj* important
**'Wichtigkeit** *f* (-; *no pl*) importance
**'wickeln** *v/t* (*ge-*, *h*) change (*baby*); ***~ in*** (*acc*) wrap in; ***~ um*** wrap (a)round
**Widder** ['vɪdɐ] *m* (*-s*; -) ZO ram; ASTR Aries; ***er ist*** (***ein***) ***~*** he's (an) Aries
**wider** ['viːdɐ] *prp* (*acc*) ***~ Willen*** against one's will; ***~ Erwarten*** contrary to expectations
**'Widerhaken** *m* barb
**'widerhallen** *v/i* (*sep*, *-ge-*, *h*) resound (***von*** with)
**wider'legen** *v/t* (*no -ge-*, *h*) refute, disprove
**'widerlich** *adj* sickening, disgusting
**'widerrechtlich** *adj* illegal, unlawful
**'Widerruf** *m* JUR revocation; withdrawal; **wider'rufen** *v/t* (*irr*, ***rufen***, *no -ge-*, *h*) revoke; withdraw
**Widersacher** ['viːdɐzaxɐ] *m* (*-s*; -) adversary, rival
**'Widerschein** *m* reflection
**wider'setzen** *v/refl* (*no -ge-*, *h*) (*dat*) oppose, resist
**'widersinnig** *adj* absurd
**widerspenstig** ['viːdɐʃpɛnstɪç] *adj* unruly, stubborn
**'widerspiegeln** *v/t* (*sep*, *-ge-*, *h*) reflect (*a. fig*); ***sich ~ in*** (*dat*) be reflected in
**wider'sprechen** *v/i* (*irr*, ***sprechen***, *no -ge-*, *h*) (*dat*) contradict
**'Widerspruch** *m* contradiction
**widersprüchlich** ['viːdɐʃprʏçlɪç] *adj* contradictory
**'widerspruchslos** *adv* without contradiction
**'Widerstand** *m* resistance (*a.* ELECTR), opposition; ***~ leisten*** offer resistance (*dat* to); **'widerstandsfähig** *adj* resistant (*a.* TECH); **wider'stehen** *v/i* (*irr*, ***stehen***, *no -ge-*, *h*) (*dat*) resist
**wider'streben** *v/i* (*no -ge-*, *h*) ***es widerstrebt mir, dies zu tun*** I hate doing *or* to do that; **~d** *adv* reluctantly
**widerwärtig** ['viːdɐvɛrtɪç] *adj* disgusting
**'Widerwille** *m* aversion (***gegen*** to), dislike (of, for); disgust (at)
**'widerwillig** *adj* reluctant, unwilling
**widmen** ['vɪtmən] *v/t* (*ge-*, *h*) dedicate; **'Widmung** *f* (-; *-en*) dedication
**wie** [viː] **1.** *interr adv* how; ***~ geht es Gordon?*** how is Gordon?; ***~ ist er?*** what's he like?; ***~ ist das Wetter?*** what's the weather like?; ***~ heißen Sie?*** what's your name?; ***~ nennt man …?*** what do you call …?; ***~ wäre*** (***ist, steht***) ***es mit …?*** what *or* how about …?; ***~ viele …?*** how many …? **2.** *cj* like; as; ***~ neu*** (***verrückt***) like new (mad); ***doppelt so … ~*** twice as … as; ***~*** (***zum Beispiel***)

such as, like; **~ *üblich*** as usual; **~ *er sagte*** as he said; ***ich zeige* (*sage*) *dir,* ~ (…)** I'll show (tell) you how (…)
**wieder** ['vi:dɐ] *adv* again; *in cpds often* re…; ***immer* ~** again and again; **~ *aufbauen*** reconstruct; **~ *aufnehmen*** resume; **~ *beleben*** MED resuscitate, revive (*a. fig*); **~ *erkennen*** recognize (***an*** *dat* by); **~ *finden*** find (what one has lost); *fig* regain; **~ *gutmachen*** make up for; **~ *herstellen*** restore; **~ *sehen*** see *or* meet again; **~ *verwendbar*** reusable; **~ *verwerten*** TECH recycle
**Wieder|'aufbau** *m* (-[*e*]*s*; *no pl*) reconstruction, rebuilding; **~'aufbereitung** *f* TECH recycling, reprocessing (*a.* NUCL); **~'aufbereitungsanlage** *f* TECH reprocessing plant; **~'aufleben** *n* (-*s*; *no pl*) revival; **~'aufnahme** *f* (-; *no pl*) resumption
**'wiederbekommen** *v/t* (*irr*, ***kommen***, *sep*, *no -ge-*, *h*) get back
**'Wieder|belebung** *f* (-; -*en*) MED resuscitation; **~belebungsversuch** *m* MED attempt at resuscitation
**'wiederbringen** *v/t* (*irr*, ***bringen***, *sep*, *-ge-*, *h*) bring back; return
**Wieder'einführung** *f* reintroduction
**'Wiederentdeckung** *f* rediscovery
**'Wiedergabe** *f* TECH reproduction, playback; **'wiedergeben** *v/t* (*irr*, ***geben***, *sep*, *-ge-*, *h*) give back, return; *fig* describe; TECH play back, reproduce
**Wieder'gutmachung** *f* (-; -*en*) reparation
**'wiederholen**[1] *v/t* (*sep*, *-ge-*, *h*) (go and) get *s.o. or s.th.* back
**wieder'holen**[2] *v/t* (*no -ge-*, *h*) repeat; PED revise, review; THEA replay; ***sich* ~** repeat o.s. (*a. fig*); **wieder'holt** *adv* repeatedly, several times
**Wieder'holung** *f* (-; -*en*) repetition; PED review; TV *etc* rerun; SPORT replay
**Wiederkehr** ['vi:dɐke:ɐ] *f* (-; *no pl*) return; recurrence; **'wiederkehren** *v/i* (*sep*, *-ge-*, *sein*) return; recur
**'wiederkommen** *v/i* (*irr*, ***kommen***, *sep*, *-ge-*, *sein*) come back, return
**'Wiedersehen** *n* (-*s*; -) seeing *s.o.* again; reunion; ***auf* ~!** goodbye!
**wiederum** ['vi:dərʊm] *adv* again; on the other hand
**'Wieder|vereinigung** *f* reunion, *esp* POL *a.* reunification; **~verkauf** *m* resale; **~verwendung** *f* reuse; **~verwertung** *f* (-; -*en*) TECH recycling; **~wahl** *f* POL re-election
**Wiege** ['vi:gə] *f* (-; -*n*) cradle
**wiegen**[1] ['vi:gən] *v/t and v/i* (*irr*, *ge-*, *h*) weigh
**'wiegen**[2] *v/t* (*ge-*, *h*) rock (***in den Schlaf*** to sleep)
**'Wiegenlied** *n* lullaby
**wiehern** ['vi:ɐn] *v/i* (*ge-*, *h*) ZO neigh
**wies** [vi:s] *pret of* ***weisen***
**Wiese** ['vi:zə] *f* (-; -*n*) meadow
**Wiesel** ['vi:zəl] *n* (-*s*; -) ZO weasel
**wieso** [vi'zo:] *interr adv* → ***warum***
**wievielt** [vi'fi:lt] *adj*: ***zum* ~*en Male?*** how many times?
**wild** [vɪlt] *adj* wild (*a. fig*) (F ***auf*** *acc* about); violent
**Wild** *n* (-[*e*]*s*; *no pl*) HUNT game; GASTR *mst* venison; **~bach** *m* torrent
**Wilde** ['vɪldə] *m*, *f* (-*n*; -*n*) savage; F ***wie ein* ~*r*** like mad
**Wilderer** ['vɪldərɐ] *m* (-*s*; -) poacher
**'wildern** *v/i* (*ge-*, *h*) poach
**'Wildhüter** *m* gamekeeper
**'Wildkatze** *f* ZO wild cat
**'Wildleder** *n* suede
**'Wildnis** *f* (-; -*se*) wilderness
**'Wild|park** *m*, **~reser,vat** *n* game park *or* reserve; **~schwein** *n* ZO wild boar
**Wille** ['vɪlə] *m* (-*ns*; -*n*) will; intention; ***s-n* ~*n durchsetzen*** have *or* get one's own way; ***j-m s-n* ~*n lassen*** let s.o. have his (own) way
**'willenlos** *adj* weak(-willed)
**'Willenskraft** *f* (-; *no pl*) willpower; ***durch* ~ *erzwingen*** will
**'willensstark** *adj* strong-willed
**willig** ['vɪlɪç] *adj* willing
**will'kommen** *adj* welcome (*a.* **~ *heißen***) (***in*** *dat* to)
**willkürlich** ['vɪlky:ɐlɪç] *adj* arbitrary; random
**wimmeln** ['vɪməln] *v/i* (*ge-*, *h*) **~ *von*** be teeming with
**wimmern** ['vɪmɐn] *v/i* (*ge-*, *h*) whimper
**Wimpel** ['vɪmpəl] *m* (-*s*; -) pennant
**Wimper** ['vɪmpɐ] *f* (-; -*n*) eyelash; ***ohne mit der* ~ *zu zucken*** without turning a hair; **'Wimperntusche** *f* mascara
**Wind** [vɪnt] *m* (-[*e*]*s*; -*e* ['vɪndə]) wind
**Winde** ['vɪndə] *f* (-; -*n*) winch, windlass, hoist
**Windel** ['vɪndəl] *f* (-; -*n*) diaper, *Br* nap-

py

**winden** ['vɪndən] *v/t* (*irr, ge-, h*) wind, TECH *a.* hoist; ***sich ~*** wind (one's way); writhe (*with pain etc*)

'**Windhund** *m* ZO greyhound

**windig** ['vɪndɪç] *adj* windy

'**Wind|mühle** *f* windmill; **~pocken** *pl* MED chickenpox; **~richtung** *f* direction of the wind; **~schutzscheibe** *f* MOT windshield, *Br* windscreen; **~stärke** *f* wind force

'**windstill** *adj*, '**Windstille** *f* calm

'**Windstoß** *m* gust

'**Windsurfen** *n* windsurfing

'**Windung** *f* (-; *-en*) bend, turn (*a.* TECH)

**Wink** [vɪŋk] *m* (-[*e*]*s*; *-e*) sign; *fig* hint

**Winkel** ['vɪŋkəl] *m* (*-s*; -) corner; MATH angle; '**winkelig** *adj* angular; crooked

**winken** ['vɪŋkən] *v/i* (*ge-, h*) wave (one's hand *etc*), signal; beckon

**winseln** ['vɪnzəln] *v/i* (*ge-, h*) whimper, whine

**Winter** ['vɪntɐ] *m* (*-s*; -) winter

'**winterlich** *adj* wintry

'**Winter|reifen** *m* MOT snow tire (*Br* tyre); **~schlaf** *m* ZO hibernation; **~spiele** *pl*: ***Olympische ~*** SPORT Winter Olympics; **~sport** *m* winter sports

**Winzer** ['vɪntsɐ] *m* (*-s*; -) winegrower

**winzig** ['vɪntsɪç] *adj* tiny, diminutive

**Wipfel** ['vɪpfəl] *m* (*-s*; -) (tree)top

**Wippe** ['vɪpə] *f* (-; *-n*), '**wippen** *v/i* (*ge-, h*) seesaw

**wir** [viːɐ] *pers pron* we; ***~ drei*** the three of us; F ***~ sind's!*** it's us!

**Wirbel** ['vɪrbəl] *m* (*-s*; -) whirl (*a. fig*); ANAT vertebra

'**wirbeln** *v/i* (*ge-, sein*) whirl

'**Wirbel|säule** *f* ANAT spinal column, spine; **~sturm** *m* cyclone, tornado; **~tier** *n* vertebrate; **~wind** *m* whirlwind

**wirken** ['vɪrkən] (*ge-, h*) **1.** *v/i* work; be effective (***gegen*** against); look; ***anregend*** *etc* **~** have a stimulating *etc* effect (***auf*** *acc* [up]on); ***~ als*** act as **2.** *v/t* weave; *fig* work (*miracles etc*)

**wirklich** ['vɪrklɪç] *adj* real, actual; true, genuine; '**Wirklichkeit** *f* (-; *-en*) reality; ***in ~*** in reality, actually

**wirksam** ['vɪrkzaːm] *adj* effective

'**Wirkung** *f* (-; *-en*) effect

'**wirkungslos** *adj* ineffective

'**wirkungsvoll** *adj* effective

**wirr** [vɪr] *adj* confused, mixed-up; *hair*: tousled; **Wirren** ['vɪrən] *pl* disorder, confusion; **Wirrwarr** ['vɪrvar] *m* (*-s*; *no pl*) confusion, mess, welter

**Wirt** [vɪrt] *m* (-[*e*]*s*; *-e*) landlord; '**Wirtin** *f* (-; *-nen*) landlady; '**Wirtschaft** *f* (-; *-en*) ECON, POL economy; business; → ***Gastwirtschaft***; '**wirtschaften** *v/i* (*ge-, h*) keep house; manage one's money *or* affairs *or* business; economize; ***gut*** (***schlecht***) **~** be a good (bad) manager; 'Wirtschafterin *f* (-; *-nen*) housekeeper; '**wirtschaftlich** *adj* economic; economical; '**Wirtschafts...** ECON *in cpds* *...gemeinschaft, ...gipfel, ...krise, ...system, ...wunder etc*: economic ...

'**Wirtshaus** *n* → ***Gastwirtschaft***

**wischen** ['vɪʃən] *v/t* (*ge-, h*) wipe; ***Staub ~*** dust

**wispern** ['vɪspɐn] *v/t and v/i* (*ge-, h*) whisper

**wissbegierig** ['vɪsbəgiːrɪç] *adj* curious

**wissen** ['vɪsən] *v/t and v/i* (*irr, ge-, h*) know; ***ich möchte ~*** I'd like to know, I wonder; ***soviel ich weiß*** as far as I know; ***weißt du*** you know; ***weißt du noch?*** (do you) remember?; ***woher weißt du das?*** how do you know?; ***man kann nie ~*** you never know; ***ich will davon*** (***von ihm***) ***nichts ~*** I don't want anything to do with it (him)

'**Wissen** *n* (*-s*; *no pl*) knowledge; know-how; ***m-s ~s*** as far as I know

'**Wissenschaft** *f* (-; *-en*) science

'**Wissenschaftler** *m* (*-s*; -), '**Wissenschaftlerin** *f* (-; *-nen*) scientist

'**wissenschaftlich** *adj* scientific

'**wissenswert** *adj* worth knowing; ***Wissenswertes*** useful facts; ***alles Wissenswerte*** (***über*** *acc*) all you need to know (about)

**wittern** ['vɪtɐn] *v/t* (*ge-, h*) scent, smell (*both a. fig*)

**Witwe** ['vɪtvə] *f* (-; *-n*) widow

**Witwer** ['vɪtvɐ] *m* (*-s*; -) widower

**Witz** [vɪts] *m* (*-es*; *-e*) joke; ***~e reißen*** crack jokes

**witzig** ['vɪtsɪç] *adj* funny; witty

**wo** [voː] *adv* where; ***~ ... doch*** when, although

**wob** [voːp] *pret of* ***weben***

**wobei** [vo'bai] *adv*: ***~ bist du?*** what are you at?; ***~ mir einfällt*** which reminds me

**Woche** ['vɔxə] *f* (-; *-n*) week

'**Wochen...** *in cpds ...lohn, ...markt, ...zeitung etc*: weekly ...; **~ende** *n* weekend; ***am ~*** on (*Br* at) the weekend
'**wochenlang 1.** *adj*: ***~es Warten*** (many) weeks of waiting **2.** *adv* for weeks
'**Wochenschau** *f film*: newsreel
'**Wochentag** *m* weekday
**wöchentlich** ['vœçəntlıç] **1.** *adj* weekly **2.** *adv* weekly, every week; ***einmal ~*** once a week
**wodurch** [vo'dʊrç] *adv* how; through which
**wofür** [vo'fyːɐ] *adv* for which; ***~?*** what (...) for?
**wog** [voːk] *pret of* ***wiegen***[1] *and* ***wägen***
**Woge** ['voːgə] *f* (-; *-n*) wave, *esp fig a.* surge; breaker; '**wogen** *v/i* (*ge-, h*) surge, heave (*both a. fig*)
**woher** [vo'heːɐ] *adv* where ... from; ***~ weißt du*** (***das***)***?*** how do you know?
**wohin** [vo'hın] *adv* where (... to)
**wohl** [voːl] *adv and cj* well; probably, I suppose; ***sich ~ fühlen → wohlfühlen***; ***~ oder übel*** willy-nilly, whether you *etc* like it or not; ***~ kaum*** hardly
**Wohl** *n* (-[*e*]*s*; *no pl*) well-being; ***auf j-s ~ trinken*** drink to s.o.('s health); ***zum ~!*** to your health!; F cheers!
'**wohlbehalten** *adv* safely
'**Wohlfahrtsstaat** *m* welfare state
'**wohlfühlen** *v/refl* (*sep, -ge-, h*): ***sich ~*** feel well, be well; feel good; feel at home ( ***bei*** with); ***ich fühle mich nicht wohl*** I don't feel well
'**wohl|gemerkt** *adv* mind you; **~genährt** *adj* well-fed; **~gesinnt** *adj*: ***j-m ~ sein*** be well-disposed towards s.o.; **~habend** *adj* well-off, well-to-do
**wohlig** ['voːlıç] *adj* snug, cozy, *Br* cosy
'**Wohl|stand** *m* (-[*e*]*s*; *no pl*) prosperity, affluence; **~standsgesellschaft** *f* affluent society
'**Wohltat** *f* (-; *no pl*) pleasure; relief; blessing; '**Wohltäter(in)** benefactor (benefactress); '**wohltätig** *adj* charitable; ***für ~e Zwecke*** for charity
'**Wohltätigkeits...** *in cpds ...ball, ...konzert etc*: charity ...
'**wohltun** *v/i* (*irr*, ***tun***, *sep, -ge-, h*): ***j-m ~*** do s.o. good
'**wohlverdient** *adj* well-deserved
'**wohlwollend** *adj* benevolent
**wohnen** ['voːnən] *v/i* (*ge-, h*) live (***in*** *dat* in; ***bei j-m*** with s.o.); stay (***in*** *dat* at; ***bei*** with)
'**Wohngebiet** *n* residential area
'**Wohngemeinschaft** *f*: (***mit j-m***) ***in e-r ~ leben*** share an apartment (*Br* a flat) *or* a house (with s.o.)
**wohnlich** ['voːnlıç] *adj* comfortable, snug, cozy, *Br* cosy
'**Wohnmo,bil** *n* (*-s*; *-e*) camper, motor home (*Br* caravan)
'**Wohn|siedlung** *f* housing development (*Br* estate); **~sitz** *m* residence; ***ohne festen ~*** of no fixed abode
'**Wohnung** *f* (-; *-en*) apartment, *Br* flat; ***m-e*** *etc* ***~*** my *etc* place
'**Wohnungs|amt** *n* housing office; **~bau** *m* (-[*e*]*s*; *no pl*) house building; **~not** *f* housing shortage
'**Wohnwagen** *m* trailer, *Br* caravan; mobile home
'**Wohnzimmer** *n* sitting *or* living room
**wölben** ['vœlbən] *v/refl* (*ge-, h*), '**Wölbung** *f* (-; *-en*) vault, arch
**Wolf** [vɔlf] *m* (-[*e*]*s*; *Wölfe* ['vœlfə]) zo wolf
**Wolke** ['vɔlkə] *f* (-; *-n*) cloud
'**Wolkenbruch** *m* cloudburst
'**Wolkenkratzer** *m* (*-s*; -) skyscraper
'**wolkenlos** *adj* cloudless
**wolkig** ['vɔlkıç] *adj* cloudy, clouded
**Woll...** [vɔl-] *in cpds ...schal, ...socken etc*: wool(l)en ...; **~decke** *f* blanket
**Wolle** ['vɔlə] *f* (-; *-n*) wool
**wollen** ['vɔlən] *v/t and v/i* (*ge-, h*) *and v/aux* (*no -ge-, h*) want (to); ***lieber ~*** prefer; ***~ wir*** (***gehen*** *etc*)*?* shall we (go *etc*)?; ***~ Sie bitte ...*** will *or* would you please ...; ***wie*** (***was, wann***) ***du willst*** as (whatever, whenever) you like; ***sie will, dass ich komme*** she wants me to come; ***ich wollte, ich wäre*** (***hätte***) ***...*** I wish I were (had) ...
**womit** [vo'mıt] *adv* with which; ***~?*** what ... with?
**Wonne** ['vɔnə] *f* (-; *-n*) joy, delight
**woran** [vo'ran] *adv*: ***~ denkst du?*** what are you thinking of?; ***~ liegt es, dass ...?*** how is it that ...?; ***~ sieht man, welche*** (***ob***) ***...?*** how can you tell which (if) ...?
**worauf** [vo'rauf] *adv* after which; on which; ***~?*** what ... on?; ***~ wartest du?*** what are you waiting for?
**woraus** [vo'raus] *adv* from which; ***~ ist es?*** what's it made of?

W

**worin** [vo'rɪn] *adv* in which; **~?** where?

**Wort** [vɔrt] *n* (-[*e*]*s*; -*e*, *Wörter* ['vœrtɐ]) word; ***mit anderen ~en*** in other words; ***sein ~ geben*** (***halten, brechen***) give (keep, break) one's word; ***j-n beim ~ nehmen*** take s.o. at his word; ***ein gutes ~ einlegen für*** put in a good word for; ***j-m ins ~ fallen*** cut s.o. short

'**Wortart** *f* LING part of speech

**Wörter|buch** ['vœrtɐbu:x] *n* dictionary; **~verzeichnis** *n* vocabulary, list of words

'**Wortführer** *m* spokesman; '**Wortführerin** *f* spokeswoman

'**wortkarg** *adj* taciturn

**wörtlich** ['vœrtlɪç] *adj* literal; ***~e Rede*** LING direct speech

'**Wort|schatz** *m* vocabulary; **~spiel** *n* pun; **~stellung** *f* LING word order

**worüber** [vo'ry:bɐ] *adv* about which; ***~ lachen Sie?*** what are you laughing at *or* about?

**worum** [vo'rʊm] *adv* about which; ***~ handelt es sich?*** what is it about?

**worunter** [vo'rʊntɐ] *adv* among which; **~?** what … under?

**wovon** [vo'fɔn] *adv* about which; ***~ redest du?*** what are you talking about?

**wovor** [vo'fo:ɐ] *adv* of which; ***~ hast du Angst?*** what are you afraid of?

**wozu** [vo'tsu:] *adv*: ***~ er mir rät*** what he advised me to do; **~?** what (…) for?; why?

**Wrack** [vrak] *n* (-[*e*]*s*; -*s*) MAR wreck (*a. fig*)

**wrang** [vraŋ] *pret of* ***wringen***

**wringen** ['vrɪŋən] *v/t* (*irr, ge-, h*) wring

**Wucher** ['vu:xɐ] *m* (-*s*; *no pl*) usury

**Wucherer** ['vu:xərɐ] *m* (-*s*; -) usurer

'**wuchern** *v/i* (*ge-, h*) grow (*fig* be) rampant; **Wucherung** ['vu:xərʊŋ] *f* (-; -*en*) MED growth

**Wuchs** [vu:ks] *m* (-*es*; *no pl*) growth; build

**wuchs** [vu:ks] *pret of* ***wachsen***[1]

**Wucht** [vʊxt] *f* (-; *no pl*) force; impact

**wuchtig** ['vʊxtɪç] *adj* massive; powerful

**wühlen** ['vy:lən] *v/i* (*ge-, h*) dig; ZO root; rummage (***in*** *dat* in, through)

**Wulst** [vʊlst] *m* (-*es*; *Wülste* ['vʏlstə], *f* -; *Wülste*) bulge; roll (*of fat*)

**wulstig** ['vʊlstɪç] *adj* bulging; thick

**wund** [vʊnt] *adj* MED sore; ***~e Stelle*** MED sore; ***~er Punkt*** *fig* sore point

**Wunde** ['vʊndə] *f* (-; -*n*) MED wound

**Wunder** ['vʊndɐ] *n* (-*s*; -) miracle, *fig a.* wonder; ***~ wirken*** work wonders; (***es ist***) ***kein ~, dass du müde bist*** no wonder you are tired; '**wunderbar** *adj* wonderful, marvel(l)ous

'**Wunderkind** *n* infant prodigy

'**wunderlich** *adj* funny, odd; senile

'**wundern** *v/refl* (*ge-, h*) be surprised *or* astonished (***über*** *acc* at)

'**wundervoll** *adj* wonderful

'**Wundstarrkrampf** *m* (-*es*; *no pl*) MED tetanus

**Wunsch** [vʊnʃ] *m* (-[*e*]*s*; *Wünsche* ['vʏnʃə]) wish; request; ***auf j-s ~*** at s.o.'s request; ***auf eigenen ~*** at one's own request; (***je***) ***nach ~*** as desired

**wünschen** ['vʏnʃən] *v/t* (*ge-, h*) wish; ***sich et.*** (***zu Weihnachten*** *etc*) ***~*** want s.th. (for Christmas *etc*); ***das habe ich mir*** (***schon immer***) ***gewünscht*** that's what I (always) wanted; ***alles, was man sich nur ~ kann*** everything one could wish for; ***ich wünschte, ich wäre*** (***hätte***) ***…*** I wish I were (had) …

'**wünschenswert** *adj* desirable

**wurde** ['vʊrdə] *pret of* ***werden***

**Würde** ['vʏrdə] *f* (-; -*n*) dignity

'**würdelos** *adj* undignified

'**Würdenträger** *m* dignitary

'**würdevoll** *adj* dignified

**würdig** ['vʏrdɪç] *adj* worthy (*gen* of); dignified; **würdigen** ['vʏrdɪgən] *v/t* (*ge-, h*) appreciate; ***j-n keines Blickes ~*** ignore s.o. completely; '**Würdigung** *f* (-; -*en*) appreciation

**Wurf** [vʊrf] *m* (-[*e*]*s*; *Würfe* ['vʏrfə]) throw; ZO litter

**Würfel** ['vʏrfəl] *m* (-*s*; -) cube (*a.* MATH); dice; '**würfeln** *v/i* (*ge-, h*) throw dice (***um*** for); play dice; GASTR dice; ***e-e Sechs ~*** throw a six

'**Würfelzucker** *m* lump sugar

'**Wurfgeschoss** *n* missile

**würgen** ['vʏrgən] *v/i and v/t* (*ge-, h*) choke; throttle *s.o.*

**Wurm** [vʊrm] *m* (-[*e*]*s*; *Würmer* ['vʏrmɐ]) ZO worm; **wurmen** ['vʊrmən] F *v/t* (*ge-, h*) gall *s.o.*; '**wurmstichig** ['vʊrmʃtɪçɪç] *adj* worm-eaten

**Wurst** [vʊrst] *f* (-; *Würste* ['vʏrstə]) sausage

**Würstchen** ['vʏrstçən] *n* (-*s*; -) small

sausage, frankfurter, wiener; hot dog
**Würze** ['vʏrtsə] *f* (-; *-n*) spice (*a. fig*)
**Wurzel** ['vʊrtsəl] *f* (-; *-n*) root (*a.* MATH); ***~n schlagen*** take root (*a. fig*)
'**wurzeln** *v/i* (*ge-*, *h*) **~ *in*** (*dat*) be rooted in (*a. fig*)
'**würzen** *v/t* (*ge-*, *h*) spice, season, flavo(u)r; **würzig** ['vʏrtsɪç] *adj* spicy, well-seasoned
**wusch** [vuːʃ] *pret of* ***waschen***
**wusste** ['vʊstə] *pret of* ***wissen***
**Wust** [vuːst] F *m* (-[*e*]*s*; *no pl*) tangled mass
**wüst** [vyːst] *adj* waste; confused; wild, dissolute
**Wüste** ['vyːstə] *f* (-; *-n*) desert
**Wut** [vuːt] *f* (-; *no pl*) rage, fury; ***e-e ~ haben*** be furious (***auf*** *acc* with)
'**Wutanfall** *m* fit of rage
**wüten** ['vyːtən] *v/i* (*ge-*, *h*) rage (*a. fig*); **~d** *adj* furious (***auf*** *acc* with; ***über*** *acc* at), F mad (at)
'**wutschnaubend** *adj* fuming

# X,Y

**X-Beine** ['ɪksbainə] *pl* knock-knees; ***sie hat ~*** she's knock-kneed
**x-beinig** ['ɪksbainɪç] *adj* knock-kneed
**x-be'liebig** *adj*: ***jede(r, -s) x-Beliebige ...*** any ... you like, F any old ...
'**x-mal** F *adv* umpteen times
**x-te** ['ɪkstə] *adj*: ***zum ~n Male*** for the umpteenth time
**Xylophon** [ksylo'foːn] *n* (*-s*; *-e*) MUS xylophone
**Yacht** [jaxt] *f* (-; *-en*) MAR yacht
**Yoga** ['joːga] *m*, *n* (-[*s*]; *no pl*) yoga

# Z

**Zacke** ['tsakə] *f* (-; *-n*), '**Zacken** *m* (*-s*; -) (sharp) point; tooth; **zackig** ['tsakɪç] *adj* serrated; jagged; *fig* smart
**zaghaft** ['tsaːkhaft] *adj* timid
**zäh** [tsɛː] *adj* tough (*a. fig*); **~flüssig** *adj* thick, viscous; *fig* slow-moving (*traffic*)
**Zähigkeit** ['tsɛːɪçkait] *f* (-; *no pl*) toughness, *fig a.* stamina
**Zahl** [tsaːl] *f* (-; *-en*) number; figure
'**zahlbar** *adj* payable (***an*** *acc* to; ***bei*** at)
**zählbar** ['tsɛːlbaːʁ] *adj* countable
**zahlen** ['tsaːlən] *v/i and v/t* (*ge-*, *h*) pay; ***~, bitte!*** the check (*Br* bill), please!
**zählen** ['tsɛːlən] *v/t and v/i* (*ge-*, *h*) count (***bis*** up to; *fig* ***auf*** *acc* on); **~ *zu*** rank with *the best etc*
'**zahlenmäßig** **1.** *adj* numerical **2.** *adv*: ***j-m ~ überlegen sein*** outnumber s.o.
**Zähler** ['tsɛːlʁ] *m* (*-s*; -) counter (*a.* TECH); MATH numerator; ELECTR *etc* meter
'**Zahlkarte** *f post* deposit (*Br* paying-in) slip
'**zahllos** *adj* countless
'**Zahlmeister** *m* MIL paymaster; MAR purser
'**zahlreich** **1.** *adj* numerous **2.** *adv* in great number
'**Zahltag** *m* payday
'**Zahlung** *f* (-; *-en*) payment
'**Zählung** *f* (-; *-en*) count; POL census
'**Zahlungs|aufforderung** *f* request for payment; **~bedingungen** *pl* terms of payment; **~befehl** *m* order to pay
'**zahlungsfähig** *adj* solvent
'**Zahlungs|frist** *f* term of payment; **~mittel** *n* currency; ***gesetzliches ~*** legal tender; **~schwierigkeiten** *pl* financial difficulties; **~ter,min** *m* date of payment
'**zahlungsunfähig** *adj* insolvent
'**Zählwerk** *n* TECH counter
'**Zahlwort** *n* LING numeral
**zahm** [tsaːm] *adj* tame (*a. fig*)
**zähmen** ['tsɛːmən] *v/t* (*ge-*, *h*) tame (*a. fig*); '**Zähmung** *f* (-; *no pl*) taming
**Zahn** [tsaːn] *m* (-[*e*]*s*; *Zähne* ['tsɛːnə]) tooth, TECH *a.* cog; **~arzt** *m*, **~ärztin** *f*

dentist, dental surgeon; **~bürste** *f* toothbrush; **~creme** *f* toothpaste
**zahnen** ['tsa:nən] *v/i* (*ge-*, *h*) cut one's teeth, teethe
'**Zahnfleisch** *n* gums
'**zahnlos** *adj* toothless
'**Zahn|lücke** *f* gap between the teeth; **~medi,zin** *f* dentistry; **~pasta**, **~paste** *f* toothpaste; **~radbahn** *f* rack railroad; **~schmerzen** *pl* toothache; **~spange** *f* MED brace; **~stein** *m* tartar; **~stocher** *m* (*-s*; -) toothpick
**Zange** ['tsaŋə] *f* (-; *-n*) TECH pliers; pincers; tongs; MED forceps; zo pincer
**zanken** ['tsaŋkən] *v/refl* (*ge-*, *h*) quarrel (***wegen*** about; ***um*** over), fight, argue (about; over)
**zänkisch** ['tsɛŋkɪʃ] *adj* quarrelsome
**Zäpfchen** ['tsɛpfçən] *n* (*-s*; -) ANAT uvula; PHARM suppository
**zapfen** ['tsapfən] *v/t* (*ge-*, *h*) tap
'**Zapfen** *m* (*-s*; -) faucet, *Br* tap; TECH peg, pin; bung; tenon; pivot; BOT cone
'**Zapfenstreich** *m* MIL tattoo, taps
'**Zapf|hahn** *m* faucet, *Br* tap; MOT nozzle; **~säule** *f* MOT gasoline (*Br* petrol) pump
**zappelig** ['tsapəlɪç] *adj* fidgety
**zappeln** ['tsapəln] *v/i* (*ge-*, *h*) fidget, wriggle
**zappen** ['zɛpən] F *v/i* (*ge-*, *h*) TV zap
**zart** [tsa:ɐt] *adj* tender; gentle; ***~ fühlend*** sensitive
'**Zartgefühl** *n* (*-[e]s*; *no pl*) delicacy (of feeling), sensitivity, tact
**zärtlich** ['tsɛ:ɐtlɪç] *adj* tender, affectionate (***zu*** with); '**Zärtlichkeit** *f* (-; *-en*) (*no pl*) tenderness, affection; caress
**Zauber** ['tsaubɐ] *m* (*-s*; -) magic, spell, charm (*all a. fig*), *fig* enchantment; **Zauberei** [tsaubə'rai] *f* (-; *-en*) magic, witchcraft; **Zauberer** ['tsaubərɐ] *m* (*-s*; -) magician, sorcerer, wizard (*a. fig*); '**zauberhaft** *fig adj* enchanting, charming; **Zauberin** ['tsaubərɪn] *f* (-; *-nen*) sorceress
'**Zauber|kraft** *f* magic power; **~künstler** *m* magician, conjurer; **~kunststück** *n* conjuring trick
'**zaubern** (*ge-*, *h*) **1.** *v/i* practise magic; do conjuring tricks **2.** *v/t* conjure (up)
'**Zauberspruch** *m* spell
**zaudern** ['tsaudɐn] *v/i* (*ge-*, *h*) hesitate

**Zaum** [tsaum] *m* (*-[e]s*; *Zäume* ['tsɔʏmə]) bridle; ***im ~ halten*** control (***sich*** o.s.), keep in check
**zäumen** ['tsɔʏmən] *v/t* (*ge-*, *h*) bridle
'**Zaumzeug** *n* (*-[e]s*; *-e*) bridle
**Zaun** [tsaun] *m* (*-[e]s*; *Zäune* ['tsɔʏnə]) fence; **~gast** *m* onlooker; **~pfahl** *m* pale
**z. B.** *abbr of* ***zum Beispiel*** e.g., for example, for instance
**Zebra** ['tse:bra] *n* (*-s*; *-s*) zo zebra
'**Zebrastreifen** *m* MOT zebra crossing
**Zeche** ['tsɛçə] *f* (-; *-n*) check, *Br* bill; (coal) mine, pit; ***die ~ bezahlen müssen*** F have to foot the bill
**Zeh** [tse:] *m* (*-s*; *-en*), ***Zehe*** ['tse:ə] *f* (-; *-n*) ANAT toe; ***große*** (***kleine***) ***~*** big (little) toe; '**Zehennagel** *m* ANAT toenail
'**Zehenspitze** *f* tip of the toe; ***auf ~n gehen*** (walk on) tiptoe
**zehn** [tse:n] *adj* ten; '**zehnfach** *adj* tenfold; '**zehnjährig** ['tse:njɛ:rɪç] *adj* ten-year-old (*boy etc*); ten-year *anniversary etc*; *absence etc* of ten years
**Zehnkampf** *m* SPORT decathlon
'**zehnmal** *adv* ten times; '**zehnte** *adj* tenth; '**Zehntel** *n* (*-s*; -) tenth; '**zehntens** *adv* tenthly
**Zeichen** ['tsaiçən] *n* (*-s*; -) sign; mark; signal; ***zum ~*** *gen* as a token of; **~block** *m* sketch pad; **~brett** *n* drawing board; **~dreieck** *n* MATH set square; **~folge** *f* IT string; **~lehrer(in)** art teacher; **~setzung** *f* (-; *no pl*) LING punctuation; **~sprache** *f* sign language; **~trickfilm** *m* (animated) cartoon
**zeichnen** ['tsaiçnən] *v/i and v/t* (*ge-*, *h*) draw; mark (*a. fig*); sign; *fig* leave its mark on *s.o.*; '**Zeichnen** *n* (*-s*; *no pl*) drawing; PED art; '**Zeichner** ['tsaiçnɐ] *m* (*-s*; -) *mst* graphic artist; draftsman, *Br* draughtsman; '**Zeichnung** *f* (-; *-en*) drawing; diagram; zo marking
**Zeigefinger** ['tsaigəfɪŋɐ] *m* ANAT forefinger, index finger; **zeigen** ['tsaigən] (*ge-*, *h*) **1.** *v/t* show (*a.* ***sich ~***); **2.** *v/i*: ***~ nach*** point to; (***mit dem Finger***) ***~ auf*** (*acc*) point (one's finger) at; **Zeiger** ['tsaigɐ] *m* (*-s*; -) hand; TECH pointer, needle; '**Zeigestock** *m* pointer
**Zeile** ['tsailə] *f* (-; *-n*) line (*a.* TV); ***j-m ein paar ~n schreiben*** drop s.o. a line
**Zeit** [tsait] *f* (-; *-en*) time; age, era; LING tense; ***vor einiger ~*** some time ago, a

while ago; ***in letzter ~*** lately, recently; ***in der*** (*or* ***zur***) ~ *gen* in the days of; ***... aller ~en*** ... of all time; ***die ~ ist um*** time's up; ***e-e ~ lang*** for some time, for a while; ***sich ~ lassen*** take one's time; ***es wird ~, dass ...*** it's time to *inf*; ***das waren noch ~en*** those were the days; ***~ raubend*** → ***zeitraubend***; → ***zurzeit***

**'Zeit|abschnitt** *m* period (of time); **~alter** *n* age; **~bombe** *f* time bomb (*a. fig*); **~druck** *m*: ***unter ~ stehen*** be pressed for time; **~fahren** *n* (*-s; no pl*) *cycling*: time trials

**'zeitgemäß** *adj* modern, up-to-date

**'Zeitgenosse** *m*, **'Zeitgenossin** *f*, **'zeitgenössisch** ['tsaitgənœsɪʃ] *adj* contemporary

**'Zeit|geschichte** *f* (*-; no pl*) contemporary history; **~gewinn** *m* (*-[e]s; no pl*) gain of time; **~karte** *f* season ticket

**'Zeitlang** *f* → ***Zeit***

**zeit'lebens** *adv* all one's life

**'zeitlich 1.** *adj* time ... **2.** *adv*: ***et. ~ planen*** *or* ***abstimmen*** time s.th.

**'zeitlos** *adj* timeless; classic

**'Zeit|lupe** *f*: ***in ~*** in slow motion; **~not** *f*: ***in ~ sein*** be pressed for time; **~punkt** *m* moment; **~raffer** *m*: ***im ~*** in quick motion

**'zeitraubend** *adj* time-consuming

**'Zeitraum** *m* period (of time)

**'Zeitschrift** *f* magazine

**Zeitung** ['tsaitʊŋ] *f* (*-; -en*) (news)paper

**'Zeitungs|abonne,ment** *n* subscription to a paper; **~ar,tikel** *m* newspaper article; **~ausschnitt** *m* (newspaper) clipping (*Br* cutting); **~junge** *m* paper boy; **~kiosk** *m* newspaper kiosk; **~no,tiz** *f* press item; **~pa,pier** *n* newspaper; **~stand** *m* newsstand; **~verkäufer(in)** newsdealer, *Br* news vendor

**'Zeitverlust** *m* (*-[e]s; no pl*) loss of time

**'Zeitverschiebung** *f* AVIAT time lag

**'Zeitverschwendung** *f* waste of time

**'Zeitvertreib** ['tsaitfɛɐtraip] *m* (*-[e]s; -e*) pastime; ***zum ~*** to pass the time

**zeitweilig** ['tsaitvailɪç] *adj* temporary

**'zeitweise** *adv* at times, occasionally

**'Zeitwort** *n* (*-[e]s; -wörter*) LING verb

**'Zeitzeichen** *n* *radio*: time signal

**'Zeitzünder** *m* MIL time fuse

**Zelle** ['tsɛlə] *f* (*-; -n*) cell

**Zellstoff** ['tsɛlʃtɔf] *m*, **Zellulose** [tsɛlu'loːzə] *f* (*-; -n*) TECH cellulose

**Zelt** [tsɛlt] *n* (*-[e]s; -e*) tent; **zelten** ['tsɛltən] *v/i* (*ge-, h*) camp; **'Zeltlager** *n* camp; **'Zeltplatz** *m* campsite

**Zement** [tse'mɛnt] *m* (*-[e]s; -e*), **zementieren** [tsemɛn'tiːrən] *v/t* (*no -ge-, h*) cement

**Zenit** [tse'niːt] *m* (*-[e]s; no pl*) zenith

**zensieren** [tsɛn'ziːrən] *v/t* (*no -ge-, h*) censor; PED mark, grade; **Zensor** ['tsɛnzoːɐ] *m* (*-s; -en* [tsɛn'zoːrən]) censor; **Zensur** [tsɛn'zuːɐ] *f* (*-; -en* [tsɛn'zuːrən]) (*no pl*) censorship; PED mark, grade

**Zentimeter** [tsɛnti'meːtɐ] *n*, *m* (*-s; -*) centimeter, *Br* centimetre

**Zentner** ['tsɛntnɐ] *m* (*-s; -*) 50 kilograms, metric hundredweight

**zentral** [tsɛn'traːl] *adj* central

**Zentrale** [tsɛn'traːlə] *f* (*-; -n*) head office; headquarters; TEL switchboard; TECH control room

**Zen'tral|heizung** *f* central heating; **~verriegelung** *f* MOT central locking

**Zentrum** ['tsɛntrʊm] *n* (*-s; Zentren*) center, *Br* centre

**Zepter** ['tsɛptɐ] *n* (*-s; -*) scepter, *Br* sceptre

**zer'brechen** *v/i* (*irr*, ***brechen***, *no -ge-, sein*) *and v/t* (*h*) break; → ***Kopf***

**zer'brechlich** *adj* fragile

**zer'bröckeln** *v/t* (*no -ge-, h*) *and v/i* (*sein*) crumble

**zer'drücken** *v/t* (*no -ge-, h*) crush

**Zeremonie** [tseremo'niː] *f* (*-; -n*) ceremony

**zeremoniell** [tseremo'njɛl] *adj*, **Zeremoni'ell** *n* (*-s; -e*) ceremonial

**Zer'fall** *m* (*-[e]s; no pl*) disintegration, decay; **zer'fallen** *v/i* (*irr*, ***fallen***, *no -ge-, sein*) disintegrate, decay; ***~ in*** (*acc*) break up into

**zer|'fetzen** *v/t* (*no -ge-, h*) tear to pieces; **~'fressen** *v/t* (*irr*, ***fressen***, *no -ge-, h*) eat (holes in); CHEM corrode; **~'gehen** *v/i* (*irr*, ***gehen***, *no -ge-, sein*) melt, dissolve; **~'hacken** *v/t* (*no -ge-, h*) chop (*a.* ELECTR)

**zerknirscht** [tsɛɐ'knɪrʃt] *adj* remorseful

**zer|'knittern** *v/t* (*no -ge-, h*) (c)rumple, crease; **~'knüllen** *v/t* (*no -ge-, h*) crumple up; **~'kratzen** *v/t* (*no -ge-, h*) scratch; **~'krümeln** *v/t* (*no -ge-, h*) crumble; ~'**lassen** *v/t* (*irr*, ***lassen***, *no -ge-*, *h*) melt; ~'**legen** *v/t* (*no -ge-*, *h*) take apart *or* to pieces; TECH dismantle; GASTR carve; CHEM, LING, *fig* analyze, *Br* analyse

**zer'lumpt** *adj* ragged, tattered

**zer'mahlen** *v/t* (*no -ge-*, *h*) grind

**zer'mürben** *v/t* (*no -ge-*, *h*) wear down

**zer'quetschen** *v/t* (*no -ge-*, *h*) crush

**Zerrbild** ['tsɛɐbɪlt] *n* caricature

**zer'reiben** *v/t* (*irr*, ***reiben***, *no -ge-*, *h*) rub to powder, pulverize

**zer'reißen** (*irr*, ***reißen***, *no -ge-*) **1.** *v/t* (*h*) tear up *or* to pieces; ***sich die Hose ~*** tear one's trousers **2.** *v/i* (*sein*) tear; break

**zerren** ['tsɛrən] (*ge-*, *h*) **1.** *v/t* tug, drag, pull (*a.* MED); **2.** *v/i*: ***~ an*** (*dat*) tug (*or* strain) at

'**Zerrung** *f* (-; *-en*) MED pulled muscle

**zerrütten** [tsɛɐ'rʏtən] *v/t* (*no -ge-*, *h*) ruin; **zer'rüttet** *adj*: ***~e Ehe*** (***Verhältnisse***) broken marriage (home)

**zer|'sägen** *v/t* (*no -ge-*, *h*) saw up; ~**schellen** [tsɛɐ'ʃɛlən] *v/i* (*no -ge-*, *sein*) be smashed, AVIAT *a.* crash; ~'**schlagen** **1.** *v/t* (*irr*, ***schlagen***, *no -ge-*, *h*) smash (to pieces); *fig* smash; ***sich ~*** come to nothing **2.** *adj*: ***sich ~ fühlen*** be (all) worn out, F be dead beat; ~'**schmettern** *v/t* (*no -ge-*, *h*) smash (to pieces), shatter (*a. fig*); ~'**schneiden** *v/t* (*irr*, ***schneiden***, *no -ge-*, *h*) cut (up); ~'**setzen** *v/t* (*no -ge-*, *h*) CHEM decompose (*a.* ***sich ~***); *fig* corrupt, undermine; ~'**splittern** *v/t* (*no -ge-*, *h*) *and v/i* (*sein*) split (up), splinter; shatter; ~'**springen** *v/i* (*irr*, ***springen***, *no -ge-*, *sein*) crack; shatter; ~'**stampfen** *v/t* (*no -ge-*, *h*) pound; GASTR mash

**zer'stäuben** *v/t* (*no -ge-*, *h*) spray; **Zerstäuber** [tsɛɐ'ʃtɔʏbɐ] *m* (*-s*; -) atomizer, sprayer

**zer'stören** *v/t* (*no -ge-*, *h*) destroy, ruin (*both a. fig*); **Zer'störer** *m* (*-s*; -) destroyer (*a.* MAR); **zer'störerisch** *adj* destructive; **Zer'störung** *f* (-; *-en*) destruction

**zer'streuen** *v/t and v/refl* (*no -ge-*, *h*) scatter, disperse; break up (*crowd etc*); *fig* take s.o.'s (*refl* one's) mind off things; **zer'streut** *fig adj* absent-minded; **Zer'streutheit** *f* (-; *no pl*) absent-mindedness; **Zer'streuung** *fig f* (-; *-en*) diversion, distraction

**zer'stückeln** *v/t* (*no -ge-*, *h*) cut up *or* (in)to pieces; dismember (*body*)

**Zertifikat** [tsɛrtifi'ka:t] *n* (-[*e*]*s*; *-e*) certificate

**zer'treten** *v/t* (*irr*, ***treten***, *no -ge-*, *h*) crush (*a. fig*)

**zer'trümmern** *v/t* (*no -ge-*, *h*) smash

**zerzaust** [tsɛɐ'tsaust] *adj* tousled, dishevel(l)ed

**Zettel** ['tsɛtəl] *m* (*-s*; -) slip (of paper); note; label, sticker

**Zeug** [tsɔʏk] *n* (-[*e*]*s*; *-e*) stuff (*a.* F); things; ***er hat das ~ dazu*** he's got what it takes; ***dummes ~*** nonsense

**Zeuge** ['tsɔʏgə] *m* (*-n*; *-n*) witness

'**zeugen**[1] *v/i* (*ge-*, *h*) JUR give evidence (***für*** for); *fig* ***~ von*** testify to

'**zeugen**[2] *v/t* (*ge-*, *h*) BIOL procreate; father

'**Zeugen|aussage** *f* JUR testimony, evidence; ~**bank** *f* (-; *-bänke*) JUR witness stand (*Br* box)

'**Zeugin** *f* (-; *-nen*) JUR (female) witness

**Zeugnis** ['tsɔʏknɪs] *n* (*-ses*; *-se*) report card, *Br* (school) report; certificate, diploma; reference; *pl* credentials

'**Zeugung** *f* (-; *-en*) BIOL procreation

**z. H(d).** *abbr of* ***zu Händen*** attn, attention

**Zickzack** ['tsɪktsak] *m* (-[*e*]*s*; *-e*) (*a.* ***im ~ fahren***) zigzag

**Ziege** ['tsi:gə] *f* (-; *-n*) ZO (nanny) goat; F *contp* (***blöde***) ~ (silly old) cow

**Ziegel** ['tsi:gəl] *m* (*-s*; -) brick; tile

'**Ziegeldach** *n* tiled roof

**Ziegelei** [tsi:gə'lai] *f* (-; *-en*) brickyard

'**Ziegelstein** *m* brick

'**Ziegen|bock** *m* ZO billy goat; ~**leder** *n* kid (leather); ~**peter** ['tsi:gənpe:tɐ] *m* (*-s*; -) MED mumps

**ziehen** ['tsi:ən] (*irr*, *-ge-*) **1.** *v/t* (*h*) pull, draw; take off *one's hat* (***vor*** *dat* to) (*a. fig*); AGR grow; pull *or* take out (***aus*** of); ***j-n ~ an*** (*dat*) pull s.o. by; ***auf sich ~*** attract (*attention etc*); ***sich ~*** run; stretch; → ***Länge, Erwägung*** **2.** *v/i* (*h*) pull (***an*** *dat* at); (*sein*) move; ZO *etc* migrate; go; travel; wander, roam; ***es zieht*** there's a draft (*Br* draught)

**Ziehharmonika** ['tsi:harmo:nika] *f* (-; *-s*) MUS accordion

'**Ziehung** *f* (-; *-en*) draw
**Ziel** [tsiːl] *n* (-[*e*]*s*; *-e*) aim, target, mark (*all a. fig*), *fig a.* goal, objective; destination; SPORT finish; ***sich ein ~ setzen*** set o.s. a goal; ***sein ~ erreichen*** reach one's goal; ***sich zum ~ gesetzt haben, et. zu tun*** aim to do *or* at doing s.th.
'**Zielband** *n* (-[*e*]*s*; *-bänder*) SPORT tape
**zielen** ['tsiːlən] *v/i* (*ge-*, *h*) (take) aim (***auf*** *acc* at)
'**Ziellinie** *f* SPORT finishing line
'**ziellos** *adj* aimless
'**Zielscheibe** *f* target, *fig a.* object
**zielstrebig** ['tsiːlʃtreːbɪç] *adj* purposeful, determined
**ziemlich** ['tsiːmlɪç] **1.** *adj* quite a **2.** *adv* rather, fairly, quite, F pretty; ***~ viele*** quite a few
**Zierde** ['tsiːɐdə] *f* (-; *-n*) (***zur*** as a) decoration; **zieren** ['tsiːrən] *v/t* (*ge-*, *h*) decorate; ***sich ~*** be coy; make a fuss
**zierlich** ['tsiːɐlɪç] *adj* dainty; petite
**Zierpflanze** ['tsiːɐpflantsə] *f* ornamental plant
**Ziffer** ['tsɪfɐ] *f* (-; *-n*) figure
'**Zifferblatt** *n* dial, face
**Zigarette** [tsiga'rɛtə] *f* (-; *-n*) cigarette
**Ziga'retten|auto,mat** *m* cigarette machine; **~stummel** *m* cigarette end, stub, butt
**Zigarre** [tsi'garə] *f* (-; *-n*) cigar
**Zimmer** ['tsɪmɐ] *n* (*-s*; -) room; apartment; **~einrichtung** *f* furniture; **~mädchen** *n* (chamber)maid; **~mann** *m* carpenter
'**zimmern** *v/t* (*ge-*, *h*) build, make
'**Zimmer|pflanze** *f* indoor plant; **~service** *m* room service; **~suche** *f*: ***auf ~ sein*** be looking (*or* hunting) for a room; **~vermittlung** *f* accommodation office
**zimperlich** ['tsɪmpɐlɪç] *adj* prudish; soft, F sissy
**Zimt** [tsɪmt] *m* (-[*e*]*s*; *-e*) cinnamon
**Zink** ['tsɪŋk] *n* (-[*e*]*s*; *no pl*) CHEM zinc
**Zinke** ['tsɪŋkə] *f* (-; *-n*) tooth; prong
**Zinn** [tsɪn] *n* (-[*e*]*s*; *no pl*) CHEM tin; pewter
**Zins** [tsɪns] *m* (*-es*; *-en*) ECON interest (*a. pl*); ***3% ~en bringen*** bear interest at 3%; '**zinslos** *adj* ECON interest-free; '**Zinssatz** *m* ECON interest rate
**Zipfel** ['tsɪpfəl] *m* (*-s*; -) corner; point; tail; GASTR end; **~mütze** *f* pointed cap
**zirka** ['tsɪrka] *adv* about, approximately
**Zirkel** ['tsɪrkəl] *m* (*-s*; -) circle (*a. fig*); MATH compasses, dividers
**zirkulieren** [tsɪrku'liːrən] *v/i* (*no -ge-*, *h*) circulate
**Zirkus** ['tsɪrkʊs] *m* (-; *-se*) circus
**zirpen** ['tsɪrpən] *v/i* (*ge-*, *h*) chirp
**zischen** ['tsɪʃən] *v/i and v/t* (*ge-*, *h*) hiss; *fat etc*: sizzle; *fig* whiz(z)
**ziselieren** [tsizə'liːrən] *v/t* (*no -ge-*, *h*) TECH chase
**Zitat** [tsi'taːt] *n* (-[*e*]*s*; *-e*) quotation, F quote; **zitieren** [tsi'tiːrən] *v/t* (*no -ge-*, *h*) quote, cite (*a.* JUR), JUR summon
**Zitrone** [tsi'troːnə] *f* (-; *-n*) BOT lemon
**Zi'tronen|limo,nade** *f* lemon soda *or* pop, *Br* (fizzy) lemonade; **~saft** *m* lemon juice; **~schale** *f* lemon peel
**zitterig** ['tsɪtərɪç] *adj* shaky; **zittern** ['tsɪtɐn] *v/i* (*ge-*, *h*) tremble, shake (*both*: ***vor*** *dat* with)
**zivil** [tsi'viːl] *adj* civil, civilian
**Zi'vil** *n* (*-s*; *no pl*) civilian clothes; ***Polizist in ~*** plainclothes policeman
**Zi'vildienst** *m* MIL alternative service (*in lieu of military service*)
**Zivilisation** [tsiviliza'tsjoːn] *f* (-; *-en*) civilization; **zivilisieren** [tsivili'ziːrən] *v/t* (*no -ge-*, *h*) civilize
**Zivilist** [tsivi'lɪst] *m* (*-en*; *-en*) civilian
**Zi'vilrecht** *n* (-[*e*]*s*; *no pl*) JUR civil law
**Zi'vilschutz** *m* civil defen|se, *Br* -ce
**Znüni** ['tsnyːni] *Swiss m*, *n* (*-s*; -) midmorning snack, tea (*or* coffee) break
**zog** [tsoːk] *pret of* ***ziehen***
**zögern** ['tsøːgɐn] *v/i* (*ge-*, *h*) hesitate; '**Zögern** *n* (*-s*; *no pl*) hesitation
**Zoll**[1] [tsɔl] *m* (-[*e*]*s*; -) inch
**Zoll**[2] *m* (-[*e*]*s*; *Zölle* ['tsœlə]) (*no pl*) customs; duty
'**Zollabfertigung** *f* customs clearance
'**Zollbeamte** *m* customs officer
'**Zollerklärung** *f* customs declaration
'**zollfrei** *adj* duty-free
'**Zollkon,trolle** *f* customs examination
'**zollpflichtig** *adj* liable to duty
'**Zollstock** *m* (folding) rule
**Zone** ['tsoːnə] *f* (-; *-n*) zone
**Zoo** [tsoː] *m* (*-s*; *-s*) zoo
'**Zoohandlung** *f* pet shop
**Zoologe** [tsoo'loːgə] *m* (*-n*; *-n*) zoologist; **Zoologie** [tsoolo'giː] *f* (-; *no pl*) zoology; **Zoo'login** *f* (-; *-nen*) zoologist; **zoo'logisch** *adj* zoological

**Zopf** [tsɔpf] *m* (-[*e*]*s*; *Zöpfe* ['tsœpfə]) plait; pigtail
**Zorn** [tsɔrn] *m* (-[*e*]*s*; *no pl*) anger
**zornig** ['tsɔrnɪç] *adj* angry
**Zote** ['tsoːtə] *f* (-; -*n*) filthy joke, obscenity
**zottelig** ['tsɔtəlɪç] *adj* shaggy
**z. T.** *abbr of* ***zum Teil*** partly
**zu** [tsuː] **1.** *prp* (*dat*) to, toward(s); at; *purpose*: for; **~ *Fuß*** (***Pferd***) on foot (horseback); **~ *Hause*** (***Ostern*** *etc*) at home (Easter *etc*); **~ *Weihnachten*** *give etc* for Christmas; ***Tür*** (***Schlüssel***) **~ ...** door (key) to ...; **~ *m-r Überraschung*** to my surprise; ***wir sind ~ dritt*** there are three of us; **~ *zweien*** two by two; **~ *zwei Euro*** at *or* for two euros; SPORT ***1 ~ 1*** one all; ***2 ~ 1 gewinnen*** win two one, win by two goals *etc* to one; → ***zum, zur*** **2.** *adv* too; F closed, shut; ***ein ~ großes Risiko*** too much of a risk; **~ *viel*** too much, too many; **~ *wenig*** too little, too few **3.** *cj* to; ***es ist ~ erwarten*** it is to be expected
**Zubehör** ['tsuːbəhøːɐ] *n* (-[*e*]*s*; -*e*) accessories
**'zubereiten** *v/t* (*sep*, *no -ge-*, *h*) prepare; **'Zubereitung** *f* (-; -*en*) preparation
**'zu|binden** *v/t* (*irr*, ***binden***, *sep*, *-ge-*, *h*) tie (up); **~bleiben** *v/i* (*irr*, ***bleiben***, *sep*, *-ge-*, *sein*) stay shut; **~blinzeln** *v/i* (*sep*, *-ge-*, *h*) (*dat*) wink at
**'Zubringer** *m* (-*s*; -), **~straße** *f* MOT feeder (road), access road
**Zucht** [tsʊxt] *f* (-; -*en*) breed; zo breeding; BOT cultivation; **züchten** ['tsʏçtən] *v/t* (*ge-*, *h*) zo breed; BOT grow, cultivate; **Züchter(in)** ['tsʏçtɐ, 'tsʏçtərɪn] *m*(*f*) (-*s*; -/-; -*nen*) zo breeder; BOT grower
**'Zuchtperle** *f* culture(d) pearl
**zucken** ['tsʊkən] *v/i* (*ge-*, *h*) jerk; twitch (***mit et.*** s.th.); wince; *lightning*: flash
**zücken** ['tsʏkən] *v/t* (*ge-*, *h*) draw (*weapon*); F pull out (*one's wallet etc*)
**Zucker** ['tsʊkɐ] *m* (-*s*; -) sugar; **~dose** *f* sugar bowl; **~guss** *m* icing, frosting
**'zuckerkrank** *adj*, **'Zuckerkranke** *m*, *f* (-*n*; -*n*) MED diabetic
**'Zuckerkrankheit** *f* MED diabetes
**'Zuckermais** *m* sweet corn
**'zuckern** *v/t* (*ge-*, *h*) sugar
**'Zuckerrohr** *n* BOT sugarcane
**'Zuckerrübe** *f* BOT sugar beet
**'Zuckerwatte** *f* candy floss
**'Zuckerzange** *f* sugar tongs
**'Zuckung** *f* (-; -*en*) twitch(ing); tic; convulsion, spasm
**'zudecken** *v/t* (*sep*, *-ge-*, *h*) cover (up)
**zudem** [tsu'deːm] *adv* besides, moreover
**'zudrehen** *v/t* (*sep*, *-ge-*, *h*) turn off; ***j-m den Rücken ~*** turn one's back on s.o.
**'zudringlich** *adj*: **~ *werden*** F get fresh (***j-m gegenüber*** with s.o.)
**'zudrücken** *v/t* (*sep*, *-ge-*, *h*) close, push *s.th.* shut; → ***Auge***
**zuerst** [tsu'ʔeːɐst] *adv* first; at first; first (of all), to begin with
**'Zufahrt** *f* approach; drive(way)
**'Zufahrtsstraße** *f* access road
**'Zufall** *m* chance; ***durch ~*** by chance, by accident; **'zufallen** *v/i* (*irr*, ***fallen***, *sep*, *-ge-*, *sein*) *door etc*: slam (shut); *fig* fall to *s.o.*; ***mir fallen die Augen zu*** I can't keep my eyes open; **'zufällig 1.** *adj* accidental, chance ... **2.** *adv* by accident, by chance; **~ *tun*** happen to do
**'Zuflucht** *f*: **~ *suchen*** (***finden***) look for (find) refuge *or* shelter (***vor*** *dat* from; ***bei*** with); (***s-e***) **~ *nehmen zu*** resort to
**zufrieden** [tsu'friːdən] *adj* content(ed), satisfied; **~ *stellen*** satisfy; **~ *stellend*** satisfactory
**zu'frieden|geben** *v/refl* (*irr*, ***geben***, *sep*, *-ge-*, *h*): ***sich ~ mit*** content o.s. with
**Zu'friedenheit** *f* (-; *no pl*) contentment, satisfaction
**zu'frieden|lassen** *v/t* (*irr*, ***lassen***, *sep*, *-ge-*, *h*) leave s.o. alone; **~stellen** *v/t* (*sep*, *-ge-*, *h*) satisfy; **~stellend** *adj* satisfactory
**'zufrieren** *v/i* (*irr*, ***frieren***, *sep*, *-ge-*, *sein*) freeze up *or* over
**'zufügen** *v/t* (*sep*, *-ge-*, *h*) do, cause; ***j-m Schaden ~*** *a.* harm s.o.
**Zufuhr** ['tsuːfuːɐ] *f* (-; -*en*) supply
**Zug** [tsuːk] *m* (-[*e*]*s*; *Züge* ['tsyːgə]) RAIL train; procession, line; parade; *fig* feature; trait; tendency; *chess etc*: move (*a. fig*); *swimming*: stroke; pull (*a.* TECH), PHYS *a.* tension; *smoking*: puff; draft, *Br* draught; PED stream; ***im ~e*** *gen* in the course of; ***in e-m ~*** at one go; **~ *um ~*** step by step; ***in groben Zügen*** in broad outlines
**'Zugabe** *f* addition; THEA encore
**'Zugang** *m* access (*a. fig*); **'zugänglich**

['tsu:gɛŋlɪç] *adj* accessible (**für** to) (*a. fig*)

'**Zugbrücke** *f* drawbridge

'**zugeben** *v/t* (*irr*, **geben**, *sep*, *-ge-*, *h*) add; *fig* admit

'**zugehen** *v/i* (*irr*, **gehen**, *sep*, *-ge-*, *sein*) F *door etc*: close, shut; **~ auf** (*acc*) walk up to, approach (*a. fig*); ***es geht auf 8 Uhr zu*** it's getting on for 8; ***es ging lustig zu*** we had a lot of fun

'**Zugehörigkeit** *f* (-; *no pl*) membership

**Zügel** ['tsy:gəl] *m* (*-s*; -) rein (*a. fig*)

'**zügeln 1.** *v/t* (*ge-*, *h*) curb, control, bridle **2.** *Swiss v/i* (*ge-*, *sein*) move

'**Zugeständnis** *n* concession

'**zugestehen** *v/t* (*irr*, **stehen**, *sep*, *no -ge-*, *h*) concede, grant

'**zugetan** *adj* attached (*dat* to)

'**Zugführer** *m* RAIL conductor, *Br* guard

**zugig** ['tsu:gɪç] *adj* drafty, *Br* draughty

'**Zugkraft** *f* TECH traction; (*no pl*) attraction, draw, appeal

'**zugkräftig** *adj*: **~ sein** be a draw

**zu'gleich** [tsu'glaiç] *adv* at the same time

'**Zugluft** *f* (-; *no pl*) draft, *Br* draught

'**Zugmaˌschine** *f* MOT tractor

'**zugreifen** *v/i* (*irr*, **greifen**, *sep*, *-ge-*, *h*) grab (at) it; *fig* grab the opportunity; ***greifen Sie zu!*** help yourself!; ***mit* ~** lend a hand

'**Zugriffscode** *m* IT access code

'**Zugriffszeit** *f* IT access time

**zugrunde** [tsu'grʊndə] *adv*: **~ *gehen*** (**an** *dat*) perish (of); ***e-r Sache et. ~ legen*** base s.th. on s.th.; **~ *richten*** ruin

**zugunsten** [tsu'gʊnstən] *prp* (*gen*) in favo(u)r of

**zu'gute** [tsu'gu:tə] *adv*: **~ *halten* → *zugutehalten***; **~ *kommen* → *zugutekommen***; **~halten** *v/t* (*irr*, **halten**, *sep*, *-ge-*, *h*): ***j-m et.* ~** give s.o. credit for s.th.; make allwances for s.o.'s …; **~kommen** *v/t* (*irr*, **kommen**, *sep*, *-ge-*, *sein*): ***j-m* ~** be for the benefit of s.o.

'**Zugvogel** *m* ZO bird of passage

'**zuhalten** *v/t* (*irr*, **halten**, *sep*, *-ge-*, *h*) keep shut; ***sich die Ohren*** (***Augen***) **~** cover one's ears (eyes) with one's hands; ***sich die Nase* ~** hold one's nose

**Zuhälter** ['tsu:hɛltɐ] *m* (*-s*; -) pimp

**Zuhause** [tsu'hauzə] *n* (*-s*; *no pl*) home

**zu'hause** *adv* → ***Haus***

'**zuhören** *v/i* (*sep*, *-ge-*, *h*) listen (*dat* to)

'**Zuhörer** *m*, '**Zuhörerin** *f* listener, *pl a. the* audience

'**zujubeln** *v/i* (*sep*, *-ge-*, *h*) cheer

'**zukleben** *v/t* (*sep*, *-ge-*, *h*) seal

'**zuknöpfen** *v/t* (*sep*, *-ge-*, *h*) button (up)

'**zukommen** *v/i* (*irr*, **kommen**, *sep*, *-ge-*, *sein*) **~ auf** (*acc*) come up to; *fig* be ahead of; ***die Dinge auf sich ~ lassen*** wait and see

**Zukunft** ['tsu:kʊnft] *f* (-; *no pl*) future (*a.* LING)

'**zukünftig 1.** *adj* future **2.** *adv* in future

'**zulächeln** *v/i* (*sep*, *-ge-*, *h*) smile at

'**Zulage** *f* bonus

'**zulangen** F *v/i* (*sep*, *-ge-*, *h*) tuck in

'**zulassen** *v/t* (*irr*, **lassen**, *sep*, *-ge-*, *h*) F keep *s.th.* closed; *fig* allow; MOT *etc* license, register; ***j-n zu et.* ~** admit s.o. to s.th.; '**zulässig** *adj* admissible (*a.* JUR); **~ *sein*** be allowed; '**Zulassung** *f* (-; *-en*) admission; MOT *etc* license, *Br* licence

'**zulegen** *v/t* (*sep*, *-ge-*, *h*) add; F ***sich …* ~** get o.s. *s.th.*; adopt (*name*)

**zu'letzt** [tsu'lɛtst] *adv* in the end; *come etc* last; finally; ***wann hast du ihn ~ gesehen?*** when did you last see him?

**zu'liebe** [tsu'li:bə] *adv*: ***j-m* ~** for s.o.'s sake

**zum** [tsʊm] *prp* ***zu dem* → *zu***; **~ *ersten Mal*** for the first time; *et.* **~ *Kaffee*** *s.th.* with one's coffee; **~ *Schwimmen*** *etc* ***gehen*** go swimming *etc*

'**zumachen** F (*sep*, *-ge-*, *h*) **1.** *v/t* close, shut; button (up) **2.** *v/i* close (down)

'**zumauern** *v/t* (*sep*, *-ge-*, *h*) brick *or* wall up

**zumutbar** ['tsu:mu:tba:ɐ] *adj* reasonable; **zu'mute** [tsu'mu:tə] *adv*: ***mir ist … ~*** I feel …; '**zumuten** *v/t* (*sep*, *-ge-*, *h*) ***j-m et.* ~** expect s.th. of s.o.; ***sich zu viel* ~** overtax o.s.; '**Zumutung** *f*: ***das ist e-e* ~** that's asking *or* expecting a bit much

**zu'nächst** [tsu'nɛ:çst] *adv* → ***zuerst***

'**zunageln** *v/t* (*sep*, *-ge-*, *h*) nail up

'**zunähen** *v/t* (*sep*, *-ge-*, *h*) sew up

**Zunahme** ['tsu:na:mə] *f* (-; *-n*) increase

'**Zuname** *m* surname

**zünden** ['tsʏndən] *v/i* (*ge-*, *h*) kindle; ELECTR, MOT ignite, fire; **~d** *fig adj* stirring

**Zünder** ['tsʏndɐ] *m* (*-s*; -) MIL fuse; *pl Austrian* matches

**Zünd|holz** ['tsʏnthɔlts] *n* match; **~kerze** *f* MOT spark plug; **~schlüssel** *m* MOT ignition key; **~schnur** *f* fuse
'**Zündung** *f* (-; *-en*) MOT ignition
'**zunehmen** *v/i* (*irr*, ***nehmen***, *sep*, *-ge-*, *h*) increase (***an*** *dat* in); put on weight; *moon*: wax; *days*: grow longer
'**Zuneigung** *f* (-; *-en*) affection
**Zunft** [tsʊnft] HIST *f* (-; *Zünfte* ['tsʏnftə]) guild
**Zunge** [tsʊŋə] *f* (-; *-n*) ANAT tongue; ***es liegt mir auf der ~*** it's on the tip of my tongue
**züngeln** ['tsʏŋəln] *v/i* (*ge-*, *h*) *flames*: lick, flicker
'**Zungenspitze** *f* tip of the tongue
'**zunicken** *v/i* (*sep*, *-ge-*, *h*) (*dat*) nod at
**zunutze** [tsu'nʊtsə] *adv*: ***sich et. ~ machen*** make (good) use of s.th.; take advantage of s.th.
**zupfen** [tsʊpfən] *v/t and v/i* (*ge-*, *h*) pull (***an*** *dat* at), pick, pluck (at) (*a.* MUS)
**zur** [tsuːɐ] *prp* ***zu der*** → ***zu***; ***~ Schule*** (***Kirche***) ***gehen*** go to school (church); ***~ Hälfte*** half (of it *or* them); ***~ Belohnung*** *etc* as a reward *etc*
'**zurechnungsfähig** *adj* JUR responsible; '**Zurechnungsfähigkeit** *f* (-; *no pl*) JUR responsibility
**zu'recht|finden** *v/refl* (*irr*, ***finden***, *sep*, *-ge-*, *h*) find one's way; *fig* cope, manage; **~kommen** *v/i* (*irr*, ***kommen***, *sep*, *-ge-*, *sein*) get along (***mit*** with); cope (with); **~legen** *v/t* (*sep*, *-ge-*, *h*) arrange; *fig* ***sich et. ~*** think s.th. out; **~machen** F *v/t* (*sep*, *-ge-*, *h*) get ready, prepare, fix; ***sich ~*** do o.s. up; **~rücken** *v/t* (*sep*, *-ge-*, *h*) put *s.th.* straight (*a. fig*)
**zu'rechtweisen** *v/t* (*irr*, ***weisen***, *sep*, *-ge-*, *h*), **Zu'rechtweisung** *f* reprimand
'**zu|reden** *v/i* (*sep*, *-ge-*, *h*) ***j-m ~*** encourage s.o.; **~reiten** *v/t* (*irr*, ***reiten***, *sep*, *-ge-*, *h*) break in; **~richten** F *fig v/t* (*sep*, *-ge-*, *h*) ***übel ~*** batter, *a.* beat *s.o.* up badly, *a.* make a mess of *s.th.*, ruin
**zurück** [tsu'rʏk] *adv* back; behind (*a. fig*); **~behalten** *v/t* (*irr*, ***halten***, *sep*, *no -ge-*, *h*) keep back, retain; **~bekommen** *v/t* (*irr*, ***kommen***, *sep*, *no -ge-*, *h*) get back; **~bleiben** *v/i* (*irr*, ***bleiben***, *sep*, *-ge-*, *sein*) stay behind, be left behind; fall behind (*a.* PED *etc*); **~blicken** *v/i* (*sep*, *-ge-*, *h*) look back (***auf*** *acc* at, *fig* on); **~bringen** *v/t* (*irr*, ***bringen***, *sep*, *-ge-*, *h*) bring *or* take back, return; **~datieren** *v/t* (*sep*, *no -ge-*, *h*) backdate (***auf*** *acc* to); **~fallen** *fig v/i* (*irr*, ***fallen***, *sep*, *-ge-*, *sein*) fall behind, SPORT *a.* drop back; **~finden** *v/i* (*irr*, ***finden***, *sep*, *-ge-*, *h*) find one's way back (***nach, zu*** to); *fig* return (to); **~fordern** *v/t* (*sep*, *-ge-*, *h*) reclaim; **~führen** *v/t* (*sep*, *-ge-*, *h*) lead back; ***~ auf*** (*acc*) attribute to; **~geben** *v/t* (*irr*, ***geben***, *sep*, *-ge-*, *h*) give back, return; **~geblieben** *fig adj* backward; retarded; **~gehen** *v/i* (*irr*, ***gehen***, *sep*, *-ge-*, *sein*) go back, return; *fig* decrease; go down, drop; **~gezogen** *fig adj* secluded; **~greifen** *v/i* (*irr*, ***greifen***, *sep*, *-ge-*, *h*) ***~ auf*** (*acc*) fall back (up)on
**zu'rückhalten** (*irr*, ***halten***, *sep*, *-ge-*, *h*) **1.** *v/t* hold back **2.** *v/refl* control o.s.; be careful; **~d** *adj* reserved
**Zu'rückhaltung** *f* (-; *no pl*) reserve
**zu'rück|kehren** *v/i* (*sep*, *-ge-*, *sein*) return; **~kommen** *v/i* (*irr*, ***kommen***, *sep*, *-ge-*, *sein*) come back, return (*both fig* ***auf*** *acc* to); **~lassen** *v/t* (*irr*, ***lassen***, *sep*, *-ge-*, *h*) leave (behind); **~legen** *v/t* (*sep*, *-ge-*, *h*) put back; put aside, save (*money*); cover, do (*miles*); **~nehmen** *v/t* (*irr*, ***nehmen***, *sep*, *-ge-*, *h*) take back (*a. fig*); **~rufen** (*irr*, ***rufen***, *sep*, *-ge-*, *h*) **1.** *v/t* call back (*a.* TEL); ECON recall; ***ins Gedächtnis ~*** recall **2.** *v/i* TEL call back; **~schlagen** (*irr*, ***schlagen***, *sep*, *-ge-*, *h*) **1.** *v/t* beat off; *tennis*: return; fold back **2.** *v/i* hit back; MIL retaliate (*a. fig*); **~schrecken** *v/i* (*sep*, *-ge-*, *sein*) ***~ vor*** (*dat*) shrink from; ***vor nichts ~*** stop at nothing; **~setzen** *v/t* (*sep*, *-ge-*, *h*) MOT back (up); *fig* neglect *s.o.*; **~stehen** *v/i* (*irr*, ***stehen***, *sep*, *-ge-*, *h*) stand aside; **~stellen** *v/t* (*sep*, *-ge-*, *h*) put back (*a. watch*); put aside; MIL defer; **~strahlen** *v/t* (*sep*, *-ge-*, *h*) reflect; **~treten** *v/i* (*irr*, ***treten***, *sep*, *-ge-*, *sein*) step *or* stand back; resign (***von e-m Amt*** [***Posten***] one's office [post]); ECON, JUR withdraw (***von*** from); **~weichen** *v/i* (*irr*, ***weichen***, *sep*, *-ge-*, *sein*) fall back (*a.* MIL); **~weisen** *v/t* (*irr*, ***weisen***, *sep*, *-ge-*, *h*) turn down; JUR dismiss; **~zahlen** *v/t* (*sep*, *-ge-*, *h*) pay back (*a. fig*); **~ziehen** *v/t* (*irr*, ***ziehen***, *sep*, *-ge-*, *h*) draw back; *fig* withdraw; ***sich ~*** retire, withdraw, MIL *a.* retreat
'**Zuruf** *m* shout; '**zurufen** *v/t* (*irr*, ***rufen***,

*sep, -ge-, h)* ***j-m et. ~*** shout s.th. to s.o.
**zur'zeit** *adv* at the moment, at present
**'Zusage** *f* promise; assent
**'zusagen** *v/i and v/t (sep, -ge-, h)* accept (an invitation); *(dat)* suit, appeal to; ***s-e Hilfe ~*** promise to help
**zusammen** [tsu'zamən] *adv* together; ***alles ~*** (all) in all; ***das macht ~ ...*** that makes ... altogether
**Zu'sammenarbeit** *f (-; no pl)* cooperation; ***in ~ mit*** in collaboration with; **zu'sammenarbeiten** *v/i (sep, -ge-, h)* cooperate, collaborate
**zu'sammenbeißen** *v/t (irr,* ***beißen****, sep, -ge-, h)* ***die Zähne ~*** clench one's teeth
**zu'sammenbrechen** *v/i (irr,* ***brechen****, sep, -ge-, sein)* break down, collapse *(both a. fig)*; **Zu'sammenbruch** *m* breakdown, collapse
**zu'sammen|fallen** *v/i (irr,* ***fallen****, sep, -ge-, sein)* coincide; **~falten** *v/t (sep, -ge-, h)* fold up
**zu'sammenfassen** *v/t (sep, -ge-, h)* summarize, sum up; **Zu'sammenfassung** *f (-; -en)* summary
**zu'sammen|fügen** *v/t (sep, -ge-, h)* join (together); **~gesetzt** *adj* compound; **~halten** *v/i and v/t (irr,* ***halten****, sep, -ge-, h)* hold together *(a. fig)*; F stick together
**Zu'sammenhang** *m (-[e]s; -hänge)* connection; context; ***im ~ stehen (mit)*** be connected (with)
**zu'sammenhängen** *v/i (irr,* ***hängen****, sep, -ge-, h)* be connected; **~d** *adj* coherent
**zu'sammenhang(s)los** *adj* incoherent, disconnected
**zu'sammen|klappen** *v/i (sep, -ge-, sein) and v/t (h)* TECH fold up; F break down; **~kommen** *v/i (irr,* ***kommen****, sep, -ge-, sein)* meet
**Zu'sammenkunft** [tsu'zamənkʊnft] *f (-; -künfte* [tsu'zamənkʏnftə]) meeting
**zu'sammen|legen** *(sep, -ge-, h)* **1.** *v/t* combine; fold up **2.** *v/i* club together; **~nehmen** *v/t (irr,* ***nehmen****, sep, -ge-, h)* muster (up); ***sich ~*** pull o.s. together; **~packen** *v/t (sep, -ge-, h)* pack up; **~passen** *v/i (sep, -ge-, h)* harmonize; match; **~rechnen** *v/t (sep, -ge-, h)* add up; **~reißen** F *v/refl (irr,* ***reißen****, sep, -ge-, h)* pull o.s. together; **~rollen** *v/t (sep, -ge-, h)* roll up; ***sich ~*** coil up; **~rotten** [tsu'zamənrɔtən] *v/refl (sep, -ge-, h)* band together; **~rücken** *(sep, -ge-)* **1.** *v/t (h)* move closer together **2.** *v/i (sein)* move up; **~schlagen** *v/t (irr,* ***schlagen****, sep, -ge-, h)* clap *(hands)*; click *(one's heels)*; beat *s.o.* up; smash (up)
**zu'sammenschließen** *v/refl (irr,* ***schließen****, sep, -ge-, h)* join, unite; **Zu'sammenschluss** *m* union
**zu'sammen|schreiben** *v/t (irr,* ***schreiben****, sep, -ge-, h)* write in one word; **~schrumpfen** *v/i (sep, -ge-, sein)* shrink
**zu'sammensetzen** *v/t (sep, -ge-, h)* put together; TECH assemble; ***sich ~ aus*** *(dat)* consist of, be composed of; **Zu'sammensetzung** *f (-; -en)* composition; CHEM, LING compound; TECH assembly
**zu'sammenstellen** *v/t (sep, -ge-, h)* put together; arrange
**Zu'sammenstoß** *m* collision *(a. fig)*, crash; impact; *fig* clash; **zu'sammenstoßen** *v/i (irr,* ***stoßen****, sep, -ge-, sein)* collide *(a. fig)*; *fig* clash; ***~ mit*** run *or* bump into; *fig* have a clash with
**zu'sammentreffen** *v/i (irr,* ***treffen****, sep, -ge-, sein)* meet, encounter; coincide (***mit*** with); **Zu'sammentreffen** *n (-s; -)* meeting; coincidence; encounter
**zu'sammen|treten** *v/i (irr,* ***treten****, sep, -ge-, sein)* meet; **~tun** *v/refl (irr,* ***tun****, sep, -ge-, h)* join (forces), F team up; **~wirken** *v/i (sep, -ge-, h)* combine; **~zählen** *v/t (sep, -ge-, h)* add up; **~ziehen** *(irr,* ***ziehen****, sep, -ge-)* **1.** *v/t and v/refl (h)* contract **2.** *v/i (sein)* move in (***mit*** with); **~zucken** *v/i (sep, -ge-, sein)* wince, flinch
**'Zusatz** *m* addition; *chemical etc* additive; **~...** *in cpds mst* additional ..., supplementary ...; auxiliary ...; **zusätzlich** ['tsu:zɛtslɪç] *adj* additional, extra
**'zuschauen** *v/i (sep, -ge-, h)* look on (***bei et.*** at s.th.); ***j-m ~*** watch s.o. (***bei et.*** doing s.th.)
**Zuschauer** ['tsu:ʃauɐ] *m (-s; -)*, **'Zuschauerin** *f (-; -nen)* spectator; TV viewer, *pl a. the* audience
**'Zuschauerraum** *m* auditorium
**'Zuschlag** *m* extra charge; RAIL *etc* excess fare; bonus; *auction*: knocking down; **'zuschlagen** *v/i (irr,* ***schlagen****,*

Z

*sep*, *-ge-*, *sein) and v/t* (*h*) *door etc*: slam *or* bang shut; *boxing etc*: hit, strike (a blow); *fig* act; ***j-m et.*** ~ *auction*: knock s.th. down to s.o.

'**zu|schließen** *v/t* (*irr*, ***schließen***, *sep*, *-ge-*, *h*) lock (up); **~schnallen** *v/t* (*sep*, *-ge-*, *h*) buckle (up); **~schnappen** *v/i* (*sep*, *-ge-*) (*h*) *dog*: snap; (*sein*) *door etc*: snap shut; **~schneiden** *v/t* (*irr*, ***schneiden***, *sep*, *-ge-*, *h*) cut out; cut (to size); **~schnüren** *v/t* (*sep*, *-ge-*, *h*) tie (*or* lace) up; **~schrauben** *v/t* (*sep*, *-ge-*, *h*) screw shut; **~schreiben** *v/t* (*irr*, ***schreiben***, *sep*, *-ge-*, *h*) ascribe *or* attribute (*dat* to)

'**Zuschrift** *f* letter

**zuschulden** [tsu'ʃʊldən] *adv*: ***sich et.*** (***nichts***) ~ ***kommen lassen*** do s.th. (nothing) wrong

'**Zuschuss** *m* allowance; subsidy

'**zuschütten** *v/t* (*sep*, *-ge-*, *h*) fill up

'**zusehen** → ***zuschauen***

**zusehends** ['tsu:se:ənts] *adv* noticeably; rapidly

'**zusetzen** (*sep*, *-ge-*, *h*) **1.** *v/t* add; lose (*money*) **2.** *v/i* lose money; ***j-m*** ~ press s.o. (hard)

'**zuspielen** *v/t* (*sep*, *-ge-*, *h*) SPORT pass

'**zuspitzen** *v/t* (*sep*, *-ge-*, *h*) point; ***sich*** ~ become critical

'**Zuspruch** *m* (*-[e]s*; *no pl*) encouragement; words of comfort

'**Zustand** *m* condition, state, F shape

**zustande** [tsu'ʃtandə] *adv*: ~ ***bringen*** bring about, manage (to do); ~ ***kommen*** come about; ***es kam nicht*** ~ it didn't come off

'**zuständig** *adj* responsible (***für*** for), in charge (of)

'**zustehen** *v/i* (*irr*, ***stehen***, *sep*, *-ge-*, *h*) ***j-m steht et.*** (***zu tun***) ***zu*** s.o. is entitled to (do) s.th.

'**zustellen** *v/t* (*sep*, *-ge-*, *h*) *post*: deliver; '**Zustellung** *f post*: delivery

'**zustimmen** *v/i* (*sep*, *-ge-*, *h*) agree (*dat* to *s.th.*; with *s.o.*); '**Zustimmung** *f* approval, consent; (***j-s***) ~ ***finden*** meet with (s.o.'s) approval

'**zustoßen** *v/i* (*irr*, ***stoßen***, *sep*, *-ge-*, *sein*) ***j-m*** ~ happen to s.o.

**zutage** [tsu'ta:gə] *adv*: ~ ***bringen*** (***kommen***) bring (come) to light

'**Zutaten** *pl* ingredients

'**zuteilen** *v/t* (*sep*, *-ge-*, *h*) assign, allot; '**Zuteilung** *f* (*-*; *-en*) allotment; ration

'**zutragen** *v/refl* (*irr*, ***tragen***, *sep*, *-ge-*, *h*) happen

'**zutrauen** *v/t* (*sep*, *-ge-*, *h*) ***j-m et.*** ~ credit s.o. with s.th.; ***sich zu viel*** ~ overrate o.s.

**zutraulich** ['tsu:traulɪç] *adj* trusting; zo friendly

'**zutreffen** *v/i* (*irr*, ***treffen***, *sep*, *-ge-*, *h*) be true; ~ ***auf*** (*acc*) apply to, go for; **~d** *adj* true, correct

'**zutrinken** *v/i* (*irr*, ***trinken***, *sep*, *-ge-*, *h*) ***j-m*** ~ drink to s.o.

'**Zutritt** *m* (*-[e]s*; *no pl*) admission; access; ~ ***verboten!*** no admittance!

**zu'ungunsten** *adv* to *s.o.'s* disadvantage

**zuverlässig** ['tsu:fɛɐlɛsɪç] *adj* reliable, dependable; safe; '**Zuverlässigkeit** *f* (*-*; *no pl*) reliability, dependability

**Zuversicht** ['tsu:fɛɐzɪçt] *f* (*-*; *no pl*) confidence; '**zuversichtlich** *adj* confident, optimistic

**zuviel** → ***zu***

**zu'vor** [tsu'fo:ɐ] *adv* before, previously; first

**zu'vorkommen** *v/i* (*irr*, ***kommen***, *sep*, *-ge-*, *sein*) anticipate; prevent; ***j-m*** ~ *a.* F beat s.o. to it; **~d** *adj* obliging; polite

**Zuwachs** ['tsu:vaks] *m* (*-es*; *no pl*) increase, growth; '**zuwachsen** *v/i* (*irr*, ***wachsen***, *sep*, *-ge-*, *sein*) become overgrown; MED close

**zu'weilen** [tsu'vailən] *adv* occasionally, now and then

'**zuweisen** *v/t* (*irr*, ***weisen***, *sep*, *-ge-*, *h*) assign

'**zuwenden** *v/t and v/refl* ([*irr*, ***wenden***,] *sep*, *-ge-*, *h*) turn to (*a. fig*)

'**Zuwendung** *f* (*-*; *-en*) payment; (*no pl*) attention; (loving) care, love, affection

**zuwenig** → ***zu***

'**zuwerfen** *v/t* (*irr*, ***werfen***, *sep*, *-ge-*, *h*) slam (shut); ***j-m et.*** ~ throw s.o. s.th.; ***j-m e-n Blick*** ~ cast a glance at s.o.

**zu'wider** [tsu'vi:dɐ] *adj*: ***… ist mir*** ~ I hate *or* detest …; **~handeln** *v/i* (*sep*, *-ge-*, *h*) (*dat*) act contrary to; violate

'**zu|winken** *v/i* (*sep*, *-ge-*, *h*) wave to; signal to; **~zahlen** *v/t* (*sep*, *-ge-*, *h*) pay extra; **~ziehen** (*irr*, ***ziehen***, *sep*, *-ge-*) **1.** *v/t* (*h*) draw (*curtains etc*); pull tight; *fig*

consult; ***sich ~*** MED catch **2.** *v/i* (*sein*) move in
**zuzüglich** ['tsu:tsy:klıç] *prp* (*gen*) plus
**Zvieri** ['tsfi:ri] *Swiss m, n* (*-s; -s*) afternoon snack, tea *or* coffee break
**zwang** [tsvaŋ] *pret of* ***zwingen***
**Zwang** *m* (*-*[*e*]*s; Zwänge* ['tsvɛŋə]) compulsion, constraint; restraint; coercion; force; ***~ sein*** be compulsory; **zwängen** ['tsvɛŋən] *v/t* (*ge-, h*) press, squeeze, force; '**zwanglos** *adj* informal; casual; '**Zwanglosigkeit** *f* (*-; no pl*) informality
'**Zwangs|arbeit** *f* JUR hard labo(u)r; **~herrschaft** *f* (*-; no pl*) despotism, tyranny; **~lage** *f* predicament
'**zwangsläufig** *adv* inevitably
'**Zwangs|maßnahme** *f* sanction; **~vollstreckung** *f* JUR compulsory execution; **~vorstellung** *f* PSYCH obsession
'**zwangsweise** *adv* by force
**zwanzig** ['tsvantsıç] *adj* twenty
'**zwanzigste** *adj* twentieth
**zwar** [tsva:ɐ] *adv*: ***ich kenne ihn ~, aber ...*** I do know him, but ..., I know him all right, but ...; ***und ~*** that is (to say), namely
**Zweck** [tsvɛk] *m* (*-*[*e*]*s; -e*) purpose, aim; ***s-n ~ erfüllen*** serve its purpose; ***es hat keinen ~*** (***zu warten*** *etc*) it's no use (waiting *etc*); '**zwecklos** *adj* useless
'**zweckmäßig** *adj* practical; wise; TECH, ARCH functional; '**Zweckmäßigkeit** *f* (*-; no pl*) practicality, functionality
**zwecks** *prp* (*gen*) for the purpose of
**zwei** [tsvai] *adj* two
**zweibeinig** ['tsvaibainıç] *adj* two-legged
'**Zweibettzimmer** *n* twin-bedded room
**zweideutig** ['tsvaidɔʏtıç] *adj* ambiguous; off-colo(u)r
**Zweier** ['tsvaiɐ] *m* (*-s; -*) *rowing*: pair
**zweierlei** ['tsvaiɐ'lai] *adj* two kinds of
'**zweifach** *adj* double, twofold
**Zweifa'milienhaus** *n* duplex, *Br* two-family house
**Zweifel** ['tsvaifəl] *m* (*-s; -*) doubt
'**zweifelhaft** *adj* doubtful, dubious
'**zweifellos** *adv* undoubtedly, no *or* without doubt
'**zweifeln** *v/i* (*ge-, h*) ***~ an*** (*dat*) doubt *s.th.*, have one's doubts about
**Zweig** [tsvaik] *m* (*-*[*e*]*s; -e*) BOT branch (*a. fig*); twig; **~geschäft** *n*, **~niederlassung** *f*, **~stelle** *f* branch
'**zweijährig** ['tsvaijɛ:rıç] *adj* two-year-old, of two (years)
'**Zweikampf** *m* duel
'**zweimal** *adv* twice
'**zweimalig** *adj* (twice) repeated
'**zwei|motorig** ['tsvaimoto:rıç] *adj* twin-engined; **~reihig** ['tsvairaiıç] *adj* double-breasted (*suit*); **~schneidig** *adj* double-edged, two-edged (*both a. fig*); **~seitig** ['tsvaizaitıç] *adj* two-sided; reversible; POL bilateral; IT double-sided
'**Zweisitzer** ['tsvaizıtsɐ] *m* (*-s; -*) *esp* MOT two-seater
'**zwei|sprachig** ['tsvaiʃpra:xıç] *adj* bilingual; **~stimmig** ['tsvaiʃtımıç] *adj* MUS ... for two voices; **~stöckig** ['tsvaiʃtœkıç] *adj* two-storied, *Br* two-storey ...
**zweit** [tsvait] *adj* second; ***ein ~er ...*** another ...; ***jede(r, -s) ~e ...*** every other ...; ***aus ~er Hand*** second-hand; ***wir sind zu ~*** there are two of us
'**zweitbeste** *adj* second-best
'**zweiteilig** *adj* two-piece (*suit etc*)
**zweitens** ['tsvaitəns] *adv* secondly
'**zweitklassig** ['tsvaitklasıç] adj, '**zweitrangig** ['tsvaitraŋıç] *adj* second-class *or* -rate
**Zwerchfell** ['tsvɛrçfɛl] *n* ANAT diaphragm
**Zwerg** [tsvɛrk] *m* (*-*[*e*]*s; -e* ['tsvɛrgə]) dwarf; gnome; *fig* midget; **~...** *in cpds* BOT dwarf ...; ZO pygmy ...
**Zwetsch(g)e** ['tsvɛtʃ(g)ə] *f* (*-; -n*) BOT plum
**zwicken** ['tsvikən] *v/t and v/i* (*ge-, h*) pinch, nip
**Zwieback** ['tsvi:bak] *m* (*-*[*e*]*s; -e, -bäcke* ['tsvi:bɛkə]) rusk, zwieback
**Zwiebel** ['tsvi:bəl] *f* (*-; -n*) GASTR onion; BOT bulb
**Zwiegespräch** ['tsvi:gəʃprɛ:ç] *n* dialog(ue)
'**Zwielicht** *n* (*-*[*e*]*s; no pl*) twilight
'**Zwiespalt** *m* (*-*[*e*]*s; -e*) conflict
'**zwiespältig** ['tsvi:ʃpɛltıç] *adj* conflicting
'**Zwietracht** *f* (*-; no pl*) discord
**Zwilling** ['tsvılıŋ] *m* (*-s; -e*) twin; *pl* ASTR Gemini; ***er ist*** (***ein***) ***~*** he's (a) Gemini
'**Zwillings|bruder** *m* twin brother;

**~schwester** *f* twin sister
**Zwinge** ['tsvɪŋə] *f* (-; -*n*) TECH clamp
**zwingen** ['tsvɪŋən] *v/t* (*irr, ge-, h*) force, compel; **~d** *adj* compelling; cogent
**Zwinger** ['tsvɪŋɐ] *m* (-*s*; -) kennels
**zwinkern** ['tsvɪŋkɐn] *v/i* (*ge-, h*) wink, blink
**Zwirn** [tsvɪrn] *m* (-[*e*]*s*; -*e*) thread, yarn, twist
**zwischen** ['tsvɪʃən] *prp* (*dat and acc*) between; among
'**zwischen'durch** F *adv* in between
'**Zwischen|ergebnis** *n* intermediate result; **~fall** *m* incident; **~händler** *m* ECON middleman; **~landung** *f* AVIAT stopover; ***ohne ~*** nonstop
'**Zwischen|raum** *m* space, interval; **~ruf** *m* (loud) interruption; *pl* heckling; **~rufer** *m* (-*s*; -) heckler; **~spiel** *n* interlude; **~stati,on** *f* stop(over); ***~ machen*** (***in*** *dat*) stop over (in); **~wand** *f* partition (wall); **~zeit** *f*: ***in der ~*** in the meantime, meanwhile
**Zwist** [tsvɪst] *m* (-[*e*]*s*; -*e*) discord
**zwitschern** ['tsvɪtʃɐn] *v/i* (*ge-, h*) twitter, chirp
**Zwitter** ['tsvɪtɐ] *m* (-*s*; -) BIOL hermaphrodite
**zwölf** [tsvœlf] *adj* twelve; ***um ~*** (***Uhr***) at twelve (o'clock); at noon; at midnight
'**zwölfte** *adj* twelfth
**Zyankali** [tsyaːn'kaːli] *n* (-*s*; *no pl*) CHEM potassium cyanide
**Zyklus** ['tsyːklʊs] *m* (-; -*klen*) cycle; series, course
**Zylinder** [tsi'lɪndɐ] *m* (-*s*; -) top hat; MATH, TECH cylinder; **zylindrisch** [tsi'lɪndrɪʃ] *adj* cylindrical
**Zyniker** ['tsyːnikɐ] *m* (-*s*; -) cynic
**zynisch** ['tsyːnɪʃ] *adj* cynical
**Zynismus** [tsy'nɪsmʊs] *m* (-; -*men*) cynicism
**Zypresse** [tsy'prɛsə] *f* (-; -*n*) BOT cypress
**Zyste** ['tsʏstə] *f* (-; -*n*) MED cyst
**z.Z(t).** *abbr of* ***zur Zeit*** at the moment, at present

# ENGLISH – GERMAN

# A

**A**, a A, a *n*; ***from A to Z*** von A bis Z

**A** *grade* Eins

**a**, *before vowel*: **an** *indef art* ein(e); per, pro, je; ***not a(n)*** kein(e); ***all of a size*** alle gleich groß; ***100 dollars a year*** 100 Dollar im Jahr; ***twice a week*** zweimal die *or* in der Woche

**a·back**: ***taken ~*** überrascht, verblüfft; bestürzt

**a·ban·don** aufgeben, preisgeben; verlassen; überlassen

**a·base** erniedrigen, demütigen

**a·base·ment** Erniedrigung *f*, Demütigung *f*

**a·bashed** verlegen

**ab·at·toir** *Br* Schlachthof *m*

**ab·bess** REL Äbtissin *f*

**ab·bey** REL Kloster *n*; Abtei *f*

**ab·bot** REL Abt *m*

**ab·bre·vi·ate** (ab)kürzen

**ab·bre·vi·a·tion** Abkürzung *f*, Kurzform *f*

**ABC** Abc *n*, Alphabet *n*

**ab·di·cate** *Amt*, *Recht etc* aufgeben, verzichten auf (*acc*); ***~ (from) the throne*** abdanken

**ab·di·ca·tion** Verzicht *m*; Abdankung *f*

**ab·do·men** ANAT Unterleib *m*

**ab·dom·i·nal** ANAT Unterleibs…

**ab·duct** JUR *j-n* entführen

**ab·er·ra·tion** Verirrung *f*

**a·bet** → ***aid*** *1*

**ab·hor** verabscheuen

**ab·hor·rence** Abscheu *m* (***of*** vor *dat*)

**ab·hor·rent** zuwider (***to*** *dat*); abstoßend

**a·bide** *v/i*: ***~ by the law*** *etc* sich an das Gesetz *etc* halten; *v/t*: ***he can't ~ him*** er kann ihn nicht ausstehen

**a·bil·i·ty** Fähigkeit *f*

**ab·jure** abschwören; entsagen (*dat*)

**a·blaze** in Flammen; *fig* glänzend, funkelnd (***with*** vor *dat*)

**a·ble** fähig; geschickt; ***be ~ to*** *inf* in der Lage sein zu *inf*, können

**a·ble-bod·ied** kräftig

**ab·norm·al** abnorm, ungewöhnlich; anomal

**a·board** an Bord; ***all ~!*** MAR alle Mann *or* Reisenden an Bord!; RAIL alles einsteigen!; ***~ a bus*** in e-m Bus; ***go ~ a train*** in e-n Zug einsteigen

**a·bode** *a.* ***place of ~*** Aufenthaltsort *m*, Wohnsitz *m*; ***of*** *or* ***with no fixed ~*** ohne festen Wohnsitz

**a·bol·ish** abschaffen, aufheben

**ab·o·li·tion** Abschaffung *f*, Aufhebung *f*

**A-bomb** → ***atom(ic) bomb***

**a·bom·i·na·ble** abscheulich, scheußlich; **a·bom·i·nate** verabscheuen; **a·bom·i·na·tion** Abscheu *m*

**ab·o·rig·i·nal** **1.** eingeboren, Ur… **2.** Ureinwohner *m*

**ab·o·rig·i·ne** Ureinwohner *m*

**a·bort** *v/t* abbrechen (*a.* MED *Schwangerschaft*); MED *Kind* abtreiben; *v/i* fehlschlagen, scheitern; MED e-e Fehlgeburt haben; **a·bor·tion** MED Fehlgeburt *f*; Schwangerschaftsabbruch *m*, Abtreibung *f*; ***have an ~*** abtreiben (lassen)

**a·bor·tive** misslungen, erfolglos

**a·bound** reichlich vorhanden sein; Überfluss haben, reich sein (***in*** an *dat*); voll sein (***with*** von)

**a·bout** **1.** *prp* um (… herum); bei (*dat*); (irgendwo) herum in (*dat*); um, gegen, etwa; im Begriff, dabei; über (*acc*) **2.** *adv* herum, umher; in der Nähe; etwa, ungefähr

**a·bove** **1.** *prp* über (*dat or acc*), oberhalb (*gen*); *fig* über, erhaben über (*acc*); ***~ all*** vor allem **2.** *adv* oben; darüber **3.** *adj* obig, oben erwähnt

**a·breast** nebeneinander; ***keep ~ of, be ~ of*** *fig* Schritt halten mit

**a·bridge** (ab-, ver)kürzen

**a·bridg(e)·ment** Kürzung *f*; Kurzfassung *f*

**a·broad** im *or* ins Ausland; überall(hin)

**a·brupt** abrupt; jäh; schroff

**ab·scess** MED Abszess *m*

**ab·sence** Abwesenheit *f*; Mangel *m*

**ab·sent** **1.** abwesend; fehlend; nicht vorhanden; ***be ~*** fehlen (***from school*** in der Schule; ***from work*** am Arbeitsplatz); **2.** ***~ o.s. from*** fernbleiben (*dat*) *or* von; **ab·sent-mind·ed** zerstreut, geistesabwesend

**ab·so·lute** absolut; unumschränkt; vollkommen; unbedingt; CHEM rein, unver-

mischt
**ab·so·lu·tion** REL Absolution *f*
**ab·solve** freisprechen, lossprechen
**ab·sorb** absorbieren, aufsaugen, einsaugen; *fig* ganz in Anspruch nehmen
**ab·sorb·ing** *fig* fesselnd, packend
**ab·stain** sich enthalten (***from*** *gen*)
**ab·ste·mi·ous** enthaltsam; mäßig
**ab·sten·tion** Enthaltung *f*; POL Stimmenthaltung *f*
**ab·sti·nence** Abstinenz *f*, Enthaltsamkeit *f*
**ab·sti·nent** abstinent, enthaltsam
**ab·stract** **1.** abstrakt **2.** *das* Abstrakte; Auszug *m* **3.** abstrahieren; entwenden
**ab·stract·ed** *fig* zerstreut
**ab·strac·tion** Abstraktion *f*; abstrakter Begriff
**ab·surd** absurd; lächerlich
**a·bun·dance** Überfluss *m*; Fülle *f*; Überschwang *m*
**a·bun·dant** reich, reichlich
**a·buse** **1.** Missbrauch *m*; Beschimpfung(en *pl*) *f*; ***~ of drugs*** Drogenmissbrauch *m*; ***~ of power*** Machtmissbrauch *m* **2.** missbrauchen; beschimpfen; **a·bu·sive** beleidigend, Schimpf…
**a·but** (an)grenzen (***on*** an *acc*)
**a·byss** Abgrund *m* (*a. fig*)
**ac·a·dem·ic** **1.** Hochschullehrer *m* **2.** akademisch; **a·cad·e·mi·cian** Akademiemitglied *n*; **a·cad·e·my** Akademie *f*; ***~ of music*** Musikhochschule *f*
**ac·cede**: ***~ to*** zustimmen (*dat*); *Amt* antreten; *Thron* besteigen
**ac·cel·e·rate** *v/t* beschleunigen; *v/i* schneller werden, MOT *a.* beschleunigen, Gas geben
**ac·cel·e·ra·tion** Beschleunigung *f*
**ac·cel·e·ra·tor** MOT Gaspedal *n*
**ac·cent** **1.** Akzent *m* (*a.* LING); **2.** → **ac·cen·tu·ate** akzentuieren, betonen
**ac·cept** annehmen; akzeptieren; hinnehmen; **ac·cept·a·ble** annehmbar; *person*: tragbar; **ac·cept·ance** Annahme *f*; Aufnahme *f*
**ac·cess** Zugang *m* (***to*** zu); *fig* Zutritt *m* (***to*** bei, zu); IT Zugriff *m* (***to*** auf *acc*)
**ac·ces·sa·ry** → ***accessory***
**ac·cess code** IT Zugriffskode *m*
**ac·ces·si·ble** (leicht) zugänglich
**ac·ces·sion** (Neu)Anschaffung *f* (***to*** für); Zustimmung *f* (***to*** zu); Antritt *m* (*e-s Amtes*); ***~ to power*** Machtübernahme *f*; ***~ to the throne*** Thronbesteigung *f*
**ac·ces·so·ry** JUR Komplize *m*, Komplizin *f*, Mitschuldige *m, f*; *mst pl* Zubehör *n*, *fashion*: *a.* Accessoires *pl*, TECH *a.* Zubehörteile *pl*
**ac·cess| road** Zufahrts- *or* Zubringerstraße *f*; **~ time** IT Zugriffszeit *f*
**ac·ci·dent** Unfall *m*, Unglück *n*, Unglücksfall *m*; NUCL Störfall *m*; ***by ~*** zufällig
**ac·ci·den·tal** zufällig; versehentlich
**ac·claim** feiern (***as*** als)
**ac·cla·ma·tion** lauter Beifall; Lob *n*
**ac·cli·ma·tize** (sich) akklimatisieren *or* eingewöhnen
**ac·com·mo·date** unterbringen; Platz haben für, fassen; anpassen (***to*** *dat or* an *acc*)
**ac·com·mo·da·tion** Unterkunft *f*, Unterbringung *f*; **~ of·fice** Zimmervermittlung *f*
**ac·com·pa·ni·ment** MUS Begleitung *f*
**ac·com·pa·ny** begleiten (*a.* MUS)
**ac·com·plice** JUR Komplize *m*, Komplizin *f*, Helfershelfer(in)
**ac·com·plish** erreichen; leisten
**ac·com·plished** fähig, tüchtig
**ac·com·plish·ment** Fähigkeit *f*, Talent *n*
**ac·cord** **1.** Übereinstimmung *f*; ***of one's own ~*** von selbst; ***with one ~*** einstimmig **2.** übereinstimmen (***with*** mit)
**ac·cord·ance**: ***in ~ with*** entsprechend (*dat*)
**ac·cord·ing**: ***~ to*** laut; nach
**ac·cord·ing·ly** folglich, also; (dem)entsprechend
**ac·cost** *j-n* ansprechen
**ac·count** **1.** ECON Rechnung *f*, Berechnung *f*; Konto *n*; Rechenschaft *f*; Bericht *m*; ***by all ~s*** nach allem, was man so hört; ***of no ~*** ohne Bedeutung; ***on no ~*** auf keinen Fall; ***on ~ of*** wegen; ***take into ~, take ~ of*** in Betracht *or* Erwägung ziehen, berücksichtigen; ***turn s.th. to (good) ~*** et. (gut) ausnutzen; ***keep ~s*** die Bücher führen; ***call to ~*** zur Rechenschaft ziehen; ***give (an) ~ of*** Rechenschaft ablegen über (*acc*); ***give an ~ of*** Bericht erstatten über (*acc*) **2.** *v/i*: ***~ for*** Rechenschaft über *et.* ablegen; (sich) erklären
**ac·count·a·ble** verantwortlich; erklärlich

**ac·coun·tant** ECON Buchhalter(in)
**ac·count·ing** ECON Buchführung *f*
**acct** *abbr of* ***account*** Konto *n*
**ac·cu·mu·late** (sich) (an)häufen *or* ansammeln
**ac·cu·mu·la·tion** Ansammlung *f*
**ac·cu·mu·la·tor** ELECTR Akkumulator *m*
**ac·cu·ra·cy** Genauigkeit *f*
**ac·cu·rate** genau
**ac·cu·sa·tion** Anklage *f*; Anschuldigung *f*, Beschuldigung *f*
**ac·cu·sa·tive** *a.* ***~ case*** LING Akkusativ *m*
**ac·cuse** JUR anklagen; beschuldigen (***of*** *gen*); ***the ~d*** der *or* die Angeklagte, die Angeklagten *pl*
**ac·cus·er** JUR Ankläger(in)
**ac·cus·ing** anklagend, vorwurfsvoll
**ac·cus·tom** gewöhnen (***to*** an *acc*)
**ac·cus·tomed** gewohnt, üblich; gewöhnt (***to*** an *acc*, zu *inf*)
**ace** Ass *n* (*a. fig*); ***have an ~ in the hole*** (*Br* ***up one's sleeve***) *fig* (noch) e-n Trumpf in der Hand haben; ***within an ~*** um ein Haar
**ache 1.** schmerzen, wehtun **2.** *anhaltender* Schmerz
**a·chieve** zustande bringen; *Ziel* erreichen; **a·chieve·ment** Zustandebringen *n*, Leistung *f*, Ausführung *f*
**ac·id 1.** sauer; *fig* beißend, bissig **2.** CHEM Säure *f*; **a·cid·i·ty** Säure *f*
**ac·id rain** saurer Regen
**ac·knowl·edge** anerkennen; zugeben; *Empfang* bestätigen
**ac·knowl·edg(e)·ment** Anerkennung *f*; (Empfangs)Bestätigung *f*; Eingeständnis *n*
**a·corn** BOT Eichel *f*
**a·cous·tics** Akustik *f*
**ac·quaint** bekannt machen; ***~ s.o. with s.th.*** j-m et. mitteilen; ***be ~ed with*** kennen; **ac·quaint·ance** Bekanntschaft *f*; Bekannte *m*, *f*
**ac·quire** erwerben; sich aneignen
**ac·qui·si·tion** Erwerb *m*; Anschaffung *f*, Errungenschaft *f*
**ac·quit** JUR freisprechen (***of*** von); ***~ o.s. well*** s-e Sache gut machen
**ac·quit·tal** JUR Freispruch *m*
**a·cre** Acre *m* (*4047 qm*)
**ac·rid** scharf, beißend
**ac·ro·bat** Akrobat(in)
**ac·ro·bat·ic** akrobatisch
**a·cross 1.** *adv* hinüber, herüber; (quer) durch; drüben, auf der anderen Seite; über Kreuz **2.** *prp* (quer) über (*acc*); (quer) durch; auf der anderen Seite von (*or gen*), jenseits (*gen*); über (*dat*); ***come ~, run ~*** *fig* stoßen auf (*acc*)
**act 1.** *v/i* handeln; sich verhalten *or* benehmen; (ein)wirken; funktionieren; (Theater) spielen; *v/t* THEA spielen (*a. fig*), *Stück* aufführen; ***~ as*** fungieren als **2.** Handlung *f*, Tat *f*; JUR Gesetz *n*; THEA Akt *m*; **act·ing** THEA Spiel(en) *n*
**ac·tion** Handlung *f* (*a.* THEA), Tat *f*; *film etc*: Action *f*; Funktionieren *n*; (Ein-) Wirkung *f*; JUR Klage *f*, Prozess *m*; MIL Gefecht *n*, Einsatz *m*; ***take ~*** handeln
**ac·tiv·ate** *v/t* aktivieren; **ac·tive** aktiv; tätig, rührig; lebhaft (*a.* ECON), rege; wirksam
**ac·tiv·ist** *esp* POL Aktivist(in)
**ac·tiv·i·ty** Tätigkeit *f*; Aktivität *f*; Betriebsamkeit *f*; *esp* ECON Lebhaftigkeit *f*; **~ va·ca·tion** Aktivurlaub *m*
**ac·tor** Schauspieler *m*
**ac·tress** Schauspielerin *f*
**ac·tu·al** wirklich, tatsächlich, eigentlich
**ac·u·men** Scharfsinn *m*
**ac·u·punc·ture** MED Akupunktur *f*
**a·cute** akut (*shortage*, *pain etc*); brennend (*problem etc*); scharf (*hearing etc*); scharfsinnig; MATH spitz (*angle*)
**ad** F → ***advertisement***
**ad·a·mant** unerbittlich
**a·dapt** anpassen (***to*** *dat or* an *acc*); *Text* bearbeiten (***from*** nach); TECH umstellen (***to*** auf *acc*); umbauen (***to*** für)
**a·dapt·a·ble** anpassungsfähig
**ad·ap·ta·tion** Anpassung *f*; Bearbeitung *f*
**a·dapt·er, a·dapt·or** ELECTR Adapter *m*
**add** *v/t* hinzufügen; ***~ up*** zusammenzählen, addieren; *v/i*: ***~ to*** vermehren, beitragen zu, hinzukommen zu; ***~ up*** MATH ergeben; F sich summieren; *fig* e-n Sinn ergeben; ***~ up to*** *fig* hinauslaufen auf (*acc*)
**ad·der** ZO Natter *f*
**ad·dict** Süchtige *m*, *f*; ***alcohol*** (***drug***) ***~*** Alkoholsüchtige (Drogen- *or* Rauschgiftsüchtige); (*Fußball- etc*) Fanatiker(in), (*Film- etc*)Narr *m*
**ad·dic·ted** süchtig, abhängig (***to*** von); ***be***

~ ***to alcohol*** (***drugs***) alkoholsüchtig (drogenabhängig *or* -süchtig) sein
**ad·dic·tion** Sucht *f*, Süchtigkeit *f*
**ad·di·tion** Hinzufügen *n*; Zusatz *m*; Zuwachs *m*; ARCH Anbau *m*; MATH Addition *f*; ***in*** ~ außerdem; ***in*** ~ ***to*** außer (*dat*)
**ad·di·tion·al** zusätzlich
**ad·dress** **1.** *Worte* richten (***to*** an *acc*), *j-n* anreden *or* ansprechen **2.** Adresse *f*, Anschrift *f*; Rede *f*, Ansprache *f*
**ad·dress·ee** Empfänger(in)
**ad·ept** erfahren, geschickt (***at, in*** in *dat*)
**ad·e·qua·cy** Angemessenheit *f*
**ad·e·quate** angemessen
**ad·here** (***to***) kleben, haften (an *dat*); *fig* festhalten (an *dat*); **ad·her·ence** Anhaften *n*; *fig* Festhalten *n*; **ad·her·ent** Anhänger(in)
**ad·he·sive** **1.** klebend **2.** Klebstoff *m*; ~ **plas·ter** MED Heftpflaster *n*; ~ **tape** Klebeband *n*, Klebstreifen *m*; MED Heftpflaster *n*
**ad·ja·cent** angrenzend, anstoßend (***to*** an *acc*); benachbart
**ad·jec·tive** LING Adjektiv *n*, Eigenschaftswort *n*
**ad·join** (an)grenzen an (*acc*)
**ad·journ** *v/t* verschieben, (*v/i* sich) vertagen; **ad·journ·ment** Vertagung *f*, Verschiebung *f*
**ad·just** anpassen; TECH einstellen, regulieren; **ad·just·a·ble** TECH verstellbar, regulierbar; **ad·just·ment** Anpassung *f*; TECH Einstellung *f*
**ad-lib** aus dem Stegreif (sprechen *or* spielen)
**ad·min·is·ter** verwalten; PHARM geben, verabreichen; ~ ***justice*** Recht sprechen
**ad·min·is·tra·tion** Verwaltung *f*; POL Regierung *f*; Amtsperiode *f*
**ad·min·is·tra·tive** Verwaltungs...
**ad·min·is·tra·tor** Verwaltungsbeamte *m*
**ad·mi·ra·ble** bewundernswert; großartig
**ad·mi·ral** MAR Admiral *m*
**ad·mi·ra·tion** Bewunderung *f*
**ad·mire** bewundern; verehren
**ad·mir·er** Verehrer *m*
**ad·mis·si·ble** zulässig
**ad·mis·sion** Eintritt *m*, Zutritt *m*; Aufnahme *f*; Eintrittsgeld *n*; Eingeständnis *n*; ~ ***free*** Eintritt frei
**ad·mit** *v/t* zugeben; (her)einlassen (***to, into*** in *acc*), eintreten lassen; zulassen (***to*** zu); **ad·mit·tance** Einlass *m*, Eintritt *m*, Zutritt *m*; ***no*** ~ Zutritt verboten
**ad·mon·ish** ermahnen; warnen (***of, against*** vor *dat*)
**a·do** Getue *n*, Lärm *m*; ***without more or further*** ~ ohne weitere Umstände
**ad·o·les·cence** Jugend *f*, Adoleszenz *f*
**ad·o·les·cent** **1.** jugendlich, heranwachsend **2.** Jugendliche *m, f*
**a·dopt** adoptieren; übernehmen; ~***ed child*** Adoptivkind *n*
**a·dop·tion** Adoption *f*
**a·dop·tive par·ents** Adoptiveltern *pl*
**a·dor·a·ble** F bezaubernd, entzückend
**ad·o·ra·tion** Anbetung *f*, Verehrung *f*
**a·dore** anbeten, verehren
**a·dorn** schmücken, zieren
**a·dorn·ment** Schmuck *m*, Verzierung *f*
**a·droit** geschickt
**ad·ult** **1.** erwachsen **2.** Erwachsene *m, f*; ~***s only*** nur für Erwachsene!; ~ **ed·uca·tion** Erwachsenenbildung *f*
**a·dul·ter·ate** verfälschen, *Wein* panschen
**a·dul·ter·er** Ehebrecher *m*
**a·dul·ter·ess** Ehebrecherin *f*
**a·dul·ter·ous** ehebrecherisch
**a·dul·ter·y** Ehebruch *m*
**ad·vance** **1.** *v/i* vordringen, vorrücken (*a. time*); Fortschritte machen; *v/t* vorrücken; *Termin etc* vorverlegen; *Argument etc* vorbringen; *Geld* vorstrecken, F vorschießen; (be)fördern; *Preis* erhöhen; *Wachstum etc* beschleunigen **2.** Vorrücken *n*, Vorstoß *m* (*a. fig*); Fortschritt *m*; ECON Vorschuss *m*; Erhöhung *f*; ***in*** ~ im Voraus
**ad·vanced** fortgeschritten; ~ ***for one's years*** weit *or* reif für sein Alter
**ad·vance·ment** Fortschritt *m*, Verbesserung *f*
**ad·van·tage** Vorteil *m* (*a.* SPORT); ~ ***rule*** SPORT Vorteilsregel *f*; ***take*** ~ ***of*** ausnutzen
**ad·van·ta·geous** vorteilhaft
**ad·ven·ture** Abenteuer *n*, Wagnis *n*
**ad·ven·tur·er** Abenteurer *m*
**ad·ven·tur·ess** Abenteu(r)erin *f*
**ad·ven·tur·ous** abenteuerlich; verwegen, kühn
**ad·verb** LING Adverb *n*, Umstandswort *n*
**ad·ver·sa·ry** Gegner(in)
**ad·ver·tise** ankündigen, bekannt ma-

chen; inserieren; Reklame machen (für)
**ad·ver·tise·ment** Anzeige *f*, Inserat *n*
**ad·ver·tis·ing** **1.** Reklame *f*, Werbung *f* **2.** Reklame…, Werbe…; *~* **a·gen·cy** Werbeagentur *f*; *~* **cam·paign** Werbefeldzug *m*
**ad·vice** Rat(schlag) *m*; ECON Benachrichtigung *f*; ***take medical ~*** e-n Arzt zu Rate ziehen; ***take my ~*** hör auf mich
**ad·vice| cen·ter**, *Br* *~* **cen·tre** Beratungsstelle *f*
**ad·vis·ab·le** ratsam
**ad·vise** *v/t j-n* beraten; *j-m* raten; *esp* ECON benachrichtigen, avisieren; *v/i* sich beraten
**ad·vis·er** *esp Br*, **ad·vis·or** Berater *m*
**ad·vi·so·ry** beratend
**ad·vo·cate** **1.** befürworten, verfechten **2.** Befürworter(in), Verfechter(in)
**aer·i·al** **1.** luftig; Luft… **2.** Antenne *f*
**aer·i·al| pho·to·graph**, *~* **view** Luftaufnahme *f*, Luftbild *n*
**aer·o…** Aero…, Luft…
**aer·o·bics** SPORT Aerobic *n*
**aer·o·drome** *esp Br* Flugplatz *m*
**aer·o·dy·nam·ic** aerodynamisch
**aer·o·dy·nam·ics** Aerodynamik *f*
**aer·o·nau·tics** Luftfahrt *f*
**aer·o·plane** *Br* Flugzeug *n*
**aer·o·sol** Spraydose *f*, Sprühdose *f*
**aes·thet·ic** *etc* → ***esthetic*** *etc*
**a·far**: ***from ~*** von weit her
**af·fair** Angelegenheit *f*, Sache *f*; F Ding *n*, Sache *f*; Affäre *f*
**af·fect** beeinflussen; MED angreifen, befallen; bewegen, rühren; e-e Vorliebe haben für; vortäuschen
**af·fec·tion** Liebe *f*, Zuneigung *f*
**af·fec·tion·ate** liebevoll, herzlich
**af·fil·i·ate** *als Mitglied* aufnehmen; angliedern
**af·fin·i·ty** Affinität *f*; (geistige) Verwandtschaft; Neigung *f* (***for, to*** zu)
**af·firm** versichern; beteuern; bestätigen;
**af·fir·ma·tion** Versicherung *f*; Beteuerung *f*; Bestätigung *f*
**af·fir·ma·tive** **1.** bejahend **2.** ***answer in the ~*** bejahen
**af·fix** (***to***) anheften, ankleben (an *acc*), befestigen (an *dat*); beifügen, hinzufügen (*dat*)
**af·flict** heimsuchen, plagen; ***~ed with*** geplagt von, leidend an (*dat*)
**af·flic·tion** Gebrechen *n*; Elend *n*, Not *f*
**af·flu·ence** Überfluss *m*; Wohlstand *m*
**af·flu·ent** reich, reichlich; *~* **so·ci·e·ty** Wohlstandsgesellschaft *f*
**af·ford** sich leisten; gewähren, bieten; ***I can ~ it*** ich kann es mir leisten
**af·front** **1.** beleidigen **2.** Beleidigung *f*
**a·float** MAR flott, schwimmend; ***set ~*** MAR flottmachen; *fig Gerücht etc* in Umlauf setzen
**a·fraid**: ***be ~ of*** sich fürchten *or* Angst haben vor (*dat*); ***I'm ~ she won't come*** ich fürchte, sie wird nicht kommen; ***I'm ~ I must go now*** leider muss ich jetzt gehen
**a·fresh** von neuem
**Af·ri·ca** Afrika *n*; **Af·ri·can** **1.** afrikanisch **2.** Afrikaner(in)
**af·ter** **1.** *adv* hinterher, nachher, danach **2.** *prp* nach; hinter (*dat*) (… her); ***~ all*** schließlich (doch) **3.** *cj* nachdem **4.** *adj* später; Nach…; *~* **ef·fect** MED Nachwirkung *f* (*a. fig*)
**af·ter·glow** Abendrot *n*
**af·ter·math** Nachwirkungen *pl*, Folgen *pl*
**af·ter·noon** Nachmittag *m*; ***this ~*** heute Nachmittag; ***good ~!*** guten Tag!
**af·ter·taste** Nachgeschmack *m*
**af·ter·thought** nachträglicher Einfall
**af·ter·ward**, *Br* **af·ter·wards** nachher, später
**a·gain** wieder; wiederum; ferner; ***~ and ~, time and ~*** immer wieder; ***as much ~*** noch einmal so viel
**a·gainst** gegen; an (*dat or acc*); ***as ~*** verglichen mit; ***he was ~ it*** er war dagegen
**age** **1.** (Lebens)Alter *n*; Zeit(alter *n*) *f*; Menschenalter *n*; (***old***) *~* (hohes) Alter; ***at the ~ of*** im Alter von; *s.o.* ***your ~*** in deinem *or* Ihrem Alter; (***come***) ***of ~*** mündig *or* volljährig (werden); ***be over ~*** die Altersgrenze überschritten haben; ***under ~*** minderjährig; unmündig; ***wait for ~s*** F e-e Ewigkeit warten **2.** alt werden *or* machen
**a·ged**[1] alt, betagt
**aged**[2]: ***~ twenty*** 20 Jahre alt
**age·less** zeitlos; ewig jung
**a·gen·cy** Agentur *f*; Geschäftsstelle *f*, Büro *n*
**a·gen·da** Tagesordnung *f*
**a·gent** Agent *m* (*a.* POL), Vertreter *m*; (*Grundstücks- etc*)Makler *m*; CHEM

Wirkstoff *m*, Mittel *n*
**ag·glom·er·ate** (sich) zusammenballen; (sich) (an)häufen
**ag·gra·vate** erschweren, verschlimmern; F ärgern
**ag·gre·gate 1.** sich belaufen auf (*acc*) **2.** gesamt **3.** Gesamtmenge *f*, Summe *f*; TECH Aggregat *n*
**ag·gres·sion** Angriff *m*
**ag·gres·sive** aggressiv, Angriffs…; *fig* energisch
**ag·gres·sor** Angreifer *m*
**ag·grieved** verletzt, gekränkt
**a·ghast** entgeistert, entsetzt
**ag·ile** flink, behend
**a·gil·i·ty** Flinkheit *f*, Behendigkeit *f*
**ag·i·tate** *v/t fig* aufregen, aufwühlen; *Flüssigkeit* schütteln; *v/i* POL agitieren, hetzen (***against*** gegen)
**ag·i·ta·tion** Aufregung *f*; POL Agitation *f*
**ag·i·ta·tor** POL Agitator *m*
**a·go**: ***a year ~*** vor e-m Jahr
**ag·o·ny** Qual *f*; Todeskampf *m*
**a·gree** *v/i* übereinstimmen; sich vertragen; einig werden, sich einigen (***on*** über *acc*); übereinkommen; ***~ to*** zustimmen (*dat*), einverstanden sein mit
**a·gree·a·ble** (***to***) angenehm (für); übereinstimmend (mit)
**a·gree·ment** Übereinstimmung *f*; Vereinbarung *f*; Abkommen *n*
**ag·ri·cul·tur·al** landwirtschaftlich
**ag·ri·cul·ture** Landwirtschaft *f*
**a·ground** MAR gestrandet; ***run ~*** stranden, auf Grund laufen
**a·head** vorwärts, voraus; vorn; ***go ~!*** nur zu!, mach nur!; ***straight ~*** geradeaus
**aid 1.** unterstützen, *j-m* helfen (***in*** bei); fördern; ***he was accused of ~ing and abetting*** JUR er wurde wegen Beihilfe angeklagt **2.** Hilfe *f*, Unterstützung *f*
**AIDS, Aids** MED Aids *n*
**ail** kränklich sein; **ail·ment** Leiden *n*
**aim 1.** *v/i* zielen (***at*** auf *acc*, nach); ***~ at*** *fig* beabsichtigen; ***be ~ing to do s.th.*** vorhaben, et. zu tun; *v/t*: ***~ at*** *Waffe etc* richten auf *or* gegen (*acc*) **2.** Ziel *n* (*a. fig*); Absicht *f*; ***take ~ at*** zielen auf (*acc*) *or* nach; **aim·less** ziellos
**air**[1] **1.** Luft *f*; Luftzug *m*; Miene *f*, Aussehen *n*; ***by ~*** auf dem Luftwege; ***in the open ~*** im Freien; ***on the ~*** im Rundfunk *or* Fernsehen; ***be on the ~*** senden; in Betrieb sein; ***go off the ~*** die Sendung beenden (*person*); sein Programm beenden (*station*); ***give o.s. ~s, put on ~s*** vornehm tun **2.** (aus)lüften; *fig* an die Öffentlichkeit bringen; erörtern
**air**[2] MUS Arie *f*, Weise *f*, Melodie *f*
**air·bag** MOT Airbag *m*
**air·base** MIL Luftstützpunkt *m*
**air·bed** Luftmatratze *f*
**air·borne** AVIAT in der Luft; MIL Luftlande…
**air·brake** TECH Druckluftbremse *f*
**air·bus** AVIAT Airbus *m*, Großraumflugzeug *n*
**air-con·di·tioned** mit Klimaanlage
**air-con·di·tion·ing** Klimaanlage *f*
**air·craft car·ri·er** MAR, MIL Flugzeugträger *m*
**air·field** Flugplatz *m*
**air force** MIL Luftwaffe *f*
**air host·ess** AVIAT Stewardess *f*
**air jack·et** Schwimmweste *f*
**air·lift** AVIAT Luftbrücke *f*
**air·line** AVIAT Fluggesellschaft *f*
**air·lin·er** AVIAT Verkehrsflugzeug *n*
**air·mail** Luftpost *f*; ***by ~*** mit Luftpost
**air·man** MIL Flieger *m*
**air·plane** Flugzeug *n*
**air·pock·et** AVIAT Luftloch *n*
**air pol·lu·tion** Luftverschmutzung *f*
**air·port** Flughafen *m*
**air raid** MIL Luftangriff *m*
**air-raid| pre·cau·tions** MIL Luftschutz *m*; **~ shel·ter** MIL Luftschutzraum *m*
**air route** AVIAT Flugroute *f*
**air·sick** luftkrank
**air·space** Luftraum *m*
**air·strip** (behelfsmäßige) Start- und Landebahn
**air ter·mi·nal** Flughafenabfertigungsgebäude *n*
**air·tight** luftdicht
**air time** Sendezeit *f*
**air traf·fic** AVIAT Flugverkehr *m*
**air-traf·fic| con·trol** AVIAT Flugsicherung *f*; **~ con·trol·ler** AVIAT Fluglotse *m*
**air·way** AVIAT Fluggesellschaft *f*
**air·wor·thy** AVIAT flugtüchtig
**air·y** luftig
**aisle** ARCH Seitenschiff *n*; Gang *m*
**a·jar** halb offen, angelehnt
**a·kin** verwandt (***to*** mit)
**a·lac·ri·ty** Bereitwilligkeit *f*

**a·larm** 1. Alarm(zeichen *n*) *m*; Wecker *m*; Angst *f* 2. alarmieren; beunruhigen; **~ clock** Wecker *m*
**al·bum** Album *n* (*a. record*)
**al·bu·mi·nous** BIOL eiweißhaltig
**al·co·hol** Alkohol *m*; **al·co·hol·ic** 1. alkoholisch 2. Alkoholiker(in)
**al·co·hol·ism** Alkoholismus *m*, Trunksucht *f*
**a·lert** 1. wachsam; munter 2. Alarm *m*; Alarmbereitschaft *f*; ***on the ~*** auf der Hut; in Alarmbereitschaft 3. warnen (***to*** vor *dat*), alarmieren
**al·ga** BOT Alge *f*
**al·ge·bra** MATH Algebra *f*
**al·i·bi** JUR Alibi *n*
**a·li·en** 1. ausländisch; fremd 2. Ausländer(in); Außerirdische *m*, *f*
**a·li·en·ate** veräußern; entfremden; *esp art*: verfremden; **a·li·en·a·tion** Entfremdung *f*; *esp art*: Verfremdung *f*
**a·light** 1. in Flammen 2. aussteigen; absteigen, absitzen; zo sich niederlassen; AVIAT landen
**a·lign** (sich) ausrichten (***with*** nach)
**a·like** 1. *adj* gleich 2. *adv* gleich, ebenso
**al·i·mo·ny** JUR Unterhalt *m*
**a·live** lebendig; (noch) am Leben; lebhaft; ***~ and kicking*** gesund und munter; ***be ~ with*** wimmeln von
**all** 1. *adj* all; ganz; jede(r, -s) 2. *pron* alles; alle *pl* 3. *adv* ganz, völlig; ***~ at once*** auf einmal; ***~ the better*** desto besser; ***~ but*** beinahe, fast; ***~ in*** F fertig, ganz erledigt; ***~ right*** in Ordnung; ***for ~ that*** dessen ungeachtet, trotzdem; ***for ~ I know*** soviel ich weiß; ***at ~*** überhaupt; ***not at ~*** überhaupt nicht; ***the score was two ~*** das Spiel stand zwei zu zwei
**all-A·mer·i·can** typisch amerikanisch; die ganzen USA vertretend
**al·lay** beruhigen; lindern
**al·le·ga·tion** *unerwiesene* Behauptung
**al·lege** behaupten
**al·leged** angeblich, vermeintlich
**al·le·giance** Treue *f*
**al·ler·gic** MED allergisch (***to*** gegen)
**al·ler·gy** MED Allergie *f*
**al·le·vi·ate** mildern, lindern
**al·ley** (enge *or* schmale) Gasse; Garten-, Parkweg *m*; *bowling*: Bahn *f*
**al·li·ance** Bündnis *n*
**al·li·ga·tor** zo Alligator *m*
**al·lo·cate** zuteilen, anweisen
**al·lo·ca·tion** Zuteilung *f*
**al·lot** zuteilen, an-, zuweisen
**al·lot·ment** Zuteilung *f*; Parzelle *f*
**al·low** erlauben, bewilligen, gewähren; zugeben; ab-, anrechnen, vergüten; ***~ for*** einplanen, berücksichtigen (*acc*)
**al·low·a·ble** erlaubt, zulässig
**al·low·ance** Erlaubnis *f*; Bewilligung *f*; Taschengeld *n*, Zuschuss *m*; Vergütung *f*; *fig* Nachsicht *f*; ***make ~(s) for s.th.*** et. berücksichtigen
**al·loy** TECH 1. Legierung *f* 2. legieren
**all-round** vielseitig
**all·round·er** Alleskönner *m*; Allroundsportler *m*, -spieler *m*
**al·lude** anspielen (***to*** auf *acc*)
**al·lure** locken, an-, verlocken
**al·lure·ment** Verlockung *f*
**al·lu·sion** Anspielung *f*
**all-wheel drive** MOT Allradantrieb *m*
**al·ly** 1. (sich) vereinigen, verbünden (***to, with*** mit); 2. Verbündete *m*, *f*, Bundesgenosse *m*, Bundesgenossin *f*; ***the Allies*** MIL die Alliierten *pl*
**al·might·y** allmächtig; ***the Almighty*** REL der Allmächtige
**al·mond** BOT Mandel *f*
**al·most** fast, beinah(e)
**alms** Almosen *n*
**a·loft** (hoch) (dr)oben
**a·lone** allein; ***let ~, leave ~*** in Ruhe lassen, bleiben lassen; ***let ~ …*** geschweige denn …
**a·long** 1. *adv* weiter, vorwärts; da; dahin; ***all ~*** die ganze Zeit; ***~ with*** (zusammen) mit; ***come ~*** mitkommen, mitgehen; ***get ~*** vorwärtskommen, weiterkommen; auskommen, sich vertragen (***with s.o.*** mit j-m); ***take ~*** mitnehmen 2. *prp* entlang (*dat*), längs (*gen*)
**a·long·side** Seite an Seite; neben
**a·loof** abseits; reserviert, zurückhaltend, verschlossen; **a·loof·ness** Reserviertheit *f*; Verschlossenheit *f*
**a·loud** laut
**al·pha·bet** Alphabet *n*
**al·pine** (Hoch)Gebirgs…, alpin
**al·read·y** bereits, schon
**al·right** → ***all right***
**Al·sa·tian** *esp Br* zo Deutscher Schäferhund
**al·so** auch, ferner
**al·tar** REL Altar *m*
**al·ter** ändern, sich (ver)ändern; ab-, um-

ändern; **al·ter·a·tion** Änderung *f* (***to*** an *dat*), Veränderung *f*

**al·ter·nate 1.** abwechseln (lassen) **2.** abwechselnd; **al·ter·nat·ing cur·rent** ELECTR Wechselstrom *m*

**al·ter·na·tion** Abwechslung *f*; Wechsel *m*

**al·ter·na·tive 1.** alternativ, wahlweise **2.** Alternative *f*, Wahl *f*, Möglichkeit *f*

**al·though** obwohl, obgleich

**al·ti·tude** Höhe *f*; ***at an ~ of*** in e-r Höhe von

**al·to·geth·er** im Ganzen, insgesamt; ganz (und gar), völlig

**al·u·min·i·um** *Br*, **a·lu·mi·num** Aluminium *n*

**al·ways** immer, stets

**am, AM** *abbr of* ***before noon*** (*Latin* ***ante meridiem***) morgens, vorm., vormittags

**a·mal·gam·ate** (sich) zusammenschließen, ECON *a.* fusionieren

**a·mass** anhäufen, aufhäufen

**am·a·teur** Amateur(in); Dilettant(in); Hobby…

**a·maze** in Erstaunen setzen, verblüffen; **a·maze·ment** Staunen *n*, Verblüffung *f*; **a·maz·ing** erstaunlich

**am·bas·sa·dor** POL Botschafter *m* (***to*** in *e-m Land*); **am·bas·sa·dress** POL Botschafterin *f* (***to*** in *e-m Land*)

**am·ber** Bernstein *m*

**am·bi·gu·i·ty** Zwei-, Mehrdeutigkeit *f*

**am·big·u·ous** zwei-, mehr-, vieldeutig

**am·bi·tion** Ehrgeiz *m*

**am·bi·tious** ehrgeizig, strebsam

**am·ble 1.** Passgang *m* **2.** im Passgang gehen *or* reiten; schlendern

**am·bu·lance** Krankenwagen *m*

**a·men** *int* REL amen

**a·mend** verbessern, berichtigen; PARL abändern, ergänzen; **a·mend·ment** Bess(e)rung *f*; Verbesserung *f*; PARL Abänderungsantrag *m*, Ergänzungsantrag *m*; Zusatzartikel *m* zur Verfassung; **a·mends** (Schaden)Ersatz *m*; ***make ~*** Schadenersatz leisten, es wieder gutmachen; ***make ~ to s.o. for s.th.*** j-n für et. entschädigen

**a·men·i·ty** *often pl* Annehmlichkeiten *pl*

**A·mer·i·ca** Amerika *n*; **A·mer·i·can 1.** amerikanisch **2.** Amerikaner(in)

**A·mer·i·can·is·m** LING Amerikanismus *m*

**A·mer·i·can·ize** (sich) amerikanisieren

**A·mer·i·can plan** Vollpension *f*

**a·mi·a·ble** liebenswürdig, freundlich

**am·i·ca·ble** freundschaftlich, *a.* JUR gütlich

**a·mid(st)** inmitten (*gen*), (mitten) in *or* unter

**a·miss** verkehrt, falsch, übel; ***take s.th. ~*** et. übel nehmen, et. verübeln

**am·mo·ni·a** CHEM Ammoniak *n*

**am·mu·ni·tion** Munition *f*

**am·nes·ty** JUR **1.** Amnestie *f* **2.** begnadigen

**a·mok**: ***run ~*** Amok laufen

**a·mong(st)** (mitten) unter, zwischen

**am·o·rous** verliebt

**a·mount 1.** (***to***) sich belaufen (auf *acc*); hinauslaufen (auf *acc*); **2.** Betrag *m*, (Gesamt)Summe *f*; Menge *f*

**am·per·age** ELECTR Stromstärke *f*

**am·ple** weit, groß, geräumig; reich, reichlich, beträchtlich

**am·pli·fi·ca·tion** Erweiterung *f*; PHYS Verstärkung *f*

**am·pli·fi·er** ELECTR Verstärker *m*

**am·pli·fy** erweitern; ELECTR verstärken

**am·pli·tude** Umfang *m*, Weite *f*, Fülle *f*; ELECTR, PHYS Amplitude *f*

**am·pu·tate** MED amputieren

**a·muck** → ***amok***

**a·muse** (***o.s.*** sich) amüsieren, unterhalten, belustigen

**a·muse·ment** Unterhaltung *f*, Vergnügen *n*, Zeitvertreib *m*; **~ park** Vergnügungspark *m*, Freizeitpark *m*

**a·mus·ing** amüsant, unterhaltend

**an** → ***a***

**an·a·bol·ic ster·oid** PHARM Anabolikum *n*

**a·nae·mi·a** *Br* → ***anemia***

**an·aes·thet·ic** *Br* → ***anesthetic***

**a·nal** ANAT anal, Anal…

**a·nal·o·gous** analog, entsprechend

**a·nal·o·gy** Analogie *f*, Entsprechung *f*

**an·a·lyse** *esp Br*, **an·a·lyze** analysieren; zerlegen

**a·nal·y·sis** Analyse *f*

**an·arch·y** Anarchie *f*, Gesetzlosigkeit *f*; Chaos *n*

**a·nat·o·mize** MED zerlegen; zergliedern; **a·nat·o·my** MED Anatomie *f*; Zergliederung *f*, Analyse *f*

**an·ces·tor** Vorfahr *m*, Ahn *m*

**an·ces·tress** Vorfahrin *f*, Ahnfrau *f*

**an·chor** MAR **1.** Anker *m*; ***at ~*** vor Anker

**2.** verankern
**an·chor·man** TV Moderator *m*
**an·chor·wom·an** TV Moderatorin *f*
**an·cho·vy** ZO Anschovis *f*, Sardelle *f*
**an·cient** **1.** alt, antik; uralt **2.** ***the ~s*** HIST die Alten, die antiken Klassiker
**and** und
**an·ec·dote** Anekdote *f*
**a·ne·mi·a** MED Blutarmut *f*, Anämie *f*
**an·es·thet·ic** MED **1.** betäubend, Narkose… **2.** Betäubungsmittel *n*
**an·gel** Engel *m*
**an·ger** **1.** Zorn *m*, Ärger *m* (***at*** über *acc*); **2.** erzürnen, (ver)ärgern
**an·gle**[1] Winkel *m* (*a.* MATH)
**an·gle**[2] angeln (***for*** nach)
**an·gler** Angler(in)
**An·gli·can** REL **1.** anglikanisch **2.** Anglikaner(in)
**An·glo-Sax·on** **1.** angelsächsisch **2.** Angelsachse *m*
**an·gry** zornig, verärgert, böse (***at, with*** über *acc*, mit *dat*)
**an·guish** Qual *f*, Schmerz *m*
**an·gu·lar** winkelig; knochig
**an·i·mal** **1.** Tier *n* **2.** tierisch; ~ **lov·er** Tierfreund *m*; ~ **shel·ter** Tierheim *n*
**an·i·mate** beleben; aufmuntern, anregen
**an·i·mat·ed** lebendig; lebhaft, angeregt; ~ **car·toon** Zeichentrickfilm *m*
**an·i·ma·tion** Lebhaftigkeit *f*; Animation *f*; Herstellung *f* von Zeichentrickfilmen; IT bewegtes Bild
**an·i·mos·i·ty** Animosität *f*, Feindseligkeit *f*
**an·kle** ANAT (Fuß)Knöchel *m*
**an·nals** Jahrbücher *pl*
**an·nex** **1.** anhängen; annektieren **2.** Anhang *m*; ARCH Anbau *m*
**an·ni·ver·sa·ry** Jahrestag *m*; Jahresfeier *f*
**an·no·tate** mit Anmerkungen versehen; kommentieren
**an·nounce** ankündigen; bekannt geben; *radio*, TV ansagen; durchsagen; **an·nounce·ment** Ankündigung *f*; Bekanntgabe *f*; *radio*, TV Ansage *f*; Durchsage *f*; **an·nounc·er** *radio*, TV Ansager(in), Sprecher(in)
**an·noy** ärgern; belästigen
**an·noy·ance** Störung *f*, Belästigung *f*; Ärgernis *n*
**an·noy·ing** ärgerlich, lästig
**an·nu·al** **1.** jährlich, Jahres… **2.** einjährige Pflanze; Jahrbuch *n*
**an·nu·i·ty** (Jahres)Rente *f*
**an·nul** für ungültig erklären, annullieren; **an·nul·ment** Annullierung *f*, Aufhebung *f*
**an·o·dyne** MED **1.** schmerzstillend **2.** schmerzstillendes Mittel
**a·noint** REL salben
**a·nom·a·lous** anomal
**a·non·y·mous** anonym
**an·o·rak** Anorak *m*
**an·oth·er** ein anderer; ein Zweiter; noch eine(r, -s)
**an·swer** **1.** *v/t et.* beantworten; *j-m* antworten; entsprechen (*dat*); *Zweck* erfüllen; TECH *dem Steuer* gehorchen; JUR *e-r Vorladung* Folge leisten; *e-r Beschreibung* entsprechen; ~ ***the bell*** *or* ***door*** (die Tür) aufmachen; ~ ***the telephone*** ans Telefon gehen; *v/i* antworten (***to*** auf *acc*); entsprechen (***to*** *dat*); ~ ***for*** einstehen für **2.** Antwort *f* (***to*** auf *acc*)
**an·swer·a·ble** verantwortlich
**an·swer·ing ma·chine** TEL Anrufbeantworter *m*
**ant** ZO Ameise *f*
**an·tag·o·nism** Feindschaft *f*
**an·tag·o·nist** Gegner(in)
**an·tag·o·nize** bekämpfen; sich *j-n* zum Feind machen
**Ant·arc·tic** antarktisch
**an·te·ced·ent** vorhergehend, früher (***to*** als)
**an·te·lope** ZO Antilope *f*
**an·ten·na**[1] ZO Fühler *m*
**an·ten·na**[2] ELECTR Antenne *f*
**an·te·ri·or** vorhergehend, früher (***to*** als); vorder
**an·them** MUS Hymne *f*
**an·ti…** Gegen…, gegen … eingestellt, Anti…, anti…
**an·ti·air·craft** MIL Fliegerabwehr…, Flugabwehr…
**an·ti·bi·ot·ic** MED Antibiotikum *n*
**an·ti·bod·y** BIOL Antikörper *m*, Abwehrstoff *m*
**an·tic·i·pate** voraussehen, ahnen; erwarten; zuvorkommen; vorwegnehmen; **an·tic·i·pa·tion** (Vor)Ahnung *f*; Erwartung *f*; Vorwegnahme *f*; Vorfreude *f*; ***in*** ~ im Voraus
**an·ti·clock·wise** *Br* entgegen dem Uhr-

zeigersinn
**an·tics** Mätzchen *pl*
**an·ti·dote** Gegengift *n*, Gegenmittel *n*
**an·ti-for·eign·er vi·o·lence** Gewalt *f* gegen Ausländer
**an·ti·freeze** Frostschutzmittel *n*
**an·ti-lock brak·ing sys·tem** MOT Antiblockiersystem *n* (*abbr* **ABS**)
**an·ti·mis·sile** MIL Raketenabwehr…
**an·ti·nu·cle·ar ac·tiv·ist** Kernkraftgegner(in)
**an·tip·a·thy** Abneigung *f*
**an·ti·quat·ed** veraltet
**an·tique 1.** antik, alt **2.** Antiquität *f*
**an·tique| deal·er** Antiquitätenhändler(in); **~ shop** *esp Br*, **~ store** Antiquitätenladen *m*
**an·tiq·ui·ty** Altertum *n*, Vorzeit *f*
**an·ti·sep·tic** MED **1.** antiseptisch **2.** antiseptisches Mittel
**ant·lers** ZO Geweih *n*
**a·nus** ANAT After *m*
**an·vil** Amboss *m*
**anx·i·e·ty** Angst *f*, Sorge *f*
**anx·ious** besorgt, beunruhigt (***about*** wegen); begierig, gespannt (***for*** auf *acc*); bestrebt (***to do*** zu tun)
**an·y 1.** *adj and pron* (irgend)eine(r, -s), (irgend)welche(r, -s); (irgend)etwas; jede(r, -s) (beliebige); einige *pl*, welche *pl*; ***not ~*** keiner **2.** *adv* irgend(wie), ein wenig, (noch) etwas
**an·y·bod·y** (irgend)jemand; jeder
**an·y·how** irgendwie; trotzdem, jedenfalls; wie dem auch sei
**an·y·one** → ***anybody***
**an·y·thing** (irgend)etwas; alles; ***~ but*** alles andere als; ***~ else?*** sonst noch etwas?; ***not ~*** nichts
**an·y·way** → ***anyhow***
**an·y·where** irgendwo(hin); überall
**a·part** einzeln, für sich; beiseite; ***~ from*** abgesehen von
**a·part·heid** POL Apartheid *f*, Politik *f* der Rassentrennung
**a·part·ment** Wohnung *f*; **~ build·ing, ~ house** Mietshaus *n*
**ap·a·thet·ic** apathisch, teilnahmslos, gleichgültig; **ap·a·thy** Apathie *f*, Teilnahmslosigkeit *f*
**ape** ZO (Menschen)Affe *m*
**ap·er·ture** Öffnung *f*
**a·pi·a·ry** Bienenhaus *n*
**a·piece** für jedes Stück, pro Stück, je
**a·pol·o·gize** sich entschuldigen (***for*** für; ***to*** bei); **a·pol·o·gy** Entschuldigung *f*; Rechtfertigung *f*; ***make an ~ (for s.th.)*** sich (für et.) entschuldigen
**ap·o·plex·y** MED Schlaganfall *m*, F Schlag *m*
**a·pos·tle** REL Apostel *m*
**a·pos·tro·phe** LING Apostroph *m*
**ap·pal(l)** erschrecken, entsetzen
**ap·pal·ling** erschreckend, entsetzlich
**ap·pa·ra·tus** Apparat *m*, Vorrichtung *f*, Gerät *n*
**ap·par·ent** offenbar; anscheinend; scheinbar
**ap·pa·ri·tion** Erscheinung *f*, Gespenst *n*
**ap·peal 1.** JUR Berufung *or* Revision einlegen, Einspruch erheben, Beschwerde einlegen; appellieren, sich wenden (***to*** an *acc*); **~ *to*** gefallen (*dat*), zusagen (*dat*), wirken auf (*acc*); *j-n* dringend bitten (***for*** um); **2.** JUR Revision *f*, Berufung *f*; Beschwerde *f*; Einspruch *m*; Appell *m* (***to*** an *acc*), Aufruf *m*; Wirkung *f*, Reiz *m*; Bitte *f* (***to*** an *acc*; ***for*** um); ***~ for mercy*** JUR Gnadengesuch *n*
**ap·peal·ing** flehend; ansprechend
**ap·pear** (er)scheinen; sich zeigen; *öffentlich* auftreten; sich ergeben *or* herausstellen; **ap·pear·ance** Erscheinen *n*; Auftreten *n*; Äußere *n*, Erscheinung *f*, Aussehen *n*; Anschein *m*, äußerer Schein; ***keep up ~s*** den Schein wahren; ***to*** *or* ***by all ~s*** allem Anschein nach
**ap·pease** besänftigen, beschwichtigen; *Durst etc* stillen; *Neugier* befriedigen
**ap·pend** an-, hinzu-, beifügen
**ap·pend·age** Anhang *m*; Anhängsel *n*
**ap·pen·di·ci·tis** MED Blinddarmentzündung *f*
**ap·pen·dix** Anhang *m*; *a.* ***vermiform ~*** ANAT Wurmfortsatz *m*, Blinddarm *m*
**ap·pe·tite** (***for***) Appetit *m* (auf *acc*); *fig* Verlangen *n* (nach)
**ap·pe·tiz·er** Appetithappen *m*, appetitanregendes Gericht *or* Getränk
**ap·pe·tiz·ing** appetitanregend
**ap·plaud** applaudieren, Beifall spenden; loben
**ap·plause** Applaus *m*, Beifall *m*
**ap·ple** BOT Apfel *m*
**ap·ple pie** (*warmer*) gedeckter Apfelkuchen
**ap·ple sauce** Apfelmus *n*; *sl* Schmus *m*,

Quatsch *m*
**ap·pli·ance** Vorrichtung *f*; Gerät *n*; Mittel *n*
**ap·plic·a·ble** anwendbar (***to*** auf *acc*)
**ap·pli·cant** Antragsteller(in), Bewerber(in) (***for*** um)
**ap·pli·ca·tion** Anwendung *f* (***to*** auf *acc*); Bedeutung *f* (***to*** für); Gesuch *n* (***for*** um); Bewerbung *f* (***for*** um)
**ap·ply** *v/t* (***to***) (auf)legen, auftragen (auf *acc*); anwenden (auf *acc*); verwenden (für); **~ *o.s. to*** sich widmen (*dat*); *v/i* (***to***) passen, zutreffen, sich anwenden lassen (auf *acc*); gelten (für); sich wenden (an *acc*); **~ *for*** sich bewerben um, *et.* beantragen
**ap·point** bestimmen, festsetzen; verabreden; ernennen (***s.o.*** *governor* j-n zum …); berufen (***to*** auf *e-n Posten*)
**ap·point·ment** Bestimmung *f*; Verabredung *f*; Termin *m*; Ernennung *f*, Berufung *f*; Stelle *f*; **~ book** Terminkalender *m*
**ap·por·tion** verteilen, zuteilen
**ap·prais·al** (Ab)Schätzung *f*
**ap·praise** (ab)schätzen, taxieren
**ap·pre·cia·ble** nennenswert, spürbar
**ap·pre·ci·ate** *v/t* schätzen, würdigen; dankbar sein für; *v/i* im Wert steigen
**ap·pre·ci·a·tion** Würdigung *f*; Dankbarkeit *f*; (richtige) Beurteilung; ECON Wertsteigerung *f*
**ap·pre·hend** ergreifen, fassen; begreifen; befürchten; **ap·pre·hen·sion** Ergreifung *f*, Festnahme *f*; Besorgnis *f*; **ap·pre·hen·sive** ängstlich, besorgt (***for*** um; ***that*** dass)
**ap·pren·tice 1.** Auszubildende *m, f*, Lehrling *m*, *Swiss* Lehrtochter *f* **2.** in die Lehre geben; **ap·pren·tice·ship** Lehrzeit *f*, Lehre *f*, Ausbildung *f*
**ap·proach 1.** *v/i* näher kommen, sich nähern; *v/t* sich nähern (*dat*); herangehen *or* herantreten an (*acc*) **2.** (Heran)Nahen *n*; Einfahrt *f*, Zufahrt *f*, Auffahrt *f*; Annäherung *f*; Methode *f*
**ap·pro·ba·tion** Billigung *f*, Beifall *m*
**ap·pro·pri·ate 1.** sich aneignen; verwenden; PARL bewilligen **2.** (***for, to***) angemessen (*dat*), passend (für, zu)
**ap·prov·al** Billigung *f*; Anerkennung *f*, Beifall *m*; **ap·prove** billigen, anerkennen; **ap·proved** bewährt
**ap·prox·i·mate** annähernd, ungefähr
**a·pri·cot** BOT Aprikose *f*
**A·pril** (*abbr* ***Apr***) April *m*
**a·pron** Schürze *f*
**apt** geeignet, passend; treffend; begabt; **~ *to*** geneigt zu
**ap·ti·tude** (***for***) Begabung *f* (für), Befähigung *f* (für), Talent *n* (zu)
**ap·ti·tude test** Eignungsprüfung *f*
**aq·ua| jog·ging** SPORT Aquajogging *n*; **~plan·ing** *Br* MOT Aquaplaning *n*
**a·quar·i·um** Aquarium *n*
**A·quar·i·us** ASTR Wassermann *m*; ***he*** (***she***) ***is*** (***an***) **~** er (sie) ist (ein) Wassermann
**a·quat·ic** Wasser…; **~ plant** Wasserpflanze *f*; **~s**, **~ sports** Wassersport *m*
**aq·ue·duct** Aquädukt *m*
**Ar·ab** Araber(in); **A·ra·bi·a** Arabien *n*
**Ar·a·bic 1.** arabisch **2.** LING Arabisch *n*
**ar·a·ble** AGR anbaufähig; Acker…
**ar·bi·tra·ry** willkürlich, eigenmächtig
**ar·bi·trate** entscheiden, schlichten
**ar·bi·tra·tion** Schlichtung *f*
**ar·bi·tra·tor** Schiedsrichter *m*; Schlichter *m*
**ar·bo(u)r** Laube *f*
**arc** Bogen *m*; ELECTR Lichtbogen *m*
**ar·cade** Arkade *f*; Lauben-, Bogengang *m*; Durchgang *m*, Passage *f*
**arch**[1] **1.** Bogen *m*; Gewölbe *n* **2.** (sich) wölben; krümmen
**arch**[2] erste(r, -s), oberste(r, -s), Haupt…, Erz…
**arch**[3] schelmisch
**ar·cha·ic** veraltet
**arch·an·gel** Erzengel *m*
**arch·bish·op** REL Erzbischof *m*
**ar·cher** Bogenschütze *m*
**ar·cher·y** Bogenschießen *n*
**ar·chi·tect** Architekt(in)
**ar·chi·tec·ture** Architektur *f*
**ar·chives** Archiv *n*
**arch·way** (Bogen)Gang *m*
**arc·tic** arktisch, nördlich, Polar…
**ar·dent** feurig, glühend; *fig* leidenschaftlich, heftig; eifrig
**ar·do(u)r** Leidenschaft *f*, Glut *f*, Feuer *n*; Eifer *m*
**are** *du* bist, *wir or sie or Sie* sind, *ihr* seid
**ar·e·a** (Boden)Fläche *f*; Gegend *f*, Gebiet *n*; Bereich *m*
**ar·e·a code** TEL Vorwahl(nummer) *f*
**a·re·na** Arena *f*
**Ar·gen·ti·na** Argentinien *n*

**Ar·gen·tine** **1.** argentinisch **2.** Argentinier(in)
**ar·gue** argumentieren; streiten; diskutieren; **ar·gu·ment** Argument *n*; Wortwechsel *m*, Auseinandersetzung *f*
**ar·id** dürr, trocken (*a. fig*)
**Ar·ies** ASTR Widder *m*; ***he*** (***she***) ***is*** (***an***) **~** er (sie) ist (ein) Widder
**a·rise** entstehen; auftauchen, auftreten
**ar·is·toc·ra·cy** Aristokratie *f*, Adel *m*
**ar·is·to·crat** Aristokrat(in), Adlige *m*, *f*
**ar·is·to·crat·ic** aristokratisch, adlig
**a·rith·me·tic**[1] Rechnen *n*
**ar·ith·met·ic**[2] arithmetisch, Rechen…
**ar·ith·met·ic u·nit** IT Rechenwerk *n*
**ark** Arche *f*; ***Noah's* ~** die Arche Noah
**arm**[1] ANAT Arm *m*; Armlehne *f*; ***keep s.o. at ~'s length*** sich j-n vom Leibe halten
**arm**[2] MIL (sich) bewaffnen; (auf)rüsten
**ar·ma·ment** MIL Bewaffnung *f*; Aufrüstung *f*
**arm·chair** Lehnstuhl *m*, Sessel *m*
**ar·mi·stice** MIL Waffenstillstand *m*
**ar·mo(u)r** **1.** MIL Rüstung *f*, Panzer *m* (*a. fig*, ZO); **2.** panzern
**ar·mo(u)red car** gepanzertes Fahrzeug
**arm·pit** ANAT Achselhöhle *f*
**arms** Waffen *pl*; Waffengattung *f*; **~ con·trol** Rüstungskontrolle *f*
**ar·my** MIL Armee *f*, Heer *n*
**a·ro·ma** Aroma *n*, Duft *m*
**ar·o·mat·ic** aromatisch, würzig
**a·round** **1.** *adv* (rings)herum, (rund-)herum, ringsumher, überall; umher, herum; in der Nähe; da **2.** *prp* um, um… herum, rund um; in (*dat*) … herum; ungefähr, etwa
**a·rouse** (auf)wecken; *fig* aufrütteln, erregen
**ar·range** (an)ordnen; festlegen, festsetzen; arrangieren (*a.* MUS); vereinbaren; MUS, THEA bearbeiten
**ar·range·ment** Anordnung *f*; Vereinbarung *f*; Vorkehrung *f*; MUS Arrangement *n*, Bearbeitung *f* (*a.* THEA)
**ar·rears** Rückstand *m*, Rückstände *pl*
**ar·rest** JUR **1.** Verhaftung *f*, Festnahme *f* **2.** verhaften, festnehmen
**ar·riv·al** Ankunft *f*; Erscheinen *n*; Ankömmling *m*; **~s** AVIAT, RAIL *etc* 'Ankunft' (*timetable*); ***day of* ~** Anreisetag;
**ar·rive** (an)kommen, eintreffen, erscheinen; **~ *at*** *fig* erreichen (*acc*), kommen zu
**ar·ro·gance** Arroganz *f*, Überheblichkeit *f*
**ar·ro·gant** arrogant, überheblich
**ar·row** Pfeil *m*
**ar·row·head** Pfeilspitze *f*
**ar·se·nic** CHEM Arsen *n*
**ar·son** JUR Brandstiftung *f*
**art** **1.** Kunst *f* **2.** Kunst…; **~ *exhibition*** Kunstausstellung *f*; → ***arts***
**ar·ter·i·al** ANAT Schlagader…
**ar·te·ri·al road** Hauptverkehrsstraße *f*, Verkehrsader *f*
**ar·ter·i·o·scle·ro·sis** MED Arteriosklerose *f*, Arterienverkalkung *f*
**ar·te·ry** ANAT Arterie *f*, Schlagader *f*; (Haupt)Verkehrsader *f*
**art·ful** schlau, verschmitzt
**art gal·le·ry** Gemäldegalerie *f*
**ar·thri·tis** MED Arthritis *f*, Gelenkentzündung *f*
**ar·ti·choke** BOT Artischocke *f*
**ar·ti·cle** Artikel *m* (*a.* LING)
**ar·tic·u·late** **1.** deutlich (aus)sprechen **2.** deutlich ausgesprochen; gegliedert
**ar·tic·u·lat·ed** Gelenk…; **~ *lorry*** *Br* MOT Sattelschlepper *m*
**ar·tic·u·la·tion** (deutliche) Aussprache; TECH Gelenk *n*
**ar·ti·fi·cial** künstlich, Kunst…; **~ *person*** juristische Person
**ar·til·le·ry** MIL Artillerie *f*
**ar·ti·san** Handwerker *m*
**art·ist** Künstler(in)
**ar·tis·tic** künstlerisch, Kunst…
**art·less** schlicht; naiv
**arts** Geisteswissenschaften *pl*; ***Arts Department***, *Br* ***Faculty of Arts*** philosophische Fakultät
**as** **1.** *adv* so, ebenso; wie; als **2.** *cj* (gerade) wie, so wie; ebenso wie; als, während; obwohl, obgleich; da, weil; **~ … ~** (eben)so … wie; **~ *for*, ~ *to*** was … (an-)betrifft; **~ *from*** von *e-m Zeitpunkt* an, ab; **~ *it were*** sozusagen; **~ *Hamlet*** THEA als Hamlet
**as·bes·tos** Asbest *m*
**as·cend** (auf)steigen; ansteigen; besteigen; **as·cen·dan·cy**, **as·cen·den·cy** Überlegenheit *f*; Einfluss *m*
**as·cen·sion** Aufsteigen *n* (*esp* ASTR); Aufstieg *m*; **As·cen·sion** (**Day**) REL Himmelfahrt(stag *m*) *f*
**as·cent** Aufstieg *m*; Besteigung *f*; Stei-

gung *f*
**as·cet·ic** asketisch
**a·sep·tic** MED **1.** aseptisch, keimfrei **2.** aseptisches Mittel
**ash**[1] BOT Esche *f*; Eschenholz *n*
**ash**[2] *a.* ***ashes*** Asche *f*
**a·shamed** beschämt; ***be ~ of*** sich schämen für (*or gen*)
**ash·en** Aschen…; aschfahl, aschgrau
**a·shore** am *or* ans Ufer *or* Land
**ash·tray** Asch(en)becher *m*
**Ash Wednes·day** Aschermittwoch *m*
**A·sia** Asien *n*; **A·sian, A·si·at·ic 1.** asiatisch **2.** Asiat(in)
**a·side** beiseite (*a.* THEA), seitwärts; ***~ from*** abgesehen von
**ask** *v/t* fragen (***s.th.*** nach et.); verlangen (***of, from s.o.*** von j-m); bitten (***s.o.*** [***for***] ***s.th.*** j-n um et.; ***that*** darum, dass); erbitten; ***~*** (***s.o.***) ***a question*** (j-m) e-e Frage stellen; *v/i* ***~ for*** bitten um; fragen nach; ***he ~ed for it*** *or* ***for trouble*** er wollte es ja so haben; ***to be had for the ~ing*** umsonst zu haben sein
**a·skew** schief
**a·sleep** schlafend; ***be*** (***fast, sound***) ***~*** (fest) schlafen; ***fall ~*** einschlafen
**as·par·a·gus** BOT Spargel *m*
**as·pect** Lage *f*; Aspekt *m*, Seite *f*, Gesichtspunkt *m*
**as·phalt 1.** Asphalt *m* **2.** asphaltieren
**as·pic** GASTR Aspik *m*, Gelee *n*
**as·pi·rant** Bewerber(in)
**as·pi·ra·tion** Ambition *f*, Bestrebung *f*
**as·pire** streben (***to, after*** nach)
**ass** zo Esel *m*
**as·sail** angreifen; ***be ~ed with doubts*** von Zweifeln befallen werden
**as·sail·ant** Angreifer(in)
**as·sas·sin** (*esp* politischer) Mörder, Attentäter *m*; **as·sas·sin·ate** *esp* POL ermorden; ***be ~d*** e-m Attentat *or* Mordanschlag zum Opfer fallen; **as·sas·sin·a·tion** (***of***) (*esp* politischer) Mord (an *dat*), Ermordung *f* (*gen*), Attentat *n* (auf *acc*)
**as·sault 1.** Angriff *m*, Überfall *m* **2.** angreifen, überfallen
**as·sem·blage** Ansammlung *f*; TECH Montage *f*; **as·sem·ble** (sich) versammeln; TECH montieren
**as·sem·bly** Versammlung *f*, Gesellschaft *f*; TECH Montage *f*; **~ line** TECH Fließband *n*
**as·sent 1.** Zustimmung *f* **2.** (***to***) zustimmen (*dat*); billigen (*acc*)
**as·sert** behaupten; geltend machen; ***~ o.s.*** sich behaupten, sich durchsetzen
**as·ser·tion** Behauptung *f*; Erklärung *f*; Geltendmachung *f*
**as·sess** *Kosten etc* festsetzen; *Einkommen etc* (zur Steuer) veranlagen (***at*** mit); *fig* abschätzen, beurteilen
**as·sess·ment** Festsetzung *f*; (Steuer)Veranlagung *f*; *fig* Einschätzung *f*
**as·set** ECON Aktivposten *m*; *fig* Plus *n*, Gewinn *m*; *pl* ECON Aktiva *pl*; JUR Vermögen(smasse *f*) *n*; Konkursmasse *f*
**as·sid·u·ous** emsig, fleißig
**as·sign** an-, zuweisen; bestimmen; zuschreiben; **as·sign·ment** An-, Zuweisung *f*; Aufgabe *f*; Auftrag *m*; JUR Abtretung *f*; Übertragung *f*
**as·sim·i·late** (sich) angleichen *or* anpassen (***to, with*** *dat*)
**as·sim·i·la·tion** Assimilation *f*, Angleichung *f*, Anpassung *f* (*all*: ***to*** an *acc*)
**as·sist** *j-m* beistehen, helfen; *j-n* unterstützen; **as·sist·ance** Beistand *m*, Hilfe *f*; **as·sist·ant 1.** stellvertretend, Hilfs… **2.** Assistent(in), Mitarbeiter(in); (***shop***) ***~*** *Br* Verkäufer(in); **~ant referee** SPORT Schiedsrichterassistent(in)
**as·so·ci·ate 1.** vereinigen, verbinden, zusammenschließen; assoziieren; ***~ with*** verkehren mit **2.** Teilhaber(in)
**as·so·ci·a·tion** Vereinigung *f*, Verbindung *f*; Verein *m*
**as·sort** sortieren, aussuchen, zusammenstellen; **as·sort·ment** ECON (***of***) Sortiment *n* (von), Auswahl *f* (an *dat*)
**as·sume** annehmen, voraussetzen; übernehmen
**as·sump·tion** Annahme *f*, Voraussetzung *f*; Übernahme *f*; ***the Assumption*** REL Mariä Himmelfahrt *f*
**as·sur·ance** Zusicherung *f*, Versicherung *f*; *esp Br* (Lebens)Versicherung *f*; Sicherheit *f*, Gewissheit *f*; Selbstsicherheit *f*; **as·sure** *j-m* versichern; *esp Br j-s Leben* versichern; **as·sured 1.** sicher **2.** *esp Br* Versicherte *m, f*; **as·sur·ed·ly** ganz gewiss
**as·te·risk** PRINT Sternchen *n*
**asth·ma** MED Asthma *n*
**as·ton·ish** in Erstaunen setzen; ***be ~ed*** erstaunt sein (***at*** über *acc*)

**as·ton·ish·ing** erstaunlich
**as·ton·ish·ment** (Er)Staunen *n*, Verwunderung *f*
**as·tound** verblüffen
**a·stray**: ***go ~*** vom Weg abkommen; *fig* auf Abwege geraten; irregehen; ***lead ~*** *fig* irreführen; verleiten
**a·stride** rittlings (***of*** auf *dat*)
**as·trin·gent** MED **1.** adstringierend **2.** Adstringens *n*
**as·trol·o·gy** Astrologie *f*
**as·tro·naut** Astronaut *m*, (Welt)Raumfahrer *m*
**as·tron·o·my** Astronomie *f*
**as·tute** scharfsinnig; schlau
**a·sun·der** auseinander, entzwei
**a·sy·lum** Asyl *n*; ***right of ~*** Asylrecht *n*
**a·sy·lum seek·er** Asylant(in), Asylbewerber(in)
**at** *prp place*: in, an, bei, auf; *direction*: auf, nach, gegen, zu; *occupation*: bei, beschäftigt mit, in; *manner, state*: in, bei, zu, unter; *price etc*: für, um; *time, age*: um, bei; ***~ the baker's*** beim Bäcker; ***~ the door*** an der Tür; ***~ school*** in der Schule; ***~ 10 dollars*** für 10 Dollar; ***~ 18*** mit 18 (Jahren); ***~ the age of*** im Alter von; ***~ 8 o'clock*** um 8 Uhr
**a·the·ism** Atheismus *m*
**ath·lete** SPORT (Leicht)Athlet(in)
**ath·let·ic** SPORT athletisch
**ath·let·ics** SPORT (Leicht)Athletik *f*
**At·lan·tic 1.** *a.* ***~ Ocean*** *der* Atlantik **2.** atlantisch
**at·mo·sphere** Atmosphäre *f* (*a. fig*)
**at·mo·spher·ic** atmosphärisch
**at·oll** Atoll *n*
**at·om** Atom *n*; **~ bomb** Atombombe *f*
**a·tom·ic** atomar, Atom…; **~ age** Atomzeitalter *n*; **~ bomb** Atombombe *f*; **~ en·er·gy** Atomenergie *f*; **~ pile** Atomreaktor *m*; **~ pow·er** Atomkraft *f*; **~-pow·ered** atomgetrieben; **~ waste** Atommüll *m*; **~ weight** CHEM Atomgewicht *n*
**at·om·ize** atomisieren; *Flüssigkeit* zerstäuben; **at·om·iz·er** Zerstäuber *m*
**a·tro·cious** grässlich; grausam
**a·troc·i·ty** Scheußlichkeit *f*; Greueltat *f*
**at sign** IT at-Zeichen *n*
**at·tach** *v/t* (***to***) anheften, ankleben (an *acc*), befestigen, anbringen (an *dat*); *Wert, Wichtigkeit etc* beimessen (*dat*); ***be ~ed to*** *fig* hängen an; **at·tach·ment** Befestigung *f*; Bindung *f* (***to*** an *acc*); Anhänglichkeit *f* (***to*** an *acc*)
**at·tack 1.** angreifen **2.** Angriff *m*; MED Anfall *m*
**at·tempt 1.** versuchen **2.** Versuch *m*; ***an ~ on s.o.'s life*** ein Mordanschlag *or* Attentat auf j-n
**at·tend** *v/t* (ärztlich) behandeln; *Kranke* pflegen; teilnehmen an (*dat*), *Schule, Vorlesung etc* besuchen; *fig* begleiten; *v/i* anwesend sein; erscheinen; ***~ to*** *j-n* (*im Laden*) bedienen; ***are you being ~ed to?*** werden Sie schon bedient?; ***~ to s.th.*** etwas erledigen; **at·tend·ance** Dienst *m*, Bereitschaft *f*; Pflege *f*; Anwesenheit *f*, Erscheinen *n*; Besucher *pl*, Teilnehmer *pl*; Besuch(erzahl *f*) *m*, Beteiligung *f*; **at·tend·ant** Begleiter(in); Aufseher(in); (*Tank-*)Wart *m*
**at·ten·tion** Aufmerksamkeit *f* (*a. fig*); ***pay ~*** aufpassen
**at·ten·tive** aufmerksam
**at·tic** Dachboden *m*; Dachkammer *f*
**at·ti·tude** (Ein)Stellung *f*; Haltung *f*
**at·tor·ney** Bevollmächtigte *m, f*; JUR (Rechts)Anwalt *m*, (Rechts)Anwältin *f*; ***power of ~*** Vollmacht *f*
**At·tor·ney Gen·e·ral** JUR Justizminister; *Br* erster Kronanwalt
**at·tract** anziehen; *Aufmerksamkeit* erregen; *fig* reizen; **at·trac·tion** Anziehung *f*, Anziehungskraft *f*, Reiz *m*; Attraktion *f*, THEA *etc* Zugnummer *f*, Zugstück *n*; **at·trac·tive** anziehend; attraktiv; reizvoll
**at·trib·ute**[1] zuschreiben (***to*** *dat*); zurückführen (***to*** auf *acc*)
**at·tri·bute**[2] Attribut *n* (*a.* LING), Eigenschaft *f*, Merkmal *n*
**at·tune**: ***~ to*** *fig* einstellen auf (*acc*)
**au·ber·gine** BOT Aubergine *f*
**au·burn** kastanienbraun
**auc·tion 1.** Auktion *f*, Versteigerung *f* **2.** *mst* ***~ off*** versteigern
**auc·tion·eer** Auktionator *m*
**au·da·cious** unverfroren, dreist
**au·dac·i·ty** Unverfrorenheit *f*, Dreistigkeit *f*
**au·di·ble** hörbar
**au·di·ence** Publikum *n*, Zuhörer *pl*, Zuschauer *pl*, Besucher *pl*, Leser(kreis *m*) *pl*; Audienz *f*
**au·di·o·vis·u·al aids** audiovisuelle Un-

terrichtsmittel *pl*
**au·dit** ECON **1.** Buchprüfung *f* **2.** prüfen
**au·di·tion** MUS Vorsingen *n*; THEA Vorsprechen *n*; ***have an ~*** vorsingen, THEA vorsprechen
**au·di·tor** ECON Buchprüfer *m*; UNIV Gasthörer(in)
**au·di·to·ri·um** Zuhörer-, Zuschauerraum *m*; Vortrags-, Konzertsaal *m*
**Aug** *abbr of* ***August*** Aug., August *m*
**au·ger** TECH großer Bohrer
**Au·gust** (*abbr* ***Aug***) August *m*
**aunt** Tante *f*
**au pair (girl)** Au-pair-Mädchen *n*
**aus·pic·es**: ***under the ~ of*** unter der Schirmherrschaft (*gen*)
**aus·tere** streng; enthaltsam; dürftig; einfach, schmucklos
**Aus·tra·li·a** Australien; **Aus·tra·li·an 1.** australisch **2.** Australier(in)
**Aus·tri·a** Österreich *n*
**Aus·tri·an 1.** österreichisch **2.** Österreicher(in)
**au·then·tic** authentisch; zuverlässig; echt
**au·thor** Urheber(in); Autor(in), Verfasser(in), Schriftsteller(in)
**au·thor·ess** Autorin *f*, Verfasserin *f*, Schriftstellerin *f*
**au·thor·i·ta·tive** gebieterisch, herrisch; maßgebend
**au·thor·i·ty** Autorität *f*; Nachdruck *m*, Gewicht *n*; Vollmacht *f*; Einfluss *m* (***over*** auf *acc*); Ansehen *n*; Quelle *f*; Autorität *f*, Kapazität *f*; *mst pl* Behörde *f*
**au·thor·ize** *j-n* autorisieren, ermächtigen, bevollmächtigen
**au·thor·ship** Urheberschaft *f*
**au·to** Auto *n*
**au·to...** auto..., selbst..., Auto..., Selbst...
**au·to·bi·og·ra·phy** Autobiografie *f*
**au·to·graph** Autogramm *n*
**au·to·mat®** Automatenrestaurant *n*
**au·to·mate** automatisieren
**au·to·mat·ic 1.** automatisch **2.** Selbstladepistole *f*, -gewehr *n*; Auto *n* mit Automatik; **~ tel·ler ma·chine** (*abbr* ***ATM***) Geld-, Bankautomat *m*
**au·to·ma·tion** TECH Automation *f*
**au·tom·a·ton** Roboter *m*
**au·to·mo·bile** Auto *n*, Automobil *n*
**au·ton·o·my** POL Autonomie *f*
**au·top·sy** MED Autopsie *f*
**au·to·tel·ler** Geld-, Bankautomat *m*
**au·tumn** Herbst *m*
**au·tum·nal** herbstlich, Herbst...
**aux·il·i·a·ry** helfend, Hilfs...
**a·vail**: ***to no ~*** vergeblich
**a·vail·a·ble** verfügbar, vorhanden; erreichbar; ECON lieferbar, vorrätig, erhältlich
**av·a·lanche** Lawine *f*
**av·a·rice** Habsucht *f*
**av·a·ri·cious** habgierig
**a·venge** rächen; **a·veng·er** Rächer(in)
**av·e·nue** Allee *f*; Boulevard *m*, Prachtstraße *f*
**av·e·rage 1.** Durchschnitt *m* **2.** durchschnittlich, Durchschnitts...
**a·verse** abgeneigt (***to*** *dat*)
**a·ver·sion** Widerwille *m*, Abneigung *f*
**a·vert** abwenden (*a. fig*)
**avian flu** Vogelgrippe *f*
**a·vi·a·ry** Vogelhaus *n*, Voliere *f*
**a·vi·a·tion** Luftfahrt *f*
**a·vi·a·tor** Flieger *m*
**av·id** gierig (***for*** nach); begeistert
**av·o·ca·do** BOT Avocado *f*
**a·void** (ver)meiden; ausweichen
**a·void·ance** Vermeidung *f*
**a·vow·al** Bekenntnis *n*, (Ein)Geständnis *n*
**a·wait** erwarten, warten auf (*acc*)
**a·wake 1.** wach, munter **2.** *a.* **a·waken** *v/t* (auf)wecken; *v/i* aufwachen, erwachen;
**a·wak·en·ing** Erwachen *n*
**a·ward 1.** Belohnung *f*; Preis *m*, Auszeichnung *f* **2.** zuerkennen, *Preis etc* verleihen
**a·ware**: ***be ~ of s.th.*** von etwas wissen, sich e-r Sache bewusst sein; ***become ~ of s.th.*** etwas merken
**a·way** weg, fort; (weit) entfernt; immer weiter, d(a)rauflos; SPORT Auswärts...; ***~ match*** SPORT Auswärtsspiel *n*
**awe 1.** Furcht *f*, Scheu *f* **2.** *j-m* (Ehr)-Furcht *or* großen Respekt einflößen
**aw·ful** furchtbar, schrecklich
**awk·ward** ungeschickt, linkisch; unangenehm; unhandlich, sperrig; ungünstig, ungelegen
**awl** Ahle *f*, Pfriem *m*
**aw·ning** Plane *f*; Markise *f*
**a·wry** schief
**ax(e)** Axt *f*, Beil *n*
**ax·is** MATH *etc* Achse *f*

B

**ax·le** TECH (Rad)Achse *f*, Welle *f*
**ay(e)** PARL Jastimme *f*
**A-Z** *Br appr* Stadtplan *m*
**az·ure** azurblau, himmelblau

# B

**B, b** B, b *n*
**b** *abbr of* ***born*** geb., geboren
**bab·ble 1.** stammeln; plappern, schwatzen; plätschern **2.** Geplapper *n*, Geschwätz *n*
**babe** kleines Kind, Baby *n*; F Puppe *f*
**ba·boon** ZO Pavian *m*
**ba·by 1.** Baby *n*, Säugling *m*, kleines Kind; F Puppe *f* **2.** Baby..., Kinder...; klein; **~ bug·gy, ~ car·riage** Kinderwagen *m*; **~-changing room** Babywickelraum *m*; **~ food** Babynahrung *f*
**ba·by·hood** Säuglingsalter *n*
**ba·by·ish** *contp* kindisch
**ba·by-mind·er** *Br* Tagesmutter *f*
**ba·by·sit** babysitten
**ba·by·sit·ter** Babysitter(in)
**bach·e·lor** Junggeselle *m*
**back 1.** Rücken *m*; Rückseite *f*; (Rück)-Lehne *f*; hinterer *or* rückwärtiger Teil; SPORT Verteidiger *m* **2.** *adj* Hinter..., Rück..., hintere(r, -s), rückwärtig; ECON rückständig; alt, zurückliegend **3.** *adv* zurück, rückwärts **4.** *v/t* mit e-m Rücken versehen; wetten *or* setzen auf (*acc*); *a.* ***~ up*** unterstützen; zurückbewegen; MOT zurückstoßen mit; ***~ up*** IT e-e Sicherungskopie machen von; *v/i often* ***~ up*** sich rückwärts bewegen, zurückgehen *or* -fahren, MOT *a.* zurückstoßen; ***~ in*(*to a parking space*)** MOT rückwärts einparken; ***~ up*** IT e-e Sicherungskopie machen
**back·ache** Rückenschmerzen *pl*
**back·bite** verleumden, schlechtmachen
**back·bone** ANAT Rückgrat *n* (*a. fig*)
**back-break·ing** erschöpfend, mörderisch
**back·chat** *Br* freche Antwort(en *pl*)
**back·comb** *Br* toupieren
**back door** Hintertür *f*; *fig* Hintertürchen *n*
**back·er** Unterstützer *m*, Geldgeber *m*
**back·fire** MOT Früh- *or* Fehlzündung haben; *fig* fehlschlagen
**back·ground** Hintergrund *m*
**back·hand** SPORT Rückhand *f*, Rückhandschlag *m*
**back·heel·er** *soccer*: Hackentrick *m*
**back·ing** Unterstützung *f*
**back num·ber** alte Nummer
**back·pack** *großer* Rucksack
**back·pack·er** Rucksacktourist(in)
**back·pack·ing** Rucksacktourismus *m*
**back-ped·al brake** *Br* Rücktritt *m*, Rücktrittbremse *f*
**back seat** MOT Rücksitz *m*
**back·side** Gesäß *n*, F Hintern *m*, Po *m*
**back·space (key)** IT Rücktaste *f*
**back stairs** Hintertreppe *f*
**back street** Seitenstraße *f*
**back·stroke** Rückenschwimmen *n*
**back talk** freche Antwort(en *pl*)
**back·track** *fig* e-n Rückzieher machen
**back·up** Unterstützung *f*; TECH Ersatzgerät *n*; IT Backup *n*, Sicherungskopie *f*; MOT Rückstau *m*
**back·ward 1.** *adj* Rück..., Rückwärts...; zurückgeblieben; rückständig; ***a ~ glance*** ein Blick zurück **2.** *adv a.* ***backwards*** rückwärts, zurück
**back·yard** Garten *m* hinter dem Haus; *Br* Hinterhof *m*
**ba·con** Speck *m*
**bac·te·ri·a** BIOL Bakterien *pl*
**bad** schlecht, böse, schlimm; ***go ~*** schlecht werden, verderben; ***he is in a ~ way*** es geht ihm schlecht; ***he is ~ly off*** es geht ihm finanziell schlecht; ***~ly wounded*** schwer verwundet; ***want ~ly*** dringend brauchen
**badge** Abzeichen *n*; Dienstmarke *f*
**bad·ger 1.** ZO Dachs *m* **2.** *j-n* plagen, *j-m* zusetzen
**bad·min·ton** Federball(spiel *n*) *m*, SPORT Badminton *n*
**bad-tempered** schlecht gelaunt
**bag 1.** Beutel *m*, Sack *m*; Tüte *f*; Tasche *f* **2.** in e-n Beutel *etc* tun; in Beutel verpacken *or* abfüllen; HUNT zur Strecke bringen; schlottern
**bag·gage** (Reise)Gepäck *n*; **~ car** RAIL

Gepäckwagen *m*; ~ **check** Gepäckschein *m*; ~ **claim** AVIAT Gepäckausgabe *f*; ~ **room** RAIL Gepäckaufbewahrung *f*
**bag·gy** bauschig; ausgebeult
**bag·pipes** MUS Dudelsack *m*
**bail 1.** Bürge *m*; JUR Kaution *f*; ***be out on*** ~ gegen Kaution auf freiem Fuß sein; ***go*** *or* ***stand*** ~ ***for s.o.*** für j-n Kaution stellen **2.** ~ ***out*** JUR *j-n* gegen Kaution freibekommen; AVIAT (mit dem Fallschirm) abspringen
**bai·liff** (Guts)Verwalter *m*; *Br* JUR Gerichtsvollzieher *m*
**bait 1.** Köder *m* (*a. fig*) **2.** mit e-m Köder versehen; *fig* ködern
**bake** backen, im (Back)Ofen braten; TECH brennen; dörren
**bak·er** Bäcker *m*
**bak·er·y** Bäckerei *f*
**bak·ing pow·der** Backpulver *n*
**bal·ance 1.** Waage *f*; Gleichgewicht *n* (*a. fig*); ECON Bilanz *f*; Saldo *m*, Kontostand *m*, Guthaben *n*; Restbetrag *m*; ***keep one's*** ~ das Gleichgewicht halten; ***lose one's*** ~ das Gleichgewicht verlieren; *fig* die Fassung verlieren; ~ ***of payments*** ECON Zahlungsbilanz *f*; ~ ***of power*** POL Kräftegleichgewicht *n*; ~ ***of trade*** ECON Handelsbilanz *f* **2.** *v/t* abwägen; im Gleichgewicht halten, balancieren; ECON ausgleichen; *v/i* balancieren; ECON sich ausgleichen; ~ ***each other*** sich die Waage halten
**bal·ance sheet** ECON Bilanz *f*
**bal·co·ny** Balkon *m* (*a.* THEA)
**bald** kahl
**bale**[1] ECON Ballen *m*
**bale**[2]: ~ ***out*** *Br* AVIAT (mit dem Fallschirm) abspringen
**bale·ful** hasserfüllt
**balk 1.** Balken *m* **2.** stutzen; scheuen
**ball**[1] **1.** Ball *m*; Kugel *f*; ANAT (Hand-, Fuß)Ballen *m*; Knäuel *m*, *n*; Kloß *m*; ***long*** ~ SPORT langer Pass **2.** ballen; sich zusammenballen
**ball**[2] Ball *m*, Tanzveranstaltung *f*
**bal·lad** Ballade *f*
**bal·last 1.** Ballast *m* **2.** mit Ballast beladen
**ball bear·ing** TECH Kugellager *n*
**bal·let** Ballett *n*
**bal·lis·tics** MIL Ballistik *f*
**bal·loon 1.** Ballon *m*; Sprech-, Denkblase *f* **2.** sich (auf)blähen
**bal·lot 1.** Stimmzettel *m*; (geheime) Wahl **2.** (***for***) stimmen (für), (in geheimer Wahl) wählen (*acc*); ~ **box** Wahlurne *f*; ~ **pa·per** Stimmzettel *m*
**ball·point** (**pen**) Kugelschreiber *m*, F Kuli *m*
**ball·room** Ballsaal *m*, Tanzsaal *m*
**balls** V Eier *pl*
**balm** Balsam *m* (*a. fig*)
**balm·y** lind, mild
**ba·lo·ney** F Quatsch *m*
**Balt·ics**: ***the*** ~ das Baltikum
**bal·us·trade** Balustrade *f*, Brüstung *f*, Geländer *n*
**bam·boo** BOT Bambus(rohr *n*) *m*
**bam·boo·zle** F betrügen, *j-n* übers Ohr hauen
**ban 1.** (amtliches) Verbot, Sperre *f*; REL Bann *m* **2.** verbieten
**ba·nal** banal, abgedroschen
**ba·na·na** BOT Banane *f*
**band 1.** Band *n*; Streifen *m*; Schar *f*, Gruppe *f*; *contp* Bande *f*; (Musik)Kapelle *f*, (Tanz-, Unterhaltungs)Orchester *n*, (*Jazz-*, *Rock*)Band *f* **2.** ~ ***together*** sich zusammentun *or* -rotten
**ban·dage** MED **1.** Bandage *f*; Binde *f*; Verband *m*; (Heft)Pflaster *n* **2.** bandagieren; verbinden
**'Band-Aid®** MED (Heft)Pflaster *n*
**B & B** *abbr of* ***bed and breakfast*** Übernachtung *f* mit Frühstück
**ban·dit** Bandit *m*
**band·lead·er** MUS Bandleader *m*
**band·mas·ter** MUS Kapellmeister *m*
**ban·dy** krumm
**ban·dy-legged** säbelbeinig, o-beinig
**bang 1.** heftiger Schlag; Knall *m*; *mst pl* Pony *m* **2.** dröhnend (zu)schlagen
**ban·gle** Armreif *m*, Fußreif *m*
**ban·ish** verbannen
**ban·ish·ment** Verbannung *f*
**ban·is·ter** *a. pl* Treppengeländer *n*
**ban·jo** MUS Banjo *n*
**bank**[1] ECON **1.** Bank *f* (*a.* MED); **2.** *v/t* bei e-r Bank einzahlen; *v/i* ein Bankkonto haben (***with*** bei)
**bank**[2] (Erd)Wall *m*; Böschung *f*; (*Fluss-etc*)Ufer *n*; (*Sand-*, *Wolken*)Bank *f*
**bank ac·count** Bankkonto *n*
**bank bill** Banknote *f*, Geldschein *m*
**bank·book** Sparbuch *n*
**bank code** ECON Bankleitzahl *f*

B

**bank·er** Bankier *m*, Banker *m*; **~'s card** Scheckkarte *f*
**bank hol·i·day** *Br* gesetzlicher Feiertag *m*
**bank·ing** ECON **1.** Bankgeschäft *n*, Bankwesen *n* **2.** Bank…
**bank note** *Br* → **bank bill**
**bank rate** ECON Diskontsatz *m*
**bank·rupt** JUR **1.** Konkursschuldner *m* **2.** bankrott; **go ~** in Konkurs gehen, Bankrott machen **3.** *j-n, Unternehmen* Bankrott machen; **bank·rupt·cy** JUR Bankrott *m*, Konkurs *m*
**bank sort·ing code** → **bank code**
**ban·ner** Transparent *n*
**banns** Aufgebot *n*
**ban·quet** Bankett *n*
**ban·ter** necken
**bap·tism** REL Taufe *f*
**bap·tize** REL taufen
**bar 1.** Stange *f*, Stab *m*; SPORT (Tor-, Quer-, Sprung)Latte *f*; Riegel *m*; Schranke *f*, Sperre *f*; *fig* Hindernis *n*; (*Gold- etc*)Barren *m*; MUS Taktstrich *m*; *ein* Takt *m*; dicker Strich; JUR (Gerichts)Schranke *f*; JUR Anwaltschaft *f*; Bar *f*; Lokal *n*, Imbissstube *f*; *pl* Gitter *n*; **a ~ of chocolate** ein Riegel *or* e-e Tafel Schokolade; **a ~ of soap** ein Stück Seife **2.** zuriegeln, verriegeln; versperren; einsperren; (ver)hindern; ausschließen
**barb** Widerhaken *m*
**bar·bar·i·an 1.** barbarisch **2.** Barbar(in)
**bar·be·cue 1.** Bratrost *m*, Grill *m*; Barbecue *n* **2.** auf dem Rost *or* am Spieß braten, grillen
**barbed wire** Stacheldraht *m*
**bar·ber** (Herren)Friseur *m*, (-)Frisör *m*
**bar code** Strichkode *m*
**bare 1.** nackt, bloß; kahl; leer **2.** entblößen
**bare·faced** unverschämt, schamlos
**bare·foot, bare·foot·ed** barfuß
**bare·head·ed** barhäuptig
**bare·ly** kaum
**bar·gain 1.** Geschäft *n*, Handel *m*; vorteilhaftes Geschäft, Gelegenheitskauf *m*; **a (dead) ~** spottbillig; **it's a ~!** abgemacht! **2.** (ver)handeln; **~ sale** Verkauf *m* zu herabgesetzten Preisen; Ausverkauf *m*
**barge 1.** Lastkahn *m* **2. ~ in** F hereinplatzen (**on** bei)
**bark**[1] BOT Borke *f*, Rinde *f*
**bark**[2] **1.** bellen; **~ up the wrong tree** F auf dem Holzweg sein; an der falschen Adresse sein **2.** Bellen *n*
**bar·ley** BOT Gerste *f*; Graupe *f*
**barn** Scheune *f*; (Vieh)Stall *m*
**ba·rom·e·ter** Barometer *n*
**bar·on** Baron *m*; Freiherr *m*
**bar·on·ess** Baronin *f*; Freifrau *f*
**bar·racks** MIL Kaserne *f*; *contp* Mietskaserne *f*
**bar·rage** Staudamm *m*; MIL Sperrfeuer *n*; *fig* (Wort- *etc*)Schwall *m*
**bar·rel** Fass *n*, Tonne *f*; (*Gewehr*)Lauf *m*; TECH Trommel *f*, Walze *f*
**bar·rel or·gan** MUS Drehorgel *f*
**bar·ren** unfruchtbar; trocken
**bar·rette** Haarspange *f*
**bar·ri·cade 1.** Barrikade *f* **2.** verbarrikadieren; sperren
**bar·ri·er** Schranke *f* (*a. fig*), Barriere *f*, Sperre *f*; Hindernis *n*
**bar·ris·ter** *Br* JUR Barrister *m*
**bar·row** Karre *f*
**bar·ter 1.** Tausch(handel) *m* **2.** tauschen (**for** gegen)
**base**[1] gemein
**base**[2] **1.** Basis *f*; Grundlage *f*; Fundament *n*; Fuß *m*; MIL Standort *m*; MIL Stützpunkt *m* **2.** gründen, stützen (**on** auf *acc*)
**base**[3] CHEM Base *f*
**base·ball** SPORT Baseball(spiel *n*) *m*
**base·board** Scheuerleiste *f*
**base·less** grundlos
**base·line** *tennis etc*: Grundlinie *f*
**base·ment** ARCH Fundament *n*; Kellergeschoss *n*
**bash·ful** scheu, schüchtern
**ba·sic**[1] **1.** Grund…, grundlegend **2.** *pl* Grundlagen *pl*
**ba·sic**[2] CHEM basisch
**ba·sic·al·ly** im Grunde
**ba·sin** Becken *n*, Schale *f*, Schüssel *f*; Tal-, Wasser-, Hafenbecken *n*
**ba·sis** Basis *f*; Grundlage *f*
**bask** sich sonnen (*a. fig*)
**bas·ket** Korb *m*
**bas·ket·ball** SPORT Basketball(spiel *n*) *m*
**bass**[1] MUS Bass *m*
**bass**[2] ZO (Fluss-, See)Barsch *m*
**bas·tard** Bastard *m*
**baste**[1] GASTR mit Fett begießen
**baste**[2] (an)heften

B

**bat**[1] zo Fledermaus *f*; ***as blind as a ~*** stockblind
**bat**[2] *baseball, cricket* **1.** Schlagholz *n*, Schläger *m*; F ***right off the ~*** sofort **2.** am Schlagen sein
**batch** Stapel *m*, Stoß *m*
**bate**: ***with ~d breath*** mit angehaltenem Atem
**bath 1.** (Wannen)Bad *n*; *pl* Bad *n*, Badeanstalt *f*; Badeort *m*; ***have a ~*** *Br*, ***take a ~*** baden, ein Bad nehmen **2.** *Br v/t j-n* baden; *v/i* baden, ein Bad nehmen
**bathe** *v/t* baden (*a.* MED); *v/i* baden, ein Bad nehmen; schwimmen
**bath foam** Badeschaum *m*
**bath·ing 1.** Baden *n* **2.** Bade…
**bath·ing suit** → ***swimsuit***
**bath·robe** Bademantel *m*; Morgenrock *m*, Schlafrock *m*
**bath·room** Badezimmer *n*; Toilette *f*
**bath·tub** Badewanne *f*
**bat·on** Stab *m*; MUS Taktstock *m*; Schlagstock *m*, Gummiknüppel *m*
**bat·tal·i·on** MIL Bataillon *n*
**bat·ten** Latte *f*
**bat·ter**[1] heftig schlagen; misshandeln; verbeulen; ***~ down, ~ in*** einschlagen
**bat·ter**[2] GASTR Rührteig *m*
**bat·ter**[3] *baseball, cricket*: Schläger *m*, Schlagmann *m*
**bat·ter·y** ELECTR Batterie *f*; JUR Tätlichkeit *f*, Körperverletzung *f*; ***assault and ~*** JUR tätliche Beleidigung
**bat·ter·y charg·er** ELECTR Ladegerät *n*
**bat·ter·y·op·e·rat·ed** ELECTR batteriebetrieben
**bat·tle 1.** MIL Schlacht *f* (***of*** bei); *fig* Kampf *m* (***for*** um); **2.** kämpfen
**bat·tle·field, bat·tle·ground** MIL Schlachtfeld *n*
**bat·tle·ments** ARCH Zinnen *pl*
**bat·tle·ship** MIL Schlachtschiff *n*
**baulk** → ***balk***
**Ba·va·ri·a** Bayern *n*
**Ba·var·i·an 1.** bay(e)risch **2.** Bayer(in)
**bawd·y** obszön
**bawl** brüllen, schreien; ***~ s.o. out*** mit j-m schimpfen
**bay**[1] GEOGR Bai *f*, Bucht *f*; ARCH Erker *m*
**bay**[2] *a.* ***~ tree*** BOT Lorbeer(baum) *m*
**bay**[3] **1.** zo bellen, Laut geben **2.** ***hold*** *or* ***keep at ~*** *j-n* in Schach halten; *et.* von sich fernhalten
**bay**[4] **1.** rotbraun **2.** zo Braune *m*
**bay·o·net** MIL Bajonett *n*
**bay·ou** GEOGR sumpfiger Flussarm
**bay win·dow** ARCH Erkerfenster *n*
**ba·zaar** Basar *m*
**BC** *abbr of* ***before Christ*** v. Chr., vor Christus
**be** sein; *to form the passive*: werden; stattfinden; ***he wants to ~ a doctor*** *etc* er möchte Arzt *etc* werden; ***how much are the shoes?*** was kosten die Schuhe?; ***that's five dollars*** das macht *or* kostet fünf Dollar; ***she is reading*** sie liest gerade; ***there is, there are*** es gibt
**beach** Strand *m*; ***~ ball*** Wasserball *m*; ***~ bug·gy*** MOT Strandbuggy *m*
**beach·wear** Strandkleidung *f*
**bea·con** Leucht-, Signalfeuer *n*
**bead** (*Glas-, Schweiß- etc*)Perle *f*; *pl* REL Rosenkranz *m*
**bead·y** klein, rund und glänzend
**beak** zo Schnabel *m*; TECH Tülle *f*
**beam 1.** Balken *m*; (Licht)Strahl *m*; AVIAT *etc* Peil-, Leit-, Richtstrahl *m* **2.** ausstrahlen; strahlen (*a. fig* ***with*** vor *dat*)
**bean** BOT Bohne *f*; ***be full of ~s*** F aufgekrazt sein; → ***spill*** *1*
**bear**[1] zo Bär *m*
**bear**[2] tragen; zur Welt bringen, gebären; ertragen, aushalten; ***I can't ~ him (it)*** ich kann ihn (es) nicht ausstehen *or* leiden; ***~ out*** bestätigen
**bear·a·ble** erträglich
**beard** Bart *m*; BOT Grannen *pl*
**beard·ed** bärtig
**bear·er** Träger(in); ECON Überbringer(in), Inhaber(in)
**bear·ing** Ertragen *n*; Betragen *n*; (Körper)Haltung *f*; *fig* Beziehung *f*; Lage *f*, Richtung *f*, Orientierung *f*; ***take one's ~s*** sich orientieren; ***lose one's ~s*** die Orientierung verlieren
**beast** (*a. wildes*) Tier; Bestie *f*
**beast·ly** scheußlich
**beast of prey** zo Raubtier *n*
**beat 1.** schlagen; (ver)prügeln; besiegen; übertreffen; F ***~ s.o. to it*** j-m zuvorkommen; ***~ it!*** F hau ab!; ***that ~s all!*** das ist doch der Gipfel *or* die Höhe!; ***that ~s me*** F das ist mir zu hoch; ***~ about the bush*** wie die Katze um den heißen Brei herumschleichen; ***~ down*** ECON drücken, herunterhan-

deln; **~ s.o. up** j-n zusammenschlagen **2.** Schlag *m*; MUS Takt(schlag) *m*; *jazz*: Beat *m*; Pulsschlag *m*; Runde *f*, Revier *n* **3.** (**dead**) **~** F wie erschlagen, fix und fertig

**beat·en track** Trampelpfad *m*; ***off the ~*** ungewohnt, ungewöhnlich

**beat·ing** (Tracht *f*) Prügel *pl*

**beau·ti·cian** Kosmetikerin *f*

**beau·ti·ful** schön

**beaut·y** Schönheit *f*; ***Sleeping Beauty*** Dornröschen *n*; **~ care** Schönheitspflege *f*; **~ par·lo(u)r**, **~ sal·on** Schönheitssalon *m*

**bea·ver** ZO Biber *m*; Biberpelz *m*

**be·cause** weil; **~ *of*** wegen (*gen*)

**beck·on** (zu)winken (*dat*)

**be·come** *v/i* werden (***of*** aus); *v/t* sich schicken für; *j-m* stehen, *j-n* kleiden

**be·com·ing** passend; schicklich; kleidsam

**bed 1.** Bett *n*; ZO Lager *n*; AGR Beet *n*; Unterlage *f*; ***~ and breakfast*** Zimmer *n* mit Frühstück **2. *~ down*** sein Nachtlager aufschlagen

**bed·clothes** Bettwäsche *f*

**bed·ding** Bettzeug *n*; AGR Streu *f*

**bed·lam** Tollhaus *n*

**bed·rid·den** bettlägerig

**bed·room** Schlafzimmer *n*

**bed·side**: ***at the ~*** am (*a. Kranken*)Bett

**bed·side lamp** Nachttischlampe *f*

**bed·sit** F, **bed·sit·ter**, **bed·sit·ting room** *Br* möbliertes Zimmer; Einzimmerappartement *n*

**bed·spread** Tagesdecke *f*

**bed·stead** Bettgestell *n*

**bed·time** Schlafenszeit *f*

**bee** ZO Biene *f*

**beech** BOT Buche *f*

**beech·nut** BOT Buchecker *f*

**beef** GASTR Rindfleisch *n*

**beef·bur·ger** GASTR *Br* Hamburger *m*

**beef tea** GASTR (Rind)Fleischbrühe *f*

**beef·y** F bullig

**bee·hive** Bienenkorb *m*, Bienenstock *m*

**bee·keep·er** Imker *m*

**bee·line**: ***make a ~ for*** F schnurstracks losgehen auf (*acc*)

**beep·er** TECH Piepser *m*

**beer** Bier *n*

**beet** BOT Runkelrübe *f*, Rote Bete, Rote Rübe

**bee·tle** ZO Käfer *m*

**beet·root** BOT *Br* Rote Bete, Rote Rübe

**be·fore 1.** *adv space*: vorn, voran; *time*: vorher, früher, schon (früher) **2.** *cj* bevor, ehe, bis **3.** *prp* vor; **be·fore·hand** zuvor, im Voraus, vorweg

**be·friend** sich *j-s* annehmen

**beg** *v/t et.* erbitten (***of s.o.*** von j-m); betteln um; *j-n* bitten; *v/i* betteln; (dringend) bitten

**be·get** (er)zeugen

**beg·gar 1.** Bettler(in); F Kerl *m* **2.** ***it ~s all description*** es spottet jeder Beschreibung

**be·gin** beginnen, anfangen

**be·gin·ner** Anfänger(in)

**be·gin·ning** Beginn *m*, Anfang *m*

**be·grudge** missgönnen

**be·guile** täuschen; betrügen (***of, out of*** um); sich *die Zeit* vertreiben

**be·half**: ***in*** (*Br* ***on***) ***~ of*** im Namen von (*or gen*)

**be·have** sich (gut) benehmen

**be·hav·io(u)r** Benehmen *n*, Betragen *n*, Verhalten *n*

**be·hav·io(u)r·al sci·ence** PSYCH Verhaltensforschung *f*

**be·head** enthaupten

**be·hind 1.** *adv* hinten, dahinter; zurück **2.** *prp* hinter (*dat or acc*) **3.** F Hinterteil *n*, Hintern *m*

**beige** beige

**be·ing** Sein *n*, Dasein *n*, Existenz *f*; (Lebe)Wesen *n*, Geschöpf *n*; *j-s* Wesen *n*, Natur *f*

**be·lat·ed** verspätet

**belch 1.** aufstoßen, rülpsen; *a.* **~ *out*** speien, ausstoßen **2.** Rülpser *m*

**bel·fry** Glockenturm *m*, -stuhl *m*

**Bel·gian 1.** belgisch **2.** Belgier(in)

**Bel·gium** Belgien *n*

**be·lief** Glaube *m* (***in*** an *acc*)

**be·liev·a·ble** glaubhaft

**be·lieve** glauben (***in*** an *acc*); ***I couldn't ~ my ears*** (***eyes***) ich traute m-n Ohren (Augen) nicht

**be·liev·er** REL Gläubige *m*, *f*

**be·lit·tle** *fig* herabsetzen

**bell** Glocke *f*; Klingel *f*

**bell·boy** *Br*, **bell·hop** (Hotel)Page *m*

**bel·lig·er·ent** kriegerisch; streitlustig, aggressiv; Krieg führend

**bel·low 1.** brüllen **2.** Gebrüll *n*

**bel·lows** Blasebalg *m*

**bel·ly 1.** Bauch *m*; Magen *m* **2. *~ out*** (an)-

schwellen lassen; bauschen
**bel·ly·ache** F Bauchweh *n*
**be·long** gehören; ~ ***to*** gehören *dat or* zu
**be·long·ings** Habseligkeiten *pl*, Habe *f*
**be·loved** **1.** (innig) geliebt **2.** Geliebte *m, f*
**be·low** **1.** *adv* unten **2.** *prp* unter (*dat or acc*)
**belt** **1.** Gürtel *m*; Gurt *m*; GEOGR Zone *f*, Gebiet *n*; TECH (Treib)Riemen *m* **2.** ~ ***out*** MUS schmettern; *a.* ~ ***up*** den Gürtel (*gen*) zumachen; ~ ***up*** MOT sich anschnallen; **belt·ed** mit e-m Gürtel
**belt·way** Umgehungsstraße *f*; Ringstraße *f*
**be·moan** betrauern, beklagen
**bench** Sitzbank *f*, Bank *f* (*a.* SPORT); TECH Werkbank *f*; JUR Richterbank *f*; Richter *m or pl*
**bend** **1.** Biegung *f*, Kurve *f*; ***drive s.o. round the*** ~ F j-n noch wahnsinnig machen **2.** (sich) biegen *or* krümmen; neigen; beugen; *fig* richten (***to, on*** auf *acc*)
**be·neath** → ***below***
**ben·e·dic·tion** REL Segen *m*
**ben·e·fac·tor** Wohltäter *m*
**be·nef·i·cent** wohltätig
**ben·e·fi·cial** wohltuend, zuträglich, nützlich
**ben·e·fit** **1.** Nutzen *m*, Vorteil *m*; Wohltätigkeitsveranstaltung *f*; (*Sozial-, Versicherungs- etc*)Leistung *f*; (*Arbeitslosen- etc*)Unterstützung *f*; (*Kranken- etc*)Geld *n* **2.** nützen; ~ ***by***, ~ ***from*** Vorteil haben von *or* durch, Nutzen ziehen aus
**be·nev·o·lence** Wohlwollen *n*
**be·nev·o·lent** wohltätig; wohlwollend
**be·nign** MED gutartig
**bent** **1.** ~ ***on doing*** entschlossen zu tun **2.** Hang *m*, Neigung *f*; Veranlagung *f*
**ben·zene** CHEM Benzol *n*
**ben·zine** CHEM Leichtbenzin *n*
**be·queath** JUR vermachen
**be·quest** JUR Vermächtnis *n*
**be·reave** berauben
**be·ret** Baskenmütze *f*
**ber·ry** BOT Beere *f*
**berth** **1.** MAR Liege-, Ankerplatz *m*; Koje *f*; RAIL (Schlafwagen)Bett *n* **2.** MAR festmachen, anlegen
**be·seech** (inständig) bitten (um); anflehen
**be·side** *prp* neben (*dat or acc*); ~ ***o.s.*** außer sich (***with*** vor); ~ ***the point***, ~ ***the question*** nicht zur Sache gehörig
**be·sides** **1.** *adv* außerdem **2.** *prp* abgesehen von, außer (*dat*)
**be·siege** belagern
**best** **1.** *adj* beste(r, -s) höchste(r, -s), größte(r, -s), meiste; ~ ***before*** GASTR haltbar bis **2.** *adv* am besten **3.** *der, die, das* Beste; ***all the*** ~***!*** alles Gute!, viel Glück!; ***to the*** ~ ***of …*** nach bestem …; ***make the*** ~ ***of*** das Beste machen aus (*dat*); ***at*** ~ bestenfalls; ***be at one's*** ~ in Hoch- *or* Höchstform sein
**best-be·fore date**, **best-by date** Mindesthaltbarkeitsdatum *n*
**bes·ti·al** *fig* tierisch, bestialisch
**be·stow** geben, verleihen (***on*** *dat*)
**best-sell·er** Bestseller *m*
**bet** **1.** Wette *f*; ***make a*** ~ e-e Wette abschließen **2.** wetten; ~ ***s.o. ten dollars*** mit j-m um zehn Dollar wetten; ***you*** ~ F und ob!
**be·tray** verraten (*a. fig*); verleiten
**be·tray·al** Verrat *m*
**be·tray·er** Verräter(in)
**bet·ter** **1.** *adj* besser; ***he is*** ~ es geht ihm besser; ~ ***and*** ~ immer besser **2.** *das* Bessere; ***get the*** ~ ***of*** die Oberhand gewinnen über (*acc*); *et.* überwinden **3.** *adv* besser; mehr; ***do*** ~ ***than*** es besser machen als; ***know*** ~ es besser wissen; ***so much the*** ~ desto besser; ***you had*** ~ ***go*** *Br*, F ***you*** ~ ***go*** es wäre besser, wenn du gingest; ~ ***off*** (finanziell) besser gestellt; ***he is*** ~ ***off than I am*** es geht ihm besser als mir **4.** *v/t* verbessern; *v/i* sich bessern
**be·tween** **1.** *adv* dazwischen; ***in*** ~ zwischendurch; F ***few and far*** ~ (ganz) vereinzelt **2.** *prp* zwischen (*dat or acc*); unter (*dat*); ~ ***you and me*** unter uns *or* im Vertrauen (gesagt)
**bev·el** TECH abkanten, abschrägen
**bev·er·age** Getränk *n*
**bev·y** zo Schwarm *m*, Schar *f*
**be·ware** (***of***) sich in Acht nehmen (vor *dat*), sich hüten (vor *dat*); ~ ***of the dog!*** Vorsicht, bissiger Hund!
**be·wil·der** verwirren
**be·wil·der·ment** Verwirrung *f*
**be·witch** bezaubern, verhexen
**be·yond** **1.** *adv* darüber hinaus **2.** *prp* jenseits (*gen*); über … (*acc*) hinaus
**bi…** zwei, zweifach, zweimal

B

**bi·as** Neigung *f*; Vorurteil *n*
**bi·as(s)ed** voreingenommen; JUR befangen
**bi·ath·lete** SPORT Biathlet *m*
**bi·ath·lon** SPORT Biathlon *n*
**bib** (Sabber)Lätzchen *n*
**Bi·ble** Bibel *f*
**bib·li·cal** biblisch, Bibel…
**bib·li·og·ra·phy** Bibliografie *f*
**bi·car·bon·ate** *a.* ~ ***of soda*** CHEM doppeltkohlensaures Natron
**bi·cen·te·na·ry** *Br*, **bi·cen·ten·ni·al** Zweihundertjahrfeier *f*
**bi·ceps** ANAT Bizeps *m*
**bick·er** sich zanken *or* streiten
**bi·cy·cle** Fahrrad *n*
**bid 1.** *auction*: bieten **2.** ECON Gebot *n*, Angebot *n*
**bi·en·ni·al** zweijährlich; BOT zweijährig; **bi·en·ni·al·ly** alle zwei Jahre
**bier** (Toten)Bahre *f*
**big** groß; dick, stark; ***talk*** ~ F den Mund voll nehmen
**big·a·my** Bigamie *f*
**big busi·ness** Großunternehmertum *n*
**big·head** F Angeber *m*
**big shot**, **big·wig** F hohes Tier
**bike** F **1.** (Fahr)Rad *n* **2.** Rad fahren
**bik·er** Motorradfahrer(in); Radfahrer(in), Radler(in)
**bi·lat·er·al** bilateral
**bile** Galle *f* (*a. fig*)
**bi·lin·gual** zweisprachig
**bill**[1] ZO Schnabel *m*
**bill**[2] ECON Rechnung *f*; POL (Gesetzes)Vorlage *f*; JUR (An)Klageschrift *f*; Plakat *n*; Banknote *f*, (Geld)Schein *m*
**bill·board** Reklametafel *f*
**bill·fold** Brieftasche *f*
**bil·li·ards** Billard(spiel) *n*
**bil·li·on** Milliarde *f*
**bill| of de·liv·er·y** ECON Lieferschein *m*; ~ **of ex·change** ECON Wechsel *m*; ~ **of sale** JUR Verkaufsurkunde *f*
**bil·low 1.** Woge *f*; (*Rauch- etc*) Schwaden *m* **2.** *a.* ~ ***out*** sich bauschen *or* blähen
**bil·ly goat** ZO Ziegenbock *m*
**bin** (großer) Behälter
**bi·na·ry** MATH, PHYS *etc* binär, Binär…
**bi·na·ry code** IT Binärcode *m*
**bi·na·ry num·ber** MATH Binärzahl *f*
**bind** *v/t* (an-, ein-, um-, auf-, fest-, ver-) binden; *a.* vertraglich binden, verpflichten; einfassen; *v/i* binden
**bind·er** (*esp Buch*)Binder(in); Einband *m*; Aktendeckel *m*
**bind·ing 1.** bindend, verbindlich **2.** Einband *m*; Einfassung *f*, Borte *f*
**bin·go** Bingo *n*
**bi·noc·u·lars**, Fern-, Opernglas *n*
**bi·o·chem·is·try** Biochemie *f*
**bi·o·de·gra·da·ble** biologisch abbaubar, umweltfreundlich
**bi·og·ra·pher** Biograf *m*
**bi·og·ra·phy** Biografie *f*
**bi·o·log·i·cal** biologisch
**bi·ol·o·gist** Biologe *m*, Biologin *f*
**bi·ol·o·gy** Biologie *f*
**bi·o·rhythms** Biorhythmus *m*
**bi·o·tope** Biotop *n*
**bi·ped** ZO Zweifüßer *m*
**birch** BOT Birke *f*
**bird** ZO Vogel *m*
**bird·cage** Vogelkäfig *m*
**bird flu** Vogelgrippe *f*
**bird of pas·sage** ZO Zugvogel *m*
**bird of prey** ZO Raubvogel *m*
**bird sanc·tu·a·ry** Vogelschutzgebiet *n*
**bird·seed** Vogelfutter *n*
**bird's-eye view** Vogelperspektive *f*
**bi·ro**® Kugelschreiber *m*
**birth** Geburt *f*; Herkunft *f*; ***give*** ~ ***to*** gebären, zur Welt bringen
**birth cer·tif·i·cate** Geburtsurkunde *f*
**birth con·trol** Geburtenregelung *f*
**birth·day** Geburtstag *m*; ***happy*** ~***!*** alles Gute *or* herzlichen Glückwunsch zum Geburtstag!
**birth·mark** Muttermal *n*
**birth·place** Geburtsort *m*
**birth·rate** Geburtenziffer *f*
**bis·cuit** *Br* Keks *m*, *n*, Plätzchen *n*
**bi·sex·u·al** bisexuell
**bish·op** REL Bischof *m*; *chess*: Läufer *m*
**bish·op·ric** REL Bistum *n*
**bi·son** ZO Bison *m*; Wisent *m*
**bit** Bisschen *n*, Stück(chen) *n*; Gebiss *n* (*am Zaum*); (Schlüssel)Bart *m*; IT Bit *n*; ***a*** (***little***) ~ ein (kleines) bisschen
**bitch** ZO Hündin *f*; F *contp* Miststück *n*, Schlampe *f*
**bit den·si·ty** IT Speicherdichte *f*
**bite 1.** Beißen *n*; Biss *m*; Bissen *m*, Happen *m*; TECH Fassen *n*, Greifen *n* **2.** (an)beißen; ZO stechen; GASTR brennen; *fig* schneiden (*cold etc*); beißen (*smoke etc*); TECH fassen, greifen
**bit·ter** bitter; *fig* verbittert

**bit·ters** GASTR Magenbitter *m*
**biz** F → ***business***
**black 1.** schwarz; dunkel; finster; ***have s.th. in ~ and white*** et. schwarz auf weiß haben *or* besitzen; ***be ~ and blue*** blaue Flecken haben; ***beat s.o. ~ and blue*** j-n grün und blau schlagen **2.** schwärzen; ***~ out*** verdunkeln **3.** Schwarz *n*; Schwärze *f*; Schwarze *m, f*
**black·ber·ry** BOT Brombeere *f*
**black·bird** ZO Amsel *f*
**black·board** (Schul-, Wand)Tafel *f*
**black box** AVIAT Flugschreiber *m*
**black cur·rant** BOT schwarze Johannisbeere
**black·en** *v/t* schwärzen; *fig* anschwärzen; *v/i* schwarz werden
**black eye** blaues Auge, Veilchen *n*
**black·head** MED Mitesser *m*
**black ice** Glatteis *n*
**black·ing** schwarze Schuhwichse
**black·leg** *Br* Streikbrecher *m*
**black·mail 1.** Erpressung *f* **2.** *j-n* erpressen; **black·mail·er** Erpresser(in)
**black mar·ket** Schwarzmarkt *m*
**black·ness** Schwärze *f*
**black·out** Verdunkelung *f*; Black-out *n, m*; ELECTR Stromausfall *m*; Ohnmacht *f*
**black pud·ding** GASTR Blutwurst *f*
**black sheep** *fig* schwarzes Schaf
**black·smith** Schmied *m*
**blad·der** ANAT Blase *f*
**blade** TECH Blatt *n*, Schaufel *f*; Klinge *f*; Schneide *f*; BOT Halm *m*
**blame 1.** Tadel *m*; Schuld *f* **2.** tadeln; ***be to ~ for*** schuld sein an (*dat*)
**blame·less** untadelig
**blanch** *v/t* bleichen; GASTR blanchieren; *v/i* erbleichen, bleich werden
**blank 1.** leer; unausgefüllt, unbeschrieben; ECON Blanko…; verdutzt **2.** Leere *f*; leerer Raum, Lücke *f*; unbeschriebenes Blatt, Formular *n*; *lottery*: Niete *f*; **~ car·tridge** Platzpatrone *f*; **~ check** (*Br* **cheque**) ECON Blankoscheck *m*
**blan·ket 1.** (Woll)Decke *f* **2.** zudecken
**blare** brüllen, plärren (*radio etc*), schmettern (*trumpet*)
**blas·pheme** lästern
**blas·phe·my** Gotteslästerung *f*
**blast 1.** Windstoß *m*; MUS Ton *m*; TECH Explosion *f*; Druckwelle *f*; Sprengung *f* **2.** sprengen; *fig* zunichtemachen; ***~ off*** (***into space***) in den Weltraum schießen; ***~ off*** abheben, starten (*rocket*); ***~!*** verdammt!; ***~ you!*** der Teufel soll dich holen!; ***~ed*** verdammt, verflucht
**blast fur·nace** TECH Hochofen *m*
**blast-off** Start *m* (*of a rocket*)
**bla·tant** offenkundig, eklatant
**blaze 1.** Flamme(n *pl*) *f*, Feuer *n*; heller Schein; *fig* Ausbruch *m* **2.** brennen, lodern; leuchten
**blaz·er** Blazer *m*
**bla·zon** Wappen *n*
**bleach** bleichen
**bleak** öde, kahl; rau; *fig* trüb, freudlos, finster
**blear·y** trübe, verschwommen
**bleat** ZO **1.** Blöken *n* **2.** blöken
**bleed** *v/i* bluten; *v/t* MED zur Ader lassen; F schröpfen
**bleed·ing** MED Blutung *f*; Aderlass *m*
**bleep 1.** Piepton *m* **2.** *j-n* anpiepsen
**bleep·er** *Br* F Piepser *m*
**blem·ish 1.** (*a.* Schönheits)Fehler *m*; Makel *m* **2.** entstellen
**blend 1.** (sich) (ver)mischen; GASTR verschneiden **2.** Mischung *f*; GASTR Verschnitt *m*
**blend·er** Mixer *m*, Mixgerät *n*
**bless** segnen; preisen; ***be ~ed with*** gesegnet sein mit; (***God***) ***~ you!*** alles Gute!; Gesundheit!; ***~ me!, ~ my heart!, ~ my soul!*** F du meine Güte!
**bless·ed** selig, gesegnet; F verflixt
**bless·ing** Segen *m*
**blight** BOT Mehltau *m*
**blind 1.** blind (*fig* ***to*** gegen[über]); unübersichtlich **2.** Rouleau *n*, Rollo *n*; ***the ~*** die Blinden *pl* **3.** blenden; *fig* blind machen (***to*** für, gegen)
**blind al·ley** Sackgasse *f*
**blind·ers** Scheuklappen *pl*
**blind·fold 1.** blindlings **2.** *j-m* die Augen verbinden **3.** Augenbinde *f*
**blind·ly** *fig* blindlings
**blind·ness** Blindheit *f*; Verblendung *f*
**blind·worm** ZO Blindschleiche *f*
**blink 1.** Blinzeln *n* **2.** blinzeln, zwinkern; blinken
**blink·ers** *Br* Scheuklappen *pl*
**bliss** Seligkeit *f*, Wonne *f*
**blis·ter** MED, TECH **1.** Blase *f* **2.** Blasen hervorrufen auf (*dat*); Blasen ziehen *or* TECH werfen
**blitz** MIL **1.** heftiger Luftangriff **2.** schwer

bombardieren

**bliz·zard** Blizzard *m*, Schneesturm *m*

**bloat·ed** (an)geschwollen, (auf)gedunsen; *fig* aufgeblasen

**bloat·er** GASTR Bückling *m*

**blob** Klecks *m*

**block** **1.** Block *m*, Klotz *m*; Baustein *m*, (Bau)Klötzchen *n*; (*Schreib-*, *Notiz-*) Block *m*; (Häuser)Block *m*; TECH Verstopfung *f*; *fig geistige etc* Sperre; **~ (*of flats*)** *Br* Wohn-, Mietshaus *n* **2.** *a.* ***~ up*** (ab-, ver)sperren, blockieren, verstopfen

**block·ade** **1.** Blockade *f* **2.** blockieren

**block·bust·er** F Kassenmagnet *m*, Kassenschlager *m*

**block·head** F Dummkopf *m*

**block let·ters** Blockschrift *f*

**blog** IT Blog *m*, *n*

**blond** **1.** Blonde *m* **2.** blond; hell (*skin*)

**blonde** **1.** blond **2.** Blondine *f*

**blood** Blut *n*; ***in cold ~*** kaltblütig; **~ bank** MED Blutbank *f*; **~ clot** MED Blutgerinnsel *n*; **~ cor·pus·cle** MED Blutkörperchen *n*

**blood·cur·dling** grauenhaft

**blood do·nor** MED Blutspender(in)

**blood group** MED Blutgruppe *f*

**blood·hound** ZO Bluthund *m*

**blood pres·sure** MED Blutdruck *m*

**blood·shed** Blutvergießen *n*

**blood·shot** blutunterlaufen

**blood test** MED Blutprobe *f*

**blood·thirst·y** blutdürstig

**blood ves·sel** ANAT Blutgefäß *n*

**blood·y** blutig; *Br* F verdammt, verflucht

**bloom** **1.** Blume *f*, Blüte *f*; *fig* Blüte(zeit) *f* **2.** blühen; *fig* (er)strahlen

**blos·som** **1.** Blüte *f* **2.** blühen; *fig* ***~ into*** erblühen zu

**blot** **1.** Klecks *m*; *fig* Makel *m* **2.** beklecksen

**blotch** Klecks *m*; Hautfleck *m*

**blotch·y** fleckig

**blot·ter** (Tinten)Löscher *m*

**blot·ting pa·per** Löschpapier *n*

**blouse** Bluse *f*

**blow**[1] Schlag *m* (*a. fig*), Stoß *m*

**blow**[2] *v/i* blasen, wehen; keuchen, schnaufen; explodieren; platzen (*tire*); ELECTR durchbrennen; ***~ up*** in die Luft fliegen; explodieren; *v/t*: ***~ one's nose*** sich die Nase putzen; ***~ out*** ausblasen; ***~ up*** sprengen; PHOT vergrößern

**blow-dry** föhnen

**blow·fly** ZO Schmeißfliege *f*

**blow·pipe** Blasrohr *n*

**blow-up** PHOT Vergrößerung *f*

**blud·geon** Knüppel *m*

**blue** **1.** blau; F melancholisch, traurig, schwermütig **2.** Blau *n*; ***out of the ~*** *fig* aus heiterem Himmel

**blue·ber·ry** BOT Blau-, Heidelbeere *f*

**blue·bot·tle** ZO Schmeißfliege *f*

**blue-col·lar work·er** Arbeiter(in)

**blues** MUS Blues *m*; F Melancholie *f*; ***have the ~*** F den Moralischen haben

**bluff**[1] Steilufer *n*

**bluff**[2] **1.** Bluff *m* **2.** bluffen

**blu·ish** bläulich

**blun·der** **1.** Fehler *m*, F Schnitzer *m* **2.** e-n (groben) Fehler machen; verpfuschen, F verpatzen

**blunt** stumpf; *fig* offen

**blunt·ly** freiheraus

**blur** [blɜː] **1.** *v/t* verwischen; verschmieren; PHOT, TV verwackeln, verzerren; *fig* trüben **2.** *v/i* verschwimmen (*a. fig*)

**blurt**: ***~ out*** herausplatzen mit

**blush** **1.** Erröten *n*, Schamröte *f* **2.** erröten, rot werden

**blus·ter** brausen (*wind*); *fig* poltern, toben

**BO** ABBR → ***body odo(u)r***

**boar** ZO Eber *m*; Keiler *m*

**board** **1.** Brett *n*; (Anschlag)Brett *n*; Konferenztisch *m*; Ausschuss *m*, Kommission *f*; Behörde *f*; Verpflegung *f*; Pappe *f*, Karton *m*; SPORT (Surf)Board *n*; ***on ~ a train*** in e-m Zug **2.** *v/t* dielen, verschalen; beköstigen; an Bord gehen; MAR entern; RAIL *etc* einsteigen in; *v/i* in Kost sein, wohnen

**board·er** Kostgänger(in); Pensionsgast *m*; Internatsschüler(in)

**board game** Brettspiel *n*

**board·ing| card** AVIAT Bordkarte *f*; **~ house** Pension *f*, Fremdenheim *n*; **~ school** Internat *n*

**board of di·rec·tors** ECON Aufsichtsrat *m*

**Board of Trade** Handelskammer *f*; *Br* Handelsministerium *n*

**board·walk** Strandpromenade *f*

**boast** **1.** Prahlerei *f* **2.** (***of, about***) sich rühmen (*gen*), prahlen (mit)

**boat** Boot *n*; Schiff *n*

B

**bob** **1.** Knicks *m*; kurzer Haarschnitt; *Br* HIST F Schilling *m* **2.** *v/t Haar* kurz schneiden; *v/i* sich auf und ab bewegen; knicksen
**bob·bin** Spule *f* (*a.* ELECTR)
**bob·sleigh** SPORT Bob *m*
**bod·ice** Mieder *n*; Oberteil *n*
**bod·i·ly** körperlich
**bod·y** Körper *m*, Leib *m*; Leiche *f*; JUR Körperschaft *f*; Hauptteil *m*; MOT Karosserie *f*; MIL Truppenkörper *m*
**bod·y·guard** Leibwache *f*; Leibwächter *m*
**bod·y| o·do(u)r** (*abbr* ***BO***) Körpergeruch *m*; **~ stock·ing** Body *m*
**bod·y·work** MOT Karosserie *f*
**Boer** **1.** Bure *m* **2.** Buren…
**bog** Sumpf *m*, Morast *m*
**bo·gus** falsch; Schwindel…
**boil**[1] MED Geschwür *n*, Furunkel *m*, *n*
**boil**[2] **1.** kochen, sieden **2.** Kochen *n*, Sieden *n*
**boil·er** (Dampf)Kessel *m*; Boiler *m*
**boil·er suit** Overall *m*
**boil·ing point** Siedepunkt *m* (*a. fig*)
**bois·ter·ous** ungestüm; heftig, laut; lärmend
**bold** kühn, verwegen; keck, dreist, unverschämt; steil; PRINT fett; *words* ***in ~ print*** fett gedruckt; **bold·ness** Kühnheit *f*, Verwegenheit *f*; Dreistigkeit *f*
**bol·ster** **1.** Keilkissen *n* **2.** ***~ up*** *fig* (unter)stützen, *j-m* Mut machen
**bolt** **1.** Bolzen *m*; Riegel *m*; Blitz(strahl) *m*; plötzlicher Satz, Fluchtversuch *m* **2.** *adv*: ***~ upright*** kerzengerade **3.** *v/t* verriegeln; F hinunterschlingen; *v/i* davonlaufen, ausreißen; zo scheuen, durchgehen
**bomb** **1.** Bombe *f*; ***the ~*** die Atombombe **2.** bombardieren; **bom·bard** bombardieren; **bomb·er** AVIAT Bomber *m*; Bombenleger *m*
**bomb·proof** bombensicher
**bomb·shell** Bombe *f* (*a. fig*)
**bo·nan·za** *fig* Goldgrube *f*
**bond** Bund *m*, Verbindung *f*; ECON Schuldverschreibung *f*, Obligation *f*; ***in ~*** ECON unter Zollverschluss
**bond·age** Hörigkeit *f*
**bonds** *fig* Bande *pl*
**bone** **1.** ANAT Knochen *m*, *pl a.* Gebeine *pl*; zo Gräte *f* **2.** die Knochen auslösen (aus); entgräten
**bon·fire** Feuer *n* im Freien; Freudenfeuer *n*
**bon·net** Haube *f*; *Br* Motorhaube *f*
**bo·nus** ECON Bonus *m*, Prämie *f*; Gratifikation *f*
**bon·y** knöchern; knochig
**boo** *int* buh!; THEA ***~ off the stage***, *soccer*: ***~ off the park*** auspfeifen
**boobs** *sl* Titten *pl*
**boo·by** F Trottel *m*
**book** **1.** Buch *n*; Heft *n*; Liste *f*; Block *m* **2.** buchen; eintragen; SPORT verwarnen; *Fahrkarte etc* lösen; *Platz etc* (vor)bestellen, reservieren lassen; *Gepäck* aufgeben; ***~ in*** *esp Br* sich (*im Hotel*) eintragen; ***~ in at*** absteigen in (*dat*); ***~ed up*** ausgebucht, ausverkauft, belegt
**book·case** Bücherschrank *m*
**book·ing** Buchen *n*, (Vor)Bestellung *f*; SPORT Verwarnung *f*; **~ clerk** Schalterbeamte *m*, -beamtin *f*; **~ of·fice** Fahrkartenausgabe *f*, -schalter *m*; THEA Kasse *f*
**book·keep·er** ECON Buchhalter(in)
**book·keep·ing** ECON Buchhaltung *f*, Buchführung *f*
**book·let** Büchlein *n*, Broschüre *f*
**book·mak·er** Buchmacher *m*
**book·mark(·er)** Lesezeichen *n*
**book·sell·er** Buchhändler(in)
**book·shelf** Bücherregal *n*
**book·shop** *esp Br*, **book·store** Buchhandlung *f*
**book·worm** *fig* Bücherwurm *m*
**boom**[1] ECON **1.** Boom *m*, Aufschwung *m*, Hochkonjunktur *f*, Hausse *f* **2.** e-n Boom erleben
**boom**[2] MAR Baum *m*, Spiere *f*; TECH (Kran)Ausleger *m*; *film*, TV (Mikrofon)Galgen *m*
**boom**[3] dröhnen, donnern
**boor·ish** ungehobelt
**boost** **1.** hochschieben; ECON in die Höhe treiben; ankurbeln; ELECTR verstärken; TECH erhöhen; *fig* stärken, Auftrieb geben (*dat*) **2.** Erhöhung *f*; Auftrieb *m*; ELECTR Verstärkung *f*
**boot**[1] Stiefel *m*; *Br* MOT Kofferraum *m*
**boot**[2]: **~ (*up*)** IT laden
**boot**[3]: ***to ~*** obendrein
**boot·ee** (*Damen*)Halbstiefel *m*
**booth** (Markt- *etc*)Bude *f*; (Messe-)Stand *m*; (Wahl- *etc*)Kabine *f*; (Tele-

B

fon)Zelle *f*

**boot·lace** Schnürsenkel *m*

**boot·y** Beute *f*

**booze** F **1.** saufen **2.** Zeug *n*; Sauferei *f*

**bor·der 1.** Rand *m*, Saum *m*, Einfassung *f*; Rabatte *f*; Grenze *f* **2.** einfassen; (um)säumen; grenzen (***on*** an *acc*)

**bore**[1] **1.** Bohrloch *n*; TECH Kaliber *n* **2.** bohren

**bore**[2] **1.** Langweiler *m*; langweilige *or* lästige Sache **2.** *j-n* langweilen; ***be ~d*** sich langweilen

**bore·dom** Lang(e)weile *f*

**bor·ing** langweilig

**bo·rough** Stadtteil *m*; Stadtgemeinde *f*; Stadtbezirk *m*

**bor·row** (sich) *et.* borgen *or* (aus)leihen

**bos·om** Busen *m*; *fig* Schoß *m*

**boss** F **1.** Boss *m*, Chef *m* **2.** *a.* ***~ about, ~ around*** herumkommandieren

**boss·y** F herrisch

**bo·tan·i·cal** botanisch

**bot·a·ny** Botanik *f*

**botch 1.** Pfusch *m* **2.** verpfuschen

**both** beide(s); ***~ … and …*** sowohl … als (auch) …

**both·er 1.** Belästigung *f*, Störung *f*, Plage *f*, Mühe *f* **2.** belästigen, stören, plagen; ***don't ~!*** bemühen Sie sich nicht!

**bot·tle 1.** Flasche *f* **2.** in Flaschen abfüllen; **~ bank** *Br* Altglascontainer *m*

**bot·tle·neck** *fig* Engpass *m*

**bot·tle o·pen·er** Flaschenöffner *m*

**bot·tom** unterster Teil, Boden *m*, Fuß *m*, Unterseite *f*; Grund *m*; F Hintern *m*, Popo *m*; ***be at the ~ of s.th.*** hinter e-r Sache stecken; ***get to the ~ of s.th.*** e-r Sache auf den Grund gehen

**bough** Ast *m*, Zweig *m*

**boul·der** Geröllblock *m*, Findling *m*

**bounce 1.** aufprallen *or* aufspringen (lassen); springen, hüpfen, stürmen; ECON F platzen (*check*) **2.** Sprung *m*, Satz *m*; F Schwung *m*

**bounc·ing** kräftig, stramm

**bound**[1] unterwegs (***for*** nach)

**bound**[2] *mst pl* Grenze *f*, *fig a.* Schranke *f*

**bound**[3] **1.** Sprung *m*, Satz *m* **2.** springen, hüpfen; auf-, abprallen

**bound·a·ry** Grenze *f*

**bound·less** grenzenlos

**boun·te·ous, boun·ti·ful** freigebig, reichlich

**boun·ty** Freigebigkeit *f*; großzügige Spende *f*; Prämie *f*

**bou·quet** Bukett *n* (*a.* GASTR), Strauß *m*; GASTR Blume *f*

**bout** SPORT (*Box-*, *Ring*)Kampf *m*; MED Anfall *m*

**bou·tique** Boutique *f*

**bow**[1] **1.** Verbeugung *f* **2.** *v/i* sich verbeugen *or* verneigen (***to*** vor *dat*); *fig* sich beugen *or* unterwerfen (***to*** *dat*); *v/t* biegen; beugen, neigen

**bow**[2] MAR Bug *m*

**bow**[3] Bogen *m*; Schleife *f*

**bow·els** ANAT Darm *m*; Eingeweide *pl*

**bowl**[1] Schale *f*, Schüssel *f*, Napf *m*; (*Zucker*)Dose *f*; Becken *n*; (*Pfeifen-*) Kopf *m*

**bowl**[2] **1.** (*Bowling-*, *Kegel- etc*)Kugel *f* **2.** kegeln; rollen (*bowling ball*); *cricket*: werfen

**bow-leg·ged** o-beinig

**bowl·er**[1] Bowlingspieler(in); Kegler(in)

**bowl·er**[2], *a.* **~ hat** *esp Br* Bowler *m*, F Melone *f*

**bowl·ing** Bowling *n*; Kegeln *n*; ***go ~*** kegeln; **~ al·ley** Kegelbahn *f*; **~ ball** Kegelkugel *f*

**box**[1] Kasten *m*, Kiste *f*; Büchse *f*, Dose *f*, Kästchen *n*; Schachtel *f*; Behälter *m*; TECH Gehäuse *n*; Postfach *n*; *Br* (Telefon)Zelle *f*; JUR Zeugenstand *m*; THEA Loge *f*; MOT, ZO Box *f*

**box**[2] **1.** SPORT boxen; F ***~ s.o.'s ears*** j-n ohrfeigen **2.** F ***a ~ on the ear*** e-e Ohrfeige

**box**[3] [bɒks] BOT Buchsbaum *m*

**box·er** Boxer *m*

**box·ing** Boxen *n*, Boxsport *m*

**Box·ing Day** *Br* der zweite Weihnachtsfeiertag

**box num·ber** Chiffre(nummer) *f*

**box of·fice** Theaterkasse *f*

**boy** Junge *m*, Knabe *m*, Bursche *m*

**boy·cott 1.** boykottieren **2.** Boykott *m*

**boy·friend** Freund *m*

**boy·hood** Knabenjahre *pl*, Jugend (-zeit) *f*

**boy·ish** jungenhaft

**boy scout** Pfadfinder *m*

**bra** BH *m* (*Büstenhalter*)

**brace 1.** TECH Strebe *f*, Stützbalken *m*; (Zahn)Klammer *f*, (-)Spange *f* **2.** TECH verstreben, versteifen, stützen

**brace·let** Armband *n*

**brac·es** *Br* Hosenträger *pl*

**brack·et** TECH Träger *m*, Halter *m*, Stütze *f*; PRINT Klammer *f*; (*esp Alters-, Steuer*)Klasse *f*; ***lower income ~*** niedrige Einkommensgruppe

**brack·ish** brackig, salzig

**brag** prahlen (***about*** mit)

**brag·gart** Prahler *m*, F Angeber *m*

**braid 1.** Zopf *m*; Borte *f*, Tresse *f* **2.** flechten; mit Borte besetzen

**brain** ANAT Gehirn *n*, *often pl fig a.* Verstand *m*, Intelligenz *f*, Kopf *m*

**brain·storm** Geistesblitz *m*

**brain·wash** *j-n* e-r Gehirnwäsche unterziehen

**brain·wash·ing** Gehirnwäsche *f*

**brain·wave** *Br* Geistesblitz *m*

**brain·y** F gescheit

**braise** GASTR schmoren

**brake** TECH **1.** Bremse *f* **2.** bremsen

**brake·light** MOT Bremslicht *n*

**bram·ble** BOT Brombeerstrauch *m*

**bran** AGR Kleie *f*

**branch 1.** Ast *m*, Zweig *m*; *fig* Fach *n*; Linie *f* (*des Stammbaumes*); ECON Zweigstelle *f*, Filiale *f* **2.** sich verzweigen; abzweigen

**brand 1.** ECON (Schutz-, Handels)Marke *f*, Warenzeichen *n*; Markenname *m*; Sorte *f*, Klasse *f*; Brandmal *n* **2.** einbrennen; brandmarken

**bran·dish** schwingen

**brand name** ECON Markenname *m*

**brand-new** nagelneu

**bran·dy** Kognak *m*, Weinbrand *m*

**brass** Messing *n*; F Unverschämtheit *f*

**brass band** MUS Blaskapelle *f*

**bras·sière** Büstenhalter *m*

**brat** *contp* Balg *m*, *n*, Gör *n*

**brave 1.** tapfer, mutig, unerschrocken **2.** trotzen; mutig begegnen (*dat*)

**brav·er·y** Tapferkeit *f*

**brawl 1.** Krawall *m*; Rauferei *f* **2.** Krawall machen; raufen

**brawn·y** muskulös

**bray 1.** ZO Eselsschrei *m* **2.** ZO schreien; *fig* wiehern

**bra·zen** unverschämt, unverfroren, frech

**Bra·zil** Brasilien *n*; **Bra·zil·ian 1.** brasilianisch **2.** Brasilianer(in)

**breach 1.** Bruch *m*; *fig* Verletzung *f*; MIL Bresche *f* **2.** e-e Bresche schlagen in (*acc*)

**bread** Brot *n*; ***brown ~*** Schwarzbrot *n*; ***know which side one's ~ is buttered*** F s-n Vorteil (er)kennen

**breadth** Breite *f*

**break 1.** Bruch *m*; Lücke *f*; Pause *f* (*Br a.* PED), Unterbrechung *f*; (plötzlicher) Wechsel, Umschwung *m*; (*Tages*)Anbruch *m*; ***give s.o. a ~*** F j-m e-e Chance geben; ***take a ~*** e-e Pause machen; ***without a ~*** ununterbrochen **2.** *v/t* (ab-, auf-, durch-, zer)brechen; zerschlagen, kaputt machen; ZO *a.* ***~ in*** zähmen, abrichten, zureiten; *Gesetz, Vertrag etc* brechen; *Kode etc* knacken; *schlechte Nachricht* (schonend) beibringen; *v/i* brechen (*a. fig*); (zer)brechen, (zer)reißen, kaputtgehen; anbrechen (*Tag*); METEOR umschlagen; *fig* ausbrechen (***into*** in *Tränen etc*); ***~ away*** ab-, losbrechen; sich losmachen *or* losreißen; ***~ down*** ein-, niederreißen, *Haus* abbrechen; zusammenbrechen (*a. fig*); versagen; MOT e-e Panne haben; *fig* scheitern; ***~ in*** einbrechen, eindringen; ***~ into*** einbrechen in (*ein Haus etc*); ***~ off*** abbrechen, *fig a.* Schluss machen mit; ***~ out*** ausbrechen; ***~ through*** durchbrechen; *fig* den Durchbruch schaffen; ***~ up*** abbrechen, beenden, schließen; (sich) auflösen; *fig* zerbrechen, auseinandergehen

**break·a·ble** zerbrechlich

**break·age** Bruch *m*

**break·a·way 1.** Trennung *f* **2.** Splitter…

**break·down** Zusammenbruch *m* (*a. fig*); TECH Maschinenschaden *m*; MOT Panne *f*; ***nervous ~*** MED Nervenzusammenbruch *m*; **~ lor·ry** *Br* MOT Abschleppwagen *m*; **~ ser·vice** *Br* MOT Pannendienst *m*, Pannenhilfe *f*; **~ truck** *Br* MOT Abschleppwagen *m*

**break·fast 1.** Frühstück *n*; ***have ~*** → **2.** frühstücken

**break·through** *fig* Durchbruch *m*

**break·up** Aufhebung *f*; Auflösung *f*

**breast** ANAT Brust *f*; Busen *m*; *fig* Herz *n*

**breast·stroke** Brustschwimmen *n*

**breath** Atem(zug) *m*; Hauch *m*; ***be out of ~*** außer Atem sein; ***waste one's ~*** in den Wind reden

**breath·a·lyse** *Br*, **breath·a·lyze** F (ins Röhrchen) blasen *or* pusten lassen

**breath·a·lys·er®** *Br*, **breath·alyz·er®** Alkoholtestgerät *n*, F Röhrchen *n*

B

**breathe** atmen
**breath·less** atemlos
**breath·tak·ing** atemberaubend
**breech·es** Kniebund-, Reithosen *pl*
**breed 1.** zo Rasse *f*, Zucht *f* **2.** *v/t* BOT, ZO züchten; *v/i* BIOL sich fortpflanzen
**breed·er** Züchter(in); Zuchttier *n*; PHYS Brüter *m*
**breed·ing** BIOL Fortpflanzung *f*; (Tier-)Zucht *f*; *fig* Erziehung *f*; (gutes) Benehmen
**breeze** Brise *f*
**breth·ren** *esp* REL Brüder *pl*
**brew** brauen; *Tee* zubereiten, aufbrühen
**brew·er** (Bier)Brauer *m*
**brew·er·y** Brauerei *f*
**bri·ar** → ***brier***
**bribe 1.** Bestechungsgeld *n*, -geschenk *n*; Bestechung *f* **2.** bestechen
**brib·er·y** Bestechung *f*
**brick** Ziegel(stein) *m*, Backstein *m*; *Br* Baustein *m*, (Bau)Klötzchen *n*
**brick·lay·er** Maurer *m*
**brick·yard** Ziegelei *f*
**brid·al** Braut…; **bride** Braut *f*
**bride·groom** Bräutigam *m*
**brides·maid** Brautjungfer *f*
**bridge 1.** Brücke *f* **2.** e-e Brücke schlagen über (*acc*); *fig* überbrücken
**bri·dle 1.** Zaum *m*; Zügel *m* **2.** (auf)zäumen; zügeln; ~ **path** Reitweg *m*
**brief 1.** kurz, bündig **2.** instruieren, genaue Anweisungen geben (*dat*)
**brief·case** Aktenmappe *f*
**briefs** Slip *m*
**bri·er** BOT Dornstrauch *m*; Wilde Rose
**bri·gade** MIL Brigade *f*
**bright** hell, glänzend; klar; heiter; lebhaft; gescheit
**bright·en** *v/t a.* ~ ***up*** heller machen, aufhellen, erhellen; aufheitern; *v/i a.* ~ ***up*** sich aufhellen
**bright·ness** Helligkeit *f*; Glanz *m*; Heiterkeit *f*; Gescheitheit *f*
**brill** *Br* F super, toll
**bril·liance**, **bril·lian·cy** Glanz *m*; *fig* Brillanz *f*
**bril·liant 1.** glänzend; hervorragend, brillant **2.** Brillant *m*
**brim 1.** Rand *m*; Krempe *f* **2.** bis zum Rande füllen *or* voll sein
**brim·ful(l)** randvoll
**brine** Sole *f*; Lake *f*
**bring** bringen, mitbringen, herbringen; *j-n* dazu bringen (***to do*** zu tun); ~ ***about*** zustande bringen; bewirken; ~ ***forth*** hervorbringen; ~ ***off*** *et.* fertigbringen, schaffen; ~ ***on*** verursachen; ~ ***out*** herausbringen; ~ ***round*** *Ohnmächtigen* wieder zu sich bringen; *Kranken* wieder auf die Beine bringen; ~ ***up*** auf-, großziehen; erziehen; zur Sprache bringen
**brink** Rand *m* (*a. fig*)
**brisk** flott; lebhaft; frisch
**bris·tle 1.** Borste *f*; (Bart)Stoppel *f* **2.** *a.* ~ ***up*** sich sträuben; zornig werden; strotzen, wimmeln (***with*** von)
**bris·tly** stoppelig, Stoppel…
**Brit** F Brite *m*, Britin *f*
**Brit·ain** Britannien *n*
**Brit·ish** britisch; ***the*** ~ die Briten *pl*
**Brit·on** Brite *m*, Britin *f*
**brit·tle** spröde, zerbrechlich
**broach** *Thema* anschneiden
**broad** breit; weit; hell; deutlich (*hint etc*); derb (*humor etc*); stark (*accent*); allgemein; weitherzig; liberal
**broad·cast 1.** im Rundfunk *or* Fernsehen bringen, ausstrahlen, übertragen; senden **2.** *radio*, TV Sendung *f*
**broad·cast·er** Rundfunk-, Fernsehsprecher(in)
**broad·en** verbreitern, erweitern
**broad jump** SPORT Weitsprung *m*
**broad·mind·ed** liberal
**bro·cade** Brokat *m*
**bro·chure** Broschüre *f*, Prospekt *m*
**brogue** fester Straßenschuh
**broil** grillen
**broke** F pleite, abgebrannt
**bro·ken** zerbrochen, kaputt; gebrochen (*a. fig*); zerrüttet
**brok·en-heart·ed** verzweifelt, untröstlich
**bro·ker** ECON Makler *m*
**bron·chi·tis** MED Bronchitis *f*
**bronze 1.** Bronze *f* **2.** bronzefarben; Bronze…
**brooch** Brosche *f*
**brood** zo **1.** Brut *f* **2.** Brut… **3.** brüten (*a. fig*)
**brook** Bach *m*
**broom** Besen *m*
**broth** GASTR Fleischbrühe *f*
**broth·el** Bordell *n*
**broth·er** Bruder *m*; ~(***s***) ***and sister***(***s***) Geschwister *pl*

**broth·er·hood** REL Bruderschaft *f*
**broth·er-in-law** Schwager *m*
**broth·er·ly** brüderlich
**brow** ANAT (Augen)Braue *f*; Stirn *f*; GEOGR Rand *m*
**brow·beat** einschüchtern
**brown 1.** braun **2.** Braun *n* **3.** bräunen; braun werden
**browse** grasen, weiden; *fig* schmökern
**bruise 1.** MED Quetschung *f*, blauer Fleck **2.** quetschen; anstoßen; MED e-e Quetschung *or* e-n blauen Fleck bekommen
**brunch** Brunch *m*
**brush 1.** Bürste *f*; Pinsel *m*; ZO (*Fuchs-*)Rute *f*; Scharmützel *n*; Unterholz *n* **2.** bürsten; fegen; streifen; **~ *against s.o.*** j-n streifen; **~ *away*, ~ *off*** wegbürsten, abwischen; **~ *aside*, ~ *away*** *et.* abtun; **~ *up* (*on*)** *fig* aufpolieren, auffrischen
**brush·wood** Gestrüpp *n*, Unterholz *n*
**brusque** brüsk, barsch
**Brus·sels sprouts** BOT Rosenkohl *m*
**bru·tal** brutal, roh
**bru·tal·i·ty** Brutalität *f*
**brute 1.** brutal; ***with ~ force*** mit roher Gewalt **2.** Vieh *n*; F Untier *n*, Scheusal *n*; Rohling *m*; **brut·ish** *fig* tierisch
**bub·ble 1.** Blase *f* **2.** sprudeln; **~ bath** Badeschaum *m*
**buck**[1] **1.** ZO Bock *m* **2.** bocken
**buck**[2] F Dollar *m*
**buck·et** Eimer *m*, Kübel *m*
**buck·le 1.** Schnalle *f*, Spange *f* **2.** *a.* **~ *up*** zu-, festschnallen; **~ *on*** anschnallen
**buck·skin** Wildleder *n*
**bud 1.** BOT Knospe *f*; *fig* Keim *m* **2.** knospen, keimen
**bud·dy** F Kamerad *m*; Kumpel *m*, Spezi *m*
**budge** *v/i* sich (von der Stelle) rühren; *v/t* (vom Fleck) bewegen
**bud·ger·i·gar** ZO Wellensittich *m*
**bud·get 1.** Budget *n*, Etat *m*; PARL Haushaltsplan *m* **2.** preisgünstig; **~ airline** Billigflieger *m*
**bud·gie** F → ***budgerigar***
**buf·fa·lo** ZO Büffel *m*
**buff·er** TECH Puffer *m*
**buf·fet**[1] schlagen; **~ *about*** durchrütteln, durchschütteln
**buf·fet**[2] Büfett *n*, Anrichte *f*
**buf·fet**[3] (*Frühstücks- etc*)Büfett *n*; Theke *f*
**bug 1.** ZO Wanze *f* (*a.* F *fig*); Insekt *n*; IT Programmfehler *m* **2.** F Wanzen anbringen in (*dat*); F ärgern
**bug·ging| de·vice** Abhörgerät *n*; **~ op·e·ra·tion** Lauschangriff *m*
**bug·gy** Kinderwagen *m*; MOT Buggy *m*
**bu·gle** MUS Wald-, Signalhorn *n*
**build 1.** (er)bauen, errichten **2.** Körperbau *m*, Figur *f*, Statur *f*; **build·er** Erbauer *m*; Bauunternehmer *m*
**build·ing 1.** (Er)Bauen *n*; Bau *m*, Gebäude *n* **2.** Bau…; **~ site** Baustelle *f*
**built-in** eingebaut, Einbau…
**built-up**: **~ *area*** bebautes Gelände *or* Gebiet; geschlossene Ortschaft
**bulb** BOT Zwiebel *f*, Knolle *f*; ELECTR (Glüh)Birne *f*
**bulge 1.** (Aus)Bauchung *f*, Ausbuchtung *f* **2.** sich (aus)bauchen; hervorquellen
**bulk** Umfang *m*, Größe *f*, Masse *f*; Großteil *m*; ***in ~*** ECON lose, unverpackt; en gros; **bulk·y** sperrig
**bull** ZO Bulle *m*, Stier *m*
**bull·dog** ZO Bulldogge *f*
**bull·doze** planieren; F einschüchtern
**bull·doz·er** TECH Bulldozer *m*, Planierraupe *f*
**bul·let** Kugel *f*
**bul·le·tin** Bulletin *n*, Tagesbericht *m*
**bul·le·tin board** Schwarzes Brett
**bul·let·proof** kugelsicher
**bull·fight** Stierkampf *m*
**bul·lion** Gold-, Silberbarren *m*
**bul·lock** ZO Ochse *m*
**bull's-eye**: ***hit the ~*** ins Schwarze treffen (*a. fig*)
**bul·ly 1.** tyrannische Person, Tyrann *m* **2.** einschüchtern, tyrannisieren
**bul·wark** Bollwerk *n* (*a. fig*)
**bum** F **1.** Gammler *m*; Tippelbruder *m*, Vagabund *m*; Nichtstuer *m* **2.** *v/t* schnorren; **~ *around*** herumgammeln
**bum·ble·bee** ZO Hummel *f*
**bump 1.** heftiger Schlag *or* Stoß; Beule *f*; Unebenheit *f* **2.** stoßen; rammen, auf *ein Auto* auffahren; zusammenstoßen; holpern; **~ *into*** *fig j-n* zufällig treffen; F **~ *s.o. off*** j-n umlegen
**bump·er** MOT Stoßstange *f*
**bump·y** holp(e)rig
**bun** süßes Brötchen; (Haar)Knoten *m*
**bunch** Bund *n*, Bündel *n*; F Verein *m*, Haufen *m*; **~ *of flowers*** Blumenstrauß

B

*m*; **~ of grapes** Weintraube *f*; **~ of keys** Schlüsselbund *m*, *n*
**bun·dle 1.** Bündel *n* (*a. fig*), Bund *n* **2.** *v/t a.* **~ up** bündeln
**bun·ga·low** Bungalow *m*
**bun·gee** elastisches Seil
**bun·gee jump·ing** Bungeespringen *n*
**bun·gle 1.** Pfusch *m* **2.** (ver)pfuschen
**bunk** Koje *f*; → **~ bed** Etagenbett *n*
**bun·ny** Häschen *n*
**buoy 1.** MAR Boje *f* **2. ~ up** *fig* Auftrieb geben (*dat*)
**bur·den 1.** Last *f*; Bürde *f* **2.** belasten
**bu·reau** *Br* Schreibtisch *m*; (Spiegel-) Kommode *f*; Büro *n*
**bu·reauc·ra·cy** Bürokratie *f*
**burg·er** GASTR Hamburger *m*
**bur·glar** Einbrecher *m*
**bur·glar·ize** einbrechen in (*acc*)
**bur·glar·y** Einbruch *m*
**bur·gle** *Br* → ***burglarize***
**bur·i·al** Begräbnis *n*
**bur·ly** stämmig, kräftig
**burn 1.** MED Verbrennung *f*, Brandwunde *f*; verbrannte Stelle **2.** (ver-, an-) brennen; **~ down** ab-, niederbrennen; **~ out** ausbrennen; **~ up** auflodern; verbrennen; verglühen (*rocket etc*)
**burn·ing** brennend (*a. fig*)
**burp** F rülpsen, aufstoßen; ein Bäuerchen machen (lassen)
**bur·row 1.** ZO Bau *m* **2.** graben; sich eingraben *or* vergraben
**burst 1.** Bersten *n*; Riss *m*; *fig* Ausbruch *m* **2.** *v/i* bersten, (zer)platzen; zerspringen; explodieren; **~ from** sich losreißen von; **~ in on *or* upon s.o.** bei j-m hereinplatzen; **~ into tears** in Tränen ausbrechen; **~ out** *fig* herausplatzen; *v/t* (auf)sprengen
**bur·y** begraben, vergraben; beerdigen
**bus** Omnibus *m*, Bus *m*
**bus driv·er** Busfahrer *m*
**bush** Busch *m*; Gebüsch *n*
**bush·el** Bushel *m*, Scheffel *m* (*Am 35,24 l, Br 36,37 l*)
**bush·y** buschig
**busi·ness** Geschäft *n*; Arbeit *f*, Beschäftigung *f*, Beruf *m*, Tätigkeit *f*; Angelegenheit *f*; Sache *f*, Aufgabe *f*; **~ of the day** Tagesordnung *f*; **on ~** geschäftlich, beruflich; **you have no ~ doing** (*or* **to do**) **that** Sie haben kein recht, das zu tun; **that's none of your ~** das geht Sie nichts an; → ***mind*** 2
**busi·ness hours** Geschäftszeit *f*
**busi·ness·like** geschäftsmäßig, sachlich
**busi·ness·man** Geschäftsmann *m*
**busi·ness trip** Geschäftsreise *f*
**busi·ness·wom·an** Geschäftsfrau *f*
**bus stop** Bushaltestelle *f*
**bust**[1] Büste *f*
**bust**[2]: **go ~** F pleitegehen
**bus·tle 1.** geschäftiges Treiben **2. ~ about** geschäftig hin und her eilen
**bus·y 1.** beschäftigt; geschäftig; fleißig (**at** bei, an *dat*); belebt (*street*); arbeitsreich (*dat*); TEL besetzt **2.** (*mst* **~ o.s.** sich) beschäftigen (**with** mit)
**bus·y·bod·y** aufdringlicher Mensch, Gschaftlhuber *m*
**bus·y sig·nal** TEL Besetztzeichen *n*
**but 1.** *cj* aber, jedoch; sondern; außer, als; ohne dass; dennoch; **~ then** and(e)rerseits; **he could not ~ laugh** er musste einfach lachen **2.** *prp* außer (*dat*); **all ~ him** alle außer ihm; **the last ~ one** der Vorletzte; **the next ~ one** der Übernächste; **nothing ~** nichts als; **~ for** wenn nicht ... gewesen wäre, ohne **3.** *adv* nur; erst, gerade; **all ~** fast, beinahe
**butch·er 1.** Fleischer *m*, Metzger *m* **2.** (*fig* ab)schlachten
**but·ler** Butler *m*
**butt**[1] **1.** (*of rifle*) (Gewehr-)Kolben *m*; (*of cigar etc*) (Zigarren-)Stummel *m* (*of cigarette*) (Zigaretten-)Kippe *f*; (*with head etc*) (Kopf-)Stoß *m* **2.** (mit dem Kopf) stoßen; **~ in** F sich einmischen (**on** in *acc*)
**butt**[2] (*of wine, beer*) Wein-, Bierfass *n*; (*rainwater tank*) Regentonne *f*
**butt**[3] (*backside*) F Hintern *m*
**but·ter 1.** Butter *f* **2.** mit Butter bestreichen
**but·ter·cup** BOT Butterblume *f*
**but·ter·fly** ZO Schmetterling *m*, Falter *m*
**but·tocks** ANAT Gesäß *n*, F *or* ZO Hinterteil *n*
**but·ton 1.** Knopf *m*; Button *m*, (Ansteck)Plakette *f*, Abzeichen *n* **2.** *mst* **~ up** zuknöpfen
**but·ton·hole** Knopfloch *n*
**but·tress** Strebepfeiler *m*
**buy 1.** F Kauf *m* **2.** (an-, ein)kaufen (**of, from** von; **at** bei); *Fahrkarte* lösen; **~ out** *j-n* abfinden, auszahlen; *Firma*

aufkaufen; ~ ***up*** aufkaufen
**buy·er** Käufer(in); ECON Einkäufer(in)
**buzz 1.** Summen *n*, Surren *n*; Stimmengewirr *n* **2.** *v/i* summen, surren; ~ ***off!*** F schwirr ab!, hau ab!
**buz·zard** ZO Bussard *m*
**buzz·er** ELECTR Summer *m*
**by 1.** *prp* (nahe *or* dicht) bei *or* an, neben (***side*** ~ ***side*** Seite an Seite); vorbei *or* vorüber an; *time*: bis um, bis spätestens (***be back*** ~ ***9.30*** sei um 9 Uhr 30 zurück); während, bei (~ ***day*** bei Tage); per, mit (~ ***bus*** mit dem Bus; ~ ***rail*** per Bahn); nach, …weise (~ ***the dozen*** dutzendweise); nach, gemäß (~ ***my watch*** nach *or* auf m-r Uhr); von (~ ***nature*** von Natur aus); von, durch (***a play*** ~ ***…*** ein Stück von …; ~ ***o.s.*** allein); um (~ ***an inch*** um e-n Zoll); MATH mal (***2*** ~ ***4***); *geteilt* durch (***6*** ~ ***3***) **2.** *adv* vorbei, vorüber (***go*** ~ vorbeigehen, -fahren; *time*: vergehen); beiseite (***put*** ~ beiseitelegen, zurücklegen); ~ ***and large*** im Großen und Ganzen
**by…** Neben…; Seiten…
**bye, bye-bye** *int* F Wiedersehen!, tschüs(s)!
**by-e·lec·tion** PARL Nachwahl *f*
**by·gone 1.** vergangen **2.** ***let*** ~***s be*** ~***s*** lass(t) das Vergangene ruhen
**by·pass 1.** Umgehungsstraße *f*; MED Bypass *m* **2.** umgehen; vermeiden
**by-prod·uct** Nebenprodukt *n*
**by·road** Nebenstraße *f*
**by·stand·er** Zuschauer(in), *pl die* Umstehenden *pl*
**byte** IT Byte *n*
**by·way** Nebenstraße *f*
**by·word** Inbegriff *m*; ***be a*** ~ ***for*** stehen für

# C

**C, c** C, c *n*
**C** *abbr of* ***Celsius*** C, Celsius; ***centigrade*** hundertgradig
**c** *abbr of* ***cent(s)*** Cent *m or pl*; ***century*** Jh., Jahrhundert *n*; ***circa*** ca., zirca, ungefähr; ***cubic*** Kubik…
**cab** Droschke *f*, Taxi *n*; RAIL Führerstand *m*; MOT Fahrerhaus *n*, *a.* TECH Führerhaus *n*
**cab·a·ret** Varieteedarbietung(en *pl*) *f*
**cab·bage** BOT Kohl *m*
**cab·in** Hütte *f*; MAR Kabine *f*, Kajüte *f*; AVIAT Kanzel *f*
**cab·i·net** Schrank *m*, Vitrine *f*; POL Kabinett *n*
**cab·i·net-mak·er** Kunsttischler *m*
**cab·i·net meet·ing** POL Kabinettssitzung *f*
**ca·ble 1.** Kabel *n*; (Draht)Seil *n* **2.** telegrafieren; *j-m Geld* telegrafisch anweisen; TV verkabeln
**ca·ble car** Kabine *f*; Wagen *m*
**ca·ble·gram** (Übersee)Telegramm *n*
**ca·ble| rail·way** Drahtseil-, Kabinenbahn *f*; ~ **tel·e·vi·sion**, ~ **TV** Kabelfernsehen *n*
**cab rank, cab·stand** Taxistand *m*
**cack·la** ZO **1.** Gegacker *n*, Geschnatter *n* **2.** gackern, schnattern
**cac·tus** BOT Kaktus *m*
**ca·dence** MUS Kadenz *f*; (Sprech-)Rhythmus *m*
**ca·det** MIL Kadett *m*
**cadge** *Br* F schnorren
**caf·é, caf·e** Café *n*
**caf·e·te·ri·a** Cafeteria *f*, Selbstbedienungsrestaurant *n*, *a.* Kantine *f*, UNIV Mensa *f*
**cage 1.** Käfig *m*; *mining*: Förderkorb *m* **2.** einsperren
**cake 1.** Kuchen *m*, Torte *f*; Tafel *f Schokolade*, Stück *n Seife* **2.** ~***d with mud*** schmutzverkrustet
**ca·lam·i·ty** großes Unglück, Katastrophe *f*
**cal·cu·late** *v/t* kalkulieren; be-, aus-, errechnen; F vermuten; *v/i*: ~ ***on*** rechnen mit *or* auf (*acc*), zählen auf (*acc*)
**cal·cu·la·tion** Berechnung *f* (*a. fig*); ECON Kalkulation *f*; *fig* Überlegung *f*
**cal·cu·la·tor** TECH (Taschen)Rechner *m*
**cal·en·dar** Kalender *m*
**calf**[1] ANAT Wade *f*
**calf**[2] ZO Kalb *n*
**calf·skin** Kalb(s)fell *n*
**cal·i·ber**, *esp Br* **cal·i·bre** Kaliber *n*

**call 1.** Ruf *m*; TEL Anruf *m*, Gespräch *n*; Ruf *m*, Berufung *f* (***to*** in *ein Amt*; auf *e-n Lehrstuhl*); Aufruf *m*, Aufforderung *f*; Signal *n*; (kurzer) Besuch; ***on ~*** auf Abruf; ***be on ~*** MED Bereitschaftsdienst haben; ***make a ~*** telefonieren **2.** *v/t* (herbei)rufen; (ein)berufen; TEL *j-n* anrufen; *j-n* berufen, ernennen (***to*** zu); nennen; *Aufmerksamkeit* lenken (***to*** auf *acc*); ***be ~ed*** heißen; ***~ s.o. names*** j-n beschimpfen, j-n beleidigen; *v/i* rufen; TEL anrufen; e-n (kurzen) Besuch machen (***on s.o., at s.o.'s*** [***house***] bei j-m); ***~ at a port*** MAR e-n Hafen anlaufen; ***~ for*** rufen nach; *et.* anfordern; *et.* abholen; ***to be ~ed for*** postlagernd; ***~ on*** sich an *j-n* wenden (***for*** wegen); appellieren an (*acc*) (***to do*** zu tun); ***~ on s.o.*** j-n besuchen

**call box** *Br* Telefonzelle *f*

**call·er** Besucher(in); TEL Anrufer(in)

**call-in** → ***phone-in***

**call·ing** Berufung *f*; Beruf *m*

**cal·lous** schwielig; *fig* gefühllos

**cal·lus** Schwiele *f*

**calm 1.** still, ruhig **2.** (Wind)Stille *f*, Ruhe *f* **3.** *often **~ down*** besänftigen, (sich) beruhigen

**cal·o·rie** Kalorie *f*; ***high*** *or* ***rich in ~s*** kalorienreich; ***low in ~s*** kalorienarm, kalorienreduziert

**cal·o·rie-con·scious** kalorienbewusst

**calve** zo kalben

**cam·cor·der** Camcorder *m*, Kamerarekorder *m*

**cam·el** zo Kamel *n*

**cam·e·o** Kamee *f*; THEA, *film*: kleine Nebenrolle, kurze Szene

**cam·e·ra** Kamera *f*, Fotoapparat *m*; **~ phone** Fotohandy *n*

**cam·o·mile** BOT Kamille *f*

**cam·ou·flage 1.** Tarnung *f* **2.** tarnen

**camp 1.** (*Zelt- etc*)Lager *n* **2.** lagern; ***~ out*** zelten, campen

**cam·paign 1.** MIL Feldzug *m* (*a. fig*); *fig* Kampagne *f*, Aktion *f*; POL Wahlkampf *m* **2.** *fig* kämpfen (***for*** für; ***against*** gegen)

**camp bed** *Br*, **camp cot** Feldbett *n*

**camp·er (van)** Campingbus *m*, Wohnmobil *n*

**camp·ground**, **camp·site** Lagerplatz *m*; Zeltplatz *m*, Campingplatz *m*

**cam·pus** Campus *m*, Universitätsgelände *n*

**can**[1] *v/aux ich* kann, *du* kannst *etc*; dürfen, können

**can**[2] **1.** Kanne *f*; (Blech-, Konserven-) Dose *f*, (-)Büchse *f* **2.** einmachen, eindosen

**Can·a·da** Kanada *n*; **Ca·na·di·an 1.** kanadisch **2.** Kanadier(in)

**ca·nal** Kanal *m* (*a.* ANAT)

**ca·nar·y** zo Kanarienvogel *m*

**can·cel** (durch-, aus)streichen; entwerten; rückgängig machen; absagen; ***be ~(l)ed*** ausfallen

**Can·cer** ASTR Krebs *m*; ***he*** (***she***) ***is*** (***a***) ***~*** er (sie) ist (ein) Krebs

**can·cer** MED Krebs *m*

**can·cer·ous** MED Krebs…, krebsbefallen

**can·cer pa·tient** MED Krebskranke *m*, *f*

**can·did** aufrichtig, offen

**can·di·date** Kandidat(in) (***for*** für), Bewerber(in) (***for*** um)

**can·died** kandiert

**can·dle** Kerze *f*; Licht *n*; ***burn the ~ at both ends*** mit s-r Gesundheit Raubbau treiben

**can·dle·stick** Kerzenleuchter *m*, Kerzenständer *m*

**can·do(u)r** Aufrichtigkeit *f*, Offenheit *f*

**can·dy 1.** Kandis(zucker) *m*; Süßigkeiten *pl* **2.** kandieren; **~ floss** Zuckerwatte *f*; **~ store** Süßwarengeschäft *n*

**cane** BOT Rohr *n*; (Rohr)Stock *m*

**ca·nine** Hunde…

**canned** Dosen…, Büchsen…; ***~ fruit*** Obstkonserven *pl*

**can·ne·ry** Konservenfabrik *f*

**can·ni·bal** Kannibale *m*

**can·non** MIL Kanone *f*

**can·ny** schlau

**ca·noe 1.** Kanu *n*, Paddelboot *n* **2.** Kanu fahren, paddeln

**can·on** Kanon *m*; Regel *f*

**can o·pen·er** Dosen-, Büchsenöffner *m*

**can·o·py** Baldachin *m*

**cant** Jargon *m*; Phrase(n *pl*) *f*

**can·tan·ker·ous** F zänkisch, mürrisch

**can·teen** *esp Br* Kantine *f*; MIL Feldflasche *f*; Besteck(kasten *m*) *n*

**can·ter 1.** Kanter *m* **2.** kantern

**can·vas** Segeltuch *n*; Zelt-, Packleinwand *f*; Segel *pl*; PAINT Leinwand *f*; Gemälde *n*

**can·vass 1.** POL Wahlfeldzug *m*; ECON Werbefeldzug *m* **2.** *v/t* eingehend untersuchen *or* erörtern *or* prüfen; POL werben um (*Stimmen*); *v/i* POL e-n Wahlfeldzug veranstalten
**can·yon** GEOGR Cañon *m*, Schlucht *f*
**cap 1.** Kappe *f*; Mütze *f*; Haube *f*; Zündkapsel *f* **2.** (mit e-r Kappe *etc*) bedecken; *fig* krönen; übertreffen
**ca·pa·bil·i·ty** Fähigkeit *f*
**cap·a·ble** fähig (***of*** zu)
**ca·pac·i·ty** (Raum)Inhalt *m*; Fassungsvermögen *n*; Kapazität *f*; Aufnahmefähigkeit *f*; (TECH Leistungs)Fähigkeit *f* (***for*** *ger* zu *inf*); ***in my ~ as*** in meiner Eigenschaft als
**cape**[1] GEOGR Kap *n*, Vorgebirge *n*
**cape**[2] Cape *n*, Umhang *m*
**ca·per 1.** Kapriole *f*, Luftsprung *m*; ***cut ~s*** → **2.** Freuden- *or* Luftsprünge machen
**ca·pil·la·ry** ANAT Haar-, Kapillargefäß *n*
**cap·i·tal 1.** ECON Kapital *n*; Hauptstadt *f*; Großbuchstabe *m* **2.** Kapital…; Tod(es)…; Haupt…; großartig, prima; **~ crime** JUR Kapitalverbrechen *n*
**cap·i·tal·ism** ECON Kapitalismus *m*
**cap·i·tal·ist** ECON Kapitalist *m*
**cap·i·tal·ize** großschreiben; ECON kapitalisieren
**cap·i·tal| let·ter** Großbuchstabe *m*; **~ pun·ish·ment** JUR Todesstrafe *f*
**ca·pit·u·late** kapitulieren (***to*** vor *dat*)
**cap·pu·cci·no** Cappucino *m*
**ca·pri·cious** launisch
**Cap·ri·corn** ASTR Steinbock *m*; ***he*** (***she***) ***is*** (***a***) **~** er (sie) ist (ein) Steinbock
**cap·size** MAR *v/i* kentern; *v/t* zum Kentern bringen
**cap·sule** Kapsel *f*
**cap·tain** (An)Führer *m*; MAR, ECON Kapitän *m*; AVIAT Flugkapitän *m*; MIL Hauptmann *m*; SPORT (Mannschafts-) Kapitän *m*, Spielführer *m*
**cap·tion** Überschrift *f*, Titel *m*; Bildunterschrift *f*; *film*: Untertitel *m*
**cap·ti·vate** *fig* gefangen nehmen, fesseln; **cap·tive 1.** gefangen; gefesselt; ***hold ~*** gefangen halten **2.** Gefangene *m, f*; **cap·tiv·i·ty** Gefangenschaft *f*
**cap·ture 1.** Eroberung *f*; Gefangennahme *f* **2.** fangen, gefangen nehmen; erobern; erbeuten; MAR kapern
**car** Auto *n*, Wagen *m*; (Eisenbahn-, Straßenbahn)Wagen *m*; Gondel *f* (*of a balloon etc*); Kabine *f*; ***by ~*** mit dem Auto, im Auto
**car·a·mel** Karamell *m*; Karamelle *f*
**car·a·van** Karawane *f*; *Br* Wohnwagen *m*; **~ site** Campingplatz *m* für Wohnwagen
**car·a·way** BOT Kümmel *m*
**car·bine** MIL Karabiner *m*
**car·bo·hy·drate** CHEM Kohle(n)hydrat *n*
**car bomb** Autobombe *f*
**car·bon** CHEM Kohlenstoff *m*; → ***carbon copy, carbon paper***
**car·bon cop·y** Durchschlag *m*
**car·bon pa·per** Kohlepapier *n*
**car·bu·ret·(t)or** MOT Vergaser *m*
**car·case** *Br*, **car·cass** Kadaver *m*, Aas *n*; GASTR Rumpf *m*
**car·cin·o·genic** MED karzinogen, krebserregend
**car·ci·no·ma** MED Krebsgeschwulst *f*
**card** Karte *f*; ***play ~s*** Karten spielen; ***have a ~ up one's sleeve*** *fig* (noch) e-n Trumpf in der Hand haben
**card·board** Pappe *f*; **~ box** Pappschachtel *f*, Pappkarton *m*
**car·di·ac** MED Herz…; **~ pace·mak·er** MED Herzschrittmacher *m*
**car·di·gan** Strickjacke *f*
**car·di·nal 1.** Grund…, Haupt…, Kardinal…; scharlachrot **2.** REL Kardinal *m*
**car·di·nal num·ber** MATH Kardinalzahl *f*, Grundzahl *f*
**card in·dex** Kartei *f*
**card phone** Kartentelefon *n*
**card·sharp·er** Falschspieler *m*
**car dump** Autofriedhof *m*
**care 1.** Sorge *f*; Sorgfalt *f*; Vorsicht *f*; Obhut *f*, Pflege *f*; ***needing ~*** MED pflegebedürftig; ***medical ~*** ärztliche Behandlung; ***take ~ of*** aufpassen auf (*acc*); versorgen; ***with ~!*** Vorsicht! **2.** Lust haben (***to*** *inf* zu *inf*); **~ *about*** sich kümmern um; **~ *for*** sorgen für, sich kümmern um; sich etwas machen aus; ***I don't ~!*** F meinetwegen!; ***I couldn't ~ less*** F es ist mir völlig egal
**ca·reer 1.** Karriere *f*, Laufbahn *f* **2.** Berufs…; Karriere… **3.** rasen
**ca·reers| ad·vice** Berufsberatung *f*; **~ ad·vi·sor** Berufsberater *m*; **~ guid·ance** Berufsberatung *f*; **~ of·fice** Berufsberatungsstelle *f*; **~ of·fi·cer** Berufsberater *m*

C

**care·free** sorgenfrei, sorglos
**care·ful** vorsichtig; sorgsam bedacht (***of*** auf *acc*); sorgfältig; ***be ~!*** pass auf!
**care·less** nachlässig, unachtsam; leichtsinnig, unvorsichtig; sorglos
**care·less·ness** Nachlässigkeit *f*, Unachtsamkeit *f*; Leichtsinn *m*; Sorglosigkeit *f*
**ca·ress 1.** Liebkosung *f*; Zärtlichkeit *f* **2.** liebkosen, streicheln
**care·tak·er** Hausmeister *m*; (Haus- *etc*) Verwalter *m*
**care·worn** abgehärmt, verhärmt
**car fer·ry** Autofähre *f*
**car·go** Ladung *f*
**car hire** *Br* Autovermietung *f*
**car·i·ca·ture 1.** Karikatur *f*, Zerrbild *n* **2.** karikieren
**car·i·ca·tur·ist** Karikaturist *m*
**car·ies**, *a.* ***dental ~*** MED Karies *f*
**car me·chan·ic** Automechaniker *m*
**car·mine** Karmin(rot) *n*
**car·nap·per** F Autoentführer *m*
**car·na·tion** BOT Nelke *f*
**car·ni·val** Karneval *m*
**car·niv·o·rous** zo fleischfressend
**car·ol** Weihnachtslied *n*
**carp**[1] zo Karpfen *m*
**carp**[2] nörgeln
**car park** *esp Br* Parkplatz *m*; Parkhaus *n*
**car·pen·ter** Zimmermann *m*
**car·pet 1.** Teppich *m*; ***fitted ~*** Teppichboden *m*; ***sweep s.th. under the ~*** *fig* et. unter den Teppich kehren **2.** mit Teppich(boden) auslegen
**car phone** Autotelefon *n*
**car pool** Fahrgemeinschaft *f*
**car pool(·ing) ser·vice** Mitfahrzentrale *f*
**car·port** MOT überdachter Abstellplatz
**car rent·al** Autovermietung *f*
**car re·pair shop** Autoreparaturwerkstatt *f*
**car·riage** Beförderung *f*, Transport *m*; Transportkosten *pl*; Kutsche *f*; *Br* RAIL (Personen)Wagen *m*
**car·riage·way** Fahrbahn *f*
**car·ri·er** Spediteur *m*; Gepäckträger *m* (*on a bicycle*); MIL Flugzeugträger *m*
**car·ri·er bag** *Br* Trag(e)tasche *f*, -tüte *f*
**car·ri·on 1.** Aas *n* **2.** Aas…
**car·rot** BOT Karotte *f*, Mohrrübe *f*
**car·ry** *v/t* bringen, führen, tragen (*a. v/i*), fahren, befördern; (bei sich) haben *or* tragen; *Ansicht* durchsetzen; *Gewinn*, *Preis* davontragen; *Ernte*, *Zinsen* tragen; (weiter)führen, *Mauer* ziehen; *Antrag* durchbringen; ***be carried*** PARL *etc* angenommen werden; ***~ s.th. too far*** et. übertreiben, et. zu weit treiben; ***get carried away*** *fig* die Kontrolle über sich verlieren; sich hinreißen lassen; ***~ forward, ~ over*** ECON übertragen; ***~ on*** fortsetzen, weiterführen; ECON betreiben; ***~ out, ~ through*** aus-, durchführen
**car·ry·cot** *Br* (Baby)Trag(e)tasche *f*
**cart 1.** Karren *m*; Wagen *m*; Einkaufswagen *m*; ***put the ~ before the horse*** *fig* das Pferd beim Schwanz aufzäumen **2.** karren
**car·ti·lage** ANAT Knorpel *m*
**cart·load** Wagenladung *f*
**car·ton** Karton *m*; ***a ~ of cigarettes*** e-e Stange Zigaretten
**car·toon** Cartoon *m*, *n*; Karikatur *f*; Zeichentrickfilm *m*
**car·toon·ist** Karikaturist *m*
**car·tridge** Patrone *f* (*a.* MIL); (Film-) Patrone *f*, (Film)Kassette *f*; Tonabnehmer *m*
**cart·wheel**: ***turn ~s*** Rad schlagen
**carve** GASTR vorschneiden, zerlegen; TECH schnitzen; meißeln
**carv·er** (Holz)Schnitzer *m*; Bildhauer *m*; GASTR Tranchierer *m*; Tranchiermesser *n*; **carv·ing** Schnitzerei *f*
**car wash** Autowäsche *f*; (Auto)Waschanlage *f*, Waschstraße *f*
**cas·cade** Wasserfall *m*
**case**[1] **1.** Behälter *m*; Kiste *f*, Kasten *m*; Etui *n*; Gehäuse *n*; Schachtel *f*; (*Glas-*) Schrank *m*; (*Kissen*)Bezug *m*; TECH Verkleidung *f* **2.** in ein Gehäuse *or* Etui stecken; TECH verkleiden
**case**[2] Fall *m* (*a.* JUR), LING *a.* Kasus *m*; MED (Krankheits)Fall *m*, Patient(in); Sache *f*, Angelegenheit *f*
**case·ment** Fensterflügel *m*; → **~ window** Flügelfenster *n*
**cash 1.** Bargeld *n*; Barzahlung *f*; ***~ down*** gegen bar; ***~ on delivery*** Lieferung *f* gegen bar; (per) Nachnahme *f* **2.** einlösen
**cash·book** ECON Kassenbuch *n*
**cash desk** Kasse *f*
**cash dis·pens·er** *esp Br* Geld-, Bankau-

tomat *m*
**cash·ier** Kassierer(in)
**cash·less** bargeldlos
**cash ma·chine** Geld-, Bankautomat *m*
**cash·mere** Kaschmir *m*
**cash·point** *Br* → ***cash machine***
**cash reg·is·ter** Registrierkasse *f*
**cas·ing** (Schutz)Hülle *f*; Verschalung *f*, Verkleidung *f*, Gehäuse *n*
**cask** Fass *n*
**cas·ket** Kästchen *n*; Sarg *m*
**cas·sette** (*Film-, Band-, Musik*)Kassette *f*; ~ **deck** Kassettendeck *n*; ~ **player** Kassettenrekorder *m*; ~ **ra·di·o** Radiorekorder *m*; ~ **re·cord·er** Kassettenrekorder *m*
**cas·sock** REL Soutane *f*
**cast 1.** Wurf *m*; TECH Guss(form *f*) *m*; Abguss *m*, Abdruck *m*; Schattierung *f*, Anflug *m*; Form *f*, Art *f*; Auswerfen *n* (*of a fishing line etc*); THEA Besetzung *f* **2.** (ab-, aus-, hin-, um-, weg)werfen; zo abwerfen (*skin*); verlieren (*teeth*); verwerfen; gestalten; TECH gießen; *a.* ~ ***up*** ausrechnen, zusammenzählen; THEA *Stück* besetzen; *Rollen* verteilen (***to*** an *acc*); ~ ***lots*** losen (***for*** um); ~ ***away*** wegwerfen; ***be ~ down*** niedergeschlagen sein; ~ ***off*** *Kleidung* ausrangieren; MAR losmachen; *Freund etc* fallen lassen; *knitting*: abketten; *v/i*: ~ ***about for***, ~ ***around for*** suchen (nach), *fig a.* sich umsehen nach
**cas·ta·net** Kastagnette *f*
**cast·a·way** Schiffbrüchige *m, f*
**caste** Kaste *f* (*a. fig*)
**cast·er** Laufrolle *f*; *Br* (*Salz-, Zucker-etc*)Streuer *m*
**cast i·ron** Gusseisen *n*
**cast-i·ron** gusseisern
**cas·tle** Burg *f*, Schloss *n*; *chess*: Turm *m*
**cast·or** → ***caster***
**cast·or oil** PHARM Rizinusöl *n*
**cas·trate** kastrieren
**cas·u·al** zufällig; gelegentlich; flüchtig; lässig
**cas·u·al·ty** Unfall *m*; Verunglückte *m, f*, Opfer *n*; MIL Verwundete *m*; Gefallene *m*; ***casualties*** Opfer *pl*, MIL *mst* Verluste *pl*; ~ **(de·part·ment)** MED Notaufnahme *f*; ~ **ward** MED Unfallstation *f*
**cas·u·al wear** Freizeitkleidung *f*
**cat** zo Katze *f*
**cat·a·log**, *esp Br* **cat·a·logue 1.** Katalog *m*; Verzeichnis *n*, Liste *f* **2.** katalogisieren
**cat·a·lyt·ic con·vert·er** MOT Katalysator *m*
**cat·a·pult** *Br* Schleuder *f*; Katapult *n, m*
**cat·a·ract** Wasserfall *m*; Stromschnelle *f*; MED grauer Star
**ca·tarrh** MED Katarr(h) *m*
**ca·tas·tro·phe** Katastrophe *f*
**catch 1.** Fangen *n*; Fang *m*, Beute *f*; Halt *m*, Griff *m*; TECH Haken *m* (*a. fig*); (Tür)Klinke *f*; Verschluss *m* **2.** *v/t* (auf-, ein)fangen; packen, fassen, ergreifen; überraschen, ertappen; *Blick etc* auffangen; F *Zug etc* (noch) kriegen, erwischen; *et.* erfassen, verstehen; *Atmosphäre etc* einfangen; sich *e-e Krankheit* holen; ~ ***(a) cold*** sich erkälten; ~ ***the eye*** ins Auge fallen; ~ ***s.o.'s eye*** j-s Aufmerksamkeit auf sich lenken; ~ ***s.o. up*** j-n einholen; ***be caught up in*** verwickelt sein in (*acc*); *v/i* sich verfangen, hängen bleiben; fassen, greifen; TECH ineinandergreifen; klemmen; einschnappen; ~ ***up with*** einholen
**catch·er** Fänger *m*
**catch·ing** packend; MED ansteckend (*a. fig*)
**catch·word** Schlagwort *n*; Stichwort *n*
**catch·y** MUS eingängig
**cat·e·chis·m** REL Katechismus *m*
**cat·e·go·ry** Kategorie *f*
**ca·ter**: ~ ***for*** Speisen und Getränke liefern für; *fig* sorgen für
**cat·er·pil·lar** zo Raupe *f*
**Cat·er·pil·lar®** MOT Raupenfahrzeug *n*; ~ **trac·tor®** MOT Raupenschlepper *m*
**cat·gut** MUS Darmsaite *f*
**ca·the·dral** Dom *m*, Kathedrale *f*
**Cath·o·lic** REL **1.** katholisch **2.** Katholik(in)
**cat·kin** BOT Kätzchen *n*
**cat·tle** Vieh *n*; ~ **breed·er** Viehzüchter *m*; ~ **breed·ing** Viehzucht *f*; ~ **dealer** Viehhändler *m*; ~ **mar·ket** Viehmarkt *m*
**ca(u)l·dron** großer Kessel
**cau·li·flow·er** BOT Blumenkohl *m*
**cause 1.** Ursache *f*; Grund *m*; Sache *f* **2.** verursachen; veranlassen
**cause·less** grundlos
**cau·tion 1.** Vorsicht *f*; Warnung *f*; Verwarnung *f* **2.** warnen; verwarnen; JUR

belehren
**cau·tious** behutsam, vorsichtig
**cav·al·ry** HIST MIL Kavallerie *f*
**cave 1.** Höhle *f* **2.** *v/i*: ~ ***in*** einstürzen
**cav·ern** (große) Höhle
**cav·i·ty** Höhle *f*; MED Loch *n*
**caw** ZO **1.** krächzen **2.** Krächzen *n*
**CD** *abbr of* ***compact disk*** CD *f*; ~ **bur·ner** CD-Brenner *m*; ~ **play·er** CD--Spieler *m*; ~**-ROM** *abbr of* ***compact disk read-only memory*** CD-ROM; ~**-ROM drive** CD-ROM-Laufwerk *n*; ~ **vid·e·o** CD-Video *n*; ~ **wri·ter** CD--Brenner *m*
**cease** aufhören; beenden
**cease·fire** MIL Feuereinstellung *f*; Waffenruhe *f*
**cease·less** unaufhörlich
**cei·ling** (Zimmer)Decke *f*; ECON Höchstgrenze *f*, oberste Preisgrenze
**cel·e·brate** feiern; **cel·e·brat·ed** gefeiert, berühmt (***for*** für, wegen)
**cel·e·bra·tion** Feier *f*
**ce·leb·ri·ty** Berühmtheit *f*
**cel·e·ry** BOT Sellerie *m*, *f*
**ce·les·ti·al** himmlisch
**cel·i·ba·cy** Ehelosigkeit *f*
**cell** BIOL Zelle *f*, ELECTR *a.* Element *n*
**cel·lar** Keller *m*
**cel·list** MUS Cellist(in)
**cel·lo** MUS (Violon)Cello *n*
**cel·lo·phane®** Cellophan® *n*
**cel·lu·lar** BIOL Zell(en)…
**cel·lu·lar phone** Handy *n*
**Cel·tic** keltisch
**ce·ment 1.** Zement *m*; Kitt *m* **2.** zementieren; (ver)kitten
**cem·e·tery** Friedhof *m*
**cen·sor 1.** Zensor *m* **2.** zensieren
**cen·sor·ship** Zensur *f*
**cen·sure 1.** Tadel *m*, Verweis *m* **2.** tadeln
**cen·sus** Volkszählung *f*
**cent** Hundert *n*; Cent *m* (*1/100 Dollar*); ***per*** ~ Prozent *n*
**cen·te·na·ry** Hundertjahrfeier *f*, hundertjähriges Jubiläum
**cen·ten·ni·al 1.** hundertjährig **2.** → ***centenary***
**cen·ter 1.** Zentrum *n*, Mittelpunkt *m*; *soccer*: Flanke *f* **2.** (sich) konzentrieren; zentrieren; ~ **back** *soccer*: Vorstopper *m*; ~ **for·ward** SPORT Mittelstürmer(in); ~ **of grav·i·ty** PHYS Schwerpunkt *m*
**cen·ti·grade**: ***10 degrees*** ~ 10 Grad Celsius
**cen·ti·me·ter**, *Br* **cen·ti·me·tre** Zentimeter *m*, *n*
**cen·ti·pede** ZO Tausendfüß(l)er *m*
**cen·tral** zentral; Haupt…, Zentral…; Mittel…; ~ **heat·ing** Zentralheizung *f*
**cen·tral·ize** zentralisieren
**cen·tral lock·ing** MOT Zentralverriegelung *f*; ~ **res·er·va·tion** *Br* MOT Mittelstreifen *m*
**cen·tre** *Br* → ***center***
**cen·tu·ry** Jahrhundert *n*
**ce·ram·ics** Keramik *f*, keramische Erzeugnisse *pl*
**ce·re·al 1.** Getreide… **2.** BOT Getreide *n*; Getreidepflanze *f*; GASTR Getreideflocken *pl*, Frühstückskost *f*
**cer·e·bral** ANAT Gehirn…
**cer·e·mo·ni·al 1.** zeremoniell **2.** Zeremoniell *n*
**cer·e·mo·ni·ous** zeremoniell; förmlich
**cer·e·mo·ny** Zeremonie *f*; Feier *f*, Feierlichkeit *f*; Förmlichkeit(en *pl*) *f*
**cer·tain** sicher, gewiss; zuverlässig; bestimmt; gewisse(r, -s); **cer·tain·ly** sicher, gewiss; *int* sicherlich, bestimmt, natürlich; **cer·tain·ty** Sicherheit *f*, Bestimmtheit *f*, Gewissheit *f*
**cer·tif·i·cate** Zeugnis *n*; Bescheinigung *f*; ~ ***of*** (***good***) ***conduct*** Führungszeugnis *n*; ***General Certificate of Education advanced level*** (***A level***) *Br* PED *appr* Abitur(zeugnis) *n*; ***General Certificate of Education ordinary level*** (***O level***) *Br* PED *appr* mittlere Reife; ***medical*** ~ ärztliches Attest
**cer·ti·fy** *et.* bescheinigen; beglaubigen
**cer·ti·tude** Sicherheit *f*, Bestimmtheit *f*, Gewissheit *f*
**CET** *abbr of* ***Central European Time*** MEZ, mitteleuropäische Zeit
**cf** (*Latin* ***confer***) *abbr of* ***compare*** vgl., vergleiche
**CFC** *abbr of* ***chlorofluorocarbon*** FCKW, Fluorchlorkohlenwasserstoff *m*
**chafe** *v/t* warm reiben; aufreiben, wund reiben; *v/i* (sich durch)reiben, scheuern
**chaff** AGR Spreu *f*; Häcksel *n*
**chaf·finch** ZO Buchfink *m*
**chag·rin 1.** Ärger *m* **2.** ärgern
**chain 1.** Kette *f*; *fig* Fessel *f* **2.** (an)ket-

ten; fesseln
**chain re·ac·tion** Kettenreaktion *f*
**chain-smoke** F Kette rauchen
**chain-smok·er** Kettenraucher(in)
**chain-smok·ing** Kettenrauchen *n*
**chain store** Kettenladen *m*
**chair** Stuhl *m*; UNIV Lehrstuhl *m*; ECON *etc* Vorsitz *m*; ***be in the ~*** den Vorsitz führen; **~ lift** Sessellift *m*
**chair·man** Vorsitzende *m*, Präsident *m*; Diskussionsleiter *m*; ECON *Br* Generaldirektor *m*
**chair·man·ship** Vorsitz *m*
**chair·wom·an** Vorsitzende *f*, Präsidentin *f*; Diskussionsleiterin *f*
**chal·ice** REL Kelch *m*
**chalk 1.** Kreide *f* **2.** mit Kreide schreiben *or* zeichnen
**chal·lenge 1.** Herausforderung *f* **2.** herausfordern
**chal·len·ger** Herausforderer *m*
**cham·ber** TECH, PARL *etc* Kammer *f*
**cham·ber·maid** Zimmermädchen *n*
**cham·ber of com·merce** ECON Handelskammer *f*
**cham·ois** ZO Gämse *f*
**cham·ois (leath·er)** Fensterleder *n*
**champ** F SPORT → ***champion***
**cham·pagne** Champagner *m*
**cham·pi·on 1.** Verfechter(in), Fürsprecher(in); SPORT Meister(in) **2.** verfechten, eintreten für; **cham·pi·on·ship** SPORT Meisterschaft *f*
**chance 1.** Zufall *m*; Chance *f*, (günstige) Gelegenheit; Aussicht *f* (***of*** auf *acc*); Möglichkeit *f*; Risiko *n*; ***by ~*** zufällig; ***take a ~*** es darauf ankommen lassen; ***take no ~s*** nichts riskieren (wollen) **2.** zufällig **3.** F riskieren
**chan·cel·lor** Kanzler(in)
**chan·de·lier** Kronleuchter *m*
**change 1.** Veränderung *f*, Wechsel *m*; Abwechslung *f*; Wechselgeld *n*; Kleingeld *n*; ***for a ~*** zur Abwechslung; ***~ for the better*** (***worse***) Bess(e)rung *f* (Verschlechterung *f*); **2.** *v/t* (ver)ändern, umändern; (aus)wechseln; (aus-, ver-) tauschen (***for*** gegen); umbuchen; MOT, TECH schalten; ***~ over*** umschalten; umstellen; ***~ trains*** umsteigen; *v/i* sich (ver)ändern, wechseln; sich umziehen
**change·a·ble** veränderlich
**change ma·chine** Münzwechsler *m*
**change·o·ver** Umstellung *f* (***to*** auf *acc*)
**chang·ing room** *esp* SPORT Umkleidekabine *f*, Umkleideraum *m*
**chan·nel 1.** Kanal *m* (*a. fig*); (*Fernseh- etc*)Kanal *m*, (*Fernseh- etc*)Programm *n*; *fig* Weg *m* **2.** *fig* lenken
**Chan·nel Tun·nel** Kanaltunnel *m*, Eurotunnel *m*
**chant 1.** (Kirchen)Gesang *m*; Singsang *m* **2.** in Sprechchören rufen
**cha·os** Chaos *n*
**chap**[1] **1.** Riss *m* **2.** rissig machen *or* werden; aufspringen
**chap**[2] *Br* F Bursche *m*, Kerl *m*
**chap·el** ARCH Kapelle *f*; REL Gottesdienst *m*
**chap·lain** REL Kaplan *m*
**chap·ter** Kapitel *n*
**char** verkohlen
**char·ac·ter** Charakter *m*; Ruf *m*, Leumund *m*; Schriftzeichen *n*, Buchstabe *m*; *novel etc*: Figur *f*, Gestalt *f*; THEA Rolle *f*; **char·ac·ter·is·tic 1.** charakteristisch (***of*** für); **2.** Kennzeichen *n*; **char·ac·ter·ize** charakterisieren
**char·coal** Holzkohle *f*
**charge 1.** *v/t* ELECTR (auf)laden; *Gewehr etc* laden; *j-n* beauftragen (***with*** mit); *j-n* beschuldigen *or* anklagen (***with*** *e-r Sache*) (*a.* JUR); ECON berechnen, verlangen, fordern (***for*** für); MIL angreifen; stürmen; ***~ s.o. with s.th.*** ECON j-m et. in Rechnung stellen; *v/i*: ***~ at s.o.*** auf j-n losgehen **2.** Ladung *f* (*a.* ELECTR *etc*); (Spreng)Ladung *f*; Beschuldigung *f*, *a.* JUR Anklage(-punkt *m*) *f*; ECON Preis *m*; Forderung *f*; Gebühr *f*; *a. pl* Unkosten *pl*, Spesen *pl*; Verantwortung *f*; Schützling *m*, Mündel *n*, *m*; ***free of ~*** kostenlos; ***be in ~ of*** verantwortlich sein für; ***take ~ of*** die Leitung *etc* übernehmen, die Sache in die Hand nehmen
**char·ger** Aufladegerät *n*
**char·i·ot** HIST Streit-, Triumphwagen *m*
**cha·ris·ma** Charisma *n*, Ausstrahlung *f*, Ausstrahlungskraft *f*
**char·i·ta·ble** wohltätig
**char·i·ty** Nächstenliebe *f*; Wohltätigkeit *f*; Güte *f*, Nachsicht *f*; milde Gabe
**char·la·tan** Scharlatan *m*; Quacksalber *m*, Kurpfuscher *m*
**charm 1.** Zauber *m*; Charme *m*, Reiz *m*; Talisman *m*, Amulett *n* **2.** bezaubern, entzücken

C

**charm·ing** charmant, bezaubernd
**chart** (*See-*, *Himmels-*, *Wetter*)Karte *f*; Diagramm *n*, Schaubild *n*; *pl* MUS Charts *pl*, Hitliste(n *pl*) *f*
**char·ter 1.** Urkunde *f*; Charta *f*; Chartern *n* **2.** chartern, mieten
**char·ter flight** Charterflug *m*
**char·wom·an** Putzfrau *f*, Raumpflegerin *f*
**chase 1.** Jagd *f*; Verfolgung *f* **2.** *v/t* jagen, hetzen; Jagd machen auf (*acc*); TECH ziselieren; *v/i* rasen, rennen
**chasm** Kluft *f*, Abgrund *m*
**chaste** keusch; schlicht
**chas·tise** züchtigen
**chas·ti·ty** Keuschheit *f*
**chat 1.** Geplauder *n*, Schwätzchen *n*, Plauderei *f*; IT Chat *m* **2.** plaudern; IT chatten
**chat show** *Br* TV Talkshow *f*
**chat show host** *Br* TV Talkmaster *m*
**chat·ter 1.** plappern; schnattern; klappern **2.** Geplapper *n*; Klappern *n*
**chat·ter·box** F Plappermaul *n*
**chat·ty** gesprächig
**chauf·feur** Chauffeur *m*
**chau·vi** F Chauvi *m*
**chau·vin·ist** Chauvinist *m*; F ***male ~ pig*** Chauvi *m*; *contp* Chauvischwein *n*
**cheap** billig; *fig* schäbig, gemein
**cheap·en** (sich) verbilligen; *fig* herabsetzen
**cheat 1.** Betrug *m*, Schwindel *m*; Betrüger(in) **2.** betrügen; F schummeln
**check 1.** Schach(stellung *f*) *n*; Hemmnis *n*, Hindernis *n* (***on*** für); Einhalt *m*; Kontrolle *f* (***on*** *gen*); Kontrollabschnitt *m*, -schein *m*; Gepäckschein *m*; Garderobenmarke *f*; ECON Scheck *m* (***for*** über); Häkchen *n* (*on a list etc*); ECON Kassenzettel *m*, Rechnung *f*; karierter Stoff **2.** *v/i* (plötzlich) innehalten; ***~ in*** sich (*in e-m Hotel*) anmelden; einstempeln; AVIAT einchecken; ***~ out*** (*aus e-m Hotel*) abreisen; ausstempeln; ***~ up*** (***on***) F (*e-e Sache*) nachprüfen, (*e-e Sache, j-n*) überprüfen; *v/t* hemmen, hindern, aufhalten; zurückhalten; checken, kontrollieren, überprüfen; *auf e-r Liste* abhaken; *Mantel etc* in der Garderobe abgeben; *Gepäck* aufgeben
**check card** ECON Scheckkarte *f*
**checked** kariert
**check·ers** Damespiel *n*
**check-in** Anmeldung *f*; Einstempeln *n*; AVIAT Einchecken *n*
**check-in| coun·ter, ~ desk** AVIAT Abfertigungsschalter *m*
**check·ing ac·count** ECON Girokonto *n*
**check·list** Check-, Kontrollliste *f*
**check·mate 1.** (Schach)Matt *n* **2.** (schach)matt setzen
**check-out** Abreise *f*; Ausstempeln *n*
**check-out coun·ter** Kasse *f*
**check·point** Kontrollpunkt *m*
**check·room** Garderobe *f*; Gepäckaufbewahrung *f*
**check·up** Überprüfung *f*; MED Check-up *m*, Vorsorgeuntersuchung *f*
**cheek** ANAT Backe *f*, Wange *f*; *Br* Unverschämtheit *f*; **cheek·y** *Br* frech
**cheer 1.** Stimmung *f*, Fröhlichkeit *f*; Hoch *n*, Hochruf *m*, Beifall *m*, Beifallsruf *m*; *pl* SPORT Anfeuerungsrufe *pl*; ***three ~s!*** dreimal hoch!; ***~s!*** prost! **2.** *v/t* mit Beifall begrüßen; *a.* ***~ on*** anspornen; *a.* ***~ up*** aufheitern; *v/i* hoch rufen, jubeln; *a.* ***~ up*** Mut fassen; ***~ up!*** Kopf hoch!; **cheer·ful** vergnügt
**cheer·i·o** *int Br* F tschüs(s)!
**cheer·lead·er** SPORT Einpeitscher *m*, Cheerleader *m*
**cheer·less** freudlos; unfreundlich
**cheer·y** vergnügt
**cheese** Käse *m*
**chee·tah** ZO Gepard *m*
**chef** Küchenchef *m*; Koch *m*
**chem·i·cal 1.** chemisch **2.** Chemikalie *f*
**chem·ist** Chemiker(in); Apotheker(in); Drogist(in)
**chem·is·try** Chemie *f*
**chem·ist's shop** Apotheke *f*; Drogerie *f*
**chem·o·ther·a·py** MED Chemotherapie *f*
**cheque** *Br* ECON Scheck *m*; ***crossed ~*** Verrechnungsscheck *m*; **~ ac·count** *Br* Girokonto *n*; **~ card** *Br* Scheckkarte *f*
**cher·ry** BOT Kirsche *f*
**chess** Schach(spiel) *n*; ***a game of ~*** e-e Partie Schach
**chess·board** Schachbrett *n*
**chess·man, chess·piece** Schachfigur *f*
**chest** Kiste *f*; Truhe *f*; ANAT Brust *f*, Brustkasten *m*; ***get s.th. off one's ~*** F sich et. von der Seele reden
**chest·nut 1.** BOT Kastanie *f* **2.** kastanienbraun
**chest of drawers** Kommode *f*

**chew** (zer)kauen
**chew·ing gum** Kaugummi *m*
**chic** schick, *Austrian* fesch
**chick** zo Küken *n*, junger Vogel; F Biene *f*, Puppe *f* (*girl*)
**chick·en** zo Huhn *n*; Küken *n*; GASTR (*Brat*)Hähnchen *n*, (*Brat*)Hühnchen *n*
**chick·en·heart·ed** furchtsam, feige
**chick·en pox** MED Windpocken *pl*
**chic·o·ry** BOT Chicorée *m, f*
**chief** **1.** oberste(r, -s), Ober…, Haupt…, Chef…; wichtigste(r, -s) **2.** Chef *m*; Häuptling *m*
**chief·ly** hauptsächlich
**chil·blain** MED Frostbeule *f*
**child** Kind *n*; **~ a·buse** JUR Kindesmisshandlung *f*; **~ ben·e·fit** *Br* Kindergeld *n*; **~birth** Geburt *f*, Niederkunft *f*; **~hood** Kindheit *f*; ***from ~*** von Kindheit an; **~ish** kindlich; kindisch; **~like** kindlich; **~mind·er** Tagesmutter *f*; **~seat** Kindersitz *m*, Babysitz *m*
**chill** **1.** kalt, frostig, kühl (*a. fig*) **2.** Frösteln *n*; Kälte *f*, Kühle *f* (*a. fig*); MED Erkältung *f* **3.** abkühlen; *j-n* frösteln lassen; kühlen
**chill·y** kalt, frostig, kühl (*a. fig*)
**chime** **1.** Glockenspiel *n*; Geläut *n* **2.** läuten; schlagen (*clock*)
**chim·ney** Schornstein *m*
**chim·ney sweep** Schornsteinfeger *m*
**chimp** F, **chim·pan·zee** zo Schimpanse *m*
**chin** ANAT Kinn *n*; ***~ up!*** Kopf hoch!, halt die Ohren steif!
**chi·na** Porzellan *n*
**Chi·na** China *n*
**Chi·nese** **1.** chinesisch **2.** Chinese *m*, Chinesin *f*; LING Chinesisch *n*; ***the ~*** die Chinesen *pl*
**chink** Ritz *m*, Spalt *m*
**chip** **1.** Splitter *m*, Span *m*, Schnitzel *n, m*; dünne Scheibe; Spielmarke *f*; IT Chip *m* **2.** *v/t* schnitzeln; anschlagen, abschlagen; *v/i* abbröckeln
**chips** (Kartoffel)Chips *pl*; *Br* Pommes frites *pl*, F Fritten *pl*
**chi·rop·o·dist** Fußpfleger(in), Pediküre *f*
**chirp** zo zirpen, zwitschern, piepsen
**chis·el** **1.** Meißel *m* **2.** meißeln
**chit-chat** Plauderei *f*
**chiv·al·rous** ritterlich
**chive(s)** BOT Schnittlauch *m*
**chlo·ri·nate** *Wasser etc* chloren
**chlo·rine** CHEM Chlor *n*
**chlo·ro·fluo·ro·car·bon** (*abbr* **CFC**) CHEM Fluorchlorkohlenwasserstoff *m* (*abbr* ***FCKW***)
**chlor·o·form** MED **1.** Chloroform *n* **2.** chloroformieren
**choc·o·late** Schokolade *f*; Praline *f*; *pl* Pralinen *pl*, Konfekt *n*
**choice** **1.** Wahl *f*; Auswahl *f* **2.** auserlesen, ausgesucht, vorzüglich
**choir** ARCH, MUS Chor *m*
**choke** **1.** *v/t* (er)würgen, (*a. v/i*) ersticken; ***~ back*** *Ärger etc* unterdrücken, *Tränen* zurückhalten; ***~ down*** hinunterwürgen; *a.* ***~ up*** verstopfen **2.** MOT Choke *m*, Luftklappe *f*
**cho·les·te·rol** MED Cholesterin *n*
**choose** (aus)wählen, aussuchen
**choos·(e)y** *esp Br* wählerisch
**chop** **1.** Hieb *m*, (Handkanten)Schlag *m*; GASTR Kotelett *n* **2.** *v/t* (zer)hacken, hauen; ***~ down*** fällen; *v/i* hacken
**chop·per** Hackmesser *n*, Hackbeil *n*; F Hubschrauber *m*
**chop·py** unruhig (*sea*)
**chop·stick** Essstäbchen *n*
**cho·ral** MUS Chor…
**cho·rale** MUS Choral *m*
**chord** MUS Saite *f*; Akkord *m*
**chore** schwierige *or* unangenehme Aufgabe; *pl* Hausarbeit *f*
**cho·rus** MUS Chor *m*; Kehrreim *m*, Refrain *m*; Tanzgruppe *f*
**Christ** REL Christus *m*
**chris·ten** REL taufen
**chris·ten·ing** REL **1.** Taufe *f* **2.** Tauf…
**Chris·tian** REL **1.** christlich **2.** Christ(in)
**Chris·ti·an·i·ty** REL Christentum *n*
**Chris·tian name** Vorname *m*
**Christ·mas** Weihnachten *n and pl*; ***at ~*** zu Weihnachten; **~ Day** erster Weihnachtsfeiertag; **~ Eve** Heiliger Abend
**chrome** Chrom *n*
**chro·mi·um** CHEM Chrom *n*
**chron·ic** chronisch; ständig, (an)dauernd
**chron·i·cle** Chronik *f*
**chron·o·log·i·cal** chronologisch
**chro·nol·o·gy** Zeitrechnung *f*; Zeitfolge *f*
**chub·by** F rundlich, pumm(e)lig; pausbäckig
**chuck** F werfen, schmeißen; ***~ out*** *j-n*

rausschmeißen; *et.* wegschmeißen; ~ **up** *Job etc* hinschmeißen
**chuck·le 1.** ~ (**to o.s.**) (stillvergnügt) in sich hineinlachen **2.** leises Lachen
**chum** F Kamerad *m*, Kumpel *m*
**chum·my** F dick befreundet
**chump** Holzklotz *m*; F Trottel *m*
**chunk** Klotz *m*, Klumpen *m*
**Chun·nel** F → ***Channel Tunnel***
**church 1.** Kirche *f* **2.** Kirch…, Kirchen…
**church ser·vice** REL Gottesdienst *m*
**church·yard** Kirchhof *m*
**churl·ish** grob, flegelhaft
**churn 1.** Butterfass *n* **2.** buttern; *Wellen* aufwühlen, peitschen
**chute** Stromschnelle *f*; Rutsche *f*, Rutschbahn *f*; F Fallschirm *m*
**ci·der** *a.* ***hard*** ~ Apfelwein *m*; (***sweet***) ~ Apfelmost *m*, Apfelsaft *m*
**ci·gar** Zigarre *f*
**cig·a·rette** Zigarette *f*
**cinch** F todsichere Sache
**cin·der** Schlacke *f*; *pl* Asche *f*
**Cin·de·rel·la** Aschenbrödel *n*, Aschenputtel *n*
**cin·der track** SPORT Aschenbahn *f*
**cin·e·cam·e·ra** (Schmal)Filmkamera *f*
**cin·e·film** Schmalfilm *m*
**cin·e·ma** *Br* Kino *n*; Film *m*
**cin·na·mon** Zimt *m*
**ci·pher** Geheimschrift *f*, Chiffre *f*; Null *f* (*a. fig*)
**cir·cle 1.** Kreis *m*; THEA Rang *m*; *fig* Kreislauf *m* **2.** (um)kreisen
**cir·cuit** Kreislauf *m*; ELECTR Stromkreis *m*; Rundreise *f*; SPORT Zirkus *m*; ***short*** ~ ELECTR Kurzschluss *m*
**cir·cu·i·tous** gewunden; weitschweifig; ~ ***route*** Umweg *m*
**cir·cu·lar 1.** kreisförmig; Kreis… **2.** Rundschreiben *n*; Umlauf *m*; (Post-) Wurfsendung *f*
**cir·cu·late** *v/i* zirkulieren, im Umlauf sein; *v/t* in Umlauf setzen
**cir·cu·lat·ing li·bra·ry** Leihbücherei *f*
**cir·cu·la·tion** (*a.* Blut)Kreislauf *m*, Zirkulation *f*; ECON Umlauf *m*; *newspaper etc*: Auflage *f*
**cir·cum·fer·ence** (Kreis)Umfang *m*
**cir·cum·nav·i·gate** umschiffen, umsegeln
**cir·cum·scribe** MATH umschreiben; *fig* begrenzen
**cir·cum·spect** umsichtig, vorsichtig
**cir·cum·stance** Umstand *m*; *pl* (Sach-) Lage *f*, Umstände *pl*; Verhältnisse *pl*; ***in*** *or* ***under no*** ~***s*** unter keinen Umständen, auf keinen Fall; ***in*** *or* ***under the*** ~***s*** unter diesen Umständen
**cir·cum·stan·tial** ausführlich; umständlich; ~ **ev·i·dence** JUR Indizien *pl*, Indizienbeweis *m*
**cir·cus** Zirkus *m*
**CIS** *abbr of* ***Commonwealth of Independent States*** *die* GUS, *die* Gemeinschaft unabhängiger Staaten
**cis·tern** Wasserbehälter *m*; Spülkasten *m*
**ci·ta·tion** Zitat *n*; JUR Vorladung *f*
**cite** zitieren; JUR vorladen
**cit·i·zen** Bürger(in); Städter(in); Staatsangehörige *m, f*
**cit·i·zen·ship** Staatsangehörigkeit *f*
**cit·y 1.** (Groß)Stadt *f*; ***the City*** die (Londoner) City **2.** städtisch, Stadt…; ~ **cen·tre** *Br* Innenstadt *f*, City *f*; ~ **coun·cil·(l)or** Stadtrat *m*, Stadträtin *f*; ~ **hall** Rathaus *n*; Stadtverwaltung *f*
**civ·ic** städtisch, Stadt…
**civ·ics** PED Staatsbürgerkunde *f*
**civ·il** staatlich, Staats…; (staats)bürgerlich, Bürger…; zivil, Zivil…; JUR zivilrechtlich; höflich
**ci·vil·i·an** Zivilist *m*
**ci·vil·i·ty** Höflichkeit *f*
**civ·i·li·za·tion** Zivilisation *f*, Kultur *f*
**civ·i·lize** zivilisieren
**civ·il rights** (Staats)Bürgerrechte *pl*; ~ **ac·tiv·ist** Bürgerrechtler(in); ~ **move·ment** Bürgerrechtsbewegung *f*
**civ·il| ser·vant** Staatsbeamte *m*, -beamtin *f*; ~ **ser·vice** Staatsdienst *m*; ~ **war** Bürgerkrieg *m*
**clad** gekleidet
**claim 1.** Anspruch *m*; Anrecht *n* (***to*** auf *acc*); Forderung *f*; Behauptung *f*; Claim *m* **2.** beanspruchen; fordern; behaupten
**clair·voy·ant 1.** hellseherisch **2.** Hellseher(in)
**clam·ber** (mühsam) klettern
**clam·my** feuchtkalt, klamm
**clam·o(u)r 1.** Geschrei *n*, Lärm *m* **2.** lautstark verlangen (***for*** nach)
**clamp** TECH Zwinge *f*
**clan** Clan *m*, Sippe *f*
**clan·des·tine** heimlich

**clang** klingen, klirren; erklingen lassen
**clank 1.** Gerassel *n*, Geklirr *n* **2.** rasseln *or* klirren (mit)
**clap 1.** Klatschen *n*; Schlag *m*, Klaps *m* **2.** schlagen *or* klatschen (mit)
**clar·et** roter Bordeaux(wein); Rotwein *m*
**clar·i·fy** *v/t* (auf)klären, klarstellen; *v/i* sich (auf)klären, klar werden
**clar·i·net** MUS Klarinette *f*
**clar·i·ty** Klarheit *f*
**clash 1.** Zusammenstoß *m*; Konflikt *m* **2.** zusammenstoßen; *fig* nicht zusammenpassen *or* harmonieren
**clasp 1.** Haken *m*, Schnalle *f*; Schloss *n*, (Schnapp) Verschluss *m*; Umklammerung *f* **2.** einhaken, zuhaken; ergreifen, umklammern
**clasp knife** Taschenmesser *n*
**class 1.** Klasse *f*; (Bevölkerungs-) Schicht *f*; (Schul)Klasse *f*; (Unterrichts)Stunde *f*; Kurs *m*; Jahrgang *m* **2.** (in Klassen) einteilen, einordnen, einstufen
**clas·sic 1.** Klassiker *m* **2.** klassisch
**clas·si·cal** klassisch
**clas·sic car** Klassiker *m*
**clas·si·fi·ca·tion** Klassifizierung *f*, Einteilung *f*
**clas·si·fied** klassifiziert; MIL, POL geheim; ~ **ad** Kleinanzeige *f*
**clas·si·fy** klassifizieren, einstufen
**class·mate** Mitschüler(in)
**class·room** Klassenzimmer *n*
**clat·ter 1.** Geklapper *n* **2.** klappern (mit)
**clause** JUR Klausel *f*, Bestimmung *f*; LING Satz(teil *n*) *m*
**claw 1.** ZO Klaue *f*, Kralle *f*; (*Krebs-*) Schere *f* **2.** (zer)kratzen; umkrallen, packen
**clay** Ton *m*, Lehm *m*
**clean 1.** *adj* rein; sauber, glatt, eben; *sl* clean **2.** *adv* völlig, ganz und gar **3.** reinigen, säubern, putzen; ~ ***out*** reinigen; ~ ***up*** gründlich reinigen; aufräumen
**clean·er** Rein(e)machefrau *f*, (*Fenster- etc*)Putzer *m*; Reinigungsmittel *n*, Reiniger *m*; ***take to the ~s*** *et.* zur Reinigung bringen; F *j-n* ausnehmen
**clean·ing**: ***do the ~*** sauber machen, putzen; ~ **la·dy**, ~ **wom·an** Putzfrau *f*
**clean·li·ness** Reinlichkeit *f*
**clean·ly 1.** *adv* sauber **2.** *adj* reinlich
**cleanse** reinigen, säubern
**cleans·er** Putzmittel *n*, Reinigungsmittel *n*, Reiniger *m*
**clear 1.** klar; hell; rein; deutlich; frei (***of*** von); ECON Netto…, Rein… **2.** *v/t* reinigen, säubern; *Wald* lichten, roden; wegräumen (*a.* ~ ***away***); *Tisch* abräumen; räumen, leeren; *Hindernis* nehmen; SPORT klären; ECON verzollen; JUR freisprechen; IT löschen; *v/i* klar *or* hell werden; METEOR aufklaren; sich verziehen (*fog*); ~ ***out*** aufräumen; ausräumen, entfernen; F abhauen; ~ ***up*** aufräumen; *Verbrechen etc* aufklären; METEOR aufklaren
**clear·ance** Räumung *f*; TECH lichter Abstand; Freigabe *f*; ~ **sale** ECON Räumungsverkauf *m*, Ausverkauf *m*
**clear·ing** Lichtung *f*
**cleave** spalten
**cleav·er** Hackmesser *n*
**clef** MUS Schlüssel *m*
**cleft** Spalt *m*, Spalte *f*
**clem·en·cy** Milde *f*, Nachsicht *f*
**clem·ent** mild (*a.* METEOR)
**clench** *Lippen etc* (fest) zusammenpressen; *Zähne* zusammenbeißen; *Faust* ballen
**cler·gy** REL Klerus *m*, *die* Geistlichen *pl*
**cler·gy·man** REL Geistliche *m*
**clerk** Verkäufer(in); (Büro- *etc*)Angestellte *m*, *f*, (Bank-, Post)Beamte *m*, (-)Beamtin *f*
**clev·er** klug, gescheit; geschickt
**click 1.** Klicken *n* **2.** *v/i* klicken; zu-, einschnappen; *mit der Zunge* schnalzen; *v/t* klicken *or* einschnappen lassen; mit *der Zunge* schnalzen; ~ ***on*** IT anklicken
**cli·ent** JUR Klient(in), Mandant(in); Kunde *m*, Kundin *f*, Auftraggeber(in)
**cliff** Klippe *f*, Felsen *m*
**cli·mate** Klima *n*
**cli·max** Höhepunkt *m*; Orgasmus *m*
**climb** klettern; (er-, be)steigen; ~ (***up***) ***a tree*** auf e-n Baum klettern
**climb·er** Kletterer *m*, Bergsteiger(in); BOT Kletterpflanze *f*
**clinch 1.** TECH sicher befestigen; (ver)nieten; *boxing*: umklammern (*v/i* clinchen); *fig* entscheiden; ***that ~ed it*** damit war die Sache entschieden **2.** *boxing*: Clinch *m*
**cling** (***to***) festhalten (an *dat*), sich klammern (an *acc*); sich (an)schmiegen (an

*acc*)
**cling·film®** *esp Br* Frischhaltefolie *f*
**clin·ic** Klinik *f*
**clin·i·cal** klinisch
**clink 1.** Klirren *n*, Klingen *n*; *sl* Knast *m* **2.** klingen *or* klirren (lassen); klimpern mit
**clip¹ 1.** ausschneiden; *Schafe etc* scheren **2.** Schnitt *m*; Schur *f*; (*Film- etc*) Ausschnitt *m*; (*Video*)Clip *m*
**clip² 1.** (Heft-, Büro- *etc*)Klammer *f*; (*Ohr*)Klipp *m* **2.** *a.* **~ on** anklammern
**clip·per:** **(a pair of) ~s** (e-e) (*Nagel- etc*)-Schere *f*, Haarschneidemaschine *f*
**clip·pings** Abfälle *pl*, Schnitzel *pl*; (*Zeitungs- etc*)Ausschnitte *pl*
**clit·o·ris** ANAT Klitoris *f*
**cloak 1.** Umhang *m* **2.** *fig* verhüllen
**cloak·room** *Br* Garderobe *f*; Toilette *f*
**clock 1.** (*Wand-*, *Stand-*, *Turm*)Uhr *f*; **9 o'clock** 9 Uhr **2.** SPORT Zeit stoppen; **~ in, ~ on** einstempeln; **~ out, ~ off** ausstempeln; **~ ra·di·o** Radiowecker *m*
**clock·wise** im Uhrzeigersinn
**clock·work** Uhrwerk *n*; **like ~** wie am Schnürchen
**clod** (Erd)Klumpen *m*
**clog 1.** (Holz)Klotz *m*; Holzschuh *m* **2.** *a.* **~ up** verstopfen
**clois·ter** ARCH Kreuzgang *m*; REL Kloster *n*
**close 1.** *adj* geschlossen; knapp (*result etc*); genau, gründlich (*inspection etc*); eng (anliegend); stickig, schwül; eng (*friend*), nah (*relative*); **keep a ~ watch on** scharf im Auge behalten (*acc*) **2.** *adv* eng, nahe, dicht; **~ by** ganz in der Nähe, nahe *or* dicht bei **3.** Ende *n*, (Ab)Schluss *m*; **come or draw to a ~** sich dem Ende nähern; Einfriedung *f* **4.** *v/t* (ab-, ver-, zu)schließen, zumachen; ECON schließen; *Straße* (ab)sperren; *v/i* sich schließen; schließen, zumachen; enden, zu Ende gehen; **~ down** *Geschäft etc* schließen, *Betrieb* stilllegen; *radio*, TV das Programm beenden, Sendeschluss haben; **~ in** bedrohlich nahe kommen; hereinbrechen (*night*); **~ up** (ab-, ver-, zu)schließen; aufschließen, aufrücken
**closed** geschlossen, F *pred* zu
**clos·et** (Wand)Schrank *m*
**close-up** PHOT, *film*: Großaufnahme *f*
**clos·ing date** Einsendeschluss *m*
**clos·ing time** Laden-, Geschäftsschluss *m*; Polizeistunde *f* (*of a pub*)
**clos·ure** Abschluss *m*; **look for ~** *mit et.* abschließen wollen
**clot 1.** Klumpen *m*, Klümpchen *n*; **~ of blood** MED Blutgerinnsel *n* **2.** gerinnen; Klumpen bilden
**cloth** Stoff *m*, Tuch *n*; Lappen *m*
**cloth·bound** in Leinen gebunden
**clothe** (an-, be)kleiden; einkleiden
**clothes** Kleider *pl*, Kleidung *f*; Wäsche *f*
**clothes bas·ket** Wäschekorb *m*
**clothes·horse** Wäscheständer *m*
**clothes·line** Wäscheleine *f*
**clothes peg** *Br*, **clothes·pin** Wäscheklammer *f*
**cloth·ing** (Be)Kleidung *f*
**cloud 1.** Wolke *f*; *fig* Schatten *m* **2.** (sich) bewölken; (sich) trüben
**cloud·burst** Wolkenbruch *m*
**cloud·less** wolkenlos
**cloud·y** bewölkt; trüb; *fig* unklar
**clout** F Schlag *m*; POL Einfluss *m*
**clove¹** GASTR (Gewürz)Nelke *f*; **~ of garlic** Knoblauchzehe *f*
**clo·ven hoof** ZO Huf *m* der Paarzeher
**clo·ver** BOT Klee *m*
**clown** Clown *m*, Hanswurst *m*
**club 1.** Keule *f*; Knüppel *m*; SPORT Schlagholz *n*; (*Golf*)Schläger *m*; Klub *m*; *pl card game*: Kreuz *n* **2.** einknüppeln auf (*acc*), niederknüppeln
**club·foot** MED Klumpfuß *m*
**cluck** ZO **1.** gackern; glucken **2.** Gackern *n*; Glucken *n*
**clue** Anhaltspunkt *m*, Fingerzeig *m*, Spur *f*
**clump 1.** Klumpen *m*; (*Baum- etc* -) Gruppe *f* **2.** trampeln
**clum·sy** unbeholfen, ungeschickt, plump
**clus·ter 1.** BOT Traube *f*, Büschel *n*; Haufen *m* **2.** sich drängen
**clutch 1.** Griff *m*; TECH Kupplung *f*; *fig* Klaue *f* **2.** (er)greifen; umklammern
**clut·ter** *fig* überladen
**c/o** *abbr of* **care of** c/o, (wohnhaft) bei
**Co** *abbr of* **company** ECON Gesellschaft *f*
**coach 1.** Reisebus *m*; *Br* RAIL (Personen)Wagen *m*; Kutsche *f*; **~ (class)** Economyclass *f*; **~ party** (*Bus*) Reisegruppe *f*; SPORT Trainer(in); PED Nach-

hilfelehrer(in) **2.** SPORT trainieren; PED *j-m* Nachhilfeunterricht geben
**coach·man** Kutscher *m*
**co·ag·u·late** gerinnen (lassen)
**coal** (Stein)Kohle *f*; ***carry ~s to Newcastle*** F *Br* Eulen nach Athen tragen
**co·a·li·tion** POL Koalition *f*; Bündnis *n*, Zusammenschluss *m*
**coal·mine, coal·pit** Kohlengrube *f*
**coarse** grob; rau; derb; ungeschliffen; gemein
**coast 1.** Küste *f* **2.** MAR die Küste entlangfahren; im Leerlauf (*car*) *or* im Freilauf (*bicycle*) fahren; rodeln
**coast·er brake** Rücktritt(bremse *f*) *m*
**coast·guard** (Angehörige *m* der) Küstenwache *f*
**coast·line** Küstenlinie *f*, -strich *m*
**coat 1.** Mantel *m*; ZO Pelz *m*, Fell *n*; (*Farb- etc*)Überzug *m*, Anstrich *m*, Schicht *f* **2.** (an)streichen, überziehen, beschichten
**coat hang·er** Kleiderbügel *m*
**coat·ing** (*Farb- etc*)Überzug *m*, Anstrich *m*; Schicht *f*; Mantelstoff *m*
**coat of arms** Wappen(schild *m*, *n*) *n*
**coax** überreden, beschwatzen
**cob** Maiskolben *m*
**cob·bled:** ~ ***street*** Straße *f* mit Kopfsteinpflaster
**cob·bler** (Flick)Schuster *m*
**cob·web** Spinn(en)gewebe *n*
**co·caine** Kokain *n*
**cock 1.** ZO Hahn *m*; V Schwanz *m* **2.** aufrichten
**cock·a·too** ZO Kakadu *m*
**cock·chaf·er** ZO Maikäfer *m*
**cock·eyed** F schielend; (krumm und) schief
**Cock·ney** Cockney *m*, waschechter Londoner
**cock·pit** AVIAT Cockpit *n*
**cock·roach** ZO Schabe *f*
**cock·sure** F übertrieben selbstsicher
**cock·tail** Cocktail *m*
**cock·y** großspurig, anmaßend
**co·co** BOT Kokospalme *f*
**co·coa** Kakao *m*
**co·co·nut** BOT Kokosnuss *f*
**co·coon** (*Seiden*)Kokon *m*
**cod** ZO Kabeljau *m*, Dorsch *m*
**COD** *abbr of* ***collect*** (*Br* ***cash***) ***on delivery*** per Nachnahme
**cod·dle** verhätscheln, verzärteln
**code 1.** Kode *m* **2.** verschlüsseln, chiffrieren; kodieren
**cod·fish** → ***cod***
**cod·ing** Kodierung *f*
**cod-liv·er oil** Lebertran *m*
**co·ed·u·ca·tion** PED Gemeinschaftserziehung *f*
**co·ex·ist** gleichzeitig *or* nebeneinander bestehen *or* leben
**co·ex·ist·ence** Koexistenz *f*
**cof·fee** Kaffee *m*; ***black*** (***white***) ~ Kaffee ohne (mit) Milch; ~ **bar** *Br* Café *n*; Imbissstube *f*; ~ **bean** Kaffeebohne *f*; ~ **grind·er** Kaffeemühle *f*; ~ **machine** Kaffeeautomat *m*
**cof·fee·mak·er** Kaffeemaschine *f*
**cof·fee| pot** Kaffeekanne *f*; ~ **shop** Café *n*; Imbissstube *f*; ~ **ta·ble** Couchtisch *m*
**cof·fin** Sarg *m*
**cog** TECH (Rad)Zahn *m*; → **cog·wheel** TECH Zahnrad *n*
**co·her·ence, co·her·en·cy** Zusammenhang *m*
**co·her·ent** zusammenhängend
**co·he·sion** Zusammenhalt *m*
**co·he·sive** (fest) zusammenhaltend
**coif·fure** Frisur *f*
**coil 1.** *a.* ~ ***up*** aufrollen, (auf)wickeln; sich zusammenrollen **2.** Spirale *f* (*a.* TECH, MED); Rolle *f*, Spule *f*
**coin 1.** Münze *f* **2.** prägen
**co·in·cide** zusammentreffen; übereinstimmen; **co·in·ci·dence** (zufälliges) Zusammentreffen; Zufall *m*
**coin-op·e·rat·ed:** ~ (***gas***, *Br* ***petrol***) ***pump*** Münztank(automat) *m*
**coke** Koks *m* (*a.* F *cocaine*)
**Coke®** F Coke *n*, Cola *n*, *f*, Coca *n*, *f*
**cold 1.** kalt **2.** Kälte *f*; MED Erkältung *f*; ***catch*** (***a***) ~ sich erkälten; ***have a*** ~ erkältet sein
**cold-blood·ed** kaltblütig
**cold cuts** GASTR Aufschnitt *m*
**cold-heart·ed** kaltherzig
**cold·ness** Kälte *f*
**cold sweat** Angstschweiß *m*; ***he broke out in a*** ~ ihm brach der Angstschweiß aus
**cold war** POL kalter Krieg
**cold wave** METEOR Kältewelle *f*
**cole·slaw** Krautsalat *m*
**col·ic** MED Kolik *f*
**col·lab·o·rate** zusammenarbeiten
**col·lab·o·ra·tion** Zusammenarbeit *f*; ***in***

C

**~ with** gemeinsam mit
**col·lapse 1.** zusammenbrechen (*a. fig*), einstürzen; umfallen; *fig* scheitern **2.** Einsturz *m*; *fig* Zusammenbruch *m*
**col·lap·si·ble** Klapp…, zusammenklappbar
**col·lar 1.** Kragen *m*; (*Hunde- etc*)Halsband *n* **2.** beim Kragen packen; *j-n* festnehmen, F schnappen
**col·lar·bone** ANAT Schlüsselbein *n*
**col·league** Kollege *m*, Kollegin *f*, Mitarbeiter(in)
**col·lect** *v/t* (ein)sammeln; *Daten* erfassen; *Geld* kassieren; *j-n or et.* abholen; *Gedanken etc* sammeln; *v/i* sich (ver)sammeln; **col·lect·ed** *fig* gefasst
**col·lect·ing box** Sammelbüchse *f*
**col·lec·tion** Sammlung *f*; ECON Eintreibung *f*; REL Kollekte *f*; Abholung *f*
**col·lec·tive** gesammelt; Sammel…; **~ bargaining** ECON Tarifverhandlungen
**col·lec·tive·ly** insgesamt; zusammen
**col·lec·tor** Sammler(in); Steuereinnehmer *m*; ELECTR Stromabnehmer *m*
**col·lege** College *n*; Hochschule *f*; höhere Lehranstalt
**col·lide** zusammenstoßen, kollidieren (*a. fig*)
**col·lie·ry** Kohlengrube *f*
**col·li·sion** Zusammenstoß *m*, Kollision *f* (*a. fig*)
**col·lo·qui·al** umgangssprachlich
**co·lon** LING Doppelpunkt *m*
**colo·nel** MIL Oberst *m*
**co·lo·ni·al·is·m** POL Kolonialismus *m*
**col·o·nize** kolonisieren, besiedeln
**col·o·ny** Kolonie *f*
**col·o(u)r 1.** Farbe *f*; *pl* MIL Fahne *f*; MAR Flagge *f*; ***what ~ is …?*** welche Farbe hat …? **2.** *v/t* färben; anmalen, bemalen, anstreichen; *fig* beschönigen; *v/i* sich (ver)färben; erröten
**col·o(u)r-blind** farbenblind
**col·o(u)red** bunt; farbig
**col·o(u)r·fast** farbecht
**col·o(u)r film** PHOT Farbfilm *m*
**col·o(u)r·ful** farbenprächtig; *fig* farbig, bunt
**col·o(u)r·ing** Färbung *f*; Farbstoff *m*; Gesichtsfarbe *f*
**col·o(u)r·less** farblos
**colt** zo (Hengst)Fohlen *n*
**col·umn** Säule *f*; PRINT Spalte *f*; MIL Kolonne *f*
**col·umn·ist** Kolumnist(in)
**comb 1.** Kamm *m* **2.** kämmen; striegeln
**com·bat 1.** Kampf *m*; ***single ~*** Zweikampf *m* **2.** kämpfen gegen, bekämpfen; **com·ba·tant** MIL Kämpfer *m*
**com·bi·na·tion** Verbindung *f*, Kombination *f*; **com·bine 1.** (sich) verbinden **2.** ECON Konzern *m*; AGR *a.* ***~ harvester*** Mähdrescher *m*
**com·bus·ti·ble 1.** brennbar **2.** Brennstoff *m*, Brennmaterial *n*
**com·bus·tion** Verbrennung *f*
**come** kommen; ***to ~*** künftig, kommend; ***~ and go*** kommen und gehen; ***~ to see*** besuchen; ***~ about*** geschehen, passieren; ***~ across*** auf *j-n or et.* stoßen; ***~ along*** mitkommen, mitgehen; ***~ apart*** auseinanderfallen; ***~ away*** sich lösen, ab-, losgehen (*button etc*); ***~ back*** zurückkommen; ***~ by s.th.*** zu et. kommen; ***~ down*** herunterkommen (*a. fig*); einstürzen; sinken (*prices*); überliefert werden; ***~ down with*** F erkranken an (*dat*); ***~ for*** abholen kommen, kommen wegen; ***~ forward*** sich melden; ***~ from*** kommen aus; kommen von; ***~ home*** nach Hause (*Austrian, Swiss a.* nachhause) kommen; ***~ in*** hereinkommen; eintreffen (*news*); einlaufen (*train*); ***~ in!*** herein!; ***~ loose*** sich ablösen, abgehen; ***~ off*** ab-, losgehen (*button etc*); ***~ on!*** los!, vorwärts!, komm!; ***~ out*** herauskommen; ***~ over*** vorbeikommen (*visitor*); ***~ round*** vorbeikommen (*visitor*); wieder zu sich kommen; ***~ through*** durchkommen; *Krankheit etc* überstehen, überleben; ***~ to*** sich belaufen auf (*acc*); wieder zu sich kommen; ***~ up to*** entsprechen (*dat*), heranreichen an (*acc*)
**come·back** Come-back *n*
**co·me·di·an** Komiker *m*
**com·e·dy** Komödie *f*, Lustspiel *n*
**come·ly** attraktiv, gut aussehend
**com·fort 1.** Komfort *m*, Bequemlichkeit *f*; Trost *m*; ***cold ~*** schwacher Trost **2.** trösten
**com·for·ta·ble** komfortabel, behaglich, bequem; tröstlich
**com·fort·er** Tröster *m*; *esp Br* Schnuller *m*; Steppdecke *f*
**com·fort·less** unbequem; trostlos
**com·fort sta·tion** Bedürfnisanstalt *f*
**com·ic** komisch; Komödien…, Lust-

spiel…; **com·i·cal** komisch, spaßig
**com·ics** Comics *pl*, Comic-Hefte *pl*
**com·ma** LING Komma *n*
**com·mand** **1.** Befehl *m*; Beherrschung *f*; MIL Kommando *n* **2.** befehlen; MIL kommandieren; verfügen über (*acc*); beherrschen
**com·mand·er** MIL Kommandeur *m*, Befehlshaber *m*; ~ **in chief** MIL Oberbefehlshaber *m*
**com·mand·ment** REL Gebot *n*
**com·mand mod·ule** Kommandokapsel *f*
**com·man·do** MIL Kommando *n*
**com·mem·o·rate** gedenken (*gen*)
**com·mem·o·ra·tion**: ***in ~ of*** zum Gedenken *or* Gedächtnis an (*acc*)
**com·mem·o·ra·tive** Gedenk…, Erinnerungs…
**com·ment** **1.** (***on***) Kommentar *m* (zu); Bemerkung *f* (zu); Anmerkung *f* (zu); ***no ~!*** kein Kommentar! **2.** *v/i* ~ ***on*** e-n Kommentar abgeben zu, sich äußern über (*acc*); *v/t* bemerken (***that*** dass)
**com·men·ta·ry** Kommentar *m* (***on*** zu)
**com·men·ta·tor** Kommentator *m*, *radio*, TV *a.* Reporter *m*
**com·merce** ECON Handel *m*
**com·mer·cial** **1.** ECON Handels…, Geschäfts…; kommerziell, finanziell **2.** *radio*, TV Werbespot *m*, Werbesendung *f*; ~ **art** Gebrauchsgrafik *f*; ~ **art·ist** Gebrauchsgrafiker(in)
**com·mer·cial·ize** kommerzialisieren
**com·mer·cial tel·e·vi·sion** Werbefernsehen *n*; kommerzielles Fernsehen
**com·mis·e·rate**: ~ ***with*** Mitleid empfinden mit
**com·mis·e·ra·tion** Mitleid *n* (***for*** mit)
**com·mis·sion** **1.** Auftrag *m*; Kommission *f*, Ausschuss *m*; ECON Kommission *f*, Provision *f*; Begehung *f* (*of a crime*) **2.** beauftragen; *et.* in Auftrag geben
**com·mis·sion·er** Beauftragte *m*, *f*; Kommissar(in)
**com·mit** anvertrauen, übergeben (***to*** *dat*); JUR *j-n* einweisen (***to*** in *acc*); *Verbrechen* begehen; *j-n* verpflichten (***to*** zu), *j-n* festlegen (***to*** auf *acc*)
**com·mit·ment** Verpflichtung *f*; Engagement *n*
**com·mit·tal** JUR Einweisung *f*
**com·mit·tee** Komitee *n*, Ausschuss *m*
**com·mod·i·ty** ECON Ware *f*, Artikel *m*
**com·mon** **1.** gemeinsam, gemeinschaftlich; allgemein; alltäglich; gewöhnlich, einfach **2.** Gemeindeland *n*; ***in ~*** gemeinsam (***with*** mit)
**com·mon·er** Bürgerliche *m*, *f*
**com·mon law** (ungeschriebenes englisches) Gewohnheitsrecht
**com·mon·place** **1.** Gemeinplatz *m* **2.** alltäglich; abgedroschen
**Com·mons**: ***the ~, the House of ~*** *Br* PARL das Unterhaus
**com·mon sense** gesunder Menschenverstand
**Com·mon·wealth**: ***the ~*** (***of Nations***) das Commonwealth
**com·mo·tion** Aufregung *f*; Aufruhr *m*, Tumult *m*
**com·mu·nal** Gemeinde…; Gemeinschafts…; **com·mune** Kommune *f*
**com·mu·ni·cate** *v/t* mitteilen; *v/i* sich besprechen; sich in Verbindung setzen (***with s.o.*** mit j-m); (durch e-e Tür) verbunden sein
**com·mu·ni·ca·tion** Mitteilung *f*; Verständigung *f*, Kommunikation *f*; Verbindung *f*; *pl* Kommunikationsmittel *pl*; Verkehrswege *pl*
**com·mu·ni·ca·tions sat·el·lite** Nachrichtensatellit *m*
**com·mu·ni·ca·tive** mitteilsam, gesprächig
**Com·mu·nion** *a.* ***Holy ~*** REL (heilige) Kommunion, Abendmahl *n*
**com·mu·nis·m** POL Kommunismus *m*
**com·mu·nist** POL **1.** Kommunist(in) **2.** kommunistisch
**com·mu·ni·ty** Gemeinschaft *f*; Gemeinde *f*
**com·mute** JUR Strafe *mildernd* umwandeln; RAIL *etc* pendeln
**com·mut·er** Pendler(in); ~ **train** Pendlerzug *m*, Nahverkehrszug *m*
**com·pact** **1.** Puderdose *f*; MOT Kleinwagen *m* **2.** *adj* kompakt; eng, klein; knapp (*style*); ~ **car** MOT Kleinwagen *m*; ~ **disk** (*abbr* ***CD***) Compact Disc *f*, CD *f*; ~ **disk play·er** CD-Player *m*, CD-Spieler *m*
**com·pan·ion** Begleiter(in); Gefährte *m*, Gefährtin *f*; Gesellschafter(in); Handbuch *n*, Leitfaden *m*
**com·pan·ion·ship** Gesellschaft *f*
**com·pa·ny** Gesellschaft *f*, ECON *a.* Firma

*f*; MIL Kompanie *f*; THEA Truppe *f*; ***keep s.o. ~*** j-m Gesellschaft leisten
**com·pa·ra·ble** vergleichbar
**com·par·a·tive 1.** vergleichend; verhältnismäßig **2.** *a.* ***~ degree*** LING Komparativ *m*; **com·par·a·tive·ly** vergleichsweise; verhältnismäßig
**com·pare 1.** *v/t* vergleichen; ***~d with*** im Vergleich zu; *v/i* sich vergleichen lassen **2.** ***beyond ~, without ~*** unvergleichlich
**com·pa·ri·son** Vergleich *m*
**com·part·ment** Fach *n*; RAIL Abteil *n*
**com·pass** Kompass *m*; ***pair of ~es*** Zirkel *m*
**com·pas·sion** Mitleid *n*
**com·pas·sion·ate** mitleidig
**com·pat·i·ble** vereinbar; ***be ~*** (***with***) passen (zu), zusammenpassen; IT *etc* kompatibel sein (mit)
**com·pat·ri·ot** Landsmann *m*, Landsmännin *f*
**com·pel** (er)zwingen
**com·pel·ling** bezwingend
**com·pen·sate** *j-n* entschädigen; *et.* ersetzen; ausgleichen
**com·pen·sa·tion** Ersatz *m*; Ausgleich *m*; Schadenersatz *m*, Entschädigung *f*; Bezahlung *f*, Gehalt *n*
**com·pere** *Br* Conférencier *m*
**com·pete** sich (mit)bewerben (***for*** um); konkurrieren; SPORT (am Wettkampf) teilnehmen
**com·pe·tence** Können *n*, Fähigkeit *f*
**com·pe·tent** fähig, tüchtig; fachkundig, sachkundig
**com·pe·ti·tion** Wettbewerb *m*; Konkurrenz *f*
**com·pet·i·tive** konkurrierend
**com·pet·i·tor** Mitbewerber(in); Konkurrent(in); SPORT (Wettbewerbs-)Teilnehmer(in)
**com·pile** kompilieren, zusammentragen, zusammenstellen
**com·pla·cence, com·pla·cen·cy** Selbstzufriedenheit *f*, Selbstgefälligkeit *f*; **com·pla·cent** selbstzufrieden, selbstgefällig
**com·plain** sich beklagen *or* beschweren (***about*** über *acc*; ***to*** bei); klagen (***of*** über *acc*)
**com·plaint** Klage *f*, Beschwerde *f*; MED Leiden *n*, *pl* MED *a.* Beschwerden *pl*
**com·ple·ment 1.** Ergänzung *f* **2.** ergänzen
**com·ple·men·ta·ry** (sich) ergänzend
**com·plete 1.** vollständig; vollzählig **2.** vervollständigen; beenden, abschließen
**com·ple·tion** Vervollständigung *f*; Abschluss *m*; **~ test** PSYCH Lückentext *m*
**com·plex 1.** zusammengesetzt; komplex, vielschichtig **2.** Komplex *m* (*a.* PSYCH)
**com·plex·ion** Gesichtsfarbe *f*, Teint *m*
**com·plex·i·ty** Komplexität *f*, Vielschichtigkeit *f*
**com·pli·ance** Einwilligung *f*; Befolgung *f*; ***in ~ with*** gemäß (*dat*)
**com·pli·ant** willfährig
**com·pli·cate** komplizieren
**com·pli·cat·ed** kompliziert
**com·pli·ca·tion** Komplikation *f* (*a.* MED)
**com·plic·i·ty** JUR Mitschuld *f*, Mittäterschaft *f* (***in*** an *dat*)
**com·pli·ment 1.** Kompliment *n*; Empfehlung *f*; Gruß *m* **2.** *v/t j-m* ein Kompliment *or* Komplimente machen (***on*** über *acc*)
**com·ply** (***with***) einwilligen (in *acc*); (*e-e Abmachung etc*) befolgen
**com·po·nent** Bestandteil *m*; TECH, ELECTR Bauelement *n*
**com·pose** zusammensetzen, -stellen; MUS komponieren; verfassen; ***be ~d of*** bestehen *or* sich zusammensetzen aus; ***~ o.s.*** sich beruhigen
**com·posed** ruhig, gelassen
**com·pos·er** MUS Komponist(in)
**com·po·si·tion** Zusammensetzung *f*; MUS Komposition *f*; PED Aufsatz *m*
**com·po·sure** Fassung *f*, (Gemüts)Ruhe *f*
**com·pound**[1] Lager *n*; Gefängnishof *m*; (Tier)Gehege *n*
**com·pound**[2] **1.** Zusammensetzung *f*; Verbindung *f*; LING zusammengesetztes Wort **2.** zusammengesetzt; ***~ interest*** ECON Zinseszinsen *pl* **3.** *v/t* zusammensetzen; steigern, *esp* verschlimmern
**com·pre·hend** begreifen, verstehen
**com·pre·hen·si·ble** verständlich
**com·pre·hen·sion** Verständnis *n*; Begriffsvermögen *n*, Verstand *m*; ***past ~*** unfassbar, unfasslich
**com·pre·hen·sive 1.** umfassend **2.** *a.* ***~ school*** *Br* Gesamtschule *f*
**com·press** zusammendrücken, -pres-

sen; **~ed air** Druckluft *f*
**com·pres·sion** PHYS Verdichtung *f*; TECH Druck *m*
**com·prise** einschließen, umfassen; bestehen aus
**com·pro·mise** **1.** Kompromiss *m* **2.** *v/t* bloßstellen, kompromittieren; *v/i* e-n Kompromiss schließen
**com·pro·mis·ing** kompromittierend; verfänglich
**com·pul·sion** Zwang *m*
**com·pul·sive** zwingend, Zwangs...; PSYCH zwanghaft
**com·pul·so·ry** obligatorisch; Pflicht..., Zwangs...
**com·punc·tion** Gewissensbisse *pl*; Reue *f*; Bedenken *pl*
**com·pute** berechnen; schätzen
**com·put·er** Computer *m*, Rechner *m*
**com·put·er|-aid·ed** computergestützt; **~-con·trolled** computergesteuert
**com·put·er| game** Computerspiel *n*; **~ graph·ics** Computergrafik *f*
**com·put·er·ize** (sich) auf Computer umstellen; computerisieren; mit Hilfe e-s Computers errechnen *or* zusammenstellen
**com·put·er| pre·dic·tion** Hochrechnung *f*; **~ sci·ence** Informatik *f*; **~ sci·en·tist** Informatiker *m*; **~ vi·rus** IT Computervirus *m*
**com·rade** Kamerad *m*; (Partei)Genosse *m*
**con**[1] → ***contra***
**con**[2] F reinlegen, betrügen
**con·ceal** verbergen; verheimlichen
**con·cede** zugestehen, einräumen
**con·ceit** Einbildung *f*, Dünkel *m*
**con·ceit·ed** eingebildet (***of*** auf *acc*)
**con·cei·va·ble** denkbar, begreiflich
**con·ceive** *v/i* schwanger werden; *v/t Kind* empfangen; sich *et.* vorstellen *or* denken
**con·cen·trate** (sich) konzentrieren
**con·cept** Begriff *m*; Gedanke *m*
**con·cep·tion** Vorstellung *f*, Begriff *m*; BIOL Empfängnis *f*
**con·cern** **1.** Angelegenheit *f*; Sorge *f*; ECON Geschäft *n*, Unternehmen *n* **2.** betreffen, angehen; beunruhigen
**con·cerned** besorgt; beteiligt (***in*** an *dat*)
**con·cern·ing** *prp* betreffend, hinsichtlich (*gen*), was ... (*acc*) (an)betrifft
**con·cert** MUS Konzert *n*
**con·cert hall** Konzerthalle *f*, -saal *m*
**con·ces·sion** Zugeständnis *n*; Konzession *f*
**con·cil·i·a·to·ry** versöhnlich, vermittelnd
**con·cise** kurz, knapp
**con·cise·ness** Kürze *f*
**con·clude** schließen, beenden; *Vertrag etc* abschließen; *et.* folgern, schließen (***from*** aus); ***to be ~d*** Schluss folgt
**con·clu·sion** (Ab)Schluss *m*, Ende *n*; Abschluss *m* (*of a contract etc*); (Schluss)Folgerung *f*; → ***jump***
**con·clu·sive** schlüssig
**con·coct** (zusammen)brauen; *fig* aushecken, ausbrüten
**con·coc·tion** Gebräu *n*; *fig* Erfindung *f*
**con·crete**[1] konkret
**con·crete**[2] **1.** Beton *m* **2.** Beton... **3.** betonieren
**con·cur** übereinstimmen
**con·cur·rence** Zusammentreffen *n*; Übereinstimmung *f*
**con·cus·sion** MED Gehirnerschütterung *f*
**con·demn** verurteilen (*a.* JUR); verdammen; für unbrauchbar *or* unbewohnbar *etc* erklären; **~ *to death*** JUR zum Tode verurteilen; **con·dem·na·tion** Verurteilung *f* (*a.* JUR); Verdammung *f*
**con·den·sa·tion** Kondensation *f*; Zusammenfassung *f*
**con·dense** kondensieren; zusammenfassen
**con·densed milk** Kondensmilch *f*
**con·dens·er** TECH Kondensator *m*
**con·de·scend** sich herablassen
**con·de·scend·ing** herablassend, gönnerhaft
**con·di·ment** Gewürz *n*, Würze *f*
**con·di·tion** **1.** Zustand *m*; (*körperlicher or* Gesundheits)Zustand *m*; SPORT Kondition *f*, Form *f*; Bedingung *f*; *pl* Verhältnisse *pl*, Umstände *pl*; ***on ~ that*** unter der Bedingung, dass; ***out of ~*** in schlechter Verfassung, in schlechtem Zustand **2.** bedingen; in Form bringen
**con·di·tion·al** **1.** (***on***) bedingt (durch), abhängig (von) **2.** *a.* **~ *clause*** LING Bedingungs-, Konditionalsatz *m*; *a.* **~ *mood*** LING Konditional *m*
**con·do** → ***condominium***
**con·dole** kondolieren (***with*** *dat*)
**con·do·lence** Beileid *n*

C

**con·dom** Kondom *n*, *m*
**con·do·min·i·um** Eigentumswohnanlage *f*; Eigentumswohnung *f*
**con·done** verzeihen, vergeben
**con·du·cive** dienlich, förderlich (***to*** *dat*)
**con·duct 1.** Führung *f*; Verhalten *n*, Betragen *n* **2.** führen; PHYS leiten; MUS dirigieren; ***~ed tour*** Führung *f* (***of*** durch); **con·duc·tor** Führer *m*, Leiter *m*; (*Bus-*, *Straßenbahn*)Schaffner *m*; RAIL Zugbegleiter *m*; MUS Dirigent *m*; PHYS Leiter *m*; ELECTR Blitzableiter *m*
**cone** Kegel *m*; GASTR Eistüte *f*; BOT Zapfen *m*
**con·fec·tion** Konfekt *n*
**con·fec·tion·er** Konditor *m*
**con·fec·tion·e·ry** Süßigkeiten *pl*, Süß-, Konditoreiwaren *pl*; Konfekt *n*; Konditorei *f*; Süßwarengeschäft *n*
**con·fed·e·ra·cy** (Staaten)Bund *m*; ***the Confederacy*** HIST die Konföderation
**con·fed·er·ate 1.** verbündet **2.** Verbündete *m*, Bundesgenosse *m* **3.** (sich) verbünden
**con·fed·er·a·tion** Bund *m*, Bündnis *n*; (Staaten)Bund *m*
**con·fer** *v/t Titel etc* verleihen (***on*** *dat*); *v/i* sich beraten
**con·fe·rence** Konferenz *f*
**con·fess** gestehen; beichten
**con·fes·sion** Geständnis *n*; REL Beichte *f*
**con·fes·sion·al** REL Beichtstuhl *m*
**con·fes·sor** REL Beichtvater *m*
**con·fi·dant(e)** Vertraute *m* (*f*)
**con·fide**: ***~ s.th. to s.o.*** j-m et. anvertrauen; ***~ in s.o.*** sich j-m anvertrauen
**con·fi·dence** Vertrauen *n*; Selbstvertrauen *n*; **~ man** → ***conman***; **~ trickster** Trickbetrüger *m*
**con·fi·dent** überzeugt, zuversichtlich
**con·fi·den·tial** vertraulich
**con·fine** begrenzen, beschränken; einsperren; ***be ~d of*** entbunden werden von; **con·fine·ment** Haft *f*; Beschränkung *f*; MED Entbindung *f*
**con·firm** bestätigen; bekräftigen; REL konfirmieren, firmen
**con·fir·ma·tion** Bestätigung *f*; REL Konfirmation *f*, Firmung *f*
**con·fis·cate** beschlagnahmen
**con·fis·ca·tion** Beschlagnahme *f*
**con·flict 1.** Konflikt *m*, Zwiespalt *m* **2.** im Widerspruch stehen (***with*** zu)
**con·flict·ing** widersprüchlich, zwiespältig
**con·form** (sich) anpassen (***to*** *dat*, an *acc*)
**con·found** verwirren, durcheinanderbringen
**con·front** gegenübertreten, -stehen (*dat*); sich stellen (*dat*); konfrontieren
**con·fron·ta·tion** Konfrontation *f*
**con·fuse** verwechseln; verwirren; **confused** verwirrt; verlegen; verworren;
**con·fu·sion** Verwirrung *f*; Verlegenheit *f*; Verwechslung *f*
**con·geal** erstarren (lassen); gerinnen (lassen)
**con·gest·ed** überfüllt; verstopft
**con·ges·tion** MED Blutandrang *m*; *a.* ***traffic ~*** Verkehrsstockung *f*, Verkehrsstörung *f*, Verkehrsstau *m*
**con·grat·u·late** beglückwünschen, *j-m* gratulieren
**con·grat·u·la·tion** Glückwunsch *m*; ***~s!*** ich gratuliere!, herzlichen Glückwunsch!
**con·gre·gate** (sich) versammeln
**con·gre·ga·tion** REL Gemeinde *f*
**con·gress** Kongress *m*; ***Congress*** PARL der Kongress
**Con·gress·man** PARL Kongressabgeordnete *m*; **Con·gress·wom·an** PARL Kongressabgeordnete *f*
**con·ic, con·i·cal** *esp* TECH konisch, kegelförmig
**co·ni·fer** BOT Nadelbaum *m*
**con·jec·ture 1.** Vermutung *f* **2.** vermuten
**con·ju·gal** ehelich
**con·ju·gate** LING konjugieren, beugen
**con·ju·ga·tion** LING Konjugation *f*, Beugung *f*
**con·junc·tion** Verbindung *f*; LING Konjunktion *f*, Bindewort *n*
**con·junc·ti·vi·tis** MED Bindehautentzündung *f*
**con·jure** zaubern; *Teufel etc* beschwören; ***~ up*** heraufbeschwören (*a. fig*)
**con·jur·er** *esp Br* → ***conjuror***
**con·jur·ing trick** Zauberkunststück *n*
**con·jur·or** Zauberer *m*, Zauberin *f*, Zauberkünstler(in)
**con·man** Betrüger *m*; Hochstapler *m*
**con·nect** verbinden; ELECTR anschließen, zuschalten; RAIL, AVIAT *etc* Anschluss haben (***with*** an *acc*)
**con·nect·ed** verbunden; (logisch) zu-

sammenhängend (*speech etc*); **be well ~** gute Beziehungen haben
**con·nec·tion**, *Br* **con·nex·ion** Verbindung *f*, Anschluss *m* (*a.* ELECTR, RAIL, AVIAT, TEL); Zusammenhang *m*; *mst pl* Beziehungen *pl*, Verbindungen *pl*; Verwandte *pl*
**con·quer** erobern; (be)siegen
**con·quer·or** Eroberer *m*
**con·quest** Eroberung *f* (*a. fig*); erobertes Gebiet
**con·science** Gewissen *n*
**con·sci·en·tious** gewissenhaft; Gewissens…; **con·sci·en·tious·ness** Gewissenhaftigkeit *f*
**con·sci·en·tious ob·jec·tor** MIL Wehrdienstverweigerer *m*
**con·scious** MED bei Bewusstsein; bewusst; **be ~ of** sich bewusst sein (*gen*)
**con·scious·ness** Bewusstsein *n* (*a.* MED)
**con·script** MIL **1.** einberufen **2.** Wehrpflichtige *m*; **con·scrip·tion** MIL Einberufung *f*; Wehrpflicht *f*
**con·se·crate** REL weihen; widmen
**con·se·cra·tion** REL Weihe *f*
**con·sec·u·tive** aufeinanderfolgend; fortlaufend
**con·sent 1.** Zustimmung *f* **2.** einwilligen, zustimmen
**con·se·quence** Folge *f*, Konsequenz *f*; Bedeutung *f*
**con·se·quent·ly** folglich, daher
**con·ser·va·tion** Erhaltung *f*; Naturschutz *m*; Umweltschutz *m*; **~ area** (Natur)Schutzgebiet *n*
**con·ser·va·tion·ist** Naturschützer(in); Umweltschützer(in)
**con·ser·va·tive 1.** erhaltend; konservativ; vorsichtig **2. *Conservative*** POL Konservative *m*, *f*
**con·ser·va·to·ry** Treibhaus *n*, Gewächshaus *n*; Wintergarten *m*
**con·serve** erhalten
**con·sid·er** *v/t* nachdenken über (*acc*); betrachten als, halten für; sich überlegen, erwägen; in Betracht ziehen, berücksichtigen; *v/i* nachdenken, überlegen
**con·sid·e·ra·ble** ansehnlich, beträchtlich; **con·sid·e·ra·bly** bedeutend, ziemlich, (sehr) viel
**con·sid·er·ate** rücksichtsvoll
**con·sid·e·ra·tion** Erwägung *f*, Überlegung *f*; Berücksichtigung *f*; Rücksicht (-nahme) *f*; ***take into ~*** in Erwägung *or* in Betracht ziehen
**con·sid·er·ing** in Anbetracht (der Tatsache, dass)
**con·sign** ECON *Waren* zusenden
**con·sign·ment** ECON (Waren)Sendung *f*; Zusendung *f*
**con·sist**: **~ *in*** bestehen in (*dat*); **~ *of*** bestehen aus
**con·sis·tence**, **con·sis·ten·cy** Konsistenz *f*, Beschaffenheit *f*; Übereinstimmung *f*; Konsequenz *f*
**con·sis·tent** übereinstimmend, vereinbar (***with*** mit); konsequent; SPORT *etc*: beständig
**con·so·la·tion** Trost *m*
**con·sole** trösten
**con·sol·i·date** festigen; *fig* zusammenschließen, -legen
**con·so·nant** LING Konsonant *m*, Mitlaut *m*
**con·spic·u·ous** deutlich sichtbar; auffallend
**con·spi·ra·cy** Verschwörung *f*
**con·spi·ra·tor** Verschwörer *m*
**con·spire** sich verschwören
**con·sta·ble** *Br* Polizist *m*
**con·stant** konstant, gleichbleibend; (be)ständig, (an)dauernd
**con·stant-care pa·tient** MED Pflegefall *m*
**con·ster·na·tion** Bestürzung *f*
**con·sti·pat·ed** MED verstopft
**con·sti·pa·tion** MED Verstopfung *f*
**con·sti·tu·en·cy** POL *Br* Wählerschaft *f*; Wahlkreis *m*
**con·sti·tu·ent** (wesentlicher) Bestandteil; POL Wähler(in)
**con·sti·tute** ernennen, einsetzen; bilden, ausmachen
**con·sti·tu·tion** POL Verfassung *f*; Konstitution *f*, körperliche Verfassung
**con·sti·tu·tion·al** konstitutionell; POL verfassungsmäßig
**con·strained** gezwungen, unnatürlich
**con·strict** zusammenziehen
**con·stric·tion** Zusammenziehung *f*
**con·struct** bauen, errichten, konstruieren
**con·struc·tion** Konstruktion *f*; Bau *m*, Bauwerk *n*; ***under ~*** im Bau (befindlich); **~ site** Baustelle *f*
**con·struc·tive** konstruktiv

C

**con·struc·tor** Erbauer *m*, Konstrukteur *m*
**con·sul** Konsul *m*
**con·su·late** Konsulat *n*; **~ gen·e·ral** Generalkonsulat *n*
**con·sul gen·e·ral** Generalkonsul *m*
**con·sult** *v/t* konsultieren, um Rat fragen; in *e-m Buch* nachschlagen; *v/i* (sich) beraten
**con·sul·tant** (fachmännischer) Berater; *Br* Facharzt *m*
**con·sul·ta·tion** Konsultation *f*, Beratung *f*, Rücksprache *f*
**con·sult·ing** beratend; **~ hours** *Br* MED Sprechstunde *f*; **~ room** *Br* MED Sprechzimmer *n*
**con·sume** *v/t Essen etc* zu sich nehmen, verzehren (*a. fig*); verbrauchen, konsumieren; zerstören, vernichten
**con·sum·er** ECON Verbraucher(in); **~ so·ci·e·ty** Konsumgesellschaft *f*
**con·sum·mate** **1.** vollendet **2.** vollenden; *Ehe* vollziehen
**con·sump·tion** Verbrauch *m*
**cont** *abbr of **continued*** Forts., Fortsetzung *f*; fortgesetzt
**con·tact** **1.** Berührung *f*; Kontakt *m*; Ansprechpartner(in), Kontaktperson *f* (*a.* MED); ***make ~s*** Verbindungen anknüpfen *or* herstellen **2.** sich in Verbindung setzen mit, Kontakt aufnehmen mit; **~ lens** Kontaktlinse *f*, -schale *f*, Haftschale *f*
**con·ta·gious** MED ansteckend (*a. fig*)
**con·tain** enthalten; *fig* zügeln, zurückhalten; **con·tain·er** Behälter *m*; ECON Container *m*; **con·tain·er·ize** ECON auf Containerbetrieb umstellen; in Containern transportieren
**con·tam·i·nate** verunreinigen; infizieren, vergiften; (*a.* radioaktiv) verseuchen; ***radioactively ~d*** verstrahlt; ***~d soil*** Altlasten *pl*; **con·tam·i·na·tion** Verunreinigung *f*; Vergiftung *f*; (*a.* radioaktive) Verseuchung
**contd** *abbr of **continued*** (→ ***cont***)
**con·tem·plate** (nachdenklich) betrachten; nachdenken über (*acc*); erwägen, beabsichtigen
**con·tem·pla·tion** (nachdenkliche) Betrachtung; Nachdenken *n*
**con·tem·pla·tive** nachdenklich
**con·tem·po·ra·ry** **1.** zeitgenössisch **2.** Zeitgenosse *m*, Zeitgenossin *f*
**con·tempt** Verachtung *f*
**con·temp·ti·ble** verachtenswert
**con·temp·tu·ous** geringschätzig, verächtlich
**con·tend** kämpfen, ringen (***for*** um; ***with*** mit); **con·tend·er** *esp* SPORT Wettkämpfer(in)
**con·tent**[1] Gehalt *m*, Aussage *f*, *pl* Inhalt *m*; (***table of***) ***~s*** Inhaltsverzeichnis *n*
**con·tent**[2] **1.** zufrieden **2.** befriedigen; ***~ o.s.*** sich begnügen
**con·tent·ed** zufrieden
**con·tent·ment** Zufriedenheit *f*
**con·test** **1.** (Wett)Kampf *m*; Wettbewerb *m* **2.** sich bewerben um; bestreiten, *a.* JUR anfechten
**con·tes·tant** Wettkämpfer(in), (Wettkampf)Teilnehmer(in)
**con·text** Zusammenhang *m*
**con·ti·nent** Kontinent *m*, Erdteil *m*; ***the Continent*** *Br* das (europäische) Festland; **con·ti·nen·tal** kontinental, Kontinental…
**con·tin·gen·cy** Möglichkeit *f*, Eventualität *f*; ***~ plan*** Notplan *m*
**con·tin·gent** **1.** ***be ~ on*** abhängen von **2.** Kontingent *n* (*a.* MIL)
**con·tin·u·al** fortwährend, unaufhörlich
**con·tin·u·a·tion** Fortsetzung *f*; Fortbestand *m*, Fortdauer *f*
**con·tin·ue** *v/t* fortsetzen, fortfahren mit; beibehalten; ***to be ~d*** Fortsetzung folgt; *v/i* fortdauern; andauern, anhalten; fortfahren, weitermachen
**con·ti·nu·i·ty** Kontinuität *f*
**con·tin·u·ous** ununterbrochen; **~ form** LING Verlaufsform *f*
**con·tort** verdrehen; verzerren
**con·tor·tion** Verdrehung *f*; Verzerrung *f*
**con·tour** Umriss *m*
**con·tra** wider, gegen
**con·tra·band** ECON Schmuggelware *f*
**con·tra·cep·tion** MED Empfängnisverhütung *f*
**con·tra·cep·tive** MED **1.** empfängnisverhütend **2.** Verhütungsmittel *n*
**con·tract** **1.** Vertrag *m* **2.** (sich) zusammenziehen; sich *e-e Krankheit* zuziehen; e-n Vertrag abschließen; sich vertraglich verpflichten
**con·trac·tion** Zusammenziehung *f*
**con·trac·tor** *a. **building ~*** Bauunternehmer *m*
**con·tra·dict** widersprechen (*dat*)

**con·tra·dic·tion** Widerspruch *m*
**con·tra·dic·to·ry** (sich) widersprechend
**con·tra·ry** **1.** entgegengesetzt (***to*** *dat*); gegensätzlich; **~ *to expectations*** wider Erwarten **2.** Gegenteil *n*; ***on the ~*** im Gegenteil
**con·trast** **1.** Gegensatz *m*; Kontrast *m* **2.** *v/t* gegenüberstellen, vergleichen; *v/i* sich abheben (***with*** von, gegen); im Gegensatz stehen (***with*** zu)
**con·trib·ute** beitragen, beisteuern; spenden (***to*** für)
**con·tri·bu·tion** Beitrag *m*; Spende *f*
**con·trib·u·tor** Beitragende *m, f*; Mitarbeiter(in)
**con·trib·u·to·ry** beitragend
**con·trite** zerknirscht
**con·trive** zustande bringen; es fertig bringen
**con·trol** **1.** Kontrolle *f*, Herrschaft *f*, Macht *f*, Gewalt *f*, Beherrschung *f*; Aufsicht *f*; TECH Steuerung *f*; *mst pl* TECH Steuervorrichtung *f*; ***get*** (***have, keep***) ***under ~*** unter Kontrolle bringen (haben, halten); ***get out of ~*** außer Kontrolle geraten; ***lose ~ of*** die Herrschaft *or* Gewalt *or* Kontrolle verlieren über **2.** beherrschen, die Kontrolle haben über (*acc*); *e-r Sache* Herr werden, (erfolgreich) bekämpfen; kontrollieren, überwachen; ECON (staatlich) lenken, *Preise* binden; ELECTR, TECH steuern, regeln, regulieren; **~ desk** ELECTR Schalt-, Steuerpult *n*; **~ pan·el** ELECTR Schalttafel *f*; **~ tow·er** AVIAT Kontrollturm *m*, Tower *m*
**con·tro·ver·sial** umstritten
**con·tro·ver·sy** Kontroverse *f*, Streit *m*
**con·tuse** MED sich *et.* prellen *or* quetschen; **con·tu·sion** MED Prellung *f*, Quetschung *f*
**con·va·lesce** gesund werden, genesen
**con·va·les·cence** Rekonvaleszenz *f*, Genesung *f*
**con·va·les·cent** **1.** genesend **2.** Rekonvaleszent(in), Genesende *m, f*
**con·vene** (sich) versammeln; zusammenkommen; *Versammlung* einberufen
**con·ve·ni·ence** Annehmlichkeit *f*, Bequemlichkeit *f*; *Br* Toilette *f*; ***all*** (***modern***) **~*s*** aller Komfort; ***at your earliest ~*** möglichst bald; **con·ve·ni·ent** bequem; günstig, passend
**con·vent** REL (Nonnen)Kloster *n*
**con·ven·tion** Zusammenkunft *f*, Tagung *f*, Versammlung *f*; Abkommen *n*; Konvention *f*, Sitte *f*; **con·ven·tion·al** herkömmlich, konventionell
**con·verge** konvergieren; zusammenlaufen, -strömen
**con·ver·sa·tion** Gespräch *n*, Unterhaltung *f*
**con·ver·sa·tion·al** Unterhaltungs…; **~ *English*** Umgangsenglisch *n*
**con·verse** sich unterhalten
**con·ver·sion** Umwandlung *f*, Verwandlung *f*; Umbau *m*; Umstellung *f* (***to*** auf *acc*); REL Bekehrung *f*, Übertritt *m*; MATH Umrechnung *f*; **~ ta·ble** Umrechnungstabelle *f*
**con·vert** (sich) umwandeln *or* verwandeln; umbauen (***into*** zu); umstellen (***to*** auf *acc*); REL *etc* (sich) bekehren; MATH umrechnen
**con·vert·er** ELECTR Umformer *m*
**con·ver·ti·ble** **1.** umwandelbar, verwandelbar; ECON konvertierbar **2.** MOT Kabrio(lett) *n*
**con·vey** befördern, transportieren, bringen; überbringen, übermitteln; *Ideen etc* mitteilen, vermitteln
**con·vey·ance** Beförderung *f*, Transport *m*; Übermittlung *f*; Verkehrsmittel *n*
**con·vey·or belt** TECH Förderband *n*
**con·vict** **1.** Verurteilte *m, f*; Strafgefangene *m, f* **2.** JUR (***of***) überführen (*gen*); verurteilen (wegen)
**con·vic·tion** Überzeugung *f*; JUR Verurteilung *f*
**con·vince** überzeugen
**con·voy** **1.** MAR Geleitzug *m*, Konvoi *m*; MOT (Wagen)Kolonne *f*; (Geleit-)Schutz *m* **2.** Geleitschutz geben (*dat*), eskortieren
**con·vul·sion** MED Zuckung *f*, Krampf *m*; **con·vul·sive** MED krampfhaft, krampfartig, konvulsiv
**coo** ZO gurren (*a. fig*)
**cook** **1.** Koch *m*; Köchin *f* **2.** kochen
**cook·book** Kochbuch *n*
**cook·er** *Br* Ofen *m*, Herd *m*
**cook·e·ry** Kochen *n*; Kochkunst *f*
**cook·e·ry book** *Br* Kochbuch *n*
**cook·ie** (süßer) Keks, Plätzchen *n*
**cook·ing** GASTR Küche *f*
**cook·y** → ***cookie***
**cool** **1.** kühl; *fig* kalt(blütig), gelassen;

abweisend; gleichgültig; F klasse, prima, cool **2.** Kühle *f*; F (Selbst)Beherrschung *f* **3.** (sich) abkühlen; *~ down, ~ off* sich beruhigen

C

**coon** F zo Waschbär *m*

**coop 1.** Hühnerstall *m* **2.** *~ up, ~ in* einsperren, einpferchen

**co-op** F Co-op *m*

**co·op·e·rate** zusammenarbeiten; mitwirken, helfen

**co·op·e·ra·tion** Zusammenarbeit *f*; Mitwirkung *f*, Hilfe *f*

**co·op·e·ra·tive 1.** zusammenarbeitend; kooperativ, hilfsbereit; ECON Gemeinschafts…, Genossenschafts… **2.** *a. ~ society* Genossenschaft *f*; Co-op *m*, Konsumverein *m*; *a. ~ store* Co-op *m*, Konsumladen *m*

**co·or·di·nate 1.** koordinieren, aufeinander abstimmen **2.** koordiniert, gleichgeordnet; **co·or·di·na·tion** Koordinierung *f*, Koordination *f*; harmonisches Zusammenspiel

**cop** F Bulle *m*

**cope**: *~ with* gewachsen sein (*dat*), fertigwerden mit

**cop·i·er** Kopiergerät *n*, Kopierer *m*

**co·pi·ous** reich(lich); weitschweifig

**cop·per 1.** MIN Kupfer *n*; Kupfermünze *f* **2.** kupfern, Kupfer…

**cop·pice, copse** Gehölz *n*

**cop·y 1.** Kopie *f*; Abschrift *f*; Nachbildung *f*; Durchschlag *m*; Exemplar *n*; (*Zeitungs*)Nummer *f*; PRINT Satzvorlage *f*; *fair ~* Reinschrift *f* **2.** kopieren; abschreiben, e-e Kopie anfertigen von; IT *Daten* übertragen; nachbilden; nachahmen

**cop·y·book** Schreibheft *n*

**cop·y·ing** Kopier…

**cop·y·right** Urheberrecht *n*, Copyright *n*

**cor·al** zo Koralle *f*

**cord 1.** Schnur *f* (*a.* ELECTR), Strick *m*; Kordsamt *m* **2.** ver-, zuschnüren

**cor·di·al**[1] Fruchtsaftkonzentrat *n*; MED Stärkungsmittel *n*

**cor·di·al**[2] herzlich

**cor·di·al·i·ty** Herzlichkeit *f*

**cord·less** schnurlos

**cord·less phone** schnurloses Telefon

**cor·don 1.** Kordon *m*, Postenkette *f* **2.** *~ off* abriegeln, absperren

**cor·du·roy** Kord *m*; (*a pair of*) *~s* (e-e) Kordhose

**core 1.** Kerngehäuse *n*; Kern *m*, *fig a. das* Innerste **2.** entkernen

**core time** ECON Kernzeit *f*

**cork 1.** Kork(en) *m* **2.** *a. ~ up* zu-, verkorken; **cork·screw** Korkenzieher *m*

**corn**[1] **1.** Korn *n*, Getreide *n*; *a. Indian ~* Mais *m* **2.** pökeln

**corn**[2] MED Hühnerauge *n*

**cor·ner 1.** Ecke *f*; Winkel *m*; *esp* MOT Kurve *f*; *soccer*: Eckball *m*, Ecke *f*; *fig* schwierige Lage, Klemme *f* **2.** Eck… **3.** in die Ecke (*fig* Enge) treiben; *~* **kick** *soccer*: Eckball *m*, Eckstoß *m*; *~* **shop** *Br* Tante-Emma-Laden *m*

**cor·net** MUS Kornett *n*; *Br* GASTR Eistüte *f*

**corn·flakes** Cornflakes *pl*

**cor·nice** ARCH Gesims *n*, Sims *m*

**cor·o·na·ry 1.** ANAT Koronar… **2.** F MED Herzinfarkt *m*

**cor·o·na·tion** Krönung *f*

**cor·o·net** Adelskrone *f*

**cor·po·ral** MIL Unteroffizier *m*

**cor·po·ral pun·ish·ment** körperliche Züchtigung

**cor·po·rate** gemeinsam; Firmen…

**cor·po·ra·tion** JUR Körperschaft *f*; Stadtverwaltung *f*; ECON (Aktien)Gesellschaft *f*

**corpse** Leichnam *m*, Leiche *f*

**cor·pu·lent** beleibt

**cor·ral 1.** Korral *m*, Hürde *f*, Pferch *m* **2.** *Vieh* in e-n Pferch treiben

**cor·rect 1.** korrekt, richtig, *a.* genau (*time*) **2.** korrigieren, verbessern, berichtigen

**cor·rec·tion** Korrektur *f*, Verbess(e)-rung *f*; Bestrafung *f*

**cor·rect·ness** Richtigkeit *f*

**cor·re·spond** (*with, to*) entsprechen (*dat*), übereinstimmen (mit); korrespondieren (*with* mit)

**cor·re·spon·dence** Übereinstimmung *f*; Korrespondenz *f*, Briefwechsel *m*; *~* **course** Fernkurs *m*

**cor·re·spon·dent 1.** entsprechend **2.** Briefpartner(in); Korrespondent(in)

**cor·re·spon·ding** entsprechend

**cor·ri·dor** Korridor *m*, Gang *m*

**cor·rob·o·rate** bekräftigen, bestätigen

**cor·rode** zerfressen; CHEM korrodieren; rosten; **cor·ro·sion** CHEM Korrosion *f*; Rost *m*; **cor·ro·sive** CHEM ätzend; *fig*

C

nagend, zersetzend
**cor·ru·gat·ed i·ron** Wellblech *n*
**cor·rupt** **1.** korrupt, bestechlich, käuflich; *moralisch* verdorben **2.** bestechen; *moralisch* verderben
**cor·rupt·i·ble** korrupt, bestechlich, käuflich
**cor·rup·tion** Verdorbenheit *f*; Unredlichkeit *f*; Korruption *f*; Bestechlichkeit *f*; Bestechung *f*
**cor·set** Korsett *n*
**cos·met·ic** **1.** kosmetisch, Schönheits… **2.** kosmetisches Mittel, Schönheitsmittel *n*
**cos·me·ti·cian** Kosmetiker(in)
**cos·mo·naut** Kosmonaut *m*, (Welt-)Raumfahrer *m*
**cos·mo·pol·i·tan** **1.** kosmopolitisch **2.** Weltbürger(in)
**cost** **1.** Preis *m*; Kosten *pl*; Schaden *m* **2.** kosten
**cost·ly** kostspielig; teuer erkauft
**cost of liv·ing** Lebenshaltungskosten *pl*
**cos·tume** Kostüm *n*, Kleidung *f*, Tracht *f*
**co·sy** *Br* → ***cozy***
**cot** Feldbett *n*; *Br* Kinderbett *n*
**cot·tage** Cottage *n*, (kleines) Landhaus; Ferienhaus *n*, Ferienhäuschen *n*
**cot·ton** **1.** Baumwolle *f*; Baumwollstoff *m*; (Baumwoll)Garn *n*, (Baumwoll-)Zwirn *m*; (Verband)Watte *f* **2.** baumwollen, Baumwoll…
**cot·ton·wood** BOT *e-e* amer. Pappel
**cot·ton wool** *Br* (Verband)Watte *f*
**couch** Couch *f*, Sofa *n*; Liege *f*
**cou·chette** RAIL Liegewagenplatz *m*; *a.* ***~ coach*** Liegewagen *m*
**cou·gar** ZO Puma *m*
**cough** **1.** Husten *m* **2.** husten
**coun·cil** Rat *m*, Ratsversammlung *f*; **~ house** *Br* gemeindeeigenes Wohnhaus
**coun·cil·(l)or** Ratsmitglied *n*, Stadtrat *m*, Stadträtin *f*
**coun·sel** **1.** Beratung *f*; Rat(schlag) *m*; *Br* JUR (Rechts)Anwalt *m*; ***~ for the defense*** (*Br* ***defence***) Verteidiger *m*; ***~ for the prosecution*** Anklagevertreter *m* **2.** *j-m* raten; zu *et.* raten; ***~ing center*** (*Br* ***~ling centre***) Beratungsstelle *f*
**coun·sel·(l)or** (*Berufs- etc*)Berater(in); JUR (Rechts)Anwalt *m*
**count**[1] Graf *m*
**count**[2] **1.** Zählung *f*; JUR Anklagepunkt *m* **2.** *v/t* (ab-, auf-, aus-, nach-, zusammen)zählen; aus-, berechnen; *fig* halten für, betrachten als; *v/i* zählen; gelten; ***~ down*** *Geld* hinzählen; den Count-down durchführen für, letzte (Start)Vorbereitungen treffen für; ***~ on*** zählen auf (*acc*), sich verlassen auf (*acc*), sicher rechnen mit
**count·down** Count-down *m*, *n*, letzte (Start)Vorbereitungen *pl*
**coun·te·nance** Gesichtsausdruck *m*; Fassung *f*, Haltung *f*
**count·er**[1] TECH Zähler *m*; *Br* Spielmarke *f*
**coun·ter**[2] Ladentisch *m*; Theke *f*; (Bank-, Post®)Schalter *m*
**coun·ter**[3] **1.** (ent)gegen, Gegen… **2.** entgegentreten (*dat*), entgegnen (*dat*), bekämpfen; abwehren
**coun·ter·act** entgegenwirken (*dat*); neutralisieren
**coun·ter·bal·ance** **1.** Gegengewicht *n* **2.** ein Gegengewicht bilden zu, ausgleichen
**coun·ter·clock·wise** entgegen dem Uhrzeigersinn
**coun·ter·es·pi·o·nage** Spionageabwehr *f*
**coun·ter·feit** **1.** falsch, gefälscht **2.** Fälschung *f* **3.** *Geld*, *Unterschrift etc* fälschen; **~ mon·ey** Falschgeld *n*
**coun·ter·foil** Kontrollabschnitt *m*
**coun·ter·mand** *Befehl etc* widerrufen; *Ware* abbestellen
**coun·ter·pane** Tagesdecke *f*
**coun·ter·part** Gegenstück *n*; genaue Entsprechung
**coun·ter·sign** gegenzeichnen
**coun·tess** Gräfin *f*
**count·less** zahllos
**coun·try** **1.** Land *n*, Staat *m*; Gegend *f*, Landschaft *f*; ***in the ~*** auf dem Lande **2.** Land…, ländlich
**coun·try·man** Landbewohner *m*; Bauer *m*; *a.* ***fellow ~*** Landsmann *m*
**coun·try road** Landstraße *f*
**coun·try·side** (ländliche) Gegend; Landschaft *f*
**coun·try·wom·an** Landbewohnerin *f*; Bäuerin *f*; *a.* ***fellow ~*** Landsmännin *f*
**coun·ty** (Land)Kreis *m*; *Br* Grafschaft *f*; **~ seat** Kreis(haupt)stadt *f*; **~ town** *Br* Grafschaftshauptstadt *f*
**coup** Coup *m*; Putsch *m*

C

**cou·ple** **1.** Paar *n*; **a ~ of** F ein paar **2.** (zusammen)koppeln; TECH kuppeln; ZO (sich) paaren
**cou·pon** Gutschein *m*; Kupon *m*, Bestellzettel *m*
**cour·age** Mut *m*
**cou·ra·geous** mutig, beherzt
**cou·ri·er** Kurier *m*, Eilbote *m*; Reiseleiter *m*
**course** AVIAT, MAR Kurs *m* (*a. fig*); SPORT (*Renn*)Bahn *f*, (*Renn*)Strecke *f*, (*Golf*)-Platz *m*; Verlauf *m*; GASTR Gang *m*; Reihe *f*, Zyklus *m*; Kurs *m*, Lehrgang *m*; ***of ~*** natürlich, selbstverständlich; ***the ~ of events*** der Gang der Ereignisse, der Lauf der Dinge
**court** **1.** Hof *m*; kleiner Platz; SPORT Platz *m*, (Spiel)Feld *n*; JUR Gericht *n*, Gerichtshof *m*; ***go to ~*** JUR prozessieren; ***take s.o. to ~*** JUR gegen j-n prozessieren; j-m den Prozess machen **2.** *j-m* den Hof machen; werben um
**cour·te·ous** höflich; **cour·te·sy** Höflichkeit *f*; ***by ~ of*** mit freundlicher Genehmigung von (*or gen*)
**court·house** Gerichtsgebäude *n*
**court·ier** Höfling *m*
**court·ly** höfisch; höflich
**court mar·tial** MIL Kriegsgericht *n*
**court-mar·tial** MIL vor ein Kriegsgericht stellen
**court·room** Gerichtssaal *m*
**court·ship** Werben *n*
**court·yard** Hof *m*
**cous·in** Cousin *m*, Vetter *m*; Cousine *f*, Kusine *f*
**cove** kleine Bucht
**cov·er** **1.** Decke *f*; Deckel *m*; Buchdeckel *m*, Einband *m*; Umschlag *m*; Titelseite *f*; Hülle *f*; Überzug *m*, Bezug *m*; Schutzhaube *f*, Schutzplatte *f*; Abdeckhaube *f*; Briefumschlag *m*; GASTR Gedeck *n*; Deckung *f*; Schutz *m*; *fig* Tarnung *f*; ***take ~*** in Deckung gehen; ***under plain ~*** in neutralem Umschlag; ***under separate ~*** mit getrennter Post **2.** (be-, zu)decken; einschlagen, einwickeln; verbergen; decken, schützen; ECON (ab)decken; versichern; *Thema* erschöpfend behandeln; *radio*, TV berichten über (*acc*); sich über *e-e Fläche etc* erstrecken; *Strecke* zurücklegen; SPORT *Gegenspieler* decken; *j-n* beschatten; ***~ up*** ab-, zudecken; *fig* verheimlichen, vertuschen; ***~ up for s.o.*** j-n decken
**cov·er·age** Berichterstattung *f* (***of*** über *acc*)
**cov·er girl** Covergirl *n*, Titelblattmädchen *n*
**cov·er·ing** Decke *f*; Überzug *m*; Hülle *f*; (*Fußboden*)Belag *m*
**cov·er sto·ry** Titelgeschichte *f*
**cow**[1] ZO Kuh *f*
**cow**[2] einschüchtern
**cow·ard** **1.** feig(e) **2.** Feigling *m*
**cow·ard·ice** Feigheit *f*
**cow·ard·ly** feig(e)
**cow·boy** Cowboy *m*
**cow·er** kauern; sich ducken
**cow·herd** Kuhhirt *m*
**cow·hide** Rind(s)leder *n*
**cow·house** Kuhstall *m*
**cowl** Mönchskutte *f*; Kapuze *f*; TECH Schornsteinkappe *f*
**cow·shed** Kuhstall *m*
**cow·slip** BOT Schlüsselblume *f*; Sumpfdotterblume *f*
**cox, cox·swain** Bootsführer *m*; *rowing*: Steuermann *m*
**coy** schüchtern, scheu
**coy·ote** ZO Kojote *m*, Präriewolf *m*
**co·zy** **1.** behaglich, gemütlich **2.** → ***egg cosy, tea cosy***
**CPU** *abbr of* ***central processing unit*** IT Zentraleinheit *f*
**crab** ZO Krabbe *f*, Taschenkrebs *m*
**crack** **1.** Knall *m*; Sprung *m*, Riss *m*; Spalt(e *f*) *m*, Ritze *f*; (heftiger) Schlag **2.** erstklassig **3.** *v/i* krachen, knallen, knacken; (zer)springen; überschnappen (*voice*); *a.* ***~ up*** zusammenbrechen; F ***~ up*** überschnappen; ***get ~ing*** F loslegen; *v/t* knallen mit (*Peitsche*), knacken mit (*Fingern*); zerbrechen; *Nuss*, F *Kode*, *Safe etc* knacken; ***~ a joke*** e-n Witz reißen; **crack·er** GASTR Cracker *m*, Kräcker *m*; Schwär-mer *m*, Knallfrosch *m*, Knallbonbon *m*, *n*
**crack·le** knattern, knistern, prasseln
**cra·dle** **1.** Wiege *f* **2.** wiegen; betten
**craft**[1] Boot(e *pl*) *n*, Schiff(e *pl*) *n*; Flugzeug(e *pl*) *n*; (Welt)Raumfahrzeug(e *pl*) *n*
**craft**[2] Handwerk *n*, Gewerbe *n*; Schlauheit *f*, List *f*
**crafts·man** (Kunst)Handwerker *m*
**craft·y** gerissen, listig, schlau

C

**crag** Klippe *f*, Felsenspitze *f*
**cram** *v/t* (voll)stopfen; nudeln, mästen; mit *j-m* pauken; *v/i* pauken, büffeln (***for*** für)
**cramp 1.** MED Krampf *m*; TECH Klammer *f*; *fig* Fessel *f* **2.** einengen, hemmen
**cran·ber·ry** BOT Preiselbeere *f*
**crane**[1] TECH Kran *m*
**crane**[2] **1.** ZO Kranich *m* **2.** den Hals recken; ~ ***one's neck*** sich den Hals verrenken (***for*** nach)
**crank 1.** TECH Kurbel *f*; TECH Schwengel *m*; F Spinner *m*, komischer Kauz **2.** (an)kurbeln
**crank·shaft** TECH Kurbelwelle *f*
**crank·y** wack(e)lig; verschroben; schlecht gelaunt
**cran·ny** Riss *m*, Ritze *f*
**crape** Krepp *m*, Flor *m*
**crash 1.** Krach *m*, Krachen *n*; MOT Unfall *m*, Zusammenstoß *m*; AVIAT Absturz *m*; ECON Zusammenbruch *m*, (Börsen)Krach *m* **2.** *v/t* zertrümmern; e-n Unfall haben mit; AVIAT abstürzen mit; *v/i* krachend einstürzen, zusammenkrachen; *esp* ECON zusammenbrechen; krachen (***against, into*** gegen); MOT zusammenstoßen, verunglücken; AVIAT abstürzen **3.** Schnell..., Sofort...; ~ **bar·ri·er** MOT Leitplanke *f*; ~ **course** Schnell-, Intensivkurs *m*; ~ **di·et** radikale Schlankheitskur; ~ **hel·met** Sturzhelm *m*
**crash-land** AVIAT e-e Bruchlandung machen (mit); **crash land·ing** AVIAT Bruchlandung *f*
**crate** (Latten)Kiste *f*
**cra·ter** Krater *m*; Trichter *m*
**crave** sich sehnen (***for, after*** nach)
**crav·ing** heftiges Verlangen
**craw·fish** → ***crayfish***
**crawl 1.** Kriechen *n* **2.** kriechen; krabbeln; kribbeln; wimmeln (***with*** von); *swimming*: kraulen; ***it makes my skin*** ~ F mir läuft e-e Gänsehaut über den Rücken
**cray·fish** ZO Flusskrebs *m*
**cray·on** Zeichen-, Buntstift *m*
**craze** Verrücktheit *f*, F Fimmel *m*; ***be the*** ~ Mode sein
**cra·zy** verrückt (***about*** nach)
**creak** knarren, quietschen
**cream 1.** GASTR Rahm *m*, Sahne *f*; Creme *f*; *fig* Auslese *f*, Elite *f* **2.** creme (-farben); **cream·y** sahnig; weich
**crease 1.** (Bügel)Falte *f* **2.** (zer)knittern
**cre·ate** (er)schaffen; hervorrufen; verursachen
**cre·a·tion** Schöpfung *f*
**cre·a·tive** schöpferisch
**cre·a·tor** Schöpfer *m*
**crea·ture** Geschöpf *n*; Kreatur *f*
**crèche** (Kinder)Krippe *f*; (Weihnachts)Krippe *f*
**cre·den·tials** Beglaubigungsschreiben *n*; Referenzen *pl*; Zeugnis *n*; Ausweis *m*, Ausweispapiere *pl*
**cred·i·ble** glaubwürdig
**cred·it 1.** Glaube(n) *m*; Ruf *m*, Ansehen *n*; Verdienst *n*; ECON Kredit *m*; Guthaben *n*; ~ (***side***) Kredit(seite *f*) *n*, Haben *n*; ***on*** ~ auf Kredit **2.** *j-m* glauben; *j-m* trauen; ECON gutschreiben; ~ ***s.o. with s.th.*** j-m et. zutrauen; j-m et. zuschreiben
**cred·i·ta·ble** achtbar, ehrenvoll (***to*** für)
**cred·it card** ECON Kreditkarte *f*
**cred·i·tor** ECON Gläubiger *m*
**cred·its** *film*: Vorspann *m*, Nachspann *m*
**cred·it·wor·thy** ECON kreditwürdig
**cred·u·lous** leichtgläubig
**creed** REL Glaubensbekenntnis *n*
**creek** Bach *m*; *Br* kleine Bucht
**creep** kriechen; schleichen (*a. fig*); ~ ***in*** (sich) hinein- *or* hereinschleichen; sich einschleichen (*mistake etc*); ***it makes my flesh*** ~ mir läuft e-e Gänsehaut über den Rücken
**creep·er** BOT Kriech-, Kletterpflanze *f*
**creep·y** unheimlich
**cre·mate** verbrennen, einäschern
**cres·cent** Halbmond *m*
**cress** BOT Kresse *f*
**crest** ZO Haube *f*, Büschel *n*; (*Hahnen-*)Kamm *m*; Bergrücken *m*, Kamm *m*; (*Wellen*)Kamm *m*; Federbusch *m*; ***family*** ~ Familienwappen *n*
**crest·fal·len** niedergeschlagen
**cre·vasse** GEOL (Gletscher)Spalte *f*
**crev·ice** GEOL Riss *m*, Spalte *f*
**crew** AVIAT, MAR Besatzung *f*, Crew *f*, MAR Mannschaft *f*
**crib 1.** (Futter)Krippe *f*; Kinderbettchen *n*; *esp Br* (Weihnachts)Krippe *f*; F PED Spickzettel *m* **2.** F abschreiben, spicken
**crick**: ***a*** ~ ***in one's back*** (***neck***) ein stei-

fer Rücken (Hals)
**crick·et**[1] zo Grille *f*
**crick·et**[2] SPORT Kricket *n*
C
**crime** JUR Verbrechen *n*; *coll* Verbrechen *pl*; ~ **nov·el** Kriminalroman *m*
**crim·i·nal** **1.** kriminell; Kriminal…, Straf… **2.** Verbrecher(in), Kriminelle *m*, *f*
**crimp** kräuseln
**crim·son** karmesinrot; puterrot
**cringe** sich ducken
**crin·kle** **1.** Falte *f*, Fältchen *n* **2.** (sich) kräuseln; knittern
**crip·ple** **1.** Krüppel *m* **2.** zum Krüppel machen; *fig* lähmen
**cri·sis** Krise *f*
**crisp** knusp(e)rig, mürbe; frisch, knackig (*vegetable*); scharf, frisch (*air*); kraus (*hair*)
**crisp·bread** Knäckebrot *n*
**crisps** *a.* ***potato*** ~ *Br* (Kartoffel)Chips *pl*
**criss-cross** **1.** Netz *n* sich schneidender Linien **2.** kreuz und quer ziehen durch; kreuz und quer (ver)laufen
**cri·te·ri·on** Kriterium *n*
**crit·ic** Kritiker(in)
**crit·i·cal** kritisch; bedenklich
**crit·i·cis·m** Kritik *f* (***of*** an *dat*)
**crit·i·cize** kritisieren; kritisch beurteilen; tadeln
**cri·tique** Kritik *f*, Besprechung *f*, Rezension *f*
**croak** zo krächzen; quaken (*both a. fig*)
**cro·chet** **1.** Häkelei *f*; Häkelarbeit *f* **2.** häkeln
**crock·e·ry** Geschirr *n*
**croc·o·dile** zo Krokodil *n*
**cro·ny** F alter Freund
**crook** **1.** Krümmung *f*; Hirtenstab *m*; F Gauner *m* **2.** (sich) krümmen *or* biegen; **crook·ed** gekrümmt krumm; F unehrlich, betrügerisch
**croon** schmachtend singen; summen
**croon·er** Schnulzensänger(in)
**crop** **1.** AGR (Feld)Frucht *f*; Ernte *f*; zo Kropf *m*; kurzer Haarschnitt; kurz geschnittenes Haar **2.** zo abfressen, abweiden; *Haar* kurz schneiden; ~ ***up*** *fig* plötzlich auftauchen
**cross** **1.** Kreuz *n* (*a. fig*); BIOL Kreuzung *f*; *soccer*: Flanke *f* **2.** böse, ärgerlich **3.** (sich) kreuzen; *Straße* überqueren; *Plan etc* durchkreuzen; BIOL kreuzen; ~ ***off***, ~ ***out*** ausstreichen, durchstreichen; ~ ***o.s.*** sich bekreuzigen; ~ ***one's arms*** die Arme verschränken; ~ ***one's legs*** die Beine übereinanderschlagen; ***keep one's fingers*** ~***ed*** den Daumen drücken
**cross·bar** SPORT Tor-, Querlatte *f*
**cross·breed** Mischling *m*, Kreuzung *f*
**cross-coun·try** Querfeldein…, Gelände…; ~ ***skiing*** Skilanglauf *m*
**cross-ex·am·i·na·tion** JUR Kreuzverhör *n*; **cross-ex·am·ine** JUR ins Kreuzverhör nehmen
**cross-eyed**: ***be*** ~ schielen
**cross·ing** (*Straßen- etc*)Kreuzung *f*; Straßenübergang *m*; *Br* Fußgängerüberweg *m*; MAR Überfahrt *f*
**cross·road** Querstraße *f*
**cross·roads** (Straßen)Kreuzung *f*; *fig* Scheideweg *m*
**cross-sec·tion** Querschnitt *m*
**cross·walk** Fußgängerüberweg *m*
**cross·wise** kreuzweise
**cross·word (puz·zle)** Kreuzworträtsel *n*
**crotch** ANAT Schritt *m*
**crotch·et** MUS *Br* Viertelnote *f*
**crouch** **1.** sich ducken **2.** Hockstellung *f*
**crow** **1.** zo Krähe *f*; Krähen *n* **2.** krähen
**crow·bar** TECH Brecheisen *n*
**crowd** **1.** (Menschen)Menge *f*; Masse *f*; Haufen *m* **2.** sich drängen; *Straßen etc* bevölkern; vollstopfen
**crowd·ed** überfüllt, voll
**crown** **1.** Krone *f* **2.** krönen; *Zahn* überkronen; ***to*** ~ ***it all*** zu allem Überfluss
**cru·cial** entscheidend, kritisch
**cru·ci·fix** REL Kruzifix *n*
**cru·ci·fix·ion** REL Kreuzigung *f*
**cru·ci·fy** REL kreuzigen
**crude** roh, unbearbeitet; *fig* roh, grob
**crude** (oil) Rohöl *n*
**cru·el** grausam; roh, gefühllos
**cru·el·ty** Grausamkeit *f*; ~ ***to animals*** Tierquälerei *f*; ***society for the prevention of*** ~ ***to animals*** Tierschutzverein *m*; ~ ***to children*** Kindesmisshandlung *f*
**cru·et** Essig-, Ölfläschchen *n*
**cruise** **1.** Kreuzfahrt *f*, Seereise *f* **2.** kreuzen, e-e Kreuzfahrt *or* Seereise machen; AVIAT, MOT mit Reisegeschwindigkeit fliegen *or* fahren; ~ **mis·sile** MIL Marschflugkörper *m*
**cruis·er** Kreuzfahrtschiff *n*; MIL MAR

Kreuzer *m*; (Funk)Streifenwagen *m*
**crumb** Krume *f*, Krümel *m*
**crum·ble** zerkrümeln, zerbröckeln
**crum·ple** *v/t* zerknittern; *v/i* knittern; zusammengedrückt werden; ~ **zone** MOT Knautschzone *f*
**crunch** geräuschvoll (zer)kauen; knirschen
**cru·sade** HIST Kreuzzug *m* (*a. fig*)
**crush 1.** Gedränge *n*; ***have a ~ on s.o.*** für j-n schwärmen, F in j-n verknallt sein **2.** *v/t* zerquetschen, zermalmen, zerdrücken; TECH zerkleinern, zermahlen; auspressen; *fig* nieder-, zerschmettern, vernichten; *v/i* sich drängen; ~ **bar·ri·er** Barriere *f*, Absperrung *f*
**crust** (Brot)Kruste *f*, (Brot)Rinde *f*
**crus·ta·cean** ZO Krebs-, Krusten-, Schalentier *n*
**crust·y** krustig
**crutch** Krücke *f*
**cry 1.** Schrei *m*, Ruf *m*; Geschrei *n*; Weinen *n* **2.** schreien, rufen (***for*** nach); weinen; heulen, jammern
**crypt** Gruft *f*, Krypta *f*
**crys·tal** Kristall *m*; Uhrglas *n*
**crys·tal·line** kristallen
**crys·tal·lize** kristallisieren
**cub** ZO Junge *n*
**cube** Würfel *m* (*a.* MATH); PHOT Blitzwürfel *m*; MATH Kubikzahl *f*
**cube root** MATH Kubikwurzel *f*
**cu·bic, cu·bi·cal** würfelförmig; kubisch; Kubik…
**cu·bi·cle** Kabine *f*
**cuck·oo** ZO Kuckuck *m*
**cu·cum·ber** BOT Gurke *f*; (***as***) ***cool as a ~*** F eiskalt, kühl und gelassen
**cud** AGR wiedergekäutes Futter; ***chew the ~*** wiederkäuen; *fig* überlegen
**cud·dle** *v/t* an sich drücken; schmusen mit; *v/i*: ~ ***up*** sich kuscheln *or* schmiegen (***to*** an *acc*)
**cud·gel 1.** Knüppel *m* **2.** prügeln
**cue**[1] THEA *etc* Stichwort *n* (*a. fig*); *fig* Wink *m*
**cue**[2] *billiards*: Queue *n*
**cuff**[1] Manschette *f*; (Hosen-, *Br* Ärmel-) Aufschlag *m*
**cuff**[2] **1.** Klaps *m* **2.** *j-m* e-n Klaps geben
**cuff link** Manschettenknopf *m*
**cui·sine** GASTR Küche *f*
**cul·mi·nate** gipfeln (***in*** in *dat*)
**cu·lottes** (***a pair of*** ein) Hosenrock
**cul·prit** Schuldige *m, f*, Täter(in)
**cul·ti·vate** AGR anbauen, bebauen; kultivieren; *Freundschaft etc* pflegen
**cul·ti·vat·ed** AGR bebaut; *fig* gebildet, kultiviert
**cul·ti·va·tion** AGR Kultivierung *f*, Anbau *m*; *fig* Pflege *f*
**cul·tu·ral** kulturell; Kultur…
**cul·ture** Kultur *f* (*a.* BIOL); ZO Zucht *f*
**cul·tured** kultiviert; gezüchtet, Zucht…
**cum·ber·some** lästig, hinderlich; klobig
**cu·mu·la·tive** sich (an)häufend, anwachsend; Zusatz…
**cun·ning 1.** schlau, listig **2.** List *f*, Schlauheit *f*
**cup 1.** Tasse *f*; Becher *m*; Schale *f*; Kelch *m*; SPORT Cup *m*, Pokal *m* **2.** *die Hand* hohl machen; ***she ~ped her chin in her hand*** sie stützte das Kinn in die Hand
**cup·board** (Geschirr-, Speise-, *Br a.* Wäsche-, Kleider)Schrank *m*
**cup·board bed** Schrankbett *n*
**cup fi·nal** SPORT Pokalendspiel *n*
**cu·po·la** ARCH Kuppel *f*
**cup tie** SPORT Pokalspiel *n*
**cup win·ner** SPORT Pokalsieger *m*
**cur** Köter *m*; Schurke *m*
**cu·ra·ble** MED heilbar
**cu·rate** REL Hilfsgeistliche *m*
**cu·ra·tive** heilkräftig; ~ ***power*** Heilkraft *f*
**curb 1.** Kandare *f* (*a. fig*); Bordstein *m* **2.** an die Kandare legen (*a. fig*); *fig* zügeln
**curd** *a. pl* Dickmilch *f*, Quark *m*
**cur·dle** *v/t Milch* gerinnen lassen; *v/i* gerinnen, dick werden; ***the sight made my blood ~*** bei dem Anblick erstarrte mir das Blut in den Adern
**cure 1.** MED Kur *f*; (Heil)Mittel *n*; Heilung *f* **2.** MED heilen; GASTR pökeln; räuchern; trocknen
**cur·few** MIL Ausgangsverbot *n*, -sperre *f*
**cu·ri·o** Rarität *f*
**cu·ri·os·i·ty** Neugier *f*; Rarität *f*
**cu·ri·ous** neugierig; wissbegierig; seltsam, merkwürdig
**curl 1.** Locke *f* **2.** (sich) kräuseln *or* locken; **curl·er** Lockenwickler *m*; **curl·y** gekräuselt; gelockt, lockig
**cur·rant** BOT Johannisbeere *f*; GASTR Korinthe *f*
**cur·ren·cy** ECON Währung *f*; ***foreign ~*** Devisen *pl*
**cur·rent 1.** laufend; gegenwärtig, aktu-

C

ell; üblich, gebräuchlich; **~ events** Tagesereignisse *pl* **2.** Strömung *f*, Strom *m* (*both a. fig*); ELECTR Strom *m*; **~ account** *Br* ECON Girokonto *n*

**cur·ric·u·lum** Lehr-, Stundenplan *m*; **~ vi·tae** Lebenslauf *m*

**cur·ry**[1] GASTR Curry *m*, *n*

**cur·ry**[2] *Pferd* striegeln

**curse** **1.** Fluch *m*, Verwünschung *f* **2.** (ver)fluchen, verwünschen

**curs·ed** verflucht

**cur·sor** IT Cursor *m*

**cur·so·ry** flüchtig, oberflächlich

**curt** knapp; barsch, schroff

**cur·tail** *Ausgaben etc* kürzen; *Rechte* beschneiden

**cur·tain** **1.** Vorhang *m*, Gardine *f*; ***draw the ~s*** die Vorhänge auf- *or* zuziehen **2.** **~ *off*** mit Vorhängen abteilen

**curt·s(e)y** **1.** Knicks *m* **2.** knicksen (***to*** vor *dat*)

**cur·va·ture** Krümmung *f*

**curve** **1.** Kurve *f*; Krümmung *f*, Biegung *f* **2.** (sich) krümmen *or* biegen

**cush·ion** **1.** Kissen *n*, Polster *n* **2.** polstern; *Stoß etc* dämpfen

**cuss** **1.** Fluch *m* **2.** (ver)fluchen

**cus·tard** Eiercreme *f*, Vanillesoße *f*

**cus·to·dy** JUR Haft *f*; Sorgerecht *n*

**cus·tom** Brauch *m*, Gewohnheit *f*; ECON Kundschaft *f*

**cus·tom·a·ry** üblich

**cus·tom-built** nach Kundenangaben gefertigt

**cus·tom·er** Kunde *m*, Kundin *f*, Auftraggeber(in)

**cus·tom house** Zollamt *n*

**cus·tom-made** maßgefertigt, Maß…

**cus·toms** Zoll *m*; **~ clear·ance** Zollabfertigung *f*; **~ of·fi·cer, ~ of·fi·cial** Zollbeamte *m*

**cut** **1.** Schnitt *m*; MED Schnittwunde *f*; GASTR Schnitte *f*, Stück *n*; (Zu)Schnitt *m* (*clothes*); TECH Schnitt *m*, Schliff *m*; Haarschnitt *m*; *fig* Kürzung *f*, Senkung *f*; *cards*: Abheben *n* **2.** schneiden; ab-, an-, auf-, aus-, be-, durch-, zer-, zuschneiden; *Edelstein etc* schleifen; *Gras* mähen, *Bäume* fällen, *Holz* hacken; MOT *Kurve* schneiden; *Löhne etc* kürzen; *Preise* herabsetzen, senken; *Karten* abheben; ***~ one's teeth*** Zähne bekommen, zahnen; ***~ s.o.*** (***dead***) *fig* F j-n schneiden; ***~ s.o. or s.th. short*** j-n *or* et. unterbrechen, j-m ins Wort fallen; ***~ across*** quer durch … gehen; ***~ back*** *Pflanze* beschneiden, stutzen; einschränken; ***~ down*** *Bäume* fällen; verringern, einschränken, reduzieren; ***~ in*** F sich einmischen, unterbrechen; ***~ in on s.o.*** MOT j-n schneiden; ***~ off*** abschneiden; unterbrechen, trennen; *Strom etc* sperren; ***~ out*** (her)ausschneiden; *Kleid etc* zuschneiden; ***be ~ out for*** wie geschaffen sein für; ***~ up*** zerschneiden

**cut·back** Kürzung *f*

**cute** F schlau; niedlich, süß

**cu·ti·cle** Nagelhaut *f*

**cut·le·ry** (Ess)Besteck *n*

**cut·let** GASTR Kotelett *n*; (*Kalbs-, Schweine*)Schnitzel *n*; Hacksteak *n*

**cut·off date** Stichtag *m*

**cut-price, cut-rate** ECON herabgesetzt, ermäßigt; Billig…

**cut·ter** Zuschneider *m*; (*Glas-, Diamant*)Schleifer *m*; Schneidemaschine *f*, -werkzeug *n*; *film*: Cutter(in); MAR Kutter *m*

**cut·throat** **1.** Mörder *m*; Killer *m* **2.** mörderisch

**cut·ting** **1.** schneidend; scharf; TECH Schneid(e)…, Fräs… **2.** Schneiden *n*; BOT Steckling *m*; *esp Br* Ausschnitt *m*

**cut·tings** Schnipsel *pl*; Späne *pl*

**cut·ting torch** TECH Schneidbrenner *m*

**Cy·ber·space** → ***virtual reality***

**cy·cle**[1] Zyklus *m*; Kreis(lauf) *m*

**cy·cle**[2] **1.** Fahrrad *n* **2.** Rad fahren

**cy·cle| path, ~ track** (Fahr)Radweg *m*

**cy·cling** Radfahren *n*

**cy·clist** Radfahrer(in); Motorradfahrer(in)

**cy·clone** Wirbelsturm *m*

**cyl·in·der** Zylinder *m*, TECH *a.* Walze *f*, Trommel *f*

**cyn·ic** Zyniker(in); **cyn·i·cal** zynisch; **cyn·i·cism** Zynismus *m*

**cy·press** BOT Zypresse *f*

**cyst** MED Zyste *f*

**czar** → ***tsar***

**Czech** **1.** tschechisch; ***~ Republic*** Tschechien *n*, Tschechische Republik **2.** Tscheche *m*, Tschechin *f*; LING Tschechisch *n*

# D

D, d D, d *n*
d *abbr of* ***died*** gest., gestorben
**dab 1.** Klecks *m*, Spritzer *m* **2.** betupfen, abtupfen
**dab·ble** bespritzen; ***~ at, ~ in*** sich oberflächlich *or contp* in dilettantischer Weise beschäftigen mit
**dachs·hund** ZO Dackel *m*
**dad** F, **dad·dy** F Papa *m*, Vati *m*
**dad·dy long·legs** ZO Schnake *f*; Weberknecht *m*
**daf·fo·dil** BOT gelbe Narzisse
**dag·ger** Dolch *m*; ***be at ~s drawn*** *fig* auf Kriegsfuß stehen (***with*** mit)
**dai·ly 1.** täglich; ***the ~ grind*** *or* ***rut*** das tägliche Einerlei **2.** Tageszeitung *f*; Putzfrau *f*
**dain·ty 1.** zierlich, reizend; wählerisch **2.** Leckerbissen *m*
**dair·y** Molkerei *f*; Milchwirtschaft *f*; Milchgeschäft *n*
**dai·sy** BOT Gänseblümchen *n*
**dal·ly:** ***~ about*** herumtrödeln
**dam 1.** (Stau)Damm *m* **2.** *a.* ***~ up*** stauen, eindämmen
**dam·age 1.** Schaden *m*, (Be)Schädigung *f*; *pl* JUR Schadenersatz *m* **2.** (be)schädigen
**dam·ask** Damast *m*
**damn 1.** verdammen; verurteilen; ***~ (it)!*** F verflucht!, verdammt! **2.** *adj and adv* F → ***damned*** **3.** ***I don't give a ~*** F das ist mir völlig gleich(gültig) *or* egal
**dam·na·tion** Verdammung *f*; REL Verdammnis *f*
**damned** F verdammt
**damn·ing** vernichtend, belastend
**damp 1.** feucht, klamm **2.** Feuchtigkeit *f* **3.** *a.* **damp·en** an-, befeuchten; dämpfen; **damp·ness** Feuchtigkeit *f*
**dance 1.** Tanz *m*; Tanzveranstaltung *f* **2.** tanzen
**danc·er** Tänzer(in)
**danc·ing 1.** Tanzen *n* **2.** Tanz…
**dan·de·li·on** BOT Löwenzahn *m*
**dan·druff** (Kopf)Schuppen *pl*
**Dane** Däne *m*, Dänin *f*
**dan·ger** Gefahr *f*; ***be out of ~*** außer Lebensgefahr sein; **~ ar·e·a** Gefahrenzone *f*, Gefahrenbereich *m*
**dan·ger·ous** gefährlich
**dan·ger zone** → ***danger area***
**dan·gle** baumeln (lassen)
**Da·nish 1.** dänisch **2.** LING Dänisch *n*
**dank** feucht, nass(kalt)
**dare** *v/i* es wagen, sich (ge)trauen; ***I ~ say*** ich glaube wohl; allerdings; ***how ~ you!*** was fällt dir ein!; untersteh dich!; *v/t et.* wagen
**dare·dev·il** Draufgänger *m*
**dar·ing 1.** kühn, verwegen, waghalsig **2.** Mut *m*, Kühnheit *f*, Verwegenheit *f*
**dark 1.** dunkel; finster; *fig* düster, trüb(e); geheim(nisvoll) **2.** Dunkel *n*, Dunkelheit *f*; ***before (at, after) ~*** vor (bei, nach) Einbruch der Dunkelheit; ***keep s.o. in the ~ about s.th.*** j-n über et. im Ungewissen lassen
**Dark Ag·es** *das* frühe Mittelalter
**dark·en** (sich) verdunkeln *or* verfinstern
**dark·ness** Dunkelheit *f*, Finsternis *f*
**dark·room** PHOT Dunkelkammer *f*
**dar·ling 1.** Liebling *m* **2.** lieb; F goldig
**darn** stopfen, ausbessern
**dart 1.** Wurfpfeil *m*; Sprung *m*, Satz *m*; ***~s*** Darts *n* **2.** *v/t* werfen, schleudern; *v/i* schießen, stürzen
**dart·board** Dartsscheibe *f*
**dash 1.** Schlag *m*; Klatschen *n*; GASTR Prise *f* (*of salt*), Schuss *m* (*of rum etc*), Spritzer *m* (*of lemon etc*); Gedankenstrich *m*; SPORT Sprint *m*; *fig* Anflug *m*; ***a ~ of blue*** ein Stich ins Blaue; ***make a ~ for*** losstürzen auf (*acc*) **2.** *v/t* schleudern, schmettern; *Hoffnung etc* zerstören, zunichtemachen; *v/i* stürmen; ***~ off*** davonstürzen
**dash·board** MOT Armaturenbrett *n*
**dash·ing** schneidig, forsch
**da·ta** Daten *pl* (*a.* IT), Angaben *pl*; **~ base** IT Datenbank *f*; **~ car·ri·er** Datenträger *m*; **~ in·put** Dateneingabe *f*; **~ me·di·um** Datenträger *m*; **~ mem·o·ry** Datenspeicher *m*; **~ output** Datenausgabe *f*; **~ pro·cess·ing** Datenverarbeitung *f*; **~ pro·tec·tion** JUR Datenschutz *m*; **~ stor·age** Datenspeicher *m*; **~ trans·fer** Datenübertragung *f*
**date**[1] BOT Dattel *f*
**date**[2] **1.** Datum *n*; Zeit *f*, Zeitpunkt *m*;

D

Termin *m*; Verabredung *f*; F (Verabredungs)Partner(in); ***out of ~*** veraltet, unmodern; ***up to ~*** zeitgemäß, modern, auf dem Laufenden **2.** datieren; F sich verabreden mit, (aus)gehen mit
**dat·ed** veraltet, überholt
**da·tive** *a.* ***~ case*** LING Dativ *m*, dritter Fall
**daub** (be)schmieren
**daugh·ter** Tochter *f*
**daugh·ter-in-law** Schwiegertochter *f*
**daunt** entmutigen
**dav·en·port** Sofa *n*
**daw** zo Dohle *f*
**daw·dle** F (herum)trödeln
**dawn 1.** (Morgen)Dämmerung *f*; ***at ~*** bei Tagesanbruch **2.** dämmern; ***~ on*** *fig j-m* dämmern
**day** Tag *m*; *often pl* (Lebens)Zeit *f*; ***any ~*** jederzeit; ***these ~s*** heutzutage; ***the other ~*** neulich; ***the ~ after tomorrow*** übermorgen; ***the ~ before yesterday*** vorgestern; ***open all ~*** durchgehend geöffnet; ***let's call it a ~!*** machen wir Schluss für heute!, Feierabend!
**day·break** Tagesanbruch *m*
**day care cen·ter** (*Br* **cen·tre**) → ***day nursery***
**day·dream 1.** Tag-, Wachtraum *m* **2.** (mit offenen Augen) träumen
**day·dream·er** Träumer(in)
**day·light** Tageslicht *n*; ***in broad ~*** am helllichten Tag
**day nur·se·ry** (Kinder)Tagesstätte *f*
**day off** freier Tag
**day re·turn** *Br* Tagesrückfahrkarte *f*
**day·time**: ***in the ~*** am Tag, bei Tage
**daze 1.** blenden; betäuben **2.** ***in a ~*** benommen, betäubt
**dead 1.** tot; unempfindlich (***to*** für); matt; blind (*window etc*); erloschen; ECON flau; tot (*capital etc*); völlig, total; ***drop ~*** tot umfallen **2.** *adv* völlig, total; plötzlich, abrupt; genau, direkt; ***~ slow*** MOT Schritt fahren!; ***~ tired*** todmüde **3.** ***the ~*** die Toten *pl*
**dead·en** abstumpfen; (ab)schwächen; dämpfen
**dead end** Sackgasse *f* (*a. fig*)
**dead heat** SPORT totes Rennen
**dead·line** letzter (Ablieferungs)Termin; Stichtag *m*
**dead·lock** *fig* toter Punkt
**dead·locked** *fig* festgefahren
**dead·ly** tödlich
**deaf 1.** taub **2.** ***the ~*** die Tauben *pl*
**deaf-and-dumb** taubstumm
**deaf·en** taub machen; betäuben
**deaf-mute** Taubstumme *m, f*
**deal 1.** F Geschäft *n*, Handel *m*; Menge *f*; ***it's a ~!*** abgemacht!; ***a good ~*** ziemlich viel; ***a great ~*** sehr viel **2.** *v/t* (aus-, ver-, zu)teilen; *j-m Karten* geben; *j-m e-n Schlag* versetzen; *v/i* handeln (***in*** mit *e-r Ware*); *sl* dealen; *cards*: geben; ***~ with*** sich befassen mit, behandeln; ECON Handel treiben mit, Geschäfte machen mit; **deal·er** ECON Händler(in); *cards*: Geber(in); *sl* Dealer *m*; **deal·ing** *mst pl* Umgang *m*, Beziehungen *pl*
**dean** REL, UNIV Dekan *m*
**dear 1.** teuer; lieb; ***Dear Sir*** Sehr geehrter Herr … **2.** Liebste *m, f*, Schatz *m*; ***my ~*** m-e Liebe, mein Lieber **3.** *int* (***oh***) ***~!, ~ me!*** F du liebe Zeit!, ach herrje!; **dear·est** sehnlichst; **dear·ly** innig, von ganzem Herzen; ECON teuer
**death** Tod *m*; Todesfall *m*
**death·bed** Sterbebett *n*
**death cer·tif·i·cate** Totenschein *m*
**death·ly** tödlich; ***~ still*** totenstill
**death war·rant** JUR Hinrichtungsbefehl *m*; *fig* Todesurteil *n*
**de·bar**: ***~ s.o. from*** j-n ausschließen aus
**de·base** erniedrigen; mindern
**de·ba·ta·ble** umstritten
**de·bate 1.** Debatte *f*, Diskussion *f* **2.** debattieren, diskutieren
**deb·it** ECON **1.** Soll *n*; (Konto)Belastung *f*; ***~ and credit*** Soll und Haben *n* **2.** *j-n, ein Konto* belasten
**deb·ris** Trümmer *pl*, Schutt *m*
**debt** Schuld *f*; ***be in ~*** Schulden haben, verschuldet sein; ***be out of ~*** schuldenfrei sein; ***get into ~*** sich verschulden, Schulden machen
**debt·or** Schuldner(in)
**de·bug** TECH, IT Fehler beseitigen
**de·but** Debüt *n*
**Dec** *abbr of* ***December*** Dez., Dezember *m*
**dec·ade** Jahrzehnt *n*
**dec·a·dent** dekadent
**de·caf·fein·at·ed** koffeinfrei
**de·camp** F verschwinden
**de·cant** abgießen; umfüllen
**de·cant·er** Karaffe *f*
**de·cath·lete** SPORT Zehnkämpfer *m*

**de·cath·lon** SPORT Zehnkampf *m*
**de·cay** **1.** zerfallen; verfaulen; kariös *or* schlecht werden (*tooth*) **2.** Zerfall *m*; Verfaulen *n*
**de·cease** *esp* JUR Tod *m*, Ableben *n*
**de·ceased** *esp* JUR **1.** ***the ~*** der *or* die Verstorbene; die Verstorbenen *pl* **2.** verstorben
**de·ceit** Betrug *m*; Täuschung *f*
**de·ceit·ful** betrügerisch
**de·ceive** betrügen; täuschen
**de·ceiv·er** Betrüger(in)
**De·cem·ber** (*abbr* ***Dec***) Dezember *m*
**de·cen·cy** Anstand *m*
**de·cent** anständig; F annehmbar, (ganz) anständig; F nett
**de·cep·tion** Täuschung *f*
**de·cep·tive** trügerisch; ***be ~*** täuschen, trügen
**de·cide** (sich) entscheiden; bestimmen; beschließen, sich entschließen
**de·cid·ed** entschieden; bestimmt; entschlossen
**dec·i·mal** MATH **1.** *a.* ***~ fraction*** Dezimalbruch *m* **2.** Dezimal…
**de·ci·pher** entziffern
**de·ci·sion** Entscheidung *f*; Entschluss *m*; Entschlossenheit *f*; ***make a ~*** e-e Entscheidung treffen; ***reach*** *or* ***come to a ~*** zu e-m Entschluss kommen
**de·ci·sive** entscheidend; ausschlaggebend; entschieden
**deck** **1.** MAR Deck *n*; Spiel *n*, Pack *m* (Spiel)Karten **2.** ***~ out*** schmücken
**deck·chair** Liegestuhl *m*
**dec·la·ra·tion** Erklärung *f*; Zollerklärung *f*; **de·clare** erklären; deklarieren, verzollen
**de·clen·sion** LING Deklination *f*
**de·cline** **1.** abnehmen, zurückgehen; fallen; verfallen; (höflich) ablehnen; LING deklinieren **2.** Abnahme *f*, Rückgang *m*, Verfall *m*
**de·cliv·i·ty** (Ab)Hang *m*
**de·clutch** MOT auskuppeln
**de·code** entschlüsseln
**de·com·pose** zerlegen; (sich) zersetzen; verwesen
**de·con·tam·i·nate** entgasen, entgiften, entseuchen, entstrahlen
**de·con·tam·i·na·tion** Entseuchung *f*
**dec·o·rate** verzieren, schmücken; tapezieren; (an)streichen; dekorieren
**dec·o·ra·tion** Verzierung *f*, Schmuck *m*, Dekoration *f*; Orden *m*
**dec·o·ra·tive** dekorativ; Zier…
**dec·o·ra·tor** Dekorateur *m*; Maler *m* und Tapezierer *m*
**dec·o·rous** anständig
**de·co·rum** Anstand *m*
**de·coy** **1.** Lockvogel *m* (*a*, *fig*); Köder *m* (*a. fig*) **2.** ködern; locken (***into*** in *acc*); verleiten (***into*** zu)
**de·crease** **1.** Abnahme *f* **2.** abnehmen; (sich) vermindern
**de·cree** **1.** Dekret *n*, Erlass *m*, Verfügung *f*; *esp* JUR Entscheid *m*, Urteil *n* **2.** verfügen
**ded·i·cate** widmen
**ded·i·cat·ed** engagiert
**ded·i·ca·tion** Widmung *f*; Hingabe *f*
**de·duce** ableiten; folgern
**de·duct** *Betrag* abziehen (***from*** von); **de·duct·i·ble**: ***tax-~*** steuerlich absetzbar;
**de·duc·tion** Abzug *m*; (Schluss)Folgerung *f*, Schluss *m*
**deed** Tat *f*; Heldentat *f*; JUR (Übertragungs)Urkunde *f*
**deep** **1.** tief (*a. fig*) **2.** Tiefe *f*
**deep·en** (sich) vertiefen, *fig a.* (sich) verstärken
**deep freeze** **1.** tiefkühlen, einfrieren **2.** Tiefkühl-, Gefriertruhe *f*
**deep-fro·zen** tiefgefroren
**deep fry** frittieren
**deep·ness** Tiefe *f*
**deer** zo Hirsch *m*; Reh *n*
**de·face** entstellen; unleserlich machen; ausstreichen
**def·a·ma·tion** Verleumdung *f*
**de·fault** **1.** JUR Nichterscheinen *n* vor Gericht; SPORT Nichtantreten *n*; ECON Verzug *m* **2.** s-n Verpflichtungen nicht nachkommen, ECON *a.* im Verzug sein; JUR nicht vor Gericht erscheinen; SPORT nicht antreten
**de·feat** **1.** Niederlage *f* **2.** besiegen, schlagen; vereiteln, zunichtemachen
**de·fect** Defekt *m*, Fehler *m*; Mangel *m*
**de·fec·tive** mangelhaft; schadhaft, defekt
**de·fence** *Br* → ***defense***
**de·fence·less** *Br* → ***defenseless***
**de·fend** (***from, against***) verteidigen (gegen), schützen (vor *dat*, gegen)
**de·fen·dant** Angeklagte *m*, *f*; Beklagte *m*, *f*
**de·fend·er** Verteidiger(in); SPORT Ab-

wehrspieler(in)
**de·fense** Verteidigung *f* (*a.* MIL, JUR, SPORT), Schutz *m*; SPORT Abwehr *f*; ***witness for the ~*** Entlastungszeuge *m*
**de·fense·less** schutzlos, wehrlos
**de·fen·sive** **1.** Defensive *f*, Verteidigung *f*, Abwehr *f* **2.** defensiv; Verteidigungs..., Abwehr...
**de·fer** aufschieben, verschieben
**de·fi·ance** Herausforderung *f*; Trotz *m*
**de·fi·ant** herausfordernd; trotzig
**de·fi·cien·cy** Unzulänglichkeit *f*; Mangel *m*
**de·fi·cient** mangelhaft, unzureichend
**def·i·cit** ECON Defizit *n*, Fehlbetrag *m*
**de·file** beschmutzen
**de·fine** definieren; erklären, bestimmen
**def·i·nite** bestimmt; endgültig, definitiv
**def·i·ni·tion** Definition *f*, Bestimmung *f*, Erklärung *f*
**de·fin·i·tive** endgültig, definitiv
**de·flect** *v/t* ablenken; *Ball* abfälschen; *v/i* abweichen
**de·form** entstellen, verunstalten
**de·formed** deformiert, verunstaltet; verwachsen
**de·for·mi·ty** Missbildung *f*
**de·fraud** betrügen (***of*** um)
**de·frost** *v/t Windschutzscheibe etc* entfrosten; *Kühlschrank etc* abtauen, *Tiefkühlkost etc* auftauen; *v/i* ab-, auftauen
**deft** geschickt, gewandt
**de·fy** herausfordern; trotzen (*dat*)
**de·gen·e·rate** **1.** entarten **2.** entartet
**deg·ra·da·tion** Erniedrigung *f*
**de·grade** erniedrigen, demütigen
**de·gree** Grad *m*; Stufe *f*; (akademischer) Grad; ***by ~s*** allmählich; ***take one's ~*** e-n akademischen Grad erwerben, promovieren
**de·hy·drate** austrocknen; TECH das Wasser entziehen (*dat*)
**de·i·fy** vergöttern; vergöttlichen
**deign** sich herablassen
**de·i·ty** Gottheit *f*
**de·jec·ted** niedergeschlagen, mutlos, deprimiert
**de·jec·tion** Niedergeschlagenheit *f*
**de·lay** **1.** Aufschub *m*; Verzögerung *f*; RAIL *etc* Verspätung *f* **2.** ver-, aufschieben; verzögern; aufhalten; ***be ~ed*** sich verzögern; RAIL *etc* Verspätung haben
**del·e·gate** **1.** abordnen, delegieren; *Vollmachten etc* übertragen **2.** Delegierte *m, f*, bevollmächtigter Vertreter
**del·e·ga·tion** Übertragung *f*; Abordnung *f*, Delegation *f*
**de·lete** (aus)streichen; IT löschen
**de·lib·e·rate** absichtlich, vorsätzlich; bedächtig, besonnen
**de·lib·e·ra·tion** Überlegung *f*; Beratung *f*; Bedächtigkeit *f*
**del·i·ca·cy** Delikatesse *f*, Leckerbissen *m*; Zartheit *f*; Feingefühl *n*, Takt *m*
**del·i·cate** delikat (*a. fig*), schmackhaft; zart; fein; zierlich; zerbrechlich; heikel; empfindlich
**del·i·ca·tes·sen** Delikatessen *pl*, Feinkost *f*; Feinkostgeschäft *n*
**de·li·cious** köstlich
**de·light** **1.** Vergnügen *n*, Entzücken *n* **2.** entzücken, erfreuen; ***~ in*** (große) Freude haben an (*dat*)
**de·light·ful** entzückend
**de·lin·quen·cy** Kriminalität *f*
**de·lin·quent** **1.** straffällig **2.** Straffällige *m, f*; → ***juvenile*** *1*
**de·lir·i·ous** MED im Delirium, fantasierend; **de·lir·i·um** MED Delirium *n*
**de·liv·er** ausliefern, (ab)liefern; *Briefe* zustellen; *Rede etc* halten; befreien, erlösen; ***be ~ed of*** MED entbunden werden von
**de·liv·er·ance** Befreiung *f*
**de·liv·er·er** Befreier(in)
**de·liv·er·y** (Ab-, Aus)Lieferung *f*; *post* Zustellung *f*; Halten *n* (*e-r Rede*); Vortrag(sweise *f*) *m*; MED Entbindung *f*
**de·liv·er·y van** *Br* MOT Lieferwagen *m*
**dell** kleines Tal
**de·lude** täuschen
**del·uge** Überschwemmung *f*; *fig* Flut *f*
**de·lu·sion** Täuschung *f*; Wahn(vorstellung *f*) *m*
**de·mand** **1.** Forderung *f* (***for*** nach); Anforderung *f* (***on*** an *acc*); Nachfrage *f* (***for*** nach), Bedarf *m* (***for*** an *dat*); ***on ~*** auf Verlangen **2.** verlangen, fordern; (*fordernd*) fragen nach; erfordern
**de·mand·ing** anspruchsvoll
**de·men·ted** wahnsinnig
**dem·i...** Halb..., halb...
**de·mil·i·ta·rize** entmilitarisieren
**dem·o** F Demo *f*
**de·mo·bi·lize** demobilisieren
**de·moc·ra·cy** Demokratie *f*
**dem·o·crat** Demokrat(in)

**dem·o·crat·ic** demokratisch
**de·mol·ish** demolieren; ab-, ein-, niederreißen; zerstören
**dem·o·li·tion** Demolierung *f*; Niederreißen *n*, Abbruch *m*
**de·mon** Dämon *m*; Teufel *m*
**dem·on·strate** demonstrieren; beweisen; zeigen; vorführen
**dem·on·stra·tion** Demonstration *f*, *a.* Kundgebung *f*, *a.* Vorführung *f*; ~ **car** *Br* Vorführwagen *m*
**dem·on·stra·tor** Demonstrant(in); Vorführer(in); MOT Vorführwagen *m*
**de·mor·al·ize** demoralisieren
**de·mote** degradieren
**de·mure** ernst, zurückhaltend
**den** zo Höhle *f* (*a. fig*); F Bude *f*
**de·ni·al** Ablehnung *f*; Leugnen *n*; Verweigerung *f*; ***official*** ~ Dementi *n*
**den·ims** Jeans *pl*
**Den·mark** Dänemark *n*
**de·nom·i·na·tion** REL Konfession *f*; ECON Nennwert *m*
**de·note** bezeichnen; bedeuten
**de·nounce** (öffentlich) anprangern
**dense** dicht; *fig* beschränkt, begriffsstutzig; **den·si·ty** Dichte *f*
**dent 1.** Beule *f*, Delle *f* **2.** ver-, einbeulen
**den·tal** Zahn…; ~ **plaque** Zahnbelag *m*; ~ **plate** (Zahn)Prothese *f*; ~ **surgeon** Zahnarzt *m*, Zahnärztin *f*
**den·tist** Zahnarzt *m*, Zahnärztin *f*
**den·tures** (Zahn)Prothese *f*, (künstliches) Gebiss
**de·nun·ci·a·tion** Denunziation *f*
**de·nun·ci·a·tor** Denunziant(in)
**de·ny** abstreiten, bestreiten, dementieren, (ab)leugnen; *j-m et.* verweigern, abschlagen
**de·o·do·rant** De(s)odorant *n*, Deo *n*
**de·part** abreisen; abfahren, abfliegen; abweichen (***from*** von)
**de·part·ment** Abteilung *f*, UNIV *a.* Fachbereich *m*; POL Ministerium *n*
**De·part·ment| of De·fense** Verteidigungsministerium *n*; ~ **of State** *a.* ***State Department*** Außenministerium *n*; ~ **of the En·viron·ment** *Br* Umweltministerium *n*; ~ **of the In·te·ri·or** Innenministerium *n*
**de·part·ment store** Kaufhaus *n*, Warenhaus *n*
**de·par·ture** Abreise *f*; RAIL *etc* Abfahrt *f*; AVIAT Abflug *m*; *fig* Abweichung *f*; **~s** AVIAT, RAIL *etc* 'Abfahrt' (*timetable*); ***day of*** ~ Abreisetag *m*; ~ **gate** AVIAT Flugsteig *m*; ~ **lounge** AVIAT Abflughalle *f*
**de·pend:** ~ ***on*** sich verlassen auf (*acc*); abhängen von; angewiesen sein auf (*acc*); ***that*** **~s** das kommt darauf an
**de·pend·a·bil·i·ty** Zuverlässigkeit *f*
**de·pend·a·ble** zuverlässig
**de·pen·dant** Angehörige *m*, *f*
**de·pen·dence** Abhängigkeit *f*; Vertrauen *n*
**de·pen·dent 1.** (***on***) abhängig (von); angewiesen (auf *acc*); **2.** → ***dependant***
**de·plor·a·ble** bedauerlich, beklagenswert; **de·plore** beklagen, bedauern
**de·pop·u·late** entvölkern
**de·port** ausweisen, *Ausländer a.* abschieben; deportieren
**de·pose** *j-n* absetzen; JUR unter Eid erklären
**de·pos·it 1.** absetzen, abstellen; CHEM, GEOL (sich) ablagern *or* absetzen; deponieren, hinterlegen; ECON *Betrag* anzahlen **2.** CHEM Ablagerung *f*, GEOL *a.* (*Erz- etc*)Lager *n*; Deponierung *f*, Hinterlegung *f*; ECON Anzahlung *f*; ***make a*** ~ e-e Anzahlung leisten (***on*** für)
**dep·ot** Depot *n*; Bahnhof *m*
**de·prave** *moralisch* verderben
**de·pre·ci·ate** an Wert verlieren
**de·press** (nieder)drücken; deprimieren, bedrücken
**de·pressed** deprimiert, niedergeschlagen; ECON flau (*market*); Not leidend (*industry*); ~ **ar·e·a** ECON Notstandsgebiet *n*
**de·press·ing** deprimierend, bedrückend
**de·pres·sion** Depression *f*, Niedergeschlagenheit *f*; ECON Depression *f*, Flaute *f*; Senke *f*, Vertiefung *f*; METEOR Tief(druckgebiet) *n*
**de·prive:** ~ ***s.o. of s.th.*** j-m et. entziehen *or* nehmen; **de·prived** benachteiligt
**dept, Dept** *abbr of* ***department*** Abt., Abteilung *f*
**depth 1.** Tiefe *f* **2.** Tiefen…
**dep·u·ta·tion** Abordnung *f*
**dep·u·tize:** ~ ***for s.o.*** j-n vertreten
**dep·u·ty** (Stell)Vertreter(in); PARL Abgeordnete *m*, *f*; *a.* ~ ***sheriff*** Hilfssheriff *m*
**de·rail:** ***be*** **~ed** entgleisen
**de·ranged** geistesgestört

D

**der·by** F Melone *f*
**der·e·lict** heruntergekommen, baufällig
**de·ride** verhöhnen, verspotten
**de·ri·sion** Hohn *m*, Spott *m*
**de·ri·sive** höhnisch, spöttisch
**de·rive** herleiten (***from*** von); (sich) ableiten (***from*** von); abstammen (***from*** von); ~ ***pleasure from*** Freude finden *or* haben an (*dat*)
**der·ma·tol·o·gist** Dermatologe *m*, Hautarzt *m*
**de·rog·a·to·ry** abfällig, geringschätzig
**der·rick** TECH Derrickkran *m*; MAR Ladebaum *m*; TECH Bohrturm *m*
**de·scend** herab-, hinabsteigen, herunter-, hinuntersteigen, -gehen, -kommen; AVIAT niedergehen; abstammen, herkommen (***from*** von); ~ ***on*** herfallen über (*acc*); überfallen (*acc*) (*visitor etc*)
**de·scen·dant** Nachkomme *m*
**de·scent** Herab-, Hinuntersteigen *n*, -gehen *n*; AVIAT Niedergehen *n*; Gefälle *n*; Abstammung *f*, Herkunft *f*
**de·scribe** beschreiben
**de·scrip·tion** Beschreibung *f*, Schilderung *f*; Art *f*, Sorte *f*; **de·scrip·tive** beschreibend; anschaulich
**des·e·crate** entweihen
**de·seg·re·gate** die Rassentrennung aufheben in (*dat*); **de·seg·re·ga·tion** Aufhebung *f* der Rassentrennung
**des·ert**[1] **1.** Wüste *f* **2.** Wüsten…
**de·sert**[2] *v/t* verlassen, im Stich lassen; *v/i* MIL desertieren
**de·sert·er** MIL Deserteur *m*
**de·ser·tion** (JUR *a.* böswilliges) Verlassen; MIL Fahnenflucht *f*
**de·serve** verdienen
**de·serv·ed·ly** verdientermaßen
**de·serv·ing** verdienstvoll
**de·sign 1.** Design *n*, Entwurf *m*, (TECH Konstruktions)Zeichnung *f*; Design *n*, Muster *n*; (*a.* böse)Absicht **2.** entwerfen, TECH konstruieren; gestalten; ausdenken; bestimmen, vorsehen (***for*** für)
**des·ig·nate** *et. or j-n* bestimmen
**de·sign·er** Designer(in); TECH Konstrukteur *m*; (*Mode*)Schöpfer(in)
**de·sir·a·ble** erwünscht, wünschenswert; begehrenswert
**de·sire 1.** Wunsch *m*, Verlangen *n*, Begierde *f* (***for*** nach); **2.** wünschen; begehren
**de·sist** Abstand nehmen (***from*** von)
**desk** Schreibtisch *m*; Pult *n*; Empfang *m*, Rezeption *f*; Schalter *m*
**desk·top| com·put·er** Desktop-Computer *m*; ~ **pub·lish·ing** (*abbr* ***DTP***) IT Desktop-Publishing *n*
**des·o·late** einsam, verlassen; trostlos
**de·spair 1.** Verzweiflung *f*; ***drive s.o. to ~*** j-n zur Verzweiflung bringen **2.** verzweifeln (***of*** an *dat*)
**de·spair·ing** verzweifelt
**de·spatch** → ***dispatch***
**des·per·ate** verzweifelt; F hoffnungslos, schrecklich
**des·per·a·tion** Verzweiflung *f*
**des·pic·a·ble** verachtenswert, verabscheuungswürdig
**de·spise** verachten
**de·spite** trotz (*gen*)
**de·spon·dent** mutlos, verzagt
**des·pot** Despot *m*, Tyrann *m*
**des·sert** Nachtisch *m*, Dessert *n*
**des·ti·na·tion** Bestimmung *f*; Bestimmungsort *m*
**des·tined** bestimmt; MAR *etc* unterwegs (***for*** nach)
**des·ti·ny** Schicksal *n*
**des·ti·tute** mittellos
**de·stroy** zerstören, vernichten; *Tier* töten, einschläfern; **de·stroy·er** Zerstörer(in); MAR MIL Zerstörer *m*
**de·struc·tion** Zerstörung *f*, Vernichtung *f*; **de·struc·tive** zerstörend, vernichtend; zerstörerisch
**de·tach** (ab-, los)trennen, (los)lösen
**de·tached** einzeln, frei *or* allein stehend; unvoreingenommen; distanziert; ~ ***house*** Einzelhaus *n*
**de·tach·ment** (Los)Lösung *f*, (Ab-)Trennung *f*; MIL (Sonder)Kommando *n*
**de·tail 1.** Detail *n*, Einzelheit *f*; MIL (Sonder)Kommando *n*; ***in ~*** ausführlich **2.** genau schildern; MIL abkommandieren
**de·tailed** detailliert, ausführlich
**de·tain** aufhalten; JUR in (Untersuchungs)Haft behalten
**de·tect** entdecken, (heraus)finden
**de·tec·tion** Entdeckung *f*
**de·tec·tive** Kriminalbeamte *m*, Detektiv *m*; ~ **nov·el**, ~ **sto·ry** Kriminalroman *m*
**de·ten·tion** JUR Haft *f*; PED Nachsitzen *n*
**de·ter** abschrecken (***from*** von)
**de·ter·gent** Reinigungs-, Wasch-, Ge-

schirrspülmittel *n*
**de·te·ri·o·rate** (sich) verschlechtern, nachlassen; verderben
**de·ter·mi·na·tion** Entschlossenheit *f*, Bestimmtheit *f*; Entschluss *m*; Feststellung *f*, Ermittlung *f*; **de·ter·mine** *et.* beschließen, bestimmen; feststellen, ermitteln; (sich) entscheiden; sich entschließen; **de·ter·mined** entschlossen
**de·ter·rence** Abschreckung *f*
**de·ter·rent** **1.** abschreckend **2.** Abschreckungsmittel *n*
**de·test** verabscheuen
**de·throne** entthronen
**de·to·nate** *v/t* zünden; *v/i* detonieren, explodieren
**de·tour** Umweg *m*; Umleitung *f*
**de·tract:** ~ ***from*** ablenken von; schmälern (*acc*)
**de·tri·ment** Nachteil *m*, Schaden *m*
**deuce** *cards etc*: Zwei *f*; *tennis*: Einstand *m*
**de·val·u·a·tion** Abwertung *f*
**de·val·ue** abwerten
**dev·a·state** verwüsten
**dev·a·stat·ing** verheerend, vernichtend; F umwerfend, toll
**de·vel·op** (sich) entwickeln; *Naturschätze, Bauland* erschließen, *Altstadt etc* sanieren; **de·vel·op·er** PHOT Entwickler *m*; (Stadt)Planer *m*
**de·vel·op·ing** Entwicklungs…; ~ **country**, ~ **na·tion** Entwicklungsland *n*
**de·vel·op·ment** Entwicklung *f*; Erschließung *f*, Sanierung *f*
**de·vi·ate** abweichen (***from*** von)
**de·vi·a·tion** Abweichung *f*
**de·vice** Vorrichtung *f*, Gerät *n*; Plan *m*, Trick *m*; ***leave s.o. to his own ~s*** j-n sich selbst überlassen
**dev·il** Teufel *m* (*a. fig*)
**dev·il·ish** teuflisch
**de·vi·ous** abwegig; gewunden; unaufrichtig; ~ ***route*** Umweg *m*
**de·vise** (sich) ausdenken
**de·void:** ~ ***of*** ohne (*acc*)
**de·vote** widmen (***to*** *dat*); **de·vot·ed** ergeben; hingebungsvoll; eifrig, begeistert; **dev·o·tee** begeisterter Anhänger; **de·vo·tion** Ergebenheit *f*; Hingabe *f*; Frömmigkeit *f*, Andacht *f*
**de·vour** verschlingen
**de·vout** fromm; sehnlichst, innig
**dew** Tau *m*; **dew·y** taufeucht, taufrisch
**dex·ter·i·ty** Gewandtheit *f*
**dex·ter·ous, dex·trous** gewandt
**di·a·bol·i·cal** teuflisch
**di·ag·nose** diagnostizieren
**di·ag·no·sis** Diagnose *f*
**di·ag·o·nal** **1.** diagonal **2.** Diagonale *f*
**di·a·gram** Diagramm *n*, grafische Darstellung
**di·al** **1.** Zifferblatt *n*; TEL Wählscheibe *f*; Skala *f* **2.** TEL wählen; ~ ***direct*** durchwählen (***to*** nach); ***direct~(l)ing*** Durchwahl *f*
**di·a·lect** Dialekt *m*, Mundart *f*
**di·al·ling code** *Br* TEL Vorwahl (-nummer) *f*
**di·a·log,** *Br* **di·a·logue** Dialog *m*, (Zwie)Gespräch *n*
**di·am·e·ter** Durchmesser *m*; ***in ~*** im Durchmesser
**di·a·mond** Diamant *m*; Raute *f*, Rhombus *m*; *cards*: Karo *n*
**di·a·per** Windel *f*
**di·a·phragm** ANAT Zwerchfell *n*; OPT Blende *f*; TEL Membran(e) *f*
**di·ar·rh(o)e·a** MED Durchfall *m*
**di·a·ry** Tagebuch *n*
**dice** **1.** Würfel *m* **2.** GASTR in Würfel schneiden; würfeln
**dic·tate** diktieren; *fig* vorschreiben
**dic·ta·tion** Diktat *n*
**dic·ta·tor** Diktator *m*
**dic·ta·tor·ship** Diktatur *f*
**dic·tion** Ausdrucksweise *f*, Stil *m*
**dic·tion·a·ry** Wörterbuch *n*
**die**[1] sterben; *zo* eingehen, verenden; ~ ***of hunger*** verhungern; ~ ***of thirst*** verdursten; ~ ***away*** sich legen (*wind*); verklingen (*sound*); ~ ***down*** nachlassen; herunterbrennen; schwächer werden; ~ ***out*** aussterben (*a. fig*)
**die**[2] Würfel *m*
**di·et** **1.** Diät *f*; Nahrung *f*, Kost *f*; ***be on a ~*** Diät leben; ***put s.o. on a ~*** j-m e-e Diät verordnen **2.** Diät leben
**di·e·ti·cian** Diätassistent(in)
**dif·fer** sich unterscheiden; anderer Meinung sein (***with, from*** als); abweichen
**dif·fe·rence** Unterschied *m*; Differenz *f*; Meinungsverschiedenheit *f*
**dif·fe·rent** verschieden; andere(r, -s); anders (***from*** als)
**dif·fe·ren·ti·ate** (sich) unterscheiden
**dif·fi·cult** schwierig

**dif·fi·cul·ty** Schwierigkeit *f*, *pl* Unannehmlichkeiten *pl*
**dif·fi·dence** Schüchternheit *f*
**dif·fi·dent** schüchtern
**dif·fuse 1.** *fig* verbreiten **2.** diffus; *esp* PHYS zerstreut; weitschweifig
**dif·fu·sion** CHEM, PHYS (Zer)Streuung *f*
**dig 1.** graben; **~ (*up*)** umgraben; **~ (*up* or *out*)** ausgraben (*a. fig*); **~ *s.o. in the ribs*** j-m e-n Rippenstoß geben **2.** F Puff *m*, Stoß *m*; Seitenhieb *m* (***at*** auf *acc*)
**di·gest 1.** verdauen; **~ *well*** leicht verdaulich sein **2.** Abriss *m*; Auslese *f*, Auswahl *f*; **di·gest·i·ble** verdaulich; **di·ges·tion** Verdauung *f*; **di·ges·tive** verdauungsfördernd; Verdauungs…
**dig·ger** (*esp* Gold)Gräber *m*
**di·git** Ziffer *f*; ***three-~ number*** dreistellige Zahl
**di·gi·tal** digital, Digital…; **~ camera** Digitalkamera *f*; **~ clock** Digitaluhr *f*; **~ television, ~ TV** Digitalfernsehen *n* **~ watch** Digitaluhr *f*
**dig·ni·fied** würdevoll, würdig
**dig·ni·ta·ry** Würdenträger(in)
**dig·ni·ty** Würde *f*
**di·gress** abschweifen
**dike 1.** Deich *m*, Damm *m*; Graben *m* **2.** eindeichen, eindämmen
**di·lap·i·dat·ed** verfallen, baufällig, klapp(e)rig
**di·late** (sich) ausdehnen *or* (aus)weiten; *Augen* weit öffnen
**dil·a·to·ry** verzögernd, hinhaltend; langsam
**dil·i·gence** Fleiß *m*
**dil·i·gent** fleißig, emsig
**di·lute 1.** verdünnen; *fig* verwässern **2.** verdünnt; *fig* verwässert
**dim 1.** (halb)dunkel, düster; undeutlich, verschwommen; schwach, trüb(e) (*light*) **2.** (sich) verdunkeln *or* verdüstern; (sich) trüben; undeutlich werden; **~ *one's headlights*** MOT abblenden
**dime** Zehncentstück *n*
**di·men·sion** Dimension *f*, Maß *n*, Abmessung *f*; *pl a.* Ausmaß *n*
**di·min·ish** (sich) vermindern *or* verringern
**di·min·u·tive** klein, winzig
**dim·ple** Grübchen *n*
**din** Getöse *n*, Lärm *m*
**dine** essen, speisen; **~ *in*** zu Hause essen; **~ *out*** auswärts essen, essen gehen
**din·er** Speisende *m*, *f*; Gast *m*; Speiselokal *n*; RAIL Speisewagen *m*
**din·ghy** MAR Jolle *f*; Dingi *n*; Beiboot *n*; Schlauchboot *n*
**din·gy** schmutzig, schmudd(e)lig
**din·ing car** RAIL Speisewagen *m*
**din·ing room** Ess-, Speisezimmer *n*
**din·ner** (Mittag-, Abend)Essen *n*; Diner *n*, Festessen *n*; **~ jack·et** Smoking *m*; **~ par·ty** Dinnerparty *f*, Abendgesellschaft *f*; **~ ser·vice, ~ set** Speiseservice *n*, Tafelgeschirr *n*
**din·ner·time** Essens-, Tischzeit *f*
**di·no** F → ***dinosaur***
**di·no·saur** zo Dinosaurier *m*
**dip 1.** *v/t* (ein)tauchen; senken; schöpfen; **~ *one's headlights*** *Br* MOT abblenden; *v/i* (unter)tauchen; sinken; sich neigen, sich senken **2.** (Ein-, Unter-)Tauchen *n*; F kurzes Bad; Senkung *f*, Neigung *f*, Gefälle *n*; GASTR Dip *m*
**diph·ther·i·a** MED Diphtherie *f*
**di·plo·ma** Diplom *n*
**di·plo·ma·cy** Diplomatie *f*
**dip·lo·mat** Diplomat *m*
**dip·lo·mat·ic** diplomatisch
**dip·per** Schöpfkelle *f*
**dire** schrecklich; höchste(r, -s), äußerste(r, -s)
**di·rect 1.** *adj* direkt; gerade; unmittelbar; offen, aufrichtig **2.** *adv* direkt, unmittelbar **3.** richten; lenken, steuern; leiten; anordnen; *j-n* anweisen; *j-m* den Weg zeigen; *Brief* adressieren; Regie führen bei; **~ cur·rent** ELECTR Gleichstrom *m*; **~ train** durchgehender Zug
**di·rec·tion** Richtung *f*; Leitung *f*, Führung *f*; *film etc*: Regie *f*; *mst pl* Anweisung *f*, Anleitung *f*; ***~s for use*** Gebrauchsanweisung *f*; ***sense of ~*** Ortssinn *m*; **~ in·di·ca·tor** MOT Fahrtrichtungsanzeiger *m*, Blinker *m*
**di·rec·tive** Anweisung *f*
**di·rect·ly 1.** *adv* sofort **2.** *cj* F sobald, sowie
**di·rec·tor** Direktor *m*; *film etc*: Regisseur(in)
**di·rec·to·ry** Adressbuch *n*
**di·rect speech** LING wörtliche Rede
**di·rect train** durchgehender Zug
**dirt** Schmutz *m*; (lockere) Erde

**dirt cheap** F spottbillig
**dirt·y 1.** schmutzig (*a. fig*) **2.** *v/t* beschmutzen; *v/i* schmutzig werden, schmutzen
**dis·a·bil·i·ty** Unfähigkeit *f*
**dis·a·bled 1.** arbeitsunfähig, erwerbsunfähig, invalid(e); MIL kriegsversehrt; *körperlich or geistig* behindert **2. the ~** die Behinderten *pl*
**dis·ad·van·tage** Nachteil *m*; Schaden *m*; **dis·ad·van·ta·geous** nachteilig, ungünstig
**dis·a·gree** nicht übereinstimmen; uneinig sein; nicht bekommen (**with s.o.** j-m); **dis·a·gree·a·ble** unangenehm; **dis·a·gree·ment** Verschiedenheit *f*, Unstimmigkeit *f*, Uneinigkeit *f*; Meinungsverschiedenheit *f*
**dis·ap·pear** verschwinden
**dis·ap·pear·ance** Verschwinden *n*
**dis·ap·point** *j-n* enttäuschen; *Hoffnungen etc* zunichtemachen
**dis·ap·point·ing** enttäuschend
**dis·ap·point·ment** Enttäuschung *f*
**dis·ap·prov·al** Missbilligung *f*
**dis·ap·prove** missbilligen; dagegen sein
**dis·arm** *v/t* entwaffnen (*a. fig*); *v/i* MIL, POL abrüsten; **dis·ar·ma·ment** Entwaffnung *f*; MIL, POL Abrüstung *f*
**dis·ar·range** in Unordnung bringen
**dis·ar·ray** Unordnung *f*
**di·sas·ter** Unglück *n*, Unglücksfall *m*, Katastrophe *f*; **~ ar·e·a** Katastrophen-, Notstandsgebiet *n*; **~ con·trol** Katastrophenschutz *m*
**di·sas·trous** katastrophal, verheerend
**dis·be·lief** Unglaube *m*; Zweifel *m* (**in** an *dat*); **dis·be·lieve** *et.* bezweifeln, nicht glauben
**disc** *Br* → **disk**
**dis·card** *Karten* ablegen, *Kleidung etc a.* ausrangieren; *Freund etc* fallen lassen
**di·scern** wahrnehmen, erkennen
**di·scern·ing** kritisch, scharfsichtig
**di·scern·ment** Scharfblick *m*
**dis·charge 1.** *v/t* entladen, ausladen; *j-n* befreien, entbinden; *j-n* entlassen; *Gewehr etc* abfeuern; von sich geben, ausströmen, -senden, -stoßen; MED absondern; *Pflicht etc* erfüllen; *Zorn etc* auslassen (**on** an *dat*); *v/i* ELECTR sich entladen; sich ergießen, münden (*river*); MED eitern **2.** MAR Entladung *f*; MIL Abfeuern *n*; Ausströmen *n*; MED Absonderung *f*, Ausfluss *m*; Ausstoßen *n*; ELECTR Entladung *f*; Entlassung *f*; Erfüllung *f* (*e-r Pflicht*)
**di·sci·ple** Schüler *m*; Jünger *m*
**dis·ci·pline 1.** Disziplin *f* **2.** disziplinieren; **well ~d** diszipliniert; **badly ~d** disziplinlos, undiszipliniert
**dis·claim** abstreiten, bestreiten; *Verantwortung* ablehnen; JUR verzichten auf (*acc*)
**dis·close** bekannt geben *or* machen; enthüllen, aufdecken
**dis·clo·sure** Enthüllung *f*
**dis·co** Disko *f*
**dis·col·o(u)r** (sich) verfärben
**dis·com·fort 1.** Unbehagen *n*; Unannehmlichkeit *f* **2.** *j-m* Unbehagen verursachen
**dis·con·cert** aus der Fassung bringen
**dis·con·nect** trennen (*a.* ELECTR); TECH auskuppeln; ELECTR *Gerät* abschalten; *Gas, Strom, Telefon* abstellen; TEL *Gespräch* unterbrechen
**dis·con·nect·ed** zusammenhang(s)los
**dis·con·so·late** untröstlich
**dis·con·tent** Unzufriedenheit *f*
**dis·con·tent·ed** unzufrieden
**dis·con·tin·ue** aufgeben, aufhören mit; unterbrechen
**dis·cord** Uneinigkeit *f*, Zwietracht *f*, Zwist *m*; MUS Missklang *m*
**dis·cord·ant** nicht übereinstimmend; MUS unharmonisch, misstönend
**dis·co·theque** Diskothek *f*
**dis·count** ECON Diskont *m*; Preisnachlass *m*, Rabatt *m*, Skonto *m*, *n*
**dis·cour·age** entmutigen; abschrecken, abhalten, *j-m* abraten (**from** von)
**dis·cour·age·ment** Entmutigung *f*; Abschreckung *f*
**dis·course 1.** Unterhaltung *f*, Gespräch *n*; Vortrag *m* **2.** e-n Vortrag halten (**on** über *acc*)
**dis·cour·te·ous** unhöflich
**dis·cour·te·sy** Unhöflichkeit *f*
**dis·cov·er** entdecken; ausfindig machen, (heraus)finden
**dis·cov·e·ry** Entdeckung *f*
**dis·cred·it 1.** Zweifel *m*; Misskredit *m*, schlechter Ruf; **bring ~ (up)on** in Verruf bringen **2.** nicht glauben; in Misskredit bringen
**di·screet** besonnen, vorsichtig; diskret, verschwiegen

D

**di·screp·an·cy** Diskrepanz *f*, Widerspruch *m*
**di·scre·tion** Ermessen *n*, Gutdünken *n*; Diskretion *f*, Verschwiegenheit *f*
**di·scrim·i·nate** unterscheiden; **~ against** benachteiligen, diskriminieren; **di·scrim·i·nat·ing** kritisch, urteilsfähig; **di·scrim·i·na·tion** unterschiedliche (*esp* nachteilige) Behandlung; Diskriminierung *f*, Benachteiligung *f*; Urteilsfähigkeit *f*
**dis·cus** SPORT Diskus *m*
**di·scuss** diskutieren, erörtern, besprechen; **di·scus·sion** Diskussion *f*, Besprechung *f*
**dis·cus| throw** SPORT Diskuswerfen *n*; **~ throw·er** SPORT Diskuswerfer(in)
**dis·ease** Krankheit *f*
**dis·eased** krank
**dis·em·bark** von Bord gehen (lassen); MAR *Waren* ausladen
**dis·en·chant·ed**: ***be ~ with*** sich keine Illusionen mehr machen über (*acc*)
**dis·en·gage** (sich) frei machen; losmachen; TECH auskuppeln, loskuppeln
**dis·en·tan·gle** entwirren; (sich) befreien
**dis·fa·vo(u)r** Missfallen *n*; Ungnade *f*
**dis·fig·ure** entstellen
**dis·grace 1.** Schande *f*; Ungnade *f* **2.** Schande bringen über (*acc*), *j-m* Schande bereiten
**dis·grace·ful** schändlich; skandalös
**dis·guise 1.** verkleiden (***as*** als); *Stimme etc* verstellen; *et.* verbergen, verschleiern **2.** Verkleidung *f*; Verstellung *f*; Verschleierung *f*; ***in ~*** maskiert, verkleidet; *fig* verkappt; ***in the ~ of*** verkleidet als
**dis·gust 1.** Ekel *m*, Abscheu *m* **2.** (an)ekeln; empören, entrüsten
**dis·gust·ing** ekelhaft
**dish 1.** flache Schüssel; (Servier)Platte *f*; GASTR Gericht *n*, Speise *f*; ***the ~es*** das Geschirr; ***wash*** *or* ***do the ~es*** abspülen, abwaschen **2. ~ *out*** F austeilen; *often* **~ *up*** *Speisen* anrichten, auftragen; F *Geschichte etc* auftischen
**dish·cloth** Geschirrtuch *n*
**dis·heart·en** entmutigen
**di·shev·el(l)ed** zerzaust
**dis·hon·est** unehrlich, unredlich
**dis·hon·est·y** Unehrlichkeit *f*, Unredlichkeit *f*
**dis·hon·o(u)r 1.** Schande *f* **2.** Schande bringen über (*acc*); ECON *Wechsel* nicht honorieren *or* einlösen
**dis·hon·o(u)·ra·ble** schändlich, unehrenhaft
**dish·wash·er** Tellerwäscher *m*, Spüler(in); TECH Geschirrspülmaschine *f*, Geschirrspüler *m*
**dish·wa·ter** Spülwasser *n*
**dis·il·lu·sion 1.** Ernüchterung *f*, Desillusion *f* **2.** ernüchtern, desillusionieren; ***be ~ed with*** sich keine Illusionen mehr machen über (*acc*)
**dis·in·clined** abgeneigt
**dis·in·fect** MED desinfizieren
**dis·in·fec·tant** Desinfektionsmittel *n*
**dis·in·her·it** JUR enterben
**dis·in·te·grate** (sich) auflösen; verfallen, zerfallen
**dis·in·terest·ed** uneigennützig, selbstlos; objektiv, unvoreingenommen
**disk** Scheibe *f*; (Schall)Platte *f*; Parkscheibe *f*; IT Diskette *f*; ANAT Bandscheibe *f*; ***slipped ~*** MED Bandscheibenvorfall *m*
**disk drive** IT Diskettenlaufwerk *n*
**disk·ette** IT Floppy *f*, Diskette *f*
**disk jock·ey** Diskjockey *m*
**disk park·ing** MOT Parken *n* mit Parkscheibe
**dis·like 1.** Abneigung *f*, Widerwille *m* (***of, for*** gegen); ***take a ~ to s.o.*** gegen j-n e-e Abneigung fassen **2.** nicht leiden können, nicht mögen
**dis·lo·cate** MED sich *den Arm etc* verrenken *or* ausrenken
**dis·loy·al** treulos, untreu
**dis·mal** trüb(e), trostlos, elend
**dis·man·tle** TECH demontieren
**dis·may 1.** Schreck(en) *m*, Bestürzung *f*; ***in ~, with ~*** bestürzt; ***to my ~*** zu m-r Bestürzung **2.** *v/t* erschrecken, bestürzen
**dis·miss** *v/t* entlassen; wegschicken; ablehnen; *Thema etc* fallen lassen; JUR abweisen; **dis·miss·al** Entlassung *f*; Aufgabe *f*; JUR Abweisung *f*
**dis·mount** *v/i* absteigen, absitzen (***from*** von); *v/t* demontieren; TECH auseinandernehmen
**dis·o·be·di·ence** Ungehorsam *m*
**dis·o·be·di·ent** ungehorsam
**dis·o·bey** nicht gehorchen, ungehorsam sein (gegen)
**dis·or·der** Unordnung *f*; Aufruhr *m*; MED Störung *f*

**dis·or·der·ly** unordentlich; ordnungswidrig; unruhig; aufrührerisch
**dis·or·gan·ize** durcheinanderbringen; desorganisieren
**dis·own** nicht anerkennen; *Kind* verstoßen; ablehnen
**di·spar·age** verächtlich machen, herabsetzen; gering schätzen
**di·spar·i·ty** Ungleichheit *f*; **~ of** *or* **in age** Altersunterschied *m*
**dis·pas·sion·ate** leidenschaftslos; objektiv
**di·spatch** **1.** schnelle Erledigung; Sendung *f*; Abfertigung *f*; Eile *f*; Botschaft *f*; Bericht *m* **2.** schnell erledigen; absenden, abschicken, *Telegramm etc* aufgeben, abfertigen
**di·spel** *Menge etc* zerstreuen (*a. fig*), *Nebel* zerteilen
**di·spen·sa·ble** entbehrlich
**di·spen·sa·ry** Werks-, Krankenhaus-, Schul-, MIL Lazarettapotheke *f*
**dis·pen·sa·tion** Austeilung *f*; Befreiung *f*; Dispens *m*; *göttliche* Fügung
**di·spense** austeilen; *Recht* sprechen; *Arzneien* zubereiten und abgeben; **~ with** auskommen ohne; überflüssig machen; **di·spens·er** Spender *m*, *a.* Abroller *m* (*for adhesive tape etc*), (*Briefmarken- etc*)Automat *m*
**di·sperse** verstreuen; (sich) zerstreuen
**di·spir·it·ed** entmutigt
**dis·place** verschieben; ablösen, entlassen; *j-n* verschleppen; ersetzen; verdrängen
**dis·play** **1.** Entfaltung *f*; (Her)Zeigen *n*; (protzige) Zurschaustellung; IT Display *n*, Bildschirm *m*, Datenanzeige *f*; ECON Display *n*, Auslage *f*; **be on ~** ausgestellt sein **2.** entfalten; zur Schau stellen; zeigen
**dis·please** *j-m* missfallen
**dis·pleased** ungehalten
**dis·plea·sure** Missfallen *n*
**dis·pos·a·ble** Einweg…; Wegwerf…
**dis·pos·al** Beseitigung *f*, Entsorgung *f*; Endlagerung *f*; Verfügung(srecht *n*) *f*; **be** (**put**) **at s.o.'s ~** j-m zur Verfügung stehen (stellen)
**dis·pose** *v/t* (an)ordnen, einrichten; geneigt machen, bewegen; *v/i*: **~ of** verfügen über (*acc*); erledigen; loswerden; wegschaffen, beseitigen; *Abfall, a. Atommüll etc* entsorgen
**dis·posed** geneigt; …gesinnt
**dis·po·si·tion** Veranlagung *f*
**dis·pos·sess** enteignen, vertreiben; berauben (**of** *gen*)
**dis·pro·por·tion·ate(·ly)** unverhältnismäßig
**dis·prove** widerlegen
**di·spute** **1.** Disput *m*, Kontroverse *f*; Streit *m*; Auseinandersetzung *f* **2.** streiten (über *acc*); bezweifeln
**dis·qual·i·fy** unfähig *or* untauglich machen; für untauglich erklären; SPORT disqualifizieren
**dis·re·gard** **1.** Nichtbeachtung *f*; Missachtung *f* **2.** nicht beachten
**dis·rep·u·ta·ble** übel; verrufen
**dis·re·pute** schlechter Ruf
**dis·re·spect** Respektlosigkeit *f*; Unhöflichkeit *f*
**dis·re·spect·ful** respektlos; unhöflich
**dis·rupt** unterbrechen
**dis·sat·is·fac·tion** Unzufriedenheit *f*
**dis·sat·is·fied** unzufrieden (**with** mit)
**dis·sect** MED sezieren, zerlegen, zergliedern (*a. fig*)
**dis·sen·sion** Meinungsverschiedenheit(en *pl*) *f*, Differenz(en *pl*) *f*; Uneinigkeit *f*
**dis·sent** **1.** abweichende Meinung **2.** anderer Meinung sein (**from** als)
**dis·sent·er** Andersdenkende *m*, *f*
**dis·si·dent** Andersdenkende *m*, *f*; POL Dissident(in), Regime-, Systemkritiker(in)
**dis·sim·i·lar** (**to**) unähnlich (*dat*); verschieden (von)
**dis·sim·u·la·tion** Verstellung *f*
**dis·si·pate** (sich) zerstreuen; verschwenden
**dis·si·pat·ed** ausschweifend, zügellos
**dis·so·ci·ate** trennen; **~ o.s.** sich distanzieren (**from** von)
**dis·so·lute** → ***dissipated***
**dis·so·lu·tion** Auflösung *f*
**dis·solve** (sich) auflösen
**dis·suade** *j-m* abraten (**from** von)
**dis·tance** **1.** Abstand *m*; Entfernung *f*; Ferne *f*; Strecke *f*; *fig* Distanz *f*, Zurückhaltung *f*; **at a ~** von weitem; in einiger Entfernung; **keep s.o. at a ~** j-m gegenüber reserviert sein **2.** hinter sich lassen; **~ race** SPORT Langstreckenlauf *m*; **~ run·ner** SPORT Langstreckenläufer(in), Langstreckler(in)

**dis·tant** entfernt; fern, Fern...; distanziert
**dis·taste** Widerwille *m*, Abneigung *f*
**dis·taste·ful** ekelerregend; unangenehm; ***be ~ to s.o.*** j-m zuwider sein
**dis·tem·per** VET Staupe *f*
**dis·tend** (sich) (aus)dehnen; (auf)blähen; sich weiten
**dis·til(l)** destillieren
**dis·tinct** verschieden; deutlich, klar
**dis·tinc·tion** Unterscheidung *f*; Unterschied *m*; Auszeichnung *f*; Rang *m*
**dis·tinc·tive** unterscheidend; kennzeichnend, bezeichnend
**dis·tin·guish** unterscheiden; auszeichnen; ***~ o.s.*** sich auszeichnen
**dis·tin·guished** berühmt; ausgezeichnet; vornehm
**dis·tort** verdrehen; verzerren
**dis·tract** ablenken; **dis·tract·ed** beunruhigt, besorgt; (***by, with*** vor *dat*) außer sich, wahnsinnig; **dis·trac·tion** Ablenkung *f*; Zerstreuung *f*; Wahnsinn *m*; ***drive s.o. to ~*** j-n wahnsinnig machen
**dis·traught** → ***distracted***
**dis·tress 1.** Leid *n*, Kummer *m*, Sorge *f*; Not(lage) *f* **2.** beunruhigen, mit Sorge erfüllen
**dis·tressed** Not leidend; **~ ar·e·a** Notstandsgebiet *n*
**dis·tress·ing** besorgniserregend
**dis·trib·ute** ver-, aus-, zuteilen; ECON *Waren* vertreiben, absetzen; *Filme* verleihen; **dis·tri·bu·tion** Ver-, Aus-, Zuteilung *f*; ECON Vertrieb *m*, Absatz *m*; *film*: Verleih *m*
**dis·trict** Bezirk *m*; Gegend *f*
**dis·trust 1.** Misstrauen *n* **2.** misstrauen (*dat*); **dis·trust·ful** misstrauisch
**dis·turb** stören; beunruhigen
**dis·turb·ance** Störung *f*; Unruhe *f*; ***~ of the peace*** JUR Störung *f* der öffentlichen Sicherheit und Ordnung; ***cause a ~*** für Unruhe sorgen; ruhestörenden Lärm machen
**dis·turbed** geistig gestört; verhaltensgestört
**dis·used** nicht mehr benutzt (*machinery etc*), stillgelegt (*colliery etc*)
**ditch** Graben *m*
**di·van** Diwan *m*; **~ bed** Bettcouch *f*
**dive 1.** (unter)tauchen; *vom Sprungbrett* springen; e-n Hecht- *or* Kopfsprung machen; hechten (***for*** nach); e-n Sturzflug machen **2.** *swimming*: Springen *n*; Kopfsprung *m*, Hechtsprung *m*; *soccer*: Schwalbe *f*; AVIAT Sturzflug *m*; F Spelunke *f*; **div·er** Taucher(in); SPORT Wasserspringer(in)
**di·verge** auseinanderlaufen; abweichen; **di·ver·gence** Abweichung *f*; **di·ver·gent** abweichend
**di·verse** verschieden; mannigfaltig
**di·ver·si·fy** verschieden(artig) *or* abwechslungsreich gestalten
**di·ver·sion** Ablenkung *f*; Zeitvertreib *m*; *Br* MOT Umleitung *f*
**di·ver·si·ty** Verschiedenheit *f*; Mannigfaltigkeit *f*
**di·vert** ablenken; *j-n* zerstreuen, unterhalten; *Br Verkehr* umleiten
**di·vide 1.** *v/t* teilen; ver-, aus-, aufteilen; trennen; MATH dividieren, teilen (***by*** durch); *v/i* sich teilen; sich aufteilen; MATH sich dividieren *or* teilen lassen (***by*** durch); **2.** GEOGR Wasserscheide *f*
**di·vid·ed** geteilt; ***~ highway*** Schnellstraße *f*
**div·i·dend** ECON Dividende *f*
**di·vid·ers** (***a pair of ~*** ein) Stechzirkel *m*
**di·vine** göttlich
**di·vine ser·vice** REL Gottesdienst *m*
**div·ing 1.** Tauchen *n*; SPORT Wasserspringen *n* **2.** Taucher...
**div·ing·board** Sprungbrett *n*
**div·ing·suit** Taucheranzug *m*
**di·vin·i·ty** Gottheit *f*; Göttlichkeit *f*; Theologie *f*
**di·vis·i·ble** teilbar
**di·vi·sion** Teilung *f*; Trennung *f*; Abteilung *f*; MIL, MATH Division *f*
**di·vorce 1.** (Ehe)Scheidung *f*; ***get a ~*** sich scheiden lassen (***from*** von); **2.** JUR *j-n*, *Ehe* scheiden; ***get ~d*** sich scheiden lassen; **di·vor·cee** Geschiedene *m*, *f*
**DIY** ABBR → ***do-it-yourself***
**DIY store** Baumarkt *m*
**diz·zy** schwind(e)lig
**do** *v/t* tun, machen; (zu)bereiten; *Zimmer* aufräumen; *Geschirr* abwaschen; *Wegstrecke* zurücklegen, schaffen; ***~ you know him? no, I don't*** kennst du ihn? nein; ***what can I ~ for you?*** was kann ich für Sie tun?, womit kann ich (Ihnen) dienen?; ***~ London*** F London besichtigen; ***have one's hair done*** sich die Haare machen *or* frisieren las-

sen; ***have done reading*** fertig sein mit Lesen; *v/i* tun, handeln; sich befinden; genügen; ***that will ~*** das genügt; ***how ~ you ~?*** guten Tag!; ***~ be quick*** beeil dich doch; ***~ you like New York? I ~*** gefällt Ihnen New York? ja; ***she works hard, doesn't she?*** sie arbeitet viel, nicht wahr?; ***~ well*** s-e Sache gut machen; gute Geschäfte machen; ***~ away with*** beseitigen, weg-, abschaffen; ***do s.o. in*** F j-n umlegen; ***I'm done in*** F ich bin geschafft; ***~ up*** *Kleid etc* zumachen; *Haus etc* instand setzen; *Päckchen* zurechtmachen; ***~ o.s. up*** sich zurechtmachen; ***I could ~ with …*** ich könnte … brauchen *or* vertragen; ***~ without*** auskommen *or* sich behelfen ohne

**doc** F → ***doctor***

**do·cile** gelehrig; fügsam

**dock**[1] stutzen, kupieren

**dock**[2] **1.** MAR Dock *n*; Kai *m*, Pier *m*; JUR Anklagebank *f* **2.** *v/t* MAR (ein)docken; *Raumschiff* koppeln; *v/i* MAR anlegen; andocken, ankoppeln (*Raumschiff*)

**dock·er** Dock-, Hafenarbeiter *m*

**dock·ing** Docking *n*, Ankopp(e)lung *f*

**dock·yard** MAR Werft *f*

**doc·tor** Doktor *m* (*a.* UNIV), Arzt *m*, Ärztin *f*

**doc·tor·al**: ***~ thesis*** UNIV Doktorarbeit *f*

**doc·trine** Doktrin *f*, Lehre *f*

**doc·u·ment 1.** Urkunde *f* **2.** (urkundlich) belegen; **doc·u·men·ta·ry 1.** urkundlich; *film etc*: Dokumentar… **2.** Dokumentarfilm *m*

**dodge** (rasch) zur Seite springen, ausweichen; F sich drücken (vor *dat*)

**dodg·er** Drückeberger *m*

**doe** zo (Reh)Geiß *f*, Ricke *f*

**dog 1.** zo Hund *m* **2.** *j-n* beharrlich verfolgen

**dog-eared** mit Eselsohren (*book*)

**dog·ged** verbissen, hartnäckig

**dog·ma** Dogma *n*; Glaubenssatz *m*

**dog·mat·ic** dogmatisch

**do-it-your·self 1.** Heimwerken *n* **2.** Heimwerker…

**do-it-your·self·er** Heimwerker *m*

**dole 1.** milde Gabe; *Br* F Stempelgeld *n*; ***go*** *or* ***be on the ~*** *Br* F stempeln gehen **2.** ***~ out*** sparsam ver- *or* austeilen

**dole·ful** traurig, trübselig

**doll** Puppe *f*

**dol·lar** Dollar *m*

**dol·phin** zo Delphin *m*

**dome** Kuppel *f*

**do·mes·tic 1.** häuslich; inländisch, einheimisch; zahm **2.** Hausangestellte *m, f*; **~ an·i·mal** Haustier *n*

**do·mes·ti·cate** *Tier* zähmen

**do·mes·tic| flight** AVIAT Inlandsflug *m*; **~ mar·ket** ECON Binnenmarkt *m*; **~ trade** ECON Binnenhandel *m*; **~ vi·olence** häusliche Gewalt

**dom·i·cile** Wohnsitz *m*

**dom·i·nant** dominierend, (vor)herrschend

**dom·i·nate** beherrschen; dominieren

**dom·i·na·tion** (Vor)Herrschaft *f*

**dom·i·neer·ing** herrisch, tyrannisch

**do·nate** schenken; stiften; spenden (*a.* MED); **do·na·tion** Schenkung *f*

**done** getan; erledigt; fertig; GASTR gar

**don·key** zo Esel *m*

**do·nor** Spender(in) (*a.* MED)

**do-noth·ing** F Nichtstuer *m*

**doom 1.** Schicksal *n*, Verhängnis *n* **2.** verurteilen, verdammen

**Dooms·day** der Jüngste Tag

**door** Tür *f*; Tor *n*; ***next ~*** nebenan

**door·bell** Türklingel *f*

**door han·dle** Türklinke *f*

**door·keep·er** Pförtner *m*

**door·knob** Türknauf *m*

**door·mat** (Fuß)Abtreter *m*

**door·step** Türstufe *f*

**door·way** Türöffnung *f*

**dope 1.** F Stoff *m* (*Rauschgift*); Betäubungsmittel *n*; SPORT Dopingmittel *n*; *sl* Trottel *m* **2.** F *j-m* Stoff geben; SPORT dopen; **~ test** SPORT Dopingkontrolle *f*

**dor·mant** schlafend, ruhend; untätig

**dor·mi·to·ry** Schlafsaal *m*; Studentenwohnheim *n*

**dor·mo·bile®** Campingbus *m*, Wohnmobil *n*

**dor·mouse** zo Haselmaus *f*

**dose 1.** Dosis *f* **2.** *j-m* e-e Medizin geben

**dot 1.** Punkt *m*; Fleck *m*; ***on the ~*** F auf die Sekunde pünktlich **2.** punktieren; tüpfeln; *fig* sprenkeln; ***~ted line*** punktierte Linie

**dote**: ***~ on*** vernarrt sein in (*acc*)

**dot·ing** vernarrt

**doub·le 1.** doppelt; Doppel…; zweifach **2.** Doppelte *n*; Doppelgänger(in); *film*, TV Double *n* **3.** (sich) verdoppeln; *film*,

TV *j-n* doubeln; *a.* ~ ***up*** falten; *Decke* zusammenlegen; ~ ***back*** kehrtmachen; ~ ***up with*** sich krümmen vor (*dat*)
**dou·ble-breast·ed** zweireihig
**dou·ble-check** genau nachprüfen
**dou·ble chin** Doppelkinn *n*
**dou·ble-cross** ein doppeltes *or* falsches Spiel treiben mit
**dou·ble-deal·ing 1.** betrügerisch **2.** Betrug *m*
**dou·ble-deck·er** Doppeldecker *m*
**dou·ble-edged** zweischneidig (*a. fig*); zweideutig
**dou·ble fea·ture** *film*: Doppelprogramm *n*
**dou·ble-park** MOT in zweiter Reihe parken
**dou·bles** *esp tennis*: Doppel *n*; ***men's*** ~ Herrendoppel *n*; ***women's*** ~ Damendoppel *n*
**dou·ble-sid·ed** IT zweiseitig
**doubt 1.** *v/i* zweifeln; *v/t* bezweifeln; misstrauen (*dat*) **2.** Zweifel *m*; ***be in*** ~ ***about*** Zweifel haben an (*dat*); ***no*** ~ ohne Zweifel
**doubt·ful** zweifelhaft
**doubt·less** ohne Zweifel
**douche 1.** Spülung *f* (*a.* MED); Spülapparat *m* **2.** spülen (*a.* MED)
**dough** Teig *m*
**dough·nut** *appr* Krapfen *m*, Berliner Pfannkuchen, Schmalzkringel *m*
**dove** ZO Taube *f*
**dow·dy** unelegant; unmodern
**dow·el** TECH Dübel *m*
**down**[1] Daunen *pl*; Flaum *m*
**down**[2] **1.** *adv* nach unten, herunter, hinunter, herab, hinab, abwärts; unten **2.** *prp* herab, hinab, herunter, hinunter; ~ ***the river*** flussabwärts **3.** *adj* nach unten gerichtet; deprimiert, niedergeschlagen; ~ ***platform*** Abfahrtsbahnsteig *m* (*in London*); ~ ***train*** Zug *m* (von London fort) **4.** *v/t* niederschlagen; *Flugzeug* abschießen; F *Getränk* runterkippen; ~ ***tools*** die Arbeit niederlegen, in den Streik treten
**down·cast** niedergeschlagen
**down·fall** Platzregen *m*; *fig* Sturz *m*
**down·heart·ed** niedergeschlagen
**down·hill 1.** *adv* bergab **2.** *adj* abschüssig; *skiing*: Abfahrts... **3.** Abhang *m*; *skiing*: Abfahrt *f*
**down pay·ment** ECON Anzahlung *f*
**down·pour** Regenguss *m*, Platzregen *m*
**down·right 1.** *adv* völlig, ganz und gar, ausgesprochen **2.** *adj* glatt (*lie etc*); ausgesprochen
**downs** Hügelland *n*
**down·stairs** die Treppe herunter *or* hinunter; (nach) unten
**down·stream** stromabwärts
**down-to-earth** realistisch
**down·town 1.** *adv* im *or* ins Geschäftsviertel **2.** *adj* im Geschäftsviertel (gelegen *or* tätig); **3.** Geschäftsviertel *n*, Innenstadt *f*, City *f*
**down·ward(s)** abwärts, nach unten
**down·y** flaumig
**dow·ry** Mitgift *f*
**doze 1.** dösen, ein Nickerchen machen **2.** Nickerchen *n*
**doz·en** Dutzend *n*
**drab** trist; düster; eintönig
**draft 1.** Entwurf *m*; (Luft)Zug *m*; Zugluft *f*; Zug *m*, Schluck *m*; MAR Tiefgang *m*; ECON Tratte *f*, Wechsel *m*; MIL Einberufung *f*; ***beer on*** ~, ~ ***beer*** Bier *n* vom Fass, Fassbier *n* **2.** entwerfen; *Brief etc* aufsetzen; MIL einberufen
**draft·ee** MIL Wehr(dienst)pflichtige *m*
**drafts·man** TECH Zeichner *m*
**drafts·wom·an** TECH Zeichnerin *f*
**draft·y** zugig
**drag 1.** Schleppen *n*, Zerren *n*; *fig* Hemmschuh *m*; F *et.* Langweiliges **2.** schleppen, zerren, ziehen, schleifen; *a.* ~ ***behind*** zurückbleiben, nachhinken; ~ ***on*** weiterschleppen; *fig* sich dahinschleppen; *fig* sich in die Länge ziehen
**drag lift** Schlepplift *m*
**drag·on** MYTH Drache *m*
**drag·on·fly** ZO Libelle *f*
**drain 1.** Abfluss(kanal) *m*, Abflussrohr *n*; Entwässerungsgraben *m* **2.** *v/t* abfließen lassen; entwässern; austrinken, leeren; *v/i*: ~ ***off***, ~ ***away*** abfließen, ablaufen; **drain·age** Abfließen *n*, Ablaufen *n*, Entwässerung *f*; Entwässerungsanlage *f*, -system *n*
**drain·pipe** Abflussrohr *n*
**drake** ZO Enterich *m*, Erpel *m*
**dram** Schluck *m*
**dra·ma** Drama *n*; **dra·mat·ic** dramatisch; **dram·a·tist** Dramatiker *m*; **dram·a·tize** dramatisieren
**drape 1.** drapieren; in Falten legen **2.**

*mst* **~s** Vorhänge *pl*
**drap·er·y** *Br* Textilien *pl*
**dras·tic** drastisch, durchgreifend
**draught** *Br* → ***draft***
**draughts** *Br* Damespiel *n*
**draughts·man** *etc* → ***draftsman*** *etc*
**draugh·ty** *Br* → ***drafty***
**draw 1.** *v/t* ziehen; *Vorhänge* auf-, zuziehen; *Atem* holen; *Tee* ziehen lassen; *fig Menge* anziehen; *Interesse* auf sich ziehen; zeichnen; *Geld* abheben; *Scheck* ausstellen; *v/i* ziehen; SPORT unentschieden spielen; **~ *back*** zurückweichen; **~ *near*** sich nähern; **~ *out*** *Geld* abheben; *fig* in die Länge ziehen; **~ *up*** *Schriftstück* aufsetzen; MOT (an)halten; vorfahren **2.** Ziehen *n*; *lottery*: Ziehung *f*; SPORT Unentschieden *n*; Attraktion *f*, Zugnummer *f*
**draw·back** Nachteil *m*, Hindernis *n*
**draw·bridge** Zugbrücke *f*
**draw·er**[1] Schublade *f*, Schubfach *n*
**draw·er**[2] Zeichner(in); ECON Aussteller(in)
**draw·ing** Zeichnen *n*; Zeichnung *f*; **~ board** Reißbrett *n*; **~ pin** *Br* Reißzwecke *f*, Reißnagel *m*, Heftzwecke *f*; **~ room** → ***living room***; Salon *m*
**drawl** gedehnt sprechen
**drawn** abgespannt; SPORT unentschieden
**dread 1.** (große) Angst, Furcht *f* **2.** (sich) fürchten
**dread·ful** schrecklich, furchtbar
**dream 1.** Traum *m* **2.** träumen
**dream·er** Träumer(in)
**dream·y** träumerisch, verträumt
**drear·y** trübselig; trüb(e); langweilig
**dredge 1.** (Schwimm)Bagger *m* **2.** (aus)baggern
**dredg·er** (Schwimm)Bagger *m*
**dregs** Bodensatz *m*; *fig* Abschaum *m*
**drench** durchnässen
**dress 1.** Kleidung *f*; Kleid *n* **2.** (sich) ankleiden *or* anziehen; schmücken, dekorieren; zurechtmachen; GASTR zubereiten, *Salat* anmachen; MED *Wunde* verbinden; *Haare* frisieren; ***get* ~*ed*** sich anziehen; **~ *s.o. down*** F j-m e-e Standpauke halten; **~ *up*** (sich) fein machen; sich kostümieren *or* verkleiden
**dress cir·cle** THEA erster Rang
**dress de·sign·er** Modezeichner(in)
**dress·er** Anrichte *f*; Toilettentisch *m*
**dress·ing** An-, Zurichten *n*; Ankleiden *n*; MED Verband *m*; GASTR Dressing *n*, Füllung *f*
**dressing-down** F Standpauke *f*
**dress·ing| gown** *esp Br* Morgenrock *m*, -mantel *m*; SPORT Bademantel *m*; **~ room** THEA *etc* (Künstler)Garderobe *f*; SPORT (Umkleide)Kabine *f*; **~ ta·ble** Toilettentisch *m*
**dress·mak·er** (Damen)Schneider(in)
**dress re·hears·al** THEA *etc* Generalprobe *f*
**drib·ble** tröpfeln (lassen); sabbern, geifern; *soccer*: dribbeln
**dried** getrocknet, Dörr…
**dri·er** → ***dryer***
**drift 1.** (Dahin)Treiben *n*; (Schnee)Verwehung *f*; Schnee-, Sandwehe *f*; *fig* Tendenz *f* **2.** (dahin)treiben; wehen; sich häufen
**drill 1.** TECH Bohrer *m*; MIL Drill *m* (*a. fig*), Exerzieren *n* **2.** bohren; MIL drillen (*a. fig*); **drill·ing site** TECH Bohrgelände *n*, Bohrstelle *f*
**drink 1.** Getränk *n* **2.** trinken; **~ *to s.o.*** j-m zuprosten *or* zutrinken
**drink-driv·ing** *Br* Trunkenheit *f* am Steuer
**drink·er** Trinker(in)
**drinks ma·chine** Getränkeautomat *m*
**drip 1.** Tröpfeln *n*; MED Tropf *m* **2.** tropfen *or* tröpfeln (lassen); triefen
**drip-dry** bügelfrei
**drip·ping** Bratenfett *n*
**drive 1.** Fahrt *f*; Aus-, Spazierfahrt *f*; Zufahrt(sstraße) *f*; (private) Auffahrt; TECH Antrieb *m*; IT Laufwerk *n*; MOT (*Links- etc*)Steuerung *f*; PSYCH Trieb *m*; *fig* Kampagne *f*; *fig* Schwung *m*, Elan *m*, Dynamik *f* **2.** *v/t* treiben; *Auto etc* fahren, lenken, steuern; (im Auto *etc*) fahren; TECH (an)treiben; *a.* **~ *off*** vertreiben; *v/i* treiben; (Auto) fahren; **~ *off*** wegfahren; ***what are you driving at?*** F worauf wollen Sie hinaus?
**drive-in 1.** Auto…; **~ *cinema*** *Br*, **~ *motion-picture theater*** Autokino *n* **2.** Autokino *n*; Drive-in-Restaurant *n*; Autoschalter *m*, Drive-in-Schalter *m*
**driv·el 1.** faseln **2.** Geschwätz *n*, Gefasel *n*
**driv·er** MOT Fahrer(in); (*Lokomotiv-*) Führer *m*
**driv·er's li·cense** Führerschein *m*

**driv·ing** (an)treibend; TECH Antriebs…, Treib…, Trieb…; MOT Fahr…
**driv·ing force** *fig* Triebkraft *f*
**driv·ing li·cence** *Br* Führerschein *m*
**driv·ing test** Fahrprüfung *f*
**driz·zle 1.** Sprühregen *m* **2.** sprühen, nieseln
**drone 1.** zo Drohne *f* (*a. fig*) **2.** summen; dröhnen
**droop** (schlaff) herabhängen
**drop 1.** Tropfen *m*; Fallen *n*, Fall *m*; *fig* Fall *m*, Sturz *m*; Bonbon *m*, *n*; ***fruit ~s*** Drops *pl* **2.** *v/t* tropfen (lassen); fallen lassen(*a. fig*); *Brief* einwerfen; *Fahrgast* absetzen; senken; ***~ s.o. a few lines*** j-m ein paar Zeilen schreiben; *v/i* tropfen; herab-, herunterfallen; umsinken, fallen; ***~ in*** (kurz) hereinschauen; ***~ off*** abfallen; zurückgehen, nachlassen; F einnicken; ***~ out*** herausfallen; aussteigen (***of*** aus); *a.* ***~ out of school*** (***university***) die Schule (das Studium) abbrechen
**drop·out** Drop-out *m*, Aussteiger *m*; (Schul-, Studien)Abbrecher *m*
**drought** Trockenkeit *f*, Dürre *f*
**drown** *v/t* ertränken; überschwemmen; *fig* übertönen; *v/i* ertrinken
**drow·sy** schläfrig; einschläfernd
**drudge** sich (ab)placken, schuften, sich schinden; **drudg·e·ry** (stumpfsinnige) Plackerei *or* Schinderei *or* Schufterei
**drug 1.** Arzneimittel *n*, Medikament *n*; Droge *f*, Rauschgift *n*; ***be on ~s*** drogenabhängig *or* drogensüchtig sein; ***be off ~s*** clean sein **2.** *j-m* Medikamente geben; *j-n* unter Drogen setzen; ein Betäubungsmittel beimischen (*dat*); betäuben (*a. fig*); **~ a·buse** Drogenmissbrauch *m*; Medikamentenmissbrauch *m*; **~ ad·dict** Drogenabhängige *m*, *f*, Drogensüchtige *m*, *f*; ***be a ~*** drogenabhängig *or* drogensüchtig sein
**drug·gist** Apotheker(in); Inhaber(in) e-s Drugstores
**drug·store** Apotheke *f*; Drugstore *m*
**drug vic·tim** Drogentote *m*, *f*
**drum 1.** MUS Trommel *f*; ANAT Trommelfell *n*; *pl* MUS Schlagzeug *n* **2.** trommeln; **drum·mer** MUS Trommler *m*; Schlagzeuger *m*
**drunk 1.** *adj* betrunken; ***get ~*** sich betrinken **2.** Betrunkene *m*, *f*; → ***drunkard***
**drunk·ard** Trinker(in), Säufer(in)
**drunk driv·ing** Trunkenheit *f* am Steuer
**drunk·en** betrunken; **~ driv·ing** *Br* Trunkenheit *f* am Steuer
**dry 1.** trocken, GASTR *a.* herb; F durstig **2.** trocknen; dörren; ***~ out*** trocknen; e-e Entziehungskur machen, F trocken werden; ***~ up*** austrocknen; versiegen
**dry-clean** chemisch reinigen
**dry clean·er's** chemische Reinigung
**dry·er** TECH Trockner *m*
**dry goods** Textilien *pl*
**du·al** doppelt, Doppel…; **~ car·riageway** *Br* Schnellstraße *f*
**dub** *Film* synchronisieren
**du·bi·ous** zweifelhaft
**duch·ess** Herzogin *f*
**duck 1.** zo Ente *f*; Ducken *n*; F Schatz *m* **2.** (unter)tauchen; (sich) ducken
**duck·ling** zo Entchen *n*
**due 1.** zustehend; gebührend; angemessen; ECON fällig; ***~ to*** wegen (*gen*); ***be ~ to*** zurückzuführen sein auf (*acc*) **2.** *adv* direkt, genau (*nach Osten etc*)
**du·el** Duell *n*
**dues** Gebühren *pl*; Beitrag *m*
**du·et** MUS Duett *n*
**duke** Herzog *m*
**dull 1.** dumm; träge, schwerfällig; stumpf; matt (*eyes etc*); schwach (*hearing*); langweilig; abgestumpft, teilnahmslos; dumpf; trüb(e); ECON flau **2.** stumpf machen *or* werden; (sich) trüben; mildern, dämpfen; *Schmerz* betäuben; *fig* abstumpfen
**du·ly** ordnungsgemäß; gebührend; rechtzeitig
**dumb** stumm; sprachlos; F doof, dumm, blöd
**dum(b)·found·ed** verblüfft, sprachlos
**dum·my** Attrappe *f*; Kleider-, Schaufensterpuppe *f*; MOT Dummy *m*, Puppe *f*; *Br* Schnuller *m*
**dump 1.** *v/t* (hin)plumpsen *or* (hin)fallen lassen; auskippen; *Schutt etc* abladen; *Schadstoffe in e-n Fluss etc* einleiten, *im Meer* verklappen (***into*** in); ECON *Waren* zu Dumpingpreisen verkaufen **2.** Plumps *m*; Schuttabladeplatz *m*, Müllkippe *f*, Müllhalde *f*, (Müll)Deponie *f*; **dump·ing** ECON Dumping *n*, Ausfuhr *f* zu Schleuderpreisen
**dune** Düne *f*

**dung** AGR **1.** Dung *m* **2.** düngen
**dun·geon** (Burg)Verlies *n*
**dupe** betrügen, täuschen
**du·plex 1.** doppelt, Doppel... **2.** *a.* ~ ***apartment*** Maisonette *f*, Maisonettewohnung *f*; *a.* ~ ***house*** Doppel-, Zweifamilienhaus *n*
**du·pli·cate 1.** doppelt; ~ ***key*** Zweit-, Nachschlüssel *m* **2.** Duplikat *n*; Zweit-, Nachschlüssel *m* **3.** doppelt ausfertigen; kopieren, vervielfältigen
**du·plic·i·ty** Doppelzüngigkeit *f*
**dur·a·ble** haltbar; dauerhaft
**du·ra·tion** Dauer *f*
**du·ress** Zwang *m*
**dur·ing** während
**dusk** (Abend)Dämmerung *f*
**dusk·y** dämmerig, düster (*a. fig*); schwärzlich
**dust 1.** Staub *m* **2.** *v/t* abstauben; (be)streuen; *v/i* Staub wischen, abstauben
**dust·bin** *Br* Abfall-, Mülleimer *m*; Abfall-, Mülltonne *f*; ~ **lin·er** *Br* Müllbeutel *m*
**dust·cart** *Br* Müllwagen *m*
**dust cov·er, dust jack·et** Schutzumschlag *m*
**dust·er** Staubtuch *n*
**dust·man** *Br* Müllmann *m*
**dust·pan** Kehrichtschaufel *f*
**dust·y** staubig
**Dutch 1.** *adj* holländisch, niederländisch **2.** *adv*: ***go*** ~ getrennte Kasse machen **3.** LING Holländisch *n*, Niederländisch *n*; ***the*** ~ die Holländer *pl*, die Niederländer *pl*
**Dutch·man** Holländer *m*, Niederländer *m*; **Dutch·wom·an** Holländerin *f*, Niederländerin *f*
**du·ti·a·ble** ECON zollpflichtig
**du·ty** Pflicht *f*; Ehrerbietung *f*; ECON Abgabe *f*; Zoll *m*; Dienst *m*; ***on*** ~ diensthabend; ***be on*** ~ Dienst haben; ***be off*** ~ dienstfrei haben; **du·ty-free** zollfrei
**DVD** *abbr of* ***Digital Versatile Disk*** DVD; ~ **player** DVD-Player *m*; ~ **recorder** DVD-Rekorder *m*
**dwarf 1.** Zwerg(in) **2.** verkleinern, klein erscheinen lassen
**dwell** wohnen; *fig* verweilen (***on*** bei)
**dwell·ing** Wohnung *f*
**dwin·dle** (dahin)schwinden, abnehmen
**dye 1.** Farbe *f*; ***of the deepest*** ~ *fig* von der übelsten Sorte **2.** färben
**dy·ing 1.** sterbend; Sterbe... **2.** Sterben *n*; ~ ***of forests*** Waldsterben *n*
**dyke** → ***dike***[1, 2]
**dy·nam·ic** dynamisch, kraftgeladen
**dy·nam·ics** Dynamik *f*
**dy·na·mite 1.** Dynamit *n* **2.** (mit Dynamit) sprengen
**dys·en·te·ry** MED Ruhr *f*
**dys·pep·si·a** MED Verdauungsstörung *f*

# E

**E, e** E, e *n*
**each** jede(r, -s); ~ ***other*** einander, sich; je, pro Person, pro Stück
**ea·ger** begierig; eifrig
**ea·ger·ness** Begierde *f*; Eifer *m*
**ea·gle** ZO Adler *m*; HIST Zehndollarstück *n*; **ea·gle-eyed** scharfsichtig
**ear** BOT Ähre *f*; ANAT Ohr *n*; Öhr *n*; Henkel *m*
**ear·ache** Ohrenschmerzen *pl*
**ear·drum** ANAT Trommelfell *n*
**earl** *englischer* Graf
**ear·lobe** ANAT Ohrläppchen *n*
**ear·ly** früh; Früh...; Anfangs..., erste(r, -s); bald(ig); ***as*** ~ ***as May*** schon im Mai; ***as*** ~ ***as possible*** so bald wie möglich; ~ ***on*** schon früh, frühzeitig
**ear·ly bird** Frühaufsteher(in)
**ear·ly warn·ing sys·tem** MIL Frühwarnsystem *n*
**ear·mark 1.** Kennzeichen *n*; Merkmal *n* **2.** kennzeichnen; zurücklegen (***for*** für)
**earn** verdienen; einbringen
**ear·nest 1.** ernst, ernstlich, ernsthaft; ernst gemeint **2.** Ernst *m*; ***in*** ~ im Ernst; ernsthaft
**earn·ings** Einkommen *n*
**ear·phones** Ohrhörer *pl*; Kopfhörer *pl*
**ear·piece** TEL Hörmuschel *f*
**ear·ring** Ohrring *m*
**ear·shot**: ***within*** (***out of***) ~ in (außer) Hörweite

E

**earth** 1. Erde *f*; Land *n* 2. *v/t* ELECTR erden
**earth·en** irden
**earth·en·ware** Steingut(geschirr) *n*
**earth·ly** irdisch, weltlich; F denkbar
**earth·quake** Erdbeben *n*
**earth·worm** ZO Regenwurm *m*
**ease** 1. Bequemlichkeit *f*; (Gemüts)Ruhe *f*; Sorglosigkeit *f*; Leichtigkeit *f*; ***at (one's) ~*** ruhig, entspannt; unbefangen; ***be** or **feel ill at ~*** sich (in s-r Haut) nicht wohlfühlen 2. *v/t* erleichtern; beruhigen; *Schmerzen* lindern; *v/i mst* ***~ off, ~ up*** nachlassen; sich entspannen (*situation etc*)
**ea·sel** Staffelei *f*
**east** 1. Ost, Osten *m* 2. *adj* östlich, Ost… 3. *adv* nach Osten, ostwärts
**Eas·ter** Ostern *n*; Oster…; **~ bun·ny** Osterhase *m*; **~ egg** Osterei *n*
**eas·ter·ly** östlich, Ost…
**east·ern** östlich, Ost…
**east·ward(s)** östlich, nach Osten
**eas·y** leicht; einfach; bequem; gemächlich, gemütlich; ungezwungen; ***go ~ on*** schonen, sparsam umgehen mit; ***go ~, take it ~*** sich Zeit lassen; ***take it ~!*** immer mit der Ruhe!
**eas·y chair** Sessel *m*
**eas·y·go·ing** gelassen; ungezwungen
**eat** essen; (zer)fressen; ***~ out*** essen gehen; ***~ up*** aufessen
**eat·a·ble** essbar, genießbar
**eat·er** Esser(in)
**eaves** Dachrinne *f*, Traufe *f*
**eaves·drop** (heimlich) lauschen *or* horchen; ***~ on*** belauschen
**ebb** 1. Ebbe *f* 2. zurückgehen; ***~ away*** abnehmen; **~ tide** Ebbe *f*
**eb·o·ny** Ebenholz *n*
**ec·cen·tric** 1. exzentrisch 2. Exzentriker *m*, Sonderling *m*
**ec·cle·si·as·tic, ec·cle·si·as·ti·cal** geistlich, kirchlich
**ech·o** 1. Echo *n* 2. widerhallen; *fig* echoen, nachsprechen
**e·clipse** ASTR (*Sonnen-, Mond*)Finsternis *f*; *fig* Niedergang *m*
**e·co·cide** Umweltzerstörung *f*
**e·co·lo·gi·cal** ökologisch, Umwelt…
**e·col·o·gist** Ökologe *m*
**e·col·o·gy** Ökologie *f*
**ec·o·nom·ic** Wirtschafts…, wirtschaftlich; ***~ growth*** Wirtschaftswachstum *n*
**e·co·nom·i·cal** wirtschaftlich, sparsam
**e·co·nom·ics** Volkswirtschaft(slehre) *f*
**e·con·o·mist** Volkswirt *m*
**e·con·o·mize** sparsam wirtschaften (mit)
**e·con·o·my** 1. Wirtschaft *f*; Wirtschaftlichkeit *f*, Sparsamkeit *f*; Einsparung *f* 2. Spar…
**e·co·sys·tem** Ökosystem *n*
**ec·sta·sy** Ekstase *f*, Verzückung *f*
**ec·stat·ic** verzückt
**ed·dy** 1. Wirbel *m* 2. wirbeln
**edge** 1. Schneide *f*; Rand *m*; Kante *f*; Schärfe *f*; ***be on ~*** nervös *or* gereizt sein 2. schärfen; (um)säumen; (sich) drängen
**edge·ways, edge·wise** seitlich, von der Seite
**edg·ing** Einfassung *f*; Rand *m*
**edg·y** scharf(kantig); F nervös; F gereizt
**ed·i·ble** essbar, genießbar
**e·dict** Edikt *n*
**ed·i·fice** Gebäude *n*
**ed·it** *Text* herausgeben, redigieren; IT editieren; *Zeitung* als Herausgeber leiten; **e·di·tion** (*Buch*)Ausgabe *f*; Auflage *f*; **ed·i·tor** Herausgeber(in); Redakteur(in); **ed·i·to·ri·al** 1. Leitartikel *m* 2. Redaktions…
**EDP** *abbr of* ***electronic data processing*** EDV, elektronische Datenverarbeitung
**ed·u·cate** erziehen; unterrichten
**ed·u·cat·ed** gebildet
**ed·u·ca·tion** Erziehung *f*; (Aus)Bildung *f*; Bildungs-, Schulwesen *n*; ***Ministry of Education*** *appr Unterrichtsministerium*
**ed·u·ca·tion·al** erzieherisch, pädagogisch, Erziehungs…; Bildungs…
**ed·u·ca·tion·(al·)ist** Pädagoge *m*
**eel** ZO Aal *m*
**ef·fect** (Aus)Wirkung *f*; Effekt *m*, Eindruck *m*; *pl* ECON Effekten *pl*; ***be in ~*** in Kraft sein; ***in ~*** in Wirklichkeit; ***take ~*** in Kraft treten; **ef·fec·tive** wirksam; eindrucksvoll; tatsächlich
**ef·fem·i·nate** verweichlicht; weibisch
**ef·fer·vesce** brausen, sprudeln
**ef·fer·ves·cent** sprudelnd, schäumend
**ef·fi·cien·cy** Leistung *f*; Leistungsfähigkeit *f*; ***~ measure*** ECON Rationalisierungsmaßnahme *f*; **ef·fi·cient** wirksam; leistungsfähig, tüchtig

**ef·flu·ent** Abwasser *n*, Abwässer *pl*
**ef·fort** Anstrengung *f*, Bemühung *f* (***at*** um); Mühe *f*; ***without ~*** → **ef·fort·less** mühelos, ohne Anstrengung
**ef·fron·te·ry** Frechheit *f*
**ef·fu·sive** überschwänglich
**egg**[1] Ei *n*; ***put all one's ~s in one basket*** alles auf eine Karte setzen
**egg**[2]: ***~ on*** anstacheln
**egg co·sy** *Br* Eierwärmer *m*
**egg·cup** Eierbecher *m*
**egg·head** F Eierkopf *m*
**egg·plant** BOT Aubergine *f*
**egg·shell** Eierschale *f*
**egg tim·er** Eieruhr *f*
**e·go·is·m** Egoismus *m*, Selbstsucht *f*
**e·go·ist** Egoist(in)
**E·gypt** Ägypten *n*; **E·gyp·tian 1.** ägyptisch **2.** Ägypter(in)
**ei·der·down** Eiderdaunen *pl*; Daunendecke *f*
**eight 1.** acht **2.** Acht *f*
**eigh·teen 1.** achtzehn **2.** Achtzehn *f*
**eigh·teenth** achtzehnte(r, -s)
**eight·fold** achtfach
**eighth 1.** achte(r, -s) **2.** Achtel *n*
**eighth·ly** achtens
**eigh·ti·eth** achtzigste(r, -s)
**eigh·ty 1.** achtzig; ***the eighties*** die Achtzigerjahre **2.** Achtzig *f*
**ei·ther** jede(r, -s) (*von zweien*): eine(r, -s) (*von zweien*); beides; ***~ ... or*** entweder ... oder; ***not ~*** auch nicht
**e·jac·u·late** *v/t Samen* ausstoßen; *v/i* ejakulieren, e-n Samenerguss haben
**e·jac·u·la·tion** Samenerguss *m*
**e·ject** *j-n* hinauswerfen; TECH ausstoßen, auswerfen
**eke**: ***~ out*** *Vorräte etc* strecken; *Einkommen* aufbessern; ***~ out a living*** sich (mühsam) durchschlagen
**e·lab·o·rate 1.** sorgfältig (aus)gearbeitet; kompliziert **2.** sorgfältig ausarbeiten
**e·lapse** verfließen, verstreichen
**e·las·tic 1.** elastisch, dehnbar; ***~ band*** *Br* → **2.** Gummiring *m*, Gummiband *n*
**e·las·ti·ci·ty** Elastizität *f*
**e·lat·ed** begeistert (***at, by*** von)
**el·bow 1.** Ellbogen *m*; (scharfe) Biegung; TECH Knie *n*; ***at one's ~*** bei der Hand **2.** mit dem Ellbogen (weg)stoßen; ***~ one's way through*** sich (mit den Ellbogen) e-n Weg bahnen durch
**el·der**[1] **1.** ältere(r, -s) **2.** der, die Ältere; (Kirchen)Älteste(r) *m*
**el·der**[2] BOT Holunder *m*
**el·der·ly** ältlich, ältere(r, -s)
**el·dest** älteste(r, -s)
**e·lect 1.** gewählt **2.** (aus-, er)wählen
**e·lec·tion** Wahl *f*; **~ vic·to·ry** POL Wahlsieg *m*; **~ win·ner** POL Wahlsieger *m*
**e·lec·tor** Wähler(in); POL Wahlmann *m*; HIST Kurfürst *m*; **e·lec·to·ral** Wähler..., Wahl...; ***~ college*** POL Wahlmänner *pl*; ***~ district*** POL Wahlkreis *m*; **elec·to·rate** POL Wähler(schaft *f*) *pl*
**e·lec·tric** elektrisch, Elektro...
**e·lec·tri·cal** elektrisch; Elektro...; **~ en·gi·neer** Elektroingenieur *m*, Elektrotechniker *m*; **~ en·gi·neer·ing** Elektrotechnik *f*
**e·lec·tric chair** elektrischer Stuhl
**e·lec·tri·cian** Elektriker *m*
**e·lec·tri·ci·ty** Elektrizität *f*
**e·lec·tric ra·zor** Elektrorasierer *m*
**e·lec·tri·fy** elektrifizieren; elektrisieren (*a. fig*)
**e·lec·tro·cute** auf dem elektrischen Stuhl hinrichten; durch elektrischen Strom töten
**e·lec·tron** Elektron *n*
**e·lec·tron·ic** elektronisch, Elektronen...; **~ da·ta pro·cess·ing** elektronische Datenverarbeitung
**e·lec·tron·ics** Elektronik *f*
**el·e·gance** Eleganz *f*; **el·egant** elegant; geschmackvoll; erstklassig
**el·e·ment** CHEM Element *n*; Urstoff *m*; (Grund)Bestandteil *m*; *pl* Anfangsgründe *pl*, Grundlage(n *pl*) *f*; Elemente *pl*, Naturkräfte *pl*
**el·e·men·tal** elementar; wesentlich
**el·e·men·ta·ry** elementar; Anfangs...; **~ school** Grundschule *f*
**el·e·phant** zo Elefant *m*
**el·e·vate** erhöhen; *fig* erheben
**el·evat·ed** erhöht; *fig* gehoben, erhaben
**el·e·va·tion** Erhebung *f*; Erhöhung *f*; Höhe *f*; Erhabenheit *f*
**el·e·va·tor** TECH Lift *m*, Fahrstuhl *m*, Aufzug *m*
**e·lev·en 1.** elf **2.** Elf *f*
**e·leventh 1.** elfte(r, -s) **2.** Elftel *n*
**elf** Elf *m*, Elfe *f*; Kobold *m*
**e·li·cit** *et.* entlocken (***from*** *dat*); ans (Tages)Licht bringen
**el·i·gi·ble** infrage kommend, geeignet, annehmbar, akzeptabel

E

**e·lim·i·nate** entfernen, beseitigen; ausscheiden; **e·lim·i·na·tion** Entfernung *f*, Beseitigung *f*; Ausscheidung *f*
**é·lite** Elite *f*; Auslese *f*
**elk** zo Elch *m*; Wapitihirsch *m*
**el·lipse** MATH Ellipse *f*
**elm** BOT Ulme *f*
**e·lon·gate** verlängern
**e·lope** (mit s-m *or* s-r Geliebten) ausreißen *or* durchbrennen
**el·o·quent** redegewandt, beredt
**else** sonst, weiter; andere(r, -s)
**else·where** anderswo(hin)
**e·lude** geschickt entgehen, ausweichen, sich entziehen *(all: dat)*; *fig* nicht einfallen *(dat)*
**e·lu·sive** schwer fassbar
**e·ma·ci·ated** abgezehrt, ausgemergelt
**em·a·nate** ausströmen; ausgehen (***from*** von); **em·a·na·tion** Ausströmen *n*; *fig* Ausstrahlung *f*
**e·man·ci·pate** emanzipieren
**e·man·ci·pa·tion** Emanzipation *f*
**em·balm** (ein)balsamieren
**em·bank·ment** (Bahn-, Straßen-) Damm *m*; (Erd)Damm *m*; Uferstraße *f*
**em·bar·go** ECON Embargo *n*, (Hafen-, Handels)Sperre *f*
**em·bark** AVIAT, MAR an Bord nehmen *or* gehen, MAR *a.* (sich) einschiffen; *Waren* verladen; ~ ***on*** *et.* anfangen, *et.* beginnen
**em·bar·rass** in Verlegenheit bringen, verlegen machen, in e-e peinliche Lage bringen; **em·bar·rass·ing** unangenehm, peinlich; verfänglich
**em·bar·rass·ment** Verlegenheit *f*
**em·bas·sy** POL Botschaft *f*
**em·bed** (ein)betten, (ein)lagern
**em·bel·lish** verschönern; *fig* ausschmücken, beschönigen
**em·bers** Glut *f*
**em·bez·zle** unterschlagen
**em·bez·zle·ment** Unterschlagung *f*
**em·bit·ter** verbittern
**em·blem** Sinnbild *n*; Wahrzeichen *n*
**em·bod·y** verkörpern; enthalten
**em·bo·lis·m** MED Embolie *f*
**em·brace 1.** (sich) umarmen; einschließen **2.** Umarmung *f*
**em·broi·der** (be)sticken; *fig* ausschmücken; **em·broi·der·y** Stickerei *f*; *fig* Ausschmückung *f*
**em·broil** verwickeln (***in*** in *acc*)
**e·mend** *Texte* verbessern, korrigieren
**em·e·rald 1.** Smaragd *m* **2.** smaragdgrün
**e·merge** auftauchen; sich herausstellen *or* ergeben
**e·mer·gen·cy 1.** Not *f*, Notlage *f*, Notfall *m*, Notstand *m*; ***state of ~*** POL Ausnahmezustand *m* **2.** Not…; **~ brake** Notbremse *f*; **~ call** Notruf *m*; **~ ex·it** Notausgang *m*; **~ land·ing** AVIAT Notlandung *f*; **~ num·ber** Notruf(nummer *f*) *m*; **~ room** MED Notaufnahme *f*
**em·i·grant** Auswanderer *m*, *esp* POL Emigrant(in)
**em·i·grate** auswandern, *esp* POL emigrieren
**em·i·gra·tion** Auswanderung *f*, *esp* POL Emigration *f*
**em·i·nence** Berühmtheit *f*, Bedeutung *f*; ***Eminence*** REL Eminenz *f*
**em·i·nent** hervorragend, berühmt; bedeutend; **~ly** ganz besonders, äußerst
**e·mis·sion** Ausstoß *m*, Ausstrahlung *f*, Ausströmen *n*; **~-free** abgasfrei
**e·mit** aussenden, ausstoßen, ausstrahlen, ausströmen; von sich geben
**e·mo·tion** (Gemüts)Bewegung *f*, Gefühl *n*, Gefühlsregung *f*; Rührung *f*
**e·mo·tion·al** emotional; gefühlsmäßig; gefühlsbetont
**e·mo·tion·al·ly** emotional, gefühlsmäßig; **~ *disturbed*** seelisch gestört
**e·mo·tion·less** gefühllos
**e·mo·tive word** PSYCH Reizwort *n*
**em·pe·ror** Kaiser *m*
**em·pha·sis** Gewicht *n*; Nachdruck *m*
**em·pha·size** nachdrücklich betonen
**em·phat·ic** nachdrücklich; deutlich; bestimmt
**em·pire** Reich *n*, Imperium *n*; Kaiserreich *n*
**em·pir·i·cal** erfahrungsgemäß
**em·ploy 1.** beschäftigen, anstellen; an-, verwenden, gebrauchen **2.** Beschäftigung *f*
**em·ploy·ee** Angestellte *m*, *f*, Arbeitnehmer(in)
**em·ploy·er** Arbeitgeber(in)
**em·ploy·ment** Beschäftigung *f*, Arbeit *f*; **~ ad** Stellenanzeige *f*; **~ a·gen·cy** *Br* Arbeitsagentur *f*; **~ of·fice** Arbeitsamt *n*
**em·pow·er** ermächtigen; befähigen
**em·press** Kaiserin *f*

**emp·ti·ness** Leere *f* (*a. fig*)
**emp·ty** **1.** leer (*a. fig*) **2.** leeren, ausleeren, entleeren; sich leeren
**em·u·late** wetteifern mit; nacheifern (*dat*); es gleichtun (*dat*)
**e·mul·sion** Emulsion *f*
**en·a·ble** befähigen, es *j-m* ermöglichen; ermächtigen
**en·act** *Gesetz* erlassen; verfügen
**e·nam·el** **1.** Email *n*, Emaille *f*; ANAT (Zahn)Schmelz *m*; Glasur *f*, Lack *m*; Nagellack *m* **2.** emaillieren; glasieren; lackieren
**en·cased**: **~ *in*** gehüllt in (*acc*)
**en·chant** bezaubern; **en·chant·ing** bezaubernd; **en·chant·ment** Bezauberung *f*; Zauber *m*
**en·cir·cle** einkreisen, umzingeln; umfassen, umschlingen
**en·close** einschließen, umgeben; beilegen, beifügen
**en·clo·sure** Einzäunung *f*; Anlage *f*
**en·code** verschlüsseln, chiffrieren; kodieren
**en·com·pass** umgeben
**en·coun·ter** **1.** Begegnung *f*; Gefecht *n* **2.** begegnen (*dat*); auf *Schwierigkeiten etc* stoßen; mit *j-m feindlich* zusammenstoßen
**en·cour·age** ermutigen; fördern
**en·cour·age·ment** Ermutigung *f*; Anfeuerung *f*; Unterstützung *f*
**en·cour·ag·ing** ermutigend
**en·croach** (***on***) eingreifen (in *j-s Recht etc*), eindringen (in *acc*); über Gebühr in Anspruch nehmen (*acc*)
**en·croach·ment** Ein-, Übergriff *m*
**en·cum·ber** belasten; (be)hindern
**en·cum·brance** Belastung *f*
**en·cy·clo·p(a)e·di·a** Enzyklopädie *f*
**end** **1.** Ende *n*; Ziel *n*, Zweck *m*; ***no ~ of*** unendlich viel(e), unzählige; ***at the ~ of May*** Ende Mai; ***in the ~*** am Ende, schließlich; ***on ~*** aufrecht; ***stand on ~*** zu Berge stehen (*hair*); ***to no ~*** vergebens; ***go off the deep ~*** F *fig* in die Luft gehen; ***make (both) ~s meet*** durchkommen, finanziell über die Runden kommen **2.** enden; beend(-ig)en
**en·dan·ger** gefährden
**en·dear** beliebt machen (***to s.o.*** bei j-m); **en·dear·ing** gewinnend; liebenswert; **en·dear·ment**: ***words of ~, ~s*** zärtliche Worte *pl*
**en·deav·o(u)r** **1.** Bestreben *n*, Bemühung *f* **2.** sich bemühen
**end·ing** Ende *n*; Schluss *m*; LING Endung *f*
**en·dive** BOT Endivie *f*
**end·less** endlos, unendlich; TECH ohne Ende
**en·dorse** ECON *Scheck etc* indossieren; *et.* vermerken (***on*** auf der Rückseite); billigen; **en·dorse·ment** Vermerk *m*; ECON Indossament *n*, Giro *n*
**en·dow** *fig* ausstatten; ***~ s.o. with s.th.*** j-m et. stiften; **en·dow·ment** Stiftung *f*; *mst pl* Begabung *f*, Talent *n*
**en·dur·ance** Ausdauer *f*; ***beyond ~, past ~*** unerträglich; **en·dure** ertragen
**end us·er** Endverbraucher *m*
**en·e·my** **1.** Feind *m* **2.** feindlich
**en·er·get·ic** energisch; tatkräftig
**en·er·gy** Energie *f*
**en·er·gy cri·sis** Energiekrise *f*
**en·er·gy-sav·ing** energiesparend
**en·er·gy sup·ply** Energieversorgung *f*
**en·fold** einhüllen; umfassen
**en·force** (mit Nachdruck, *a.* gerichtlich) geltend machen; *Gesetz etc* durchführen; durchsetzen, erzwingen
**en·force·ment** ECON, JUR Geltendmachung *f*; Durchsetzung *f*, Erzwingung *f*
**en·fran·chise** *j-m* das Wahlrecht verleihen
**en·gage** *v/t j-s Aufmerksamkeit* auf sich ziehen; TECH einrasten lassen; MOT *e-n Gang* einlegen; *j-n* einstellen, anstellen, *Künstler* engagieren; *v/i* TECH einrasten, greifen; ***~ in*** sich einlassen auf (*acc*) *or* in (*acc*); sich beschäftigen mit
**en·gaged** verlobt (***to*** mit); beschäftigt (***in, on*** mit); besetzt (*a. Br* TEL); ***~ tone** or **signal*** *Br* TEL Besetztzeichen *n*
**en·gage·ment** Verlobung *f*; Verabredung *f*; MIL Gefecht *n*
**en·gag·ing** einnehmend; gewinnend
**en·gine** Maschine *f*; Motor *m*; RAIL Lokomotive *f*; **~ driv·er** *Br* RAIL Lokomotivführer *m*
**en·gi·neer** **1.** Ingenieur *m*, Techniker *m*, Mechaniker *m*; RAIL Lokomotivführer *m*; MIL Pionier *m* **2.** bauen; *fig* (geschickt) in die Wege leiten
**en·gi·neer·ing** Technik *f*, Ingenieurwesen *n*, Maschinen- und Gerätebau *m*
**En·gland** England *n*
**En·glish** **1.** englisch **2.** LING Englisch *n*;

***the ~*** die Engländer *pl*; ***in plain ~*** *fig* unverblümt
**Eng·lish·man** Engländer *m*
**Eng·lish·wom·an** Engländerin *f*
**en·grave** (ein)gravieren, (ein)meißeln, (ein)schnitzen; *fig* einprägen
**en·grav·er** Graveur *m*
**en·grav·ing** (Kupfer-, Stahl)Stich *m*; Holzschnitt *m*

E

**en·grossed**: ~ ***in*** (voll) in Anspruch genommen von, vertieft *or* versunken in (*acc*)
**en·hance** erhöhen, verstärken, steigern
**e·nig·ma** Rätsel *n*
**en·ig·mat·ic** rätselhaft
**en·joy** sich erfreuen an (*dat*); genießen; ***did you ~ it?*** hat es Ihnen gefallen?; ***~ o.s.*** sich amüsieren, sich gut unterhalten; ***~ yourself!*** viel Spaß!; ***I ~ my dinner*** es schmeckt mir; **en·joy·a·ble** angenehm, erfreulich; **en·joy·ment** Vergnügen *n*, Freude *f*; Genuss *m*
**en·large** (sich) vergrößern *or* erweitern, ausdehnen; PHOT vergrößern; sich verbreiten *or* auslassen (***on*** über *acc*)
**en·large·ment** Erweiterung *f*; Vergrößerung *f* (*a.* PHOT)
**en·light·en** aufklären, belehren
**en·light·en·ment** Aufklärung *f*
**en·list** MIL *v/t* anwerben; *v/i* sich freiwillig melden
**en·liv·en** beleben
**en·mi·ty** Feindschaft *f*
**en·no·ble** adeln; veredeln
**e·nor·mi·ty** Ungeheuerlichkeit *f*
**e·nor·mous** ungeheuer
**e·nough** genug
**en·quire, en·qui·ry** → ***inquire, inquiry***
**en·rage** wütend machen
**en·raged** wütend (***at*** über *acc*)
**en·rap·ture** entzücken, hinreißen
**en·rap·tured** entzückt, hingerissen
**en·rich** bereichern; anreichern
**en·rol(l)** (sich) einschreiben *or* eintragen; UNIV (sich) immatrikulieren
**en·sign** MAR *esp* (National)Flagge *f*; MIL Leutnant *m* zur See
**en·sue** (darauf-, nach)folgen
**en·sure** sichern
**en·tail** mit sich bringen, zur Folge haben
**en·tan·gle** verwickeln
**en·ter** *v/t* hinein-, hereingehen, -kommen, -treten in (*acc*), eintreten, einsteigen in (*acc*), betreten; einreisen in (*acc*); MAR, RAIL einlaufen, einfahren in (*acc*); eindringen in (*acc*); *Namen etc* eintragen, einschreiben; SPORT melden, nennen (***for*** für); *fig* eintreten in (*acc*), beitreten (*dat*); IT eingeben; *v/i* eintreten, herein-, hineinkommen, herein-, hineingehen; THEA auftreten; sich eintragen *or* einschreiben *or* anmelden (***for*** für); SPORT melden, nennen (***for*** für)
**en·ter key** IT Eingabetaste *f*
**en·ter·prise** Unternehmen *n* (*a.* ECON); ECON Unternehmertum *n*; Unternehmungsgeist *m*; **en·ter·pris·ing** unternehmungslustig; wagemutig; kühn
**en·ter·tain** unterhalten; bewirten
**en·ter·tain·er** Entertainer(in), Unterhaltungskünstler(in)
**en·ter·tain·ment** Unterhaltung *f*; Entertainment *n*; Bewirtung *f*
**en·thral(l)** fesseln, bezaubern
**en·throne** inthronisieren
**en·thu·si·asm** Begeisterung *f*, Enthusiasmus *m*; **en·thu·si·ast** Enthusiast(in); **en·thu·si·as·tic** begeistert, enthusiastisch
**en·tice** (ver)locken
**en·tice·ment** Verlockung *f*, Reiz *m*
**en·tire** ganz, vollständig; ungeteilt
**en·tire·ly** völlig; ausschließlich
**en·ti·tle** betiteln; berechtigen (***to*** zu)
**en·ti·ty** Einheit *f*
**en·trails** ANAT Eingeweide *pl*
**en·trance** Eintreten *n*, Eintritt *m*; Eingang *m*, Zugang *m*; Zufahrt *f*; Einlass *m*, Eintritt *m*, Zutritt *m*
**en·trance| ex·am(·i·na·tion)** Aufnahmeprüfung *f*; ~ **fee** Eintritt *m*, Eintrittsgeld *n*; Aufnahmegebühr *f*
**en·treat** inständig bitten, anflehen
**en·trea·ty** dringende *or* inständige Bitte
**en·trench** MIL verschanzen (*a. fig*)
**en·tre·pre·neur** ECON Unternehmer(in); **en·tre·pre·neu·ri·al** ECON unternehmerisch
**en·trust** anvertrauen (***s.th. to s.o.*** j-m et.); *j-n* betrauen (***with*** mit)
**en·try** Eintreten *n*, Eintritt *m*; Einreise *f*; Beitritt *m* (***into*** zu); Einlass *m*, Zutritt *m*; Zugang *m*, Eingang *m*, Einfahrt *f*; Eintrag(ung *f*) *m*; Stichwort *n*; SPORT Nennung *f*, Meldung *f*; ***no ~!*** Zutritt verboten!, MOT keine Einfahrt!

**en·try per·mit** Einreiseerlaubnis *f*, -genehmigung *f*
**en·try·phone** Türsprechanlage *f*
**en·try vi·sa** Einreisevisum *n*
**en·twine** ineinander schlingen
**e·nu·me·rate** aufzählen
**en·vel·op** (ein)hüllen, einwickeln
**en·ve·lope** Briefumschlag *m*
**en·vi·a·ble** beneidenswert
**en·vi·ous** neidisch
**en·vi·ron·ment** Umgebung *f*, *a.* Milieu *n*; Umwelt *f*; **en·vi·ron·men·tal** Milieu...; Umwelt...; **en·vi·ron·mental·ist** Umweltschützer(in)
**en·vi·ron·men·tal| law** Umweltschutzgesetz *n*; **~ pol·lu·tion** Umweltverschmutzung *f*
**en·vi·ron·ment friend·ly** umweltfreundlich
**en·vi·rons** Umgebung *f*
**en·vis·age** sich *et.* vorstellen
**en·voy** Gesandte *m*, Gesandtin *f*
**en·vy 1.** Neid *m* **2.** beneiden
**ep·ic 1.** episch **2.** Epos *n*
**ep·i·dem·ic** MED **1.** seuchenartig; ***~ disease*** → **2.** Epidemie *f*, Seuche *f*
**ep·i·der·mis** ANAT Oberhaut *f*
**ep·i·lep·sy** MED Epilepsie *f*
**ep·i·log**, *Br* **ep·i·logue** Epilog *m*, Nachwort *n*
**e·pis·co·pal** REL bischöflich
**ep·i·sode** Episode *f*
**ep·i·taph** Grabinschrift *f*
**e·poch** Epoche *f*, Zeitalter *n*
**eq·ua·ble** ausgeglichen (*a.* METEOR)
**e·qual 1.** gleich; gleichmäßig; ***~ to*** *fig* gewachsen (*dat*); ***~ opportunities*** Chancengleichheit *f*; ***~ rights for women*** Gleichberechtigung *f* der Frau **2.** Gleiche *m*, *f* **3.** gleichen (*dat*)
**e·qual·i·ty** Gleichheit *f*
**e·qual·i·za·tion** Gleichstellung *f*; Ausgleich *m*; **e·qual·ize** gleichmachen, gleichstellen, angleichen; SPORT ausgleichen; **e·qual·iz·er** SPORT Ausgleich *m*, Ausgleichstor *n*, -treffer *m*
**eq·ua·nim·i·ty** Gleichmut *m*
**e·qua·tion** MATH Gleichung *f*
**e·qua·tor** Äquator *m*
**e·qui·lib·ri·um** Gleichgewicht *n*
**e·quip** ausrüsten
**e·quip·ment** Ausrüstung *f*, Ausstattung *f*; TECH Einrichtung *f*; *fig* Rüstzeug *n*
**e·quiv·a·lent 1.** gleichwertig, äquivalent; gleichbedeutend (***to*** mit); **2.** Äquivalent *n*, Gegenwert *m*
**e·ra** Zeitrechnung *f*; Zeitalter *n*
**e·rad·i·cate** ausrotten
**e·rase** ausradieren, ausstreichen, löschen (*a.* IT); *fig* auslöschen
**e·ras·er** Radiergummi *m*
**e·rect 1.** aufrecht **2.** aufrichten; *Denkmal etc* errichten; aufstellen
**e·rec·tion** Errichtung *f*; MED Erektion *f*
**er·mine** ZO Hermelin *n*
**e·rode** GEOL erodieren
**e·ro·sion** GEOL Erosion *f*
**e·rot·ic** erotisch
**err** (sich) irren
**er·rand** Botengang *m*, Besorgung *f*; ***go on an ~, run an ~*** e-e Besorgung machen
**er·rat·ic** sprunghaft, unstet, unberechenbar
**er·ro·ne·ous** irrig
**er·ror** Irrtum *m*, Fehler *m* (*a.* IT); ***in ~*** irrtümlicherweise; ***~ of judg(e)ment*** Fehleinschätzung *f*; ***~s excepted*** ECON Irrtümer vorbehalten; **~ mes·sage** IT Fehlermeldung *f*
**e·rupt** ausbrechen (*volcano etc*); durchbrechen (*teeth*); **e·rup·tion** (*Vulkan-*) Ausbruch *m*; MED Ausschlag *m*
**ESA** *abbr of* ***European Space Agency*** Europäische Weltraumbehörde
**es·ca·late** eskalieren; ECON steigen, in die Höhe gehen
**es·ca·la·tion** Eskalation *f*
**es·ca·la·tor** Rolltreppe *f*
**es·ca·lope** GASTR (*esp* Wiener) Schnitzel *n*
**es·cape 1.** entgehen (*dat*); entkommen, entrinnen (*both dat*); entweichen; *j-m* entfallen **2.** Entrinnen *n*; Entweichen *n*; Flucht *f*; ***have a narrow ~*** mit knapper Not davonkommen
**es·cape chute** AVIAT Notrutsche *f*
**es·cape key** IT Escape-Taste *f*
**es·cort 1.** MIL Eskorte *f*; Geleit(schutz *m*) *n* **2.** MIL eskortieren; AVIAT, MAR Geleit(schutz) geben; geleiten
**es·cutch·eon** Wappenschild *m*, *n*
**es·pe·cial** besondere(r, -s);
**es·pe·cial·ly** besonders
**es·pi·o·nage** Spionage *f*
**es·pla·nade** (*esp* Strand)Promenade *f*
**es·say** Aufsatz *m*, kurze Abhandlung, Essay *m*, *n*

**es·sence** Wesen *n*; Essenz *f*; Extrakt *m*
**es·sen·tial 1.** wesentlich; unentbehrlich **2.** *mst pl das* Wesentliche
**es·sen·tial·ly** im Wesentlichen, in der Hauptsache
**es·tab·lish** einrichten, errichten; **~ *o.s.*** sich etablieren *or* niederlassen; beweisen, nachweisen; **es·tab·lish·ment** Einrichtung *f*, Errichtung *f*; ECON Unternehmen *n*, Firma *f*; ***the Establishment*** das Establishment, die etablierte Macht, die herrschende Schicht
**es·tate** (großes) Grundstück, Landsitz *m*, Gut *n*; JUR Besitz *m*, (Erb)Masse *f*, Nachlass *m*; ***housing* ~** (Wohn)Siedlung *f*; ***industrial* ~** Industriegebiet *n*; ***real* ~** Liegenschaften *pl*; **~ a·gent** *Br* Grundstücks-, Immobilienmakler *m*; **~ car** *Br* MOT Kombiwagen *m*
**es·teem 1.** Achtung *f*, Ansehen *n* (***with*** bei); **2.** achten, (hoch) schätzen
**es·thet·ic** ästhetisch
**es·thet·ics** Ästhetik *f*
**es·ti·mate 1.** (ab-, ein)schätzen; veranschlagen **2.** Schätzung *f*; (Kosten)Voranschlag *m*; **es·ti·ma·tion** Meinung *f*; Achtung *f*, Wertschätzung *f*
**es·tranged** entfremdet
**es·trange·ment** Entfremdung *f*
**es·tu·a·ry** weite Flussmündung
**etch** ätzen; radieren
**etch·ing** Radierung *f*; Kupferstich *m*
**e·ter·nal** ewig
**e·ter·ni·ty** Ewigkeit *f*
**e·ther** Äther *m*
**e·the·re·al** ätherisch (*a. fig*)
**eth·i·cal** sittlich, ethisch
**eth·ics** Sittenlehre *f*, Ethik *f*
**eu·ro** Euro *m*
**Eu·rope** Europa *n*
**Eu·ro·pe·an 1.** europäisch **2.** Europäer(in); **~ Union** (*abbr* ***EU***) Europäische Union (*abbr* EU)
**e·vac·u·ate** entleeren; evakuieren; *Haus etc* räumen
**e·vade** (geschickt) ausweichen (*dat*); umgehen
**e·val·u·ate** schätzen; abschätzen, bewerten, beurteilen
**e·vap·o·rate** verdunsten, verdampfen (lassen); **~d milk** Kondensmilch *f*
**e·vap·o·ra·tion** Verdunstung *f*, Verdampfung *f*
**e·va·sion** Umgehung *f*, Vermeidung *f*; (*Steuer*)Hinterziehung *f*; Ausflucht *f*
**e·va·sive** ausweichend; ***be* ~** ausweichen
**eve** Vorabend *m*; Vortag *m*; ***on the* ~ *of*** unmittelbar vor (*dat*), am Vorabend (*gen*)
**e·ven 1.** *adj* eben, gleich; gleichmäßig; ausgeglichen; glatt; gerade (*Zahl*); ***get* ~ *with s.o.*** es j-m heimzahlen **2.** *adv* selbst, sogar, auch; ***not* ~** nicht einmal; **~ *though*, ~ *if*** wenn auch **3. ~ *out*** sich einpendeln; sich ausgleichen
**eve·ning** Abend *m*; ***in the* ~** am Abend, abends; **~ class·es** Abendkurs *m*, Abendunterricht *m*; **~ dress** Gesellschaftsanzug *m*; Frack *m*, Smoking *m*; Abendkleid *n*
**e·ven·song** REL Abendgottesdienst *m*
**e·vent** Ereignis *n*; Fall *m*; SPORT Disziplin *f*; SPORT Wettbewerb *m*; ***at all* ~*s*** auf alle Fälle; ***in the* ~ *of*** im Falle (*gen*)
**e·vent·ful** ereignisreich
**e·ven·tu·al(·ly)** schließlich
**ev·er** immer (wieder); je(mals); **~ *after*, ~ *since*** seitdem; **~ *so*** F sehr, noch so; ***for* ~** für immer, auf ewig; ***Yours* ~, ..., *Ever yours*, ...** Viele Grüße, dein(e) *or* Ihr(e), ...; ***have you* ~ *been to Boston?*** bist du schon einmal in Boston gewesen?
**ev·er·green 1.** immergrün; unverwüstlich, *esp* immer wieder gern gehört **2.** immergrüne Pflanze; MUS Evergreen *m*, *n*
**ev·er·last·ing** ewig
**ev·er·more**: (***for***) **~** für immer
**ev·ery** jede(r, -s); alle(r, -s); **~ *now and then*** von Zeit zu Zeit, dann und wann; **~ *one of them*** jeder von ihnen; **~ *other day*** jeden zweiten Tag, alle zwei Tage
**ev·ery·bod·y** jeder(mann)
**ev·ery·day** Alltags...
**ev·ery·one** jeder(mann)
**ev·ery·thing** alles
**ev·ery·where** überall(hin)
**e·vict** JUR zur Räumung zwingen; *j-n* gewaltsam vertreiben
**ev·i·dence** Beweis(material *n*) *m*, Beweise *pl*; (Zeugen)Aussage *f*; ***give* ~** (als Zeuge) aussagen; **ev·i·dent** augenscheinlich, offensichtlich
**e·vil 1.** übel, schlimm, böse **2.** Übel *n*; *das* Böse; **e·vil-mind·ed** bösartig
**e·voke** (herauf)beschwören; *Erinnerungen* wachrufen

**ev·o·lu·tion** Entwicklung *f*; BIOL Evolution *f*
**e·volve** (sich) entwickeln
**ewe** ZO Mutterschaf *n*
**ex** *prp* ECON ab; ~ ***works*** ab Werk
**ex...** Ex..., ehemalig
**ex·act** **1.** exakt, genau **2.** fordern, verlangen; **ex·act·ing** streng, genau; aufreibend, anstrengend; **ex·act·ly** exakt, genau; ~**!** ganz recht!, genau!
**ex·act·ness** Genauigkeit *f*
**ex·ag·ge·rate** übertreiben
**ex·ag·ge·ra·tion** Übertreibung *f*
**ex·am** F Examen *n*
**ex·am·i·na·tion** Examen *n*, Prüfung *f*; Untersuchung *f*; JUR Vernehmung *f*, Verhör *n*; **ex·am·ine** untersuchen; JUR vernehmen, verhören; PED *etc* prüfen (***in*** in *dat*; ***on*** über *acc*)
**ex·am·ple** Beispiel *n*; Vorbild *n*, Muster *n*; ***for*** ~ zum Beispiel
**ex·as·pe·rate** wütend machen
**ex·as·pe·rat·ing** ärgerlich
**ex·ca·vate** ausgraben, ausheben, ausschachten
**ex·ceed** überschreiten; übertreffen
**ex·ceed·ing** übermäßig
**ex·ceed·ing·ly** außerordentlich, überaus
**ex·cel** *v/t* übertreffen; *v/i* sich auszeichnen
**ex·cel·lence** ausgezeichnete Qualität
**Ex·cel·lency** Exzellenz *f*
**ex·cel·lent** ausgezeichnet, hervorragend
**ex·cept** **1.** ausnehmen, ausschließen **2.** *prp* ausgenommen, außer; ~ ***for*** abgesehen von, bis auf (*acc*)
**ex·cept·ing** *prp* ausgenommen
**ex·cep·tion** Ausnahme *f*; Einwand *m* (***to*** gegen); ***make an*** ~ e-e Ausnahme machen; ***take*** ~ ***to*** Anstoß nehmen an (*dat*); ***without*** ~ ohne Ausnahme, ausnahmslos; **ex·cep·tion·al** außergewöhnlich; **ex·cep·tion·al·ly** ungewöhnlich, außergewöhnlich
**ex·cerpt** Auszug *m*
**ex·cess** **1.** Übermaß *n*; Überschuss *m*; Ausschweifung *f* **2.** Mehr...; ~ **baggage** AVIAT Übergepäck *n*; ~ **fare** (Fahrpreis)Zuschlag *m*
**ex·ces·sive** übermäßig, übertrieben
**ex·cess| lug·gage** → ***excess baggage***; ~ **post·age** Nachgebühr *f*
**ex·change** **1.** (aus-, ein-, um)tauschen (***for*** gegen); wechseln **2.** (Aus-, Um-) Tausch *m*; (*esp* Geld)Wechsel *m*; ECON *a.* ***bill of*** ~ Wechsel *m*; Börse *f*; Wechselstube *f*; TEL Fernsprechamt *n*; ECON ***foreign*** ~**(*s*)** Devisen *pl*; ***rate of*** ~ → ***exchange rate***; ~ **of·fice** Wechselstube *f*; ~ **rate** Wechselkurs *m*; ~ **student** Austauschschüler(in), Austauschstudent(in)
**Ex·cheq·uer**: ***Chancellor of the*** ~ *Br* Finanzminister *m*
**ex·cise** Verbrauchssteuer *f*
**ex·ci·ta·ble** reizbar, (leicht) erregbar
**ex·cite** erregen, anregen; reizen
**ex·cit·ed** erregt, aufgeregt
**ex·cite·ment** Aufregung *f*, Erregung *f*
**ex·cit·ing** erregend, aufregend, spannend
**ex·claim** (aus)rufen
**ex·cla·ma·tion** Ausruf *m*, (Auf)Schrei *m*; ~ **mark** *Br*, ~ **point** Ausrufe-, Ausrufungszeichen *n*
**ex·clude** ausschließen
**ex·clu·sion** Ausschließung *f*, Ausschluss *m*; **ex·clu·sive** ausschließlich; exklusiv; Exklusiv...; ~ ***of*** abgesehen von, ohne
**ex·com·mu·ni·cate** REL exkommunizieren; **ex·com·mu·ni·ca·tion** REL Exkommunikation *f*
**ex·cre·ment** Kot *m*
**ex·crete** MED ausscheiden
**ex·cur·sion** Ausflug *m*
**ex·cu·sa·ble** entschuldbar
**ex·cuse** **1.** entschuldigen; ~ ***me*** entschuldige(n Sie) **2.** Entschuldigung *f*
**ex·di·rec·to·ry num·ber** *Br* TEL Geheimnummer *f*
**ex·e·cute** ausführen; vollziehen; MUS vortragen; hinrichten; JUR *Testament* vollstrecken; **ex·e·cu·tion** Ausführung *f*; Vollziehung *f*; JUR (Zwangs-) Vollstreckung *f*; Hinrichtung *f*; MUS Vortrag *m*; ***put*** *or* ***carry a plan into*** ~ e-n Plan ausführen *or* verwirklichen
**ex·e·cu·tion·er** JUR Henker *m*, Scharfrichter *m*
**ex·ec·u·tive** **1.** vollziehend, ausübend, POL Exekutiv...; ECON leitend **2.** POL Exekutive *f*, vollziehende Gewalt; ECON *der*, *die* leitende Angestellte; ~ **board** Geschäftsleitung *f*;
**ex·em·pla·ry** vorbildlich

E

**ex·em·pli·fy** veranschaulichen
**ex·empt** **1.** befreit, frei **2.** ausnehmen, befreien
**ex·er·cise** **1.** Übung *f*; Ausübung *f*; PED Übung(sarbeit) *f*, Schulaufgabe *f*; MIL Manöver *n*; (körperliche) Bewegung; ***do one's ~s*** Gymnastik machen; ***take ~*** sich Bewegung machen **2.** üben; ausüben; (sich) bewegen; sich Bewegung machen; MIL exerzieren
**ex·er·cise book** Schul-, Schreibheft *n*
**ex·ert** *Einfluss etc* ausüben; ***~ o.s.*** sich anstrengen *or* bemühen; **ex·er·tion** Ausübung *f*; Anstrengung *f*, Strapaze *f*
**ex·hale** ausatmen; *Gas, Geruch etc* verströmen; *Rauch* ausstoßen
**ex·haust** **1.** erschöpfen; *Vorräte* ver-, aufbrauchen **2.** TECH Auspuff *m*; *a.* ***~ fumes*** TECH Auspuff-, Abgase *pl*
**ex·haust·ed** erschöpft, aufgebraucht (*supplies*), vergriffen (*book*)
**ex·haus·tion** Erschöpfung *f*
**ex·haus·tive** erschöpfend
**ex·haust pipe** TECH Auspuffrohr *n*
**ex·hib·it** **1.** ausstellen; vorzeigen; *fig* zeigen, zur Schau stellen **2.** Ausstellungsstück *n*; JUR Beweisstück *n*
**ex·hi·bi·tion** Ausstellung *f*; Zurschaustellung *f*
**ex·hil·a·rat·ing** erregend, berauschend
**ex·hort** ermahnen
**ex·ile** **1.** Exil *n*; im Exil Lebende *m, f* **2.** ins Exil schicken
**ex·ist** existieren; vorhanden sein; leben; bestehen; **ex·ist·ence** Existenz *f*; Vorhandensein *n*, Vorkommen *n*; Leben *n*, Dasein *n*; **ex·ist·ent** vorhanden
**ex·it** **1.** Abgang *m*; Ausgang *m*; (Autobahn)Ausfahrt *f*; Ausreise *f* **2.** *v/i* verlassen; IT (das Programm) beenden; ***~ Macbeth*** THEA Macbeth (geht) ab
**ex·o·dus** Auszug *m*; Abwanderung *f*; ***general ~*** allgemeiner Aufbruch
**ex·on·e·rate** entlasten, entbinden, befreien
**ex·or·bi·tant** übertrieben, maßlos; unverschämt (*price etc*)
**ex·or·cize** *böse Geister* beschwören, austreiben (***from*** aus); befreien (***of*** von)
**ex·ot·ic** exotisch; fremd(artig)
**ex·pand** ausbreiten; (sich) ausdehnen *or* erweitern; ECON *a.* expandieren
**ex·panse** weite Fläche, Weite *f*
**ex·pan·sion** Ausbreitung *f*; Ausdehnung *f*, Erweiterung *f*
**ex·pan·sive** mitteilsam
**ex·pat·ri·ate** *j-n* ausbürgern, *j-m* die Staatsangehörigkeit aberkennen
**ex·pect** erwarten; F annehmen; ***be ~ing*** in anderen Umständen sein
**ex·pec·tant** erwartungsvoll; ***~ mother*** werdende Mutter
**ex·pec·ta·tion** Erwartung *f*; Hoffnung *f*, Aussicht *f*
**ex·pe·dient** **1.** zweckdienlich, zweckmäßig; ratsam **2.** (Hilfs)Mittel *n*, (Not)Behelf *m*
**ex·pe·di·tion** Expedition *f*, (Forschungs)Reise *f*
**ex·pe·di·tious** schnell
**ex·pel** (***from***) vertreiben (aus); ausweisen (aus); ausschließen (von, aus)
**ex·pen·di·ture** Ausgaben *pl*, (Kosten-)Aufwand *m*
**ex·pense** Ausgaben *pl*; *pl* ECON Unkosten *pl*, Spesen *pl*, Auslagen *pl*; ***at the ~ of*** auf Kosten (*gen*)
**ex·pen·sive** kostspielig, teuer
**ex·pe·ri·ence** **1.** Erfahrung *f*; (Lebens-)Praxis *f*; Erlebnis *n* **2.** erfahren, erleben; **ex·pe·rienced** erfahren
**ex·per·i·ment** **1.** Versuch *m* **2.** experimentieren; **ex·per·i·men·tal** Versuchs…
**ex·pert** **1.** erfahren, geschickt; fachmännisch **2.** Fachmann *m*; Sachverständige *m, f*
**ex·pi·ra·tion** Ablauf *m*, Ende *n*; Verfall *m*
**ex·pire** ablaufen, erlöschen; verfallen
**ex·plain** erklären
**ex·pla·na·tion** Erklärung *f*
**ex·pli·cit** ausdrücklich; ausführlich; offen, deutlich; (***sexually***) ***~*** freizügig (*film etc*)
**ex·plode** *v/t* zur Explosion bringen; *v/i* explodieren; *fig* ausbrechen (***with*** in *acc*), platzen (***with*** vor); *fig* sprunghaft ansteigen
**ex·ploit** **1.** (Helden)Tat *f* **2.** ausbeuten; *fig* ausnutzen
**ex·ploi·ta·tion** Ausbeutung *f*, Auswertung *f*, Verwertung *f*, Abbau *m*
**ex·plo·ra·tion** Erforschung *f*
**ex·plore** erforschen
**ex·plor·er** Forscher(in); Forschungsreisende *m, f*

**ex·plo·sion** Explosion *f*; *fig* Ausbruch *m*; *fig* sprunghafter Anstieg
**ex·plo·sive 1.** explosiv; *fig* aufbrausend; *fig* sprunghaft ansteigend **2.** Sprengstoff *m*
**ex·po·nent** MATH Exponent *m*, Hochzahl *f*; Vertreter(in), Verfechter(in)
**ex·port** ECON **1.** exportieren, ausführen **2.** Export *m*, Ausfuhr *f*; *mst pl* Export-, Ausfuhrartikel *m*
**ex·por·ta·tion** ECON Ausfuhr *f*
**ex·port·er** ECON Exporteur *m*
**ex·pose** aussetzen; PHOT belichten; *Waren* ausstellen; *j-n* entlarven, bloßstellen, *et.* aufdecken
**ex·po·si·tion** Ausstellung *f*
**ex·po·sure** Aussetzen *n*, Ausgesetztsein *n* (***to*** *dat*); *fig* Bloßstellung *f*, Aufdeckung *f*, Enthüllung *f*, Entlarvung *f*; PHOT Belichtung *f*; PHOT Aufnahme *f*; ***die of ~*** an Unterkühlung sterben; **~ me·ter** PHOT Belichtungsmesser *m*
**ex·press 1.** ausdrücklich, deutlich; Express…, Eil… **2.** Eilbote *m*; Schnellzug *m*; ***by ~*** → **3.** *adv* durch Eilboten; als Eilgut **4.** äußern, ausdrücken
**ex·pres·sion** Ausdruck *m*
**ex·pres·sion·less** ausdruckslos
**ex·pres·sive** ausdrucksvoll; ***be ~ of*** *et.* ausdrücken
**ex·press let·ter** *Br* Eilbrief *m*
**ex·press·ly** ausdrücklich, eigens
**ex·press train** Schnellzug *m*
**ex·press·way** Schnellstraße *f*
**ex·pro·pri·ate** JUR enteignen
**ex·pul·sion** (***from***) Vertreibung *f* (aus); Ausweisung *f* (aus)
**ex·pur·gate** reinigen
**ex·qui·site** erlesen; fein
**ex·tant** noch vorhanden
**ex·tem·po·re** aus dem Stegreif
**ex·tem·po·rize** aus dem Stegreif sprechen *or* spielen
**ex·tend** (aus)dehnen, (aus)weiten; *Hand etc* ausstrecken; *Betrieb etc* vergrößern, ausbauen; *Frist, Pass etc* verlängern; sich ausdehnen *or* erstrecken
**ex·tend·ed fam·i·ly** Großfamilie *f*
**ex·ten·sion** Ausdehnung *f*, Vergrößerung *f*, Erweiterung *f*; (Frist)Verlängerung *f*; ARCH Erweiterung *f*, Anbau *m*; TEL Nebenanschluss *m*, (-)Apparat *m*; *a.* ***~ cord*** (*Br* ***lead***) ELECTR Verlängerungskabel *n*, -schnur *f*
**ex·ten·sive** ausgedehnt, umfassend
**ex·tent** Ausdehnung *f*; Umfang *m*, (Aus)Maß *n*, Grad *m*; ***to some ~, to a certain ~*** bis zu e-m gewissen Grade; ***to such an ~ that*** so sehr, dass
**ex·ten·u·ate** abschwächen, mildern; beschönigen; ***extenuating circumstances*** JUR mildernde Umstände *pl*
**ex·te·ri·or 1.** äußerlich, äußere(r, -s), Außen… **2.** *das* Äußere; Außenseite *f*; äußere Erscheinung
**ex·ter·mi·nate** ausrotten (*a. fig*), vernichten, *Ungeziefer, Unkraut a.* vertilgen
**ex·ter·nal** äußere(r, -s), äußerlich, Außen…
**ex·tinct** erloschen; ausgestorben
**ex·tinc·tion** Erlöschen *n*; Aussterben *n*, Untergang *m*; Vernichtung *f*, Zerstörung *f*
**ex·tin·guish** (aus)löschen; vernichten
**ex·tin·guish·er** (*Feuer*)Löscher *m*
**ex·tort** erpressen (***from*** von)
**ex·tra 1.** *adj* zusätzlich, Extra…, Sonder…; ***be ~*** gesondert berechnet werden **2.** *adv* extra, besonders; ***charge ~ for*** *et.* gesondert berechnen **3.** Sonderleistung *f*; *esp* MOT Extra *n*; Zuschlag *m*; Extrablatt *n*; THEA, *film*: Statist(in)
**ex·tract 1.** Auszug *m* **2.** (heraus)ziehen; herauslocken; ableiten, herleiten
**ex·trac·tion** (Heraus)Ziehen *n*; Herkunft *f*
**ex·tra·dite** ausliefern; *j-s* Auslieferung erwirken;
**ex·tra·di·tion** Auslieferung *f*
**extra·or·di·na·ry** außerordentlich; ungewöhnlich; Sonder…
**ex·tra pay** Zulage *f*
**ex·tra·ter·res·tri·al** außerirdisch
**ex·tra time** SPORT (Spiel)Verlängerung *f*
**ex·trav·a·gance** Übertriebenheit *f*; Verschwendung *f*; Extravaganz *f*
**ex·trav·a·gant** übertrieben, überspannt; verschwenderisch; extravagant
**ex·treme 1.** äußerste(r, -s), größte(r, -s), höchste(r, -s); außergewöhnlich; ***~ right*** POL rechtsextrem(istisch); ***~ right wing*** POL rechtsradikal **2.** *das* Äußerste; Extrem *n*; höchster Grad
**ex·treme·ly** äußerst, höchst
**ex·trem·ism** POL Extremismus *m*
**ex·trem·ist** POL Extremist(in)

E

**ex·trem·i·ties** Gliedmaßen *pl*, Extremitäten *pl*
**ex·trem·i·ty** *das* Äußerste; höchste Not; äußerste Maßnahme
**ex·tri·cate** herauswinden, herausziehen, befreien
**ex·tro·vert** Extrovertierte *m, f*
**ex·u·be·rance** Fülle *f*; Überschwang *m*;
**ex·u·be·rant** reichlich, üppig; überschwänglich; ausgelassen
**ex·ult** frohlocken, jubeln
**eye 1.** ANAT Auge *n*; Blick *m*; Öhr *n*; Öse *f*; ***see ~ to ~ with s.o.*** mit j-m völlig übereinstimmen; ***be up to the ~s in work*** bis über die Ohren in Arbeit stecken; ***with an ~ to s.th.*** im Hinblick auf et. **2.** ansehen; mustern
**eye·ball** ANAT Augapfel *m*
**eye·brow** ANAT Augenbraue *f*
**eye-catch·ing** ins Auge fallend, auffallend
**eye doc·tor** F Augenarzt *m*, -ärztin *f*
**eye·glass·es** *a. **pair of ~*** Brille *f*
**eye·lash** ANAT Augenwimper *f*
**eye·lid** ANAT Augenlid *n*
**eye·lin·er** Eyeliner *m*
**eye-o·pen·er**: ***that was an ~ to me*** das hat mir die Augen geöffnet
**eye shad·ow** Lidschatten *m*
**eye·sight** Augen(licht *n*) *pl*, Sehkraft *f*
**eye·sore** F Schandfleck *m*
**eye spe·cial·ist** Augenarzt *m*, -ärztin *f*
**eye·strain** Ermüdung *f or* Überanstrengung *f* der Augen
**eye·wit·ness** Augenzeuge *m*, -zeugin *f*

# F

**F, f** F, f *n*
**fa·ble** Fabel *f*; Sage *f*
**fab·ric** Gewebe *n*, Stoff *m*; Struktur *f*
**fab·ri·cate** fabrizieren (*mst fig*)
**fab·u·lous** sagenhaft, der Sage angehörend; fabelhaft
**fa·cade, fa·çade** ARCH Fassade *f*
**face 1.** Gesicht *n*; Gesichtsausdruck *m*, Miene *f*; (Ober)Fläche *f*; Vorderseite *f*; Zifferblatt *n*; ***~ to ~ with*** Auge in Auge mit; ***save*** (***lose***) ***one's ~*** das Gesicht wahren (verlieren); ***on the ~ of it*** auf den ersten Blick; ***pull a long ~*** ein langes Gesicht machen; ***have the ~ to do s.th.*** die Stirn haben, et. zu tun **2.** *v/t* ansehen; gegenüberstehen (*dat*); (hinaus)gehen auf (*acc*); die Stirn bieten (*dat*); einfassen; ARCH bekleiden; *v/i*: ***~ about*** sich umdrehen
**face·cloth**, *Br* **face flan·nel** Waschlappen *m*
**face·lift** Facelifting *n*, Gesichtsstraffung *f*; *fig* Renovierung *f*, Verschönerung *f*
**fa·ce·tious** witzig
**fa·cial 1.** Gesichts… **2.** Gesichtsbehandlung *f*
**fa·cile** leicht; oberflächlich
**fa·cil·i·tate** erleichtern
**fa·cil·i·ty** Leichtigkeit *f*; Oberflächlichkeit *f*; *mst pl* Erleichterung(en *pl*) *f*; Einrichtung(en *pl*) *f*, Anlage(n *pl*) *f*
**fac·ing** TECH Verkleidung *f*; *pl* Besatz *m*
**fact** Tatsache *f*, Wirklichkeit *f*, Wahrheit *f*; Tat *f*; *pl* Daten; ***in ~*** in der Tat, tatsächlich
**fac·tion** *esp* POL Splittergruppe *f*; Zwietracht *f*
**fac·ti·tious** künstlich
**fac·tor** Faktor *m*
**fac·to·ry** Fabrik *f*
**fac·ul·ty** Fähigkeit *f*; Kraft *f*; *fig* Gabe *f*; UNIV Fakultät *f*; Lehrkörper *m*
**fad** Mode *f*, Modeerscheinung *f*, -torheit *f*; (vorübergehende) Laune
**fade** (ver)welken (lassen); verschießen, verblassen (*color*); schwinden; immer schwächer werden (*person*); *film, radio*, TV ***~ in*** auf- *or* eingeblendet werden; auf- *or* einblenden; ***~ out*** aus- *or* abgeblendet werden; aus- *or* abblenden; ***~d jeans*** ausgewaschene Jeans *pl*
**fail 1.** *v/i* versagen; misslingen, fehlschlagen; versiegen; nachlassen; durchfallen (*candidate*); *v/t* im Stich lassen; *j-n in e-r Prüfung* durchfallen lassen **2.** ***without ~*** mit Sicherheit, ganz bestimmt; **fail·ure** Versagen *n*; Fehlschlag *m*, Misserfolg *m*; Versäumnis *n*; Versager *m*, F Niete *f*
**faint 1.** schwach, matt **2.** ohnmächtig

werden, in Ohnmacht fallen (***with*** vor); **3.** Ohnmacht *f*
**faint-heart·ed** verzagt
**fair**[1] gerecht, ehrlich, anständig, fair; recht gut, ansehnlich; schön (*weather*); klar (*sky*); blond (*hair*); hell (*skin*); ***play*** ~ fair spielen; *fig* sich an die Spielregeln halten
**fair**[2] (Jahr)Markt *m*; Volksfest *n*; Ausstellung *f*, Messe *f*
**fair game** *fig* Freiwild *n*
**fair·ground** Rummelplatz *m*
**fair·ly** gerecht; ziemlich
**fair·ness** Gerechtigkeit *f*, Fairness *f*
**fair play** SPORT *and fig* Fair Play *n*, Fairness *f*
**fai·ry** Fee *f*; Zauberin *f*; Elf *m*, Elfe *f*
**fai·ry·land** Feen-, Märchenland *n*
**fai·ry| sto·ry, ~ tale** Märchen *n* (*a. fig*)
**faith** Glaube *m*; Vertrauen *n*; **faith·ful** treu (***to*** *dat*); ***Yours ~ly*** Hochachtungsvoll (*letter*); **faith·less** treulos
**fake 1.** Schwindel *m*; Fälschung *f*; Schwindler *m* **2.** fälschen; imitieren, nachmachen; vortäuschen, simulieren **3.** gefälscht; fingiert
**fal·con** zo Falke *m*
**fall 1.** Fallen *n*, Fall *m*; Sturz *m*; Verfall *m*; Einsturz *m*; Herbst *m*; ECON Sinken *n* (*of prices etc*); Gefälle *n*; *mst pl* Wasserfall *m* **2.** fallen, stürzen; ab-, einfallen; sinken; sich legen (*wind*); *in e-n Zustand* verfallen; ***~ ill, ~ sick*** krank werden; ***~ in love with*** sich verlieben in (*acc*); ***~ short of*** *den Erwartungen etc* nicht entsprechen; ***~ back*** zurückweichen; ***~ back on*** *fig* zurückgreifen auf (*acc*); ***~ for*** hereinfallen auf (*acc*); F sich in *j-n* verknallen; ***~ off*** zurückgehen (*business*, *demand etc*), nachlassen; ***~ on*** herfallen über (*acc*); ***~ out*** sich streiten (***with*** mit); ***~ through*** durchfallen (*a. fig*); ***~ to*** reinhauen, tüchtig zugreifen
**fal·la·cious** trügerisch
**fal·la·cy** Trugschluss *m*
**fall guy** F *der* Lackierte, *der* Dumme
**fal·li·ble** fehlbar
**fall·ing star** Sternschnuppe *f*
**fall·out** Fall-out *m*, radioaktiver Niederschlag
**fal·low** zo falb; AGR brach(liegend)
**false** falsch
**false·hood**, **false·ness** Falschheit *f*; Unwahrheit *f*
**false start** Fehlstart *m*
**fal·si·fi·ca·tion** (Ver)Fälschung *f*
**fal·si·fy** (ver)fälschen
**fal·si·ty** Falschheit *f*, Unwahrheit *f*
**fal·ter** schwanken; stocken (*voice*); stammeln; *fig* zaudern
**fame** Ruf *m*, Ruhm *m*
**famed** berühmt (***for*** wegen)
**fa·mil·i·ar 1.** vertraut; gewohnt; familiär **2.** Vertraute *m*, *f*
**fa·mil·i·ar·i·ty** Vertrautheit *f*; (plumpe) Vertraulichkeit
**fa·mil·i·ar·ize** vertraut machen
**fam·i·ly 1.** Familie *f* **2.** Familien…, Haus…; **~ al·low·ance** → ***child benefit***; **~ doc·tor** Hausarzt *m*; **~ name** Familien-, Nachname *m*; **~ plan·ning** Familienplanung *f*; **~ tree** Stammbaum *m*
**fam·ine** Hungersnot *f*; Knappheit *f* (***of*** an *dat*)
**fam·ished** verhungert; ***be ~*** F am Verhungern sein
**fa·mous** berühmt
**fan**[1] **1.** Fächer *m*; Ventilator *m* **2.** (zu)fächeln; anfachen; *fig* entfachen
**fan**[2] (*Sport- etc*)Fan *m*
**fa·nat·ic** Fanatiker(in)
**fa·nat·i·cal** fanatisch
**fan belt** TECH Keilriemen *m*
**fan·ci·er** BOT, zo Liebhaber(in), Züchter(in)
**fan·ci·ful** fantastisch
**fan club** Fanklub *m*
**fan·cy 1.** Fantasie *f*; Einbildung *f*; plötzlicher Einfall, Idee *f*; Laune *f*; Vorliebe *f*, Neigung *f* **2.** ausgefallen; Fantasie… **3.** sich vorstellen; sich einbilden; ***~ that!*** stell dir vor!, denk nur!; sieh mal einer an!
**fan·cy| ball** Kostümfest *n*, Maskenball *m*; **~ dress** (Masken)Kostüm *n*
**fan·cy-free** → ***footloose***
**fan·cy goods** Modeartikel *pl*, -waren *pl*
**fan·cy·work** Stickerei *f*
**fang** zo Reiß-, Fangzahn *m*; Hauer *m*; Giftzahn *m*
**fan mail** Fanpost *f*, Verehrerpost *f*
**fan·tas·tic** fantastisch
**fan·ta·sy** Fantasie *f*
**far 1.** *adj* fern, entfernt, weit **2.** *adv* fern; weit; (sehr) viel; ***as ~ as*** bis; ***in so ~ as*** insofern als
**far·a·way** weit entfernt

**fare** 1. Fahrgeld *n*; Fahrgast *m*; Verpflegung *f*, Kost *f* 2. *gut* leben; ***he ~d well*** es (er)ging ihm gut
**fare dodg·er** Schwarzfahrer(in)
**fare·well** 1. *int* lebe(n Sie) wohl! 2. Abschied *m*, Lebewohl *n*
**far·fetched** *fig* weit hergeholt, gesucht
**farm** 1. Bauernhof *m*, Gut *n*, Gehöft *n*, Farm *f* 2. *Land, Hof* bewirtschaften
**farm·er** Bauer *m*, Landwirt *m*, Farmer *m*
**farm·hand** Landarbeiter(in)
**farm·house** Bauernhaus *n*
**farm·ing** 1. Acker…, landwirtschaftlich 2. Landwirtschaft *f*
**farm·stead** Bauernhof *m*, Gehöft *n*
**farm·yard** Wirtschaftshof *m*
**far-off** entfernt, fern
**far right** POL rechtsgerichtet
**far·sight·ed** weitsichtig, *fig a.* weitblickend
**fas·ci·nate** faszinieren
**fas·ci·nat·ing** faszinierend
**fas·ci·na·tion** Zauber *m*, Reiz *m*, Faszination *f*
**fas·cism** POL Faschismus *m*
**fas·cist** POL 1. Faschist *m* 2. faschistisch
**fash·ion** Mode *f*; Art *f* und Weise *f*; ***be in ~*** in Mode sein; ***out of ~*** unmodern; **fash·ion·a·ble** modisch, elegant; in Mode
**fash·ion| pa·rade, ~ show** Modenschau *f*
**fast**[1] 1. Fasten *n* 2. fasten
**fast**[2] schnell; fest; treu; echt, beständig (*color*); flott; ***be ~*** vorgehen (*watch*)
**fast·back** MOT (Wagen *m* mit) Fließheck *n*
**fast breed·er (re·ac·tor)** PHYS Schneller Brüter
**fas·ten** befestigen, festmachen, anheften, anschnallen, anbinden, zuknöpfen, zu-, verschnüren; *Blick etc* richten (***on*** auf *acc*); sich festmachen *or* schließen lassen; **fas·ten·er** Verschluss *m*
**fast food** Schnellgericht(e *pl*) *n*
**fast-food res·tau·rant** Schnellimbiss *m*, Schnellgaststätte *f*
**fas·tid·i·ous** anspruchsvoll, heikel, wählerisch, verwöhnt
**fast lane** MOT Überholspur *f*
**fat** 1. fett; dick; fettig, fetthaltig 2. Fett *n*; ***be low in ~*** fettarm sein
**fa·tal** tödlich; verhängnisvoll, fatal (***to*** für); **fa·tal·i·ty** Verhängnis *n*; tödlicher Unfall; (Todes)Opfer *n*
**fate** Schicksal *n*; Verhängnis *n*
**fa·ther** Vater *m*
**Fa·ther Christ·mas** *esp Br* der Weihnachtsmann, der Nikolaus
**fa·ther·hood** Vaterschaft *f*
**fa·ther-in-law** Schwiegervater *m*
**fa·ther·less** vaterlos
**fa·ther·ly** väterlich
**fath·om** 1. MAR Faden *m* 2. MAR loten; *fig* ergründen
**fath·om·less** unergründlich
**fa·tigue** 1. Ermüdung *f*; Strapaze *f* 2. ermüden
**fat·ten** dick *or contp* fett machen *or* werden; mästen; **fat·ty** fett; fettig
**fau·cet** TECH (Wasser)Hahn *m*
**fault** Fehler *m*; Defekt *m*; Schuld *f*; ***find ~ with*** et. auszusetzen haben an (*dat*); ***be at ~*** Schuld haben
**fault·less** fehlerfrei, fehlerlos
**fault·y** fehlerhaft, TECH *a.* defekt
**fa·vo(u)r** 1. Gunst *f*; Gefallen *m*; Begünstigung *f*; ***in ~ of*** zu Gunsten von (*or gen*); ***do s.o. a ~*** j-m e-n Gefallen tun 2. begünstigen; bevorzugen, vorziehen; wohlwollend gegenüberstehen; SPORT favorisieren; **fa·vo(u)r·a·ble** günstig; **fa·vo(u)r·ite** 1. Liebling *m*; SPORT Favorit *m* 2. Lieblings…
**fawn** 1. ZO (Reh)Kitz *n*; Rehbraun *n* 2. rehbraun
**fax** 1. Fax *n* 2. faxen; ***~ s.th. (through) to s.o.*** j-m et. faxen
**fax (ma·chine)** Faxgerät *n*
**fear** 1. Furcht *f* (***of*** vor *dat*); Befürchtung *f*; Angst *f* 2. (be)fürchten; sich fürchten vor (*dat*)
**fear·ful** furchtsam; furchtbar
**fear·less** furchtlos
**fea·si·ble** durchführbar
**feast** 1. REL Fest *n*, Feiertag *m*; Festessen *n*; *fig* Fest *n*, (Hoch)Genuss *m* 2. *v/t* festlich bewirten; *v/i* sich gütlich tun (***on*** an *dat*), schlemmen
**feat** große Leistung; (Helden)Tat *f*
**fea·ther** 1. Feder *f*; *a. pl* Gefieder *n*; ***birds of a ~*** Leute vom gleichen Schlag; ***birds of a ~ flock together*** Gleich und Gleich gesellt sich gern; ***that is a ~ in his cap*** darauf kann er stolz sein 2. mit Federn polstern *or* schmücken; *Pfeil* fiedern
**feath·er·bed** verhätscheln

**feath·er·brained** F hohlköpfig
**feath·ered** zo gefiedert
**feath·er·weight** SPORT Federgewicht *n*, Federgewichtler *m*; Leichtgewicht *n* (*person*)
**feath·er·y** gefiedert; federleicht
**fea·ture 1.** (Gesichts)Zug *m*; (charakteristisches) Merkmal; *radio*, TV *etc* Feature *n*; Haupt-, Spielfilm *m* **2.** groß herausbringen; *film*: in der Hauptrolle zeigen; ~ **film** Haupt-, Spielfilm *m*
**Feb** *abbr of* ***February*** Febr., Februar *m*
**Feb·ru·a·ry** (*abbr* ***Feb***) Februar *m*
**fed·e·ral** POL Bundes…
**Fed·e·ral Re·pub·lic of Ger·man·y** *die* Bundesrepublik Deutschland (*abbr* ***BRD***)
**fed·e·ra·tion** POL Bundesstaat *m*; Föderation *f*, Staatenbund *m*; ECON, SPORT *etc* (Dach)Verband *m*
**fee** Gebühr *f*; Honorar *n*; (Mitglieds-) Beitrag *m*; Eintrittsgeld *n*
**fee·ble** schwach
**feed 1.** Futter *n*; Nahrung *f*; Fütterung *f*; TECH Zuführung *f*, Speisung *f* **2.** *v/t* füttern; ernähren; TECH *Maschine* speisen; IT eingeben; AGR weiden lassen; ***be fed up with s.o.*** (***s.th.***) j-n (et.) satthaben; ***well fed*** wohlgenährt; *v/i* (fr)essen; sich ernähren; weiden
**feed·back** ELECTR Feed-back *n*, Rückkoppelung *f*; *radio*, TV Reaktion *f*
**feed·er** Esser *m*
**feed·er road** Zubringer(straße *f*) *m*
**feed·ing bot·tle** (Saug)Flasche *f*
**feel 1.** (sich) fühlen; befühlen; empfinden; sich anfühlen; ***~ sorry for s.o.*** j-n bedauern *or* bemitleiden **2.** Gefühl *n*; Empfindung *f*; **feel·er** zo Fühler *m*; **feel·ing** Gefühl *n*
**feign** *Interesse etc* vortäuschen, *Krankheit a.* simulieren
**feint** Finte *f*
**fell** niederschlagen; fällen
**fel·low 1.** Gefährte *m*, Gefährtin *f*, Kamerad(in); Gegenstück *n*; F Kerl *m*; ***old ~*** F alter Knabe; ***the ~ of a glove*** der andere Handschuh **2.** Mit…; ~ **be·ing** Mitmensch *m*; ~ **cit·i·zen** Mitbürger *m*; ~ **coun·try·man** Landsmann *m*
**fel·low·ship** Gemeinschaft *f*; Kameradschaft *f*
**fel·low trav·el·(l)er** Mitreisende *m*, *f*, Reisegefährte *m*, -gefährtin *f*; POL Mitläufer(in)
**fel·on** JUR Schwerverbrecher *m*
**fel·o·ny** JUR (schweres) Verbrechen, Kapitalverbrechen *n*
**felt** Filz *m*; ~ **pen**, ~ **tip**, **~-tip(ped) pen** Filzstift *m*, Filzschreiber *m*
**fe·male 1.** weiblich **2.** *contp* Weib *n*, Weibsbild *n*; zo Weibchen *n*
**fem·i·nine** weiblich, Frauen…; feminin
**fem·i·nism** Feminismus *m*
**fem·i·nist 1.** Feminist(in) **2.** feministisch
**fen** Fenn *n*, Sumpf-, Marschland *n*
**fence 1.** Zaun *m*; *sl* Hehler *m* **2.** *v/t*: ***~ in*** einzäunen, umzäunen; einsperren; ***~ off*** abzäunen; *v/i* SPORT fechten; **fenc·er** SPORT Fechter *m*; **fenc·ing 1.** Einfriedung *f*; SPORT Fechten *n* **2.** Fecht…
**fend**: ***~ off*** abwehren; ***~ for o.s.*** für sich selbst sorgen
**fend·er** Schutzvorrichtung *f*; Schutzblech *n*; MOT Kotflügel *m*; Kamingitter *n*, Kaminvorsetzer *m*
**fen·nel** BOT Fenchel *m*
**fer·ment 1.** Ferment *n*; Gärung *f* **2.** gären (lassen)
**fer·men·ta·tion** Gärung *f*
**fern** BOT Farn(kraut *n*) *m*
**fe·ro·cious** wild; grausam
**fe·roc·i·ty** Wildheit *f*
**fer·ret 1.** zo Frettchen *n*; *fig* Spürhund *m* **2.** herumstöbern; ***~ out*** aufspüren, aufstöbern
**fer·ry 1.** Fähre *f* **2.** übersetzen
**fer·ry·boat** Fährboot *n*, Fähre *f*
**fer·ry·man** Fährmann *m*
**fer·tile** fruchtbar; reich (***of, in*** an *dat*)
**fer·til·i·ty** Fruchtbarkeit *f* (*a. fig*)
**fer·ti·lize** fruchtbar machen; befruchten; AGR düngen; **fer·ti·liz·er** AGR (*esp* Kunst)Dünger *m*, Düngemittel *n*
**fer·vent** glühend, leidenschaftlich
**fer·vo(u)r** Glut *f*; Inbrunst *f*
**fes·ter** MED eitern
**fes·ti·val** Fest *n*; Festival *n*, Festspiele *pl*
**fes·tive** festlich
**fes·tiv·i·ty** Festlichkeit *f*
**fes·toon** Girlande *f*
**fetch** holen; *Preis* erzielen; *Seufzer* ausstoßen; **fetch·ing** F reizend
**fete, fête 1.** Fest *n*; ***village ~*** Dorffest *n* **2.** feiern
**fet·id** stinkend
**fet·ter 1.** Fessel *f* **2.** fesseln
**feud** Fehde *f*

**feud·al** Feudal..., Lehns...
**feu·dal·ism** Feudalismus *m*, Feudal-, Lehnssystem *n*
**fe·ver** MED Fieber *n*; **fe·ver·ish** MED fieb(e)rig, fieberhaft (*a. fig*)
**few** wenige; ***a*** **~** ein paar, einige; ***no fewer than*** nicht weniger als; ***quite a*** **~**, ***a good*** **~** e-e ganze Menge
**fi·an·cé** Verlobte *m*
**fi·an·cée** Verlobte *f*
**fi·as·co** Fiasko *n*
**fib** F **1.** Flunkerei *f*, Schwindelei *f* **2.** schwindeln, flunkern
**fi·ber**, *Br* **fi·bre** Faser *f*
**fi·ber·glass** TECH Fiberglas *n*, Glasfaser *f*
**fi·brous** faserig
**fick·le** wankelmütig; unbeständig
**fic·tion** Erfindung *f*; Prosaliteratur *f*, Belletristik *f*; Romane *pl*
**fic·tion·al** erdichtet; Roman...
**fic·ti·tious** erfunden, fiktiv
**fid·dle 1.** Fiedel *f*, Geige *f*; ***play first*** (***second***) **~** *esp fig* die erste (zweite) Geige spielen; (***as***) ***fit as a*** **~** kerngesund **2.** MUS fiedeln; *a.* **~** ***about*** *or* ***around*** (***with***) herumfingern (an *dat*), spielen (mit)
**fid·dler** Geiger(in)
**fi·del·i·ty** Treue *f*; Genauigkeit *f*
**fid·get** F nervös machen; (herum)zappeln; **fid·get·y** zapp(e)lig, nervös
**field** Feld *n*; SPORT Spielfeld *n*; Arbeitsfeld *n*; Gebiet *n*; Bereich *m*; **~** ***of vision*** OPT Gesichtsfeld *n*; **~ e·vents** SPORT Sprung- und Wurfdisziplinen *pl*; **~ glass·es** *a.* ***pair of*** **~** Feldstecher *m*, Fernglas *n*; **~ mar·shal** MIL Feldmarschall *m*
**field·work** praktische (wissenschaftliche) Arbeit, *a.* Arbeit *f* im Gelände; ECON Feldarbeit *f*
**fiend** Satan *m*, Teufel *m*; F (*Frischluft-etc*)Fanatiker(in)
**fiend·ish** teuflisch, boshaft
**fierce** wild; scharf; heftig; **fierce·ness** Wildheit *f*, Schärfe *f*; Heftigkeit *f*
**fi·er·y** feurig; hitzig
**fif·teen 1.** fünfzehn **2.** Fünfzehn *f*
**fif·teenth** fünfzehnte(r, -s)
**fifth 1.** fünfte(r, -s) **2.** Fünftel *n*
**fifth·ly** fünftens
**fif·ti·eth** fünfzigste(r, -s)
**fif·ty 1.** fünfzig **2.** Fünfzig *f*
**fif·ty·fif·ty** F halbe-halbe
**fig** BOT Feige *f*
**fight 1.** Kampf *m*; MIL Gefecht *n*; Schlägerei *f*; *boxing*: Kampf *m*, Fight *m* **2.** *v/t* bekämpfen; kämpfen gegen *or* mit, SPORT *a.* boxen gegen; *v/i* kämpfen, sich schlagen; SPORT boxen
**fight·er** Kämpfer *m*; SPORT Boxer *m*, Fighter *m*; *a.* **~** ***plane*** MIL Jagdflugzeug *n*
**fight·ing** Kampf *m*
**fig·u·ra·tive** bildlich
**fig·ure 1.** Figur *f*; Gestalt *f*; Zahl *f*, Ziffer *f*; Preis *m*; ***be good at*** **~*s*** ein guter Rechner sein **2.** *v/t* abbilden, darstellen; F meinen, glauben; sich *et.* vorstellen; **~** ***out*** *Problem* lösen, F rauskriegen; verstehen; **~** ***up*** zusammenzählen; *v/i* erscheinen, vorkommen; **~** ***on*** rechnen mit; **~ skat·er** Eiskunstläufer(in); **~ skat·ing** Eiskunstlauf *m*
**fil·a·ment** ELECTR Glühfaden *m*
**filch** F klauen, stibitzen
**file**[1] **1.** Ordner *m*; Karteikasten *m*; Akte *f*, Akten *pl*; Ablage *f*; IT Datei *f*; Reihe *f*; MIL Rotte *f*; ***on*** **~** bei den Akten **2.** *v/t Briefe etc* ablegen, zu den Akten nehmen, einordnen; *Antrag* einreichen, *Berufung* einlegen; *v/i* hintereinander marschieren
**file**[2] TECH **1.** Feile *f* **2.** feilen
**file| man·age·ment** IT Dateiverwaltung *f*; **~ pro·tec·tion** IT Schreibschutz *m*
**fil·et** GASTR Filet *n*
**fi·li·al** kindlich, Kindes...
**fil·ing** Ablegen *n*
**fil·ing cab·i·net** Aktenschrank *m*
**fill 1.** (sich) füllen; an-, aus-, erfüllen, vollfüllen; *Pfeife* stopfen; *Zahn* füllen, plombieren; **~** ***in*** einsetzen; **~** ***out*** (*Br* ***in***) *Formular* ausfüllen; **~** ***up*** vollfüllen; sich füllen **2.** Füllung *f*
**fil·let** → ***filet***
**fill·ing** Füllung *f*; MED (Zahn)Füllung *f*, Plombe *f*; **~ sta·tion** Tankstelle *f*
**fil·ly** ZO Stutenfohlen *n*
**film 1.** Häutchen *n*; Membran(e) *f*; Film *m* (*a.* PHOT); ***take*** *or* ***shoot a*** **~** e-n Film drehen **2.** (ver)filmen; sich verfilmen lassen; **~ star** *esp Br* Filmstar *m*
**fil·ter 1.** Filter *m* **2.** filtern
**fil·ter tip** Filter *m*; Filterzigarette *f*
**fil·ter-tipped**: **~** ***cigarette*** Filterzigarette *f*

**filth** Schmutz *m*
**filth·y** schmutzig; *fig* unflätig
**fin** zo Flosse *f*; SPORT Schwimmflosse *f*
**fi·nal 1.** letzte(r, -s); End…, Schluss…; endgültig **2.** SPORT Finale *n*; *mst pl* Schlussexamen *n*, -prüfung *f*
**fi·nal dis·pos·al** Endlagerung *f*
**fi·nal·ist** SPORT Finalist(in)
**fi·nal·ly** endlich, schließlich; endgültig
**fi·nal whis·tle** SPORT Schlusspfiff *m*, Abpfiff *m*
**fi·nance 1.** Finanzwesen *n*; *pl* Finanzen *pl* **2.** finanzieren
**fi·nan·cial** finanziell
**fi·nan·cier** Finanzier *m*
**finch** zo Fink *m*
**find 1.** finden; (an)treffen; herausfinden; JUR *j-n* für (*nicht*) *schuldig* erklären; beschaffen, besorgen; **~ *out*** *v/t et.* herausfinden; *v/i* es herausfinden **2.** Fund *m*, Entdeckung *f*; **find·ings** Befund *m*; JUR Feststellung *f*, Spruch *m*
**fine[1] 1.** *adj* fein; schön; ausgezeichnet, großartig; ***I'm ~*** mir geht es gut **2.** *adv* F sehr gut, bestens
**fine[2] 1.** Geldstrafe *f*, Bußgeld *n* **2.** zu e-r Geldstrafe verurteilen
**fin·ger 1.** ANAT Finger *m*; → ***cross*** *3* **2.** betasten, (herum)fingern an (*dat*)
**fin·ger·nail** ANAT Fingernagel *m*
**fin·ger·print** Fingerabdruck *m*
**fin·ger·tip** Fingerspitze *f*
**fin·i·cky** pedantisch; wählerisch
**fin·ish 1.** (be)enden, aufhören (mit); *a.* **~ *off*** vollenden, zu Ende führen, erledigen, *Buch etc* auslesen; *a.* **~ *off*, ~ *up*** aufessen, austrinken **2.** Ende *n*, Schluss *m*; SPORT Endspurt *m*, Finish *n*; Ziel *n*; Vollendung *f*, letzter Schliff
**fin·ish·ing line** SPORT Ziellinie *f*
**Fin·land** Finnland *n*
**Finn** Finne *m*, Finnin *f*
**Finn·ish 1.** finnisch **2.** LING Finnisch *n*
**fir** *a.* **~ *tree*** BOT Tanne *f*
**fir cone** BOT Tannenzapfen *m*
**fire 1.** Feuer *n*; ***be on ~*** in Flammen stehen, brennen; ***catch ~*** Feuer fangen, in Brand geraten; ***set on ~, set ~ to*** anzünden **2.** *v/t* anzünden, entzünden; *fig* anfeuern; abfeuern; *Ziegel etc* brennen; F *j-n* rausschmeißen; heizen; *v/i* Feuer fangen (*a. fig*); feuern
**fire a·larm** Feueralarm *m*; Feuermelder *m*
**fire·arms** Schusswaffen *pl*
**fire bri·gade** *Br* Feuerwehr *f*
**fire·bug** F Feuerteufel *m*
**fire·crack·er** Knallfrosch *m*; Knallbonbon *m*, *n*
**fire de·part·ment** Feuerwehr *f*
**fire en·gine** *Br* Löschfahrzeug *n*
**fire es·cape** Feuerleiter *f*, -treppe *f*
**fire ex·tin·guish·er** Feuerlöscher *m*
**fire fight·er** Feuerwehrmann *m*
**fire·guard** *Br* Kamingitter *n*
**fire hy·drant** *Br* Hydrant *m*
**fire·man** Feuerwehrmann *m*; Heizer *m*
**fire·place** (offener) Kamin
**fire·plug** Hydrant *m*
**fire·proof** feuerfest
**fire-rais·ing** *Br* Brandstiftung *f*
**fire·screen** Kamingitter *n*
**fire ser·vice** *Br* Feuerwehr *f*
**fire·side** (offener) Kamin
**fire sta·tion** Feuerwache *f*
**fire truck** Löschfahrzeug *n*
**fire·wood** Brennholz *n*
**fire·works** Feuerwerk *n*
**fir·ing squad** MIL Exekutionskommando *n*
**firm[1]** fest; hart; standhaft
**firm[2]** Firma *f*
**first 1.** *adj* erste(r, -s); beste(r, -s) **2.** *adv* erstens; zuerst; **~ *of all*** an erster Stelle; zu allererst **3.** Erste(r, -s); ***at ~*** zuerst, anfangs; ***from the ~*** von Anfang an
**first aid** MED Erste Hilfe; **~ box, ~ kit** Verband(s)kasten *m*
**first·born** erstgeborene(r, -s), älteste(r, -s)
**first class** RAIL *etc* 1. Klasse
**first-class** erstklassig
**first floor** Erdgeschoss *n*, *Br* erster Stock; → ***second floor***
**first·hand** aus erster Hand
**first leg** SPORT Hinspiel *n*
**first·ly** erstens
**first name** Vorname *m*
**first-rate** erstklassig
**firth** Förde *f*, Meeresarm *m*
**fish 1.** zo Fisch *m* **2.** fischen, angeln
**fish·bone** Gräte *f*
**fish·er·man** Fischer *m*
**fish·e·ry** Fischerei *f*
**fish fin·ger** *Br* GASTR Fischstäbchen *n*
**fish·hook** Angelhaken *m*
**fish·ing** Fischen *n*, Angeln *n*; **~ line** Angelschnur *f*; **~ rod** Angelrute *f*; **~ tack-**

le Angelgerät *n*
**fish·mon·ger** *esp Br* Fischhändler *m*
**fish stick** GASTR Fischstäbchen *n*
**fish·y** Fisch…; F verdächtig
**fis·sion** PHYS Spaltung *f*
**fis·sure** GEOL Spalt *m*, Riss *m*
**fist** Faust *f*
**fit**[1] **1.** geeignet, passend; tauglich; SPORT fit, (gut) in Form; ***keep ~*** sich fit halten **2.** *v/t* passend machen (***for*** für), anpassen; TECH einpassen, einbauen; anbringen; ***~ in*** *j-m* e-n Termin geben, *j-n*, *et.* einschieben; *a.* ***~ on*** anprobieren; *a.* ***~ out*** ausrüsten, ausstatten, einrichten (***with*** mit); *a.* ***~ up*** einrichten (***with*** mit); montieren, installieren; *v/i* passen, sitzen (*dress etc*) **3.** Sitz *m*
**fit**[2] MED Anfall *m*; ***give s.o. a ~*** F j-n auf die Palme bringen; j-m e-n Schock versetzen
**fit·ful** unruhig (*sleep etc*)
**fit·ness** Tauglichkeit *f*; *esp* SPORT Fitness *f*, (gute) Form; ***~ cen·ter*** (*Br* ***cen·tre***) Fitnesscenter *n*
**fit·ted** zugeschnitten; ***~ carpet*** Spannteppich *m*, Teppichboden *m*; ***~ kitchen*** Einbauküche *f*
**fit·ter** Monteur *m*; Installateur *m*
**fit·ting 1.** passend; schicklich **2.** Montage *f*, Installation *f*; *pl* Ausstattung *f*; Armaturen *pl*
**five 1.** fünf **2.** Fünf *f*
**fix 1.** befestigen, anbringen (***to*** an *dat*); *Preis* festsetzen; fixieren; *Blick etc* richten (***on*** auf *acc*); *Aufmerksamkeit etc* fesseln; reparieren, in Ordnung bringen (*a. fig*); *Essen* zubereiten **2.** F Klemme *f*; *sl* Fix *m*
**fixed** fest; starr
**fix·ings** GASTR Beilagen *pl*
**fix·ture** Inventarstück *n*; ***lighting ~*** Beleuchtungskörper *m*
**fizz** zischen, sprudeln
**flab·ber·gast** F verblüffen; ***be ~ed*** F platt sein
**flab·by** schlaff
**flac·cid** schlaff, schlapp
**flag**[1] **1.** Fahne *f*, Flagge *f* **2.** beflaggen
**flag**[2] **1.** (Stein)Platte *f*, Fliese *f* **2.** mit (Stein)Platten *or* Fliesen belegen, fliesen
**flag**[3] nachlassen, erlahmen
**flag·pole**, **flag·staff** Fahnenstange *f*
**flag·stone** (Stein)Platte *f*, Fliese *f*
**flake 1.** Flocke *f*; Schuppe *f* **2.** *mst* ***~ off*** abblättern; F ***~ out*** schlappmachen
**flak·y** flockig; blätt(e)rig
**flak·y pas·try** GASTR Blätterteig *m*
**flame 1.** Flamme *f* (*a. fig*); ***be in ~s*** in Flammen stehen **2.** flammen, lodern
**flam·ma·ble** TECH brennbar, leicht entzündlich, feuergefährlich
**flan** GASTR Obst-, Käsekuchen *m*
**flank 1.** Flanke *f* **2.** flankieren
**flan·nel** Flanell *m*; *Br* Waschlappen *m*; *pl Br* Flanellhose *f*
**flap 1.** Flattern *n*, (Flügel)Schlag *m*; Klappe *f* **2.** mit *den Flügeln etc* schlagen; flattern
**flare 1.** flackern; sich weiten; ***~ up*** aufflammen; *fig* aufbrausen **2.** Lichtsignal *n*
**flash 1.** Aufblitzen *n*, Aufleuchten *n*, Blitz *m*; *radio etc*: Kurzmeldung *f*; PHOT F Blitz *m*; F Taschenlampe *f*; ***like a ~*** wie der Blitz; ***in a ~*** im Nu; ***a ~ of lightning*** ein Blitz **2.** (auf)blitzen *or* aufleuchten (lassen); zucken; rasen, flitzen
**flash·back** *film*: Rückblende *f*
**flash freeze** GASTR schnell einfrieren
**flash·light** PHOT Blitzlicht *n*; Taschenlampe *f*
**flash·y** protzig; auffallend
**flask** Taschenflasche *f*
**flat**[1] **1.** flach, eben, platt; schal; ECON flau; MOT platt (*tire*) **2.** *adv* ***fall ~*** danebengehen; ***sing ~*** zu tief singen **3.** Fläche *f*, Ebene *f*; flache Seite; Flachland *n*, Niederung *f*; MOT Reifenpanne *f*
**flat**[2] *Br* Wohnung *f*
**flat-foot·ed** plattfüßig
**flat·mate** *Br* Mitbewohner(in)
**flat·ten** (ein)ebnen; abflachen; *a.* ***~ out*** flach(er) werden
**flat·ter** schmeicheln (*dat*)
**flat·ter·er** Schmeichler(in)
**flat·ter·y** Schmeichelei *f*
**fla·vo(u)r 1.** Geschmack *m*; Aroma *n*; Blume *f*; *fig* Beigeschmack *m*; Würze *f* **2.** würzen
**fla·vo(u)r·ing** Würze *f*, Aroma *n*
**flaw** Fehler *m*, TECH *a.* Defekt *m*
**flaw·less** einwandfrei, tadellos
**flax** BOT Flachs *m*
**flea** ZO Floh *m*
**flea mar·ket** Flohmarkt *m*
**fleck** Fleck(en) *m*; Tupfen *m*

**fledged** zo flügge
**fledg(e)·ling** zo Jungvogel *m*; *fig* Grünschnabel *m*
**flee** fliehen; meiden
**fleece 1.** Vlies *n*, *esp* Schafsfell *n* **2.** F *j-n* neppen
**fleet** MAR Flotte *f*
**flesh** Fleisch *n*; **flesh·y** fleischig; dick
**flex**[1] *esp* ANAT biegen
**flex**[2] *esp Br* ELECTR (Anschluss-, Verlängerungs)Kabel *n*, (-)Schnur *f*
**flex·i·ble** flexibel, biegsam; *fig* anpassungsfähig; **~ *working hours*** Gleitzeit *f*
**flex·i·time** *Br*, **flex·time** Gleitzeit *f*
**flick** schnippen; schnellen
**flick·er 1.** flackern; TV flimmern **2.** Flackern *n*; TV Flimmern *n*
**fli·er** AVIAT Flieger *m*; Reklamezettel *m*
**flight** Flucht *f*; Flug *m* (*a. fig*); zo Schwarm *m*; *a.* **~ *of stairs*** Treppe *f*; ***put to*** **~** in die Flucht schlagen; ***take*** (***to***) **~** die Flucht ergreifen; **~ at·tend·ant** AVIAT Flugbegleiter(in); **~ con·nec·tion** AVIAT Flugverbindung *f*
**flight·less** zo flugunfähig
**flight| num·ber** AVIAT Flugnummer *f*; **~ re·cord·er** AVIAT Flugschreiber *m*
**flight·y** flatterhaft
**flim·sy** dünn; zart; *fig* fadenscheinig
**flinch** (zurück)zucken, zusammenfahren; zurückschrecken (***from*** vor *dat*)
**fling 1.** werfen, schleudern; **~ *o.s.*** sich stürzen; **~ *open*** (***to***) *Tür etc* aufreißen (zuschlagen) **2.** ***have a*** **~** sich austoben; ***have a*** **~ *at*** es versuchen *or* probieren mit
**flint** Feuerstein *m*
**flip** schnippen, schnipsen; *Münze* hochwerfen
**flip·pant** respektlos, F schnodd(e)rig
**flip·per** zo Flosse *f*; Schwimmflosse *f*
**flirt 1.** flirten **2.** ***be a*** **~** gern flirten
**flir·ta·tion** Flirt *m*
**flit** flitzen, huschen
**float 1.** *v/i* (auf dem Wasser) schwimmen, (im Wasser) treiben; schweben; *a.* ECON in Umlauf sein; *v/t* schwimmen *or* treiben lassen; MAR flottmachen; ECON *Wertpapiere etc* in Umlauf bringen; *Währung* floaten, den Wechselkurs (*gen*) freigeben **2.** Festwagen *m*
**float·ing 1.** schwimmend, treibend; ECON umlaufend; frei (*exchange rate*); frei konvertierbar (*currency*) **2.** ECON Floating *n*
**float·ing vot·er** POL Wechselwähler(in)
**flock 1.** zo Herde *f* (*a.* REL); Menge *f*, Schar *f* **2.** *fig* strömen
**floe** (treibende) Eisscholle
**flog** prügeln, schlagen
**flog·ging** Tracht *f* Prügel
**flood 1.** *a.* **~ *tide*** Flut *f*; Überschwemmung *f* **2.** überfluten, überschwemmen
**flood·gate** Schleusentor *n*
**flood·lights** ELECTR Flutlicht *n*
**floor 1.** (Fuß)Boden *m*; Stock *m*, Stockwerk *n*, Etage *f*; Tanzfläche *f*; → ***first floor, second floor***; ***take the*** **~** das Wort ergreifen **2.** e-n (Fuß)Boden legen in; zu Boden schlagen; *fig* F *j-n* umhauen
**floor·board** (Fußboden)Diele *f*
**floor cloth** Putzlappen *m*
**floor·ing** (Fuß)Bodenbelag *m*
**floor lamp** Stehlampe *f*
**floor lead·er** PARL Fraktionsführer *m*
**floor-length** bodenlang
**floor show** Nachtklubvorstellung *f*
**floor·walk·er** Aufsicht *f*
**flop 1.** sich (hin)plumpsen lassen; F durchfallen, danebengehen, ein Reinfall sein **2.** Plumps *m*; F Flop *m*, Reinfall *m*, Pleite *f*; Versager *m*
**flop·py (disk)** IT Floppy Disk *f*, Diskette *f*
**flor·id** rot, gerötet
**flor·ist** Blumenhändler(in)
**floun·der**[1] zo Flunder *f*
**floun·der**[2] zappeln; strampeln; *fig* sich verhaspeln
**flour** (feines) Mehl
**flour·ish 1.** Schnörkel *m*; MUS Tusch *m* **2.** *v/i* blühen, gedeihen; *v/t* schwenken
**flow 1.** fließen, strömen; wallen **2.** Fluß *m*, Strom *m* (*both a. fig*)
**flow·er 1.** Blume *f*; Blüte *f* (*a. fig*) **2.** blühen
**flow·er·bed** Blumenbeet *n*
**flow·er·pot** Blumentopf *m*
**flu** F MED Grippe *f*
**fluc·tu·ate** schwanken
**fluc·tu·a·tion** Schwankung *f*
**flue** Rauchfang *m*, Esse *f*
**flu·en·cy** Flüssigkeit *f*; (Rede)Gewandtheit *f*; **flu·ent** flüssig; gewandt; ***speak*** **~ *French*** fließend Französisch sprechen
**fluff 1.** Flaum *m*; Staubflocke *f* **2.** zo auf-

F

plustern; **fluff·y** flaumig

**flu·id 1.** flüssig **2.** Flüssigkeit *f*

**flunk** F durchfallen (lassen)

**flu·o·res·cent** fluoreszierend

**flu·o·ride** CHEM Fluor *n*

**flu·o·rine** CHEM Fluor *n*

**flur·ry** Windstoß *m*; (*Regen-*, *Schnee-*) Schauer *m*; *fig* Aufregung *f*, Unruhe *f*

**flush 1.** (Wasser)Spülung *f*; Erröten *n*; Röte *f* **2.** *v/t a.* ~ ***out*** (aus)spülen; ~ ***down*** hinunterspülen; ~ ***the toilet*** spülen; *v/i* erröten, rot werden; spülen **3.** ***be*** ~ F gut bei Kasse sein

**flus·ter 1.** nervös machen *or* werden **2.** Nervosität *f*

**flute** MUS **1.** Flöte *f* **2.** (auf der) Flöte spielen

**flut·ter 1.** flattern **2.** Flattern *n*; *fig* Erregung *f*

**flux** *fig* Fluss *m*

**fly**[1] zo Fliege *f*

**fly**[2] Hosenschlitz *m*; Zeltklappe *f*

**fly**[3] fliegen (lassen); stürmen, stürzen; flattern, wehen; (ver)fliegen (*time*); *Drachen* steigen lassen; ~ ***at s.o.*** auf j-n losgehen; ~ ***into a passion*** *or* ***rage*** in Wut geraten; **fly·er** → ***flier***

**fly·ing** fliegend; Flug…; ~ **sau·cer** fliegende Untertasse; ~ **squad** Überfallkommando *n*; ~ **time** AVIAT Flugzeit *f*; ~ **vis·it** F Stippvisite *f*

**fly·o·ver** *Br* (Straßen-, Eisenbahn-) Überführung *f*

**fly·screen** Fliegenfenster *n*

**fly·weight** *boxing*: Fliegengewicht *n*, Fliegengewichtler *m*

**fly·wheel** TECH Schwungrad *n*

**foal** zo Fohlen *n*

**foam 1.** Schaum *m* **2.** schäumen; ~ **ex·tin·guish·er** Schaumlöscher *m*, -löschgerät *n*; ~ **rub·ber** Schaumgummi *m*

**foam·y** schaumig

**fo·cus 1.** Brennpunkt *m*, *fig a.* Mittelpunkt *m*; OPT, PHOT Scharfeinstellung *f* **2.** OPT, PHOT scharf einstellen; *fig* konzentrieren (***on*** auf *acc*)

**fod·der** AGR (Trocken)Futter *n*

**foe** POET Feind *m*, Gegner *m*

**fog** (dichter) Nebel

**fog·gy** neb(e)lig; *fig* nebelhaft

**foi·ble** (kleine) Schwäche

**foil**[1] Folie *f*; *fig* Hintergrund *m*

**foil**[2] vereiteln

**foil**[3] *fencing*: Florett *n*

**fold**[1] **1.** Falte *f*; Falz *m* **2.** …fach, …fältig **3.** (sich) falten; falzen; *Arme* verschränken; einwickeln; *often* ~ ***up*** zusammenfalten, -legen, -klappen

**fold**[2] AGR Schafhürde *f*, Pferch *m*; REL Herde *f*

**fold·er** Aktendeckel *m*; Schnellhefter *m*; Faltprospekt *m*, -blatt *n*, Broschüre *f*

**fold·ing** zusammenlegbar; Klapp…; ~ **bed** Klappbett *n*; ~ **bi·cy·cle** Klapprad *n*; ~ **boat** Faltboot *n*; ~ **chair** Klappstuhl *m*; ~ **door(s)** Falttür *f*

**fo·li·age** BOT Laub *n*, Laubwerk *n*

**folk 1.** Leute *pl*; *pl* F *m-e etc* Leute *pl* **2.** Volks…

**folk·lore** Volkskunde *f*; Volkssagen *pl*; Folklore *f*

**folk mu·sic** Volksmusik *f*

**folk song** Volkslied *n*; Folksong *m*

**fol·low** folgen (*dat*); folgen auf (*acc*); befolgen; verfolgen; *s-m Beruf etc* nachgehen; ~ ***through*** *Plan etc* bis zum Ende durchführen; ~ ***up*** *e-r Sache* nachgehen; *e-e Sache* weiterverfolgen; ***as*** ~***s*** wie folgt; **fol·low·er** Nachfolger(in); Verfolger(in); Anhänger(in); **fol·low·ing 1.** Anhängerschaft *f*, Anhänger *pl*; Gefolge *n*; ***the*** ~ das Folgende; die Folgenden *pl* **2.** folgende(r, -s) **3.** im Anschluss an (*acc*)

**fol·ly** Torheit *f*

**fond** zärtlich; vernarrt (***of*** in *acc*); ***be*** ~ ***of*** gernhaben, lieben

**fon·dle** liebkosen; streicheln; (ver)hätscheln

**fond·ness** Zärtlichkeit *f*; Vorliebe *f*

**font** REL Taufstein *m*, Taufbecken *n*

**food** Nahrung *f*, Essen *n*; Nahrungs-, Lebensmittel *pl*; AGR Futter *n*

**fool 1.** Narr *m*, Närrin *f*, Dummkopf *m*; ***make a*** ~ ***of s.o.*** j-n zum Narren halten; ***make a*** ~ ***of o.s.*** sich lächerlich machen **2.** zum Narren halten; betrügen (***out of*** um); ~ ***about***, ~ ***around*** herumtrödeln; Unsinn machen, herumalbern

**fool·har·dy** tollkühn

**fool·ish** dumm, töricht; unklug

**fool·ish·ness** Dummheit *f*

**fool·proof** kinderleicht; todsicher

**foot 1.** ANAT Fuß *m* (*a. linear measure = 30,48 cm*); Fußende *n*; ***on*** ~ zu Fuß **2.** F *Rechnung* bezahlen; ***have to*** ~ ***the bill*** die Zeche bezahlen müssen; ~ ***it*** zu Fuß

gehen
**foot·ball** Football(spiel *n*) *m*; *Br* Fußball(spiel *n*) *m*; Football-Ball *m*; *Br* Fußball *m*
**foot·bal·ler** *Br* Fußballer *m*
**foot·ball| hoo·li·gan** *Br* Fußballrowdy *m*; ~ **play·er** *Br* Fußballspieler *m*
**foot·bridge** Fußgängerbrücke *f*
**foot·fall** Tritt *m*, Schritt *m*
**foot·hold** fester Stand, Halt *m*
**foot·ing** Halt *m*, Stand *m*; *fig* Grundlage *f*, Basis *f*; ***be on a friendly ~ with s.o.*** ein gutes Verhältnis zu j-m haben; ***lose one's ~*** den Halt verlieren
**foot·lights** THEA Rampenlicht(er *pl*) *n*
**foot·note** Fußnote *f*
**foot·path** (Fuß)Pfad *m*, (Fuß)Weg *m*
**foot·print** Fußabdruck *m*, *pl a.* Fußspur(en *pl*) *f*
**foot·sore**: ***be ~*** wunde Füße haben
**foot·step** Tritt *m*, Schritt *m*; Fußstapfe *f*
**foot·wear** Schuhwerk *n*, Schuhe *pl*
**fop** Geck *m*, F Fatzke *m*
**for 1.** *prp mst* für; *purpose, direction*: zu; nach; *warten, hoffen etc* auf (*acc*); *sich sehnen etc* nach; *cause*: aus, vor (*dat*), wegen; *time*: ***~ three days*** drei Tage (lang); seit drei Tagen; *distance*: ***I walked ~ a mile*** ich ging eine Meile (weit); *exchange*: (an)statt; als; ***I ~ one*** ich zum Beispiel; ***~ sure*** sicher!, gewiss! **2.** *cj* denn, weil
**for·age** *a.* ***~ about*** (herum)stöbern, (herum)wühlen (***in*** in *dat*; ***for*** nach)
**for·ay** MIL Einfall *m*, Überfall *m*; *fig* Ausflug *m* (***into*** *politics* in *die Politik*)
**for·bid** verbieten; hindern
**for·bid·ding** abstoßend
**force 1.** Stärke *f*, Kraft *f*, Gewalt *f*, Wucht *f*; ***the (police) ~*** die Polizei; ***(armed) ~s*** MIL Streitkräfte *pl*; ***by ~*** mit Gewalt; ***come*** *or* ***put into ~*** in Kraft treten *or* setzen **2.** *j-n* zwingen; *et.* erzwingen; zwängen; drängen; *Tempo* beschleunigen; ***~ s.th. on s.o.*** j-m et. aufzwingen *or* aufdrängen; ***~ o.s. on s.o.*** sich j-m aufdrängen; ***~ open*** aufbrechen
**forced** erzwungen; gezwungen, gequält; ~ **land·ing** AVIAT Notlandung *f*
**force·ful** energisch, kraftvoll; eindrucksvoll, überzeugend
**for·ceps** MED Zange *f*
**for·ci·ble** gewaltsam; eindringlich
**ford 1.** Furt *f* **2.** durchwaten
**fore 1.** vorder, Vorder…; vorn **2.** Vorderteil *m*, Vorderseite *f*, Front *f*
**fore·arm** ANAT Unterarm *m*
**fore·bear** *mst pl* Vorfahren *pl*, Ahnen *pl*
**fore·bod·ing** (böses) Vorzeichen; (*böse*) (Vor)Ahnung
**fore·cast 1.** voraussagen, vorhersehen; *Wetter* vorhersagen **2.** Voraussage *f*; METEOR Vorhersage *f*
**fore·fa·ther** Vorfahr *m*
**fore·fin·ger** ANAT Zeigefinger *m*
**fore·foot** zo Vorderfuß *m*
**fore·gone con·clu·sion** ausgemachte Sache; ***be a ~*** *a.* von vornherein feststehen
**fore·ground** Vordergrund *m*
**fore·hand** SPORT **1.** Vorhand *f*, Vorhandschlag *m* **2.** Vorhand…
**fore·head** ANAT Stirn *f*
**for·eign** fremd, ausländisch, Außen…, Auslands…; ~ **af·fairs** Außenpolitik *f*; ~ **aid** Auslandshilfe *f*
**for·eign·er** Ausländer(in)
**for·eign| lan·guage** Fremdsprache *f*; ~ **min·is·ter** POL Außenminister *m*
**For·eign Of·fice** *Br* POL Außenministerium *n*
**for·eign pol·i·cy** Außenpolitik *f*
**For·eign Sec·re·ta·ry** *Br* POL Außenminister *m*
**for·eign trade** ECON Außenhandel *m*
**for·eign work·er** Gastarbeiter(in)
**fore·knowl·edge** vorherige Kenntnis
**fore·leg** zo Vorderbein *n*
**fore·man** TECH Vorarbeiter *m*, Polier *m*; Werkmeister *m*; JUR Sprecher *m*
**fore·most** vorderste(r, -s), erste(r, -s)
**fore·name** Vorname *m*
**fo·ren·sic** JUR Gerichts…; ~ **me·dicine** Gerichtsmedizin *f*
**fore·run·ner** Vorläufer(in)
**fore·see** vorhersehen, voraussehen
**fore·see·a·ble** vorhersehbar
**fore·shad·ow** ahnen lassen, andeuten
**fore·sight** Weitblick *m*; (weise) Voraussicht
**for·est** Wald *m* (*a. fig*); Forst *m*
**fore·stall** *et.* vereiteln; *j-m* zuvorkommen
**for·est·er** Förster *m*
**for·est·ry** Forstwirtschaft *f*
**fore·taste** Vorgeschmack *m*
**fore·tell** vorhersagen

F

**for·ev·er, for ev·er** für immer
**fore·wom·an** TECH Vorarbeiterin *f*
**fore·word** Vorwort *n*
**for·feit** verwirken; einbüßen
**forge 1.** Schmiede *f* **2.** fälschen; schmieden
**forg·er** Fälscher *m*
**for·ge·ry** Fälschen *n*; Fälschung *f*
**for·ge·ry-proof** fälschungssicher
**for·get** vergessen
**for·get·ful** vergesslich
**for·get-me-not** BOT Vergissmeinnicht *n*
**for·give** vergeben, verzeihen
**for·give·ness** Verzeihung *f*; Vergebung *f*
**for·giv·ing** versöhnlich; nachsichtig
**fork 1.** Gabel *f* **2.** (sich) gabeln
**fork·lift truck** MOT Gabelstapler *m*
**form 1.** Form *f*; Gestalt *f*; Formular *n*, Vordruck *m*; *Br* (Schul)Klasse *f*; Formalität *f*; Kondition *f*, Verfassung *f*; ***in great ~*** gut in Form **2.** (sich) formen, (sich) bilden, gestalten
**for·mal** förmlich; formell
**for·mal dress** Gesellschaftskleidung *f*
**for·mal·i·ty** Förmlichkeit *f*; Formalität *f*
**for·mat 1.** Aufmachung *f*; Format *n* **2.** IT formatieren
**for·ma·tion** Bildung *f*
**form·a·tive** bildend; gestaltend; ***~ years*** Entwicklungsjahre *pl*
**for·mat·ting** IT Formatierung *f*
**for·mer 1.** früher; ehemalig **2.** ***the ~*** der *or* die *or* das Erstere
**for·mer·ly** früher
**for·mi·da·ble** furchterregend; gewaltig, riesig, gefährlich, schwierig
**form teach·er** *Br* Klassenlehrer(in), Klassenleiter(in)
**for·mu·la** Formel *f*; Rezept *n*
**for·mu·late** formulieren
**for·sake** aufgeben; verlassen
**for·swear** abschwören, entsagen (*dat*)
**fort** MIL Fort *n*, Festung *f*
**forth** weiter, fort; (her)vor; ***and so ~*** und so weiter
**forth·com·ing** bevorstehend, kommend; in Kürze erscheinend (*book*) *or* anlaufend (*film*)
**for·ti·eth** vierzigste(r, -s)
**for·ti·fi·ca·tion** Befestigung *f*
**for·ti·fy** MIL befestigen; *fig* (ver)stärken
**for·ti·tude** (innere) Kraft *or* Stärke
**fort·night** *esp Br* vierzehn Tage
**for·tress** MIL Festung *f*
**for·tu·i·tous** zufällig
**for·tu·nate** glücklich; ***be ~*** Glück haben;
**for·tu·nate·ly** glücklicherweise
**for·tune** Vermögen *n*; (glücklicher) Zufall, Glück *n*; Schicksal *n*
**for·tune-tell·er** Wahrsager(in)
**for·ty 1.** vierzig **2.** Vierzig *f*
**for·ward 1.** *adv* nach vorn, vorwärts **2.** *adj* Vorwärts…; fortschrittlich; vorlaut, dreist **3.** *soccer*: Stürmer *m* **4.** befördern, (ver)senden, schicken; *Brief etc* nachsenden
**for·ward·ing a·gent** Spediteur *m*
**fos·sil** GEOL Fossil *n* (*a.* F), Versteinerung *f*
**fos·ter-child** Pflegekind *n*
**fos·ter-par·ents** Pflegeeltern *pl*
**foul 1.** stinkend, widerlich; verpestet, schlecht (*air, water*); GASTR verdorben, faul; schmutzig, verschmutzt; METEOR stürmisch, schlecht; SPORT regelwidrig; *esp Br* F mies **2.** SPORT Foul *n*, Regelverstoß *m*; ***vicious ~*** böses *or* übles Foul **3.** beschmutzen, verschmutzen; SPORT foulen
**found**[1] gründen; stiften
**found**[2] TECH gießen
**foun·da·tion** ARCH Grundmauer *f*, Fundament *n*; *fig* Gründung *f*, Errichtung *f*; (gemeinnützige) Stiftung; *fig* Grundlage *f*, Basis *f*
**found·er**[1] Gründer(in); Stifter(in)
**foun·der**[2] MAR sinken; *fig* scheitern
**found·ling** JUR Findelkind *n*
**foun·dry** TECH Gießerei *f*
**foun·tain** Springbrunnen *m*; (*Wasser-*) Strahl *m*; **~ pen** Füllfederhalter *m*
**four 1.** vier **2.** Vier *f*; *rowing*: Vierer *m*; ***on all ~s*** auf allen vieren
**four star** *Br* F Super *n*
**four-star pet·rol** *Br* Superbenzin *n*
**four-stroke en·gine** Viertaktmotor *m*
**four·teen 1.** vierzehn **2.** Vierzehn *f*
**four·teenth** vierzehnte(r, -s)
**fourth 1.** vierte(r, -s) **2.** Viertel *n*
**fourth·ly** viertens
**four-wheel drive** MOT Vierradantrieb *m*
**fowl** ZO Geflügel *n*
**fox** ZO Fuchs *m*
**fox·glove** BOT Fingerhut *m*
**fox·y** schlau, gerissen
**frac·tion** Bruchteil *m*; MATH Bruch *m*
**frac·ture** MED **1.** (Knochen)Bruch *m* **2.**

brechen
**fra·gile** zerbrechlich
**frag·ment** Bruchstück *n*
**fra·grance** Wohlgeruch *m*, Duft *m*
**fra·grant** wohlriechend, duftend
**frail** gebrechlich; zerbrechlich; zart, schwach; **frail·ty** Zartheit *f*; Gebrechlichkeit *f*; Schwäche *f*
**frame 1.** Rahmen *m*; (*Brillen- etc*)Gestell *n*; Körper(bau) *m*; **~ of mind** (Gemüts)Verfassung *f*, (-)Zustand *m* **2.** (ein)rahmen; bilden, formen, bauen; *a.* **~ up** F *j-m* et. anhängen
**frame-up** F abgekartetes Spiel; Intrige *f*
**frame·work** TECH Gerüst *n*; *fig* Struktur *f*, System *n*
**franc** Franc *m*; Franken *m*
**France** Frankreich *n*
**fran·chise** POL Wahlrecht *n*; ECON Konzession *f*
**frank 1.** frei(mütig), offen; **~ly (speaking)** offen gesagt **2.** *Brief* freistempeln
**frank·fur·ter** GASTR Frankfurter (Würstchen *n*) *f*
**frank·ness** Offenheit *f*
**fran·tic** hektisch; **be ~** außer sich sein
**fra·ter·nal** brüderlich
**fra·ter·ni·ty** Brüderlichkeit *f*; Vereinigung *f*, Zunft *f*; UNIV Verbindung *f*
**frat·er·ni·za·tion** Verbrüderung *f*
**frat·er·nize** sich verbrüdern
**fraud** Betrug *m*; F Schwindel *m*
**fraud·u·lent** betrügerisch
**fray** ausfransen, (sich) durchscheuern
**freak 1.** Missgeburt *f*; Laune *f*; *in cpds* F …freak *m*, …fanatiker *m*; Freak *m*, irrer Typ; **~ of nature** Laune *f* der Natur **2.** F *a.* **~ out** durchdrehen, die Nerven verlieren
**freck·le** Sommersprosse *f*
**freck·led** sommersprossig
**free 1.** frei; ungehindert; ungebunden; kostenlos, zum Nulltarif; freigebig; **~ and easy** zwanglos; sorglos; **set ~** freilassen **2.** befreien; freilassen
**free climb·ing** Freeclimbing *n*
**free·dom** Freiheit *f*
**free fares** Nulltarif *m*
**free·lance** frei, freiberuflich tätig, freischaffend
**Free·ma·son** Freimaurer *m*
**free skat·ing** Kür *f*
**free·style** SPORT Freistil *m*
**free time** Freizeit *f*
**free trade** ECON Freihandel *m*; **~ ar·e·a** ECON Freihandelszone *f*
**free·way** Schnellstraße *f*
**free·wheel** im Freilauf fahren
**freeze 1.** *v/i* (ge)frieren; erstarren; *v/t* gefrieren lassen; GASTR einfrieren (*a.* ECON), tiefkühlen **2.** Frost *m*, Kälte *f*; ECON, POL Einfrieren *n*; **wage ~, ~ on wages** ECON Lohnstopp *m*
**freeze-dried** gefriergetrocknet
**freeze-dry** gefriertrocknen
**freez·er** Gefriertruhe *f*, Tiefkühl-, Gefriergerät *n*; Gefrierfach *n*
**freez·ing** eisig; Gefrier…; **~ compartment** Gefrierfach *n*; **~ point** Gefrierpunkt *m*
**freight 1.** Fracht *f*; Frachtgebühr *f* **2.** Güter… **3.** beladen; verfrachten
**freight car** RAIL Güterwagen *m*
**freight·er** MAR Frachter *m*, Frachtschiff *n*; AVIAT Transportflugzeug *n*
**freight train** Güterzug *m*
**French 1.** französisch **2.** LING Französisch *n*; **the ~** die Franzosen *pl*
**French doors** Terrassen-, Balkontür *f*
**French fries** GASTR Pommes frites *pl*
**French·man** Franzose *m*
**French win·dows** → ***French doors***
**French·wom·an** Französin *f*
**fren·zied** wahnsinnig, rasend (**with** vor *dat*); hektisch; **fren·zy** Wahnsinn *m*; Ekstase *f*; Raserei *f*
**fre·quen·cy** Häufigkeit *f*; ELECTR Frequenz *f*
**fre·quent 1.** häufig **2.** (oft) besuchen
**fresh** frisch; neu; unerfahren; frech; **fresh·en** auffrischen (*wind*); **~ (o.s.) up** sich frisch machen
**fresh·man** UNIV Student(in) im ersten Jahr
**fresh·ness** Frische *f*; Frechheit *f*
**fresh wa·ter** Süßwasser *n*
**fresh·wa·ter** Süßwasser…
**fret** sich Sorgen machen;
**fret·ful** verärgert, gereizt; quengelig
**FRG** *abbr of* ***Federal Republic of Germany*** Bundesrepublik *f* Deutschland
**Fri** *abbr of* ***Friday*** Fr., Freitag *m*
**fri·ar** REL Mönch *m*
**fric·tion** TECH *etc* Reibung *f* (*a. fig*)
**Fri·day** (*abbr* ***Fri***) Freitag *m*; **on ~** (am) Freitag; **on ~s** freitags
**fridge** F Kühlschrank *m*
**friend** Freund(in); Bekannte *m*, *f*; ***make***

**~s with** sich anfreunden mit, Freundschaft schließen mit
**friend·ly** 1. freund(schaft)lich 2. *esp Br* SPORT Freundschaftsspiel *n*
**friend·ship** Freundschaft *f*
**fries** F GASTR Fritten *pl*
**frig·ate** MAR Fregatte *f*
**fright** Schreck(en) *m*; ***look a ~*** F verboten aussehen; **fright·en** erschrecken; ***be ~ed*** erschrecken (***at, by, of*** vor *dat*); Angst haben (***of*** vor *dat*)
**fright·ful** schrecklich, fürchterlich
**fri·gid** PSYCH frigid(e); kalt, frostig
**frill** Krause *f*, Rüsche *f*
**fringe** 1. Franse *f*; Rand *m*; Pony *m* 2. mit Fransen besetzen; **~ ben·e·fits** ECON Gehalts-, Lohnnebenleistungen *pl*; **~ e·vent** Randveranstaltung *f*; **~ group** *soziale* Randgruppe *f*
**frisk** herumtollen; F *j-n* filzen, durchsuchen; **frisk·y** lebhaft, munter
**friz·zle** F GASTR verbrutzeln
**frizz·y** gekräuselt, kraus
**fro**: ***to and ~*** hin und her
**frock** REL Kutte *f*
**frog** ZO Frosch *m*
**frog·man** Froschmann *m*, MIL *a.* Kampfschwimmer *m*
**frol·ic** herumtoben, herumtollen
**from** von; aus; von … aus *or* her; von … (an), seit; aus, vor (*dat*); ***~ 9 to 5 (o'clock)*** von 9 bis 5 (Uhr)
**front** 1. Vorderseite *f*; Front *f* (*a.* MIL); ***at the ~, in ~*** vorn; ***in ~ of*** vor; ***be in ~*** in Führung sein 2. Vorder… 3. *a.* ***~ on, ~ to(wards)*** gegenüberstehen, gegenüberliegen
**front·age** ARCH (Vorder)Front *f*
**front cov·er** Titelseite *f*
**front door** Haustür *f*, Vordertür *f*
**front en·trance** Vordereingang *m*
**fron·tier** 1. (Landes)Grenze *f*; HIST Grenzland *n*, Grenze *f* 2. Grenz…
**front-page** F wichtig, aktuell
**front-wheel drive** MOT Vorderradantrieb *m*
**frost** 1. Frost *m*; *a.* ***hoar ~, white ~*** Reif *m* 2. mit Reif überziehen; *Glas* mattieren; GASTR glasieren, mit Zuckerguss überziehen; mit (Puder)Zucker bestreuen
**frost·bite** MED Erfrierung *f*
**frost·bit·ten** MED erfroren
**frost·ed glass** Matt-, Milchglas *n*
**frost·y** eisig, frostig (*a. fig*)
**froth** 1. Schaum *m* 2. schäumen; zu Schaum schlagen
**froth·y** schäumend; schaumig
**frown** 1. Stirnrunzeln *n*; ***with a ~*** stirnrunzelnd 2. *v/i* die Stirn runzeln
**fro·zen** *adj* (eis)kalt; (ein-, zu)gefroren; Gefrier…
**fro·zen foods** Tiefkühlkost *f*
**fru·gal** sparsam; bescheiden; einfach
**fruit** Frucht *f*; Früchte *pl*; Obst *n*
**fruit·er·er** Obsthändler *m*
**fruit·ful** fruchtbar
**fruit juice** Fruchtsaft *m*
**fruit·less** unfruchtbar; erfolglos
**fruit·y** fruchtartig; fruchtig (*wine*)
**frus·trate** vereiteln; frustrieren
**frus·tra·tion** Vereitelung *f*; Frustration *f*
**fry** braten; ***fried eggs*** Spiegeleier *pl*; ***fried potatoes*** Bratkartoffeln *pl*
**fry·ing pan** Bratpfanne *f*
**fuch·sia** BOT Fuchsie *f*
**fuck** V ficken, vögeln; ***~ off!*** verpiss dich!; ***get ~ed!*** der Teufel soll dich holen!; **fuck·ing** V Scheiß…, verflucht; ***~ hell!*** verdammte Scheiße!
**fudge** GASTR Fondant *m*
**fu·el** 1. Brennstoff *m*; MOT Treib-, Kraftstoff *m* 2. MOT, AVIAT (auf)tanken
**fu·el in·jec·tion en·gine** MOT Einspritzmotor *m*
**fu·gi·tive** 1. flüchtig (*a. fig*) 2. Flüchtling *m*
**ful·fil** *Br*, **ful·fill** erfüllen; vollziehen; **ful·fil·(l)ing** befriedigend; **ful·fil(l)·ment** Erfüllung *f*, Ausführung *f*
**full** 1. voll; ganz; Voll…; ***~ of*** voll von, voller; ***~ (up)*** (voll) besetzt (*bus etc*); F voll, satt; ***house ~!*** THEA ausverkauft!; ***~ of o.s.*** (ganz) von sich eingenommen 2. *adv* völlig, ganz 3. ***in ~*** vollständig, ganz; ***write out in ~*** *Wort etc* ausschreiben
**full board** Vollpension *f*
**full dress** Gesellschaftskleidung *f*
**full-fledged** ZO flügge; *fig* richtig
**full-grown** ausgewachsen
**full-length** in voller Größe; bodenlang; abendfüllend (*film etc*)
**full moon** Vollmond *m*
**full stop** LING Punkt *m*
**full time** SPORT Spielende *n*
**full-time** ganztägig, Ganztags…; **~ job** Ganztagsbeschäftigung *f*

**ful·ly** voll, völlig, ganz
**ful·ly-fledged** *Br* → ***full-fledged***
**ful·ly-'grown** *Br* → ***full-grown***
**fum·ble** tasten; fummeln
**fume** wütend sein
**fumes** Dämpfe *pl*, Rauch *m*; Abgase *pl*
**fum·ing** wutschnaubend
**fun** Scherz *m*, Spaß *m*; ***for*** ~ aus *or* zum Spaß; ***make*** ~ ***of*** sich lustig machen über (*acc*), verspotten
**func·tion 1.** Funktion *f*; Aufgabe *f*; Veranstaltung *f* **2.** funktionieren
**func·tion·a·ry** Funktionär *m*
**func·tion key** IT Funktionstaste *f*
**fund** ECON Fonds *m*; Geld(mittel *pl*) *n*
**fun·da·men·tal 1.** Grund…, grundlegend **2.** ~**s** Grundlage *f*, Grundbegriffe *pl*
**fun·da·men·tal·ist** Fundamentalist *m*
**fu·ne·ral** Begräbnis *n*, Beerdigung *f*; ~ **march** MUS Trauermarsch *m*; ~ **oration** Trauerrede *f*; ~ **pro·ces·sion** Trauerzug *m*; ~ **ser·vice** Trauerfeier *f*
**fun·fair** Rummelplatz *m*
**fun·gus** BOT Pilz *m*, Schwamm *m*
**fu·nic·u·lar** *a.* ~ ***railway*** (Draht)Seilbahn *f*
**funk·y** F irre, schräg, schrill
**fun·nel** Trichter *m*; MAR, RAIL Schornstein *m*
**fun·nies** F Comics *pl*
**fun·ny** komisch, lustig, spaßig; sonderbar
**fur** Pelz *m*, Fell *n*; MED Belag *m*; TECH Kesselstein *m*
**fu·ri·ous** wütend
**furl** *Fahne*, *Segel* aufrollen, einrollen; *Schirm* zusammenrollen
**fur·nace** TECH Schmelzofen *m*, Hochofen *m*; (Heiz)Kessel *m*
**fur·nish** einrichten, möblieren; liefern; versorgen, ausrüsten, ausstatten (***with*** mit)
**fur·ni·ture** Möbel *pl*; ***sectional*** ~ Anbaumöbel *pl*
**furred** MED belegt, pelzig
**fur·ri·er** Kürschner *m*
**fur·row 1.** Furche *f* **2.** furchen
**fur·ry** pelzig; flauschig
**fur·ther 1.** weiter **2.** fördern, unterstützen; ~ **ed·u·ca·tion** *Br* Fortbildung *f*, Weiterbildung *f*
**fur·ther·more** *fig* weiter, überdies
**fur·ther·most** entfernteste(r, -s), äußerste(r, -s)
**fur·tive** heimlich, verstohlen
**fu·ry** Wut *f*, Zorn *m*
**fuse 1.** Zünder *m*; ELECTR Sicherung *f*; Zündschnur *f* **2.** schmelzen; ELECTR durchbrennen
**fuse box** ELECTR Sicherungskasten *m*
**fu·se·lage** (Flugzeug)Rumpf *m*
**fu·sion** Verschmelzung *f*, Fusion *f*; PHYS ***nuclear*** ~ Kernfusion *f*
**fuss 1.** (unnötige) Aufregung; Wirbel *m*, F Theater *n* **2.** sich (unnötig) aufregen; viel Aufhebens machen (***about*** um, von); **fuss·y** aufgeregt, hektisch; kleinlich, pedantisch; heikel, wählerisch
**fus·ty** muffig; *fig* verstaubt
**fu·tile** nutzlos, zwecklos
**fu·ture 1.** (zu)künftig **2.** Zukunft *f*; LING Futur *n*, Zukunft *f*; ***in*** ~ in Zukunft, künftig
**fuzz** feiner Flaum
**fuzz·y** kraus, wuschelig; unscharf, verschwommen; flaumig, flauschig

# G

**G, g** G, g *n*
**gab** F Geschwätz *n*; ***have the gift of the*** ~ ein gutes Mundwerk haben
**gab·ble 1.** Geschnatter *n*, Geschwätz *n* **2.** schnattern, schwatzen
**ga·ble** ARCH Giebel *m*
**gad·fly** ZO Bremse *f*
**gad·get** TECH Apparat *m*, Gerät *n*, Vorrichtung *f*; *often contp* technische Spielerei
**gag 1.** Knebel *m* (*a. fig*); F Gag *m* **2.** knebeln; *fig* mundtot machen
**gage 1.** Eichmaß *n*; TECH Messgerät *n*, Lehre *f*; TECH Stärke *f*, Dicke *f*; RAIL Spur(weite) *f* **2.** TECH eichen; (ab-, aus)messen
**gai·e·ty** Fröhlichkeit *f*
**gain 1.** gewinnen; erreichen, bekom-

G

men; zunehmen an (*dat*); vorgehen (um) (*watch*); ~ ***speed*** schneller werden; ~ ***5 pounds*** 5 Pfund zunehmen; ~ ***in*** zunehmen an (*dat*) **2.** Gewinn *m*; Zunahme *f*; ~ ***of time*** Zeitgewinn *m*
**gait** Gang *m*, Gangart *f*; Schritt *m*
**gai·ter** Gamasche *f*
**gal** F Mädchen *n*
**ga·la** **1.** Festlichkeit *f*; Gala(-veranstaltung) *f* **2.** Gala…
**gal·ax·y** ASTR Milchstraße *f*, Galaxis *f*
**gale** Sturm *m*
**gall**[1] Frechheit *f*
**gall**[2] **1.** wund geriebene Stelle **2.** wund reiben *or* scheuern; *fig* (ver)ärgern
**gal·lant** tapfer; galant, höflich
**gal·lan·try** Tapferkeit *f*; Galanterie *f*
**gall blad·der** ANAT Gallenblase *f*
**gal·le·ry** Galerie *f*; Empore *f*
**gal·ley** MAR Galeere *f*; Kombüse *f*; *a.* ~ ***proof*** PRINT Fahne *f*, Fahnenabzug *m*
**gal·lon** Gallone *f* (*3,79 l*, *Br 4,55 l*)
**gal·lop** **1.** Galopp *m* **2.** galoppieren (lassen)
**gal·lows** Galgen *m*
**gal·lows hu·mo(u)r** Galgenhumor *m*
**ga·lore** in rauen Mengen
**gam·ble** **1.** (um Geld) spielen **2.** Glücksspiel *n*
**gam·bler** (Glücks)Spieler(in)
**gam·bol** **1.** Luftsprung *m* **2.** (herum-)tanzen, (herum)hüpfen
**game** (Karten-, Ball- *etc*)Spiel *n*; (einzelnes) Spiel (*a. fig*); HUNT Wild *n*; Wildbret *n*; *pl* Spiele *pl*; PED Sport *m*
**game·keep·er** Wildhüter *m*
**game| park**, ~ **re·serve** Wildpark *m*; Wildreservat *n*
**gan·der** zo Gänserich *m*
**gang** **1.** (Arbeiter)Trupp *m*; Gang *f*, Bande *f*; Clique *f*; Horde *f* **2.** ~ ***up*** sich zusammentun, *contp* sich zusammenrotten
**gan·gling** schlaksig
**gang·ster** Gangster *m*
**gang| war**, ~ **war·fare** Bandenkrieg *m*
**gang·way** Gang *m*; AVIAT, MAR Gangway *f*
**gaol**, **gaol·bird**, **gaol·er** *Br* → ***jail*** *etc*
**gap** Lücke *f*; Kluft *f*; Spalte *f*
**gape** gähnen; klaffen; gaffen
**gar·age** **1.** Garage *f*; (Reparatur)Werkstatt *f* (und Tankstelle *f*); **2.** *Auto* in e-r Garage ab- *or* unterstellen; *Auto* in die Garage fahren
**gar·bage** Abfall *m*, Müll *m*; ~ **bag** Müllbeutel *m*; ~ **can** Abfalleimer *m*, Mülleimer *m*; Abfalltonne *f*, Mülltonne *f*; ~ **truck** Müllwagen *m*
**gar·den** Garten *m*
**gar·den·er** Gärtner(in)
**gar·den·ing** Gartenarbeit *f*
**gar·gle** gurgeln
**gar·ish** grell, auffallend
**gar·land** Girlande *f*
**gar·lic** BOT Knoblauch *m*
**gar·ment** Kleidungsstück *n*; Gewand *n*
**gar·nish** GASTR garnieren
**gar·ret** Dachkammer *f*
**gar·ri·son** MIL Garnison *f*
**gar·ter** Strumpfband *n*; Sockenhalter *m*; Strumpfhalter *m*, Straps *m*
**gas** Gas *n*; F Benzin *n*, Sprit *m*
**gas·e·ous** gasförmig
**gash** klaffende Wunde
**gas·ket** TECH Dichtung(sring *m*) *f*
**gas me·ter** Gasuhr *f*, Gaszähler *m*
**gas·o·lene**, **gas·o·line** Benzin *n*; ~ **pump** Zapfsäule *f*
**gasp** **1.** keuchen, röcheln; ~ (***for breath***) nach Atem ringen, F nach Luft schnappen **2.** Keuchen *n*, Röcheln *n*
**gas sta·tion** Tankstelle *f*
**gas stove** Gasofen *m*, Gasherd *m*
**gas·works** TECH Gaswerk *n*
**gate** Tor *n*; Pforte *f*; Schranke *f*, Sperre *f*; AVIAT Flugsteig *m*
**gate·crash** F uneingeladen kommen (zu); sich ohne zu bezahlen hineinschmuggeln (in *acc*)
**gate·post** Tor-, Türpfosten *m*
**gate·way** Tor(weg *m*) *n*, Einfahrt *f*
**gate·way drug** Einstiegsdroge *f*
**gath·er** *v/t* sammeln, *Informationen* einholen, einziehen; *Personen* versammeln; ernten, pflücken; zusammenziehen, kräuseln; *fig* folgern, schließen (***from*** aus); ~ ***speed*** schneller werden; *v/i* sich (ver)sammeln; sich (an)sammeln; **gath·er·ing** Versammlung *f*; Zusammenkunft *f*
**gau·dy** auffällig, bunt, grell; protzig
**gauge** *Br* → ***gage***
**gaunt** hager; ausgemergelt
**gaunt·let** Schutzhandschuh *m*
**gauze** Gaze *f*; MED Bandage *f*, Binde *f*
**gav·el** Hammer *m*
**gaw·ky** linkisch

**gay 1.** lustig, fröhlich; bunt, (farben-) prächtig; F schwul **2.** F Schwule *m*
**gaze 1.** (starrer) Blick **2.** starren; ~ ***at*** starren auf (*acc*), anstarren
**ga·zelle** zo Gazelle *f*
**ga·zette** Amtsblatt *n*
**gear** TECH Getriebe *n*; MOT Gang *m*; *mst in cpds* Vorrichtung *f*, Gerät *n*; F Kleidung *f*, Aufzug *m*; ***shift*** (*esp Br* ***change***) ~(***s***) MOT schalten; ***shift*** (*esp Br* ***change***) ***into second*** ~ MOT in den zweiten Gang schalten
**gear·box** MOT Getriebe *n*
**gear le·ver** *Br*, **gear shift**, **gear stick** *Br* MOT Schalthebel *m*
**Gei·ger count·er** PHYS Geigerzähler *m*
**geld·ing** zo Wallach *m*
**gem** Edelstein *m*
**Gem·i·ni** ASTR Zwillinge *pl*; ***he*** (***she***) ***is*** (***a***) ~ er (sie) ist (ein) Zwilling
**gen·der** LING Genus *n*, Geschlecht *n*
**gene** BIOL Gen *n*, Erbfaktor *m*
**gen·e·ral 1.** allgemein; Haupt..., General... **2.** MIL General *m*; ***in*** ~ im Allgemeinen; ~ **de·liv·er·y**: (***in care of***) ~ postlagernd; ~ **e·lec·tion** *Br* POL Parlamentswahlen *pl*
**gen·e·ral·ize** verallgemeinern
**gen·er·al·ly** im Allgemeinen, allgemein
**gen·e·ral prac·ti·tion·er** (*abbr* ***GP***) *appr* Arzt *m or* Ärztin *f* für Allgemeinmedizin
**gen·e·rate** erzeugen; **gen·e·ra·tion** Erzeugung *f*; Generation *f*
**gen·e·ra·tor** ELECTR Generator *m*; MOT Lichtmaschine *f*
**gen·e·ros·i·ty** Großzügigkeit *f*
**gen·e·rous** großzügig; reichlich
**ge·net·ic** genetisch; ~ **code** BIOL Erbanlage *f*; ~ **en·gin·eer·ing** Gentechnologie *f*; ~ **fin·ger·print** genetischer Fingerabdruck
**ge·net·ics** BIOL Genetik *f*, Vererbungslehre *f*
**ge·ni·al** freundlich
**gen·i·tive** *a.* ~ ***case*** LING Genitiv *m*, zweiter Fall
**ge·ni·us** Genie *n*
**gen·o·cide** Völkermord *m*
**gent** F *esp Br* Herr *m*; ***gents*** *Br* F Herrenklo *n*
**gen·tle** sanft, zart, sacht; mild
**gen·tle·man** Gentleman *m*; Herr *m*
**gen·tle·man·ly** gentlemanlike, vornehm
**gen·tle·ness** Sanftheit *f*, Zartheit *f*; Milde *f*
**gen·try** *Br* niederer Adel; Oberschicht *f*
**gen·u·ine** echt; aufrichtig
**ge·og·ra·phy** Geografie *f*
**ge·ol·o·gy** Geologie *f*
**ge·om·e·try** Geometrie *f*
**germ** BIOL, BOT Keim *m*; MED Bazillus *m*, Bakterie *f*, (Krankheits)Erreger *m*
**Ger·man 1.** deutsch **2.** Deutsche *m, f*; LING Deutsch *n*; ~ **shep·herd** zo Deutscher Schäferhund
**Ger·man·y** Deutschland *n*
**ger·mi·nate** BIOL, BOT keimen (lassen)
**ger·und** LING Gerundium *n*
**ges·tic·u·late** gestikulieren
**ges·ture** Geste *f*, Gebärde *f*
**get** *v/t* bekommen, erhalten; sich *et.* verschaffen *or* besorgen; erwerben, sich aneignen; holen; bringen; F erwischen; F kapieren, verstehen, checken; *j-n* dazu bringen (***to do*** zu tun); *with pp*: lassen; ~ ***one's hair cut*** sich die Haare schneiden lassen; ~ ***going*** in Gang bringen; ~ ***s.th. ready*** et. fertig machen; ***have got*** haben; ***have got to*** müssen; *v/i* kommen, gelangen; *with pp or adj*: werden; ~ ***tired*** müde werden, ermüden; ~ ***going*** in Gang kommen; *fig* in Schwung kommen; ~ ***home*** nach Hause kommen; ~ ***ready*** sich fertig machen; ~ ***about*** herumkommen; sich herumsprechen *or* verbreiten (*rumor etc*); ~ ***ahead of*** übertreffen (*acc*); ~ ***along*** vorwärts-, vorankommen; auskommen (***with*** mit *j-m*); zurechtkommen (***with*** mit *et.*); ~ ***at*** herankommen an (*acc*); ***what is he getting at?*** worauf will er hinaus?; ~ ***away*** loskommen; entkommen; ~ ***away with*** davonkommen mit; ~ ***back*** zurückkommen; *et.* zurückbekommen; ~ ***in*** hinein-, hereinkommen; einsteigen (in *acc*); ~ ***off*** aussteigen (aus); davonkommen (***with*** mit); ~ ***on*** einsteigen (in *acc*); → ***get along***; ~ ***out*** herausgehen, hinausgehen; aussteigen (***of*** aus); *et.* herausbekommen; ~ ***over s.th.*** über et. hinwegkommen; ~ ***to*** kommen nach; ~ ***together*** zusammenkommen; ~ ***up*** aufstehen
**get·a·way** Flucht *f*; ~ ***car*** Fluchtauto *n*
**get·up** Aufmachung *f*
**gey·ser** GEOL Geysir *m*; *Br* TECH Durchlauferhitzer *m*

**ghast·ly** grässlich; schrecklich; (toten-) bleich
**gher·kin** Gewürzgurke *f*
**ghet·to** Getto *n*
**ghost** Geist *m*, Gespenst *n*; *fig* Spur *f*
**ghost·ly** geisterhaft
**gi·ant 1.** Riese *m* **2.** riesig
**gib·ber·ish** Kauderwelsch *n*
**gib·bet** Galgen *m*
**gibe 1.** spotten (***at*** über *acc*); **2.** höhnische Bemerkung, Stichelei *f*
**gib·lets** GASTR Hühner-, Gänseklein *n*
**gid·di·ness** MED Schwindel(gefühl *n*) *m*;
**gid·dy** schwindelerregend; ***I feel ~*** mir ist schwind(e)lig
G
**gift** Geschenk *n*; Talent *n*
**gift·ed** begabt
**gift| vouch·er** Geschenkgutschein *m*; **~ wrap** Geschenkpapier *n*
**gig** F MUS Gig *m*, Auftritt *m*, Konzert *n*
**gi·gan·tic** gigantisch, riesenhaft, riesig, gewaltig
**gig·gle 1.** kichern **2.** Gekicher *n*
**gild** vergolden
**gill** ZO Kieme *f*; BOT Lamelle *f*
**gim·mick** F Trick *m*; Spielerei *f*
**gin** Gin *m*
**gin·ger 1.** Ingwer *m* **2.** rötlich *or* gelblich braun;
**gin·ger·bread** Lebkuchen *m*, Pfefferkuchen *m*
**gin·ger·ly** behutsam, vorsichtig
**gip·sy** *Br* → ***gypsy***
**gi·raffe** ZO Giraffe *f*
**gir·der** TECH Tragbalken *m*
**gir·dle** Hüfthalter *m*, Hüftgürtel *m*
**girl** Mädchen *n*
**girl·friend** Freundin *f*
**girl guide** *Br* Pfadfinderin *f*
**girl·hood** Mädchenjahre *pl*, Jugend *f*, Jugendzeit *f*
**girl·ish** mädchenhaft; Mädchen…
**girl scout** Pfadfinderin *f*
**girth** (Sattel)Gurt *m*; (*a.* Körper)Umfang *m*
**gist** *das* Wesentliche, Kern *m*
**give** geben; schenken; spenden; *Leben* hingeben, opfern; *Befehl etc* geben, erteilen; *Hilfe* leisten; *Schutz* bieten; *Grund etc* angeben; THEA *etc* geben, aufführen; *Vortrag* halten; *Schmerzen* bereiten, verursachen; *Grüße etc* übermitteln; ***~ her my love*** bestelle ihr herzliche Grüße von mir; ***~ birth to*** zur Welt bringen; ***~ s.o. to understand that*** j-m zu verstehen geben, dass; ***~ way*** nachgeben; *Br* MOT die Vorfahrt lassen (*dat*); ***~ away*** hergeben, weggeben, verschenken; *j-n, et.* verraten; ***~ back*** zurückgeben; ***~ in*** *Gesuch etc* einreichen; *Prüfungsarbeit etc* abgeben; nachgeben; aufgeben; ***~ off*** *Geruch* verbreiten; ausstoßen; ausströmen, verströmen; ***~ on(to)*** führen auf *or* nach, gehen nach; ***~ out*** aus-, verteilen; *esp Br* bekannt geben; zu Ende gehen (*supplies, strength etc*); F versagen (*engine etc*); ***~ up*** aufgeben; aufhören mit; *j-n* ausliefern; ***~ o.s. up*** sich (freiwillig) stellen (***to the police*** der Polizei)
**give-and-take** beiderseitiges Entgegenkommen, Kompromiss(bereitschaft *f*) *m*
**giv·en**: ***be ~ to*** neigen zu (*dat*)
**giv·en name** Vorname *m*
**gla·cial** eisig; Eis…
**gla·ci·er** Gletscher *m*
**glad** froh, erfreut; ***be ~ of*** sich freuen über (*acc*); **glad·ly** gern(e)
**glam·o(u)r** Zauber *m*, Glanz *m*
**glam·o(u)r·ous** bezaubernd, reizvoll
**glance 1.** (schneller *or* flüchtiger) Blick (***at*** auf *acc*); ***at a ~*** auf e-n Blick **2.** (schnell *or* flüchtig) blicken (***at*** auf *acc*)
**gland** ANAT Drüse *f*
**glare 1.** grell scheinen *or* leuchten; wütend starren; ***~ at s.o.*** j-n wütend anstarren **2.** greller Schein, grelles Leuchten; wütender Blick
**glar·ing** *fig* schreiend
**glass 1.** Glas *n*; (Trink)Glas *n*; Glas (-gefäß) *n*; (Fern-, Opern)Glas *n*; *Br* F Spiegel *m*; *Br* Barometer *n*; (***a pair of***) ***~es*** (e-e) Brille **2.** gläsern; Glas… **3. *~ in, ~ up*** verglasen
**glass case** Vitrine *f*; Schaukasten *m*
**glass·ful** *ein* Glas (voll)
**glass·house** Gewächs-, Treibhaus *n*
**glass·ware** Glaswaren *pl*
**glass·y** gläsern; glasig
**glaze 1.** *v/t* verglasen; glasieren; *v/i*: *a.* ***~ over*** glasig werden (*eyes*) **2.** Glasur *f*
**gla·zi·er** Glaser *m*
**gleam 1.** schwacher Schein, Schimmer *m* **2.** leuchten, schimmern
**glean** *v/t* sammeln; *v/i* Ähren lesen
**glee** Fröhlichkeit *f*
**glee club** Gesangverein *m*

**glee·ful** ausgelassen, fröhlich
**glen** enges Bergtal *n*
**glib** gewandt; schlagfertig
**glide 1.** gleiten; segeln **2.** Gleiten *n*; AVIAT Gleitflug *m*; **glid·er** Segelflugzeug *n*; **glid·ing** Segelfliegen *n*
**glim·mer 1.** schimmern **2.** Schimmer *m*
**glimpse 1.** (nur) flüchtig zu sehen bekommen **2.** flüchtiger Blick
**glint 1.** glitzern, glänzen **2.** Glitzern *n*, Glanz *m*
**glis·ten** glitzern, glänzen
**glit·ter 1.** glitzern, funkeln, glänzen **2.** Glitzern *n*, Funkeln *n*, Glanz *m*
**glo·bal** Welt…, global, weltumspannend; umfassend; ~ **warm·ing** Erwärmung *f* der Erdatmosphäre
**globe** (Erd)Kugel *f*; Globus *m*
**gloom** Düsterkeit *f*; Dunkelheit *f*; düstere *or* gedrückte Stimmung
**gloom·y** düster; hoffnungslos; niedergeschlagen; trübsinnig, trübselig
**glo·ri·fi·ca·tion** Verherrlichung *f*
**glo·ri·fy** verherrlichen
**glo·ri·ous** ruhmreich, glorreich; herrlich, prächtig
**glo·ry** Ruhm *m*; Herrlichkeit *f*, Pracht *f*
**gloss 1.** Glanz *m*; LING Glosse *f* **2.** ~ ***over*** beschönigen, vertuschen
**glos·sa·ry** Glossar *n*
**gloss·y** glänzend
**glove** Handschuh *m*; ~ **com·part·ment** MOT Handschuhfach *n*
**glow 1.** glühen **2.** Glühen *n*; Glut *f*
**glow·er** finster blicken
**glow-worm** ZO Glühwürmchen *n*
**glu·cose** Traubenzucker *m*
**glue 1.** Leim *m* **2.** kleben
**glum** bedrückt
**glut·ton** *fig* Vielfraß *m*
**glut·ton·ous** gefräßig, unersättlich
**gnarled** knorrig; knotig (*hands etc*)
**gnash** knirschen (mit)
**gnat** ZO (Stech)Mücke *f*
**gnaw** (zer)nagen; (zer)fressen
**gnome** Gnom *m*; Gartenzwerg *m*
**go 1.** gehen, fahren, reisen (***to*** nach); (fort)gehen; gehen, führen (***to*** nach) (*road etc*); sich erstrecken, gehen (***to*** bis zu); verkehren, fahren (*bus etc*); TECH gehen, laufen, funktionieren; vergehen (*time*); harmonieren (***with*** mit), passen (***with*** zu); ausgehen, ablaufen, ausfallen; werden (~ ***mad***; ~ ***blind***); ***be ~ing to*** *inf* im Begriff sein zu *inf*, *tun* wollen, *tun* werden; ~ ***swimming*** schwimmen gehen; ***it is ~ing to rain*** es gibt Regen; ***I must be ~ing*** ich muss gehen; ~ ***for a walk*** e-n Spaziergang machen, spazieren gehen; ~ ***to bed*** ins Bett gehen; ~ ***to school*** zur Schule gehen; ~ ***to see*** besuchen; ***let*** ~ loslassen; ~ ***after*** nachlaufen (*dat*); sich bemühen um; ~ ***ahead*** vorangehen; vorausgehen, vorausfahren; ~ ***ahead with*** beginnen mit; fortfahren mit; ~ ***at*** losgehen auf (*acc*); ~ ***away*** weggehen; ~ ***between*** vermitteln zwischen (*dat*); ~ ***by*** vorbeigehen, vorbeifahren; vergehen (*time*); *fig* sich halten an (*acc*), sich richten nach; ~ ***down*** untergehen (*sun*); ~ ***for*** holen; ~ ***in*** hineingehen; ~ ***in for an examination*** e-e Prüfung machen; ~ ***off*** fortgehen, weggehen; losgehen (*gun etc*); ~ ***on*** weitergehen, weiterfahren; *fig* fortfahren (***doing*** zu tun); *fig* vor sich gehen, vorgehen; ~ ***out*** hinausgehen; ausgehen (***with*** mit); ausgehen (*light etc*); ~ ***through*** durchgehen, durchnehmen; durchmachen; ~ ***up*** steigen; hinaufgehen, -steigen; ~ ***without*** sich behelfen ohne, auskommen ohne **2.** F Schwung *m*, Schmiss *m*; *esp Br* F Versuch *m*; ***it's my*** ~ *esp Br* F ich bin dran *or* an der Reihe; ***it's a ~!*** F abgemacht!; ***have a ~ at s.th.*** *Br* F et. probieren
**goad** *fig* anstacheln
**go-a·head**[1]: ***get the*** ~ grünes Licht bekommen; ***give s.o. the*** ~ j-m grünes Licht geben
**go-a·head**[2] *Br* zielstrebig; unternehmungslustig
**goal** Ziel *n* (*a. fig*); SPORT Tor *n*; ***keep*** ~ im Tor stehen; ***score a*** ~ ein Tor schießen *or* erzielen; ***consolation*** ~ Ehrentreffer *m*; ***own*** ~ Eigentor *n*, Eigentreffer *m*; ***shot at*** ~ Torschuss *m*
**goal·ie** F, **goal·keep·er** SPORT Torwart *m*, Torhüter *m*
**goal kick** *soccer*: Abstoß *m*
**goal line** SPORT Torlinie *f*
**goal·mouth** SPORT Torraum *m*
**goal·post** SPORT Torpfosten *m*
**goat** ZO Ziege *f*, Geiß *f*
**gob·ble** schlingen; *mst* ~ ***up*** verschlingen (*a. fig*)
**go-be·tween** Vermittler(in), Mittels-

mann *m*
**gob·lin** Kobold *m*
**god** REL ***God*** Gott *m*; *fig* Abgott *m*
**god·child** Patenkind *n*
**god·dess** Göttin *f*
**god·fa·ther** Pate *m* (*a. fig*), Taufpate *m*
**god·for·sak·en** *contp* gottverlassen
**god·head** Gottheit *f*
**god·less** gottlos
**god·like** gottähnlich; göttlich
**god·moth·er** (Tauf)Patin *f*
**god·pa·rent** (Tauf)Pate, (Tauf)Patin *f*
**god·send** Geschenk *n* des Himmels
**gog·gle** glotzen
**gog·gle box** *Br* F TV Glotze *f*
**gog·gles** Schutzbrille *f*
**go·ings-on** F Treiben *n*, Vorgänge *pl*
**gold 1.** Gold *n* **2.** golden
**gold·en** *mst fig* golden, goldgelb
**gold·finch** ZO Stieglitz *m*
**gold·fish** ZO Goldfisch *m*
**gold·smith** Goldschmied *m*
**golf 1.** Golf(spiel) *n* **2.** Golf spielen
**golf club** Golfschläger *m*; Golfklub *m*
**golf course, golf links** Golfplatz *m*
**gon·do·la** Gondel *f*
**gone** *adj* fort; F futsch; vergangen; tot; F hoffnungslos
**good 1.** gut; artig; gütig; gründlich; ***~ at*** geschickt *or* gut in (*dat*); ***real ~*** F echt gut **2.** Nutzen *m*, Wert *m*; *das* Gute; ***do*** (***no***) ***~*** (nichts) nützen; ***for ~*** für immer; F ***what ~ is ...?*** was nützt ...?
**good·by(e) 1.** ***wish s.o. ~, say ~ to s.o.*** j-m Auf Wiedersehen sagen **2.** *int* (auf) Wiedersehen!
**Good Fri·day** REL Karfreitag *m*
**good-hu·mo(u)red** gut gelaunt; gutmütig
**good·look·ing** gut aussehend
**good·na·tured** gutmütig
**good·ness** Güte *f*; ***thank ~!*** Gott sei Dank!; (***my***) ***~!, ~ gracious!*** du meine Güte!, du lieber Himmel!; ***for ~' sake*** um Himmels willen!; ***~ knows*** weiß der Himmel
**goods** ECON Waren *pl*, Güter *pl*
**good·will** gute Absicht, guter Wille; ECON Firmenwert *m*
**good·y** F Bonbon *m*, *n*
**goose** ZO Gans *f*
**goose·ber·ry** BOT Stachelbeere *f*
**goose·flesh, goose pim·ples** *fig* Gänsehaut *f*
**go·pher** ZO Taschenratte *f*; Ziesel *m*
**gore** durchbohren, aufspießen
**gorge 1.** ANAT Kehle *f*, Schlund *m*; GEOGR enge (Fels)Schlucht **2.** verschlingen; schlingen, (sich) vollstopfen
**gor·geous** prächtig
**go·ril·la** ZO Gorilla *m*
**gor·y** F blutrünstig
**gosh** *int* F Mensch!, Mann!
**gos·ling** ZO junge Gans
**go-slow** *Br* ECON Bummelstreik *m*
**Gos·pel** REL Evangelium *n*
**gos·sa·mer** Altweibersommer *m*
**gos·sip 1.** Klatsch *m*, Tratsch *m*; Klatschbase *f* **2.** klatschen, tratschen
**gos·sip·y** geschwätzig; voller Klatsch und Tratsch (*letter etc*)
**Goth·ic** ARCH **1.** gotisch; ***~ novel*** Schauerroman *m* **2.** Gotik *f*
**gourd** BOT Kürbis *m*
**gout** MED Gicht *f*
**gov·ern** *v/t* regieren; lenken, leiten; *v/i* herrschen
**gov·ern·ess** Erzieherin *f*
**gov·ern·ment** Regierung *f*; Staat *m*
**gov·er·nor** Gouverneur *m*; Direktor *m*, Leiter *m*; F Alte *m*
**gown** Kleid *n*; Robe *f*, Talar *m*
**grab 1.** packen, (hastig *or* gierig) ergreifen, fassen **2.** (hastiger *or* gieriger) Griff; TECH Greifer *m*
**grace 1.** Anmut *f*, Grazie *f*; Anstand *m*; ECON Frist *f*, Aufschub *m*; Gnade *f*; REL Tischgebet *n* **2.** zieren, schmücken
**grace·ful** anmutig
**grace·less** ungraziös
**gra·cious** gnädig
**gra·da·tion** Abstufung *f*
**grade 1.** Grad *m*, Rang *m*; Stufe *f*; ECON Qualität *f*; RAIL *etc* Steigung *f*, Gefälle *n*; PED Klasse *f*; Note *f*, Zensur *f* **2.** sortieren, einteilen; abstufen
**grade cross·ing** RAIL schienengleicher Bahnübergang
**grade school** Grundschule *f*
**gra·di·ent** *Br* RAIL *etc* Steigung *f*, Gefälle *n*
**grad·u·al** stufenweise, allmählich
**grad·u·al·ly** nach und nach; allmählich
**grad·u·ate 1.** UNIV Hochschulabsolvent(in), Akademiker(in); Graduierte *m*, *f*; PED Schulabgänger(in) **2.** abstufen, staffeln; UNIV graduieren; PED die Abschlussprüfung bestehen

**grad·u·a·tion** Abstufung *f*, Staffelung *f*; UNIV Graduierung *f*; PED Absolvieren *n* (***from*** *gen*)
**graf·fi·ti** Graffiti *pl*, Wandschmierereien *pl*
**graft 1.** MED Transplantat *n*; AGR Pfropfreis *n* **2.** MED *Gewebe* verpflanzen, transplantieren; AGR pfropfen
**grain** (Samen-, *esp* Getreide)Korn *n*; Getreide *n*; (*Sand- etc*)Körnchen *n*, (-)Korn *n*; Maserung *f*
**gram** Gramm *n*
**gram·mar** Grammatik *f*
**gram·mar school** Grundschule *f*; *Br appr* (humanistisches) Gymnasium
**gram·mat·i·cal** grammatisch, Grammatik…
**gramme** → ***gram***
**gra·na·ry** Kornspeicher *m*
**grand 1.** *fig* großartig; erhaben; groß; Groß…, Haupt… **2.** F Riese *m* (*1000 dollars or pounds*)
**grand·child** Enkel *m*, Enkelin *f*
**grand·daugh·ter** Enkelin *f*
**gran·deur** Größe *f*, Erhabenheit *f*; Großartigkeit *f*
**grand·fa·ther** Großvater *m*
**gran·di·ose** großartig
**grand·moth·er** Großmutter *f*
**grand·par·ents** Großeltern *pl*
**grand·son** Enkel *m*
**grand·stand** SPORT Haupttribüne *f*
**gran·ny** F Oma *f*
**grant 1.** bewilligen, gewähren; *Erlaubnis etc* geben; *Bitte etc* erfüllen; *et.* zugeben; ***take s.th. for ~ed*** et. als selbstverständlich betrachten *or* hinnehmen **2.** Stipendium *n*; Bewilligung *f*, Unterstützung *f*
**gran·u·lat·ed** körnig, granuliert; ***~ sugar*** Kristallzucker *m*
**gran·ule** Körnchen *n*
**grape** BOT Weinbeere *f*, Weintraube *f*
**grape·fruit** BOT Grapefruit *f*, Pampelmuse *f*
**grape·vine** BOT Weinstock *m*
**graph** grafische Darstellung
**graph·ic** grafisch; anschaulich; ***~ arts*** Grafik *f*; **graph·ics** IT Grafik *f*
**grap·ple**: ***~ with*** kämpfen mit, *fig a.* sich herumschlagen mit
**grasp 1.** (er)greifen, packen; *fig* verstehen, begreifen **2.** Griff *m*; Reichweite *f* (*a. fig*); *fig* Verständnis *n*
**grass** Gras *n*; Rasen *m*; Weide(land *n*) *f*; *sl.* Grass *n* (*marijuana*)
**grass·hop·per** ZO Heuschrecke *f*
**grass roots** POL Basis *f*
**grass wid·ow** Strohwitwe *f*
**grass wid·ow·er** Strohwitwer *m*
**gras·sy** grasbedeckt, Gras…
**grate 1.** (Kamin)Gitter *n*; (Feuer)Rost *m* **2.** reiben, raspeln; knirschen (mit); ***~ on s.o.'s nerves*** an j-s Nerven zerren
**grate·ful** dankbar
**grat·er** Reibe *f*
**grat·i·fi·ca·tion** Befriedigung *f*; Freude *f*; **grat·i·fy** erfreuen; befriedigen
**grat·ing**[1] kratzend, knirschend, quietschend; schrill; unangenehm
**grat·ing**[2] Gitter(werk) *n*
**grat·i·tude** Dankbarkeit *f*
**gra·tu·i·tous** unentgeltlich; freiwillig
**gra·tu·i·ty** Abfindung *f*; Gratifikation *f*; Trinkgeld *n*
**grave**[1] ernst; (ge)wichtig; gemessen
**grave**[2] Grab *n*
**grave·dig·ger** Totengräber *m*
**grav·el 1.** Kies *m* **2.** mit Kies bestreuen
**grave·stone** Grabstein *m*
**grave·yard** Friedhof *m*
**grav·i·ta·tion** PHYS Gravitation *f*, Schwerkraft *f*
**grav·i·ty** PHYS Schwerkraft *f*; Ernst *m*
**gra·vy** Bratensaft *m*; Bratensoße *f*
**gray 1.** grau **2.** Grau *n* **3.** grau machen *or* werden
**gray·hound** ZO Windhund *m*
**graze**[1] *Vieh* weiden (lassen); (ab)weiden; (ab)grasen
**graze**[2] **1.** streifen; schrammen; *Haut* (ab-, auf)schürfen, (auf)schrammen **2.** Abschürfung *f*, Schramme *f*; Streifschuss *m*
**grease 1.** Fett *n*; TECH Schmierfett *n*, Schmiere *f* **2.** (ein)fetten; TECH schmieren; **greas·y** fett(ig), ölig; speckig; schmierig
**great** groß; Ur(groß)…; F großartig, super
**Great Brit·ain** Großbritannien *n*
**great-grand·child** Urenkel(in)
**great-grand·par·ents** Urgroßeltern *pl*
**great·ly** sehr
**great·ness** Größe *f*
**Greece** Griechenland *n*
**greed** Gier *f*; **greed·y** gierig (***for*** auf *acc*, nach); habgierig; gefräßig

G

**Greek** 1. griechisch 2. Grieche *m*, Griechin *f*; LING Griechisch *n*
**green** 1. grün; *fig* grün, unerfahren 2. Grün *n*; Grünfläche *f*, Rasen *m*; *pl* grünes Gemüse, Blattgemüse *n*
**green·back** F Dollar *m*
**green belt** Grüngürtel *m*
**green card** Arbeitserlaubnis *f*
**green·gro·cer** *esp Br* Obst- und Gemüsehändler(in)
**green·horn** F Greenhorn *n*, Grünschnabel *m*
**green·house** Gewächs-, Treibhaus *n*; ~ **ef·fect** Treibhauseffekt *m*
**green·ish** grünlich
**greet** grüßen; **greet·ing** Begrüßung *f*, Gruß *m*; *pl* Grüße *pl*
**gre·nade** MIL Granate *f*
**grey** *Br* → ***gray***
**grid** Gitter *n*; ELECTR *etc* Versorgungsnetz *n*; Gitter(netz) *n* (*map etc*)
**grid·i·ron** Bratrost *m*
**grief** Kummer *m*
**griev·ance** (Grund *m* zur) Beschwerde *f*; Missstand *m*
**grieve** *v/t* betrüben, bekümmern; *v/i* bekümmert sein; ~ ***for*** trauern um
**griev·ous** schwer, schlimm
**grill** 1. grillen 2. Grill *m*; Bratrost *m*; GASTR *das* Gegrillte *n*
**grim** grimmig; schrecklich; erbittert; F schlimm
**gri·mace** 1. Fratze *f*, Grimasse *f* 2. Grimassen schneiden
**grime** Schmutz *m*; Ruß *m*
**grim·y** schmutzig; rußig
**grin** 1. Grinsen *n* 2. grinsen
**grind** 1. *v/t* (zer)mahlen, zerreiben, zerkleinern; *Messer etc* schleifen; *Fleisch* durchdrehen; ~ ***one's teeth*** mit den Zähnen knirschen; *v/i* F schuften; pauken, büffeln 2. Schinderei *f*, F Schufterei *f*; ***the daily*** ~ das tägliche Einerlei
**grind·er** (Messer- *etc*)Schleifer *m*; TECH Schleifmaschine *f*; TECH Mühle *f*
**grind·stone** Schleifstein *m*
**grip** 1. packen (*a. fig*) 2. Griff *m*; *fig* Gewalt *f*, Herrschaft *f*; Reisetasche *f*
**grip·ping** spannend
**gris·ly** grässlich, schrecklich
**gris·tle** GASTR Knorpel *m*
**grit** 1. Kies *m*, (grober) Sand; *fig* Mut *m* 2. streuen; ~ ***one's teeth*** die Zähne zusammenbeißen
**griz·zly (bear)** ZO Grislibär *m*, Graubär *m*
**groan** 1. stöhnen, ächzen 2. Stöhnen *n*, Ächzen *n*
**gro·cer** Lebensmittelhändler *m*
**gro·cer·ies** Lebensmittel *pl*
**gro·cer·y** Lebensmittelgeschäft *n*
**grog·gy** F groggy, schwach *or* wackelig (auf den Beinen)
**groin** ANAT Leiste *f*, Leistengegend *f*
**groom** 1. Pferdepfleger *m*, Stallbursche *m*; Bräutigam *m* 2. *Pferde* versorgen, striegeln; pflegen
**groove** Rinne *f*, Furche *f*; Rille *f*, Nut *f*
**grope** tasten; F *Mädchen* befummeln
**gross** 1. dick, feist; grob, derb; ECON Brutto… 2. Gros *n*
**gro·tesque** grotesk
**ground**[1] gemahlen (*coffee etc*); ~ ***meat*** Hackfleisch *n*
**ground**[2] 1. (Erd)Boden *m*, Erde *f*; Boden *m*, Gebiet *n*; SPORT (*Spiel*)Platz *m*; ELECTR Erdung *f*; (Boden)Satz *m*; *fig* Beweggrund *m*; *pl* Grundstück *n*, Park *m*, Gartenanlage *f*; ***on the*** ~***(s) of*** aufgrund (*gen*); ***hold*** *or* ***stand one's*** ~ sich behaupten 2. MAR auflaufen; ELECTR erden; *fig* gründen, stützen; ~ **crew** AVIAT Bodenpersonal *n*; ~ **floor** *esp Br* Erdgeschoss *n*; ~ **forc·es** MIL Bodentruppen *pl*, Landstreitkräfte *pl*
**ground·hog** ZO Amer. Waldmurmeltier *n*
**ground·ing** ELECTR Erdung *f*; Grundlagen *pl*, Grundkenntnisse *pl*
**ground·keep·er** SPORT Platzwart *m*
**ground·less** grundlos
**ground·nut** *Br* BOT Erdnuss *f*
**grounds·man** *Br* SPORT Platzwart *m*
**ground| staff** *Br* AVIAT Bodenpersonal *n*; ~ **sta·tion** Bodenstation *f*
**ground·work** *fig* Grundlage *f*, Fundament *n*
**group** 1. Gruppe *f* 2. (sich) gruppieren
**group·ie** F Groupie *n*
**group·ing** Gruppierung *f*
**grove** Wäldchen *n*, Gehölz *n*
**grov·el** (am Boden) kriechen
**grow** *v/i* wachsen; (allmählich) werden; ~ ***up*** aufwachsen, heranwachsen; *v/t* BOT anpflanzen, anbauen, züchten; ~ ***a beard*** sich e-n Bart wachsen lassen
**grow·er** Züchter *m*, Erzeuger *m*
**growl** knurren, brummen

**grown-up 1.** erwachsen **2.** Erwachsene *m, f*
**growth** Wachsen *n*, Wachstum *n*; Wuchs *m*, Größe *f*; *fig* Zunahme *f*, Anwachsen *n*; MED Gewächs *n*, Wucherung *f*
**grub 1.** ZO Larve *f*, Made *f*; F Futter *n* **2.** graben
**grub·by** schmudd(e)lig
**grudge 1.** missgönnen (***s.o. s.th.*** j-m et.); **2.** Groll *m*
**grudg·ing·ly** widerwillig
**gru·el** Haferschleim *m*
**gruff** grob, schroff, barsch, unwirsch
**grum·ble** murren, F meckern (***über*** *acc* about, at); ***~ at*** schimpfen über (*acc*)
**grump·y** F schlecht gelaunt, mürrisch, missmutig, verdrießlich, verdrossen
**grun·gy** F schmudd(e)lig-schlampig; MUS schlecht und laut
**grunt 1.** grunzen; brummen; stöhnen **2.** Grunzen *n*; Stöhnen *n*
**guar·an·tee 1.** Garantie *f*; Kaution *f*, Sicherheit *f* **2.** (sich ver)bürgen für; garantieren
**guar·an·tor** JUR Bürge *m*, Bürgin *f*
**guar·an·ty** JUR Garantie *f*; Sicherheit *f*
**guard 1.** Wache *f*, (Wacht)Posten *m*, Wächter *m*; Wärter *m*, Aufseher *m*; Wache *f*, Bewachung *f*; *Br* Zugbegleiter *m*; Schutz(vorrichtung *f*) *m*; Garde *f*; ***be on ~*** Wache stehen; ***be on*** (***off***) ***one's ~*** (nicht) auf der Hut sein **2.** *v/t* bewachen, (be)schützen (***from*** vor *dat*); *v/i* sich hüten *or* in Acht nehmen *or* schützen (***against*** vor *dat*)
**guard·ed** vorsichtig, zurückhaltend
**guard·i·an 1.** JUR Vormund *m* **2.** Schutz...
**guard·i·an·ship** JUR Vormundschaft *f*
**gue(r)·ril·la** MIL Guerilla *m*
**gue(r)·ril·la war·fare** Guerillakrieg *m*
**guess 1.** (er)raten; vermuten; schätzen; glauben, meinen **2.** Vermutung *f*
**guess·work** (reine) Vermutung(en *pl*)
**guest** Gast *m*
**guest·house** (Hotel)Pension *f*, Fremdenheim *n*
**guest·room** Gäste-, Fremdenzimmer *n*
**guf·faw 1.** schallendes Gelächter **2.** schallend lachen
**guid·ance** Führung *f*; (An)Leitung *f*
**guide 1.** (Reise-, Fremden)Führer(in); (Reise- *etc*)Führer *m* (*book*); Handbuch (***to*** *gen*); ***a ~ to London*** ein London-Führer **2.** leiten; führen; lenken
**guide·book** (Reise- *etc*)Führer *m*
**guid·ed tour** Führung *f*
**guide·lines** Richtlinien *pl* (***on*** *gen*)
**guild** HIST Gilde *f*, Zunft *f*
**guile·less** arglos
**guilt** Schuld *f*
**guilt·less** schuldlos, unschuldig (***of*** an *dat*)
**guilt·y** schuldig (***of*** *gen*); schuldbewusst
**guin·ea pig** ZO Meerschweinchen *n*; *fig* Versuchsperson *f*, F Versuchskaninchen *n*
**guise** *fig* Gestalt *f*, Maske *f*
**gui·tar** MUS Gitarre *f*
**gulch** GEOGR tiefe Schlucht, Klamm *f*
**gulf** GEOGR Golf *m*; *fig* Kluft *f*
**gull** ZO Möwe *f*
**gul·let** ANAT Speiseröhre *f*; Gurgel *f*, Kehle *f*
**gulp 1.** (großer) Schluck **2.** *often* ***~ down*** *Getränk* hinunterstürzen, *Speise* hinunterschlingen
**gum¹** ANAT *mst pl* Zahnfleisch *n*
**gum² 1.** Gummi *m, n*; Klebstoff *m*; Kaugummi *m*; (Frucht)Gummi *m* **2.** kleben
**gump·tion** F Grips *m*; Schneid *m*
**gun 1.** Gewehr *n*; Pistole *f*, Revolver *m*; Geschütz *n*, Kanone *f* **2.** ***~ down*** niederschießen
**gun·fight** Feuergefecht *n*, Schießerei *f*
**gun·fire** Schüsse *pl*; MIL Geschützfeuer *n*
**gun li·cence** *Br*, **gun li·cense** Waffenschein *m*
**gun·man** Bewaffnete *m*
**gun·point**: ***at ~*** mit vorgehaltener Waffe, mit Waffengewalt
**gun·pow·der** Schießpulver *n*
**gun·run·ner** Waffenschmuggler *m*
**gun·run·ning** Waffenschmuggel *m*
**gun·shot** Schuss *m*; ***within*** (***out of***) ***~*** in (außer) Schussweite
**gur·gle 1.** gurgeln, gluckern, glucksen **2.** Gurgeln *n*, Gluckern *n*, Glucksen *n*
**gush 1.** strömen, schießen (***from*** aus); **2.** Schwall *m*, Strom *m* (*a. fig*)
**gust** Windstoß *m*, Bö *f*
**gust** F Eingeweide *pl*; Schneid *m*, Mumm *m*
**gut·ter** Gosse *f* (*a. fig*), Rinnstein *m*; Dachrinne *f*

G

**guy** F Kerl *m*, Typ *m*
**guz·zle** F saufen; fressen
**gym** F Fitnesscenter *n*; → ***gymnasium***; → ***gymnastics***
**gym·na·si·um** Turn-, Sporthalle *f*
**gym·nast** Turner(in)
**gym·nas·tics** Turnen *n*, Gymnastik *f*
**gym shirt** Turnhemd *n*
**gym shorts** Turnhose *f*
**gy·n(a)e·col·o·gist** Gynäkologe *m*, Gynäkologin *f*, Frauenarzt *m*, -ärztin *f*
**gy·n(a)e·col·o·gy** Gynäkologie *f*, Frauenheilkunde *f*
**gyp·sy** Zigeuner *m*, Zigeunerin *f*
**gy·rate** kreisen, sich (im Kreis) drehen, (herum)wirbeln

# H

**H, h** H, h *n*
**hab·it** (An)Gewohnheit *f*; *esp* (Ordens-)Tracht *f*; ***get into*** (***out of***) ***the ~ of smoking*** sich das Rauchen angewöhnen (abgewöhnen); **ha·bit·u·al** gewohnheitsmäßig, Gewohnheits…
**hack**[1] hacken
**hack**[2] *contp* Schreiberling *m*
**hack**[3] *contp* Klepper *m*
**hack·er** IT Hacker *m*
**hack·neyed** abgedroschen
**had·dock** zo Schellfisch *m*
**h(a)e·mor·rhage** MED Blutung *f*
**hag** hässliches altes Weib, Hexe *f*
**hag·gard** abgespannt; verhärmt, abgehärmt; hager
**hag·gle** feilschen, handeln
**hail** **1.** Hagel *m* **2.** hageln
**hail·stone** Hagelkorn *n*
**hail·storm** Hagelschauer *m*
**hair** *einzelnes* Haar; *coll* Haar *n*, Haare *pl*; ***let one's ~ down*** F aus sich herausgehen; ***without turning a ~*** ohne mit der Wimper zu zucken
**hair·breadth** → ***hair's breadth***
**hair·brush** Haarbürste *f*
**hair·cut** Haarschnitt *m*
**hair·do** F Frisur *f*
**hair·dress·er** Friseur(in)
**hair·dri·er**, **hair·dry·er** Trockenhaube *f*; Haartrockner *m*, Föhn *m*
**hair·grip** *Br* Haarklammer *f*, Haarklemme *f*
**hair·less** ohne Haare, kahl
**hair·pin** Haarnadel *f*; **~ bend** MOT Haarnadelkurve *f*
**hair-rais·ing** haarsträubend
**hair's breadth**: ***by a ~*** um Haaresbreite
**hair slide** *Br* Haarspange *f*
**hair-split·ting** Haarspalterei *f*
**hair·spray** Haarspray *m*, *n*
**hair·style** Frisur *f*
**hair styl·ist** Hair-Stylist *m*, Damenfriseur *m*
**hair·y** behaart, haarig
**half** **1.** Hälfte *f*; ***go halves*** halbe-halbe machen, teilen **2.** halb; ***~ an hour*** e-e halbe Stunde; ***~ a pound*** ein halbes Pfund; ***~ past ten*** halb elf (Uhr); ***~ way up*** auf halber Höhe
**half-breed** Halbblut *n*
**half-broth·er** Halbbruder *m*
**half-caste** *esp contp* Mischling *m*
**half-heart·ed** halbherzig
**half time** SPORT Halbzeit *f*; **~ score** SPORT Halbzeitstand *m*
**half·way** halb; auf halbem Weg, in der Mitte; **~ line** *soccer*: Mittellinie *f*
**half-wit·ted** schwachsinnig
**hal·i·but** zo Heilbutt *m*
**hall** Halle *f*, Saal *m*; Flur *m*, Diele *f*; *esp Br* Herrenhaus *n*; *Br* UNIV Speisesaal *m*; *Br* ***~ of residence*** Studentenheim *n*
**hall·mark** *fig* Kennzeichen *n*
**Hal·low·e'en** Abend *m* vor Allerheiligen
**hal·lu·ci·na·tion** Halluzination *f*
**hall·way** Halle *f*, Diele *f*; Korridor *m*
**ha·lo** ASTR Hof *m*; Heiligenschein *m*
**halt** **1.** Halt *m* **2.** (an)halten
**hal·ter** Halfter *m*, *n*
**halt·ing** zögernd, stockend
**halve** halbieren
**ham** Schinken *m*; ***~ and eggs*** Schinken mit (Spiegel)Ei
**ham·burg·er** GASTR Hamburger *m*; Rinderhack *n*
**ham·let** Weiler *m*
**ham·mer** **1.** Hammer *m* **2.** hämmern
**ham·mock** Hängematte *f*

**ham·per**[1] (Deckel)Korb *m*; Präsentkorb *m*; Wäschekorb *m*
**ham·per**[2] (be)hindern
**ham·ster** zo Hamster *m*
**hand 1.** Hand *f* (*a. fig*); Handschrift *f*; (Uhr)Zeiger *m*; *often in cpds* Arbeiter *m*; Fachmann *m*; *card game*: Blatt *n*, Karten *pl*; ***change ~s*** den Besitzer wechseln; ***give*** *or* ***lend a ~*** mit zugreifen, *j-m* helfen (***with*** by); ***shake ~s with*** *j-m* die Hand schütteln *or* geben; ***at ~*** in Reichweite; nahe; bei der *or* zur Hand; ***at first ~*** aus erster Hand; ***by ~*** mit der Hand; ***on the one ~*** einerseits; ***on the other ~*** andererseits; ***on the right ~*** rechts; ***~s off!*** Hände weg!; ***~s up!*** Hände hoch! **2.** aushändigen, (über)geben, (über)reichen; ***~ around*** herumreichen; ***~ down*** weitergeben, überliefern; ***~ in*** *Prüfungsarbeit etc* abgeben; *Bericht, Gesuch etc* einreichen; ***~ on*** weiterreichen, weitergeben; überliefern; ***~ out*** austeilen, verteilen; ***~ over*** übergeben, aushändigen (***to*** *dat*); ***~ up*** hinauf-, heraufreichen; **~·bag** Handtasche *f*; **~ bag·gage** Handgepäck *n*; **~·ball** SPORT Handball *m*; *soccer*: Handspiel *n*; **~·bill** Handzettel *m*, Flugblatt *n*; **~·book** Handbuch *n*; **~·brake** TECH Handbremse *f*; **~·cart** Handwagen *m*; **~·cuffs** Handschellen *pl*; **~·ful** Handvoll *f*; F Plage *f*
**hand·i·cap 1.** Handikap *n*, MED *a.* Behinderung *f*, SPORT *a.* Vorgabe *f*; → ***mental handicap, physical handicap*** **2.** behindern, benachteiligen; **hand·i·capped 1.** gehandikapt, behindert, benachteiligt; → ***mental, physical*** **2.** ***the ~*** MED die Behinderten *pl*
**hand·ker·chief** Taschentuch *n*
**han·dle 1.** Griff *m*; Stiel *m*; Henkel *m*; Klinke *f*; ***fly off the ~*** F wütend werden **2.** anfassen, berühren; hantieren *or* umgehen mit; behandeln; **~·bar(s)** Lenkstange *f*
**hand|·lug·gage** Handgepäck *n*; **~·made** handgearbeitet; **~·out** Handzettel *m*; Hand-out *n*, Informationsmaterial *n*; **~·rail** Geländer *n*; **~s-free·kit** Freisprechanlage *f*; **~·shake** Händedruck *m*
**hand·some** gut aussehend; *fig* ansehnlich, beträchtlich (*sum etc*)
**hands-on** praktisch
**hand|·spring** Handstandüberschlag *m*; **~·stand** Handstand *m*; **~·writ·ing** Handschrift *f*; **~·writ·ten** handgeschrieben
**hand·y** zur Hand; geschickt; handlich, praktisch; nützlich; ***come in ~*** sich als nützlich erweisen; (sehr) gelegen kommen; **~·man** Handwerker *m*; ***be a ~*** *a.* handwerklich geschickt sein
**hang** (auf-, be-, ein)hängen; *Tapete* ankleben; *j-n* (auf)hängen; ***~ o.s.*** sich erhängen; ***~ about, ~ around*** herumlungern; ***~ on*** sich klammern (***to*** an *acc*) (*a. fig*), festhalten (***to*** *acc*); TEL am Apparat bleiben; ***~ up*** TEL einhängen, auflegen; ***she hung up on me*** sie legte einfach auf
**han·gar** Hangar *m*, Flugzeughalle *f*
**hang·er** Kleiderbügel *m*
**hang glid·er** SPORT (Flug)Drachen *m*; Drachenflieger(in)
**hang glid·ing** SPORT Drachenfliegen *n*
**hang·ing 1.** Hänge… **2.** (Er)Hängen *n*
**hang·ings** Tapete *f*, Wandbehang *m*, Vorhang *m*
**hang·man** Henker *m*
**hang·nail** MED Niednagel *m*
**hang·o·ver** Katzenjammer *m*, Kater *m*
**han·ker** F sich sehnen (***after, for*** nach)
**han·kie, han·ky** F Taschentuch *n*
**hap·haz·ard** willkürlich, planlos, wahllos
**hap·pen** (zufällig) geschehen; sich ereignen, passieren, vorkommen
**hap·pen·ing** Ereignis *n*, Vorkommnis *n*; Happening *n*
**hap·pi·ly** glücklich(erweise)
**hap·pi·ness** Glück *n*
**hap·py** glücklich; erfreut
**hap·py-go-luck·y** unbekümmert, sorglos
**ha·rangue 1.** (Straf)Predigt *f* **2.** *v/t j-m* e-e Strafpredigt halten
**har·ass** ständig belästigen; schikanieren; aufreiben, zermürben
**har·ass·ment** ständige Belästigung; Schikane(n *pl*) *f*; → ***sexual harassment***
**har·bo(u)r 1.** Hafen *m*; Zufluchtsort *m* **2.** *j-m* Zuflucht *or* Unterschlupf gewähren; *Groll etc* hegen
**hard** hart (*a. fig*); fest; schwer, schwierig; heftig, stark; streng (*a. winter*); *fig* nüchtern (*facts etc*); ***give s.o. a ~ time***

H

j-m das Leben schwer machen; ~ ***of hearing*** schwerhörig; ***be ~ on s.th.*** et. strapazieren; ~ ***up*** F in (Geld)-Schwierigkeiten, knapp bei Kasse; F ***the ~ stuff*** die harten Sachen (*alcohol, drugs*)
**hard·back** gebundene Ausgabe
**hard-boiled** GASTR hart (gekocht); F *fig* hart, unsentimental, nüchtern
**hard cash** Bargeld *n*; klingende Münze
**hard core** harter Kern; **hard-core** zum harten Kern gehörend; hart
**hard court** *tennis*: Hartplatz *m*
**hard·cov·er 1.** gebunden **2.** Hard Cover *n*, gebundene Ausgabe
**hard cur·ren·cy** ECON harte Währung
**hard disk** IT Festplatte *f*
**hard·en** härten; hart machen *or* werden; (sich) abhärten
**hard hat** Schutzhelm *m*
**hard-head·ed** nüchtern, praktisch; starrköpfig, dickköpfig
**hard-heart·ed** hartherzig
**hard la·bo(u)r** JUR Zwangsarbeit *f*
**hard line** *esp* POL harter Kurs
**hard-line** *esp* POL hart, kompromisslos
**hard·ly** kaum
**hard·ness** Härte *f*; Schwierigkeit *f*
**hard·ship** Not *f*; Härte *f*; Strapaze *f*
**hard shoul·der** *Br* MOT Standspur *f*
**hard·top** MOT Hardtop *n, m*
**hard·ware** Eisenwaren *pl*; Haushaltswaren *pl*; IT Hardware *f*
**hard·wear·ing** strapazierfähig
**har·dy** zäh, robust, abgehärtet; BOT winterhart, winterfest
**hare** ZO Hase *m*
**hare·bell** BOT Glockenblume *f*
**hare·brained** verrückt
**hare·lip** MED Hasenscharte *f*
**harm 1.** Schaden *m* **2.** verletzen; schaden (*dat*)
**harm·ful** schädlich
**harm·less** harmlos
**har·mo·ni·ous** harmonisch
**har·mo·nize** harmonieren; in Einklang sein *or* bringen
**har·mo·ny** Harmonie *f*
**har·ness 1.** (*Pferde- etc*)Geschirr *n* **2.** anschirren; anspannen (***to*** an *acc*)
**harp 1.** MUS Harfe *f* **2.** MUS Harfe spielen
**har·poon 1.** Harpune *f* **2.** harpunieren
**har·row** AGR **1.** Egge *f* **2.** eggen
**har·row·ing** quälend, qualvoll, erschütternd
**harsh** rau; grell; streng; schroff, barsch
**hart** ZO Hirsch *m*
**har·vest 1.** Ernte(zeit) *f*; (Ernte)Ertrag *m* **2.** ernten
**har·vest·er** MOT Mähdrescher *m*
**hash**[1] GASTR Haschee *n*
**hash**[2] F Hasch *n*
**hash browns** GASTR Brat-, Röstkartoffeln *pl*
**hash·ish** Haschisch *n*
**hasp** TECH Haspe *f*
**haste** Eile *f*, Hast *f*
**has·ten** *j-n* antreiben; (sich be)eilen; *et.* beschleunigen
**hast·y** eilig, hastig, überstürzt; voreilig
**hat** Hut *m*
**hatch**[1]: *a.* ~ ***out*** ZO ausbrüten; ausschlüpfen
**hatch**[2] Durchreiche *f*; AVIAT, MAR Luke *f*
**hatch·back** MOT (Wagen *m* mit) Hecktür *f*
**hatch·et** Beil *n*; ***bury the ~*** das Kriegsbeil begraben
**hate 1.** Hass *m* **2.** hassen
**hate·ful** verhasst; abscheulich
**ha·tred** Hass *m*
**haugh·ty** hochmütig, überheblich
**haul 1.** ziehen, zerren; schleppen; befördern, transportieren **2.** Ziehen *n*; Fischzug *m*, *fig* F *a.* Fang *m*; Beförderung *f*, Transport *m*; Transportweg *m*
**haul·age** Beförderung *f*, Transport *m*
**haul·er**, *Br* **haul·i·er** Transportunternehmer *m*
**haunch** ANAT Hüfte *f*, Hüftpartie *f*, Hinterbacke *f*; GASTR Keule *f*
**haunt 1.** spuken in (*dat*); häufig besuchen; *fig* verfolgen, quälen **2.** häufig besuchter Ort; Schlupfwinkel *m*
**haunt·ing** quälend; unvergesslich, eindringlich
**have** *v/t* haben; erhalten, bekommen; essen, trinken; ~ ***breakfast*** frühstücken; ~ ***a cup of tea*** e-n Tee trinken; *with inf*: müssen (***I ~ to go now*** ich muss jetzt gehen); *with object and pp*: lassen (***I had my hair cut*** ich ließ mir die Haare schneiden); ~ ***back*** zurückbekommen; ~ ***on*** *Kleidungsstück* anhaben, *Hut* aufhaben; *v/aux* haben; *v/i often* sein; ***I ~ come*** ich bin gekommen
**ha·ven** Hafen *m* (*mst fig*)
**hav·oc** Verwüstung *f*, Zerstörung *f*; ***play***

~ **with** verwüsten, zerstören; *fig* verheerend wirken auf (*acc*)
**hawk**[1] zo Habicht *m*, Falke *m*
**hawk**[2] hausieren mit; auf der Straße verkaufen; **hawk·er** Hausierer(in); Straßenhändler(in); Drücker(in)
**haw·thorn** BOT Weißdorn *m*
**hay** Heu *n*
**hay fe·ver** MED Heuschnupfen *m*
**hay·loft** Heuboden *m*
**hay·stack** Heuhaufen *m*
**haz·ard** Gefahr *f*, Risiko *n*
**haz·ard·ous** gewagt, gefährlich, riskant; ~ **waste** Sonder-, Giftmüll *m*
**haze** Dunst(schleier) *m*
**ha·zel 1.** BOT Hasel(nuss)strauch *m* **2.** (hasel)nussbraun
**ha·zel·nut** BOT Haselnuss *f*
**haz·y** dunstig, diesig; *fig* unklar, verschwommen
**H-bomb** H-Bombe *f*, Wasserstoffbombe *f*
**he 1.** er **2.** Er *m*; zo Männchen *n*; ***~-goat*** Ziegenbock *m*
**head 1.** Kopf *m*; (Ober)Haupt *n*; Chef *m*; (An)Führer(in), Leiter(in); Spitze *f*; Kopf(ende *n*) *m*; Kopf *m* (*of a page, nail etc*); Vorderseite *f*; Überschrift *f*; ***20 dollars a ~ or per ~*** zwanzig Dollar pro Kopf *or* Person; ***40 ~ (of cattle)*** 40 Stück (Vieh); ***~s or tails?*** Kopf oder Zahl?; ***at the ~ of*** an der Spitze (*gen*); ***~ over heels*** kopfüber; bis über beide Ohren (*verliebt sein*); ***bury one's ~ in the sand*** den Kopf in den Sand stecken; ***get it into one's ~ that …*** es sich in den Kopf setzen, dass; ***lose one's ~*** den Kopf *or* die Nerven verlieren **2.** Ober…, Haupt…, Chef…, oberste(r, -s), erste(r, -s) **3.** *v/t* anführen, an der Spitze stehen von (*or gen*); voran-, vorausgehen (*dat*); (an)führen, leiten; *soccer*: köpfen; *v/i* (**for**) gehen, fahren (nach); lossteuern, losgehen (auf *acc*); MAR Kurs halten (auf *acc*)
**head·ache** Kopfweh *n*
**head·band** Stirnband *n*
**head·dress** Kopfschmuck *m*
**head·er** Kopfsprung *m*; *soccer*: Kopfball *m*
**head·first** kopfuber, mit dem Kopf voran; *fig* ungestüm, stürmisch
**head·gear** Kopfbedeckung *f*
**head·ing** Überschrift *f*, Titel(zeile *f*) *m*
**head·land** Landspitze *f*, Landzunge *f*
**head·light** MOT Scheinwerfer *m*
**head·line** Schlagzeile *f*; ***news ~s*** *radio*, TV *das* Wichtigste in Schlagzeilen
**head·long** kopfüber; *fig* ungestüm
**head·mas·ter** *Br* PED Direktor *m*, Rektor *m*
**head·mis·tress** *Br* PED Direktorin *f*, Rektorin *f*
**head-on** frontal, Frontal…; ***~ collision*** MOT Frontalzusammenstoß *m*
**head·phones** Kopfhörer *pl*
**head·quar·ters** (*abbr* ***HQ***) MIL Hauptquartier *n*; Zentrale *f*
**head·rest** MOT Kopfstütze *f*
**head·set** Kopfhörer *pl*
**head start** SPORT Vorgabe *f*, Vorsprung *m* (*a. fig*)
**head·strong** halsstarrig
**head teach·er** → ***headmaster, headmistress, principal***
**head·wa·ters** GEOGR Quellgebiet *n*
**head·way** Fortschritt(e *pl*) *m*; ***make ~*** (gut) vorankommen
**head·word** Stichwort *n*
**head·y** zu Kopfe steigend, berauschend
**heal** heilen; ***~ over, ~ up*** (zu)heilen
**heal·ing** Heilung *f*; ***~ power*** Heilkraft *f*
**health** Gesundheit *f*; ~ **cer·tif·i·cate** Gesundheitszeugnis *n*; ~ **club** Fitnessklub *m*, Fitnesscenter *n*; ~ **food** Reform-, Biokost *f*; ~ **food shop** *Br*, ~ **food store** Reformhaus *n*, Bioladen *m*
**health·ful** gesund; heilsam
**health| in·su·rance** Krankenversicherung *f*; ~ **re·sort** Kurort *m*; ~ **service** Gesundheitsdienst *m*
**health·y** gesund
**heap 1.** Haufe(n) *m* **2.** *a.* ***~ up*** aufhäufen, *fig a.* anhäufen
**hear** hören; anhören, *j-m* zuhören; *Zeugen* vernehmen; *Lektion* abhören
**hear·er** (Zu)Hörer(in)
**hear·ing** Gehör *n*; Hören *n*; JUR Verhandlung *f*; JUR Vernehmung *f*; *esp* POL Hearing *n*, Anhörung *f*; ***within (out of) ~*** in (außer) Hörweite
**hear·ing aid** Hörgerät *n*
**hear·say** Gerede *n*; ***by ~*** vom Hörensagen *n*
**hearse** Leichenwagen *m*
**heart** ANAT Herz *n* (*a. fig*); Kern *m*; *card games*: Herz(karte *f*) *n*, *pl* Herz *n*; ***lose ~*** den Mut verlieren; ***take ~*** sich ein

Herz fassen; ***take s.th. to ~*** sich et. zu Herzen nehmen; ***with a heavy ~*** schweren Herzens
**heart·ache** Kummer *m*
**heart at·tack** MED Herzanfall *m*; Herzinfarkt *m*
**heart·beat** Herzschlag *m*
**heart·break** Leid *n*, großer Kummer
**heart·break·ing** herzzerreißend
**heart·brok·en** gebrochen, verzweifelt
**heart·burn** MED Sodbrennen *n*
**heart·en** ermutigen
**heart fail·ure** MED Herzversagen *n*
**heart·felt** innig, tief empfunden
**hearth** Kamin *m*
**heart·less** herzlos
**heart·rend·ing** herzzerreißend
**heart trans·plant** MED Herzverpflanzung *f*, Herztransplantation *f*
**heart·y** herzlich; gesund; herzhaft
**heat 1.** Hitze *f*; PHYS Wärme *f*; Eifer *m*; zo Läufigkeit *f*; SPORT (Einzel)Lauf *m*; ***preliminary ~*** Vorlauf *m* **2.** *v/t* heizen; *a.* ***~ up*** erhitzen, aufwärmen; *v/i* sich erhitzen (*a. fig*); **heat·ed** geheizt; heizbar; erhitzt, *fig a.* erregt
**heat·er** Heizgerät *n*, Heizkörper *m*
**heath** Heide *f*, Heideland *n*
**hea·then** REL **1.** Heide *m*, Heidin *f* **2.** heidnisch
**heath·er** BOT Heidekraut *n*; Erika *f*
**heat·ing 1.** Heizung *f* **2.** Heiz…
**heat·proof** hitzebeständig
**heat shield** Hitzeschild *m*
**heat·stroke** MED Hitzschlag *m*
**heat wave** Hitzewelle *f*
**heave** *v/t* (hoch)stemmen, (hoch)hieven; *Anker* lichten; *Seufzer* ausstoßen; *v/i* sich heben und senken, wogen
**heav·en** Himmel *m*
**heav·en·ly** himmlisch
**heav·y** schwer; stark (*rain*, *smoker*, *drinker*, *traffic etc*); hoch (*fine*, *taxes etc*); schwer (verdaulich); drückend, lastend; Schwer…
**heav·y cur·rent** ELECTR Starkstrom *m*
**heav·y-du·ty** TECH Hochleistungs…; strapazierfähig
**heav·y-hand·ed** ungeschickt
**heav·y·weight** *boxing*: Schwergewicht *n*, Schwergewichtler *m*
**He·brew 1.** hebräisch **2.** Hebräer(in); LING Hebräisch *n*
**heck·le** *Redner* durch Zwischenrufe *or* Zwischenfragen stören; **heck·ler** Zwischenrufer *m*; **heck·ling** Zwischenrufe
**hec·tic** hektisch
**hedge 1.** Hecke *f* **2.** *v/t*: *a.* ***~ in*** mit e-r Hecke einfassen; *v/i fig* ausweichen
**hedge·hog** zo Stachelschwein *n*; *Br* Igel *m*
**hedge·row** Hecke *f*
**heed 1.** beachten, Beachtung schenken (*dat*) **2.** ***give*** *or* ***pay ~ to, take ~ of*** → 1
**heed·less**: ***be ~ of*** nicht beachten, *Warnung etc* in den Wind schlagen
**heel 1.** ANAT Ferse *f*; Absatz *m*; ***down at ~*** *fig* abgerissen; heruntergekommen **2.** Absätze machen auf (*acc*)
**hef·ty** kräftig, stämmig; mächtig (*blow etc*), gewaltig; F saftig (*prices*, *fine etc*)
**heif·er** zo Färse *f*, junge Kuh
**height** Höhe *f*; (Körper)Größe *f*; Anhöhe *f*; *fig* Höhe(punkt *m*) *f*
**height·en** erhöhen; vergrößern
**heir** Erbe *m*; ***~ to the throne*** Thronerbe *m*, Thronfolger *m*
**heir·ess** Erbin *f*
**heir·loom** Erbstück *n*
**hel·i·cop·ter** AVIAT Hubschrauber *m*, Helikopter *m*
**hel·i·port** AVIAT Hubschrauberlandeplatz *m*
**hell 1.** Hölle *f*; ***a ~ of a noise*** F ein Höllenlärm; ***what the ~ …?*** F was zum Teufel …? **2.** Höllen… **3.** *int* F verdammt!, verflucht!; **hell·ish** F höllisch
**hel·lo** *int* hallo!
**helm** MAR Ruder *n*, Steuer *n*
**hel·met** Helm *m*
**helms·man** MAR Steuermann *m*
**help 1.** Hilfe *f*; Hausangestellte *f*; ***a call*** *or* ***cry for ~*** ein Hilferuf, ein Hilfeschrei **2.** helfen; ***~ o.s.*** sich bedienen, zulangen; ***I cannot ~ it*** ich kann es nicht ändern; ***I could not ~ laughing*** ich musste einfach lachen
**help·er** Helfer(in)
**help·ful** hilfreich; nützlich
**help·ing** Portion *f*
**help·less** hilflos
**help·less·ness** Hilflosigkeit *f*
**help men·u** IT Hilfemenü *n*
**hel·ter-skel·ter 1.** *adv* holterdiepolter, Hals über Kopf **2.** *adj* überstürzt
**helve** Stiel *m*, Griff *m*
**Hel·ve·tian** Schweizer …
**hem 1.** Saum *m* **2.** säumen; ***~ in*** ein-

schließen
**hem·i·sphere** GEOGR Halbkugel *f*, Hemisphäre *f*
**hem·line** Saum *m*
**hem·lock** BOT Schierling *m*
**hemp** BOT Hanf *m*
**hem·stitch** Hohlsaum *m*
**hen** ZO Henne *f*, Huhn *n*; Weibchen *n*
**hence** daher; ***a week ~*** in e-r Woche
**hence·forth** von nun an
**hen house** Hühnerstall *m*
**hen·pecked hus·band** Pantoffelheld *m*
**her** sie; ihr; ihr(e); sich
**her·ald** **1.** HIST Herold *m* **2.** ankündigen
**her·ald·ry** Wappenkunde *f*, Heraldik *f*
**herb** BOT Kraut *n*; Heilkraut *n*
**her·ba·ceous** BOT krautartig; ***~ plant*** Staudengewächs *n*
**herb·al** BOT Kräuter..., Pflanzen...
**her·bi·vore** ZO Pflanzenfresser *m*
**herd** **1.** Herde *f* (*a. fig*), Rudel *n* **2.** *v/t Vieh* hüten; *v/i*: *a.* ***~ together*** in e-r Herde leben; sich zusammendrängen
**herds·man** Hirt *m*
**here** hier; hierher; ***~ you are*** hier (bitte); ***~'s to you!*** auf dein Wohl!
**here·a·bout(s)** hier herum, in dieser Gegend
**here·af·ter** **1.** künftig **2.** *das* Jenseits
**here·by** hiermit
**he·red·i·ta·ry** BIOL erblich, Erb...
**he·red·i·ty** BIOL Erblichkeit *f*; ererbte Anlagen *pl*, Erbmasse *f*
**here·in** hierin
**here·of** hiervon
**her·e·sy** REL Ketzerei *f*
**her·e·tic** REL Ketzer(in)
**here·up·on** hierauf, darauf(hin)
**here·with** hiermit
**her·i·tage** Erbe *n*
**her·maph·ro·dite** BIOL Zwitter *m*
**her·met·ic** TECH hermetisch
**her·mit** Einsiedler *m*
**he·ro** Held *m*
**he·ro·ic** heroisch, heldenhaft, Helden...
**her·o·in** Heroin *n*
**her·o·ine** Heldin *f*
**her·o·is·m** Heldentum *n*
**her·on** ZO Reiher *m*
**her·ring** ZO Hering *m*
**hers** ihrs, ihre(r, -s)
**her·self** sie selbst, ihr selbst; sich (selbst); ***by ~*** von selbst, allein, ohne Hilfe
**hes·i·tant** zögernd, zaudernd, unschlüssig; **hes·i·tate** zögern, zaudern, unschlüssig sein, Bedenken haben; **hes·i·ta·tion** Zögern *n*, Zaudern *n*, Unschlüssigkeit *f*; ***without ~*** ohne zu zögern, bedenkenlos
**heterosexual** heterosexuell
**hew** hauen, hacken; ***~ down*** fällen, umhauen
**hey** *int* F he!, heda!
**hey·day** Höhepunkt *m*, Gipfel *m*; Blüte (-zeit) *f*
**hi** *inf* F hallo!
**hi·ber·nate** ZO Winterschlaf halten
**hic·cough**, **hic·cup** **1.** Schluckauf *m* **2.** den Schluckauf haben
**hide**[1] (sich) verbergen, verstecken; verheimlichen
**hide**[2] Haut *f*, Fell *n*
**hide-and-seek** Versteckspiel *n*
**hide·a·way** F Versteck *n*
**hid·e·ous** abscheulich, scheußlich
**hide·out** Versteck *n*
**hid·ing**[1] F Tracht *f* Prügel
**hid·ing**[2]: ***be in ~*** sich versteckt halten; ***go into ~*** untertauchen
**hid·ing place** Versteck *n*
**hi-fi** Hi-Fi *n*, Hi-Fi-Gerät *n*, -Anlage *f*
**high** **1.** hoch; groß (*hopes etc*); GASTR angegangen; F blau; F high; ***be in ~ spirits*** in Hochstimmung sein; ausgelassen *or* übermütig sein **2.** METEOR Hoch *n*; Höchststand *m*; High School *f*
**high·brow** F **1.** Intellektuelle *m*, *f* **2.** (betont) intellektuell
**high-cal·o·rie** kalorienreich
**high-class** erstklassig
**high·er ed·u·ca·tion** Hochschulausbildung *f*
**high fi·del·i·ty** High Fidelity *f*
**high·grade** hochwertig; erstklassig
**high-hand·ed** anmaßend, eigenmächtig
**high-heeled** hochhackig
**high jump** SPORT Hochsprung *m*
**high jump·er** SPORT Hochspringer(in)
**high·land** Hochland *n*
**high·light** **1.** Höhe-, Glanzpunkt *m* **2.** hervorheben
**high·ly** *fig* hoch; ***think ~ of*** viel halten von; **high·ly-strung** reizbar, nervös
**high·ness** *mst fig* Höhe *f*; ***Highness*** Hoheit *f* (*title*)
**high-pitched** schrill; steil (*roof*)

**high-pow·ered** TECH Hochleistungs…; *fig* dynamisch
**high-pres·sure** METEOR, TECH Hochdruck…
**high-rank·ing** hochrangig
**high rise** Hochhaus *n*
**high road** *esp Br* Hauptstraße *f*
**high school** High School *f*
**high sea·son** Hochsaison *f*
**high so·ci·e·ty** High Society *f*
**high-spir·it·ed** übermütig, ausgelassen
**high street** *Br* Hauptstraße *f*
**high tea** *Br* frühes Abendessen
**high tech·nol·o·gy** Hochtechnologie *f*
**high ten·sion** ELECTR Hochspannung *f*
**high tide** Flut *f*
**high time**: ***it is ~*** es ist höchste Zeit
**high wa·ter** Hochwasser *n*
**high·way** Highway *m*, Haupt(verkehrs)straße *f*; **High·way Code** *Br* Straßenverkehrsordnung *f*
**hi·jack 1.** *Flugzeug* entführen; *j-n*, *Geldtransport etc* überfallen **2.** (Flugzeug-)Entführung *f*; Überfall *m*
**hi·jack·er** Räuber *m*; (Flugzeug)Entführer(in)
**hike 1.** wandern **2.** Wanderung *f*
**hik·er** Wanderer *m*, Wanderin *f*
**hik·ing** Wandern *n*
**hi·lar·i·ous** ausgelassen
**hi·lar·i·ty** Ausgelassenheit *f*
**hill** Hügel *m*, Anhöhe *f*
**hill·bil·ly** *contp* Hinterwäldler *m*
**hill·ock** kleiner Hügel
**hill·side** (Ab)Hang *m*
**hill·top** Hügelspitze *f*
**hill·y** hügelig
**hilt** Heft *n*, Griff *m*
**him** ihn; ihm; F er; sich
**him·self** er *or* ihm *or* ihn selbst; sich; sich (selbst); ***by ~*** von selbst, allein, ohne Hilfe
**hind**[1] ZO Hirschkuh *f*
**hind**[2] Hinter…
**hin·der** hindern (***from*** an *dat*); hemmen
**hind·most** hinterste(r, -s), letzte(r, -s)
**hin·drance** Hindernis *n*
**Hin·du** Hindu *m*
**Hin·du·ism** Hinduismus *m*
**hinge 1.** TECH (Tür)Angel *f*, Scharnier *n* **2.** ***~ on*** *fig* abhängen von
**hint 1.** Wink *m*, Andeutung *f*; Tipp *m*; Anspielung *f*; ***take a ~*** e-n Wink verstehen **2.** andeuten; anspielen (***at*** auf *acc*)
**hip**[1] ANAT Hüfte *f*
**hip**[2] BOT Hagebutte *f*
**hip·po** F → **hip·po·pot·a·mus** ZO Flusspferd *n*, Nilpferd *n*
**hire 1.** *Br Auto etc* mieten, *Flugzeug etc* chartern; *j-n* anstellen; *j-n* engagieren, anheuern; ***~ out*** *Br* vermieten **2.** Miete *f*; Lohn *m*; ***for ~*** zu vermieten; frei
**hire car** *Br* Leih-, Mietwagen *m*
**hire pur·chase**: ***on ~*** *Br* ECON auf Abzahlung, auf Raten
**his** sein(e); seins, seine(r, -s)
**hiss 1.** zischen; fauchen (*cat*); auszischen **2.** Zischen *n*; Fauchen *n*
**his·to·ri·an** Historiker(in)
**his·tor·ic** historisch, geschichtlich (bedeutsam); **his·tor·i·cal** historisch, geschichtlich (belegt *or* überliefert); Geschichts…; ***~ novel*** historischer Roman
**his·to·ry** Geschichte *f*; ***~ of civilization*** Kulturgeschichte *f*; ***contemporary ~*** Zeitgeschichte *f*
**hit 1.** schlagen; treffen (*a. fig*); MOT *etc* *j-n*, *et.* anfahren, *et.* rammen; F ***~ it off*** (***with s.o.***) sich (mit j-m) gut vertragen; ***~ on*** (zufällig) auf *et.* stoßen, *et.* finden **2.** Schlag *m*; *fig* (Seiten)Hieb *m*; (Glücks)Treffer *m*; Hit *m*
**hit-and-run**: ***~ driver*** (unfall)flüchtiger Fahrer; ***~ offense*** (*Br* ***offence***) Fahrerflucht *f*
**hitch 1.** befestigen, festmachen, festhaken, anbinden, ankoppeln (***to*** an *acc*); ***~ up*** hochziehen; ***~ a ride*** *or* ***lift*** im Auto mitgenommen werden **2.** Ruck *m*, Zug *m*; Schwierigkeit *f*, Haken *m*; ***without a ~*** glatt, reibungslos;
**hitch·hike** per Anhalter fahren, trampen; **hitch·hik·er** Anhalter(in), Tramper(in)
**hi-tech** → ***high tech***
**HIV**: ***~ carrier*** HIV-Positive *m, f*; ***~ negative*** HIV-negativ; ***~ positive*** HIV-positiv
**hive** Bienenstock *m*; Bienenschwarm *m*
**hoard 1.** Vorrat *m*, Schatz *m* **2.** *a.* ***~ up*** horten, hamstern; **hoard·ing** Bauzaun *m*; *Br* Reklametafel *f*
**hoar·frost** (Rau)Reif *m*
**hoarse** heiser, rau
**hoax 1.** Falschmeldung *f*; (übler) Scherz **2.** *j-n* hereinlegen
**hob·ble** humpeln, hinken

**hob·by** Hobby *n*, Steckenpferd *n*
**hob·by·horse** Steckenpferd *n* (*a. fig*)
**hob·gob·lin** Kobold *m*
**ho·bo** F Landstreicher *m*
**hock**[1] weißer Rheinwein
**hock**[2] zo Sprunggelenk *n*
**hock·ey** SPORT Eishockey *n*; *esp Br* Hockey *n*
**hodge·podge** Mischmasch *m*
**hoe** AGR **1.** Hacke *f* **2.** hacken
**hog** zo (Haus-, Schlacht)Schwein *n*
**hoist 1.** hochziehen; hissen **2.** TECH Winde *f*, (Lasten)Aufzug *m*
**hold 1.** halten; festhalten; *Gewicht etc* tragen, aushalten; zurück-, abhalten (***from*** von); *Wahlen*, *Versammlung etc* abhalten; *Stellung* halten; SPORT *Meisterschaft etc* austragen; *Aktien*, *Rechte etc* besitzen; *Amt* bekleiden; *Platz* einnehmen; *Rekord* halten; fassen, enthalten; Platz bieten für; der Ansicht sein (***that*** dass); halten für; *fig* fesseln, in Spannung halten; (sich) festhalten; anhalten, andauern (*a. fig*); ***~ one's ground, ~ one's own*** sich behaupten; ***~ the line*** TEL am Apparat bleiben; ***~ responsible*** verantwortlich machen; ***~ still*** still halten; ***~ s.th. against s.o.*** j-m et. vorhalten *or* vorwerfen; j-m et. übel nehmen *or* nachtragen; ***~ back*** (sich) zurückhalten; *fig* zurückhalten mit; ***~ on*** (sich) festhalten (***to*** an *dat*); aus-, durchhalten; andauern; TEL am Apparat bleiben; ***~ out*** aus-, durchhalten; reichen (*supplies etc*); ***~ up*** hochheben; hochhalten; hinstellen (***as*** als); aufhalten, verzögern; *j-n*, *Bank etc* überfallen **2.** Griff *m*, Halt *m*; Stütze *f*; Gewalt *f*, Macht *f*, Einfluss *m*; MAR Laderaum *m*, Frachtraum *m*; ***catch*** (***get, take***) ***~ of s.th.*** et. ergreifen, et. zu fassen bekommen
**hold·er** TECH Halter *m*; *esp* ECON Inhaber(in)
**hold·ing** Besitz *m*; **~ com·pa·ny** ECON Holding-, Dachgesellschaft *f*
**hold·up** (Verkehrs)Stockung *f*; (bewaffneter) (Raub)Überfall
**hole 1.** Loch *n*; Höhle *f*, Bau *m*; *fig* F Klemme *f* **2.** durchlöchern
**hol·i·day** Feiertag *m*; freier Tag; *esp Br mst pl* Ferien *pl*, Urlaub *m*; ***be on ~*** im Urlaub sein, Urlaub machen; **~ home** Ferienhaus *n*, Ferienwohnung *f*
**hol·i·day·mak·er** Urlauber(in)
**hol·i·ness** Heiligkeit *f*; ***His Holiness*** Seine Heiligkeit
**hol·ler** F schreien
**hol·low 1.** hohl **2.** Hohlraum *m*, (Aus)Höhlung *f*; Mulde *f*, Vertiefung *f* **3.** ***~ out*** aushöhlen
**hol·ly** BOT Stechpalme *f*
**hol·o·caust** Massenvernichtung *f*, Massensterben *n*, (*esp* Brand)Katastrophe *f*; ***the Holocaust*** HIST der Holocaust
**hol·ster** (Pistolen)Halfter *m*, *n*
**ho·ly** heilig
**ho·ly wa·ter** REL Weihwasser *n*
**Ho·ly Week** REL Karwoche *f*
**home 1.** Heim *n*; Haus *n*; Wohnung *f*; Zuhause *n*; Heimat *f*; ***at ~*** zu Hause; ***make oneself at ~*** es sich bequem machen; ***at ~ and abroad*** im In- und Ausland **2.** *adj* häuslich, Heim… (*a.* SPORT); inländisch, Inlands…; Heimat… **3.** *adv* heim, nach Hause; zu Hause; daheim; *fig* ins Ziel, ins Schwarze; ***return ~*** heimkehren; ***strike ~*** sitzen, treffen
**home ad·dress** Privatanschrift *f*
**home com·put·er** Heimcomputer *m*
**home·less** heimatlos; obdachlos; ***~ person*** Obdachlose *m*, *f*; ***shelter for the ~*** Obdachlosenasyl *n*
**home·ly** einfach; unscheinbar, reizlos
**home·made** selbst gemacht, Hausmacher…
**home mar·ket** ECON Binnenmarkt *m*
**Home| Of·fice** *Br* POL Innenministerium *n*; **~ Sec·re·ta·ry** *Br* POL Innenminister *m*
**home·sick**: ***be ~*** Heimweh haben
**home·sick·ness** Heimweh *n*
**home team** SPORT Gastgeber *pl*
**home·ward** *adj* Heim…, Rück…
**home·ward(s)** *adv* nach Hause
**home·work** Hausaufgabe(n *pl*) *f*; ***do one's ~*** s-e Hausaufgaben machen (*a. fig*)
**hom·i·cide** JUR Mord *m*; Totschlag *m*; Mörder(in)
**hom·i·cide squad** Mordkommission *f*
**ho·mo·ge·ne·ous** homogen, gleichartig
**ho·mo·sex·u·al 1.** homosexuell **2.** Homosexuelle *m*, *f*
**hone** TECH fein schleifen
**hon·est** ehrlich, rechtschaffen; aufrichtig; **hon·es·ty** Ehrlichkeit *f*, Rechtschaffenheit *f*; Aufrichtigkeit *f*

**hon·ey** Honig *m*; Liebling *m*, Schatz *m*
**hon·ey·comb** (Honig)Wabe *f*
**hon·eyed** *fig* honigsüß
**hon·ey·moon** **1.** Flitterwochen *pl*, Hochzeitsreise *f* **2.** ***be ~ing*** auf Hochzeitsreise sein
**hon·ey·suck·le** BOT Geißblatt *n*
**honk** MOT hupen
**hon·or·ar·y** Ehren…; ehrenamtlich
**hon·o(u)r** **1.** Ehre *f*; Ehrung *f*, Ehre(n *pl*) *f*; *pl* besondere Auszeichnung(en *pl*); ***Your Hono(u)r*** JUR Euer Ehren **2.** ehren; auszeichnen; ECON *Scheck etc* honorieren, einlösen
**hon·o(u)r·a·ble** ehrenvoll, ehrenhaft; ehrenwert
**hood** Kapuze *f*; MOT Verdeck *n*; (Motor)Haube *f*; TECH (Schutz)Haube *f*
**hood·lum** F Rowdy *m*; Ganove *m*
**hood·wink** *j-n* hinters Licht führen
**hoof** ZO Huf *m*
**hook** **1.** Haken *m*; Angelhaken *m* **2.** an-, ein-, fest-, zuhaken; angeln (*a. fig*)
**hooked** krumm, Haken…; F süchtig (***on*** nach) (*a. fig*); ***~ on heroin*** (***television***) heroinsüchtig (fernsehsüchtig)
**hook·er** F Nutte *f*
**hoo·li·gan** Rowdy *m*
**hoo·li·gan·ism** Rowdytum *n*
**hoop** Reif(en) *m*
**hoot** **1.** ZO Schrei *m* (*a. fig*); MOT Hupen *n* **2.** *v/i* heulen; johlen; ZO schreien; MOT hupen; *v/t* auspfeifen, auszischen
**Hoo·ver®** *Br* **1.** Staubsauger *m* **2.** *mst* ***hoover*** (staub)saugen
**hop¹** **1.** hüpfen, hopsen; hüpfen über (*acc*); ***be ~ping mad*** F e-e Stinkwut haben **2.** Sprung *m*
**hop²** BOT Hopfen *m*
**hope** **1.** Hoffnung *f* (***of*** auf *acc*); **2.** hoffen (***for*** auf *acc*); ***~ for the best*** das Beste hoffen; ***I ~ so, let's ~ so*** hoffentlich
**hope·ful**: ***be ~ that*** hoffen, dass
**hope·ful·ly** hoffnungsvoll; hoffentlich
**hope·less** hoffnungslos; verzweifelt
**horde** Horde *f* (*often contp*)
**ho·ri·zon** Horizont *m*
**hor·i·zon·tal** horizontal, waag(e)recht
**hor·mone** BIOL Hormon *n*
**horn** ZO Horn *n*, *pl* Geweih *n*; MOT Hupe *f*
**hor·net** ZO Hornisse *f*
**horn·y** schwielig; V geil
**hor·o·scope** Horoskop *n*
**hor·ri·ble** schrecklich, furchtbar, scheußlich
**hor·rid** *esp Br* grässlich, abscheulich; schrecklich
**hor·rif·ic** schrecklich, entsetzlich
**hor·ri·fy** entsetzen
**hor·ror** Entsetzen *n*; Abscheu *m*, Horror *m*; F Gräuel *m*
**horse** ZO Pferd *n*; Bock *m*, Gestell *n*; ***wild ~s couldn't drag me there*** keine zehn Pferde bringen mich dort hin
**horse·back**: ***on ~*** zu Pferde, beritten
**horse chest·nut** BOT Rosskastanie *f*
**horse·hair** Rosshaar *n*
**horse·man** (geübter) Reiter
**horse·pow·er** TECH Pferdestärke *f*
**horse race** Pferderennen *n*
**horse rac·ing** Pferderennen *n or pl*
**horse·rad·ish** BOT Meerrettich *m*
**horse·shoe** Hufeisen *n*
**horse·wom·an** (geübte) Reiterin
**hor·ti·cul·ture** Gartenbau *m*
**hose¹** Schlauch *m*
**hose²** Strümpfe *pl*, Strumpfwaren *pl*
**ho·sier·y** Strumpfwaren *pl*
**hos·pice** Sterbeklinik *f*
**hos·pi·ta·ble** gastfreundlich
**hos·pi·tal** Krankenhaus *n*, Klinik *f*; ***in the ~*** im Krankenhaus
**hos·pi·tal·i·ty** Gastfreundschaft *f*
**hos·pi·tal·ize** ins Krankenhaus einliefern *or* einweisen
**host¹** **1.** Gastgeber *m*; BIOL Wirt *m*; *radio*, TV Talkmaster *m*, Showmaster *m*, Moderator(in); ***your ~ was …*** durch die Sendung führte Sie … **2.** *radio*, TV F *Sendung* moderieren
**host²** Menge *f*, Masse *f*
**host³** REL *often* ***Host*** Hostie *f*
**hos·tage** Geisel *m*, *f*; ***take s.o. ~*** j-n als Geisel nehmen
**hos·tel** *esp Br* UNIV (Wohn)Heim *n*; *mst* ***youth ~*** Jugendherberge *f*
**host·ess** Gastgeberin *f*; Hostess *f* (*a.* AVIAT); AVIAT Stewardess *f*
**hos·tile** feindlich; feindselig (***to*** gegen); ***~ to foreigners*** ausländerfeindlich
**hos·til·i·ty** Feindseligkeit *f* (***to*** gegen); ***~ to foreigners*** Ausländerfeindlichkeit *f*
**hot** heiß (*a. fig and sl*); GASTR scharf; warm (*meal*); *fig* hitzig, heftig; ganz neu *or* frisch (*news etc*); ***I am or feel ~*** mir ist heiß
**hot·bed** Mistbeet *n*; *fig* Brutstätte *f*

**hotch·potch** *Br* → ***hodgepodge***
**hot dog** GASTR Hot Dog *n*, *m*
**ho·tel** Hotel *n*
**hot·head** Hitzkopf *m*
**hot·house** Treib-, Gewächshaus *n*
**hot line** POL heißer Draht; TEL Hotline *f*
**hot·plate** Kochplatte *f*
**hot spot** *esp* POL Unruhe-, Krisenherd *m*
**hot spring** Thermalquelle *f*
**hot-tem·pered** jähzornig
**hot-wa·ter bot·tle** Wärmflasche *f*
**hound** ZO Jagdhund *m*
**hour** Stunde *f*; *pl* (*Arbeits*)Zeit *f*, (*Geschäfts*)Stunden *pl*; **hour·ly** stündlich
**house 1.** Haus *n* **2.** unterbringen
**house·bound** ans Haus gefesselt
**house·break·ing** Einbruch *m*
**house·hold 1.** Haushalt *m* **2.** Haushalts…
**house hus·band** Hausmann *m*
**house·keep·er** Haushälterin *f*
**house·keep·ing** Haushaltung *f*, Haushaltsführung *f*
**house·maid** Hausangestellte *f*, Hausmädchen *n*
**house·man** *Br* MED Assistenzarzt *m*, -ärztin *f*
**House of Lords** *Br* PARL Oberhaus *n*
**house plant** Zimmerpflanze *f*
**house-warm·ing** Hauseinweihung *f*, Einzugsparty *f*
**house·wife** Hausfrau *f*
**house·work** Hausarbeit *f*
**hous·ing** Wohnung *f*; **~ de·vel·opment**, *Br* **~ es·tate** Wohnsiedlung *f*
**hov·er** schweben; herumlungern; *fig* schwanken
**hov·er·craft** Hovercraft *n*, Luftkissenfahrzeug *n*
**how** wie; ***~ are you?*** wie geht es dir?; ***~ about …?*** wie steht's mit …?, wie wäre es mit …?; ***~ do you do?*** guten Tag!; ***~ much?*** wie viel?; ***~ many*** wie viele?
**how·ev·er 1.** *adv* wie auch (immer) **2.** *cj* jedoch
**howl 1.** heulen; brüllen, schreien **2.** Heulen *n*; **howl·er** F grober Schnitzer
**hub** TECH (Rad)Nabe *f*; *fig* Mittelpunkt *m*, Angelpunkt *m*
**hub·bub** Stimmengewirr *n*; Tumult *m*
**hub·by** F (Ehe)Mann *m*
**huck·le·ber·ry** BOT amerikanische Heidelbeere
**hud·dle**: ***~ together*** (sich) zusammendrängen; ***~d up*** zusammengekauert
**hue**[1] Farbe *f*; (Farb)Ton *m*
**hue**[2]: ***~ and cry*** *fig* großes Geschrei, heftiger Protest
**huff**: ***in a ~*** verärgert, verstimmt
**hug 1.** (sich) umarmen; an sich drücken **2.** Umarmung *f*
**huge** riesig, riesengroß
**hulk** F Koloss *m*; sperriges Ding
**hull 1.** BOT Schale *f*, Hülse *f*; MAR Rumpf *m* **2.** enthülsen, schälen
**hul·la·ba·loo** Lärm *m*, Getöse *n*
**hul·lo** *int* hallo!
**hum** summen; brummen
**hu·man 1.** menschlich, Menschen… **2.** *a.* ***~ being*** Mensch *m*
**hu·mane** human, menschlich
**hu·man·i·tar·i·an** humanitär, menschenfreundlich
**hu·man·i·ty** die Menschheit, die Menschen *pl*; Humanität *f*, Menschlichkeit *f*; *pl* Geisteswissenschaften *pl*; Altphilologie *f*
**hu·man·ly**: ***~ possible*** menschenmöglich
**hu·man rights** Menschenrechte *pl*
**hum·ble 1.** demütig; bescheiden **2.** demütigen; **hum·ble·ness** Demut *f*
**hum·drum** eintönig, langweilig
**hu·mid** feucht, nass
**hu·mid·i·ty** Feuchtigkeit *f*
**hu·mil·i·ate** demütigen, erniedrigen
**hu·mil·i·a·tion** Demütigung *f*, Erniedrigung *f*
**hu·mil·i·ty** Demut *f*
**hum·ming·bird** ZO Kolibri *m*
**hu·mor·ous** humorvoll, komisch
**hu·mo(u)r 1.** Humor *m*; Komik *f* **2.** *j-m* s-n Willen lassen; eingehen auf (*acc*)
**hump** ZO Höcker *m*; MED Buckel *m*
**hump·back(ed)** → ***hunchback(ed)***
**hunch 1.** → ***hump***; dickes Stück; (Vor)Ahnung *f* **2.** *a.* ***~ up*** krümmen; ***~ one's shoulders*** die Schultern hochziehen
**hunch·back** Buckel *m*; Bucklige *m*, *f*
**hunch·backed** buck(e)lig
**hun·dred 1.** hundert **2.** Hundert *f*
**hun·dredth 1.** hundertste(r, -s) **2.** Hundertstel *n*
**hun·dred·weight** *appr* Zentner *m* (= *50,8 kg*)
**Hun·ga·ri·an 1.** ungarisch **2.** Ungar(in); LING Ungarisch *n*

**Hun·ga·ry** Ungarn *n*
**hun·ger 1.** Hunger *m* (*a. fig* ***for*** nach); **2.** *fig* hungern (***for, after*** nach)
**hun·ger strike** Hungerstreik *m*
**hun·gry** hungrig
**hunk** dickes *or* großes Stück
**hunt 1.** jagen; Jagd machen auf (*acc*); verfolgen; suchen (***for, after*** nach); **~ *down*** zur Strecke bringen; **~ *for*** Jagd machen auf (*acc*); **~ *out*, ~ *up*** aufspüren **2.** Jagd *f* (*a. fig*), Jagen *n*; Verfolgung *f*; Suche *f* (***for, after*** nach)
**hunt·er** Jäger *m*; Jagdpferd *n*
**hunt·ing 1.** Jagen *n* **2.** Jagd…
**hunt·ing ground** Jagdrevier *n*
**hur·dle** SPORT Hürde *f* (*a. fig*)
**hur·dler** SPORT Hürdenläufer(in)
**hur·dle race** SPORT Hürdenrennen *n*
**hurl** schleudern; **~ *abuse at s.o.*** j-m Beleidigungen ins Gesicht schleudern
**hur·rah, hur·ray** *int* hurra!
**hur·ri·cane** Hurrikan *m*, Wirbelsturm *m*; Orkan *m*
**hur·ried** eilig, hastig, übereilt
**hur·ry 1.** *v/t* schnell *or* eilig befördern *or* bringen; *often* **~ *up*** *j-n* antreiben, hetzen; *et.* beschleunigen; *v/i* eilen, hasten; **~ (*up*)** sich beeilen; **~ *up!*** (mach) schnell! **2.** (große) Eile, Hast *f*; ***be in a* ~** es eilig haben
**hurt** verletzen, verwunden (*a. fig*); schmerzen, wehtun; schaden (*dat*)
**hurt·ful** verletzend
**hus·band** (Ehe)Mann *m*
**hush 1.** *int* still! **2.** Stille *f* **3.** zum Schweigen bringen; **~ *up*** vertuschen, totschweigen
**hush mon·ey** Schweigegeld *n*
**husk** BOT **1.** Hülse *f*, Schote *f*, Schale *f* **2.** enthülsen, schälen
**hus·tle 1.** (*in aller Eile*) *wohin* bringen *or* schicken; hasten, hetzen; sich beeilen **2. ~ *and bustle*** Gedränge *n*; Gehetze *n*; Betrieb *m*, Wirbel *m*
**hut** Hütte *f*
**hutch** Stall *m*
**hy·a·cinth** BOT Hyazinthe *f*
**hy·(a)e·na** ZO Hyäne *f*
**hy·brid** BIOL Mischling *m*, Kreuzung *f*
**hy·drant** Hydrant *m*
**hy·draul·ic** hydraulisch
**hy·draul·ics** hydraulik *f*
**hy·dro…** Wasser…
**hy·dro·car·bon** CHEM Kohlenwasserstoff *m*
**hy·dro·chlor·ic ac·id** CHEM Salzsäure *f*
**hy·dro·foil** MAR Tragflächenboot *n*, Tragflügelboot *n*
**hy·dro·gen** CHEM Wasserstoff *m*; **~ *bomb*** Wasserstoffbombe
**hy·dro·plane** AVIAT Wasserflugzeug *n*; MAR Gleitboot *n*
**hy·dro·plan·ing** MOT Aquaplaning *n*
**hy·e·na** ZO Hyäne *f*
**hy·giene** Hygiene *f*
**hy·gien·ic** hygienisch
**hymn** Kirchenlied *n*, Choral *m*
**hype** F **1.** *a.* **~ *up*** (übersteigerte) Publicity machen für **2.** (übersteigerte) Publicity; ***media* ~** Medienrummel *m*
**hy·per…** hyper…, übermäßig
**hy·per·mar·ket** *Br* Groß-, Verbrauchermarkt *m*
**hy·per·sen·si·tive** überempfindlich (***to*** gegen)
**hy·phen** Bindestrich *m*
**hy·phen·ate** mit Bindestrich schreiben
**hyp·no·tize** hypnotisieren
**hy·po·chon·dri·ac** Hypochonder *m*
**hy·poc·ri·sy** Heuchelei *f*
**hyp·o·crite** Heuchler(in); **hyp·o·crit·i·cal** heuchlerisch, scheinheilig
**hy·poth·e·sis** Hypothese *f*
**hys·te·ri·a** MED Hysterie *f*
**hys·ter·i·cal** hysterisch
**hys·ter·ics** hysterischer Anfall; ***go into* ~** hysterisch werden

# I

**I, i** I, i *n*
**I** ich; ***it is* ~** ich bin es
**ice 1.** Eis *n* **2.** *Getränke etc* mit *or* in Eis kühlen; GASTR glasieren, mit Zuckerguss überziehen; **~*d over*** zugefroren (*lake etc*); **~*d up*** vereist (*road*)
**ice age** Eiszeit *f*
**ice·berg** Eisberg *m* (*a. fig*)

**ice·bound** eingefroren
**ice cream** (Speise)Eis *n*
**ice-cream par·lo(u)r** Eisdiele *f*
**ice cube** Eiswürfel *m*
**iced** eisgekühlt
**ice floe** Eisscholle *f*
**ice hock·ey** SPORT Eishockey *n*
**ice lol·ly** *Br* Eis *n* am Stiel
**ice rink** (Kunst)Eisbahn *f*
**ice show** Eisrevue *f*
**ice skate** Schlittschuh *m*
**ice-skate** Schlittschuh laufen
**i·ci·cle** Eiszapfen *m*
**ic·ing** GASTR Glasur *f*, Zuckerguss *m*; ***the ~ on the cake*** das Tüpfelchen auf dem i
**i·con** REL Ikone *f*; IT Icon *n*, (Bild)Symbol *n*
**i·cy** eisig; vereist
**ID** *abbr of* ***identity*** Identität *f*; ***ID card*** (Personal)Ausweis *m*
**i·dea** Idee *f*, Vorstellung *f*, Begriff *m*; Gedanke *m*, Idee *f*; ***have no ~*** keine Ahnung haben
**i·deal 1.** ideal **2.** Ideal *n*
**i·deal·ism** Idealismus *m*
**i·deal·ize** idealisieren
**i·den·ti·cal** identisch (***to, with*** mit); **~ twins** eineiige Zwillinge *pl*
**i·den·ti·fi·ca·tion** Identifizierung *f*; **~ (pa·pers)** Ausweis(papiere *pl*) *m*
**i·den·ti·fy** identifizieren; ***~ o.s.*** sich ausweisen
**i·den·ti·kit® pic·ture** *Br* JUR Phantombild *n*
**i·den·ti·ty** Identität *f*; **~ card** (Personal)Ausweis *m*
**i·de·o·log·i·cal** ideologisch
**i·de·ol·o·gy** Ideologie *f*
**id·i·om** Idiom *n*, idiomatischer Ausdruck, Redewendung *f*
**id·i·o·mat·ic** idiomatisch
**id·i·ot** Idiot(in), *contp a.* Trottel *m*
**id·i·ot·ic** idiotisch, F *a.* blödsinnig, schwachsinnig
**i·dle 1.** untätig; faul, träge; nutzlos; leer, hohl (*talk*); TECH stillstehend, außer Betrieb; MOT leerlaufend, im Leerlauf **2.** faulenzen; MOT leerlaufen; *mst* ***~ away*** *Zeit* vertrödeln
**i·dol** Idol *n* (*a. fig*); Götzenbild *n*
**i·dol·ize** abgöttisch verehren, vergöttern
**i·dyl·lic** idyllisch
**if** wenn, falls; ob; ***~ I were you*** wenn ich du wäre

**ig·loo** Iglu *m*, *n*
**ig·nite** anzünden, (sich) entzünden; MOT zünden; **ig·ni·tion** MOT Zündung *f*
**ig·ni·tion key** MOT Zündschlüssel *m*
**ig·no·rance** Unkenntnis *f*, Unwissenheit *f*; **ig·no·rant**: ***be ~ of s.th.*** et. nicht wissen *or* kennen, nichts wissen von et.
**ig·nore** ignorieren, nicht beachten
**ill** krank; schlimm, schlecht; ***fall ~*** krank werden, erkranken
**ill-ad·vised** schlecht beraten; unklug
**ill-bred** schlecht erzogen; ungezogen
**il·le·gal** verboten; JUR illegal, ungesetzlich; ***~ parking*** Falschparken *n*
**il·le·gi·ble** unleserlich
**il·le·git·i·mate** unehelich; unrechtmäßig
**ill feel·ing** Verstimmung *f*; ***cause ~*** böses Blut machen
**ill-hu·mo(u)red** schlecht gelaunt
**il·li·cit** unerlaubt, verboten
**il·lit·e·rate** ungebildet
**ill-man·nered** ungehobelt, ungezogen
**ill-na·tured** boshaft, bösartig
**ill·ness** Krankheit *f*
**ill-tem·pered** schlecht gelaunt
**ill-timed** ungelegen, unpassend
**ill-treat** misshandeln
**il·lu·mi·nate** beleuchten
**il·lu·mi·nat·ing** aufschlussreich
**il·lu·mi·na·tion** Beleuchtung *f*; *pl* Illumination *f*, Festbeleuchtung *f*
**il·lu·sion** Illusion *f*, Täuschung *f*
**il·lu·sive**, **il·lu·so·ry** illusorisch, trügerisch
**il·lus·trate** illustrieren; bebildern; erläutern, veranschaulichen
**il·lus·tra·tion** Erläuterung *f*; Illustration *f*; Bild *n*, Abbildung *f*
**il·lus·tra·tive** erläuternd
**il·lus·tri·ous** berühmt
**ill will** Feindschaft *f*
**im·age** Bild *n*; Ebenbild *n*; Image *n*; bildlicher Ausdruck, Metapher *f*
**im·age·ry** Bildersprache *f*, Metaphorik *f*
**i·ma·gi·na·ble** vorstellbar, denkbar
**i·ma·gi·na·ry** eingebildet, imaginär
**i·ma·gi·na·tion** Einbildung(skraft) *f*; Vorstellungskraft *f*, -vermögen *n*
**i·ma·gi·na·tive** ideenreich, einfallsreich; fantasievoll
**i·ma·gine** sich *j-n or et.* vorstellen; sich *et.* einbilden
**im·bal·ance** Unausgewogenheit *f*; POL *etc* Ungleichgewicht *n*

**im·be·cile** Idiot *m*, Trottel *m*
**im·i·tate** nachahmen, nachmachen, imitieren; **im·i·ta·tion** **1.** Nachahmung *f*, Imitation *f* **2.** nachgemacht, unecht, künstlich, Kunst…
**im·mac·u·late** unbefleckt, makellos; tadellos, fehlerlos
**im·ma·te·ri·al** unwesentlich, unerheblich (***to*** für)
**im·ma·ture** unreif
**im·mea·su·ra·ble** unermesslich
**im·me·di·ate** unmittelbar; sofortig, umgehend; nächste(r, -s) (*family*)
**im·me·di·ate·ly** unmittelbar; sofort
**im·mense** riesig, *fig a.* enorm, immens
**im·merse** (ein)tauchen; ***~ o.s. in*** sich vertiefen in (*acc*)
**im·mer·sion** Eintauchen *n*
**im·mer·sion heat·er** Tauchsieder *m*
**im·mi·grant** Einwanderer *m*, Einwanderin *f*, Immigrant(in); **im·mi·grate** einwandern, immigrieren (***into*** in *dat*); **im·mi·gra·tion** Einwanderung *f*, Immigration *f*
**im·mi·nent** nahe bevorstehend; ***~ danger*** drohende Gefahr
**im·mo·bile** unbeweglich
**im·mod·e·rate** maßlos
**im·mod·est** unbescheiden; schamlos, unanständig
**im·mor·al** unmoralisch
**im·mor·tal** **1.** unsterblich **2.** Unsterbliche *m, f*
**im·mor·tal·i·ty** Unsterblichkeit *f*
**im·mo·va·ble** unbeweglich; *fig* unerschütterlich; hart, unnachgiebig
**im·mune** MED immun (***to*** gegen); geschützt (***from*** vor, gegen); **~ sys·tem** MED Immunsystem *n*
**im·mu·ni·ty** MED Immunität *f*
**im·mu·nize** MED immunisieren, immun machen (***against*** gegen)
**imp** Kobold *m*; F Racker *m*
**im·pact** Zusammenprall *m*, Anprall *m*; Aufprall *m*; Wucht *f*; *fig* (Ein)Wirkung *f*, (starker) Einfluss (***on*** auf *acc*)
**im·pair** beeinträchtigen
**im·part** (***to*** *dat*) mitteilen; vermitteln
**im·par·tial** unparteiisch, unvoreingenommen; **im·par·ti·al·i·ty** Unparteilichkeit *f*, Objektivität *f*
**im·pass·a·ble** unpassierbar
**im·passe** *fig* Sackgasse *f*; ***reach an ~*** in e-e Sackgasse geraten
**im·pas·sioned** leidenschaftlich
**im·pas·sive** teilnahmslos; ungerührt; gelassen
**im·pa·tience** Ungeduld *f*
**im·pa·tient** ungeduldig
**im·peach** JUR anklagen (***for, of, with*** *gen*); JUR anfechten; infrage stellen, in Zweifel ziehen
**im·pec·ca·ble** untadelig, einwandfrei
**im·pede** (be)hindern
**im·ped·i·ment** Hindernis *n* (***to*** für); Behinderung *f*
**im·pel** antreiben; zwingen
**im·pend·ing** nahe bevorstehend, drohend
**im·pen·e·tra·ble** undurchdringlich; *fig* unergründlich
**im·per·a·tive** **1.** unumgänglich, unbedingt erforderlich; gebieterisch; LING Imperativ… **2.** *a.* ***~ mood*** LING Imperativ *m*, Befehlsform *f*
**im·per·cep·ti·ble** nicht wahrnehmbar, unmerklich
**im·per·fect** **1.** unvollkommen; mangelhaft **2.** *a.* ***~ tense*** LING Imperfekt *n*, 1. Vergangenheit
**im·pe·ri·al·ism** POL Imperialismus
**im·pe·ri·al·ist** POL Imperialist *m*
**im·per·il** gefährden
**im·pe·ri·ous** herrisch, gebieterisch
**im·per·me·a·ble** undurchlässig
**im·per·son·al** unpersönlich
**im·per·so·nate** *j-n* imitieren, nachahmen; verkörpern, THEA *etc* darstellen
**im·per·ti·nence** Unverschämtheit *f*, Frechheit *f*
**im·per·ti·nent** unverschämt, frech
**im·per·tur·ba·ble** unerschütterlich, gelassen
**im·per·vi·ous** undurchlässig; *fig* unzugänglich (***to*** für)
**im·pe·tu·ous** ungestüm, heftig; impulsiv; vorschnell
**im·pe·tus** TECH Antrieb *m*, Impuls *m*
**im·pi·e·ty** Gottlosigkeit *f*; Pietätlosigkeit *f*, Respektlosigkeit *f* (***to*** gegenüber)
**im·pinge**: ***~ on*** sich auswirken auf (*acc*), beeinflussen (*acc*)
**im·pi·ous** gottlos; pietätlos, respektlos (***to*** gegenüber)
**im·plac·a·ble** unversöhnlich
**im·plant** MED implantieren, einpflanzen; *fig* einprägen

**im·plau·si·ble** unglaubwürdig
**im·ple·ment 1.** Werkzeug *n*, Gerät *n* **2.** ausführen
**im·pli·cate** *j-n* verwickeln, hineinziehen (***in*** in *acc*); **im·pli·ca·tion** Verwicklung *f*; Folge *f*; Andeutung *f*
**im·pli·cit** vorbehaltlos, bedingungslos; impliziert, (stillschweigend *or* mit) inbegriffen
**im·plore** *j-n* anflehen; *et.* erflehen
**im·ply** implizieren, einbeziehen, mit enthalten; andeuten; bedeuten
**im·po·lite** unhöflich
**im·pol·i·tic** unklug
**im·port** ECON **1.** importieren, einführen **2.** Import *m*, Einfuhr *f*
**im·por·tance** Wichtigkeit *f*, Bedeutung *f*; **im·por·tant** wichtig, bedeutend
**im·por·ta·tion** → ***import*** *2*
**im·port du·ty** ECON Einfuhrzoll *m*
**im·port·er** ECON Importeur *m*
**im·pose** auferlegen, aufbürden (***on*** *dat*); *Strafe* verhängen (***on*** gegen); *et.* aufdrängen, aufzwingen (***on*** *dat*); ***~ o.s. on s.o.*** sich j-m aufdrängen
**im·pos·ing** imponierend, eindrucksvoll, imposant
**im·pos·si·bil·i·ty** Unmöglichkeit *f*
**im·pos·si·ble** unmöglich
**im·pos·ter**, *Br* **im·pos·tor** Betrüger(in), *esp* Hochstapler(in)
**im·po·tence** Unvermögen *n*, Unfähigkeit *f*; Hilflosigkeit *f*; MED Impotenz *f*
**im·po·tent** unfähig; hilflos; MED impotent
**im·pov·e·rish** arm machen; ***be ~ed*** verarmen; verarmt sein
**im·prac·ti·ca·ble** undurchführbar; unpassierbar
**im·prac·ti·cal** unpraktisch; undurchführbar
**im·preg·na·ble** uneinnehmbar
**im·preg·nate** imprägnieren, tränken; BIOL schwängern
**im·press** aufdrücken, einprägen (*a. fig*); *j-n* beeindrucken; ***be ~ed with*** beeindruckt sein von
**im·pres·sion** Eindruck *m*; Abdruck *m*; ***under the ~ that*** in der Annahme, dass
**im·pres·sive** eindrucksvoll
**im·print 1.** (auf)drücken (***on*** auf *acc*); ***~ s.th. on s.o.'s memory*** j-m et. ins Gedächtnis einprägen **2.** Abdruck *m*, Eindruck *m*; PRINT Impressum *n*
**im·pris·on** JUR inhaftieren
**im·pris·on·ment** Freiheitsstrafe *f*, Gefängnis(strafe *f*) *n*, Haft *f*
**im·prob·a·ble** unwahrscheinlich
**im·prop·er** ungeeignet, unpassend; unanständig, unschicklich; unrichtig
**im·pro·pri·e·ty** Unschicklichkeit *f*
**im·prove** *v/t* verbessern; *Wert etc* erhöhen, steigern; ***~ on*** übertreffen; *v/i* sich (ver)bessern, besser werden, sich erholen; **im·prove·ment** (Ver)Bess(e)rung *f*; Steigerung *f*; Fortschritt *m* (***on*** gegenüber *dat*)
**im·pro·vise** improvisieren
**im·pru·dent** unklug
**im·pu·dence** Unverschämtheit *f*
**im·pu·dent** unverschämt
**im·pulse** Impuls *m* (*a. fig*); Anstoß *m*, Anreiz *m*; **im·pul·sive** impulsiv
**im·pu·ni·ty**: ***with ~*** straflos, ungestraft
**im·pure** unrein (*a.* REL), schmutzig; *fig* schlecht, unmoralisch
**im·pu·ri·ty** Unreinheit *f*
**im·pute**: ***~ s.th. to s.o.*** j-n e-r Sache bezichtigen; j-m et. unterstellen
**in 1.** *prp place*: in (*dat or acc*), an (*dat*), auf (*dat*): ***~ New York*** in New York; ***~ the street*** auf der Straße; ***put it ~ your pocket*** steck es in deine Tasche; *time*: in (*dat*), an (*dat*): ***~ 1999*** 1999; ***~ two hours*** in zwei Stunden; ***~ the morning*** am Morgen; *state, manner*: in (*dat*), auf (*acc*), mit; ***~ English*** auf Englisch; *activity*: in (*dat*), bei, auf (*dat*): ***~ crossing the road*** beim Überqueren der Straße; *author*: bei: ***~ Shakespeare*** bei Shakespeare; *direction*: in (*acc, dat*), auf (*acc*), zu: ***have confidence ~*** Vertrauen haben zu; *purpose*: in (*dat*), zu, als: ***~ defense of*** zur Verteidigung *or* zum Schutz von; *material*: in (*dat*), aus, mit: ***dressed ~ blue*** in Blau (gekleidet); *amount etc*: in, von, aus, zu: ***three ~ all*** insgesamt *or* im Ganzen drei; ***one ~ ten*** eine(r, -s) von zehn; nach, gemäß: ***~ my opinion*** m-r Meinung nach **2.** *adv* innen, drinnen; hinein, herein; da, (an)gekommen; da, zu Hause **3.** *adj* F in (Mode)
**in·a·bil·i·ty** Unfähigkeit *f*
**in·ac·ces·si·ble** unzugänglich, unerreichbar (***to*** für *or dat*)
**in·ac·cu·rate** ungenau
**in·ac·tive** untätig

**in·ac·tiv·i·ty** Untätigkeit *f*
**in·ad·e·quate** unangemessen; unzulänglich, ungenügend
**in·ad·mis·si·ble** unzulässig, unstatthaft
**in·ad·ver·tent** unbeabsichtigt, versehentlich; **~ly** *a.* aus Versehen
**in·an·i·mate** leblos; langweilig
**in·ap·pro·pri·ate** unpassend, ungeeignet (***for, to*** für)
**in·apt** ungeeignet, unpassend
**in·ar·tic·u·late** unartikuliert, undeutlich (ausgesprochen), unverständlich; unfähig(, deutlich) zu sprechen
**in·at·ten·tive** unaufmerksam
**in·au·di·ble** unhörbar
**in·au·gu·ral** **1.** Eröffnungs…, Antritts…; **~ *speech*** → **2.** Antrittsrede *f*
**in·au·gu·rate** *j-n* (feierlich) (in sein Amt) einführen; einweihen, eröffnen; einleiten; **in·au·gu·ra·tion** Amtseinführung *f*; Einweihung *f*, Eröffnung *f*; Beginn *m*; ***Inauguration Day*** Tag *m* der Amtseinführung des neu gewählten Präsidenten der USA
**in·born** angeboren
**in·cal·cu·la·ble** unberechenbar; unermesslich
**in·can·des·cent** (weiß) glühend
**in·ca·pa·ble** unfähig (***of*** zu *inf or gen*), nicht imstande (***of doing*** zu tun)
**in·ca·pa·ci·tate** unfähig *or* untauglich machen; **in·ca·pac·i·ty** Unfähigkeit *f*, Untauglichkeit *f*
**in·car·nate** leibhaftig; personifiziert
**in·cau·tious** unvorsichtig
**in·cen·di·a·ry** Brand…; *fig* aufwiegelnd, aufhetzend
**in·cense**[1] REL Weihrauch *m*
**in·cense**[2] in Wut bringen, erbosen
**in·cen·tive** Ansporn *m*, Anreiz *m*
**in·ces·sant** ständig, unaufhörlich
**in·cest** Inzest *m*, Blutschande *f*
**inch** **1.** Inch *m* (*2,54 cm*), Zoll *m* (*a. fig*); ***by ~es, ~ by ~*** allmählich; ***every ~*** durch und durch **2.** (sich) zentimeterweise *or* sehr langsam bewegen
**in·ci·dence** Vorkommen *n*
**in·ci·dent** Vorfall *m*, Ereignis *n*; POL Zwischenfall *m*
**in·ci·den·tal** nebensächlich, Neben…; beiläufig; **in·ci·den·tal·ly** nebenbei bemerkt, übrigens
**in·cin·e·rate** verbrennen
**in·cin·e·ra·tor** TECH Verbrennungsofen *m*; Verbrennungsanlage *f*
**in·cise** einschneiden; aufschneiden; einritzen, einschnitzen
**in·ci·sion** (Ein)Schnitt *m*
**in·ci·sive** schneidend, scharf; *fig* treffend
**in·ci·sor** ANAT Schneidezahn *m*
**in·cite** anstiften; aufwiegeln, aufhetzen
**in·cite·ment** Anstiftung *f*; Aufhetzung *f*, Aufwieg(e)lung *f*
**in·clem·ent** rau
**in·cli·na·tion** Neigung *f* (*a. fig*)
**in·cline** **1.** *v/i* sich neigen (***to, towards*** nach); *fig* neigen (***to, towards*** zu); *v/t* neigen; *fig* veranlassen **2.** Gefälle *n*; (Ab)Hang *m*
**in·close, in·clos·ure** → ***enclose, enclosure***
**in·clude** einschließen, enthalten; aufnehmen (***in*** in *e-e Liste etc*); ***the group ~d several …*** zu der Gruppe gehörten einige …; ***tax ~d*** inklusive Steuer
**in·clud·ing** einschließlich
**in·clu·sion** Einschluss *m*, Einbeziehung *f*; **in·clu·sive** einschließlich, inklusive (***of*** *gen*); ***be ~ of*** einschließen (*acc*)
**in·co·her·ent** unzusammenhängend, unklar, unverständlich
**in·come** ECON Einkommen *n*, Einkünfte *pl*; **~ tax** ECON Einkommensteuer *f*
**in·com·ing** hereinkommend; ankommend; nachfolgend, neu; **~ *mail*** Posteingang *m*
**in·com·mu·ni·ca·tive** verschlossen
**in·com·pa·ra·ble** unvergleichlich; unvergleichbar
**in·com·pat·i·ble** unvereinbar; unverträglich; inkompatibel
**in·com·pe·tence** Unfähigkeit *f*; Inkompetenz *f*; **in·com·pe·tent** unfähig; nicht fachkundig *or* sachkundig; unzuständig, inkompetent
**in·com·plete** unvollständig; unvollendet
**in·com·pre·hen·si·ble** unbegreiflich, unfassbar
**in·com·pre·hen·sion** Unverständnis *n*
**in·con·cei·va·ble** unbegreiflich, unfassbar; undenkbar
**in·con·clu·sive** nicht überzeugend; ergebnislos, erfolglos
**in·con·gru·ous** nicht übereinstimmend; unvereinbar
**in·con·se·quen·tial** unbedeutend

**in·con·sid·e·ra·ble** unbedeutend
**in·con·sid·er·ate** unüberlegt; rücksichtslos
**in·con·sis·tent** unvereinbar; widersprüchlich; inkonsequent
**in·con·so·la·ble** untröstlich
**in·con·spic·u·ous** unauffällig
**in·con·stant** unbeständig, wankelmütig
**in·con·test·a·ble** unanfechtbar
**in·con·ti·nent** MED inkontinent
**in·con·ve·ni·ence 1.** Unbequemlichkeit *f*; Unannehmlichkeit *f*, Ungelegenheit *f* **2.** *j-m* lästig sein; *j-m* Umstände machen; **in·con·ve·ni·ent** unbequem; ungelegen, lästig
**in·cor·po·rate** (sich) vereinigen *or* zusammenschließen; (mit) einbeziehen; enthalten; eingliedern; *Ort* eingemeinden; ECON, JUR als Aktiengesellschaft eintragen (lassen)
**in·cor·po·rat·ed com·pa·ny** ECON Aktiengesellschaft *f*
**in·cor·po·ra·tion** Vereinigung *f*, Zusammenschluss *m*; Eingliederung *f*; Eingemeindung *f*; ECON, JUR Eintragung *f* als Aktiengesellschaft
**in·cor·rect** unrichtig, falsch; inkorrekt
**in·cor·ri·gi·ble** unverbesserlich
**in·cor·rup·ti·ble** unbestechlich
**in·crease 1.** zunehmen, (an)wachsen; steigen; vergrößern, vermehren, erhöhen **2.** Vergrößerung *f*, Erhöhung *f*, Zunahme *f*, Zuwachs *m*, (An)Wachsen *n*, Steigerung *f*; **in·creas·ing·ly** immer mehr; **~ *difficult*** immer schwieriger
**in·cred·i·ble** unglaublich
**in·cre·du·li·ty** Ungläubigkeit *f*
**in·cred·u·lous** ungläubig, skeptisch
**in·crim·i·nate** *j-n* belasten
**in·cu·bate** ausbrüten; **in·cu·ba·tor** Brutapparat *m*; MED Brutkasten *m*
**in·cur** sich *et.* zuziehen, auf sich laden; *Schulden* machen; *Verluste* erleiden
**in·cu·ra·ble** unheilbar
**in·cu·ri·ous** nicht neugierig, gleichgültig, uninteressiert
**in·cur·sion** (feindlicher) Einfall; Eindringen *n*
**in·debt·ed** (zu Dank) verpflichtet; ECON verschuldet
**in·de·cent** unanständig, anstößig; JUR unsittlich, unzüchtig; **~ *assault*** JUR Sittlichkeitsverbrechen *n*
**in·de·ci·sion** Unentschlossenheit *f*
**in·de·ci·sive** unentschlossen; unentschieden; unbestimmt, ungewiss
**in·deed 1.** *adv* in der Tat, tatsächlich, wirklich; allerdings; ***thank you very much ~!*** vielen herzlichen Dank! **2.** *int* ach wirklich?
**in·de·fat·i·ga·ble** unermüdlich
**in·de·fen·si·ble** unhaltbar
**in·de·fi·na·ble** undefinierbar, unbestimmbar
**in·def·i·nite** unbestimmt; unbegrenzt
**in·def·i·nite·ly** auf unbestimmte Zeit
**in·del·i·cate** taktlos; unfein, anstößig
**in·dem·ni·fy** *j-n* entschädigen, *j-m* Schadenersatz leisten (***for*** für)
**in·dem·ni·ty** Entschädigung *f*
**in·dent** (ein)kerben, auszacken; PRINT *Zeile* einrücken
**in·de·pen·dence** Unabhängigkeit *f*; Selbstständigkeit *f*; ***Independence Day*** Unabhängigkeitstag *m*
**in·de·pen·dent** unabhängig; selbstständig
**in·de·scri·ba·ble** unbeschreiblich
**in·de·struc·ti·ble** unzerstörbar; unverwüstlich
**in·de·ter·mi·nate** unbestimmt; unklar, vage
**in·dex** Index *m*, (Inhalts-, Namens-, Stichwort)Verzeichnis *n*, (Sach)Register *n*; (An)Zeichen *n*; ***cost of living ~*** Lebenshaltungsindex *m*
**in·dex card** Karteikarte *f*
**in·dex fin·ger** ANAT Zeigefinger *m*
**In·di·a** Indien *n*
**In·di·an 1.** indisch; *neg!* indianisch, Indianer... **2.** Inder(in); ***American ~*** Indianer(in); **~ corn** BOT Mais *m*; **~ *file*: *in ~*** im Gänsemarsch; **~ sum·mer** Altweibersommer *m*, Nachsommer *m*
**in·di·a rub·ber** Gummi *n*, *m*; Radiergummi *m*
**in·di·cate** deuten *or* zeigen auf (*acc*); TECH anzeigen; MOT blinken; *fig* hinweisen *or* hindeuten auf (*acc*); andeuten; **in·di·ca·tion** (An)Zeichen *n*, Hinweis *m*, Andeutung *f*, Indiz *n*
**in·dic·a·tive** *a.* **~ *mood*** LING Indikativ *m*
**in·di·ca·tor** TECH Anzeiger *m*; MOT Richtungsanzeiger *m*, Blinker *m*
**in·dict** JUR anklagen (***for*** wegen)
**in·dict·ment** JUR Anklage *f*
**in·dif·fer·ence** Gleichgültigkeit *f*
**in·dif·fer·ent** gleichgültig (***to*** gegen);

mittelmäßig
**in·di·gent** arm
**in·di·ges·ti·ble** unverdaulich
**in·di·ges·tion** MED Verdauungsstörung *f*, Magenverstimmung *f*
**in·dig·nant** entrüstet, empört, ungehalten (***about, at, over*** über *acc*)
**in·dig·na·tion** Entrüstung *f*, Empörung *f* (***about, at, over*** über *acc*)
**in·dig·ni·ty** Demütigung *f*, unwürdige Behandlung
**in·di·rect** indirekt; ***by ~ means*** *fig* auf Umwegen
**in·dis·creet** unbesonnen, unbedacht; indiskret; **in·dis·cre·tion** Unbesonnenheit *f*; Indiskretion *f*
**in·dis·crim·i·nate** kritiklos; wahllos
**in·di·spen·sa·ble** unentbehrlich, unerlässlich
**in·dis·posed** indisponiert, unpässlich; abgeneigt; **in·dis·po·si·tion** Unpässlichkeit *f*; Abneigung *f* (***to do*** zu tun)
**in·dis·pu·ta·ble** unbestreitbar, unstreitig
**in·dis·tinct** undeutlich; unklar, verschwommen
**in·dis·tin·guish·a·ble** nicht zu unterscheiden(d) (***from*** von)
**in·di·vid·u·al** **1.** individuell, einzeln, Einzel…; persönlich **2.** Individuum *n*, Einzelne *m*, *f*
**in·di·vid·u·al·ism** Individualismus *m*
**in·di·vid·u·al·ist** Individualist(in)
**in·di·vid·u·al·i·ty** Individualität *f*, (persönliche) Note
**in·di·vid·u·al·ly** einzeln, jede(r, -s) für sich; individuell
**in·di·vis·i·ble** unteilbar
**in·dom·i·ta·ble** unbezähmbar, nicht unterzukriegen(d)
**in·door** Haus…, Zimmer…, Innen…, SPORT Hallen…
**in·doors** im Haus, drinnen; ins Haus (hinein); SPORT in der Halle
**in·dorse** → ***endorse*** *etc*
**in·duce** *j-n* veranlassen; verursachen, bewirken; **in·duce·ment** Anreiz *m*
**in·duct** einführen, -setzen; **in·duc·tion** Herbeiführung *f*; Einführung *f*, Einsetzung *f*; ELECTR Induktion *f*
**in·dulge** nachsichtig sein gegen; *e-r Neigung etc* nachgeben; ***~ in s.th.*** sich et. gönnen *or* leisten; **in·dul·gence** Nachsicht *f*; Luxus *m*; REL Ablass *m*
**in·dul·gent** nachsichtig, nachgiebig
**in·dus·tri·al** industriell, Industrie…, Gewerbe…, Betriebs…
**in·dus·tri·al ar·e·a** Industriegebiet *n*
**in·dus·tri·al·ist** Industrielle *m*, *f*
**in·dus·tri·al·ize** industrialisieren
**in·dus·tri·ous** fleißig
**in·dus·try** Industrie(zweig *m*) *f*; Gewerbe(zweig *m*) *n*; Fleiß *m*
**in·ed·i·ble** ungenießbar, nicht essbar
**in·ef·fec·tive, in·ef·fec·tu·al** unwirksam, wirkungslos; unfähig, untauglich
**in·ef·fi·cient** ineffizient; unfähig, untauglich; unrationell, unwirtschaftlich
**in·el·e·gant** unelegant
**in·el·i·gi·ble** nicht berechtigt
**in·ept** unpassend; ungeschickt; albern, töricht
**in·e·qual·i·ty** Ungleichheit *f*
**in·ert** PHYS träge (*a. fig*); inaktiv
**in·er·tia** PHYS Trägheit *f* (*a. fig*)
**in·es·cap·a·ble** unvermeidlich
**in·es·sen·tial** unwesentlich, unwichtig (***to*** für)
**in·es·ti·ma·ble** unschätzbar
**in·ev·i·ta·ble** unvermeidlich
**in·ev·i·ta·bly** zwangsläufig
**in·ex·act** ungenau
**in·ex·cu·sa·ble** unverzeihlich, unentschuldbar
**in·ex·haus·ti·ble** unerschöpflich; unermüdlich
**in·ex·o·ra·ble** unerbittlich
**in·ex·pe·di·ent** unzweckmäßig; nicht ratsam
**in·ex·pen·sive** billig, preiswert
**in·ex·pe·ri·ence** Unerfahrenheit *f*
**in·ex·pe·ri·enced** unerfahren
**in·ex·pert** unerfahren; ungeschickt
**in·ex·plic·a·ble** unerklärlich
**in·ex·pres·si·ble** unaussprechlich, unbeschreiblich
**in·ex·pres·sive** ausdruckslos
**in·ex·tri·ca·ble** unentwirrbar
**in·fal·li·ble** unfehlbar
**in·fa·mous** berüchtigt; schändlich, niederträchtig; **in·fa·my** Ehrlosigkeit *f*; Schande *f*; Niedertracht *f*
**in·fan·cy** frühe Kindheit; ***be in its ~*** *fig* in den Kinderschuhen stecken
**in·fant** Säugling *m*; kleines Kind, Kleinkind *n*; **in·fan·tile** kindlich; Kindes…, Kinder…; infantil, kindisch
**in·fan·try** MIL Infanterie *f*

**in·fat·u·at·ed** vernarrt (***with*** in *acc*)
**in·fect** MED *j-n, et.* infizieren, *j-n* anstecken (*a. fig*); verseuchen, verunreinigen; **in·fec·tion** MED Infektion *f*, Ansteckung *f* (*a. fig*); **in·fec·tious** MED infektiös, ansteckend (*a. fig*)
**in·fer** folgern, schließen (***from*** aus)
**in·fer·ence** (Schluss)Folgerung *f*, (Rück)Schluss *m*
**in·fe·ri·or** **1.** untergeordnet (***to*** *dat*), niedriger (***to*** als); weniger wert (***to*** als); minderwertig; ***be ~ to s.o.*** j-m untergeordnet sein; j-m unterlegen sein **2.** Untergebene *m, f*
**in·fe·ri·or·i·ty** Unterlegenheit *f*; Minderwertigkeit *f*; **~ com·plex** PSYCH Minderwertigkeitskomplex *m*
**in·fer·nal** höllisch, Höllen…
**in·fer·no** Inferno *n*, Hölle *f*
**in·fer·tile** unfruchtbar
**in·fest** verseuchen, befallen; *fig* überschwemmen (***with*** mit)
**in·fi·del·i·ty** (*esp* eheliche) Untreue
**in·fil·trate** einsickern in (*acc*); einschleusen (***into*** in *acc*); POL unterwandern
**in·fi·nite** unendlich
**in·fin·i·tive** *a.* **~ *mood*** LING Infinitiv *m*, Nennform *f*
**in·fin·i·ty** Unendlichkeit *f*
**in·firm** schwach, gebrechlich
**in·fir·ma·ry** Krankenhaus *n*; PED *etc* Krankenzimmer *n*
**in·fir·mi·ty** Schwäche *f*, Gebrechlichkeit *f*
**in·flame** entflammen (*mst fig*); erregen; ***become ~d*** MED sich entzünden
**in·flam·ma·ble** brennbar, leicht entzündlich; feuergefährlich
**in·flam·ma·tion** MED Entzündung *f*
**in·flam·ma·to·ry** MED entzündlich; *fig* aufrührerisch, Hetz…
**in·flate** aufpumpen, aufblasen, aufblähen (*a. fig*); ECON *Preise etc* in die Höhe treiben
**in·fla·tion** ECON Inflation *f*
**in·flect** LING flektieren, beugen
**in·flec·tion** LING Flexion *f*, Beugung *f*
**in·flex·i·ble** unbiegsam, starr (*a. fig*); *fig* inflexibel, unbeweglich, unbeugsam
**in·flex·ion** *Br* → ***inflection***
**in·flict** (***on***) *Leid, Schaden etc* zufügen (*dat*); *Wunde etc* beibringen (*dat*); *Strafe* auferlegen (*dat*), verhängen (über *acc*); aufbürden, aufdrängen (*dat*)
**in·flic·tion** Zufügung *f*; Verhängung *f*; Plage *f*
**in·flu·ence** **1.** Einfluss *m* **2.** beeinflussen; **in·flu·en·tial** einflussreich
**in·flux** Zustrom *m*, Zufluss *m*, (*Waren-*) Zufuhr *f*
**in·form** benachrichtigen, unterrichten (***of*** von), informieren (***of*** über *acc*); **~ *against*** *or* ***on s.o.*** j-n anzeigen; j-n denunzieren
**in·for·mal** formlos, zwanglos
**in·for·mal·i·ty** Formlosigkeit *f*; Ungezwungenheit *f*
**in·for·ma·tion** Auskunft *f*, Information *f*; Nachricht *f*
**in·for·ma·tive** informativ; lehrreich; mitteilsam
**in·form·er** Denunziant(in); Spitzel *m*
**in·fra·struc·ture** Infrastruktur *f*
**in·fre·quent** selten
**in·fringe**: **~ *on*** *Rechte, Vertrag etc* verletzen, verstoßen gegen
**in·fu·ri·ate** wütend machen
**in·fuse** *Tee* aufgießen
**in·fu·sion** Aufguss *m*; MED Infusion *f*
**in·ge·ni·ous** genial; einfallsreich; raffiniert; **in·ge·nu·i·ty** Genialität *f*; Einfallsreichtum *m*
**in·gen·u·ous** offen, aufrichtig; naiv
**in·got** (*Gold- etc*)Barren *m*
**in·gra·ti·ate**: **~ *o.s. with s.o.*** sich bei j-m beliebt machen
**in·grat·i·tude** Undankbarkeit *f*
**in·gre·di·ent** Bestandteil *m*; GASTR Zutat *f*
**in·hab·it** bewohnen, leben in (*dat*)
**in·hab·it·a·ble** bewohnbar
**in·hab·i·tant** Bewohner(in); Einwohner(in)
**in·hale** einatmen, MED *a.* inhalieren
**in·her·ent** innewohnend, eigen (***in*** *dat*)
**in·her·it** erben; **in·her·i·tance** Erbe *n*
**in·hib·it** hemmen (*a.* PSYCH), (ver)hindern; **in·hib·it·ed** PSYCH gehemmt; **in·hi·bi·tion** PSYCH Hemmung *f*
**in·hos·pi·ta·ble** ungastlich; unwirtlich (*region etc*)
**in·hu·man** unmenschlich
**in·hu·mane** inhuman, menschenunwürdig
**in·im·i·cal** feindselig (***to*** gegen); nachteilig (***to*** für)
**in·im·i·ta·ble** unnachahmlich
**i·ni·tial** **1.** anfänglich, Anfangs… **2.** Initi-

ale *f*, (großer) Anfangsbuchstabe
**i·ni·tial·ly** am *or* zu Anfang, anfänglich
**i·ni·ti·ate** in die Wege leiten, ins Leben rufen; einführen
**i·ni·ti·a·tion** Einführung *f*
**i·ni·tia·tive** Initiative *f*, erster Schritt; ***take the ~*** die Initiative ergreifen; ***on one's own ~*** aus eigenem Antrieb
**in·ject** MED injizieren, einspritzen
**in·jec·tion** MED Injektion *f*, Spritze *f*
**in·ju·di·cious** unklug, unüberlegt
**in·junc·tion** JUR gerichtliche Verfügung
**in·jure** verletzen, verwunden; schaden (*dat*); kränken; **in·jured 1.** verletzt **2.** ***the ~*** die Verletzten *pl*
**in·ju·ri·ous** schädlich; ***be ~ to*** schaden (*dat*); ***~ to health*** gesundheitsschädlich
**in·ju·ry** MED Verletzung *f*; Kränkung *f*; **~ time** *Br esp soccer*: Nachspielzeit *f*
**in·jus·tice** Ungerechtigkeit *f*, Unrecht *n*; ***do s.o. an ~*** j-m unrecht tun
**ink** Tinte *f*
**ink·ling** Andeutung *f*; dunkle *or* leise Ahnung
**ink pad** Stempelkissen *n*
**ink·y** Tinten…; tinten-, pechschwarz
**in·laid** eingelegt, Einlege…; ***~ work*** Einlegearbeit *f*
**in·land 1.** *adj* inländisch, einheimisch; ECON Binnen… **2.** *adv* landeinwärts
**In·land Rev·e·nue** *Br* Finanzamt *n*
**in·lay** Einlegearbeit *f*; MED (Zahn)Füllung *f*, Plombe *f*
**in·let** GEOGR schmale Bucht; TECH Eingang *m*, Einlass *m*
**in-line skate** Inliner *m*, Inline Skate *m*
**in·mate** Insasse *m*, Insassin *f*; Mitbewohner(in)
**in·most** innerste(r, -s) (*a. fig*)
**inn** Gasthaus *n*, Wirtshaus *n*
**in·nate** angeboren
**in·ner** innere(r, -s); Innen…; verborgen
**in·ner·most** → ***inmost***
**in·nings** *cricket*, *baseball*: Spielzeit *f*
**inn·keep·er** Gastwirt(in)
**in·no·cence** Unschuld *f*; Harmlosigkeit *f*; Naivität *f*; **in·no·cent** unschuldig; harmlos; arglos, naiv
**in·noc·u·ous** harmlos
**in·no·va·tion** Neuerung *f*
**in·nu·en·do** (versteckte) Andeutung *f*
**in·nu·me·ra·ble** unzählig, zahllos
**i·noc·u·late** MED impfen
**i·noc·u·la·tion** MED Impfung *f*
**in·of·fen·sive** harmlos
**in·op·e·ra·ble** MED inoperabel, nicht operierbar; undurchführbar (*plan etc*)
**in·op·por·tune** inopportun, unangebracht, ungelegen
**in·or·di·nate** unmäßig
**in·pa·tient** MED stationärer Patient, stationäre Patientin
**in·put** Input *m*, *n*, IT *a.* (Daten)Eingabe *f*, ELECTR *a.* Eingangsleistung *f*
**in·quest** JUR gerichtliche Untersuchung
**in·quire** fragen *or* sich erkundigen (nach); ***~ into*** *et.* untersuchen, prüfen
**in·quir·ing** forschend; wissbegierig
**in·quir·y** Erkundigung *f*, Nachfrage *f*; Untersuchung *f*; Ermittlung *f*; ***make inquiries*** Erkundigungen einziehen
**in·qui·si·tion** (amtliche) Untersuchung; Verhör *n*; ***Inquisition*** REL HIST Inquisition *f*
**in·quis·i·tive** neugierig, wissbegierig
**in·roads** (***in***[***to***], ***on***) Eingriff *m* (in *acc*), Übergriff *m* (auf *acc*)
**in·sane** geisteskrank, wahnsinnig
**in·san·i·ta·ry** unhygienisch
**in·san·i·ty** Geisteskrankheit *f*, Wahnsinn *m*
**in·sa·tia·ble** unersättlich
**in·scrip·tion** Inschrift *f*, Aufschrift *f*; Widmung *f*
**in·scru·ta·ble** unerforschlich, unergründlich
**in·sect** zo Insekt *n*; **in·sec·ti·cide** Insektenvertilgungsmittel *n*, Insektizid *n*
**in·se·cure** unsicher; nicht sicher *or* fest
**in·sen·si·ble** unempfindlich (***to*** gegen); bewusstlos; unempfänglich (***of, to*** für), gleichgültig (***of, to*** gegen); unmerklich
**in·sen·si·tive** unempfindlich (***to*** gegen); unempfänglich (***of, to*** für), gleichgültig (***of, to*** gegen)
**in·sep·a·ra·ble** untrennbar; unzertrennlich
**in·sert 1.** einfügen, einsetzen, einführen, (hinein)stecken, *Münze* einwerfen; inserieren **2.** (Zeitungs)Beilage *f*, (Buch)Einlage *f*
**in·ser·tion** Einfügen *n*, Einsetzen *n*, Einführen *n*, Hineinstecken *n*; Einfügung *f*; Einwurf *m*; Anzeige *f*, Inserat *n*
**in·sert key** IT Einfügetaste *f*
**in·shore** an *or* nahe der Küste; Küsten…

**in·side 1.** Innenseite *f*; *das* Innere; ***turn ~ out*** umkrempeln; auf den Kopf stellen **2.** *adj* innere(r, -s), Innen…; Insider… **3.** *adv* im Inner(e)n, innen, drinnen; ***~ of*** F innerhalb (*gen*) **4.** *prp* innerhalb, im Inner(e)n

**in·sid·er** Insider(in), Eingeweihte *m, f*

**in·sid·i·ous** heimtückisch

**in·sight** Einsicht *f*, Einblick *m*; Verständnis *n*

**in·sig·ni·a** Insignien *pl*; Abzeichen *pl*

**in·sig·nif·i·cant** bedeutungslos; unbedeutend

**in·sin·cere** unaufrichtig

**in·sin·u·ate** andeuten, anspielen auf (*acc*); unterstellen; ***~ that s.o. …*** j-m unterstellen, dass er …

**in·sin·u·a·tion** Anspielung *f*, Andeutung *f*, Unterstellung *f*

**in·sip·id** geschmacklos, fad

**in·sist** bestehen, beharren (***on*** auf *dat*)

**in·sis·tence** Bestehen *n*, Beharren *n*; Beharrlichkeit *f*

**in·sis·tent** beharrlich, hartnäckig

**in·sole** Einlegesohle *f*; Brandsohle *f*

**in·so·lent** unverschämt

**in·sol·u·ble** unlöslich (*substance etc*); unlösbar (*problem etc*)

**in·sol·vent** ECON zahlungsunfähig, insolvent

**in·som·ni·a** Schlaflosigkeit *f*

**in·spect** untersuchen, prüfen, nachsehen; besichtigen, inspizieren

**in·spec·tion** Prüfung *f*, Untersuchung *f*, Kontrolle *f*; Inspektion *f*

**in·spec·tor** Aufsichtsbeamte *m*, Inspektor *m*; (Polizei)Inspektor *m*, (Polizei)-Kommissar *m*

**in·spi·ra·tion** Inspiration *f*, (plötzlicher) Einfall; **in·spire** inspirieren, anregen; *Gefühl etc* auslösen

**in·stall** TECH installieren, einrichten, aufstellen, einbauen, *Leitung* legen; *j-n in ein Amt etc* einsetzen

**in·stal·la·tion** TECH Installation *f*, Einrichtung *f*, Einbau *m*; TECH *fertige* Anlage *f*; *fig* Einsetzung *f*, Einführung *f*

**in·stall·ment, in·stal·ment** *Br* ECON Rate *f*; (Teil)Lieferung *f*; Fortsetzung *f*; *radio*, TV Folge *f*

**in·stall·ment plan**: ***buy on the ~*** ECON auf Abzahlung *or* Raten kaufen

**in·stance** Beispiel *n*; (besonderer) Fall; JUR Instanz *f*; ***for ~*** zum Beispiel

**in·stant 1.** Moment *m*, Augenblick *m* **2.** sofortig, augenblicklich

**in·stan·ta·ne·ous** sofortig, augenblicklich; ***death was ~*** der Tod trat sofort ein

**in·stant| cam·e·ra** PHOT Sofortbildkamera *f*; **~ cof·fee** GASTR Pulver-, Instantkaffee *m*

**in·stant·ly** sofort, augenblicklich

**in·stead** stattdessen, dafür; ***~ of*** anstelle von, (an)statt

**in·step** ANAT Spann *m*, Rist *m*

**in·sti·gate** anstiften; aufhetzen; veranlassen; **in·sti·ga·tor** Anstifter(in); (Auf)Hetzer(in)

**in·stil** *Br*, **in·still** beibringen, einflößen (***into*** *dat*)

**in·stinct** Instinkt *m*

**in·stinc·tive** instinktiv

**in·sti·tute** Institut *n*

**in·sti·tu·tion** Institution *f*, Einrichtung *f*; Institut *n*; Anstalt *f*

**in·struct** unterrichten, -weisen; ausbilden, schulen; informieren; anweisen

**in·struc·tion** Unterricht *m*; Ausbildung *f*, Schulung *f*, Unterweisung *f*; Anweisung *f*, Instruktion *f*; IT Befehl *m*; ***~s for use*** Gebrauchsanweisung *f*; ***operating ~s*** Bedienungsanleitung *f*

**in·struc·tive** instruktiv, lehrreich

**in·struc·tor** Lehrer *m*; Ausbilder *m*

**in·struc·tress** Lehrerin *f*; Ausbilderin *f*

**in·stru·ment** Instrument *n* (*a.* MUS); Werkzeug *n* (*a. fig*)

**in·stru·men·tal** MUS Instrumental…; behilflich

**in·sub·or·di·nate** aufsässig

**in·sub·or·di·na·tion** Auflehnung *f*, Aufsässigkeit *f*

**in·suf·fe·ra·ble** unerträglich, unausstehlich

**in·suf·fi·cient** unzulänglich, ungenügend

**in·su·lar** Insel…; *fig* engstirnig

**in·su·late** isolieren; **in·su·la·tion** Isolierung *f*; Isoliermaterial *n*

**in·sult 1.** Beleidigung *f* **2.** beleidigen

**in·sur·ance** Versicherung *f*; Versicherungssumme *f*; Absicherung *f* (***against*** gegen); **~ com·pa·ny** Versicherungsgesellschaft *f*; **~ pol·i·cy** Versicherungspolice *f*

**in·sure** versichern (***against*** gegen)

**in·sured**: ***the ~*** der *or* die Versicherte

**in·sur·gent 1.** aufständisch **2.** Aufstän-

dische *m*, *f*
**in·sur·moun·ta·ble** *fig* unüberwindlich
**in·sur·rec·tion** Aufstand *m*
**in·tact** intakt, unversehrt, unbeschädigt, ganz
**in·take** (*Nahrungs- etc*)Aufnahme *f*; (Neu)Aufnahme(n *pl*) *f*, (Neu)Zugänge *pl*; TECH Einlass(öffnung *f*) *m*
**in·te·gral** ganz, vollständig; wesentlich
**in·te·grate** (sich) integrieren; zusammenschließen; eingliedern, einbeziehen; ***~d circuit*** ELECTR integrierter Schaltkreis
**in·te·gra·tion** Integration *f*
**in·teg·ri·ty** Integrität *f*; Vollständigkeit *f*; Einheit *f*
**in·tel·lect** Intellekt *m*, Verstand *m*
**in·tel·lec·tual** **1.** intellektuell, Verstandes…, geistig **2.** Intellektuelle *m*, *f*
**in·tel·li·gence** Intelligenz *f*; nachrichtendienstliche Informationen *pl*
**in·tel·li·gent** intelligent, klug
**in·tel·li·gi·ble** verständlich (***to*** für)
**in·tem·per·ate** unmäßig
**in·tend** beabsichtigen, vorhaben, planen; ***~ed for*** bestimmt für *or* zu
**in·tense** intensiv, stark, heftig
**in·ten·si·fy** intensivieren; (sich) verstärken
**in·ten·si·ty** Intensität *f*
**in·ten·sive** intensiv, gründlich; **~ care unit** MED Intensivstation *f*
**in·tent** **1.** gespannt, aufmerksam; ***~ on*** fest entschlossen zu (*dat*); konzentriert auf (*acc*) **2.** Absicht *f*, Vorhaben *n*
**in·ten·tion** Absicht *f*; JUR Vorsatz *m*
**in·ten·tion·al** absichtlich, vorsätzlich
**in·ter** bestatten
**in·ter…** zwischen, Zwischen…; gegenseitig, einander
**in·ter·act** aufeinander (ein)wirken, sich gegenseitig beeinflussen
**in·ter·ac·tion** Wechselwirkung *f*
**in·ter·cede** vermitteln, sich einsetzen (***with*** bei; ***for*** für)
**in·ter·cept** abfangen
**in·ter·ces·sion** Fürsprache *f*
**in·ter·change** **1.** austauschen **2.** Austausch *m*; MOT Autobahnkreuz *n*
**in·ter·com** Sprechanlage *f*
**in·ter·course** Verkehr *m*; *a.* ***sexual ~*** (Geschlechts)Verkehr *m*
**in·terest** **1.** Interesse *n* (***in*** an *dat*, für); Wichtigkeit *f*, Bedeutung *f*; Vorteil *m*, Nutzen *m*; ECON Anteil *m*, Beteiligung *f*; ECON Zins(en *pl*) *m*; ***take an ~ in*** sich interessieren für **2.** interessieren (***in*** für *et*); **in·terest·ed** interessiert (***in*** an *dat*); ***be ~ in*** sich interessieren für
**in·terest·ing** interessant
**in·terest rate** ECON Zinssatz *m*
**in·ter·face** IT Schnittstelle *f*
**in·ter·fere** sich einmischen (***with*** in *acc*); stören; **in·ter·fer·ence** Einmischung *f*; Störung *f*
**in·te·ri·or** **1.** innere(r, -s), Innen…; Binnen…; Inlands… **2.** *das* Innere; Interieur *n*; POL innere Angelegenheiten *pl*; → ***Department of the Interior***; **~ dec·o·ra·tor** Innenarchitekt(in)
**in·ter·ject** *Bemerkung* einwerfen
**in·ter·jec·tion** Einwurf *m*; Ausruf *m*; LING Interjektion *f*
**in·ter·lace** (sich) (ineinander) verflechten
**in·ter·lop·er** Eindringling *m*
**in·ter·lude** Zwischenspiel *n*; Pause *f*; ***~s of bright weather*** zeitweilig schön
**in·ter·me·di·a·ry** Vermittler(in), Mittelsmann *m*
**in·ter·me·di·ate** in der Mitte liegend, Mittel…, Zwischen…; PED für fortgeschrittene Anfänger
**in·ter·ment** Beerdigung *f*, Bestattung *f*
**in·ter·mi·na·ble** endlos
**in·ter·mis·sion** Unterbrechung *f*; THEA *etc* Pause *f*
**in·ter·mit·tent** mit Unterbrechungen, periodisch (auftretend); ***~ fever*** MED Wechselfieber *n*
**in·tern¹** internieren
**in·tern²** Assistenzarzt *m*, -ärztin *f*
**in·ter·nal** innere(r, -s); einheimisch, Inlands…
**in·ter·nal-com·bus·tion en·gine** Verbrennungsmotor *m*
**in·ter·na·tion·al** **1.** international; Auslands… **2.** SPORT Internationale *m*, *f*, Nationalspieler(in); internationaler Wettkampf; Länderspiel *n*; **~ call** TEL Auslandsgespräch *n*; **~ law** JUR Völkerrecht *n*
**In·ter·net** Internet *n*; **~ac·cess** Internetzugang *m*; **~ auc·tion** Internetauktion *f*; **~ caf·é** Internetcafé *n*; **~ con·nec·tion** Internetanschluss *m*
**in·tern·ist** MED Internist *m*
**in·ter·per·son·al** zwischenmenschlich

**in·ter·pret** interpretieren, auslegen, erklären; dolmetschen
**in·ter·pre·ta·tion** Interpretation *f*, Auslegung *f*
**in·ter·pret·er** Dolmetscher(in)
**in·ter·ro·gate** verhören, vernehmen; (be)fragen; **in·ter·ro·ga·tion** Verhör *n*, Vernehmung *f*; Frage *f*
**in·ter·rog·a·tive** LING Interrogativ..., Frage...
**in·ter·rupt** unterbrechen
**in·ter·rup·tion** Unterbrechung *f*
**in·ter·sect** (durch)schneiden; sich schneiden *or* kreuzen; **in·ter·sec·tion** Schnittpunkt *m*; (Straßen)Kreuzung *f*
**in·ter·sperse** einstreuen, hier und da einfügen
**in·ter·state** **1.** zwischenstaatlich **2.** *a.* ~ ***highway*** Autobahn *f*
**in·ter·twine** (sich ineinander) verschlingen, sich verflechten
**in·ter·val** Intervall *n* (*a.* MUS), Abstand *m*; *Br* Pause *f* (*a.* THEA *etc*); ***at regular ~s*** in regelmäßigen Abständen
**in·ter·vene** eingreifen, einschreiten, intervenieren; dazwischenkommen
**in·ter·ven·tion** Eingreifen *n*, Einschreiten *n*, Intervention *f*
**in·ter·view** **1.** Interview *n*; Einstellungsgespräch *n* **2.** interviewen; ein Einstellungsgespräch führen mit
**in·ter·view·ee** Interviewte *m*, *f*
**in·ter·view·er** Interviewer(in)
**in·ter·weave** (miteinander) verweben
**in·tes·tate**: ***die ~*** JUR ohne Hinterlassung e-s Testaments sterben
**in·tes·tine** ANAT Darm *m*; *pl* Eingeweide *pl*; ***large ~*** Dickdarm *m*; ***small ~*** Dünndarm *m*
**in·ti·ma·cy** Intimität *f*, Vertrautheit *f*; (*a. plumpe*) Vertraulichkeit; intime (*sexuelle*) Beziehungen *pl*
**in·ti·mate** **1.** intim (*a. sexually*); vertraut, eng (*friends etc*); (*a.* plump)vertraulich; innerste(r, -s); gründlich, genau (*knowledge etc*) **2.** Vertraute *m*, *f*
**in·tim·i·date** einschüchtern
**in·tim·i·da·tion** Einschüchterung *f*
**in·to** in (*acc*), in (*acc*) ... hinein; gegen (*acc*); MATH in (*acc*); ***4 ~ 20 goes five times*** 4 geht fünfmal in 20
**in·tol·e·ra·ble** unerträglich
**in·tol·e·rance** Intoleranz *f*, Unduldsamkeit (***of*** gegen)
**in·tol·e·rant** intolerant, unduldsam (***of*** gegen)
**in·to·na·tion** MUS Intonation *f*, LING *a.* Tonfall *m*
**in·tox·i·cat·ed** berauscht, betrunken
**in·tox·i·ca·tion** Rausch *m* (*a. fig*)
**in·trac·ta·ble** eigensinnig; schwer zu handhaben(d)
**in·tran·si·tive** LING intransitiv
**in·tra·ve·nous** MED intravenös
**in tray**: ***in the ~*** im Posteingang *etc*
**in·trep·id** unerschrocken
**in·tri·cate** verwickelt, kompliziert
**in·trigue** **1.** Intrige *f* **2.** faszinieren, interessieren; intrigieren
**in·tro·duce** vorstellen (***to*** *dat*), *j-n* bekannt machen (***to*** mit); einführen
**in·tro·duc·tion** Vorstellung *f*; Einführung *f*; Einleitung *f*, Vorwort *n*; ***letter of ~*** Empfehlungsschreiben *n*
**in·tro·duc·to·ry** Einführungs...; einleitend, Einleitungs...
**in·tro·spec·tion** Selbstbeobachtung *f*
**in·tro·vert** PSYCH introvertierter Mensch; **in·tro·vert·ed** PSYCH introvertiert, in sich gekehrt
**in·trude** (sich) aufdrängen; stören; ***am I intruding?*** störe ich?; **in·trud·er** Eindringling *m*, Störenfried *m*
**in·tru·sion** Störung *f*
**in·tru·sive** aufdringlich
**in·tu·i·tion** Intuition *f*
**in·tu·i·tive** intuitiv
**In·u·it** *a.* ***Innuit*** Inuit *m*, Eskimo *m*
**in·un·date** überschwemmen, überfluten (*a. fig*)
**in·vade** eindringen in (*acc*), einfallen in (*acc*), MIL *a.* einmarschieren in (*acc*); *fig* überlaufen, überschwemmen
**in·vad·er** Eindringling *m*
**in·va·lid**[1] **1.** krank; invalid(e) **2.** Kranke *m*; *f*; Invalide *m*, *f*
**in·val·id**[2] (rechts)ungültig
**in·val·i·date** JUR für ungültig erkären
**in·val·u·a·ble** *fig* unschätzbar, unbezahlbar
**in·var·i·a·ble** unveränderlich
**in·var·i·a·bly** ausnahmslos
**in·va·sion** Invasion *f* (*a.* MIL), Einfall *m*, MIL *a.* Einmarsch *m*; *fig* Eingriff *m*, Verletzung *f*
**in·vec·tive** Schmähung(en *pl*) *f*, Beschimpfung(en *pl*) *f*
**in·vent** erfinden

I

**in·ven·tion** Erfindung *f*
**in·ven·tive** erfinderisch; einfallsreich
**in·ven·tor** Erfinder(in)
**in·ven·tory** Inventar *n*, Bestand *m*; Bestandsliste *f*; Inventur *f*
**in·verse 1.** umgekehrt **2.** Umkehrung *f*, Gegenteil *n*; **in·ver·sion** Umkehrung *f*; LING Inversion *f*; **in·vert** umkehren
**in·ver·te·brate** ZO **1.** wirbellos **2.** wirbelloses Tier
**in·vert·ed com·mas** LING Anführungszeichen *pl*
**in·vest** ECON investieren, anlegen
**in·ves·ti·gate** untersuchen; überprüfen; Untersuchungen *or* Ermittlungen anstellen (***into*** über *acc*), nachforschen
**in·ves·ti·ga·tion** Untersuchung *f*; Ermittlung *f*, Nachforschung *f*
**in·ves·ti·ga·tor**: ***private ~*** Privatdetektiv *m*
**in·vest·ment** ECON Investition *f*, (Kapital)Anlage *f*
**in·ves·tor** ECON Anleger *m*
**in·vet·e·rate** unverbesserlich; hartnäckig
**in·vid·i·ous** gehässig, boshaft, gemein
**in·vig·o·rate** stärken, beleben
**in·vin·ci·ble** unbesiegbar; unüberwindlich
**in·vi·o·la·ble** unantastbar
**in·vis·i·ble** unsichtbar
**in·vi·ta·tion** Einladung *f*; Aufforderung *f*
**in·vite** einladen; auffordern; *Gefahr etc* herausfordern; ***~ s.o. in*** j-n hereinbitten; **in·vit·ing** einladend, verlockend
**in·voice** ECON **1.** (Waren)Rechnung *f* **2.** in Rechnung stellen, berechnen
**in·voke** flehen um; *Gott etc* anrufen; beschwören
**in·vol·un·ta·ry** unfreiwillig; unabsichtlich; unwillkürlich
**in·volve** verwickeln, hineinziehen (***in*** in *acc*); *j-n, et.* angehen, betreffen; zur Folge haben, mit sich bringen
**in·volved** kompliziert, verworren
**in·volve·ment** Verwicklung *f*; Beteiligung *f*
**in·vul·ne·ra·ble** unverwundbar; *fig* unanfechtbar
**in·ward 1.** *adj* innere(r, -s), innerlich **2.** *adv mst* ***~s*** einwärts, nach innen
**i·o·dine** CHEM Jod *n*
**i·on** PHYS Ion *n*
**IOU** (= ***I owe you***) Schuldschein *m*
**IQ** *abbr of* ***intelligence quotient*** IQ, Intelligenzquotient *m*
**I·ran** Iran *m*; **I·ra·ni·an 1.** iranisch **2.** Iraner(in); LING Iranisch *n*
**I·raq** Irak *m*; **I·ra·qi 1.** irakisch **2.** Iraker(in); LING Irakisch *n*
**i·ras·ci·ble** jähzornig
**i·rate** zornig, wütend
**Ire·land** Irland *n*
**ir·i·des·cent** schillernd
**i·ris** ANAT Regenbogenhaut *f*, Iris *f*; BOT Schwertlilie *f*, Iris *f*
**I·rish 1.** irisch **2.** LING Irisch *n*; ***the ~*** die Iren *pl*
**I·rish·man** Ire *m*
**I·rish·wom·an** Irin *f*
**i·ron 1.** Eisen *n*; Bügeleisen *n*; ***strike while the ~ is hot*** *fig* das Eisen schmieden, solange es heiß ist **2.** eisern (*a. fig*), Eisen…, aus Eisen **3.** bügeln; ***~ out*** ausbügeln
**I·ron Cur·tain** POL HIST Eiserner Vorhang
**i·ron·ic, i·ron·i·cal** ironisch, spöttisch
**i·ron·ing board** Bügelbrett *n*
**i·ron·mon·ger** *Br* Eisenwarenhändler *m*
**i·ron·works** TECH Eisenhütte *f*
**i·ron·y** Ironie *f*
**ir·ra·tion·al** irrational, unvernünftig
**ir·rec·on·ci·la·ble** unversöhnlich; unvereinbar
**ir·re·cov·e·ra·ble** unersetzlich; unwiederbringlich
**ir·re·fut·a·ble** unwiderlegbar
**ir·reg·u·lar** unregelmäßig; ungleichmäßig; regelwidrig, vorschriftswidrig
**ir·rel·e·vant** irrelevant, unerheblich, belanglos (***to*** für)
**ir·rep·a·ra·ble** irreparabel, nicht wieder gutzumachen(d)
**ir·re·place·a·ble** unersetzlich
**ir·re·pres·si·ble** nicht zu unterdrücken(d); unbezähmbar
**ir·re·proach·a·ble** einwandfrei, untadelig
**ir·re·sist·i·ble** unwiderstehlich
**ir·res·o·lute** unentschlossen
**ir·re·spec·tive**: ***~ of*** ohne Rücksicht auf (*acc*); unabhängig von
**ir·re·spon·si·ble** unverantwortlich; verantwortungslos
**ir·re·trie·va·ble** unwiederbringlich, unersetzlich
**ir·rev·e·rent** respektlos

**ir·rev·o·ca·ble** unwiderruflich, endgültig
**ir·ri·gate** bewässern
**ir·ri·ga·tion** Bewässerung *f*
**ir·ri·ta·ble** reizbar
**ir·ri·tant** Reizmittel *n*
**ir·ri·tate** reizen; (ver)ärgern
**ir·ri·tat·ing** ärgerlich
**ir·ri·ta·tion** Reizung *f*; Verärgerung *f*; Ärger *m* (***at*** über *acc*)
**is** *er, sie, es* ist
**Is·lam** der Islam
**is·land** Insel *f*; *a.* ***traffic ~*** Verkehrsinsel *f*; **is·land·er** Inselbewohner(in)
**isle** POET Insel *f*
**i·so·late** absondern; isolieren
**i·so·lat·ed** isoliert, abgeschieden; einzeln; ***become ~*** vereinsamen
**i·so·la·tion** Isolierung *f*, Absonderung *f*; ***~ ward*** MED Isolierstation *f*
**Is·rael** Israel *n*
**Is·rae·li** **1.** israelisch **2.** Israeli *m, f*
**is·sue** **1.** Streitfrage *f*, Streitpunkt *m*; Ausgabe *f*; Erscheinen *n*; JUR Nachkommen(schaft *f*) *pl*; *fig* Ausgang *m*, Ergebnis *n*; ***be at ~*** zur Debatte stehen; ***point at ~*** strittiger Punkt **2.** *v/t Zeitung etc* herausgeben; *Banknoten etc* ausgeben; *Dokument etc* ausstellen; *v/i* herauskommen, hervorkommen; herausfließen, herausströmen
**it** es; *s.th. previously mentioned*: es, er, ihn, sie
**I·tal·i·an** **1.** italienisch **2.** Italiener(in); LING Italienisch *n*
**i·tal·ics** PRINT Kursivschrift *f*
**It·a·ly** Italien *n*
**itch** **1.** Jucken *n*, Juckreiz *m* **2.** jucken, kratzen; ***I ~ all over*** es juckt mich überall; ***be ~ing for s.th.*** F et. unbedingt (haben) wollen; ***be ~ing to*** *inf* F darauf brennen zu *inf*
**itch·y** juckend; kratzend
**i·tem** Punkt *m* (*on the agenda etc*), Posten *m* (*on a list*); Artikel *m*, Gegenstand *m*; (*Presse-, Zeitungs*)Notiz *f*, (*a. radio*, TV) Nachricht *f*, Meldung *f*
**i·tem·ize** einzeln angeben *or* aufführen
**i·tin·e·ra·ry** Reiseweg *m*, Reiseroute *f*; Reiseplan *m*
**its** sein(e), ihr(e)
**it·self** sich; sich selbst; selbst; ***by ~*** (für sich) allein; von selbst; ***in ~*** an sich
**i·vo·ry** Elfenbein *n*
**i·vy** BOT Efeu *m*

# J

**J, j** J, j *n*
**jab** **1.** (hinein)stechen, (hinein)stoßen **2.** Stich *m*, Stoß *m*
**jab·ber** F (daher)plappern
**jack** **1.** TECH Hebevorrichtung *f*; MOT Wagenheber *m*; *cards*: Bube *m* **2.** ***~ up*** *Auto* aufbocken
**jack·al** ZO Schakal *m*
**jack·ass** ZO Esel *m* (*a. fig*)
**jack·daw** ZO Dohle *f*
**jack·et** Jacke *f*, Jackett *n*; TECH Mantel *m*; (Schutz)Umschlag *m*; (*Platten*)Hülle *f*; ***~ potatoes, potatoes (boiled) in their ~s*** Pellkartoffeln *pl*
**jack knife** **1.** Klappmesser *n* **2.** zusammenklappen, zusammenknicken
**jack-of-all-trades** Hansdampf *m* in allen Gassen
**jack·pot** Jackpot *m*, Hauptteffer *m*; ***hit the ~*** F den Jackpot gewinnen; *fig* das große Los ziehen
**jade** MIN Jade *m, f*; Jadegrün *n*
**jag** Zacken *m*
**jag·ged** gezackt, zackig; schartig
**jag·u·ar** ZO Jaguar *m*
**jail** **1.** Gefängnis *n* **2.** einsperren
**jail·bird** F Knastbruder *m*
**jail·er** Gefängnisaufseher *m*
**jail·house** Gefängnis *n*
**jam**[1] Konfitüre *f*, Marmelade *f*
**jam**[2] **1.** *v/t* (hinein)pressen, (hinein-) quetschen, (hinein)zwängen, *Menschen a.* (hinein)pferchen; (ein)klemmen, (ein)quetschen; *a.* ***~ up*** blockieren, verstopfen; *Funkempfang* stören; ***~ on the brakes*** MOT voll auf die Bremse treten; *v/i* sich (hinein)drängen *or* (hinein-) quetschen; TECH sich verklemmen, *brake*: blockieren **2.** Gedränge *n*; TECH Blockierung *f*; Stauung

*f*, Stockung *f*; ***traffic ~*** Verkehrsstau *m*; ***be in a ~*** F in der Klemme stecken
**jamb** (Tür-, Fenster)Pfosten *m*
**jam·bo·ree** Jamboree *n*, Pfadfindertreffen *n*; Fest *n*
**Jan** *abbr of* ***January*** Jan., Januar *m*
**jan·gle** klimpern *or* klirren (mit)
**jan·i·tor** Hausmeister *m*
**Jan·u·a·ry** (ABBR *of* ***Jan***) Januar *m*
**Ja·pan** Japan *n*; **Jap·a·nese 1.** japanisch **2.** Japaner(in); LING Japanisch *n*; ***the ~*** die Japaner *pl*
**jar**[1] Gefäß *n*, Krug *m*; (Marmelade- *etc*)-Glas *n*
**jar**[2]: ***~ on*** wehtun (*dat*)
**jar·gon** Jargon *m*, Fachsprache *f*
**jaun·dice** MED Gelbsucht *f*
**jaunt 1.** Ausflug *m*, MOT Spritztour *f* **2.** e-n Ausflug *or* e-e Spritztour machen
**jaun·ty** unbeschwert, unbekümmert; flott
**jav·e·lin** SPORT Speer *m*; ***~ (throw)***, ***throwing the ~*** SPORT Speerwerfen *n*
**jav·e·lin throw·er** SPORT Speerwerfer(in)
**jaw** ANAT Kiefer *m*; *pl* ZO Rachen *m*, Maul *n*; TECH Backen *pl*; ***lower ~*** ANAT Unterkiefer *m*; ***upper ~*** ANAT Oberkiefer; **jaw·bone** ANAT Kieferknochen *m*
**jay** ZO Eichelhäher *m*
**jay·walk·er** unachtsamer Fußgänger
**jazz** MUS Jazz *m*
**jazz·y** F poppig
**jeal·ous** eifersüchtig (***of*** auf acc); neidisch; **jeal·ous·y** Eifersucht *f*; Neid *m*
**jeans** Jeans *pl*
**jeer 1.** (***at***) höhnische Bemerkung(en) machen (über *acc*); höhnisch lachen (über *acc*); ***~ (at)*** verhöhnen **2.** höhnische Bemerkung; Hohngelächter *n*
**jel·lied** GASTR in Aspik, in Sülze
**jel·ly** Gallert(e *f*) *n*; GASTR Gelee *n*; Aspik *m*, *n*, Sülze *f*; Götterspeise *f*; ***~ baby*** *Br* Gummibärchen *n*; ***~ bean*** Gummi-, Geleebonbon *m*, *n*
**jel·ly·fish** ZO Qualle *f*
**jeop·ar·dize** gefährden
**jerk 1.** ruckartig ziehen an (*dat*); (zusammen)zucken; sich ruckartig bewegen **2.** (plötzlicher) Ruck; Sprung *m*, Satz *m*; MED Zuckung *f*
**jerk·y** ruckartig; holprig; rüttelnd
**jer·sey** Pullover *m*
**jest 1.** Scherz *m*, Spaß *m* **2.** scherzen, spaßen; **jest·er** HIST (Hof)Narr *m*
**jet 1.** (Wasser-, Gas- *etc*)Strahl *m*; TECH Düse *f*; AVIAT Jet *m* **2.** (heraus-, hervor)-schießen (***from*** aus); AVIAT F jetten; ***~ en·gine*** AVIAT Düsen-, Strahltriebwerk *n*; ***~ plane*** AVIAT Düsenflugzeug *n*, Jet *m*
**jet-pro·pelled** AVIAT mit Düsenantrieb, Düsen…
**jet pro·pul·sion** AVIAT Düsen-, Strahlantrieb *m*
**jet·ty** MAR (Hafen)Mole *f*
**Jew** Jude *m*, Jüdin *f*
**jew·el** Juwel *n*, *m*, Edelstein *m*
**jew·el·er**, *Br* **jew·el·ler** Juwelier *m*
**jew·el·lery** *Br*, **jew·el·ry** Juwelen *pl*; Schmuck *m*
**Jew·ess** Jüdin *f*
**Jew·ish** jüdisch
**jif·fy**: F ***in a ~*** im Nu, sofort
**jig·saw** Laubsäge *f*; → **jig·saw puz·zle** Puzzle(spiel) *n*
**jin·gle 1.** klimpern (mit), bimmeln (lassen) **2.** Klimpern *n*, Bimmeln *n*; Werbesong *m*, Werbespruch *m*
**jit·ters**: F ***the ~*** Bammel *m*, e-e Heidenangst; **jit·ter·y** F nervös; ängstlich
**job 1.** (*einzelne*) Arbeit; Beruf *m*, Beschäftigung *f*, Stellung *f*, Stelle *f*, Arbeit *f*, Job *m* (*a.* IT); Arbeitsplatz *m*; Aufgabe *f*, Sache *f*, Angelegenheit *f*; *a.* ***~ work*** Akkordarbeit *f*; ***by the ~*** im Akkord; ***out of a ~*** arbeitslos **2.** ***~ around*** jobben; ***~ ad***, ***~ ad·ver·tisement*** Stellenanzeige *f*
**job·ber** *Br* ECON Börsenspekulant *m*
**job cen·tre** *Br* Arbeitsamt *n*
**job hop·ping** häufiger Arbeitsplatzwechsel
**job·hunt·ing** Arbeitssuche *f*; ***be ~*** auf Arbeitssuche sein
**job·less** arbeitslos
**jock·ey** Jockei *m*
**jog 1.** stoßen an (*acc*) *or* gegen, *j-n* anstoßen; *mst* ***~ along, ~ on*** dahintrotten, dahinzuckeln; SPORT joggen **2.** (leichter) Stoß, Stups *m*; Trott *m*; SPORT Trimmtrab *m*
**jog·ger** SPORT Jogger(in)
**jog·ging** SPORT Joggen *n*, Jogging *n*
**join 1.** *v/t* verbinden, vereinigen, zusammenfügen; sich anschließen (*dat or* an *acc*), sich gesellen zu; eintreten in (*acc*), beitreten; teilnehmen *or* sich beteiligen an (*dat*), mitmachen bei; ***~ in*** ein-

stimmen in; *v/i* sich vereinigen *or* verbinden; ~ ***in*** teilnehmen *or* sich beteiligen (an *dat*), mitmachen (bei) **2.** Verbindungsstelle *f*, Naht *f*

**join·er** Tischler *m*, Schreiner *m*

**joint 1.** Verbindungs-, Nahtstelle *f*; ANAT, TECH Gelenk *n*; BOT Knoten *m*; *Br* GASTR Braten *m*; F Laden *m*; Bude *f*, Spelunke *f*; *sl* Joint *m*; ***out of*** ~ MED ausgerenkt; *fig* aus den Fugen **2.** gemeinsam, gemeinschaftlich; Mit…

**joint·ed** gegliedert; Glieder…

**joint-stock com·pa·ny** *Br* ECON Kapital- *or* Aktiengesellschaft *f*

**joint ven·ture** ECON Gemeinschaftsunternehmen *n*

**joke 1.** Witz *m*; Scherz *m*, Spaß *m*; ***practical*** ~ Streich *m*; ***play a ~ on s.o.*** j-m e-n Streich spielen **2.** scherzen, Witze machen; **jok·er** Spaßvogel *m*, Witzbold *m*; *cards*: Joker *m*

**jol·ly 1.** *adj* lustig, fröhlich, vergnügt **2.** *adv Br* F ganz schön; ~ ***good*** prima

**jolt 1.** e-n Ruck *or* Stoß geben; durchrütteln, durchschütteln; rütteln, holpern (*vehicle*); *fig* aufrütteln **2.** Ruck *m*, Stoß *m*; *fig* Schock *m*

**joss stick** Räucherstäbchen *n*

**jos·tle** (an)rempeln; dränge(l)n

**jot 1.** ***not a*** ~ keine Spur **2.** ~ ***down*** sich schnell *et.* notieren

**joule** PHYS Joule *n*

**jour·nal** Journal *n*; (Fach)Zeitschrift *f*; Tagebuch *n*

**jour·nal·ism** Journalismus *m*

**jour·nal·ist** Journalist(in)

**jour·ney 1.** Reise *f* **2.** reisen

**jour·ney·man** Geselle *m*

**joy** Freude *f*; ***for*** ~ vor Freude

**joy·ful** freudig; erfreut

**joy·less** freudlos, traurig

**joy·stick** AVIAT Steuerknüppel *m*; IT Joystick *m*

**jub·i·lant** jubelnd, überglücklich

**ju·bi·lee** Jubiläum *n*

**judge 1.** JUR Richter(in); SPORT Kampf-, Schieds-, Preisrichter(in); *fig* Kenner(in) **2.** JUR *Fall* verhandeln; urteilen, ein Urteil fällen; beurteilen, einschätzen

**judg·ment** JUR Urteil *n*; Urteilsvermögen *n*; Meinung *f*, Ansicht *f*; göttliches (Straf)Gericht; ***the Last Judgment*** REL das Jüngste Gericht

**Judgment Day**, *a.* ***Day of Judgment*** REL Tag *m* des Jüngsten Gerichts, Jüngster Tag

**ju·di·cial** JUR gerichtlich, Justiz…; richterlich

**ju·di·cia·ry** JUR Richter *pl*

**ju·di·cious** klug, weise

**ju·do** SPORT Judo *n*

**jug** Krug *m*; Kanne *f*, Kännchen *n*

**jug·gle** jonglieren (mit); ECON *Bücher etc* frisieren; **jug·gler** Jongleur *m*

**juice** Saft *m*; MOT F Sprit *m*

**juic·y** saftig; F pikant (*story etc*); F gepfeffert (*price etc*)

**juke·box** Musikbox *f*, Musikautomat *m*

**Jul** *abbr of* ***July*** Juli *m*

**Ju·ly** (*abbr* ***Jul***) Juli *m*

**jum·ble 1.** *a.* ~ ***together***, ~ ***up*** durcheinanderbringen *or* durcheinanderwerfen **2.** Durcheinander *n*; ~ **sale** *Br* Wohltätigkeitsbasar *m*

**jum·bo 1.** riesig, Riesen… **2.** AVIAT F Jumbo *m*; ~ **jet** AVIAT Jumbo-Jet *m*

**jum·bo-sized** riesig

**jump 1.** *v/i* springen; hüpfen; zusammenzucken, -fahren, hochfahren (***at*** bei); ~ ***at the chance*** mit beiden Händen zugreifen; ~ ***to conclusions*** voreilige Schlüsse ziehen; *v/t* (hinweg)springen über (*acc*); überspringen; ~ ***the queue*** *Br* sich vordränge(l)n; ~ ***the lights*** bei Rot über die Kreuzung fahren **2.** Sprung *m*

**jump·er**[1] SPORT (*Hoch- etc*)Springer(in)

**jump·er**[2] Trägerrock *m*, Trägerkleid *n*; *Br* Pullover *m*

**jump·ing jack** Hampelmann *m*

**jump·y** nervös

**Jun** *abbr of* ***June*** Juni *m*

**junc·tion** (Straßen)Kreuzung *f*; RAIL Knotenpunkt *m*

**junc·ture**: ***at this*** ~ zu diesem Zeitpunkt

**June** (*abbr* ***Jun***) Juni *m*

**jun·gle** Dschungel *m*

**ju·ni·or 1.** junior; jüngere(r, -s); untergeordnet; SPORT Junioren…, Jugend… **2.** Jüngere *m, f*; ~ **school** *Br* Grundschule *f* (*for children aged 7 to 11*)

**junk**[1] MAR Dschunke *f*

**junk**[2] F Trödel *m*; Schrott *m*; Abfall *m*; *sl* Stoff *m*

**junk food** F Junk-Food *n*

**junk·ie**, **junk·y** *sl* Junkie *m*, Fixer(in)

**junk·yard** Schuttabladeplatz *m*;

J

Schrottplatz *m*
**jur·is·dic·tion** JUR Gerichtsbarkeit *f*; Zuständigkeit(sbereich *m*) *f*
**ju·ris·pru·dence** Rechtswissenschaft *f*
**ju·ror** JUR Geschworene *m, f*
**ju·ry** JUR *die* Geschworenen *pl*; SPORT *etc* Jury *f*, Preisrichter *pl*
**ju·ry·man** JUR Geschworene *m*
**ju·ry·wom·an** JUR Geschworene *f*
**just 1.** *adj* gerecht; berechtigt; angemessen **2.** *adv* gerade, (so)eben; genau, eben; gerade (noch), ganz knapp; nur, bloß; **~ *about*** ungefähr, etwa; **~ *like that*** einfach so; **~ *now*** gerade (jetzt), (so)eben
**jus·tice** Gerechtigkeit *f*; JUR Richter *m*; ***Justice of the Peace*** Friedensrichter *m*; ***court of ~*** Gericht *n*, Gerichtshof *m*
**jus·ti·fi·ca·tion** Rechtfertigung *f*
**jus·ti·fy** rechtfertigen
**just·ly** mit *or* zu Recht
**jut**: **~ *out*** vorspringen, herausragen
**ju·ve·nile 1.** jugendlich; Jugend… **2.** Jugendliche *m, f*; **~ court** JUR Jugendgericht *n*; **~ de·lin·quen·cy** JUR Jugendkriminalität *f*; **~ de·lin·quent** JUR straffälliger Jugendlicher, jugendlicher Straftäter

# K

**K, k** K, k *n*
**kan·ga·roo** ZO Känguru *n*
**ka·ra·te** SPORT Karate *n*
**keel** MAR **1.** Kiel *m* **2. ~ *over*** umschlagen, kentern
**keen** scharf (*a. fig*); schneidend (*cold*); heftig, stark; lebhaft (*interest*); groß (*appetite etc*); begeistert, leidenschaftlich; **~ *on*** versessen *or* scharf auf (*acc*)
**keep 1.** *v/t* (auf-, fest-, zurück)halten; (bei)behalten, bewahren; *Gesetze etc* einhalten, befolgen; *Ware* führen; *Geheimnis* für sich behalten; *Versprechen, Wort* halten; ECON *Buch* führen; aufheben, aufbewahren; abhalten, hindern (***from*** von); *Tiere* halten; *Bett* hüten; ernähren, erhalten, unterhalten; **~ *early hours*** früh zu Bett gehen; **~ *one's head*** die Ruhe bewahren; **~ *one's temper*** sich beherrschen; **~ *s.o. company*** j-m Gesellschaft leisten; **~ *s.th. from s.o.*** j-m et. vorenthalten *or* verschweigen *or* verheimlichen; **~ *time*** richtig gehen (*watch*); MUS Takt halten; *v/i* bleiben; sich halten; **~ *going*** weitergehen; **~ *smiling*** immer nur lächeln!; **~ (*on*) *talking*** weitersprechen; **~ (*on*) *trying*** es weiterversuchen, es immer wieder versuchen; **~ *s.o. waiting*** j-n warten lassen; **~ *away*** (sich) fernhalten (***from*** von); **~ *back*** zurückhalten (*a. fig*); **~ *from doing s.th.*** et. nicht tun; **~ *in*** *Schüler(in)* nachsitzen lassen; **~ *off*** (sich) fern halten; **~ *off!*** Betreten verboten!; **~ *on*** *Kleidungsstück* anbehalten, anlassen, *Hut* aufbehalten; *Licht* brennen lassen; ***keep on doing*** fortfahren zu tun; **~ *out*** nicht hinein- *or* hereinlassen; **~ *out!*** Zutritt verboten!; **~ *to*** sich halten an (*acc*); **~ *up*** *fig* aufrechterhalten; *Mut* nicht sinken lassen; fortfahren mit, weitermachen; **~ *s.o. up*** j-n nicht schlafen lassen; **~ *it up*** so weitermachen; **~ *up with*** Schritt halten mit; **~ *up with the Joneses*** nicht hinter den Nachbarn zurückstehen (wollen) **2.** (Lebens)Unterhalt *m*; ***for ~s*** F für immer
**keep·er** Wärter(in), Wächter(in), Aufseher(in); *mst in cpds*: Inhaber(in), Besitzer(in); **keep·ing** Verwahrung *f*; Obhut *f*; ***be in*** (***out of***) **~ *with …*** (nicht) übereinstimmen mit …
**keep·sake** Andenken *n*
**keg** Fässchen *n*, kleines Fass
**ken·nel** Hundehütte *f*; **~s** Hundezwinger *m*; Hundepension *f*
**kerb** *Br* → ***curb***
**ker·chief** (Hals-, Kopf)Tuch *n*
**ker·nel** BOT Kern *m* (*a. fig*)
**ker·o·sene** Petroleum *n*
**ket·tle** Kessel *m*
**ket·tle·drum** MUS (Kessel)Pauke *f*
**key 1.** Schlüssel *m* (*a. fig*); (*Schreibmaschinen-, Klavier- etc*)Taste *f*; MUS Tonart *f* **2.** Schlüssel… **3.** anpassen (***to*** an *acc*); **~ *in*** IT *Daten* eingeben; **~*ed up*** nervös, aufgeregt, überdreht

**key·board** Tastatur *f*
**key·hole** Schlüsselloch *n*
**key·note** MUS Grundton *m*; *fig* Grundgedanke *m*, Tenor *m*
**key ring** Schlüsselring *m*
**key·stone** ARCH Schlussstein *m*; *fig* Grundpfeiler *m*
**key·word** Schlüssel-, Stichwort *n*
**kick 1.** (mit dem Fuß) stoßen, treten, e-n Tritt geben *or* versetzen (*dat*); *soccer*: schießen, treten, kicken; strampeln; ausschlagen (*horse*); *~ off* von sich schleudern; *soccer*: anstoßen; *~ out* F rausschmeißen; *~ up* hochschleudern; *~ up a fuss or row* F Krach schlagen **2.** (Fuß)Tritt *m*; Stoß *m*; *soccer*: Schuss *m*; *free ~* Freistoß *m*; *for ~s* F zum Spaß; *they get a ~ out of it* es macht ihnen e-n Riesenspaß
**kick·off** *soccer*: Anstoß *m*
**kick·out** *soccer*: Abschlag *m*
**kid**[1] ZO Zicklein *n*, Kitz *n*; Ziegenleder *n*; F Kind *n*; *~ brother* F kleiner Bruder
**kid**[2] *v/t j-n* auf den Arm nehmen; *~ s.o.* j-m et. vormachen; *v/i* Spaß machen; *he is only ~ding* er macht ja nur Spaß; *no ~ding!* im Ernst!
**kid gloves** Glacéhandschuhe *pl* (*a. fig*)
**kid·nap** entführen, kidnappen
**kid·nap·(p)er** Entführer(in), Kidnapper(in)
**kid·nap·(p)ing** Entführung *f*, Kidnapping *n*
**kid·ney** ANAT Niere *f*; *~* **bean** BOT Kidneybohne *f*, rote Bohne; *~* **ma·chine** MED künstliche Niere
**kill** töten (*a. fig*), umbringen, ermorden; vernichten; ZO schlachten; HUNT erlegen, schießen; *be ~ed in an accident* tödlich verunglücken; *~ time* die Zeit totschlagen; **kill·er** Mörder(in), Killer(in); **kill·ing** mörderisch, tödlich
**kill·joy** Spielverderber *m*
**kiln** TECH Brennofen *m*
**ki·lo** F Kilo *n*
**kil·o·gram(me)** Kilogramm *n*
**kil·o·me·ter**, *Br* **kil·o·me·tre** Kilometer *m*
**kilt** Kilt *m*, Schottenrock *m*
**kin** Verwandtschaft *f*, Verwandte *pl*; *next of ~ der, die* nächste Verwandte, *die* nächsten Angehörigen *pl*
**kind**[1] freundlich, liebenswürdig, nett; herzlich
**kind**[2] Art *f*, Sorte *f*; Wesen *n*; *all ~s of* alle möglichen, allerlei; *nothing of the ~* nichts dergleichen; *~ of* F ein bisschen
**kin·der·gar·ten** Kindergarten *m*
**kind-heart·ed** gütig
**kin·dle** anzünden, (sich) entzünden; *Interesse etc* wecken
**kind·ly 1.** *adj* freundlich, liebenswürdig, nett **2.** *adv* → 1; freundlicherweise, liebenswürdigerweise, netterweise
**kind·ness** Freundlichkeit *f*, Liebenswürdigkeit *f*; Gefälligkeit *f*
**kin·dred** verwandt; *~ spirits* Gleichgesinnte *pl*
**king** König *m*
**king·dom** Königreich *n*; REL Reich *n* Gottes; *fig* Reich *n*; *animal ~* Tierreich *n*; *vegetable ~* Pflanzenreich *n*
**king·ly** königlich
**king-size(d)** Riesen…
**kink** Knick *m*; *fig* Tick *m*, Spleen *m*
**kink·y** spleenig; pervers
**ki·osk** Kiosk *m*; *Br* Telefonzelle *f*
**kip·per** GASTR Räucherhering *m*
**kiss 1.** Kuss *m* **2.** (sich) küssen
**kit** Ausrüstung *f*; Arbeitsgerät *n*, Werkzeug(e *pl*) *n*; Werkzeugtasche *f*, -kasten *m*; Bastelsatz *m*; **kit bag** Seesack *m*
**kitch·en 1.** Küche *f* **2.** Küchen…
**kitch·en·ette** Kleinküche *f*, Kochnische *f*
**kitch·en gar·den** Küchen-, Gemüsegarten *m*
**kite** Drachen *m*; ZO Milan *m*; *fly a ~* e-n Drachen steigen lassen
**kit·ten** ZO Kätzchen *n*
**knack** Kniff *m*, Trick *m*, F Dreh *m*; Geschick *n*, Talent *n*
**knave** *card games*: Bube *m*, Unter *m*
**knead** kneten; massieren
**knee** ANAT Knie *n*; TECH Knie(stück) *n*
**knee·cap** ANAT Kniescheibe *f*
**knee-deep** knietief, bis an die Knie (reichend)
**knee joint** ANAT Kniegelenk *n* (*a.* TECH)
**kneel** knien (*to* vor *dat*)
**knee-length** knielang
**knell** Totenglocke *f*
**knick·er·bock·ers** Knickerbocker *pl*, Kniehosen *pl*
**knick·ers** *Br* F (Damen)Schlüpfer *m*
**knick-knack** Nippsache *f*
**knife 1.** Messer *n* **2.** mit e-m Messer ste-

K

chen *or* verletzen; erstechen

**knight** 1. Ritter *m*; *chess*: Springer *m* 2. zum Ritter schlagen

**knight·hood** Ritterwürde *f*, -stand *m*

**knit** *v/t* stricken; *a.* ~ ***together*** zusammenfügen, verbinden; ~ ***one's brows*** die Stirn runzeln; *v/i* stricken; MED zusammenwachsen

**knit·ting** 1. Stricken *n*; Strickzeug *n* 2. Strick...; ~ **nee·dle** Stricknadel *f*

**knit·wear** Strickwaren *pl*

**knob** Knopf *m*, Knauf *m*, *runder* Griff; GASTR Stück(chen) *n*

**knock** 1. schlagen, stoßen; pochen, klopfen; ~ ***at the door*** an die Tür klopfen; ~ ***about***, ~ ***around*** herumstoßen; F sich herumtreiben; F herumliegen; ~ ***down*** *Gebäude etc* abreißen; umstoßen, umwerfen; niederschlagen; anfahren, umfahren; überfahren; mit *dem Preis* heruntergehen; *auction*: *et.* zuschlagen (***to s.o.*** j-m); ***be ~ed down*** überfahren werden; ~ ***off*** herunter-, abschlagen; F *et.* hinhauen; F aufhören (mit); F Feierabend *or* Schluss machen; ~ ***out*** herausschlagen, -klopfen, *Pfeife* ausklopfen; *j-n* bewusstlos schlagen; *boxing*: k.o. schlagen; *fig* betäuben (*drug etc*); *fig* F umhauen, schocken; ~ ***over*** umwerfen, umstoßen; überfahren; ***be ~ed over*** überfahren werden 2. Schlag *m*, Stoß *m*; Klopfen *n*; ***there is a ~*** (***on*** [*Br* ***at***] ***the door***) es klopft

**knock·er** Türklopfer *m*

**knock-kneed** x-beinig

**knock·out** *boxing*: K.o. *m*

**knoll** Hügel *m*

**knot** 1. Knoten *m*; BOT Astknoten *m*; MAR Knoten *m*, Seemeile *f* 2. (ver-)knoten, (ver)knüpfen; **knot·ty** knotig; knorrig; *fig* verwickelt, kompliziert

**know** wissen; können; kennen; erfahren, erleben; (wieder) erkennen; verstehen; ~ ***French*** Französisch können; ~ ***one's way around*** sich auskennen in (*a place etc*); ~ ***all about it*** genau Bescheid wissen; ***get to ~*** kennenlernen; ~ ***one's business***, ~ ***the ropes***, ~ ***a thing or two***, ~ ***what's what*** F sich auskennen, Erfahrung haben; ***you ~*** wissen Sie

**know-how** Know-how *n*, (Sach-, Spezial)Kenntnis(se *pl*) *f*

**know·ing** klug, gescheit; schlau; verständnisvoll; **know·ing·ly** wissend; wissentlich, absichtlich, bewusst

**knowl·edge** Kenntnis(se *pl*) *f*; Wissen *n*; ***to my ~*** meines Wissens; ***have a good ~ of*** viel verstehen von, sich gut auskennen in (*dat*)

**knowl·edge·a·ble**: ***be very ~ about*** viel verstehen von

**knuck·le** 1. ANAT (Finger)Knöchel *m* 2. ~ ***down to work*** sich an die Arbeit machen

**Krem·lin**: POL ***the ~*** der Kreml

# L

**L**, **l** L, l *n*

**L** *abbr of* ***large*** (***size***) groß

**lab** F Labor *n*

**la·bel** 1. Etikett *n*, (Klebe- *etc*)Zettel *m*, (-)Schild(chen) *n*; (Schall)Plattenfirma *f* 2. etikettieren, beschriften; *fig* abstempeln als

**la·bor** 1. (schwere) Arbeit; Mühe *f*; Arbeiter *pl*, Arbeitskräfte *pl*; MED Wehen *pl* 2. (schwer) arbeiten; sich bemühen, sich abmühen, sich anstrengen

**la·bor·a·to·ry** Labor(atorium) *n*; ~ **assis·tant** Laborant(in)

**la·bored** schwerfällig (*style etc*); mühsam (*breathing etc*)

**la·bor·er** (*esp* Hilfs)Arbeiter *m*

**la·bo·ri·ous** mühsam; schwerfällig

**la·bor u·ni·on** Gewerkschaft *f*

**la·bour** *Br* → ***labor***

**Labour** *Br* POL die Labour Party

**la·boured**, **la·bour·er** *Br* → ***labored***, ***laborer***

**La·bour Par·ty** *Br* POL Labour Party *f*

**lace** 1. Spitze *f*; Borte *f*; Schnürsenkel *m* 2. ~ ***up*** (zu-, zusammen)schnüren; *Schuh* zubinden; ***~d with brandy*** mit e-m Schuss Weinbrand

**la·ce·rate** zerschneiden, zerkratzen, aufreißen; *j-s Gefühle* verletzen

**lack** 1. (***of***) Fehlen *n* (von), Mangel *m* (an

*dat*); **2.** *v/t* nicht haben; ***he ~s money*** es fehlt ihm an Geld; *v/i* ***be ~ing*** fehlen; ***he is ~ing in courage*** ihm fehlt der Mut
**lack·lus·ter**, *Br* **lack·lus·tre** glanzlos, matt
**la·con·ic** lakonisch, wortkarg
**lac·quer** **1.** Lack *m*; Haarspray *m*, *n* **2.** lackieren
**lad** Bursche *m*, Junge *m*
**lad·der** Leiter *f*; *Br* Laufmasche *f*
**lad·der·proof** (lauf)maschenfest
**la·den** (schwer) beladen
**la·dle** **1.** (Schöpf-, Suppen)Kelle *f*, Schöpflöffel *m* **2.** ***~ out*** *Suppe* austeilen
**la·dy** Dame *f*; ***Lady*** Lady *f*; ***~ doctor*** Ärztin *f*; ***Ladies' room***, *Br* ***Ladies(')*** Damentoilette *f*
**la·dy·bird** ZO Marienkäfer *m*
**la·dy·like** damenhaft
**lag** **1.** *mst* ***~ behind*** zurückbleiben **2.** → ***time lag***
**la·ger** Lagerbier *n*
**la·goon** Lagune *f*
**lair** ZO Lager *n*, Höhle *f*, Bau *m*
**la·i·ty** Laien *pl*
**lake** See *m*
**lamb** ZO **1.** Lamm *n* **2.** lammen
**lame** **1.** lahm (*a. fig*) **2.** lähmen
**la·ment** **1.** jammern, (weh)klagen; trauern **2.** Jammer *m*, (Weh)Klage *f*
**lam·en·ta·ble** beklagenswert; kläglich
**lam·en·ta·tion** (Weh)Klage *f*
**lam·i·nat·ed** laminiert, geschichtet, beschichtet; ~ **glass** Verbundglas *n*
**lamp** Lampe *f*; Laterne *f*
**lamp·post** Laternenpfahl *m*
**lamp·shade** Lampenschirm *m*
**lance** Lanze *f*
**land** **1.** Land *n*, AGR *a.* Boden *m*, POL *a.* Staat *m*; ***by ~*** auf dem Landweg **2.** landen, MAR *a.* anlegen; *Güter* ausladen, MAR *a.* löschen
**land a·gent** AGR Gutsverwalter *m*
**land·ed** Land..., Grund...; ***~ gentry*** Landadel *m*; ***~ property*** Grundbesitz *m*
**land·ing** AVIAT Landung *f*, Landen *n*, MAR *a.* Anlegen *n*; Treppenabsatz *m*; ~ **field** AVIAT Landeplatz *m*; ~ **gear** AVIAT Fahrgestell *n*; ~ **stage** MAR Landungsbrücke *f*, -steg *m*; ~ **strip** AVIAT Landeplatz *m*
**land·la·dy** Vermieterin *f*; Wirtin *f*
**land·lord** Vermieter *m*; Wirt *m*; Grundbesitzer *m*
**land·lub·ber** MAR *contp* Landratte *f*
**land·mark** Wahrzeichen *n*; *fig* Meilenstein *m*
**land·own·er** Grundbesitzer(in)
**land·scape** Landschaft *f* (*a. paint*)
**land·slide** Erdrutsch *m* (*a.* POL); ***a ~ victory*** POL ein überwältigender Wahlsieg
**land·slip** (kleiner) Erdrutsch
**lane** (Feld)Weg *m*; Gasse *f*, Sträßchen *n*; MAR Fahrrinne *f*; AVIAT Flugschneise *f*; SPORT (*einzelne*) Bahn; MOT (Fahr-) Spur *f*; ***change ~s*** MOT die Spur wechseln; ***get in ~*** MOT sich einordnen
**lan·guage** Sprache *f*
**lan·guid** matt; träg(e)
**lank** glatt
**lank·y** schlaksig
**lan·tern** Laterne *f*
**lap**[1] Schoß *m*
**lap**[2] SPORT **1.** Runde *f*; ***~ of hono(u)r*** Ehrenrunde *f* **2.** *Gegner* überrunden; e-e Runde zurücklegen
**lap**[3] *v/t*: ***~ up*** auflecken, aufschlecken; *v/i* plätschern
**la·pel** Revers *n*, *m*, Aufschlag *m*
**lapse** **1.** Versehen *n*, (kleiner) Fehler *or* Irrtum; Vergehen *n*; Zeitspanne *f*; JUR Verfall *m*; ***~ of memory, memory ~*** Gedächtnislücke *f* **2.** verfallen; JUR verfallen, erlöschen
**lar·ce·ny** JUR Diebstahl *m*
**larch** BOT Lärche *f*
**lard** **1.** Schweinefett *n*, Schweineschmalz *n* **2.** *Fleisch* spicken
**lar·der** Speisekammer *f*, -schrank *m*
**large** groß; beträchtlich, reichlich; umfassend, weitgehend; ***at ~*** in Freiheit, auf freiem Fuß; *fig* (sehr) ausführlich; in der Gesamtheit
**large·ly** großenteils, größtenteils
**large-mind·ed** aufgeschlossen, tolerant
**large·ness** Größe *f*
**lar·i·at** Lasso *n*, *m*
**lark**[1] ZO Lerche *f*
**lark**[2] F Jux *m*, Spaß *m*
**lark·spur** BOT Rittersporn *m*
**lar·va** ZO Larve *f*
**lar·yn·gi·tis** MED Kehlkopfentzündung *f*; **lar·ynx** ANAT Kehlkopf *m*
**las·civ·i·ous** geil, lüstern
**la·ser** PHYS Laser *m*; ~ **beam** PHYS Laserstrahl *m*; ~ **print·er** IT Laserdrucker *m*; ~ **tech·nol·o·gy** Lasertechnik *f*

L

**lash 1.** Peitschenschnur *f*; (Peitschen-) Hieb *m*; Wimper *f* **2.** peitschen (mit); (fest)binden; schlagen; **~ *out*** (wild) um sich schlagen
**las·so** Lasso *n, m*
**last**[1] **1.** *adj* letzte(r, -s); vorige(r, -s); **~ *but one*** vorletzte(r, -s); **~ *night*** gestern Abend; letzte Nacht **2.** *adv* zuletzt, an letzter Stelle; **~ *but not least*** nicht zuletzt, nicht zu vergessen **3.** *der, die, das* Letzte; ***at* ~** endlich; ***to the* ~** bis zum Schluss
**last**[2] (an-, fort)dauern; (sich) halten; (aus)reichen
**last**[3] (Schuhmacher)Leisten *m*
**last·ing** dauerhaft; beständig
**last·ly** zuletzt, zum Schluss
**latch 1.** Schnappriegel *m*; Schnappschloss *n* **2.** einklinken, zuklinken
**latch·key** Haus-, Wohnungsschlüssel *m*
**late** spät; jüngste(r, -s), letzte(r, -s), frühere(r, -s), ehemalig; verstorben; ***be* ~** zu spät kommen, sich verspäten; RAIL *etc* Verspätung haben; ***as* ~ *as*** noch, erst; ***of* ~** kürzlich; ***later on*** später
**late·ly** kürzlich
**lath** Latte *f*, Leiste *f*
**lathe** TECH Drehbank *f*
**la·ther 1.** (Seifen)Schaum *m* **2.** *v/t* einseifen; *v/i* schäumen
**Lat·in** LING **1.** lateinisch; südländisch **2.** Latein(isch) *n*; **~ A·mer·i·ca** Lateinamerika *n*; **~ A·mer·i·can 1.** lateinamerikanisch **2.** Lateinamerikaner(in)
**lat·i·tude** GEOGR Breite *f*
**lat·ter** Letztere(r, -s)
**lat·tice** Gitter(werk) *n*
**lau·da·ble** lobenswert
**laugh 1.** lachen (***at*** über *acc*); **~ *at s.o. a.*** j-n auslachen **2.** Lachen *n*, Gelächter *n*
**laugh·a·ble** lächerlich, lachhaft
**laugh·ter** Lachen *n*, Gelächter *n*
**launch**[1] **1.** MAR vom Stapel lassen; MIL abschießen, *Rakete a.* starten; *fig Projekt etc* in Gang setzen, starten **2.** MAR Stapellauf *m*; MIL Abschuss *m*, Start *m*
**launch**[2] MAR Barkasse *f*
**launch·ing** → ***launch***[1] 2; **~ pad** Abschussrampe *f*; **~ site** Abschussbasis *f*
**launch pad** → ***launching pad***
**laun·der** *Wäsche* waschen (und bügeln); F *esp Geld* waschen
**laun·der·ette, laun·drette** *esp Br*, **laun·dro·mat**® Waschsalon *m*
**laun·dry** Wäscherei *f*; Wäsche *f*
**laur·el** BOT Lorbeer *m* (*a. fig*)
**la·va** GEOL Lava *f*
**lav·a·to·ry** Toilette *f*, Klosett *n*; ***public* ~** Bedürfnisanstalt *f*
**lav·en·der** BOT Lavendel *m*
**lav·ish 1.** sehr freigebig, verschwenderisch **2.** **~ *s.th. on s.o.*** j-n mit et. überhäufen *or* überschütten
**law** Gesetz(e *pl*) *n*; Recht *n*, Rechtssystem *n*; Rechtswissenschaft *f*, Jura; F Bullen *pl* (*police*); F Bulle *m* (*policeman*); Gesetz *n*, Vorschrift *f*; **~ *and order*** Recht *or* Ruhe und Ordnung
**law-a·bid·ing** gesetzestreu
**law·court** Gericht *n*, Gerichtshof *m*
**law·ful** gesetzlich; rechtmäßig, legitim; rechtsgültig
**law·less** gesetzlos; gesetzwidrig; zügellos
**lawn** Rasen *m*
**lawn·mow·er** Rasenmäher *m*
**law·suit** JUR Prozess *m*
**law·yer** JUR (Rechts)Anwalt *m*, (Rechts)Anwältin *f*
**lax** locker, schlaff; lax, lasch
**lax·a·tive** MED **1.** abführend **2.** Abführmittel *n*
**lay**[1] REL weltlich; Laien...
**lay**[2] *v/t* legen; *Teppich* verlegen; belegen, auslegen (***with*** mit); *Tisch* decken; zo *Eier* legen; vorlegen (***before*** *dat*), bringen (***before*** vor *acc*); *Schuld etc* zuschreiben, zur Last legen (*dat*); *v/i* zo (Eier) legen; **~ *aside*** beiseitelegen, zurücklegen; **~ *off*** *Arbeiter* (*esp* vorübergehend) entlassen; *Arbeit* einstellen; **~ *open*** darlegen; **~ *out*** ausbreiten, auslegen; *Garten etc* anlegen; entwerfen, planen; PRINT das Layout (*gen*) machen; **~ *up*** anhäufen, (an)sammeln; ***be laid up*** das Bett hüten müssen
**lay-by** *Br* MOT Parkbucht *f*, Parkstreifen *m*; Parkplatz *m*, Rastplatz *m*
**lay·er** Lage *f*, Schicht *f*; BOT Ableger *m*
**lay·man** Laie *m*
**lay-off** ECON (*esp* vorübergehende) Entlassung
**lay·out** Grundriss *m*, Lageplan *m*; PRINT Layout *n*, Gestaltung *f*
**la·zy** faul, träg(e)
**LCD** *abbr of* ***liquid crystal display*** Flüssigkristallanzeige *f*
**lead**[1] **1.** *v/t* führen; (an)führen, leiten; da-

zu bringen, veranlassen (***to do*** zu tun); *v/i* führen; vorangehen; SPORT an der Spitze *or* in Führung liegen; **~ *off*** anfangen, beginnen; **~ *on*** *j-m* et. vormachen *or* weismachen; **~ *to*** *fig* führen zu; **~ *up to*** *fig* (allmählich) führen zu **2.** Führung *f*; Leitung *f*; Spitzenposition *f*; Vorbild *n*, Beispiel *n*; THEA Hauptrolle *f*; Hauptdarsteller(in); (Hunde)Leine *f*; Hinweis *m*, Tipp *m*, Anhaltspunkt *m*; SPORT *and fig* Führung *f*, Vorsprung *m*; ***be in the* ~** in Führung sein; ***take the* ~** in Führung gehen, die Führung übernehmen

**lead**[2] CHEM Blei *n*; MAR Lot *n*

**lead·ed** verbleit, bleihaltig

**lead·en** bleiern (*a. fig*), Blei…

**lead·er** (An)Führer(in), Leiter(in); Erste *m, f*; *Br* Leitartikel *m*

**lead·er·ship** Führung *f*, Leitung *f*

**lead-free** bleifrei

**lead·ing** leitend; führend; Haupt…

**leaf 1.** BOT, PRINT Blatt *n*; (*Tür- etc*)Flügel *m*; (*Tisch*)Klappe *f*, Ausziehplatte *f* **2. ~ *through*** durchblättern

**leaf·let** Hand-, Reklamezettel *m*; Prospekt *m*

**league** POL Bund *m*; SPORT Liga *f*

**leak 1.** lecken, leck sein; tropfen; **~ *out*** auslaufen; *fig* durchsickern **2.** Leck *n*, undichte Stelle (*a. fig*)

**leak·age** Auslaufen *n*

**leak·y** leck, undicht

**lean**[1] (sich) lehnen; (sich) neigen; **~ *on*** sich verlassen auf (*acc*)

**lean**[2] **1.** mager (*a. fig*) **2.** GASTR das Magere; **~ man·age·ment** ECON schlanke Unternehmensstruktur

**leap 1.** springen; **~ *at*** *fig* sich stürzen auf (*acc*) **2.** Sprung *m*

**leap·frog** Bockspringen *n*

**leap year** Schaltjahr *n*

**learn** (er)lernen; erfahren, hören

**learn·ed** gelehrt

**learn·er** Anfänger(in); Lernende *m, f*; **~ *driver*** *Br* MOT Fahrschüler(in)

**learn·ing** Gelehrsamkeit *f*

**lease 1.** Pacht *f*, Miete *f*; Pacht-, Mietvertrag *m* **2.** pachten, mieten; leasen; **~ *out*** verpachten, vermieten

**leash** (Hunde)Leine *f*

**least 1.** *adj* geringste(r, -s), mindeste(r, -s), wenigste(r, -s) **2.** *adv* am wenigsten; **~ *of all*** am allerwenigsten **3.** *das* Mindeste, *das* wenigste; ***at* ~** wenigstens; ***to say the* ~** gelinde gesagt

**leath·er 1.** Leder *n* **2.** ledern; Leder…

**leave 1.** *v/t* (hinter-, über-, ver-, zurück)lassen, übrig lassen; liegen *or* stehen lassen, vergessen; vermachen, vererben; ***be left*** übrig bleiben, übrig sein; *v/i* (fort-, weg)gehen, abreisen, abfahren, abfliegen; **~ *alone*** allein lassen; *j-n, et.* in Ruhe lassen; **~ *behind*** zurücklassen; **~ *on*** anlassen; **~ *out*** draußen lassen; auslassen, weglassen **2.** Erlaubnis *f*; Urlaub *m*; Abschied *m*; ***on* ~** auf Urlaub

**leav·en** Sauerteig *m*

**leaves** BOT Laub *n*

**leav·ings** Überreste *pl*

**lech·er·ous** geil, lüstern

**lec·ture 1.** UNIV Vorlesung *f* (***über*** *acc* on); Vortrag *m*; Strafpredigt *f* **2.** *v/i* UNIV e-e Vorlesung *or* Vorlesungen halten (***über*** *acc* on; ***vor*** *dat* to); e-n Vortrag *or* Vorträge halten; *v/t j-m* e-e Strafpredigt halten

**lec·tur·er** UNIV Dozent(in); Redner(in)

**ledge** Leiste *f*, Sims *m, n*

**leech** ZO Blutegel *m*

**leek** BOT Lauch *m*, Porree *m*

**leer 1.** anzüglicher *or* lüsterner Seitenblick **2.** anzüglich *or* lüstern blicken *or* schielen (***at*** nach)

**left 1.** *adj* linke(r, -s), Links… **2.** *adv* links; ***turn* ~** (sich) nach links wenden; MOT links abbiegen **3.** *die* Linke (*a.* POL, *boxing*), linke Seite; ***on the* ~** links, auf der linken Seite; ***to the* ~** (nach) links; ***keep to the* ~** sich links halten; links fahren

**left-hand** linke(r, -s)

**left-hand drive** MOT Linkssteuerung *f*

**left-hand·ed** linkshändig; für Linkshänder; ***be* ~** Linkshänder(in) sein

**left lug·gage of·fice** *Br* RAIL Gepäckaufbewahrung *f*

**left·o·vers** (Speise)Reste *pl*

**left-wing** POL dem linken Flügel angehörend, links…, Links…

**leg** ANAT Bein *n*; GASTR Keule *f*; MATH Schenkel *m*; ***pull s.o.'s* ~** F j-n auf den Arm nehmen; ***stretch one's*** sich die Beine vertreten

**leg·a·cy** *fig* Vermächtnis *n*, Erbe *n*

**le·gal** legal, gesetzmäßig; gesetzlich, rechtlich; juristisch, Rechts…

**le·gal·i·za·tion** Legalisierung *f*
**le·gal·ize** legalisieren
**le·gal pro·tec·tion** Rechtsschutz *m*
**le·ga·tion** POL Gesandtschaft *f*
**le·gend** Legende *f*, Sage *f*
**le·gen·da·ry** legendär
**le·gi·ble** leserlich
**le·gis·la·tion** Gesetzgebung *f*
**le·gis·la·tive** POL **1.** gesetzgebend, legislativ **2.** Legislative *f*, gesetzgebende Gewalt
**le·gis·la·tor** POL Gesetzgeber *m*
**le·git·i·mate** legitim; gesetzmäßig, rechtmäßig; ehelich
**lei·sure** freie Zeit; Muße *f*; ***at ~*** ohne Hast; **~ cen·tre** *Br* Freizeitzentrum *n*
**lei·sure·ly** gemächlich
**lei·sure time** Freizeit *f*
**lei·sure-time ac·tiv·i·ties** Freizeitbeschäftigung *f*, -gestaltung *f*
**lei·sure·wear** Freizeitkleidung *f*
**lem·on** BOT **1.** Zitrone *f* **2.** Zitronen…
**lem·on·ade** Zitronenlimonade *f*
**lend** *j-m et.* (ver-, aus)leihen
**length** Länge *f*; Strecke *f*; (Zeit)Dauer *f*; ***at ~*** ausführlich
**length·en** verlängern, länger machen; länger werden
**length·ways**, **length·wise** der Länge nach
**length·y** sehr lang
**le·ni·ent** mild(e), nachsichtig
**lens** ANAT, PHOT, PHYS Linse *f*; PHOT Objektiv *n*
**Lent** REL Fastenzeit *f*
**len·til** BOT Linse *f*
**Le·o** ASTR Löwe *m*; ***he (she) is (a) ~*** er (sie) ist (ein) Löwe
**leop·ard** ZO Leopard *m*
**le·o·tard** (Tänzer)Trikot *n*
**lep·ro·sy** MED Lepra *f*
**les·bi·an** **1.** lesbisch **2.** Lesbierin *f*, F Lesbe *f*
**less** **1.** *adj and adv* kleiner, geringer, weniger **2.** *prp* weniger, minus, abzüglich
**less·en** (sich) vermindern *or* verringern; abnehmen; herabsetzen
**less·er** kleiner, geringer
**les·son** Lektion *f*; (Unterrichts)Stunde *f*; *fig* Lehre *f*; *pl* Unterricht *m*
**let** lassen; *esp Br* vermieten, verpachten; ***~ alone*** *j-n, et.* in Ruhe lassen; geschweige denn; ***~ down*** hinunterlassen, herunterlassen; *Kleider* verlängern; *j-n* im Stich lassen, F *j-n* sitzen lassen; enttäuschen; ***~ go*** loslassen; ***~ o.s. go*** sich gehenlassen; ***~'s go*** gehen wir!; ***~ in*** (her)einlassen; ***~ o.s. in for s.th.*** sich et. einbrocken, sich auf et. einlassen
**le·thal** tödlich; Todes…
**leth·ar·gy** Lethargie *f*
**let·ter** Buchstabe *m*; PRINT Type *f*; Brief *m*
**let·ter·box** *esp Br* Briefkasten *m*
**let·ter car·ri·er** Briefträger *m*
**let·tuce** BOT (*esp* Kopf)Salat *m*
**leu·k(a)e·mia** MED Leukämie *f*
**lev·el** **1.** *adj* eben; gleich (*a. fig*); ausgeglichen; ***be ~ with*** auf gleicher Höhe sein mit; ***my ~ best*** F mein Möglichstes **2.** Ebene *f* (*a. fig*), ebene Fläche; Höhe *f* (*a.* GEOGR), (*Wasser- etc*)Spiegel *m*, (-)Stand *m*, (-)Pegel *m*; Wasserwaage *f*; *fig* Niveau *n*, Stufe *f*; ***sea ~*** Meeresspiegel *m*; ***on the ~*** F ehrlich, aufrichtig **3.** (ein)ebnen, planieren; dem Erdboden gleichmachen; ***~ at*** *Waffe* richten auf (*acc*); *Beschuldigungen* erheben gegen (*acc*) **4.** *adv*: ***~ with*** in Höhe (*gen*)
**lev·el cross·ing** *Br* schienengleicher Bahnübergang
**lev·el-head·ed** vernünftig, nüchtern
**le·ver** Hebel *m*
**lev·y** **1.** Steuer *f*, Abgabe *f* **2.** *Steuern* erheben
**lewd** geil, lüstern; unanständig, obszön
**li·a·bil·i·ty** ECON, JUR Verpflichtung *f*, Verbindlichkeit *f*; ECON, JUR Haftung *f*, Haftpflicht *f*; Neigung *f* (***to*** zu), Anfälligkeit *f* (***to*** für); **li·a·ble** ECON, JUR haftbar, haftpflichtig; ***be ~ for*** haften für; ***be ~ to*** neigen zu, anfällig sein für
**li·ar** Lügner(in)
**li·bel** JUR **1.** (*schriftliche*) Verleumdung *or* Beleidigung **2.** (*schriftlich*) verleumden *or* beleidigen
**lib·e·ral** **1.** liberal (*a.* POL), aufgeschlossen; großzügig; reichlich **2.** Liberale *m*, *f* (*a.* POL)
**lib·e·rate** befreien; **lib·e·ra·tion** Befreiung *f*; **lib·e·ra·tor** Befreier *m*
**lib·er·ty** Freiheit *f*; ***take liberties with*** sich Freiheiten gegen *j-n* herausnehmen; willkürlich mit *et.* umgehen; ***be at ~*** frei sein
**Li·bra** ASTR Waage *f*; ***he (she) is (a) ~*** er (sie) ist (eine) Waage

**li·brar·i·an** Bibliothekar(in)
**li·bra·ry** Bibliothek *f*; Bücherei *f*
**li·cence 1.** *Br* → ***license 1*** **2.** e-e Lizenz *or* Konzession erteilen (*dat*); *behördlich* genehmigen
**li·cense 1.** Lizenz *f*, Konzession *f*; (*Führer-*, *Jagd-*, *Waffen- etc*)Schein *m* **2.** *Br* → ***licence 2***
**li·cense plate** MOT Nummernschild *n*
**li·chen** BOT Flechte *f*
**lick 1.** Lecken *n*; Salzlecke *f* **2.** *v/t* ab-, auflecken; F verdreschen, verprügeln; F schlagen, besiegen; *v/i* lecken; züngeln (*flames*)
**lic·o·rice** Lakritze *f*
**lid** Deckel *m*; ANAT (Augen)Lid *n*
**lie**[1] **1.** lügen; ***~ to s.o.*** j-n belügen, j-n anlügen **2.** Lüge *f*; ***tell ~s, tell a ~*** lügen; ***give the ~ to*** *j-n*, *et.* Lügen strafen
**lie**[2] **1.** liegen; ***let sleeping dogs ~*** schlafende Hunde soll man nicht wecken; ***~ behind*** *fig* dahinter stecken; ***~ down*** sich hinlegen **2.** Lage *f* (*a. fig*)
**lie-down** *Br* F Nickerchen *n*
**lie-in**: ***have a ~*** *esp Br* F sich gründlich ausschlafen
**lieu**: ***in ~ of*** anstelle von (*or gen*)
**lieu·ten·ant** MIL Leutnant *m*
**life** Leben *n*; JUR lebenslängliche Freiheitsstrafe; ***all her ~*** ihr ganzes Leben lang; ***for ~*** fürs (ganze) Leben; *esp* JUR lebenslänglich
**life as·sur·ance** *Br* → ***life insurance***
**life belt** Rettungsgürtel *m*
**life·boat** Rettungsboot *n*
**life·guard** Bademeister *m*; Rettungsschwimmer *m*
**life im·pris·on·ment** JUR lebenslängliche Freiheitsstrafe
**life in·sur·ance** Lebensversicherung *f*
**life jack·et** Schwimmweste *f*
**life·less** leblos; matt, schwung-, lustlos
**life·like** lebensecht
**life·long** lebenslang
**life pre·serv·er** Schwimmweste *f*; Rettungsgürtel *m*
**life sen·tence** JUR lebenslängliche Freiheitsstrafe
**life·time** Lebenszeit *f*
**lift 1.** *v/t* (hoch-, auf)heben; erheben; *Verbot etc* aufheben; *Gesicht etc* liften, straffen; F klauen; *v/i* sich heben, steigen (*a. fog*); ***~ off*** starten (*rocket*), AVIAT abheben **2.** (Hoch-, Auf)Heben *n*; PHYS, AVIAT Auftrieb *m*; *Br* Lift *m*, Aufzug *m*, Fahrstuhl *m*; ***give s.o. a ~*** j-n (im Auto) mitnehmen; F j-n aufmuntern, j-m Auftrieb geben
**lift-off** Start *m*, Abheben *n*
**lig·a·ment** ANAT Band *n*
**light**[1] **1.** Licht *n* (*a. fig*); Beleuchtung *f*; Schein *m*; Feuer *n*; *fig* Aspekt *m*; *Br mst pl* (Verkehrs)Ampel *f*; ***do you have*** (*Br* ***have you got***) ***a ~?*** haben Sie Feuer? **2.** *v/t* beleuchten, erleuchten; *a.* ***~ up*** anzünden; *v/i* sich entzünden; ***~ up*** *fig* aufleuchten **3.** hell, licht
**light**[2] leicht (*a. fig*); ***make ~ of s.th.*** et. leichtnehmen; et. bagatellisieren
**light·en**[1] *v/t* erhellen; aufhellen; *v/i* hell(er) werden, sich aufhellen
**light·en**[2] leichter machen *or* werden; erleichtern
**light·er** Anzünder *m*; Feuerzeug *n*
**light-head·ed** (leicht) benommen; leichtfertig, töricht
**light-heart·ed** fröhlich, unbeschwert
**light·house** Leuchtturm *m*
**light·ing** Beleuchtung *f*
**light·ness** Leichtheit *f*; Leichtigkeit *f*
**light·ning** Blitz *m*; ***like ~*** wie der Blitz; (***as***) ***quick as ~*** blitzschnell
**light·ning| con·duc·tor** *Br*, **~ rod** ELECTR Blitzableiter *m*
**light·weight** SPORT Leichtgewicht *n*, Leichtgewichtler *m*
**like**[1] **1.** *v/t* gernhaben, mögen; ***I ~ it*** es gefällt mir; ***I ~ her*** ich kann sie gut leiden; ***how do you ~ it?*** wie gefällt es dir?, wie findest du es?; ***I ~ that!*** *iro* das hab ich gern!; ***I should*** *or* ***would ~ to know*** ich möchte gern wissen; *v/i* wollen; (***just***) ***as you ~*** (ganz) wie du willst; ***if you ~*** wenn du willst **2.** ***~s and dislikes*** Neigungen und Abneigungen *pl*
**like**[2] **1.** gleich; wie; ähnlich; ***~ that*** so; ***feel ~*** Lust haben auf (*acc*) *or* zu; ***what is he ~?*** wie ist er?; ***that is just ~ him!*** das sieht ihm ähnlich! **2.** *der*, *die*, *das* Gleiche; ***his ~*** seinesgleichen; ***the ~*** dergleichen; ***the ~s of you*** Leute wie du
**like·li·hood** Wahrscheinlichkeit *f*
**like·ly 1.** *adj* wahrscheinlich; geeignet **2.** *adv* wahrscheinlich; ***not ~!*** F bestimmt nicht!
**like·ness** Ähnlichkeit *f*; Abbild *n*
**like·wise** ebenso

**lik·ing** Vorliebe *f*
**li·lac 1.** lila **2.** BOT Flieder *m*
**lil·y** BOT Lilie *f*
**lil·y of the val·ley** BOT Maiglöckchen *n*
**limb** ANAT (*Körper*)Glied *n*; BOT Ast *m*
**lime**[1] Kalk *m*
**lime**[2] BOT Linde *f*; Limone *f*
**lime·light** *fig* Rampenlicht *n*
**lim·it 1.** Limit *n*, Grenze *f*; ***within ~s*** in Grenzen; ***off ~s*** Zutritt verboten (***to*** für); ***that is the ~!*** F das ist der Gipfel!, das ist (doch) die Höhe!; ***go to the ~*** bis zum Äußersten gehen **2.** beschränken (***to*** auf *acc*)
**lim·i·ta·tion** Beschränkung *f*; *fig* Grenze *f*; JUR Verjährung *f*
**lim·it·ed** beschränkt, begrenzt; ***~ (liability) company*** *Br* ECON Gesellschaft *f* mit beschränkter Haftung
**lim·it·less** grenzenlos
**limp**[1] **1.** hinken, humpeln **2.** Hinken *n*, Humpeln *n*
**limp**[2] schlaff, schlapp, F lappig
**line**[1] **1.** Linie *f*, Strich *m*; Zeile *f*; Falte *f*, Runzel *f*; Reihe *f*; (Menschen-, *a.* Auto)Schlange *f*; (Abstammungs)Linie *f*; (*Verkehrs-*, *Eisenbahn- etc*)Linie *f*, Strecke *f*; (*Flug- etc*)Gesellschaft *f*; *esp* TEL Leitung *f*; MIL Linie *f*; Fach *n*, Gebiet *n*, Branche *f*; SPORT (*Ziel- etc*)Linie *f*; Leine *f*; Schnur *f*; Linie *f*, Richtung *f*; *fig* Grenze *f*; *pl* THEA Rolle *f*, Text *m*; ***the ~*** der Äquator; ***draw the ~*** Halt machen, die Grenze ziehen (***at*** bei); ***the ~ is busy*** *or* ***engaged*** TEL die Leitung ist besetzt; ***hold the ~*** TEL bleiben Sie am Apparat; ***stand in ~*** anstehen, Schlange stehen (***for*** um, nach); **2.** lin(i)ieren; *Gesicht* zeichnen, (zer)furchen; *Straße etc* säumen; ***~ up*** (sich) in e-r Reihe *or* Linie aufstellen, SPORT sich aufstellen; sich anstellen (***for*** um, nach)
**line**[2] *Kleid etc* füttern; TECH auskleiden, ausschlagen; MOT *Bremsen etc* belegen
**lin·e·ar** linear; Längen…
**lin·en 1.** Leinen *n*; (*Bett-*, *Tisch- etc* -)Wäsche *f* **2.** leinen, Leinen…
**lin·en| clos·et**, *Br* **~ cup·board** Wäscheschrank *m*
**lin·er** MAR Linienschiff *n*; AVIAT Verkehrsflugzeug *n*
**lines·man** SPORT Linienrichter *m*
**lines·wom·an** SPORT Linienrichterin *f*
**line-up** SPORT Aufstellung *f*; Gegenüberstellung *f* (zur Identifizierung)
**lin·ger** verweilen, sich aufhalten; *a.* ***~ on*** dahinsiechen; ***~ on*** noch dableiben; *fig* fortleben
**lin·ge·rie** Damenunterwäsche *f*
**lin·ing** Futter(stoff *m*) *n*; TECH Auskleidung *f*; MOT (*Brems- etc*)Belag *m*
**link 1.** (Ketten)Glied *n*; Manschettenknopf *m*; *fig* (Binde)Glied *n*, Verbindung *f* **2.** *a.* ***~ up*** (sich) verbinden
**links** → ***golf links***
**link·up** Verbindung *f*
**lin·seed** BOT Leinsamen *m*
**lin·seed oil** Leinöl *n*
**li·on** ZO Löwe *m*
**li·on·ess** ZO Löwin *f*
**lip** ANAT Lippe *f*; (*Tassen- etc*)Rand *m*; F Unverschämtheit *f*
**lip·stick** Lippenstift *m*
**liq·ue·fy** (sich) verflüssigen
**liq·uid 1.** Flüssigkeit *f* **2.** flüssig; ***~ soap*** Flüssigseife *f*
**liq·ui·date** liquidieren (*a.* ECON); *Schulden* tilgen
**liq·uid·ize** zerkleinern, pürieren
**liq·uid·iz·er** Mixgerät *n*, Mixer *m*
**liq·uor** *Br* alkoholische Getränke *pl*, Alkohol *m*; Schnaps *m*, Spirituosen *pl*
**liq·uo·rice** *Br* → ***licorice***
**lisp 1.** lispeln **2.** Lispeln *n*
**list 1.** Liste *f*, Verzeichnis *n*; MAR Schlagseite *f* **2.** (in e-e Liste) eintragen, erfassen; MAR ***be ~ing*** Schlagseite haben
**lis·ten** hören; ***~ in*** Radio hören; ***~ in to*** *et.* im Radio (an)hören; ***~ in on*** *Telefongespräch etc* abhören *or* mithören; ***~ to*** anhören (*acc*), zuhören (*dat*); hören auf (*acc*)
**lis·ten·er** Zuhörer(in); (Rundfunk)Hörer(in)
**list·less** teilnahmslos, lustlos
**li·ter** Liter *m*, *n*
**lit·e·ral** (wort)wörtlich; genau; prosaisch
**lit·e·ra·ry** literarisch, Literatur…
**lit·e·ra·ture** Literatur *f*
**lithe** geschmeidig, gelenkig
**li·tre** *Br* → ***liter***
**lit·ter 1.** (*esp Papier*)Abfall *m*; AGR Streu *f*; ZO Wurf *m*; Trage *f*; Sänfte *f* **2.** *et.* herumliegen lassen in (*dat*) *or* auf (*dat*); ***be ~ed with*** übersät sein mit
**lit·ter| bas·ket**, **~ bin** Abfallkorb *m*
**lit·tle 1.** *adj* klein; wenig; ***the ~ ones*** die

Kleinen *pl* **2.** *adv* wenig, kaum **3.** Kleinigkeit *f*; ***a ~*** ein wenig, ein bisschen; ***~ by ~*** (ganz) allmählich, nach und nach; ***not a ~*** nicht wenig

**live**[1] leben; wohnen (***with*** bei); ***~ to see*** erleben; ***~ on*** leben von; weiterleben; ***~ up to*** *s-n Grundsätzen etc* gemäß leben; *Erwartungen etc* entsprechen; ***~ with*** mit *j-m* zusammenleben; mit *et.* leben

**live**[2] **1.** *adj* lebend, lebendig; richtig, echt; ELECTR Strom führend; *radio*, TV Direkt..., Live-... **2.** *adv* direkt, original, live

**live·li·hood** (Lebens)Unterhalt *m*

**live·li·ness** Lebhaftigkeit *f*

**live·ly** lebhaft, lebendig; aufregend

**liv·er** ANAT Leber *f* (*a.* GASTR)

**liv·e·ry** Livree *f*

**live·stock** Vieh *n*, Viehbestand *m*

**liv·id** bläulich; F fuchsteufelswild

**liv·ing 1.** lebend; ***the ~ image of*** das genaue Ebenbild (*gen*) **2.** Leben *n*, Lebensweise *f*; Lebensunterhalt *m*; ***the ~*** die Lebenden *pl*; ***standard of ~*** Lebensstandard *m*; ***earn** or **make a ~*** (sich) s-n Lebensunterhalt verdienen

**liv·ing room** Wohnzimmer *n*

**liz·ard** zo Eidechse *f*

**load 1.** Last *f* (*a. fig*); Ladung *f*; Belastung *f* **2.** *j-n* überhäufen (***with*** mit); *Schusswaffe* laden; *a.* ***~ up*** (auf-, be-, ein)laden

**loaf**[1] Laib *m* (Brot); Brot *n*

**loaf**[2] *a.* ***~ about, ~ around*** F herumlungern

**loaf·er** Müßiggänger(in)

**loam** Lehm *m*; **loam·y** lehmig

**loan 1.** (Ver)Leihen *n*; ECON Kredit *m*, Darlehen *n*; Leihgabe *f*; ***on ~*** leihweise **2.** ***~ s.o. s.th., ~ s.th. to s.o.*** j-m et. (aus)leihen; et. an j-n verleihen

**loath**: ***be ~ to do s.th.*** et. nur (sehr) ungern tun

**loathe** verabscheuen, hassen

**loath·ing** Abscheu *m*

**lob** *esp tennis*: Lob *m*

**lob·by 1.** Vorhalle *f*; THEA, *film*: Foyer *n*; Wandelhalle *f*; POL Lobby *f*, Interessengruppe *f* **2.** POL *Abgeordnete etc* beeinflussen

**lobe** ANAT, BOT Lappen *m*

**lob·ster** zo Hummer *m*

**lo·cal 1.** örtlich, Orts..., lokal, Lokal... **2.** Ortsansässige *m, f*, Einheimische *m, f*; *Br* F Stammkneipe *f*; ***~ call*** TEL Ortsgespräch *n*; ***~ e·lec·tions*** POL Kommunalwahlen *pl*; ***~ gov·ern·ment*** Gemeindeverwaltung *f*; ***~ time*** Ortszeit *f*; ***~ traf·fic*** Orts-, Nahverkehr *m*

**lo·cate** ausfindig machen; orten; ***be ~d*** gelegen sein, liegen, sich befinden

**lo·ca·tion** Lage *f*; Standort *m*; Platz *m* (***for*** für); *film*, TV Gelände *n* für Außenaufnahmen; ***on ~*** auf Außenaufnahme

**lock**[1] **1.** (*Tür-, Gewehr- etc*)Schloss *n*; Schleuse(nkammer) *f*; Verschluss *m*; Sperrvorrichtung *f* **2.** *v/t* zu-, verschließen, zu-, versperren (*a.* ***~ up***); umschlingen, umfassen; TECH sperren; *v/i* schließen; abschließbar *or* verschließbar sein; MOT *etc* blockieren; ***~ away*** wegschließen; ***~ in*** einschließen, einsperren; ***~ out*** aussperren; ***~ up*** abschließen; wegschließen; einsperren

**lock**[2] (Haar)Locke *f*

**lock·er** Spind *m*, Schrank *m*; Schließfach *n*; ***~ room*** *esp* SPORT Umkleidekabine *f*, Umkleideraum *m*

**lock·et** Medaillon *n*

**lock·out** ECON Aussperrung *f*

**lock·smith** Schlosser *m*

**lock·up** Arrestzelle *f*

**lo·cust** zo Heuschrecke *f*

**lodge 1.** Portier-, Pförtnerloge *f*; (*Jagd-, Ski- etc*)Hütte *f*; Sommer-, Gartenhaus *n*; (*Freimaurer*)Loge *f* **2.** *v/i* logieren, (*esp* vorübergehend *or* in Untermiete) wohnen; stecken (bleiben) (*bullet etc*); *v/t* aufnehmen, beherbergen, (für die Nacht) unterbringen; *Beschwerde etc* einreichen; *Berufung, Protest* einlegen

**lodg·er** Untermieter(in); **lodg·ing** Unterkunft *f*; *pl esp* möbliertes Zimmer

**loft** (Dach)Boden *m*; Heuboden *m*; Empore *f*; (***converted***) ***~*** Loft *m*, Fabriketage *f*

**loft·y** hoch; erhaben; stolz, hochmütig

**log** (Holz)Klotz *m*; (*gefällter*) Baumstamm; (Holz)Scheit *n*; → **log·book** MAR Logbuch *n*; AVIAT Bordbuch *n*; MOT Fahrtenbuch *n*

**log cab·in** Blockhaus *n*, Blockhütte *f*

**log·ger·heads**: ***be at ~*** sich streiten, sich in den Haaren liegen (***with*** mit)

**lo·gic** Logik *f*; **lo·gic·al** logisch

**loin** GASTR Lende(nstück *n*) *f*; *pl* ANAT Lende *f*

L

**loi·ter** trödeln; herumlungern
**loll** hängen (*head*), heraushängen (*tongue*); **~ *around*** *or* ***about*** F sich rekeln *or* lümmeln
**lol·li·pop** GASTR Lutscher *m*; *esp Br* Eis *n* am Stiel; **~ *man*** *Br* Schülerlotse *m*; **~ *woman***, **~ *lady*** *Br* Schülerlotsin *f*
**lol·ly** GASTR F Lutscher *m*; ***ice* ~** Eis *n* am Stiel
**lone·li·ness** Einsamkeit *f*
**lone·ly** einsam; ***become* ~** vereinsamen
**lone·some** einsam
**long**[1] **1.** *adj* lang; weit; langfristig **2.** *adv* lang(e); ***as*** *or* ***so* ~ *as*** solange wie; vorausgesetzt, dass; **~ *ago*** vor langer Zeit **3.** (e-e) lange Zeit; ***for* ~** lange; ***take* ~** lange brauchen *or* dauern
**long**[2] sich sehnen (***for*** nach)
**long-dis·tance** Fern…, Langstrecken…; ~ **call** TEL Ferngespräch *n*; ~ **run·ner** SPORT Langstreckenläufer(in)
**long·hand** Schreibschrift *f*
**long·ing 1.** sehnsüchtig **2.** Sehnsucht *f*, Verlangen *n*
**lon·gi·tude** GEOGR Länge *f*
**long johns** lange Unterhose
**long jump** SPORT Weitsprung *m*
**long-life milk** *esp Br* H-Milch *f*
**long-range** MIL, AVIAT Fern…, Langstrecken…; langfristig
**long·shore·man** Dock-, Hafenarbeiter *m*
**long·sight·ed** *esp Br* weitsichtig, *fig a.* weitblickend
**long-stand·ing** seit langer Zeit bestehend; alt
**long-term** langfristig, auf lange Sicht
**long wave** ELECTR Langwelle *f*
**long·wear·ing** strapazierfähig
**long·wind·ed** langatmig
**look 1.** sehen, blicken, schauen (***at, on*** auf *acc*, nach); nachschauen, nachsehen; *krank etc* aussehen; nach *e-r Richtung* liegen, gehen (*window etc*); **~ *here!*** schau mal (her); hör mal (zu)!; **~ *like*** aussehen wie; ***it* ~*s as if*** es sieht (so) aus, als ob; **~ *after*** aufpassen auf (*acc*); sich kümmern um, sorgen für, *den Haushalt etc* versehen; **~ *ahead*** nach vorne sehen; *fig* vorausschauen; **~ *around*** sich umsehen; **~ *at*** ansehen; **~ *back*** sich umsehen; *fig* zurückblicken; **~ *down*** herab-, heruntersehen (*a. fig* ***on s.o.*** auf j-n); **~ *for*** suchen; **~ *forward to*** sich freuen auf (*acc*); **~ *in*** F hereinschauen (***on*** bei); **~ *into*** untersuchen, prüfen; **~ *on*** zusehen, zuschauen (*dat*); betrachten, ansehen (***as*** als); **~ *onto*** liegen zu, (hinaus)gehen auf (*acc*) (*window etc*); **~ *out*** hinaus-, heraussehen; aufpassen, sich vorsehen; ausschauen *or* Ausschau halten (***for*** nach); **~ *over*** *et.* durchsehen; *j-n* mustern; **~ *round*** sich umsehen; **~ *through*** *et.* durchsehen; **~ *up*** aufblicken, aufsehen; *et.* nachschlagen; *j-n* aufsuchen **2.** Blick *m*; Miene *f*, (Gesichts)Ausdruck *m*; (***good***) **~*s*** gutes Aussehen; ***have a* ~ *at s.th.*** sich et. ansehen; ***I don't like the* ~ *of it*** es gefällt mir nicht
**look·ing glass** Spiegel *m*
**look·out** Ausguck *m*; Ausschau *f*; *fig* F Aussicht(en *pl*) *f*; ***be on the* ~ *for*** Ausschau halten nach
**loom**[1] Webstuhl *m*
**loom**[2] *a.* **~ *up*** undeutlich sichtbar werden *or* auftauchen
**loop 1.** Schlinge *f*, Schleife *f*; Schlaufe *f*; Öse *f*; AVIAT Looping *m*, *n*; IT Schleife *f* **2.** (sich) schlingen
**loop·hole** MIL Schießscharte *f*; *fig* Hintertürchen *n*; ***a* ~ *in the law*** e-e Gesetzeslücke
**loose 1.** los(e); locker; weit; frei; ***let* ~** loslassen; freilassen **2.** ***be on the* ~** frei herumlaufen
**loos·en** (sich) lösen *or* lockern; **~ *up*** SPORT Lockerungsübungen machen
**loot 1.** Beute *f* **2.** plündern
**lop** *Baum* beschneiden, stutzen; **~ *off*** abhauen, abhacken
**lop·sid·ed** schief; *fig* einseitig
**lord** Herr *m*, Gebieter *m*; *Br* Lord *m*; ***the Lord*** REL Gott *m* (der Herr); ***the Lord's Prayer*** REL das Vaterunser; ***the Lord's Supper*** REL das (heilige) Abendmahl; ***House of Lords*** *Br* POL Oberhaus *n*
**Lord Mayor** *Br* Oberbürgermeister *m*
**lor·ry** *Br* MOT Last(kraft)wagen *m*, Lastauto *n*, Laster *m*
**lose** verlieren; verpassen, versäumen; nachgehen (*watch*); **~ *o.s.*** sich verirren; sich verlieren; **los·er** Verlierer(in); **loss** Verlust *m*; Schaden *m*; ***at a* ~** ECON mit Verlust; ***be at a* ~** in Verlegenheit sein (***for*** um); **lost** verloren; ***be* ~** sich verirrt haben, sich nicht mehr zurecht-

finden (*a. fig*); **be ~ in thought** in Gedanken versunken sein; **get ~** sich verirren; **get ~!** *sl* hau ab!

**lost-and-found (of·fice)**, *Br* **lost prop·er·ty of·fice** Fundbüro *n*

**lot** Los *n*; Parzelle *f*; Grundstück *n*; ECON Partie *f*, Posten *m*; Gruppe *f*, Gesellschaft *f*; Menge *f*, Haufen *m*; Los *n*, Schicksal *n*; **the ~** alles, das Ganze; **a ~ of** F, **~s of** F viel, e-e Menge; **a bad ~** F ein übler Kerl; **cast** *or* **draw ~s** losen

**loth** → **loath**

**lo·tion** Lotion *f*

**lot·te·ry** Lotterie *f*

**loud** laut; *fig* schreiend, grell

**loud·mouth** *contp* Schwätzer *m*

**loud·speak·er** Lautsprecher *m*

**lounge 1.** Wohnzimmer *n*; Aufenthaltsraum *m*, Lounge *f* (*a.* AVIAT); Wartehalle *f* **2.** F *contp* sich flegeln; **~ about, ~ around** herumlungern

**louse** zo Laus *f*

**lou·sy** verlaust; F miserabel, saumäßig

**lout** Flegel *m*, Lümmel *m*, Rüpel *m*

**lov·a·ble** liebenswert; reizend

**love 1.** Liebe *f* (**of, for, to, towards** zu); Liebling *m*, Schatz *m*; *tennis*: null; **be in ~ with s.o.** in j-n verliebt sein; **fall in ~ with s.o.** sich in j-n verlieben; **make ~** sich lieben, miteinander schlafen; **give my ~ to her** grüße sie herzlich von mir; **send one's ~ to** *j-n* grüßen lassen; **~ from ...** herzliche Grüße von ... **2.** lieben; gern mögen

**love af·fair** Liebesaffäre *f*

**love·ly** (wunder)schön; nett, reizend; F prima

**lov·er** Liebhaber *m*, Geliebte *m, f*; (*Musik- etc*)Liebhaber(in), (-)Freund(in); *pl* Liebende *pl*, Liebespaar *n*

**lov·ing** liebevoll, liebend

**low 1.** *adj* niedrig (*a. fig*); tief (*a. fig*); knapp (*supplies etc*); gedämpft, schwach (*light*); tief (*sound*); leise (*sound, voice*); *fig* gering(schätzig); ordinär; niedergeschlagen, deprimiert **2.** *adv* niedrig; tief (*a. fig*); leise **3.** METEOR Tief(druckgebiet) *n*; *fig* Tief(punkt *m*) *n*

**low·brow** F **1.** geistig Anspruchslose *m, f*, Unbedarfte *m, f* **2.** geistig anspruchslos, unbedarft

**low-cal·o·rie** kalorienarm, -reduziert

**low-e·mis·sion** schadstoffarm

**low·er 1.** niedriger; tiefer; untere(r, -s), Unter... **2.** niedriger machen; herab-, herunterlassen; *Augen*, *Stimme*, *Preis etc* senken; *Standard* herabsetzen; *fig* erniedrigen

**low-fat** fettarm

**low-fly·ing plane** AVIAT Tiefflieger *m*

**low·land** Tief-, Flachland *n*

**low·ly** niedrig

**low-necked** (tief) ausgeschnitten

**low-pitched** MUS tief

**low-pres·sure** METEOR Tiefdruck...; TECH Niederdruck...

**low-rise** ARCH niedrig (gebaut)

**low-spir·it·ed** niedergeschlagen

**low tide** Ebbe *f*

**low wa·ter** Niedrigwasser *n*

**loy·al** loyal, treu

**loy·al·ty** Loyalität *f*, Treue *f*

**loz·enge** MATH Raute *f*, Rhombus *m*; GASTR Pastille *f*

**lu·bri·cant** TECH Schmiermittel *n*

**lu·bri·cate** TECH schmieren, ölen

**lu·bri·ca·tion** TECH Schmieren *n*, Ölen *n*

**lu·cid** klar

**luck** Schicksal *n*; Glück *n*; **bad ~, hard ~, ill ~** Unglück *n*, Pech *n*; **good ~** Glück *n*; **good ~!** viel Glück!; **be in (out of) ~** (kein) Glück haben

**luck·i·ly** glücklicherweise, zum Glück

**luck·y** glücklich, Glücks...; **be ~** Glück haben; **~ day** Glückstag *m*; **~ fellow** Glückspilz *m*

**lu·cra·tive** einträglich, lukrativ

**lu·di·crous** lächerlich

**lug** zerren, schleppen

**luge** SPORT Rennrodeln *n*; Rennrodel *m*, Rennschlitten *m*

**lug·gage** *esp Br* (Reise)Gepäck *n*; **~ rack** *esp Br* RAIL *etc* Gepäcknetz *n*, Gepäckablage *f*; **~ van** *Br* RAIL Gepäckwagen *m*

**luke·warm** lau(warm); *fig* lau, mäßig, halbherzig

**lull 1.** beruhigen; sich legen (*storm*); *mst* **~ to sleep** einlullen **2.** Pause *f*; MAR Flaute *f* (*a. fig*)

**lul·la·by** Wiegenlied *n*

**lum·ba·go** MED Hexenschuss *m*

**lum·ber**[1] schwerfällig gehen; (dahin-)rumpeln (*vehicle*)

**lum·ber**[2] **1.** Bau-, Nutzholz *n*; *esp Br* Gerümpel *n* **2.** *v/t* **~ s.o. with s.th.** *Br* F j-m

et. aufhalsen
**lum·ber·jack** Holzfäller *m*, -arbeiter *m*
**lum·ber mill** Sägewerk *n*
**lum·ber room** *esp Br* Rumpelkammer *f*
**lum·ber·yard** Holzplatz *m*, Holzlager *n*
**lu·mi·na·ry** *fig* Leuchte *f*, Koryphäe *f*
**lu·mi·nous** leuchtend, Leucht…
**lu·mi·nous di·splay** Leuchtanzeige *f*
**lu·mi·nous paint** Leuchtfarbe *f*
**lump** **1.** Klumpen *m*; Schwellung *f*, Beule *f*; MED Geschwulst *f*, Knoten *m*; GASTR Stück *n*; ***in the ~*** in Bausch und Bogen, pauschal **2.** *v/t*: ***~ together*** *fig* zusammenwerfen; in e-n Topf werfen; *v/i* Klumpen bilden, klumpen
**lump sug·ar** Würfelzucker *m*
**lump sum** Pauschalsumme *f*
**lump·y** klumpig
**lu·na·cy** Wahnsinn *m*
**lu·nar** ASTR Mond…
**lu·nar mod·ule** Mond(lande)fähre *f*
**lu·na·tic** *fig* **1.** wahnsinnig, verrückt **2.** Wahnsinnige *m, f*, Verrückte *m, f*
**lunch**, *formal* **lun·cheon** **1.** Lunch *m*, Mittagessen *n* **2.** zu Mittag essen
**lunch hour, lunch time** Mittagszeit *f*, Mittagspause *f*
**lung** ANAT Lungenflügel *m*; *pl* die Lunge
**lunge** sich stürzen (***at*** auf *acc*)
**lurch** **1.** taumeln, torkeln **2.** ***leave s.o. in the ~*** j-n im Stich lassen, F j-n sitzen lassen
**lure** **1.** Köder *m*; *fig* Lockung *f* **2.** ködern, (an)locken
**lu·rid** grell; grässlich, schauerlich
**lurk** lauern; ***~ about, ~ around*** herumschleichen
**lus·cious** köstlich, lecker; üppig; F knackig
**lush** saftig, üppig
**lust** **1.** sinnliche Begierde, Lust *f*; Gier *f* **2.** ***~ after, ~ for*** begehren; gierig sein nach
**lus·ter**, *Br* **lus·tre** Glanz *m*, Schimmer *m*; **lus·trous** glänzend, schimmernd
**lust·y** kräftig, robust, vital
**lute** MUS Laute *f*
**Lu·ther·an** REL lutherisch
**lux·u·ri·ant** üppig
**lux·u·ri·ate** schwelgen (***in*** in *dat*)
**lux·u·ri·ous** luxuriös, Luxus…
**lux·u·ry** **1.** Luxus *m*; Komfort *m*; Luxusartikel *m* **2.** Luxus…
**lye** Lauge *f*
**ly·ing** lügnerisch, verlogen
**lymph** MED Lymphe *f*
**lynch** lynchen; ***~ law*** Lynchjustiz *f*
**lynx** ZO Luchs *m*
**lyr·ic** **1.** lyrisch **2.** lyrisches Gedicht; *pl* Lyrik *f*; (Lied)Text *m*
**lyr·i·cal** lyrisch, gefühlvoll; schwärmerisch

M

# M

**M, m** M, m *n*
**M** *abbr of* ***medium*** (***size***) mittelgroß
**ma** F Mama *f*, Mutti *f*
**ma'am** → ***madam***
**ma·cad·am** Asphalt *m*
**mac·a·ro·ni** Makkaroni *pl*
**ma·chine** **1.** Maschine *f* **2.** maschinell herstellen
**ma·chine·gun** Maschinengewehr *n*
**ma·chine-read·a·ble** IT maschinenlesbar
**ma·chin·e·ry** Maschinen *pl*; Maschinerie *f*
**ma·chin·ist** TECH Maschinist *m*
**mach·o** *contp* Macho *m*
**mack·e·rel** ZO Makrele *f*
**mac·ro…** Makro…, (sehr) groß
**mad** wahnsinnig, verrückt; VET tollwütig; F wütend; *fig* ***be ~ about*** wild *or* versessen sein auf (*acc*), verrückt sein nach; ***drive s.o. ~*** j-n verrückt machen; ***go ~*** verrückt werden; ***like ~*** wie verrückt
**mad·am** gnädige Frau
**mad·cap** verrückt
**mad cow dis·ease** VET Rinderwahn (-sinn) *m*
**mad·den** verrückt *or* rasend machen
**mad·den·ing** unerträglich; verrückt *or* rasend machend
**made**: ***~ of gold*** aus Gold
**made-to-meas·ure** maßgeschneidert
**made-up** geschminkt; erfunden
**mad·house** *fig* F Irrenhaus *n*

**mad·ly** wie verrückt; F wahnsinnig, schrecklich
**mad·man** Verrückte *m*
**mad·ness** Wahnsinn
**mad·wom·an** Verrückte *f*
**mag·a·zine** Magazin *n* (*a.* PHOT, MIL), Zeitschrift *f*; Lagerhaus *n*
**mag·got** ZO Made *f*
**Ma·gi**: ***the*** (***three***) ~ die (drei) Weisen aus dem Morgenland, die Heiligen Drei Könige
**ma·gic 1.** Magie *f*, Zauberei *f*; Zauber *m*; *fig* Wunder *n* **2.** *a.* ***magical*** magisch, Zauber…
**ma·gi·cian** Magier *m*, Zauberer *m*; Zauberkünstler *m*
**ma·gis·trate** (Friedens)Richter(in)
**mag·na·nim·i·ty** Großmut *f*
**mag·nan·i·mous** großmütig
**mag·net** Magnet *m*
**mag·net·ic** magnetisch, Magnet…
**mag·nif·i·cent** großartig, prächtig
**mag·ni·fy** vergrößern
**mag·ni·fy·ing glass** Vergrößerungsglas *n*, Lupe *f*
**mag·ni·tude** Größe *f*; Wichtigkeit *f*
**mag·pie** ZO Elster *f*
**ma·hog·a·ny** Mahagoni(holz) *n*
**maid** (Dienst)Mädchen *n*, Hausangestellte *f*; ~ ***of hono(u)r*** Hofdame *f*; (erste) Brautjungfer
**maid·en** Jungfern…, Erstlings…
**maid·en name** Mädchenname *m*
**mail 1.** Post(sendung) *f*; ***by*** ~ mit der Post® **2.** mit der Post® (zu)schicken, aufgeben, *Brief* einwerfen
**mail·bag** Postsack *m*; Posttasche *f*
**mail·box** Briefkasten *m*
**mail car·ri·er, mail·man** Briefträger *m*, Postbote *m*
**mail or·der** Bestellung *f* bei e-m Versandhaus
**mail-or·der| firm,** ~ **house** Versandhaus *n*
**maim** verstümmeln
**main 1.** Haupt…, wichtigste(r, -s); hauptsächlich; ***by*** ~ ***force*** mit äußerster Kraft **2.** *mst pl* Hauptleitung *f*, Hauptgas-, Hauptwasser-, Hauptstromleitung *f*; (Strom)Netz *n*; ***in the*** ~ in der Hauptsache, im Wesentlichen
**main·frame** IT Großrechner *m*
**main·land** Festland *n*
**main·ly** hauptsächlich
**main mem·o·ry** IT Hauptspeicher *m*; Arbeitsspeicher *m*
**main men·u** IT Hauptmenü *n*
**main road** Haupt(verkehrs)straße *f*
**main·spring** TECH Hauptfeder *f*; *fig* (Haupt)Triebfeder *f*
**main·stay** *fig* Hauptstütze *f*
**main street** Hauptstraße *f*
**main·tain** (aufrecht)erhalten, beibehalten; instand halten, pflegen, TECH *a.* warten; *Familie etc* unterhalten, versorgen; *et.* behaupten
**main·te·nance** (Aufrecht)Erhaltung *f*; Instandhaltung *f*, Pflege *f*, TECH *a.* Wartung *f*; Unterhalt *m*
**maize** *esp Br* BOT Mais *m*
**ma·jes·tic** majestätisch
**ma·jes·ty** Majestät *f*; ***His*** (***Her, Your***) ***Majesty*** Seine (Ihre, Eure) Majestät
**ma·jor 1.** größere(r, -s), *fig a.* bedeutend, wichtig; JUR volljährig; ***C*** ~ MUS C-Dur *n* **2.** MIL Major *m*; JUR Volljährige *m, f*; UNIV Hauptfach *n*; MUS Dur *n*; ~ **gen·e·ral** MIL Generalmajor *m*
**ma·jor·i·ty** Mehrheit *f*, Mehrzahl *f*; JUR Volljährigkeit *f*
**ma·jor league** *baseball*: oberste Spielklasse
**ma·jor road** Haupt(verkehrs)straße *f*
**make 1.** machen; anfertigen, herstellen, erzeugen; (zu)bereiten; (er)schaffen; ergeben, bilden; machen zu; ernennen zu; *Geld* verdienen; sich erweisen als, abgeben (*person*); schätzen auf (*acc*); *Geschwindigkeit* erreichen; *Fehler* machen; *Frieden etc* schließen; *e-e Rede* halten; F *Strecke* zurücklegen; *with inf*: *j-n* lassen, veranlassen zu, bringen zu, zwingen zu; ~ ***it*** es schaffen; ~ ***do with s.th.*** mit et. auskommen, sich mit et. behelfen; ***what do you*** ~ ***of it?*** was halten Sie davon?; ~ ***believe*** vorgeben; ~ ***friends with*** sich anfreunden mit; ~ ***good*** wieder gutmachen; *Versprechen etc* halten; ~ ***way*** Platz machen; ~ ***for*** zugehen auf (*acc*); sich aufmachen nach; ~ ***into*** verarbeiten zu; ~ ***off*** sich davonmachen, sich aus dem Staub machen; ~ ***out*** *Rechnung, Scheck etc* ausstellen; ausmachen, erkennen; aus *j-m, e-r Sache* klug werden; ~ ***over*** *Eigentum* übertragen; ~ ***up*** *et.* zusammenstellen; sich *et.* ausdenken, *et.* erfinden; (sich) zurechtma-

M

chen *or* schminken; **~ it up** sich versöhnen *or* wieder vertragen (**with** mit); **~ up one's mind** sich entschließen; **be made up of** bestehen aus, sich zusammensetzen aus; **~ up for** nachholen, aufholen; für *et.* entschädigen **2.** Machart *f*, Bauart *f*; Fabrikat *n*, Marke *f*

**make-be·lieve** Schein *m*, Fantasie *f*

**mak·er** Hersteller *m*; **Maker** REL Schöpfer *m*

**make·shift 1.** Notbehelf *m* **2.** behelfsmäßig, Behelfs...

**make-up** Make-up *n*, Schminke *f*; Aufmachung *f*; Zusammensetzung *f*

**mak·ing** Erzeugung *f*, Herstellung *f*, Fabrikation *f*; **be in the ~** noch in Arbeit sein; **have the ~s of** das Zeug haben zu

**mal·ad·just·ed** nicht angepasst, verhaltensgestört, milieugestört

**mal·ad·min·i·stra·tion** schlechte Verwaltung; POL Misswirtschaft *f*

**mal·con·tent 1.** unzufrieden **2.** Unzufriedene *m*, *f*

**male 1.** männlich **2.** Mann *m*; ZO Männchen *n*

**male nurse** (Kranken)Pfleger *m*

**mal·for·ma·tion** Missbildung *f*

**mal·ice** Bosheit *f*; Groll *m*; JUR böse Absicht, Vorsatz *m*

**ma·li·cious** boshaft; böswillig

**ma·lign** verleumden

**ma·lig·nant** bösartig (*a.* MED); boshaft

**mall** Einkaufszentrum *n*

**mal·le·a·ble** TECH verformbar; *fig* formbar

**mal·let** Holzhammer *m*; (Krocket-, Polo)Schläger *m*

**mal·nu·tri·tion** Unterernährung *f*; Fehlernährung *f*

**mal·o·dor·ous** übel riechend

**mal·prac·tice** Vernachlässigung *f* der beruflichen Sorgfalt; MED falsche Behandlung, (ärztlicher) Kunstfehler

**malt** Malz *n*

**mal·treat** schlecht behandeln; misshandeln

**mam·mal** ZO Säugetier *n*

**mam·moth 1.** ZO Mammut *n* **2.** Mammut..., Riesen..., riesig

**mam·my** F Mami *f*

**man 1.** Mann *m*; Mensch(en *pl*) *m*; Menschheit *f*; F (Ehe)Mann *m*; F Geliebte *m*; (*Schach*)Figur *f*; (*Dame*)Stein *m*; **the ~ on** (*Br* **in**) **the street** der Mann auf der Straße **2.** (*Raum*)*Schiff etc* bemannen; *Büro etc* besetzen

**man·age** *v/t Betrieb etc* leiten, führen; *Künstler*, *Sportler etc* managen; *et.* zustande bringen; es fertigbringen (**to do** zu tun); umgehen (können) mit; mit *j-m*, *et.* fertigwerden; F *Arbeit*, *Essen etc* bewältigen, schaffen; *v/i* auskommen (**with** mit; **without** ohne); F es schaffen, zurechtkommen; F es einrichten, es ermöglichen

**man·age·a·ble** handlich; lenksam

**man·age·ment** Verwaltung *f*; ECON Management *n*, Unternehmensführung *f*; Geschäftsleitung *f*, Direktion *f*

**man·ag·er** Verwalter *m*; ECON Manager *m* (*a.* THEA *etc*); Geschäftsführer *m*, Leiter *m*, Direktor *m*; SPORT (Chef-) Trainer *m*; **be a good ~** gut *or* sparsam wirtschaften können

**man·a·ge·ri·al** ECON geschäftsführend, leitend; **~ position** leitende Stellung; **~ staff** leitende Angestellte *pl*

**man·ag·ing** ECON geschäftsführend, leitend; **~ di·rec·tor** Generaldirektor *m*, leitender Direktor

**man·date** Mandat *n*; Auftrag *m*; Vollmacht *f*

**man·da·to·ry** obligatorisch, zwingend

**mane** ZO Mähne *f* (*a.* F)

**ma·neu·ver** *a. fig* **1.** Manöver *n* **2.** manövrieren

**mange** VET Räude *f*

**man·ger** AGR Krippe *f*

**man·gle 1.** (Wäsche)Mangel *f* **2.** mangeln; *j-n* übel zurichten, zerfleischen; *fig Text* verstümmeln

**mang·y** VET räudig; *fig* schäbig

**man·hood** Mannesalter *n*; Männlichkeit *f*

**ma·ni·a** Wahnsinn *m*; *fig* (**for**) Sucht *f* (nach), Leidenschaft *f* (für), Manie *f*, Fimmel *m*; **ma·ni·ac** F Wahnsinnige *m*, *f*, Verrückte *m*, *f*; *fig* Fanatiker(in)

**man·i·cure** Maniküre *f*, Handpflege *f*

**man·i·fest 1.** offenkundig **2.** *v/t* offenbaren, manifestieren

**man·i·fold** mannigfaltig, vielfältig

**ma·nip·u·late** manipulieren; (geschickt) handhaben

**ma·nip·u·la·tion** Manipulation *f*

**man·kind** die Menschheit, die Menschen *pl*

**man·ly** männlich

M

**man-made** vom Menschen geschaffen, künstlich; ~ ***fiber*** Kunstfaser *f*
**man·ner** Art *f* (und Weise *f*); Betragen *n*, Auftreten *n*; *pl* Benehmen *n*, Umgangsformen *pl*, Manieren *pl*; Sitten *pl*
**ma·noeu·vre** *Br* → ***maneuver***
**man·or** *Br* (Land)Gut *n*; → **man·or house** Herrenhaus *n*
**man·pow·er** menschliche Arbeitskraft; Arbeitskräfte *pl*
**man·sion** (herrschaftliches) Wohnhaus
**man·slaugh·ter** JUR Totschlag *m*, fahrlässige Tötung
**man·tel·piece, man·tel·shelf** Kaminsims *m*
**man·u·al** **1.** Hand…; mit der Hand (gemacht) **2.** Handbuch *n*
**man·u·fac·ture** **1.** erzeugen, herstellen **2.** Herstellung *f*, Fertigung *f*; Erzeugnis *n*, Fabrikat *n*
**man·u·fac·tur·er** Hersteller *m*, Erzeuger *m*
**man·u·fac·tur·ing** Herstellungs…
**ma·nure** AGR **1.** Dünger *m*, Mist *m*, Dung *m* **2.** düngen
**man·u·script** Manuskript *n*
**man·y** **1.** viel(e); ~ ***a*** manche(r, -s), manch eine(r, -s); ~ ***times*** oft; ***as*** ~ ebenso viel(e) **2.** viele; ***a good*** ~ ziemlich viel(e); ***a great*** ~ sehr viele
**map** **1.** (Land- *etc*)Karte *f*; (Stadt- *etc*)-Plan *m* **2.** e-e Karte machen von; auf e-r Karte eintragen; ~ ***out*** *fig* (bis in die Einzelheiten) (voraus)planen
**ma·ple** BOT Ahorn *m*
**mar** beeinträchtigen; verderben
**Mar** *abbr of* ***March*** März *m*
**mar·a·thon** SPORT **1.** *a.* ~ ***race*** Marathonlauf *m* **2.** Marathon… (*a. fig*)
**ma·raud** plündern
**mar·ble** **1.** Marmor *m*; Murmel *f* **2.** marmorn
**march** **1.** marschieren; *fig* fortschreiten **2.** Marsch *m*; *fig* (Fort)Gang *m*; ***the*** ~ ***of events*** der Lauf der Dinge
**March** (*abbr* ***Mar***) März *m*
**mare** ZO Stute *f*
**mar·ga·rine**, *Br* F **marge** Margarine *f*
**mar·gin** Rand *m* (*a. fig*); Grenze *f* (*a. fig*); *fig* Spielraum *m*; (*Gewinn-, Verdienst*)Spanne *f*; ***by a wide*** ~ mit großem Vorsprung; **mar·gin·al** Rand…; ~ ***note*** Randbemerkung *f*
**mar·i·hua·na, mar·i·jua·na** Marihuana *n*
**ma·ri·na** Boots-, Jachthafen *m*
**ma·rine** Marine *f*; MIL Marineinfanterist *m*
**mar·i·ner** Seemann *m*
**mar·i·tal** ehelich, Ehe…
**mar·i·tal sta·tus** Familienstand *m*
**mar·i·time** See…; Küsten…; Schifffahrts…
**mark**[1] **1.** Marke *f*, Markierung *f*; (Kenn)-Zeichen *n*, Merkmal *n*; (Körper)Mal *n*; Ziel *n* (*a. fig*); Spur *f* (*a. fig*); Fleck *m*; (*Fabrik-, Waren*)Zeichen *n*, (*Schutz-, Handels*)Marke *f*; ECON Preisangabe *f*; PED Note *f*, Zensur *f*, Punkt *m*; SPORT Startlinie *f*; *fig* Zeichen *n*; *fig* Norm *f*; ***be up to the*** ~ den Anforderungen gewachsen sein (*person*) *or* genügen (*performance etc*); *gesundheitlich* auf der Höhe sein; ***be wide of the*** ~ weit danebenschießen; *fig* sich gewaltig irren; weit danebenliegen (*estimate etc*); ***hit the*** ~ (das Ziel) treffen; *fig* ins Schwarze treffen; ***miss the*** ~ danebenschießen, das Ziel verfehlen (*a. fig*) **2.** markieren, anzeichnen; anzeigen; kennzeichnen; *Waren* auszeichnen; *Preis* festsetzen; Spuren hinterlassen auf (*dat*); Flecken machen auf (*dat*); PED benoten, zensieren; SPORT *Gegenspieler* decken, markieren; ~ ***my words*** denk an m-e Worte; ***to*** ~ ***the occasion*** zur Feier des Tages; ~ ***time*** auf der Stelle treten (*a. fig*); ~ ***down*** notieren, vermerken; *im Preis* herabsetzen; ~ ***off*** abgrenzen; *auf e-r Liste* abhaken; ~ ***out*** *durch Striche etc* markieren; bestimmen (***for*** für); ~ ***up*** *im Preis* heraufsetzen
**mark**[2] *hist* (*former monetary unit of Germany*) (Deutsche) Mark
**marked** deutlich, ausgeprägt
**mark·er** Markierstift *m*; Lesezeichen *n*; SPORT Bewacher(in)
**mar·ket** **1.** Markt *m*; Marktplatz *m*; (Lebensmittel)Geschäft *n*, Laden *m*; ECON Absatz *m*; (***for***) Nachfrage *f* (nach), Bedarf *m* (an *dat*); ***on the*** ~ auf dem Markt *or* im Handel; ***put on the*** ~ auf den Markt *or* in den Handel bringen; (zum Verkauf) anbieten **2.** *v/t* auf den Markt *or* in den Handel bringen; verkaufen, vertreiben
**mar·ket·a·ble** ECON marktgängig

M

**mar·ket gar·den** *Br* Gemüse- und Obstgärtnerei *f*
**mar·ket·ing** ECON Marketing *n*
**mark·ing** Markierung *f*; zo Zeichnung *f*; SPORT Deckung *f*; ***man-to-man ~*** Manndeckung *f*
**marks·man** guter Schütze
**mar·ma·lade** *esp* Orangenmarmelade *f*
**mar·mot** zo Murmeltier *n*
**ma·roon** **1.** kastanienbraun **2.** *auf e-r einsamen Insel* aussetzen **3.** Leuchtrakete *f*
**mar·quee** Festzelt *n*
**mar·quis** Marquis *m*
**mar·riage** Heirat *f*, Hochzeit *f* (***to*** mit); Ehe *f*; ***civil ~*** standesamtliche Trauung
**mar·ria·ge·a·ble** heiratsfähig
**mar·riage cer·tif·i·cate** Trauschein *m*, Heiratsurkunde *f*
**mar·ried** verheiratet; ehelich, Ehe…; ***~ couple*** Ehepaar *n*; ***~ life*** Ehe(leben *n*) *f*
**mar·row** ANAT (Knochen)Mark *n*; *fig* Kern *m*, *das* Wesentliche
**mar·ry** *v/t* heiraten; *Paar* trauen; ***be married*** verheiratet sein (***to*** mit); ***get married*** heiraten; sich verheiraten (***to*** mit); *v/i* heiraten
**marsh** Sumpf(land *n*) *m*, Marsch *f*
**mar·shal** **1.** MIL Marschall *m*; Bezirkspolizeichef *m* **2.** ordnen; führen
**marsh·y** sumpfig
**mar·ten** zo Marder *m*
**mar·tial** kriegerisch; Kriegs…, Militär…; **~ arts** asiatische Kampfsportarten *pl*; **~ law** Kriegsrecht *n*
**mar·tyr** REL Märtyrer(in) (*a. fig*)
**mar·vel** **1.** Wunder *n* **2.** sich wundern, staunen; **mar·vel·(l)ous** wunderbar; fabelhaft, fantastisch
**mar·zi·pan** Marzipan *n*, *m*
**mas·ca·ra** Wimperntusche *f*
**mas·cot** Maskottchen *n*
**mas·cu·line** männlich; Männer…; maskulin (*a.* LING)
**mash** zerdrücken, zerquetschen
**mashed po·ta·toes** Kartoffelbrei *m*
**mask** **1.** Maske *f* (*a.* IT); **2.** maskieren; *fig* verbergen, verschleiern
**masked** maskiert; ***~ ball*** Maskenball *m*
**ma·son** Steinmetz *m*; *mst* ***Mason*** Freimaurer *m*; **ma·son·ry** Mauerwerk *n*
**masque** THEA HIST Maskenspiel *n*
**mas·que·rade** **1.** Maskerade *f* (*a. fig*); Verkleidung *f* **2.** sich ausgeben (***as*** als, für)
**mass** **1.** Masse *f*; Menge *f*; Mehrzahl *f*; ***the ~es*** die (breite) Masse **2.** (sich) (an)sammeln *or* (an)häufen **3.** Massen…
**Mass** REL Messe *f*
**mas·sa·cre** **1.** Massaker *n* **2.** niedermetzeln
**mas·sage** **1.** Massage *f* **2.** massieren
**mas·seur** Masseur *m*
**mas·seuse** Masseurin *f*, Masseuse *f*
**mas·sif** (Gebirgs)Massiv *n*
**mas·sive** massiv; groß, gewaltig
**mass me·di·a** Massenmedien *pl*
**mass-pro·duce** serienmäßig herstellen
**mass pro·duc·tion** Massen-, Serienproduktion *f*
**mast** MAR Mast *m*; *Br* ELECTR Sendemast *m*
**mas·ter** **1.** Meister *m* (*a.* PAINT); Herr *m*; *esp Br* Lehrer *m*; Original(kopie *f*) *n*; UNIV Magister *m*; ***Master of Arts*** (*abbr* ***MA***) Magister *m* Artium; ***~ of ceremonies*** Conférencier *m* **2.** Meister…; Haupt…; ***~ copy*** Originalkopie *f*; ***~ tape*** TECH Mastertape *n*, Originaltonband *n* **3.** Herr sein über (*acc*); *Sprache etc* beherrschen; *Aufgabe etc* meistern
**mas·ter key** Hauptschlüssel *m*
**mas·ter·ly** meisterhaft, virtuos
**mas·ter·piece** Meisterstück *n*, -werk *n*
**mas·ter·y** Herrschaft *f*; Oberhand *f*; Beherrschung *f*
**mas·tur·bate** masturbieren, onanieren
**mat**[1] **1.** Matte *f*; Untersetzer *m* **2.** sich verfilzen
**mat**[2] mattiert, matt
**match**[1] Streichholz *n*, Zündholz *n*
**match**[2] **1.** *der, die, das* Gleiche; (dazu) passende Sache *or* Person, Gegenstück *n*; (*Fußball- etc*)Spiel *n*, (*Box- etc* -)Kampf *m*, (*Tennis- etc*)Match *n*, *m*; Heirat *f*; *gute etc* Partie (*person*); ***be a*** (***no***) ***~ for s.o.*** j-m (nicht) gewachsen sein; ***find or meet one's ~*** s-n Meister finden **2.** *v/t j-m, e-r Sache* ebenbürtig *or* gewachsen sein, gleichkommen; *j-m, e-r Sache* entsprechen, passen zu; *v/i* zusammenpassen, übereinstimmen, entsprechen; ***gloves to ~*** dazu passende Handschuhe
**match·box** Streichholz-, Zündholzschachtel *f*

M

**match·less** unvergleichlich, einzigartig
**match·mak·er** Ehestifter(in)
**match point** *tennis etc*: Matchball *m*
**mate**[1] → ***checkmate***
**mate**[2] **1.** (Arbeits)Kamerad *m*, (-)Kollege *m*; zo Männchen *n*, Weibchen *n*; MAR Maat *m* **2.** zo (sich) paaren
**ma·te·ri·al 1.** Material *n*, Stoff *m*; ***writing ~s*** Schreibmaterial(ien *pl*) *n* **2.** materiell; leiblich; wesentlich
**ma·ter·nal** mütterlich, Mutter…; mütterlicherseits
**ma·ter·ni·ty 1.** Mutterschaft *f* **2.** Schwangerschafts…, Umstands…
**ma·ter·ni·ty| leave** Mutterschaftsurlaub *m*; **~ ward** Entbindungsstation *f*
**math** F Mathe *f*
**math·e·ma·ti·cian** Mathematiker(in)
**math·e·mat·ics** Mathematik *f*
**maths** *Br* F Mathe *f*
**mat·i·née** THEA *etc* Nachmittagsvorstellung *f*
**ma·tric·u·late** (sich) immatrikulieren
**mat·ri·mo·ni·al** ehelich, Ehe…
**mat·ri·mo·ny** Ehe *f*, Ehestand *m*
**ma·trix** TECH Matrize *f*
**ma·tron** *Br* MED Oberschwester *f*; Hausmutter *f*; Matrone *f*
**mat·ter 1.** Materie *f*, Material *n*, Substanz *f*, Stoff *m*; MED Eiter *m*; Sache *f*, Angelegenheit *f*; ***printed ~*** Drucksache *f*; ***what's the ~ (with you)?*** was ist los (mit dir)?; ***no ~ who*** gleichgültig, wer; ***for that ~*** was das betrifft; ***a ~ of course*** e-e Selbstverständlichkeit; ***a ~ of fact*** e-e Tatsache; ***as a ~ of fact*** tatsächlich, eigentlich; ***a ~ of form*** e-e Formsache; ***a ~ of time*** e-e Frage der Zeit **2.** von Bedeutung sein (***to*** für); ***it doesn't ~*** es macht nichts
**mat·ter-of-fact** sachlich, nüchtern
**mat·tress** Matratze *f*
**ma·ture 1.** reif (*a. fig*) **2.** (heran)reifen, reif werden
**ma·tu·ri·ty** Reife *f* (*a. fig*)
**maud·lin** rührselig
**maul** übel zurichten; *fig* verreißen
**Maun·dy Thurs·day** Gründonnerstag *m*
**mauve** malvenfarbig, mauve
**mawk·ish** rührselig
**max·i…** Maxi…, riesig, Riesen…
**max·im** Grundsatz *m*
**max·i·mum 1.** Maximum *n* **2.** maximal, Maximal…, Höchst…
**May** Mai *m*
**may** *v/aux ich* kann / mag / darf *etc*, *du* kannst / magst / darfst etc
**may·be** vielleicht
**may·bug** zo Maikäfer *m*
**May Day** der 1. Mai
**may·on·naise** Mayonnaise *f*
**mayor** Bürgermeister(in)
**may·pole** Maibaum *m*
**maze** Irrgarten *m*, Labyrinth *n* (*a. fig*)
**me** mich; mir; F ich
**mead·ow** Wiese *f*, Weide *f*
**mea·ger**, *Br* **mea·gre** mager (*a. fig*), dürr; dürftig
**meal**[1] Mahl(zeit *f*) *n*; Essen *n*
**meal**[2] Schrotmehl *n*
**mean**[1] gemein, niederträchtig; geizig, knauserig; schäbig
**mean**[2] meinen; sagen wollen; bedeuten; beabsichtigen, vorhaben; ***be meant for*** bestimmt sein für; ***~ well (ill)*** es gut (schlecht) meinen
**mean**[3] **1.** Mitte *f*, Mittel *n*, Durchschnitt *m* **2.** mittlere(r, -s), Mittel…, durchschnittlich, Durchschnitts…
**mean·ing 1.** Sinn *m*, Bedeutung *f* **2.** bedeutungsvoll, bedeutsam
**mean·ing·ful** bedeutungsvoll; sinnvoll
**mean·ing·less** sinnlos
**means** Mittel *n or pl*, Weg *m*; ECON Mittel *pl*, Vermögen *n*; ***by all ~*** auf alle Fälle, unbedingt; ***by no ~*** keineswegs, auf keinen Fall; ***by ~ of*** durch, mit
**mean·time 1.** inzwischen **2.** ***in the ~*** inzwischen
**mean·while** inzwischen
**mea·sles** MED Masern *pl*
**mea·sur·a·ble** messbar
**mea·sure 1.** Maß *n* (*a. fig*); TECH Messgerät *n*; MUS Takt *m*; *fig* Maßnahme *f*; ***beyond ~*** über alle Maßen; ***in a great ~*** großenteils; ***take ~s*** Maßnahmen treffen *or* ergreifen **2.** (ab-, aus-, ver)messen; *j-m* Maß nehmen; ***~ up to*** den Ansprüchen (*gen*) genügen; **measured** gemessen; wohlüberlegt; maßvoll
**mea·sure·ment** (Ver)Messung *f*; Maß *n*; **~ of ca·pac·i·ty** Hohlmaß *n*
**mea·sur·ing tape** → ***tape measure***
**meat** GASTR Fleisch *n*; ***cold ~*** kalter Braten
**meat·ball** GASTR Fleischklößchen *n*
**me·chan·ic** Mechaniker(in)

M

**me·chan·i·cal** mechanisch; Maschinen...
**me·chan·ics** PHYS Mechanik *f*
**mech·a·nism** Mechanismus *m*
**mech·a·nize** mechanisieren
**med·al** Medaille *f*; Orden *m*
**med·al·(l)ist** SPORT Medaillengewinner(in)
**med·dle** sich einmischen (***with, in*** in *acc*); **med·dle·some** aufdringlich
**me·di·a** Medien *pl*
**med·i·ae·val** → ***medieval***
**me·di·an** *a.* ~ ***strip*** MOT Mittelstreifen *m*
**me·di·ate** vermitteln
**me·di·a·tion** Vermittlung *f*
**me·di·a·tor** Vermittler *m*
**med·ic** MIL Sanitäter *m*
**med·i·cal 1.** medizinisch, ärztlich **2.** ärztliche Untersuchung
**med·i·cal cer·tif·i·cate** ärztliches Attest
**med·i·cated** medizinisch
**me·di·ci·nal** medizinisch, heilkräftig, Heil...
**medi·cine** Medizin *f*, *a.* Arznei *f*, *a.* Heilkunde *f*
**med·i·e·val** mittelalterlich
**me·di·o·cre** mittelmäßig
**med·i·tate** *v/i* (***on***) nachdenken (über *acc*); meditieren (über *acc*); *v/t* erwägen
**med·i·ta·tion** Nachdenken *n*; Meditation *f*
**med·i·ta·tive** nachdenklich
**Med·i·ter·ra·ne·an** Mittelmeer...
**me·di·um 1.** Mitte *f*; Mittel *n*; Medium *n* **2.** mittlere(r, -s), Mittel..., *a.* mittelmäßig; GASTR medium, halb gar
**med·ley** Gemisch *n*; MUS Medley *n*, Potpourri *n*
**meek** sanft(mütig), bescheiden
**meet** *v/t* treffen, sich treffen mit; begegnen (*dat*); *j-n* kennenlernen; *j-n* abholen; zusammentreffen mit, stoßen *or* treffen auf (*acc*); *Wünschen* entgegenkommen, entsprechen; *e-r Forderung, Verpflichtung* nachkommen; *v/i* zusammenkommen, -treten; sich begegnen, sich treffen; (*feindlich*) zusammenstoßen; SPORT aufeinandertreffen; sich kennenlernen; ~ ***with*** zusammentreffen mit; sich treffen mit; stoßen auf (*Schwierigkeiten etc*); erleben, erleiden
**meet·ing** Begegnung *f*, (Zusammen-) Treffen *n*; Versammlung *f*, Konferenz *f*, Tagung *f*; ~ **place** Tagungs-, Versammlungsort *m*; Treffpunkt *m*
**mel·an·chol·y 1.** Melancholie *f*, Schwermut *f*, Trübsinn *m* **2.** melancholisch, traurig, trübsinnig, wehmütig
**mel·low 1.** reif, weich; sanft, mild (*light*), zart (*colors*); *fig* gereift (*person*) **2.** reifen (lassen) (*a. fig*); weich *or* sanft werden
**me·lo·di·ous** melodisch
**mel·o·dra·mat·ic** melodramatisch
**mel·o·dy** MUS Melodie *f*
**mel·on** BOT Melone *f*
**melt** (zer)schmelzen; ~ ***down*** einschmelzen
**mem·ber** Mitglied *n*, Angehörige *m*, *f*; ANAT Glied *n*, Gliedmaße *f*; (männliches) Glied; ***Member of Parliament*** *Br* Mitglied *n* des Unterhauses, Unterhausabgeordnete *m*, *f*; **mem·ber·ship** Mitgliedschaft *f*; Mitgliederzahl *f*
**mem·brane** Membran(e) *f*
**mem·o** Memo *n*
**mem·oirs** Memoiren *pl*
**mem·o·ra·ble** denkwürdig
**me·mo·ri·al** Denkmal *n*, Ehrenmal *n*, Gedenkstätte *f* (***to*** für); Gedenkfeier *f* (***to*** für)
**mem·o·rize** auswendig lernen, sich *et.* einprägen
**mem·o·ry** Gedächtnis *n*; Erinnerung *f*; Andenken *n*; IT Speicher *m*; ***in ~ of*** zum Andenken an (*acc*)
**men·ace 1.** (be)drohen **2.** (Be)Drohung *f*
**mend 1.** *v/t* (ver)bessern; ausbessern, reparieren, flicken; ~ ***one's ways*** sich bessern; *v/i* sich bessern **2.** ausgebesserte Stelle; ***on the*** ~ auf dem Wege der Bess(e)rung
**men·di·cant** REL Bettelmönch *m*
**me·ni·al** niedrig, untergeordnet
**men·in·gi·tis** MED Meningitis *f*, Hirnhautentzündung *f*
**men·o·pause** MED Wechseljahre *pl*
**men·stru·ate** menstruieren
**men·stru·a·tion** Menstruation *f*
**men·tal** geistig, Geistes...; seelisch, psychisch; ~ **a·rith·me·tic** Kopfrechnen *n*; ~ **hand·i·cap** geistige Behinderung; ~ **hos·pi·tal** psychiatrische Klinik
**men·tal·i·ty** Mentalität *f*
**men·tal·ly**: ~ ***handicapped*** geistig behindert; ~ ***ill*** geisteskrank
**men·tion 1.** erwähnen; ***don't ~ it!*** keine

Ursache! **2.** Erwähnung *f*

**men·u** Speise(n)karte *f*; IT Menü *n*

**me·ow** ZO miauen

**mer·can·tile** Handels…

**mer·ce·na·ry 1.** geldgierig **2.** MIL Söldner *m*

**mer·chan·dise 1.** Ware(n *pl*) *f* **2.** vermarkten

**mer·chan·dis·ing** Vermarktung *f*

**mer·chant 1.** (Groß)Händler *m*, (Groß)Kaufmann *m* **2.** Handels…

**mer·ci·ful** barmherzig, gnädig

**mer·ci·less** unbarmherzig, erbarmungslos

**mer·cu·ry** CHEM Quecksilber *n*

**mer·cy** Barmherzigkeit *f*, Erbarmen *n*, Gnade *f*

**mere, mere·ly** bloß, nur

**merge** verschmelzen (***into, with*** mit); ECON fusionieren

**merg·er** ECON Fusion *f*

**me·rid·i·an** GEOGR Meridian *m*; *fig* Gipfel *m*, Höhepunkt *m*

**mer·it 1.** Verdienst *n*; Wert *m*; Vorzug *m* **2.** verdienen

**mer·maid** Meerjungfrau *f*, Nixe *f*

**mer·ri·ment** Fröhlichkeit *f*; Gelächter *n*, Heiterkeit *f*

**mer·ry** lustig, fröhlich, ausgelassen; ***Merry Christmas!*** fröhliche *or* frohe Weihnachten

**mer·ry-go-round** Karussell *n*

**mesh 1.** Masche *f*; *fig often pl* Netz *n*, Schlingen *pl*; ***be in ~*** TECH (ineinander)greifen **2.** TECH (ineinander)greifen; *fig* passen (***with*** zu), zusammenpassen

**mess 1.** Unordnung *f*, Durcheinander *n*; Schmutz *m*, F Schweinerei *f*; F Patsche *f*, Klemme *f*; MIL Messe *f*, Kasino *n*; ***make a ~ of*** F *fig* verpfuschen, ruinieren, *Pläne etc* über den Haufen werfen **2. *~ about, ~ around*** F herumspielen, herumbasteln (***with*** an *dat*); herumgammeln; ***~ up*** in Unordnung bringen, durcheinanderbringen; *fig* F verpfuschen, ruinieren, *Pläne etc* über den Haufen werfen

**mes·sage** Mitteilung *f*, Nachricht *f*; Anliegen *n*, Aussage *f*; ***can I take a ~?*** kann ich etwas ausrichten?; ***get the ~*** F kapieren; **mes·sen·ger** Bote *m*

**mess·y** unordentlich; unsauber, schmutzig

**me·tab·o·lis·m** MED Stoffwechsel *m*

**met·al** Metall *n*

**me·tal·lic** metallisch; Metall…

**met·a·mor·pho·sis** Metamorphose *f*, Verwandlung *f*

**met·a·phor** Metapher *f*

**me·tas·ta·sis** MED Metastase *f*

**me·te·or** Meteor *m*

**me·te·or·o·log·i·cal** meteorologisch, Wetter…, Witterungs…; **~ of·fice** Wetteramt *n*

**me·te·o·rol·o·gy** Meteorologie *f*, Wetterkunde *f*

**me·ter**[1] TECH Messgerät *n*, Zähler *m*

**me·ter**[2] Meter *m*, *n*; Versmaß *n*

**meth·od** Methode *f*, Verfahren *n*; System *n*; **me·thod·i·cal** methodisch, systematisch, planmäßig

**me·tic·u·lous** peinlich genau, übergenau

**me·tre** *Br* → ***meter***[2]

**met·ric** metrisch; **~ sys·tem** metrisches (Maß- und Gewichts)System

**me·trop·o·lis** Weltstadt *f*

**met·ro·pol·i·tan** … der Hauptstadt

**met·tle** Eifer *m*, Mut *m*, Feuer *n*

**mew** ZO miauen

**Mex·i·can 1.** mexikanisch **2.** Mexikaner(in)

**Mex·i·co** Mexiko *n*

**mi·aow** ZO miauen

**mi·cro…** Mikro…, (sehr) klein

**mi·cro·chip** Mikrochip *m*

**mi·cro·e·lec·tron·ics** Mikroelektronik *f*

**mi·cro·film** Mikrofilm *m*

**mi·cro·or·gan·ism** BIOL Mikroorganismus *m*

**mi·cro·phone** Mikrofon *n*

**mi·cro·pro·ces·sor** Mikroprozessor *m*

**mi·cro·scope** Mikroskop *n*

**mi·cro·scop·ic** mikroskopisch

**mi·cro·wave** Mikrowelle *f*; **~ ov·en** Mikrowellenherd *m*

**mid** mittlere(r, -s), Mitt(el)…

**mid·air**: ***in ~*** in der Luft

**mid·day 1.** Mittag *m* **2.** mittägig, Mittag(s)…

**mid·dle 1.** mittlere(r, -s), Mittel… **2.** Mitte *f*

**mid·dle-aged** mittleren Alters

**Mid·dle Ag·es** HIST Mittelalter *n*

**mid·dle class(·es)** Mittelstand *m*

**mid·dle·man** ECON Zwischenhändler *m*; Mittelsmann *m*

M

**mid·dle name** zweiter Vorname *m*
**mid·dle-sized** mittelgroß
**mid·dle·weight** *boxing*: Mittelgewicht *n*, Mittelgewichtler *m*
**mid·dling** F mittelmäßig, Mittel…; leidlich
**mid·field** *esp soccer*: Mittelfeld *n*
**mid·field·er, mid·field play·er** *esp soccer*: Mittelfeldspieler *m*
**midge** zo Mücke *f*
**midg·et** Zwerg *m*, Knirps *m*
**mid·night** Mitternacht *f*; ***at** ~* um Mitternacht
**midst**: ***in the** ~ **of*** mitten in (*dat*)
**mid·sum·mer** Hochsommer *m*; ASTR Sommersonnenwende *f*
**mid·way** auf halbem Wege
**mid·wife** Hebamme *f*
**mid·win·ter** Mitte *f* des Winters; ASTR Wintersonnenwende *f*; ***in** ~* mitten im Winter
**might** Macht *f*, Gewalt *f*; Kraft *f*
**might·y** mächtig, gewaltig
**mi·grate** (aus)wandern, (fort)ziehen (*a.* zo)
**mi·gra·tion** Wanderung *f* (*a.* zo)
**mi·gra·to·ry** Wander…; zo Zug…
**mike** F Mikrofon *n*
**mild** mild, sanft, leicht
**mil·dew** BOT Mehltau *m*
**mild·ness** Milde *f*
**mile** Meile *f* (*1,6 km*)
**mile·age** zurückgelegte Meilenzahl *or* Fahrtstrecke; Meilenstand *m*; *a.* ***~ allowance*** Meilengeld *n*, *appr* Kilometergeld *n*
**mile·stone** Meilenstein *m* (*a. fig*)
**mil·i·tant** militant; streitbar, kriegerisch
**mil·i·ta·ry** **1.** militärisch, Militär… **2.** ***the** ~* das Militär; **~ gov·ern·ment** Militärregierung *f*; **~ po·lice** (*abbr* ***MP***) Militärpolizei *f*
**mi·li·tia** Miliz *f*, Bürgerwehr *f*
**milk** **1.** Milch *f*; ***it's no use crying over spilt** ~* geschehen ist geschehen **2.** *v/t* melken; *v/i* Milch geben; **~ choc·olate** Vollmilchschokolade *f*
**milk·man** Milchmann *m*
**milk pow·der** Milchpulver *n*, Trockenmilch *f*
**milk shake** Milchmixgetränk *n*
**milk tooth** ANAT Milchzahn *m*
**milk·y** milchig; Milch…
**Milky Way** ASTR Milchstraße *f*
**mill** **1.** Mühle *f*; Fabrik *f* **2.** *Korn etc* mahlen; *Metall* verarbeiten; *Münze* rändeln
**mil·le·pede** → ***millipede***
**mill·er** Müller *m*
**mil·let** BOT Hirse *f*
**mil·li·ner** Hutmacherin *f*, Putzmacherin *f*, Modistin *f*
**mil·lion** Million *f*
**mil·lion·aire** Millionär(in)
**mil·lionth** **1.** millionste(r, -s) **2.** Millionstel *n*
**mil·li·pede** zo Tausendfüß(l)er *m*
**mill·stone** Mühlstein *m*; ***be a** ~ **round s.o.'s neck*** *fig* j-m ein Klotz am Bein sein
**milt** zo Milch *f*
**mime** **1.** Pantomime *f*; Pantomime *m* **2.** (panto)mimisch darstellen; **mim·ic** **1.** mimisch; Schein… **2.** Imitator *m* **3.** nachahmen; nachäffen; **mim·ic·ry** Nachahmung *f*; zo Mimikry *f*
**mince** **1.** *v/t* zerhacken, (zer)schneiden; ***he does not** ~ **matters** or **his words*** er nimmt kein Blatt vor den Mund; *v/i* tänzeln, trippeln **2.** *a.* ***~d meat*** Hackfleisch *n*; **minc·er** Fleischwolf *m*
**mind** **1.** Sinn *m*, Gemüt *n*, Herz *n*; Verstand *m*, Geist *m*; Ansicht *f*, Meinung *f*; Absicht *f*, Neigung *f*, Lust *f*; Erinnerung *f*, Gedächtnis *n*; ***be out of one's** ~* nicht (recht) bei Sinnen sein; ***bear** or **keep in** ~* (immer) denken an (*acc*), *et.* nicht vergessen; ***change one's** ~* es sich anders überlegen, s-e Meinung ändern; ***enter s.o.'s** ~* j-m in den Sinn kommen; ***give s.o. a piece of one's** ~* j-m gründlich die Meinung sagen; ***have** (**half**) **a** ~ **to** inf* (nicht übel) Lust haben zu *inf*; ***lose one's** ~* den Verstand verlieren; ***make up one's** ~* sich entschließen, e-n Entschluss fassen; ***to my** ~* meiner Ansicht nach **2.** *v/t* achtgeben auf (*acc*); sehen nach, aufpassen auf (*acc*); et. haben gegen; ***~ the step!*** Vorsicht, Stufe!; ***~ your own business!*** kümmere dich um deine eigenen Angelegenheiten!; ***do you** ~ **if I smoke?, do you** ~ **my smoking?*** haben Sie et. dagegen *or* stört es Sie, wenn ich rauche?; ***would you** ~ **opening the window?*** würden Sie bitte das Fenster öffnen?; ***would you** ~ **coming*** würden Sie bitte kommen?; *v/i* aufpassen; et. dage-

gen haben; ~ (***you***) wohlgemerkt, allerdings; ***never ~!*** macht nichts!, ist schon gut!; ***I don't ~*** meinetwegen, von mir aus

**mind·less** gedankenlos, blind; unbekümmert (***of*** um), ohne Rücksicht (***of*** auf *acc*)

**mine**[1] meins; ***that's ~*** das gehört mir

**mine**[2] **1.** Bergwerk *n*, Mine *f*, Zeche *f*, Grube *f*; MIL Mine *f*; *fig* Fundgrube *f* **2.** *v/i* schürfen, graben (***for*** nach); *v/t Erz, Kohle* abbauen; MIL verminen

**min·er** Bergmann *m*, Kumpel *m*

**min·e·ral** **1.** Mineral *n*; *pl Br* Mineralwasser *n* **2.** Mineral…; **~ oil** Mineralöl *n*; **~ wa·ter** Mineralwasser *n*

**min·gle** *v/t* (ver)mischen; *v/i* sich mischen *or* mengen (***with*** unter)

**min·i…** Mini…, Klein(st)…; → ***miniskirt***

**min·i·a·ture** **1.** Miniatur(gemälde *n*) *f* **2.** Miniatur…; Klein…; **~ cam·e·ra** Kleinbildkamera *f*

**min·i·mize** auf ein Mindestmaß herabsetzen; herunterspielen, bagatellisieren

**min·i·mum** **1.** Minimum *n*, Mindestmaß *n* **2.** minimal, Mindest…

**min·ing** **1.** Bergbau *m* **2.** Berg(bau)…, Bergwerks…; Gruben…

**min·i·skirt** Minirock *m*

**min·is·ter** POL Minister(in); Gesandte *m*; REL Geistliche *m*; **min·is·try** POL Ministerium *n*; REL geistliches Amt

**mink** ZO Nerz *m*

**mi·nor** **1.** kleinere(r, -s), *fig a.* unbedeutend, geringfügig; JUR minderjährig; ***A ~*** MUS a-Moll *n*; ***~ key*** MUS Moll(tonart *f*) *n* **2.** JUR Minderjährige *m, f*; UNIV Nebenfach *n*; MUS Moll *n*; **mi·nor·i·ty** Minderheit *f*; JUR Minderjährigkeit *f*

**min·ster** *Br* Münster *n*

**mint**[1] **1.** Münze *f*, Münzanstalt *f* **2.** prägen

**mint**[2] BOT Minze *f*

**min·u·et** MUS Menuett *n*

**mi·nus** **1.** *prp* minus, weniger; F ohne **2.** *adj* Minus… **3.** Minus *n*, *fig a.* Nachteil *m*

**min·ute**[1] Minute *f*; Augenblick *m*; ***in a ~*** sofort; ***just a ~!*** Moment mal!

**mi·nute**[2] winzig; sehr genau

**min·utes** Protokoll *n*; ***take*** (*or* ***keep***) ***the ~*** (das) Protokoll führen

**mir·a·cle** Wunder *n*

**mi·rac·u·lous** wunderbar

**mi·rac·u·lous·ly** wie durch ein Wunder

**mi·rage** Luftspiegelung *f*, Fata Morgana *f*

**mire** Schlamm *m*; ***drag through the ~*** *fig* in den Schmutz ziehen

**mir·ror** **1.** Spiegel *m* **2.** (wider)spiegeln (*a. fig*)

**mis…** miss…, falsch, schlecht

**mis·ad·ven·ture** Missgeschick *n*; Unglück *n*, Unglücksfall *m*

**mis·an·thrope**, **mis·an·thro·pist** Menschenfeind(in)

**mis·ap·ply** falsch an- *or* verwenden

**mis·ap·pre·hend** missverstehen

**mis·ap·pro·pri·ate** unterschlagen, veruntreuen

**mis·be·have** sich schlecht benehmen

**mis·cal·cu·late** falsch berechnen; sich verrechnen (in *dat*)

**miscar·riage** MED Fehlgeburt *f*; Misslingen *n*, Fehlschlag(en *n*) *m*; ***~ of justice*** JUR Fehlurteil *n*

**mis·car·ry** MED e-e Fehlgeburt haben; misslingen, scheitern

**mis·cel·la·ne·ous** gemischt, vermischt; verschiedenartig

**mis·cel·la·ny** Gemisch *n*; Sammelband *m*

**mis·chief** Schaden *m*; Unfug *m*; Übermut *m*

**mis·chie·vous** boshaft, mutwillig; schelmisch

**mis·con·ceive** falsch auffassen, missverstehen

**mis·con·duct** schlechtes Benehmen; schlechte Führung; Verfehlung *f*

**mis·con·strue** falsch auslegen, missdeuten

**mis·de·mea·no(u)r** JUR Vergehen *n*

**mis·di·rect** fehlleiten, irreleiten; *Brief etc* falsch adressieren

**mise-en-scène** THEA Inszenierung *f*

**mi·ser** Geizhals *m*

**mis·e·ra·ble** erbärmlich, kläglich, elend; unglücklich

**mi·ser·ly** geizig, F knick(e)rig

**mis·e·ry** Elend *n*, Not *f*

**mis·fire** versagen (*gun*); MOT fehlzünden, aussetzen; *fig* danebengehen

**mis·fit** Außenseiter(in)

**mis·for·tune** Unglück *n*, Unglücksfall *m*; Missgeschick *n*

M

**mis·giv·ing** Befürchtung *f*, Zweifel *m*
**mis·guid·ed** irregeleitet, irrig, unangebracht
**mis·hap** Unglück *n*; Missgeschick *n*; ***without ~*** ohne Zwischenfälle
**mis·in·form** falsch unterrichten
**mis·in·ter·pret** missdeuten, falsch auffassen *or* auslegen
**mis·lay** *et.* verlegen
**mis·lead** irreführen, täuschen; verleiten
**mis·man·age** schlecht verwalten *or* führen *or* handhaben
**mis·place** *et.* an e-e falsche Stelle legen *or* setzen; *et.* verlegen; ***~d*** *fig* unangebracht, deplatziert
**mis·print 1.** verdrucken **2.** Druckfehler *m*
**mis·read** falsch lesen; falsch deuten, missdeuten
**mis·rep·re·sent** falsch darstellen; entstellen, verdrehen
**miss 1.** *v/t* verpassen, versäumen, verfehlen; übersehen, nicht bemerken; überhören; nicht verstehen *or* begreifen; vermissen; *a.* ***~ out*** auslassen, übergehen, überspringen; *v/i* nicht treffen; missglücken; ***~ out on*** *et.* verpassen **2.** Fehlschuss *m*, Fehlstoß *m*, Fehlwurf *m etc*; Verpassen *n*, Verfehlen *n*
**Miss** Fräulein *n*
**mis·shap·en** missgebildet
**mis·sile 1.** Geschoss *n*; Rakete *f* **2.** Raketen…
**miss·ing** fehlend; ***be ~*** fehlen, verschwunden *or* weg sein; (MIL *a.* ***~ in action***) vermisst; ***be ~*** MIL vermisst sein *or* werden
**mis·sion** (*Militär- etc*)Mission *f*; *esp* POL Auftrag *m*, Mission *f* (*a.* REL); MIL, AVIAT Einsatz *m*
**mis·sion·a·ry** REL Missionar *m*
**mis·spell** falsch buchstabieren *or* schreiben
**mis·spend** falsch verwenden; vergeuden
**mist 1.** (feiner *or* leichter) Nebel **2.** ***~ over*** sich trüben; ***~ up*** (sich) beschlagen
**mis·take 1.** verwechseln (***for*** mit); verkennen, sich irren in (*dat*); falsch verstehen, missverstehen **2.** Irrtum *m*, Versehen *n*, Fehler *m*; ***by ~*** aus Versehen, irrtümlich; **mis·tak·en** irrig, falsch (verstanden); ***be ~*** sich irren
**mis·tle·toe** BOT Mistel *f*
**mis·tress** Herrin *f*; *esp Br* Lehrerin *f*; Geliebte *f*
**mis·trust 1.** misstrauen (*dat*) **2.** Misstrauen *n* (***of*** gegen)
**mis·trust·ful** misstrauisch
**mist·y** (leicht) neb(e)lig; *fig* unklar, verschwommen
**mis·un·der·stand** missverstehen; *j-n* nicht verstehen; **mis·un·der·stand·ing** Missverständnis *n*
**mis·use 1.** missbrauchen; falsch gebrauchen **2.** Missbrauch *m*
**mite** ZO Milbe *f*; kleines Ding, Würmchen *n*; ***a ~*** F ein bisschen
**mi·ter**, *Br* **mi·tre** REL Mitra *f*, Bischofsmütze *f*
**mitt** *baseball*: Fanghandschuh *m*; → **mit·ten** Fausthandschuh *m*
**mix 1.** (ver)mischen, vermengen; *Getränke* mixen; sich (ver)mischen; sich mischen lassen; verkehren (***with*** mit); ***~ well*** kontaktfreudig sein; ***~ up*** zusammenmischen, durcheinander mischen; (völlig) durcheinanderbringen; verwechseln (***with*** mit); ***be ~ed up*** verwickelt sein *or* werden (***in*** in *acc*); (*geistig*) ganz durcheinander sein **2.** Mischung *f*
**mixed** gemischt (*a. fig*); vermischt, Misch…
**mix·er** Mixer *m*; TECH Mischmaschine *f*; *radio*, TV *etc*: Mischpult *n*
**mix·ture** Mischung *f*; Gemisch *n*
**mix-up** F Verwechs(e)lung *f*
**moan 1.** Stöhnen *n* **2.** stöhnen
**moat** (Burg-, Stadt)Graben *m*
**mob 1.** Mob *m*, Pöbel *m* **2.** herfallen über (*acc*); *j-n* bedrängen, belagern
**mo·bile 1.** beweglich; MIL mobil, motorisiert; *fig* lebhaft **2.** → ***mobile phone*** *or* ***telephone***; ~ **home** Wohnwagen *m*; ~ **phone**, ~ **tel·e·phone** Mobiltelefon *n*, Handy *n*
**mo·bil·ize** mobilisieren, MIL *a.* mobil machen
**moc·ca·sin** Mokassin *m*
**mock 1.** *v/t* verspotten; nachäffen; *v/i* sich lustig machen, spotten (***at*** über *acc*); **2.** nachgemacht, Schein…
**mock·e·ry** Spott *m*, Hohn *m*; Gespött *n*
**mock·ing·bird** ZO Spottdrossel *f*
**mode** (Art *f* und) Weise *f*; IT Modus *m*,

M

Betriebsart *f*
**mod·el** **1.** Modell *n*; Muster *n*; Vorbild *n*; Mannequin *n*; Model *n*, (Foto)Modell *n*; TECH Modell *n*, Typ *m*; ***male** ~* Dressman *m* **2.** Modell..., Muster... **3.** *v/t* modellieren, *a. fig* formen; *Kleider etc* vorführen; *v/i* Modell stehen *or* sitzen; als Mannequin *or* (Foto)Modell *or* Dressman arbeiten
**mo·dem** IT Modem *m, n*
**mod·e·rate** **1.** (mittel)mäßig; gemäßigt; vernünftig, angemessen **2.** (sich) mäßigen
**mod·e·ra·tion** Mäßigung *f*
**mod·ern** modern, neu
**mod·ern·ize** modernisieren
**mod·est** bescheiden
**mod·es·ty** Bescheidenheit *f*
**mod·i·fi·ca·tion** (Ab-, Ver)Änderung *f*
**mod·i·fy** (ab-, ver)ändern
**mod·u·late** modulieren
**mod·ule** TECH Modul *n*, ELECTR *a.* Baustein *m*; (*Kommando- etc*)Kapsel *f*
**moist** feucht
**moist·en** *v/t* anfeuchten, befeuchten; *v/i* feucht werden
**mois·ture** Feuchtigkeit *f*
**mo·lar** ANAT Backenzahn *m*
**mo·las·ses** Sirup *m*
**mold**[1] Schimmel *m*; Moder *m*; Humus (-boden) *m*
**mold**[2] TECH **1.** (Gieß-, Guss-, Press-) Form *f* **2.** gießen; formen
**mol·der** *a.* ***~ away*** vermodern; zerfallen
**mold·y** verschimmelt, schimm(e)lig; mod(e)rig
**mole**[1] ZO Maulwurf *m*
**mole**[2] Muttermal *n*, Leberfleck *m*
**mole**[3] Mole *f*, Hafendamm *m*
**mol·e·cule** Molekül *n*
**mole·hill** Maulwurfshügel *m*; ***make a mountain out of a ~*** aus e-r Mücke e-n Elefanten machen
**mo·lest** belästigen
**mol·li·fy** besänftigen, beschwichtigen
**mol·lusc** *Br*, **mol·lusk** ZO Weichtier *n*
**mol·ly·cod·dle** F verhätscheln, verzärteln
**molt** (sich) mausern; *Haare* verlieren
**mol·ten** geschmolzen
**mom** F Mami *f*, Mutti *f*
**mom-and-pop store** Tante-Emma-Laden *m*
**mo·ment** Moment *m*, Augenblick *m*; Bedeutung *f*; PHYS Moment *n*
**mo·men·ta·ry** momentan, augenblicklich
**mo·men·tous** bedeutsam, folgenschwer
**mo·men·tum** PHYS Moment *n*; Schwung *m*
**Mon** *abbr of* ***Monday*** Mo., Montag *m*
**mon·arch** Monarch(in), Herrscher(in)
**mon·ar·chy** Monarchie *f*
**mon·as·tery** REL (Mönchs)Kloster *n*
**Mon·day** (*abbr* ***Mon***) Montag *m*; ***on ~*** (am) Montag; ***on ~s*** montags
**mon·e·ta·ry** ECON Währungs...; Geld...
**mon·ey** Geld *n*
**mon·ey·box** *Br* Sparbüchse *f*
**mon·ey·chang·er** (Geld)Wechsler *m*; TECH Wechselautomat *m*
**mon·ey or·der** Post- *or* Zahlungsanweisung *f*
**mon·grel** ZO Bastard *m*, *esp* Promenadenmischung *f*
**mon·i·tor** **1.** Monitor *m*; Kontrollgerät *n*, -schirm *m* **2.** abhören; überwachen
**monk** REL Mönch *m*
**mon·key** **1.** ZO Affe *m*; F (kleiner) Schlingel; ***make a ~ (out) of s.o.*** F j-n zum Deppen machen **2.** ***~ about, ~ around*** F (herum)albern; ***~ about*** *or* ***around with*** F herumspielen mit *or* an (*dat*) herummurksen an (*dat*); ***~ wrench*** TECH Engländer *m*, Franzose *m*; ***throw a ~ into s.th.*** F et. behindern
**mon·o** **1.** Mono *n*; F Monogerät *n* **2.** Mono...
**mon·o...** ein..., mono...
**mon·o·log**, *esp Br* **mon·o·logue** Monolog *m*
**mo·nop·o·lize** monopolisieren; *fig* an sich reißen
**mo·nop·o·ly** Monopol *n* (***of*** auf *acc*)
**mo·not·o·nous** monoton, eintönig
**mo·not·o·ny** Monotonie *f*
**mon·soon** Monsun *m*
**mon·ster** **1.** Monster *n*, Ungeheuer *n* (*a. fig*); Monstrum *n* **2.** Riesen...
**mon·stros·i·ty** Ungeheuerlichkeit *f*; Monstrum *n*; **mon·strous** ungeheuer; *mst contp* ungeheuerlich; scheußlich
**month** Monat *m*; **month·ly** **1.** monatlich, Monats... **2.** Monatsschrift *f*
**mon·u·ment** Monument *n*, Denkmal *n*
**mon·u·ment·al** monumental; F kolossal, Riesen...; Gedenk...
**moo** ZO muhen

**mooch** F schnorren
**mood** Stimmung *f*, Laune *f*; ***be in a good*** (***bad***) ~ gute (schlechte) Laune haben, gut (schlecht) aufgelegt sein
**mood·y** launisch; schlecht gelaunt
**moon 1.** ASTR Mond *m* **2.** ~ ***about***, ~ ***around*** F herumtrödeln; F ziellos herumstreichen
**moon·light** Mondlicht *n*, -schein *m*
**moon·lit** mondhell
**moor**[1] (Hoch)Moor *n*
**moor**[2] MAR vertäuen, festmachen
**moor·ings** MAR Vertäuung *f*; Liegeplatz *m*
**moose** ZO *nordamerikanischer* Elch
**mop 1.** Mopp *m*; F (Haar)Wust *m* **2.** wischen; ~ ***up*** aufwischen
**mope** Trübsal blasen
**mo·ped** *Br* MOT Moped *n*
**mor·al 1.** moralisch; Moral..., Sitten... **2.** Moral *f*, Lehre *f*; *pl* Moral *f*, Sitten *pl*
**mo·rale** Moral *f*, Stimmung *f*
**mor·al·ize** moralisieren (***about, on*** über *acc*)
**mor·bid** morbid, krankhaft
**more 1.** *adj* mehr; noch (mehr); ***some*** ~ ***tea*** noch etwas Tee **2.** *adv* mehr; noch; ~ ***and*** ~ immer mehr; ~ ***or less*** mehr oder weniger; ***once*** ~ noch einmal; ***the*** ~ ***so because*** umso mehr, da; ~ ***important*** wichtiger; ~ ***often*** öfter **3.** Mehr *n* (***of*** an *dat*); ***a little*** ~ etwas mehr
**mo·rel** BOT Morchel *f*
**more·o·ver** außerdem, weiter, ferner
**morgue** Leichenschauhaus *n*; F (Zeitungs)Archiv *n*
**morn·ing** Morgen *m*; Vormittag *m*; ***good*** ~***!*** guten Morgen!; ***in the*** ~ morgens, am Morgen; vormittags, am Vormittag; ***tomorrow*** ~ morgen früh *or* Vormittag
**mo·rose** mürrisch, verdrießlich
**mor·phi·a**, **mor·phine** PHARM Morphium *n*
**mor·sel** Bissen *m*, Happen *m*; ***a*** ~ ***of*** ein bisschen
**mor·tal 1.** sterblich; tödlich; Tod(es)... **2.** Sterbliche *m, f*
**mor·tal·i·ty** Sterblichkeit *f*
**mor·tar**[1] Mörtel *m*
**mor·tar**[2] Mörser *m*
**mort·gage 1.** Hypothek *f* **2.** mit e-r Hypothek belasten, e-e Hypothek aufnehmen auf (*acc*)
**mor·ti·cian** Leichenbestatter *m*
**mor·ti·fi·ca·tion** Kränkung *f*; Ärger *m*, Verdruss *m*
**mor·ti·fy** kränken; ärgern, verdrießen
**mor·tu·a·ry** Leichenhalle *f*
**mo·sa·ic** Mosaik *n*
**Mos·lem** → ***Muslim***
**mosque** Moschee *f*
**mos·qui·to** ZO Moskito *m*; Stechmücke *f*
**moss** BOT Moos *n*
**moss·y** BOT moosig, bemoost
**most 1.** *adj* meiste(r, -s), größte(r, -s); die meisten; ~ ***people*** die meisten Leute **2.** *adv* am meisten; ~ ***of all*** am allermeisten; *before adj*: höchst, äußerst; ***the*** ~ ***important point*** der wichtigste Punkt **3.** *das* meiste, *das* Höchste; das meiste, der größte Teil; die meisten *pl*; ***at*** (***the***) ~ höchstens; ***make the*** ~ ***of*** *et.* nach Kräften ausnutzen, das Beste herausholen aus
**most·ly** hauptsächlich, meist(ens)
**mo·tel** Motel *n*
**moth** ZO Motte *f*
**moth-eat·en** mottenzerfressen
**moth·er 1.** Mutter *f* **2.** bemuttern
**moth·er coun·try** Vaterland *n*, Heimatland *n*; Mutterland *n*
**moth·er·hood** Mutterschaft *f*
**moth·er-in-law** Schwiegermutter *f*
**moth·er·ly** mütterlich
**moth·er-of-pearl** Perlmutter *f*, *n*, Perlmutt *n*
**moth·er tongue** Muttersprache *f*
**mo·tif** Motiv *n*
**mo·tion 1.** Bewegung *f*; PARL Antrag *m*; ***in quick*** ~ ***film***: im Zeitraffer; ***in slow*** ~ ***film***: in Zeitlupe; ***put*** *or* ***set in*** ~ in Gang bringen (*a. fig*), in Bewegung setzen **2.** *v/t j-n* durch e-n Wink auffordern, *j-m* ein Zeichen geben; *v/i* winken
**mo·tion·less** bewegungslos, unbeweglich
**mo·tion pic·ture** Film *m*
**mo·ti·vate** motivieren, anspornen
**mo·ti·va·tion** Motivation *f*, Ansporn *m*
**mo·tive 1.** Motiv *n*, Beweggrund *m* **2.** treibend (*a. fig*)
**mot·ley** bunt
**mo·to·cross** SPORT Motocross *n*
**mo·tor 1.** Motor *m*, *fig a.* treibende Kraft **2.** Motor...

**mo·tor·bike** Moped *n*; *Br* F Motorrad *n*
**mo·tor·boat** Motorboot *n*
**mo·tor·cade** Auto-, Wagenkolonne *f*
**mo·tor·car** *Br* Kraftfahrzeug *n*
**mo·tor car·a·van** *Br* Wohnmobil *n*
**mo·tor·cy·cle** Motorrad *n*
**mo·tor·cy·clist** Motorradfahrer(in)
**mo·tor home** Wohnmobil *n*
**mo·tor·ing** Autofahren *n*; ***school of ~*** Fahrschule *f*
**mo·tor·ist** Autofahrer(in)
**mo·tor·ize** motorisieren
**mo·tor launch** Motorbarkasse *f*
**mo·tor·way** *Br* Autobahn *f*
**mot·tled** gefleckt, gesprenkelt
**mould**[1] *Br* → ***mold***[1]
**mould**[2] *Br* → ***mold***[2]
**moul·der** *Br* → ***molder***
**mould·y** *Br* → ***moldy***
**moult** *Br* → ***molt***
**mound** Erdhügel *m*, Erdwall *m*
**mount 1.** *v/t Pferd etc* besteigen, steigen auf (*acc*); montieren; anbringen, befestigen; *Bild etc* aufziehen, aufkleben; *Edelstein* fassen; ***~ed police*** berittene Polizei; *v/i* aufsitzen (*rider*); steigen, *fig a.* (an)wachsen; ***~ up to*** sich belaufen auf (*acc*) **2.** Gestell *n*; Fassung *f*; Reittier *n*, Reitpferd *n*
**moun·tain 1.** Berg *m*, *pl a.* Gebirge *n* **2.** Berg…, Gebirgs…
**moun·tain bike** Mountainbike *n*
**moun·tain·eer** Bergsteiger(in)
**moun·tain·eer·ing** Bergsteigen *n*
**moun·tain·ous** bergig, gebirgig
**mourn** *v/i* trauern (***for, over*** um); *v/t* betrauern, trauern um
**mourn·er** Trauernde *m, f*
**mourn·ful** traurig
**mourn·ing** Trauer *f*; Trauerkleidung *f*
**mouse** ZO Maus *f* (*a.* IT)
**mous·tache** → ***mustache***
**mouth** Mund *m*; ZO Maul *n*, Schnauze *f*; GEOGR Mündung *f*; Öffnung *f*
**mouth·ful** *ein* Mundvoll; Bissen *m*
**mouth or·gan** F Mundharmonika *f*
**mouth·piece** Mundstück *n*; *fig* Sprachrohr *n*
**mouth·wash** Mundwasser *n*
**mo·va·ble** beweglich
**move 1.** *v/t* (weg)rücken; transportieren; bewegen, rühren (*both a. fig*); *chess etc*: e-n Zug machen mit; PARL beantragen; ***~ house*** umziehen; ***~ heaven and earth*** Himmel und Hölle in Bewegung setzen; *v/i* sich (fort)bewegen; sich rühren; umziehen (***to*** nach); *chess etc*: e-n Zug machen; ***~ away*** weg-, fortziehen; ***~ in*** einziehen; ***~ off*** sich in Bewegung setzen; ***~ on*** weitergehen; ***~ out*** ausziehen **2.** Bewegung *f*; Umzug *m*; *chess etc*: Zug *m*; *fig* Schritt *m*; ***on the ~*** in Bewegung; auf den Beinen; ***get a ~ on!*** F Tempo!, mach(t) schon!, los!
**move·a·ble** → ***movable***
**move·ment** Bewegung *f* (*a. fig*); MUS Satz *m*; TECH Werk *n*
**mov·ie 1.** Film *m*; Kino *n* **2.** Film…, Kino…; **~ cam·e·ra** Filmkamera *f*; **~ star** Filmstar *m*; **~ thea·ter** Kino *n*
**mov·ing** sich bewegend, beweglich; *fig* rührend; **~ stair·case** Rolltreppe *f*; **~ van** Möbelwagen *m*
**mow** mähen
**mow·er** Mähmaschine *f*, *esp* Rasenmäher *m*
**MP3 player** MP3–Player *m*
**Mr.** *abbr of* ***Mister*** Herr *m*
**Mrs.** Frau *f*
**Ms.** Frau *f*
**much 1.** *adj* viel **2.** *adv* sehr; viel; ***~ better*** viel besser; ***very ~*** sehr; ***I thought as ~*** das habe ich mir gedacht **3.** große Sache; ***nothing ~*** nichts Besonderes; ***make ~ of*** viel Wesens machen von; ***think ~ of*** viel halten von; ***I am not ~ of a dancer*** F ich bin kein großer Tänzer
**muck** F *Br* AGR Mist *m*, Dung *m*; *fig* Dreck *m*, Schmutz *m*; F *contp* Fraß *m*
**mu·cus** (Nasen)Schleim *m*
**mud** Schlamm *m*, Matsch *m*; Schmutz *m* (*a. fig*)
**mud·dle 1.** Durcheinander *n*; ***be in a ~*** durcheinander sein **2.** *a.* ***~ up*** durcheinanderbringen; ***~ through*** F sich durchwursteln
**mud·dy** schlammig, trüb; schmutzig; *fig* wirr
**mud·guard** Kotflügel *m*; Schutzblech *n*
**mues·li** Müsli *n*
**muff** Muff *m*
**muf·fle** *Ton etc* dämpfen; *often* ***~ up*** einhüllen, einwickeln
**muf·fler** (dicker) Schal; MOT Auspufftopf *m*
**mug**[1] Krug *m*; Becher *m*; große Tasse; F

M

Visage *f*; V Fresse *f*
**mug**[2] F überfallen und ausrauben
**mug·ger** F (Straßen)Räuber *m*
**mug·ging** F Raubüberfall *m*, *esp* Straßenraub *m*
**mug·gy** schwül
**mul·ber·ry** BOT Maulbeerbaum *m*; Maulbeere *f*
**mule** ZO Maultier *n*; Maulesel *m*
**mulled**: ~ ***wine*** Glühwein *m*
**mul·li·on** ARCH Mittelpfosten *m*
**mul·ti...** viel..., mehr..., Mehrfach..., Multi...
**mul·ti·cul·tur·al** multikulturell
**mul·ti·far·i·ous** mannigfaltig, vielfältig
**mul·ti·lat·e·ral** vielseitig; POL multilateral, mehrseitig
**mul·ti·me·di·a** multimedial
**mul·ti·na·tion·al** ECON multinationaler Konzern, F Multi *m*
**mul·ti·ple** **1.** vielfach, mehrfach **2.** MATH Vielfache *n*
**mul·ti·pli·ca·tion** Vermehrung *f*; MATH Multiplikation *f*; ~ **table** Einmaleins *n*
**mul·ti·pli·ci·ty** Vielfalt *f*; Vielzahl *f*
**mul·ti·ply** (sich) vermehren, (sich) vervielfachen; MATH multiplizieren, malnehmen (***by*** mit)
**mul·ti·pur·pose** Mehrzweck...
**mul·ti·sto·rey** *Br* mehrstöckig; ~ **car park** *Br* Park(hoch)haus *n*
**mul·ti·tude** Vielzahl *f*
**mul·ti·tu·di·nous** zahlreich
**mum**[1] *Br* F Mami *f*, Mutti *f*
**mum**[2] **1.** *int*: ~***'s the word*** Mund halten!, kein Wort darüber! **2.** *adj*: ***keep*** ~ nichts verraten, den Mund halten
**mum·ble** murmeln, F nuscheln; mümmeln
**mum·mi·fy** mumifizieren
**mum·my**[1] Mumie *f*
**mum·my**[2] *Br* F Mami *f*, Mutti *f*
**mumps** MED Ziegenpeter *m*, Mumps *m*
**munch** mampfen
**mun·dane** alltäglich; weltlich
**mu·ni·ci·pal** städtisch, Stadt..., kommunal, Gemeinde...; ~ ***council*** Stadt-, Gemeinderat *m*
**mu·ni·ci·pal·i·ty** Kommunalbehörde *f*; Stadtverwaltung *f*
**mu·ral** Wandgemälde *n*
**mur·der** **1.** Mord *m*, Ermordung *f* **2.** Mord... **3.** ermorden; F verschandeln
**mur·der·er** Mörder *m*
**mur·der·ess** Mörderin *f*
**mur·der·ous** mörderisch
**murk·y** dunkel, finster
**mur·mur** **1.** Murmeln *n*; Gemurmel *n*; Murren *n* **2.** murmeln; murren
**mus·cle** Muskel *m*
**mus·cu·lar** Muskel...; muskulös
**muse**[1] (nach)sinnen, (nach)grübeln (***on, over*** über *acc*)
**muse**[2] *a.* ***Muse*** Muse *f*
**mu·se·um** Museum *n*
**mush** Brei *m*, Mus *n*; Maisbrei *m*
**mush·room** **1.** BOT Pilz *m*, *esp* Champignon *m* **2.** rasch wachsen; ~ ***up*** *fig* (wie Pilze) aus dem Boden schießen
**mu·sic** Musik *f*; Noten *pl*; ***put*** or ***set to*** ~ vertonen
**mu·sic·al** **1.** musikalisch; Musik... **2.** Musical *n*; ~ **box** *esp Br* Spieldose *f*; ~ **in·stru·ment** Musikinstrument *n*
**mu·sic| box** Spieldose *f*; ~ **cen·ter** (*Br* **cen·ter**) Kompaktanlage *f*; ~ **hall** *Br* Varietee(theater) *n*
**mu·si·cian** Musiker(in)
**mu·sic stand** Notenständer *m*
**musk** Moschus *m*
**musk·rat** ZO Bisamratte *f*; Bisampelz *m*
**Mus·lim** **1.** Muslim *m*, Moslem *m* **2.** muslimisch, moslemisch
**mus·sel** ZO (Mies)Muschel *f*
**must**[1] **1.** *v/aux ich* muss, *du* musst *etc*; ***you*** ~ ***not*** (F ***mustn't***) du darfst nicht **2.** Muss *n*
**must**[2] Most *m*
**mus·tache** Schnurrbart *m*
**mus·tard** Senf *m*
**mus·ter** **1.** ~ ***up*** *s-e Kraft etc* aufbieten; *s-n Mut* zusammennehmen **2.** ***pass*** ~ *fig* Zustimmung finden (***with*** bei); den Anforderungen genügen
**must·y** mod(e)rig, muffig
**mu·ta·tion** Veränderung *f*; BIOL Mutation *f*
**mute** **1.** stumm **2.** Stumme *m, f*; MUS Dämpfer *m*
**mu·ti·late** verstümmeln
**mu·ti·la·tion** Verstümmelung *f*
**mu·ti·neer** Meuterer *m*
**mu·ti·nous** meuternd; rebellisch
**mu·ti·ny** **1.** Meuterei *f* **2.** meutern
**mut·ter** **1.** murmeln; murren **2.** Murmeln *n*; Murren *n*
**mut·ton** GASTR Hammel-, Schaffleisch *n*; ***leg of*** ~ Hammelkeule *f*

**mut·ton chop** GASTR Hammelkotelett *n*
**mu·tu·al** gegenseitig; gemeinsam
**muz·zle 1.** ZO Maul *n*, Schnauze *f*; Mündung *f* (*of a gun*); Maulkorb *m* **2.** e-n Maulkorb anlegen (*dat*), *fig a. j-n* mundtot machen
**my** mein(e)
**myrrh** BOT Myrrhe *f*
**myr·tle** BOT Myrte *f*
**my·self** ich, mich *or* mir selbst; mich; mich (selbst); ***by ~*** allein
**mys·te·ri·ous** rätselhaft, unerklärlich; geheimnisvoll, mysteriös
**mys·te·ry** Geheimnis *n*, Rätsel *n*; REL Mysterium *n*; ***~ tour*** Fahrt *f* ins Blaue
**mys·tic 1.** Mystiker(in) **2.** → **mystic·al** mystisch
**mys·ti·fy** verwirren, vor ein Rätsel stellen; ***be mystified*** vor e-m Rätsel stehen
**myth** Mythos *m*, Sage *f*
**my·thol·o·gy** Mythologie *f*

# N

**N, n** N, n *n*
**nab** F schnappen, erwischen
**na·dir** ASTR Nadir *m*; *fig* Tiefpunkt *m*
**nag[1] 1.** nörgeln; ***~ (at)*** herumnörgeln an (*dat*) **2.** Nörgler(in)
**nag[2]** F Gaul *m*, Klepper *m*
**nail 1.** ANAT, TECH Nagel *m* **2.** (an-)nageln (***to*** an *acc*); **~ pol·ish** Nagellack *m*; **~ scis·sors** Nagelschere *f*; **~ var·nish** *Br* Nagellack *m*
**na·ive, na·ïve** naiv (*a. art*)
**na·ked** nackt, bloß; kahl; *fig* ungeschminkt; **nak·ed·ness** Nacktheit *f*
**name 1.** Name *m*; Ruf *m*; ***by ~*** mit Namen, namentlich; ***by the ~ of ...*** namens ...; ***what's your ~?*** wie heißen Sie?; ***call s.o. ~s*** j-n beschimpfen **2.** (be)nennen; erwähnen; ernennen zu
**name·less** namenlos; unbekannt
**name·ly** nämlich
**name·plate** Namens-, Tür-, Firmenschild *n*
**name·sake** Namensvetter *m*, Namensschwester *f*
**name tag** Namensschild *n*
**nan·ny** Kindermädchen *n*
**nan·ny goat** ZO Geiß *f*, Ziege *f*
**nap 1.** Schläfchen *n*; ***have or take a ~*** → **2.** ein Nickerchen machen
**nape** *mst* ***~ of the neck*** ANAT Genick *n*, Nacken *m*
**nap·kin** Serviette *f*
**nap·py** *Br* Windel *f*
**nar·co·sis** MED Narkose *f*
**nar·cot·ic 1.** narkotisch, betäubend, einschläfernd; Rauschgift...; ***~ addiction*** Rauschgiftsucht *f* **2.** Narkotikum *n*, Betäubungsmittel *n*; *often pl* Rauschgift *n*; ***~s squad*** Rauschgiftdezernat *n*
**nar·rate** erzählen; berichten, schildern
**nar·ra·tion** Erzählung *f*
**nar·ra·tive 1.** Erzählung *f*; Bericht *m*, Schilderung *f* **2.** erzählend
**nar·ra·tor** Erzähler(in)
**nar·row 1.** eng, schmal; beschränkt; knapp **2.** enger *or* schmäler werden *or* machen, (sich) verengen; beschränken, einschränken; **nar·row·ly** mit knapper Not; **nar·row-mind·ed** engstirnig, beschränkt; **nar·row·ness** Enge *f*; Beschränktheit *f*
**na·sal** nasal; Nasen...
**nas·ty** ekelhaft, eklig, widerlich (*smell*, *sight etc*); abscheulich (*weather etc*); böse, schlimm (*accident etc*); hässlich (*character*, *behavior etc*); gemein, fies; schmutzig, zotig (*language*)
**na·tal** Geburts...
**na·tion** Nation *f*, Volk *n*
**na·tion·al 1.** national, National..., Landes..., Volks... **2.** Staatsangehörige *m, f*; **~ an·them** Nationalhymne *f*
**na·tion·al·i·ty** Nationalität *f*, Staatsangehörigkeit *f*
**na·tion·al·ize** ECON verstaatlichen
**na·tion·al| park** Nationalpark *m*; **~ so·cial·ism** HIST POL Nationalsozialismus *m*; **~ so·cial·ist** HIST POL Nationalsozialist *m*; **~ team** SPORT Nationalmannschaft *f*
**na·tion-wide** landesweit
**na·tive 1.** einheimisch, Landes...; heimatlich, Heimat...; eingeboren, Eingeborenen...; angeboren **2.** Eingebo-

rene *m*, *f*; Einheimische *m*, *f*; ~ **lan·guage** Muttersprache *f*; ~ **speak·er** Muttersprachler(in)
**Na·tiv·i·ty** REL *die* Geburt Christi
**nat·ty** F schick, *Austrian* fesch
**nat·u·ral** natürlich; angeboren; Natur…; ~ **gas** Erdgas *n*
**nat·u·ral·ize** naturalisieren, einbürgern
**nat·u·ral·ly** natürlich; von Natur (aus)
**nat·u·ral| re·sourc·es** Boden- u. Naturschätze *pl*; ~ **sci·ence** Naturwissenschaft *f*
**na·ture** Natur *f*; ~ **con·ser·va·tion** Naturschutz *m*; ~ **re·serve** Naturschutzgebiet *n*; ~ **trail** Naturlehrpfad *m*
**naugh·ty** unartig; unanständig
**nau·se·a** Übelkeit *f*, Brechreiz *m*
**nau·se·ate**: ~ ***s.o.*** j-m Übelkeit verursachen; *fig* j-n anwidern
**nau·se·at·ing** ekelerregend, widerlich
**nau·ti·cal** nautisch, See…
**na·val** MIL Flotten…, Marine…; See…; ~ **base** MIL Flottenstützpunkt *m*; ~ **offi·cer** MIL Marineoffizier *m*; ~ **pow·er** MIL Seemacht *f*
**nave** ARCH Mittel-, Hauptschiff *n*
**na·vel** ANAT Nabel *m* (*a. fig*)
**nav·i·ga·ble** schiffbar
**nav·i·gate** MAR befahren; AVIAT, MAR steuern, lenken
**nav·i·ga·tion** Schifffahrt *f*; AVIAT, MAR Navigation *f*
**nav·i·ga·tor** AVIAT, MAR Navigator *m*
**na·vy** (Kriegs)Marine *f*; Kriegsflotte *f*
**na·vy blue** Marineblau *n*
**nay** PARL Gegen-, Neinstimme *f*
**Na·zi** HIST POL *contp* Nazi *m*
**Na·zism** HIST POL *contp* Nazismus *m*
**near 1.** *adj* nahe; kurz; nahe (verwandt); ***in the ~ future*** in naher Zukunft; ***be a ~ miss*** knapp scheitern **2.** *adv* nahe, in der Nähe (*a.* ~ ***at hand***); nahe (bevorstehend) (*a.* ~ ***at hand***); beinahe, fast; ~ ***the station*** *etc* in der Nähe des Bahnhofs *etc*; ~ ***you*** in deiner Nähe **3.** *prp* nahe (*dat*), in der Nähe von (*or gen*) **4.** sich nähern, näher kommen (*dat*)
**near·by 1.** *adj* nahe (gelegen) **2.** *adv* in der Nähe
**near·ly** beinahe, fast; annähernd
**near·sight·ed** kurzsichtig
**neat** ordentlich; sauber; gepflegt; pur (*whisky etc*)
**neb·u·lous** verschwommen
**ne·ces·sar·i·ly** notwendigerweise; ***not ~*** nicht unbedingt
**ne·ces·sa·ry** notwendig, nötig; unvermeidlich
**ne·ces·si·tate** *et.* erfordern, verlangen
**ne·ces·si·ty** Notwendigkeit *f*; (dringendes) Bedürfnis; Not *f*
**neck 1.** ANAT Hals *m* (*a. of bottle etc*); Genick *n*, Nacken *m*; ***be ~ and ~*** F Kopf an Kopf liegen (*a. fig*); ***be up to one's ~ in debt*** F bis zum Hals in Schulden stecken **2.** F knutschen, schmusen
**neck·er·chief** Halstuch *n*
**neck·lace** Halskette *f*
**neck·let** Halskettchen *n*
**neck·line** Ausschnitt *m*
**neck·tie** Krawatte *f*, Schlips *m*
**née**: ~ ***Smith*** geborene Smith
**need 1.** (***of, for***) (dringendes) Bedürfnis (nach), Bedarf *m* (an *dat*); Notwendigkeit *f*; Mangel *m* (***of, for*** an *dat*); Not *f*; ***be in ~ of s.th.*** et. dringend brauchen; ***in ~*** in Not; ***in ~ of help*** hilfs-, hilfebedürftig **2.** *v/t* benötigen, brauchen; *v/aux* brauchen, müssen
**nee·dle 1.** Nadel *f* (*a.* BOT, MED); Zeiger *m* **2.** F *j-n* aufziehen, hänseln
**need·less** unnötig, überflüssig
**nee·dle·wom·an** Näherin *f*
**nee·dle·work** Handarbeit *f*
**need·y** bedürftig, arm
**ne·ga·tion** Verneinung *f*
**neg·a·tive 1.** negativ; verneinend **2.** Verneinung *f*; PHOT Negativ *n*; ***answer in the ~*** verneinen
**ne·glect 1.** vernachlässigen; es versäumen (***doing, to do*** zu tun); **2.** Vernachlässigung *f*; Nachlässigkeit *f*
**neg·li·gence** Nachlässigkeit *f*, Unachtsamkeit *f*; **neg·li·gent** nachlässig, unachtsam; lässig, salopp
**neg·li·gi·ble** unbedeutend
**ne·go·ti·ate** verhandeln (über *acc*)
**ne·go·ti·a·tion** Verhandlung *f*
**ne·go·ti·a·tor** Unterhändler(in)
**neigh** ZO **1.** wiehern **2.** Wiehern *n*
**neigh·bo(u)r** Nachbar(in)
**neigh·bo(u)r·hood** Nachbarschaft *f*, Umgebung *f*
**neigh·bo(u)r·ing** benachbart, Nachbar…, angrenzend
**neigh·bo(u)r·ly** (gut)nachbarlich
**nei·ther 1.** *adj and pron* keine(r, -s) (von beiden) **2.** *cj* ~ … ***nor*** weder … noch

**ne·on** CHEM Neon *n*; **~ lamp** Neonlampe *f*; **~ sign** Neon-, Leuchtreklame *f*
**neph·ew** Neffe *m*
**nep·o·tism** *contp* Vetternwirtschaft *f*
**nerd** F Trottel *m*; Computerfreak *m*
**nerve** Nerv *m*; Mut *m*, Stärke *f*, Selbstbeherrschung *f*; F Frechheit *f*; ***get on s.o.'s ~s*** j-m auf die Nerven gehen *or* fallen; ***lose one's ~*** den Mut *or* die Nerven verlieren; ***you've got a ~!*** F Sie haben Nerven!; **nerve·less** kraftlos; mutlos; ohne Nerven, kaltblütig
**ner·vous** nervös; Nerven…
**ner·vous·ness** Nervosität *f*
**nest 1.** Nest *n* **2.** nisten
**nes·tle** (sich) schmiegen *or* kuscheln (***against, on*** an *acc*); *a.* ***~ down*** sich behaglich niederlassen, es sich bequem machen (***in*** in *dat*)
**net**[1] **1.** Netz *n*; ***~ curtain*** Store *m* **2.** mit e-m Netz fangen *or* abdecken
**net**[2] **1.** netto, Netto…, Rein… **2.** netto einbringen
**Neth·er·lands** *die* Niederlande *pl*
**net·tle 1.** BOT Nessel *f* **2.** F *j-n* ärgern
**net·work** Netz *n* (*a.* IT), Netzwerk *n*; (*Straßen- etc*)Netz *n*; *radio*, TV Sendernetz *n*; ***be in the ~*** IT am Netz sein
**neu·ro·sis** MED Neurose *f*; **neu·rot·ic** MED **1.** neurotisch **2.** Neurotiker(in)
**neu·ter 1.** LING sächlich; geschlechtslos **2.** LING Neutrum *n*
**neu·tral 1.** neutral **2.** Neutrale *m, f*; *a.* ***~ gear*** MOT Leerlauf(stellung *f*) *m*
**neu·tral·i·ty** Neutralität *f*
**neu·tral·ize** neutralisieren
**neu·tron** PHYS Neutron *n*
**nev·er** nie, niemals; **nev·er-end·ing** endlos, nicht enden wollend, unendlich
**nev·er·the·less** nichtsdestoweniger, dennoch, trotzdem
**new** neu; frisch; unerfahren; ***nothing ~*** nichts Neues
**new·born** neugeboren
**new·com·er** Neuankömmling *m*; Neuling *m*
**new·ly** kürzlich; neu
**news** Neuigkeit(en *pl*) *f*, Nachricht(en *pl*) *f*
**news·a·gent** Zeitungshändler(in)
**news·boy** Zeitungsjunge *m*, Zeitungsausträger *m*
**news bul·le·tin** Kurznachricht(en *pl*) *f*
**news·cast** *radio*, TV Nachrichtensendung *f*; **news·cast·er** *radio*, TV Nachrichtensprecher(in)
**news deal·er** Zeitungshändler(in)
**news·flash** *radio*, TV Kurzmeldung *f*
**news·let·ter** Rundschreiben *n*
**news·pa·per** Zeitung *f*
**news·print** Zeitungspapier *n*
**news·read·er** *esp Br* → ***newscaster***
**news·reel** *film*: Wochenschau *f*
**news·room** Nachrichtenredaktion *f*
**news·stand** Zeitungskiosk *m*, -stand *m*
**news·ven·dor** *esp Br* Zeitungsverkäufer(in)
**new year** Neujahr *n*, *das* neue Jahr; ***New Year's Day*** Neujahrstag *m*; ***New Year's Eve*** Silvester(abend *m*) *m, n*
**next 1.** *adj* nächste(r, -s); (***the***) ***~ day*** am nächsten Tag; ***~ door*** nebenan; ***~ but one*** übernächste(r, -s); ***~ to*** gleich neben *or* nach; beinahe, fast *unmöglich etc* **2.** *adv* als Nächste(r, -s); demnächst, das nächste Mal **3.** *der, die, das* Nächste; → ***kin***
**next-door** (von) nebenan
**nib·ble** *v/i* knabbern (***at*** an *dat*); *v/t Loch etc* nagen, knabbern (***in*** in *acc*)
**nice** nett, freundlich; hübsch, schön; *fig* fein (*detail etc*)
**nice·ly** gut, fein; genau, sorgfältig
**ni·ce·ty** Feinheit *f*; Genauigkeit *f*
**niche** Nische *f*
**nick 1.** Kerbe *f* **2.** (ein)kerben; *j-n* streifen (*bullet*); *Br* F *et.* klauen; *Br* F *j-n* schnappen
**nick·el 1.** MIN Nickel *n*; Fünfcentstück *n* **2.** TECH vernickeln
**nick·el-plate** TECH vernickeln
**nick-nack** → ***knick-knack***
**nick·name 1.** Spitzname *m* **2.** *j-m* den Spitznamen … geben
**niece** Nichte *f*
**nig·gard** Geizhals *m*
**nig·gard·ly** geizig, knaus(e)rig; schäbig, kümmerlich
**night** Nacht *f*; Abend *m*; ***at ~, by ~, in the ~*** in der Nacht, nachts
**night·cap** Schlummertrunk *m*
**night·club** Nachtklub *m*, Nachtlokal *n*
**night·dress** (Damen-, Kinder)Nachthemd *n*
**night·fall**: ***at ~*** bei Einbruch der Dunkelheit
**night·gown** → ***nightdress***

**night·ie** F → ***nightdress***
**nigh·tin·gale** zo Nachtigall *f*
**night·ly** (all)nächtlich; (all)abendlich; jede Nacht; jeden Abend
**night·mare** Albtraum *m* (*a. fig*)
**night school** Abendschule *f*
**night shift** Nachtschicht *f*
**night·shirt** (Herren)Nachthemd *n*
**night·time**: ***in the ~, at ~*** nachts
**night watch·man** Nachtwächter *m*
**night·y** F → ***nightdress***
**nil** Nichts *n*, Null *f*; ***our team won two to ~*** *or* ***by two goals to ~ (2-0)*** unsere Mannschaft gewann zwei zu null (2:0)
**nim·ble** flink, gewandt; geistig beweglich
**nine 1.** neun; ***~ to five*** normale Dienststunden (von 9-5); ***a ~-to-five job*** e-e (An)Stellung mit geregelter Arbeitszeit **2.** Neun *f*
**nine·pins** Kegeln *n*
**nine·teen 1.** neunzehn **2.** Neunzehn *f*
**nine·teenth** neunzehnte(r, -s)
**nine·ti·eth** neunzigste(r, -s)
**nine·ty 1.** neunzig **2.** Neunzig *f*
**ninth 1.** neunte(r, -s) **2.** Neuntel *n*
**ninth·ly** neuntens
**nip[1] 1.** kneifen, zwicken; F flitzen, sausen; ***~ off*** F abknipsen; ***~ in the bud*** *fig* im Keim ersticken **2.** Kneifen *n*, Zwicken *n*; ***it was ~ and tuck*** F es war ganz knapp; ***there's a ~ in the air today*** heute ist es ganz schön kalt
**nip[2]** Schlückchen *n* (*of brandy etc*)
**nip·per**: (***a pair of***) ***~s*** (e-e) (Kneif)Zange *f*
**nip·ple** ANAT Brustwarze *f*; (Gummi-) Sauger *m*; TECH Nippel *m*
**ni·ter**, *Br* **ni·tre** CHEM Salpeter *m*
**ni·tro·gen** CHEM Stickstoff *m*
**no 1.** *adv* nein; nicht **2.** *adj* kein(e); ***~ one*** keiner, niemand; ***in ~ time*** im Nu, im Handumdrehen **3.** Nein *n*
**no·bil·i·ty** (Hoch)Adel *m*; *fig* Adel *m*
**no·ble** adlig; edel, nobel; prächtig
**no·ble·man** Adlige *m*
**no·ble·wom·an** Adlige *f*
**no·bod·y 1.** niemand, keiner **2.** *fig* Niemand *m*, Null *f*
**no-cal·o·rie di·et** Nulldiät *f*
**noc·tur·nal** nächtlich, Nacht…
**nod 1.** nicken (mit); ***~ off*** einnicken; ***have a ~ding acquaintance with s.o.*** j-n flüchtig kennen **2.** Nicken *n*
**node** BOT, MED Knoten *m*
**noise 1.** Krach *m*, Lärm *m*; Geräusch *n* **2.** ***~ about*** (***abroad, around***) *Gerücht etc* verbreiten; **noise·less** geräuschlos; **nois·y** laut, geräuschvoll
**no·mad** Nomade *m*, Nomadin *f*
**nom·i·nal** nominell; ***~ value*** ECON Nennwert *m*
**nom·i·nate** ernennen; nominieren, (zur Wahl) vorschlagen; **nom·i·na·tion** Ernennung *f*; Nominierung *f*
**nom·i·na·tive** *a.* ***~ case*** LING Nominativ *m*, erster Fall
**nom·i·nee** Kandidat(in)
**non…** nicht…, Nicht…, un…
**non·al·co·hol·ic** alkoholfrei
**non·a·ligned** POL blockfrei
**non·com·mis·sioned of·fi·cer** MIL Unteroffizier *m*
**non·com·mit·tal** unverbindlich
**non·con·duc·tor** ELECTR Nichtleiter *m*
**non·de·script** nichtssagend; unauffällig
**none 1.** *pron* keine(r, -s), niemand **2.** *adv* in keiner Weise, keineswegs
**non·en·ti·ty** *fig* Null *f*
**none·the·less** nichtsdestoweniger, dennoch, trotzdem
**non·ex·ist·ence** Nichtvorhandensein *n*, Fehlen *n*
**non·ex·ist·ent** nicht existierend
**non·fic·tion** Sachbücher *pl*
**non·flam·ma·ble, non·in·flam·mable** nicht brennbar
**non·in·ter·fer·ence, non·in·ter·vention** POL Nichteinmischung *f*
**non-i·ron** bügelfrei
**no-non·sense** nüchtern, sachlich
**non·par·ti·san** POL überparteilich; unparteiisch
**non·pay·ment** ECON Nicht(be)zahlung *f*
**non·plus** verblüffen
**non·pol·lut·ing** umweltfreundlich
**non·prof·it**, *Br* **non-prof·it·mak·ing** gemeinnützig
**non·res·i·dent 1.** nicht (orts)ansässig; nicht im Hause wohnend **2.** Nichtansässige *m, f*; nicht im Hause Wohnende *m, f*
**non·re·turn·a·ble** Einweg…; ***~ bot·tle*** Einwegflasche *f*
**non·sense** Unsinn *m*, dummes Zeug
**non-skid** rutschfest, rutschsicher
**non·smok·er** Nichtraucher(in)
**non·smok·ing** Nichtraucher…

**non·stick** mit Antihaftbeschichtung
**non·stop** nonstop, ohne Unterbrechung; RAIL durchgehend; AVIAT ohne Zwischenlandung; ~ ***flight*** *a.* Nonstop-Flug *m*
**non·u·nion** nicht (gewerkschaftlich) organisiert
**non·vi·o·lence** (Politik *f* der) Gewaltlosigkeit *f*
**non·vi·o·lent** gewaltlos
**noo·dle** Nudel *f*
**nook** Ecke *f*, Winkel *m*
**noon** Mittag(szeit *f*) *m*; ***at*** ~ um 12 Uhr (mittags)
**noose** Schlinge *f*
**nope** F ne(e), nein
**nor** → ***neither*** *2*; auch nicht
**norm** Norm *f*
**nor·mal** normal
**nor·mal·ize** (sich) normalisieren
**north** **1.** Nord, Norden *m* **2.** *adj* nördlich, Nord… **3.** *adv* nach Norden, nordwärts
**north·east** **1.** Nordost, Nordosten *m* **2.** *a.* ***northeastern*** nordöstlich
**nor·ther·ly, nor·thern** Nord…, nördlich
**North Pole** Nordpol *m*
**north·ward(s)** *adv* nördlich, nach Norden
**north·west** **1.** Nordwest, Nordwesten *m* **2.** *a.* ***northwestern*** nordwestlich
**Nor·way** Norwegen *n*
**Nor·we·gian** **1.** norwegisch **2.** Norweger(in); LING Norwegisch *n*
**nose** **1.** Nase *f*; zo Schnauze *f*; *fig* Gespür *n* **2.** *Auto etc* vorsichtig fahren; *a.* ~ ***about***, ~ ***around*** *fig* F herumschnüffeln (in *dat*) (***for*** nach)
**nose·bleed** Nasenbluten *n*; ***have a*** ~ Nasenbluten haben
**nose·dive** AVIAT Sturzflug *m*
**nos·ey** → ***nosy***
**nos·tal·gia** Nostalgie *f*
**nos·tril** ANAT Nasenloch *n*, *esp* zo Nüster *f*
**nos·y** F neugierig
**not** nicht; ~ ***a*** kein(e)
**no·ta·ble** bemerkenswert; beachtlich
**no·ta·ry** *mst* ~ ***public*** Notar *m*
**notch** **1.** Kerbe *f*; GEOL Engpass *m* **2.** (ein)kerben
**note** (*mst pl*) Notiz *f*, Aufzeichnung *f*; Anmerkung *f*; Vermerk *m*; Briefchen *n*, Zettel *m*; (diplomatische) Note; Banknote *f*, Geldschein *m*; MUS Note *f*; *fig* Ton *m*; ***take*** ~***s*** (***of***) sich Notizen machen (über *acc*); **note·book** Notizbuch *n*; IT Notebook *n*
**not·ed** bekannt, berühmt (***for*** wegen)
**note·pa·per** Briefpapier *n*
**note·wor·thy** bemerkenswert
**noth·ing** nichts; ~ ***but*** nichts als, nur; ~ ***much*** F nicht viel; ***for*** ~ umsonst; ***to say*** ~ ***of*** ganz zu schweigen von; ***there is*** ~ ***like*** es geht nichts über (*acc*)
**no·tice** **1.** Ankündigung *f*, Bekanntgabe *f*, Mitteilung *f*, Anzeige *f*; Kündigung(sfrist) *f*; Beachtung *f*; ***give*** *or* ***hand in one's*** ~ kündigen (***to*** bei); ***give s.o.*** ~ j-m kündigen; ***give s.o.*** ~ ***to quit*** j-m kündigen; ***at six months'*** ~ mit halbjährlicher Kündigungsfrist; ***take*** (***no***) ~ ***of*** (keine) Notiz nehmen von, (nicht) beachten; ***at short*** ~ kurzfristig; ***until further*** ~ bis auf Weiteres; ***without*** ~ fristlos **2.** (es) bemerken; (besonders) beachten *or* achten auf (*acc*)
**no·tice·a·ble** erkennbar, wahrnehmbar; bemerkenswert
**no·tice·board** *Br* schwarzes Brett
**no·ti·fy** *et.* anzeigen, melden, mitteilen; *j-n* benachrichtigen
**no·tion** Begriff *m*, Vorstellung *f*; Idee *f*
**no·tions** Kurzwaren *pl*
**no·to·ri·ous** berüchtigt (***for*** für)
**not·with·stand·ing** trotz (*gen*)
**nought** *Br*: ***0.4*** (~ ***point four***) 0,4
**noun** LING Substantiv *n*, Hauptwort *n*
**nour·ish** (er)nähren; *fig* hegen
**nour·ish·ing** nahrhaft
**nour·ish·ment** Ernährung *f*; Nahrung *f*
**Nov** *abbr of* ***November*** Nov., November *m*
**nov·el** **1.** Roman *m* **2.** (ganz) neu(artig)
**nov·el·ist** Romanschriftsteller(in)
**no·vel·la** Novelle *f*
**nov·el·ty** Neuheit *f*
**No·vem·ber** (*abbr* ***Nov***) November *m*
**nov·ice** Anfänger(in), Neuling *m*; REL Novize *m*, Novizin *f*
**now** **1.** *adv* nun, jetzt; ~ ***and again***, (***every***) ~ ***and then*** von Zeit zu Zeit, dann und wann; ***by*** ~ inzwischen; ***from*** ~ (***on***) von jetzt an; ***just*** ~ gerade eben **2.** *cj a.* ~ ***that*** nun da; **now·a·days** heutzutage
**no·where** nirgends
**nox·ious** schädlich
**noz·zle** TECH Schnauze *f*; Stutzen *m*; Düse *f*; Zapfpistole *f*

N

**nu·ance** Nuance *f*
**nub** springender Punkt
**nu·cle·ar** Kern…, Atom…, atomar, nuklear, Nuklear…; **~ en·er·gy** PHYS Atomenergie *f*, Kernenergie *f*; **~ fis·sion** PHYS Kernspaltung *f*
**nu·cle·ar-free** atomwaffenfrei
**nu·cle·ar| fu·sion** PHYS Kernfusion *f*; **~ phys·ics** Kernphysik *f*; **~ pow·er** PHYS Atomkraft *f*, Kernkraft *f*
**nu·cle·ar-pow·ered** atomgetrieben
**nu·cle·ar| pow·er plant** ELECTR Atomkraftwerk *n*, Kernkraftwerk *n*; **~ re·ac·tor** PHYS Atomreaktor *m*, Kernreaktor *m*; **~ war** Atomkrieg *m*; **~ war·head** MIL Atomsprengkopf *m*; **~ waste** Atommüll *m*; **~ weap·ons** MIL Atomwaffen *pl*, Kernwaffen *pl*
**nu·cle·us** BIOL, PHYS Kern *m* (*a. fig*)
**nude 1.** nackt **2.** *art*: Akt *m*
**nudge 1.** *j-n* anstoßen, (an)stupsen **2.** Stups(er) *m*
**nug·get** (*esp* Gold)Klumpen *m*
**nui·sance** Plage *f*, Ärgernis *n*; Nervensäge *f*, Quälgeist *m*; ***what a ~!*** wie ärgerlich!; ***be a ~ to s.o.*** j-m lästig fallen, F j-n nerven; ***make a ~ of o.s.*** den Leuten auf die Nerven gehen *or* fallen
**nukes** F Atom-, Kernwaffen *pl*
**null**: ***~ and void*** *esp* JUR null und nichtig
**numb 1.** starr (***with*** vor), taub; *fig* wie betäubt (***with*** vor); **2.** starr *or* taub machen
**num·ber 1.** Zahl *f*, Ziffer *f*; Nummer *f*; (An)Zahl *f*; Ausgabe *f*; (*Bus- etc*)Linie *f*; ***sorry, wrong ~*** TEL falsch verbunden! **2.** nummerieren; zählen; sich belaufen auf (*acc*)
**num·ber·less** zahllos
**num·ber·plate** *esp Br* MOT Nummernschild *n*
**nu·me·ral** Ziffer *f*; LING Zahlwort *n*
**nu·me·ra·tor** MATH Zähler *m*
**nu·me·rous** zahlreich
**nun** REL Nonne *f*
**nun·ne·ry** REL Nonnenkloster *n*
**nurse 1.** (Kranken-, Säuglings)Schwester *f*; Kindermädchen *n*; (Kranken-)Pflegerin *f*; → ***male nurse***; *a.* ***wet ~*** Amme *f* **2.** stillen; pflegen; hegen; als Krankenschwester *or* -pfleger arbeiten; ***~ s.o. back to health*** j-n gesund pflegen
**nur·se·ry** Tagesheim *n*, Tagesstätte *f*; Baum-, Pflanzschule *f*; **~ rhyme** Kinderlied *n*, Kinderreim *m*; **~ school** *Br* Vorschule *f*; **~ slope** *skiing*: F Idiotenhügel *m*
**nurs·ing** Stillen *n*; (Kranken)Pflege *f*; **~ bot·tle** (Saug)Flasche *f*; **~ home** Pflegeheim *n*
**nut** BOT Nuss *f*; TECH (Schrauben)Mutter *f*; F verrückter Kerl; F Birne *f* (*head*)
**nut·crack·er(s)** Nussknacker *m*
**nut·meg** BOT Muskatnuss *f*
**nu·tri·ent 1.** Nährstoff *m* **2.** nahrhaft
**nu·tri·tion** Ernährung *f*
**nu·tri·tious, nu·tri·tive** nahrhaft
**nut·shell** Nussschale *f*; (***to put it***) ***in a ~*** F kurz gesagt, mit e-m Wort
**nut·ty** voller Nüsse, nussig; Nuss…; F verrückt
**ny·lon®** Nylon® *n*; **~ stock·ings** Nylonstrümpfe® *pl*
**nymph** Nymphe *f*

# O

**O, o** O, o *n*
**o** Null *f*
**oaf** Lümmel *m*, Flegel *m*
**oak** BOT Eiche *f*
**oar** Ruder *n*
**oars·man** SPORT Ruderer *m*
**oars·wom·an** SPORT Ruderin *f*
**o·a·sis** Oase *f* (*a. fig*)
**oath** Eid *m*, Schwur *m*; Fluch *m*; ***take an ~*** e-n Eid leisten *or* schwören; ***be on*** *or* ***under ~*** JUR unter Eid stehen; ***take the ~*** JUR schwören
**oat·meal** Hafermehl *n*, Hafergrütze *f*
**o·be·di·ence** Gehorsam *m*
**o·be·di·ent** gehorsam
**o·bese** fett, fettleibig
**o·bes·i·ty** Fettleibigkeit *f*
**o·bey** gehorchen (*dat*), folgen (*dat*); *Befehl etc* befolgen
**o·bit·u·a·ry** Nachruf *m*; *a.* ***~ notice*** To-

desanzeige *f*
**ob·ject** **1.** Objekt *n* (*a.* LING); Gegenstand *m*; Ziel *n*, Zweck *m*, Absicht *f* **2.** einwenden; et. dagegen haben
**ob·jec·tion** Einwand *m*, Einspruch *m* (*a.* JUR); **ob·jec·tion·a·ble** nicht einwandfrei; unangenehm; anstößig
**ob·jec·tive** **1.** objektiv, sachlich **2.** Ziel *n*; **ob·jec·tive·ness** Objektivität *f*
**ob·li·ga·tion** Verpflichtung *f*; ***be under an ~ to s.o.*** j-m (zu Dank) verpflichtet sein; ***be under an ~ to do*** verpflichtet sein, *et.* zu tun; **ob·lig·a·to·ry** verpflichtend, verbindlich
**o·blige** nötigen, zwingen; (zu Dank) verpflichten; ***~ s.o.*** j-m e-n Gefallen tun; ***much ~d*** besten Dank
**o·blig·ing** entgegenkommend, gefällig
**o·blique** schief, schräg; *fig* indirekt
**o·blit·er·ate** auslöschen; vernichten, völlig zerstören; verdecken
**o·bliv·i·on** Vergessen(heit *f*) *n*; ***fall into ~*** in Vergessenheit geraten
**o·bliv·i·ous**: ***be ~ of*** *or* ***to s.th.*** sich e-r Sache nicht bewusst sein; et. nicht bemerken *or* wahrnehmen
**ob·long** rechteckig; länglich
**ob·nox·ious** widerlich
**ob·scene** obszön, unanständig
**ob·scure** **1.** dunkel, *fig a.* unklar; unbekannt **2.** verdunkeln, verdecken
**ob·scu·ri·ty** Unbekanntheit *f*; Unklarheit *f*
**ob·se·quies** Trauerfeier(lichkeiten *pl*) *f*
**ob·ser·va·ble** wahrnehmbar, merklich; **ob·ser·vance** Beachtung *f*, Befolgung *f*; **ob·ser·vant** aufmerksam; **ob·ser·va·tion** Beobachtung *f*, Überwachung *f*; Bemerkung *f* (***on*** über *acc*); **ob·ser·va·to·ry** Observatorium *n*, Sternwarte *f*; **ob·serve** beobachten; überwachen; *Vorschrift etc* beachten, befolgen, einhalten; bemerken, äußern; **ob·serv·er** Beobachter(in)
**ob·sess**: ***be ~ed by*** *or* ***with*** besessen sein von; **ob·ses·sion** PSYCH Besessenheit *f*, fixe Idee, Zwangsvorstellung *f*; **ob·ses·sive** PSYCH zwanghaft
**ob·so·lete** veraltet
**ob·sta·cle** Hindernis *n*
**ob·sti·na·cy** Starrsinn *m*
**ob·sti·nate** hartnäckig; halsstarrig, eigensinnig, starrköpfig
**ob·struct** verstopfen, versperren; blockieren; behindern
**ob·struc·tion** Verstopfung *f*; Blockierung *f*; Behinderung *f*
**ob·struc·tive** blockierend; hinderlich
**ob·tain** erhalten, bekommen, sich *et.* beschaffen; **ob·tain·a·ble** erhältlich
**ob·tru·sive** aufdringlich
**ob·vi·ous** offensichtlich, klar, einleuchtend
**oc·ca·sion** Gelegenheit *f*; Anlass *m*; Veranlassung *f*; (festliches) Ereignis; ***on the ~ of*** anlässlich (*gen*)
**oc·ca·sion·al** gelegentlich; vereinzelt
**oc·ca·sion·al·ly** gelegentlich, manchmal
**Oc·ci·dent** *der* Westen, *der* Okzident, *das* Abendland
**oc·ci·den·tal** abendländisch, westlich
**oc·cu·pant** Bewohner(in); Insasse *m*, Insassin *f*
**oc·cu·pa·tion** Beruf *m*; Beschäftigung *f*; MIL, POL Besetzung *f*, Besatzung *f*, Okkupation *f*
**oc·cu·py** in Besitz nehmen, MIL, POL besetzen; *Raum* einnehmen; in Anspruch nehmen; beschäftigen; ***be occupied*** bewohnt sein; besetzt sein (*seat*)
**oc·cur** sich ereignen; vorkommen; ***it ~red to me that*** es fiel mir ein *or* mir kam der Gedanke, dass
**oc·cur·rence** Vorkommen *n*; Ereignis *n*; Vorfall *m*
**o·cean** Ozean *m*, (Welt)Meer *n*
**o'clock**: (***at***) ***five ~*** (um) fünf Uhr
**Oct** *abbr of* ***October*** Okt., Oktober *m*
**Oc·to·ber** (*abbr* ***Oct***) Oktober *m*
**oc·u·lar** Augen...
**oc·u·list** Augenarzt *m*, Augenärztin *f*
**OD** F *v/i*: ***~ on heroin*** an e-r Überdosis Heroin sterben
**odd** sonderbar, seltsam, merkwürdig; einzeln, Einzel...; ungerade (*number*); gelegentlich, Gelegenheits...; ***~ jobs*** Gelegenheitsarbeiten *pl*; F ***30 ~*** (et.) über 30, einige 30
**odds** (Gewinn)Chancen *pl*; ***the ~ are 10 to 1*** die Chancen stehen 10 zu 1; ***the ~ are that*** es ist sehr wahrscheinlich, dass; ***against all ~*** wider Erwarten, entgegen allen Erwartungen; ***be at ~*** uneins sein (***with*** mit); ***~ and ends*** Krimskrams *m*; **odds-on** hoch, klar (*favorite*), aussichtsreichst (*candidate*

O

etc); F ***it's ~ that*** es sieht ganz so aus, als ob ...

**ode** Ode *f*

**o·do(u)r** Geruch *m*

**o·do(u)r·less** geruchlos

**of** *prp* von; *origin*: von, aus; *material*: aus; um (***cheat s.o. ~ s.th.*** j-n um et. betrügen); *cause*: an (*dat*) (***die ~*** sterben an); aus (***~ charity*** aus Nächstenliebe); vor (*dat*) (***be afraid ~*** Angst haben vor); auf (*acc*) (***be proud ~*** stolz sein auf); über (*acc*) (***be glad ~*** sich freuen über); nach (***smell ~*** riechen nach); von, über (*acc*) (***speak ~ s.th.*** von *or* über et. sprechen); an (*acc*) (***think ~ s.th.*** an et. denken); ***the city ~ London*** die Stadt London; ***the works ~ Dickens*** Dickens' Werke; ***your letter ~ ...*** Ihr Schreiben vom ...; ***five minutes ~ twelve*** fünf Minuten vor zwölf

**off 1.** *adv* fort(...), weg(...); ab(...), ab, abgegangen (*button etc*); weg, entfernt (***3 miles ~***); ELECTR *etc* aus(...), aus-, abgeschaltet; TECH zu; aus(gegangen), alle; aus, vorbei; verdorben (*food*); frei; ***I must be ~*** ich muss gehen *or* weg; ***~ with you!*** fort mit dir!; ***be ~*** ausfallen, nicht stattfinden; ***10% ~*** ECON 10% Nachlass; ***~ and on*** ab und zu, hin und wieder; ***take a day ~*** sich e-n Tag freinehmen; ***be well*** (***badly***) ***~*** gut (schlecht) d(a)ran *or* gestellt *or* situiert sein **2.** *prp* fort von, weg von, von (..., ab, weg, herunter); abseits von (*or gen*), von ... weg; MAR vor *der Küste etc*; ***be ~ duty*** nicht im Dienst sein, dienstfrei haben; ***be ~ smoking*** nicht mehr rauchen **3.** *adj* frei, arbeits-, dienstfrei; *fig* ***have an ~ day*** e-n schlechten Tag haben

**of·fal** GASTR Innereien *pl*

**off-col·o(u)r** schlüpfrig, zweideutig

**of·fence** *Br* → ***offense***

**of·fend** beleidigen, kränken; verstoßen (***against*** gegen); **of·fend·er** (Übel-, Misse)Täter(in); ***first ~*** JUR nicht Vorbestrafte *m, f*, Ersttäter(in)

**of·fense** Vergehen *n*, Verstoß *m*; JUR Straftat *f*; Beleidigung *f*, Kränkung *f*; ***take ~*** Anstoß nehmen (***at*** an *dat*)

**of·fen·sive 1.** beleidigend, anstößig; widerlich (*smell etc*); MIL Offensiv..., Angriffs... **2.** MIL Offensive *f* (*a. fig*)

**of·fer 1.** *v/t* anbieten (*a.* ECON); *Preis, Möglichkeit etc* bieten; *Preis, Belohnung* aussetzen; sich bereit erklären (***to do*** zu tun); *Widerstand* leisten; *v/i* es *or* sich anbieten **2.** Angebot *n*

**off·hand 1.** *adj* lässig; Stegreif...; ***be ~ with s.o.*** F mit j-m kurz angebunden sein **2.** *adv* auf Anhieb, so ohne weiteres

**of·fice** Büro *n*, Geschäftsstelle *f*, (*Anwalts*)Kanzlei *f*; (*esp* öffentliches) Amt, Posten *m*; *mst* ***Office*** *esp Br* Ministerium *n*; **~ block** *Br*, **~ build·ing** Bürohaus *n*; **~ hours** Dienstzeit *f*; Geschäfts-, Öffnungszeiten *pl*

**of·fi·cer** MIL Offizier *m*; (*Polizei- etc*)Beamte *m*, (-)Beamtin *f*

**of·fi·cial 1.** Beamte *m*, Beamtin *f* **2.** offiziell, amtlich, dienstlich

**of·fi·ci·ate** amtieren

**of·fi·cious** übereifrig

**off-licence** *Br* Wein- und Spirituosenhandlung *f*

**off-line** IT offline, Offline..., rechnerunabhängig

**off-peak**: ***~ electricity*** Nachtstrom *m*; ***~ hours*** verkehrsschwache Stunden *pl*

**off sea·son** Nebensaison *f*

**off·set** ECON ausgleichen; verrechnen (***against*** mit)

**off·shoot** BOT Ableger *m*, Spross *m*

**off·shore** vor der Küste

**off·side** SPORT abseits; ***~ position*** Abseitsposition *f*, Abseitsstellung *f*; ***~ trap*** Abseitsfalle *f*

**off·spring** Nachkomme *m*, Nachkommenschaft *f*

**off-the-peg** *Br*, **off-the-rack** Konfektions..., ... von der Stange

**off-the-rec·ord** inoffiziell

**of·ten** oft(mals), häufig

**oh** *int* oh!

**oil 1.** Öl *n*; Erdöl *n* **2.** (ein)ölen, schmieren (*a. fig*)

**oil change** MOT Ölwechsel *m*

**oil·cloth** Wachstuch *n*

**oil·field** Ölfeld *n*

**oil paint·ing** Ölmalerei *f*; Ölgemälde *n*

**oil pan** MOT Ölwanne *f*

**oil plat·form** → ***oilrig***

**oil pol·lu·tion** Ölpest *f*

**oil-pro·duc·ing coun·try** Ölförderland *n*

**oil pro·duc·tion** Ölförderung *f*

**oil re·fin·e·ry** Erdölraffinerie *f*

**oil·rig** (Öl)Bohrinsel *f*
**oil·skins** Ölzeug *n*
**oil slick** Ölteppich *m*
**oil well** Ölquelle *f*
**oil·y** ölig; *fig* schmierig, schleimig
**oint·ment** Salbe *f*
**OK, o·kay** F **1.** *adj and int* okay(!), o.k.(!), in Ordnung(!) **2.** genehmigen, *e-r Sache* zustimmen **3.** Okay *n*, O.K. *n*, Genehmigung *f*, Zustimmung *f*
**old 1.** alt **2.** ***the ~*** die Alten *pl*
**old age** (hohes) Alter; **~ pen·sion** Rente *f*, Pension *f*; **~ pen·sion·er** Rentner(in), Pensionär(in)
**old-fash·ioned** altmodisch
**old·ish** ältlich
**old peo·ple's home** Altersheim *n*, Altenheim *n*
**ol·ive** BOT Olive *f*; Olivgrün *n*
**O·lym·pic Games** SPORT Olympische Spiele *pl*
**om·i·nous** unheilvoll
**o·mis·sion** Auslassung *f*; Unterlassung *f*; Versäumnis *n*
**o·mit** auslassen, weglassen; unterlassen
**om·nip·o·tent** allmächtig
**om·nis·ci·ent** allwissend
**on 1.** *prp* auf (*acc or dat*) (***~ the table*** auf dem *or* den Tisch); an (*dat*) (***~ the wall*** an der Wand); in (***~ TV*** im Fernsehen); *direction, target*: auf (*acc*) … (hin), an (*acc*), nach (*dat*) … (hin); *fig* auf (*acc*) … (hin) (***~ demand*** auf Anfrage); *time*: an (*dat*) (***~ Sunday*** am Sonntag; ***~ the 1st of April*** am 1. April); (gleich) nach, bei (***~ his arrival***); *gehörig* zu, *beschäftigt* bei (***be ~ a committee*** e-m Ausschuss angehören; ***be ~ the „Daily Mail"*** bei der "Daily Mail" beschäftigt sein); *state*: in (*dat*), auf (*dat*) (***~ duty*** im Dienst; ***be ~ fire*** in Flammen stehen); *subject*: über (*acc*) (***talk ~ a subject*** über ein Thema sprechen); nach (*dat*) (***~ this model*** nach diesem Modell); von (*dat*) (***live ~ s.th.*** von et. leben); ***~ the street*** auf der Straße; ***~ a train*** in e-m Zug; ***~ hearing it*** als ich *etc* es hörte; ***have you any money ~ you?*** hast du Geld bei dir? **2.** *adj and adv* an (-geschaltet) (*light etc*), eingeschaltet (*radio etc*), auf (*faucet etc*); (dar)auf(*legen, -schrauben etc*); an(*haben, -ziehen*) (***have a coat ~*** e-n Mantel anhaben); auf(*behalten*) (***keep one's hat ~*** den Hut aufbehalten); weiter(*gehen, -sprechen etc*); ***and so ~*** und so weiter; ***~ and ~*** immer weiter; ***from this day ~*** von dem Tage an; ***be ~*** THEA gegeben werden; *film*: laufen; *radio*, TV gesendet werden; ***what's ~?*** was ist los?
**once 1.** einmal; einst; ***~ again, ~ more*** noch einmal; ***~ in a while*** ab und zu, hin und wieder; ***~ and for all*** ein für alle Mal; ***not ~*** kein einziges Mal, keinmal; ***at ~*** sofort; auf einmal, gleichzeitig; ***all at ~*** plötzlich; ***for ~*** diesmal, ausnahmsweise; ***this ~*** dieses eine Mal; ***~ upon a time there was …*** es war einmal … **2.** sobald
**one** ein(e); einzig; man; Eins *f*, eins; ***~'s*** sein(e); ***~ day*** eines Tages; ***~ another*** sich (gegenseitig), einander; ***~ by ~, ~ after another, ~ after the other*** e-r nach dem andern; ***I for ~*** ich zum Beispiel; ***the little ~s*** die Kleinen *pl*
**one-horse town** F *contp* Nest *n*
**one·self** sich (selbst); sich selbst; (***all***) ***by ~*** ganz allein; ***to ~*** ganz für sich (allein)
**one-sid·ed** einseitig
**one·time** ehemalig, früher
**one-track mind**: ***have a ~*** immer nur dasselbe im Kopf haben
**one-two** *soccer*: Doppelpass *m*
**one-way** Einbahn…; **~ street** Einbahnstraße *f*; **~ tick·et** RAIL *etc* einfache Fahrkarte, AVIAT einfaches Ticket; **~ traf·fic** MOT Einbahnverkehr *m*
**on·ion** BOT Zwiebel *f*
**on·line** IT online, Online…, rechnerabhängig
**on·look·er** Zuschauer(in)
**on·ly 1.** *adj* einzige(r, -s) **2.** *adv* nur, bloß; erst; ***~ yesterday*** erst gestern **3.** *cj* F nur, bloß
**on·rush** Ansturm *m*
**on·set** Beginn *m*; MED Ausbruch *m*
**on·slaught** (heftiger) Angriff (*a. fig*)
**on·to** auf (*acc*)
**on·ward(s)** *adv* vorwärts, weiter; ***from now ~*** von nun an
**ooze** *v/i* sickern; ***~ away*** *fig* schwinden; *v/t* absondern; *fig* ausstrahlen, verströmen
**o·paque** undurchsichtig; *fig* unverständlich
**o·pen 1.** offen, *a.* geöffnet, *a.* frei (*country etc*); öffentlich; *fig* offen, *a.* unentschieden, *a.* freimütig; *fig* zugänglich,

aufgeschlossen (***to*** für *or dat*); **~ *all day*** durchgehend geöffnet; ***in the ~ air*** im Freien **2.** *golf, tennis*: offenes Turnier; ***in the ~*** im Freien; ***come out into the ~*** *fig* an die Öffentlichkeit treten **3.** *v/t* öffnen, aufmachen, *Buch etc a.* aufschlagen; eröffnen; *v/i* sich öffnen, aufgehen; öffnen, aufmachen (*store*); anfangen, beginnen; **~ *into*** führen nach *or* in (*acc*); **~ *onto*** hinausgehen auf (*acc*)

**o·pen-air** im Freien

**o·pen-end·ed** zeitlich unbegrenzt

**o·pen·er** (*Dosen- etc*)Öffner *m*

**o·pen-eyed** mit großen Augen, staunend

**o·pen-hand·ed** freigebig, großzügig

**o·pen-heart·ed** offenherzig

**o·pen·ing 1.** Öffnung *f*; ECON freie Stelle; Eröffnung *f*, Erschließung *f*, Einstieg *m* **2.** Eröffnungs…; Öffnungs…

**o·pen-mind·ed** aufgeschlossen

**o·pen·ness** Offenheit *f*

**op·e·ra** Oper *f*; **~ glass·es** Opernglas *n*; **~ house** Opernhaus *n*, Oper *f*

**op·e·rate** *v/i* wirksam sein *or* werden; TECH arbeiten, in Betrieb sein, laufen (*machine etc*); MED operieren (***on s.o.*** j-n); *v/t Maschine* bedienen, *Schalter etc* betätigen; *Unternehmen, Geschäft* betreiben, führen

**op·e·rat·ing| room** MED Operationssaal *m*; **~ sys·tem** IT Betriebssystem *n*; **~ thea·tre** *Br* MED Operationssaal *m*

**op·e·ra·tion** TECH Betrieb *m*, Lauf *m*; Bedienung *f*; ECON Tätigkeit *f*, Unternehmen *n*; MED, MIL Operation *f*; ***in ~*** TECH in Betrieb; ***have an ~*** MED operiert werden

**op·e·ra·tive** wirksam; MED operativ

**op·e·ra·tor** TECH Bedienungsperson *f*; IT Operator *m*; TEL Vermittlung *f*

**o·pin·ion** Meinung *f*, Ansicht *f*; Gutachten *n* (***on*** über *acc*); ***in my ~*** meines Erachtens

**op·po·nent** Gegner(in)

**op·por·tune** günstig, passend; rechtzeitig

**op·por·tu·ni·ty** (günstige) Gelegenheit

**op·pose** sich widersetzen (*dat*)

**op·posed** entgegengesetzt; ***be ~ to*** gegen … sein

**op·po·site 1.** Gegenteil *n*, Gegensatz *m* **2.** *adj* gegenüberliegend; entgegengesetzt **3.** *adv* gegenüber (***to*** *dat*); **4.** *prp* gegenüber (*dat*)

**op·po·si·tion** Widerstand *m*, Opposition *f* (*a.* PARL); Gegensatz *m*

**op·press** unterdrücken

**op·pres·sion** Unterdrückung *f*

**op·pres·sive** (be)drückend; hart, grausam; schwül (*weather*)

**op·tic** Augen…, Seh…; → **op·ti·cal** optisch; **op·ti·cian** Optiker(in)

**op·ti·mism** Optimismus *m*

**op·ti·mist** Optimist(in)

**op·ti·mis·tic** optimistisch

**op·tion** Wahl *f*; ECON Option *f*, Vorkaufsrecht *n*; MOT Extra *n*

**op·tion·al** freiwillig; Wahl…; ***be an ~ extra*** MOT gegen Aufpreis erhältlich sein; **~ sub·ject** PED *etc* Wahlfach *n*

**or** oder; **~ *else*** sonst

**o·ral** mündlich; Mund…

**or·ange 1.** BOT Orange *f*, Apfelsine *f* **2.** orange(farben)

**or·ange·ade** Orangenlimonade *f*

**o·ra·tion** Rede *f*, Ansprache *f*

**or·a·tor** Redner(in)

**or·bit 1.** Kreisbahn *f*, Umlaufbahn *f*; ***get*** *or* ***put into ~*** in e-e Umlaufbahn gelangen *or* bringen **2.** *v/t die Erde etc* umkreisen; *v/i* die Erde *etc* umkreisen, sich auf e-r Umlaufbahn bewegen

**or·chard** Obstgarten *m*

**or·ches·tra** MUS Orchester *n*; THEA Parkett *n*

**or·chid** BOT Orchidee *f*

**or·dain**: **~ *s.o.*** (***priest***) j-n zum Priester weihen

**or·deal** Qual *f*, Tortur *f*

**or·der 1.** Ordnung *f*; Reihenfolge *f*; Befehl *m*, Anordnung *f*; ECON Bestellung *f*, Auftrag *m*; PARL *etc* (Geschäfts)Ordnung *f*; REL *etc* Orden *m*; **~ *to pay*** ECON Zahlungsanweisung *f*; ***in ~ to*** *inf* um zu *inf*; ***out of ~*** TECH nicht in Ordnung, defekt; außer Betrieb; ***make to ~*** auf Bestellung *or* nach Maß anfertigen **2.** *v/t j-m* befehlen (***to do*** zu tun), *et.* befehlen, anordnen; *j-n* schicken, beordern; MED *j-m et.* verordnen; ECON bestellen; *fig* ordnen, in Ordnung bringen; *v/i* bestellen (*in restaurant*)

**or·der·ly 1.** ordentlich; *fig* gesittet, friedlich **2.** MED Hilfspfleger *m*

**or·di·nal** *a.* **~ *number*** MATH Ordnungszahl *f*

**or·di·nary** üblich, gewöhnlich, normal
**ore** MIN Erz *n*
**or·gan** ANAT Organ *n* (*a. fig*); MUS Orgel *f*; **~ do·nor** MED Organspender *m*
**or·gan·ic** organisch
**or·gan·ism** Organismus *m*
**or·gan·i·za·tion** Organisation *f*
**or·gan·ize** organisieren; sich (gewerkschaftlich) organisieren
**or·gan·iz·er** Organisator(in)
**or·gan recip·i·ent** MED Organempfänger(in) *m(f)*
**or·gasm** Orgasmus *m*
**o·ri·ent 1. *Orient*** *der* Osten, *der* Orient, *das* Morgenland **2.** orientieren
**o·ri·en·tal 1.** orientalisch, östlich **2. *Oriental*** Orientale *m*, Orientalin *f*
**o·ri·en·tate** orientieren
**or·i·gin** Ursprung *m*, Abstammung *f*, Herkunft *f*
**o·rig·i·nal 1.** ursprünglich; Original…; originell **2.** Original *n*
**o·rig·i·nal·i·ty** Originalität *f*
**o·rig·i·nal·ly** ursprünglich; originell
**o·rig·i·nate** *v/t* schaffen, ins Leben rufen; *v/i* zurückgehen (***from*** auf *acc*), (her)stammen (***from*** von, aus)
**or·na·ment 1.** Ornament(e *pl*) *n*, Verzierung(en *pl*) *f*, Schmuck *m*; *fig* Zier(de) *f* (***to*** für *or gen*); **2.** verzieren, schmücken (***with*** mit)
**or·na·men·tal** dekorativ, schmückend, Zier…
**or·nate** *fig* überladen
**or·phan 1.** Waise *f*, Waisenkind *n* **2. *be ~ed*** Waise werden
**or·phan·age** Waisenhaus *n*
**or·tho·dox** orthodox
**os·cil·late** PHYS schwingen; *fig* schwanken (***between*** zwischen *dat*)
**os·prey** ZO Fischadler *m*
**os·ten·si·ble** angeblich, vorgeblich
**os·ten·ta·tion** (protzige) Zurschaustellung; Protzerei *f*, Prahlerei *f*
**os·ten·ta·tious** protzend, prahlerisch
**os·tra·cize** ächten
**os·trich** ZO Strauß *m*
**oth·er** andere(r, -s); ***the ~ day*** neulich; ***the ~ morning*** neulich morgens; ***every ~ day*** jeden zweiten Tag, alle zwei Tage
**oth·er·wise** anders; sonst
**ot·ter** ZO Otter *m*
**ought** *v/aux ich* sollte, *du* solltest *etc*; ***you ~ to have done it*** Sie hätten es tun sollen
**ounce** Unze *f* (*28,35 g*)
**our** unser
**ours** unsere(r, -s)
**our·selves** wir *or* uns selbst; uns (selbst)
**oust** verdrängen, hinauswerfen (***from*** aus); *j-n s-s Amtes* entheben
**out 1.** *adv*, *adj* aus; hinaus(*gehen*, *-werfen etc*); heraus(*kommen etc*); aus(*brechen etc*); draußen, im Freien; nicht zu Hause; SPORT aus, draußen; aus, vorbei; aus, erloschen; ausverkauft; F out, aus der Mode; ***~ of*** aus (… heraus); zu … hinaus; außerhalb von (*or gen*); außer *Reichweite etc*; außer *Atem*, *Übung etc*; (hergestellt) aus; aus *Furcht etc*; ***be ~ of bread*** kein Brot mehr haben; ***in nine ~ of ten cases*** in neun von zehn Fällen **2.** *prp* F aus (… heraus); zu … hinaus **3.** outen
**out·bal·ance** überwiegen
**out·bid** überbieten
**out·board mo·tor** Außenbordmotor *m*
**out·break** MED, MIL Ausbruch *m*
**out·build·ing** Nebengebäude *n*
**out·burst** *fig* Ausbruch *m*
**out·cast 1.** ausgestoßen **2.** Ausgestoßene *m*, *f*, Verstoßene *m*, *f*
**out·come** Ergebnis *n*
**out·cry** Aufschrei *m*, Schrei *m* der Entrüstung
**out·dat·ed** überholt, veraltet
**out·dis·tance** hinter sich lassen
**out·do** übertreffen
**out·door** *adj* im Freien, draußen
**out·doors** *adv* draußen, im Freien
**out·er** äußere(r, -s)
**out·er·most** äußerste(r, -s)
**out·er space** Weltraum *m*
**out·fit** Ausrüstung *f*, Ausstattung *f*; Kleidung *f*; F (Arbeits)Gruppe *f*
**out·fit·ter** Ausstatter *m*; ***men's ~*** Herrenausstatter *m*
**out·go·ing** (aus dem Amt) scheidend
**out·grow** herauswachsen aus (*dat*); *Angewohnheit etc* ablegen; größer werden als
**out·house** Nebengebäude *n*
**out·ing** Ausflug *m*; Outing *n*
**out·land·ish** befremdlich, sonderbar
**out·last** überdauern, überleben
**out·law** HIST Geächtete *m*, *f*
**out·lay** (Geld)Auslagen *pl*, Ausgaben *pl*
**out·let** Abfluss *m*, Abzug *m*; *fig* Ventil *n*

O

**out·line** **1.** Umriss *m*; Überblick *m* **2.** umreißen, skizzieren
**out·live** überleben
**out·look** (Aus)Blick *m*, (Aus)Sicht *f*; Einstellung *f*, Auffassung *f*
**out·ly·ing** abgelegen, entlegen
**out·num·ber** in der Überzahl sein; ***be ~ed by s.o.*** j-m zahlenmäßig unterlegen sein
**out-of-date** veraltet, überholt
**out-of-the-way** abgelegen, entlegen; *fig* ungewöhnlich
**out·pa·tient** MED ambulanter Patient, ambulante Patientin
**out·post** Vorposten *m*
**out·pour·ing** (Gefühls)Erguss *m*
**out·put** ECON Output *m*, Produktion *f*, Ausstoß *m*, Ertrag *m*; IT (Daten)Ausgabe *f*
**out·rage** **1.** Gewalttat *f*, Verbrechen *n*; Empörung *f* **2.** grob verletzen; *j-n* empören; **out·ra·geous** abscheulich; empörend, unerhört
**out·right** **1.** *adj* völlig, gänzlich, glatt (*lie etc*) **2.** *adv* auf der Stelle, sofort; ohne Umschweife
**out·run** schneller laufen als; *fig* übersteigen, übertreffen
**out·set** Anfang *m*, Beginn *m*
**out·shine** überstrahlen, *fig a.* in den Schatten stellen
**out·side** **1.** Außenseite *f*; SPORT Außenstürmer(in); ***at the*** (***very***) ***~*** (aller)höchstens; ***~ left*** (***right***) SPORT Linksaußen (Rechtsaußen) *m* **2.** *adj* äußere(r, -s), Außen… **3.** *adv* draußen; heraus, hinaus **4.** *prp* außerhalb
**out·sid·er** Außenseiter(in)
**out·size** **1.** Übergröße *f* **2.** übergroß
**out·skirts** Stadtrand *m*, Außenbezirke *pl*
**out·spo·ken** offen, freimütig
**out·spread** ausgestreckt, ausgebreitet
**out·stand·ing** hervorragend; ECON ausstehend; ungeklärt (*problem*); unerledigt (*work*)
**out·stay** länger bleiben als; → ***welcome*** *4*
**out·stretched** ausgestreckt
**out·strip** überholen; *fig* übertreffen
**out tray**: ***in the ~*** im Postausgang *etc*
**out·vote** überstimmen
**out·ward** **1.** äußere(r, -s); äußerlich **2.** *adv mst* ***outwards*** auswärts, nach außen; **out·ward·ly** äußerlich
**out·weigh** *fig* überwiegen
**out·wit** überlisten, F reinlegen
**out·worn** veraltet, überholt
**o·val** **1.** oval **2.** Oval *n*
**o·va·tion** Ovation *f*; ***give s.o. a standing ~*** j-m stehende Ovationen bereiten, j-m stehend Beifall klatschen
**ov·en** Backofen *m*, Bratofen *m*
**ov·en-read·y** bratfertig
**o·ver** **1.** *prp* über; über (*acc*), über (*acc*) … (hin)weg; über (*dat*), auf der anderen Seite von (*or gen*); über (*acc*), mehr als **2.** *adv* hinüber, herüber (***to*** zu); drüben; darüber, mehr; zu Ende, vorüber, vorbei; über…, um…: *et.* über(*geben etc*); über(*kochen etc*); um(*fallen*, *-werfen etc*); herum(*drehen etc*); von Anfang bis Ende, durch(*lesen etc*); (gründlich) über(*legen etc*); (***all***) ***~ again*** noch einmal; ***all ~*** ganz vorbei; ***~ and ~*** (***again***) immer wieder; ***~ and above*** obendrein, überdies
**o·ver·age** zu alt
**o·ver·all** **1.** gesamt, Gesamt…; allgemein; insgesamt **2.** *Br* Arbeitsmantel *m*, Kittel *m*; (*Br* ***~s***) Overall *m*, Arbeitsanzug *m*; Arbeitshose *f*
**o·ver·awe** einschüchtern
**o·ver·bal·ance** umstoßen, umkippen; das Gleichgewicht verlieren
**o·ver·bear·ing** anmaßend
**o·ver·board** MAR über Bord
**o·ver·bur·den** *fig* überlasten
**o·ver·cast** bewölkt, bedeckt
**o·ver·charge** überlasten, ELECTR *a.* überladen; ECON *j-m* zu viel berechnen; *Betrag* zu viel verlangen
**o·ver·coat** Mantel *m*
**o·ver·come** überwinden, überwältigen; ***be ~ with emotion*** von s-n Gefühlen übermannt werden
**o·ver·crowd·ed** überfüllt; überlaufen
**o·ver·do** übertreiben; GASTR zu lange kochen *or* braten; ***overdone*** *a.* übergar
**o·ver·dose** Überdosis *f*
**o·ver·draft** ECON (Konto)Überziehung *f*; *a.* ***~ facility*** Überziehungskredit *m*
**o·ver·draw** ECON *Konto* überziehen (***by*** um)
**o·ver·dress** (sich) zu fein anziehen; ***~ed*** overdressed, zu fein angezogen
**o·ver·drive** MOT Overdrive *m*, Schongang *m*

**o·ver·due** überfällig
**o·ver·eat** zu viel essen
**o·ver·es·ti·mate** zu hoch schätzen *or* veranschlagen; *fig* überschätzen
**o·ver·ex·pose** PHOT überbelichten
**o·ver·feed** überfüttern
**o·ver·flow** **1.** *v/t* überfluten, überschwemmen; *v/i* überlaufen, überfließen; überquellen (***with*** von); **2.** TECH Überlauf *m*; Überlaufen *n*, -fließen *n*
**o·ver·grown** BOT überwachsen, überwuchert
**o·ver·hang** *v/t* über (*dat*) hängen; *v/i* überhängen
**o·ver·haul** *Maschine* überholen
**o·ver·head** **1.** *adv* oben, droben **2.** *adj* Hoch…, Ober…; ECON ~ ***expenses*** *or* ***costs*** Gemeinkosten *pl*; SPORT Überkopf…; ~ ***kick*** *soccer*: Fallrückzieher *m* **3.** ECON *esp Br a. pl* Gemeinkosten *pl*
**o·ver·hear** (zufällig) hören
**o·ver·heat·ed** überhitzt, überheizt; TECH heiß gelaufen
**o·ver·joyed** überglücklich
**o·ver·lap** (sich) überlappen; sich überschneiden
**o·ver·leaf** umseitig, umstehend
**o·ver·load** überlasten (*a.* ELECTR), überladen
**o·ver·look** übersehen; ~***ing the sea*** mit Blick aufs Meer
**o·ver·night** **1.** über Nacht; ***stay*** ~ über Nacht bleiben, übernachten **2.** Nacht…, Übernachtungs…; ~ ***bag*** Reisetasche *f*
**o·ver·pass** (Straßen-, Eisenbahn-) Überführung *f*
**o·ver·pay** zu viel (be)zahlen
**o·ver·pop·u·lat·ed** übervölkert
**o·ver·pow·er** überwältigen; ~***ing*** *fig* überwältigend
**o·ver·rate** überbewerten, überschätzen
**o·ver·reach**: ~ ***o.s.*** sich übernehmen
**o·ver·re·act** überreagieren, überzogen reagieren (***to*** auf *acc*)
**o·ver·re·ac·tion** Überreaktion *f*, überzogene Reaktion
**o·ver·ride** sich hinwegsetzen über (*acc*)
**o·ver·rule** *Entscheidung etc* aufheben, *Einspruch etc* abweisen
**o·ver·run** länger dauern als vorgesehen; *Signal* überfahren; ***be*** ~ ***with*** wimmeln von
**o·ver·seas** **1.** *adj* überseeisch, Übersee… **2.** *adv* in *or* nach Übersee
**o·ver·see** beaufsichtigen, überwachen
**o·ver·shad·ow** *fig* überschatten, in den Schatten stellen
**o·ver·sight** Versehen *n*
**o·ver·size(d)** übergroß, überdimensional, in Übergröße(n)
**o·ver·sleep** verschlafen
**o·ver·staffed** (personell) überbesetzt
**o·ver·state** übertreiben
**o·ver·state·ment** Übertreibung *f*
**o·ver·stay** länger bleiben als; → ***welcome 4***
**o·ver·step** *fig* überschreiten
**o·ver·take** überholen; *j-n* überraschen
**o·ver·tax** zu hoch besteuern; *fig* überbeanspruchen, überfordern
**o·ver·throw** **1.** *Regierung etc* stürzen **2.** (Um)Sturz *m*
**o·ver·time** ECON Überstunden *pl*; SPORT (Spiel)Verlängerung *f*; ***do*** ~, ***work*** ~ Überstunden machen
**o·ver·tired** übermüdet
**o·ver·ture** MUS Ouvertüre *f*; Vorspiel *n*
**o·ver·turn** *v/t* umwerfen, umstoßen; *Regierung etc* stürzen; *v/i* umkippen, MAR kentern
**o·ver·view** *fig* Überblick *m* (***of*** über *acc*)
**o·ver·weight** **1.** Übergewicht *n* **2.** übergewichtig (*person*), zu schwer (***by*** um); ***be five pounds*** ~ fünf Pfund Übergewicht haben
**o·ver·whelm** überwältigen (*a. fig*)
**o·ver·whelm·ing** überwältigend
**o·ver·work** sich überarbeiten; überanstrengen
**o·ver·wrought** überreizt
**o·ver·zeal·ous** übereifrig
**owe** *j-m et.* schulden, schuldig sein; *et.* verdanken
**ow·ing**: ~ ***to*** infolge, wegen
**owl** ZO Eule *f*
**own** **1.** eigen; ***my*** ~ mein Eigentum; (***all***) ***on one's*** ~ allein **2.** besitzen; zugeben, (ein)gestehen
**own·er** Eigentümer(in), Besitzer(in)
**own·er-oc·cu·pied** *esp Br* eigengenutzt; ~ ***flat*** Eigentumswohnung *f*
**own·er·ship** Besitz *m*; Eigentum *n*; Eigentumsrecht *n*
**ox** ZO Ochse *m*
**ox·ide** CHEM Oxid *n*, Oxyd *n*
**ox·i·dize** CHEM oxidieren

O

**ox·y·gen** CHEM Sauerstoff *m*; **~ ap·pa·ra·tus** MED Sauerstoffgerät *n*; **~ tent** MED Sauerstoffzelt *n*
**oy·ster** ZO Auster *f*
**o·zone** CHEM Ozon *n*
**o·zone-friend·ly** FCKW-frei, ohne Treibgas
**o·zone| hole** Ozonloch *n*; **~ lay·er** Ozonschicht *f*; **~ lev·els** Ozonwerte *pl*; **~ shield** Ozonschild *m*

# P

**P, p** P, p *n*
**pace 1.** Tempo *n*, Geschwindigkeit *f*; Schritt *m*; Gangart *f* (*of a horse*) **2.** *v/t Zimmer etc* durchschreiten; *a.* **~ *out*** abschreiten; *v/i* (einher)schreiten; **~ *up and down*** auf und ab gehen
**pace·mak·er** SPORT Schrittmacher(in); MED Herzschrittmacher *m*
**pace·set·ter** SPORT Schrittmacher(in)
**Pa·cif·ic** *a.* **~ *Ocean*** *der* Pazifik, *der* Pazifische *or* Stille Ozean
**pac·i·fi·er** Schnuller *m*
**pac·i·fist** Pazifist(in)
**pac·i·fy** beruhigen, besänftigen
**pack 1.** Pack(en) *m*, Paket *n*, Bündel *n*; Packung *f*, Schachtel *f*; ZO Meute *f*; Rudel *n*; *contp* Pack *n*, Bande *f*; MED *etc* Packung *f*; (Karten)Spiel *n*; ***a ~ of lies*** ein Haufen Lügen **2.** *v/t* ein-, zusammenpacken, abpacken, verpacken (*a.* **~ *up***); zusammenpferchen; vollstopfen; *Koffer etc* packen; **~ *off*** F fort-, wegschicken; *v/i* packen; (sich) drängen (***into*** in *acc*); **~ *up*** zusammenpacken; ***send s.o. ~ing*** j-n fort- *or* wegjagen
**pack·age** Paket *n*; Packung *f*; ***software* ~** IT Software-, Programmpaket *n*
**pack·age| deal** F Pauschalangebot *n*, -arrangement *n*; **~ hol·i·day** Pauschalurlaub *m*; **~ tour** Pauschalreise *f*
**pack·et** Päckchen *n*; Packung *f*, Schachtel *f*
**pack·ing** Packen *n*; Verpackung *f*
**pact** Pakt *m*, POL *a.* Vertrag *m*
**pad 1.** Polster *n*; SPORT (*Knie- etc*)Schützer *m*; (*Schreib- etc*)Block *m*; (*Stempel*)Kissen *n*; ZO Ballen *m*; (*Abschuss-*) Rampe *f* **2.** (aus)polstern, wattieren
**pad·ding** Polsterung *f*, Wattierung *f*
**pad·dle 1.** Paddel *n*; MAR (Rad)Schaufel *f* **2.** paddeln; plan(t)schen
**pad·dock** (Pferde)Koppel *f*
**pad·lock** Vorhängeschloss *n*
**pa·gan 1.** Heide *m*, Heidin *f* **2.** heidnisch
**page**[1] **1.** Seite *f* **2.** paginieren
**page**[2] **1.** (Hotel)Page *m* **2.** *j-n* ausrufen (lassen)
**pag·eant** (*a.* historischer) Festzug
**pa·gin·ate** paginieren
**pail** Eimer *m*, Kübel *m*
**pain 1.** Schmerz(en *pl*) *m*; Kummer *m*; *pl* Mühe *f*, Bemühungen *pl*; ***be in (great)* ~** (große) Schmerzen haben; ***be a ~ (in the neck)*** F e-m auf den Wecker gehen; ***take ~s*** sich Mühe geben **2.** *esp fig* schmerzen; **pain·ful** schmerzhaft, schmerzend; *fig* schmerzlich; peinlich
**pain·kill·er** Schmerzmittel *n*
**pain·less** schmerzlos
**pains·tak·ing** sorgfältig, gewissenhaft
**paint 1.** Farbe *f*; Anstrich *m* **2.** *v/t* anmalen, bemalen; (an)streichen; *Auto etc* lackieren; *v/i* malen
**paint·box** Malkasten *m*
**paint·brush** (Maler)Pinsel *m*
**paint·er** (*a.* Kunst)Maler(in), Anstreicher(in)
**paint·ing** Malerei *f*; Gemälde *n*, Bild *n*
**pair 1.** Paar *n*; ***a ~ of ...*** ein Paar ..., ein(e) ...; ***a ~ of scissors*** e-e Schere **2.** *v/i* zo sich paaren; *a.* **~ *off*, ~ *up*** Paare bilden; *v/t a.* **~ *off*, ~ *up*** paarweise anordnen; **~ *off*** *zwei Leute* zusammenbringen, verkuppeln
**pa·ja·ma(s)** (***a pair of*) ~s** (ein) Schlafanzug *m*, (ein) Pyjama *m*
**pal** Kamerad *m*, F Kumpel *m*, Spezi *m*
**pal·ace** Palast *m*, Schloss *n*
**pal·a·ta·ble** schmackhaft (*a. fig*)
**pal·ate** ANAT Gaumen *m*; *fig* Geschmack *m*
**pale**[1] **1.** blass, *a.* bleich, *a.* hell (*color*) **2.** blass *or* bleich werden

**pale**[2] Pfahl *m*; *fig* Grenzen *pl*
**pale·ness** Blässe *f*
**Pal·es·tin·i·an** **1.** palästinensisch **2.** Palästinenser(in)
**pal·ings** Lattenzaun *m*
**pal·i·sade** Palisade *f*; *pl* Steilufer *n*
**pal·let** TECH Palette *f*
**pal·lid** blass; **pal·lor** Blässe *f*
**palm**[1] *a.* ***~ tree*** BOT Palme *f*
**palm**[2] **1.** ANAT Handfläche *f* **2.** *et.* in der Hand verschwinden lassen; ***~ s.th. off on s.o.*** F j-m et. andrehen
**pal·pa·ble** fühlbar, greifbar
**pal·pi·tate** MED klopfen, pochen
**pal·pi·ta·tions** MED Herzklopfen *n*
**pal·sy** MED Lähmung *f*
**pal·try** armselig
**pam·per** verwöhnen
**pam·phlet** Broschüre *f*
**pan** Pfanne *f*; Topf *m*
**pan·a·ce·a** Allheilmittel *n*
**pan·cake** Pfannkuchen *m*
**pan·da** ZO Panda *m*
**pan·da car** *Br* (Funk)Streifenwagen *m*
**pan·de·mo·ni·um** Hölle *f*, Höllenlärm *m*, Tumult *m*, Chaos *n*
**pan·der** Vorschub leisten (***to*** *dat*)
**pane** (*Fenster*)Scheibe *f*
**pan·el** **1.** (*Tür*)Füllung *f*, (*Wand*)Täfelung *f*; ELECTR, TECH Instrumentenbrett *n*, (*Schalt-*, *Kontroll-* *etc*)Tafel *f*; JUR Liste *f* der Geschworenen; Diskussionsteilnehmer *pl*, Diskussionsrunde *f*; Rateteam *n* **2.** täfeln
**pang** stechender Schmerz; ***~s of hunger*** nagender Hunger; ***~s of conscience*** Gewissensbisse *pl*
**pan·han·dle** **1.** Pfannenstiel *m*; GEOGR schmaler Fortsatz **2.** F betteln
**pan·ic** **1.** panisch **2.** Panik *f* **3.** in Panik versetzen *or* geraten
**pan·ick·y**: F ***be ~*** in Panik sein
**pan·ic-strick·en** von Panik erfasst *or* erfüllt
**pan·o·ra·ma** Panorama *n*, Ausblick *m*
**pan·sy** BOT Stiefmütterchen *n*
**pant** keuchen, schnaufen, nach Luft schnappen
**pan·ther** ZO Panther *m*; Puma *m*; Jaguar *m*
**pan·ties** (Damen)Schlüpfer *m*, Slip *m*; Höschen *n*
**pan·to·mime** THEA Pantomime *f*; *Br* F Weihnachtsspiel *n*
**pan·try** Speisekammer *f*
**pants** Hose *f*; *Br* Unterhose *f*; *Br* Schlüpfer *m*
**pant·suit** Hosenanzug *m*
**pan·ty·hose** Strumpfhose *f*
**pan·ty·lin·er** Slipeinlage *f*
**pap** Brei *m*
**pa·pal** päpstlich
**pa·per** **1.** Papier *n*; Zeitung *f*; (Prüfungs)Arbeit *f*; UNIV Klausur(arbeit) *f*; Aufsatz *m*; Referat *n*; Tapete *f*; *pl* (Ausweis)Papiere *pl* **2.** tapezieren
**pa·per·back** Taschenbuch *n*, Paperback *n*
**pa·per bag** (Papier)Tüte *f*
**pa·per·boy** Zeitungsjunge *m*
**pa·per clip** Büro-, Heftklammer *f*
**pa·per cup** Pappbecher *m*
**pa·per·hang·er** Tapezierer *m*
**pa·per knife** *Br* Brieföffner *m*
**pa·per mon·ey** Papiergeld *n*
**pa·per·weight** Briefbeschwerer *m*
**par**: ***at ~*** zum Nennwert; ***be on a ~ with*** gleich *or* ebenbürtig sein (*dat*)
**par·a·ble** Parabel *f*, Gleichnis *n*
**par·a·chute** Fallschirm *m*
**par·a·chut·ist** Fallschirmspringer(in)
**pa·rade** **1.** Umzug *m*, *esp* MIL Parade *f*; *fig* Zurschaustellung *f*; ***make a ~ of*** *fig* zur Schau stellen **2.** ziehen (***through*** durch); MIL antreten (lassen), vorbeimarschieren (lassen); zur Schau stellen; ***~*** (***through***) stolzieren durch
**par·a·dise** Paradies *n*
**par·af·fin** *Br* Petroleum *n*
**par·a·glid·er** SPORT Gleitschirm *m*; Gleitschirmflieger(in); **par·a·glid·ing** SPORT Gleitschirmfliegen *n*
**par·a·gon** Muster *n* (***of*** an *dat*)
**par·a·graph** Absatz *m*, Abschnitt *m*; (Zeitungs)Notiz *f*
**par·al·lel** **1.** parallel (***to, with*** zu); **2.** MATH Parallele *f* (*a. fig*); ***without ~*** ohne Parallele, ohnegleichen **3.** entsprechen (*dat*), gleichkommen (*dat*)
**par·a·lyse** *Br*, **par·a·lyze** MED lähmen, *fig a.* lahmlegen, zum Erliegen bringen; ***~d with*** *fig* starr *or* wie gelähmt vor (*dat*)
**pa·ral·y·sis** MED Lähmung *f*, *fig a.* Lahmlegung *f*
**par·a·med·ic** MED Sanitäter *m*
**par·a·mount** größte(r, -s), übergeordnet; ***of ~ importance*** von (aller)größter

Bedeutung *or* Wichtigkeit

**par·a·pet** Brüstung *f*

**par·a·pher·na·li·a** (persönliche) Sachen *pl*; Ausrüstung *f*; *esp Br* F Scherereien *pl*

**par·a·phrase** **1.** umschreiben **2.** Umschreibung *f*

**par·a·site** Parasit *m*, Schmarotzer *m*

**par·a·troop·er** MIL Fallschirmjäger *m*; *pl* Fallschirmjägertruppe *f*

**par·boil** halb gar kochen, ankochen

**par·cel** **1.** Paket *n*; Parzelle *f* **2.** ~ ***out*** aufteilen; ~ ***up*** (als Paket) verpacken

**parch** ausdörren, austrocknen; vertrocknen

**parch·ment** Pergament *n*

**par·don** **1.** JUR Begnadigung *f*; ***I beg your*** ~ Entschuldigung!, Verzeihung!; erlauben Sie mal!, ich muss doch sehr bitten!; *a.* ~**?** F (wie) bitte? **2.** verzeihen; vergeben; JUR begnadigen; ~ ***me*** → ***I beg your pardon***; F (wie) bitte?

**par·don·a·ble** verzeihlich

**pare** sich *die Nägel* schneiden; *Apfel etc* schälen

**par·ent** Elternteil *m*, Vater *m*, Mutter *f*; *pl* Eltern *pl*; **par·ent·age** Abstammung *f*, Herkunft *f*; **pa·ren·tal** elterlich

**pa·ren·the·ses** (runde) Klammer

**par·ents-in-law** Schwiegereltern *pl*

**par·ent-teach·er meet·ing** PED Elternabend *m*

**par·ings** Schalen *pl*

**par·ish** REL Gemeinde *f*

**par·ish church** REL Pfarrkirche *f*

**pa·rish·ion·er** REL Gemeindemitglied *n*

**park** **1.** Park *m*, (Grün)Anlage(n *pl*) *f* **2.** MOT parken; ***look for somewhere to*** ~ ***the car*** e-n Parkplatz suchen

**par·ka** Parka *m*, *f*

**park·ing** MOT Parken *n*; ***no*** ~ Parkverbot, Parken verboten; ~ **disk** Parkscheibe *f*; ~ **fee** Parkgebühr *f*; ~ **garage** Park(hoch)haus *n*; ~ **lot** Parkplatz *m*; ~ **lot at·tend·ant** Parkwächter *m*; ~ **me·ter** Parkuhr *f*; ~ **of·fend·er** Parksünder(in); ~ **space** Parkplatz *m*, Parklücke *f*; ~ **tick·et** Strafzettel *m*

**par·ley** *esp* MIL Verhandlung *f*

**par·lia·ment** Parlament *n*

**par·lia·men·tar·i·an** Parlamentarier(in)

**par·lia·men·ta·ry** parlamentarisch, Parlaments…

**par·lo(u)r** *mst in cpds* Salon *m*

**pa·ro·chi·al** REL Pfarr…, Gemeinde…; *fig* engstirnig, beschränkt

**par·o·dy** **1.** Parodie *f* **2.** parodieren

**pa·role** JUR **1.** Hafturlaub *m*; bedingte Haftentlassung **2.** ~ ***s.o.*** j-m Hafturlaub gewähren; j-n bedingt entlassen

**par·quet** Parkett *n* (*a.* THEA)

**par·quet floor** Parkett(fuß)boden *m*

**par·rot** **1.** ZO Papagei *m* (*a. fig*) **2.** *et.* (wie ein Papagei) nachplappern

**par·ry** abwehren, parieren

**par·si·mo·ni·ous** geizig

**pars·ley** BOT Petersilie *f*

**par·son** REL Pfarrer *m*

**par·son·age** REL Pfarrhaus *n*

**part** **1.** Teil *m*; TECH Teil *n*, Bau-, Ersatzteil *n*; Anteil *m*; Seite *f*, Partei *f*; THEA, *fig* Rolle *f*; MUS Stimme *f*, Partie *f*; GEOGR Gegend *f*, Teil *m*; (Haar)Scheitel *m*; ***for my*** ~ was mich betrifft; ***for the most*** ~ größtenteils; meistens; ***in*** ~ teilweise, zum Teil; ***on the*** ~ ***of*** vonseiten, seitens (*gen*); ***on my*** ~ von m-r Seite; ***take*** ~ ***in s.th.*** an e-r Sache teilnehmen; ***take s.th. in good*** ~ et. nicht übel nehmen **2.** *v/t* trennen; (ab-, zer)teilen; einteilen; *Haar* scheiteln; ~ ***company*** sich trennen (***with*** von); *v/i* sich trennen (***with*** von); **3.** *adj* Teil… **4.** *adv*: ~ ***…***, ~ teils …, teils

**par·tial** Teil…, teilweise; parteiisch, voreingenommen (***to*** für)

**par·ti·al·i·ty** Parteilichkeit *f*, Voreingenommenheit *f*; Schwäche *f*, besondere Vorliebe (***for*** für)

**par·tial·ly** teilweise, zum Teil

**par·tic·i·pant** Teilnehmer(in)

**par·tic·i·pate** teilnehmen, sich beteiligen (*both*: ***in*** an *dat*)

**par·tic·i·pa·tion** Teilnahme *f*, Beteiligung *f*

**par·ti·ci·ple** LING Partizip *n*, Mittelwort *n*

**par·ti·cle** Teilchen *n*

**par·tic·u·lar** **1.** besondere(r, -s), speziell; genau, eigen, wählerisch **2.** Einzelheit *f*; *pl* nähere Umstände *pl or* Angaben *pl*; Personalien *pl*; ***in*** ~ insbesondere;

**par·tic·u·lar·ly** besonders

**part·ing** **1.** Trennung *f*, Abschied *m*; *esp Br* (Haar)Scheitel *m* **2.** Abschieds…

**par·ti·san** **1.** Parteigänger(in); MIL Partisan(in) **2.** parteiisch

**par·ti·tion** **1.** Teilung *f*; Trennwand *f* **2.** ~

P

***off*** abteilen, abtrennen
**part·ly** teilweise, zum Teil
**part·ner** Partner(in), ECON *a.* Teilhaber(in); **part·ner·ship** Partnerschaft *f*, ECON *a.* Teilhaberschaft *f*
**part-own·er** Miteigentümer(in)
**par·tridge** ZO Rebhuhn *n*
**part-time 1.** *adj* Teilzeit…, Halbtags…; ***~ worker*** → ***part-timer*** **2.** *adv* halbtags
**part-tim·er** F Teilzeitbeschäftigte *m, f*, Halbtagskraft *f*
**par·ty** Partei *f* (*a.* POL); (*Arbeits-, Reise-*) Gruppe *f*; (*Rettungs- etc*)Mannschaft *f*; MIL Kommando *n*, Trupp *m*; Party *f*, Gesellschaft *f*; Teilnehmer(in), Beteiligte *m, f*; **~ line** POL Parteilinie *f*; **~ pol·i·tics** Parteipolitik *f*
**pass 1.** *v/i* vorbeigehen, -fahren, -kommen, -ziehen *etc* (***by*** an *dat*); übergehen (***to*** auf *acc*), fallen (***to*** an *acc*); vergehen (*pain etc, time*); durchkommen, (die Prüfung) bestehen; gelten (***as, for*** als), gehalten werden (***as, for*** für); PARL Rechtskraft erlangen; unbeanstandet bleiben; SPORT (den Ball) abspielen *or* passen (***to*** zu); *card game*: passen (*a. fig*); ***let s.o. ~*** j-n vorbeilassen; ***let s.th. ~*** et. durchgehen lassen; *v/t* vorbeigehen, -fahren, -fließen, -kommen, -ziehen *etc* an (*dat*); überholen; *Prüfung* bestehen; *Prüfling* durchkommen lassen; (*mit der Hand*) streichen (***over*** über *acc*); *j-m et.* reichen, geben, *et.* weitergeben; SPORT *Ball* abspielen, passen (***to*** zu); *Zeit* verbringen; PARL *Gesetz* verabschieden; *Urteil* abgeben, fällen, JUR *a.* sprechen (***on*** über *acc*); *fig* hinausgehen über (*acc*), übersteigen, übertreffen; ***~ away*** sterben; ***~ off*** *j-n, et.* ausgeben (***as*** als); *gut etc* verlaufen; ***~ out*** ohnmächtig werden **2.** Passierschein *m*; Bestehen *n* (*examination*); SPORT Pass *m*, Zuspiel *n*; (*Gebirgs*)Pass *m*; ***free ~*** Frei(fahr)karte *f*; ***things have come to such a ~ that*** F die Dinge haben sich derart zugespitzt, dass; ***make a ~ at*** F Annäherungsversuche machen bei
**pass·a·ble** passierbar, befahrbar; passabel, leidlich
**pas·sage** Passage *f*, Korridor *m*, Gang *m*; Durchgang *m*; (See-, Flug)Reise *f*; Durchfahrt *f*, Durchreise *f*; Passage *f* (*a.* MUS), Stelle *f*; ***bird of ~*** Zugvogel *m*
**pass·book** ECON Sparbuch *n*
**pas·sen·ger** Passagier *m*, Fahrgast *m*, Fluggast *m*, Reisende *m, f*, MOT Insasse *m*, Insassin *f*
**pass·er-by** Passant(in)
**pas·sion** Leidenschaft *f*; Wut *f*, Zorn *m*; ***Passion*** REL Passion *f*; ***~s ran high*** die Erregung schlug hohe Wellen
**pas·sion·ate** leidenschaftlich
**pas·sive** passiv; LING passivisch
**Pass·o·ver** REL Passah(fest) *n*
**pass·port** (Reise)Pass *m*
**pass·word** Kennwort *n* (*a.* IT), MIL *a.* Parole *f*, Losung *f*
**past 1.** *adj* vergangen; frühere(r, -s); ***be ~*** *a.* vorüber sein; ***for some time ~*** seit einiger Zeit; ***~ tense*** LING Vergangenheit *f*, Präteritum *n* **2.** *adv* vorüber, vorbei; ***go ~*** vorbeigehen **3.** *prp time*: nach, über (*acc*); über … (*acc*) hinaus; an … (*dat*) vorbei; ***half ~ two*** halb drei; ***~ hope*** hoffnungslos **4.** Vergangenheit *f* (*a.* LING)
**pas·ta** Teigwaren *pl*
**paste 1.** Paste *f*; Kleister *m*; Teig *m* **2.** kleben (***to, on*** an *acc*); ***~ up*** ankleben
**paste·board** Karton *m*, Pappe *f*
**pas·tel** Pastell(zeichnung *f*) *n*
**pas·teur·ize** pasteurisieren
**pas·time** Zeitvertreib *m*, Freizeitbeschäftigung *f*
**pas·tor** REL Pastor *m*, Pfarrer *m*, Seelsorger *m*; **pas·tor·al** REL seelsorgerisch, pastoral; ***~ care*** Seelsorge *f*
**pas·try** GASTR (*Blätter-, Mürbe*)Teig *m*; Feingebäck *n*; **~ cook** Konditor *m*
**pas·ture 1.** Weide(land *n*) *f* **2.** *v/t* weiden (lassen); *v/i* grasen, weiden
**pas·ty**[1] *esp Br* GASTR (Fleisch)Pastete *f*
**past·y**[2] blass, F käsig
**pat 1.** Klaps *m*; GASTR Portion *f* **2.** tätscheln; klopfen
**patch 1.** Fleck *m*; Flicken *m*; kleines Stück Land; ***in ~es*** stellenweise **2.** flicken
**pa·tent 1.** offenkundig; patentiert; Patent… **2.** Patent *n*; ***take out a ~ for s.th.*** (sich) et. patentieren lassen **3.** *et.* patentieren lassen
**pa·tent·ee** Patentinhaber(in)
**pa·tent leath·er** Lackleder *n*
**pa·ter·nal** väterlich; väterlicherseits
**pa·ter·ni·ty** JUR Vaterschaft *f*
**path** Pfad *m*; Weg *m*

**pa·thet·ic** mitleiderregend; kläglich, miserabel
**pa·tience** Geduld *f*; *esp Br* Patience *f*
**pa·tient**[1] geduldig
**pa·tient**[2] MED Patient(in)
**pat·i·o** Terrasse *f*; Innenhof *m*, Patio *m*
**pat·ri·ot** Patriot(in)
**pat·ri·ot·ic** patriotisch
**pa·trol 1.** Patrouille *f* (*a.* MIL), Streife *f*, Runde *f*; ***on ~*** auf Patrouille, auf Streife **2.** abpatrouillieren, auf Streife sein in (*dat*), s-e Runde machen in (*dat*)
**pa·trol car** (Funk)Streifenwagen *m*
**pa·trol·man** Streifenpolizist *m*; *Br* motorisierter Pannenhelfer
**pa·tron** Schirmherr *m*; Gönner *m*, Förderer *m*; (Stamm)Kunde *m*; Stammgast *m*; **pat·ron·age** Schirmherrschaft *f*; Förderung *f*; **pat·ron·ess** Schirmherrin *f*; Gönnerin *f*, Förderin *f*; **pat·ron·ize** fördern; (Stamm)Kunde *or* Stammgast sein bei *or* in (*dat*); gönnerhaft *or* herablassend behandeln
**pa·tron saint** REL Schutzheilige *m*, *f*
**pat·ter** prasseln (*rain*); trappeln (*feet*)
**pat·tern 1.** Muster *n* (*a. fig*); Schema *n* **2.** bilden, formen (***after, on*** nach)
**paunch** (dicker) Bauch
**pau·per** Arme *m*, *f*
**pause 1.** Pause *f* **2.** innehalten, e-e Pause machen
**pave** pflastern; ***~ the way for*** *fig* den Weg ebnen für
**pave·ment** Fahrbahn *f*; Belag *m*, Pflaster *n*; *Br* Bürgersteig *m*, Gehsteig *m*
**pave·ment ca·fé** *Br* Straßencafé *n*
**paw 1.** zo Pfote *f*, Tatze *f* **2.** *v/t Boden* scharren; scharren an (*dat*); F betatschen; *v/i* scharren (***at*** an *dat*)
**pawn**[1] *chess*: Bauer *m*; *fig* Schachfigur *f*
**pawn**[2] **1.** verpfänden, versetzen **2.** ***be in ~*** verpfändet *or* versetzt sein
**pawn·bro·ker** Pfandleiher *m*
**pawn·shop** Leihhaus *n*, Pfandhaus *n*
**pay 1.** *v/t et.* (be)zahlen; *j-n* bezahlen; *Aufmerksamkeit* schenken; *Besuch* abstatten; *Kompliment* machen; ***~ attention*** achtgeben auf (*acc*); PED aufpassen; ***~ cash*** bar bezahlen; *v/i* zahlen; *fig* sich lohnen; ***~ for*** (*fig* für) *et.* bezahlen; *fig* büßen; ***~ in*** einzahlen; ***~ into*** einzahlen auf (*acc*); ***~ off*** *et.* ab(be)zahlen; *j-n* auszahlen **2.** Bezahlung *f*, Gehalt *n*, Lohn *m*
**pay·a·ble** zahlbar, fällig
**pay·day** Zahltag *m*
**pay·ee** Zahlungsempfänger(in)
**pay en·ve·lope** Lohntüte *f*
**pay·ing** lohnend
**pay·mas·ter** MIL Zahlmeister *m*
**pay·ment** (Be)Zahlung *f*
**pay pack·et** *Br* Lohntüte *f*
**pay phone** *Br* Münzfernsprecher *m*
**pay·roll** Lohnliste *f*
**pay·slip** Lohn-, Gehaltsstreifen *m*
**PC** *abbr of* ***personal computer*** PC *m*, Personal Computer *m*; ***PC user*** PC-Benutzer *m*
**pea** BOT Erbse *f*
**peace** Friede(n) *m*; Ruhe *f*; JUR öffentliche Ruhe und Ordnung; ***at ~*** in Frieden
**peace·a·ble** friedlich, friedfertig
**peace·ful** friedlich
**peace·lov·ing** friedliebend
**peace move·ment** Friedensbewegung *f*
**peace·time** Friedenszeiten *pl*
**peach** BOT Pfirsich(baum) *m*
**pea·cock** zo Pfau *m*, Pfauhahn *m*
**pea·hen** zo Pfauhenne *f*
**peak** Spitze *f*, Gipfel *m*; Schirm *m*; *fig* Höhepunkt *m*, Höchststand *m*
**peaked cap** Schirmmütze *f*
**peak hours** Hauptverkehrszeit *f*, Stoßzeit *f*; ELECTR Hauptbelastungszeit *f*
**peak| time**, **~ viewing hours** *Br* TV Haupteinschaltzeit *f*, Hauptsendezeit *f*, beste Sendezeit
**peal 1.** (*Glocken*)Läuten *n*; (*Donner-*)Schlag *m*; ***~s of laughter*** schallendes Gelächter **2.** *a.* ***~ out*** läuten; krachen
**pea·nut** BOT Erdnuss *f*; *pl* F lächerliche Summe
**pear** BOT Birne *f*; Birnbaum *m*
**pearl 1.** Perle *f*; Perlmutter *f*, Perlmutt *n* **2.** Perlen…
**pearl·y** perlenartig, Perlen…
**peas·ant** Kleinbauer *m*
**peat** Torf *m*
**peb·ble** Kiesel(stein) *m*
**peck** picken, hacken; ***~ at one's food*** im Essen herumstochern
**pe·cu·li·ar** eigen, eigentümlich, typisch; eigenartig, seltsam
**pe·cu·li·ar·i·ty** Eigenheit *f*, Eigentümlichkeit *f*
**ped·a·go·gic** pädagogisch
**ped·al 1.** Pedal *n* **2.** das Pedal treten;

(mit dem Rad) fahren, strampeln
**pe·dan·tic** pedantisch
**ped·es·tal** Sockel *m*
**pe·des·tri·an** **1.** Fußgänger(in) **2.** Fußgänger…; **~ cross·ing** Fußgängerübergang *m*; **~ mall**, *esp Br* **~ pre·cinct** Fußgängerzone *f*
**ped·i·cure** Pediküre *f*
**ped·i·gree** Stammbaum *m* (*a.* zo)
**ped·lar** *Br* → ***peddler***
**pee** F **1.** pinkeln **2.** ***have*** (*or* ***go for***) ***a ~*** pinkeln (gehen)
**peek** **1.** kurz *or* verstohlen gucken (***at*** auf *acc*); **2.** ***have*** *or* ***take a ~ at*** e-n kurzen *or* verstohlenen Blick werfen auf (*acc*)
**peel** **1.** *v/t* schälen; *a.* ***~ off*** abschälen, *Folie*, *Tapete etc* abziehen, ablösen; *Kleid* abstreifen; *v/i a.* ***~ off*** sich lösen (*wallpaper etc*), abblättern (*paint etc*), sich schälen (*skin*) **2.** BOT Schale *f*
**peep**[1] **1.** kurz *or* verstohlen gucken (***at*** auf *acc*); *mst* ***~ out*** (her)vorschauen **2.** ***take a ~ at*** e-n kurzen *or* verstohlenen Blick werfen auf (*acc*)
**peep**[2] **1.** Piep(s)en *n*; F Piepser *m* **2.** piep(s)en
**peep·hole** Guckloch *n*; (Tür)Spion *m*
**peer** angestrengt schauen, spähen; ***~ at s.o.*** j-n anstarren
**peer·less** unvergleichlich, einzigartig
**peev·ish** verdrießlich, gereizt
**peg** **1.** (Holz)Stift *m*, Zapfen *m*, Pflock *m*; (Kleider)Haken *m*; *Br* (*Wäsche-*) Klammer *f*; (*Zelt*)Hering *m*; ***take s.o. down a ~*** (***or two***) F j-m e-n Dämpfer aufsetzen **2.** anpflocken; *Wäsche* anklammern, festklammern
**pel·i·can** zo Pelikan *m*; **~ cross·ing** *Br* Ampelübergang *m*
**pel·let** Kügelchen *n*; Schrotkorn *n*
**pelt**[1] *v/t* bewerfen, *v/i*: ***it's ~ing*** (***down***), *esp Br* ***it's ~ing with rain*** es gießt in Strömen
**pelt**[2] zo Fell *n*, Pelz *m*
**pel·vis** ANAT Becken *n*
**pen**[1] (*Schreib*)Feder *f*; Füller *m*; Kugelschreiber *m*
**pen**[2] **1.** Pferch *m*, (*Schaf*)Hürde *f* **2.** ***~ in***, ***~ up*** *Tiere* einpferchen, *Personen* zusammenpferchen
**pe·nal** JUR Straf…; strafbar
**pe·nal code** JUR Strafgesetzbuch *n*
**pe·nal·ize** bestrafen
**pen·al·ty** Strafe *f*, SPORT *a.* Strafpunkt *m*; *soccer*: Elfmeter *m*; **~ ar·e·a**, **~ box** F *soccer*: Strafraum *m*; **~ goal** *soccer*: Elfmetertor *n*; **~ kick** *soccer*: Elfmeter *m*, Strafstoß *m*; **~ shoot-out** *soccer*: Elfmeterschießen *n*; **~ spot** *soccer*: Elfmeterpunkt *m*
**pen·ance** REL Buße *f*
**pen·cil** **1.** Bleistift *m* **2.** (mit Bleistift) markieren *or* schreiben *or* zeichnen; *Augenbrauen* nachziehen
**pen·cil case** Federmäppchen *n*
**pen·cil sharp·en·er** Bleistiftspitzer *m*
**pen·dant, pen·dent** (Schmuck)Anhänger *m*
**pend·ing** **1.** *prp* bis zu **2.** *adj esp* JUR schwebend
**pen·du·lum** Pendel *n*
**pen·e·trate** *v/t* eindringen in (*acc*); dringen durch, durchdringen; *v/i* eindringen (***into*** in *acc*); **pen·e·trat·ing** durchdringend; *fig* scharf; scharfsinnig;
**pen·e·tra·tion** Durchdringen *n*, Eindringen *n*; *fig* Scharfsinn *m*
**pen friend** *Br* Brieffreund(in)
**pen·guin** zo Pinguin *m*
**pe·nin·su·la** Halbinsel *f*
**pe·nis** ANAT Penis *m*
**pen·i·tence** Buße *f*, Reue *f*
**pen·i·tent** **1.** reuig, bußfertig **2.** REL Büßer(in)
**pen·i·ten·tia·ry** (Staats)Gefängnis *n*, Strafanstalt *f*
**pen·knife** Taschenmesser *n*
**pen name** Schriftstellername *m*, Pseudonym *n*
**pen·nant** Wimpel *m*
**pen·ni·less** (völlig) mittellos
**pen·ny** *Br* Penny *m*
**pen pal** Brieffreund(in)
**pen·sion** **1.** Rente *f*, Pension *f* **2.** ***~ off*** pensionieren, in den Ruhestand versetzen
**pen·sion·er** Rentner(in), Pensionär(in)
**pen·sive** nachdenklich
**pen·tath·lete** SPORT Fünfkämpfer(in)
**pen·tath·lon** SPORT Fünfkampf *m*
**Pen·te·cost** REL Pfingsten *n*
**pent·house** Penthouse *n*, Penthaus *n*
**pent-up** auf-, angestaut (*emotions*)
**pe·o·ny** BOT Pfingstrose *f*
**peo·ple** **1.** Volk *n*, Nation *f*; die Menschen *pl*, die Leute *pl*; Leute *pl*, Personen *pl*; man; ***the ~*** das (*gemeine*) Volk

2. besiedeln, bevölkern (***with*** mit)
**peo·ple's re·pub·lic** Volksrepublik *f*
**pep** F **1.** Pep *m*, Schwung *m* **2.** *mst* ~ ***up*** *j-n or et.* in Schwung bringen, aufmöbeln
**pep·per 1.** Pfeffer *m*; BOT Paprikaschote *f* **2.** pfeffern
**pep·per cast·er** Pfefferstreuer *m*
**pep·per·mint** BOT Pfefferminze *f*; Pfefferminz *n*
**pep·per·y** pfeff(e)rig; *fig* hitzig
**pep·pill** F Aufputschpille *f*
**per** per, durch; pro, für, je
**per·ceive** (be)merken, wahrnehmen; erkennen
**per cent, per·cent** Prozent *n*
**per·cen·tage** Prozentsatz *m*; F Prozente *pl*, (An)Teil *m*
**per·cep·ti·ble** wahrnehmbar, merklich; **per·cep·tion** Wahrnehmung *f*; Auffassung *f*, Auffassungsgabe *f*
**perch**[1] **1.** (Sitz)Stange *f* **2.** (***on***) sich setzen (auf *acc*), sich niederlassen (auf *acc*, *dat*); F hocken (***on*** auf *dat*); ~ ***o.s.*** F sich hocken (***on*** auf *acc*)
**perch**[2] zo Barsch *m*
**per·co·la·tor** Kaffeemaschine *f*
**per·cus·sion** Schlag *m*; Erschütterung *f*; MUS Schlagzeug *n*; ~ **drill** TECH Schlagbohrer *m*; ~ **in·stru·ment** MUS Schlaginstrument *n*
**pe·remp·to·ry** herrisch
**pe·ren·ni·al** ewig, immer während; BOT mehrjährig
**per·fect 1.** perfekt, vollkommen, vollendet; gänzlich, völlig **2.** vervollkommnen **3.** *a.* ~ ***tense*** LING Perfekt *n*
**per·fec·tion** Vollendung *f*; Vollkommenheit *f*, Perfektion *f*
**per·fo·rate** durchbohren, -löchern
**per·form** *v/t* verrichten, durchführen, tun; *Pflicht etc* erfüllen; THEA, MUS aufführen, spielen, vortragen; *v/i* THEA *etc* e-e Vorstellung geben, auftreten, spielen; **per·form·ance** Verrichtung *f*, Durchführung *f*; Leistung *f*; THEA, MUS Aufführung *f*, Vorstellung *f*, Vortrag *m*; **per·form·er** THEA, MUS Darsteller(in), Künstler(in)
**per·fume 1.** Duft *m*; Parfüm *n* **2.** parfümieren; **per·fum·er·y** Parfümerie *f*
**per·haps** vielleicht
**per·il** Gefahr *f*; **per·il·ous** gefährlich
**pe·ri·od** Periode *f*, Zeit *f*, Zeitdauer *f*, Zeitraum *m*, Zeitspanne *f*; (Unterrichts)Stunde *f*; MED Periode *f*; LING Punkt *m*; ~ **fur·ni·ture** Stilmöbel *pl*
**pe·ri·od·ic** periodisch
**pe·ri·od·i·cal 1.** periodisch **2.** Zeitschrift *f*
**pe·riph·e·ral** IT Peripheriegerät *n*; ~ **e·quip·ment** IT Peripheriegeräte *pl*
**pe·riph·e·ry** Peripherie *f*, Rand *m*
**per·ish** umkommen; GASTR schlecht werden, verderben; TECH verschleißen
**per·ish·a·ble** leicht verderblich
**per·ish·a·bles** leicht verderbliche Lebensmittel
**per·jure**: ~ ***o.s.*** JUR e-n Meineid leisten
**per·ju·ry** JUR Meineid *m*; ***commit*** ~ e-n Meineid leisten
**perk**: ~ ***up*** *v/i* aufleben, munter werden; *v/t j-n* munter machen, F aufmöbeln
**perk·y** F munter, lebhaft; keck, selbstbewusst
**perm 1.** Dauerwelle *f*; ***get a*** ~ → **2.** ***get one's hair ~ed*** sich e-e Dauerwelle machen lassen
**per·ma·nent 1.** (be)ständig, dauerhaft, Dauer… **2.** *a.* ~ ***wave*** Dauerwelle *f*
**per·me·a·ble** durchlässig (***to*** für)
**per·me·ate** durchdringen; dringen (***into*** in *acc*; ***through*** durch)
**per·mis·si·ble** zulässig, erlaubt
**per·mis·sion** Erlaubnis *f*
**per·mis·sive** liberal; (sexuell) freizügig; ~ **so·ci·e·ty** tabufreie Gesellschaft
**per·mit 1.** erlauben, gestatten **2.** Genehmigung *f*
**per·pen·dic·u·lar** senkrecht; rechtwink(e)lig (***to*** zu)
**per·pet·u·al** fortwährend, ständig, ewig
**per·plex** verwirren
**per·plex·i·ty** Verwirrung *f*
**per·se·cute** verfolgen
**per·se·cu·tion** Verfolgung *f*
**per·se·cu·tor** Verfolger(in)
**per·se·ver·ance** Ausdauer *f*, Beharrlichkeit *f*
**per·se·vere** beharrlich weitermachen
**per·sist** beharren (***in*** auf *dat*); anhalten
**per·sis·tence** Beharrlichkeit *f*
**per·sis·tent** beharrlich; anhaltend
**per·son** Person *f* (*a.* LING)
**per·son·al** persönlich (*a.* LING); Personal…; Privat…; ~ **com·pu·ter** (*abbr* ***PC***) Personal Computer *m*; ~ **da·ta** Personalien *pl*

P

**per·son·al·i·ty** Persönlichkeit *f*; *pl* anzügliche *or* persönliche Bemerkungen *pl*
**per·son·al| or·ga·ni·zer** Notizbuch *n*, Adressbuch *n* und Taschenkalender *m etc* (*in einem*); ~ **pro·noun** LING Personalpronomen *n*; ~ **ster·e·o** Walkman® *m*
**per·son·i·fy** personifizieren, verkörpern
**per·son·nel** Personal *n*, Belegschaft *f*; die Personalabteilung; ~ **de·part·ment** Personalabteilung *f*; ~ **man·ager** Personalchef *m*
**per·spec·tive** Perspektive *f*; Fernsicht *f*
**per·spi·ra·tion** Transpirieren *n*, Schwitzen *n*; Schweiß *m*
**per·spire** transpirieren, schwitzen
**per·suade** überreden; überzeugen
**per·sua·sion** Überredung(skunst) *f*; Überzeugung *f*
**per·sua·sive** überzeugend
**pert** keck, kess; schnippisch
**per·tain**: ~ ***to s.th.*** et. betreffen
**per·ti·nent** sachdienlich, relevant, zur Sache gehörig
**per·turb** beunruhigen
**per·vade** durchdringen, erfüllen
**per·verse** pervers; eigensinnig
**per·ver·sion** Verdrehung *f*; Perversion *f*
**per·ver·si·ty** Perversität *f*; Eigensinn *m*
**per·vert** **1.** pervertieren; verdrehen **2.** perverser Mensch
**pes·sa·ry** MED Pessar *n*
**pes·si·mism** Pessimismus *m*
**pes·si·mist** Pessimist(in)
**pes·si·mis·tic** pessimistisch
**pest** zo Schädling *m*; F Nervensäge *f*; F Plage *f*; ~ **con·trol** Schädlingsbekämpfung *f*
**pes·ter** F *j-n* belästigen, *j-m* keine Ruhe lassen
**pes·ti·cide** Pestizid *n*, Schädlingsbekämpfungsmittel *n*
**pet** **1.** (zahmes) (Haus)Tier; *often contp* Liebling *m* **2.** Lieblings…; Tier… **3.** streicheln; F Petting machen
**pet·al** BOT Blütenblatt *n*
**pet food** Tiernahrung *f*
**pe·ti·tion** **1.** Eingabe *f*, Gesuch *n*, (schriftlicher) Antrag **2.** ersuchen; ein Gesuch einreichen (***for*** um), e-n Antrag stellen (***for*** auf *acc*)
**pet name** Kosename *m*
**pet·ri·fy** versteinern
**pet·rol** *Br* Benzin *n*
**pe·tro·le·um** Erdöl *n*, Mineralöl *n*
**pet·rol| pump** *Br* Zapfsäule *f*; ~ **station** *Br* Tankstelle *f*
**pet shop** Tierhandlung *f*, Zoogeschäft *n*
**pet·ti·coat** Unterrock *m*
**pet·ting** F Petting *n*
**pet·tish** launisch, gereizt
**pet·ty** belanglos, unbedeutend, JUR *a.* geringfügig; engstirnig; ~ **cash** Portokasse *f*; ~ **lar·ce·ny** JUR einfacher Diebstahl
**pet·u·lant** launisch, gereizt
**pew** (Kirchen)Bank *f*
**pew·ter** Zinn *n*; *a.* ~ ***ware*** Zinn(-geschirr) *n*
**phan·tom** Phantom *n*; Geist *m*
**phar·ma·cist** Apotheker(in)
**phar·ma·cy** Apotheke *f*
**phase** Phase *f*
**pheas·ant** zo Fasan *m*
**phe·nom·e·non** Phänomen *n*, Erscheinung *f*
**phi·lan·thro·pist** Philanthrop(in), Menschenfreund(in)
**phil·is·tine** F *contp* **1.** Spießer *m* **2.** spießig
**phi·lol·o·gist** Philologe *m*, Philologin *f*
**phi·lol·o·gy** Philologie *f*
**phi·los·o·pher** Philosoph(in)
**phi·los·o·phy** Philosophie *f*
**phlegm** MED Schleim *m*
**phone** **1.** Telefon *n*; ***answer the*** ~ ans Telefon gehen; ***by*** ~ telefonisch; ***on the*** ~ am Telefon; ***be on the*** ~ Telefon haben; am Telefon sein **2.** telefonieren, anrufen; ~ **book** Telefonbuch *n*; ~ **booth**, *Br* ~ **box** Telefonzelle *f*; ~ **call** Anruf *m*, Gespräch *n*
**phone·card** Telefonkarte *f*
**phone-in** *radio*, TV Sendung *f* mit telefonischer Zuhörer- *or* Zuschauerbeteiligung
**phone num·ber** Telefonnummer *f*
**pho·net·ics** Phonetik *f*
**pho·n(e)y** F **1.** Fälschung *f*; Schwindler(in) **2.** falsch, gefälscht, unecht; Schein…
**phos·pho·rus** CHEM Phosphor *m*
**pho·to** F Foto *n*, Bild *n*; ***in the*** ~ auf dem Foto; ***take a*** ~ ein Foto machen (***of*** von)
**pho·to·cop·i·er** Fotokopiergerät *n*
**pho·to·cop·y** **1.** Fotokopie *f* **2.** fotokopieren

**pho·to·graph 1.** Fotografie *f* **2.** fotografieren
**pho·tog·ra·pher** Fotograf(in)
**pho·tog·ra·phy** Fotografie *f*
**phras·al verb** LING Verb *n* mit Adverb (und Präposition)
**phrase 1.** (Rede)Wendung *f*, Redensart *f*, idiomatischer Ausdruck **2.** ausdrücken; **phrase·book** Sprachführer *m*
**phys·i·cal 1.** physisch, körperlich; physikalisch; ***~ly handicapped*** körperbehindert **2.** ärztliche Untersuchung; **~ ed·u·ca·tion** Leibeserziehung *f*, Sport *m*; **~ ex·am·i·na·tion** ärztliche Untersuchung; **~ hand·i·cap** Körperbehinderung *f*; **~ train·ing** Leibeserziehung *f*, Sport *m*
**phy·si·cian** Arzt *m*, Ärztin *f*
**phys·i·cist** Physiker(in)
**phys·ics** Physik *f*
**phy·sique** Körper(bau) *m*, Statur *f*
**pi·a·nist** MUS Pianist(in)
**pi·an·o** MUS Klavier *n*
**pick 1.** (auf)hacken; (auf)picken; auflesen, aufnehmen; pflücken; *Knochen* abnagen; bohren *or* stochern in (*dat*); F *Schloss* knacken; aussuchen, auswählen; ***~ one's nose*** in der Nase bohren; ***~ one's teeth*** in den Zähnen (herum)stochern; ***~ s.o.'s pocket*** j-n bestehlen; ***have a bone to ~ with s.o.*** mit j-m ein Hühnchen zu rupfen haben; ***~ out*** (sich) *et.* auswählen; ausmachen, erkennen; ***~ up*** aufheben, auflesen, aufnehmen; aufpicken; *Spur* aufnehmen; *j-n* abholen; *Anhalter* mitnehmen; F *Mädchen* aufreißen; *Kenntnisse, Informationen etc* aufschnappen; sich *e-e Krankheit etc* holen; *a.* ***~ up speed*** MOT schneller werden **2.** (Spitz)Hacke *f*, Pickel *m*; (Aus)Wahl *f*; ***take your ~*** suchen Sie sich etwas aus
**pick-a-back** huckepack
**pick·ax**, *Br* **pick·axe** (Spitz)Hacke *f*, Pickel *m*
**pick·et 1.** Pfahl *m*; Streikposten *m* **2.** Streikposten aufstellen vor (*dat*), mit Streikposten besetzen; Streikposten stehen; **~ fence** Lattenzaun *m*; **~ line** Streikpostenkette *f*
**pick·le** GASTR **1.** Salzlake *f*; Essigsoße *f*; Essig-, Gewürzgurke *f*; *mst pl esp Br* Pickles *pl*; ***be in a*** (***pretty***) ***~*** F (ganz schön) in der Patsche sitzen *or* sein *or* stecken **2.** einlegen
**pick·lock** Einbrecher *m*; TECH Dietrich *m*
**pick·pock·et** Taschendieb(in)
**pick-up** Tonabnehmer *m*; Kleintransporter *m*; F (Zufalls)Bekanntschaft *f*
**pick·y** F wählerisch (***in*** *dat* about)
**pic·nic 1.** Picknick *n* **2.** ein Picknick machen, picknicken
**pic·ture 1.** Bild *n*; Gemälde *n*; PHOT Aufnahme *f*; Film *m*; *pl esp Br* Kino *n* **2.** darstellen, malen; *fig* sich *j-n, et.* vorstellen; **~ book** Bilderbuch *n*; **~ post·card** Ansichtskarte *f*
**pic·tur·esque** malerisch
**pie** (*Fleisch- etc*)Pastete *f*; (*mst* gedeckter) (*Apfel- etc*)Kuchen
**piece 1.** Stück *n*; Teil *n* (*of a machine etc*); Teil *m* (*of a set etc*); *chess*: Figur *f*; *board game*: Stein *m*; (Zeitungs)Artikel *m*, (-)Notiz *f*; ***by the ~*** stückweise; ***a ~ of advice*** ein Rat; ***a ~ of news*** e-e Neuigkeit; ***give s.o. a ~ of one's mind*** j-m gründlich die Meinung sagen; ***go to ~s*** F zusammenbrechen; ***take to ~s*** auseinandernehmen **2. *~ together*** zusammensetzen, zusammenstückeln; *fig* zusammenfügen
**piece·meal** schrittweise
**piece·work** Akkordarbeit *f*; ***do ~*** im Akkord arbeiten
**pier** MAR Pier *m*, Landungsbrücke *f*; TECH Pfeiler *m*
**pierce** durchbohren, durchstechen, durchstoßen; durchdringen
**pierc·ing** durchdringend, (*Kälte etc a.*) schneidend, (*Schrei a.*) gellend, (*Blick, Schmerz etc a.*) stechend
**pi·e·ty** Frömmigkeit *f*
**pig** ZO Schwein *n* (*a.* F); F Ferkel *n*; *sl contp* Bulle *m*
**pi·geon** ZO Taube *f*
**pi·geon·hole 1.** Fach *n* **2.** ablegen
**pig·gy** F Schweinchen *n*
**pig·gy·back** huckepack
**pig·gy bank** Sparschwein(chen) *n*
**pig·head·ed** dickköpfig, stur
**pig·let** ZO Ferkel *n*
**pig·sty** Schweinestall *m*, F *contp* Saustall *m*
**pig·tail** Zopf *m*
**pike**[1] ZO Hecht *m*
**pike**[2] → ***turnpike***
**pile**[1] **1.** Stapel *m*, Stoß *m*; F Haufen *m*,

P

Menge *f*; (***atomic***) ~ Atommeiler *m* **2.** ~ ***up*** (an-, auf)häufen, (auf)stapeln, aufschichten; sich anhäufen; MOT F aufeinander auffahren
**pile**[2] Flor *m*
**pile**[3] Pfahl *m*
**piles** *Br* F MED Hämorrhoiden *pl*
**pile·up** MOT Massenkarambolage *f*
**pil·fer** stehlen, klauen
**pil·grim** Pilger(in)
**pil·grim·age** Pilgerfahrt *f*, Wallfahrt *f*
**pill** PHARM Pille *f*; ***the*** ~ F die (*Antibaby*)-Pille; ***be on the*** ~ die Pille nehmen
**pil·lar** Pfeiler *m*; Säule *f*
**pil·li·on** MOT Soziussitz *m*
**pil·lo·ry** **1.** HIST Pranger *m* **2.** *fig* anprangern
**pil·low** (Kopf)Kissen *n*
**pil·low·case, pil·low slip** (Kopf)Kissenbezug *m*
**pi·lot** **1.** AVIAT Pilot *m*; MAR Lotse *m* **2.** Versuchs…, Pilot… **3.** lotsen; steuern; ~ **film** TV Pilotfilm *m*; ~ **scheme** Versuchs-, Pilotprojekt *n*
**pimp** Zuhälter *m*
**pim·ple** MED Pickel *m*, Pustel *f*
**pin** **1.** (Steck)Nadel *f*; (*Haar-, Krawatten- etc*)Nadel *f*; Brosche *f*; TECH Bolzen *m*, Stift *m*; *bowling*: Kegel *m*; Pin *m*; (*Wäsche*)Klammer *f*; *Br* (*Reiß*)Nagel *m*, (-)Zwecke *f* **2.** (an)heften, anstecken (***to*** an *acc*), befestigen (***to*** an *dat*); pressen, drücken (***against, to*** gegen, an *acc*)
**PIN** *a.* ~ ***number*** *abbr of* ***personal identification number*** PIN, persönliche Geheimzahl
**pin·a·fore** Schürze *f*
**pin·ball** Flippern *n*; ***play*** ~ flippern
**pin·ball ma·chine** Flipper(automat) *m*
**pin·cers**: (***a pair of*** ~ e-e) (Kneif)Zange
**pinch** **1.** *v/t* kneifen, zwicken; F klauen; *v/i* drücken **2.** Kneifen *n*, Zwicken *n*; Prise *f*; *fig* Not(lage) *f*
**pin·cush·ion** Nadelkissen *n*
**pine**[1] BOT Kiefer *f*, Föhre *f*
**pine**[2] sich sehnen (***for*** nach)
**pine·ap·ple** BOT Ananas *f*
**pine cone** BOT Kiefernzapfen *m*
**pine·tree** BOT Kiefer *f*, Föhre *f*
**pin·ion** ZO Schwungfeder *f*
**pink** **1.** rosa(farben) **2.** Rosa *n*; BOT Nelke *f*
**pint** Pint *n* (*0,47 l, Br 0,57 l*); *Br* F Halbe *f*
**pi·o·neer** **1.** Pionier *m* **2.** den Weg bahnen (für)
**pi·ous** fromm, religiös
**pip**[1] *Br* (*Apfel-, Orangen- etc*)Kern *m*
**pip**[2] (Piep)Ton *m*
**pip**[3] *on cards etc*: Auge *n*, Punkt *m*
**pipe** **1.** TECH Rohr *n*, Röhre *f*; (*Tabaks*)-Pfeife *f*; MUS (*Orgel*)Pfeife *f*; *pl Br* F Dudelsack *m* **2.** (durch Rohre) leiten
**pipe·line** Rohrleitung *f*; Pipeline *f*
**pip·er** MUS Dudelsackpfeifer *m*
**pip·ing** **1.** Rohrleitung *f*, Rohrnetz *n* **2.** ~ ***hot*** kochend heiß, siedend heiß
**pi·quant** pikant (*a. fig*)
**pique** **1.** ***in a fit of*** ~ gekränkt, verletzt, pikiert **2.** kränken, verletzen; ***be ~d*** *a.* pikiert sein
**pi·rate** **1.** Pirat *m*, Seeräuber *m* **2.** unerlaubt kopieren *or* nachdrucken *or* nachpressen
**pi·rate ra·di·o** Piratensender *m or pl*
**Pis·ces** ASTR Fische *pl*; ***he*** (***she***) ***is*** (***a***) ~ er (sie) ist (ein) Fisch
**piss** V **1.** Pisse *f*; ***take the*** ~ ***out of s.o.*** j-n verarschen **2.** pissen; ~ ***off!*** verpiss dich!
**pis·tol** Pistole *f*
**pis·ton** TECH Kolben *m*
**pit**[1] **1.** Grube *f* (*a.* ANAT), MIN *a.* Zeche *f*; *esp Br* THEA Parkett *n*; *a.* ***orchestra*** ~ THEA Orchestergraben *m*; MED (*esp* Pocken)Narbe *f*; *car racing*: Box *f*; ~ ***stop*** Boxenstopp *m* **2.** mit Narben bedecken
**pit**[2] **1.** BOT Kern *m*, Stein *m* **2.** entkernen, entsteinen
**pitch**[1] **1.** *v/t Zelt, Lager* aufschlagen; werfen, schleudern; MUS (an)stimmen; *v/i* stürzen, fallen; MAR stampfen; sich neigen (*roof etc*); ~ ***in*** F sich ins Zeug legen; kräftig zulangen **2.** *esp Br* SPORT (Spiel)Feld *n*; MUS Tonhöhe *f*; *fig* Grad *m*, Stufe *f*; *esp Br* Stand(platz) *m*; MAR Stampfen *n*; Neigung *f* (*of a roof etc*)
**pitch**[2] Pech *n*
**pitch-black, pitch-dark** pechschwarz; stockdunkel
**pitch·er**[1] Krug *m*
**pitch·er**[2] *baseball*: Werfer *m*
**pitch·fork** Heugabel *f*, Mistgabel *f*
**pit·e·ous** kläglich
**pit·fall** Fallgrube *f*; *fig* Falle *f*
**pith** BOT Mark *n*; weiße innere Haut; *fig* Kern *m*; **pith·y** markig, prägnant
**pit·i·a·ble** → ***pitiful***

**pit·i·ful** mitleiderregend, bemitleidenswert; erbärmlich, jämmerlich
**pit·i·less** unbarmherzig, erbarmungslos
**pit·ta bread** Fladenbrot *n*
**pit·y 1.** Mitleid *n* (***on*** mit); ***it is a*** (***great***) **~** es ist (sehr) schade; ***what a ~!*** wie schade! **2.** bemitleiden, bedauern
**piv·ot 1.** TECH Drehzapfen *m*; *fig* Dreh- und Angelpunkt *m* **2.** sich drehen; **~ *on*** *fig* abhängen von
**pix·el** IT Pixel *m*
**piz·za** Pizza *f*
**plac·ard 1.** Plakat *n*; Transparent *n* **2.** mit Plakaten bekleben
**place 1.** Platz *m*, Ort *m*, Stelle *f*; Stätte *f*; Haus *n*, Wohnung *f*; Wohnort *m*; (*Arbeits-*, *Lehr*)Stelle *f*; ***in the first ~*** erstens; ***in third ~*** SPORT *etc* auf dem dritten Platz; ***in ~ of*** anstelle von (*or gen*); ***out of ~*** fehl am Platz; ***take ~*** stattfinden; ***take s.o.'s ~*** j-s Stelle einnehmen **2.** stellen, legen, setzen; *Auftrag* erteilen (***with*** *dat*), *Bestellung* aufgeben (***with*** bei); ***be ~d*** SPORT sich platzieren (***second*** an zweiter Stelle)
**place mat** Platzdeckchen *n*, Set *n*, *m*
**place·ment test** Einstufungsprüfung *f*
**place name** Ortsname *m*
**plac·id** ruhig; gelassen
**pla·gia·rize** plagiieren
**plague 1.** Seuche *f*; Pest *f*; Plage *f* **2.** plagen
**plaice** ZO Scholle *f*
**plaid** Plaid *n or m*
**plain 1.** *adj* einfach schlicht; klar (und deutlich); offen (und ehrlich); unscheinbar, wenig anziehend; rein, völlig (*nonsense etc*) **2.** *adv* F (ganz) einfach **3.** Ebene *f*, Flachland *n*
**plain choc·olate** *Br* (zart)bittere Schokolade
**plain-clothes** … in Zivil
**plain·tiff** JUR Kläger(in)
**plain·tive** traurig, klagend
**plait** *esp Br* **1.** Zopf *m* **2.** flechten
**plan 1.** Plan *m* **2.** planen; beabsichtigen
**plane**[1] Flugzeug *n*; ***by ~*** mit dem Flugzeug; ***go by ~*** fliegen
**plane**[2] **1.** flach, eben **2.** MATH Ebene *f*; *fig* Stufe *f*, Niveau *n*
**plane**[3] **1.** Hobel *m* **2.** hobeln; **~ *down*** abhobeln
**plan·et** ASTR Planet *m*
**plank** Planke *f*, Bohle *f*; **~ bed** Pritsche *f*
**plank·ing** Planken *pl*
**plant 1.** BOT Pflanze *f*; ECON Werk *n*, Betrieb *m*, Fabrik *f* **2.** (an-, ein)pflanzen; bepflanzen; *Garten etc* anlegen; aufstellen, postieren; **~ *s.th. on s.o*** F j-m et. (*Belastendes*) unterschieben
**plan·ta·tion** Plantage *f*, Pflanzung *f*; Schonung *f*
**plant·er** Plantagenbesitzer(in), Pflanzer(in); Pflanzmaschine *f*; Übertopf *m*
**plaque** Gedenktafel *f*; MED Zahnbelag *m*
**plas·ter 1.** MED Pflaster *n*; (Ver)Putz *m*; *a.* **~ *of Paris*** Gips *m*; ***have one's leg in ~*** MED das Bein in Gips haben **2.** verputzen; bekleben; **~ cast** Gipsabguss *m*, Gipsmodell *n*; MED Gipsverband *m*
**plas·tic 1.** plastisch; Plastik… **2.** Plastik *n*, Kunststoff *m*; → **~ mon·ey** F Plastikgeld *n*, Kreditkarten *pl*; **~ wrap** Frischhaltefolie *f*
**plate 1.** Teller *m*; Platte *f*; (*Namens-*, *Nummern- etc*)Schild *n*; (Bild)Tafel *f*; (Druck)Platte *f*; Gegenstände *pl* aus Edelmetall; Doublé *n*, Dublee *n* **2.** ***~d with gold, gold-plated*** vergoldet
**plat·form** Plattform *f*; RAIL Bahnsteig *m*; (Redner)Tribüne *f*, Podium *n*; POL Plattform *f*; MOT Pritsche *f*; ***party ~*** POL Parteiprogramm *n*; ***election ~*** POL Wahlprogramm *n*
**plat·i·num** CHEM Platin *n*
**pla·toon** MIL Zug *m*
**plat·ter** (Servier)Platte *f*
**plau·si·ble** plausibel, glaubhaft
**play 1.** Spiel *n*; Schauspiel *n*, (Theater)Stück *n*; TECH Spiel *n*; *fig* Spielraum *m*; ***at ~*** beim Spiel(en); ***in ~*** im Spiel (*ball*); ***out of ~*** im Aus (*ball*) **2.** *v/i* spielen (*a.* SPORT, THEA *etc*); *v/t Karten, Rolle, Stück etc* spielen, SPORT *Spiel* austragen; **~ *s.o.*** SPORT gegen j-n spielen; **~ *the guitar*** Gitarre spielen; **~ *a trick on s.o.*** j-m e-n Streich spielen; **~ *back*** *Ball* zurückspielen (***to*** zu); *Tonband* abspielen; **~ *s.th. down*** verharmlosen, herunterspielen; **~ *off*** *fig* ausspielen (***against*** gegen); **~ *on*** *fig j-s Schwächen* ausnutzen
**play·back** Play-back *n*, Wiedergabe *f*, Abspielen *n*
**play·er** MUS, SPORT Spieler(in)

**play·fel·low** *Br* → ***playmate***
**play·ful** verspielt; scherzhaft
**play·go·er** Theaterbesucher(in)
**play·ground** Spielplatz *m* (*a. fig*); Schulhof *m*
**play·group** *Br* Spielgruppe *f*
**play·house** THEA Schauspielhaus *n*; Spielhaus *n* (*for children*)
**play·ing card** Spielkarte *f*
**play·ing field** Sportplatz *m*, Spielfeld *n*
**play·mate** Spielkamerad(in)
**play·pen** Laufgitter *n*, Laufstall *m*
**play·thing** Spielzeug *n*
**play·wright** Dramatiker(in)
**plc, PLC** *Br econ abbr of* ***public limited company*** AG, Aktiengesellschaft *f*
**plea**: ***enter a ~ of*** (***not***) ***guilty*** JUR sich schuldig bekennen (s-e Unschuld erklären)
**plead** *v/i* (dringend) bitten (***for*** um); ~ (***not***) ***guilty*** JUR sich schuldig bekennen (s-e Unschuld erklären); *v/t a.* JUR zu s-r Verteidigung *or* Entschuldigung anführen, geltend machen; ~ ***s.o.'s case*** sich für j-n einsetzen; JUR j-n vertreten
**pleas·ant** angenehm, erfreulich; freundlich; sympathisch
**please 1.** *j-m* gefallen; *j-m* zusagen, *j-n* erfreuen; zufriedenstellen; ***only to ~ you*** nur dir zuliebe; ~ ***o.s.*** tun, was man will; ~ ***yourself!*** mach, was du willst! **2.** *int* bitte; (***yes***,) ~ (ja,) bitte; (oh ja,) gerne; ~ ***come in!*** bitte, treten Sie ein!
**pleased** erfreut, zufrieden; ***be ~ about*** sich freuen über (*acc*); ***be ~ with*** zufrieden sein mit; ***I am ~ with it*** es gefällt mir; ***be ~ to do s.th.*** et. gern tun; ~ ***to meet you!*** angenehm!
**pleas·ing** angenehm
**plea·sure** Vergnügen *n*; ***at*** (***one's***) ~ nach Belieben
**pleat** (Plissee)Falte *f*
**pleat·ed skirt** Faltenrock *m*
**pledge 1.** Pfand *n*; *fig* Unterpfand *n*; Versprechen *n* **2.** versprechen, zusichern
**plen·ti·ful** reichlich
**plen·ty 1.** Überfluss *m*; ***in ~*** im Überfluss, in Hülle und Fülle; ~ ***of*** e-e Menge, viel(e), reichlich **2.** F reichlich
**pleu·ri·sy** MED Brustfell-, Rippenfellentzündung *f*
**pli·a·ble, pli·ant** biegsam; *fig* flexibel; *fig* leicht beeinflussbar
**pli·ers** (***a pair of ~*** e-e) Beißzange *f*
**plight** Not *f*, Notlage *f*
**plim·soll** *Br* Turnschuh *m*
**plod** *a.* ~ ***along*** sich dahinschleppen; ~ ***away*** sich abplagen (***at*** mit), schuften
**plop** F **1.** Plumps *m*, Platsch *m* **2.** plumpsen, (*ins Wasser*) platschen
**plot 1.** Stück *n* Land, Parzelle *f*, Grundstück *n*; THEA, *film etc*: Handlung *f*; Komplott *n*, Verschwörung *f*; IT grafische Darstellung **2.** *v/i* sich verschwören (***against*** gegen); *v/t* planen; einzeichnen
**plot·ter** IT Plotter *m*
**plough** *Br*, **plow** AGR **1.** Pflug *m* **2.** (um)pflügen; **plough·share** *Br*, **plowshare** AGR Pflugschar *f*
**pluck 1.** *v/t Geflügel* rupfen; *mst* ~ ***out*** ausreißen, ausrupfen, auszupfen; MUS *Saiten* zupfen; ~ ***up*** (***one's***) ***courage*** Mut *or* sich ein Herz fassen; *v/i* zupfen (***at*** an *dat*); **2.** F Mut *m*, Schneid *m*
**pluck·y** F mutig
**plug 1.** Stöpsel *m*; ELECTR Stecker *m*, F Steckdose *f*; F MOT (*Zünd*)Kerze *f* **2.** *v/t* F für *et.* Schleichwerbung machen; *a.* ~ ***up*** zustöpseln; zustopfen, verstopfen; ~ ***in*** ELECTR anschließen, einstecken
**plug·ging** F Schleichwerbung *f*
**plum** BOT Pflaume *f*; Zwetsch(g)e *f*
**plum·age** Gefieder *n*
**plumb 1.** (Blei)Lot *n* **2.** ausloten, *fig a.* ergründen; ~ ***in*** *esp Br Waschmaschine etc* anschließen **3.** *adj* lotrecht, senkrecht **4.** *adv* F (haar)genau
**plumb·er** Klempner *m*, Installateur *m*
**plumb·ing** Klempner-, Installateurarbeit *f*; Rohre *pl*, Rohrleitungen *pl*
**plume** (Schmuck)Feder *f*; Federbusch *m*; (*Rauch*)Fahne *f*
**plump 1.** *adj* drall, mollig, rund(lich), F pumm(e)lig **2.** ~ ***down*** fallen *or* plumpsen (lassen)
**plum pud·ding** *Br* Plumpudding *m*
**plun·der 1.** plündern **2.** Plünderung *f*; Beute *f*
**plunge 1.** (ein-, unter)tauchen; (sich) stürzen (***into*** in *acc*); MAR stampfen **2.** (Kopf)Sprung *m*; ***take the ~*** *fig* den entscheidenden Schritt wagen
**plu·per·fect** *a.* ~ ***tense*** LING Plusquam-

P

perfekt *n*, Vorvergangenheit *f*

**plu·ral** LING Plural *m*, Mehrzahl *f*

**plus 1.** *prp* plus, und, *esp* ECON zuzüglich **2.** *adj* Plus…; **~ sign** MATH Plus *n*, Pluszeichen *n* **3.** MATH Plus *n* (*a.* F), Pluszeichen *n*; F Vorteil *m*

**plush** Plüsch *m*

**ply**[1] *regelmäßig* verkehren, fahren (**between** zwischen *dat*)

**ply**[2] *mst in cpds* TECH Lage *f*, Schicht *f*; **three-~** dreifach (*thread etc*); dreifach gewebt (*carpet*)

**ply·wood** Sperrholz *n*

**pm, PM** *abbr of* **after noon** (*Latin* **post meridiem**) nachm., nachmittags, abends

**pneu·mat·ic** Luft…, pneumatisch; TECH Druck…, Pressluft…

**pneu·mat·ic drill** Pressluftbohrer *m*

**pneu·mo·ni·a** MED Lungenentzündung *f*

**poach**[1] GASTR pochieren; **~ed eggs** verlorene Eier *pl*

**poach**[2] wildern

**poach·er** Wilddieb *m*, Wilderer *m*

**PO Box** Postfach *n*; **write to ~ 225** schreiben Sie an Postfach 225

**pock** MED Pocke *f*, Blatter *f*

**pock·et 1.** (Hosen- *etc*)Tasche *f* **2.** *adj* Taschen… **3.** einstecken, in die Tasche stecken; *fig* in die eigene Tasche stecken; **pock·et·book** Notizbuch *n*; Brieftasche *f*

**pock·et| cal·cu·la·tor** Taschenrechner *m*; **~ knife** Taschenmesser *n*; **~ money** Taschengeld *n*

**pod** BOT Hülse *f*, Schote *f*

**po·di·a·trist** Fußpfleger(in)

**po·em** Gedicht *n*

**po·et** Dichter(in)

**po·et·ic** dichterisch

**po·et·i·cal** dichterisch

**po·et·ic jus·tice** *fig* ausgleichende Gerechtigkeit

**po·et·ry** Gedichte *pl*; Poesie *f* (*a. fig*), Dichtkunst *f*, Dichtung *f*

**poi·gnant** schmerzlich; ergreifend

**point 1.** Spitze *f*; GEOGR Landspitze *f*; LING, MATH, PHYS, SPORT *etc* Punkt *m*; MATH (Dezimal)Punkt *m*; Grad *m*; MAR (*Kompass*)Strich *m*; *fig* Punkt *m*, Stelle *f*, Ort *m*; Zweck *m*; Ziel *n*, Absicht *f*; springender Punkt; Pointe *f*; **two ~ five** (**2.5**) 2,5; **~ of view** Stand-, Gesichtspunkt *m*; **be on the ~ of doing s.th.** im Begriff sein, et. zu tun; **to the ~** zur Sache gehörig; **off** *or* **beside the ~** nicht zur Sache gehörig; **come to the ~** zur Sache kommen; **that's not the ~** darum geht es nicht; **what's the ~?** wozu?; **win on ~s** SPORT nach Punkten gewinnen; **winner on ~s** SPORT Punktsieger *m* **2.** *v/t* (zu)spitzen; *Waffe etc* richten (**at** auf *acc*); **~ one's finger at s.o.** (mit dem Finger) auf j-n zeigen; **~ out** zeigen; *fig* hinweisen *or* aufmerksam machen auf (*acc*); *v/i* (mit dem Finger) zeigen (**at, to** auf *acc*); **~ to** nach *e-r Richtung* weisen *or* liegen; *fig* hinweisen auf (*acc*)

**point·ed** spitz; Spitz…; *fig* scharf (*remark etc*); ostentativ

**point·er** Zeiger *m*; Zeigestock *m*; ZO Pointer *m*, Vorstehhund *m*

**point·less** sinnlos, zwecklos

**points** *Br* RAIL Weiche *f*

**poise 1.** (Körper)Haltung *f*; *fig* Gelassenheit *f* **2.** balancieren; **be ~d** schweben

**poi·son 1.** Gift *n* **2.** vergiften

**poi·son·ous** giftig (*a. fig*)

**poke 1.** *v/t* stoßen; *Feuer* schüren; stecken; *v/i* **~ about, ~ around** F (herum-) stöbern, (-)wühlen (**in** in *dat*); **2.** Stoß *m*

**pok·er** Schürhaken *m*

**pok·y** F eng; schäbig

**Po·land** Polen *n*

**po·lar** polar; **~ bear** ZO Eisbär *m*

**pole**[1] GEOGR Pol *m*

**pole**[2] Stange *f*; Mast *m*; Deichsel *f*; SPORT (Sprung)Stab *m*

**Pole** Pole *m*, Polin *f*

**pole·cat** ZO Iltis *m*; F Skunk *m*, Stinktier *n*

**po·lem·ic, po·lem·i·cal** polemisch

**pole star** ASTR Polarstern *m*

**pole vault** SPORT Stabhochsprung *m*, Stabhochspringen *n*

**pole-vault** SPORT stabhochspringen

**pole vault·er** SPORT Stabhochspringer(in)

**po·lice 1.** Polizei *f* **2.** überwachen

**po·lice car** Polizeiauto *n*

**po·lice·man** Polizist *m*

**po·lice| of·fi·cer** Polizeibeamte *m*, -beamtin *f*, Polizist(in); **~ sta·tion** Polizeiwache *f*, Polizeirevier *n*

**po·lice·wom·an** Polizistin *f*

P

**pol·i·cy** Politik *f*; Taktik *f*; Klugheit *f*; (Versicherungs)Police *f*
**po·li·o** MED Polio *f*, Kinderlähmung *f*
**pol·ish 1.** polieren; *Schuhe* putzen; **~ up** aufpolieren (*a. fig*) **2.** Politur *f*; (*Schuh*)Creme *f*; *fig* Schliff *m*
**Pol·ish 1.** polnisch **2.** LING Polnisch *n*
**po·lite** höflich
**po·lite·ness** Höflichkeit *f*
**po·lit·i·cal** politisch
**pol·i·ti·cian** Politiker(in)
**pol·i·tics** Politik *f*
**pol·ka** MUS Polka *f*
**pol·ka-dot** gepunktet, getupft
**poll 1.** (*Meinungs*)Umfrage *f*; Wahlbeteiligung *f*; *a. pl* Stimmabgabe *f*, Wahl *f* **2.** befragen; *Stimmen* erhalten
**pol·len** BOT Pollen *m*, Blütenstaub *m*
**poll·ing** Stimmabgabe *f*; Wahlbeteiligung *f*; **~ booth** *esp Br* Wahlkabine *f*; **~ day** Wahltag *m*; **~ place**, *esp Br* **~ station** Wahllokal *n*
**polls** Wahl *f*; Wahllokal *n*
**poll·ster** Demoskop(in), Meinungsforscher(in)
**pol·lut·ant** Schadstoff *m*; **pol·lute** beschmutzen, verschmutzen; verunreinigen; **pol·lut·er** *a.* ***environmental* ~** Umweltsünder(in); **pol·lu·tion** (*Luft-, Wasser- etc*)Verschmutzung *f*; Verunreinigung *f*
**po·lo** SPORT Polo *n*
**po·lo neck** *a.* **~ *sweater*** *esp Br* Rollkragenpullover *m*
**pol·yp** ZO, MED Polyp *m*
**pol·y·sty·rene®** Styropor® *n*
**pom·mel** (Sattel- *etc*)Knopf *m*
**pomp** Pomp *m*, Prunk *m*
**pom·pous** aufgeblasen, wichtigtuerisch; schwülstig (*speech*)
**pond** Teich *m*, Weiher *m*
**pon·der** *v/i* nachdenken (***on, over*** über *acc*); *v/t* überlegen
**pon·der·ous** schwerfällig; schwer
**pon·toon** Ponton *m*
**pon·toon bridge** Pontonbrücke *f*
**po·ny** ZO Pony *n*
**po·ny·tail** Pferdeschwanz *m*
**poo·dle** ZO Pudel *m*
**pool**[1] Teich *m*, Tümpel *m*; Pfütze *f*, (*Blut- etc*)Lache *f*; (*Schwimm*)Becken *n*, (*Swimming*)Pool *m*
**pool**[2] **1.** (*Arbeits-, Fahr*)Gemeinschaft *f*; (*Mitarbeiter- etc*)Stab *m*; (*Fuhr*)Park *m*; (*Schreib*)Pool *m*; ECON Pool *m*, Kartell *n*; *card games*: Gesamteinsatz *m*; Poolbillard *n* **2.** *Geld*, *Unternehmen etc* zusammenlegen; *Kräfte etc* vereinen
**pool hall, pool·room** Billardspielhalle *f*
**pools** *a.* ***football* ~** *Br* (Fußball)Toto *n*, *m*
**poor 1.** arm; dürftig, mangelhaft, schwach **2.** ***the* ~** die Armen *pl*
**poor·ly 1.** *adj esp Br* F kränklich, unpässlich **2.** *adv* ärmlich, dürftig, schlecht, schwach
**pop**[1] **1.** *v/t* zerknallen; F schnell *wohin* tun *or* stecken; *v/i* knallen; (zer)platzen; **~ *in*** F auf e-n Sprung vorbeikommen; **~ *up*** (plötzlich) auftauchen **2.** Knall *m*; F Limo *f*
**pop**[2] MUS **1.** Pop *m* **2.** Schlager…; Pop…
**pop**[3] F Paps *m*, Papa *m*
**pop**[4] *abbr of* ***population*** Einw., Einwohner *pl*; Einwohnerzahl *f*
**pop con·cert** MUS Popkonzert *n*
**pop·corn** Popcorn *n*, Puffmais *m*
**Pope** REL Papst *m*
**pop-eyed** F glotzäugig
**pop group** MUS Popgruppe *f*
**pop·lar** BOT Pappel *f*
**pop mu·sic** Popmusik *f*
**pop·py** BOT Mohn *m*
**pop·u·lar** populär, beliebt; volkstümlich; allgemein
**pop·u·lar·i·ty** Popularität *f*, Beliebtheit *f*; Volkstümlichkeit *f*
**pop·u·late** bevölkern, besiedeln; bewohnen
**pop·u·la·tion** Bevölkerung *f*
**pop·u·lous** dicht besiedelt, dicht bevölkert
**porce·lain** Porzellan *n*
**porch** überdachter Vorbau; Portal *n*; Veranda *f*
**por·cu·pine** ZO Stachelschwein *n*
**pore**[1] Pore *f*
**pore**[2]: **~ *over*** vertieft sein in (*acc*), *et.* eifrig studieren
**pork** GASTR Schweinefleisch *n*
**porn** F → ***porno***
**por·no** F **1.** Porno *m* **2.** Porno…
**por·nog·ra·phy** Pornografie *f*
**po·rous** porös
**por·poise** ZO Tümmler *m*
**por·ridge** Porridge *m*, *n*, Haferbrei *m*
**port**[1] Hafen *m*; Hafenstadt *f*

P

**port**[2] AVIAT, MAR Backbord *n*
**port**[3] IT Port *m*, Anschluss *m*
**port**[4] Portwein *m*
**por·ta·ble** tragbar
**por·ter** (Gepäck)Träger *m*; *esp Br* Pförtner *m*, Portier *m*; RAIL Schlafwagenschaffner *m*
**port·hole** MAR Bullauge *n*
**por·tion 1.** (An)Teil *m*; GASTR Portion *f* **2.** **~ *out*** aufteilen, verteilen (***among, between*** unter *acc*)
**port·ly** korpulent
**por·trait** Porträt *n*, Bild *n*, Bildnis *n*
**por·tray** porträtieren; darstellen; schildern; **por·tray·al** THEA Verkörperung *f*, Darstellung *f*; Schilderung *f*
**Por·tu·gal** Portugal *n*
**Por·tu·guese 1.** portugiesisch **2.** Portugiese *m*, Portugiesin *f*; LING Portugiesisch *n*; ***the ~*** die Portugiesen *pl*
**pose 1.** *v/t* aufstellen; *Problem*, *Frage* aufwerfen, *Bedrohung*, *Gefahr etc* darstellen; *v/i* Modell sitzen *or* stehen; **~ *as*** sich ausgeben als *or* für **2.** Pose *f*
**posh** *esp Br* F schick, piekfein
**po·si·tion 1.** Position *f*, Lage *f*, Stellung *f* (*a. fig*); Stand *m*; *fig* Standpunkt *m* **2.** (auf)stellen
**pos·i·tive 1.** positiv; bestimmt, sicher, eindeutig; greifbar, konkret; konstruktiv **2.** PHOT Positiv *n*
**pos·sess** besitzen; *fig* beherrschen
**pos·sessed** *fig* besessen
**pos·ses·sion** Besitz *m*; *fig* Besessenheit *f*
**pos·ses·sive** besitzergreifend; LING possessiv, besitzanzeigend
**pos·si·bil·i·ty** Möglichkeit *f*
**pos·si·ble** möglich
**pos·si·bly** möglicherweise, vielleicht; ***if I ~ can*** wenn ich irgend kann; ***I can't ~ do this*** ich kann das unmöglich tun
**post**[1] **1.** (*Tür-*, *Tor-*, *Ziel- etc*)Pfosten *m*; Pfahl *m* **2.** *a.* **~ *up*** *Plakat etc* anschlagen, ankleben; ***be ~ed missing*** AVIAT, MAR als vermisst gemeldet werden
**post**[2] *esp Br* **1.** Post® *f*; Postsendung *f*; ***by ~*** mit der Post® **2.** mit der Post® (zu-) schicken, aufgeben, *Brief* einwerfen
**post**[3] **1.** Stelle *f*, Job *m*; Posten *m* **2.** aufstellen, postieren; *esp Br* versetzen, MIL abkommandieren (***to*** nach)
**post...** nach..., Nach...
**post·age** Porto *n*; **~ stamp** Postwertzeichen *n*, Briefmarke *f*
**post·al** postalisch, Post®...; **~ or·der** *Br* ECON Postanweisung *f*; **~ vote** POL Briefwahl *f*
**post·bag** *esp Br* Postsack *m*
**post·box** *esp Br* Briefkasten *m*
**post·card** Postkarte *f*; *a.* ***picture ~*** Ansichtskarte *f*
**post·code** *Br* Postleitzahl *f*
**post·er** Plakat *n*; Poster *n*, *m*
**poste res·tante** *Br* **1.** Abteilung *f* für postlagernde Sendungen **2.** postlagernd
**pos·te·ri·or** HUMOR Hinterteil *n*
**pos·ter·i·ty** die Nachwelt
**post-free** *esp Br* portofrei
**post·hu·mous** post(h)um
**post·man** *esp Br* Briefträger *m*, Postbote *m*
**post·mark 1.** Poststempel *m* **2.** stempeln, abstempeln
**post of·fice** Post® *f*; Postamt *n*, -filiale *f*
**post of·fice box** → ***PO Box***
**post-paid** portofrei
**post·pone** verschieben, aufschieben
**post·pone·ment** Verschiebung *f*, Aufschub *m*
**post·script** Postskript(um) *n*, Nachschrift *f*
**pos·ture 1.** (Körper)Haltung *f*; Stellung *f* **2.** *fig* sich aufspielen
**post·war** Nachkriegs...
**post·wom·an** *esp Br* Briefträgerin *f*, Postbotin *f*
**po·sy** Sträußchen *n*
**pot 1.** Topf *m*; Kanne *f*; Kännchen *n* (*Tee etc*); SPORT F Pokal *m* **2.** *Pflanze* eintopfen
**po·tas·si·um cy·a·nide** CHEM Zyankali *n*
**po·ta·to** Kartoffel *f*; → ***chips, crisps***
**pot·bel·ly** Schmerbauch *m*
**po·ten·cy** Stärke *f*; Wirksamkeit *f*, Wirkung *f*; MED Potenz *f*
**po·tent** PHARM stark; MED potent
**po·ten·tial 1.** potenziell, möglich **2.** Potenzial *n*, Leistungsfähigkeit *f*
**pot·hole** MOT Schlagloch *n*
**po·tion** Trank *m*
**pot·ter**[1] *Br*: **~ *about*** herumwerkeln
**pot·ter**[2] Töpfer(in)
**pot·ter·y** Töpferei *f*; Töpferware(n *pl*) *f*
**pouch** Beutel *m* (*a.* ZO); ZO (*Backen*)Tasche *f*

**poul·tice** MED (warmer) Umschlag *m*
**poul·try** Geflügel *n*
**pounce 1.** sich stürzen (***on*** auf *acc*); **2.** Satz *m*, Sprung *m*
**pound**[1] Pfund *n* (*453,59 g*); *~* (***sterling***) (*abbr* **£**) Pfund *n*
**pound**[2] Tierheim *n*; Abstellplatz *m* für (polizeilich) abgeschleppte Fahrzeuge
**pound**[3] *v/t* zerstoßen, zerstampfen; trommeln *or* hämmern auf (*acc*) *or* an (*acc*) *or* gegen; *v/i* hämmern (***with*** vor *dat*)
**pour** *v/t* gießen, schütten; *~* ***out*** ausgießen, ausschütten; *Getränk* eingießen; *v/i* strömen (*a. fig*)
**pout** *v/t Lippen* schürzen; *v/i* e-n Schmollmund machen; schmollen
**pov·er·ty** Armut *f*
**pow·der 1.** Pulver *n*; Puder *m* **2.** pulverisieren; (sich) pudern; *~* **puff** Puderquaste *f*; *~* **room** (Damen)Toilette *f*
**pow·er 1.** Kraft *f*; Macht *f*; Fähigkeit *f*, Vermögen *n*; Gewalt *f*; JUR Befugnis *f*, Vollmacht *f*; MATH Potenz *f*; ELECTR Strom *m*; ***in*** *~* POL an der Macht **2.** TECH antreiben; *~* **cut** ELECTR Stromsperre *f*; *~* **fail·ure** ELECTR Stromausfall *m*, Netzausfall *m*
**pow·er·ful** stark, kräftig; mächtig
**pow·er·less** kraftlos; machtlos
**pow·er| plant** Elektrizitäts-, Kraftwerk *n*; *~* **pol·i·tics** Machtpolitik *f*; *~* **sta·tion** *Br* Elektrizitäts-, Kraftwerk *n*
**prac·ti·ca·ble** durchführbar
**prac·ti·cal** praktisch; *~* **joke** Streich *m*
**prac·ti·cal·ly** so gut wie
**prac·tice 1.** Praxis *f*; Übung *f*; Gewohnheit *f*, Brauch *m*; ***it is common*** *~* es ist allgemein üblich; ***put into*** *~* in die Praxis umsetzen **2.** *v/t* (ein)üben; *als Beruf* ausüben; *~* ***law*** (***medicine***) als Anwalt (Arzt) praktizieren; *v/i* praktizieren; üben
**prac·ticed** geübt (***in*** in *dat*)
**prac·tise** *Br* → ***practice*** *2*
**prac·tised** → ***practiced***
**prac·ti·tion·er**: ***general*** *~* praktischer Arzt
**prai·rie** Prärie *f*
**prai·rie schoo·ner** HIST Planwagen *m*
**praise 1.** loben, preisen **2.** Lob *n*
**praise·wor·thy** lobenswert
**pram** *Br* Kinderwagen *m*
**prance** sich aufbäumen, steigen (*horse*); tänzeln (*horse*); stolzieren
**prank** Streich *m*
**prat·tle**: *~* ***on*** plappern (***about*** von)
**prawn** ZO Garnele *f*
**pray** beten (***to*** zu; ***for*** für, um)
**prayer** REL Gebet *n*; *often pl* Andacht *f*; ***the Lord's Prayer*** das Vaterunser
**prayer book** REL Gebetbuch *n*
**preach** predigen (***to*** zu, vor *dat*)
**preach·er** Prediger(in)
**pre·am·ble** Einleitung *f*
**pre·ar·range** vorher vereinbaren
**pre·car·i·ous** prekär, unsicher; gefährlich
**pre·cau·tion** Vorsichtsmaßnahme *f*; ***as a*** *~* vorsorglich; ***take*** *~****s*** Vorsichtsmaßnahmen treffen; **pre·cau·tion·a·ry** vorbeugend; vorsorglich
**pre·cede** voraus-, vorangehen (*dat*)
**pre·ce·dence** Vorrang *m*
**pre·ce·dent** Präzedenzfall *m*
**pre·cept** Regel *f*, Richtlinie *f*
**pre·cinct** (*Wahl*)Bezirk *m*; (*Polizei*)Revier *n*; *pl* Gelände *n*; *esp Br* (*Einkaufs*)-Viertel *n*; (*Fußgänger*)Zone *f*
**pre·cious 1.** *adj* kostbar, wertvoll; Edel… (*stone etc*) **2.** *adv*: *~* ***little*** F herzlich wenig
**pre·ci·pice** Abgrund *m*
**pre·cip·i·tate 1.** *v/t* (hinunter-, herunter)schleudern; CHEM ausfällen; beschleunigen; stürzen (***into*** in *acc*); *v/i* CHEM ausfallen **2.** *adj* überstürzt **3.** CHEM Niederschlag *m*
**pre·cip·i·ta·tion** CHEM Ausfällung *f*; METEOR Niederschlag *m*; Überstürzung *f*, Hast *f*
**pre·cip·i·tous** steil (abfallend); überstürzt
**pré·cis** Zusammenfassung *f*
**pre·cise** genau, präzis
**pre·ci·sion** Genauigkeit *f*; Präzision *f*
**pre·clude** ausschließen
**pre·co·cious** frühreif; altklug
**pre·con·ceived** vorgefasst
**pre·con·cep·tion** vorgefasste Meinung
**pre·cur·sor** Vorläufer(in)
**pred·a·to·ry** ZO Raub…
**pre·de·ces·sor** Vorgänger(in)
**pre·des·ti·na·tion** Vorherbestimmung *f*; **pre·des·tined** prädestiniert, vorherbestimmt (***to*** für, zu)
**pre·de·ter·mine** vorherbestimmen; vorher vereinbaren

P

**pre·dic·a·ment** missliche Lage, Zwangslage *f*
**pred·i·cate** LING Prädikat *n*, Satzaussage *f*; **pre·dic·a·tive** LING prädikativ
**pre·dict** vorhersagen, voraussagen
**pre·dic·tion** Vorhersage *f*, Voraussage *f*; ***computer ~*** Hochrechnung *f*
**pre·dis·pose** geneigt machen, einnehmen (***in favor of*** für); *esp* MED anfällig machen (***to*** für)
**pre·dis·po·si·tion**: ***~ to*** Neigung *f* zu, *esp* MED *a.* Anfälligkeit *f* für
**pre·dom·i·nant** (vor)herrschend, überwiegend
**pre·dom·i·nate** vorherrschen, überwiegen; die Oberhand haben
**pre·em·i·nent** hervorragend, überragend
**pre·emp·tive** ECON Vorkaufs…; MIL Präventiv…
**preen** ZO *sich or das Gefieder* putzen
**pre·fab** F Fertighaus *n*
**pre·fab·ri·cate** vorfabrizieren, vorfertigen; ***~d house*** Fertighaus *n*
**pref·ace 1.** Vorwort *n* (***to*** zu); **2.** *Buch, Rede etc* einleiten (***with*** mit)
**pre·fect** *Br* PED Aufsichts-, Vertrauensschüler(in)
**pre·fer** vorziehen (***to*** *dat*), lieber mögen (***to*** als), bevorzugen
**pref·e·ra·ble**: ***be ~*** (***to***) vorzuziehen sein (*dat*), besser sein (als)
**pref·e·ra·bly** vorzugsweise, lieber, am liebsten
**pref·e·rence** Vorliebe *f* (***for*** für); Vorzug *m*
**pre·fix** LING Präfix *n*, Vorsilbe *f*
**preg·nan·cy** MED Schwangerschaft *f*; ZO Trächtigkeit *f*
**preg·nant** MED schwanger; ZO trächtig
**pre·heat** *Backofen etc* vorheizen
**pre·judge** *j-n* vorverurteilen; vorschnell beurteilen
**prej·u·dice 1.** Vorurteil *n*, Voreingenommenheit *f*, Befangenheit *f*; ***to the ~ of*** zum Nachteil *or* Schaden (*gen*) **2.** einnehmen (***in favo[u]r of*** für; ***against*** gegen); schaden (*dat*), beeinträchtigen
**prej·u·diced** (vor)eingenommen, befangen
**pre·lim·i·na·ry 1.** vorläufig, einleitend, Vor… **2.** *pl* Vorbereitungen *pl*
**prel·ude** Vorspiel *n* (*a.* MUS)
**pre·mar·i·tal** vorehelich
**pre·ma·ture** vorzeitig, verfrüht; *fig* voreilig
**pre·med·i·tat·ed** JUR vorsätzlich
**pre·med·i·ta·tion**: ***with ~*** JUR vorsätzlich
**prem·i·er** POL Premier(minister) *m*
**prem·i·ere, prem·i·ère** THEA *etc* Premiere *f*, Ur-, Erstaufführung *f*
**prem·is·es** Gelände *n*, Grundstück *n*, (*Geschäfts*)Räume *pl*; ***on the ~*** an Ort und Stelle, im Haus, im Lokal
**pre·mi·um** Prämie *f*, Bonus *m*
**pre·mi·um (gas·o·line)** MOT Super *n*, Superbenzin *n*
**pre·mo·ni·tion** (böse) Vorahnung
**pre·oc·cu·pa·tion** Beschäftigung *f* (***with*** mit)
**pre·oc·cu·pied** gedankenverloren, geistesabwesend
**pre·oc·cu·py** (stark) beschäftigen
**prep** *Br* F PED Hausaufgabe(n *pl*) *f*
**pre·packed, pre·pack·aged** abgepackt
**pre·paid** *post* frankiert, freigemacht; **~ envelope** Freiumschlag *m*
**prep·a·ra·tion** Vorbereitung *f* (***for*** auf *acc*, für); Zubereitung *f*; CHEM, MED Präparat *n*
**pre·par·a·to·ry** vorbereitend
**pre·pare** *v/t* vorbereiten; GASTR zubereiten; *v/i*: ***~ for*** sich vorbereiten auf (*acc*); Vorbereitungen treffen für; sich gefasst machen auf (*acc*)
**pre·pared** vorbereitet; bereit
**prep·o·si·tion** LING Präposition *f*, Verhältniswort *n*
**pre·pos·sess·ing** einnehmend, anziehend
**pre·pos·ter·ous** absurd; lächerlich, grotesk
**pre·pro·gram(me)** vorprogrammieren
**pre·req·ui·site** Vorbedingung *f*, Voraussetzung *f*
**pre·rog·a·tive** Vorrecht *n*
**pre·school** Vorschule *f*
**pre·scribe** *et.* vorschreiben; MED *j-m et.* verschreiben; **pre·scrip·tion** Verordnung *f*, Vorschrift *f*; MED Rezept *n*
**pres·ence** Gegenwart *f*, Anwesenheit *f*; **~ of mind** Geistesgegenwart *f*
**pres·ent**[1] Geschenk *n*
**pre·sent**[2] präsentieren; (über)reichen, (über)bringen, (über)geben; schenken; vorbringen, vorlegen; zeigen, vorführen, THEA *etc* aufführen; schildern, darstellen; *j-n*, *Produkt etc* vorstellen;

*Programm etc* moderieren
**pres·ent**[3] **1.** anwesend; vorhanden; gegenwärtig, jetzig; laufend; vorliegend (*case etc*); **~ tense** LING Präsens *n*, Gegenwart *f* **2.** Gegenwart *f*, LING *a.* Präsens *n*; **at ~** gegenwärtig, zurzeit; **for the ~** vorerst, vorläufig
**pre·sen·ta·tion** Präsentation *f*; Überreichung *f*; Vorlage *f*; Vorführung *f*, THEA *etc* Aufführung *f*; Schilderung *f*, Darstellung *f*; Vorstellung *f*; *radio*, TV Moderation *f*
**pres·ent-day** heutig, gegenwärtig, modern
**pre·sent·er** *esp Br radio*, TV Moderator(in)
**pre·sen·ti·ment** (böse) Vorahnung
**pres·ent·ly** zurzeit, jetzt; *Br* bald
**pres·er·va·tion** Bewahrung *f*; Erhaltung *f*; GASTR Konservierung *f*
**pre·ser·va·tive** GASTR Konservierungsmittel *n*
**pre·serve 1.** bewahren, (be)schützen; erhalten; GASTR konservieren, *Obst etc* einmachen, einkochen **2.** (*Jagd*)Revier *n*; *fig* Ressort *n*, Reich *n*; *mst pl* GASTR *das* Eingemachte
**pre·side** den Vorsitz haben (**at, over** bei); **pres·i·den·cy** POL Präsidentschaft *f*; Amtszeit *f*; **pres·i·dent** Präsident *m*; ECON Generaldirektor *m*
**press 1.** *v/t* drücken, pressen; *Frucht* (aus)pressen; drücken auf (*acc*); bügeln; drängen; *j-n* (be)drängen; bestehen auf (*dat*); *v/i* drücken; drängen (*time etc*); (sich) drängen; **~ for** dringen *or* drängen auf (*acc*); **~ on** (zügig) weitermachen **2.** Druck *m* (*a. fig*); (Wein*etc*)Presse *f*; Bügeln *n*; *die* Presse; *a.* **printing ~** Druckerpresse *f*
**press a·gen·cy** Presseagentur *f*
**press box** Pressetribüne *f*
**press con·fe·rence** Pressekonferenz *f*
**press·ing** dringend
**press of·fice** Pressebüro *n*, Pressestelle *f*; **press of·fi·cer** Pressereferent(in)
**press re·lease** Pressemitteilung *f*
**press stud** *Br* Druckknopf *m*
**press-up** *esp Br* SPORT Liegestütz *m*
**pres·sure** PHYS, TECH *etc* Druck *m* (*a. fig*); **~ cook·er** Dampfkochtopf *m*, Schnellkochtopf *m*
**pres·tige** Prestige *n*, Ansehen *n*
**pre·su·ma·bly** vermutlich
**pre·sume** *v/t* annehmen, vermuten; sich erdreisten *or* anmaßen (**to do** zu tun); *v/i* annehmen, vermuten; anmaßend sein; **~ on** *et.* ausnützen, *et.* missbrauchen
**pre·sump·tion** Annahme *f*, Vermutung *f*; Anmaßung *f*
**pre·sump·tu·ous** anmaßend, vermessen
**pre·sup·pose** voraussetzen
**pre·sup·po·si·tion** Voraussetzung *f*
**pre·tence** *Br* → **pretense**; **pre·tend** vortäuschen, vorgeben; sich verstellen; Anspruch erheben (**to** auf *acc*); **she is only ~ing** sie tut nur so; **pre·tend·ed** vorgetäuscht, gespielt; **pre·tense** Verstellung *f*, Vortäuschung *f*; Anspruch *m* (**to** auf *acc*); **pre·ten·sion** Anspruch *m* (**to** auf *acc*); Anmaßung *f*
**pre·ter·it(e)** LING Präteritum *n*
**pre·text** Vorwand *m*
**pret·ty 1.** *adj* hübsch **2.** *adv* ziemlich, ganz schön
**pret·zel** Brezel *f*
**pre·vail** vorherrschen, weit verbreitet sein; siegen (**over, against** über *acc*)
**pre·vail·ing** (vor)herrschend
**pre·vent** verhindern, verhüten, *e-r Sache* vorbeugen; *j-n* hindern (**from** an *dat*)
**pre·ven·tion** Verhinderung *f*, Verhütung *f*, Vorbeugung *f*
**pre·ven·tive** vorbeugend
**pre·view** *film*, TV Voraufführung *f*; Vorbesichtigung *f*; *film*, TV *etc*: Vorschau *f* (**of** auf *acc*)
**pre·vi·ous** vorhergehend, vorausgehend, vorherig, vorig; **~ to** bevor, vor (*dat*); **~ knowledge** Vorkenntnisse *pl*
**pre·vi·ous·ly** vorher, früher
**pre-war** Vorkriegs…
**prey 1.** zo Beute *f*, Opfer *n* (*a. fig*); **be easy ~ for** *or* **to** *fig* e-e leichte Beute sein für **2. ~ on** zo Jagd machen auf (*acc*); *fig* nagen an (*dat*); **~ on s.o.'s mind** j-m keine Ruhe lassen
**price 1.** Preis *m* **2.** den Preis festsetzen für; auszeichnen (**at** mit)
**price·less** unbezahlbar
**price tag** Preisschild *n*
**prick 1.** Stich *m*; V Schwanz *m*; **~s of conscience** Gewissensbisse *pl* **2.** *v/t* (auf-, durch)stechen, stechen in (*acc*); **her conscience ~ed her** sie hatte Ge-

P

wissensbisse; ~ ***up one's ears*** die Ohren spitzen; *v/i* stechen
**prick·le** BOT, ZO Stachel *m*, Dorn *m*
**prick·ly** stach(e)lig; prickelnd, kribbelnd
**pride 1.** Stolz *m*; Hochmut *m*; ***take*** (***a***) ~ ***in*** stolz sein auf (*acc*) **2.** ~ ***o.s. on*** stolz sein auf (*acc*)
**priest** REL Priester *m*
**prig** Tugendbold *m*
**prig·gish** tugendhaft
**prim** steif; prüde
**pri·mae·val** *esp Br* → ***primeval***
**pri·ma·ri·ly** in erster Linie, vor allem
**pri·ma·ry 1.** wichtigste(r, -s), Haupt…; grundlegend, elementar, Grund…; Anfangs…, Ur… **2.** POL Vorwahl *f*
**pri·ma·ry school** *Br* Grundschule *f*
**prime 1.** MATH Primzahl *f*; *fig* Blüte(zeit) *f*; ***in the*** ~ ***of life*** in der Blüte s-r Jahre; ***be past one's*** ~ s-e besten Jahre hinter sich haben **2.** *adj* erste(r, -s), wichtigste(r, -s), Haupt…; erstklassig **3.** *v/t* TECH grundieren; *j-n* instruieren, vorbereiten; ~ **min·is·ter** (*abbr* POL F ***PM***) Premierminister(in), Ministerpräsident(in); ~ **num·ber** MATH Primzahl *f*
**prim·er** Fibel *f*, Elementarbuch *n*
**prime time** TV Haupteinschaltzeit *f*, Hauptsendezeit *f*, beste Sendezeit
**pri·me·val** urzeitlich, Ur…
**prim·i·tive** erste(r, -s), ursprünglich, Ur…; primitiv
**prim·rose** BOT Primel *f*, *esp* Schlüsselblume *f*
**prince** Fürst *m*; Prinz *m*
**prin·cess** Fürstin *f*; Prinzessin *f*
**prin·ci·pal 1.** wichtigste(r, -s), hauptsächlich, Haupt… **2.** PED Direktor(in), Rektor(in); THEA Hauptdarsteller(in); MUS Solist(in)
**prin·ci·pal·i·ty** Fürstentum *n*
**prin·ci·ple** Prinzip *n*, Grundsatz *m*; ***on*** ~ grundsätzlich, aus Prinzip
**print 1.** PRINT Druck *m* (*a. art*); Gedruckte *n*; (*Finger- etc*)Abdruck *m*; PHOT Abzug *m*; bedruckter Stoff; ***in*** ~ gedruckt; ***out of*** ~ vergriffen **2.** *v/i* drucken; *v/t* (ab-, auf-, be)drucken; in Druckbuchstaben schreiben; *fig* einprägen (***on*** *dat*); *a.* ~ ***off*** PHOT abziehen; ~ ***out*** IT ausdrucken
**print·ed mat·ter** *post* Drucksache *f*
**print·er** Drucker *m* (*a.* TECH); ~***'s error*** Druckfehler *m*; ~***'s ink*** Druckerschwärze *f*; **print·ers** Druckerei *f*
**print·ing** Drucken *n*; Auflage *f*; ~ **ink** Druckerschwärze *f*; ~ **press** Druckerpresse *f*
**print·out** IT Ausdruck *m*
**pri·or** frühere(r, -s); vorrangig
**pri·or·i·ty** Priorität *f*, Vorrang *m*; MOT Vorfahrt *f*; ***give s.th.*** ~ et. vordringlich behandeln
**prise** *esp Br* → ***prize***[2]
**prism** Prisma *n*
**pris·on** Gefängnis *n*, Strafanstalt *f*
**pris·on·er** Gefangene *m*, *f*, Häftling *m*; ***hold*** ~, ***keep*** ~ gefangen halten; ***take*** ~ gefangen nehmen
**pri·va·cy** Intim-, Privatsphäre *f*; Geheimhaltung *f*
**pri·vate 1.** privat, Privat…; vertraulich; geheim; ~ ***parts*** Geschlechtsteile *pl* **2.** MIL gemeiner Soldat; ***in*** ~ privat; unter vier Augen
**pri·va·tion** Entbehrung *f*
**priv·i·lege** Privileg *n*; Vorrecht *n*
**priv·i·leged** privilegiert
**priv·y**: ***be*** ~ ***to*** eingeweiht sein in (*acc*)
**prize**[1] **1.** (Sieger-, Sieges)Preis *m*, Prämie *f*, Auszeichnung *f*; (*Lotterie*)Gewinn *m* **2.** preisgekrönt; Preis… **3.** (hoch) schätzen
**prize**[2]: ~ ***open*** aufbrechen, aufstemmen
**prize·win·ner** Preisträger(in)
**pro**[1] F Profi *m*
**pro**[2]: ***the*** ~***s and cons*** das Pro und Kontra, das Für und Wider
**prob·a·bil·i·ty** Wahrscheinlichkeit *f*; ***in all*** ~ höchstwahrscheinlich
**prob·a·ble** *adj* wahrscheinlich
**prob·a·bly** *adv* wahrscheinlich
**pro·ba·tion** Probe *f*, Probezeit *f*; JUR Bewährung *f*, Bewährungsfrist *f*
**pro·ba·tion of·fi·cer** JUR Bewährungshelfer(in)
**probe 1.** MED, TECH Sonde *f*; *fig* Untersuchung *f* (***into*** *gen*); **2.** sondieren; (gründlich) untersuchen
**prob·lem** Problem *n*; MATH *etc* Aufgabe *f*; **prob·lem·at·ic**, **prob·lem·at·i·cal** problematisch
**pro·ce·dure** Verfahren *n*, Verfahrensweise *f*, Vorgehen *n*
**pro·ceed** (weiter)gehen, (weiter)fahren; sich begeben (***to*** nach, zu); *fig* weitergehen; *fig* fortfahren; *fig* vorgehen;

P

*~ from* kommen *or* herrühren von; *~ to do s.th.* sich anschicken *or* daranmachen, et. zu tun
**pro·ceed·ing** Verfahren *n*, Vorgehen *n*
**pro·ceed·ings** Vorgänge *pl*, Geschehnisse *pl*; ***start*** *or* ***take*** (***legal***) *~ **against*** JUR (gerichtlich) vorgehen gegen
**pro·ceeds** ECON Erlös *m*, Ertrag *m*, Einnahmen *pl*
**pro·cess** **1.** Prozess *m*, Verfahren *n*, Vorgang *m*; ***in the ~*** dabei; ***be in ~*** im Gange sein; ***in ~ of construction*** im Bau (befindlich) **2.** TECH *etc* bearbeiten, behandeln; IT *Daten* verarbeiten; PHOT *Film* entwickeln
**pro·ces·sion** Prozession *f*
**pro·ces·sor** IT Prozessor *m*; (*Wort-, Text*)Verarbeitungsgerät *n*
**pro·claim** proklamieren, ausrufen
**proc·la·ma·tion** Proklamation *f*, Bekanntmachung *f*
**pro·cure** (sich) *et.* beschaffen *or* besorgen; verkuppeln
**prod** **1.** stoßen; *fig* anstacheln, anspornen (***into*** zu); **2.** Stoß *m*
**prod·i·gal** **1.** verschwenderisch **2.** F Verschwender(in)
**pro·di·gious** erstaunlich, großartig
**prod·i·gy** Wunder *n*; ***child ~*** Wunderkind *n*
**pro·duce**[1] ECON produzieren (*a. film*, TV), herstellen, erzeugen (*a. fig*); hervorholen (***from*** aus); *Ausweis etc* (vor)zeigen; *Beweise etc* vorlegen; *Zeugen etc* beibringen; *Gewinn etc* (er)bringen, abwerfen; THEA inszenieren; *fig* hervorrufen, *Wirkung* erzielen
**prod·uce**[2] *esp* (*Agrar*)Produkt(e *pl*) *n*, (*Agrar*)Erzeugnis(se *pl*) *n*
**pro·duc·er** Produzent(in) (*a. film*, TV), Hersteller(in); THEA Regisseur(in)
**prod·uct** Produkt *n*, Erzeugnis *n*
**pro·duc·tion** ECON Produktion *f* (*a. film*, TV), Erzeugung *f*, Herstellung *f*; Produkt *n*, Erzeugnis *n*; Hervorholen *n*; Vorzeigen *n*, Vorlegen *n*, Beibringung *f*; THEA Inszenierung *f*
**pro·duc·tive** produktiv (*a. fig*), ergiebig, rentabel; *fig* schöpferisch
**pro·duc·tiv·i·ty** Produktivität *f*
**prof** F Prof *m*
**pro·fa·na·tion** Entweihung *f*
**pro·fane** **1.** (gottes)lästerlich; profan, weltlich **2.** entweihen
**pro·fan·i·ty**: ***profanities*** Flüche *pl*, Lästerungen *pl*
**pro·fess** vorgeben, vortäuschen; behaupten (***to be*** zu sein); erklären
**pro·fessed** erklärt (*enemy etc*); angeblich
**pro·fes·sion** (*esp akademischer*) Beruf; Berufsstand *m*
**pro·fes·sion·al** **1.** Berufs…, beruflich; Fach…, fachlich; fachmännisch; professionell **2.** Fachmann *m*, Profi *m*; Berufsspieler(in), -sportler(in), Profi *m*
**pro·fes·sor** Professor(in); Dozent(in)
**pro·fi·cien·cy** Können *n*, Tüchtigkeit *f*
**pro·fi·cient** tüchtig (***at, in*** in *dat*)
**pro·file** Profil *n*; ***keep a low ~*** Zurückhaltung üben
**prof·it** **1.** Gewinn *m*, Profit *m*; Vorteil *m*, Nutzen *m* **2.** ***~ by, ~ from*** Nutzen ziehen aus, profitieren von
**prof·it·a·ble** gewinnbringend, einträglich; nützlich, vorteilhaft
**prof·it·eer** *contp* Profitmacher *m*, Schieber *m*
**prof·it shar·ing** ECON Gewinnbeteiligung *f*
**prof·li·gate** verschwenderisch
**pro·found** *fig* tief; tiefgründig; profund (*knowledge etc*)
**pro·fuse** (über)reich; verschwenderisch; **pro·fu·sion** Überfülle *f*; ***in ~*** in Hülle und Fülle
**prog·e·ny** Nachkommen(schaft *f*) *pl*
**prog·no·sis** MED Prognose *f*
**pro·gram** **1.** Programm *n* (*a.* IT); *radio*, TV *a.* Sendung *f* **2.** (vor)programmieren; planen; IT programmieren
**pro·gram·er** IT Programmierer(in)
**pro·gramme** *Br* → ***program***
'**pro·gram·mer** *Br* → ***programer***
**pro·gress** **1.** Fortschritt(e *pl*) *m*; ***make slow ~*** (nur) langsam vorankommen; ***be in ~*** im Gange sein **2.** fortschreiten; Fortschritte machen
**pro·gres·sive** progressiv, fortschreitend; fortschrittlich
**pro·hib·it** verbieten; verhindern
**pro·hi·bi·tion** Verbot *n*
**pro·hib·i·tive** Schutz… (*Zoll etc*); unerschwinglich
**proj·ect**[1] Projekt *n*, Vorhaben *n*
**pro·ject**[2] *v/i* vorspringen, vorragen, vorstehen; *v/t* werfen, schleudern; planen; projizieren

**pro·jec·tile** Projektil *n*, Geschoss *n*
**pro·jec·tion** Vorsprung *m*, vorspringender Teil; Werfen *n*, Schleudern *n*; Planung *f*; *film*: Projektion *f*
**pro·jec·tion·ist** Filmvorführer *m*
**pro·jec·tor** *film*: Projektor *m*
**pro·le·tar·i·an 1.** proletarisch **2.** Proletarier(in)
**pro·lif·ic** fruchtbar
**pro·log**, *esp Br* **pro·logue** Prolog *m*
**pro·long** verlängern
**prom·e·nade 1.** (Strand)Promenade *f* **2.** promenieren
**prom·i·nent** vorspringend, vorstehend; *fig* prominent
**pro·mis·cu·ous** sexuell freizügig
**prom·ise 1.** Versprechen *n*; *fig* Aussicht *f* **2.** versprechen
**prom·is·ing** vielversprechend
**prom·on·to·ry** GEOGR Vorgebirge *n*
**pro·mote** *j-n* befördern; *Schüler* versetzen; ECON werben für; *Boxkampf, Konzert etc* veranstalten; *et.* fördern; ***be ~d*** SPORT *esp Br* aufsteigen (***to*** in *acc*)
**pro·mot·er** Promoter(in), Veranstalter(in); ECON Verkaufsförderer *m*
**pro·mo·tion** Beförderung *f*; PED Versetzung *f*; SPORT Aufstieg *m*; ECON Verkaufsförderung *f*, Werbung *f*
**pro·mo·tion(·al) film** Werbefilm *m*
**prompt 1.** *j-n* veranlassen (***to do*** zu tun); führen zu, *Gefühle etc* wecken; *j-m* vorsagen; THEA *j-m* soufflieren **2.** prompt, umgehend, unverzüglich; pünktlich
**prompt·er** THEA Souffleur *m*, Souffleuse *f*
**prone** auf dem Bauch *or* mit dem Gesicht nach unten liegend; ***be ~ to*** *a.* MED neigen zu, anfällig sein für
**prong** Zinke *f*; (*Geweih*)Sprosse *f*
**pro·noun** LING Pronomen *n*, Fürwort *n*
**pro·nounce** aussprechen; erklären für; JUR *Urteil* verkünden
**pro·nun·ci·a·tion** Aussprache *f*
**proof 1.** Beweis(e *pl*) *m*, Nachweis *m*; Probe *f*; PRINT Korrekturfahne *f*, *a.* PHOT Probeabzug *m* **2.** *adj in cpds* …fest, …beständig, …dicht, …sicher; → ***heatproof, soundproof, waterproof***; ***be ~ against*** geschützt sein vor (*dat*) **3.** imprägnieren
**proof·read** PRINT Korrektur lesen
**proof·read·er** PRINT Korrektor(in)
**prop 1.** Stütze *f* (*a. fig*) **2.** *a.* ***~ up*** stützen; *sich or et.* lehnen (***against*** gegen)
**prop·a·gate** BIOL sich fortpflanzen *or* vermehren; verbreiten
**prop·a·ga·tion** Fortpflanzung *f*, Vermehrung *f*; Verbreitung *f*
**pro·pel** (an)treiben; **pro·pel·lant, pro·pel·lent** Treibstoff *m*; Treibgas *n*
**pro·pel·ler** AVIAT Propeller *m*, MAR *a.* Schraube *f*
**pro·pel·ling pen·cil** Drehbleistift *m*
**pro·pen·si·ty** *fig* Neigung *f*
**prop·er** richtig, passend, geeignet; anständig, schicklich; echt, wirklich, richtig; eigentlich; eigen(tümlich); *esp Br* F ordentlich, tüchtig, gehörig
**prop·er| name, ~ noun** Eigenname *m*
**prop·er·ty** Eigentum *n*, Besitz *m*; Landbesitz *m*, Grundbesitz *m*; Grundstück *n*; *fig* Eigenschaft *f*
**proph·e·cy** Prophezeiung *f*
**proph·e·sy** prophezeien
**proph·et** Prophet *m*
**pro·por·tion 1.** Verhältnis *n*; (An)Teil *m*; *pl* Größenverhältnisse *pl*, Proportionen *pl*; ***in ~ to*** im Verhältnis zu **2.** (***to***) in das richtige Verhältnis bringen (mit, zu); anpassen (*dat*)
**pro·por·tion·al** proportional; → ***proportionate***
**pro·por·tion·ate** (***to***) im richtigen Verhältnis (zu), entsprechend (*dat*)
**pro·pos·al** Vorschlag *m*; (Heirats)Antrag *m*; **pro·pose** *v/t* vorschlagen; beabsichtigen, vorhaben; *Toast* ausbringen (***to*** auf *acc*); ***~ s.o.'s health*** auf j-s Gesundheit trinken; *v/i*: ***~ to*** *j-m* e-n (Heirats)Antrag machen
**prop·o·si·tion** Behauptung *f*; Vorschlag *m*, ECON *a.* Angebot *n*
**pro·pri·e·ta·ry** ECON gesetzlich *or* patentrechtlich geschützt; *fig* besitzergreifend
**pro·pri·e·tor** Eigentümer *m*, Besitzer *m*, Geschäftsinhaber *m*
**pro·pri·e·tress** Eigentümerin *f*, Besitzerin *f*, Geschäftsinhaberin *f*
**pro·pri·e·ty** Anstand *m*; Richtigkeit *f*
**pro·pul·sion** TECH Antrieb *m*
**pro·sa·ic** prosaisch, nüchtern, sachlich
**prose** Prosa *f*
**pros·e·cute** JUR strafrechtlich verfolgen, (gerichtlich) belangen (***for*** wegen)
**pros·e·cu·tion** JUR strafrechtliche Verfolgung, Strafverfolgung *f*; ***the ~*** die

Staatsanwaltschaft, die Anklage (-behörde)

**pros·e·cu·tor** *a.* ***public*** **~** JUR Staatsanwalt *m*, Staatsanwältin *f*

**pros·pect 1.** Aussicht *f* (*a. fig*); Interessent *m*, ECON möglicher Kunde, potenzieller Käufer **2. ~ *for*** *mining*: schürfen nach; bohren nach

**pro·spec·tive** voraussichtlich

**pro·spec·tus** (Werbe)Prospekt *m*

**pros·per** gedeihen; ECON blühen, florieren; **pros·per·i·ty** Wohlstand *m*; **pros·per·ous** ECON erfolgreich, blühend, florierend; wohlhabend

**pros·ti·tute** Prostituierte *f*, Dirne *f*; ***male*** **~** Strichjunge *m*

**pros·trate 1.** hingestreckt; *fig* am Boden liegend; erschöpft; **~ *with grief*** gramgebeugt **2.** niederwerfen; *fig* erschöpfen; *fig* niederschmettern

**pros·y** langweilig; weitschweifig

**pro·tag·o·nist** Vorkämpfer(in); THEA Hauptfigur *f*, Held(in)

**pro·tect** (be)schützen (***from*** vor *dat*; ***against*** gegen)

**pro·tec·tion** Schutz *m*; F Schutzgeld *n*; **~ *of animals*** Tierschutz; **~ *of endangered species*** Artenschutz *m*; **~ mon·ey** F Schutzgeld *n*; **~ rack·et** F Schutzgelderpressung *f*

**pro·tec·tive** (be)schützend; Schutz…; **~ cloth·ing** Schutzkleidung *f*; **~ cus·to·dy** JUR Schutzhaft *f*; **~ du·ty, ~ tar·iff** ECON Schutzzoll *m*

**pro·tec·tor** Beschützer *m*; (*Brust- etc -*) Schutz *m*

**pro·tec·to·rate** POL Protektorat *n*

**pro·test 1.** Protest *m*; Einspruch *m* **2.** *v/i* protestieren (***against*** gegen); *v/t* protestieren gegen; beteuern

**Prot·es·tant** REL **1.** protestantisch **2.** Protestant(in)

**prot·es·ta·tion** Beteuerung *f*; Protest *m* (***against*** gegen)

**pro·to·col** Protokoll *n*

**pro·to·type** Prototyp *m*

**pro·tract** in die Länge ziehen, hinziehen

**pro·trude** herausragen, vorstehen (***from*** aus); **pro·trud·ing** vorstehend (*a. teeth*), vorspringend (*chin*)

**proud** stolz (***of*** auf *acc*)

**prove** *v/t* be-, er-, nachweisen; *v/i*: **~ (*to be*)** sich herausstellen *or* erweisen als

**prov·en** bewährt

**prov·erb** Sprichwort *n*

**pro·vide** *v/t* versehen, versorgen, beliefern; zur Verfügung stellen, bereitstellen; JUR vorsehen, vorschreiben (***that*** dass); *v/i*: **~ *against*** Vorsorge treffen gegen; JUR verbieten; **~ *for*** sorgen für; vorsorgen für; JUR *et.* vorsehen

**pro·vid·ed: ~ (*that*)** vorausgesetzt(, dass)

**pro·vid·er** Ernährer(in)

**prov·ince** Provinz *f*; (Aufgaben-, Wissens)Gebiet *n*; **pro·vin·cial 1.** Provinz…, provinziell, *contp* provinzlerisch **2.** *contp* Provinzler(in)

**pro·vi·sion** Bereitstellung *f*, Beschaffung *f*; Vorkehrung *f*, Vorsorge *f*; Bestimmung *f*, Vorschrift *f*; *pl* Proviant *m*, Verpflegung *f*; ***with the*** **~ *that*** unter der Bedingung, dass

**pro·vi·sion·al** provisorisch, vorläufig

**pro·vi·so** Bedingung *f*, Vorbehalt *m*; ***with the*** **~ *that*** unter der Bedingung, dass

**prov·o·ca·tion** Provokation *f*

**pro·voc·a·tive** provozierend, (*a. sexually*) aufreizend

**pro·voke** provozieren, reizen

**prowl 1.** *v/i a.* **~ *about*, ~ *around*** herumschleichen, herumstreifen; *v/t* durchstreifen **2.** Herumstreifen *n*

**prowl car** (Funk)Streifenwagen *m*

**prox·im·i·ty** Nähe *f*

**prox·y** (Handlungs)Vollmacht *f*; (Stell)Vertreter(in), Bevollmächtigte *m, f*; ***by*** **~** durch e-n Bevollmächtigten

**prude: *be a*** **~** prüde sein

**pru·dence** Klugheit *f*, Vernunft *f*; Besonnenheit *f*

**pru·dent** klug, vernünftig; besonnen

**prud·ish** prüde

**prune**[1] BOT (be)schneiden

**prune**[2] Backpflaume *f*

**prus·sic ac·id** CHEM Blausäure *f*

**pry**[1] neugierig sein; **~ *about*** herumschnüffeln; **~ *into*** s-e Nase stecken in (*acc*)

**pry**[2] → ***prize***[2]

**psalm** REL Psalm *m*

**pseu·do·nym** Pseudonym *n*, Deckname *m*

**psy·chi·a·trist** Psychiater(in)

**psy·chi·a·try** Psychiatrie *f*

**psy·cho·a·nal·y·sis** Psychoanalyse *f*

**psy·cho·log·i·cal** psychologisch

**psy·chol·o·gist** Psychologe *m*, Psycho-

login *f*
**psy·chol·o·gy** Psychologie *f*
**psy·cho·so·mat·ic** psychosomatisch
**pub** *Br* Pub *n, m*, Kneipe *f*
**pu·ber·ty** Pubertät *f*
**pu·bic hair** Schamhaare *pl*
**pub·lic 1.** öffentlich; allgemein bekannt; ***make*** ~ bekannt machen, an die Öffentlichkeit bringen **2.** *die* Öffentlichkeit, *das* Publikum; ***in*** ~ öffentlich, in aller Öffentlichkeit
**pub·li·ca·tion** Bekanntgabe *f*, Bekanntmachung *f*; Publikation *f*, Veröffentlichung *f*
**pub·lic| con·ve·ni·ence** *Br* öffentliche Bedürfnisanstalt; ~ **en·e·my** Staatsfeind *m*; ~ **health** öffentliches Gesundheitswesen; ~ **hol·i·day** gesetzlicher Feiertag
**pub·lic·i·ty** Publicity *f*, *a.* Bekanntheit *f*, ECON *a.* Reklame *f*, Werbung *f*; ~ **depart·ment** Werbeabteilung *f*
**pub·lic| li·bra·ry** Leihbücherei *f*; ~ **relations** (*abbr* ***PR***) Public Relations *pl*, Öffentlichkeitsarbeit *f*; ~ **school** staatliche Schule; *Br* Public School *f*; ~ **trans·port** *esp Br*, ~ **trans·por·tation** öffentliche Verkehrsmittel *pl*
**pub·lish** bekannt geben *or* machen; publizieren, veröffentlichen; *Buch etc* verlegen, herausgeben
**pub·lish·er** Verleger(in), Herausgeber(in); Verlag *m*, Verlagshaus *n*
**pub·lish·er's, pub·lish·ers, publishing house** Verlag *m*, Verlagshaus *n*
**puck·er** *a.* ~ ***up*** (sich) verziehen, (sich) runzeln
**pud·ding** *Br* GASTR Nachspeise *f*, Nachtisch *m*; (*Reis- etc*)Auflauf *m*; (*Art*) Fleischpastete *f*; Pudding *m*
**pud·dle** Pfütze *f*
**pu·er·ile** infantil, kindisch
**puff 1.** *v/i* schnaufen, keuchen; *a.* ~ ***away*** paffen (***at*** an *dat*); ~ ***up*** (an)schwellen; *v/t Rauch* blasen; ~ ***out*** *Kerze etc* ausblasen; *Rauch etc* ausstoßen; *Brust* herausdrücken **2.** Zug *m*; (*Wind-*) Hauch *m*, (*Wind*)Stoß *m*; (*Puder*)Quaste *f*; F Puste *f*
**puffed sleeve** Puffärmel *m*
**puff pas·try** GASTR Blätterteig *m*
**puff·y** (an)geschwollen; aufgedunsen
**pug** ZO Mops *m*
**puke** F (aus)kotzen
**pull 1.** Ziehen *n*; Zug *m*, Ruck *m*; Anstieg *m*, Steigung *f*; Zuggriff *m*, Zugleine *f*; F Beziehungen *pl* **2.** ziehen; ziehen an (*dat*); zerren; reißen; *Pflanze* ausreißen; *esp Br Bier* zapfen; *fig* anziehen; ~ ***ahead of*** vorbeiziehen an (*dat*), MOT überholen (*acc*); ~ ***away*** anfahren (*bus etc*); ~ ***down*** *Gebäude* abreißen; ~ ***in*** einfahren (*train*); anhalten; ~ ***off*** F *et.* zustande bringen, schaffen; ~ ***out*** herausziehen (***of*** aus); *Tisch* ausziehen; RAIL abfahren; MOT ausscheren; *fig* sich zurückziehen, aussteigen (***of*** aus); ~ ***over*** (s-n Wagen) an die *or* zur Seite fahren; ~ ***round*** MED durchbringen; durchkommen; ~ ***through*** *j-n* durchbringen; ~ ***o.s. together*** sich zusammennehmen, F sich zusammenreißen; ~ ***up*** MOT anhalten; (an)halten; ~ ***up to***, ~ ***up with*** SPORT *j-n* einholen
**pull date** Mindesthaltbarkeitsdatum *n*
**pul·ley** TECH Flaschenzug *m*
**pull-in** *Br* F Raststätte *f*, Rasthaus *n*
**pull·o·ver** Pullover *m*
**pull-up** SPORT Klimmzug *m*; ***do a*** ~ e-n Klimmzug machen
**pulp 1.** Fruchtfleisch *n*; Brei *m* **2.** Schund…; ~ ***novel*** Schundroman *m*
**pul·pit** Kanzel *f*
**pulp·y** breiig
**pul·sate** pulsieren, vibrieren
**pulse** Puls *m*; Pulsschlag *m*
**pul·ver·ize** pulverisieren
**pu·ma** ZO Puma *m*
**pum·mel** mit den Fäusten bearbeiten
**pump 1.** Pumpe *f*; (*Zapf*)Säule *f* **2.** pumpen; F *j-n* aushorchen; ~ ***up*** aufpumpen; ~ **at·tend·ant** Tankwart *m*
**pump·kin** BOT Kürbis *m*
**pun 1.** Wortspiel *n* **2.** Wortspiele *or* ein Wortspiel machen
**punch**[1] **1.** boxen, (mit der Faust) schlagen **2.** (Faust)Schlag *m*
**punch**[2] **1.** lochen; *Loch* stanzen (***in*** in *acc*); ~ ***in*** einstempeln; ~ ***out*** ausstempeln **2.** Locher *m*; Lochzange *f*; Locheisen *n*
**punch**[3] Punsch *m*
**Punch** *appr* Kasper *m*, Kasperle *n, m*; ***be as pleased*** *or* ***proud as*** ~ sich freuen wie ein Schneekönig; ~ **and Ju·dy show** Kasperletheater *n*
**punc·tu·al** pünktlich
**punc·tu·al·i·ty** Pünktlichkeit *f*

P

**punc·tu·ate** interpunktieren
**punc·tu·a·tion** LING Interpunktion *f*; **~ mark** LING Satzzeichen *n*
**punc·ture 1.** (Ein)Stich *m*, Loch *n*; MOT Reifenpanne *f* **2.** durchstechen, durchbohren; ein Loch bekommen, platzen; MOT e-n Platten haben
**pun·gent** scharf, stechend, beißend (*smell, taste*); scharf, bissig (*remark etc*)
**pun·ish** *j-n* (be)strafen
**pun·ish·a·ble** strafbar
**pun·ish·ment** Strafe *f*; Bestrafung *f*
**punk** Punk *m* (*a.* MUS); Punk(er) *m*
**pu·ny** schwächlich
**pup** ZO Welpe *m*, junger Hund
**pu·pa** ZO Puppe *f*
**pu·pil**[1] Schüler(in)
**pu·pil**[2] ANAT Pupille *f*
**pup·pet** Handpuppe *f*; Marionette *f* (*a. fig*)
**pup·pe·teer** Puppenspieler(in)
**pup·pet show** Marionettentheater *n*, Puppenspiel *n*
**pup·py** ZO Welpe *m*, junger Hund
**pur·chase 1.** kaufen; *fig* erkaufen **2.** Kauf *m*; ***make ~s*** Einkäufe machen
**pur·chas·er** Käufer(in)
**pure** rein; pur
**pure·bred** ZO reinrassig
**pur·ga·tive** MED **1.** abführend **2.** Abführmittel *n*
**pur·ga·to·ry** REL Fegefeuer *n*
**purge 1.** *Partei etc* säubern (***of*** von); **2.** Säuberung *f*, Säuberungsaktion *f*
**pu·ri·fy** reinigen
**pu·ri·tan** (HIST ***Puritan***) **1.** Puritaner(in) **2.** puritanisch
**pu·ri·ty** Reinheit *f*
**purl 1.** linke Masche **2.** links stricken
**pur·ple** purpurn, purpurrot
**pur·pose 1.** Absicht *f*, Vorsatz *m*; Zweck *m*, Ziel *n*; Entschlossenheit *f*; ***on ~*** absichtlich; ***to no ~*** vergeblich **2.** beabsichtigen, vorhaben
**pur·pose·ful** entschlossen, zielstrebig
**pur·pose·less** zwecklos; ziellos
**pur·pose·ly** absichtlich
**purr** ZO schnurren; MOT summen, surren
**purse**[1] Geldbeutel *m*, Geldbörse *f*, Portemonnaie *n*; Handtasche *f*; SPORT Siegprämie *f*; *boxing*: Börse *f*
**purse**[2]: ***~ (up) one's lips*** die Lippen schürzen
**purs·er** MAR Zahlmeister *m*
**pur·su·ance**: ***in (the) ~ of his duty*** in Ausübung s-r Pflicht
**pur·sue** verfolgen; *s-m Studium etc* nachgehen; *Absicht, Politik etc* verfolgen; *Angelegenheit etc* weiterführen
**pur·su·er** Verfolger(in)
**pur·suit** Verfolgung *f*; Weiterführung *f*
**pur·vey** *Lebensmittel etc* liefern
**pur·vey·or** Lieferant *m*
**pus** MED Eiter *m*
**push 1.** stoßen, F schubsen; schieben; *Taste etc* drücken; drängen; (an)treiben; F *Rauschgift* pushen; *fig j-n* drängen (***to do*** zu tun); *fig* Reklame machen für; ***~ one's way*** sich drängen (***through*** durch); ***~ ahead with*** *Plan etc* vorantreiben; ***~ along*** F sich auf die Socken machen; ***~ around*** F herumschubsen; ***~ for*** drängen auf (*acc*); ***~ forward with*** → ***push ahead with***; ***~ o.s. forward*** *fig* sich in den Vordergrund drängen *or* schieben; ***~ in*** F sich vordrängeln; ***~ off!*** F hau ab!; ***~ on with*** → ***push ahead with***; ***~ out*** *fig j-n* hinausdrängen; ***~ through*** *et.* durchsetzen; ***~ up*** *Preise etc* hochtreiben **2.** Stoß *m*, F Schubs *m*; (*Werbe*)-Kampagne *f*; F Durchsetzungsvermögen *n*, Energie *f*, Tatkraft *f*
**push but·ton** TECH Druckknopf *m*, Drucktaste *f*
**push·chair** *Br* Sportwagen *m*
**push·er** F *contp* Rauschgifthändler *m*
**push·o·ver** F Kinderspiel *n*
**push-up** SPORT Liegestütz *m*
**puss** F ZO Mieze *f*
**pus·sy** *a.* ***~ cat*** F Miezekatze *f*
**pus·sy·foot**: F ***~ about, ~ around*** leisetreten, sich nicht festlegen wollen
**put** legen, setzen, stecken, stellen, tun; *j-n in e-e Lage etc, et. auf den Markt, in Ordnung etc* bringen; *et. in Kraft, in Umlauf etc* setzen; SPORT *Kugel* stoßen; unterwerfen, unterziehen (***to*** *dat*); *et.* ausdrücken, *in Worte* fassen; übersetzen (***into German*** ins Deutsche); *Schuld* geben (***on*** *dat*); ***~ right*** in Ordnung bringen; ***~ s.th. before s.o.*** *fig* j-m et. vorlegen; ***~ to bed*** ins Bett bringen; ***~ to school*** zur Schule schicken; ***~ about*** *Gerüchte* verbreiten, in Umlauf setzen; ***~ across*** *et.* verständlich machen; ***~ ahead*** SPORT in Führung bringen; ***~ aside*** beiseitelegen; *Ware* zu-

P

rücklegen; *fig* beiseiteschieben; ~ ***away*** weglegen, wegtun; auf-, wegräumen; ~ ***back*** zurücklegen, -stellen, -tun; *Uhr* zurückstellen (***by*** um); ~ ***by*** *Geld* zurücklegen; ~ ***down*** *v/t* hinlegen, niederlegen, hinsetzen, hinstellen; *j-n* absetzen, aussteigen lassen; (auf-, nieder-) schreiben, eintragen; zuschreiben (***to*** *dat*); *Aufstand* niederschlagen; (*a. v/i*) AVIAT landen; ~ ***forward*** *Plan etc* vorlegen; *Uhr* vorstellen (***by*** um); *fig* vorverlegen (***two days*** um zwei Tage; ***to*** auf *acc*); ~ ***in*** *v/t* hineinlegen, -stecken, -stellen, *Kassette etc* einlegen; installieren; *Gesuch etc* einreichen, *Forderung etc a.* geltend machen; *Antrag* stellen; *Arbeit, Zeit* verbringen (***on*** mit); *Bemerkung* einwerfen; *v/i* MAR einlaufen (***at*** in *acc*); ~ ***off*** *et.* verschieben (***until*** auf *acc*); *j-m* absagen; *j-n* hinhalten (***with*** mit), *j-n* vertrösten; *j-n* aus dem Konzept bringen; ~ ***on*** *Kleider etc* anziehen, *Hut, Brille* aufsetzen; *Licht, Radio etc* anmachen, einschalten; *Sonderzug* einsetzen; THEA *Stück etc* herausbringen; *et.* vortäuschen; F *j-n* auf den Arm nehmen; ~ ***on airs*** sich aufspielen; ~ ***on weight*** zunehmen; ~ ***out*** *v/t* hinauslegen, -setzen, -stellen; *Hand etc* ausstrecken; *Feuer* löschen; *Licht, Radio etc* ausmachen (*a. cigarette*), ab-, ausschalten; veröffentlichen, herausgeben; *radio*, TV bringen, senden; *j-n* aus der Fassung bringen; *j-n* verärgern; *j-m* Ungelegenheiten bereiten; *j-m* Umstände machen; sich *den Arm etc* verrenken *or* ausrenken; *v/i* MAR auslaufen; ~ ***over*** → ***put across***; ~ ***through*** TEL *j-n* verbinden (***to*** mit); durch-, ausführen; ~ ***together*** zusammenbauen, -setzen, -stellen; ~ ***up*** *v/t* hinauflegen, -stellen; *Hand* (hoch)heben; *Zelt etc* aufstellen; *Gebäude* errichten; *Bild etc* aufhängen; *Plakat, Bekanntmachung etc* anschlagen; *Schirm* aufspannen; *zum Verkauf* anbieten; *Preis* erhöhen; *Widerstand* leisten; *Kampf* liefern; *j-n* unterbringen, (bei sich) aufnehmen; *v/i* ~ ***up at*** absteigen in (*dat*); ~ ***up with*** sich gefallen lassen; sich abfinden mit

**pu·tre·fy** (ver)faulen, verwesen

**pu·trid** faul, verfault, verwest; F scheußlich, saumäßig

**put·ty 1.** Kitt *m* **2.** kitten

**put-up job** F abgekartetes Spiel

**puz·zle 1.** Rätsel *n*; Geduld(s)spiel *n* **2.** *v/t j-n* vor ein Rätsel stellen; verwirren; ***be ~d*** vor e-m Rätsel stehen; ~ ***out*** herausfinden, herausbringen, F austüfteln; *v/i* sich den Kopf zerbrechen (***about, over*** über *dat or acc*)

**pyg·my 1.** Pygmäe *m*, Pygmäin *f*; Zwerg(in) **2.** *esp* zo Zwerg…

**py·ja·mas** *Br* → ***pajamas***

**py·lon** TECH Hochspannungsmast *m*

**pyr·a·mid** Pyramide *f*

**pyre** Scheiterhaufen *m*

**py·thon** zo Python(schlange) *f*

**pyx** REL Hostienbehälter *m*

# Q

**Q, q** Q, q *n*

**quack¹** zo **1.** quaken **2.** Quaken *n*

**quack²** *a.* ~ ***doctor*** Quacksalber *m*, Kurpfuscher *m*; **quack·er·y** Quacksalberei *f*, Kurpfuscherei *f*

**quad·ran·gle** Viereck *n*

**quad·ran·gu·lar** viereckig

**quad·ra·phon·ic** quadrophon(isch)

**quad·rat·ic** MATH quadratisch

**quad·ri·lat·er·al** MATH **1.** vierseitig **2.** Viereck *n*

**quad·ro·phon·ic** → ***quadraphonic***

**quad·ru·ped** zo Vierfüß(l)er *m*; Vierbeiner *m*

**quad·ru·ple 1.** vierfach **2.** (sich) vervierfachen

**quad·ru·plets** Vierlinge *pl*

**quads** Vierlinge *pl*

**quag·mire** Morast *m*, Sumpf *m*

**quail** zo Wachtel *f*

**quaint** idyllisch, malerisch

**quake 1.** zittern, beben (***with, for*** vor *dat*; ***at*** bei); **2.** F Erdbeben *n*

**Quak·er** REL Quäker(in)

**qual·i·fi·ca·tion** Qualifikation *f*, Befähigung *f*, Eignung *f* (**for** für, zu); Voraussetzung *f*; Einschränkung *f*
**qual·i·fied** qualifiziert, geeignet, befähigt (**for** für); berechtigt; bedingt, eingeschränkt; **qual·i·fy** *v/t* qualifizieren, befähigen (**for** für, zu); berechtigen (**to do** zu tun); einschränken, abschwächen, mildern; *v/i* sich qualifizieren *or* eignen (**for** für; **as** als); SPORT sich qualifizieren (**for** für)
**qual·i·ty** Qualität *f*; Eigenschaft *f*
**qualms** Bedenken *pl*, Skrupel *pl*
**quan·da·ry**: ***be in a ~ about what to do*** nicht wissen, was man tun soll
**quan·ti·ty** Quantität *f*, Menge *f*
**quan·tum** PHYS **1.** Quant *n* **2.** Quanten…
**quar·an·tine 1.** Quarantäne *f* **2.** unter Quarantäne stellen
**quar·rel 1.** Streit *m*, Auseinandersetzung *f* **2.** (sich) streiten
**quar·rel·some** streitsüchtig, zänkisch
**quar·ry**¹ Steinbruch *m*
**quar·ry**² HUNT Beute *f*, *a. fig* Opfer *n*
**quart** Quart *n* (*abbr* ***qt***) (*0,95 l*, *Br 1,14 l*)
**quar·ter 1.** Viertel *n*, vierter Teil; Quartal *n*, Vierteljahr *n*; Viertelpfund *n*; Vierteldollar *m*; SPORT (Spiel)Viertel *n*; (Himmels)Richtung *f*; Gegend *f*, Teil *m*; (Stadt)Viertel *n*; GASTR (*esp* Hinter)Viertel *n*; Gnade *f*, Pardon *m*; *pl* Quartier *n*, Unterkunft *f* (*a.* MIL); ***a ~ of an hour*** e-e Viertelstunde; ***a ~ of*** (*Br* ***to***) ***five*** (ein) Viertel vor fünf (*4.45*); ***a ~ after*** (*Br* ***past***) ***five*** (ein) Viertel nach fünf (*5.15*); ***at close ~s*** in *or* aus nächster Nähe; ***from official ~s*** von amtlicher Seite **2.** vierteln; *esp* MIL einquartieren (**on** bei)
**quar·ter·deck** MAR Achterdeck *n*
**quar·ter·fi·nals** SPORT Viertelfinale *n*
**quar·ter·ly 1.** vierteljährlich **2.** Vierteljahresschrift *f*
**quar·tet(te)** MUS Quartett *n*
**quartz** MIN Quarz *m*; **~ clock** Quarzuhr *f*; **~ watch** Quarz(armband)uhr *f*
**qua·ver 1.** *v/i* zittern; *v/t et.* mit zitternder Stimme sagen **2.** Zittern *n*
**quay** MAR Kai *m*
**quea·sy**: ***I feel ~*** mir ist übel *or* F mulmig
**queen** Königin *f*; *card game*, *chess*: Dame *f*; F Schwule *m*, Homo *m*
**queen bee** ZO Bienenkönigin *f*
**queen·ly** wie e-e Königin, königlich
**queer** komisch, seltsam; F wunderlich; F schwul
**quench** *Durst* löschen, stillen
**quer·u·lous** nörglerisch
**que·ry 1.** Frage *f*; Zweifel *m* **2.** infrage stellen, in Zweifel ziehen
**quest 1.** Suche *f* (**for** nach); ***in ~ of*** auf der Suche nach **2.** suchen (***after, for*** nach)
**ques·tion 1.** Frage *f*, *a.* Problem *n*, *a.* Sache *f*, *a.* Zweifel *m*; ***only a ~ of time*** nur e-e Frage der Zeit; ***this is not the point in ~*** darum geht es nicht; ***there is no ~ that, it is beyond ~ that*** es steht außer Frage, dass; ***there is no ~ about this*** daran besteht kein Zweifel; ***be out of the ~*** nicht infrage kommen **2.** befragen (**about** über *acc*); JUR vernehmen, verhören (**about** zu); bezweifeln, in Zweifel ziehen, infrage stellen
**ques·tion·a·ble** fraglich, zweifelhaft; fragwürdig
**ques·tion·er** Fragesteller(in)
**ques·tion| mark** Fragezeichen *n*; **~ master** *esp Br* Quizmaster *m*
**ques·tion·naire** Fragebogen *m*
**queue** *esp Br* **1.** Schlange *f*; → ***jump*** **2.** *mst* **~ up** Schlange stehen, anstehen, sich anstellen
**quib·ble** sich herumstreiten (***with*** mit; ***about, over*** wegen)
**quick 1.** *adj* schnell, rasch; aufbrausend, hitzig (*temper*); ***be ~!*** mach schnell!, beeil dich! **2.** *adv* schnell, rasch **3.** ***cut s.o. to the ~*** *fig* j-n tief verletzen
**quick·en** (sich) beschleunigen
**quick·sand** Treibsand *m*
**quick-tem·pered** aufbrausend, hitzig
**quick-wit·ted** schlagfertig; geistesgegenwärtig
**qui·et 1.** ruhig, still; ***~, please*** Ruhe, bitte; ***be ~!*** sei still! **2.** Ruhe *f*, Stille *f*; ***on the ~*** F heimlich **3.** *v/t a.* ***~ down*** *j-n* beruhigen; *v/i a.* ***~ down*** sich beruhigen
**qui·et·en** *Br* → ***quiet 3***
**qui·et·ness** Ruhe *f*, Stille *f*
**quill** ZO (Schwung-, Schwanz)Feder *f*; Stachel *m*
**quilt** Steppdecke *f*; **quilt·ed** Stepp…
**quince** BOT Quitte *f*
**quin·ine** PHARM Chinin *n*
**quint** F Fünfling *m*
**quin·tes·sence** Quintessenz *f*; Inbegriff *m*

**quin·tet(te)** MUS Quintett *n*
**quin·tu·ple 1.** fünffach **2.** (sich) verfünffachen
**quin·tu·plets** Fünflinge *pl*
**quip 1.** geistreiche *or* witzige Bemerkung **2.** witzeln, spötteln
**quirk** Eigenart *f*, Schrulle *f*; ***by some ~ of fate*** durch e-e Laune des Schicksals, durch e-n verrückten Zufall
**quit** F *v/t* aufhören mit; ***~ one's job*** kündigen; *v/i* aufhören; kündigen
**quite** ganz, völlig; ziemlich; ***~ a few*** ziemlich viele; ***~ nice*** ganz nett, recht nett; ***~ (so)!*** *esp Br* genau, ganz recht; ***be ~ right*** völlig recht haben; ***she's ~ a beauty*** sie ist e-e wirkliche Schönheit
**quits** F quitt (***with*** mit); ***call it ~*** es gut sein lassen
**quit·ter**: F ***be a ~*** schnell aufgeben
**quiv·er**[1] zittern (***with*** vor *dat*; ***at*** bei)
**quiv·er**[2] Köcher *m*
**quiz 1.** Quiz *n*; Prüfung *f*, Test *m* **2.** ausfragen (***about*** über *acc*)
**quiz·mas·ter** Quizmaster *m*
**quiz·zi·cal** spöttisch-fragend
**quo·ta** Quote *f*, Kontingent *n*
**quo·ta·tion** Zitat *n*; ECON Notierung *f*; Kostenvoranschlag *m*; **~ marks** LING Anführungszeichen *pl*
**quote** zitieren; *Beispiel etc* anführen; *Preis* nennen; ***be ~d at*** ECON notieren mit
**quo·tient** MATH Quotient *m*

# R

**R, r** R, r *n*
**rab·bi** REL Rabbiner *m*
**rab·bit** ZO Kaninchen *n*
**rab·ble** Pöbel *m*, Mob *m*
**rab·ble-rous·ing** Hetz..., aufwieglerisch
**rab·id** VET tollwütig; *fig* fanatisch
**ra·bies** VET Tollwut *f*
**rac·coon** ZO Waschbär *m*
**race**[1] Rasse *f*, Rassenzugehörigkeit *f*; (*Menschen*)Geschlecht *n*
**race**[2] **1.** (Wett)Rennen *n*, (Wett)Lauf *m* **2.** *v/i* an (e-m) Rennen teilnehmen; um die Wette laufen *or* fahren *etc*; rasen, rennen; MOT durchdrehen; *v/t* um die Wette laufen *or* fahren *etc* mit; rasen mit
**race car** MOT Rennwagen *m*
**race·course** Rennbahn *f*
**race·horse** Rennpferd *n*
**rac·er** Rennpferd *n*; Rennrad *n*, Rennwagen *m*
**race ri·ots** Rassenunruhen *pl*
**race·track** Rennbahn *f*
**ra·cial** rassisch, Rassen...
**rac·ing 1.** Rennsport *m* **2.** Renn...
**rac·ing car** *Br* MOT Rennwagen *m*
**ra·cism** Rassismus *m*
**ra·cist 1.** Rassist(in) **2.** rassistisch
**rack 1.** Gestell *n*, (*Geschirr-, Zeitungs- etc*)Ständer *m*, RAIL (*Gepäck*)Netz *n*, MOT (*Dach*)Gepäckständer *m*; HIST Folter(bank) *f* **2.** ***be ~ed by*** *or* ***with*** geplagt *or* gequält werden von; ***~ one's brains*** sich das Hirn zermartern, sich den Kopf zerbrechen
**rack·et**[1] *tennis etc*: Schläger *m*
**rack·et**[2] F Krach *m*, Lärm *m*; Schwindel *m*, Gaunerei *f*; (*Drogen- etc*)Geschäft *n*; organisierte Erpressung
**rack·et·eer** Gauner *m*; Erpresser *m*
**ra·coon** → ***raccoon***
**rac·y** spritzig, lebendig; gewagt (*joke*)
**ra·dar** TECH Radar *m, n*; **~ screen** Radarschirm *m*; **~ speed check** MOT Radarkontrolle *f*; **~ sta·tion** Radarstation *f*; **~ trap** MOT Radarkontrolle *f*
**ra·di·al 1.** radial, Radial..., strahlenförmig **2.** MOT Gürtelreifen *m*
**ra·di·al| tire**, *Br* **~ tyre** → ***radial*** 2
**ra·di·ant** strahlend, leuchtend (*a. fig* ***with*** vor *dat*)
**ra·di·ate** ausstrahlen; strahlenförmig ausgehen (***from*** von)
**ra·di·a·tion** Ausstrahlung *f*
**ra·di·a·tor** Heizkörper *m*; MOT Kühler *m*
**rad·i·cal 1.** radikal (*a.* POL); MATH Wurzel... **2.** POL Radikale *m, f*
**ra·di·o 1.** Radio(apparat *m*) *n*; Funk *m*; Funkgerät *n*; ***by ~*** über Funk; ***on the ~*** im Radio **2.** funken
**ra·di·o·ac·tive** radioaktiv; **~ waste**

R

Atommüll *m*, radioaktiver Abfall
**ra·di·o·ac·tiv·i·ty** Radioaktivität *f*
**ra·di·o| ham** Funkamateur *m*; **~ play** Hörspiel *n*; **~ set** Radioapparat *m*; **~ sta·tion** Funkstation *f*; Rundfunksender *m*, -station *f*; **~ ther·a·py** MED Strahlentherapie *f*, Röntgentherapie *f*; **~ tow·er** Funkturm *m*
**rad·ish** BOT Rettich *m*; Radieschen *n*
**ra·di·us** MATH Radius *m*
**raf·fle 1.** Tombola *f* **2.** *a.* ***~ off*** verlosen
**raft** Floß *n*
**raf·ter** (Dach)Sparren *m*
**rag** Lumpen *m*, Fetzen *m*; Lappen *m*; ***in ~s*** zerlumpt
**rage 1.** Wut *f*, Zorn *m*; ***fly into a ~*** wütend werden; ***the latest ~*** F der letzte Schrei; ***be all the ~*** F große Mode sein **2.** wettern (***against, at*** gegen); wüten, toben
**rag·ged** zerlumpt; struppig; *fig* stümperhaft
**raid 1.** (***on***) Überfall *m* (auf *acc*), MIL *a.* Angriff *m* (gegen); Razzia *f* (in *dat*); **2.** überfallen, MIL *a.* angreifen; e-e Razzia machen in (*dat*)
**rail 1.** Geländer *n*; Stange *f*; (*Handtuch*)-Halter *m*; (Eisen)Bahn *f*; RAIL Schiene *f*, *pl a.* Gleis *n*; ***by ~*** mit der Bahn **2.** ***~ in*** einzäunen; ***~ off*** abzäunen
**rail·ing** *often pl* (Gitter)Zaun *m*
**rail·road** Eisenbahn *f*; **~ line** Bahnlinie *f*; **~ sta·tion** Bahnhof *m*
**rail·way** *Br* → ***railroad***
**rain 1.** Regen *m*, *pl* Regenfälle *pl*; ***the ~s*** die Regenzeit **2.** regnen; ***it never ~s but it pours*** es kommt immer gleich knüppeldick, ein Unglück kommt selten allein
**rain·bow** Regenbogen *m*
**rain·coat** Regenmantel *m*
**rain·fall** Niederschlag(smenge *f*) *m*
**rain for·est** GEOGR Regenwald *m*
**rain·proof** regendicht, wasserdicht
**rain·y** regnerisch, verregnet, Regen…
**raise 1.** heben; hochziehen; erheben; *Denkmal etc* errichten; *Staub etc* aufwirbeln; *Gehalt*, *Miete etc* erhöhen; *Geld* zusammenbringen, beschaffen; *Kinder* aufziehen, großziehen; *Tiere* züchten; *Getreide etc* anbauen; *Frage* aufwerfen, *et.* zur Sprache bringen; *Blockade etc*, *a. Verbot* aufheben **2.** Lohn- *or* Gehaltserhöhung *f*
**rai·sin** Rosine *f*
**rake 1.** Rechen *m*, Harke *f* **2.** *v/t*: **~ (*up*)** (zusammen)rechen, (zusammen)harken; F ***~ in*** scheffeln; *v/i*: ***~ about, ~ around*** herumstöbern
**rak·ish** flott, keck, verwegen
**ral·ly 1.** (sich) (wieder) sammeln; sich erholen (***from*** von) (*a.* ECON); ***~ round*** sich scharen um **2.** Kundgebung *f*, (Massen)Versammlung *f*; MOT Rallye *f*; *tennis etc*: Ballwechsel *m*
**ram 1.** zo Widder *m*, Schafbock *m*; TECH Ramme *f* **2.** rammen
**ram·ble 1.** wandern, umherstreifen; abschweifen **2.** Wanderung *f*; **ram·bler** Wanderer *m*; BOT Kletterrose *f*
**ram·bling** weitschweifig; weitläufig; **~ rose** BOT Kletterrose *f*
**ramp** Rampe *f*; MOT (Autobahn)Auffahrt *f*; (Autobahn)Ausfahrt *f*
**ram·page 1.** ***~ through*** (wild *or* aufgeregt) trampeln durch (*elephant etc*); → **2.** ***go on the ~ through*** randalierend ziehen durch
**ram·pant**: ***be ~*** wuchern (*plant*); grassieren (***in*** in *dat*)
**ram·shack·le** baufällig (*building*); klapp(e)rig (*vehicle*)
**ranch** Ranch *f*; (*Geflügel- etc*)Farm *f*
**ranch·er** Rancher *m*; (*Geflügel- etc*) Züchter *m*
**ran·cid** ranzig
**ran·co(u)r** Groll *m*, Erbitterung *f*
**ran·dom 1.** *adj* ziellos, wahllos; zufällig, Zufalls…; ***~ sample*** Stichprobe *f* **2.** ***at ~*** aufs Geratewohl
**range 1.** Reich-, Schuss-, Tragweite *f*; Entfernung *f*; *fig* Bereich *m*, *a.* Spielraum *m*, *a.* Gebiet *n*; (*Schieß*)Stand *m*, (-)Platz *m*; (*Berg*)Kette *f*; offenes Weidegebiet; ECON Kollektion *f*, Sortiment *n*; Küchenherd *m*; ***at close ~*** aus nächster Nähe; ***within ~ of vision*** in Sichtweite; ***a wide ~ of …*** eine große Auswahl an … (*dat*) **2.** *v/i*: ***~ from … to …, ~ between … and …*** sich zwischen … und … bewegen (*prices etc*); *v/t* aufstellen, anordnen
**range find·er** PHOT Entfernungsmesser *m*
**rang·er** Förster *m*; Ranger *m*
**rank[1] 1.** Rang *m* (*a.* MIL), (soziale) Stellung; Reihe *f*; (*Taxi*)Stand *m*; ***of the first ~*** *fig* erstklassig; ***the ~ and file***

R

*fig* die Basis; ***the ~s*** *fig* das Heer, die Masse **2.** *v/t* rechnen, zählen (***among*** zu); stellen (***above*** über *acc*); *v/i* zählen, gehören (***among*** zu); gelten (***as*** als)

**rank**[2] BOT (üppig) wuchernd; übel riechend, übel schmeckend; *fig* krass (*outsider*), blutig (*beginner*)

**ran·kle** *fig* nagen, wehtun, F wurmen

**ran·sack** durchwühlen, durchsuchen; plündern

**ran·som 1.** Lösegeld *n* **2.** freikaufen, auslösen

**rap 1.** Klopfen *n*; Klaps *m* **2.** klopfen (an *acc*, auf *acc*)

**ra·pa·cious** habgierig

**rape**[1] **1.** vergewaltigen **2.** Vergewaltigung *f*

**rape**[2] BOT Raps *m*

**rap·id** schnell, rasch

**ra·pid·i·ty** Schnelligkeit *f*

**rap·ids** GEOGR Stromschnellen *pl*

**rapt**: ***with ~ attention*** mit gespannter Aufmerksamkeit

**rap·ture** Entzücken *n*, Verzückung *f*; ***go into ~s*** in Verzückung geraten

**rare**[1] selten, rar; dünn (*air*); F Mords…

**rare**[2] GASTR blutig (*steak*)

**rar·e·fied** dünn (*air*)

**rar·i·ty** Seltenheit *f*; Rarität *f*

**ras·cal** Schlingel *m*

**rash**[1] voreilig, vorschnell, unbesonnen

**rash**[2] MED (Haut)Ausschlag *m*

**rash·er** dünne Speckscheibe

**rasp 1.** raspeln; kratzen **2.** Raspel *f*; Kratzen *n*

**rasp·ber·ry** BOT Himbeere *f*

**rat** ZO Ratte *f* (*a. contp*); F ***smell a ~*** Lunte *or* den Braten riechen

**rate 1.** Quote *f*, Rate *f*, (*Geburten-*, *Sterbe*)Ziffer *f*; (*Steuer-*, *Zins- etc*)Satz *m*; (*Wechsel*)Kurs *m*; Geschwindigkeit *f*, Tempo *n*; ***at any ~*** auf jeden Fall **2.** einschätzen, halten (***as*** für); *Lob etc* verdienen; ***be ~d as*** gelten als

**rate of ex·change** ECON (Umrechnungs-, Wechsel)Kurs *m*

**rate of in·terest** ECON Zinssatz *m*

**ra·ther** ziemlich; eher, vielmehr, besser gesagt; ***~!*** *esp Br* F und ob!; ***I would or had ~ go*** ich möchte lieber gehen

**rat·i·fy** POL ratifizieren

**rat·ing** Einschätzung *f*; *radio*, TV Einschaltquote *f*

**ra·ti·o** MATH Verhältnis *n*

**ra·tion 1.** Ration *f* **2.** *et.* rationieren; ***~ out*** zuteilen (***to*** *dat*)

**ra·tion·al** rational; vernunftbegabt; vernünftig; verstandesmäßig

**ra·tion·al·i·ty** Vernunft *f*

**ra·tion·al·ize** rational erklären; ECON rationalisieren

**rat race** F endloser Konkurrenzkampf

**rat·tle 1.** klappern; rasseln *or* klimpern (mit); prasseln (***on*** auf *acc*) (*rain etc*); rattern, knattern (*vehicle*); rütteln an (*dat*); F *j-n* verunsichern; ***~ at*** rütteln an (*dat*); ***~ off*** F *Gedicht etc* herunterrasseln; F ***~ on*** quasseln (***about*** über *acc*); F ***~ through*** *Rede etc* herunterrasseln **2.** Klappern *n* (*etc* → 1); Rassel *f*, Klapper *f*

**rat·tle·snake** ZO Klapperschlange *f*

**rau·cous** heiser, rau

**rav·age** verwüsten

**rav·ag·es** Verwüstungen *pl*, *a. fig* verheerende Auswirkungen *pl*

**rave** fantasieren, irrereden; toben; wettern (***against, at*** gegen); schwärmen (***about*** von)

**rav·el** (sich) verwickeln *or* verwirren

**ra·ven** ZO Rabe *m*

**rav·e·nous** ausgehungert, heißhungrig

**ra·vine** Schlucht *f*, Klamm *f*

**rav·ing mad** tobsüchtig

**rav·ings** irres Gerede, Delirien *pl*

**rav·ish·ing** *fig* hinreißend

**raw** GASTR roh, ECON, TECH *a.* Roh…; MED wund; METEOR nasskalt; *fig* unerfahren; ***~ vegetables and fruit*** Rohkost *f*

**raw-boned** knochig, hager

**raw·hide** Rohleder *n*

**raw ma·te·ri·al** Rohstoff *m*

**ray** Strahl *m*; *fig* Schimmer *m*

**ray·on** Kunstseide *f*

**ra·zor** Rasiermesser *n*; Rasierapparat *m*; ***electric ~*** Elektrorasierer *m*

**ra·zor blade** Rasierklinge *f*

**ra·zor('s) edge** *fig* kritische Lage; ***be on a ~*** auf des Messers Schneide stehen

**re...** wieder, noch einmal, neu

**reach 1.** *v/t* erreichen; reichen *or* gehen bis an (*acc*) *or* zu; ***~ down*** herunter-, hinunterreichen (***from*** von); ***~ out*** *Arm etc* ausstrecken; *v/i* reichen, gehen, sich erstrecken; *a.* ***~ out*** greifen, langen (***for*** nach); ***~ out*** die Hand ausstrecken **2.** Reichweite *f*; ***within*** (***out of***) ***~*** in (au-

R

ßer) Reichweite; ***within easy ~*** leicht erreichbar

**re·act** reagieren (***to*** auf *acc*; CHEM ***with*** mit); **re·ac·tion** Reaktion *f* (*a.* CHEM)

**re·ac·tor** PHYS Reaktor *m*

**read** lesen; TECH (an)zeigen; *Zähler etc* ablesen; UNIV studieren; deuten, verstehen (***as*** als); sich *gut etc* lesen (lassen); lauten; ***~*** (***s.th.***) ***to s.o.*** j-m (et.) vorlesen

**read·a·ble** lesbar; leserlich; lesenswert

**read·er** Leser(in); Lektor(in); Lesebuch *n*

**read·i·ly** bereitwillig, gern; leicht, ohne weiteres

**read·i·ness** Bereitschaft *f*

**read·ing 1.** Lesen *n*; Lesung *f* (*a.* PARL); TECH Anzeige *f*, (*Thermometer- etc -*) Stand *m*; Auslegung *f* **2.** Lese…; ***~ matter*** Lesestoff *m*

**re·ad·just** TECH nachstellen, korrigieren; ***~*** (***o.s.***) ***to*** sich wieder anpassen (*dat*) *or* an (*acc*), sich wieder einstellen auf (*acc*)

**read·y** bereit, fertig; bereitwillig; im Begriff (***to do*** zu tun); schnell, schlagfertig; ***~ for use*** gebrauchsfertig; ***get ~*** (sich) fertig machen

**read·y cash** → ***ready money***

**read·y-made** Konfektions…

**read·y meal** Fertiggericht *n*

**read·y mon·ey** Bargeld *n*

**real** echt; wirklich, tatsächlich, real; F ***for ~*** echt, im Ernst

**real es·tate** Grundbesitz *m*, Immobilien *pl*; ***~ a·gent*** Grundstücks-, Immobilienmakler *m*

**re·a·lism** Realismus *m*

**re·al·ist** Realist(in)

**re·al·is·tic** realistisch

**re·al·i·ty** Realität *f*, Wirklichkeit *f*

**re·a·li·za·tion** Erkenntnis *f*; Realisierung *f* (*a.* ECON), Verwirklichung *f*

**re·al·ize** sich klarmachen, erkennen, begreifen, einsehen; realisieren (*a.* ECON), verwirklichen

**real·ly** wirklich, tatsächlich; ***well, ~!*** ich muss schon sagen!; ***~?*** im Ernst?

**realm** Königreich *n*; *fig* Reich *n*

**real·tor** Grundstücks-, Immobilienmakler *m*

**reap** *Getreide etc* schneiden; *Feld* abernten; *fig* ernten

**re·ap·pear** wieder erscheinen

**rear 1.** *v/t Kind*, *Tier* aufziehen, großziehen; *Kopf* heben; *v/i* sich aufbäumen (*horse*) **2.** Rückseite *f*, Hinterseite *f*, MOT Heck *n*; ***in*** (***Br at***) ***the ~ of*** hinter (*dat*); ***bring up the ~*** die Nachhut bilden **3.** hinter, Hinter…, Rück…, MOT *a.* Heck…

**rear-end col·li·sion** MOT Auffahrunfall *m*

**rear·guard** MIL Nachhut *f*

**rear light** MOT Rücklicht *n*

**re·arm** MIL (wieder) aufrüsten

**re·ar·ma·ment** MIL (Wieder)Aufrüstung *f*

**rear·most** hinterste(r, -s)

**rear·view mir·ror** MOT Rückspiegel *m*

**rear·ward 1.** *adj* hintere(r, -s), rückwärtig **2.** *adv a.* ***rearwards*** rückwärts

**rear-wheel drive** MOT Hinterradantrieb *m*

**rear win·dow** MOT Heckscheibe *f*

**rea·son 1.** Grund *m*; Verstand *m*; Vernunft *f*; ***by ~ of*** wegen; ***for this ~*** aus diesem Grund; ***it stands to ~ that*** es leuchtet ein, dass **2.** *v/i* vernünftig *or* logisch denken; vernünftig reden (***with*** mit); *v/t* folgern, schließen (***that*** dass); ***~ s.o. into*** (***out of***) ***s.th.*** j-m et. einreden (ausreden); **rea·son·a·ble** vernünftig; günstig (*price*); ganz gut, nicht schlecht

**re·as·sure** beruhigen

**re·bate** ECON Rabatt *m*, (Preis)Nachlass *m*; Rückzahlung *f*

**reb·el**[1] **1.** Rebell(in); Aufständische *m*, *f* **2.** aufständisch

**re·bel**[2] rebellieren, sich auflehnen (***against*** gegen)

**re·bel·lion** Rebellion *f*, Aufstand *m*

**re·bel·lious** rebellisch, aufständisch

**re·birth** Wiedergeburt *f*

**re·bound 1.** abprallen, zurückprallen (***from*** von); *fig* zurückfallen (***on*** auf *acc*.); **2.** SPORT Abpraller *m*

**re·buff 1.** schroffe Abweisung, Abfuhr *f* **2.** schroff abweisen

**re·build** wieder aufbauen (*a. fig*)

**re·buke 1.** rügen, tadeln **2.** Rüge *f*, Tadel *m*

**re·call 1.** zurückrufen, abberufen; MOT (in die Werkstatt) zurückrufen; sich erinnern an (*acc*); erinnern an (*acc*) **2.** Zurückrufung *f*, Abberufung *f*; Rückrufaktion *f*; ***have total ~*** das absolute Ge-

R

dächtnis haben; ***beyond ~, past ~*** unwiederbringlich *or* unwiderruflich vorbei

**re·ca·pit·u·late** rekapitulieren, (kurz) zusammenfassen

**re·cap·ture** wieder einfangen (*a. fig*); *Häftling* wieder fassen; MIL zurückerobern

**re·cast** TECH umgießen; umformen, neu gestalten; THEA *etc* umbesetzen, neu besetzen

**re·cede** schwinden; ***receding chin*** fliehendes Kinn

**re·ceipt** *esp* ECON Empfang *m*, Eingang *m*; Quittung *f*; *pl* Einnahmen *pl*

**re·ceive** bekommen, erhalten; empfangen; *j-n* aufnehmen (***into*** in *acc*); *radio*, TV empfangen; **re·ceiv·er** Empfänger(in); TEL Hörer *m*; JUR Hehler(in); *a.* ***official ~*** *Br* JUR Konkursverwalter *m*

**re·cent** neuere(r, -s); jüngste(r, -s)

**re·cent·ly** kürzlich, vor kurzem

**re·cep·tion** Empfang *m*; Aufnahme *f* (***into*** in *acc*); *radio*, TV Empfang *m*; *a.* ***~ desk*** *hotel*: Rezeption *f*, Empfang *m*

**re·cep·tion·ist** Empfangsdame *f*, -chef *m*; MED Sprechstundenhilfe *f*

**re·cep·tive** aufnahmefähig; empfänglich (***to*** für)

**re·cess** Unterbrechung *f*, (Schul)Pause *f*; PARL, JUR Ferien *pl*; Nische *f*

**re·ces·sion** ECON Rezession *f*

**re·ci·pe** (Koch)Rezept *n*

**re·cip·i·ent** Empfänger(in)

**re·cip·ro·cal** wechselseitig, gegenseitig

**re·cip·ro·cate** *v/i* TECH sich hin- und herbewegen; sich revanchieren; *v/t Einladung etc* erwidern

**re·cit·al** Vortrag *m*, (*Klavier- etc*)Konzert *n*, (*Lieder*)Abend *m*; Schilderung *f*; **re·ci·ta·tion** Aufsagen *n*, Hersagen *n*; Vortrag *m*; **re·cite** aufsagen, hersagen; vortragen; aufzählen

**reck·less** rücksichtslos

**reck·on** *v/t* (aus-, be)rechnen; glauben, schätzen; ***~ up*** zusammenrechnen; *v/i*: ***~ on*** rechnen mit; ***~ with*** rechnen mit; ***~ without*** nicht rechnen mit

**reck·on·ing** (Be)Rechnung *f*; ***be out in one's ~*** sich verrechnet haben

**re·claim** zurückfordern; *Gepäck etc* abholen; *dem Meer etc Land* abgewinnen; TECH wiedergewinnen

**re·cline** sich zurücklehnen

**re·cluse** Einsiedler(in)

**rec·og·ni·tion** (Wieder)Erkennen *n*; Anerkennung *f*

**rec·og·nize** (wieder) erkennen; anerkennen; zugeben, eingestehen

**re·coil 1.** zurückschrecken (***from*** vor *dat*); **2.** Rückstoß *m*

**rec·ol·lect** sich erinnern an (*acc*)

**rec·ol·lec·tion** Erinnerung *f* (***of*** an *acc*)

**rec·om·mend** empfehlen (***as*** als; ***for*** für)

**rec·om·men·da·tion** Empfehlung *f*

**rec·om·pense 1.** entschädigen (***for*** für); **2.** Entschädigung *f*

**rec·on·cile** versöhnen, aussöhnen; in Einklang bringen (***with*** mit)

**rec·on·cil·i·a·tion** Versöhnung *f*, Aussöhnung *f* (***between*** zwischen *dat*; ***with*** mit)

**re·con·di·tion** TECH (general)überholen

**re·con·nais·sance** MIL Aufklärung *f*, Erkundung *f*

**re·con·noi·ter**, *Br* **re·con·noi·tre** MIL erkunden, auskundschaften

**re·con·sid·er** noch einmal überdenken

**re·con·struct** wieder aufbauen (*a. fig*); *Verbrechen etc* rekonstruieren

**re·con·struc·tion** Wiederaufbau *m*; Rekonstruktion *f*

**rec·ord**[1] Aufzeichnung *f*; JUR Protokoll *n*; Akte *f*; (Schall)Platte *f*; SPORT Rekord *m*; ***off the ~*** inoffiziell; ***have a criminal ~*** vorbestraft sein

**re·cord**[2] aufzeichnen, aufschreiben, schriftlich niederlegen; JUR protokollieren, zu Protokoll nehmen; *auf Schallplatte, Tonband etc* aufnehmen, *Sendung a.* aufzeichnen, mitschneiden

**re·cord·er** (*Kassetten*)Rekorder *m*; (*Tonband*)Gerät *n*; MUS Blockflöte *f*

**re·cord·ing** Aufnahme *f*, Aufzeichnung *f*, Mitschnitt *m*

**rec·ord play·er** Plattenspieler *m*

**re·count** erzählen

**re·cov·er** *v/t* wiedererlangen, wiederbekommen, wieder finden; *Kosten etc* wiedereinbringen; *Fahrzeug, Verunglückten etc* bergen; ***~ consciousness*** MED wieder zu sich kommen, das Bewusstsein wiedererlangen; *v/i* sich erholen (***from*** von); **re·cov·er·y** Wiedererlangen *n*; Wiederfinden *n*; Bergung *f*; Genesung *f*; Erholung *f*

**rec·re·a·tion** Entspannung *f*; Unterhal-

R

tung *f*, Freizeitbeschäftigung *f*
**re·cruit 1.** MIL Rekrut *m*; Neue *m*, *f*, neues Mitglied **2.** MIL rekrutieren; *Personal* einstellen; *Mitglieder* werben
**rec·tan·gle** MATH Rechteck *n*
**rec·tan·gu·lar** rechteckig
**rec·ti·fy** ELECTR gleichrichten
**rec·tor** REL Pfarrer *m*
**rec·to·ry** REL Pfarrhaus *n*
**re·cu·pe·rate** sich erholen (***from*** von) (*a. fig*)
**re·cur** wiederkehren, wieder auftreten
**re·cur·rence** Wiederkehr *f*
**re·cur·rent** wiederkehrend
**re·cy·cla·ble** TECH recycelbar, wiederverwertbar; **re·cy·cle** TECH *Abfälle* recyceln, wieder verwerten; ***~d paper*** Recyclingpapier *n*, Umwelt(schutz)papier *n*; **re·cy·cling** TECH Recycling *n*, Wiederverwertung *f*
**red 1.** rot **2.** Rot *n*; ***be in the ~*** ECON in den roten Zahlen sein
**red·breast** → ***robin***
**Red Cres·cent** Roter Halbmond
**Red Cross** Rotes Kreuz
**red·cur·rant** BOT Rote Johannisbeere
**red·den** röten, rot färben; rot werden
**red·dish** rötlich
**re·dec·o·rate** *Zimmer etc* neu streichen *or* tapezieren
**re·deem** *Pfand*, *Versprechen etc* einlösen; REL erlösen
**Re·deem·er** REL Erlöser *m*, Heiland *m*
**re·demp·tion** Einlösung *f*; REL Erlösung *f*
**re·de·vel·op** *Gebäude*, *Stadtteil* sanieren
**red-faced** verlegen, mit rotem Kopf
**red-hand·ed**: ***catch s.o. ~*** j-n auf frischer Tat ertappen
**red·head** F Rotschopf *m*, Rothaarige *f*
**red-head·ed** rothaarig
**red her·ring** *fig* falsche Fährte *or* Spur
**red-hot** rot glühend; *fig* glühend; F brandaktuell (*news etc*)
**Red In·di·an** *contp* Indianer(in)
**red-let·ter day** Freuden-, Glückstag *m*
**red·ness** Röte *f*
**re·dou·ble** verdoppeln
**red tape** Bürokratismus *m*, F Amtsschimmel *m*
**re·duce** verkleinern; *Geschwindigkeit*, *Risiko etc* verringern, *Steuern etc* senken, *Preis*, *Waren etc* herabsetzen, reduzieren (***from ... to*** von ... auf *acc*), *Gehalt etc* kürzen; verwandeln (***to*** in *acc*), machen (***to*** zu); reduzieren, zurückführen (***to*** auf *acc*); **re·duc·tion** Verkleinerung *f*; Verringerung *f*, Senkung *f*, Herabsetzung *f*, Reduzierung *f*, Kürzung *f*
**re·dun·dant** überflüssig
**reed** BOT Schilf(rohr) *n*
**re·ed·u·cate** umerziehen
**re·ed·u·ca·tion** Umerziehung *f*
**reef** (Felsen)Riff *n*
**reek 1.** Gestank *m* **2.** stinken (***of*** nach)
**reel**[1] **1.** Rolle *f*, Spule *f* **2.** ***~ off*** abrollen, abspulen; *fig* herunterrasseln
**reel**[2] sich drehen; (sch)wanken, taumeln, torkeln; ***my head ~ed*** mir drehte sich alles
**re-e·lect** wieder wählen
**re-en·ter** wieder eintreten in (*acc*), wieder betreten; **re-en·try** Wiedereintreten *n*, Wiedereintritt *m*
**ref** F SPORT Schiri *m*
**re·fer**: ***~ to*** verweisen *or* hinweisen auf (*acc*); *j-n* verweisen an (*acc*); sich beziehen auf (*acc*); anspielen auf (*acc*); erwähnen (*acc*); nachschlagen in (*dat*)
**ref·er·ee** SPORT Schiedsrichter *m*, Unparteiische *m*; *boxing*: Ringrichter *m*
**ref·er·ence** Verweis *m*, Hinweis *m* (***to*** auf *acc*); Verweisstelle *f*; Referenz *f*, Empfehlung *f*, Zeugnis *n*; Bezugnahme *f* (***to*** auf *acc*); Anspielung *f* (***to*** auf *acc*); Erwähnung *f* (***to*** *gen*); Nachschlagen *n* (***to*** in *dat*); ***list of ~s*** Quellenangabe *f*; **~ book** Nachschlagewerk *n*; **~ li·bra·ry** Handbibliothek *f*; **~ num·ber** Aktenzeichen *n*
**ref·e·ren·dum** POL Referendum *n*, Volksentscheid *m*
**re·fill 1.** wieder füllen, nachfüllen, auffüllen **2.** (*Ersatz*)Mine *f*; (*Ersatz*)Patrone *f*
**re·fine** TECH raffinieren; *fig* verfeinern, kultivieren; ***~ on*** verbessern, verfeinern
**re·fined** TECH raffiniert; *fig* kultiviert, vornehm
**re·fine·ment** TECH Raffinierung *f*; *fig* Verbess(e)rung *f*, Verfeinerung *f*; Kultiviertheit *f*, Vornehmheit *f*
**re·fin·e·ry** TECH Raffinerie *f*
**re·flect** *v/t* reflektieren, zurückwerfen, -strahlen, (wider)spiegeln; ***be ~ed in*** sich (wider)spiegeln in (*dat*) (*a. fig*);

*v/i* nachdenken (**on** über *acc*); **~ (badly) on** sich nachteilig auswirken auf (*acc*); ein schlechtes Licht werfen auf (*acc*)
**re·flec·tion** Reflexion *f*, Zurückwerfung *f*, -strahlung *f*, (Wider)Spiegelung *f* (*a. fig*); Spiegelbild *n*; Überlegung *f*; Betrachtung *f*; **on ~** nach einigem Nachdenken
**re·flec·tive** reflektierend; nachdenklich
**re·flex** Reflex *m*; **~ ac·tion** Reflexhandlung *f*; **~ cam·e·ra** PHOT Spiegelreflexkamera *f*
**re·flex·ive** LING reflexiv, rückbezüglich
**re·form 1.** reformieren, verbessern; sich bessern **2.** Reform *f* (*a.* POL), Besserung *f*; **ref·or·ma·tion** Reformierung *f*; Besserung *f*; ***the Reformation*** REL die Reformation; **re·form·er** *esp* POL Reformer *m*; REL Reformator *m*
**re·fract** *Strahlen etc* brechen
**re·frac·tion** (*Strahlen- etc*)Brechung *f*
**re·frain**[1]: **~ *from*** sich enthalten (*gen*), unterlassen (*acc*)
**re·frain**[2] Kehrreim *m*, Refrain *m*
**re·fresh** (***o.s.*** sich) erfrischen, stärken; *Gedächtnis* auffrischen
**re·fresh·ing** erfrischend (*a. fig*)
**re·fresh·ment** Erfrischung *f*
**re·fri·ge·rate** TECH kühlen
**re·fri·ge·ra·tor** Kühlschrank *m*
**re·fu·el** auftanken
**ref·uge** Zuflucht *f*, Zufluchtsstätte *f*; *Br* Verkehrsinsel *f*
**ref·u·gee** Flüchtling *m*
**ref·u·gee camp** Flüchtlingslager *n*
**re·fund 1.** Rückzahlung *f*, Rückerstattung *f* **2.** *Geld* zurückzahlen, zurückerstatten; *Auslagen* ersetzen
**re·fur·bish** aufpolieren (*a. fig*); renovieren
**re·fus·al** Ablehnung *f*; Weigerung *f*; Verweigerung *f*
**re·fuse**[1] *v/t* ablehnen; verweigern; sich weigern, es ablehnen (***to do*** zu tun); *v/i* ablehnen; sich weigern
**ref·use**[2] Abfall *m*, Abfälle *pl*, Müll *m*
**ref·use dump** Müllabladeplatz *m*
**re·fute** widerlegen
**re·gain** wieder-, zurückgewinnen
**re·gale**: **~ *s.o. with s.th.*** j-n mit et. erfreuen *or* ergötzen
**re·gard 1.** Achtung *f*; Rücksicht *f*; *pl* Grüße *pl*; ***in this ~*** in dieser Hinsicht; ***with ~ to*** im Hinblick auf (*acc*); hinsichtlich (*gen*); ***with kind ~s*** mit freundlichen Grüßen **2.** betrachten (*a. fig*), ansehen; **~ *as*** betrachten als, halten für; ***as ~s ...*** was ... betrifft
**re·gard·ing** bezüglich, hinsichtlich (*gen*)
**re·gard·less**: **~ *of*** ohne Rücksicht auf (*acc*), ungeachtet (*gen*)
**regd** *abbr of* ***registered*** ECON eingetragen; *post* eingeschrieben
**re·gen·e·rate** (sich) erneuern *or* regenerieren
**re·gent** Regent(in)
**re·gi·ment 1.** MIL Regiment *n*, *fig a.* Schar *f* **2.** reglementieren, bevormunden
**re·gion** Gegend *f*, Gebiet *n*, Region *f*
**re·gion·al** regional, örtlich, Orts...
**re·gis·ter 1.** Register *n*, Verzeichnis *n*, (*Wähler- etc*)Liste *f* **2.** *v/t* registrieren, eintragen (lassen); *Messwerte* anzeigen; *Brief etc* einschreiben lassen; *v/i* sich eintragen (lassen)
**re·gis·tered let·ter** Einschreib(e)brief *m*, Einschreiben *n*
**re·gis·tra·tion** Registrierung *f*, Eintragung *f*; MOT Zulassung *f*; **~ fee** Anmeldegebühr *f*; **~ num·ber** MOT (polizeiliches) Kennzeichen
**re·gis·try** Registratur *f*
**re·gis·try of·fice** *esp Br* Standesamt *n*
**re·gret 1.** bedauern; bereuen **2.** Bedauern *n*; Reue *f*; **re·gret·ful** bedauernd; **re·gret·ta·ble** bedauerlich
**reg·u·lar 1.** regelmäßig; geregelt, geordnet; richtig; normal; MIL Berufs...; **~ *gas*** (*Br* ***petrol***) MOT Normalbenzin *n* **2.** F Stammkunde *m*, Stammkundin *f*; Stammgast *m*; SPORT Stammspieler(in); MIL Berufssoldat *m*; MOT Normal(-benzin) *n*
**reg·u·lar·i·ty** Regelmäßigkeit *f*
**reg·u·late** regeln, regulieren; TECH einstellen, regulieren
**reg·u·la·tion** Reg(e)lung *f*, Regulierung *f*; TECH Einstellung *f*; Vorschrift *f*
**reg·u·la·tor** TECH Regler *m*
**re·hears·al** MUS, THEA Probe *f*
**re·hearse** MUS, THEA proben
**reign 1.** Regierung *f*, *a. fig* Herrschaft *f* **2.** herrschen, regieren
**re·im·burse** *Auslagen* erstatten, vergüten
**rein 1.** Zügel *m* **2. ~ *in*** *Pferd etc* zügeln; *fig* bremsen

**rein·deer** zo Ren *n*, Rentier *n*
**re·in·force** verstärken
**re·in·force·ment** Verstärkung *f*
**re·in·state** *j-n* wieder einstellen (***as*** als; ***in*** in *dat*)
**re·in·sure** rückversichern
**re·it·e·rate** (ständig) wiederholen
**re·ject** *j-n*, *et.* ablehnen, *Bitte* abschlagen, *Plan etc* verwerfen; *j-n* ab-, zurückweisen; MED *Organ etc* abstoßen
**re·jec·tion** Ablehnung *f*; Verwerfung *f*; Zurückweisung *f*; MED Abstoßung *f*
**re·joice** sich freuen, jubeln (***at, over*** über *acc*); **re·joic·ing(s)** Jubel *m*
**re·join**[1] wieder zusammenfügen; wieder zurückkehren zu
**re·join**[2] erwidern
**re·ju·ve·nate** verjüngen
**re·kin·dle** *Feuer* wieder anzünden; *fig* wieder entfachen
**re·lapse 1.** zurückfallen, wieder verfallen (***into*** in *acc*); rückfällig werden; MED e-n Rückfall bekommen **2.** Rückfall *m*
**re·late** *v/t* erzählen, berichten; in Verbindung *or* Zusammenhang bringen (***to*** mit); *v/i* sich beziehen (***to*** auf *acc*); zusammenhängen (***to*** mit)
**re·lat·ed** verwandt (***to*** mit)
**re·la·tion** Verwandte *m*, *f*; Beziehung *f* (***between*** zwischen *dat*; ***to*** zu); *pl diplomatische*, *geschäftliche* Beziehungen *pl*; ***in*** *or* ***with ~ to*** in Bezug auf (*acc*)
**re·la·tion·ship** Verwandtschaft *f*; Beziehung *f*, Verhältnis *n*
**rel·a·tive**[1] Verwandte *m*, *f*
**rel·a·tive**[2] relativ, verhältnismäßig; bezüglich (***to*** *gen*); LING Relativ…, bezüglich
**rel·a·tive pro·noun** LING Relativpronomen *n*, bezügliches Fürwort
**re·lax** *v/t Muskeln etc* entspannen; *Griff etc* lockern; *fig* nachlassen in (*dat*); *v/i* sich entspannen, *fig a.* ausspannen; sich lockern
**re·lax·a·tion** Entspannung *f*; Erholung *f*; Lockerung *f*
**re·laxed** entspannt, zwanglos
**re·lay**[1] **1.** Ablösung *f*; SPORT Staffel *f*; *radio*, TV Übertragung *f*; ELECTR Relais *n* **2.** *radio*, TV übertragen
**re·lay**[2] *Kabel*, *Teppich* neu verlegen
**re·lay race** SPORT Staffel *f*
**re·lease 1.** entlassen, freilassen; loslassen; freigeben, herausbringen, veröffentlichen; MOT *Handbremse* lösen; *fig* befreien, erlösen **2.** Entlassung *f*, Freilassung *f*; Befreiung *f*; Freigabe *f*; Veröffentlichung *f*; TECH, PHOT Auslöser *m*; *film*: *often* ***first ~*** Uraufführung *f*
**rel·e·gate** verbannen; ***be ~d*** SPORT absteigen (***to*** in *acc*)
**re·lent** nachgeben; nachlassen
**re·lent·less** unbarmherzig; anhaltend
**rel·e·vant** relevant, erheblich, wichtig; sachdienlich, zutreffend
**re·li·a·bil·i·ty** Zuverlässigkeit *f*
**re·li·a·ble** zuverlässig
**re·li·ance** Vertrauen *n*; Abhängigkeit *f* (***on*** von)
**rel·ic** Relikt *n*, Überrest *m*; REL Reliquie *f*
**re·lief** Erleichterung *f*; Unterstützung *f*, Hilfe *f*; Sozialhilfe *f*; Ablösung *f*; Relief *n*; **~ map** GEOGR Reliefkarte *f*
**re·lieve** *Schmerz*, *Not* lindern, *j-n*, *Gewissen* erleichtern; *j-n* ablösen
**re·li·gion** Religion *f*
**re·li·gious** Religions…; religiös; gewissenhaft
**rel·ish 1.** *fig* Gefallen *m*, Geschmack *m* (***for*** an *dat*); GASTR Würze *f*; Soße *f*; ***with ~*** mit Genuss **2.** genießen, sich *et.* schmecken lassen; Geschmack *or* Gefallen finden an (*dat*)
**re·luc·tance** Widerstreben *n*; ***with ~*** widerwillig, ungern
**re·luc·tant** widerstrebend, widerwillig
**re·ly**: ***~ on*** sich verlassen auf (*acc*)
**re·main 1.** (ver)bleiben; übrig bleiben **2.** *pl* (Über)Reste *pl*
**re·main·der** Rest *m*; Restbetrag *m*
**re·make 1.** wieder *or* neu machen **2.** Remake *n*, Neuverfilmung *f*
**re·mand** JUR **1.** ***be ~ed in custody*** in Untersuchungshaft bleiben **2.** ***be on ~*** in Untersuchungshaft sein; ***prisoner on ~*** Untersuchungsgefangene *m*, *f*
**re·mark 1.** *v/t* bemerken, äußern; *v/i* sich äußern (***on*** über *acc*, zu); **2.** Bemerkung *f*
**re·mark·a·ble** bemerkenswert; außergewöhnlich
**rem·e·dy 1.** (Heil-, Hilfs-, Gegen)Mittel *n*; (Ab)Hilfe *f* **2.** *Schaden etc* beheben; *Missstand* abstellen; *Situation* bereinigen

**re·mem·ber** sich erinnern an (*acc*); denken an (*acc*); ***please ~ me to her*** grüße sie bitte von mir
**re·mem·brance** Erinnerung *f*; ***in ~ of*** zur Erinnerung an (*acc*)
**re·mind** erinnern (***of*** an *acc*)
**re·mind·er** Mahnung *f*
**rem·i·nis·cences** Erinnerungen *pl* (***of*** an *acc*); **rem·i·nis·cent**: ***be ~ of*** erinnern an (*acc*)
**re·mit** *Schulden, Strafe* erlassen; *Sünden* vergeben; *Geld* überweisen (***to*** *dat or* an *acc*); **re·mit·tance** ECON Überweisung *f* (***to*** an *acc*)
**rem·nant** (Über)Rest *m*
**re·mod·el** umformen, umgestalten
**re·morse** Gewissensbisse *pl*, Reue *f* (***über*** *acc* for)
**re·morse·ful** zerknirscht, reumütig
**re·morse·less** unbarmherzig
**re·mote** fern, entfernt; abgelegen, entlegen; **~ con·trol** TECH Fernlenkung *f*, Fernsteuerung *f*; Fernbedienung *f*
**re·mov·al** Entfernung *f*; Umzug *m*
**re·mov·al van** Möbelwagen *m*
**re·move** *v/t* entfernen (***from*** von); *Hut, Deckel etc* abnehmen; *Kleidung* ablegen; beseitigen, aus dem Weg räumen; *v/i* (um)ziehen (***from*** von; ***to*** nach)
**re·mov·er** (*Flecken- etc*)Entferner *m*
**Re·nais·sance** *die* Renaissance
**ren·der** *berühmt, schwierig, möglich etc* machen; *Dienst* erweisen; *Gedicht, Musikstück* vortragen; übersetzen, übertragen (***into*** in *acc*); *mst* ***~ down*** *Fett* auslassen
**ren·der·ing** *esp Br* → ***rendition***
**ren·di·tion** MUS *etc* Vortrag *m*; Übersetzung *f*, Übertragung *f*
**re·new** erneuern; *Gespräch etc* wieder aufnehmen; *Kraft etc* wiedererlangen; *Vertrag, Pass* verlängern (lassen)
**re·new·al** Erneuerung *f*; Verlängerung *f*
**re·nounce** verzichten auf (*acc*); *s-m Glauben etc* abschwören
**ren·o·vate** renovieren
**re·nown** Ruhm *m*; **re·nowned** berühmt (***as*** als; ***for*** wegen, für)
**rent**[1] **1.** Miete *f*; Pacht *f*; Leihgebühr *f*; ***for ~*** zu vermieten, zu verleihen **2.** mieten, pachten (***from*** von); *a.* ***~ out*** vermieten, verpachten (***to*** an *acc*); ***~ed car*** Miet-, Leihwagen *m*
**rent**[2] Riss *m*
**rent·al** Miete *f*; Pacht *f*; Leihgebühr *f*; ***~ car*** Miet-, Leihwagen *m*
**re·nun·ci·a·tion** Verzicht *m* (***of*** auf *acc*); Abschwören *n*
**re·pair 1.** reparieren, ausbessern; *fig* wieder gutmachen **2.** Reparatur *f*; Ausbesserung *f*; *pl* Instandsetzungsarbeiten *pl*; ***beyond ~*** nicht mehr zu reparieren; ***in good*** (***bad***) ***~*** in gutem (schlechtem) Zustand; ***be under ~*** in Reparatur sein; ***the road is under ~*** an der Straße wird gerade gearbeitet
**rep·a·ra·tion** Wiedergutmachung *f*; Entschädigung *f*; *pl* POL Reparationen *pl*
**rep·ar·tee** Schlagfertigkeit *f*; schlagfertige Antwort(en *pl*) *f*
**re·pay** *et.* zurückzahlen; *Besuch* erwidern; *et.* vergelten; *j-n* entschädigen
**re·pay·ment** Rückzahlung *f*
**re·peal** *Gesetz etc* aufheben
**re·peat 1.** *v/t* wiederholen; nachsprechen; ***~ o.s.*** sich wiederholen; *v/i* F aufstoßen (***on s.o.*** j-m) (*food*) **2.** *radio*, TV Wiederholung *f*; **re·peat·ed** wiederholt; **re·peat·ed·ly** verschiedentlich
**re·pel** *Angriff, Feind* zurückschlagen; *Wasser etc, fig j-n* abstoßen
**re·pel·lent** abstoßend
**re·pent** bereuen
**re·pent·ance** Reue *f* (***for*** über *acc*)
**re·pen·tant** reuig, reumütig
**re·per·cus·sion** *mst pl* Auswirkungen *pl* (***on*** auf *acc*)
**rep·er·toire** THEA *etc* Repertoire *n*
**rep·er·to·ry the·a·ter** (*Br* **the·a·tre**) Repertoiretheater *n*
**rep·e·ti·tion** Wiederholung *f*
**re·place** an *j-s* Stelle treten, *j-n, et.* ersetzen; TECH austauschen, ersetzen
**re·place·ment** TECH Austausch *m*; Ersatz *m*
**re·plant** umpflanzen
**re·play 1.** SPORT *Spiel* wiederholen; *Tonband-, Videoaufname etc* abspielen **2.** SPORT Wiederholung *f*
**re·plen·ish** (wieder) auffüllen
**re·plete** satt; angefüllt, ausgestattet (***with*** mit)
**rep·li·ca** *art*: Originalkopie *f*; Kopie *f*, Nachbildung *f*
**re·ply 1.** antworten, erwidern (***to*** auf *acc*); **2.** Antwort *f*, Erwiderung *f* (***to*** auf *acc*); ***in ~ to*** (als Antwort) auf (*acc*)

**re·ply cou·pon** Rückantwortschein *m*
**re·ply-paid en·ve·lope** Freiumschlag *m*
**re·port 1.** Bericht *m*; Meldung *f*, Nachricht *f*; Gerücht *n*; Knall *m*; ~ **card** PED Zeugnis *n* **2.** berichten (über *acc*); (sich) melden; anzeigen; ***it is ~ed that*** es heißt, dass; ***~ed speech*** LING indirekte Rede; **re·port·er** Reporter(in), Berichterstatter(in)
**re·pose** Ruhe *f*; Gelassenheit *f*
**re·pos·i·to·ry** (Waren)Lager *n*; *fig* Fundgrube *f*, Quelle *f*
**rep·re·sent** *j-n*, *Wahlbezirk* vertreten; darstellen; hinstellen (***as, to be*** als)
**rep·re·sen·ta·tion** Vertretung *f*; Darstellung *f*
**rep·re·sen·ta·tive 1.** repräsentativ (*a.* POL), typisch (***of*** für); **2.** (Stell)Vertreter(in); ECON (Handels)Vertreter(in); PARL Abgeordnete *m*, *f*; ***House of Representatives*** Repräsentantenhaus *n*
**re·press** unterdrücken; PSYCH verdrängen; **re·pres·sion** Unterdrückung *f*; PSYCH Verdrängung *f*
**re·prieve** JUR **1.** ***he was ~d*** er wurde begnadigt; s-e Urteilsvollstreckung wurde ausgesetzt **2.** Begnadigung *f*; Vollstreckungsaufschub *m*
**rep·ri·mand 1.** rügen, tadeln (***for*** wegen); **2.** Rüge *f*, Tadel *m*, Verweis *m*
**re·print 1.** neu auflegen *or* drucken, nachdrucken **2.** Neuauflage *f*, Nachdruck *m*
**re·pri·sal** Repressalie *f*, Vergeltungsmaßnahme *f*
**re·proach 1.** Vorwurf *m* **2.** vorwerfen (***s.o. with s.th.*** j-m et.); Vorwürfe machen; **re·proach·ful** vorwurfsvoll
**rep·ro·bate** verkommenes Subjekt
**re·pro·cess** NUCL wieder aufbereiten
**re·pro·cess·ing** TECH Wiederaufbereitung *f*; ~ **plant** TECH Wiederaufbereitungsanlage *f*
**re·pro·duce** *v/t* *Ton etc* wiedergeben; *Bild etc* reproduzieren; ***~ o.s.*** → *v/i* BIOL sich fortpflanzen, sich vermehren
**re·pro·duc·tion** BIOL Fortpflanzung *f*; Reproduktion *f*; Wiedergabe *f*; PED Nacherzählung *f*
**re·pro·duc·tive** BIOL Fortpflanzungs…
**re·proof** Rüge *f*, Tadel *m*
**re·prove** rügen, tadeln (***for*** wegen)
**rep·tile** ZO Reptil *n*
**re·pub·lic** Republik *f*
**re·pub·li·can 1.** republikanisch **2.** Republikaner(in)
**re·pug·nant** widerlich, abstoßend
**re·pulse 1.** *j-n*, *Angebot etc* zurückweisen; MIL *Angriff* zurückschlagen **2.** MIL Zurückschlagen *n*; Zurückweisung *f*
**re·pul·sion** Abscheu *m*, Widerwille *m*; PHYS Abstoßung *f*
**re·pul·sive** abstoßend, widerlich, widerwärtig; PHYS abstoßend
**rep·u·ta·ble** angesehen
**rep·u·ta·tion** (guter) Ruf, Ansehen *n*
**re·pute** (guter) Ruf
**re·put·ed** angeblich
**re·quest 1.** (***for***) Bitte *f* (um), Wunsch *m* (nach); ***at the ~ of s.o., at s.o.'s ~*** auf j-s Bitte hin; ***on ~*** auf Wunsch **2.** um *et.* bitten *or* ersuchen; *j-n* bitten, ersuchen (***to do*** zu tun)
**re·quest stop** *Br* Bedarfshaltestelle *f*
**re·quire** erfordern; benötigen, brauchen; verlangen; ***if ~d*** wenn nötig
**re·quire·ment** Erfordernis *n*, Bedürfnis *n*; Anforderung *f*
**req·ui·site 1.** erforderlich **2.** *mst pl* Artikel *pl*
**req·ui·si·tion 1.** Anforderung *f*; MIL Requisition *f*, Beschlagnahme *f*; ***make a ~ for*** *et.* anfordern **2.** anfordern; MIL requirieren, beschlagnahmen
**re·sale** Wieder-, Weiterverkauf *m*
**re·scind** JUR *Gesetz*, *Urteil etc* aufheben
**res·cue 1.** retten (***from*** aus, vor *dat*); **2.** Rettung *f*; Hilfe *f* **3.** Rettungs…
**re·search 1.** Forschung *f* **2.** forschen; *et.* erforschen
**re·search·er** Forscher(in)
**re·sem·blance** Ähnlichkeit *f* (***to*** mit; ***between*** zwischen *dat*)
**re·sem·ble** ähnlich sein, ähneln (*both*: *dat*)
**re·sent** übel nehmen, sich ärgern über (*acc*); **re·sent·ful** ärgerlich (***of, at*** über *acc*); **re·sent·ment** Ärger *m* (***against, at*** über *acc*)
**res·er·va·tion** Reservierung *f*, Vorbestellung *f*; Vorbehalt *m*; (*Indianer*)Reservat(ion *f*) *n*; (*Wild*)Reservat *n*
**re·serve 1.** (sich) *et.* aufsparen (***for*** für); sich vorbehalten; reservieren (lassen), vorbestellen **2.** Reserve *f* (*a.* MIL); Vorrat *m*; (*Naturschutz-*, *Wild*)Reservat *n*; SPORT Reservespieler(in); Reserviert-

heit *f*, Zurückhaltung *f*
**re·served** zurückhaltend, reserviert
**res·er·voir** Reservoir *n* (*a. fig* ***of*** an *dat*)
**re·set** *Uhr* umstellen; *Zeiger etc* zurückstellen (***to*** auf *acc*)
**re·set·tle** umsiedeln
**re·side** wohnen, ansässig sein, s-n Wohnsitz haben
**res·i·dence** Wohnsitz *m*, Wohnort *m*; Aufenthalt *m*; Residenz *f*; ***official ~*** Amtssitz *m*; **~ per·mit** Aufenthaltsgenehmigung *f*, -erlaubnis *f*
**res·i·dent 1.** wohnhaft, ansässig **2.** Bewohner(in), *in a town etc a.* Einwohner(in); (Hotel)Gast *m*; MOT Anlieger(in)
**res·i·den·tial** Wohn...; **~ ar·e·a** Wohngebiet *n*, Wohngegend *f*
**re·sid·u·al** übrig (geblieben), restlich, Rest...; **~ pol·lu·tion** Altlasten *pl*
**res·i·due** Rest *m*, CHEM *A.* Rückstand *m*
**re·sign** *v/i* zurücktreten (***from*** von); *v/t* *Amt etc* niederlegen; aufgeben; verzichten auf (*acc*); ***~ o.s. to*** sich fügen in (*acc*), sich abfinden mit
**res·ig·na·tion** Rücktritt *m*; Resignation *f*
**re·signed** ergeben, resigniert
**re·sil·i·ence** Elastizität *f*; *fig* Zähigkeit *f*;
**re·sil·i·ent** elastisch; *fig* zäh
**res·in** Harz *n*
**re·sist** widerstehen (*dat*); Widerstand leisten, sich widersetzen (*both*: *dat*)
**re·sist·ance** Widerstand *m* (*a.* ELECTR); MED Widerstandskraft *f*; (*Hitze- etc* -)Beständigkeit *f*, (*Stoß- etc*)Festigkeit *f*
**re·sist·ant** widerstandsfähig; (*hitze- etc*)beständig, (*stoß- etc*)fest
**res·o·lute** resolut, entschlossen
**res·o·lu·tion** Beschluss *m*, PARL *etc a.* Resolution *f*; Vorsatz *m*; Entschlossenheit *f*; Lösung *f*
**re·solve 1.** beschließen; *Problem etc* lösen; (sich) auflösen; ***~ on*** sich entschließen zu **2.** Vorsatz *m*; Entschlossenheit *f*
**res·o·nance** Resonanz *f*; voller Klang
**res·o·nant** voll(tönend); widerhallend
**re·sort 1.** Erholungsort *m*, Urlaubsort *m*; ***have ~ to*** → **2.** ***~ to*** Zuflucht nehmen zu
**re·sound** widerhallen (***with*** von)
**re·source** Mittel *n*, Zuflucht *f*; Ausweg *m*; Einfallsreichtum *m*; *pl* Mittel *pl*; (*natürliche*) Reichtümer *pl*, (*Boden-, Natur*)Schätze *pl*
**re·source·ful** einfallsreich, findig
**re·spect 1.** Achtung *f*, Respekt *m* (*both*: ***for*** vor *dat*); Rücksicht *f* (***for*** auf *acc*); Beziehung *f*, Hinsicht *f*; ***with ~ to ...*** was ... anbelangt *or* betrifft; ***in this ~*** in dieser Hinsicht; ***give my ~s to ...*** e-e Empfehlung an ... (*acc*) **2.** *v/t* respektieren, *a.* achten, *a.* berücksichtigen, beachten
**re·spect·a·ble** ehrbar, anständig, geachtet; F ansehnlich, beachtlich
**re·spect·ful** respektvoll, ehrerbietig
**re·spec·tive** jeweilig; ***we went to our ~ places*** jeder ging zu seinem Platz
**re·spec·tive·ly** beziehungsweise
**res·pi·ra·tion** Atmung *f*
**res·pi·ra·tor** Atemschutzgerät *n*
**re·spite** Pause *f*; Aufschub *m*, Frist *f*; ***without ~*** ohne Unterbrechung
**re·splen·dent** glänzend, strahlend
**re·spond** antworten, erwidern (***to*** auf *acc*; ***that*** dass); reagieren, MED *a.* ansprechen (***to*** auf *acc*)
**re·sponse** Antwort *f*, Erwiderung *f* (***to*** auf *acc*); *fig* Reaktion *f* (***to*** auf *acc*)
**re·spon·si·bil·i·ty** Verantwortung *f*; ***on one's own ~*** auf eigene Verantwortung; ***sense of ~*** Verantwortungsgefühl *n*; ***take (full) ~ for*** die (volle) Verantwortung übernehmen für
**re·spon·si·ble** verantwortlich; verantwortungsbewusst; verantwortungsvoll
**rest**[1] **1.** Ruhe(pause) *f*; Erholung *f*; TECH Stütze *f*; (*Telefon*)Gabel *f*; ***have or take a ~*** sich ausruhen; ***set s.o.'s mind at ~*** j-n beruhigen **2.** *v/i* ruhen; sich ausruhen; lehnen (***against, on*** an *dat*); ***let s.th. ~*** et. auf sich beruhen lassen; ***~ on*** ruhen auf (*dat*) (*a. fig*); *fig* beruhen auf (*dat*); *v/t* (aus)ruhen (lassen); lehnen (***against*** gegen; ***on*** an *acc*)
**rest**[2] Rest *m*; ***all the ~ of them*** alle Übrigen; ***for the ~*** im Übrigen
**rest ar·e·a** MOT Rastplatz *m*
**res·tau·rant** Restaurant *n*, Gaststätte *f*
**rest·ful** ruhig, erholsam
**rest home** Altenpflegeheim *n*; Erholungsheim *n*
**res·ti·tu·tion** ECON Rückgabe *f*, Rückerstattung *f*
**res·tive** unruhig, nervös
**rest·less** ruhelos, rastlos; unruhig

R

**res·to·ra·tion** Wiederherstellung *f*; Restaurierung *f*; Rückgabe *f*, Rückerstattung *f*; **re·store** wiederherstellen; restaurieren; zurückgeben, -erstatten; ***be ~d* (*to health*)** wieder gesund sein

**re·strain (*from*)** zurückhalten (von), hindern an (*dat*); ***I had to ~ myself*** ich musste mich beherrschen (***from doing s.th.*** um nicht et. zu tun)

**re·strained** beherrscht; dezent (*color*)

**re·straint** Beherrschung *f*, Zurückhaltung *f*; ECON Be-, Einschränkung *f*

**re·strict** ECON beschränken (***to*** auf *acc*), einschränken

**re·stric·tion** ECON Be-, Einschränkung *f*; ***without ~s*** uneingeschränkt

**rest room** Toilette *f*

**re·struc·ture** umstrukturieren

**re·sult 1.** Ergebnis *n*, Resultat *n*; Folge *f*; ***as a ~ of*** als Folge von (*or gen*); ***without ~*** ergebnislos **2.** folgen, sich ergeben (***from*** aus); ***~ in*** zur Folge haben (*acc*), führen zu

**re·sume** wieder aufnehmen; fortsetzen; *Platz* wieder einnehmen

**re·sump·tion** Wiederaufnahme *f*; Fortsetzung *f*

**Res·ur·rec·tion** REL Auferstehung *f*

**re·sus·ci·tate** MED wieder beleben

**re·sus·ci·ta·tion** MED Wiederbelebung *f*

**re·tail** ECON **1.** Einzelhandel *m*; ***by ~*** im Einzelhandel **2.** Einzelhandels… **3.** *adv* im Einzelhandel **4.** *v/t* im Einzelhandel verkaufen (***at, for*** für); *v/i* im Einzelhandel verkauft werden (***at, for*** für); **re·tail·er** ECON Einzelhändler(in)

**re·tain** (be)halten, bewahren; *Wasser, Wärme* speichern

**re·tal·i·ate** Vergeltung üben, sich revanchieren; **re·tal·i·a·tion** Vergeltung *f*, Vergeltungsmaßnahmen *pl*

**re·tard** verzögern, aufhalten, hemmen; **(*mentally*) *~ed*** (geistig) zurückgeblieben

**retch** würgen

**re·tell** nacherzählen

**re·think** *et.* noch einmal überdenken

**re·ti·cent** schweigsam, zurückhaltend

**ret·i·nue** Gefolge *n*

**re·tire** *v/i* in Rente *or* Pension gehen, sich pensionieren lassen; sich zurückziehen; ***~ from business*** sich zur Ruhe setzen; *v/t* in den Ruhestand versetzen, pensionieren; **re·tired** pensioniert, im Ruhestand (lebend); ***be ~*** *a.* in Rente *or* Pension sein; **re·tire·ment** Pensionierung *f*, Ruhestand *m*

**re·tir·ing** zurückhaltend

**re·tort 1.** (scharf) entgegnen *or* erwidern **2.** (scharfe) Entgegnung *or* Erwiderung

**re·touch** PHOT retuschieren

**re·trace** *Tathergang etc* rekonstruieren; ***~ one's steps*** denselben Weg zurückgehen

**re·tract** *v/t Angebot* zurückziehen; *Behauptung* zurücknehmen; *Geständnis* widerrufen; TECH, ZO einziehen; *v/i* TECH, ZO eingezogen werden

**re·train** umschulen

**re·tread** MOT **1.** *Reifen* runderneuern **2.** runderneuerter Reifen

**re·treat 1.** MIL Rückzug *m*; Zufluchtsort *m* **2.** sich zurückziehen; zurückweichen (***from*** vor *dat*)

**ret·ri·bu·tion** Vergeltung *f*

**re·trieve** zurückholen, wiederbekommen; *Fehler, Verlust etc* wieder gutmachen; HUNT apportieren

**ret·ro·ac·tive** JUR rückwirkend

**ret·ro·grade** rückschrittlich

**ret·ro·spect**: ***in ~*** im Rückblick

**ret·ro·spec·tive** rückblickend; JUR rückwirkend

**re·try** JUR *Fall* erneut verhandeln; neu verhandeln gegen *j-n*

**re·turn 1.** *v/i* zurückkehren, zurückkommen; zurückgehen; ***~ to*** auf *ein Thema etc* zurückkommen; in *e-e Gewohnheit etc* zurückfallen; in *e-n Zustand etc* zurückkehren; *v/t* zurückgeben (***to*** *dat*); zurückbringen (***to*** *dat*); zurückschicken, -senden (***to*** *dat or* an *acc*); zurücklegen, -stellen; erwidern; *Gewinn etc* abwerfen; → ***verdict*** **2.** Rückkehr *f*; *fig* Wiederauftreten *n*; Rückgabe *f*; Zurückbringen *n*; Zurückschicken *n*, -senden *n*; Zurücklegen *n*, -stellen *n*; Erwiderung *f*; (*Steuer*)Erklärung *f*; *tennis etc*: Return *m*, Rückschlag *m*; ECON *a. pl* Gewinn *m*; *Br* → ***return ticket***; *Br* ***many happy ~s* (*of the day*)** herzlichen Glückwunsch zum Geburtstag; ***by ~* (*of post*)** umgehend, postwendend; ***in ~ for*** (als Gegenleistung) für **3.** *adj* Rück…

**re·turn·a·ble** *in cpds* Mehrweg…; ***~ bot-***

R

***tle*** Pfandflasche *f*
**return| game, ~ match** SPORT Rückspiel *n*; **re·turn key** IT Eingabetaste *f*; **~ tick·et** *Br* RAIL Rückfahrkarte *f*; AVIAT Rückflugticket *n*
**re·u·ni·fi·ca·tion** POL Wiedervereinigung *f*
**re·u·nion** Treffen *n*, Wiedersehensfeier *f*; Wiedervereinigung *f*
**re·us·a·ble** wieder verwendbar
**rev** F MOT **1.** Umdrehung *f*; ***~ counter*** Drehzahlmesser *m* **2.** *a.* ***~ up*** aufheulen (lassen)
**re·val·ue** ECON *Währung* aufwerten
**re·veal** den Blick freigeben auf (*acc*), zeigen; *Geheimnis etc* enthüllen, aufdecken; **re·veal·ing** aufschlussreich (*remark etc*); offenherzig (*dress etc*)
**rev·el**: ***~ in*** schwelgen in (*dat*); sich weiden an (*dat*)
**rev·e·la·tion** Enthüllung *f*; REL Offenbarung *f*
**re·venge 1.** Rache *f*; *esp* SPORT Revanche *f*; ***in ~ for*** aus Rache für; ***take ~ on s.o. for s.th.*** sich an j-m für et. rächen **2.** rächen; **re·venge·ful** rachsüchtig
**rev·e·nue** Staatseinkünfte *pl*, Staatseinnahmen *pl*
**re·ver·be·rate** nach-, widerhallen
**re·vere** (ver)ehren; **rev·e·rence** Verehrung *f*; Ehrfurcht *f* (***for*** vor *dat*)
**Rev·e·rend** REL Hochwürden *m*
**rev·e·rent** ehrfürchtig, ehrfurchtsvoll
**rev·er·ie** (Tag)Träumerei *f*
**re·vers·al** Umkehrung *f*; Rückschlag *m*
**re·verse 1.** *adj* umgekehrt; ***in ~ order*** in umgekehrter Reihenfolge **2.** *Wagen* im Rückwärtsgang fahren *or* rückwärtsfahren; *Reihenfolge etc* umkehren; *Urteil etc* aufheben; *Entscheidung etc* umstoßen **3.** Gegenteil *n*; MOT Rückwärtsgang *m*; Rückseite *f*, Kehrseite *f* (*of a coin*); Rückschlag *m*; **~ gear** MOT Rückwärtsgang *m*; **~ side** linke (*Stoff*)Seite
**re·vers·i·ble** doppelseitig (tragbar)
**re·vert**: ***~ to*** in *e-n Zustand* zurückkehren; in *e-e Gewohnheit etc* zurückfallen; auf *ein Thema* zurückkommen
**re·view 1.** Überprüfung *f*; Besprechung *f*, Kritik *f*, Rezension *f*; MIL Parade *f*; PED (Stoff)Wiederholung *f* (***for*** für *e-e Prüfung*); **2.** überprüfen; besprechen, rezensieren; MIL besichtigen, inspizieren; PED *Stoff* wiederholen (***for*** für *e-e Prüfung*)
**re·view·er** Kritiker(in), Rezensent(in)
**re·vise** revidieren, *Ansicht* ändern, *Buch etc* überarbeiten; *Br* PED *Stoff* wiederholen (***for*** für *e-e Prüfung*)
**re·vi·sion** Revision *f*, Überarbeitung *f*; überarbeitete Ausgabe; *Br* PED (Stoff-) Wiederholung *f* (***for*** für *e-e Prüfung*)
**re·viv·al** Wiederbelebung *f*; Wiederaufleben *n*
**re·vive** wieder beleben; wieder aufleben (lassen); *Erinnerungen* wachrufen; MED wieder zu sich kommen; sich erholen
**re·voke** widerrufen, zurücknehmen, rückgängig machen
**re·volt 1.** *v/i* sich auflehnen, revoltieren (***against*** gegen); Abscheu empfinden, empört sein (***against, at, from*** über *acc*); *v/t* mit Abscheu erfüllen, abstoßen **2.** Revolte *f*, Aufstand *m*
**re·volt·ing** abscheulich, abstoßend
**rev·o·lu·tion** Revolution *f*, Umwälzung *f*; ASTR Umlauf *m* (***round*** um); TECH Umdrehung *f*; ***number of ~s*** Drehzahl *f*; ***~ counter*** Drehzahlmesser *m*; **rev·o·lu·tion·a·ry 1.** revolutionär; Revolutions... **2.** POL Revolutionär(in)
**rev·o·lu·tion·ize** revolutionieren
**re·volve** sich drehen (***on, round*** um); ***~ around*** *fig* sich drehen um
**re·volv·er** Revolver *m*
**re·volv·ing** Dreh...; ***~ door(s)*** Drehtür *f*
**re·vue** THEA Revue *f*; Kabarett *n*
**re·vul·sion** Abscheu *m*
**re·ward 1.** Belohnung *f* **2.** belohnen
**re·ward·ing** lohnend
**re·write** neu schreiben, umschreiben
**rhap·so·dy** MUS Rhapsodie *f*
**rhe·to·ric** Rhetorik *f*
**rheu·ma·tism** MED Rheumatismus *m*, F Rheuma *n*
**rhi·no** F, **rhi·no·ce·ros** ZO Rhinozeros *n*, Nashorn *n*
**rhu·barb** BOT Rhabarber *m*
**rhyme 1.** Reim *m*; Vers *m*
**rhyth·m** Rhythmus *m*
**rhyth·mic, rhyth·mi·cal** rhythmisch
**rib** ANAT Rippe *f*
**rib·bon** (*a.* Farb-, Ordens)Band *n*; Streifen *m*; Fetzen *m*
**rib cage** ANAT Brustkorb *m*
**rice** BOT Reis *m*

**rice pud·ding** GASTR Milchreis *m*
**rich** **1.** reich (***in*** an *dat*); prächtig, kostbar; GASTR schwer; AGR fruchtbar, fett (*soil*); voll (*sound*); satt (*color*); **~ (*in calories*)** kalorienreich **2.** ***the ~*** die Reichen *pl*
**rick** (Stroh-, Heu)Schober *m*
**rick·ets** MED Rachitis *f*
**rick·et·y** F *fig* gebrechlich; wack(e)lig
**rid** befreien (***of*** von); ***get ~ of*** loswerden
**rid·den** *in cpds* geplagt von
**rid·dle**[1] Rätsel *n*
**rid·dle**[2] **1.** grobes Sieb, Schüttelsieb *n* **2.** sieben; durchlöchern, durchsieben
**ride** **1.** *v/i* reiten; fahren (***on*** auf *e-m Fahrrad etc*; ***on*** *or Br* ***in*** in *e-m Bus etc*); *v/t* reiten (auf *dat*); *Fahrrad, Motorrad* fahren, fahren auf (*dat*) **2.** Ritt *m*; Fahrt *f*; **rid·er** Reiter(in); (*Motorrad-, Rad*)Fahrer(in)
**ridge** GEOGR (*Gebirgs*)Kamm *m*, Grat *m*; ARCH (*Dach*)First *m*
**rid·i·cule** **1.** Spott *m* **2.** lächerlich machen, spotten über (*acc*), verspotten
**ri·dic·u·lous** lächerlich
**rid·ing** Reit…
**ri·fle**[1] Gewehr *n*
**ri·fle**[2] durchwühlen
**rift** Spalt *m*, Spalte *f*; *fig* Riss *m*
**rig** **1.** *Schiff* auftakeln; ***~ out*** *j-n* ausstaffieren; ***~ up*** F (behelfsmäßig) zusammenbauen (***from*** aus); **2.** MAR Takelage *f*; TECH Bohrinsel *f*; F Aufmachung *f*
**rig·ging** MAR Takelage *f*
**right** **1.** *adj* recht; richtig; rechte(r, -s), Rechts…; ***all ~!*** in Ordnung!, gut!; ***that's all ~!*** das macht nichts!, schon gut!, bitte!; ***that's ~!*** richtig!, ganz recht!, stimmt!; ***be ~*** recht haben; ***put ~, set ~*** in Ordnung bringen; berichtigen, korrigieren **2.** *adv* (nach) rechts; richtig, recht; genau; gerade (-wegs), direkt; ganz, völlig; ***~ away*** sofort; ***~ now*** im Moment; sofort; ***~ on*** geradeaus; ***turn ~*** (sich) nach rechts wenden; MOT rechts abbiegen **3.** Recht *n*; *die* Rechte (*a.* POL, *boxing*), rechte Seite; ***on the ~*** rechts, auf der rechten Seite; ***to the ~*** (nach) rechts; ***keep to the ~*** sich rechts halten; MOT rechts fahren **4.** aufrichten; *et.* wieder gutmachen; in Ordnung bringen
**right an·gle** MATH rechter Winkel
**right-an·gled** MATH rechtwink(e)lig
**right·eous** gerecht (*anger etc*)
**right·ful** rechtmäßig
**right-hand** rechte(r, -s); **~ drive** MOT Rechtssteuerung *f*
**right-hand·ed** rechtshändig; für Rechtshänder; ***be ~*** Rechtshänder(in) sein
**right·ly** richtig; mit Recht
**right of way** MOT Vorfahrt *f*, Vorfahrtsrecht *n*; Durchgangsrecht *n*
**right-wing** POL dem rechten Flügel angehörend, Rechts…
**rig·id** starr, steif; *fig* streng, strikt
**rig·or·ous** streng; genau
**rig·o(u)r** Strenge *f*, Härte *f*
**rile** F ärgern, reizen
**rim** Rand *m*; TECH Felge *f*
**rim·less** randlos
**rind** (*Zitronen- etc*)Schale *f*; (*Käse*)Rinde *f*; (*Speck*)Schwarte *f*
**ring**[1] **1.** Ring *m*; Kreis *m*; Manege *f*; (Box)Ring *m*; (Spionage- *etc*)Ring *m* **2.** umringen, umstellen; *Vogel* beringen
**ring**[2] **1.** läuten; klingeln; klingen (*a. fig*); *Br* TEL anrufen; ***the bell is ~ing*** es läutet *or* klingelt; ***~ the bell*** läuten, klingeln; ***~ back*** *Br* TEL zurückrufen; ***~ for*** nach *j-m*, *et.* läuten; *Arzt etc* rufen; ***~ off*** *Br* TEL (den Hörer) auflegen, Schluss machen; ***~ s.o.* (*up*)** j-n *or* bei j-m anrufen **2.** Läuten *n*, Klingeln *n*; *fig* Klang *m*; *Br* TEL Anruf *m*; F ***give s.o. a ~*** j-n anrufen
**ring bind·er** Ringbuch *n*
**ring fin·ger** Ringfinger *m*
**ring·lead·er** Rädelsführer(in)
**ring·let** (Ringel)Löckchen *n*
**ring road** *Br* Umgehungsstraße *f*; Ringstraße *f*
**ring·side**: ***at the ~*** *boxing*: am Ring
**rink** (Kunst)Eisbahn *f*; Rollschuhbahn *f*
**rinse** *a.* ***~ out*** (aus)spülen
**ri·ot** **1.** Aufruhr *m*; Krawall *m*; ***run ~*** randalieren; ***run ~ through*** randalierend ziehen durch **2.** Krawall machen, randalieren; **ri·ot·er** Aufrührer(in); Randalierer(in); **ri·ot·ous** aufrührerisch; randalierend; ausgelassen, wild
**rip** **1.** *a.* ***~ up*** zerreißen; ***~ open*** aufreißen; F ***~ s.o. off*** j-n neppen **2.** Riss *m*
**ripe** reif; **rip·en** reifen (lassen)
**rip-off** F Nepp *m*
**rip·ple** **1.** (sich) kräuseln; plätschern, rie-

seln **2.** kleine Welle; Kräuselung *f*; Plätschern *n*, Rieseln *n*

**rise 1.** aufstehen, sich erheben; REL auferstehen; aufsteigen (*smoke etc*); sich heben (*curtain, spirits*); ansteigen (*road, river etc*), anschwellen (*river etc*); (an)steigen (*temperature etc*), *prices etc*: *a.* anziehen; stärker werden (*wind etc*); aufgehen (*sun etc, bread etc*); entspringen (*river etc*); *fig* aufsteigen; *fig* entstehen (***from, out of*** aus); *a.* ***~ up*** sich erheben (***against*** gegen); ***~ to the occasion*** sich der Lage gewachsen zeigen **2.** (An)Steigen *n*; Steigung *f*; Anhöhe *f*; ASTR Aufgang *m*; *Br* Lohn- *or* Gehaltserhöhung *f*; *fig* Anstieg *m*; Aufstieg *m*; ***give ~ to*** verursachen, führen zu

**ris·er**: ***early ~*** Frühaufsteher(in)

**ris·ing 1.** Aufstand *m* **2.** aufstrebend

**risk 1.** Gefahr *f*, Risiko *n*; ***at one's own ~*** auf eigene Gefahr; ***at the ~ of doing s.th.*** auf die Gefahr hin, et. zu tun; ***be at ~*** gefährdet sein; ***run the ~ of doing s.th.*** Gefahr laufen, et. zu tun; ***run a ~, take a ~*** ein Risiko eingehen **2.** wagen, riskieren; **risk·y** riskant

**rite** Ritus *m*; Zeremonie *f*

**rit·u·al 1.** rituell; Ritual… **2.** Ritual *n*

**ri·val 1.** Rivale *m*, Rivalin *f*, Konkurrent(in) **2.** Konkurrenz…, rivalisierend **3.** rivalisieren *or* konkurrieren mit; **ri·val·ry** Rivalität *f*; Konkurrenz *f*; Konkurrenzkampf *m*

**riv·er** Fluss *m*; Strom *m*; **riv·er·side** Flussufer *n*; ***by the ~*** am Fluss

**riv·et 1.** TECH Niet *m*, *n*, Niete *f* **2.** TECH (ver)nieten; *fig Aufmerksamkeit, Blick* richten (**on** auf *acc*)

**road** (Auto-, Land)Straße *f*; *fig* Weg *m*; ***on the ~*** auf der Straße; unterwegs; THEA auf Tournee

**road ac·ci·dent** Verkehrsunfall *m*

**road·block** Straßensperre *f*

**road hog** F Verkehrsrowdy *m*

**road map** Straßenkarte *f*

**road safe·ty** Verkehrssicherheit *f*

**road·side** Straßenrand *m*; ***at the ~, by the ~*** am Straßenrand

**road toll** Straßenbenutzungsgebühr *f*

**road·way** Fahrbahn *f*

**road works** Straßenarbeiten *pl*

**road·wor·thi·ness** Verkehrssicherheit *f*; **road·wor·thy** verkehrssicher

**roam** *v/i* (umher)streifen, (-)wandern; *v/t* streifen *or* wandern durch

**roar 1.** Brüllen *n*, Gebrüll *n*; Brausen *n*, Krachen *n*, Donnern *n*; ***~s of laughter*** brüllendes Gelächter **2.** brüllen; brausen; donnern (*truck, gun etc*)

**roast** GASTR **1.** *v/t* braten (*a. v/i*); *Kaffee etc* rösten **2.** Braten *m* **3.** *adj* gebraten

**roast beef** GASTR Rinderbraten *m*

**rob** *Bank etc* überfallen; *j-n* berauben

**rob·ber** Räuber *m*

**rob·ber·y** Raubüberfall *m*, (*Bank-*)Raub *m*, (*Bank*)Überfall *m*

**robe** *a. pl* Robe *f*, Talar *m*

**rob·in** ZO Rotkehlchen *n*

**ro·bot** Roboter *m*

**ro·bust** robust, kräftig

**rock**[1] schaukeln, wiegen; erschüttern (*a. fig*)

**rock**[2] Fels(en) *m*; Felsen *pl*; GEOL Gestein *n*; Felsbrocken *m*; Stein *m*; *Br* Zuckerstange *f*; *pl* Klippen *pl*; F ***on the ~s*** in ernsten Schwierigkeiten (*business etc*); kaputt (*marriage etc*); GASTR mit Eis

**rock**[3] *a.* ***~ music*** Rock(musik *f*) *m*; → ***rock 'n' roll***

**rock·er** Kufe *f*; Schaukelstuhl *m*; *Br* Rocker *m*; ***off one's ~*** F übergeschnappt

**rock·et 1.** Rakete *f* **2.** rasen, schießen; *a.* ***~ up*** hochschnellen, in die Höhe schießen (*prices*)

**rock·ing chair** Schaukelstuhl *m*

**rock·ing horse** Schaukelpferd *n*

**rock 'n' roll** MUS Rock 'n' Roll *m*

**rock·y** felsig; steinhart

**rod** Rute *f*; TECH Stab *m*, Stange *f*

**ro·dent** ZO Nagetier *n*

**ro·de·o** Rodeo *m*, *n*

**roe** ZO *a.* ***hard ~*** Rogen *m*; *a.* ***soft ~*** Milch *f*

**roe·buck** ZO Rehbock *m*

**roe deer** ZO Reh *n*

**rogue** Schurke *m*, Gauner *m*; Schlingel *m*, Spitzbube *m*

**ro·guish** schelmisch, spitzbübisch

**role** THEA *etc* Rolle *f* (*a. fig*)

**roll 1.** *v/i* rollen; sich wälzen; fahren; MAR schlingern; (g)rollen (*thunder*); *v/t et.* rollen; auf-, zusammenrollen; *Zigarette* drehen; ***~ down*** *Ärmel* herunterkrempeln; MOT *Fenster* herunterkurbeln; ***~ out*** ausrollen; ***~ up*** aufrollen; (sich) zusammenrollen; *Ärmel* hoch-

R

krempeln; MOT *Fenster* hochkurbeln **2.** Rolle *f*; GASTR Brötchen *n*, Semmel *f*; Namens-, Anwesenheitsliste *f*; (G)Rollen *n* (*of thunder*); (*Trommel*)-Wirbel *m*; MAR Schlingern *n*

**roll call** Namensaufruf *m*

**roll·er** (Locken)Wickler *m*; TECH Rolle *f*, Walze *f*

**roll·er coast·er** Achterbahn *f*

**roll·er skate** Rollschuh *m*

**roll·er-skate** Rollschuh laufen

**roll·er-skat·ing** Rollschuhlaufen *n*

**roll·er tow·el** Rollhandtuch *n*

**roll·ing pin** Nudelholz *n*

**roll-on** Deoroller *m*

**Ro·man** **1.** römisch **2.** Römer(in)

**ro·mance** Abenteuer-, Liebesroman *m*; Romanze *f*; Romantik *f*

**Ro·mance** LING romanisch

**Ro·ma·ni·a** Rumänien *n*

**Ro·ma·ni·an** **1.** rumänisch **2.** Rumäne *m*, Rumänin *f*; LING Rumänisch *n*

**ro·man·tic** **1.** romantisch **2.** Romantiker(in)

**ro·man·ti·cism** Romantik *f*

**romp** *a.* ~ ***about***, ~ ***around*** herumtollen, herumtoben

**romp·ers** Spielanzug *m*

**roof** **1.** Dach *n*; MOT Verdeck *n* **2.** mit e-m Dach versehen; ~ ***in***, ~ ***over*** überdachen

**roof·ing felt** Dachpappe *f*

**roof-rack** MOT Dachgepäckträger *m*

**rook**[1] ZO Saatkrähe *f*

**rook**[2] *chess*: Turm *m*

**rook**[3] F *j-n* betrügen (***of*** um)

**room** **1.** Raum *m*, *a.* Zimmer *n*, *a.* Platz *m*; *fig* Spielraum *m* **2.** wohnen

**room·er** Untermieter(in)

**room·ing-house** Fremdenheim *n*, Pension *f*

**room·mate** Zimmergenosse *m*, -genossin *f*

**room ser·vice** Zimmerservice *m*

**room·y** geräumig

**roost** **1.** (Hühner)Stange *f*; ZO Schlafplatz *m* **2.** auf der Stange *etc* sitzen *or* schlafen

**roost·er** ZO (Haus)Hahn *m*

**root** **1.** Wurzel *f*; ***take*** ~ Wurzeln schlagen (*a. fig*) **2.** *v/i* Wurzeln schlagen; wühlen (***for*** nach); ~ ***about*** herumwühlen (***among*** in *dat*); *v/t* ~ ***out*** *fig* ausrotten; ~ ***up*** mit der Wurzel ausreißen

**root·ed**: ***deeply*** ~ *fig* tief verwurzelt; ***stand*** ~ ***to the spot*** wie angewurzelt dastehen

**rope** **1.** Seil *n*; MAR Tau *n*; Strick *m*; (*Perlen- etc*)Schnur *f*; ***give s.o. plenty of*** ~ j-m viel Freiheit *or* Spielraum lassen; ***know the*** ~***s*** F sich auskennen; ***show s.o. the*** ~***s*** F j-n einarbeiten **2.** festbinden (***to*** an *dat or acc*); ~ ***off*** (durch ein Seil) absperren *or* abgrenzen; ~ **ladder** Strickleiter *f*

**ro·sa·ry** REL Rosenkranz *m*

**rose** **1.** BOT Rose *f*; Brause *f* **2.** rosarot, rosenrot

**ros·trum** Redner-, Dirigentenpult *n*

**ros·y** rosig (*a. fig*)

**rot** **1.** *v/t* (ver)faulen *or* verrotten lassen; *v/i a.* ~ ***away*** (ver)faulen, verrotten, morsch werden **2.** Fäulnis *f*

**ro·ta·ry** rotierend, sich drehend; Rotations…, Dreh…; **ro·tate** rotieren (lassen), (sich) drehen; turnusmäßig (aus-) wechseln; **ro·ta·tion** Rotation *f*, Drehung *f*; Wechsel *m*

**ro·tor** TECH Rotor *m*

**rot·ten** verfault, faul; verrottet, morsch; *fig* miserabel; gemein; ***feel*** ~ F sich mies fühlen

**ro·tund** rund und dick

**rough** **1.** *adj* rau; uneben (*road etc*); stürmisch (*sea, crossing, weather*); grob; barsch; hart; grob, ungefähr (*estimate etc*); roh, Roh… **2.** *adv* ***sleep*** ~ im Freien übernachten; ***play*** ~ SPORT hart spielen **3.** *golf*: Rough *n*; ***write it out in*** ~ ***first*** zuerst ins Unreine schreiben **4.** ~ ***it*** F primitiv *or* anspruchslos leben; ~ ***out*** entwerfen, skizzieren; ~ ***up*** F *j-n* zusammenschlagen

**rough·age** MED Ballaststoffe *pl*

**rough·cast** ARCH Rauputz *m*

**rough| cop·y** Rohentwurf *m*, Konzept *n*; ~ **draft** Rohfassung *f*

**rough·en** rau werden; rau machen, anrauen, aufrauen

**rough·ly** grob, *fig a.* ungefähr

**rough·neck** F Schläger *m*

**rough·shod**: ***ride*** ~ ***over*** *j-n* rücksichtslos behandeln; sich rücksichtslos über *et.* hinwegsetzen

**round** **1.** *adj* rund; ***a*** ~ ***dozen*** ein rundes Dutzend; ***in*** ~ ***figures*** aufgerundet, abgerundet, rund(e) … **2.** *adv* rund(her)um, rings(her)um; überall, auf *or* von *or* nach allen Seiten; ***turn ~*** sich umdrehen; ***invite s.o. ~*** j-n zu sich einladen; ***~ about*** F ungefähr; ***all*** (***the***) ***year ~*** das ganze Jahr hindurch *or* über; ***the other way ~*** umgekehrt **3.** *prp* (rund) um, um (*acc* … herum); in *or* auf (*dat*) … herum; ***trip ~ the world*** Weltreise *f* **4.** Runde *f*, *a.* Rundgang *m*, MED Visite *f*, *a.* Lage *f* (*beer etc*); Schuss *m*; *esp Br* Scheibe *f* (*bread etc*); MUS Kanon *m* **5.** rund machen, (ab)runden, *Lippen* spitzen; umfahren, fahren um, *Kurve* nehmen; ***~ down*** *Zahl etc* abrunden (***to*** auf *acc*); ***~ off*** *Essen etc* abrunden, beschließen (***with*** mit); *Zahl etc* auf- *or* abrunden (***to*** auf *acc*); ***~ up*** *Vieh* zusammentreiben; *Leute etc* zusammentrommeln; *Zahl etc* aufrunden (***to*** auf *acc*)

**round·a·bout** **1.** *Br* MOT Kreisverkehr *m*; *Br* Karussell *n* **2.** ***take a ~ route*** e-n Umweg machen; ***in a ~ way*** *fig* auf Umwegen

**round trip** Hin- und Rückfahrt *f*; Hin- und Rückflug *m*

**round-trip tick·et** Rückfahrkarte *f*; Rückflugticket *n*

**round·up** Razzia *f*

**rouse** *j-n* wecken; *fig j-n* aufrütteln, wach rütteln; *j-n* erzürnen, reizen

**route** Route *f*, Strecke *f*, Weg *m*, (*Bus-etc*)Linie *f*

**rou·tine** **1.** Routine *f*; ***the same old*** (***daily***) ***~*** das (tägliche) ewige Einerlei **2.** üblich, routinemäßig, Routine…

**rove** (umher)streifen, (umher)wandern

**row**[1] Reihe *f*

**row**[2] **1.** rudern **2.** Kahnfahrt *f*

**row**[3] *Br* F **1.** Krach *m*; (lauter) Streit **2.** (sich) streiten

**row·boat** Ruderboot *n*

**row·er** Ruderer *m*, Ruderin *f*

**row house** Reihenhaus *n*

**row·ing boat** *Br* Ruderboot *n*

**roy·al** königlich, Königs…

**roy·al·ty** die königliche Familie; Tantieme *f* (***on*** auf *acc*)

**rub** **1.** *v/t* reiben; abreiben; polieren; ***~ dry*** trocken reiben; ***~ it in*** *fig* F darauf herumreiten; ***~ shoulders with*** F verkehren mit; *v/i* reiben, scheuern (***against, on*** an *dat*); ***~ down*** abreiben, trocken reiben; abschmirgeln, abschleifen; ***~ off*** abreiben; abgehen (*paint etc*); ***~ off on***(***to***) *fig* abfärben auf (*acc*); ***~ out*** *Br* ausradieren **2.** ***give s.th. a ~*** et. abreiben *or* polieren

**rub·ber** Gummi *n*, *m*; *esp Br* Radiergummi *m*; Wischtuch *n*; F Gummi *m*

**rub·ber band** Gummiband *n*

**rub·ber din·ghy** Schlauchboot *n*

**rub·ber·neck** F **1.** neugierig gaffen **2.** *a.* ***rubbernecker*** Gaffer(in), Schaulustige *m*, *f*

**rub·ber·y** gummiartig; zäh

**rub·bish** *Br* Abfall *m*, Abfälle *pl*, Müll *m*; F Schund *m*; Quatsch *m*, Blödsinn *m*; ***~ bin*** *Br* Mülleimer *m*; ***~ chute*** *Br* Müllschlucker *m*

**rub·ble** Schutt *m*; Trümmer *pl*

**ru·by** Rubin *m*; Rubinrot *n*

**ruck·sack** *esp Br* Rucksack *m*

**rud·der** AVIAT, MAR Ruder *n*

**rud·dy** frisch, gesund

**rude** unhöflich, grob; unanständig (*joke etc*); bös (*shock etc*)

**ru·di·men·ta·ry** elementar, Anfangs…; primitiv

**ru·di·ments** Anfangsgründe *pl*

**rue·ful** reuevoll, reumütig

**ruff** Halskrause *f* (*a.* ZO)

**ruf·fle** **1.** kräuseln; *Haar* zerzausen; *Federn* sträuben; ***~ s.o.'s composure*** j-n aus der Fassung bringen **2.** Rüsche *f*

**rug** Vorleger *m*, Brücke *f*; *esp Br* dicke Wolldecke

**rug·by** *a.* ***~ football*** SPORT Rugby *n*

**rug·ged** GEOGR zerklüftet, schroff; TECH robust, stabil; zerfurcht (*face*)

**ru·in** **1.** Ruin *m*; *mst pl* Ruine(n *pl*) *f*, Trümmer *pl* **2.** ruinieren, zerstören

**ru·in·ous** ruinös

**rule** **1.** Regel *f*; Spielregel *f*; Vorschrift *f*; Herrschaft *f*; Lineal *n*; ***against the ~s*** regelwidrig; verboten; ***as a ~*** in der Regel; ***as a ~ of thumb*** als Faustregel; ***work to ~*** Dienst nach Vorschrift tun **2.** *v/t* herrschen über (*acc*); *esp* JUR entscheiden; *Papier* lin(i)ieren; *Linie* ziehen; ***be ~d by*** *fig* sich leiten lassen von; beherrscht werden von; ***~ out*** *et.* ausschließen; *v/i* herrschen (***over*** über *acc*); *esp* JUR entscheiden

**rul·er** Herrscher(in); Lineal *n*

**rum** Rum *m*

**rum·ble** rumpeln (*vehicle*); (g)rollen (*thunder*); knurren (*stomach*)

**ru·mi·nant** ZO Wiederkäuer *m*

R

**ru·mi·nate** zo wiederkäuen

**rum·mage** F **1.** *a.* **~ *about*** herumstöbern, herumwühlen (***among, in, through*** in *dat*); **2.** Ramsch *m*; **~ sale** Wohltätigkeitsbasar *m*

**ru·mo(u)r** **1.** Gerücht *n*; **~ *has it that*** es geht das Gerücht, dass **2.** ***it is ~ed that*** es geht das Gerücht, dass; ***he is ~ed to be …*** man munkelt, er sei …

**rump** F Hinterteil *n*

**rum·ple** zerknittern, zerknüllen, zerwühlen; *Haar* zerzausen

**run** **1.** *v/i* laufen (*a.* SPORT), rennen; fahren, verkehren, gehen (*train, bus etc*); laufen, fließen; zerfließen, zerlaufen (*butter, paint etc*); TECH laufen (*engine*), in Betrieb *or* Gang sein; verlaufen (*road etc*); *esp* JUR gelten, laufen (***for one year*** ein Jahr); THEA *etc* laufen (***for three months*** drei Monate lang); lauten (*text*); gehen (*melody*); POL kandidieren (***for*** für); **~ *dry*** austrocknen; **~ *low*** knapp werden; **~ *short*** knapp werden; **~ *short of gas*** (*Br* ***petrol***) kein Benzin mehr haben; *v/t Strecke, Rennen* laufen; *Zug, Bus* fahren *or* verkehren lassen; *Wasser, Maschine etc* laufen lassen; *Geschäft, Hotel etc* führen, leiten; *Zeitungsartikel etc* abdrucken, bringen; **~ *s.o. home*** F j-n nach Hause bringen *or* fahren; → ***errand***; **~ *across*** *j-n* zufällig treffen; stoßen auf (*acc*); **~ *after*** hinterherlaufen, nachlaufen (*dat*); **~ *along!*** F ab mit dir!; **~ *away*** davonlaufen (***from*** vor *dat*); **~ *away with*** durchbrennen mit; durchgehen mit (*feelings etc*); **~ *down*** MOT anfahren, umfahren; F schlechtmachen; ausfindig machen; ablaufen (*watch*); leer werden (*battery*); **~ *in*** *Wagen etc* einfahren; F *Verbrecher* schnappen; **~ *into*** laufen *or* fahren gegen; *j-n* zufällig treffen; *fig* geraten in (*acc*); *fig* sich belaufen auf (*acc*); **~ *off with*** → ***run away with***; **~ *on*** weitergehen, sich hinziehen (***until*** bis); F unaufhörlich reden (***about*** über *acc*, von); **~ *out*** ablaufen (*time etc*); ausgehen, zu Ende gehen (*supplies etc*); **~ *out of gas*** (*Br* ***petrol***) kein Benzin mehr haben; **~ *over*** MOT überfahren; überlaufen, überfließen; **~ *through*** überfliegen, durchgehen, durchlesen; **~ *up*** *Flagge* hissen; *hohe Rechnung, Schulden* machen; **~ *up against*** stoßen auf (*acc*) **2.** Lauf *m* (*a.* SPORT); Fahrt *f*; Spazierfahrt *f*; Ansturm *m*, ECON *a.* Run *m* (***on*** auf *acc*); THEA *etc* Laufzeit *f*; Laufmasche *f*; Gehege *n*; Auslauf *m*, (*Hühner*)Hof *m*; SPORT (*Bob-*, *Rodel-*) Bahn *f*; (*Ski*)-Hang *m*; **~ *of good*** (***bad***) ***luck*** Glückssträhne *f* (Pechsträhne *f*); ***in the long ~*** auf die Dauer; ***in the short ~*** zunächst; ***on the ~*** auf der Flucht

**run·a·bout** F MOT Stadt-, Kleinwagen *m*

**run·a·way** Ausreißer(in)

**rung** Sprosse *f*

**run·ner** SPORT Läufer(in); Rennpferd *n*; *mst in cpds* Schmuggler(in); (*Schlitten-*, *Schlittschuh*)Kufe *f*; Tischläufer *m*; TECH (Gleit)Schiene *f*; BOT Ausläufer *m*; **~ bean** *Br* BOT grüne Bohne

**run·ning** **1.** Laufen *n*, Rennen *n*; Führung *f*, Leitung *f* **2.** fließend; SPORT Lauf…; ***two days ~*** zwei Tage hintereinander; **~ costs** ECON Betriebskosten *pl*, laufende Kosten *pl*

**run·ny** F flüssig; laufend (*nose*), tränend (*eyes*)

**run-off** POL Stichwahl *f*

**run-up** SPORT Zweite *m*, *f*, Vizemeister(in)

**run·way** AVIAT Start- und Landebahn *f*, Rollbahn *f*, Piste *f*

**rup·ture** **1.** Bruch *m* (*a.* MED *and fig*), Riss *m* **2.** bersten, platzen; (zer)reißen; **~ *o.s.*** MED sich e-n Bruch heben *or* zuziehen

**ru·ral** ländlich

**ruse** List *f*, Trick *m*

**rush**[1] **1.** *v/i* hasten, hetzen, stürmen, rasen; **~ *at*** losstürzen *or* sich stürzen auf (*acc*); **~ *in*** hineinstürzen, hineinstürmen, hereinstürzen, hereinstürmen; **~ *into*** *fig* sich stürzen in (*acc*); *et.* überstürzen; *v/t* antreiben, drängen, hetzen; schnell bringen; *Essen* hinunterschlingen; losstürmen auf (*acc*); ***don't ~ it*** lass dir Zeit dabei **2.** Ansturm *m*; Hast *f*, Hetze *f*; Hochbetrieb *m*; ECON stürmische Nachfrage; ***what's all the ~?*** wozu diese Eile *or* Hetze?

**rush**[2] BOT Binse *f*

**rush hour** Rushhour *f*, Hauptverkehrszeit *f*, Stoßzeit *f*

**rush-hour traf·fic** Stoßverkehr *m*

**rusk** *esp Br* Zwieback *m*

**Rus·sia** Russland *n*

**Rus·sian 1.** russisch **2.** Russe *m*, Russin *f*; LING Russisch *n*
**rust 1.** Rost *m* **2.** *v/t* (ein-, ver)rosten lassen; *v/i* (ein-, ver)rosten
**rus·tic** ländlich, bäuerlich; rustikal
**rus·tle 1.** rascheln (mit), knistern; *Vieh* stehlen **2.** Rascheln *n*
**rust·proof** rostfrei, nicht rostend
**rust·y** rostig; *fig* eingerostet
**rut**[1] **1.** (Rad)Spur *f*, Furche *f*; *fig* (alter) Trott; ***the daily ~*** das tägliche Einerlei **2.** furchen; ***rutted*** ausgefahren
**rut**[2] ZO Brunft *f*, Brunst *f*
**ruth·less** unbarmherzig; rücksichtslos, skrupellos
**rye** BOT Roggen *m*

# S

**S, s** S, s *n*
**S** *abbr of* ***small*** (***size***) klein
**sa·ber**, *Br* **sa·bre** Säbel *m*
**sa·ble** ZO Zobel *m*; Zobelpelz *m*
**sab·o·tage 1.** Sabotage *f* **2.** sabotieren
**sack 1.** Sack *m*; ***get the ~*** *Br* F rausgeschmissen werden; ***give s.o. the ~*** *Br* F j-n rausschmeißen; ***hit the ~*** F sich in die Falle *or* Klappe hauen **2.** in Säcke füllen, einsacken; *Br* F *j-n* rausschmeißen
**sack·cloth, sack·ing** Sackleinen *n*
**sac·ra·ment** REL Sakrament *n*
**sa·cred** geistlich (*music etc*); heilig
**sac·ri·fice 1.** Opfer *n* **2.** opfern
**sac·ri·lege** REL Sakrileg *n*; Frevel *m*
**sac·ris·ty** REL Sakristei *f*
**sad** traurig; schmerzlich; schlimm
**sad·dle 1.** Sattel *m* **2.** satteln
**sa·dism** Sadismus *m*
**sa·dist** Sadist(in)
**sa·dis·tic** sadistisch
**sad·ness** Traurigkeit *f*
**sa·fa·ri** Safari *f*; **~ park** Safaripark *m*
**safe 1.** sicher **2.** Safe *m, n*, Tresor *m*, Geldschrank *m*
**safe con·duct** freies Geleit
**safe de·pos·it** Tresor *m*
**safe-de·pos·it box** Schließfach *n*
**safe·guard 1.** Schutz *m* (***against*** gegen, vor *dat*); **2.** schützen (***against, from*** gegen, vor *dat*)
**safe·keep·ing** sichere Verwahrung
**safe·ty 1.** Sicherheit *f* **2.** Sicherheits...; **~ belt** → ***seat belt***; **~ is·land** Verkehrsinsel *f*; **~ lock** Sicherheitsschloss *n*; **~ mea·sure** Sicherheitsmaßnahme *f*; **~ pin** Sicherheitsnadel *f*
**sag** sich senken, absacken; durchhängen; (herab)hängen (*shoulders*); *fig* sinken (*morale*); nachlassen (*interest etc*)
**sa·ga·cious** scharfsinnig
**sa·ga·ci·ty** Scharfsinn *m*
**sage** BOT Salbei *m, f*
**Sa·git·tar·i·us** ASTR Schütze *m*; ***he*** (***she***) ***is*** (***a***) ***~*** er (sie) ist (ein) Schütze
**sail 1.** Segel *n*; Segelfahrt *f*; (*Windmühlen*)Flügel *m*; ***set ~*** auslaufen (***for*** nach); ***go for a ~*** segeln gehen **2.** *v/i* MAR segeln, fahren; auslaufen (***for*** nach); gleiten, schweben; ***go ~ing*** segeln gehen; *v/t* MAR befahren; *Schiff* steuern, *Boot* segeln
**sail·board** Surfbrett *n*
**sail·boat** Segelboot *n*
**sail·ing** Segeln *n*; Segelsport *m*; ***when is the next ~ to ...?*** wann fährt das nächste Schiff nach ...?; **~ boat** *Br* Segelboot *n*; **~ ship** Segelschiff *n*
**sail·or** Seemann *m*, Matrose *m*; ***be a good*** (***bad***) ***~*** (nicht) seefest sein
**sail·plane** Segelflugzeug *n*
**saint** Heilige *m, f*
**saint·ly** heilig, fromm
**sake**: ***for the ~ of ...*** um ... (*gen*) willen; ***for my ~*** meinetwegen; ***for God's ~*** F um Gottes willen
**sal·a·ble** verkäuflich
**sal·ad** Salat *m*; **~ dress·ing** Dressing *n*, Salatsoße *f*
**sal·a·ried**: ***~ employee*** Angestellte *m, f*, Gehaltsempfänger(in)
**sal·a·ry** Gehalt *n*
**sale** Verkauf *m*; Absatz *m*, Umsatz *m*; (Saison)Schlussverkauf *m*; Auktion *f*, Versteigerung *f*; ***for ~*** zu verkaufen; ***not for ~*** unverkäuflich; ***be on ~*** verkauft werden, erhältlich sein
**sale·a·ble** → ***salable***

**sales·clerk** (Laden)Verkäufer(in)
**sales·girl** (Laden)Verkäuferin *f*
**sales·man** Verkäufer *m*; (Handels-) Vertreter *m*
**sales rep·re·sen·ta·tive** Handlungsreisende *m, f*; (Handels)Vertreter(in)
**sales slip** ECON Quittung *f*
**sales tax** ECON Umsatzsteuer *f*
**sales·wom·an** Verkäuferin *f*; (Handels)Vertreterin *f*
**sa·line** salzig, Salz…
**sa·li·va** Speichel *m*
**sal·low** gelblich
**salm·on** ZO Lachs *m*
**sal·on** (*Schönheits- etc*)Salon *m*
**sa·loon** *Br* MOT Limousine *f*; HIST Saloon *m*; MAR Salon *m*
**sa·loon car** *Br* MOT Limousine *f*
**salt 1.** Salz *n* **2.** salzen; (ein)pökeln, einsalzen (*a.* **~ down**); *Straße etc* (mit Salz) streuen **3.** Salz…; gepökelt; salzig, gesalzen
**salt·cel·lar** *Br* Salzstreuer *m*
**salt·pe·ter**, *esp Br* **salt·pe·tre** CHEM Salpeter *m*
**salt shak·er** Salzstreuer *m*
**salt wa·ter** Salzwasser *n*
**salt·y** salzig
**sal·u·ta·tion** Gruß *m*, Begrüßung *f*; Anrede *f*; **sa·lute 1.** MIL salutieren; (be)grüßen **2.** Gruß *m*; MIL Ehrenbezeugung *f*; Salut *m*
**sal·vage 1.** Bergung *f*; Bergungsgut *n* **2.** bergen (***from*** aus); retten (*a. fig*)
**sal·va·tion** Rettung *f*; REL Erlösung *f*; (Seelen)Heil *n*
**Sal·va·tion Ar·my** Heilsarmee *f*
**salve** (Heil)Salbe *f*
**same**: ***the ~*** derselbe, dieselbe, dasselbe; ***all the ~*** trotzdem; ***it is all the ~ to me*** es ist mir ganz egal
**sam·ple 1.** Muster *n*, Probe *f* **2.** kosten, probieren
**san·a·to·ri·um** Sanatorium *n*
**sanc·ti·fy** heiligen
**sanc·tion 1.** Billigung *f*, Zustimmung *f*; *mst pl* Sanktionen *pl* **2.** billigen, sanktionieren
**sanc·ti·ty** Heiligkeit *f*
**sanc·tu·a·ry** Zuflucht *f*, Asyl *n*; ZO Schutzgebiet *n*
**sand 1.** Sand *m*; *pl* Sandfläche *f* **2.** *Straße etc* mit Sand (be)streuen; TECH schmirgeln
**san·dal** Sandale *f*
**sand·bag** Sandsack *m*
**sand·bank** GEOGR Sandbank *f*
**sand·box** Sandkasten *m*
**sand·cas·tle** Sandburg *f*
**sand·man** Sandmännchen *n*
**sand·pa·per** Sand-, Schmirgelpapier *n*
**sand·pip·er** ZO Strandläufer *m*
**sand·pit** *Br* Sandkasten *m*; Sandgrube *f*
**sand·stone** GEOL Sandstein *m*
**sand·storm** Sandsturm *m*
**sand·wich 1.** Sandwich *n* **2.** ***be ~ed between*** eingekeilt sein zwischen (*dat*); ***~ s.th. in between*** *fig* et. einschieben zwischen (*acc or dat*)
**sand·y** sandig; rotblond
**sane** geistig gesund; JUR zurechnungsfähig; vernünftig
**san·i·tar·i·um** → ***sanatorium***
**san·i·ta·ry** hygienisch; Gesundheits…; **~ nap·kin**, *Br* **~ tow·el** (Damen)Binde *f*
**san·i·ta·tion** sanitäre Einrichtungen *pl*; Kanalisation *f*
**san·i·ty** geistige Gesundheit; JUR Zurechnungsfähigkeit *f*
**San·ta Claus** der Weihnachtsmann, der Nikolaus
**sap**[1] BOT Saft *m*
**sap**[2] schwächen
**sap·phire** Saphir *m*
**sar·casm** Sarkasmus *m*
**sar·cas·tic** sarkastisch
**sar·dine** ZO Sardine *f*
**sash**[1] Schärpe *f*
**sash**[2] Fensterrahmen *m*
**sash win·dow** Schiebefenster *n*
**sas·sy** frech
**Sat** *abbr of* ***Saturday*** Sa., Samstag *m*, Sonnabend *m*
**Sa·tan** der Satan
**satch·el** (Schul)Ranzen *m*; Schultasche *f*
**sat·ed** *fig* übersättigt
**sat·el·lite 1.** Satellit *m*; ***by or via ~*** über Satellit **2.** Satelliten…; **~ *dish*** F Satellitenschüssel *f*
**sat·in** Satin *m*
**sat·ire** Satire *f*
**sat·ir·ic**, **sat·ir·i·cal** satirisch
**sat·i·rist** Satiriker(in)
**sat·ir·ize** verspotten
**sat·is·fac·tion** Befriedigung *f*; Genugtuung *f*, Zufriedenheit *f*
**sat·is·fac·to·ry** befriedigend, zufrieden-

stellend

**sat·is·fy** befriedigen, zufrieden stellen; überzeugen; ***be satisfied that*** davon überzeugt sein, dass

**sat·u·rate** (durch)tränken (***with*** mit); CHEM sättigen (*a. fig*)

**Sat·ur·day** Sonnabend *m*, Samstag *m*; ***on ~*** (am) Sonnabend *or* Samstag; ***on ~s*** sonnabends, samstags

**sauce** Soße *f*

**sauce·pan** Kochtopf *m*

**sau·cer** Untertasse *f*

**sauc·y** *Br* frech

**saun·ter** bummeln, schlendern

**saus·age** Wurst *f*; *a.* ***small ~*** Würstchen *n*

**sav·age 1.** wild; unzivilisiert **2.** Wilde *m*, *f*; **sav·ag·e·ry** Wildheit *f*; Rohheit *f*, Grausamkeit *f*

**save 1.** retten (***from*** vor *dat*); *Geld*, *Zeit etc* (ein)sparen; *et.* aufheben, aufsparen (***for*** für); *j-m et.* ersparen; IT (ab)speichern, sichern; SPORT *Schuss* halten, parieren, *Tor* verhindern **2.** SPORT Parade *f*

**sav·er** Retter(in); ECON Sparer(in)

**sav·ings** ECON Ersparnisse *pl*; **~ account** Sparkonto *n*; **~ bank** Sparkasse *f*; **~ de·pos·it** Spareinlage *f*

**sa·vio(u)r** Retter(in); ***the Savio(u)r*** REL der Erlöser, der Heiland

**sa·vo(u)r** mit Genuss essen *or* trinken; ***~ of*** *fig* e-n Beigeschmack haben von

**sa·vo(u)r·y** schmackhaft

**saw 1.** Säge *f* **2.** sägen

**saw·dust** Sägemehl *n*, Sägespäne *pl*

**saw·mill** Sägewerk *n*

**Sax·on 1.** (Angel)Sachse *m*, (Angel-)Sächsin *f* **2.** (angel)sächsisch

**say 1.** sagen; aufsagen; *Gebet* sprechen, *Vaterunser* beten; ***~ grace*** das Tischgebet sprechen; ***what does your watch ~?*** wie spät ist es auf deiner Uhr?; ***he is said to be …*** er soll … sein; ***it ~s*** es lautet (*letter etc*); ***it ~s here*** hier heißt es; ***it goes without ~ing*** es versteht sich von selbst; ***no sooner said than done*** gesagt, getan; ***that is to ~*** das heißt; ***(and) that's ~ing s.th.*** (und) das will was heißen; ***you said it*** du sagst es; ***you can ~ that again!*** das kannst du laut sagen!; ***I ~*** sag(en Sie) mal!; ich muss schon sagen!; ***I can't ~*** das kann ich nicht sagen **2.** Mitspracherecht *n* (***in*** bei); ***have one's ~*** s-e Meinung äußern, zu Wort kommen; ***he always has to have his ~*** er muss immer mitreden

**say·ing** Sprichwort *n*, Redensart *f*; ***as the ~ goes*** wie man so (schön) sagt

**scab** MED, BOT Schorf *m*; *contp* Streikbrecher(in)

**scaf·fold** (Bau)Gerüst *n*; Schafott *n*

**scaf·fold·ing** (Bau)Gerüst *n*

**scald 1.** sich *die Zunge etc* verbrühen; *Milch* abkochen; ***~ing hot*** kochend heiß **2.** MED Verbrühung *f*

**scale**[1] **1.** Skala *f* (*a. fig*), Grad- *or* Maßeinteilung *f*; MATH, TECH Maßstab *m* (*a. fig*); Waage *f*; MUS Skala *f*, Tonleiter *f*; *fig* Ausmaß *n*, Umfang *m* **2.** erklettern; ***~ down*** *fig* verringern; ***~ up*** *fig* erhöhen

**scale**[2] Waagschale *f*; ***(a pair of) ~s*** (e-e) Waage

**scale**[3] **1.** ZO Schuppe *f*; TECH Kesselstein *m*; ***the ~s fell from my eyes*** es fiel mir wie Schuppen von den Augen **2.** *Fisch* (ab)schuppen

**scal·lop** ZO Kammmuschel *f*

**scalp 1.** Kopfhaut *f*; Skalp *m* **2.** skalpieren

**scal·y** ZO schuppig (*a. fig*)

**scamp** F Schlingel *m*, (kleiner) Strolch

**scam·per** trippeln; huschen

**scan 1.** *et.* absuchen (***for*** nach); *Zeitung etc* überfliegen; IT, *radar*, TV abtasten, scannen **2.** MED *etc* Scanning *n*

**scan·dal** Skandal *m*; Klatsch *m*

**scan·dal·ize**: ***be ~d at s.th.*** über et. empört *or* entrüstet sein

**scan·dal·ous** skandalös; ***be ~*** *a.* ein Skandal sein (***that*** dass)

**Scan·di·na·vi·a** Skandinavien *n*

**Scan·di·na·vi·an 1.** skandinavisch **2.** Skandinavier(in)

**scan·ner** TECH Scanner *m*

**scant** dürftig, gering

**scant·y** dürftig, kärglich, knapp

**scape·goat** Sündenbock *m*

**scar** MED **1.** Narbe *f* (*a. fig*) **2.** e-e Narbe *or* Narben hinterlassen auf (*dat*) *or fig* bei *j-m*; ***~ over*** vernarben

**scarce** knapp (*food etc*); selten; ***be ~*** Mangelware sein (*a. fig*); **scarce·ly** kaum; **scar·ci·ty** Mangel *m*, Knappheit *f* (***of*** an *dat*)

**scare 1.** erschrecken; ***be ~d*** Angst haben (***of*** vor *dat*); **~ *away,* ~ *off*** verjagen, -scheuchen **2.** Schreck(en) *m*; Panik *f*

**scare·crow** Vogelscheuche *f* (*a. fig*)

**scarf** Schal *m*; Hals-, Kopf-, Schultertuch *n*

**scar·let** scharlachrot; **~ fe·ver** MED Scharlach *m*

**scarred** narbig

**scath·ing** bissig (*remark etc*); vernichtend (*criticism etc*)

**scat·ter** (sich) zerstreuen (*crowd*); ausstreuen, verstreuen; auseinanderstieben (*birds etc*)

**scat·ter·brained** F schusselig, schusslig

**scat·tered** verstreut; vereinzelt

**scav·enge**: **~ *on*** zo leben von; **~ *for*** suchen (nach)

**scene** Szene *f*; Schauplatz *m*; *pl* THEA Kulissen *pl*

**sce·ne·ry** Landschaft *f*, Gegend *f*; THEA Bühnenbild *n*, Kulissen *pl*

**scent 1.** Duft *m*, Geruch *m*; *esp Br* Parfüm *n*; HUNT Witterung *f*; Fährte *f*, Spur *f* (*a. fig*) **2.** wittern; *esp Br* parfümieren;

**scent·less** geruchlos

**scep·ter**, *Br* **scep·tre** Zepter *n*

**scep·tic, scep·ti·cal** *Br* → ***skeptic*** *etc*

**sched·ule 1.** Aufstellung *f*, Verzeichnis *n*; (*Arbeits-*, *Stunden-*, *Zeit- etc*)Plan *m*; Fahr-, Flugplan *m*; ***ahead of* ~** dem Zeitplan voraus, früher als vorgesehen; ***be behind* ~** Verspätung haben; im Verzug *or* Rückstand sein; ***on* ~** (fahr-) planmäßig, pünktlich **2.** ***the meeting is ~d for Monday*** die Sitzung ist für Montag angesetzt; ***it is ~d to take place tomorrow*** es soll morgen stattfinden

**sched·uled| de·par·ture** (fahr)planmäßige Abfahrt; **~ flight** Linienflug *m*

**scheme 1.** *esp Br* Programm *n*, Projekt *n*; Schema *n*, System *n*; Intrige *f*, Machenschaft *f* **2.** intrigieren

**schmaltz·y** F schnulzig

**schnit·zel** GASTR Wiener Schnitzel *n*

**schol·ar** Gelehrte *m*, *f*; UNIV Stipendiat(in); **schol·ar·ly** gelehrt

**schol·ar·ship** Gelehrsamkeit *f*; UNIV Stipendium *n*

**school**[1] **1.** Schule *f* (*a. fig*); UNIV Fakultät *f*; Hochschule *f*; ***at* ~** auf *or* in der Schule; ***go to* ~** in die *or* zur Schule gehen **2.** *j-n* schulen, unterrichten; *Tier* dressieren

**school**[2] zo Schule *f*, Schwarm *m*

**school·bag** Schultasche *f*

**school·boy** Schüler *m*

**school·child** Schulkind *n*

**school·fel·low** → ***schoolmate***

**school·girl** Schülerin *f*

**school·ing** (Schul)Ausbildung *f*

**school·mate** Mitschüler(in), Schulkamerad(in)

**school·teach·er** (Schul)Lehrer(in)

**school·yard** Schulhof *m*

**schoo·ner** MAR Schoner *m*

**sci·ence** Wissenschaft *f*; *a.* ***natural* ~** Naturwissenschaft(en *pl*) *f*; **~ fic·tion** (*abbr* ***SF***) Sciencefiction *f*

**sci·en·tif·ic** (natur)wissenschaftlich; exakt, systematisch

**sci·en·tist** (Natur)Wissenschaftler(in)

**sci-fi** F Sciencefiction *f*

**scis·sors**: (***a pair of* ~** e-e) Schere

**scoff 1.** spotten (***at*** über *acc*); **2.** spöttische Bemerkung

**scold** schimpfen (mit)

**scoop 1.** Schöpfkelle *f*; (*Mehl- etc* -) Schaufel *f*; (*Eis- etc*)Portionierer *m*; Kugel *f* (*icecream*); *newspaper, radio,* TV Exklusivmeldung *f*, F Knüller *m* **2.** schöpfen, schaufeln; **~ *up*** aufheben, hochheben

**scoot·er** (Kinder)Roller *m*; (*Motor-*) Roller *m*

**scope** Bereich *m*; Spielraum *m*

**scorch** *v/t* ansengen, versengen, verbrennen; ausdörren; *v/i Br* MOT F rasen

**score 1.** SPORT (Spiel)Stand *m*, (-)Ergebnis *n*; MUS Partitur *f*; Musik *f*; 20 (Stück); *a.* **~ *mark*** Kerbe *f*, Rille *f*; ***what is the* ~?** wie steht es *or* das Spiel?; ***the* ~ *stood at*** *or* ***was 3-2*** das Spiel stand 3:2; ***keep* (*the*) ~** anschreiben; ***~s of*** e-e Menge; ***four* ~ *and ten*** neunzig; ***on that* ~** deshalb, in dieser Hinsicht; ***have a* ~ *to settle with s.o.*** e-e alte Rechnung mit j-m zu begleichen haben **2.** *v/t* SPORT *Punkte*, *Treffer* erzielen, *Tor a.* schießen; *Erfolg*, *Sieg* erringen; MUS instrumentieren; die Musik schreiben zu *or* für; einkerben; *v/i* SPORT e-n Treffer *etc* erzielen, ein Tor schießen; erfolgreich sein

**score·board** SPORT Anzeigetafel *f*

**scor·er** SPORT Torschütze *m*, Torschützin *f*; Anschreiber(in)

**scorn** Verachtung *f*

S

**scorn·ful** verächtlich
**Scor·pi·o** ASTR Skorpion *m*; ***he*** (***she***) ***is*** (***a***) ~ er (sie) ist (ein) Skorpion
**Scot** Schotte *m*, Schottin *f*
**Scotch 1.** schottisch **2.** Scotch *m*
**scot-free**: F ***get off*** ~ ungeschoren davonkommen
**Scot·land** Schottland *n*
**Scots** schottisch; **Scotsman** Schotte *m*; **Scots·wom·an** Schottin *f*
**Scot·tish** schottisch
**scoun·drel** Schurke *m*
**scour**[1] scheuern, schrubben
**scour**[2] *Gegend* absuchen, durchkämmen (***for*** nach)
**scourge 1.** Geißel *f* (*a. fig*) **2.** geißeln, *fig a.* heimsuchen
**scout 1.** *esp* MIL Kundschafter *m*; *Br* motorisierter Pannenhelfer; *a.* ***boy*** ~ Pfadfinder *m*; *a.* ***girl*** ~ Pfadfinderin *f*; *a.* ***talent*** ~ Talentsucher(in) **2.** ~ ***about***, ~ ***around*** sich umsehen (***for*** nach); *a.* ~ ***out*** MIL auskundschaften
**scowl 1.** finsteres Gesicht **2.** finster blicken; ~ ***at s.o.*** j-n böse *or* finster anschauen
**scram·ble 1.** klettern; sich drängeln (***for*** zu); **2.** Kletterei *f*; Drängelei *f*
**scram·bled eggs** Rührei(er *pl*) *n*
**scrap**[1] **1.** Stückchen *n*, Fetzen *m*; Altmaterial *n*; Schrott *m*; *pl* Abfall *m*, Speisereste *pl* **2.** verschrotten; ausrangieren; *Plan etc* aufgeben, fallen lassen
**scrap**[2] F **1.** Streiterei *f*; Balgerei *f* **2.** sich streiten; sich balgen
**scrap·book** Sammelalbum *n*
**scrape 1.** (ab)kratzen, (ab)schaben; sich *die Knie etc* aufschürfen; *Wagen etc* ankratzen; scheuern (***against*** an *dat*); (entlang)streifen; scharren **2.** Kratzen *n*; Kratzer *m*, Schramme *f*; *fig* Klemme *f*
**scrap heap** Schrotthaufen *m*
**scrap met·al** Altmetall *n*, Schrott *m*
**scrap pa·per** *esp Br* Schmierpapier *n*
**scrap val·ue** Schrottwert *m*
**scrap·yard** Schrottplatz *m*
**scratch 1.** (zer)kratzen; abkratzen; *s-n Namen etc* einkratzen; (sich) kratzen; scharren **2.** Kratzer *m*, Schramme *f*; Gekratze *n*; Kratzen *n*; ***from*** ~ F ganz von vorn **3.** (bunt) zusammengewürfelt
**scratch·pad** Notiz-, Schmierblock *m*
**scratch pa·per** Schmierpapier *n*
**scrawl 1.** kritzeln **2.** Gekritzel *n*
**scraw·ny** dürr
**scream 1.** schreien (***with*** vor *dat*); *a.* ~ ***out*** schreien; ~ ***with laughter*** vor Lachen brüllen **2.** Schrei *m*; ~***s of laughter*** brüllendes Gelächter; ***be a*** ~ F zum Schreien (komisch) sein
**screech 1.** kreischen (*a. fig*), (gellend) schreien **2.** Kreischen *n*; (gellender) Schrei
**screen 1.** Wand-, Ofen-, Schutzschirm *m*; *film*: Leinwand *f*; *radar*, TV, IT Bildschirm *m*; Fliegenfenster *n*, -gitter *n*; *fig* Tarnung *f* **2.** abschirmen; *film* zeigen, *Fernsehprogramm a.* senden; *fig j-n* decken; *fig j-n* überprüfen; ~ ***off*** abtrennen
**screen·play** Drehbuch *n*
**screen sav·er** IT Bildschirmschoner *m*
**screw 1.** TECH Schraube *f*; ***he has a*** ~ ***loose*** F bei ihm ist e-e Schraube locker **2.** (an)schrauben (***to*** an *acc*); V bumsen, vögeln; ~ ***up*** *Gesicht* verziehen; *Augen* zusammenkneifen; ~ ***up one's courage*** sich ein Herz fassen
**screw·ball** F Spinner(in)
**screw·driv·er** Schraubenzieher *m*
**screw top** Schraubverschluss *m*
**scrib·ble 1.** (hin)kritzeln **2.** Gekritzel *n*
**scrimp**: ~ ***and save*** jeden Cent zweimal umdrehen
**script** Manuskript *n*; film, TV Drehbuch *n*, Skript *n*; THEA Text *m*, Textbuch *n*; Schrift(zeichen *pl*) *f*; *Br* UNIV (schriftliche) Prüfungsarbeit
**Scrip·ture** *a.* ***the*** ~***s*** REL die Heilige Schrift
**scroll 1.** Schriftrolle *f* **2.** ~ ***down*** (***up***) IT zurückrollen (vorrollen)
**scro·tum** ANAT Hodensack *m*
**scrub**[1] **1.** schrubben, scheuern **2.** Schrubben *n*, Scheuern *n*
**scrub**[2] Gebüsch *n*, Gestrüpp *n*
**scru·ple 1.** Skrupel *m*, Zweifel *m*, Bedenken *pl* **2.** Bedenken haben
**scru·pu·lous** gewissenhaft
**scru·ti·nize** genau prüfen; mustern
**scru·ti·ny** genaue Prüfung; prüfender Blick
**scu·ba div·ing** (Sport)Tauchen *n*
**scuf·fle 1.** Handgemenge *n*, Rauferei *f* **2.** sich raufen
**scull 1.** Skull *n*; Skullboot *n* **2.** rudern, skullen

**sculp·tor** Bildhauer *m*
**sculp·ture** **1.** Bildhauerei *f*; Skulptur *f*, Plastik *f* **2.** hauen, meißeln, formen
**scum** Schaum *m*; *fig* Abschaum *m*
**scurf** (Kopf)Schuppen *pl*
**scur·ri·lous** beleidigend; verleumderisch
**scur·ry** huschen; trippeln
**scur·vy** MED Skorbut *m*
**scut·tle**: ***~ away, ~ off*** davonhuschen
**scythe** Sense *f*
**sea** Meer *n* (*a. fig*), See *f*; ***at ~*** auf See; ***by ~*** auf dem Seeweg; ***by the ~*** am Meer
**sea·food** GASTR Meeresfrüchte *pl*
**sea·gull** ZO Seemöwe *f*
**seal**[1] ZO Robbe *f*, Seehund *m*
**seal**[2] **1.** Siegel *n*; TECH Plombe *f*; TECH Dichtung *f* **2.** (ver)siegeln; TECH plombieren; abdichten; *fig* besiegeln; ***~ed envelope*** verschlossener Briefumschlag; ***~ off*** *Gegend etc* abriegeln
**sea lev·el**: ***above*** (***below***) ***~*** über (unter) dem Meeresspiegel
**seal·ing wax** Siegellack *m*
**seam** Naht *f*; Fuge *f*; GEOL Flöz *n*
**sea·man** Seemann *m*
**seam·stress** Näherin *f*
**sea·plane** Wasserflugzeug *n*
**sea·port** Seehafen *m*; Hafenstadt *f*
**sea pow·er** Seemacht *f*
**search** **1.** *v/i* suchen (***for*** nach); ***~ through*** durchsuchen; *v/t j-n, et.* durchsuchen (***for*** nach) **2.** Suche *f* (***for*** nach); Fahndung *f* (***for*** nach); Durchsuchung *f*; ***in ~ of*** auf der Suche nach; **search·ing** prüfend (*look*); eingehend (*examination*)
**search·light** (Such)Scheinwerfer *m*
**search par·ty** Suchmannschaft *f*
**search war·rant** JUR Haussuchungs-, Durchsuchungsbefehl *m*
**sea·shore** Meeresküste *f*
**sea·sick** seekrank
**sea·side**: ***at*** *or* ***by the ~*** am Meer; ***go to the ~*** ans Meer fahren
**sea·side re·sort** Seebad *n*
**sea·son**[1] Jahreszeit *f*; Saison *f*, THEA *etc a.* Spielzeit *f*, (*Jagd-*, *Urlaubs- etc*)Zeit *f*; ***in*** (***out of***) ***~*** in (außerhalb) der (Hoch)Saison; ***cherries are now in ~*** jetzt ist Kirschenzeit; ***Season's Greetings!*** Frohe Weihnachten!; ***with the compliments of the ~*** mit den besten Wünschen zum Fest
**sea·son**[2] *Speise* würzen (***with*** mit); *Holz* ablagern
**sea·son·al** saisonbedingt, Saison…
**sea·son·ing** GASTR Gewürz *n*
**sea·son tick·et** RAIL *etc* Dauer-, Zeitkarte *f*; THEA Abonnement *n*
**seat** **1.** Sitz(gelegenheit *f*) *m*; (Sitz)Platz *m*; Sitz(fläche *f*) *m*; Hosenboden *m*; Hinterteil *n*; (*Geschäfts-*, *Regierungs- etc*)Sitz *m*; PARL Sitz *m*; ***take a ~*** Platz nehmen; ***take one's ~*** s-n Platz einnehmen **2.** *j-n* setzen; Sitzplätze bieten für; ***be ~ed*** sitzen; ***please be ~ed*** bitte nehmen Sie Platz; ***remain ~ed*** sitzen bleiben
**seat belt** AVIAT, MOT Sicherheitsgurt *m*; ***fasten one's ~*** sich anschnallen
**sea ur·chin** ZO Seeigel *m*
**sea·ward(s)** seewärts
**sea·weed** BOT (See)Tang *m*
**sea·wor·thy** seetüchtig
**sec** F Augenblick *m*, Sekunde *f*; ***just a ~*** Augenblick(, bitte)!
**se·cede** sich abspalten (***from*** von)
**se·ces·sion** Abspaltung *f*, Sezession *f* (***from*** von)
**se·clud·ed** abgelegen, abgeschieden (*place*); zurückgezogen (*life*)
**se·clu·sion** Abgeschiedenheit *f*; Zurückgezogenheit *f*
**sec·ond**[1] **1.** *adj* zweite(r, -s); ***every ~ day*** jeden zweiten Tag, alle zwei Tage; ***~ to none*** unerreicht, unübertroffen; ***but on ~ thought*** (*Br* ***thoughts***) aber wenn ich es mir so überlege **2.** *adv* als Zweite(r, -s) **3.** *der*, *die*, *das* Zweite; MOT zweiter Gang; Sekundant *m*; *pl* F ECON Waren *pl* zweiter Wahl **4.** *Antrag etc* unterstützen
**sec·ond**[2] Sekunde *f*; *fig* Augenblick *m*, Sekunde *f*; ***just a ~*** Augenblick(, bitte)!
**sec·ond·a·ry** sekundär, zweitrangig; PED höher
**sec·ond-best** zweitbeste(r, -s)
**sec·ond class** RAIL *etc* zweiter Klasse
**sec·ond-class** zweitklassig
**sec·ond floor** erster (*Br* zweiter) Stock
**sec·ond hand** Sekundenzeiger *m*
**sec·ond-hand** aus zweiter Hand; gebraucht; antiquarisch
**sec·ond·ly** zweitens
**sec·ond-rate** zweitklassig
**se·cre·cy** Verschwiegenheit *f*; Geheimhaltung *f*

**se·cret 1.** geheim, Geheim...; heimlich; verschwiegen **2.** Geheimnis *n*; ***in ~*** heimlich, im Geheimen; ***keep s.th. a ~*** et. geheim halten (***from*** vor *dat*); ***can you keep a ~?*** kannst du schweigen?
**se·cret a·gent** Geheimagent(in)
**sec·re·ta·ry** Sekretär(in); POL Minister(in)
**Sec·re·ta·ry of State** POL Außenminister(in); *Br* Minister(in)
**se·crete** MED absondern; **se·cre·tion** MED Sekret *n*; Absonderung *f*
**se·cre·tive** verschlossen
**se·cret·ly** heimlich
**se·cret ser·vice** Geheimdienst *m*
**sec·tion** Teil *m*; Abschnitt *m*; JUR Paragraf *m*; Abteilung *f*; MATH, TECH Schnitt *m*
**sec·tor** Sektor *m*, Bereich *m*
**sec·u·lar** weltlich
**se·cure 1.** sicher (***against, from*** vor *dat*); **2.** *Tür etc* fest verschließen; *et.* sichern (***against, from*** vor *dat*)
**se·cu·ri·ty** Sicherheit *f*; *pl* ECON Wertpapiere *pl*; **~ check** Sicherheitskontrolle *f*; **~ mea·sure** Sicherheitsmaßnahme *f*; **~ risk** Sicherheitsrisiko *n*
**se·dan** MOT Limousine *f*
**se·date** ruhig, gelassen
**sed·a·tive** *mst* MED **1.** beruhigend **2.** Beruhigungsmittel *n*
**sed·i·ment** (Boden)Satz *m*
**se·duce** verführen
**se·duc·er** Verführer(in)
**se·duc·tion** Verführung *f*
**se·duc·tive** verführerisch
**see**[1] *v/i* sehen; nachsehen; ***I ~!*** (ich) verstehe!, ach so!; ***you ~*** weißt du; ***let me ~*** warte mal, lass mich überlegen; ***we'll ~*** mal sehen; *v/t* sehen; besuchen; *j-n* aufsuchen, *j-n* konsultieren; ***~ s.o. home*** j-n nach Hause bringen *or* begleiten; ***~ you!*** bis dann!, auf bald!; ***~ about*** sehen nach, sich kümmern um; ***~ off*** *j-n* verabschieden (***at*** am *Bahnhof etc*); ***~ out*** *j-n* hinausbringen, hinausbegleiten; ***~ through*** *j-n*, *et.* durchschauen; *j-m* hinweghelfen über (*acc*); ***~ to it that*** dafür sorgen, dass
**see**[2] REL Bistum *n*, Diözese *f*; ***Holy See*** *der* Heilige Stuhl
**seed 1.** BOT Same(n) *m*; AGR Saat *f*, Saatgut *n*; (*Apfel- etc*)Kern *m*; SPORT gesetzter Spieler, gesetzte Spielerin; ***go*** *or* ***run to ~*** BOT schießen; ***go to ~*** F herunterkommen, verkommen **2.** *v/t* besäen; entkernen; SPORT *Spieler* setzen; *v/i* BOT in Samen schießen
**seedless** BOT kernlos
**seed·y** F heruntergekommen
**seek** *Schutz, Wahrheit etc* suchen
**seem** scheinen; **seem·ing** scheinbar
**seep** sickern
**see·saw** Wippe *f*, Wippschaukel *f*
**seethe** schäumen (*a. fig*); *fig* kochen
**see-through** durchsichtig
**seg·ment** Teil *m*, *n*; Stück *n*; Abschnitt *m*; Segment *n*
**seg·re·gate** trennen
**seg·re·ga·tion** Rassentrennung *f*
**seize** *j-n*, *et.* packen, ergreifen; *Macht etc* an sich reißen; *et.* beschlagnahmen; *et.* pfänden; **sei·zure** Beschlagnahme *f*; Pfändung *f*; MED Anfall *m*
**sel·dom** *adv* selten
**se·lect 1.** (aus)wählen **2.** ausgewählt; exklusiv; **se·lec·tion** (Aus)Wahl *f*; ECON Auswahl *f* (***of*** an *dat*)
**self** Ich *n*, Selbst *n*
**self-as·sured** selbstbewusst, -sicher
**self-cen·tered**, *Br* **self-cen·tred** egozentrisch
**self-col·o(u)red** einfarbig
**self-con·fi·dence** Selbstbewusstsein *n*, Selbstvertrauen *n*
**self-con·fi·dent** selbstbewusst
**self-con·scious** befangen, gehemmt, unsicher
**self-con·tained** (in sich) abgeschlossen; *fig* verschlossen; ***~ flat*** *Br* abgeschlossene Wohnung
**self-con·trol** Selbstbeherrschung *f*
**self-crit·i·cal** selbstkritisch
**self-de·fence** *Br*, **self-de·fense** Selbstverteidigung *f*; ***in ~*** in *or* aus Notwehr
**self-de·ter·mi·na·tion** POL Selbstbestimmung *f*
**self-em·ployed** selbstständig
**self-es·teem** Selbstachtung *f*
**self-ev·i·dent** selbstverständlich; offensichtlich
**self-gov·ern·ment** POL Selbstverwaltung *f*
**self-help** Selbsthilfe *f*; **~ group** Selbsthilfegruppe *f*
**self-im·por·tant** überheblich
**self-in·dul·gent** nachgiebig gegen sich

selbst; zügellos
**self-in·terest** Eigennutz *m*
**self·ish** selbstsüchtig, egoistisch
**self-knowl·edge** Selbsterkenntnis *f*
**self-pit·y** Selbstmitleid *n*
**self-por·trait** Selbstportät *n*
**self-pos·sessed** selbstbeherrscht
**self-re·li·ant** selbstständig
**self-re·spect** Selbstachtung *f*
**self-right·eous** selbstgerecht
**self-sat·is·fied** selbstzufrieden
**self-serv·ice** **1.** mit Selbstbedienung, Selbstbedienungs… **2.** Selbstbedienung *f*
**self-stud·y** Selbststudium *n*
**self-suf·fi·cient** ECON autark
**self-sup·port·ing** finanziell unabhängig
**self-willed** eigensinnig, eigenwillig
**sell** *v/t* verkaufen; *v/i* verkauft werden (***at, for*** für); sich *gut etc* verkaufen (lassen), gehen; ***~ by…*** mindestens haltbar bis …; ***~ off*** (*esp* billig) abstoßen; ***~ out*** ausverkaufen; ***be sold out*** ausverkauft sein; ***~ up*** *esp Br sein Geschäft etc* verkaufen; **sell-by date** Mindesthaltbarkeitsdatum *n*; **sell·er** Verkäufer(in); ***good ~*** ECON gut gehender Artikel
**sem·blance** Anschein *m* (***of*** von)
**se·men** MED Samen(flüssigkeit *f*) *m*, Sperma *n*
**se·mes·ter** UNIV Semester *n*
**sem·i…** halb…, Halb…
**sem·i·cir·cle** Halbkreis *m*
**sem·i·co·lon** LING Semikolon *n*, Strichpunkt *m*
**sem·i·con·duc·tor** ELECTR Halbleiter *m*
**sem·i·de·tached (house)** *Br* Doppelhaushälfte *f*
**sem·i·fi·nals** SPORT Semi-, Halbfinale *n*
**sem·i·nar·y** Priesterseminar *n*
**sem·i·pre·cious**: ***~ stone*** Halbedelstein *m*
**sem·i-skilled** angelernt
**sem·o·li·na** Grieß *m*
**sen·ate** POL Senat *m*
**sen·a·tor** POL Senator *m*
**send** *et., a. Grüße, Hilfe etc* senden, schicken (***to*** *dat or* an *acc*); *Ware etc* versenden, verschicken (***to*** an *acc*); *j-n* schicken (***to*** ins *Bett etc*); *with adj or pp*: machen; ***~ word to s.o.*** j-m Nachricht geben; ***~ away*** fort-, wegschicken; *Brief etc* absenden, abschicken; ***~ down*** *Preise etc* fallen lassen; ***~ for*** nach *j-m* schicken, *j-n* kommen lassen; sich *et.* kommen lassen, *et.* anfordern; ***~ in*** einsenden, einschicken, einreichen; ***~ off*** fort-, wegschicken; *Brief etc* absenden, abschicken; SPORT *j-n* vom Platz stellen; ***~ on*** *Brief etc* nachsenden, nachschicken (***to*** an *acc*); *Gepäck etc* vorausschicken; ***~ out*** hinausschicken; *Einladungen etc* verschicken; ***~ up*** *Preise etc* steigen lassen
**send·er** Absender(in)
**se·nile** senil; **se·nil·i·ty** Senilität *f*
**se·ni·or** **1.** senior; älter (***to*** als); dienstälter; rangälter; Ober… **2.** Ältere *m*, *f*; UNIV Student(in) im letzten Jahr; ***he is my ~ by a year*** er ist ein Jahr älter als ich; **~ cit·i·zens** ältere Mitbürger *pl*, Senioren *pl*
**se·ni·or·i·ty** (höheres) Alter; (höheres) Dienstalter; (höherer) Rang
**se·ni·or part·ner** ECON Seniorpartner *m*
**sen·sa·tion** Empfindung *f*; Gefühl *n*; Sensation *f*
**sen·sa·tion·al** F großartig, fantastisch; sensationell, Sensations…
**sense** **1.** Sinn *m*; Verstand *m*; Vernunft *f*; Gefühl *n*; Bedeutung *f*; ***bring s.o. to his ~s*** j-n zur Besinnung *or* Vernunft bringen; ***come to one's ~s*** zur Besinnung *or* Vernunft kommen; ***in a ~*** in gewisser Hinsicht; ***make ~*** e-n Sinn ergeben; vernünftig sein; ***~ of duty*** Pflichtgefühl *n*; ***~ of security*** Gefühl *n* der Sicherheit **2.** fühlen, spüren
**sense·less** bewusstlos; sinnlos
**sen·si·bil·i·ty** Empfindlichkeit *f*; *a. pl* Empfindsamkeit *f*, Zartgefühl *n*
**sen·si·ble** vernünftig; spürbar, merklich; *esp Br* praktisch (*clothes etc*)
**sen·si·tive** empfindlich; sensibel, empfindsam, feinfühlig
**sen·sor** TECH Sensor *m*
**sen·su·al** sinnlich
**sen·su·ous** sinnlich
**sen·tence** **1.** LING Satz *m*; JUR Strafe *f*, Urteil *n*; ***pass or pronounce ~*** das Urteil fällen (***on*** über *acc*); **2.** JUR verurteilen (***to*** zu)
**sen·ti·ment** Gefühle *pl*; Sentimentalität *f*; *a. pl* Ansicht *f*, Meinung *f*
**sen·ti·ment·al** sentimental; gefühlvoll
**sen·ti·men·tal·i·ty** Sentimentalität *f*
**sen·try** MIL Wache *f*, (Wach[t])Posten *m*

S

**sep·a·ra·ble** trennbar; **sep·a·rate 1.** (sich) trennen; (auf-, ein-, zer)teilen (***into*** in *acc*); **2.** getrennt, separat; einzeln; **sep·a·ra·tion** Trennung *f*; (Auf-, Ein-, Zer)Teilung *f*

**Sept** *abbr of* ***September*** Sept., September *m*

**Sep·tem·ber** September *m*

**sep·tic** MED vereitert, septisch

**se·quel** Nachfolgeroman *m*, -film *m*, Fortsetzung *f*; *fig* Folge *f*; Nachspiel *n*

**se·quence** (Aufeinander-, Reihen)Folge *f*; *film*, TV Sequenz *f*, Szene *f*; ***~ of tenses*** LING Zeitenfolge *f*

**ser·e·nade** MUS **1.** Serenade *f*, Ständchen *n* **2.** *j-m* ein Ständchen bringen

**se·rene** klar; heiter; gelassen

**ser·geant** MIL Feldwebel *m*; (Polizei-) Wachtmeister *m*

**se·ri·al 1.** Fortsetzungsroman *m*; (*Rundfunk-, Fernseh*)Serie *f* **2.** serienmäßig, Serien..., Fortsetzungs...

**se·ries** Serie *f*, Reihe *f*, Folge *f*; (*Buch*)-Reihe *f*; (*Rundfunk-, Fernseh*)Serie *f*, Sendereihe *f*

**se·ri·ous** ernst, ernsthaft; ernstlich; schwer (*illness, damage, crime etc*); ***be ~*** es ernst meinen (***about*** mit)

**se·ri·ous·ness** Ernst *m*, Ernsthaftigkeit *f*; Schwere *f*

**ser·mon** REL Predigt *f*; F Moral-, Strafpredigt *f*

**ser·pen·tine** gewunden, kurvenreich

**ser·rat·ed** zackig, gezackt

**se·rum** MED Serum *n*

**ser·vant** Diener(in) (*a. fig*); Dienstmädchen *n*; → ***civil servant***

**serve 1.** *v/t j-m, s-m Land etc* dienen; *Dienstzeit* (*a.* MIL) ableisten, *Amtszeit etc* durchlaufen; *j-n, et.* versorgen (***with*** mit); *Essen* servieren; *Alkohol* ausschenken; *j-n* (*im Laden*) bedienen; JUR *Strafe* verbüßen; *e-m Zweck* dienen; *e-n Zweck* erfüllen; JUR *Vorladung etc* zustellen (***on s.o.*** j-m); *tennis etc*: aufschlagen; ***are you being ~d?*** werden Sie schon bedient?; (***it***) ***~s him right*** F (das) geschieht ihm ganz recht; *v/i esp* MIL dienen; servieren; dienen (***as, for*** als); *tennis etc*: aufschlagen; ***XY to ~*** *tennis etc*: Aufschlag XY; ***~ on a committee*** e-m Ausschuss angehören **2.** *tennis etc*: Aufschlag *m*

**serv·er** *tennis etc*: Aufschläger(in); GASTR Servierlöffel *m*

**ser·vice 1.** Dienst *m* (***to*** an *dat*); Dienstleistung *f*; (*Post-, Staats-, Telefon- etc-*) Dienst *m*; (*Zug- etc*)Verkehr *m*; ECON Service *m*, Kundendienst *m*; Bedienung *f*; Betrieb *m*; REL Gottesdienst *m*; TECH Wartung *f*, MOT *a.* Inspektion *f*; (*Tee- etc*)Service *n*; JUR Zustellung *f* (*e-r Vorladung*); *tennis etc*: Aufschlag *m*; *pl* MIL Streitkräfte *pl* **2.** TECH warten

**ser·vice·a·ble** brauchbar; strapazierfähig

**ser·vice| ar·e·a** MOT (Autobahn)Raststätte *f*; **~ charge** Bedienung *f*, Bedienungszuschlag *m*; **~ sta·tion** Tankstelle *f*; (Reparatur)Werkstatt *f*

**ser·vi·ette** *esp Br* Serviette *f*

**ser·vile** sklavisch (*a. fig*); servil, unterwürfig

**serv·ing** Portion *f*

**ser·vi·tude** Knechtschaft *f*; Sklaverei *f*

**ses·sion** Sitzung *f*; Sitzungsperiode *f*; ***be in ~*** JUR, PARL tagen

**set 1.** *v/t* setzen, stellen, legen; *in e-n Zustand* versetzen; veranlassen (***doing*** zu tun); TECH einstellen, *Uhr* stellen (***by*** nach), *Wecker* stellen (***for*** auf *acc*); *Tisch* decken; *Preis, Termin etc* festsetzen, festlegen; *Rekord* aufstellen; *Edelstein* fassen (***in*** in *dat*); *Ring etc* besetzen (***with*** mit); *Flüssigkeit* erstarren lassen; *Haar* legen; *Knochen* einrenken, einrichten; MUS vertonen; PRINT absetzen; *Aufgabe, Frage* stellen; ***~ at ease*** beruhigen; ***~ an example*** ein Beispiel geben; ***~ s.o. free*** j-n freilassen; ***~ going*** in Gang setzen; ***~ s.o. thinking*** j-m zu denken geben; ***~ one's hopes on*** s-e Hoffnung setzen auf (*acc*); ***~ s.o.'s mind at rest*** j-n beruhigen; ***~ great*** (***little***) ***store by*** großen (geringen) Wert legen auf (*acc*); ***the novel is ~ in*** der Roman spielt in (*dat*); *v/i* ASTR untergehen; fest werden, erstarren; HUNT vorstehen; ***~ about doing s.th.*** sich daranmachen, et. zu tun; ***~ about s.o.*** F über j-n herfallen; ***~ aside*** beiseitelegen; JUR *Urteil etc* aufheben; ***~ back*** verzögern; *j-n, et.* zurückwerfen (***by two months*** um zwei Monate); ***~ in*** einsetzen; ***~ off*** aufbrechen, sich aufmachen; hervorheben, betonen; *et.* auslösen; ***~ out*** arrangieren, herrichten; aufbrechen, sich aufmachen; ~

***out to do s.th.*** sich daranmachen, et. zu tun; ~ ***up*** errichten; *Gerät etc* aufbauen; *Firma etc* gründen; *et.* auslösen, verursachen; *j-n* versorgen (***with*** mit); sich niederlassen; ~ ***o.s. up as*** sich ausgeben für **2.** *adj* festgesetzt, festgelegt; F bereit, fertig; starr (*smile etc*); ~ ***lunch** or* ***meal*** *Br* Menü *n*; ~ ***phrase*** feststehender Ausdruck; ***be ~ on doing s.th.*** (fest) entschlossen sein, et. zu tun; ***be all ~*** F startklar sein **3.** Satz *m*; (*Möbel- etc*)Garnitur *f*, (*Tee- etc*)Service *n*; (*Fernseh-, Rundfunk-*)Apparat *m*, (-)Gerät *n*; THEA Bühnenbild *n*; *film*, TV Set *n*, *m*; *tennis etc*: Satz *m*; (Personen)Kreis *m*, Clique *f*; (*Kopf- etc*)Haltung *f*; ***have a shampoo and ~*** sich die Haare waschen und legen lassen

**set·back** Rückschlag *m* (***to*** für)

**set·square** *Br* Winkel *m*, Zeichendreieck *n*

**set·tee** Sofa *n*

**set the·o·ry** MATH Mengenlehre *f*

**set·ting** ASTR Untergang *m*; TECH Einstellung *f*; Umgebung *f*; *film etc*: Schauplatz *m*; (*Gold- etc*)Fassung *f*

**set·ting lo·tion** Haarfestiger *m*

**set·tle** *v/i* sich niederlassen (***on*** auf *acc or dat*), sich setzen (***on*** auf *acc*) (*a.* ~ ***down***); sich niederlassen (***in*** in *dat*); sich legen (*dust*); sich setzen (*coffee etc*); sich senken (*building etc*); sich beruhigen (*person, stomach etc*), sich legen (*a.* ~ ***down***); sich einigen; *v/t j-n*, *Nerven etc* beruhigen; vereinbaren; *Frage etc* klären, entscheiden; *Streit etc* beilegen; *Land* besiedeln; *Leute* ansiedeln; *Rechnung* begleichen, bezahlen; *Konto* ausgleichen; *Schaden* regulieren; *s-e Angelegenheiten* in Ordnung bringen; ~ ***o.s.*** sich niederlassen (***on*** auf *acc or dat*), sich setzen (***on*** auf *acc*); ***that ~s it*** damit ist der Fall erledigt; ***that's ~d then*** das ist also klar; ~ ***back*** sich (gemütlich) zurücklehnen; ~ ***down*** → *v/i*; sesshaft werden; ~ ***down to*** sich widmen (*dat*); ~ ***for*** sich zufriedengeben *or* begnügen mit; ~ ***in*** sich einleben *or* eingewöhnen; ~ ***on*** sich einigen auf (*acc*); ~ ***up*** (be)zahlen; abrechnen (***with*** mit)

**set·tled** fest (*ideas etc*); geregelt (*life*); beständig (*weather*)

**set·tle·ment** Vereinbarung *f*; Klärung *f*; Beilegung *f*; Einigung *f*; Siedlung *f*; Besiedlung *f*; Begleichung *f*, Bezahlung *f*; ***reach a ~*** sich einigen

**set·tler** Siedler(in)

**sev·en 1.** sieben **2.** Sieben *f*

**sev·en·teen 1.** siebzehn **2.** Siebzehn *f*

**sev·en·teenth** siebzehnte(r, -s)

**sev·enth 1.** siebente(r, -s), siebte(r, -s) **2.** Siebentel *n*, Siebtel *n*

**sev·enth·ly** siebentens, siebtens

**sev·en·ti·eth** siebzigste(r, -s)

**sev·en·ty 1.** siebzig **2.** Siebzig *f*

**sev·er** durchtrennen; abtrennen; *Beziehungen* abbrechen; (zer)reißen

**sev·er·al** mehrere

**sev·er·al·ly** einzeln, getrennt

**se·vere** schwer (*injuries, setback etc*); stark (*pain*); hart, streng (*winter*); streng (*person, discipline etc*); scharf (*criticism etc*); **se·ver·i·ty** Schwere *f*; Stärke *f*; Härte *f*; Strenge *f*; Schärfe *f*

**sew** nähen

**sew·age** Abwasser *n*

**sew·age works** Kläranlage *f*

**sew·er** Abwasserkanal *m*

**sew·er·age** Kanalisation *f*

**sew·ing 1.** Nähen *n*; Näharbeit *f* **2.** Näh…; ~ **ma·chine** Nähmaschine *f*

**sex** Geschlecht *n*; Sexualität *f*; Sex *m*; Geschlechtsverkehr *m*

**sex·ism** Sexismus *m*

**sex·ist 1.** sexistisch **2.** Sexist(in)

**sex·ton** Küster *m* (und Totengräber *m*)

**sex·u·al** sexuell, Sexual…, geschlechtlich, Geschlechts…; ~ **har·ass·ment** sexuelle Belästigung; ~ **in·ter·course** Geschlechtsverkehr *m*

**sex·u·al·i·ty** Sexualität *f*

**sex·y** F sexy, aufreizend

**shab·by** schäbig

**shack** Hütte *f*, Bude *f*; F *contp* Schuppen *m*

**shack·les** Fesseln *pl*, Ketten *pl* (*both a. fig*)

**shade 1.** Schatten *m* (*a. fig*); (*Lampen-*)Schirm *m*; Schattierung *f*; Rouleau *n*; *fig* Nuance *f*; ***a ~*** *fig* ein kleines bisschen, e-e Spur **2.** abschirmen (***from*** gegen); schattieren; ~ ***off*** allmählich übergehen (***into*** in *acc*)

**shad·ow 1.** Schatten *m* (*a. fig*); ***there's not a** or* ***the ~ of a doubt about it*** daran besteht nicht der geringste Zweifel **2.** *j-n* beschatten

**shad·ow·y** schattig, dunkel; verschwommen, vage, schemenhaft
**shad·y** schattig; Schatten spendend; F zwielichtig, fragwürdig
**shaft** (*Pfeil- etc*)Schaft *m*; (*Hammer- etc*)Stiel *m*; TECH Welle *f*; (*Aufzugs-, Bergwerks- etc*)Schacht *m*; (*Sonnen- etc*)Strahl *m*
**shag·gy** zottig, struppig
**shake 1.** *v/t* schütteln; rütteln an (*dat*); erschüttern; **~ *hands*** sich die Hand geben *or* schütteln; *v/i* zittern, beben, wackeln (***with*** vor *dat*); **~ *down*** herunterschütteln; durchsuchen, F filzen; *Br* F kampieren; **~ *off*** abschütteln; *Erkältung etc* loswerden; **~ *up*** *Kissen etc* aufschütteln; *Flasche, Flüssigkeit* (durch-) schütteln; *fig* erschüttern **2.** Schütteln *n*; F Milchshake *m*; **~ *of the head*** Kopfschütteln *n*
**shake·down** F Erpressung *f*; Durchsuchung *f*, Filzung *f*; *Br* (Not)Lager *n*
**shak·en** *a.* **~ *up*** erschüttert
**shak·y** wack(e)lig; zitt(e)rig
**shall** *v/aux future*: *ich* werde, *wir* werden; *in questions*: soll *ich* ...?, sollen *wir* ...?; **~ *we go?*** gehen wir?
**shal·low** seicht, flach, *fig a.* oberflächlich; **shal·lows** seichte *or* flache Stelle, Untiefe *f*
**sham 1.** Farce *f*; Heuchelei *f* **2.** unecht, falsch; vorgetäuscht, geheuchelt **3.** *v/t* *Mitgefühl etc* vortäuschen, heucheln; *Krankheit etc* simulieren; *v/i* sich verstellen, heucheln; ***he's only ~ming*** er tut nur so
**sham·bles** F Schlachtfeld *n*, wüstes Durcheinander, Chaos *n*
**shame 1.** Scham *f*, Schamgefühl *n*; Schande *f*; **~*!*** pfui!; **~ *on you!*** pfui!; schäm dich!; ***put to ~*** → **2.** beschämen; Schande machen (*dat*)
**shame·faced** betreten, verlegen
**shame·ful** beschämend; schändlich
**shame·less** schamlos
**sham·poo 1.** Shampoo *n*, Schampon *n*, Schampun *n*; Haarwäsche *f*; → ***set*** *3* **2.** *Haare* waschen; *j-m* die Haare waschen; *Teppich etc* schamponieren
**shank** TECH Schaft *m*; GASTR Hachse *f*
**shan·ty**¹ Hütte *f*, Bude *f*
**shan·ty**² Shanty *n*, Seemannslied *n*
**shan·ty·town** Elendsviertel *n*
**shape 1.** Form *f*; Gestalt *f*; Verfassung *f*, Zustand *m*; ***in good*** (***bad***) **~** in gutem (schlechtem) Zustand; ***in*** (***out of***) **~** SPORT (nicht) gut in Form; ***take ~*** *fig* Gestalt annehmen **2.** *v/t* formen; gestalten; *v/i a.* **~ *up*** sich *gut etc* machen
**shape·less** formlos; ausgebeult
**shape·ly** wohlgeformt
**share 1.** Anteil *m* (***in, of*** an *dat*); *esp Br* ECON Aktie *f*; ***go ~s*** teilen; ***have a*** (***no***) **~ *in*** (nicht) beteiligt sein an (*dat*) **2.** *v/t* (sich) *et.* teilen (***with*** mit); *a.* **~ *out*** verteilen (***among, between*** an *acc*, unter *acc*); *v/i* teilen; **~ *in*** sich teilen in (*acc*)
**share·hold·er** *esp Br* ECON Aktionär(in)
**shark** ZO Hai(fisch) *m*
**sharp 1.** *adj* scharf (*a. fig*); spitz; abrupt; schneidend (*wind, frost, command, voice, etc*); beißend (*cold, smell etc*); stechend, heftig (*pain*); gescheit; MUS (*um e-n Halbton*) erhöht; ***C ~*** MUS Cis *n* **2.** *adv* scharf, abrupt; MUS zu hoch; pünktlich, genau; ***at eight o'clock ~*** Punkt 8 (Uhr)
**sharp·en** *Messer etc* schärfen, schleifen; *Bleistift etc* spitzen
**sharp·en·er** (*Messer- etc*)Schärfer *m*; (*Bleistift*)Spitzer *m*
**sharp·ness** Schärfe *f* (*a. fig*)
**sharp·shoot·er** Scharfschütze *m*
**sharp-sight·ed** scharfsichtig
**sharp-wit·ted** scharfsinnig
**shat·ter** *v/t* zerschmettern, zerschlagen; *Hoffnungen etc* zerstören; *v/i* zerspringen, zersplittern
**shat·ter·ing** vernichtend; erschütternd
**shat·ter·proof** splitterfrei
**shave 1.** (sich) rasieren; (glatt) hobeln; *j-n, et.* streifen **2.** Rasur *f*; ***have a ~*** sich rasieren; ***that was a close ~*** das war knapp, das ist gerade noch einmal gut gegangen!; **shav·en** kahl geschoren
**shav·er** (*esp* elektrischer) Rasierapparat *m*
**shav·ing 1.** Rasieren *n* **2.** Rasier...; **~ bag** Kulturbeutel *m*; **~ brush** Rasierpinsel *m*; **~ cream** Rasiercreme *f*
**shav·ings** Späne *pl*
**shawl** Umhängetuch *n*; Kopftuch *n*
**she 1.** *pron* sie **2.** Sie *f*; ZO Weibchen *n* **3.** *adj in cpds* ZO ...weibchen *n*; ***~-bear*** Bärin *f*
**sheaf** Bündel *n*; AGR Garbe *f*
**shear 1.** scheren **2.** (***a pair of***) ***~s*** (e-e)

S

große Schere
**sheath** (*Schwert- etc*)Scheide *f*; Hülle *f*; *Br* Kondom *n*, *m*; **sheathe** *Schwert etc* in die Scheide stecken; TECH umhüllen, verkleiden, ummanteln
**shed**[1] Schuppen *m*; Stall *m*
**shed**[2] *Tränen etc* vergießen; *Blätter etc* verlieren; *fig Hemmungen etc* ablegen; **~ *its skin*** sich häuten; **~ *a few pounds*** ein paar Pfund abnehmen
**sheen** Glanz *m*
**sheep** ZO Schaf *n*
**sheep·dog** ZO Schäferhund *m*
**sheep·ish** verlegen
**sheep·skin** Schaffell *n*
**sheer** rein, bloß; steil, (fast) senkrecht; hauchdünn
**sheet** Betttuch *n*, (Bett)Laken *n*, Leintuch *n*; (*Glas-*, *Metall- etc*)Platte *f*; Blatt *n*, Bogen *m*; weite (*Eis- etc*)Fläche; ***the rain was coming down in ~s*** es regnete in Strömen
**sheet light·ning** Wetterleuchten *n*
**shelf** (Bücher-, Wand- *etc*)Brett *n*, (-)Bord *n*; GEOGR Riff *n*; *pl* Regal *n*; ***off the ~*** gleich zum Mitnehmen
**shell** **1.** (*Austern-*, *Eier-*, *Nuss- etc*) Schale *f*; BOT (*Erbsen- etc*)Hülse *f*; ZO Muschel *f*; (*Schnecken*)Haus *n*; ZO Panzer *m*; MIL Granate *f*; (Geschoss-, Patronen)Hülse *f*; Patrone *f*; TECH Rumpf *m*, Gerippe *n*, ARCH *a.* Rohbau *m* **2.** schälen, enthülsen; mit Granaten beschießen
**shell·fish** ZO Schal(en)tier *n*
**shel·ter** **1.** Zuflucht *f*, Schutz *m*; Unterkunft *f*, Obdach *n*; MIL Unterstand *m*; ***run for ~*** Schutz suchen; ***take ~*** sich unterstellen (***under*** unter *dat*); ***bus ~*** Wartehäuschen *n* **2.** *v/t* schützen (***from*** vor *dat*); *v/i* sich unterstellen
**shelve** *v/t Bücher* in ein Regal stellen; *Plan etc* aufschieben, zurückstellen; *v/i* sanft abfallen (*garden etc*)
**shep·herd** **1.** Schäfer *m*, Hirt *m* **2.** *j-n* führen
**sher·iff** Sheriff *m*
**shield** **1.** Schild *m* **2.** *j-n* (be)schützen (***from*** vor *dat*); *j-n* decken
**shift** **1.** *v/t et.* bewegen, schieben, *Möbelstück a.* (ver)rücken; *Schuld etc* (ab-) schieben (***onto*** auf *acc*); **~ *gear(s)*** MOT schalten; *v/i* sich bewegen; umspringen (*wind*); *fig* sich verlagern *or* verschieben *or* wandeln; MOT schalten (***into, to*** in *acc*); **~ *from one foot to the other*** von e-m Fuß auf den anderen treten; **~ *on one's chair*** auf s-m Stuhl *ungeduldig etc* hin und her rutschen **2.** *fig* Verlagerung *f*, Verschiebung *f*, Wandel *m*; ECON Schicht *f*; **~ key** TECH Umschalttaste *f*; **~ work·er** Schichtarbeiter(in)
**shift·y** F verschlagen
**shim·mer** schimmern; flimmern
**shin** **1.** *a.* ***~bone*** ANAT Schienbein *n* **2.** **~ *up*** hinaufklettern; **~ *down*** herunterklettern
**shine** **1.** *v/i* scheinen; leuchten; glänzen (*a. fig*); *v/t Schuhe etc* polieren **2.** Glanz *m*
**shin·gle**[1] grober Strandkies
**shin·gle**[2] (Dach)Schindel *f*
**shin·gles** MED Gürtelrose *f*
**shin·y** blank, glänzend
**ship** **1.** Schiff *n* **2.** verschiffen; ECON verfrachten, versenden
**ship·ment** ECON Ladung *f*; Verschiffung *f*, Verfrachtung *f*, Versand *m*
**ship·own·er** Reeder *m*; Schiffseigner *m*
**ship·ping** Schifffahrt *f*; Schiffsbestand *m*; ECON Verschiffung *f*, Verfrachtung *f*, Versand *m*
**ship·wreck** Schiffbruch *m*
**ship·wrecked** **1.** ***be ~*** Schiffbruch erleiden **2.** schiffbrüchig
**ship·yard** (Schiffs)Werft *f*
**shirk** sich drücken (vor *dat*)
**shirk·er** Drückeberger(in)
**shirt** Hemd *n*
**shirt·sleeve** **1.** Hemdsärmel *m*; ***in (one's) ~s*** in Hemdsärmeln, hemdsärmelig **2.** hemdsärmelig
**shish ke·bab** GASTR Schaschlik *m*, *n*
**shit** V **1.** Scheiße *f* (*a. fig*); *fig* Scheiß *m* **2.** (voll)scheißen
**shiv·er** **1.** zittern (***with*** vor *dat*); **2.** Schauer *m*; *pl* MED F Schüttelfrost *m*; ***the sight send ~s (up and) down my spine*** bei dem Anblick überlief es mich eiskalt
**shoal**[1] Untiefe *f*; Sandbank *f*
**shoal**[2] ZO Schwarm *m*
**shock**[1] **1.** Schock *m* (*a.* MED); Wucht *f*; ELECTR Schlag *m*, (*a.* MED Elektro-) Schock *m*; ***be in (a state of) ~*** unter Schock stehen **2.** schockieren, empören; *j-m* e-n Schock versetzen

S

**shock**[2] (~ ***of hair*** Haar)Schopf *m*
**shock ab·sorb·er** TECH Stoßdämpfer *m*
**shock·ing** schockierend, empörend, anstößig; F scheußlich
**shod·dy** minderwertig (*goods*); gemein, schäbig (*trick etc*)
**shoe 1.** Schuh *m*; Hufeisen *n* **2.** *Pferd* beschlagen
**shoe·horn** Schuhanzieher *m*, -löffel *m*
**shoe·lace** Schnürsenkel *m*
**shoe·mak·er** Schuhmacher *m*, Schuster *m*
**shoe·shine boy** Schuhputzer *m*
**shoe store** (*Br* **shop**) Schuhgeschäft *n*
**shoe·string** Schnürsenkel *m*
**shoot 1.** *v/t* schießen, HUNT *a.* erlegen; abfeuern, abschießen; erschießen; *Riegel* vorschieben; *j-n* fotografieren, aufnehmen, *Film* drehen; *Heroin etc* spritzen; ~ ***the lights*** MOT bei Rot fahren; *v/i* schießen (***at*** auf *acc*); jagen; *fig* schießen, rasen; *film*, TV drehen, filmen; BOT sprießen, treiben **2.** BOT Trieb *m*; Jagd *f*; Jagdrevier *n*
**shoot·er** F Schießeisen *n*
**shoot·ing 1.** Schießen *n*; Schießerei *f*; Erschießung *f*; Anschlag *m*; Jagd *f*; *film*, TV Dreharbeiten *pl*, Aufnahmen *pl* **2.** stechend (*pain*); ~ **gal·le·ry** Schießbude *f*; ~ **range** Schießstand *m*; ~ **star** ASTR Sternschnuppe *f*
**shop 1.** *Br* Laden *m*, Geschäft *n*; Werkstatt *f*; Betrieb *m*; ***talk*** ~ fachsimpeln **2.** *mst* ***go shopping*** einkaufen gehen
**shop as·sis·tant** *Br* Verkäufer(in)
**shop·keep·er** *Br* Ladenbesitzer(in), Ladeninhaber(in)
**shop·lift·er** Ladendieb(in)
**shop·lift·ing** Ladendiebstahl *m*
**shop·per** Käufer(in)
**shop·ping 1.** Einkauf *m*, Einkaufen *n*; Einkäufe *pl* (*items bought*); ***do one's*** ~ *Br* einkaufen, (s-e) Einkäufe machen **2.** Einkaufs...; ~ **bag** Einkaufsbeutel *m*, -tasche *f*; ~ **cart** Einkaufswagen *m*; ~ **cen·ter** (*Br* **cen·tre**) Einkaufszentrum *n*; ~ **list** Einkaufsliste *f*, -zettel *m*; ~ **mall** Einkaufszentrum *n*; ~ **precinct** *Br* Fußgängerzone *f*; ~ **street** Geschäfts-, Ladenstraße *f*
**shop stew·ard** ECON gewerkschaftlicher Vertrauensmann
**shop·walk·er** *Br* Aufsicht(sperson) *f*
**shop win·dow** Schaufenster *n*
**shore**[1] Küste *f*; (*See*)Ufer *n*; ***on*** ~ an Land
**shore**[2]: ~ ***up*** (ab)stützen
**short 1.** *adj* kurz; klein (*person*); kurz angebunden, barsch, schroff (***with*** zu); GASTR mürbe; ***be*** ~ ***for*** die Kurzform sein von; ***be*** ~ ***of ...*** nicht genügend ... haben **2.** *adv* plötzlich, abrupt; ~ ***of*** außer; ***cut*** ~ plötzlich unterbrechen; ***fall*** ~ ***of*** *et.* nicht erreichen; ***stop*** ~ plötzlich innehalten, stutzen; ***stop*** ~ ***of*** *or* ***at*** zurückschrecken vor (*dat*); → ***run*** *1* **3.** F Kurzfilm *m*; ELECTR Kurze *m*; ***called ... for*** ~ kurz ... genannt; ***in*** ~ kurz(um)
**short·age** Knappheit *f*, Mangel *m* (***of*** an *dat*)
**short·com·ings** Unzulänglichkeiten *pl*, Mängel *pl*, Fehler *pl*
**short cut** Abkürzung *f*; ***take a*** ~ (den Weg) abkürzen
**short·en** *v/t* (ab-, ver)kürzen; *v/i* kürzer werden
**short·hand** Kurzschrift *f*, Stenografie *f*
**short·ly** bald; barsch, schroff; mit wenigen Worten
**short·ness** Kürze *f*; Schroffheit *f*
**shorts** *a.* ***pair of*** ~ Shorts *pl*; (Herren)Unterhose *f*
**short·sight·ed** *esp Br* kurzsichtig (*a. fig*)
**short sto·ry** Kurzgeschichte *f*
**short-tem·pered** aufbrausend, hitzig
**short-term** ECON kurzfristig
**short time** ECON Kurzarbeit *f*
**short wave** ELECTR Kurzwelle *f*
**short-wind·ed** kurzatmig
**shot** Schuss *m*; Schrot(kugeln *pl*) *m*, *n*; SPORT Kugel *f*; *guter etc* Schütze *m*; *soccer etc*: Schuss *m*; *basketball etc*: Wurf *m*; *tennis*, *golf*: Schlag *m*; PHOT Schnappschuss *m*, Aufnahme *f*; *film*, TV Aufnahme *f*, Einstellung *f*; MED F Spritze *f*; F Schuss *m* (*of drugs*); *fig* F Versuch *m*; ***a*** ~ ***of rum*** ein Schluck Rum; ***I'll have a*** ~ ***at it*** ich probier's mal; ***not by a long*** ~ F noch lange nicht; → ***big shot***
**shot·gun** Schrotflinte *f*
**shot·gun wed·ding** F Mussheirat *f*
**shot put** SPORT Kugelstoßen *n*
**shot put·ter** SPORT Kugelstoßer(in)
**shoul·der 1.** ANAT Schulter *f*; MOT Standspur *f* **2.** schultern; *Kosten*, *Verantwortung etc* übernehmen; (mit der Schul-

ter) stoßen; ~ **bag** Schulter-, Umhängetasche *f*; ~ **blade** ANAT Schulterblatt *n*; ~ **strap** Träger *m*; Tragriemen *m*

**shout 1.** *v/i* rufen, schreien (***for*** nach; ***for help*** um Hilfe); ~ ***at s.o.*** j-n anschreien; *v/t* rufen, schreien **2.** Ruf *m*, Schrei *m*

**shove 1.** stoßen, F schubsen; *et.* schieben, stopfen **2.** Stoß *m*, F Schubs *m*

**shov·el 1.** Schaufel *f* **2.** schaufeln

**show 1.** *v/t* zeigen, vorzeigen, anzeigen; *j-n* bringen, führen (***to*** zu); ausstellen; zeigen, *film etc a.* vorführen, TV *a.* bringen; *v/i* zu sehen sein; ***be ~ing*** gezeigt werden, laufen; ~ ***around*** herumführen; ~ ***in*** herein-, hineinführen, herein-, hineinbringen; ~ ***off*** angeben *or* protzen (mit); vorteilhaft zur Geltung bringen; ~ ***out*** heraus-, hinausführen, heraus-, hinausbringen; ~ ***round*** herumführen; ~ ***up*** *v/t* herauf-, hinaufführen, herauf-, hinaufbringen; sichtbar machen; *j-n* entlarven, bloßstellen; *et.* aufdecken; *j-n* in Verlegenheit bringen; *v/i* zu sehen sein; F aufkreuzen, auftauchen **2.** THEA *etc* Vorstellung *f*; Show *f*; *radio*, TV Sendung *f*; Ausstellung *f*; Zurschaustellung *f*, Demonstration *f*; *fig leerer* Schein; ***be on ~*** ausgestellt *or* zu besichtigen sein; ***steal the ~ from s.o.*** *fig* j-m die Schau stehlen; ***make a ~ of*** *Anteilnahme*, *Interesse etc* heucheln; ***put up a poor ~*** F e-e schwache Leistung zeigen; ***be in charge of the whole ~*** F den ganzen Laden schmeißen **3.** Muster…

**show·biz** F, **show busi·ness** Showbusiness *n*, Showgeschäft *n*, Unterhaltungsindustrie *f*

**show·case** Schaukasten *m*, Vitrine *f*

**show·down** Kraft-, Machtprobe *f*

**show·er 1.** (Regen- *etc*)Schauer *m*; (*Funken*)Regen *m*; (*Wasser-*, *Wort-etc*)Schwall *m*; Dusche *f*; (Geschenk-) Party *f*; ***have*** *or* ***take a ~*** duschen **2.** *v/t j-n mit et.* überschütten *or* überhäufen; *v/i* duschen; ~ ***down*** niederprasseln

**show jump·er** SPORT Springreiter(in)

**show jump·ing** SPORT Springreiten *n*

**show-off** F Angeber(in)

**show·room** Ausstellungsraum *m*

**show tri·al** JUR Schauprozess *m*

**show·y** auffallend

**shred 1.** Fetzen *m* **2.** zerfetzen; in (schmale) Streifen schneiden, schnitzeln, schnetzeln; in den Papier- *or* Reißwolf geben; **shred·der** Schnitzelmaschine *f*; Papier-, Reißwolf *m*

**shrewd** scharfsinnig; schlau

**shriek 1.** (gellend) aufschreien; ~ ***with laughter*** vor Lachen kreischen **2.** (schriller) Schrei

**shrill** schrill; *fig* heftig, scharf, lautstark

**shrimp** ZO Garnele *f*; *fig contp* Knirps *m*

**shrine** Schrein *m*

**shrink 1.** (ein-, zusammen)schrumpfen (lassen); einlaufen; *fig* abnehmen **2.** F Klapsdoktor *m*

**shrink·age** Schrumpfung *f*; Einlaufen *n*; *fig* Abnahme *f*

**shrink-wrap** einschweißen

**shriv·el** schrumpfen (lassen); runz(e)lig werden (lassen)

**shroud 1.** Leichentuch *n* **2.** *fig* hüllen

**Shrove Tues·day** Fastnachts-, Faschingsdienstag *m*

**shrub** Strauch *m*, Busch *m*

**shrub·be·ry** BOT Strauch-, Buschwerk *n*, Gebüsch *n*

**shrug 1.** *a.* ~ ***one's shoulders*** mit den Achseln *or* Schultern zucken **2.** Achselzucken *n*, Schulterzucken *n*

**shuck** BOT **1.** Hülse *f*, Schote *f*; Schale *f* **2.** enthülsen; schälen

**shud·der 1.** schaudern **2.** Schauder *m*

**shuf·fle 1.** *v/t Karten* mischen; *Papiere etc* umordnen, hierhin oder dorthin legen; ~ ***one's feet*** schlurfen; *v/i* schlurfen; *Karten* mischen **2.** Schlurfen *n*, schlurfender Gang; Mischen *n*

**shun** *j-n*, *et.* meiden

**shunt** *Zug etc* rangieren, verschieben; *a.* ~ ***off*** F *j-n* abschieben (***to*** in *acc*, nach)

**shut** (sich) schließen; zumachen; ~ ***down*** *Fabrik etc* schließen; ~ ***off*** *Wasser*, *Gas*, *Maschine etc* abstellen; ~ ***up*** einschließen; einsperren; *Geschäft* schließen; ~ ***up!*** F halt die Klappe!

**shut·ter** Fensterladen *m*; PHOT Verschluss *m*

**shut·tle 1.** Pendelverkehr *m*; (*Raum-*) Fähre *f*, (-)Transporter *m*; TECH Schiffchen *n* **2.** hin- und herbefördern

**shut·tle·cock** SPORT Federball *m*

**shut·tle ser·vice** Pendelverkehr *m*

**shy 1.** scheu; schüchtern **2.** scheuen (***at*** vor *dat*); ~ ***away from*** *fig* zurückschrecken vor (*dat*)

**shy·ness** Scheu *f*; Schüchternheit *f*
**sick 1.** krank; ***be ~*** *esp Br* sich übergeben; ***she was*** *or* ***felt ~*** ihr war schlecht; ***get ~*** krank werden; ***be off ~*** krank (geschrieben) sein; ***report ~*** sich krank melden; ***be ~ of s.th.*** F et. satthaben; ***it makes me ~*** F mir wird schlecht davon, *a. fig* es ekelt *or* widert mich an **2.** ***the ~*** die Kranken *pl*
**sick·bed** Krankenbett *n*
**sick·en** *v/t j-n* anekeln, anwidern; *v/i esp Br* krank werden
**sick·le** ['sɪkl] Sichel *f*
**sick leave**: ***be on ~*** krank (geschrieben) sein, wegen Krankheit fehlen
**sick·ly** kränklich; ungesund; matt; widerlich (*smell etc*)
**sick·ness** Krankheit *f*; Übelkeit *f*; **~ ben·e·fit** *Br* Krankengeld *n*
**side 1.** Seite *f*; *esp Br* SPORT Mannschaft *f*; ***~ by ~*** nebeneinander; ***take ~s*** Partei ergreifen (***with*** für; ***against*** gegen); **2.** Seiten…; Neben… **3.** Partei ergreifen (***with*** für; ***against*** gegen)
**side·board** Anrichte *f*, Sideboard *n*
**side·car** MOT Bei-, Seitenwagen *m*
**side dish** GASTR Beilage *f*
**side·long** seitlich; Seiten…; **~ glance** Seitenblick *m*
**side street** Nebenstraße *f*
**side·swipe** Seitenhieb *m*
**side·track** *j-n* ablenken; F *et.* abbiegen; RAIL *etc* rangieren, verschieben
**side·walk** Bürgersteig *m*, Gehsteig *m*
**side·walk ca·fé** Straßencafé *n*
**side·ways** seitlich; seitwärts, nach der *or* zur Seite
**sid·ing** RAIL Nebengleis *n*
**si·dle**: ***~ up to s.o.*** sich an j-n heranschleichen
**siege** MIL Belagerung *f*; ***lay ~ to*** belagern (*a. fig*)
**sieve 1.** Sieb *n* **2.** (durch)sieben
**sift** (durch)sieben; *a.* ***~ through*** *fig* sichten, durchsehen, prüfen
**sigh 1.** seufzen **2.** Seufzer *m*
**sight 1.** Sehvermögen *n*, Sehkraft *f*, Augenlicht *n*; Anblick *m*; Sicht(weite) *f*; *pl* Visier *n*; Sehenswürdigkeiten *pl*; ***at ~, on ~*** sofort; ***at the ~ of*** beim Anblick von (*or gen*); ***at first ~*** auf den ersten Blick; ***catch ~ of*** erblicken; ***know by ~*** vom Sehen kennen; ***lose ~ of*** aus den Augen verlieren; ***be (with)in ~*** in Sicht sein (*a. fig*) **2.** sichten
**sight-read** MUS vom Blatt singen *or* spielen
**sight·see·ing** Sightseeing *n*, Besichtigung *f* von Sehenswürdigkeiten; ***go ~*** sich die Sehenswürdigkeiten anschauen; **~ tour** Sightseeingtour *f*, Besichtigungstour *f*, (Stadt)Rundfahrt *f*
**sight·se·er** Tourist(in)
**sight test** Sehtest *m*
**sign 1.** Zeichen *n*; (*Hinweis-*, *Warn- etc*)-Schild *n*; *fig* (An)Zeichen *n* **2.** unterschreiben, unterzeichnen; *Scheck* ausstellen; ***~ in*** sich eintragen; ***~ out*** sich austragen
**sig·nal 1.** Signal *n* (*a. fig*); Zeichen *n* (*a. fig*) **2.** (ein) Zeichen geben; signalisieren
**sig·na·to·ry** Unterzeichner(in)
**sig·na·ture** Unterschrift *f*; Signatur *f*; **~ tune** *radio*, TV Kennmelodie *f*
**sign·board** (Aushänge)Schild *n*
**sign·er** Unterzeichnete *m*, *f*
**sig·net** Siegel *n*
**sig·nif·i·cance** Bedeutung *f*, Wichtigkeit *f*; **sig·nif·i·cant** bedeutend, bedeutsam, wichtig; bezeichnend
**sig·ni·fy** bedeuten; andeuten
**sign·post** Wegweiser *m*
**si·lence 1.** Stille *f*; Schweigen *n*; ***~!*** Ruhe!; ***in ~*** schweigend; ***reduce to ~*** → **2.** zum Schweigen bringen
**si·lenc·er** TECH Schalldämpfer *m*; *Br* MOT Auspufftopf *m*
**si·lent** still; schweigend; schweigsam; stumm; **~ part·ner** ECON stiller Teilhaber
**sil·i·con** CHEM Silizium *n*
**sil·i·cone** CHEM Silikon *n*
**silk 1.** Seide *f* **2.** Seiden…
**silk·worm** ZO Seidenraupe *f*
**silk·y** seidig; samtig (*voice*)
**sill** (*Fenster*)Brett *n*
**sil·ly 1.** albern, töricht, dumm **2.** F Dummerchen *n*
**sil·ver 1.** Silber *n* **2.** silbern, Silber… **3.** versilbern
**sil·ver-plat·ed** versilbert
**sil·ver·ware** Tafelsilber *n*
**sil·ver·y** silberglänzend; *fig* silberhell
**sim·i·lar** ähnlich (***to*** *dat*)
**sim·i·lar·i·ty** Ähnlichkeit *f*
**sim·i·le** Gleichnis *n*, Vergleich *m*
**sim·mer** leicht kochen, köcheln; ***~ with***

*fig* kochen vor (*rage etc*), fiebern vor (*excitement etc*); ~ ***down*** F sich beruhigen, F sich abregen
**sim·per** albern *or* affektiert lächeln
**sim·ple** einfach, schlicht; leicht; dumm, einfältig; naiv; ***the ~ fact is that …*** es ist einfach e-e Tatsache, dass …
**sim·ple-mind·ed** dumm; naiv
**sim·pli·ci·ty** Einfachheit *f*, Schlichtheit *f*; Dummheit *f*; Naivität *f*
**sim·pli·fi·ca·tion** Vereinfachung *f*
**sim·pli·fy** vereinfachen
**sim·ply** einfach; bloß, nur
**sim·u·late** vortäuschen; MIL, TECH simulieren
**sim·ul·ta·ne·ous** simultan, gleichzeitig
**sin 1.** Sünde *f* **2.** sündigen
**since 1.** *adv a.* ***ever ~*** seitdem, seither **2.** *prp* seit (*dat*) **3.** *cj* seit(dem); da
**sin·cere** aufrichtig, ehrlich, offen
**sin·cer·i·ty** Aufrichtigkeit *f*; Offenheit *f*
**sin·ew** ANAT Sehne *f*
**sin·ew·y** sehnig; *fig* kraftvoll
**sin·ful** sündig, sündhaft
**sing** singen; ~ ***s.th. to s.o.*** j-m et. vorsingen
**singe** (sich *et.*) ansengen *or* versengen
**sing·er** Sänger(in)
**sing·ing** Singen *n*, Gesang *m*
**sin·gle 1.** einzig; einzeln, Einzel…; einfach; ledig, unverheiratet; ***in ~ file*** im Gänsemarsch **2.** *Br* RAIL *etc* einfache Fahrkarte, AVIAT einfaches Ticket (*both a.* ~ ***ticket***); Single *f*; Single *m*, Unverheiratete *m*, *f* **3.** ~ ***out*** sich herausgreifen
**sin·gle-breast·ed** einreihig
**sin·gle-en·gined** AVIAT einmotorig
**sin·gle fam·i·ly home** Einfamilienhaus *n*
**sin·gle fa·ther** allein erziehender Vater
**sin·gle-hand·ed** eigenhändig, allein
**sin·gle-lane** MOT einspurig
**sin·gle-mind·ed** zielstrebig, -bewusst
**sin·gle moth·er** allein erziehende Mutter
**sin·gle pa·rent** Alleinerziehende *m*, *f*
**sin·gle room** Einzelzimmer *n*
**sin·gles** *esp tennis*: Einzel *n*; ***a ~ match*** ein Einzel; ***men's ~*** Herreneinzel *n*; ***women's ~*** Dameneinzel *n*
**sin·glet** *Br* ärmelloses Unterhemd *or* Trikot
**sin·gle-track** eingleisig, einspurig
**sin·gu·lar 1.** einzigartig, einmalig **2.** LING Singular *m*, Einzahl *f*
**sin·is·ter** finster, unheimlich
**sink 1.** *v/i* sinken, untergehen; sich senken; ~ ***in*** eindringen (*a. fig*); *v/t* versenken; *Brunnen etc* bohren; *Zähne etc* vergraben (***into*** in *acc*); **2.** Spülbecken *n*, Spüle *f*; Waschbecken *n*
**sin·ner** Sünder(in)
**sip 1.** Schlückchen *n* **2.** *v/t* nippen an (*dat*) *or* von; schlückchenweise trinken; *v/i* nippen (***at*** an *dat or* von)
**sir** mein Herr; ***Dear Sir or Madam*** Sehr geehrte Damen und Herren (*address in letters*)
**sire** zo Vater *m*, Vatertier *n*
**si·ren** Sirene *f*
**sis·sy** F Weichling *m*
**sis·ter** Schwester *f*; *Br* MED Oberschwester *f*; REL (Ordens)Schwester *f*
**sis·ter·hood** Schwesternschaft *f*
**sis·ter-in-law** Schwägerin *f*
**sis·ter·ly** schwesterlich
**sit** *v/i* sitzen; sich setzen; tagen; *v/t j-n* setzen; *esp Br Prüfung* ablegen, machen; ~ ***down*** sich setzen; ~ ***for*** *Br Prüfung* ablegen, machen; ~ ***in*** ein Sit-in veranstalten; an e-m Sit-in teilnehmen; ~ ***in for*** *j-n* vertreten; ~ ***in on*** als Zuhörer teilnehmen an (*dat*); ~ ***on*** sitzen auf (*dat*) (*a. fig*); ~ ***on a committee*** e-m Ausschuss angehören; ~ ***out*** das Ende (*gen*) abwarten; *Krise etc* aussitzen; ~ ***up*** sich *or j-n* aufrichten *or* aufsetzen; aufrecht sitzen; aufbleiben
**sit·com** → ***situation comedy***
**sit-down** *a.* ~ ***strike*** Sitzstreik *m*; *a.* ~ ***demonstration*** *or* F ***demo*** Sitzblockade *f*
**site** Platz *m*, Ort *m*, Stelle *f*; (*Ausgrabungs*)Stätte *f*; Baustelle *f*
**sit-in** Sit-in *n*, Sitzstreik *m*
**sit·ting** Sitzung *f*
**sit·ting room** *esp Br* Wohnzimmer *n*
**sit·u·at·ed**: ***be ~*** liegen, gelegen sein
**sit·u·a·tion** Lage *f*, Situation *f*; ~ **com·e·dy** TV *etc* Situationskomödie *f*
**six 1.** sechs **2.** Sechs *f*
**six·teen 1.** sechzehn **2.** Sechzehn *f*
**six·teenth** sechzehnte(r, -s)
**sixth 1.** sechste(r, -s) **2.** Sechstel *n*
**sixth·ly** sechstens
**six·ti·eth** sechzigste(r, -s)

S

**six·ty** 1. sechzig 2. Sechzig *f*
**size** 1. Größe *f*, *fig a.* Ausmaß *n*, Umfang *m* 2. ~ ***up*** F abschätzen
**siz(e)·a·ble** beträchtlich
**siz·zle** brutzeln
**skate** 1. Schlittschuh *m*; Rollschuh *m* 2. Schlittschuh laufen, eislaufen; Rollschuh laufen
**skate·board** Skateboard *n*
**skat·er** Eisläufer(in), Schlittschuhläufer(in); Rollschuhläufer(in)
**skat·ing** Eislaufen *n*, Schlittschuhlaufen *n*; Rollschuhlaufen *n*; ***free*** ~ Kür *f*, Kürlauf *m*; ~ **rink** (Kunst)Eisbahn *f*; Rollschuhbahn *f*
**skel·e·ton** Skelett *n*, Gerippe *n*
**skep·tic** Skeptiker(in)
**skep·ti·cal** skeptisch
**sketch** 1. Skizze *f*; THEA *etc* Sketch *m* 2. skizzieren
**skew·er** 1. (Brat)Spieß *m* 2. (auf)spießen
**ski** 1. Ski *m* 2. Ski... 3. Ski fahren *or* laufen
**skid** 1. MOT rutschen, schleudern 2. MOT Rutschen *n*, Schleudern *n*; TECH Kufe *f*
**skid mark(s)** MOT Bremsspur *f*
**ski·er** Skifahrer(in), Skiläufer(in)
**ski goggles** Skibrille *f*
**ski·ing** Skifahren *n*, Skilaufen *n*, Skisport *m*
**ski jump** (Sprung)Schanze *f*
**ski jump·er** Skispringer *m*
**ski jump·ing** Skispringen *n*
**skil·ful** *Br* → ***skillful***
**ski lift** Skilift *m*
**skill** Geschicklichkeit *f*, Fertigkeit *f*
**skilled** geschickt (***at, in*** in *dat*)
**skilled work·er** Facharbeiter(in)
**skill·ful** geschickt
**skim** *Fett etc* abschöpfen (*a.* ~ ***off***); *Milch* entrahmen; (hin)gleiten über (*acc*); *a.* ~ ***over***, ~ ***through*** *Bericht etc* überfliegen
**skim(med) milk** Magermilch *f*
**skimp** *a.* ~ ***on*** sparen an (*dat*)
**skimp·y** dürftig; knapp
**skin** 1. ANAT Haut *f*; ZO Fell *n*; BOT Schale *f* 2. *Tier* abhäuten; *Zwiebel etc* schälen; sich *das Knie etc* aufschürfen
**skin-deep** (nur) oberflächlich
**skin div·ing** Sporttauchen *n*
**skin·flint** Geizhals *m*
**skin·ny** F dürr, mager
**skin·ny-dip** F nackt baden
**skip** 1. *v/i* hüpfen, springen; seilhüpfen, seilspringen; *v/t et.* überspringen, aus lassen 2. Hüpfer *m*
**skip·per** MAR, SPORT Kapitän *m*
**skir·mish** Geplänkel *n*
**skirt** 1. Rock *m* 2. *a.* ~ ***(a)round*** umgeben; *Problem etc* umgehen
**skirt·ing board** *Br* Scheuerleiste *f*
**ski| run** Skipiste *f*; ~ **tow** Schlepplift *m*
**skit·tle** Kegel *m*
**skulk** sich herumdrücken, herumschleichen
**skull** ANAT Schädel *m*
**skul(l)·dug·ge·ry** F fauler Zauber
**skunk** ZO Skunk *m*, Stinktier *n*
**sky** *a.* ***skies*** Himmel *m*
**sky·jack** *Flugzeug* entführen
**sky·jack·er** Flugzeugentführer(in)
**sky·lark** ZO Feldlerche *f*
**sky·light** Dachfenster *n*
**sky·line** Skyline *f*, Silhouette *f*
**sky·rock·et** F hochschnellen, in die Höhe schießen
**sky·scrap·er** Wolkenkratzer *m*
**slab** (*Stein- etc*)Platte *f*; dickes Stück
**slack** 1. locker; ECON flau; *fig* lax, lasch, nachlässig 2. bummeln; ~ ***off***, ~ ***up*** *fig* nachlassen, (*person a.*) abbauen
**slack·en** *v/t* lockern; verringern; ~ ***speed*** langsamer werden; *v/i* locker werden; *a.* ~ ***off*** nachlassen
**slacks** F Hose *f*
**slag** TECH Schlacke *f*
**sla·lom** SPORT Slalom *m*
**slam** 1. *a.* ~ ***shut*** zuschlagen, F zuknallen; *a.* ~ ***down*** F *et.* knallen (***on*** auf *acc*); ~ ***on the brakes*** F MOT auf die Bremse steigen 2. Zuschlagen *n*; Knall *m*
**slan·der** 1. Verleumdung *f* 2. verleumden; **slan·der·ous** verleumderisch
**slang** 1. Slang *m*; Jargon *m* 2. *esp Br* F *j-n* wüst beschimpfen
**slant** 1. schräg legen *or* liegen; sich neigen 2. schräge Fläche; Abhang *m*; *fig* Einstellung *f*; ***at*** *or* ***on a*** ~ schräg
**slant·ing** schräg
**slap** 1. Klaps *m*, Schlag *m* 2. e-n Klaps geben (*dat*); schlagen; klatschen (***down on*** auf *acc*; ***against*** gegen)
**slap·stick** THEA Slapstick *m*, Klamauk *m*; ~ **com·e·dy** Slapstickkomödie *f*
**slash** 1. auf-, zerschlitzen; *Preise* drastisch herabsetzen; *Ausgaben etc* dras-

S

tisch kürzen; ~ ***at*** schlagen nach **2.** Hieb *m*; Schlitz *m*
**slate 1.** Schiefer *m*; Schiefertafel *f*; POL Kandidatenliste *f* **2.** mit Schiefer decken; *j-n* vorschlagen (***for, to be*** als); *et.* planen (***for*** für)
**slaugh·ter 1.** Schlachten *n*; *fig* Blutbad *n*, Gemetzel *n* **2.** schlachten; *fig* niedermetzeln; **slaugh·ter·house** Schlachthaus *n*, Schlachthof *m*
**Slav 1.** Slawe *m*, Slawin *f* **2.** slawisch
**slave 1.** Sklave *m*, Sklavin *f* (*a. fig*) **2.** *a.* ~ ***away*** sich abplagen, F schuften
**slav·er** geifern, sabbern
**sla·ve·ry** Sklaverei *f*
**slav·ish** sklavisch
**sleaze** unsaubere Machenschaften; Kumpanei *f*; F POL Filz *m*
**slea·zy** schäbig, heruntergekommen; anrüchig
**sled 1.** (*a.* Rodel)Schlitten *m* **2.** Schlitten fahren, rodeln
**sledge** *Br* → ***sled***
**sledge·ham·mer** TECH Vorschlaghammer *m*
**sleek 1.** glatt, glänzend; geschmeidig; MOT schnittig **2.** glätten
**sleep 1.** Schlaf *m*; ***I couldn't get to*** ~ ich konnte nicht einschlafen; ***go to*** ~ einschlafen (F *a. leg etc*); ***put to*** ~ *Tier* einschläfern **2.** *v/i* schlafen; ~ ***late*** lang *or* länger schlafen; ~ ***on*** *Problem etc* überschlafen; ~ ***with s.o.*** mit j-m schlafen; *v/t* Schlafgelegenheit bieten für
**sleep·er** Schlafende *m*, *f*, Schläfer(in); *Br* RAIL Schwelle *f*; RAIL Schlafwagen *m*
**sleep·ing bag** Schlafsack *m*
**Sleep·ing Beau·ty** Dornröschen *n*
**sleep·ing| car** RAIL Schlafwagen *m*; ~ **part·ner** *Br* ECON stiller Teilhaber; ~ **pill** PHARM Schlaftablette *f*, -mittel *n*; ~ **sick·ness** MED Schlafkrankheit *f*
**sleep·less** schlaflos
**sleep·walk·er** Schlafwandler(in)
**sleep·y** schläfrig, müde; verschlafen
**sleep·y·head** F Schlafmütze *f*
**sleet 1.** Schneeregen *m*; Graupelschauer *m* **2.** ***it's*** ~***ing*** es gibt Schneeregen; es graupelt
**sleeve** Ärmel *m*; TECH Manschette *f*, Muffe *f*; *esp Br* (*Platten*)Hülle *f*
**sleeve·less** ärmellos
**sleigh** (*esp* Pferde)Schlitten *m*
**sleight of hand** Fingerfertigkeit *f*; *fig* (Taschenspieler)Trick *m*
**slen·der** schlank; *fig* mager, dürftig; schwach (*hope etc*)
**slice 1.** Scheibe *f*, Stück *n*; *fig* Anteil *m* (***of*** an *dat*); **2.** *a.* ~ ***up*** in Scheiben *or* Stücke schneiden; ~ ***off*** *Stück* abschneiden (***from*** von)
**slick 1.** gekonnt; geschickt, raffiniert; glatt (*road etc*) **2.** F (*Öl*)Teppich *m* **3.** ~ ***down*** *Haar* glätten, F anklatschen
**slick·er** Regenmantel *m*
**slide 1.** gleiten (lassen); rutschen; schlüpfen; schieben; ***let things*** ~ *fig* die Dinge schleifenlassen **2.** Gleiten *n*, Rutschen *n*; Rutsche *f*, Rutschbahn *f*; TECH Schieber *m*; PHOT Dia *n*; Objektträger *m*; (*Erd- etc*)Rutsch *m*; *Br* (*Haar*)Spange *f*; ~ **rule** Rechenschieber *m*; ~ **tack·le** *soccer*: Grätsche *f*
**slid·ing door** Schiebetür *f*
**slight 1.** leicht, gering(fügig), unbedeutend **2.** beleidigen, kränken **3.** Beleidigung *f*, Kränkung *f*
**slim 1.** schlank; *fig* gering **2.** *a.* ***be slimming, be on a slimming diet*** e-e Schlankheitskur machen, abnehmen
**slime** Schleim *m*
**slim·y** schleimig (*a. fig*)
**sling 1.** aufhängen; F schleudern **2.** Schlinge *f*; Tragriemen *m*; Tragetuch *n*; Schleuder *f*
**slip**[1] **1.** *v/i* rutschen, schlittern; ausgleiten, ausrutschen; schlüpfen; *v/t* sich losreißen von; ~ ***s.th. into s.o.'s hand*** j-m et. in die Hand schieben; ~ ***s.o. s.th.*** j-m et. zuschieben; ~ ***s.o.'s attention*** j-m *or* j-s Aufmerksamkeit entgehen; ~ ***s.o.'s mind*** j-m entfallen; ***she has*** ~***ped a disk*** MED sie hat e-n Bandscheibenvorfall; ~ ***by***, ~ ***past*** verstreichen (*time*); ~ ***off***, ~ ***out of*** schlüpfen aus; ~ ***on*** überstreifen, schlüpfen in (*acc*) **2.** Ausgleiten *n*, (Aus)Rutschen *n*; Versehen *n*; Unterrock *m*; (*Kissen*)-Bezug *m*; ~ ***of the tongue*** Versprecher *m*; ***give s.o. the*** ~ F j-m entwischen
**slip**[2] *a.* ~ ***of paper*** Zettel *m*
**slip·case** Schuber *m*
**slip-on 1.** *adj* ~ ***shoe*** → **2.** Slipper *m*
**slipped disk** MED Bandscheibenvorfall *m*
**slip·per** Hausschuh *m*, Pantoffel *m*
**slip·per·y** glatt, rutschig, glitschig
**slip road** *Br* MOT → ***ramp***

S

**slip·shod** schlampig
**slit 1.** Schlitz *m* **2.** schlitzen; **~ *open*** aufschlitzen
**slith·er** gleiten, rutschen
**sliv·er** (*Glas- etc*)Splitter *m*
**slob·ber** sabbern
**slo·gan** Slogan *m*
**sloop** MAR Schaluppe *f*
**slop 1.** *v/t* verschütten; *v/i* überschwappen; schwappen (***over*** über *acc*); **2.** *a. pl* schlabb(e)riges Zeug; (*Tee-, Kaffee-*) Rest(e *pl*) *m*; *esp Br* Schmutzwasser *n*
**slope 1.** (Ab)Hang *m*; Neigung *f*, Gefälle *n* **2.** sich neigen, abfallen
**slop·py** schlampig; F gammelig; F rührselig
**slot** Schlitz *m*, (Münz)Einwurf *m*; IT Steckplatz *m*
**sloth** ZO Faultier *n*
**slot ma·chine** (Waren-, Spiel)Automat *m*
**slouch 1.** krumme Haltung; F latschiger Gang **2.** krumm dasitzen *or* dastehen; F latschen
**slough**[1]: **~ *off*** *Haut* abstreifen, ZO sich häuten
**slough**[2] Sumpf *m*, Sumpfloch *n*
**Slo·vak 1.** slowakisch **2.** Slowake *m*, Slowakin *f*; LING Slowakisch *n*
**Slo·va·ki·a** Slowakei *f*
**slov·en·ly** schlampig
**slow 1.** *adj* langsam; begriffsstutzig; ECON schleppend; ***be*** (***ten minutes***) **~** (zehn Minuten) nachgehen **2.** *adv* langsam **3.** *v/t often* **~ *down***, **~ *up*** *Geschwindigkeit* verringern; *v/i often* **~ *down***, **~ *up*** langsamer fahren *or* gehen *or* werden
**slow·coach** *Br* → ***slowpoke***
**slow·down** ECON Bummelstreik *m*
**slow lane** MOT Kriechspur *f*
**slow mo·tion** Zeitlupe *f*
**slow-mov·ing** kriechend (*traffic*)
**slow·poke** Langweiler(in)
**slow·worm** ZO Blindschleiche *f*
**sludge** Schlamm *m*
**slug**[1] ZO Nacktschnecke *f*
**slug**[2] F (*Gewehr- etc*)Kugel *f*; Schluck *m* (*whisky etc*)
**slug**[3] F *j-m* e-n Faustschlag versetzen
**slug·gish** träge; ECON schleppend
**sluice** TECH Schleuse *f*
**slum** *a. pl* Slums *pl*, Elendsviertel *n or pl*
**slum·ber** POET **1.** schlummern **2.** *a. pl* Schlummer *m*
**slump 1.** ECON stürzen (*prices*), stark zurückgehen (*sales etc*); ***sit* ~*ed over*** zusammengesunken sitzen über (*dat*); **~ *into a chair*** sich in e-n Sessel fallen lassen **2.** ECON starker Konjunkturrückgang; **~ *in prices*** Preissturz *m*
**slur**[1] **1.** MUS *Töne* binden; **~ *one's speech*** undeutlich sprechen; lallen **2.** undeutliche Aussprache
**slur**[2] **1.** verleumden **2. ~ *on s.o.'s reputation*** Rufschädigung *f*
**slurp** F schlürfen
**slush** Schneematsch *m*; F Kitsch *m*
**slush·y** F kitschig
**slut** Schlampe *f*; Nutte *f*
**sly** gerissen, schlau, listig; ***on the* ~** heimlich
**smack**[1] **1.** *j-m* e-n Klaps geben; **~ *one's lips*** sich (geräuschvoll) die Lippen lecken; **~ *down*** F *et.* hinklatschen **2.** klatschendes Geräusch, Knall *m*; F Schmatz *m* (*kiss*); F Klaps *m*
**smack**[2]: **~ *of*** *fig* schmecken *or* riechen nach
**small 1.** *adj and adv* klein; **~ *wonder*** (***that***) kein Wunder, dass; ***feel* ~** *fig* sich klein (und hässlich) vorkommen **2. ~ *of the back*** ANAT Kreuz *n*; **~ ad** Kleinanzeige *f*; **~ arms** Handfeuerwaffen *pl*; **~ change** Kleingeld *n*; **~ hours**: ***in the* ~** in den frühen Morgenstunden
**small-mind·ed** engstirnig; kleinlich
**small·pox** MED Pocken *pl*
**small print** *das* Kleingedruckte
**small talk** Small Talk *m, n*, oberflächliche Konversation; ***make* ~** plaudern
**small-time** F klein, unbedeutend; *in cpds* Schmalspur…
**small town** Kleinstadt *f*
**smart 1.** schick, fesch; smart, schlau, clever **2.** wehtun; brennen **3.** (brennender) Schmerz; **~ al·eck** F Besserwisser(in), Klugscheißer(in)
**smart·ness** Schick *m*; Schlauheit *f*, Cleverness *f*
**smash 1.** *v/t* zerschlagen (*a.* **~ *up***); schmettern (*a. tennis etc*); *Aufstand etc* niederschlagen, *Drogenring etc* zerschlagen; **~ *up one's car*** s-n Wagen zu Schrott fahren; *v/i* zerspringen; **~ *into*** prallen an (*acc*) *or* gegen, krachen gegen **2.** Schlag *m*; *tennis etc*: Schmetterball *m*; → ***smash hit, smash-up***

S

**smash hit** Hit *m*
**smash-up** MOT, RAIL schwerer Unfall
**smear 1.** Fleck *m*; MED Abstrich *m*; Verleumdung *f* **2.** (ein-, ver)schmieren; (sich) verwischen; verleumden
**smell 1.** *v/i* riechen (***at*** an *dat*); duften; stinken; *v/t* riechen (an *dat*); **2.** Geruch *m*; Gestank *m*; Duft *m*
**smell·y** übel riechend, stinkend
**smelt** *Erz* schmelzen
**smile 1.** Lächeln *n* **2.** lächeln; ***~ at*** *j-n* anlächeln, *j-m* zulächeln; *j-n, et.* belächeln, lächeln über (*acc*); ***~ to o.s.*** schmunzeln
**smiley** Smiley *n*
**smirk** (selbstgefällig *or* schadenfroh) grinsen
**smith** Schmied *m*
**smith·e·reens**: ***smash (in)to ~*** F in tausend Stücke schlagen *or* zerspringen
**smith·y** Schmiede *f*
**smit·ten** verliebt, F verknallt (***with*** in *acc*); ***be ~ by*** *or* ***with*** *fig* gepackt werden von
**smock** Kittel *m*
**smog** Smog *m*
**smoke 1.** Rauch *m*; ***have a ~*** eine rauchen **2.** rauchen; räuchern
**smok·er** Raucher(in); RAIL Raucher *m*, Raucherabteil *n*
**smoke·stack** Schornstein *m*
**smok·ing** Rauchen *n*; ***no ~*** Rauchen verboten; ***~ com·part·ment*** RAIL Raucher *m*, Raucherabteil *n*
**smok·y** rauchig; verräuchert
**smooch** F schmusen
**smooth 1.** glatt (*a. fig*); ruhig (*a. journey etc*); mild (*wine*); *fig* (aal)glatt **2.** *a.* ***~ out*** glätten, glatt streichen; ***~ away*** *Falten etc* glätten; *Schwierigkeiten etc* aus dem Weg räumen; ***~ down*** glatt streichen
**smoth·er** ersticken
**smo(u)l·der** glimmen, schwelen
**smudge 1.** Schmutzfleck *m* **2.** (be-, ver)schmieren; (sich) verwischen
**smug** selbstgefällig
**smug·gle** schmuggeln (***into*** nach; in *acc*); **smug·gler** Schmuggler(in)
**smut** Rußflocke *f*; Schmutz *m* (*a. fig*)
**smut·ty** *fig* schmutzig
**snack** Snack *m*, Imbiss *m*; ***have a ~*** e-e Kleinigkeit essen
**snack bar** Snackbar *f*, Imbissstube *f*
**snag 1.** *fig* Haken *m* **2.** mit *et.* hängen bleiben (***on*** an *dat*)
**snail** zo Schnecke *f*
**snake** zo Schlange *f*
**snap 1.** *v/i* (zer)brechen, (zer)reißen; *a.* ***~ shut*** zuschnappen; ***~ at*** schnappen nach; *j-n* anschnauzen; ***~ out of it!*** F Kopf hoch!, komm, komm!; ***~ to it!*** mach fix!; *v/t* zerbrechen; PHOT F knipsen; ***~ one's fingers*** mit den Fingern schnalzen; ***~ one's fingers at*** *fig* keinen Respekt haben vor (*dat*), sich hinwegsetzen über (*acc*); ***~ off*** abbrechen; ***~ up*** *et.* schnell entschlossen kaufen; ***~ it up!*** mach fix! **2.** Krachen *n*, Knacken *n*, Knall *m*; PHOT F Schnappschuss *m*; Druckknopf *m*; F Schwung *m*; ***cold ~*** Kälteeinbruch *m*
**snap fas·ten·er** Druckknopf *m*
**snap·pish** *fig* bissig
**snap·py** modisch, schick; ***make it ~!*** F mach fix!
**snap·shot** PHOT Schnappschuss *m*
**snare 1.** Schlinge *f*, Falle *f* (*a. fig*) **2.** in der Schlinge fangen; F *et.* ergattern
**snarl 1.** knurren; ***~ at s.o.*** j-n anknurren **2.** Knurren *n*
**snatch 1.** *v/t et.* packen; *Gelegenheit* ergreifen; *ein paar Stunden Schlaf etc* ergattern; ***~ s.o.'s handbag*** j-m die Handtasche entreißen; *v/i* ***~ at*** (schnell) greifen nach; *Gelegenheit* ergreifen **2.** ***make a ~ at*** (schnell) greifen nach; ***~ of conversation*** Gesprächsfetzen *m*
**sneak 1.** *v/i* (sich) schleichen; *Br* F petzen; *v/t* F stibitzen **2.** *Br* F Petze *f*
**sneak·er** Turnschuh *m*
**sneer 1.** höhnisch *or* spöttisch grinsen (***at*** über *acc*); spotten (***at*** über *acc*); **2.** höhnisches *or* spöttisches Grinsen; höhnische *or* spöttische Bemerkung
**sneeze 1.** niesen **2.** Niesen *n*
**snick·er** kichern (***at*** über *acc*)
**sniff 1.** *v/i* schniefen; schnüffeln (***at*** an *dat*); ***~ at*** *fig* die Nase rümpfen über (*acc*); *v/t Klebstoff etc* schnüffeln, *Kokain etc* schnupfen **2.** Schniefen *n*
**snif·fle 1.** schniefen **2.** Schniefen *n*; ***she's got the ~s*** F ihr läuft dauernd die Nase
**snig·ger** *esp Br* → ***snicker***
**snip 1.** Schnitt *m* **2.** durchschnippeln; ***~ off*** abschnippeln

**snipe**[1] zo Schnepfe *f*
**snipe**[2] aus dem Hinterhalt schießen (***at*** auf *acc*)
**snip·er** Heckenschütze *m*
**sniv·el** greinen, jammern
**snob** Snob *m*; **snob·bish** versnobt
**snoop**: ~ ***about***, ~ ***around*** F herumschnüffeln
**snoop·er** F Schnüffler(in)
**snooze** F **1.** ein Nickerchen machen **2.** Nickerchen *n*
**snore 1.** schnarchen **2.** Schnarchen *n*
**snor·kel 1.** Schnorchel *m* **2.** schnorcheln
**snort 1.** schnauben **2.** Schnauben *n*
**snot·ty nose** F Rotznase *f*
**snout** zo Schnauze *f*, Rüssel *m*
**snow 1.** Schnee *m* (*a. sl cocaine*) **2.** schneien; ***be ~ed in*** *or* ***up*** eingeschneit sein
**snow·ball** Schneeball *m*; ~ **fight** Schneeballschlacht *f*
**snow·board** Snowboard *n*; **~ing** Snowboardfahren *n*
**snow·bound** eingeschneit
**snow-capped** schneebedeckt
**snow·drift** Schneewehe *f*
**snow·drop** BOT Schneeglöckchen *n*
**snow·fall** Schneefall *m*
**snow·flake** Schneeflocke *f*
**snow line** Schneegrenze *f*
**snow·man** Schneemann *m*
**snow·mo·bile** Schneemobil *n*
**snow·plough** *Br*, **snow·plow** Schneepflug *m*
**snow·storm** Schneesturm *m*
**snow-white** schneeweiß
**Snow White** Schneewittchen *n*
**snow·y** schneereich; verschneit
**snub** *j-n* brüskieren, *j-n* vor den Kopf stoßen
**snub nose** Stupsnase *f*
**snuff**[1] Schnupftabak *m*
**snuff**[2] *Kerze* ausdrücken, löschen; ~ ***out*** *Leben* auslöschen
**snuf·fle** schnüffeln, schniefen
**snug** gemütlich, behaglich; *clothing*: gut sitzend; eng (anliegend)
**snug·gle**: ~ ***up to s.o.*** sich an j-n kuscheln; ~ ***down in bed*** sich ins Bett kuscheln
**so** so; deshalb; → ***hope*** 2, ***think***; ***is that ~?*** wirklich?; ***an hour or ~*** etwa e-e Stunde; ***she is tired - ~ am I*** sie ist müde - ich auch; ~ ***far*** bisher

**soak** *v/t* einweichen (***in*** in *dat*); durchnässen; ~ ***up*** aufsaugen; *v/i* sickern
**soak·ing** *a.* ~ ***wet*** völlig durchnässt, F klatschnass
**soap 1.** Seife *f*; F → ***soap opera*** **2.** (sich) einseifen
**soap op·e·ra** *radio*, TV Seifenoper *f*
**soap·y** Seifen...; seifig; *fig* F schmeichlerisch
**soar** (hoch) aufsteigen; hochragen; zo, AVIAT segeln, gleiten; *fig* in die Höhe schnellen (*prices etc*)
**sob 1.** schluchzen **2.** Schluchzen *n*
**so·ber 1.** nüchtern (*a. fig*) **2.** ernüchtern; ~ ***up*** nüchtern machen *or* werden
**so-called** sogenannt
**soc·cer** Fußball *m*
**soc·cer hoo·li·gan** Fußballrowdy *m*
**so·cia·ble** gesellig
**so·cial** sozial, Sozial...; gesellschaftlich, Gesellschafts...; zo gesellig; ~ **democrat** POL Sozialdemokrat(in); ~ **insurance** Sozialversicherung *f*
**so·cial·ism** Sozialismus *m*
**so·cial·ist 1.** Sozialist(in) **2.** sozialistisch
**so·cial·ize** *v/i* gesellschaftlich verkehren (***with*** mit); *v/t* sozialisieren
**so·cial| sci·ence** Sozialwissenschaft *f*; ~ **se·cu·ri·ty** *Br* Sozialhilfe *f*; ***be on ~*** Sozialhilfe beziehen; ~ **ser·vic·es** *esp Br* Sozialeinrichtungen; ~ **work** Sozialarbeit *f*; ~ **work·er** Sozialarbeiter(in)
**so·ci·e·ty** Gesellschaft *f*; Verein *m*
**so·ci·ol·o·gy** Soziologie *f*
**sock** Socke *f*
**sock·et** ELECTR Steckdose *f*; Fassung *f*; (Anschluss)Buchse *f*; ANAT (*Augen-*)Höhle *f*
**so·da** Soda(wasser) *n*; (*Orangen- etc*)Limonade *f*
**sod·den** aufgeweicht (*ground*); durchweicht (*clothes*)
**so·fa** Sofa *n*
**soft** weich; sanft; leise; gedämpft (*light etc*); F leicht, angenehm, ruhig (*job etc*); alkoholfrei (*drink*); F verweichlicht
**soft drink** Soft Drink *m*, alkoholfreies Getränk
**soft·en** *v/t* weich machen; *Wasser* enthärten; *Ton*, *Licht*, *Stimme etc* dämpfen; ~ **up** F *j-n* weich machen; *v/i* weich(er) *or* sanft(er) *or* mild(er) werden
**soft·heart·ed** weichherzig
**soft land·ing** weiche Landung

S

**soft·ware** IT Software *f*; ~ **pack·age** IT Softwarepaket *n*
**soft·y** F Softie *m*, Weichling *m*
**sog·gy** aufgeweicht, matschig
**soil**[1] Boden *m*, Erde *f*
**soil**[2] beschmutzen, schmutzig machen
**so·lar** Sonnen…; ~ **en·er·gy** Solar-, Sonnenenergie *f*; ~ **pan·el** Sonnenkollektor *m*; ~ **sys·tem** Sonnensystem *n*
**sol·der** TECH (ver)löten
**sol·dier** Soldat *m*
**sole**[1] **1.** (Fuß-, Schuh)Sohle *f* **2.** besohlen
**sole**[2] zo Seezunge *f*
**sole**[3] einzig; alleinig, Allein…
**sole·ly** (einzig und) allein, ausschließlich
**sol·emn** feierlich; ernst
**so·lic·it** bitten um
**so·lic·i·tous** besorgt (***about, for*** um)
**sol·id** **1.** fest; stabil; massiv; MATH körperlich; gewichtig, triftig (*reason etc*), stichhaltig (*argument etc*); solid(e), gründlich (*work etc*); einmütig, geschlossen; ***a ~ hour*** F e-e geschlagene Stunde **2.** MATH Körper *m*; *pl* feste Nahrung
**sol·i·dar·i·ty** Solidarität *f*
**so·lid·i·fy** fest werden (lassen); *fig* (sich) festigen
**so·lil·o·quy** Selbstgespräch *n*, *esp* THEA Monolog *m*
**sol·i·taire** Solitär *m*; Patience *f*
**sol·i·ta·ry** einsam, (*Leben a.*) zurückgezogen, (*Ort etc a.*) abgelegen; einzig; ~ **con·fine·ment** JUR Einzelhaft *f*
**so·lo** MUS Solo *n*; AVIAT Alleinflug *m*
**so·lo·ist** MUS Solist(in)
**sol·u·ble** CHEM löslich; *fig* lösbar
**so·lu·tion** CHEM Lösung *f*; *fig* (Auf)Lösung *f*
**solve** *Fall etc* lösen
**sol·vent** **1.** ECON zahlungsfähig **2.** CHEM Lösungsmittel *n*
**som·ber**, *Br* **som·bre** düster, trüb(e); *fig* trübsinnig
**some** (irgend)ein; *pl* einige, ein paar; manche; etwas, ein wenig, ein bisschen; ungefähr; ***~ 20 miles*** etwa 20 Meilen; ***~ more cake*** noch ein Stück Kuchen; ***to ~ extent*** bis zu e-m gewissen Grade
**some·bod·y** jemand
**some·day** eines Tages
**some·how** irgendwie
**some·one** jemand
**some·place** irgendwo, irgendwohin
**som·er·sault** **1.** Salto *m*; Purzelbaum *m*; ***turn a ~*** → **2.** e-n Salto machen; e-n Purzelbaum schlagen
**some·thing** etwas; ***~ like*** ungefähr
**some·time** irgendwann
**some·times** manchmal
**some·what** ein bisschen, ein wenig
**some·where** irgendwo(hin)
**son** Sohn *m*; ***~ of a bitch*** V Scheißkerl *m*
**so·na·ta** MUS Sonate *f*
**song** MUS Lied *n*; Gesang *m*
**song·bird** zo Singvogel *m*
**son·ic** Schall…; ~ **bang** *Br*, ~ **boom** Überschallknall *m*
**son-in-law** Schwiegersohn *m*
**son·net** Sonett *n*
**so·nor·ous** sonor, volltönend
**soon** bald; ***as ~ as*** sobald; ***as ~ as possible*** so bald wie möglich
**soon·er** eher, früher; ***~ or later*** früher oder später; ***the ~ the better*** je eher, desto besser; ***no ~ … than*** kaum … als; ***no ~ said than done*** gesagt, getan
**soot** Ruß *m*
**soothe** beruhigen, beschwichtigen (*a.* ***~ down***); *Schmerzen* lindern, mildern
**sooth·ing** beruhigend; lindernd
**soot·y** rußig
**sop**[1] Beschwichtigungsmittel *n* (***to*** für)
**sop**[2]: ***~ up*** aufsaugen
**so·phis·ti·cat·ed** anspruchsvoll, kultiviert; intellektuell; TECH raffiniert, hoch entwickelt
**soph·o·more** Student(in) im zweiten Jahr
**sop·o·rif·ic** einschläfernd
**sop·ping** *a.* ***~ wet*** F klatschnass
**sor·cer·er** Zauberer *m*, Hexenmeister *m*, Hexer *m*
**sor·cer·ess** Zauberin *f*, Hexe *f*
**sor·cer·y** Zauberei *f*, Hexerei *f*
**sor·did** schmutzig; schäbig
**sore** **1.** weh, wund (*a. fig*); entzündet; F *fig* sauer; ***I'm ~ all over*** mir tut alles weh; ***~ throat*** Halsentzündung *f*; ***have a ~ throat*** *a.* Halsschmerzen haben **2.** wunde Stelle, Wunde *f*
**sor·rel**[1] BOT Sauerampfer *m*
**sor·rel**[2] **1.** zo Fuchs *m* (*horse*) **2.** rotbraun
**sor·row** Kummer *m*, Leid *n*, Schmerz *m*, Trauer *f*

**sor·row·ful** traurig, betrübt
**sor·ry** 1. *adj* traurig, jämmerlich; ***be** or **feel ~ for s.o.*** j-n bedauern *or* bemitleiden; ***I'm ~ for her*** sie tut mir leid; ***I am ~ to say*** ich muss leider sagen; ***I'm ~*** → 2. *int* (es) tut mir leid!; Entschuldigung!, Verzeihung!; ***~?*** *esp Br* wie bitte?
**sort** 1. Sorte *f*, Art *f*; ***~ of*** F irgendwie; ***of a ~, of ~s*** F so etwas Ähnliches wie; ***all ~s of things*** alles Mögliche; ***nothing of the ~*** nichts dergleichen; ***what ~ of (a) man is he?*** wie ist er?; ***be out of ~s*** F nicht auf der Höhe *or* auf dem Damm sein; ***be completely out of ~s*** SPORT F völlig außer Form sein 2. sortieren; ***~ out*** aussortieren; *Problem etc* lösen, *Frage etc* klären
**SOS** SOS *n*; ***send an ~*** ein SOS funken; ***~ call** or **message*** SOS-Ruf *m*
**soul** Seele *f* (*a. fig*); MUS Soul *m*
**sound**[1] 1. Geräusch *n*; Laut *m*; PHYS Schall *m*; *radio*, TV Ton *m*; MUS Klang *m*, Sound *m* 2. *v/i* (er)klingen, (er)tönen; sich *gut etc* anhören; *v/t* LING (aus)sprechen; MAR (aus)loten; MED abhorchen; ***~ one's horn*** MOT hupen
**sound**[2] gesund; intakt, in Ordnung; solid(e), stabil, sicher; klug, vernünftig (*person, advice etc*); gründlich (*training etc*); gehörig (*beating*); vernichtend (*defeat*); fest, tief (*sleep*)
**sound| bar·ri·er** Schallgrenze *f*, Schallmauer *f*; **~ film** Tonfilm *m*
**sound·less** lautlos
**sound·proof** schalldicht
**sound·track** Filmmusik *f*; Tonspur *f*
**sound wave** Schallwelle *f*
**soup** 1. Suppe *f* 2. ***~ up*** F *Motor* frisieren
**sour** 1. sauer; *fig* mürrisch 2. sauer werden (lassen); *fig* trüben, verbittern
**source** Quelle *f*, *fig a.* Ursache *f*, Ursprung *m*
**south** 1. Süd, Süden *m* 2. *adj* südlich, Süd… 3. *adv* nach Süden, südwärts
**south·east** 1. Südost, Südosten *m* 2. *a.* **south·east·ern** südöstlich
**south·er·ly, south·ern** südlich, Süd…
**south·ern·most** südlichste(r, -s)
**South Pole** Südpol *m*
**south·ward(s)** südlich, nach Süden
**south·west** 1. Südwest, Südwesten *m* 2. *a.* **south·west·ern** südwestlich
**sou·ve·nir** Souvenir *n*, Andenken *n* (***of*** an *acc*)
**sove·reign** 1. Monarch(in), Landesherr(in) 2. POL souverän
**sove·reign·ty** Souveränität *f*
**So·vi·et** HIST POL sowjetisch, Sowjet…
**sow**[1] (aus)säen
**sow**[2] ZO Sau *f*
**soy bean** BOT Sojabohne *f*
**spa** (Heil)Bad *n*
**space** 1. Raum *m*, Platz *m*; (Welt-) Raum *m*; Zwischenraum *m*; Zeitraum *m* 2. *a.* ***~ out*** in Abständen anordnen; PRINT sperren
**space age** Weltraumzeitalter *n*
**space bar** TECH Leertaste *f*
**space cap·sule** Raumkapsel *f*
**space cen·ter** (*Br* **cen·tre**) Raumfahrtzentrum *n*
**space·craft** (Welt)Raumfahrzeug *n*
**space flight** (Welt)Raumflug *m*
**space·lab** Raumlabor *n*
**space·man** F Raumfahrer *m*; Außerirdische *m*
**space probe** (Welt)Raumsonde *f*
**space re·search** (Welt)Raumforschung *f*
**space·ship** Raumschiff *n*
**space shut·tle** Raumfähre *f*, Raumtransporter *m*
**space sta·tion** (Welt)Raumstation *f*
**space·suit** Raumanzug *m*
**space walk** Weltraumspaziergang *m*
**space·wom·an** F (Welt)Raumfahrerin *f*; Außerirdische *f*
**spa·cious** geräumig
**spade** Spaten *m*; *card game*: Pik *n*, Grün *n*; ***king of ~s*** Pikkönig *m*; ***call a ~ a ~*** das Kind beim (rechten) Namen nennen
**Spain** Spanien *n*
**span** 1. Spanne *f*; Spannweite *f* 2. *Fluss etc* überspannen; *fig* sich erstrecken über (*acc*)
**span·gle** 1. Flitter *m*, Paillette *f* 2. mit Flitter *or* Pailletten besetzen; *fig* übersäen (***with*** mit)
**Span·iard** Spanier(in)
**span·iel** ZO Spaniel *m*
**Span·ish** 1. spanisch 2. LING Spanisch *n*; ***the ~*** die Spanier *pl*
**spank** *j-m* den Hintern versohlen
**spank·ing** Tracht *f* Prügel
**span·ner** *esp Br* Schraubenschlüssel *m*; ***put** or **throw a ~ in the works*** F j-m in die Quere kommen

S

**spar** *boxing*: sparren (***with*** mit); *fig* sich ein Wortgefecht liefern (***with*** mit)
**spare 1.** *j-n*, *et.* entbehren; *Geld*, *Zeit etc* übrig haben; *keine Kosten*, *Mühen etc* scheuen; **~ *s.o. s.th.*** j-m et. ersparen **2.** Ersatz…, Reserve…; überschüssig **3.** MOT Ersatz-, Reservereifen *m*; *esp Br* → **~ part** TECH Ersatzteil *n*, *m*
**spare room** Gästezimmer *n*
**spare time** Freizeit *f*
**spar·ing** sparsam; ***use ~ly*** sparsam umgehen mit
**spark 1.** Funke(n) *m* (*a. fig*) **2.** Funken sprühen
**spark·ing plug** *Br* → ***spark plug***
**spar·kle 1.** funkeln, blitzen (***with*** vor *dat*); perlen (*drink*) **2.** Funkeln *n*, Blitzen *n*; **spar·kling** funkelnd, blitzend; (geist)sprühend, spritzig; **~ *wine*** Sekt *m*, Schaumwein *m*
**spark plug** MOT Zündkerze *f*
**spar·row** ZO Spatz *m*, Sperling *m*
**spar·row·hawk** ZO Sperber *m*
**sparse** spärlich, dünn
**spasm** MED Krampf *m*; Anfall *m*
**spas·mod·ic** MED krampfartig; *fig* sporadisch, unregelmäßig
**spas·tic** MED **1.** spastisch **2.** Spastiker(in)
**spa·tial** räumlich
**spat·ter** (be)spritzen
**spawn 1.** ZO laichen; *fig* hervorbringen **2.** ZO Laich *m*
**speak** *v/i* sprechen, reden (***to, with*** mit; ***about*** über *acc*); sprechen (***to*** vor *dat*; ***about, on*** über *acc*); ***so to ~*** sozusagen; ***speaking!*** TEL am Apparat!; **~ *up*** lauter sprechen; *v/t* sprechen, sagen; *Sprache* sprechen
**speak·er** Sprecher(in), Redner(in)
**spear 1.** Speer *m* **2.** aufspießen; durchbohren
**spear·head** Speerspitze *f*; MIL Angriffsspitze *f*; SPORT (Sturm-, Angriffs)Spitze *f*
**spear·mint** BOT Grüne Minze
**spe·cial 1.** besondere(r, -s); speziell; Sonder…; Spezial… **2.** Sonderbus *m*, Sonderzug *m*; *radio*, TV Sondersendung *f*; ECON F Sonderangebot *n*; ***be on ~*** ECON im Angebot sein
**spe·cial·ist** Spezialist(in), MED *a.* Facharzt *m*, Fachärztin *f* (***in*** für)
**spe·ci·al·i·ty** *Br* → ***specialty***
**spe·cial·ize** sich spezialisieren (***in*** auf *acc*)
**spe·cial·ty** Spezialgebiet *n*; GASTR Spezialität *f*
**spe·cies** Art *f*, Spezies *f*
**spe·cif·ic** konkret, präzis; spezifisch, speziell, besondere(r, -s); eigen (***to*** *dat*)
**spe·ci·fy** genau beschreiben *or* angeben *or* festlegen
**spe·ci·men** Exemplar *n*; Probe *f*, Muster *n*
**speck** kleiner Fleck, (*Staub*)Korn *n*; Punkt *m* (***on the horizon*** am Horizont)
**speck·led** gefleckt, gesprenkelt
**spec·ta·cle** Schauspiel *n*; Anblick *m*; (***a pair of***) **~*s*** (e-e) Brille
**spec·tac·u·lar 1.** spektakulär **2.** große (*Fernseh- etc*)Show
**spec·ta·tor** Zuschauer(in)
**spec·ter** (*fig a. Schreck*)Gespenst *n*
**spec·tral** geisterhaft, gespenstisch
**spec·tre** *Br* → ***specter***
**spec·u·late** spekulieren, Vermutungen anstellen (***about, on*** über *acc*); ECON spekulieren (***in*** mit); **spec·u·la·tion** Spekulation *f* (*a.* ECON), Vermutung *f*; **spec·u·la·tive** spekulativ, ECON *a.* Spekulations…; **spec·u·la·tor** ECON Spekulant(in)
**speech** Sprache *f*; Rede *f*, Ansprache *f*; ***make a ~*** e-e Rede halten
**speech day** *Br* PED (Jahres)Schlussfeier *f*
**speech·less** sprachlos (***with*** vor *dat*)
**speed 1.** Geschwindigkeit *f*, Tempo *n*, Schnelligkeit *f*; TECH Drehzahl *f*; PHOT Lichtempfindlichkeit *f*; *sl* Speed *n*; MOT *etc* Gang *m*; ***five-speed gearbox*** Fünfganggetriebe *n*; ***at a ~ of*** mit e-r Geschwindigkeit von; ***at full or top ~*** mit Höchstgeschwindigkeit **2.** *v/i* rasen; ***be ~ing*** MOT zu schnell fahren; **~ *up*** beschleunigen, schneller werden; *v/t* rasch bringen *or* befördern; **~ *up*** *et.* beschleunigen
**speed·boat** Rennboot *n*
**speed·ing** MOT zu schnelles Fahren, Geschwindigkeitsüberschreitung *f*
**speed lim·it** MOT Geschwindigkeitsbegrenzung *f*, Tempolimit *n*
**speed·om·e·ter** MOT Tachometer *m*, *n*
**speed trap** MOT Radarfalle *f*
**speed·y** schnell, (*reply etc a.*) prompt
**spell**[1] *a.* **~ *out*** buchstabieren; (*orthographisch* richtig) schreiben

S

**spell**[2] Weile *f*; (*Husten- etc*)Anfall *m*; ***for a ~*** e-e Zeit lang; ***a ~ of fine weather*** e-e Schönwetterperiode; ***hot ~*** Hitzewelle *f*
**spell**[3] Zauber *m* (*a. fig*)
**spell·bound** wie gebannt
**spell·er** IT Speller *m*, Rechtschreibsystem *n*; ***be a good (bad) ~*** in Rechtschreibung gut (schlecht) sein
**spell·ing** Buchstabieren *n*; Rechtschreibung *f*, Schreibung *f*, Schreibweise *f*; **~ mis·take** (Recht)Schreibfehler *m*
**spend** *Geld* ausgeben (***on*** für); *Urlaub, Zeit* verbringen
**spend·ing** Ausgaben *pl*
**spend·thrift** Verschwender(in)
**spent** verbraucht
**sperm** BIOL Sperma *n*, Samen *m*
**sphere** Kugel *f*; *fig* (*Einfluss- etc*)Sphäre *f*, (*Einfluss- etc*)Bereich *m*, Gebiet *n*
**spher·i·cal** kugelförmig
**spice 1.** Gewürz *n*; *fig* Würze *f* **2.** würzen
**spick-and-span** blitzsauber
**spic·y** gut gewürzt, würzig; *fig* pikant
**spi·der** ZO Spinne *f*
**spike 1.** Spitze *f*; Dorn *m*; Stachel *m*; SPORT Spike *m*, Dorn *m*; *pl* Spikes *pl*, Rennschuhe *pl* **2.** aufspießen
**spill 1.** *v/t* ausschütten, verschütten; ***~ the beans*** F alles ausplaudern, singen; → ***milk*** *1*; *v/i fig* strömen (***out of*** aus); ***~ over*** überlaufen; *fig* übergreifen (***into*** auf *acc*); **2.** F Sturz *m*
**spin 1.** *v/t* drehen; *Wäsche* schleudern; *Münze* hochwerfen; *Fäden, Wolle etc* spinnen; ***~ out*** *Arbeit etc* in die Länge ziehen; *Geld etc* strecken; *v/i* sich drehen; spinnen; ***my head was ~ning*** mir drehte sich alles; ***~ along*** MOT dahinrasen; ***~ round*** herumwirbeln **2.** (schnelle) Drehung; SPORT Effet *m*; TECH Schleudern *n*; AVIAT Trudeln *n*; ***be in a (flat) ~*** *esp Br* F am Rotieren sein; ***go for a ~*** MOT F e-e Spritztour machen
**spin·ach** BOT Spinat *m*
**spin·al** ANAT Rückgrat…; **~ col·umn** ANAT Wirbelsäule *f*, Rückgrat *n*; **~ cord**, **~ mar·row** ANAT Rückenmark *n*
**spin·dle** Spindel *f*
**spin-dri·er** (Wäsche)Schleuder *f*
**spin-dry** *Wäsche* schleudern
**spin-dry·er** → ***spin-drier***
**spine** ANAT Wirbelsäule *f*, Rückgrat *n*; ZO Stachel *m*, BOT *a.* Dorn *m*; (*Buch*-) Rücken *m*
**spin·ning| mill** TECH Spinnerei *f*; **~ top** Kreisel *m*; **~ wheel** Spinnrad *n*
**spin·ster** ältere unverheiratete Frau, *contp* alte Jungfer, spätes Mädchen
**spin·y** ZO stach(e)lig, BOT *a.* dornig
**spi·ral 1.** spiralförmig, Spiral… **2.** (*a.* ECON *Preis- etc*)Spirale *f*
**spi·ral stair·case** Wendeltreppe *f*
**spire** (*Kirch*)Turmspitze *f*
**spir·it** Geist *m*; Stimmung *f*, Einstellung *f*; Schwung *m*; Elan *m*; CHEM Spiritus *m*; *mst pl* Spirituosen *pl*
**spir·it·ed** energisch; erregt (*debate etc*)
**spir·it·less** temperamentlos; mutlos
**spir·its** Laune *f*, Stimmung *f*; ***be in high ~*** in Hochstimmung sein; ausgelassen *or* übermütig sein; ***be in low ~*** niedergeschlagen sein
**spir·i·tu·al 1.** geistig; geistlich **2.** MUS Spiritual *n*
**spit**[1] **1.** spucken; knistern (*fire*), brutzeln (*meat etc*); *a.* ***~ out*** ausspucken; ***~ at s.o.*** j-n anspucken; ***it is ~ting (with rain)*** es tröpfelt **2.** Spucke *f*
**spit**[2] (Brat)Spieß *m*; GEOGR Landzunge *f*
**spite 1.** Bosheit *f*, Gehässigkeit *f*; ***out of*** *or* ***from pure ~*** aus reiner Bosheit; ***in ~ of*** trotz (*gen*) **2.** *j-n* ärgern
**spite·ful** boshaft, gehässig
**spit·ting im·age** Ebenbild *n*; ***she is the ~ of her mother*** sie ist ihrer Mutter wie aus dem Gesicht geschnitten
**spit·tle** Speichel *m*, Spucke *f*
**splash 1.** (be)spritzen; klatschen; plan(t)schen; platschen; ***~ down*** wassern **2.** Klatschen *n*, Platschen *n*; Spritzer *m*, Spritzfleck *m*; *esp Br* GASTR Spritzer *m*, Schuss *m*
**splash·down** Wasserung *f*
**splay** *a.* ***~ out*** *Finger, Zehen* spreizen
**spleen** ANAT Milz *f*
**splen·did** großartig, herrlich, prächtig
**splen·do(u)r** Pracht *f*
**splice** miteinander verbinden, *Film etc* (zusammen)kleben
**splint** MED Schiene *f*; ***put in a ~, put in ~s*** schienen
**splin·ter 1.** Splitter *m* **2.** (zer)splittern; ***~ off*** absplittern; *fig* sich abspalten (***from*** von)
**split 1.** *v/t* (zer)spalten; zerreißen; *a.* ***~ up*** aufteilen (***between*** unter *acc*; ***into*** in *acc*); sich *et.* teilen; ***~ hairs*** Haarspal-

S

terei treiben; **~ one's sides** F sich vor Lachen biegen; *v/i* sich spalten; zerreißen; sich teilen (**into** in *acc*); *a.* **~ up** (**with**) Schluss machen (mit), sich trennen (von) **2.** Riss *m*; Spalt *m*; Aufteilung *f*; *fig* Bruch *m*; *fig* Spaltung *f*
**split·ting** heftig, rasend (*headache etc*)
**splut·ter** stottern (*a.* MOT); zischen
**spoil 1.** *v/t* verderben; ruinieren; *j-n* verwöhnen, *Kind a.* verziehen; *v/i* verderben, schlecht werden **2.** *mst pl* Beute *f*
**spoil·er** MOT Spoiler *m*
**spoil·sport** F Spielverderber(in)
**spoke** TECH Speiche *f*
**spokes·man** Sprecher *m*
**spokes·wom·an** Sprecherin *f*
**sponge 1.** Schwamm *m*; Schnorrer(in); *Br* → **sponge cake 2.** *v/t a.* **~ down** (mit e-m Schwamm) abwaschen; **~ off** weg-, abwischen; **~ (up)** aufsaugen, aufwischen (**from** von); *et.* schnorren (**from, off, on** von, bei); *v/i* schnorren (**from, off, on** bei)
**sponge cake** Biskuitkuchen *m*
**spong·er** Schnorrer(in)
**spong·y** schwammig; weich
**spon·sor 1.** Bürge *m*, Bürgin *f*; Sponsor(in), Geldgeber(in); Spender(in) **2.** bürgen für; sponsern
**spon·ta·ne·ous** spontan
**spook** F Geist *m*
**spook·y** F gespenstisch, unheimlich
**spool** Spule *f*; **~ of thread** Garnrolle *f*
**spoon 1.** Löffel *m* **2.** löffeln
**spoon-feed** *Kind etc* füttern
**spoon·ful** (*ein*) Löffel (voll)
**spo·rad·ic** sporadisch, gelegentlich
**spore** BOT Spore *f*
**sport 1.** Sport *m*; Sportart *f*; F feiner Kerl; *pl* Sport *m* **2.** herumlaufen mit; protzen mit
**sports** Sport…; **~ car** MOT Sportwagen *m*; **~ cen·ter** (*Br* **cen·tre**) Sportzentrum *n*
**sports·man** Sportler *m*
**sports·wear** Sportkleidung *f*
**sports·wom·an** Sportlerin *f*
**spot 1.** Punkt *m*, Tupfen *m*; Fleck *m*; MED Pickel *m*; Ort *m*, Platz *m*, Stelle *f*; *radio*, TV (Werbe)Spot *m*; F Spot *m*; **a ~ of** *Br* F ein bisschen; **on the ~** auf der Stelle, sofort; zur Stelle; an Ort und Stelle, vor Ort; auf der Stelle; **soft ~** *fig* Schwäche *f* (**for** für); **tender ~** empfindliche Stelle; **weak ~** schwacher Punkt; Schwäche *f* **2.** entdecken, sehen
**spot check** Stichprobe *f*
**spot·less** tadellos sauber; *fig* untad(e)-lig
**spot·light** Spotlight *n*, Scheinwerfer *m*; Scheinwerferlicht *n*
**spot·ted** getüpfelt; fleckig
**spot·ter** Beobachter *m*
**spot·ty** pick(e)lig
**spouse** Gatte *m*, Gattin *f*, Gemahl(in)
**spout 1.** *v/t Wasser etc* (heraus)spritzen; *v/i* spritzen (**from** aus); **2.** Schnauze *f*, Tülle *f*; (*Wasser- etc*)Strahl *m*
**sprain** MED **1.** sich *et.* verstauchen **2.** Verstauchung *f*
**sprat** ZO Sprotte *f*
**sprawl** ausgestreckt liegen *or* sitzen (*a.* **~ out**); sich ausbreiten
**spray 1.** (be)sprühen; spritzen; sich *die Haare* sprayen; *Parfüm etc* versprühen, zerstäuben **2.** Sprühnebel *m*; Gischt *m*, *f*; Spray *m*, *n*; → **sprayer**
**spray can** → **spray·er** Sprüh-, Spraydose *f*, Zerstäuber *m*
**spread 1.** *v/t* ausbreiten, *Arme a.* ausstrecken, *Finger etc* spreizen (*all a.* **~ out**); *Furcht*, *Krankheit*, *Nachricht etc* verbreiten, *Gerücht a.* ausstreuen; *Butter etc* streichen (**on** auf *acc*); *Brot etc* (be)streichen (**with** mit); *v/i* sich ausbreiten (*a.* **~ out**); sich erstrecken (**over** über *acc*); sich verbreiten, übergreifen (**to** auf *acc*); sich streichen lassen (*butter etc*) **2.** Ausbreitung *f*, Verbreitung *f*; Ausdehnung *f*; Spannweite *f*; GASTR Aufstrich *m*
**spread·sheet** IT Tabellenkalkulation *f*, Tabellenkalkulationsprogramm *n*
**spree**: **go (out) on a ~** F e-e Sauftour machen; **go on a buying** (*or* **shopping, spending**) **~** wie verrückt einkaufen
**sprig** BOT kleiner Zweig
**spright·ly** lebhaft; rüstig
**spring 1.** *v/i* springen; **~ from** herrühren von; **~ up** aufkommen (*wind*); aus dem Boden schießen (*building etc*); *v/t*: **~ a leak** ein Leck bekommen; **~ a surprise on s.o.** j-n überraschen **2.** Frühling *m*, Frühjahr *n*; Quelle *f*; TECH Feder *f*; Elastizität *f*; Federung *f*; Sprung *m*, Satz *m*; **in (the) ~** im Frühling
**spring·board** Sprungbrett *n*
**spring-clean** gründlich putzen, Früh-

S

jahrsputz machen (in *dat*)
**spring tide** Springflut *f*
**spring·time** Frühling *m*, Frühlingszeit *f*, Frühjahr *n*
**spring·y** elastisch, federnd
**sprin·kle 1.** *Wasser etc* sprengen (**on** auf *acc*); *Salz etc* streuen (**on** auf *acc*); *et.* (be)sprengen *or* bestreuen (**with** mit); ***it is sprinkling*** es tröpfelt **2.** Sprühregen *m*
**sprin·kler** (*Rasen*)Sprenger *m*; Sprinkler *m*, Berieselungsanlage *f*
**sprin·kling**: ***a ~ of*** ein bisschen, ein paar
**sprint** SPORT **1.** sprinten; spurten **2.** Sprint *m*; Spurt *m*
**sprint·er** SPORT Sprinter(in)
**sprite** Kobold *m*
**sprout** BOT **1.** sprießen (*a. fig*), keimen; wachsen lassen **2.** Spross *m*; (***Brussels***) ***~s*** Rosenkohl *m*
**spruce**[1] BOT Fichte *f*; Rottanne *f*
**spruce**[2] adrett
**spry** rüstig, lebhaft
**spur 1.** Sporn *m* (*a.* ZO); *fig* Ansporn *m* (**to** zu); ***on the ~ of the moment*** spontan **2.** *e-m Pferd* die Sporen geben; *often* ***~ on*** *fig* anspornen (**to** zu)
**spurt**[1] **1.** spurten, sprinten **2.** plötzliche Aktivität, (*Arbeits*)Anfall *m*; Spurt *m*, Sprint *m*
**spurt**[2] **1.** spritzen (**from** aus); **2.** (*Wasser- etc*)Strahl *m*
**sput·ter** stottern (*a.* MOT); zischen
**spy 1.** Spion(in) **2.** spionieren, Spionage treiben (**for** für); ***~ into*** *fig* herumspionieren in (*dat*); ***~ on*** *j-m* nachspionieren
**spy·hole** (Tür)Spion *m*
**squab·ble** (sich) streiten (***about, over*** um, wegen)
**squad** Mannschaft *f*, Trupp *m*; (*Überfall- etc*)Kommando *n*; Dezernat *n*
**squad car** (Funk)Streifenwagen *m*
**squad·ron** MIL, AVIAT Staffel *f*; MAR Geschwader *n*
**squal·id** schmutzig, verwahrlost, verkommen, armselig
**squall** Bö *f*
**squan·der** *Geld*, *Zeit etc* verschwenden, *Chance* vertun
**square 1.** Quadrat *n*; Viereck *n*; *öffentlicher* Platz; MATH Quadrat(zahl *f*) *n*; *board game*: Feld *n*; TECH Winkel(maß *n*) *m* **2.** quadratisch, Quadrat…; viereckig; rechtwink(e)lig; eckig (*shoulders etc*); *fig* fair, gerecht; ***be*** (***all***) ***~*** quitt sein **3.** quadratisch *or* rechtwink(e)lig machen (*a.* ***~ off*** *or* ***up***); in Quadrate einteilen (*a.* ***~ off***); MATH *Zahl* ins Quadrat erheben; *Schultern* straffen; *Konto* ausgleichen; *Schulden* begleichen; *fig* in Einklang bringen *or* stehen (**with** mit); ***~ up*** F abrechnen; ***~ up to*** sich *j-m*, *e-m Problem etc* stellen
**square root** MATH Quadratwurzel *f*
**squash**[1] **1.** zerdrücken, zerquetschen; quetschen, zwängen (**into** in *acc*); ***~ flat*** flach drücken, F platt walzen **2.** Gedränge *n*; SPORT Squash *n*
**squash**[2] BOT Kürbis *m*
**squat 1.** hocken, kauern; *leer stehendes Haus* besetzen; ***~ down*** sich (hin)kauern *or* (hin)hocken **2.** gedrungen, untersetzt; **squat·ter** Hausbesetzer(in)
**squaw** Squaw *f*
**squawk** kreischen, schreien; F lautstark protestieren (**about** gegen)
**squeak 1.** piep(s)en (*mouse etc*); quietschen (*door etc*) **2.** Piep(s)en *n*; Piep(s) *m*; Quietschen *n*; **squeak·y** piepsig (*voice*); quietschend (*door etc*)
**squeal 1.** kreischen (**with** vor *dat*); ***~ on s.o.*** *fig* F j-n verpfeifen **2.** Kreischen *n*; Schrei *m*
**squeam·ish** empfindlich, zart besaitet
**squeeze 1.** drücken; auspressen, ausquetschen; (sich) quetschen *or* zwängen (**into** in *acc*); **2.** Druck *m*; GASTR Spritzer *m*; Gedränge *n*
**squeez·er** (Frucht)Presse *f*
**squid** ZO Tintenfisch *m*
**squint** schielen; blinzeln
**squirm** sich winden
**squir·rel** ZO Eichhörnchen *n*
**squirt 1.** (be)spritzen **2.** Strahl *m*
**stab 1.** *v/t* niederstechen; ***be ~bed in the arm*** e-n Stich in den Arm bekommen; *v/i* stechen (**at** nach); **2.** Stich *m*
**sta·bil·i·ty** Stabilität *f*; *fig* Dauerhaftigkeit *f*; Ausgeglichenheit *f*
**sta·bil·ize** (sich) stabilisieren
**sta·ble**[1] stabil; *fig* dauerhaft; ausgeglichen
**sta·ble**[2] Stall *m*
**stack 1.** Stapel *m*, Stoß *m*; ***~s of, a ~ of*** F jede Menge *Arbeit etc* **2.** stapeln; voll stapeln (**with** mit); ***~ up*** aufstapeln
**sta·di·um** SPORT Stadion *n*

S

**staff 1.** Stab *m*; Mitarbeiter(stab *m*) *pl*; Personal *n*, Belegschaft *f*; Lehrkörper *m*; MIL Stab *m* **2.** besetzen (***with*** mit)

**staff room** Lehrerzimmer *n*

**stag** ZO Hirsch *m*

**stage 1.** THEA Bühne *f* (*a. fig*); Etappe *f* (*a. fig*), (Reise)Abschnitt *m*; Teilstrecke *f*, Fahrzone *f* (*bus etc*); *fig* Stufe *f*, Stadium *n*, Phase *f* **2.** THEA inszenieren; veranstalten

**stage·coach** Postkutsche *f*

**stage| di·rec·tion** THEA Regieanweisung *f*; **~ fright** Lampenfieber *n*; **~ man·ag·er** THEA Inspizient *m*

**stag·ger 1.** *v/i* (sch)wanken, taumeln, torkeln; *v/t j-n* sprachlos machen, F umhauen; *Arbeitszeit etc* staffeln **2.** Wanken *n*, Schwanken *n*, Taumeln *n*

**stag·nant** stehend (*water*); *esp* ECON stagnierend

**stag·nate** *esp* ECON stagnieren

**stain 1.** *v/t* beflecken; (ein)färben; *Holz* beizen; *Glas* bemalen; *v/i* Flecken bekommen, schmutzen **2.** Fleck *m*; TECH Färbemittel *n*; (*Holz*)Beize *f*; Makel *m*

**stained glass** Bunt-, Farbglas *n*

**stain·less** nicht rostend, rostfrei

**stair** (Treppen)Stufe *f*; *pl* Treppe *f*

**stair·case, stair·way** Treppe *f*; Treppenhaus *n*

**stake**[1] **1.** Pfahl *m*, Pfosten *m*; HIST Marterpfahl *m* **2.** **~ *off*, ~ *out*** abstecken

**stake**[2] **1.** Anteil *m*, Beteiligung *f* (***in*** an *dat*) (*a.* ECON); (Wett- *etc*)Einsatz *m*; ***be at* ~** *fig* auf dem Spiel stehen **2.** *Geld etc* setzen (***on*** auf *acc*); *Ruf etc* riskieren, aufs Spiel setzen

**stale** alt(backen); abgestanden, *beer etc*: *a.* schal, *air etc*: *a.* verbraucht

**stalk**[1] BOT Stängel *m*, Stiel *m*, Halm *m*

**stalk**[2] *v/t* sich heranpirschen an (*acc*); verfolgen, hinter *j-m*, *et.* herschleichen; *v/i* stolzieren

**stall**[1] **1.** (*Obst- etc*)Stand *m*, (*Markt- etc*) Bude *f*; AGR Box *f*; *pl* REL Chorgestühl *n*; *Br* THEA Parkett *n* **2.** *v/t Motor* abwürgen; *v/i* MOT absterben

**stall**[2] *v/i* Ausflüchte machen; Zeit schinden; *v/t j-n* hinhalten; *et.* hinauszögern

**stal·li·on** ZO (Zucht)Hengst *m*

**stal·wart** kräftig, robust; *esp* POL treu

**stam·i·na** Ausdauer *f*; Durchhaltevermögen *n*, Kondition *f*

**stam·mer 1.** stottern, stammeln **2.** Stottern *n*, Stammeln *n*

**stamp 1.** *v/i* sta(m)pfen, trampeln; *v/t Pass etc* (ab)stempeln; *Datum etc* aufstempeln (***on*** auf *acc*); *Brief etc* frankieren; *fig j-n* abstempeln (***as*** als, zu); **~ *one's foot*** aufstampfen; **~ *out*** *Feuer* austreten; TECH ausstanzen **2.** (Brief-) Marke *f*; (*Steuer- etc*)Marke *f*; Stempel *m*; **~*ed addressed envelope*** Freiumschlag *m*

**stam·pede 1.** ZO wilde Flucht; wilder Ansturm, Massenansturm *m* (***for*** auf *acc*); **2.** *v/i* ZO durchgehen; *v/t* in Panik versetzen

**stanch** treu, zuverlässig

**stand 1.** *v/i* stehen; aufstehen; *fig fest- etc* bleiben; **~ *still*** still stehen; *v/t* stellen (***on*** auf *acc*); aushalten, ertragen; *e-r Prüfung etc* standhalten; *Probe* bestehen; *Chance* haben; *Drink etc* spendieren; ***I can't* ~ *him*** (*or* ***it***) ich kann ihn (*or* das) nicht ausstehen *or* leiden; **~ *around*** herumstehen; **~ *back*** zurücktreten; **~ *by*** danebenstehen; *fig* zu *j-m* halten; zu *et.* stehen; **~ *idly by*** tatenlos zusehen; **~ *down*** verzichten; zurücktreten; JUR den Zeugenstand verlassen; **~ *for*** stehen für, bedeuten; sich *et.* gefallen lassen, *et.* dulden; *esp Br* kandidieren für; **~ *in*** einspringen (***for*** für); **~ *in for s.o.*** *a.* j-n vertreten; **~ *on*** (*fig* be)stehen auf (*dat*); **~ *out*** hervorstechen; sich abheben (***against*** gegen, von); **~ *over*** überwachen, aufpassen auf (*acc*); **~ *together*** zusammenhalten, -stehen; **~ *up*** aufstehen, sich erheben; **~ *up for*** eintreten *or* sich einsetzen für; **~ *up to*** *j-m* mutig gegenübertreten, *j-m* die Stirn bieten **2.** (*Obst-*, *Messe- etc*)Stand *m*; (*Schirm-*, *Noten-etc*)Ständer *m*; SPORT *etc* Tribüne *f*; (*Taxi*)Stand(platz) *m*; JUR Zeugenstand *m*; ***take a* ~** *fig* Position beziehen (***on*** zu)

**stan·dard**[1] **1.** Norm *f*, Maßstab *m*; Standard *m*, Niveau *n*; **~ *of living, living* ~** Lebensstandard *m* **2.** normal, Normal…; durchschnittlich, Durchschnitts…; Standard…

**stan·dard**[2] Standarte *f*, MOT Stander *m*; HIST Banner *n*

**stan·dard·ize** vereinheitlichen, *esp* TECH standardisieren, normen

S

**stan·dard lamp** *Br* Stehlampe *f*

**stand·by 1.** Reserve *f*; AVIAT Stand-by *n*; ***be on ~*** in Bereitschaft stehen **2.** Reserve…, Not…; AVIAT Stand-by…

**stand-in** *film*, TV Double *n*; Ersatzmann *m*; Vertreter(in)

**stand·ing 1.** stehend; *fig* ständig; → ***ovation*** **2.** Rang *m*, Stellung *f*; Ansehen *n*, Ruf *m*; Dauer *f*; ***of long ~*** alt, seit langem bestehend; **~ or·der** ECON Dauerauftrag *m*; **~ room**: ***~ only*** nur noch Stehplätze

**stand·off·ish** F (sehr) ablehnend, hochnäsig

**stand·point** *fig* Standpunkt *m*

**stand·still** Stillstand *m*; ***be at a ~*** stehen (*car etc*); ruhen (*production etc*); ***bring to a ~*** *Auto etc* zum Stehen bringen; *Produktion etc* zum Erliegen bringen

**stand-up** Steh…; **~ *fight*** Schlägerei *f*

**stan·za** Strophe *f*

**sta·ple**[1] **1.** Hauptnahrungsmittel *n*; ECON Haupterzeugnis *n* **2.** Haupt…; üblich

**sta·ple**[2] **1.** Heftklammer *f*; Krampe *f* **2.** heften

**sta·pler** TECH (Draht)Hefter *m*

**star 1.** ASTR Stern *m*; PRINT Sternchen *n*; THEA, SPORT *etc* Star *m* **2.** *v/t* PRINT mit e-m Sternchen kennzeichnen; ***~ring …*** in der Hauptrolle *or* in den Hauptrollen …; ***a film ~ring …*** ein Film mit … in der Hauptrolle *or* den Hauptrollen; *v/i* die *or* e-e Hauptrolle spielen (***in*** in *dat*)

**star·board** AVIAT, MAR Steuerbord *n*

**starch 1.** (*Kartoffel- etc*)Stärke *f*; stärkereiches Nahrungsmittel; (*Wäsche-*) Stärke *f* **2.** *Wäsche* stärken

**stare 1.** starren; **~ *at*** *j-n* anstarren **2.** (starrer) Blick, Starren *n*

**stark 1.** *adj fig* nackt; ***be in ~ contrast to*** in krassem Gegensatz stehen zu **2.** *adv*: F ***~ naked*** splitternackt; ***~ raving mad***, ***~ staring mad*** total verrückt

**star·light** ASTR Sternenlicht *n*

**star·ling** ZO Star *m*

**star·lit** stern(en)klar

**star·ry** Stern…, Sternen…

**star·ry-eyed** F blauäugig, naiv

**start 1.** *v/i* anfangen, beginnen (*a.* ***~ off***); aufbrechen (***for*** nach) (*a.* ***~ off***, ***~ out***); RAIL *etc* abfahren, MAR ablegen, AVIAT abfliegen, starten; MOT anspringen; TECH anlaufen; SPORT starten; zusammenfahren, -zucken (***at*** bei); ***to ~ with*** anfangs, zunächst; erstens; ***~ from scratch*** ganz von vorn anfangen; *v/t* anfangen, beginnen (*a.* ***~ off***); in Gang setzen *or* bringen, *Motor etc a.* anlassen, starten **2.** Anfang *m*, Beginn *m*, (*esp* SPORT) Start *m*; Aufbruch *m*; Auffahren *n*, Aufschrecken *n*; ***at the ~*** am Anfang; SPORT am Start; ***for a ~*** erstens; ***from ~ to finish*** von Anfang bis Ende

**start·er** SPORT Starter(in); MOT Anlasser *m*, Starter *m*; *esp Br* GASTR F Vorspeise *f*; ***for ~s*** zunächst einmal

**start·le** erschrecken; überraschen, bestürzen

**starv·a·tion** Hungern *n*; ***die of ~*** verhungern; **~ *diet*** F Fasten-, Hungerkur *f*, Nulldiät *f*

**starve** hungern (lassen); **~ (*to death*)** verhungern (lassen); ***I'm starving!*** *Br* F, ***I'm ~d!*** F ich komme um vor Hunger!

**state 1.** Zustand *m*; Stand *m*, Lage *f*; POL (Bundes-, Einzel)Staat *m*; *often* ***State*** POL Staat *m* **2.** Staats…, staatlich **3.** angeben, nennen; erklären, JUR aussagen (***that*** dass); festlegen, festsetzen

**State De·part·ment** POL Außenministerium *n*

**state·ly** gemessen, würdevoll; prächtig

**state·ment** Statement *n*, Erklärung *f*; Angabe f; JUR Aussage *f*; ECON (*Bank-*, *Konto*)Auszug *m*; ***make a ~*** e-e Erklärung abgeben

**state-of-the-art** TECH neuest, modernst

**states·man** POL Staatsmann *m*

**stat·ic** statisch

**sta·tion 1.** (*a. Bus-*, *U-*)Bahnhof *m*, Station *f*; (*Forschungs-*, *Rettungs- etc*)Station *f*; Tankstelle *f*; (*Feuer*)Wache *f*; (*Polizei*)Revier *n*; (*Wahl*)Lokal *n*; *radio*, TV Sender *m*, Station *f* **2.** aufstellen, postieren; MIL stationieren

**sta·tion·ar·y** stehend

**sta·tion·er** Schreibwarenhändler(in); **sta·tion·er's (shop)** Schreibwarenhandlung *f*; **sta·tion·er·y** Schreibwaren *pl*; Briefpapier *n*

**sta·tion·mas·ter** RAIL Stations-, Bahnhofsvorsteher *m*

**sta·tion wag·on** MOT Kombiwagen *m*

**sta·tis·ti·cal** statistisch

**stat·is·ti·cian** Statistiker *m*

**sta·tis·tics** Statistik(en *pl*) *f*

**stat·ue** Statue *f*, Standbild *n*

**sta·tus** Status *m*, Rechtsstellung *f*; (*Fa-*

S

*milien*)Stand *m*; Stellung *f*, Rang *m*, Status *m*; **~ line** IT Statuszeile *f*
**stat·ute** Gesetz *n*; Statut *n*, Satzung *f*
**stat·ute of lim·i·ta·tions** JUR Verjährungsfrist *f*; ***come under the ~*** verjähren
**staunch**[1] *Br* → ***stanch***
**staunch**[2] *Blutung* stillen
**stay 1.** bleiben (***with s.o.*** bei j-m); wohnen (***at*** in *dat*; ***with s.o.*** bei j-m); **~ *put*** F sich nicht (vom Fleck) rühren; **~ *away*** wegbleiben, sich fernhalten (***from*** von); **~ *up*** aufbleiben **2.** Aufenthalt *m*; JUR Aussetzung *f*, Aufschub *m*
**stead·fast** treu, zuverlässig; fest
**stead·y 1.** *adj* fest; stabil; ruhig (*hand*), gut (*nerves*); gleichmäßig **2.** (sich) beruhigen **3.** *int a.* **~ *on!*** *Br* F Vorsicht! **4.** *adv*: ***go ~ with s.o.*** (fest) mit j-m gehen **5.** feste Freundin, fester Freund
**steak** GASTR Steak *n*; (*Fisch*)Filet *n*
**steal** stehlen (*a. fig*); sich stehlen, (sich) schleichen (***out of*** aus)
**stealth**: ***by ~*** heimlich, verstohlen
**stealth·y** heimlich, verstohlen
**steam 1.** Dampf *m*; Dunst *m*; ***let off ~*** Dampf ablassen, *fig a.* sich Luft machen **2.** Dampf... **3.** *v/i* dampfen; **~ *up*** beschlagen (*mirror etc*); *v/t* GASTR dünsten, dämpfen
**steam·boat** Dampfboot *n*, Dampfer *m*
**steam·er** Dampfer *m*, Dampfschiff *n*; Dampf-, Schnellkochtopf *m*
**steam·ship** Dampfer *m*, Dampfschiff *n*
**steel 1.** Stahl *m* **2. ~ *o.s. for*** sich wappnen gegen
**steel·work·er** Stahlarbeiter *m*
**steel·works** Stahlwerk *n*
**steep**[1] steil; *fig* stark (*rise etc*); F happig
**steep**[2] eintauchen (***in*** in *acc*); *Wäsche* (ein)weichen
**stee·ple** Kirchturm *m*
**stee·ple·chase** *horse racing*: Hindernisrennen *n*; SPORT Hindernislauf *m*
**steer**[1] ZO (junger) Ochse
**steer**[2] steuern, lenken
**steer·ing col·umn** MOT Lenksäule *f*
**steer·ing wheel** MOT Lenkrad *n*, *a.* MAR Steuerrad *n*
**stein** Maßkrug *m*
**stem 1.** BOT Stiel *m* (*a. of a wine glass etc*), Stängel *m*; LING Stamm *m* **2. ~ *from*** stammen *or* herrühren von
**stench** Gestank *m*
**sten·cil** Schablone *f*; PRINT Matrize *f*
**ste·nog·ra·pher** Stenotypistin *f*
**step 1.** Schritt *m* (*a. fig*); Stufe *f*; Sprosse *f*; (***a pair of***) **~*s*** (e-e) Tritt- *or* Stufenleiter; ***mind the ~!*** Vorsicht, Stufe!; **~ *by ~*** Schritt für Schritt; ***take ~s*** Schritte *or* et. unternehmen **2.** gehen; treten (***in*** in *acc*; ***on*** auf *acc*); **~ *on it***, **~ *on the gas*** MOT F Gas geben, auf die Tube drücken; **~ *aside*** zur Seite treten; *fig* Platz machen; **~ *down*** *fig* Platz machen; **~ *up*** *Produktion etc* steigern
**step-by-step** *fig* schrittweise
**step·fa·ther** Stiefvater *m*
**step·lad·der** Tritt-, Stufenleiter *f*
**step·moth·er** Stiefmutter *f*
**steppes** GEOGR Steppe *f*
**step·ping-stone** *fig* Sprungbrett *n* (***to*** für)
**ster·e·o 1.** Stereo *n*; Stereogerät *n*, Stereoanlage *f* **2.** Stereo...; **~ sys·tem** MUS Kompaktanlage *f*
**ster·ile** steril (*a. fig*), *a.* unfruchtbar, MED *a.* keimfrei
**ste·ril·i·ty** Sterilität *f* (*a. fig*), Unfruchtbarkeit *f*
**ster·il·ize** MED sterilisieren
**ster·ling** das Pfund Sterling
**stern**[1] streng
**stern**[2] MAR Heck *n*
**stew 1.** *Fleisch, Gemüse* schmoren, *Obst* dünsten; ***~ed apples*** Apfelkompott *n* **2.** Eintopf *m*; ***be in a ~*** in heller Aufregung sein
**stew·ard** Ordner *m*; AVIAT, MAR Steward *m*
**stew·ard·ess** AVIAT, MAR Stewardess *f*
**stick**[1] trockener Zweig; Stock *m*; ([*Eis*]-*Hockey*)Schläger *m*; (*Besen- etc-*) Stiel *m*; AVIAT (*Steuer*)Knüppel *m*; Stück *n*, Stange *f*, (*Lippen- etc*)Stift *m*, Stäbchen *n*
**stick**[2] *v/t* mit *e-r Nadel etc* stechen (***into*** in *acc*); *et.* kleben (***on*** auf, an *acc*); an-, festkleben (***with*** mit); stecken; F tun, stellen, setzen, legen; ***I can't ~ him*** (*or* ***it***) *esp Br* F ich kann ihn (*or* das) nicht ausstehen *or* leiden; *v/i* kleben; kleben bleiben (***to*** an *dat*); stecken bleiben; **~ *at nothing*** vor nichts zurückschrecken; **~ *by*** F bleiben bei; F zu *j-m* halten; **~ *out*** vorstehen; abstehen; *et.* ausstrecken *or* vorstrecken; **~ *to*** bleiben bei

**stick·er** Aufkleber *m*
**stick·ing plas·ter** *Br* Heftpflaster *n*
**stick·y** klebrig (***with*** von); F heikel, unangenehm
**stiff 1.** *adj* steif; F stark (*drink etc*); schwer, hart (*task, penalty etc*); hartnäckig (*resistance*); F happig, gepfeffert, gesalzen (*price*); ***keep a ~ upper lip*** *fig* Haltung bewahren **2.** *adv* äußerst; höchst; ***be bored ~*** F sich zu Tode langweilen; ***be scared ~*** e-e wahnsinnige Angst haben; ***be worried ~*** sich furchtbare Sorgen machen
**stiff·en** *v/t Wäsche* stärken; versteifen; verstärken; *v/i* steif werden; sich verhärten *or* versteifen
**sti·fle** ersticken; *fig* unterdrücken
**stile** Zauntritt *m*
**sti·let·to** Stilett *n*; **~ heel** Bleistift-, Pfennigabsatz *m*
**still**[1] **1.** *adv* (immer) noch, noch immer; *with comparative*: noch **2.** *cj* dennoch, trotzdem
**still**[2] **1.** *adj* still; ruhig; GASTR ohne Kohlensäure **2.** *film*, TV Standfoto *n*
**still·born** MED tot geboren
**still life** PAINT Stillleben *n*
**stilt** Stelze *f*; **stilt·ed** *fig* gestelzt
**stim·u·lant** MED Stimulans *n*, Anregungs-, Aufputschmittel *n*; *fig* Anreiz *m*, Ansporn *m* (***to*** für)
**stim·u·late** MED stimulieren (*a. fig*), anregen, *fig a.* anspornen
**stim·u·lus** Reiz *m*; *fig* Anreiz *m*, Ansporn *m* (***to*** für)
**sting 1.** stechen (*insect*); brennen (auf *or* in *dat*); **2.** Stachel *m*; Stich *m*; Brennen *n*, brennender Schmerz
**stin·gy** F knaus(e)rig, knick(e)rig (*person*); mick(e)rig (*meal etc*)
**stink 1.** stinken (***of*** nach); **~ *up*** (*Br* ***out***) verpesten **2.** Gestank *m*
**stint**: **~ *o.s.*** (***of s.th.***) sich einschränken (mit et.); **~** (***on***) ***s.th.*** sparen mit et.
**stip·u·late** zur Bedingung machen; festsetzen, vereinbaren; **stip·u·la·tion** Bedingung *f*; Vereinbarung *f*
**stir 1.** (um)rühren; (sich) rühren *or* bewegen; *j-n* aufwühlen; **~ *up*** *Unruhe* stiften; *Streit* entfachen; *Erinnerungen* wachrufen **2.** ***give s.th. a ~*** et. umrühren; ***cause*** (*or* ***create***) ***a ~*** für Aufsehen sorgen
**stir·rup** Steigbügel *m*
**stitch 1.** Stich *m*; Masche *f*; MED Seitenstechen *n* **2.** zunähen, *Wunde* nähen (*a.* **~ *up***); heften
**stock 1.** Vorrat *m* (***of*** an *dat*); GASTR Brühe *f*; *a.* ***live~*** Viehbestand *m*; (*Gewehr*)Schaft *m*; *fig* Abstammung *f*, Herkunft *f*; ECON Aktie(n *pl*) *f*; *pl* Aktien *pl*, Wertpapiere *pl*; ***have s.th. in ~*** ECON et. vorrätig *or* auf Lager haben; ***take ~*** ECON Inventur machen; ***take ~ of*** *fig* sich klar werden über (*acc*) **2.** ECON *Ware* vorrätig haben, führen; **~ *up*** sich eindecken *or* versorgen (***on, with*** mit); **3.** Serien…; Standard…; stereotyp
**stock·breed·er** AGR Viehzüchter *m*
**stock·breed·ing** AGR Viehzucht *f*
**stock·brok·er** ECON Börsenmakler *m*
**stock ex·change** ECON Börse *f*
**stock·hold·er** ECON Aktionär(in)
**stock·ing** Strumpf *m*
**stock mar·ket** ECON Börse *f*
**stock·pile 1.** Vorrat *m* (***of*** an *dat*); **2.** e-n Vorrat anlegen an (*dat*)
**stock·still** regungslos
**stock·tak·ing** ECON Inventur *f*; *fig* Bestandsaufnahme *f*
**stock·y** stämmig, untersetzt
**stol·id** gleichmütig
**stom·ach 1.** ANAT Magen *m*; Bauch *m*; *fig* Appetit *m* (***for*** auf *acc*); **2.** vertragen (*a. fig*)
**stom·ach·ache** MED Magenschmerzen *pl*, Bauchschmerzen *pl*, Bauchweh *n*
**stom·ach up·set** MED Magenverstimmung *f*
**stone 1.** Stein *m*, BOT *a.* Kern *m*; (*Hagel*)Korn *n* **2.** mit Steinen bewerfen; steinigen; entkernen, entsteinen
**stone·ma·son** Steinmetz *m*
**stone·ware** Steingut *n*
**ston·y** steinig; steinern (*face etc*), eisig (*silence*)
**stool** Hocker *m*, Schemel *m*; MED Stuhl *m*, Stuhlgang *m*
**stool·pi·geon** F (Polizei)Spitzel *m*
**stoop 1.** *v/i* sich bücken (*a.* **~ *down***); gebeugt gehen; **~ *to*** *fig* sich herablassen *or* hergeben zu **2.** gebeugte Haltung
**stop 1.** *v/i* (an)halten, stehen bleiben (*a. watch etc*), stoppen; aufhören; *esp Br* bleiben; **~ *dead*** plötzlich *or* abrupt stehen bleiben; **~ *at nothing*** vor nichts zurückschrecken; **~ *short of doing***, **~**

***short at*** *s.th.* zurückschrecken vor (*dat*); *v/t* anhalten, stoppen; aufhören mit; ein Ende machen *or* setzen (*dat*); *Blutung* stillen; *Arbeiten, Verkehr etc* zum Erliegen bringen; *et.* verhindern; *j-n* abhalten (***from*** von), hindern (***from*** an *dat*); *Rohr etc* verstopfen (*a.* ~ ***up***); *Zahn* füllen, plombieren; *Scheck* sperren (lassen); ~ ***by*** vorbeischauen; ~ ***in*** vorbeischauen (***at*** bei); ~ ***off*** F kurz Halt machen; ~ ***over*** kurz Halt machen; Zwischenstation machen **2.** Halt *m*; (*Bus*)Haltestelle *f*; PHOT Blende *f*; *mst* ***full*** ~ LING Punkt *m*

**stop·gap** Notbehelf *m*

**stop·light** MOT Bremslicht *n*; rotes Licht

**stop·o·ver** Zwischenstation *f*; AVIAT Zwischenlandung *f*

**stop·page** Unterbrechung *f*, Stopp *m*; Verstopfung *f*; Streik *m*; *Br* (Gehalts-, Lohn)Abzug *m*

**stop·per** Stöpsel *m*

**stop sign** MOT Stoppschild *n*

**stop·watch** Stoppuhr *f*

**stor·age** ECON Lagerung *f*; Lagergeld *n*; IT Speicher *m*

**store 1.** (ein)lagern; *Energie* speichern; IT (ab)speichern, sichern; *a.* ~ ***up*** sich e-n Vorrat anlegen an (*dat*) **2.** Vorrat *m*; Lager *n*, Lagerhalle *f*, Lagerhaus *n*; Laden *m*, Geschäft *n*, *esp Br* Kaufhaus *n*, Warenhaus *n*

**store·house** Lagerhaus *n*; *fig* Fundgrube *f*

**store·keep·er** Ladenbesitzer(in)

**store·room** Lagerraum *m*

**sto·rey** *Br* → ***story²***

**...sto·reyed** *Br*, **...sto·ried** mit ... Stockwerken, ...stöckig

**stork** ZO Storch *m*

**storm 1.** Unwetter *n*; Gewitter *n*; Sturm *m* **2.** *v/t* MIL *etc* stürmen; *v/i* stürmen, stürzen; **storm·y** stürmisch

**sto·ry¹** Geschichte *f*; Märchen *n* (*a. fig*); Story *f*, *a.* Handlung *f*, *a.* Bericht *m* (***on*** über *acc*)

**sto·ry²** Stock *m*, Stockwerk *n*, Etage *f*

**stout** korpulent, vollschlank; *fig* unerschrocken; entschieden

**stove** Ofen *m*, Herd *m*

**stow** *a.* ~ ***away*** verstauen

**stow·a·way** AVIAT, MAR blinder Passagier

**strad·dle** rittlings sitzen auf (*dat*)

**strag·gle** verstreut liegen *or* stehen; BOT *etc* wuchern; ~ ***in*** F einzeln eintrudeln

**strag·gler** Nachzügler(in)

**strag·gly** verstreut (liegend); BOT *etc* wuchernd; struppig (*mustache etc*)

**straight 1.** *adj* gerade; glatt (*hair*); pur (*whisky etc*); aufrichtig, offen, ehrlich; *sl* hetero(*sexuell*); *sl* clean, sauber; ***put*** ~ in Ordnung bringen **2.** *adv* gerade; genau, direkt; klar; ehrlich, anständig; ~ ***ahead*** geradeaus; ~ ***off*** F sofort; ~ ***on*** geradeaus; ~ ***out*** F offen, rundheraus **3.** SPORT (*Gegen-*, *Ziel*)Gerade *f*

**straight·en** *v/t* gerade machen, (gerade) richten; ~ ***out*** in Ordnung bringen; *v/i a.* ~ ***out*** gerade werden; ~ ***up*** sich aufrichten

**straight·for·ward** aufrichtig; einfach

**strain 1.** *v/t Seil etc* (an)spannen; *sich, Augen etc* überanstrengen; sich *e-n Muskel etc* zerren; *Gemüse, Tee etc* abgießen; *v/i* sich anstrengen; ~ ***at*** zerren *or* ziehen an (*dat*) **2.** Spannung *f*; Anspannung *f*; Strapaze *f*; *fig* Belastung *f*; MED Zerrung *f*; **strained** MED gezerrt; gezwungen (*smile etc*); gespannt (*relations*); ***look*** ~ abgespannt aussehen

**strain·er** Sieb *n*

**strait** GEOGR Meerenge *f*, Straße *f*; *pl fig* Notlage *f*

**strait·ened**: ***live in ~ circumstances*** in beschränkten Verhältnissen leben

**strand** Strang *m*; Faden *m*; (*Kabel-*) Draht *m*; (*Haar*)Strähne *f*

**strand·ed**: ***be*** ~ MAR gestrandet sein; ***be*** (***left***) ~ *fig* festsitzen (***in*** in *dat*)

**strange** merkwürdig, seltsam, sonderbar; fremd; **strang·er** Fremde *m, f*

**stran·gle** erwürgen

**strap 1.** Riemen *m*, Gurt *m*; (*Uhr*)Armband *n*; Träger *m* **2.** festschnallen; anschnallen

**stra·te·gic** strategisch

**strat·e·gy** Strategie *f*

**stra·tum** GEOL Schicht *f* (*a. fig*)

**straw** Stroh *n*; Strohhalm *m*

**straw·ber·ry** BOT Erdbeere *f*

**stray 1.** (herum)streunen; sich verirren; *fig* abschweifen (***from*** von); **2.** verirrtes *or* streunendes Tier **3.** verirrt (*bullet, dog etc*); streunend (*dog etc*); vereinzelt

**streak 1.** Streifen *m*; Strähne *f*; (Charakter)Zug *m*; ***a ~ of lightning*** ein Blitz; ***lucky*** ~ Glückssträhne *f* **2.** flitzen;

streifen
**streak·y** streifig; GASTR durchwachsen
**stream 1.** Bach *m*; Strömung *f*; *fig* Strom *m* **2.** strömen; flattern, wehen
**stream·er** Luft-, Papierschlange *f*; Wimpel *m*; IT Streamer *m*
**street 1.** Straße *f*; ***on*** (*esp Br* ***in***) ***the ~*** auf der Straße **2.** Straßen…
**street·car** Straßenbahn(wagen *m*) *f*
**street sweep·er** Straßenkehrer *m*
**strength** Stärke *f*, Kraft *f*, Kräfte *pl*
**strength·en** *v/t* (ver)stärken; *v/i* stärker werden
**stren·u·ous** anstrengend, strapaziös; unermüdlich
**stress 1.** *fig* Stress *m*; PHYS, TECH Beanspruchung *f*, Belastung *f*, Druck *m*; LING Betonung *f*; *fig* Nachdruck *m* **2.** betonen
**stress·ful** stressig, aufreibend
**stretch 1.** *v/t* strecken; (aus)weiten, dehnen; spannen; *fig* es nicht allzu genau nehmen mit; ***~ out*** ausstrecken; ***be fully ~ed*** *fig* richtig gefordert werden; voll ausgelastet sein; *v/i* sich dehnen, *a.* länger *or* weiter werden; sich dehnen *or* recken *or* strecken; sich erstrecken; ***~ out*** sich ausstrecken **2.** Dehnbarkeit *f*, Elastizität *f*; Strecke *f*; SPORT (*Gegen-, Ziel*)Gerade *f*; Zeit *f*, Zeitraum *m*, Zeitspanne *f*; ***have a ~*** sich dehnen *or* recken *or* strecken
**stretch·er** Trage *f*
**strick·en** schwer betroffen; ***~ with*** befallen *or* ergriffen von
**strict** streng, strikt; genau; ***~ly*** (***speaking***) genau genommen
**strict·ness** Strenge *f*
**stride 1.** schreiten, mit großen Schritten gehen **2.** großer Schritt
**strife** Streit *m*
**strike 1.** *v/t* schlagen; treffen; einschlagen in (*acc*) (*lightning*); *Streichholz* anzünden; MAR auflaufen auf (*acc*); streichen (***from, off*** aus *dat*, von); stoßen auf (*acc*); *j-n* beeindrucken; *j-m* einfallen, in den Sinn kommen; *Münze* prägen; *Saite etc* anschlagen; *Lager, Zelt* abbrechen; *Flagge, Segel* streichen; ***~ out*** (aus)streichen; ***~ up*** *Lied etc* anstimmen; *Freundschaft etc* schließen; *v/i* schlagen; einschlagen; ECON streiken; ***~ (out) at s.o.*** auf j-n einschlagen **2.** ECON Streik *m*; (*Öl- etc*)Fund *m*; MIL Angriff *m*; *soccer*: Schuss *m*; ***be on ~*** streiken; ***go on ~*** streiken, in den Streik treten; ***a lucky ~*** ein Glückstreffer
**strik·er** ECON Streikende *m, f*; *soccer*: Stürmer(in)
**strik·ing** apart; auffallend
**string 1.** Schnur *f*, Bindfaden *m*; (*Schürzen-, Schuh- etc*)Band *n*; (*Puppenspiel*) Faden *m*, Draht *m*; (*Perlen- etc*)Schnur *f*; MUS, SPORT Saite *f*; (*Bogen*)Sehne *f*; BOT Faser *f*; IT Zeichenfolge *f*; *fig* Reihe *f*, Serie *f*; ***the ~s*** MUS die Streichinstrumente *pl*, die Streicher *pl*; ***pull a few ~s*** *fig* ein paar Beziehungen spielen lassen; ***with no ~s attached*** *fig* ohne Bedingungen **2.** *Perlen etc* aufreihen; *Gitarre etc* besaiten, *Tennisschläger etc* bespannen; *Bohnen* abziehen **3.** MUS Streich…; **string bean** BOT grüne Bohne
**strin·gent** streng
**string·y** fas(e)rig
**strip 1.** *v/i*: *a.* ***~ off*** sich ausziehen (***to*** bis auf *acc*); *v/t* ausziehen; *Farbe etc* abkratzen, *Tapete etc* abreißen (***from, off*** von); *a.* ***~ down*** TECH zerlegen, auseinandernehmen; ***~ s.o. of s.th.*** j-m et. rauben *or* wegnehmen **2.** (*Land-, Papier- etc*)Streifen *m*; Strip *m*
**stripe** Streifen *m*; **striped** gestreift
**strive**: ***~ for*** *or* ***after*** streben nach
**stroke 1.** streicheln; streichen über (*acc*) **2.** Schlag *m* (*a.* SPORT); MED Schlag(-anfall) *m*; (*Pinsel*)Strich *m*; *swimming*: Zug *m*; TECH Hub *m*; → ***four-stroke engine***; ***~ of lightning*** Blitzschlag *m*; ***a ~ of luck*** *fig* ein glücklicher Zufall, ein Glücksfall
**stroll 1.** bummeln, spazieren **2.** Bummel *m*, Spaziergang *m*
**stroll·er** Bummler(in), Spaziergänger(in); Sportwagen *m*
**strong** stark (*a.* GASTR, PHARM); kräftig; mächtig; stabil; fest; robust
**strong·box** (Geld-, Stahl)Kassette *f*
**strong·hold** Festung *f*; Stützpunkt *m*; *fig* Hochburg *f*
**strong-mind·ed** willensstark
**strong room** Tresor(raum) *m*
**struc·ture** Struktur *f*; (Auf)Bau *m*, Gliederung *f*; Bau *m*, Konstruktion *f*
**strug·gle 1.** kämpfen, ringen (***with*** mit; ***for*** um); sich abmühen; sich winden, zappeln; ***~ against*** sich sträuben gegen

2. Kampf *m*
**strum** klimpern auf (*dat*) (*or* ***on*** auf *dat*)
**strut**[1] stolzieren
**strut**[2] TECH Strebe *f*; Stütze *f*
**stub 1.** (*Bleistift-*, *Zigaretten- etc*)Stummel *m*; Kontrollabschnitt *m* **2.** sich *die Zehe* anstoßen; ***~ out*** *Zigarette* ausdrücken
**stub·ble** Stoppeln *pl*
**stub·bly** stoppelig
**stub·born** eigensinnig, stur; hartnäckig
**stub·born·ness** Starrsinn *m*
**stuck-up** F hochnäsig
**stud**[1] **1.** (*Kragen-*, *Manschetten*)Knopf *m*; *soccer*: Stollen *m*; Beschlagnagel *m*; Ziernagel *m*; *pl* MOT Spikes *pl* **2.** ***be ~ded with*** besetzt sein mit; übersät sein mit; ***~ded tires*** Spikesreifen *pl*
**stud**[2] Gestüt *n*
**stu·dent** Student(in); Schüler(in)
**stud farm** Gestüt *n*
**stud horse** zo Zuchthengst *m*
**stud·ied** wohlüberlegt; gesucht
**stu·di·o** Studio *n*; Atelier *n*; *a.* ***~ apartment***, *Br* ***~ flat*** Studio *n*, Einzimmerappartement *n*; **~ couch** Schlafcouch *f*
**stu·di·ous** fleißig
**stud·y 1.** Studium *n*; Studie *f*, Untersuchung *f*; Arbeitszimmer *n*; *pl* Studium *n* **2.** studieren; lernen (***for*** für)
**stuff 1.** Zeug *n* **2.** (aus)stopfen, stopfen, vollstopfen; füllen (*a.* GASTR); ***~ o.s.*** F sich vollstopfen; **stuff·ing** Füllung *f* (*a.* GASTR)
**stuff·y** stickig; spießig; prüde
**stum·ble 1.** stolpern (***on, over***, *fig* ***at, over*** über *acc*); ***~ across, ~ on*** stoßen auf (*acc*) **2.** Stolpern *n*
**stump 1.** Stumpf *m*; Stummel *m* **2.** stampfen, stapfen
**stump·y** F kurz und dick
**stun** betäuben; *fig* sprachlos machen
**stun·ning** fantastisch; unglaublich
**stunt**[1] (das Wachstum *gen*) hemmen; ***~ed*** BIOL verkümmert; ***become ~ed*** BIOL verkümmern
**stunt**[2] (*Film*)Stunt *m*; (*gefährliches*) Kunststück; (*Reklame*)Gag *m*
**stunt| man** *film*, TV Stuntman *m*, Double *n*; **~ wom·an** *film*, TV Stuntwoman *f*, Double *n*
**stu·pid** dumm; F blöd
**stu·pid·i·ty** Dummheit *f*
**stu·por** Betäubung *f*; ***in a drunken ~*** im Vollrausch
**stur·dy** kräftig, stämmig; *fig* entschlossen, hartnäckig
**stut·ter 1.** stottern (*a.* MOT); stammeln **2.** Stottern *n*, Stammeln *n*
**sty**[1] → ***pigsty***
**sty**[2], **stye** MED Gerstenkorn *n*
**style 1.** Stil *m*; Ausführung *f*; Mode *f* **2.** entwerfen; gestalten
**styl·ish** stilvoll; modisch, elegant
**styl·ist** Stilist(in)
**Sty·ro·foam®** Styropor® *n*
**suave** verbindlich
**sub·con·scious** Unterbewusstsein *n*; ***~ly*** im Unterbewusstsein
**sub·di·vi·sion** Unterteilung *f*; Unterabteilung *f*
**sub·due** unterwerfen; *Ärger etc* unterdrücken; **sub·dued** gedämpft (*light*, *voice etc*); ruhig, still (*person*)
**sub·ject 1.** Thema *n*; PED, UNIV Fach *n*; LING Subjekt *n*, Satzgegenstand *m*; Untertan(in); Staatsangehörige *m*, *f*, -bürger(in) **2.** *adj*: ***~ to*** anfällig für; ***be ~ to*** *a.* neigen zu; ***be ~ to*** unterliegen (*dat*); abhängen von; ***prices ~ to change*** Preisänderungen vorbehalten **3.** unterwerfen; ***~ to*** *e-m Test etc* unterziehen; *der Kritik etc* aussetzen
**sub·jec·tion** Unterwerfung *f*; Abhängigkeit *f* (***to*** von)
**sub·ju·gate** unterjochen, unterwerfen
**sub·junc·tive** LING *a.* ***~ mood*** Konjunktiv *m*
**sub·lease, sub·let** untervermieten, weitervermieten
**sub·lime** großartig; *fig* total
**sub·ma·chine gun** Maschinenpistole *f*
**sub·ma·rine 1.** unterseeisch **2.** Unterseeboot *n*, U-Boot *n*
**sub·merge** tauchen; (ein)tauchen (***in*** in *acc*)
**sub·mis·sion** Einreichung *f*; *boxing etc*: Aufgabe *f*; Unterwerfung *f* (***to*** unter); **sub·mis·sive** unterwürfig
**sub·mit** *Gesuch etc* einreichen (***to*** *dat or* bei); sich fügen (***to*** *dat or* in *acc*); *boxing etc*: aufgeben
**sub·or·di·nate 1.** untergeordnet (***to*** *dat*); **2.** Untergebene *m*, *f* **3.** ***~ to*** unterordnen (*dat*), zurückstellen (hinter *acc*); **~ clause** LING Nebensatz *m*
**sub·scribe** *v/t Geld* gegen, spenden (***to*** für); *v/i*: ***~ to*** *Zeitung etc* abonnieren;

S

**sub·scrib·er** Abonnent(in); TEL Teilnehmer(in); **sub·scrip·tion** Abonnement *n*; (Mitglieds)Beitrag *m*
**sub·se·quent** später
**sub·side** sich senken (*building, road etc*); zurückgehen (*flood, demand etc*), sich legen (*storm, anger etc*)
**sub·sid·i·a·ry 1.** Neben...; *~ question* Zusatzfrage *f* **2.** ECON Tochtergesellschaft *f*
**sub·si·dize** subventionieren
**sub·si·dy** Subvention *f*
**sub·sist** leben, existieren (***on*** von)
**sub·sis·tence** Existenz *f*
**sub·stance** Substanz *f* (*a. fig*), Stoff *m*; *das* Wesentliche, Kern *m*
**sub·stan·dard** minderwertig
**sub·stan·tial** solid (*furniture etc*); beträchtlich (*salary etc*), (*changes etc a.*) wesentlich; reichlich, kräftig (*meal*)
**sub·stan·ti·ate** beweisen
**sub·stan·tive** LING Substantiv *n*, Hauptwort *n*
**sub·sti·tute 1.** Ersatz *m*; Stellvertreter(in), Vertretung *f*; SPORT Auswechselspieler(in), Ersatzspieler(in) **2.** *~ s.th. for s.th.* et. durch et. ersetzen, et. gegen et. austauschen *or* auswechseln; *~ for* einspringen für, *j-n* vertreten
**sub·sti·tu·tion** Ersatz *m*; SPORT Austausch *m*, Auswechslung *f*
**sub·ter·fuge** List *f*
**sub·ter·ra·ne·an** unterirdisch
**sub·ti·tle** Untertitel *m*
**sub·tle** fein (*differences etc*); raffiniert (*plan etc*); scharf (*mind*); scharfsinnig
**sub·tract** MATH abziehen, subtrahieren (***from*** von); **sub·trac·tion** MATH Abziehen *n*, Subtraktion *f*
**sub·trop·i·cal** subtropisch
**sub·urb** Vorort *m*, Vorstadt *f*
**sub·ur·ban** Vorort..., vorstädtisch, Vorstadt...
**sub·ver·sive** umstürzlerisch, subversiv
**sub·way** Unterführung *f*; U-Bahn *f*
**suc·ceed** *v/i* Erfolg haben, erfolgreich sein, (*plan etc a.*) gelingen; *~ to* in *e-m Amt* nachfolgen; *~ to the throne* auf dem Thron folgen; *v/t*: *~ s.o. as* j-s Nachfolger werden als
**suc·cess** Erfolg *m*
**suc·cess·ful** erfolgreich
**suc·ces·sion** Folge *f*; Erb-, Nach-, Thronfolge *f*; ***five times in ~*** fünfmal hintereinander; ***in quick ~*** in rascher Folge; **suc·ces·sive** aufeinanderfolgend; **suc·ces·sor** Nachfolger(in); Thronfolger(in)
**suc·cu·lent** GASTR saftig
**such** solche(r, -s); derartige(r, -s); so; derart; *~ a* so ein(e)
**suck 1.** *v/t* saugen; lutschen (an *dat*); *v/i* saugen (***at*** an *dat*); **2.** ***have*** *or* ***take a ~ at*** saugen *or* lutschen an (*dat*)
**suck·er** ZO Saugnapf *m*, Saugorgan *n*; TECH Saugfuß *m*; BOT Wurzelschössling *m*, Wurzelspross *m*; F Trottel *m*, Simpel *m*; Lutscher *m*
**suck·le** säugen, stillen
**suc·tion** (An)Saugen *n*; Saugwirkung *f*; **~ pump** TECH Saugpumpe *f*
**sud·den** plötzlich, unvermittelt; ***all of a ~*** F ganz plötzlich
**sud·den·ly** plötzlich
**suds** Seifenschaum *m*
**sue** JUR *j-n* verklagen (***for*** auf *acc*, wegen); klagen (***for*** auf *acc*)
**suede, suède** Wildleder *n*, Velours (-leder) *n*
**su·et** GASTR Nierenfett *n*, Talg *m*
**suf·fer** *v/i* leiden (***from*** an *dat*, unter *dat*); darunter leiden; *v/t* erleiden; *Folgen* tragen; **suf·fer·er** Leidende *m, f*; **suf·fer·ing** Leiden *n*; Leid *n*
**suf·fi·cient** genügend, genug, ausreichend; ***be ~*** genügen, (aus)reichen
**suf·fix** LING Suffix *n*, Nachsilbe *f*
**suf·fo·cate** ersticken
**suf·frage** POL Wahl-, Stimmrecht *n*
**suf·fuse** durchfluten (*light etc*); überziehen (*color etc*)
**sug·ar 1.** Zucker *m* **2.** zuckern
**sug·ar beet** BOT Zuckerrübe *f*
**sug·ar bowl** Zuckerdose *f*
**sug·ar·cane** BOT Zuckerrohr *n*
**sug·ar tongs** Zuckerzange *f*
**sug·ar·y** süß; *fig* süßlich
**sug·gest** vorschlagen, anregen; hindeuten *or* hinweisen auf (*acc*), schließen lassen auf (*acc*); andeuten
**sug·ges·tion** Vorschlag *m*, Anregung *f*; Anflug *m*, Spur *f*; Andeutung *f*; PSYCH Suggestion *f*
**sug·ges·tive** zweideutig (*remark etc*), vielsagend (*look etc*)
**su·i·cide** Selbstmord *m*; Selbstmörder(in); ***commit ~*** Selbstmord begehen
**suit 1.** Anzug *m*; Kostüm *n*; *card game*:

Farbe *f*; JUR Prozess *m*; ***follow ~*** *fig* dem Beispiel folgen, dasselbe tun **2.** *v/t j-m* passen (*date etc*); *j-n* kleiden, *j-m* stehen; *et.* anpassen (**to** *dat*); **~ s.th., be ~ed to s.th.** geeignet sein *or* sich eignen für; **~ yourself!** mach, was du willst!
**sui·ta·ble** passend, geeignet (**for, to** für)
**suit·case** Koffer *m*
**suite** (*Möbel-, Sitz*)Garnitur *f*; Suite *f*, Zimmerflucht *f*; MUS Suite *f*; Gefolge *n*
**sul·fur** CHEM Schwefel *m*
**sul·fu·ric ac·id** CHEM Schwefelsäure *f*
**sulk** schmollen, F eingeschnappt sein
**sulk·y** schmollend, F eingeschnappt
**sul·len** mürrisch, verdrossen
**sul·phur** *Br* → **sulfur**
**sul·phu·ric ac·id** *Br* → **sulfuric acid**
**sul·try** schwül; aufreizend (*look etc*)
**sum 1.** Summe *f*; Betrag *m*; (einfache) Rechenaufgabe; **do ~s** rechnen **2. ~ up** zusammenfassen; *j-n, et.* abschätzen
**sum·mar·ize** zusammenfassen
**sum·ma·ry** Zusammenfassung *f*, (kurze) Inhaltsangabe
**sum·mer** Sommer *m*; **in** (**the**) **~** im Sommer; **~ camp** Ferienlager *n*; **~ hol·i·days** *Br* Sommerferien *pl*; **~ school** Ferienkurs *m*
**sum·mer·time** Sommer *m*, Sommerszeit *f*; **in** (**the**) **~** im Sommer
**sum·mer| time** *esp Br* Sommerzeit *f*; **~ va·ca·tion** Sommerferien *pl*
**sum·mer·y** sommerlich, Sommer…
**sum·mit** Gipfel *m* (*a.* ECON, POL, *fig*); **~ con·fe·rence** POL Gipfelkonferenz *f*; **~ meet·ing** POL Gipfeltreffen *n*
**sum·mon** auffordern; *Versammlung etc* einberufen; JUR vorladen; **~ up** *Kraft, Mut etc* zusammenehmen
**sum·mons** JUR Vorladung *f*
**sump** *Br* MOT Ölwanne *f*
**sump·tu·ous** luxuriös, aufwändig
**sun 1.** Sonne *f* **2.** Sonnen… **3. ~ o.s.** sich sonnen
**Sun** *abbr of* **Sunday** So., Sonntag *m*
**sun·bathe** sich sonnen, ein Sonnenbad nehmen
**sun·beam** Sonnenstrahl *m*
**sun·bed** Sonnenbank *f*
**sun·burn** Sonnenbrand *m*
**sun cream** Sonnencreme *f*
**sun·dae** GASTR Eisbecher *m*
**Sun·day** (*abbr* **Sun**) Sonntag *m*; **on ~** (am) Sonntag; **on ~s** sonntags
**sun·dial** Sonnenuhr *f*
**sun·dries** Diverses, Verschiedenes
**sun·dry** diverse, verschiedene
**sun·glass·es** (**a pair of ~** e-e) Sonnenbrille *f*
**sunk·en** MAR gesunken, versunken; versenkt; tief liegend; eingefallen (*cheeks*), (*a. eyes*) eingesunken
**sun·light** Sonnenlicht *n*
**sun·lit** sonnenbeschienen
**sun·ny** sonnig
**sun·rise** Sonnenaufgang *m*; **at ~** bei Sonnenaufgang
**sun·roof** Dachterrasse *f*; MOT Schiebedach *n*
**sun·set** Sonnenuntergang *m*; **at ~** bei Sonnenuntergang
**sun·shade** Sonnenschirm *m*
**sun·shine** Sonnenschein *m*
**sun·stroke** MED Sonnenstich *m*
**sun·tan** (Sonnen)Bräune *f*; **~ lo·tion** Sonnenschutz *m*, Sonnencreme *f*; **~ oil** Sonnenöl *n*
**su·per** F super, spitze, klasse
**su·per...** Über…, über…
**su·per·a·bun·dant** überreichlich
**su·per·an·nu·at·ed** pensioniert, im Ruhestand
**su·perb** ausgezeichnet
**su·per·charg·er** MOT Kompressor *m*
**su·per·cil·i·ous** hochmütig, F hochnäsig
**su·per·fi·cial** oberflächlich
**su·per·flu·ous** überflüssig
**su·per·hu·man** übermenschlich
**su·per·im·pose** überlagern; *Bild etc* einblenden (**on** in *acc*)
**su·per·in·tend** die (Ober)Aufsicht haben über (*acc*), überwachen; leiten
**su·per·in·tend·ent** Aufsicht *f*, Aufsichtsbeamter *m*, -beamtin *f*; *Br* Kriminalrat *m*
**su·pe·ri·or 1.** ranghöher (**to** als); überlegen (**to** *dat*), besser (**to** als); ausgezeichnet, hervorragend; überheblich, überlegen; **Father Superior** REL Superior *m*; **Mother Superior** REL Oberin *f* **2.** Vorgesetzte *m, f*; **su·peri·or·i·ty** Überlegenheit *f* (**over** gegenüber)
**su·per·la·tive 1.** höchste(r, -s), überragend **2.** *a.* **~ degree** LING Superlativ *m*
**su·per·mar·ket** Supermarkt *m*
**su·per·nat·u·ral** übernatürlich

**su·per·nu·me·ra·ry** zusätzlich
**su·per·sede** ablösen, ersetzen, verdrängen
**su·per·son·ic** AVIAT, PHYS Überschall…
**su·per·sti·tion** Aberglaube *m*
**su·per·sti·tious** abergläubisch
**su·per·store** Großmarkt *m*
**su·per·vene** dazwischenkommen
**su·per·vise** beaufsichtigen, überwachen; **su·per·vi·sion** Beaufsichtigung *f*, Überwachung *f*; ***under s.o.'s ~*** unter j-s Aufsicht; **su·per·vi·sor** Aufseher(in), Aufsicht *f*
**sup·per** Abendessen *n*; ***have ~*** zu Abend essen; → ***lord***
**sup·plant** verdrängen
**sup·ple** gelenkig, geschmeidig, biegsam
**sup·ple·ment 1.** Ergänzung *f*; Nachtrag *m*, Anhang *m*; Ergänzungsband *m*; (*Zeitungs- etc*)Beilage *f* **2.** ergänzen; **sup·ple·men·ta·ry** ergänzend, zusätzlich
**sup·pli·er** ECON Lieferant(in), *a. pl* Lieferfirma *f*
**sup·ply 1.** liefern; stellen, sorgen für; *j-n, et.* versorgen, ECON beliefern (***with*** mit); **2.** Lieferung *f* (***to*** an *acc*); Versorgung *f*; ECON Angebot *n*; *mst pl* Vorrat *m* (***of*** an *dat*), *a.* Proviant *m*, MIL Nachschub *m*; ***~ and demand*** ECON Angebot und Nachfrage
**sup·port 1.** (ab)stützen, *Gewicht etc* tragen; *Währung* stützen; unterstützen; unterhalten, sorgen für **2.** Stütze *f*; TECH Träger *m*; *fig* Unterstützung *f*
**sup·port·er** Anhänger(in) (*a.* SPORT), Befürworter(in)
**sup·pose 1.** annehmen, vermuten; ***be ~d to …*** sollen; ***what is that ~d to mean?*** was soll denn das?; ***I ~ so*** ich nehme es an, vermutlich **2.** *cj* angenommen; wie wäre es, wenn
**sup·posed** angeblich, vermeintlich
**sup·pos·ing** → ***suppose*** *2*
**sup·po·si·tion** Annahme *f*, Vermutung *f*
**sup·pos·i·to·ry** PHARM Zäpfchen *n*
**sup·press** unterdrücken
**sup·pres·sion** Unterdrückung *f*
**sup·pu·rate** MED eitern
**su·prem·a·cy** Vormachtstellung *f*
**su·preme** höchste(r, -s), oberste(r, -s), Ober…; größte(r, -s)
**sur·charge 1.** Nachporto *or* e-n Zuschlag erheben (***on*** auf *acc*); **2.** Aufschlag *m*, Zuschlag *m* (***on*** auf *acc*); Nach-, Strafporto *n* (***on*** auf *acc*)
**sure 1.** *adj* sicher; ***~ of o.s.*** selbstsicher; ***~ of winning*** siegessicher; ***~ thing!*** F (aber) klar!; ***be*** *or* ***feel ~*** sicher sein; ***be ~ to …*** vergiss nicht zu …; ***for ~*** ganz sicher *or* bestimmt; ***make ~ that*** sich (davon) überzeugen, dass; ***to be ~*** sicher(lich) **2.** *adv* F sicher, klar; ***~ enough*** tatsächlich
**sure·ly** sicher(lich)
**sur·e·ty** JUR Bürge *m*, Bürgin *f*; Bürgschaft *f*, Sicherheit *f*; ***stand ~ for s.o.*** für j-n bürgen
**surf 1.** Brandung *f* **2.** SPORT surfen
**sur·face 1.** Oberfläche *f*; (*Straßen*)Belag *m* **2.** auftauchen; *Straße* mit e-m Belag versehen **3.** Oberflächen…; *fig* oberflächlich; ***~ mail*** gewöhnliche Post
**surf·board** Surfboard *n*, Surfbrett *n*
**surf·er** Surfer(in), Wellenreiter(in)
**surf·ing** Surfen *n*, Wellenreiten *n*
**surge 1.** *fig* Welle *f*, Woge *f*, (*Gefühls*)-Aufwallung *f* **2.** (vorwärts-)drängen; ***~ (up)*** aufwallen
**sur·geon** MED Chirurg(in)
**sur·ge·ry** MED Chirurgie *f*; operativer Eingriff, Operation *f*; *Br* Sprechzimmer *n*; *Br* Sprechstunde *f*; *a.* ***doctor's ~*** Arztpraxis *f*; ***~ hours*** MED *Br* Sprechstunde(n *pl*) *f*
**sur·gi·cal** MED chirurgisch
**sur·ly** mürrisch, unwirsch
**sur·name** Familienname *m*, Nachname *m*, Zuname *m*
**sur·pass** *Erwartungen etc* übertreffen
**sur·plus 1.** Überschuss *m* (***of*** an *dat*); **2.** überschüssig
**sur·prise 1.** Überraschung *f*, Verwunderung *f*; ***take s.o. by ~*** j-n überraschen **2.** überraschen; ***be ~d at*** *or* ***by*** überrascht sein über (*acc*)
**sur·ren·der 1.** *v/i* ***~ to*** MIL, *a. fig* sich ergeben (*dat*), kapitulieren vor (*dat*); ***~ to the police*** sich der Polizei stellen; *v/t et.* übergeben, ausliefern (***to*** *dat*); aufgeben, verzichten auf (*acc*); ***~ o.s. to the police*** sich der Polizei stellen **2.** MIL Kapitulation *f* (*a. fig*); Aufgabe *f*, Verzicht *m*
**sur·ro·gate** Ersatz *m*
**sur·ro·gate moth·er** Leihmutter *f*
**sur·round** umgeben; umstellen
**sur·round·ing** umliegend

**sur·round·ings** Umgebung *f*
**sur·vey 1.** (sich) *et.* betrachten (*a. fig*); *Haus etc* begutachten; *Land* vermessen **2.** Umfrage *f*; Überblick *m* (***of*** über *acc*); Begutachtung *f*; Vermessung *f*
**sur·vey·or** Gutachter *m*; Land(ver)-messer *m*
**sur·viv·al** Überleben *n* (*a. fig*); Überbleibsel *n*; ~ **in·stinct** Selbsterhaltungstrieb *m*; ~ **kit** Überlebensausrüstung *f*; ~ **train·ing** Überlebenstraining *n*
**sur·vive** überleben; *Feuer etc* überstehen; erhalten bleiben *or* sein
**sur·vi·vor** Überlebende *m*, *f* (***from, of*** *gen*)
**sus·cep·ti·ble** empfänglich, anfällig (*both*: ***to*** für)
**sus·pect 1.** *j-n* verdächtigen (***of*** *gen*); *et.* vermuten; *et.* anzweifeln, *et.* bezweifeln **2.** Verdächtige *m*, *f* **3.** verdächtig, suspekt
**sus·pend** *Verkauf, Zahlungen etc* (vorübergehend) einstellen; JUR *Verfahren, Urteil* aussetzen; *Strafe* zur Bewährung aussetzen; *j-n* suspendieren; vorübergehend ausschließen (***from*** aus); SPORT *j-n* sperren; (auf)hängen; ***be ~ed*** schweben; **sus·pend·er** *Br* Strumpfhalter *m*, Straps *m*; Sockenhalter *m*; (*a.* ***a pair of***) ***~s*** Hosenträger *pl*
**sus·pense** Spannung *f*; ***in*** ~ gespannt, voller Spannung
**sus·pen·sion** (vorübergehende) Einstellung; Suspendierung *f*; vorübergehender Ausschluss; SPORT Sperre *f*; MOT *etc* Aufhängung *f*; ~ **bridge** Hängebrücke *f*; ~ **rail·way** *esp Br* Schwebebahn *f*
**sus·pi·cion** Verdacht *m*; Verdächtigung *f*; Argwohn *m*, Misstrauen *n*; *fig* Hauch *m*, Spur *f*; **sus·pi·cious** verdächtig; argwöhnisch, misstrauisch; ***become*** ~ Verdacht schöpfen
**sus·tain** *j-n* stärken; *Interesse etc* aufrechterhalten; *Schaden, Verlust* erleiden; JUR *e-m Einspruch etc* stattgeben
**swab** MED **1.** Tupfer *m*; Abstrich *m* **2.** *Wunde* abtupfen
**swad·dle** *Baby* wickeln
**swag·ger** stolzieren
**swal·low**[1] **1.** schlucken (*a.* F); hinunterschlucken; ~ ***up*** *fig* schlucken, verschlingen **2.** Schluck *m*
**swal·low**[2] zo Schwalbe *f*
**swamp 1.** Sumpf *m* **2.** überschwemmen; ***be ~ed with*** *fig* überschwemmt werden mit; **swamp·y** sumpfig
**swan** zo Schwan *m*
**swank 1.** F *esp Br* angeben **2.** F *esp Br* Angeber(in); Angabe *f* **3.** F piekfein
**swank·y** F piekfein; *esp Br* angeberisch
**swap** F **1.** (ein)tauschen **2.** Tausch *m*
**swarm 1.** zo Schwarm *m* (*a. fig*) **2.** zo schwärmen, *fig a.* strömen; *a. fig* wimmeln (***with*** von)
**swar·thy** dunkel (*skin*), dunkelhäutig (*person*)
**swas·ti·ka** Hakenkreuz *n*
**swat** *Fliege etc* totschlagen
**sway 1.** *v/i* sich wiegen, schaukeln; ***~ between*** *fig* schwanken zwischen (*dat*); *v/t* hin- und herbewegen, schwenken, *s-n Körper* wiegen; beeinflussen **2.** Schwanken *n*, Schaukeln *n*
**swear** fluchen; schwören; ~ ***at s.o.*** j-n wüst beschimpfen; ~ ***by*** *fig* F schwören auf (*acc*); ~ ***s.o. in*** JUR j-n vereidigen
**sweat 1.** *v/i* schwitzen (***with*** vor *dat*); v/t: ~ ***out*** *Krankheit* ausschwitzen; ~ ***blood*** F sich abrackern (***over*** mit); **2.** Schweiß *m*; F Schufterei *f*; ***get in(to) a*** ~ *fig* F ins Schwitzen geraten *or* kommen
**sweat·er** Pullover *m*
**sweat·shirt** Sweatshirt *n*
**sweat·y** schweißig, verschwitzt; nach Schweiß riechend, Schweiß...; schweißtreibend
**Swede** Schwede *m*, Schwedin *f*
**Swe·den** Schweden *n*
**Swe·dish 1.** schwedisch **2.** LING Schwedisch *n*
**sweep 1.** *v/t* kehren, fegen; *fig* fegen über (*acc*) (*storm etc*); *Horizont etc* absuchen (***for*** nach); *fig Land etc* überschwemmen; ~ ***along*** mitreißen; *v/i* kehren, fegen; rauschen (*person*) **2.** Kehren *n*, Fegen *n*; Hieb *m*, Schlag *m*; F Schornsteinfeger *m*, Kaminkehrer *m*; ***give the floor a good*** ~ den Boden gründlich kehren *or* fegen; ***make a clean*** ~ gründlich aufräumen; SPORT gründlich abräumen
**sweep·er** (*Straßen*)Kehrer *m*; Kehrmaschine *f*; *soccer*: Libero *m*
**sweep·ing** durchgreifend (*changes etc*); pauschal, zu allgemein
**sweep·ings** Kehricht *m*

S

**sweet** **1.** süß (*a. fig*); lieblich; lieb; ~ ***nothings*** Zärtlichkeiten *pl*; ***have a ~ tooth*** gern naschen **2.** *Br* Süßigkeit *f*, Bonbon *m*, *n*; *Br* Nachtisch *m*; ~ **corn** *esp Br* BOT Zuckermais *m*
**sweet·en** süßen
**sweet·heart** Schatz *m*, Liebste *m*, *f*
**sweet pea** BOT Gartenwicke *f*
**sweet shop** *esp Br* Süßwarengeschäft *n*
**swell** **1.** *v/i a.* ~ ***up*** MED (an)schwellen; *a.* ~ ***out*** sich blähen; *v/t fig Zahl etc* anwachsen lassen; *a.* ~ ***out*** *Segel* blähen **2.** MAR Dünung *f* **3.** F klasse
**swell·ing** MED Schwellung *f*
**swel·ter** vor Hitze fast umkommen
**swerve** **1.** schwenken (***to the left*** nach links), e-n Schwenk machen; *fig* abweichen (***from*** von); **2.** Schwenk *m*, Schwenkung *f*, MOT *etc a.* Schlenker *m*
**swift** schnell
**swim** **1.** *v/i* schwimmen; *fig* verschwimmen; ***my head was ~ming*** mir drehte sich alles; *v/t Strecke* schwimmen; *Fluss etc* durchschwimmen **2.** Schwimmen *n*; ***go for a ~*** schwimmen gehen
**swim·mer** Schwimmer(in)
**swim·ming** Schwimmen *n*; ~ **bath(s)** *Br* Schwimmbad *n*, *esp* Hallenbad *n*; ~ **cap** Badekappe *f*, Bademütze *f*; ~ **costume** Badeanzug *m*; ~ **gear** Badezeug *n*; ~ **pool** Swimmingpool *m*, Schwimmbecken *n*; ~ **things** Badesachen *pl*; ~ **trunks** Badehose *f*
**swim·suit** Badeanzug *m*
**swin·dle** **1.** *j-n* beschwindeln (***out of*** um); **2.** Schwindel *m*
**swine** zo Schwein *n* (*a.* F *fig*)
**swing** **1.** *v/i* (hin- und her)schwingen; sich schwingen; einbiegen, -schwenken (***into*** in *acc*); MUS schwungvoll spielen (*band etc*); Schwung haben (*music*); ~ ***round*** sich ruckartig umdrehen; ~ ***shut*** zuschlagen (*door etc*); *v/t* et., *die Arme etc* schwingen **2.** Schwingen *n*; Schaukel *f*; *fig* Schwung *m*; *fig* Umschwung *m*; ***in full ~*** in vollem Gang
**swing door** Pendeltür *f*
**swin·ish** ekelhaft
**swipe** **1.** Schlag *m* **2.** schlagen (***at*** nach)
**swirl** **1.** wirbeln **2.** Wirbel *m*
**swish**[1] **1.** *v/i* sausen, zischen; rascheln (*silk etc*); *v/t* mit *dem Schwanz* schlagen **2.** Sausen *n*, Zischen *n*; Rascheln *n*; Schlagen *n*
**swish**[2] *Br* feudal, schick
**Swiss** **1.** schweizerisch, eidgenössisch, Schweizer… **2.** Schweizer(in); ***the ~*** die Schweizer *pl*
**switch** **1.** ELECTR, TECH Schalter *m*; RAIL Weiche *f*; Gerte *f*, Rute *f*; *fig* Umstellung *f* **2.** ELECTR, TECH (um)schalten (*a.* ~ ***over***) (***to*** auf *acc*); RAIL rangieren; wechseln (***to*** zu); ~ ***off*** abschalten, ausschalten; ~ ***on*** anschalten, einschalten
**switch·board** ELECTR Schalttafel *f*; (Telefon)Zentrale *f*
**Swit·zer·land** die Schweiz
**swiv·el** (sich) drehen
**swiv·el chair** Drehstuhl *m*
**swoon** in Ohnmacht fallen
**swoop** **1.** *fig* F zuschlagen (*police etc*); *a.* ~ ***down*** zo herabstoßen (***on*** auf *acc*); ~ ***on*** F herfallen über (*acc*) **2.** Razzia *f*
**swop** F → ***swap***
**sword** Schwert *n*
**syc·a·more** BOT Bergahorn *m*; Platane *f*
**syl·la·ble** Silbe *f*
**syl·la·bus** PED, UNIV Lehrplan *m*
**sym·bol** Symbol *n*
**sym·bol·ic** symbolisch
**sym·bol·is·m** Symbolik *f*
**sym·bol·ize** symbolisieren
**sym·met·ri·cal** symmetrisch
**sym·me·try** Symmetrie *f*
**sym·pa·thet·ic** mitfühlend; verständnisvoll; wohlwollend
**sym·pa·thize** mitfühlen; sympathisieren
**sym·pa·thiz·er** Sympathisant(in)
**sym·pa·thy** Mitgefühl *n*; Verständnis *n*
**sym·pho·ny** MUS Sinfonie *f*; ~ **orches·tra** MUS Sinfonieorchester *n*
**symp·tom** Symptom *n*
**syn·chro·nize** *v/t* aufeinander abstimmen; *Uhren*, *Film* synchronisieren; *v/i* synchron gehen *or* sein
**syn·o·nym** Synonym *n*
**sy·non·y·mous** synonym; gleichbedeutend
**syn·tax** LING Syntax *f*, Satzlehre *f*
**syn·the·sis** Synthese *f*
**syn·thet·ic** CHEM synthetisch; ~ **fi·ber** (*Br* **fi·bre**) Kunstfaser *f*
**Syr·i·a** Syrien *n*
**sy·ringe** MED Spritze *f*
**syr·up** Sirup *m*

S

**sys·tem** System *n*; (*Straßen- etc*)Netz *n*; Organismus *m*

**sys·te·mat·ic** systematisch

**sys·tem er·ror** IT Systemfehler *m*

# T

**T, t** T, t *n*

**tab** Aufhänger *m*, Schlaufe *f*; Lasche *f*; Etikett *n*, Schildchen *n*; Reiter *m*; F Rechnung *f*

**ta·ble 1.** Tisch *m*; (Tisch)Runde *f*; Tabelle *f*, Verzeichnis *n*; MATH Einmaleins *n*; ***at ~*** bei Tisch; ***at the ~*** am Tisch; ***turn the ~s*** (***on s.o.***) *fig* den Spieß umdrehen **2.** *fig* auf den Tisch legen; *esp fig* zurückstellen

**ta·ble·cloth** Tischdecke *f*, Tischtuch *n*

**ta·ble·land** GEOGR Tafelland *n*, Plateau *n*, Hochebene *f*

**ta·ble lin·en** Tischwäsche *f*

**ta·ble·mat** Untersetzer *m*

**ta·ble·spoon** Esslöffel *m*

**tab·let** PHARM Tablette *f*; Stück *n*; (*Stein- etc*)Tafel *f*

**ta·ble ten·nis** SPORT Tischtennis *n*

**ta·ble·top** Tischplatte *f*

**ta·ble·ware** Geschirr *n* und Besteck *n*

**tab·loid** Boulevardblatt *n*, -zeitung *f*

**tab·loid press** Boulevardpresse *f*

**ta·boo 1.** tabu **2.** Tabu *n*

**tab·u·lar** tabellarisch

**tab·u·late** tabellarisch (an)ordnen

**tab·u·la·tor** Tabulator *m*

**tach·o·graph** MOT Fahrtenschreiber *m*

**ta·chom·e·ter** MOT Drehzahlmesser *m*

**ta·cit** stillschweigend

**ta·ci·turn** schweigsam, wortkarg

**tack 1.** Stift *m*, (Reiß)Zwecke *f*; Heftstich *m* **2.** heften (***to*** an *acc*); ***~ on*** anfügen (***to*** *dat*)

**tack·le 1.** *Problem etc* angehen; *soccer etc*: *ballführenden Gegner* angreifen; *j-n* zur Rede stellen (***about*** wegen); **2.** TECH Flaschenzug *m*; (*Angel*)Gerät(e *pl*) *n*; *soccer etc*: Angriff *m*

**tack·y** klebrig; F schäbig

**tact** Takt *m*, Feingefühl *n*

**tact·ful** taktvoll

**tac·tics** Taktik *f*

**tact·less** taktlos

**tad·pole** ZO Kaulquappe *f*

**taf·fe·ta** Taft *m*

**taf·fy** Sahnebonbon *m*, *n*, Toffee *n*

**tag 1.** Etikett *n*; (*Namens-*, *Preis*)Schild *n*; (Schnürsenkel)Stift *m*; stehende Redensart *f*; *a.* ***question ~*** LING Frageanhängsel *n* **2.** etikettieren; *Waren* auszeichnen; anhängen; ***~ along*** F mitgehen, mitkommen; ***~ along behind s.o.*** F hinter j-m hertrotten

**tail 1.** Schwanz *m*; Schweif *m*; hinterer Teil; F Schatten *m*, Beschatter(in); *pl* Rück-, Kehrseite *f*; Frack *m*; ***put a ~ on*** *j-n* beschatten lassen; ***turn ~*** *fig* sich auf dem Absatz umdrehen; ***with one's ~ between one's legs*** *fig* mit eingezogenem Schwanz **2.** F *j-n* beschatten; ***~ back*** *esp Br* MOT sich stauen (***to*** bis zu); ***~ off*** schwächer werden, abnehmen, nachlassen

**tail·back** *esp Br* MOT Rückstau *m*

**tail·coat** Frack *m*

**tail end** Ende *n*, Schluss *m*

**tail·light** MOT Rücklicht *n*

**tai·lor 1.** Schneider *m* **2.** schneidern

**tai·lor-made** Maß…; maßgeschneidert (*a. fig*)

**tail pipe** TECH Auspuffrohr *n*

**tail·wind** Rückenwind *m*

**taint·ed** GASTR verdorben

**take 1.** *v/t* nehmen; (weg)nehmen; mitnehmen; bringen; MIL, MED einnehmen; *chess etc*: *Figur*, *Stein* schlagen; *Gefangene*, *Prüfung etc* machen; UNIV studieren; *Preis etc* erringen; *Scheck etc* (an)nehmen; *Rat* annehmen; *et.* hinnehmen; fassen, Platz bieten für; *et.* aushalten, ertragen; PHOT *et.* aufnehmen, *Aufnahme* machen; *Temperatur* messen; *Notiz* machen, niederschreiben; *ein Bad*, *Zug*, *Bus*, *Weg etc* nehmen; *Gelegenheit*, *Maßnahmen* ergreifen; *Mut* fassen; *Zeit*, *Geduld etc* erfordern, brauchen; *Zeit* dauern; ***it took her four hours*** sie brauchte vier Stunden; ***I ~ it that*** ich nehme an, dass; ***~ it or leave it*** F mach, was du willst; ***~n all in all*** im Großen (und) Ganzen; ***this seat***

***is* ~*n*** dieser Platz ist besetzt; ***be* ~*n by*** *or* ***with*** angetan sein von; ***be* ~*n ill*** *or* ***sick*** erkranken, krank werden; ~ ***to bits*** *or* ***pieces*** *et.* auseinandernehmen, zerlegen; ~ ***the blame*** die Schuld auf sich nehmen; ~ ***care*** vorsichtig sein, aufpassen; ~ ***care!*** F mach's gut!; → ***care*** *1*; ~ ***hold of*** ergreifen; ~ ***part*** teilnehmen (***in*** an *dat*); → ***part*** *1*; ~ ***pity on*** Mitleid haben mit; ~ ***a walk*** e-n Spaziergang machen; ~ ***my word for it*** verlass dich drauf; → ***advice, bath*** *1*, ***break*** 1, ***lead***[1] 2, ***message, oath, offense, place*** 1, ***prisoner, risk*** 1, ***seat*** 1, ***step*** 1, ***trouble*** 1, ***turn*** 2, *etc*; *v/i* MED wirken, anschlagen; ~ ***after*** *j-m* nachschlagen, ähneln; ~ ***along*** mitnehmen; ~ ***apart*** auseinandernehmen (*a. fig* F), zerlegen; ~ ***away*** wegnehmen (***from s.o.*** j-m); ... ***to*** ~ ***away*** *Br* ... zum Mitnehmen; ~ ***back*** zurückbringen; zurücknehmen; bei *j-m* Erinnerungen wachrufen; *j-n* zurückversetzen (***to*** in *acc*); ~ ***down*** herunternehmen, abnehmen; *Hose* herunterlassen; auseinandernehmen, zerlegen; (sich) *et.* aufschreiben *or* notieren; sich *Notizen* machen; ***what do you*** ~ ***me for?*** wofür hältst du mich eigentlich?; ~ ***from*** *j-m et.* wegnehmen; MATH abziehen von; ~ ***in*** *j-n* (bei sich) aufnehmen; *fig et.* einschließen; *Kleidungsstück* enger machen; *et.* begreifen; *j-n* hereinlegen, F *j-n* aufs Kreuz legen; ***be* ~*n in by*** hereinfallen auf (*acc*); ~ ***off*** *Kleidungsstück* ablegen, ausziehen, *Hut etc* abnehmen; *et.* ab-, wegnehmen; abziehen; AVIAT abheben; SPORT abspringen; F sich davonmachen; ~ ***a day off*** sich e-n Tag freinehmen; ~ ***on*** *j-n* einstellen; *Arbeit etc* annehmen, übernehmen; *Farbe*, *Ausdruck etc* annehmen; sich anlegen mit; ~ ***out*** herausnehmen, *Zahn* ziehen; *j-n* ausführen, ausgehen mit *j-m*; *Versicherung* abschließen; *s-n Frust etc* auslassen (***on*** an *dat*); ~ ***over*** *Amt*, *Macht*, *Verantwortung etc* übernehmen; die Macht übernehmen; ~ ***to*** Gefallen finden an (*dat*); ~ ***to doing s.th.*** anfangen, et. zu tun; ~ ***up*** *Vorschlag etc* aufgreifen; *Zeit etc* in Anspruch nehmen, *Platz* einnehmen; *Erzählung etc* aufnehmen; ~ ***up doing s.th.*** anfangen, sich mit et. zu beschäftigen; ~ ***up with*** sich einlassen mit **2.** *film*, TV Einstellung *f*; F Einnahmen *pl*

**take·a·way** *Br* **1.** Essen *n* zum Mitnehmen **2.** Restaurant *n* mit Straßenverkauf

**take·off** AVIAT Abheben *n*, Start *m*; SPORT Absprung *m*

**tak·ings** Einnahmen *pl*

**tale** Erzählung *f*; Geschichte *f*; Lüge *f*, Lügengeschichte *f*, Märchen *n*; ***tell* ~*s*** petzen

**tal·ent** Talent *n*, Begabung *f*

**tal·ent·ed** talentiert, begabt

**tal·is·man** Talisman *m*

**talk 1.** *v/i* reden, sprechen, sich unterhalten (***to, with*** mit; ***about*** über *acc*; ***of*** von); ~ ***about s.th.*** *a.* et. besprechen; ***s.o. to*** ~ ***to*** Ansprechpartner(in); *v/t Unsinn etc* reden; reden *or* sprechen *or* sich unterhalten über (*acc*); ~ ***s.o. into s.th.*** j-n zu et. überreden; ~ ***s.o. out of s.th.*** j-m et. ausreden; ~ ***s.th. over*** *Problem etc* besprechen (***with*** mit); ~ ***round*** *j-n* bekehren (***to*** zu), umstimmen **2.** Gespräch *n*, Unterhaltung *f* (***with*** mit; ***about*** über *acc*); Vortrag *m*; Sprache *f*, Sprechweise *f*; Gerede *n*, Geschwätz *n*; ***give a*** ~ e-n Vortrag halten (***to*** vor *dat*; ***about, on*** über *acc*); ***be the*** ~ ***of the town*** Stadtgespräch sein; ***baby*** ~ Babysprache *f*, kindliches Gebabbel; → ***small talk***

**talk·a·tive** gesprächig, redselig

**talk·er**: ***be a good*** ~ gut reden können

**talk·ing-to** F Standpauke *f*; ***give s.o. a*** ~ j-m e-e Standpauke halten

**talk show** TV Talkshow *f*

**talk-show host** TV Talkmaster *m*

**tall** groß (*person*), hoch (*building etc*)

**tal·low** Talg *m*

**tal·ly**[1] SPORT *etc* Stand *m*; ***keep a*** ~ ***of*** Buch führen über (*acc*)

**tal·ly**[2] übereinstimmen (***with*** mit); *a.* ~ ***up*** zusammenrechnen, -zählen

**tal·on** ZO Kralle *f*, Klaue *f*

**tame 1.** ZO zahm; *fig* fad(e), lahm **2.** ZO zähmen (*a. fig*)

**tam·per**: ~ ***with*** sich zu schaffen machen an (*dat*)

**tam·pon** MED Tampon *m*

**tan 1.** *Fell* gerben; bräunen; braun werden **2.** Gelbbraun *n*; (Sonnen)Bräune *f* **3.** gelbbraun

**tang** (scharfer) Geruch *or* Geschmack
**tan·gent** MATH Tangente *f*; ***fly** or **go off at a ~*** plötzlich (vom Thema) abschweifen
**tan·ge·rine** BOT Mandarine *f*
**tan·gi·ble** greifbar, *fig a.* handfest, klar
**tan·gle 1.** (sich) verwirren *or* verheddern, durcheinanderbringen; durcheinanderkommen **2.** Gewirr *n*, *fig a.* Wirrwarr *m*, Durcheinander *n*
**tank** MOT *etc* Tank *m*; MIL Panzer *m*
**tank·ard** (Bier)Humpen *m*
**tank·er** MAR Tanker *m*, Tankschiff *n*; AVIAT Tankflugzeug *n*; MOT Tankwagen *m*
**tan·ner** Gerber *m*
**tan·ne·ry** Gerberei *f*
**tan·ta·lize** *j-n* aufreizen
**tan·ta·liz·ing** verlockend
**tan·ta·mount**: ***be ~ to*** gleichbedeutend sein mit, hinauslaufen auf (*acc*)
**tan·trum** Wut-, Tobsuchtsanfall *m*
**tap[1] 1.** TECH Hahn *m*; ***beer on ~*** Bier *n* vom Fass **2.** *Naturschätze etc* erschließen; *Vorräte etc* angreifen; *Telefon (-leitung)* abhören, F anzapfen; *Fass* anzapfen, anstechen
**tap[2] 1.** mit *den Fingern, Füßen* klopfen, mit *den Fingern* trommeln (***on*** auf *acc*); antippen; ***~ s.o. on the shoulder*** j-m auf die Schulter klopfen; ***~ on*** (leicht) klopfen an (*acc*) *or* auf (*acc*) *or* gegen **2.** (leichtes) Klopfen; Klaps *m*
**tap dance** Stepptanz *m*
**tape 1.** (schmales) Band; Kleb(e)streifen *m*; (Magnet-, Video-, Ton)Band *n*; (*Video- etc*)Kassette *f*; (Band)Aufnahme *f*; TV Aufzeichnung *f*; SPORT Zielband *n*; → ***red tape*** **2.** (auf Band) aufnehmen; TV aufzeichnen; *a.* ***~ up*** (mit Klebeband) zukleben
**tape deck** Tapedeck *n*
**tape meas·ure** Bandmaß *n*, Maßband *n*, Messband *n*
**ta·per** *a.* ***~ off*** spitz zulaufen, sich verjüngen; *fig* langsam nachlassen
**tape re·cord·er** Tonbandgerät *n*
**tape re·cord·ing** Tonbandaufnahme *f*
**ta·pes·try** Gobelin *m*, Wandteppich *m*
**tape·worm** ZO Bandwurm *m*
**taps** MIL Zapfenstreich *m*
**tap wa·ter** Leitungswasser *n*
**tar 1.** Teer *m* **2.** teeren
**tare** ECON Tara *f*
**tar·get** (Schieß-, Ziel)Scheibe *f*; MIL Ziel *n* (*a. fig*), ECON *a.* Soll *n*; *fig* Zielscheibe *f*; **~ ar·e·a** MIL Zielbereich *m*; **~ group** Zielgruppe *f*
**tar·iff** ECON Zoll(tarif) *m*; *esp Br* Preisverzeichnis *n*
**tar·mac** Asphalt *m*; AVIAT Rollfeld *n*, Rollbahn *f*
**tar·nish** *v/i* anlaufen; *v/t Ansehen etc* beflecken
**tart[1]** *esp Br* Obstkuchen *m*; Obsttörtchen *n*; F Flittchen *n*, *sl* Nutte *f*
**tart[2]** herb, sauer; scharf (*a. fig*)
**tar·tan** Tartan *m*; Schottenstoff *m*; Schottenmuster *n*
**tar·tar** MED Zahnstein *m*; CHEM Weinstein *m*
**task** Aufgabe *f*; ***take s.o. to ~*** *fig* j-n zurechtweisen (***for*** wegen); **~ force** MIL *etc* Sonder-, Spezialeinheit *f*
**tas·sel** Troddel *f*, Quaste *f*
**taste 1.** Geschmack *m* (*a. fig*), Geschmackssinn *m*; Kostprobe *f*; Vorliebe *f* (***for*** für); **2.** *v/t* kosten, probieren; schmecken; *v/i* schmecken (***of*** nach)
**taste·ful** *fig* geschmackvoll
**taste·less** geschmacklos (*a. fig*)
**tast·y** schmackhaft
**tat·tered** zerlumpt
**tat·ters** Fetzen *pl*; ***in ~*** zerfetzt, in Fetzen; *fig* ruiniert
**tat·too[1] 1.** Tätowierung *f* **2.** (ein)tätowieren
**tat·too[2]** MIL Zapfenstreich *m*
**taunt 1.** verhöhnen, verspotten **2.** höhnische *or* spöttische Bemerkung
**Tau·rus** ASTR Stier *m*; ***he*** (***she***) ***is*** (***a***) **~** er (sie) ist (ein) Stier
**taut** straff; *fig* angespannt
**taw·dry** (billig und) geschmacklos
**taw·ny** gelbbraun
**tax 1.** Steuer *f* (***on*** auf *acc*); **2.** besteuern; *j-s Geduld etc* strapazieren
**tax·a·ble** steuerpflichtig
**tax·a·tion** Besteuerung *f*
**tax e·va·sion** Steuerhinterziehung *f*
**tax·i 1.** Taxi *n*, Taxe *f* **2.** AVIAT rollen
**tax·i driv·er** Taxifahrer(in)
**tax·i rank, tax·i stand** Taxistand *m*
**tax of·fi·cer** Finanzbeamte *m*
**tax·pay·er** Steuerzahler(in)
**tax re·duc·tion** Steuersenkung *f*
**tax re·turn** Steuererklärung *f*
**T-bar** Bügel *m*; *a.* ***~ lift*** Schlepplift *m*

**tea** Tee *m*; ***have a cup of ~*** e-n Tee trinken; ***make some ~*** e-n Tee machen *or* kochen
**tea·bag** Teebeutel *m*, Aufgussbeutel *m*
**teach** lehren, unterrichten (in *dat*); *j-m et.* beibringen; unterrichten (***at*** an *dat*)
**teach·er** Lehrer(in)
**tea co·sy** Teewärmer *m*
**tea·cup** Teetasse *f*; ***a storm in a ~*** *fig* ein Sturm im Wasserglas
**team** Team *n*, *a.* Arbeitsgruppe *f*, SPORT *a.* Mannschaft *f*, *soccer*: *a.* Elf *f*
**team·ster** MOT LKW-Fahrer *m*
**team·work** Zusammenarbeit *f*, Teamwork *n*; Zusammenspiel *n*
**tea·pot** Teekanne *f*
**tear**[1] Träne *f*; ***in ~s*** weinend, in Tränen (aufgelöst)
**tear**[2] **1.** *v/t* zerreißen; sich *et.* zerreißen (***on*** an *dat*); weg-, losreißen (***from*** von); *v/i* (zer)reißen; F rasen, sausen; ***~ down*** *Plakat etc* herunterreißen; *Haus etc* abreißen; ***~ off*** abreißen; sich *Kleidung* vom Leib reißen; ***~ out*** (her)ausreißen; ***~ up*** aufreißen; zerreißen **2.** Riss *m*
**tear·drop** Träne *f*
**tear·ful** weinend; tränenreich
**tear·jerk·er** F Schnulze *f*
**tea·room** Teestube *f*
**tease** necken, hänseln; ärgern
**tea·spoon** Teelöffel *m*
**teat** ZO Zitze *f*; *Br* (Gummi)Sauger *m*
**tech·ni·cal** technisch; fachlich, Fach…
**tech·ni·cal·i·ty** technische Einzelheit; reine Formsache
**tech·ni·cian** Techniker(in)
**tech·nique** Technik *f*, Verfahren *n*
**tech·nol·o·gy** Technologie *f*; Technik *f*
**ted·dy bear** Teddybär *m*
**te·di·ous** langweilig, ermüdend
**teem**: ***~ with*** wimmeln von, strotzen von *or* vor (*dat*)
**teen·age(d)** im Teenageralter; für Teenager; **teen·ag·er** Teenager *m*
**teens**: ***be in one's ~*** im Teenageralter sein
**tee·ny(-wee·ny)** F klitzeklein, winzig
**tee shirt** → ***T-shirt***
**teethe** zahnen
**tee·to·tal·(l)er** Abstinenzler(in)
**tel·e·cast** Fernsehsendung *f*
**tel·e·com·mu·ni·ca·tions** Telekommunikation *f*, Fernmeldewesen *n*
**tel·e·gram** Telegramm *n*
**tel·e·graph** **1.** ***by ~*** telegrafisch **2.** telegrafieren
**tel·e·graph·ic** telegrafisch
**te·leg·ra·phy** Telegrafie *f*
**tel·e·phone** **1.** Telefon *n* **2.** telefonieren; anrufen; **~ booth, ~ box** *Br* Telefonzelle *f*, Fernsprechzelle *f*; **~ call** Telefonanruf *n*, Telefongespräch *n*; **~ di·rec·to·ry** → ***phone book***; **~ number** Telefonnummer *f*
**te·leph·o·nist** *esp Br* Telefonist(in)
**tel·e·pho·to lens** PHOT Teleobjektiv *n*
**tel·e·print·er** Fernschreiber *m*
**tel·e·scope** Teleskop *n*, Fernrohr *n*
**tel·e·text** Teletext *m*, Videotext *m*
**tel·e·type·writ·er** Fernschreiber *m*
**tel·e·vise** im Fernsehen übertragen *or* bringen; **tel·e·vi·sion** **1.** Fernsehen *n*; *a.* ***~ set*** Fernsehapparat *m*, -gerät *n*, F Fernseher *m*; ***on ~*** im Fernsehen; ***watch ~*** fernsehen **2.** Fernseh…
**tel·ex** **1.** Telex *n*, Fernschreiben *n* **2.** telexen (***to*** an *acc*), ein Telex schicken (*dat*)
**tell** *v/t* sagen; erzählen; erkennen (***by*** an *dat*); *Namen etc* nennen; *et.* anzeigen; *j-m* sagen, befehlen (***to do*** zu tun); ***I can't ~ one from the other, I can't ~ them apart*** ich kann sie nicht auseinanderhalten; *v/i* sich auswirken (***on*** bei, auf *acc*), sich bemerkbar machen; ***who can ~?*** wer weiß?; ***you can never ~, you never can ~*** man kann nie wissen; ***~ against*** sprechen gegen; von Nachteil sein für; ***~ s.o. off*** F mit j-m schimpfen (***for*** wegen); ***~ on s.o.*** j-n verpetzen *or* verraten
**tell·er** Kassierer(in)
**tell·ing** aufschlussreich
**tell·tale** **1.** verräterisch **2.** F Petze *f*
**tel·ly** *Br* F Fernseher *m*
**te·mer·i·ty** Frechheit *f*, Kühnheit *f*
**tem·per** **1.** Temperament *n*, Wesen *n*, Wesensart *f*; Laune *f*, Stimmung *f*; TECH Härte(grad *m*) *f*; ***keep one's ~*** sich beherrschen, ruhig bleiben; ***lose one's ~*** die Beherrschung verlieren **2.** TECH *Stahl* härten
**tem·pe·ra·ment** Temperament *n*, Naturell *n*, Wesen *n*, Wesensart *f*
**tem·pe·ra·men·tal** launisch; von Natur aus
**tem·pe·rate** gemäßigt (*climate*, *region*)

**tem·pe·ra·ture** Temperatur *f*; ***have a ~*** MED erhöhte Temperatur *or* Fieber haben
**tem·pest** POET (heftiger) Sturm
**tem·ple**[1] Tempel *m*
**tem·ple**[2] ANAT Schläfe *f*
**tem·po·ral** weltlich; LING temporal, der Zeit
**tem·po·ra·ry** vorübergehend, zeiweilig
**tempt** *j-n* in Versuchung führen; *j-n* verführen (***to*** zu); **temp·ta·tion** Versuchung *f*, Verführung *f*; **tempt·ing** verführerisch
**ten 1.** zehn **2.** Zehn *f*
**ten·a·ble** *fig* haltbar
**te·na·cious** hartnäckig, zäh
**ten·ant** Pächter(in), Mieter(in)
**tend** neigen, tendieren (***to*** zu); ***~ upwards*** e-e steigende Tendenz haben
**ten·den·cy** Tendenz *f*; Neigung *f*
**ten·der**[1] empfindlich, *fig a.* heikel; GASTR zart, weich; sanft, zart, zärtlich
**ten·der**[2] RAIL, MAR Tender *m*
**ten·der**[3] ECON **1.** Angebot *n*; ***legal ~*** gesetzliches Zahlungsmittel **2.** ein Angebot machen (***for*** für)
**ten·der·foot** F Neuling *m*, Anfänger *m*
**ten·der·loin** GASTR zartes Lendenstück
**ten·der·ness** Zartheit *f*; Zärtlichkeit *f*
**ten·don** ANAT Sehne *f*
**ten·dril** BOT Ranke *f*
**ten·e·ment** Mietshaus *n*, *contp* Mietskaserne *f*
**ten·nis** Tennis *n*; **~ court** Tennisplatz *m*; **~ play·er** Tennisspieler(in)
**ten·or** MUS, JUR Tenor *m*, JUR *a.* Wortlaut *m*, Sinn *m*; Verlauf *m*
**tense**[1] LING Zeit(form) *f*, Tempus *n*
**tense**[2] gespannt, straff (*rope etc*), (an)gespannt (*a. fig*); (über)nervös, verkrampft (*person*)
**ten·sion** Spannung *f* (*a.* ELECTR)
**tent** Zelt *n*
**ten·ta·cle** zo Tentakel *m*, *n*, Fangarm *m*
**ten·ta·tive** vorläufig; vorsichtig, zaghaft
**tenth 1.** zehnte(r, -s) **2.** Zehntel *n*
**tenth·ly** zehntens
**ten·u·ous** *fig* lose (*link*, *relationship etc*)
**ten·ure** Besitz *m*, Besitzdauer *f*; ***~ of office*** Amtsdauer *f*, Dienstzeit *f*
**tep·id** lau(warm)
**term 1.** Zeit *f*, Zeitraum *m*, Dauer *f*; JUR Laufzeit *f*; PED, UNIV Semester *n*, *esp Br* Trimester *n*; Ausdruck *m*, Bezeichnung *f*; ***~ of office*** Amtsdauer *f*, Amtsperiode *f*, Amtszeit *f*; *pl* Bedingungen *pl*; ***be on good*** (***bad***) ***~s with*** gut (schlecht) auskommen mit; ***they are not on speaking ~s*** sie sprechen nicht (mehr) miteinander; ***come to ~s*** sich einigen (***with*** mit); **2.** nennen, bezeichnen als
**ter·mi·nal 1.** End…; letzte(r, -s); MED unheilbar; im Endstadium; ***~ly ill*** unheilbar krank **2.** RAIL *etc* Endstation *f*; Terminal *m*, *n*; ELECTR Pol *m*; IT Terminal *n*, Datenendstation *f*
**ter·mi·nate** *v/t* beenden; *Vertrag* kündigen, lösen; MED *Schwangerschaft* unterbrechen; *v/i* enden; ablaufen (*contract*)
**ter·mi·na·tion** Beendigung *f*; Kündigung *f*, Lösung *f*; Ende *n*; Ablauf *m*
**ter·mi·nus** RAIL *etc* Endstation *f*
**ter·race** Terrasse *f*; Häuserreihe *f*; *mst pl esp Br* SPORT Ränge *pl*
**ter·raced house** *Br* Reihenhaus *n*
**ter·res·tri·al** irdisch; Erd…; esp BOT, ZO Land…
**ter·ri·ble** schrecklich
**ter·rif·ic** F toll, fantastisch; irre (*speed*, *heat etc*)
**ter·ri·fy** *j-m* schreckliche Angst einjagen
**ter·ri·to·ri·al** territorial, Gebiets…
**ter·ri·to·ry** Territorium *n*, (*a.* Hoheits-, Staats)Gebiet *n*
**ter·ror** Entsetzen *n*; Schrecken *m*; POL Terror *m*; F Landplage *f*; ***in ~*** in panischer Angst
**ter·ror·is·m** Terrorismus *m*
**ter·ror·ist** Terrorist(in)
**ter·ror·ize** terrorisieren
**terse** *fig* knapp, kurz (und bündig)
**test 1.** Test *m*, Prüfung *f*; Probe *f* **2.** testen, prüfen; probieren; *j-s Geduld etc* auf e-e harte Probe stellen
**tes·ta·ment**: ***last will and ~*** JUR Letzter Wille, Testament *n*
**test an·i·mal** Versuchstier *n*
**test card** TV Testbild *n*
**test drive** MOT Probefahrt *f*
**tes·ti·cle** ANAT Hoden *m*
**tes·ti·fy** JUR aussagen
**tes·ti·mo·ni·al** Referenz *f*
**tes·ti·mo·ny** JUR Aussage *f*; Beweis *m*
**test pi·lot** AVIAT Testpilot *m*
**test tube** CHEM Reagenzglas *n*
**tes·ty** gereizt

**tet·a·nus** MED Tetanus *m*, Wundstarrkrampf *m*
**teth·er 1.** Strick *m*; Kette *f*; ***at the end of one's ~*** *fig* mit s-n Kräften *or* Nerven am Ende sein **2.** *Tier* anbinden; anketten
**text 1.** Text *m*; TEL SMS *f*; Kurzmitteilung *f* **2.** eine SMS schicken / schreiben; ***I'll ~ you*** ich schicke dir eine SMS
**text·book** Lehrbuch *n*
**tex·tile 1.** Stoff *m*, *pl* Textilien *pl* **2.** Textil…
**text message** TEL SMS *f*; Kurzmitteilung *f*; ***I'll send you a ~*** ich schicke dir eine SMS
**tex·ture** Textur *f*, Gewebe *n*; Beschaffenheit *f*; Struktur *f*
**than** als
**thank 1.** *j-m* danken, sich bei *j-m* bedanken (***for*** für); ***~ you*** danke; ***~ you very much*** vielen Dank; ***no, ~ you*** nein, danke; (***yes***,) ***~ you*** ja, bitte **2.** ***~s*** Dank *m*; ***~s*** danke (schön); ***no, ~s*** nein, danke; ***~s to*** dank (*gen*), wegen (*gen*)
**thank·ful** dankbar
**thank·less** undankbar
**that 1.** *pron and adj* das; jene(r, -s), der, die, das, derjenige, diejenige, dasjenige **2.** *relative pron* der, die, das, welche(r, -s) **3.** *cj* dass **4.** *adv* F so, dermaßen; ***it's ~ simple*** so einfach ist das
**thatch 1.** mit Stroh *or* Reet decken **2.** (Dach)Stroh *n*, Reet *n*; Strohdach *n*, Reetdach *n*
**thaw 1.** (auf)tauen **2.** Tauwetter *n*; (Auf)Tauen *n*
**the 1.** der, die, das, *pl* die **2.** *adv*: ***~ … ~ …*** je … desto …; ***~ sooner ~ better*** je eher, desto besser
**the·a·ter** Theater *n*; UNIV (*Hör*)Saal *m*; MIL (Kriegs)Schauplatz *m*
**the·a·ter·go·er** Theaterbesucher(in)
**the·a·tre** *Br* → ***theater***; MED Operationssaal *m*
**the·at·ri·cal** Theater…; *fig* theatralisch
**theft** Diebstahl *m*
**their** ihr(e)
**theirs** der (die, das) ihrige *or* ihre
**them** sie (*acc pl*); ihnen (*dat*)
**theme** Thema *n*
**them·selves** sie (*acc pl*) selbst; sich (selbst)
**then 1.** *adv* dann; da; damals; ***by ~*** bis dahin; ***from ~ on*** von da an; → ***every, now 1, there 2.*** *adj* damalig
**the·o·lo·gian** Theologe *m*, Theologin *f*
**the·ol·o·gy** Theologie *f*
**the·o·ret·i·cal** theoretisch
**the·o·rist** Theoretiker *m*
**the·o·ry** Theorie *f*
**ther·a·peu·tic** therapeutisch; F wohltuend; gesund
**ther·a·pist** Therapeut(in)
**ther·a·py** Therapie *f*
**there 1.** da, dort; (da-, dort)hin; ***~ is, ~ are*** es gibt, es ist, *pl* es sind; ***~ and then*** auf der Stelle; ***~ you are*** hier bitte; siehst du!, na also! **2.** *int* so; siehst du!, na also!; ***~, ~*** ist ja gut!
**there·a·bout(s)** so ungefähr
**there·af·ter** danach
**there·by** dadurch
**there·fore** deshalb, daher; folglich
**there·up·on** darauf(hin)
**ther·mal 1.** thermisch, Thermo…, Wärme… **2.** Thermik *f*
**ther·mom·e·ter** Thermometer *n*
**ther·mos®** Thermosflasche® *f*
**the·sis** These *f*; UNIV Dissertation *f*, Doktorarbeit *f*
**they** sie *pl*; man
**thick 1.** *adj* dick, (*fog etc a.*) dicht; F dumm; F dick befreundet; ***be ~ with*** wimmeln von; ***~ with smoke*** verräuchert; ***that's a bit ~!*** *esp Br* F das ist ein starkes Stück! **2.** *adv* dick, dicht; ***lay it on ~*** F dick auftragen **3.** ***in the ~ of*** mitten in (*dat*); ***through ~ and thin*** durch dick und dünn; **thick·en** dicker werden, (*fog etc a.*) dichter werden; GASTR eindicken, binden
**thick·et** Dickicht *n*
**thick·head·ed** F strohdumm
**thick·ness** Dicke *f*; Lage *f*, Schicht *f*
**thick·set** gedrungen, untersetzt
**thick-skinned** *fig* dickfellig
**thief** Dieb(in)
**thigh** ANAT (Ober)Schenkel *m*
**thim·ble** Fingerhut *m*
**thin 1.** *adj* dünn; dürr; spärlich, dürftig; schütter (*hair*); schwach, (*excuse etc a.*) fadenscheinig **2.** *adv* dünn **3.** verdünnen; dünner werden, (*fog, hair a.*) sich lichten
**thing** Ding *n*; Sache *f*; *pl* Sachen *pl*, Zeug *n*; *fig* Dinge *pl*, Lage *f*, Umstände *pl*; ***I couldn't see a ~*** ich konnte überhaupt nichts sehen; ***another ~*** et. ande-

T

res; ***the right* ~** das Richtige

**thing·a·ma·jig** F Dings(bums) *m, f, n*

**think** *v/i* denken (***of*** an *acc*); nachdenken (***about*** über *acc*); ***I ~ so*** ich glaube *or* denke schon; ***I'll ~ about it*** ich überlege es mir; ***~ of*** sich erinnern an (*acc*); ***~ of doing s.th.*** beabsichtigen *or* daran denken, et. zu tun; ***what do you ~ of or about …?*** was halten Sie von …?; *v/t* denken, glauben, meinen; *j-n, et.* halten für; ***~ over*** nachdenken über (*acc*), sich *et.* überlegen; ***~ up*** sich *et.* ausdenken

**think tank** Beraterstab *m*, Sachverständigenstab *m*, Denkfabrik *f*

**third 1.** dritte(r, -s) **2.** Drittel *n*

**third·ly** drittens

**third·rate** drittklassig

**Third World** Dritte Welt

**thirst** Durst *m*

**thirst·y** durstig; ***be ~*** Durst haben, durstig sein

**thir·teen 1.** dreizehn **2.** Dreizehn *f*

**thir·teenth** dreizehnte(r, -s)

**thir·ti·eth** dreißigste(r, -s)

**thir·ty 1.** dreißig **2.** Dreißig *f*

**this** diese(r, -s); ***~ morning*** heute Morgen; ***~ is John speaking*** TEL hier (spricht) John

**this·tle** BOT Distel *f*

**thong** (Leder)Riemen *m*

**thorn** Dorn *m*

**thorn·y** dornig; *fig* schwierig, heikel

**thor·ough** gründlich, genau; fürchterlich (*mess etc*)

**thor·ough·bred** zo Vollblüter *m*

**thor·ough·fare** Hauptverkehrsstraße *f*; ***no ~!*** Durchfahrt verboten!

**though 1.** *cj* obwohl; (je)doch; ***as ~*** als ob **2.** *adv* dennoch, trotzdem

**thought** Denken *n*; Gedanke *m* (***of*** an *acc*); ***on second ~*** wenn ich es mir (recht) überlege

**thought·ful** nachdenklich; rücksichtsvoll, aufmerksam

**thought·les** gedankenlos; rücksichtslos

**thou·sand 1.** tausend **2.** Tausend *n*

**thou·sandth 1.** tausendste(r, -s) **2.** Tausendstel *n*

**thrash** verdreschen, verprügeln; SPORT F *j-m* e-e Abfuhr erteilen; ***~ about, ~ around*** sich *im Bett etc* hin und her werfen; um sich schlagen; zappeln (*fish*); ***~ out*** *Problem etc* ausdiskutieren

**thrash·ing** Dresche *f*, Tracht *f* Prügel

**thread 1.** Faden *m* (*a. fig*); Garn *n*; TECH Gewinde *n* **2.** *Nadel* einfädeln; *Perlen etc* auffädeln, aufreihen

**thread·bare** abgewetzt, abgetragen; *fig* abgedroschen

**threat** Drohung *f*; Bedrohung *f*, Gefahr *f* (***to*** *gen or* für)

**threat·en** (be)drohen

**threat·en·ing** drohend

**three 1.** drei **2.** Drei *f*

**three·fold** dreifach

**three-ply** → ***ply²***

**three·score** sechzig

**three-stage** dreistufig

**thresh** AGR dreschen

**thresh·ing ma·chine** AGR Dreschmaschine *f*

**thresh·old** Schwelle *f*

**thrift** Sparsamkeit *f*

**thrift·y** sparsam

**thrill 1.** prickelndes Gefühl; Nervenkitzel *m*; aufregendes Erlebnis **2.** *v/t* ***be ~ed*** (ganz) hingerissen sein (***at, about*** von)

**thrill·er** Thriller *m*, F Reißer *m*

**thrill·ing** spannend, fesselnd, packend

**thrive** gedeihen; *fig* blühen, florieren

**throat** ANAT Kehle *f*, Gurgel *f*; Rachen *m*; Hals *m*; ***clear one's ~*** sich räuspern; → ***sore 1***

**throb 1.** hämmern (*machine*), (*heart etc a.*) pochen, schlagen; pulsieren (*pain*) **2.** Hämmern *n*, Pochen *n*, Schlagen *n*

**throm·bo·sis** MED Thrombose *f*

**throne** Thron *m*

**throng 1.** Schar *f*, Menschenmenge *f* **2.** sich drängen (in *dat*)

**throt·tle 1.** erdrosseln; ***~ down*** MOT, TECH drosseln, Gas wegnehmen **2.** TECH Drosselklappe *f*

**through 1.** *prp* durch (*acc*); bis (einschließlich); ***Monday ~ Friday*** von Montag bis Freitag **2.** *adv* durch; ***~ and ~*** durch und durch; ***put s.o. ~ to*** TEL j-n verbinden mit; ***wet ~*** völlig durchnässt **3.** *adj* durchgehend (*train etc*); Durchgangs…

**through·out 1.** *prp*: ***~ the night*** die ganze Nacht hindurch; ***~ the country*** im ganzen Land, überall im Land **2.** *adv* ganz, überall; die ganze Zeit (hindurch)

T

**through traf·fic** Durchgangsverkehr *m*

**through·way** *Br* → **thruway**

**throw 1.** werfen; *Hebel etc* betätigen; *Reiter* abwerfen; *Party* geben, F schmeißen; **~ a four** e-e Vier würfeln; **~ off** *Jacke etc* abwerfen; *Verfolger* abschütteln; *Krankheit* loswerden; **~ on** sich *e-e Jacke etc* (hastig) überwerfen; **~ out** hinauswerfen; wegwerfen; **~ up** *v/t* hochwerfen; F *Job etc* hinschmeißen; F (er)brechen; *v/i* F (sich er)brechen **2.** Wurf *m*

**throw·a·way** Wegwerf…, Einweg…; **~ pack** Einwegpackung *f*

**throw-in** *soccer*: Einwurf *m*

**thru** F → **through**

**thrum** → **strum**

**thrush** zo Drossel *f*

**thrust 1.** *j-n, et.* stoßen (**into** in *acc*); *et.* stecken, schieben (**into** in *acc*); **~ at** stoßen nach; **~ s.th. upon s.o.** j-m et. aufdrängen **2.** Stoß *m*; MIL Vorstoß *m*; PHYS Schub *m*, Schubkraft *f*

**thru·way** Schnellstraße *f*

**thud 1.** dumpfes Geräusch, Plumps *m* **2.** plumpsen

**thug** Verbrecher *m*, Schläger *m*

**thumb 1.** ANAT Daumen *m* **2. ~ a lift** *or* **ride** per Anhalter fahren, trampen (**to** nach); **~ through a book** ein Buch durchblättern; **well-thumbed** abgegriffen

**thumb·tack** Reißzwecke *f*, Reißnagel *m*, Heftzwecke *f*

**thump 1.** *v/t j-m* e-n Schlag versetzen; **~ out** *Melodie* herunterhämmern (**on the piano** auf dem Klavier); *v/i* (heftig) schlagen *or* hämmern *or* pochen (*a. heart*); plumpsen; trampeln **2.** dumpfes Geräusch, Plumps *m*; Schlag *m*

**thun·der 1.** Donner *m*, Donnern *n* **2.** donnern

**thun·der·bolt** Blitz *m* und Donner *m*

**thun·der·clap** Donnerschlag *m*

**thun·der·cloud** Gewitterwolke *f*

**thun·der·ous** donnernd (*applause*)

**thun·der·storm** Gewitter *n*, Unwetter *n*

**thun·der·struck** wie vom Donner gerührt

**Thur(s)** *abbr of* **Thursday** Do., Donnerstag *m*

**Thurs·day** (*abbr* **Thur, Thurs**) Donnerstag *m*; **on ~** (am) Donnerstag; **on ~s** donnerstags

**thus** so, auf diese Weise; folglich, somit; **~ far** bisher

**thwart** durchkreuzen, vereiteln

**thyme** BOT Thymian *m*

**thy·roid (gland)** ANAT Schilddrüse *f*

**tick**[1] **1.** Ticken *n*; Haken *m*, Häkchen *n* **2.** *v/i* ticken; *v/t mst* **~ off** ab-, anhaken

**tick**[2] zo Zecke *f*

**tick**[3]: **on ~** *Br* F auf Pump

**tick·er·tape pa·rade** Konfettiparade *f*

**tick·et 1.** Fahrkarte *f*, Fahrschein *m*; Flugkarte *f*, Flugschein *m*, Ticket *n*; (*Eintritts-, Theater- etc*)Karte *f*; (*Gepäck*)Schein *m*; Etikett *n*, (*Preis- etc* -) Schild *n*; POL Wahl-, Kandidatenliste *f*; (*a.* **parking ~**) MOT Strafzettel *m* **2.** etikettieren; bestimmen, vorsehen (**for** für)

**tick·et-can·cel·(l)ing ma·chine** (Fahrschein)Entwerter *m*

**tick·et| col·lec·tor** (Bahnsteig)Schaffner(in); **~ machine** Fahrkartenautomat *m*; **~ of·fice** RAIL Fahrkartenschalter *m*

**tick·ing** Inlett *n*; Matratzenbezug *m*

**tick·le** kitzeln

**tick·lish** kitz(e)lig, *fig a.* heikel

**tid·al wave** Flutwelle *f*

**tid·bit** Leckerbissen *m*

**tide 1.** Gezeiten *pl*; Flut *f*; *fig* Strömung *f*, Trend *m*; **high ~** Flut *f*; **low ~** Ebbe *f* **2. ~ over** *fig j-m* hinweghelfen über (*acc*); *j-n* über Wasser halten

**ti·dy 1.** sauber, ordentlich, aufgeräumt; F hübsch, beträchtlich (*Sum etc*) **2.** *a.* **~ up** in Ordnung bringen, (*Zimmer a.*) aufräumen; **~ away** wegräumen, aufräumen

**tie 1.** Krawatte *f*, Schlips *m*; Band *n*; Schnur *f*; Stimmengleichheit *f*; SPORT Unentschieden *n*; (*Pokal*)Spiel *n*; RAIL Schwelle *f*; *mst pl fig* Bande *pl* **2.** *v/t* an-, festbinden; (sich) *Krawatte etc* binden; *fig* verbinden; **the game was ~d** SPORT das Spiel ging unentschieden aus; *v/i*: **they ~d for second place** SPORT *etc* sie belegten gemeinsam den zweiten Platz; **~ down** *fig* (an)binden; *j-n* festlegen (**to** auf *acc*); **~ in with** übereinstimmen mit, passen zu; verbinden *or* koppeln mit; **~ up** *Paket etc* verschnüren; *et.* in Verbindung bringen (**with** mit); *Verkehr etc* lahmlegen; **be ~d up** ECON fest angelegt sein (**in** in *dat*)

T

**tie·break(·er)** *tennis*: Tie-Break *m, n*
**tie-in** (enge) Verbindung, (enger) Zusammenhang; ECON Kopplungsgeschäft *n*; ***a book movie ~*** *appr* das Buch zum Film
**tie-on** Anhänge…
**tie·pin** Krawattennadel *f*
**tier** (Sitz)Reihe *f*; Lage *f*, Schicht *f*; *fig* Stufe *f*
**tie-up** (enge) Verbindung, (enger) Zusammenhang; ECON Fusion *f*
**ti·ger** ZO Tiger *m*
**tight 1.** *adj* fest (sitzend), fest angezogen; straff (*rope etc*); eng (*a. dress etc*); knapp (*a. fig*); F knick(e)rig; F blau; ***be in a ~ corner*** in der Klemme sein *or* sitzen *or* stecken **2.** *adv* fest; F gut; ***hold ~*** festhalten; ***sleep ~!*** F schlaf gut!
**tight·en** festziehen, anziehen; *Seil etc* straffen; ***~ one's belt*** *fig* den Gürtel enger schnallen; ***~ up*** (***on***) *Gesetz etc* verschärfen
**tight·fist·ed** F knick(e)rig
**tights** (*Tänzer-, Artisten*)Trikot *n*; *esp Br* Strumpfhose *f*
**ti·gress** ZO Tigerin *f*
**tile 1.** (Dach)Ziegel *m*; Fliese *f*, Kachel *f* **2.** (mit Ziegeln) decken; fliesen, kacheln
**til·er** Dachdecker *m*; Fliesenleger *m*
**till**[1] → ***until***
**till**[2] (Laden)Kasse *f*
**tilt 1.** kippen; sich neigen **2.** Kippen *n*; ***at a ~*** schief, schräg; (***at***) ***full ~*** F mit Volldampf
**tim·ber** *Br* Bau-, Nutzholz *n*; Baumbestand *m*, Bäume *pl*; Balken *m*
**time 1.** Zeit *f*; Uhrzeit *f*; MUS Takt *m*; Mal *n*; ***~ after ~, ~ and again*** immer wieder; ***every ~ I …*** jedes Mal, wenn ich …; ***how many ~s?*** wie oft?; ***next ~*** nächstes Mal; ***this ~*** diesmal; ***three ~s*** dreimal; ***three ~s four equals*** *or* ***is twelve*** drei mal vier ist zwölf; ***what's the ~?*** wie spät ist es?; ***what ~?*** um wie viel Uhr?; ***all the ~*** die ganze Zeit; ***at all ~s, at any ~*** jederzeit; ***at the ~*** damals; ***at the same ~*** gleichzeitig; ***at ~s*** manchmal; ***by the ~*** wenn; als; ***for a ~*** e-e Zeit lang; ***for the ~ being*** vorläufig, fürs Erste; ***from ~ to ~*** von Zeit zu Zeit; ***have a good ~*** sich gut unterhalten *or* amüsieren; ***in ~*** rechtzeitig; ***in no ~ (at all)*** im Nu; ***on ~*** pünktlich; ***some ~ ago*** vor einiger Zeit; ***to pass the ~*** zum Zeitvertreib; ***take one's ~*** sich Zeit lassen **2.** *et.* timen (*a.* SPORT); (ab)stoppen; zeitlich abstimmen, den richtigen Zeitpunkt wählen *or* bestimmen für
**time| card** Stechkarte *f*; **~ clock** Stechuhr *f*; **~ lag** Zeitdifferenz *f*
**time-lapse** *film*: Zeitraffer…
**time·less** immer während, ewig; zeitlos
**time lim·it** Frist *f*
**time·ly** (recht)zeitig
**time sheet** Stechkarte *f*
**time sig·nal** *radio*: Zeitzeichen *n*
**time·ta·ble** *Br* Fahrplan *m*, Flugplan *m*; Stundenplan *m*; Zeitplan *m*
**tim·id** ängstlich, furchtsam, zaghaft
**tim·ing** Timing *n*
**tin 1.** Zinn *n*; *Br* (Blech-, Konserven)Dose *f*, (-)Büchse *f* **2.** verzinnen; *Br* einmachen, eindosen
**tinc·ture** Tinktur *f*
**tin·foil** Stanniol(papier) *n*; Alufolie *f*
**tinge 1.** tönen; ***be ~d with*** *fig* e-n Anflug haben von **2.** Tönung *f*; *fig* Anflug *m*, Spur *f* (***of*** von)
**tin·gle** prickeln, kribbeln
**tink·er** herumpfuschen, herumbasteln (***at*** an *dat*)
**tin·kle** bimmeln; klirren
**tinned** *Br* Dosen…, Büchsen…
**tinned fruit** *Br* Obstkonserven *pl*
**tin o·pen·er** *Br* Dosenöffner *m*, Büchsenöffner *m*
**tin·sel** Lametta *n*; Flitter *m*
**tint 1.** (Farb)Ton *m*, Tönung *f* **2.** tönen
**ti·ny** winzig
**tip**[1] **1.** Spitze *f*; Filter *m*; ***it's on the ~ of my tongue*** *fig* es liegt mir auf der Zunge **2.** mit e-r Spitze versehen
**tip**[2] **1.** *esp Br* (aus)kippen, schütten; kippen; ***~ over*** umkippen **2.** *esp Br* (*Schutt- etc*)Abladeplatz *m*, (-)Halde *f*; *Br fig* F Saustall *m*
**tip**[3] **1.** Trinkgeld *n* **2.** *j-m* ein Trinkgeld geben
**tip**[4] **1.** Tipp *m*, Rat(schlag) *m* **2.** tippen auf (*acc*) (***as*** als); ***~ s.o. off*** j-m e-n Tipp *or* Wink geben
**tip·sy** angeheitert
**tip·toe 1.** ***on ~*** auf Zehenspitzen **2.** auf Zehenspitzen gehen
**tire**[1] MOT Reifen *m*
**tire**[2] ermüden, müde machen *or* werden

**tired** müde; ***be ~ of*** *j-n, et.* satt haben
**tire·less** unermüdlich
**tire·some** ermüdend; lästig
**tis·sue** BIOL Gewebe *n*; Papier(taschen)-tuch *n*; → ***~*** **pa·per** Seidenpapier *n*
**tit**[1] F *contp* Titte *f*
**tit**[2] zo Meise *f*
**tit·bit** *esp Br* → ***tidbit***
**tit·il·late** *j-n (sexuell)* anregen
**ti·tle** Titel *m*; JUR (Rechts)Anspruch *m* (***to*** auf *acc*)
**ti·tle·hold·er** SPORT Titelhalter(in)
**ti·tle page** Titelseite *f*
**ti·tle role** THEA *etc* Titelrolle *f*
**tit·mouse** zo Meise *f*
**tit·ter 1.** kichern **2.** Kichern *n*
**to 1.** *prp* zu; an (*acc*), auf (*acc*), für, in (*acc*), in (*dat*), nach; (im Verhältnis *or* im Vergleich) zu, gegen(über); *extent, limit, degree*: bis, (bis) zu, (bis) an (*acc*); *time*: bis, bis zu, bis gegen, vor (*dat*); ***from Monday ~ Friday*** von Montag bis Freitag; ***a quarter ~ one*** (ein) Viertel vor eins, drei viertel eins; ***go ~ Italy*** nach Italien fahren; ***go ~ school*** in die *or* zur Schule gehen; ***have you ever been ~ Rome?*** bist du schon einmal in Rom gewesen?; ***~ me*** *etc* mir *etc*; ***here's ~ you!*** auf Ihr Wohl!, prosit! **2.** *adv* zu; ***pull ~*** *Tür etc* zuziehen; ***come ~*** (wieder) zu sich kommen; ***~ and fro*** hin und her, auf und ab **3.** *with infinitive*: zu; *intention, aim*: um zu; ***~ go*** gehen; ***easy ~ learn*** leicht zu lernen; ***... ~ earn money*** ... um Geld zu verdienen
**toad** zo Kröte *f*, Unke *f*
**toad·stool** BOT ungenießbarer Pilz; Giftpilz *m*
**toad·y 1.** Kriecher(in) **2.** ***~ to s.o.*** *fig* vor j-m kriechen
**toast**[1] **1.** Toast *m* **2.** toasten; rösten
**toast**[2] **1.** Toast *m*, Trinkspruch *m* **2.** auf *j-n or j-s* Wohl trinken
**toast·er** TECH Toaster *m*
**to·bac·co** Tabak *m*; **to·bac·co·nist** Tabak(waren)händler(in)
**to·bog·gan 1.** (Rodel)Schlitten *m* **2.** Schlitten fahren, rodeln
**to·day 1.** *adv* heute; heutzutage; ***a week ~, ~ week*** heute in e-r Woche, heute in acht Tagen **2.** ***~'s paper*** die heutige Zeitung, die Zeitung von heute; ***of ~, ~'s*** von heute, heutig
**tod·dle** auf wack(e)ligen *or* unsicheren Beinen gehen
**to-do** F *fig* Theater *n*
**toe** ANAT Zehe *f*; Spitze *f*
**toe·nail** ANAT Zehennagel *m*
**tof·fee, tof·fy** Sahnebonbon *m, n*, Toffee *n*
**to·geth·er** zusammen; gleichzeitig
**toi·let** Toilette *f*; ***~*** **pa·per** Toilettenpapier *n*; ***~*** **roll** *esp Br* Rolle *f* Toilettenpapier
**to·ken** Zeichen *n*; ***as a ~, in ~ of*** als *or* zum Zeichen (*gen*); zum Andenken an (*acc*); ***~*** **strike** Warnstreik *m*
**tol·e·ra·ble** erträglich
**tol·e·rance** Toleranz *f*; Nachsicht *f*
**tol·e·rant** tolerant (***of, towards*** gegenüber)
**tol·e·rate** tolerieren, dulden; ertragen
**toll**[1] Benutzungsgebühr *f*, Maut *f*; ***heavy death ~*** große Zahl an Todesopfern; ***take its ~*** (***on***) *fig* s-n Tribut fordern (von); s-e Spuren hinterlassen (bei)
**toll**[2] läuten
**toll-free** TEL gebührenfrei
**toll road** gebührenpflichtige Straße, Mautstraße *f*
**tom** F → ***tomcat***
**to·ma·to** BOT Tomate *f*
**tomb** Grab *n*; Grabmal *n*; Gruft *f*
**tom·boy** Wildfang *m*
**tomb·stone** Grabstein *m*
**tom·cat** zo Kater *m*
**tom·fool·e·ry** Unsinn *m*
**to·mor·row 1.** *adv* morgen; ***a week ~, ~ week*** morgen in e-r Woche, morgen in acht Tagen; ***~ morning*** morgen früh; ***~ night*** morgen Abend **2.** ***the day after ~*** übermorgen; ***of ~, ~'s*** von morgen
**ton** (*abbr* ***t, tn***) Tonne *f*
**tone 1.** Ton *m*; Klang *m*; (Farb)Ton *m*; MUS Note *f*; MED Tonus *m*; *fig* Niveau *n* **2.** ***~ down*** abschwächen; ***~ up*** *Muskeln etc* kräftigen
**ton·er** *for cleansing the face* Gesichtswasser *n*; PRINT Toner *m*
**tongs** (***a pair of ~*** e-e) Zange *f*
**tongue** ANAT, TECH Zunge *f*; (*Mutter*)-Sprache *f*; Klöppel *m* (*e-r Glocke*); ***hold one's ~*** den Mund halten
**ton·ic** Tonikum *n*, Stärkungsmittel *n*; Tonic *n*; MUS Grundton *m*
**to·night** heute Abend *or* Nacht
**ton·sil** ANAT Mandel *f*

T

**ton·sil·li·tis** MED Mandelentzündung *f*; Angina *f*
**too** zu; zu, sehr; auch (noch)
**tool** Werkzeug *n*, Gerät *n*; ~ **bag** Werkzeugtasche *f*; ~ **box** Werkzeugkasten *m*; ~ **kit** Werkzeug *n*
**tool·mak·er** Werkzeugmacher *m*
**tool·shed** Geräteschuppen *m*
**toot** *esp* MOT hupen
**tooth** Zahn *m*
**tooth·ache** Zahnschmerzen *pl*, Zahnweh *n*
**tooth·brush** Zahnbürste *f*
**tooth·less** zahnlos
**tooth·paste** Zahncreme *f*, Zahnpasta *f*
**tooth·pick** Zahnstocher *m*
**top**[1] **1.** oberer Teil; GEOGR Gipfel *m*, Spitze *f*; BOT Krone *f*, Wipfel *m*; Kopfende *n*, oberes Ende; Oberteil *n*; Oberfläche *f*; Deckel *m*; Verschluss *m*; MOT Verdeck *n*; MOT höchster Gang; ***at the ~ of the page*** oben auf der Seite; ***at the ~ of one's voice*** aus vollem Hals; ***on ~*** oben(auf); darauf, F drauf; ***on ~ of*** (oben) auf (*dat or acc*), über (*dat or acc*) **2.** oberste(r, -s); Höchst…, Spitzen…, Top… **3.** bedecken (***with*** mit); *fig* übersteigen, übertreffen; ~ ***up*** *Tank etc* auffüllen; F *j-m* nachschenken
**top**[2] Kreisel *m* (*toy*)
**top hat** Zylinder *m*
**top-heav·y** kopflastig (*a. fig*)
**top·ic** Thema *n*; **top·ic·al** aktuell
**top·ple**: *mst* ~ ***over*** umkippen; ~ ***the government*** die Regierung stürzen
**top·sy-tur·vy** in e-r heillosen Unordnung
**torch** *Br* Taschenlampe *f*; Fackel *f*
**torch·light** Fackelschein *m*; ~ ***procession*** Fackelzug *m*
**tor·ment 1.** Qual *f* **2.** quälen, peinigen, plagen
**tor·na·do** Tornado *m*, Wirbelsturm *m*
**tor·pe·do** MIL **1.** Torpedo *m* **2.** torpedieren (*a. fig*)
**tor·rent** reißender Strom; *fig* Schwall *m*
**tor·ren·tial**: ~ ***rain*** sintflutartige Regenfälle *pl*
**tor·toise** ZO Schildkröte *f*
**tor·tu·ous** gewunden
**tor·ture 1.** Folter *f*, Folterung *f*; *fig* Qual *f*, Tortur *f* **2.** foltern; *fig* quälen
**toss 1.** *v/t* werfen; *Münze* hochwerfen; GASTR schwenken; ~ ***off*** F *Bild etc* hinhauen; *v/i a.* ~ ***about,*** ~ ***and turn*** sich *im Schlaf* hin und her werfen; *a.* ~ ***up*** e-e Münze hochwerfen; ~ ***for s.th.*** um et. losen; ~ ***one's head*** den Kopf zurückwerfen **2.** Wurf *m*; Zurückwerfen *n*; Hochwerfen *n*
**tot** F Knirps *m*
**to·tal 1.** völlig, total; ganz, gesamt, Gesamt… **2.** Gesamtbetrag *m*, -menge *f* **3.** sich belaufen auf (*acc*); ~ ***up*** zusammenrechnen, -zählen
**tot·ter** schwanken, wanken
**touch 1.** (sich) berühren; anfassen; *Essen etc* anrühren; *fig* herankommen an (*acc*); *fig* rühren; ~ ***wood!*** toi, toi, toi!; ~ ***down*** AVIAT aufsetzen; ~ ***up*** ausbessern; PHOT retuschieren **2.** Tastempfindung *f*; Berührung *f*, MUS *etc* Anschlag *m*; (*Pinsel- etc*)Strich *m*; GASTR Spur *f*; Verbindung *f*, Kontakt *m*; *fig* Note *f*; *fig* Anflug *m*; ***a ~ of flu*** e-e leichte Grippe; ***get in ~ with s.o.*** sich mit j-m in Verbindung setzen
**touch-and-go** F kritisch, riskant, prekär; ***it was ~ whether*** es stand auf des Messers Schneide, ob
**touch·down** AVIAT Aufsetzen *n*, Landung *f*
**touched** gerührt; F leicht verrückt
**touch·ing** rührend
**touch·line** *soccer*: Seitenlinie *f*
**touch·stone** Prüfstein *m* (***of*** für)
**touch·y** empfindlich; heikel (*subject etc*)
**tough** zäh; widerstandsfähig; *fig* hart; schwierig (*problem, negotiations etc*)
**tough·en** *a.* ~ ***up*** hart *or* zäh machen *or* werden
**tour 1.** Tour *f* (***of*** durch), (Rund)Reise *f*, (Rund)Fahrt *f*; Ausflug *m*; Rundgang *m* (***of*** durch); THEA Tournee *f* (*a.* SPORT); ***go on ~*** auf Tournee gehen; → ***conduct*** *2* **2.** bereisen, reisen durch
**tour·is·m** Tourismus *m*, Fremdenverkehr *m*
**tour·ist 1.** Tourist(in) **2.** Touristen…; ~ **class** AVIAT, MAR Touristenklasse *f*; ~ **in·dus·try** Tourismusgeschäft *n*; ~ **in·for·ma·tion of·fice**, ~ **of·fice** Verkehrsverein *m*; ~ **sea·son** Reisesaison *f*, Reisezeit *f*
**tour·na·ment** Turnier *n*
**tou·sled** zerzaust
**tow 1.** *Boot etc* schleppen, *Auto etc a.* abschleppen **2.** ***give s.o. a ~*** j-n abschlep-

T

pen; ***take in** ~* *Auto etc* abschleppen
**to·ward**, *esp Br* **to·wards** auf (*acc*) … zu, (in) Richtung, zu; *time*: gegen; *fig* gegenüber
**tow·el 1.** Handtuch *n*, (*Bade- etc*)Tuch *n* **2.** (mit e-m Handtuch) abtrocknen *or* abreiben
**tow·er 1.** Turm *m* **2.** ***~ above, ~ over*** überragen; **~ block** *Br* Hochhaus *n*
**tow·er·ing** turmhoch; *fig* überragend; ***in a ~ rage*** rasend vor Zorn
**town** Stadt *f*; Kleinstadt *f*; ***go into ~*** in die Stadt gehen; **~ cen·tre** *Br* Innenstadt *f*, City *f*; **~ coun·cil** *Br* Stadtrat *m*; **~ coun·ci(l)·lor** *Br* Stadtrat *m*, Stadträtin *f*; **~ hall** Rathaus *n*
**town·ie** F Städter(in), Stadtmensch *m*
**town| plan·ner** Stadtplaner(in); **~ plan·ning** Stadtplanung *f*
**towns·peo·ple** Städter *pl*, Stadtbevölkerung *f*
**tow·rope** MOT Abschleppseil *n*
**tox·ic** toxisch, giftig; Gift…
**tox·ic waste** Giftmüll *m*
**tox·ic waste dump** Giftmülldeponie *f*
**toy 1.** Spielzeug *n*, *pl a.* Spielsachen *pl*, ECON Spielwaren *pl* **2.** Spielzeug…; Miniatur…; Zwerg… **3.** ***~ with*** spielen mit (*a. fig*)
**trace 1.** (durch)pausen; *j-n*, *et.* ausfindig machen, aufspüren, *et.* finden; *a.* ***~ back*** *et.* zurückverfolgen (***to*** bis zu); ***~ s.th. to*** et. zurückführen auf (*acc*) **2.** Spur *f* (*a. fig*)
**track 1.** Spur *f* (*a. fig*), Fährte *f*; Pfad *m*, Weg *m*; RAIL Gleis *n*, Geleise *n*; TECH Raupe *f*, Raupenkette *f*; SPORT (Renn-, Aschen)Bahn *f*, (*Renn*)Strecke *f*; *tape etc*: Spur *f*; Nummer *f* (*on an LP etc*) **2.** verfolgen; ***~ down*** aufspüren; auftreiben
**track and field** SPORT Leichtathletik *f*
**track e·vent** SPORT Laufdisziplin *f*
**track·ing sta·tion** Bodenstation *f*
**track·suit** Trainingsanzug *m*
**tract** Fläche *f*, Gebiet *n*; ANAT (*Verdauungs*)Trakt *m*, (*Atem*)Wege *pl*
**trac·tion** Ziehen *n*, Zug *m*
**trac·tion en·gine** Zugmaschine *f*
**trac·tor** Traktor *m*, Trecker *m*
**trade 1.** Handel *m*; Branche *f*, Gewerbe *n*; (*esp* Handwerks)Beruf *m* **2.** Handel treiben, handeln; ***~ on*** ausnutzen; **~ a·gree·ment** Handelsabkommen *n*
**trade·mark** Warenzeichen *n*
**trade name** Markenname *m*, Handelsbezeichnung *f*
**trade price** Großhandelspreis *m*
**trad·er** Händler(in)
**trades·man** (Einzel)Händler *m*; Ladeninhaber *m*; Lieferant *m*
**trade(** *Br* **trades)| u·nion** Gewerkschaft *f*; **~ u·nion·ist** Gewerkschaftler(in)
**tra·di·tion** Tradition *f*; Überlieferung *f*
**tra·di·tion·al** traditionell
**traf·fic 1.** Verkehr *m*; (*esp* illegaler) Handel (***in*** mit); **2.** (*esp* illegal) handeln (***in*** mit); **~ cir·cle** MOT Kreisverkehr *m*; **~ in·struc·tion** Verkehrsunterricht *m*; **~ is·land** Verkehrsinsel *f*; **~ jam** (Verkehrs)Stau *m*, Verkehrsstockung *f*; **~ light(s)** Verkehrsampel *f*; **~ offend·er** Verkehrssünder(in); **~ of·fense** (*Br* **offence**) Verkehrsdelikt *n*; **~ reg·u·la·tions** Straßenverkehrsordnung *f*; **~ sign** Verkehrszeichen *n*, -schild *n*; **~ sig·nal** → ***traffic light(s)***; **~ war·den** *Br* Parküberwacher *m*, Politesse *f*
**tra·ge·dy** Tragödie *f*
**tra·gic** tragisch
**trail 1.** *v/t et.* nachschleifen lassen; verfolgen; SPORT zurückliegen hinter (*dat*) (***by*** um); *v/i* sich schleppen; BOT kriechen; SPORT zurückliegen (***by 3-0*** 0:3); ***~ (along) behind s.o.*** hinter j-m herschleifen **2.** Spur *f* (*a. fig*), Fährte *f*; Pfad *m*, Weg *m*; ***~ of blood*** Blutspur *f*; ***~ of dust*** Staubwolke *f*
**trail·er** MOT Anhänger *m*; Wohnwagen *m*, Caravan *m*; *film*, TV Trailer *m*, Vorschau *f*; **~ park** Standplatz *m* für Wohnwagen
**train 1.** RAIL Zug *m*; Kolonne *f*, Schlange *f*; Schleppe *f*; *fig* Folge *f*, Kette *f*; ***by ~*** mit der Bahn, mit dem Zug; ***~ of thought*** Gedankengang *m* **2.** *v/t j-n* ausbilden (***as*** als, zum), schulen; SPORT trainieren; *Tier* abrichten, dressieren; *Kamera etc* richten (***on*** auf *acc*); *v/i* ausgebildet werden (***as*** als, zum); SPORT trainieren (***for*** für)
**train·ee** Auszubildende *m*, *f*
**train·er** Ausbilder(in); ZO Abrichter(in), Dompteur *m*, Dompteuse *f*; SPORT Trainer(in); *Br* Turnschuh *m*
**train·ing** Ausbildung *f*, Schulung *f*; Abrichten *n*, Dressur *f*; SPORT Training *n*
**trait** (Charakter)Zug *m*

T

**trai·tor** Verräter *m*
**tram** *Br* Straßenbahn(wagen *m*) *f*
**tram·car** *Br* Straßenbahnwagen *m*
**tramp 1.** sta(m)pfen *or* trampeln (durch) **2.** Tramp *m*, Landstreicher *m*, Vagabund *m*; Wanderung *f*; Flittchen *n*; **tram·ple** (zer)trampeln
**trance** Trance *f*
**tran·quil** ruhig, friedlich
**tran·quil·(l)i·ty** Ruhe *f*, Frieden *m*
**tran·quil·(l)ize** beruhigen
**tran·quil·(l)iz·er** PHARM Beruhigungsmittel *n*
**trans·act** *Geschäft* abwickeln, *Handel* abschließen
**trans·ac·tion** Abwicklung *f*, Abschluss *m*; Geschäft *n*, Transaktion *f*
**trans·at·lan·tic** transatlantisch, Transatlantik…, Übersee…
**tran·scribe** abschreiben, kopieren; *Stenogramm etc* übertragen
**tran·script** Abschrift *f*, Kopie *f*
**tran·scrip·tion** Umschreibung *f*, Umschrift *f*; Abschrift *f*, Kopie *f*
**trans·fer 1.** *v/t* (**to**) *Betrieb etc* verlegen (nach); *j-n* versetzen (nach); SPORT *Spieler* transferieren (zu), abgeben (an *acc*); *Geld* überweisen (an *acc*, auf *acc*); JUR *Eigentum*, *Recht* übertragen (auf *acc*); *v/i* SPORT wechseln (**to** zu); umsteigen (***from … to …*** von … auf … *acc*); **2.** Verlegung *f*; Versetzung *f*; SPORT Transfer *m*, Wechsel *m*; ECON Überweisung *f*; JUR Übertragung *f*; Umsteige(fahr)karte *f*
**trans·fer·a·ble** übertragbar
**trans·fixed** *fig* versteinert, starr
**trans·form** umwandeln, verwandeln
**trans·for·ma·tion** Umwandlung *f*, Verwandlung *f*
**trans·form·er** ELECTR Transformator *m*
**trans·fu·sion** MED Bluttransfusion *f*, Blutübertragung *f*
**trans·gress** verletzen, verstoßen gegen
**tran·sient** flüchtig, vergänglich
**tran·sis·tor** Transistor *m*
**tran·sit** Transit-, Durchgangsverkehr *m*; ECON Transport *m*; ***in ~*** unterwegs, auf dem Transport
**tran·si·tion** Übergang *m*
**tran·si·tive** LING transitiv
**tran·si·to·ry** → ***transient***
**trans·late** übersetzen (***from English into German*** aus dem Englischen ins Deutsche)
**trans·la·tion** Übersetzung *f*
**trans·la·tor** Übersetzer(in)
**trans·lu·cent** lichtdurchlässig
**trans·mis·sion** MED Übertragung *f*; *radio*, TV Sendung *f*; MOT Getriebe *n*
**trans·mit** *Signale* (aus)senden; *radio*, TV senden; PHYS *Wärme etc* leiten, *Licht etc* durchlassen; MED *Krankheit* übertragen
**trans·mit·ter** Sender *m*
**trans·par·en·cy** Durchsichtigkeit *f* (*a. fig*); *fig* Durchschaubarkeit *f*; Dia (-positiv) *n*; Folie *f*; **trans·par·ent** durchsichtig (*a. fig*); *fig* durchschaubar
**tran·spire** transpirieren, schwitzen; *fig* durchsickern; F passieren
**trans·plant 1.** umpflanzen, verpflanzen (*a.* MED); MED transplantieren **2.** MED Transplantation *f*, Verpflanzung *f*; Transplantat *n*
**trans·port 1.** Transport *m*, Beförderung *f*; Beförderungs-, Verkehrsmittel *n or pl*; MIL Transportschiff *n*, -flugzeug *n*, (*Truppen*)Transporter *m* **2.** transportieren, befördern
**trans·port·a·ble** transportabel, transportfähig
**trans·por·ta·tion** Transport *m*, Beförderung *f*
**trap 1.** Falle *f* (*a. fig*); ***set a ~ for s.o.*** j-m e-e Falle stellen; ***shut one's ~, keep one's ~ shut*** F die Schnauze halten **2.** (in *or* mit e-r Falle) fangen; *fig* in e-e Falle locken; ***be ~ped*** eingeschlossen sein
**trap·door** Falltür *f*; THEA Versenkung *f*
**tra·peze** Trapez *n*
**trap·per** Trapper *m*, Fallensteller *m*, Pelztierjäger *m*
**trap·pings** Rangabzeichen *pl*; *fig* Drum und Dran *n*
**trash** F Schund *m*; Quatsch *m*, Unsinn *m*; Abfall *m*, Abfälle *pl*, Müll *m*; Gesindel *n*
**trash·can** Abfall-, Mülleimer *m*; Abfall-, Mülltonne *f*
**trash·y** Schund…
**trav·el 1.** *v/i* reisen; fahren; TECH *etc* sich bewegen; *fig* sich verbreiten; *fig* schweifen, wandern; *v/t* bereisen; *Strecke* zurücklegen, fahren **2.** Reisen *n*; *pl* (*esp* Auslands)Reisen *pl*; **~ a·gen·cy** Reisebüro *n*; **~ a·gent** Reisebüroinha-

T

ber(in); Angestellte *m, f* in e-m Reisebüro; **~ a·gent's, ~ bu·reau** Reisebüro *n*
**trav·el·(l)er** Reisende *m, f*
**trav·el·(l)er's check** (*Br* **cheque**) Reise-, Travellerscheck *m*
**trav·el·(l)ing| bag** Reisetasche *f*; **~ expens·es** Reisekosten *pl*
**trav·el sick·ness** Reisekrankheit *f*
**trav·es·ty** Zerrbild *n*
**trawl 1.** Schleppnetz *n* **2.** mit dem Schleppnetz fischen
**trawl·er** MAR Trawler *m*
**tray** Tablett *n*; Ablagekorb *m*
**treach·er·ous** verräterisch; tückisch
**treach·er·y** Verrat *m*
**trea·cle** *esp Br* Sirup *m*
**tread 1.** treten (**on** auf *acc*; in *acc*); *Pfad etc* treten **2.** Gang *m*; Schritt(e *pl*) *m*; (Reifen)Profil *n*
**tread·mill** Tretmühle *f* (*a. fig*)
**trea·son** Landesverrat *m*
**trea·sure 1.** Schatz *m* **2.** sehr schätzen; in Ehren halten
**trea·sur·er** Schatzmeister(in)
**trea·sure trove** Schatzfund *m*
**Trea·su·ry** *Br*, **~ De·part·ment** Finanzministerium *n*
**treat 1.** *j-n, et.* behandeln; umgehen mit; *et.* ansehen, betrachten (**as** als); MED *j-n* behandeln (**for** gegen); *j-n* einladen (**to** zu); **~ s.o. to s.th.** *a.* j-m et. spendieren; **~ o.s. to s.th.** sich et. leisten *or* gönnen; **be ~ed for** MED in ärztlicher Behandlung sein wegen **2.** (besondere) Freude *or* Überraschung; ***this is my ~*** das geht auf meine Rechnung, ich lade dich *etc* ein
**trea·tise** Abhandlung *f*
**treat·ment** Behandlung *f*
**treat·y** Vertrag *m*
**tre·ble**[1] **1.** dreifach **2.** (sich) verdreifachen
**tre·ble**[2] MUS Knabensopran *m*; *radio*: (Ton)Höhe *f*
**tree** BOT Baum *m*
**tre·foil** BOT Klee *m*
**trel·lis** BOT Spalier *n*
**trem·ble** zittern (**with** vor *dat*)
**tre·men·dous** gewaltig, enorm; F klasse, toll
**trem·or** Zittern *n*; Beben *n*
**trench** Graben *m*; MIL Schützengraben *m*

**trend** Trend *m*, Entwicklung *f*, Tendenz *f*; Mode *f*
**trend·y** F **1.** modern, modisch; **be ~** als schick gelten, in sein **2.** *esp Br contp* Schickimicki *m*
**tres·pass 1. ~ on** *Grundstück etc* unbefugt betreten; *j-s Zeit etc* über Gebühr in Anspruch nehmen; ***no ~ing*** Betreten verboten! **2.** unbefugtes Betreten
**tres·pass·er**: ***~s will be prosecuted*** Betreten bei Strafe verboten!
**tres·tle** Bock *m*, Gestell *n*
**tri·al 1.** JUR Prozess *m*, (Gerichts)Verhandlung *f*, (-)Verfahren *n*; Erprobung *f*, Probe *f*, Prüfung *f*, Test *m*; Plage *f*; ***on ~*** auf *or* zur Probe; ***be on ~*** erprobt *or* getestet werden; ***be on ~, stand ~*** vor Gericht stehen (**for** wegen); ***by way of ~*** versuchsweise **2.** Versuchs…, Probe…
**tri·an·gle** Dreieck *n*; Winkel *m*, Zeichendreieck *n*
**tri·an·gu·lar** dreieckig
**tri·ath·lon** SPORT Triathlon *n, m*, Dreikampf *m*
**trib·al** Stammes…
**tribe** (Volks)Stamm *m*
**tri·bu·nal** JUR Gericht(shof *m*) *n*
**trib·u·ta·ry** GEOGR Nebenfluss *m*
**trib·ute**: ***be a ~ to*** *j-m* Ehre machen; ***pay ~ to*** *j-m* Anerkennung zollen
**trick 1.** Trick *m*; (*Karten- etc*)Kunststück *n*; Streich *m*; *card game*: Stich *m*; (merkwürdige) Angewohnheit, Eigenart *f*; ***play a ~ on s.o.*** j-m e-n Streich spielen **2.** Trick…; ***~ question*** Fangfrage *f* **3.** überlisten, F reinlegen
**trick·e·ry** Tricks *pl*
**trick·le 1.** tröpfeln; rieseln **2.** Tröpfeln *n*; Rinnsal *n*
**trick·ster** Betrüger(in), Schwindler(in)
**trick·y** heikel, schwierig; durchtrieben, raffiniert
**tri·cy·cle** Dreirad *n*
**tri·dent** Dreizack *m*
**tri·fle 1.** Kleinigkeit *f*; Lappalie *f*; ***a ~*** ein bisschen, etwas **2. ~ *with*** *fig* spielen mit; ***he is not to be ~d with*** er lässt nicht mit sich spaßen
**tri·fling** geringfügig, unbedeutend
**trig·ger** Abzug *m*; ***pull the ~*** abdrücken
**trig·ger-hap·py** F schießwütig
**trill 1.** Triller *m* **2.** trillern
**trim 1.** *Hecke etc* stutzen, beschneiden, sich *den Bart etc* stutzen; *Kleidungs-*

T

*stück* besetzen (***with*** mit); ***~med with fur*** pelzbesetzt, mit Pelzbesatz; ***~ off*** abschneiden **2.** ***give s.th. a ~*** et. stutzen, et. (be)schneiden; ***be in good ~*** F gut in Form sein **3.** gepflegt
**trim·mings** Besatz *m*; GASTR Beilagen *pl*
**Trin·i·ty** REL Dreieinigkeit *f*
**trin·ket** (*esp* billiges) Schmuckstück
**trip 1.** *v/i* stolpern (***over*** über *acc*); (e-n) Fehler machen; *v/t a.* ***~ up*** *j-m* ein Bein stellen (*a. fig*) **2.** (kurze) Reise; Ausflug *m*, Trip *m* (*a. sl*); Stolpern *n*, Fallen *n*
**tripe** GASTR Kaldaunen *pl*, Kutteln *pl*
**trip·le 1.** dreifach **2.** verdreifachen
**trip·le jump** SPORT Dreisprung *m*
**trip·lets** Drillinge *pl*
**trip·li·cate 1.** dreifach **2.** ***in ~*** in dreifacher Ausfertigung
**tri·pod** PHOT Stativ *n*
**trip·per** *esp Br* (*esp Tages*)Ausflügler(in)
**trite** abgedroschen, banal
**tri·umph 1.** Triumph *m*, *fig* Sieg *m* (***over*** über *acc*); **2.** triumphieren (***over*** über *acc*)
**tri·um·phal** Triumph…
**tri·um·phant** triumphierend
**triv·i·al** unbedeutend, bedeutungslos; trivial, alltäglich
**trol·ley** *esp Br* Einkaufswagen *m*; Gepäckwagen *m*, Kofferkuli *m*; (*Tee- etc*)-Wagen *m*; (***supermarket***) ***~*** Einkaufswagen *m*; ***shopping ~*** Einkaufsroller *m*
**trol·ley·bus** Oberleitungsbus *m*, Obus *m*
**trom·bone** MUS Posaune *f*
**troop 1.** Schar *f*; *pl* MIL Truppen *pl* **2.** (*herein- etc*)strömen; ***~ the colour*** *Br* MIL e-e Fahnenparade abhalten
**troop·er** MIL Kavallerist *m*; Panzerjäger *m*; Polizist *m*
**tro·phy** Trophäe *f*
**trop·ic** ASTR, GEOGR Wendekreis *m*; ***the ~ of Cancer*** der Wendekreis des Krebses; ***the ~ of Capricorn*** der Wendekreis des Steinbocks
**trop·i·cal** tropisch, Tropen…
**trop·ics** Tropen *pl*
**trot 1.** Trab *m*; Trott *m* **2.** traben (lassen); ***~ along*** F losziehen
**trou·ble 1.** Schwierigkeit *f*, Problem *n*, Ärger *m*; Mühe *f*; MED Beschwerden *pl*; *a. pl* POL Unruhen *pl*; *pl* Unannehmlichkeiten *pl*; ***be in ~*** in Schwierigkeiten sein; ***get into ~*** Schwierigkeiten *or* Ärger bekommen; *j-n* in Schwierigkeiten bringen; ***get*** *or* ***run into ~*** in Schwierigkeiten geraten; ***have ~ with*** Schwierigkeiten *or* Ärger haben mit; ***put s.o. to ~*** j-m Mühe *or* Umstände machen; ***take the ~ to do s.th.*** sich die Mühe machen, et. zu tun **2.** *v/t* *j-n* beunruhigen; *j-m* Mühe *or* Umstände machen; *j-n* bemühen (***for*** um), bitten (***for*** um; ***to do*** zu tun); ***be ~d by*** geplagt werden von, leiden an (*dat*); *v/i* sich bemühen (***to do*** zu tun), sich Umstände machen (***about*** wegen)
**trou·ble·mak·er** Störenfried *m*, Unruhestifter(in)
**trou·ble·some** lästig
**trou·ble spot** *esp* POL Krisenherd *m*
**trough** Trog *m*; Wellental *n*
**trounce** SPORT haushoch besiegen
**troupe** THEA Truppe *f*
**trou·ser:** (***a pair of***) ***~s*** (e-e) Hose *f*
**trou·ser suit** *Br* Hosenanzug *m*
**trous·seau** Aussteuer *f*
**trout** ZO Forelle *f*
**trow·el** (Maurer)Kelle *f*
**tru·ant** Schulschwänzer(in); ***play ~*** *Br* (die Schule) schwänzen
**truce** MIL Waffenstillstand *m* (*a. fig*)
**truck 1.** MOT Lastwagen *m*; Fernlaster *m*; *Br* RAIL (offener) Güterwagen; Transportkarren *m* **2.** auf *or* mit Lastwagen transportieren
**truck driv·er, truck·er** MOT Lastwagenfahrer *m*; Fernfahrer *m*
**truck farm** ECON Gemüse- und Obstgärtnerei *f*
**trudge** (mühsam) stapfen
**true** wahr; echt, wirklich; treu (***to*** *dat*); ***be ~*** wahr sein, stimmen; ***come ~*** in Erfüllung gehen; wahr werden; ***~ to life*** lebensecht
**tru·ly** wahrheitsgemäß; wirklich, wahrhaft; aufrichtig
**trump 1.** Trumpf(karte *f*) *m*; *pl* Trumpf *m* **2.** mit e-m Trumpf stechen; ***~ up*** erfinden
**trum·pet 1.** MUS Trompete *f* **2.** trompeten; *fig* ausposaunen
**trun·cheon** (Gummi)Knüppel *m*, Schlagstock *m*
**trun·dle** *Karren etc* ziehen
**trunk** (Baum)Stamm *m*; Schrankkoffer *m*; ZO Rüssel *m*; ANAT Rumpf *m*; MOT

Kofferraum *m*; ~ **road** *Br* Fernstraße *f*
**trunks** (*a.* ***a pair of*** ~ e-e) (*Bade*)Hose *f*; SPORT Shorts *pl*
**truss 1.** *a.* ~ **up** *j-n* fesseln; GASTR *Geflügel etc* dressieren **2.** MED Bruchband *n*
**trust 1.** Vertrauen *n* (**in** zu); JUR Treuhand *f*; ECON Trust *m*; Großkonzern *m*; ***hold s.th. in*** ~ et. treuhänderisch verwalten (**for** für); ***place s.th. in s.o.'s*** ~ j-m et. anvertrauen **2.** *v/t* (ver)trauen (*dat*); sich verlassen auf (*acc*); (zuversichtlich) hoffen; ~ ***him!*** das sieht ihm ähnlich!; *v/i*: ~ **in** vertrauen auf (*acc*); ~ **to** sich verlassen auf (*acc*)
**trust·ee** JUR Treuhänder(in); Sachverwalter(in)
**trust·ful, trust·ing** vertrauensvoll
**trust·wor·thy** vertrauenswürdig, zuverlässig
**truth** Wahrheit *f*
**truth·ful** wahr; wahrheitsliebend
**try 1.** *v/t* versuchen; *et.* (aus)probieren; JUR (über) *e-e Sache* verhandeln; *j-m* den Prozess machen (**for** wegen); *j-n*, *j-s Geduld*, *Nerven etc* auf e-e harte Probe stellen; ~ *s.th.* **on** *Kleid etc* anprobieren; ~ *s.th.* **out** *et.* ausprobieren; *v/i* es versuchen; ~ **for** *Br*, ~ **out for** sich bemühen um **2.** Versuch *m*; ***give*** *s.o.*, *s.th.* **a** ~ es mit *j-m*, *et.* versuchen; ***have a*** ~ es versuchen; **try·ing** anstrengend
**tsar** HIST Zar *m*
**T-shirt** T-Shirt *n*
**tub** Bottich *m*, Zuber *m*, Tonne *f*; Becher *m*; F (Bade)Wanne *f*
**tub·by** F pumm(e)lig
**tube** Röhre *f* (*a.* ANAT), Rohr *n*; Schlauch *m*; Tube *f*; *Br* F U-Bahn *f* (*in London*); F Röhre *f*, Glotze *f*
**tube·less** schlauchlos
**tu·ber** BOT Knolle *f*
**tu·ber·cu·lo·sis** MED Tuberkulose *f*
**tu·bu·lar** röhrenförmig
**tuck 1.** stecken; ~ **away** F wegstecken; ~ **in** *esp Br* F reinhauen, zulangen; ~ **up** (**in bed**) *Kind* ins Bett packen **2.** Biese *f*; Saum *m*; Abnäher *m*
**Tue(s)** *abbr of* ***Tuesday*** Di., Dienstag *m*
**Tues·day** (*abbr* ***Tue, Tues***) Dienstag *m*; **on** ~ (am) Dienstag; **on** ~**s** dienstags
**tuft** (*Gras-*, *Haar- etc*)Büschel *n*
**tug 1.** zerren *or* ziehen (an *dat or* **at** an *dat*); **2. give** *s.th.* **a** ~ zerren *or* ziehen an (*dat*)
**tug-of-war** SPORT Tauziehen *n* (*a. fig*)
**tu·i·tion** Unterricht *m*; Unterrichtsgebühr(en *pl*) *f*
**tu·lip** BOT Tulpe *f*
**tum·ble 1.** fallen, stürzen; purzeln (*a. fig*) **2.** Fall *m*, Sturz *m*
**tum·ble·down** baufällig
**tum·bler** (Trink)Glas *n*
**tu·mid** MED geschwollen
**tum·my** F Bauch *m*, Bäuchlein *n*
**tu·mo(u)r** MED Tumor *m*
**tu·mult** Tumult *m*
**tu·mul·tu·ous** tumultartig, (*applause etc*) stürmisch
**tu·na** ZO Thunfisch *m*
**tune 1.** MUS Melodie *f*; ***be out of*** ~ verstimmt sein **2.** *v/t mst* ~ **in** *Radio etc* einstellen (**to** auf *acc*); *a.* ~ **up** MUS stimmen; *a.* ~ **up** *Motor* tunen; *v/i*: ~ **in** (das Radio *etc*) einschalten; ~ **up** MUS (die Instrumente) stimmen
**tune·ful** melodisch
**tune·less** unmelodisch
**tun·er** *radio*, TV Tuner *m*
**tun·nel 1.** Tunnel *m* **2.** *Berg* durchtunneln; *Fluss etc* untertunneln
**tun·ny** ZO Thunfisch *m*
**tur·ban** Turban *m*
**tur·bid** trüb (*water*); dick, dicht (*smoke etc*); *fig* verworren, wirr
**tur·bine** TECH Turbine *f*
**tur·bo** F, **tur·bo·charg·er** MOT Turbolader *m*
**tur·bot** ZO Steinbutt *m*
**tur·bu·lent** turbulent
**tu·reen** (Suppen)Terrine *f*
**turf 1.** Rasen *m*; Sode *f*, Rasenstück *n*; ***the*** ~ die (Pferde)Rennbahn; der Pferderennsport **2.** mit Rasen bedecken
**tur·gid** MED geschwollen
**Turk** Türke *m*, Türkin *f*
**Tur·key** die Türkei
**tur·key** ZO Truthahn *m*, Truthenne *f*, Pute *f*, Puter *m*; ***talk*** ~ F offen *or* sachlich reden
**Turk·ish 1.** türkisch **2.** LING Türkisch *n*
**tur·moil** Aufruhr *m*
**turn 1.** *v/t* drehen, herum-, umdrehen; (um)wenden; *Seite* umblättern; *Schlauch etc* richten (**on** auf *acc*); *Antenne* ausrichten (**toward**[**s**] auf *acc*); *Aufmerksamkeit* zuwenden (**to** *dat*); verwandeln (**into** in *acc*); *Laub etc* färben; *Milch* sauer werden lassen; TECH

T

formen, drechseln; ~ ***the corner*** um die Ecke biegen; ~ ***loose*** los-, freilassen; ~ ***s.o.'s stomach*** j-m den Magen umdrehen; → ***inside*** *1*, ***upside down, somersault*** 1; *v/i* sich (um)drehen; abbiegen; einbiegen (***onto*** auf *acc*; ***into*** in *acc*); MOT wenden; *blass, sauer etc* werden; sich verwandeln, *fig a.* umschlagen (***into, to*** in *acc*); → ***left*** *2*, ***righ*** 2; ~ ***against*** *j-n* aufbringen *or* aufhetzen gegen; *fig* sich wenden gegen; ~ ***away*** (sich) abwenden (***from*** von); *j-n* abweisen, wegschicken; ~ ***back*** umkehren; *j-n* zurückschicken; *Uhr* zurückstellen; ~ ***down*** *Radio etc* leiser stellen; *Gas etc* klein(er) stellen; *Heizung etc* runterschalten; *j-n, Angebot etc* ablehnen; *Kragen* umschlagen; *Bettdecke* zurückschlagen; ~ ***in*** *v/t* zurückgeben; *Gewinn etc* erzielen, machen; *Arbeit* einreichen, abgeben; ~ ***o.s. in*** sich stellen; *v/i* F sich aufs Ohr legen; ~ ***off*** *v/t Gas, Wasser etc* abdrehen; *Licht, Radio etc* ausmachen, ausschalten; *Motor* abstellen; F *j-n* anwidern; F *j-m* die Lust nehmen; *v/i* abbiegen; ~ ***on*** *Gas, Wasser etc* aufdrehen; *Gerät* anstellen; *Licht, Radio etc* anmachen, an-, einschalten; F *j-n* antörnen, anmachen; ~ ***out*** *v/t Licht* ausmachen, ausschalten; *j-n* hinauswerfen; F *Waren* ausstoßen; *Tasche etc* (aus)leeren; *v/i* kommen (***for*** zu); sich erweisen *or* herausstellen als; ~ ***over*** (sich) umdrehen; *Seite* umblättern; wenden; *et.* umkippen; sich *et.* überlegen; *j-n, et.* übergeben (***to*** *dat*); *Waren* umsetzen; ~ ***round*** sich umdrehen; ~ ***one's car round*** wenden; ~ ***to*** sich an *j-n* wenden; sich zuwenden (*dat*); ~ ***up*** *Kragen* hochschlagen; *Ärmel, Saum etc* umschlagen; *Radio etc* lauter stellen; *Gas etc* aufdrehen; *fig* auftauchen **2.** (Um)Drehung *f*; Biegung *f*, Kurve *f*, Kehre *f*; Abzweigung *f*; *fig* Wende *f*, Wendung *f*; ***at every*** ~ auf Schritt und Tritt; ***by*** ~***s*** abwechselnd; ***in*** ~ der Reihe nach; abwechselnd; ***it is my*** ~ ich bin an der Reihe *or* F dran; ***make a left*** ~ (nach) links abbiegen; ***take*** ~***s*** sich abwechseln (***at*** bei); ***take a*** ~ ***for the better*** (***worse***) sich bessern (sich verschlimmern); ***do s.o. a good*** (***bad***) ~ j-m e-n guten (schlechten) Dienst erweisen

**turn·coat** Abtrünnige *m, f*, Überläufer(in); (***political***) ~ F Wendehals *m*

**turn·er** Drechsler *m*; Dreher *m*

**turn·ing** *esp Br* Abzweigung *f*

**turn·ing cir·cle** MOT Wendekreis *m*

**turn·ing point** *fig* Wendepunkt *m*

**tur·nip** BOT Rübe *f*

**turn-off** Abzweigung *f*

**turn·out** Besucher(zahl *f*) *pl*, Beteiligung *f*; Wahlbeteiligung *f*; F Aufmachung *f*

**turn·o·ver** ECON Umsatz *m*; Personalwechsel *m*, Fluktuation *f*

**turn·pike** (**road**) gebührenpflichtige Schnellstraße

**turn·stile** Drehkreuz *n*

**turn·ta·ble** Plattenteller *m*

**turn-up** *Br* (Hosen)Aufschlag *m*

**tur·pen·tine** CHEM Terpentin *n*

**tur·quoise** MIN Türkis *m*

**tur·ret** ARCH Ecktürmchen *n*; MIL (Panzer)Turm *m*; MAR Gefechtsturm *m*, Geschützturm *m*

**tur·tle** ZO (See)Schildkröte *f*

**tur·tle·dove** ZO Turteltaube *f*

**tur·tle·neck** Rollkragen(pullover) *m*

**tusk** ZO Stoßzahn *m*; Hauer *m*

**tus·sle** F Gerangel *n*

**tus·sock** Grasbüschel *n*

**tu·te·lage** (An)Leitung *f*; JUR Vormundschaft *f*

**tu·tor** Privat-, Hauslehrer(in); *Br* UNIV Tutor(in), Studienleiter(in)

**tu·to·ri·al** *Br* UNIV Tutorenkurs *m*

**tux·e·do** Smoking *m*

**TV 1.** TV *n*, Fernsehen *n*; Fernsehgerät *n*, F Fernseher *m*; ***on*** ~ im Fernsehen; ***watch*** ~ fernsehen **2.** Fernseh…

**twang 1.** Schwirren *n*; *mst* ***nasal*** ~ näselnde Aussprache **2.** schwirren (lassen)

**tweak** F zwicken, kneifen

**tweet** ZO piep(s)en

**tweez·ers** (***a pair of*** ~ e-e) Pinzette *f*

**twelfth 1.** zwölfte(r, -s) **2.** Zwölftel *n*

**twelve 1.** zwölf **2.** Zwölf *f*

**twen·ti·eth** zwanzigste(r, -s)

**twen·ty 1.** zwanzig **2.** Zwanzig *f*

**twice** zweimal

**twid·dle** (herum)spielen mit (*or* ***with*** mit); ~ ***one's thumbs*** Däumchen drehen

**twig** BOT dünner Zweig, Ästchen *n*

**twi·light** (*esp* Abend)Dämmerung *f*; Zwielicht *n*, Dämmerlicht *n*
**twin 1.** Zwilling *m*; *pl* Zwillinge *pl* **2.** Zwillings…; doppelt **3. be ~ned with** die Partnerstadt sein von
**twin-bed·ded room** Zweibettzimmer *n*
**twin beds** zwei Einzelbetten
**twin broth·er** Zwillingsbruder *m*
**twine 1.** Bindfaden *m*, Schnur *f* **2.** (sich) schlingen *or* winden (**round** um); *a.* **~ together** zusammendrehen
**twin-en·gined** AVIAT zweimotorig
**twinge** stechender Schmerz, Stechen *n*; **a ~ of conscience** Gewissensbisse *pl*
**twin·kle 1.** glitzern (*stars*), (*a. eyes*) funkeln (**with** vor *dat*); **2.** Glitzern *n*, Funkeln *n*; **with a ~ in one's eye** augenzwinkernd
**twin sis·ter** Zwillingsschwester *f*
**twin town** Partnerstadt *f*
**twirl 1.** (herum)wirbeln; wirbeln (**round** über *acc*); **2.** Wirbel *m*
**twist 1.** *v/t* drehen; wickeln (**round** um); *fig* verdrehen; **~ off** abdrehen, *Deckel* abschrauben; **~ one's ankle** (mit dem Fuß) umknicken, sich den Fuß vertreten; **her face was ~ed with pain** ihr Gesicht war schmerzverzerrt; *v/i* sich winden, (*river etc a.*) sich schlängeln **2.** Drehung *f*; Biegung *f*; (*überraschende*) Wendung; MUS Twist *m*
**twitch 1.** *v/t* zucken (mit); *v/i* zucken (**with** vor); zupfen (**at** an *dat*); **2.** Zucken *n*; Zuckung *f*
**twit·ter 1.** zwitschern **2.** Zwitschern *n*, Gezwitscher *n*; **be all of a ~** F ganz aufgeregt sein
**two 1.** zwei; **the ~ cars** die beiden Autos; **the ~ of us** wir beide; **in ~s** zu zweit, paarweise; **cut in ~** in zwei Teile schneiden; **put ~ and ~ together** zwei und zwei zusammenzählen **2.** Zwei *f*
**two-edged** zweischneidig
**two-faced** falsch, heuchlerisch
**two·fold** zweifach
**two·pence** *Br* zwei Pence *pl*
**two·pen·ny** *Br* F für zwei Pence
**two-piece** zweiteilig; **~ dress** Jackenkleid *n*
**two-seat·er** AVIAT, MOT Zweisitzer *m*
**two-sid·ed** zweiseitig
**two-sto·ried**, *Br* **two-sto·rey** zweistöckig
**two-way traf·fic** MOT Gegenverkehr *m*
**ty·coon** (*Industrie- etc*)Magnat *m*
**type 1.** Art *f*, Sorte *f*; Typ *m*; PRINT Type *f*, Buchstabe *m* **2.** *v/t et.* mit der Maschine schreiben, tippen; *v/i* Maschine schreiben, tippen
**type·writ·er** Schreibmaschine *f*
**type·writ·ten** maschine(n)geschrieben
**ty·phoid (fe·ver)** MED Typhus *m*
**ty·phoon** Taifun *m*
**ty·phus** MED Flecktyphus *m*, -fieber *n*
**typ·i·cal** typisch, bezeichnend (**of** für)
**typ·i·fy** typisch sein für, kennzeichnen; verkörpern
**typ·ing er·ror** Tippfehler *m*
**typ·ing pool** ECON Schreibzentrale *f*
**typ·ist** Schreibkraft *f*; Maschinenschreiber(in)
**ty·ran·ni·cal** tyrannisch
**tyr·an·nize** tyrannisieren
**tyr·an·ny** Tyrannei *f*
**ty·rant** Tyrann(in)
**tyre** *Br* → **tire**[1]
**tzar** → **tsar**

# U

**U, u** U, u *n*
**ud·der** zo Euter *n*
**ug·ly** hässlich (*a. fig*); bös(e), schlimm (*wound etc*)
**ul·cer** MED Geschwür *n*
**ul·te·ri·or**: **~ motive** Hintergedanke *m*
**ul·ti·mate** letzte(r, -s), End…; höchste(r, -s)
**ul·ti·mate·ly** letztlich; schließlich
**ul·ti·ma·tum** Ultimatum *n*; **deliver an ~ to s.o.** j-m ein Ultimatum stellen
**ul·tra·high fre·quen·cy** ELECTR Ultrakurzwelle *f*
**ul·tra·ma·rine** ultramarin
**ul·tra·son·ic** Ultraschall…
**ul·tra·sound** PHYS Ultraschall *m*
**ul·tra·vi·o·let** ultraviolett
**um·bil·i·cal cord** ANAT Nabelschnur *f*

**um·brel·la** (Regen)Schirm *m*; *fig* Schutz *m*
**um·pire** SPORT **1.** Schiedsrichter(in) **2.** als Schiedsrichter(in) fungieren (bei)
**un·a·bashed** unverfroren
**un·a·bat·ed** unvermindert
**un·a·ble** unfähig, außerstande, nicht in der Lage
**un·ac·cept·a·ble** unzumutbar
**un·ac·count·a·ble** unerklärlich
**un·ac·cus·tomed** ungewohnt
**un·ac·quaint·ed**: ***be ~ with s.th.*** et. nicht kennen, mit e-r Sache nicht vertraut sein
**un·ad·vised** unbesonnen, unüberlegt
**un·af·fect·ed** natürlich, ungekünstelt; ***be ~ by*** nicht betroffen sein von
**un·aid·ed** ohne Unterstützung, (ganz) allein
**un·al·ter·a·ble** unabänderlich
**u·nan·i·mous** einmütig; einstimmig
**un·an·nounced** unangemeldet
**un·an·swer·a·ble** unwiderlegbar; nicht zu beantworten(d)
**un·ap·pe·tiz·ing** unappetitlich
**un·ap·proach·a·ble** unnahbar
**un·armed** unbewaffnet
**un·asked** ungestellt (*question*); unaufgefordert, ungebeten (*guest etc*)
**un·as·sist·ed** ohne (fremde) Hilfe, (ganz) allein
**un·as·sum·ing** bescheiden
**un·at·tached** ungebunden, frei
**un·at·tend·ed** unbeaufsichtigt
**un·at·trac·tive** unattraktiv, wenig anziehend, reizlos
**un·au·thor·ized** unberechtigt, unbefugt
**un·a·void·a·ble** unvermeidlich
**un·a·ware**: ***be ~ of s.th.*** sich e-r Sache nicht bewusst sein, et. nicht bemerken
**un·a·wares**: ***catch*** *or* ***take s.o. ~*** j-n überraschen
**un·bal·ance** *j-n* aus dem (seelischen) Gleichgewicht bringen
**un·bal·anced** unausgeglichen, labil
**un·bar** aufriegeln, entriegeln
**un·bear·a·ble** unerträglich; *person*: unausstehlich
**un·beat·a·ble** unschlagbar
**un·beat·en** ungeschlagen, unbesiegt
**un·be·com·ing** unvorteilhaft
**un·be·known(st)**: ***~ to s.o.*** ohne j-s Wissen
**un·be·liev·a·ble** unglaublich
**un·bend** gerade biegen; sich aufrichten; *fig* aus sich herausgehen, auftauen
**un·bend·ing** unbeugsam
**un·bi·as(s)ed** unvoreingenommen; JUR unbefangen
**un·bind** losbinden
**un·blem·ished** makellos
**un·born** ungeboren
**un·break·a·ble** unzerbrechlich
**un·bri·dled** *fig* ungezügelt, zügellos; ***~ tongue*** lose Zunge
**un·bro·ken** ununterbrochen; heil, unversehrt; nicht zugeritten (*horse*)
**un·buck·le** aufschnallen, losschnallen
**un·bur·den**: ***~ o.s. to s.o.*** j-m sein Herz ausschütten
**un·but·ton** aufknöpfen
**un·called-for** ungerechtfertigt; unnötig; unpassend
**un·can·ny** unheimlich
**un·cared-for** vernachlässigt
**un·ceas·ing** unaufhörlich
**un·ce·re·mo·ni·ous** brüsk, unhöflich; überstürzt
**un·cer·tain** unsicher, ungewiss, unbestimmt; vage; METEOR unbeständig
**un·cer·tain·ty** Unsicherheit *f*, Ungewissheit *f*
**un·chain** losketten
**un·changed** unverändert
**un·chang·ing** unveränderlich
**un·char·i·ta·ble** unfair
**un·checked** ungehindert; ungeprüft
**un·chris·tian** unchristlich
**un·civ·il** unhöflich
**un·civ·i·lized** unzivilisiert
**un·cle** Onkel *m*
**un·com·fort·a·ble** unbequem; ***feel ~*** sich unbehaglich fühlen
**un·com·mon** ungewöhnlich
**un·com·mu·ni·ca·tive** wortkarg, verschlossen
**un·com·pre·hend·ing** verständnislos
**un·com·pro·mis·ing** kompromisslos
**un·con·cerned**: ***be ~ about*** sich keine Gedanken *or* Sorgen machen über (*acc*); ***be ~ with*** uninteressiert sein an (*dat*)
**un·con·di·tion·al** bedingungslos
**un·con·firmed** unbestätigt
**un·con·scious** unbewusst; unbeabsichtigt; MED bewusstlos; ***be ~ of*** sich *e-r Sache* nicht bewusst sein, nicht bemerken; **un·con·scious·ness** MED Be-

wusstlosigkeit *f*
**un·con·sti·tu·tion·al** verfassungswidrig
**un·con·trol·la·ble** unkontrollierbar; nicht zu bändigen(d); unbändig (*rage etc*); **un·con·trolled** unkontrolliert
**un·con·ven·tion·al** unkonventionell
**un·con·vinced**: ***be ~*** nicht überzeugt sein (***about*** von)
**un·con·vinc·ing** nicht überzeugend
**un·cooked** ungekocht, roh
**un·cork** entkorken
**un·count·a·ble** unzählbar
**un·coup·le** abkoppeln
**un·couth** *fig* ungehobelt
**un·cov·er** aufdecken, *fig a.* enthüllen
**un·crit·i·cal** unkritisch; ***be ~ of s.th.*** e-r Sache unkritisch gegenüberstehen
**unc·tion** REL Salbung *f*
**unc·tu·ous** salbungsvoll
**un·cut** ungekürzt (*film, novel etc*); ungeschliffen (*diamond etc*)
**un·dam·aged** unbeschädigt, unversehrt, heil
**un·dat·ed** undatiert, ohne Datum
**un·daunt·ed** unerschrocken, furchtlos
**un·de·cid·ed** unentschieden, offen; unentschlossen
**un·de·mon·stra·tive** zurückhaltend, reserviert
**un·de·ni·a·ble** unbestreitbar
**un·der 1.** *prp* unter (*dat or acc*) **2.** *adv* unten; darunter
**un·der·age** minderjährig
**un·der·bid** unterbieten
**un·der·brush** → ***undergrowth***
**un·der·car·riage** AVIAT Fahrwerk *n*, Fahrgestell *n*
**un·der·charge** zu wenig berechnen; zu wenig verlangen
**un·der·clothes, un·der·cloth·ing** → ***underwear***
**un·der·coat** Grundierung *f*
**un·der·cov·er**: ***~ agent*** verdeckter Ermittler
**un·der·cut** *j-n* (im Preis) unterbieten
**un·der·de·vel·oped** unterentwickelt; ***~ country*** Entwicklungsland *n*
**un·der·dog** Benachteiligte *m, f*
**un·der·done** nicht durchgebraten
**un·der·es·ti·mate** zu niedrig schätzen *or* veranschlagen; *fig* unterschätzen
**un·der·ex·pose** PHOT unterbelichten
**un·der·fed** unterernährt
**un·der·go** erleben, durchmachen; MED sich *e-r Operation etc* unterziehen
**un·der·grad** F, **un·der·grad·u·ate** Student(in)
**un·der·ground 1.** *adv* unterirdisch, unter der Erde **2.** *adj* unterirdisch; *fig* Untergrund... **3.** *esp Br* Untergrundbahn *f*, U-Bahn *f*; ***by ~*** mit der U-Bahn
**un·der·growth** Unterholz *n*
**un·der·hand, un·der·hand·ed** heimlich; hinterhältig
**un·der·line** unterstreichen (*a. fig*)
**un·der·ling** *contp* Untergebene *m, f*
**un·der·ly·ing** zugrunde liegend
**un·der·mine** unterspülen; *fig* untergraben, unterminieren
**un·der·neath 1.** *prp* unter (*dat or acc*) **2.** *adv* darunter
**un·der·nour·ished** unterernährt
**un·der·pants** Unterhose *f*
**un·der·pass** Unterführung *f*
**un·der·pay** *j-m* zu wenig bezahlen, *j-n* unterbezahlen
**un·der·priv·i·leged** unterprivilegiert, benachteiligt
**un·der·rate** unterbewerten, -schätzen
**un·der·sec·re·ta·ry** POL Staatssekretär *m*
**un·der·sell** ECON *Ware* verschleudern, unter Wert verkaufen; ***~ o.s.*** *fig* sich schlecht verkaufen
**un·der·shirt** Unterhemd *n*
**un·der·side** Unterseite *f*
**un·der·signed**: ***the ~*** der *or* die Unterzeichnete, die Unterzeichneten *pl*
**un·der·size**(d) zu klein
**un·der·staffed** (personell) unterbesetzt
**un·der·stand** verstehen; erfahren *or* gehört haben (***that*** dass); ***make o.s. understood*** sich verständlich machen; ***am I to ~ that*** soll das heißen, dass; ***give s.o. to ~ that*** j-m zu verstehen geben, dass
**un·der·stand·a·ble** verständlich
**un·der·stand·ing 1.** Verstand *m*; Verständnis *n*; Abmachung *f*; Verständigung *f*; ***come to an ~*** e-e Abmachung treffen (***with*** mit); ***on the ~ that*** unter der Voraussetzung, dass **2.** verständnisvoll
**un·der·state** untertreiben, untertrieben darstellen; **un·der·state·ment** Understatement *n*, Untertreibung *f*
**un·der·take** *et.* übernehmen; sich verpflichten (***to do*** zu tun)

U

**un·der·tak·er** Leichenbestatter *m*; Beerdigungs-, Bestattungsinstitut *n*
**un·der·tak·ing** Unternehmen *n*; Zusicherung *f*
**un·der·tone** *fig* Unterton *m*; ***in an ~*** mit gedämpfter Stimme
**un·der·val·ue** unterbewerten
**un·der·wa·ter** **1.** *adj* Unterwasser… **2.** *adv* unter Wasser
**un·der·wear** Unterwäsche *f*
**un·der·weight** **1.** Untergewicht *n* **2.** untergewichtig, zu leicht (***by*** um); ***she is five pounds ~*** sie hat fünf Pfund Untergewicht
**un·der·world** Unterwelt *f*
**un·de·served** unverdient
**un·de·sir·a·ble** unerwünscht
**un·de·vel·oped** unerschlossen (*area*); unentwickelt
**un·dies** F (Damen)Unterwäsche *f*
**un·dig·ni·fied** würdelos
**un·di·min·ished** unvermindert
**un·dis·ci·plined** undiszipliniert
**un·dis·cov·ered** unentdeckt
**un·dis·guised** unverhohlen
**un·dis·put·ed** unbestritten
**un·dis·turbed** ungestört
**un·di·vid·ed** ungeteilt
**un·do** aufmachen, öffnen; *fig* zunichtemachen; **un·do·ing**: ***be s.o.'s ~*** j-s Ruin *or* Verderben sein; **un·done** unerledigt; offen; ***come ~*** aufgehen
**un·doubt·ed** unbestritten
**un·doubt·ed·ly** zweifellos, ohne (jeden) Zweifel
**un·dreamed-of**, **un·dreamt-of** ungeahnt
**un·dress** sich ausziehen; *j-n* ausziehen
**un·due** übermäßig
**un·du·lat·ing** sanft (*hills*)
**un·dy·ing** ewig
**un·earned** *fig* unverdient
**un·earth** ausgraben, *fig a.* ausfindig machen, aufstöbern
**un·earth·ly** überirdisch; unheimlich; ***at an ~ hour*** F zu e-r unchristlichen Zeit
**un·eas·i·ness** Unbehagen *n*
**un·eas·y** unruhig (*sleep*); unsicher (*peace*); ***feel ~*** sich unbehaglich fühlen; ***I'm ~ about*** mir ist nicht wohl bei
**un·e·co·nom·ic** unwirtschaftlich
**un·ed·u·cat·ed** ungebildet
**un·e·mo·tion·al** leidenschaftslos, kühl, beherrscht
**un·em·ployed** **1.** arbeitslos **2.** ***the ~*** die Arbeitslosen *pl*
**un·em·ploy·ment** Arbeitslosigkeit *f*; **~ a·gen·cy** *Am* Arbeitsagentur *f*; **~ ben·e·fit** *Br*, **~ com·pen·sa·tion** Arbeitslosengeld *n*
**un·end·ing** endlos
**un·en·dur·a·ble** unerträglich
**un·en·vi·a·ble** wenig beneidenswert
**un·e·qual** ungleich (*a. fig*), unterschiedlich; *fig* einseitig; ***be ~ to*** *e-r Aufgabe etc* nicht gewachsen sein
**un·e·qual(l)ed** unerreicht, unübertroffen
**un·er·ring** unfehlbar
**un·e·ven** uneben; ungleich(mäßig); ungerade (*number*)
**un·e·vent·ful** ereignislos
**un·ex·am·pled** beispiellos
**un·ex·pec·ted** unerwartet
**un·ex·posed** PHOT unbelichtet
**un·fail·ing** unerschöpflich; nie versagend
**un·fair** unfair, ungerecht
**un·faith·ful** untreu (***to*** *dat*)
**un·fa·mil·i·ar** ungewohnt; unbekannt; nicht vertraut (***with*** mit)
**un·fas·ten** aufmachen, öffnen; losbinden
**un·fa·vo(u)r·a·ble** ungünstig; unvorteilhaft (***for, to*** für); negativ, ablehnend
**un·feel·ing** gefühllos, herzlos
**un·fin·ished** unvollendet; unfertig; unerledigt
**un·fit** nicht fit, nicht in Form; ungeeignet, untauglich; unfähig
**un·flag·ging** unermüdlich, unentwegt
**un·flap·pa·ble** F nicht aus der Ruhe zu bringen(d)
**un·fold** auffalten, auseinanderfalten; darlegen, enthüllen; sich entfalten
**un·fore·seen** unvorhergesehen, unerwartet
**un·for·get·ta·ble** unvergesslich
**un·for·got·ten** unvergessen
**un·for·tu·nate** unglücklich; unglückselig; bedauerlich
**un·for·tu·nate·ly** leider
**un·found·ed** unbegründet
**un·friend·ly** unfreundlich (***to, towards*** zu)
**un·furl** *Fahne* aufrollen, entrollen, *Segel* losmachen
**un·fur·nished** unmöbliert

**un·gain·ly** linkisch, unbeholfen
**un·god·ly** gottlos; ***at an ~ hour*** F zu e-r unchristlichen Zeit
**un·gra·cious** ungnädig; unfreundlich
**un·grate·ful** undankbar
**un·guard·ed** unbewacht; unbedacht, unüberlegt
**un·hap·pi·ly** unglücklicherweise, leider; **un·hap·py** unglücklich
**un·harmed** unversehrt
**un·health·y** kränklich, nicht gesund; ungesund; *contp* krankhaft, unnatürlich
**un·heard**: ***go ~*** keine Beachtung finden, unbeachtet bleiben; **un·heard-of** noch nie da gewesen, beispiellos
**un·hinge**: ***~ s.o.('s mind)*** *fig* j-n völlig aus dem Gleichgewicht bringen
**un·ho·ly** F furchtbar, schrecklich
**un·hoped-for** unverhofft, unerwartet
**un·hurt** unverletzt
**u·ni·corn** Einhorn *n*
**un·i·den·ti·fied** unbekannt, nicht identifiziert
**u·ni·fi·ca·tion** Vereinigung *f*
**u·ni·form 1.** Uniform *f* **2.** gleichmäßig; einheitlich
**u·ni·form·i·ty** Einheitlichkeit *f*
**u·ni·fy** verein(ig)en; vereinheitlichen
**u·ni·lat·e·ral** *fig* einseitig
**un·i·ma·gin·a·ble** unvorstellbar
**un·i·ma·gin·a·tive** fantasielos, einfallslos
**un·im·por·tant** unwichtig
**un·im·pressed**: ***remain ~*** unbeeindruckt bleiben (***by*** von)
**un·in·formed** nicht unterrichtet *or* eingeweiht
**un·in·hab·it·a·ble** unbewohnbar
**un·in·hab·it·ed** unbewohnt
**un·in·jured** unverletzt
**un·in·tel·li·gi·ble** unverständlich
**un·in·ten·tion·al** unabsichtlich, unbeabsichtigt
**un·in·terest·ed** uninteressiert (***in*** an *dat*); ***be ~ in*** *a.* sich nicht interessieren für; **un·in·terest·ing** uninteressant
**un·in·ter·rupt·ed** ununterbrochen
**u·nion** Vereinigung *f*; Union *f*; Gewerkschaft *f*; **u·nion·ist** Gewerkschaftler(in); **u·nion·ize** (sich) gewerkschaftlich organisieren
**u·nique** einzigartig; einmalig
**u·ni·son**: ***in ~*** gemeinsam
**u·nit** Einheit *f*; PED Unit *f*, Lehreinheit *f*; MATH Einer *m*; TECH (Anbau)Element *n*, Teil *n*; ***~ furniture*** Anbaumöbel *pl*
**u·nite** verbinden, vereinigen; sich vereinigen *or* zusammentun
**u·nit·ed** vereinigt, vereint
**U·nit·ed King·dom** *das* Vereinigte Königreich (*England, Scotland, Wales and Northern Ireland*)
**U·nit·ed States of A·mer·i·ca** *die* Vereinigten Staaten von Amerika
**u·ni·ty** Einheit *f*; MATH Eins *f*
**u·ni·ver·sal** allgemein; universal, universell; Welt…
**u·ni·verse** Universum *n*, Weltall *n*
**u·ni·ver·si·ty** Universität *f*, Hochschule *f*; **~ grad·u·ate** Akademiker(in)
**un·just** ungerecht
**un·kempt** ungekämmt (*hair*); ungepflegt (*clothes etc*)
**un·kind** unfreundlich
**un·known 1.** unbekannt (***to*** *dat*); **2.** *der, die, das* Unbekannte; **~ quan·ti·ty** MATH unbekannte Größe (*a. fig*), Unbekannte *f*
**un·law·ful** ungesetzlich, gesetzwidrig
**un·lead·ed** bleifrei
**un·learn** *Ansichten etc* ablegen, aufgeben
**un·less** wenn … nicht, außer wenn …, es sei denn …
**un·like** *prp* im Gegensatz zu; ***he is very ~ his father*** er ist ganz anders als sein Vater; ***that is very ~ him*** das sieht ihm gar nicht ähnlich
**un·like·ly** unwahrscheinlich
**un·lim·it·ed** unbegrenzt
**un·list·ed**: ***be ~*** nicht im Telefonbuch stehen; **~ num·ber** TEL Geheimnummer *f*
**un·load** entladen, abladen, ausladen; MAR *Ladung* löschen
**un·lock** aufschließen
**un·loos·en** losmachen; lockern; lösen
**un·loved** ungeliebt
**un·luck·y** unglücklich; ***be ~*** Pech haben
**un·made** ungemacht
**un·manned** unbemannt
**un·marked** nicht gekennzeichnet; SPORT ungedeckt, frei
**un·mar·ried** unverheiratet, ledig
**un·mask** *fig* entlarven
**un·matched** unübertroffen, unvergleichlich
**un·men·tio·na·ble** Tabu…; ***be ~*** tabu

sein
**un·mis·tak·a·ble** unverkennbar, unverwechselbar, untrüglich
**un·mo·lest·ed** unbehelligt
**un·moved** ungerührt; ***she remained ~ by it*** es ließ sie kalt
**un·mu·si·cal** unmusikalisch
**un·named** ungenannt
**un·nat·u·ral** unnatürlich; widernatürlich
**un·ne·ces·sa·ry** unnötig
**un·nerve** entnerven
**un·no·ticed** unbemerkt
**un·num·bered** unnummeriert
**un·ob·tru·sive** unauffällig, unaufdringlich
**un·oc·cu·pied** leer (stehend), unbewohnt; unbeschäftigt
**un·of·fi·cial** inoffiziell
**un·pack** auspacken
**un·paid** unbezahlt; *post* unfrei
**un·par·al·leled** einmalig, beispiellos
**un·par·don·a·ble** unverzeihlich
**un·per·turbed** gelassen, ruhig
**un·pick** *Naht etc* auftrennen
**un·placed**: ***be ~*** SPORT sich nicht platzieren können
**un·play·a·ble** SPORT unbespielbar
**un·pleas·ant** unangenehm, unerfreulich; unfreundlich
**un·plug** den Stecker (*gen*) herausziehen
**un·pol·ished** unpoliert; *fig* ungehobelt
**un·pol·lut·ed** sauber, unverschmutzt
**un·pop·u·lar** unpopulär, unbeliebt
**un·pop·u·lar·i·ty** Unbeliebtheit *f*
**un·prac·ti·cal** unpraktisch
**un·prac·ticed**, *Br* **un·prac·tised** ungeübt
**un·pre·ce·dent·ed** beispiellos, noch nie da gewesen
**un·pre·dict·a·ble** unvorhersehbar; unberechenbar (*person*)
**un·prej·u·diced** unvoreingenommen; JUR unbefangen
**un·pre·med·i·tat·ed** nicht vorsätzlich; unüberlegt
**un·pre·pared** unvorbereitet
**un·pre·ten·tious** bescheiden, einfach, schlicht
**un·prin·ci·pled** skrupellos, gewissenlos
**un·prin·ta·ble** nicht druckfähig *or* druckreif
**un·pro·duc·tive** unproduktiv, unergiebig
**un·pro·fes·sion·al** unprofessionell; unfachmännisch
**un·prof·it·a·ble** unrentabel
**un·pro·nounce·a·ble** unaussprechbar
**un·pro·tect·ed** ungeschützt
**un·proved**, **un·prov·en** unbewiesen
**un·pro·voked** grundlos
**un·pun·ished** unbestraft, ungestraft; ***go ~*** straflos bleiben
**un·qual·i·fied** unqualifiziert, ungeeignet (***for*** für); uneingeschränkt
**un·ques·tion·a·ble** unbestritten
**un·ques·tion·ing** bedingungslos
**un·quote**: ***quote … ~*** Zitat … Zitat Ende
**un·rav·el** (sich) auftrennen (*pullover etc*); entwirren
**un·read·a·ble** nicht lesenswert, unlesbar, *a.* unleserlich
**un·re·al** unwirklich
**un·rea·lis·tic** unrealistisch
**un·rea·son·a·ble** unvernünftig; übertrieben, unzumutbar
**un·rec·og·niz·a·ble** nicht wieder zu erkennen(d)
**un·re·lat·ed**: ***be ~*** in keinem Zusammenhang stehen (***to*** mit)
**un·re·lent·ing** unvermindert
**un·re·li·a·ble** unzuverlässig
**un·re·lieved** ununterbrochen, ständig
**un·re·mit·ting** unablässig, unaufhörlich
**un·re·quit·ed**: ***~ love*** unerwiderte Liebe
**un·re·served** uneingeschränkt; nicht reserviert
**un·rest** POL *etc* Unruhen *pl*
**un·re·strained** hemmungslos, ungezügelt
**un·re·strict·ed** uneingeschränkt
**un·ripe** unreif
**un·ri·val(l)ed** unerreicht, unübertroffen, einzigartig
**un·roll** (sich) aufrollen *or* entrollen; sich entfalten
**un·ruf·fled** gelassen, ruhig
**un·ru·ly** ungebärdig, wild; widerspenstig (*hair*)
**un·sad·dle** *Pferd* absatteln; *Reiter* abwerfen
**un·safe** unsicher, nicht sicher
**un·said** unausgesprochen
**un·sal(e)·a·ble** unverkäuflich
**un·salt·ed** ungesalzen
**un·san·i·tar·y** unhygienisch
**un·sat·is·fac·to·ry** unbefriedigend

**un·sat·u·rat·ed** CHEM ungesättigt
**un·sa·vo(u)r·y** anrüchig, unerfreulich
**un·scathed** unversehrt, unverletzt
**un·screw** abschrauben, losschrauben
**un·scru·pu·lous** skrupellos, gewissenlos
**un·seat** *Reiter* abwerfen; *j-n* s-s Amtes entheben
**un·seem·ly** ungebührlich
**un·self·ish** selbstlos, uneigennützig
**un·set·tle** durcheinanderbringen; beunruhigen; aufregen
**un·set·tled** ungeklärt, offen (*question etc*); unsicher (*situation etc*); METEOR unbeständig
**un·shak(e)·a·ble** unerschütterlich
**un·shav·en** unrasiert
**un·shrink·a·ble** nicht eingehend *or* einlaufend
**un·sight·ly** unansehnlich; hässlich
**un·skilled**: ***~ worker*** ungelernter Arbeiter
**un·so·cia·ble** ungesellig
**un·so·cial**: ***work ~ hours*** außerhalb der normalen Arbeitszeit arbeiten
**un·so·lic·it·ed** unaufgefordert ein- *or* zugesandt, ECON *a.* unbestellt
**un·solved** ungelöst (*problem etc*)
**un·so·phis·ti·cat·ed** einfach, schlicht; TECH unkompliziert
**un·sound** nicht gesund; nicht in Ordnung; morsch; unsicher, schwach; nicht stichhaltig (*argument etc*); ***of ~ mind*** JUR unzurechnungsfähig
**un·spar·ing** großzügig, freigebig, verschwenderisch; schonungslos, unbarmherzig
**un·speak·a·ble** unbeschreiblich, entsetzlich
**un·spoiled**, **un·spoilt** unverdorben; nicht verwöhnt *or* verzogen
**un·sta·ble** instabil; unsicher, schwankend; labil (*person*)
**un·stead·y** wack(e)lig, schwankend, unsicher; unbeständig; ungleichmäßig, unregelmäßig
**un·stop** *Abfluss etc* frei machen; *Flasche* entstöpseln
**un·stressed** LING unbetont
**un·stuck**: ***come ~*** abgehen, sich lösen; *fig* scheitern
**un·stud·ied** ungekünstelt, natürlich
**un·suc·cess·ful** erfolglos, ohne Erfolg; vergeblich
**un·suit·a·ble** unpassend, ungeeignet; unangemessen
**un·sure** unsicher; ***~ of o.s.*** unsicher
**un·sur·passed** unübertroffen
**un·sus·pect·ed** unverdächtig; unvermutet; **un·sus·pect·ing** nichts ahnend, ahnungslos
**un·sus·pi·cious** arglos; unverdächtig, harmlos
**un·sweet·ened** ungesüßt
**un·swerv·ing** unbeirrbar, unerschütterlich
**un·tan·gle** entwirren (*a. fig*)
**un·tapped** unerschlossen (*resource etc*)
**un·teach·a·ble** unbelehrbar (*person*); nicht lehrbar
**un·ten·a·ble** unhaltbar (*theory etc*)
**un·think·a·ble** undenkbar, unvorstellbar; **un·think·ing** gedankenlos
**un·ti·dy** unordentlich
**un·tie** aufknoten, *Knoten etc* lösen; losbinden
**un·til** *prp*, *cj* bis; ***not ~*** erst; erst wenn, nicht bevor
**un·time·ly** vorzeitig, verfrüht; unpassend, ungelegen
**un·tir·ing** unermüdlich
**un·told** *fig* unermesslich
**un·touched** unberührt, unangetastet
**un·true** unwahr, falsch
**un·trust·wor·thy** unzuverlässig, nicht vertrauenswürdig
**un·used**[1] unbenutzt, ungebraucht
**un·used**[2]: ***be ~ to s.th.*** an et. nicht gewöhnt sein, et. nicht gewohnt sein; ***be ~ to doing s.th.*** es nicht gewohnt sein, et. zu tun
**un·u·su·al** ungewöhnlich
**un·var·nished** *fig* ungeschminkt
**un·var·y·ing** unveränderlich, gleichbleibend
**un·veil** *Denkmal etc* enthüllen
**un·versed** unbewandert, unerfahren (***in*** in *dat*)
**un·voiced** unausgesprochen
**un·want·ed** unerwünscht, ungewollt
**un·war·rant·ed** ungerechtfertigt
**un·washed** ungewaschen
**un·wel·come** unwillkommen
**un·well**: ***be*** *or* ***feel ~*** sich unwohl fühlen *or* nicht wohlfühlen
**un·whole·some** ungesund (*a. fig*)
**un·wield·y** unhandlich, sperrig
**un·will·ing** widerwillig; ungern; ***be ~ to***

***do s.th.*** et. nicht tun wollen
**un·wind** (sich) abwickeln; F abschalten, sich entspannen
**un·wise** unklug
**un·wit·ting** unwissentlich; unbeabsichtigt
**un·wor·thy** unwürdig; ***he*** (***she***) ***is ~ of it*** er (sie) verdient es nicht, er (sie) ist es nicht wert
**un·wrap** auswickeln, auspacken
**un·writ·ten** ungeschrieben
**un·yield·ing** unnachgiebig
**un·zip** den Reißverschluss (*gen*) aufmachen
**up 1.** *adv* herauf, hinauf, aufwärts, nach oben, hoch, in die Höhe; oben; ***~ there*** dort oben; ***jump ~ and down*** hüpfen; ***walk ~ and down*** auf und ab gehen, hin und her gehen; ***~ to*** bis zu; ***be ~ to s.th.*** F et. vorhaben, et. im Schilde führen; ***not to be ~ to s.th.*** e-r Sache nicht gewachsen sein; ***it's ~ to you*** das liegt bei dir **2.** *prp* herauf, hinauf; oben auf (*dat*); ***~ the river*** flussaufwärts **3.** *adj* nach oben (gerichtet), Aufwärts…; ASTR aufgegangen; ECON gestiegen; *time*: abgelaufen, um; aufgestanden, F auf; ***the ~ train*** der Zug nach London; ***be ~ and about*** F wieder auf den Beinen sein; ***what's ~?*** F was ist los? **4.** F *v/t Angebot, Preis etc* erhöhen **5. *the ~s and downs*** F die Höhen und Tiefen *pl* (***of life*** des Lebens)
**up-and-com·ing** aufstrebend, vielversprechend
**up·bring·ing** Erziehung *f*
**up·com·ing** bevorstehend
**up·coun·try** landeinwärts; im Landesinneren
**up·date 1.** auf den neuesten Stand bringen; aktualisieren **2.** Lagebericht *m*
**up·end** hochkant stellen
**up·grade** *j-n* befördern
**up·heav·al** *fig* Umwälzung *f*
**up·hill** aufwärts, bergan; bergauf führend; *fig* mühsam
**up·hold** *Rechte etc* schützen, wahren; JUR *Urteil* bestätigen
**up·hol·ster** *Möbel* polstern
**up·hol·ster·er** Polsterer *m*
**up·hol·ster·y** Polsterung *f*; Bezug *m*; Polsterei *f*
**up·keep** Instandhaltung(skosten *pl*) *f*; Unterhalt(ungskosten *pl*) *m*
**up·land** *mst pl* Hochland *n*
**up·lift 1.** *j-n* aufrichten, *j-m* Auftrieb geben **2.** Auftrieb *m*
**up·on** → ***on, once 1***
**up·per** obere(r, -s), Ober…;
**up·per·most 1.** *adj* oberste(r, -s), größte(r, -s), höchste(r, -s); ***be ~*** oben sein; *fig* an erster Stelle stehen **2.** *adv* nach oben
**up·right** aufrecht, *a.* gerade, *fig a.* rechtschaffen
**up·ris·ing** Aufstand *m*
**up·roar** Aufruhr *m*; **up·roar·i·ous** lärmend, laut; schallend (*laughter*)
**up·root** ausreißen, entwurzeln; *fig j-n* herausreißen (***from*** aus)
**up·set** umkippen, umstoßen, umwerfen; *Pläne etc* durcheinanderbringen, stören; *j-n* aus der Fassung bringen; ***the fish has ~ me*** *or* ***my stomach*** ich habe mir durch den Fisch den Magen verdorben; ***be ~*** aufgeregt sein; aus der Fassung *or* durcheinander sein; gekränkt *or* verletzt sein
**up·shot** Ergebnis *n*
**up·side down** verkehrt herum; *fig* drunter und drüber; ***turn ~*** umdrehen, *a. fig* auf den Kopf stellen
**up·stairs 1.** die Treppe herauf *or* hinauf, nach oben; oben **2.** im oberen Stockwerk (gelegen), obere(r, -s)
**up·start** Emporkömmling *m*
**up·state** im Norden (e-s Bundesstaats)
**up·stream** fluss-, stromaufwärts
**up·take**: F ***be quick*** (***slow***) ***on the ~*** schnell begreifen (schwer von Begriff sein)
**up-to-date** modern; aktuell, auf dem neuesten Stand
**up·town** in den Wohnvierteln; in die Wohnviertel
**up·turn** Aufschwung *m*
**up·ward(s)** aufwärts, nach oben
**u·ra·ni·um** CHEM Uran *n*
**ur·ban** städtisch, Stadt…
**ur·ban·i·za·tion** Verstädterung *f*
**ur·chin** Bengel *m*
**urge 1.** *j-n* drängen (***to do*** zu tun); drängen auf (*acc*); *a.* ***~ on*** *j-n* drängen, antreiben **2.** Drang *m*, Verlangen *n*
**ur·gen·cy** Dringlichkeit *f*
**ur·gent** dringend; ***be ~*** *a.* eilen
**u·ri·nate** urinieren; **u·rine** Urin *m*
**urn** Urne *f*

**us** uns; ***all of ~*** wir alle; ***both of ~*** wir beide
**us·age** Sprachgebrauch *m*; Behandlung *f*; Verwendung *f*, Gebrauch *m*
**USB flash drive** IT USB-Stick *m*
**use 1.** *v/t* benutzen, gebrauchen, anwenden, verwenden; (ver)brauchen; ***~ up*** auf-, verbrauchen; *v/i*: ***I ~d to live here*** ich habe früher hier gewohnt **2.** Benutzung *f*, Gebrauch *m*, Verwendung *f*; Nutzen *m*; ***be of ~*** nützlich *or* von Nutzen sein (***to*** für); ***it's no ~*** *doing* es ist nutzlos *or* zwecklos *zu inf*; → ***milk*** *1*
**used**[1]: ***be ~ to s.th.*** an et. gewöhnt sein, et. gewohnt sein; ***be ~ to doing s.th.*** es gewohnt sein, et. zu tun
**used**[2] gebraucht; **~ car** Gebrauchtwagen *m*; **~ car deal·er** Gebrauchtwagenhändler(in)
**use·ful** nützlich
**use·less** nutzlos, zwecklos
**us·er** Benutzer(in); Verbraucher(in)
**us·er-friend·ly** benutzer- *or* verbraucherfreundlich
**us·er in·ter·face** IT Benutzeroberfläche *f*
**ush·er 1.** Platzanweiser *m*; Gerichtsdiener *m* **2.** *j-n* führen, geleiten (***into*** in *acc*; ***to*** zu)
**ush·er·ette** Platzanweiserin *f*
**u·su·al** gewöhnlich, üblich
**u·su·al·ly** (für) gewöhnlich, normalerweise
**u·sur·er** Wucherer *m*
**u·su·ry** Wucher *m*
**u·ten·sil** Gerät *n*
**u·te·rus** ANAT Gebärmutter *f*
**u·til·i·ty** Nutzen *m*; *pl* Leistungen *pl* der öffentlichen Versorgungsbetriebe
**u·til·ize** nutzen
**ut·most** äußerste(r, -s), größte(r, -s), höchste(r, -s)
**u·to·pi·an** utopisch
**ut·ter**[1] total, völlig
**ut·ter**[2] äußern, *Seufzer etc* ausstoßen, *Wort* sagen
**U-turn** MOT Wende *f*; *fig* Kehrtwendung *f*
**u·vu·la** ANAT (Gaumen)Zäpfchen *n*

# V

**V, v** V, v *n*
**va·can·cy** freie *or* offene Stelle; ***vacancies*** Zimmer frei; ***no vacancies*** belegt
**va·cant** leer stehend, unbewohnt; frei (*seat etc*); frei, offen (*job*); *fig* leer (*expression, stare etc*)
**va·cate** *Hotelzimmer* räumen; *Stelle etc* aufgeben
**va·ca·tion 1.** Ferien *pl*, Urlaub *m*; *esp Br* UNIV Semesterferien *pl*; JUR Gerichtsferien *pl*; ***be on ~*** im Urlaub sein, Urlaub machen **2.** Urlaub machen, die Ferien verbringen
**va·ca·tion·er, va·ca·tion·ist** Urlauber(in)
**vac·cin·ate** MED impfen
**vac·cin·a·tion** MED (Schutz)Impfung *f*
**vac·cine** MED Impfstoff *m*
**vac·il·late** *fig* schwanken
**vac·u·um 1.** PHYS Vakuum *n* **2.** F *Teppich, Zimmer etc* saugen; **~ bot·tle** Thermosflasche® *f*; **~ clean·er** Staubsauger *m*; **~ flask** *Br* Thermosflasche® *f*; **~-packed** vakuumverpackt
**vag·a·bond** Vagabund *m*, Landstreicher(in)
**va·ga·ry** *mst pl* Laune *f*; wunderlicher Einfall
**va·gi·na** ANAT Vagina *f*, Scheide *f*
**va·gi·nal** ANAT vaginal, Scheiden…
**va·grant** Nichtsesshafte *m, f*, Landstreicher(in)
**vague** verschwommen; vage; unklar
**vain** eingebildet, eitel; vergeblich; ***in ~*** vergebens, vergeblich
**val·en·tine** Valentinskarte *f*
**va·le·ri·an** BOT, PHARM Baldrian *m*
**val·et** (Kammer)Diener *m*
**val·id** stichhaltig, triftig; gültig (***for two weeks*** zwei Wochen); JUR rechtsgültig, rechtskräftig; ***be ~*** *a.* gelten
**va·lid·i·ty** (JUR Rechts)Gültigkeit *f*; Stichhaltigkeit *f*, Triftigkeit *f*
**val·ley** Tal *n*
**val·u·a·ble 1.** wertvoll **2.** *pl* Wertgegenstände *pl*, Wertsachen *pl*

**val·u·a·tion** Schätzung *f*; Schätzwert *m* (***on*** *gen*)

**val·ue 1.** Wert *m*; ***be of ~*** wertvoll sein (***to*** für); ***get ~ for money*** reell bedient werden **2.** *Haus etc* schätzen (***at*** auf *acc*); *j-n, j-s Rat etc* schätzen

**val·ue-ad·ded tax** *Br* ECON (*abbr* ***VAT***) Mehrwertsteuer *f*

**val·ue·less** wertlos

**valve** TECH, MUS Ventil *n*; ANAT (*Herz-etc*)Klappe *f*

**vam·pire** Vampir *m*

**van** MOT Lieferwagen *m*, Transporter *m*; *Br* RAIL (geschlossener) Güterwagen

**van·dal** Wandale *m*, Vandale *m*

**van·dal·ism** Wandalismus *m*, Vandalismus *m*

**van·dal·ize** mutwillig beschädigen *or* zerstören

**vane** TECH (*Propeller- etc*)Flügel *m*; (*Wetter*)Fahne *f*

**van·guard** MIL Vorhut *f*

**va·nil·la** Vanille *f*

**van·ish** verschwinden

**van·i·ty** Eitelkeit *f*; **~ bag** Kosmetiktäschchen *n*; **~ case** Kosmetikkoffer *m*

**va·por·ize** verdampfen; verdunsten (lassen)

**va·po(u)r** Dampf *m*, Dunst *m*; **~ trail** AVIAT Kondensstreifen *m*

**var·i·a·ble 1.** variabel, veränderlich; unbeständig, wechselhaft; TECH einstellbar, regulierbar **2.** MATH, PHYS Variable *f*, veränderliche Größe (*both a. fig*)

**var·i·ance**: ***be at ~ with*** im Gegensatz *or* Widerspruch stehen zu

**var·i·ant 1.** abweichend, verschieden **2.** Variante *f*; **var·i·a·tion** Abweichung *f*; Schwankung *f*; MUS Variation *f*

**var·i·cose veins** MED Krampfadern *pl*

**var·ied** unterschiedlich; abwechslungsreich

**va·ri·e·ty** Abwechslung *f*; Vielfalt *f*; ECON Auswahl *f*, Sortiment *n* (***of*** an *dat*); BOT, ZO Art *f*; Varietee *n*; ***for a ~ of reasons*** aus den verschiedensten Gründen

**var·i·ous** verschieden; mehrere, verschiedene

**var·nish 1.** Lack *m* **2.** lackieren

**var·si·ty team** SPORT Universitäts-, College-, Schulmannschaft *f*

**var·y** *v/i* sich (ver)ändern; variieren, auseinandergehen (*opinions etc*) (***on*** über *acc*); ***~ in size*** verschieden groß sein; *v/t* (ver)ändern; variieren

**vase** Vase *f*

**vast** gewaltig, riesig, (*area a.*) ausgedehnt, weit; **vast·ly** gewaltig, weitaus

**vat** (großes) Fass, Bottich *m*

**VAT** *abbr of* ***value-added tax*** ECON Mehrwertsteuer *f*

**vau·de·ville** Varietee(theater) *n*

**vault**[1] ARCH Gewölbe *n*; *a. pl* Stahlkammer *f*, Tresorraum *m*; (Keller)Gewölbe *n*; Gruft *f*

**vault**[2] **1. ~** (***over***) springen über (*acc*) **2.** *esp* SPORT Sprung *m*

**vault·ing| horse** *gymnastics*: Pferd *n*; **~ pole** SPORT Sprungstab *m*

**VCR** *abbr of* ***video cassette recorder*** Videorekorder *m*, Videogerät *n*

**veal** GASTR Kalbfleisch *n*; ***~ chop*** Kalbskotelett *n*; ***~ cutlet*** Kalbsschnitzel *n*; ***roast ~*** Kalbsbraten *m*

**veer** (sich) drehen; MOT ausscheren; ***~ to the right*** das Steuer nach rechts reißen

**veg·e·ta·ble 1.** *mst pl* Gemüse *n* **2.** Gemüse…; Pflanzen…

**veg·e·tar·i·an 1.** Vegetarier(in) **2.** vegetarisch

**veg·e·tate** (dahin)vegetieren

**veg·e·ta·tion** Vegetation *f*

**ve·he·mence** Vehemenz *f*, Heftigkeit *f*; **ve·he·ment** vehement, heftig

**ve·hi·cle** Fahrzeug *n*; *fig* Medium *n*

**veil 1.** Schleier *m* **2.** verschleiern (*a. fig*)

**vein** ANAT Vene *f*, Ader *f* (*a.* BOT, GEOL, *fig*); *fig* (*Charakter*)Zug *m*; Stimmung *f*

**ve·loc·i·ty** TECH Geschwindigkeit *f*

**ve·lour(s)** Velours *m*

**vel·vet** Samt *m*; **vel·vet·y** samtig

**vend·er** → ***vendor***

**vend·ing ma·chine** (Verkaufs-, Waren)-Automat *m*

**vend·or** (*Straßen*)Händler(in), (*Zeitungs- etc*)Verkäufer(in)

**ve·neer 1.** Furnier *n*; *fig* Fassade *f* **2.** furnieren

**ven·e·ra·ble** ehrwürdig

**ven·e·rate** verehren

**ven·e·ra·tion** Verehrung *f*

**ve·ne·re·al dis·ease** MED Geschlechtskrankheit *f*

**Ve·ne·tian 1.** Venezianer(in) **2.** venezianisch; **~ blind** (Stab)Jalousie *f*

**ven·geance** Rache *f*; ***take ~ on*** sich rächen an (*dat*); ***with a ~*** mächtig, F wie verrückt

**ve·ni·al** entschuldbar, verzeihlich; REL lässlich

**ven·i·son** GASTR Wildbret *n*

**ven·om** ZO Gift *n*, *fig a.* Gehässigkeit *f*

**ven·om·ous** giftig, *fig a.* gehässig

**ve·nous** MED venös

**vent** **1.** *v/t s-m Zorn etc* Luft machen, *s-e Wut etc* auslassen, abreagieren (***on*** an *dat*); **2.** Schlitz *m* (*in a coat etc*); TECH (Abzugs)Öffnung *f*; ***give ~ to*** *s-m Ärger etc* Luft machen

**ven·ti·late** (be)lüften; *fig* äußern

**ven·ti·la·tion** (Be)Lüftung *f*, Ventilation *f*

**ven·ti·la·tor** Ventilator *m*

**ven·tri·cle** ANAT Herzkammer *f*

**ven·tril·o·quist** Bauchredner(in)

**ven·ture** **1.** *esp* ECON Wagnis *n*, Risiko *n*; ECON Unternehmen *n*; → ***joint venture*** **2.** sich wagen; riskieren

**ven·ue** SPORT Austragungsort *m*

**verb** LING Verb *n*, Zeitwort *n*

**verb·al** mündlich; wörtlich, Wort…

**ver·dict** JUR (Urteils)Spruch *m*; *fig* Urteil *n*; ***bring in*** *or* ***return a ~ of*** (***not***) ***guilty*** JUR auf (nicht) schuldig erkennen

**ver·di·gris** Grünspan *m*

**verge** **1.** Rand *m* (*a. fig*); ***be on the ~ of*** kurz vor (*dat*) stehen; ***be on the ~ of despair*** (***tears***) der Verzweiflung (den Tränen) nahe sein **2.** ***~ on*** *fig* grenzen an (*acc*)

**ver·i·fy** bestätigen; nachweisen; (über-) prüfen

**ver·i·ta·ble** wahr

**ver·mi·cel·li** Fadennudeln *pl*

**ver·mi·form ap·pen·dix** ANAT Wurmfortsatz *m*, Blinddarm *m*

**ver·mil·i·on** **1.** zinnoberrot **2.** Zinnoberrot *n*

**ver·min** Ungeziefer *n*; Schädlinge *pl*; *fig* Gesindel *n*, Pack *n*

**ver·min·ous** voller Ungeziefer

**ver·nac·u·lar** Dialekt *m*, Mundart *f*; ***in the ~*** im Volksmund

**ver·sa·tile** vielseitig; vielseitig verwendbar

**verse** Versdichtung *f*; Vers *m*; Strophe *f*

**versed**: ***be*** (***well***) ***~ in*** beschlagen *or* bewandert sein in (*dat*)

**ver·sion** Version *f*; TECH Ausführung *f*; Darstellung *f* (*of an event*); Fassung *f* (*of a film etc*); Übersetzung *f*

**ver·sus** (*abbr* **v., vs.**) SPORT, JUR gegen

**ver·te·bra** ANAT Wirbel *m*

**ver·te·brate** ZO Wirbeltier *n*

**ver·ti·cal** vertikal, senkrecht

**ver·ti·go** MED Schwindel *m*; ***suffer from ~*** an *or* unter Schwindel leiden

**verve** Elan *m*, Schwung *m*

**ver·y** **1.** *adv* sehr; aller…; ***I ~ much hope that*** ich hoffe sehr, dass; ***the ~ best*** das Allerbeste; ***for the ~ last time*** zum allerletzten Mal **2.** *adj* ***the ~*** genau der *or* die *or* das; ***the ~ opposite*** genau das Gegenteil; ***the ~ thing*** genau das Richtige; ***the ~ thought of*** schon der *or* der bloße Gedanke an (*acc*)

**ves·i·cle** MED Bläschen *n*

**ves·sel** ANAT, BOT Gefäß *n*; Schiff *n*

**vest** Weste *f*; *Br* Unterhemd *n*; *kugelsichere* Weste

**ves·ti·bule** (Vor)Halle *f*

**ves·tige** *fig* Spur *f*

**vest·ment** Ornat *n*, Gewand *n*, Robe *f*

**ves·try** REL Sakristei *f*

**vet**[1] F Tierarzt *m*, Tierärztin *f*

**vet**[2] *esp Br* F überprüfen

**vet**[3] MIL F Veteran *m*

**vet·e·ran** **1.** MIL Veteran *m* (*a. fig*) **2.** altgedient; erfahren; **~ car** *Br* Oldtimer *m* (*built before 1905*)

**vet·e·ri·nar·i·an** Tierarzt *m*, -ärztin *f*

**vet·e·ri·na·ry** tierärztlich; **~ sur·geon** *Br* Tierarzt *m*, Tierärztin *f*

**ve·to** **1.** Veto *n* **2.** sein Veto einlegen gegen

**vexed ques·tion** leidige Frage

**vi·a** über (*acc*), via

**vi·a·duct** Viadukt *m*, *n*

**vi·al** (*esp* Arznei)Fläschchen *n*

**vibes** F Atmosphäre *f*

**vi·brant** kräftig (*color etc*); pulsierend (*city etc*)

**vi·brate** *v/i* vibrieren, zittern; flimmern; *fig* pulsieren; *v/t* in Schwingungen versetzen; **vi·bra·tion** Vibrieren *n*, Zittern *n*; *pl* F Atmosphäre *f*

**vic·ar** REL Pfarrer *m*

**vic·ar·age** Pfarrhaus *n*

**vice**[1] Laster *n*

**vice**[2] *esp Br* Schraubstock *m*

**vice…** Vize…, stellvertretend

**vice squad** Sittendezernat *n*, Sittenpolizei *f*; Rauschgiftdezernat *n*

**vi·ce ver·sa**: ***and ~*** und umgekehrt
**vi·cin·i·ty** Nähe *f*; Nachbarschaft *f*
**vi·cious** brutal; bösartig
**vi·cis·si·tudes** *das* Auf und Ab, *die* Wechselfälle *pl*
**vic·tim** Opfer *n*
**vic·tim·ize** (ungerechterweise) bestrafen, ungerecht behandeln; schikanieren
**vic·to·ri·ous** siegreich
**vic·to·ry** Sieg *m*
**vid·e·o** **1.** Video *n*; Videokassette *f*; F Videoband *n*; *esp Br* Videorekorder *m*, Videogerät *n*; ***on ~*** auf Video **2.** Video... **3.** *esp Br* auf Video aufnehmen, aufzeichnen; **~ cam·e·ra** Videokamera *f*; **~ cas·sette** Videokassette *f*; **~ cassette re·cord·er** → ***video recorder***; **~ clip** Videoclip *m*
**vid·eo·disk** Bildplatte *f*
**vid·e·o| game** Videospiel *n*; **~ li·brary** Videothek *f*; **~ re·cord·er** Videorekorder *m*, Videogerät *n*; **~ re·cord·ing** Videoaufnahme *f*, Videoaufzeichnung *f*; **~ shop** *Br*, **~ store** Videothek *f*
**vid·e·o·tape** **1.** Videokassette *f*; Videoband *n* **2.** auf Video aufnehmen, aufzeichnen
**vid·e·o·text** Bildschirmtext *m*
**vie** wetteifern (***with*** mit; ***for*** um)
**Vi·en·nese** **1.** Wiener(in) **2.** wienerisch, Wiener...
**view** **1.** Sicht *f* (***of*** auf *acc*); Aussicht *f*, (Aus)Blick *m* (***of*** auf *acc*); Ansicht *f* (*a.* PHOT), Meinung *f* (***about, on*** über *acc*); *fig* Überblick *m* (***of*** über *acc*); ***a room with a ~*** ein Zimmer mit schöner Aussicht; ***be on ~*** ausgestellt *or* zu besichtigen sein; ***be hidden from ~*** nicht zu sehen sein; ***come into ~*** in Sicht kommen; ***in full ~ of*** direkt vor *j-s* Augen; ***in ~ of*** *fig* angesichts (*gen*); ***in my ~*** m-r Ansicht nach; ***keep in ~*** et. im Auge behalten; ***with a ~ to*** *fig* mit Blick auf (*acc*) **2.** *v/t Haus etc* besichtigen; *fig* betrachten (***as*** als); *v/i* fernsehen
**view·da·ta** Bildschirmtext *m*
**view·er** Fernsehzuschauer(in), F Fernseher(in); TECH (*Dia*)Betrachter *m*
**view·find·er** PHOT Sucher *m*
**view·point** Gesichts-, Standpunkt *m*
**vig·il** (Nacht)Wache *f*
**vig·i·lance** Wachsamkeit *f*
**vig·i·lant** wachsam
**vig·or·ous** energisch; kräftig
**vig·o(u)r** Energie *f*
**Vi·king** **1.** Wikinger *m* **2.** Wikinger...
**vile** gemein, niederträchtig; F scheußlich
**vil·lage** Dorf *n*; **~ green** Dorfanger *m*
**vil·lag·er** Dorfbewohner(in)
**vil·lain** Bösewicht *m*, Schurke *m*; *Br* F Ganove *m*
**vin·di·cate** *j-n* rehabilitieren; *et.* rechtfertigen; *et.* Bestätigen
**vin·dic·tive** rachsüchtig, nachtragend
**vine** BOT (Wein)Rebe *f*; Kletterpflanze *f*
**vin·e·gar** Essig *m*
**vine·grow·er** Winzer *m*
**vine·yard** Weinberg *m*
**vin·tage** **1.** Weinernte *f*, Weinlese *f*; GASTR Jahrgang *m* **2.** GASTR Jahrgangs...; *fig* hervorragend, glänzend; ***a 1999 ~*** ein 1999er Jahrgang *or* Wein
**vin·tage car** *esp Br* Oldtimer *m* (*built between 1919 and 1930*)
**vi·o·la** MUS Bratsche *f*
**vi·o·late** *Vertrag etc* verletzen, *a. Versprechen* brechen, *Gesetz etc* übertreten; *Ruhe etc* stören; *Grab etc* schänden; **vi·o·la·tion** Verletzung *f*, Bruch *m*, Übertretung *f*
**vi·o·lence** Gewalt *f*; Gewalttätigkeit *f*; Ausschreitungen *pl*; Heftigkeit *f*
**vi·o·lent** gewalttätig; gewaltsam; heftig
**vi·o·let** **1.** BOT Veilchen *n* **2.** violett
**vi·o·lin** MUS Geige *f*, Violine *f*
**vi·o·lin·ist** Geiger(in), Violinist(in)
**VIP** *abbr of* ***very important person*** VIP *f*
**vi·per** ZO Viper *f*, Natter *f*
**VIP lounge** AVIAT *etc* VIP-Lounge *f*; SPORT Ehrentribüne *f*
**vir·gin** **1.** Jungfrau *f* **2.** jungfräulich, unberührt (*both a. fig*)
**Vir·go** ASTR Jungfrau *f*; ***he*** (***she***) ***is*** (***a***) ***~*** er (sie) ist Jungfrau
**vir·ile** männlich; potent
**vi·ril·i·ty** Männlichkeit *f*; Potenz *f*
**vir·tu·al** eigentlich, praktisch
**vir·tu·al·ly** praktisch, so gut wie
**vir·tu·al re·al·i·ty** IT virtuelle Realität
**vir·tue** Tugend *f*; Vorzug *m*, Vorteil *m*; ***by*** *or* ***in ~ of*** aufgrund (*gen*), kraft (*gen*); ***make a ~ of necessity*** aus der Not e-e Tugend machen
**vir·tu·ous** tugendhaft
**vir·u·lent** MED (akut und) bösartig;

schnell wirkend (*poison*); *fig* bösartig, gehässig
**vi·rus** MED Virus *n*, *m*
**vi·sa** Visum *n*, Sichtvermerk *m*
**vis·cose** Viskose *f*
**vis·cous** dickflüssig, zähflüssig
**vise** TECH Schraubstock *m*
**vis·i·bil·i·ty** Sicht *f*, Sichtverhältnisse *pl*, Sichtweite *f*
**vis·i·ble** sichtbar; (er)sichtlich
**vi·sion** Sehkraft *f*; Weitblick *m*; Vision *f*
**vi·sion·a·ry 1.** weitblickend; eingebildet, unwirklich **2.** Fantast(in), Träumer(in); Seher(in)
**vis·it 1.** *v/t j-n* besuchen, *Schloss etc a.* besichtigen; *et.* inspizieren; *v/i*: ***be ~ing*** auf Besuch sein (***with*** bei) **2.** Besuch *m*, Besichtigung *f* (***to*** *gen*); Plauderei *f*; ***for*** *or* ***on a ~*** auf Besuch; ***have a ~ from*** Besuch haben von; ***pay a ~ to*** *j-n* besuchen, *j-m* e-n Besuch abstatten; *Arzt* aufsuchen
**vis·it·ing hours** MED Besuchszeit *f*
**vis·it·or** Besucher(in), Gast *m*
**vi·sor** Visier *n*; Schirm *m*; MOT (*Sonnen-*)Blende *f*
**vis·u·al** Seh…; visuell; **~ aids** PED Anschauungsmaterial *n*, Lehrmittel *pl*; **~ dis·play u·nit** IT Bildschirmgerät *n*, Datensichtgerät *n*; **~ in·struc·tion** PED Anschauungsunterricht *m*
**vis·u·al·ize** sich *et.* vorstellen
**vi·tal** vital, Lebens…; lebenswichtig; unbedingt notwendig; ***of ~ importance*** von größter Wichtigkeit
**vi·tal·i·ty** Vitalität *f*
**vit·a·min** Vitamin *n*; **~ de·fi·cien·cy** Vitaminmangel *m*
**vit·re·ous** Glas…
**vi·va·cious** lebhaft, temperamentvoll
**viv·id** hell (*light*); kräftig, leuchtend (*color*); anschaulich (*description*); lebhaft (*imagination*)
**vix·en** ZO Füchsin *f*
**V-neck** V-Ausschnitt *m*
**V-necked** mit V-Ausschnitt
**vo·cab·u·la·ry** Vokabular *n*, Wortschatz *m*; Wörterverzeichnis *n*
**vo·cal** Stimm…; F lautstark; MUS Vokal…, Gesang…; **~ cords** ANAT Stimmbänder *pl*
**vo·cal·ist** Sänger(in)
**vo·ca·tion** Begabung *f* (***for*** für); Berufung *f*
**vo·ca·tion·al** Berufs…; **~ ed·u·ca·tion** Berufsausbildung *f*; **~ guid·ance** Berufsberatung *f*; **~ train·ing** Berufsausbildung *f*
**vogue** Mode *f*; ***be in ~*** Mode sein
**voice 1.** Stimme *f*; ***active ~*** LING Aktiv *n*; ***passive ~*** LING Passiv *n* **2.** zum Ausdruck bringen; LING (stimmhaft) aussprechen; **voiced** LING stimmhaft; **voice·less** LING stimmlos
**void 1.** leer; JUR ungültig; ***~ of*** ohne **2.** (Gefühl *n* der) Leere *f*
**vol** *abbr of* ***volume*** Bd., Band *m*
**vol·a·tile** cholerisch (*person*); explosiv (*situation etc*); CHEM flüchtig
**vol·ca·no** Vulkan *m*
**vol·ley 1.** Salve *f*; (*Geschoss- etc*)Hagel *m* (*a. fig*); *tennis*: Volley *m*, Flugball *m*; *soccer*: Volleyschuss *m* **2.** *Ball* volley schießen
**vol·ley·ball** SPORT Volleyball *m*
**volt** ELECTR Volt *n*
**volt·age** ELECTR Spannung *f*
**vol·u·ble** redselig; wortreich
**vol·ume** Band *m*; Volumen *n*, Rauminhalt *m*; Umfang *m*, große Menge; Lautstärke *f*
**vo·lu·mi·nous** bauschig (*dress etc*); geräumig; umfangreich (*notes etc*)
**vol·un·ta·ry** freiwillig; unbezahlt
**vol·un·teer 1.** *v/i* sich freiwillig melden (***for*** zu) (*a.* MIL); *v/t Hilfe etc* anbieten; *et.* von sich aus sagen, F herausrücken mit **2.** Freiwillige *m, f*; freiwilliger Helfer
**vo·lup·tu·ous** sinnlich (*lips etc*); aufreizend (*gesture etc*); üppig (*body etc*); kurvenreich (*woman*)
**vom·it 1.** *v/t* erbrechen; *v/i* (sich er)brechen, sich übergeben **2.** Erbrochene *n*
**vo·ra·cious** unersättlich (*appetite etc*)
**vote 1.** Abstimmung *f* (***about, on*** über *acc*); (Wahl)Stimme *f*; Stimmzettel *m*; *a. pl* Wahlrecht *n*; ***~ of no confidence*** Misstrauensvotum *n*; ***take a ~ on s.th.*** über et. abstimmen **2.** *v/i* wählen; ***~ for*** (***against***) stimmen für (gegen); ***~ on*** abstimmen über (*acc*); *v/t* wählen; *et.* bewilligen; ***~ out of office*** abwählen
**vot·er** Wähler(in)
**vot·ing booth** Wahlkabine *f*
**vouch**: ***~ for*** (sich ver)bürgen für
**vouch·er** Gutschein *m*, Kupon *m*

**vow 1.** Gelöbnis *n*; Gelübde *n*; ***take a ~, make a ~*** ein Gelöbnis *or* Gelübde ablegen **2.** geloben, schwören (***to do*** zu tun)
**vow·el** LING Vokal *m*, Selbstlaut *m*
**voy·age** (See)Reise *f*
**vul·gar** vulgär, ordinär; geschmacklos
**vul·ne·ra·ble** *fig* verletzbar, verwundbar; verletzlich; anfällig (***to*** für)
**vul·ture** ZO Geier *m*

# W

**W, w** W, w *n*
**wad** (*Watte- etc*)Bausch *m*; Bündel *n*; (*Papier- etc*)Knäuel *m, n*
**wad·ding** Einlage *f*, Füllmaterial *n*
**wad·dle** watscheln
**wade** *v/i* waten; ***~ through*** waten durch; F sich durchkämpfen durch, *et.* durchackern; *v/t* durchwaten
**wa·fer** (*esp* Eis)Waffel *f*; Oblate *f*; REL Hostie *f*
**waf·fle**[1] Waffel *f*
**waf·fle**[2] *Br* F schwafeln
**waft** *v/i* ziehen (*smell etc*); *v/t* wehen
**wag 1.** wedeln (mit) **2.** ***with a ~ of its tail*** schwanzwedelnd
**wage**[1] *mst pl* (Arbeits)Lohn *m*
**wage**[2]: ***~ (a) war against*** *or* ***on*** MIL Krieg führen gegen; *fig* e-n Feldzug führen gegen
**wage| earn·er** Lohnempfänger(in); Verdiener(in); **~ freeze** Lohnstopp *m*; **~ ne·go·ti·a·tions** Tarifverhandlungen *pl*
**wa·ger** Wette *f*
**wage rise** Lohnerhöhung *f*
**wag·gle** F wackeln (mit)
**wag·gon** *Br* → **wag·on** Fuhrwerk *n*, Wagen *m*; *Br* RAIL (offener) Güterwagen; (*Tee- etc*)Wagen *m*
**wag·tail** ZO Bachstelze *f*
**wail 1.** jammern; heulen (*siren, wind*) **2.** Jammern *n*; Heulen *n*
**wain·scot** (Wand)Täfelung *f*
**waist** Taille *f*
**waist·coat** *esp Br* Weste *f*
**waist·line** Taille *f*
**wait 1.** *v/i* warten (***for, on*** auf *acc*); ***~ for s.o.*** *a.* j-n erwarten; ***keep s.o. ~ing*** j-n warten lassen; ***~ and see!*** warte es ab!; ***~ on s.o.*** j-n bedienen; ***~ up*** F aufbleiben (***for*** wegen); *v/t*: ***~ one's chance*** auf e-e günstige Gelegenheit warten (***to do*** zu tun); ***~ one's turn*** warten, bis man an der Reihe ist **2.** Wartezeit *f*; ***have a long ~*** lange warten müssen; ***lie in ~ for s.o.*** j-m auflauern
**wait·er** Kellner *m*, Ober *m*; ***~, the check*** (*Br* ***bill***), ***please!*** (Herr) Ober, bitte zahlen!
**wait·ing** Warten *n*; ***no ~*** MOT Halt(e)verbot *n*; **~ list** Warteliste *f*; **~ room** MED *etc* Wartezimmer *n*; RAIL Wartesaal *m*
**wait·ress** Kellnerin *f*, Bedienung *f*; ***~, the check*** (*Br* ***bill***), ***please!*** Fräulein, bitte zahlen!
**wake**[1] *v/i a.* ***~ up*** aufwachen, wach werden; *v/t a.* ***~ up*** (auf)wecken; *fig* wachrufen, wecken
**wake**[2] MAR Kielwasser *n*; ***follow in the ~ of*** *fig* folgen auf (*acc*)
**wake·ful** schlaflos
**wak·en** *v/i a.* ***~ up*** aufwachen, wach werden; *v/t a.* ***~ up*** (auf)wecken
**walk 1.** *v/i* (zu Fuß) gehen, laufen; spazieren gehen; wandern; *v/t Strecke* gehen, laufen; *j-n* bringen (***to*** zu; ***home*** nach Hause); *Hund* ausführen; *Pferd* im Schritt gehen lassen; ***~ away*** → ***walk off***; ***~ in*** hineingehen, hereinkommen; ***~ off*** fort-, weggehen; ***~ off with*** F abhauen mit; F *Preis etc* locker gewinnen; ***~ out*** hinausgehen; (unter Protest) den Saal *etc* verlassen; ECON streiken, in (den) Streik treten; ***~ out on s.o.*** F j-n verlassen, j-n im Stich lassen; ***~ up*** hinaufgehen, heraufkommen; ***~ up to s.o.*** auf j-n zugehen; ***~ up!*** treten Sie näher! **2.** Spaziergang *m*; Wanderung *f*; Spazier-, Wanderweg *m*; ***go for a ~, take a ~*** e-n Spaziergang machen, spazieren gehen; ***an hour's ~*** e-e Stunde Fußweg *or* zu Fuß; ***from all ~s of life*** *Leute* aus allen Berufen *or* Schichten
**walk·a·way** F Spaziergang *m*, leichter Sieg

**walk·er** Spaziergänger(in); Wanderer *m*, Wand(r)erin *f*; SPORT Geher(in); ***be a good ~*** gut zu Fuß sein
**walk·ie-talk·ie** Walkie-Talkie *n*, tragbares Funksprechgerät
**walk·ing** Gehen *n*, Laufen *n*; Spazierengehen *n*; Wandern *n*; **~ pa·pers**: ***get one's ~*** F den Laufpass bekommen; **~ shoes** Wanderschuhe *pl*; **~ stick** Spazierstock *m*; **~ tour** Wanderung *f*
**Walk·man**® Walkman® *m*
**walk·out** Auszug *m* (***by, of*** *e-r Delegation etc*); ECON Ausstand *m*, Streik *m*
**walk·over** → ***walkaway***
**walk-up** F (Miets)Haus *n* ohne Fahrstuhl; Wohnung *f or* Büro *n etc* in e-m Haus ohne Fahrstuhl
**wall 1.** Wand *f*; Mauer *f* **2.** *a.* ***~ in*** mit e-r Mauer umgeben; ***~ up*** zumauern
**wall cal·en·dar** Wandkalender *m*
**wall·chart** Wandkarte *f*
**wal·let** Brieftasche *f*
**wall·flow·er** F Mauerblümchen *n*
**wal·lop** F *j-m* ein Ding verpassen; SPORT *j-n* erledigen, vernichten (***at*** in *dat*)
**wal·low** sich wälzen; *fig* schwelgen, sich baden (***in*** in *dat*)
**wall·pa·per 1.** Tapete *f* **2.** tapezieren
**wall-to-wall**: ***~ carpet(ing)*** Spannteppich *m*, Teppichboden *m*
**wal·nut** BOT Walnuss(baum *m*) *f*
**wal·rus** ZO Walross *n*
**waltz 1.** Walzer *m* **2.** Walzer tanzen
**wand** (*Zauber*)Stab *m*
**wan·der** (herum)wandern, herumlaufen, umherstreifen; *fig* abschweifen; fantasieren
**wane 1.** ASTR abnehmen; *fig* schwinden **2.** ***be on the ~*** *fig* im Schwinden begriffen sein
**wan·gle** F deichseln, hinkriegen; ***~ s.th. out of s.o.*** j-m et. abluchsen; ***~ one's way out of*** sich herauswinden aus
**want 1.** *v/t et.* wollen; *j-n* brauchen; *j-n* sprechen wollen; F *et.* brauchen, nötig haben; ***be ~ed*** (*polizeilich*) gesucht werden (***for*** wegen); *v/i* wollen; ***I don't ~ to*** ich will nicht; ***he does not ~ for anything*** es fehlt ihm an nichts **2.** Mangel *m* (***of*** an *dat*); Bedürfnis *n*, Wunsch *m*; Not *f*; **~ ad** Kleinanzeige *f*
**want·ed** (*polizeilich*) gesucht
**wan·ton** mutwillig
**war** Krieg *m* (*a. fig*); *fig* Kampf *m* (***against*** gegen)
**war·ble** zo trillern
**ward 1.** MED Station *f*; *Br* POL Stadtbezirk *m*; JUR Mündel *n* **2.** ***~ off*** *Schlag etc* abwehren, *Gefahr etc* abwenden
**war·den** Aufseher(in); Heimleiter(in); (Gefängnis)Direktor(in)
**ward·er** *Br* Aufsichtsbeamte *m*, -beamtin *f*
**war·drobe** Kleiderschrank *m*; Garderobe *f*
**ware·house** Lager(haus) *n*
**war·fare** Krieg *m*; Kriegführung *f*
**war·head** MIL Spreng-, Gefechtskopf *m*
**war·like** kriegerisch; Kriegs…
**warm 1.** *adj* warm, *fig a.* herzlich; ***I am ~, I feel ~*** mir ist warm **2.** *v/t a.* ***~ up*** wärmen, sich *die Hände etc* wärmen; *Motor* warm laufen lassen; *v/i a.* ***~ up*** warm *or* wärmer werden, sich erwärmen;
**warmth** Wärme *f*
**warm-up** SPORT Aufwärmen *n*
**warn** warnen (***against, of*** vor *dat*); *j-n* verständigen
**warn·ing** Warnung *f* (***of*** vor *dat*); Verwarnung *f*; ***without ~*** ohne Vorwarnung; **~ sig·nal** Warnsignal *n*
**warp** sich verziehen *or* werfen
**war·rant 1.** JUR (Durchsuchungs-, Haft-*etc*)Befehl *m* **2.** *et.* rechtfertigen; **~ of ar·rest** JUR Haftbefehl *m*
**war·ran·ty** ECON Garantie(erklärung) *f*; ***it's still under ~*** darauf ist noch Garantie
**war·ri·or** Krieger *m*
**war·ship** Kriegsschiff *n*
**wart** MED Warze *f*
**war·y** vorsichtig
**was** *ich, er, sie, es* war; *passive*: *ich, er, sie, es* wurde
**wash 1.** *v/t* waschen, sich *die Hände etc* waschen; *v/i* sich waschen; sich *gut etc* waschen (lassen); ***~ up*** *v/i Br* abwaschen, (das) Geschirr spülen; *v/t* anschwemmen, anspülen; ***~ one's dirty linen*** schmutzige Wäsche waschen **2.** Wäsche *f*; MOT Waschanlage *f*, Waschstraße *f*; ***be in the ~*** in der Wäsche sein; ***give s.th. a ~*** et. waschen; ***have a ~*** sich waschen
**wash·a·ble** (ab)waschbar
**wash-and-wear** bügelfrei; pflegeleicht
**wash·ba·sin** *Br*, **wash·bowl** Waschbecken *n*

W

**wash·cloth** Waschlappen *m*
**wash·er** Waschmaschine *f*; TECH Unterlegscheibe *f*
**wash·ing** **1.** Wäsche *f* **2.** Wasch…
**wash·ing| ma·chine** Waschmaschine *f*; **~ pow·der** Waschpulver *n*, -mittel *n*
**washing-up** *Br* Abwasch *m*; ***do the ~*** den Abwasch machen
**wash·room** Toilette *f*
**wasp** ZO Wespe *f*
**waste** **1.** Verschwendung *f*; Abfall *m*; Müll *m*; ***~ of time*** Zeitverschwendung *f*; ***hazardous ~, special toxic ~*** Sondermüll *m*; ***special ~ dump*** Sondermülldeponie *f* **2.** *v/t* verschwenden, vergeuden; *j-n* auszehren; *v/i* ***~ away*** immer schwächer werden (*person*) **3.** überschüssig; Abfall…; brachliegend, öde; ***lay ~*** verwüsten
**waste dis·pos·al** Abfall-, Müllbeseitigung *f*; Entsorgung *f*; **~ site** Deponie *f*
**waste·ful** verschwenderisch
**waste| gas** Abgas *n*; **~ pa·per** Abfallpapier *n*; Altpapier *n*
**waste·pa·per bas·ket** Papierkorb *m*
**waste pipe** Abflussrohr *n*
**watch** **1.** *v/i* zuschauen; ***~ for*** warten auf (*acc*); ***~ out!*** pass auf!, Vorsicht!; ***~ out for*** Ausschau halten nach; sich in Acht nehmen vor (*dat*); *v/t* beobachten; zuschauen bei, sich *et.* ansehen; → ***television*** **2.** (*Armband-*, *Taschen*)Uhr *f*; Wache *f*; ***keep ~*** Wache halten, wachen (***over*** über *acc*); ***be on the ~ for*** Ausschau halten nach; auf der Hut sein vor (*dat*); ***keep (a) careful*** *or* ***close ~ on*** genau beobachten, scharf im Auge behalten
**watch·dog** Wachhund *m*
**watch·ful** wachsam
**watch·mak·er** Uhrmacher(in)
**watch·man** Wachmann *m*, Wächter *m*
**watch·tow·er** Wach(t)turm *m*
**wa·ter** **1.** Wasser *n* **2.** *v/t Blumen* gießen, *Rasen etc* sprengen; *Vieh* tränken; ***~ down*** verdünnen, verwässern; *fig* abschwächen; *v/i* tränen (*eyes*); ***make s.o.'s mouth ~*** j-m den Mund wässerig machen
**wa·ter bird** ZO Wasservogel *m*
**wa·ter·col·o(u)r** Wasser-, Aquarellfarbe *f*; Aquarellmalerei *f*; Aquarell *n*
**wa·ter·course** Wasserlauf *m*
**wa·ter·cress** BOT Brunnenkresse *f*
**wa·ter·fall** Wasserfall *m*
**wa·ter·front** Hafenviertel *n*; ***along the ~*** am Wasser entlang
**wa·ter·hole** Wasserloch *n*
**wa·ter·ing can** Gießkanne *f*
**wa·ter jump** SPORT Wassergraben *m*
**wa·ter lev·el** Wasserstand *m*
**wa·ter lil·y** BOT Seerose *f*
**wa·ter·mark** Wasserzeichen *n*
**wa·ter·mel·on** BOT Wassermelone *f*
**wa·ter| pol·lu·tion** Wasserverschmutzung *f*; **~ po·lo** SPORT Wasserball(spiel *n*) *m*
**wa·ter·proof** **1.** wasserdicht **2.** *Br* Regenmantel *m* **3.** imprägnieren
**wa·ters** Gewässer *pl*; Wasser *pl*
**wa·ter·shed** GEOGR Wasserscheide *f*; *fig* Wendepunkt *m*
**wa·ter·side** Ufer *n*
**wa·ter ski·ing** SPORT Wasserskilaufen *n*
**wa·ter·tight** wasserdicht, *fig a.* hieb- und stichfest
**wa·ter·way** Wasserstraße *f*
**wa·ter·works** Wasserwerk *n*; ***turn on the ~*** F zu heulen anfangen
**wa·ter·y** wäss(e)rig
**watt** ELECTR Watt *n*
**wave** **1.** *v/t* schwenken; winken mit; *Haar* wellen, in Wellen legen; ***~ one's hand*** winken; ***~ s.o. aside*** j-n beiseitewinken; *v/i* winken; wehen (*flag etc*); sich wellen (*hair*); ***~ at s.o., ~ to s.o.*** j-m zuwinken **2.** Welle *f* (*a. fig*); Winken *n*
**wave·length** PHYS Wellenlänge *f* (*a. fig*)
**wa·ver** flackern; schwanken
**wav·y** wellig, gewellt
**wax**[1] **1.** Wachs *n*; (*Ohren*)Schmalz *n* **2.** wachsen; bohnern
**wax**[2] ASTR zunehmen
**wax·en** wächsern
**wax·works** Wachsfigurenkabinett *n*
**wax·y** wächsern
**way** **1.** Weg *m*; Richtung *f*, Seite *f*; Entfernung *f*, Strecke *f*; Art *f*, Weise *f*; ***~s and means*** Mittel und Wege *pl*; ***~ back*** Rückweg *m*, Rückfahrt *f*; ***~ home*** Heimweg *m*; ***~ in*** Eingang *m*; ***~ out*** Ausgang *m*; ***be on the ~ to, be on one's ~ to*** unterwegs sein nach; ***by ~ of*** über (*acc*), via; *esp Br* statt; ***by the ~*** übrigens; ***give ~*** nachgeben; *Br* MOT die Vorfahrt lassen; ***in a ~*** in gewisser Hinsicht; ***in no ~*** in keiner Weise;

***lead the ~*** vorangehen; ***let s.o. have his*** (***own***) ~ j-m s-n Willen lassen; ***lose one's ~*** sich verlaufen *or* verirren; ***make ~*** Platz machen (***for*** für); ***no ~!*** F kommt überhaupt nicht in Frage!; ***out of the ~*** ungewöhnlich; ***this ~*** hierher; hier entlang **2.** *adv* weit
**way·bill** ECON Frachtbrief *m*
**way·lay** *j-m* auflauern; *j-n* abfangen, abpassen
**way·ward** eigensinnig, launisch
**we** wir *pl*
**weak** schwach (***at, in*** in *dat*), GASTR *a.* dünn; **weak·en** *v/t* schwächen (*a. fig*); *v/i* schwächer werden; *fig* nachgeben; **weak·ling** Schwächling *m*, F Schlappschwanz *n*; **weak·ness** Schwäche *f*
**weal** Striemen *m*
**wealth** Reichtum *m*; *fig* Fülle *f* (***of*** von)
**wealth·y** reich
**wean** entwöhnen; ***~ s.o. from*** *or* ***off s.th.*** j-m et. abgewöhnen
**weap·on** Waffe *f* (*a. fig*)
**wear 1.** *v/t Bart, Brille, Schmuck etc* tragen, *Mantel etc a.* anhaben, *Hut etc a.* aufhaben; abnutzen, abtragen; ***~ an angry expression*** verärgert dreinschauen; *v/i* sich abnutzen, verschleißen; sich gut *etc* halten; ***s.th. to ~*** et. zum Anziehen; ***~ away*** (sich) abtragen *or* abschleifen; ***~ down*** (sich) abtreten (*stairs*), (sich) ablaufen (*heels*), (sich) abfahren (*tires*); abschleifen; *j-n* zermürben; ***~ off*** nachlassen (*pain etc*); ***~ on*** sich hinziehen (***all day*** über den ganzen Tag); ***~ out*** (sich) abnutzen *or* abtragen; *fig j-n* erschöpfen **2.** *often in cpds* Kleidung *f*; *a.* ***~ and tear*** Abnutzung *f*, Verschleiß *m*; ***the worse for ~*** abgenutzt, verschlissen; F lädiert
**wear·i·some** ermüdend; langweilig; lästig
**wear·y** erschöpft, müde; ermüdend, anstrengend; ***be ~ of s.th.*** F et. satthaben
**wea·sel** ZO Wiesel *n*
**weath·er 1.** Wetter *n*; Witterung *f* **2.** *v/t* dem Wetter aussetzen; *fig Krise etc* überstehen; *v/i* verwittern
**weath·er-beat·en** verwittert
**weath·er| chart** METEOR Wetterkarte *f*; **~ fore·cast** METEOR Wettervorhersage *f*; Wetterbericht *m*
**weath·er·man** *radio*, TV Wetteransager *m*
**weath·er·proof 1.** wetterfest **2.** wetterfest machen
**weath·er| re·port** METEOR Wetterbericht *m*; **~ sta·tion** METEOR Wetterwarte *f*; **~ vane** Wetterfahne *f*
**weave** weben; *Netz* spinnen; *Korb* flechten; ***~ one's way through*** sich schlängeln durch; **weav·er** Weber(in)
**web** Netz *n* (*a. fig*), Gewebe *n*; ZO Schwimmhaut *f*
**wed** heiraten
**Wed(s)** *abbr of* ***Wednesday*** Mi., Mittwoch *m*
**wed·ding 1.** Hochzeit *f* **2.** Hochzeits…, Braut…, Ehe…, Trau…
**wed·ding ring** Ehering *m*, Trauring *m*
**wedge 1.** Keil *m* **2.** verkeilen, mit e-m Keil festklemmen; ***~ in*** einkeilen, einzwängen
**Wednes·day** (*abbr* ***Wed, Weds***) Mittwoch *m*; ***on ~*** (am) Mittwoch; ***on ~s*** mittwochs
**wee**[1] F klein, winzig; ***a ~ bit*** ein (kleines) bisschen
**wee**[2] F **1.** Pipi machen **2.** ***do*** *or* ***have a ~*** Pipi machen
**weed 1.** Unkraut *n* **2.** jäten
**weed·kill·er** Unkrautvertilgungsmittel *n*
**weed·y** voll Unkraut; F schmächtig; F rückgratlos
**week** Woche *f*; ***~ after ~*** Woche um Woche; ***a ~ today, today ~*** heute in e-r Woche *or* in acht Tagen; ***every other ~*** jede zweite Woche; ***for ~s*** wochenlang; ***four times a ~*** viermal die Woche; ***in a ~('s time)*** in e-r Woche
**week·day** Wochentag *m*
**week·end** Wochenende *n*; ***on*** (*Br* ***at***) ***the ~*** am Wochenende; **week·end·er** Wochenendausflügler(in)
**week·ly 1.** Wochen…; wöchentlich **2.** Wochenblatt *n*, Wochen(zeit)schrift *f*, Wochenzeitung *f*
**weep** weinen (***for*** um *j-n*; ***over*** über *acc*); MED nässen
**weep·ing wil·low** BOT Trauerweide *f*
**weep·y** F weinerlich; rührselig
**wee-wee** F → ***wee***[2]
**weigh** *v/t* (ab)wiegen; *fig* abwägen (***against*** gegen); ***~ anchor*** MAR den Anker lichten; ***be ~ed down with*** *fig* niedergedrückt werden von; *v/i … Kilo etc* wiegen; ***~ on*** *fig* lasten auf (*dat*)

**weight 1.** Gewicht *n*; Last *f* (*a. fig*); *fig* Bedeutung *f*; ***gain ~, put on ~*** zunehmen; ***lose ~*** abnehmen **2.** beschweren
**weight·less** schwerelos
**weight·less·ness** Schwerelosigkeit *f*
**weight lift·er** SPORT Gewichtheber *m*
**weight lift·ing** SPORT Gewichtheben *n*
**weight·y** schwer; *fig* schwerwiegend
**weir** Wehr *n*
**weird** unheimlich; F sonderbar, verrückt
**wel·come 1.** *int* ***~ back!, ~ home!*** willkommen zu Hause!; ***~ to England!*** willkommen in England! **2.** *v/t* begrüßen (*a. fig*), willkommen heißen **3.** *adj* willkommen; ***you are ~ to do it*** Sie können es gerne tun; ***you're ~!*** nichts zu danken!, keine Ursache!, bitte sehr! **4.** Empfang *m*, Willkommen *n*; ***outstay** or **overstay one's ~*** j-s Gastfreundschaft überstrapazieren *or* zu lange in Anspruch nehmen
**weld** TECH schweißen
**wel·fare** Wohl(ergehen) *n*; Sozialhilfe *f*; ***be on ~*** Sozalhilfe beziehen; **~ state** Wohlfahrtsstaat *m*; **~ work** Sozialarbeit *f*; **~ work·er** Sozialarbeiter(in)
**well**[1] **1.** *adv* gut; gründlich; ***as ~*** ebenso, auch; ***as ~ as ...*** sowohl ... als auch ...; nicht nur ..., sondern auch ...; ***very ~*** also gut, na gut; ***~ done!*** bravo!; → ***off** 1* **2.** *int* nun, also; ***~, ~!*** na so was! **3.** *adj* gesund; ***feel ~*** sich wohlfühlen
**well**[2] **1.** Brunnen *m*; (*Öl*)Quelle *f*; (*Aufzugs- etc*)Schacht *m* **2.** *a.* ***~ out*** quellen (***from*** aus); ***tears ~ed (up) in their eyes*** die Tränen stiegen ihnen in die Augen
**well-bal·anced** ausgeglichen (*person*); ausgewogen (*diet*)
**well-be·haved** artig, gut erzogen
**well·be·ing** Wohl(befinden) *n*
**well-dis·posed:** ***be ~ towards s.o.*** j-m wohlgesinnt sein
**well-done** GASTR durchgebraten
**well-earned** wohlverdient
**well-fed** gut genährt
**well-found·ed** (wohl) begründet
**well-in·formed** gut unterrichtet; gebildet
**well-known** (wohl) bekannt
**well-mean·ing** wohlmeinend, gut gemeint; **well-meant** gut gemeint
**well-off 1.** wohlhabend, vermögend, bessergestellt; ***be ~ for*** gut versorgt sein mit **2.** ***the ~*** die Wohlhabenden *pl*
**well-read** belesen
**well-timed** (zeitlich) günstig, im richtigen Augenblick
**well-to-do** wohlhabend, reich
**well-worn** abgetragen; *fig* abgedroschen
**Welsh 1.** walisisch **2.** LING Walisisch *n*; ***the ~*** die Waliser *pl*
**welt** Striemen *m*
**wel·ter** Wirrwarr *m*, Durcheinander *n*
**wel·ter·weight** SPORT Weltergewicht *n*; Weltergewichtler *m*
**were** *du* warst, *Sie* waren, *wir, sie* waren, *ihr* wart
**west 1.** West, Westen *m*; ***the West*** POL der Westen; die Weststaaten *pl* **2.** *adj* westlich, West... **3.** *adv* nach Westen, westwärts; **west·er·ly** West..., westlich; **west·ern 1.** westlich, West... **2.** Western *m*; **west·ward(s)** westlich, nach Westen
**wet 1.** nass, feucht **2.** Nässe *f* **3.** nass machen, anfeuchten
**weth·er** ZO Hammel *m*
**wet nurse** Amme *f*
**whack** (knallender) Schlag; F Anteil *m*
**whacked** F fertig, erledigt
**whack·ing 1.** *Br* F Mords... **2.** (Tracht *f*) Prügel *pl*
**whale** ZO Wal *m*
**wharf** Kai *m*
**what 1.** *pron* was; ***~ about ...?*** wie wärs mit ...?; ***~ for?*** wozu?; ***so ~?*** na und?; ***know ~'s ~*** F wissen, was Sache ist **2.** *adj* was für ein(e), welche(r, -s); alle, die; alles, was
**what·cha·ma·call·it** F → ***whatsit***
**what·ev·er 1.** *pron* was (auch immer); alles, was; egal, was **2.** *adj* welche(r, -s) ... auch (immer); ***no ... ~*** überhaupt kein(e) ...
**whats·it** F Dings(bums, -da) *m, f, n*
**what·so·ev·er** → ***whatever***
**wheat** BOT Weizen *m*
**whee·dle** beschwatzen; ***~ s.th. out of s.o.*** j-m et. abschwatzen
**wheel 1.** Rad *n*; MOT, MAR Steuer *n* **2.** schieben, rollen; kreisen; ***~ about, ~ (a)round*** herumfahren, herumwirbeln
**wheel·bar·row** Schubkarre(n *m*) *f*
**wheel·chair** Rollstuhl *m*
**wheel clamp** MOT Parkkralle *f*
**wheeled** mit Rädern; fahrbar; *in cpds*

...räd(e)rig
**wheeze** keuchen, pfeifend atmen
**whelp** zo Welpe *m*, Junge *n*
**when** wann; als; wenn; obwohl; ***since ~?*** seit wann?
**when·ev·er** wann auch (immer); jedes Mal, wenn
**where** wo; wohin; **~ ... (*from*)?** woher?; **~ ... (*to*)?** wohin?; **where·a·bouts 1.** *adv* wo etwa **2.** Verbleib *m*; Aufenthalt *m*, Aufenthaltsort *m*
**where·as** während, wohingegen
**where·by** wodurch, womit; wonach
**where·u·pon** worauf, woraufhin
**wher·ev·er** wo *or* wohin auch (immer); ganz gleich wo *or* wohin
**whet** *Messer etc* schärfen; *fig Appetit* anregen
**wheth·er** ob
**whey** Molke *f*
**which** welche(r, -s); der, die, das; was; ***~ of you?*** wer von euch?
**which·ev·er** welche(r, -s) auch (immer); ganz gleich, welche(r, -s)
**whiff** Luftzug *m*; Hauch *m* (*a. fig* ***of*** von); Duft *m*, Duftwolke *f*
**while 1.** Weile *f*; ***for a ~*** e-e Zeit lang **2.** *cj* während; obwohl **3.** *mst* ***~ away*** sich *die Zeit* vertreiben (***by doing s.th.*** mit et.)
**whim** Laune *f*
**whim·per 1.** wimmern; zo winseln **2.** Wimmern *n*; zo Winseln *n*
**whim·si·cal** wunderlich; launisch
**whine 1.** zo jaulen; jammern (***about*** über *acc*); **2.** zo Jaulen *n*; Gejammer *n*
**whin·ny** zo **1.** wiehern **2.** Wiehern *n*
**whip 1.** Peitsche *f*; GASTR Creme *f* **2.** *v/t* (aus)peitschen; GASTR schlagen; *v/i* sausen, flitzen, (*wind*) fegen
**whipped| cream** Schlagsahne *f*, Schlagrahm *m*; **~ eggs** Eischnee *m*
**whip·ping** (Tracht *f*) Prügel *pl*
**whip·ping boy** Prügelknabe *m*
**whip·ping cream** Schlagsahne *f*, Schlagrahm *m*
**whir** → ***whirr***
**whirl 1.** wirbeln; ***my head is ~ing*** mir schwirrt der Kopf **2.** Wirbeln *n*; Wirbel *m* (*a. fig*); ***my head's in a ~*** mir schwirrt der Kopf
**whirl·pool** Strudel *m*; Whirlpool *m*
**whirl·wind** Wirbelsturm *m*
**whirr** schwirren
**whisk 1.** schnelle Bewegung; Wedel *m*; GASTR Schneebesen *m* **2.** GASTR schlagen; ***~ its tail*** zo mit dem Schwanz schlagen; ***~ away*** *Fliegen etc* verscheuchen *or* wegscheuchen; *et.* schnell verschwinden lassen *or* wegnehmen
**whis·ker** zo Schnurr- *or* Barthaar *n*; *pl* Backenbart *m*
**whis·k(e)y** Whisky *m*
**whis·per 1.** flüstern **2.** Flüstern *n*; ***say s.th. in a ~*** et. im Flüsterton sagen
**whis·tle 1.** Pfeife *f*; Pfiff *m* **2.** pfeifen
**white 1.** weiß **2.** Weiß(e) *n*; Weiße *m*, *f*; Eiweiß *n*; **~ bread** Weißbrot *n*; **~ coffee** *Br* Milchkaffee *m*, Kaffee *m* mit Milch
**white-col·lar work·er** (Büro)Angestellte *m*, *f*
**white lie** Notlüge *f*
**whit·en** weiß machen *or* werden
**white·wash 1.** Tünche *f* **2.** tünchen, anstreichen; weißen; *fig* beschönigen
**whit·ish** weißlich
**Whit·sun** Pfingstsonntag *m*; Pfingsten *n or pl*
**Whit Sunday** Pfingstsonntag *m*
**Whit·sun·tide** Pfingsten *n or pl*
**whit·tle** (zurecht)schnitzen; ***~ away*** *Gewinn etc* allmählich aufzehren; ***~ down*** *et.* reduzieren (***to*** auf *acc*)
**whiz(z)** F **1.** ***~ by, ~ past*** vorbeizischen, vorbeidüsen **2.** Ass *n*, Kanone *f* (***at*** in *dat*); **~ kid** F Senkrechtstarter(in)
**who** wer; wen; wem; welche(r, -s); der, die, das
**who·dun·(n)it** F Krimi *m*
**who·ev·er** wer *or* wen *or* wem auch (immer); egal, wer *or* wen *or* wem
**whole 1.** *adj* ganz **2.** *das* Ganze; ***the ~ of London*** ganz London; ***on the ~*** im Großen (und) Ganzen
**whole-heart·ed** ungeteilt (*attention*), voll (*support*), ernsthaft (*effort etc*)
**whole-heart·ed·ly** uneingeschränkt, voll und ganz
**whole·meal** Vollkorn...; ***~ bread*** Vollkornbrot *n*
**whole·sale** ECON **1.** Großhandel *m* **2.** Großhandels...; **~ mar·ket** ECON Großmarkt *m*
**whole·sal·er** ECON Großhändler *m*
**whole·some** gesund
**whole wheat** → ***wholemeal***
**whol·ly** gänzlich, völlig
**whoop 1.** schreien, *esp* jauchzen; ***~ it up*** F auf den Putz hauen **2.** (*esp* Freuden)-

W

Schrei *m*
**whoop·ee**: F ***make ~*** auf den Putz hauen
**whoop·ing cough** MED Keuchhusten *m*
**whore** Hure *f*
**why** warum, weshalb; ***that's ~*** deshalb
**wick** Docht *m*
**wick·ed** gemein, niederträchtig
**wick·er·work** Korbwaren *pl*
**wick·et** *cricket*: Tor *n*
**wide 1.** *adj* breit; weit offen, aufgerissen (*eyes*); *fig* umfangreich (*knowledge etc*), vielfältig (*interests etc*) **2.** *adv* weit; ***go ~*** danebengehen; ***go ~ of the goal*** SPORT am Tor vorbeigehen
**wide-an·gle lens** PHOT Weitwinkelobjektiv *n*
**wide-a·wake** hellwach; *fig* aufgeweckt, wach
**wide-eyed** mit großen *or* aufgerissenen Augen; naiv
**wid·en** verbreitern; breiter werden
**wide-o·pen** weit offen, aufgerissen (*eyes*)
**wide·spread** weit verbreitet
**wid·ow** Witwe *f*
**wid·owed** verwitwet; ***be ~*** verwitwet sein; Witwe(r) werden
**wid·ow·er** Witwer *m*
**width** Breite *f*; Bahn *f*
**wield** *Einfluss etc* ausüben
**wife** (Ehe)Frau *f*, Gattin *f*
**wig** Perücke *f*
**wild 1.** *adj* wild; stürmisch (*wind, applause etc*); außer sich (***with*** vor *dat*); verrückt (*idea etc*); ***make a ~ guess*** einfach drauflosraten; ***be ~ about*** (ganz) verrückt sein nach **2.** *adv*: ***go ~*** ausflippen **3.** ***in the ~*** in freier Wildbahn; ***the ~s*** die Wildnis
**wild·cat** zo Wildkatze *f*
**wild·cat strike** ECON wilder Streik
**wil·der·ness** Wildnis *f*
**wild·fire**: ***spread like ~*** sich wie ein Lauffeuer verbreiten
**wild·life** Tier- und Pflanzenwelt *f*
**wil·ful** *Br* → ***willful***
**will**[1] *v/aux ich, du* will(st) *etc*; *ich* werde … *etc*
**will**[2] Wille *m*; Testament *n*; ***of one's own free ~*** aus freien Stücken
**will**[3] durch Willenskraft erzwingen; JUR vermachen
**will·ful** eigensinnig; absichtlich, *esp* JUR vorsätzlich
**will·ing** bereit (***to do*** zu tun); (bereit)willig
**will-o'-the-wisp** Irrlicht *n*
**wil·low** BOT Weide *f*
**wil·low·y** *fig* gertenschlank
**will·pow·er** Willenskraft *f*
**wil·ly-nil·ly** wohl oder übel
**wilt** verwelken, welk werden
**wi·ly** gerissen, raffiniert
**wimp** F Schlappschwanz *m*
**win 1.** *v/t* gewinnen; ***~ s.o. over*** *or* ***round to*** j-n gewinnen für; *v/i* gewinnen, siegen; ***OK, you ~*** okay, du hast gewonnen **2.** *esp* SPORT Sieg *m*
**wince** zusammenzucken (***at*** bei)
**winch** TECH Winde *f*
**wind**[1] **1.** Wind *m*; Atem *m*, Luft *f*; MED Blähungen *pl*; ***the ~*** MUS die Bläser *pl* **2.** *j-m* den Atem nehmen *or* verschlagen; HUNT wittern
**wind**[2] **1.** *v/t* drehen (an *dat*); *Uhr etc* aufziehen; wickeln (***round*** um); *v/i* sich winden *or* schlängeln; ***~ down*** *Autofenster etc* herunterdrehen, -kurbeln; *Produktion etc* reduzieren; sich entspannen; ***~ up*** *v/t Autofenster etc* hochdrehen, -kurbeln; *Uhr etc* aufziehen; *Versammlung etc* schließen (***with*** mit); *Unternehmen* liquidieren, auflösen; *v/i* F enden, landen; (*esp* s-e Rede) schließen (***by saying*** mit den Worten); **2.** Umdrehung *f*
**wind·bag** F Schwätzer(in)
**wind·fall** BOT Fallobst *n*; unverhofftes Geschenk; unverhoffter Gewinn
**wind·ing** gewunden
**wind·ing stairs** Wendeltreppe *f*
**wind in·stru·ment** MUS Blasinstrument *n*
**wind·lass** TECH Winde *f*
**wind·mill** Windmühle *f*
**win·dow** Fenster *n*; Schaufenster *n*; Schalter *m*; ~ **clean·er** Fensterputzer *m*; ~ **dress·er** Schaufensterdekorateur(in); ~ **dress·ing** Schaufensterdekoration *f*; *fig* F Mache *f*
**win·dow·pane** Fensterscheibe *f*
**win·dow seat** Fensterplatz *m*
**win·dow shade** Rouleau *n*
**win·dow-shop**: ***go window-shopping*** e-n Schaufensterbummel machen
**win·dow·sill** Fensterbank *f*, -brett *n*
**wind·pipe** ANAT Luftröhre *f*
**wind·screen** *Br* MOT Windschutzschei-

be *f*; ~ **wip·er** *Br* MOT Scheibenwischer *m*
**wind·shield** MOT Windschutzscheibe *f*; ~ **wip·er** MOT Scheibenwischer *m*
**wind·surf·ing** SPORT Windsurfing *n*, Windsurfen *n*
**wind·y** windig; MED blähend
**wine** Wein *m*; ~ **cel·lar** Weinkeller *m*; ~ **list** Weinkarte *f*; ~ **mer·chant** Weinhändler *m*
**win·er·y** Weinkellerei *f*
**wine tast·ing** Weinprobe *f*
**wing** zo Flügel *m*, Schwinge *f*; *Br* MOT Kotflügel *m*; AVIAT Tragfläche *f*; AVIAT MIL Geschwader *n*; *pl* THEA Seitenkulisse *f*
**wing·er** SPORT Außenstürmer(in), Flügelstürmer(in)
**wink 1.** zwinkern; ~ ***at*** *j-m* zuzwinkern; *et.* geflissentlich übersehen; ~ ***one's lights*** *Br* MOT blinken **2.** Zwinkern *n*; ***I didn't get a ~ of sleep last night, I didn't sleep a ~ last night*** ich habe letzte Nacht kein Auge zugetan; → ***forty*** *1*
**win·ner** Gewinner(in), *esp* SPORT Sieger(in)
**win·ning 1.** einnehmend, gewinnend **2.** *pl* Gewinn *m*
**win·ter 1.** Winter *m*; ***in (the) ~*** im Winter **2.** überwintern; den Winter verbringen; ~ **sports** Wintersport *m*
**win·ter·time** Winter *m*; Winterzeit *f*; ***in (the) ~*** im Winter
**win·try** winterlich; *fig* frostig
**wipe** (ab-, auf)wischen; ~ ***off*** ab-, wegwischen; ~ ***out*** auswischen; auslöschen, ausrotten; ~ ***up*** aufwischen
**wip·er** MOT (*Scheiben*)Wischer *m*
**wire 1.** Draht *m*; ELECTR Leitung *f*; Telegramm *n* **2.** Leitungen verlegen in (*dat*) (*a.* ~ ***up***); *j-m* ein Telegramm schicken; *j-m et.* telegrafieren
**wire·less** drahtlos, Funk...
**wire net·ting** Maschendraht *m*
**wire-tap** *j-n*, *j-s Telefon* abhören
**wir·y** *fig* drahtig
**wis·dom** Weisheit *f*, Klugheit *f*
**wis·dom tooth** Weisheitszahn *m*
**wise** weise, klug
**wise·crack** F **1.** Witzelei *f* **2.** witzeln
**wise guy** F Klugscheißer *m*
**wish 1.** wünschen; wollen; ~ ***s.o. well*** j-m alles Gute wünschen; ***if you ~ (to)*** wenn du willst; ~ ***for s.th.*** sich et. wünschen **2.** Wunsch *m* (***for*** nach)
**wish·ful think·ing** Wunschdenken *n*
**wish·y-wash·y** F labb(e)rig, wäss(e)rig; *fig* lasch (*person*); verschwommen
**wisp** (*Gras-*, *Haar*)Büschel *n*
**wist·ful** wehmütig
**wit** Geist *m*, Witz *m*; geistreicher Mensch; *a. pl* Verstand *m*; ***be at one's ~s' end*** mit s-r Weisheit am Ende sein
**witch** Hexe *f*
**witch·craft** Hexerei *f*
**with** mit; bei; vor (*dat*)
**with·draw** *v/t Geld* abheben (***from*** von); *Angebot etc* zurückziehen, *Anschuldigung etc* zurücknehmen; MIL *Truppen* zurückziehen, abziehen; *v/i* sich zurückziehen; zurücktreten (***from*** von)
**with·draw·al** Rücknahme *f*; *esp* MIL Abzug *m*, Rückzug *m*; Rücktritt *m* (***from*** von), Ausstieg *m* (***from*** aus); MED Entziehung *f*, Entzug *m*; ***make a ~*** Geld abheben (***from*** von); ~ **cure** MED Entziehungskur *f*; ~ **symp·toms** MED Entzugserscheinungen *pl*
**with·er** eingehen *or* verdorren *or* (ver)welken (lassen)
**with·hold** zurückhalten; ~ ***s.th. from s.o.*** j-m et. vorenthalten
**with·in** innerhalb (*gen*)
**with·out** ohne (*acc*)
**with·stand** *e-m Angriff etc* standhalten; *Beanspruchung etc* aushalten
**wit·ness 1.** Zeuge *m*, Zeugin *f*; ~ ***for the defense*** (*Br* ***defence***) JUR Entlastungszeuge *m*, -zeugin *f*; ~ ***for the prosecution*** JUR Belastungszeuge *m*, -zeugin *f* **2.** Zeuge sein von *et.*; *et.* bezeugen, *Unterschrift* beglaubigen; ~ ***box*** *Br*, ~ **stand** JUR Zeugenstand *m*
**wit·ti·cis·m** geistreiche *or* witzige Bemerkung; **wit·ty** geistreich, witzig
**wiz·ard** Zauberer *m*; *fig* Genie *n* (***at*** in *dat*)
**wiz·ened** verhutzelt
**wob·ble** *v/i* wackeln, zittern (*a. voice*), schwabbeln; MOT flattern; *fig* schwanken; *v/t* wackeln an (*dat*)
**woe·ful** traurig; bedauerlich
**wolf 1.** zo Wolf *m*; ***lone ~*** *fig* Einzelgänger(in) **2.** *a.* ~ ***down*** F *Essen* hinunterschlingen
**wom·an** Frau *f*; ~ **doc·tor** Ärztin *f*; ~ **driv·er** Frau *f* am Steuer

**wom·an·ish** weibisch
**wom·an·ly** fraulich; weiblich
**womb** ANAT Gebärmutter *f*
**women's| lib·ber** F Emanze *f*; **~ move·ment** Frauenbewegung *f*; **~ ref·uge** *Br*, **~ shel·ter** Frauenhaus *n*
**won·der 1.** neugierig *or* gespannt sein, gern wissen mögen; sich fragen, überlegen; sich wundern, erstaunt sein (***about*** über *acc*); ***I ~ if you could help me*** vielleicht können Sie mir helfen **2.** Staunen *n*, Verwunderung *f*; Wunder *n*; ***do*** *or* ***work ~s*** wahre Wunder vollbringen, Wunder wirken (***for*** bei)
**won·der·ful** wunderbar, wundervoll
**wont 1.** ***be ~ to do s.th.*** et. zu tun pflegen **2.** ***as was his ~*** wie es s-e Gewohnheit war
**woo** umwerben, werben um
**wood** Holz *n*; Holzfass *n*; *a. pl* Wald *m*, Gehölz *n*; ***touch ~!*** unberufen!, toi, toi, toi!; ***he can't see the ~ for the trees*** er sieht den Wald vor lauter Bäumen nicht
**wood·cut** Holzschnitt *m*
**wood·cut·ter** Holzfäller *m*
**wood·ed** bewaldet
**wood·en** hölzern (*a. fig*), aus Holz, Holz...
**wood·peck·er** ZO Specht *m*
**wood·wind**: ***the ~*** MUS die Holzblasinstrumente *pl*, die Holzbläser *pl*; ***~ instrument*** Holzblasinstrument *n*
**wood·work** Holzarbeit *f*
**wood·y** waldig; BOT holzig
**wool** Wolle *f*
**wool·(l)en 1.** wollen, Woll... **2.** *pl* Wollsachen *pl*, Wollkleidung *f*
**wool·(l)y 1.** wollig; *fig* schwammig **2.** *pl* F Wollsachen *pl*
**word 1.** Wort *n*; Nachricht *f*; Losung *f*, Losungswort *n*; Versprechen *n*; Befehl *m*; *pl* MUS *etc* Text *m*; ***have a ~*** *or* ***a few ~s with s.o.*** mit j-m sprechen **2.** *et.* ausdrücken, *Text* abfassen, formulieren;
**word·ing** Wortlaut *m*
**word| or·der** LING Wortstellung *f*; **~ pro·cess·ing** IT Textverarbeitung *f*; **~ pro·ces·sor** IT Textverarbeitungsgerät *n*
**word·y** wortreich, langatmig
**work 1.** Arbeit *f*; Werk *n*; *pl* TECH Werk *n*, Getriebe *n*; ECON Werk *n*, Fabrik *f*; ***at ~*** bei der Arbeit; ***be in ~*** Arbeit haben; ***be out of ~*** arbeitslos sein; ***go*** *or* ***set to ~*** an die Arbeit gehen **2.** *v/i* arbeiten (***at, on*** an *dat*); TECH funktionieren (*a. fig*); wirken; ***~ to rule*** Dienst nach Vorschrift tun; *v/t j-n* arbeiten lassen; *Maschine etc* bedienen, *et.* betätigen; *et.* bearbeiten; bewirken, herbeiführen; ***~ one's way*** sich durcharbeiten *or* durchkämpfen; ***~ off*** *Schulden* abarbeiten; *Wut etc* abreagieren; ***~ out*** *v/t* ausrechnen; *Aufgabe* lösen; *Plan etc* ausarbeiten; *fig* sich *et.* zusammenreimen; *v/i* gut gehen, F klappen; aufgehen; F SPORT trainieren; ***~ up*** *Zuhörer etc* aufpeitschen, aufwühlen; *et.* ausarbeiten (***into*** zu); ***be ~ed up*** aufgeregt *or* nervös sein (***about*** wegen)
**work·a·ble** formbar; *fig* durchführbar
**work·a·day** Alltags...
**work·a·hol·ic** F Arbeitssüchtige *m, f*
**work·bench** TECH Werkbank *f*
**work·book** PED Arbeitsheft *n*
**work·day** Arbeitstag *m*; Werktag *m*; ***on ~s*** werktags
**work·er** Arbeiter(in); Angestellte *m, f*
**work ex·pe·ri·ence** Erfahrung *f*
**work·ing** werktätig; Arbeits...; ***~ knowledge*** Grundkenntnisse *pl*; ***in ~ order*** in betriebsfähigem Zustand; **~ class** Arbeiterklasse *f*; **~ day** → ***workday***; **~ hours** Arbeitszeit *f*
**work·ings** Arbeits-, Funktionsweise *f*
**work·man** Handwerker *m*
**work·man·like** fachmännisch
**work·man·ship** fachmännische Arbeit
**work of art** Kunstwerk *n*
**work·out** F SPORT Training *n*
**work·place** Arbeitsplatz *m*; ***at the ~*** am Arbeitsplatz
**works coun·cil** Betriebsrat *m*
**work·sheet** PED *etc* Arbeitsblatt *n*
**work·shop** Werkstatt *f*; Workshop *m*
**work·shy** arbeitsscheu
**work·sta·tion** IT Bildschirmarbeitsplatz *m*
**work-to-rule** *Br* Dienst *m* nach Vorschrift
**world 1.** Welt *f*; ***all over the ~*** in der ganzen Welt; ***bring into the ~*** auf die Welt bringen; ***do s.o. a*** *or* ***the ~ of good*** j-m unwahrscheinlich guttun; ***mean all the ~ to s.o.*** j-m alles bedeuten; ***they are ~s apart*** zwischen ihnen liegen Welten; ***think the ~ of*** große Stücke halten von; ***what in the ~ ...?*** was um alles in

der Welt …? **2.** Welt…; **~ cham·pi·on** SPORT Weltmeister *m*; **~ cham·pi·onship** SPORT Weltmeisterschaft *f*
**World Cup** Fußballweltmeisterschaft *f*; *skiing*: Weltcup *m*
**world-fa·mous** weltberühmt
**world lit·er·a·ture** Weltliteratur *f*
**world·ly** weltlich; irdisch
**world·ly·wise** weltklug
**world| mar·ket** ECON Weltmarkt *m*; **~ pow·er** POL Weltmacht *f*; **~ rec·ord** SPORT Weltrekord *m*; **~ trip** Weltreise *f*; **~ war** Weltkrieg *m*
**world·wide** weltweit; auf der ganzen Welt
**worm 1.** ZO Wurm *m* **2.** *Hund etc* entwurmen; ***~ one's way through*** sich schlängeln *or* zwängen durch; ***~ o.s. into s.o.'s confidence*** sich in j-s Vertrauen einschleichen; ***~ s.th. out of s.o.*** j-m et. entlocken
**worm-eat·en** wurmstichig
**worm's-eye view** Froschperspektive *f*
**worn-out** abgenutzt, abgetragen; *fig* erschöpft
**wor·ried** besorgt, beunruhigt
**wor·ry 1.** beunruhigen; (sich) Sorgen machen; ***don't ~!*** keine Angst!, keine Sorge! **2.** Sorge *f*
**worse** schlechter, schlimmer; ***~ still*** was noch schlimmer ist; ***to make matters ~*** zu allem Übel
**wors·en** schlechter machen *or* werden, (sich) verschlechtern
**wor·ship 1.** Verehrung *f*; Gottesdienst *m* **2.** *v/t* anbeten, verehren; *v/i* den Gottesdienst besuchen
**wor·ship·(p)er** Anbeter(in), Verehrer(in); Kirchgänger(in)
**worst 1.** *adj* schlechteste(r, -s), schlimmste(r, -s) **2.** *adv* am schlechtesten, am schlimmsten **3.** *der, die, das* Schlechteste *or* Schlimmste; ***at (the) ~*** schlimmstenfalls
**wor·sted** Kammgarn *n*
**worth 1.** wert; ***~ reading*** lesenswert **2.** Wert *m*; **worth·less** wertlos
**worth·while** lohnend; ***be ~*** sich lohnen
**worth·y** würdig
**would-be** Möchtegern…
**wound 1.** Wunde *f*, Verletzung *f* **2.** verwunden, verletzen
**wow** *int* F wow!, Mensch!, toll!
**wran·gle 1.** (sich) streiten **2.** Streit *m*
**wrap 1.** *v/t a.* ***~ up*** (ein)packen, (ein)wickeln (***in*** in *dat*); *et.* wickeln (***[a]round*** um); *v/i*: ***~ up*** sich warm anziehen **2.** Umhang *m*
**wrap·per** (Schutz)Umschlag *m*
**wrap·ping** Verpackung *f*; **~ pa·per** Einwickel-, Pack-, Geschenkpapier *n*
**wrath** Zorn *m*
**wreath** Kranz *m*
**wreck 1.** MAR Wrack *n* (*a. fig*) **2.** *Pläne etc* zunichtemachen; ***be ~ed*** MAR zerschellen; Schiffbruch erleiden
**wreck·age** Trümmer *pl* (*a. fig*), Wrackteile *pl*
**wreck·er** MOT Abschleppwagen *m*
**wreck·ing| com·pa·ny** Abbruchfirma *f*; **~ ser·vice** MOT Abschleppdienst *m*
**wren** ZO Zaunkönig *m*
**wrench 1.** MED sich *das Knie etc* verrenken; ***~ s.th. from*** *or* ***out of s.o.'s hands*** j-m et. aus den Händen winden, j-m et. entwinden; ***~ off*** *et.* mit e-m Ruck abreißen *or* wegreißen; ***~ open*** aufreißen **2.** Ruck *m*; MED Verrenkung *f*; *Br* TECH Schraubenschlüssel *m*
**wrest**: ***~ s.th. from*** *or* ***out of s.o.'s hands*** j-m et. aus den Händen reißen, j-m et. entreißen *or* entwinden
**wres·tle** *v/i* SPORT ringen (***with*** mit), *fig a.* kämpfen (***with*** mit); *v/t* SPORT ringen gegen; **wres·tler** SPORT Ringer *m*; **wres·tling** SPORT Ringen *n*
**wretch** *often* HUMOR Schuft *m*, Wicht *m*
**wretch·ed** elend; (tod)unglücklich; scheußlich; verdammt, verflixt
**wrig·gle** *v/i* sich winden; zappeln; ***~ out of*** *fig* F sich herauswinden aus; F sich drücken vor (*dat*); *v/t* mit *den Zehen* wackeln
**wring** *j-m die Hand* drücken; *die Hände* ringen; *den Hals* umdrehen; ***~ out*** *Wäsche etc* auswringen; ***~ s.o.'s heart*** j-m zu Herzen gehen
**wrin·kle 1.** Falte *f*, Runzel *f* **2.** runzeln; *Nase* krausziehen, rümpfen; faltig *or* runz(e)lig werden
**wrist** ANAT Handgelenk *n*
**wrist·band** Bündchen *n*, (Hemd)Manschette *f*; Armband *n*
**wrist·watch** Armbanduhr *f*
**writ** JUR Befehl *m*, Verfügung *f*
**write** schreiben; ***~ down*** auf-, niederschreiben; ***~ off*** *j-n*, ECON *et.* abschreiben; ***~ out*** *Namen etc* ausschreiben;

*Bericht etc* ausarbeiten; *j-m e-e Quittung etc* ausstellen; ~ **pro·tec·tion** IT Schreibschutz *m*
**writ·er** Schreiber(in), Verfasser(in), Autor(in); Schriftsteller(in)
**writhe** sich krümmen *or* winden (***in, with*** vor *dat*)
**writ·ing 1.** Schreiben *n*; (Hand)Schrift *f*; Schriftstück *n*; *pl* Werke *pl*; ***in*** ~ schriftlich **2.** Schreib...; ~ **case** Schreibmappe *f*; ~ **desk** Schreibtisch *m*; ~ **pad** Schreibblock *m*; ~ **pa·per** Briefpapier *n*, Schreibpapier *n*
**writ·ten** schriftlich
**wrong 1.** *adj* falsch; unrecht; ***be*** ~ falsch sein, nicht stimmen; unrecht haben; falsch gehen (*watch*); ***be on the*** ~ ***side of forty*** über 40 (Jahre alt) sein; ***is anything*** ~***?*** ist et. nicht in Ordnung?; ***what's*** ~ ***with her?*** was ist los mit ihr?, was hat sie? **2.** *adv* falsch; ***get*** ~ *j-n, et.* falsch verstehen; ***go*** ~ e-n Fehler machen; kaputtgehen; *fig* F schiefgehen **3.** Unrecht *n*; ***be in the*** ~ im Unrecht sein **4.** *j-m* unrecht tun
**wrong·ful** ungerechtfertigt; gesetzwidrig
**wrong-way driv·er** MOT F Geisterfahrer(in)
**wrought i·ron** Schmiedeeisen *n*
**wrought-i·ron** schmiedeeisern
**wry** süßsauer (*smile*); ironisch, sarkastisch (*humor etc*)
**wt** *abbr of* ***weight*** Gew., Gewicht *n*
**WWF** *abbr of* ***World Wide Fund for Nature*** WWF *m*
**WYSIWYG** *abbr of* ***what you see is what you get*** IT was du (*auf dem Bildschirm*) siehst, bekommst du (*auch ausgedruckt*)

# X

**X, x** X, x *n*
**xen·o·pho·bi·a** Fremdenhass *m*; Ausländerfeindlichkeit *f*
**XL** *abbr of* ***extra large*** (***size***) extragroß
**X·mas** F → ***Christmas***
**X-ray** MED **1.** röntgen **2.** Röntgenstrahl *m*; Röntgenaufnahme *f*, -bild *n*; Röntgenuntersuchung *f*
**xy·lo·phone** MUS Xylophon *n*

# Y

**Y, y** Y, y *n*
**yacht** MAR **1.** (Segel)Boot *n*; Jacht *f* **2.** segeln; ***go*** ~***ing*** segeln gehen
**yacht club** Segelklub *m*, Jachtklub *m*
**yacht·ing** Segeln *n*, Segelsport *m*
**Yan·kee** F Yankee *m*, Ami *m*
**yap** kläffen; F quasseln
**yard**[1] (*abbr* ***yd***) Yard *n* (*91, 44 cm*)
**yard**[2] Hof *m*; (*Bau-, Stapel- etc*)Platz *m*; Garten *m*
**yard·stick** *fig* Maßstab *m*
**yarn** Garn *n*
**yawn 1.** gähnen **2.** Gähnen *n*
**yeah** F ja
**year** Jahr *n*; ***all the*** ~ ***round*** das ganze Jahr hindurch; ~ ***after*** ~ Jahr für Jahr; ~ ***in*** ~ ***out*** jahraus, jahrein; ***this*** ~ dieses Jahr; ***this*** ~***'s*** diesjährige(r, -s)
**year·ly** jährlich
**yearn** sich sehnen (***for*** nach; ***to do*** danach, zu tun); **yearn·ing 1.** Sehnsucht *f* **2.** sehnsüchtig
**yeast** Hefe *f*
**yell 1.** schreien, brüllen (***with*** vor *dat*); ~ ***at s.o.*** j-n anschreien *or* anbrüllen; ~ (***out***) *et.* schreien, brüllen **2.** Schrei *m*
**yel·low 1.** gelb; F feig(e) **2.** Gelb *n*; ***at*** ~ MOT bei Gelb **3.** (sich) gelb färben; gelb werden; vergilben
**yel·low fe·ver** MED Gelbfieber *n*
**yel·low·ish** gelblich
**Yel·low Pag·es**® TEL *die* Gelben Seiten *pl*, Branchenverzeichnis *n*
**yel·low press** Sensationspresse *f*

**yelp 1.** (auf)jaulen; aufschreien **2.** (Auf)Jaulen *n*; Aufschrei *m*
**yes 1.** ja; doch **2.** Ja *n*
**yes·ter·day** gestern; **~ *morning* (*afternoon*)** gestern Morgen (Nachmittag); ***the day before* ~** vorgestern
**yet 1.** *adv in questions*: schon; noch; (doch) noch; doch, aber; ***as* ~** bis jetzt, bisher; ***not* ~** noch nicht **2.** *cj* aber, doch
**yew** BOT Eibe *f*
**yield 1.** *v/t Früchte* tragen; *Gewinn* abwerfen; *Resultat etc* ergeben, liefern; *v/i* nachgeben; **~ *to*** MOT *j-m* die Vorfahrt lassen **2.** Ertrag *m*
**yip·pee** *int* F hurra!
**yo·del 1.** jodeln **2.** Jodler *m*
**yo·ga** Joga *m, n*, Yoga *m, n*
**yog·h(o)urt, yog·urt** Jog(h)urt *m, n*
**yoke** Joch *n* (*a. fig*)
**yolk** (Ei)Dotter *m, n*, Eigelb *n*
**you** du, ihr, Sie; (*dat*) dir, euch, Ihnen; (*acc*) dich, euch, Sie; man
**young 1.** jung **2.** ZO Junge *pl*; ***with* ~** ZO trächtig; ***the* ~** die jungen Leute *pl*, die Jugend
**young·ster** Junge *m*
**your** dein(e); *pl* euer, eure; Ihr(e) (*a. pl*)
**yours** deine(r, -s); *pl* euer eure(s); Ihre(r, -s) (*a. pl*); ***a friend of* ~** ein Freund von dir; ***Yours, Bill*** Dein Bill
**your·self** selbst; dir, dich, sich; ***by* ~** allein
**youth** Jugend *f*; Jugendliche *m*
**youth club** Jugendklub *m*
**youth·ful** jugendlich
**youth hos·tel** Jugendherberge *f*
**yuck·y** F *contp* scheußlich
**Yu·go·slav** HIST **1.** jugoslawisch **2.** Jugoslawe *m*, Jugoslawin *f*; **Yu·go·sla·vi·a** HIST Jugoslawien *n*
**yup·pie, yup·py** *abbr of* ***young upwardly-mobile*** *or* ***urban professional*** junger, aufstrebender *or* städtischer Karrieremensch, Yuppie *m*

# Z

**Z, z** Z, z *n*
**zap** F *esp computer game etc*: abknallen, fertigmachen; MOT beschleunigen (***from … to …*** von … auf *acc* …); jagen, hetzen; TV *Fernbedienung* bedienen; TV zappen, umschalten; **~ *off*** abzischen; **~ *to*** düsen *or* jagen *or* hetzen nach
**zap·per** TV F Fernbedienung *f*
**zap·py** *Br* F voller Pep, schmissig, fetzig
**zeal** Eifer *m*
**zeal·ot** Fanatiker(in), Eiferer *m*, Eiferin *f*; **zeal·ous** eifrig; ***be* ~ *to do s.th.*** eifrig darum bemüht sein, et. zu tun
**ze·bra** ZO Zebra *n*
**ze·bra cross·ing** *Br* Zebrastreifen *m*
**zen·ith** Zenit *m* (*a. fig*)
**ze·ro 1.** Null *f*; Nullpunkt *m*; ***20 degrees below* ~** 20 Grad unter Null **2.** Null…; **~ *growth*** Nullwachstum *n*; **~ *op·tion*** POL Nulllösung *f*
**zest** *fig* Würze *f*; Begeisterung *f*; **~ *for life*** Lebensfreude *f*
**zig·zag 1.** Zickzack *m* **2.** Zickzack… **3.** im Zickzack fahren, laufen *etc*, zickzackförmig verlaufen
**zinc** CHEM Zink *n*
**zip**[1] **1.** Reißverschluss *m* **2.** **~ *the bag open* (*shut*)** den Reißverschluss der Tasche aufmachen (zumachen); **~ *s.o. up*** j-m den Reißverschluss zumachen
**zip**[2] **1.** Zischen *n*, Schwirren *n*; F Schwung *m* **2.** zischen, schwirren; **~ *by*, ~ *past*** vorbeiflitzen
**zip code** Postleitzahl *f*
**zip fas·ten·er** *esp Br* → ***zipper***
**zip·per** Reißverschluss *m*
**zo·di·ac** ASTR Tierkreis *m*; ***signs of the* ~** Tierkreiszeichen *pl*
**zone** Zone *f*
**zoo** Zoo *m*, Tierpark *m*
**zo·o·log·i·cal** zoologisch; **~ *gar·dens*** Tierpark *m*, zoologischer Garten
**zo·ol·o·gist** Zoologe *m*, Zoologin *f*
**zo·ol·o·gy** Zoologie *f*
**zoom 1.** surren; F sausen; F *fig* in die Höhe schnellen; PHOT zoomen; **~ *by*, ~ *past*** F vorbeisausen; **~ *in on*** PHOT *et.* heranholen **2.** Surren *n*; *a.* **~ *lens*** PHOT Zoom *n*, Zoomobjektiv *n*

# APPENDICES

# States of the Federal Republic of Germany

**Baden-Württemberg** ['ba:dən'vʏrtəmbɛrk] Baden-Württemberg
**Bayern** ['baɪɐn] Bavaria
**Berlin** [bɛr'li:n] Berlin
**Brandenburg** ['brandənbʊrk] Brandenburg
**Bremen** ['bre:mən] Bremen
**Hamburg** ['hambʊrk] Hamburg
**Hessen** ['hɛsən] Hesse
**Mecklenburg-Vorpommern** ['me:klənbʊrk'fo:ɐpɔmɐn] Mecklenburg-Western Pomerania
**Niedersachsen** ['ni:dɐzaksən] Lower Saxony
**Nordrhein-Westfalen** ['nɔrtraɪnvɛst'fa:lən] North Rhine-Westphalia
**Rheinland-Pfalz** ['raɪnlant'pfalts] Rhineland-Palatinate
**Saarland** ['za:ɐlant]: ***das*** ~ the Saarland
**Sachsen** ['zaksən] Saxony
**Sachsen-Anhalt** ['zaksən'anhalt] Saxony-Anhalt
**Schleswig-Holstein** ['ʃle:svɪç'hɔlʃtaɪn] Schleswig-Holstein
**Thüringen** ['ty:rɪŋən] Thuringia

# States of the Republic of Austria

**Burgenland** ['bʊrgənlant]: ***das*** ~ the Burgenland
**Kärnten** ['kɛrntən] Carinthia
**Niederösterreich** ['ni:dɐˀø:stəraɪç] Lower Austria
**Oberösterreich** ['o:bɐˀø:stəraɪç] Upper Austria
**Salzburg** ['zaltsbʊrk] Salzburg
**Steiermark** ['ʃtaɪɐmark]: ***die*** ~ Styria
**Tirol** [ti'ro:l] Tyrol
**Vorarlberg** ['fo:ɐˀarlbɛrk] Vorarlberg
**Wien** [vi:n] Vienna

# Cantons of the Swiss Confederation

**Aargau** ['a:ɐgaʊ]: ***der*** ~ the Aargau
**Appenzell** [apən'tsɛl] Appenzell
**Basel** ['ba:zəl] Basel, Basle
**Bern** [bɛrn] Bern(e)
**Freiburg** ['fraɪbʊrk], *French* **Fribourg** [fri'bu:r] Fribourg
**Genf** [gɛnf], *French* **Genève** [ʒə'nɛ:v] Geneva
**Glarus** ['gla:rʊs] Glarus
**Graubünden** [graʊ'bʏndən] Graubünden, Grisons
**Jura** ['ju:ra]: ***der*** ~ the Jura
**Luzern** [lu'tsɛrn] Lucerne
**Neuenburg** ['nɔyənbʊrk], *French* **Neuchâtel** [nøʃa'tɛl] Neuchâtel
**St. Gallen** [zaŋkt 'galən] St Gallen, St Gall
**Schaffhausen** [ʃaf'haʊzən] Schaffhausen
**Schwyz** [ʃvi:ts] Schwyz
**Solothurn** ['zo:lotʊrn] Solothurn
**Tessin** [tɛ'si:n]: ***der*** ~ the Ticino, *Italian* **Ticino** [ti'tʃi:no]: ***das*** ~ the Ticino
**Thurgau** ['tu:ɐgaʊ]: ***der*** ~ the Thurgau
**Unterwalden** ['ʊntɐvaldən] Unterwalden
**Uri** ['u:ri] Uri
**Waadt** [va(:)t], *French* **Vaud** [vo] Vaud
**Wallis** ['valɪs], *French* **Valais** [va'lɛ]: ***das*** ~ the Valais, Wallis
**Zug** [tsu:k] Zug
**Zürich** ['tsy:rɪç] Zurich

# European currency

## Germany and Austria

1 euro (€) = 100 cent (ct)

**coins**

1 ct
2 ct
5 ct
10 ct
20 ct
50 ct
€ 1
€ 2

**bills (*Br* bank notes)**

€ 5
€ 10
€ 20
€ 50
€ 100
€ 200
€ 500

## Switzerland

1 Swiss franc (Sfr) = 100 Rappen (Rp) / centimes (c)

**coins**

1 Rp
5 Rp
10 Rp
20 Rp
½ Sfr (50 Rp)
1 Sfr
2 Sfr
5 Sfr

**bills (*Br* bank notes)**

10 Sfr
20 Sfr
50 Sfr
100 Sfr
200 Sfr
1000 Sfr

# Numbers

## Cardinal numbers

**0** null *nought*, *zero*
**1** eins *one*
**2** zwei *two*
**3** drei *three*
**4** vier *four*
**5** fünf *five*
**6** sechs *six*
**7** sieben *seven*
**8** acht *eight*
**9** neun *nine*
**10** zehn *ten*
**11** elf *eleven*
**12** zwölf *twelve*
**13** dreizehn *thirteen*
**14** vierzehn *fourteen*
**15** fünfzehn *fifteen*
**16** sechzehn *sixteen*
**17** siebzehn *seventeen*
**18** achtzehn *eighteen*
**19** neunzehn *nineteen*
**20** zwanzig *twenty*
**21** einundzwanzig *twenty-one*
**22** zweiundzwanzig *twenty-two*
**30** dreißig *thirty*
**31** einunddreißig *thirty-one*
**40** vierzig *forty*
**41** einundvierzig *forty-one*
**50** fünfzig *fifty*
**51** einundfünfzig *fifty-one*
**60** sechzig *sixty*
**61** einundsechzig *sixty-one*
**70** siebzig *seventy*
**71** einundsiebzig *seventy-one*
**80** achtzig *eighty*
**81** einundachtzig *eighty-one*
**90** neunzig *ninety*
**91** einundneunzig *ninety-one*
**100** hundert *a* or *one hundred*
**101** hunderteins *a hundred and one*
**200** zweihundert *two hundred*
**300** dreihundert *three hundred*
**572** fünfhundertzweiundsiebzig *five hundred and seventy-two*
**1000** tausend *a* / *one thousand*
**1999** neunzehnhundertneunundneunzig *nineteen* (*hundred and*) *ninety-nine*
**2000** zweitausend *two thousand*
**2010** *as year*: zweitausendzehn *two thousand* (*and*) *ten*
**5044** TEL fünfzig vierundvierzig *five O* (or *zero*) *double four*
**1,000,000** eine Million *one million*
**2,000,000** zwei Millionen *two million*
**1,000,000,000** eine Milliarde *a* / *one billion*

## Ordinal numbers

**1.** erste *first* (*1st*)
**2.** zweite *second* (*2nd*)
**3.** dritte *third* (*3rd*)
**4.** vierte *fourth* (*4th*)
**5.** fünfte *fifth* (*5th*) *etc*.
**6.** sechste *sixth*
**7.** siebente *seventh*
**8.** achte *eighth*
**9.** neunte *ninth*
**10.** zehnte *tenth*
**11.** elfte *eleventh*
**12.** zwölfte *twelfth*
**13.** dreizehnte *thirteenth*
**14.** vierzehnte *fourteenth*
**15.** fünfzehnte *fifteenth*
**16.** sechzehnte *sixteenth*
**17.** siebzehnte *seventeenth*
**18.** achtzehnte *eighteenth*
**19.** neunzehnte *nineteenth*
**20.** zwanzigste *twentieth*
**21.** einundzwanzigste *twenty-first*
**22.** zweiundzwanzigste *twenty-second*
**23.** dreiundzwanzigste *twenty-third*
**30.** dreißigste *thirtieth*
**31.** einunddreißigste *thirty-first*
**40.** vierzigste *fortieth*
**41.** einundvierzigste *forty-first*
**50.** fünfzigste *fiftieth*
**51.** einundfünfzigste *fifty-first*
**60.** sechzigste *sixtieth*
**61.** einundsechzigste *sixty-first*
**70.** siebzigste *seventieth*
**71.** einundsiebzigste *seventy-first*
**80.** achtzigste *eightieth*
**81.** einundachtzigste *eighty-first*
**90.** neunzigste *ninetieth*
**100.** hundertste (*one*) *hundredth*
**101.** hundert(und)erste (*one*) *hundred and first*
**200.** zweihundertste *two hundredth*
**300.** dreihundertste *three hundredth*
**572.** fünfhundert(und)zweiundsiebzigste *five hundred and seventy-second*
**1000.** tausendste (*one*) *thousandth*
**1970.** neunzehnhundert(und)siebzigste *nineteen hundred and seventieth*
**500 000.** fünfhunderttausendste *five hundred thousandth*
**1 000 000.** millionste (*one*) *millionth*

## Fractions, decimals and mathematical calculation methods

$^1/_2$ halb *one / a half*
$^1/_2$ eine halbe Meile *half a mile*
$1^1/_2$ anderthalb / eineinhalb *one and a half*
$2^1/_2$ zweieinhalb *two and a half*
$^1/_3$ ein Drittel *one / a third*
$^2/_3$ zwei Drittel *two thirds*
$^1/_4$ ein Viertel *one fourth, one / a quarter*
$^3/_4$ drei Viertel *three fourths, three quarters*
$1^1/_4$ ein und eine viertel Stunde *one hour and a quarter*
$^1/_5$ ein Fünftel *one / a fifth*
$3^4/_5$ drei vier Fünftel *three and four fifths*
0,4 null Komma vier *point four (.4)*
2,5 zwei Komma fünf *two point five (2.5)*

einfach *single*
zweifach *double, twofold*
dreifach *threefold, treble, triple*
vierfach *fourfold, quadruple*
fünffach *fivefold, quintuple*

einmal *once*
zweimal *twice*
dreimal *three times*
viermal *four times*
fünfmal *five times*
zweimal so viel (so viele) *twice as much (many)*

erstens *first(ly), in the first place*
zweitens *secondly; in the second place*
drittens *thirdly; in the third place*

2 × 3 = 6 zwei mal drei ist sechs, zwei multipliziert mit drei ist sechs *two threes are six, two multiplied by three is six*

7 + 8 = 15 sieben plus acht ist fünfzehn *seven plus eight is fifteen*

10 – 3 = 7 zehn minus drei ist sieben *ten minus three is seven*

20 : 5 = 4 zwanzig (dividiert) durch fünf ist vier *twenty divided by five is four*

# German weights and measures

## I linear measure

**1 mm** ***Millimeter*** millimeter, *Br* millimetre
= $^{1}/_{1000}$ meter (*Br* metre)
= 0.003 feet
= 0.039 inches

**1 cm** ***Zentimeter*** centimeter, *Br* centimetre
= $^{1}/_{100}$ meter (*Br* metre)
= 0.39 inches

**1 dm** ***Dezimeter*** decimeter, *Br* decimetre
= $^{1}/_{10}$ meter (*Br* metre)
= 3.94 inches

**1 m** ***Meter*** meter, *Br* metre
= 1.094 yards
= 3.28 feet
= 39.37 inches

**1 km** ***Kilometer*** kilometer, *Br* kilometre
= 1,000 meters (*Br* metres)
= 1,093.637 yards
= 0.621 (statute) miles

**1 sm** ***Seemeile*** nautical mile
= 1,852 meters (*Br* metres)

## II square measure

**1 mm²** ***Quadratmillimeter*** square millimeter (*Br* millimetre)
= 0.0015 square inches

**1 cm²** ***Quadratzentimeter*** square centimeter (*Br* centimetre)
= 0.155 square inches

**1 m²** ***Quadratmeter*** square meter (*Br* metre)
= 1.195 square yards
= 10.76 square feet

**1 a** ***Ar*** are
= 100 square meters (*Br* metres)
= 119.59 square yards
= 1,076.40 square feet

**1 ha** ***Hektar*** hectare
= 100 ares
= 10,000 square meters (*Br* metres)
= 11,959.90 square yards
= 2.47 acres

**1 km²** ***Quadratkilometer*** square kilometer (*Br* kilometre)
= 100 hectares
= 1,000,000 square meters (*Br* metres)
= 247.11 acres
= 0.386 square miles

## III cubic measure

**1 cm³** ***Kubikzentimeter*** cubic centimeter (*Br* centimetre)
= 1,000 cubic millimeters (*Br* millimetres)
= 0.061 cubic inches

**1 dm³** ***Kubikdezimeter*** cubic decimeter (*Br* decimetre)
= 1,000 cubic centimeters (*Br* centimetres)
= 61.025 cubic inches

**1 m³** ***Kubikmeter***
**1 rm** ***Raummeter***
**1 fm** ***Festmeter***
} cubic meter (*Br* metre)
= 1,000 cubic decimeters (*Br* decimetres)
= 1.307 cubic yards
= 35.31 cubic feet

**1 RT** ***Registertonne*** register ton
= 2.832 m³
= 100 cubic feet

## IV measure of capacity

**1 l** ***Liter*** liter, *Br* litre
= 10 deciliters (*Br* decilitres)
= 2.11 pints (*Am*)
= 8.45 gills (*Am*)
= 1.06 quarts (*Am*)
= 0.26 gallons (*Am*)
= 1.76 pints (*Br*)
= 7.04 gills (*Br*)
= 0.88 quarts (*Br*)
= 0.22 gallons (*Br*)

**1 hl** ***Hektoliter*** hectoliter, *Br* hectolitre
= 100 liters (*Br* litres)
= 26.42 gallons (*Am*)
= 2.84 bushels (*Am*)
= 22.009 gallons (*Br*)
= 2.75 bushels (*Br*)

## V weight

**1 mg** ***Milligramm*** milligram(me)
= 1/1000 gram(me)
= 0.015 grains

**1 g** ***Gramm*** gram(me)
= 1/1000 kilogram(me)
= 15.43 grains

**1 Pfd** ***Pfund*** pound (German)
= 1/2 kilogram(me)
= 500 gram(me)s
= 1.102 pounds (1b)

**1 kg** ***Kilogramm***, ***Kilo*** kilogram(me)
= 1,000 gram(me)s
= 2.204 pounds (1b)

**1 Ztr.** ***Zentner*** centner
= 100 pounds (German)
= 50 kilogram(me)s
= 110.23 pounds (1b)
= 1.102 US hundredweights
= 0.98 British hundredweights

**1 t** ***Tonne*** ton
= 1,000 kilogram(me)s
= 1.102 US tons
= 0.984 British tons

# Conversion tables for temperatures

| °C (Celsius) | °F (Fahrenheit) |
|---|---|
| 100 | 212 |
| 95 | 203 |
| 90 | 194 |
| 85 | 185 |
| 80 | 176 |
| 75 | 167 |
| 70 | 158 |
| 65 | 149 |
| 60 | 140 |
| 55 | 131 |
| 50 | 122 |
| 45 | 113 |
| 40 | 104 |
| 35 | 95 |
| 30 | 86 |
| 25 | 77 |
| 20 | 68 |
| 15 | 59 |
| 10 | 50 |
| 5 | 41 |
| 0 | 32 |
| – 5 | 23 |
| –10 | 14 |
| –15 | 5 |
| –17.8 | 0 |
| –20 | – 4 |
| –25 | –13 |
| –30 | –22 |
| –35 | –31 |
| –40 | –40 |
| –45 | –49 |
| –50 | –58 |

# Clinical thermometer

| °C (Celsius) | °F (Fahrenheit) |
|---|---|
| 42.0 | 107.6 |
| 41.8 | 107.2 |
| 41.6 | 106.9 |
| 41.4 | 106.5 |
| 41.2 | 106.2 |
| 41.0 | 105.8 |
| 40.8 | 105.4 |
| 40.6 | 105.1 |
| 40.4 | 104.7 |
| 40.2 | 104.4 |
| 40.0 | 104.0 |
| 39.8 | 103.6 |
| 39.6 | 103.3 |
| 39.4 | 102.9 |
| 39.2 | 102.6 |
| 39.0 | 102.2 |
| 38.8 | 101.8 |
| 38.6 | 101.5 |
| 38.4 | 101.1 |
| 38.2 | 100.8 |
| 38.0 | 100.4 |
| 37.8 | 100.0 |
| 37.6 | 99.7 |
| 37.4 | 99.3 |
| 37.2 | 99.0 |
| 37.0 | 98.6 |
| 36.8 | 98.2 |
| 36.6 | 97.9 |

## How to convert Celsius into Fahrenheit and vice versa

To convert Celsius into Fahrenheit multiply by 9, divide by 5 and add 32.

To convert Fahrenheit into Celsius subtract 32, multiply by 5 and divide by 9.

# German irregular verbs

## infinitive – 3rd person singular – past tense – past participle

**backen** – backt/bäckt – backte – gebacken
**bedingen** – bedingt – bedang (bedingte) – bedungen (*conditional*: bedingt)
**befehlen** – befiehlt – befahl – befohlen
**beginnen** – beginnt – begann – begonnen
**beißen** – beißt – biss – gebissen
**bergen** – birgt – barg – geborgen
**bersten** – birst – barst – geborsten
**bewegen** – bewegt – bewog – bewogen
**biegen** – biegt – bog – gebogen
**bieten** – bietet – bot – geboten
**binden** – bindet – band – gebunden
**bitten** – bittet – bat – gebeten
**blasen** – bläst – blies – geblasen
**bleiben** – bleibt – blieb – geblieben
**bleichen** – bleicht – blich – geblichen
**braten** – brät – briet – gebraten
**brauchen** – braucht – brauchte – gebraucht (*v/aux* brauchen)
**brechen** – bricht – brach – gebrochen
**brennen** – brennt – brannte – gebrannt
**bringen** – bringt – brachte – gebracht
**denken** – denkt – dachte – gedacht
**dreschen** – drischt – drosch – gedroschen
**dringen** – dringt – drang – gedrungen
**dürfen** – darf – durfte – gedurft (*v/aux* dürfen)
**empfangen** – empfängt – empfing – empfangen
**empfehlen** – empfiehlt – empfahl – empfohlen
**empfinden** – empfindet – empfand – empfunden
**erlöschen** – erlischt – erlosch – erloschen
**erschrecken** – erschrickt – erschrak – erschrocken
**essen** – isst – aß – gegessen
**fahren** – fährt – fuhr – gefahren
**fallen** – fällt – fiel – gefallen
**fangen** – fängt – fing – gefangen
**fechten** – ficht – focht – gefochten
**finden** – findet – fand – gefunden
**flechten** – flicht – flocht – geflochten
**fliegen** – fliegt – flog – geflogen
**fliehen** – flieht – floh – geflohen
**fließen** – fließt – floss – geflossen
**fressen** – frisst – fraß – gefressen
**frieren** – friert – fror – gefroren
**gären** – gärt – gor (*esp fig* gärte) – gegoren (*esp fig* gegärt)
**gebären** – gebärt (gebiert) – gebar – geboren
**geben** – gibt – gab – gegeben
**gedeihen** – gedeiht – gedieh – gediehen
**gehen** – geht – ging – gegangen
**gelingen** – gelingt – gelang – gelungen
**gelten** – gilt – galt – gegolten
**genesen** – genest – genas – genesen
**genießen** – genießt – genoss – genossen
**geschehen** – geschieht – geschah – geschehen
**gewinnen** – gewinnt – gewann – gewonnen
**gießen** – gießt – goss – gegossen
**gleichen** – gleicht – glich – geglichen
**gleiten** – gleitet – glitt – geglitten
**glimmen** – glimmt – glomm – geglommen
**graben** – gräbt – grub – gegraben
**greifen** – greift – griff – gegriffen
**haben** – hat – hatte – gehabt
**halten** – hält – hielt – gehalten
**hängen** – hängt – hing – gehangen
**hauen** – haut – haute (hieb) – gehauen
**heben** – hebt – hob – gehoben
**heißen** – heißt – hieß – geheißen
**helfen** – hilft – half – geholfen
**kennen** – kennt – kannte – gekannt
**klingen** – klingt – klang – geklungen
**kneifen** – kneift – kniff – gekniffen
**kommen** – kommt – kam – gekommen
**können** – kann – konnte – gekonnt (*v/aux* können)
**kriechen** – kriecht – kroch – gekrochen
**laden** – lädt – lud – geladen
**lassen** – lässt – ließ – gelassen (*v/aux* lassen)
**laufen** – läuft – lief – gelaufen
**leiden** – leidet – litt – gelitten
**leihen** – leiht – lieh – geliehen

**lesen** – liest – las – gelesen
**liegen** – liegt – lag – gelegen
**lügen** – lügt – log – gelogen
**mahlen** – mahlt – mahlte – gemahlen
**meiden** – meidet – mied – gemieden
**melken** – melkt – melkte (molk) – gemolken (gemelkt)
**messen** – misst – maß – gemessen
**misslingen** – misslingt – misslang – misslungen
**mögen** – mag – mochte – gemocht (*v/aux* mögen)
**müssen** – muss – musste – gemusst (*v/aux* müssen)
**nehmen** – nimmt – nahm – genommen
**nennen** – nennt – nannte – genannt
**pfeifen** – pfeift – pfiff – gepfiffen
**preisen** – preist – pries – gepriesen
**quellen** – quillt – quoll – gequollen
**raten** – rät – riet – geraten
**reiben** – reibt – rieb – gerieben
**reißen** – reißt – riss – gerissen
**reiten** – reitet – ritt – geritten
**rennen** – rennt – rannte – gerannt
**riechen** – riecht – roch – gerochen
**ringen** – ringt – rang – gerungen
**rinnen** – rinnt – rann – geronnen
**rufen** – ruft – rief – gerufen
**salzen** – salzt – salzte – gesalzen (gesalzt)
**saufen** – säuft – soff – gesoffen
**saugen** – saugt – sog – gesogen
**schaffen** – schafft – schuf – geschaffen
**schallen** – schallt – schallte (scholl) – geschallt (*for* ***erschallen*** *a.* erschollen)
**scheiden** – scheidet – schied – geschieden
**scheinen** – scheint – schien – geschienen
**scheißen** – scheißt – schiss – geschissen
**scheren** – schert – schor – geschoren
**schieben** – schiebt – schob – geschoben
**schießen** – schießt – schoss – geschossen
**schinden** – schindet – schund – geschunden
**schlafen** – schläft – schlief – geschlafen
**schlagen** – schlägt – schlug – geschlagen
**schleichen** – schleicht – schlich – geschlichen
**schleifen** – schleift – schliff – geschliffen
**schließen** – schließt – schloss – geschlossen
**schlingen** – schlingt – schlang – geschlungen
**schmeißen** – schmeißt – schmiss – geschmissen
**schmelzen** – schmilzt – schmolz – geschmolzen
**schneiden** – schneidet – schnitt – geschnitten
**schreiben** – schreibt – schrieb – geschrieben
**schreien** – schreit – schrie – geschrie(e)n
**schreiten** – schreitet – schritt – geschritten
**schweigen** – schweigt – schwieg – geschwiegen
**schwellen** – schwillt – schwoll – geschwollen
**schwimmen** – schwimmt – schwamm – geschwommen
**schwinden** – schwindet – schwand – geschwunden
**schwingen** – schwingt – schwang – geschwungen
**schwören** – schwört – schwor – geschworen
**sehen** – sieht – sah – gesehen
**sein** – ist – war – gewesen
**senden** – sendet – sandte – gesandt
**sieden** – siedet – sott – gesotten
**singen** – singt – sang – gesungen
**sinken** – sinkt – sank – gesunken
**sinnen** – sinnt – sann – gesonnen
**sitzen** – sitzt – saß – gesessen
**sollen** – soll – sollte – gesollt (*v/aux* sollen)
**spalten** – spaltet – spaltete – gespalten (gespaltet)
**speien** – speit – spie – gespie(e)n
**spinnen** – spinnt – spann – gesponnen
**sprechen** – spricht – sprach – gesprochen
**sprießen** – sprießt – spross – gesprossen
**springen** – springt – sprang – gesprungen
**stechen** – sticht – stach – gestochen
**stecken** – steckt – steckte (stak) – gesteckt
**stehen** – steht – stand – gestanden
**stehlen** – stiehlt – stahl – gestohlen
**steigen** – steigt – stieg – gestiegen
**sterben** – stirbt – starb – gestorben
**stinken** – stinkt – stank – gestunken

**stoßen** – stößt – stieß – gestoßen
**streichen** – streicht – strich – gestrichen
**streiten** – streitet – stritt – gestritten
**tragen** – trägt – trug – getragen
**treffen** – trifft – traf – getroffen
**treiben** – treibt – trieb – getrieben
**treten** – tritt – trat – getreten
**trinken** – trinkt – trank – getrunken
**trügen** – trügt – trog – getrogen
**tun** – tut – tat – getan
**überwinden** – überwindet – überwand – überwunden
**verderben** – verdirbt – verdarb – verdorben
**verdrießen** – verdrießt – verdross – verdrossen
**vergessen** – vergisst – vergaß – vergessen
**verlieren** – verliert – verlor – verloren
**verschleißen** – verschleißt – verschliss – verschlissen
**verschwinden** – verschwindet – verschwand – verschwunden
**verzeihen** – verzeiht – verzieh – verziehen
**wachsen** – wächst – wuchs – gewachsen
**wägen** – wägt – wog (*rare* wägte) – gewogen (*rare* gewägt)
**waschen** – wäscht – wusch – gewaschen
**weben** – webt – wob – gewoben
**weichen** – weicht – wich – gewichen
**weisen** – weist – wies – gewiesen
**wenden** – wendet – wandte – gewandt
**werben** – wirbt – warb – geworben
**werden** – wird – wurde – geworden (worden*)
**werfen** – wirft – warf – geworfen
**wiegen** – wiegt – wog – gewogen
**winden** – windet – wand – gewunden
**wissen** – weiß – wusste – gewusst
**wollen** – will – wollte – gewollt (*v/aux* wollen)
**wringen** – wringt – wrang – gewrungen
**ziehen** – zieht – zog – gezogen
**zwingen** – zwingt – zwang – gezwungen

* only in connection with the past participles of other verbs, *e.g.* ***er ist gesehen worden*** he has been seen.

# English irregular verbs

## infinitive – past tense – past participle

**arise** – arose – arisen
**awake** – awoke – awoke*
**be** – was – been
**bear** – bore – *getragen*: borne – *geboren*: born
**beat** – beat – beaten, beat
**become** – became – become
**beget** – begot – begotten
**begin** – began – begun
**bend** – bent – bent
**bereave** – bereft* – bereft*
**beseech** – besought – besought
**bet** – bet * – bet*
**bid** – bade, bid – bidden, bid
**bide** – bode* – bided
**bind** – bound – bound
**bite** – bit – bitten
**bleed** – bled – bled
**bless** – blest* – blest*
**blow** – blew – blown
**break** – broke – broken
**breed** – bred – bred
**bring** – brought – brought
**build** – built – built
**burn** – burnt* – burnt*
**burst** – burst – burst
**buy** – bought – bought
**cast** – cast – cast
**catch** – caught – caught
**choose** – chose – chosen
**cleave** – cleft, clove* – cleft, cloven*
**cling** – clung – clung
**clothe** – clad* – clad*
**come** – came – come
**cost** – cost – cost
**creep** – crept – crept
**crow** – crew* – crowed
**cut** – cut – cut
**deal** – dealt – dealt
**dig** – dug – dug
**dive** – dived, *a.* dove – dived
**do** – did – done
**draw** – drew – drawn
**dream** – dreamt* – dreamt*
**drink** – drank – drunk
**drive** – drove – driven
**dwell** – dwelt* – dwelt*
**eat** – ate – eaten
**fall** – fell – fallen
**feed** – fed – fed
**feel** – felt – felt
**fight** – fought – fought
**find** – found – found
**fit** – fitted, *a.* fit – fitted, *a.* fit
**flee** – fled – fled
**fling** – flung – flung
**fly** – flew – flown
**forbid** – forbade – forbidden
**forget** – forgot – forgotten
**forsake** – forsook – forsaken
**freeze** – froze – frozen
**get** – got – got, *a.* gotten
**give** – gave – given
**go** – went – gone
**grind** – ground – ground
**grow** – grew – grown
**hang** – hung – hung
**have** – had – had
**hear** – heard – heard
**heave** – hove* – hove*
**hew** – hewed – hewn*
**hide** – hid – hidden
**hit** – hit – hit
**hold** – held – held
**hurt** – hurt – hurt
**keep** – kept – kept
**kneel** – knelt* – knelt*
**knit** – knit* – knit*
**know** – knew – known
**lay** – laid – laid
**lead** – led – led
**lean** – leant* – leant*
**leap** – leapt* – leapt*
**learn** – learnt* – learnt*
**leave** – left – left
**lend** – lent – lent
**let** – let – let
**lie** – lay – lain
**light** – lit* – lit*
**lose** – lost – lost
**make** – made – made
**mean** – meant – meant
**meet** – met – met
**mow** – mowed – mown*
**pay** – paid – paid
**plead** – pleaded, *a.* pled – pleaded, *a.* pled

**put** – put – put
**read** – read – read
**rid** – rid – rid
**ride** – rode – ridden
**ring** – rang – rung
**rise** – rose – risen
**run** – ran – run
**saw** – sawed – sawn*
**say** – said – said
**see** – saw – seen
**seek** – sought – sought
**sell** – sold – sold
**send** – sent – sent
**set** – set – set
**sew** – sewed – sewn*
**shake** – shook – shaken
**shave** – shaved – shaven*
**shear** – sheared – shorn
**shed** – shed – shed
**shine** – shone – shone
**shit** – shit – shit
**shoe** – shod – shod
**shoot** – shot – shot
**show** – showed – shown*
**shrink** – shrank – shrunk
**shut** – shut – shut
**sing** – sang – sung
**sink** – sank – sunk
**sit** – sat – sat
**slay** – slew – slain
**sleep** – slept – slept
**slide** – slid – slid
**sling** – slung – slung
**slink** – slunk – slunk
**slit** – slit – slit
**smell** – smelt* – smelt*
**sow** – sowed – sown*
**speak** – spoke – spoken
**speed** – sped* – sped*
**spell** – spelt* – spelt*
**spend** – spent – spent
**spill** – spilt* – spilt*
**spin** – spun – spun
**spit** – spat – spat
**split** – split – split
**spoil** – spoilt* – spoilt*
**spread** – spread – spread
**spring** – sprang, *a.* sprung – sprung
**stand** – stood – stood
**stave** – stove* – stove*
**steal** – stole – stolen
**stick** – stuck – stuck
**sting** – stung – stung
**stink** – stank, stunk – stunk
**strew** – strewed – strewn*
**stride** – strode – stridden
**strike** – struck – struck
**string** – strung – strung
**strive** – strove – striven
**swear** – swore – sworn
**sweat** – sweat* – sweat*
**sweep** – swept – swept
**swell** – swelled – swollen
**swim** – swam – swum
**swing** – swung – swung
**take** – took – taken
**teach** – taught – taught
**tear** – tore – torn
**tell** – told – told
**think** – thought – thought
**thrive** – throve* – thriven*
**throw** – threw – thrown
**thrust** – thrust – thrust
**tread** – trod – trodden, trod
**wake** – woke* – woke(n)*
**wear** – wore – worn
**weave** – wove – woven
**wed** – wedded, wed – wedded, wed
**weep** – wept – wept
**wet** – wet* – wet*
**win** – won – won
**wind** – wound – wound
**wring** – wrung – wrung
**write** – wrote – written

Irregular forms marked with asterisks (*)
can be exchanged for the regular forms.

# German declension and conjugation

## A. Declension

Order of cases: *nom*, *gen*, *dat*, *acc*, *sg* and *pl*. – Compound nouns and adjectives (e.g. *Eisbär*, *Ausgang*, *abfällig* etc.) inflect like their last elements (*Bär*, *Gang*, *fällig*). *dem* = demonstrative, *imp* = imperative, *ind* = indicative, *perf* = perfect, *pres* = present, *pres p* = present participle, *rel* = relative, *su* = substantive.

## I. Nouns

| | | | | |
|---|---|---|---|---|
| **1** | Bild | ~(e)s[1] | ~(e) | ~ |
| | Bilder[2] | ~ | ~n | ~ |

[1] **es *only*:** Geist, Geistes.
[2] **a, o, u > ä, ö, ü:** Rand, Ränder; Haupt, Häupter; Dorf, Dörfer; Wurm, Würmer.

| | | | | |
|---|---|---|---|---|
| **2** | Reis* | ~es ['-zəs] | ~(e) | ~ |
| | Reiser[1] ['-zɐ] | ~ | ~n | ~ |

[1] **a, o > ä, ö:** Glas, Gläser ['glɛːzɐ]; Haus, Häuser ['hɔʏzɐ]; Fass, Fässer; Schloss, Schlösser.

* Fass, Fasse(s).

| | | | | |
|---|---|---|---|---|
| **3** | Arm | ~(e)s[1, 2] | ~(e)[1] | ~ |
| | Arme[3] | ~ | ~n | ~ |

[1] ***without* e:** Billard, Billard(s).
[2] **es *only*:** Maß, Maßes.
[3] **a, o, u > ä, ö, ü:** Gang, Gänge; Saal, Säle; Gebrauch, Gebräuche [gə'brɔʏçə]; Sohn, Söhne; Hut, Hüte.

| | | | | |
|---|---|---|---|---|
| **4** | Greis[1]* | ~es ['-zəs] | ~(e) | ~ |
| | Greise[2] ['-zə] | ~ | ~n | ~ |

[1] **s > ss:** Kürbis, Kürbisse(s).
[2] **a, o, u > ä, ö, ü:** Hals, Hälse; Bass, Bässe; Schoß, Schöße; Fuchs, Füchse; Schuss, Schüsse.

* Ross, Rosse(s).

| | | | | |
|---|---|---|---|---|
| **5** | Strahl | ~(e)s[1, 2] | ~(e)[2] | ~ |
| | Strahlen[3] | ~ | ~ | ~ |

[1] **es *only*:** Schmerz, Schmerzes.
[2] ***without* e:** Juwel, Juwel(s).
[3] Sporn, Sporen.

| | | | | |
|---|---|---|---|---|
| **6** | Lappen | ~s | ~ | ~* |
| | Lappen[1] | ~ | ~ | ~ |

[1] **a, o > ä, ö:** Graben, Gräben; Boden, Böden.

* ***Infinitives used as nouns have no*** *pl*: Geschehen, Befinden etc.

| | | | | |
|---|---|---|---|---|
| **7** | Maler | ~s | ~ | ~ |
| | Maler[1] | ~ | ~n | ~ |

[1] **a, o, u > ä, ö, ü:** Vater, Väter; Kloster, Klöster; Bruder, Brüder.

| | | | | |
|---|---|---|---|---|
| **8** | Untertan | ~s | ~ | ~ |
| | Untertanen[1, 2] | ~ | ~ | ~ |

[1] ***with change of accent*:** Pro'fessor, Profes'soren [-'soːrən]; 'Dämon ['dɛːmɔn], Dä'monen [dɛ'moːnən].
[2] *pl* **ien** [-jən]: Kolleg, Kollegien [-'leːgjən]; Mineral, Mineralien.

| | | | | |
|---|---|---|---|---|
| **9** | Studium | ~s | ~ | ~ |
| | Studien[1, 2] ['-djən] | ~ | ~ | ~ |

[1] **a *and* o(n) > en:** Drama, Dramen; Stadion, Stadien.
[2] **on *and* um > a:** Lexikon, Lexika; Neutrum, Neutra.

| | | | | |
|---|---|---|---|---|
| **10** | Auge | ~s | ~ | ~ |
| | Augen | ~ | ~ | ~ |

| | | | | |
|---|---|---|---|---|
| **11** | Genie | ~s[1*] | ~ | ~ |
| | Genies[2*] | ~ | ~ | ~ |

[1] ***without inflection***: Bouillon etc.

[2] *pl* **s *or* ta:** Komma, Kommas ***or*** Kommata; ***but***: 'Klima, Klimate [kli'ma:tə] (3).

* **s *is pronounced***: [ʒe'ni:s].

| | | | | |
|---|---|---|---|---|
| **12** | Bär* | ~en[1] | ~en[1] | ~en[1] |
| | Bären | ~ | ~ | ~ |

[1] Herr, *sg mst* Herrn; Herz, *gen* Herzens, *acc* Herz.

* **...'log *as well as* ... 'loge** (13), e.g. Biolog(e).

| | | | | |
|---|---|---|---|---|
| **13** | Knabe | ~n[1] | ~n | ~n |
| | Knaben | ~ | ~ | ~ |

[1] **ns:** Name, Namens.

| | | | | |
|---|---|---|---|---|
| **14** | Trübsal | ~ | ~ | ~ |
| | Trübsale[1,2,3] | ~ | ~n | ~ |

[1] **a, o, u > ä, ö, ü:** Hand, Hände; Braut, Bräute; Not, Nöte; Luft, Lüfte; Nuss, Nüsse; ***without* e:** Tochter, Töchter; Mutter, Mütter.

[2] **s > ss:** Kenntnis, Kenntnisse; Nimbus, Nimbusse.

[3] **is *or* us > e:** Kultus, Kulte; ***with change of accent***: Di'akonus, Dia'kone [-'ko:nə].

| | | | | |
|---|---|---|---|---|
| **15** | Blume | ~ | ~ | ~ |
| | Blumen | ~ | ~ | ~ |

**...ee:** e:, *pl* e:ən, *e.g.* I'dee, I'deen.

**...ie** { ***stressed syllable***: i:, *pl* i:ən, *e.g.* Batte'rie(n). ***unstressed syllable***: jə, *pl* jən, *e.g.* Ar'terie(n).

| | | | | |
|---|---|---|---|---|
| **16** | Frau | ~ | ~ | ~ |
| | Frauen[1,2,3] | ~ | ~ | ~ |

[1] **in > innen:** Freundin, Freundinnen.

[2] **a, is, os *and* us > en:** Firma, Firmen; Krisis, Krisen; Epos, Epen; Genius, Genien; ***with change of accent***: 'Heros, He'roen [he'ro:ən]; Di'akonus, Dia'konen [-'ko:nən].

[3] **s > ss:** Kirmes, Kirmessen.

## II. Proper nouns

**17** ***In general proper nouns have no*** *pl.*

***The following form the*** *gen sg* ***with* s:**

1. ***Proper nouns without a definite article***: Friedrichs, Paulas, (Friedrich von) Schillers, Deutschlands, Berlins;
2. ***Proper nouns, masculine and neuter*** (***except the names of countries***) ***with a definite article and an adjective***: des braven Friedrichs Bruder, des jungen Deutschlands (Söhne).

***After* s, sch, ß, tz, x, *and* z *the*** *gen sg* ***ends in* -ens** *or* **'** (***instead of* ' *it is more advisable to use the definite article or* von**), e.g. die Werke des [*or* von] Sokrates, Voß *or* Sokrates', Voß' [***not*** Sokratessens, ***seldom*** Vossens] Werke; ***but***: die Umgebung von Mainz. ***Feminine names ending in a consonant or the vowel* e *form the*** *gen sg* ***with* (en)s *or* (n)s; *in the*** *dat* ***and*** *acc sg* ***such names may end in* (e)n** (*pl* = ***a***).

***If a proper noun is followed by a title, only the following forms are inflected***:

1. ***the title when used*** with ***a definite article***:

| | | |
|---|---|---|
| der Kaiser Karl | | (der Große) |
| des | ~s ~ | (des ~n) |

etc.

| | |
|---|---|
| 2. ***the*** (***last***) ***name when used*** with-out ***an article***: | Kaiser Karl (der Große)<br>~ **~s** (des **~n**) etc.<br>(***but***: Herrn Lehmanns Brief). |

## III. Adjectives and participles (also used as nouns*), pronouns, etc.

**18**

| | | *m* | *f* | *n* | *pl* | |
|---|---|---|---|---|---|---|
| **a**) gut | | er[1,2] | ~e | ~es | ~e° | ***without article, after prepositions, personal pronouns, and invariables*** |
| | | en** | ~er | ~en** | ~er | |
| | | em | ~er | ~em | ~en | |
| | | en | ~e | ~es | ~e | |
| **b**) gut | | e[1,2] | ~e | ~e | ~en | ***with definite article*** (22) ***or with pronoun*** (21) |
| | | en | ~en | ~en | ~en | |
| | | en | ~en | ~en | ~en | |
| | | en | ~e | ~e | ~en | |
| **c**) gut | | er[1,2] | ~e | ~es | ~en | ***with indefinite article or with pronoun*** (20) |
| | | en | ~en | ~en | ~en | |
| | | en | ~en | ~en | ~en | |
| | | en | ~e | ~es | ~en | |

[1] krass, krasse(r, ~s, ~st etc.).

[2] **a, o, u > ä, ö, ü *when forming the*** *comp* ***and*** *sup*: alt, älter(e, ~es etc.), ältest (der ~e, am ~en); grob, gröber(e, ~es etc.), gröbst (der ~e, am ~en); kurz, kürzer(e, ~es etc.), kürzest (der ~e, am ~en).

* e.g. Böse(r) *su*: der (die, eine) Böse, ein Böser; Böse(s) *n*: das Böse, ***without article*** Böses; ***in the same way*** Abgesandte(r) *su*, Angestellte(r) *su* etc.; ***in some cases the use varies.***

** ***Sometimes the*** *gen sg* ***ends in ~es instead of ~en***: gutes (***or*** gut**en**) Mutes sein.

° ***In*** böse, böse(r, ~s, ~st etc.) ***one* e *is dropped.***

## The grades of comparison

***The endings of the*** *comparative* ***and*** *superlative* ***are***:

| | | | |
|---|---|---|---|
| | reich | schön | ***inflected according to*** (18[2]). |
| *comp* | reicher | schöner | |
| *sup* | reichst | schönst | |

***After vowels*** (***except* e** [18°]) ***and after*** d, s, sch, ß, st, t, tz, x, y, z ***the*** *sup* ***ends in ~est, but in unstressed syllables after* d, sch *and* t *generally in ~st***: blau, 'blau**est**; rund, 'rund**est**; rasch, 'rasch**est** etc.; ***but***: 'dringend, 'dringend**st**; 'närrisch, 'närrisch**st**; ge'eignet, ge'eignet**st**.

*Note*. – ***The adjectives ending in ~el, ~en*** (***except ~nen***) ***and ~er*** (e.g. dunk**el**, eb**en**, heit**er**), ***and also the possessive adjectives*** unser ***and*** euer ***generally drop* e.**

| ***Inflection***: | ~e | ~em | ~en | ~er | ~es, ***and*** |
|---|---|---|---|---|---|
| **~el** > | ~le | ~lem* | ~len* | ~ler | ~les |
| **~en** > | ~(e)ne | ~(e)nem | ~(e)nen | ~(e)ner° | ~(e)nes |
| **~er** > | ~(e)re | ~rem* | ~ren* | ~(e)rer° | ~(e)res |

* ***or*** ~elm, ~eln, ~erm, ~ern; e.g. **dunk|el:** ~le, ~lem (***or*** ~elm), ~len (***or*** ~eln), ~ler, ~les; **eb|en:** ~(e)ne, ~(e)nem etc.; **heit|er:** ~(e)re, ~rem (***or*** ~erm) etc.

° ***The inflected*** *comp* ***ends in*** ~ner ***and*** ~rer ***only***: eben, ebnere(r, ~s etc.); heiter, heitrere(r, ~s etc.); ***but*** *sup* ebenst, heiterst.

**19**

| | ***1st pers.*** | ***2nd pers.*** | ***3rd pers.*** | | |
|---|---|---|---|---|---|
| | *m, f, n* | *m, f, n* | *m* | *f* | *n* |
| *sg* | ich | du | er | sie | es |
| | meiner* | deiner* | seiner* | ihrer | seiner* |
| | mir | dir | ihm | ihr | ihm° |
| | mich | dich | ihn | sie | es° |
| *pl* | wir | ihr | sie | (Sie) | |
| | unser | euer | ihrer | (Ihrer) | |
| | uns | euch | ihnen | (Ihnen)° | |
| | uns | euch | sie | (Sie)° | |

* ***In poetry sometimes without inflection***: gedenke mein!; ***also*** **es** ***instead of*** seiner *n* (= *e-r Sache*): ich bin es überdrüssig.

° ***Reflexive form***: sich.

**20**

| | *m* | *f* | *n* | *pl* |
|---|---|---|---|---|
| mein | | ~e | ~ | ~e* |
| dein | es | ~er | ~es | ~er |
| sein | em | ~er | ~em | ~en |
| (k)ein | en | ~e | ~ | ~e |

* ***The indefinite article*** ein ***has no*** *pl*. – ***In poetry*** mein, dein ***and*** sein ***may stand behind the*** *su* ***without inflection***: die Mutter (Kinder) mein, ***or as predicate***: *der Hut* [*die Tasche, das Buch*] *ist* mein; ***without*** *su*: meiner *m*, meine *f*, mein(e)s *n*, meine *pl* etc.: *wem gehört der Hut* [*die Tasche, das Buch*]*? es ist* meiner (meine, mein[e]s); ***or with definite article***: der (die, das) meine, *pl* die meinen (18b). ***Regarding*** unser ***and*** euer ***see note*** (18).

[1] **welche(r, s)** ***as*** *rel pron*: *gen sg* dessen, deren, *gen pl* deren, *dat pl* denen (23).

* ***Used as*** *su*, dies ***is preferable to*** dieses.

** manch, solch, welch ***frequently are uninflected***:

| | | | |
|---|---|---|---|
| manch | gut**er** | (ein gut**er**) | Mann |
| solch | **~en** | ( **~es** **~en**) | **~es** |
| welch | **~em** | ( **~em** **~en**) | **~e** |
| | etc. (18) | | |

***Similarly*** all:

all der (dies**er**, mein ) Schmerz
~ des ( **~es**, **~es**) **~es**

**21**

| | *m* | *f* | *n* | *pl* |
|---|---|---|---|---|
| dies | er | ~e | ~es* | ~e** |
| jen | es | ~er | ~es | ~er[1] |
| manch | em | ~er | ~em | ~en[1] |
| welch | en | ~e | ~es* | ~e |

**22**

| *m* | *f* | *n* | *pl* | |
|---|---|---|---|---|
| der | die | das | die[1] | |
| des | der | des | der | ***definite*** |
| dem | der | dem | den | ***article*** |
| den | die | das | die | |

[1] derjenige, derselbe – desjenigen, demjenigen, desselben, demselben etc. (18b).

[1] ***also*** derer, ***when used as*** *dem pron*
* ***also*** des.

**23** ***Relative pronoun***

| *m* | *f* | *n* | *pl* |
|---|---|---|---|
| der | die | das | die |
| dessen* | deren | dessen* | deren[1] |
| dem | der | dem | denen |
| den | die | das | die |

**24**

| wer | was | jemand, niemand |
|---|---|---|
| wessen* | wessen | ~(e)s |
| wem | – | ~(em°) |
| wen | was | ~(en°) |

* ***also*** wes.
° ***preferably without inflection.***

## B. Conjugation

In the conjugation tables (25–30) only the simple verbs may be found; in the alphabetical list of the German irregular verbs compound verbs are only included when no simple verb exists (e.g. **beginnen;** *ginnen* does not exist). In order to find the conjugation of any compound verb (with separable or inseparable prefix, regular or irregular) look up the respective simple verb.

Verbs with separable and stressed prefixes such as **'ab-, 'an-, 'auf-, 'aus-, 'bei-, be'vor-, 'dar-, 'ein-, em'por-, ent'gegen-, 'fort-, 'her-, he'rab-** etc. and also *'klar-[legen], 'los-[schießen], 'sitzen [bleiben], über'hand [nehmen]* etc. (but not the verbs derived from compound nouns as *be'antragen* or *be'ratschlagen* from *Antrag* and *Ratschlag* etc.) take the preposition **zu** (in the *inf* and the *pres p*) and the syllable **ge** (in the *pp* and in the passive voice) between the stressed prefix and their root.

Verbs with inseparable and unstressed prefixes such as **be-, emp-, ent-, er-, ge-, ver-, zer-** and generally **miss-** (in spite of its being stressed) take the preposition **zu** before the prefix and drop the syllable **ge** in the *pp* and in the passive voice. The prefixes **durch-, hinter-, über-, um-, unter-, voll-, wi(e)der-** are separable when stressed and inseparable when unstressed, e.g.

**geben:** *zu geben, zu gebend; gegeben; ich gebe, du gibst* etc.;

**'abgeben:** *'abzugeben, 'abzugebend; 'abgegeben; ich gebe* (*du gibst* etc.) *ab*;

**ver'geben:** *zu ver'geben, zu ver'gebend; ver'geben; ich ver'gebe, du ver'gibst* etc.;

**'umgehen:** *'umzugehen, 'umzugehend; 'umgegangen; ich gehe* (*du gehst* etc.) *um*;

**um'gehen:** *zu um'gehen, zu um'gehend; um'gangen; ich um'gehe, du um'gehst* etc.

The same rules apply to verbs with two prefixes, e.g.

**zu'rückbehalten** [see *halten*]: *zu'rückzubehalten, zu'rückzubehaltend; zu'rückbehalten; ich behalte* (*du behältst* etc.) *zurück*;

**wieder 'aufheben** [see *heben*]: *wieder 'aufzuheben, wieder 'aufzuhebend; wieder 'aufgehoben; ich hebe* (*du hebst* etc.) *wieder auf*.

The forms in parentheses ( ) follow the same rules.

## a) 'Weak' conjugation

### 25 loben

| | | | |
|---|---|---|---|
| *pres ind* | lobe | lobst | lobt |
| | loben | lobt | loben |
| *pres subj* | lobe | lobest | lobe |
| | loben | lobet | loben |
| *pret ind* and *subj* | lobte | lobtest | lobte |
| | lobten | lobtet | lobten |

*imp sg* lob(e), *pl* lob(e)t, loben Sie; *inf pres* loben; *inf perf* gelobt haben; *pres p* lobend; *pp* gelobt (18; 29**).

### 26 reden

| | | | |
|---|---|---|---|
| *pres ind* | rede | redest | redet |
| | reden | redet | reden |
| *pres subj* | rede | redest | rede |
| | reden | redet | reden |
| *pret ind* and *subj* | redete | redetest | redete |
| | redeten | redetet | redeten |

*imp sg* rede, *pl* redet, reden Sie; *inf pres* reden; *inf perf* geredet haben; *pres p* redend; *pp* geredet (18; 29**).

### 27 reisen

| | | | |
|---|---|---|---|
| *pres ind* | reise | rei(se)st* | reist |
| | reisen | reist | reisen |
| *pres subj* | reise | reisest | reise |
| | reisen | reiset | reisen |
| *pret ind* and *subj* | reiste | reistest | reisten |
| | reisten | reistet | reisten |

*imp sg* reise, *pl* reist, reisen Sie; *inf pres* reisen; *inf perf* gereist sein *or now rare* haben; *pres p* reisend; *pp* gereist (18; 29**).

* **sch:** naschen, nasch(e)st; **ß:** spaßen, spaßt (spaßest); **tz:** ritzen, ritzt (ritzest); **x:** hexen, hext (hexest); **z:** reizen, reizt (reizest); faulenzen, faulenzt (faulenzest).

### 28 fassen

| | | | |
|---|---|---|---|
| *pres ind* | fasse | fasst (fassest) | fasst |
| | fassen | fasst | fassen |
| *pres subj* | fasse | fassest | fasse |
| | fassen | fasset | fassen |
| *pret ind* and *subj* | fasste | fasstest | fasste |
| | fassten | fasstet | fassten |

*imp sg* fasse (fass), *pl* fasst, fassen Sie; *inf pres* fassen; *inf perf* gefasst haben; *pres p* fassend; *pp* gefasst (18; 29**).

### 29 handeln

| | | |
|---|---|---|
| | *pres ind* | |
| handle* | handelst | handelt |
| handeln | handelt | handeln |
| | *pres subj* | |
| handle* | handelst | handle* |
| handeln | handelt | handeln |
| | *pret ind* and *subj* | |
| handelte | handeltest | handelte |
| handelten | handeltet | handelten |

*imp sg* handle, *pl* handelt, handeln Sie; *inf pres* handeln; *inf perf* gehandelt haben; *pres p* handelnd; *pp* gehandet (18).

* ***Also*** handele; wandern, wand(e)re; bessern, bessere (bessre); donnern, donnere.

** ***Without* ge*, when the first syllable is unstressed,*** e.g. be'grüßen, be'grüßt; ent'stehen, ent'standen; stu'dieren, studiert (***not*** gestudiert); trom'peten, trom'petet (***also when preceded by a stressed prefix***: 'austrompeten, 'austrompetet, ***not*** 'ausgetrompetet). ***In some weak verbs the** pp **ends in en instead of* t,** e.g. mahlen, gemahlen. ***With the verbs*** brauchen, dürfen, heißen, helfen, hören, können, lassen, lehren, lernen, machen, mögen, müssen, sehen, sollen, wollen ***the** pp **is replaced by** inf* (***without*** ge), ***when used in connection with another*** *inf*, e.g. ich habe ihn singen hören, du hättest es tun können, er hat gehen müssen, ich hätte ihn laufen lassen sollen.

## b) 'Strong' conjugation

**30** **fahren**

| | | | |
|---|---|---|---|
| *pres ind* | fahre | fährst | fährt |
| | fahren | fahrt | fahren |
| *pres subj* | fahre | fahrest | fahre |
| | fahren | fahret | fahren |
| *pret ind* | fuhr | fuhr(e)st | fuhr |
| | fuhren | fuhrt | fuhren |
| *pres subj* | führe | führest | führe |
| | führen | führet | führen |

*imp sg* fahr(e), *pl* fahr(e)t, fahren Sie; *inf pres* fahren; *inf perf* gefahren haben **or** sein; *pres p* fahrend; *pp* gefahren (18; 29**).

# Proper names

**Aachen** ['a:xən] Aachen, Aix-la-Chapelle
**Adler** ['a:dlɐ] *Austrian psychologist*
**Adria** ['a:dria]: ***die*** ~ the Adriatic (Sea)
**Afrika** ['a:frika] Africa
**Ägäis**[ɛ'gɛ:ɪs]: ***die*** ~ the Aegean (Sea)
**Ägypten** [ɛ'gʏptən] Egypt
**Albanien** [al'ba:njən] Albania
**Algerien** [al'ge:rjən] Algeria
**Algier** ['alʒi:ɐ] Algiers
**Allgäu** ['algɔʏ]: ***das*** ~ the Al(l)gäu (*region of Bavaria, Germany*)
**Alpen** ['alpən]: ***die*** ~ *pl* the Alps
**Amerika** [a'me:rika] America
**Anden** ['andən]: ***die*** ~ *pl* the Andes
**Antillen** [an'tɪlən]: ***die*** ~ *pl* the Antilles
**Antwerpen** [ant'vɛrpən] Antwerp
**Apenninen** [ape'ni:nən]: ***die*** ~ *pl* the Apennines
**Argentinien** [argɛn'ti:njən] Argentina, the Argentine
**Ärmelkanal** ['ɛrməlkana:l]: ***der*** ~ the English Channel, the Channel
**Asien** ['a:zjən] Asia
**Athen** [a'te:n] Athens
**Äthiopien** [ɛ'tjo:pjən] Ethiopia
**Atlantik** [at'lantɪk]: ***der*** ~ the Atlantic (Ocean)
**Australien** [aʊs'tra:ljən] Australia

**Bach** [bax] *German composer*
**Barlach** ['barlax] *German sculptor*
**Basel** ['ba:zəl] Basel, Basle
**Bayern** ['baɪɐn] Bavaria
**Beethoven** ['be:tho:fən] *German composer*
**Belgien** ['bɛlgjən] Belgium
**Berlin** [bɛr'li:n] *German city*
**Bern** [bɛrn] Bern(e)
**Bloch** [blɔx] *German philosopher*
**Böcklin** ['bœkli:n] *German painter*
**Bodensee** ['bo:dənze:]: ***der*** ~ Lake Constance
**Böhm** [bø:m] *Austrian conductor*
**Böhmen** ['bø:mən] *hist* Bohemia
**Böll** [bœl] *German author*
**Bonn** [bɔn] *German city*
**Brahms** [bra:ms] *German composer*
**Brasilien** [bra'zi:ljən] Brazil
**Braunschweig** ['braʊnʃvaɪk] Braunschweig, Brunswick
**Brecht** [brɛçt] *German dramatist*
**Bremen** ['bre:mən] *German city*
**Bruckner** ['brʊknɐ] *Austrian composer*
**Brüssel** ['brʏsəl] Brussels
**Budapest** ['bu:dapɛst] *Hungarian city*
**Bukarest** ['bu:karɛst] Bucharest
**Bulgarien** [bʊl'ga:rjən] Bulgaria

**Calais** [ka'lɛ:]: ***die Straße von*** ~ the Straits of Dover
**Calvin** [kal'vi:n] *Swiss religious reformer*
**Chile** ['tʃi:le] Chile
**China** ['çi:na] China

**Daimler** ['daɪmlɐ] *German inventor*
**Dänemark** ['dɛ:nəmark] Denmark
**Deutschland** ['dɔʏtʃlant] Germany
**Diesel** ['di:zəl] *German inventor*
**Döblin** ['dø:bli:n] *German author*
**Dolomiten** [dolo'mi:tən]: ***die*** ~ *pl* the Dolomites
**Donau** ['do:naʊ]: ***die*** ~ the Danube
**Dortmund** ['dɔrtmʊnt] *German city*
**Dresden** ['dre:sdən] *German city*
**Dünkirchen** ['dy:nkɪrçən] Dunkirk
**Dürer** ['dy:rɐ] *German painter*
**Dürrenmatt** ['dʏrənmat] *Swiss dramatist*
**Düsseldorf** ['dʏsəldɔrf] *German city*

**Egk** [ɛk] *German composer*
**Eichendorff** ['aɪçəndɔrf] *German poet*
**Eiger** ['aɪgɐ] *Swiss mountain*
**Einstein** ['aɪnʃtaɪn] *German physicist*
**Elbe** ['ɛlbə]: ***die*** ~ (*German river*)
**Elsass** ['ɛlzas]: ***das*** ~ Alsace
**England** ['ɛŋlant] England
**Essen** ['ɛsən] *German city*
**Europa** [ɔʏ'ro:pa] Europe

**Finnland** ['fɪnlant] Finland
**Florenz** [flo'rɛnts] Florence
**Fontane** [fɔn'ta:nə] *German author*
**Franken** ['fraŋkən] Franconia
**Frankfurt am Main** ['fraŋkfʊrt am 'maɪn] Frankfurt on the Main
**Frankfurt an der Oder** ['fraŋkfʊrt an

deːɐ 'oːdɐ] Frankfurt on the Oder
**Frankreich** ['fraŋkraɪç] France
**Freud** [frɔyt] *Austrian psychologist*
**Frisch** [frɪʃ] *Swiss author*

**Garmisch** ['garmɪʃ] *health resort in Bavaria, Germany*
**Genf** [gɛnf] Geneva; **~er See** Lake Geneva
**Genua** ['geːnua] Genoa
**Goethe** ['gøːtə] *German poet*
**Grass** [gras] *German author*
**Griechenland** ['griːçənlant] Greece
**Grillparzer** ['grɪlpartsɐ] *Austrian dramatist*
**Grönland** ['grøːnlant] Greenland
**Gropius** ['groːpjʊs] *German architect*
**Großbritannien** [groːsbri'tanjən] (Great) Britain
**Großglockner** ['groːsglɔknɐ]: **der ~** (*Austrian mountain*)
**Grünewald** ['gryːnəvalt] *German painter*

**Haag** [haːk]: **Den ~** The Hague
**Hahn** [haːn] *German chemist*
**Hamburg** ['hambʊrk] *German city*
**Händel** ['hɛndəl] Handel (*German composer*)
**Hannover** [ha'noːfɐ] Hanover
**Harz** [haːɐts]: **der ~** the Harz (Mountains)
**Hauptmann** ['haʊptman] *German dramatist*
**Haydn** ['haɪdən] *Austrian composer*
**Hegel** ['heːgəl] *German philosopher*
**Heidegger** ['haɪdɛgɐ] *German philosopher*
**Heidelberg** ['haɪdəlbɛrk] *German city*
**Heine** ['haɪnə] *German poet*
**Heisenberg** ['haɪzənbɛrk] *German physicist*
**Heißenbüttel** ['haɪsənbʏtəl] *German poet*
**Helgoland** ['hɛlgolant] Hel(i)goland
**Helsinki** ['hɛlzɪŋki] *Finnish city*
**Hesse** ['hɛsə] *German poet*
**Hindemith** ['hɪndəmɪt] *German composer*
**Hölderlin** ['hœldɐliːn] *German poet*
**Holland** ['hɔlant] Holland

**Indien** ['ɪndjən] India
**Inn** [ɪn]: **der ~** (*affluent of the Danube*)
**Innsbruck** ['ɪnsbrʊk] *Austrian city*
**Irak** [i'raːk]: **der ~** Iraq
**Iran** [i'raːn]: **der ~** Iran
**Irland** ['ɪrlant] Ireland
**Island** ['iːslant] Iceland
**Israel** ['ɪsraɛl] Israel
**Italien** [i'taːljən] Italy

**Japan** ['jaːpan] Japan
**Jaspers** ['jaspɐs] *German philosopher*
**Jordanien** [jɔr'daːnjən] Jordan
**Jung** [jʊŋ] *Swiss psychologist*
**Jungfrau** ['jʊŋfraʊ]: **die ~** (*Swiss mountain*)

**Kafka** ['kafka] *Czech author*
**Kanada** ['kanada] Canada
**Kant** [kant] *German philosopher*
**Karlsruhe** ['karlsruːə] *German city*
**Kärnten** ['kɛrntən] Carinthia
**Kästner** ['kɛstnɐ] *German author*
**Kiel** [kiːl] *German city*
**Klee** [kleː] *Swiss-born painter*
**Kleist** [klaɪst] *German poet*
**Koblenz** ['koːblɛnts] Koblenz, Coblenz
**Kokoschka** [ko'kɔʃka] *Austrian painter*
**Köln** [kœln] Cologne
**Kolumbien** [ko'lʊmbjən] Colombia
**Kolumbus** [ko'lʊmbʊs] Columbus
**Konstanz** ['kɔnstants] Constance
**Kopenhagen** [koːpən'haːgən] Copenhagen
**Kordilleren** [kɔrdɪl'jeːrən]: **die ~** *pl* the Cordilleras
**Kreml** ['kreːməl]: **der ~** the Kremlin

**Leibniz** ['laɪbnɪts] *German philosopher*
**Leipzig** ['laɪptsɪç] Leipzig, Leipsic
**Lessing** ['lɛsɪŋ] *German poet*
**Libanon** ['liːbanɔn]: **der ~** (the) Lebanon
**Liebig** ['liːbɪç] *German chemist*
**Lissabon** ['lɪsabɔn] Lisbon
**London** ['lɔndɔn] London
**Lothringen** ['loːtrɪŋən] Lorraine
**Lübeck** ['lyːbɛk] *German city*
**Luther** ['lʊtɐ] *German religious reformer*
**Luxemburg** ['lʊksəmbʊrk] Luxemb(o)urg
**Luzern** [lu'tsɛrn] Lucerne

**Maas** [maːs]: **die ~** the Meuse, the Maas
**Madrid** [ma'drɪt] Madrid
**Mahler** ['maːlɐ] *Austrian composer*

**Mailand** ['maɪlant] Milan
**Main** [maɪn]: ***der*** ~ (*German river*)
**Mainz** [maɪnts] *German city*
**Mann** [man] *name of three German authors*
**Marokko** [ma'rɔko] Morocco
**Matterhorn** ['matɐhɔrn]: ***das*** ~ (*Swiss mountain*)
**Meißen** ['maɪsən] Meissen
**Menzel** ['mɛntsəl] *German painter*
**Mexiko** ['mɛksiko] Mexico
**Mies van der Rohe** ['miːs fan deːɐ 'roːə] *German architect*
**Mittelmeer** ['mɪtəlmeːɐ]: ***das*** ~ the Mediterranean (Sea)
**Moldau** ['mɔldaʊ]: ***die*** ~ the Vltava; *hist* the Moldau (*Bohemian river*)
**Mörike** ['møːrɪkə] *German poet*
**Mosel** ['moːzəl]: ***die*** ~ the Moselle
**Mössbauer** ['mœsbauɐ] *German physicist*
**Moskau** ['mɔskaʊ] Moscow
**Mozart** ['moːtsart] *Austrian composer*
**München** ['mʏnçən] Munich

**Neapel** [ne'aːpəl] Naples
**Neiße** ['naɪsə]: ***die*** ~ (*German river*)
**Neufundland** [nɔʏ'fʊntlant] Newfoundland
**Neuseeland** [nɔʏ'zeːlant] New Zealand
**Niederlande** ['niːdɐlandə]: ***die*** ~ *pl* the Netherlands
**Nietzsche** ['niːtʃə] *German philosopher*
**Nil** [niːl]: ***der*** ~ the Nile
**Nordamerika** ['nɔrtʔa'meːrika] North America
**Nordsee** ['nɔrtzeː]: ***die*** ~ the North Sea
**Normandie** [nɔrman'diː]: ***die*** ~ Normandy
**Norwegen** ['nɔrveːgən] Norway
**Nürnberg** ['nʏrnbɛrk] Nuremberg

**Oder** ['oːdɐ]: ***die*** ~ (*German river*)
**Orff** [ɔrf] *German composer*
**Oslo** ['ɔslo] Oslo
**Ostende** [ɔst'ʔɛndə] Ostend
**Österreich** ['øːstəraɪç] Austria
**Ostsee** ['ɔstzeː]: ***die*** ~ the Baltic (Sea)

**Palästina** [palɛs'tiːna] Palestine
**Paris** [pa'riːs] Paris
**Pfalz** [pfalts]: ***die*** ~ the Palatinate
**Philippinen** [fɪlɪ'piːnən]: ***die*** ~ *pl* the Philippines
**Planck** [plaŋk] *German physicist*
**Polen** ['poːlən] Poland
**Porsche** ['pɔrʃə] *German inventor*
**Portugal** ['pɔrtugal] Portugal
**Prag** [praːk] Prague
**Preußen** ['prɔʏsən] *hist* Prussia
**Pyrenäen** [pyre'nɛːən]: ***die*** ~ *pl* the Pyrenees

**Rhein** [raɪn]: ***der*** ~ the Rhine
**Rilke** ['rɪlkə] *Austrian poet*
**Rom** [roːm] Rome
**Röntgen** ['rœntgən] *German physicist*
**Ruhr** [ruːɐ]: ***die*** ~ (*German river*); **Ruhrgebiet** ['ruːɐgəbiːt]: ***das*** ~ (*industrial center of Germany*)
**Rumänien** [ru'mɛːnjən] Rumania, Ro(u)mania
**Russland** ['rʊslant] Russia

**Saale** ['zaːlə]: ***die*** ~ (*German river*)
**Saar** [zaːɐ]: ***die*** ~ (*affluent of the Moselle*)
**Salzburg** ['zaltsbʊrk] *Austrian city*
**Schiller** ['ʃɪlɐ] *German poet*
**Schönberg** ['ʃøːnbɛrk] *Austrian composer*
**Schottland** ['ʃɔtlant] Scotland
**Schubert** ['ʃuːbɐt] *Austrian composer*
**Schumann** ['ʃuːman] *German composer*
**Schwaben** ['ʃvaːbən] Swabia
**Schwarzwald** ['ʃvartsvalt]: ***der*** ~ the Black Forest
**Schweden** ['ʃveːdən] Sweden
**Schweiz** [ʃvaɪts]: ***die*** ~ Switzerland
**Sibirien** [zi'biːrjən] Siberia
**Siemens** ['ziːməns] *German inventor*
**Sizilien** [zi'tsiːljən] Sicily
**Skandinavien** [skandi'naːvjən] Scandinavia
**Slowakei** [slova'kai]: ***die*** ~ Slovakia
**Sofia** ['zɔfja] Sofia
**Spanien** ['ʃpaːnjən] Spain
**Spitzweg** ['ʃpɪtsveːk] *German painter*
**Spranger** ['ʃpraŋɐ] *German philosopher*
**Stifter** ['ʃtɪftɐ] *Austrian author*
**Stockholm** ['ʃtɔkhɔlm] Stockholm
**Storm** [ʃtɔrm] *German poet*
**Straßburg** ['ʃtraːsbʊrk] Strasbourg
**Strauß** [ʃtraʊs] *Austrian composer*
**Strauss** [ʃtraʊs] *German composer*
**Südamerika** ['zyːtʔa'meːrika] South America

**Syrien** ['zy:rjən] Syria

**Themse** ['tɛmzə]: ***die*** ~ the Thames
**Tirol** [ti'ro:l] (the) Tyrol
**Tschechien** ['tʃɛçjən] Czech Republic
**Türkei** [tʏr'kaɪ]: ***die*** ~ Turkey

**Ungarn** ['ʊŋgarn] Hungary
**Ural** [u'ra:l]: ***der*** ~ the Urals

**Venedig** [ve'ne:dɪç] Venice
**Vereinigte Staaten (von Amerika)** [fɛr'ʔaɪnɪçtə 'ʃta:tən (fɔn a'me:rika)]: ***die Vereinigten Staaten*** (***von Amerika***) the United States (of America)
**Vierwaldstätter See** [fi:ɐ'valtʃtɛtɐ 'ze:]: ***der*** ~ Lake Lucerne

**Wagner** ['va:gnɐ] *German composer*
**Wankel** ['vaŋkəl] *German inventor*
**Warschau** ['varʃaʊ] Warsaw
**Weichsel** ['vaɪksəl]: ***die*** ~ the Vistula
**Weiß** [vaɪs] *German dramatist*
**Werfel** ['vɛrfəl] *Austrian author*
**Weser** ['ve:zɐ]: ***die*** ~ (*German river*)
**Wien** [vi:n] Vienna
**Wiesbaden** ['vi:sba:dən] German city

**Zuckmayer** ['tsʊkmaɪɐ] *German dramatist*
**Zweig** [tsvaɪk] *Austrian author*
**Zürich** ['tsy:rɪç] Zurich
**Zypern** ['tsy:pɐn] Cyprus

# German abbreviations

**Abb.** ***Abbildung*** illustration
**Abf.** ***Abfahrt*** departure, *abbr* dep.
**Abt.** ***Abteilung*** department, *abbr* dept.
**a. D.** ***außer Dienst*** retired
**ADAC** ***Allgemeiner Deutscher Automobil-Club*** General German Automobile Association
**AG** ***Aktiengesellschaft*** (stock) corporation, joint-stock company
**allg.** ***allgemein*** general
**Ank.** ***Ankunft*** arrival
**atü** ***Atmosphärenüberdruck*** atmospheric excess pressure

**Bd.** ***Band*** volume, *abbr* vol.; **Bde.** ***Bände*** volumes, *abbr* vols.
**Betr.** ***Betreff, betrifft*** *letter* : subject, re
**BRD** ***Bundesrepublik Deutschland*** Federal Republic of Germany

**CDU** ***Christlich-Demokratische Union*** Christian Democratic Union
**CSU** ***Christlich-Soziale Union*** Christian Social Union

**DB** ***Deutsche Bahn*** *Germany's main railway operator*
**DDR** *hist* ***Deutsche Demokratische Republik*** German Demoratic Republic
**DGB** ***Deutscher Gewerkschaftsbund*** Federation of German Trade Unions
**d. h.** ***das heißt*** that is, *abbr* i. e.
**DIN** ***Deutsche Industrie-Norm(en)*** German Industrial Standards
**DM** *hist* ***Deutsche Mark*** German Mark(s)
**dpa** ***Deutsche Presse-Agentur*** German Press Agency
**Dr.** ***Doktor*** Doctor, *abbr* Dr.
**DRK** ***Deutsches Rotes Kreuz*** German Red Cross

**EDV** ***Elektronische Datenverarbeitung*** electronic data processing, *abbr* EDP
**EM** ***Europameisterschaft*** European championship(s)
**EU** ***Europäische Union*** European Union, *abbr* EU
**e. V.** ***eingetragener Verein*** registered association, incorporated, *abbr* inc.

**FDP** ***Freie Demokratische Partei*** Liberal Democratic Party
**Forts.** ***Fortsetzung*** continuation

**geb.** ***geboren*** born; ***geborene ...*** née; ***gebunden*** bound
**Ges.** ***Gesellschaft*** association, company; society
**gez.** ***gezeichnet*** signed, *abbr* sgd
**GmbH** ***Gesellschaft mit beschränkter Haftung*** private limited liability company

**h. c.** ***honoris causa*** = ehrenhalber; *academic title* : honorary
**Hrsg.** ***Herausgeber*** editor, *abbr* ed.

**i. A.** ***im Auftrage*** for, by order, under instruction
**Ing.** ***Ingenieur*** engineer
**Inh.** ***Inhaber*** proprietor
**inkl.** ***inklusive, einschließlich*** inclusive
**'Interpol** ***Internationale Kriminalpolizeiliche Organisation*** International Criminal Police Commission
**IOK** ***Internationales Olympisches Komitee*** International Olympic Committee, *abbr* IOC
**ISBN** ***Internationale Standardbuchnummer*** international standard book number, *abbr* ISBN
**i. V.** ***in Vertretung*** by proxy, as a substitute

**jr., jun.** ***junior, der Jüngere*** junior *abbr* jr, jun.

**Kat** ***Katalysator*** catalytic converter, catalyst, *abbr* cat.
**Kfz.** ***Kraftfahrzeug*** motor vehicle
**KG** ***Kommanditgesellschaft*** limited

partnership
**Kl.** ***Klasse*** class; *school*: form
**'Kripo** ***Kriminalpolizei*** Criminal Investigation Department, *abbr* CID
**Kto.** ***Konto*** account, *abbr* a/c

**lfd.** ***laufend*** current, running
**Lfg., Lfrg.** ***Lieferung*** delivery; instal(l)-ment, part
**Lkw, LKW** ***Lastkraftwagen*** truck, lorry
**lt.** ***laut*** according to

**MdB** ***Mitglied des Bundestages*** Member of the Bundestag
**MEZ** ***mitteleuropäische Zeit*** Central European Time
**MS, Ms.** ***Manuskript*** manuscript, *abbr* MS, ms.
**mtl.** ***monatlich*** monthly

**n. Chr.** ***nach Christus*** after Christ, *abbr* AD
**No., Nr.** ***Numero, Nummer*** number, *abbr* No., no

**o. B.** ***ohne Befund*** MED without findings
**OEZ** ***osteuropäische Zeit*** Eastern European Time, *abbr* EET

**PDS** *hist* ***Partei des Demokratischen Sozialismus*** Party of Democratic Socialism
**Pf** *hist* ***Pfennig*** *former German coin* : pfennig
**Pfd.** ***Pfund*** *German weight* : pound
**PKW, Pkw** ***Personenkraftwagen*** car
**PLZ** ***Postleitzahl*** zip code, *Br* post – code
**Prof.** ***Professor*** professor
**PS** ***Pferdestärke(n)*** horse-power, *abbr* HP, h.p.; ***postscriptum, Nachschrift*** postscript, *abbr* PS

**Rel.** ***Religion*** religion

**S.** ***Seite*** page
**s.** ***siehe*** see, *abbr* v., vid. (= vide)
**Sa.** ***Summa, Summe*** sum, total
**sen.** ***senior, der Ältere*** senior
**s. o.** ***siehe oben*** see above
**sog.** ***so genannt*** so-called
**SPD** ***Sozialdemokratische Partei Deutschlands*** Social Democratic Party of Germany
**St.** ***Stück*** piece; ***Sankt*** Saint
**Std.** ***Stunde*** hour, *abbr* h
**Str.** ***Straße*** street, *abbr* St.
**StVO** ***Straßenverkehrsordnung*** (road) traffic regulations, *in GB* : Highway Code
**s. u.** ***siehe unten*** see below

**tägl.** ***täglich*** daily, per day
**Tel.** ***Telefon*** telephone
**TH** ***Technische Hochschule*** college *or* institute of technology
**TU** ***Technische Universität*** technical university; college *or* institute of technology
**TÜV** ***Technischer Überwachungs – Verein*** safety standards authority

**u. a.** ***und andere(s)*** and others; ***unter anderem*** *or* ***anderen*** among other things, inter alia
**UKW** ***Ultrakurzwelle*** ultra-short wave, very high frequency, *abbr* VHF

**V** ***Volt*** volt; ***Volumen*** volume
**v. Chr.** ***vor Christus*** before Christ, *abbr* BC
**vgl.** ***vergleiche*** confer, *abbr* cf.

**WAA** ***Wiederaufbereitungsanlage*** reprocessing plant
**WEZ** ***westeuropäische Zeit*** Greenwich Mean Time, *abbr* GMT
**WG** ***Wohngemeinschaft*** flat share, flat sharing (community)
**WM** ***Weltmeisterschaft*** world championship(s); *soccer*: World Cup

**z. B.** ***zum Beispiel*** for instance, *abbr* e.g.
**z. H(d).** ***zu Händen*** attention of, to be delivered to, care of, *abbr* c/o
**z. T.** ***zum Teil*** partly
**zus.** ***zusammen*** together
**z. Z(t).** ***zur Zeit*** at the time, at present, for the time being